ACKNOWLEDGMENTS

National Journal Inc. and the authors of the 1988 *Almanac of American Politics* would like to give special thanks to four people for their contributions to this edition. Their commitment to excellence and willingness to work long hours were indispensable to the publication of this book.

Almanac Executive Director: Eleanor Evans
Editorial Director: Sarah Orrick
Research Director: Gary Cohen
Senior Researcher: Isobel Ellis

We wish also to thank those people whose additional research and production support made this book possible: Sheila Dwyer, Chip Long, Lisa Cherubini, Denise Westray, George Cannon, Colin Hood, Steve Koehler, Amy Dreifuss, William Ellis, Greta Waller, Janie Blackman, Jackie Meering, Everett Lee and Kerry Corrigan.

Additionally, National Journal Inc. would like to acknowledge the following organizations for the services they provided: Rebetsky & Company, Foxon-Maddocks Associates, The Response Group, U.S. Bureau of the Census, and the Federal Election Commission.

CONTENTS

The States & Congressional Districts:
Their Governors, Senators & Representatives

DISTRICTS AT-A-GLANCE

Districts At-A-Glance is a guide to the geographic area represented by a Member of Congress. Senators will not have a specific location listed next to their name since they represent the entire state.

ALABAMA

Senate		Heflin (D)	
		Shelby (D)	
House	1	Callahan (R)	*Mobile*
	2	Dickinson (R)	*Montgomery*
	3	Nichols (D)	*Anniston*
	4	Bevill (D)	*Jasper*
	5	Flippo (D)	*Huntsville*
	6	Erdreich (D)	*Birmingham*
	7	Harris (D)	*Tuscaloosa*

ALASKA

Senate		Stevens (R)	
		Murkowski (R)	
House	1	Young, D. (R)	*At Large*

ARIZONA

Senate		DeConcini (D)	
		McCain (R)	
House	1	Rhodes (R)	*Tempe*
	2	Udall (D)	*Phoenix*
	3	Stump (R)	*Flagstaff*
	4	Kyl (R)	*Scottsdale*
	5	Kolbe (R)	*Tucson*

ARKANSAS

Senate		Bumpers (D)	
		Pryor (D)	
House	1	Alexander (D)	*Jonesboro*
	2	Robinson (D)	*Little Rock*
	3	Hammerschmidt (R)	*Fort Smith*
	4	Anthony (D)	*Pine Bluff*

CALIFORNIA

Senate		Cranston (D)	
		Wilson, P. (R)	
House	1	Bosco (D)	*Santa Rosa*
	2	Herger (R)	*Chico*
	3	Matsui (D)	*Sacramento*
	4	Fazio (D)	*Sacramento*
	5	Pelosi (D)	*San Francisco*
	6	Boxer (D)	*Marin County*
	7	Miller, G. (D)	*Richmond*
	8	Dellums (D)	*Oakland*
	9	Stark (D)	*Hayward*
	10	Edwards, D. (D)	*San Jose*
	11	Lantos (D)	*San Mateo County*
	12	Konnyu (R)	*Sunnyvale*
	13	Mineta (D)	*San Jose*
	14	Shumway (R)	*Stockton*
	15	Coelho (D)	*Modesto*
	16	Panetta (D)	*Monterey*
	17	Pashayan (R)	*Fresno*
	18	Lehman, R. (D)	*Fresno*
	19	Lagomarsino (R)	*Santa Barbara*
	20	Thomas, W. (R)	*Bakersfield*
	21	Gallegly (R)	*Thousand Oaks*
	22	Moorhead (R)	*Pasadena*
	23	Beilenson (D)	*Beverly Hills*
	24	Waxman (D)	*Hollywood*
	25	Roybal (D)	*Los Angeles*
	26	Berman (D)	*Van Nuys*
	27	Levine (D)	*Santa Monica*
	28	Dixon (D)	*Culver City*
	29	Hawkins (D)	*Los Angeles*
	30	Martinez (D)	*El Monte*
	31	Dymally (D)	*Compton*
	32	Anderson (D)	*Long Beach*
	33	Dreier (R)	*Pomona*
	34	Torres (D)	*West Covina*
	35	Lewis, J. (R)	*Redlands*
	36	Brown, G. (D)	*Riverside*
	37	McCandless (R)	*Palm Springs*
	38	Dornan (R)	*Santa Ana*
	39	Dannemeyer (R)	*Anaheim*
	40	Badham (R)	*Newport Beach*
	41	Lowery (R)	*San Diego*
	42	Lungren (R)	*Long Beach*
	43	Packard (R)	*Carlsbad*
	44	Bates (D)	*San Diego*
	45	Hunter (R)	*Coronado*

COLORADO

Senate		Armstrong (R)	
		Wirth (D)	
House	1	Schroeder (D)	*Denver*
	2	Skaggs (D)	*Boulder*
	3	Campbell (D)	*Pueblo*
	4	Brown, H. (R)	*Greeley*
	5	Hefley (R)	*Colorado Springs*
	6	Schaefer (R)	*Lakewood*

CONNECTICUT

Senate		Weicker (R)	
		Dodd (D)	
House	1	Kennelly (D)	*Hartford*
	2	Gejdenson (D)	*New London*
	3	Morrison, B. (D)	*New Haven*
	4	McKinney (R)	*Stamford*
	5	Rowland, J. (R)	*Waterbury*
	6	Johnson (R)	*New Britain*

DELAWARE

Senate		Roth, W. (R)	
		Biden (D)	
House	1	Carper (D)	*At Large*

FLORIDA

Senate		Chiles (D)	
		Graham (D)	
House	1	Hutto (D)	*Pensacola*
	2	Grant (D)	*Tallahassee*
	3	Bennett (D)	*Jacksonville*
	4	Chappell (D)	*Daytona Beach*
	5	McCollum (R)	*Orlando*
	6	MacKay (D)	*Ocala*
	7	Gibbons (D)	*Tampa*
	8	Young, B. (R)	*St. Petersburg*
	9	Bilirakis (R)	*Clearwater*
	10	Ireland (R)	*Winter Haven*
	11	Nelson (D)	*Melbourne*
	12	Lewis, T. (R)	*N. Palm Beach*
	13	Mack (R)	*Ft. Myers*
	14	Mica (D)	*W. Palm Beach*
	15	Shaw (R)	*Ft. Lauderdale*
	16	Smith, L. (D)	*Hollywood*
	17	Lehman, W. (D)	*N. Miami Beach*
	18	Pepper (D)	*Miami*
	19	Fascell (D)	*Coral Gables*

GEORGIA

Senate		Nunn (D)	
		Fowler (D)	
House	1	Thomas, R. (D)	*Savannah*
	2	Hatcher (D)	*Albany*
	3	Ray (D)	*Columbus*
	4	Swindall (R)	*Dunwoody*
	5	Lewis, John (D)	*Atlanta*
	6	Gingrich (R)	*Carrollton*
	7	Darden (D)	*Marietta*
	8	Rowland, R. (D)	*Macon*
	9	Jenkins (D)	*Dalton*
	10	Barnard (D)	*Augusta*

HAWAII

Senate		Inouye (D)	
		Matsunaga (D)	
House	1	Saiki (R)	*Honolulu*
	2	Akaka (D)	*Outer Islands*

IDAHO

Senate		McClure (R)	
		Symms (R)	
House	1	Craig (R)	*Boise*
	2	Stallings (D)	*Pocatello*

ILLINOIS

Senate		Dixon, A. (D)	
		Simon (D)	
House	1	Hayes (D)	*Chicago*
	2	Savage (D)	*S. Chicago*
	3	Russo (D)	*Oak Lawn*
	4	Davis, J. (R)	*Joliet*
	5	Lipinski (D)	*Chicago*
	6	Hyde (R)	*Wheaton*
	7	Collins (D)	*Chicago*
	8	Rostenkowski (D)	*Chicago*
	9	Yates (D)	*Chicago*
	10	Porter (R)	*Evanston*
	11	Annunzio (D)	*Chicago*
	12	Crane (R)	*Palatine*
	13	Fawell (R)	*Oak Brook*
	14	Hastert (R)	*Elgin*
	15	Madigan (R)	*Bloomington*
	16	Martin, L. (R)	*Rockford*
	17	Evans, L. (D)	*Moline*
	18	Michel (R)	*Peoria*
	19	Bruce (D)	*Danville*
	20	Durbin (D)	*Springfield*
	21	Price (D)	*East St. Louis*
	22	Gray, K. (D)	*Carbondale*

INDIANA

Senate	Lugar (R)	
	Quayle (R)	
House	1 Visclosky (D)	Gary
	2 Sharp (D)	Muncie
	3 Hiler (R)	South Bend
	4 Coats (R)	Fort Wayne
	5 Jontz (D)	Kokomo
	6 Burton (R)	Indianapolis
	7 Myers (R)	Terre Haute
	8 McCloskey (D)	Evansville
	9 Hamilton (D)	Bloomington
	10 Jacobs (D)	Indianapolis

IOWA

Senate	Grassley (R)	
	Harkin (D)	
House	1 Leach (R)	Davenport
	2 Tauke (R)	Cedar Rapids
	3 Nagle (D)	Waterloo
	4 Smith, N. (D)	Des Moines
	5 Lightfoot (R)	Council Bluffs
	6 Grandy (R)	Sioux City

KANSAS

Senate	Dole (R)	
	Kassebaum (R)	
House	1 Roberts (R)	Dodge City
	2 Slattery (D)	Topeka
	3 Meyers (R)	Kansas City
	4 Glickman (D)	Wichita
	5 Whittaker (R)	Emporia

KENTUCKY

Senate	Ford, W. (D)	
	McConnell (R)	
House	1 Hubbard (D)	Paducah
	2 Natcher (D)	Owensboro
	3 Mazzoli (D)	Louisville
	4 Bunning (R)	Covington
	5 Rogers (R)	Somerset
	6 Hopkins (R)	Lexington
	7 Perkins (D)	Ashland

LOUISIANA

Senate	Johnston (D)	
	Breaux (D)	
House	1 Livingston (R)	New Orleans
	2 Boggs (D)	New Orleans
	3 Tauzin (D)	New Iberia
	4 Roemer (D)	Shreveport
	5 Huckaby (D)	Monroe
	6 Baker (R)	Baton Rouge
	7 Hayes, J. (D)	Lafayette
	8 Holloway (R)	Alexandria

MAINE

Senate	Cohen (R)	
	Mitchell, G. (D)	
House	1 Brennan (D)	Portland
	2 Snowe (R)	Bangor

MARYLAND

Senate	Sarbanes (D)	
	Mikulski (D)	
House	1 Dyson (D)	Eastern Shore
	2 Bentley (R)	Towson
	3 Cardin (D)	Baltimore
	4 McMillen (D)	Annapolis
	5 Hoyer (D)	Landover
	6 Byron (D)	Hagerstown
	7 Mfume (D)	Baltimore
	8 Morella (R)	Montgomery County

MASSACHUSETTS

Senate	Kennedy, E. (D)	
	Kerry (D)	
House	1 Conte (R)	Pittsfield
	2 Boland (D)	Springfield
	3 Early (D)	Worcester
	4 Frank (D)	Newton
	5 Atkins (D)	Lowell
	6 Mavroules (D)	Lynn
	7 Markey (D)	Malden
	8 Kennedy, J. (D)	Cambridge
	9 Moakley (D)	Boston
	10 Studds (D)	Cape Cod
	11 Donnelly (D)	Boston

MICHIGAN

Senate	Riegle (D)	
	Levin, C. (D)	
House	1 Conyers (D)	Detroit
	2 Pursell (R)	Ann Arbor
	3 Wolpe (D)	Lansing
	4 Upton (R)	Benton Harbor
	5 Henry (R)	Grand Rapids
	6 Carr (D)	Pontiac
	7 Kildee (D)	Flint
	8 Traxler (D)	Bay City
	9 Vander Jagt (R)	Traverse City
	10 Schuette (R)	Midland
	11 Davis (R)	Upper Peninsula

			Port Huron
12		Bonior (D)	Port Huron
13		Crockett (D)	Detroit
14		Hertel (D)	Warren
15		Ford, W. (D)	Wayne
16		Dingell (D)	Dearborn
17		Levin, S. (D)	Southfield
18		Broomfield (R)	Birmingham

MINNESOTA

Senate		Durenberger (R)	
		Boschwitz (R)	
House	1	Penny (D)	Rochester
	2	Weber (R)	Willmar
	3	Frenzel (R)	Bloomington
	4	Vento (D)	St. Paul
	5	Sabo (D)	Minneapolis
	6	Sikorski (D)	Stillwater
	7	Stangeland (R)	St. Cloud
	8	Oberstar (D)	Duluth

MISSISSIPPI

Senate		Stennis (D)	
		Cochran (R)	
House	1	Whitten (D)	Oxford
	2	Espy (D)	Vicksburg
	3	Montgomery (D)	Meridian
	4	Dowdy (D)	Jackson
	5	Lott (R)	Pascagoula

MISSOURI

Senate		Danforth (R)	
		Bond (R)	
House	1	Clay (D)	St. Louis
	2	Buechner (R)	Kirkwood
	3	Gephardt (D)	St. Louis
	4	Skelton (D)	Jefferson City
	5	Wheat (D)	Kansas City
	6	Coleman, T. (R)	St. Joseph
	7	Taylor (R)	Springfield
	8	Emerson (R)	Cape Girardeau
	9	Volkmer (D)	Hannibal

MONTANA

Senate		Melcher (D)	
		Baucus (D)	
House	1	Williams, P. (D)	Helena
	2	Marlenee (R)	Billings

NEBRASKA

Senate		Exon (D)	
		Karnes (R)	
House	1	Bereuter (R)	Lincoln
	2	Daub (R)	Omaha
	3	Smith, V. (R)	Grand Island

NEVADA

Senate		Hecht (R)	
		Reid (D)	
House	1	Bilbray (D)	Las Vegas
	2	Vucanovich (R)	Reno

NEW HAMPSHIRE

Senate		Humphrey (R)	
		Rudman (R)	
House	1	Smith, R. (R)	Manchester
	2	Gregg (R)	Concord

NEW JERSEY

Senate		Bradley (D)	
		Lautenberg (D)	
House	1	Florio (D)	Pine Hill
	2	Hughes (D)	Ocean City
	3	Howard (D)	Toms River
	4	Smith, C. (R)	Trenton
	5	Roukema (R)	Ridgewood
	6	Dwyer (D)	Edison
	7	Rinaldo (R)	Union
	8	Roe (D)	Paterson
	9	Torricelli (D)	Hackensack
	10	Rodino (D)	Newark
	11	Gallo (R)	Parsippany
	12	Courter (R)	Hackettstown
	13	Saxton (R)	Bordentown
	14	Guarini (D)	Jersey City

NEW MEXICO

Senate		Domenici (R)	
		Bingaman (D)	
House	1	Lujan (R)	Albuquerque
	2	Skeen (R)	Picacho
	3	Richardson (D)	Santa Fe

NEW YORK

Senate		Moynihan (D)	
		D'Amato (R)	
House	1	Hochbrueckner (D)	E. Long Island
	2	Downey (D)	Babylon
	3	Mrazek (D)	Huntington
	4	Lent (R)	E. Rockaway
	5	McGrath (R)	Valley Stream
	6	Flake (D)	Jamaica

7	Ackerman (D)	*Flushing*
8	Scheuer (D)	*Queens*
9	Manton (D)	*Astoria*
10	Schumer (D)	*Flatbush*
11	Towns (D)	*Brooklyn*
12	Owens (D)	*Brooklyn*
13	Solarz (D)	*Brooklyn*
14	Molinari (R)	*Staten Island*
15	Green (R)	*Manhattan*
16	Rangel (D)	*Harlem*
17	Weiss (D)	*Manhattan*
18	Garcia (D)	*Bronx*
19	Biaggi (D)	*Bronx*
20	DioGuardi (R)	*Westchester*
21	Fish (R)	*Poughkeepsie*
22	Gilman (R)	*Middletown*
23	Stratton (D)	*Albany*
24	Solomon (R)	*Saratoga Springs*
25	Boehlert (R)	*Utica*
26	Martin, D. (R)	*Watertown*
27	Wortley (R)	*Syracuse*
28	McHugh (D)	*Binghamton*
29	Horton (R)	*Rochester*
30	Slaughter (D)	*Rochester*
31	Kemp (R)	*Buffalo*
32	LaFalce (D)	*Niagara Falls*
33	Nowak (D)	*Buffalo*
34	Houghton (R)	*Corning*

NORTH CAROLINA

Senate		Helms (R)	
		Sanford (D)	
House	1	Jones, W. (D)	*Greenville*
	2	Valentine (D)	*Durham*
	3	Lancaster (D)	*Goldsboro*
	4	Price (D)	*Raleigh*
	5	Neal (D)	*Winston-Salem*
	6	Coble (R)	*Greensboro*
	7	Rose (D)	*Willimington*
	8	Hefner (D)	*Salisbury*
	9	McMillan (R)	*Charlotte*
	10	Ballenger (R)	*Hickory*
	11	Clarke (D)	*Asheville*

NORTH DAKOTA

Senate		Burdick (D)	
		Andrews, M. (R)	
House	1	Dorgan (D)	*At Large*

OHIO

Senate		Glenn (D)	
		Metzenbaum (D)	
House	1	Luken (D)	*Cincinnati*
	2	Gradison (R)	*Cincinnati*
	3	Hall, T. (D)	*Dayton*
	4	Oxley (R)	*Findlay*
	5	Latta (R)	*Bowling Green*
	6	McEwen (R)	*Portsmouth*
	7	DeWine (R)	*Springfield*
	8	Lukens (R)	*Hamilton*
	9	Kaptur (D)	*Toledo*
	10	Miller, C. (R)	*Lancaster*
	11	Eckart (D)	*Cleveland*
	12	Kasich (R)	*Columbus*
	13	Pease (D)	*Oberlin*
	14	Sawyer (D)	*Akron*
	15	Wylie (R)	*Columbus*
	16	Regula (R)	*Canton*
	17	Traficant (D)	*Youngstown*
	18	Applegate (D)	*Steubenville*
	19	Feighan (D)	*Cleveland*
	20	Oakar (D)	*Cleveland*
	21	Stokes (D)	*Cleveland*

OKLAHOMA

Senate		Boren (D)	
		Nickles (R)	
House	1	Inhofe (R)	*Tulsa*
	2	Synar (D)	*Muskogee*
	3	Watkins (D)	*Ada*
	4	McCurdy (D)	*Norman*
	5	Edwards, M. (R)	*Bartlesville*
	6	English (D)	*Oklahoma City*

OREGON

Senate		Hatfield (R)	
		Packwood (R)	
House	1	AuCoin (D)	*Portland*
	2	Smith, B. (R)	*Medford*
	3	Wyden (D)	*Portland*
	4	DeFazio (D)	*Eugene*
	5	Smith, D. (R)	*Salem*

PENNSYLVANIA

Senate		Heinz (R)	
		Specter (R)	
House	1	Foglietta (D)	*Philadelphia*
	2	Gray, W. (D)	*Philadelphia*
	3	Borski (D)	*Philadelphia*
	4	Kolter (D)	*New Castle*
	5	Schulze (R)	*Chester*
	6	Yatron (D)	*Reading*
	7	Weldon (R)	*Swarthmore*

8	Kostmayer (D)	*Bucks County*
9	Shuster (R)	*Altoona*
10	McDade (R)	*Scranton*
11	Kanjorski (D)	*Wilkes Barre*
12	Murtha (D)	*Johnstown*
13	Coughlin (R)	*Villanova*
14	Coyne (D)	*Pittsburgh*
15	Ritter (R)	*Allentown*
16	Walker (R)	*Lancaster*
17	Gekas (R)	*Harrisburg*
18	Walgren (D)	*Pittsburgh*
19	Goodling (R)	*York*
20	Gaydos (D)	*McKeesport*
21	Ridge (R)	*Erie*
22	Murphy (D)	*Monangahela*
23	Clinger (R)	*Warren*

RHODE ISLAND

Senate		Pell (D)	
		Chafee (R)	
House	1	St Germain (D)	*Providence*
	2	Schneider (R)	*Warwick*

SOUTH CAROLINA

Senate		Thurmond (R)	
		Hollings (D)	
House	1	Ravenel (R)	*Charleston*
	2	Spence (R)	*Columbia*
	3	Derrick (D)	*Aiken*
	4	Patterson (D)	*Spartanburg*
	5	Spratt (D)	*Rock Hill*
	6	Tallon (D)	*Florence*

SOUTH DAKOTA

Senate		Pressler (R)	
		Daschle (D)	
House	1	Johnson (D)	*At Large*

TENNESSEE

Senate		Sasser (D)	
		Gore (D)	
House	1	Quillen (R)	*Kingsport*
	2	Duncan (R)	*Knoxville*
	3	Lloyd (D)	*Chattanooga*
	4	Cooper (D)	*Shelbyville*
	5	Boner (D)	*Nashville*
	6	Gordon (D)	*Murfreesboro*
	7	Sundquist (R)	*Memphis*
	8	Jones, E. (D)	*Jackson*
	9	Ford, H. (D)	*Memphis*

TEXAS

Senate		Bentsen (D)	
		Gramm (R)	
House	1	Chapman (D)	*Texarkana*
	2	Wilson, C. (D)	*Lufkin*
	3	Bartlett (R)	*Dallas*
	4	Hall, R. (D)	*Tyler*
	5	Bryant (D)	*Dallas*
	6	Barton (R)	*Ennis*
	7	Archer (R)	*Houston*
	8	Fields (R)	*Humble*
	9	Brooks (D)	*Beaumont*
	10	Pickle (D)	*Austin*
	11	Leath (D)	*Waco*
	12	Wright (D)	*Fort Worth*
	13	Boulter (R)	*Amarillo*
	14	Sweeney (R)	*Victoria*
	15	de la Garza (D)	*McAllen*
	16	Coleman, R. (D)	*El Paso*
	17	Stenholm (D)	*Abilene*
	18	Leland (D)	*Houston*
	19	Combest (R)	*Lubbock*
	20	Gonzalez (D)	*San Antonio*
	21	Smith (R)	*Midland*
	22	DeLay (R)	*Houston*
	23	Bustamante (D)	*San Antonio*
	24	Frost (D)	*Dallas*
	25	Andrews, M. (D)	*Houston*
	26	Armey (R)	*Arlington*
	27	Ortiz (D)	*Corpus Christi*

UTAH

Senate		Garn (R)	
		Hatch (R)	
House	1	Hansen (R)	*Ogden*
	2	Owens (D)	*Salt Lake City*
	3	Nielson (R)	*Provo*

VERMONT

Senate		Stafford (R)	
		Leahy (D)	
House	1	Jeffords (R)	*At Large*

VIRGINIA

Senate		Warner (R)	
		Trible (R)	
House	1	Bateman (R)	*Newport News*
	2	Pickett (D)	*Norfolk*
	3	Bliley (R)	*Richmond*
	4	Sisisky (D)	*Portsmouth*
	5	Daniel (D)	*Danville*

6	Olin (D)	*Roanoke*
7	Slaughter (R)	*Charlottesville*
8	Parris (R)	*Alexandria*
9	Boucher (D)	*Blacksburg*
10	Wolf (R)	*Arlington*

WASHINGTON

Senate		Evans, D. (R)	
		Adams (D)	
House	1	Miller, J. (R)	*Seattle*
	2	Swift (D)	*Everett*
	3	Bonker (D)	*Olympia*
	4	Morrison, S. (R)	*Yakima*
	5	Foley (D)	*Spokane*
	6	Dicks (D)	*Tacoma*
	7	Lowry (D)	*Seattle*
	8	Chandler (R)	*Seattle*

WEST VIRGINIA

Senate		Byrd (D)	
		Rockefeller (D)	
House	1	Mollohan (D)	*Wheeling*
	2	Staggers (D)	*Morgantown*
	3	Wise (D)	*Charleston*
	4	Rahall (D)	*Huntington*

WISCONSIN

Senate		Proxmire (D)	
		Kasten (R)	
House	1	Aspin (D)	*Kenosha*
	2	Kastenmeier (D)	*Madison*
	3	Gunderson (R)	*Eau Claire*
	4	Kleczka (D)	*Milwaukee*
	5	Moody (D)	*Wauwatosa*
	6	Petri (R)	*Oshkosh*
	7	Obey (D)	*Wausau*
	8	Roth, T. (R)	*Green Bay*
	9	Sensenbrenner (R)	*Sheboygan*

WYOMING

Senate		Wallop (R)	
		Simpson (R)	
House	1	Cheney (R)	*At Large*

GUIDE TO USAGE

The Almanac of American Politics is designed to be self-explanatory. The following guide provides a brief description of each section and a list of sources from which information was derived, both of which serve as a road map to understanding the meaning behind the figures.

The People

Population. All population figures are from the Bureau of the Census, U.S. Department of Commerce, Washington, D.C. 20233 (301) 763-4040. The 1980 Census figures regarding population, education, poverty, ancestry, households and voting age can be found in the following publications: Congressional Districts of the 98th Congress, Congressional Districts of the 99th Congress (redistricted states: CA, HI, LA, ME, MS, MT, NJ, NY, TX, and WA), and Congressional Districts of the 100th Congress (redistricted state: OH), PHC–80. The 1986 population figures are provisional estimates as of July 1, 1986.

Education. The level of higher education is measured by the Census from persons over 25 years of age who have pursued vocational, public, or private forms of college education not necessarily leading to graduation.

Poverty. Poverty level statistics are current as of the 1980 Census. These figures represent the percentage of persons under the poverty level in 1979. Poverty level statistics are updated annually to reflect changes in the Consumer Price Index, but these "poverty thresholds" (published in a Census series called *Current Population Reports*), are arrived at using different analytical methods than those used for the 1980 Census. Comparisons between the two sets of numbers, therefore, have not been made.

Ancestry. For the 1980 Census, the Census Bureau simply asked people what their ancestry was; these figures indicate the percentage that responded that they were members of a particular group and only that group. Those that indicated that their ancestry was of a mixed heritage are not reflected in these figures. The *Almanac* uses the single ancestry statistics because identification with a particular ancestry (Irish, Italian, etc.) is more politically relevant. Only those groups that round up to one percent of the population are listed.

Households. A family consists of a head of household and one or more individuals related by birth, marriage, or adoption to the head of the household. Children are defined as those persons under eighteen years of age that are related to the head of the household by birth, marriage, or adoption. Married couple households are those where the head of the household and spouse are counted as members of the same household. Percentage of housing units rented is determined by relating figures for all owner-occupied housing units to the total amount of housing units. (By Census definition, a housing unit is a "separate living quarter" whether occupied or vacant, if intended for occupancy. Tents, caves, boats, vans, and the like are included only if occupied.) Monthly rent includes the rent agreed to, or contracted for, even if furnishings, utilities, or services are part of the package. Median house value is determined through usual residence costs, including mortgage payments, deeds or trusts, real estate taxes, fire and hazard insurance, utilities and fuels. Condominiums, mobile homes, trailers, and boats are not included.

Voting Age Population. A tally of persons at least eighteen years of age who are eligible to vote, the voting age population is a measurement of the voter potential in a district. Figures are current as of the 1980 Census. The ethnic breakdown relates to the voting age population only, not to the overall population. The concept of race as defined by the Census Bureau reflects self-identification and not clear-cut biological or scientific definitions. An ethnic breakdown is provided if the ethnic population in relation to the voting age population rounds off to one percent or more.

Registered Voters. The voter registration totals were provided by state Secretaries of State and Boards of Elections. Different states have different cut-off dates for registration—the *Almanac* has tried to list those totals closest to Election Day.

Federal Tax Burden. The federal tax burden is determined by the Tax Foundation, Inc., a non-partisan, non-profit organization located at One Thomas Circle, N.W., Suite 500, Washington, DC 20005, 202-822-9050. The Tax Foundation uses federal-fund taxes (individual, corporate, alcohol, tobacco, etc.) and trust-fund taxes as bases to determine a more accurate picture of the tax burden than Treasury Department tax collection data.

Federal Expenditures. For fiscal year 1986, the Census Bureau compiled statistics on federal expenditures amounting to $830 billion. Not included in these figures are interest on federal debts, international payments and foreign aid, and expenditures for selected federal agencies (i.e. CIA and National Security Agency). *Federal Expenditures by State for Fiscal Year 1986* (March 1987) by the Department of Commerce contains an in-depth discussion of the categories composing the total federal expenditure.

Political Lineup. This block includes the names of top state elected officials as well as a breakdown by party of the State Senate and State House of Representatives. The names of U.S. Senators and a party breakdown of the state's Congressional delegation are also provided.

Presidential Vote. The 1980 and 1984 presidential vote is included for each state; the 1984 vote for each congressional district. Presidential vote on the state level was drawn from the Federal Election Commission and from state election returns. Presidential vote by congressional district was derived from state, county, and precinct results. In the following cases, the presidential vote was provided by the Republican National Committee: FL 14-16; IL 2-3, 5-7,9,11,13-22; KY 3-4; MS 1-5; NC 2-3,8-11; OR 1-5; WI 1-9. Discrepancies exist between the state and district figures because of inconsistent reporting methods employed by the counties, the states, and the FEC, and because of different tallying methods used by the RNC and the *Almanac* (the RNC figures do not include candidates other than Reagan and Mondale in the total vote count). Results of the presidential primaries were provided by the states.

Biographies. This section lists when each Governor, Senator, and Representative was elected (and when the Governor's and Senator's seats are up), his or her birth date and birthplace, home, college education (if any), religion, marital status and, if applicable, spouse's name. Also listed is a brief outline of the politician's career, and his or her office addresses and telephone numbers. Committee and subcommittee assignments are provided as well. (Note: On many committees, the chairman and ranking minority member are ex officio members of each subcommittee on which they do not hold a regular assignment.)

Ratings

Rating Groups. The congressional rating statistics of 10 lobby groups are used to provide an idea of a legislator's general ideology and the degree to which the legislator represents different groups' interests. Not just a record of liberal/conservative voting behavior, these ratings come from a range of groups concerned with everything from single issues (defense spending) to those that focus on the political interests of a particular group (e.g., consumers). The order of the groups is such that the more "liberal " ones are on the left and the more "conservative" are on the right. Four groups, NSI, ACLU, LCV and CEI release ratings only once every two years, the duration of one full congressional session. Following is a general description of each organization, its address and telephone number.

ADA   Americans for Democratic Action
815 15th St., N.W., Ste. 711, Washington, DC 20005, 202-638-6447.
  Liberal: Since its founding in 1947, ADA members have pushed for legislation designed to reduce inequality, curtail rising defense spending, prevent encroachments on civil liberties, and promote international human rights. The ADA uses a broad spectrum of issues for its vote analysis.

ACLU   American Civil Liberties Union
122 Maryland Ave., S.E., Washington, DC 20002, 202-544-1681.
  Pro-individual liberties: ACLU seeks to protect individuals from legal, executive, and congressional infringement on basic rights guaranteed by the Bill of Rights. The ACLU ratings are published for every Congress; the 1986 ratings include the years 1985 and 1986.

COPE   Committee on Political Education of the AFL-CIO
815 16th St., N.W., Washington, DC 20006, 202-637-5101.
  Liberal-Labor: As the powerful and well-funded arm of the AFL-CIO, COPE is concerned with the economic interests of the American worker. While COPE covers a broad spectrum of issues, it monitors few votes on foreign policy and defense spending.

CFA   Consumer Federation of America
1424 16th St., N.W., Ste. 604, Washington, DC 20036, 202-387-6121.
  Pro-Consumer: CFA is a group spawned in the mid-sixties as a pro-consumer counterweight to various business-oriented lobbies. Their voting record concentrates on pocketbook consumer issues and health and safety concerns.

LCV   League of Conservation Voters
320 4th St., N.E., Washington, DC 20002, 202-547-7200.
  Environmental: Formed in 1970, LCV lobbies for legislation and executive action favoring the environment and opposing those who despoil it. A steering committee composed of leaders from major national environmental groups determine the key votes for LCV's ratings.

ACU   American Conservative Union
38 Ivy St., S.E., Washington, DC 20003, 202-546-6555.
  Conservative: Since 1971, the ACU ratings have provided a means of gauging the conservatism of Members of Congress. Foreign policy, social, and budgetary issues are their primary concerns.

NTU   National Taxpayers Union
713 Maryland Ave. N.E., Washington, DC 20002, 202-543-1300.
  Anti-governmental spending: Founded in 1969, NTU seeks reductions in taxes, government waste, and government spending. Their vote selection includes every roll-call vote that affects the amount of federal spending.

NSI   National Security Index of the American Security Council
499 S. Capitol St., S.W., Ste. 500, Washington, DC 20003, 202-484-1676.
  Pro-strong defense: Founded in 1965, the Council feels that American security is best preserved by developing and maintaining large weapons systems to achieve strategic military superiority. The NSI rates members on their support of defense and foreign policy issues that affect the NSI strategy of peace through strength.

COC   Chamber of Commerce of the United States
1615 H Street, N.W., Washington, DC 20062, 202-659-6000.
  Pro-business: Founded in 1912 as a voice for organized business, COC represents local, regional, and state chambers of commerce in addition to trade and professional organizations.

CEI   Competitive Enterprise Institute
2039 New Hampshire Ave., N.W., Ste. 206, Washington, DC 20009, 202-547-1010

Pro-free enterprise: Founded in 1984, CEI's purpose is to advance the principles of free enterprise and limited government. CEI focuses primarily on deficit reduction and tax reform, deregulation and privatization, free market approaches to environmental problems, anti-trust reform and international trade.

National Journal Ratings. *National Journal's* rating system establishes a relatively objective method of analyzing congressional voting. Editors of *National Journal* and *The Baron Report* annually canvass the congressional roll-call votes identified by a wide variety of interest groups as key votes for the preceding year. In the first session of the 99th Congress (1985), 50 Senate votes and 47 House votes were chosen on 1) economic, 2) social and 3) foreign policy and defense issues; in the second session (1986), 40 Senate votes and 46 House votes were chosen. The interrelationship of these votes was shown by a statistical procedure called "principal components analysis," which revealed which "yea" votes and which "nay" votes fit a liberal or a conservative pattern. The votes in each of the three subject areas were computer-weighted to reflect the degree they fit the common pattern. All members of Congress who participated in at least half of the votes in each area received ratings; those who missed more that half the votes were not scored (shown as *). Absences and abstentions were not counted.

Members of Congress were then ranked according to relative liberalism and conservatism. Finally, they were assigned percentiles showing their rank relative to others in their chamber. Suppose that a Senator received a rating of 94% Liberal and 4% Conservative on economic issues. His or her voting behavior is 94% more liberal and 4% more conservative than all of the other Senators. Often the numbers add up to less than 99%; the difference is the percentage of senators who are tied at that same rank. In this example, the Senator was tied with 1% of the body (one other Senator). This also means that because of ties, the top score on an index could be less than 99%.

Votes

Key Votes. The Key Votes section is an attempt to illustrate a legislator's stance on important votes where he or she must vote for or against a national issue. The process grossly oversimplifies the legislative system where months of debate, amendment, pressure, persuasion, and compromise go into a final floor vote. However, the voting record remains the best indication of a member's position on specific issues and his or her general ideological persuasions.

Following is a list of key votes used. A member who was absent, voted present, or who was not in office at the time of a particular vote receives a dash. A vote FOR indicates the member was in favor of the issue; a vote AGN indicates disapproval.

Key votes were drawn from Legi-Slate , a computer system that tracks legislation, voting attendance, committee schedules, etc. For information about Legi-Slate or about their vote recording process, please contact: Legi-Slate, 111 Massachusetts Ave., N.W., Ste. 520, Washington, DC 20001, 202-898-2300.

Senate Votes:

1) **Ease Gun Control** Firearm Owners Protection Act (S 49)—July 9, 1985. Bill to ease firearms restrictions contained in 1968 Gun Control Act. Passed 79-15 (D:30–13; R:49-2).

2) **Immig Reform** Immigration Reform and Control Act (S 1200)—September 19, 1985. Bill revising and reforming the Immigration and Nationality Act. Passed 69-30 (D:28–19; R:41-11).

3) **Limit Text Imp** Textile and Apparel Trade Enforcement Act (HR 1562)—November 13, 1985. Bill restricting textile and apparel imports. Passed 60–39 (D:35–11; R:25–28).

4) **Aid Tobac Ind** Omnibus Budget Reconciliation Act, Fiscal 1986 (S 1730)—November 14, 1985. Motion to table amendment allowing the tobacco industry to buy back U.S. tobacco reserves. Passed 66–33 (D:24–22; R:42–11).

5) **Grm-Rdmn Def Red**   Balanced Budget and Emergency Deficit Control Act (HJR 372)—December 11, 1985. Conference report on joint resolution establishing maximum limits on the federal deficit. Adopted 61–31 (D:22–22; R:39–9).

6) **Contra Aid**   Nicaraguan Resistance Assistance (SJR 283)—March 27, 1986. Amendment to provide $100 million in aid and lift restrictions on U.S. involvement with guerilla forces in Nicaragua. Adopted 53–47 (D:11–36; R:42–11).

7) **SDI Funding**   Defense Procurement Improvement Act (S 2638)—August 5, 1986. Motion to table amendment to reduce funding for the strategic defense initiative. Adopted 50–49 (D:9–38; R:41–11).

8) **Limit PAC Contrib**   Campaign Finance/PAC Spending (S 655)—August 11, 1986. Amendment to limit money that political action committees can contribute to congressional candidates. Adopted 69–30 (D:43–3; R:26–27).

9) **Rehnquist Nom**   Nomination of William H. Rehnquist to be Chief Justice of the U.S. Supreme Court. September 17, 1986. Confirmed 65–33 (D:16–31; R:49–2).

10) **Tax Reform**   Tax Reform Act of 1986 (HR 3838)—September 27, 1986. Conference report on bill making extensive changes in the tax system. Adopted 74–23 (D:33–12; R:41–11).

11) **Drug Death Pen**   Omnibus Drug Enforcement, Education and Control Act (HR 5484)—September 27, 1986. Motion to kill amendment authorizing the death penalty for certain drug-related murders. Rejected 25–60 (D:15–25; R:10–35).

12) **S Africa Sanc**   Anti-Apartheid Act (HR 4868)—October 2, 1986. Attempt to override President's veto of bill to impose sanctions on South African government. Passed 78–21 (D:47–0; R:31–21).

House Votes:

1) **Lmt Cln Water Act**   Water Quality Renewal Act (HR 8)—July 23, 1985. Amendment to freeze funding for the Clean Air Act through 1990. Rejected 207–219 (D:68–177; R:139–42).

2) **Rpl Tobac Sub**   Food Security Act (HR 2100)—October 8, 1985. Amendment to repeal the federal tobacco price support program. Rejected 195–230 (D:94–154; R:101–76).

3) **Grm-Rdmn Def Red**   Balanced Budget and Emergency Deficit Control Act (HJR 372)—December 11, 1985. Conference report on joint resolution establishing maximum limits on the federal deficit. Adopted 271–154 (D:118–130; R:153–24).

4) **Ban Polygraph**   Employee Polygraph Protection Act (HR 1524)—March 12, 1986. Bill to prohibit the use of polygraph tests as a condition for employment. Passed 236–173 (D:197–41; R:39–132).

5) **Retain Gun Cont**   Federal Firearms Law Reform Act (HR 4332)—April 9, 1986. Amendment to continue prohibitions on the sale of handguns. Rejected 176–248 (D:136–110; R:40–138).

6) **Contra Aid**   Resolution Concerning Funding for Nicaragua Democratic Resistance (HJR 540)—March 20, 1986. Joint resolution to approve the President's request for $100 million in aid to the Nicaraguan contras and to lift restrictions on CIA and Defense Department involvement. Rejected 210–222 (D:46–206; R:164–16).

7) **Limit Text Imp**   Textile and Apparel Trade Enforcement Act (HR 1562)—August 8, 1986. Attempt to override veto of bill restricting textile and apparel imports. Failed 276–149 (⅔ margin required) (D:205–43; R:71–106).

8) **Limit SDI**   Department of Defense Authorization Act, Fiscal 1987 (HR 4428)—August 12, 1986. Amendment to limit funds for the strategic defense initiative. Adopted 239–176 (D:206–34; R:33–142).

9) **Aid Angola Reb** Intelligence Authorization Act, Fiscal 1987 (HR 4759)—September 17, 1986. Amendment continuing covert aid to UNITA rebels in Angola. Adopted 229–186 (D:63–179; R:166–7).

10) **Tax Reform** Tax Reform Act of 1986 (HR 3838)—September 25, 1986. Conference report on bill making extensive changes in the tax system. Adopted 292–136 (D:176–74; R:116–62).

11) **S Africa Sanc** Anti-Apartheid Act (HR 4868)—September 29, 1986. Attempt to override veto of bill imposing sanctions on South African government. Passed 313–83 (D:232–4; R:81–79).

12) **Immig Reform** Immigration Reform and Control Act (S 1200)—October 15, 1986. Conference report on bill revising and reforming the Immigration and Nationality Act. Adopted 238–172 (D:161–80; R:77–93).

Election Results

Election Results. Listed for each member of the House are results of the 1986 general, runoff, and primary elections, as well as the 1984 general elections (results of any special elections are also listed). Gubernatorial and Senatorial results are presented in a like manner (dependent, of course, on the year in which the Governor or Senator was elected or re-elected). Votes and percentages are included, indicating the margin of victory (due to the process of rounding up and rounding down; some percentages may equal more or less than 100%). Dollar amounts listed to the right of the vote totals are campaign expenditures as reported by the candidate to the Federal Election Commission. Election returns were provided by state Secretaries of State and Boards of Elections.

Campaign Finance

All data are derived from candidates' campaign finance reports and party reports, as well as other official studies available from the Federal Election Commission (FEC), 999 E St., N.W., Washington, D.C., 20463, 202-376-5140 (toll-free, 1-800-424-9530).

Receipts and disbursement activity covers the period beginning January 1, 1985, and ending December 31, 1986, for House members and Senators elected in 1986. Receipt and disbursement activity for Senators elected in 1982 and 1984 are already stated.

Receipts, Expenditures and Cash-on-Hand/Debt. These three figures give a good overview of a winning candidate's campaign finances for the 1986 elections (primary, runoff and general). Funds raised and spent for special elections in the House of Representatives in order to fill vacancies caused by death or resignation are not included. Transfer payments from affiliated committees have not been included to avoid double-counting. The data was taken directly from candidate reports.

Receipts. Receipts constitute all incoming funds as reported by the candidate for the 1986 campaign. Candidate committees, both principal and authorized, report semi-annually in non-election years and six times in election years. They report all incoming funds either in the form of contributions received from individuals, political parties, PACs, and the candidate themselves, as well as loans, or receipts in the form of earnings on previously received funds (interest, dividends) and rebates (such as the sale of a previously purchased campaign vehicle). These receipts are for the 1985-86 election cycle only.

Expenditures. Expenditures constitute all outgoing funds spent by the candidate committees, including loan repayments and contributions by the committee to other candidates or committees. As in the Receipts category, refunds of contributions have been subtracted from the total.

Cash-on-Hand. Unspent funds refer to a campaign's leftover cash-on-hand, less any reported debts, as of December 31, 1986. In many cases, this figure does not represent the difference between the receipts and expenditures listed. An incumbents campaign report often begins with the Cash-on-Hand (or debt if that is the case) remaining from a previous campaign.

Direct Contributions. For greater accuracy the breakdown of campaign contributions have been obtained from a variety of sources at the FEC. The total of all the direct contribution categories does not equal the total receipts because it does not detail all of the candidates receipts (for example, they do not include income from interest, dividends and rebates).

Individual Contributions. This figure is taken directly from candidate reports for year-end 1985 and 1986 and represents the amount received in personal contributions from individual donors.

Party Contributions. The figure for Party Contributions includes only those organizations that have been registered under the Federal Election Campaign Act. Donations can come either in the form of funds or contributions of goods and services to a campaign. Independent party expenditures spent on behalf of a candidate (*i.e.*, not directly contributed to a candidate committee) are not included in the *Almanac's* section on Direct Contributions.

Political Action Committees (PACS). Political Action Committees are groups that are not affiliated directly with a candidate or political party. PAC figures represent donations of money or in-kind goods and services to a congressional campaign. Total PAC contributions listed are only from those committees registered under the Federal Election Campaign Act.

Candidate Contributions. This figure includes direct candidate contributions, both candidate-secured loans and all other types of loans, and transfers from *other* authorized committees .

PACs Breakdown. The following catagories have been chosen by the FEC to identify PAC donations.

CORP   *Corporations.* Includes specific corporate PACs (*e.g.*, AT&T and Boeing).

LABOR   *Labor.* Includes unions and teacher organizations (*e.g.*, United Steelworkers and National Education Association).

IDEO   *Ideological.* Includes a broad range of interests groups (*e.g.*, National Council to Preserve Social Security, PAC's of former Presidents).

T/M/H   *Trade/Membership/Health.* Includes PACs for professional associations in the fields of business, health and trade.

AGR   *Agriculture.* Includes cooperatives such as Mid-American Dairymen and Sunkist Growers.

CWOS   *Corporations Without Capital Stock.* Includes corporations (*i.e.*, New York Life Insurance Co., Handgun Control and The Council for National Defense).

ABBREVIATIONS

AA	Administrative Assistant	Crt.	Court
ACLU	American Civil Liberties Union	CT	Connecticut
ACU	American Conservative Union	Ctr.	Center
ADA	Americans for Democratic Action	CWOS	Corporations Without Capital Stock
Admin.	Administration		
Adv.	Advertising		
Agcy.	Agency	D	Democrat
AGN	Against	DC	District of Columbia
Agric.	Agriculture	DE	Delaware
AI	Alaska Independent Party	Dem.	Democratic
AK	Alaska	Dept.	Department
AL	Alabama	DFL	Democratic–Farmer–Labor Party (Minnesota)
Amer.	American		
AR	Arkansas	Dir.	Director
AS	American Samoa	Dist.	District
Asst.	Assistant	DNC	Democratic National Committee
Atty.	Attorney	DOE	Department of Energy
AZ	Arizona	DOT	Department of Transportation
		Dpty.	Deputy
Bd.	Board	DSOB	Dirksen Senate Office Building
Bus.	Business		
		Econ.	Economic
C	Conservative Party (New York)	ECP	Effective Congress Party
CA	California	EPA	Environmental Protection Agency
CA	Carroll Arms Building	Expend.	Expenditure/s
CAB	Civil Aeronautics Board		
Cand.	Candidate	FCC	Federal Communications Commission
CEI	Competitive Enterprise Institute		
CFA	Consumer Federation of America	FEC	Federal Election Commission
CG	Coast Guard	Fed.	Federal
Chmn.	Chairman	FL	Florida
CHOB	Cannon House Office Building	FTC	Federal Trade Commission
Chwmn.	Chairwoman	FTP	Fair Trade Party
CIA	Central Intelligence Agency		
Cmtee.	Committee	GA	Georgia
Cncl.	Council	GU	Guam
Cnty.	County		
CO	Colorado	H	Capitol Building—House side
COC	Chamber of Commerce of the United States	HHS	Department of Health and Human Services
COH	Cash-On-Hand	HI	Hawaii
Col.	College	Hlth.	Health
Comm.	Commission	HSOB	Hart Senate Office Building
COPE	Committee on Political Education (AFL-CIO)	I, Indep.	Independent
Corp.	Corporation	IA	Iowa

ID	Idaho
Ideo.	Ideological
IL	Illinois
IN	Indiana
Indiv.	Individual
IR	Independent-Republican Party (Minnesota)
IV	Independent Vote
KS	Kansas
KY	Kentucky
L	Liberal Party (New York)
LA	Louisiana
Lbr.	Labor
LCV	League of Conservation Voters
Ldr.	Leader
LHOB	Longworth House Office Building
Libert	Libertarian Party
LU	Liberty Union Party (Vermont)
LWV	League of Women Voters
MA	Massachusetts
MD	Maryland
ME	Maine
MI	Michigan
MN	Minnesota
MO	Missouri
MS	Mississippi
MT	Montana
NC	North Carolina
NCPAC	National Conservative PAC
ND	North Dakota
NE	Nebraska
NH	New Hampshire
NJ	New Jersey
NM	New Mexico
NSC	National Security Council
NSI	National Security Index of the American Security Council
NTU	National Taxpayers Union
NV	Nevada
NY	New York
OH	Ohio
OK	Oklahoma
OMB	Office of Management and Budget
OR	Oregon
ORRTL	Oregon Right-to-Life
PA	Pennsylvania

PAC	Political Action Committee
PBP	People Before Profits
POP	Populist Party
PR	Puerto Rico
ProL	Pro-Life
Prof.	Professional
Pub.	Public
Publ.	Publisher
R, Repub.	Republican
RC	Rainbow Coalition
Rep./s	Representative/s
Repub.	Republican
RHOB	Rayburn House Office Building
RI	Rhode Island
RNC	Republican National Committee
RSOB	Russell Senate Office Building
RTL	Right-to-Life
S	Capitol Building—Senate side
SBA	Small Business Administration
SC	South Carolina
Sch.	School
SD	South Dakota
Secy.	Secretary
Sen.	Senator
Spkr.	Speaker
St.	State
Ste.	Suite
SWP	Socialist Workers Party
T/M/H	Trade/Membership/Health
TN	Tennessee
TX	Texas
U.	University
USAF	United States Air Force
USAFR	United States Air Force Reserve
USMC	United States Marine Corps
USN	United States Navy
UT	Utah
VA	Veterans Administration
VA	Virginia
VI	Virgin Islands
VT	Vermont
WA	Washington
WI	Wisconsin
WL	Workers League
WV	West Virginia
WY	Wyoming

THE NATION

The Political Year: Looking for a Formula. Americans approach the 1988 election year knowing that it will change our politics and, to some extent, our national life—but no one is sure just how. There is more than the usual uncertainty here, more than the usual inability to know who will win each party nomination and which party's nomination will turn out to be worth winning. That uncertainty was one of the things that made 1960 so thrilling that it inspired the highest voter turnout of the 20th century and Theodore White's first *Making of the President*.

But we follow a presidential election not just for the reasons we watch the Super Bowl. We know that the results of elections will make a difference in people's lives. The difficulty with the 1988 election is that we cannot be sure of what those differences will be. In 1959 and 1960 we had a fairly clear idea of what the domestic policies of a Democratic and a Republican administration would be; we knew enough about their foreign policies to know that they would be more similar than different; we knew that both were exceedingly cautious about interfering with Americans' cultural mores, including racial segregation. We knew that Kennedy Democrats would race the economy a little faster than Nixon Republicans and give unions a bit more of an edge in their negotiations with management. Americans in 1960 were unhappy with the facts around them: the economy was in its third year of recession; American power in the world seemed to be slipping behind the Soviet Union's. But voters felt confident that there was a formula for governing. If the out-party candidate was promising the "get the country moving again," and the in-party candidate was saying he'd do that better, both did so knowing that most Americans were pretty sure that we knew how that could be done.

Americans approach the 1988 election in just the opposite frame of mind. They have been reasonably pleased with the facts around them. But they have no confidence that anyone has a formula for governing. Satisfaction with government, politics, and other institutions has been on the rise in the 1980s, even before the economic recovery began in 1983; the dips in confidence in late 1986 and early 1987 have not produced the kind of dissatisfaction seen in the 1970s. Yet Americans feel distinctly uneasy about the future, not because they are sure it will be dreadful, but because they're not quite certain what it will be like.

This has not always been so. On the economy, the Americans of 1960 knew that you voted for Democrats to provide a Keynesian fiscal stimulus to combat recession and you called in Republicans for a little fiscal austerity to stop inflation. Big labor was the countervailing power to big business; the wage level was set in the steel or auto negotiations and ratified by Congress ratcheting up the minimum wage. In effect, the two parties offered a slightly different mix of the same formula. For 1988 no one has a macroeconomic theory that explains what has happened to our economy over the last dozen years—much less one that anyone is comfortable relying on to prescribe policy for the future. With low inflation, huge job growth, and negligible unemployment of heads of household, the American economy in early 1987 could be labelled a success. With enormous federal budget deficits, widening trade deficits, and mounting personal and corporate debt, it could be depicted as tottering on the edge of failure. But no one was sure how to sustain the successes or avert what some feel is impending doom.

On foreign policy, the formula in 1960 was for the United States to use nuclear power to deter an attack on Western Europe and to use conventional forces where necessary to combat Communist aggression. But Americans were threatened by what looked menacingly like Soviet technical superiority (Sputnik and the bogus missile gap) and more rapid economic growth (Khrushchev's promise, then widely believed, that Russia would equal America's standard of living by 1970). Today, Americans find the facts more encouraging: the United States no longer seems, as it did in 1979, at bay in the Middle East, Latin America, East Asia, and Western Europe. But a formula for stability, not to speak of steady advance, is not apparent.

On race, the Americans of 1960 were prepared to take small steps to assure blacks the right to vote, but otherwise were willing to let events take their course: the North was still unwilling to interfere with institutionalized segregation in the South. Most voters were not pleased with the facts—they disliked segregation and the Freedom Riders, southern sheriffs and lunch counter sit-ins—but they were satisfied with the formula being applied. In the years since Americans have made great strides in racial fairness, and have no desire to retreat to a status quo that was for most quite bearable in 1960. But they are dissatisfied with the facts, with the continued existence of forms of racial preference, and with the persistence of a violent and parasitic racial underclass.

On cultural issues, the formula of the Americans of conformist 1960 was to have no formula at all: government should not challenge or even comment upon cultural behavior, except to reinforce the conventional mores that were taken for granted. Within a decade beginning in the late 1960s, government acted to legalize, openly or covertly, abortion, marijuana, pornography, prostitution, teenage drinking, and homosexuality. Within a decade beginning in the late 1970s, individuals began to exercise more restraint on themselves and on others; visible forms include a levelling off of abortion and divorce rates, lower alcohol and drug use, stricter drunk driving laws, enforcement of child support obligations, and diminished extramarital sex if only in response to AIDS. Americans are adjusting the facts to their satisfaction. But they lack a formula for government's rule in setting rules and limiting or allowing choices.

Satisfaction, sometimes guarded satisfaction, with the facts; anxiety about the absence of formulas for governing: this is the mood in which Americans approach 1988. They have been pleased with the trends and leadership they have had in the 1980s, but they understand they will not be precisely replicated in the 1990s, and they do not want them to be replicated precisely anyway; they can easily think of an improvement here or a different solution there. Satisfied with Ronald Reagan's leadership for most of his two terms, they were less happy with him after the Iran-contra scandal broke; their unease may be limited by the knowledge that he soon will be out of office in any case, and a replacement can be chosen who shows a greater attention to detail and less penchant for off-the-wall mistakes like arming Khomeini's Iran.

The good results of the 1980s have come mostly from a divided government, and voters understand instinctively not only that it will be difficult to replace Ronald Reagan with a President who has all his positive qualities plus some that he lacks, but also that it will be hard to strike the same balance between the Reagan Administration, the Howard Baker-Bob Dole Senate, and the Tip O'Neill House that existed for six of the first seven years of the 1980s. What is striking on looking back is that this divided government produced solutions for problems that politicians were supposed to be unable to solve. Inflation was reduced from nearly 20% to almost zero. The giddy and constant rise in domestic government spending, a rise that seemed to be sucking growth out of the private economy, was slowed. Social Security benefits were cut, after the Democrats won the 1982 elections by promising never to cut them, by raising the retirement age. The gasoline tax was raised. Energy prices were decontrolled—and fell. Congress passed tax reform, lowering rates and eliminating most tax preferences. Congress even managed to increase its own pay. Not all problems were addressed. Budget deficits remained high as the White House was occupied by the only President America has ever had or ever will have who paid 91% income tax rates. But in early 1987 Congress and the Administration, though distracted by the Iran-contra affair, were at least thinking about devising some sort of workfare to replace the welfare system. And it was even possible that they would revise the system of financing congressional elections.

This is not to say that Americans are suddenly bursting with pride about their politicians. But they are quite proud about their country, and they are bursting with pride about many of their states and local communities, and they have been giving higher job ratings to their politicians and their government than they have since the years of Vietnam and Watergate. Ronald Reagan's job rating since the trough of recession in 1982 has been as high as any President's, and bobbed back upward to levels well above those of other Presidents similarly beleaguered. Tip

O'Neill's job rating, after the longest consecutive service as speaker of the House in American history, was higher even than the President's.

In 1976 and 1980 Americans sought Presidents who lacked the defects of those who preceded: ordinary citizens rather than Washington insiders, honest ingenues rather than wily political manueverers. Hence the spectacle, which surely people in the future will think odd, of the richest and most powerful country in the world electing as its President a peanut farmer and a movie actor. In 1984 Americans, for the first time in 20 years, enthusiastically and ungrudgingly reelected their President, and looked ahead for a successor who shared his strengths rather than one who lacked his weaknesses. In 1986 they cast a vote for governing, reelecting the third highest number of House members in American history, ousting the Republicans from control of the Senate but casting almost precisely the same number of votes for each candidate of both parties as they had when the same seats were up six years before. They also installed in governor's mansions leaders who had proven in state capitals and city halls their competence at governing. In an America full of local patriotisms and bubbling optimism, Americans in early November 1986 once again had confidence in their government (an ironic result of the Reagan governmental minimalism) and their political leaders. That confidence was at least somewhat shaken by revelations later that month about the arms deal with Iran and the diversion of the money to the Nicaraguan contras. By pointing up Reagan's inattention to detail and penchant for off-the-wall ideas, the Iran-contra affair prompted voters to add to their list of qualifications greater command of detail and more conventional thinking on issues. In much the same way the Americans of 1960 wanted a President who had all of Dwight D. Eisenhower's experience, gravity, and sense of command, plus the liveliness and taste for adventure he plainly lacked— even though they were displeased with the results of the shooting down of the U-2 and the collapse of the Paris summit.

The problem voters face for 1988 is that they must choose from a field of candidates who are, collectively and individually, less well known to the public than any field of candidates at least since 1976 and quite possibly long before that. George Bush, to be sure, is a familiar figure as Vice President, and is said to be a useful and involved adviser to the President, as was Walter Mondale before him. But because Bush has loyally kept to himself his own views and contributions, voters do not see him actively governing. Robert Dole, who went up in the polls as he attained visibility as Senate Majority Leader, now leads the minority instead, probably less conspicuously. Jack Kemp is a member of the heavily outnumbered minority party in a House that, resigning his leadership position, will be mostly campaigning, not governing. Howard Baker, as he seemed about to enter the race, was grabbed up by the President to replace Donald Regan as White House Chief of Staff; he got the opportunity to manage the White House for two years in return for giving up a slender chance to occupy it himself for four or eight. Totally out of office is Pete du Pont, whose record as governor is familiar to only 600,000 of the 242 million Americans he seeks to lead.

The Democrats have similar problems. Joseph Biden and Richard Gephardt have about 600,000 constituents and fairly important perches on Capitol Hill; Michael Dukakis is busy governing in the State House in Boston. Bruce Babbitt used to be governor of a state with 3 million people that is at least 1,000 miles from where two-thirds of Americans live; Paul Simon and Albert Gore, Jr., are junior Senators; while Jesse Jackson has never held public office.

Moreover, voters will have little time in which to reach informed judgments about these candidates. Michigan Republican precinct delegates, elected in August 1986, meet in county conventions in mid-January, 1988, to select delegates to the state convention which, two weeks later, will choose national convention delegates. On Monday night, February 8, perhaps 100,000 Democrats and 100,000 Republicans will troop to firehalls and living rooms across Iowa for their precinct caucuses. Eight days later, February 16, perhaps 250,000 New Hampshire voters, will vote in what is still the nation's first primary. A week later, under a schedule new for 1988, comes the South Dakota primary. Republican caucuses in six small states west of the Mississippi are expected to be scheduled some time in February. Then on Tuesday, March 1, Vermont's non-binding Democratic primary; on Saturday, March 5, Wyoming's Democratic caucuses and South Carolina's Republican primary. Then Super Tuesday, March 8: primaries in 14 more or less southern states (as far north as Maryland, Kentucky, Missouri, and Oklahoma) plus the South Carolina Democratic caucuses; the Massachusetts and Rhode Island primaries plus Democratic caucuses in Alaska, Hawaii, and Nevada, and caucuses in both parties in Washington. Those are followed by weekend contests in Delaware and North Dakota, while scheduled for Tuesday, March 15, are the Illinois and Ohio primaries and Minnesota caucuses—a kind of Great Lakes contest.

It is entirely possible that half the delegates will be chosen by then, certain that both parties' fields will be seriously winnowed down, and likely—but, tantalizingly, not certain—that both nominations will be determined within five weeks of the Iowa caucuses. Yet something on the

1988 REPUBLICAN PRIMARY AND CAUCUS SCHEDULE
Schedule is tentative and subject to change.
States holding primaries are in roman type, caucuses in italics.

January 27	Wednesday	*Hawaii*
29	Friday	*Michigan*
February 8	*Monday*	*Iowa*
16	Tuesday	New Hampshire
23	Tuesday	South Dakota
28	Sunday	*Maine*
March 1	Tuesday	Vermont
5	Saturday	*South Carolina, Wyoming*
8	Super Tuesday	Alabama, Alaska, Arkansas, Florida, Georgia, Kentucky, Louisiana, Maryland, Massachusetts, Mississippi, Missouri, North Carolina, Oklahoma, Rhode Island, Tennessee, Texas, Virginia, *Washington*
15	Tuesday	Illinois, *Minnesota*, Ohio
20	Sunday	*Puerto Rico*
29	Tuesday	Connecticut
April 4	Monday	*Colorado*
5	Tuesday	New York, Wisconsin
15	Friday	*Nevada*
25	Monday	*Utah*
26	Tuesday	Pennsylvania
May 3	Tuesday	Washington, D.C., Indiana
10	Tuesday	Nebraska, West Virginia
17	Tuesday	Oregon
24	Tuesday	Idaho
June 7	Tuesday	California, Montana, New Jersey, New Mexico
14	Tuesday	North Dakota

order of 15 million of the 175 million adult Americans will have taken part by this time, and something like 25 million by the time the primaries end in June.

The tables on these two pages show the *tentative* dates for primaries and caucuses—tentative because they can be changed by legislatures and parties, and in some cases may very well be. However, by June 1987 most of the candidates were proceeding on the assumption that the schedule was pretty well set.

This, many think, is a wacky way to choose the two candidates one of whom will occupy the most important position in the most important government in the world. Some will call for a return to the day when political bosses chose the nominees. But there are no political bosses whose gravity is tested by the responsibility of managing government any more, since party organizations are mostly moribund or technician-led, and officeholders mostly run on their own;

1988 DEMOCRATIC PRIMARY AND CAUCUS SCHEDULE

Schedule is tentative and subject to change.
States holding primaries are in roman type, caucuses in italics.

February	8	Monday	*Iowa*
	16	Tuesday	New Hampshire
	23	Tuesday	South Dakota
	28	Sunday	*Maine*
March	1	Tuesday	Vermont
	5	Saturday	*Wyoming*
	8	Super Tuesday	Alabama, Alaska, Arkansas, Florida, Georgia, *Hawaii*, *Idaho*, Kentucky, Louisiana, Maryland, Massachusetts, Mississippi, Missouri, *Nevada*, North Carolina, Oklahoma, Rhode Island, Tennessee, Texas, Virginia, *Washington*
	11	Friday	*Delaware*
	12	Saturday	*South Carolina*
	14	Monday	*North Dakota*
	15	Tuesday	Illinois, *Minnesota*, Ohio
	19	Saturday	*Kansas*
	20	Sunday	*Puerto Rico*
	26	Saturday	*Michigan*
	29	Tuesday	Connecticut
April	2	Saturday	*Virgin Islands*
	4	Monday	*Colorado*
	5	Tuesday	New York, Wisconsin
	18	Monday	*Utah*
	26	Tuesday	Pennsylvania
May	3	Tuesday	Washington, D.C., Indiana
	10	Tuesday	Nebraska, West Virginia
	17	Tuesday	Oregon
June	7	Tuesday	California, Montana, New Jersey, New Mexico

you can't have responsible party leaders unless ordinary citizens will vote straight tickets and thus make local politicians accountable for their nominees for high office. Others will call for a single national primary; the bunching of southern and other primaries early in the season produces a set of regional primaries. But the current system, as revised mainly by the southern regional primary movement in 1985 and 1986, accomplishes something close to this result.

This much can be said for the system as it seems likely to work. The campaign subjects the candidates to an intense if brief examination of their capacity and character: people get a chance to see them operate under pressure. And it gives the parties, if they are lucky, nominees chosen early, long before the conventions, so that they have time to operate as the head of the shadow cabinet does in a parliamentary system. That gives the voters more time to test their mettle and to try to get a sense of what their formula will be, the lessons they draw from the facts they see around them, and the way they will try to apply those lessons in the future.

Politics: The Search for Community. The rhetoric of political campaigning usually focuses on the negative—on problems that need solving, conditions that cannot be tolerated, crises that threaten to undermine our security. Yet a formula for governing must also appreciate what is right, the more so when the voters whose support candidates seek have showed appreciation for the way the system has been working.

Start with the first thing that future historians will probably say about our time, but which is seldom noted today: we are a nation at peace. And not only—though this is the most important reason—because we are not at war, but because we are not likely to be involved in a major war any time soon. We have a large defense establishment, but no draft, and little contact between career military and civilians; since 1940 we have never been less militarized.

We are also a nation at peace, to an extent greater than we realize, with ourselves. Beneath the turmoil and clash of everyday American politics, beneath the sometimes apocalyptic rhetoric, we have reached something like a consensus about basic values and policies, and something close to a consensus on the differences we are willing to tolerate in each other. The fashionable talk of a politics of alienation, angst, and anomie has faded, as the 1984 and 1986 elections revealed Americans to themselves as reasonably pleased with the nation they have come to be.

We are also a nation that is rich, even while so much of the political debate consists of complaints about the economy. But the fact is that the American economy, which seemed stalled in the 1970s, has grown in the 1980s. By 1986, an economy that floundered in two recessions in 1978–82 was producing a gross national product 18% above the 1978 level, while population was up 8% over the same period. And inflation, which once seemed headed over 20%, was down to negligible levels. The American economy generated 11 million more jobs over that period, and fully 61% of Americans over 15 were in the work force—higher than ever before. Since the end of the supposedly prosperous 1960s, GNP was up in real terms more than 50%, GNP per capita was up 35%, and income per head was up 39%. True, family income did not rise as fast—partly because individuals were using their higher incomes to create new household units: older people and students choosing more often to live alone, married people choosing more often to get divorced. People were using affluence to buy cultural variety.

War fosters big government and cultural unity. Peace and prosperity foster less government and cultural variety. The formula that Americans developed by 1960 was derived from their success in dealing with the economic collapse of the 1930s and the total war of the 1940s. That formula was predictably less successful in dealing with the economic boom since the early 1960s and the era of peace since the early 1970s. The old formula took cultural unity for granted: it was crafted for a nation of conformists. There was no need to foster a communitarian spirit; the old formula was required to limit the extent to which central government and local institutions could enforce conformity. The new formula, toward which Americans are groping in the late 1980s, has a different requirement. It can afford to—must, since it can't be changed by fiat—accept cultural variety as a given. What it needs to do is to foster the communitarian spirit that is conspicuously lacking in American politics.

This communitarian spirit has been flagging in both political parties. The Democrats' historic impulse to redistribute income and wealth has little vitality. Walter Mondale in 1984 found that voters resisted a tax increase, even while acknowledging a deficit they know is harmful. Other Democrats now are restrained by that deficit from even suggesting programs which will require larger outlays. None of the likely candidates for 1988, Jesse Jackson aside, believes as strongly in government spending and economic redistribution as Mondale. Certainly there are no proposals for national health insurance, no calls for a guaranteed annual income, no demand for the federal government to guarantee every American a job—the stated purpose of the Humphrey-Hawkins bill which every Democratic candidate in 1976 was required to endorse. Meanwhile, leading Democrats like Bill Bradley and Dan Rostenkowski in fashioning the tax reform passed in 1986 recognized that steeply progressive tax rates were no longer sustainable during an extended period of peace in a free society. Out in the Farm Belt in 1986 you could hear on the campaign trail echoes of the 1890s Populist line that the big interests were squeezing the little guy and had to be contained by policies like Tom Harkin's plan for government controls on grain production. But in an economy where big units have been ailing and small businesses have been flowering and account for most of the nation's economic growth, the argument against corporate giants rings hollow; and, anyway, farm crop and land prices seemed headed upward in early 1987. The Democratic Leadership Council in 1985 and 1986 struck a chord when it called for a politics that encouraged economic production rather than distribution, and most of the Democratic candidates in 1987 were talking about encouraging the production of wealth, not directing the distribution of it.

For the Republicans, the communitarian impulse in the 1980s has taken the form of using government to strengthen personal morality. This has not been without its successes: drug and alcohol use have dropped and errant fathers are now forced more often to pony up child support. But mostly the hopes of the moralizers have been disappointed. Abortion is not likely to be outlawed in the United States, even if the Supreme Court returns the issue to state legislatures; 14 legislatures in states with 41% of the nation's population had already liberalized their abortion laws when the Supreme Court legalized abortion nationally in 1973. Extramarital sex may be less common than it was, but not on the television and movie screens: showbiz remains the domain of celebrators of liberation from traditional mores. School children may some day be dragooned into prayer sessions, but these are not likely to produce the kind of piety their advocates hope for; in the meantime, they see on TV in the afternoon or in the family hour at night expletives and innuendo which used to get Jack Paar kicked off the Tonight show. In short, in a nation where peace and affluence allow cultural variety, attempts to impose cultural uniformity are bound to fail. Ronald Reagan, America's first divorced President, gave vivid rhetorical support to the moral platform of the New Right. But none of the likely candidates for 1988, Pat Robertson aside, seems to have as strong a personal commitment to these positions.

Government: Groping Toward Communitarian Ideas. As 1987 began, the cry heard everywhere on the political spectrum was "competitiveness." Alarmed by the trade deficit, fearful of being stampeded into destructive protectionism, worried that the long economic recovery could not be sustained, politicians of both parties were trying to come up with lists of proposals that would be seen as making America more competitive in world markets. Implicit was a sense that the Reagan policy of encouraging production through purely individual incentives was not enough to produce continuing and widespread economic growth, any more than the Democrats' policy of redistributing income through government action. If wages had been propped up too high and the quality of workmanship allowed to deteriorate too much in the 1970s to make American products competitive in a world market, then it was still not obvious that at least some of the most visible characteristics of the Reagan market-driven economy were repairing the damage. In an environment in which the nation's biggest arbitrageur, Ivan Boesky, was a kind of folk hero until his downfall in November 1986; where leveraged buyouts, followed by going public, gave corporate executives the windfalls that occupants of rent-controlled apartments get when they go condominium; where the best-paid graduates were first lawyers and then investment bankers, the paradigmatic "paper entrepreneur." In such an environment no one feels confident that the pursuit of short-term market signals by individuals produces long-term growth and prosperity for the nation.

The more so, when you consider that the model—and the threat—Americans are contemplating is the success of Japan and East Asia: success that depends heavily on unified national efforts to achieve common goals. By contrast, the models which caught Americans' eyes around 1960 came from Europe and even Soviet Russia. American liberals cast longing eyes on Western Europe's generous welfare states and argued that the United States was backward for not having them. Liberals and conservatives alike worried that Europe was growing more rapidly than the United States (it was still making up ground lost in World War II) and, taking Soviet statistics at face value, argued that Russia was growing faster too. At that point Japan and East Asia did not present alternative models. Japan, where leftist riots prevented President Eisenhower from visiting in 1960, seemed to be going the way of Western Europe. The other countries of the East Asia rim seemed impoverished and, bereft of resources, without hope of ever feeding their populations. Americans looked across the Atlantic, and decided that they needed more state involvement in the economy, more social welfare protections, more pumping money into the hands of middle- and lower-income citizens to stimulate consumer demand. The European, Keynesian, social democratic model seemed the wave of the future.

Quite the opposite today. Western Europe's economies have quit growing, have not generated new jobs in a decade, and seem clearly overburdened with social obligations. The Soviet model is a shambles, dependent on American grain and credit, with even its public sector so decrepit that life expectancy has been growing shorter—in a system whose proudest boast once was that at least it provided universal medical care. As the bestseller lists show, Americans are fascinated with the Japanese success, and particularly the tendency of various groups and social strata of Japanese to work together: government planning with business, labor cooperating with management. Americans are looking across the Pacific, and deciding that they need somewhat less state involvement in the economy, no more social welfare protections, greater savings and investment, and more cooperation and fewer adversary relationships between segments of society. The East Asian, cooperative, capitalistic model seems to be the wave of the future.

What is interesting about the response of politicians to the "competitiveness" idea is that no real dispute exists between the parties. All the candidates are talking about similar goals: beefing up America, opening up markets in Japan and East Asia, driving down the federal and trade deficits. Politics no longer seemed to be a matter of one party advocating one policy and the other another. Rather, the parties are competing to see which one can become most closely identified with the same set of ideas. Much the same thing happened on tax reform. It was first advanced by Democrats Bill Bradley and Richard Gephardt, then by Republican Jack Kemp. The Reagan Administration picked it up, gingerly, lest Walter Mondale steal a march by endorsing it; when he didn't, they continued. In the end neither party got the advantage, because both were divided. Reagan was for it, but the House Republicans nearly ditched it; Bradley and Dan Rostenkowski played leading roles in getting it enacted, but so did Bob Packwood, while none of the best-known presidential Democrats—Mondale, Gary Hart, Jesse Jackson, Mario Cuomo—showed much interest in the issue.

If competitiveness is one area where a desire for communitarian action has surfaced, another possible area may be where the communitarian economic and moral impulses intersect. This is workfare: moving welfare mothers toward jobs by providing economic aid (child care, medical insurance) and moral guidance (work habits, abstinence from drugs and extramarital sex). The idea, best articulated by Lawrence Mead—that there are reciprocal obligations here, society's and the welfare recipient's—has struck a chord with Republicans and Democrats alike. Congress may have a hard time passing a workfare law. But presidential candidates will be talking the issue up and officeholders in the state will continue experimenting with it.

Then there is education. The insistence on minimum standards was pioneered in the South, where educational levels have long been low and politicians and voters realized they must upgrade their labor forces if they want continuing economic growth; the same lesson is now being applied in the North, where for some years the idea gained ground that the purpose of education was to liberate a child's instincts to allow him untrammelled self-expression. Now Americans may be reaching consensus on other educational issues. Advocates of making English the national language are coming to understand that that implies an obligation to teach English to those who speak other languages; advocates of welcoming immigrants to the United States have come to understand that they must be schooled in the nation's language and culture if they are to have a fair chance to rise. Sources as antagonistic as William Bennett's Department of Education and Norman Lear's People For the American Way are groping toward agreement that children should be taught to understand respectfully America's traditions of religious expression and tolerance of diversity.

Americans discontented with policies that aid and therefore seem to encourage sociopathic and deviant conduct—multiple teenage pregnancies, heavy drug use, rampant crime—are beginning to rediscover the American tradition of government aiding and therefore encouraging and honoring those who are upwardly mobile. This tradition is embodied in the fabulously successful post-World War II policies of the G.I. Bill of Rights, FHA home mortgage guarantees, and the family allowances created by steeply progressive income tax rates combined with generous exemptions for dependents: three policies which helped change the grade-school-educated, renter, economically stagnant America of the 1930s into the college-educated, homeowner, economically dynamic America of the 1960s. These specific policies, of course, cannot be precisely replicated in today's different nation. But they suggest the direction a communitarian-minded politics might go.

As we approach 1988, a communitarian politics still goes against the grain in the atomistic, culturally various nation created by a generation or more of peace and prosperity. Americans are not ready to be called upon to commit themselves to some form of national service, nor will you hear very much talk about a military draft. The national pride Ronald Reagan did so much to foster in the 1980s, symbolized by the Olympic ceremonies of 1984 and the Statue of Liberty commemoration of 1986, has this weakness: it asks too little from the nation's citizens. True, it is not the ordinary habit of political candidates to ask things anyway; they usually promise. But there are times—1960 was one of them—when satisfaction with the system places the premium not just on the candidate who promises but even more on the one who inspires. Americans' satisfaction with the facts they see around them gives the politicians of 1988 an opportunity— quite possibly gives them the incentive—to come up with a formula for governing that goes beyond addressing individual grievances and asserts a communitarian purpose. Who will do it?

THE REGIONS

An Age of Hustle. The 1980s have been for Americans an age of hustle. In the first 30 years after World War II, they had grown accustomed to the verities of lifetime employment, cheap energy, and regulated transportation. In their economic life, they lived in a "society of segments," in historian Robert Wiebe's words, "whose arrangements were fundamentally social rather than economic," placing "compartmental autonomy and insular peace above economic rationality— yet remain[ing] prosperous [as] a luxury of America's unprecedented wealth." Oil prices were propped by the Texas Railroad Commission and import quotas, Pittsburgh steel plants were favored by the Pittsburgh basing point system, rates were set by mutual agreement for railroads and airlines and truckers, the Big Three auto companies, secure against competition foreign and domestic, were the beneficiaries of the interstate highway program.

The vision of Adolf Berle and Gardiner Means, popularized by John Kenneth Galbraith and Arthur Schlesinger, Jr., politicized by Franklin D. Roosevelt and the Wagner labor act, became reality: an economy of big units, managed by professionals free from control by stockholders, with countervailing power in the hands of big government and big labor. All these things changed by the late 1970s. Stunning increases in oil and fuel prices, the collapse of the auto and steel industries, then the dizzying fall in oil prices, the decaying of big business units and the sudden rise of thousands of small ones, the decline of the big labor unions, deregulation of airlines and railroads and trucking—all these developments got Americans hustling, to and then from the Oil Patch, closer to and then farther away from central city cores, out of and then into small towns.

The good news is that all this hustling resulted in greater economic production. The bad news is that many ordinary people were uprooted from comfortable niches. The good news is that inefficiency and incompetence were again being penalized after years of tolerance. The bad news is that sharp dealing, self-serving paper entrepreneurship, out-and-out fraud—hustling in the pejorative sense of the word—were too often rewarded.

The oscillations of the economy—oil price hikes, then falls; auto sales down, then back up— have sent Americans scurrying from one part of the country to the other, although the effect shouldn't be overestimated: there was actually much more migration in the 1950s, just after war had loosened so many Americans from their moorings and unexpected economic growth provided opportunity in unexpected quarters, than there has been in the 1980s. Still, it's worth tracking the movements by dividing the country into eight sections, not along the standard historical lines, but according to economic regions important in the 1980s. A certain imprecision is inevitable in using state lines; the Philadelphia area should be in the North Atlantic region, for example, and most of Upstate New York with the Great Lakes. Still the boundaries indicated in the adjoining map can be illuminating.

The economic, migrational, and cultural flux of recent years has changed the politics of each of the eight regions spotlighted here. In looking ahead through the fog of uncertainty to the 1988 election, a review of each of the regions might provide some guideposts. The responses of each region to national politics has, on the surface, been more similar than different: Ronald Reagan carried all eight of them against both Jimmy Carter and Walter Mondale, and all eight gave most of their votes to Democrats in House races in 1982, 1984, and 1986, with the single exception of the Southwest in 1984. There has been a consensus for both the Reagan presidency and the Democratic House.

Yet each has developed a distinctive politics, with key ramifications for 1988. Each region seems to be moving toward a consensus politics, symbolized in each by a national figure who is not running for president; and so in looking at the presidential race, and in trying to peer farther

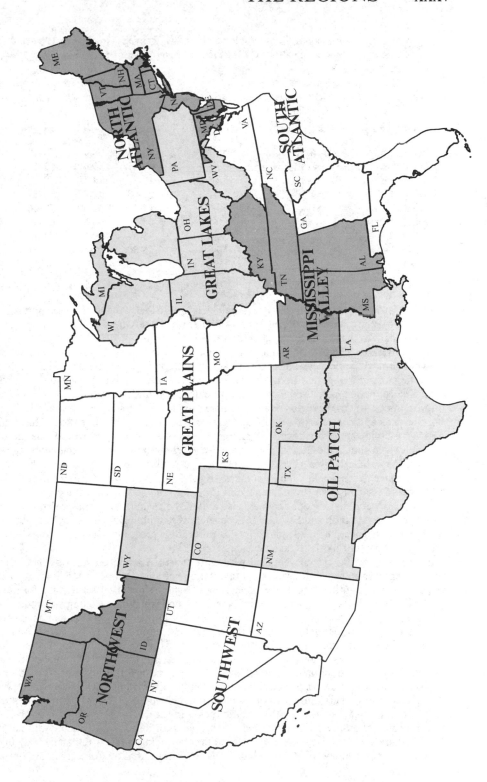

Percentages for Reagan-Carter-Anderson in 1980, Reagan-Mondale in 1984 and for
Democratic and Republican candidates for House of Representatives 1980, 1982, 1984, 1986.

Region	Reagan-Carter Anderson 1980	Reagan-Mondale 1984	House of Representatives Democratic-Republican			
			1980	1982	1984	1986
UNITED STATES	51-41-7%	59-41%	50-48%	55-43%	52-47%	53-47%
North Atlantic	46-42-10	55-44	52-46	58-41	54-45	52-46
Great Lakes	48-40-6	57-42	48-51	55-44	52-48	52-48
Great Plains	52-39-7	58-42	49-51	52-48	50-49	53-47
Northwest	52-36-10	58-41	51-48	52-47	53-47	55-45
South Atlantic	51-44-4	63-37	54-45	57-42	53-46	56-44
Mississippi Valley	49-48-4	60-39	54-43	60-39	62-37	58-42
Oil Patch	55-39-4	64-36	55-44	60-38	53-46	51-49
Southwest	54-34-8	59-39	46-50	50-47	47-51	51-49

ahead toward the politics of the 1990s, it may be useful to look at each of these eight politicians, and see how they have developed consensus politics out of the economic, migrational, and cultural changes that have occurred around them.

North Atlantic. The pattern seen in New England in the late 1970s has now spread down the whole North Atlantic coast: gentrification. Growth in high-income and high tech jobs is attracting talented migrants from outside the region, while many natives of the area with less skills and education have been moving out: the low-income outmigration is larger numerically, but the process leaves the region richer and more productive. Population grew only 1.6% in 1980-84, but per capita incomes rose 13% and are now the highest in the nation. This is also the nation's leading singles area, with a high percentage of working women; and it is these young graduates who stay in the Boston or New York or Washington areas who are reaping the highest rewards more than the area's high and by now long-established populations of blacks and Puerto Ricans. Sharp drops in state and local taxes, triggered by New York City's near-bankruptcy in 1975 and Massachusetts's Proposition 2½ in 1980, have helped to spark the growth that the old higher taxes were choking off, and have also muted the region's longtime preference, rooted in the days when Al Smith and Franklin D. Roosevelt were building a pioneer welfare state in New York, for high government spending. In this prosperous area, Democratic House percentages have gone down during the Reagan era.

In the early 1970s, the conventional wisdom in North Atlantic politics was that the task of government was to use high progressive taxes and generous domestic spending to redistribute the income and wealth, which has been clearly visible here since the 19th century, for the benefit of those left at the bottom of the ladder. Now the emphasis is on encouraging production and, while holding taxes down, trying to restore the level of public services that help productivity—maintaining the infrastructure, improving higher education—while keeping spending under control. Important figures here include Governors Hugh Carey, Mario Cuomo, Michael Dukakis, and Thomas Kean, and Mayor Edward Koch. But the North Atlantic politician with the biggest impact so far on national policy has been Senator Bill Bradley of New Jersey. As in his basketball career, he has picked his shots carefully. His first initiative in the Senate was to fill America's strategic petroleum reserve—a move that helped lower the energy costs that had such a devastating impact on the North Atlantic region in the 1970s. His second initiative was tax reform: eliminating preferences that helped the well-positioned (who typically did not include North Atlantic entrepreneurs and innovators) and flattening rates, with particularly big drops for the affluent and the poor (both numerous in North Atlantic America). Bradley's latest initiative is on the debt crisis, to restore order to international banking and trade. He surprised many by quietly supporting aid to the Nicaraguan contras, but a dovish foreign policy may no longer be required in the North Atlantic: in Montgomery County, Maryland's Michael Barnes, the leader of opposition to Reagan Central America policy as a House subcommittee chairman, was replaced when he ran for the Senate by a Republican who made a point of supporting contra aid.

It's not clear whether Bradley's New Jersey constituents appreciate every subtlety of his policy strategies, any more than most basketball fans understood all the subtleties of his play. But everybody knows the score. Reelected with 64% in 1984, 25% ahead of Walter Mondale, with no likelihood of serious competition in the future, Bradley has become one of America's consensus politicians, achieving success because he staked out and laid claim to a policy and an approach that Americans were prepared to accept.

Great Lakes. In the early 1980s, as auto and steel workers came to the end of their 65 weeks of unemployment benefits, outmigration from the auto-and-steel Great Lakes region became a rush. Population actually declined in several of the biggest American states. The auto and steel labor forces were suffering, inadvertently, from what the coal labor force suffered from deliberately 20 years before: decisions to force higher wages even if that meant a vastly reduced number of jobs. But the population drop ended in 1983 and a rise began then—a pattern accentuated in the most hard-hit Great Lakes state, Michigan, which had a bigger percentage drop and a bigger rise than its neighbors. The damage to particular communities—to a Flint, Michigan, or a Youngstown, Ohio—was vast: housing values collapsed, civic institutions were dismantled, young residents with initiative and ambition left and those left behind were dispirited. But the unexpected disaster also forced Great Lakes residents to get out of bad habits and to explore new possibilities, as MIT economist David Birch has documented. It took Lowell, Massachusetts, 50 years to replace its textile mills with a high tech boom and Scranton, Pennsylvania, 40 years to replace anthracite mining jobs with low-wage apparel factory work.

The Great Lakes region seems to be moving faster. These states lost hundreds of thousands of jobs in Big Three auto factories and in steel mills during the last decade. But the total number of jobs in 1980–84 was up, and per capita incomes were up a less-than-disastrous 6%—a rise made possible by the fact that many people went to Texas or California or back home to the South. The Great Lakes region seems to have learned the lesson that it must use the ingenuity and enterprise of the old-fashioned tinkerers—Thomas Edison and Henry Ford, Charles Kettering and Walter Chrysler—who made the Great Lakes the world center of manufacturing. It seems to realize that its strength lies not in highly-paid low-skill labor, but in high-skill labor that produces things that earn good pay. The work force is descended in large part from migrants who came from the same parts of Germany and Eastern Europe. There are trouble spots still, in the central cities of Detroit and Chicago and Cleveland, where underclass blacks, left behind after everyone able to has fled, imposed a sort of reign of terror. Here are factories still dark and scheduled for the wrecker and families who lost the equity in their houses. But there are also signs of revival, in the booming white-collar suburbs, and in smaller factory towns like Akron and Lansing and Muncie as well, justification again for optimism and the locus again of innovation and creativity.

The politician whose work symbolizes best what has been happening in the Great Lakes region is Michigan Governor James Blanchard, who was elected with a low percentage, a Democrat in a state where the traditional policies of the Democrats—support for big unions and high wages—seemed plainly unsustainable. Known primarily as the House manager of the Chrysler bailout bill, Blanchard did not seem likely to pioneer a new strategy of government and politics. But he has. His predecessor, William Milliken, governed for 14 years by brokering the state's big interests, and in Michigan you could get them around one table: the Big Three auto companies, the UAW, the two or three major utilities, a few other big companies like Burroughs and Bendix and Dow Chemical. All backed high spending to maintain state institutions and prop up high wages, and high taxes to pay for them. It was assumed that the cost of all this, and of free dental care and exceedingly generous workmen's compensation could be passed along to the rest of the nation, who after all had to buy a new American car every other year, or to less well-placed Michiganians: in the 1970s Michigan passed a business activities tax, which the Big Three and UAW members didn't have to pay, but small business units—the only growing part of the economy—did.

Blanchard understood the bankruptcy of this approach. He did raise taxes when he came to office, in order to maintain basic state institutions, especially the excellent universities; but he paid a political price for that (losing control of the state Senate), and ended up repealing the tax rise as he promised. More important, he worked to attract and encourage small business and little employers, cutting the burden of doing business and positioning Michigan to be, not another high tech state, but a specialist in high-skill manufacturing. Other Great Lakes governors followed similar approaches, though Illinois's much ballyhooed James Thompson followed the Milliken strategy and, against fatally weakened opposition and with the support of the state AFL-CIO, got only 53% of the vote. Blanchard got 68%—12% more than any Democrat has since Michigan became a state.

Great Plains. Swept again and again by farm revolts, the Farm Belt is the part of America most suspicious of capitalism—because it has so many capitalists. Only 3% of Americans are still farmers, and only 9% in the Great Plains region, but the farm economy permeates everything here; and that economy depends on the fate of the farmer-entrepreneur. And for the entrepreneur who must be ever alert to downside risks, everything threatens disaster: bad weather will reduce his yields and good weather will lower his prices, too much rain will destroy his crops and too little will destroy them too. The 1970s were good years for farmers (though even then there were farm revolts), as land prices rose giddily and exports surged. This lured many farmers into taking on too much debt; and when crop prices and land prices plummeted in the 1980s, many were ruined. Little of this is reflected in overall statistics: the Great Plains's population has risen steadily in the 1980s (although population in Iowa and adjacent downstate Illinois, where the farm machinery factories are centered, is down), job growth has kept pace with population growth, and per capita income is up 10%. But that doesn't measure loss of equity. The land is still being worked, but it matters to the farmer where he owns land worth $500,000 or simply works on the land for wages or crop shares. The New Deal majority was swelled with urban Americans who had been upwardly mobile in the 1920s but whose equity in stock and city real estate was wiped out by the depression of the 1930s. The farmer-entrepreneurs of the Great Plains, accustomed to call on the government to protect them against downside risk, are facing the same situation and if it continues may move toward the same solution.

There is some historical basis for this: the Great Plains are heavily German (44%) and Scandinavian (16%), and both groups brought over traditions of cooperative enterprise and scientifically guided government intervention in the economy. This they applied in Bob LaFollette's Wisconsin, Farmer-Labor Minnesota, and, with the help of Great Plainsmen in Washington, in the U.S.D.A. But it's not clear that the Great Plains feels confident the government can help any more. The cost of farm programs escalated so rapidly in the early 1980s that everyone recognized they would have to be scaled back in the 1985 farm bill, and they were, despite continuing bankruptcies. Iowa's Senator Tom Harkin has been stumping for a bill that would allow farmers to vote for grain production controls, putting the government into micromanagement of individual farms and raising food prices for consumers. But even in Iowa candidates pushing Harkin–Gephardt had no great success. The 1986 elections suggest there is a sullen recognition that government can no more restore farmers' equity than it could stop urban crime. Signs that crop and land prices were at last rising again in 1987 could, if those trends materialize, dampen the demand for change.

Political trends in the Great Plains are best summarized by Iowa's Republican Senator Charles Grassley. With delivery so down home that he sounds like he just stepped off a tractor, Grassley attacks Reagan Administration farm programs without promising his own can accomplish much; he attacks wasteful Pentagon spending—attacks popular in a part of the country always thrifty and, since the days of German-American isolationism, hostile to American military involvement abroad; and he champions traditional cultural values, in a part of the country with one of the highest marriage rates and where women outside the big Minneapolis-St. Paul, St. Louis, and Kansas City metropolitan areas have not gotten heavily into the labor force. Grassley was one of the Republican Senators who beat a Democratic incumbent by a narrow margin in 1980; in 1986 he was reelected with 66% of the vote—more than any Iowa Senator has ever received.

Northwest. Separated from every other part of the country by hundreds of miles of wilderness, the Northwest is a kind of echt-America. There are still fewer than 10 million Americans out here, most of them clustered in urban strips along Puget Sound or the Willamette River. Population growth slowed down as the 1980s went on, and incomes in the region were hurt by the slump in the lumber industry and fluctuations in Washington's largest employer, Boeing; the Northwest went from above to below the national average income. There are few blacks and almost as many Asians as Hispanics here; the major ethnic stocks are British, German, Irish, and Scandinavian. Culturally liberal, the Northwest in its day was one of the most economically liberal parts of the country; much of its growth depended on cheap power developed by federal dams on the Columbia River. But the Washington public power system went bankrupt because of mismanagement in the early 1980s, and power rates have risen, slowing growth further. This is one region that has seemed to move toward the Democrats during the Reagan years The prototypical politician is probably Washington Governor Booth Gardner, a Democrat elected in 1984, who has been highly popular; he is engaging, has a sense of command, and has worn well in a state whose recent leaders have been lackluster or bizarre.

South Atlantic. The surprise boom region of the United States—a surprise even to some people who live there— is the South Atlantic. The marshy barrier islands from Florida to Virginia's Hampton Roads, where the descendants of slaves still speak Gullah and suffered from malnutrition when Senator Ernest Hollings visited them in the 1960s seem an unlikely setting for rapid economic growth; but grown it has. Condominiums galore, on the model of Hilton Head, have been built up and down the Atlantic Coast, Florida-izing much of the Carolinas; one of the nation's fastest-growing high tech economies has been growing around North Carolina's Research Triangle Park, established by Governor Luther Hodges in the 1950s between Raleigh, Durham, and Chapel Hill, metropolitan Atlanta has been spreading far out into the Georgia hills, affluent and swaggering with prosperity; and Florida continues to grow prodigiously, as the well-off and only mildly well-off elderly of every state from Maine to Iowa funnel down to the winter sun.

The South Atlantic has had sustained, solid growth in the 1980s, and not just of retirees; jobs rose 18% in the first four years of the decade, and incomes rose enough to place this once impoverished area within 7% of the national average. This is the most heavily black of the eight regions—21%—but blacks' incomes have risen substantially too, and there is no longer any "chicken bone special" in the Carolinas any more—the bus that every black high school graduate would get on, with several pieces of fried chicken, to go up to New York or Philadelphia to get a job. Culturally, too, the South Atlantic is getting more diverse; marriage rates, thanks to retirement condos and suburban singles complexes, are much lower than they used to be, and women, whose longtime high participation in the labor force used to be as "Norma Raes" in textile and apparel factories, are now working more often in white-collar jobs. Metropolitan Atlanta, in fact, has one of the highest rates of working women in the country: the boom gives young couples the chance to make more money than they'd ever thought possible.

The South Atlantic has had many governors who have stimulated growth not by giving away plant sites, but by raising education levels, improving universities, and actively courting higher paying and higher skill businesses than most of the South Atlantic was able to attract before the 1970s. But most of the outstanding ones are out of office now: Jim Hunt of North Carolina, Richard Riley of South Carolina, Bob Graham of Georgia, Charles Robb of Virginia; Robb's able successor, Gerald Baliles, is another. But perhaps most symbolic is Georgia's Governor Joe Frank Harris. He has the name of a good old boy and the look of a dour church deacon; he is deeply religious, a veteran of the state legislature, a conservative temperamentally and otherwise. Little was expected of him when he was elected, but he has proved competent and has presided over one of the most sophisticated and explosive booms in America today and has come up with his own education reform program. He is another consensus politician: reelected to his second term with 71% of the vote, carrying all 159 counties.

Mississippi Valley. Proof that the so-called Sun Belt boom does not extend evenly across the South can readily be found in the five states of the Mississippi Valley. For most of the nation's history they have been the poorest part of the United States, and they are still. For years southerners boasted of their industrial growth, and cited as their chief example Birmingham, Alabama, founded after the Civil War beneath a red mountain made of iron ore and one of the nation's leading steel producers. But by the 1980s most of the mills had closed and Birmingham's biggest employer was the university medical center. Still, outmigration from Mississippi Valley pretty well stopped in the 1970s and has been only slight in the 1980s, nothing like the streams of blacks, and many whites as well, who lit out of Mississippi or Kentucky or Arkansas for Chicago or Detroit or St. Louis from 1940 to 1970. Income levels too remained steady—low, but only about 20% behind the national average, instead of the 40% or so they lagged in the 1950s and early 1960s. Mississippi Valley remains the most unethnic of American regions, with the population divided mainly by race in the lowlands along the Mississippi River; when the land gets higher, however, you find hardly any blacks, and just 19% of the region's residents in 1980 were black. Culturally, the Mississippi Valley is the most tradition-bound region of the country, where the fewest women work; though one suspects many more would, as their cousins do in metro Atlanta or the Dallas-Fort Worth Metroplex, if there were more jobs.

Politically, this was the strongest region for Jimmy Carter in 1980; he came within a hair of winning each of the five states, and it probably could be competitive again for Democrats. It has no million-plus metro areas, full of new Republican voters enraptured with the workings of the free market; it has long looked for government largesse, in the form of dams and military bases and cotton subsidies and highway money, for steady work. It has no principled objection to an economically redistributive government. Nor does its white majority have an ineradicable opposition to any politician who backs civil rights. Black endorsements are no longer the kiss of death, and if Walter Mondale could muster no more than 39% of the vote here, that was only 2% below his national average. But culturally this is conservative country, resentful of any aspersion cast on family values or traditional religion, and on foreign policy the region is surely the most hawkish part of America.

The dominant politician here is probably former Tennessee Governor Lamar Alexander, though you could hear some votes for Arkansas's Bill Clinton and Mississippi's William Winter. Operating from Nashville, the biggest boom town in the region, Alexander orchestrated one of the South's most venturesome education reforms and he also choreographed in his last year in office a statewide celebration of Tennessee that went far beyond routine ceremonies and highlighted some of the region's genuine strengths: its traditional values, its tight-knit communities where families have lived and can trace their roots back 200 years, its openness to economic innovation and its increased levels of skills. The Mississippi Valley is frustrated because it remains at the bottom of the national rankings. But it has gained much ground over the past quarter-century and, given its resource base, it has shown considerable strength by holding even with national growth in the 1980s.

Oil Patch. For a moment in the early 1980s—a delicious moment in Houston, a sickening one in Detroit—the Oil Patch bid fair to become the richest and fast-growing region in the United States. It was also the newest region, for what did Louisiana and Colorado have in common before OPEC's price fixing made the oil they produce worth so much? In the first four years of the 1980s the Oil Patch was the fastest growing part of America, with population up 10%, jobs up 13%, income levels at parity with the national average—a great improvement for historically impoverished states like Texas and Louisiana. Economic change has produced vast cultural change in the Oil Patch. In 1970, before the big oil price hikes, this was one of the most heavily tradition-minded parts of the country. It still may be tradition-*minded*, but its behavior has changed: more than half the women here are in the labor force, and the marriage rate is not much above the national average. If you look at the most affluent parts of the Oil Patch—north Dallas, west Houston, Denver suburbs—you will find some of the highest percentages of working women in the nation. They may believe the doctrine of Phyllis Schlafly, but they are living the life of Geraldine Ferraro.

Ethnically, the Oil Patch is more than one-eighth black, Hispanic, Irish, German; there are even more exotic groups, like the Spanish-speaking Indians of New Mexico and the French-speaking Cajuns of Louisiana. Yet the tone is set, except perhaps in urban Colorado and sparsely populated Wyoming, by the white male Texan, in blue jeans and drawl, a fanatic football fan with a picturesque turn of phrase. They strengthen the Oil Patch's cultural conservatism and set the tone for its macho attitudes on foreign policy: Texas Governor Mark White made a point of being photographed in fatigues attending National Guard manuevers in Honduras. Texas and most of the Oil Patch was settled by dirt-poor farmers who couldn't make it in places like Arkansas; it is almost bereft of an hereditary aristocracy. Yet it is full of fabulously successful millionaires, convinced that it was the free market and their own exertions, not government-managed oil prices or favorable federal tax treatment that produced that wealth. Politically the Oil Patch has become the most free market part of the country, and the one region which increasingly seems to call for the Republicans, not the Democrats, to produce economic growth. It was 64% for Ronald Reagan in 1984, the highest in the nation, and, although much of the rural Oil Patch retains an ancestral Democratic preference, it produced rather small margins for the Democrats in the House elections of 1984 and 1986.

The most influential politician here is former Texas Governor Mark White. Unlike the leading politicians in the other seven regions, he has not developed a consensus politics which resulted in his overwhelming reelection; quite to the contrary, after a career of giantkiller victories, over James Baker for attorney general of Texas in 1978 and incumbent Governor Bill Clements in 1982, he was beaten soundly by Clements in a rematch in 1986. White's problem is that he is all too visibly an instinctive political animal, scrambling to avoid unpopular moves and sloppily seeking momentary advantage until, at the last minute, he seems forced by circumstances to do the right thing; his unpopular moves were enough to convince Texas voters that he lacked the steadiness and conviction they wanted for the job, even though they readily conceded that the big things he did were right.

So too did Bill Clements, although you'll never hear him say so. White appointed billionaire H. Ross Perot to come up with education reforms, and then pushed Perot's package through a balky legislature—balky not only at higher taxes, but at the no-pass-no-play rule he promulgated for high school football and other extracurricular activities. This, in a state where one Dallas suburb chartered a pair of 727s so fans could attend a high school playoff game in Midland. Then, as revenues slackened in 1986, White after much hesitation called for more taxes. Clements backs no-pass-no-play and, though he says he's against higher taxes, may have to accept some, to keep Texas's education system from deteriorating; he seems to accept White's belief that in education, and not in oil reserves, lies Texas's long-range future.

Southwest. Into the interstices between ocean, desert, and sea, on America's edge of the Pacific Rim, has grown in what was almost entirely vacant territory 120 years ago a civilization more creative and productive and economically buoyant than any the world has ever seen. On the dry lands of the Central Valley and other interstitial flatlands Americans have developed the most productive agriculture in the world; they have created in the Los Angeles Basin and hugging the edges of San Francisco Bay they have created cities with the highest income levels in human history. Growing more slowly than the Oil Patch in the early 1980s, almost matched by the South Atlantic's growth rate in the middle 1980s, it has nonetheless grown more rapidly than any other region during the decade—15% through 1986. Its 34 million people are about one-third the population of Japan and more than half the population of Britain or France or West Germany or Italy; set apart from the rest of the world by vacant expanses of water and sand, it is of national magnitude by itself.

The key to the growth of the Southwest (most of which of course is California) is and always has been immigration. In the 1980s that has meant immigration of rich retirees and, far more important, high-skill graduates from the rest of the United States, and it has meant increasingly immigration from Latin America (mainly, but by no means entirely Mexico) and East Asia. In 1980, 17% of the population here was Hispanic and 6% Asian; by the late 1980s more than one-quarter of the region's people will be from these two groups. It should not be said that they are a sodden mass, lying there in poverty and amassing grievances against the Anglo capitalist order. Quite the contrary, they are moving up fast, and are in many cases politically to the right. Vast immigration has depressed average wage levels only a bit: incomes remain well above the national average. Many immigrants have been high-skill technical pioneers, but larger numbers have set to work and created a vast low-wage labor force that outperforms East Asia and keeps costs down to reasonable levels. Americans instinctively recoil at wide disparities in income and at such two-tiered wage systems; and yet they have accompanied and undoubtedly contributed to most of the episodes of exceedingly rapid economic growth in world history—New York in 1913, Los Angeles in 1987. They are bearable if they provide plenty of opportunity for rapid upward mobility, and this the Southwest, with its rapid and sustained growth rates, has done in the 1980s. That has strengthened the movement, already apparent in 1980, of Mexican-Americans out of the East Los Angeles staging area and into the San Fernando Valley, eastern Los Angeles Basin, and Orange County, and the upward climb of Asians into middle-class neighborhoods everywhere in the state. The upward mobility is aided by California's cultural liberalism and tolerance, probably the greatest in the nation.

Economically the Southwest believes in market economics and sees little need for government interference; culturally, it brooks little messing around in its personal lives, though it is ready to talk endlessly about them; on foreign policy, it is of two minds, with affluent liberals still regarding American intervention as about the worst thing that can happen to a virtuous Third World country, in the face of evidence to the contrary from Afghanistan to the Philippines, and with affluent conservatives ready to call for military intervention on any whim, careless about the imprecision of war in achieving its aims and of the reluctance of their fellow citizens to give their lives to such adventures.

The key political figure here is California's Governor George Deukmejian—a fact that surely must surprise even him. Deukmejian is the mousiest of politicians, a dull foil to his endlessly interesting predecessor Jerry Brown, a stolid and uninspiring conservative who beat a black woman for attorney general in 1978 and a black man for governor in 1982 (and then so barely that he won only because of the Republican absentee ballot drive) and in 1986. Deukmejian still has a Democratic legislature (though his Republicans have gained seats) which he usually ignores and with which he usually refuses to negotiate—and ends up with almost all of what he wants. Deukmejian has prevented tax rises, has appointed tough-minded judges (including a chief justice to replace Brown's Rose Bird, thrown out by a 2 to 1 margin by voters in 1986), has modulated his predecessor's commitment to environmental restraints and bilingual education while still maintaining the principles that the environment is not entirely to be spoiled and that California's children must be taught basic fundamentals so they are proficient in English. In national elections, the Southwest hasn't swung heavily to Reagan or Republicans since 1980, but mostly because it was already for them by solid margins then and, despite its cultural liberalism, remains so now; it gave House Democrats their narrowest margin in 1986. Democrats, by running good candidates, by brilliantly skillful legislative districting, by sheer political skill, have won more than their share of victories here. But it is hard to see what natural advantages they have for carrying the Southwest in future presidential elections.

The Bottom Line. In this country, which political party has the natural advantage? It is an impossible question to answer. At various stages in our history analysts have identified natural party majorities. The brilliant journalist and electoral analyst Samuel Lubell identified and described the natural Democratic majority that became apparent after Harry Truman's surprise victory in 1948; Washington lobbyist Horace Busby identified and described a natural Republican advantage in the electoral college after the surprise election of Ronald Reagan in 1980. The problem, at least in a nation at peace and characterized by vast cultural variety, is that there is not likely to be a natural majority for any party, because voters make their decisions for different reasons, and different reasons produce different results.

Consider President Reagan's victories in 1980 and 1984. He managed to get most economic conservatives to vote for him regardless of their views on cultural issues (though many are liberation-minded), and he managed to get most cultural conservatives to vote for him regardless of their views on economic issues (which are sometimes favorable toward government intervention). Does that mean a Republican lock? Not if a Democrat could get most economic liberals to vote on economics and most cultural liberals to vote on culture. But if economic and cultural issues tend to pit the coasts against the heartlands, with each region favoring different parties on different issues, foreign policy tends to complicate things further: it tends to split the nation between a dovish North (especially the far northern tier of states) and a hawkish South (culminating in the arch-hawkish crescent around the Gulf of Mexico).

Or look at the division of the nation into coastal and heartland America. This was publicized by David Obey's Joint Economic Committee and by House Democratic Campaign Committee Chairman Tony Coelho in 1986: their theme was that the heartland was falling behind the coasts economically, and would therefore prove favorable to the Democrats. But actually the heartland voted about the same as the coastal areas in 1986, and in 1984 as well. The reason is that the coastal areas tend to be more liberation-minded on cultural issues. Similarly, if you divide the electorate along lines of age, the Democrats have the advantage with older voters on economic issues, but with younger voters on cultural issues; with the Republicans having just the opposite.

It can probably be said that the Democrats have a disadvantage in the electoral college. It is hard, on the basis of the last five elections, to count up how any Democratic presidential candidate, absent major Republican mistakes, can capture more than about 320 electoral votes. That leaves very little margin for error in amassing the 270 needed to win. Yet if the Democratic nominee gets 54% of the vote—which somehow does not seem impossible—he cannot fail to carry a solid majority of the electoral votes.

So instead of finding a natural majority for anyone in 1988, we see a sort of eerie equipoise in American politics: any advantage you can see for one party or one approach is balanced off by an advantage you can see for the other. This strengthens the view that the task of political strategists in 1988 is not to stake out the winning sides of a set of divisive issues, but to capture the voters' imaginations with their approach to the unifying issues. Americans are not sure what is coming next economically, culturally, in foreign policy; they have no formulas to tell them. But they do know what kind of facts they like, and they have some sense of the direction they want to see American government and American politicians go: toward a communitarian politics that builds economic growth and produces a common national effort at a time when the nation seems dangerously fragmented and atomized. In their search for a leader who can move the country in this direction the betting here is that they will be less impressed with position papers or even slogans, and more concerned about finding a candidate with the right attributes of character. The reward could be great. In states across the nation governors of both parties who successfully pursued consensus policies that the public was seeking were rewarded with overwhelming reelection not only at the top of their ticket but often for their party. A President who pursues successful consensus policies nationally might have a chance to capture the imagination and allegiance of the nation's voters for much of the 1990s and to establish, for a moment anyway, the closest thing to a natural advantage for his party—and it could be either party—we are likely to see in the America of the very late 20th century.

The picture that emerges is a good bit more complex than the rule used hastily (and not entirely accurately) to sum up the demographic changes of the last two decades, that the South

1980-86 Regional Populations and Population Growth 1980-83 and 1983-86.
(in thousands and percentages)

Region	1980 Census	1983 Estimate	1986 Estimate	1980-83 % Growth	1983-86 % Growth
UNITED STATES	226,546	234,023	241,077	3.3%	3.0%
A. North Atlantic	42,720	43,141	43,851	1.0	1.6
B. Great Lakes	55,497	55,329	55,547	−.3	.4
C. Great Plains	17,972	18,228	18,482	1.4	1.4
D. Northwest	8,111	8,428	8,698	3.9	3.2
E. South Atlantic	29,560	31,362	33,275	6.1	6.1
F. Mississippi Valley	16,953	17,256	17,581	1.8	1.9
G. Oil Patch	26,123	28,590	29,741	9.4	4.0
H. Southwest	29,612	31,689	33,988	7.0	7.3
ABCD Snow Belt	124,300	125,126	126,578	.7	1.2
EFGH Sun Belt	102,248	108,897	114,585	6.5	5.2
ADEH Coast	110,003	114,620	119,812	4.2	4.5
BCFG Interior	116,545	119,403	121,351	2.5	1.6

and the West have gained at the expense of the East and the Midwest. To be sure, the Sun Belt has grown much faster than the Snow Belt in the 1980s, but the gap narrowed after 1983, and the Mississippi Valley now is growing no faster than the Snow Belt and only marginally faster than the North Atlantic. Nor do we see the stark contrast between a yuppified coastal America and an impoverished heartland. There is a significant gap, and it widened after 1983, largely because of the slowdown in growth of the Oil Patch; but the other three parts of the heartland revived or stayed steady after the turnaround.

Those conclusions are strengthened when looking at the trends in jobs and incomes. With just one exception, in the Great Plains, jobs and incomes have risen perceptibly faster than population in each region for the first half of the 1980s. Snow Belt incomes remain slightly

1980-84 Regional Population Growth, Job Growth, and Per Capita Income Growth.

Region	Pop. Growth	Job Growth	Income Growth	Income as % U.S. 1980	Income as % U.S. 1984
UNITED STATES	4.2%	8.0%	8.7%	100%	100%
A. North Atlantic	1.6	4.9	13.1	109	113
B. Great Lakes	−.1	.8	6.1	101	98
C. Great Plains	2.0	2.1	10.1	97	98
D. Northwest	4.1	6.5	1.7	104	97
E. South Atlantic	8.0	17.9	11.5	91	93
F. Mississippi Valley	2.5	5.8	9.7	78	79
G. Oil Patch	10.5	17.5	7.1	98	97
H. Southwest	9.0	13.1	4.8	112	108
ABCD Snow Belt	1.2	2.8	8.6	103	103
EFGH Sun Belt	8.0	14.5	8.1	97	96
ADEH Coast	5.6	10.5	8.9	105	105
BCFG Interior	3.0	5.4	7.3	96	97

higher than Sun Belt incomes, but the most striking thing about regional variation is how little there is. Aside from the Mississippi Valley, long the most impoverished region in the nation, and the only one with no metropolitan areas with populations over one million, per capita incomes ranged in 1986 between 91% and 119% of the national average. The Great Lakes and Great Plains, for all their woes, stayed close to the national average, which is to say that real incomes rose; the smallest rise occurred in the smallest region, the Northwest, but so great are its attractions to its residents that it had little population outflow. Only in the Oil Patch in the middle 1980s was there a real fall.

But the great story in America today is not of outmigration but of millions of people moving to

Percentage of Blacks, Hispanics, Asians, and self-identified Irish, Scandinavian, Italian, and Eastern European Ancestry, 1980 Census.

Region	Black	Hispanic	Asian	Irish	German	Scandinavian	Italian	East European
UNITED STATES	12%	6%	2%	18%	23%	5%	5%	7%
North Atlantic	12	6	1	19	16	2	14	10
Great Lakes	10	2	1	18	33	4	5	12
Great Plains	4	1	1	19	41	16	2	6
Northwest	2	3	2	20	28	14	2	3
South Atlantic	21	4	1	16	14	2	2	3
Mississippi Valley	19	1	—	18	11	1	1	1
Oil Patch	13	15	1	17	17	2	2	3
Southwest	7	17	6	15	19	6	4	4

America, hustling, and making their way upward. It is a story more American than apple pie. This nation created by successive waves of immigration is now being shaped anew by a new wave unforeseen by futurists, academics, politicians, journalists, and leaders of ethnic groups.

The first wave, from 1630 to the early 1700s and then in the dozen years before the Revolution, came mostly from the British Isles and, involuntarily, West Africa, with some from Germany and Holland. The second wave, from 1840 to 1924, came first from Britain and Ireland, then Germany, then southern, northern, and eastern Europe, with substantial numbers from the British Isles throughout. The third wave of immigration began around 1970 and gives no signs of having crested. Between the second and third waves, there was a massive movement within the United States of black Americans, from the rural South to the big industrial cities of the North and between 1940 and 1970; curiously, black and white migration from South to North was negligible before 1940 and has been roughly balanced by movement in the opposite direction since 1970.

The results of all these migrations are evidenced in the percentages in the table, of the first distinctive ethnic group, blacks; of the 1880–1924 migrants who have been politically distinctive, Irish, Germans, Scandinavians, Italians, and East Europeans (not including Russians, a category which turns out to be mostly Jewish and includes the Volga Germans of North Dakota); and of the most recent migrants, Hispanics and Asians. Note that the dispersal of blacks has gone far enough that the black percentage is about as large in the booming North Atlantic region as in the mostly southern Oil Patch. Note also that Irish are scattered all over the country, but Germans and Scandinavians are concentrated in the northern interior; Italians are still heavily concentrated in the North Atlantic; and East Europeans are most heavily represented in the Great Lakes and North Atlantic—the northern American plains end up with a population ethnically similar to that of the northern European plains. Hispanics are already the most notable ethnic group in the fast-growing Southwest and Oil Patch, and one out of 16 residents in the Southwest, one of the two most affluent parts of the country, is Asian. Periodically reformers mount platforms and urge that government guide immigrants to places where they can find jobs and do well. But immigrants, who are betting their lives on their decisions, seem to do better on their own.

Another way in which Americans have been hustling is evidenced by their personal lives. American women have been going out increasingly into the workplace, while men and women both have stayed single longer and gotten divorced more often. The percentage of women age 16 and over in the work force rose from 41% to 50% in the 1970s, while the percentage of Americans 15 and over who were married or widowed—the percentage *not* separated, divorced, or single—dropped from 77% to 62%. For women below retirement age, working has become the norm; while being unattached has become almost as common as being married or remaining married until one spouse dies.

	% Married		% In Labor Force	
Region	1970	1980	1970	1980
UNITED STATES	**77%**	**65%**	**41%**	**50%**
North Atlantic	75	62	42	51
Great Lakes	78	66	41	49
Great Plains	79	66	41	51
Northwest	79	66	41	51
South Atlantic	79	66	43	50
Mississippi Valley	80	69	38	46
Oil Patch	79	67	39	50
Southwest	75	62	42	52

There are some regional variations: the Coasts, primarily because of large blocs of singles in New York City and Los Angeles, have the lowest married percentage. Rapid economic growth has drawn more women into jobs in the Oil Patch and on the Pacific Coast, while sluggish growth even in the 1970s in the blue-collar Great Lakes has meant a smaller increase in jobs for women. Traditional mores—women married and not on the job—are most pronounced in the Mississippi Valley, which is also the region with by far the lowest levels of income. Economic growth, after all, is disruptive, changing traditional cultural behavior as much as it does economic inefficiency; a society, as J. W. Anderson of the *Washington Post* says, "has only as much economic growth as it can stand." But regional differences are overshadowed by national change.

There is no overlap: a larger percentage of adults were married in North Atlantic or Southwest in 1970 than in the Mississippi Valley in 1980; a larger percentage of women were in the labor force in every region in 1980 than in any region in 1970. And all these changes seem to have continued in the same direction well into the 1980s; the percentage of women in the work force rose to 54% in 1985, while the percentage married and widowed appears to have fallen from 65% to 63%.

THE PRESIDENCY

No nation has come up with a completely satisfactory way to choose leaders. Those who complain about the American presidential process should remember that there are demonstrably worse systems: hereditary monarchy, for example, which produced in the two most populous nations of Europe before World War I, two leaders, one mentally unstable and the other mentally deficient, who took power in their 20s and held it for 30 and 23 years, and made decisions that led proximately to a world war and the installation of Communist and Nazi regimes. The Iowa caucuses and the New Hampshire primary have not done as badly as that. Nor do the much-vaunted parliamentary systems of Europe produce results that are so pleasing. Britain's system of vesting all power in a prime minister with a parliamentary majority means, with the current multi-party system, that the leader of a party which is the first choice of maybe 36 percent of the voters but hated by 60 percent can pass any law it wants—can leave the NATO alliance or confiscate private property—and no one can do anything about it for five years. There's no way anything like that can happen in the American system.

For 1988 the American system of choosing the leader who dominates our government and public life will be tested as it has not been at least since 1960. Voting for president is the most personal decision any voter makes, yet Americans will be asked in 1988 to choose from a large field of candidates who range from unfamiliar to unknown, and to choose in a very short period of time. Effectively, much of the races for the nominations will take place in calendar year 1987, when voters can watch candidates act and react under stress and pressure. The contests, after the opening races in Iowa, New Hampshire, and a few other states, will come with staccato speed. Yet so much emphasis has been put on the mostly (but not entirely) southern primaries of Super Tuesday that the candidates who survive, if they still have competition, will be at a loss as to how to campaign or to finance their campaigns in the big states of Illinois, Ohio, Pennsylvania, and New York.

The races for the nominations are likely to have three stages. First come the contests in Iowa and New Hampshire, in South Dakota and among Michigan Republican precinct delegates. The electorates are small and often heavily concentrated among party activists, and the candidates must engage in what columnist Mark Shields christened "retail politics," talking directly to voters, courting leaders of small groups who can swing small blocs, organizing voters to turn out on election day. The second stage is Super Tuesday. All of a sudden the electorate becomes huge, spread out among more than 100 media markets. Candidates cannot make a reasonable pretense of visiting in person each state, much less each local community. Unpaid media—network and perhaps local television newscasts, newspaper stories—become critical media, and it's possible that paid media—television or other advertisements—may play a role here too. Mistakes are heavily penalized; the ability to state an attractive message succinctly, preferably in a 10- or 20-second sound bite, is highly rewarded. The third stage is the later primaries, if serious contests remain—or even if they don't, for presumptive nominees will be subject to close scrutiny. Here the danger is that the candidate's need to repeat his message, to get through to a mostly uninterested electorate, runs up against the press's need for novelty, for a new angle or a new story to report. The novelty usually appears, and usually turns out to be negative.

Finally comes the convention. Once upon a time party conventions were truly deliberative bodies, where politicians who weren't in constant touch with each other—even as assiduous a delegate-hunter as Franklin Roosevelt's Jim Farley didn't make many long distance phone calls—met once every four years, tried to gauge various candidates' strengths, and made deals and decisions. Now all that information is gathered and the deals are made long before anyone gets to the convention hall. The convention takes place electronically long before, as pols trade information and votes over the phone and as TV network delegate counters can tell you, with accuracy Farley or John Kennedy's Larry O'Brien would have marveled at, how many votes each candidate has on any given day. Once in the hall the delegates, unable to watch on TV and waiting for the phone calls from their candidates' trailers to tell them what to do, know less about what is going on than any interested person anywhere else in America. These developments are no longer very new. They were apparent by 1976, when the delegate counters had their totals exactly right in the exceedingly close Ford-Reagan contest and when outsider Jimmy Carter clinched the Democratic nomination not because he won by himself an absolute majority of delegates but because he was far enough ahead that within a few days after the last primary he had collected the endorsements of Scoop Jackson, Mayor Daley, and George Wallace. A deadlocked convention in 1988? A deadlock, perhaps, but one likely to be broken well before the Democrats get to Atlanta or the Republicans to New Orleans.

At last the general election. It is fought with an intensity you won't find elsewhere in American politics, for the stakes are so great; it is fought out primarily over television screens, not so much in the ads the candidates present, but in the two- or three- or sometimes five-minute stories run on the network newscasts each week night. Each campaign's job is to get the single message it wants across on that day, and it will fight hard to do that. In the meantime, the candidate goes through the motions of giving speeches and shaking hands with voters, though functionally the audiences and voters are nothing more than props for the television cameras; the rallies are just "visuals" designed to look good for viewers. This sounds cynical, but isn't necessarily: politics goes where the voters are. Once upon a time tens of thousands of voters would stand outside for three hours to listen to a candidate speak; on Labor Day as recently as 1960, 125,000 came to Detroit's Cadillac (later Kennedy) Square to cheer John F. Kennedy as he started his campaign. Eight years later the Democrats didn't bother holding a Labor Day kickoff in Detroit; the UAW leaders said too many members were up at their cottages. In the late 1980s voters don't especially want to see or listen to politicians, so politicians must go where they are—gathered around the set to watch evening newscasts or *Dallas* and *Miami Vice*.

Party and positions on issues matter a lot to voters; but in presidential races character usually matters more. And for good reason: a President is not bound by party platforms or bosses and his job amounts to more than just running down a checklist of issues and voting yea and nay. Presidents can set the national agenda, they must make many tough decisions, they affect the tone of our national life. In all these things character is the critical variable. Voters understand that and try to get what clues to character they can. Television, often reviled as a medium of political communication, has the advantage of putting candidates out there for all to see, often in unrehearsed and stressful situations; it provides a basis for accurate insights into character. And voters have not been deceived as often as commentators—and the voters themselves—would like to think. Americans did not reelect Richard Nixon in 1972 because they thought he was trustworthy (they had well-founded doubts about that), they did not elect Jimmy Carter in 1976 because they thought he knew how to handle insider politicians (they wanted a President who was an outsider), and they did not elect Ronald Reagan in 1980 or 1984 because they admired his attention to detail (they knew it was hazy at best). They voted for each of these men for positive traits which they do in fact possess and they got some of the kinds of results (the Vietnam treaty and detente, the Camp David accords and racial liberalism, the quashing of inflation and military buildup) they wanted.

Until Americans start caucusing and voting, it's too early to be absolutely sure what qualities they will seek and which they will find in the dozen or so politicians who will seek the presidency in 1988. It is the least-known field in recent American history, and voters will have to make quick judgments. But it is possible to set forth here thumbnail sketches of those who said by May 1987 they were going to run and of several other politicians who may turn out to be added starters. America goes through candidates quickly these days: of the nine serious candidates for President in 1984, only one is running again in 1988; and of the 12 running in May 1987 most will not be seriously in the race by May 1988, and quite possibly someone not on the list will.

REPUBLICANS

George Bush. The best known candidate in the 1988 race is undoubtedly Vice President George Bush, yet how well do voters know him? For that matter, how well do most Republican political insiders know him? As a Vice President who is said to be involved in all major White House decisions, as Walter Mondale was before him, Bush may be one of the best-informed candidates of all time. Yet it is in the nature of the vice presidential office that we do not see its holder at work; we have no opportunity to see him perform under pressure; we get no sense of where he differs with the President on issues, and which issues he would emphasize if he were in the Oval Office and not just near it. George Bush began his political career after heroic service as a pilot in World War II and after blazing success in the always risky and rough-and-ready oil business in Texas, far from the green lawns of Greenwich, Connecticut where he grew up. (Much is made of his supposedly aristocratic background, but his father grew up in Columbus, Ohio, and made his own success as an investment banker and U.S. Senator: a meritocrat, not an aristocrat.) George Bush's electoral record was less dazzling. He lost two races for the Senate in Texas, was elected twice to the House from the west Houston district which is one of the dozen most Republican seats in the country, and after a fast start lost the New Hampshire primary and the presidential nomination to Ronald Reagan in 1980.

The case for Bush depends on his service as Vice President in the 1980s and in sensitive posts like director of the CIA and ambassador to China in the 1970s. His habit of speaking in sentence fragments and his occasional cornball phrases make it hard for many voters to take him as seriously as many who have seen him from the inside do. His convictions seem to be those of a conventional conservative Republican of the late 1960s—not those of the eastern Nelson Rockefeller Republicans with whom many erroneously identify him. He is not a generous spender and the phrase he used in 1980 to describe Reagan's supply-side philosophy, "voodoo economics," still infuriates many Republicans who believe he would readily raise taxes to get the budget closer to balance. He has switched toward an anti-abortion position—a cynical move, many believe, but possibly one example (and probably the Reagan tax and budget cuts are another) where his mind has genuinely been changed by arguments he heard in the Reagan White House. He believes in high defense budgets, sturdy support of the CIA, an assertive foreign policy—though he is harmed by his apparent concurrence in the Iran-contra arms deal. He sometimes seems clumsy, but he has great persistence. He is not likely to leave the race for the nomination even if he receives grave setbacks. For all his youthful appearance as he jogs each morning, he has been seeking the presidency for many years now, and if he wins in 1988 he will be the fifth oldest man to take office.

The schedule does not help Bush. He could be stymied from winning a majority of delegates in Michigan by a coalition of Robertson foot soldiers and Kemp officers; in Iowa he runs in the state with the lowest Reagan job ratings during most of the second Reagan term; South Dakota is full of disaffected farmers; in New Hampshire he has been reviled for nearly a decade by the *Manchester Union-Leader* (it was Bush's appearance at a banquet for the paper's publisher that prompted George Will to call his bark "a thin, tinny 'arf' of a lapdog"). Nor, despite his years in Texas, is there any reason in polls or previous primaries to think he has any special strength in the South. But if he can get through the first contests with creditable vote totals and his dignity, his chances improve. For the general election, his greatest asset and liability are the same: his association with the Reagan Administration.

Robert Dole. Of all the candidates in the field, Dole has the most Washington experience: he was first elected to Congress in 1960 and was sworn in to the House in time to serve the last 17 days of the Eisenhower Administration. He was elected Senator in 1968, served as Republican national chairman in the first Nixon term, was nearly defeated in 1974 and, as Gerald Ford's running mate in 1976, ran a campaign that prompted many to call him a hatchet man. His 1980 presidential campaign was a fiasco. Yet in the 1980s he has been hailed as a mature, sensitive, effective leader.

There is evidence to support all these views. But it's important to remember that Bob Dole has been tested in a way none of the other presidential candidates of 1988 have been. He was grievously wounded in World War II, his right arm was shattered, he spent years lying on his back and recovering. That experience has made him a champion of the handicapped and has given him a compassion that comes out on many issues; it has also caused a bitterness that came out in his "Democrat wars" comment in the 1976 vice presidential debate. Dole is a hard worker and has an extensive and constructive legislative record. With George McGovern, he was the architect of the successful food stamp program. He played a larger role than any other Senator in shaping the 1981 and 1985 farm bills. As chairman of the Senate Finance Committee for four years, he supported the Reagan tax cuts, then through sheer effort pushed through the tax rise of 1982, and helped pass the gas-tax-and-highways bill later that year. It is widely assumed that he would raise taxes to get closer to balancing the budget, and he has been scathing in his criticism of supply-side economics; in response, Newt Gingrich once called him "the tax collector for the welfare state."

As Senate Majority Leader in 1985 and 1986, Dole was successful in helping tax reform through and at the same time actively cultivated the New Right. He is not a master of parliamentary procedure, but he has shown a sure touch for the pithy, candid sound-bite, and he has used it to show both his sympathy with the Reagan Administration and his unwillingness to be servile to it. As a farm state Senator who knows farm issues, he presumably has an advantage in the early contests in Iowa and South Dakota; he didn't participate in the Michigan precinct delegate contest in August 1986 and so little will be expected of him there. Then he faces tests in low-tax New Hampshire and in the Super Tuesday contests which will stretch the capacity of his not very deep organization. Dole is not a bookish man or one who relies much on staff: the advantage is that his personal imprint is unmistakable in so much of what he does, the disadvantage is he is not used to delegating and yet being a candidate and being a President requires delegation. Dole's wit is a good clue to how things are going for him. It is almost always funny and to the point, but when it becomes biting then things are not going well for him.

Pete du Pont. It would have been preposterous in the class-conscious America of two generations ago to expect that voters would elect a candidate named Pierre S. du Pont IV who proposed creating alternatives to Social Security, abolishing AFDC, and phasing out all payments to farmers. In that class-conscious America, he would have been labelled a hard-hearted rich man insensitive to the plight of the working man and that, even in Republican primaries, would have been that. It is not quite so simple in 1988. Pete du Pont certainly begins as a long-shot for the Republican nomination; but he cannot be ruled out. He brings to the race a capacity for crisp articulation of ideas about reducing the role of government and letting markets create more economic growth, and he brings a record as governor of Delaware for eight years in which he claims those principles brought good results. He has the zeal of a convert: he was a more conventional, sometimes even liberal, Republican when he served in the House in the 1970s; but he's been convinced that markets work better than government and that the ideas he championed, which would have been labelled retrograde in the days of some of the earlier Pierre du Ponts, are instead the wave of the future.

As a long shot, du Pont has little to lose by taking risks, and he has taken plenty. His position on farm programs is considered a handicap in Iowa and South Dakota; his Social Security plank has been denounced by Jack Kemp and will presumably not play in St. Petersburg. More generally, du Pont is running in a year when voters may think they have had enough of the Reagan revolution rather than that it is time for the next step. His strategy presumably is to squeeze out Kemp and get enough votes to go one-on-one with Bush or Dole, in the hope of capturing the nation's imagination in the moments he is in the spotlight. It might just work.

Alexander Haig. The case for Alexander Haig is that he has held more powerful positions in the White House than anyone else in the race, that he knows the job. The case against is that he worked for Richard Nixon during the Watergate cover-up, that his service as Ronald Reagan's Secretary of State was characterized by clumsy power grabs and eventual failure, and that his mangling of syntax and taste for grating neologisms are evidence of a disorderly mind. Haig stands ready to refute all these points, but he probably won't get the opportunity. Few Republican politicians and activists seem interested in his candidacy. His only strategy is to go over their heads to the voters, but for that he must survive the early contests. In Michigan the delegates are already taken and in Iowa even Republicans are dovish; New Hampshire is presumably his make-or-break state.

Jack Kemp. For years Jack Kemp aimed to run for President in 1988 as the logical heir to Ronald Reagan, the man whose ideas—notably supply-side economics and the Kemp-Roth tax cut—helped to produce Reagan's political victories and his policy revolution. Shoved aside by White House operatives, who seemed to think that Administration policy was to support George Bush, he soldiered on, often independently of White House strategy. Sometimes he was purer than the Administration, as when he attacks the IMF or the World Bank; sometimes he was less bold, as when he hesitated to fight against the overwhelming desire of his House Republican colleagues to sink Dan Rostenkowski's tax reform bill in December 1985. Then in November 1986 came the Iran-contra scandal, and suddenly the Republican race became something other than a contest to establish who is the closest thing to a Reagan clone. With that change Kemp has had some trouble adjusting.

On the one hand, the religious-based Right is uneasy with him, suspecting that his fervent opposition to abortion is less important to him than his advocacy of tax cuts and economic freedom. Business interests mistrust his economic theories, like his advocacy of something like a gold standard, and are puzzled by his genuine interest in doing something for blacks and the poor—the genesis for his enterprise zones proposal. He has worked more closely with more blacks than any other candidate and seems dedicated to achieving racial justice; but Republicans have a hard time attracting any black votes. His desire to appeal to the great masses is jeopardized by his opposition to protectionism and fervent support of free trade. It is not clear whether his strong support of Reagan's Strategic Defense Initiative will help him in a Republican field where all the candidates wholeheartedly support SDI. His surging, uplifting optimism may or may not be in tune with voters' basic mood in 1988.

It is possible that Jack Kemp is being left behind by history just as many liberal Democrats were—in both cases, not because of their failures but because of their successes. He has long since gotten past the need to argue that he is more than a former football quarterback, to point out that he headed the players' union (as Reagan did the actors' union) and studied economics in between games; he is now a tested and veteran politician, a congressman since 1970, a national leader since 1978, a once scorned backbencher who has achieved stunning successes. Kemp has succeeded in what 10 years ago seemed a quixotic crusade against high tax rates: the top income tax rate has declined from 70% to 28%. With Bill Bradley and Dick Gephardt, he was one of the early and ultimately successful promoters of preference-eliminating, rate-cutting tax reform. His positions on other issues—defense, abortion, SDI—which were once considered odd are now widely accepted. He speaks eloquently and with great force and has mastered the substance of issues some of his detractors are unable to discuss. Yet in 1986 and early 1987 his showings in polls stayed in single digits. He had yet to mobilize the conservative movement—assuming there is a conservative movement out there to be mobilized, now that so many of his objects have been achieved and others seem to have proven unachievable. Kemp won fewer precinct delegates in Michigan than he would have liked, but has a crucial presence there; his operatives have forged an alliance with Pat Robertson's many delegates which threatens to outvote George Bush's bloc. In the farm states his ideas don't seem strong. So New Hampshire and the southern regional primary seem his make-or-break ground.

Paul Laxalt. President Reagan's best friend in the Senate for most of the 1980s; Reagan's colleague when they were the governors of adjoining California and Nevada from 1967 to 1970; the only outsider Howard Hughes talked to when he bought up the Las Vegas casinos; a sometimes casino owner himself who in the second Reagan term sued the *Sacramento Bee* for articles it ran about skimming (though neither the *Bee* nor anyone else had accused Laxalt of skimming or any other illegal activity and the suit was settled out of court in May of 1987). All these things are Paul Laxalt, and the first two explain why he was saying in early 1987 that he was running for President. He was a governor for 4 years, a Senator for 12; he was "general chairman" of the Republican Party from 1981–85; for his friend in the White House, he undertook successfully such delicate missions as journeying to the Philippines and explaining to Ferdinand Marcos that it was time to go.

Laxalt can claim plausibly to be as close to Ronald Reagan on the issues and as similar in temperament as any presidential candidate. But there are minuses as well as pluses here. His strategy for winning the nomination must depend on winning support from conservative activists around the country. But after 13 years in the capital, this pleasant and tolerant man seems to find Washington more congenial than they do. Voters everywhere are looking for a candidate harder working and more attentive to detail than Reagan. But Laxalt does not give the appearance of being a grind, and he has left two offices he might have easily won again, the governorship in 1970 and the Senate seat in 1986, only to see Democrats win them. More likely, the success of the Laxalt candidacy depends on the ability of a candidate who has spent the last seven years comfortably in Washington to convince the true believers out on the hustings that he is their man.

Pat Robertson. Is the Republican Party ready to nominate a television evangelist—a religious broadcaster, in his terms—for President? No one would have thought to ask the question as recently as 1980. Pat Robertson raises it for 1988. He has other claims beyond his success as proprietor and star of the Christian Broadcasting Network. He is the son of a Senator, Willis Robertson in Virginia, who knew Capitol Hill when Lyndon Johnson was a young bull in the Senate and John Kennedy a bachelor congressman. He is a Yale Law graduate and was once an Adlai Stevenson campaign worker in New York. He is well-informed on the issues and speaks articulately and unthreateningly. He has built up a large audience on television as an interviewer, commentator, and charismatic preacher, and he has backing around the country from thousands of evangelicals and fundamentalists.

The problem is converting that into a Republican nomination. By early 1987 Robertson had mastered the mechanics of the early contests as much as any candidate. He elected a large bloc of precinct delegates in Michigan in August 1986, perhaps enough in coalition with Jack Kemp's followers to choose a majority of the delegation. His followers have overturned the Republican organization in Polk County (Des Moines) and elsewhere in Iowa and might well be able to marshal squadrons of followers to the state's precinct caucuses. He surely hopes to score victories in southern primaries, where Republican turnout has historically been low and where traditional Republicans could be overwhelmed if hundreds of thousands of new voters surge into their contests (and most states don't have registration laws that would stop them).

For Robertson's followers seem threatening to many. "The Christians are coming!" they proclaimed after filing day in Michigan in 1986; where voters had a choice on election day they voted for delegates that opposed Robertson. The use of the word "Christian" in a way that excludes most Americans who would describe themselves as such cannot be an asset; and it seems clear that many of Robertson's followers, like many of the followers of George McGovern in the early 1970s, are in politics less to change government than to proclaim and champion beliefs and views which they know are not shared by the great majority of their fellow countrymen. It is cathartic to proclaim, as some McGovernites did, that the United States is the great aggressor in the world or, as some Robertson followers do, that most Americans are in the grip of Satan—but it is politically self-defeating.

Robertson has two other handicaps. One is the libel suit he has brought against Representative Andrew Jacobs and former Representative Pete McCloskey, for saying he escaped combat duty in Korea through political influence. Robertson does not claim to have been under fire, but has stated that he served in what the military technically calls a combat zone, and asserts that he made no effort to get out of combat duty through his father's pull. Also undercutting Robertson's appeal in early 1987 was the scandal involving Jim and Tammy Faye Bakker.

Robertson is not in any way involved (though his CBN put Bakker on the air years ago), but the scandal reinforces the suspicions most Americans have about the integrity and sincerity of television preachers who are always asking for contributions. Disgust with the Bakkers could not only impair Robertson's ability to attract a broader constituency but undermine the morale of his core group. Yet even if these things happen, his organizational work gives him the potential of being a player in Republican presidential politics.

DEMOCRATS

Bruce Babbitt. Governor of Arizona for nine years, Bruce Babbitt has bicycled across Iowa and climbed Mount Washington in his attempts to win recognition from early state Democrats. He has come out with proposals that would have been considered startling from a Democrat a few years ago: for taxing Social Security benefits more than at present, for performance testing in education, for encouraging sharing of businesses' profits and of losses by their employees. He brings to the dissection of the details of public policy a passion which politicians ordinarily reserve for handicapping the next election.

Babbitt has the virtues, and perhaps the defects, of the small state governor he was. In a Rocky Mountain state like Arizona, voters know their governors closely and depend on them to make fundamental decisions on policies which are vital to their lives—like providing enough water in Arizona—and putting them into effect. Medium-sized states, with ongoing institutions that pretty well run themselves, may be able to afford mediocrities in governors' offices; the smaller states of the West, whose institutions and infrastructure still need to be created, insist on smart leaders. Babbitt came to the governorship in Arizona accidentally in 1978, when the incumbent resigned and his replacement died, but after pushing through a groundwater plan for the 21st century, declaring one year totally devoted to problems of children, and managing affairs generally with competence, he became politically unbeatable. His background is unusual: he is from a family of traders and landowners from the deserts of northern Arizona; he was a geology student originally; he studied extensively in Latin America, has kept in close touch with Mexican politicians, and speaks good Spanish. He is not shy of showing contempt for politicians whom he considers just plain stupid, and he speaks with an intensity that doesn't lend itself to small talk. Yet he is at the least an interesting and provocative candidate.

The Babbitt strategy revolves heavily around the first contests and particularly Iowa. He spent much of the summer of 1986 in Iowa and was running a TV commercial there in May 1987. He hopes his early start gives him an edge in the precinct caucuses, where organization is essential: ordinary citizens don't go trooping into someone else's house or union hall to declare openly their support of a presidential candidate unless they're sure someone else they know is going too, and making sure all those someone elses go is the major job of Iowa organizers. Babbitt's task is the harder because he won't have the support of organized teachers (who dislike performance testing) or of unions (which resent him for dispatching the National Guard to a copper strike in 1983). The hope is to make a good enough showing to give him a moment in the spotlight, where this interesting candidate with his interesting ideas will have a chance to capture America's imagination.

Joseph Biden. Few other candidates have ever brought to presidential politics the level of emotional intensity of Joe Biden. His natural medium is the spoken word: he often seems to be thinking out loud as he talks, circling around an issue and interjecting emotion-laden asides, then rising to an emotional pitch that sweeps up his listener—and yet, when his words are reduced to cold print, are usually intellectually defensible. Joseph Biden has been a Senator since 1972, but not one with conspicuous legislative accomplishments; much of his first term he passed in the shadow of his first wife's and daughter's deaths in an auto accident, and most of his second term was spent on the minority side of the aisle. He is known to the public for his agonized cross-examinations of Edwin Meese and his angry denunciation of George Shultz. But he has been exposed to the top policymakers in Washington for most of two decades and has been systematically studying with leading policy thinkers. Those who deny that he has accomplished much admit that he's smart and learns fast.

Biden has certainly demonstrated that he has an instinctive understanding for electoral politics. He comes from the suburbs of Wilmington, a small city but one with a vivid contrast between the rich du Ponts in their chateau country just beyond the city limits and the close-packed rowhouse neighborhoods of blacks, Italians, and Poles circling the downtown towers. As a Catholic and a Democrat who was a senior in a Catholic high school when the first Catholic President was elected, Biden identifies with the working class side of his town, and sees himself as a tribune for those who started with little money and as the victims of discrimination and who have worked their way up, with varying success, in urban America. Running for the Senate at age 29, in 1972, he was able to relate as well to quasi-southern downstate Delaware, beating a popular incumbent in a state where person-to-person retail politics was and is still important. His voting record puts him in line with most Washington liberals, but his sympathies are instinctively with the families he knows from Wilmington row houses and downstate crossroads towns.

In the presidential race, Biden's strategy seems to be built around the inspirational speech, in which he summons up memories of John F. Kennedy and calls on this generation of Americans to work together to solve their problems. As a young politician in the past, he has been free to sound the themes of protest and complaint; seeking the presidency, he must show the vision of the future and ability to govern that voters in the late 1980s have been seeking. The speeches, of course, are heard by only small percentages even of the small electorates of Iowa and New Hampshire. Personal contact and word of mouth can spread his message more, but at some point Biden's campaign must figure out how this hot politician can communicate his message over the cool medium of television.

Michael Dukakis. In 1962 the commonwealth of Massachusetts elected the 30-year-old brother of the President of the United States to the U.S. Senate and the voters of the town of Brookline elected a 29-year-old son of a Greek immigrant state representative. In 1987 it was the latter, not the former, who was Massachusetts' candidate for President. Edward Kennedy's slogan was "he can do more for Massachusetts" in 1962, when the state's economy was still lagging from the flight of the textile mills, wages were low, and the skyline of Boston had only one major building that went up after World War II. By the late 1980s, Massachusets' economy was arguably leading the nation into a surge of high tech growth. The state's revenues grew 16% between 1985 and 1986, the highest growth in the nation; its unemployment was below 4%, one of the lowest in the nation; the high-skill labor force continued to expand day by day.

That surging growth, more than anything else, explains the presidential candidacy of Governor Michael Dukakis. He cannot claim all the credit, and doesn't: Massachusetts' high tech economy owes much to Harvard and MIT, and its growth owes something to the tax cuts put through under Edward King, who in 1978 upset Dukakis after his first term and then was beaten in a return bout in 1982. But he argues that even before 1978 he began using state government to stimulate economic growth, that he increased tax revenues through a tax amnesty program and tougher enforcement enough to allow him to lower tax rates, that his Employment and Training program helped place 23,000 welfare recipients in jobs. In a time when politicians of both parties are straining to prove that they know how to use government to stimulate private economic growth, Dukakis begins with strong credentials.

His campaign strategy hinges heavily on New Hampshire. There, thanks to Boston TV, he is almost as well known as in Massachusetts and, partly because his refusal to approve an evacuation plan stopped the Seabrook nuclear plant in 1986, he is highly popular with local Democratic voters. By early 1987, even before Hart's weekends with a Florida actress were publicized, Dukakis was leading Hart in New Hampshire primary polls. Nor can a strong Dukakis showing there be dismissed as just local pride. Voters don't support local candidates reflexively, but only when they genuinely respect their work; the last incumbent governor to run, Jerry Brown in 1980, got only 4% in his home state. For the states beyond New Hampshire,

Dukakis is crisp and trained in TV (he was a moderator on the public TV program *The Advocates*), culturally liberal but personally austere (he likes to ride the trolley to the State House), and the only candidate who is close to the immigrant experience symbolized by the revival of Ellis Island and the Statue of Liberty: his father came from a Greek village in Turkey to Manchester, New Hampshire, in 1912 speaking no English, and eight years later enrolled in medical school.

Richard Gephardt. For six years the only branch of the federal government controlled by Democrats was the House; yet only one House Democrat is running for President, Richard Gephardt. He can legitimately claim to be a leader there. And not just by virtue of position—after only eight years in the House, he was unanimously elected Democratic Caucus Chairman—but also by virtue of substantive achievement. He has taken on one tough issue after another, starting with the national debt ceiling, going on to hospital cost controls, the income tax system, and most recently international trade, and has come up with new positions for his party—positions which have won Democratic majorities in the House and have proved attractive to voters. With his boyish good looks, his Eagle Scout demeanor, he makes all this look easy: but there is nothing harder in politics than to take a complex issue and come up with a solution that can be explained not only in simple terms to colleagues and voters but also can be defended intellectually to experts and critics. Gephardt has proved he can do that over and over again.

Gephardt is part of the generation that came of age in the 1960s, but he seems to have missed the campus rebellions, the civil rights revolution, and the anti-Vietnam war movement altogether; by 1965 he was a lawyer in a big St. Louis firm, a husband and homeowner on the city's south side who was dabbling in local politics. He was elected alderman in 1971 and congressman in 1976, and got a seat on Ways and Means as a freshman. His rise in the House is all the more striking because he leaves few resentful colleagues in his wake. His candidacy is supported by dozens of House members, and many congressmen of quite different views freely express their admiration of him.

Gephardt's rise in the House came partly because he eschewed big-government solutions for every problem. Yet his presidential campaign strategy seems designed to appeal to specific groups which are important in the process. Although he was co-sponsor of the Bradley-Gephardt tax plan, and thus an originator of the 1986 tax reform, he downplayed the tax issue as early as 1985 and emphasized trade; that was perhaps out of deference to Dan Rostenkowski, but he bucked Rostenkowski in April 1987 when he got his retaliatory trade bill through the House 218–214. Trade is the number one issue for many unions these days, especially the UAW which has many members in Iowa. Then there is abortion, on which he switched from pro-life to pro-choice positions; that will help with the feminists who are so numerous at Democratic conventions. Finally, he is co-sponsor of the Harkin–Gephardt farm bill, which would allow grain farmers to vote in mandatory production controls, to hold up farm incomes (and increase prices for consumers). Gephardt has a ready defense for all these positions, but cynicism persists. It remains clear that Iowa is central to his effort to become one of the leading Democratic candidates.

Albert Gore, Jr. The first Vietnam veteran to run for President, and if he is selected in Atlanta the youngest major party nominee since William Jennings Bryan won at 36 in 1896, is Albert Gore, Jr., who turns 40 three weeks after Super Tuesday. He has served in Congress since 1976, and as the son of a Senator has been a close observer of the Washington scene and of electoral politics since childhood; he is, moreover, an original thinker who is well respected by the voters who know him best. In the House he served on a leading committee, Energy and Commerce, and did outstanding work on other subjects, including arms control; with Les Aspin, he was part of the group that got the MX missile approved in the early 1980s in return for Administration concessions on arms control, and he convinced none less than Henry Kissinger that it was a mistake to have allowed MIRVing under SALT I. He became an expert on organ transplants while in the House and for 1988 promises to emphasize the danger to the ozone layer.

Gore attacks issues by studying them intensively, mastering the details, and thinking up his own solutions; he proceeds deliberately enough to bring colleagues along rather than antagonize them. He got into the race after being approached by Nathan Landow and other fundraisers who interviewed several candidates, were impressed by Gore, and reportedly promised to raise $2.5 million. This looks unseemly to some. But these days the people who raise big money for both parties are in it for no more selfish reason than to get invited to White House dinners; most of them are as public-spirited as the young hotshots who run shabby campaign offices with their laundry piled in the corner and more knowledgeable about the society they seek to serve. Gore's serious demeanor, his command of facts, his gravity may turn out to be as appealing to voters as they were to insiders.

Obviously Gore would like to strike a spark in the southern states that vote on Super Tuesday. But it seems likely that he will have to show he can win some votes in Iowa and New Hampshire if he is to do so. Neither Gore himself nor southern Democratic primary voters are so parochial as they used to be in the days when race and civil rights divided the two regions; and Gore's strong standing in Tennessee, where he was elected overwhelmingly to the Senate when Howard Baker retired in 1984, is probably not transferable across state lines.

Jesse Jackson. It is hard to capture in print what makes Jesse Jackson such an electrifying political figure. He was not, despite some claims, the first black presidential candidate in 1984; Shirley Chisholm was, back in 1972. He was not the first candidate to win the votes of virtually all black voters; Robert Kennedy did that in 1968, and won a lot of others besides. He was not at Martin Luther King, Jr.'s side when he died, as has been claimed, and he was more of a foot soldier than a leader in the civil rights revolution of the 1960s. His chances of becoming President seem nil: the large majority of Americans would never vote for him. Yet in 1984 he was a solid third-place finisher in the Democratic primaries; after starting off by sharing the black vote with Walter Mondale in early primaries like Alabama's, he ended up sweeping it in New York and afterwards.

Perhaps the reason is that his appeal partakes of the traditional and of the radical in black politics. His speaking style, impassioned and rhythmic, filled with rhymes and incantations, is derived from the ancient and noble tradition of fiery black preachers. And parts of his philosophy—his imprecations against drug taking, his calling on babies to stop having babies—come straight out of old-fashioned preachers' morality. The radical can be seen in his sympathetic comments about Castro's Cuba and Yasir Arafat's Palestine Liberation Organization, which seems to come out of a sense that American blacks have a stake in solidarity with oppressed peoples in the Third World and that Socialist regimes, even authoritarian or totalitarian ones, represent in some respects a progressive form of government when compared to right-wing oligarchies or dictatorships. These views led him into some troublesome waters in 1984: his reference to New York as "Hymietown" and his refusal for weeks to renounce Louis Farrakhan (on the patently ridiculous ground that to do so would infringe on Farrakhan's First Amendment freedoms) convinced many Americans that he was anti-semitic. The uncomfortable fact is that by the end of the Democratic primaries almost all blacks were voting for Jesse Jackson and almost no whites were—a degree of polarization the party had not seen at least since George Wallace's candidacy collapsed in the 1976 Florida primary.

For 1988 Jackson has taken great pains to mend relations with American Jews and to campaign extensively among whites; in early 1987 he opened a headquarters in Greenfield, Iowa. He talks of assembling a coalition of those with economic discontents, including not only blacks, but farmers who have been ruined by the collapse in prices and factory workers whose jobs have migrated elsewhere. This is the kind of populist black-white coalition liberals have been talking about wistfully since the days of Franklin D. Roosevelt, and which had come closest to actuality in presidential politics in 1976. Jackson's appeal looks to be vulnerable to an uptick in farm prices or the surge that by 1986 was apparent in Great Lakes industrial economies. But more importantly, his strategy rests on an assumption that a large mass of low-income Americans see themselves as a bloc with interests antithetical to those with more money. In the economically polarized America just before and after World War II, when everyone had given up on economic growth, that assumption seemed plausible. It seems more dubious now in the more fragmented and various America in which almost every region and sector has experienced some growth, though at different times and a different pace, in the 1980s.

Jackson's core of black support, plus some white votes he is likely to get, can nevertheless give him impressive percentages, and perhaps some victories, in primaries south and north; if whites don't turn out heavily (as they did not in 1984), a state like Alabama can easily have a Democratic electorate that is 40% black and a state like Illinois can have one that is 25% black. The question is what can he do with such showings. Jackson loves to negotiate with white powerholders; it is the primary work he has done for his PUSH organization and he spent days and nights on the phone negotiating with Mondale aides in 1984. He can negotiate another chance to make a big convention speech, as he did in 1984; but it's not likely that a nominee will want to be seen agreeing to put Jackson in the Cabinet or to consult with him on all major appointments. Jackson has some useful and interesting messages and a brilliant ability to deliver them. The question he will have to answer after 1988 if not before is whether a presidential campaign is the right vehicle for delivering them.

Paul Simon. The crusading publisher of a small-town newspaper as long ago as 1948, elected to the Illinois legislature in 1954, a nearly successful candidate for governor in 1972, Paul Simon has the longest history in politics of any of the candidates. Yet he is still in his 50s and in the prime of his political life. He is instinctively a liberal reformer who sometimes takes unorthodox positions; a tilter against the local powers to statewide and even national acclaim when he edited the *Troy Tribune* and one who was endorsed for governor by Mayor Richard J. Daley; a legislator for 26 of the last 36 years whose highest executive office was lieutenant governor and who now is running for Chief Executive.

Simon's candidacy was one of the more unexpected developments of the 1987 campaign season, and came about after those counted as supporters of traditional big-government Democratic programs—Edward Kennedy, Mario Cuomo—bowed out. Simon knew that Downstate Illinois, which he carried against Charles Percy, was in similar economic shape with much of Iowa; and he hoped that the big contributors, who backed him in that 1984 contest because they disliked Percy's views on Israel as chairman of the Senate Foreign Relations Committee, would back him again. "I am not a neo-anything," he said in one of the more appealing lines of the season. "I am a Democrat."

Conventional wisdom says that this bow-tied journalist who writes his own newsletters and has written 11 books—the latest on workfare, a hot topic for 1987—can't make it. But Simon has the confidence of a politician who has rebounded from defeat and beaten the odds before. In 1972 he was the favorite to beat Republican Governor Richard Ogilvie, but he was upset by anti-Daley walking candidate Daniel Walker in the primary. Two years later, he was elected to the House seat vacated by Ken Gray. After 10 productive years in the House, Simon took the risk of another statewide race, taking on the undefeated Percy in a year when Ronald Reagan swept 49 states. Simon won a multicandidate primary and beat Percy. He enters the race with the optimism about politics of a man who met his wife when they were both members of the Illinois legislature.

DEMOCRATS: POSSIBLE ADDED STARTERS

Bill Clinton. Pondering a presidential candidacy in the spring of 1987 was Arkansas' Governor Bill Clinton. Barely 40, he has served as governor for six of the preceding eight years; he pushed through a major education program in 1983, including testing of teachers, which earned him the hostility of the teachers' unions but the approval of the voters, for Arkansas has been a poor state which urgently needs to upgrade its labor force if it is to grow economically. Clinton has no federal government experience, but has been a familiar speaker at national events; he is an orator whose hot style can dazzle a live audience and whose cool style can reassure television viewers. Talk of Clinton's candidacy began when Arkansas' Senator Dale Bumpers took himself out of the race in the winter of 1987; with Sam Nunn and Chuck Robb out, there was for a moment no authentic southerner in a race in which the southern states voting on Super Tuesday could play a decisive role. But quickly Albert Gore jumped in, and candidates like Bruce Babbitt, Joseph Biden, and Richard Gephardt made claims of coming from the periphery of the South. The question is whether there is an opening for Clinton—particularly if, as a result of any weakening of Gary Hart or for other reasons, Sam Nunn or Charles Robb moves to enter the race.

Mario Cuomo. In February 1987, at the end of a call-in show on WCBS, Mario Cuomo stunned New Yorkers, Democrats, and voters who follow these things by announcing that he wasn't running for President in 1988; he also flummoxed the press, with which he had been feuding during his 1986 campaign, by making his announcement when they couldn't cross-examine him until after their deadlines. Cuomo's stewardship of the affairs of New York gave him the highest percentage in history for reelection as governor in 1986; his argumentativeness also got him into a few arguments he would better have avoided. Cuomo brings to politics the skills of a superb appellate lawyer: the ability to frame questions favorably to his cause; the ability to argue the facts or the law and to turn questions to his advantage; a tenaciousness in seeking his goals that is second to none. He is the one American politician who, it is probably fair to say, every other American politician would be fearful about debating. He is too New Yorky in his aggressiveness and abrasiveness, say some, and too unacquainted with the rest of the country; his Italian ancestry, say some others, would be a handicap. Both these arguments are surely wrong. Cuomo's immigrant heritage gives special meaning to his metaphor of society as a family, in which stronger members take care of the weak, and in knowledge and insight he is anything but parochial. This is a serious politician, who if he changes his mind and runs will be assessed as such by the voters.

Sam Nunn. In February 1987 Sam Nunn took himself out of the race, but saved the possibility of running later. Experts scoffed that that would be too late, but maybe not. Nunn's strength nationally is as an expert on defense, and that strength is maximized by his remaining an active Chairman of the Senate Armed Services Committee, not by attending picnics in dovish Iowa or fish fries in anti-nuclear power New Hampshire. He is one Democrat with a distinctively southern record—more conservative on economic and especially cultural and foreign issues than his northern colleagues—and whose candidacy might prompt as many southern whites to vote in Democratic presidential primaries as vote in Democratic primaries for governor. Nunn made some points with other Democrats in 1987 by disagreeing pointedly with the Reagan Administration's interpretation of the ABM treaty; he is not unacceptable to northern liberals, as he would have been in 1984 or any earlier year. But his strength is in the South where he would be the favorite in the Super Tuesday primaries no matter how late he entered: for what will matter there is not your precinct organization (there must be more than 100,000 precincts voting that one day) but what voters see of you on television newscasts and advertisements.

Charles Robb. Taking himself out of the race effectively even before 1987 was former Virginia Governor Charles Robb. He was one of the founders of the Democratic Leadership Conference, and one of those candidates southern legislators had in mind when they created the southern regional primary. Robb's success in Virginia was impressive. Elected narrowly in 1981 in a state that had not voted Democratic for governor or Senator in 15 years, he brought blacks into public life and got state government stimulating economic growth to such an impressive degree that the whole Democratic ticket won in 1985, including a black lieutenant governor and a woman attorney general. Robb started off not as a politician but as a Marine, who met Lynda Byrd Johnson while on duty at the White House, married her, and served in combat in Vietnam; if his speaking style sometimes seems wooden and his manner anything but easy, he also carries himself with an air of command. Comparatively young and with no government experience in foreign policy, Robb has not thrust himself forward. But if he should do so, he would be an especially strong candidate in the South.

THE DEMOCRATIC HOUSE

For six years in the 1980s the House of Representatives was held by Democrats while the Senate and the Presidency were held by Republicans—the only such extended period in which this has been so. This naturally breeds certain institutional habits and tends to produce certain kinds of leadership. In the House it strengthened certain trends that were already apparent in the 1970s, to the point that the House in the 1980s has operated almost entirely differently from the House of the 1960s. And that will be true now that there is a Democratic Senate and even if a Democratic President is elected in 1988.

The Speaker. The first and most obvious change has been in leadership. The leaders in the early 1970s were elderly men clearly past their best years who were elevated to one place because they had been elevated to the one below many years before. Thus John McCormack became speaker in 1962, at age 70, because he had been chosen majority leader in 1940, at age 48; Carl Albert became Speaker in 1971, at age 62, because he had been chosen whip in 1953, at 44. McCormack and Albert, like Sam Rayburn in the 1950s, felt obliged to honor the prerogatives of committee chairmen and never dared to threaten in any way the operation of the seniority system, which after all protected them too. As a result, any time the Democrats had fewer than 290 House members of 435, the speaker lacked working control.

This changed because Tip O'Neill and most of his colleagues wanted it to. O'Neill, who had served on the Rules Committee for years when speakers couldn't control even that crucial body, determined that he always would and the new younger Democrats, especially the huge class elected in 1974 and, with just two or three exceptions, reelected in 1976, were not weighed down with committee loyalties and trusted O'Neill. O'Neill in turn, though he was 64 when he became speaker, was anything but tired. He had the old-fashioned pol's talent for listening to his colleagues and sensing their drift plus the master politician's knack for knowing when the times were changing and how to change with them: he knew how to listen and how to count. He was genuinely interested in the younger members, quick to spot talent among them (and challenges, too); he had seen Carl Albert leave the Speaker's chair two years earlier than he had planned because he could not handle the new House, and he was determined he wouldn't leave under similar circumstances.

On policy O'Neill's initial impulse was to follow the lead of the Democratic Administration, which he did in 1977 on energy: he assembled a special committee which put through a bill much like what Jimmy Carter wanted. But as time went on, the Administration failed to provide a lead; and then the victory of Ronald Reagan and the Republican capture of the Senate made O'Neill the de facto leader of the Democratic Party. He responded brilliantly. He positioned his party during each Congress so as to maximize its numbers in the next election, confronting the Administration on the budget, taxes, and Social Security to make a record for recessionary 1982; reaching compromises on the gas tax, highways, and Social Security to make a record for pro-incumbent 1984; sitting back and letting the Republicans advocate tax hikes and defense cuts and opposing contra aid and the MX for incumbent-prone but uneasy 1986. As a result, there were more House Democrats in the last Reagan years than in the first ones, though only one election in the 1980s has come in a recession year.

Jim Wright seems determined to maintain and extend the gains O'Neill won for the speakership. He entered office with a specific agenda in mind—difficult issues like trade legislation, workfare, campaign finance reform—and he came out more strongly for higher taxes than anyone else in Washington. Wright is an old-fashioned FDR Democrat who believes in federal spending at home and abroad: he supported unfashionable causes like dam building and the Vietnam war as well as antipoverty programs and the international lending agencies; and if he smiles on special provisions for Texas oil men and Texas savings and loans, that is part of an old tradition that goes back to Lyndon Johnson and Sam Rayburn and John Nance Garner and Jesse Jones. Wright is not as comfortable conversing with his colleagues as O'Neill was and is more guarded. But he seems to be using the power of the Speaker at least as vigorously as O'Neill did. So with just 258 Democrats he has working control of the House.

The committee chairmen. The single most effective House reform of the 1970s was the election of committee chairmen by all House Democrats, and of subcommittee chairmen by committee Democrats. One effect is to make committee chairmen responsible to their colleagues of the majority party. Another effect is to make the majority party responsible, in elections in every district, for what its committee chairmen do. The first effect can plainly be seen in the career of Jamie Whitten, dean of the House now and Chairman since 1979 of the Appropriations Committee. In the 1960s Whitten was already powerful as chairman of the Agriculture Appropriations Committee—he has held that post, except for two years of Republican control, since 1949—and voted on most issues with the conservative alliance of Republicans and southern segregationists. In the middle 1970s his rating from organized labor jumped from about 10% to about 40%. It's been up over 50% in the 1980s. When committee chairmen were first required to be elected, in 1975, Whitten won by only 157–88, though there was no opposition; a switch of 35 votes would have beaten him. More recently, he has almost no opposition. He supports Democratic leadership programs (which are in turn not as liberal as they once were) and, as a highly competent chairman, he is supported in return.

The obverse side of this is that House Democrats remove chairmen who are no longer up to the job. Wright Patman of Banking lost in 1976 and Mel Price of Armed Services in 1984 not because their views were out of line of their colleagues', but because House Democrats didn't want voters back in their districts to see their party represented by old men who didn't seem up to their duties. Similarly, the move in 1986 to oust Price's successor, Les Aspin, lost steam partly because House Democrats recognized that he represented them competently on national issues—even if he didn't keep them informed of his policy switches the way they would like.

There was criticism, particularly from the Senate, during the Aspin imbroglio of the election of chairmen, on the grounds that it consumes so much time and produces so much uncertainty. But the legislative process is not meant to be efficient or relaxing. The election of chairmen has produced competent and accountable leaders on every committee. Few reforms have done so much good and so little harm.

The subcommittee entrepreneurs. Criticism has also been levelled at the proliferation of subcommittees and the uncertainty caused by the election of subcommittee chairmen. Neither point is well taken. Not all subcommittees are created equal: in any two years in the House there are a dozen or so subcommittees that really make a difference, and a great many others—some with grand-sounding titles and sweeping jurisdiction—don't make much difference at all. The difference is in the political and legislative abilities of the chairmen and, sometimes, of the ranking Republicans. Chairmen who can get things done, who can forge majorities in full committee and carry bills on the floor, who know their substance and their procedure, can make an immense difference in the House; so, for that matter, can junior and minority members who know how to work with their subcommittee chairmen. Others will not do so well. The House in the 1980s is a kind of meritocracy, where power goes mostly to those who are competent, and powerlessness (or a quiet retirement) is the lot of those who are not adept at legislating.

The following is an attempt to list the 12 House members who are likely to be most powerful and influential in 1987 and 1988. Like all such efforts, it is inevitably impressionistic and subject to error, and should not be taken too seriously.

Most are on because of their obvious leadership or committee positions. Gephardt will presumably spend only limited time in the House as the Iowa caucuses and New Hampshire primary approach; yet he had a signal and impressive victory on his trade bill in April 1987. Swift is chairman of the House Democrats' task force on campaign finance reform, and could end up determining whether such a bill passes or not.

House Leadership

Congressman	Party/State District	Committee/ Subcommittee	Year Elected	%
Jim Wright	D-TX 12	Speaker	1954	69
Dan Rostenkowski	D-IL 8	Chmn., Ways & Means	1958	79
John Dingell	D-MI 16	Chmn., Energy & Commerce	1955	78
Thomas Foley	D-WA 5	Majority Leader	1964	75
William Gray	D-PA 2	Chmn., Budget	1978	100
Tony Coehlo	D-CA 15	Majority Whip	1978	72
Jamie Whitten	D-MS 1	Chmn., Appropriations	1941	66
Richard Gephardt	D-MO 3	Chmn., Dem. Caucus	1976	69
Les Aspin	D-WI 1	Chmn., Armed Services	1970	75
Robert Michel	R-IL 18	Minority Leader	1956	62
Henry Waxman	D-CA 24	Chmn., Health & Envir. Sbcmte.	1974	100
Al Swift	D-WA 2	Chmn., Tsk. Force on Camp. Fin. Rfm.	1978	72

Lobbying. As recently as a decade ago, lobbying before the Congress was a bilateral business. On one side was organized labor, primarily the brilliant lobbyists of the AFL–CIO, sometimes joined by representatives of any Democratic administration. On the other side was the lobbyists of the Republican administration, backed up by a centralized cadre of business lobbyists. Of course specific special interests did have representation. But on the big bills going through Congress, the two big lobbies were usually what mattered. Most members were signed up on one team or the other, and the two sides fought for the few in the middle.

The game is different now. The AFL–CIO made the fatal mistake in 1977, the first Carter year, of making their top priority their least appealing issue: common situs picketing. The Congress, filled now with Democrats who got there more through their revulsion at Richard Nixon and the Vietnam war than at their opposition to Herbert Hoover and economic royalists, rejected labor's common situs bill and, soon after, its much more important and appealing labor law reform as well. Ralph Nader's consumer protection agency, vetoed by President Ford, was beaten in the Democratic House. The progressive tax reform bill House Democrats brought out was amended by Republican William Steiger to cut the tax on capital gains. The labor/liberal lobby has never been the same.

Nor has the conservative/business lobby done so well after the first Reagan years. It is one of the casualties, perhaps, of Reagan's desire to fight big government by running a big deficit: it is not needed to oppose new spending programs (since no one is seriously proposing any); it is barred from cutting the deficit (because it doesn't want to increase taxes); and it is unable to champion the fictitious Reagan budgets which don't have half a dozen votes in the House.

The result is a proliferation of lobbying and interests represented, and a kind of meritocracy in the lobbies as well as on the floor and in the committee and subcommittee rooms. That puts a premium on the skill of legislators who, like Dan Rostenkowski and John Dingell, can put together bills that serve a lot of purposes and hold them together to passage.

Elections. House Republicans may be the most frustrated politicians in Washington. They see their fellow Republicans dominant in the White House, controlling the Senate for most of the decade, and producing far more than their share of new ideas and policy initiatives. Yet they seem permanently mired in the minority in the House. No wonder they yell with glee when they win a procedural victory, even if, as in December 1985, it risks destroying the major policy initiative of their own President.

Why do the Democrats maintain control? First, because Tip O'Neill saw that they adopted the right posture—confrontation or statesmanship—for the election, and not just in the weeks before it but during the whole biennium. Second, because the Democratic Party just seems to produce more natural politicians, more people who like politics enough and are good enough at it to win elections where the odds are against them. Democrats today hold at least 50 seats which, if no incumbent were running, the Republicans would have an excellent chance to win. Third is redistricting, which the Republicans overestimate but still gives the Democrats an extra 15 seats—not unimportant when they have just 40 more than the majority of 218.

Fourth, the Democrats have learned to play the money game brilliantly in the 1980s. In 1981 the word was that the Republican Party had a huge money advantage and that it was going to get all the business PACs to work together to support only Republicans and produce a Republican House in 1982. It wasn't such a wacky idea as it now seems. But Tony Coelho, the Democrats' campaign committee chairman, put the kibosh on it. He went into the offices of PAC after PAC, told them he expected them to be bipartisan, provided them with lists of Democratic incumbents and challengers who were good on their issues, and reminded them that the Democrats controlled all subcommittee chairmanships and knew how to keep score. The PACs kept channeling money to the Democrats, the recession came along, and the dream (or nightmare) of a Republican House vanished for a decade. As the 1980s went on, Coelho brilliantly funneled PAC money where it was needed so that in the large majority of close races the Democrat outspent or spent as much as the Republican. By 1986 the Democrats had turned the Republicans' money advantage upside down.

But the Democrats do not control the House just because they're better at manipulating the system; they also control it because the voters want them to. There is a strong and sensible desire, in an era when presidential nominating processes give an advantage to extremists or enthusiasts of both parties, to dividing the control of government, for having Tip O'Neill's or Jim Wright's Democrats there to check and balance Ronald Reagan's Republicans. Proof: many more serious Democratic House candidates argue checks-and-balances than serious Republican candidates argue support-your-President. In fact, divided government has become the rule in the advanced democracies in the 1980s: France has cohabitation, Italy and Japan are ruled always by coalitions of parties and factions, in West Germany the Free Democrats decide which party rules, and in Canada power is shared by a federal government led by one party and provincial governments which are mostly led by others. Even in Britain a three-party system, and so a potential sharing of power, has developed. The United States simply has divided government in its most sophisticated, complex, and exquisitely sensitive form.

Does that mean the Republicans can never capture the House? On the contrary, it means they can. Three factors may be working for them in the 1990s which are not operating today: the Democrats' redistricting edge may be reduced (particularly if Speaker Willie Brown's unpopularity means the Republicans win control of the California legislature), there will be inevitable attrition among the Watergate class of 1974, and the current Democratic advantage in fundraising may not hold up. It is entirely possible, though by no means assured, that we will spend much of the next decade with a Republican House checking and balancing a Democratic President and Senate—the exact opposite of the situation for most of the 1980s. Events, personalities, changes in demographics—all these will matter. But we can be reasonably sure that the House will provide an accurate representation of what the country wants, biased and distorted somewhat toward those with superior political ability.

THE DEMOCRATIC SENATE

With only 100 members, with a set of arcane rules that probably no member has fully mastered, the Senate is a uniquely human institution, as antique as the inkwells and blotting sand on Senators' desks, but as prone to sudden and transforming change as human institutions can be when there is heavy turnover in the people that make them up. Because party control of the Senate has changed twice in the 1980s, it is tempting to contrast the Democratic with the Republican Senate. But that's probably not the useful divide. The Senate, which likes to emphasize that it is a continuing body, with two-thirds of its members in one Congress entitled to return to the next, changes more slowly than that. Over the adult lifetimes of most active politicians, three stages in the life of the Senate can be discerned.

The first is the Senate of the 1950s as described by *New York Times* reporter William S. White in his book *The Citadel.* White, a Texan and a conservative, admired the insiders of the Senate club of the time, and described them better than anyone else: Richard Russell of Georgia, the master of the rules, who quieted the national furor when Harry Truman fired Douglas MacArthur; John Stennis, the former judge and master of propriety; Robert Kerr and Lyndon Johnson, the hard-charging young leaders from the oil states, eager to make their regions and themselves rich. White's Senate was run by perhaps a dozen of the then 96 Senators, all able men, almost all southerners, most conservatives. Yet it is misleading to suppose that only southerners or conservatives could join the club. Back in the 1940s Robert Wagner, the liberal from New York, was certainly a member, because—and these were always the criteria—he was a brilliant legislator, a fine judge of men, a man who could respect his colleagues even as he opposed them. But Wagner retired in 1949, and the postwar liberals—Hubert Humphrey, Paul Douglas, Joseph Clark—while able men experienced in public life, were painfully naive about the Senate when they arrived in Washington and utterly unequipped with legislative instinct. Wagner, who had served for years in the New York Senate, took the trouble to learn the birthdays and the favorite sports, the interests and the soft spots of each of his colleagues; Humphrey, Douglas, and Clark, who had never served in a legislature, got started by insulting senior members and in pursuit of causes that got them nowhere.

The end of White's Senate came in the middle 1960s, when Lyndon Johnson, who was chosen Democratic leader by Richard Russell, insisted on jamming through the Senate the one measure which threatened the life and, in most cases, the core beliefs, and undermined the cherished filibuster, of the leading southerners in the club, and Russell in particular: the Civil Rights Act of 1964. The civil rights bills which Johnson as Majority Leader got through the Senate in 1957 and 1960, in contrast, were far less threatening; and Johnson's other dazzling achievements in the Senate were achieved with the help or at least at the sufferance of Russell and the club. But by the 1960s their numbers were dwindling, and they recruited no new members from the huge new class of liberal Democrats elected in 1958. The liberals had a hard time legislating at first. But by the time Russell died in 1971, control of the Senate had gone over to the liberals—or, rather, to no one in particular.

This is the second stage of the Senate, when the liberals of both parties were in the majority, but when no one was really in control. Majority Leader Mike Mansfield believed that a leader should not coerce or cajole Senators, but treat them respectfully as utterly independent entities, respecting their committee jurisdictions, their home state's interests, their particular beliefs, and their quirks. The result was a Senate with dozens of highly competent members who could get legislation through, but in which no one did so consistently. It was a Senate liberal enough to vote at various times to shut down the Vietnam war and to reject a President's choices for the Supreme Court; but it was not a Senate determined enough to make those choices stick and ended up funding the war and approving nominees whose views were similar to those who were rejected. Mansfield retired in 1976 and was replaced by Robert Byrd, who as Whip had done a brilliant job of making other Senators' lives easier, and who as Leader saw himself as a servant of the incumbent Democratic Administration and of his Democratic colleagues. Yet as time went on there was attrition in the liberal Senate. The number of liberals did not much decline, but Senators in the middle 1970s became the focal points of Americans' discontent with government, and in the 1976 and 1978 elections more than half of the Senators with serious opposition were defeated. Then, quite unexpectedly in 1980, almost all the Democrats who had serious opposition (and some who didn't) were beaten, turning over control to the Republicans.

This was also the clear beginning of the third stage in the life of the Senate, though in retrospect the signs were apparent from 1976 on, as high turnover produced a less senior and arguably less distinguished Senate. The liberals' Senate turned into the leaders' Senate. In the liberals' Senate dozens of Senators made important differences in policy. In the leaders' Senate only a handful did. Partly this was a result of the leaders' skills. Majority Leaders Howard Baker, Robert Dole, and, it appears, Robert Byrd, installed again after the Democrats' recapture of the Senate, have set agendas for the body and pretty well determined how it will stand on issues. They have worked hard and used their particular and in each case rather different skills to hold almost all of their own parties together and to fashion positions which can command a few votes from the other side when necessary. In this they have had good cooperation from committee chairmen, particularly Robert Dole, Bob Packwood, and, it appears, Lloyd Bentsen of Finance, and of Pete Domenici and Lawton Chiles of Budget.

Going beyond that, it has been hard to compile lists of the dozen most powerful Senators in the 1980s. A few names pop up, and some Senators have made an impact on a particular question. But the majority of Senators at any given time have had little seniority, have had limited legislative skills, have had trouble developing the detailed knowledge they need to legislate of how government and society work. Some in particular of the Republican class of 1980 were weak in basic skills. It always used to be said that in conference committees the House members had an advantage because they knew more of the details of legislation; now it is often the case that they have a broader view of the problem and a more generous understanding of society than their Senate counterparts. This point of view can be carried too far: Senators are mostly able men and women, and as the 1980s continue they may get the seasoning they need to match their counterparts of the past. But after the 1986 elections they still had a ways to go.

The change from the liberals' to the leaders' Senate can most clearly be seen in the conduct of Robert Byrd, who came to the Senate when it was still run by William S. White's club. Byrd was a relatively passive Majority Leader in the 1970s, a man who knew the details of procedure and of legislation as well—he prides himself on getting the Panama Canal treaty through, but he decided to support it only after reading up extensively about it. But in 1987 he seemed to be operating in a different manner. He seemed to have learned from Howard Baker and Robert Dole the need to provide strong leadership and guidance on substance. He seemed to have learned from Tip O'Neill the need to set a posture for his party in which it can be seen to govern and from which it can advantageously fight the next election. And he added to this his own ability to hone in on important details and get them right. In early 1987 Byrd was actively working to see that Democratic Party policy was set on arms control, campaign finance reform, and trade—all areas in which the details of legislation are of paramount importance. He was working with committee chairmen and sponsors of key bills, but he was also putting his own imprint on matters.

Byrd, who grew up as a coal miner's son, and who worked as a produce man, a butcher, and a welder before he went into politics, seems to be proving that he can learn a new leadership style and adapt to new legislative times even as he approaches the age of 70. Through most of the 1980s there was talk that the Democrats wanted to replace Byrd, who was considered untelegenic and a weak leader, and candidates arose against him. There was little such talk in early 1987.

What follows is a list of the 12 Senators likely to be most powerful in the 100th Congress. Drawing up such lists, it should not be necessary to add, is an utterly impressionistic and unscientific enterprise, and no one should take them too seriously.

Senate Leadership

Senator	Party/State	Committee	Term Exp.	%
Robert Byrd	D-WV	Majority Leader	1988	69-31
Lloyd Bentsen	D-TX	Chmn., Finance	1988	59-40
San Nunn	D-GA	Chmn., Armed Services	1990	80-20
Daniel Inouye	D-HI	Chmn., Select Cmte. on Iran	1992	74-26
David Boren	D-OK	Chmn., Intelligence	1990	76-23
Lawton Chiles	D-FL	Chmn, Budget	1988	62-38
Edward Kennedy	D-MA	Chmn., Labor	1988	61-38
Ernest Hollings	D-SC	Chmn., Commerce	1992	64-36
Christopher Dodd	D-CT	Member, Foreign Relations	1992	65-35
Robert Dole	R-KS	Minority Leader	1992	70-30
Howard Metzenbaum	D-OH	Chmn., Labor Sbcmte.	1988	57-41
Jesse Helms	R-NC	Ranking, Foreign Relations	1990	52-48

There is a big falloff in power after position three or four. Boren is on because he is the chief sponsor of the campaign finance law and chairs Intelligence as well. Chiles chairs Budget. Kennedy at Human Resoures and Hollings at Commerce may try to revive or revise traditional Democratic welfare programs and regulatory schemes. Dodd chairs the Latin American Subcommittee and is an articulate opponent of aiding the Nicaraguan contras. Dole is Minority Leader, and a smart one. Metzenbaum and Helms are on as negative forces, Metzenbaum because he knows the rules and makes a practice of bottling up bills he doesn't like, Helms because as ranking Republican on Foreign Relations he will try to hog-tie foreign policy appointments and initiatives he doesn't like. The fact that negative forces could end up on this list shows how few positive forces there are besides the leadership.

How will the 1988 elections change the Senate? No one of course can be sure: few people expected the Republicans to win control in 1980 or the Democrats to win control by such a wide margin in 1986, but in both cases almost all the close races went to one party, and so control changed hands. That could happen again in 1988, although initially the numbers seem to favor the Democrats. They have more seats up, but fewer seem vulnerable, while initial indications are that Republican Senators who would otherwise easily win may be drawing challengers who can defeat them. (See 1988 Senate Elections Chart on page LXVI.)

Regardless of the party outcome, however, this is liable to remain a leaders' Senate, at least for another two years.

1988 SENATE ELECTIONS

State	Senator	Age 1986	Year App'd or Elected	1982 %
Democrats				
EAST				
ME	George Mitchell	53	1980	61-39
MD	Paul Sarbanes	53	1976	63-37
MA	Edward Kennedy	54	1962	61-38
NJ	Frank Lautenberg	62	1982	51-48
NY	Daniel Patrick Moynihan	59	1976	65-34
SOUTH				
FL	Lawton Chiles	56	1970	62-38
MS	John Stennis	85	1978	64-36
TN	James Sasser	50	1976	62-38
WV	Robert Byrd	69	1958	69-31
MIDWEST				
MI	Donald Riegle	48	1976	58-41
ND	Quentin Burdick	78	1960	62-34
OH	Howard Metzenbaum	69	1976	57-41
WI	William Proxmire	71	1957	64-34
WEST				
AZ	Dennis DeConcini	49	1976	59-41
HI	Spark Matsunaga	70	1976	80-17
NM	Jeff Bingaman	43	1982	54-46
MT	John Melcher	62	1976	54-42
TX	Lloyd Bentsen	65	1970	59-40
Republicans				
EAST				
CT	Lowell Weicker	55	1970	50-46
DE	William Roth	65	1970	56-44
PA	John Heinz	48	1976	59-39
RI	John Chafee	64	1976	51-49
VT	Robert Stafford*	73	1971	51-48
SOUTH				
VA	Paul Trible	40	1982	51-49
MIDWEST				
IN	Richard Lugar	54	1976	54-46
MN	David Durenberger	52	1978	53-47
MO	John Danforth	50	1976	51-49
NE	David Karnes	38	1987	
WEST				
CA	Pete Wilson	53	1982	52-45
NV	Chic Hecht	58	1982	50-48
UT	Orrin Hatch	52	1976	58-41
WA	Daniel Evans	61	1983	55-45

*Retiring at end of term.

ALABAMA

The trees' buds are out and the early leaves are the same lacy light green in early springtime, the rivers still wind gently over the fertile Black Belt toward the Gulf, the statue of Vulcan on Red Mountain still looks down over Birmingham in the valley; Alabama physically looks no different. But you don't have to listen long to people talking—to politicians or just to ordinary folks—to get the sense that something is seriously wrong in Alabama. While most southern states are bustling economically and bursting with pride over their education reforms and their quality of life, Alabama senses that it is slipping farther behind. When other southern states are producing national leaders and presidential candidates for both parties, Alabama is conspicuous for having on the average the lowest quality of politicians of any state in the union.

Why is Alabama in trouble? One reason is economic. In the days when "industry" was synonymous with economic growth, Alabama was the premier heavy industry state in the South. Birmingham, the state's largest city, sits in a valley beneath a red mountain made of iron ore, not far from Appalachian coal mines—the best natural location for steel mills in the United States. In 1960 Birmingham was one of the largest cities in the South, and its steel mills, plus the smaller factories tucked here and there in the hardscrabble red hills of central and northern Alabama, made this the leading manufacturing state in the South. But the 1970s and 1980s were not a good time for heavy industry, and Alabama has not yet found anything to replace steel as a provider of paychecks. In the 1980s Alabama had some of the nation's highest unemployment rates and negative economic growth.

Alabama has also suffered from its political leadership. For most of the 24 years from 1962, when he was first elected governor, until 1986, when he retired, George Wallace set the style and tone of public life in Alabama. In his declining years, Wallace was a sad figure, crippled by gunshot wounds, unable to hear much, often in dreadful pain; his once superb political talents were not much in evidence. He inspired sympathy by seeking the support of the blacks he had once scorned, and for saying "The South has changed, and for the better." Yet he could not undo the damage caused by his earlier deeds. By sweeping to victory in 1962 on the platform of "segregation forever," by standing ostentatiously (though ineffectively) in the schoolhouse door to prevent integration in 1963, by campaigning effectively in the North in the 1964 and 1972 Democratic primaries and as a third-party candidate in the 1968 presidential race, Wallace kept the cause of opposition to civil rights in the forefront of public life in Alabama and the nation. "Send them a message!" Wallace cried, and he shrewdly tailored his own message to local causes and local complaints. His force as a national politician was spent by 1976, when he was beaten by Jimmy Carter in the Florida primary. But he remained the key figure in Alabama, retiring in 1978 but returning to office in 1982 after his successor, Fob James, proved inept and decided not to seek reelection.

Wallace made himself Alabama's leading political figure in the early 1960s by adopting the feisty tone and populist rhetoric which have long been trademarks of Alabama politics. But in the late 1980s, it's not clear that this old tone serves the state's economic interests or that this old rhetoric resonates with most Alabama voters. Alabama's reputation was besmirched in the 1960s by Bull Connor's police dogs and shaped in the 1970s by Wallace's rough-hewn politics; neither staunch stands for segregation nor the threat (if not the reality) of populistic legislation has attracted businesses or generated many jobs. George Wallace has left Alabama with a gritty blue collar job base that is shrinking and with state and local government that provides few services (this is the last state without a full kindergarten program, for example) but whose taxes as of early 1987 seemed sure to be raised.

He has also left state politics in the hands of politicians with great flaws and limited

ALABAMA — **Congressional Districts, Counties, and Selected Places** — *(7 Districts)*

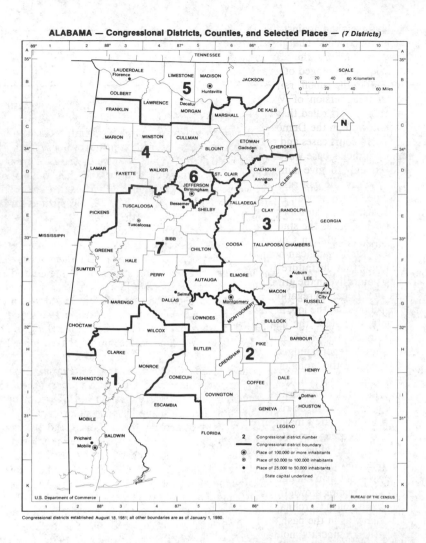

Congressional districts established August 18, 1981; all other boundaries are as of January 1, 1980.

competence. Alabama's vibrant populist tradition was once championed by men like Senator Hugo Black, later a Supreme Court justice, Senators Lister Hill and John Sparkman, and half a dozen congressmen who supported New Deal economic programs. Their politics took economic growth for granted and concentrated on the redistribution of wealth—from stockholders to steel workers, from the rich Northeast to the poor Tennessee Valley, from the "Big Mules" who owned the banks and utilities and factories to the independent-minded white farmers in the red hills. In 1986 this tradition was represented by Bill Baxley, candidate for governor, who had the eloquence and habits (tobacco chewing) but also the flaws (a penchant for gambling, womanizing, and paying his taxes late) of the stereotypical populist politician. For all his experience (two terms as attorney general and one as lieutenant governor) and accomplishments (convictions in the 1963 Birmingham bombing case, consumer fraud work), Baxley could not parley his populism into anything better than 37% in the first primary, a second-place finish in the runoff (8,756 votes behind), and (after he was given the nomination by his allies on the state Democratic executive committee) a defeat by an apparently unqualified Republican in the general. Baxley inveighed against the "Big Mules," but those attacks were persuasive to fewer voters than his opponents' charges that he was a captive of the "special interests"—black organizations, labor unions, the teachers associations, trial lawyers.

Against Baxley were ranged other politicians with different appeals. Charles Graddick, who ran ahead of him in the runoff, ran as a conservative supporter of school prayer and scourge of crime—an updated version of Wallace's old segregation strategy. But Graddick lost the nomination after a court ruled that he used his powers as attorney general to allow Republican primary voters to vote in the Democratic runoff, contrary to state law, and though he struggled through at least 14 court cases and ran a write-in campaign, he withdrew in the last week before the election. Graddick's base was among strongly religious and tradition-minded whites, but it wasn't large enough to give him a clear victory. A third appeal—that of the successful businessman who says he can restore the state's economy—was sounded by former Governor and plastic barbell entrepreneur, Fob James. But he got only 21% of the vote in the Democratic primary—a devastating result for a former incumbent. The default of the various Democrats and their strategies left as the state's governor Republican Guy Hunt, a former probate judge from Holly Pond in Cullman County, a lay Primitive Baptist preacher and former Amway salesman who as the Republican nominee won all of 26% of the vote against James in 1978.

One could argue that the failure of these strategies shows that Alabama has solved some of its problems. Few voters live in the grinding poverty that made the Big Mules such useful targets 40 and 60 years ago. Legal segregation has ended, and Alabama whites have long since accepted integration in schools, on the job, in restaurants, and at the shopping mall. They no longer mind that blacks vote, and since the late 1970s black support has not cost a candidate all white support. The religious fervor which led Fob James to sponsor a predictably futile school prayer law and led a Mobile federal judge to rule that textbooks, by omitting information about religion and morals, promoted the "religion" of secular humanism does not sway a majority of voters.

Political cleavages now run mostly on economic lines, with Democrats carrying the lower income vote—the black neighborhoods in the cities, the smaller white farm counties—while the Republicans do better with the rising affluent class of whites, carrying not only country club precincts but all of the state's major urban centers and the counties encircling the cities and the corridors of counties along the interstate highways where young families in search of country atmosphere, traditional values, and job opportunities have flocked. These are the fastest-growing part of the states, and the most heavily Republican. But neither party dominates. Alabama's Democratic base is not firm enough to give the party reliable victories (like those in Tennessee) nor has the affluent sector grown fast enough to make the Republican party label an advantage (as it seems to be in South Carolina). Democratic primaries still attract the lion's share of voters, though not as many as in the past, and Democrats still hold most legislative and minor offices; but so weak is the Democrats' hold on many voters that even those candidates unopposed by Republicans in the 1986 election ran well behind Democratic primary turnout. In fact, in the governor's race the county-by-county percentages in the Democratic runoff and the general election were uncannily similar; Alabamians have no compunction about voting in the primary and then deserting the Democratic nominee, and they evidently saw the Baxley-Graddick and Baxley-Hunt choices as similar.

Unfortunately, the political competition generated by this close division has inspired raucous candidates who cannot sustain their appeal, negative campaigns, and a plethora of candidates with few other assets than familiar names. The new lieutenant governor is Jim Folsom, Jr., son of a one-time populist governor; the new state treasurer is George Wallace, Jr. Perhaps the most talented politician in the state is Birmingham Mayor Richard Arrington, who helped carry Alabama's crucial early 1984 primary for Walter Mondale; he and Alabama Democratic Conference Chairman Joe Reed were among the few black politicians (Mayor Coleman Young of Detroit was another) able to persuade blacks to choose Mondale over Jesse Jackson. But Alabama does not seem ready for a black leader statewide, and so Arrington's influence will be limited.

Not all of what is amiss in Alabama can be blamed on its politicians, and some of its economic problems may be beyond the capacity of government to solve. There is only so much the most energetic state government can do to redirect a state's economy. But it is obvious that Alabama's politicians—and voters—can do better. George Wallace has accustomed Alabamians to a politics of rhetoric and little follow-through, of appeals to the prejudices and parochialism and neglect of long-term interests. So long as Alabamians keep voting for politicians who are, in Charlie Graddick's self-description, "attackin', cussin', fussin'," for demagogues who denounce the Big Mules or secular humanists but have little in the way of positive programs, they are not likely to get better politics or government than they have had.

Governor. The man Alabamians have chosen to lead them in the computer age lives on a 140-acre farm on a leafy country road in Holly Pond and, before he beat the gravely flawed Bill Baxley, had never won a higher office than Cullman County probate judge. He was born when almost no Alabama farms had electricity and few had running water; he became governor when a hospital center supplanted U.S. Steel as the state's largest employer. Hunt seemed almost comically unprepared for the job, yet in his first months showed some sureness of foot. He hired former Democratic speakers as legislative lobbyists and sealed an alliance with the current speaker, a conservative Democrat; he hired long-time Republicans who have lost statewide campaigns, like John Grenier (Senate 1966) and one-term Congressman Jim Martin (Senate 1962 and 1978, governor 1966). Hunt and the speaker were the targets when 2,500 blacks, led by Richard Arrington and Joe Reed and joined by Jesse Jackson, marched in Montgomery to protest the low number of black appointees; but most Alabama blacks had supported the losing candidates. Hunt will have difficulty achieving his goals of stimulating the state's economy while balancing the budget and avoiding new taxes. Improving the business climate would seem to require lower taxes; upgrading the labor force might require higher. Hunt's experience as a lay preacher and a stalwartly conservative Republican activist have given him practice in spouting the kind of feisty rhetoric Alabama voters have enjoyed listening to. Whether he will do anything more than that is not clear.

Senators. Alabama's two Senators, both Democrats, stand well above the run of the state's politicians. Howell Heflin, elected in 1978 and reelected in 1984, is a man of substance, who could be a pivotal figure in some of the hardest fights of the 100th Congress. Richard Shelby, the winner by a narrow margin over Republican Jeremiah Denton in 1986, helps to swell the Democratic majority, but it is not clear whether he will be a reliably partisan Democrat or a potential ally of the Republicans on closely fought issues.

Heflin, a huge man with the look of a country storekeeper, is in fact a careful lawyer, who picks at and tinkers with the rules of law with the delicate touch of a watch repairman. He served in the 1960s as president of the state bar and in 1970, as an anti-Wallace candidate, was elected chief justice of the state Supreme Court; he got a legal reform referendum passed over Wallace's opposition. Despite his pedigree (his uncle, "Cotton Tom" Heflin, was a fierce segregationist who served in the Senate from 1920 to 1931 and once shot a black on a Washington streetcar), this was his first elective office. When he ran for the Senate in 1978, he expected Wallace to be his opponent; but Wallace declined to run. Heflin beat Representative Walter Flowers in the primary by running against "the Washington crowd"—a slogan used by Alabama candidates of all political stripes.

In the 100th Congress Heflin is in the uncomfortable position of being a pivotal vote on the floor and in the Judiciary Committee—uncomfortable, that is, for a man who does not crave clout and finds many issues and judicial nominations to be close questions. Heflin tends to hold his counsel until he has studied an issue; when he does take to the floor, he is listened to by other senators who understand that he has plowed through the detail work. When he reaches a conclusion he can carry all before him, as he did when as ranking minority member he led the way in making the case for the expulsion of Senator Harrison Williams on Abscam charges. But he sometimes has a hard time making up his mind. He has missed crucial votes on issues like immigration reform and abortion. On the Agriculture Committee he has not taken a lead role in writing farm legislation, concentrating instead on advancing Alabama interests.

On Judiciary, though he has done yeoman work on difficult technical issues like regulatory reform and bankruptcy, he has often hung back on controversial judicial nominations. He finally ended up voting for Daniel Manion and against Alabamian Jefferson Sessions in 1986; Sessions had been accused of making racially insensitive remarks, and Heflin was attacked as a "traitor" by a Mobile newspaper for opposing him. But Heflin said he had "reasonable doubts" that Sessions would be a fair judge. This vote did not attract much attention, but others in 1987 and 1988 might. The Democrats have an 8-6 edge on Judiciary, which means that Republicans, if united, must win two Democratic votes to get any nomination to the floor. So Heflin can block any controversial judicial nominee. On issues on the floor his vote can also be important, though it won't be so noticeable. Heflin often votes with his party on economic issues; he less often lines up with liberals on foreign and cultural issues.

On most issues Heflin is in line with most other southern Democratic Senators—a bloc now as large as it has been in the generation since the filibuster of the Civil Rights Act of 1964 was beaten. Electorally he appears to be in a strong position. He won his first term with no Republican opposition and his second, in 1984, with 63% of the vote against a one-term Birmingham congressman who had been unable to win reelection in 1982. But in Alabama he cannot be regarded as absolutely safe. In 1984 he did no better than split the white vote against weak and underfinanced opposition, and the anti-Washington themes that helped him get elected in the first place tends to undermine what would in most states be the asset of incumbency. So long as Alabama shows a taste for feisty, demagogic politicians, the craftsman-like and genial Heflin cannot be regarded as utterly safe.

Heflin's seat had been held for 32 years before him by John Sparkman; Alabama's other Senate seat had five occupants in eight years: James Allen, the conservative master of the Senate rules, who died suddenly in 1978 after leading the unsuccessful fight against the Panama Canal Treaties; his unexpectedly spunky widow, Maryon Allen, who lost the 1978 primary; Donald Stewart, a populist young lawyer who was upset in the 1980 runoff; Admiral Jeremiah Denton, a prisoner of war in Vietnam for seven years, who surprised almost everyone by winning the seat in 1980; and Representative Richard Shelby, who beat Denton narrowly in 1986. Of all these senators Shelby is the least colorful and the most in line with the current bloc of southern Democratic Senators.

For a man who has been in public life for nearly two decades—eight years in the state Senate and eight in the U.S. House—Shelby has revealed surprisingly little about his deep convictions and political priorities. His pedigree is conservative: he was a law partner of Walter Flowers, who represented the 7th district before him, and won his critical congressional runoff in 1978 against a black candidate with the support of white conservatives. On economic issues he is more conservative than other north Alabama Democrats; on foreign policy quite conservative— despite the large number of blacks in his district, he voted against the Voting Rights Act extension and the Martin Luther King holiday. He served on one of the most active House committees, Energy and Commerce, but without making any great impact.

His 1986 campaign was largely negative. He managed to get Secretary of State Don Siegelman to drop out of the primary and attacked his one late-entering primary opponent, James Allen Jr., for his driving record, and with 51% in a five-candidate field barely avoided a runoff against him. In the general his TV ads attacked Denton for voting to cut Social Security and for faking invoices to raise campaign money, voting to raise his pay while cutting veterans' benefits, and driving two Mercedes. The obvious intent was to deprive Denton of his greatest political asset, his good faith. No one would deny that Denton, who blinked out "torture" in Morse code when he was interviewed while a POW, is a genuine hero; and as a senator he combined a quixotic desire to bolster traditional values and a gift for gaffes with a compassionate concern for the plight of Amerasian babies. But his constituency services were weak, he did not return often to the state ("I can't be down here patting babies on the butt and get things done in Washington"), and he told staffers back in 1981 that he probably wouldn't win a second term.

What is surprising is that he came so close. The Democrats' disarray in the governors' race, with their nomination being bandied about in court from July to October and ultimately being handed to the candidate who won fewer votes in the runoff, hurt Shelby and helped Denton maintain his lead into the last weeks. But Shelby's Social Security attacks hurt him on that issue and on the broader question of credibility, and this 50%–47% winner in 1980 became a 50.3%–49.7% loser.

With his narrow margins and vague commitment to "put Alabama's needs on the top of his priority list," Shelby enters the Senate without any clear specific goals. On that basis he seems likely to be a conservative Democrat who makes few waves and concentrates on his local base rather than national issues.

Presidential politics. Alabama played a pivotal part in the 1984 presidential election, when it was one of three southern primaries on Super Tuesday, and gave Walter Mondale his first primary victory with 35% of the vote, to 21% each for John Glenn and Gary Hart and 20% for Jesse Jackson. Two things are interesting, and portentous, about the result. First, the turnout: more than one million Alabamians used to turn out for seriously contested gubernatorial and senatorial Democratic primaries, and 940,000 did in 1986; but only 428,000 voted in the much ballyhooed contest on Super Tuesday. Second, the importance of black voters and politicians: Richard Arrington and Joe Reed endorsed Mondale early and stuck with him under great pressure from Jesse Jackson and his supporters. Jackson would have won here if he'd had the near-unanimous support he got from blacks later.

Congressional districting. The state's seven congressional districts were changed only slightly for 1982 and could easily be unchanged for 1992 as well. The state's Black Belt is split among four districts, and most of it could be combined with Montgomery to make a seat with a near-black majority and a 49% Mondale vote in 1984. However, the shapes of adjacent districts would be notably more grotesque than under the current plan.

The People: Est. Pop. 1986: 4,053,000; Pop. 1980: 3,893,888, up 4.1% 1980–86 and 13.1% 1970–80; 1.68% of U.S. total, 22d largest. 12% with 1–3 yrs. col., 13% with 4+ yrs. col.; 18.9% below poverty level. Single ancestry: 22% English, 6% Irish, 3% German, 1% French. Households (1980): 77% family, 43% with children, 63% married couples; 29.9% housing units rented; median monthly rent: $119; median house value: $33,900. Voting age pop. (1980): 2,731,640; 23% Black, 1% Spanish origin. Registered voters (1986): 2,362,361; no party registration.

1986 Share of Federal Tax Burden: $9,526,000,000; 1.27% of U.S. total, 24th largest.

1986 Share of Federal Expenditures

	Total		Non-Defense		Defense	
Total Expend	$13,097m	(1.58%)	$9,689m	(1.61%)	$3,408m	(1.48%)
St/Lcl Grants	1,759m	(1.56%)	1,755m	(1.56%)	3m	(0%)
Salary/Wages	2,423m	(2.01%)	1,019m	(1.74%)	1,403m	(2.27%)
Pymnts to Indiv	6,437m	(1.77%)	6,026m	(1.74%)	412m	(2.32%)
Procurement	2,266m	(1.10%)	667m	(1.22%)	1,589m	(1.06%)
Research/Other	213m	(0.80%)	212m	(0.80%)	0m	(0%)

Political Lineup: Governor, Guy Hunt (R); Lt. Gov., Jim Folsom, Jr. (D); Secy. of State, Glenn Browder (D); Atty. Gen., Don Siegelman (D); Treasurer, George Wallace, Jr. (D); Auditor, Jan Cook (D). State Senate, 35 (31 D, 4 R); State House of Representatives, 105 (89 D, 16 R). Senators, Howell Heflin (D) and Richard C. Shelby (D). Representatives, 7 (5 D and 2 R).

1984 Presidential Vote

Reagan (R)	872,849	(61%)
Mondale (D)	551,899	(38%)

1980 Presidential Vote

Reagan (R)	654,192	(49%)
Carter (D)	636,730	(47%)
Anderson (I)	16,481	(1%)

1984 Democratic Presidential Primary

Mondale	148,165	(35%)
Glenn	89,286	(21%)
Hart	88,465	(21%)
Jackson	83,787	(20%)
Four others, uncomm.	18,580	(4%)

1984 Republican Presidential Primary

Reagan	unopposed

GOVERNOR

Gov. Guy Hunt (R)

Elected 1986, term expires Jan. 1992; b. June 17, 1933, Holly Pond; home, Holly Pond; Baptist; married (Helen).

Career: Army Air Corps, WWII: Probate Judge, 1964-76; Candidate for Repub. Nomination for Gov., 1978; State Executive Dir., Agricultural Stabilization and Conservation Service, U.S.D.A., 1981-1985.

Office: State Capitol, Montgomery 36130, 205-261-2500.

Election Results

1986 gen.	Guy Hunt (R)	696,203	(56%)
	William J. Baxley (D)	537,163	(44%)
1986 prim.	Guy Hunt (R)	20,823	(60%)
	Doug Carter (R)	8,371	(40%)
1982 gen.	George Wallace (D)	650,538	(58%)
	Emory Folmar (R)	440,815	(39%)

SENATORS

Sen. Howell Heflin (D)

Elected 1978, seat up 1990; b. June 19, 1921, Poulan, GA; home, Tuscumbia; Birmingham-Southern Col., B.A. 1941, U. of AL, J.D. 1948; United Methodist; married (Elizabeth Ann).

Career: USMC, WWII; Practicing atty., 1948–71, 1977–79; Chief Justice, AL Supreme Crt., 1971–77.

Offices: 728 HSOB 20510, 202-224-4124. Also B-29 Fed. Crthse., 15 Lee St., Montgomery 36104, 205-832-7287; P.O. Box 228, Tuscumbia 35674, 205-381-7060; 1800 5th Ave., N., Birmingham 35203, 205-254-1500; and 437 Fed. Crthse. Bldg., Mobile 36602, 205-690-3167.

Committees: *Agriculture, Nutrition, and Forestry* (5th of 10 D). Subcommittees: Rural Development and Rural Electrification (Chairman); Agricultural Production and Stabilization of Prices; Agricultural Research, Conservation, Forestry and General Legislation. *Judiciary* (7th of 8 D). Subcommittees: Antitrust, Monopolies and Business Rights; Courts and Administrative Practice (Chairman); Patents, Copyright and Trademarks. *Select Committee on Ethics* (Chairman of 3 D).

Group Ratings

	ADA	ACLU	COPE	CFA	LCV	ACU	NTU	NSI	COC	CEI
1986	25	28	59	33	8	65	44	100	58	48
1985	25	—	60	33	—	74	34	—	45	—

National Journal Ratings

	1986 LIB — 1986 CONS	1985 LIB — 1985 CONS
Economic	62% — 35%	61% — 38%
Social	45% — 52%	28% — 68%
Foreign	30% — 65%	31% — 66%

Key Votes

1) Ease Gun Cont	FOR	5) Grm-Rdmn Def Red	FOR	9) Rehnquist Nom	FOR
2) Immig Reform	AGN	6) Contra Aid	FOR	10) Tax Reform	AGN
3) Lmt Text Imp	FOR	7) SDI Funding	FOR	11) Drug Death Pen	AGN
4) Aid Tobac Ind	FOR	8) Lmt PAC Contrib	FOR	12) S Africa Sanc	FOR

Election Results

1984 general	Howell Heflin (D)	860,535	(63%)	($2,001,386)
	Albert Lee Smith (R)	498,508	(36%)	($574,382)
1984 primary	Howell Heflin (D)	399,817	(83%)	
	Charles Wayne Borden (D)	47,463	(10%)	
	Mrs. Frank Ross Stewart (D)	33,114	(7%)	
1978 general	Howell Heflin (D)	547,054	(94%)	($1,059,113)
	Jerome B. Couch (ProL)	34,951	(6%)	

Campaign Contributions and Expenditures

1979-84		Direct Cont. 1979-84		PACS Breakdown 1979-84			
Receipts	$2,391,192	Indiv.	$1,315,791	Corp.	$444,566	T/M/H	$269,870
Expend.	$2,001,386	PACS	$945,293	Labor	$110,600	Agr.	$13,600
Unspent	$484,533			Ideo.	$79,550	CWOS	$20,350

Sen. Richard C. Shelby (D)

Elected 1986, seat up 1992; b. May 6, 1934, Birmingham; home, Tuscaloosa; U. of AL, B.A. 1957; U. of AL, LL.B. 1963; Presbyterian; married (Annette).

Career: Practicing atty., 1963–78; AL Senate, 1970–78; U.S. House of Reps., 1978–1986.

Offices: 313 HSOB 20510, 202-224-5744. Also 3280 Dauphin St., Ste. B121, Mobile 36616, 205-690-3222.

Committees: *Armed Services* (9th of 10 D). Subcommittees: Conventional Forces and Alliance Defense; Manpower and Personnel; Projection Forces and Regional Defense. *Banking, Housing and Urban Affairs* (9th of 10 D). Subcommittees: Consumer Affairs; Securities. *Special Committee on Aging* (9th of 10 D).

Group Ratings (as Member of U.S. House of Representatives)

	ADA	ACLU	COPE	CFA	LCV	ACU	NTU	NSI	COC	CEI
1986	40	20	44	58	33	55	29	100	39	30
1985	25	—	39	25	—	67	30	—	57	—

National Journal Ratings (as Member of U.S. House of Representatives)

	1986 LIB — 1986 CONS		1985 LIB — 1985 CONS	
Economic	58% —	41%	48% —	52%
Social	41% —	58%	34% —	64%
Foreign	31% —	69%	24% —	66%

Key Votes (as Member of U.S. House of Representatives)

1) Lmt Cln Water Act	FOR	5) Retain Gun Cont	AGN	9) Aid Angola Reb	FOR
2) Rpl Tobac Sub	AGN	6) Contra Aid	FOR	10) Tax Reform	FOR
3) Grm-Rdmn Def Red	FOR	7) Lmt Text Imp	FOR	11) S Africa Sanc	FOR
4) Ban Polygraph	FOR	8) Lmt SDI	AGN	12) Immig Reform	AGN

Election Results

1986 general	Richard C. Shelby (D)	609,360	(50%)	($2,259,167)
	Jeremiah Denton (R)	602,537	(49%)	($4,621,163)
1986 primary	Richard C. Shelby (D)	420,155	(51%)	
	Jim Allen, Jr. (D)	294,206	(35%)	
	Four others (D)	114,229	(14%)	
1980 general	Jeremiah Denton (R)	650,362	(50%)	($855,346)
	Jim Folsom, Jr. (D)	617,175	(47%)	($356,647)

Campaign Contributions and Expenditures

1985-86		Direct Cont. 1985-86		PACS Breakdown 1985-86			
Receipts	$2,400,488	Indiv.	$686,727	Corp	$315,438	T/M/H	$210,300
Expend.	$2,259,167	Party	$17,499	Labor	$257,274	Agr.	$ 12,500
Unspent	$141,319	PACS	$891,434	Ideo.	$ 86,922	CWOS	$ 9,000
		Cand.	$696,104				

FIRST DISTRICT

Mobile, Alabama's opening to the sea, is one of the oldest towns on the Gulf Coast; the British governor who took it over from the Spanish in 1763, according to historian Bernard Bailyn, reported "the state of the town in filth, nastiness and brushwood running over the houses is hardly to be credited"; it was "the most unhealthy place on the face of the earth." As civilization has channeled filth into underground pipes, protected building materials against rot and mildew, and conquered tropical diseases, Mobile has mellowed. A more recent British visitor, Nigel Nicolson in 1986, found "a southern city as lovely as Charleston or Savannah, lovelier than New Orleans. There is something unmistakably French about it, with a touch of Spain. Great live-oaks rise from perfect lawns, and around them are gathered large houses with double porches, one above the other. Low lights glow from within. Squirrels dance across the lawns. The heat, even after dark, is that of a tropical glasshouse." There is another Mobile as well, the industrial town of docks and shipyards, the black working class neighborhoods nearby, the glare of fast food and motel signs on the roads into town. But even this is not a picture of misery. Incomes are higher than a generation ago, vastly higher than two generations ago.

Mobile is in the center of America's Gulf Coast, a region that was once the southern seaboard of the Confederacy, was long part of the solidly Democratic South, and is now part of the Republican heartland in national elections. From boutique- and stockbroker-thronged Florida retirement towns to the white suburbs of New Orleans to the oil-pumping towns of south Texas, the Gulf has delivered solid majorities for every Republican presidential candidate since the 1960s, even when the Democrats nominated southerners. Mobile is no exception: with Baldwin County across the river, it provides the largest vote base in Alabama for Republicans and for conservative candidates in Democratic primaries. Blacks vote heavily Democratic, but country club whites are joined in most elections by blue-collar and country-born whites whose lives are centered on tradition-minded religions. In the mid-1960s Mobile-area whites were united in defense of segregation and enthusiastic for George Wallace. By the mid-1980s they had long since accepted integration, but their affluence had made them suspicious of domestic government programs, and something—reliance on Pentagon spending, their position on America's border, native bellicosity—had made them, like other Gulf Coast voters, among the most hawkish of Americans. In national elections they overwhelmingly supported Ronald Reagan. In state elections they have favored Mobile-based candidates like Charlie Graddick, who as attorney general trumpeted his support of capital punishment, and Jeremiah Denton, a hero after his seven years as a prisoner of war in Vietnam.

Mobile forms the heart of Alabama's 1st Congressional District. The district extends to the north, along the lazily flowing Tombigbee and Alabama rivers, near the old forts and mansions and miles of fields that once grew cotton and are more likely now to be producing soybeans or scrub pine; and, to the south, along the shores of the Gulf of Mexico, and off the highways and waterways headed there, are the condominiums which are the final homes of thousands of affluent but not genuinely rich southerners.

The 1st District got a new congressman in 1984, when Jack Edwards, a beneficiary of the Goldwater landslide and the respected ranking Republican on the Defense Appropriations Subcommittee, retired. The favorite for the seat was former Mobile state Senator Sonny Callahan, a nominal Democrat and supporter of Reagan policies, who was wooed by both parties. Yet Callahan turned out to be a weak candidate, winning with just 61% in the Republican primary and squeaking through with 51% against the Democrat, a local lawyer named Frank McRight, who got a black candidate out of the race, tied Callahan to a local government establishment then tinged by scandal, and carried Mobile County. But in Baldwin County, which includes a suburban area across the harbor from Mobile and the Gulf Coast condominium areas, Callahan won 61% of the votes—and the election.

Callahan in Washington has been one of the most solidly conservative of Republicans on most issues. Yet his political chances have been helped by government money channeled into the district. The Tennessee-Tombigbee Waterway, completed in 1985, connecting Mobile with the Tennessee River, has been a disappointment commercially. But the Navy's home port program has assigned Mobile two frigates, two guided missile cruisers, and a minesweeper. Callahan served on Merchant Marine and Public Works Committees in his first term, and was strong enough that he had no opposition in primary or general election in 1986. After the election, he got with colleague Bill Dickinson's help a seat on Energy and Commerce—a real plum, with its broad legislative jurisdiction and the ability of its members to raise lots of campaign dollars. After the close race of 1984, this is beginning to look like a safe Republican seat again.

The People: Pop. 1980: 563,905, up 14.7% 1970–1980. Households (1980): 78% family, 46% with children, 62% married couples; 29.4% housing units rented; median monthly rent: $127; median house value: $35,600. Voting age pop. (1980): 384,289; 28% Black, 1% Spanish origin, 1% American Indian.

1984 Presidential Vote: Reagan (R) 134,551   (64%)
Mondale (D) 72,298   (34%)

Rep. H.L. (Sonny) Callahan (R)

Elected 1984; b. Sept. 11, 1932, Mobile; home, Mobile; U. of AL, Mobile Extension; Roman Catholic; married (Karen).

Career: Navy, 1952–54; Finch Co. (trucking, real estate, warehousing), Pres., 1964–85; AL House of Reps., 1970–78; AL Senate, 1978–82.

Offices: 1232 LHOB 20515, 202-225-4931. Also 2970 Cottage Hill Rd., Ste. 126, Mobile 36602, 205-690-2811.

Committees: *Energy and Commerce* (17th of 17 R). Subcommittees: Energy and Power; Transportation, Tourism and Hazardous Materials.

Group Ratings

	ADA	ACLU	COPE	CFA	LCV	ACU	NTU	NSI	COC	CEI
1986	0	5	19	25	11	95	49	100	89	73
1985	0	—	12	25	—	86	55	—	86	—

National Journal Ratings

	1986 LIB — 1986 CONS		1985 LIB — 1985 CONS	
Economic	13%	— 85%	9%	— 88%
Social	11%	— 85%	0%	— 76%
Foreign	0%	— 86%	0%	— 76%

Key Votes

1) Lmt Cln Water Act	FOR	5) Retain Gun Cont	AGN	9) Aid Angola Reb	FOR
2) Rpl Tobac Sub	FOR	6) Contra Aid	FOR	10) Tax Reform	FOR
3) Grm-Rdmn Def Red	FOR	7) Lmt Text Imp	FOR	11) S Africa Sanc	AGN
4) Ban Polygraph	AGN	8) Limit SDI	AGN	12) Immig Reform	AGN

Election Results

1986 general	H.L. (Sonny) Callahan (R)..............	96,469	(100%)	($144,314)
1986 primary	H.L. (Sonny) Callahan (R) (unopposed)			
1984 general	H.L. (Sonny) Callahan (R).............	102,479	(51%)	($554,557)
	Frank McRight (D)	98,455	(49%)	($582,198)

Campaign Contributions and Expenditures

1985-86		Direct Cont. 1985-86		PACS Breakdown 1985-86			
Receipts	$296,605	Indiv.	$167,492	Corp.	$52,600	T/M/H	$26,521
Expend.	$144,314	Party	$ 5,178	Labor	$10,000	Agr.	$250
Unspent	$156,236	PACS	$102,621	Ideo.	$13,250	CWOS	$0

SECOND DISTRICT

Montgomery, Alabama, is the Cradle of the Confederacy and the birthplace of the civil rights movement, the home base in the 1950s of Martin Luther King, Jr., and in the 1960s of George C. Wallace. Its landmarks include the first Confederate White House and the Baptist chruch where King in 1955 became spokesman for the bus boycott that began when Rosa Parks was asked to move to the back of a bus and refused. Much history and much racial hatred and fear has been packed into a few square miles here, where the land rises above the Alabama River floodplain in the heart of Alabama's fertile Black Belt. A kind of conclusion was marked in early 1986, when blacks active in the boycott and whites active in opposing it met to commemorate it in a program sponsored by the state department of archives and history. Some movements do succeed, and some healers do heal. Henceforth Montgomery may come to be known as much for the Alabama Shakespeare Festival, in the Palladian theater built on his estate by former Postmaster General Winton Blount.

The 2d Congressional District of Alabama, which covers the southeast corner of the state, includes Montgomery, the eastern part of the Black Belt, and the piney woods counties to the south. Since the Voting Rights Act of 1965, the Black Belt has been solidly Democratic, and Montgomery, nearly evenly divided between the races, has been nearly evenly divided between the parties. The biggest change in political attitudes in recent decades has been in the mostly white counties to the south. In the 1950s and early 1960s they were solidly segregationist and solidly Democratic—not a contradiction in terms at the time, but the way things had been for 80 years. They switched to civil rights law opponent Barry Goldwater in 1964, supported George Wallace's third party bid in 1968, and went for Richard Nixon and Republicans in 1972. In the middle 1970s they went back to Jimmy Carter's Democrats. By the middle 1980s they were becoming solidly Republican again, and not just in national elections, but also in fiercely contested state races like the governor and Senate contests in 1986.

The change can be linked to foreign and military policy. This is one of the most hawkish parts of the United States, supportive of Franklin Roosevelt's interventionism in the 1940s and Lyndon Johnson's in the 1960s. Voters here rejected Carter's dovish policies and embraced Reagan's assertiveness. Cynics would add that the presence of military bases—Montgomery's Maxwell Air Force Base, Fort Rucker near Dothan in the southeast corner of the state—also made a difference, and certainly these have contributed to the general rise in the area's economy since the stagnant 1950s. But similar changes in attitude took place in parts of the non-metropolitan South with no military presence at all.

The congressman from the 2d District is Bill Dickinson, a Republican elected in an upset in the local Goldwater landslide of 1964 (when few, if any, blacks voted here), reelected sometimes (1972, 1976, 1978, 1982) by tenuous margins, and now one of the most senior and potentially most powerful Republicans in the House. Since the 1980 election, he has been ranking Republican on the House Armed Services Committee. During the first Reagan term, he often dominated and in effect chaired the committee, since the elderly chairman, Mel Price of Illinois, exerted little influence. After the 1984 election, Les Aspin of Wisconsin ousted Price, and took command, depriving Dickinson of some power. Aspin's difficulties in holding onto the chairmanship may have given Dickinson more leverage.

Armed Services is a difficult committee to dominate. It has a single staff, steeped in expertise and experience, on which members of both parties necessarily rely. The lion's share of the defense budget is driven by previous years' commitments, and the leeway for effective action—for promoting new initiatives or squelching old ones—is limited. Nevertheless Dickinson is in a position to exert important influence. If he is no longer the conduit between Defense Secretary Caspar Weinberger and the House, as he was between 1981 and 1984, he is still the administration's lead man on votes where Republicans are in conflict with the Democrats. At a time when Congress and the voters are tired of defense spending increases, Dickinson still has an emotional commitment to higher military spending: in 1987 he was so moved during one committee meeting that he lifted the American flag from its holder and paraded around the room with it to demonstrate his resolve. That may look buffoonish in certain precincts in Washington, but it doesn't in southern Alabama, where Dickinson's support for military spending remains highly popular. Nearly defeated in 1982, he now seems solidly entrenched.

The People: Pop. 1980: 549,505, up 11.7% 1970–80. Households (1980): 76% family, 43% with children, 61% married couples; 31.9% housing units rented; median monthly rent: $110; median house value: $31,700. Voting age pop. (1980): 383,150; 27% Black, 1% Spanish origin.

1984 Presidential Vote: Reagan (R) 130,370   (63%)
                       Mondale (D) 73,603   (36%)

Rep. William L. Dickinson (R)

Elected 1964; b. June 5, 1925, Opelika; home, Montgomery; U. of AL, LL.B. 1950; United Methodist; married (Barbara).

Career: Navy, WWII; Practicing atty., 1950–63; Judge, Opelika City Crt., Lee Cnty. Crt. of Common Pleas, and Juvenile Crt., 5th Judicial Circuit; Asst. V.P., Southern Railway System.

Offices: 2406 RHOB 20515, 202-225-2901. Also 301 Fed. Crt. Bldg., Montgomery 36104, 205-832-7292.

Committees: *Armed Services* (Ranking Member of 21 R). Subcommittees: Military Installations and Facilities; Research and Development (Ranking Member). *House Administration* (2d of 7 R). Subcommittees: Office Systems; Personnel amd Police.

Group Ratings

	ADA	ACLU	COPE	CFA	LCV	ACU	NTU	NSI	COC	CEI
1986	15	26	12	0	10	86	51	100	73	61
1985	10	—	11	17	—	65	50	—	82	—

National Journal Ratings

	1986 LIB — 1986 CONS		1985 LIB — 1985 CONS	
Economic	23% —	77%	20% —	79%
Social	37% —	61%	51% —	49%
Foreign	0% —	86%	0% —	76%

Key Votes

1) Lmt Cln Water Act	FOR	5) Retain Gun Cont	AGN	9) Aid Angola Reb	FOR
2) Rpl Tobac Sub	AGN	6) Contra Aid	FOR	10) Tax Reform	FOR
3) Grm-Rdmn Def Red	AGN	7) Lmt Text Imp	FOR	11) S Africa Sanc	AGN
4) Ban Polygraph	FOR	8) Limit SDI	AGN	12) Immig Reform	AGN

Election Results

1986 general	William L. Dickinson (R)	115,302	(67%)	($245,555)
	Mercer Stone (D)	57,568	(33%)	($10,015)
1986 primary	William L. Dickinson (R) (unopposed)			
1984 general	William L. Dickinson (R)	118,153	(60%)	($339,800)
	Larry G. Lee (D)	75,506	(39%)	($60,790)

Campaign Contributions and Expenditures

1985-86		Direct Cont. 1985-86		PACS Breakdown 1985-86			
Receipts	$381,367	Indiv.	$147,545	Corp.	$132,857	T/M/H	$39,100
Expend.	$245,555	Party	$4,201	Labor	$1,250	Agr.	$500
Unspent	$351,585	PACS	$178,209	Ideo.	$3,300	CWOS	$1,202

THIRD DISTRICT

From the Black Belt in the south to the red clay hills in the north, across land that is densely populated but without a single city of any size, stretches the 3d Congressional District of Alabama. In the south is Tuskegee, a black-majority town in a black-majority county, and the home of Booker T. Washington's Tuskegee Institute. Also in the southern part is Phenix City, a one-time Alabama "sin city" across the Chattahoochee River from Georgia's huge Fort Benning. A mid-1950s cleanup of Phenix City propelled a young prosecutor, John Patterson, into the governor's chair in 1958; he beat George Wallace in the Democratic primary, the one time Wallace allowed himself to be "out-segged." Equidistant from Tuskegee and Phenix City is Auburn, home of Auburn University, with its nationally renowned veterinary school and athletic teams (not to mention the fraternity where former first mother Lillian Carter was once a housemother). In the northern part of the district is the small industrial city of Anniston, where there is a distinguished local newspaper and the Army's Fort McClellan. At the western and southern edges of the district are counties increasingly filled up with small subdivisions amid the peanut fields and red hills, inhabited by young families who work at the edges of Birmingham or Montgomery but want to raise their children in an environment that is recognizably country.

The 3d District's congressman for more than 20 years has been Bill Nichols, the kind of retiring and tradition-minded southerner who has accumulated seniority and quietly made a major impact on national policy from the House. Nichols came to Washington in 1966 with a Wallace label; he was a Wallace floor leader in the legislature, and that helped him easily beat a Republican who won in the local Goldwater landslide. But Nichols's legislative career began in 1958, four years before Wallace was elected governor; and now he has outlasted Wallace's tenure. In Washington Nichols has long since emerged from under his shadow.

Most of Nichols's congressional energy has been spent on things military. "I put in a little time in the service—combat time," he once said, not mentioning that he lost a leg in a land mine explosion in World War II; and he has served two decades on the House Armed Services Committee. In the Vietnam years he had low seniority, was a solid supporter of the war, and naturally helped tend Alabama's military bases. Seniority propelled him upward, and he became chairman of the subcommittee that handled personnel matters, pay and benefits—handling issues full of tricky details that can have great impact on the quality of the military. After the 1982 election he became chairman of the Investigations Subcommittee, a forum long desired by Pentagon critics but one in which Nichols was expected to be a solid Pentagon supporter.

That is not the way it turned out. Nichols probed procurement practices, did not like what he saw, and drew up a reform bill. He visited the Marine barracks near Beirut, said he was worried about their defenses—and then was appalled when a truck bomb penetrated them and killed 241 servicemen. From that grew a desire to change the basic structure of the Pentagon. Sam Nunn and Barry Goldwater got more publicity in the Senate with their military reform package centralizing authority in the Chairman of the Joint Chiefs of Staff. But Nichols got the House to vote provisions centralizing operating authority in combat commanders. He also insisted on merging the staffs of each service secretary with those of the service's military commander. The Nichols reforms generally prevailed in 1986 and were a substantial accomplishment for a man who has given much in the line of duty to his country.

Such achievements might not have been possible in the early 1970s, when military issues tended to be polarized on hawk-and-dove lines. But in the 1980s, within the confines of Armed Services with its long-experienced staff and without, the real issues became how to enable the military services to do their jobs. On these matters Nichols has been able to work with members of the committee from California's Ronald Dellums to his Alabama neighbor Bill Dickinson. Nichols refused to challenge elderly Chairman Melvin Price after the 1984 election, and must have resented the elevation of the considerably less senior Les Aspin to the chair ahead of him, which ended any chance Nichols has of chairing the full committee; he opposed Aspin on the chairmanship vote in 1987. But he was also able to work effectively if a bit gingerly with him.

Before its moment of political turbulence in the mid-1960s, the 3d District was one of those southern constituencies who elected a conservative Democrat young and kept him in till he got lots of seniority. That is in effect what the district has done with Nichols, whose record on economics is mixed but who is generally conservative on cultural issues and almost always favors the conservative side on such foreign issues as come to a vote. He has encountered almost no opposition, and has won without any serious campaigning when he has. He seems likely to remain in the House and in his Armed Services chair as long as he wants.

The People: Pop. 1980: 555,321, up 15.5% 1970–80. Households (1980): 77% family, 43% with children, 62% married couples; 29.6% housing units rented; median monthly rent: $103; median house value: $29,400. Voting age pop. (1980): 390,418; 25% Black, 1% Spanish origin.

1984 Presidential Vote:

Reagan (R)	113,641	(60%)
Mondale (D)	70,024	(37%)

Rep. Bill Nichols (D)

Elected 1966; b. Oct. 16, 1918, Becker, MS; home, Sylacauga; Auburn U., B.S. 1939, M.S. 1941; United Methodist; married (Carolyn).

Career: Army, WW II; V.P., Parker Fertilizer Co., Pres., Parker Gin Co., 1947–66; AL Senate, 1963–67.

Offices: 2405 RHOB 20515, 202-225-3261. Also Fed. Bldg., Anniston 36202, 205-236-5655.

Committees: *Armed Services* (5th of 21 D). Subcommittees: Investigations (Chairman); Readiness; Military Personnel and Compensation.

Group Ratings

	ADA	ACLU	COPE	CFA	LCV	ACU	NTU	NSI	COC	CEI
1986	10	10	31	33	4	63	30	100	73	36
1985	10	—	31	17	—	67	36	—	71	—

National Journal Ratings

	1986 LIB — 1986 CONS		1985 LIB — 1985 CONS	
Economic	40% —	60%	40% —	60%
Social	34% —	65%	24% —	72%
Foreign	16% —	79%	0% —	76%

Key Votes

1) Lmt Cln Water Act	FOR	5) Retain Gun Cont	—	9) Aid Angola Reb	FOR
2) Rpl Tobac Sub	AGN	6) Contra Aid	FOR	10) Tax Reform	FOR
3) Grm-Rdmn Def Red	FOR	7) Lmt Text Imp	FOR	11) S Africa Sanc	FOR
4) Ban Polygraph	FOR	8) Limit SDI	AGN	12) Immig Reform	—

Election Results

1986 general	Bill Nichols (D)	115,127	(81%)	($110,555)
	Whit Guerin (R)	27,769	(19%)	($30,578)
1986 primary	Bill Nichols (D) (unopposed)			
1984 general	Bill Nichols (D)	120,357	(96%)	($33,040)
	Mark Thornton (Libertarian)	4,745	(4%)	

Campaign Contributions and Expenditures

1985-86		Direct Cont. 1985-86		PACS Breakdown 1985-86			
Receipts	$206,234	Indiv.	$61,346	Corp.	$44,694	T/M/H	$14,750
Expend.	$110,555	PACS	$65,994	Labor	$5,800	Agr.	$250
Unspent	$356,616			Ideo.	$500	CWOS	$0

FOURTH DISTRICT

If there is an equivalent of the industrial "black country" of western Pennsylvania around Pittsburgh anywhere in the South, it is in the red hill country of northern Alabama around Birmingham that makes up the state's 4th Congressional District. Even the terrain is similar, and it should be, for the chains of ridges that peter out in western Alabama's Tombigbee River valley extend north and northeast all the way to western Pennsylvania and beyond. Birmingham and Pittsburgh are America's two premier steel cities, North and South. The hill country around them was populated by feisty Scotch-Irish farmers in the years between the Revolution and the Civil War, and their populations are still almost all-white to this day; after the Civil War, large factories were built along the river bottoms and smaller workshops and factories burgeoned in the small cities and towns in the valleys and on the hillsides.

Yet politically these two regions have been almost mirror images of each other. Western Pennsylvania within a 100-mile radius of Pittsburgh was overwhelmingly Republican until the 1930s, while northern Alabama within a 100-mile radius of Birmingham was, with the exception of a few mountain communities that remained loyal to the Union during the Civil War, solidly Democratic through the 1950s. Then they changed. Western Pennsylvania became Democratic in the New Deal and, though conservative on cultural issues, became with the collapse of the steel industry one of the nation's most Democratic areas, voting for Walter Mondale in 1984. Northern Alabama repudiated national Democrats during the civil rights era, voting for Goldwater, Wallace, and Nixon. And although it supported Jimmy Carter in 1976, it has moved Republican in the 1980s, as people move out from the Birmingham area, seeking a country setting, traditional values, and a job at one of the factories or office centers proliferating along the interstates or four-lane highways radiating from the metropolis. This movement is not as heavy, because the local economy is not as prosperous, as in the 100-mile radius around Atlanta or on North Carolina's Piedmont. But it is large enough to make a difference here, and to change the hill counties that used to vote for populists who berated Alabama's "Big Mules" to strongholds for Republicans who back school prayer and capital punishment.

Alabama's 4th Congressional District is situated in these hills. It extends from the gritty factory town of Gadsden in the east, still often Democratic, across the increasingly Republican counties around Birmingham, to the hill counties of the west represented by one-time (1937–40) Speaker William Bankhead. The Republican trend is apparent here. As late as 1980 the district went for Jimmy Carter; in 1986 it failed to go for Democratic governor candidate Bill Baxley and gave only the barest of margins to Senator Richard Shelby. In congressional politics, however, the district has not veered from its traditional Democratic fold since it replaced a 1964 Goldwater landslide victor with Democrat Tom Bevill.

Tom Bevill is an old-fashioned kind of Democratic politician. He chairs the Appropriations Subcommittee on Energy and Water Development—a fancy name for public works, or the pork barrel. He adheres to the philosophy that government should spend liberally on projects to build dams and public buildings and, in the process, to provide public service jobs. In an historically low-wage, rural area like the 4th District, such programs were an unalloyed good: local communities desperately needed the facilities, and local people needed the jobs. Now the need for them is problematic and the political support for them less fervent. An example is the Tennessee-Tombigbee Waterway project which passes through western Alabama. Bevill struggled hard to save Tennessee-Tombigbee from congressional opponents and had the satisfaction of seeing it open in 1985. But it was never clear that American industry needed another water route from Tennessee to the Gulf beyond what nature already provided (the Mississippi River), and traffic on the waterway has been embarrassingly below projections. Nor does it generate any more construction jobs. Bevill has had to struggle hard to prevent economy- and environment-minded Congresses and administrations from shutting down water projects all over the nation, and he has had his successes. But often he seems to be fighting more to cut losses than to make gains, and it may just be that the United States has run out of useful sites for dams and canals.

On economic issues Bevill's stands are as close to those of northern Democrats as any member of the Alabama delegation, and as a member of the Democratic Steering and Policy Committee and as part of the whip organization, he is part of the Democratic leadership rather than an opponent of it. He tends to favor high defense spending and has limited sympathy for liberal positions on most cultural issues. Well suited at least to the historical Democratic preference of his district, he has been returned to Congress for two decades now with no more than token opposition.

The People: Pop. 1980: 562,088, up 19.7% 1970–80. Households (1980): 81% family, 44% with children, 70% married couples; 23.1% housing units rented; median monthly rent: $92; median house value: $28,000. Voting age pop. (1980): 397,076; 6% Black, 1% Spanish origin.

1984 Presidential Vote:

Reagan (R)	118,750	(59%)
Mondale (D)	80,187	(40%)

Rep. Tom Bevill (D)

Elected 1966; b. Mar. 27, 1921, Townley; home, Jasper; U. of AL, B.S. 1943, LL.B. 1948; Baptist; married (Lou).

Career: Army, WWII; Practicing atty., 1948–66; AL House of Reps., 1958–66.

Offices: 2302 RHOB 20515, 202-225-4876. Also 107 Fed. Bldg., Gadsden 35901, 205-546-0201; 1804 4th Ave., Jasper 35501, 205-221-2310; and 102 Fed. Bldg., Cullman 35055, 205-734-6043.

Committees: *Appropriations* (9th of 35 D). Subcommittees: Energy and Water Development (Chairman); Interior; Military Construction.

Group Ratings

	ADA	ACLU	COPE	CFA	LCV	ACU	NTU	NSI	COC	CEI
1986	40	25	57	33	23	50	23	80	29	20
1985	25	—	56	50	—	57	25	—	35	—

National Journal Ratings

	1986 LIB — 1986 CONS		1985 LIB — 1985 CONS	
Economic	55% —	44%	53% —	47%
Social	44% —	54%	41% —	56%
Foreign	34% —	64%	24% —	66%

Key Votes

1) Lmt Cln Water Act	AGN	5) Retain Gun Cont	AGN	9) Aid Angola Reb	AGN
2) Rpl Tobac Sub	AGN	6) Contra Aid	FOR	10) Tax Reform	FOR
3) Grm-Rdmn Def Red	FOR	7) Lmt Text Imp	FOR	11) S Africa Sanc	FOR
4) Ban Polygraph	FOR	8) Limit SDI	AGN	12) Immig Reform	AGN

Election Results

1986 general	Tom Bevill (D)	132,881	(78%)	($149,263)
	Al De Shazo (R).....................	38,588	(22%)	($10,287)
1986 primary	Tom Bevill (D) (unopposed)			
1984 general	Tom Bevill (D)	120,106	(100%)	($100,281)

Campaign Contributions and Expenditures

1985-86		Direct Cont. 1985-86		PACS Breakdown 1985-86			
Receipts	$228,724	Indiv.	$52,305	Corp.	$57,650	T/M/H	$20,570
Expend.	$149,263	PACS	$100,470	Labor	$19,500	Agr.	$1,500
Unspent	$437,485	Cand.	$3,000	Ideo.	$1,250	CWOS	$0

FIFTH DISTRICT

Seldom has one federal program shaped the life of a particular congressional district as much as the Tennessee Valley Authority has shaped the life of the 5th District of Alabama. Fifty-odd years ago the Tennessee River coursed through the northern counties of Alabama and every spring flooded the farm country and small towns along its banks. Then TVA—an idea prompted by the need to do something with the government's World War I munitions plant at Muscle Shoals—was created in 1933. The agency dammed the wild river for most of its length, controlled the flooding, and produced cheap public power. This part of Alabama has had a populist streak since it was first settled in the time of Andrew Jackson, and since the coming of TVA it has been the part of the state most likely to support generous federal spending. It has also consistently elected congressmen inclined to support such programs, including John Sparkman, who represented what now is the 5th Congressional District from 1937 through 1946 before spending 32 years in the Senate, and Bob Jones, who represented the 5th from 1946 until his retirement in 1976 and ended up chairing the House Public Works Committee.

These men helped to bring to the 5th benefits from the federal government, and the changes in the district have been striking. In 1950 Huntsville, the metropolis of these parts, was just a sleepy hill town of 14,000. Today its population is more than ten times that, and growing. The main reason has been the space program. In the 1950s Werner von Braun was designing Army rockets at the the Redstone Missile Arsenal here, with considerable success, and space has mushroomed since then. The federal government, most visibly through TVA and the missile program but also through other, more broadly targeted programs, has in 50 years transformed this backward, impoverished area into a place whose standard of living and level of sophistication is up to or above the national average.

But these big government programs have not always maintained their levels of competence. TVA is plagued by unwise major investments in nuclear power and on environmental quality is not notably superior to private utilities. Huntsville's Marshall Space Center was the place where NASA officials pressured Morton Thiokol engineers to give the go-ahead for the *Challenger* space shuttle that exploded in January 1986. Once poor and hard-working, the Tennessee Valley shows signs of being flabby, self-satisfied, and selfish. Its politics has changed at the same time. The counties east and west of Huntsville remain TVA Democratic, but by lesser margins than they once were. The fast-growing area around Huntsville has an increasing number of technology-loving Republicans, to the point that in the close 1986 Senate race the 5th District delivered only the narrowest of margins to Democrat Richard Shelby.

The congressman from the 5th district comes from the TVA tradition, but he has hinted at moving on to other things. Ronnie Flippo was first elected in 1976, and after six years of minding district interests on the Public Works and Science Committees, he got a seat on Ways and Means after the 1982 election. There he found himself in the middle of the action in 1985 and 1986. Like most committee Democrats he ended up supporting Chairman Dan Rostenkowski's thoroughgoing tax reform plan. But he spent much of his time lobbying to maintain provisions whose benefits have become an integral part of life in areas like his. These included keeping non-taxable status for industrial revenue municipal bonds and for workmen's compensation benefits—which enabled Flippo himself to go to college after he was seriously injured at age 24 while working as an ironworker on a TVA generating plant. He is one of the few congressmen of his generation with an authentic working class background.

In the House Flippo, like his northern Alabama colleagues Tom Bevill and Ben Erdreich, has been mostly a team player in the Democratic caucus, relatively generous on economic issues, more cautious on cultural and foreign questions. He has kept an eye cocked on Alabama politics, and gave some thought to running for governor in 1982 and 1986. He decided not to make either race, and one could argue that this accountant who has concentrated on technical issues in Congress would not make an exciting candidate. But every indication is that Alabama has had its fill of exciting candidates, and that Flippo's combination of political ability and grass-roots experience would have made him superior to any of the leading candidates in the 1986 race.

The People: Pop. 1980: 549,844, up 12.3% 1970–80. Households (1980): 80% family, 46% with children, 68% married couples; 28.0% housing units rented; median monthly rent: $143; median house value: $37,400. Voting age pop. (1980): 385,388; 13% Black, 1% Spanish origin.

1984 Presidential Vote: Reagan (R) 119,034   (59%)
Mondale (D) 80,039   (40%)

Rep. Ronnie G. Flippo (D)

Elected 1976; b. Aug. 15, 1937, Florence; home, Florence; U. of N. AL, B.S. 1965; U. of AL, M.A. 1966; Church of Christ; married (Faye).

Career: CPA, 1966–77; AL House of Reps., 1971–75; AL Senate, 1975–77.

Offices: 334 RHOB 20515, 202-225-4801. Also 301 N. Seminary St., Florence 35630, 205-766-7692; and Huntsville-Madison Cnty. Jetport, P.O. Box 6065, Huntsville 35806, 205-772-0244.

Committees: *Ways and Means* (16th of 23 D). Subcommittees: Oversight; Select Revenue Measures.

Group Ratings

	ADA	ACLU	COPE	CFA	LCV	ACU	NTU	NSI	COC	CEI
1986	40	29	42	50	47	33	23	54	29	31
1985	35	—	55	58	—	58	28	—	43	—

National Journal Ratings

	1986 LIB — 1986 CONS		1985 LIB — 1985 CONS	
Economic	69%	— 31%	50%	— 49%
Social	44%	— 54%	51%	— 48%
Foreign	45%	— 54%	34%	— 65%

Key Votes

1) Lmt Cln Water Act	AGN	5) Retain Gun Cont	AGN	9) Aid Angola Reb	—
2) Rpl Tobac Sub	AGN	6) Contra Aid	FOR	10) Tax Reform	FOR
3) Grm-Rdmn Def Red	FOR	7) Lmt Text Imp	FOR	11) S Africa Sanc	FOR
4) Ban Polygraph	FOR	8) Limit SDI	—	12) Immig Reform	AGN

Election Results

1986 general	Ronnie G. Flippo (D)	125,406	(79%)	($172,356)
	Herb McCarley (R)).	33,528	(21%)	
1986 primary	Ronnie G. Flippo (D)	100,857	(90%)	
	Pryor (Fess) Sandlin (D).	7,386	(7%)	
	Zachary Wakefield (D).	3,729	(3%)	
1984 general	Ronnie G. Flippo (D)	140,452	(96%)	($127,962)
	D.M. (Sam) Samsil (Libertarian).	6,033	(4%)	

Campaign Contributions and Expenditures

1985-86		Direct Cont. 1985-86		PACS Breakdown 1985-86			
Receipts	$438,287	Indiv.	$81,288	Corp.	$142,200	T/M/H	$94,941
Expend.	$172,356	PACS	$292,941	Labor	$26,000	Agr.	$2,500
Unspent	$603,947			Ideo.	$19,300	CWOS	$8,000

SIXTH DISTRICT

Standing above the city of Birmingham, atop Red Mountain, is a statue of Vulcan, the Roman god of fire and metal working. It is an appropriate place and symbol. The mountain is red because it is made of iron ore, and Birmingham, a city that lies in a curving valley between two mountain chains, would not exist without iron and steel. This is one of the few major southern cities that was not founded until after the Civil War, and since the 1870s it has had the South's largest concentration of heavy industry. But in the last two decades the steel industry has declined, and Atlanta—the same size as Birmingham in 1950—has become the cultural and commercial capital of the South. That has left Birmingham pondering how to get its economy moving—and how to remove the stigma it earned in 1963 when police commissioner Bull Connor set dogs and firehoses against peaceful civil rights demonstrators and Ku Klux Klansmen bombed a black church and killed four young girls.

Even though Birmingham's population has long since spread past its city limits, to the steel mill country in the Bessemer Cutoff and the country club suburbs over the mountain, the task of reestablishing Birmingham's economy and image has fallen largely to its mayor, Richard Arrington. He has helped to stimulate spending for culture and the arts, even as the University of Alabama Medical Center has replaced U.S. Steel as the biggest local employer, and the evil-looking air that used to hover in the valley is now mostly clear. And as the first black mayor of this city he is not only a symbol, but has shown more political skill and nerve than most recent statewide candidates in this state. Birmingham has an image of being a rough workingman's town, but politically the more important impulse has been a white collar, upscale distaste for populist-tone politics. In the early days the steel mills were manned mainly by blacks, and even today there is a smaller white working class, proportionately, than in the big steel manufacturing centers of the North. Birmingham is the part of Alabama least hospitable to George Wallace—it voted against him many times—and Jefferson County has not voted for a Democratic presidential candidate since 1952. The white-collar and professional population of Alabama is heavily concentrated in this one urban center (although it is spilling over into adjacent Shelby and St. Clair Counties as well), and it votes heavily against the blue-collar and farm electorates of the small counties.

Birmingham and most of its Jefferson County suburbs form Alabama's 6th Congressional District, a seat which has had serious contests—and has elected three different congressmen—in the last four elections. The incumbent, Ben Erdreich, was the first Democrat elected here in 20 years when he won in 1982; he was helped by redistricting (which added some industrial and heavily black suburbs west of the city), by high turnout among blacks, and by division among the Republicans. The district's long-time Republican congressman, John Buchanan, could probably have won general elections as long as he wanted; as a Baptist minister increasingly sympathetic to blacks, he was beaten in the 1980 Republican primary. Later in the 1980s he became one of the leaders of Norman Lear's People for the American Way. His successor, Albert Lee Smith, won in the Reagan year of 1980, but lost in 1982, and was soundly beaten statewide by Senator Howell Heflin in 1984.

Erdreich, like many younger Democratic congressmen, has a background in local government: as a state legislator he sponsored Alabama's Clean Air Act, and as a county commissioner he became well enough known to be a creditable candidate for Congress. His politics have no roots in the old segregationist South, but neither is he likely to support the kind of big-spending Democratic politics once standard in the North. He is used to assembling a biracial coalition, but in an environment where blacks and whites, voters and activists, are all aware that they cannot get everything they want; he is used to working with business and labor, in an economic setting where both are often desperate to save their common stake. He has concentrated heavily on issues of local importance, like the plight of the steel industry, and he has devoted himself heavily to constituency service. He serves on the Banking Committee, which handles several aid-to-cities programs like UDAG, and on Government Operations. To an extent not widely appreciated, it is members like Erdreich who have set the tone of the House through most of the 1980s.

Politically, Erdreich seems on his way to making this a safe seat. He is a beneficiary of high black turnout and the political competence of Mayor Richard Arrington's organization; the high-income vote is irrevocably Republican, but not enough to prevail by itself. The 1984 Republican candidate, Jabo Waggoner, made a bid for white working-class votes, but Erdreich won with 60%. In 1986, against weaker opposition, and while Democrat Bill Baxley was losing Jefferson County in the governor's race, Erdreich won with 73%.

The People: Pop. 1980: 554,156, up 3.3% 1970–80. Households (1980): 73% family, 39% with children, 56% married couples; 37.8% housing units rented; median monthly rent: $151; median house value: $40,000. Voting age pop. (1980): 404,782; 31% Black, 1% Spanish origin.

1984 Presidential Vote:

Reagan (R)	130,184	(59%)
Mondale (D)	89,841	(41%)

Rep. Ben Erdreich (D)

Elected 1982; b. Dec. 9, 1938, Birmingham; home, Birmingham; Yale U., B.A. 1960; U. of AL Law Sch., J.D. 1963; Jewish; married (Ellen).

Career: Army, 1963–65; Practicing atty., 1965–73; AL House of Reps., 1970–74; Jefferson Cnty. Comm., 1974–82.

Offices: 439 CHOB 20515, 202-225-4921. Also 105 Fed. Crthse., Birmingham 35203, 205-254-0956.

Committees: *Banking, Finance and Urban Affairs* (17th of 31 D). Subcommittees: Domestic Monetary Policy; Economic Stabilization; Housing and Community Development. *Government Operations* (17th of 24 D). Subcommittees: Commerce, Consumer, and Monetary Affairs; Intergovernmental Relations & Human Resources. *Select Committee on Aging* (27th of 39 D). Subcommittees: Human Services.

Group Ratings

	ADA	ACLU	COPE	CFA	LCV	ACU	NTU	NSI	COC	CEI
1986	55	25	73	67	53	78	28	80	50	32
1985	35	—	68	75	—	52	33	—	45	—

National Journal Ratings

	1986 LIB — 1986 CONS			1985 LIB — 1985 CONS		
Economic	59%	—	40%	57%	—	41%
Social	39%	—	59%	59%	—	40%
Foreign	44%	—	56%	35%	—	63%

Key Votes

1) Lmt Cln Water Act	FOR	5) Retain Gun Cont	AGN	9) Aid Angola Reb	FOR
2) Rpl Tobac Sub	FOR	6) Contra Aid	FOR	10) Tax Reform	FOR
3) Grm-Rdmn Def Red	FOR	7) Lmt Text Imp	FOR	11) S Africa Sanc	FOR
4) Ban Polygraph	FOR	8) Limit SDI	AGN	12) Immig Reform	AGN

Election Results

1986 general	Ben Erdreich (D)	139,608	(73%)	($216,526)
	L. Morgan Williams (R)...............	51,924	(27%)	($5,534)
1986 primary	Ben Erdreich (D) (unopposed)			
1984 general	Ben Erdreich (D)	130,973	(60%)	($567,118)
	J.T. (Jabo) Waggoner (R)..............	87,550	(40%)	($355,295)

Campaign Contributions and Expenditures

1985-86		Direct Cont. 1985-86		PACS Breakdown 1985-86			
Receipts	$342,883	Indiv.	$121,575	Corp.	$65,871	T/M/H	$63,100
Expend.	$216,526	Party	$261	Labor	$63,825	Agr.	$5,250
Unspent	$146,955	PACS	$207,446	Ideo.	$500	CWOS	$8,900

SEVENTH DISTRICT

Spanning a cultural cross-section of the state is the 7th Congressional District of Alabama. It includes a significant part of metropolitan Birmingham, including the steel mill suburb of Bessemer, with its black majority, and Black Belt counties with the highest black percentages and lowest incomes in Alabama. Here is Selma, the old small city where Sheriff Jim Clark's brutal treatment of blacks seeking to register to vote in 1965 led to the march on Montgomery and passage of the Voting Rights Act. Between Birmingham and the Black Belt is Tuscaloosa, the geographical center of the district, a middle-sized city, home of the University of Alabama.

The racial balance here is not the same as it is statewide, however. The 7th District has one of the largest black percentages of any Alabama district, but until 1986 it was represented by conservative Democrats responsive to the well-to-do whites who run local businesses and governments and consider themselves the only people in the community competent to do so. Two were even law partners: Walter Flowers, first elected in 1968, and Richard Shelby, who succeeded him by beating a Birmingham-area black in the 1978 runoff; Shelby narrowly won the 1986 Senate race, and only because of overwhelming support from blacks.

The 1986 race to succeed him produced a surprise winner. Initial attention focused on District Attorney Billy Hill, a conservative Democrat from a fast-growing county outside Birmingham, and Bill McFarland, a Tuscaloosa developer who switched to the Republican party in 1985. But neither managed to beat Tuscaloosa Democrat Claude Harris. With almost unanimous (81%) backing in Tuscaloosa County and running even with a black candidate in the Black Belt counties, he led Hill in the first primary; in the runoff his home strength and support from blacks was enough to prevail. In the general election he lost the Birmingham area counties only narrowly, while running better than 2 to 1 in Tuscaloosa and the Black Belt. His background was anything but anti-establishment: he spent 19 years as a prosecutor and judge, and is a lieutenant colonel in the National Guard. But in campaigning he declined to run away from the national Democratic record in the House, as Flowers and Shelby usually did. His voting record is likely to be similar to those of other northern Alabama Democrats: fairly generous on economic issues, more cautious on cultural and foreign policy. His apparent political talent and popularity make him a good bet to hold onto this district despite the Republican trend in the counties outside Birmingham.

The People: Pop. 1980: 559,069, up 15.5% 1970–80. Households (1980): 78% family, 45% with children, 62% married couples; 28.8% housing units rented; median monthly rent: $108; median house value: $34,400. Voting age pop. (1980): 386,537; 30% Black, 1% Spanish origin.

1984 Presidential Vote:

Reagan (R)	126,319	(59%)
Mondale (D)	85,907	(40%)

Rep. Claude Harris, Jr. (D)

Elected 1986; b. June 29, 1940, Bessemer; home, Tuscaloosa; U. of AL, B.S. 1962, LL.B. 1965; Baptist; married (Barbara).

Career: Asst. Dist. Atty., 1965–76; Circuit Judge, 1977–85.

Offices: 1009 LHOB 20515, 202-225-2665. Also Fed. Bldg., Rm. 133, Tuscaloosa 35403, 205-752-3578; 103 Courthouse, Bessemer 35020, 205-425-5031; and Fed. Bldg., Selma 36701, 205-872-2684.

Committees: *Agriculture* (24th of 26 D). Subcommittees: Cotton, Rice and Sugar; Forests, Family Farms and Energy; Livestock, Dairy and Poultry. *Veterans' Affairs* (17th of 21 D). Subcommittees: Hospitals and Health Care; Housing and Memorial Affairs.

Group Ratings and Key Votes: Newly Elected

Election Results

1986 general	Claude Harris, Jr. (D)	108,126	(60%)	($485,880)
	Bill McFarland (R)	72,777	(40%)	($299,220)
1986 primary	Claude Harris, Jr. (D)	44,300	(35%)	
	Billy Hill (D)	41,730	(33%)	
	William Branch (D)	17,612	(14%)	
	Aubrey Green (D)	7,326	(6%)	
	Three others (D)	14,033	(12%)	
1984 general	Richard C. Shelby (D)	135,834	(97%)	($69,487)
	Charles Ewing (Libertarian)	4,498	(3%)	

Campaign Contributions and Expenditures

1985-86		Direct Cont. 1985-86		PACS Breakdown 1985-86			
Receipts	$484,220	Indiv.	$104,096	Corp.	$34,850	Trade	$32,000
Expend.	$485,880	Party	$4,242	Labor	$88,625	Agr.	$1,500
Unspent	$1,501	PACS	$190,925	Ideo.	$33,950	CWOS	$0

ALASKA

Alaska, nearly 30 years after statehood, remains an improbable state—a gigantic land mass at the northern edge of the Pacific Rim, straddling the Arctic Circle, the only part of the United States with a boundary on the Soviet Union, so vast that if superimposed on the Lower 48 it would stretch from Florida to Los Angeles to Lake Superior. Yet it only has half a million residents, most of them concentrated in two cities. It is a land where darkness at noon and winter windchill factors bring on cabin fever and outright emotional depression. Also here are the tallest mountains in North America and thousands of miles of rugged seacoast. The airport at Anchorage is a stopoff on flights from New York to Tokyo and Paris to Seoul—it was here that KAL 007 last touched down before it was shot down by the Soviets—and for dozens of small planes that will land on unmarked airstrips you can't find on the map or will skitter to a stop on one of Alaska's thousands of lakes and inlets.

Most of Alaska's physical expanse still belongs to nature, remaining the home of the caribou and an occasional Native hunter. Dreams of sudden riches still bring men to Alaska (a frontier state in which men still outnumber women), but riches are hard to find and harder, given the high cost of living, to keep. The lone trapper or miner and the laid-off pipeline worker are not the typical Alaskans; Alaska has a high birth rate and lots of young families with small children. Public life is conducted by men who have been far more successful than they ever dreamed possible, and Alaska's politicians—like its businessmen and labor leaders—have the self-assurance and optimism of the newly rich. Yet life here is difficult, one measure of which is that there is a substantially lower proportion of people over 65 here, by a wide margin, than in any other state. However much people may say they love Alaska, after a while things seem to get too rough, and they tend to move back south.

For most of its first three decades, Alaska saw major decisions about its future made elsewhere: in the Congress in Washington and the Interior Department, in the boardrooms of giant oil companies. Now, in its second generation, the decisions may be less momentous but they are being made, with one major exception, by Alaskans. At statehood in 1959 Alaska was still a ward of the federal government, with a private economy based tenuously on extractive industries—fishing, timber—but dependent on federal spending and management. Then came the rapid economic development of East Asia, Alaska's natural market (even its oil would be mostly shipped there but for an economically nonsensical prohibition voted by Congress in the energy crisis hysteria of the 1970s). But the opportunities it opened up were mostly obscured by the discovery of the vast, remote North Slope oil field in 1968. But first Alaska had to wait for others to make decisions that would shape its development as surely as the Northwest Ordinance did Ohio's or the Homestead Act, Nebraska's.

The first was to determine who owned Alaska's land, a decision deferred by the Statehood Act and rendered critical by the land claims of Alaska's Natives. The Statehood law let the state gain ownership by selecting 103 million acres (of 375 million), but in 1966 the Interior Department imposed a freeze, preventing the state from claiming mineral-rich lands. In 1971 Congress passed the Alaska Native Claims Act, setting up 12 regional and 220 village Native corporations, and giving them $962 million and time to select their own 44 million acres. The freeze was ended, but the Native corporations had until the middle 1980s to select their lands.

Then came the question of how to get the North Slope oil out. A pipeline was the only feasible way, but environmentalists charged that the pipeline as originally designed would destroy the permafrost (land that remains frozen year round except for a few inches at the top), would interfere with caribou migrations, and would otherwise irreparably injure Alaska's unique and fragile environment. They got a 1973 court ruling halting pipeline construction; Alaskans got

ALASKA — Congressional District, Boroughs, Census Areas, and Selected Places — *(1 At Large)*

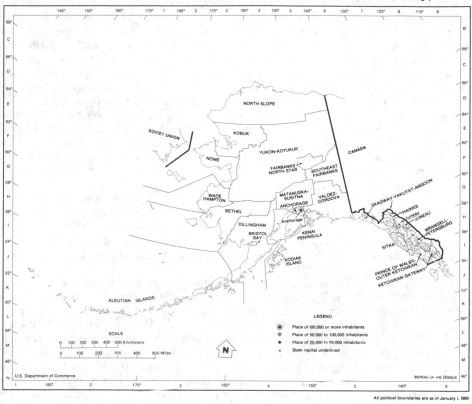

All political boundaries are as of January 1, 1980

that reversed in Congress, with a one-vote margin in the Senate. The delay may have been a boon: the redesign did protect the caribou and the permafrost, and the pipeline was not completed until 1977, when oil prices were soon to hit their peak.

Finally Congress had to decide which Alaska lands should be set aside as wilderness or otherwise protected from development. Environmentalists from the Lower 48 rallied around the issue, and lobbied the Congress brilliantly; Congress passed, over the objections of Alaska's two senators and in the face of tears from its congressman, the Alaska Lands Act of 1980, which protected 159 million acres.

So the Natives were compensated, the pipeline built, the parks and wilderness areas set aside (altogether, 49% of Alaska's land is set aside in some way), the oil dollars came gushing in. From this point in the early 1980s Alaskans have been making their own decisions, less momentous perhaps, but still critical to the state's future. They do so with a bias that is boomer rather than a greenie—Alaskan for development-minded and environmentalist. Democrats as well as Republicans, union leaders as much as real estate developers, libertarians as well as advocates of more federal projects here—all favor development and most believe the more untrammelled the better. Zoning is a dirty word, and even Anchorage, which contains 40% of Alaska's people, is a hodgepodge of a city, with businesses and apartments next to single-family houses and trash left outside during the long freezing winter.

The first decision the state had to make was what to do with its oil revenues—well over $2 billion at their peak—and its answer was a combination of libertarianism and socialism. Quite quickly Alaska abolished its sales and income taxes: oil by the mid-1980s provided 85% of its revenue. But Governor Jay Hammond, a bush pilot elected by narrow margins in 1974 and 1978, insisted on setting up a Permanent Fund for most of the oil money, which accumulated some $8 billion by the mid-1980s, and insisted that only the interest could be disbursed and only in the form of checks to each Alaska citizen. So in late 1986 each Alaskan got a check for $556—and each voter has a stake in preventing legislators from dipping into the Permanent Fund and raising the states's long-term wealth to meet short-term needs. It has worked. Alaska's state government has lavished all kinds of benefits on its mostly affluent citizens (the cost of living differential from the Lower 48 is much less than it used to be and incomes nearly 50% higher): it employs one out of ten employed Alaskans; it subsidizes mortgage interest so rates are 3% below the market; it makes low-interest loans to Alaskan college and graduate students, and forgives half the debt if they return to the state for five years; it subsidizes housing for old people who have been in Alaska 25 years. But revenues have slumped with lower oil prices, and since 1984 governors have submitted budgets with huge slashes in state spending. There was even talk in 1987 of bringing back the state income tax.

Alaskans also had to decide an issue long since settled in the other 49 states: where the state capital should be. In 1974 and 1976 referenda voters decided to move it from tiny Juneau—two time zones away from most state residents, inaccessible by car, with an airport that is often fogged in—to a site near Anchorage. But in 1982 they voted against providing the money for the move. So the capital stays in Juneau, which has had its own little building boom, and whose population is zooming up to 30,000.

Another decision has to be made about the future of the Native corporations. These fascinating entities have been operating on uncharted waters. Some have tried to promote traditional though uneconomic activities; others have sought a higher return; one is on the *Fortune* 1000 list. The Native Claims Act allows stock in these corporations to become transferable in 1991. But most Natives fear this would change their character as Native entities, and at their behest the Alaska delegation asked Congress to bar stock transfers to non-Natives unless most shareholders agree. The measure passed the House, but stumbled in the Senate when the Interior Department asked for a provision allowing minority shareholders to be able to sell their stock back to the corporations and Native leaders balked. The issue is likely to return to the 100th Congress; Senator Ted Stevens and Representative Don Young have said they'll sponsor any bill that has a consensus among Natives.

Alaskans also have to weigh continually the claims of resources versus the environment. Should the Forest Service subsidize logging in the Tongass rain forest on the Panhandle south of Juneau? Should oil drilling be allowed in Bristol Bay and other offshore areas? Should—and this was the most pressing question in early 1987—oil exploration be allowed in the Arctic National Wildlife Reserve, on the coastal plain where 180,000 caribou now graze in summer? The Reagan administration wants to see drilling, and so would most Alaskans. But Congress will decide, and in early 1987 there were complicated negotiations for trades of mineral rights between the federal government, the state, and Native corporations: probably everyone will have to be satisfied, and the caribou provided for, before Congress will give any go-ahead.

It should be apparent that political issues in Alaska are starkly different from those in other states, and not surprisingly Lower 48 political alignments mean very little here. Alaska has weak or non-existent party organizations, it has no party registration and like Washington State allows voters to select candidates of different parties in primaries, it has a Libertarian party which has elected legislators and won 15% of the vote for governor (though it did poorly in 1984 and 1986), and as in most small states many voters know the candidates personally and character counts for much more than party or ideological label. In national elections it is now heavily Republican. But by the middle 1970s, Alaska began voting mainly on Alaska, not national issues, and as a result became one of the most Republican states in presidential and congressional elections. But its two most recent governors have been Democrats—and fierce political adversaries.

There are regional partisan patterns, however. Greater Anchorage, with nearly half the state's population, is prosperous and tends to be Republican. It is not utterly dependent on oil; its port and airport make it the one place in Alaska where services and amenities are generally available. The smaller settlements in a 200-mile arc around Anchorage are places where boomers from the Lower 48 arrived to seek their fortunes—the Matanuska Valley, one of the few places in Alaska where farming is possible, Seward, the Kenai peninsula, the little port of Valdez at the southern terminus of the pipeline—tend to go Republican. So does the second largest city, Fairbanks, a pipeline and mineral service center deep in the interior, unprotected from the Arctic winds in winter and fierce crowds of mosquitoes in its brief but hot summer. Vast beds of coal and other minerals as well lie under Fairbanks, but the physical environment puts up formidable obstacles to commercial development—obstacles quite unfamiliar to most Americans, who assume technology always triumphs over nature.

The older Alaska and Native Alaska, with far less of the population, tend to go Democratic. The old Alaska, first settled by Russians, can be seen in the fishing towns of the Panhandle and Juneau, located on an inlet of the Pacific up against a steep mountain. Far away to the north and west is the Alaska of the Bush, the villages where Natives—Indians, Aleuts, Eskimos—live, often in poverty. Natives make up 16% of Alaska's population, and 70% in the vast lands north and west of Anchorage and Fairbanks. But they are only 51,000 people living in an area larger than the northeast United States. Almost all of Alaska remains physically vacant, devoid of human habitation, perhaps unseen by human eyes. What to do with this vast expanse and with the oil and other minerals which are or may be there is the continuing and dominant question of Alaska politics.

Governor. The small-town character of Alaska politics was never so clear as in the summer of 1985 when the Alaska Senate held hearings on the impeachment of Governor Bill Sheffield. The hearings were prompted by a grand jury which declined to indict him but suggested—though surely it was not legally authorized to do so—that the legislature impeach him on grounds he steered a state building contract to a political contributor. But the facts were murky, it was not at all clear that Sheffield had done more than use poor judgment, and the Senate (which in Alaska decides whether to impeach; the House holds any trial) voted 12-8 not to impeach. Poor judgment, however, is grounds for political defeat. Sheffield, a successful hotel operator who never before held public office, spent much of his time in office raising money to pay off the debts owed himself by his campaign committee.

The 1986 race was a rip-roaring contest on both sides. Sheffield was defeated soundly by Steve Cowper, a Fairbanks lawyer who lost the 1982 nomination by 260 votes. Republican Arliss Sturgulewski beat former Governor (1967-69) and Interior Secretary (1969-70) Walter Hickel after charging him with conflict of interest because he owned stock in a company seeking to build a natural gas pipeline. She was helped by the last-minute endorsement of Jay Hammond, who beat Hickel in two primaries himself. Both Cowper (pronounced cooper) and Sturgulewski (pronounced sturjoolooskee) were colorful candidates; both wanted to scale down spending; both favor minimal interference with development.

Cowper—mustachioed, thrice-married, war correspondent in Vietnam, underwater diver— was one of the legislators who pushed through the Permanent Fund. He extolls entrepreneurs, believes the day of big oil exploration projects is over, and feels, in David Broder's words, that "new jobs must be developed from the state's abundant supply of young, well-educated immigrants tuned to trade possibilities with the Pacific Rim." It is a plausible, even inspiring vision, but it could be frustrated if Democrats in Congress build trade barriers across the Pacific. Alaska does have a talented labor supply, important natural resources, and the stability of the U.S. flag off in a corner of the Pacific and in time zones halfway between Washington and Tokyo. But in the meantime low oil prices were forcing Cowper in 1987 to propose a 27% cut in state spending.

Senators. Alaska's leading representative in Washington is its senior Senator, Ted Stevens. Being a senator from Alaska is a different kind of job from being a senator from any other state: however much an Alaska Senator gets involved in issues of national scope, much of his time and energy are necessarily consumed in dealing with parochial Alaska issues. Stevens has spent most of his adult lifetime on Alaska issues, from his service in the Eisenhower administration Interior Department and his representation of Native groups as an Anchorage lawyer in the 1950s. He probably knows the details of Alaska legislation better than anyone else. He has been the senior senator almost since he was appointed, in 1968, to fill a vacancy created by the death of Bob Bartlett; the other senator, Ernest Greuning, had been defeated and was about to be replaced by Democrat Mike Gravel, whose grandstanding on Alaska issues aroused Stevens's fierce temper and again and again until Gravel's defeat in the 1980 primary.

But then Stevens's temper has become as legendary as his expertise on matters Alaskan, and he gets especially furious when an exhaustively negotiated compromise has been rejected by people who, in Stevens's view, have only a superficial knowledge of and no practical stake in Alaska matters. His version of the Alaska lands bill was rejected, for instance; and, on a much less important matter, Howard Metzenbaum of Ohio prevented the Senate from passing in 1982 a bill to give the federally owned Alaska Railroad to the state government, which finally bought it under Stevens's terms in 1985. His temper may have cost Stevens the Senate majority leadership after the 1984 election. Stevens had been party whip for four years under Howard Baker, and was one of four candidates to succeed him; he did better than expected, but finally lost 28-25 to Bob Dole. That has left him free to concentrate on Alaska issues and on the Defense Appropriations Subcommittee he chaired when Republicans had a majority and where he is now ranking minority member. Stevens has generally been a supporter of higher defense budgets, but has become less than an enthusiast for Caspar Weinberger's Pentagon. It has fallen on him to defend, at various stages in the appropriations process, challenged weapons systems like the MX missile and challenged operations like aid to the Nicaraguan contras. He also plays a constructive role in civil service issues—one fraught with at least a little political risk in a state with high federal employment. He chaired the Commerce subcommittee on Merchant Marine, and has generally supported the current complex system of subsidies and regulations; naturally, he has taken particular interest in Pacific coastal shipping. He also closely follows fishing law— important in Alaska—where fishing is the second industry after oil. He sponsored legislation to preserve the Alaska Native land settlement by extending restrictions on the sale or transfer of Native corporation stock, thus protecting the land from taxation. Stevens also backs a measure to compensate Alaska's Aleuts for having been removed from their land by the Army during World War II; this is similar to the issue of Japanese-American redress, on which Stevens also could be active.

Any politician who sustains a defeat, particularly one at the hands of his colleagues, as Stevens did in November 1984, faces a crossroads in his career. Will he withdraw from the fray and indulge his temper, or will he get back to work and become a more accomplished and productive senator? Stevens seems to have taken the second course. At home, his occasional defeats on Alaskan issues have not mattered, and he has been reelected by wide margins, most recently in 1984.

Stevens now has a colleague he can work comfortably with in Alaska's junior Senator, Frank Murkowski. He was first elected in 1980, but was not part of the crop of New Right Republicans that year; he is a Fairbanks banker who favors opening up and developing Alaska's resources, and like many Alaskans, he is a little skeptical of government interference in personal as well as economic life. In his first term he served on the bread-and-butter committees of Energy (the old Interior) and Environment (the old Public Works). In 1983 he left Environment to go to Foreign Relations, and chaired the East Asian and Pacific Affairs Subcommittee. In 1985 he became chairman of the Veterans Committee. Murkowski was named by *National Journal* as one of the least productive members of Congress. But as a Stevens ally in line with the state on most issues, he was considered a cinch for reelection. He received more spirited opposition than expected, from Glenn Olds, president of Alaska Pacific University. But he prevailed by a comfortable margin nonetheless.

Congressman. Representative Don Young also tends to work well with Stevens. First elected in 1973, after his Democratic opponent Nick Begich was killed in a 1972 plane crash, Young is a Republican from the Bush. A former teacher in the winter and riverboat captain in the summer, he is a man of directness, fluent in the salty language in which much of Alaska politics is conducted, fervent in his boomerism and emotional in his appeals. Since 1985 he has been ranking Republican on the Interior Committee; he previously held that position on the subcommittee which handled the Alaska Lands Act. These are frustrating assignments for a congressman of Young's views, for Democratic environmentalists have a comfortable majority on the committee, a solid command of the facts, and a considerable ability to conciliate and influence wavering colleagues. Young, in contrast, tends to be angry, bombastic, even tearful— and often self-defeating. He may also be frustrated and often seems to spend more time on his Merchant Marine assignment than on Interior. On issues he probably represents Alaska's majority views. But his political base has seemed surprisingly weak when he has had significant opposition. In 1978, for example, he won with just 55% of the vote, and in 1984 and 1986, against Pegge Begich, the widow of his predecessor, he won with similarly unimpressive percentages. Will this apparent weakness stimulate more serious competition in 1988?

Presidential Politics. Alaska's reaction against the environmental movement and economic regulation have made it one of the most Republican states in presidential politics. In the very close elections of 1960 and 1968, Alaska came eerily close to the national average in its preferences. In the last three elections, however, it has been one of the most Republican—and least Democratic — states. In 1984 Walter Mondale lost it by more than 2–1 and in 1980 Jimmy Carter got only 26% of the vote and in some places ran behind Libertarian Ed Clark. Alaska has no presidential primary. No presidential candidate is going to take time off to campaign way up here for so few delegates.

The People: Est. Pop. 1986: 534,000; Pop. 1980: 401,851, up 32.8% 1980–86 and 32.8% 1970–80; 0.22% of U.S. total, 50th largest. 22% with 1–3 yrs. col., 22% with 4+ yrs. col.; 10.7% below poverty level. Single ancestry: 9% English, 8% German, 4% Irish, 2% Norwegian, French, 1% Swedish, Scottish, Italian, Dutch, Polish. Households (1980): 73% family, 49% with children, 61% married couples; 41.7% housing units rented; median monthly rent: $338; median house value: $75,200. Voting age pop. (1980): 271,106; 14% American Indian, 3% Black, 2% Spanish origin, 2% Asian origin. Registered voters (1986): 290,808; 65,187 D (22%), 61,431 R (21%), 155,617 unaffiliated (54%), 8,582 minor parties (3%).

1986 Share of Federal Tax Burden: $2,489,000,000; 0.33% of U.S. total, 44th largest.

1986 Share of Federal Expenditures

	Total		Non-Defense		Defense	
Total Expend	$2,719m	(0.33%)	$1,532m	(0.26%)	$1,187m	(0.52%)
St/Lcl Grants	664m	(0.59%)	663m	(0.59%)	0m	(.90%)
Salary/Wages	887m	(0.74%)	326m	(0.56%)	561m	(0.91%)
Ind Payments	388m	(0.11%)	331m	(0.10%)	58m	(0.33%)
Procurement	759m	(0.37%)	192m	(0.35%)	567m	(0.38%)
Research/Other	20m	(0.07%)	20m	(0.08%)	0m	(0%)

Political Lineup: Governor, Steve Cowper (D); Lt. Gov., Stephen McAlpine (D); Atty. Gen., Grace Schaible (D); Commissioner of Revenue, Hugh Malone (D). State Senate, 20 (12 R and 8 D); State House of Representatives, 40 (24 D, 16 R).Senators, Ted Stevens (R) and Frank H. Murkowski (R). Representative, 1 R at large.

1984 Presidential Vote

Reagan (R)	138,377	(67%)
Mondale (D)	62,007	(30%)

1980 Presidential Vote

Reagan (R)	85,364	(62%)
Carter (D)	41,228	(30%)
Clark (L)	18,389	(12%)
Anderson (I)	10,988	(7%)

GOVERNOR

Gov. Steve Cowper (D)

Elected 1986, term expires Dec. 1990; b. August 21, 1938, Petersburg, VA; home, Fairbanks; U. of NC, B.A. 1960, LL.B. 1963; Episcopalian; married (Michael Margaret).

Career: Army Air Corps, 1946–49; Sears, Roebuck and Co., 1952–62; Bd. Chmn., Sheffield Enterprises, 1962–82.

Office: Box A, Juneau 99811, 907-465-3500.

Election Results

1986 gen.	Steve Cowper (D)............	84,943	(47%)
	Arliss Sturgulewski (R)	76,515	(43%)
	Joe Vogler (AI)..............	10,013	(6%)
1986 prim.	Steve Cowper (D)............	36,233	(57%)
	William Sheffield (D).........	26,935	(42%)
1982 gen.	William Sheffield (D).........	89,259	(46%)
	Thomas A. Fink (R)..........	71,949	(37%)
	Richard L. Randolph (L)	28,981	(15%)

SENATORS

Sen. Ted Stevens (R)

Appointed Dec. 24, 1968, elected 1970, seat up 1990; b. Nov. 18, 1923, Indianapolis, IN; home, Girdwood; U. of CA at Los Angeles, A.B. 1947, Harvard U., LL.B. 1950; Episcopalian; married (Catherine).

Career: Air Force, WWII; Practicing atty., 1950–53, 1961–68; U.S. Atty., 1953–56; U.S. Dept. of Interior, Legis. counsel, 1956–58, Asst. to the Secy., 1958–60, Solicitor 1960–61; AK House of Reps., 1964–68.

Offices: 522 HSOB 20510, 202-224-3004. Also Fed. Bldg., Box 4, 101 12th Ave., Fairbanks 99701, 907-456-0261; Fed. Bldg., Box 149, Juneau 99802, 907-586-7400; 120 Trading Bay Rd., Kenai 99611, 907-283-5808; and Front St., Ketchikan 99901, 907-225-6880.

Committees: *Appropriations* (2d of 13 R). Subcommittees: Commerce, Justice, State, and Judiciary; Defense (Ranking Member); Interior; Labor, Health and Human Services, Education; Military Construction. *Commerce, Science, and Transportation* (5th of 9 R). Subcommittees: Aviation; Communications; Merchant Marine (Ranking Member); National Ocean Policy Study. *Governmental Affairs* (2d of 6 R). Subcommittees: Federal Services, Post Office and Civil Service (Ranking Member); Federal Spending, Budget and Accounting; Government Management; Investigations. *Rules and Administration* (Ranking Member of 7 R). *Joint Committee on the Library. Joint Committee on Printing.*

Group Ratings

	ADA	ACLU	COPE	CFA	LCV	ACU	NTU	NSI	COC	CEI
1986	15	30	42	07	8	71	40	100	74	59
1985	10	—	43	20	—	64	46	—	74	—

National Journal Ratings

	1986 LIB — 1986 CONS		1985 LIB — 1985 CONS	
Economic	36% —	60%	29% —	70%
Social	37% —	61%	54% —	45%
Foreign	18% —	77%	22% —	70%

Key Votes

1) Ease Gun Cont	FOR	5) Grm-Rdmn Def Red	FOR	9) Rehnquist Nom	FOR
2) Immig Reform	FOR	6) Contra Aid	FOR	10) Tax Reform	FOR
3) Lmt Text Imp	AGN	7) SDI Funding	FOR	11) Drug Death Pen	AGN
4) Aid Tobac Ind	FOR	8) Lmt PAC Contrib	AGN	12) S Africa Sanc	AGN

Election Results

1984 general	Ted Stevens (R)	146,919	(71%)	($1,323,218)
	John E. Havelock (D)..................	58,804	(29%)	($90,685)
1984 primary	Ted Stevens (R)	65,522	(100%)	
1978 general	Ted Stevens (R)	92,783	(76%)	($346,837)
	Donald W. Hobbs (D).................	29,574	(24%)	($21,234)

Campaign Contributions and Expenditures

1979-84		Direct Cont. 1979-84		PACS Breakdown 1979-84			
Receipts	$1,418,819	Indiv.	$650,846	Corp.	$393,106	T/M/H	$149,994
Expend.	$1,323,218	Party	$15,981	Labor	$64,018	Agr.	$2,000
Unspent	$184,289	PACS	$660,019	Ideo.	$45,074	CWOS	$4,200

Sen. Frank H. Murkowski (R)

Elected 1980, seat up 1992; b. Mar. 28, 1933, Seattle, WA; home, Fairbanks; U. of Santa Clara, Seattle U., B.A. 1955; Roman Catholic; married (Nancy).

Career: Coast Guard, 1955–56; AK Commissioner of Econ. Develop., 1966–70; Pres., AK Natl. Bank of the North, 1971–80.

Offices: 709 HSOB 20510, 202-224-6665. Also Fed. Bldg, 701 C St., Box 1, Anchorage 99513, 907-271-3735.

Committees: *Energy and Natural Resources* (6th of 9 R). Subcommittees: Mineral Resources Development and Production; Public Lands, National Parks and Forests; Water and Power. *Foreign Relations* (6th of 9 R). Subcommittees: International Economic Policy, Trade, Oceans and Environment; East Asian and Pacific Affairs (Ranking Member); Terrorism, Narcotics and International Communications. *Veterans' Affairs* (Ranking Member). *Select Committee on Indian Affairs* (2d of 3 R). *Select Committee on Intelligence* (4th of 7 R).

Group Ratings

	ADA	ACLU	COPE	CFA	LCV	ACU	NTU	NSI	COC	CEI
1986	20	7	23	20	8	78	37	100	65	61
1985	0	—	20	07	—	82	54	—	84	—

National Journal Ratings

	1986 LIB — 1986 CONS		1985 LIB — 1985 CONS	
Economic	53% —	46%	27% —	71%
Social	23% —	76%	0% —	83%
Foreign	38% —	59%	0% —	88%

Key Votes

1) Ease Gun Cont	FOR	5) Grm-Rdmn Def Red	FOR	9) Rehnquist Nom	FOR
2) Immig Reform	FOR	6) Contra Aid	FOR	10) Tax Reform	FOR
3) Lmt Text Imp	AGN	7) SDI Funding	FOR	11) Drug Death Pen	AGN
4) Aid Tobac Ind	FOR	8) Lmt PAC Contrib	FOR	12) S Africa Sanc	FOR

Election Results

1986 general	Frank H. Murkowski (R)	97,674	(54%)	($1,389,056)
	Glenn Olds (D)	79,727	(44%)	($412,074)
1986 primary	Frank H. Murkowski (R)	91,705	(100%)	
1980 general	Frank H. Murkowski (R)	84,159	(54%)	($697,387)
	Clark Gruening (D)	72,007	(46%)	($507,445)

Campaign Contributions and Expenditures

1985-1986		Direct Cont. 1985-86		PACS Breakdown 1985-86			
Receipts	$1,425,261	Indiv.	$738,750	Corp. $336,640		T/M/H	$149,717
Expend.	$1,389,056	Party	$17,885	Labor $37,550		Agr.	$2,750
Unspent	$53,848	PACS	$594,206	Ideo. $56,387		CWOS	$11,162
		Cand.	$15,853				

Rep. Don Young (R)

Elected Mar. 6, 1973; b. June 9, 1933, Meridian, CA; home, Fort Yukon; Chico St. Col., B.A. 1956; Episcopalian; married (Lu).

Career: Construction work, 1959; Teacher, 1960–69; Riverboat captain; Fort Yukon City Cncl., 1960–64; Mayor of Fort Yukon, 1964–68; AK House of Reps., 1966–70; AK Senate, 1970–73.

Offices: 2331 RHOB, 202-225-5765. Also 115 Fed. Bldg., Anchorage 99501, 907-279-1587.

Committees: *Interior and Insular Affairs* (Ranking Member of 15 R). Subcommittees: Energy and the Environment; Water and Power. *Merchant Marine and Fisheries* (2nd of 17 R). Subcommittees: Coast Guard and Navigation; Fish and Wildlife (Ranking Member); Merchant Marine; Panama Canal. *Post Office and Civil Service* (6th of 8 R). Subcommittees: Postal Operations and Services; Postal Personnel and Modernization (Ranking Member).

Group Ratings

	ADA	ACLU	COPE	CFA	LCV	ACU	NTU	NSI	COC	CEI
1986	20	23	42	8	16	65	36	100	56	39
1985	30	—	41	33	—	62	34	—	45	—

National Journal Ratings

	1986 LIB — 1986 CONS			1985 LIB — 1985 CONS		
Economic	28%	—	71%	46%	—	53%
Social	33%	—	66%	32%	—	67%
Foreign	16%	—	79%	24%	—	66%

Key Votes

1) Lmt Cln Water Act	AGN	5) Retain Gun Cont	AGN	9) Aid Angola Reb	FOR
2) Rpl Tobac Sub	AGN	6) Contra Aid	FOR	10) Tax Reform	AGN
3) Grm-Rdmn Def Red	FOR	7) Lmt Text Imp	AGN	11) S Africa Sanc	FOR
4) Ban Polygraph	FOR	8) Lmt SDI	AGN	12) Immig Reform	AGN

Election Results

1986 general	Don Young (R)	101,799	(56%)	($487,261)
	Pegge Begich (D)	74,053	(41%)	($269,560)
1986 primary	Don Young (R)	86,021	(92%)	
	Three others (R)	86,052	(8%)	
1984 general	Don Young (R)	113,582	(55%)	($486,799)
	Pegge Begich (D)	86,052	(42%)	($359,345)

Campaign Contributions and Expenditures

1985-86		Direct Cont. 1985-86		PACS Breakdown 1985-86			
Receipts	$495,429	Indiv.	$223,827	Corp.	$105,044	T/M/H	$68,000
Expend.	$487,261	Party	$16,359	Labor	$39,700	Agr.	$3,400
Unspent	$12,010	PACS	$235,264	Ideo.	$15,820	CWOS	$3,300

ARIZONA

Arizona today is almost entirely a creation of post-World War II America: a series of grid streets laid out over deserts, shopping centers and schools clustered where not long ago there was nothing but sagebrush, water piped over hundreds of miles of barren land and pumped up nearly 3,000 feet in elevation to irrigate farms and swimming pools, fountains and artificial wave machines, in a region of dry river beds and relentless sun. The older Arizona was demographically negligible—only 550,000 people in 1940, spread out over Indian reservations, crowded into a few sleepy railroad junction towns, and isolated in a couple of company-owned copper mining towns. Then Arizona was exotic. Americans had heard stories about the fierce Apache and had seen pictures of the Grand Canyon; moviegoers glimpsed U.S. 66 and saw the sun set behind giant Saguaro cactuses in the movies. Then the jet airliner and the airconditioner changed everything. Jets made Arizona accessible first for vacationers and then for businessmen. Air conditioning made life here bearable in the hot summer months. From the Midwest in particular, from the East and South and lately even from California, people have been pouring in and creating this new Arizona. By the middle 1980s there were more than three million Arizonans, 56% of them in metropolitan Phoenix and another 21% in metropolitan Tucson.

The new Arizona is a fresh start, a chance to make a new and quintessentially American civilization where there was none before. In their city planning—mile-square street grids proceeding right up to the base of the mountain outcroppings that loom over Phoenix and Tucson—and in their politics, Arizonanas have gone back to first principles and abstract ideas. Most newcomers here like to think of themselves as upholders of traditional values, but Phoenix, glaringly contemporary with its glass and chrome buildings, humming always with the sound of air-conditioners, is not an old conservative city, like Philadelphia or Cincinnati, where things are done according to custom and tradition and old connections are more important than new deals. In this new Arizona citizens face squarely first questions—government or free enterprise, development or environment, regulation or freedom—and tend to come out squarely on one side or the other.

Yet there is something vibrant about chaotic life in Phoenix—the absence of an established order and, often, of established standards of legality and fair play. The establishment occupies a very thin layer atop local society; there are no really old families here, and the men who have guided the destiny of the city and state are businessmen and lawyers whose names are not widely known. Underneath that top layer, there is plenty of money but few standards. The lure of Arizona has brought in big corporations, and for years there was low unemployment; contrary to popular impression, Arizona is not just a retirement haven and has a percentage of elderly near the national average. Arizona has also attracted many unscrupulous con men and fast-buck artists: drifters and grifters who would have been at home in Raymond Chandler's Los Angeles (though not in the more mature and sophisticated Los Angeles of today). Chandler might have scripted the 1976 murder of investigative reporter Don Bolles, for which the trigger man fingered a prominent developer who was convicted, got the conviction reversed on appeal, and sued the police for $605 million for prosecuting him; who ordered the murder remains unknown. Nor would Chandler have been surprised to learn that the publisher of the Phoenix newspapers, Darrow Tully, was forced to resign in 1985 when it was revealed that the war record he claimed as a fighter pilot in Korea and Vietnam was a fake; there is a marvelous picture showing Tully in a black tie with epaulets and medals. Chandler might also have loved knowing that Tully was exposed by county prosecutor Thomas Collins, a political ally of an antipornography crusader, even though there was no criminal charge to provide a legal basis for his investigation.

Naturally Arizona's sudden growth transformed the state's politics—from an old-fashioned, practical-minded Democratic state to a brash, abstract Republican one. In the old Arizona the key task of politicians was to funnel government subsidies to the state's struggling economy. So Carl Hayden, Democratic congressman from statehood, Senator from 1927 to 1969, tried to keep up the price of copper and secure water—more precious here than oil—for the cotton, citrus, and cattle farmers. Hayden first proposed the Central Arizona Project in 1947, saw it enacted in his last full year in Congress in 1968, and would have seen its completion date of 1992 only if he had lived to 125. At a cost of some $3.5 billion, the CAP diverts Colorado River water up to the Phoenix and Tucson areas, and originally almost all of that was intended for farming. But that won't always be true. Arizona has been pumping more groundwater than it replaces, which threatens literally to undermine its urban civilization: in time, the CAP water will go to Phoenix and Tucson, and the green circles of irrigated cultivation you can see from the air will turn back into desert.

If Hayden helped give the old Arizona critical water, another longtime Senator, Barry Goldwater, helped give the new Arizona its characteristic philosophy. Proprietor of his family's department store in the 1940s, he was elected to the Phoenix council in 1949 and then upset the Senate Majority Leader, oldtime Democrat Ernest McFarland, in 1952. (That opened the way for a 44-year-old Texan named Lyndon Johnson to become Senate Democratic leader.) In the middle 1950s Goldwater authored *The Conscience of a Conservative,* won reelection by a large margin in 1958, a bad year for his party elsewhere, and became the spiritual leader of Republicans who wanted to roll back the New Deal and pursue, at least in Asia and the Pacific, an aggressive foreign policy. His frank, often blunt and impolitic articulation of his beliefs brought him so much devotion and volunteer support from all over the country that he won the 1964 Republican presidential nomination despite his malapropisms, his modesty, and his evident distaste for running. His defeat that year set the stage for later conservative victories, but not quite in the way he intended. The resulting Democratic landslide made possible Lyndon Johnson's Great Society. In the years since, the popular New Deal programs have remained unchallenged, a part of history, while critics of the less popular Great Society, like Ronald Reagan, have thrived.

Goldwater's insistence on reexamining first principles did, however, appeal to the new Arizonans seeking to root a new American society in desert soil. They found the old "pinto" Democrats unappealing—dusty, rural, old, and more concerned about a few federal dollars when the real growth of the local economy seemed to come from private business. They found the Goldwater Republicans appealing—including some young Arizonans who became prominent in Washington: John Rhodes, William Rehnquist, Richard Kleindienst, Sandra Day O'Connor. So the years 1958 to 1972 were almost entirely Republican in Arizona—the only state which has gone Republican in every presidential election since 1948, a state where Republicans held the governorship for all but two years in the 1958–74 period, whose congressional delegation was, with the exception of Morris Udall, entirely Republican during the entire Nixon and Ford Administrations.

Arizona Republicans have not won all local elections, however. Democrats were elected

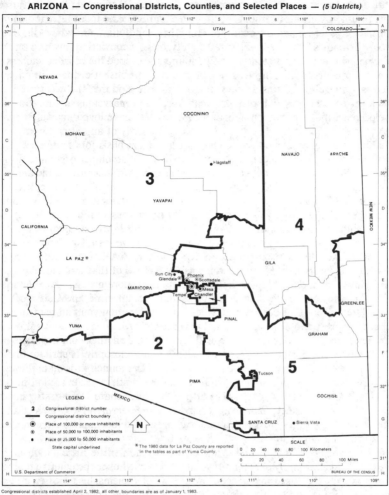

ARIZONA — Congressional Districts, Counties, and Selected Places — (5 Districts)

governor in 1974, 1978, and 1982, and a Democrat is mayor of Phoenix. Democrats hold statewide office and one of the two Senate seats. Yet overall this is still a very Republican state. That is evident in presidential elections, it is evident from the Republican majorities in the legislature and from the success of Republican candidates in local elections in the big countries. Their failure to monopolize the top officials is due in part to the talent of the Democrats who have held them, but it can be ascribed as well to a kind of abdication. Successful young men and women of Republican views here do not see high office as the way to success or achievement: accomplishment comes through private enterprise. For these free market philosophers of the desert, government and politics are not where it's at. That leaves the field open often enough to talented young Democrats who are interested in government, like Bruce Babbitt, governor from 1978 to 1986.

Governor. For years Arizona didn't seem to need — and didn't get — much state government. It was the last state to participate in the Medicaid program, the last state with a state park system; its governor and legislature had just about no staff at all. For eight years Arizona did have a state government capable of spawning controversies and a governor who ranked among the nations brainiest and most original. But Bruce Babbitt came to the office only after the resignation of one governor and the death four months later of another. Babbitt likes to stress his Arizona roots: he comes from an old Flagstaff family, he goes backpacking with his family in the Grand Canyon, he remains unpretentious and unflappable despite his political success. And if he is from the old, pre-airconditioning Arizona, he respects the new Arizona built up since World War II, and saw himself as setting a course for yet another Arizona for the future. He loves the nuts and bolts of government, and spent one year devising programs to help children, another on water development, most of another on health care, and other time on developing finally a state park system.

What Babbitt was not able to do was to choose a successor. He would have been pleased to be followed by Democrat Bill Schulz, a Phoenix apartment developer who nearly beat Barry Goldwater in 1980. But Schulz pulled out of the race in 1985 because of his daughter's poor health. Then Babbitt's endorsed candidate, Tony Mason, lost the Democratic primary to Superintendent of Public Construction Carolyn Warner. That result was less startling than the defeat in the Republican primary of Senate Majority Leader Burton Barr, a competent political craftsman, by Phoenix-area auto dealer Evan Mecham, a perennial candidate whose only claim on the office was a reputation for being more conservative than Barr. Six days afer the primary, Schulz got back into the race as an independent, and for a while it was a genuine three-way contest in the polls. Ultimately Mecham won with 40% of the vote, to 36% for Warner and 26% for Schulz. Many Democrats blamed Schulz for splitting the vote. But a comparison of the results with those in other races suggests that Schulz got most of his votes from those who backed Republicans for other offices, and Mecham might have won in a two-way race.

Mecham has proved to be a controversial governor. He rescinded Babbitt's proclamation of Martin Luther King's birthday as a state holiday; a technicality, he said, the governor can't proclaim holidays. He barred one reporter from his press conferences, saying he was a "nonperson." He refused to appoint the choice of an advisory panel to the state Supreme Court. His education advisor defended parents' right to oppose teaching of evolution in the schools. Civil rights leaders threatened to start a recall drive, but he seems certain to stay in office; like a mirror in a funhouse, he reflects in an exaggerated way the conservative beliefs of a majority of voters in the state. It's just not clear that a majority of the voters will choose this mirror in 1990, just as a majority did not in 1986.

Senators. In 1986, 34 years after he was first elected to the Senate, Barry Goldwater retired at age 77. He won his last term by only a hair, yet it turned out to be a productive one for him. He was able to serve for the first time since 1954 as part of the Senate majority; he chaired the Intelligence Committee and kept a rein on William Casey and his operatives; he chaired the Senate Armed Services Committee, and pushed through a major Pentagon reform centralizing authority in the Chairman of the Joint Chiefs of Staff, to reduce service autonomy, and placing more power in the hands of theater commanders—over the opposition of Caspar Weinberger's Pentagon. But Goldwater was as ready to flay lazy generals, or Reagan appointees, or New Right conservatives who insist that their candidates be born-again Christians as he was to denounce the works of Franklin D. Roosevelt and Walter Reuther.

Arizona's Democratic Senator, Dennis DeConcini, is in the midst of his second term. DeConcini is part of a fairly large bloc in the Senate: a group of Democrats not from the South but from states that are Republican in national elections—Arizona, Nebraska, Montana, North Dakota—whose instincts on many issues are conservative and who in the Senate of 1987 and 1988 are as likely to be key swing votes as southern Democrats or liberal Republicans. Unlike the northern Democrats of the late 1960s and early 1970s, DeConcini is not a sure vote for organized labor, environmental activists, the civil right lobby, or opponents of Pentagon spending or American military intervention abroad. DeConcini demonstrated this early in his first term, on the Panama Canal Treaties, when he insisted on making public his own interpretation that the United States was not pledging to refrain from using military force to keep the canal open in the future. This was a point which the Carter administration wanted to fudge and which Panama's Omar Torrijos also wanted to obscure; bringing it out in the open hurt everyone politically, including DeConcini, who was attacked at home for giving away the Canal.

But this was characteristic of his penchant for detail: he is a lawyer who likes his t's crossed and i's dotted, and who is not persuaded by airy assurances that messy little details will be worked out later. On other issues DeConcini has proceeded similarily. A former criminal prosecutor, he has been a stickler for detail on the proposed federal criminal code and on other issues in the Judiciary Committee. There he supports tough sentencing and crackdowns on organized crime, and claims success in cracking down on drug smuggling through the Arizona-Mexico boarder; as ranking Democrat on the Constitution Subcommittee, he supports measures to mandate a balanced budget. He also serves, as Carl Hayden did, on the Appropriations Committee—another good spot for detail work. DeConcini is less prone to generalization, although it's apparent he feels a distaste for the politics of the kind of national Democrats who, for example, dominated the party's 1984 convention in San Francisco. He sides with them sometimes on economic issues, less often on cultural and foreign matters.

DeConcini will be on the spot in the 100th Congress on Reagan judicial nominations: his party loyalty may lead him one way, his often conservative inclinations and his political standing in Arizona the other. He is up for reelection in 1988, and although he once said he would retire in 1988 he probably will run (Barry Goldwater, after all, reconsidered a long-standing promise to retire in 1980). DeConcini's Democratic allegiance comes from family tradition, and his political success has come from a combination of hard work and fortunate circumstances. As member of an active political family and county prosecutor in Tucson in the 1970s, he became known as a hardliner; as the Democratic Senate nominee in 1976, he was helped when the Republicans had a bitter primary. In that race Representative John Conlan, an evangelical Christian, bitterly and aggressively attacked Representative Sam Steiger, who is Jewish—with nasty implications that Barry Goldwater, for one, complained about; nonetheless, when Steiger won the nomination, he was in trouble and DeConcini won easily. He won again in 1982, a good Democratic year, against a weaker-than-expected opponent. For 1988 possible opponents include Congressmen Bob Stump and Jim Kolbe and Attorney General Bob Corbin.

Goldwater's successor is John McCain, who only moved to Arizona in 1981 but is now one of the most popular politicians in the state. He is one of the very few career military men in Congress, and a very distinguished one at that: son and grandson of admirals, Navy fighter pilot, prisoner of war in North Vietnam for 5½ years. As McCain put it, when challenged for not having lived long in the state, "The longest place I ever lived in was Hanoi." McCain has other qualifications: he spent his last four years in the Navy as a congressional liaison, and so has been on Capitol Hill for most of the last 10 years. His crucial race was in 1982, when he won a four-way Republican primary to succeed John Rhodes by a 32%–26% margin. Reelection was easy, and he was strong enough a contender for the Senate that he drew no serious Republican primary opposition and Governor Bruce Babbitt, interested in the White House, declined in March 1985 to make the Senate race.

Yet McCain's campaign was not wholly smooth. He is a personable man but also has a temper, and he got riled when Democrat Richard Kimball accused him of being bought by Pentagon contractors because of their PAC contributions. He also had to go to Leisure World and apologize to its elderly residents for having called their home "seizure world." But he was able to make a convincing case that he is not a patsy for every policy of the Reagan Pentagon: he voted against sending Marines to Lebanon, for example, voted to kill the troubled Bradley fighting vehicle, and has been involved with the right-and-left caucus on military reform. And he added to his vigorous support for an assertive foreign policy to his support of some liberal stands on environmental and cultural issues. By election day, after a drop in the polls, he was back up and won a 60%–40% victory. With a seat he has reason to regard as safe, with his aggressiveness and probing mind, McCain has the potential to be an interesting and useful Senator.

Presidential politics. If any state is likely to go Republican in the 1988 presidential election, Arizona is: it is the only state that has voted for every Republican presidential nominee since 1948. As a result no sensible candidate spends much—or any—time there. Nor does anyone pay much attention to Arizona's delegate selection process, which resulted in an early and, as it turned out, the only victory for John Lindsay in the 1972 Democratic race.

Congressional districting. Arizona gained one congressional district from the 1980 census, as it has in each of the last four decades, giving it five. The Republican legislature, with enough votes to override Governor Babbitt's veto, enacted a plan which split the Phoenix metropolitan area among four districts, three of them solidly Republican. Tucson—as it happens, the perfect size for one district—was also split, and Morris Udall chose to run in the solidly Democratic Phoenix-to-Tucson 2d, leaving the marginal Tucson-and-southeast 5th District to close races in 1982 and 1984. With their capture of the 5th in 1984, and the party switch of the third's Bob Stump in 1982, and the election of two freshmen—both sons of longtime Republican congressmen—Arizona now has four Republican congressmen in five seats.

The People: Est. Pop. 1986: 3,317,000; Pop. 1980: 2,718,215, up 22.1% 1980–86 and 53.1% 1970–80; 1.38% of U.S. total, 25th largest. 21% with 1–3 yrs. col., 17% with 4+ yrs. col.; 13.2% below poverty level. Single ancestry: 10% English, 7% German, 4% Irish, 2% Italian, 1% Polish, French, Swedish, Scottish, Dutch, Norwegian. Households (1980): 74% family, 39% with children, 62% married couples; 31.7% housing units rented; median monthly rent: $228; median house value: $56,600. Voting age pop. (1980): 1,926,728; 13% Spanish origin, 4% American Indian, 3% Black, 1% Asian origin. Registered voters (1986): 1,596,079; 687,605 D (43%), 726,199 R (46%), 182,275 unaffiliated and minor parties (11%).

1986 Share of Federal Tax Burden: $8,789,000,000; 1.17% of U.S. total, 27th largest.

1986 Share of Federal Expenditures

	Total		Non-Defense		Defense	
Total Expend	$11,403m	(1.37%)	$7,514m	(1.25%)	$3,888m	(1.69%)
St/Lcl Grants	1,206m	(1.07%)	1,199m	(1.07%)	7m	(6.31%)
Salary/Wages	1,563m	(1.30%)	759m	(1.29%)	804m	(1.30%)
Pymts to Indiv	5,166m	(1.42%)	4,715m	(1.36%)	451m	(2.54%)
Procurement	3,253m	(1.58%)	628m	(1.13%)	1,625m	(1.75%)
Research/Other	214m	(0.80%)	214m	(1.80%)	0m	(0.46%)

Political Lineup: Governor, Evan Mecham (R); Secy. of State, Rose Mofford (D); Atty. Gen., Bob Corbin (R); Treasurer, Ray Rottas (R). State Senate, 30 (19 R and 11 D); State House of Representatives, 60 (36 R and 24 D). Senators, Dennis DeConcini (D) and John McCain (R). Representatives, 5 (4 R and 1 D).

1984 Presidential Vote

Reagan (R) 681,416 (66%)
Mondale (D) 333,854 (33%)

1980 Presidential Vote

Reagan (R) 529,688 (61%)
Carter (D) 246,843 (28%)
Anderson (I) 76,952 (9%)

GOVERNOR

Gov. Evan Mecham (D)

Elected 1986, term expires Jan. 1991; b. May 12, 1924, Duchesne, UT; home, Glendale; AZ St. U.; Mormon; married (Florence).

Career: USAF, WWII; Auto dealer, 1954–86; AZ Sen., 1961–62; Repub. Nominee for for U.S. Sen., 1962; newspaper publisher, 1967–69; Repub. nominee for Gov., 1978.

Office: Capitol Bldg., 9th Flr., Phoenix 85007, 602-225-4311.

Election Results

1986 gen.	Evan Mecham (R)	....	343,913	(40%)
	Carolyn Warner (D)	....	298,986	(34%)
	Bill Schulz (I)	....	224,085	(26%)
1986 prim.	Evan Mecham (R)	....	121,614	(54%)
	Burton S. Barr (R)	....	104,682	(46%)
1982 gen.	Bruce E. Babbitt (D)	....	455,760	(62%)
	Leo Corbet (R)	....	236,857	(32%)
	Sam Steiger (I)	....	36,680	(5%)

SENATORS

Sen. Dennis DeConcini (D)

Elected 1976, seat up 1988; b. May 8, 1937, Tucson; home, Tucson; U. of AZ, B.A. 1959, LL.B. 1963; Roman Catholic; married (Susan).

Career: Army, 1959–60; Practicing atty., 1963–65, 1968–73; Special Counsel, A.A. to Gov. Samuel P. Goddard, 1965–67; Pima Cnty. Atty., 1973–76.

Offices: 328 HSOB 20510, 202-224-4521. Also 700 E. Jefferson, Ste. 200, Phoenix 85034, 602-261-6756; 97 E. Congress, Ste. 120, Tucson 85701, 602-629-6831; and 20 E. Main, Ste. 315, Mesa 85201, 602-261-4998.

Committees: *Appropriations* (11th of 16 D). Subcommittees: Defense; Energy and Water Development; Foreign Operations; Interior; Treasury, Postal Service, and General Government (Chairman). *Judiciary* (5th of 8 D). Subcommittees: Antitrust, Monopolies and Business Rights; Constitution; Courts and Administrative Practices; Patents, Copyrights and Trademarks (Chairman); Technology and the Law. *Rules and Administration* (5th of 9 D). *Veterans' Affairs* (3d of 6 D). *Select Committee on Indian Affairs* (3d of 5 D). *Select Committee on Intelligence* (8th of 8 D). *Joint Committee on the Library. Joint Committee on Printing.*

Group Ratings

	ADA	ACLU	COPE	CFA	LCV	ACU	NTU	NSI	COC	CEI
1986	45	38	61	60	63	52	45	56	38	39
1985	45	—	61	53	—	38	38	—	45	—

National Journal Ratings

	1986 LIB — 1986 CONS			1985 LIB — 1985 CONS		
Economic	62%	—	35%	58%	—	41%
Social	39%	—	60%	43%	—	55%
Foreign	60%	—	38%	57%	—	41%

Key Votes

1) Ease Gun Cont	FOR	5) Grm-Rdmn Def Red	AGN	9) Rehnquist Nom	FOR
2) Immig Reform	AGN	6) Contra Aid	AGN	10) Tax Reform	AGN
3) Lmt Text Imp	FOR	7) SDI Funding	AGN	11) Drug Death Pen	AGN
4) Aid Tobac Ind	FOR	8) Lmt PAC Contrib	FOR	12) S Africa Sanc	FOR

Election Results

1982 general	Dennis DeConcini (D)................	413,951	(59%)	($2,086,401)
	Pete Dunn (R).......................	292,638	(41%)	($884,517)
1982 primary	Dennis DeConcini (D)................	140,328	(84%)	
	Caroline P. Killeen (D)	25,909	(16%)	
1976 general	Dennis DeConcini (D)................	400,334	(54%)	($597,405)
	Sam Steiger (R)	321,236	(43%)	($679,384)

Campaign Contributions and Expenditures

1979-82		Direct Cont. 1981-82		PACS Breakdown			
Receipts	$2,093,816	Indiv.	$1,406,258	Agr	$40,075	Ideo	$47,575
Expend.	$2,086,401	Party	$17,500	Bus	$237,711	Lbr	$107,450
Unspent	$107,324	PACS	$541,585	Hlth	$30,500	Prof	$18,950

Sen. John McCain (R)

Elected 1986, seat up 1992; b. Aug. 29, 1936, Panama Canal Zone; home, Tempe; U.S. Naval Acad., 1958, Natl. War Col., 1973–74; Episcopalian; married (Cindy).

Career: Navy, 1958–80; Dir., Navy Senate Liaison Office, 1976–80; U.S. House of Reps., 1982–1986.

Offices: 111 RSOB 20510, 202-224-2235. Also 5353 N. 16th St., Ste. 190, Phoenix 85016, 602-241-2567; 2675 E. Broadway, Tucson 85716, 602-241-2567; and 151 N. Centennial Way, Ste. 1000, Mesa 85201, 602-835-8994.

Committees: *Armed Services* (9th of 9 R). Subcommittees: Manpower and Personnel; Projection Forces and Regional Defense; Readiness, Sustainability and Support. *Commerce, Science and Transportation* (9th of 9 R). Subcommittees: Aviation; Communications; Consumer (Ranking Member). *Select Committee on Indian Affairs* (3rd of 3 R).

Group Ratings (as Member of U.S. House of Representatives)

	ADA	ACLU	COPE	CFA	LCV	ACU	NTU	NSI	COC	CEI
1986	10	15	16	33	27	73	47	100	60	68
1985	5	—	17	25	—	81	55	—	91	—

National Journal Ratings (as Member of U.S. House of Representatives)

	1986 LIB — 1986 CONS			1985 LIB — 1985 CONS		
Economic	26%	—	73%	16%	—	81%
Social	43%	—	57%	34%	—	64%
Foreign	32%	—	67%	0%	—	76%

Key Votes (as Member of U.S. House of Representatives)

1) Lmt Cln Water Act	FOR	5) Retain Gun Cont	AGN	9) Aid Angola Reb	FOR
2) Rpl Tobac Sub	AGN	6) Contra Aid	FOR	10) Tax Reform	FOR
3) Grm-Rdmn Def Red	FOR	7) Lmt Text Imp	AGN	11) S Africa Sanc	FOR
4) Ban Polygraph	AGN	8) Lmt SDI	AGN	12) Immig Reform	AGN

Election Results

1986 general	John McCain (R)	521,850	(60%)	($2,228,498)
	Richard Kimball (D).	340,965	(40%)	($657,908)
1986 primary	John McCain (R)	205,965	(100%)	
1980 general	Barry Goldwater (R).	432,371	(50%)	($949,992)
	Bill Schulz (D)	422,972	(49%)	($2,073,232)

Campaign Contributions and Expenditures

1985-86		Direct Cont. 1985-86		PACS Breakdown 1985-86			
Receipts	$2,549,080	Indiv.	$1,441,759	Corp.	$438,337	T/M/H	$169,728
Expend.	$2,228,498	Party	$23,107	Labor	$16,500	Agr.	$6,500
Unspent	$287,217	PACS	$765,678	Ideo.	$123,675	CWOS	$10,938
		Cand.	$214,406				

FIRST DISTRICT

In the past 40 years, great cities—agglomerations of millions of people—have sprouted in America's subtropics. One of these is Phoenix, Arizona. It is the archetype of the American Sun Belt city, an almost instant metropolis created not in response to geographical imperative but in spite of it. Phoenix is almost totally the product of the air conditioned years after World War II. In 1940 Phoenix had 65,000 residents; in 1950, 106,000; by 1970 the metropolitan area had nearly one million and in 1980 1.5 million. There is little evidence of tradition or heritage here: almost every building is new, and the concessions to Indian or Mexican styles are mostly in the idiom of the 1970s. Many people think Phoenix is a giant retirement village, and there is one huge retirement development, Del Webb's Sun City, nearby. But statistically, metropolitan Phoenix is a young city, full of energetic young people with growing families, eager to work their way up from whatever level of society they were born into. And there are all kinds of opportunities: top-level executive and professional jobs, white-collar and engineering opportunities in many high-tech industries, including the giants of the semiconductor business, Motorola and Intel. There are also lots of low-wage jobs for immigrants from south of the border and elsewhere.

Technologically advanced, Phoenix is politically conservative. Not conservative in the Burkean sense, however: this is not a place that seeks to maintain ancient institutions, tightly knit communities, or webs of interlocking relationships that go back generations. On the contrary, most Phoenix residents have left these behind. Here conservatism means devotion to abstract principle, to the ideal of the untrammeled free market, opposition to unionization and minimum wages, abhorrence of government welfare programs. Of all the nation's states, Arizona probably comes closest to this conservative ideal, but it is still that, an ideal. Phoenix, reluctantly, drinks and swims in federally provided water, complains that it has too few 90%-federally-financed freeways, enjoys easy access to federally protected national parks and monuments. But most idealists understand the need to compromise with the practical world. Such abstract politics come naturally, it seems, to engineers and technicians, whose work it is to make unruly nature conform to concrete principle and abstract rule, and to upwardly mobile migrants, who have staked their lives on change and movement and who believe—or want to—that the system works fairly.

The 1st Congressional District of Arizona is the only one wholly within the Phoenix metropolitan area. It includes some of the comfortable neighborhoods east of downtown Phoenix and north of Sky Harbor Airport. The district dips south of the almost-always-dry Salt River and includes some black and low-income neighborhoods, but it also extends to the high-income areas near the Arizona Biltmore and takes in the southern half of high-income Scottsdale. To the south and east it includes two East Valley suburbs, each with more than 100,000 people—Tempe, home of Arizona State University and the Fiesta Bowl, and Mesa, whose central focus is one of the nation's few Mormon temples. Here are dozens of 1960s and 1970s subdivisions with curved streets and cul-de-sacs; income levels are high, although you won't find many members of Phoenix's establishment in this part of town. To the south is the old desert town of Chandler, which is becoming part of suburbia now that freeways bring it within easy driving distance of Phoenix.

Although the 1st does include a few Democratic precincts in Phoenix, this is a solidly Republican district. It has had distinguished representation for 30 years. John Rhodes, first elected in the Eisenhower landslide of 1952, was House Minority Leader from 1973 to 1980; he stepped down voluntarily from that position, and retired from the House in 1982. He was replaced, after a vigorous Republican primary, by John McCain, one-time prisoner of war in Vietnam, who was elected Senator in 1986. The latest congressman, chosen in effect in a seriously contested Republican primary, is none other than Jay Rhodes, son of his predecessor's predecessor.

The younger Rhodes, though he lived for years in the Washington area and went to Yale, served in the military in Vietnam and went back to Arizona for law school and stayed. He raised his family and became active in civic affairs in Mesa. While McCain tends to concentrate on national and military issues, Rhodes seems likely to hone in on local causes—making sure there is enough water for the Phoenix area, building more freeways, and the like. There seems to be no reason he cannot be reelected indefinitely.

The People: Pop. 1980: 543,747, up 47.8% 1970–80. Households (1980): 69% family, 35% with children, 58% married couples; 36.0% housing units rented; median monthly rent: $257; median house value: $60,600. Voting age pop. (1980): 399,698; 9% Spanish origin, 3% Black, 1% American Indian, 1% Asian origin.

1984 Presidential Vote: Reagan (R) 154,845   (72%)
Mondale (D)   58,492   (27%)

Rep. John J. Rhodes III (R)

Elected 1986; b. Sept. 8, 1943, Mesa; home, Tempe; Yale U., B.A. 1965, U. of AZ, J.D. 1968; Presbyterian; married (Ann).

Career: Army, 1968–70; Practicing atty.; Mesa School Bd., 1972–76.

Offices: 510 CHOB 20515, 202-225-2635. Also 2345 S. Alma School, Mesa 85202, 602-831-6433.

Committees: *Interior and Insular Affairs* (13th of 15 R). Subcommittees: Energy and the Enfironment; National Parks and Public Lands; Water and Power Resources. *Small Business* (14th of 17 R). Subcommittees: Antitrust, Impact of Deregulation and Privatization; Procurement, Innovation and Minority Enterprise Development.

Group Ratings and Key Votes: Newly Elected

Election Results

1986 general	John J. Rhodes III (R)	127,370	(71%)	($493,182)
	Harry W. Braun III (D)	51,163	(29%)	($31,528)
1986 primary	John J. Rhodes III (R)	25,091	(44%)	
	Ray Russell (R).	20,720	(37%)	
	Two others (R)	10,629	(19%)	
1984 general	John McCain (R)	162,418	(78%)	($522,141)
	Harry W. Braun III (D)	45,609	(22%)	($2,770)

Campaign Contributions and Expenditures

1985-86		Direct Cont. 1985-86		PACS Breakdown 1985-86			
Receipts	$498,408	Indiv.	$274,674	Corp.	$51,850	T/M/H	$40,480
Expend.	$493,182	Party	$9,795	Labor	$10,500	Agr.	$2,000
Unspent	$5,226	PACS	$120,142	Ideo.	$10,800	CWOS	$4,512
		Cand.	$86,675				

SECOND DISTRICT

Not all of Arizona's two major cities are glitteringly new. Not far from the skyscrapers of downtown Phoenix and downtown Tucson, across dry river beds and in the shadow of giant outcroppings of mountains, along the railroad tracks that were for decades Arizona's only connection with the rest of the United States, are the dilapidated and shabby neighborhoods, with the vacant lots between the small stucco houses and the gaudy roadside establishments that could easily grow back into small patches of desert, where the poor people of Phoenix and Tucson live. These neighborhoods, plus some better-off adjacent areas, are connected together incongruously into Arizona's 2d Congressional District. It owes its shape to politics: the Republican legislature wanted to concentrate as many of the state's Democratic precincts as possible in this one district, while other districts include the more affluent and Republican parts of greater Phoenix and Tucson. Also included is Yuma, 180 miles across the desert southwest of Phoenix, an agricultural center on the Colorado River and on many days of every year the hottest place in the United States. The few towns connecting these three points have mostly been excised from the 2d, leaving a few Indian reservations and a lot of desert. That leaves a district in which 30% of the adults are of Spanish origin, 5% Black, and 4% Indian.

Nearly half the district's population is in Phoenix, including the city's downtown and the state Capitol, but it also includes most of Tuscon, except for the affluent fringe. Overshadowed demographically by Phoenix, Tucson has always been the more Democratic of the two cities—somewhat more blue collar, more Mexican-American (the 2d's part of Tucson is 42% Hispanic), less high tech, not blessed with so many corporate headquarters, with a Democratic Pulitzer rather than a Republican Pulliam newspaper.

Morris Udall, one of the leading and most productive Democratic politicians of his generation, is the congressman from the 2d District. First elected to Congress in 1961, to replace his brother Stewart who became Secretary of the Interior, Mo Udall has many legislative accomplishments. One is our current campaign finance law, the source of much carping, but a measure which has substantially improved the political process. Another is the civil service reform of 1978. Udall labored for years in the dull vineyards of the Post Office and Civil Service Committee; this bill moved, finally, at least a little toward making government employees more accountable. Udall's most noted efforts have been in the environmental field. Since 1977 he has chaired the Interior Committee, which has jurisdiction over national parks, mining and mineral exploration, government land, Indian tribes, and American overseas possessions. He has always been counted as a friend, though not an automatic vote, by environmentalists. During the Carter years, when the committee and the administration were of similar views, he had a number of accomplishments, most notably a comprehensive strip mining law and the Alaska Lands Act. In the Reagan years, Udall and his committee have been at odds with the administration, but he did manage to get through a wilderness act in 1984, and he has been riding herd on the James Watt and Donald Hodel Interior Departments. He led deliberations over the potentially awesome issue of nuclear plant liability, taking a stand between those of the nuclear industry and the environmentalists.

Udall has also had his disappointments, the foremost of which was the lack of success of his 1976 presidential campaign: he finished second in six primaries, but never first. In the House he was unable to persuade even a heavily Democratic Congress to pass postcard voter registration. His proposals for public financing of congressional elections languished in the late 1970s. He encountered spirited opposition at home on his proposals for changing the mining laws, and ultimately he backed down. His national stature seems to have hurt rather than helped him at home, and he had an uncomfortably close call in the 1978 election. Only after extensive personal campaigning and expensive TV advertising was he able to win convincingly in 1980. In 1982 he had his choice of districts and, faced with Parkinson's disease and less than eager for an endless series of close races, he chose the safe 2d—even though it meant his campaigning for the first time in Phoenix. He was reelected easily in 1984 and 1986, but he has visibly slowed up and though he retains his sense of humor—one of Washington's best—he does not speak as forcefully as he used to. Yet he is still formidable legislatively in the House and politically in the 2d District. Tucson state senator Luis Gonzalez ran against him in the 1986 primary and was soundly beaten; there was no serious Republican candidate. There have been rumors for several years that Udall was about to retire, and if he does he will probably be succeeded by one of the Hispanic legislators from the area. But so far this most productive member of his generation is fighting to work on, and winning.

The People: Pop. 1980: 543,187, up 21.9% 1970–80. Households (1980): 71% family, 42% with children, 56% married couples; 39.8% housing units rented; median monthly rent: $185; median house value: $40,300. Voting age pop. (1980): 372,734; 30% Spanish origin, 5% Black, 4% American Indian, 1% Asian origin.

1984 Presidential Vote: Reagan (R)   71,001   (51%)
                                Mondale (D)   66,596   (48%)

Rep. Morris K. Udall (D)

Elected May 2, 1961; b. June 15, 1922, St. Johns; home, Tucson; U. of AZ, J.D. 1949; Mormon; married (Ella).

Career: Air Force, WWII; Pro basketball player, Denver Nuggets, 1948–49; Practicing atty., 1949–61; Pima Cnty. Atty., 1952–54.

Offices: 235 CHOB 20515, 202-225-4065. Also 373 S. Meyer, Tucson 85701, 602-629-6404; and 522 W. Roosevelt, Phoenix 85003, 602-261-3018.

Committees: *Foreign Affairs* (21st of 27 D). Subcommittees: Arms Control, International Security and Science. *Interior and Insular Affairs* (Chairman of 26 D). Subcommittees: Energy and the Environment (Chairman); Insular and International Affairs; Mining and Natural Resources; National Parks and Public Lands; General Oversight and Investigations. *Post Office and Civil Service* (13th of 14 D).

Group Ratings

	ADA	ACLU	COPE	CFA	LCV	ACU	NTU	NSI	COC	CEI
1986	85	95	86	75	69	25	24	11	13	19
1985	80	—	86	67	—	0	26	—	20	—

National Journal Ratings

	1986 LIB — 1986 CONS			1985 LIB — 1985 CONS		
Economic	80%	—	19%	89%	—	0%
Social	79%	—	19%	85%	—	0%
Foreign	73%	—	26%	75%	—	25%

Key Votes

1) Lmt Cln Water Act	AGN	5) Retain Gun Cont	AGN	9) Aid Angola Reb	AGN
2) Rpl Tobac Sub	AGN	6) Contra Aid	AGN	10) Tax Reform	FOR
3) Grm-Rdmn Def Red	AGN	7) Lmt Text Imp	FOR	11) S Africa Sanc	FOR
4) Ban Polygraph	FOR	8) Limit SDI	FOR	12) Immig Reform	FOR

Election Results

1986 general	Morris K. Udall (D)	77,239	(73%)	($447,112)
	Sheldon Clark (R).	24,522	(23%)	
1986 primary	Morris K. Udall (D)	29,798	(73%)	
	Luis Armando Gonzales (D).	11,131	(27%)	
1984 general	Morris K. Udall (D)	106,332	(88%)	($226,553)
	Lorenzo Torrez (PBP).	14,869	(12%)	

Campaign Contributions and Expenditures

1985-86		Direct Cont. 1985-86		PACS Breakdown 1985-86			
Receipts	$403,554	Indiv.	$240,179	Corp.	$38,880	T/M/H	$26,025
Expend.	$447,112	PACS	$128,480	Labor	$51,875	Agr.	$1,250
Unspent	$12,916			Ideo.	$10,450	CWOS	$0

THIRD DISTRICT

Most of western Arizona is in the state's 3d Congressional District, but the apparent regularity of the lines masks the area's diversity. Before World War II, this was desert punctuated with dude ranches and dusty towns that were little more than two gas stations facing each other. The ancestral politics was mostly Democratic, but there were few voters here. Then after World War II the population of small pleasant towns like Flagstaff and Prescott swelled. But more important, Phoenix spread out into the current boundaries of the 3d, and today some 60% of the district's residents live in Phoenix and Maricopa County. In addition, vast retirement communities were built in the 1960s and 1970s—Sun City just northwest of Phoenix, Lake Havasu City (whose developer purchased and transplanted the London Bridge) on the Colorado River.

Thus this one geographical expanse has changed from old-time Democrats to several different kinds of Republicans. Sun City and Lake Havasu City are heavily Republican; these are relatively affluent Midwesterners and others who (since no one under 50 can live in Sun City) started voting in many cases in the prosperous 1920s and have not abandoned their party since. The district's part of Phoenix, a strip along the northwest side that is affluent, although not fashionable, and the next-door suburb of Glendale, with nearly 100,000 people, are filled mainly by families with children—a reminder of the suburbia that was so common in the 1950s; similar except for climate to the neighborhoods in which Sun City residents raised their families 30 years ago. Voters here are heavily Republican too. Interestingly, about 13% of the residents of these areas are of Spanish origin: it is a mistake to picture Mexican-Americans in Phoenix as huddled in an impoverished ghetto, for most live in rather pleasant, and diverse, neighborhoods like this.

The congressman from the 3d District, Bob Stump, has a political career which resembles that of the area he represents. He started off as a cotton and grain farmer, in the rich irrigated lands west of Phoenix: the green splotches you see from the air as you bank toward Sky Harbor. He was what Arizonans call a pinto Democrat, elected to the state legislature at 29 in 1958, when Democrats were still the majority party there; he was state Senate president in 1975–76, when the 1974 election gave them a majority again. His politics have been solidly conservative; although his farm benefited from subsidized federal water, he has been a foe of government spending generally. When the 3d District's Sam Steiger ran for the Senate in 1976, Stump won a close race for the Democratic nomination and won the general election easily.

In the House, Stump always seemed to belong more with the Republicans than the Democrats, and in 1981 he voted for the Reagan budget and tax plans and for administration policies generally. So that year he decided to switch parties and put on the label that most of his constituency had long since worn. It was a successful move. He won 64% as a Democrat in 1980 and 63% as a Republican in 1982—one of the smoothest party switches of all time. His only possible vulnerability before was in the Democratic primary, and now he was safe from that. Republicans gave him a seat on the Armed Services Committee, where he is one of the most reliable supporters of the Pentagon. Generally Stump is a congressman who quietly adds his one vote to the legislative balance, on the side most of his constituents want, and makes few waves, even when he holds a position, which he achieved in 1985, like ranking minority member of the Permanent Select Committee on Intelligence. His fervor seems directed mostly at foreign policy issues. He sponsored a successful amendment to remove restrictions on U.S. aid to the UNITA rebels in Angola. He fervently supports the Nicaraguan contras. He ballyhoos the fight against terrorism and, at home in the national security establishment, he advocates the use of lie detectors (although one wonders whether he would use them to track down the truth in the Iran-to-Nicaragua arms-and-money transfers).

Stump does not appear to be an original thinker on these matters; his statements are written in a military-ese seldom composed outside five-sided buildings. But he does advance with obvious sincerity views which are surely shared by the 3d District that is happy to reelect him overwhelmingly. He has been mentioned as a candidate against Senator Dennis DeConcini in 1988, although they were Democratic colleagues for most of the preceding 12 years.

The People: Pop. 1980: 544,870, up 90.8% 1970–80. Households (1980): 78% family, 39% with children, 69% married couples; 24.3% housing units rented; median monthly rent: $222; median house value: $58,300. Voting age pop. (1980): 389,150; 9% Spanish origin, 4% American Indian, 1% Black, 1% Asian origin.

1984 Presidential Vote:	Reagan (R) 156,030	(71%)
	Mondale (D) 60,382	(28%)

Rep. Bob Stump (R)

Elected 1976; b. Apr. 4, 1927, Phoenix; home, Tolleson; AZ St. U., B.S. 1951; Seventh Day Adventist; divorced.

Career: Navy, WWII; Cotton and grain farmer; AZ House of Reps., 1959–67; AZ Senate, 1967–76, Senate Pres., 1975–76.

Offices: 211 CHOB 20515, 202-225-4576. Also 5001 Fed. Bldg., Phoenix 85025, 602-261-6923.

Committees: *Armed Services* (4th of 21 R). Subcommittees: Investigations; Research and Development. *Veterans Affairs* (4th of 13 R). Subcommittees: Housing and Memorial Affairs; Oversight and Investigations.

Group Ratings

	ADA	ACLU	COPE	CFA	LCV	ACU	NTU	NSI	COC	CEI
1986	0	5	10	8	11	100	69	100	79	88
1985	0	—	9	67	—	100	70	—	95	—

National Journal Ratings

	1986 LIB — 1986 CONS	1985 LIB — 1985 CONS
Economic	0% — 94%	0% — 95%
Social	0% — 89%	0% — 76%
Foreign	0% — 86%	24% — 66%

Key Votes

1) Lmt Cln Water Act	FOR	5) Retain Gun Cont	AGN	9) Aid Angola Reb	FOR
2) Rpl Tobac Sub	AGN	6) Contra Aid	FOR	10) Tax Reform	FOR
3) Grm-Rdmn Def Red	FOR	7) Lmt Text Imp	AGN	11) S Africa Sanc	AGN
4) Ban Polygraph	AGN	8) Limit SDI	AGN	12) Immig Reform	AGN

Election Results

1986 general	Bob Stump (R)	146,462	(100%)	($135,636)
1986 primary	Bob Stump (R)	51,985	(100%)	
1984 general	Bob Stump (R)	156,686	(72%)	($230,938)
	Bob Schuster (D)	57,748	(26%)	($64,411)

Campaign Contributions and Expenditures

1985-86		Direct Cont. 1985-86		PACS Breakdown 1985-86			
Receipts	$233,689	Indiv.	$121,407	Corp.	$60,560	T/M/H	$25,050
Expend.	$135,636	Party	$2,036	Labor	$250	Agr.	$1,000
Unspent	$170,179	PACS	$90,710	Ideo.	$3,100	CWOS	$750

FOURTH DISTRICT

It's hard to think of two parts of Arizona where life is more dissimilar than the affluent and comfortable neighborhoods in northeastern Phoenix and its suburbs and the Indian reservations over the mountains in the far northeast corner of the state. Yet both areas are in Arizona's 4th Congressional District. In Phoenix and Scottsdale and Paradise Valley, in the shadow of and behind Camelback Mountain and Squaw Peak, the sunlight falls on the desert with a kind of hush; the careful landscaping of houses and condominiums contrasts with the bluff stone of the mountains that punctuate Phoenix's plain and with the brown earth and vagrant cactus plants on the land that has been left undeveloped. Shopping centers affect western decor here, and galleries are full of paintings depicting the Old West; but inside the houses you can find furniture of just about any period you want. The planting of such a comfortable and secure civilization in such an inhospitable environment—it seldom rains, but when it does anything near a usually dry creek bed can get washed away—is one of the generally unappreciated triumphs of American civilization.

One of the not much more appreciated failures of American civilization is apparent in the reservation country, the failure of the cultures native to North America to adjust to the stresses and conflicts caused by the progress of the dominant civilization. The terrain is familiar: you can see it on any Scottsdale coffee table in the latest edition of *Arizona Highways*. But the 130,000 Navajos and 5,000 Hopi live in grim, patched-together houses, often without electricity; they struggle to make a living herding sheep. The Navajo, the nation's largest organized tribe, have an active politics, fiercely contested tribal elections (in 1982 tribal chairman Peter McDonald lost to Peterson Zah; in 1986, Zah lost 51%–49% to McDonald), and a tribal budget well into nine figures.

The Navajo and the Hopi have been fighting over land, partly because of the coal lease income, but also to maintain their native traditions and landholdings; the Hopi agreed to a 1974 law ceding much of its large reservation back to the Navajo, but when the 1986 deadline came and went for the 250 to 1,000 Navajo families living on land retained by the Hopi, they refused to go or even to sell. The Navajo have been painted as martyrs here, but the law is squarely on the Hopi side; demonstrators have flocked to the reservation to protest ("wannabe Indians," one Indian calls them—people who want to be Indians), but against whom? There are equities on all sides, and each side has worked in what it reasonably considers good faith to reach a fair solution. When cultures collide, sometimes there is no good solution. The Navajo-Hopi fight has become a political issue, with Barry Goldwater antagonizing his longtime Navajo friends by taking the Hopi side and Dennis DeConcini siding with the Navajo.

The cultural conflict is matched by political differences. The Navajos have increasingly been registering to vote in regular elections, and have become heavily Democratic; Zah was a delegate to the 1984 Democratic convention in San Francisco. The 4th District's portion of Phoenix and its suburbs is one of the most heavily Republican parts of the country. In between, the 4th hops northeast over the Mazatzal Mountains and the Sierra Ancha to pick up the copper mining towns of Globe and Miami; the Fort Apache Indian Reservation; the dusty Route 66 towns of Holbrook and Winslow, lined with gas stations; and the reservations to the north. This is mixed political terrain, with some Democratic patches. But 79% of the votes are on the Phoenix side of the mountains, and in most elections the 4th District is heavily Republican.

There were, however, serious Democratic challenges when the district was created in 1972 and when Republican congressman John Conlan left it to run for the Senate in 1976. But both times Republicans won. This time Democrat Phil Davis, a successful developer, hoped to wage a strong campaign. He might have if the Republican primary winner had been Conlan, for the former congressman is not only very religious but seriously antagonized any number of Republicans by his political tactics. Barry Goldwater, apparently still bothered by the way Conlan ran his 1976 Senate race, made a surprise endorsement of Jon Kyl, the winning candidate. Kyl, son of a Republican congressman from Iowa, has become very much a part of the Phoenix business and civic establishment since graduating from the University of Arizona Law School in 1966. He was head of the Phoenix Chamber of Commerce, active in many Republican campaigns, and as a lawyer specialized in water law, which is of course crucial to this desert metropolis. Pleasant, unflamboyantly conservative, well-financed, Kyl was able to prevail over Conlan's enthusiasts in the primary and to frustrate Davis's efforts to make a real contest of the general. The two new Phoenix congressmen elected in 1986 have astonishing similarities: both are sons of congressmen, they overlapped at law school, they have pursued their entire careers in Phoenix though they grew up elsewhere, and they are very much part of the business establishment, not the enthusiastic right of the Republican party.

The People: Pop. 1980: 543,493, up 65.9% 1970–80. Households (1980): 76% family, 42% with children, 64% married couples; 27.6% housing units rented; median monthly rent: $267; median house value: $66,200. Voting age pop. (1980): 375,192; 12% American Indian, 4% Spanish origin, 1% Asian origin, 1% Black.

1984 Presidential Vote: Reagan (R) 155,112   (71%)
Mondale (D) 61,600   (28%)

Rep. Jon Kyl (R)

Elected 1986; b. April 25, 1942, Oakland; home, Phoenix; U. of AZ, B.A. 1964, LL.B. 1966; Presbyterian; married (Caryll).

Career: Practicing atty., 1966–86; Chmn., Metro. Phoenix Chamber of Commerce, 1985–86.

Offices: 313 CHOB 20515, 202-225-3361. Also 4250 E. Camelback Rd., Phoenix 85018, 602-840-1891.

Committees: *Armed Services* (19th of 21 R). Subcommittees: Investigations; Military Personnel and Compensation. *Government Operations* (13th of 15 R). Subcommittees: Employment and Housing; Environment, Energy and Natural Resources.

Group Ratings and Key Votes: Newly Elected

Election Results

1986 general	Jon Kyl (R)	121,939	(65%)	($1,010,914)
	Philip R. Davis (D)	66,894	(35%)	($822,030)
1986 primary	Jon Kyl (R)	35,482	(60%)	
	John B. Conlan (R)	16,802	(28%)	
	Mark Dioguardi (R)	7,418	(12%)	
1984 general	Eldon Rudd (R)	167,558	(100%)	($156,438)

Campaign Contributions and Expenditures

1985-86		Direct Cont. 1985-86		PACS Breakdown 1985-86			
Receipts	$1,019,967	Indiv.	$747,359	Corp.	$117,006	T/M/H	$69,196
Expend.	$1,010,914	Party	$644	Labor	$0	Agr.	$3,500
Unspent	$9,053	PACS	$231,747	Ideo.	$35,561	CWOS	$6,484
		Cand.	$21,378				

FIFTH DISTRICT

The southeast corner of Arizona, its little towns tucked into the valleys just north of the Mexican border, was really the first part of the state to be settled, and for many years the critical part: for this is where most of Arizona's copper has been found. Copper prices have been in a slump for most of a decade now, and Arizona's mines have had to lay off workers because the market is swamped by foreign production. But the pit mines outside Bisbee and Morenci, and the spirited little towns that grew up alongside them and nearby—Tombstone and Douglas, Clifton and even in its early days Tucson—are evidence of the importance of copper to Arizona.

Arizona's 5th Congressional District includes this copper country and, much more populous, the whole east side of the city of Tucson and its suburbs. This was a new district created after the 1980 Census, as the predecessors of the 4th, 3d, and 2d Districts were created after the 1970, 1960, and 1950 Censuses. It was intended by the Republican legislature to be a Republican district; it includes the prosperous east side of Tucson, so Republican that it gave Morris Udall a scare in the late 1970s when it was still part of his 2d district, and the Republican communities around Davis-Monthan Air Force Base and Green Valley to the south. As intended, the 5th was Republican in 1986; but in 1982 it elected a Democrat, and in both 1982 and 1984 it was one of the prime marginal districts in the nation.

The Republican candidate in all three of its races has been Jim Kolbe, who won a reputation—which was not too hard to do—as a moderate in the Arizona legislature, spurring

Arizona to finally enter the Medicaid program and moving forward ground-water legislation. In 1982, however, he lost 50%–48% to Democrat Jim McNulty, also a talented legislator, with a base in Bisbee (though an accent from Boston); McNulty did just about everything he could to hold the district, to the point of getting a water resources research bill passed over the President's veto. But Kolbe was able to wage a vigorous campaign in 1984 and win 51%–48%. He has strengths as well. His 1984 campaign focused on economic issues; he championed a balanced-budget constitutional amendment and a line-item veto for the President. Kolbe charged that McNulty, like Walter Mondale, would raise taxes, and he decried the condition of the copper industry. In 1986 McNulty decided not to run again, and Kolbe, having amassed a large war chest, won easily.

The problem before him, now that he has a reasonably safe seat, is how to make a legislative impact in Washington as he did in Phoenix. Kolbe is not regarded with much enthusiasm by some Washington-based conservatives (he declines to oppose abortions, for example), though he is a regular enough Republican; he does not have great seniority, though he did get on the Appropriations Committee his second term; he is part of a party that seems stuck indefinitely in the minority of the House. It's possible that Kolbe might challenge Senator DeConcini in 1988, although he's likely to have a more conservative opponent in the Republican primary if he runs.

The People: Pop. 1980: 542,918, up 55.6% 1970–80. Households (1980): 75% family, 39% with children, 64% married couples; 30.8% housing units rented; median monthly rent: $216; median house value: $57,800. Voting age pop. (1980): 389,954; 14% Spanish origin, 2% Black, 1% Asian origin, 1% American Indian.

1984 Presidential Vote:

Reagan (R) 144,428	(62%)
Mondale (D) 86,784	(37%)

Rep. Jim Kolbe (R)

Elected 1984; b. June 28, 1942, Evanston, IL; home, Tucson; Northwestern U., B.A. 1965, Stanford U., M.B.A. 1967; United Methodist; married (Sarah).

Career: Navy, Vietnam; Asst. to IL Bldg. Authority Architect, 1970–72; Asst. to IL Gov. Ogilvie, 1972–73; Vice Pres., land planning firm; Real estate consultant; AZ Senate 1977–82.

Offices: 1222 LHOB 20515, 202-225-2542. Also 1661 N. Swan, Ste. 112, Tucson 85712, 602-322-3555.

Committees: *Appropriations* (22d of 22 R). Subcommittees: Commerce, Justice, State and Judiciary; Military Installations and Facilities.

Group Ratings

	ADA	ACLU	COPE	CFA	LCV	ACU	NTU	NSI	COC	CEI
1986	20	25	6	25	38	73	59	100	88	79
1985	0	—	6	42	—	76	60	—	95	—

National Journal Ratings

	1986 LIB — 1986 CONS		1985 LIB — 1985 CONS	
Economic	6%	— 90%	0%	— 95%
Social	37%	— 61%	59%	— 40%
Foreign	32%	— 67%	35%	— 65%

Key Votes

1) Lmt Cln Water Act	FOR	5) Retain Gun Cont	AGN	9) Aid Angola Reb	FOR
2) Rpl Tobac Sub	FOR	6) Contra Aid	FOR	10) Tax Reform	FOR
3) Grm-Rdmn Def Red	FOR	7) Lmt Text Imp	AGN	11) S Africa Sanc	FOR
4) Ban Polygraph	AGN	8) Limit SDI	AGN	12) Immig Reform	AGN

Election Results

1986 general	Jim Kolbe (R)......................	119,647	(65%)	($619,296)
	Joel Ireland (D)......................	64,848	(35%)	($31,166)
1986 primary	Jim Kolbe (R)........................	34,166	(100%)	
1984 general	Jim Kolbe (R).......................	116,075	(51%)	($740,444)
	Jim McNulty (D)	109,871	(48%)	($734,299)

Campaign Contributions and Expenditures

1985-86		Direct Cont. 1985-86		PACS Breakdown 1985-86			
Receipts	$629,526	Indiv.	$384,712	Corp.	$92,571	T/M/H	$63,110
Expend.	$619,296	Party	$10,291	Labor	$550	Agr.	$2,500
Debts	$21,725	PACS	$177,663	Ideo.	$15,500	CWOS	$3,432
		Cand.	$39,094				

ARKANSAS

Geographically the smallest state between the Mississippi and the Pacific, in population the smallest state in the South, not blessed with any major industry or great commercial metropolis, Arkansas has always hovered near the bottom of the list of states in nearly everything. The terrain is what was left in between when the states of Louisiana and Missouri were admitted from the Louisiana Purchase territories and the land that is now Oklahoma was fenced off as Indian territory. It was settled by poor farmers from Tennessee, Mississippi, and points east, men and women with large families, few slaves, and little cash. History has left Arkansas—the marshy lowlands west of the Mississippi River, the hills that rise to mountains in the northwest—with handicaps which it has been working hard the past two decades to overcome. For most of the last 20 years, since Winthrop Rockefeller was elected governor in 1966, it has made progress toward an economically vibrant and politically enlightened future.

Now it seems poised at the brink of success—or failure. For if Arkansas is part of the Sun Belt which has been growing faster than the national average, it is still far from having caught up with national income and education levels. It is part of the Mississippi Valley, the central core of the nation, which was hit harder than most other regions by the recessions of 1979–83 and which recovered more sluggishly than the rest of the country. Politically, Arkansas has maintained the progressive tradition begun by Rockefeller. His predecessor, Orval Faubus, made national headlines (and kept himself in office beyond the traditional two terms) when he tried to stop the integration of Little Rock's Central High School in 1957; Rockefeller was one of the first southern governors to endorse integration and bring blacks into political life. His celebrity and recruiting efforts helped attract business and jobs. His political success helped encourage other progressive politicians—mostly Democrats, but some Republicans as well.

In many respects Arkansas has caught up with the rest of the nation. It is still one of the lowest states in income, but today that leaves it less than 20% below the national average. When you factor in the low cost of living, that means Arkansans' standard of living is not much different from that of Americans in the more affluent states of the North and West—something that was definitely not true 30 years ago. It even has the man named in the 1986 *Forbes* 400 as the richest American—Sam Walton, the proprietor of Wal-Mart, a discount store with branches all over the South and Southwest who, despite his success, still lives in Bentonville and drives a beat-up Chevrolet with dog-teeth marks on the steering wheel. With several other southern states, Arkansas has led the nation in education reform: Governor Bill Clinton's 1983 education reform package included competency tests not only for new but for working teachers, a teacher pay raise, and a sales tax increase to pay for it. But teachers' groups vociferously opposed the tests and, since Arkansas seems to have missed out on the economic revival of the middle 1980s, it was not clear in 1986 whether the sales tax hike would generate enough money to fulfill Clinton's promises. There has been an unmistakable boom in the hill country of northern and northwestern Arkansas, with thousands of retirees from big cities coming to enjoy the equable climate and low cost of living. But retirement communities can only do so much for a state's economy. They can even make it harder to spend the additional money on education that a state like Arkansas needs to train a high-skill work force. Arkansas has much going for it. But the question is whether it will be enough.

If Arkansas's economic future is unsettled, its political future seems reasonably clear. This is perhaps the most safely Democratic of southern states. Oddly, the credit may go to a Republican, Winthrop Rockefeller, who by beating the Orval Faubus wing of the Democratic party opened it up to the likes of Dale Bumpers, who beat Rockefeller himself in 1970, and David Pryor, who succeeded him as governor in 1974; both went on to the Senate, in 1974 and 1978. The Democrats hold most major offices here now, and have won them by solid margins; in 1986 they held a House seat that seemed endangered, and in 1984 they regained one held by a Republican for three terms. Still, Arkansas does not necessarily cotton to national Democrats. Jimmy Carter carried the state easily in 1976 and would have again in 1980 but for the furor over the housing of Cuban refugees in Fort Chaffee. But Walter Mondale was no stronger here than in other southern states. Dale Bumpers considered running for president in 1983 and 1987, but decided both times not to run. Bill Clinton has been mentioned often as a national candidate. Arkansas would probably lead the South if they or another southern candidate were nominated. But it's not clear that Arkansas is ready to cast its six electoral votes for any other kind of Democrat.

Governor. Bill Clinton's convincing victory in 1986 over the man who beat him in 1980, Republican Frank White, and his even more convincing primary victory over the 76-year-old Orval Faubus established his strength in Arkansas, without bringing him the national acclaim he got after he was first elected to the office in 1978. He was then 32, a graduate of Yale Law, a Rhodes Scholar, with a wife who is a lawyer and used her maiden name; he was quickly mentioned as a candidate for national office. But he was defeated in 1980 because of two of the most local of issues—the Cubans at Fort Chaffee and a rise in license tag fees. Since then he has seemed more Arkansas: he has a shorter haircut, his wife now calls herself Clinton, and his speaking style is often loud and homey. Out of office, he turned down an offer to run for Democratic national chairman.

Clinton still generates controversy, but there can be no doubt he has been a successful governor. His 1983 education package was followed by a 1985 jobs program that focused on upgrading the Arkansas work force and helping small in-state employers to create more jobs—a refreshing contrast with the efforts of so many states to bid wildly for highly-visible projects of out-of-state firms which end up producing more publicity than jobs. He has also pushed a "good beginnings" program for infant and child health care and education. Clinton has been mentioned as a candidate for other office, though not usually the Senate (there is no plausible rationale for him to challenge the likeminded Bumpers or Pryor), but for the presidency. With Bumpers out of the race and Clinton installed as the new chairman of the governors' conference in 1987, he has a sort of platform; he is well known to the national press and Democratic pols; he has a creditable record (though in a state few national reporters even visit); he is southern, in a race that has no southern candidates but lots of early southern primaries; he is acceptable to liberals while being more post-liberal himself; he is capable of both television-cool articulation and old-time oratory, an officeholder of some accomplishment but of limited national ambitions.

ARKANSAS — Congressional Districts, Counties, and Selected Places — *(4 Districts)*

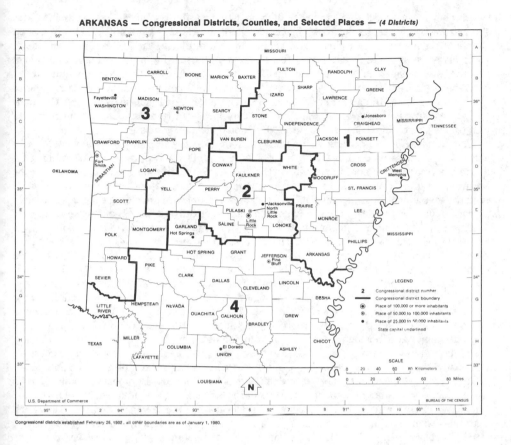

Congressional districts established February 26, 1902, all other boundaries are as of January 1, 1980.

He turns 42 a month after the 1988 Democratic convention, which would make him the youngest nominee since William Jennings Bryan (just a few months older than Thomas E. Dewey was in 1944). Will he run?

Senators. Arkansas has a habit of holding in office for many years pairs of senators of similar but distinguishable outlooks. For 30 years it was represented by John McClellan and William Fulbright, the one conservative and a master of pork barrel politics, the other skeptical and an expert on foreign policy. McClellan got the government to make the Arkansas River navigable for seagoing ships; nearly beaten by David Pryor in the 1972 primary, he was about to retire when he died in 1978. Fulbright was for years the leading opponent of the Vietnam war, who through hearings and speeches made his views first politically acceptable and later almost mandatory; he was beaten in the 1974 primary by Dale Bumpers. Bumpers and Pryor are both from small towns, both served two terms as governor, and both have always been pro-civil rights. But they have fashioned different voting records and different careers.

Dale Bumpers, mentioned in 1983 and 1987 as a possible presidential candidate, sprang from a small town law practice straight to the governorship, and from there straight to the Senate. He has not had major committee positions and has not stamped his name on any major piece of legislation; yet he is taken seriously as a national candidate, and not just because he is good on television. It's true that his fluent speaking style impressed consultant Delos Walker, who found him practicing law in Charleston, and managed his first campaign for governor. But it would be a mistake to see him simply as the product of political packaging. Bumpers is pleasant, fluent, sincere but not cloying, able to master difficult issues easily. But, like most politicians with staying power, he has a solid rock of convictions. Bumpers is a genuine Franklin Roosevelt Democrat, a man who, growing up in small town Arkansas in the 1930s, saw the federal government as *the* major force working for the ordinary person. From that definition he did not exclude blacks: while Faubus was posturing in Little Rock, Bumpers was helping to integrate the local schools in Charleston. He made a successful career as a country trial lawyer, talking juries into his way of seeing things. He has a streak of stubbornness, and is not easily lobbied. He seems instinctively to mistrust smooth-talking advocates of measures right and left, a country lawyer who prides himself on always seeing through the city slickers' games.

That has made him something of an "aginner" in the Senate. Despite his liberal views, he cast a critical vote killing the AFL–CIO's labor law reform bill in the Carter years, something for which labor leaders had not forgiven him in the middle 1980s. He sponsored a bill to remove the presumption in federal courts that federal regulations are valid—a measure some think would produce government-by-litigation. But he has caustically opposed amending the Constitution to prevent abortions or allow school prayer, and has practically dared opponents to come into Arkansas and fight him on them. On the Energy Committee he fought oil companies in the losing battle to prevent price decontrol. He was one of the three senators (Bradley and Hollings were the others) who voted for the 1981 Reagan budget cuts and against the 1981 tax cuts—a set of positions which, if adopted, would have just about eliminated the deficit right there. He is one of four senators (Chafee, Heinz, and Leahy were the others) who publicly urged President Reagan to get the United States back into compliance with the never-ratified SALT II treaty.

There is a kind of country cussedness in Bumpers's voting record—and also in the way he is happy to defend it in Arkansas. In 1980 he was caught a little unawares by the Fort Chaffee imbroglio, and was reelected with 59% of the vote—low for him. In 1986, he was opposed by Asa Hutchinson, an attractive young U.S. Attorney (and graduate of fundamentalist Bob Jones University) who won fame for leading a raid, dressed in a flak jacket, of a white supremacist group called the Covenant, the Sword, and the Arm of the Lord. But Bumpers campaigned hard, and Hutchinson was not able to make a dent. In the 100th Congress, Bumpers will for the first time have high committee positions, chairing Small Business and ranking second on Energy and Natural Resources. But Small Business has a very limited jurisdiction, and energy issues have largely been settled. So it's unclear whether this talented politician will find legislative work on which he can play a major role.

If Bumpers doesn't like playing traditional games in the Senate, he doesn't care for the rules laid down in the 1970s have mandated in national elections. He has declined twice to run for president, in December 1983 and March 1987, partly because he didn't want to spend the time that seemed necessary campaigning and raising money; and he declined to seek the vice presidential nomination in 1984, because he didn't cotton to the idea of trooping up with others, not all of them serious contenders, to Walter Mondale's house in North Oaks, Minnesota. A campaign would mean "a total disruption of the closeness my family has cherished," he said in 1987. If presidential candidates could be drafted, as Adlai Stevenson and Dwight Eisenhower were in 1952, then many professional Democrats these days might choose Bumpers. But it didn't come close to happening in 1984, and doesn't seem likely to in 1988 either.

David Pryor, first elected to Congress at age 32 as a small town lawyer and editor, made a name for himself as one of the most liberal of southern representatives. That was in 1966 and 1967. It was news then when Pryor worked in a nursing home and then set up informal hearings in a trailer when he was denied subcommittee hearings on the subject; it was news when, coming from a district that supported Goldwater and Wallace for president, he voted for civil rights legislation; it was news when he voted at the 1968 national convention against the seating of the regular Mississippi delegation. Given that record, it is striking how close Pryor came to beating John McClellan in 1972 and how easily he won the governorship in 1974 and 1976.

Yet now Pryor seems more skeptical about government's ability to solve problems or even spend money wisely than he seemed in those Great Society days. His experiences in Arkansas in the middle 1970s seem to have been chastening. He lost the 1972 Senate runoff to John McClellan. Then, when he was elected governor in 1974, he found himself at the head of a state government less in need of reform than of penny-pinching. He won a tough three-candidate primary-and-runoff fight for the Senate in 1978, a year when many of the trends that worked for Republicans nationally in 1980 were already apparent in the electorate. In the Senate he has been both more cautious and somewhat more conservative than Bumpers. His tightfistedness carries over from domestic into military matters; he has attacked Pentagon procurement methods and led the fight against binary chemical weapons (though they would be produced in Arkansas).

Pryor has spent most of his Senate career with low seniority and as a member of the minority. But in 1985 and 1986 as a member of the Finance Committee he was suddenly a player on the hottest issue on Capitol Hill, tax reform. He was one of the Democrats on the committee who, more than the Republicans at some points, provided support for the rate-lowering-preference-cutting approach championed by Bill Bradley and adopted dramatically by Chairman Bob Packwood. He stayed with the measure when it was threatened, and can claim some credit for what is one of the major achievements of Congresss in the 1980s.

His reelection campaign in 1984 was, in line with his cautious approach, very much pitched to local issues: "Arkansas comes first," was his slogan and he stressed his seat on the Agriculture Committee. His opponent was Republican Representative Ed Bethune, a former law school classmate, a one time protégé of Winthrop Rockefeller who had held his House seat for three terms; with his exposure in Little Rock media, he was about as strong a candidate as the Republicans could have run. But his attempt to tie Pryor to unpopular Democratic stands on national issues did not succeed. Pryor won with 57%, a margin that may prove enough to deter a major Republican effort in the future.

Presidential politics. Arkansas is a good litmus test for the Democrats: if their national ticket can't win here, it's not likely to win many electoral votes in the South—or to win the election. Arkansas used to have a presidential primary late in the season, which almost everyone ignored; it was cancelled in favor of a caucus in 1984. In 1987 the legislature voted to join the southern regional primary for 1988.

Congressional districting. Unchanged since 1982 and little changed since 1962, when the delegation was reduced from six to four seats.

The People: Est. Pop. 1986: 2,372,000; Pop. 1980: 2,286,435, up 3.8% 1980–86 and 18.9% 1970–1980; 0.98% of U.S. total, 33d largest. 11% with 1–3 yrs. col., 10% with 4+ yrs. col.; 19.0% below poverty level. Single ancestry: 18% English, 6% Irish, 4% German, 1% French. Households (1980): 77% family, 41% with children, 65% married couples; 29.5% housing units rented; median monthly rent: $129; median house value: $31,100. Voting age pop. (1980): 1,615,061; 14% Black, 1% Spanish origin. Registered voters (1986): 1,267,912; no party registration.

1986 Share of Federal Tax Burden: $5,308,000,000; 0.71% of U.S. total, 32d largest.

1986 Share of Federal Expenditures

	Total		Non-Defense		Defense	
Total Expend	$7,179m	(0.86%)	$5,705m	(0.95%)	$1,474m	(0.64%)
St/Lcl Grants	1,123m	(1.00%)	1,121m	(1.00%)	2m	(1.80%)
Salary/Wages	766m	(0.64%)	407m	(0.69%)	359m	(0.58%)
Pymts to Indiv	3,960m	(1.09%)	3,734m	(1.08%)	226m	(1.27%)
Procurement	1,021m	(.50%)	135m	(0.24%)	887m	(0.59%)
Research/Other	308m	(1.15%)	308m	(1.16%)	0m	(0%)

Political Lineup: Governor, Bill Clinton (D); Lt. Gov., Winston Bryant (D); Secy. of State, Bill McCuen (D); Atty. Gen., Steve Clark (D); Treasurer, Jimmie Lou Fisher (D); Auditor, Julia Hughes Jones (D). State Senate, 35 (31 D and 4 R); State House of Representatives, 100 (91 D and 9 R). Senators, Dale Bumpers (D) and David Pryor (D). Representatives, 4 (3 D and 1 R).

1984 Presidential Vote

Reagan (R) 534,774   (60%)
Mondale (D) 338,646   (38%)

1980 Presidential Vote

Reagan (R) 403,164   (48%)
Carter (D) 398,041   (48%)
Anderson (I) 22,468   (3%)

GOVERNOR
Gov. Bill Clinton (D)

Elected 1986, term expires Jan. 1991; b. Aug. 19, 1946, Hope; home, Little Rock; Georgetown U., B.S.F.S. 1968, Rhodes Scholar, Oxford U., 1968–70, Yale U., J.D. 1973; Baptist; married (Hillary).

Career: Professor, U. of AR, 1974–76; Dem. Nominee for U.S. House of Reps., 1974; Atty. Gen. of AR, 1977–79; Gov. of AR, 1979–81; Practicing atty., 1981–82.

Office: State Capitol, Little Rock 72201, 501-371-2345.

Election Results

1986 gen.	Bill Clinton (D)	439,851	(64%)
	Frank White (R)	248,415	(36%)
1986 prim.	Bill Clinton (D)	315,397	(61%)
	Orval E. Faubus (D).	174,402	(33%)
	W. Dean Goldsby (D).	30,829	(6%)
1984 gen.	Bill Clinton (D)	554,561	(63%)
	Woody Freeman (R).	331,987	(37%)

SENATORS
Sen. Dale Bumpers (D)

Elected 1974, seat up 1992; b. Aug. 12, 1925, Charleston; home, Charleston; U. of AR, Northwestern U., LL.B. 1951; Methodist; married (Betty).

Career: USMC, WWII; Practicing atty., 1951–70; Gov. of AR, 1970–74.

Offices: 229 DSOB 20510, 202-224-4843. Also 2527 Fed. Bldg., 700 W. Capitol, Little Rock 72201, 501-378-6286.

Committees: *Appropriations* (12th of 16 D). Subcommittees: Agriculture, Rural Development and Related Agencies; Commerce, Justice, State, and Judiciary; Interior; Labor, Health and Human Services, Education; Legislative Branch (Chairman). *Energy and Natural Resources* (2d of 10 D). Subcommittees: Energy Research and Development; Energy Research and Development; Public Lands, National Parks and Forests (Chairman). *Small Business* (Chairman of 10 D). Subcommittees: Export and Expansion; Competition and Antitrust Enforcement.

Group Ratings

	ADA	ACLU	COPE	CFA	LCV	ACU	NTU	NSI	COC	CEI
1986	70	64	65	60	54	22	47	11	47	40
1985	70	—	65	73	—	13	32	—	45	—

National Journal Ratings

	1986 LIB — 1986 CONS		1985 LIB — 1985 CONS	
Economic	66% —	32%	65% —	31%
Social	55% —	43%	68% —	28%
Foreign	64% —	33%	73% —	26%

Key Votes

1) Ease Gun Cont	FOR	5) Grm-Rdmn Def Red	FOR	9) Rehnquist Nom	FOR
2) Immig Reform	FOR	6) Contra Aid	AGN	10) Tax Reform	FOR
3) Lmt Text Imp	FOR	7) SDI Funding	AGN	11) Drug Death Pen	AGN
4) Aid Tobac Ind	FOR	8) Lmt PAC Contrib	FOR	12) S Africa Sanc	FOR

Election Results

1986 general	Dale Bumpers (D)	433,092	(62%)	($1,672,432)
	Asa Hutchinson (R)	262,300	(38%)	($939,342)
1986 primary	Dale Bumpers (D) unopposed			
1980 general	Dale Bumpers (D)	477,905	(59%)	($220,861)
	Bill Clark (R)	330,576	(41%)	($119,196)

Campaign Contributions and Expenditures

1985-86		Direct Cont. 1985-86		PACS Breakdown 1985-86			
Receipts	$1,726,383	Indiv.	$1,132,857	Corp.	$154,275	T/M/H	$169,146
Expend.	$1,672,432	Party	$3,250	Labor	$77,150	Agr.	$22,000
Unspent	$124,978	PACS	$503,831	Ideo.	$69,260	CWOS	$12,000

Sen. David Pryor (D)

Elected 1978, seat up 1990; b. Aug. 29, 1934, Camden; home, Little Rock; U. of AR, B.A. 1957, LL.B. 1964; Presbyterian; married (Barbara).

Career: Ed. and Publ., *Ouachita Citizen*, Camden, 1957–61; AR House of Reps., 1960–66; Practicing atty., 1964–66; U.S. House of Reps., 1967–72; Cand. for Dem. Nomination for U.S. Senate, 1972; Gov. of AR, 1975–79.

Office: 185 DSOB 20510, 202-224-2353. Also 3030 Fed. Bldg., Little Rock 72201, 501-378-6336.

Committees: *Agriculture, Nutrition, and Forestry* (4th of 10 D). Subcommittees: Agricultural Production and Stabilization of Prices; Domestic and Foreign Marketing and Product Promotion (Chairman). *Finance* (8th of 11 D). Subcommittees: Health; Private Retirement and Internal Revenue Service (Chairman); Taxation and Debt Management. *Governmental Affairs* (6th of 8 D). Subcommittees: Federal Services, Post Office and Civil Service (Chairman); Government Management; Investigations. *Select Committee on Ethics* (2d of 3 D). *Special Committee on Aging* (3d of 10 D).

Group Ratings

	ADA	ACLU	COPE	CFA	LCV	ACU	NTU	NSI	COC	CEI
1986	60	76	58	60	50	33	48	11	53	39
1985	80	—	60	67	—	4	29	—	41	—

National Journal Ratings

	1986 LIB — 1986 CONS			1985 LIB — 1985 CONS	
Economic	54%	—	45%	69%	—	30%
Social	64%	—	34%	68%	—	28%
Foreign	75%	—	0%	78%	—	19%

Key Votes

1) Ease Gun Cont	FOR	5) Grm-Rdmn Def Red	AGN	9) Rehnquist Nom	FOR
2) Immig Reform	AGN	6) Contra Aid	AGN	10) Tax Reform	—
3) Lmt Text Imp	FOR	7) SDI Funding	AGN	11) Drug Death Pen	—
4) Aid Tobac Ind	FOR	8) Lmt PAC Contrib	FOR	12) S Africa Sanc	FOR

Election Results

1984 general	David Pryor (D)	502,341	(57%)	($1,838,352)
	Ed Bethune (R)......................	373,615	(43%)	($1,072,879)
1984 primary	David Pryor (D) unopposed			
1978 general	David Pryor (D)	395,506	(77%)	($774,824)
	Thomas Kelly, Jr. (R)	84,308	(16%)	($16,208)
	John G. Black (I)	37,211	(7%)	($32,863)

Campaign Contributions and Expenditures

1979-84		Direct Cont. 1979-84		PACS Breakdown 1979-84			
Receipts	$1,981,197	Indiv.	$1,162,696	Corp.	$234,774	T/M/H	$216,514
Expend.	$1,838,352	Party	$24,030	Labor	$106,900	Agr.	$36,250
Unspent	$174,188	PACS	$685,982	Ideo.	$103,334	CWOS	$14,050

FIRST DISTRICT

Flat as far as the eye can see, stretching past rows of telephone poles and ribbons of asphalt in the shimmering heat: this is the land, just west of the Mississippi River, of eastern Arkansas. Far beyond the horizon are the green hills that begin to rise around Little Rock, or the cool green Ozarks farther west; here the climate, meteorologically and culturally, is deep southern. Physically, eastern Arkansas is more like the Mississippi Delta than the Arkansas hills; economically it is more tied to Memphis than to Little Rock. Some of this land was plantation country before the Civil War, but much of it was not developed till later, when business-minded planters drained the marshy fields, recruited blacks to work them, and planted cotton. But that wore out the soil, and the main crops here now are soybeans and rice; both are major export crops, and this part of Arkansas is export-conscious.

Eastern Arkansas was never a hotbed of upcountry populism, but it has always retained at least a nominal Democratic allegiance. Today, with segregation gone and other old antagonisms forgotten, eastern Arkansas remains the most Democratic part of the state. It went solidly for Jimmy Carter in his losing race in 1980, and gave Walter Mondale a respectable percentage in 1984. Eastern Arkansas forms about half of Arkansas's 1st Congressional District, which also includes some hill counties to the northwest, added after the 1970 and 1980 censuses. Nonetheless, this is basically an agricultural area. Its largest cities are West Memphis, a hamlet staring across the levees and the river, barely able to make out the towers of Memphis, Tennessee in the distance; and Jonesboro, home of Arkansas State University.

The 1st District's congressman, Bill Alexander, is a politician who has not lived up to his early promise. In 1976, when still a junior member of the Appropriations Committee, he was chosen by the new Speaker, Tip O'Neill, and the new Majority Leader, Jim Wright, to be a deputy whip; in 1980, after Whip John Brademas was defeated, Alexander was picked by O'Neill and Wright to the number four leadership position of chief deputy whip (oddly enough, that was still an appointive post; it became elective in 1982). By traditional criteria, Alexander seemed an ideal choice. He is from the Deep South, from a district represented for years by a Dixiecrat—quite a contrast from Tip O'Neill's North Cambridge or even Jim Wright's gritty, cowpoke's city of Fort Worth. Alexander's voting record on economic issues has for some time been not too far distant from those of northern Democrats; on foreign and cultural issues, somewhat farther. He is articulate, presentable on television, generally loyal to the leadership but independent in his own thinking.

But once installed he made mistakes. Some charged that he was lackadaisical about his duties, and wasn't a good vote-counter. He deserted the Democrats on a difficult vote on the Appropriations Committee in 1982, voting to report to the floor a measure the leadership opposed; he switched and opposed the MX missile in 1985. He did stake out a position for himself as the leadership's man on Central America, opposing aid to the contras but at the same time trying not to seem to be totally undercutting American interests there. But then in August 1985, he requisitioned an Air Force plane for a trip to Brazil for what he said would be a delegation of five lawmakers; but only one member, Alexander, came aboard, and it's not clear that any of the others were ever interested in going. Republicans filmed the almost-empty airliner as it returned to Washington on its $50,000 trip. O'Neill criticized him, and others recalled a *Wall Street Journal* story in 1985 that depicted him holding an African spear and saying "boogaloo" when a lobbyist came to his office. Alexander had his responses. He said he'd said "Jambo," the Swahili word for hello, but Republicans started calling him Boogaloo Bill anyway. And he argued that he is a genuine expert on Brazil and gasohol and that his trip had been useful and issued a single-spaced 15-page report on it.

All plausible points, perhaps. But nothing is more damaging for a politician than to look ridiculous. Alexander wanted to move up and become whip when O'Neill retired in 1986 and Wright and Whip Thomas Foley moved up; by September his chances had evaporated. Back home, he was under attack from Republicans (who asked 1st District voters to fill out a questionnaire on Alexander's travels and expenses and become eligible for a prize of free air fare for anywhere in the world and $2,000 for travel expenses) and from conservative Democratic state Senator Jim Wood. "While eastern Arkansas suffered through record high unemployment and recession," a Wood ad said, Alexander "took 19 foreign trips." Wood came within a hairsbreadth of unseating Alexander in the May primary, and by early July Alexander left the whip race, saying "I am no longer a national Democrat, I am an Arkansas Democrat." That may have helped his local standing, and the Republicans, who did so much to raise the junketeering issue against him, had an inexperienced 27-year-old candidate who ended up with barely more than one-third of a vote.

That gives Alexander a chance to rebuild his congressional career. He has a high-ranking seat on the Appropriations Committee and the seniority to seek a subcommittee chairmanship, perhaps that of Military Construction, held in the 99th Congress by the more junior Bill Hefner of North Carolina. Alexander remains interested in Central America—and has reason to feel that his warnings about a "secret war" there have been vindicated by the Iran-contra scandal. But he is likely also to attend conspicuously to flood control and public works projects, the fate of the rice and soybean industries, and other matters of special import to eastern Arkansas.

The People: Pop. 1980: 573,551, up 9.5% 1970–80. Households (1980): 78% family, 43% with children, 65% married couples; 32.3% housing units rented; median monthly rent: $99; median house value: $28,000. Voting age pop. (1980): 396,107; 16% Black, 1% Spanish origin.

1984 Presidential Vote: Reagan (R) 114,091   (57%)
                                Mondale (D) 86,741   (43%)

Rep. Bill Alexander (D)

Elected 1968; b. Jan 16, 1934, Memphis, TN; home, Osceola; U. of AR, Southwestern U. at Memphis, B.A. 1957, Vanderbilt U., LL.B. 1960; Episcopalian; divorced.

Career: Army, 1951–53; Law clerk, Fed. Judge Marion Boyd, 1960–61; Practicing atty., 1961–68.

Offices: 233 CHOB 20515, 202-225-4076. Also 211-A Fed. Bldg., Jonesboro 72401, 501-972-4600.

Committees: *Appropriations* (11th of 35 D). Subcommittees: Commerce, Justice, State, and Judiciary; Legislative; Military Construction.

Group Ratings

	ADA	ACLU	COPE	CFA	LCV	ACU	NTU	NSI	COC	CEI
1986	75	70	67	83	55	24	121	25	29	12
1985	70	—	65	50	—	5	20	—	23	—

National Journal Ratings

	1986 LIB — 1986 CONS	1985 LIB — 1985 CONS
Economic	87% — 0%	71% — 28%
Social	57% — 40%	79% — 19%
Foreign	59% — 40%	61% — 39%

Key Votes

1) Lmt Cln Water Act	AGN	5) Retain Gun Cont	AGN	9) Aid Angola Reb	AGN
2) Rpl Tobac Sub	AGN	6) Contra Aid	AGN	10) Tax Reform	AGN
3) Grm-Rdmn Def Red	AGN	7) Lmt Text Imp	FOR	11) S Africa Sanc	FOR
4) Ban Polygraph	FOR	8) Limit SDI	FOR	12) Immig Reform	FOR

Election Results

1986 general	Bill Alexander (D)	105,733	(64%)	($703,571)
	Rick Albin (R)	58,937	(36%)	($52,708)
1986 primary	Bill Alexander (D)	81,409	(52%)	
	Jim Wood (D).........................	74,701	(48%)	
1984 general	Bill Alexander (D)	121,047	(97%)	($270,294)
	Peter Cochran (R).....................	3,481	(3%)	

Campaign Contributions and Expenditures

1985-86		Direct Cont. 1985-86		PACS Breakdown 1985-86			
Receipts	$630,461	Indiv.	$217,619	Corp.	$64,475	T/M/H	$72,700
Expend.	$703,571	Party	$1,729	Labor	$130,575	Agr.	$13,000
Unspent	$8,540	PACS	$302,500	Ideo.	$19,750	CWOS	$2,000

SECOND DISTRICT

Little Rock is, geographically and in most other ways, the center of Arkansas. It dominates the public life of its state as do only a few other state capitals, and all of them—Boston, Providence, Atlanta, Denver, Honolulu—are much larger. Little Rock has the state's dominant newspaper, the *Arkansas Gazette*, and its pesky and more conservative competitor, the *Arkansas Democrat*. It has television stations that reach nearly to the state's boundaries. It has the state government and is the home of the Stephens brothers, two of the nation's richest investment bankers who are politically involved with both parties. Little Rock made for a time an international name for itself forcibly resisting integration of Central High School in 1957; President Eisenhower had to send in federal troops when Governor Orval Faubus refused to enforce the court order. But electorally today Little Rock is usually a progressive force in a state with widely divergent political tendencies; unlike most southern cities, Little Rock is not the Republican bastion of the state, and stuck with Jimmy Carter even in 1980 when he failed to carry the state.

The 2d Congressional District of Arkansas includes Little Rock and surrounding Pulaski County, plus smaller counties on almost all sides. A little more than half the district's people live in Pulaski County, including the state capital of Little Rock, with its large black and affluent white neighborhoods, and North Little Rock, a kind of industrial suburb across the Arkansas River known informally for years as Dog Town, because at the turn of the century Little Rock officials, peeved that North Little Rock was allowed to incorporate separately, dumped all their stray dogs there. The 2d also includes several hill counties to the north and, in the southeast, part of the flat, cotton, rice, and soybean-growing Mississippi plain. It supported Republican Governor Winthrop Rockefeller and his three Democratic successors, Dale Bumpers, David Pryor, and Bill Clinton; it has elected progressive candidates at about every level.

Yet the last two congressmen from this district, represented for 38 years by longtime Ways and Means Chairman Wilbur Mills, have been a Republican and a bombastic sheriff. The reason may be media: for years campaigns were conducted person to person, and southern districts like this chose a smart young man and stayed with him while he accumulated seniority so he could bring home the bacon; now television is the medium of political campaigning, and a district like this goes for the most interesting candidate, only to lose him when he runs soon after for statewide office. The Republican congressman here was Ed Bethune, who ran against Senator David Pryor in 1984 and lost. The sheriff is the current incumbent, Tommy Robinson, who ran a riproaring race in 1984 and now—since no avenues to statewide office seem open—seems to be settling in to represent the district more quietly.

As Sheriff, Robinson was quoted as claiming to feed black prisoners "watermelon and chicken"; he accused President Reagan of trying to "starve this country out." Despite or because of his bizarre behavior, he edged out Secretary of State Paul Riviere in the 1984 runoff and beat Judy Petty—whose 15 minutes of national fame came when she was the Republican nominee against Mills in 1974, year of the Fanne Fox scandal—in the general, while a liberal Independent got 11% of the vote.

In the House Robinson seems to be having a more conventional career. He was chosen whip for his freshman class (one of the smallest in years) and got seats on Veterans' Affairs and Armed Services. He served in the Navy himself, directly out of high school (he became a policeman afterwards, and got his college degree while working), and seems temperamentally among the most hawkish of members. But he did waver before supporting the MX missile. Robinson's big project of the 99th Congress, however, was not legislative but financial: paying off his 1984 campaign debt. In 1984 he spent over $911,000 in the primary, runoff, and general election races, and spent $441,000 of his own money, all borrowed, to do it. By fall 1986 he had raised $635,000, including $243,000 from political action committees, and spent nearly $500,000 of it to retire his 1984 debt. In retrospect his borrowings show a breathtaking nerve: how would he have paid back the debts if he had lost? But that is just a theoretical question now. He had no serious opposition in 1986, and seems likely to be able to hold the seat indefinitely—or until he decides to run for statewide office.

The People: Pop. 1980: 569,116, up 24.5% 1970–80. Households (1980): 75% family, 43% with children, 63% married couples; 32.4% housing units rented; median monthly rent: $160; median house value: $37,300. Voting age pop. (1980): 401,104; 15% Black, 1% Spanish origin.

1984 Presidential Vote: Reagan (R) 133,093   (60%)
                                               Mondale (D) 87,447   (40%)

Rep. Tommy F. Robinson (D)

Elected 1984; b. Mar. 7, 1942, Little Rock; home, Jacksonville; U. of AR at Fayetteville, U. of Central AR, U. of AR at Little Rock, B.A. 1976; United Methodist; married (Carolyn).

Career: AR St. Police Dept., 1966–68; N. Little Rock Police Dept., 1968–71; U.S. Marshall Srvc., 1971–74; Dir., Public Safety, U. of AR Med. Sciences, Asst. Dir., Public Safety, U. of AR at Fayetteville, 1974–75; Police chief, Jacksonville, 1975–79; AR Dir. of Public Safety, 1979–80; Sheriff, Pulaski Cnty., 1980–84.

Offices: 1541 LHOB 20515, 202-225-2506. Also 1527 Fed. Bldg., 700 W. Capitol, Little Rock 72201, 501-378-5941; 411 N. Spruce St., Searcy 72143, 501-268-4287; and P.O. Box 431, Lonoke Cnty. Crthse., Lonoke 72086, 501-676-6403.

Committees: *Armed Services* (26th of 31 D). Subcommittees: Military Installations and Facilities; Readiness. *Education and Labor* (8th of 21 D). Subcommittees: Elementary, Secondary and Vocational Education; Labor Standards; Postsecondary Education. *Veterans' Affairs* (15th of 21 D). Subcommittees: Compensation, Pension, and Insurance; Hospitals and Health Care. *Select Committee On Aging* (35th of 39 D). Subcommittee: Human Services.

Group Ratings

	ADA	ACLU	COPE	CFA	LCV	ACU	NTU	NSI	COC	CEI
1986	25	25	73	33	51	68	30	80	44	29
1985	40	—	63	67	—	57	33	—	45	—

National Journal Ratings

	1986 LIB — 1986 CONS		1985 LIB — 1985 CONS	
Economic	46%	— 53%	50%	— 50%
Social	23%	— 74%	47%	— 52%
Foreign	21%	— 77%	37%	— 60%

Key Votes

1) Lmt Cln Water Act	AGN	5) Retain Gun Cont	AGN	9) Aid Angola Reb	FOR
2) Rpl Tobac Sub	AGN	6) Contra Aid	FOR	10) Tax Reform	AGN
3) Grm-Rdmn Def Red	FOR	7) Lmt Text Imp	FOR	11) S Africa Sanc	FOR
4) Ban Polygraph	FOR	8) Limit SDI	AGN	12) Immig Reform	AGN

Election Results

1986 general	Tommy Robinson (D)	128,814	(76%)	($740,921)
	Keith Hamaker (R).	11,244	(24%)	($81,863)
1986 primary	Tommy Robinson (D)	80,699	(78%)	
	Alan Lindsay (D)	22,694	(22%)	
1984 general	Tommy Robinson (D)	103,165	(47%)	($911,450)
	Judy Petty (R)	90,841	(41%)	($399,822)
	Jim Taylor (I)	25,073	(11%)	($17,628)

Campaign Contributions and Expenditures

1985-86		Direct Cont. 1985-86		PACS Breakdown 1985-86			
Receipts	$786,273	Indiv.	$413,438	Corp.	$119,707	T/M/H	$106,940
Expend.	$740,921	Party	$1,148	Labor	$23,250	Agr.	$5,750
Unspent	$49,367	PACS	$277,197	Ideo.	$11,000	CWOS	$10,550
		Cand.	$68,075				

THIRD DISTRICT

West of Little Rock, the hills of Arkansas rise and soon enough become mountains—not Rockies or even Appalachians, but ruggedly beautiful and spotted with farmhouses and little towns. These mountains—the Ozarks and the Ouachita Range—are the heart of the 3d congressional District of Arkansas, which occupies the northwest and western part of the state. For long years this was a poor area; now it is somewhat better off, thanks to retirees and young people attracted by the area's mild climate, its scenic mountains and reservoirs, by its jobs in small industries, by its low-keyed pace of life, and by its fidelity to traditional values. The cities of the 3d are medium-sized, the kind of place most Americans say they would like to live in. Among them are Fort Smith, on the Oklahoma border, which erupted in anger and fear when nearby Fort Chaffee was filled with Cuban refugees in 1980; Fayetteville, site of the University of Arkansas; Bentonville, up near the Missouri border. The last is the headquarters of the Wal-Mart discount chain whose success in small towns across the South and Midwest has made its owner, Sam Walton, and his family worth some $2.3 billion.

The hills of northwestern Arkansas have always harbored more Republicans than any other part of the state, and for most of the 20th century this was the only part of Arkansas with two-party politics. The Republicanism here was the ornery type, often encountered in southern hill country, a vestige of opposition to slavery and the Civil War. Republicans won a House election in these parts in 1868, but although they were competitive in a few elections since, they didn't finally win the district in a congressional election for 98 years, until 1966.

The winner then and still congressman is John Paul Hammerschmidt, head of his family's local lumber business in Harrison and now one of the most senior Republicans on Capitol Hill. Hammerschmidt is neither very partisan nor very ideological, however, and is not often a contributor to debate on national issues. His heart seems to be where his roots are, in the hills of Arkansas. He is ranking Republican on Public Works and has been ranking member on Veterans' Affairs. On the latter committee the debate, when there is one, is more generational than partisan, with Hammerschmidt mildly inclined to favor his fellow World War II veterans. On Public Works, the question historically is whose district gets the projects, and Hammerschmidt has been effective at getting some for the Arkansas 3d. He does not, however, try hard to be a power to see who gets the rest, though he does oppose efforts by market-minded conservatives to cut pork barrel programs generally. By virtue of his committee position, he was one of the leaders of the successful moves to override President Reagan's vetoes of the water projects and highway bills in 1987.

On national issues, Hammerschmidt is a bit more generous than other Republicans with federal spending, representing as he does an historically poor district; on foreign and cultural issues, he is solidly conservative. Overall he represents the strengths and weaknesses of Republican House members over the years. He has strong roots in his local community, a sense of decency and responsibility, integrity and attention to duty. But he is not an aggressive partisan nor an accomplished pugilist in the battle of ideas. Electorally, his only tough test came in the Watergate year of 1974, when a 28-year-old law professor at the University of Arkansas named Bill Clinton challenged him; Clinton held Hammerschmidt to 52% and has been elected governor three times since. Since then Hammerschmidt has won easily, sometimes with no opposition at all.

The People: Pop. 1980: 572,937, up 33.3% 1970–80. Households (1980): 77% family, 39% with children, 68% married couples; 26.0% housing units rented; median monthly rent: $147; median house value: $32,200. Voting age pop. (1980): 414,806; 2% Black, 1% American Indian, 1% Spanish origin.

1984 Presidential Vote:

Reagan (R)	165,217	(70%)
Mondale (D)	69,974	(30%)

Rep. John Paul Hammerschmidt (R)

Elected 1966; b. May 4, 1922, Harrison; home, Harrison; The Citadel, OK A&M Col., U. of AR; Presbyterian; married (Virginia).

Career: Army Air Corps, WWII; Bd. Chmn., Hammerschmidt Lumber Co.; Chmn., Repub. State Central Cmtee., 1964–66.

Offices: 2207 RHOB 20515, 202-225-4301. Also Main P.O. Bldg., Rm. 248, Ft. Smith 72901, 501-782-7787.

Committees: *Public Works and Transportation* (Ranking Member of 20 R). *Veterans' Affairs* (2d of 13 R). Subcommittee: Hospitals and Health Care (Ranking Member). *Select Committee on Aging* (2d of 26 R). Subcommittee: Housing and Consumer Interests (Ranking Member).

Group Ratings

	ADA	ACLU	COPE	CFA	LCV	ACU	NTU	NSI	COC	CEI
1986	5	5	15	42	21	82	39	100	78	53
1985	25	—	15	17	—	81	46	—	77	—

National Journal Ratings

	1986 LIB — 1986 CONS			1985 LIB — 1985 CONS		
Economic	21%	—	77%	36%	—	63%
Social	11%	—	85%	0%	—	76%
Foreign	0%	—	86%	0%	—	76%

Key Votes

1) Lmt Cln Water Act	AGN	5) Retain Gun Cont	AGN	9) Aid Angola Reb	FOR
2) Rpl Tobac Sub	AGN	6) Contra Aid	FOR	10) Tax Reform	AGN
3) Grm-Rdmn Def Red	FOR	7) Lmt Text Imp	FOR	11) S Africa Sanc	AGN
4) Ban Polygraph	AGN	8) Limit SDI	AGN	12) Immig Reform	AGN

Election Results

1986 general	John Paul Hammerschmidt (R)	115,113	(80%)	($63,341)
	Su Sargent (D)	36,726	(20%)	($11,837)
1986 primary	John Paul Hammerschmidt (R) unopposed			
1984 general	John Paul Hammerschmidt (R) unopposed			($57,510)

Campaign Contributions and Expenditures

1985-86		Direct Cont. 1983-84		PACS Breakdown 1983-84			
Receipts	$159,238	Indiv.	$44,063	Corp.	$44,600	T/M/H	$40,300
Expend.	$63,341	PACS	$99,800	Labor	$3,700	Agr.	$4,600
Unspent	$168,435	Cand.	$13,800	Ideo.	$2,100	CWOS	$4,500

FOURTH DISTRICT

From the flat Delta lands along the Mississippi River, west across rolling hills to the resort town of Hot Springs and to Texarkana, a city situated so squarely on the Texas-Arkansas border that the state line runs through City Hall, stretches the 4th Congressional District of Arkansas. The principal towns in the district are, with the exception of Hot Springs (once home to a major illegal gambling industry), quiet places: El Dorado (with a long A), just north of Louisiana and a center of oil production; Camden, the home of Senator David Pryor and of the late Senator John McClellan; Arkadelphia; and Pine Bluff, an old agricultural center with a large black population on the flat banks of the Arkansas River. Pine Bluff is the home town of Martha Mitchell, the vocal wife of Richard Nixon's attorney general who caused so much political uproar in the early 1970s; Pine Bluff has built a statue of her and named U.S. 65 the Martha Mitchell Freeway.

Southern Arkansas, together with the flatlands west of the Mississippi, to the north is the section of Arkansas most clearly part of the Deep South. In racial makeup (24% black), economic base (cotton, oil, rice), mores (traditional Dixie), and political leanings (solidly Democratic for years, interrupted by enthusiasm for candidates like Barry Goldwater and George Wallace), the 4th District is the most indisputably southern part of Arkansas.

The congressman from this district is Beryl Anthony, who in late 1986 suddenly became an important Democratic leader in the House after eight years of quieter service. For it was just after the new leadership elections that Anthony was chosen by Speaker Jim Wright to chair the Democratic Congressional Campaign Committee. Outgoing chairman, Tony Coelho, did a brilliant job of raising money, erasing the Democrats' debt, building a new party headquarters and media center, and of electing new members and returning old ones—so brilliant that he was elected Democratic Whip. Anthony had been cultivating Coelho and has long been close to Wright, and he has made a name for himself as a big fundraiser. But it was still a surprise when he was chosen over Vic Fazio, who had the disadvantage of coming, as Coelho does, from California.

Anthony actually has little experience beating Republicans; there are seldom any serious Republican candidates in southern Arkansas. But he has considerable experience staying close with the Democratic leadership and raising money. When he came to the House after a tough primary contest in 1978, he seemed likely to be more conservative than previous 4th District representatives; he comes from an El Dorado family in the timber business, is a former prosecutor, was inclined to look favorably on incentives for business (including oil, which El Dorado produces) and unfavorably on federal interference on local matters. But in the House he worked closely with Jim Wright and was rewarded with seats first on Budget and later on Ways and Means.

On Budget he voted with the Democrats, not the Republicans, on the Reagan budget and tax cuts of 1981; this set him pretty solidly with House Democrats when it counts. On Ways and Means he was influential for a junior member, lobbying Chairman Dan Rostenkowski at one point for a shorter holding period for capital gains, back when rates on capital gains were much lower than on ordinary incomes, and looking after the interests of timber and oil producers. During the protracted consideration of the tax reform bill, he also looked after parochial issues, but ended up, as he does generally, supporting his chairman. Having a seat on Ways and Means when Congress is pondering tax reform doesn't hurt when it comes to raising campaign money; he accumulated some $350,000 of unspent campaign funds in 1986. The one time the

Republicans did make a point of challenging him was in the Democratic year of 1982, and he got 66% of the vote.

The 1988 elections will provide a good test of his acumen as Campaign Committee Chairman. House elections will mostly be ignored by the press, and paid little heed by most politicians: the key will be to encourage good challengers in races where Republicans are weak, raise money for such challengers and early money for incumbent Democrats to deter Republican competition, and to frame national issues in ways that help House Democrats. It requires tremendous energy and mastery of detail as well as the fundraising ability and political instinct Anthony has already shown. The score will be kept: as of early 1987 there were no macropolitical factors saying the Democrats should make major gains or suffer major losses; the key will probably be in the details, as it was in 1986. If Anthony does as well as Coelho, he could be headed for an even higher position.

The People: Pop. 1980: 570,831, up 11.4% 1970–80. Households (1980): 76% family, 40% with children, 62% married couples; 27.4% housing units rented; median monthly rent: $102; median house value: $26,200. Voting age pop. (1980): 403,044; 25% Black, 1% Spanish origin.

1984 Presidential Vote:

Reagan (R)	122,373	(56%)
Mondale (D)	94,484	(44%)

Rep. Beryl F. Anthony, Jr. (D)

Elected 1978; b. Feb. 21, 1938, El Dorado; home, El Dorado; U. of AR, B.S., B.A. 1961, J.D. 1963; Episcopalian; married (Sheila).

Career: Asst. Atty. Gen. of AR, 1964–65; Dpty. Union Cnty. Prosecutor, 1966–70; Prosecuting Atty., 13th Judicial Dist., 1971–76; Legal Counsel, Anthony Forest Products Co., 1977.

Offices: 1117 LHOB 20515, 202-225-3772. Also 206 Fed. Bldg., El Dorado 71730, 501-863-0121; 2521 Fed. Bldg., Pine Bluff 71601, 501-536-3376; and 201 Fed. Bldg., Hot Springs 71901, 501-624-1011.

Committees: *Ways and Means* (15th of 23 D). Subcommittees: Oversight; Health. *Select Committee on Children, Youth, and Families* (7th of 18 D). Task Forces: Crisis Intervention.

Group Ratings

	ADA	ACLU	COPE	CFA	LCV	ACU	NTU	NSI	COC	CEI
1986	50	60	52	75	57	30	27	22	40	27
1985	55	—	52	50	—	33	34	—	32	—

National Journal Ratings

	1986 LIB — 1986 CONS		1985 LIB — 1985 CONS	
Economic	47% —	53%	67% —	32%
Social	61% —	37%	69% —	28%
Foreign	56% —	43%	58% —	40%

Key Votes

1) Lmt Cln Water Act	AGN	5) Retain Gun Cont	FOR	9) Aid Angola Reb	FOR
2) Rpl Tobac Sub	AGN	6) Contra Aid	AGN	10) Tax Reform	FOR
3) Grm-Rdmn Def Red	FOR	7) Lmt Text Imp	FOR	11) S Africa Sanc	—
4) Ban Polygraph	FOR	8) Limit SDI	FOR	12) Immig Reform	FOR

Election Results

1986 general	Beryl F. Anthony, Jr. (D)...............	115,335	(78%)	($179,169)
	Lamar Keels (R)......................	22,980	(15%)	($23,134)
	Stephen Bitely (I).....................	10,604	(7%)	
1986 primary	Beryl F. Anthony, Jr. (D) unopposed			
1984 general	Beryl F. Anthony, Jr. (D)...............	117,123	(98%)	($93,041)
	Roy Rood (I).........................	2,516	(2%)	

Campaign Contributions and Expenditures

1985-86		Direct Cont. 1985-86		PACS Breakdown 1985-86			
Receipts	$390,697	Indiv.	$78,325	Corp.	$137,207	T/M/H	$106,940
Expend.	$179,169	Party	$1,148	Labor	$5,750	Agr.	$5,750
Unspent	$337,764	PACS	$277,197	Ideo.	$11,000	CWOS	$10,550

CALIFORNIA

Who could have predicted, 150 years ago as industrial democracy was just dawning in lands on both sides of the Atlantic, where the richest and most dynamic parts of the world would be today? Few people in the late 1830s would have guessed that Switzerland, a land of mountain shepherds, would be the richest part of Europe, or that Japan, two decades before Commodore Perry opened it up to intercourse with the rest of the world, would be the world's most innovative manufacturer and premier exporter. Hardly any thought that California would have the richest and most rapidly growing economy in the world. California was almost empty then, with less than 10,000 inhabitants in land that now holds 26 million. A British explorer sailing past Point Lobos and through the Golden Gate into San Francisco Bay saw thousands of cattle roaming untended on the hills—"California in a nutshell, nature doing everything and man nothing"— and others were disgusted to see Californians slaughtering cattle for their hides, leaving the meat to rot in the sun. Yet the same explorer foresaw that this autonomous province of Mexico, thousands of miles from Mexico City and Washington, must become "English, in some sense of the word," British or American. "In the hands of an enterprising people," the New Englander Richard Henry Dana wrote in 1840, "what a country this might be!"

And so it is. California is not the nation's cultural capital, but it is its entertainment capital; it is not the financial capital, but it is its biggest and strongest engine of economic growth; it is not the political capital, but it is one place where political trends are made and where presidents come from (Nixon, Reagan) or go after they retire (Ford, Eisenhower). It is not surrounded by a heavily populated industrial hinterland as the East Coast cities are, but by thousands of miles of sparsely populated desert, mountains, and ocean. Looking out from Point Lobos or from Los Angeles International, there is only a vast expanse of ocean between you and China. This is America's very substantial foothold on the Pacific Rim, where millions of human beings packed into enormous cities in the seismically active interstices between mountain and ocean have produced the world's fastest economic growth for three decades.

Off by itself, California is watched by all the rest of the world. By the early 1980s California had become the number one immigrant destination in the world, so attractive to so many people that the Russians, fearful of mass defections, refused to send their team to the 1984 Los Angeles Olympics. The Olympics itself—the ceremonies, the pomp, the American victories—were one of the central events of the first optimistic presidential election year since 1960, central enough to make their organizer, Peter Ueberroth, *Time*'s Man of the Year. Yet California's outlook has not always been so sunny. A dozen years before, in the early 1970s, California was suffering from smog and reeling after earthquakes. Its aerospace industry was on the rocks as defense spending plummeted, and its microchip industry was in infancy. Moreover, for the first time in a century, outmigration was coming close to equal the inflow of new residents. Its students were rebellious and rejecting the values of their elders, and many of the elders themselves were unsure that they had values worth defending. Abortion, pornography, marijuana—all were effectively legalized in a few years. Show business, always a reflector of certain Californian if not national values, mocked chastity and patriotism, and celebrated challenges to the establishment and to middle class morality.

Presiding over California's government then, to be sure, was that defender of traditional American values, Ronald Reagan. But he was politically beleaguered. His 1966 margin had been cut in half in 1970 by an underfinanced opponent; his campaign to maintain a Republican majority in the legislature had been frustrated; his efforts to hold down state spending and prevent tax increases had failed; his chances of winning a third term or of getting elected to the Senate in 1974 seemed iffy. In 1972, a Californian in the White House won a record reelection margin, but he failed to engage the sympathies or capture the imaginations of ordinary Americans; in his administration domestic government grew and defense spending was cut, and when he was forced out of office by the Watergate scandal almost no one, in California or elsewhere, regretted his political demise.

How to account for the change? What explains the rise in national confidence and pride? A look at changes in California, the prototypical trendsetter state, over the last dozen years suggests some answers.

First, the economy has changed. Californians have for some years lived in a nation-state whose affluence can hardly be overstated. Yet the basis for its affluence used to seem mysterious—and under threat. The standard explanation for years was that some boom industry—entertainment (first the movies, later TV and records, more recently video games and electronic toys), defense (first aircraft, then aerospace)—was the engine of growth. The corrollary was that disaster was looming when the latest boom went bust.

But over the long term California has grown rapidly despite wide oscillations in the health of particular industries. Urbanologist Jane Jacobs has pointed out that in 18 months at the end of World War II, metropolitan Los Angeles lost 230,000 jobs in defense industries, and every expert predicted depression and depopulation of the Los Angeles Basin in the postwar years. Exactly the opposite happened. In 1945–55 Los Angeles was the fastest growing metro area in the nation and generated one out of eight new jobs in the United States. Standard economic analysis tells us that growth comes where there are basic resources and access to markets. But the 26 million people of California are separated by almost two thousand miles of desert and mountain, punctuated by a few other California-like metropolitan areas, from any other significant market, and its basic resources are limited. It has been a net importer of oil since the 1950s (although it is a significant producer as well), it is hundreds of miles from basic fuels like coal and raw materials like iron ore; southern California is always in danger of running short of water. California has only one basic industry dependent on its physical endowment: agriculture (although that depends on irrigation as well). The answer is that California's economy, like the thriving economies on the other side of the Pacific Rim, is growing largely because the people there want it to. But the big difference is that California, unlike Japan or South Korea or Singapore, welcomes immigrants and owes much of its growth to their ingenuity and enterprise.

Economists of the right, supply-siders like Arthur Laffer, would explain all of California's recent growth as the result of cuts in taxes and restraint in government spending. The private sector, they say, has been given room to grow by Proposition 13 and other tax cuts in the late 1970s and early 1980s. This, like the boom-and-bust theory, explains some things, but leaves even more unexplained. For California has been growing rapidly for a very long time, and during most of that time it has been a big-government, high-tax state. That has been true at least since the 1940s, when Earl Warren deliberately kept taxes high during World War II. He anticipated vast population growth after the war, and wanted to be able to build schools, highways, and

CALIFORNIA — Congressional Districts, Counties, and Selected Places — *(45 Districts)*

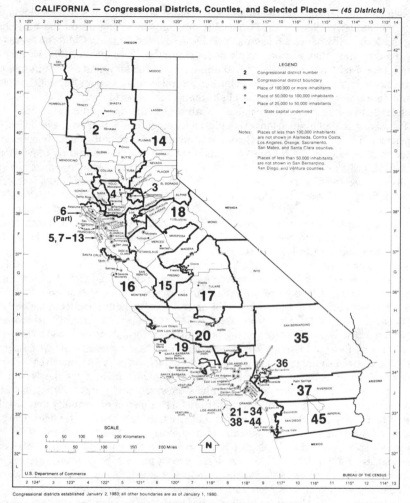

See pages 1369-1374 for additional metropolitan area maps.

water mains for the new residents; seldom has a public official been so right. California thus did not grow as a tax haven, as a giant New Hampshire. It grew despite high taxes (they're still pretty high, even after Proposition 13 and its progeny) and in part because of what the taxes bought: a vast freeway system, an awe-inspiring water delivery system, a higher educational system that every year nonchalantly takes in more than half the state's young people.

California's affluence thus depends on free enterprise and government, on one boom-and-bust industry after another and on an underlying, prosaic economy that is much more solid than anyone thinks. Californians have used government intervention and market mechanisms, natural endowments and technological improvements—whatever comes to hand—to build a society whose affluence is genuinely awesome. As an ex-governor running for president, Ronald Reagan liked to say that if California were an independent country, it would have the seventh largest gross national product in the world. He might have added that it would have one of the fastest-growing GNPs in the world and, except for a few resource-rich enclaves, by far the highest GNP per capita. California's success is all the more striking, because unlike some other high-GNP areas (Switzerland, Japan, Massachusetts) it has had massive immigration, beginning just at that time in the early 1970s when fashionable opinion was giving up on the possibility and denying the desirability of economic growth. Then the eyes of southern California were focused, literally, on the smog that was one result of four decades in which the Los Angeles Basin's population increased from 2.5 million to 10 million. Now the air quality in California is much better, thanks in large part to stringent pollution controls which Reagan Republicans tended to resist, and growth is seen less often as a blight than as an opportunity.

Which leads to the second major change in California's life during the last dozen years—or, rather, two changes which are seldom thought of together, but which both symbolize California's openness. These are the vast technological advances, especially the development of the computer chip industry in the Silicon Valley, and the vast migrations, mostly of Mexicans and Asians, to California over the past two decades. California has succeeded in spawning a vigorous high-tech industry, growing though beleaguered by Japanese competition, and a sprawling low-wage (but high upwardly-mobile) economy, both at the same time. In the early 1970s California was just one of many areas with some high-tech development, and in-migration had trickled almost to a standstill. By the middle 1980s California still had the premier high-tech economy in the world and had spawned hundreds of thousands of jobs for immigrants who are moving upward more rapidly, probably, than any migrants in American history.

Neither development was anticipated by any sizeable body of experts, and especially not by the doomsayers of the early 1970s who saw technology as a threat and growth as nothing but an environmental threat. Yet both are very much in line with California's history and tradition. California's economic growth has always built on technological advance, from the early miners to the Central Valley's farmers, from the movie moguls to the aircraft assemblers. The microchip is just the latest chapter in a long saga. And California's economic growth has always depended on vast flows of migrants. These people—from Massachusetts and Mississippi, Iowa and Oklahoma, from southern Ireland and southern Italy, from Jewish enclaves in New York and Chicago, from south China and rural Japan, from Armenia in Turkey, and now from Mexico and the Philippines, El Salvador and Indochina—powered that growth. What has attracted them, it seems, and what they in turn have fostered, is a sense of opportunity and possibility, a willingness to let people try things their way and to give heed to their pleas for help. The common ingredient to both is openness to people and to new ideas.

California's scientific and technological surge attracted favorable, if usually belated, notice from journalists and politicians. Governor Jerry Brown made a point of his interest in space exploration, and by the early 1980s Apple Computer founder Steve Jobs was on the cover of *Time*. Generally high tech was seen as an advantage, although occasionally observers succumbed to the temptation of seeing any change in society as a problem: one writer lamented that the University of California at Berkeley was being overrun by Asian mathematics and computer whizzes, as if every university in the land wouldn't want a similar problem. As one chip executive put it, "It's our Chinese-American kids against their Japanese kids."

Immigration, on the other hand, was seen almost always as a problem and a burden. Government statistics and journalists' stories have been unable to keep up with the rapid upward mobility of these people: they begin their life in America in what look to journalists like ghetto neighborhoods, but they quickly begin to make comfortable livings and to move up in the world—not to Beverly Hills, but to the San Fernando Valley and Orange County (the comparative absence of upwardly mobile migrants on the west side of Los Angeles makes them invisible to people in the entertainment business, and thus we don't see much of them on television or in movies). Los Angeles is to the nation today what New York was in 1913: the great entry port for people seeking—and finding—opportunity. Nor is this the result of simple geographic proximity. Los Angeles is close to the Mexican border, to be sure, but it is 1,000 miles away from any significant concentration of population in Mexico except for the border towns. And while it is true that the West Coast is the part of the continental United States closest to Asia, that is not what makes Asian migrants stay here: they fly in, and could just as easily fly to the Midwest or the South. In California and in Washington, immigration is treated as a problem and immigrants are considered people in distress. But the continuing large immigration to California is a sure sign that its economy is buoyant and for the immigrants themselves the move is their big opportunity. Why else would they come?

Opportunity is what California has always represented to migrants, and this is a state largely built by outsiders. They may have been attracted, initially, by the climate, which for most Americans is well-nigh perfect (or was, until smog was noticed in the 1950s). For post-1945 migrants from the Midwest and South, the cultural atmosphere was good: except for San Francisco, all California then had the small-town atmosphere most Americans consider ideal. Today it is far more cosmopolitan: Los Angeles produced Rodeo Drive just as New York in 1913 had Fifth Avenue. Many Californians find such an atmosphere unfriendly; they have moved farther out, to suburbs in Orange County, and increasingly to small towns and subdivisions 50 and 80 miles from the large metro areas or even, in the last 10 years, to the foothills of the Sierras. As California grew more affluent, its cultural habits grew more diverse: it supports not only Rodeo Drive, but decorated vans and weekend skydiving and skiing and surfing and Jacuzzi thermal baths. The new migrants will pioneer—are already pioneering—other cultural styles. The chance to do such pioneering, in turn, is part of what attracts people of talent and initiative to California and keeps them there.

Which leads to the third major change in California life over the last dozen years: the emergence of a confident acceptance of the state's cultural diversity. There is an unmistakably less abrasive tone to public and to private life today in California than there was 20 years ago. In those days of student rebellions and ghetto riots, of uptight fathers and long-haired sons, of a wartime draft and a langorous peacetime affluence, Californians of all ages and backgrounds thought their beliefs were under attack and, if only in defense, attacked the beliefs of those who they thought were their attackers. Politicians joined in. Ronald Reagan sent in the National Guard to Berkeley while Robert Kennedy listened sympathetically, almost apologetically, to rebellious students. Reagan didn't hesitate to attack ghetto rioters while Hubert Humphrey said that if he were subjected to such conditions he might riot too. When politicians wore flags on their lapels or let their hair grow, they were sending signals that cheered or infuriated hundreds of thousands of voters.

Californians and Americans generally in the late 1960s and early 1970s were operating against a background of cultural homogeneity. Whatever their own cultural style, they agreed that there could be only one prevailing cultural tone to society, and that those who behaved in another way would be subject to attack as abnormal or dangerous. This is in fact how the war-united America of the 1940s and 1950s behaved. But what the cultural warriors circa 1970 didn't foresee is that they were entering an era of cultural diversity, a time when affluence would permit Americans to live by all manner of different rules and no universal military conflict would require that everyone be treated the same way. By the early 1980s it became clear that cultural diversity was possible, and the fact that the people in the next subdivision or three miles away lived an entirely different lifestyle wasn't much of a threat against your own. California discovered, or rediscovered, the old American rule of live and let live.

How have these developments changed California politics? The cultural warfare and—this is the right word for it—malaise of California life in the early 1970s swept away from memory for a moment the state's nonpartisan political heritage. Government has played an important part in California's growth from the time the United States went to war with Mexico to win it. Water programs, subsidies to the first railroads, the freeways, schools and universities—all are examples of government spending without which it seems unlikely that California would be nearly as affluent or productive as it is. But support for these measures has usually been bipartisan, and many of the most important—the Los Angeles Aqueduct, Earl Warren's and Pat Brown's support of higher education—were pushed through without much debate. As Governor, Reagan spouted anti-government rhetoric, but did not really change the thrust of government programs; instead, he supported the state's largest (to then) tax increase, and his attempt to get the voters to approve a tax limitation referendum in 1973 failed. The real cuts in spending occurred after Proposition 13 in 1978, and even then the thrust was to put limits on what seemed to be runaway increases in government spending levels. Reagan's political role was to stand for one side in the cultural warfare, a stand that cost rather than gained him popularity: his victory margin as governor was cut in half between 1966 and 1970.

Standing on one of the other sides was his successor as Governor, Jerry Brown. It's hard to remember how popular Brown was in his early years in office, and how fresh and innovative he was. Personifying the affluent, skeptical young products of the baby boom generation who were suddenly a huge part of the California electorate, Brown pioneered, and applied to the actual business of government, a politics that is the exact reverse of the politics produced by the New Deal in most parts of America. That traditional New Deal politics—you can find it best exemplified in a Pennsylvania factory town—is liberal on economic issues and conservative on cultural issues, because most people in that community regard themselves as economically deprived and as part of a deep-rooted cultural community. Affluent, shallow-rooted California produced a politics conservative on economic issues and liberal on cultural issues. It was traditional American politics turned upside down.

But this politics turned out to have rather shallow roots itself. Brown lost his hold on the imagination of the electorate in 1978, when he campaigned against Proposition 13, spouting standard big-government arguments, and then, when it passed 2 to 1, flip-flopped and posed as its chief supporter. That destroyed any belief that he was a uniquely candid, sincere politician; the man who won 59% in California's Democratic 1976 presidential primary won only 4% four years later. Brown's passion for innovation came to seem only a reflex against the past, an echo of his desire not to replicate his father's policies (although in so many ways he has replicated his father's career); his rigorous skepticism came to seem only corrosive cynicism. He was reelected in 1978 against an opponent whose mistakes he shrewdly and cynically exploited. His rejection in the 1982 Senate election was no fluke and certainly not the result of enthusiasm for his opponent; it was a good indication of where he and his politics stood in voters' regard.

George Deukmejian stands for a very different kind of politics, more Reaganite than Reagan in standing against tax increases and seeking to replace welfare with workfare, but not interested in dismantling the government which has served California so well. Standing for still other varieties of politics are Thomas Bradley, the Mayor of Los Angeles, who nearly won the 1982 governor election but was shellacked in 1986, and the Democrats who won statewide office in 1986: Lieutenant Governor Leo McCarthy, an old-fashioned liberal; Attorney General John Van de Kamp, a crusader against crime; Secretary of State March Fong Eu, who was herself mugged in 1986; Controller Gray Davis, a former top aide to Jerry Brown; and Treasurer Jesse Unruh, who as custodian of a huge portfolio of pension funds has made himself one of the leading investment decision-makers in America.

This variety reflects a movement away from ideology by California's primary voters. In the 1960s and 1970s Democrats tended to favor the most liberal candidates: George McGovern in 1972, Robert Kennedy and Eugene McCarthy in 1968. But by the 1980s they were less enthusiastic than voters elsewhere in backing an economic liberal like Walter Mondale, and the contests in statewide races could not be classified as liberal-conservative battles. The conventional wisdom about California Republican primary voters from the time Barry Goldwater beat Nelson Rockefeller in 1964 is that they are heavily conservative. Yet in the last two Senate races, they have tended to prefer candidates classified as moderates. Pete Wilson and Pete McCloskey shared 64% of the primary voter in 1982, running against Barry Goldwater Jr., Robert Dornan, and Maureen Reagan, and in 1986, Ed Zschau beat Bruce Herschensohn 39%–31%, with the vote among other candidates split in a way making it plausible that Zschau could have won a runoff. The Republican electorate today is younger than the voters that chose Goldwater over Rockefeller and Reagan over the now forgotten San Francisco Mayor George Christopher two years later, it is less likely to come from the Midwest and more likely to have grown up in California, less opposed to Franklin Roosevelt than it is dedicated to saving the environment. Republican registration has been growing, and 45% of the 1986 primary vote was cast outside southern California, in counties where Zschau led Herschensohn 56%–13%.

Californians are voting for divided government, pitting Speaker Willie Brown against Governor Deukmejian, Democratic Mayor Bradley against a conservative Board of Supervisors in Los Angeles County, a Democratic U.S. House delegation and Senator Alan Cranston against a California Republican president. The result is a government fiscally restrained and culturally tolerant, but ready at the same time to pump more money into education and to insist on sterner standards for students and sterner restrictions on drug use.

These results represent a consensus that is inconsistent by the ideological standards of 20 years ago. That is underlined by the results on recent ballot referenda in this state where the voters often have the last say over legislators and governors. Californians insisted on local property tax cuts in 1978, but balked at deeper tax and spending cuts in 1982 and 1984. They overwhelmingly opposed the limits on their right to have guns in a 1982 proposition that became central to that year's campaign, and provided enough votes to defeat Thomas Bradley and elect George Deukmejian. But they delivered an overwhelming majority in 1986 against the AIDS proposition authorizing quarantines put on the ballot by followers of Lyndon LaRouche.

They have overwhelmingly supported the death penalty and in 1986 voted out Chief Justice Rose Bird (who voted to overturn convictions in all 65 death penalty cases she considered) and two other Jerry Brown appointees to the Supreme Court; they did not want Brown's judicial activists to control state policy for decades after they had tired of him and his politics. At the same time they heavily supported a toxic waste proposal put on the ballot by Democrats to help Bradley's campaign and rejected a move to cap elected officials' salaries. They voted by an even greater margin to establish English as the official language of state government. But far from being a bigoted rejection of outsiders, this amounts to little more than a ratification of the status quo, for the immigrants themselves are rapidly learning English and show no substantial support for the "bilingual" education programs designed by Brown appointees to keep their children in Spanish-language classes even after they become competent in English. This is in line with the policies of Superintendent of Public Instruction Bill Honig, first elected in 1982, who has insisted on higher standards of instruction and has helped to turn around what was in the 1970s a sharp decline in the quality of California's hitherto superb system of public education.

A few years ago some Californians thought the state was about to become a sort of Third World commonwealth, with a black-Hispanic-Asian majority. But they failed to understand that these three groups would not make up one cohesive bloc just because they were all, once and in different ways, the subjects of discrimination. Most Hispanic and Asian voters, for example, voted to recall Chief Justice Rose Bird in 1986; near-majorities voted for George Deukmejian rather than Tom Bradley; over 40% of Hispanics voted to make English the official state language. California in the 1980s, for all its outre lifestyles, is a success story squarely in the American tradition. Its upwardly mobile new immigrants are no more going to make California the image of the places they left behind than its affluent residents are going to dismantle the government structures and programs which have contributed so much to its private economy's successes. Its supple and strong economy, its capacity and willingness to welcome newcomers and help them rise, its tolerance of eccentricity but insistence on standards, are all in the best of American traditions. What the success and the confidence of California in the 1980s helps to show is what many Americans in the 1960s and 1970s forgot: that America works.

Governor. Elected by the narrowest of margins in 1982—he actually lost among people who went to the polls, and won only because the Republicans took brilliant advantage of a Democratic law allowing anyone to vote absentee—Deukmejian was reelected in 1986, against the same opponent, with a higher percentage than Ronald Reagan has ever won in California. The result cannot be ascribed to racism; after all, in 1982 48% of the voters in a 7% black state voted for a black candidate for governor. It was an endorsement of the decisions Deukmejian has made and the manner in which he has handled the office. Those decisions and that manner have infuriated many other California politicians. In his first year as governor, Deukmejian stopped the Democratic legislature from raising taxes, arguing that economic growth would produce enough revenue; that turned out to be right, and the governor resists tax increases still. Orderly and aloof, a believer in pomp and ceremony, Deukmejian is not close to other officials, not even Republicans though he spent four years as attorney general and 16 years in the legislature in Sacramento; he sticks closely to a tight-knit staff. He professes no grand goals for his second term, but is in a position to continue his experiments with workfare, keep control of the budget (which must be approved by two-thirds votes in the legislature, and hence is usually the product of compromise), and appoint a majority on the Supreme Court. These are just the things—the aloofness, the lack of programs to target, the fact that he turned out to be right—politicians cannot stand in a rival. He spurned those who urged him in 1987 to become a favorite son presidential candidate, but at the same time set up his own organization, Citizens for Common Sense, to help him travel around the country and the world to further his goals.

Sacramento has become a kind of smaller Washington, a city where competent legislators work year-round and actually live, flying back to their districts on weekends, a city full of lawyers and lobbyists who raise most of the campaign money for legislators and in turn are well-positioned to ask for their support. It is at once cynical and competent, full of Democratic politicians and of talented bureaucrats who regard Republican campaign rhetoric as hogwash, but they find themselves unaccustomedly on the defensive. The Democrats' margin in the Assembly is down to 44–36, their hold on several seats is weak, and Speaker Willie Brown is widely unpopular; one Democratic assemblyman was convicted of mail fraud in 1987 in a case involving a lobbyist who provided cash and prostitutes to legislators and another, Speaker Pro-Tem Mike Roos, was under investigation in the same case. Republicans could put on a major drive to capture control in 1988, as another Republican governor did in 1968. The Democrats are in a little better shape in the Senate, controlling it 24–15, with one Independent and several seats held only by incumbents' personal popularity. On the minds of both parties is the opportunity for redistricting after the 1990 Census. Democrats led by Representative Phillip Burton redistricted after the 1970 and 1980 Censuses, to their political profit; Republicans would love to control the governorship and legislature after 1990, and turn the tables. That would have national implications. The Democrats' current 27–18 edge in the House delegation might be reversed, and the incumbency of several nationally prominent Democrats threatened.

The other statewide offices in California have duties of varying importance; politically, their function is to give their occupants the visibility and name identification necessary to make a run for a really important office like governor or senator. Every governor since the 1940s except Reagan has come from one of these offices. Among the current occupants, all Democrats, are several likely candidates. Leo McCarthy, a former Speaker who solved many of Jerry Brown's legislative problems while the governor stayed up late at night and worried about space, is one; he could also run against Senator Pete Wilson in 1988. Attorney General John Van de Kamp, formerly Los Angeles County District Attorney, started his political career by losing a special House election to Barry Goldwater, Jr., in 1969, but he is highly popular now, and could be elected governor in 1990. Gray Davis, with experience in the Assembly, a statewide victory, and as Jerry Brown's chief of staff, can make a plausible case for himself. Only Jesse Unruh seems sure not to run for higher office: he lost to Reagan in the 1970 gubernatorial race, and has made himself a figure of national stature as treasurer.

As for George Deukmejian, despite his plodding, pedestrian style, he is mentioned sometimes by his admirers—including some with top-level Washington experience—as a presidential candidate. But he is not known outside California, and is anchored in his present office by his reluctance to turn it over to his Democratic lieutenant governor.

Senators. The biggest upset in the 1986 Senate elections, coming after one of the shrewdest campaigns of recent times, was the reelection of California's Alan Cranston. After the 1984 campaign, he looked like a goner. He had just finished a humiliating presidential campaign in which his supposedly national stature netted him nothing more than a victory in a 1983 Wisconsin straw poll—and a $2 million debt. He would be 72 on election day 1986 and he looked gaunt and haggard, though he has always been in excellent physical shape, and made himself ridiculous by dying his hair a shade of orange. His views on issues seemed out of line with California: his longtime support of disarmament seemed irrelevant when the contrary policies of Ronald Reagan seemed to be bringing peace, and his longtime support of generous government spending at home seemed foolish to young affluent voters who believe that markets and entrepreneurs, not governments and regulators, produce economic growth. And finally, the Republicans nominated the strongest possible candidate to oppose him, Silicon Valley Representative Ed Zschau, a successful entrepreneur himself, well-financed, tolerant on cultural issues, assertive on foreign policy, market-oriented on economics.

But Cranston was not daunted. In 1984 he set about methodically raising money, phone call by phone call; he eradicated his debt (while Gary Hart and John Glenn, with much better political prospects, could not eradicate theirs) and by 1986 raised another $10 million or so besides. He criss-crossed California's small towns in 1985 and remained on the campaign trail—which these days means in TV studios and raising money personally on the phone and in parties—in 1986. The day after the Republican primary, he had ads on the air attacking Zschau for flip-flopping on issues, and kept a running attack on them through November. At the same time, he used Ansel Adams photographs to identify himself with all the best things in California, and at the last minute sent out 250,000 letters to coastal households on environmental issues. Zschau, a business school graduate who approached campaigning as a management exercise, eventually counterattacked by calling Cranston a liberal and an opponent of the death penalty and tough drug laws. But he never got the footing to get across his own positive message. In the last weeks Ronald Reagan came back twice to California and scathingly attacked Cranston. Some conservatives had been attacking Zschau as too liberal, yet he was not able to carry his home territory on the Peninsula south of San Francisco. Only Zschau could win with a positive message, but Cranston succeeded early in establishing a negative tone. In that negative environment, turnout was low (8% below 1982), and neither candidate got a majority. But Cranston won 50%–47%.

That means another six years for what is already one of California's longest political careers. Though 3 years younger than Ronald Reagan, he has been active in public affairs longer. As a young journalist in the 1930s he published an unexpurgated version of Hitler's *Mein Kampf*, and in the years after World War II he was a founder of the California Democratic Council, the leading liberal political force in the state. Cranston was elected state controller in 1958 and 1962 and U.S. Senator in 1968, and reelected three times—in 1980 with the most votes any senator has ever received in American history. His career has had its ups and downs: he was defeated for controller in the 1966 Reagan landslide, and he won the Senate seat only when the moderate incumbent, Thomas Kuchel, was defeated in the primary by right-winger Max Rafferty. (Was he thinking about running a flip-flop campaign against moderate Republican Kuchel as he did against Zschau?) It is a measure of the strength of the Reagan movement then that even after certain facts about Rafferty's past came out—he sat out World War II with an alleged injury and then threw away his crutches on VJ Day—Cranston still won with only 52%. Six years later, opinion turned, and Cranston might have beaten Reagan had he run.

All this seems implausible when you see Cranston. He is quiet, almost shy, calculating rather than magnetic. He is hard for many to get a handle on: part dreamy idealist, part shrewd political operator—and neither role is very attractive to voters. His manner is quiet and cool; he was an Olympic-class sprinter, though he did not make the team for the 1932 Olympics in Los Angeles or the 1936 Olympics in Berlin, and he still runs and holds records for his age group. Cranston got into politics, in the 1930s and 1940s, as an opponent of fascism and an advocate of world government. He remains more interested in arms control than any other issue. He eagerly supported the nuclear freeze and is always ready to discuss the arcana of disarmament. He favors some form of national service, not necessarily military, for young people. He supports basically Keynesian economics.

But Cranston is also an operator. For 15 years his California colleagues in the Senate were men with rather abstract interests or limited attention spans, and so California interests—farmers, aerospace companies, banks and savings and loans, labor unions, the entertainment industry, the new Silicon Valley industries—went to Cranston when they needed help in the Senate. Cranston delivered. When Lockheed needed a federal loan guarantee to stay in business, Cranston produced the critical vote on the floor by persuading a colleague who later admitted a drinking problem to change his mind. He has no bias against business; he was a successful real estate developer himself. On the Banking Committee he looks out for the state's savings and loans. Perhaps more than anyone else in Washington, Cranston understands how the incredibly productive economy of California works, and who the major players are. That knowledge paid off in 1986, enabling him to match the Republicans' fundraising. In Washington, he has nurtured friendships not so much with the strongest, best-known senators, as with those who are obscure and in some cases of limited talents. That helped to make him a good vote-counter and helped him win the position of Democratic Whip in 1977.

Now he is once again majority rather than minority whip—a position he relished, although Majority Leader Byrd gives him a rather cold shoulder. Byrd has said he will give up the leadership after the 1988 election, but Cranston has not been mentioned as a competitor for the post. But if he has no great boosters for that post, he seems to have no great enemies in the one he has, and he might very well keep it whoever succeeds Byrd. There is a general assumption that Cranston is serving his last term: he turns 78 in 1992. But he has work he wants to do and things he wants to get done, and one lesson of the 1986 campaign is that there is more than one tenant in the political graveyard who underestimated the determination and political skills of Alan Cranston.

One problem Cranston faces confronts every California senator: it's hard to stay in close touch with 26 million people who live 2,600 miles away from where you work (especially when local newscasts in Los Angeles and San Francisco are not going to do anything as un-with-it as presenting 30 seconds of footage of a U.S. Senator). That problem will be faced in 1988 by Senator Pete Wilson. He occupies a seat to which no one has been reelected since 1952; William Knowland, Clair Engle, Pierre Salinger, George Murphy, John Tunney, S.I. Hayakawa—all lost or retired when they could not win. Will Wilson break the string?

With a bland speaking style, a handsome but unremarkable appearance, a common name, Pete Wilson is one of the more anonymous people in American politics. During most of his term one-third of California voters were unable even to rate his performance. He made his pre-Senate career in a media market with only 8% of California's population, and he won his Senate seat mainly because of the unpopularity of his opponent, Jerry Brown. Yet he has had a successful and, by now, long career. He was a competent member of the California Assembly, a body full of skilled legislators; he was a very successful mayor of San Diego, a rapidly growing city that decided under his leadership to control its growth a little more strictly than it had in the past. He was bold enough to endorse Gerald Ford over Ronald Reagan in the 1976 presidential campaign—an endorsement that left Reagan so cool that he could hardly bear to pronounce Wilson's name when he made a speech in his behalf in 1982. But Senator Wilson has been one of the Reagan Administration's more faithful supporters in the Senate. He even showed up one day in pajamas, while recovering from surgery, to cast a decisive vote for the balanced budget constitutional amendment. George Will called him "a rarity: a conservative who understands the discriminating, but vigorous use of government power for conservative purposes."

Unlike Cranston's previous four colleagues, Wilson has spent time and effort on parochial California problems and, with more friends in the administration than Cranston can count on, has had some successes. He was the lead advocate of amendments to the immigration bill allowing in more guestworkers for California growers; he took on chief sponsor Alan Simpson and won. With less success he tried in 1984 to increase tuna tariffs (the U.S. tuna fleet is based in San Diego). He worked with Cranston and against some Republicans on the California wilderness bill and was the chief Senate sponsor of the "wine equity act." On Armed Services, he calls for increased shipbuilding and rehabilitation on the Pacific Coast and generally supports

Caspar Weinberger's Pentagon. On Commerce, a committee assignment he picked up in 1987, he will have an opportunity to vote many regulatory issues (which doesn't hurt when it comes time to raise campaign money), but sometimes he may be pressed to take sides in fights between California interests, as in the fight between cable TV operators and movie studios over copyright law and compensation.

In California politicians were lining up in late 1986 to run against Wilson for what many regard as this jinxed seat. He is not likely to have a serious Republican primary opponent, although there are mutterings on the right that he is dangerously moderate. Democrats named as possible opponents include Lieutenant Governor Leo McCarthy, Representative Robert Matsui, Attorney General John Van de Kamp, and San Francisco Mayor Dianne Feinstein (who must leave that office in 1987); Secretary of State March Fong Eu said she was running in early 1987. Their party's stands on national issues are a mixed blessing, and Wilson in early 1987 had already raised $2.9 million. But Wilson so far lacks that strong identification with one or two issues which can define a senator for his public and provide him the strength to win in foul years and fair.

Presidential politics. California has become a reliable Republican state in national elections— in many political strategists' views. Others would only say that it comes close to matching the nationwide percentages: in the close contests of 1960, 1968, and 1976 California ended up Republican each time by small margins. Culturally California may be a harbinger of trends; on election day it often knows the result before it votes, but that doesn't produce any bandwagon effect: California more often than not has produced a higher than average percentage for the *loser* of the presidential election.

The great days of California's presidential primaries—when its conservative Republicans picked Barry Goldwater in 1964 and its liberal Democrats Robert Kennedy and George McGovern in 1968 and 1972—are now part of the distant past. Once both parties' electorates were extreme in the national context, the Republicans on the right and the Democrats on the left; now both are more normal. The timing which once worked for California now usually works against: recent nominations have been decided by the time its last-in-the-nation primary is held. Thus Gary Hart's good showing in the popular vote and excellent showing in the delegate count here in 1984 availed him nothing. Governor George Deukmejian in early 1987 was under pressure from Democrats to make the primary earlier and from some Republicans to become a favorite son candidate himself. But with the steadfastness typical of his career he spurned both ideas.

Congressional districting. California's House delegation of 45 is the largest since New York had that many districts in the 1940s; it is lopsidedly (27-18) Democratic. That is attributed to the redistricting plans drawn up by the late San Francisco Representative Phillip Burton and Michael Berman, an aide to Representative Henry Waxman and brother of former Assembly Majority Leader and now U.S. Representative Howard Berman. For this the Republicans have themselves at least partly to blame; in early 1981 they turned down overtures for a bipartisan incumbent-protection plan on the dim hope that they could get Hispanic assemblymen to support their plan. Then the Republicans turned to referenda, and failed again. They won at the polls in 1982, only to have Burton draw another plan before Jerry Brown left office; their effort to create a commission of retired judges to draw the district lines was turned down by the voters in 1984. The history of redistricting in California tells us, in any case, that the Democrats' advantage will dissipate over the 10 years the Burton plans are in effect, just as the Republicans' own advantage did in the 1950s and the Democrats' advantages did in the 1960s and 1970s. The fights of the 1980s are history anyway, and the talk in Sacramento is now over the redistricting fights of the 1990s, although the Republicans in late 1986 filed a last-gasp lawsuit against the current plan.

In the meantime, almost every House member has a safe seat and the ability to accumulate seniority and concentrate on legislation. And, though they diverge widely on many issues, California Democrats and Republicans do sometimes cooperate, and effectively, as in their continuing battle against Interior Secretary Donald Hodel to limit or prevent offshore oil drilling on the California coast.

The People: Est. Pop. 1986: 26,981,000; Pop. 1980: 23,667,902, up 14% 1980–86 and 18.5% 1970–80; 11.19% of U.S. total, 1st largest. 23% with 1–3 yrs. col., 20% with 4+ yrs. col.; 11.4% below poverty level. Single ancestry: 8% English, 5% German, 3% Irish, 2% Italian, 1% French, Russian, Portuguese, Polish, Swedish, Dutch, Scottish, Norwegian. Households (1980): 69% family, 37% with children, 55% married couples; 44.1% housing units rented; median monthly rent: $253; median house value: $84,700. Voting age pop. (1980): 17,278,944; 16% Spanish origin, 7% Black, 5% Asian origin, 1% American Indian. Registered voters (1986): 12,833,920; 6,524,496 D (51%), 4,912,581 R (36%); 183,798 unaffiliated (9%), 245,880 minor parties (2%).

1986 Share of Federal Tax Burden: $91,441,000,000; 12.16% of U.S. total, largest.

1986 Share of Federal Expenditures

	Total		Non-Defense		Defense	
Total Expend	$100,860m	(12.15%)	$60,556m	(10.09%)	$40,304m	(17.53%)
St/Lcl Grants	11,291m	(10.03%)	11,284m	(10.03%)	7m	(6.31%)
Salary/Wages	15,052m	(12.48%)	5,396m	(9.19%)	9,656m	(15.60%)
Pymts to Indiv	36,960m	(10.13%)	34,327m	(9.89%)	2,633m	(14.82%)
Procurement	35,228m	(17.13%)	7,223m	(12.99%)	28,005m	(18.66%)
Research/Other	2,328m	(8.73%)	2,325m	(8.73%)	3m	(9.19%)

Political Lineup: Governor, George Deukmejian (R); Lt. Gov., Leo T. McCarthy (D); Secy. of State, March Fong Eu (D); Atty. Gen., John Van De Camp (D); Treasurer, Jesse M. Unruh (D); Controller, Gray Davis (D). State Senate, 40 (23 D and 16 R); State Assembly, 80 (44 D and 36 R). Senators, Alan Cranston (D) and Pete Wilson (R). Representatives, 45 (27 D and 18 R).

1984 Presidential Vote			1980 Presidential Vote		
Reagan (R)	5,467,009	(58%)	Reagan (R)	4,524,835	(53%)
Mondale (D)	3,922,519	(41%)	Carter (D)	3,083,652	(36%)
			Anderson (I)	739,832	(9%)

1984 Democratic Presidential Primary			1984 Republican Presidential Primary		
Hart	6,606,198	(38%)	Reagan	1,874,897	(100%)
Mondale	6,091,690	(35%)			
Jackson	3,589,248	(21%)			
Three others	927,795	(5%)			

GOVERNOR

Gov. George Deukmejian (R)

Elected 1982, term expires 1991; b. June 6, 1928, Menands, NY; home, Long Beach; Sienna Col., B.A. 1949, St. Johns U. Law Sch., J.D. 1952; Episcopalian; married (Gloria).

Career: Practicing atty., 1952–53, 1958–62; Army, 1953–55; Texaco Inc., 1955–58; CA Assembly, 1963–67; CA Senate, 1967–79; CA Atty. General, 1979–83.

Office: State Capitol Bldg., Sacramento 95814, 916-445-2841.

Election Results

1986 gen.	George Deukmejian (R)	4,506,601	(61%)
	Tom Bradley (D)	2,781,714	(37%)
1986 prim.	George Deukmejian (R)	1,927,290	(94%)
	William H. R. Clark (R)	132,126	(6%)
1982 gen.	George Deukmejian (R)	3,881,014	(49%)
	Tom Bradley (D)	3,787,669	(48%)

SENATORS

Sen. Alan Cranston (D)

Elected 1968, seat up 1992; b. June 19, 1914, Palo Alto; home, Los Angeles; Pomona Col., U. of Mexico, Stanford U., B.A. 1936; Protestant; married (Norma).

Career: Foreign Correspondent, Intl. News Srvc., 1936–38; Lobbyist, Common Council for American Unity, 1939; Army, WWII; Real estate business, 1947–67; Pres., United World Federalists, 1949–52; State Comptroller of CA, 1958–66.

Offices: 112 HSOB 20510, 202-224-3553. Also 45 Polk St., San Francisco 94102, 415-556-8449; 5757 W. Century Blvd., #515, Los Angeles 90045, 213-215-2186; and 880 Front St., #5S31, San Diego 92188, 619-293-5014.

Committees: *Majority Whip. Banking, Housing and Urban Affairs* (2d of 11 D). Subcommittees: Housing and Urban Affairs (Chairman); Securities. *Foreign Relations* (4th of 11 D). Subcommittees: Near Eastern and South Asian Affairs; East Asian and Pacific Affairs (Chairman); Western Hemisphere and Peace Corps Affairs. *Veterans' Affairs* (Chairman). *Select Committee on Intelligence* (7th of 8 D).

Group Ratings

	ADA	ACLU	COPE	CFA	LCV	ACU	NTU	NSI	COC	CEI
1986	95	92	91	67	98	10	38	0	32	31
1985	100	—	92	87	—	4	31	—	21	—

National Journal Ratings

	1986 LIB — 1986 CONS		1985 LIB — 1985 CONS	
Economic	85% —	8%	77% —	19%
Social	92% —	0%	88% —	0%
Foreign	75% —	0%	88% —	0%

Key Votes

1) Ease Gun Cont	AGN	5) Grm-Rdmn Def Red	AGN	9) Rehnquist Nom	AGN
2) Immig Reform	AGN	6) Contra Aid	AGN	10) Tax Reform	FOR
3) Lmt Text Imp	AGN	7) SDI Funding	AGN	11) Drug Death Pen	FOR
4) Aid Tobac Ind	FOR	8) Lmt PAC Contrib	AGN	12) S Africa Sanc	FOR

Election Results

1986 general	Alan Cranston (D)	3,646,672	(50%)	($11,037,707)
	Ed Zschau (R)	3,541,804	(47%)	($11,781,316)
1986 primary	Alan Cranston (D)	1,807,244	(81%)	
	Charles Greene (D).................	165,594	(7%)	
	John Hancock Abbott (D)	124,218	(6%)	
	Two others (D)	142,193	(6%)	
1980 general	Alan Cranston (D)	4,705,399	(57%)	($2,823,462)
	Paul Gann (R).....................	3,093,426	(37%)	($1,705,523)

Campaign Contributions and Expenditures

1985-86		Direct Cont. 1985-86		PACS Breakdown 1985-86			
Receipts	$10,851,596	Indiv.	$8,874,482	Corp.	$360,332	T/M/H	$262,357
Expend.	$11,037,707	Party	$19,523	Labor	$302,292	Agr.	$25,600
Unspent	$11,593	PACS	$1,373,466	Ideo	$380,874	CWOS	$42,011
		Cand.	$375,250				

Sen. Pete Wilson (R)

Elected 1982, seat up 1988; b. Aug. 23, 1933, Lake Forest, IL; home, San Diego; Yale U., B.A. 1955, U. of CA at Berkeley, J.D. 1962; Protestant; married (Gayle).

Career: USMC, 1955–58; Practicing atty., 1963–66; CA Assembly, 1966–71, Minor. Whip, 1967–69; Mayor of San Diego, 1971–83.

Offices: 720 HSOB 20510, 202-224-3841. Also Fed. Bldg., 450 Golden Gate Ave., San Francisco 94102, 415-556-4307; 11111 Santa Monica Blvd., #915, Los Angeles 90025, 213-209-6765; Fed. Bldg., 1130 O St., Rm. 4015, Fresno 93721, 209-487-5727; and 840 Newport Center Dr., #240, Newport Beach 92660, 714-720-1474.

Committees: *Agriculture, Nutrition, and Forestry* (8th of 9 R). Subcommittees: Agricultural Production and Stabilization of Prices; Agricultural Research, Conservation, Forestry, and General Legislation; Domestic and Foreign Marketing and Production Promotion. *Armed Services* (6th of 9 R). Subcommittees: Conventional Forces and Alliance Defense; Manpower and Personnel (Ranking Member); Strategic Forces and Nuclear Defense. *Commerce, Science and Transportation* (8th of 9 R). Subcommittees: Communications; Foreign Commerce and Tourism; Science, Technology and Space. *Special Committee on Aging* (5th of 9 R). *Joint Economic Committee.* Subcommittees: National Security and Economics; Economic Goals and Intergovernmental Policy; Education and Health.

Group Ratings

	ADA	ACLU	COPE	CFA	LCV	ACU	NTU	NSI	COC	CEI
1986	5	21	8	14	42	83	52	100	89	80
1985	10	—	9	13	—	77	66	—	93	—

National Journal Ratings

	1986 LIB — 1986 CONS		1985 LIB — 1985 CONS	
Economic	16%	— 76%	0%	— 86%
Social	37%	— 61%	45%	— 52%
Foreign	30%	— 65%	21%	— 78%

Key Votes

1) Ease Gun Cont	FOR	5) Grm-Rdmn Def Red	FOR	9) Rehnquist Nom	FOR
2) Immig Reform	FOR	6) Contra Aid	FOR	10) Tax Reform	FOR
3) Lmt Text Imp	AGN	7) SDI Funding	FOR	11) Drug Death Pen	AGN
4) Aid Tobac Ind	FOR	8) Lmt PAC Contrib	FOR	12) S Africa Sanc	FOR

Election Results

1982 general	Pete Wilson (R).....................	4,022,565	(52%)	($7,082,651)
	Edmund G. Brown, Jr. (D)............	3,494,968	(45%)	($5,367,931)
1982 primary	Pete Wilson (R).....................	851,292	(38%)	
	Paul N. (Pete) McCloskey, Jr. (R).......	577,267	(26%)	
	Barry Goldwater, Jr. (R)..............	408,308	(18%)	
	Robert K. Dornan (R)................	181,970	(8%)	
	Maureen E. Reagan (R)..............	118,326	(5%)	
1976 general	S.I. Hayakawa (R)	3,748,973	(50%)	($1,184,624)
	John Tunney (D)....................	3,502,862	(47%)	($1,940,988)

Campaign Contributions and Expenditures

1981-82		Direct Cont. 1981-82		PACS Breakdown			
Receipts	$7,190,985	Indiv.	$5,894,693	Agr	$127,944	Ideo	$73,115
Expend.	$7,082,651	Party	$28,796	Bus	$855,795	Lbr	$16,450
Unspent	$108,080	PACS	$1,182,432	Hlth	$32,850	Prof	$20,750

FIRST DISTRICT

The north coast of California is a world unto itself, sealed off from the rest of the United States and in most places from the Pacific itself by various ridges of the Coast Range: the people here tend to cluster in fertile inland valleys. This is wet country, with some of the highest rainfall in the United States—higher as you get toward Oregon—a moist, rainy land of massive trees and rounded mountains, of small towns with filigreed Victorian houses and lumber mills. The Redwood Empire some call it, after the giant trees which grow up and down the coast, nourished most of the year by drizzle and fog. The first white settlers here were Russians, who left little behind them but interesting place names (the Russian River, Sebastopol). They were followed, in the years after the California Gold Rush, by lumbermen and fishermen. By the late 19th century great fortunes had been made in lumber from the redwoods and Douglas firs, as the Victorian mansions still standing in Eureka attest. This Redwood Empire, beginning in the south around Santa Rosa (and, over a hill, in Napa) and continuing all the way up to the Oregon border, forms California's 1st Congressional District.

It is as distinctive politically as it is physically. Its towns appear so quintessentially Middle American that Hollywood directors have often used them as sets for movies, but the population is more diverse. There are the descendants of original settlers, many of them lumbermen and farmers still, and there are veterans of the counterculture, attracted by the scenery and the unaffected cultural atmosphere. There are people who tend the vineyards and wineries in the Sonoma and Alexander Valleys. And of course there are the lumber folk in the northern part of the district. In the 1980s the rural and small town interior of California has become more Republican because of the influx of conservatively-minded families from the big metropolitan areas. But in the same years the more liberal and even radical migrants to the coastal counties have made them more Democratic. In the close 1986 Senate election, Democrat Alan Cranston carried every coastal county from the Big Sur south of San Francisco north to Eureka. But in the interior, aside from the Sacramento area, he carried only one county and ran far behind Ed Zschau in most.

This is a sharp reversal of political tradition, and one which has benefited 1st District Representative Doug Bosco. Throughout his career he seems to have had the knack of being at the right place at the right time. In the 1960s he left New York (which has been losing congressional districts) for school on the West Coast (which has been gaining); in the 1970s he moved to Sonoma County, near the coast north of San Francisco, ran for Congress and lost, and was elected to the Assembly in 1978; in 1982, he ran for Congress just as the 1st District was moving away, after 20 years, from the politics of Republican Representative Don Clausen. He had the good fortune to be running in a recession year, when his support for the lumber and fishing industries was particularly appreciated in the northern part of the district, and when Democrats were ballyhooing the nuclear freeze, a surefire way to enthuse the counterculture migrants in the south.

Bosco has a mixed record and a demonstrated ability to please the rather different parts of his district. Coming from Sonoma County, he has wooed the Redwood Empire, and his seats on the Public Works and Merchant Marine Committees have helped. Timing again helped: the California wilderness bill is a divisive issue in this district, but it passed (with Bosco's support) in his first year in the House and is no longer around to bother him. Now Bosco seems to concentrate on local issues—Sonoma County sewage, Cache Creek and Clear Lake flood control, Eel River flood control, Noyo harbor dredging—and only occasionally surfacing on national issues, as he did with his much-criticized protectionist proposal to require that 50% of the steel in offshore drilling rigs be produced in this country. But then neither the old fishermen nor the new migrants want to see drilling rigs in their part of the Pacific anyway. Again Bosco's timing has been brilliant: in 1984 and 1986 he got the biggest percentages any Redwood Empire congressman has in 20 years.

The People: Pop. 1980: 525,986, up 33.1% 1970–80. Households (1980): 69% family, 35% with children, 57% married couples; 36.4% housing units rented; median monthly rent: $233; median house value: $73,500. Voting age pop. (1980): 390,186; 5% Spanish origin, 2% American Indian, 1% Asian origin, 1% Black.

1984 Presidential Vote:
Reagan (R)	134,358	(52%)
Mondale (D)	119,330	(46%)

Rep. Douglas H. Bosco (D)

Elected 1982; b. July 28, 1946, New York, NY; home, Occidental; Willamette U., B.A. 1968, J.D. 1971; Roman Catholic; single.

Career: Practicing atty., 1971–78; CA Assembly, 1978–82.

Offices: 408 CHOB 20515, 202-225-3311. Also Fed. Bldg., Ste. 329, 777 Sonoma Ave., Santa Rosa 95405, 707-525-4235; and Eureka Inn, Ste. 216, 7th and F Sts., Eureka 95501, 707-445-2055.

Committees: *Merchant Marine and Fisheries* (17th of 25 D). Subcommittees: Fish and Wildlife Conservation and the Environment; Oceanography; Panama Canal and Outer Continental Shelf. *Public Works and Transportation* (12th of 32 D). Subcommittees: Aviation; Surface Transportation; Water Resources.

Group Ratings

	ADA	ACLU	COPE	CFA	LCV	ACU	NTU	NSI	COC	CEI
1986	70	76	78	58	77	15	30	10	23	27
1985	65	—	72	58	—	19	37	—	33	—

National Journal Ratings

	1986 LIB — 1986 CONS		1985 LIB — 1985 CONS	
Economic	79% —	21%	64% —	35%
Social	69% —	31%	73% —	23%
Foreign	70% —	29%	67% —	32%

Key Votes

1) Lmt Cln Water Act	AGN	5) Retain Gun Cont	AGN	9) Aid Angola Reb	AGN
2) Rpl Tobac Sub	AGN	6) Contra Aid	—	10) Tax Reform	AGN
3) Grm-Rdmn Def Red	FOR	7) Lmt Text Imp	FOR	11) S Africa Sanc	FOR
4) Ban Polygraph	FOR	8) Limit SDI	FOR	12) Immig Reform	FOR

Election Results

1986 general	Douglas H. Bosco (D).................	138,174	(68%)	($219,608)
	Floyd G. Sampson (R).................	54,436	(27%)	
	Elden McFarland (Peace & Freedom).....	12,149	(6%)	($9,421)
1986 primary	Douglas H. Bosco (D).................	55,709	(75%)	
	Mike Keopf (D)......................	10,497	(14%)	
	Richard M. Davis (D)..................	8,572	(11%)	
1984 general	Douglas H. Bosco (D).................	157,037	(62%)	($215,009)
	David Redick (R)....................	95,186	(38%)	($48,332)

Campaign Contributions and Expenditures

1985-86		Direct Cont. 1985-86		PACS Breakdown 1985-86			
Receipts	$197,849	Indiv.	$24,210	Corp.	$26,811	T/M/H	$23,050
Expend.	$219,608	PACS	$99,222	Labor	$42,150	Agr.	$2,000
Unspent	$653	Cand.	$6,978	Ideo.	$4,711	CWOS	$500

SECOND DISTRICT

The great valley of California—the bowl of almost perfectly flat land, divided into geometric parcels by land but only within the limits established by the ranges of velvetly brown and green mountains—extends not only south from Sacramento but north. This Sacramento Valley is less heavily populated than the Central Valley in the south, and does not cultivate so many different kinds of agricultural products. But it is still wonderfully productive. And, in contrast to the San Joaquin Valley to the south, it has a plentiful supply of what may be California's most precious and often scarcest resource: water. The Sacramento Valley is hemmed in on three sides by mountains: the Coast Range on the west, the Sierra Nevada on the east, and the gigantic volcanoes, Mount Lassen and Mount Shasta, on the north. The mountains get plenty of rainfall that drops from the moisture-laden clouds that sweep in from the warm Pacific, and from their slopes flow the waters that become the Sacramento River and the waters are distributed over an ingenious set of canals and aqueducts to the Central Valley and the Los Angeles Basin, where they sustain the most productive part of western civilization. The Sacramento Valley has always guarded its water jealously and in the days before one-person-one-vote it had enough seats in the California Senate to veto water decisions it didn't like; today it still retains a plentiful supply for its own use.

For years the Sacramento Valley was lightly populated. But since the mid-1970s it has been one of the fastest growing parts of California. Young people from the big metropolitan areas came up here to be closer to nature; young families came here to raise their children in a small town atmosphere, where people still go to neighborhood churches and you don't have to worry about drugs in the schools.

The 2d Congressional District of California occupies most of the Sacramento Valley north of the state capital. It takes in the sparsely populated agricultural lands in the western part of the valley, and the more thickly populated land that starts sloping gently up toward the Sierras on the east. The district also includes, west over a small range of mountains, part of the wine-growing Napa Valley, including the mansion that appears under the credits of *Falcon Crest*.

Partisan traditions here vary: some counties are heavily Republican, some heavily Democratic. But all parts of the district are moving toward the Republicans. Turnout here zoomed in 1982, as new voters came out to oppose the gun control referendum and incidentally to vote against Tom Bradley, who supported it; turnout was down in 1986, but more than 70% who did vote voted for Governor George Deukmejian and against Bradley. Most of this area was represented for years by Democrat Harold Johnson, who specialized in bringing in public works projects into the area. But Johnson was defeated in 1980 by a Republican Eugene Chappie, a salty legislative veteran who himself retired in 1986 "before they have to issue me a wheelchair."

The new congressman, Wally Herger, has deep roots in the southern part of the district, only 20 miles from Sacramento, but represents aptly the values of the new residents of the area. In his early 40s, he has eight children; he is a businessman and rancher who was elected to the Assembly in 1978 as a "Proposition 13 baby," and has been part of the New Right group there. He had tough primary opposition from the mayor of Redding, far to the north, and in the general election from a county supervisor also from Shasta County. He has every chance to make this a safe seat, and what may be hardest for him is to choose between the traditional approach for Sacramento Valley congressmen—funneling in every possible federal dollar—and adherence to his own low-tax, low-spending principles. His success in winning a seat on the Agriculture Committee suggests he will follow the second approach in at least some respects.

The People: Pop. 1980: 526,009, up 34.2% 1970–80. Households (1980): 72% family, 37% with children, 62% married couples; 34.7% housing units rented; median monthly rent: $186; median house value: $58,100. Voting age pop. (1980): 384,601; 5% Spanish origin, 2% American Indian, 1% Asian origin, 1% Black.

1984 Presidential Vote:
Reagan (R)	150,641	(63%)
Mondale (D)	83,085	(35%)

Rep. Wally Herger (R)

Elected 1986; b. May 20, 1945, Yuba City; home, Rio Oso; American River Commun. Col., A.A. 1968; CA St. U., 1968–69; Mormon; married (Pamela).

Career: Rancher, Owner, Herger Gas, Inc. 1969–80; CA Assembly, 1981–86.

Offices: 1630 LHOB 20515, 202-225-3076. Also 20 Declaration Dr., Ste. 10, Chico 95991, 916-893-8363; 2400 Washington Ave., Ste. 410, Redding 96001, 916-246-5172; and 951 Live Oak Blvd., Ste. 10, Yuba City 95991, 916-673-7182.

Committees: *Agriculture* (16th of 17 R). Subcmtees: Cotton, Rice and Sugar; Domestic Marketing, Consumer Relations, and Nutrition; Forests, Family Farms and Energy. *Merchant Marine and Fisheries* (16th of 17 R). Subcmtees: Coast Guard and Navigation; Fish and Wildlife; Panama Canal and Outer Continental Shelf.

Group Ratings and Key Votes: Newly Elected

Election Results

1986 general	Wally Herger (R)	109,758	(58%)	($628,361)
	Stephen C. Swendiman (D)	74,602	(40%)	($244,097)
1986 primary	Wally Herger (R)	47,123	(72%)	
	Howard D Kirkpatrick (R).	15,373	(24%)	
	Robert B. Wareham (R)	2,896	(4%)	
1984 general	Eugene A. Chappie (R)	158,679	(69%)	($366,566)
	Harry W. Cozad (D)	69,793	(31%)	($38,449)

Campaign Contributions and Expenditures

1985-86		Direct Cont. 1985-86		PACS Breakdown 1985-86			
Receipts	$646,951	Indiv.	$298,455	Corp.	$59,622	T/M/H	$67,662
Expend.	$628,361	Party	$10,466	Labor	$4,750	Agr.	$9,330
Unspent	$18,589	PACs	$194,484	Ideo.	$45,420	CWOS	$7,700
		Cand.	$67,377				

THIRD DISTRICT

Sacramento is perhaps America's purest political city. Even more than Washington, it depends on politics and government for its livelihood. And more than Washington, it operates out of the day-to-day scrutiny of the constituents it serves. This frontier outpost burst suddenly into the American consciousness when gold was discovered at Sutter's mill in 1849. In the Gold Rush, it was the natural choice to be California's capital, halfway between the Mother Lode country in the foothills of the Sierras and San Francisco Bay, and in the middle of California's vast valley. Sacramento has been an important agricultural and food processing center, like the other cities in the valley; but government has been its main business. California's gleaming Capitol is as impressive as any in the nation; its state government generally is conducted with a competence and often with an esprit that should be the envy of most other governments in the world.

And, in the past few decades—and despite the intentions of Ronald Reagan—it has gotten vastly bigger. In the 1940s Sacramento was a hangout for a few fabled lobbyists; in the 1980s it is headquarters for a vast army of lobbyists, lawyers, and consultants exceeded in size only by those in Washington, D.C. California's highly competent legislators and their large staffs in effect live year-round in Sacramento, although they usually keep legal residences elsewhere; so good a job do they do in keeping in touch with both constituents and lobbyists that the best way to get elected to the legislature now is to have been a staffer. Legislators control much of the flow of information to their constituents through free mail and expensive campaigns, and so Sacramento has become an almost self-contained engine of government, situated in a huge valley, serving primarily two hugely populous metropolitan areas situated in niches between mountains and ocean. In the process it has grown, from a medium-sized provincial city to a metropolitan area that can claim, with the right boundaries, one million residents, the site since spring 1987 of a new trolley system that will reach 18 miles into the suburbs, the home of a major league sports team, albeit not a winning one, the Sacramento Kings.

Oddly, as government has gotten bigger, Sacramento has become more Republican. Sacramento resisted Governor Ronald Reagan in 1966 and 1970, but by 1980 it was voting for President Reagan, and the Sacramento area voted for George Deukmejian over Thomas Bradley in 1982 and 1986. Civil servants and the *Sacramento Bee* once made Sacramento Democratic. But the increasing strength of the private sector here, growing affluence, and in-migration from elsewhere have helped Republicans. Since Proposition 13 in 1978 they seem to have soured on the same big government which is the foundation of their local economy.

The 3d Congressional District of California consists of the main part of the city of Sacramento and its suburbs east of the Sacramento River and south of the American River. It includes the Capitol, downtown, and most of the more affluent parts of the Sacramento area. Historically, it is heavily Democratic; in recent elections, less so. The congressman from the 3d, Robert Matsui, is a Democrat, first elected in a close contest in 1978, returned easily since then. Matsui is a generally loyal member of the Democratic Caucus, with strong liberal records on most issues. He is also a sharp practical politician, aware of the needs of California interests, capable of raising money, and receptive to new ideas.

One of those new ideas is rate-lowering-preference-cutting tax reform, and Matsui was in a position to do something about it. He is a member of the Ways and Means Committee who has been careful to work closely with Chairman Dan Rostenkowski; as a result, he played a major role in shaping the House's version of tax reform in 1985 and 1986. It is not the first time Matsui has been found on the right committee at the right time; he was on Energy and Commerce in 1981 and 1982, when it was stopping much of the deregulatory initiatives of the early Reagan administration.

Matsui is not entirely content, even with a safe seat and a first-rate committee assignment. He wants to play a leading role in the redefinition of American liberalism—and perhaps already has. Seemingly diffident, Matsui has contributed to American public life some of the celebrated virtues of the Samurai: he is skilled, tough and principled. A party-line Democrat on most issues, Matsui, who spent his infancy and early childhood in a Japanese-American detention camp, also thoughtfully appreciates the strengths and virtues of American society. For this reason, perhaps, Matsui, a thoroughly professional politician, is personally committed to redress for Japanese–Americans who in 1942 were clear victims of racial hysteria and economic expropriation and who spent four years in desert internment camps.

Matsui is considered a possible candidate for the Senate in 1988, for the seat held by Republican Pete Wilson. There will likely be a primary fight for the Democratic nomination, but Matsui if he runs, and he has given every indication he might, is likely to be one of the top contenders. The interesting question for the 3d District then becomes whether the Republicans will, as in 1978, make a serious attempt to win this district. In their favor is the underlying partisan trend, but against them is the political savvy of the Democrats, like veteran state Senator Leroy Greene who beat back Republican Sandy Smoley, Matsui's 1978 opponent, in her attempt to unseat him in 1986.

The People: Pop. 1980: 525,774, up 21.5% 1970–80. Households (1980): 67% family, 35% with children, 53% married couples; 41.2% housing units rented; median monthly rent: $217; median house value: $67,100. Voting age pop. (1980): 390,354; 8% Spanish origin, 7% Black, 6% Asian origin, 1% American Indian.

1984 Presidential Vote:

Reagan (R) 139,564	(55%)
Mondale (D) 112,714	(44%)

Rep. Robert T. Matsui (D)

Elected 1978; b. Sept. 17, 1941, Sacramento; home, Sacramento; U. of CA, A.B. 1963, Hastings Col. of Law, U. of CA, J.D. 1966; United Methodist; married (Doris).

Career: Practicing atty., 1967–78; Sacramento City Cncl., 1971–78.

Offices: 2419 RHOB 20515, 202-225-7163. Also 8058 Fed. Bldg., 650 Capitol Mall, Sacramento 95814, 916-440-3543.

Committees: *Ways and Means* (14th of 23 D). Subcommittees: Public Assistance; Trade. *Select Committee on Narcotics Abuse and Control* (8th of 15 D).

Group Ratings

	ADA	ACLU	COPE	CFA	LCV	ACU	NTU	NSI	COC	CEI
1986	95	90	90	92	82	5	25	0	17	16
1985	90	—	89	75	—	5	29	—	18	—

National Journal Ratings

	1986 LIB — 1986 CONS		1985 LIB — 1985 CONS	
Economic	74% —	23%	89% —	0%
Social	89% —	0%	85% —	0%
Foreign	80% —	0%	75% —	21%

Key Votes

1) Lmt Cln Water Act	AGN	5) Retain Gun Cont	FOR	9) Aid Angola Reb	AGN
2) Rpl Tobac Sub	AGN	6) Contra Aid	AGN	10) Tax Reform	FOR
3) Grm-Rdmn Def Red	AGN	7) Lmt Text Imp	AGN	11) S Africa Sanc	FOR
4) Ban Polygraph	FOR	8) Limit SDI	FOR	12) Immig Reform	FOR

Election Results

1986 general	Robert T. Matsui (D)	158,709	(76%)	($563,150)
	Lowell Landowski (R).	50,265	(24%)	($3,043)
1986 primary	Robert T. Matsui (D)	73,337	(100%)	
1984 general	Robert T. Matsui (D)	131,369	(100%)	($233,661)

Campaign Contributions and Expenditures

1985-86		**Direct Cont. 1985-86**		**PACS Breakdown 1985-86**			
Receipts	$659,793	Indiv.	$300,853	Corp.	$121,325	T/M/H	$98,347
Expend.	$563,150	PACS	$305,758	Labor	$51,025	Agr.	$11,950
Unspent	$374,464			Ideo.	$11,411	CWOS	$121,325

FOURTH DISTRICT

The low, flat delta lands where the Sacramento and San Joaquin Rivers empty into San Francisco Bay; the rich fruit-growing land of the lower Sacramento Valley; the northern and southern suburbs of Sacramento, and a part of the city itself—these make up the 4th Congressional District of California. The delta is the district's central geographical focus, although it is scarcely inhabited: the river byways bend around curves and irrigate rice fields, whose farmers wonder if the California water system is going to divert too much water from the delta. The delta and the 4th District generally are separated from the weather—and the cultural ambience—of the San Francisco Bay area by a ridge of mountains only barely interrupted by the river making its way to the sea. The farmlands and suburbs here are one part of California with large numbers of young families with children, a kind of Middle America set off near Baghdad. The district's major university, California at Davis, started as an agricultural school, became a countercultural haven for a time, and now is quieter again, its bike paths thronged with bicycles.

The 4th District is and has been Democratic country for many years. Half its population is in Sacramento County, traditionally heavily Democratic though recently less so; the 4th District has some of the lower income, less elite parts of the county—the industrial suburbs north of the American River, the heavily Mexican-American towns on the flatlands across the Sacramento River from the city's historic landing. Davis and the agricultural area around it are Democratic; so is the area farther west, around Fairfield and Suisun.

This Sacramento area district is represented, appropriately, by a man who is literally a legislator's legislator, and who was voted the best in the 45-member California House delegation in *California* magazine. Vic Fazio used to serve in the California Assembly; before that, he was an Assembly staffer and founder of the estimable *California Journal*. That means that he was learning the legislative business from some of the best teachers in the country, in one of the best schools. He won the 4th District House seat in 1978, when incumbent Robert Leggett prudently retired (it was revealed that he had been maintaining two families for years, and he nearly lost in 1976). And Fazio brought to Washington the lessons he learned in Sacramento.

He is in a good position to apply them, as chairman of the Legislative Appropriations Subcommittee and as a high-ranking member of the Budget Committee. The Legislative Subcommittee is an obscure body, which controls the budgets of House members, committees, and their staffs. It has a lot to say about what work can get done by whom and under which circumstances. It also handles the politically difficult matter of the congressional salary. Fazio got an increase voted in the lame duck session in 1982—earning himself credit from grateful members and party leaders—and is the architect of the current system, under which Congress gets a raise unless it votes early in the session to deny itself one. The House hoped to avoid a vote in early 1987, but when the Senate voted the raise down, Speaker Jim Wright promised there would be a roll-call vote—but it came beyond the deadline and the raise became law with a large majority of House members in the politically advantageous position of being recorded against.

On Appropriations, Fazio also serves on the Energy and Water Development Subcommittee—a body more politically useful to him, considering how much water flows into, around, down, and under his district, and he attends to Travis Air Force Base and other local problems. On Budget, Fazio tends to go along with Chairman William Gray, who in turn works closely with the House leadership. He is respected by colleagues and appreciated as a member who can and will solve political problems for them, and give them the credit.

Fazio did, however, have one major disappointment after the 1986 campaign: he was not chosen as chairman of the House Democrats' campaign committee. Many members thought he was better prepared than anyone else to step quickly into the shoes of Tony Coelho, who vastly increased the committee's fundraising capabilities and did a brilliant job of challenging Republicans. But two Californians in a row may have been too much. Fazio managed Coelho's successful campaign for Democratic Whip, the number three position, and then Speaker Jim Wright turned and appointed Beryl Anthony of Arkansas to head the campaign committee. Fazio did not react bitterly, and he is likely to remain busy with his other positions.

Back home the major issue Republicans raise against him every two years is the congressional pay raise—so far, in this district filled with government employees, without much success.

The People: Pop. 1980: 525,764, up 34.3% 1970–80. Households (1980): 73% family, 42% with children, 60% married couples; 38.5% housing units rented; median monthly rent: $216; median house value: $64,200. Voting age pop. (1980): 374,278; 10% Spanish origin, 5% Black, 4% Asian origin, 1% American Indian.

1984 Presidential Vote:

Reagan (R) 127,252	(56%)
Mondale (D) 96,775	(43%)

Rep. Vic Fazio (D)

Elected 1978; born Oct. 11, 1942, Winchester, MA; home, West Sacramento; Union Col., B.A. 1965, CA State U.; Episcopalian; married (Judy).

Career: Cong. and Legis. Consultant, 1966–75; Cofounder, *The California Journal*; Consultant and Asst. to CA Assembly Spkr., 1971; CA Assembly, 1975–78.

Offices: 2433 RHOB 20515, 202-225-5716. Also 4811 Chippendale Dr., Ste. 503, Sacramento 95841, 916-484-4174; 844B Union Ave., Fairfield 94533, 707-426-4333; and 117 W. Main St., Woodland 95695, 916-666-5521.

Committees: *Appropriations* (22d of 35 D). Subcommittees: Energy and Water Development; Legislative (Chairman); Military Construction. *Budget* (9th of 21 D). Task Forces: Budget Process; Community and Natural Resources; Defense and International Affairs (Chairman); Income Security. *Standards of Official Conduct* (2d of 6 D). *Select Committee on Hunger* (5th of 16 D). Task Force: International Task Force.

Group Ratings

	ADA	ACLU	COPE	CFA	LCV	ACU	NTU	NSI	COC	CEI
1986	80	95	87	67	47	9	21	20	24	6
1985	75	—	86	50	—	14	23	—	32	—

National Journal Ratings

	1986 LIB — 1986 CONS	1985 LIB — 1985 CONS
Economic	84% — 13%	73% — 26%
Social	85% — 14%	81% — 15%
Foreign	60% — 39%	58% — 40%

Key Votes

1) Lmt Cln Water Act	AGN	5) Retain Gun Cont	FOR	9) Aid Angola Reb	AGN
2) Rpl Tobac Sub	AGN	6) Contra Aid	AGN	10) Tax Reform	AGN
3) Grm-Rdmn Def Red	AGN	7) Lmt Text Imp	FOR	11) S Africa Sanc	FOR
4) Ban Polygraph	FOR	8) Limit SDI	FOR	12) Immig Reform	FOR

Election Results

1986 general	Vic Fazio (D)	128,364	(70%)	($386,346)
	Jack D. Hite (R)	54,596	(30%)	($9,344)
1986 primary	Vic Fazio (D)	61,885	(100%)	
1984 general	Vic Fazio (D)	130,109	(61%)	($565,569)
	Roger B. Canfield (R)	77,773	(37%)	($84,739)

Campaign Contributions and Expenditures

1985-86		Direct Cont. 1985-86		PACS Breakdown 1985-86			
Receipts	$634,656	Indiv.	$140,346	Corp.	$115,475	T/M/H	$87,051
Expend.	$386,346	PACS	$336,125	Labor	$90,199	Agr.	$10,525
Unspent	$285,596			Ideo.	$24,875	CWOS	$8,000

FIFTH DISTRICT

San Francisco is the most American city and the most exotic American city; a city created in an instant, growing from nothing to a major city in the single year of 1850, and a city that is changing every year. Its American settlers built regular American grids of streets named after politicians and local developers over some of the steepest hills in any American city, but white non-Hispanic non-gay Americans make up only a small percentage of its population today. San Francisco has its own literary traditions, from the days around the turn of the last century when Jack London, Ambrose Bierce, and Frank Norris were writing here, and its own artistic traditions, dating from the Arts and Crafts movement of the same era. It has always been particularly fond of itself and particularly hospitable to outsiders, from the Beats of North Beach in the 1950s to the hippies who thronged Haight-Ashbury in 1967 and the gays of Castro Street in the 1970s and 1980s.

But San Francisco's taste for the exotic and the arts has always rested on the success of a prosaic yet booming economy. It is based on everything from food (the Bay Area remains the national outlet for the cornucopia of California's Central Valley) to finance (despite the current troubles of Bank of America) to high tech (much of Silicon Valley is financed in San Francisco). Fifty years ago, the economy was dominated by the port, and this was a burly town, with a general strike led in 1934 by Communist sympathizers—some feared it was the outbreak of a revolution in the United States. Today San Francisco's economy is based primarily on its booming downtown, with a high-skill service economy.

Historically, San Francisco was a progressive Republican town, the home base of Governor and Senator Hiram Johnson, a strong supporter of Teddy Roosevelt's Progressive candidacy in 1912, always sympathetic to the conservation movement, prone to elect Republican congressmen and legislators with support from labor as well as business. But in the 1930s San Francisco came as close as any American city to class warfare, as the rich in their mansions in Pacific Heights or their stucco Spanish-style houses out in St. Francis Wood suddenly found themselves surrounded by the cloth-capped workingmen on the docks and the Irish and Italian and nativestock working families in the little frame houses on streets coming down from the hills. The progressive Republican tradition survived and thrived in the era of Earl Warren in California; the working-class tradition made San Francisco Democratic in national elections by the 1950s. More recently its local politics has fallen on different lines. For a time in the mid-1970s it seemed that a culturally liberal coalition—environmentalists opposing high-rise buildings, gays seeking sanction of their lifestyle, counterculture veterans—would dominate city politics, outvoting the Catholic family vote in the outer neighborhoods; in 1975 the liberal coalition elected George Moscone mayor. But in 1978 Moscone and gay Supervisor Harvey Milk were murdered by Dan White, former policeman and supervisor, and Dianne Feinstein—sympathetic to gays, but willing to veto their gay marriage ordinance—became mayor and was reelected with wide support in 1979 and 1983. In early 1987, with Feinstein ineligible, it was not clear who would succeed her. There were signs that the 1970s liberal coalition was being threatened by the emergence of Hispanics and Asians as the majority of the city's now growing population. But two things have changed in the intervening years. AIDS has undermined the élan and cruelly stripped the ranks of the gay community. And the biggest minority in this city of minorities is no longer gay or black or Hispanic, but Asian. These new San Franciscans do not share the liberals' yearning for a slowdown in economic growth or disdain for family values, while the tragic AIDS epidemic may be undermining the liberals' belief that the good life is to be found in the rejection of traditional restraints.

The 5th Congressional District of California takes in three-fourths of San Francisco. It includes most of the rich areas of the city: Nob Hill, Russian Hill, and Pacific Heights overlooking the Bay; the Marina district down by the water's edge; Presidio Heights with its leafy palms; St. Francis Wood, below Twin Peaks, the home of the city's Catholic elite. It includes the city's middle income Sunset district, with its older houses amid unburied telephone and electric wires, lying on curving hills that were once sand dunes, stretching out toward the ocean. And it includes lower income areas: the sunny Mission District, shielded from the ocean clouds by Twin Peaks; Portrero Hill, with restored houses overlooking downtown; the farther reaches of the city, with their varicolored pastel houses strewn out along grid streets hugging the steep hills. For two decades the politics of this district was dominated by Phillip Burton, who represented the 5th from 1965 until his death in 1983. Burton was an old-fashioned labor-liberal Democrat, an opponent of the Vietnam war from the beginning, who started off on the left wing of the House and ended up the architect of its reforms and who lost, by only one vote, the race for House majority leader in the Democratic Caucus in 1976. He had other accomplishments, before and after: the expansion of welfare laws and the election of House committee chairmen, the biggest wilderness bill in history and two decades of redistricting the California House delegation and legislature. After his sudden death, he was succeeded by his wife, Sala Burton, a political force in her own right, who was the host House member for the 1984 Democratic National Convention and won a seat on the House Rules Committee. In 1986 she had cancer surgery but was reelected; a few days before her death she announced her retirement and endorsed as her successor Nancy Pelosi.

Pelosi went on to win the Democratic nomination in the April 7 special primary which was tantamount to election in the June 2 runoff. She has a fine political pedigree herself: she is the daughter of Thomas D'Alessandro, who served in the House from 1939 to 1947 and was mayor of Baltimore for 12 years after that; her brother Thomas D'Alessandro, Jr., was mayor from 1967 to 1971; she was California Democratic chairman in the early 1980s, the head of the Democrats' delegate rules compliance for 1984, the chief fundraiser for the Senate Democrats. She was attacked by some as a rich woman who lived outside the district. But she has the energy and shrewdness of one who has handled the most delicate political chores and the charm and unflappability of one who has been at the same time the parent of five children. Her chief opponent for the Democratic nomination was Harry Britt, a gay former minister who succeeded Harvey Milk on the Board of Supervisors; with the gay community desperate for a cure for AIDS and well-organized politically, he won 31% of the total vote cast to Pelosi's 35%. But

Pelosi also had gay support and promised to work hard to find a cure for AIDS. Although she will be the least senior member of Congress, Pelosi gives every sign of being able and effective and of aptly representing this most American of cities as it undergoes yet another American transformation.

The People: Pop. 1980: 525,971, dn. 4.8% 1970–80. Households (1980): 48% family, 21% with children, 35% married couples; 63.5% housing units rented; median monthly rent: $264; median house value: $98,900. Voting age pop. (1980): 434,190; 20% Asian origin, 12% Spanish origin, 9% Black.

1984 Presidential Vote:

Mondale (D)	142,282	(65%)
Reagan (R)	72,437	(33%)

Rep. Nancy Pelosi (D)

Elected June 2, 1987; b. March 26, 1940, Baltimore, MD; home, San Francisco; Trinity College, B.A. 1962; Roman Catholic; married (Paul).

Career: San Francisco Library Comm., 1974–76; Northern Chmn., State Chmn., DNC, 1976–83; Chairwoman, Dem. Natl. Convention, 1983–84; Dem. Senatorial Campaign Cmtee., 1984–86; public relations exec., Ogilvy and Mather, 1984–86.

Office: House Office Bldg., 20515, 202-225-4965.

Committees: *Banking, Finance and Urban Affairs* (30th of 30 D). *Government Operations* (24th of 24 D). Subcommittees unavailable.

Group Ratings and Key Votes: Newly Elected

Election Results

1987 general	Nancy Pelosi (D).	45,770	(67%)	($1,033,072)
	Harriet Ross (R).	22,188	(33%)	($7,547)
1987 primary	Nancy Pelosi (D).	38,927	(35%)	
	Harry Britt (D).	35,008	(31%)	
	Bill Maher (D)	19,355	(17%)	
	Doris Ward (I)	6,498	(6%)	
	Harriet Ross (R).	3,016	(3%)	
	Nine others	8,872	(8%)	
1986 general	Sala Burton (D).	122,688	(75%)	($388,026)
	Mike Garza (R)	36,039	(22%)	

SIXTH DISTRICT

At the western end of the continent, tucked away between mountains and bay, is Marin County, a string of affluent suburbs with only one-tenth of 1% of the nation's population but with an important place in the national consciousness. For Marin occupies the odd corner on the national matrix of political attitudes: liberal on cultural issues, conservative on economics. It is, all at the same time, trendy and affluent, liberal though not totally permissive on cultural issues, conservative and sometimes downright stingy and selfish on economic matters. "Trendy Marin" in the 1970s has been captured for history in Cyra McFadden's *The Serial* and the pattern continues today: people in Marin may be me-centered, but they do not seem very self-conscious. In tune with the times, they are less permissive about drugs than they used to be, and more accepting of making money. But trendiness has become a tradition. In their Volvo-filled parking lots, in their rustic redwood-sided contemporary homes, in their evergreen-shaded Jacuzzi thermal baths, Marin Countians continue to keep up with the latest fads and fashions and to believe almost devoutly in their own virtue for doing so.

Marin has not, however, turned out to be the harbinger of America's future that many Marinites and others thought, and for many Americans Marin's combination of personal liberation and economic laissez-faire has come to seem more like self-indulgence and selfishness. In presidential elections Marin has been almost as perfect an indicator as Maine and Vermont were in 1936. A longtime Republican stronghold, it came within a hairsbreadth of going for George McGovern in 1972. Then it turned around and voted solidly for Gerald Ford in 1976. In 1980 it refused to give Ronald Reagan a majority and gave John Anderson one of his highest percentages in the nation. In 1984 it switched and gave a majority to Walter Mondale.

Marin County forms about half of California's 6th Congressional District. The other half is a hodgepodge: a bit of southern Sonoma County, the working class port of Vallejo, and part of San Francisco. But all are strongly Democratic. Southern Sonoma, the bucolic country around Sebastopol, Cotati, and Petaluma, seems to be the place where the hippies of yesteryear went when they grew up; not so hemmed in by mountains and bay, stretching out over rolling countryside, it seems to be a somewhat more mellow, less trendy, less affluent Marin. Vallejo is the site of a naval shipyard, the sort of working-class town that Socialists of the Jack London era hoped would be the vanguard of a socialist America. The 6th District's portion of San Francisco includes the mostly black Fillmore and Western Addition areas; Haight-Ashbury, once the bedraggled center of hippiedom and now another gentrifying San Francisco neighborhood; and the middle income Richmond area, stretching out north of Golden Gate Park toward the ocean, with its many Chinese residents; also there is high-income Sea Cliff on the hills overlooking the Golden Gate Bridge. The district was originally drawn, with more grotesque boundaries, for Representative John Burton; but to the surprise of everyone, including his late brother, he announced his retirement before the 1982 elections.

That led to the victory of the present congresswoman, Barbara Boxer, who is a fitting personification of Marin County politics. Originally from New York, she was elected to the Marin County Board of Supervisors as an environmentalist in 1976. In her first election the odd makeup of the district helped her. Marin provided most of the votes to give her the 1982 Democratic nomination, while in the general against a serious (and Marin-based) Republican she needed the Democratic margins from Vallejo and the Fillmore in order to win. Since then she has won easily.

Contrary to what many House members must have expected of a Marin County Supervisor, Boxer has not proved to be quirky or difficult to get along with. She is a team player, a member usually loyal to the Democratic leadership, to feminist causes, to caucus groups representing significant constituencies in her district. A prominent member of the congressional military reform caucus, Boxer gained national attention in 1984 for disclosing that the Air Force had paid $7,622 for a coffee pot. She summed up the issue in the offshore oil drilling controversy after Interior Secretary Donald Hodel reneged on his agreement with the California delegation by saying he was playing a new game, "Let's Break a Deal." Her committee assignments her first term were not particularly good—Government Operations and Merchant Marine and Fisheries. But she has used Gov Ops to take the lead on Pentagon procurement reform, and after the 1984 elections she got a seat on the Budget Committee; she finally got a seat on Armed Services after the 1986 election. In 1986 she put into a defense authorization bill a requirement that Pentagon contractors keep records of production costs; she also has a bill to eliminate "cost of money" reimbursement for defense contractors. These are not popular with defense contractors but match perfectly the predelictions of her district. On Budget she is one of many Democrats who want to hold defense spending increases down and, because of the deficit, are wary of raising domestic spending very much. This puts her in line with majority opinion in the House and the 6th District. Marin may not be in the national mainstream, but its congresswoman seems to be in the mainstream in the House.

The People: Pop. 1980: 526,020, up 5.8% 1970–80. Households (1980): 59% family, 30% with children, 46% married couples; 50.4% housing units rented; median monthly rent: $285; median house value: $119,900. Voting age pop. (1980): 409,204; 9% Asian origin, 9% Black, 5% Spanish origin, 1% American Indian.

1984 Presidential Vote:

Mondale (D)	....	141,884	(56%)
Reagan (R)	....	106,610	(42%)

Rep. Barbara Boxer (D)

Elected 1982; b. Nov. 11, 1940, Brooklyn, NY; home, Greenbrae; Brooklyn Col., B.A. 1962; Jewish; married (Stewart).

Career: Stockbroker, researcher, 1962–65; Journalist, *Pacific Sun,* 1972–74; District aide to U.S. Rep. John Burton, 1974–76; Marin Cnty. Bd. of Sprvsrs., 1976–82, Pres., 1980–81.

Offices: 315 CHOB 20515, 202-225-5161. Also 450 Golden Gate Ave., San Francisco 94102, 415-556-1333; 823 Marin, Rm. 8, Vallejo 94590, 707-552-0720; and 88 Belvedere St., San Rafael 94901, 415-457-7272.

Committees: *Armed Services* (28th of 31 D). Subcommittees: Investigations; Research and Development. *Budget* (14th of 21 D). Task Forces: Defense and International Affairs; Income Security; State and Local Government. *Select Committee on Children, Youth, and Families* (8th of 18 D). Task Force: Prevention Strategies.

Group Ratings

	ADA	ACLU	COPE	CFA	LCV	ACU	NTU	NSI	COC	CEI
1986	90	89	98	67	100	5	30	0	13	14
1985	95	—	98	92	—	5	34	—	26	—

National Journal Ratings

	1986 LIB — 1986 CONS			1985 LIB — 1985 CONS		
Economic	79%	—	21%	89%	—	0%
Social	72%	—	27%	85%	—	0%
Foreign	80%	—	0%	92%	—	0%

Key Votes

1) Lmt Cln Water Act	AGN	5) Retain Gun Cont	FOR	9) Aid Angola Reb	AGN
2) Rpl Tobac Sub	FOR	6) Contra Aid	AGN	10) Tax Reform	FOR
3) Grm-Rdmn Def Red	AGN	7) Lmt Text Imp	FOR	11) S Africa Sanc	FOR
4) Ban Polygraph	FOR	8) Limit SDI	FOR	12) Immig Reform	AGN

Election Results

1986 general	Barbara Boxer (D)	142,946	(74%)	($279,727)
	Franklin Ernst III (R).................	50,606	(26%)	($10,171)
1986 primary	Barbara Boxer (D)	60,057	(90%)	
	James Legare (D)	6,425	(10%)	
1984 general	Barbara Boxer (D)	162,511	(68%)	($457,791)
	Douglas F. Binderup (R)...............	71,011	(30%)	($70,264)

Campaign Contributions and Expenditures

1985-86		Direct Cont. 1985-86		PACS Breakdown 1985-86			
Receipts	$358,015	Indiv.	$184,509	Corp.	$16,060	T/M/H	$30,475
Expend.	$279,727	Party	$785	Labor	$89,250	Agr.	$4,000
Unspent	$134,467	PACS	$150,016	Ideo.	$8,881	CWOS	$1,350

SEVENTH DISTRICT

Just across the water from the city, the East Bay is not nearly so well known nationally as San Francisco. Yet just as many people live on the east side of San Francisco Bay as on the west—nearly two million if you count all the way down to San Jose. There are four East Bay congressional districts, represented by perhaps the most liberal bloc of congressmen in the nation. The northernmost of them is the 7th District. It includes most of Contra Costa County, a diverse jurisdiction, jumping over several rugged chains of mountains to include very different kinds of suburbs. Facing the Bay in the 7th is Richmond; much of this was an instant town, housing put up for the workers at the Kaiser Shipyard in World War II. About half of Richmond's residents are black, and the area is heavily Democratic.

Separated from Richmond by the Berkeley Hills and the San Pablo Ridge are several industrial towns on the Bay (Pinole, Hercules, Rodeo); over more hills is the county seat of Martinez, on the Bay where it becomes an arm of the Sacramento River, and the inland suburbs of Concord and Pleasant Hill. These are white collar in character, politically marginal in elections; they are far enough out from the Bay—nearly 20 miles from downtown San Francisco by freeway or BART—to feature housing prices that are affordable for young couples; this is where many, hoping to move some place more fashionable later, start out. Another ridge separates Concord from the industrial towns of Pittsburg and Antioch, near the Sacramento River delta.

The 7th leans Democratic, but not overwhelmingly. Its congressman is George Miller, one of the most important members of the Democratic class of 1974. Miller, whose father was a powerful state senator, got his legislative training in Sacramento; in the House he was a protégé and ally of San Francisco's Phillip Burton. Miller is not burdened with the doubts some members of the class of 1974 express about the wisdom of government spending programs; he generally supports them, and with some enthusiasm and skill. Like many older Democrats, he regards his duty as keeping the rich from getting too greedy and seeing that the poor and middle class enjoy economic security and get their share of society's wealth. Physically imposing, with a hearty temper, Miller is a formidable opponent of what he considers ripoffs.

Miller has spent much of his time on water issues, oppposing the heavy subsidies farmers in the Central Valley and elsewhere get from the federal government, using the leverage of the long unenforced 1902 limit of 160 acres for subsidized water-users to get them to pay more. This gets him in fights with others in the California delegation, notably Tony Coelho from the Valley, but Miller operates from a position of strength as chairman of the Water and Power Resources Subcommittee. He is next in line to chair the full Interior Committee, if Morris Udall, who has Parkinson's disease, retires. Miller is likely to be a forceful chairman, but he is not a dogmatic environmentalist and is not likely to run roughshod over others with different views.

Miller has two other interesting committee assignments. He is a high-ranking member of the Budget Committee and chairman of the Select Committee on Children, Youth, and Families. On budget matters in 1984 he advanced a "pay-as-you-go" budget, embraced by House Democrats, to force budgeters to balance higher spending with cuts in other programs or higher taxes. Miller himself would like higher domestic spending, but he is ready to pay for it. On the special committee he faces squarely another problem: that we are increasingly a nation of rich adults and poor children. He favors more government aid to the needy, but is not under the illusion that what the poor need is liberation from restraint. He has the perspective of a man who has raised a family himself, not the view of a rebellious teenager within it. Miller gave up his high-ranking seat on Education and Labor to serve on Budget in 1984; he will likely take it back when he has served his three terms on Budget.

Miller has won reelection by wide margins since 1976. He was helped by Phil Burton's redistricting plan: Ronald Dellums of the next door 8th District would surely have liked to have Richmond in his district, but Burton made sure that its heavy Democratic margins would go to his friend Miller.

The People: Pop. 1980: 525,990, up 16.9% 1970–80. Households (1980): 72% family, 40% with children, 59% married couples; 34.4% housing units rented; median monthly rent: $261; median house value: $84,600. Voting age pop. (1980): 379,409; 10% Black, 8% Spanish origin, 4% Asian origin, 1% American Indian.

1984 Presidential Vote:

Reagan (R)	126,001	(52%)
Mondale (D)	114,148	(47%)

Rep. George Miller (D)

Elected 1974; b. May 17, 1945, Richmond; home, Martinez; Diablo Valley Col., San Fran. St. Col., B.A. 1968, U. of CA at Davis, J.D. 1972; Roman Catholic; married (Cynthia).

Career: Legis. Aide to CA Sen. Major. Ldr., 1969–74; Practicing atty., 1972–74.

Offices: 2228 RHOB 20515 202-225-2095. Also 367 Civic Dr., Pleasant Hill 94523, 415-687-3260; and 3220 Blume Dr., #218, Richmond 94806, 415-222-4212.

Committees: *Budget* (2d of 21 D). Task Forces: Budget Process; Defense and International Affairs; Income Security; State and Local Government (Chairman). *Interior and Insular Affairs* (2d of 26 D). Subcommittees: Energy and the Environment; General Oversight and Investigations; Mining and Natural Resources; Water and Power Resources (Chairman). *Select Committee on Children, Youth, and Families* (Chairman of 18 D).

Group Ratings

	ADA	ACLU	COPE	CFA	LCV	ACU	NTU	NSI	COC	CEI
1986	90	94	89	58	85	6	33	0	15	20
1985	95	—	89	83	—	10	36	—	19	—

National Journal Ratings

	1986 LIB — 1986 CONS			1985 LIB — 1985 CONS		
Economic	71%	—	29%	83%	—	15%
Social	83%	—	15%	85%	—	0%
Foreign	80%	—	0%	92%	—	0%

Key Votes

1) Lmt Cln Water Act	AGN	5) Retain Gun Cont	FOR	9) Aid Angola Reb	AGN
2) Rpl Tobac Sub	FOR	6) Contra Aid	AGN	10) Tax Reform	FOR
3) Grm-Rdmn Def Red	AGN	7) Lmt Text Imp	AGN	11) S Africa Sanc	—
4) Ban Polygraph	FOR	8) Limit SDI	FOR	12) Immig Reform	FOR

Election Results

1986 general	George Miller (D)...................	124,174	(67%)	($312,522)
	Rosemary Thakar (R).................	62,379	(33%)	($92,496)
1986 primary	George Miller (D)....................	56,839	(100%)	
1984 general	George Miller (D)...................	158,306	(67%)	($180,614)
	Rosemary Thakar (R)................	78,985	(33%)	($130,206)

Campaign Contributions and Expenditures

1985-86		Direct Cont. 1985-86		PACS Breakdown 1985-86			
Receipts	$391,356	Indiv.	$207,308	Corp.	$27,850	T/M/H	$26,453
Expend.	$312,522	Party	$50	Labor	$78,419	Agr.	$2,500
Unspent	$257,437	PACS	$149,868	Ideo.	$13,196	CWOS	$1,450

EIGHTH DISTRICT

More than 20 years ago, in 1964, the streets of Berkeley were thronged by University of California students rioting in the so-called Free Speech Movement. The spirit of student rebellion and elements of unreality have been part of politics in Berkeley and adjacent parts of the East Bay. From the hillier parts of the lush Berkeley campus you can look out over the San Francisco Bay, and take in with one gaze one of the most affluent and culturally most liberated places in the world. It takes a fevered adolescent imagination to see a land of oppression and poverty. But sometimes the protestors' complaints are justified; sometimes the standard ways of doing things are unjust, and the protests prompt the rest of us suddenly to see the injustice, and to change. Yet politics in Berkeley can get a little silly and self-indulgent—there was a ballot measure ordering the mayor and council to ask the President to reduce aid to Israel, for example, and rent control is less helpful to the oppressed proletariat than it is to highly educated but underpaid professionals who want to live near stores that stock the right kind of goat cheese.

That spirit still seems to dominate the politics of the 8th District, even though it animates a relatively small percentage of its voters. About one-quarter of the district's residents live in Berkeley and three similar suburbs (Albany, Kensington, El Cerrito); about half live in Oakland; and another quarter live over the Berkeley Hills, in highly affluent suburbs. Oakland is very much a divided city: 43% of its residents in the 8th District are black, living again on the flatland spreading north and south from the city's downtown; most of the rest are affluent whites, living on curving streets in the hills or in the enclave suburb of Piedmont or in the modest neighborhood where Attorney General Edwin Meese, son and grandson of Oakland civil servants, grew up. The Contra Costa suburbs over the hills—whether woodsy and rustic like Orinda, Moraga, and Lafayette, or full of newly minted subdivisions with pricey houses on treeless streets like Alamo, Danville, and San Ramon—are unsympathetic to anything smacking of radical politics.

The 8th District's congressman, Ronald Dellums, a product of its radical tradition, has succeeded in making a significant impact on national policy in the House. A former social worker and Berkeley councilman, he won the seat in 1970, beating a Democrat with a near-perfect liberal record by charging that he was not anti-war and anti-establishment enough. He infuriates many voters, not all of them Republicans, and there is a rock-solid 40% anti-Dellums vote; but there is also a rock-hard 55–60% pro-Dellums vote. Typically, in November he loses the suburbs east of the hills by a 2–1 margin or more, but still manages to hold the seat comfortably.

Dellums's world view is very much that of the protestors of the 1960s. He believes, as civil rights marchers did, that American society is infected with racism; he believes, as poverty warriors originally did, that government should be much more generous to the poor; he believes, as Vietnam war protestors did, that American military spending is excessive and threatens world peace. His scathing denunciation of the Grenada invasion suggests that he sees virtue in the income-redistribution policies of Socialist countries and no harm in their military connections with the Soviet Union, though certainly he would not endorse their suppressions of civil liberties. He is eloquent in his denunciations of the hideous acts of the South African government.

And sometimes with success. In June 1986, he was startled when the House adopted by voice vote his amendment placing an embargo on South Africa and ordering all American firms there to leave. The bill ultimately passed by Congress did not have such drastic sanctions, but Dellums's amendment did make vivid the House's disgust with the South African regime and its own willingness to act. Others argued that his bill would hurt South African blacks, but similar arguments can be made against any anti-apartheid measure; sadly, no obvious way exists for the United States to produce a good outcome there. Dellums is entitled to satisfaction for having led the way for America to take a stand against injustice.

Dellums surprised some colleagues when he came out vociferously for conservative Marvin Leath for House Armed Services Committee chairman and nominated him in a moving speech before the Democratic Caucus. But this was not a departure for Dellums. Like many on the fringes of either party, he supports the seniority system which protects his positions, and he supported elderly Chairman Mel Price against Aspin in 1984. Moreover, on military and budget issues Dellums and some of his friends had startling success forging joint party positions with Leath and some of his friends; and such experiences can bond otherwise unlike politicians together. Leath did not win, but Dellums made his point, and in the process established himself as a force to be reckoned within the caucus. In the meantime, his seniority makes him Chairman of the House District of Columbia Committee—less important than it was before the District got home rule in 1973—and of the Armed Services subcommittee on Military Installations and Facilities (will some historian 100 years hence argue that Dellums sought this post to protect the interests of Oakland's big military bases?), whose affairs he has conducted with businesslike competence.

The People: Pop. 1980: 525,646, dn. 1.8% 1970–80. Households (1980): 57% family, 29% with children, 42% married couples; 51.1% housing units rented; median monthly rent: $218; median house value: $107,900. Voting age pop. (1980): 409,168; 24% Black, 8% Asian origin, 6% Spanish origin.

1984 Presidential Vote:

Mondale (D)	173,055	(65%)
Reagan (R)	88,833	(34%)

Rep. Ronald V. Dellums (D)

Elected 1970; b. Nov. 24, 1935, Oakland; home, Berkeley; Oakland City Col., A.A. 1958, San Fran. St. Col., B.A. 1960, U. of CA, M.S.W. 1962; Protestant; married (Leola).

Career: USMC, 1954–56; Psychiatric social worker, CA Dept. of Mental Hygiene, 1962–64; Prog. Dir., Bayview Community Ctr., 1964–65; Dir., Hunter's Pt. Bayview Youth Opp. Ctr., 1965–66; Plng. consult., Bay Area Social Plng. Cncl., 1966–67; Dir., San Fran. Econ. Opp. Council's Concentrated Empl. Prog., 1967–68; Berkeley City Cncl., 1967–71; Sr. consultant, Social Dynamics, Inc. (manpower programs), 1968–70.

Offices: 2136 RHOB 20515, 202-225-2661. Also 1720 Oregon St., Rm. 6, Berkeley 94703, 415-548-7767; 201 13th St., Ste. 105, Oakland 94617; and 3730 Mt. Diablo Blvd., Rm. 160, Lafayette 94549, 415-763-0370.

Committees: *Armed Services* (8th of 31 D). Subcommittees: Investigations; Military Installations and Facilities (Chairman). *District of Columbia* (Chairman of 8 D). Subcommittee: Fiscal Affairs and Health.

Group Ratings

	ADA	ACLU	COPE	CFA	LCV	ACU	NTU	NSI	COC	CEI
1986	100	89	91	100	95	0	33	0	12	16
1985	95	—	92	92	—	5	39	—	19	—

National Journal Ratings

	1986 LIB — 1986 CONS	1985 LIB — 1985 CONS
Economic	84% — 13%	79% — 19%
Social	86% — 11%	85% — 0%
Foreign	80% — 0%	92% — 0%

Key Votes

1) Lmt Cln Water Act	AGN	5) Retain Gun Cont	FOR	9) Aid Angola Reb	AGN
2) Rpl Tobac Sub	FOR	6) Contra Aid	AGN	10) Tax Reform	FOR
3) Grm-Rdmn Def Red	AGN	7) Lmt Text Imp	FOR	11) S Africa Sanc	FOR
4) Ban Polygraph	FOR	8) Limit SDI	FOR	12) Immig Reform	AGN

Election Results

1986 general	Ronald V. Dellums (D)	121,790	(60%)	($1,223,490)
	Steven Eigenberg (R)	76,850	(38%)	($74,567)
1986 primary	Ronald V. Dellums (D)	67,696	(83%)	
	Ruth L. Williams (D)	14,378	(17%)	
1984 general	Ronald V. Dellums (D)	144,316	(60%)	($981,747)
	Charles Connor (R)	94,907	(40%)	($169,356)

Campaign Contributions and Expenditures

1985-86		Direct Cont. 1985-86		PACS Breakdown 1985-86			
Receipts	$1,370,820	Indiv.	$1,063,709	Corp.	$12,570	T/M/H	$11,820
Expend.	$1,223,490	PACS	$91,286	Labor	$58,790	Agr.	$600
Unspent	$153,259	Cand.	$175,777	Ideo.	$7,506	CWOS	$0

NINTH DISTRICT

As you look out on the East Bay from the skyscrapers of downtown San Francisco, your eyes go first to the Bay Bridge, then to the big Navy and Army bases and the port of Oakland, up a little to the skyscrapers of Oakland, then over to the left of the Bridge to see if you can make out the towers of the campus in Berkeley. Those are the landmarks: you don't look much to the right, or south, of downtown Oakland, to see the expanse of East Bay neighborhoods and suburbs spreading out down to where the Bay itself spreads out to the width of a miniature sea and is spanned by the causeway-like San Mateo Bridge. If you were looking there, though, what you would be seeing is most of the 9th Congressional District of California.

The 9th District includes the old city of Alameda, resolutely middle class despite its proximity to Navy bases and the Oakland ghetto; it includes some mostly black neighborhoods in Oakland itself; it passes south and includes the modest working-class suburbs of San Leandro, San Lorenzo, and Hayward. The terrain here is not much different from other places in the Bay Area; the houses are built of the same materials, mostly stucco; the shopping centers to outward appearances are what you see all over. But there are discount chains rather than Saks, bargain drugstores rather than boutiques. Housing prices here are among the least unreasonable in the Bay Area, and this is where working people, mostly white but many Mexican-Americans as well, live. Over the mountains, where you can't see if you are looking from San Francisco, it includes the upper middle-income suburbs of Pleasanton and Livermore, in a valley outside the Bay Area orbit.

The military is a presence here, from the Oakland waterfront to the Livermore Laboratories, long headed by Edward Teller, which is one of the leading centers for research on President

Reagan's Strategic Defense Initiative. But the 9th District votes mostly for Democrats, and usually liberal Democrats at that. The congressman here is Fortney (Pete) Stark, first elected in 1972 when he beat an elderly incumbent who supported the Vietnam war. Stark is by nature a kind of insurgent: he started a bank in nearby Walnut Creek and attracted deposits from all over the Bay Area by putting a giant peace symbol atop his headquarters and peace symbol motifs on all the checks. He spent liberally on his own campaign and, reversing what was then the usual practice, got rid of his bank stock before taking a seat on the House Banking Committee; other members used to acquire bank stock, often for nominal amounts, at that point.

Now Stark has become one of the leading Democrats in the House. He has risen to a subcommittee chairmanship on Ways and Means, and in 1985 and 1986 he was one of Chairman Dan Rostenkowski's chief supporters on tax reform. At first glance the alliance and the cause might seem unusual. Stark's experience has been that it's easy to make money, and that you don't need to give people incentives to do it; but even in the first Reagan term he was proposing to lower tax rates in return for getting rid of preferences in the tax code—the essential tradeoff of reform. And he was already a Rostenkowski ally before tax reform; these two politicians who came up through very different routes (though both went to high school in Wisconsin) are a good example of a committee and a subcommittee chairman supporting each other to their mutual benefit. Rostenkowski supported the detail work Stark did on a Special Revenues Subcommittee and his health legislation on the Health Subcommittee, and was careful to include Stark on the vital tax conference committee.

Stark often has a puckish demeanor and can even seem flip. Yet he has been grave enough to get some hard and often detailed work done as subcommittee chairman. He has been hostile to the idea of raising payroll taxes—regressive, after all—to finance Social Security, and so has a special incentive to hold down Medicare costs; this is difficult work, and may be his biggest challenge in years ahead. In 1987 he came out with his own catastrophic health insurance bill, co-sponsored by Republican Bill Gradison, which would expand coverage by taxing the insurance value of Medicare for those with enough income to pay taxes; he is likely to be the House's leading member on this major issue.

Stark has not had many serious political challenges in the 9th District since first winning it in 1972; the closest the Republicans have come was holding him to 55% of the vote in 1980. The American Medical Association's PAC made some $200,000 of independent expenditures against him in 1986, but they failed to help the hapless Republican candidate and do not seem likely to deter Stark from opposing AMA stands on the Health Subcommittee.

The People: Pop. 1980: 526,234, up 2.8% 1970–80. Households (1984): 71% family, 38% with children, 57% married couples; 40.5% housing units rented; median monthly rent: $258; median house value: $82,800. Voting age pop. (1980): 388,528; 12% Spanish origin, 10% Black, 6% Asian origin, 1% American Indian.

1984 Presidential Vote: Reagan (R) 107,925   (50%)
Mondale (D) 106,640   (49%)

Rep. Fortney H. (Pete) Stark (D)

Elected 1972; b. Nov. 11, 1931, Milwaukee, WI; home, Oakland; MIT, B.S. 1953, U. of CA, M.B.A. 1960; Unitarian; divorced.

Career: Air Force, 1955–57; Founder, Beacon Savings and Loan Assn., 1961; Founder and Pres., Security Natl. Bank, Walnut Creek, 1963–72.

Offices: 1125 LHOB 20515, 202-225-5065. Also 22300 Foothill Blvd., Hayward 94541, 415-635-1092.

Committees: *District of Columbia* (4th of 8 D). Subcommittees: Fiscal Affairs and Health; Government Operations and Metropolitan Affairs. *Ways and Means* (5th of 23 D). Subcommittees: Health (Chairman); Select Revenue Measures. *Select Committee on Narcotics Abuse and Control* (3d of 15 D). *Joint Economic Committee.* Subcommittees: Economic Growth, Trade and Taxes; Fiscal and Monetary Policy; Education and Health.

Group Ratings

	ADA	ACLU	COPE	CFA	LCV	ACU	NTU	NSI	COC	CEI
1986	95	85	93	50	98	5	34	0	12	21
1985	90	—	91	92	99	11	39	—	14	—

National Journal Ratings

	1986 LIB — 1986 CONS	1985 LIB — 1985 CONS
Economic	72% — 27%	89% — 0%
Social	85% — 15%	85% — 0%
Foreign	80% — 0%	92% — 0%

Key Votes

1) Lmt Cln Water Act	AGN	5) Retain Gun Cont	FOR	9) Aid Angola Reb	AGN
2) Rpl Tobac Sub	FOR	6) Contra Aid	AGN	10) Tax Reform	FOR
3) Grm-Rdmn Def Red	AGN	7) Lmt Text Imp	AGN	11) S Africa Sanc	FOR
4) Ban Polygraph	FOR	8) Limit SDI	FOR	12) Immig Reform	FOR

Election Results

1986 general	Fortney H. (Pete) Stark (D)	113,490	(70%)	($533,314)
	David M. Williams (R)	49,300	(30%)	($61,483)
1986 primary	Fortney H. (Pete) Stark (D)	56,282	(89%)	
	Evelyn K. Lantz (D)	6,990	(11%)	
1984 general	Fortney H. (Pete) Stark (D)	136,511	(70%)	($570,639)
	J.T. Eager Beaver (R)	51,399	(26%)	

Campaign Contributions and Expenditures

1985-86		Direct Cont. 1985-86		PACS Breakdown 1985-86			
Receipts	$566,745	Indiv.	$182,667	Corp.	$105,557	T/M/H	$117,897
Expend.	$533,314	PACS	$354,096	Labor	$70,760	Agr.	$3,500
Debts	$37,565	Cand.	$26,400	Ideo.	$22,596	CWOS	$33,786

TENTH DISTRICT

Nowhere is the growth of post-World War II America more vividly illustrated than in San Jose, California. As the war ended, and troops unloaded at the docks of the big cities of San Francisco and Oakland, San Jose was a sleepy farm town 50 miles to the south, just beyond the marshlands at the south end of San Francisco Bay, surrounded by lush orchards and fields of crops. It had, even then, a significant Mexican-American population (as the smaller California farm towns of Salinas and Hollister still do today). Few people anticipated then what was about to happen: that San Jose would become the focus of the most massive population growth in the San Francisco Bay Area. Today there are almost as many people in the irregular bounds of San Jose as in the tip of the peninsula that is San Francisco, and there are more people living along the freeways within a few mile of San Jose than there are in San Francisco and the suburbs just below it up to San Bruno Mountain, where the quite different Peninsula suburbs begin. In 1945 all this seemed quite improbable. San Jose seemed no more likely to become a metropolis than Salinas or Bakersfield. How would people make a living down there?

The answer is, off everything from old-fashioned farming to the most up-to-date high technology. San Jose's growth came from two directions. From the east, people moved down from working-class East Bay neighborhoods. Factories were built on vacant land, and employees flocked to the new subdivisions nearby. The east side of San Jose is thus largely blue collar, as are the East Bay suburbs to the north: Fremont, Newark, Union City. In the late 1970s they came on hard times, as when General Motors closed its Fremont assembly plant. But the 1980s saw revival, as the plant became the site of GM's much ballyhooed joint venture with Toyota.

The other stream of migration to San Jose came from the northwest. Here, along U.S. 101 and Interstate 280, is the Silicon Valley, the heart of the nation's microelectronics industry. People here are highly educated, affluent, addicted to Perrier, bicycling, and jogging. The heart of the Silicon Valley is a dozen miles or so up the freeways from downtown San Jose, but the entire area has benefited from the prosperity and growth that the now threatened industry has generated. Santa Clara County, which includes San Jose and many of the Silicon Valley towns, has increased in population from 290,000 in 1950 to 1.3 million in 1980.

California's 10th Congressional District consists of eastern and central San Jose, suburban areas nearby, and the East Bay cities just to the north. It spans the southern edge of the Bay from Hayward to the border between San Jose and Sunnyvale. The 10th has the largest Spanish origin population in the Bay Area (28%), some concentrated in old Mexican neighborhoods in San Jose, but many scattered about the district, as are many products of earlier waves of immigration. This used to be a solidly Democratic district, solid enough to have voted for George McGovern in 1972. Now it is more marginal in national elections; like most of California, it spurned Jimmy Carter in 1980 and, thanks to Ronald Reagan's inroads among Mexican-American voters, went for him over Walter Mondale in 1984.

For more than 20 years this part of California has been represented by Democratic Congressman Don Edwards. He has a conservative background: he was once an FBI agent, and he got rich because his family owned the only title company in Santa Clara County during its years of great expansion. But by the time he was elected to Congress in 1962, he was one of its most liberal members: one of the early opponents of the Vietnam war and an advocate of abolition of the House Un-American Activities Committee. Today he continues to be one of its most liberal members—and also a competent and accomplished legislator.

Edwards, the fourth-ranking Democrat on the Judiciary Committee and a trusted colleague of Chairman Peter Rodino, is chairman of its Civil and Constitutional Rights Subcommittee. This is a hot seat: the committee has jurisdiction over all constitutional amendments, to ban abortion and to enforce school prayer, to declare that Congress must balance the budget and to ban school busing. Edwards opposes all these amendments, and has no compunction about using his margin on the subcommittee to make sure that they are not reported out to the full Judiciary Committee or get onto the floor. This often means he takes the heat for killing attractive-sounding measures that a majority of the House in most cases would oppose on a secret ballot but doesn't want to vote on.

Edwards does more than stop measures he doesn't like. He works closely with the civil rights lobby and has been lead sponsor of most of its top priority bills. He is one of the leading sponsors of the bill to reverse the *Grove City College* decision and broaden what the Supreme Court has said is the ambit of the government's anti-discrimination mandate to colleges. He was the chief sponsor of the renewal of the Voting Rights Act in 1982 and succeeded in getting his measure passed despite opposition from the Reagan Administration on important provisions. Edwards also sponsored the Fair Housing Act that passed the House in 1980, and he is ready to press a similar measure if the Reagan Administration can agree on terms with the civil rights lobby. He is a wary watcher of Reagan-appointed judges. He is quick to oppose overreliance on lie detector tests, FBI surveillance of Nicaragua aid opponents, and other government actions which he sees as undermining civil liberties. In the rush to pass antidrug legislation in 1986, Edwards stood up and opposed the death penalty and measures to involve the military for the first time in civilian law enforcement.

Edwards also spends time as the second-ranking Democrat on the Veterans' Affairs Committee. He has a friendly relationship with Chairman Sonny Montgomery, but sometimes opposes him, as he did in 1986 by pushing to allow veterans to go to court to appeal denial of VA benefits. He is dean of the California Democratic delegation, the largest such group in the House and one which contains many able members some of whom are jealous of others. Edwards, with his reputation for fairness and candor, is able to bridge gaps. Edwards has a deserved reputation for being scrupulously fair when it comes to procedure, and he is pleasant on a personal level; though he is past 70, he remains a good athlete and is in superb physical shape. But he also fights hard for what he believes in and does not make concessions easily.

In the 10th District he is reelected routinely without significant opposition.

The People: Pop. 1980: 525,882, up 39.0% 1970–80. Households (1980): 76% family, 48% with children, 61% married couples; 37.7% housing units rented; median monthly rent: $276; median house value: $88,700. Voting age pop. (1980): 360,334; 24% Spanish origin, 10% Asian origin, 5% Black, 1% American Indian.

1984 Presidential Vote:

Reagan (R)	87,529	(51%)
Mondale (D)	82,340	(48%)

Rep. Don Edwards (D)

Elected 1962; b. Jan. 6, 1915, San Jose; home, San Jose; Stanford U., A.B. 1936, Stanford U. Law Sch., 1936–38; Unitarian; married (Edith).

Career: FBI Agent, 1940–41; Navy, WWII; Pres., Valley Title Co.

Offices: 2307 RHOB 20515, 202-225-3072. Also 1042 W. Hedding St., Ste. 110, San Jose 95125, 408-247-1711; and 38750 Paseo Padre Pkwy., Fremont 94536, 415-792-5320.

Committees: *Judiciary* (4th of 21 D). Subcommittees: Civil and Constitutional Rights (Chairman); Criminal Justice; Monopolies and Commercial Law. *Veterans' Affairs* (2d of 21 D). Subcommittee: Oversight and Investigations.

Group Ratings

	ADA	ACLU	COPE	CFA	LCV	ACU	NTU	NSI	COC	CEI
1986	100	100	93	100	89	0	32	0	12	19
1985	100	—	93	83	—	0	36	—	18	—

National Journal Ratings

	1986 LIB — 1986 CONS		1985 LIB — 1985 CONS	
Economic	87% —	0%	89% —	0%
Social	86% —	11%	85% —	0%
Foreign	80% —	0%	92% —	0%

Key Votes

1) Lmt Cln Water Act	AGN	5) Retain Gun Cont	FOR	9) Aid Angola Reb	AGN
2) Rpl Tobac Sub	FOR	6) Contra Aid	AGN	10) Tax Reform	FOR
3) Grm-Rdmn Def Red	AGN	7) Lmt Text Imp	FOR	11) S Africa Sanc	FOR
4) Ban Polygraph	FOR	8) Limit SDI	FOR	12) Immig Reform	AGN

Election Results

1986 general	Don Edwards (D)	84,240	(71%)	($156,410)
	Michael R. La Crone (R)	31,826	(27%)	
1986 primary	Don Edwards (D)	38,447	(100%)	
1984 general	Don Edwards (D)	102,469	(62%)	($140,812)
	Bob Herriott (R)	56,256	(34%)	($86,078)

Campaign Contributions and Expenditures

1985-86		Direct Cont. 1985-86		PACS Breakdown 1985-86			
Receipts	$188,165	Indiv.	$70,838	Corp.	$19,750	T/M/H	$27,070
Expend.	$156,410	PACS	$112,881	Labor	$57,700	Agr.	$600
Unspent	$46,556			Ideo.	$7,461	CWOS	$300

ELEVENTH DISTRICT

As late as the 1920s most of the level land between San Francisco Bay and the mountains that run along the Peninsula south of San Francisco was given over to apricot orchards; now it is some of the highest-value suburban land in the United States. Connecting San Francisco and the Silicon Valley, it is hemmed in by natural obstacles, and lies almost on top of the San Andreas Fault, which runs right down the middle of the Peninsula. On top of the fault are San Francisco's reservoirs; to the west the land is mountainous enough to have prevented development south of the suburb of Pacifica, which clings to the foggy mountainsides above the ocean, a few miles south of San Francisco. Most of the Peninsula's population is packed into neat little suburbs between the fault and the salt flats and industrial parks on the landfill along San Francisco Bay.

There are two distinct sets of Peninsula suburbs. In the north, adjacent to the city and encircling San Bruno Mountain, are towns that, demographically and politically, are extensions of the city neighborhoods just to the north. Daly City, at the southern extension of the BART lines, has substantial numbers of Mexican-Americans and Asians as well as whites of varying descent; South San Francisco proclaims itself "the industrial city" in big letters on San Bruno Mountain near the Bayshore Freeway; the streets lined with boxy houses in Pacifica and San Bruno wind over sweeping hillsides facing the cemeteries where so many San Franciscans and veterans of Pacific wars have been buried. People in these neighborhoods are mostly from working-class backgrounds, although most are upwardly mobile; they are ancestral Democrats, although they sometimes vote Republican; their orientation is to the urban pace of San Francisco, not the life of the Peninsula suburbs south of the airport.

There the atmosphere is different. For one thing, the weather is warmer and sunnier, because the mountains protect the towns from the ocean clouds and fogs. The people here are more likely to have white-collar jobs, to be college educated, to be from backgrounds both Protestant and Republican. The weather is perfect for outdoor sports, and there are more jogging and bicycle paths and tennis courts here, in the string of suburbs south from Millbrae to Los Altos, than anywhere else in the United States. Cultural attitudes here tend to be liberal; people want to save the environment, oppose Vietnam-like wars, and in some cases even legalize marijuana. On economic issues, however, they are not especially interested in redistributing income nor much concerned with unemployment. The federal government is as much a threat as a source of help.

Most of the Peninsula makes up California's 11th congressional district, which includes all of the Peninsula from the San Francisco city limits down to Redwood City except the very high-income suburbs of Hillsborough, Woodside, Portola Valley, and Atherton. Nationally, it is a closely divided district, only narrowly favoring Ronald Reagan in 1980 and 1984. The Peninsula, under various district boundaries, has also been the scene of some closely contested congressional elections; the 11th was picked up by the Republicans in a 1979 election after the death of Representative Leo Ryan in Jonestown, Guyana, and was recaptured by the Democrats in 1980—one of only four Republican districts they picked up that year.

The congressman is Tom Lantos, who for years taught economics at San Francisco State. Lantos is one of the few members of Congress—ex-POW Senator John McCain is another—who has personal experience living under tyranny. Lantos was born in Hungary and fought as a teenager in the underground against the Nazis; he was one of the Jews saved by the Swedish diplomat Raoul Wallenberg. Lantos devotes much of his attention to his work on the Foreign Affairs Committee. Like almost all the other Democrats there, he has been an opponent of aid to the Nicaraguan contras; but he does not seem to bring to his work the same instinctive mistrust of administration policy or doubts of American good intentions you get from many other post-Watergate Democrats. He made something of a stir in December 1986 when he promised to contribute to Lt. Col. Oliver North's legal defense fund—because, he said, he didn't want North, who wore his Marine uniform and decorations to the committee room where he took the Fifth Amendment, to be a scapegoat for those higher up. Lantos is among the most enthusiastic supporters of Israel, and was the co-sponsor of the measure, which became controversial in the 1984 presidential campaign, to move the U.S. embassy in Israel from Tel Aviv to Jerusalem. He strongly mistrusts the Soviets and in 1982 labored unsuccessfully to persuade the Swedes to use the leverage they gained by trapping a Soviet submarine in their waters to get more information about Wallenberg, who many think has been a Soviet prisoner since 1945.

On domestic issues Lantos, after opposing some Democratic positions early in his tenure, has lately been voting pretty much with his party.

After his first victory, Lantos was determined to make this marginal seat safe. He raised and spent $1.1 million in 1982, won handily, and has not had serious competition since.

The People: Pop. 1980: 525,981, up 5.9% 1970–80. Households (1980): 68% family, 34% with children, 55% married couples; 42.2% housing units rented; median monthly rent: $311; median house value: $117,100. Voting age pop. (1980): 400,549; 12% Spanish origin, 9% Asian origin, 6% Black.

1984 Presidential Vote:

Reagan (R)	112,986	(50%)
Mondale (D)	109,053	(49%)

Rep. Tom Lantos (D)

Elected 1980; b. Feb. 1, 1928, Budapest, Hungary; home, Burlingame; U. of WA, B.A. 1949, M.A. 1950, U. of CA, Ph.D. 1953; Jewish; married (Annette).

Career: Economist, Bank of America, 1952–53; Television Commentator, San Francisco, 1955–63; Dir. of Intl. Programs, CA St. U. system, 1962–71; Econ.-Foreign Policy Adviser to U.S. Sen. Joseph R. Biden Jr., 1978–79; Member, Pres. Task Force on Defense and Foreign Policy, 1976; Faculty, San. Fran. St. U., 1950–80.

Offices: 1707 LHOB 20515, 202-225-3531. Also 520 El Camino Real, Ste. 800, San Mateo 94402, 415-342-0300.

Committees: *Foreign Affairs* (12th of 27 D). Subcommittees: Arms Control, International Security and Science; Europe and the Middle East; Human Rights and International Organizations. *Government Operations* (11th of 24 D). Subcommittees: Employment and Housing (Chairman). *Select Committee on Aging* (19th of 39 D). Subcommittees: Housing and Consumer Interests; Human Services.

Group Ratings

	ADA	ACLU	COPE	CFA	LCV	ACU	NTU	NSI	COC	CEI
1986	70	65	93	83	74	18	22	10	31	18
1985	70	—	91	83	—	5	32	—	22	—

National Journal Ratings

	1986 LIB — 1986 CONS		1985 LIB — 1985 CONS	
Economic	79% —	20%	75% —	22%
Social	67% —	32%	81% —	15%
Foreign	64% —	34%	71% —	26%

Key Votes

1) Lmt Cln Water Act	—	5) Retain Gun Cont	FOR	9) Aid Angola Reb	FOR
2) Rpl Tobac Sub	FOR	6) Contra Aid	AGN	10) Tax Reform	FOR
3) Grm-Rdmn Def Red	FOR	7) Lmt Text Imp	FOR	11) S Africa Sanc	FOR
4) Ban Polygraph	FOR	8) Limit SDI	FOR	12) Immig Reform	FOR

Election Results

1986 general	Tom Lantos (D)	112,380	(74%)	($325,435)
	G. M. (Bill) Quraishi (R)	39,315	(26%)	($63,996)
1986 primary	Tom Lantos (D)	58,269	(100%)	
1984 general	Tom Lantos (D)	147,607	(70%)	($288,064)
	John J. (Jack) Hickey (R)	59,625	(28%)	($800)

Campaign Contributions and Expenditures

1985-86		Direct Cont. 1985-86		PACS Breakdown 1985-86			
Receipts	$299,231	Indiv.	$164,733	Corp.	$9,200	T/M/H	$14,460
Expend.	$325,435	Party	$304	Labor	$29,750	Agr.	$600
Unspent	$353,277	PACS	$56,571	Ideo.	$2,311	CWOS	$250

TWELFTH DISTRICT

If you had to pick one congressional district as the center of American high technology, you would pick the 12th District of California. The 12th's boundaries follow almost uncannily the unofficial boundaries of California's Silicon Valley. In the north, nearest San Francisco, it includes the center of the Peninsula, taking in Hillsborough, Woodside, Portola Valley, and Atherton—the highest income suburbs of San Francisco, the places where Silicon Valley instant millionaires bought houses for a once remarkable $1 million. It includes Palo Alto and the neighboring Menlo Park, the home country of Stanford University and of the conservatively inclined Hoover Institution and Stanford Research Institute—the places that formulate the theoretical and ideological implications of the microchip revolution.

Farther south, where Interstate 280 dips below the hills to the string of towns on the flatlands below, the 12th reaches the town of Cupertino, next to San Jose; with only 34,000 people, Cupertino is nonetheless a giant city in the microcomputer business, the headquarters of Apple Computer and other firms less well known outside. The district includes also the high-income hillside suburbs of Los Altos, Saratoga, and Monte Sereno. It then curves around San Jose, avoiding the city and its east side Mexican-American suburban fringe, and includes part of Santa Cruz County and several agricultural towns south of San Jose, notably Gilroy, the garlic capital of America.

Why is high tech here? Not because of any need for bulky raw materials or ready access to particular energy sources. Partly because of Stanford, surely, which has encouraged its faculty to experiment with—and profit from—high tech breakthroughs, and because some of the earliest high tech companies, like Hewlett-Packard, are in Palo Alto. Then there is IBM's decision in the 1950s to site a major facility in San Jose. But these aren't the full explanation. There are no comparable high tech centers around midwestern universities; the University of Illinois, for example, with one of the strongest electrical engineering departments in the country, has little industry around it. Another thing that may have brought the Valley's collection of chemists, physicists and electrical engineers and software programmers to critical mass was the proximity of financial resources that were virtually unavailable to would-be entrepreneurs in academic communities elsewhere. Hot venture capital firms and old Nob Hill and Pacific Heights money was put at risk, often with marvelous returns: high tech and old money.

Plus ambiance. This part of California also has a natural attraction for innovative, creative, restless people. Not for veterans of the counterculture, who seem to cluster around Berkeley and Santa Cruz and to be migrating to the coastal counties north of Marin. The Silicon Valley attracts tinkerers, wonderers, people who may combine the squarest and most traditional of values with eccentricity and a fascination with mathematics and machinery. They work in squat and rectilinear offices and factories set in unpretentious lots on what was, 20 or 40 years ago, exceedingly fertile fruit and vegetable croplands, on the flat Peninsula lands radiating southeast from what was once Leland Stanford's farm. They live, if they are successful, in the hills where the first settlers here built mills and farmhouses, in stark contemporary houses amid huge live oak and eucalyptus trees. There is a sort of pure Americanness here: these communities were rustic but never poor, rural but never bigoted, country-like but still easily accessible to all the luxuries of civilization, culturally interesting but without ethnic discrimination. People here were ahead of the rest of the nation in fighting to preserve the environment, in favoring natural over processed foods, in indulging in systematic exercise, and in appreciating the possibilities of computers and microcircuitry. Unfettered by convention, they have been ready to accept—and anticipate and create—the latest fashion as well as the latest innovation.

By 1984 the computer boom of the early 1980s had gone bust, inspiring wry jokes and sending some entrepreneurs temporarily to the unemployment offices, back to their garages, or to Washington to ask politicians to do something about the Japanese. But the faith in private enterprise seems to remain. In the late 1960s and early 1970s, this area trended Democratic and came surprisingly close to going for George McGovern in 1972. In congressional elections it chose Pete McCloskey, an environmentalist and opponent of the Vietnam War, over Shirley Temple Black in a special 1967 Republican primary. Since then it has moved toward the mainstream of Republican conservatism—or vice versa. When McCloskey ran for the Senate in 1982, he was replaced by Ed Zschau, a young entrepreneur who made his fortune manufacturing disc storage systems. Zschau lobbied Congress in the late 1970s and helped get capital gains rates lowered, which Silicon Valley businessmen will tell you played a key role in stimulating their industry and which represented a sharp and evidently permanent change in American public policy. When the seat came open, Zschau won the Republican nomination unopposed and easily won the general election. His record in the House was conservative—against government regulation, spending, and taxing—and mixed on cultural and foreign issues

When Zschau ran for the Senate in 1986, he was replaced in this district by a rather different kind of Republican. Ernest Konnyu, like the 11th District's congressman Tom Lantos, is a native of Hungary with a special hatred for totalitarian regimes. He has served in the California Assembly, where he was an adversary of Speaker Willie Brown and his Democratic majority, and he is a strong advocate of an assertive American foreign policy. He was one of the few candidates in 1986, for example, to speak critically of Philippines President Corazon Aquino. Konnyu had some difficulty in the Republican primary but won with 60% of the vote against a businessman who used to be a Democrat. He won easily against a weak Democratic candidate in 1986. Konnyu's politics may have raised some hackles in the Silicon Valley and in the hills above. But so strong is the Republican trend here on economic issues that he won handily, and probably will have a safe seat.

The People: Pop. 1980: 525,731, up 13.0% 1970–80. Households (1980): 69% family, 35% with children, 59% married couples; 38.3% housing units rented; median monthly rent: $320; median house value: $150,300. Voting age pop. (1980): 397,900; 8% Spanish origin, 6% Asian origin, 2% Black.

1984 Presidential Vote:

Reagan (R)	148,724	(57%)
Mondale (D)	108,069	(41%)

Rep. Ernest L. Konnyu (R)

Elected 1986; b. May 17, 1937, Tamasi, Hungary; home, Saratoga; OH St. U., B.S. 1965; Roman Catholic; married (Lillian).

Career: Air Force, 1959–1969; Auditor, 1972–80; CA State Assembly, 1980–86.

Offices: 511 CHOB 20515, 202-225-5411. Also 1008 N. Wolfe Rd., SW Bldg. 3, Ste. 210, Cupertino 95014, 408-257-7051.

Committees: *Government Operations* (14th of 15 R). Subcommittees: Commerce, Consumer and Monetary Affairs; Employment and Housing; Human Resources and Intergovernmental Relations. *Science, Space and Technology* (15th of 18 R). Subcommittees: Space Science and Applications; Energy Research and Development; Investigations and Oversight.

Group Ratings and Key Votes: Newly Elected

Election Results

1986 general	Ernest L. Konnyu (R)................ 111,252	(60%)	($950,447)
	Lance T. Weil (D)..................... 69,564	(37%)	($62,377)
	Bill White (L)......................... 6,227	(3%)	
1986 primary	Ernest L. Konnyu (R)................. 33,093	(53%)	
	Tom Skornia (R)...................... 16,401	(26%)	
	Laddie W. Hughes (R)................. 7,472	(12%)	
	John Mercer (R)...................... 5,730	(9%)	
1984 general	Ed Zschau (R) 155,795	(62%)	($308,274)
	Martin Carnoy (D)................... 91,026	(36%)	($69,132)

Campaign Contributions and Expenditures

1985-86		Direct Cont. 1985-86		PACS Breakdown 1985-86			
Receipts	$960,536	Indiv.	$473,271	Corp.	$81,161	T/M/H	$69,521
Expend.	$950,447	Party	$7,252	Labor	$2,500	Agr.	$1,000
Unspent	$4,139	PACS	$202,734	Ideo.	$46,002	CWOS	$2,550
		Cand.	$220,139				

THIRTEENTH DISTRICT

Twenty-five years ago, most of what is now the 13th Congressional District of California was acres of vineyards and fruit orchards below the mountains of the Coast Range near San Jose. This was one of the richest agricultural areas in the country, but it was also in the path of some of the most explosive growth the country has ever seen. Santa Clara County, which includes San Jose and the 13th District, grew from 290,000 people in 1950 to 1,064,000 in 1970 and 1,297,000 in 1980. In the 1960s and 1970s the 13th District just about tripled in population—a rate of growth exceeded by only a few other districts in the United States.

Two-thirds of the people in the district live within the city limits of San Jose—almost as many as live in San Francisco. But San Jose's boundaries are considerably more irregular, having been extended, in jagged fashion, hundreds of times; growth was so rapid that for a while someone every day had to paste on top of the city government's own map inserts adding new streets and subdivisions. The 13th District includes the southern and southwestern parts of the city, areas basically suburban, white Anglo, and white collar in character. They are farther out than some of the more expensive Silicon Valley suburbs, though similar in outward appearances. Most of the rest of the people in the 13th live in Santa Clara, an old suburban town just west of downtown San Jose, with its own mission and university. The 13th also includes the suburb of Campbell, surrounded by and indistinguishable from San Jose, and Los Gatos, a higher income town going up into the hills.

The congressman from the 13th is Norman Mineta, one of the leaders of the large class of Democrats first elected in 1974. As mayor Mineta made a name in San Jose in the early 1970s for slowing up the development that had transformed a market town of 95,000 to a city of 445,000 in 20 years; he was popular enough to succeed a Republican congressman when he retired in 1974. The district is actually not all that Democratic; Republicans have carried it in the last five presidential elections. Nevertheless, Mineta has consistently won by wide margins.

Mineta is now a high-ranking member of the Public Works Committee, and chairs the Aviation Subcommittee. He has been in effect one of the government's chief policymakers on aviation issues, from noise regulation to financing airport expansion. He has supported airline deregulation—one of the reforms of the Carter years—but has been keeping a close and critical watch on the FAA's work on safety regulation in the Reagan years. Naturally he has also worked to bring home the bacon for San Jose.

Mineta is one of those Democrats who gets special assignments. He served three terms on the Budget Committee early in his career, and was one of the key Democrats there in 1981 and 1982, fighting at first unsuccessfully and then with more success against the Reagan budget cuts. More recently he was a member of the Intelligence Committee, where he was critical of former CIA Director William Casey and opposed military or "humanitarian" aid to the Nicaraguan contras. In addition, he is a deputy majority whip, and thus a part of the Democratic leadership. As a child, Mineta was one of 120,000 Americans of Japanese descent interred in detention camps, and he has been one of the leaders in the attempt to have the government apologize for this act and redress its victims. Mineta was slowed down in his sixth term by a heart attack, but had returned to a full schedule in late 1986 as one of the workhorses of the House.

The People: Pop. 1980: 526,281, up 21.6% 1970–80. Households (1980): 71% family, 41% with children, 58% married couples; 39.3% housing units rented; median monthly rent: $331; median house value: $104,900. Voting age pop. (1980): 380,270; 10% Spanish origin, 6% Asian origin, 2% Black, 1% American Indian.

1984 Presidential Vote:

Reagan (R)	126,585	(58%)
Mondale (D)	89,789	(41%)

Rep. Norman Y. Mineta (D)

Elected 1974; b. Nov. 12, 1931, San Jose; home, San Jose; U. of CA at Berkeley, B.S. 1953; United Methodist; married (May).

Career: Army, 1953–56; Owner/Agent, Mineta Insur. Agcy.; San Jose City Cncl., 1967–71, Vice Mayor, 1968–71, Mayor, 1971–74.

Offices: 2350 RHOB 20515, 202-225-2631. Also 1245 S. Winchester Blvd., Ste. 310, San Jose 95128, 408-984-6045.

Committees: *Public Works and Transportation* (4th of 32 D). Subcommittees: Aviation (Chairman); Investigations and Oversight; Surface Transportation. *Science, Space and Technology* (11th of 27 D). Subcommittees: Science, Research and Technology; Space Science and Applications.

Group Ratings

	ADA	ACLU	COPE	CFA	LCV	ACU	NTU	NSI	COC	CEI
1986	95	95	88	92	68	5	23	0	18	17
1985	80	—	89	83	—	5	30	—	18	—

National Journal Ratings

	1986 LIB — 1986 CONS			1985 LIB — 1985 CONS		
Economic	77%	—	20%	89%	—	0%
Social	86%	—	11%	85%	—	0%
Foreign	75%	—	20%	85%	—	8%

Key Votes

1) Lmt Cln Water Act	AGN	5) Retain Gun Cont	FOR	9) Aid Angola Reb	AGN
2) Rpl Tobac Sub	FOR	6) Contra Aid	AGN	10) Tax Reform	FOR
3) Grm-Rdmn Def Red	AGN	7) Lmt Text Imp	AGN	11) S Africa Sanc	FOR
4) Ban Polygraph	FOR	8) Limit SDI	FOR	12) Immig Reform	AGN

Election Results

1986 general	Norman Y. Mineta (D)	107,696	(70%)	($443,822)
	Bob Nash (R)	46,754	(30%)	($33,297)
1986 primary	Norman Y. Mineta (D)	42,657	(100%)	
1984 general	Norman Y. Mineta (D)	139,851	(65%)	($421,789)
	John D. (Jack) Williams (R)	70,666	(33%)	($14,720)

Campaign Contributions and Expenditures

1985-86		Direct Cont. 1985-86		PACS Breakdown 1985-86			
Receipts	$546,210	Indiv.	$279,094	Corp.	$85,085	T/M/H	$52,639
Expend.	$443,822	PACS	$224,098	Labor	$68,273	Agr.	$3,000
Unspent	$265,856			Ideo.	$11,351	CWOS	$3,750

FOURTEENTH DISTRICT

The Mother Lode country, where the Central Valley of California begins rising toward the Sierra Nevada, has been one of the fastest-growing parts of California in the last decade—one of those trends that no one predicted but the reasons for which become obvious to almost everyone soon after. Here the reasons seem to be that a lot of Californians, from the smog-filled middle-class suburbs of the Los Angeles Basin and the San Francisco Bay Area, and from the vast flat expanse of the Central Valley, were looking for a more pleasant, small town, tradition-minded environment—and found it not far away, where the land began to rise. They came to an area that hasn't grown much since the Gold Rush of 1849, when many men (and only a few women) sprinted to these fast-flowing creeks and rivers from all over the world to make their fortunes. Some actually did, and others spent them, and in the process they built good-sized towns complete with opera houses in places that a year before no white man had seen. Placerville, Nevada City, Angels Camp, Poker Flat—the names recall a way of life made immortal by Mark Twain and Bret Harte and that then abruptly vanished. The mining towns were abandoned quickly when the ore gave out; some parts of the Mother Lode country had more people in 1850 than they have had ever since. They left behind Victorian houses and commercial buildings, set amidst beautiful hills and mountains, which are now, 100 years later, suddenly the focus of fashion and locus of growth.

In big cities, the renovators of Victorian houses are often those with liberation-minded cultural values. That's not true of those who converged on these Victorian towns. Many came from metropolitan California, where their children grew up as parts of vast peer groups, taught by teachers who often wanted them to rebel against their parent's values more than anything else, interested in everything from drugs to cult religions. In the Mother Lode country, migrants felt they could keep an eye on their children's upbringing and have more say in how they grew up.

So this has proved to be more a conservative than a liberal migration. By 1980 the effect was plain in partisan elections: these traditionally Democratic counties were swinging to the Republicans. In 1982, the gun control referendum brought to the polls thousands of people who had not voted before: young fathers in plaid flannel shirts and down-filled jackets, who strongly opposed gun control and voted for Republicans up and down the ballot. In 1986 turnout did not rise, but George Deukmejian carried the Mother Lode country well-nigh unanimously—a clear indication that the change was permanent. The many younger and some older people in California seem to be re-creating in the Sierra foothills the kind of communities their parents or grandparents left behind years ago in the Midwest.

The Mother Lode country is large enough now to rate a congressional district of its own. Under the current redistricting plan, the Mother Lode area from Amador County in the north and the sparsely populated mountain counties in the northeast corner of the state account for two-thirds of the population of California's 14th Congressional District. The rest is in the Central Valley, and includes the more Republican parts of the city of Stockton and Lodi, a Republican town settled almost entirely by North Dakotans.

This is a Republican district, designed for Representative Norman Shumway. Shumway was a member of the board of supervisors in Stockton in 1978 when he beat John McFall, who had been House Democratic whip from 1972 to 1976; McFall made the mistake in 1974 of taking $3,000 from Korean lobbyist Tongsun Park, depositing it in his office account, and using it for personal business. Shumway's reelection since then, in two quite different-shaped districts, shows the distinct Republican trend in the Mother Lode country. A devout Mormon and firm believer in free enterprise, Shumway has a solid conservative voting record on most issues; on the Banking Committee he even made a point of opposing a bill that would limit bank service charges, something no voter likes. He is the prime House sponsor of the measure, much opposed by trial lawyers, to establish a uniform and not particularly generous product liability law for the nation—an interesting example of conservatives opposing state's rights. He opposes protectionist legislation.

Not an opponent of all public works measures, he is proud of the work he has done channeling money to the port of Stockton, which is now open through channels in the Sacramento Delta, to oceangoing ships. He has opposed sanctions on South Africa. A strong backer of establishing English as our official language, he was happy to see California voters approve such a measure in 1986—although he himself speaks Japanese and has been learning Spanish. He has been the major opponent of Democrat John LaFalce's industrial policy bill, a measure that isn't going anywhere but which sounds attractive. On many issues he has shown himself willing to take tough stands that antagonize important constituency groups or could irritate many voters.

Perhaps one or more of these stands will cause him problems some day; they have not so far. On the contrary, he has won reelection in the 1980s by overwhelming margins, and seems even more firmly established in the Mother Lode country than in his own home area around Stockton.

The People: Pop. 1980: 526,030, up 50.8% 1970–80. Households (1980): 75% family, 39% with children, 65% married couples; 32.1% housing units rented; median monthly rent: $220; median house value: $71,200. Voting age pop. (1980): 381,713; 7% Spanish origin, 2% Asian origin, 1% Black, 1% American Indian.

Presidential Vote:

Reagan (R)	162,239	(64%)
Mondale (D)	86,619	(34%)

Rep. Norman D. Shumway (R)

Elected 1978; b. July 28, 1934, Phoenix, AZ; home, Stockton; U. of UT, B.S. 1960, Hastings Col. of Law, J.D. 1963; Mormon; married (Luana).

Career: Practicing atty., 1964–78; San Joaquin Cnty. Bd. of Sprvsrs., 1974–78, Chmn., 1978.

Offices: 1203 LHOB 20515, 202-225-2511. Also 1150 W. Robinhood, Ste. 1-A, Stockton 95207, 209-957-7773; and 11899 Edgewood Rd., Ste. B, Auburn 95603, 916-885-3737.

Committees: *Banking, Finance and Urban Affairs* (4th of 20 R). Subcommittees: Economic Stabilization (Ranking Member); Financial Institutions Supervision, Regulation and Insurance; International Finance, Trade, and Monetary Policy. *Merchant Marine and Fisheries* (4th of 17 R). Subcommittees: Merchant Marine; Oceanography (Ranking Member); Panama Canal and Outer Continental Shelf. *Select Committee on Aging* (4th of 26 R). Subcommittee: Human Services; Retirement Income and Employment.

Group Ratings

	ADA	ACLU	COPE	CFA	LCV	ACU	NTU	NSI	COC	CEI
1986	0	5	7	0	16	95	68	100	94	86
1985	15	—	7	17	—	95	72	—	91	—

National Journal Ratings

	1986 LIB — 1986 CONS			1985 LIB — 1985 CONS		
Economic	13%	—	85%	5%	—	92%
Social	11%	—	85%	0%	—	76%
Foreign	0%	—	86%	0%	—	76%

Key Votes

1) Lmt Cln Water Act	FOR	5) Retain Gun Cont	AGN	9) Aid Angola Reb	FOR
2) Rpl Tobac Sub	FOR	6) Contra Aid	FOR	10) Tax Reform	AGN
3) Grm-Rdmn Def Red	AGN	7) Lmt Text Imp	AGN	11) S Africa Sanc	AGN
4) Ban Polygraph	AGN	8) Limit SDI	FOR	12) Immig Reform	FOR

Election Results

1986 general	Norman D. Shumway (R)	146,906	(72%)	($257,431)
	Bill Steele (D)	53,597	(26%)	
1986 primary	Norman D. Shumway (R)	61,241	(100%)	
1984 general	Norman D. Shumway (R)	179,238	(73%)	($292,131)
	Ruth (Paula) Carlson (D)	58,384	(24%)	

Campaign Contributions and Expenditures

1985-86		Direct Cont. 1985-86		PACS Breakdown 1985-86			
Receipts	$323,671	Indiv.	$166,745	Corp.	$66,215	T/M/H	$44,690
Expend.	$257,431	PACS	$141,443	Labor	$11,750	Agr.	$3,750
Unspent	$139,098			Ideo.	$7,750	CWOS	$7,288

FIFTEENTH DISTRICT

When white men first saw the Central Valley of California it seemed barren, almost a desert—a vast flat dry expanse between the Sierra Nevada and the Coast Range, extending up and down the state from Tehachapi, north of Los Angeles, almost to the Oregon border. Today the Valley is incredibly productive, the nation's leading producer of vegetables and fruits (though hurt now by the worldwide glut in agricultural commodities), and a major cotton producer as well. The Valley as it is today is the joint creation of man, technology, free enterprise, and government.

Nowhere is that more evident than in the 15th Congressional District of California. Here, between Modesto and Fresno, are some of the Valley's most productive farmlands and some of its larger cities. Fresno, the largest next to Sacramento, is mostly in other districts, but some of its suburban fringe and all of its western agricultural region are in the district. Here in the flat lands west of Route 99 as it goes from Fresno to Modesto you can sees the Valley's greatest riches, in the Westlands, the real agricultural heart of the Valley. Vast, largely unpopulated, the site of huge corporate farms, they are exceedingly productive and profitable. But they would be worth nothing without the heavily subsidized water which the federal and state governments provide. Federal reclamation projects and the California Aqueduct channel the plentiful waters that flow down from the Sierras into the Westlands, from channels that begin as far away as the northern Sacramento River, 300 miles away.

Politically, the 15th District remains Democratic in an increasingly Republican Valley. Nearly one-quarter of its residents are of Spanish origin, and probably about the same number are of white southern ancestry; both groups tend to be Democrats on economic issues. But on cultural issues the 15th and the neighboring 17th Districts are also the most family- and children-oriented parts of California, except for a couple of suburban Los Angeles districts; the 15th has a higher than national average percentage of children, married couples, and families. Voters here have never been very positive toward the liberal referenda promoted by coastal Californians, from gun control to marijuana decriminalization and coastal zone preservation, and in 1986 they overwhelmingly rejected the urban Thomas Bradley in favor of quiet, reassuring, stubbornly conservative George Deukmejian.

The 15th District has one of the most powerful and most competent members of the House, a man who in eight years' time moved up from freshman status to the number three position in the Democratic leadership. He is Tony Coelho, chairman of the Democratic Congressional Campaign Committee from 1981 to 1986 and elected after the 1986 election as majority whip. Coelho began his career with deep roots in the Valley, where he was raised on a dairy farm. In college he discovered he had epilepsy, was renounced by his parents and rejected for the priesthood. Bob Hope's wife heard about his plight and Hope took him under his arm and suggested that if he couldn't serve the public as a priest he could do so on Capitol Hill instead; and so Coelho got a job with Fresno Representative B. F. Sisk. He stayed with Sisk for 15 years; he learned the politics of agriculture and water at a master's knee.

Elected in his own right in 1978, when Sisk retired, Coelho's first order of business was the Valley. He got seats on the Agriculture and Interior Committees and worked hard for Valley and Westlands water interests. He fought Bay Area Democrat George Miller in his desire to enforce a long-waived 160-acre limit on farmers who receive subsidized water; eventually Coelho produced the compromise under which owners would pay a higher price for the water and still keep their land. In just a few years the veteran congressmen from the Valley all were leaving— John McFall was beaten in 1978, Sisk retired that year, Harold Johnson lost in 1980. That left Coelho as one of the senior congressmen from the Valley and, by common consent, the Valley's key man on all agricultural and water issues, one of the people who keeps this wondrously productive, if not always logical, system working.

All that he accomplished in just a few years. But he took on a greater challenge as chairman of the House Democratic Campaign Committee. It seemed a thankless post. The incumbent had just lost to a Republican. The committee had little money in the bank and had been outraised 10 to 1 by its Republican counterpart. It had a puny direct mail list, relied on a single dinner for most of its money, and did little more than funnel a few dollars to incumbents who often didn't need the help. The Republicans had just won the White House and Senate in stunning upsets and seemed within striking range of winning control of the House. The word was out that the new Reaganites expected Republican-leaning PACs to contribute solely to Republican candidates and free themselves from Democratic control of the House once and for all in 1982.

Systematically Coelho went about preventing that from happening. He started the long work of building up direct mail fundraising lists and went around the country courting businessmen and entrepreneurs. He provided unprecedented kinds of aid to candidates. He built a press relations staff second to none in Washington. He modeled much of his operation after the successful work of Republicans, and unblushingly. Most important, he went door to door to PACS all over Washington and let them know he expected them to be bipartisan in their giving—and that if they didn't know of any Democrats they could support, he would be happy to supply them with a list of those who were right on their issue. "Just remember," he would say, "that we control every committee and subcommittee in the House, and we keep score."

His strategy worked. The campaign committee was able to provide critical money and advice to challenger candidates. Democratic candidates for the House raised more PAC money than Republican candidates for the House. Some observers—and some Democratic congressmen— criticized Coelho for shaking down business interests and hitching congressional Democrats to business interests which, in this view, they should be opposing. But of course those interests would have been better served if Republicans had maintained working control or had won nominal control of the House. Instead they lost ground. The Democrats picked up 26 House seats in 1982, when many had expected the Republicans to make more gains. They lost only 15 seats in 1984, when President Reagan was winning reelection with 59% of the vote. They won a net of five seats in 1986, despite a lack of strong challengers, and lost only a single incumbent. In race after race, even in Republican open seats, Democrats led Republicans in PAC contributions, many of them steered that way by Coelho. Through the Reagan years, when most of the major issues were working for the Republicans, Coelho played a major role, second perhaps only to that of Tip O'Neill, in keeping the House of Representatives in Democratic control.

He did it with an attention to detail and a passion for orderliness that seems to carry all before it. Coelho jots down notes on his 3x5 cards and then proceeds to touch every base and make every phone call. He checks and rechecks all his commitments and never hesitates to ask for contributions from outsiders and help from colleagues. Through all his work on the campaign committee, he maintained his superintendency of Valley issues and also chaired the Agriculture Livestock, Dairy and Poultry Subcommittee, successfully managing a dairy subsidy bill (milk money, as it has been for many years, is one of the cements that holds the Democratic majority together). He took the trouble to apply for membership in the Hispanic Caucus and, in 1985, was finally admitted after arguing that the Roman "Hispania" included what is now Portugal and pointing out that he is of Portuguese descent. He stage-managed the ultimately successful but arduous fight to seat Indiana Democrat Frank McCloskey rather than his Republican opponent after the 1984 election. His thoroughness and his record of helping colleagues enabled him to win the whip post by an overwhelming margin over as attractive an opponent as Charles Rangel of New York.

Coelho comes to the whip position with not a particularly good reputation in Washington: the sense is that he is a fixer, without principles, who sometimes sells out his party. Yet he could not have done his campaign work successfully without a mastery of the substance of legislation; he had to learn the legislative goals of every lobby and every member. Also, he has helped to set party strategy, which means taking positions on substantive issues—trade and the Nicaraguan contras, to name two—that can be sustained over the long haul. His own voting record is not as liberal as those of Bay Area Democrats, but is in line with that of other Democratic leaders, and he was happy to join a dozen other Democrats sleeping out on Capitol Hill to publicize the issue of the homeless. Like Tip O'Neill and Jim Wright, he is little interested in bipartisan efforts on most issues. As whip he is likely to be aggressive and combative, determined to beat the Republicans on big issues and small, in the long term and the short. But Coelho may not be wedded to the system he has exploited. In late 1986 he was hinting that he was ready to support thoroughgoing campaign finance reform, and he has a seat on House Administration to keep a close eye on the issue. If he is convinced that the old system must go, his success in exploiting it probably gives him confidence he can learn to exploit whatever comes next.

Coelho may be handicapped by his sometimes breathtaking frankness in a business that likes to put the best face on things. He admits his partisan motives and is open about his strategy. His success as whip and his possibilities for advancement when Speaker Jim Wright or Majority Leader Thomas Foley retire depend on his matching his electoral and political accomplishments with more solid legislative work and using his political skills for the achievement of more than political gain.

The People: Pop. 1980: 525,949, up 30.8% 1970–80. Households (1980): 77% family, 44% with children, 64% married couples; 39.4% housing units rented; median monthly rent: $192; median house value: $57,100. Voting age pop. (1980): 361,570; 20% Spanish origin, 2% Black, 2% Asian origin, 1% American Indian.

1984 Presidential Vote: Reagan (R) 101,657   (59%)
Mondale (D) 70,069   (40%)

Rep. Tony L. Coelho (D)

Elected 1978; b. June 15, 1942, Los Banos; home, Merced; Loyola U., L.A., B.A. 1964; Roman Catholic; married (Phyllis).

Career: Staff of U.S. Rep. B. F. Sisk, 1965–78, A. A., 1970–78.

Offices: 403 CHOB 20515, 202-225-6131. Also Fed. Bldg., 415 W. 18th St., Merced 95340, 209-383-4455; 900 H St., Ste. B, Modesto 95354, 209-527-1914; and 419 S. Madera, Kerman 93630, 209-846-7705.

Committees: *Majority Whip. Agriculture* (10th of 26 D). Subcommittee: Conservation, Credit and Rural Development; Cotton, Rice and Sugar; Domestic Marketing, Consumer Relations, and Nutrition; Livestock, Dairy, and Poultry. *House Administration* (8th of 12 D). Subcommittees: Accounts; Elections; Personnel and Police. *Interior and Insular Affairs* (10th of 26 D). Subcommittees: National Parks and Public Lands; Water and Power Resources.

Group Ratings

	ADA	ACLU	COPE	CFA	LCV	ACU	NTU	NSI	COC	CEI
1986	70	80	85	50	48	14	24	0	14	12
1985	80	—	83	50	—	0	10	—	26	—

National Journal Ratings

	1986 LIB — 1986 CONS	1985 LIB — 1985 CONS
Economic	87% — 0%	79% — 21%
Social	57% — 40%	69% — 28%
Foreign	73% — 26%	71% — 26%

Key Votes

1) Lmt Cln Water Act	AGN	5) Retain Gun Cont	FOR	9) Aid Angola Reb	AGN
2) Rpl Tobac Sub	AGN	6) Contra Aid	AGN	10) Tax Reform	FOR
3) Grm-Rdmn Def Rcd	AGN	7) Lmt Text Imp	FOR	11) S Africa Sanc	FOR
4) Ban Polygraph	FOR	8) Limit SDI	FOR	12) Immig Reform	FOR

Election Results

1986 general	Tony L. Coelho (D)	93,600	(71%)	($655,211)
	Carol Harner (R)	35,793	(27%)	
1986 primary	Tony L. Coelho (D)	39,144	(100%)	
1984 general	Tony L. Coelho (D)	109,590	(65%)	($482,891)
	Carol Harner (R)	54,730	(33%)	($8,814)

Campaign Contributions and Expenditures

1985-86		Direct Cont. 1985-86		PACS Breakdown 1985-86			
Receipts	$726,304	Indiv.	$353,676	Corp.	$104,750	T/M/H	$98,000
Expend.	$655,211	PACS	$353,645	Labor	$87,025	Agr.	$37,820
Unspent	$232,032			Ideo.	$15,800	CWOS	$10,250

SIXTEENTH DISTRICT

Following the coastline of California, from the bare green hills north of Santa Cruz past Monterey and Carmel and down the Big Sur coast past William Randolph Hearst's San Simeon is the 16th Congressional District of California. This coastline boasts some of the nation's most spectacular scenery, from the Monterey cypresses at Carmel's Pebble Beach through the barren mountains of the Big Sur as they plunge down into the surf to the gaudy architecture of Hearst's mansion. The district extends inland as well, into sunny valleys sheltered from the ocean mists.

Just a few miles from some of the nation's richest farmland: the lettuce fields of the Salinas Valley, the artichoke fields around Castroville. This is John Steinbeck country: he grew up in Salinas, and his Cannery Row, four decades after the bay's sardines disappeared, now has luxury hotels and one of the nation's finest aquariums.

If most of the interior of America has moved toward the Republicans over the past quarter-century, most coastal areas have become more Democratic; and so it is here. The older residents—landowners in Salinas and the townspeople who sympathize with them, retirees in Santa Cruz and the Monterey Peninsula—still vote Republican. But as the focus in the 1970s shifted from economic to cultural issues, the coast moved to the left. Environmental issues are one reason. Population shifts—an influx of liberation-minded young people—is another. The coast seems to attract migrants who, while affluent, subscribe to liberal magazines and buy Sierra Club calendars. Also, the branch of the University of California at Santa Cruz is so liberal (97% for McGovern in 1972) that it changed the political balance of the whole county. Sometimes the shift has gone too far: the artsy-craftsy ocean village of Carmel, after its mayor and council insisted on banning the sale of ice cream cones, elected conservative movie star Clint Eastwood as mayor in 1986.

In congressional elections, however, the 16th District has proved loyal to its now longtime Democratic congressman, Leon Panetta. That loyalty must have been particularly welcome in 1986, for Panetta had just gone through an arduous term. Coming out of the 1984 election, he looked like the favorite to become the new Budget Committee chairman. For four years he had been one of the leading Democrats on budget issues, doing all the necessary detail work and deal-making to weld a united Democratic front on this most difficult of issues. A little less free-spending than traditional northern liberals, operating with extensive experience in government and an instinctive understanding of how it works, he built up credibility on both sides of the aisle. But not quite everywhere. Speaker O'Neill and Majority Leader Wright in late 1984 worried that he might challenge their authority, and they persuaded the Democratic caucus not to waive the three-term limit on Budget Committee membership. That automatically ruled out Panetta and the incumbent chairman Jim Jones as well, and opened the way for O'Neill's choice, William Gray.

Then O'Neill delivered an even nastier stroke, picking Panetta as chairman of the task force conducting a recount of the disputed Indiana 8th election. Panetta insisted that he was behaving fairly, and could argue that he was leaning over backwards to do so, but when he ruled that Democrat Frank McCloskey won by four votes, the Republicans were enraged. Panetta was attacked on the floor, and his bipartisan reputation was tarnished.

Fortunately for Panetta, he had other things to keep him busy. He was the House's chief advocate of guestworker amendments to immigration bills, to provide cheap labor for California's fruit and vegetable growers, and after he got one such amendment through in 1984 over the objections of organized labor and most Democrats it became clear that the House would not pass an immigration bill without one. He also serves on the Agriculture Committee, which allows him to tend to district interests as well as to push for more generous nutrition programs and to keep California's rigorous anti-pesticide laws from being superseded by weaker federal standards. He has been the Democrats' leading negotiator in the uncharacteristically bipartisan effort of the California delegation to limit offshore oil drilling—an effort in which they have been at odds with Interior Secretary Donald Hodel, and in which the major fights come over the Interior appropriation battle each year. Panetta's career in the House is an illustration of the new rhythm of House politics: instead of rising slowly over the decades to a position of power, Panetta rose quickly because of his talents to a national policymaking role, then receded after some setbacks and concentrated more on local and committee matters. He may well be heard on major national issues again.

In the meantime, he remains extremely popular at home. Like many residents of the 16th District, he was once a Republican—a Nixon Administration appointee, in fact, who resigned over policy as head of the Office of Civil Rights at the Department of Health, Education and

Welfare in 1970. He switched parties after that, and back home he ran for the House in 1976, beating a starchy conservative Republican. His combination of mixed votes on economic issues and generally liberal stands on cultural and foreign policy has been in line with the shifts of opinion along this coast, and his hard work and pleasant personality have cemented his hold on the district. In 1986, after all the travail of the past two years, he was reelected with 78% of the vote.

The People: Pop. 1980: 526,120, up 26.1% 1970–80. Households (1980): 68% family, 36% with children, 56% married couples; 46.1% housing units rented; median monthly rent: $263; median house value: $87,400. Voting age pop. (1980): 391,002; 18% Spanish origin, 5% Asian origin, 4% Black, 1% American Indian.

Presidential Vote:

Reagan (R) 111,375	(53%)
Mondale (D) 98,292	(46%)

Rep. Leon E. Panetta (D)

Elected 1976; b. June 28, 1938, Monterey; home, Carmel Valley; U. of Santa Clara, B.A. 1960, J.D. 1963; Roman Catholic; married (Sylvia).

Career: Army, 1963–65; Legis. Asst. to U.S. Sen. Thomas Kuchel, 1966–69; Dir., U.S. Ofc. of Civil Rights, Dept. of H.E.W., 1969–70; Exec. Asst. to Mayor of New York City, 1970–71; Practicing atty., 1971–76.

Offices: 339 CHOB 20515, 202-225-2861. Also 380 Alvarado St., Monterey 93940, 408-649-3555; and 100 W. Alisal, Salinas 93901, 408-424-2229.

Committees: *Agriculture* (7th of 26 D). Subcommittees: Department Operations, Research, and Foreign Agriculture; Domestic Marketing, Consumer Relations, and Nutrition (Chairman); Forests, Family Farms, and Energy. *House Administration* (5th of 12 D). Subcommittees: Accounts; Elections; Personnel and Police (Chairman). *Select Committee on Hunger* (4th of 16 D). Task Force: Domestic Task Force (Chairman).

Group Ratings

	ADA	ACLU	COPE	CFA	LCV	ACU	NTU	NSI	COC	CEI
1986	85	84	72	58	82	11	31	0	31	19
1985	75	—	71	75	—	14	39	—	32	—

National Journal Ratings

	1986 LIB — 1986 CONS		1985 LIB — 1985 CONS	
Economic	66% —	32%	68% —	30%
Social	72% —	27%	81% —	15%
Foreign	80% —	0%	85% —	8%

Key Votes

1) Lmt Cln Water Act	AGN	5) Retain Gun Cont	FOR	9) Aid Angola Reb	AGN
2) Rpl Tobac Sub	AGN	6) Contra Aid	AGN	10) Tax Reform	FOR
3) Grm-Rdmn Def Red	FOR	7) Lmt Text Imp	AGN	11) S Africa Sanc	—
4) Ban Polygraph	FOR	8) Limit SDI	FOR	12) Immig Reform	FOR

Election Results

1986 general	Leon E. Panetta (D) 128,151	(78%)	($114,446)
	Louis Darrigo (R) 31,386	(19%)	($9,557)
1986 primary	Leon E. Panetta (D) 53,568	(94%)	
	Arthur V. Dunn (D) 3,407	(6%)	
1984 general	Leon E. Panetta (D) 153,377	(71%)	($279,887)
	Patricia Smith Ramsey (R) 60,065	(28%)	($425,277)

Campaign Contributions and Expenditures

1985-86		Direct Cont. 1985-86		PACS Breakdown 1985-86			
Receipts	$166,791	Indiv.	$80,839	Corp.	$13,825	T/M/H	$29,150
Expend.	$115,446	PACS	$87,786	Labor	$21,750	Agr.	$7,500
Unspent	$116,169			Ideo.	$12,561	CWOS	$3,000

SEVENTEENTH DISTRICT

Grapes, cotton, alfalfa, cantaloupes, plums, peaches, lima beans, tomatoes, sugar beets, walnuts, olives, poultry, dairy products: these are some of the crops grown in the southern part of the Central Valley, between Fresno and Bakersfield, that makes up California's 17th Congressional District. This is some of the richest agricultural land in the world. Almost all the crops here are produced by very large farming operations that bear little resemblance to the stereotypical family farm: these are serious medium-sized and large businesses. The producers pride themselves on their success through free enterprise, but like most entrepreneurs they are happy to have the government provide safety nets, in the form of crop subsidies, agricultural research, irrigation systems, and subsidized water. It's hard to make a theoretical case for such a mixed system, and no one person would have designed it from scratch. But it works. It has made Central Valley agriculture exceedingly productive; and if it has helped some producers get rich, they can argue they deserve it for the work they do and what they produce.

The congressman from the 17th District is Chip Pashayan, a son of the Fresno area's large and conspicuously successful Armenian-American community and a staunch Republican conservative. Pashayan first won his seat in 1978 by upsetting a Democratic incumbent when the district included more of Fresno than it does now; in retrospect this was one harbinger of the conservative trend that saw the election of Ronald Reagan and a Republican Senate in 1980. Pashayan is a determined and often contentious Republican, of a very different mold from the get-along-go-along Democrats who tended to the Valley's special interests for so many years. Pashayan has a seat on the Interior Committee and on the Water Subcommittee, which is of such vital importance to the district. Though he fought vociferously for the area's water users, the key work was done by Democrat Tony Coelho of the next-door 15th District.

Since he first won the district, Pashayan has been helped by redistricting, which removed most of Democratic Fresno and moved the district so far south that it now includes all of the Valley counties of Tulare (half the district's population and heavily Republican) and Kings (much smaller and formerly Democratic) and dips down into Kern County to Bakersfield. That last area, which includes Delano, the headquarters of Cesar Chavez's United Farm Workers, is usually Republican; the UFW is rather unpopular, in the manner of insurgent unions, except with its own membership. Pashayan has been a target of Democrats several times, and in 1982 they held him to 54%. But in 1986 he won against a well-financed opponent by a 60%–40% margin. That, plus his additional seniority on committees important to the district, suggest he has made this once marginal district a safe seat.

The People: Pop. 1980: 526,033, up 34.6% 1970–80. Households (1980): 79% family, 47% with children, 66% married couples; 36.2% housing units rented; median monthly rent: $189; median house value: $56,800. Voting age pop. (1980): 356,229; 23% Spanish origin, 3% Asian origin, 2% Black, 1% American Indian.

1984 Presidential Vote:
Reagan (R) 116,975   (63%)
Mondale (D) 65,892   (36%)

Rep. Charles (Chip) Pashayan, Jr. (R)

Elected 1978; b. Mar. 27, 1941, Fresno; home, Fresno; Pomona Col., B.A. 1963, U. of CA, J.D. 1968, Oxford U., M. Litt. 1977; Congregational; married (Sallie).

Career: Army, 1968–70; Practicing atty., 1969–78; Spec. Asst. to Gen. Counsel, U.S. Dept. of H.E.W., 1973–75.

Offices: 129 CHOB 20515, 202-225-3341. Also 1702 E. Bullard Ave., #103, Fresno 93710, 209-487-5500; 804 N. Irwin, Hanford 93230, 209-582-2896; 831 W. Center St., Visalia 93291, 209-627-2700; and 201 High St., Delano 93215, 805-725-7371.

Committees: *Interior and Insular Affairs* (6th of 15 R). Subcommittees: Energy and the Environment; National Parks and Public Lands; Water and Power Resources (Ranking Member). *Post Office and Civil Service* (3d of 8 R). Subcommittees: Civil Service (Ranking Member); Postal Operations and Services. *Standards of Official Conduct* (4th of 6 R).

Group Ratings

	ADA	ACLU	COPE	CFA	LCV	ACU	NTU	NSI	COC	CEI
1986	25	15	28	33	21	64	34	100	56	40
1985	5	—	23	25	—	80	52	—	85	—

National Journal Ratings

	1986 LIB — 1986 CONS		1985 LIB — 1985 CONS	
Economic	38%	— 61%	19%	— 81%
Social	37%	— 61%	0%	— 76%
Foreign	25%	— 74%	0%	— 76%

Key Votes

1) Lmt Cln Water Act	AGN	5) Retain Gun Cont	AGN	9) Aid Angola Reb	FOR
2) Rpl Tobac Sub	AGN	6) Contra Aid	FOR	10) Tax Reform	FOR
3) Grm-Rdmn Def Red	—	7) Lmt Text Imp	FOR	11) S Africa Sanc	FOR
4) Ban Polygraph	FOR	8) Limit SDI	AGN	12) Immig Reform	FOR

Election Results

1986 general	Charles (Chip) Pashayan, Jr. (R)	88,787	(60%)	($304,194)
	John Hartnett (D)	58,682	(40%)	($228,592)
1986 primary	Charles (Chip) Pashayan, Jr. (R)	41,777	(100%)	
1984 general	Charles (Chip) Pashayan, Jr. (R)	128,802	(72%)	($288,264)
	Simon Lakritz (D)	48,888	(28%)	($21,803)

Campaign Contributions and Expenditures

1985-86		Direct Cont. 1985-86		PACS Breakdown 1985-86			
Receipts	$307,169	Indiv.	$185,230	Corp.	$40,345	T/M/H	$42,750
Expend.	$304,194	Party	$2,884	Labor	$4,901	Agr.	$11,750
Unspent	$60,440	PACS	$113,649	Ideo.	$8,175	CWOS	$5,728

EIGHTEENTH DISTRICT

Fresno is one of those American cities that doesn't get much respect. The 1986 TV miniseries *Fresno* poked tasteless fun at the town and told anyone who didn't already know that it is the nation's leading raisin producer. One of those ratings of cities placed Fresno dead last in 1984 as a place to live. Californians from the Los Angeles Basin or the San Francisco Bay use "Fresno" as a synonym for a hopelessly out-of-touch backwater. Statistics tell another story: Fresno is prosperous and rapidly growing, hot in the summer perhaps, but with warm winters, accessible to desert and mountain, but situated itself square in the center of the richest agricultural land in the United States, California's Central Valley. If it is more tradition-minded than California's bigger cities, that is something more and more Americans like, and it has given a warm welcome to immigrants from the Armenians earlier in the century to Mexicans and Vietnamese today.

Fresno is the largest component of California's 18th congressional district, but not exactly its center; in fact, nothing is, since this is one of the most grotesquely-shaped districts in America today. The Fresno portion of the 18th, carefully excised of affluent suburbs, is connected to a similar portion of the smaller Central Valley city of Stockton, 105 miles northwest, by largely uninhabited land on the other side of the Sierra Nevada. Appended to the Fresno end is the agricultural land around the town of Sanger, home of the current congressman, Richard Lehman. The 18th was designed by the late Phillip Burton to accommodate Lehman, one of those young idealistic political maneuverers that the California legislature seems to nurture in such abundance.

Lehman combines a desire to move the country a bit left on economic and environmental policy with a readiness to nurture the interests of the agricultural business which is almost the sole basis of the economies of both halves of his district. He votes generally with other House Democrats on most issues and is generally a team player. He irritated some farming interests by backing a successful bill to keep several remaining rivers in the mountains undammed, but he also defends strenuously agribusiness's eagerness to import otherwise illegal migrants to work their fields.

In 1982, at age 34, he won his Democratic primary without opposition and, with huge hometown support from Fresno County, won the general election easily. In the House he won assignment to the Interior Committee, which handles issues relating to water, which is so precious to the Valley. He has won reelection twice easily and has become a regional whip, laying the groundwork for what could be a long congressional career representing disparate parts of the Central Valley. Lehman is one of those young Democrats who make politics look easy, and whose skills explain, more than any other single factor, why their party has continued to have such large majorities in the House and in most of America's legislatures in the Reagan years of the 1980s.

The People: Pop. 1980: 525,990, up 14.2% 1970–80. Households (1980): 70% family, 38% with children, 55% married couples; 42.0% housing units rented; median monthly rent: $186; median house value: $54,500. Voting age pop. (1980): 376,078; 21% Spanish origin, 6% Black, 4% Asian origin, 1% American Indian.

1984 Presidential Vote:

Reagan (R)	102,593	(51%)
Mondale (D)	98,163	(48%)

Rep. Richard H. Lehman (D)

Elected 1982; b. July 20, 1948, Sanger; home, Sanger; Fresno City Col., CA State U., U. of CA at Santa Cruz; Lutheran; married (Patricia).

Career: A. A. to CA St. Sen. George N. Zenovich, 1970–76; CA Assembly, 1976–82.

Offices: 1319 LHOB 20515, 202-225-4540. Also 1900 Mariposa Mall, Ste. 301, Fresno 93721, 209-487-5760; 48 W. Yaney Ave., Sonora 95370, 209-533-1426; and 209 W. Yosemite, Rm. W-1, Madera 93637, 209-661-4084.

Committees: *Banking, Finance, and Urban Affairs* (15th of 31 D). Subcommittees: Financial Institutions Supervision, Regulation and Insurance; Housing and Community Development; International Finance, Trade and Monetary Policy. *Interior and Insular Affairs* (15th of 26 D). Subcommittees: National Parks and Public Lands; Water and Power Resources.

Group Ratings

	ADA	ACLU	COPE	CFA	LCV	ACU	NTU	NSI	COC	CEI
1986	75	73	92	50	63	10	26	0	25	11
1985	80	—	89	50	—	0	33	—	30	—

National Journal Ratings

	1986 LIB — 1986 CONS		1985 LIB — 1985 CONS	
Economic	79%	— 20%	79%	— 21%
Social	63%	— 36%	73%	— 27%
Foreign	75%	— 20%	75%	— 21%

Key Votes

1) Lmt Cln Water Act	AGN	5) Retain Gun Cont	FOR	9) Aid Angola Reb	AGN
2) Rpl Tobac Sub	AGN	6) Contra Aid	AGN	10) Tax Reform	AGN
3) Grm-Rdmn Def Red	AGN	7) Lmt Text Imp	FOR	11) S Africa Sanc	FOR
4) Ban Polygraph	FOR	8) Limit SDI	FOR	12) Immig Reform	FOR

Election Results

1986 general	Richard H. Lehman (D)	101,480	(71%)	($290,626)
	David C. Crevelt (R)	40,907	(28%)	($32,503)
1986 primary	Richard H. Lehman (D)	49,086	(100%)	
1984 general	Richard H. Lehman (D)	128,186	(67%)	($194,660)
	Dale L. Ewen (R)	62,339	(33%)	($14,389)

Campaign Contributions and Expenditures

1985-86		Direct Cont. 1985-86		PACS Breakdown 1985-86			
Receipts	$253,791	Indiv.	$94,537	Corp.	$41,900	T/M/H	$60,110
Expend.	$290,626	Party	$307	Labor	$29,200	Agr.	$4,550
Unspent	$7,099	PACS	$147,371	Ideo.	$4,761	CWOS	$6,850

NINETEENTH DISTRICT

A president of the United States can vacation just about anywhere in the country he wants; the president for most of the 1980s, Ronald Reagan, chooses to vacation in a ranch in the hills above Santa Barbara, California. He is not the only rich American in his later years who chooses to live in the Santa Barbara area: this has been one of the favorite retirement areas of the wealthy since the 1920s. Yet Santa Barbara still looks much as it did early in the century; the town has rigid architectural controls and almost all its buildings are in the Mission style complete with red tile roofs. The mountains, dotted just occasionally with subdivisions and ranches, look much as they did when Father Junipero Serra came here and built the Santa Barbara Mission in 1786. Some of the towns around Santa Barbara have grown and changed. There is a University of California branch in Isla Vista, where students in the long-ago 1970s burned the Bank of America branch, and to the east is the industrial town of Oxnard, burgeoning around its oil refineries. But Santa Barbara, its population limited, its buildings controlled, its real estate prices ever higher, remains much the same: the center of a kind of American Riviera, a place where those who ponder the smog of Los Angeles can understand what brought so many millions of Americans to southern California decades ago.

Politically, Santa Barbara has been conservative, as befits a city that lives off capital; but it has also been determined to preserve its near-perfect environment. The world's first offshore drilling began six miles east of Santa Barbara in 1895, but the blowout of an underwater well in 1969 helped to launch the environmental movement as a national political force in the 1970s, and Santa Barbara in the 1980s is still determined to resist the oil companies' and Interior Secretary Donald Hodel's proposals for offshore drilling.

Santa Barbara is the epicenter of the 19th Congressional District of California. Politically, it is still a little leftward on the political spectrum from where it was when Ronald Reagan was first elected governor in 1966; cultural issues have chiseled, a bit, into Republican margins here. It elects a Democrat named Gary Hart (no relation) to the California Senate, for instance. But the new California farther east on the coast is increasingly Republican, and the 19th District as a whole seems to be solidly so, as does the valley west of Santa Barbara where Vandenberg Air Force Base and Lompoc Federal Prison are situated.

The congressman here is Robert Lagomarsino, an adept and intelligent veteran politician who won the district under difficult circumstances and has held it with seeming ease. He was the only Republican in a 1974 special election to hold a district for his party, despite Watergate; he was shrewd enough to say that he would not support Richard Nixon if he deserved to be impeached. On cultural issues he has a mixed voting record, in line with district preferences; on economic and cultural matters he is pretty solidly conservative. His two committee assignments—Interior and Foreign Affairs—give him opportunity to strike both attitudes. On Interior he served as ranking minority member on the Insular Affairs Subcommittee, a body of great importance to Puerto Rico, the Virgin Islands, Guam, and American Samoa, but of virtually no interest to anyone who votes in congressional elections—a workhorse assignment. He has since become ranking Republican on National Parks and Recreation, a panel better suited for a congressman from the California coast.

Since 1983 he has occupied one of the hot seats in the House, as ranking Republican on what is now the Western Hemisphere Affairs Subcommittee. Almost all the Democrats on the subcommittee and full committee are hotly opposed to the Reagan administration's policy in Central America. Lagomarsino is left with the task of defending administration policy in committee rooms and on the floor—or, another frustrating role, to be the messenger of bad news back to the White House. He himself, though a faithful and enthusiastic supporter of administration policy, is certainly not a zealot for it.

Lagomarsino has been easily reelected in the 19th District every two years, though the district could be seriously contested if he retires.

The People: Pop. 1980: 526,032, up 17.3% 1970–80. Households (1980): 70% family, 38% with children, 57% married couples; 45.3% housing units rented; median monthly rent: $268; median house value: $88,200. Voting age pop. (1980): 384,025; 21% Spanish origin, 3% Asian origin, 3% Black, 1% American Indian.

1984 Presidential Vote: Reagan (R) 141,327   (62%)
Mondale (D) 82,697   (37%)

Rep. Robert J. Lagomarsino (R)

Elected Mar. 5, 1974; b. Sept. 4, 1926, Ventura; home, Ventura; U. of CA at Santa Barbara, B.A. 1950, U. of Santa Clara Law Sch., LL.B. 1953; Roman Catholic; married (Norma Jean).

Career: Navy, WWII; Practicing atty., 1954–74; Ojai City Cncl., 1958, Mayor, 1958–61; CA Senate, 1961–74.

Offices: 2332 RHOB 20515, 202-225-3601. Also 814 State St., Studio 121, Santa Barbara 93101, 805-963-1708; 5740 Ralston, Ste. 101, Ventura 93003, 805-642-2200; and 104 E. Boone St., Ste. E, Santa Maria 93454, 805-922-2131.

Committees: *Foreign Affairs* (3d of 18 R). Subcommittees: Asian and Pacific Affairs; International Economic Policy and Trade; Western Hemisphere Affairs (Ranking Member). *Interior and Insular Affairs* (3d of 15 R). Subcommittees: Insular and International Affairs (Ranking Member); National Parks and Public Lands.

Group Ratings

	ADA	ACLU	COPE	CFA	LCV	ACU	NTU	NSI	COC	CEI
1986	5	15	12	17	26	86	56	100	89	81
1985	5	—	12	33	—	90	88	—	82	—

National Journal Ratings

	1986 LIB — 1986 CONS			1985 LIB — 1985 CONS		
Economic	13%	—	85%	19%	—	81%
Social	31%	—	67%	0%	—	76%
Foreign	25%	—	74%	0%	—	76%

Key Votes

1) Lmt Cln Water Act	FOR	5) Retain Gun Cont	AGN	9) Aid Angola Reb	FOR
2) Rpl Tobac Sub	FOR	6) Contra Aid	FOR	10) Tax Reform	FOR
3) Grm-Rdmn Def Red	FOR	7) Lmt Text Imp	AGN	11) S Africa Sanc	FOR
4) Ban Polygraph	AGN	8) Limit SDI	AGN	12) Immig Reform	FOR

Election Results

1986 general	Robert J. Lagomarsino (R)	122,578	(72%)	($333,464)
	Wayne B Norris (D)	45,619	(27%)	($16,041)
1986 primary	Robert J. Lagomarsino (R)	50,478	(100%)	
1984 general	Robert J. Lagomarsino (R)	153,187	(67%)	($288,682)
	James C. Carey, Jr. (D)	70,278	(31%)	($43,870)

Campaign Contributions and Expenditures

1985-86		Direct Cont. 1985-86		PACS Breakdown 1985-86			
Receipts	$341,497	Indiv.	$231,379	Corp.	$28,120	T/M/H	$24,101
Expend.	$333,464	Party	$3,402	Labor	$1,000	Agr.	$1,500
Unspent	$272,488	PACS	$63,434	Ideo.	$6,865	CWOS	$1,848

TWENTIETH DISTRICT

The Central Valley of California stands out clearly on a relief map—a swath of green down the middle of the state, surrounded by brown: a vast, flat expanse bounded by rugged mountains. The Valley's heavily irrigated flatlands are probably the world's most productive farmland. In the south, the mountains form a kind of semicircle, separating the Valley from the desert on the east, the Los Angeles Basin more than 50 miles to the south, and from the valleys of San Luis

Obispo to the west. The 20th Congressional District of California includes parts of three of these regions: most of the southern end of the Valley around Bakersfield, a portion of the desert, and most of San Luis Obispo County all the way to the ocean.

Half the district's population, and its center of political gravity, is in the Valley around Bakersfield. In the 1930s, Bakersfield was a kind of Canaan: the first green land that the Dust Bowl migrants from Oklahoma and Kansas saw after 1,500 miles of travel in rickety cars across the desert on U.S. 66. This is still the part of California where you are likely to find the most southern accents; Bakersfield is even a country music center, the home of Merle Haggard. As in Oklahoma, the political heritage here is Democratic, voting habits increasingly Republican since the late 1960s.

A surprisingly large number of people—about 140,000—live in the 20th District east of the Tehachapi Pass, in the desert. Here you find giant military installations, first put out here because of the dry climate and to keep them isolated and out of sight: the China Lake Naval Weapons Center and Edwards Air Force Base, where most of the space shuttles have landed. South of Edwards—in northern Los Angeles County, but in the desert, not the Los Angeles Basin—are the fast-growing towns of Lancaster and Palmdale. In subdivisions and shopping centers sprouting quickly from the desert, young people with families have been moving here, to work at Lockheed or other local businesses, or even to commute the 35 freeway miles to the San Fernando Valley. Political attitudes here are ultraconservative: strongly pro-defense, for the free market and traditional family values.

About the same number of people live in the 20th District's portion of San Luis Obispo County. Ranching is still important in these hills (former Interior Secretary and top Reagan aide William Clark has a ranch here), though people have been flocking here from California's metropolitan areas. San Luis Obispo County remains, as it has been for many years, mildly Republican.

The 20th District's congressman, Bill Thomas, was elected after the incumbent died quite suddenly in the summer of 1978. A former college teacher and four-year veteran of the California Assembly, he seems to be one of those people who instinctively knows how to go about being a legislator. He got a seat on the Agriculture Committee in his first term—a plum assignment for a Bakersfield representative—and now sits on the Ways and Means Committee. There he is more the practical politician than the free-market theorist, favoring import restrictions on avocadoes and pushing for the Wine Equity Act. He mustered minority support for increasing the retirement age in the 1983 Social Security amendments.

Thomas is also one of his party's leading political tacticians. He was the California Republicans' leading (and unsuccessful) strategist for redistricting. He sits on the House Administration Committee, a dull body unless you are interested in serving as a watchdog for your party's interests in campaign finance legislation. He was entrusted with a seat on the House Ethics Committee. He was the Republican on the three-member panel to look into the dispute over the election result in the 8th District of Indiana, and led a hard and heated charge against the Democrats when they ruled their colleague Frank McCloskey had won by four votes. On that occasion and others he has shown a heated temper. But he is also a good detail man. While other Republicans are interested in theories and exotic ideas, Thomas is inclined to forge practical compromises. He won a seat on the Budget Committee in 1987, where he is unlikely to be influential immediately but could be a force in the post-Reagan years after 1988.

This evidently suits his constituents in the 20th District fine. Thomas's hardest battle was winning the Republican nomination in a convention when incumbent William Ketchum died after the June primary. He has won general elections by very impressive margins. With a safe seat, he has become one of the leading Republicans in the House.

The People: Pop. 1980: 525,750, up 31.9% 1970–80. Households (1980): 75% family, 41% with children, 63% married couples; 36.0% housing units rented; median monthly rent: $215; median house value: $63,600. Voting age pop. (1980): 371,945; 12% Spanish origin, 4% Black, 2% American Indian, 2% Asian origin.

1984 Presidential Vote: Reagan (R) 151,080 (69%)
Mondale (D) 64,244 (30%)

Rep. William M. Thomas (R)

Elected 1978; b. Dec. 6, 1941, Wallace, ID; home, Bakersfield; Santa Ana Commun. Col., A.A. 1959, San Fran. St. U., B.A. 1963, M.A. 1965; Baptist; married (Sharon).

Career: Prof., Bakersfield Commun. Col., 1965–74; CA Assembly, 1974–78.

Offices: 2402 RHOB 20515, 202-225-2915. Also 1830 Truxtun Ave., #200, Bakersfield 93301, 805-327-3611; 858 W. Jackman St., #115, Lancaster 93534, 805-948-2634; and 1390 Price St., #203, Pismo Beach 93449, 805-773-2533.

Committees: *Budget* (8th of 14 R). Task Forces: Budget Process; Economic Policy; Income Security. *House Administration* (5th of 7 R). Subcommittees: Accounts; Elections (Ranking Member); Office Systems (Ranking Member). *Ways and Means* (8th of 13 R). Subcommittee: Oversight.

Group Ratings

	ADA	ACLU	COPE	CFA	LCV	ACU	NTU	NSI	COC	CEI
1986	10	25	10	17	27	85	56	90	93	65
1985	10	—	9	17	—	86	54	—	95	—

National Journal Ratings

	1986 LIB — 1986 CONS	1985 LIB — 1985 CONS
Economic	21% — 77%	16% — 81%
Social	42% — 58%	56% — 43%
Foreign	16% — 84%	0% — 76%

Key Votes

1) Lmt Cln Water Act	FOR	5) Retain Gun Cont	AGN	9) Aid Angola Reb	FOR
2) Rpl Tobac Sub	AGN	6) Contra Aid	FOR	10) Tax Reform	AGN
3) Grm-Rdmn Def Red	FOR	7) Lmt Text Imp	FOR	11) S Africa Sanc	—
4) Ban Polygraph	AGN	8) Limit SDI	AGN	12) Immig Reform	FOR

Election Results

1986 general	William M. Thomas (R)	129,989	(73%)	($255,261)
	Jules H. Moquin (D)	49,027	(27%)	($5,573)
1986 primary	William M. Thomas (R)	55,544	(100%)	
1984 general	William M. Thomas (R)	151,732	(71%)	($179,898)
	Michael T. Le Sage (D)	62,307	(29%)	($22,747)

Campaign Contributions and Expenditures

1985-86		Direct Cont. 1985-86		PACS Breakdown 1985-86			
Receipts	$260,680	Indiv.	$30,356	Corp.	$94,150	T/M/H	$73,710
Expend.	$255,261	Party	$1,314	Labor	$1,500	Agr.	$2,500
Unspent	$220,486	PACS	$192,704	Ideo.	$10,500	CWOS	$10,344

TWENTY-FIRST DISTRICT

Demographically, Los Angeles has become a city very much like those back east, with population concentrations of the elderly and minorities, immigrants and old-timers, the very rich and the very poor. This trend is apparent even in the San Fernando Valley, the huge 12-by-20 mile expanse that is the Los Angeles showbiz synonym for suburbia (and the inspiration for the phrase "Valley girls"). In the 1950s the Valley was filling up with young families: working fathers, homemaker mothers, two or three or four kids walking every day to the local public school. These were almost entirely white Anglo people, few of them Jewish or members of any self-conscious minority group. By the 1980s the the Valley had become a rather different place. Erstwhile young parents are now living alone—often divorced. Young married couples both work and have few if any children. The whites who remained in the 1970s often withdrew their children from L.A. public schools because of a busing order that was later overturned. Substantial numbers of Mexican-Americans and some blacks live in the Valley now, as well as large numbers of Jews.

What most resembles the Valley of the 1950s is the collection of communities that form the 21st Congressional District of California. This includes the fringes of the Valley: parts of Woodland Hills on the west, Northridge and Granada Hills on the north and, separated by mountains but still within the Los Angeles city limits, the communities of Sunland and Tujunga on the east. But almost two-thirds of the district's residents live beyond the mountains that ring the Valley; the Valley has in effect moved beyond its own geographic limits. The typical 21st District voter now lives in the string of communities enclosed by mountains and connected with the northern San Fernando Valley by freeway: Simi Valley, Moorpark, Thousand Oaks (known locally as T.O.), and Camarillo. These areas have grown fast; there were very few people here in 1960. The district also includes, farther north in Ventura County, the more established communities of Fillmore and Ojai.

This is a family district: fully 80% of the households in this district are occupied by families, 69% by married couples, and 47% have children. These figures are well above the national average and are exceeded in California only by the predominantly Mexican-American 34th district, on the other side of the Los Angeles Basin. While the divorce rate may be higher here than it was in the Valley 20 years ago, life has probably undergone less change than you would guess judging by outward appearances. Politically, this is an area of economic upward mobility and cultural caution, of salary-earners skeptical of government intervention in the economy, of parents fearful of cultural libertinism yet not eager for their own lives to be interfered with, of patriots admiring an assertive foreign policy but with the Vietnam example in their minds worried about the consequences.

The congressional representation of the 21st District, like most of its residents, has moved out from the Valley into Ventura County. Elected in a 1980 upset was Bobbi Fiedler, an opponent of busing in the Valley who got elected to the citywide school board and beat Representative James Corman in 1980. She ran for the Senate in 1986, but in January her campaign manager was charged with bribery under an obsolete state law never previously invoked and applied here to the legitimate political tactic of urging state Senator Ed Davis, also of the Valley, to withdraw and promising to help him pay off his debts if he would. In February the indictment was dropped, but not before damaging Fiedler's camapign beyond repair; her only consolation was that Davis was hurt too, and she ended up ahead of him, 8% to 7%.

In the meantime, her successor was being determined in the 21st's Republican primary. The favorite was Tony Hope, son of comedian Bob Hope, whose longtime home is in Toluca Lake, in a corner of the Valley; but Tony Hope had spent most of the last decade in Washington and concentrated most of his 90-day campaign in the Valley. The winner was Elton Gallegly, the mayor of Simi Valley in Ventura County, a city that scarcely existed in the early 1960s and now has over 100,000 people and is the center of its own urbanized area. A self-made man who made his fortune in real estate and his political career in a typically nonpartisan, efficient local government in California, Gallegly seems likely to be a practical-minded congressman, looking for a major committee assignment soon and in the House for the long haul.

The People: Pop. 1980: 525,880, up 41.4% 1970–80. Households (1980): 80% family, 47% with children, 69% married couples; 25.2% housing units rented; median monthly rent: $331; median house value: $114,100. Voting age pop. (1980): 367,604; 9% Spanish origin, 3% Asian origin, 2% Black, 1% American Indian.

1984 Presidential Vote:

Reagan (R)	177,196	(72%)
Mondale (D)	65,617	(27%)

Rep. Elton Gallegly (R)

Elected 1986; b. Mar. 7, 1944, Huntington Park; home, Simi Valley; Los Angeles St. Col., 1962–63; Protestant; married (Janice).

Career: Owner and operator of real estate firm; Simi Valley City Cncl., 1979–80; Mayor of Simi Valley, 1980–86.

Offices: 1020 LHOB 20515, 202-225-5811. Also 21053 Devonshire St., Chatsworth 91311, 818-341-2121.

Committees: *Interior and Insular Affairs* (14th of 15 R). Subcommittees: Insular and International Affairs; National Parks and Public Lands; Water and Power Resources. *Small Business* (17th of 17 R). Subcommittees: Energy and Agriculture; Procurement, Innovation and Minority Enterprise Development.

Group Ratings and Key Votes: Newly Elected

Election Results

1986 general	Elton Gallegly (R)	132,090	(68%)	($591,018)
	Gilbert R. Saldana (D)	54,497	(28%)	($65,501)
1986 primary	Elton Gallegly (R)	34,109	(50%)	
	Anthony J. Hope (R)	23,242	(34%)	
	Thomas La Porte (R)	10,591	(16%)	
1984 general	Bobbi Fiedler (R)	173,504	(72%)	($175,140)
	Charles (Charlie) Davis (D)	62,085	(26%)	($69,113)

Campaign Contributions and Expenditures

1985-86		Direct Cont. 1985-86		PACS Breakdown 1985-86			
Receipts	$631,425	Indiv.	$341,902	Corp.	$64,322	T/M/H	$57,337
Expend.	$591,018	Party	$10,849	Labor	$1,500	Agr.	$4,500
Unspent	$40,407	PACS	$153,090	Ideo.	$21,513	CWOS	$3,918
		Cand.	$123,827				

TWENTY-SECOND DISTRICT

The 22d Congressional District of California consists of three distinct parts of Los Angeles County, united by political affiliation but separated by the awesome San Gabriel Mountains. One is centered on Glendale, an old suburb nestled just below the mountains and almost directly north of downtown Los Angeles. The population here tends to be elderly, Wasp Republicans. So too the surrounding towns: a jagged-demarked section of Burbank and the mountain-surrounded suburbs of La Canada and La Crescenta.

The second section, which also includes about 40% of the district's voters, is demographically similar. This is a string of towns running east from Los Angeles beneath the mountains. These started off as stations on the Santa Fe Railroad line, then became separate little towns, then finally high-income suburbs: Monrovia (starting from the east), Arcadia, Sierra Madre, Temple City, San Marino, most of Pasadena, and South Pasadena. These suburbs have fewer Mexican-Americans (though in many cases more than 10%) than the suburbs farther south from the mountains; their incomes are high, though with the exception of San Marino not the highest in the Los Angeles metropolitan area; their residents tend to be older than average, with grown rather than young families.

The third part of the district includes the communities of Saugus and Newhall nestled in the mountains north of the San Fernando Valley. This has a much younger population, but all three parts of the district are heavily Republican.

When the 22d's lines were drawn, two Republican congressmen lived in the district. One, John Rousselot, in an act of unusual political unselfishness, moved to the Democratic 30th District, where he nearly won. The other, Carlos Moorhead, who had represented Glendale and Pasadena for 10 years, ran here and won easily. Moorhead, a high-ranking member of the Judiciary and Energy and Commerce Committees, is not a particularly assertive or articulate politician. Much of his legislative work has been done on Patent and Copyright, useful but scarcely fascinating matters like protecting American patent rights abroad, protecting the privacy of electronic mail, and extending drug patents to give time for regulatory approval. He is dean of the California Republican delegation, second ranking Republican on the Judiciary Committee, and a member of Energy and Commerce as well, a pleasant but not very aggressive man who has been a legislator in Sacramento and Washington for more than 20 years. He is reelected without difficulty in the 22d District.

The People: Pop. 1980: 525,939, up 3.3% 1970-80. Households (1980): 66% family, 31% with children, 54% married couples. 43.1% housing units rented; median monthly rent: $267; median house value: $110,100. Voting age pop. (1980): 403,471; 11% Spanish origin, 4% Asian origin, 2% Black, 1% American Indian.

Presidential Vote:

Reagan (R)	175,164	(72%)
Mondale (D)	63,874	(26%)

Rep. Carlos J. Moorhead (R)

Elected 1972; b. May 6, 1922, Long Beach; home, Glendale; U. of CA at Los Angeles, B.A. 1943, U. of Southern CA, J.D. 1949; Presbyterian; married (Valery).

Career: Army, WWII; Practicing atty.; CA Assembly, 1967–72.

Offices: 2346 RHOB 20515, 202-225-4176. Also 420 N. Brand Blvd., Ste. 304, Glendale 91203, 818-247-8445; and 301 E. Colorado Blvd., #618, Pasadena 91101, 818-792-6168.

Committees: *Energy and Commerce* (3d of 17 R). Subcommittees: Energy and Power (Ranking Member); Telecommunications and Finance. *Judiciary* (2d of 14 R). Subcommittees: Courts, Civil Liberties, and the Administration of Justice (Ranking Member); Monopolies and Commercial Law.

Group Ratings

	ADA	ACLU	COPE	CFA	LCV	ACU	NTU	NSI	COC	CEI
1986	0	5	8	8	22	95	62	100	100	80
1985	5	—	8	25	—	90	69	—	88	—

National Journal Ratings

	1986 LIB — 1986 CONS	1985 LIB — 1985 CONS
Economic	0% — 94%	0% — 95%
Social	11% — 85%	0% — 76%
Foreign	0% — 86%	0% — 76%

Key Votes

1) Lmt Cln Water Act	FOR	5) Retain Gun Cont	AGN	9) Aid Angola Reb	FOR
2) Rpl Tobac Sub	FOR	6) Contra Aid	FOR	10) Tax Reform	AGN
3) Grm-Rdmn Def Red	FOR	7) Lmt Text Imp	AGN	11) S Africa Sanc	AGN
4) Ban Polygraph	AGN	8) Limit SDI	AGN	12) Immig Reform	FOR

Election Results

1986 general	Carlos J. Moorhead (R)	141,096	(74%)	($144,132)
	John G. Simmons (D)..................	44,036	(23%)	($26,490)
1986 primary	Carlos J. Moorhead (R)	56,764	(100%)	
1984 general	Carlos J. Moorhead (R)	184,981	(85%)	($106,402)
	Michael B. Yauch (Libert.).	32,036	(15%)	($6,824)

Campaign Contributions and Expenditures

1985-86		Direct Cont. 1985-86		PACS Breakdown 1985-86			
Receipts	$315,365	Indiv.	$88,496	Corp.	$86,450	T/M/H	$55,350
Expend.	$144,132	Party	$2,000	Labor	$1,000	Agr.	$1,000
Unspent	$460,138	PACS	$148,751	Ideo.	$2,625	CWOS	$2,236

TWENTY-THIRD DISTRICT

Is Rodeo Drive the center of the world? You might think so, to hear showbiz types and the hosts of *Lifestyles of the Rich and Famous* talk. Actually this instant Fifth Avenue (a quite ordinary shopping street 15 years ago) is not even the center of life for most people in Beverly Hills who, while quite comfortably affluent, are not able to shop there regularly. The southern side of Beverly Hills, the flatlands south of Wilshire Boulevard, are more typical of the political constituency of which they are a party, the 23d Congressional District of California. On the south side of the Santa Monica Mountains the 23d stretches from the newly incorporated city of West Los Angeles, with its gay mayor, through Beverly Hills to the veterans home in West Los Angeles and the Pacific Palisades neighborhood where Ronald Reagan lived until 1980. On the north side of the mountains, there are the hillside communities of Encino and Woodland Hills, and the middle-class Valley neighborhoods of Van Nuys, Reseda, and Canoga Park, stretching four and five miles north of Ventura Boulevard on their mile-square grid avenues, below. Twenty years ago these streets were filled with children; now more often they are quiet. The boundaries at the edge of the district are jagged so as to enclose the maximum number of Democratic votes.

You can find plenty of exotic areas here, from Rodeo Drive to Malibu, and in the winter the movie theaters all have signs inviting Academy members in to see nominated films. But the typical neighborhood here is modestly affluent, with many Jewish residents and many professionals, liberal and Democratic in its political tradition, but willing sometimes these days to consider Republicans.

The congressman from this district is Anthony Beilenson, who has represented Beverly Hills and surrounding areas since he was elected to the California Assembly in 1962 at age 30. He went to the California Senate in 1966 and to the House, when incumbent Thomas Rees retired, in 1976. He is an accomplished legislative strategist and tactician himself, one of the real pros in the House. Yet he is also relatively quiet, more of a loner than a team player, and almost entirely unglitzy. He got the California seat on Rules in 1978 against the wishes of his delegation, and was not happy with the political leanings of the district Phil Burton gave him after the 1980 Census. But he has generally been a leadership man on Rules and has been reelected easily.

Rules is a committee best suited to a legislator willing to remain anonymous; it allows a skilled operator to exert important influence on many different kinds of legislation, but often silently and seldom with any fanfare. Thus Beilenson has been the House's closest student of the budget process, proposing changes in the early 1980s that were not adopted then but which he advanced later when Gramm-Rudman came up, and he urged the House to prepare a plan to erase the budget deficit by 1989. On politics he is the House's leading advocate of full public financing of congressional elections—a lonely cause up through 1986, but which seemed to be gathering more supporters in 1987. Beilenson's independence comes out on other roll call votes; he is one who seems to vote almost entirely on the merits of legislation, without much regard to who is backing or opposing it. This makes him a potentially moderating force on Rules, a member who is well placed to put the kibosh on a too partisan procedural rule and to insist on a rational and fair legislative process.

Beilenson is now a member of the Intelligence Committee, a sensitive and critical assignment. He has had some particular legislative successes, notably on setting up a Santa Monica Mountains National Recreation Area. But mostly his imprint is hard to see. He ranks fourth in seniority on Rules today, behind octogenarian Claude Pepper, Boston's Joe Moakley, and Butler Derrick, and so could conceivably be chairman some day; he already is a player on many key legislative issues. He has the luxury of a safe seat. His new district boundaries inspired a tough challenge in 1982 from a professor who opposed school busing. But Beilenson won with 60% and has gotten 62% and 66%, although his opponents have matched his spending each time. Barring redistricting problems after the 1990 Census, he seems to have a long and useful legislative career ahead of him.

The People: Pop. 1980: 525,936, up 3.6% 1970–80. Households (1980): 59% family, 26% with children, 47% married couples; 51.8% housing units rented; median monthly rent: $334; median house value: $135,300. Voting age pop. (1980): 422,708; 8% Spanish origin, 3% Asian origin, 3% Black.

1984 Presidential Vote: Reagan (R) 129,010   (53%)
                            Mondale (D) 113,020   (46%)

Rep. Anthony C. Beilenson (D)

Elected 1976; b. Oct. 26, 1932, New Rochelle, NY; home, Los Angeles; Harvard Col., A.B. 1954, LL.B. 1957; Jewish; married (Dolores).

Career: Practicing atty., 1957–59; Counsel, CA Assembly Cmtee. on Finance and Insur., 1960; Staff atty., CA Comp. and Insur. Fund, 1961–62; CA Assembly, 1963–66; CA Senate, 1967–77.

Offices: 1025 LHOB 20515, 202-225-5911. Also 11000 Wilshire Blvd., Ste. 14223, Los Angeles 90024, 213-209-7801; and 18401 Burbank Blvd., Ste. 222, Tarzana 91356, 818-345-1560.

Committees: *Rules* (4th of 9 D). Subcommittee: Rules of the House. *Permanent Select Committee on Intelligence* (3d of 11 D). Subcommittee: Oversight and Evaluation (Chairman).

Group Ratings

	ADA	ACLU	COPE	CFA	LCV	ACU	NTU	NSI	COC	CEI
1986	80	83	76	75	88	9	33	0	18	34
1985	95	—	78	92	—	5	37	—	24	—

National Journal Ratings

	1986 LIB — 1986 CONS		1985 LIB — 1985 CONS	
Economic	49%	— 50%	89%	— 0%
Social	79%	— 19%	85%	— 0%
Foreign	71%	— 28%	92%	— 0%

Key Votes

1) Lmt Cln Water Act	AGN	5) Retain Gun Cont	FOR	9) Aid Angola Reb	AGN
2) Rpl Tobac Sub	FOR	6) Contra Aid	AGN	10) Tax Reform	FOR
3) Grm-Rdmn Def Red	AGN	7) Lmt Text Imp	AGN	11) S Africa Sanc	FOR
4) Ban Polygraph	FOR	8) Limit SDI	FOR	12) Immig Reform	FOR

Election Results

1986 general	Anthony C. Beilenson (D)............	121,468	(66%)	($215,076)
	George Woolverton (R)...............	58,746	(32%)	($220,313)
1986 primary	Anthony C. Beilenson (D)............	52,866	(88%)	
	Eric C. Jacobson (D)	4,512	(8%)	
	William J. Kurdi (D)	2,625	(4%)	
1984 general	Anthony C. Beilenson (D)............	140,461	(62%)	($157,880)
	Claude Parrish (R)	84,093	(37%)	($149,486)

Campaign Contributions and Expenditures

1985-86		Direct Cont. 1985-86		PACS Breakdown 1985-86			
Receipts	$195,166	Indiv.	$186,146	Corp.	$300	T/M/H	$500
Expend.	$215,076	PACS	$1,861	Labor	$0	Agr.	$0
Unspent	$5,678	Cand.	$5,000	Ideo.	$1,061	CWOS	$0

TWENTY-FOURTH DISTRICT

West and north of downtown Los Angeles, roughly along the route of the Hollywood Freeway, is the middle-class core of what is now the nation's second largest metropolitan area. Over the past 60 years here, the land has changed from vacant lots and barren hills to carefully tended subdivisions and houses perched on hillsides—and sometimes back again, for this part of Los Angeles has gone through many changes. Fifty years ago, this was mostly standard middle-class territory, populated by families with roots in places like Protestant Iowa and Nebraska, comfortable residential neighborhoods stretched out along the interurban lines and the wide avenues that made one of America's first automobile cities. But this was also Hollywood, the center of America's showbiz industry, and as time went on newly formed middle-class families moved out along the freeways and settled elsewhere—West Los Angeles on the other side of Beverly Hills, the San Fernando Valley over the Santa Monica Mountains, Orange County far to the southeast on the Santa Ana Freeway. The Fairfax area near Beverly Hills and North Hollywood, off the freeway just over the mountains, became one of Los Angeles's major Jewish neighborhoods. Rich neighborhoods like Hancock Park and Los Feliz kept their tone, but Hollywood itself became seedy, and the Hollywood Hills became the home of the single and the unusual, the soap-opera actress busy finding herself.

But this west side of Los Angeles was not dragged down by decline as similar parts of midwestern cities have been. The fabulous growth of the showbiz industry, fueled by the demand of an economically growing nation (and world) for entertainment, helped to turn around many of even the tackiest parts of Hollywood, and today the boulevards are full of glass and chrome buildings filled with gold-chained and polo-shirted executives, and one previously obscure street after another is now the home of restaurants so chic that their phone numbers are unlisted. But other change is in sight. Along the avenues closer to downtown are less affluent neighborhoods filling up with Latin and Asian immigrants, especially Koreans. They are rising so rapidly in income and seem so thoroughly imbued with respect for order and hard work that they pose little threat to the affluence of the blocks farther west. But there is no question that these latest migrants will play a major role in shaping Los Angeles's future.

This is the land of California's 24th Congressional District, which stretches almost from MacArthur Park and downtown Los Angeles to the limits of Beverly Hills, includes all of Hollywood, Hancock Park, and Los Feliz, and goes north over the mountains with the Hollywood sign to take in hill neighborhoods, Universal City, and North Hollywood. Politically, these neighborhoods which were solidly Republican 40 years ago now form one of the leading liberal constituencies in America. Jewish voters are especially important here, since they tend to turn out when others do not (as in 1986, when turnout in Latin and Asian neighborhoods was close to zero). Gay voters are an important force also. Some day Mexican-Americans, Korean-Americans and other Asian groups may be large voting blocs here: in 1980 the district's population was 22% Hispanic and 11% Asian, and its children were 44% Hispanic and 15% Asian. This new mixture causes some friction; there was a dispute over Los Angeles city council lines between incumbents Michael Woo and Richard Alatorre, settled only when another incumbent died and both Woo and Alatorre got safe districts. But among both groups turnout is still low, and many of the children may end up raising their families in less glitzy and less expensive neighborhoods.

The congressman from this district, Henry Waxman, has become one of the most powerful and competent members of the House. He was first elected to the California Assembly in 1968 at age 29, and in his second term chaired the Reapportionment Committee; he went to Congress in 1974 in a district designed, he likes to point out, not by his committee but by a court. Waxman's big break came after the 1978 election, when he was elected chairman of the Energy and Commerce Committee's Health Subcommittee. This was one of the first times House Democrats decided not to observe seniority in handing out subcommittee chairs, and Waxman's opponent moreover was popular, competent, and widely respected. Nevertheless he argued his case on the issues and also made campaign contributions to other Democrats on the full committee and won the post 15–12.

The campaign contributions were no accident. Waxman and his friends Howard Berman and Mel Levine, now also area congressmen, have built their own political machine in Los Angeles. Its power comes not from patronage but from fund raising and savvy: they raise money from affluent liberals in Los Angeles and put it to good use all over the country and in direct mail campaigns in southern California, where TV ads are usually too expensive.

In the House Waxman has built his power less on money than through his work on substantive issues. He is now the number three Democrat on the committee which after the 1982 and 1986 elections was the most sought-after assignment for Democrats (in 1984 there were no vacancies), Energy and Commerce; and on the full committee and Health Subcommittee he has been an exceptionally productive and knowledgeable legislator. He is the House's chief packager of acid rain legislation, for example, a difficult assignment requiring him to weigh the interests of industrial areas against those of other regions. He has dominated all House action on the Clean Air Act since his bravura performance in 1981 and 1982, when he prevented the united forces of the Reagan Administration and Energy and Commerce Chairman John Dingell from relaxing the Clean Air Act, delaying action for months while Dingell and allies had a majority, and eventually splitting their forces apart. His performance on the Clean Air Act in 1981 and 1982 was a clear example. Yet on other issues he has remained a staunch Dingell ally. On health matters he has led the charge for money for AIDS research, pushed to passage the law providing damages to children injured by required immunizations, sponsored measures to deal with the problem of adolescent pregnancies, expanded the availability of generic drugs, extended patent protection for drugs during part of the regulatory process, is working to legalize heroin to reduce the pain of terminal cancer patients, oversees the National Institutes of Health—the list goes on and on.

Waxman brings to all these tasks an instinct for the legislative process that is second to none, a thorough knowledge of the rules and willingness to exploit every one, and a temperament that is all but unflappable. He considers issues on the merits and sometimes surprises everyone, as he does by opposing the Los Angeles subway on which construction has begun in the district. Short, readily recognizable with his moustache, he makes his arguments calmly and cheerfully, even when opponents are thundering and screaming. Waxman's career shows how the House has changed in the last dozen years. It is more of a meritocracy now; important positions are given not just to senior members, but to those most capable of using them in the way the majority wants.

At home Waxman's district seems exceedingly pleased with him: he is probably the first congressman from Los Angeles, and certainly the first liberal congressman from Los Angeles, to be both a legislative power in the House and a political power back home.

The People: Pop. 1980: 525,918, up 12.8% 1970–80. Households (1980): 47% family, 22% with children, 34% married couples; 76.4% housing units rented; median monthly rent: $235; median house value: $111,700. Voting age pop. (1980): 429,288; 22% Spanish origin, 11% Asian origin, 6% Black.

| Presidential Vote | Mondale (D) .... | 88,680 | (55%) |
| | Reagan (R) .... | 70,370 | (44%) |

Rep. Henry A. Waxman (D)

Elected 1974; b. Sept. 12, 1939, Los Angeles; home, Los Angeles; UCLA, B.A. 1961, J.D. 1964; Jewish; married (Janet).

Career: Practicing atty., 1965–68; CA Assembly, 1968–74.

Offices: 2418 RHOB 20515, 202-225-3976. Also 8425 W. 3d St., Ste. 400, Los Angeles 90048, 213-651-1040.

Committees: *Energy and Commerce* (3d of 25 D). Subcommittees: Commerce, Consumer Protection and Competitiveness; Health and the Environment (Chairman). *Government Operations* (5th of 24 D). Subcommittees: Environment, Energy and Natural Resources; Human Resources and Intergovernmental Personnel. *Select Committee on Aging* (14th of 39 D). Subcommittee: Health and Long-Term Care.

Group Ratings

	ADA	ACLU	COPE	CFA	LCV	ACU	NTU	NSI	COC	CEI
1986	95	88	88	100	100	5	28	0	20	24
1985	95	—	94	100	—	16	34	—	27	—

National Journal Ratings

	1986 LIB — 1986 CONS		1985 LIB — 1985 CONS	
Economic	81% —	18%	85% —	11%
Social	89% —	0%	85% —	0%
Foreign	80% —	0%	79% —	20%

Key Votes

1) Lmt Cln Water Act	AGN	5) Retain Gun Cont	FOR	9) Aid Angola Reb	AGN
2) Rpl Tobac Sub	FOR	6) Contra Aid	AGN	10) Tax Reform	FOR
3) Grm-Rdmn Def Red	AGN	7) Lmt Text Imp	AGN	11) S Africa Sanc	FOR
4) Ban Polygraph	FOR	8) Limit SDI	FOR	12) Immig Reform	FOR

Election Results

1986 general	Henry A. Waxman (D)................	103,914	(88%)	($136,807)
	George Abrahams (Libertarian)..........	8,871	(7%)	
	James Green (Peace & Freedom).........	5,388	(5%)	($300)
1986 primary	Henry A. Waxman (D).................	41,868	(100%)	
1984 general	Henry A. Waxman (D).................	97,340	(63%)	($117,831)
	Jerry Zerg (R)......................	51,010	(33%)	($133,765)

Campaign Contributions and Expenditures

1985-86		Direct Cont. 1985-86		PACS Breakdown 1985-86			
Receipts	$146,746	Indiv.	$30,304	Corp.	$32,825	T/M/H	$53,167
Expend.	$136,807	PACS	$125,198	Labor	$27,370	Agr.	$1,850
Unspent	$101,881			Ideo.	$8,236	CWOS	$1,750

TWENTY-FIFTH DISTRICT

Downtown Los Angeles, long the butt of jokes and derision, is now recognizably the center of one of the great cities of the world. Giant towers, some owned by Japanese interests, jut up not gracefully perhaps but still quite assertively from the bowl of land surrounded by freeways, hills, and the cement-lined Los Angeles River where the center of this pueblo was established just over 200 years ago and which is now one of the nation's biggest office centers and, thanks to the new Museum of Modern Art, one of its cultural centers as well. Downtown Los Angeles is geographically the most noticeable part of California's 25th Congressional District, but not demographically. For the 25th is California's most heavily Latin district. Across the river from Los Angeles is Boyle Heights and, farther out, East Los Angeles, the entry points for many migrants just in from Mexico and parts south; the Highland Park neighborhood to the north has also become heavily Mexican-American. The district also proceeds north into part of Pasadena which has a large black population.

Are these central Mexican-American areas, in the shadow of downtown L.A.'s new towers, a hopeless ghetto, where residents are condemned to live in misery by poverty and discrimination? Apparently not. Hispanics have been able to move pretty freely all over the Los Angeles metropolitan area: every congressional district there, every suburb and enclave of the city, had a significant Spanish origin population of 3% or more—in most cases, quite a bit more in 1980, and the figures have probably been rising since. Boyle Heights and East Los Angeles seem to be the first stops on a well-trodden trail from certain states of central and northern Mexico to the San Fernando Valley, the eastern Los Angeles Basin, and Orange County. In Hispanic neighborhoods in the 25th immigrants are received by relatives or friends, live doubled up in houses or apartments, find their first jobs—and then, mostly, move on. These are equivalents not of the black ghettoes but of the early Irish and Italian neighborhoods of New York or Philadelphia or Chicago.

Moreover, these are not desperately poor neighborhoods. Compared to peasants in central Mexico, almost everyone in East Los Angeles is affluent indeed, and even by U.S. standards, people here aren't in hopeless straits. A drive through the area shows not empty storefronts, but busy shops with new signs; not housing riddled with vandalism and neglect, but houses newly painted and with carefully tended gardens. Americans are used to seeing their lowest income neighborhoods nearly abandoned, but East Los Angeles is thronged with people, and especially with children. Housing prices tell an interesting story. According to the Census Bureau, housing prices in 1980 in mostly black Watts were about $42,000. But in East Los Angeles they were $53,000 and in the Los Angeles portion of the 25th, $65,000 (the same as prices in the comfortable suburbs of Philadelphia). You can't afford to buy or rent housing of that price, even if two families act together, on welfare payments or the minimum wage. What we are seeing in these areas are not people who are failures but people who are in the process of becoming successes.

Yet Hispanics, with the conspicuous and unusual exception of 25th District Representative Edward Roybal, have not elected many of their own to office. They do not even vote much: less than 80,000 residents of the 25th voted for a congressman in 1986, compared to 185,000 in the next-door 22d. Mexican-Americans for a long time didn't see politics as their way up in the world. There are now two Hispanic council members in Los Angeles, Richard Alatorre and Gloria Molina, both former members of the Assembly and political rivals. But the Hispanic vote is not necessarily leftish: Molina's big issue is her opposition to a new prison in East Los Angeles; Mexican–Americans voted to recall Chief Justice Rose Bird and were evenly divided on making English the official state language. They are not the first ethnic group in America to move up mainly through private sector jobs, largely ignoring politics. Moving up rapidly economically, hobbled less by segregation and discrimination, they don't need as much from government as do blacks.

Representative Roybal, first elected in 1962, comes not of Mexican stock, but from northern New Mexico, where the Spanish-speaking community dates back from before Plymouth Rock. He is one of California's senior congressmen now, but he has not had the most distinguished record in the House. In 1978 the Ethics Committee recommended that he be censured for having lied about a $1,000 campaign contribution from Tongsun Park that he converted to his own use. Roybal admitted taking the money, but his supporters, some of whom thought him the victim of discrimination, persuaded the House that he should be reprimanded rather than censured. In 1982 and 1984 he led the opposition to the immigration reform bill, charging with some passion that the employer sanction provisions would result in discrimination against Hispanic Americans. He failed to persuade the House on employer sanctions, but played a part in stopping the bill in those years. But in 1986 Roybal and other Hispanic congressmen, fearful that a more onerous bill might pass, did not interpose great objections and the House finally passed, and the President signed, a bill with employer sanctions, toughened border controls, and a broad exemption for agricultural guestworkers.

Roybal has two important committee assignments. A senior member of Appropriations, he chairs the Treasury, Postal Service, General Government Subcommittee, ordinarily one of the less controversial units, though he has sometimes had problems with his bill on the floor. He succeeded Claude Pepper as chairman of the Select Committee on Aging, and has championed Social Security there, though not as passionately as Pepper (but who could?). Roybal is a man of intellectual ability, but sometimes seems cynical. He has a solidly liberal voting record and has no problems winning reelection, though he has had no serious primary opposition for many years. Although past 70, he has shown no sign of retiring; his daughter was in 1987 the early favorite to win a seat in the California Assembly.

The People: Pop. 1980: 526,013, up 9.5% 1970–80. Households (1980): 70% family, 44% with children, 49% married couples; 62.0% housing units rented; median monthly rent: $176; median house value: $65,500. Voting age pop. (1980): 358,659; 57% Spanish origin, 10% Black, 8% Asian origin, 1% American Indian.

Presidential Vote: Mondale (D) 65,974   (60%)
Reagan (R) 42,375   (39%)

Rep. Edward R. Roybal (D)

Elected 1962; b. Feb. 10, 1916, Albuquerque, NM; home, Los Angeles; U. of CA at Los Angeles, Southwestern U.; Roman Catholic; married (Lucille).

Career: Army, WWII; Dir. of Health Educ., L.A. Cnty. Tuberculosis & Health Assn., 1945–49; L.A. City Cncl., 1949–62, Pres. Pro Tem, 1961–62.

Offices: 2211 RHOB 20515, 202-225-6235. Also 300 N. Los Angeles St., Rm. 7106, Los Angeles 90012, 213-688-4870.

Committees: *Appropriations* (7th of 35 D). Subcommittees: Labor–Health and Human Services–Education; Treasury–Postal Service–General Government (Chairman). *Select Committee on Aging* (Chairman of 39 D). Subcommittee: Retirement Income and Employment (Chairman).

Group Ratings

	ADA	ACLU	COPE	CFA	LCV	ACU	NTU	NSI	COC	CEI
1986	95	100	93	75	66	5	27	0	19	14
1985	95	—	94	75	—	5	30	—	15	—

National Journal Ratings

	1986 LIB — 1986 CONS			1985 LIB — 1985 CONS		
Economic	81%	—	18%	83%	—	15%
Social	78%	—	21%	85%	—	0%
Foreign	73%	—	26%	92%	—	0%

Key Votes

1) Lmt Cln Water Act	AGN	5) Retain Gun Cont	FOR	9) Aid Angola Reb	AGN
2) Rpl Tobac Sub	AGN	6) Contra Aid	AGN	10) Tax Reform	FOR
3) Grm-Rdmn Def Red	AGN	7) Lmt Text Imp	FOR	11) S Africa Sanc	FOR
4) Ban Polygraph	FOR	8) Limit SDI	FOR	12) Immig Reform	AGN

Election Results

1986 general	Edward R. Roybal (D)	62,692	(76%)	($63,996)
	Gregory L. Hardy (R)	17,588	(21%)	
1986 primary	Edward R. Roybal (D)	31,481	(89%)	
	Dorothy Andromidas (D)	3,878	(11%)	
1984 general	Edward R. Roybal (D)	74,261	(72%)	($74,290)
	Roy D. (Bill) Bloxom (R)	24,968	(24%)	($18,360)

Campaign Contributions and Expenditures

1985-86		Direct Cont. 1985-86		PACS Breakdown 1985-86			
Receipts	$98,919	Indiv.	$21,814	Corp.	$5,300	T/M/H	$11,700
Expend.	$63,996	PACS	$45,925	Labor	$21,200	Agr.	$2,250
Unspent	$225,526	Cand.	$12,465	Ideo.	$5,475	CWOS	$0

TWENTY-SIXTH DISTRICT

If you stood at the crest of the Santa Monica Mountains in 1910—when you would have had to climb on foot to get there—and looked north, you would have seen spread out before you, almost totally empty and barren, 20 miles wide and 12 miles deep, the San Fernando Valley. Its history has been recounted, with surprisingly little distortion, in the movie *Chinatown*. So close to a city that even then was growing explosively, the Valley inspired great plans. Civic leaders like Harry

Chandler of the *Los Angeles Times* encouraged city engineer William Mulholland to build a huge aqueduct from the Owens Valley to give Los Angeles water and got the city to annex most of the Valley, large chunks of which they had, with foresight, already acquired. The land is just about all built up now, except for the few remaining movie ranches and flood control areas, and is changing slowly from suburban to urban in character. Its population is becoming older and consists more frequently of identifiable minorities; it is more liberal politically. The San Fernando Valley now has more than one million people, enough to constitute the major part of two congressional districts and minor parts of three others. One of them is the 26th Congressional District of California.

This is a district created for and by a particular congressman, Howard Berman. It begins in his political base in the Hollywood Hills, above West Hollywood and Beverly Hills. Here expensive houses are built off the roads that twist up hillsides; nestled under steep overhangs or looking out, from atop a scraped-off hillside, on the whole city. In the early 1960s, the Hollywood Hills were affluent, family-oriented, and Republican, voting on economic issues; today they are affluent, singles- (and sometimes gay-) oriented, and Democratic, primarily because of cultural issues. The politician who first perceived and acted on the change was Howard Berman. In 1972, supposedly a terrible year for Democrats, Berman at 27 ran for the seat in the Hollywood Hills district represented by the Assembly Republican leader—and won handily. He became majority leader in the Assembly himself, an active legislator (the chief sculptor of the farm labor law), and, unwilling to wait for him to leave that office in two years, challenged his erstwhile ally Leo McCarthy for the speakership in 1980. The McCarthy forces engineered the election of Willie Brown instead, and Berman, deciding to leave the Assembly, made sure that Phil Burton drew a congressional district for him.

The 26th District created for Berman proceeds directly north from the Hollywood Hills into the heart of the San Fernando Valley. It includes the Democratic middle-class neighborhoods of Van Nuys and Panorama City, goes northwest to take in, within a jagged boundary, the more Democratic parts of Granada Hills, takes in the black neighborhood of Pacoima and the heavily Mexican-American neighborhoods on either side of the Golden State Freeway, and dips a little south to include a carefully selected set of precincts in Burbank. Altogether this is a district with a large and growing—and upwardly mobile—Mexican-American population, one whose leaning toward Ronald Reagan put the 26th District in the Reagan column in 1984 but whose political leanings make this a Democratic district in other contests.

Berman has been an active legislator in the House. Long an ally of Cesar Chavez's United Farm Workers, he opposed Leon Panetta's guestworker amendment to the immigration bill in 1982 and 1984. In 1986 he and Charles Schumer worked up a compromise on the issue, allowing in a large number of guestworkers and opening the way up for them to become U.S. citizens, which at first stymied and then, altered, helped to facilitate the passage of the immigration law that year. Berman acted there from his seat on Judiciary, where he is also able to tend to the interests of showbiz types in copyright and licensing laws. He also serves on Foreign Affairs, where he has taken a hand in crafting anti-apartheid legislation and a law allowing imposition of arms embargoes on nations that support terrorism.

Berman also serves on the Steering and Policy Committee, which makes committee assignments; this seat he got in 1982 with the help of his longtime ally Henry Waxman. With Waxman and colleague Mel Levine and his political consultant brother Michael, Berman heads an unusual political machine that raises money in Los Angeles for campaigns there and elsewhere. He has had little trouble getting elected here himself, although the boundaries of the district, by including many tradition-minded neighborhoods in the Valley as well as the self-consciously liberal hills, have prevented him from getting a 2 to 1 victory yet.

The People: Pop. 1980: 525,995, up 2.4% 1970–80. Households (1980): 68% family, 34% with children, 54% married couples; 44.5% housing units rented; median monthly rent: $282; median house value: $96,200. Voting age pop. (1980): 392,919; 20% Spanish origin, 4% Black, 3% Asian origin, 1% American Indian.

Presidential Vote:

Reagan (R) 108,528	(54%)
Mondale (D) 90,429	(45%)

Rep. Howard L. Berman (D)

Elected 1982; b. Apr. 15, 1941, Los Angeles; home, Los Angeles; U. of CA at Los Angeles, B.A. 1962, LL.B. 1965; Jewish; married (Janis).

Career: Practicing atty., 1966–72; CA Assembly, 1973–82.

Offices: 137 CHOB 20515, 202-225-4695. Also 14600 Roscoe Blvd., Ste. 506, Panorama City 91402, 818-891-0543.

Committees: *Foreign Affairs* (16th of 27 D). Subcommittees: Arms Control, International Security and Science; International Economic Policy and Trade. *Judiciary* (17th of 21 D). Subcommittees: Administrative Law and Governmental Relations; Courts, Civil Liberties, and the Administration of Justice; Criminal Justice; Immigration, Refugees, and International Law.

Group Ratings

	ADA	ACLU	COPE	CFA	LCV	ACU	NTU	NSI	COC	CEI
1986	95	94	88	83	93	5	30	0	19	26
1985	100	—	87	83	—	10	32	—	24	—

National Journal Ratings

	1986 LIB — 1986 CONS			1985 LIB — 1985 CONS		
Economic	84%	—	16	89%	—	0%
Social	89%	—	0%	85%	—	0%
Foreign	80%	—	0%	85%	—	8%

Key Votes

1) Lmt Cln Water Act	AGN	5) Retain Gun Cont	FOR	9) Aid Angola Reb	AGN
2) Rpl Tobac Sub	FOR	6) Contra Aid	AGN	10) Tax Reform	FOR
3) Grm-Rdmn Def Red	AGN	7) Lmt Text Imp	AGN	11) S Africa Sanc	FOR
4) Ban Polygraph	FOR	8) Limit SDI	FOR	12) Immig Reform	FOR

Election Results

1986 general	Howard L. Berman (D)	98,091	(65%)	($272,956)
	Robert M. Kerns (R)	52,662	(35%)	($10,314)
1986 primary	Howard L. Berman (D)	47,606	(100%)	
1984 general	Howard L. Berman (D)	117,080	(63%)	($204,227)
	Miriam Ojeda (R)...................	69,372	(37%)	($6,545)

Campaign Contributions and Expenditures

	1985-86	Direct Cont. 1985-86		PACS Breakdown 1985-86			
Receipts	$277,688	Indiv.	$128,650	Corp.	$34,100	T/M/H	$32,600
Expend.	$272,956	Party	$227	Labor	$51,975	Agr.	$2,600
Debts	$21,273	PACS	$133,261	Ideo.	$10,436	CWOS	$1,550
		Cand.	$15,000				

TWENTY-SEVENTH DISTRICT

The beach district, the 27th Congressional District of California, is a long, thin swath of land along the Pacific Coast, from Pacific Palisades in the north almost to Palos Verdes in the south. It takes in most of Los Angeles's beachfront plus some odd-shaped salients inland. The cool ocean breezes give the area its own microclimate, cooler than the rest of Los Angeles in the summer, a little less cool but damper in the winter. The beach communities are about as diverse as can be imagined. Pacific Palisades, on its cliffs overlooking the ocean and the huge Getty Museum, was once the home of Ronald Reagan. Santa Monica and Venice, full of young people living in cheap housing and fearful that they will be expelled for higher-paying tenants or condominium buyers, have generated in Santa Monica's case an indigenous leftish political movement (Tom Hayden's Committee for Economic Democracy lost control of Santa Monica City Hall in 1983 but Hayden has been elected to the Assembly since 1982 and casts himself as something of a neoliberal) and in Venice's case a countercultural lifestyle full of enthusiasm for roller skating or breakdancing or whatever is the latest craze. Next is Los Angeles International Airport (known by its three letter code, LAX), followed by the beach suburbs of El Segundo (named after Socal's second refinery), Manhattan Beach (more yuppified lately), Hermosa Beach (like Venice, but not as bizarre), and Redondo Beach (with different beachfront and inland sections). The tightly packed frame houses here were originally the homes of elderly retirees; by the 1970s they were inhabited more often by groups of young singles.

Politically, the beach communities do have some things in common: a Republican heritage, dating from their original settlement by midwestern retirees, and liberal cultural attitudes, brought in by the suntanned, pot-smoking residents of the 1970s. To this should be added the atmosphere created by CED's temporary capture of the Santa Monica city government, based primarily on the rent control issue: young renters celebrating themselves as proletarians because they want to continue to rent apartments a few blocks from the beach for $175 a month when others would pay much more. But altogether the 27th would be a marginal Republican district—as it was before 1982—without the inland territory: odd-shaped fingers of land some four miles inland into a heavily black part of West Los Angeles, half of the prosperous black-majority suburb of Inglewood, the mostly Mexican-American suburbs of Lennox behind the airport and Lawndale behind the South Bay beach towns, and a slice of the mostly-black several-blocks-wide corridor of Los Angeles which connects the port of San Pedro with the rest of the city. These areas, heavily Democratic, have made this a safe district for Rep. Mel Levine.

Since his days as valedictorian at Berkeley, Levine has been tabbed as a rising politician through Princeton's Woodrow Wilson School, Harvard Law, seven years of law practice, and three terms in the California Assembly. Rich and articulate, pleasant but hard-driving, he has been a political ally of Howard Berman and Henry Waxman since the 1970s. When Phillip Burton's redistricting changed the 27th District from Republican to Democratic, sending fiery conservative Robert Dornan into the 1982 Senate race and ultimately to the 38th district in Orange County, Levine ran for the House and won easily. He was surprised in 1984 to be held to 55% by evangelical Republican (and former Los Angeles Ram) Rob Scribner, but this time Scribner's religiosity alienated voters. Levine "is diametrically opposed to nearly everything the Lord's Church stands for in this nation," he wrote district pastors in 1985, "I hope you will agree to link arms with us as we literally 'take territory' for our Lord Jesus Christ." Levine won in this not overwhelmingly Democratic district by nearly 2 to 1; he was confident enough to leave $310,000 in the bank when the campaign was over.

In the House Levine serves on the Interior Committee, where he has stoutly opposed oil drilling in Santa Monica Bay in the running dispute between the California delegation and Interior Secretary Donald Hodel, and he is on Foreign Affairs, where he is a champion of the cause of Israel. He also co-chaired the Military Reform Caucus, a position of some interest since many major defense contractors—Hughes, Northrop, Rockwell, TRW—have big installations in or near the 27th District; the reform group wants to reexamine defense contracts critically.

Levine is said to have statewide ambitions, but decided not to run for the Senate in 1988. He could run for Alan Cranston's seat in 1992, especially if the Democrats do not control redistricting as they did in the 1970s and 1980s and there are not enough congressional districts for Levine and his close friends and allies Henry Waxman and Howard Berman.

The People: Pop. 1980: 525,929, dn. 4.4% 1970–80. Households (1980): 54% family, 27% with children, 40% married couples; 63.4% housing units rented; median monthly rent: $310; median house value: $121,600. Voting age pop. (1980): 415,975; 12% Spanish origin, 9% Black, 5% Asian origin, 1% American Indian.

Presidential Vote:

Reagan (R) 117,634	(52%)
Mondale (D) 104,031	(46%)

Rep. Mel Levine (D)

Elected 1982; b. June 7, 1943, Los Angeles; home, Los Angeles; U. of CA at Berkeley, A.B. 1964, Princeton U., M.P.A. 1966, Harvard Law Sch., J.D. 1969; Jewish; married (Jan).

Career: Practicing atty., 1969–71, 1973–77; Legis. Asst. to U.S. Sen. John V. Tunney, 1971–73; CA Assembly, 1977–82.

Offices: 132 CHOB 20515, 202-225-6451. Also 5250 W. Century Blvd., Ste. 447, Los Angeles 90045, 213-215-2035.

Committees: *Foreign Affairs* (17th of 27 D) Subcommittees: Europe and the Middle East; International Economic Policy and Trade. *Interior and Insular Affairs* (21st of 26 D). Subcommittees: Energy and the Environment; National Parks and Public Lands; Water Resources and Power. *Select Committee on Narcotics Abuse and Control* (12th of 15 D).

Group Ratings

	ADA	ACLU	COPE	CFA	LCV	ACU	NTU	NSI	COC	CEI
1986	85	94	94	92	89	5	29	0	15	26
1985	100	—	90	92	—	0	34	—	27	—

National Journal Ratings

	1986 LIB — 1986 CONS		1985 LIB — 1985 CONS	
Economic	73% —	26%	85% —	11%
Social	89% —	0%	85% —	0%
Foreign	80% —	0%	85% —	8%

Key Votes

1) Lmt Cln Water Act	AGN	5) Retain Gun Cont	FOR	9) Aid Angola Reb	AGN
2) Rpl Tobac Sub	FOR	6) Contra Aid	AGN	10) Tax Reform	FOR
3) Grm-Rdmn Def Red	AGN	7) Lmt Text Imp	AGN	11) S Africa Sanc	FOR
4) Ban Polygraph	FOR	8) Limit SDI	FOR	12) Immig Reform	FOR

Election Results

1986 general	Mel Levine (D)	110,403	(64%)	($498,833)
	Robert B. Scribner (R)	59,410	(34%)	($393,860)
1986 primary	Mel Levine (D)	51,891	(100%)	
1984 general	Mel Levine (D)	116,933	(55%)	($282,914)
	Robert B. Scribner (R)	88,896	(42%)	($167,360)

Campaign Contributions and Expenditures

1985-86		Direct Cont. 1985-86		PACS Breakdown 1985-86			
Receipts	$711,129	Indiv.	$537,220	Corp.	$38,150	T/M/H	$17,950
Expend.	$498,833	PACS	$126,908	Labor	$34,400	Agr.	$1,750
Unspent	$310,765			Ideo.	$34,158	CWOS	$500

TWENTY-EIGHTH DISTRICT

If you want to get a sense of where prosperous, upwardly mobile black Americans are going politically, perhaps the best place to go in the United States is the 28th Congressional District of California. Stretching from downtown Los Angeles to Los Angeles International Airport, from the park around the Coliseum where the 1984 Olympic ceremonies were held to the MGM studios in Culver City, the district covers a wide swath of the Los Angeles Basin. Forty years ago, there were only a few blacks living within these bounds, along its eastern edges near the Coliseum and the University of Southern California. Beginning in the 1950s, Los Angeles area blacks began moving west from the core ghetto area south of downtown, across the nondescript neighborhoods on bent-grid streets south of Wilshire Boulevard, out toward the Crenshaw neighborhood with its art deco May Company shopping center, southwest toward the then lightly populated suburb of Inglewood and the unpopulated Fox Hills and Ladera Heights. Many of these neighborhoods were affluent and comfortable when the first blacks moved in, and still are today.

In fact, what's striking about this area is not its racial change but racial stability. Someone looking ahead from 1970, when its population was about 38% black and 12% Spanish origin, might have predicted a rapid increase in the black percentage in the next decade. But actually it has not increased much at all; it is the Spanish origin that has risen (but no one is sure by quite how much, since the categories in the two censuses are not commensurate). The Mexican-Americans do not seem to be concentrated in just a few neighborhoods; neither, to a surprising extent considering our history of neighborhood segregation, do blacks. Culver City, once virtually all white, is now 8% black; but there is no established ghetto there. Inglewood is now 57% black, but there are no signs that the whites there are about to move out en masse. This slower, more relaxed pace of change seems to have prevented the sort of feverish politics and wildly fluctuating housing prices often seen in racially changing neighborhoods. In any case, this is a solidly Democratic area: not only the blacks, but a majority of the whites, regularly vote Democratic. With relatively little fuss the mostly white voters have elected black Democrats: first Yvonne Brathwaite Burke and, since 1978, Julian Dixon.

Dixon, who served six years in the California Assembly, is a competent and shrewd politician. In his first term he won a seat on the Appropriations Committee. In his second he became chairman of the District of Columbia Appropriations Subcommittee. In his third term he chaired both the Congressional Black Caucus and the Democratic national convention committee before which Jesse Jackson made his challenge to the legitimacy of the party rules. In his fourth term Dixon became chairman of the House's ethics committee. Each assignment he has handled carefully, taking time to learn the facts, and then moving quickly to get what he wants. This is a politician who quietly becomes sure of his ground and then pounces like a tiger.

On District of Columbia matters, for example, he is sympathetic but not sycophantic to the city government and Mayor Marion Barry. On his other Appropriations subcommittee, Foreign

Operations, he moved early to pressure South Africa to abandon apartheid and to help black African states. As Black Caucus chairman, he declined to push vehemently for a separate Caucus budget resolution, though he did advance one in 1984. As for the Democratic convention, his committee produced a unanimous report which was accepted without demur on the floor.

On Ethics, Dixon has proceeded with characteristic quietness and thoroughness. The committee ruled against Virginia Democrat Dan Daniel for accepting free plane rides but voted no harsh punishment; but no one thinks Daniel acted culpably. Dixon did not hesitate to issue new interpretations of House assets reporting requirements which many members complained bitterly about, and he made it clear he expected his views to be followed. His committee acted reasonably expeditiously in the case involving Oregon's James Weaver (who lost funds from his campaign account in commodities speculation) and seems to have pursued the case of Banking Chairman Fernand St Germain (who seems to have made a lot of money thanks to below-market-interest bank loans). Dixon's Ethics Committee does not work as rapidly or punish as roughly as some critics would like. But it when it docs take a stand it does not have to back down.

Dixon has not had serious competition at home since he won the 1978 primary. He was helped then by Henry Waxman and Howard Berman and is considered their ally on many matters.

The People: Pop. 1980: 525,993, up 6.2% 1970–80. Households: (1980): 60% family, 33% with children, 39% married couples; 67.0% housing units rented; median monthly rent: $198; median house value: $82,600. Voting age pop. (1980): 395,349; 37% Black, 24% Spanish origin, 8% Asian origin.

1984 Presidential Vote:

Mondale (D)	108,287	(67%)
Reagan (R)	51,069	(32%)

Rep. Julian C. Dixon (D)

Elected 1978; b. Aug. 8, 1934, Washington, D.C.; home, Culver City; CA St. U. at L.A., B.S. 1962, Southwestern U., LL.B. 1967; Episcopalian; married (Betty).

Career: Army, 1957–60; Practicing atty., 1960–73; CA Assembly, 1972–78.

Offices: 2400 RHOB 20515, 202-225-7084. Also 111 N. LaBrea Ave., Ste. 301, Inglewood 90301, 213-678-5424.

Committees: *Appropriations* (21st of 35 D). Subcommittees: District of Columbia (Chairman); Foreign Operations. *Standards of Official Conduct* (Chairman of 6 D).

Group Ratings

	ADA	ACLU	COPE	CFA	LCV	ACU	NTU	NSI	COC	CEI
1986	85	94	96	67	66	0	21	0	25	7
1985	80	—	96	58	—	0	25	—	15	—

National Journal Ratings

	1986 LIB — 1986 CONS		1985 LIB — 1985 CONS	
Economic	87% —	0%	89% —	0%
Social	89% —	0%	85% —	0%
Foreign	80% —	0%	84% —	15%

Key Votes

1) Lmt Cln Water Act	AGN	5) Retain Gun Cont	FOR	9) Aid Angola Reb	AGN
2) Rpl Tobac Sub	AGN	6) Contra Aid	AGN	10) Tax Reform	AGN
3) Grm-Rdmn Def Red	AGN	7) Lmt Text Imp	FOR	11) S Africa Sanc	FOR
4) Ban Polygraph	FOR	8) Limit SDI	—	12) Immig Reform	FOR

Election Results

1986 general	Julian C. Dixon (D)	92,635	(76%)	($103,442)
	George Adams (R)	25,858	(21%)	($39,341)
1986 primary	Julian C. Dixon (D)	52,205	(93%)	
	Joe Alcoset (D)	4,138	(7%)	
1984 general	Julian C. Dixon (D)	113,076	(76%)	($105,907)
	Beatrice M. Jett (R)	33,511	(22%)	

Campaign Contributions and Expenditures

1985-86		Direct Cont. 1985-86		PACS Breakdown 1985-86			
Receipts	$148,385	Indiv.	$46,199	Corp.	$27,075	T/M/H	$22,950
Expend.	$103,442	PACS	$101,186	Labor	$43,925	Agr.	$1,250
Unspent	$80,527			Ideo.	$5,986	CWOS	$0

TWENTY-NINTH DISTRICT

It has been more than 20 years since Watts, the center of Los Angeles's black community, has been in the headlines. For a few weeks in 1965 it became the center of national attention as rioters ranged the streets, fires burned, and stores were looted of their merchandise. East Coast writers, familiar with Harlem, had a hard time understanding Watts, with its small frame double- and single-family houses along wide streets, and took some time grasping that this poor neighborhood, like five-story tenement neighborhoods in eastern cities, had few good schools or hospitals, parks or strong community institutions, that much of the territory around Watts wasn't part of the city of Los Angeles at all, and the city had no intention of annexing it. Not very much seems to have changed in two decades. The area's most distinctive feature is still the Watts Tower, a weird sculpture of bits of broken glass and scrap metal, assembled over 30 years by Italian immigrant Simon Rodia, who gave it to the city free, while other cities spend huge sums for less attractive and more obtrusive pieces. But there has been substantial population movement. Watts's successful sons and daughters have moved west or south into middle and upper income black and integrated neighborhoods and even occasionally into the working class suburbs to the east, across Alameda Street, which for years were all white but as the whites have moved or died have become heavily Mexican-American.

Watts is also the center of California's 29th Congressional District, which sprawls east, west, and north from Watts: east through working class Huntington Park and South Gate to take in part of white collar Downey, and west toward middle income Inglewood, and north toward the Los Angeles Coliseum and the Los Angeles Convention Center. It is still predominantly a black district, but the black population has been falling and in the 1970s the number of Hispanic within these boundaries rose by more than 100,000. As a result the Democratic percentages here have declined somewhat. But this is still California's most Democratic congressional district.

The congressman from the 29th is Augustus Hawkins, chairman of the House Education and Labor Committee, senior member of the Congressional Black Caucus and the senior black legislator in the United States. For 28 years, from 1934 to 1962, he served in the California Assembly, for most of the time as its only black member; in 1959 he was nearly elected speaker. But California was apparently not ready for that then, and so Hawkins had to settle for a seat in Congress in 1962. He has been an active member of Education and Labor for many years, and even though he was 76 when he succeeded Carl Perkins as chairman in 1984, he remains in full command of his powers and firm in his convictions.

His problem is that the nation, and even the Democratic House, seem to have lost faith in the programs he remains devoted to. Hawkins believes that government programs can help, and have helped, the poor and the middle class; that aid to education has strengthened the nation and helped to make more equal the opportunities open to each child; that federal job programs have made the difference between a productive life and an idle one for hundreds of thousands of Americans; that the government has a responsibility to give jobs to those who cannot find employment in the private sector. His sympathies, it should be added, are by no means confined to blacks, but extend to all that he considers in economic need.

So during most of the 1980s he has been pushing against the tide. His most conspicuous previous success, the Humphrey-Hawkins Act of 1978, was not actually the federal job guarantee he wanted, and is pretty much a dead letter; no one expects unemployment ever to fall to its goal of 4%. Humphrey-Hawkins was a kind of litmus test for Democratic candidates in 1976; in 1988 it seems more likely that they will have to prove their realism by rejecting rather than embracing federal jobs programs. Hawkins has been unsuccessful in other endeavors, on a youth jobs bill for example; and his fight to protect the minimum wage against exceptions, while successful, seems to have become moot as even the lowest-paying employers like fast food outlets are being driven in tighter labor markets to pay more than the minimum wage anyway.

But after more than 50 years of legislating, Hawkins is not going to quit now. He is ready for the late 1980s with bills to spend more on early childhood education and adult illiteracy, to raise the minimum wage from $3.35 to $4.65. Education and Labor remains packed with Democrats sympathetic to his views (as it has been ever since organized labor lost a key vote on the labor bill there in 1959), even if on occasion some of its seats have gone begging; and given a more favorable political climate, Hawkins is ready to work up and report out the kind of legislation he has always backed. He will be helped, as he has been before, by his scrupulous courtesy and unfailing concern for the rights of other legislators.

At home Hawkins is always reelected without difficulty. One likely successor, should he retire, is Assemblywoman Maxine Waters, though she may have been weakened a bit by the defeat of her son by a Republican in a nearby Assembly district in 1986.

The People: Pop. 1980: 525,938, up 4.9% 1970–80. Households: (1980): 72% family, 47% with children, 43% married couples; 60.0% housing units rented; median monthly rent: $161; median house value: $52,700. Voting age pop. (1980): 339,585; 51% Black, 32% Spanish origin, 1% Asian origin.

1984 Presidential Vote:

Mondale (D)	103,221	(77%)
Reagan (R)	29,106	(22%)

Rep. Augustus F. Hawkins (D)

Elected 1962; b. Aug. 31, 1907, Shreveport, LA; home, Los Angeles; U. of CA at Los Angeles, A.B. 1931; U. of Southern CA Institute of Govt.; United Methodist; married (Elsie).

Career: Real estate business; CA Assembly, 1935–62.

Offices: 2371 RHOB 20515, 202-225-2201. Also 2710 Zoe Ave., Huntington Park 90255, 213-587-0421; and 4509 S. Broadway, Los Angeles 90037, 213-750-0260.

Committees: *Education and Labor* (Chairman of 21 D). Subcommittee: Elementary, Secondary, and Vocational Education (Chairman). *Joint Economic Committee.* Subcommittees: Economic Goals and Intergovernmental Policy; Investment, Jobs and Prices; Education and Health.

Group Ratings

	ADA	ACLU	COPE	CFA	LCV	ACU	NTU	NSI	COC	CEI
1986	85	94	96	67	53	0	26	0	15	9
1985	85	—	96	75	—	0	27	—	22	—

National Journal Ratings

	1986 LIB — 1986 CONS	1985 LIB — 1985 CONS
Economic	87% — 0%	79% — 19%
Social	83% — 17%	85% — 0%
Foreign	80% — 0%	83% — 16%

Key Votes

1) Lmt Cln Water Act	AGN	5) Retain Gun Cont	FOR	9) Aid Angola Reb	AGN
2) Rpl Tobac Sub	AGN	6) Contra Aid	AGN	10) Tax Reform	FOR
3) Grm-Rdmn Def Red	AGN	7) Lmt Text Imp	FOR	11) S Africa Sanc	FOR
4) Ban Polygraph	FOR	8) Limit SDI	FOR	12) Immig Reform	AGN

Election Results

1986 general	Augustus F. Hawkins (D)	78,132	(85%)	($34,061)
	John Van de Brooke (R)	13,432	(15%)	
1986 primary	Augustus F. Hawkins (D)	108,777	(93%)	
	Mervin Evans (R)......................	3,418	(7%)	
1984 general	Augustus F. Hawkins (D)	108,777	(87%)	($48,495)
	Echo Y. Goto (R)	16,781	(13%)	

Campaign Contributions and Expenditures

1985-86		Direct Cont. 1985-86		PACS Breakdown 1985-86			
Receipts	$87,403	Indiv.	$7,065	Corp.	$10,300	T/M/H	$16,438
Expend.	$34,061	PACS	$73,281	Labor	$40,750	Agr.	$2,350
Unspent	$111,442			Ideo.	$3,193	CWOS	$250

THIRTIETH DISTRICT

The 30th Congressional District of California is one of two suburban Los Angeles County districts running from northeast to southwest, in the valley east of downtown Los Angeles. Both the 30th and the 34th were designed to be Mexican-American districts, though in neither is a majority of the adult population of Spanish origin, and in both Mexican-American voters are not just concentrated in a couple of enclosed ghettos, but in fact are dispersed through a wide variety of neighborhoods. The heaviest Mexican-American concentrations, on the order of 60%, in the 30th District are in industrial suburbs: young Mexican families have replaced aging whites in the factory and warehouse suburbs of Vernon, Maywood, Commerce, Bell, and Bell Gardens directly south of Boyle Heights, on either side of the usually dry, cement-channeled Los Angeles River. The towns directly adjacent to East Los Angeles have lower Mexican percentages. In some cases, as in Montebello and Monterey Park, this is because they also have sizable numbers of Korean and other Asian inhabitants; Monterey Park, which has produced two congressmen, has even had some interesting Asian vs. Latin and Asian vs. Asian politics. In other towns, like Alhambra and San Gabriel, the economic level is a little higher. But even here the population in 1980 was 38% Spanish origin. From there the 30th sweeps far northeast, through the valley's blue-collar suburb of El Monte to Azusa, at the foot of the giant San Gabriel Mountains.

This has always been a basically Democratic area, even when there were few Mexican-Americans there. What is fascinating is that the steady dispersal of Mexican-Americans (and Asians) outward, in a kind of Brownian movement, from the East Los Angeles and Boyle Heights concentrations, has not increased the Democratic percentages as some predicted—and in fact may end up lowering them. The Democratic percentage in the 30th and 34th Districts were stable between the 1980 and 1984 elections. But the Reagan percentages rose to robust majorities. Monterey Park, long Democratic, went for Reagan; Montebello only barely went for Mondale. Mexicans and Koreans, Salvadoreans and Chinese: this generation of immigrants seems more upwardly mobile and more Republican than the white working-class people who lived in the same places 20 and 30 years ago. Working their way upward in small businesses, they are not attracted by a Democratic party that puts its faith in big government; made aware by terrible personal histories of the decency and security of life in America, they are turned off by a party so many of whose supporters and candidates seem skeptical or ironic about the virtues of the country they seek to represent.

The congressman from the 30th District is a Democrat who has had the advantage of being in the right place at the right time. When Marty Martinez, owner of an upholstery company, was elected to the Monterey Park Council in 1974, he seemed unlikely to end up in Congress. But in 1980 Howard Berman, running for Assembly speaker, tabbed Martinez to run against an Anglo incumbent, raised money for him, superintended his direct mail campaigning, and saw him elected. For the 1982 election California's master redistricter Phillip Burton wanted to forestall Republicans who were seeking an alliance with Hispanics at the Democrats' expense. So where no one thought it possible he created two Hispanic districts, the 30th and 34th. Martinez, a friend of Berman's and therefore of Burton's, became the Democratic nominee.

That should have made him an easy winner. But he had a game opponent in John Rousselot, longtime Republican incumbent and John Birch Society organizer, who passed up an easy chance to beat a fellow Republican incumbent and worked hard enough to hold Martinez to a 54%–46% victory. Two years later he soundly beat Gladys Danielson, wife of former Representative George Danielson, in the primary. But Montebello lawyer Richard Gomez, though little known, held him to 52% in the general. In 1986 Martinez did better, with 63% against an unknown foe; even so, this was the second lowest percentage for any incumbent in Los Angeles County. Even the congressional races here have been closer than anyone expected.

Martinez's major committee assignment is Education and Labor, and after the 1984 election, he became chairman of the Employment Opportunities Subcommittee. That may be parochially advantageous but is not otherwise terribly important panel these days; its writ includes superintendency of a long-bedraggled Equal Employment Opportunity Commission. Martinez has not been a particularly active or voluble legislator.

The People: Pop. 1980: 526,018, up 10.4% 1970–80. Households: (1980): 74% family, 44% with children, 56% married couples; 53.4% housing units rented; median monthly rent: $234; median house value: $73,700. Voting age pop. (1980): 360,738; 48% Spanish origin, 9% Asian origin, 1% Black, 1% American Indian.

1984 Presidential Vote: Reagan (R)   71,658   (55%)
                               Mondale (D)   56,598   (44%)

Rep. Matthew G. Martinez (D)

Elected July 13, 1982; b. Feb. 14, 1929, Walsenburg, CO; home, Monterey Park; Los Angeles Trade Technical Sch.; Roman Catholic; divorced.

Career: USMC, 1947–50; Small businessman (furniture and upholstery), 1957–82; Monterey Park Planning Comm., 1971–74; Monterey Park City Cncl., 1974–76; Mayor of Monterey Park, 1976–80; CA Assembly, 1980–82.

Offices: 109 CHOB 20515, 202-225-5464. Also 1712 W. Beverly Blvd., Montebello 90640, 213-722-7731.

Committees: *Education and Labor* (9 of 21 D). Subcommittees: Elementary, Secondary, and Vocational Education; Employment Opportunities (Chairman); Postsecondary Education. *Government Operations* (20th of 24 D). Subcommittees: Commerce, Consumer and Monetary Affairs; Environment, Energy and Natural Resources. *Select Committee on Children, Youth, and Families* (14th of 18 D). Task Force: Economic Security.

Group Ratings

	ADA	ACLU	COPE	CFA	LCV	ACU	NTU	NSI	COC	CEI
1986	85	83	99	75	77	10	23	10	7	14
1985	80	—	96	75	—	5	31	—	19	—

National Journal Ratings

	1986 LIB — 1986 CONS	1985 LIB — 1985 CONS
Economic	77% — 22%	89% — 0%
Social	57% — 43%	85% — 0%
Foreign	80% — 0%	71% — 26%

Key Votes

1) Lmt Cln Water Act	—	5) Retain Gun Cont	—	9) Aid Angola Reb	AGN
2) Rpl Tobac Sub	AGN	6) Contra Aid	AGN	10) Tax Reform	FOR
3) Grm-Rdmn Def Red	AGN	7) Lmt Text Imp	FOR	11) S Africa Sanc	FOR
4) Ban Polygraph	FOR	8) Limit SDI	FOR	12) Immig Reform	AGN

Election Results

1986 general	Matthew G. Martinez (D)	59,369	(63%)	($135,854)
	John W. Almquist (R)	33,705	(36%)	($70,955)
1986 primary	Matthew G. Martinez (D)	27,161	(81%)	
	Gilbert Barron (D)	4,079	(12%)	
	George Trivich (D)	2,179	(7%)	
1984 general	Matthew G. Martinez (D)	64,378	(52%)	($212,969)
	Richard Gomez (R)	53,900	(43%)	($152,872)
	Houston A. Meyers (Am.-Indep.)	6,055	(5%)	

Campaign Contributions and Expenditures

1985-86		Direct Cont. 1985-86		PACS Breakdown 1985-86			
Receipts	$165,641	Indiv.	$45,084	Corp.	$8,750	T/M/H	$7,350
Expend.	$135,854	PACS	$116,931	Labor	$83,220	Agr.	$800
Debts	$42,524			Ideo.	$16,811	CWOS	$0

THIRTY-FIRST DISTRICT

The 31st Congressional District of California is a patch of fairly typical 1940s and 1950s Los Angeles County suburban territory, on both sides of the Harbor Freeway between downtown Los Angeles and the port at San Pedro. Most of it is made up of neat single-family stucco houses, in natural tan or different pastels, often with an above-ground swimming pool and some slightly shabby lawn furniture. There are parcels of still vacant land here and newly laid out subdivisions, and next to them the overgrown lots of factory workers' widows who are just getting by on Social Security. The 31st also contains sparkling steel-and-glass shopping centers and the fading pink stucco commercial strips of the 1940s. Undergirding the economy are huge defense plants and other factories spread out along the Harbor and San Diego Freeways.

The 31st sits directly south of the Watts black neighborhood, and over the past few decades some of its suburbs—Willowbrook, Compton—have changed from white to black. But in the 1970s and 1980s the pace of racial change has been less than the other ethnic changes. The suburbs of Lynwood and Paramount, southeast of Watts, have become more Mexican than black; Bellflower, directly north of Long Beach, is still mostly white Anglo. Gardena, just west of the Harbor Freeway, has the most varied mix, with roughly equal parts white Anglo, black, Spanish, and Japanese. (Gardena has another distinction: it is permitted by California law to license poker clubs at which some of the most cutthroat poker in the country is played.)

This part of Los Angeles County has been solidly Democratic since the 1930s, when it was almost entirely white. It is not, however, a coherent political community. The 31st is the kind of congressional district where people can get elected to legislative office by putting up billboards that say "Charles Wilson is a good guy." In fact there was a Charles Wilson who was elected congressman here for 18 years and was finally beaten after it was revealed that he lied about a $600 wedding gift from Tongsun Park (he got only 15% in his last primary).

The current representative is a more vivid political figure, a talented man with a chip on his shoulder, former Lieutenant Governor Mervyn Dymally. He has a distinctive speaking style and accent from his native Trinidad. His reputation was damaged in the 1970s by never-proven allegations of wrongdoing (subsequently never proved), and he was defeated for reelection as lieutenant governor in 1978 by Republican Mike Curb, than whom there is no more unsavory and plastic a figure in California politics. There is justice: Curb lost the 1982 governor primary to George Deukmejian and an attempted 1986 comeback was thwarted when he lost to his successor as lieutenant governor, Democrat Leo McCarthy. And Dymally made a striking comeback in 1980 in the 31st District, by winning 49% of the vote in a primary against four other candidates (including Wilson and former 34th District Congressman Mark Hannaford), in a district no more than one-third of whose voters were black. The redrawn district lines decrease rather than increase the black percentage, but Dymally has won since by overwhelming margins.

As lieutenant governor, Dymally liked to say that California would soon have a "Third World majority." True in the sense that Asians, Latins, and (the smallest group of the three) blacks may become a majority; false, if it means that they share the anti-American reflex of some Third World politicians. Leaders and voters in Dymally's native eastern Caribbean may welcome American action against Castro and the Communist regime in Grenada, but Dymally tends to see the United States as more part of the problem than the solution in the Third World, and he decries the lack of American aid to Caribbean countries other than El Salvador and Honduras. On Middle Eastern matters he seems more sympathetic to some Arab causes than to Israel. He sits on no less than four committees—Education and Labor, Foreign Affairs, Post Office and Civil Service, District of Columbia—and there and on the floor his record is solidly liberal on most issues. He has contributed to the Higher Education Act and drug abuse bills and has worked on a host of other lightly publicized issues from civil rights in Micronesia to giving minority firms a share in oil and gas leases on federal lands.

The People: Pop. 1980: 525,939, up 0.1% 1970–80. Households (1980): 75% family, 47% with children, 54% married couples; 46.6% housing units rented; median monthly rent: $237; median house value: $68,500. Voting age pop. (1980): 354,360; 31% Black, 21% Spanish origin, 8% Asian origin, 1% American Indian.

1984 Presidential Vote:

Mondale (D)	87,740	(58%)
Reagan (R)	61,006	(41%)

Rep. Mervyn M. Dymally (D)

Elected 1980; b. May 12, 1926, Cedros, Trinidad, West Indies; home, Compton; CA St. U., B.A. 1954, M.A. 1969, U.S. Intl. U., Ph.D. 1978; Episcopalian; married (Alice).

Career: Teacher, L.A. Schls., 1955–61; Coord., CA Disaster Ofc., 1961–62; CA Assembly, 1962–66; CA Senate, 1966–75; Lt. Gov. of CA, 1975–79.

Offices: 1717 LHOB 20515, 202-225-5425. Also 322 W. Compton Blvd., Ste. 102, Compton 90220, 213-536-6930.

Committees: *District of Columbia* (6th of 8 D). Subcommittee: Judiciary (Chairman). *Foreign Affairs* (11th of 27 D). Subcommittees: Asian and Pacific Affairs; International Operations. *Post Office and Civil Service* (12th of 14 D). Subcommittees: Census and Population (Chairman); Postal Personnel and Modernization.

Group Ratings

	ADA	ACLU	COPE	CFA	LCV	ACU	NTU	NSI	COC	CEI
1986	100	95	93	83	72	0	28	0	19	17
1985	90	—	93	50	—	10	32	—	24	—

National Journal Ratings

	1986 LIB — 1986 CONS		1985 LIB — 1985 CONS	
Economic	87% —	0%	83% —	17%
Social	85% —	14%	73% —	23%
Foreign	80% —	0%	92% —	0%

Key Votes

1) Lmt Cln Water Act	AGN	5) Retain Gun Cont	FOR	9) Aid Angola Reb	AGN
2) Rpl Tobac Sub	AGN	6) Contra Aid	AGN	10) Tax Reform	AGN
3) Grm-Rdmn Def Red	AGN	7) Lmt Text Imp	FOR	11) S Africa Sanc	FOR
4) Ban Polygraph	FOR	8) Limit SDI	FOR	12) Immig Reform	AGN

Election Results

1986 general	Mervyn M. Dymally (D).	77,126	(70%)	($385,063)
	Jack McMurray (R)	30,322	(28%)	($41,875)
1986 primary	Mervyn M. Dymally (D).	40,339	(85%)	
	Kevin Zondervan (D)	7,394	(15%)	
1984 general	Mervyn M. Dymally (D).	100,658	(71%)	($332,361)
	Henry C. Minturn (R)	41,691	(29%)	

Campaign Contributions and Expenditures

1985-86		Direct Cont. 1985-86		PACS Breakdown 1985-86			
Receipts	$386,427	Indiv.	$227,130	Corp.	$20,700	T/M/H	$23,245
Expend.	$385,063	Party	$658	Labor	$70,900	Agr.	$4,500
Unspent	$3,788	PACS	$129,945	Ideo.	$10,350	CWOS	$250
		Cand.	$19,000				

THIRTY-SECOND DISTRICT

Nature did not intend for Los Angeles to be America's biggest port on the Pacific, but man—or at least the city fathers of Los Angeles just after the turn of the century—did, and they succeeded in their purpose. They started off with nothing more than the mouth of a river that was dry most of the year, 20 miles downstream from a farm market and railroad depot center of 100,000 people or so. In the same years they were building the aqueduct system that brings fresh water hundreds of miles over the mountains to Los Angeles, they also built one, or rather two, man-made harbors—one west of Terminal Island built by the city of Los Angeles and the other on the east by the city of Long Beach. In the years since, they outhustled San Francisco with its complacent merchant class and militant unions, and made this the biggest port on the West Coast, a triumph of man-made channels and breakwaters and dredging over the superb harbors nature sculpted in San Francisco, San Diego, and Seattle. Here are berthed also the Queen Mary, now the biggest tourist attraction of Long Beach, and the Spruce Goose, the huge cargo seaplane that was piloted just once across this harbor by its builder, Howard Hughes.

The focus of the 32d Congressional District of California is on this port area. Technically, the port itself is outside the district, a thin land-bridge connecting two disparate Republican areas into a single 42d District and preventing them from contaminating districts which are, like the 32d, Democratic. The area around the port is one of the few recognizably working-class areas of Los Angeles, where someone nostalgic for the ethnic neighborhoods of the northeast might, amid scruffy palm trees and stucco storefronts, still feel at home. You can find a Yugoslav-American community here in San Pedro, or groups of Italian-American families who still send husbands and fathers out in fishing boats. The 32d District includes relatively few blacks and Mexican-Americans, though the 1980s will likely see them move in in fair numbers; the district's boundaries fence off, in jagged lines, the Democratic parts of the Los Angeles port area, Long Beach, and, to the northeast, the suburbs of Lakewood (mostly white Anglo) and Hawaiian Gardens (mostly Mexican-American).

Like eastern working class areas, the 32d District is ancestrally Democratic, but often attracted in major races to Republican candidates, especially on cultural issues. In congressional elections, however, it stays faithful to a congressman, Glenn Anderson, who seems to fit it like a glove, though his political base used to be in other Los Angeles suburbs. Actually Anderson could fit a great many districts: a 1986 study by *Washington Monthly* shows that the ratings he receives from disparate interest groups add up to the largest total in the House. He is adept, in other words, in keeping almost every special interest happy. Some are clearly more important to him than others, however. Anderson has been a strong union supporter for many years now, and as a top-ranking Democrat on the Public Works and Transportation (number two) and the Merchant Marine and Fisheries (number three) Committees, he is in an excellent position to advance public works projects that provide jobs—especially in the Los Angeles port area. He is perfectly positioned to see that federal monies go to the port, that construction projects around it are funded, that the interests of shipping companies, seamen, and fishermen are protected and subsidized. As chairman of the Surface Transportation Subcommittee he plays a key role on highway legislation, inserting such measures as the 21 drinking age and child seat-belt laws into it; he has backed moves to open up the highway trust fund to mass transit. He is one of the leading political enforcers on Public Works, doling out projects to other members but making sure they support the committee's bills in return. In that capacity he had some sweet revenge on Ronald Reagan, who helped end his career in state government, when the House overrode the President's vetoes of water and highway bills in early 1987.

Anderson is best known in California outside his district for his role as lieutenant governor during the Watts riots of 1965, when some charged he was tardy at sending in the National Guard. He is best known in Washington as a supporter of most public works projects, both because of what they do for local communities and because they put people to work. But in the 32d District he is probably far better known for what he has done for the port and other local interests.

Anderson's most recent tough race came in 1982, when redistricting left him with new territory and a serious opponent in 28-year-old policeman Brian Lungren, brother of 42d District congressman, Dan Lungren. But Anderson won that race 58%–40%. By 1986 he had raised his margin to 69%–29%. Anderson is past 70, at an age when many members choose to retire, but he is in good health and perhaps the tantalizing prospect of a committee chairmanship keeps him going: James Howard of New Jersey has an iffy seat, and if he loses Anderson will become chairman of Public Works. That would be a fitting cap to the career of a man who was elected to the California Assembly in 1942 and once dreamed, plausibly, of being governor of the most populous state in the union.

The People: Pop. 1980: 525,922, up 0.6% 1970–80. Households (1980): 66% family, 36% with children, 51% married couples; 53.1% housing units rented; median monthly rent: $229; median house value: $78,900. Voting age pop. (1980): 383,383; 19% Spanish origin, 7% Black, 5% Asian origin, 1% American Indian.

1984 Presidential Vote:

Reagan (R) 103,902	(58%)
Mondale (D) 71,926	(40%)

Rep. Glenn M. Anderson (D)

Elected 1968; b. Feb. 21, 1913, Hawthorne; home, San Pedro; U. of CA at Los Angeles, B.A. 1936; Episcopalian; married (Lee).

Career: Mayor of Hawthorne, 1940–43; CA Assembly, 1943, 1945–51; Army, WWII; Lt. Gov. of CA, 1958–67.

Offices: 2329 RHOB 20515, 202-225-6676. Also 300 Long Beach Blvd., Long Beach 90801, 213-437-7665.

Committees: *Merchant Marine and Fisheries* (3d of 25 D). Subcommittees: Fisheries and Wildlife Conservation and the Environment; Merchant Marine; Panama Canal and Outer Continental Shelf. *Public Works and Transportation* (2d of 32 D). Subcommittees: Aviation; Surface Transportation (Chairman); Water Resources.

Group Ratings

	ADA	ACLU	COPE	CFA	LCV	ACU	NTU	NSI	COC	CEI
1986	75	65	84	42	68	23	23	30	28	24
1985	70	—	84	75	—	38	29	—	19	—

National Journal Ratings

	1986 LIB — 1986 CONS		1985 LIB — 1985 CONS	
Economic	58% —	41%	81% —	17%
Social	57% —	43%	81% —	15%
Foreign	60% —	39%	53% —	46%

Key Votes

1) Lmt Cln Water Act	AGN	5) Retain Gun Cont	FOR	9) Aid Angola Reb	AGN
2) Rpl Tobac Sub	FOR	6) Contra Aid	AGN	10) Tax Reform	FOR
3) Grm-Rdmn Def Red	AGN	7) Lmt Text Imp	AGN	11) S Africa Sanc	FOR
4) Ban Polygraph	AGN	8) Limit SDI	FOR	12) Immig Reform	FOR

Election Results

1986 general	Glenn M. Anderson (D)	90,739	(69%)	($417,066)
	Joyce M. Robertson (R)	39,003	(29%)	($11,742)
1986 primary	Glenn M. Anderson (D)	42,673	(91%)	
	Margaret E. Thrasher (D)	4,329	(9%)	
1984 general	Glenn M. Anderson (D)	102,961	(61%)	($408,381)
	Roger E. Fiola (R)	62,176	(37%)	($63,989)

Campaign Contributions and Expenditures

1985-86		Direct Cont. 1985-86		PACS Breakdown 1985-86			
Receipts	$457,477	Indiv.	$215,528	Corp.	$95,011	T/M/H	$46,222
Expend.	$417,066	PACS	$216,983	Labor	$63,150	Agr.	$850
Debts	$46,556	Cand.	$10,000	Ideo.	$10,250	CWOS	$1,500

THIRTY-THIRD DISTRICT

The 33d Congressional District of California, in its present lines, is pretty much the lineal descendant of the 12th district that in 1946 ousted New Deal Democrat Jerry Voorhis and elected 33-year-old Republican Richard Nixon. It is the eastern end of Los Angeles County, far enough east that the percentage of Mexican-Americans is not much higher than in Nixon's time. One part of the district, with about one-third of its population, is centered around Nixon's home town of Whittier, a onetime Quaker settlement and now a pleasant suburban town with its own civic institutions and colleges, above-average housing prices, and a Mexican-American population of 23%. The other heavily populated part of the district, separated from the Whittier area by the low Puente Hills, is centered on another old college town, Pomona, laid out in the flat lands directly east of Los Angeles, on the last leg of the Santa Fe Railroad on its long trek from Chicago. Just north are the Claremont colleges, which are among other things a center for conservative scholarship, and the above-average income suburbs of LaVerne, San Dimas, Covina, and Glendora, above the valley floor and not far below the glaring San Gabriel Mountains.

Whittier, Pomona, the smaller towns—all were creations of pious Protestants, transplanting their civilization, their street grids, and their Republican politics from the hardy flatlands of the Midwest to the sunny mountainous land of California. Swept along by the New Deal, they went for Voorhis and the Democrats; but from Richard Nixon's time to this they have stuck with their ancestral Republicanism.

The vagaries of redistricting have made the history of representation here a little confusing between Nixon's House years and those of David Dreier, the current incumbent. Dreier was one of those young conservative ideologues elected in 1980, beating a seemingly safe Democratic incumbent; after redistricting, he beat a fellow Republican in the 1982 primary, a man more interested in local affairs who was later elected to the California Assembly and in early 1987 was running for a vacancy in the state Senate.

Dreier's approach is more theoretical. Before coming to Congress, he spent most of his adult life on the Claremont campus, and he came to Washington less to pass bills than repeal them (though he does take stands against local polluters). The interesting question is how successful has he been, now that he has a safe seat? He took intellectually rigorous and gutsy stands, as when he was the first member on the Small Business Committee to come out wholeheartedly for the Reagan proposal to abolish the Small Business Administration. But after six Reagan years SBA still stands. He is pleased about deregulation of trucking, airlines, and natural gas. But advocates of reregulation are gathering steam. He devotes much of his time to the Banking Committee, which has been considering deregulation bills. But not even Milton Friedman considers banking a part of the economy in which government has no business, and so the choices are not so pure. Suburban California, for example, is filled with rich owners of savings and loans; Dreier supports S&Ls (often a favorite of Democrats) on some issues but not others. But he is out of favor with more practical-minded senior Republicans on Banking.

He has held his House seat without difficulty, raising so much money that after the 1986 election he had $949,000 in cash-on-hand—more than any other member of the House. But he does not seem about to run statewide nor is he likely to have much opposition in the 33d, so it's hard to see what he'll do with it. This is a politician who has had considerable political success, but who still must find the House a frustrating place.

The People: Pop. 1980: 525,348, up 15.5% 1970–80. Households (1980): 78% family, 44% with children, 65% married couples; 29.1% housing units rented; median monthly rent: $262; median house value: $86,700. Voting age pop. (1980): 370,470; 16% Spanish origin, 5% Black, 4% Asian origin, 1% American Indian.

1984 Presidential Vote:

Reagan (R) 152,606	(70%)
Mondale (D) 63,307	(29%)

Rep. David Dreier (R)

Elected 1980; b. July 5, 1952, Kansas City, MO; home, La Verne; Claremont McKenna Col., B.A. 1975, M.A. 1976; Christian Science; single.

Career: Dir. of Corp. Relations, Claremont McKenna Col., 1975–79; Dir. of Pub. Affairs, Industrial Hydrocarbons, 1979–80.

Offices: 410 CHOB 20515, 202-225-2305. Also 112 N. 2d Ave., Covina 91723, 818-339-9078.

Committees: *Banking, Finance and Urban Affairs* (10th of 20 R). Subcommittees: Financial Institutions Supervision, Regulation and Insurance; General Oversight and Investigations; Housing and Community Development. *Small Business* (6th of 17 R). Subcommittees: Energy and Agriculture (Ranking Member).

Group Ratings

	ADA	ACLU	COPE	CFA	LCV	ACU	NTU	NSI	COC	CEI
1986	0	5	1	8	37	95	69	100	100	89
1985	10	—	1	25	—	90	75	—	95	—

National Journal Ratings

	1986 LIB — 1986 CONS		1985 LIB — 1985 CONS	
Economic	0% —	94%	0% —	95%
Social	0% —	89%	0% —	76%
Foreign	0% —	86%	0% —	76%

Key Votes

1) Lmt Cln Water Act	FOR	5) Retain Gun Cont	AGN	9) Aid Angola Reb	FOR
2) Rpl Tobac Sub	FOR	6) Contra Aid	FOR	10) Tax Reform	AGN
3) Grm-Rdmn Def Red	FOR	7) Lmt Text Imp	AGN	11) S Africa Sanc	AGN
4) Ban Polygraph	AGN	8) Limit SDI	AGN	12) Immig Reform	AGN

Election Results

1986 general	David Dreier (R).....................	118,541	(72%)	($148,242)
	Monty Hempel (D)...................	44,312	(27%)	
1986 primary	David Dreier (R).....................	40,608	(100%)	
1984 general	David Dreier (R).....................	147,363	(71%)	($101,803)
	Claire K. McDonald (D)...............	54,147	(26%)	($40,121)

Campaign Contributions and Expenditures

1985-86		Direct Cont. 1985-86		PACS Breakdown 1985-86			
Receipts	$491,587	Indiv.	$218,727	Corp.	$69,170	T/M/H	$29,600
Expend.	$148,242	Party	$2,201	Labor	$1,000	Agr.	$0
Unspent	$949,829	PACS	$104,670	Ideo.	$2,500	CWOS	$2,400

THIRTY-FOURTH DISTRICT

If you want to see the shape of the future of much of California, the place to come to is the 34th Congressional District. This is a barbell-shaped hunk of suburban Los Angeles County, on either side of the San Gabriel River, south and southeast of downtown Los Angeles. It includes the middle-income suburb of West Covina and the working-class suburbs of Baldwin Park, La Puente, and Industry in its northern section; and the basically blue-collar suburbs of Pico Rivera, Santa Fe Springs, South Whittier, and Norwalk, all strung out along the Santa Ana Freeway, on the southern section. Connecting them is a narrow corridor through the industrial town of South El Monte.

This area provides a preview of the future of California because it has the largest number of children of any congressional district in the state. The white middle-class children of the 1950s, educated in the schools that burgeoned in every new suburb and finally on the culturally liberal campuses of the University of California, are the adults of California today: technologically capable, relatively high income, culturally liberal if not liberated. They take affluence and economic growth for granted; they concentrate much of their psychic energy on making life pleasant for themselves.

The children of the 34th District, growing up on some of the same terrain, have a different background. Some 59% of them are of Spanish origin; they come from parents or grandparents who are immigrants from another culture. They are part of large families—not a sign of their parents' ignorance, but of the same optimism which brought them to America, and out to the suburbs of eastern Los Angeles County—the same optimism which produced the large Anglo families of the baby-boom years. Some of them start off speaking little else but Spanish, but most know English, and they are entirely capable of absorbing instruction in it provided that the political authorities (and Mexican-American lobbying groups) don't keep them confined in classes where the instruction is in a language which will not prepare them for most good jobs. People here are not impoverished: the median house price, according to the Census, was $69,000 in 1980; people have jobs and very few live below the poverty level. You will see some of the youths here parading down avenues on Friday night in souped-up cars, just as you would have seen white teenagers doing the same thing, with similar cars, 25 years ago; that doesn't mean, in either case, that they won't grow up to hold solid and even high level jobs. The history of America is largely a history of the rapid progress of children of immigrant groups. Why should the history of the Mexican-American residents of California be any different from the history of the Italian-American residents of New York?

The 34th District was newly created by Representative Phillip Burton from the results of the 1980 Census. It was Burton's *piece de resistance*. The Republicans had hoped to get crucial Mexican-American votes in the California Assembly and pass a districting plan that had more Mexican-American districts than the Democrats could come up with—and of course more Republican districts as well. But Burton, by creating this district which is 48% Spanish origin, in addition to the 54% Spanish origin 30th and the 64% Spanish origin 25th, did the Republicans one better. From that point there was nothing to stop the Democratic legislature and governor from approving Burton's plans.

Nor was there much that anyone could do to stop Democrat Esteban Torres from being elected to Congress. Torres had tried once before, in 1974, against George Danielson in the old 30th District, and fallen short; Mexican-Americans do not invariably vote for Mexican-Americans, presumably because they do not feel deprived of fair representation when they have an Anglo congressman. But Torres does have a positive appeal. He rose from an auto assembly line, through the ranks of the United Auto Workers, to head an antipoverty program in East Los Angeles; in the Carter Administration he was a White House aide and ambassador to UNESCO. He had financial support from the local machine of Henry Waxman and Howard Berman. He won a solid primary victory against former Representative Jim Lloyd, whose base is in West Covina, and won the general election by a 57%–43% margin. Torres, who sits on the Banking and Small Business Committees, has positions on economic issues that are about what you would expect from a UAW veteran; he is, however, opposed to abortion. He represents, after all, the number one family district in Los Angeles, a place where people have committed themselves to family patterns and where their large hopes for the future depend on the progress of their children in schools and in jobs. They are interested in having a secure government safety net, but they seem to believe that their children will get somewhere—as their parents or grandparents emerged from rural Mexico—largely through their own efforts.

Torres's percentage has crept upward only slowly from 57% in 1982 to 60% in 1986—a small increase for an incumbent. The Republicans with their championing of free enterprise and family values seem to be making gains here; Ronald Reagan carried this heretofore Democratic district with an impressive 59% in 1984. For the immediate future, the political leanings of this district seem fairly clear: Democratic for Congress, Republican or about even in statewide elections. But the tantalizing question for the future is this: who is capturing—or will capture the imaginations of the multitudes of children growing up here? Will it be Democrats like Torres, with their support of big government programs and sympathy for Third World causes? Or will it be Republicans like Reagan, with their enthusiasm for a surging private economy and an assertive American foreign policy abroad? A few years ago, no one would have thought those were questions worth asking. Now, no matter what the final verdict on the Reagan Administration, they are worth pondering.

The People: Pop. 1980: 526,665, up 2.1% 1970–80. Households (1980): 83% family, 53% with children, 68% married couples; 29.3% housing units rented; median monthly rent: $276; median house value: $68,700. Voting age pop. (1980): 348,515; 42% Spanish origin, 4% Asian origin, 2% Black, 1% American Indian.

1984 Presidential Vote: Reagan (R) 89,795   (59%)
Mondale (D) 60,961   (40%)

Rep. Esteban E. Torres (D)

Elected 1982; b. Jan. 30, 1930, Miami, AZ; home, La Puente; E. Los Angeles Commun. Col., A.A. 1959, CA State U. at Los Angeles, B.A. 1963, U. of MD, 1965, American U., 1966; No religious affiliation; married (Arcy).

Career: Army, Korea; Assembly-line worker, Chrysler Corp., 1953–63; Chief Steward, Local 230 UAW, 1961–63; UAW Intl. Rep., Region 6, 1963–64; Inter-Amer. Rep., 1965–68; Dir., E. Los Angeles Commun. Union, 1968–74; Asst. Dir., Intl. Affairs Dept., 1974–77; U.S. Permanent Rep., UNESCO, 1977–79; Special Asst. to the Pres., 1979–81; Pres., Intl. Enterprise and Develop. Corp., 1981–82.

Offices: 1740 LHOB 20515, 202-225-5256. Also 8819 Whittier Blvd., Ste. 101, Pico Rivera 90660, 213-695-0702, 818-961-3978.

Committees: *Banking, Finance and Urban Affairs* (20th of 31 D). Subcommittees: Financial Institutions Supervision, Regulation and Insurance; Housing and Community Development; International Development Institutions and Finance. *Small Business* (14th of 27 D). Subcommittees: Regulation and Business Opportunities; SBA and the General Economy; Procurement, Innovation and Minority Enterprise Development.

Group Ratings

	ADA	ACLU	COPE	CFA	LCV	ACU	NTU	NSI	COC	CEI
1986	90	84	97	75	74	5	22	0	18	14
1985	75	—	98	83	—	10	28	—	24	—

National Journal Ratings

	1986 LIB — 1986 CONS		1985 LIB — 1985 CONS	
Economic	87%	— 0%	85%	— 11%
Social	81%	— 19%	85%	— 0%
Foreign	80%	— 0%	84%	— 15%

Key Votes

1) Lmt Cln Water Act	AGN	5) Retain Gun Cont	—	9) Aid Angola Reb	AGN
2) Rpl Tobac Sub	AGN	6) Contra Aid	AGN	10) Tax Reform	FOR
3) Grm-Rdmn Def Red	FOR	7) Lmt Text Imp	FOR	11) S Africa Sanc	FOR
4) Ban Polygraph	FOR	8) Limit SDI	FOR	12) Immig Reform	FOR

Election Results

1986 general	Esteban E. Torres (D)	66,404	(60%)	($111,685)
	Charles M. House (R)	43,659	(40%)	($81,759)
1986 primary	Esteban E. Torres (D)	32,692	(100%)	
1984 general	Esteban E. Torres (D)	87,060	(60%)	($182,096)
	Paul R. Jackson (R)	58,467	(40%)	($28,946)

Campaign Contributions and Expenditures

1985-86		Direct Cont. 1985-86		PACS Breakdown 1985-86			
Receipts	$181,729	Indiv.	$84,930	Corp.	$22,751	T/M/H	$27,000
Expend.	$111,685	Party	$100	Labor	$32,800	Agr.	$1,250
Unspent	$124,694	PACS	$88,412	Ideo.	$2,811	CWOS	$1,800

THIRTY-FIFTH DISTRICT

The 35th Congressional District of California includes most of San Bernardino County, geographically the largest county in the United States, with ghost towns and weapons testing systems in the desert, tiny towns dominated by huge gas station signs built to catch the eyes of motorists on their five hours' journey across the desert to Las Vegas, mountains and lakes, the Joshua Tree National Monument and the Twentynine Palms Marine Corps Base. It has some of the nation's hottest temperatures (in Needles, on the Colorado River across from Arizona) and some of its lowest rainfall. Yet most of its citizens live not in this expanse, but clustered in the southwest corner of San Bernardino County, in the eastern end of the Los Angeles Basin, in mostly affluent suburbs on the plains running east from Los Angeles and in the foothills of the mountains. Even so, more than 150,000 people live in the desert—in tiny gas station towns, now swelled with people who have left the city behind; in trailer parks scattered a few miles away; in military bases and the neat geometrical towns that grow up beside them.

The 35th was designed to be a Republican district. It bypasses the heavily Democratic towns in the flatlands often choked with smog at the eastern end of the Los Angeles Basin, and includes those up higher, near the mountains, or with higher real estate prices: Upland, Montclair, and Chino in western San Bernardino County, Redlands, Highland, and Loma Linda (a Seventh Day Adventist town) east of the city of San Bernardino.

The congressman from the 35th is Jerry Lewis (no relation to the comedian), a former insurance agent and California Assemblyman with the blown-dry look of a stereotypical candidate. Actually, Lewis is a thoughtful Republican of some considerable political skill. He won the district (with rather different boundaries) in 1978 with not much problem, and has retained it easily ever since. Legislatively, he is rather quiet, since he works as a minority member on the Appropriations Committee, and still has rather low seniority; his accomplishments include the bill authorizing the issuance of gold coins and highway money for the entry roads to Ontario airport. He is the chief opponent of Senator Alan Cranston's desert protection bill.

But he has made his mark in other ways. He is chairman of the House Republican Research Committee, an informal group that produces policy papers from time to time. It has become more difficult, as Congress and the nation have accepted what were considered not long ago farfetched Republican ideas for change, to keep producing something original; but Lewis and his colleagues continue to make the effort. Debating policy, speaking the lingo of OMB bureaucrats and policy mavens as well as home-town Rotaries and Chambers of Commerce, they try to maintain the Republicans' hard-won status as the party of ideas. Also they try to goad the Democrats to action; Lewis feels they forced them to allow a vote on the death penalty in the 1986 drug bill. Lewis has another important position in his party: he beat out Bill Thomas for the California seat on the Republican Committee on Committees. On this body sits one Republican from each state casting as many votes as there are Republicans in the House delegation; California has 18, and so Lewis casts more votes than any other committee member. He comes from a state with a tradition of ideological conservative Republicans, but in the House he is a close ally of Republican leader Robert Michel, and a possible Republican leader or whip himself some day.

In the early 1980s Lewis thought about running for lieutenant governor in 1982, a position that gives little power but does give its holder enough statewide name identification to become, some day, a plausible candidate for governor; doubtless running through his head were the fantasies that motivate so many politicians of finding their way some day to a spot on their party's national ticket. But Lewis did not take that particular plunge, and nothing more has been heard about his running statewide. He has interesting work to do in the House and seems likely to continue doing it.

The People: Pop. 1980: 525,956, up 46.3% 1970–80. Households (1980): 77% family, 43% with children, 66% married couples; 29.6% housing units rented; median monthly rent: $235; median house value: $68,000. Voting age pop. (1980): 371,311; 12% Spanish origin, 3% Black, 2% Asian origin, 1% American Indian.

1984 Presidential Vote:

Reagan (R)	154,583	(71%)
Mondale (D)	59,824	(28%)

Rep. Jerry Lewis (R)

Elected 1978; b. Oct. 21, 1934, Seattle, WA; home, Redlands; U. of CA at Los Angeles, B.A. 1956; Presbyterian; married (Arlene).

Career: Life insur. agent, 1959–78; Field Rep. to U.S. Rep. Jerry Pettis, 1968; CA Assembly, 1968–78.

Offices: 326 CHOB 20515, 202-225-5861. Also 1826 Orange Tree Lane, Ste. 104, Redlands 92374, 714-862-6030.

Committees: *Appropriations* (14th of 22 R). Subcommittees: Foreign Operations; HUD-Independent Agencies; Legislative (Ranking Member).

Group Ratings

	ADA	ACLU	COPE	CFA	LCV	ACU	NTU	NSI	COC	CEI
1986	0	5	14	8	22	88	43	100	64	58
1985	10	—	14	25	—	76	39	—	62	—

National Journal Ratings

	1986 LIB — 1986 CONS		1985 LIB — 1985 CONS	
Economic	33% —	67%	33% —	66%
Social	29% —	70%	40% —	59%
Foreign	0% —	86%	24% —	66%

Key Votes

1) Lmt Cln Water Act	AGN	5) Retain Gun Cont	AGN	9) Aid Angola Reb	FOR
2) Rpl Tobac Sub	—	6) Contra Aid	FOR	10) Tax Reform	FOR
3) Grm-Rdmn Def Red	AGN	7) Lmt Text Imp	AGN	11) S Africa Sanc	AGN
4) Ban Polygraph	AGN	8) Limit SDI	—	12) Immig Reform	FOR

Election Results

1986 general	Jerry Lewis (R)	127,235	(77%)	($91,355)
	R. (Sarge) Hall (D)	38,322	(23%)	
1986 primary	Jerry Lewis (R)	48,421	(100%)	
1984 general	Jerry Lewis (R)	176,477	(85%)	($159,517)
	Kevin Akin (Peace & Freedom)	29,990	(15%)	

Campaign Contributions and Expenditures

1985-86		Direct Cont. 1985-86		PACS Breakdown 1985-86			
Receipts	$141,143	Indiv.	$21,072	Corp.	$49,350	T/M/H	$36,000
Expend.	$91,355	Party	$2,106	Labor	$5,750	Agr.	$2,350
Unspent	$223,268	PACS	$106,498	Ideo.	$10,550	CWOS	$2,498

THIRTY-SIXTH DISTRICT

At the far east end of the Los Angeles Basin, where the smog piles up against the mountains, are two cities with their own historical beginnings, situated near the eastern end of the strip that extends westward more than 50 miles to Los Angeles and the sea. These are San Bernardino and Riverside, county seats of the counties with the same names, old agricultural towns and railroad stops. Parts of each city and of several suburbs in the immediate vicinity and to the east make up the 36th Congressional District of California. The district includes industrial suburbs—Colton, Rialto, and Fontana with its once thriving Kaiser Steel plant—and the city of Ontario, west toward Los Angeles, which has its own airport where you can catch a jet to Chicago or Dallas-Fort Worth. Riverside is still a major center for the citrus industry, and its University of California branch is one of the leading sources of research on citrus.

Surrounded by Republican territory, the 36th District is nonetheless Democratic. There is a substantial Mexican-American population in each of these towns, totaling almost one-fourth of the district's population; there are a fair number of blacks in each town as well. Union membership is higher in some of these precincts than in most of southern California, and working-class consciousness is perhaps fed by the poor air quality: if you could afford to move to a higher and more expensive area, you probably would.

The 36th District was designed for, and is represented by, a congressman with a long career that has benefited, stage by stage, from redistricting. George Brown was a councilman from Monterey Park, far west of here, when he was first elected to the California Assembly in 1958; he had the good fortune to be placed on the Reapportionment Committee, and when California gained eight House seats in 1962, he was elected to one of them. He ran for the Senate in 1970 and almost beat John Tunney in the primary; if he had, this longtime peacenik—a scientist with a Quaker upbringing who cares deeply about arms control issues—might have beaten George Murphy and made his way to the Senate. He found a new district in 1972, here in the eastern part of the valley, and in redistricting it has been altered and shaped for him.

Brown's committee assignments would seem to be useful ones for the district—Agriculture; Science, Space, and Technology—even though in 1985 he gave up an Agriculture subcommittee chairmanship in an unsuccessful attempt to chair the Space Science and Applications panel. He spends much time on environmental issues, including the cleanup of the Stringfellow Acid Pits toxic waste dump in Riverside County, and he pushes for civilian rather than military exploration of space. His very liberal politics has helped attract serious Republican competition. Religious fundamentalist John Paul Stark held him to 53% and 54% in 1980 and 1982; in 1984 Brown got 57% against him, and in 1986 he won 57% against a businessman from Colton who ran a serious but underfinanced campaign. Republicans have been sniping at Brown for many years now, but he is one of only 41 House members who served when the Great Society legislation was passed more than 20 years ago. Brown was serving in Congress, threatened by serious Republican challenges, when Ronald Reagan's political career began, and, though still threatened, he is still serving as Reagan's political career approaches its end. He is not quite a power in the House, not even yet, but he is a persistent and competent advocate of his own particular and special views, and one determined not to be silenced.

The People: Pop. 1980: 525,987, up 15.1% 1970–80. Households (1980): 74% family, 44% with children, 59% married couples; 36.5% housing units rented; median monthly rent: $214; median house value: $58,900. Voting age pop. (1980): 362,108; 20% Spanish origin, 7% Black, 1% Asian origin, 1% American Indian.

1984 Presidential Vote: Reagan (R) 103,809   (56%)
                              Mondale (D) 80,504   (43%)

Rep. George E. Brown, Jr. (D)

Elected 1972; b. Mar. 6, 1920, Holtville; home, Riverside; U. of CA at Los Angeles, B.A. 1946; United Methodist; widowed.

Career: Army, WWII; Monterey Park City Cncl., Mayor, 1954–58; Personnel, Engineering, and Management Consultant, City of Los Angeles, 1957–61; CA Assembly, 1959–62; U.S. House of Reps., 1962–70; Cand. for Dem. Nomination for U.S. Senate, 1970.

Offices: 2256 RHOB 20515, 202-225-6161. Also 657 La Cadena Dr., Colton 92324, 714-825-2472.

Committees: *Agriculture* (4th of 26 D). Subcommittee: Department Operations, Research and Foreign Agriculture (Chairman). *Science, Space and Technology* (2d of 27 D). Subcommittees: Investigations and Oversight; Natural Resources, Agriculture Research and Development; Science Research and Technology; Space Science and Applications. *Permanent Select Committee on Intelligence* (7th of 11 D). Subcommittees: Oversight and Evaluation; Program and Budget Authorization.

Group Ratings

	ADA	ACLU	COPE	CFA	LCV	ACU	NTU	NSI	COC	CEI
1986	95	94	90	58	85	0	21	0	21	20
1985	85	—	90	92	—	6	18	—	28	—

National Journal Ratings

	1986 LIB — 1986 CONS		1985 LIB — 1985 CONS	
Economic	87%	0%	89%	0%
Social	89%	0%	85%	0%
Foreign	80%	0%	79%	21%

Key Votes

1) Lmt Cln Water Act	AGN	5) Retain Gun Cont	FOR	9) Aid Angola Reb	AGN
2) Rpl Tobac Sub	FOR	6) Contra Aid	AGN	10) Tax Reform	FOR
3) Grm-Rdmn Def Red	AGN	7) Lmt Text Imp	FOR	11) S Africa Sanc	FOR
4) Ban Polygraph	—	8) Limit SDI	FOR	12) Immig Reform	FOR

Election Results

1986 general	George E. Brown, Jr. (D) 78,118	(57%)	($534,733)
	Bob Henley (R)........................ 58,660	(43%)	($210,003)
1986 primary	George E. Brown, Jr. (D) 39,077	(100%)	
1984 general	George E. Brown, Jr. (D) 104,438	(57%)	($612,018)
	John Paul Stark (R) 80,212	(43%)	($374,384)

Campaign Contributions and Expenditures

1985-86		Direct Cont. 1985-86		PACS Breakdown 1985-86			
Receipts	$570,729	Indiv.	$297,602	Corp.	$18,700	T/M/H	$42,881
Expend.	$534,733	Party	$10,000	Labor	$102,660	Agr.	$1,500
Debts	$37,388	PACS	$220,499	Ideo.	$54,258	CWOS	$500
		Cand.	$30,903				

THIRTY-SEVENTH DISTRICT

Who would have thought, 25 or 125 years ago, that the desert would be one of the fastest-growing and most glamorous parts of America? For years the vast desert of eastern California was land you had to go through, in steel-hot Pullmans or about-to-boil-over cars on U.S. 66, on your way to the green valleys and pleasant seacoasts. In the days before World War II, when California was much more a retirement haven than it is now, the elderly headed to the sea, the modestly-off from Iowa to Long Beach, the rich to La Jolla, old families to Santa Barbara. In recent decades older migrants have avoided the crowded, smoggy beaches, with their damp winters, and have headed instead inland, to the clean, dry, roomy desert. What was once just the site of a few winter resorts has now, become the year-round home for some half a million people.

The 1980s is the first time when the desert has had enough population for a congressman of its own, the representative elected by the 37th Congressional District. Just east of Riverside, the district takes a series of geologically fascinating valleys, some rather affluent, some noticeably threadbare, which have large numbers of retirees. Altogether, nearly 200,000 people live here now—approximately double 1970. Further east, through the San Gorgonio Pass, you come to the desert proper, with a year-round population, in the 37th District, of 145,000 people. Here the days are almost always crystal clear, the sky usually blue and cloudless. The desert can be fertile farmland, as it is in the Coachella Valley; almost all of America's dates are produced near Indio, east of Palm Springs. But constant irrigation is necessary for most crops; without daily doses of water almost any plant will wilt and die in the heat. The first white settlers in the desert were prospectors, and some ghost towns still stand. They are quite a contrast with Palm Springs and Palm Desert, which are outposts of affluence (Palm Springs is more showbiz, Palm Desert more Waspy). It is too hot here in the summer for most people, even though the heat is dry, but the winter weather is almost ideal. Two presidents have retired within the confines of the 37th District, Eisenhower in Palm Desert for the winters, Ford in nearby Rancho Mirage—which is also the home of Frank Sinatra and Spiro Agnew.

The 37th District also includes the more affluent and Republican parts of the city of Riverside, plus the towns of Norco and Corona immediately to the east. Overall, this is a Republican district; the most Democratic parts of the Riverside area were cropped off carefully and put into the 36th. There have been Democrats elected to the legislature from the desert, but the last one was nearly defeated in 1986. Both parties' primaries were seriously contested when no incumbent congressman chose to run in this district in 1982. But the easy winner of the general election, and still congressman, is Republican Al McCandless.

McCandless is a son of the desert, born in Imperial County; he had a successful auto dealership; he moved upward politically as the desert has grown more populous, to a seat on the Riverside County Board of Supervisors in 1970 and Congress in 1982. The representative of the place—the Palm Springs home of Walter Annenberg—where Ronald Reagan spends every New Year's Eve, he is one of the most faithful supporters of the Reagan administration on Capitol Hill. He is a member of the Banking and Government Operations Committees and is ranking Republican on the latter panel's Government Activities and Transportation Subcommittee; he is proud of his successful 1986 amendment knocking allowable travel costs for federal contractors down closer to the rates allowed for federal employees. The only real threat to his tenure is state Senator Robert Presley, a moderate Democrat, but so far he has not run.

The People: Pop. 1980: 525,938, up 55.8% 1970–80. Households (1980): 74% family, 35% with children, 64% married couples; 29.1% housing units rented; median monthly rent: $235; median house value: $69,300. Voting age pop. (1980): 383,799; 15% Spanish origin, 3% Black, 1% Asian origin, 1% American Indian.

1984 Presidential Vote:

Reagan (R)	153,832	(65%)
Mondale (D)	80,012	(34%)

Rep. Alfred A. (Al) McCandless (R)

Elected 1982; b. July 23, 1927, Brawley; home, Bermuda Dunes; U. of CA at Los Angeles, B.A. 1951; Protestant; married (Gail).

Career: USMC, 1945–46, Korea; Automobile dealer, 1959–75; Riverside Cnty. Sprvsr., 1970–82.

Offices: 435 CHOB 20515, 202-225-5330. Also 6529 Riverside Ave., Ste. 165, Riverside 92506, 714-682-7127; and P.O. Box 1495, Palm Desert 92261, 619-340-2900.

Committees: *Banking, Finance and Urban Affairs* (15th of 20 R). Subcommittees: Economic Stabilization; Financial Institutions Supervision, Regulation and Insurance; General Oversight and Investigations; International Development Institutions and Finance. *Government Operations* (4th of 15 R). Subcommittee: Government Information, Justice and Agriculture (Ranking Member).

Group Ratings

	ADA	ACLU	COPE	CFA	LCV	ACU	NTU	NSI	COC	CEI
1986	5	15	2	8	16	95	62	100	94	79
1985	5	—	0	8	—	86	63	—	91	—

National Journal Ratings

	1986 LIB — 1986 CONS		1985 LIB — 1985 CONS	
Economic	0% —	94%	0% —	95%
Social	23% —	74%	41% —	56%
Foreign	0% —	86%	0% —	76%

Key Votes

1) Lmt Cln Water Act	FOR	5) Retain Gun Cont	AGN	9) Aid Angola Reb	FOR
2) Rpl Tobac Sub	—	6) Contra Aid	FOR	10) Tax Reform	AGN
3) Grm-Rdmn Def Red	FOR	7) Lmt Text Imp	AGN	11) S Africa Sanc	AGN
4) Ban Polygraph	AGN	8) Limit SDI	AGN	12) Immig Reform	FOR

Election Results

1986 general	Alfred A. (Al) McCandless (R)	122,416	(64%)	($127,793)
	David E. (Dave) Skinner (D)	69,808	(36%)	($56,185)
1986 primary	Alfred A. (Al) McCandless (R)	50,954	(85%)	
	Bud Mathewson (R)	9,082	(15%)	
1984 general	Alfred A. (Al) McCandless (R)	149,955	(64%)	($99,747)
	David E. (Dave) Skinner (D)	85,908	(36%)	($39,524)

Campaign Contributions and Expenditures

1985-86		Direct Cont. 1985-86		PACS Breakdown 1985-86			
Receipts	$151,438	Indiv.	$75,328	Corp.	$30,700	T/M/H	$31,500
Expend.	$127,793	Party	$2,042	Labor	$0	Agr.	$2,500
Unspent	$51,783	PACS	$71,616	Ideo.	$4,000	CWOS	$2,916

THIRTY-EIGHTH DISTRICT

Between the Santa Ana and San Diego Freeways, in the longest-developed slice of California's Orange County, is a congressional district, the 38th, that has produced some of the most fiercely contested congressional elections in the United States. To the participants, anyway, great things have seemed to be at stake, in this geographically compact and now entirely settled segment of urban America. Roughly speaking, the 38th District includes that portion of Orange County between the Santa Ana and San Diego Freeways, bounded by the Los Angeles County border on the west and the Newport Freeway on the east. Since the 1960 Census, Democratic legislators have tried to draw a Democratic district in Orange County, and for most of that time they have succeeded. But they have been undercut by reverberations from the other side of the Pacific Rim. One Democratic congressman, Richard Hanna, retired in 1974 and eventually went to jail for taking money from Korean businessman Tongsun Park. And his successor, Democrat Jerry Patterson, was defeated in 1984 in part because of the near-unanimous support for Republicans by the district's rising number of Vietnamese-American voters.

For this central core of Orange County seems to be the number one district destination for Vietnamese migrants to this country. It may seem odd that they have come to an area that is well above average in income and has long described as unrelievedly white, with the implication that residents of other races would not be welcome. But refugees and migrants from Vietnam, Laos, and Cambodia have proved themselves hard workers, with every family member pitching in so that the family can afford to buy one of the stucco houses you see as you zoom by on the freeway or, for the moment, to rent an apartment in one of the many low-rise complexes that you see on the straight streets leading from Disneyland or Knott's Berry Farm to the beaches. And bigotry is not much in evidence in southern California. In 1980 the 38th District was already about 25% Hispanic, mostly Mexican-Americans scattered through different neighborhoods. There is a solidly Mexican area in southern Santa Ana, just as Westminster has the heaviest concentration of Vietnamese. But this new community, this county which was almost entirely rural and unsettled as recently as 1950, has not hesitated to give a home to the latest new Americans.

For some time observers thought Hispanics and Asians would be Democrats, eager for government to act against discrimination and to aid the needy. But unlike earlier Japanese and Chinese immigrants, these Orange Countians don't seem to encounter much discrimination and don't consider themselves needy. They seem rather to share many of the values and attitudes of the people they have chosen as neighbors. Some may feel them more intensely: Mexicans who have struggled to get to a clear-aired corner of the Los Angeles Basin, Vietnamese who have found safety and prosperity on the other side of the Pacific may have a more explicit American patriotism, a deeper appreciation for the strengths and virtues of the United States, than their somewhat more jaded and blasé neighbors who have long taken America's bounty for granted.

The political beneficiary of these changes is one of America's stormiest and most flamboyant congressmen, onetime fighter pilot and talk show host Robert K. Dornan. First elected from the Los Angeles coastal district in 1976, he was reelected in 1978 and 1980 against an opponent he called "a sick, pompous little ass"; the 1980 race was the most expensive in the country. In 1982, hurt by redistricting, he raised $1 million from his mailing list and ran for the Senate, winning only 8% of the vote. In 1983 he spent time touting President Reagan's Strategic Defense Initiative, but failed to get an arms control post when Republican Representative Jack Edwards pointed out he would cost the Administration votes in the House. In 1984 he journeyed down the

California coast, got a residence in the 38th District, and took on Democrat Patterson, a skillful politician and advocate for southern California savings and loans on the Banking Committee. The tone of the campaign was not elevated: Dornan called Patterson "a sneaky little dirtbag." In 1986 Dornan was a prime target of Democratic campaign chairman Tony Coelho. But Coelho's candidate, former Judge and Vietnam veteran David Carter, lost the primary, and the winner, Assemblyman Richard Robinson, though well-known, well-financed, and popular, got only 42% of the vote to Dornan's 55%.

Dornan has described himself in his younger years as "a gung-ho, crazy kid," and many of his political adversaries think the description still fits. In his early years in the House he made such an impassioned speech for the B-1 bomber that he became known as "B-1 Bob," and in a debate on abortion he gave graphic descriptions of the Charles Manson murders. When he returned to the House in 1985 he approached New York Democrat Tom Downey, who had been quoted as gloating when Dornan's arms control appointment fell through, Dornan called Downey a "draft-dodging wimp" and grabbed his collar and tie. Downey did not retaliate in kind. He wrote later, "despite recent reports from the House floor, the masked marvel of professional wrestling is not your congressman." Dornan claimed, lamely, that he was just straightening Downey's tie.

This kind of bullying prompted Democrats to look closely at Dornan's record and to do a little tie-straightening of their own. Dornan, they claimed, sat out the Korean war in college and did not serve as a wartime fighter pilot. Dornan did spend most of the war at Loyola, but he left school without graduating and enlisted in the Air Force in March 1953. That was just three months before the armistice, the Democrats pointed out. But no one knew then that there would be an armistice, and so Dornan was putting himself in line for combat and did serve five years in the not undangerous work of being a peacetime fighter pilot. His claims later to have flown "combat missions" in Vietnam, when he went there as a TV talk show host, are obviously stretching matters. But does his hawkish politics put him under a moral obligation to have rejoined the Air Force to fight in Vietnam at age 32? Dornan has invited more criticism than he deserves.

Legislatively, Dornan is certainly not ready to become an elder statesman, and is not about to be treated as such in a Democratic House; yet he was pragmatic enough to endorse George Bush for 1988, which may have hurt him with Republican Whip Trent Lott who is an ally of Jack Kemp. Dornan successfully pushed an amendment restricting abortions in the District of Columbia and for inmates of federal prisons and ballyhooed the 1986 push to amend the 22d Amendment to allow Ronald Reagan to serve a third term—all cheap shots. But given his long record of flamboyance he has little chance to become a workhorse legislator. His duty, as he evidently sees it, is to dramatize the causes he believes in and to goad the opposition. These things he does to the evident satisfaction of most of his constituents, looking out from the American grid streets of Orange County across the vast ocean to the turbulence and threats, growth and gore at the other side of the Pacific Rim.

The People: Pop. 1980: 525,919, up 14.2% 1970–80. Households (1980): 77% family, 46% with children, 62% married couples; 43.1% housing units rented; median monthly rent: $299; median house value: $85,100. Voting age pop. (1980): 364,684; 25% Spanish origin, 6% Asian origin, 2% Black, 1% American Indian.

1984 Presidential Vote:

Reagan (R)	....	114,786	(69%)
Mondale (D)	....	48,856	(30%)

Rep. Robert K. (Bob) Dornan (R)

Elected 1984; b. April 3, 1933, New York, NY; home, Garden Grove; Loyola U.; Roman Catholic; married (Sallie).

Career: Air Force, 1953–58; Broadcast Journalist, 1965–69; Talk show host, 1969–73; U.S. House of Reps., 1976–82; Cand. for U.S. Senate, 1982.

Offices: 301 CHOB 20515, 202-225-2965. Also 12387 Lewis St., Garden Grove 92640, 714-971-9292.

Committees: *Foreign Affairs* (10th of 18 R). Subcommittees: Africa; International Economic Policy and Trade; Western Hemisphere Affairs. *Veterans' Affairs* (11th of 13 R). Subcommittees: Education, Training and Employment; Oversight and Investigations. *Select Committee on Narcotics Abuse and Control* (7th of 10 R).

Group Ratings

	ADA	ACLU	COPE	CFA	LCV	ACU	NTU	NSI	COC	CEI
1986	5	15	8	0	16	95	54	100	81	80
1985	10	—	12	33	—	95	63	—	81	—

National Journal Ratings

	1986 LIB — 1986 CONS		1985 LIB — 1985 CONS	
Economic	10%	— 90%	24%	— 74%
Social	34%	— 65%	0%	— 76%
Foreign	16%	— 79%	0%	— 76%

Key Votes

1) Lmt Cln Water Act	FOR	5) Retain Gun Cont	AGN	9) Aid Angola Reb	FOR
2) Rpl Tobac Sub	FOR	6) Contra Aid	FOR	10) Tax Reform	FOR
3) Grm-Rdmn Def Red	AGN	7) Lmt Text Imp	AGN	11) S Africa Sanc	AGN
4) Ban Polygraph	—	8) Limit SDI	AGN	12) Immig Reform	FOR

Election Results

1986 general	Robert K. (Bob) Dornan (R)	66,032	(55%)	($1,174,637)
	Richard Robinson (D)	50,625	(42%)	($581,864)
1986 primary	Robert K. (Bob) Dornan (R)	26,481	(100%)	
1984 general	Robert K. (Bob) Dornan (R)	86,545	(53%)	($1,017,853)
	Jerry M. Patterson (D)	73,231	(45%)	($698,747)

Campaign Contributions and Expenditures

1985-86		Direct Cont. 1985-86		PACS Breakdown 1985-86			
Receipts	$1,190,237	Indiv.	$1,017,170	Corp.	$74,835	T/M/H	$44,501
Expend.	$1,174,637	Party	$19,791	Labor	$500	Agr.	$2,450
Debts	$39,508	PACS	$170,947	Ideo.	$41,411	CWOS	$7,250

THIRTY-NINTH DISTRICT

As World War II ended, Orange County, California, had all the political notoriety of a few thousand acres of citrus trees; today, "Orange County" has become a synonym across the nation, and perhaps the world, for American-style political conservatism. In 1950 there were only 216,000 people living in this prime agricultural real estate; but this eastern end of the Los Angeles Basin, a mass of flat land surrounded by mountains and sea, was directly in the path of settlement of the most explosively growing metropolitan area in the United States. Population increased ninefold in 30 years: by 1960 there were 703,000 people there; in 1970, 1,421,000; in 1980, 1,931,000. And most of that migration was, politically, Republican. In the 1960s and 1970s Orange County consistently turned in the highest Republican percentages of any major California county. Ronald Reagan liked to begin and end his campaigns in Orange County and no wonder: it was the county that gave him his largest vote margins—353,000 in 1980 and 428,000 in 1984—in the nation. Yet Orange County is not as uniformly affluent or as monolithically conservative and Republican as is supposed. Democrats have been competitive here in many elections, although they are now losing ground in the lower-middle income precincts now filling up with anti-Communist Asian-Americans.

The northern section of the heavily populated part of Orange County forms the 39th Congressional District of California, one of three districts wholly within this jurisdiction whose name has become synonymous with conservatism. It includes Anaheim, home of Disneyland, the amusement park whose opening here in 1955 introduced millions to Orange County, and Anaheim Stadium, where the California Angels and Los Angeles Rams now play (though these landmarks sit just a block outside the district's boundaries). In tiny Yorba Linda, where the subdivisions end and the scrubby hills begin, is the birthplace of Richard Nixon, a man whose career moved back and forth in and out of Orange County for several decades.

What kind of communities are these? It's a mistake to think of Orange County as just a collection of suburbs, although they would not have the economic vitality they do were they not part of a larger metropolitan expanse. In their grid street patterns and square moral outlooks, in their comfortable but far from showy affluence and their industriousness, in their apparent ethnic homogeneity and their adherence to traditional family patterns, they resemble those midwestern towns 40 and 60 miles away from Chicago, which are classed as part of the Chicago metropolitan area by the Census Bureau but in their own residents' minds are places apart. These places also share a strong allegiance to the Republican Party and a conviction that they represent the typical American community—although, in political terms at least, they haven't for many years in post-New Deal, Democrat-majority America. Many of the people here actually come from towns like these in the Midwest and Illinois, at the other end of the Santa Fe Railroad and U.S. 66, and have brought their attitudes with them. If their view of themselves and America is statistically not accurate, there is a sense in which almost all Americans believe it to be true: this is, for more than Orange Countians, how typical Americans live.

And so you have a county, and especially the 39th District, that may not be the most affluent part of the country but is certainly one of the most Republican; its residents' children may be grown, and many more of them than expected may have gotten divorces, but they still believe fiercely in family values; there may be more renters here, in the apartment complexes that line the main streets behind painted cement block walls, but they believe in the kind of strong communities that are nurtured by home-ownership. The 39th is, in election after election, one of the strongest Republican districts in the country; it went 77% for Ronald Reagan in 1984.

The current congressman, William Dannemeyer, was once, oddly enough, a Democrat; he comes from a working class suburb of Los Angeles, and he was elected as an Orange County Democrat to the California Assembly in 1962 and 1964. But he switched parties when he lost a race for the state Senate, and eventually went back to the Assembly term as a Republican; and now he seems thoroughly in line with the predilections of the 39th District. Dannemeyer is a member of the important Energy and Commerce Committee, where he favors reducing regulation on business, and in 1985 became a member of Judiciary, where he can champion conservative constitutional amendments. One of his few disagreements with the Administration has come on a Food and Drug Administration proposal to ban raw, or unpasteurized, milk; he was once an attorney for a firm in his district that manufactures the product.

But his greatest fervor he saves for his battle against AIDS. More than any other member of the Congress he has been pushing measures to isolate the general population from this disease. Some of his proposals seem no more than common sense and have been widely accepted: closing the bathhouses where the disease has been spread by promiscuous homosexual contacts, testing blood in blood banks for the AIDS virus, barring high-risk persons from donating blood. Despite the lack of evidence that the disease is spread except through the blood or sexual contact, Dannemeyer wants to permit hospital personnel to take any steps they want to protect themselves from contact with AIDS patients and to allow parents to keep their children home from schools which AIDS victims attend. But though his position can be defended on neutral grounds—"if we're going to err, let's err on the side of being careful," he says—he insists on raising the issue of whether homosexual conduct is a sin: God's "plan for man," he says, is "Adam and Eve, not Adam and Steve." He opens himself up to charges that he is trying to stir up hatred and persecution of homosexuals; his view that AIDS victims "emit spores" that can spread the disease has received no scientific backing.

Dannemeyer was elected to the House in 1978 when Charles Wiggins, Richard Nixon's brilliant defender in the House Judiciary Committee impeachment hearings, retired. He has as safe a district as anyone in the House, but he has a reputation even among Republicans for going too far and lost out in 1987 to two freshmen for a seat on the Budget Committee despite his interest in the subject.

The People: Pop. 1980: 525,858, up 33.0% 1970–80. Households (1980): 75% family, 41% with children, 63% married couples; 38.1% housing units rented; median monthly rent: $318; median house value: $106,300. Voting age pop. (1980): 380,058; 11% Spanish origin, 3% Asian origin, 1% Black, 1% American Indian.

1984 Presidential Vote: Reagan (R) 185,491   (77%)
                             Mondale (D) 52,591   (22%)

Rep. William E. Dannemeyer (R)

Elected 1978; b. Sept. 22, 1929, Los Angeles; home, Fullerton; Valparaiso U., B.A. 1950, U. of CA, Hastings Law Sch., J.D. 1952; Lutheran; married (Evelyn).

Career: Army, Korea; Practicing atty.; Fullerton Dpty. Dist. Atty., 1955–57; Asst. City Atty., Fullerton, 1959–62; CA Assembly, 1963–66, 1976–77.

Offices: 1214 LHOB 20515, 202-225-4111. Also 1235 N. Harbor Blvd., Ste. 100, Fullerton 92632, 714-992-0141.

Committees: *Energy and Commerce* (5th of 17 R). Subcommittees: Commerce, Consumer Protection and Competitiveness (Ranking Member); Energy and Power; Health and the Environment. *Judiciary* (10th of 14 R). Subcommittees: Civil and Constitutional Rights; Monopolies and Commercial Law.

Group Ratings

	ADA	ACLU	COPE	CFA	LCV	ACU	NTU	NSI	COC	CEI
1986	5	10	5	0	10	95	72	100	87	84
1985	10	—	6	8	—	90	72	—	95	—

National Journal Ratings

	1986 LIB — 1986 CONS		1985 LIB — 1985 CONS	
Economic	0%	— 94%	9%	— 88%
Social	26%	— 74%	0%	— 76%
Foreign	0%	— 86%	0%	— 76%

Key Votes

1) Lmt Cln Water Act	FOR	5) Retain Gun Cont	AGN	9) Aid Angola Reb	FOR
2) Rpl Tobac Sub	FOR	6) Contra Aid	FOR	10) Tax Reform	AGN
3) Grm-Rdmn Def Red	FOR	7) Lmt Text Imp	AGN	11) S Africa Sanc	AGN
4) Ban Polygraph	AGN	8) Limit SDI	AGN	12) Immig Reform	FOR

Election Results

1986 general	William E. Dannemeyer (R).	131,603	(75%)	($260,009)
	David C. Vest (D).	42,377	(24%)	($7,473)
1986 primary	William E. Dannemeyer (R).	61,018	(100%)	
1984 general	William E. Dannemeyer (R).	175,788	(76%)	($318,065)
	Robert E. Ward (D)	54,889	(24%)	($31,237)

Campaign Contributions and Expenditures

1985-86		Direct Cont. 1985-86		PACS Breakdown 1985-86			
Receipts	$264,037	Indiv.	$98,423	Corp.	$72,675	T/M/H	$38,400
Expend.	$260,009	Party	$3,147	Labor	$0	Agr.	$1,450
Unspent	$80,989	PACS	$126,570	Ideo.	$11,995	CWOS	$2,050
		Cand.	$17,450				

FORTIETH DISTRICT

In the early 1960s, the land that is now the 40th Congressional District of California was almost entirely vacant. Most of it was part of the totally undeveloped Irvine Ranch, a swathe of land that extended 10 miles along the Pacific Ocean south from Newport Beach and 22 miles inland, over orange groves and vegetable fields, to the mountains. Now the land is beginning to be filled up, and not just with stucco-housed subdivisions. Near Newport Beach is the 1,000 acres the Irvine developers donated for a local branch of the University of California; at the edge of the property, the small airport of 1960 has become John Wayne Orange County Airport; just to the east is Costa Mesa's South Coast Plaza, the highest-volume shopping center in southern California standing in what not too long ago was a lima bean field; and almost everywhere are the gleaming office towers that indicate that here—in the new city of Irvine, in Newport Beach, even down past where the Santa Ana and San Diego Freeways meet—is one of America's largest office centers. Development here is only spurred by the few remnants of the old days: the artsy settlement on the coast in Laguna Beach, locked in by hills, a few of the older streets in Newport Beach, the Marine Corps air base at El Toro.

This is almost uniformly an affluent area. The subdivisions are walled off from the surrounding roads and freeways, with access limited to a few roads; the old grid street patterns do not provide enough privacy and security for the affluent residents here. The underlying street patterns however, are geometrical, as if people were trying to impose a predictable order on the lush and unpredictable California landscape of mountain, coast, and desert. Such attempts do not always succeed, just as the efforts of the conservative Republicans whom voters here inevitably prefer do not always succeed: Richard Nixon retired in disgrace and Ronald Reagan has not been able to completely dismantle the welfare state. But Reagan's themes of traditional values and technological progress remain highly popular in this newest of Americas.

The 40th District has been represented by a member of the John Birch Society and by a former county assessor who went to jail. Its congressman since 1976, Robert Badham, has been a more conventional politician but has had his political troubles too. His politics are solidly conservative Republican, but he is not flamboyant like Robert Dornan or obsessed with a specific issue like William Dannemeyer. He is a member of the Armed Services Committee and an advocate of large increases in defense spending; he is on House Administration as well. But he does not spend as much time and energy on the tedious—and usually critical—routine of subcommittee business as do many of his colleagues; he seems more interested in his position as vice chairman of the Travel and Tourism Caucus, and some consider him not especially hard-working. Certainly he is among the most widely-traveled of congressmen; one Republican colleague said he'd get on anything that has jet engines and is heading out of town. In 1984 he was attacked as a junketeer, and his Democratic opponent held him to 64% of the vote—a low score indeed for a Republican in this district. In 1986 he was opposed in the Republican primary by Nathan Rosenberg, a fringe candidate who is the brother of *est* founder Werner Erhard, and who got 34% in the heart of Orange County nonetheless; in the general election, he was held to 61% of the vote—a real rebuke here. Unless Badham changes his work habits he will be vulnerable indeed in 1988.

The People: Pop. 1980: 525,935, up 58.6% 1970–80. Households: (1980): 65% family, 33% with children, 54% married couples; 39.6% housing units rented; median monthly rent: $366; median house value: $130,400. Voting age pop. (1980): 399,759; 7% Spanish origin, 4% Asian origin, 1% Black.

1984 Presidential Vote:

Reagan (R) 198,338	(75%)
Mondale (D) 63,210	(24%)

Rep. Robert E. Badham (R)

Elected 1976; b. June 9, 1929, Los Angeles; home, Newport Beach Occidental Col., 1947–48, Stanford U., B.A. 1951; Lutheran married (Anne).

Career: Navy, Korea; Secy. and Vice Pres., Hoffman Hardware Los Angeles, 1954–69; CA Assembly, 1962–76.

Offices: 2427 RHOB 20515, 202-225-5611. Also 180 Newport Center Dr., Ste. 240, Newport Beach 92660, 714-644-4040.

Committees: *Armed Services* (3d of 21 R). Subcommittees: Procurement and Military Nuclear Systems (Ranking Member) Seapower and Strategic and Critical Materials. *House Administration* (3d of 7 R). Subcommittees: Accounts (Ranking Member) Procurement and Printing. *Joint Committee on Printing.*

Group Ratings

	ADA	ACLU	COPE	CFA	LCV	ACU	NTU	NSI	COC	CEI
1986	0	11	10	0	10	89	57	100	100	93
1985	0	—	10	17	—	95	63	—	89	—

National Journal Ratings

	1986 LIB — 1986 CONS		1985 LIB — 1985 CONS	
Economic	0%	— 94%	9%	— 91%
Social	23%	— 77%	36%	— 64%
Foreign	0%	— 86%	0%	— 76%

Key Votes

1) Lmt Cln Water Act	FOR	5) Retain Gun Cont	AGN	9) Aid Angola Reb	FOR
2) Rpl Tobac Sub	FOR	6) Contra Aid	FOR	10) Tax Reform	AGN
3) Grm-Rdmn Def Red	FOR	7) Lmt Text Imp	AGN	11) S Africa Sanc	—
4) Ban Polygraph	AGN	8) Limit SDI	AGN	12) Immig Reform	—

Election Results

1986 general	Robert E. Badham (R)	119,829	(60%)	($418,975)
	Bruce W. Sumner (D)	75,664	(38%)	($169,872)
1986 primary	Robert E. Badham (R)	53,068	(66%)	
	Nathan Owen Rosenberg (R)	27,872	(34%)	
1984 general	Robert E. Badham (R)	164,257	(64%)	($172,133)
	Carol Ann Bradford (D)	86,748	(34%)	($129,689)

Campaign Contributions and Expenditures

1985-86		Direct Cont. 1985-86		PACS Breakdown 1985-86			
Receipts	$360,300	Indiv.	$153,744	Corp.	$123,405	T/M/H	$46,170
Expend.	$418,975	Party	$5,363	Labor	$4,500	Agr.	$800
Unspent	$1,660	PACS	$185,096	Ideo.	$9,739	CWOS	$482

FORTY-FIRST DISTRICT

Before World War II, San Diego was a sleepy resort town with a fine natural harbor and a few Navy installations. Then the United States fought a war in the Pacific, and San Diego was forever changed. It became the Navy's West Coast headquarters and naval installations proliferated. Later its pleasant climate—arguably the most pleasant in the continental United States—made it a favorite retirement place for Navy officers and for others as well. But San Diego, like most Sun Belt cities, is far more than a collection of retirement villages. It has developed a significant industrial base, largely on high-skill businesses; its metropolitan area population has reached nearly two million.

San Diego was evenly divided politically before 1945, split between the well-to-do Republican north side and the more modest and sometimes working-class south side. In the years following the war, the heavy immigration gave both the city and county of San Diego a very Republican, conservative complexion. Over the years it has been more raffish and scandal-prone than other California cities. Richard Nixon for years regarded this as his "lucky city"—until the unfolding ITT scandal caused him to cancel plans to have the 1972 Republican National Convention here. And Roger Hedgecock, a young Republican elected mayor in 1985, was forced from office when convicted on felony charges of receiving $360,000 in illegal campaign contributions from convicted financier J. David Dominelli and then lying about them. In his place was elected Democrat Maureen O'Connor, who with some of her 12 siblings won fame first as swimmers and then as politicians and opponents of further growth.

On growth issues and on preventing scandals she seems to follow in the footsteps of San Diego's best-known mayor, Pete Wilson, who is now United States senator from California. Bringing a conservative record from the legislature, Wilson nonetheless challenged big developers and insisted on regulating growth; he became one of the most popular politicians around and carried the city easily in general elections. He also made it easier for his kind of Republicans to win the votes of young, affluent voters who were conservative on economic issues but liberal on cultural matters. In the middle 1970s San Diego was voting for Democrats in many contests. But in the 1980s it has become once again pretty solidly Republican.

California's 41st Congressional District takes in the north side of San Diego where Wilson's politics were most popular and is represented by a political ally of Wilson's, Bill Lowery. The north side includes affluent beach communities (La Jolla, Pacific Beach, Mission Bay) as well as inland, comfortable sections of San Diego. Much of the city's land is still vacant, held that way to some extent by city policies but more by nature: these hillsides are too steep for condominiums, too precipitous for subdivision houses. Although this may seem odd to many, the 41st District has a very small Mexican-American population that is, despite the proximity of Mexico, lower in percentage than in affluent Los Angeles area districts; the reason seems to be that Mexicans who want to work at San Diego wages can cross the border each day and live more cheaply in Tijuana.

Lowery has solid roots in San Diego; his lifespan coincides almost exactly with San Diego's growth from a provincial Navy town to a major American city. He served in the 1970s as a councilman and then as Pete Wilson's Deputy Mayor. When Bob Wilson, for 28 years the 41st District's congressman and senior member of the Armed Services Committee, retired in 1980, Lowery ran and edged out two tough candidates, Dan MacKinnon (later chairman of the Civil Aeronautics Board until it was deregulated out of existence) in the primary and a Democratic state senator named Bob Wilson in the general. He has been reelected easily ever since, with his toughest challenge coming in the heavily Republican year of 1984.

In his first term Lowery didn't get Wilson's Armed Services seat; it went to fellow San Diegoan, and upset winner, Duncan Hunter instead. But after the 1984 election Lowery got a seat on Appropriations, a spot from which he should be able to look after San Diego's military and other parochial interests. His views on national issues are reliably conservative, and he makes a point of fighting proposals for offshore oil drilling (on which he has been the leading Republican in the California delegation's fight against Interior Secretary Donald Hodel), getting money to sweep the Tierrasanta area near San Diego Stadium for World War II shells, and backing research on Alzheimer's disease. He has been the leading Republican in the long-run negotiations with Interior Secretary Donald Hodel on offshore drilling, and in 1987 he gained a seat on the Interior Appropriations Subcommittee which should give him greater leverage in this battle. This seems to be a winning formula and he seems to be settling in for a long run of representing San Diego.

The People: Pop. 1980: 526,043, up 30.0% 1970–80. Households (1980): 60% family, 29% with children, 49% married couples; 49.8% housing units rented; median monthly rent: $273; median house value: $106,800. Voting age pop. (1980): 412,731; 6% Spanish origin, 4% Asian origin, 2% Black.

1984 Presidential Vote: Reagan (R) 171,535   (64%)
Mondale (D) 92,994   (35%)

Rep. Bill Lowery (R)

Elected 1980; b. May 2, 1947, San Diego; home, San Diego; San Diego St. Col.; Roman Catholic; married (Kathleen).

Career: Pub. Rel. and Adv.; San Diego City Cncl., 1977–80, Dpty. Mayor, 1980.

Offices: 225 CHOB 20515, 202-225-3201. Also 880 Front St., Rm. 6-S-15, San Diego 92188, 619-231-0957.

Committees: *Appropriations* (19th of 22 R). Subcommittees: Interior; Military Construction (Ranking Member); Treasury—Postal Service—General Government.

Group Ratings

	ADA	ACLU	COPE	CFA	LCV	ACU	NTU	NSI	COC	CEI
1986	5	10	5	17	21	74	41	100	75	62
1985	5	—	5	42	—	81	46	—	86	—

National Journal Ratings

	1986 LIB — 1986 CONS			1985 LIB — 1985 CONS		
Economic	15%	—	84%	16%	—	81%
Social	23%	—	74%	0%	—	76%
Foreign	25%	—	74%	0%	—	76%

Key Votes

1) Lmt Cln Water Act	AGN	5) Retain Gun Cont	AGN	9) Aid Angola Reb	FOR
2) Rpl Tobac Sub	FOR	6) Contra Aid	FOR	10) Tax Reform	FOR
3) Grm-Rdmn Def Red	FOR	7) Lmt Text Imp	AGN	11) S Africa Sanc	FOR
4) Ban Polygraph	AGN	8) Limit SDI	AGN	12) Immig Reform	FOR

Election Results

1986 general	Bill Lowery (R).....................	133,566	(68%)	($401,730)
	Dan Kripke (D).....................	59,816	(30%)	($153,732)
1986 primary	Bill Lowery (R).....................	61,582	(100%)	
1984 general	Bill Lowery (R).....................	161,068	(63%)	($399,959)
	Bob Simmons (D).....................	85,475	(34%)	($126,295)

Campaign Contributions and Expenditures

1985-86		Direct Cont. 1985-86		PACS Breakdown 1985-86			
Receipts	$389,021	Indiv.	$221,482	Corp.	$78,724	T/M/H	$32,475
Expend.	$401,730	Party	$2,228	Labor	$6,750	Agr.	$1,050
Unspent	$71,707	PACS	$130,413	Ideo.	$8,550	CWOS	$2,865

FORTY-SECOND DISTRICT

The 42d Congressional District of California is the descendant of several districts based in the city of Long Beach, a sort of mini-central city almost directly south of downtown Los Angeles, a city large enough to constitute most of a district by itself. But less than one-fifth of the residents of the current 42d live in Long Beach or the nearby harbor area of Los Angeles. Rather, a few blocks of Long Beach and the harbor area form a kind of land bridge, as if the Queen Mary and Howard Hughes's Spruce Goose, both moored in Long Beach harbor, were tying together two heavily Republican areas that redistricter Phillip Burton wanted to keep out of Democratic districts.

One is centered on the Palos Verdes Peninsula and the suburb of Torrance just to the north. Palos Verdes is a mountainous peninsula jutting up above the flat plain of the Los Angeles Basin and staring out over the ocean to Santa Catalina Island; all but its most seismically active parts are filled with spacious ranch houses built on, for the Los Angeles area, generous-sized lots. The population here is affluent and highly Republican; perhaps Palos Verdes's best-known resident is Arthur Laffer, the conceiver, on a paper napkin, of the now-famous Laffer Curve. Torrance, down on the plain, is much more prosaic in appearance and is criss-crossed by railroads, with warehouses and factories and U.S. headquarters of Japanese firms. Nonetheless, it is a higher than average income (and Republican) suburb.

The other part of the district, connected by a thin strip of waterfront going inland a distance in Long Beach, is in Orange County: the retirement development of Rossmoor and nearby Seal Beach; the spread-out suburb of Huntington Beach, affluent but with many renters as well as homeowners; the by now long-settled suburbs of Cypress and Los Alamitos and part of Westminster, with their comfortable stucco houses inhabited increasingly by families who 10 or 15 years ago lived precarious lives in Vietnam.

The congressman from the 42d District is Dan Lungren, as enthusiastic a young Republican as one could find and an accomplished legislator as well. His father was Richard Nixon's personal physician; he worked on the staffs of Senators George Murphy and Bill Brock. After a few years of law practice in Long Beach, he challenged a Democrat elected in 1974, lost in 1976, then came back and won in 1978. Lungren jammed down his opponent's throat his opposition to Proposition 13 and won rather easily. He has been reelected without difficulty ever since.

By chance and by temperament, Lungren has become one of the most legislatively accomplished of the young Republican members of Congress. The chance was his assignment to the liberal Judiciary Committee. He worked hard on the criminal code reform and on immigration reform. Lungren worked hard to reach bipartisan agreement with the Democrats on most provisions in the bill, including those which cause many Republican businessmen and conservative ideologues problems, like those granting amnesty to immigrants who got here illegally several years ago. When the bill, delayed by Mexican-American lobbying groups, the Democratic leadership, and the Reagan administration, reached the floor in 1984, Lungren assisted ably in managing it, and delivered huge—on many issues, near-unanimous—blocs of Republican votes for its major provisions. He helped get the bill through the House in 1984, though it died in conference. Then in 1986, when the bill seemed to die half-a-dozen deaths, Lungren kept plugging; and in the last days of the session it passed and became law. To those who say that divided government and ideology-minded politicians cannot respond affirmatively to society's challenges, his performance on this issue is a refutation.

Lungren has also had other successes, notably in using parliamentary legerdemain to get an omnibus crime bill passed in 1984. He is aggressive and tenacious but is also unpretentious and hard-working. He has contemplated making a statewide race, but in huge California that is always an iffy proposition. More likely he will keep holding this safe seat and honing his considerable legislative talents.

The People: Pop. 1980: 525,909, up 15.0% 1970–80. Households (1980): 67% family, 34% with children, 56% married couples; 40.3% housing units rented; median monthly rent: $336; median house value: $131,500. Voting age pop. (1980): 400,256; 6% Spanish origin, 5% Asian origin, 1% Black, 1% American Indian.

1984 Presidential Vote: Reagan (R) 183,392   (72%)
Mondale (D) 67,480   (27%)

Rep. Daniel E. (Dan) Lungren (R)

Elected 1978; b. Sept. 22, 1946, Long Beach; home, Long Beach; Notre Dame U., B.A. 1964, U. of Southern CA, Georgetown U., J.D. 1971; Roman Catholic; married (Barbara).

Career: Staff of U.S. Sen. George Murphy, 1969–70; Staff of U.S. Sen. Bill Brock of TN, 1971; Spec. Asst., Repub. Natl. Cmtee., 1971–72; Practicing atty., 1973–78.

Offices: 2440 RHOB 20515, 202-225-2415. Also 555 E. Ocean Blvd., Ste. 505, Long Beach 90802, 213-436-9133.

Committees: *Judiciary* (4th of 14 R). Subcommittee: Courts; Monopolies and Commercial Law. *Permanent Select Committee on Intelligence* (5th of 6 R). Subcommittees: Legislative; Program and Budget Authority.

Group Ratings

	ADA	ACLU	COPE	CFA	LCV	ACU	NTU	NSI	COC	CEI
1986	0	15	5	8	32	95	68	100	100	88
1985	5	—	5	33	—	90	73	—	90	—

National Journal Ratings

	1986 LIB — 1986 CONS			1985 LIB — 1985 CONS		
Economic	0%	—	94%	0%	—	95%
Social	27%	—	71%	0%	—	76%
Foreign	0%	—	86%	0%	—	76%

Key Votes

1) Lmt Cln Water Act	FOR	5) Retain Gun Cont	FOR	9) Aid Angola Reb	FOR
2) Rpl Tobac Sub	FOR	6) Contra Aid	FOR	10) Tax Reform	FOR
3) Grm-Rdmn Def Red	FOR	7) Lmt Text Imp	AGN	11) S Africa Sanc	AGN
4) Ban Polygraph	AGN	8) Limit SDI	AGN	12) Immig Reform	FOR

Election Results

1986 general	Daniel E. (Dan) Lungren (R)	140,364	(73%)	($215,940)
	Michael P. Blackburn (D)	47,586	(25%)	($17,606)
1986 primary	Daniel E. (Dan) Lungren (R)	56,314	(100%)	
1984 general	Daniel E. (Dan) Lungren (R)	177,783	(73%)	($151,248)
	Mary Lou Brophy (D)	60,025	(25%)	($54,673)

Campaign Contributions and Expenditures

1985-86		Direct Cont. 1985-86		PACS Breakdown 1985-86			
Receipts	$214,698	Indiv.	$65,579	Corp.	$36,600	T/M/H	$29,600
Expend.	$215,940	Party	$2,126	Labor	$500	Agr.	$1,650
Unspent	$101,231	PACS	$76,839	Ideo.	$7,575	CWOS	$914
		Cand.	$50,742				

FORTY-THIRD DISTRICT

One of America's most comfortable environments, and one largely undiscovered by the mass media—though not by affluent migrants from all over the nation—is the country north of San Diego. The coastline was pretty well settled, all the way from the Marine Corps's Camp Pendleton south to La Jolla several decades ago, but it is only in the last dozen years that there has been major settlement inland. Here, amid dry but not desert landscape, you can see miles of rolling hills, with occasional surrealistic trees and sagebrush-like bushes; mountains clump up not in ridges but here and there, almost at random. Upon this, developers have planted, rather than standard subdivisions, whole little communities, existing alone in the mountains. Many but by no means all their residents are retirees; and while some may miss the urbanity and busyness of big cities (or even a metropolitan area like Orange County) most don't. The climate is close to ideal, the air remains clear, there is little fear of crime.

Yet condominiums and houses here cost less—roughly 50% less—than in the more regimented developments like Mission Viejo in southern Orange County. Northern San Diego County is one of the real bargains left in the United States. Why do the media ignore it (except for the Teamsters' luxurious La Costa development)? Partly because it is outside the ambit of one of our really big metropolitan areas, partly because it is not fashionable in the way Malibu or the Hamptons are. And partly, perhaps, because the very existence of such a place, and the fact that quite ordinary people can afford to live here, contradicts the pessimistic picture of America in which so many in the media have a psychological stake.

Most of northern San Diego County, plus the southern tip of Orange County (including San Clemente and San Juan Capistrano of Nixon and swallows fame, respectively) form the 43d Congressional District of California. The people who have moved here are heavily Republican: affluent enough to identify with the party of property, conventional enough in their personal lives to identify with what describes itself as the party of the family, unscarred enough by ethnic differences to identify with the party that fancies it is made up of an unethnic majority.

The 43d District was a new creation for the 1982 election, evidence that even the most assiduous Democratic redistricter, like the late Phillip Burton, was constrained by the equal-population standard to draw at least one new Republican district. But oddly, the new congressman wasn't chosen in the Republican primary—at least, not exactly. That contest attracted 18 entrants (which made it theoretically possible for a candidate to win with 6%), and its winner, Johnnie Crean, struck most of the other contenders—and many others—as a despicable candidate. Crean spent some $500,000 of his own money on television advertising that implied that he was the choice of President Reagan, and on direct mail that charged one of his opponents, spuriously, with vote fraud. He won the primary by only 92 votes out of 83,000 cast, and the second place finisher, Carlsbad Mayor and dentist Ron Packard, ran as a write-in candidate. He won: this is a highly literate district, and the Republican party was encouraging supporters of George Deukmejian to vote absentee ballots, on which write-ins are easy. Packard had the blessing of most local Republican officials, who were even willing to risk a Democratic victory to stop Crean. The final score: Packard, 37%; Democrat Roy Archer, 32%; Crean, 31%.

That wild and woolly contest will probably turn out to be the last seriously contested election—and the last question about its regular Republicanism—the 43d District sees for some time. Packard, seated as a Republican, sits now on the Public Works and Science and Technology Committees. Considered a moderate Republican out in California, his voting record in Washington is impeccably conservative. Packard is personable, without previous high-level political experience, and seems to be the kind of citizen-politician voters in these parts want. He is a consensus-builder rather than an ideologue in the House, bringing the style of California's nonpartisan, efficiency-minded municipal politics to a chamber and a delegation usually more confrontation-prone. He has concentrated on nitty-gritty issues like the Santa Ana River flood control project and the handling on untreated sewage from across the border in Mexico. He was reelected easily in 1984 and 1986 and seems likely to remain in the House as long as he likes.

The People: Pop. 1980: 525,956, up 99.4% 1970–80. Households (1980): 75% family, 38% with children, 64% married couples; 35.7% housing units rented; median monthly rent: $291; median house value: $109,800. Voting age pop. (1980): 387,050; 11% Spanish origin, 2% Black, 2% Asian origin, 1% American Indian.

1984 Presidential Vote:

Reagan (R)	176,550	(74%)
Mondale (D)	58,918	(25%)

Rep. Ronald C. Packard (R)

Elected 1982; b. Jan. 19, 1931, Meridian, ID; home, Oceanside; Brigham Young U., Portland State U., U. of OR, D.M.D. 1957; Mormon; married (Roma Jean).

Career: Navy, 1957–59; Dentist; Carlsbad Sch. Dist. Bd., 1960–72; Carlsbad City Cncl., 1976–78; Mayor of Carlsbad, 1978–82.

Offices: 316 CHOB 20515, 202-225-3906. Also 2121 Palomar Airport Rd., Ste. 105, Carlsbad 92008, 619-438-0443.

Committees: *Public Works and Transportation* (12th of 20 R). Subcommittees: Aviation; Surface Transportation; Water Resources. *Space, Science and Technology* (9th of 18 R). Subcommittees: International Science Cooperation; Investigations and Oversight; Space, Science and Applications. *Select Committee on Children, Youth and Families* (8th of 12 R). Subcommittee: Prevention Strategies.

Group Ratings

	ADA	ACLU	COPE	CFA	LCV	ACU	NTU	NSI	COC	CEI
1986	5	10	5	17	16	91	53	100	94	78
1985	10	—	4	17	—	86	60	—	95	—

National Journal Ratings

	1986 LIB — 1986 CONS	1985 LIB — 1985 CONS
Economic	0% — 94%	5% — 92%
Social	30% — 70%	0% — 76%
Foreign	16% — 79%	0% — 76%

Key Votes

1) Lmt Cln Water Act	AGN	5) Retain Gun Cont	AGN	9) Aid Angola Reb	FOR
2) Rpl Tobac Sub	FOR	6) Contra Aid	FOR	10) Tax Reform	FOR
3) Grm-Rdmn Def Red	FOR	7) Lmt Text Imp	AGN	11) S Africa Sanc	AGN
4) Ban Polygraph	AGN	8) Limit SDI	AGN	12) Immig Reform	FOR

Election Results

1986 general	Ronald C. Packard (R)................	137,341	(73%)	($132,967)
	Joseph Chirra (D).....................	45,078	(24%)	($26,367)
1986 primary	Ronald C. Packard (R)................	64,401	(100%)	
1984 general	Ronald C. Packard (R)................	165,643	(74%)	($356,474)
	Lois E. Humphreys (D)	50,966	(23%)	($16,268)

Campaign Contributions and Expenditures

1985-86		Direct Cont. 1985-86		PACS Breakdown 1985-86			
Receipts	$179,593	Indiv.	$72,957	Corp.	$41,350	T/M/H	$41,200
Expend.	$132,967	Party	$2,268	Labor	$3,750	Agr.	$500
Unspent	$99,131	PACS	$95,640	Ideo.	$8,200	CWOS	$640

FORTY-FOURTH DISTRICT

Like most Sun Belt cities, San Diego has its second side. To many, San Diego evokes images of La Jolla, its shopping streets lined with boutiques and stockbrokers' offices, or Mission Bay, with its comfortable homes of retired Navy officers, or the magnificent Balboa Park Zoo. But just a short distance away is another San Diego, down by the harbor, along the hills running inland, and on the flat, dusty land going down to Tijuana. This is the south side where the city's blacks live in neighborhoods stretching east from the city's gleaming downtown and where Mexican-Americans are scattered in various parts of the city, from Encanto and Chollas Park in the east down through the blue-collar suburbs of National City and Chula Vista to the south. They live also, unobtrusively here and there, in mostly Anglo neighborhoods like East San Diego and suburbs like Lemon Grove. Indeed, the Mexican-American percentage here is not as large as most people would guess, given the proximity of Mexico. One reason is that immigrants come to the United States less to get residency and qualify for welfare than they do to get jobs; and Mexicans in the San Diego area can live in Tijuana, which is cheaper and culturally more comfortable, and cross the border each day as thousands do to commute to jobs in San Diego.

This central and southern part of San Diego, enclosed by a jagged line drawn to maximize its Democratic percentage, makes up California's 44th Congressional District. Its boundaries were very carefully sculpted, because most of its precincts were in the old 42d District that surprised everyone and elected a Republican congressman, Duncan Hunter, in 1980. Heavily Republican areas, like the old beach resort of Coronado and the pleasant neighborhood around Balboa Park, were split off and put into a new 45th District, safe for Hunter; the rest, with some new parts added, was made a safe Democratic seat.

This left a district ripe for San Diego County Supervisor Jim Bates. A onetime Republican with 11 years in local government, he was well known for insisting that welfare recipients work, but he was no across-the-board conservative: he first became a Democrat because he opposed the Vietnam war and supported Eugene McCarthy in 1968. In 1982 Bates won both the primary and the general election by wide margins. Since then he has done better, winning reelection easily, though his percentage dipped a bit in Democratic 1986.

In the House he is hard to classify. He was adroit enough to win a seat on the Energy and Commerce Committee, beating in the process a Los Angeles freshman backed by Health Subcommittee Chairman Henry Waxman, in 1983. But he irritated Speaker O'Neill and many other Democrats for not supporting the party position on the budget. He sees himself as an independent thinker, willing to buck the big guys, approaching each issue thoughtfully, ready to advocate unpopular stands like the legalization of some drugs in 1986. But there is a thin boundary between that and being unpredictable and unreliable, and many serious House members think he has crossed that line. He is criticized bitterly if anonymously for treating his staff capriciously and cruelly. He can say that congressmen are paid to serve constituents, not staff members, and Bates has managed to amass a large core of enthusiastic supporters in San Diego and to win elections by substantial margins. He is a man who has risen far from difficult circumstances, but he needs to discipline himself and focus his talents more steadily if he is to come close to achieving his potential in Congress.

The People: Pop. 1980: 525,868, up 17.2% 1970–80. Households (1980): 69% family, 41% with children, 52% married couples; 51.9% housing units rented; median monthly rent: $225; median house value: $70,300. Voting age pop. (1980): 379,593; 22% Spanish origin, 13% Black, 7% Asian origin, 1% American Indian.

1984 Presidential Vote:

Reagan (R)	79,269	(52%)
Mondale (D)	71,160	(47%)

Rep. Jim Bates (D)

Elected 1982; b. July 21, 1941, Denver, CO; home, San Diego; San Diego State U., B.A. 1974; Congregationalist; married (Marilyn).

Career: USMC, 1959–63; Bank loan officer, 1963–68; Aerospace administrator, 1968–69; Store mgr., Heavenly Donuts, 1970; San Diego City Cncl., 1971–74; Member, San Diego Cnty. Bd. of Sprvsrs., 1975–82, Chmn., 1982.

Offices: 1404 LHOB 20515, 202-225-5452. Also 3450 College Ave., #231, San Diego 92115, 619-287-8851; and 430 Davidson St., Ste. A, Chula Vista 92010, 619-691-1166.

Committees: *Energy and Commerce* (22d of 25 D). Subcommittees: Commerce, Consumer Protection and Competitiveness; Health and the Environment; Transportation, Tourism and Hazardous Materials. *House Administration* (9th of 12 D). Subcommittees: Elections; Procurement and Printing.

Group Ratings

	ADA	ACLU	COPE	CFA	LCV	ACU	NTU	NSI	COC	CEI
1986	90	80	82	75	95	0	44	10	44	34
1985	80	—	81	92	—	29	32	—	41	—

National Journal Ratings

	1986 LIB — 1986 CONS		1985 LIB — 1985 CONS	
Economic	62% —	35%	63% —	36%
Social	67% —	32%	81% —	15%
Foreign	75% —	20%	69% —	30%

Key Votes

1) Lmt Cln Water Act	FOR	5) Retain Gun Cont	FOR	9) Aid Angola Reb	AGN
2) Rpl Tobac Sub	FOR	6) Contra Aid	AGN	10) Tax Reform	FOR
3) Grm-Rdmn Def Red	FOR	7) Lmt Text Imp	FOR	11) S Africa Sanc	FOR
4) Ban Polygraph	FOR	8) Limit SDI	FOR	12) Immig Reform	FOR

Election Results

1986 general	Jim Bates (D)	70,557	(64%)	($410,133)
	Bill Mitchell (R)	36,359	(33%)	($134,980)
1986 primary	Jim Bates (D)	38,898	(100%)	
1984 general	Jim Bates (D)	99,378	(70%)	($272,454)
	Neil R. Campbell (R).................	39,977	(28%)	($9,123)

Campaign Contributions and Expenditures

1985-86		Direct Cont. 1985-86		PACS Breakdown 1985-86			
Receipts	$410,133	Indiv.	$211,681	Corp.	$33,950	T/M/H	$57,310
Expend.	$410,017	PACS	$187,937	Labor	$75,250	Agr.	$1,200
Debts	$377	Cand.	$11,425	Ideo.	$17,452	CWOS	$2,775

FORTY-FIFTH DISTRICT

One of the fastest-growing metropolitan areas in the United States in the last two decades was San Diego, and as a result this city and its suburbs, represented a generation ago by just one congressman, now elect four—as many as (depending on how you draw metropolitan area lines) Cleveland or Minneapolis–St. Paul. The most recently created of these is California's 45th Congressional District. Although its boundaries seem regular on the map, its population concentrations are oddly dispersed. One is right on the coast: the old beach suburb of Coronado, with its delightful Victorian hotel, a favorite of retired Navy officers, on a narrow peninsula connected by bridge to downtown San Diego and lined at each end by Navy installations.

Another, connected by a land bridge sweeping south through Imperial Beach and the southern edge of the city, runs along the eastern edge of suburban settlement. These are pleasant suburbs nestled between mountains, not terribly high income, but conservative on both economic and cultural issues. The 45th includes the sparsely populated interior of San Diego County, with its small Indian reservations—some of the last traces of the people who populated the state, very lightly, before Junipero Serra set up his missions along the coast. Farther inland, outside San Diego County, is the Imperial Valley, an agricultural area in the desert created entirely by irrigation; the majority of the people here are Mexican, with more huddling in Mexicali, right on the border; the political power is in the hands of the growers.

This is a solidly Republican district, created by Phillip Burton to entice freshman Duncan Hunter out of the otherwise Democratic 44th, most of which he had been representing and which he, alone of San Diego area Republicans, might have won. The strategy worked. Hunter may have had some misgivings: before his election he was a storefront lawyer in a low-income neighborhood, and he was proud of his ability to win votes, often through door-to-door campaigning, among Democrats. But the prospect of having to court a basically contrary constituency indefinitely must have been daunting. So Hunter ran in the 45th and won easily.

Hunter is also a Vietnam veteran and a believer in strong national defense who brings the aggressiveness of a veteran of helicopter combat assaults in Vietnam and the brashness of a poverty lawyer to his work. He went against the conventional wisdom by running against 18-year incumbent Lionel Van Deerlin in 1980, when Van Deerlin chaired a subcommittee both important and capable of generating vast campaign contributions. But Hunter outcampaigned the Democrat and won. Once in Washington, he took on his fellow 1980 San Diego freshman Bill Lowery and won a seat on the Armed Services Committee. There he has made some impact on decisions local and national. He led the fight against homeporting, Navy Secretary John Lehman's plan, naturally unpopular in San Diego. He was also a lead sponsor of the amendment (which Caspar Weinberger called "pretty absurd") to use military forces to intercept drug shipments. He pushed through a "return-to-sender" system to intercept sewage flows from across the border in Tijuana and return them to Mexico before sewage can enter the Tijuana River and pollute San Diego beaches. He is one of the most aggressive leaders of the Conservative Opportunity Society group, always ready to take on Democrats or stand-patters. Hunter is not always the smoothest operator and often he plunges in despite institutional barriers and received wisdom. But he is one young Republican whose fervor has made a difference in the House and seems likely to do so for some years to come.

The People: Pop. 1980: 525,927, up 43.3% 1970–80. Households (1980): 76% family, 42% with children, 63% married couples; 36.9% housing units rented; median monthly rent: $257; median house value: $88,200. Voting age pop. (1980): 373,038; 14% Spanish origin, 2% Asian origin, 2% Black, 1% American Indian.

1984 Presidential Vote:

Reagan (R) 149,282	(71%)
Mondale (D) 58,141	(28%)

Rep. Duncan L. Hunter (R)

Elected 1980; b. May 31, 1948, Riverside; home, Coronado; Western St. U., B.S.L. 1976, J.D. 1976; Baptist; married (Lynne).

Career: Army, Vietnam; Practicing atty., 1976–80.

Offices: 133 CHOB 20515, 202-225-5672. Also 366 S. Pierce St., El Cajon 92020, 619-579-3001; and 1101 Airport Rd., Imperial 92251, 619-353-5420.

Committees: *Armed Services* (8th of 21 R). Subcommittees: Research and Development; Seapower and Strategic and Critical Materials. *Select Committee on Narcotics Abuse and Control* (6th of 10 R).

Group Ratings

	ADA	ACLU	COPE	CFA	LCV	ACU	NTU	NSI	COC	CEI
1986	0	0	24	17	21	82	53	100	100	74
1985	10	—	23	17	—	86	61	—	76	—

National Journal Ratings

	1986 LIB — 1986 CONS		1985 LIB — 1985 CONS	
Economic	13% —	85%	19% —	80%
Social	16% —	83%	0% —	76%
Foreign	0% —	86%	0% —	76%

Key Votes

1) Lmt Cln Water Act	AGN	5) Retain Gun Cont	AGN	9) Aid Angola Reb	FOR
2) Rpl Tobac Sub	FOR	6) Contra Aid	FOR	10) Tax Reform	FOR
3) Grm-Rdmn Def Red	AGN	7) Lmt Text Imp	FOR	11) S Africa Sanc	AGN
4) Ban Polygraph	AGN	8) Limit SDI	AGN	12) Immig Reform	AGN

Election Results

1986 general	Duncan L. Hunter (R)	118,900	(77%)	($400,612)
	Hewitt Fitts Ryan (D).................	32,800	(21%)	($21,875)
1986 primary	Duncan L. Hunter (R)	46,465	(100%)	
1984 general	Duncan L. Hunter (R)	149,011	(75%)	($272,431)
	David W. Guthrie (D).................	45,325	(23%)	($229)

Campaign Contributions and Expenditures

1985-86		Direct Cont. 1985-86		PACS Breakdown 1985-86			
Receipts	$401,076	Indiv.	$217,383	Corp.	$72,815	T/M/H	$37,440
Expend.	$400,612	Party	$2,567	Labor	$12,500	Agr.	$600
Unspent	$122,032	PACS	$138,735	Ideo.	$14,500	CWOS	$880

COLORADO

Anyone who has driven Interstate 70 across the country knows that there are few sights more thrilling than coming over an incline on a clear day and seeing, suddenly in the distance, the Front Range of the Rocky Mountains as they tower over an ocean-like expanse of dry, brown, flat plateau. Then, as you get closer to the mountains, you see as well the man-made ramparts, the cluster of high-rise buildings that in the 1970s made downtown Denver one of the fastest-growing and in the 1980s one of the most overbuilt office centers in the nation. Together, these two sights symbolize Colorado, what has made it attractive to migrants from all over the nation, and what has made it a kind of national trend-setter. On the one hand you have the pristine beauty and awesome abruptness of a physical environment many people consider the best in the country. On the other hand you have an advanced, post-industrial economy which is the envy of most of the rest of the world.

Nowhere else in the world is there a city of Denver's magnitude sitting on parched plains at the edge of towering mountains. By any traditional standard it is an improbable place for an advanced civilization. The High Plains just to the east are too arid for crops and have no dependable supply of water. The rivers are mere trickles, if that, except in flood season, and even the Plains Indians had a hard time here. The mountains behind the Front Range—the Western Slope—get plenty of precipitation, but their terrain is forbidding. There are dozens of peaks over 10,000 feet and scarcely a patch of level ground, but nothing much grows at these altitudes anyway. Yet Denver and Colorado—for 80% of the people in the state live along this Front Range—have been the biggest population cluster between the Missouri River and San Francisco Bay not just since the 1960s, but going back well into the 19th century.

For much of that time, and most conspicuously in the past two decades, Colorado has been a harbinger of the nation's future. Its economic trends, its political proclivities, and most of all its cultural attitudes have eerily presaged changes that have swept the nation a few years later. But as the 1980s turn into 1990s, Colorado's future is suddenly not so clear. The familiar patterns of the 1970s and 1980s are disappearing, and in the smog that hangs over Denver and the Front Range on a dismayingly large number of days, it's hard to make out the new patterns that are emerging—and not certain that those patterns will then appear elsewhere.

One change is that Colorado is getting a new set of leaders: Governor Richard Lamm and Senator Gary Hart, the most illustrious of the young liberals who have led the Democratic party here since 1970, did not run for reelection in 1986; while their longtime conservative adversaries, people like brewer Joseph Coors, who are of an older generation, are also passing off the baton to others. Also, the issues politicians are fighting about are changing. For years the Democrats have campaigned for limits on growth and the Republicans have campaigned for traditional values. Both battles seem to have been won now, pushed about as far as either can be, and the question is what comes next.

That question is rendered more difficult by changes in the economy. For two decades Colorado grew much more rapidly than the nation, attracting newcomers not just because of its environment (though that has certainly helped) but because of its opportunities. But in 1986, for the first time in years, more people moved out of Colorado than in. Government jobs and defense contracts, which helped fuel growth in the 1970s and early 1980s respectively, are not growth industries any more. Energy exploration and the oil business generally have been devastated by lower prices here: those Denver skyscrapers were supposed to fill up with energy companies, but have stayed empty instead. Marvin Davis, the Denver-based, Brooklyn-born oil man, shrewdly sold out many of his buildings at the energy price top, and became a Hollywood movie mogul. The same energy depression has affected the entire "Empty Quarter," as Joel Garreau calls the energy-producing expanse of the Rockies in *The Nine Nations of North America,* of which Denver has since the 1870s been the commercial center, transportation hub, and supply depot. Public discourse in Colorado had focused on the question of how to respond to economic growth. What does it do if there is not much economic growth any more? When development-minded conservatives arranged to have the 1976 Winter Olympics in Colorado, the young liberals, led by Richard Lamm, protested, put the issue on the 1972 ballot, and voted the Olympics out. Such fights still occur: some Denverites opposed Mayor Federico Peña's plan to build a convention center near the railway yards along the (usually dry) South Platte River.

During the years of rapid growth, Colorado voters were again and again uncannily ahead of the nation. Conservative Republicans swept the state in 1962, profiting from affluent voters' resentment of big government in Washington—presaging the Goldwater nomination of 1964 and the Republican victories of 1966 and beyond. In the wake of the Olympics referendum, an affluent younger population eager to protect the environment it had come to enjoy, elected new style Democrats like Hart, Lamm, Patricia Schroeder, Tim Wirth—forshadowing the success of new-style and environmentalist Democrats like Jimmy Carter in 1976 and Gary Hart himself when he almost won the Democratic presidential nomination in 1984. By the late 1970s, Colorado's affluent voters, fed up with federal regulation of their energy industry and eager for economic growth, elected Bill Armstrong Senator and gave the Republicans two-thirds margins in the legislature—presaging the Reagan and Republican victories of 1980 and 1984.

In contrast, the 1986 results look inconclusive: Democrats won the governorship and close races for the Senate and two House seats less because of their stands on issues than because of their superior political skills. No ideas swept the state for either side. For two decades Colorado voters, unfettered by pressing economic need, with no deep roots in the community, swung wildly from right to left and back again. In the late 1980s Colorado voters, suddenly queasy about the future of their economy, and now that in-migration has ended suddenly with roots in this community, seemed to swing less far in either direction and to choose cautiously the side of competence and safety. Colorado politics used to be battles between different segments of the state's population with a very clear idea of who they were and what they wanted. "If she wins, we win," Pat Schroeder's buttons read in 1972, when American troops were still in Vietnam; "They've had their turn; now it's our turn," said Gary Hart's slogan in 1974, when a candidate's hair length was a political statement. Now as we approach the 1990s, it's less apparent in Colorado who "we" are and whose turn it is now. Is that the harbinger the nation will follow?

Governor. In a state like Colorado, with great population and economic growth, a governor can set an agenda and a tone in a way not usually possible in more settled and stable states. Colorado's governor for 12 years, Dick Lamm, did just that. He not only proclaimed but celebrated an "era of limits," was hostile to population growth and immigration, concentrated on protecting the environment, against the federal government as well as local developers and potential Japanese investors whom Lamm regarded as worse than agents of the Kremlin. He was outspokenly liberal on cultural issues, sponsoring one of the nation's first liberalized abortion

COLORADO — Congressional Districts, Counties, and Selected Places — (6 Districts)

Congressional districts established June 3, 1982; all other boundaries are as of January 1, 1980.

laws in 1967 and saying in 1984 that certain old people had a "duty to die." That's all very well for affluent young people who don't want to be bothered having to spend their ski vacation or Acapulco money on some unwanted baby or oldster: but will Colorado's baby boomers as they get older, with fewer youngsters to care for them and some of them eager to get them out of the way, share Lamm's outlook as they do now?

The new governor is Roy Romer, a Democrat who served as Lamm's chief of staff and whom Lamm appointed state Treasurer. But Romer does not share all of Lamm's views, and certainly not his pungency; and his own political career and roots in Colorado go back longer and down deeper than Lamm's. Romer grew up on the eastern plains of Colorado, has seven children, went into business as long ago as World War II, and was first elected to the legislature in 1958. Few of the nation's current governors have such long experience in their state capitols.

Running in a year when Republican registration topped Democratic for the first time in 20 years, Romer had the good fortune to run against state Senator Ted Strickland, a controversial Texas native who after making several mistakes lost 2 to 1 to Lamm in 1978. Strickland made mistakes this time too. In August he said America should become a "Christian-centered" nation and emphasized his strong oppositon to abortion. In October he ran an ad linking Romer with Angela Davis, the once prominent Communist whom many voters probably had no memory of. On a statewide broadcast the night the Davis ad started—the candidates met face-to-face more than 30 times—Romer offered to take all his negative spots off the air, and Strickland declined. Evidently voters decided Strickland was ungubernatorial, and Romer won 58%–41%. His priorities after the election sounded different from Lamm's: stimulating the Colorado economy and bringing in jobs (and Japanese investors), improving the state's higher education, building a new Denver airport and the convention center; he had promised not to run the state's tax reform windfall, but spend it on education, highways, water projects, and economic development. He had hopes of getting along better with Republican legislators and, since Republicans lost their ⅔ margin in the state House, can probably prevent his vetoes from being overridden.

Senators. Colorado senators are getting into the habit of running for president. Gary Hart, having nearly won the Democratic nomination in 1984, followed the course of conventional wisdom—that you have to be out of office to have enough time to campaign—and declined to run for reelection in 1986. In April 1987 he announced he was running, although it was not so clear that being out of office was an advantage at a time when Americans seemed to be looking for competence at governing. For a time there was a chance Hart would be joined in the race by his former colleague, Republican Bill Armstrong, touted by some on the New Right as a presidential candidate. And it would surprise no one entirely if newly elected Senator Tim Wirth should in some future year try to run for president himself.

Bill Armstrong, after nearly a decade in the Senate, remains not much known to the general public. He combines the conservatism of one whose politics is rooted in deep religious faith with a certain practicality and ability to deal with the world as it is. He is a businessman who has made his fortune in broadcasting (ironically, a heavily regulated industry), but he has spent most of his adult life in public office. He was elected to the Colorado House in 1962, at age 25; to the United States House, in a new district whose boundaries he helped draw, in 1972; to the Senate in 1978, beating Democrat Floyd Haskell whose base had never been strong and who won in an upset himself six years before. In each case Armstrong came to office just as his party came or was coming to power and as its ideas seemed to be carrying all before them; in each case there has been a certain disappointment afterwards, as there almost inevitably is in politics.

Armstrong's work in the Senate has been mostly on economic issues. He got seats on the money committees—Finance, Budget, the President's Social Security Commission—and used them to advance his positions. His biggest achievement is probably income tax indexing, which he insisted on putting in the 1981 tax bill although others urged him to try it another time. As a result, and because he made it plain he would oppose fiercely any attempt to repeal it, indexing went into effect in 1985 and has probably become a permanent part of the tax code. So far the effect has been slight, because inflation is low. But indexing means that any boost in inflation will not boost government revenues, as happened in the 1970s, and push individuals into the high tax brackets. You can question whether any one index factor can reflect inflation accurately and fairly (the Consumer Price Index overstated inflation in the late 1970s—one of the reasons why Social Security, which is indexed, got into financial trouble); but it's hard to argue that Armstrong's perseverance here has not made a difference.

That Armstrong was also willing to fight had already been demonstrated in 1981 on the budget and in 1983 on Social Security. On taxes, Armstrong led a group of Republican conservatives against the Reagan budget in 1981, arguing presciently that the Administration was not providing long-term savings and cuts needed to hold down deficits. Their unexpected defection forced the Administration—and the Democrats—to fashion a compromise closer to their position. On Social Security, Armstrong led three dissenters on the Commission. He objected, reasonably given his perspective, that the commission closed the Social Security gap mostly by raising taxes rather than cutting promised future benefits; and he argued, that in a recession particularly, the tax burden is simply too high. Although Armstrong does not want Social Security dismantled, it seems clear that he thinks society would be better off with more savings in the private sector (*i.e.,* in investments and savings that would abet capital formation), and less in the public sector (*i.e.,* in Social Security that fosters consumption). He had the courage to take a stand, in what for him was an election year, on this very sensitive issue—rather than just writing an article about it.

Armstrong has concentrated mostly on economic issues, but his convictions have led him into other fields. He is, for example, the Senate's leading advocate of a return to the generosity of the post-World War II G.I. Bill of Rights. After the 1984 election he was elected chairman of the Senate Republican Policy Committee—the only strong conservative to win a leadership position. Behind all his stands are his deeply-held religious beliefs. These, as much as his specific stands on issues and his willingness to combat conventional wisdom, led several New Right leaders to urge that he run for president. But in January 1987 he announced he would not run. The demand in any case was not very strong, and came not from those who were convinced that this man should run, but from those who thought Armstrong was the closest thing they could find to the kind of candidate they had in mind. He remains highly popular in Colorado. He won his seat easily in 1978 and defended it even more easily, against Lieutenant Governor Nancy Dick, in 1984. Given Colorado's conservative leanings on national issues, he has one of the safer seats up in 1990, unless Dick Lamm runs; in early 1987 Lamm said the chances were 50–50 he would.

Colorado's junior Senator is Democrat Tim Wirth, tabbed as an up-and-comer when he was first elected to the House in 1974, one of the busiest and most powerful members of the House in the Carter and Reagan years, and now, after a breathtakingly close win over Republican Ken Kramer, a member of the Senate and, some say, maybe someday—after he has made an impact in that body—a candidate for national office. He was one of the first Democrats who seemed to come from the liberal wing of the party but took conservative positions on economic issues, such as when he opposed price controls on oil and gas. This was not a popular position among House Energy and Commerce Committee Democrats, but it was vindicated over time. Similarly, on the Budget Committee, he was part of a key bloc of middle votes, not a supporter of ever-greater spending. After the 1980 election he got the chairmanship of the Telecommunications, Consumer Protection and Finance Subcommittee, with jurisdiction over TV networks, the telephone industry, and Wall Street. This gave him immense clout (and ability to raise campaign dollars), but it also gave him responsibility for some tough problems: in 1982 his AT&T divestiture bill was beaten after AT&T lobbied its stockholders, and he got into unseemly hassles bludgeoning the networks over early evening election projections.

For all his prominence in Washington, Wirth could not take his suburban-Denver-and-Boulder district for granted. He had tough races in 1976, 1978, and 1984, and spent much time in the district and putting on (he seems to have originated these) a series of annual Washington seminars for interested constituents. The Senate race was a risk, and Wirth could probably have remained a powerful member of the House. But his constituency was demanding and his workload heavy; now he has a six-year term and pointedly did not seek committee assignments similar to Energy and Commerce.

The race between Wirth and Kramer was one of those 1986 contests hailed as unedifying, and there were some undignified comments made. But both candidates had a fair chance to present their cases. Kramer made a virtue of his frizzy-haired, disorganized appearance by running ads saying that he was "not slick, just good." He won the nomination at the June party convention by holding two opponents, a woman state Senator and the son-in-law of the state Republican chairman, to less than 20% of the delegate votes. He got a further break when Ronald Reagan's performance at Reykjavik in October 1986 made his Strategic Defense Initiative. Kramer was one of SDI's original enthusiasts, and much of it is to be deployed in his Colorado Springs home base. But Kramer was vulnerable to attack as an extremist: he was part of a group called "the crazies" in the legislature, and is given to provocative statements which are easier to defend intellectually than politically. Wirth, smoother both in appearance and demeanor, nonetheless made statements he had to apologize for. It turned out to be an exceedingly tight race, with Wirth carrying the Denver media market by enough to carry the state despite Kramer's better than 2 to 1 margin in his home area of Colorado Springs. The difference, oddly, may have come from an issue hardly aired: the same farm discontent which helped Democrats win Senate seats in the Dakotas. Wirth ran even in the wheat- and beef-producing northeast part of the state and well ahead in the beef-producing and Hispanic southeast, running in both areas well ahead of

Gary Hart's pace six years before.

Presidential politics. For all its trend-setting reputation, Colorado does not bulk large in presidential campaigning. Its national convention delegates are chosen by party caucuses. This has meant Coors Republicans and Hart Democrats. In close general elections over the past 40 years Colorado has been Republican. It was the only western state to go against FDR twice (1940, 1944); it went easily for Nixon in 1960 and 1968 and for Ford in 1976. It was solidly for Ronald Reagan in 1980, with one of the larger John Anderson percentages, and was only 3% less for Reagan in 1984 than the indubitably conservative state of Arizona.

Congressional districting. Control over congressional districting for the 1980s was split between the Republican legislature and Democratic Governor Lamm. After lengthy argument, they couldn't agree, and a federal court came up with one of the more sensible plans around the country—and a vast improvement from what Colorado had before. Virtually the whole Western Slope was placed in one district (the 3d), instead of being split in two. Ditto for most of the eastern plains, which were combined with Front Range towns north of Denver, places with which they have something in common. The new 6th District was placed entirely in the Denver suburbs. Colorado in 1986 elected three Democrats and three Republicans, but all of the Republicans are solid, while two of the Democrats are freshmen elected by narrow margins. They are both politically talented and will try to establish their holds on their districts, but the Republicans may very well counterattack in 1988.

The People: Est. Pop. 1986: 3,267,000; Pop. 1980: 2,889,964, up 13.1% 1980–86 and 30.8% 1970–80; 1.36% of U.S. total, 27th largest. 21% with 1–3 yrs. col., 23% with 4+ yrs. col.; 10.1% below poverty level. Single ancestry: 11% German, 9% English, 4% Irish, 2% Italian, 1% Swedish, French, Dutch, Polish, Scottish, Norwegian. Households (1980): 70% family, 39% with children, 59% married couples; 35.5% housing units rented; median monthly rent: $225; median house value: $64,600. Voting age pop. (1980): 2,081,151; 10% Spanish origin, 3% Black, 1% Asian origin, 1% American Indian. Registered voters (1986): 1,810,998; 599,214 D (33%), 560,942 R (31%), 650,842 unaffiliated (36%), 624 minor parties.

1986 Share of Federal Tax Burden: $10,799,000,000; 1.44% of U.S. total, 23d largest.

1986 Share of Federal Expenditures

	Total		Non-Defense		Defense	
Total Expend	$19,496m	(1.38%)	$7,968m	(1.33%)	$3,528m	(1.53%)
St/Lcl Grants	1,220m	(1.08%)	1,220m	(1.08%)	0m	(0.06%)
Salary/Wages	2,296m	(1.90%)	1,137m	(1.94%)	1,159m	(1.87%)
Pymnts to Indiv	4,068m	(1.12%)	3,594m	(1.04%)	473m	(2.66%)
Procurement	3,555m	(1.73%)	1,662m	(2.99%)	1,893m	(1.26%)
Ressearch/Other	356m	(1.33%)	354m	(1.33%)	2m	(5.41%)

Political Lineup: Governor, Roy R. Romer (D); Lt. Gov., Mike Callihan (D); Secy. of State, Natalie Meyer (R); Atty. Gen., Duane Woodard (R); Treasurer, Gail Schoettler (D). State Senate, 35 (24 R and 11 D); State House of Representatives, 65 (47 R and 18 D). Senators, William L. Armstrong (R) and Timothy E. Wirth (D). Representatives, 6 (3 R and 3 D).

1984 Presidential Vote

Reagan (R)	821,817	(63%)
Mondale (D)	454,975	(35%)

1980 Presidential Vote

Reagan (R)	652,264	(55%)
Carter (D)	368,009	(31%)
Anderson (I)	130,633	(11%)

GOVERNOR

Gov. Roy R. Romer (D)

Elected 1986, term expires Jan. 1991; b. Oct. 31, 1928, Garden City, KS; home, Denver; CO St. U, B.S. 1950, U. of CO, LL.B. 1952; Presbyterian; married (Bea).

Career: CO House of Reps., 1958–62, Asst. Minor. Ldr., 1964–66; CO Senate, 1962–1966; CO Agric. Commissioner, 1975; Chief of Staff, Gov. Richard D. Lamm, 1975–1977, 1982–1983; CO Treasurer, 1977–1986.

Offices: 136 State Capitol, Denver 80203, 303-866-2471.

Election Results

1986 gen.	Roy R. Romer (D)	616,325	(58%)
	Ted Strickland (R)	434,420	(41%)
1986 prim.	Roy R. Romer (D)	101,992	(100%)
1982 gen.	Richard D. Lamm (D)	627,960	(66%)
	John Fuhr (R)	302,740	(32%)

SENATORS

Sen. William L. Armstrong (R)

Elected 1978, seat up 1990; b. Mar. 16, 1937, Fremont, NE; home, Englewood; Tulane U., U. of MN; Lutheran; married (Ellen).

Career: Pres., KEZW-Radio, KPVI-TV; CO House of Reps., 1963–64; CO Senate, 1965–72, Major. Ldr., 1969–72; U.S. House of Reps., 1973–78.

Offices: 528 HSOB 20510, 202-224-5941. Also 311 Steele St., Ste. 103, Denver 80206, 303-398-0831; 228 N. Cascade, Ste. 106, Colorado Springs 80903, 303-634-6071; 722 Thatcher Bldg., 5th and Main, Pueblo 81022, 303-545-9751; and 215 Fed. Bldg., 400 Rood Ave., Grand Junction 81501, 303-245-9553.

Committees: *Banking, Housing, and Urban Affairs* (3d of 9 R). Subcommittees: International Finance and Monetary Policy; Securities (Ranking Member). *Budget* (2d of 11R). *Finance* (9th of 9 R). Subcommittees: Energy and Agricultural Taxation; International Trade; Social Security and Family Policy.

Group Ratings

	ADA	ACLU	COPE	CFA	LCV	ACU	NTU	NSI	COC	CEI
1986	0	7	1	7	17	96	65	100	100	91
1985	0	—	1	7	—	90	69	—	92	—

National Journal Ratings

	1986 LIB — 1986 CONS			1985 LIB — 1985 CONS		
Economic	0%	—	84%	0%	—	86%
Social	0%	—	91%	0%	—	83%
Foreign	0%	—	86%	0%	—	88%

Key Votes

1) Ease Gun Cont	—	5) Grm-Rdmn Def Red	FOR	9) Rehnquist Nom	FOR
2) Immig Reform	AGN	6) Contra Aid	FOR	10) Tax Reform	FOR
3) Lmt Text Imp	AGN	7) SDI Funding	FOR	11) Drug Death Pen	AGN
4) Aid Tobac Ind	FOR	8) Lmt PAC Contrib	AGN	12) S Africa Sanc	AGN

Election Results

1984 general	William L. Armstrong (R)	833,821	(64%)	($3,098,129
	Nancy Dick (D)	449,327	(35%)	($840,595
1984 primary	William L. Armstrong (R)	105,870	(100%)	
1978 general	William L. Armstrong (R)	480,596	(59%)	($1,081,944
	Floyd K. Haskell (D)	330,247	(40%)	($664,249

Campaign Contributions and Expenditures

1979-84		Direct Cont. 1979-84		PACS Breakdown 1979-84			
Receipts	$3,169,764	Indiv.	$2,134,536	Corp.	$454,593	T/M/H	$226,45
Expend.	$3,098,129	Party	$15,418	Labor	$9,750	Agr.	$4,70
Unspent	$173,373	PACS	$837,784	Ideo.	$98,070	CWOS	$7,85
		Cand.	$10,000				

Sen. Timothy E. Wirth (D)

Elected 1986, seat up 1992; b. Sept. 22, 1939, Santa Fe, NM; home, Boulder; Harvard U., A.B. 1961, M. Ed. 1964, Stanford U. Ph.D. 1973; Episcopalian; married (Wren).

Career: White House Fellow, U.S. Dept. of HEW, Spec. Asst. to Secy., 1967–68; Dpty. Asst. Secy. of Educ., HEW 1969–70; Businessman, 1970–74; U.S. House of Reps., 1974–86.

Offices: 380 RSOB 20510, 202-224-5852. Also 1129 Pennsylvania St., Denver 80203, 303-866-1900.

Committees: *Armed Services* (10th of 11 D). Subcmtee.: Conventional Forces and Alliance Defense; Defense Ind. and Tech. Readiness, Sustainability and Support. *Banking, Housing and Urban Affairs* (11th of 11 D). *Budget* (10th of 13 D). *Energy and Natural Resources* (8th of 10 D). Subcmtee.: Energy Research and Devel.; Mineral Resources Devel. and Production; Public Lands, Natl. Parks and Forests; Water and Power.

Group Ratings (as Member of the House of Representatives)

	ADA	ACLU	COPE	CFA	LCV	ACU	NTU	NSI	COC	CEI
1986	75	76	88	67	80	0	41	10	54	34
1985	70	—	76	50	—	10	39	—	38	—

National Journal Ratings (as Member of U.S. House of Representatives)

	1986 LIB — 1986 CONS		1985 LIB — 1985 CONS	
Economic	60% —	40%	65% —	33%
Social	77% —	23%	79% —	19%
Foreign	67% —	30%	80% —	17%

Key Votes (as Member of U.S. House of Representatives)

1) Lmt Cln Water Act	AGN	5) Retain Gun Cont	FOR	9) Aid Angola Reb	AGN
2) Rpl Tobac Sub	FOR	6) Contra Aid	AGN	10) Tax Reform	FOR
3) Grm-Rdmn Def Red	FOR	7) Lmt Text Imp	AGN	11) S Africa Sanc	FOR
4) Ban Polygraph	FOR	8) Lmt SDI	FOR	12) Immig Reform	AGN

Election Results

1986 general	Timothy E. Wirth (D).	529,449	(50%)	($3,787,202)
	Ken Kramer (R)	512,994	(48%)	($3,785,577)
1986 primary	Timothy E. Wirth (D).	97,044	(100%)	
1980 general	Gary W. Hart (D)	590,501	(50%)	($1,142,304)
	Mary Estill Buchanan (R)	571,295	(49%)	($1,099,945)

Campaign Contributions and Expenditures

1985-86		Direct Cont. 1985-86		PACS Breakdown 1985-86			
Receipts	$3,819,308	Indiv.	$2,613,318	Corp.	$180,540	T/M/H	$130,346
Expend.	$3,787,202	Party	$17,500	Labor	$262,758	Agr.	$1,950
Unspent	$32,106	PACS	$842,038	Ideo.	$245,144	CWOS	$21,300
		Cand.	$319,946				

FIRST DISTRICT

The city of Denver is the center, the focus, of the entire Rocky Mountain region. The old gold dome on the state capitol, the gleaming new skyscrapers pushing up—these are the tangible symbols of Denver's riches, first from mining, more recently from oil. Surrounded by hundreds of miles of mountains on one side and High Plains on the other, Denver has become one of the nation's major metropolises. In the process, development has spread far beyond its original city limits and the city itself; the 1st Congressional District, which is almost precisely coterminous, contains less than one-third of the metropolitan area's 1.6 million people.

Still, it remains clearly the center —and a center wondering about the future. For perhaps half the office space in the newest high rises is going unrented; hotels are empty and even the venerable Brown Palace was threatening in 1986 to close down; multimillionaire Marvin Davis's plan to revitalize the stockyards was still a plan and the city was struggling to build a convention center (to compete with Kansas City) down by the usually dry South Platte River. Residential Denver still looks like a comfortable, orderly suburb. But the aging yuppies with all the right hiking and running shoes and the Mexican-American families may be wondering if their children are going to be able to rise in the world. Not many miles away on the freeway, you can see the city suddenly end and the high plains or the mountains begin where the water lines abruptly run out: Denverites, more than most Americans, can see precisely the difference between the natural environment and civilization. But this is only on clear days; in the 1980s Denver has had the nastiest and filthiest air of any major American city except Los Angeles, with an angry brown cloud hanging over the city most of the time and carbon monoxide levels almost three times the maximum allowed by the Clean Air Act.

That same environment is what has attracted so many young people to the Denver area—producing great population growth and a quiet transformation of the central city. Denver increasingly is a city of the rich and poor, or at least the comfortable and the struggling; of large families of migrants and of young singles and older empty-nesters. Only one in four households here has children, and less than half include a married couple—one of the lowest figures in America. Demographically, Denver has come to look a little like San Francisco.

In the 1950s and 1960s Denver was more Democratic than Colorado because it had more union members and low income voters. Now it is more Democratic because it has more singles. Denver from 1950 to 1970 elected a Trumanish Democrat to Congress. Since 1972, Denver has elected a prime representative of Colorado's baby boom generation liberal movement, and one of the Congress's leading feminists, Representative Patricia Schroeder. She was an oddity when she was first elected in 1972: not only a woman and a feminist, but an opponent of the Vietnam war who got herself, over the objection of Chairman Edward Hébert, a seat on the House Armed Services Committee.

Schroeder has become, after a dozen years in Washington, a national political figure. She is a leading sponsor of legislation sought by feminist groups; in 1987 she was pushing a bill to require employers to give child-care leave to employees who are parents. She has been a co-chairman—and an unusually visible one—of Gary Hart's 1984 and 1988 presidential campaigns. Her flip demeanor puts some people off, but behind it is a politician with a wide range of knowledge and an impressive command of argument. And also one with wit: it was Schroeder who described Ronald Reagan as "the Teflon president," because criticisms simply did not stick to him, and it was Schroeder who said that George Bush wouldn't choose a female running mate because "Then people would say, 'We need a man on the ticket.'" But there is also a certain Teflon-like and aggressive quality to Schroeder and the cultural niche in America she represents, an imperviousness to contrary arguments and a self-assurance that only uninformed or ill-intentioned people could disagree with their feminist, dovish views. The thought that one could reasonably believe that tradition has things to teach us and that there are external threats which may not be amenable to negotiation does not seem to cross their minds. Patricia Schroeder seems to have no more self-doubt—maybe less—than the elderly hawks she serves with on the Armed Services Committee.

Schroeder's main committee assignment remains Armed Services, and she is perhaps not so unlikely a member as some think. Her father was an aviation insurance adjuster, and she herself is a pilot; she has interested herself in the situation of women in the military and in the wives of servicemen, and has done much useful work for them. On more deadly issues, she is an opponent of most controversial weapons systems, to get chemical weaponry out of the Rocky Mountain Arsenal near Denver.

Such opposition is seldom successful on the committee, most of whose members believe in high defense spending and tend to trust the Pentagon's recommendations. But Schroeder's views have, in the middle 1970s and perhaps again in the middle 1980s, found support on the floor. Schroeder is not one of the weightiest of Pentagon opponents when it comes to swaying opinion on the floor, but she is well enough prepared not to be disregarded either. She also serves on the Judiciary Committee, where she is a solid vote against an anti-abortion constitutional amendment and for the Equal Rights Amendment. And she chairs the Civil Service Subcommittee of Post Office and Civil Service, in which capacity she is likely to be a champion of federal workers. Denver is one of the federal government's major regional centers, and has a large number of well-organized federal employees.

The People: Pop. 1980: 481,672, dn. 5.5% 1970–80. Households (1980): 55% family, 26% with children, 42% married couples; 50.7% housing units rented; median monthly rent: $214; median house value: $63,600. Voting age pop. (1980): 373,579; 15% Spanish origin, 11% Black, 1% Asian origin, 1% American Indian.

1984 Presidential Vote: Mondale (D) 104,299   (53%)
                                Reagan (R) 94,321   (47%)

Rep. Patricia Schroeder (D)

Elected 1972; b. July 30, 1940, Portland, OR; home, Denver; U. of MN, B.A. 1961, Harvard U., J.D. 1964; United Church of Christ; married (James).

Career: Field Atty., Natl. Labor Relations Bd., 1964–66; Practicing atty.; Lecturer, Law instructor, Commun. Col. of Denver, 1969–70, U. of Denver, Denver Ctr., 1969, Regis Col., 1970–72; Hearing officer, CO Dept. of Personnel, 1971–72; Legal Counsel, CO Planned Parenthood.

Offices: 2410 RHOB 20515, 202-225-4431. Also Denver Fed. Bldg., 1767 High St., Denver 80218, 303-398-0970.

Committees: *Armed Services* (9th of 31 D). Subcommittees: Military Personnel and Compensation; Research and Development. *Judiciary* (9th of 21 D). Subcommittees: Civil and Constitutional Rights; Courts, Civil Liberties, and the Administration of Justice. *Post Office and Civil Service* (3d of 14 D). Subcommittee: Civil Service (Chairman). *Select Committee on Children, Youth and Families* (3d of 18 D). Task Force: Economic Security (Chairman).

Group Ratings

	ADA	ACLU	COPE	CFA	LCV	ACU	NTU	NSI	COC	CEI
1986	95	85	74	92	100	5	47	10	29	36
1985	80	—	74	100	—	19	56	—	55	—

National Journal Ratings

	1986 LIB — 1986 CONS		1985 LIB — 1985 CONS	
Economic	72%	— 27%	57%	— 41%
Social	69%	— 28%	81%	— 15%
Foreign	67%	— 30%	85%	— 8%

Key Votes

1) Lmt Cln Water Act	AGN	5) Retain Gun Cont	FOR	9) Aid Angola Reb	AGN
2) Rpl Tobac Sub	FOR	6) Contra Aid	AGN	10) Tax Reform	AGN
3) Grm-Rdmn Def Red	AGN	7) Lmt Text Imp	FOR	11) S Africa Sanc	FOR
4) Ban Polygraph	FOR	8) Limit SDI	FOR	12) Immig Reform	AGN

Election Results

1986 general	Patricia Schroeder (D)	106,113	(68%)	($156,237)
	Joy Wood (R)	49,095	(32%)	($13,251)
1986 primary	Patricia Schroeder (D)	17,311	(100%)	
1984 general	Patricia Schroeder (D)	126,348	(62%)	($237,488)
	Mary Downs (R)...................	73,993	(36%)	($79,725)

Campaign Contributions and Expenditures

1985-86		Direct Cont. 1985-86		PACS Breakdown 1985-86			
Receipts	$243,383	Indiv.	$113,229	Corp.	$16,450	T/M/H	$29,636
Expend.	$156,237	Party	$1,362	Labor	$39,050	Agr.	$250
Unspent	$203,758	PACS	$101,102	Ideo.	$14,966	CWOS	$750

SECOND DISTRICT

From the flats around the mostly dry South Platte River, up in a breathtakingly short 10 miles to the 12,000-plus foot towering crags of the Rockies, is the 2d Congressional District of Colorado. This is one of two districts consisting entirely of Denver's suburbs, which also make up important parts of still two more districts. Like most American suburban districts, it is a mixture of communities. The most distinctive is Boulder, 25 miles northwest of downtown Denver, the home of the University of Colorado perched literally at the edge of the Front Range. Twenty years ago this was an affluent Republican town; then students got the vote in 1972 and it turned sharply left; by the early 1980s the students had grown more conservative, but the now grown-up Vietnam era generation—graduate students, young homeowners with backpacking gear spilling out of their closets—with their concern for the environment if not their sympathy with the economic underdogs intact, are still an important political force there. They are behind, for example, the city's design plan that discourages stucco surfaces and Astroturf, drive-in windows, New Orleans railings, and Swiss chalets.

East of Boulder, down on the flats running north from Denver along Interstate 25 and the river, are working class suburbs like Westminster, Thornton, and Northglenn, with increasing numbers of Mexican-Americans, not isolated in small barrios but moving, mostly unnoticed, into various middle-class neighborhoods in upwardly mobile fashion, like similar immigrant groups before them. West, toward the mountains, is the higher income suburb of Arvada, and in the mountains themselves, near the remnants of what were once mining towns, are subdivisions of contemporary homes amid the rocks and firs.

In national elections this 2d District is heavily Republican; even Boulder went for Ronald Reagan over Walter Mondale. In Colorado elections, it is a swing district, willing to vote for Dick Lamm and Roy Romer for Governor, for example, or for native son Tim Wirth for Senator in 1986. Wirth was congressman for 12 years here, beating an incumbent Republican in 1974, holding on by close margins in 1976, 1978, and 1984, and always needing to raise lots of money and to campaign intensively. Those demands, on top of his major legislative duties, seem to have prompted him to run for Gary Hart's Senate seat.

That left the House seat as one of the Republicans' major targets for 1986. National issues seemed to be with them and their candidate, Mike Norton, had given Wirth serious competition in 1984. But victory went not to Norton but to former Wirth aide David Skaggs. Norton campaigned long and hard, but Skaggs, Wirth's administrative assistant in his first term and a Colorado legislator since 1980, outmanuevered him, calling for a positive campaign in August and then attacking Norton in October for taking positions in his campaign different from those he had advocated as a lobbyist. A Vietnam veteran, Skaggs emphasized the need for government support for education and scientific research—themes that resonated in Boulder and the Denver suburbs. He and Norton both spent over $450,000; Skaggs, like so many Democrats, raised considerably more PAC money, and was also the beneficiary of $108,000 of independent advertising from the American Medical Association's PAC.

Skaggs is part of the same generation of Democratic migrants who came to Colorado about 20 years ago and began dominating its politics in the 1970s. In the manner of 19th century California Gold Rush—where the same generation of migrants held most major offices for 40 years, from 1850 when they were in their 30s to the 1890s when they were in their 70s—this pre-Baby Boom generation of politicians may monopolize at least the Democrats's share of offices for most of their adult lives. This district cannot be considered safe for a national Democrat. But the skill with which Skaggs obtained the seat, and the example Wirth set in holding it, give the incumbent a good chance to stay in the House as long as his predecessor.

The People: Pop. 1980: 481,617, up 50.4% 1970–80. Households (1980): 73% family, 44% with children, 62% married couples; 31.2% housing units rented; median monthly rent: $266; median house value: $70,500. Voting age pop. (1980): 339,617; 7% Spanish origin, 1% Asian origin, 1% Black.

1984 Presidential Vote: Reagan (R) 128,573   (61%)
Mondale (D) 82,590   (39%)

Rep. David E. Skaggs (D)

Elected 1986; b. Feb. 22, 1943, Cincinnati, OH; home, Boulder; Wesleyan U., B.A. 1964, M. Ed. 1964, Yale U., L.L.B. 1967; Congregationalist; married (Laura).

Career: Marine Corps, 1968–71; CO House of Reps., 1980–86, Dem. Minor. Ldr. 1982–85; A.A. to Rep. Timothy E. Wirth, 1975–77, Campaign Dir., 1976; Practicing Attorney, 1977–86.

Offices: 1723 LHOB 20515, 202-225-2161. Also 9101 Harlan, Ste. 130, Westminster 80030, 303-650-7886.

Committees: *Public Works and Transportation* (30th of 32 D). Subcommittees: Aviation; Public Buildings and Grounds; Water Resources. *Science, Space and Technology* (27 of 27 D). Subcommittees: Space, Science and Applications; Science, Research and Technology. *Select Committee on Children, Youth and Families* (18th of 18 D). Task Force: Prevention Strategies.

Group Ratings and Key Votes: Newly Elected

Election Results

1986 general	David E. Skaggs (D)	91,223	(51%)	($519,307)
	Michael J. (Mike) Norton (R)	86,032	(49%)	($491,329)
1986 primary	David E. Skaggs (D)	10,681	(58%)	
	Polly Baca (D)	7,665	(42%)	
1984 general	Timothy E. Wirth (D)	118,580	(53%)	($587,725)
	Michael J. (Mike) Norton (R)	101,488	(46%)	($149,914)

Campaign Contributions and Expenditures

1985-86		Direct Cont. 1985-86		PACS Breakdown 1985-86			
Receipts	$522,375	Indiv.	$235,902	Corp.	$5,430	T/M/H	$45,317
Expend.	$519,307	Party	$5,579	Labor	$115,400	Agr.	$0
Unspent	$3,068	PACS	$253,644	Ideo.	$84,497	CWOS	$3,000
		Cand.	$22,750				

THIRD DISTRICT

The Western Slope is the oldest and newest part of Colorado. The mountains west of the Front Range—Coloradans call the whole region the Western Slope—are what originally attracted settlers here. Mountain men and trappers were the first, leaving little trace but the lore of their trails. Then came the miners, who tracked gold and silver and lead ores and built Victorian towns with opera houses and gingerbread storefronts in valleys and defiles scarcely accessible to the outside world. Later came more prosaic prospectors, looking for uranium in the 1950s and oil shale in the 1960s and 1970s. For the last 20 years, the new settlers have clustered in condominium villages of which Aspen and Vail are the prototypes.

All of which leaves the Western Slope politically as one of the most variegated of regions. Aspen and Telluride, with its countercultural substratum and Victorian houses, is liberal and Democratic; Vail and Crested Butte, with contemporary-styled condominiums and affluent empty-nesters like the Gerald Fords, are conservative and Republican. The rough-handed mining area around Grand Junction, where piles of tailings still crackle with radioactivity, is hostile to environmentalists, as is the oil shale area—once booming and now gone bust—up around the Utah and Wyoming borders. Cattle-raising counties are now switching to the care and feeding of tourists, with unclear partisan consequences. The small Hispanic and Indian communities in the south vote heavily, when they vote at all, for the Democrats.

The Western Slope forms more than half of Colorado's 3d Congressional District; the other part is around the small industrial city of Pueblo. There, on the banks of the Arkansas River, is one of the few major steel factories west of the Mississippi, first built in the years before World War I when the Rockefellers were big investors in Colorado; it is still operating today, but Pueblo is prey to many of the problems of steel towns back east, though here in the west it has weathered them better. Pueblo is heavily Democratic, and so are the Hispanic counties just to the south. Hispanic, not Mexican-American: the Spanish-speaking people here, like those in northern New Mexico, have been living here for generations.

The 3d District has been the scene of vigorous contests going back to the 1970s, and often between colorful candidates; currently the Democrats hold the seat. They benefited from the personal financial problems of Mike Strang, Republican incumbent elected in 1984; the onetime captain of the Princeton polo team and lifelong Colorado ranch resident was two years and $106,000 delinquent on a loan from the Farmers Home Administration. But Strang's white Stetson and conservative record were enough to enable him to carry the Western Slope. Democrat Ben Nighthorse Campbell was even more noteworthy: half Cheyenne Indian, an Olympic gold medalist in judo, a state legislator who used to wear his hair in a pony tail. He attacked Strang's record more on economic than environmental issues. That was shrewd strategy, for the environmentalist position remains unpopular in the uranium and oil shale pockets of the Western Slopes, and is not a particularly big vote-winner in blue collar Pueblo. Campbell, though outspent, raised as much PAC money as Strang. He ran close to Strang in the Western Slope and won 63% in Pueblo County, enough to win.

Will this be a seriously contested seat again in 1988, as it has been in every election since 1976? Quite possibly. Campbell will have his opportunity to use the powers of incumbency to make the district safe. But as Strang showed, they are not always enough.

The People: Pop. 1980: 481,854, up 29.5% 1970–80. Households (1980): 72% family, 40% with children, 62% married couples; 30.5% housing units rented; median monthly rent: $198; median house value: $48,900. Voting age pop. (1980): 345,175; 15% Spanish origin, 1% American Indian, 1% Black.

1984 Presidential Vote:

Reagan (R)	131,951	(63%)
Mondale (D)	76,642	(37%)

Rep. Ben Nighthorse Campbell (D)

Elected 1986; b. April 13, 1933, Auburn, CA; home, Ignacio; San Jose St. U., B.A. 1958, Meisi U., Japan; no religious affiliation; married (Linda).

Career: Air Force, 1952–54; CO House of Reps., 1982–86; Horse Breeder and Trainer, Jewelry Manufacturer.

Offices: 1724 LHOB 20515, 303-225-4761. Also 720 N. Main St., Ste. 400, Pueblo 81003, 303-543-9621; 115 N. 5th St., Ste. 520, Grand Junction 81501, 303-242-2400; and 835 2d Ave., Ste. 105, Durango 81301, 303-247-9300.

Committees: *Agriculture* (25th of 26 D). Subcommittees: Forests, Family Farms and Energy; Livestock, Dairy and Poultry. *Interior and Insular Affairs* (25th of 26 D). Subcommittees: Mining and Natural Resources; Water and Power Resources. *Small Business* (24th of 27 D). Subcommittees: Exports, Tourism and Special Problems.

Group Ratings and Key Votes: Newly Elected

Election Results

1986 general	Ben Nighthorse Campbell (D)	95,353	(52%)	($396,799)
	Michael L. Strang (R)	88,508	(48%)	($566,439)
1986 primary	Ben Nighthorse Campbell (D)	29,422	(100%)	
1984 general	Michael L. Strang (R)	122,669	(57%)	($455,837)
	W Mitchell (D)	90,063	(42%)	($508,623)

Campaign Contributions and Expenditures

1985-86		Direct Cont. 1985-86		PACS Breakdown 1985-86			
Receipts	$407,861	Indiv.	$142,060	Corp.	$8,500	T/M/H	$21,400
Expend.	$396,799	Party	$999	Labor	$140,150	Agr.	$550
Unspent	$11,062	PACS	$204,153	Ideo.	$31,553	CWOS	$2,000
		Cand.	$36,429				

FOURTH DISTRICT

Eastern Colorado is the dusty, brown plains and gently rolling plateaus that seem flat but are really sloping downward imperceptibly toward the Mississippi River. This is the farthest west extension of America's agricultural plains, and despite its fallow appearance it is actually rich land. But its richness is precarious. Rainfall is scarce, the rivers—even the Arkansas River, the biggest of the lot—most of the year are just a trickle, and in many places groundwater is scarce: it's hard to find enough water to irrigate wheatlands or swab out a feedlot. With enough water the land will produce excellent yields of wheat, and this is one of the foremost beef cattle regions of the country. But wheat exports have fallen far below the levels of the late 1970s, and beef prices have been notoriously volatile and demand has fallen since the middle 1970s. It is not too surprising, then, that eastern Colorado has been on occasion the spawning grounds of national farm rebellions, like the American Agricultural Movement that sent farmers and their tractors in to Washington, D.C., in the late 1970s—years that, ironically, a great many farmers look back on now as a kind of golden age.

The 4th Congressional District of Colorado contains almost all of the state's eastern plains, plus the medium-sized towns of Greeley, Fort Collins, and Loveland near the Front Range of the Rockies and several of Denver's northern suburbs as well. By heritage and usually by inclination, this is Republican territory. The major cities here, Greeley and Fort Collins, have universities, but they are not so liberal culturally or politically as Boulder; in most years, in most elections they, like the High Plains, vote Republican. So do the string of towns along Interstate 25 running south from Fort Collins to Denver. The only Democratic part of the 4th is its small segment of the Denver metropolitan area, the working-class suburb of Commerce City and once completely agricultural Brighton, both with large Mexican-American populations.

The congressman from the 4th is a Republican with deep roots in Colorado. Hank Brown was born in Denver, went to college in Boulder, served in Vietnam, and went to work for Ken Monfort, the nation's biggest cattle feedlot operator and a maverick Democrat who ran for the Senate and nearly won the Democratic nomination in 1968. Brown himself was active in Republican politics, and served in the legislature in the 1970s; he was well enough established to be an easy winner in 1980 when the incumbent retired; he didn't even have any competition in the Republican primary.

In Congress Brown has been a successful Republican even though, on some important issues, he has been out of line with Republican trends in the 1980s. He was elected president of the Republican freshmen elected in 1980—the largest Republican freshman group since 1966—even though many of them were sympathetic to the New Right and he is pro-choice on abortion and liberal on some foreign policy issues. On economics he tends to oppose government intervention and prefers the operation of the free market—though he has been ready to retaliate in kind against countries that bar U.S. beef. On the Interior Committee, he was not as development-minded as some Republicans, and worked on difficult issues like the disposal of nuclear waste.

Brown has been disappointed, as when his fellow Republicans passed over him for a seat on Ways and Means after the 1984 election; he got a seat on Budget instead. For a time in 1985 he toyed with the idea of running for governor, but soon decided not to make the race. But after the 1986 election he won a Ways and Means seat easily; there was a widespread feeling he'd been unjustly passed over. In 1987 he was suddenly ranking Republican on the subcommittee handling welfare reform; he opposes Democrat Harold Ford's bill, criticizing it for concentrating on raising benefits in low-benefit states, but optimistic nonetheless that a bill more to his liking could be passed.

Brown has been reelected easily since 1980, running even or better in Democratic areas and carrying the rest of the district easily.

The People: Pop. 1980: 481,512, up 29.6% 1970–80. Households (1980): 73% family, 41% with children, 64% married couples; 32.9% housing units rented; median monthly rent: $191; median house value: $54,000. Voting age pop. (1980): 342,745; 11% Spanish origin, 1% Asian origin.

1984 Presidential Vote:

Reagan (R)	139,048	(68%)
Mondale (D)	64,939	(32%)

Rep. Hank Brown (R)

Elected 1980; b. Feb. 12, 1940, Denver; home, Greeley; U. of CO, B.S. 1961, J.D. 1969; United Church of Christ; married (Nan).

Career: Navy, Vietnam; Accountant, 1968–69; Vice Pres., Monfort of CO, Inc., 1969–80; CO Senate, 1972–76, Asst. Major. Ldr., 1974–76; Greeley City Planning Comm., 1979.

Offices: 1424 LHOB 20515, 202-225-4676. Also 1015 37th Ave. Ct., Ste. 101A, Greeley 80634, 303-352-4112; 203 Fed. Bldg., Ft. Collins 80521, 303-493-9132; 230 Main St., Rm. 9, Ft. Morgan 80701, 303-867-8909; and 243 P.O. Bldg., La Junta 81050, 303-384-7370.

Committees: *Ways and Means* (12th of 13 R). Subcommittees: Public Assistance (Ranking Member); Select Revenue Measures.

Group Ratings

	ADA	ACLU	COPE	CFA	LCV	ACU	NTU	NSI	COC	CEI
1986	10	15	7	0	32	77	79	80	94	78
1985	30	—	7	17	—	67	72	—	82	—

National Journal Ratings

	1986 LIB	—	1986 CONS		1985 LIB	—	1985 CONS
Economic	0%	—	94%		9%	—	88%
Social	0%	—	89%		47%	—	52%
Foreign	39%	—	60%		37%	—	60%

Key Votes

1) Lmt Cln Water Act	FOR	5) Retain Gun Cont	AGN	9) Aid Angola Reb	FOR
2) Rpl Tobac Sub	FOR	6) Contra Aid	FOR	10) Tax Reform	FOR
3) Grm-Rdmn Def Red	FOR	7) Lmt Text Imp	AGN	11) S Africa Sanc	FOR
4) Ban Polygraph	AGN	8) Limit SDI	FOR	12) Immig Reform	AGN

Election Results

1986 general	Hank Brown (R)	117,089	(70%)	($212,172)
	David Sprague (D)	50,672	(30%)	($22,273)
1986 primary	Hank Brown (R)	27,510	(100%)	
1984 general	Hank Brown (R)	146,469	(71%)	($139,053)
	Mary Fagan Bates (D)	56,462	(27%)	($60,946)

Campaign Contributions and Expenditures

1985-86		Direct Cont. 1985-86		PACS Breakdown 1985-86			
Receipts	$184,809	Indiv.	$79,098	Corp.	$33,250	T/M/H	$21,631
Expend.	$212,172	Party	$2,318	Labor	$650	Agr.	$500
Unspent	$109,720	PACS	$59,781	Ideo.	$3,750	CWOS	$0
		Cand.	$19,200				

FIFTH DISTRICT

Colorado Springs is the second largest city in Colorado, standing almost precisely at the base of Pike's Peak. Far smaller than Denver, and once just a small town, it is now the center of a metropolitan area of more than 300,000 people. It is known as a tourist attraction: people come to drive the Pike's Peak road, to see the Garden of the Gods, to stay at the Broadmoor, one of America's grand old resort hotels. But the real economic mainstay of Colorado Springs for many years has been the military. Colorado Springs has been the home for years of the Army's Fort Carson, and just to the north is the Air Force Academy, its striking modern buildings silhouetted against the mountains. Not far away is Falcon Air Force Base, the central planning site for Ronald Reagan's Strategic Defense Initiative, and Cheyenne Mountain, where NORAD in its underground headquarters patrols the skies for invading planes or missiles. In its surrealistic setting, on the high plains, beneath the craggy Rockies, with its lack of regional accent and identifiable ethnicity, with its local residents drawn from Midwestern stock and its service families living in neighborhoods filled with military personnel who have spent their lives moving from base to base, but mixing always with similar and sometimes with the same people, Colorado Springs is a quintessentially American community. Politically it tends to favor the party long favored by people who feel they are quintessentially American, even if numerically they have often not been the majority, the Republicans.

Colorado Springs is the heart and geographical center of Colorado's 5th Congressional District. It reaches north to the Denver metropolitan area and includes some of its suburbs: Golden, west of the city, an old mining town with a mining school and the Coors brewery, and some of the new suburbs at the southern edge of settlement, where the water lines have just been laid in and the pavement and sidewalks laid out off what was until recently an empty, dusty plain. The 5th District also proceeds east across the High Plains to the gas station junction of Limon and west into the Rockies to the old mining town of Leadville.

The 5th District, since it was created after the 1970 Census, has always elected a conservative Republican. One, Bill Armstrong, was elected to the Senate in 1978; another, Ken Kramer, nearly joined him in 1986. The current incumbent seems less ideological and more deeply based in his community than either of his predecessors. He is Joel Hefley, a native of Oklahoma who made his way from the Panhandle of Texas to Colorado Springs in 1965; he is older than either Armstrong or Kramer. For 20 years Hefley was a professional civic father, executive director of the Community Planning and Research Council in Colorado Springs. The crucial contest in the 1986 House race was the Republican primary, and there Hefley's heavy home town support in Colorado Springs and surrounding El Paso County was enough to enable him to overcome the bid of a rich suburban Denver businessman. The general election was anticlimactic.

In the House Hefley can be counted on to champion, as Kramer did, the Strategic Defense Initiative, important parts of which are produced or would be deployed in Colorado Springs, and other defense spending. But he is unlikely to bring to that task the fervor or occasional imprudence Kramer did.

The People: Pop. 1980: 481,627, up 60.6% 1970–80. Households (1980): 76% family, 46% with children, 66% married couples; 32.2% housing units rented; median monthly rent: $209; median house value: $66,100. Voting age pop. (1980): 335,156; 6% Spanish origin, 4% Black, 1% Asian origin.

1984 Presidential Vote:	Reagan (R)	154,780	(75%)
	Mondale (D)	50,465	(25%)

Rep. Joel Hefley (R)

Elected 1986; b. April 18, 1935, Ardmore, OK; home, Colorado Springs; OK Baptist U., B.A. 1957, OK St. U., M.S. 1962; Presbyterian; married (Lynn).

Career: CO House of Reps., 1977–78; CO Senate, 1979–86; Exec. Dir., Community Planning and Research Cncl., 1966–86.

Offices: 508 CHOB 20515, 202-225-4422. Also 2190A Vickers Dr., Colorado Springs 80907, 303-531-5555.

Committees: *Small Business* (15th of 17 R). Subcommittees: Procurement, Innovation and Minority Enterprise Development; SBA and the General Economy. *Science, Space and Technology* (17th of 18 R). Subcommittees: Natural Resources, Agriculture Research and Environment; Space Science and Applications.

Group Ratings and Key Votes: Newly Elected

Election Results

1986 general	Joel Hefley (R)	121,153	(70%)	($283,404)
	Bill Story (D)	52,488	(30%)	($51,253)
1986 primary	Joel Hefley (R)	24,160	(57%)	
	Hal Krause (R)	17,907	(43%)	
1984 general	Ken Kramer (R)	163,654	(79%)	($350,229)
	William Geffen (D)	44,588	(21%)	($3,281)

Campaign Contributions and Expenditures

1985–86		Direct Cont. 1985–86		PACS Breakdown 1985–86			
Receipts	$298,717	Indiv.	$163,430	Corp.	$57,822	T/M/H	$39,370
Expend.	$283,404	Party	$3,063	Labor	$1,500	Agr.	$1,350
Unspent	$15,282	PACS	$111,619	Ideo.	$10,077	CWOS	$1,500
		Cand.	$6,000				

SIXTH DISTRICT

The 6th Congressional District of Colorado was created anew from the Denver suburbs after the 1980 Census: this was the political dividend the state got from its rapidly growing population, and it came at an appropriate place and in an appropriate political form. The 6th District forms a kind of U around the city of Denver. In the south, at the bottom of the U, are Englewood and Littleton, directly south of downtown Denver. These were the city's main high-income suburbs in the 1940s and 1950s; today they are older, still pleasant but no longer the place where you expect to find Denver's elite. Farther to the south and east are newer suburbs and subdivisions, with names like Columbine Valley, Dream House Acres, and Cherry Knolls. West of Denver are Lakewood and Wheat Ridge, creations of the 1960s, high income but for the most part not elite suburbs with winding streets and, stuck incongruously on a highway in Lakewood, the gigantic

Denver Federal Center. East of Denver, just beyond Stapleton Airport and Lowry Air Force Base, is Aurora. Bisected by the garish signs of the East Colfax strip, Aurora is the creation of the 1960s and 1970s. On the socioeconomic scale it does not rank as high as, say, Lakewood or Englewood; but in its voting habits it is comfortably Republican.

In fact, all of the 6th District is comfortably Republican in most elections. These are regions of upward mobility, places people usually not from Denver have worked their way up to. Their occupations tend to be technical or managerial, their moral values and family patterns traditional; they may pride themselves on their concern for the environment, but they also respect the need for economic growth and scientific innovation—both of which they think environmentalists and Democrats are too inclined to take for granted. The voters' experience has persuaded them that orderliness and predictability are important virtues, all the more so in a new environment where neither they nor anyone else has deep roots. The politics of Reagan Republicanism—disciplining domestic spending, honoring traditional family patterns—seems to provide some of this orderliness, and voters here seem to accept it.

In its brief history the 6th District has elected two men to Congress. The first, astronaut Jack Swigert, showed courage both when he brought a disabled Apollo capsule back to earth and when, after a diagnosis of cancer, he campaigned with only the most minor interruptions for chemotherapy; he died after winning the 1982 election but before he could take office. The winner of the March 1983 special election was Dan Schaefer, a public relations consultant who had served six years in the legislature and was a Republican leader in the Senate. In the House he became, for a moment, number 435 out of 435 in seniority, and got assigned to the Government Operations and Small Business Committees. After the 1984 elections, he moved to a much more coveted post, a seat on the Energy and Commerce Committee. On foreign and cultural issues, he had as solid a conservative record as anyone in the Colorado delegation; on economics, this son of a blue collar worker was occasionally a bit more liberal.

A solidly conservative Republican, Schaefer has gotten along well on his side of the House and in the 6th District, and he did not even have a Democratic opponent in 1984.

The People: Pop. 1980: 481,682, up 43.2% 1970–80. Households (1980): 73% family, 41% with children, 62% married couples; 32.3% housing units rented; median monthly rent: $261; median house value: $73,200. Voting age pop. (1980): 344,879; 4% Spanish origin, 2% Black, 1% Asian origin.

1984 Presidential Vote:

Reagan (R)	148,667	(69%)
Mondale (D)	65,629	(31%)

Rep. Dan Schaefer (R)

Elected Mar. 29, 1983; b. Jan. 25, 1936, Gutenberg, IA; home, Lakewood; Niagara U., B.A. 1961, Potsdam U.; Roman Catholic; married (Mary).

Career: USMC, 1955–57; Educator, 1961–67; Public Affairs Consultant, 1967–83; CO House of Reps., 1977–78; CO Senate, 1979–83.

Offices: 1317 LHOB 20515, 202-225-7882. Also 3615 S. Huron St., Ste. 101, Englewood 80110, 303-762-8890.

Committees: *Energy and Commerce* (15th of 17 R). Subcommittees: Energy and Power; Oversight and Investigations; Transportation, Tourism and Hazardous Materials.

Group Ratings

	ADA	ACLU	COPE	CFA	LCV	ACU	NTU	NSI	COC	CEI
1986	0	5	11	17	16	95	61	89	88	66
1985	0	—	9	8	—	80	83	—	91	—

National Journal Ratings

	1986 LIB	—	1986 CONS	1985 LIB	—	1985 CONS
Economic	19%	—	79%	21%	—	78%
Social	15%	—	84%	0%	—	76%
Foreign	27%	—	70%	0%	—	76%

Key Votes

1) Lmt Cln Water Act	AGN	5) Retain Gun Cont	AGN	9) Aid Angola Reb	FOR
2) Rpl Tobac Sub	FOR	6) Contra Aid	FOR	10) Tax Reform	AGN
3) Grm-Rdmn Def Red	FOR	7) Lmt Text Imp	AGN	11) S Africa Sanc	AGN
4) Ban Polygraph	AGN	8) Limit SDI	AGN	12) Immig Reform	FOR

Election Results

1986 general	Dan Schaefer (R)	104,359	(65%)	($125,435)
	Chuck Norris (D)	53,834	(34%)	
1986 primary	Dan Schaefer (R)	22,192	(100%)	
1984 general	Dan Schaefer (R)	171,427	(89%)	($458,853)*
	John Heckman (D)	20,333	(11%)	($1,000)

Campaign Contributions and Expenditures

1985-86		Direct Cont. 1985-86		PACS Breakdown 1985-86			
Receipts	$144,328	Indiv.	$33,310	Corp.	$54,476	T/M/H	$32,090
Expend.	$125,435	Party	$2,183	Labor	$6,500	Agr.	$2,100
Unspent	$44,428	PACS	$99,994	Ideo.	$4,500	CWOS	$328

*Includes expenditures for the 1983 special election.

CONNECTICUT

Alexis de Tocqueville, journeying in the United States in 1831, was struck by how Connecticut—a mere spot on the map—gave America "the clock-peddler, the schoolmaster, and the senator. The first gives you time, the second tells you what to do with it, and the third makes your law and civilization." He was talking when Connecticut was already almost 200 years old, and well known as a quaint backwater—and as a cradle of civilization and hive of ingenuity that had placed its peculiar imprint on American civilization. The stony hills rising from the shores of Long Island Sound, the fast-flowing brooks and occasional meadows along the Connecticut River—there were none of the natural resources here that are supposed to be necessary for economic growth. Connecticut had only timber, falling water and rocky farmland. Yet for nearly 350 years now Connecticut has been one of the most prosperous and productive areas of North America.

This has always been a state of tinkerers and innovators, a place whose people—from the stern Congregational Yankees of the 17th century to the ethnic melange of today—have worked with vast ingenuity and unusual precision. Connecticut has produced Eli Whitney's rifle made of interchangeable components and his cotton gin; Colt Industries; the brass fabrication business and hats made of felt; Sikorsky helicopters, Pratt and Whitney jet engines and United Technologies, to the point that this small state has one of the largest shares of Pentagon spending; Perkin Elmer, the high tech company that makes the machines that make semiconductor chips with lines no wider than a micron, one millionth of a centimeter. The industries here from time to time decline and are replaced by something else. Thanks to its ingenuity, Connecticut has always generated plenty of capital to export, in anonymous private placements and through the well-publicized medium of some of the nation's largest insurance companies, long headquartered in Hartford, and it has enjoyed high incomes—with per capita incomes in 1986 the highest in the nation, 33% above the average.

Connecticut's politics has been a struggle between the conservative tendencies fostered by its economic success and the more liberal proclivities which stem from its ethnic history. For much of the 20th century, politics was an arena in which ethnic conflicts and rivalries were played out; now it seems that economic concerns are becoming paramount instead. Once the state was populated almost entirely by the kind of "Connecticut Yankees" celebrated by Mark Twain. If you drive around the state today, you still see towns with saltbox colonial houses, tourist attraction whaling ships, and low green mountains, and you can still talk to old Yankees with slightly dry New England accents (though theirs are not nearly so distinctive as those in Massachusetts). But Yankees are no longer the majority in Connecticut, and haven't been for years. In the 19th century Connecticut's Yankees, more ornery and parochial than those in other parts of New England, were the last voters loyal to the Federalists and the Whigs; they were loyal enough to the Republicans who succeeded them to make Connecticut one of the few states to vote for Herbert Hoover in 1932.

Yet in the years that followed, Connecticut became more Democratic—even as it grew more affluent. You can understand why if you look again at 1932, when a majority of the state's adults were Protestant, but a majority of its children were Catholic. Catholics had been Democrats since they settled here and found the Republican Party dominated by WASPs; their allegiance was cemented by the Al Smith candidacy in 1928. From that point it was only a matter of time. The Catholic/Democratic dominance of the state's politics was accelerated by the skill of John Bailey, Democratic State Chairman from 1946 to 1975. He was a master legislative strategist and ticket-balancer, and Connecticut's strong party and straight ticket voting traditions enabled him to exercise more clout than he could have in Massachusetts or New York. Bailey had a brilliant sense of timing: he endorsed, early, the state's first Jewish governor, Abraham Ribicoff, in 1954 and the nation's first Catholic president, John Kennedy. Bailey and his Democrats also gave the state honest and thrifty government: Connecticut does not have a state income tax nor a big bureaucracy like those of its neighbors.

Connecticut had throughout the Democratic ascendancy a vital Republican party, a strong enough organization to have generated a couple of Republican national chairmen. It elected senators in the 1950s (including Vice President George Bush's father), and it swept the board when the Democrats were split on the Vietnam war and cultural issues in 1970. And that election produced, among others, Senator Lowell Weicker. In the 1980s Connecticut has tipped first one way and then another. It has voted Republican in the last four presidential elections, not narrowly but by solid margins. It has tilted heavily to Republican congressmen in some years (1972, 1980, 1984) but toward Democrats in others (1982, 1986). It threw out a Democratic majority in the legislature in 1984 and threw out the Republican majority in 1986. Connecticut has had Democratic governors for all but four of the last 30 years, and has one Democratic senator, elected in 1980, and a Republican who ostentatiously opposes the Reagan Administration on all manner of issues. But it would shock no one to see Connecticut move to Republicans for one or all of these offices.

One reason is the role of the defense industry. Defense contractors have been prominent in Connecticut since World War II, but it has only been since the defense buildup, begun in the last Carter years and accelerated in the early Reagan Administration, that the defense business has become as important and visible as it now is. Its success draws on New England's strength in high tech industries a strength that has its historical analogues in Connecticut's success as the first mass producer of rifles and cannons in the 1840s and its capacity for precision work ever

CONNECTICUT — Congressional Districts, Counties, County Subdivisions (Towns), and Places — *(6 Districts)*

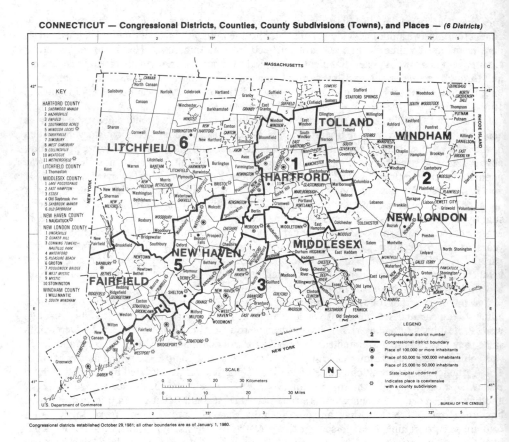

since. Connecticut's unemployment rates have been among the lowest in the country in the 1980s, and it would be hard for one living here to ignore the connection between defense work and economic recovery. As it happens, Reagan percentages in the 1980s rose most rapidly in places with significant defense business—the corridor running southwest from Hartford down to Fairfield County—and sagged most noticeably in the eastern part of the state and around New Haven, where the concentration of defense business is lower. Yet Connecticut's Democrats in Congress, and Lowell Weicker too, find it easy—and, so far, politically profitable—to oppose major defense programs and Reagan foreign policy initiatives even as they continue to lobby, with some embarrassment, for local companies' defense contracts. It's a situation that refutes any Marxist notion of the economic determination of politics, and seems unsustainable over the long run. Yet it's been sustained for quite a long time now.

Governor. Connecticut's governor, William O'Neill, is a man with a very traditional Democratic background. A bar owner in the town of East Hampton, on the lower Connecticut River, he got active in local Democratic politics in the 1950s when he returned from the Air Force. In 1966 he was elected to the legislature—not a difficult feat since Connecticut's lower house has many seats and a district is about the size of a neighborhood. He got his current job less for his leadership ability than for his loyalty. Governor Ella Grasso made him chairman of the state Democratic Party when John Bailey died, and when her lieutenant governor ran against her in the 1978 primary, she chose the faithful O'Neill as his successor. When Grasso resigned in late 1980 just before her death, O'Neill became Governor.

O'Neill has won the job in his own right now twice, and both times against opposition that initially looked formidable. In 1982 he withstood a primary challenge from state legislative leader Ernest Abate and then won with only 53% against Republican legislator Lewis Rome in the general election. In 1986 he did better, holding challenger Toby Moffett—a onetime Nader's raider and four-term congressmen, at the state convention to less than the 20% he needed to get on the ballot; and then beating Republican Julie Belaga, a Weicker ally, in the general election by a 58%–41% margin. O'Neill has now been elected to serve as long as John Dempsey, who succeeded to the governorship when Abraham Ribicoff became Secretary of Health, Education and Welfare in 1961 and held the office through 1970. Dempsey had a surer political touch and support from a strong state chairman who was also the state's premier legislative lobbyist. But the strength of Connecticut's economy, and the possibilities it offers him to increase popular spending programs, seems to be working in O'Neill's favor.

Senators. Lowell Weicker is now Connecticut's senior officeholder, but he remains very much a maverick and a loner in Washington. His politics has turned out to be well suited to this state: an aggressive, independent Republicanism, which gives him high marks from organized labor and Common Cause. But for years Weicker did not have much patience for cultivating constituents or local politicians. That, more than anything else, was why he was in trouble at the beginning of 1982. His reelection cut against the odds: the denouement of a perils of Pauline saga. He seemed vulnerable in the Republican convention or, if not there, certainly in the primary, to the candidacy of Prescott Bush, Jr., son of a former Senator and brother of the Vice President. But Bush proved to be a naive candidate, given to embarrassing statements; after qualifying for the ballot, he abruptly withdrew from the primary, apparently at the request of the White House. Weicker's general election opponent, Toby Moffett, was formidable, though he lost his biggest issue when Congress in 1980 voted to phase out price controls on oil, and he won 46% of the vote (later he left politics and became a Hartford TV anchor). But Weicker carried most of the state outside its central cities, and in mostly suburban Connecticut this was enough.

In the course of his campaign, Weicker took control of the Republican party apparatus and held it up through the 1986 election. Its delegation to the 1984 national convention was notably out of step in Ronald Reagan's Dallas, he got the party to nominate his candidate for governor in 1986, and he even won a Supreme Court case 5–4 allowing voters who haven't registered in either party to vote in Republican primaries (Connecticut Democrats, however, said that Independents would have to register as Democrats to vote in theirs). But the Weickerites failure to win the governorship and their loss of both houses of the legislature in 1986 undercut the argument always made by liberal Republicans—that they can win more votes than conservatives—and Weicker's state chairman was ousted in early 1987.

In Washington Weicker has the committee posts—Appropriations, Energy, Labor—to be an important Senator, and while the Republicans had control he made a lot of policy. Much of it was through his chairmanship of the Labor, Health and Human Services, and Education Appropriations Subcommittee: this plus a critical vote on the Labor Committee made him a kind of czar over literally hundreds of federal programs that affect the lives of millions. More than the ranking Democrat, William Proxmire, he is inclined to be generous and liberal on spending for many such programs, and was able to overcome the contrary inclinations of most other Republican Senators. As a member of the minority again, Weicker will have less clout on these issues. But he is a voice—often a loud and bellowing one—for generosity here, and one which will probably often be heard and heeded.

Weicker's minority status will make it if anything easier for him to continue his crusades against anti-abortion and school prayer amendments—if their proponents muster the votes and the nerve to bring them up. Those who belittle Weicker because of his temperament ("an excitable kid," Nixon aide John Ehrlichman called him during Watergate) should remember that he won on these issues through perseverance and genuine skill as well as outrage—and the same may be said, if you want to go back to it, to his work on the Senate Watergate Committee in 1973. Still, it is easy to understand why many colleagues regard him as unreliable or at least as someone who refuses to play ball, and he is not personally popular.

There is marvelous political irony in Weicker's career. He owed his first election to the Nixon Administration (which may have helped persuade Thomas Dodd to run as an independent, splitting the Democratic vote) and he owed much in 1982 to the Reagan Administration (for yanking Bush) and to Howard Baker (who came in to campaign for him despite his uncooperativeness on many issues). But Weicker has never acknowledged, much less honored, these debts—out of high principle or just stubbornness. He owes his current power in the Senate, which he exerts for liberal causes, to the conservative seniority system—in whose behalf he announced he'd vote in 1987 for Jesse Helms to be ranking Republican on Foreign Relations. For 1988, assuming he runs again, he will have to rely on his own resources. It doesn't seem likely he will control the party apparatus any more, and he may have primary competition from brash young Representative John Rowland. Weicker remains popular with voters. But the possibility of primary competition or a loss makes this race attractive to many strong Democrats, as the race against Weicker was in 1982; among those who might be interested are Representatives Bruce Morrison and Sam Gejdenson and Attorney General Joseph Lieberman. Or—no one can ever be sure about him—Weicker might retire, in which case Representative Nancy Johnson would probably run.

Connecticut's other Senator, Christopher Dodd, has succeeded to a position of national power and prominence. He was a Watergate baby, first elected to Congress in 1974; in 1980, when Senator Abraham Ribicoff retired, he faced down Toby Moffett and got the Democratic nomination uncontested. He easily beat his Republican opponent, former New York Senator James Buckley. His name helped: Dodd's father served Connecticut in the Senate for two terms, and was even mentioned as a vice presidential candidate by Lyndon Johnson in 1964. Dodd Sr. was notably conservative on some foreign and cultural issues, and had a following among the state's more tradition-minded voters. He was censured by the Senate for misuse of campaign funds in 1967 and left the Senate a broken man. Chris Dodd's election was a much happier moment for the family.

Dodd's major work in the Senate now is on foreign policy. When the Democrats were in the minority, his Foreign Relations seat and interest in the issue—he served in Latin America in the Peace Corps—made him one of his party's leading spokesmen against Reagan Administration policy in Central America. He has consistently worked against U.S. aid to and involvement with what he sees as right-wing forces in the area. On El Salvador, he pushed the measure barring economic aid unless the president certified progress in human rights, and then opposed the certifications when Reagan made them. The decline of right-wing death squad activity and the election of President Jose Napoleon Duarte in 1984 seems to have proven Dodd's fears unfounded, but he can argue that those results would not have been attained without the pressure he brought. On Nicaragua, he was one of the first opponents of aid to the contras, and has visited often with the Sandinista leaders; in 1986 he brought home the captured Eugene Hasenfus. On Central America generally, he seems more concerned about Vietnam-type involvement by the United States on the side of what he considers unprogressive forces than he does with human rights violations by El Salvadorian guerrillas or the Sandinista government. Domestically, he is known for his sponsorship of the bill to require employers to give parents child-care leave—an admirable aim, but a method that puts all the cost on a private sector which most Americans think today has only a limited capacity to pay for such good things.

Dodd also achieved headlines when he became the first Senator to support the presidential candidacy of Gary Hart. He is a friend of Hart's and finds himself in sympathy with many of his views, though not all since Dodd is a more conventional Democrat. He probably helped Hart to his resounding primary victory in Connecticut, which was *not* due to its yuppified population; Connecticut remains if anything an older, more ethnic, and more traditional state than the average.

Dodd himself proved exceedingly popular in Connecticut in 1986. Against a respectable, but politically weak opponent, Dodd won 65% of the vote—an impressive margin, and particularly for a dovish Senator in a big-defense state.

Presidential politics. In the final days of the 1960 campaign, John Kennedy was scheduled to finish his day with a rally in Waterbury. He was far behind schedule (in those days when rallies weren't all staged before 6:30 so as to be on the TV news), but a crowd of 100,000 waited up past midnight to cheer him wildly. It was the clearest example of the enthusiasm Kennedy aroused in the Catholic voters of the Northeast, and of John Bailey's shrewdness in endorsing him early. In 1984, the crowds in Waterbury—not as large, certainly not so late, but still enthusiastic—came out not for Walter Mondale but for Ronald Reagan. There was not the fervor for him and his Republicans that there was for Kennedy and the Democrats, but the results were pretty clear. For all the success of Democrats and liberals in statewide elections, Republican presidential candidates have carried Connecticut in the past four elections pretty solidly. The disconnection between state and national preference may get bigger. In 1986 voters by a 50.4%–49.6% margin outlawed the straight-party levers which for years dominated Connecticut politics. Straight-ticket voting was once required in Connecticut: until 1965 you had to pull one party's lever to activate the machine, and only then could fiddle with the levers down below to split your ticket. So the party with the winning presidential or gubernatorial candidate tended to sweep the state. Even in the 1980s Connecticut's highly educated voters split their tickets far less often than most Americans. Now that is likely to change.

As for primaries, here you find a vestige of Connecticut's old machines: registration on both sides is low, because the machines used conventions rather than primaries for nominating statewide and congressional candidates, and didn't encourage uncontrollables to vote in what primaries there were. This has been changing only slowly: there have been statewide primaries, but not all that many, since 1970, and the 1986 Supreme Court case opens up the Republican primary to independents. But it's not true that either the Democratic or Republican electorates here are dominated by young upwardly mobile professionals. Gary Hart's victory here, for example, seems less similar to his wins in yuppie neighborhoods than it does to his winning margins in most areas—from Orange County, California, to Florida's space center—where defense industries are a mainstay of the local economy. Voters there, and in parts of Connecticut, may have perceived Hart as the Democrat most interested in (if not universally supportive of) defense spending, and the one who seemed to welcome rather than fear technological advance. And it's not clear that Lowell Weicker's kind of Republicans could carry the state for their kind of candidate.

Congressional districting. The boundaries of Connecticut's six congressional districts received only marginal adjustments for the 1980s.

The People: Est. Pop. 1986: 3,189,000; Pop. 1980: 3,107,576, up 2.6% 1980–86 and 2.5% 1970–80; 1.32% of U.S. total, 28th largest. 16% with 1–3 yrs. col., 21% with 4+ yrs. col.; 8% below poverty level. Single ancestry: 11% Italian, 7% English, 6% Irish, 5% Polish, 3% French, German, 1% Russian, Portuguese, Swedish, Hungarian, Scottish, Greek. Households (1980): 74% family, 38% with children, 61% married couples; 36.1% housing units rented; median monthly rent: $203; median house value: $67,400. Voting age pop. (1980): 2,284,657; 6% Black, 3% Spanish origin, 1% Asian origin. Registered voters (1986): 1,672,949; 670,468 D (40%), 445,745 R (27%), 555,795 unaffiliated (33%), 8,941 minor parties.

1986 Share of Federal Tax Burden: 14,097,000,000; 1.87% of U.S. total, 19th largest.

1986 Share of Federal Expenditures

	Total		Non-Defense		Defense	
Total Expend	$13,491m	(1.62%)	$7,496m	(1.25%)	$5,995m	(2.61%)
St/Lcl Grants	1,501m	(1.33%)	1,501m	(1.33%)	0m	(0.02%)
Salary/Wages	1,000m	(0.83%)	554m	(0.94%)	446m	(0.72%)
Pymnts to Indiv	4,643m	(1.27%)	4,526m	(1.30%)	117m	(0.66%)
Procurement	5,848m	(2.84%)	416m	(1.75%)	5,432m	(3.62%)
Research/Other	498m	(1.87%)	498m	(1.87%)	0m	(0.86%)

Political Lineup: Governor, William A. O'Neill (D); Lt. Gov., Joseph J. Fauliso (D); Secy. of State, Julia H. Tashjian (D); Atty. Gen., Joe Lieberman (D); Treasurer, Francisco L. Borges (D); Comptroller, J. Edward Caldwell (D). State Senate, 36 (25 R and 11 D); State House of Representatives, 151 (92 D and 59 R). Senators, Lowell P. Weicker, Jr. (R) and Christopher J. Dodd (D). Representatives, 6 (3 D, 2 R and 1 vacancy.)

1984 Presidential Vote

Reagan (R)	890,877	(61%)
Mondale (D)	569,597	(39%)

1984 Democratic Presidential Primary

Hart	116,286	(53%)
Mondale	64,230	(29%)
Jackson	26,395	(12%)
Five others, uncomm.	13,931	(6%)

1980 Presidential Vote

Reagan (R)	677,210	(48%)
Carter (D)	541,732	(39%)
Anderson (I)	171,807	(12%)

GOVERNOR

Gov. William A. O'Neill (D)

Assumed office 1980, term expires Jan. 1991; b. Aug. 11, 1930, Hartford; home, East Hampton; New Britain Teacher's Col., U. of Hartford; Roman Catholic; married (Natalie).

Career: USAF, Korea; Dem. East Hampton Town Cmtee., 1954–80; CT House of Reps., 1966–78; Chmn., CT Dem. Central Cmtee., 1975–78; Lt. Gov. of CT, 1978–80.

Office: State Capitol, 210 Capitol Ave., Hartford 06106, 203-566-4840.

Election Results

1986 gen.	William A. O'Neill (D)	575,638	(58%)
	Julie D. Belaga (R)	408,489	(41%)
1986 prim.	William A. O'Neill (D)	unopposed	
1982 gen.	William A. O'Neill (D)	578,264	(53%)
	Lewis B. Rome (R)	497,773	(46%)

SENATORS

Sen. Lowell P. Weicker, Jr. (R)

Elected 1970, seat up 1988; b. May 16, 1931, Paris, France; home, Greenwich; Yale U., B.A. 1953, U. of VA, LL.B. 1958; Episcopalian; married (Claudia).

Career: Army, 1953–55; Practicing atty.; CT Gen. Assembly, 1962–68; U.S. House of Reps., 1969–71.

Offices: 225 RSOB 20510, 202-224-4041. Also One Corporate Ctr., 11th Flr., Hartford 06103, 203-722-2882; 915 Lafayette Blvd., Bridgeport 06604, 203-579-5830; and 100 Grand St., 3d Flr., Waterbury 06702, 203-575-9537.

Committees: *Appropriations* (3d of 13 R). Subcommittees: Commerce, Justice, State, and Judiciary; Defense; Interior; Labor, Health and Human Services, Education (Ranking Member); Transportation. *Energy and Natural Resources* (3d of 9 R). Subcommittees: Energy Regulation and Conservation; Energy Research and Development; Public Lands, National Parks and Forests. *Labor and Human Services* (5th of 7 R). Subcommittees: Aging; Education, Arts, and Humanities; Handicapped (Ranking Member). *Small Business* (Ranking Member of 9 R). Subcommittees: Innovation, Technology and Productivity.

Group Ratings

	ADA	ACLU	COPE	CFA	LCV	ACU	NTU	NSI	COC	CEI
1986	80	85	64	53	48	14	48	11	50	39
1985	70	—	64	33	—	13	20	—	50	—

National Journal Ratings

	1986 LIB — 1986 CONS		1985 LIB — 1985 CONS	
Economic	61%	— 38%	49%	— 49%
Social	69%	— 30%	64%	— 32%
Foreign	75%	— 0%	82%	— 15%

Key Votes

1) Ease Gun Cont	FOR	5) Grm-Rdmn Def Red	AGN	9) Rehnquist Nom	AGN
2) Immig Reform	FOR	6) Contra Aid	AGN	10) Tax Reform	AGN
3) Lmt Text Imp	FOR	7) SDI Funding	AGN	11) Drug Death Pen	FOR
4) Aid Tobac Ind	FOR	8) Lmt PAC Contrib	AGN	12) S Africa Sanc	FOR

Election Results

1982 general	Lowell P. Weicker, Jr. (R)	545,987	(50%)	($2,306,615)
	Anthony Toby Moffett (D)	499,146	(46%)	($1,368,147)
1982 primary	Lowell P. Weicker, Jr. (R) unopposed			
1982 pre-primary	Prescott S. Bush, Jr. (R)			($1,503,209)
1976 general	Lowell P. Weicker, Jr. (R)	785,683	(58%)	($480,709)
	Gloria Schaffer (D)	561,018	(41%)	($306,104)

Campaign Contributions and Expenditures

1980-82		Direct Cont. 1980-82		PACS Breakdown			
Receipts	$2,308,888	Indiv.	$1,474,396	Agr	$10,250	Ideo	$57,975
Expend.	$2,306,615	Party	$36,748	Bus	$216,744	Lbr	$110,825
Unspent	$2,273	PACS	$444,954	Hlth	$26,100	Prof	$3,300
		Cand.	$236,000				

Sen. Christopher J. Dodd (D)

Elected 1980, seat up 1992; b. May 27, 1944, Willimantic; home, East Haddam; Providence Col., B.A. 1966, U. of Louisville, J.D. 1972; Roman Catholic; divorced.

Career: Peace Corps, Dominican Republic, 1966–68; Army, 1969–75; Practicing atty., 1972–74; U.S. House of Reps., 1975–81.

Offices: 444 RSOB 20510, 202-224-2823. Also Putnam Park, 100 Great Meadow Rd., Wheathersfield 06109, 203-722-3920.

Committees: *Banking, Housing and Urban Affairs* (5th of 11 D). Subcommittees: Consumer Affairs (Chairman); Housing and Urban Affairs. *Budget* (13th of 13 D). *Foreign Relations* (5th of 11 D). Subcommittees: East Asian and Pacific Affairs; International Economic Policy, Trade, Oceans and Environment; Western Hemisphere and Peace Corps Affairs (Chairman). *Labor and Human Resources* (5th of 9 D). Subcommittees: Aging; Children, Family, Drugs, and Alcoholism (Chairman); Education, Arts, and Humanities. *Rules and Administration* (8th of 9 D).

Group Ratings

	ADA	ACLU	COPE	CFA	LCV	ACU	NTU	NSI	COC	CEI
1986	85	85	98	73	72	17	46	20	44	29
1985	85	—	100	87	—	0	34	—	41	—

National Journal Ratings

	1986 LIB — 1986 CONS	1985 LIB — 1985 CONS
Economic	73% — 22%	81% — 17%
Social	86% — 11%	88% — 0%
Foreign	71% — 25%	74% — 23%

Key Votes

1) Ease Gun Cont	AGN	5) Grm-Rdmn Def Red	FOR	9) Rehnquist Nom	AGN
2) Immig Reform	FOR	6) Contra Aid	AGN	10) Tax Reform	AGN
3) Lmt Text Imp	FOR	7) SDI Funding	AGN	11) Drug Death Pen	AGN
4) Aid Tobac Ind	AGN	8) Lmt PAC Contrib	FOR	12) S Africa Sanc	FOR

Election Results

1986 general	Christopher J. Dodd (D)..............	632,695	(65%)	($2,276,764)
	Roger W. Eddy (R)...................	340,438	(35%)	($183,632)
1986 primary	Christopher J. Dodd (D).............	unopposed		
1980 general	Christopher J. Dodd (D)..............	763,969	(56%)	($1,403,672)
	James L. Buckley (R)................	581,884	(43%)	($1,652,672)

Campaign Contributions and Expenditures

1985-86		Direct Cont. 1985-86		PACS Breakdown 1985-86			
Receipts	$2,395,798	Indiv.	$1,551,211	Corp.	$218,009	T/M/H	$166,370
Expend.	$2,276,764	Party	$14,973	Labor	$199,700	Agr.	$8,000
Unspent	$266,781	PACS	$721,289	Ideo.	$113,360	CWOS	$15,850

FIRST DISTRICT

Hartford is Connecticut's first city, the center of its largest urban area, the state capital, and its economic capital as well. Superficially Hartford's history and location resemble those of many bedraggled mill towns, but over the years it has proved economically adaptable and productive. Like all of southern New England, this was a land of Yankee ingenuity, of tinkerers in the early

1800s—tinkerers who built machines and factories to produce things like the Colt revolver, whose big factory still stands on the Connecticut River south of downtown Hartford. Such precision mass-production industries gave Hartford its growth and prosperity in the early 19th century. The insurance companies came later, growing naturally in the part of the country with the most surplus capital. The relatively steady business of insurance still contributes significantly to Hartford's well-being, bringing up to date the reputation it had in colonial days as "the land of steady habits." More recently, Hartford became the center of one of the nation's leading defense contractors, United Technologies, which produces a large percentage of the world's jet engines in the Pratt & Whitney plant in East Hartford. State government also provides Hartford with a stable employment base, but not a large one in thrifty Connecticut.

We are speaking here of metropolitan Hartford, for this city has long since outgrown the limits it had as a colonial town. Metropolitan Hartford is, give or take a few suburbs, coterminous with Connecticut's 1st Congressional District. Politically, this is the most Democratic part of the state, less because of the leanings of an industrial proletariat than because of its ethnic history and local political leadership. Hartford's Irish-, Italian-, French Canadian-, Polish-, and Jewish-Americans far outnumber its Yankees (and its small black community); they were enrolled in the Democratic Party early, and they and their children have stayed with it pretty much ever since. They were strengthened in their resolve by John Bailey, longtime state (1946–75) and national (1961–68) Democratic chairman, an old-fashioned political boss who had a career free of scandal and who promoted a raft of first-class candidates.

It is fitting that today the 1st District is represented in Congress by Bailey's daughter, Barbara Kennelly. She first won in a January 1982 special election, against Ann Uccello, a former Hartford mayor. By November 1982 the Republicans gave up on this district, and Kennelly won by a 2 to 1 margin. She seems now to have a safe seat.

Kennelly is a professional politician in her own right, and she has shown her mettle in a number of ways. First, she won a seat on the Ways and Means Committee in early 1983. This is a prized position: Ways and Means has jurisdiction over taxes—a matter of concern to virtually every economic interest—and especially for Hartford's insurance industry. Kennelly shrewdly accomplished this in tandem with Alabama's Ronnie Flippo, a politician of somewhat different views and very different cultural background. Second, Kennelly was the chief House sponsor of the successful bill to use the federal tax system to enforce child support payments. For years no one had thought to do this: there are good reasons to be reluctant about using the IRS to enforce state laws, and many legislators probably did not think non-paying ex-husbands were doing anything all that reprehensible. By focusing hard on the issue, and by coming up with a workable plan, Kennelly and the other members of the Women's Legislative Caucus who worked on this issue were able to turn around opinion on both counts. Aside from budget bills, this was one of the major legislative accomplishments of the 98th Congress. On the 1986 tax reform bill, Kennelly concentrated on getting a high deduction for single heads of household and saving the historic preservation and rehabilitation tax credit.

So far Kennelly has shown sure political instincts, and has made herself a valuable member of women's groups, of the Connecticut delegation, and of the House Democratic Caucus generally. Temperamentally, she can be counted on as a down-the-line supporter of each of these groups. She comes from a family of team players, not apostates; and she has demonstrated she knows how to play with the best of them.

The People: Pop. 1980: 516,232, dn. 1.7% 1970–80. Households (1980): 71% family, 36% with children, 56% married couples; 42.2% housing units rented; median monthly rent: $205; median house value: $65,700. Voting age pop. (1980): 383,559; 10% Black, 5% Spanish origin, 1% Asian origin.

1984 Presidential Vote Reagan (R) 129,384 (53%)
  Mondale (D) 115,174 (47%)

Rep. Barbara B. Kennelly (D)

Elected 1982; b. July 10, 1936, Hartford; home, Hartford; Trinity Col. (Washington, D.C.), B.A. 1958, Trinity Col. (Hartford, CT), M.A., 1971; Roman Catholic; married (James).

Career: Vice Chmn., Hartford Comm. on Aging, 1971–75; Hartford Crt. of Common Cncl., 1975–79; CT Secy. of State, 1979–82.

Offices: 1230 LHOB 20515, 202-225-2265. Also Abraham A. Ribicoff Fed. Bldg., 450 Main St., Ste. 618, Hartford 06103, 203-722-2383.

Committees: *Ways and Means* (18th of 23 D). Subcommittees: Public Assistance; Select Revenue Measures. *Permanent Select Committee on Intelligence* (11th of 11 D). Subcommittees: Legislative; Oversight and Evaluation.

Group Ratings

	ADA	ACLU	COPE	CFA	LCV	ACU	NTU	NSI	COC	CEI
1986	85	84	89	92	89	0	28	0	38	23
1985	85	—	88	100	—	10	35	—	27	—

National Journal Ratings

	1986 LIB — 1986 CONS		1985 LIB — 1985 CONS	
Economic	74%	— 26%	85%	— 11%
Social	89%	— 0%	78%	— 21%
Foreign	80%	— 0%	85%	— 8%

Key Votes

1) Lmt Cln Water Act	AGN	5) Retain Gun Cont	FOR	9) Aid Angola Reb	AGN
2) Rpl Tobac Sub	AGN	6) Contra Aid	AGN	10) Tax Reform	FOR
3) Grm-Rdmn Def Red	AGN	7) Lmt Text Imp	FOR	11) S Africa Sanc	FOR
4) Ban Polygraph	FOR	8) Limit SDI	FOR	12) Immig Reform	FOR

Election Results

1986 general	Barbara B. Kennelly (D)...............	128,930	(74%)	($388,045)
	Herschel A. Klein (R)..................	44,122	(25%)	($6,705)
1986 primary	Barbara B. Kennelly (D) unopposed			
1984 general	Barbara B. Kennelly (D)...............	147,748	(62%)	($361,300)
	Herschel A. Klein (R)..................	90,823	(38%)	($22,295)

Campaign Contributions and Expenditures

1985-86		Direct Cont. 1985-86		PACS Breakdown 1985-86			
Receipts	$456,997	Indiv.	$175,203	Corp.	$68,368	T/M/H	$92,288
Expend.	$388,045	Party	$396	Labor	$60,609	Agr.	$1,000
Unspent	$123,599	PACS	$247,380	Ideo.	$15,545	CWOS	$9,570

SECOND DISTRICT

Eastern Connecticut, with its Yankee villages and high-income summer and retirement colonies with names like Old Saybrook and Old Lyme, does not look like one of the industrial centers of the United States. But it is. In colonial times its small cities of New London and Norwich were among the 13 colonies' leading workshops and ports, and in the 19th century factories sprang up there and in the little villages on fast-flowing rivers that provided waterpower—mill towns like Danielson, Putnam, Jewett City, and Willimantic. But none of these places turned into a metropolis. Instead, they remain a size the Founding Fathers would have found comprehensible—about as big as New York City was in 1790.

Yet they have also changed, in their population and their economies. In Groton, across the Thames River from New London, is General Dynamics's Electric Boat Company, the major producer of the nuclear submarines which do so much to maintain nuclear stability; but building submarines is a messy business and, as Patrick Tyler's *Running Critical* documents, subject to tremendous cost overruns and bad decisions even by the legendary Admiral Rickover.

The landscape here may be colonial or early industrial; but the people are as often descended from the immigrants of 1840–1924 as from the Yankees who lived here during the Revolution. This mixture of mostly Protestant Yankees and mostly Catholic immigrants has produced a politics in which neither party has enjoyed a clear edge in this district. The Republican trend of the 1980s, which seems to accompany the increasing importance of defense industries in the state's economic recovery, is less apparent here: outside the New London area, there are fewer defense jobs than in any other part of the state. Over the last 25 years the 2d District has been represented by both Republicans and Democrats, although none has actually lost an election: they usually have run for other offices. The most recent example is Senator Christopher Dodd, who with a well-known name and after representing the 2d District for six years, became well enough known on Hartford and New Haven television (each of which covers part of the district) to be a formidable statewide candidate.

The current congressman, Sam Gejdenson, started off with a name not only not well-known, but difficult to pronounce (gay-den-son). A young liberal running in a Republican year, a not-at-all affluent former state legislator running at a time when campaigns cost a great deal of money—he did not seem like a particularly hot prospect. But he turned out to have assets not apparent on his resume: an ability to organize a campaign, an instinctive feel for communicating issues to voters, a wry sense of humor, and the willingness to campaign hard personally. In the 1980 primary he beat John Dempsey, son of a former governor; in the general election he beat a Republican of Italian descent with 53% of the vote. It took him a while to raise this to the level most incumbents like to attain: he got 56% in 1982, sagged to 54% in 1984—a danger sign—but then got 67% in 1986, carrying every city and town except for the affluent Republican stronghold of Lyme. This showing was achieved against former high FBI official Francis (Bud) Mullen, who turned out to be a weaker candidate than many conservatives hoped. Mullen's moment in the national limelight came in the hearings on the nomination of Labor Secretary Raymond Donovan, when Mullen told Senator Orrin Hatch that the FBI had no evidence linking Donovan to organized crime—when in fact, and as Mullen later admitted—the FBI did have such evidence. Why conservatives should think withholding of evidence and giving at best misleading testimony to a congressional committee, and one chaired by a leading conservative, should recommend a candidate is unclear, unless they are suckers for anyone with an FBI pedigree; but sources in the Bureau could have told them that Mullen was known there as "an empty suit." Mullen was able to spend only $173,000, while Gejdenson raised and spent more than $900,000—a phenomenal amount that enabled him to buy time on all the different media markets that reach eastern Connecticut.

Conservatives must be infuriated that this typical American district continues to elect a congressman who takes outspokenly liberal positions on national and international issues. He is part of that generation of Democratic politicos who came of age during the Vietnam war, and he is the son of refugees from Nazism as well; his own biography is a reminder that many people are not lucky enough to escape history. His own politics, on foreign affairs particularly, is along the liberal lines: he tends to oppose U.S. military involvement in Central America and to favor lower military budgets than does the Reagan Administration. But Gejdenson spends plenty of time keeping in touch with constituents and handling local matters, from loans to Connecticut flood victims to settling Indian land claims, and he gets into bigger issues like getting another Trident launched and trying to diversify the district's economy. He has not switched to a more powerful committee: he hasn't wanted to go onto Armed Services, where his views are in the minority, and he lost a bid after the 1984 election to get onto Appropriations. But his pleasant personality and good sense of humor help keep him popular at home. The interesting question for 1988 is whether his 1986 showing was evidence of his own strength or of Mullen's special weakness or both.

The People: Pop. 1980: 518,244, up 6.4% 1970–80. Households (1980): 74% family, 40% with children, 63% married couples; 35.2% housing units rented; median monthly rent: $202; median house value: $56,800. Voting age pop. (1980): 378,132; 3% Black, 1% Spanish origin, 1% Asian origin.

1984 Presidential Vote:

Reagan (R)	141,593	(61%)
Mondale (D)	90,869	(39%)

Rep. Samuel Gejdenson (D)

Elected 1980; b. May 20, 1948, Eschwege, Germany; home, Bozrah; Mitchell Col., A.S. 1966, U. of CT, B.A. 1970; Jewish; married (Karen).

Career: CT House of Reps., 1974–78; Legis. Liaison to Gov. of CT, 1979–80.

Offices: 1410 LHOB 20515, 202-225-2076. Also P.O. Box 2000, Norwich 06360, 203-886-0139; and 94 Court St., Middletown 06457, 203-346-1123.

Committees: *Foreign Affairs* (10th of 27 D). Subcommittees: International Economic Policy and Trade; Western Hemisphere Affairs. *House Administration* (11th of 12 D). Subcommittees: Accounts; Libraries and Memorials; Office Systems. *Interior and Insular Affairs* (13th of 26 D). Subcommittees: Energy and the Environment; General Oversignt and Investigations. *Select Committee on Hunger* (6th 16 D). Task Force: International Task Force.

Group Ratings

	ADA	ACLU	COPE	CFA	LCV	ACU	NTU	NSI	COC	CEI
1986	95	90	89	83	95	0	27	0	41	24
1985	90	—	94	100	—	10	37	—	23	—

National Journal Ratings

	1986 LIB — 1986 CONS		1985 LIB — 1985 CONS	
Economic	69% —	30%	85% —	11%
Social	89% —	0%	81% —	15%
Foreign	80% —	0%	85% —	8%

Key Votes

1) Lmt Cln Water Act	AGN	5) Retain Gun Cont	FOR	9) Aid Angola Reb	AGN
2) Rpl Tobac Sub	FOR	6) Contra Aid	AGN	10) Tax Reform	AGN
3) Grm-Rdmn Def Red	FOR	7) Lmt Text Imp	FOR	11) S Africa Sanc	FOR
4) Ban Polygraph	FOR	8) Limit SDI	FOR	12) Immig Reform	FOR

Election Results

1986 general	Samuel Gejdenson (D)	109,229	(67%)	($987,167)
	Bud Mullen (R)	52,869	(33%)	($145,336)
1986 primary	Samuel Gejdenson (D) unopposed			
1984 general	Samuel Gejdenson (D)	124,110	(54%)	($526,021)
	Roberta F. Koontz (R)	103,119	(45%)	($53,804)

Campaign Contributions and Expenditures

1985-86		Direct Cont. 1985-86		PACS Breakdown 1985-86			
Receipts	$975,785	Indiv.	$541,031	Corp.	$25,320	T/M/H	$31,900
Expend.	$987,167	Party	$3,923	Labor	$141,100	Agr.	$6,750
Unspent	$6,586	PACS	$284,835	Ideo.	$77,865	CWOS	$1,900
		Cand.	$76,433				

THIRD DISTRICT

New Haven, once the state's largest and most industrialized major city and the home of one of Connecticut's best known institutions, Yale University, is the center of Connecticut's 3d Congressional District. Today you can still see the remains of New Haven's turn-of-the-century factories, but the descendants of the Irish, Italian, and Polish immigrants have long since spread out from their old neighborhoods of frame houses, huddled within walking distance of the factories, to the close-in suburbs and beyond. New Haven's politics for years were structured around ethnic rivalries: the Irish became Democrats because the Yankee Republicans would have nothing to do with them; the Italians became Republicans because the Democratic Party was controlled by the Irish. (In all this Yale played only a minor part: despite its national reputation, it has a relatively small enrollment and, except for a few blocks near the campus, New Haven is not really a college town.) But over time ethnic origin has come to matter less. There are probably still clubs and social circles Italian-Americans cannot aspire to; but they certainly have the opportunity to make a good living, join a profession, build a strong business, even go to Yale. As real incomes rose in the 1950s, 1960s, and 1970s, people of various ethnic backgrounds moved to suburbs where they would have felt unwelcome before and married into families that would have been reluctant to have them a generation before. Others were left behind in the old houses in New Haven and the relatively low-income suburbs of East Haven and West Haven. The fierce political battles of the early 1980s in Connecticut's 3d Congressional District tended to divide voters along economic rather than ethnic lines.

The undisputed winner of those battles, and one of the more ingenious young politicians around, is Representative Bruce Morrison. To his first race in 1982 he seemed to bring no great advantages. His name was Waspy in a district represented for 30 years by men named DeNardis, Giaimo, and Cretella. He did not grow up in New Haven, but came there to go to Yale Law. He was not part of the local political network, but was director of the local poverty law agency—not a good base, you would think, from which to raise the money necessary for a serious candidacy. To win the primary he had to beat the president of the New Haven Council and to win the general he had to beat incumbent Lawrence DeNardis, who had held elective office in the New Haven area for 12 years and had earned a reputation as a critic of at least some of the Reagan economic policies.

Yet Morrison managed to raise as much as DeNardis, over $300,000, and won 50%–49%. In a 1984 rematch he raised $1.1 million, one of the biggest warchests in the country, and won 53%–47%. Against weak opposition in 1986 he won 70%–30%, carrying every city and town in the district. Morrison won in 1982 by stressing economic issues, by contrasting Democratic fairness with trickle-down Reaganomics, by charging DeNardis with voting to weaken Social Security. The 3d, served primarily by two Connecticut TV stations, permits unusually spirited and specific campaigning, with plenty of charges and countercharges on TV, and Morrison prepared clever and memorable TV and radio ads in a district where the congressional race has more prominence than in most parts of America.

In Congress Morrison has been one of the most liberal of young Democrats on economic issues particularly; he is a special favorite of unions. He used his legal skills to good advantage as well, as the chief architect of the clause prohibiting corporations from voiding union contracts by declaring bankruptcy (as Continental Airlines had done). He has not been afraid to rile his party's leadership, and has been passed over for a seat on the Budget Committee three times. In early 1987 he was arguing that Congress should think about whether George Bush should be impeached. But his emphasis on housing programs and the elderly helped solidify his position in the district, and he took care to provide good constituency services and to help 3d District businessmen. It's possible that the Republicans will make a serious challenge in this district again, but not terribly likely: who can hope to beat a liberal who campaigns so shrewdly and can raise $1 million?

The People: Pop. 1980: 518,677, up 1.6% 1970–80. Households (1980): 73% family, 36% with children, 59% married couples; 37.0% housing units rented; median monthly rent: $212; median house value: $65,400. Voting age pop. (1980): 387,740; 9% Black, 2% Spanish origin, 1% Asian origin.

1984 Presidential Vote:

Reagan (R) 146,171	(59%)
Mondale (D) 101,877	(41%)

Rep. Bruce A. Morrison (D)

Elected 1982; b. Oct. 8, 1944, New York, NY; home, Hamden; MA Institute of Technology, S.B. 1965, U. of IL, M.S. 1970, Yale U., J.D. 1973; Lutheran; married (Jane).

Career: New Haven Legal Assistance Assn., Staff atty., 1973–74, Managing atty., 1974–76, Exec. Dir., 1976–81.

Offices: 437 CHOB 20515, 202-225-3661. Also 85 Church St., New Haven 06510, 203-773-2325.

Committees: *Banking, Finance and Urban Affairs* (16th of 31 D). Subcommittees: Consumer Affairs and Coinage; Financial Institutions Supervision, Regulation and Insurance; Housing and Community Development; International Development Institutions and Finance. *Judiciary* (14th of 21 D). Subcommittees: Administrative Law and Government Relations; Courts, Civil Liberties, and the Administration of Justice; Immigration, Refugees and International Law. *Select Committee on Children, Youth and Families* (10th of 18 D). Task Force: Economic Security.

Group Ratings

	ADA	ACLU	COPE	CFA	LCV	ACU	NTU	NSI	COC	CEI
1986	80	95	86	92	88	0	27	0	27	26
1985	90	—	94	91	—	5	43	—	24	—

National Journal Ratings

	1986 LIB — 1986 CONS		1985 LIB — 1985 CONS	
Economic	74% —	23%	85% —	11%
Social	89% —	0%	85% —	0%
Foreign	80% —	0%	85% —	8%

Key Votes

1) Lmt Cln Water Act	FOR	5) Retain Gun Cont	FOR	9) Aid Angola Reb	AGN
2) Rpl Tobac Sub	FOR	6) Contra Aid	AGN	10) Tax Reform	FOR
3) Grm-Rdmn Def Red	AGN	7) Lmt Text Imp	FOR	11) S Africa Sanc	FOR
4) Ban Polygraph	FOR	8) Limit SDI	—	12) Immig Reform	FOR

Election Results

1986 general	Bruce A. Morrison (D)	114,276	(70%)	($567,868)
	Ernest J. Diette, Jr. (R)	49,806	(30%)	($14,307)
1986 primary	Bruce A. Morrison (D) unopposed			
1984 general	Bruce A. Morrison (D)	129,230	(53%)	($1,125,532)
	Lawrence J. DeNardis (R)	115,939	(47%)	($555,682)

Campaign Contributions and Expenditures

1985-86		Direct Cont. 1985-86		PACS Breakdown 1985-86			
Receipts	$598,976	Indiv.	$344,462	Corp.	$31,325	T/M/H	$55,799
Expend.	$567,868	Party	$2,353	Labor	$103,500	Agr.	$1,000
Unspent	$47,294	PACS	$223,054	Ideo.	$28,930	CWOS	$2,500

FOURTH DISTRICT

Fairfield County, the southwest corner of the state dangling down toward New York City, has been the Republican stronghold in state politics for more than 40 years. It has long been one of the most affluent counties in the nation, a land of broad, well-manicured lawns sweeping down to Long Island Sound, of woodsy New Canaan and artsy-craftsy Westport, of commuters driving down to the station to take the newly refurbished Metro North line into Manhattan. That is the stereotypical image, going back at least to the 1940s; the more recent reality is of mirrored-glass corporate headquarters, stuck in downtown Stamford near the bedraggled station or on some grassy knoll, and of luxury condominiums sprouting up near the shore or in the woods. Meanwhile, the focus here is always on New York, not Connecticut. People watch New York, not New Haven or Hartford, TV stations; they are Yankees, not Red Sox, fans; and their political attitudes, more than in other parts of the state, are shaped by what is happening in the City. Many people here have little idea what is happening in politics or government in Connecticut; Hartford is a lot farther away than Grand Central Station.

Most of Fairfield County is in the 4th Congressional District, a string of high-income, traditionally Republican towns along Long Island Sound—Greenwich, Stamford, Darien, Norwalk, Westport, Fairfield—up to the old industrial (but also park-laden) city of Bridgeport. Politics here was once a battle between factory workers and railroad commuters, back in the 1940s when Clare Boothe Luce won the seat and used her platform to denounce Franklin D. Roosevelt. Nowadays there are fewer factory workers and not so many commuters, and politics is more complicated. High-income voters in artsy-craftsy Westport are more liberal on cultural and foreign issues than blue collar voters in Bridgeport; economic hard times may affect middle-income neighborhoods in Fairfield but not woodsy New Canaan; new rich are always replacing old rich in Greenwich, the Henry Luces and Prescott Bushes (new rich in their time) giving way to the David Stockmans and the Ivan Lendls.

After a long and constructive House career, Stewart McKinney, the congressman from the 4th District, died on May 8, 1987, of pneumonia brought on by AIDS. Lucie McKinney, the Representative's wife, said in a statement released following his death: "Stewart and I had long communications before he died and knew that his death would be used by certain people. The children knew him as a very good father, and I knew him as a wonderful husband who was very caring for people. I know that right now he would have liked us to look forward and not behind, and get help in finding a cure for this disease, however we look at how people get it." McKinney was a classic liberal Republican, a man with some family money who went into public service to help his community and those who are less fortunate but who did not want to cozy up too much to the big city ethnic politicians and labor bosses who have traditionally called the shots on the Democratic side. McKinney was elected to the House in 1970, when Lowell Weicker moved up to the Senate. As second ranking Republican on the Banking Committee, he supported the Chrysler and New York City loan guarantees, and the synfuels corporation; he was an enthusiast for Community Development Block Grants and Urban Development Action Grants. He was also wary of the consequences of a sudden and complete deregulation of banking. McKinney also served as ranking minority member on the House District of Columbia Committee, which in 1985 he recommended be abolished, for the sensible reason that since Congress voted the District home rule in 1972 there isn't a full committee's worth of work left to do. McKinney himself worked hard and constructively on District affairs, though they were of no conceivable political benefit to him.

All this left McKinney as the odd man out in Ronald Reagan's Washington. While younger House members called for guerrilla warfare against Democrats, he worked with them; when congressional Republicans have been united as never before, he voted the party line less often than almost any other House Republican. For years liberal Republicans won easily in districts like McKinney's by holding their own high-income base and adding some Democratic blue-collar workers and ethnics as well. But in 1986 McKinney faced an opponent, state legislator Christine Niedermeier, who built on the Democratic base in Bridgeport, where she grew up, and cut into the Republican vote in the suburbs, where she like so many other upwardly mobile residents moved from the city and won her legislative elections. Niedermeier is young, arguably more conservative on cultural issues, and not particularly a free spender; she is also determined, well organized, and well-financed. She carried Bridgeport solidly and ran even in Fairfield, Norwalk, and Stamford, winning 47% district-wide.

Niedermeier was helped by the strong showings of Governor William O'Neill and Senator Christopher Dodd, both of whom carried the 4th District, and by the straight-party lever which carried some of their strength to the races below. In 1988 O'Neill and Dodd won't be on the ballot and there won't be a straight party lever. But Niedermeier raised a serious amount of campaign money and could raise even more if her 1986 performance gets her on the PACs' A-list this time. She is a strong favorite to win the special election to be held in August 1987.

The People: Pop. 1980: 518,577, dn. 4.8% 1970–80. Households (1980): 74% family, 37% with children, 59% married couples; 38.8% housing units rented; median monthly rent: $230; median house value: $98,500. Voting age pop. (1980): 384,352; 9% Black, 6% Spanish origin, 1% Asian origin.

1984 Presidential Vote:

Reagan (R)	154,515	(63%)
Mondale (D)	88,941	(36%)

Rep. Stewart B. McKinney (R)

Elected 1970; b. Jan. 30, 1931, Pittsburgh, PA, d. May 8, 1987; home, Westport; Princeton U., 1949–51, Yale U., B.A. 1958; Episcopalian; married (Lucie).

Career: Air Force, 1951–55; Pres., CMF Tires, Inc.; Real estate development; CT House of Reps., 1966–70.

Offices: 237 CHOB 20515, 202-225-5541. Also Fed. Bldg., 915 Lafayette Blvd., Bridgeport 06604, 203-579-5870; and 500 Summer St., Stamford 06901, 203-357-8277.

Committees: *Banking, Finance and Urban Affairs* (2d of 20 R). Subcommittees: Economic Stabilization; Financial Institutions Supervision, Regulation and Insurance; Housing and Community Development (Ranking Member). *District of Columbia* (Ranking Member of 3 R). Subcommittees: Fiscal Affairs and Health; Government Operations and Metropolitan Affairs. *Select Committee on Narcotics Abuse and Control* (8th of 10 R).

Group Ratings

	ADA	ACLU	COPE	CFA	LCV	ACU	NTU	NSI	COC	CEI
1986	50	73	60	42	58	0	32	10	47	28
1985	63	—	58	42	—	13	43	—	57	—

National Journal Ratings

	1986 LIB — 1986 CONS		1985 LIB — 1985 CONS	
Economic	60%	40%	61%	38%
Social	74%	23%	78%	22%
Foreign	80%	0%	64%	33%

Key Votes

1) Lmt Cln Water Act	FOR	5) Retain Gun Cont	FOR	9) Aid Angola Reb	AGN
2) Rpl Tobac Sub	—	6) Contra Aid	AGN	10) Tax Reform	AGN
3) Grm-Rdmn Def Red	—	7) Lmt Text Imp	FOR	11) S Africa Sanc	FOR
4) Ban Polygraph	FOR	8) Limit SDI	FOR	12) Immig Reform	FOR

Election Results

1986 general	Stewart B. McKinney (R). . . . . ,	77,212	(54%)	($534,663)
	Christine M. Niedermeier (D)	69,666	(46%)	($305,822)
1986 primary	Stewart B. McKinney (R) unopposed			
1984 general	Stewart B. McKinney (R).	165,644	(70%)	($377,750)
	John M. Orman (D)	69,666	(30%)	($16,312)

Campaign Contributions and Expenditures

1985-86		Direct Cont. 1985-86		PACS Breakdown 1985-86			
Receipts	$534,691	Indiv.	$253,176	Corp.	$76,234	T/M/H	$87,712
Expend.	$534,663	Party	$9,187	Labor	$56,650	Agr.	$0
Unspent	$26,991	PACS	$249,102	Ideo.	$25,750	CWOS	$2,756

FIFTH DISTRICT

The 5th Congressional District of Connecticut is a slice of the state that takes in some of its prettiest rural towns, some of its most affluent suburbs, and some of those small industrial cities where ingenious Connecticut Yankees built factories and businesses that made—and often still make—the state one of the nation's most prosperous. The biggest of these cities, Waterbury, was until recently the nation's largest producer of brass products and one of its major clockmakers; the last of the city's Big Three brass fabricators shut down in 1985, leaving less than 1,000 workers in a local industry that once employed 20,000 here. Danbury, near the New York border, was known for years for its hats, and is now headquarters to troubled Union Carbide. The towns of the Naugatuck Valley, along a fast-flowing river, made a variety of products. Yet this middle part of Connecticut still thrives. Heavy defense spending has created many jobs, and Connecticut ingenuity and hustle has created others, so that this region has one of the nation's lowest levels of unemployment.

Industrial development and ethnic immigration changed the political complexion of this part of Connecticut—for a time. Originally, this part of Connecticut, between New Haven and Long Island Sound on one side and Hartford and Litchfield County on the other, was contrary Yankee country. Its voters—first Federalists, later Whigs, then Republicans—were men who wanted to stop foolish populists like Thomas Jefferson and Andrew Jackson from putting into effect their newfangled ideas, even as they themselves, in their factories, were injecting into the economy newfangled machines and products. By the 1940s they were in a political minority, replaced by Democrats who went to Mass, lived in traditional ethnic neighborhoods, supported the New Deal, and revered John F. Kennedy. Now, as ethnic discrimination vanishes and market capitalism (and the Pentagon) produces new and unanticipated prosperity, this part of

Connecticut has been moving perceptibly to the right again. In the Kennedy and Johnson years this was a solidly Democratic district. More recently, with the Democratic factory towns balanced off by the smaller, still Yankee rural towns and by the wide Republican margins in the high-income woodsy suburbs of Weston, Wilton, and Ridgefield, it has become marginal or even Republican. Party control changed hands in 1972, 1978, and again in 1984.

The current congressman is John Rowland, a Republican from Waterbury elected in 1984 at age 27—the youngest member, then and after the 1986 election as well, in the House. John Rowland describes himself as a "Waterbury rat." One year out of college, while working in his father's insurance business, he ran for the legislature and ousted a veteran Democrat; two years later he was a minority whip; two years after that the youngest congressman. Rowland is the kind of candidate and congressman the Republicans wish they had more of: a brash self-starter generally faithful to the party but who also stakes out his own positions and builds up his own popularity. He campaigned as a supporter of family values and opponent of abortion and as a supporter of Ronald Reagan, who came to his district in 1984; but he was quick to say in 1985 about the President, "I don't owe him a damn thing." He speaks in the authentic language of the vast American middle class, eager to get ineligibles off the welfare rolls, determined not to deny college loans to students in families with incomes over $32,500. In 1984 Rowland was helped by the sag in Democratic fortunes in this part of Connecticut and by Ronald Reagan's 2 to 1 win in the district. But in 1986 it was the Democrats on the top of the ticket, Governor O'Neill and Senator Dodd, who were carrying the district, albeit by lesser margins; and Rowland's opponent's campaign was well financed. Yet Rowland ran 16% ahead of O'Neill and won with 61%; Waterbury, which he lost by 15 votes in 1984, he carried with 56% in 1986. With that he seems launched, on a long House career—unless he should decide, and he has been careful not to rule the possibility out, to run for Lowell Weicker's seat in 1988.

The People: Pop. 1980: 518,700, up 8.2% 1970–80. Households (1980): 78% family, 42% with children, 65% married couples; 32.2% housing units rented; median monthly rent: $179; median house value: $70,200. Voting age pop. (1980): 372,002; 4% Black, 3% Spanish origin.

1984 Presidential Vote: Reagan (R) 163,371   (67%)
Mondale (D) 80,816   (33%)

Rep. John G. Rowland (R)

Elected 1984; b. May 24, 1957, Waterbury; home, Waterbury; Villanova U., B.S. 1979; Roman Catholic; married (Deborah).

Career: Insur. agent, 1979–84; CT House of Reps., 1981–85.

Offices: 512 CHOB 20515, 202-225-3822. Also 135 Grand St., Waterbury 06701, 203-573-1418.

Committees: *Armed Services* (17th of 21 R). Subcommittees: Procurement and Military Nuclear Systems; Readiness. *Veterans' Affairs* (10th of 13 R). Subcommittees: Hospitals and Health Care; Housing and Memorial Affairs.

Group Ratings

	ADA	ACLU	COPE	CFA	LCV	ACU	NTU	NSI	COC	CEI
1986	50	25	48	42	53	64	37	90	72	59
1985	67	—	24	42	—	76	55	—	86	—

National Journal Ratings

	1986 LIB — 1986 CONS			1985 LIB — 1985 CONS		
Economic	42%	—	58%	27%	—	71%
Social	35%	—	64%	32%	—	67%
Foreign	39%	—	61%	37%	—	60%

Key Votes

1) Lmt Cln Water Act	FOR	5) Retain Gun Cont	AGN	9) Aid Angola Reb	FOR
2) Rpl Tobac Sub	FOR	6) Contra Aid	AGN	10) Tax Reform	FOR
3) Grm-Rdmn Def Red	FOR	7) Lmt Text Imp	AGN	11) S Africa Sanc	FOR
4) Ban Polygraph	FOR	8) Limit SDI	AGN	12) Immig Reform	FOR

Election Results

1986 general	John G. Rowland (R)	98,664	(61%)	($425,746)
	Jim Cohen (D)	63,371	(39%)	($344,285)
1986 primary	John G. Rowland (R) unopposed			
1984 general	John G. Rowland (R)	130,700	(54%)	($236,923)
	William R. Ratchford (D)	109,425	(45%)	($523,460)

Campaign Contributions and Expenditures

1985-86		Direct Cont. 1985-86		PACS Breakdown 1985-86			
Receipts	$426,187	Indiv.	$210,481	Corp.	$67,430	T/M/H	$62,218
Expend.	$425,746	Party	$16,547	Labor	$29,875	Agr.	$250
Unspent	$3,779	PACS	$174,820	Ideo.	$13,506	CWOS	$1,541
		Cand.	$135				

SIXTH DISTRICT

Some congressional districts seem to be made up of territory left over after everyone else has constructed his own constituency. Such a district is the 6th of Connecticut. Its population concentrations are widely dispersed, at just about opposite ends of the district. Enfield and Windsor Locks, in the far northeast corner, are predominantly Italian-American and part of the Hartford-to-Springfield, Massachusetts, industrial corridor along the Connecticut River. In the southeast corner are New Britain and Bristol, old mill towns, the latter predominantly Polish-American. In the north central part of the district, amid the mountains, are the much smaller mill towns of Torrington and Winsted, the latter the hometown of Ralph Nader. These Democratic areas are separated by much larger (geographically) and much smaller (in population) Yankee Republican towns of Litchfield County, whose proud houses bear witness to its prosperity in the Revolutionary era, and whose hills and lakes, small towns and hidden estates are now some of America's most valuable real estate. The 6th also includes several high-income suburbs of Hartford: Farmington (site of the famous Miss Porter's School and—politically more significant—the headquarters of United Technologies), Avon, and Simsbury.

The 6th District was created in the 1960s to elect a Democrat, but in fact it has proved to be a bipartisan district: in its 20 years of existence it has elected two Republicans and three Democrats. An unusual number of them have gone on to win, or run for, statewide office: Republican Thomas Meskill was elected governor in 1970, Democrat Ella Grasso was elected governor in 1974 and 1978, and Democrat Toby Moffett ran a close but unsuccessful race for the Senate in 1982. The current incumbent, Republican Nancy Johnson, has been mentioned several times as a statewide candidate herself.

For good reason. Elected in a close race in 1982, she has turned what was a safe Democratic district in the 1970s into a safe—as long as she runs, anyway, Republican seat in the 1980s. Johnson, a doctor's wife and a teacher, raised three children and was active in charitable and community affairs. In 1976 she won a seat in the Connecticut Senate from a district centered on the heavily Democratic industrial city of New Britain. In some elections, being a woman is a disadvantage; it may have helped Johnson, first to get her known and second to suggest (correctly) that she would be somewhat more compassionate and generous than most Republicans. Johnson was certainly the Republicans' strongest possible candidate in the recession year of 1982, and she beat a nuclear freeze organizer—one of those young antiwar activists that prevailed in a lot of districts in the mid-1970s but have been less successful in the mid-1980s. Evidently people decided that Johnson's experience in charitable and community affairs over several years taught her more about the fabric of life than did the few campaigns of canvassing and caucusing that were the sum of her opponent's experience.

On some issues Johnson has compiled a record midway between standard Republicans and Democrats. She worked with Augustus Hawkins to get a 25% tax credit for retraining. She belongs to the House Wednesday Group, the Ripon Society, and the 92 Group. Still, she was one of the first Connecticut Republicans to support Ronald Reagan, even before the 1980 campaign. On foreign policy she was a hardliner in her first term, supporting most Reagan Administration positions on Central America and defense spending. But she voted against the MX missile and against aid to the contras in her second term. On economics, she combines an enthusiasm for free markets with a record of working to protect and further Connecticut's machine tool and other precision industries. On cultural issues too her record is mixed, and not easily categorized. She has worked to come up with a proposal to expand the tax deductio for day care. Yet she is obviously more comfortable with the thrust of Reagan era policies than was her traditionally liberal Republican colleague Stewart McKinney. Yet she is often a dissenter from Republican ranks, a vote that must be sought by the Republican leadership and cannot be taken for granted.

Her electoral performance has been spectacular. Against a strong opponent in 1984 and a somewhat weaker one in 1986, she won with 64% of the vote, carrying New Britain and in 1986 every city and town in the district. She would be a logical Republican candidate, and a strong one, if Lowell Weicker should choose not to run for reelection in 1988; she has been mentioned as a candidate for governor as well. In the meantime she obviously has a safe seat.

The People: Pop. 1980: 517,146, up 6.4% 1970–80. Households (1980): 77% family, 39% with children, 65% married couples; 30.6% housing units rented; median monthly rent: $185; median house value: $63,300. Voting age pop. (1980): 378,872; 2% Black, 2% Spanish origin.

1984 Presidential Vote;

Reagan (R)	155,843	(63%)
Mondale (D)	91,920	(37%)

Rep. Nancy L. Johnson (R)

Elected 1982; b. Jan. 5, 1935, Chicago, IL; home, New Britain; U. of Chicago, 1953, Radcliffe Col., B.A. 1957, U. of London, 1958; Unitarian; married (Theodore).

Career: Pres., Sheldon Commun. Guidance Clinic; Adjunct Prof., Central CT St. Col.; CT Senate; 1976–82.

Offices: 119 CHOB 20515, 202-225-4476. Also One Grove St., New Britain 06053, 203-223-8412; and 92 High St., Enfield 06082, 203-745-5722.

Committees: *Budget* (11th of 14 R). Task Forces: Economic Policy; Health (Ranking Member); Human Resources. *Public Works and Transportation* (11th of 20 R). Subcommittees: Economic Development; Investigations and Oversight; Water Resources. *Select Committee on Children, Youth and Families* (4th of 12 R). Task Force: Crisis Intervention.

Group Ratings

	ADA	ACLU	COPE	CFA	LCV	ACU	NTU	NSI	COC	CEI
1986	67	42	52	33	63	55	36	50	72	51
1985	67	—	43	42	—	48	49	—	64	—

National Journal Ratings

	1986 LIB — 1986 CONS			1985 LIB — 1985 CONS		
Economic	48%	—	51%	46%	—	53%
Social	60%	—	39%	63%	—	33%
Foreign	47%	—	53%	53%	—	46%

Key Votes

1) Lmt Cln Water Act	AGN	5) Retain Gun Cont	FOR	9) Aid Angola Reb	FOR
2) Rpl Tobac Sub	FOR	6) Contra Aid	FOR	10) Tax Reform	FOR
3) Grm-Rdmn Def Red	FOR	7) Lmt Text Imp	AGN	11) S Africa Sanc	FOR
4) Ban Polygraph	FOR	8) Limit SDI	AGN	12) Imig Reform	FOR

Election Results

1986 general	Nancy L. Johnson (R)................	111,304	(64%)	($425,553)
	Paul S. Amenta (D)	62,133	(36%)	($41,840)
1986 primary	Nancy L. Johnson (R)...............	unopposed		
1984 general	Nancy L. Johnson (R)...............	155,422	(64%)	($529,207)
	Arthur H. House (D)	87,489	(36%)	($265,691)

Campaign Contributions and Expenditures

1985-86		Direct Cont. 1985-86		PACS Breakdown 1985-86			
Receipts	$428,767	Indiv.	$284,766	Corp.	$60,025	T/M/H	$51,239
Expend.	$425,553	Party	$2,469	Labor	$23,500	Agr.	$1,250
Unspent	$28,865	PACS	$144,064	Ideo.	$6,950	CWOS	$1,100

DELAWARE

Even as the Framers were drawing up the Constitution 200 years ago, it was apparent that Delaware was a tiny state: the Delaware delegation in nearby Philadelphia was under strict orders to insist on equal representation for every state, no matter how tiny. Those patriots would be as surprised as Americans are today to see that this small state has produced two plausible candidates for president in 1988, Senator Joseph Biden and former Governor Pete du Pont. For Delaware has been an oddity from its beginnings. Delaware owes its existence to a footnote in American history. In the 17th century America was settled by ship, and the three counties along the Delaware River split away from William Penn's Pennsylvania over some long-forgotten squabble. It hung on to its independence by pitting Anglican London against Quaker Pennsylvania, by standing tough in the Constitutional Convention, and then by rushing to beat Pennsylvania and New Jersey by a few days to become the first state to ratify the Constitution in 1787. Today Delaware is a mostly prosperous chunk of the eastern United States not much larger, in population or area, than the average congressional district. Most of the people live in one medium-sized metropolitan area, Wilmington; but downstate you could almost imagine yourself in the rural South.

Delaware's separate existence—plus the du Ponts—have helped to make it prosperous. In the 19th century the legislature passed liberal incorporation laws, allowed corporate owners and managers maximum flexibility, and Delaware courts have mostly been careful to enforce those laws correctly and predictably. Delaware today is still, technically, the home of many of the nation's leading corporations: they exist because of a few sheets of paper in a Georgian state office building in the small state capital of Dover. Delaware is also the home, this time in a real sense, of the Du Pont Company. It is by far the state's largest employer, and of course its size dwarfs state government. Du Pont was founded by a French emigré, an impractical inventor whose sons had an aptitude for business. For years it grew by monopolizing the gunpowder trade, and later by pioneering in its remarkably productive industrial R&D labs new plastics and other synthetics. In the 1980s it branched out in another direction, acquiring Conoco for its oil reserves and a source of cheap chemical feedstock, so now a large percentage of its revenues come from low-priced oil and a large hunk of it is owned by the Canadian-American Bronfman family. But the company remains a colossus in Delaware.

Wealthy members of the du Pont family—there are more than 2,000 du Ponts—and corporate executives of course have considerable influence in Delaware. For eight years, until 1984, the governor was Pierre du Pont IV. A few years ago some Naderites wrote a book breathlessly charging that du Ponts, family and corporation, were powerful in Delaware. How could it be otherwise? What does not follow from this is that the corporation or the more politically troglodytic of the du Pont cousins always get their way. In fact Governor du Pont began his career by opposing the company on some environmental issues, and the company was headed through most of the 1970s by a prominent Democrat, Irving Shapiro. And Delaware for years had one of the nation's most sharply graduated state income taxes.

The politics of this small state (49th in area, 48th in population), it can be argued, is a microcosm of the nation. Wilmington is an old-fashioned industrial city with distinct Polish, Italian, black, and rich Waspy neighborhoods; it is heavily Democratic but only casts 10% of the state's votes. The two downstate counties, Kent and Sussex, have a southern air about them; they were once segregationist, have always been hawkish, and cast one-third of the state's votes. Most of the voters live in suburban New Castle County, in all manner of suburbs, from the working-class environs around a steel mill to the "chateau country" where du Ponts and their friends live—as thick a gathering of multimillionaires in as lush an area, with narrow roads passing between stone fences over gentle hills and wooded lanes, as you will find anywhere in the United States. Thanks to high wages as well as the concentration of the rich, Delaware has had above average incomes for many years, and a solid Republican base; Delaware went for Hoover in 1932, for Dewey in 1948, and trended Republican in the 1960s. But Wilmington and the downstate counties, the southern-oriented whites and blacks (14% of the population) provide a solid base for the Democrats, and they have won their share of victories too; Delaware went for Kennedy in 1960, and has elected as many Democrats as Republicans to Congress and the governorship.

Governor. If Delaware has one potential presidential candidate in the Senate, it has another who declined to run for it: former Governor Pierre S. du Pont IV, who understandably prefers to be called Pete. Despite the majesty of the name, he is not an offshoot of the richest part of the family and never came close to running (though he did work in) the Du Pont company. He was elected to Congress in 1970 when Roth ran for the Senate and was easily reelected in 1972 and 1974; he ran for governor in 1976 when both Senate seats seemed taken for some time. He made a splash by opposing the company on some environmental laws, but he is by no means anti-business. One of his major achievements is a revision of Delaware's banking laws to encourage out-of-state banks to move some of their operations here. In personal style du Pont looks straight from *The Preppy Handbook,* but he is anything but stuffy: he is friendly and affable, crisply articulate, at ease with and curious about people from all parts of society. His early reputation was as a moderate Republican. But in Congress and as governor he became convinced that government needed pruning and that the private economy needed to be liberated from overgovernance to be productive. He cut taxes sharply and became Delaware's version of a supply-sider, and was reelected in 1980 with 71% of the vote. Barred from seeking a third term, he helped his lieutenant governor, Mike Castle, succeed him with 55% even while Democrats were carrying most of the other statewide races. Castle has continued the du Pont policies and as

DELAWARE - Congressional District, Counties, and Selected Places — *(1 At Large)*

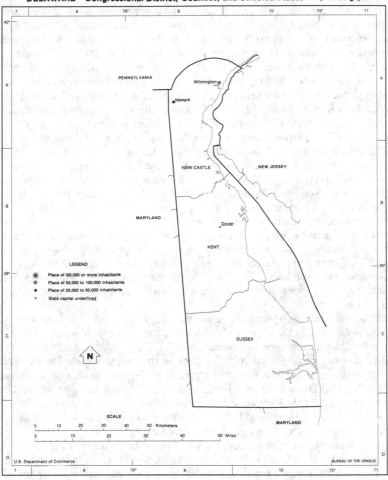

LEGEND

◉ Place of 100,000 or more inhabitants
◉ Place of 50,000 to 100,000 inhabitants
● Place of 25,000 to 50,000 inhabitants
* State capital underlined

N

SCALE

0   10   20   30   40   50 Kilometers
0   10   20   30   40   50 Miles

U.S. Department of Commerce   BUREAU OF THE CENSUS

All political boundaries are as of January 1, 1980

chairman of the Governors' Conference Committee on Welfare, has a chance to make his impression on a critical national issue. He seems to be the favorite now for reelection in 1988.

Senators. Delaware's senior statewide official is Senator William Roth, a Republican first elected to the House in 1966 and to the Senate in 1970. Roth is a party stalwart, a man who came to national politics as the Republicans were ruing their failure to stop Lyndon Johnson's Great Society legislation. He is not the sort to strike observers as a deep thinker, but in fact he sponsored, in the late 1970s, several of the major initiatives against what he considered negative trends: a case in point for the proposition that Republicans seized the legislative initiative and were winning the battle of ideas even before they won the presidency and control of the Senate in the 1980 elections. Roth's initiatives include a tax credit (of $250 per student) for college tuitions, an antibusing proposal, and the Roth-Kemp bill (as it is known in the Senate) to cut tax rates 10% per year for three straight years. He continues now to sponsor what he calls "the Roth reforms," including what amount to tax-free savings accounts up to $6,000 a year, IRAs for housewives, and bigger business deductions for capital spending combined with what amounts to a value-added tax.

Roth is trying to steer American society toward having a smaller share of the economy in the public sector and a larger share in the private—a preoccupation of many conservative intellectuals. But he is acting not only in line with theory but in response to the affluent society he sees around him in Delaware. The upwardly mobile residents of New Castle County want their children to do at least as well as they have, and they resent it when they are ordered bused to what they consider, often rightly, inferior schools; they feel threatened by high tuition fees; they resent high tax rates that seem to take away money desperately needed. From this you get the major planks of Roth's career: opposition to busing, support of tuition tax credits, the Kemp-Roth tax cut, his latest Roth reforms, his robust exposure of wasteful spending by the Pentagon and other agencies. His proposals are open to criticism. The tax cut, largely enacted, has left huge deficits that leave many Republicans appalled; his antibusing measure was of dubious constitutionality; ditto for tuition tax credits, which can also be attacked as a very generous subsidy for the relatively rich; and you may look askance at a program which aims its first benefits to the well-to-do. But Roth can reply that his ideas help the large mass of his constituents, that they are popular, and that the success of some of his ideas has given the nation a more secure prosperity which works in everyone's favor.

Despite this productivity, Roth is not a famous Senator, nor does he seem much stronger politically than when he came to the Senate. Legislatively, he occupies important positions on the Finance Committee and is the ranking Republican on Governmental Affairs. But he did not play a major role in the 1984 tax reform; and Governmental Affairs, theoretically a good place to gain visibility, always seems mired in issues of government organization that turn out to matter very little.

Roth has run well, but not spectacularly, in the past. In 1976 and 1982 he won by identical margins, 56%–44%, against Democrats who were able to raise enough money to be competitive. That's more now than it used to be. Delaware has no VHF TV stations of its own, and candidates in the 1970s didn't buy much Philadelphia TV time; in the 1980s, they do. Roth will raise plenty of money for 1988 and should start off well ahead, and it's possible that he won't get a strong opponent. But if one of Delaware's presidential candidates is nominated, bets should be off: a du Pont nomination should shoo Roth in, a Biden nomination might give him trouble. All that is assuming Roth runs, as Republicans hope; if he chooses to retire at age 67, this could be an opening for Democratic Congressman-at-Large Tom Carper.

Delaware's junior Senator, without any major legislation to his name, is nonetheless one of the leading candidates for the 1988 Democratic nomination—the first Delaware Democrat since James Bayard (Cleveland's first secretary of state) to be a serious candidate for president. He is also, with the Democrats in the majority again, an important senator. Biden was elected to the Senate in 1972 when he was 29 (although he turned 30 by the time the term began); he campaigned against an incumbent who, the voters sensed accurately, would have preferred to retire. Biden had the advantages of energy, a skillful handling of the issues, and an attractive extended family; tragically his first wife and daughter died in an auto accident just after the election. He won reelection comfortably in 1978 and again in 1984, despite the Republican tendencies of those years.

Biden's number one political asset is his articulateness. He speaks easily and fluently, in sentences that parse, with ideas that stand up to scrutiny, and usually with an emotional fervor that carries his audience along where he wants it to go. In an era dominated by the cool political medium of television, he is a hot politician. But he is not all mouth: he also has an acute political ear, to which he owes his initial election and much of his popularity in Delaware. He has a sure instinct for what is troubling voters, a talent for articulating their complaints, and the ability to come up with plausible ways to attack problems. He was the first incumbent senator to back Jimmy Carter in 1976, and he was one of the first to criticize Carter later when things were not working out well.

Biden has the gut Democratic instincts that come from growing up Catholic and middle class in an industrial city where the elite is Protestant and Republican and at the time (he was a junior in a Catholic boys school) when John F. Kennedy was elected President. On issues he follows a course similar, though not identical, to Kennedy's—not the mythical Kennedy who was liberal on everything, but the actual Kennedy, a skeptic but not a cynic who could argue both sides of a lot of issues but who could also summon up his followers' enthusiasm for the course he would follow. Biden made a point in 1986 and 1987 of assembling various experts on policies foreign and domestic around him, but he still seems to rely heavily on his own political instincts to decide where he will stand.

On economic issues Biden has followed the mainstream of his party, voting for the more generous domestic spending alternatives but expressing some doubts about the effectiveness of government action. On foreign policy, he is a skeptic about American military involvement abroad, a critic of many American allies (but a supporter of Israel), an opponent of some military spending programs. In the Carter years he became an authentic expert on and supporter of the SALT II Treaty. In the first six Reagan years he has not taken a lead role on the major foreign policy issues, although he has the potential to be a force on less publicized ones. With his high-ranking seat on Foreign Relations and his presidential ambitions, he will almost have to take a lead role in 1987 and 1988. On cultural issues, he often does not support positions associated with liberal Democrats. He has joined with Roth in sponsoring measures to limit the ability of federal courts to issue busing orders and has supported them if anything more vociferously. But he is with the Senate majority against a constitutional amendment to ban abortion.

In the Senate now Biden's most visible role is as chairman of the Judiciary Committee, a position he got somewhat unexpectedly when Edward Kennedy, who has 10 years' more seniority, decided to chair Labor and Public Welfare instead. Biden has made a specialty of impassioned statements and interrogations of leading Reagan officials, anguishing in public about his decision to oppose the nomination of Attorney General Edwin Meese, dramatizing his opposition to Chief Justice William Rehnquist. But he has also taken care to remain on good terms with his Republican predecessor, Strom Thurmond, and points out that he has voted for the lion's share of Reagan's nominations. Judiciary could prove a hot seat for him. He can win plaudits from liberals any time for opposing a Reagan nomination, and there may be some that will be unpopular with the general public as well. But Biden knows enough about voters' sentiments to know that most of them would be even less pleased to see the courts staffed by the kind of nominees they sense Reagan's liberal opponents would put there. On Foreign Relations, the other plum committee assignment he got early in his career, he faces similar problems. He has every reason to believe that the Reagan policy of aiding the Nicaraguan contras is unpopular. But he needs to be able to signal voters that he does not favor the kind of foreign policy that throws up its hands and says that a supine America is just going to have to live with whatever the Soviets and Third World terrorists want to do.

Congressman. Delaware's only congressman is Democrat Thomas Carper, who has beaten two very well-known Republicans in tough and occasionally bitter contests. He won the seat in 1982 by beating Thomas Evans, one of the congressional casualties of the Paula Parkinson scandal (she was the lobbyist whose picture appeared in *Playboy* and who was rumored, incorrectly, to have videotaped affairs with 17 congressmen). Carper won by a large margin in 1984, against Elise du Pont, the wife of the outgoing governor and an AID administrator in her own right; he won by an even bigger margin in 1986 against a hapless Republican who apologized to veterans' groups for having sought conscientious objector status in the Vietnam war.

In the House Carper has low-ranking positions on rather dull though, for a Delaware representative, politically useful committees (Banking, Merchant Marine); Banking is particularly important, since Delaware owes much of its growth to the state government's enticements to the financial service industry. Carper has carried the water for the big financial interests of Delaware; he has not taken a front-row leadership position on any major bill.

Presidential politics. Delaware chooses its small number of national convention delegates by caucus. In the general election, it is often one of the nation's most closely contested states, and in close elections it has gone with the winner since 1948. Yet Delaware voters are not heavily wooed in presidential elections, for the good reason that there are not very many of them. Commercials on Philadelphia TV stations reach almost the entire state, so there is not much reason for a candidate to come here—unless, as will be the case if the Republicans nominate Pete du Pont or the Democrat Joe Biden, he happens to live here.

The People: Est. Pop. 1986: 633,000; Pop. 1980: 594,338, up 6.5% 1980–86 and 8.4% 1970–80; 0.26% of U.S. total, 47th largest. 14% with 1–3 yrs. col., 16% with 4+ yrs. col.; 11.9% below poverty level. Single ancestry: 13% English, 6% Irish, German, 4% Italian, 2% Polish, 1% French, Scottish. Households (1980): 75% family, 41% with children, 61% married couples; 30.9% housing units rented; median monthly rent: $202; median house value: $44,600. Voting age pop. (1980): 427,743; 14% Black, 1% Spanish origin, 1% Asian origin. Registered voters (1986): 296,436; 132,044 D (44%), 102,527 R (35%); 61,805 unaffiliated (21%).

1986 Share of Federal Tax Burden: $2,113,000,000; 0.28% of U.S. total, 47th largest.

1986 Share of Federal Expenditures

	Total		Non-Defense		Defense	
Total Expend	$1,786m	(0.22%)	$1,358m	(0.23%)	$428m	(0.19%)
St/Lcl Grants	314m	(0.28%)	313m	(0.28%)	1m	(.90%)
Salary/Wages	253m	(0.21%)	104m	(0.18%)	149m	(0.24%)
Pymts to Indiv	927m	(0.25%)	874m	(0.25)	52m	(0.29%)
Procurement	260m	(0.13%)	35m	(0.06%)	224m	(0.15%)
Research/Other	32m	(0.12%)	32m	(0.12%)	0m	(0%)

Political Lineup: Governor, Michael N. Castle (R); Lt. Gov., S. B. Woo (D); Secy. of State, Michael E. Harkins (R); Atty. Gen., Charles M. Oberly, III (D); Treasurer, Janet C. Rzewnicki (R); Auditor, Dennis E. Greenhouse (D). State Senate, 21 (13 D and 8 R); State House of Representatives, 41 (22 R and 19 D). Senators, William V. Roth, Jr. (R) and Joseph R. Biden, Jr. (D). Representative, 1 D at large.

1984 Presidential Vote			1980 Presidential Vote		
Reagan (R)	152,190	(60%)	Reagan (R)	111,252	(47%)
Mondale (D)	101,656	(40%)	Carter (D)	105,754	(45%)
			Anderson (I)	6,754	(7%)

GOVERNOR

Gov. Michael N. Castle (R)

Elected 1984, term expires Jan. 1989; b. July 2, 1935, Wilmington; home, Dover; Hamilton Col., B.A. 1961, Georgetown U., LL.B. 1964; Roman Catholic; single.

Career: DE Dpty. Atty. Gen., 1965–66; DE House of Reps., 1966–68; DE Senate, 1968–76, Minor. Ldr., 1975–76; DE Lt. Gov., 1980–84.

Offices: Legislative Hall, Dover 19901, 302-736-4101.

Election Results

1984 gen.	Michael N. Castle (R)	135,250	(56%)
	William T. Quillen (D)	108,315	(44%)
1984 prim.	Michael N. Castle (R) nominated by convention		
1980 gen.	Pierre S. du Pont IV (R)	159,004	(71%)
	William J. Gordy (D)	64,217	(29%)

SENATORS

Sen. William V. Roth, Jr. (R)

Elected 1970, seat up 1988; b. July 22, 1921, Great Falls, MT; home, Wilmington; U. of OR, B.A. 1944, Harvard U., M.B.A. 1947, LL.B. 1947; Episcopalian; married (Jane).

Career: Army, WWII; Practicing atty.; Chmn., DE Repub. State Cmtee., 1961-64; U.S. House of Reps., 1967-71.

Offices: 104 HSOB 20510, 202-224-2441. Also 3021 Fed. Bldg., 844 King St., Wilmington 19801, 302-573-6291; 2215 Fed. Bldg., 300 S. New St., Dover 19901, 302-674-3308; and 2 S. Bedford St., Georgetown 19947, 302-856-7690.

Committees: *Finance* (3d of 9 R). Subcommittees: International Debt (Ranking Member); International Trade; Taxation and Debt Management. *Governmental Affairs* (Ranking Member of 6 R). Subcommittee: Investigations (Ranking Member). *Select Committee on Intelligence* (2d of 7 R). *Joint Economic Committee.*
Subcommittees: International Economic Policy; Economic Growth, Trade and Taxes; Economic Goals and Intergovernmental Policy.

Group Ratings

	ADA	ACLU	COPE	CFA	LCV	ACU	NTU	NSI	COC	CEI
1986	15	21	18	33	68	78	58	80	82	64
1985	20	—	18	33	—	70	72	—	83	—

National Journal Ratings

	1986 LIB — 1986 CONS		1985 LIB — 1985 CONS	
Economic	30% —	69%	14% —	83%
Social	35% —	63%	35% —	62%
Foreign	30% —	65%	34% —	63%

Key Votes

1) Ease Gun Cont	FOR	5) Grm-Rdmn Def Red	AGN	9) Rehnquist Nom	FOR
2) Immig Reform	FOR	6) Contra Aid	FOR	10) Tax Reform	AGN
3) Lmt Text Imp	FOR	7) SDI Funding	FOR	11) Drug Death Pen	AGN
4) Aid Tobac Ind	AGN	8) Lmt PAC Contrib	AGN	12) S Africa Sanc	FOR

Election Results

1982 general	William V. Roth, Jr. (R)	105,472	(56%)	($797,516)
	David N. Levinson (D)	83,722	(44%)	($777,819)
1982 primary	William V. Roth, Jr. (R) unopposed			
1976 general	William V. Roth, Jr. (R)	125,454	(56%)	($322,080)
	Thomas Maloney (D)	98,042	(44%)	($211,258)

Campaign Contributions and Expenditures

1979-82		Direct Cont. 1981-82		PACS Breakdown			
Receipts	$843,047	Indiv.	$423,656	Agr.	$3,200	Ideo.	$38,600
Expend.	$797,516	Party	$18,066	Bus.	$261,870	Lbr.	$7,500
Unspent	$48,019	PACS	$353,444	Hlth.	$26,250	Prof.	$14,250

Sen. Joseph R. Biden, Jr. (D)

Elected 1972, seat up 1990; b. Nov. 20, 1942, Scranton, PA; home, Wilmington; U. of DE, B.A. 1965, Syracuse U., J.D. 1968; Roman Catholic; married (Jill).

Career: Practicing atty., 1968–72; New Castle Cnty. Cncl., 1970–72.

Offices: 489 RSOB 20510, 202-224-5042. Also Fed. Bldg., 844 King St., Wilmington 19801, 302-573-6345; 1101 Fed. Bldg, 300 S. New St., Dover 17901, 302-678-9483; and Box 109, The Circle, Georgetown 19901, 302-856-9275.

Committees: *Foreign Relations* (2d of 11 D). Subcommittee: European Affairs (Chairman). *Judiciary* (Chairman).

Group Ratings

	ADA	ACLU	COPE	CFA	LCV	ACU	NTU	NSI	COC	CEI
1986	80	92	80	80	86	6	41	10	38	28
1985	75	—	80	60	—	10	29	—	37	—

National Journal Ratings

	1986 LIB — 1986 CONS		1985 LIB — 1985 CONS	
Economic	84%	— 15%	76%	— 23%
Social	85%	— 14%	80%	— 18%
Foreign	75%	— 0%	74%	— 23%

Key Votes

1) Ease Gun Cont	FOR	5) Grm-Rdmn Def Red	—	9) Rehnquist Nom	AGN
2) Immig Reform	AGN	6) Contra Aid	AGN	10) Tax Reform	FOR
3) Lmt Text Imp	FOR	7) SDI Funding	AGN	11) Drug Death Pen	AGN
4) Aid Tobac Ind	AGN	8) Lmt PAC Contrib	—	12) S Africa Sanc	FOR

Election Results

1984 general	Joseph R. Biden, Jr. (D) 147,831	(60%)	($1,602,052)
	John M. Burris (R) 98,101	(40%)	($816,484)
1984 primary	Joseph R. Biden, Jr. (D) nominated by convention		
1978 general	Joseph R. Biden, Jr. (D. 93,930	(58%)	($494,718)
	James H. Baxter, Jr. (R). 66,479	(41%)	($206,250)

Campaign Contributions and Expenditures

1979-84		Direct Cont. 1979-84		PACS Breakdown 1979-84			
Receipts	$1,627,215	Indiv.	$1,101,130	Corp.	$61,880	T/M/H	$72,879
Expend.	$1,602,052	Party	$22,500	Labor	$191,184	Agr.	$1,000
Unspent	$24,489	PACS	$433,947	Ideo.	$99,330	CWOS	$2,500

REPRESENTATIVE

Rep. Thomas R. Carper (D)

Elected 1982; b. Jan. 23, 1947, Beckley, WV; home, New Castle; OH State U., B.A. 1968, U. of DE, M.B.A. 1975; Presbyterian; married (Martha).

Career: Naval Flight Officer, 1968–73; Treas., James R. Soles for Congress Campaign, 1974; Industrial Develop., DE Div. of Econ. Develop., 1975–76; State Treas., 1976–82.

Offices: 131 CHOB 20515, 202-225-4165. Also 5021 Fed. Bldg., Wilmington 19801, 302-573-6181; and Fed. Bldg., 300 S. New St., Dover 19901, 302-736-1666.

Committees: *Banking, Finance and Urban Affairs* (19th of 31 D). Subcommittees: Financial Institutions Supervision, Regulation and Insurance; Housing and Community Development; International Finance, Trade and Monetary Policy. *Merchant Marine and Fisheries* (16th of 25 D). Subcommittees: Coast Guard and Navigation; Fisheries and Wildlife Conservation and the Environment.

Group Ratings

	ADA	ACLU	COPE	CFA	LCV	ACU	NTU	NSI	COC	CEI
1986	55	50	69	75	84	27	36	20	50	39
1985	55	—	64	67	—	24	52	—	50	—

National Journal Ratings

	1986 LIB — 1986 CONS		1985 LIB — 1985 CONS	
Economic	50%	— 48%	51%	— 48%
Social	61%	— 37%	63%	— 33%
Foreign	56%	— 43%	64%	— 33%

Key Votes

1) Lmt Cln Water Act	FOR	5) Retain Gun Cont	FOR	9) Aid Angola Reb	FOR
2) Rpl Tobac Sub	FOR	6) Contra Aid	AGN	10) Tax Reform	FOR
3) Grm-Rdmn Def Red	FOR	7) Lmt Text Imp	FOR	11) S Africa Sanc	FOR
4) Ban Polygraph	FOR	8) Lmt SDI	FOR	12) Immig Reform	FOR

Election Results

1986 general	Thomas R. Carper (D)	106,351	(66%)	($307,300)
	Thomas S. Neuberger (R)	53,767	(34%)	($270,563)
1986 primary	Thomas R. Carper (D) unopposed			
1984 general	Thomas R. Carper (D)	142,070	(58%)	($354,502)
	Elise du Pont (R)	100,650	(41%)	($704,403)

Campaign Contributions and Expenditures

1985-86		Direct Cont. 1985-86		PACS Breakdown 1985-86			
Receipts	$326,795	Indiv.	$161,726	Corp.	$36,320	T/M/H	$47,763
Expend.	$307,300	PACS	$159,912	Labor	$67,125	Agr.	$0
Debts	$32,784			Ideo.	$8,704	CWOS	$0

DISTRICT OF COLUMBIA

The most political of American cities is also the least political: Washington, D.C., the nation's capital, has a local politics that is underdeveloped—and seems to be getting more so. This is not all Washingtonians' fault. The framers of the Constitution were wary of vesting political power in the citizens of a capital city: they remembered how the London mob had threatened Parliament in the Gordon riots, and they would see a few years later how the Paris mob would bring down the government of France. So the Constitution gave the federal government power over a capital district, not to exceed ten miles square, and George Washington picked a site close to his own Mount Vernon. In the 200 years since, Congress has allowed Washington self-government for less than two decades.

One reason is race: Washington had the nation's largest free black population before the Civil War and was a magnet for blacks in years afterwards. Republicans, who won most black votes then, gave the District self-government in the 1870s; Republican Governor Alexander Shepherd built great public works and spent the District into bankruptcy. Exit self-government. Then during the civil rights revolution of the 1960s, it came to seem absurd to deny Washington, which officially became majority-black in 1960, the vote. And so in 1964 Washingtonians began to cast three electoral votes for president; in 1968 they could vote for school board; in 1971 they finally got to elect a non-voting delegate to Congress; in 1974, after the defeat of longtime House District Committee Chairman John McMillan in his 1972 primary in South Carolina, they got home rule and could, like residents of every other American city, vote for mayor and council.

Still, the results of Washington's electoral politics have been disappointing. One reason is that Washington has proved to be out of sync with national opinion through most of the 1970s and 1980s. It voted 86% for Walter Mondale in 1984 while the rest of the country was voting 59% for Ronald Reagan. The District is not only more Democratic than any American state; it is more Democratic than any American *county*. Another reason for Washington's political underdevelopment is the sense that not much is at stake. Congress retains, under the Constitution, final authority over the District, can always threaten to overturn D.C. laws, and has in fact threatened to undo some particularly silly ones. Congress must approve every year a federal payment in lieu of the huge property taxes the government would pay if it were not exempt: this gives even the sympathetic members of the District Committee a responsibility to question D.C. officials on local affairs. Also, the District's prosecutor and judges are federal appointees, not responsible to the voter; there are federal police forces that patrol federal buildings, embassies, parks, Capitol Hill. Finally, District politicians can never become voting members of Congress. The current prime minister of France used to be mayor of Paris; in Britain one possible future Labor party leader is the former head of the Greater London Council.

But even taken together these factors do not explain Washington's failure to develop a stronger political culture. Neither does race. Blacks in other American cities have developed a dynamic and competitive politics, and Washington's black community has especially deep roots and vast talents. Howard University and Freedmen's Hospital date back to Reconstruction, and there are old black families here who have been producing leaders for generations. Moreover, there is no significant white voting bloc that wants to take power away from blacks. Washington has not had a significant white working-class or ethnic population since the 1950s. Its affluent whites west of Rock Creek Park or in gentrified neighborhoods like Capitol Hill, Adams-Morgan, and Mount Pleasant, do not imagine that they will ever form a majority in the city, or should; neither do the city's Latin and Asian immigrants.

Yet even so, black Washington is generating few candidates and, for most of the 1980s, no effective competition for Mayor Marion Barry. Many talented blacks seem to head away from

DISTRICT OF COLUMBIA — Delegate District,
Quadrants, and Place — *(1 Delegate At Large)*

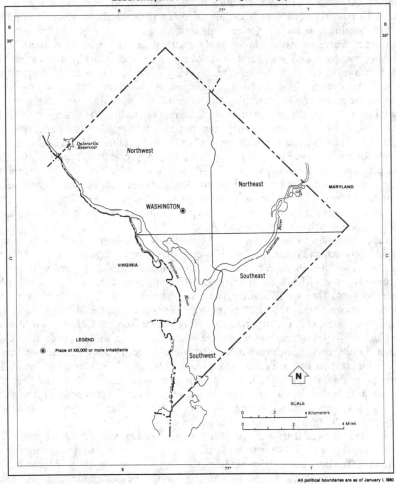

All political boundaries are as of January I, 1960

seeking office and into comfortable and well-paid positions as lawyers, lobbyists, and consultants. Setting the tone is Mayor Barry. He was known as a militant when he started an organization called Pride, Inc., in the 1960s; in the 1970s he ran for the school board and got citywide recognition. In 1978 he won a close three-way primary over incumbent Walter Washington and City Council President Sterling Tucker; in 1982 he won a second term by defeating his main challenger, former HUD and HEW/HHS Secretary Patricia Roberts Harris, who died in 1985. In 1986 he did not have serious primary opposition, but he was held to an unusually low percentage in the general election by Republican Council member Carol Schwartz.

As time has gone on, scandal has accumulated around Barry. His first wife went to jail for skimming money from Pride, Inc. His top aide in his first years as mayor, Ivanhoe Donaldson, went to jail for channeling hundreds of thousands of city dollars to himself. Other former top aides are under investigation. The Mayor himself was under investigation for some time, but no charges resulted. Barry has been careful to condemn misconduct, but he often seems more agonized by the trouble these scandals have caused him than by the betrayal of community responsibility they show. His own conduct is anything but austere. He staged several gala inaugural balls over three days to begin his third term. When the city failed to make even a beginning of clearing the snow away after a gigantic snowstorm in January 1987, Barry called in from California, where he was spending six days attending the Super Bowl, to say that he had been working too hard and was going to take more vacation time in the future. When he returned, he surveyed the snow by helicopter, saying it would take him too long to go by car.

With no serious competition, and with a competent record in some respects—he fixed the city's chaotic accounting, for example, and streamlined some city services, got a start on reducing infant mortality—Barry seems able to be mayor-for-life. Yet when difficulties arise, he responds by sloughing off responsibility: the busy signals on the 911 line are the fault of consultants; the lack of shelter for the homeless is a federal problem. He lacks the uncompromising demand for performance that is the hallmark of any successful executive and the austere intolerance for misbehavior that is a necessity if a political leader is to set a high moral tone. The problems associated with the black underclass—high crime, high illegitimacy—come because many poor blacks feel no obligation to adhere to basic standards of morality. A leader, no matter how talented, of a black majority city if he does not reinforce those standards runs a terrible risk of seeing sociopathic behavior spread and grow.

In the meantime many Washingtonians of both races have been disturbed by an apparently growing gulf between the races. In the 1974 and 1978 mayoral races, blacks and whites cast votes for the candidates in almost identical proportions; Barry may very well owe his 1978 election to whites west of Rock Creek Park. In 1986, in contrast, Schwartz led Barry by a wide margin west of Rock Creek Park, while Barry won overwhelmingly among black voters. Many Washington blacks note that the black percentage is not rising in the city any more, that young black families are moving to the suburbs, especially Prince Georges County, Maryland, and that whites are gentrifying new neighborhoods; they fear there is a white agenda to take over city government. Oddly enough, whites do hold citywide office, notably Council President David Clarke. But his support comes heavily from black voters, and the idea of an anti-black white takeover is preposterous; city government does not impinge that much on the lives of affluent whites for them to bother. But whites are coming to regard the District government, and perhaps the majority who elects it, with contempt—a contempt that often exaggerates its shortcomings and loses sight totally of its considerable achievements.

One of them is to at least nurture, if not single-handedly produce, the economic growth which continues through the 1980s to surge through Washington. People are renovating houses and apartments; the business district has been thriving and moving eastward into territory land developers once shunned, though in the middle 1980s the east downtown was temporarily overbuilt; property values are still climbing not only in affluent white areas but in many of the city's comfortable black neighborhoods as well. The District's new Convention Center, a Barry project, is thriving and stimulating a big hotel-building boom in what was a bedraggled area. But all this growth could be threatened if the city government and the city's political culture do not provide a more elevated tone of leadership.

The District has one member of Congress, Delegate Walter Fauntroy, who necessarily spends a lot of time on District affairs. Like other nonvoting members, he can vote in committee, and he is now the number two Democrat on the House District of Columbia Committee. He first won his seat in a special 1971 election, and the real contest was in the Democratic primary; he has had no serious opposition since. Fauntroy gets on fairly well now with Mayor Barry, although they have not always been allies; he defers to Barry often in sticky negotiations with Congress or the Administration. He seems not to have any ambition to run for mayor himself, though he would surely run for the Senate if Washington got representation there. A minister with a proud past in the civil rights movement, he is a pleasant, self-effacing man.

Fauntroy has had varied success when he has ventured beyond local matters, however. He succeeded in making an impact on national policy on South Africa and moving even the Reagan

Administration in his direction when he became the first congressman to be arrested demonstrating in front of the South African embassy in November 1984. Fauntroy's strength—and weakness—is his tendency to treat issues as simple moral questions of racial justice. When that matches the facts, as in South Africa or during his work in the civil rights movement, he has a genuine ability to focus moral indignation against evil and get results. When the facts are less clear or more complicated, however—when he finds himself defending the PLO after Andrew Young was fired or when he attacks the issuance of a traffic ticket to a black politician as evidence of racism—he squanders some of the moral capital he has earned.

On one of the causes dearest to his heart, he has not been successful. In 1978 he got the Congress to approve a constitutional amendment giving the District full representation in the Congress, which in practical terms would mean the addition of two senators and a vote as well as a voice for the city's congressman. But the amendment died when far fewer than the required number of state legislatures voted to ratify it.

Fauntroy is a member of the Banking Committee, in which he was probably first interested because of its jurisdiction over housing programs. He has spent some time and done some serious and creditable work on the Monetary Policy Subcommittee. He is now the fourth ranking Democrat, behind a chairman who has been investigated by the ethics committee and two other Democrats who are nearly two decades older; it is conceivable that Fauntroy could become chairman of this committee, with its important though often technical legislation. So it may be that a District of Columbia representative, without even the right to vote on the floor, could become an important national policymaker.

The People: Est. Pop. 1986: 626,000; Pop. 1980: 638,333, dn. 1.9% 1980–86 and 15.6% 1970–80; 0.26% of U.S. total, 48th largest. 14% with 1–3 yrs. col., 28% with 4+ yrs. col.; 18.6% below poverty level. Households: 53% family, 29% with children, 30% married couples; 64.5% housing units rented; median monthly rent: $208; median house value: $70,700. Voting age pop. (1980): 494,842; 66% Black, 3% Spanish origin, 1% Asian origin. Registered voters (1986): 281,999; 226,023 D (80%); 22,874 R (8%); 31,256 unaffiliated (12%), 1,846 minor parties (1%).

1986 Share of Federal Tax Burden $2,657,000,000; 0.35% of U.S. total, 43d largest.

1986 Share of Federal Expenditures

	Total		Non-Defense		Defense	
Total Expend	$14,436m	(1.74%)	$12,705m	(2.12%)	$1,732m	(0.75%)
St/Lcl Grants	1,423m	(1.26%)	1,423m	(1.27%)	0m	(0%)
Salary/Wages	7,453m	(6.18%)	6,532m	(11.12%)	921m	(1.49%)
Pymts to Indiv	1,499m	(0.41%)	1,453m	(0.42%)	45m	(0.25%)
Procurement	2,759m	(1.34%)	1,994m	(3.59%)	765m	(0.51%)
Research/Other	1,302m	(4.88%)	1,302m	(4.89%)	0m	(0%)

Political Lineup: Representative, 1 D at large.

1984 Presidential Vote

Mondale (D)	180,408	(85%)
Reagan (R)	29,009	(14%)

1980 Presidential Vote

Carter (D)	130,231	(75%)
Reagan (R)	23,313	(13%)
Anderson (I)	16,131	(9%)

1984 Democratic Presidential Primary

Jackson	69,106	(67%)
Mondale	26,320	(26%)
Hart	7,305	(7%)

1984 Republican Presidential Primary

Reagan	5,692	(100%)

REPRESENTATIVE

Rep. Walter E. Fauntroy (D)

Elected Mar. 23, 1971; b. Feb. 6, 1933, Washington, D.C.; home, Washington, D.C.; VA Union U., B.A. 1955, Yale U., B.D. 1958; Baptist; married (Dorothy).

Career: Pastor, New Bethel Baptist Church, 1958–present; Founder and former Dir., Model Inner City Commun. Org.; Dir., Washington Bureau, SCLC, 1960–71; Coordinator, Selma to Montgomery March, 1965; Vice Chmn., DC City Cncl., 1967–79; Natl. Coordinator, Poor Peoples Campaign, 1969; Chmn., Bd. of Dirs., Martin Luther King, Jr., Ctr. for Social Change, 1969–present.

Offices: 2135 RHOB 20515, 202-225-8050. Also 2041 Martin Luther King, Jr., Ave., S.E., Ste. 311, Washington, D.C. 20020, 202-426-2530.

Committees: *Banking, Finance and Urban Affairs* (4th of 31 D). Subcommittees: Domestic Monetary Policy; Housing and Community Development; International Development Institutions and Finance (Chairman); International Finance, Trade, and Monetary Policy. *District of Columbia* (2d of 8 D). Subcommittees: Fiscal Affairs and Health (Chairman); Government Operations and Metropolitan Affairs. *Select Committee on Narcotics Abuse and Control* (10th of 15 D).

Group Ratings and Key Votes: Does Not Vote

Election Results

1986 general	Walter E. Fauntroy (D)	101,604	(80%)	($74,681)
	Mary L. H. King (R)	17,643	(14%)	
	Julie McCall (Statehood)	6,122	(5%)	
1986 primary	Walter E. Fauntroy (D) unopposed	66,019	(100%)	
1984 general	Walter E. Fauntroy (D)	154,583	(96%)	($61,427)

Campaign Contributions and Expenditures

1985-86		Direct Cont. 1985-86		PACS Breakdown 1985-86			
Receipts	$83,593	Indiv.	$124,824	Corp.	$9,598	T/M/H	$7,675
Expend.	$74,681	PACS	$26,898	Labor	$5,975	Agr.	$0
Unspent	$15,543			Ideo.	$900	CWOS	$2,750

FLORIDA

"America at its best," one candidate for governor in 1986 called Florida. Some will quibble with that, but Florida is certainly America at its newest. Some time before 1990 Florida will welcome its 12 millionth resident and become the nation's fourth most populous state, after California, New York, and Texas. That is something almost no one would have predicted in the 1940s, when Florida was still, as it had been for years, a steamy, sparsely populated backwater, one of the least developed parts of the Deep South. The land did not seem intended for dense human habitation. The climate, Florida's greatest attraction today, was in all but the winter months considered intolerable by most Americans until air conditioning became common. The state's few citizens were mostly poor, disease-ridden, uneducated, insular, and bigoted. Florida then as now had no important mineral resources (except phosphates in the central part of the state), and its agricultural potential (except for citrus) went unrecognized for years. Geographically it was not close to anything, except the farmlands and swamps of south Georgia and, across the sea, Cuba and the Bahamas. Its long shoreline has surprisingly few natural ports.

But Florida has always had warm weather, and over the last four decades, since the development of the room air conditioner, Florida's population has zoomed from 2 million to 12 million. As one cohort of older Americans after another has migrated from the cold industrial belt from Boston to St. Louis down to the funnel of the Florida peninsula, a new megastate has grown. Fully 90% of Florida's housing units have been built since 1945, hundreds of square miles of swampland have been drained, miles and miles of roads and parking lots have been laid down, shopping centers and restaurants and luxury resorts and trailer parks have been built. For millions of Americans, Florida has been a chance to start over, to create the kind of community they have always wanted to live in, to build if not a city on the hill then a suburb in what was until quite recently a swamp.

The result is a population and an electorate as diverse as any in America—but not in the same proportions. The old, pre-migration Florida, located almost entirely within the northern part of the state and extending a little way down the peninsula, was heavily Democratic, strongly segregationist, and interested in state politics because its shrewd legislators could bring money and jobs to impoverished local communities. To that Florida was added two distinct streams of migration. Starting in the late 1940s, affluent and mostly Protestant northerners, from pleasant suburbs and prosperous small towns, started moving to Florida to retire. They were joined, not too long after, by ethnic and blue-collar northerners—Jews moving to Miami were the most visible, but they included Catholics as well—who were mostly New Deal Democrats. Both streams continued in large volume, with some younger migrants as well; but Florida remains easily the most elderly of states, and the constant turnover in its elderly population has made for constant demographic and political change. And now Florida is becoming the home for much of what appears to be a third wave of migration to this country: not only the Cubans who came here first in the 1960s and then again in 1980 as refugees from Castro's dictatorship, but also people from Haiti and Nicaragua, Colombia and Jamaica.

This diversity produced some cultural conflict and has had political repercussions. The emergence of Miami not only as the center for Latin American commerce but also for a huge and murderous drug trade has made it the most cynical and politically alienated of American cities. Blacks have rioted in Miami, in part because of resentment over the more rapid economic progress of the Cubans and other Latins; Jews and other migrants from the East Coast have moved north into Broward and Palm Beach County; Wasps have settled in new condominium communities farther north or on the Gulf Coast. Similarly rapid though less turbulent migration has affected almost every part of the state.

The result is that relatively few Florida voters have any longstanding connection with the civic culture of the state; they know nothing of the antics of Governor Claude Kirk (1967–70), or how Reubin Askew came to office, or how the legislature was dominated for years by conservatives from north Florida called the Pork Chop Gang. Yet for all their diversity and newness Floridians have some things in common. They have an unfocused concern about Florida's physical environment, though the Florida they live in is anything but pristine. They are against any income tax and favor a high sales tax instead (because one-third of the revenue comes from tourists). They are cautious about proposals for casino gambling and wary of big-money crime.

Also contributing to Florida's political instability is its geographical size and the briefness of its political season. There are eight media markets here, none of them dominant; Miami's Dade County casts only 12% of its votes, and together with the other Gold Coast counties of Broward and Palm Beach only 30%. Another major metropolitan area has two contrasting central cities, bustling Tampa and retiree-haven St. Petersburg. Jacksonville is big enough to be significant in the state's economy and politics, and so is Orlando, the home of Disney World and its Epcot Center as well as the center of the state's citrus industry. There are, moreover, literally dozens of

FLORIDA — Congressional Districts, Counties, and Selected Places — (19 Districts)

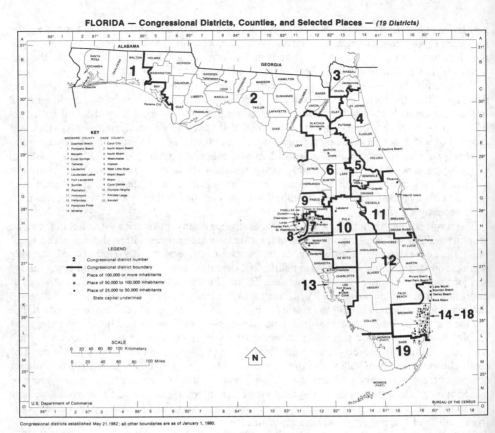

See pages 1369-1374 for additional metropolitan area maps.

small cities, from Pensacola to Naples and Key West that, for most of their residents, are Florida, and most are growing more rapidly than the big centers. Then too, no single dominant newspaper and a capital (tiny Tallahassee) tucked away in a corner of the state, more than a comfortable day's drive from where most voters live, state government and what sense of unity it may provide elsewhere is often invisible. Finally, to complete the sense of helter-skleter, Florida's political campaigns are decided in a rush: in 1986 the primary was September 2, the runoff (and there were gubernatorial runoffs in both parties) was September 30, followed five weeks later by the general election.

All these factors make Florida elections subject to startling fluctuations. In presidential races it trended Republican after 1948, went for Jimmy Carter in 1976, then turned sharply toward Ronald Reagan in 1980 and 1984. In state politics Republicans became competitive in the mid-1960s but saw Democrats win most elections in the 1970s and 1980s—until Democrat-turned-Republican Bob Martinez was elected governor in 1986. For a time anyway there seemed to be a predictable pattern for success in Florida politics. A little-known moderate state legislator would edge into second place in the Democratic primary, then run away with the runoff, and win the general elections: thus were Lawton Chiles and Reubin Askew elected Senator and governor in 1970 and Bob Graham, governor in 1978. But no one has won this way since: Buddy MacKay in the 1980 Senate race, Harry Johnston in the 1986 governor's race, and Tom Gallagher in that same race on the Republican side all finished a close third, missing runoffs that could have put them in statewide office for years.

One reason may have been luck. But another was the change in the balance of party registration: as recently as 1982 it was 64% Democratic and 30% Republican, but by fall 1986 it was 57%–36%, with Democrats adding just 127,000 voters and Republicans 609,000. The result is a Democratic primary electorate less tilted toward southern-accented moderates and a Republican primary electorate more representative of the voters generally. Republicans have ended up with candidates more saleable statewide, like Paula Hawkins and Martinez, while Democrats tend to choose liberal candidates who seem almost as out of line with majority opinion here as the party's presidential nominees.

The trends here reflect attitudinal changes and the migration patterns of the 1980s. Republicans have been helped by increased registration among Miami-area Cuban-Americans, by rapid growth in the affluent Gulf coast south of St. Petersburg and Atlantic coast north of Palm Beach, by Republican trends in family-oriented central Florida around Orlando, and by the continuing Republican trend in the heavily military panhandle around Pensacola and Panama City. These shifts are only partially offset by Democratic trends in less affluent retirement areas on the Gulf coast north of St. Petersburg, the Atlantic coast between Cape Canaveral and Jacksonville, and in and around Tallahassee.

Governor. Governor Bob Martinez entered the 1986 race with severe handicaps. He was a Republican, still the minority party here; he had spirited primary opposition in a party he had joined only in 1963; he is Hispanic in a state whose most heavily Hispanic area, Miami's Dade County, voted resoundingly for making English its only official language. Yet Martinez won, and handily. He was well positioned on the issues, he proved he was qualified for the office, and he had luck. In the Republican primary, he had the advantage of national backing and ballyhoo, and ran well ahead of the field; the strongest runoff opponent, hard-charging Tom Gallagher, was narrowly beaten by former Representative Louis Frey, who had spent little time in Florida after losing the 1980 Senate runoff to Paula Hawkins. In the general election, Martinez was helped because Jim Smith, the conservative attorney general, was beaten by liberal legislator Steve Pajcic by a 51%–49% margin. Smith was handicapped by political missteps (in 1985 he started running for governor as a Democrat, then said he was considering becoming a Republican and even went to the White House, then said he was staying a Democrat and not running for governor, then ran for lieutenant governor on Harry Johnston's ticket, then flirted with a congressional race, then ran for governor as a Democrat). But Pajcic was also handicapped by Smith ads attacking him for opposing the death penalty—a burning issue in Florida, which has one of the nation's most crowded death rows—and voting against a bill to keep pornography out of convenience stores.

Meanwhile, Martinez, who grew up in Tampa, not Miami or Cuba, and talks with a decidedly southern accent, campaigned as an experienced public official, a stern opponent of crime, and pledged to trim $800 million of waste from the state's $16 billion budget. Pajcic's considerable abilities as a legislator and campaign fundraiser were not enough to put him ahead in more than Broward County, his native Jacksonville, and several north Florida counties around Tallahassee and Gainesville. Martinez, aided by an unusually strong Republican Cuban-American vote, carried Dade County, long a Democratic stronghold, the Tampa Bay area, and most of the state's rural areas.

Martinez, like every Florida governor, holds an office with few institutional powers; many decisions are made by vote of the cabinet of elected officials, and he must deal with a Democratic legislature. But the most difficult issues facing Florida—from controlling growth to casino gambling and insurance liability—don't split legislators along party lines, and in his first months Martinez showed a command over the agenda. Having called for budget cuts, he promptly switched directions and called for extending the sales tax to services (also being considered in Texas, Illinois, and Washington); and he put together a coalition of leaders of the Democratic House plus the coalition of conservative Democrats and Republicans in the state Senate that beat the Democrats' choice for Senate president and installed a conservative instead. He ruffled some Republican feathers by appointing Jim Smith his chief of staff; also he made Jeb Bush, son of the Vice President and Dade County party chairman, commerce secretary.

Senators. Florida, represented by the same U.S. Senators in the 1950s and 1960s, has retired Senators often since; only one, Lawton Chiles, the state's senior Senator, has been reelected since 1964. Chiles, a Democrat whose origin and politics are part of an old Florida tradition, is from Lakeland, an old community in the central part of the state, and his politics can be described as small-town Democratic. He is a very religious man, and an earnest one, but congenial enough in temperament not to be cloying. Chiles does not appear to be an elbows-out aggressive politician, but he has taken risks to advance himself that few politicians would, from his first race for the Senate in 1970 (in which he invented the tactic, since widely copied, of walking across the state) to his resoundingly unsuccessful campaign for the Senate minority leadership in late 1984. He has been one of the spark plugs of the Democratic Leadership Council, setting up hearings in various states and making a positive case for new policies but against the big-spending mistakes of the past. But characteristically he has gone about this work quietly and without promoting his own career.

Chiles has been ranking Democrat on the Budget Committee since 1983 and became chairman in 1987. It is a position of more responsibility than reward: Budget does not have the clout of committees that actually hand out money, and in an era of high deficits more often is put in the position of denying funds than granting them. Chiles's problem is to come up with a plausible budget after the Reagan Administration sends up, as it has since 1981, budgets with almost zero support on Capitol Hill. In the 98th and 99th Congresses, Chiles worked cooperatively with Republican chairman Pete Domenici, who wanted to see the deficit cut; when Domenici and other Republicans deferred making their own proposals while seeking compromise with the Administration, Chiles was able to come up with his own budget resolutions which won near-unanimous support among the usually fractious Senate Democrats. As chairman, he found unity more difficult to achieve, sending four budgets to the floor in early 1987, as Ernest Hollings, who was chairman in 1980, insisted on consideration of his proposal to increase taxes some $34 billion. That left Chiles's budget vulnerable to the Republicans on the floor. With far fewer big spenders among the Democrats than when he entered the Senate, Chiles seems well positioned to come up with a successful budget resolution; but the path he is following is full of political landmines, not the least of which is that this Senator about to seek reelection will in this high-visibility position be seeking a tax increase.

Chiles's political standing in Florida has seemed strong since his walking campaign in 1970 and his victories in 1976 and 1982 with more than 60% of the vote. Yet as his seat comes up in 1988, Republican strategists do not regard him as home free. Personally pleasant, unobjectionable to most voters on most issues, he seems in strong shape. But he has not had strong opposition since 1970, and Florida is large and changing. You can't meet that many voters walking, and most of the electorate he'll face in 1988 wasn't voting in Florida when he first won. Some of Chiles's most endearing qualities—his self-effacing modesty, his aversion to publicity, his refusal (which he reaffirmed in 1987) to take contributions over $100 or any money from PACs or individuals outside Florida—may work against him if he should draw a serious Republican opponent. In early 1987 the well-known Republicans were dropping out of the race in numbers: Paula Hawkins, Representatives Connie Mack, Andy Ireland, and Bill McCollum, and Jim Smith. Orlando financier Phil Handy, Martinez's chief fundraiser in 1986, may be interested; so may Tom Gallagher.

The first Florida governor to win a Senate seat in 40 years is Bob Graham, now the state's junior Senator after 8 years in Tallahassee. He won primarily because voters felt he did a good job as governor. On many issues he represents the more liberal strain in Florida politics, backing some tax increases and setting up a water quality trust fund and passing a wetlands protection act; but he was always solidly conservative on the basics, opposing any income tax and, as a capital punishment backer, signing death warrants. His long anticipated race against Paula Hawkins—Florida governors are barred from seeking a third consecutive term—was one of the nation's most expensive, fought out mostly in TV ads; and for all of Graham's advantages Hawkins made it a contest. "Unique and irreplaceable," her ads called her, capitalizing on her spunky, assertive personality which drove many other Senators bonkers, and pointing up her work as sponsor of the Missing Child Assistance Act and crusader against child abuse. Graham replied that it's easy to work against things no one is for, but Hawkins had a point: there's room for Senators who specialize in issues that aren't on anyone else's front burner, even if they irritate colleagues in the process. Hawkins had much publicized surgery to repair a back injury during the campaign, but more damaging was her rambling performance in her late October debate with Graham; behind then, she gained no further ground. Graham, in contrast, is always methodical, careful, knowledgeable, and very boosterish about Florida, an exceedingly orderly man who was criticized by Hawkins as a "robot"; but the length of his career and the persistence of his striving suggests there are passions underneath. Graham won 55%–45%, although Hawkins would probably have beaten any other Democrat.

In national politics, Graham was a vehement Jimmy Carter backer in 1980; now he will probably be one of the moderate Democrats who will sit at the fulcrum of the Senate in the late 1980s. He is able and articulate and better known to voters in vast Florida than almost any other politician; his prospect for a long Senate career is good. But he holds a jinxed seat: not since George Smathers's last victory in 1962 has a Senator been reelected to it.

Presidential politics. Will Florida ever vote for a Democrat for President again? A decade ago it seemed likely to: it voted for Jimmy Carter in 1976; it would likely have gone against him by only 6% in 1980 had it not been for the sudden influx of 125,000 Cuban refugees into Miami earlier that year; it has been getting more blue collar-retirees in a decade when Republicans' support of Social Security has been challenged. But the trends here since 1980 have clearly been Republican, in party registration, in the state legislature and in statewide elections. It was Bob Graham, not Bob Martinez, who won in 1986 thanks to personal appeal and despite party proclivities.

Florida's presidential primary, as one of the nation's earliest, attracted national attention, especially when the state voted for George Wallace in 1972 and then rejected him for Jimmy Carter four years later. But now Florida is only one part of the huge southern regional primary, and not even the largest state voting that day (Texas is). Changes in each party's electorates make results hard to predict: Gary Hart won one of his early victories in this fast-growing but scarcely young state, and the Republican electorate is not monolithically conservative as it once was.

Congressional districting. Florida gained four House seats in the 1980 Census, more than any other state, and it will probably gain more than any other state again in the 1990 count. The Democrats drew the lines last time, but the one-person-one-vote limited their ability to help themselves, and two of the four new seats went Republican. Next time the Republicans may have more leverage, if Martinez remains Governor and Republicans have enough votes in the legislature to keep Democrats from overriding his veto. In the meantime, the state's House delegation, which had only six members, all conservative Democrats, in 1950, now has 19, of all political descriptions. They include two important committee chairmen, both from the Miami area, Claude Pepper of Rules and Dante Fascell of Foreign Affairs. With Miami firmly established as the economic capital of Latin America, Florida seems to have an unusually strong interest in foreign policy: it is one state where it is politic to support aid to the Nicaraguan contras just as it is to support aid to Israel.

The People: Est. Pop. 1986: 11,675,000; Pop. 1980: 9,746,324, up 19.8% 1980–84 and 43.5% 1970–80; 4.84% of U.S. total, 5th largest. 17% with 1–3 yrs. col., 15% with 4+ yrs. col.; 13.5% below poverty level. Single ancestry: 12% English, 6% German, 4% Irish, 3% Italian, 1% Polish, Russian, French, Scottish, Dutch. Households (1980): 72% family, 33% with children, 59% married couples; 31.7% housing units rented; median monthly rent: $209; median house value: $45,300. Voting age pop. (1980): 7,386,688; 11% Black, 9% Spanish origin, 1% Asian origin. Registered voters (1986): 5,631,188; 3,214,753 D (57%), 2,038,831 R (36%), 377,604 minor parties (7%).

1986 Share of Federal Tax Burden: $35,271,800,000; 4.69% of U.S. total, 6th largest.

1986 Share of Federal Expenditures

	Total		Non-Defense		Defense	
Total Expend	$39,537m	(4.76%)	$29,171m	(4.86%)	$10,366m	(4.51%)
St/Lcl Grants	3,244m	(2.88%)	3,242m	(2.88%)	2m	(1.80%)
Salary/Wages	4,988m	(4.14%)	2,071m	(3.53%)	2,917m	(4.71%)
Pymnts to Indivs	23,669m	(6.49%)	21,884m	(6.31%)	1,785m	(10.05%)
Procurement	7,223m	(3.51%)	1,562m	(2.81%)	5,661m	(3.77%)
Research/Other	412m	(1.54%)	412m	(1.55%)	0m	(1.46%)

Political Lineup: Governor, Bob Martinez (R); Lt. Gov., Bobby Brantley (R); Secy. of State, George Firestone (D); Atty. Gen., Robert A. Butterworth (D); Treasurer/Comm. of Insurance, Bill Gunter (D); Comptroller, Gerald Lewis (D). State Senate, 40 (25 D and 15 R); State House of Representatives, 120 (75 D, 45 R). Senators, Lawton Chiles (D) and Bob Graham (D). Representatives, 19 (12 D, 7 R).

1984 Presidential Vote

Reagan (R) 2,730,350 (65%)
Mondale (D) 1,448,816 (35%)

1980 Presidential Vote

Reagan (R) 2,046,951 (56%)
Carter (D) 1,419,475 (39%)
Anderson (I) 189,692   (5%)

1984 Democratic Presidential Primary

Hart 463,799 (39%)
Mondale 394,350 (33%)
Jackson 144,263 (12%)
Glenn. 128,209 (11%)
Six others 51,569   (4%)

1984 Republican Presidential Primary

Reagan 344,150 (100%)

GOVERNOR

Gov. Bob Martinez (R)

Elected 1986, term expires Jan. 1991; b. Dec. 25, 1934, Tampa; home, Tampa; U. of Tampa, B.A. 1957, U. of IL, M.A. 1964; Roman Catholic; married (Mary Jane).

Career: Teacher, 1952–62, 1963–66; Labor Relations Consultant, 1963–67; Exec. Dir., Hillsboro Cnty. Classroom Teachers Assoc., 1966–75; Restaurant owner/manager, 1975–83; Mayor of Tampa, 1979–86.

Office: The Capitol, Tallahassee 32301, 904-488-2272.

Election Results

1986 gen.	Bob Martinez (R)	1,847,525	(55%)
	Steve Pajcic (D)	1,538,620	(45%)
1986 runoff	Bob Martinez (R)	131,652	(34%)
	Lou Frey, Jr. (R)	259,333	(66%)
1986 prim.	Bob Martinez (R)	244,499	(44%)
	Lou Frey, Jr. (R)	138,017	(25%)
	Tom Gallagher (R)	127,709	(23%)
	Chester Clem (R)	44,438	(8%)
1982 gen.	Robert (Bob) Graham (D)	1,739,553	(65%)
	Lewis A. Bafalis (R).	949,023	(35%)

SENATORS

Sen. Lawton Chiles (D)

Elected 1970, seat up 1988; b. Apr. 3, 1930, Lakeland; home, Lakeland; U. of FL, B.S. 1952, LL.B. 1955; Presbyterian; married (Rhea).

Career: Army, Korea; Practicing atty., 1955–71; Instructor, FL Southern Col., 1955–58; FL House of Reps., 1958–66; FL Senate, 1966–70.

Offices: 250 RSOB 20510, 202-224-5274. Also Fed. Bldg., Lakeland 33801, 813-688-6681; 931 Fed. Bldg., 51 S.W. 1st Ave., Miami 33130, 305-536-4891; and U.S. Post and Crthse., 110 E. Park Ave. A, #24, Tallahassee 32301, 904-681-7514.

Committees: *Appropriations* (6th of 16 D). Subcommittees: Agriculture and Related Agencies; Commerce, Justice, State, and Judiciary; Defense; Labor, Health and Human Services, Education (Chairman); Transportation. *Budget* (Chairman of 13 D). *Governmental Affairs* (2d of 8 D). Subcommittees: Federal Spending, Budget and Accounting (Chairman); Oversight of Governmental Management; Investigations. *Special Committee on Aging* (3d of 10 D).

Group Ratings

	ADA	ACLU	COPE	CFA	LCV	ACU	NTU	NSI	COC	CEI
1986	40	42	53	67	72	52	52	70	58	39
1985	55	—	53	87	—	37	—	—	31	—

National Journal Ratings

	1986 LIB — 1986 CONS	1985 LIB — 1985 CONS
Economic	33% — 64%	62% — 36%
Social	60% — 36%	73% — 26%
Foreign	51% — 47%	49% — 49%

Key Votes

1) Ease Gun Cont	FOR	5) Grm-Rdmn Def Red	—	9) Rehnquist Nom	FOR
2) Immig Reform	FOR	6) Contra Aid	FOR	10) Tax Reform	AGN
3) Lmt Text Imp	—	7) SDI Funding	AGN	11) Drug Death Pen	AGN
4) Aid Tobac Ind	—	8) Lmt PAC Contrib	FOR	12) S Africa Sanc	FOR

Election Results

1982 general	Lawton Chiles (D)	1,636,857	(62%)	($806,629)
	Van B. Poole (R)	1,014,551	(38%)	($472,505)
1982 primary	Lawton Chiles (D) unopposed			
1976 general	Lawton Chiles (D)	1,799,518	(63%)	($362,235)
	John Grady (R)	1,057,886	(37%)	($394,574)

Campaign Contributions and Expenditures

1981-82		Direct Cont. 1981-82		PACS Breakdown			
Receipts	$848,266	Indiv.	$821,117	Agr	$200	Ideo	$1,600
Expend.	$806,629	Party	$5,813	Bus	$5,758	Lbr	$2,100
Unspent	$41,646	PACS	$10,358	Hlth	$100	Prof	$600

Sen. Robert (Bob) Graham (D)

Elected 1986, seat up 1992; b. Nov. 9, 1936, Coral Gables; home, Miami Lakes; U. of FL, B.A. 1959, Harvard U., LL.B. 1962; United Church of Christ; married (Adele).

Career: V.P., Graham Co., cattle and dairy production; Chmn., Sengra Development Corp., land developers; FL House of Reps., 1966–70; FL Senate, 1970–78; Gov. of FL, 1979–1986.

Offices: 241 DSOB 20510, 202-224-3041. Also 501 44 W. Flagler St., Miami 33130, 305-536-7293; and 325 John Knox Rd., Bldg. 600, Tallahassee 32308, 904-681-7726.

Committees: *Banking, Housing and Urban Affairs* (10th of 10 D). Subcommittees: Consumer Affairs; International Finance and Monetary Policy. *Environment and Public Works* (9th of 9 D) Subcommittees: Environmental Protection; Hazardous Wastes and Toxic Substances; Water Resources, Transportation and Infrastructure. *Veterans' Affairs* (6th of 6 D).

Group Ratings and Key Votes: Newly Elected

Election Results

1986 general	Robert (Bob) Graham (D)	1,877,231	(55%)	($6,173,663)
	Paula Hawkins (R)	1,551,888	(45%)	($6,723,729)
1986 primary	Robert (Bob) Graham (D)	851,586	(85%)	
	Robert P. (Bob) Kunst (D)	149,797	(15%)	
1980 general	Paula Hawkins (R)	1,822,460	(52%)	($696,969)
	Bill Gunter (D)	1,705,409	(48%)	($2,164,560)

Campaign Contributions and Expenditures

1985-86		Direct Cont. 1985-86		PACS Breakdown 1985-86			
Receipts	$6,215,914	Indiv.	$5,226,130	Corp.	$324,219	T/M/H	$159,330
Expend.	$6,173,663	Party	$19,619	Labor	$305,037	Agr.	$20,500
Unspent	$42,247	PACS	$926,157	Ideo.	$93,471	CWOS	$23,600

FIRST DISTRICT

No part of the American coast of the Gulf of Mexico bristles with more military installations than the panhandle of Florida. This has always been militarily important land: John Quincy Adams persuaded Spain to sell Florida to the United States in 1819 in order to get the port of Pensacola, and the United States Navy has been there (except for a spot of trouble in the 1860s) ever since. Pensacola Naval Air Station was the setting for much of the action in Herman Wouk's *The Winds of War*, and it remains one of several bases here, the most important of which is Eglin Air Force Base, which spreads over the lion's share of three counties. For years the bases propped up the local economy, and even today they are exceedingly important. But the beaches and the towns just inland have developed their own private economy and, though never fashionable to northerners, have drawn many settlers from inland counties of the South.

More than 1,000 miles from Miami, Pensacola and the panhandle economically, culturally, and politically have little to do with the rest of Florida; they are part of the Gulf Coast crescent that goes west through the southern tips of Alabama and Mississippi to the oil-rig precincts of Louisiana and Texas. Politically, this entire region's voting trends are clearly Republican and conservative. You can ascribe this to the military influence, but you should also remember that the Gulf Coast and the panhandle, as much as any part of America, is young family country. People here live in small houses, not stucco condominium villages; they shop, at least sometimes, on old main streets as well as in air-conditioned shopping malls. Their conservatism is not based on economics—they understand that the government pumps a lot of money in here—and their support for things military is not just selfish; they believe that American military power helps build a better world. But the essence of their conservatism is cultural. They may have left their old communities behind, they may have violated some of the rules themselves, but they still yearn to live in a community where people honor those who follow the old rules. So they have voted solidly Republican in national elections for 20 years, and have been voting Republican in Florida elections as well. The panhandle was one of the few parts of the state that voted for Senator Paula Hawkins in 1986 and it gave Governor Bob Martinez a solid margin as well.

The 1st Congressional District of Florida covers the western end of the Panhandle, including Pensacola and Panama City. Congressman Bob Sikes, first elected in 1940 and for years chairman the Military Construction Appropriations Subcommittee, pumped in money for years until he was reprimanded formally by the House for unethical practices in 1976, was stripped of his chairmanship by the Democratic Caucus in 1977, and retired in 1978. He was replaced by Earl Hutto, a Democrat and a former state legislator and TV sportscaster, who beat a serious Republican challenger that year and has held onto the district ever since. Hutto's formula is simple. On national issues, he stays close to the district's views, a little mixed on economics, solidly conservative on foreign and cultural issues. He serves on Armed Services and devotes much attention to maintaining the flow of money to panhandle military facilities. Otherwise he has made few waves and has been reelected easily.

The People: Pop. 1980: 512,821, up 22.6% 1970–80. Households (1980): 78% family, 44% with children, 64% married couples; 31.5% housing units rented; median monthly rent: $162; median house value: $35,500. Voting age pop. (1980): 362,491; 12% Black, 2% Spanish origin, 1% Asian origin, 1% American Indian.

1984 Presidential Vote:

Reagan (R)	....	159,173	(76%)
Mondale (D)	....	50,052	(24%)

Rep. Earl Dewitt Hutto (D)

Elected 1978; b. May 12, 1926, Midland City, AL; home, Panama City; Troy St. U., B.S. 1949, Northwestern U., 1951; Baptist; married (Nancy).

Career: Navy, WWII; Pres., Earl Hutto Advertising Agency, 1974–78; Founder and former Pres., WPEX Radio, 1960–65; TV Sports Dir., WEAR, WSFA, WJHG, 1954–72; FL House of Reps., 1972–78.

Offices: 2435 RHOB 20515, 202-225-4136. Also Fed. Bldg., Panama City 32401, 904-763-0709; and Olde Townhouse Sq., Ste. 110-B, 15 Strong St., Pensacola 32501, 904-432-6179.

Committees: *Armed Services* (12th of 31 D). Subcommittees: Military Installations and Facilities; Readiness; Seapower and Strategic and Critical Materials. *Merchant Marine and Fisheries* (9th of 25 D). Subcommittees: Coast Guard and Navigation (Chairman); Fisheries and Wildlife Conservation and the Environment.

Group Ratings

	ADA	ACLU	COPE	CFA	LCV	ACU	NTU	NSI	COC	CEI
1986	5	5	35	33	33	76	34	100	89	37
1985	15	—	36	8	—	82	—	—	86	—

National Journal Ratings

	1986 LIB — 1986 CONS			1985 LIB — 1985 CONS		
Economic	33%	—	66%	35%	—	65%
Social	27%	—	71%	0%	—	76%
Foreign	0%	—	86%	0%	—	76%

Key Votes

1) Lmt Cln Water Act	FOR	5) Retain Gun Cont	AGN	9) Aid Angola Reb	FOR
2) Rpl Tobac Sub	AGN	6) Contra Aid	FOR	10) Tax Reform	AGN
3) Grm-Rdmn Def Red	FOR	7) Lmt Text Imp	FOR	11) S Africa Sanc	AGN
4) Ban Polygraph	AGN	8) Limit SDI	AGN	12) Immig Reform	FOR

Election Results

1986 general	Earl Dewitt Hutto (D)	97,465	(64%)	($134,745)
	Greg Neubeck (R)	55,415	(36%)	($54,046)
1986 primary	Earl Dewitt Hutto (D) unopposed			
1984 general	Earl Dewitt Hutto (D) unopposed			($40,444)

Campaign Contributions and Expenditures

1985-86		Direct Cont. 1985-86		PACS Breakdown 1985-86			
Receipts	$85,465	Indiv.	$12,529	Corp.	$26,500	T/M/H	$28,750
Expend.	$134,745	PACS	$59,458	Labor	$2,000	Agr.	$0
Unspent	$53,805			Ideo.	$2,000	CWOS	$208

SECOND DISTRICT

Catfish farms, large families, small towns with big churches black and white—what you see in the northernmost counties of Florida looks like the southernmost extension of the Deep South. Yet Florida, with its millions of immigrants from the industrial North, is expanding its influence into the rural counties between Jacksonville and the panhandle. The key catalyst here is Tallahassee, the tiny state capital located here in the 19th century when it seemed unlikely that any non-Seminole would penetrate the swampy vastness south of Jacksonville. With a fast-growing state government, plus Florida State University, Tallahassee has boomed and with surrounding Leon County now is approaching 200,000 in population. Tallahassee has not attained the critical mass of the capitals of the three clearly more populous states, Albany, Austin, and Sacramento, but it may very well be on its way. In the meantime its influence is spreading out into surrounding counties, which never suffered the depopulation and decay of many Dixie counties to the north.

Tallahassee's growth has changed the political complexion of the 2d Congressional District of Florida, which extends westward almost to Panama City and eastward almost to Jacksonville. Once upon a time this was a Dixiecrat district, segregationist and southern, its blacks outvoted heavily by whites. But Tallahassee's growth has given the district a significant bloc of white voters who believe in affirmative government and are disposed to vote, if not for George McGovern or Walter Mondale, then for Jimmy Carter and the kind of moderate Democratic governors who presided in Tallahassee for the 16 years up to 1986. Leon and several adjacent counties now tend to vote for the more liberal candidate in Democratic primaries, like the 1986 gubernatorial runoff between Steve Pajcic and Jim Smith, and they support mostly Democrats in general elections. The 2d District went solidly for Bob Graham in the 1986 Senate contest, and came within a few hundred votes of being one of the few Florida districts to go for Pajcic over Republican Bob Martinez.

The 1986 congressional election also saw a shift in congressional politics from the old Dixie to the new Tallahassee. Representative Don Fuqua, after 24 years in office and despite his chairmanship of the Science and Technology Committee, decided to retire. Fuqua served in the legislature in the old days when it was dominated by north Florida's Pork Chop Gang; he was elected to the House in 1962 when a major issue in these parts was opposition to civil rights. Over time he adapted to the new House and the new district, but nearly got forced into a runoff in 1976 and had serious primary opposition again in 1982. Science and Technology, once a glamor committee, seemed more of a chore after the *Challenger* disaster and at a time when Americans seem to be losing their wonderment at scientific achievements. So Fuqua retired at age 53.

The contest to succeed him took place in the Democratic primary; there was no Republican candidate at all. The winner was Bill Grant, a banker from Madison County just east of Tallahassee and a member of the Florida Senate for four years. He won a big vote in Tallahassee and got 51% in a five-candidate field, way ahead of any single opponent and enough to win without a runoff. Grant seems well adapted to the new political balance in the district, which leaves him in turn well situated to be a team player in the House Democratic Caucus.

The People: Pop. 1980: 513,127, up 33.5% 1970–80. Households (1980): 74% family, 42% with children, 60% married couples; 29.0% housing units rented; median monthly rent: $142; median house value: $30,700. Voting age pop. (1980): 363,447; 22% Black, 1% Spanish origin.

1984 Presidential Vote:

Reagan (R)	126,656	(62%)
Mondale (D)	78,549	(38%)

Rep. Bill Grant (D)

Elected 1986; b. Feb. 22, 1943, Lake City; home, Madison; FL St. U., B.A. 1963; Baptist; single.

Career: Bank pres., 1973–86; FL Senate, 1982–86.

Offices: 1331 RHOB 20515, 202-225-5235. 930 Thomasville Rd., Ste. 103, Tallahassee 32303, 904-681-7434; 1990-A S. 1st St., Lake City 32055, 904-755-5657; and P.O. Bldg., #109, Marianna 32446, 904-526-3525.

Committees: *Government Operations* (24th of 24 D). Subcommittees: Employment and Housing; Government Information, Justice and Agriculture. *Public Works* (29th of 32 D). Subcommittees: Public Buildings and Grounds; Surface Transportation; Water Resources.

Group Ratings and Key Votes: Newly Elected

Election Results

1986 general	Bill Grant (D)	110,120	(100%)	($266,070)
1986 primary	Bill Grant (D)	60,408	(51%)	
	Pete Skinner (D)	23,560	(20%)	
	Barbara Greadington (D)	19,902	(17%)	
	Ernie Padgett (D)	12,268	(10%)	
1984 general	Don Fuqua (D) unopposed			($696,969)

Campaign Contributions and Expenditures

1985-86		Direct Cont. 1985-86		PACS Breakdown 1985-86			
Receipts	$266,579	Indiv.	$151,340	Corp.	$35,050	T/M/H	$48,857
Expend.	$266,070	PACS	$114,957	Labor	$4,500	Agr.	$2,500
Unspent	$508			Ideo.	$24,050	CWOS	$0

THIRD DISTRICT

Jacksonville is a border city between the Old South and the boom lands of central Florida. Once Florida's largest metropolitan area, it is technically still the state's largest city because of the annexation of surrounding Duval County. Jacksonville is also the closest thing in Florida to a typical American industrial and commercial center. It is an important port, paper manufacturer, and banking and insurance center; and if the central city did not grow much in the 1970s, the surrounding areas within commuter distance have. Because of its coolish winter climate, Jacksonville has not attracted as many retirees or northern migrants as have Florida cities and towns farther south, but it does have the largest black percentage of any major Florida city and a large population of southern white origin.

The 3d Congressional District of Florida includes almost all of Jacksonville and the one Florida county to the north. It has one of the most senior congressmen in the House, Charles Bennett, a Democrat first elected in 1948. A punctilious man and a stickler for propriety, he has served his country and the House at considerable personal cost. He is one of the last World War II veterans in Congress; he enlisted after he was 30, performed heroically, and contracted polio in the service. He once set a record for consecutive roll calls, although he has difficulty walking. Bennett was a pioneer supporter in the 1950s of ethical codes and disclosure of congressmen's finances; but it was years before his code of ethics was applied to federal employees, and when the House finally did set up an Ethics Committee in 1967, he was pointedly not asked to serve on it for years. House leaders feared, justifiably, that he would not be understanding of members' difficulties. Finally, in 1978, with the Koreagate scandal looming and Bennett the committee's senior member, the chair could no longer be denied him. He oversaw the Abscam investigation and headed the 10 to 2 majority that recommended and secured the expulsion of Representative Ozzie Myers from the House.

Bennett's major committee is Armed Services, and here too he has suffered his disappointments. He does chair its Seapower subcommittee, but in 1983 lost on secret ballot a bid for the procurement subcommittee chair. After the 1984 election he supported aging Chairman Mel Price, and after he was voted out by the Democratic Caucus sought the chair himself. But he was beaten by Les Aspin, who came to the House 22 years after Bennett did. Again his scruples hurt: he refused to lobby for votes while Price was in the race. After the 1986 election, he opposed Aspin again, and was again painfully rejected, as the main opposition to the chairman came from the much less senior Marvin Leath. Bennett seems unable to get political benefit out of the unusual combination of positions he takes: he has led the House opposition to the MX missile, he is skeptical about President Reagan's Strategic Defense Initiative, but he strongly supports the 600-ship Navy.

To Bennett's bitterness at losing out on a chairmanship he has longed for must be added his continued anguish over the death of his 22-year-old son from a drug overdose in 1977. "It was the greatest wound in my life," he said, and in the 1980s championed a measure to require the military to interdict drug traffickers outside U.S. borders; "I have violent feelings about this bill." Opposed by the Defense Department, contrary to the principle of separation of the military from civilian life, it was rejected in the early 1980s but adopted by an overwhelming vote in the House in 1985. On this issue and on seemingly unrelated matters Bennett has become movingly but also embarrassingly emotional.

He continues, however, to tend to the needs of Jacksonville and his district, and the Seapower

Subcommittee is a good place to do it. The naval base at Mayport, at the mouth of Jacksonville's St. Johns River, is second in importance only to Norfolk for the Atlantic Fleet, and the 3d District has a naval air station as well; military spending is an important component of the Jacksonville economy. Bennett has remained very popular in the 3d District over the years and has won reelection easily. If he should choose to retire, the 3d District will likely have a seriously contested Democratic primary and perhaps a serious Republican candidacy as well.

The People: Pop. 1980: 512,692, up 4.7% 1970–80. Households (1980): 73% family, 42% with children, 55% married couples; 36.6% housing units rented; median monthly rent: $165; median house value: $29,900. Voting age pop. (1980): 362,272; 25% Black, 2% Spanish origin, 1% Asian origin.

1984 Presidential Vote: Reagan (R) 103,133   (59%)
Mondale (D) 71,347   (41%)

Rep. Charles E. Bennett (D)

Elected 1948; b. Dec. 2, 1910, Canton, NY; home, Jacksonville; U. of FL, B.A., J.D. 1934; Disciples of Christ; married (Jean).

Career: Practicing atty., 1934–42, 1947–48; FL House of Reps., 1941–42; Army, WWII.

Offices: 2107 RHOB 20515, 202-225-2501. Also 314 Palmetto St., Jacksonville 32202, 904-791-2587.

Committees: *Armed Services* (3d of 31 D). Subcommittees: Procurement and Military Nuclear Systems; Seapower and Strategic and Critical Materials (Chairman). *Merchant Marine and Fisheries* (21st of 25 D). Subcommittees: Coast Guard; Merchant Marine.

Group Ratings

	ADA	ACLU	COPE	CFA	LCV	ACU	NTU	NSI	COC	CEI
1986	55	40	46	75	63	27	25	50	50	18
1985	70	—	46	58	—	19	32	—	32	—

National Journal Ratings

	1986 LIB — 1986 CONS		1985 LIB — 1985 CONS	
Economic	50%	— 50%	65%	— 33%
Social	47%	— 52%	59%	— 40%
Foreign	51%	— 48%	54%	— 45%

Key Votes

1) Lmt Cln Water Act	AGN	5) Retain Gun Cont	FOR	9) Aid Angola Reb	AGN
2) Rpl Tobac Sub	AGN	6) Contra Aid	FOR	10) Tax Reform	FOR
3) Grm-Rdmn Def Red	AGN	7) Lmt Text Imp	AGN	11) S Africa Sanc	FOR
4) Ban Polygraph	AGN	8) Limit SDI	FOR	12) Immig Reform	FOR

Election Results

1986 general	Charles E. Bennett (D) unopposed	($19,564)
1986 primary	Charles E. Bennett (D) unopposed	
1984 general	Charles E. Bennett (D) unopposed	($5,230)

Campaign Contributions and Expenditures

1985-86		Direct Cont. 1985-86		PACS Breakdown 1985-86			
Receipts	$125,752	Indiv.	$23,596	Corp.	$35,991	T/M/H	$17,750
Expend.	$19,564	Party	$300	Labor	$14,350	Agr.	$1,500
Unspent	$217,345	PACS	$74,841	Ideo.	$5,250	CWOS	$0

FOURTH DISTRICT

Along the hard sand beaches from Jacksonville south through Daytona toward Cape Canaveral, and inland 20 or 30 miles through the orange grove country along the St. Johns River, extends the 4th Congressional District of Florida. It is a part of America in transition. The beach, which has attracted northern migrants since the Spanish settled St. Augustine in the 16th century and the British set up their disastrous experiment in New Smyrna in the 18th century, is sprouting huge new developments attracting modest-income retirees. Inland the orange groves, hit by four disastrous frosts and bad prices for juice in the 1980s, are being sold off to developers too. Over the past 40 years the district has been an in-between part of Florida, the marchland between northern migrants and Dixie natives. For the future its character will be determined by who moves in: the target of the marketing pitches of the big subdividers—white Southern Baptists or northern Episcopalians, southern country clubbers or factory-town ethnics—will set the tone of the 4th District for the 1990s.

In the meantime, this is a marginally southern and marginally Democratic district represented by a veteran of southern Democratic politics. He is Bill Chappell, who has spent most of his adult life in elective office. He was elected to the legislature in 1954, served as speaker of the Florida House back in the early 1960s when the legislature was still dominated by Dixie conservatives—the Pork Chop Gang—from the northern part of the state, and was elected to Congress in 1968.

Chappell is an important member of the House as chairman of the Defense Appropriations Subcommittee, a post he succeeded to on the death of New York's Joseph Addabbo in April 1986. This is the small subcommittee that actually marks up the Pentagon appropriations bill. Chappell served in the Navy in World War II and was in the Navy Reserves for years afterwards; he is a solid supporter of things naval and of the reserves in particular. Like many tradition-minded southerners who have served on this subcommittee or on Armed Services. In general he tends to favor the big, sophisticated defense systems proposed by the Pentagon—the B-1 bomber, giant aircraft carriers, technologically advanced Navy fighter planes. He has used his influence of course to beef up Jacksonville's Mayport Naval Base, but more important is the support he tends to give career military men's judgment over that of their civilian controllers. Addabbo tended to be skeptical of big defense spending except when it helped New York contractors; Chappell leads the subcommittee in quite another direction.

Chappell spends most of his time on defense matters and seems to have shaped the rest of his work on the Hill to safeguarding his incumbency and his chairmanship. His political opposition at home came initially from Republicans, but they have not challenged him since he got some seniority; now if he is vulnerable anywhere it is in the Democratic primary. In 1982 he was forced into a runoff by Democrat Reid Hughes, who accused Chappell of voting to cut Social Security; Claude Pepper endorsed the challenger. Chappell was the runoff by only 54%–46%. Since then this enthusiastic supporter of the Reagan budget and tax cuts has voted most of the time with Democrats on economic issues and emphasizes his support of Social Security; this backer of the Cross-Florida Barge Canal, stresses his work for the environment. The result has been that little opposition has appeared at home and, when Addabbo died, his fellow Democrats on Appropriations elected Chappell to the chair. For the moment at least he seems strongly entrenched in his district and his important subcommittee chair.

The People: Pop. 1980: 512,672, up 56.8% 1970–80. Households (1980): 72% family, 33% with children, 61% married couples; 28.7% housing units rented; median monthly rent: $196; median house value: $41,800. Voting age pop. (1980): 385,967; 9% Black, 2% Spanish origin.

1984 Presidential Vote: Reagan (R) 151,528   (67%)
Mondale (D) 74,921   (33%)

Rep. Bill Chappell, Jr. (D)

Elected 1968; b. Feb. 3, 1922, Kendrick; home, Ormond Beach; U. of FL, B.A. 1947, LL.B. 1949, J.D. 1967; Methodist; married (Jeane).

Career: Navy, WWII; Marion Cnty. Prosecuting Atty., 1950–54; FL House of Reps., 1954–64, 1967–68, Spkr., 1961–63.

Offices: 2468 RHOB 20515, 202-225-4035. Also 575 N. Halifax Ave., Daytona Beach 32018, 904-253-7632; and 8789 San Jose Blvd., Ste. 4, Jacksonville 32217, 904-731-4236.

Committees: *Appropriations* (10th of 35 D). Subcommittees: Defense (Chairman); Energy and Water Development.

Group Ratings

	ADA	ACLU	COPE	CFA	LCV	ACU	NTU	NSI	COC	CEI
1986	30	23	35	58	27	52	19	100	31	22
1985	40	—	34	33	—	57	21	—	33	—

National Journal Ratings

	1986 LIB — 1986 CONS		1985 LIB — 1985 CONS	
Economic	80%	— 19%	61%	— 39%
Social	34%	— 65%	57%	— 43%
Foreign	31%	— 69%	24%	— 66%

Key Votes

1) Lmt Cln Water Act	AGN	5) Retain Gun Cont	AGN	9) Aid Angola Reb	FOR
2) Rpl Tobac Sub	AGN	6) Contra Aid	FOR	10) Tax Reform	AGN
3) Grm-Rdmn Def Red	AGN	7) Lmt Text Imp	FOR	11) S Africa Sanc	FOR
4) Ban Polygraph	AGN	8) Limit SDI	AGN	12) Immig Reform	AGN

Election Results

1986 general	Bill Chappell, Jr. (D) unopposed			($139,758)
1986 primary	Bill Chappell, Jr. (D) unopposed			
1984 general	Bill Chappell, Jr. (D)	134,694	(65%)	($399,169)
	Alton H. (Bill) Starling (R)	73,218	(35%)	($22,670)

Campaign Contributions and Expenditures

1985-86		Direct Cont. 1985-86		PACS Breakdown 1985-86			
Receipts	$279,117	Indiv.	$88,235	Corp.	$120,701	T/M/H	$37,600
Expend.	$139,758	PACS	$181,123	Labor	$16,350	Agr.	$1,000
Unspent	$156,899			Ideo.	$5,250	CWOS	$222

FIFTH DISTRICT

Who would have thought, 40 years ago when it was a town of 40,000 that Orlando would become the number one tourist destination in the world? Or that this center of the citrus industry—the county seat of Orange County—would develop a diversified high tech and office economy? Or that it would become home to one million people, few of them retirees, most of them young families with children from both the South and the North? Yet all that has happened over 40 years here in Orlando. Much of Orlando's growth can be traced to the decision and vision of one man. Walt Disney invented the theme park in the flatlands of Orange County, California, but he perfected it in the 17,000 acres of swamp and lakes outside Orlando he quietly bought up. It is hard to remember now, but when Disney began, there was no such thing as a year-round family amusement center, and no one thought of organizing it around themes relating to the nation's past and future. Nor did anyone think to organize the logistics of this make-believe city in so sophisticated a manner, or reflect that to work properly a high tech world that accommodated so many people would have to be labor-intensive. Some Orlando residents criticize Disney World for being too self-contained, for trying to monopolize tourists and keep them away from other area attractions like Sea World, yet demanding roads and infrastructure to accommodate them. But even so, the fact is that Disney World has done much to make Orlando the boom town it is.

The 5th Congressional District of Florida includes most of the Orlando metropolitan area; Disney World is just to the south, but most of the 17,000 people who work there live in the district. In the north and into Seminole County are high-income suburbs like Maitland and Altamonte Springs in a string leading to the citrus town of Sanford; to the west, across the lakes that dot central Florida, is Winter Garden. The 5th on balance is basically Republican; it went only narrowly for Democrat Bob Graham in the 1986 Senate race (although his vote may have been held down because his opponent Paula Hawkins lives in Maitland).

The 5th's congressman is Bill McCollum, who has become one of the more prominent members of the large Republican class elected in 1980. Little in his background suggested his prominence. He is not one of his party's speculative thinkers nor one of its blow-dry-handsome media stars. His base is local, not ideological, and he won in 1980 largely because he geared up to oppose in the primary incumbent Richard Kelly, one of the less bright members of Congress, who was videotaped stuffing Abscam money into his pockets. In the House, McCollum got seats on non-sought-after committees—Judiciary and Banking—and made the most of them. Some time he spent looking after local interests, which Florida has plenty of on banking. But more importantly, McCollum waded into substantive issues. He was the lead spokesman in the debate on the immigration bill against an amnesty for illegal aliens; but when the House voted one, he continued to support the reform bill. He took a part in saving but also curbing the Legal Services Corporation. He organized a volunteer airlift of medical supplies to El Salvador in 1983. His proficiency at detail work and popularity among younger and older Republicans help explain why Minority Leader Robert Michel chose him as one of the Republicans on the Iran-Contra investigating committee.

McCollum seems to have made the 5th District a safe seat. After dispatching Kelly he had to beat another Republican in the 1980 runoff and then narrowly won over a Democrat who had nearly beaten Kelly two years before in a district which by then had more than one million residents. After redistricting, he had another significant opponent in 1982, but won 59%–41%. Since then he has been unopposed. His stress on his status as a family man, and his proclaimed belief in traditional values together with his earnestness have made him a popular politician in this middle American city that Walt Disney helped to make.

The People: Pop. 1980: 513,005, up 47.0% 1970–80. Households (1980): 73% family, 38% with children, 59% married couples; 33.9% housing units rented; median monthly rent: $200; median house value: $45,400. Voting age pop. (1980): 373,987; 14% Black, 3% Spanish origin, 1% Asian origin.

1984 Presidential Vote:

Reagan (R)	134,122	(71%)
Mondale (D)	53,580	(28%)

Rep. Bill McCollum (R)

Elected 1980; b. July 12, 1944, Brooksville; home, Altamonte Springs; U. of FL, B.A. 1965, J.D. 1968; Episcopalian; married (Ingrid).

Career: Navy, 1969–72; Practicing atty., 1973–81; Chmn., Seminole Cnty. Repub. Exec. Cmttees., 1976.

Offices: 1507 LHOB 20515, 202-225-2176. Also 1801 Lee Rd., Ste. 301, Winter Park 32789, 305-645-3100.

Committees: *Banking, Finance and Urban Affairs* (6th of 20 R). Subcommittees: Domestic Monetary Policy (Ranking Member); Financial Institutions Supervision, Regulation and Insurance; Housing and Community Development. *Judiciary* (6th of 14 R). Subcommittees: Crime (Ranking Member); Immigration, Refugees and International Law.

Group Ratings

	ADA	ACLU	COPE	CFA	LCV	ACU	NTU	NSI	COC	CEI
1986	0	5	7	17	42	82	60	100	82	76
1985	5	—	8	25	—	90	63	—	90	—

National Journal Ratings

	1986 LIB — 1986 CONS		1985 LIB — 1985 CONS	
Economic	0% —	94%	8% —	91%
Social	11% —	85%	0% —	76%
Foreign	14% —	84%	0% —	76%

Key Votes

1) Lmt Cln Water Act	FOR	5) Retain Gun Cont	AGN	9) Aid Angola Reb	FOR
2) Rpl Tobac Sub	FOR	6) Contra Aid	FOR	10) Tax Reform	FOR
3) Grm-Rdmn Def Red	FOR	7) Lmt Text Imp	AGN	11) S Africa Sanc	AGN
4) Ban Polygraph	AGN	8) Limit SDI	AGN	12) Immig Reform	FOR

Election Results

1986 general	Bill McCollum (R) unopposed	($121,052)
1986 primary	Bill McCollum (R) unopposed	
1984 general	Bill McCollum (R) unopposed	

Campaign Contributions and Expenditures

1985-86		Direct Cont. 1985-86		PACS Breakdown 1985-86			
Receipts	$165,986	Indiv.	$46,596	Corp.	$40,050	T/M/H	$39,850
Expend.	$121,052	Party	$1,293	Labor	$2,000	Agr.	$600
Unspent	$222,029	PACS	$88,504	Ideo.	$5,500	CWOS	$504

SIXTH DISTRICT

The grasslands of central Florida, complete with bluegrass horse farms; the small university town of Gainesville, where such a large percentage of this huge state's political elite went to school together at the University of Florida; and the rapidly growing swampy, lake-strewn land west of Orlando, clear to the new condominium and trailer park communities of the Gulf coast well north of St. Petersburg—this is the 6th Congressional District of Florida. It is one of four new districts created after the 1980 Census, reflecting the growth of central Florida, the slow march up Florida's peninsula of in-migrants seeking sun and pleasant places to retire or to make their livings.

Historically, the political tradition here is Democratic, southern style. But today local politics reflects more the origins of recent settlers. The horse farm country around Ocala, like the bluegrass land around Lexington, Kentucky, is trending Republican, while Gainesville, like Ann Arbor, Michigan, is liberal and Democratic. The Gulf Coast counties of Citrus and Hernando have been growing rapidly, filling up with relatively low income retirees and other migrants who bring with them from points north and south a willingness to vote Democratic. The 6th District was not only designed to be Democratic, but to elect a particular Democrat, and it has.

He is Buddy MacKay, a 12-year veteran of the Florida legislature who came within 5% of making the runoff in the 1980 primary for U.S. Senator—a runoff which he would probably have won and which might have propelled him to victory over Paula Hawkins in the general election and to a Senate seat he would probably prominently hold today. Instead, he went to the House from the 6th District, unopposed in the 1982 primary, and became one of the leading members of the largest class of Democratic freshmen in the last decade. As co-chairman of the freshman group on the budget, he supported an across-the-board freeze even if it meant freezing the cost-of-living increase for Social Security; he moved the Democrats to take a stand when the leadership wanted to hang back and let the Republicans take the heat. Yet at the same time MacKay made friends among the leadership and after the 1984 election won a seat on the Budget Committee himself. There he has championed the popular end of cutting the budget deficit and the unpopular (but necessary) means of raising taxes and cutting spending. Not one to avoid a hot seat, he has also taken a place on the increasingly polarized Western Hemisphere Affairs Subcommittee of Foreign Affairs; he was one of two Floridians who opposed aid to the contras in 1986.

In the Florida legislature MacKay championed "sunshine" and "sunset" laws. Florida has the nation's most comprehensive disclosure (sunshine) measures, which prevent public business from being done in private; it also originated the idea that government programs should have a specific expiration (sunset) date. In Congress, impressed with the fact-gathering of the Northeast-Midwest Coalition, MacKay started a Sun Belt Institute, with a budget goal of $400,000, to provide data for southern and southwestern members. In general, he has been a model for a new kind of Democrat, not wedded to big-spending programs and not interested in using federal leverage to promote liberation-minded cultural mores, but clearly more generous on spending and open to government involvement than Republicans.

There was some talk of MacKay running statewide in 1986. But he decided to stay in the House, and he has held his seat since 1982 without significant opposition.

The People: Pop. 1980: 512,950, up 70.9% 1970–80. Households (1980): 73% family, 31% with children, 62% married couples; 27.0% housing units rented; median monthly rent: $174; median house value: $37,500. Voting age pop. (1980): 394,134; 12% Black, 2% Spanish origin.

1984 Presidential Vote: Reagan (R) 154,985   (64%)
                                 Mondale (D) 85,603   (36%)

Rep. Kenneth H. (Buddy) MacKay (D)

Elected 1982; b. Mar. 22, 1933, Ocala; home, Ocala; Davidson Col., U. of FL, B.S. 1954, LL.B. 1961; Presbyterian; married (Anne).

Career: Air Force, 1954–58; Practicing atty., 1961–82; FL House of Reps., 1969–75; FL Senate, 1975–81.

Offices: 330 CHOB 20515, 202-225-5744. Also 207 N.W. 2d St., Rm. 256, Ocala 32670, 904-351-8777; and 401 S.E. 1st Ave., Rm. 316, Gainesville 32601, 904-372-0382.

Committees: *Budget* (15th of 21 D). Task Forces: Budget Process; Defense and International Affairs; Economic Policy; Health. *Science, Space and Technology* (12th of 27 D). Subcommittees: International Scientific Cooperation; Science, Research and Technology; Space, Science and Applications. *Select Committee on Aging* (28th of 39 D). Subcommittee: Health and Long-Term Care.

Group Ratings

	ADA	ACLU	COPE	CFA	LCV	ACU	NTU	NSI	COC	CEI
1986	55	35	48	75	84	36	36	10	61	41
1985	50	—	49	83	—	38	47	—	62	—

National Journal Ratings

	1986 LIB — 1986 CONS	1985 LIB — 1985 CONS
Economic	45% — 54%	45% — 55%
Social	49% — 49%	63% — 33%
Foreign	64% — 34%	64% — 33%

Key Votes

1) Lmt Cln Water Act	FOR	5) Retain Gun Cont	AGN
2) Rpl Tobac Sub	FOR	6) Contra Aid	AGN
3) Grm-Rdmn Def Red	FOR	7) Lmt Text Imp	AGN
4) Ban Polygraph	AGN	8) Limit SDI	FOR

9) Aid Angola Reb	FOR
10) Tax Reform	FOR
11) S Africa Sanc	FOR
12) Immig Reform	FOR

Election Results

1986 general	Kenneth H. (Buddy) MacKay (D)	143,583	(70%)	($462,732)
	Larry Gallagher (R)	61,053	(30%)	($14,522)
1986 primary	Kenneth H. (Buddy) MacKay (D)	63,027	(85%)	
	Ken Stepp (D).........................	10,702	(15%)	
1984 general	Kenneth H. (Buddy) MacKay (D)	167,409	(99%)	($129,525)

Campaign Contributions and Expenditures

1985-86		Direct Cont. 1985-86		PACS Breakdown 1985-86			
Receipts	$528,712	Indiv.	$251,089	Corp.	$52,000	T/M/H	$61,565
Expend.	$462,732	Party	$9,000	Labor	$22,150	Agr.	$950
Unspent	$101,932	PACS	$152,965	Ideo.	$15,700	CWOS	$600

SEVENTH DISTRICT

One of the surprise cities of Florida is Tampa. In the early 1970s, it looked like a place left behind by the Florida boom, a one-time cigar-making center and maritime city out of place in the new and gleaming state growing up all around. For many years Tampa seemed eclipsed by the growth around St. Petersburg and Clearwater, across Tampa Bay. But by the 1980s St. Petersburg was pretty filled up, while Tampa was just starting to grow again. Its downtown has been spruced up, its neighborhoods have spread in all directions across swamps and lowlands, and traffic jams have clogged many of its intersections. Unlike St. Petersburg and so many other Florida cities, Tampa is a working rather than a retirement town, a city of families and younger people, a place with a blue-collar past which is fast moving upscale as it expands.

Tampa and most of surrounding Hillsborough County forms the 7th Congressional District of Florida. This district has had the same congressman since it was created in 1962, Democrat Sam Gibbons. Historically Tampa has been as Democratic as St. Petersburg has been Republican, but in the 1980s its growing population has moved in tandem with Florida voters generally; and so as St. Petersburg becomes more Democratic the two sides of the bay are, politically, converging. In legislative and local elections Tampa usually backs Democrats. But one of its Democratic mayors, Bob Martinez, turned Republican and was elected governor of Florida in 1986.

Sam Gibbons has deep roots in Tampa and in the Democratic Party. He has the look of an old-fashioned southern congressman, but in his first years in the House he usually supported the national Democratic administration. He got a seat on Ways and Means, where he supported progressive tax reform. He supported civil rights bills. He championed reforms to open up House procedures, and he ran a quixotic and aborted race for majority leader against Tip O'Neill in 1972. Yet Gibbons was never in sync with the liberal Democrats who emerged as powers in the House in the later 1970s. He was not a vociferous opponent of the Vietnam war nor was he a champion of liberated cultural values. He became more concerned about holding down government spending.

For many years he also adhered to one of the Democratic party's old traditions, free trade. He is chairman of the Trade Subcommittee of Ways and Means, and worked to hold up restrictive trade bills or, when they seem to have enough votes to pass, let them go through hoping they'll be vetoed. But Gibbons's position leverage weakened by his lack of closeness to Ways and Means Chairman Dan Rostenkowski. Gibbons had hoped Rostenkowski would become party whip in 1981 and leave the chairmanship to him; Rostenkowski, who supports his other subcommittee chairmen, seems cool to Gibbons. Gibbons played virtually no part in the 1985 and 1986 tax reform bill, and Rostenkowski pointedly left him off the conference committee on the bill. In the 100th Congress the action on trade is likely to take place outside his subcommittee. Perhaps in response, but presumably also out of changes in circumstances, Gibbons by early 1987 was, while still arguing for freer trade, maintaining that "Japan has some adjustments of its own to make." It is a sympton of Japan's political weakness on trade in the United States that it is being criticized by one of the few congressmen with the position and inclination to stoutly oppose protectionism.

Gibbons is also determined, however. That showed back in Tampa, when he got serious competition in 1984 from Republican Michael Kavouklis, a Tampa judge. He held Gibbons to 59% of the vote—a comfortable win, but far below earlier showings, and the veteran congressman vowed to spend more time in the district and more money on campaigns. That paid off in 1986 when no Republican filed against him; Gibbons has nonetheless worked hard to make himself well known in the district once again, raising $903,000 in 1985 and 1986, more than $500,000 of it from PACs, spending $563,000, and keeping $390,000 in cash just to give any potential opponent something to think about.

The People: Pop. 1980: 512,905, up 25.3% 1970–80. Households (1980): 71% family, 37% with children, 56% married couples; 35.1% housing units rented; median monthly rent: $188; median house value: $35,800. Voting age pop. (1980): 376,478; 13% Black, 11% Spanish origin, 1% Asian origin.

1984 Presidential Vote:			
	Reagan (R)	119,135	(63%)
	Mondale (D)	70,645	(37%)

Rep. Sam M. Gibbons (D)

Elected 1962; b. Jan. 20, 1920, Tampa; home, Tampa; U. of FL, J.D. 1947; Presbyterian; married (Martha).

Career: Army, WWII; Practicing atty., 1947–62; FL House of Reps., 1952–58; FL Senate, 1958–62.

Offices: 2204 RHOB 20515, 202-225-3376. 101 E. Kennedy Blvd., Tampa 33602, 813-228-2101; abd 201 S. Kings Ave., #6, Brandon 33511, 813-689-2847.

Committees: *Ways and Means* (2d of 23 D). Subcommittees: Social Security; Trade (Chairman). *Joint Committee on Taxation.*

Group Ratings

	ADA	ACLU	COPE	CFA	LCV	ACU	NTU	NSI	COC	CEI
1986	50	42	54	83	66	45	37	40	57	45
1985	40	—	55	50	—	38	31	—	50	—

National Journal Ratings

	1986 LIB — 1986 CONS			1985 LIB — 1985 CONS		
Economic	36%	—	63%	46%	—	53%
Social	57%	—	43%	56%	—	43%
Foreign	53%	—	46%	57%	—	42%

Key Votes

1) Lmt Cln Water Act	FOR	5) Retain Gun Cont	FOR	9) Aid Angola Reb	AGN
2) Rpl Tobac Sub	FOR	6) Contra Aid	FOR	10) Tax Reform	FOR
3) Grm-Rdmn Def Red	FOR	7) Lmt Text Imp	AGN	11) S Africa Sanc	FOR
4) Ban Polygraph	AGN	8) Limit SDI	FOR	12) Immig Reform	FOR

Election Results

1986 general	Sam M. Gibbons (D) unopposed			($563,509)
1986 primary	Sam M. Gibbons (D) unopposed			
1984 general	Sam M. Gibbons (D)	100,430	(59%)	($292,805)
	Michael N. Kavouklis (R)	70,280	(41%)	($194,218)

Campaign Contributions and Expenditures

1985-86		Direct Cont. 1985-86		PACS Breakdown 1985-86			
Receipts	$903,485	Indiv.	$305,601	Corp.	$307,045	T/M/H	$150,699
Expend.	$563,509	PACS	$571,019	Labor	$23,150	Agr.	$5,000
Unspent	$390,559			Ideo.	$61,675	CWOS	$23,450

EIGHTH DISTRICT

When somebody says St. Petersburg, almost everyone thinks of elderly retirees sitting on park benches or playing shuffleboard in the Florida sun. And reasonably so. St. Petersburg and its suburbs to the north and west do have some light manufacturing, and some young families live here with children. But not many. In the 8th Congressional District, which includes St. Petersburg and Pinellas County suburbs as far north as Clearwater, only 23% of households contain children; 34% of adults are 65 or older—the highest percentage in any congressional district in the country. There are more than 40,000 people over 65 living alone in the constituency, accounting for one out of every six households.

Most of these people were not born in St. Petersburg, which had fewer than 20,000 residents 65 years ago. They are immigrants from some other part of the South or, more frequently, from the North. The large Yankee concentration here produced Florida's first center of Republican strength. The migrants of the 1940s and 1950s were people of at least modest affluence—blue-collar workers at the time didn't get much in the way of pensions—and the new residents continued to vote in St. Petersburg as they had back in Oak Park or Garden City. They carried Pinellas County for Eisenhower, and in 1954 elected a Republican congressman.

More recently, St. Petersburg has been trending Democratic. In 1976 Pinellas County almost went for Carter and in the elections of the 1980s its Republican percentage was around—or higher than—the statewide average. In 1986 it gave Bob Graham a large margin over Paula Hawkins and almost went for Democrat Steve Pajcic over its Tampa Bay neighbor Bob Martinez. Why? Inevitably there is a turnover in this area's elderly population; very few of the elderly voters who made this area Republican are still alive today. In the 1960s and 1970s people with blue-collar—and Democratic—backgrounds increasingly could afford to retire in Florida. They settled in St. Petersburg, while their more affluent counterparts went to the newer, more glittery retirement towns.

This trend has not changed the 8th District's representation in Congress, however. Bill Young—ironic name—has been representing St. Petersburg for more than 25 years, first as an aide to its first Republican congressman, then as a legislator in Tallahassee, and finally as congressman since 1970. Yet he is still only approaching his constituents' median age. Through careful attention to the district, and devotion to the Social Security system (he opposes a freeze for cost of living allowances on Social Security, for example), Young has gained a reputation for political strength, and has encountered no serious challenges. With an apparently safe seat and no serious challenges, he has passed by opportunities to run for statewide office.

In Washington he has been able to concentrate on national and international issues. For some years he worked on the Foreign Operations Appropriations Subcommittee, a body with the unpleasant task of managing the foreign aid bill; usually Young took the politically attractive course and opposed the foreign aid bill on the floor or tried to impose restrictions on international lending agencies. In 1981 he switched to Defense Appropriations, now chaired by Florida's Bill Chappell; he has supported generous defense spending and an assertive foreign policy. He also serves on the Intelligence Committee, and is a strong advocate of U.S. aid to those who want to overthrow the Sandinista regime.

The People: Pop. 1980: 512,909, up 30.3% 1970–80. Households (1980): 65% family, 23% with children, 54% married couples; 28.7% housing units rented; median monthly rent: $201; median house value: $39,600. Voting age pop. (1980): 413,853; 7% Black, 1% Spanish origin.

1984 Presidential Vote: Reagan (R) 153,584   (63%)
                                Mondale (D) 91,393   (37%)

Rep. C. W. (Bill) Young (R)

Elected 1970; b. Dec. 16, 1930, Harmarville, PA; home, Largo; United Methodist; married (Marian).

Career: Aide to U.S. Rep. William C. Cramer, 1957–60; FL Senate, 1960–70, Minor. Ldr., 1966–70.

Offices: 2407 RHOB 20515, 202-225-5961. Also 627 Fed. Bldg., St. Petersburg 33701, 813-893-3191.

Committees: *Appropriations* (6th of 22 R). Subcommittees: Defense; Labor–Health and Human Services–Education.

Group Ratings

	ADA	ACLU	COPE	CFA	LCV	ACU	NTU	NSI	COC	CEI
1986	5	26	15	25	26	95	47	100	67	72
1985	5	—	15	50	—	71	54	—	76	—

National Journal Ratings

	1986 LIB — 1986 CONS		1985 LIB — 1985 CONS	
Economic	21%	— 77%	24%	— 74%
Social	0%	— 89%	0%	— 76%
Foreign	0%	— 86%	0%	— 76%

Key Votes

1) Lmt Cln Water Act	FOR	5) Retain Gun Cont	AGN	9) Aid Angola Reb	FOR
2) Rpl Tobac Sub	FOR	6) Contra Aid	FOR	10) Tax Reform	FOR
3) Grm-Rdmn Def Red	AGN	7) Lmt Text Imp	AGN	11) S Africa Sanc	AGN
4) Ban Polygraph	AGN	8) Limit SDI	AGN	12) Immig Reform	AGN

Election Results

1986 general	C. W. (Bill) Young (R) unopposed		($96,142)
1986 primary	C. W. (Bill) Young (R) unopposed		
1984 general	C. W. (Bill) Young (R) 184,553	(80%)	($104,143)
	Robert Kent (D) 45,393	(20%)	($7,921)

Campaign Contributions and Expenditures

1985-86		Direct Cont. 1985-86		PACS Breakdown 1985-86			
Receipts	$214,687	Indiv.	$83,140	Corp.	$55,055	T/M/H	$26,470
Expend.	$96,142	Party	$1,092	Labor	$2,500	Agr.	$800
Unspent	$306,907	PACS	$90,325	Ideo.	$4,000	CWOS	$1,500

NINTH DISTRICT

In the early 1950s you could have driven U.S. 19 north from St. Petersburg's Pinellas County and never noticed much more than the swamp. The road passed through intersections marked by gas stations, and every so often there was a sleepy little town, with low brick buildings constructed in some northern style, baking in the Florida sun. There weren't many people here.

The coastline that looks so tempting on the map was then under the kind of water that fills a swamp. Any large development would have required investment in infrastructure—water and sewer lines, underground electricity—that would have seemed hopelessly uneconomical.

Today all that investment has been made, and the Gulf Coast for 50 miles north of St. Petersburg is home now to half a million people (and that doesn't include the 350,000 right around St. Petersburg). This is not the Florida where the rich of Greenwich and Winnetka retire; it is the final home of more modest people, many of them blue-collar, most of them probably with Democratic rather than Republican heritages. Most of this area is in the 9th Congressional District, one of the four new districts created by the Florida legislature after the 1980 Census. The district begins in Largo and Clearwater, some eight miles from St. Petersburg, and continues up past the old resort of Tarpon Springs to the new condominium communities of Holiday, Elfers, New Port Richey, Bayonet Point, and Hudson in Pasco County. It also sweeps inland, circling Tampa and including the agricultural center of Plant City inland; but more than two-thirds of its population is along the coast.

Politically, the 9th District is one of the most evenly balanced districts in the state. It was expected to elect a Democrat when it was created in 1982, but by a narrow margin chose Republican Michael Bilirakis instead, and has now reelected him twice with over 70% of the vote. Bilirakis has much in common with many of his constituents. Though a native of the Greek-American community in Tarpon Springs, he grew up in Pittsburgh and worked his way through college toiling in a steel mill; he served in the Air Force during the Korean War; he is, like many self-made men, an ardent free enterpriser. He is a foe in general of government spending and profligacy, but is all for generous Social Security benefits and government-funded research on Alzheimer's disease.

Bilirakis has an important committee assignment, Energy and Commerce, but is not a front-rank legislator. He had his tough races in 1982, when he won the Republican runoff with 54% of the vote and the general election with 51%; he seems solidly entrenched now.

The People: Pop. 1980: 513,191, up 91.6% 1970–80. Households (1980): 74% family, 27% with children, 65% married couples; 22.2% housing units rented; median monthly rent: $208; median house value: $44,600. Voting age pop. (1980): 404,361; 3% Black, 2% Spanish origin.

1984 Presidential Vote:

Reagan (R) 187,534	(67%)
Mondale (D) 90,468	(33%)

Rep. Michael Bilirakis (R)

Elected 1982; b. July 16, 1930, Tarpon Springs; home, Palm Harbor; U. of Pittsburgh, B.S. 1959, U. of FL, J.D. 1963; Greek Orthodox; married (Evelyn).

Career: Air Force, Korea; Steelworker, 1955–59; Govt. contract negotiator, 1959–60; Petroleum engineer, 1960–63; Practicing atty., 1969–83.

Offices: 1130 LHOB 20515, 202-225-5755. Also 1100 Cleveland St., Ste. 1103, Clearwater 33515, 813-441-3721.

Committees: *Energy and Commerce* (14th of 17 R). Subcommittees: Energy and Power; Oversight and Investigations; Transportation, Tourism and Hazardous Material. *Veterans' Affairs* (8th of 21 R). Subcommittees: Compensation, Pensions and Insurance; Hospitals and Health Care.

Group Ratings

	ADA	ACLU	COPE	CFA	LCV	ACU	NTU	NSI	COC	CEI
1986	15	15	26	33	27	86	53	100	67	69
1985	10	—	26	33	—	71	59	—	77	—

National Journal Ratings

	1986 LIB — 1986 CONS		1985 LIB — 1985 CONS	
Economic	35%	64%	12%	85%
Social	18%	78%	24%	72%
Foreign	0%	86%	0%	76%

Key Votes

1) Lmt Cln Water Act	FOR	5) Retain Gun Cont	AGN	9) Aid Angola Reb	FOR
2) Rpl Tobac Sub	AGN	6) Contra Aid	FOR	10) Tax Reform	FOR
3) Grm-Rdmn Def Red	AGN	7) Lmt Text Imp	FOR	11) S Africa Sanc	AGN
4) Ban Polygraph	AGN	8) Limit SDI	AGN	12) Immig Reform	AGN

Election Results

1986 general	Michael Bilirakis (R)	166,504	(71%)	($509,321)
	Gabe Cazares (D).....................	68,574	(29%)	($83,619)
1986 primary	Michael Bilirakis (R) unopposed			
1984 general	Michael Bilirakis (R)	191,343	(79%)	($311,938)
	Jack Wilson (D)	52,150	(21%)	($14,680)

Campaign Contributions and Expenditures

1985-86		Direct Cont. 1985-86		PACS Breakdown 1985-86			
Receipts	$471,612	Indiv.	$298,143	Corp.	$69,950	T/M/H	$59,854
Expend.	$509,321	Party	$4,423	Labor	$5,300	Agr.	$1,550
Unspent	$12,063	PACS	$152,531	Ideo.	$12,806	CWOS	$3,071

TENTH DISTRICT

If you want to see what Florida looked like before the huge growth of the last 30 years, the best way is to drive inland from the coast and look at the parts of the state that have changed least. One such area is the citrus country of central Florida, south of Orlando. Of course there has been growth here: the population figures have grown by percentages unheard of in the Northeast; new shopping malls have sprung up on four-lane highways leading out of the old downtowns, and most people live in small, air-conditioned stucco houses or apartments built since 1950.

Yet a visitor from that year would not find utterly unrecognizable Lakeland or Winter Haven or Lake Wales or the citrus fields lying between these towns and the dozens of lakes of central Florida. None of these towns has grown to metropolitan size. None has reclaimed and built on hundreds of acres of swamp, as has been done in so many other parts of Florida. Nor would attitudes here be totally unrecognizable to our hypothetical visitor. Racial segregation, once firmly embedded in central Florida, is of course gone. But political attitudes associated with rural southern Democrats are not. People here tend to be southern in origin, faithful churchgoers, believers in traditional mores, sympathetic to the idea of government intervention in the economy to help the ordinary person (though not always the poor). They still register Democratic and, even though not as often, vote for Democrats.

But over the years they have become increasingly used to voting Republican. This is the country that forms most of Florida's 10th Congressional District, the home of Congressman Andy Ireland, who switched in 1984 from the Democratic Party to the Republican and was reelected comfortably. Most of the 10th district's people live in Polk County; it also extends to the Gulf Coast, taking in Bradenton, one of the more modest and least Yankeefied towns on the Gulf Coast. Before 1982 this district also included high-income, heavily Republican Sarasota;

now that city is in the heavily Republican 13th District. This district and its predecessors have been a natural target for Republican strategists since the early 1970s. But they always failed in elections and succeeded finally because Ireland got fed up with the Democrats and switched.

Ireland's background has always seemed more Republican anyway: he is from the Republican city of Cincinnati, went to prep school and the Ivy League, and is a banker by trade (as are two other Florida congressmen). From his base in Winter Haven he ran for Congress as a Democrat in 1976 when the incumbent retired; but he won, when the district included Sarasota, largely because of his conservative views and style, and in the House he found himself supporting the Republicans as often as just about any Democrat. Unlike some other party switchers, Ireland does not seem to have acted out of opportunism; when he switched in 1984, his seat was safer than ever, he had seniority and committee assignments he liked, and he had no ambitions for statewide office. A quiet and pleasant man, he seems to have felt shunted aside by the Democratic leadership, but at a time when many other southern conservatives felt welcomed by then. He seems to have acted entirely out of conviction and somewhat against his own political interest.

But only somewhat. He did lose his seat on Foreign Affairs, kept one of his committee assignments—Small Business—and got an important though temporary one, Intelligence. As a Democrat Ireland had not been highly visible on major issues anyway. Back home, the new party label was no handicap in 1984, a very good year for Republicans, nor in 1986, when Bob Graham at the top of the Democratic ticket carried the 10th District. In an age when voters split tickets and switch party preferences themselves freely, party-switching is looked down on only when it seems opportunistic. National Republicans took care to see that Ireland was well financed in 1984, and he won with 62% of the vote; against weaker opposition he got 71% in 1986—more than the best he had done as a Democrat (69% in 1980). In his quiet, thoughtful way Ireland seems to have made his once safe Democratic seat safely Republican.

The People: Pop. 1980: 512,890, up 44.3% 1970–80. Households (1980): 75% family, 35% with children, 63% married couples; 27.9% housing units rented; median monthly rent: $170; median house value: $38,100. Voting age pop. (1980): 381,628; 11% Black, 3% Spanish origin.

1984 Presidential Vote:

Reagan (R)	150,110	(71%)
Mondale (D)	60,788	(29%)

Rep. Andy Ireland (R)

Elected 1976; b. Aug. 23, 1930, Cincinnati, OH; home, Winter Haven; Yale U., B.S. 1952, Columbia Business Sch., LA St. U.; Episcopalian; married (Nancy).

Career: Banker, 1960–70; Chmn. of the Bd., Barnett Banks of Winter Haven, Cypress Gardens, and Auburndale, 1970–76; Mbr., Winter Haven City Comm., 1966–68.

Offices: 2416 RHOB 20515, 202-225-5015. Also 120 W. Central Ave., Winter Haven 33883, 813-299-4041; 1101 6th Ave., W., Bradenton 33506, 813-746-0766; and 1803 Richmond Rd., P.O. Box 8758, Lakeland 33803, 813-687-8015.

Committees: *Armed Services* (15th of 21 R). Subcommittees: Investigations; Procurement and Military Nuclear Systems. *Small Business* (4th of 17 R). Subcommittee: Export Opportunities and Special Small Business Problems (Ranking Member).

Group Ratings

	ADA	ACLU	COPE	CFA	LCV	ACU	NTU	NSI	COC	CEI
1986	0	0	15	17	22	80	58	100	100	83
1985	5	—	16	33	—	90	62	—	82	—

National Journal Ratings

	1986 LIB — 1986 CONS	1985 LIB — 1985 CONS
Economic	0% — 94%	12% — 85%
Social	15% — 84%	0% — 76%
Foreign	16% — 79%	0% — 76%

Key Votes

1) Lmt Cln Water Act	FOR	5) Retain Gun Cont	AGN	9) Aid Angola Reb	FOR
2) Rpl Tobac Sub	FOR	6) Contra Aid	FOR	10) Tax Reform	FOR
3) Grm-Rdmn Def Red	FOR	7) Lmt Text Imp	AGN	11) S Africa Sanc	FOR
4) Ban Polygraph	AGN	8) Limit SDI	AGN	12) Immig Reform	FOR

Election Results

1986 general	Andy Ireland (R)	122,368	(71%)	($402,873)
	David Higginbottom (D)................	49,559	(29%)	($12,903)
1986 primary	Andy Ireland (R) unopposed			
1984 general	Andy Ireland (R)	126,206	(62%)	($620,115)
	Patricia M. (Pat) Glass (D)	77,635	(38%)	($108,457)

Campaign Contributions and Expenditures

1985-86		Direct Cont. 1985-86		PACS Breakdown 1985-86			
Receipts	$463,554	Indiv.	$284,106	Corp.	$77,975	T/M/H	$75,501
Expend.	$402,873	Party	$2,007	Labor	$1,000	Agr.	$1,600
Unspent	$127,819	PACS	$168,966	Ideo.	$9,550	CWOS	$3,340

ELEVENTH DISTRICT

In the 1940s, Cape Canaveral was chosen as the nation's rocket testing site for two reasons: it was on the Atlantic coast (projectiles have to be launched eastward, so the spent rocket casings will drop into the ocean) and the location was virtually unpopulated. There were only 20,000 people then in all of Brevard County, which stretches along 60 miles of the coast and includes the Cape. Florida's warm weather plus the high tech economy of the Cape, have produced such rapid growth that today, although Brevard County has no major city, about 300,000 people live there. They are generally found not on the beach (a lot of that, after all, is restricted government property), but in towns west of the channel (here called the Indian River) that separates all of Florida's Atlantic coastal barrier islands from the mainland. It is a new kind of urban community, and even has a new kind of newspaper, *Florida Today,* Gannett's attempt to adapt *USA Today's* format to a local paper.

Brevard County forms the heart of Florida's 11th Congressional District. The district also extends westward into booming metropolitan Orlando to include Walt Disney World—the world's number one tourist attraction, but with almost no registered voters. To the south, the 11th extends as far as Vero Beach, once an old Dixie town with a large black community and now bristling with condominiums full of retirees from the affluent suburbs of the North. Most of this territory has trended Republican since the 1960s. Gratitude to the Kennedy Administration for its commitment to space is scanty, and locals spurred their politicians to get the cape's name changed back to Canaveral (though it's still the John F. Kennedy Space Center). Engineers and high tech workers typically like the order and certitude of traditional Republican fiscal policy and traditional religious mores, and as long ago as 1962, Brevard and Orlando's Orange County, then a single district, elected a Republican congressman (Edward Gurney, later of Senate Watergate Committee fame). In the 1970s there was some movement toward Democrats, who were able to win many local offices, but in national and statewide elections this area remains Republican.

In congressional elections, however, it elects Democrat Bill Nelson. He is part of the generation of Democrats that came to the House in the 1970s: handsome, well educated, ambitious, and able to finance much of his own campaign. He was elected at 30 to the Florida legislature; by the time he won his seat in Congress, in 1978 at 36, he was a political veteran. He is also not freighted with the baggage of old political ideologies. Unlike the liberal Democrats of the 1950s, he does not see politics as inevitably a struggle between rich and poor, or between business and labor; nor does he see a large federal government as the answer to every problem. In his first term in office, he was politically shrewd enough to win appointment to the Budget Committee. But once there he was in a quandary over the Reagan budget and tax bills and, under pressure, wobbled and gave the Administration some votes he came to regret in 1982 and 1983. From the onset of recession in 1982, he has tended to support the Democratic leadership on many, though not all, issues. But his chances for leadership on the Budget Committee disappeared. After the 1984 election, the Democratic Caucus declined to change the rule limiting Budget Committee service to three terms, and Nelson rotated off.

Since then he has dissented more often from his copartisans and has concentrated on an issue that in this district is local: space. Scrambling for committee assignments after rotating off Budget, he got on Banking, of major importance in booming Florida; and on Science and Technology he got his fellow Democrats to vote him rather than California's George Brown as head of the Space Science Subcommittee. Brown, a longtime dove, wanted to stop military uses of space; Nelson's inclination seems to be to encourage space exploration of all kinds. In early January, 1986 he went up in the space shuttle himself, after several delays, and landed safely. Then, weeks later, the next shuttle, *Challenger*, blew up.

The Rogers Commission's investigation highlighted the specific problems that led to the explosion, notably the O-rings that went rigid in Florida's January freeze, and spotlighted the shortcomings of NASA administrators and contractors. Nelson's subcommittee was in no position to add much to that record. But Nelson is confronted with uncomfortable questions about the shuttle. Even if the O-rings are fixed and management tightened up, the shuttle program seems certain not to produce anything like the commercial revenues projected, and its usefulness—and the usefulness of manned space exploration generally—seem limited given the huge expense. Yet Nelson and others recognize that manned spaceflight generates an enthusiasm for exploring the unknown that is a national asset in a blasé and cynical society. It would be handy politically for Nelson to simply be a cheerleader for the space program. But events have put before him more difficult tasks.

Just as he had to switch off Budget, Nelson also had to face spirited opposition at home, from Republican Rob Quartel in 1984. Spending liberally, stressing his roots in the district, Nelson won 61% against Quartel, a former George Bush aide, and seems to have proved that this Republican-leaning district is safe for him. But at the same time he seems to have relinquished the ambitions he once undoubtedly had to run statewide, just as he has shifted from national to local issues. Certainly he made no moves to run for governor or other office in 1986, likely to be the last opening for a Democrat in some time.

The People: Pop. 1980: 512,691, up 39.8% 1970–80. Households (1980): 76% family, 37% with children, 64% married couples; 30.8% housing units rented; median monthly rent: $219; median house value: $47,400. Voting age pop. (1980): 380,011; 6% Black, 3% Spanish origin, 1% Asian origin.

1984 Presidential Vote: Reagan (R) 182,952   (74%)
Mondale (D) 63,214   (26%)

Rep. Bill Nelson (D)

Elected 1978; b. Sept. 29, 1942, Miami; home, Melbourne; Yale U., B.A. 1965, U. of VA, J.D. 1968; Episcopalian; married (Grace).

Career: Army, 1968–70; Practicing atty., 1970–72; FL House of Reps., 1972–78.

Offices: 2404 RHOB 20515, 202-225-3671. Also 65 E. NASA Blvd., Ste. 202, Melbourne 32901, 305-724-1978; 780 S. Appollo Blvd., Ste. 12, Melbourn 32901, 305-676-1176; and Fed. Bldg., Ste. 300, Orlando 32801, 305-841-1776.

Committees: *Banking, Finance and Urban Affairs* (22d of 31 D). Subcommittees: Financial Institutions Supervision, Regulation and Insurance. *Science, Space and Technology* (8th of 27 D). Subcommittees: Space Science and Applications (Chairman); Transportation, Aviation and Materials.

Group Ratings

	ADA	ACLU	COPE	CFA	LCV	ACU	NTU	NSI	COC	CEI
1986	15	11	38	58	60	77	28	80	61	43
1985	30	—	37	42	—	71	41	—	54	—

National Journal Ratings

	1986 LIB — 1986 CONS		1985 LIB — 1985 CONS	
Economic	43%	56%	43%	57%
Social	27%	71%	29%	70%
Foreign	32%	67%	24%	66%

Key Votes

1) Lmt Cln Water Act	AGN	5) Retain Gun Cont	AGN	9) Aid Angola Reb	FOR
2) Rpl Tobac Sub	FOR	6) Contra Aid	FOR	10) Tax Reform	FOR
3) Grm-Rdmn Def Red	—	7) Lmt Text Imp	AGN	11) S Africa Sanc	FOR
4) Ban Polygraph	AGN	8) Limit SDI	AGN	12) Immig Reform	FOR

Election Results

1986 general	Bill Nelson (D)	149,036	(73%)	($304,914)
	Scott Ellis (R)	55,904	(27%)	($11,896)
1986 primary	Bill Nelson (D) unopposed			
1984 general	Bill Nelson (D)	145,764	(61%)	($349,549)
	Rob Quartel (R)	95,115	(39%)	($150,758)

Campaign Contributions and Expenditures

1985-86		Direct Cont. 1985-86		PACS Breakdown 1985-86			
Receipts	$349,335	Indiv.	$123,265	Corp.	$70,980	T/M/H	$43,825
Expend.	$304,914	Party	$300	Labor	$12,000	Agr.	$750
Unspent	$113,738	PACS	$137,668	Ideo.	$8,375	CWOS	$1,738

TWELFTH DISTRICT

The history of the settlement of Florida's Gold Coast is one that begins in south Florida, in Miami, and, counterintuitively, marches north along the Atlantic coast. At each step this northward migration has encountered and then eclipsed the small southern towns found in its way. Thus Fort Lauderdale, once a sleepy southern crossroads, is now the center of a Yankee metropolis; likewise, West Palm Beach. Now the migration is moving north of Palm Beach, into what is now Florida's 12th Congressional District. The north side of West Palm and neighboring

Riviera Beach include most of that area's black population. Farther north, surrounding the old aristocratic resort of Hobe Sound, are several major condominium developments, ranging from high to very high income. They are reaching up past Stuart, in Martin County, to St. Lucie County, where Fort Pierce, a good-sized town with a black near-majority, has as its neighbors developments filled with affluent Yankees. The same is true of Vero Beach, even farther north. This stretch of coast includes three-fourths of the 12th District's population.

The rest is spread over a much vaster expanse of land, all the way across to Naples on the Gulf Coast. The district also takes in the town of Sebring, in whimsically named Highlands County, where a Grand Prix auto race is held yearly. In the middle is Lake Okeechobee, not so much a resort area as the center of an agricultural empire. In cleared and drained swampland, acres of crops are planted, raised, sprayed, and finally harvested, mostly by blacks and Mexican-Americans whose wages and working conditions have long been among America's worst.

This is essentially a Republican district, certainly in national elections; but its boundaries were crafted by a Democratic legislature in the wistful—though, as it happened, almost realized—hope that it would elect a Democrat. The Republican candidate, Tom Lewis, had many assets: as a state senator, he had represented most of the new 12th and had won high ratings for competence; he steadfastly professed his opposition to Social Security cuts. Democrat Brad Culverhouse spent liberally of his own money and had labor endorsements; he carried Palm Beach County (with its big black vote) and the interior counties. But Lewis had enough votes in the coastal counties north of Palm Beach and in Naples to win. Literally, this was a triumph for Republican Yankees.

Lewis has backgrounds both in the military and in local government. After serving in the Air Force for 11 years, he was an executive for Pratt & Whitney, the jet engine manufacturers. His career in local government goes back almost 20 years. Neither has made him an insurgent or a believer in lost causes: he is a man who has worked his way up through competent organizations, and seems likely to believe in orderly, sober conservatism. A bit unpredictable on cultural and foreign issues, he is solidly conservative on economics. Bills he has sponsored include establishing clearinghouses for missing children and adding 136,000 acres to the Big Cypress National Preserve in the Florida Everglades. His initial committee assignments—Government Operations, Science and Technology—did not suggest a high profile; after the 1984 election he switched off Gov Ops to the Agriculture Committee. Stolid, hardworking, Lewis seems to have made this a safe district; he was unopposed in 1984 and 1986.

The People: Pop. 1980: 513,121, up 67.0% 1970–80. Households (1980): 73% family, 32% with children, 61% married couples; 30.3% housing units rented; median monthly rent: $190; median house value: $47,700. Voting age pop. (1980): 384,221; 16% Black, 4% Spanish origin.

1984 Presidential Vote: Reagan (R) 158,850   (67%)
Mondale (D) 78,830   (33%)

Rep. Tom Lewis (R)

Elected 1982; b. Oct. 26, 1924, Philadelphia, PA; home, North Palm Beach; Palm Beach Jr. Col., 1956–57, U. of FL, 1958–59; United Methodist; married (Marian).

Career: Air Force, WWII and Korea; Corp. Exec., Pratt & Whitney Aircraft, 1957–73; Mayor/Councilman, North Palm Beach, 1964–71; FL House of Reps., 1972–80; FL Senate 1980–82.

Offices: 1216 LHOB 20515, 202-225-5792. Also 2500 Midport Rd., Ste. 120, Port St. Lucie, 305-627-6192, 305-465-3710.

Committees: *Agriculture* (11th of 17 R). Subcommittees: Cotton, Rice and Sugar; Domestic Marketing, Consumer Relations, and Nutrition; Livestock Dairy, and Poultry. *Science, Space and Technology* (6th of 18 R). Subcommittee: Space Science and Applications; Transportation, Aviation and Materials.

Group Ratings

	ADA	ACLU	COPE	CFA	LCV	ACU	NTU	NSI	COC	CEI
1986	10	20	16	25	27	70	51	90	76	59
1985	5	—	15	17	—	77	53	—	86	—

National Journal Ratings

	1986 LIB — 1986 CONS		1985 LIB — 1985 CONS	
Economic	27%	72%	0% —	95%
Social	0% —	89%	36% —	60%
Foreign	25% —	74%	24% —	66%

Key Votes

1) Lmt Cln Water Act	FOR	5) Retain Gun Cont	AGN
2) Rpl Tobac Sub	AGN	6) Contra Aid	FOR
3) Grm-Rdmn Def Red	FOR	7) Lmt Text Imp	AGN
4) Ban Polygraph	AGN	8) Limit SDI	AGN

9) Aid Angola Reb	—
10) Tax Reform	AGN
11) S Africa Sanc	FOR
12) Immig Reform	AGN

Election Results

1986 general	Tom Lewis (R)	150,222	(100%)	($285,685)
1986 primary	Tom Lewis (R) unopposed			
1984 general	Tom Lewis (R) unopposed			

Campaign Contributions and Expenditures

1985-86		Direct Cont. 1985-86		PACS Breakdown 1985-86			
Receipts	$309,923	Indiv.	$196,155	Corp.	$29,400	T/M/H	$33,950
Expend.	$285,685	Party	$4,729	Labor	$3,500	Agr.	$7,350
Unspent	$150,369	PACS	$85,202	Ideo.	$8,750	CWOS	$2,252

THIRTEENTH DISTRICT

Florida's Gulf Coast is probably the closest thing there is in the continental United States to a tropical paradise. The weather, hot and humid in the summer, is pleasant most of the rest of the year. The geography here is more varied than on the Atlantic coast, with its monotonous barrier islands. There are barrier islands on the Gulf, too; but there are also major gaps between them, wide estuaries, and places where the swampy lowlands seem to proceed directly into the ocean. And, perhaps most important, the sea is not blocked by miles of high-rise apartments. There are, to be sure, some high-rises on the Gulf Coast; but the favored building height here is only two stories, and the favored community is not the high-rise, but the sprawling, city-sized development like Cape Coral or Port Charlotte.

The Gulf Coast, Sarasota south to Naples, is Florida's 13th Congressional District. It is, like much of America's Sun Belt, a creature of the air conditioner: 40 years ago, before air conditioning was widely available, some 45,000 people lived here; by 1980, 513,000 did. The population of the district is heavily tilted toward retirees: only 24% of households include children, and 33% of the adults are over 65—one of the highest percentages in the country. The population is also almost entirely white and usually affluent, people who populated the Waspy suburbs of Chicago and New York and Detroit and Philadelphia in the 1950s and 1960s. Not surprisingly, this is the most Republican congressional district in Florida, perhaps one of the most solidly Republican in the nation.

The 13th District's congressman, Connie Mack III, is a Republican who has quickly become one of the leaders of his party. His aggressiveness and political skills have a pedigree: he is the grandson not only of his namesake, the longtime manager and owner of the Philadelphia Athletics, but also of Texas Senator (1913–41) Morris Sheppard. In 1983 he won a seat on the Budget Committee as a freshman, and with Newt Gingrich, Vin Weber, and others formed the informal Conservative Opportunity Society, championing innovative approaches to issues and hazing the Democrats. They seized on the tactic of using the House's special orders procedure, a time for speechmaking after the legislative day is over, to attack Democrats for the growing audience on the C-SPAN cable service. In 1985 Mack and his allies seemed to stumble when they poured their energies into the fight over the contested Indiana 8th election; they wanted to cast doubt on the legitimacy of the Democrats' control of the House but only succeeded in getting off on a sidetrack away from substantive issues that interest the public and onto inside-baseball procedural matters of interest to no one off Capitol Hill. But later in the year Mack recovered and became the House's lead sponsor of the budget-cutting initiative usually known by the names of its Senate originators, Phil Gramm and Warren Rudman. With little institutional memory, with a sense of urgency as the Reagan years went on, Mack seized this opportunity to change the course of American public policy.

Gifted with movie star good looks and an affable temperament, Mack looks nothing like a man who would turn American politics upside down. Back in Cape Coral he was a bank president—a job that enables a man in a fast-growing community to meet many people and learn how they make their livings—who had not held public office when he ran; he was attacked, curiously enough, as insufficiently conservative in the 1982 Republican primary. But he led in the primary 29%–22% and won the runoff 58%–42%. He has a safe seat. In early 1987 he seemed poised to run against Senator Lawton Chiles, but in April he announced he wouldn't. The risks were evidently too great and the satisfaction of service in the House, where he has good committee positions and congenial allies, if not a sympathetic majority, was great enough.

The People: Pop. 1980: 513,048, up 86.5% 1970–80. Households (1980): 73% family, 24% with children, 65% married couples; 23.3% housing units rented; median monthly rent: $238; median house value: $53,700. Voting age pop. (1980): 413,477; 4% Black, 2% Spanish origin.

| **1984 Presidential Vote:** | Reagan (R) . . . . 221,828 | (74%) |
| | Mondale (D) . . . . 77,085 | (26%) |

Rep. Connie Mack III (R)

Elected 1982; b. Oct. 29, 1940, Philadelphia, PA; home, Cape Coral; U. of FL, B.A. 1966; Roman Catholic; married (Priscilla).

Career: Banker, 1966–82.

Offices: 228 CHOB 20515, 202-225-2536. Also 106 Fed. Bldg., Fort Myers 33901, 813-334-4424; and 4000 S. Tamiami Trail, Snelling Pl., Ste. 208, Sarasota 33581, 813-923-8084.

Committees: *Budget* (3d of 14 R). Task Forces: Defense and International Affairs; Health; Income Security (Ranking Member). *Foreign Affairs* (12th of 18 R). Subcommittees: International Operations; Western Hemisphere Affairs.

Group Ratings

	ADA	ACLU	COPE	CFA	LCV	ACU	NTU	NSI	COC	CEI
1986	0	15	11	17	26	100	70	100	100	92
1985	10	—	13	25	—	95	69	—	86	—

National Journal Ratings

	1986 LIB — 1986 CONS		1985 LIB — 1985 CONS	
Economic	0%	— 94%	9%	— 88%
Social	0%	— 89%	0%	— 76%
Foreign	0%	— 86%	0%	— 76%

Key Votes

1) Lmt Cln Water Act	FOR	5) Retain Gun Cont	AGN	9) Aid Angola Reb	FOR
2) Rpl Tobac Sub	FOR	6) Contra Aid	FOR	10) Tax Reform	FOR
3) Grm-Rdmn Def Red	FOR	7) Lmt Text Imp	AGN	11) S Africa Sanc	AGN
4) Ban Polygraph	AGN	8) Limit SDI	AGN	12) Immig Reform	AGN

Election Results

1986 general	Connie Mack III (R)	187,794	(75%)	($313,639)
	Addison S. Gilbert III (D)	62,694	(25%)	($42,898)
1986 primary	Connie Mack III (R) unopposed			
1984 general	Connie Mack III (R) unopposed			($450,701)

Campaign Contributions and Expenditures

1985-86		Direct Cont. 1985-86		PACS Breakdown 1985-86			
Receipts	$456,462	Indiv.	$327,616	Corp.	$48,750	T/M/H	$51,650
Expend.	$313,639	Party	$1,953	Labor	$6,500	Agr.	$250
Unspent	$183,351	PACS	$124,526	Ideo.	$11,876	CWOS	$5,500

FOURTEENTH DISTRICT

When Henry Flagler built his railroad south to Palm Beach, he had a vision—of a grand Mediterranean resort for the few Americans who could afford it. That dream has been realized in Palm Beach, across Lake Worth from the railroad terminus in West Palm Beach. In the 1920s grand palaces were built along the Atlantic, and America's most exclusive shops followed their clients down to Worth Avenue for the winter. Palm Beach then was almost the only resort in south Florida: Miami was just being developed, Fort Lauderdale was a crossroads, the Gulf Coast was still swamp. But even today, Palm Beach remains something special, even if many of its ethnic barriers are gone and its streets are lined less often with marble palaces than with million dollar condominiums. This remains the premier winter resort for the very rich.

What would have surprised Flagler is what has happened to the land around, up and down the narrow barrier island on which Palm Beach sits and on the flat land running west from Lake Worth to the still unreclaimed swamp. For most of the past two decades, Palm Beach County has been one of the fastest-growing parts of the United States, spawning subdivisions and condominiums and even whole suburbs faster than the mapmakers can draw. In effect two paths of migration have converged here. One is the southward movement of retirees and of young working families as well to Florida's warm climate and suddenly growing high tech and service economy (Palm Beach County is where IBM developed its PC). The other is the northward movement along Florida's Gulf Coast, of older and middle-aged residents looking for the quiet ambiance and crime-free atmosphere they can no longer find in Miami's Dade County or even Fort Lauderdale's Broward.

This is the land of Florida's 14th Congressional District, by some measures the fastest-growing district in the nation in the 1980s. The 14th extends along the coast from Palm Beach and West Palm down to ultra-expensive Boca Raton. It also goes about 12 miles inland, where the fastest recent growth is taking place, in places like Florida Gardens, Country Club Acres, and, to the south along Broward County's Sawgrass Expressway, in Margate and Tamarac. Palm Beach County's politics are as volatile as its demographics. Solidly Republican in national elections in the 1980s, it was 3% more Democratic than the state as a whole in the key 1986 elections. The long-term trend may be toward the Democrats, since the Palm Beach area now seems to be getting more Jews moving in from Broward County than Cuban-Americans from Dade.

The congressman from the 14th District is Dan Mica, a Democrat first elected in 1978, who has already had an eventful House career. He got the district as a kind of inheritance, succeeding the man on whose staff he worked for 10 years, Paul Rogers, who in turn had succeeded his father. But Mica's victory was not automatic, and he had to win a tough primary in 1978 and to fight tough Republican challenges in the district in 1978, 1980, and 1984. In the House, he got a seat on the Foreign Affairs Committee immediately and that has been the focus of his legislative work. In the 1970s the committee was a stronghold of older hawks; as they retired they were replaced by young doves, and by Dan Mica. After the Reagan Republican victories in 1981, Foreign Affairs became one of the liberal strongholds of Congress. But Mica, out of conviction and as the representative of a Florida district acutely conscious of the consequences of Communist gains in Latin America, disagreed on many issues with his fellow Democrats. In 1981 committee Democrats voted out Latin America subcommittee chairman Gus Yatron, and then, although Mica had seniority by virtue of a coin toss, rejected him for his fellow sophomore, Michael Barnes, by a 10–9 vote. That put into a key chair a harsh critic of Reagan Latin American policy rather than one who at least partially favored it.

Mica was openly bitter and that year voted with Reagan on budget and tax cuts. But over time he moved back toward positions not far out of line with those of most Democrats. In 1984, when committee chairman Clement Zablocki's death opened up the Foreign Operations subcommittee chair, Mica won it. In that capacity he has been the House's lead man on legislation to protect American embassies and installations from terrorists, and he has had the duty of floor managing the State Department authorization bill, which always attracts a lot of politically attractive-sounding amendments. He has provided key support to the National Endowment for Democracy. In the 100th Congress, with the House poised to cut out all aid to the Nicaraguan contras, Mica may find himself again at odds with most other Democrats. But he will approach such battles with better party credentials and with the sympathy and support of the current Foreign Affairs chairman, his fellow Floridian Dante Fascell.

It's hard to say how secure Mica's position is in the 14th District. A serious Republican challenger held him to 55% in 1984, but he got over 70% in 1986, and the Palm Beach County returns for other offices must be encouraging. Mica may be looking ahead to redistricting: an area with high concentrations of population, like Florida's Gold Coast, provides maximum flexibility for redistricters, particularly here, where he is liable to lose nearly half his constituency because of population gains.

The People: Pop. 1980: 512,803, up 126.3% 1970–80. Households (1980): 74% family, 27% with children, 65% married couples; 22.0% housing units rented; median monthly rent: $278; median house value: $62,200. Voting age pop. (1980): 406,873; 4% Spanish origin, 3% Black.

1984 Presidential Vote:

Reagan (R)	....	171,663	(61%)
Mondale (D)	....	110,775	(39%)

Rep. Daniel (Dan) Mica (D)

Elected 1978; b. Feb. 4, 1944, Binghamton, NY; home, Lake Worth; U. of FL, Miami Dade Jr. Col., A.A., 1965, FL Atlantic U., B.A. 1966; Roman Catholic; married (Martha).

Career: Pub. sch. teacher, 1966–68; A.A. to U.S. Rep. Paul Rogers, 1968–78.

Offices: 2455 RHOB 20515, 202-225-3001. Also 639 E. Ocean Ave., Ste. 303, Boynton Beach 33435, 305-732-4000.

Committees: *Foreign Affairs* (7th of 27 D). Subcommittees: International Economic Policy and Trade; International Operations (Chairman). *Veterans' Affairs* (4th of 21 D). Subcommittees: Compensation, Pension, and Insurance; Hospitals and Health Care; Oversight and Investigations. *Select Committee on Aging* (13th of 39 D). Subcommittee: Health and Long-Term Care.

Group Ratings

	ADA	ACLU	COPE	CFA	LCV	ACU	NTU	NSI	COC	CEI
1986	55	27	56	75	51	32	23	60	47	23
1985	45	—	55	58	—	48	31	—	48	—

National Journal Ratings

	1986 LIB — 1986 CONS		1985 LIB — 1985 CONS	
Economic	53% —	47%	50% —	49%
Social	60% —	39%	63% —	33%
Foreign	52% —	47%	49% —	50%

Key Votes

1) Lmt Cln Water Act	AGN	5) Retain Gun Cont	FOR	9) Aid Angola Reb	FOR
2) Rpl Tobac Sub	AGN	6) Contra Aid	FOR	10) Tax Reform	AGN
3) Grm-Rdmn Def Red	FOR	7) Lmt Text Imp	AGN	11) S Africa Sanc	FOR
4) Ban Polygraph	FOR	8) Limit SDI	FOR	12) Immig Reform	FOR

Election Results

1986 general	Daniel (Dan) Mica (D)	171,961	(74%)	($386,905)
	Rick Martin (R)	61,185	(26%)	($11,072)
1984 primary	Daniel (Dan) Mica (D) unopposed			
1984 general	Daniel (Dan) Mica (D)	153,935	(55%)	($439,511)
	Don Ross (R)	123,926	(45%)	($336,994)

Campaign Contributions and Expenditures

1985-86		Direct Cont. 1985-86		PACS Breakdown 1985-86			
Receipts	$562,421	Indiv.	$336,290	Corp.	$82,732	T/M/H	$61,795
Expend.	$386,905	Party	$437	Labor	$24,600	Agr.	$7,700
Unspent	$196,645	PACS	$215,202	Ideo.	$34,750	CWOS	$3,625

FIFTEENTH DISTRICT

Just about smack in the middle of Florida's Gold Coast—the strip of Atlantic Coast from somewhere south of Miami to somewhere north of Palm Beach, with three million people—is the city of Fort Lauderdale. In its rather short life, the city has gone through a number of transformations. As late as 1950, when Fort Lauderdale had 36,000 people (with 83,000 in all of Broward County), almost no one had heard of it. Ten years later it was famous nationally for its college spring sand-and-beer vacations—celebrated in the book and movie, *Where the Boys Are*. Among a more select company, Fort Lauderdale had won a reputation as an agreeable place to retire or, perhaps, make a living: a city cosmopolitan but small, with interesting canals and (with air conditioning) a pleasant climate. Here also were wide beaches and good shopping and at least some of the cultural attractions you would expect in a big metropolitan area.

Most of Fort Lauderdale's early residents were from the high-income suburbs of the East and Midwest, the Locust Valleys and Winnetkas of America. Through the middle 1960s, Fort Lauderdale tended to exclude Jews: this was the WASPy part of south Florida. Its politics was straight out of the old *Chicago Tribune*: solidly Republican, conservative, unchanging. Then in the late 1960s restrictions against Jews eased in Broward County. Hollywood, just south of Fort Lauderdale, became a mostly Jewish city; Fort Lauderdale itself acquired many Jewish residents. At the same time, there was vast growth, in beach towns to the north and especially in the newly created cities to the west in reclaimed swampland. All this made the Fort Lauderdale area culturally more varied and politically more closely—and sometimes bitterly—contested. In 1964 Broward County went for Barry Goldwater, in 1976 for Jimmy Carter—the first time it had gone Democratic for president since 1944. In 1984, for the first time in modern history, it was more Democratic than Miami's Dade County—and cast almost as many votes; in 1986 it backed the Democratic candidate for governor while Dade went for Republican Bob Martinez.

The 15th Congressional District of Florida, entirely within Broward County, is centered on Fort Lauderdale. On the coast it goes past Pompano Beach and Deerfield Beach up to the Palm Beach County line; inland it includes golf-course-laden suburbs like Plantation, Lauderhill, and Lauderdale Lakes past and just beyond the newly built Sawgrass Expressway. It does not include Hollywood or the towns just to the west: this is the more Republican section of Broward County.

Its congressman is a Republican, Clay Shaw, who won it in 1980. His involvement in city government goes back to 1968, when he was not yet 30; he served as mayor from 1975 to 1980. Shaw won the seat after a series of tumultuous contests in districts rendered politically precarious because of demographic change. J. Herbert Burke, a *Tribune* Republican first elected in 1966, was defeated in 1978 following an arrest for disorderly behavior; Ed Stack, the 68-year-old Broward County Sheriff who won was in turn beaten in the Democratic primary in 1980; the primary winner, Miami-area legislator Alan Becker, was not even from Broward County and had other problems, and lost to Shaw. In the 1980s things have cooled down. Shaw won in 1982 over Ed Stack, by a 57%–43% margin; he won by nearly 2 to 1 in 1984 and had no Democratic opponent in 1986.

So the Fort Lauderdale area seems finally to have found a congressman it is comfortable with. Shaw is a quiet congressman who votes predictably with his fellow Republicans. He serves on the nuts-and-bolts Public Works Committee, from which he hopes to derive some benefit for the new airport Fort Lauderdale is building. On Judiciary, he has made a point of opposing illegal aliens and drugs—mandatory positions in Fort Lauderdale and Broward, which are not so far from Miami's vices; but his major amendments on immigration amnesty were unsuccessful, and some but not all of his anti-drug proposals were included in the House omnibus anti-drug bill in 1986. He did get through a requirement that high schools receiving federal aid run drug abuse programs, and he championed the death penalty for drug dealers who commit murder. Shaw considered running for governor in 1986, and if he had done so, and had had Bob Martinez's luck, he might have won. But he didn't, and seems comfortably ensconced in the House.

The People: Pop. 1980: 512,950, up 34.0% 1970–80. Households (1980): 65% family, 24% with children, 53% married couples; 33.2% housing units rented; median monthly rent: $261; median house value: $59,900. Voting age pop. (1980): 411,582; 13% Black, 3% Spanish origin.

1984 Presidential Vote:

Reagan (R)	117,110	(59%)
Mondale (D)	81,906	(41%)

Rep. E. Clay Shaw, Jr. (R)

Elected 1980; b. Apr. 19, 1939, Miami; home, Ft. Lauderdale; Stetson U., B.A. 1961, U. of AL, M.B.A. 1963, Stetson U., J.D. 1966; Roman Catholic; married (Emilie).

Career: Practicing atty., 1966–68; Ft. Lauderdale Asst. City Atty., 1968; Chf. City Prosecutor, 1968–69, Assoc. Munic. Judge, 1969–71, City Commissioner, 1971–73, Vice Mayor, 1973–75, Mayor, 1975–80.

Offices: 440 CHOB 20515, 202-225-3026. Also Broward Fed. Bldg., 299 E. Broward Blvd., Ft. Lauderdale 33301, 305-522-1800.

Committees: *Judiciary* (7th of 14 R). Subcommittees: Administrative Law and Government Relations (Ranking Member); Crime. *Public Works and Transportation* (7th of 20 R). Subcommittees: Economic Development (Ranking Member); Surface Transportation; Water Resources. *Select Committee on Narcotics Abuse and Control* (3d of 10 R).

Group Ratings

	ADA	ACLU	COPE	CFA	LCV	ACU	NTU	NSI	COC	CEI
1986	5	0	8	25	27	82	51	100	87	78
1985	5	—	9	42	—	81	55	—	81	—

National Journal Ratings

	1986 LIB — 1986 CONS			1985 LIB — 1985 CONS		
Economic	18%	—	82%	20%	—	79%
Social	17%	—	82%	0%	—	76%
Foreign	14%	—	84%	0%	—	76%

Key Votes

1) Lmt Cln Water Act	FOR	5) Retain Gun Cont	AGN	9) Aid Angola Reb	FOR
2) Rpl Tobac Sub	FOR	6) Contra Aid	FOR	10) Tax Reform	FOR
3) Grm-Rdmn Def Red	FOR	7) Lmt Text Imp	AGN	11) S Africa Sanc	AGN
4) Ban Polygraph	AGN	8) Limit SDI	AGN	12) Immig Reform	FOR

Election Results

1986 general	E. Clay Shaw, Jr. (R) unopposed			($102,671)
1986 primary	E. Clay Shaw, Jr. (R) unopposed			
1984 general	E. Clay Shaw, Jr. (R)	128,097	(66%)	($371,855)
	Bill Humphrey (D)	66,833	(34%)	($97,923)

Campaign Contributions and Expenditures

1985-86		Direct Cont. 1985-86		PACS Breakdown 1985-86			
Receipts	$203,765	Indiv.	$109,501	Corp.	$38,100	T/M/H	$29,550
Expend.	$102,671	Party	$1,176	Labor	$7,000	Agr.	$0
Unspent	$120,811	PACS	$80,851	Ideo.	$5,250	CWOS	$951

SIXTEENTH DISTRICT

Forty years ago the Florida land that is now its 16th Congressional District was almost entirely uninhabited: some empty coastal land between Miami and the small town of Fort Lauderdale and thousands of acres of unreclaimed Everglades that started just west of Miami and continued for miles inland. Today more than half a million people live here, in closely packed subdivisions, around new golf courses, or in high-rise condominiums. And some of the most explosive growth in south Florida is taking place here, on either side of the new Sawgrass Expressway in Broward County, 12 to 15 miles west of the ocean, built in record time to meet the demand for development, and in the former swamplands west of the Palmetto Expressway that used to mark the edge of urban settlement in Miami's Dade County.

The 16th was the new district south Florida's Gold Coast got after the 1980 Census (the 17th, 18th, and 19th are descendants of the new districts the area got after the 1950, 1960, and 1970 Censuses respectively). In effect the 16th includes the products of two migrations. The first, and larger, is the migration of Jews and others who originally came from New York and the Northeast out from Dade County and into Broward. The most populous city here now is Hollywood, whose high-rise condominiums facing the ocean are full of former New Yorkers and Miamians; and similar populations live in Pembroke Pines to the west, Hallandale to the south, and Miramar to the southwest. Condominium activists are the big political force here. Large high-rise condominiums bring into one handy location, to which access can be controlled, hundreds and sometimes even thousands of voters. In many cases, they are articulate people with organizational literacy, an interest in issues, a knack for politics, and plenty of time on their hands. Properly organized, a condominium can give an endorsed candidate a margin of hundreds of votes—a huge advantage in a closely contested primary where most ordinary precincts are carried by 10 or 20 votes. In partisan politics this part of Broward County is heavily Democratic—perhaps the most Democratic part of Florida these days.

The second part of the 16th District is in Miami's Dade County, not directly south of the Broward County portion of the 16th, but to the west. There it stretches south past the Tamiami Trail, also known as Southwest 8th Street or, to Cubans, Calle Ocho. Between 60% and 80% of the residents here are of Spanish origin, living, around and behind Miami International Airport, in upwardly mobile communities like Westchester and Westwood Lakes. Altogether the Dade County portion of the 16th District is 60% Spanish. It votes heavily Republican: the Cubans know the evils of Communism, appreciate the virtues of free enterprise, cherish traditional moral values, and prefer Republicans to Democrats on all these counts.

Demographically, Broward formed just 59% of the district in 1980; politically, because many Cubans are still not citizens or not registered to vote, Broward casts three-quarters of the district's votes (and cast 83% in the so-far decisive 1982 Democratic primary). That makes the district basically Democratic, but there is also a large and enthusiastic Republican base, and that has made for some strenuously contested elections.

The congressman from the 16th is Larry Smith, brought up in Brooklyn and Long Island, and possessed of a zest for argument and a brash New York style. He turns off some colleagues and constituents, but others are attracted by his enthusiasm and verve; he is never stale or blasé. Like several other young Florida congressmen, he sought a seat on Foreign Affairs, and in this district filled with residents who themselves or whose parents or grandparents fled tyranny, and who now live on a peninsula thrust downward toward Latin America, foreign issues arouse more passion than domestic. Smith is one of the House's leading and most aggressive backers of aid to Israel and led opposition to sale of weapons to Jordan and Saudi Arabia so aggressively that the proposals were dropped. On Central America he supported after initially opposing aid to the Nicaraguan contras; he is more skeptical about their prospects for success than some Florida colleagues, but has never been a romantic admirer of the Sandinistas like so many of his Democratic copartisans. He serves also on Judiciary, where he sponsored and pushed to passage the bill outlawing Quaaludes. It would be easy to dismiss Smith's record as catering to the prejudices of his constituents, concerned about Israel, worried about Central America, cautious about leaving their condominium compounds for fear of drug-driven crime. But Smith seems to share their passions and fears, and seems determined to do something about them.

Although he has won by large percentages in two of his three races, Smith's political status at home is still tenuous. His first primary, in 1982, was fought out almost entirely in Broward County, and he won 55%–45% a battle decided in the condominiums. He won 72% of the vote in the fall, but only barely carried Dade County. In 1984 Republicans targeted the district, running a fundamentalist who wanted creationism taught in the schools; although he seemed to have little cultural affinity with either of the district's two major ethnic groups, he held Smith to 56%, 64% in Broward but only 33% in Dade, where turnout rose from 27,000 to 47,000. In 1986, against less well-funded opposition, Smith won with 70%, 76% in Broward and 49% in Dade. The big increase in turnout here, while turnout nationally was slumping, is evidence of the explosive growth in this part of south Florida: from 1982 to 1986 turnout in the Broward portion of the 16th was up from 108,000 to 134,000 and in the Dade portion from 27,000 to 40,000.

In the long run the growth of the Cuban vote here might threaten Smith. But there is no long run in Florida districts: Smith has to run within these boundaries only twice more, and then there will be redistricting. It's possible then that a heavily Cuban district will be created, leaving him mostly in Broward County and with a safe seat. In the meantime he has shored up his position by raising and spending more than $800,000 for the 1986 election.

The People: Pop. 1980: 513,365, up 74.6% 1970–80. Households (1980): 74% family, 33% with children, 63% married couples; 25.8% housing units rented; median monthly rent: $278; median house value: $62,500. Voting age pop. (1980): 396,409; 20% Spanish origin, 4% Black, 1% Asian origin.

1984 Presidential Vote:
Reagan (R)	123,441	(61%)
Mondale (D)	78,576	(39%)

Rep. Lawrence J. (Larry) Smith (D)

Elected 1982; b. Apr. 25, 1941, Brooklyn, NY; home, Hollywood; NYU, Brooklyn Law Sch., LL.B. 1964, Jewish; married (Sheila).

Career: Practicing atty., 1964–82; Hollywood Planning and Zoning Board, 1974–78, Chmn., 1975–78; Broward Cnty. Advisory Board, 1978; FL House of Reps., 1978–82; Governor's Task Force on Criminal Justice Systems, 1980–81.

Offices: 113 CHOB 20515, 202-225-7931. Also 4747 Hollywood Blvd., Hollywood 33021, 305-987-6484.

Committees: *Foreign Affairs* (15th of 27 D). Subcommittees: Europe and the Middle East; International Operations. *Judiciary* (16th of 21 D). Subcommittees: Crime; Monopolies and Commercial Law. *Select Committee on Narcotics Abuse and Control* (14th of 15 D).

Group Ratings

	ADA	ACLU	COPE	CFA	LCV	ACU	NTU	NSI	COC	CEI
1986	65	50	93	75	82	24	26	33	27	18
1985	55	—	91	92	—	35	32	—	33	—

National Journal Ratings

	1986 LIB — 1986 CONS			1985 LIB — 1985 CONS		
Economic	68%	—	31%	64%	—	35%
Social	56%	—	44%	85%	—	0%
Foreign	54%	—	45%	57%	—	42%

Key Votes

1) Lmt Cln Water Act	FOR	5) Retain Gun Cont	FOR	9) Aid Angola Reb	FOR
2) Rpl Tobac Sub	FOR	6) Contra Aid	FOR	10) Tax Reform	FOR
3) Grm-Rdmn Def Red	FOR	7) Lmt Text Imp	FOR	11) S Africa Sanc	FOR
4) Ban Polygraph	FOR	8) Limit SDI	FOR	12) Immig Reform	FOR

Election Results

1986 general	Lawrence J. (Larry) Smith (D)	121,213	(70%)	($878,922)
	Mary Collins (R).....................	52,807	(30%)	($60,337)
1986 primary	Lawrence J. (Larry) Smith (D) unopposed			
1984 general	Lawrence J. (Larry) Smith (D)	108,410	(56%)	($554,223)
	Tom Bush (R)	83,903	(44%)	($113,435)

Campaign Contributions and Expenditures

1985-86		Direct Cont. 1985-86		PACS Breakdown 1985-86			
Receipts	$848,821	Indiv.	$429,804	Corp.	$46,907	T/M/H	$69,356
Expend.	$878,922	Party	$6,010	Labor	$118,606	Agr.	$3,600
Unspent	$57,030	PACS	$308,935	Ideo.	$67,116	CWOS	$3,350
		Cand.	$74,345				

SEVENTEENTH DISTRICT

Florida's 17th Congressional District is the northern part of Dade County—an almost square portion between the beach above Bal Harbour to the new town suburb of Miami Lakes developed by Senator Bob Graham in the west. The district includes only a small part of the city of Miami itself, but in many ways is the heart of the metropolitan area—a status reflected in the fact that the Miami Dolphins' new 73,000-seat stadium was sited here. It is about one-quarter Cuban: the once white working-class suburb of Hialeah, around the race track, is now mostly Cuban. The 17th is also about one-quarter black: just as Cubans move out from Miami along Southwest 8th Street, blacks tend to move north in a corridor between Northwest 7th and 27th Avenues. Yet the dominant political tone in the 17th is set by a group less numerous than either: the Jews, who tend to live in the communities along Biscayne Bay, especially North Miami and North Miami Beach (which is not on the beach at all). They turn out in Democratic primaries, which are tantamount to election here; they organize in condominium and neighborhood associations, which can deliver large margins to candidates.

The congressman from the 17th is William Lehman. He was first elected in 1972, when the district was newly created; he had been active on the school board. Before that he had a long and successful career selling used cars. Lehman entered Congress when he was almost 60, and is now one of the House's oldest members. He serves rather quietly on the Appropriations Committee, and since 1982 he has been chairman of the Transportation Subcommittee. This is a position of potentially vast influence, but Lehman, a pleasant man, does not seem to have the aggressiveness and ambition to make high policy, although he has been successful in advancing Miami's Metrorail mass transit system and downtown Metromover. On other issues he votes with liberal

Democrats more often than any other Florida congressman; he was one of only two in the delegation to oppose contra aid in 1986. At home, he has not had serious competition since his first campaign.

The People: Pop. 1980: 513,048, up 25.6% 1970–80. Households (1980): 72% family, 35% with children, 55% married couples; 38.3% housing units rented; median monthly rent: $237; median house value: $46,700. Voting age pop. (1980): 385,199; 24% Spanish origin, 22% Black, 1% Asian origin.

1984 Presidential Vote:

Mondale (D)	93,545	(54%)
Reagan (R)	80,780	(46%)

Rep. William Lehman (D)

Elected 1972; b. Oct. 5, 1913, Selma, AL; home, Biscayne Park; U. of AL, B.S. 1934; Jewish; married (Joan).

Career: Auto dealer, 1936–72; Teacher, Pub. Schools, 1963; Miami Dade Jr. Col., 1964–66; Dade Cnty. Sch. Bd., 1964–70, Chmn., 1971.

Offices: 2347 RHOB 20515, 202-225-4211. Also 2020 N.E. 163rd St., N. Miami Beach 33162, 305-945-7518; and 3275 N.W. 79th St., Miami 33147, 305-836-3141.

Committees: *Appropriations* (19th of 35 D). Subcommittees: Foreign Operations (Chairman); Transportation. *Select Committee on Children, Youth, and Families* (2d of 18 D). Task Force: Prevention Strategies (Chairman).

Group Ratings

	ADA	ACLU	COPE	CFA	LCV	ACU	NTU	NSI	COC	CEI
1986	100	95	87	75	51	0	26	0	20	18
1985	95	—	87	92	—	5	30	—	24	—

National Journal Ratings

	1986 LIB — 1986 CONS		1985 LIB — 1985 CONS	
Economic	80% —	19%	85% —	11%
Social	89% —	0%	85% —	0%
Foreign	80% —	0%	75% —	21%

Key Votes

1) Lmt Cln Water Act	AGN	5) Retain Gun Cont	FOR	9) Aid Angola Reb	AGN
2) Rpl Tobac Sub	FOR	6) Contra Aid	AGN	10) Tax Reform	FOR
3) Grm-Rdmn Def Red	AGN	7) Lmt Text Imp	FOR	11) S Africa Sanc	FOR
4) Ban Polygraph	FOR	8) Limit SDI	FOR	12) Immig Reform	FOR

Election Results

1986 general	William Lehman (D) unopposed	($172,800)
1986 primary	William Lehman (D) unopposed	
1984 general	William Lehman (D) unopposed	($150,477)

Campaign Contributions and Expenditures

1985-86		Direct Cont. 1985-86		PACS Breakdown 1985-86			
Receipts	$215,286	Indiv.	$89,463	Corp.	$42,228	T/M/H	$18,000
Expend.	$172,800	PACS	$114,228	Labor	$39,900	Agr.	$1,000
Unspent	$153,854			Ideo.	$8,650	CWOS	$4,450

EIGHTEENTH DISTRICT

Miami lies at one extremity of the United States—geographically, economically, culturally, and politically. Geographically, it is at the far southeast extremity of the United States. Economically, it is in effect the economic capital of Latin America and the center of the who-knows-how-big drug trade as well. Culturally, it is part Latin, part North American, a city with prominent Jewish and Cuban accents that has become a favorite of British and European tourists, the locale of the surrealistic *Miami Vice* and of equally surrealistic drug-dealer wars and random violence. Miami—technically a city of 350,000 people, but also the major metropolis in Florida's Gold Coast, with about 10 times that population—since its abrupt beginnings in the 1920s has always been on its way to becoming something else, and today that process of transformation is especially striking—and painful. Miami is not a city most Americans would like to live in any more, or perhaps even visit. But it is a mecca for millions to the south, east, and west, and especially to its half a million Cubans whose hard work and fierce ambition have done so much to create its vibrant economy.

Politically, Miami is a city filled with ardent cynicism—and passionate beliefs. The cynics tend to be those who come from the north, who are wary of the crime, alarmed by drugs, uncomfortable with Latin accents and Spanish speech. Many of Miami's old residents have moved north, to non-Latin suburbs in northern Dade County or to Broward or even Palm Beach Counties. They are ready to try any expedient to improve things, from voting for casino gambling—a referendum issue that loses overwhelmingly elsewhere in Florida, most recently in 1986—to ousting an incumbent mayor, as Maurice Ferré was ousted in 1985. The non-Cuban vote in Miami still tends to be solidly Democratic. But it is not as credulous in its liberalism as it once was.

The Cuban-Americans, in contrast, are believers. They come not from a society of well-ordered suburbs, but from a culture in which property is routinely confiscated, in which people who make any conspicuous success are liable to have their money and their freedom taken away by dictators of the left or right, where taxes of 100% and 200% are imposed on almost every imported product so that black markets and smuggling are common, where the currency is subject to sudden devaluation and bank accounts can one day be frozen. Miami means stability and reliability and freedom. Miami's Cuban-American voters, many of whom were born after their parents fled Castro, retain an affection for their native land and a desire to change its government. But they are also realistic enough to know that after nearly 30 years an old society cannot be restored, and contented enough in their new country to be patriotic Americans themselves. Miami's Cuban-Americans are less interested in U.S. government wars on poverty than its wars against Latin American Communists; they are ardently Republican in most elections. Their leading political spokesman now is Xavier Suarez, who was elected Mayor of Miami in 1985, winning a large majority of Cuban but very few black votes; Suarez endorsed President Reagan, but has been careful not to identify with either one of the major parties.

Florida's 18th Congressional District covers most of the city of Miami; all of Miami Beach, Bal Harbour, and Key Biscayne; the high-income suburb of Coral Gables. Its center is Southwest 8th Street—Calle Ocho—which extends west from downtown and becomes the Tamiami Trail; this is the main street of the Cuban community. There are still many Jewish residents here, though perhaps more in Miami Beach than on the mainland; there are blacks in the ghetto running north from downtown. But the overall ethnic flavor is distinctly Cuban. Fully 50% of the district's residents are of Spanish origin, almost all of them Cuban.

The 18th is represented by the oldest man in Congress, Claude Pepper, who has been a pivotal figure in American politics and government over a longer span of time than probably anyone else in American history. Pepper was born in 1900 in Alabama, moved to Florida after Harvard Law School, was elected to the legislature in 1928, ran for the Senate and lost in 1934, and was elected to the Senate to fill a vacancy in 1936. In 1938 Pepper was a vocal supporter of Franklin Roosevelt's minimum wage bill, which was thought unpopular in the South and which seemed to threaten his chances to win a full term. But he campaigned hard for it, and won 58% of the vote against an incumbent congressman and a former governor—a victory so impressive that Congress passed the stalled bill within weeks. Pepper quickly became known as a brilliant orator, given to the most grandiloquent of southern courtesy but also capable of silencing and bringing tears to the eyes of hard-bitten Yankee politicos. He was persuasive too: none less than Robert Taft, no admirer of his New Deal politics, said he always made it a point to be on the floor when Pepper spoke because the man had a first-class mind. When Lyndon Johnson set about to provide speakers for Democratic House candidates in 1940, one of those most in demand was Senator Claude Pepper.

Pepper was also a force on foreign affairs, an opponent of isolationism before World War II and a skeptic about the cold war afterwards. That, plus his continuing support for unfashionable New Deal measures and his support of civil rights (he came out for an anti-lynching bill in the 1930s), made him vulnerable to challenge, and he was beaten 55%–45% by George Smathers in a bitter primary in 1950. Today Smathers has long since (1968) retired, and Claude Pepper is again one of the most senior members of Congress. When Miami got a second House seat after the 1960 Census, Pepper was the obvious man to fill it, and he won easily. His constituency then tended to be elderly, with many Jewish and Catholic migrants from the Northeast; it has changed since, but he continues to win reelection easily.

In the House, Pepper was from the beginning among the strongest of liberals from the South; but he did some floundering about, chairing a special subcommittee on crime, which made some recommendations and finally died. Then he got a seat on, and eventually became chairman of, the Select Committee on Aging. Here he finally found a good match of conviction and position. Pepper is still a New Dealer: he believes that government should do more to help the aged and infirm and to give them choices to lead their lives as they wish. He wants Social Security maintained and strengthened—allowing people to live in comfort—and looks with suspicion on all proposals to cut it back. And he pushed to passage the 1978 law raising the minimum mandatory retirement age for most jobs from 65 to 70 and the 1986 law banning any compulsory retirement age—allowing people to work longer. By the early 1980s Pepper was a major national figure once again. His was one of the most sought-after of endorsements in 1982 House races, and he was one of the most active campaigners for Democrats around the country in 1982, 1984, and 1986.

He also became, after Richard Bolling retired in 1982, chairman of the House Rules Committee. He is not an aficionado of procedural issues, but he is quite capable of handling them; and while he generally worked in tandem with Tip O'Neill and Jim Wright, he was ready to go out on his own or to let other Democrats on Rules do so. Pepper insisted on a roll call vote on raising the Social Security retirement age in 1983, although he lost it; he went along with the leadership on contra aid, although that hurt the chances of his position (in favor of the aid) prevailing; he was ready to give Dan Rostenkowski a closed rule limiting amendments on tax reform in 1985 and 1986. He has floor managed debates on tricky rules on the tax bill and immigration reform bills capably and patiently for hours on end. House observers look for signs that Pepper in his late 80s is flagging. He is hard of hearing. But he is still capable of understanding and explaining the complexities of legislation and procedure, and he is capable sometimes of flights of eloquence that move members of Congress as he did 50 years ago. He has spent all of this century developing superb political skills and instincts, and he can still summon them up.

Pepper's lead role on Social Security obviously doesn't hurt him politically in a district where 30% of the adults are 65 or over, and his fervent support of contra aid and Radio Martí has given him strong support from the 18th District's Cuban-Americans. Nor do his efforts to bring money into Miami for mass transit and a bayfront park hurt. But no one in cynical Miami thinks there is any cynicism in Pepper's views; he is not naive about the machinations of his fellow politicians, but each of these positions is consistent with stands he has taken for more than 50 years. Republicans have considered targeting him, but Cuban-American Republicans could do no better than 37% in 1978 and 40% in 1980. He was reelected with 74% in 1986, and some detected signs of nervousness because he raised $1 million; but most of that went to pay the cost of a less successful than planned direct mail campaign. In the late 1980s Claude Pepper seems more firmly entrenched than ever, and has been taking steps to make sure that he gets a favorable district after the 1990 Census. As much as any politician in American history, this is a man who perseveres.

The People: Pop. 1980: 513,250, up 6.4% 1970–80. Households (1980): 62% family, 25% with children, 46% married couples; 64.7% housing units rented; median monthly rent: $210; median house value: $53,500. Voting age pop. (1980): 416,969; 50% Spanish origin, 13% Black, 1% Asian origin.

1984 Presidential Vote:

Reagan (R)	91,297	(60%)
Mondale (D)	59,926	(40%)

Rep. Claude Pepper (D)

Elected 1962; b. Sept. 8, 1900, Chambers Cnty., AL; home, Miami; U. of AL, A.B. 1921, Harvard U., LL.B. 1924; Baptist; widowed.

Career: Instructor in Law, U. of AR, 1924–25; Practicing atty., 1925–36, 1951–62; FL House of Reps., 1929–30; FL Bd. of Pub. Welfare, 1931–32; FL Bd. of Law Examiners, 1933–34; U.S. Senate, 1937–51.

Offices: 2239 RHOB 20515, 202-225-3931. Also 300 Courthouse Tower, 44 W. Flagler St., Miami 33130, 305-536-5565.

Committees: *Rules* (Chairman of 9 D). Subcommittees: Rules of the House; The Legislative Process. *Select Committee on Aging* (2d of 39 D). Subcommittee: Health and Long-Term Care (Chairman).

Group Ratings

	ADA	ACLU	COPE	CFA	LCV	ACU	NTU	NSI	COC	CEI
1986	70	68	94	83	60	16	18	70	25	13
1985	60	—	93	75	—	32	18	—	15	

National Journal Ratings

	1986 LIB — 1986 CONS		1985 LIB — 1985 CONS	
Economic	87% —	0%	89% —	0%
Social	89% —	0%	77% —	23%
Foreign	50% —	49%	50% —	50%

Key Votes

1) Lmt Cln Water Act	AGN	5) Retain Gun Cont	FOR	9) Aid Angola Reb	FOR
2) Rpl Tobac Sub	AGN	6) Contra Aid	FOR	10) Tax Reform	FOR
3) Grm-Rdmn Def Red	AGN	7) Lmt Text Imp	—	11) S Africa Sanc	FOR
4) Ban Polygraph	FOR	8) Limit SDI	FOR	12) Immig Reform	FOR

Election Results

1986 general	Claude Pepper (D)	80,047	(74%)	($1,395,549)
	Tom Brodie (R).......................	28,803	(26%)	($15,888)
1986 primary	Claude Pepper (D) unopposed			
1984 general	Claude Pepper (D)	76,404	(61%)	($269,368)
	Ricardo Nunez (R)....................	49,818	(39%)	($47,858)

Campaign Contributions and Expenditures

1985-86		Direct Cont. 1985-86		PACS Breakdown 1985-86			
Receipts	$1,448,167	Indiv.	$1,110,221	Corp.	$93,150	T/M/H	$69,270
Expend.	$1,395,549	Party	$473	Labor	$115,701	Agr.	$4,450
Unspent	$52,780	PACS	$316,371	Ideo.	$26,050	CWOS	$7,750

NINETEENTH DISTRICT

The southernmost outpost of metropolitan civilization on the continental 48 states lies on both sides of U.S. 1 as it heads southwest from Miami toward the Florida Keys Highway. Not so long ago this road was a narrow ribbon of highway passing between acres of Everglades swamp, a road for tourists, with every so often a tourist attraction (the Serpentarium, Monkey Jungle, Coral Castle). In the past 30 years much of this land has been reclaimed and subdivided and became as a result the part of the Miami area closest to the typical middle-class American ideal. This is Florida's 19th Congressional District, which starts in Miami's Coconut Grove area and passes through Coral Gables, planned as a ritzy suburb in the 1920s, to newer offspring of Miami like Kendall, Olympia Heights, Richmond Heights, and Perrine. In one way this constituency is not typical: 22% of its population is of Spanish origin. But if the Cubans still speak Spanish at home and at work, they also are upwardly striving, young, and family-oriented (40% of the households here contain children, one of the highest figures in Florida). More than many Americans whose immigrant ancestors are more remote, they are believers in the American dream.

The political tone here is still set mainly by Anglos, but Cubans are now entering the electorate in significant numbers. For 40 years south Dade County has generally been Democratic. But some of the white residents have been moving to the Republicans, and Cuban-Americans tend to vote heavily Republican in serious contests. In congressional elections, however, the south Dade County district (numbered 4th in the 1950s, 12th in the 1960s, and 15th in the 1970s) has since 1954 regularly elected Dante Fascell. He is now Chairman of the House Foreign Affairs Committee and a member as well of the special committee investigating the Iran/Contra affair. These are strategic posts for a man who has been interested in—and a force in—foreign policy for many years and who, unlike most members of the House, has a district with two constituency groups strongly interested in foreign policy matters. With their views Fascell has always been in sympathy: he is pro-Israel and anti-Castro.

Institutionally, Fascell's chairmanship does not confer great power. The House is usually overshadowed in foreign policy by the Senate, with its power to approve treaties and nominations, and Fascell's predecessor as chairman, Clement Zablocki, who died suddenly in 1983, had allowed Foreign Affairs subcommittee chairmen, most of them young liberals, to pretty much have their way. Fascell agrees with them on many issues, but not on Latin America, where he has strongly opposed Fidel Castro and strongly favors aid to the Nicaraguan contras; nor does he share the mistrust many of the politicians who came of age during the Vietnam era seem to have in any assertion of American power in the Third World. Having exerted his influence against a cutoff of economic and military aid to El Salvador, Fascell has been part of the process which has strengthened President Jose Napoleon Duarte there against both the local military and the rebels in the hills. Fascell, in his support for the National Endowment for Democracy and for Radio Marti, has shown a desire to propagate the ideas of democracy, and a faith that the values

America stands for are better than those espoused by Marxist-leaning Third World politicos. On some issues Fascell may be outvoted in his own committee. But, fierce and ready to bellow with outrage, he is a force to be reckoned with on the House floor, determined and aggressive and well-informed.

On the special committee, Fascell will be in a particularly dicey position: he is one member with strong commitments to both Israel and the Contras, who may be embarrassed by what is disclosed; yet Fascell temperamentally is not one to cover up (in fact he was a procedural reformer in the House in the 1950s and 1960s). On other foreign policy issues, and particularly on the sticky problem of foreign aid, Fascell will probably continue to be a congressional workhorse.

At home he has been reelected by wide margins, despite Republican inroads in other contests in south Dade. His last serious opponent was TV newscaster Glenn Rinker in 1982, who held him to 59%, and it's possible he'll get another serious challenger again; some Republicans are talking about new state Senator Dexter Lehtinen. But if voters in the Miami area area interested in maximizing their clout and fighting Communism in Latin America, they could hardly be better represented than by the two committee chairmen who represent them now, Fascell and the 18th District's Claude Pepper. Fascell is capable of raising plenty of money and after 1986 had $426,000 in his campaign treasury—an attempt obviously to improve the already good chances he'll be reelected indefinitely.

The People: Pop. 1980: 512,886, up 45.0% 1970–80. Households (1980): 73% family, 40% with children, 60% married couples; 33.3% housing units rented; median monthly rent: $263; median house value: $69,900. Voting age pop. (1980): 373,329; 21% Spanish origin, 10% Black, 1% Asian origin.

1984 Presidential Vote:

Reagan (R)	124,180	(65%)
Mondale (D)	68,079	(35%)

Rep. Dante B. Fascell (D)

Elected 1954; b. Mar. 9, 1917, Bridgehampton, L.I., NY; home, Miami; U. of Miami, J.D. 1938; Protestant; married (Jeanne-Marie).

Career: Practicing atty., 1938–42, 1946–54; Army, WWII; Legal Attache, Dade Cnty. St. Legis. Delegation, 1947–50; FL House of Reps., 1950–54; Mbr., U.S. Delegation to U.N., 1969.

Offices: 2354 RHOB 20515, 202-225-4506. Also 7855 S.W. 104 St., Ste. 220, Miami 33156, 305-536-5301.

Committees: *Foreign Affairs* (Chairman of 27 D). Subcommittee: Arms Control, International Security and Science (Chairman). *Select Committee on Narcotics Abuse and Control* (9th of 15 D).

Group Ratings

	ADA	ACLU	COPE	CFA	LCV	ACU	NTU	NSI	COC	CEI
1986	70	55	83	92	79	23	21	40	24	13
1985	60	—	82	75	—	24	13	—	11	—

National Journal Ratings

	1986 LIB — 1986 CONS		1985 LIB — 1985 CONS	
Economic	82%	16%	75%	22%
Social	67%	32%	85%	0%
Foreign	54%	45%	51%	48%

Key Votes

1) Lmt Cln Water Act	AGN	5) Retain Gun Cont	FOR	9) Aid Angola Reb	FOR
2) Rpl Tobac Sub	AGN	6) Contra Aid	FOR	10) Tax Reform	FOR
3) Grm-Rdmn Def Red	FOR	7) Lmt Text Imp	FOR	11) S Africa Sanc	FOR
4) Ban Polygraph	FOR	8) Limit SDI	FOR	12) Immig Reform	FOR

Election Results

1986 general	Dante B. Fascell (D)	99,203	(69%)	($293,227)
	Bill Flanagan (R)	44,455	(31%)	(359,382)
1986 primary	Dante B. Fascell (D) unopposed			
1984 general	Dante B. Fascell (D)	115,631	(64%)	($285,362)
	Bill Flanagan (R)	64,317	(36%)	

Campaign Contributions and Expenditures

1985-86		Direct Cont. 1985-86		PACS Breakdown 1985-86			
Receipts	$473,480	Indiv.	$278,805	Corp.	$48,750	T/M/H	$33,000
Expend.	$293,227	Party	$184	Labor	$34,300	Agr.	$600
Unspent	$426,393	PACS	$142,650	Ideo.	$24,500	CWOS	$1,500

GEORGIA

Georgia is the heart of the South—whether you're talking about the New South or the Old South, the Deep South or the civil rights South, the South of the poor white or of the black elite. One reason is geography: the Appalachian chain that separates the Atlantic coastal states from the Mississippi Valley turns into hills and then into gently rolling farmland in Georgia, and Atlanta, a little railroad junction in the Civil War, is situated nearer to the geographical center of the South than any other significant city. Georgia's history has not always been auspicious. Its first settlers were mainly convicts, recruited by philanthropist James Oglethorpe to settle in his rule-restricted colony; but of his dreams of a new and orderly world little but the street grid of Savannah survived. Much of its later history is tragic: whites driving thousands of slaves in the hot flatlands of south Georgia, Andrew Jackson's troops driving the civilized Cherokee tribe west over the Trail of Tears, General Sherman's troops marching through, burning Atlanta and dozens of plantations. But out of tragedy the South has distilled pride, and out of a heritage of poverty it has built something that looks very much like booming economic growth. The same Atlanta that Scarlett O'Hara saw burning became in time the center of southern industry (of Coca Cola, long the biggest southern firm, and Delta Airlines, long one of the best-run) and of the civil rights movement, the cultural, intellectual and political center of the South. The same Georgia that was home base to the most powerful segregationist strategist in the civil rights years, Senator Richard Russell, was also the home base of the first president produced from a southern statehouse in American history, Jimmy Carter, who began his career as governor calling for an end to segregation and to give the benediction at his first national convention called on the Rev. Martin Luther King, Sr.

Georgia, even more than the rest of the South, has been a political stronghold of the Democratic Party throughout its history—and in 1988 Atlanta will be host to the Democratic national convention. But, like other southern states, it found itself tossing between the parties in the difficult years during and after the civil rights revolution. Georgia was the most Democratic state in the old "solid South," and as late as 1960 it gave John F. Kennedy his second highest percentage in the country, higher than Massachusetts. But in 1964 it switched to Republican Barry Goldwater and in 1968, even after the Voting Rights Act gave southern blacks the vote, it voted for George Wallace. Well before the civil rights movement, Atlanta was the preeminent urban center in the Deep South. But Georgia's unit rule system, which gave each of the state's 159 counties 2, 4, or 6 votes in the decisive Democratic primary, reduced Atlanta's political influence to nothing until it was finally thrown out by the U.S. Supreme Court in the early 1960s.

The turning point in Georgia—and southern—politics was the election of Jimmy Carter in 1970. Carter, like Lester Maddox and other segregationists, campaigned as a spokesman of the rural areas against cosmopolitan Atlanta—a winning strategy since metro Atlanta cast only 25% of the votes in the Democratic primary and rural voters, aware of Atlanta's large black electorate and of its whites' pride in being "a city too busy to hate," were always ready to vote against its candidates. But against a serious Republican candidate Carter won despite having black support—the first time after the civil rights revolution that candidates supported by blacks did not automatically forfeit white support (Atlanta blacks used to send out endorsements in letters to arrive on election day, so that white voters wouldn't know whom they were backing). On taking office Carter pointedly announced that the days of segregation were gone and put a picture of Martin Luther King, Jr., on the wall of the Georgia Capitol. Similarly, Carter's election as president six years later marked the first time white southerners had voted in large numbers for a black-backed nominee, as well as the first time blacks had enthusiastically backed a white candidate from the Deep South. Today those breakthroughs are taken for granted. But Georgia—and the nation—owe a debt to Carter for moving the South into a new and better political era at a time when what we now take for granted seemed to be quite impossible.

Carter's success was also the beginning of the end, though no one could be sure at the time, of the Georgia politics that pitted city against country, south Georgia and other rural areas against metropolitan Atlanta. Up through Carter's term as governor, Atlanta tended to favor candidates who favored civil rights, who were close to their national parties, whose accents were broadcaster-neutral and whose clothes and bearing reflected the sophistication which Atlanta prides itself on. Rural Georgia tended to oppose such candidates and, since it outvoted Atlanta (especially in Democratic primaries), usually beat them. Jimmy Carter won the 1970 Democratic primary by campaigning as a "redneck" from south Georgia; the only candidate who lived in Atlanta and won a major office was Lester Maddox, who symbolized rural values. Senator Sam Nunn also ran as a south Georgian when he won his Senate seat in 1972, in the primary against an Atlanta lawyer appointed by Carter to fill a vacancy, in the general election against an Atlanta congressman so unfriendly to blacks that he refused to appear before a black audience though nearly half his constituents were black.

By the late 1970s the dichotomy between Atlanta and rural Georgia was fading. The state's most successful politicians continued to be Democrats from out-of-the-way places, like Governors George Busbee (1974–82) of Albany and Joe Frank Harris of Bartow County. But increasingly the rest of the state has been voting like metropolitan Atlanta—or vice versa. In the 1982 Democratic primary for governor, for example, there simply were not the sharp differences between Atlanta and the rural counties, between blacks and whites which characterized Georgia elections in the past. In 1984, Carter's vice president Walter Mondale got a lower share of the vote in greater Atlanta (38%) than outside it (41%). And in the ultra-close general election for U.S. Senator in 1986, Democrat Wyche Fowler, a congressman from Atlanta, got 51% of the vote in metropolitan Atlanta and 51% in the state's other 144 counties. Fowler had won the Democratic primary 50%–32% over former Carter aide Hamilton Jordan who made a point of stressing his rural roots and opposition to big city liberal values.

Georgia politics no longer cleaves along the lines of city versus country—nor does that of other southern states. The intense conflicts over civil rights and between metropolitan and rural areas seem to have disappeared, as desegregation has been accepted and the cultural styles of city and country blend—or at least coexist. The rapid economic growth of the South is nowhere more apparent than in Georgia, where metropolitan Atlanta surges ahead, recession or no, with effects radiating outward not 50 but 100 miles, and counties even farther out, planning a second

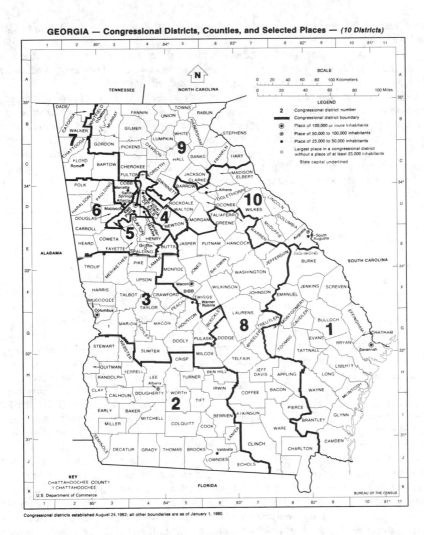

GEORGIA — Congressional Districts, Counties, and Selected Places — (10 Districts)

perimeter highway even as new city-sized office clusters develop along the current perimeter. In the Georgia of today, living with levels of affluence and comfort unthinkable 40 years ago, political attitudes tend to run along economic and cultural lines, not metropolitan borders. The young Georgians who have been expanding the Atlanta metro area over the north Georgia countryside, filling the rolling landscape punctuated by a few craggy mountains with freeways, huge shopping centers, pleasant colonial-style subdivisions, and contemporary condominium developments, tend to vote heavily Republican; they are family people, hoping to root down in this new setting the values they remember from elsewhere. But closer in to Atlanta, not only within the city but in DeKalb County, where young people are moving close to universities and cultural institutions, high-toned shopping centers and black neighbors, the movement is toward the Democrats. Similar movements are taking place outside the big metropolitan area. Republicans are making their biggest gains in once entirely rural counties which are now filling up with blue and white collar breadwinners willing to commute 20 or 50 miles to raise their children in a country atmosphere. Democrats are making their gains in counties where low-income whites or those raised with more liberal values—the progeny of Miss Lillian Carter, if you will—are an important force.

Religion plays a role here too. Consider the importance of religion to the state's two most visible political executives, Governor Joe Frank Harris and Atlanta Mayor Andrew Young. Harris made his strong Christian views on issues and his abstemious personal behavior the centerpiece of his campaign; Young is a minister whose understanding of the Gospel led to his civil rights work and influenced his political stands. For that matter, Jimmy Carter owes much of his rise to religion as well, for it was religious conviction, apparently, that led him to repudiate segregation—without which he never could have been a national candidate. If you could separate Georgians—and other southerners—by religion, with tradition-minded voters on one side and liberation-minded voters on the other, you would probably have as good a predictor of voting behavior as any. And we are talking not just about whites but blacks too. Heretofore their religion, while usually based firmly on a fundamentalist reading of the Bible, has also looked for liberation. But there are signs that some black voters are moving the other way, and that blacks—still solidly Democratic and liberal in most elections here—may become as flexible and even volatile as the once segregationist white voters have become.

Governor. Georgia's last two governors, presiding over a state with rapid economic growth, emphasizing orderly administration, improvement of education, and the attraction of business, have ended up immensely popular. It helped that both—George Busbee and Joe Frank Harris—were, unlike Jimmy Carter, veteran leaders in the state legislature; and that both came along at a time, ushered in by Carter, when being from rural Georgia didn't mean you had to be against everything Atlanta was for. Joe Frank Harris came to office after winning a runoff over Savannah-area Congressman Bo Ginn with the reputation of being dominated by House Speaker Thomas Murphy and being extremely religious. He pledged early and often that he would impose no new state taxes. He remains dour, serious, dignified, and not well connected or comfortable outside the world of Georgia politics. But he has had a major achievement, enacting in 1985 a $200 million-plus educational reform package that did not call for a tax increase. This came after similar initiatives in other southern states, but was popular nonetheless. In 1986 he won his primary with 85% of the vote and beat a Republican with 71%, carrying every one of the state's 159 counties. For his second term he promised to battle illiteracy, better access to health services, and a "growth strategy" that might mean regulation of development.

Senators. Senator Sam Nunn, after years as a respected insider in government, is now a major public figure, Chairman of the Senate Armed Services Committee, and a possible future president. Until the middle-1980s his career had much in common with those of older southern members of the House Armed Services Committee—men like his great-uncle, Carl Vinson, who came to Congress in 1914 and was chairman first of the Naval Affairs and then of the Armed Services Committee. Like Vinson, Nunn came from a small south Georgia town, served in the legislature, was elected to Congress at a young age, devoted most of his attention to military affairs, and by force of intellect and attention to detail, and despite an aversion for publicity and self-promotion, became a power in American government. What is striking in retrospect is how close a thing Nunn's election to the Senate was. When he ran, in 1972 at age 34 against Jimmy Carter's choice to replace longtime Senate Armed Services and Appropriations Chairman Richard Russell, he was little known and he got a place in the runoff by edging a former governor 23%–21%—an 18,000-vote margin. He won the runoff and the general election by unspectacular 54%–46% margins. It was not an easy year for even the most conservative of Democrats. He shunned George McGovern and courted George Wallace and emphasized how "tough" he was. Since then he has become unbeatable—unchallengeable, really—in Georgia.

Nunn entered a Senate that had been voting against the major defense and war policies of the Administration, got a seat on the Armed Services Committee, and soon made himself one of the Senate's most respected experts on military policy. His secret was hard work. He actually reads and absorbs all the detailed information which most members leave to their staffs. He has always believed in a strong military and usually in increased defense spending. But he always has a critical interest in what the money is spent on. He was one of the sponsors, with Barry Goldwater, of the 1986 military reform centralizing theater commands and the power of the chairman of the Joint Chiefs of Staff. In the 1980s he has favored the MX missile, and has worked with others, including House Armed Services Chairman Les Aspin, who came from the wing of the Democratic party against the Vietnam war and skeptical of the Pentagon, to come up with an alternative that could pass both houses in Congress and strengthen rather than weaken deterrence. Nunn is not afraid to point out any unclothed emperor. After the Reykjavik summit, he was the first to point out that Reagan's proposals for getting rid of nuclear weapons would have left Europe undefended. Although supporting research on Ronald Reagan's Strategic Defense Initiative, he was quick to point out that it could never be an effective shield for the whole population, as Reagan implied. And in March 1987 he changed the whole SDI debate by his own analysis of the ABM treaty, rejecting and largely discrediting the administration's interpretation of the ABM treaty as allowing untrammelled SDI development. Nunn, who has backed cuts in U.S. military forces in Europe in order to stimulate countries there to spend more, is definitely not in favor of trusting the freedom of western Europe to Communist good intentions. Nunn's statements carry so much weight because they are based on close factual knowledge and because he is always intellectually honest—thoughtful, candid, never given to cheap shots.

Nunn's accession to the Armed Services chair is one argument for the seniority system. Yet his influence goes beyond his position. Even when the Republicans controlled the Senate he was the most influential voice on military policy. On many issues he is probably more distant from many of his Democratic colleagues than from most Republicans—though dovish Democrats do not have anything like a majority in the Senate today. Respectful of every President but not a reliable ally for any, Nunn criticizes some of the Reagan Administration's defense plans and made no secret of the fact that he thought his fellow Georgian Jimmy Carter (with whom he was not close) was cutting defense spending to dangerously low levels.

Nunn's record on non-military issues seems almost incidental, though he approaches them with the hard work and seriousness he does military matters. His basic instincts are conservative, particularly on cultural issues; and on many issues his voting record looks like that of an old Dixiecrat. But he is not a knee-jerk vote for anything and is open to persuasion on most domestic issues. Politically, he stayed distant for years from his fellow Democrats, refusing to campaign for others; his jargon-laden, precise verbal style was not much use on the stump anyway. But in 1986 he changed course. After hinting that he wouldn't do much to oppose his Georgia colleague, Republican Mack Mattingly, he made a strong endorsement of Democrat Wyche Fowler—although Fowler's record on military issues is notably more liberal than his. Democrats across the country were able to use Nunn endorsements to counter charges they were anti-defense: this was particularly effective for Timothy Wirth in Colorado, and a Nunn endorsement was used by that longtime enthusiast for disarmament, Alan Cranston of California.

Suddenly, after the 1986 elections, there was a groundswell for a Nunn presidential candidacy, and in some of the unlikeliest quarters. The Iran-Contra scandal put a premium on his grasp of detail and intellectual rigor. His opposition to many liberal positions suddenly seemed of little importance. But in February 1987 he announced that he was not running, though he was careful to retain the option, a difficult one in these days of long campaigns, of deciding to run later.

Georgia's other senator is a Democrat who owes his seat to his own well-honed political talents—and to some help from Sam Nunn. He is Wyche Fowler, who is politically adept enough to have been elected for nine years to represent the black-majority 5th Congressional District in Atlanta and then to have won seriously contested statewide primary and general elections. Fowler won the primary against Hamilton Jordan, one of America's premier political strategists, whose candidacy was strengthened by his gallant recovery from cancer and an absence of the arrogance that so many detected in him when he was Jimmy Carter's campaign manager and chief of staff. But Jordan relied too much on the stale anti-Atlanta theme and in the last weeks

Fowler, with more money by then, was able to campaign as the only candidate with experience in the Army and Congress and to tell voters to pronounce his name "Wyche—ch as in church." Fowler got 50.2%, avoiding a runoff.

Incumbent Senator Mack Mattingly immediately lambasted Fowler with charges of absenteeism, citing House votes with the refrain "Fowler—absent for Georgia." But this theme proved unsustainable. Mattingly, a former IBM salesman from Indiana who had upset scandal-tarred Herman Talmadge in 1980, had made a respectable record in the Senate, managing Ted Stevens's nearly successful campaign for majority leader and championing the President's proposal for a legislative veto. But few would call Mattingly, as many would Fowler, a hard worker or skilled political operator. Interestingly, Mattingly's reliance on the absenteeism issue—a favorite of the national Republican Party in 1986, because of its success in different circumstances in Kentucky in 1984—meant that he did not much attack Fowler's liberal voting record in south Georgia.

Fowler in contrast showed a mastery of campaign tactics. In both primary and general he showed steely discipline and husbanded his money for late media bursts produced by consultant Frank Greer; and in both cases Fowler was successful by narrow margins. He won the general election 51%–49%, with similar margins in metro Atlanta and outstate. His old congressional district gave him nearly a 2 to 1 majority, but just as striking was his carrying the 2d, 3d, and 8th Districts in south Georgia. Altogether he won nearly 4 in 10 white votes, a stunning percentage for a candidate with a generally liberal record in a state where, when Sam Nunn got his start, Democratic presidential nominees were doing well to win 1 in 10.

Fowler served on the Ways and Means in the House although, as a Senate candidate, he was not a front-row player on the 1985–86 tax bill. He was generally counted as a liberal in the House, but tempered his record, especially in 1985 and 1986; now with a constituency mostly hawkish on foreign policy and tradition-minded on cultural issues, and with the example of Nunn beside him, he can be expected to be middle-of-the-road.

Presidential politics. There has been a Georgian on two of the last three Democratic presidential tickets, and the Democrats' nominees for 1988 will be chosen in Georgia; for all the glitter of its metropolitan prosperity, Georgia has become, even with no Georgian running in the last presidential election, one of the closest things to a national Democratic state in the South. More than residual local pride is involved here, though that is one factor; but something more is going on when a Mondale–Ferraro ticket can carry a town like Macon and run well enough in rural areas that it exerts no particular downdraft on other candidates. The tantalizing question for the national Democrats is whether it's possible, absent a Nunn candidacy, for them to rise the still considerable distance from Mondale's 40% showing to real contention for Georgia's—and most of the South's—electoral votes.

In 1984 Georgia was one of the Super Tuesday states, and was the key unknown; Florida was conceded to Gary Hart, Alabama to Mondale, and so Mondale's narrow victory in Georgia kept him in the race. In 1988 Georgia, as one of more than a dozen southern states voting the same week, will probably not be as pivotal. But media coverage and campaign management may be centered in Atlanta, and the state contains a good cross-section of the South, so it will probably be more closely watched than most. The Republican primary remains an uninteresting, small, country club contest.

Congressional redistricting. After the 1980 Census, a federal court redrew Georgia's district lines to make the Atlanta-based 5th District 65% black. It's not clear they needed to bother: Atlanta and Georgia are well past the days when white officeholders were implacably hostile to black constituents. This was the district once represented by Andrew Young (who won it when it had a white majority); he was replaced by Wyche Fowler (who held it easily, sometimes against serious competition, when it had a black majority) and, after Fowler ran for the Senate in 1986, by John Lewis. One side effect: the removal of blacks from the 5th enabled Pat Swindall, a Republican of the evangelical right, to win in the next-door 4th District in 1984 and 1986. The 1990 Census could conceivably bring Georgia a new district, and the interesting question is whether a presumably Democratic legislature will create a heavily Republican district in the fast-growing suburban ring around Atlanta.

The People: Est. Pop. 1986: 6,104,000; Pop. 1980: 5,463,105, up 11.7% 1980–86 and 19.1% 1970–80; 2.53% of U.S. total, 11th largest. 13% with 1–3 yrs. col., 15% with 4+ yrs. col.; 16.6% below poverty level. Single ancestry: 21% English, 5% Irish, 3% German, 1% French. Households (1980): 76% family, 44% with children, 61% married couples; 35.0% housing units rented; median monthly rent: $153; median house value: $36,900. Voting age pop. (1980): 3,816,975; 24% Black, 1% Spanish origin. Registered voters (1986): 2,575,815; no party registration.

1986 Share of Federal Tax Burden: $16,343,000,000; 2.17% of U.S. total, 12th largest.

1986 Share of Federal Expenditures

	Total		Non-Defense		Defense	
Total Expend	$18,506m	(2.23%)	$12,068m	(2.01%)	$6,438m	(2.80%)
St/Lcl Grants	2,732m	(2.43%)	2,726m	(2.42%)	6m	(5.41%)
Salary/Wages	3,728m	(3.09%)	1,391m	(2.37%)	2,337m	(3.78%)
Pymnts to Indiv	7,799m	(2.14%)	7,215m	(2.08%)	584m	(3.29%)
Procurement	3,957m	(1.92%)	449m	(0.81%)	3,508m	(2.34%)
Research/Other	292m	(1.09%)	288m	(1.08%)	3m	(12.26%)

Political Lineup: Governor, Joe Frank Harris (D); Lt. Gov., Zell Miller (D); Secy. of State, Max Cleland (D); Atty. Gen., Michael J. Bowers (D). State Senate, 53 (44 D and 9 R); State House of Representatives, 180 (153 D and 27 R). Senators, Sam Nunn (D) and Wyche Fowler (D). Representatives, 10 (8 D and 2 R).

1984 Presidential Vote

Reagan (R)	1,068,722	(60%)
Mondale (D)	706,628	(40%)

1980 Presidential Vote

Carter (D)	890,733	(56%)
Reagan (R)	654,168	(41%)
Anderson (I)	36,055	(2%)

1984 Democratic Presidential Primary

Mondale	208,588	(30%)
Hart	186,903	(27%)
Jackson	143,730	(21%)
Glenn	122,744	(18%)
Five others, uncomm.	22,576	(3%)

1984 Republican Presidential Primary

Reagan	50,793	(100%)

GOVERNOR

Gov. Joe Frank Harris (D)

Elected 1982, term expires Jan. 1991; b. Feb. 16, 1936, Bartow County; home, Cartersville; U. of GA, B.B.A. 1958; United Methodist; married (Elizabeth).

Career: Army, 1958–64; Concrete business, 1964–82; GA House of Reps., 1965–83.

Offices: 203 State Capitol, Atlanta 30334, 404-656-1776.

Election Results

1986 gen.	Joe Frank Harris (D)	828,461	(71%)
	Guy Davis (R)	346,508	(29%)
1986 prim.	Joe Frank Harris (D)	521,704	(85%)
	Kenneth B. Quarterman (D)	89,759	(15%)
1982 gen.	Joe Frank Harris (D)	732,686	(63%)
	Robert H. Bell (R)	434,204	(37%)

SENATORS

Sen. Sam Nunn (D)

Elected 1972, seat up 1990; b. Sept. 8, 1938, Perry; home, Perry; Emory U., A.B. 1960, LL.B. 1962; United Methodist; married (Colleen).

Career: Coast Guard, 1959–60; Farmer, practicing atty., 1963–72; GA House of Reps., 1968–72.

Offices: 303 DSOB 20510, 202-224-3521. Also 930 Fed. Bldg., 275 Peachtree St. N.E., Atlanta 30303, 404-331-4811; 915 Main St., Perry 31069, 912-987-1458; 130 Fed. Bldg., Gainesville 30501, 404-532-9976; 101 P.O. Bldg., Columbus 31902, 404-327-3270; 361 Fed. Bldg., 600 E. 1st St., Rome 30161, 404-291-5696; and Fed. Bldg., 126 Bull St., Savannah 31402, 912-944-4300.

Committees: *Armed Services* (Chairman of 11 D). *Governmental Affairs* (3d of 8 D). Subcommittees: Federal Spending, Budget and Accounting; Investigations (Chairman). *Small Business* (2d of 10 D). Subcommittees: Export and Expansion; Rural Economy and Family Farming. *Select Committee on Intelligence* (4th of 8 D).

Group Ratings

	ADA	ACLU	COPE	CFA	LCV	ACU	NTU	NSI	COC	CEI
1986	30	35	38	53	38	55	45	90	74	41
1985	30	—	37	47	—	57	40	—	59	—

National Journal Ratings

	1986 LIB — 1986 CONS	1985 LIB — 1985 CONS
Economic	40% — 55%	48% — 51%
Social	60% — 36%	56% — 38%
Foreign	47% — 51%	34% — 63%

Key Votes

1) Ease Gun Cont	FOR	5) Grm-Rdmn Def Red	FOR	9) Rehnquist Nom	FOR
2) Immig Reform	FOR	6) Contra Aid	FOR	10) Tax Reform	AGN
3) Lmt Text Imp	FOR	7) SDI Funding	FOR	11) Drug Death Pen	AGN
4) Aid Tobac Ind	FOR	8) Lmt PAC Contrib	FOR	12) S Africa Sanc	FOR

Election Results

1984 general	Sam Nunn (D)	1,344,104	(80%)	($843,891)
	Mike Hicks (R).....................	337,196	(20%)	
1984 primary	Sam Nunn (D)	801,412	(90%)	
	Jim Boyd (D)	86,973	(10%)	
1978 general	Sam Nunn (D)	536,320	(83%)	($548,814)
	John W. Stokes (R).................	108,808	(17%)	

Campaign Contributions and Expenditures

1979-84		Direct Cont. 1979-84		PACS Breakdown 1979-84			
Receipts	$1,360,247	Indiv.	$760,453	Corp.	$232,194	T/M/H	$96,970
Expend.	$843,891	Party	$850	Labor	$19,050	Agr.	$5,000
Unspent	$676,199	PACS	$386,546	Ideo.	$29,100	CWOS	$4,600

Sen. Wyche Fowler (D)

Elected 1986, seat up 1992; b. Oct 6, 1940, Atlanta; home, Atlanta; Davidson Col., A.B. 1962, Emory U., J.D. 1969; Presbyterian; divorced.

Career: Army, 1962–64; Chief Asst. to U.S. Rep. Charles Weltner, 1965–66; Night Mayor for the City of Atlanta, 1968–69; Mbr., Atlanta Bd. of Aldermen, 1970–74; Pres., Atlanta City Cncl., 1974–77; Practicing atty., 1970–77; U.S. House of Reps., 1977–87.

Offices: 204 RSOB 20510, 202-224-3643. Also 10 Park Place S., Ste. 210, Atlanta 30303, 404-688-8207.

Committees *Agriculture, Nutrition and Forestry* (8th of 10 D). Subcommittees: Agricultural Production and Stabilization of Prices; Agricultural Research, Conservation , Forestry and General Legislation; Rural Development and Rural Electrification. *Budget* (11th of 13 D). *Energy and Natural Resources* (9th of 10 D). Subcommittees: Energy Regulation and Conservation; Public Lands, Natural Parks and Forests.

Group Ratings (as Member of U.S. House of Representatives)

	ADA	ACLU	COPE	CFA	LCV	ACU	NTU	NSI	COC	CEI
1986	15	45	65	25	66	44	30	33	94	31
1985	50	—	66	67	—	26	34	—	50	—

National Journal Ratings (as Member of U.S. House of Representatives)

	1986 LIB — 1986 CONS			1985 LIB — 1985 CONS		
Economic	*	—	*	54%	—	45%
Social	*	—	*	63%	—	37%
Foreign	*	—	*	61%	—	39%

Key Votes (as Member of U.S. House of Representatives)

1) Lmt Cln Water Act	FOR	5) Retain Gun Cont	AGN
2) Rpl Tobac Sub	AGN	6) Contra Aid	AGN
3) Grm-Rdmn Def Red	FOR	7) Lmt Text Imp	FOR
4) Ban Polygraph	AGN	8) Lmt SDI	—

9) Aid Angola Reb	—
10) Tax Reform	FOR
11) S Africa Sanc	—
12) Immig Reform	—

Election Results

1986 general	Wyche Fowler (D)	623,705	(51%)	($2,779,297)
	Mack Mattingly (R)	601,235	(49%)	($5,119,249)
1986 primary	Wyche Fowler (D)	314,787	(50%)	
	Hamilton Jordan (D).	196,307	(32%)	
	John D. Russell (D)	100,307	(16%)	
1980 general	Mack Mattingly (R)	803,677	(51%)	($504,016)
	Herman E. Talmadge (D).............	776,025	(49%)	($2,213,289)

Campaign Contributions and Expenditures

1985-86		Direct Cont. 1985-86		PACS Breakdown 1985-86			
Receipts	$2,912,638	Indiv.	$1,423,393	Corp.	$97,675	T/M/H	$84,445
Expend.	$2,779,297	Party	$24,400	Labor	$222,432	Agr.	$9,250
Unspent	$133,342	PACS	$596,601	Ideo.	$173,049	CWOS	$9,750
		Cand.	$50,000				

FIRST DISTRICT

The southeast corner of Georgia, along the Savannah River and the Atlantic Ocean, was the site of the 13th British colony in North America, named after a king who spoke English with a German accent. The proprietor, James Oglethorpe, enlisted compliant convicts in his plan to establish an orderly, closely regulated, and presumably rehabilitative society. But the attempt failed, as the settlers sensibly refused to follow detailed instructions from London. Something of Oglethorpe's vision remains, however, in the rectangular street plan of Savannah, with its 19 parks, imposed on the marshy landscape of south Georgia. For 100 years Savannah was Georgia's only major city, and its cotton exchange one of the leading emporia of southern commerce. But in the later 19th century it was eclipsed by Atlanta. Today, many of Savannah's old houses have been restored and its squares are kept more tidily than they probably were in their antebellum heyday. With its variety of architectural styles, its occasional pastel buildings, its trees hanging with Spanish moss, Savannah suggests the tropics; and the kind of social structure it has developed over the years is almost tropical. It has little of Atlanta's economic diversity: cotton has been replaced, by peanuts and wood pulp and tobacco. There are a few rich people, while the great majority of the population has income levels as low as anywhere in the United States; there are beautiful mansions, but most people live in modest dwellings within sight or smell of the Union Camp paper mills and the chemical plants outside the city.

Savannah and surrounding Chatham County comprise more than one-third of the 1st Congressional District of Georgia; the rest consists of adjacent rural counties, a few running down the coast (including Georgia's resort-and-retirement islands) and most inland. This part of the South was parched in the drought of 1986, although that turned out to be good weather for the Vidalia onions which are grown only near the town of that name, 80 miles west of Savannah. Politically, there seems to be an antipathy, or at least a lack of perceived common interest, between Savannah and its hinterland. It is as if the small farmers, black and white, of the rural counties suppose that everyone in Savannah lives in a grand mansion, enjoying the profits made from the sweat of their own brows. The real division in elections here then is between town and country, not—as it seemed likely to be 15 years ago—between black and white.

The incumbent congressman, Lindsay Thomas, has a curriculum vitae that spans that division, and that probably is why he was elected when incumbent Bo Ginn ran for governor in 1982. Thomas was born in the rural areas, spent seven years in Savannah as a banker and in civic affairs, then ran a family farm operation for nine years. He had held no political office, but he had good connections throughout the district and enough money to get his campaign started. That enabled him to build up big margins in the rural counties and a respectable vote in Savannah—enough to get him by a Savannah aristocrat in the primary and a Republican in the general election.

Many House members reach a point in their careers when they must decide whether to go statewide or to stay rooted in the House. Thomas reached one such point in the middle 1980s. He could have taken on the risks of running against Senator Mack Mattingly, but decided not to. Now, with two Democrats in the Senate, the next opening is likely to be the governorship in 1990. In the House Thomas has concentrated on Agriculture Committee business, and in rewriting farm legislation has been less than eager to cut subsidies. He also serves on Merchant Marine and Fisheries, a useful seat for a member from a port district. On other issues he has turned out to be one of those middle-of-the-road Democrats who, increasingly, tend to chart the course for their congressional party. His political success—he has not had significant opposition since 1982—shows that his constituents, if not Washington observers and campaign strategists, understand that Democrats like Thomas, and House Democrats generally, are not the wild big-spenders and radical liberationists of partisan caricature. Thomas and his counterparts are not Republicans-in-disguise either. They are far less likely to vote to cut budgets for domestic programs and willing on occasion to entertain arguments against weapons systems or foreign involvements. They are, in the current Democratic House, the real balance wheels.

The People: Pop. 1980: 541,180, up 15.9% 1970–80. Households (1980): 77% family, 45% with children, 61% married couples; 36.0% housing units rented; median monthly rent: $125; median house value: $32,900. Voting age pop. (1980): 375,257; 30% Black, 1% Spanish origin, 1% Asian origin.

1984 Presidential Vote:

Reagan (R)	100,525	(59%)
Mondale (D)	69,408	(41%)

Rep. Robert Lindsay Thomas (D)

Elected 1982; b. Nov. 20, 1943, Waycross; home, Statesboro; U. of GA, B.A. 1966; United Methodist; married (Melinda).

Career: Investment banker, 1966–73; Farmer, 1973–82.

Offices: 431 CHOB 20515, 202-225-5831. Also 240 Old P.O. Bldg., Savannah 31412, 912-944-4074; P.O. Box 333, Statesboro 30458, 912-489-8797; 304 Fed. Bldg., Brunswick 31520, 912-264-4040; and 161 N. Macon St., Jesup 31545, 912-427-9231.

Committees: *Agriculture* (17th of 26 D). Subcommittees: Conservation, Credit, and Rural Development; Tobacco and Peanuts. *Merchant Marine and Fisheries* (19th of 25 D). Subcommittees: Coast Guard; Fisheries and Wildlife Conservation and the Environment; Merchant Marine.

Group Ratings

	ADA	ACLU	COPE	CFA	LCV	ACU	NTU	NSI	COC	CEI
1986	25	25	46	42	53	68	25	80	50	23
1985	25	—	47	50	—	67	29	—	45	—

National Journal Ratings

	1986 LIB — 1986 CONS			1985 LIB — 1985 CONS		
Economic	54%	—	45%	44%	—	56%
Social	35%	—	64%	69%	—	28%
Foreign	37%	—	62%	24%	—	66%

Key Votes

1) Lmt Cln Water Act	AGN	5) Retain Gun Cont	AGN	9) Aid Angola Reb	FOR
2) Rpl Tobac Sub	AGN	6) Contra Aid	FOR	10) Tax Reform	AGN
3) Grm-Rdmn Def Red	FOR	7) Lmt Text Imp	FOR	11) S Africa Sanc	FOR
4) Ban Polygraph	AGN	8) Limit SDI	AGN	12) Immig Reform	FOR

Election Results

1986 general	Robert Lindsay Thomas (D)	69,440	(100%)	($201,603)
1986 primary	Robert Lindsay Thomas (D)	39,959	(100%)	
1984 general	Robert Lindsay Thomas (D)	126,082	(82%)	($239,604)
	Erie Lee Downing (R)	28,460	(18%)	($30,312)

Campaign Contributions and Expenditures

1985-86		Direct Cont. 1985-86		PACS Breakdown 1985-86			
Receipts	$244,400	Indiv.	$102,860	Corp.	$46,700	T/M/H	$45,500
Expend.	$201,603	Party	$278	Labor	$14,750	Agr.	$10,050
Unspent	$85,580	PACS	$125,900	Ideo.	$7,050	CWOS	$1,850
		Cand.	$4,000				

SECOND DISTRICT

The 2d Congressional District, the southwest corner of Georgia, is one of the lowest income parts of the United States, and statistically one of the most rural and backward. But those are statistics which mean something quite different from what they meant at the end of World War II. Then places like southwest Georgia had little more than subsistence farming economies; diseases like pellagra and rickets were rife; children were malnourished enough to stunt their growth and received little or no schooling; indoor plumbing and electricity were the exception rather than the rule.

Today the 2d District may rank as low on national statistics, but everyday life has changed almost radically. Endemic diseases have been wiped out, and infant mortality reduced to near-national levels. Electricity and indoor plumbing, washing machines and refrigerators and television are universal. Given the low cost of living, average incomes here are now in real dollars similar to what the very few local rich people made before the war. In one other important respect life has changed. Legal segregation has disappeared, despite predictions that whites would never tolerate integration; schools, restaurants, and shops are integrated; old forms of address are no longer required, though the sometimes elaborate politeness of the Deep South has not altogether vanished.

Accompanying this socioeconomic change, but not precisely in tandem, has been political change. In Franklin Roosevelt's day, south Georgia was one of the most Democratic parts of the United States: blacks didn't vote, and whites still hated the Republicans for Reconstruction and liked New Deal welfare, rural electrification, and farm programs, which pumped money into these otherwise moribund areas. Whites' preference for national Democrats vanished in the early 1960s, as they became associated with civil rights; blacks, when they could vote, went Democratic, but remained a minority here. What's surprising, as time went on, is that the Republican movement among whites didn't go deeper, and farther down the ballot. Beginning around the middle 1960s, economic growth here accelerated, and the southern standard of living became recognizably American; and voters here became economically more conservative.

But not completely. They supported Democrats like their neighbor Jimmy Carter in state and presidential races, against more parsimonious, cut-spending Republicans. Even Walter Mondale got above his national average here. And in congressional races they have elected House members who are not free market purists. The current incumbent, Democrat Charles Hatcher, supports spending programs on close votes more than half the time, and quietly votes with most other House Democrats most of the time—more often than any other rural Georgia congressman. On the Agriculture Committee he is held accountable for the continuation of peanut subsidies. Like many southern Democrats he is a supporter of the food stamp program, which, because need is determined on a national basis, is particularly generous to the South. Behind the surface talk of support for the free market, there seems to be a residual support for many government programs. That's not so surprising when you reflect that government programs played a vital role in changing people's everyday lives here from what they were 50 years ago. For in a mature welfare-state society, the true conservative course is to preserve the protections and subsidies people have come to expect and which they depend on when they make long-range plans for their lives. That's one reason Atlanta Democrat Wyche Fowler was able to carry this district in the 1986 Senate race over fiscally conservative Republican Mack Mattingly.

Charles Hatcher has a conventional background for an area like this. He was first elected to the legislature in 1972, at 33; he represented Albany, the largest city in the 2d District, but he is from an elite family in a small town, like the Carters. He became an assistant floor leader with the help of his south Georgia neighbor, George Busbee, who was elected governor to follow Carter; with Busbee's patronage, he was elected to Congress in 1980 when the 2d District incumbent, Dawson Mathis, ran unsuccessfully for the Senate. In 1982 Mathis returned and ran in the 2d again; Hatcher held on in the primary with 52% of the vote. That hurdle passed, he seems safely entrenched and has been unopposed since. He appears little interested in statewide races, and instead concentrates heavily on his Agriculture work, particularly on the Tobacco and Peanuts Subcommittee.

The People: Pop. 1980: 549,977, up 13.7% 1970–80. Households (1980): 78% family, 46% with children, 61% married couples; 35.1% housing units rented; median monthly rent: $100; median house value: $30,200. Voting age pop. (1980): 369,606; 32% Black, 1% Spanish origin.

1984 Presidential Vote:			
Reagan (R)	....	88,306	(58%)
Mondale (D)	....	62,974	(42%)

Rep. Charles F. Hatcher (D)

Elected 1980; b. July 1, 1939, Doerun; home, Newton; GA Southern Col., Statesboro, B.S. 1965, U. of GA, J.D. 1969; Episcopalian; married (Ellen).

Career: Air Force, 1958–62; Practicing atty.; GA House of Reps., 1973–80.

Offices: 405 CHOB 20515, 202-225-3631. Also P.O. Box 1932, Albany 31702, 912-439-8067; P.O. Box 2966, Thomasville 31799, and 912-228-7359; and P.O. Box 1626, Valdosta 31603, 912-247-9705.

Committees: *Agriculture* (13th of 26 D). Subcommittees: Department Operations, Research, and Foreign Agriculture; Forests, Family Farms, and Energy; Tobacco and Peanuts. *Small Business* (8th of 27 D). Subcommittee: Energy and Agriculture (Chairman).

Group Ratings

	ADA	ACLU	COPE	CFA	LCV	ACU	NTU	NSI	COC	CEI
1986	30	23	58	58	36	56	25	75	58	24
1985	35	—	57	50	—	52	23	—	42	—

National Journal Ratings

	1986 LIB — 1986 CONS			1985 LIB — 1985 CONS		
Economic	55%	—	44%	52%	—	47%
Social	35%	—	65%	69%	—	31%
Foreign	43%	—	57%	37%	—	60%

Key Votes

1) Lmt Cln Water Act	FOR	5) Retain Gun Cont	FOR	9) Aid Angola Reb	FOR
2) Rpl Tobac Sub	AGN	6) Contra Aid	FOR	10) Tax Reform	FOR
3) Grm-Rdmn Def Red	FOR	7) Lmt Text Imp	FOR	11) S Africa Sanc	—
4) Ban Polygraph	—	8) Limit SDI	FOR	12) Immig Reform	FOR

Election Results

1986 general	Charles F. Hatcher (D)	72,482	(100%)	($140,185)
1986 primary	Charles F. Hatcher (D)	58,033	(100%)	
1984 general	Charles F. Hatcher (D)	110,561	(100%)	($162,831)

Campaign Contributions and Expenditures

1985-86		Direct Cont. 1985-86		PACS Breakdown 1985-86			
Receipts	$164,810	Indiv.	$48,748	Corp.	$38,500	T/M/H	$38,893
Expend.	$140,185	Party	$273	Labor	$12,550	Agr.	$10,250
Debts	$29,786	PACS	$110,593	Ideo.	$9,800	CWOS	$600
		Cand.	$18,850				

THIRD DISTRICT

The 3d Congressional District of Georgia is Jimmy Carter's home district, and Sam Nunn's—a large hunk of rural and small-town south Georgia. This was once cotton land, with some big plantations and plenty of smaller farmers; now it is devoted to soybeans, peanuts, and the softwood pine trees which grow almost as fast as cotton bolls in the warm, humid South. Since the Civil War, this has been a poor area, with a few rich families in each town, but the large majority living on incomes northern city-dwellers would regard as pathetically low. Fort Benning, the giant Army training base which takes up most of one county, was one mainstay of the local economy for years; so, increasingly were low-wage factories like the textile and apparel mills that began appearing along the highways after World War II.

But real economic growth here did not happen until the 1960s. One reason may have been the civil rights revolution, which made life in the South more attractive for blacks: in the 1960s black outmigration slowed significantly, and income levels rose very rapidly. Another reason was improved education and the rise in skills of the local work force. A third was the construction of interstate highways and the increasing importance of truck transportation. Conservative orators like to attribute the growth of the South to free enterprise. But the South had free enterprise long before it had widespread affluence. Here government—through civil rights, education, highways—played a critical role.

Jimmy Carter's district has remained faithful to him—it gave him a solid majority in 1980—and to his party. Wyche Fowler, for example, got 55% of the vote here in his close Senate race in 1986. Whatever the success of Democrats elsewhere in the South in constructing a majority of blacks and low-income whites, they have been successful here in south Georgia.

But Carter himself has never been active in congressional politics here. As a young state senator, he passed up a chance to run for Congress in 1966, making an unsuccessful race for governor instead; the winner, Jack Brinkley, was a quiet conservative who served on the Armed Services Committee and retired in 1982.

The congressman today is Richard Ray, a Democrat whose prime credential was ten years' service as administrative assistant to Senator Sam Nunn. Ray is in fact older than Nunn, almost Carter's age, a pesticide business owner who was mayor of Perry, Georgia, for six years, when Nunn was city attorney. Ray, in his late 50s, is part of an older generation of Georgia politicians, of the pre- rather than post-Carter generation. His instincts on economic issues are conservative, which is to say in today's environment for cutting spending on most domestic programs. His instincts on defense policy are to support generous defense spending but to be a stickler for details. He serves on Armed Services and on its Readiness and Military Installations Subcommittees—good assignments for this district—and does his homework.

Ray won the seat in the 1982 primary with little difficulty and has held it since with less. The district would probably support a less rigorously conservative congressman, and a challenger did get 32% in the 1984 primary; but Ray seems to have a safe seat.

The People: Pop. 1980: 540,865, up 8.9% 1970–80. Households (1980): 78% family, 46% with children, 61% married couples; 35.6% housing units rented; median monthly rent: $117; median house value: $30,200. Voting age pop. (1980): 376,128; 31% Black, 2% Spanish origin, 1% Asian origin.

1984 Presidential Vote:			
Reagan (R)	....	83,658	(55%)
Mondale (D)	....	68,149	(45%)

Rep. Richard B. Ray (D)

Elected 1982; b. Feb. 2, 1927, Fort Valley; home, Perry; United Methodist; married (Barbara).

Career: Navy, WWII; Farmer, 1946–50; Owner, Ray Services Inc. (pest control), 1950–62; S.E. Mngr., Getz Inc., 1962–72; Cnclmn. of Perry, 1962–64; Mayor of Perry, 1964–70; Pres., GA Municipal Assoc., 1969; A.A. to Sen. Sam Nunn, 1973–82.

Offices: 331 CHOB 20515, 202-225-5901. Also 301 15th St., Columbus 31901, 404-324-0292; 200 Carl Vinson Pkwy., Warner Robins 31056, 912-929-2764; and 200 Ridley Ave., LaGrange 30240, 404-882-9214.

Committees: *Armed Services* (21st of 31 D). Subcommittees: Military Personnel and Compensation; Procurement and Military Nuclear Systems; Readiness. *Small Business* (17th of 27 D). Subcommittee: Energy and Agriculture.

Group Ratings

	ADA	ACLU	COPE	CFA	LCV	ACU	NTU	NSI	COC	CEI
1986	10	25	25	50	37	71	48	100	47	47
1985	15	—	24	33	—	71	48	—	82	—

National Journal Ratings

	1986 LIB — 1986 CONS			1985 LIB — 1985 CONS		
Economic	26%	—	73%	21%	—	78%
Social	27%	—	71%	44%	—	54%
Foreign	37%	—	62%	24%	—	66%

Key Votes

1) Lmt Cln Water Act	FOR	5) Retain Gun Cont	AGN	9) Aid Angola Reb	FOR
2) Rpl Tobac Sub	AGN	6) Contra Aid	AGN	10) Tax Reform	AGN
3) Grm-Rdmn Def Red	FOR	7) Lmt Text Imp	FOR	11) S Africa Sanc	FOR
4) Ban Polygraph	AGN	8) Limit SDI	FOR	12) Immig Reform	AGN

Election Results

1986 general	Richard B. Ray (D)	....	75,850	(100%)	($150,796)
1986 primary	Richard B. Ray (D)	....	50,209	(100%)	
1984 general	Richard B. Ray (D)	....	111,061	(81%)	($508,335)
	Mitch Cantu (R)	....	25,410	(19%)	

Campaign Contributions and Expenditures

1985-86		Direct Cont. 1985-86		PACS Breakdown 1985-86			
Receipts	$291,691	Indiv.	$138,991	Corp.	$77,095	T/M/H	$26,800
Expend.	$150,796	PACS	$118,043	Labor	$8,700	Agr.	$2,500
Debts	$165,621	Cand.	$20,000	Ideo.	$2,250	CWOS	$698

FOURTH DISTRICT

The Atlanta metropolitan area, largest in the Deep South, is coming to resemble northern metropolises—as they were a decade or two ago. It has a central city with a booming downtown and a black majority in its neighborhoods. Its outlying reaches, still seemingly rural along the highways, are filling with subdivisions among the farmland where young white parents are raising families in something like traditional surroundings. And it has an inner core of suburbs, which include some fading neighborhoods—and the neighborhoods where the city's richest and most prominent people live. The 4th Congressional District is made up almost entirely of inner suburban Atlanta. Its southwestern reaches do touch on the city's black ghetto, and its black population is rising in adjacent areas, and its farther reaches, especially in Rockdale and Newton Counties are exurban. But most of the district is made up of DeKalb County and a small chunk of affluent north Atlanta. Here you find the old city of Decatur, the super-affluent neighborhoods on the north side, and the mostly Jewish area around Emory University and the Center for Disease Control. But most of the people here live in comfortable subdivisions built in the 1950s and 1960s, when this was the farthest edge of greater Atlanta.

For years this was the most Republican part of Georgia: DeKalb County elected Republicans to the Georgia legislature while almost all the rest of Georgia elected Democrats. But now the farther-out suburbs are more Republican, and DeKalb, still mostly white and more affluent than ever, is a battleground between cultural conservatives and cultural liberals—the same kind of battle you find in so many suburban counties in the North.

Only here it seems to be waged with special intensity, and the cultural conservatives are winning. Their champion is Representative Pat Swindall, an evangelical Republican who won an upset victory in 1984 and held onto the district in 1986. Swindall has won with aggressive tactics. Running against 10-year Democratic incumbent Elliott Levitas in 1984, Swindall charged that his opponent's voting record was similar to Geraldine Ferraro's, although Levitas, father of the legislative veto, was in fact more market- than government-oriented on economics; he toted a "biblical scorecard" and campaigned as a Christian fundamentalist. He also played effective hardball. When a Treasury undersecretary cancelled plans to attend a Swindall fundraiser because Levitas threatened to withdraw his support for an Administration bill to refinance Washington's Kennedy Center, Swindall called the Treasury to protest and taped the conversation, and charged that Levitas's threats constituted a felony. That seemed naive, but Levitas was suddenly a political insider on the defensive and Swindall an idealistic young opponent. The challenger won 53%–47%.

Swindall is a pleasant, sincere man with a conservative record in the House. He seems less interested in positive legislative initiatives than in things like insisting on a roll call on whether to fire the House's 14 elevator operators. He is one of those House Republicans dedicated to challenging the legitimacy of the Democrats' control of the House. Yet his own hold on the 4th District is not yet secure. In 1986 he was challenged by Democrat Ben Jones, the actor who plays the mechanic, Cooter, on *The Dukes of Hazzard*. He was not considered a strong candidate and raised and spent only $118,000. But Jones (who pointed out that Cooter in southern slang means turtle) held Swindall, who raised $753,000 and spent $627,000, to 51% in DeKalb County and 53% districtwide. This is not a strong showing for an incumbent, and suggests that his evangelical and aggressive brand of politics abrades on the sensibilities of at least some of the constituents who like his views on economics. These are people who shop in the best stores and fly directly from Atlanta to Europe; to them, Republicanism stands for modernity, sophistication, erudition, and good taste, and they want no part of southern Democrats who ran as "rednecks" nor of Republicans who run as religious enthusiasts. Ironically, Swindall may owe his victory to the Voting Rights Act and a successful suit brought by Atlanta blacks to take black voters from the 4th and put them into the 5th District. That suit has not affected results in the 5th District, but it may have given Swindall enough votes to win both times. Whether it will a third time is unclear. The close margin has gotten a lot of politicians, including Jones (who announced in February 1987 he'd run), Levitas, state legislator Cathy Steinberg, and prosecutor Bob Wilson, to think about running here in 1988, and national Democrats are as sure to pour money into this district as Swindall is to raise plenty more from evangelicals and cultural conservatives.

The People: Pop. 1980: 542,368, up 24.1% 1970–80. Households (1980): 71% family, 38% with children, 58% married couples; 39.2% housing units rented; median monthly rent: $253; median house value: $57,100. Voting age pop. (1980): 399,703; 11% Black, 2% Spanish origin, 1% Asian origin.

1984 Presidential Vote:

Reagan (R)	148,469	(66%)
Mondale (D)	77,481	(34%)

Rep. Patrick L. Swindall (R)

Elected 1984; b. Oct. 18, 1950, Gadsden, AL; home, Dunwoody; U. of GA, B.A. 1972, J.D. 1975; Presbyterian; married (Kimberly).

Career: Practicing atty., 1975–84; Owner, furniture co.

Offices: 508 CHOB 20515, 202-225-4272. Also 160 Clairmont Ave., Ste. 140, Decatur 30030, 404-373-3509.

Committees: *Banking, Finance and Urban Affairs* (18th of 20 R). Subcommittees: Economic Stabilization; Housing and Community Development; International Development Institutions and Finance; International Finance, Trade and Monetary Policy. *Judiciary* (11th of 14 R). Subcommittees: Administrative Law and Governmental Relations; Criminal Justice; Immigration, Refugees and International Law (Ranking Member). *Select Committee on Aging* (20th of 26 R). Subcommittee: Retirement Income and Employment.

Group Ratings

	ADA	ACLU	COPE	CFA	LCV	ACU	NTU	NSI	COC	CEI
1986	0	0	10	8	32	91	64	100	47	80
1985	5	—	6	25	—	86	69	—	95	—

National Journal Ratings

	1986 LIB — 1986 CONS		1985 LIB — 1985 CONS	
Economic	6% —	90%	0% —	95%
Social	0% —	89%	0% —	76%
Foreign	0% —	86%	0% —	76%

Key Votes

1) Lmt Cln Water Act	FOR	5) Retain Gun Cont	AGN	9) Aid Angola Reb	FOR
2) Rpl Tobac Sub	AGN	6) Contra Aid	FOR	10) Tax Reform	AGN
3) Grm-Rdmn Def Red	FOR	7) Lmt Text Imp	FOR	11) S Africa Sanc	AGN
4) Ban Polygraph	AGN	8) Limit SDI	AGN	12) Immig Reform	AGN

Election Results

1986 general	Patrick L. Swindall (R)	86,366	(53%)	($627,655)
	Ben Jones (D)	75,892	(47%)	($118,085)
1986 primary	Patrick L. Swindall (R)	13,778	(100%)	
1984 general	Patrick L. Swindall (R)	120,456	(53%)	($535,729)
	Elliott H. Levitas (D)	106,376	(47%)	($382,557)

Campaign Contributions and Expenditures

1985-86		Direct Cont. 1985-86			PACS Breakdown 1985-86		
Receipts	$753,889	Indiv.	$519,513	Corp.	$86,016	T/M/H	$76,569
Expend.	$627,655	Party	$18,339	Labor	$850	Agr.	$5,550
Debts	$147,970	PACS	$187,962	Ideo.	$17,605	CWOS	$1,372

FIFTH DISTRICT

Stuck smack in the Deep South—and, by just about any definition, the capital of the region—is Atlanta, "the city," it used to boast, "too busy to hate." Atlanta owes some of its prosperity to its central position, to its role as a transportation hub (it was a key railroad junction, and not much else, during the Civil War, and now has the nation's second busiest airport), and to the success of some local businesses (notably Coca-Cola, founded in 1886). But, ironically, it owes much of its status as capital of the South to its longstanding reputation for tolerance and its central importance to the civil rights movement. Under longtime Mayors William Hartsfield and Ivan Allen, and with the leadership of Coke's Robert Woodruff, Atlanta avoided resistance to integration, and thereby became the kind of peaceful, uncontroversial environment which investors and big corporations like. With the nation's largest black middle class and long-established black institutions, Atlanta was a natural choice as the headquarters for Martin Luther King, Jr., and other leaders of the civil rights movement. That brought the media and when the movement was successful, Atlanta seemed the natural center for a New South. So Atlanta owes its status as the center of the South to its own refusal to join whites in the region resisting integration.

Yet today Atlantans, white and black, are not quite as smug about their success as they used to be. The city's business district continues to be important, but it has suffered from periodic overbuilding; growth has gone mostly to the suburbs and farther out counties, and aside from the rich north side, Atlanta has been left with mostly low-income residents. A city which once prided itself on a degree of neighborhood integration—with blacks living in close proximity to whites—is now mostly all black. Blacks are left a majority in a central city on whose government increasing demands are made with fewer resources left to meet them. One of Atlanta's most distinguished blacks, Andrew Young—former congressman, former ambassador to the United Nations—was first elected mayor in 1981. His election was marred by blatantly racial appeals by his partisans, including outgoing Mayor Maynard Jackson, and he was criticized afterwards for his extensive travels. But Young makes a good case that these have promoted Atlanta as a world economic center, and he has worked closely with white businessmen to build the city's economy. In national politics he remains an important, but not always decisive, figure. In 1983 he was skeptical about a black presidential candidacy and in 1984 he let it be known he was really for Walter Mondale, but dared not say so for fear of irritating Jesse Jackson's supporters (who include Maynard Jackson). Yet at the Democratic National Convention it was Andrew Young, not forthright Mondale supporters like Richard Arrington of Birmingham or Coleman Young of Detroit, who was booed by blacks when he spoke out for a Mondale platform plank.

The 5th Congressional District of Georgia includes most of Atlanta, and some diverse suburban territory, from posh Sandy Spring in the north to middle-class East Point, to which blacks have been moving in the last decade; to the rural precincts of southwest Fulton and mostly black southwest DeKalb counties. Its current boundaries were set by a federal court, which decided that the Georgia legislature's district did not contain enough blacks to satisfy the Voting Rights Act. The Justice Department standard, requiring that a district be 65% black to be counted as black, is pretty silly; if blacks are allowed to vote, as they have been for years now in Atlanta, then a majority black district should be one where the majority of adult residents are black. The result was ironic: a 5th District with a white majority elected Andrew Young congressman in 1972, 1974, and 1976, while in 1982 and 1984 a 5th District with a court-augmented black majority elected and reelected Wyche Fowler, who is white. Fowler, as was generally expected, ran for the Senate in 1986 and, as was not generally expected, won.

The new congressman from the 5th District, selected in the Democratic runoff, is John Lewis. He comes to Congress already as an important maker of American history. In 1959 and 1960 Lewis, then 19, helped organize the first lunch counter sit-ins. In 1961, he was one of the leaders of the Freedom Rides, and while riding on a public bus was viciously beaten in Rock Hill, South Carolina, and Montgomery, Alabama. In 1963 he became leader of the Student Non-Violent Coordinating Committee and spoke at the March on Washington. In 1964 he helped coordinate the Mississippi Freedom Project. In 1965 he led the Selma-to-Montgomery march to petition for voting rights and was beaten by policemen using clubs, whips, and tear gas. Modestly, quietly, with incredible grace under pressure, maintaining his poise and good judgment under the harshest of circumstance, Lewis was one of the people who made the civil rights revolution happen. *Time* called him a "living saint." "Probably none has paid a higher price to help change this country than John Lewis," David Broder wrote.

Lewis has also had his disappointments. His decade as head of the Voter Education Project in Atlanta and his stint at ACTION in the Carter Administration did not give him the publicity and fame that, for example, made Jesse Jackson, whose credentials in the civil rights movement are so much thinner, a national celebrity. When Young left the House, Lewis ran for his seat and was soundly beaten by Fowler. In 1981 he won a seat on the Atlanta Council. But in the Democratic primary for Congress in 1986, he trailed in the first primary 47%–35%. It looked like he would lose again, this time to Julian Bond, who has his own illustrious record: he was denied his seat in the Georgia legislature in 1967 because of his opposition to the Vietnam war; he was nominated, when well under age, for vice president at the Democrats' 1968 convention; he had served for nearly 20 years in the legislature, and with a smooth and articulate style was a star of the national speaker circuit and his own syndicated TV show. Yet it was Lewis and not Bond who won, and in a curious way: Bond won over 60% of the black votes, but Lewis won nearly 90% of the whites. One reason was that he concentrated on local issues like zoning and city ethics; another was his record of hard work, compared with Bond's apparent boredom in the legislature. A bizarre footnote: in early 1987 Bond's estranged wife charged him and others, including Mayor Andrew Young, with using cocaine; she retracted the charges, and Bond and Young angrily denied them.

Lewis enters the 100th Congress with special prestige for a freshman and with what looks to be a safe seat in the 5th District. There was talk after the election that Bond would run again, but it's hard to come up with a rationale for ousting a competent incumbent.

The People: Pop. 1980: 550,070, dn. 6.4% 1970–80. Households (1980): 66% family, 40% with children, 41% married couples; 53.5% housing units rented; median monthly rent: $154; median house value: $34,500. Voting age pop. (1980): 390,138; 60% Black, 1% Spanish origin.

1984 Presidential Vote: Mondale (D) 124,006   (67%)
                              Reagan (R) 60,150   (33%)

Rep. John Lewis (D)

Elected 1986; b. Feb. 21, 1940, Troy, AL; home, Atlanta; Amer. Baptist Theological Seminary, B.A. 1961, Fisk U, B.A. 1963; Baptist; married (Lillian).

Career: Chmn., Student Nonviolent Coordinating Cmtee., 1963–66; Staff Member, Field Foundation, 1966–67; Dir. of Community Organization, Southern Regional Cncl., 1967–70; Exec. Dir., Voter Education Project, 1970–76; Assoc. Dir., ACTION, 1977–80; Dir. of Community Affairs, Natl. Cooperative Bank, 1980–82; Member, Atlanta City Cncl., 1982–86.
Offices: 501 CHOB 20515, 202-225-3801. Also Equitable Bldg. Ste. 750, 100 Peach Tree St., N.W., Atlanta 30303, 404-659-0116.
Committees: *Interior and Insular Affairs* (24th of 26 D). Subcommittees: Insular and International Affairs; National Parks and Public Lands. *Public Works and Transportation* (26th of 32 D). Subcommittees: Economic Development; Public Buildings and Grounds; Water Resources.

Group Ratings and Key Votes: Newly Elected
Election Results

1986 general	John Lewis (D)	93,229	(75%)	($380,314)
	Portia A. Scott (R)	30,562	(25%)	($75,862)
1986 runoff	John Lewis (D)	35,142	(52%)	
	Julian Bond (D)	32,447	(48%)	
1986 primary	Julian Bond (D)	31,911	(47%)	
	John Lewis (D)	23,622	(35%)	
	Charles Johnson (D)	5,756	(8%)	
	Four others (D)	6,693	(8%)	
1984 general	Wyche Fowler, Jr. (D)	151,233	(100%)	($254,826)

Campaign Contributions and Expenditures

1985-86		Direct Cont. 1985-86		PACS Breakdown 1985-86			
Receipts	$381,754	Indiv.	$204,707	Corp.	$29,630	T/M/H	$25,300
Expend.	$380,314	Party	$280	Labor	$114,656	Agr.	$1,500
Unspent	$1,437	PACS	$215,329	Ideo.	$43,393	CWOS	$850
		Cand.	$8,000				

SIXTH DISTRICT

As metropolitan Atlanta moves out into the red earth of the north Georgia countryside, a new kind of community—urban in its amenities, rural in its ambiance—is being created, and a new political constituency comes into existence. Such a constituency is the 6th Congressional District of Georgia, which is almost entirely within the metropolitan ambit of Atlanta and yet sees itself distinct and apart from that city. The district includes Atlanta's huge airport and the close-in suburbs of College Park and Hapeville, with increasing black populations. But more typical is Clayton County just to the south and the counties further south and west where you can almost see metropolitan Atlanta growing out along the freeways. Small towns and rural counties which were once a full day's travel from the capital are now within 60 minutes' drive of I-285 around Atlanta; so you can work in Atlanta or a close-in suburb and live in Newnan or Griffin or Carroll County. This is politically conservative country, full of younger men and women with young families, almost all white, who have climbed some distance on the economic ladder and hope to climb some more. They like the homier, culturally more conservative atmosphere of the smaller counties, where most people still attend church and the high school kids don't use drugs. The political tradition here is Democratic, but increasingly this is Republican territory: Senator Mack Mattingly increased his percentage in the 6th District outside Fulton County from 52% in

1980 to 55% in 1986, even as his share of the vote went down statewide.

The congressman from the 6th District is Newt Gingrich: history professor, transplanted Yankee, conservative intellectual, Republican, temperamentally a gadfly in a state which has valued in its Representatives a kind of dull faithfulness to duty. His first election way back in 1978 was more a forecast of what the district would become than an reflection of what it then was. Actually, he almost won it twice before, against scandal-plagued Democrat John Flynt in 1974 and 1976. He was reelected by respectable margins in 1980 and 1982, by an overwhelming margin in 1984, and in 1986 with 60% against a hard-charging Democrat heavily backed by his state and national party, Clayton County Administrator Crandle Bray. The Democrats added blacks to the 6th, but that did not hurt Gingrich, and the growth generally helps him. By now he has had quite a long career in congressional politics.

And a successful one. In the late 1970s Gingrich was one of those young Republicans who, with David Stockman and Jack Kemp, set the tone and agenda for Republicans and the nation, and their proposals—the Kemp-Roth tax cut, decontrol of oil prices, higher defense spending—which seemed quixotic when Gingrich was first elected were law a few years later. Gingrich and allies also moved aggressively. Before then, House Republican ranks were no place for the intellectually adventurous; they were filled with middle-aged products of college fraternity and small town Rotary bonhomie. Congeniality was highly valued, and getting along with your colleagues (including your Democrats); your positions on issues were predictable, taken for granted, not the subject of much interest. It was assumed that, on the major issues, the tide of history was in the Democrats' favor and they would sooner or later prevail; your job was to slow them down a bit.

Gingrich favored something like guerrilla warfare. He and other junior Republicans started using the House's special order procedure, after the finish of legislative business, to raise issues and attack the Democrats, at least to the C-SPAN cable TV audience. Gingrich's group was embarrassed when Speaker O'Neill ordered the House cameras to pan around, while they were reading a foreign policy document prepared by a Gingrich staffer, to show that the House chamber the Republicans were addressing was empty. But O'Neill himself looked worse when he attacked Gingrich on the floor of the House and was ruled out of order for insulting him. O'Neill believed that Gingrich was attacking Democratic members' patriotism. But Gingrich argues convincingly that he was calling the Democrats' judgment, not their patriotism, into question for consistently minimizing the risks and negative effects of Soviet aggression. Gingrich's aim is not always true. He seized on the contest over the Indiana 8th election in 1985, to point up what he considers the illegitimacy of the Democrats' control of the House. But he did little to shake the Democratic majority, and whatever the accuracy of the Indiana 8th count the fact is that Democrats control the House because they consistently get more votes than Republicans, as frustrating as that is to a Republican who believes most Americans accept or are ready to accept his ideas.

What are those ideas? They might be summed up in the phrase, high tech and traditional values. Gingrich, who lived as an Army brat in France, is something of an American Gaullist. He insists on the need for an assertive foreign policy and a high-tech, expensive defense to combat Communists. But he is sympathetic both to technical innovations and to the need for shrewd strategy and venturesome tactics: he is more with the military reformers than the Weinberger Pentagon. He favors liberating markets from government regulation, but he also believes in major state enterprises, like a manned space program, which he hopes will stimulate technological innovation and by capturing the national imagination inspire national pride. He is untethered by the need traditional and especially southern conservatives felt to justify racial segregation, and made a point—and got some conservative flak for—opposing apartheid. He calls for a Conservative Opportunity Society—a name he coined as the opposite of what he regards as a failed liberal welfare state.

The 1986 election results and the Iran-contra scandal cowed some conservatives; not Gingrich. He came forward with a proposal to replace the Social Security tax and trust fund with a value-added tax and Individual Retirement Accounts, with all current benefits currently accrued guaranteed for life; it was his solution to the problems of the trade deficit, low savings, and Social Security's fiscal plight. For welfare he came forward with a proposal for workfare, retraining, and making all parents financially responsible for their children up to age 18. For education, drugs, and almost everything else he had an original position paper. He knows that most people regard his ideas as politically unviable. So he wants to prove that they are by selling them in the 6th district.

It is not a bad forum, in part because Gingrich, on being targeted by Democrats, spent much time in the district and on local issues. He is still not an active or effective legislator in Washington. His biggest frustration is that few like-minded and politically savvy Republican candidates have arisen in districts across the land. But he has the satisfaction of being on the cutting edge of new ideas and of representing a district that is on the cutting edge of demographic growth in the nation—and which, as he showed in his 1986 race, seems to be receptive to what he regards as his cutting edge politics.

The People: Pop. 1980: 548,959, up 41.4% 1970–80. Households (1980): 80% family, 49% with children, 67% married couples; 29.9% housing units rented; median monthly rent: $177; median house value: $38,200. Voting age pop. (1980): 375,209; 14% Black, 1% Spanish origin.

1984 Presidential Vote: Reagan (R) 117,764   (69%)
Mondale (D) 53,929   (31%)

Rep. Newt Gingrich (R)

Elected 1978; b. June 17, 1943, Harrisburg, PA; home, Jonesboro; Emory U., B.A. 1965, Tulane U., M.A. 1968, Ph.D. 1971; Baptist; married (Marianne).

Career: Prof., West GA Col., 1970–78; Repub. Nominee for U.S. House of Reps., 1974, 1976.

Offices: 2438 RHOB 20515, 202-225-4501. Also 6351 Jonesboro Rd., Ste. E, Morrow 30260, 404-968-3219; Carroll Cnty. Crthse., Carrollton 30117, 404-834-6398; P.O. Box 848, Griffin Fed. Bldg., Griffin 30224, 404-228-0389; and Cnty. Office Bldg., 15 E. Washington St., Newnan 30263, 404-253-8355.

Committees: *House Administration* (4th of 7 R). Subcommittees: Libraries and Memorials (Ranking Member); Procurement and Printing (Ranking Member). *Public Works and Transportation* (4th of 20 R). Subcommittees: Aviation (Ranking Member); Investigations and Oversight; Surface Transportation.

Group Ratings

	ADA	ACLU	COPE	CFA	LCV	ACU	NTU	NSI	COC	CEI
1986	0	10	8	17	33	81	56	100	94	68
1985	10	—	7	17	—	81	57	—	95	—

National Journal Ratings

	1986 LIB — 1986 CONS		1985 LIB — 1985 CONS	
Economic	10%	— 90%	16%	— 81%
Social	26%	— 74%	0%	— 76%
Foreign	27%	— 73%	0%	— 76%

Key Votes

1) Lmt Cln Water Act	FOR	5) Retain Gun Cont	AGN	9) Aid Angola Reb	FOR
2) Rpl Tobac Sub	AGN	6) Contra Aid	FOR	10) Tax Reform	FOR
3) Grm-Rdmn Def Red	FOR	7) Lmt Text Imp	FOR	11) S Africa Sanc	FOR
4) Ban Polygraph	AGN	8) Limit SDI	AGN	12) Immig Reform	FOR

Election Results

1986 general	Newt Gingrich (R)	75,583	(60%)	($736,607)
	Crandle Bray (D)	51,352	(40%)	($251,751)
1986 primary	Newt Gingrich (R)	9,481	(100%)	
1984 general	Newt Gingrich (R)	116,655	(69%)	($479,131)
	Gerald L. Johnson (D)	52,061	(31%)	($74,940)

Campaign Contributions and Expenditures

1985-86		Direct Cont. 1985-86		PACS Breakdown 1985-86			
Receipts	$738,258	Indiv.	$478,223	Corp.	$117,724	T/M/H	$63,600
Expend.	$736,607	Party	$14,937	Labor	$7,200	Agr.	$2,250
Unspent	$11,731	PACS	$213,750	Ideo.	$22,645	CWOS	$331
		Cand.	$38,023				

SEVENTH DISTRICT

Running northwest from Atlanta, toward Chattanooga and ultimately to Chicago, is U.S. 41. Its four lanes go up and down the red hills of northern Georgia, which are part of the southern end of the Appalachian chain. This is a part of Georgia which never saw a plantation culture and whose population to this day is almost all white; it was also one of the first industrialized parts of Georgia, with textile mills and carpet factories springing up here starting about 60 years ago, near its swift flowing rivers, its railroads, the newly paved U.S. 41, and a plentiful low-wage labor supply. This was George Wallace country back in the days of segregation and the civil rights revolution, and labor unions and liberal politicians have never had much foothold here. It is a place where people's politics remains Democratic, but in presidential races only nominally; it is a place where people characterize themselves as conservatives, but in loud country boy tones that can as easily sound populist as conservative.

These northwestern Georgia counties form a little less than half of the 7th Congressional District. The rest is in Cobb County, around and in Marietta. Though only 20 miles from Atlanta and part of its metropolitan area according to government definition, Marietta has a separate consciousness of its own; it is the center of what in the 1980s has been one of the South's fast-growing new communities. In the past Marietta's economy depended heavily on the giant Lockheed plant here, but increasingly it has attracted high tech firms and office parks of all kinds and an educated but not entirely upscale and very tradition-minded new population. Politically Marietta and surrounding Cobb County have become the most Republican part of Georgia.

The most famous congressman from this district by far was Larry McDonald, who in 1983 was shot down by the Soviets in Korean Airlines flight 007—the first American congressman ever to be murdered by a foreign power. McDonald was the most right-wing of Democrats, a urologist who got into politics through the John Birch Society and who spun conspiracy theories that made even many of his political allies wince. In a career filled with ironies, McDonald came to Congress with the liberal Watergate class of 1974 (he won by beating an incumbent who had a drinking problem), had several close calls thereafter, but would probably be stronger than ever in the district as it is today.

He was succeeded, however, by George (Buddy) Darden, a different breed of Democrat—one of those practical, experienced, savvy politicians who keeps in touch with his district and chooses his issues shrewdly—that helps explain why the Democrats hold a majority in the House.

Darden was elected county prosecutor in 1972, at age 28, and to the legislature in 1980 and 1982; when McDonald died, he was able to build on his local base and beat McDonald's widow by a solid 59%–41% margin.

In the House Darden has one of those middle-of-the-road voting records which are common in southern delegations. You wouldn't mistake him for a northern big-city Democrat, but you wouldn't mistake him for a Republican either. He has McDonald's old seat on the Armed Services Committee and is careful to vote for big defense budgets and an assertive foreign policy; he boasts, as do so many Democrats, that his record is similar to Senator Sam Nunn's. Darden's political advantage is his base in Cobb County; his disadvantage is that Cobb County is so heavily Republican. In 1984, against an airline pilot who ran a few years before in Massachusetts, Darden won with just 55% of the vote—not an overwhelming percentage. In 1986, he was opposed by Joe Morecraft, a minister who delivered the eulogy at McDonald's funeral. A Birch Society member and of a philosophy called Theonomy, which holds God's laws above man (it sounds like William H. Seward's higher law), Morecraft bitterly attacked Darden as a liberal; Darden said Morecraft had a "fake and fraudulent" theology degree. Morecraft seems to have bombed, winning only 38% in Cobb County, where Darden had run only even two years before, while Darden got 74% in the rest of the district, for a 66% win. This does not mean Darden has an utterly safe seat, but it is testimony to his political adeptness and to the lack of appeal, even in a place like Cobb County, of a politics that is too fundamentalist and too far right.

The People: Pop. 1980: 545,913, up 32.2% 1970–80. Households (1980): 78% family, 45% with children, 67% married couples; 30.2% housing units rented; median monthly rent: $207; median house value: $41,200. Voting age pop. (1980): 385,552; 5% Black, 1% Spanish origin.

1984 Presidential Vote:

Reagan (R)	144,315	(73%)
Mondale (D)	53,882	(27%)

Rep. George (Buddy) Darden (D)

Elected Nov. 8, 1983; b. Nov. 22, 1943, Hancock Cnty.; home, Marietta; N. GA Col., Geo. Wash. U., U. of GA, B.A. 1965, J.D. 1967; United Methodist; married (Lillian).

Career: Asst. Dist. Atty., Cobb Cnty., 1967–72; Dist. Atty., 1973–77; Practicing atty., 1977–83; GA House of Reps., 1980–83.

Offices: 1330 LHOB 20515, 202-225-2931. Also 366 Powder Springs St., Marietta 30064, 404-422-4480; 301 Fed. Bldg., Rome 30161, 404-291-7777; and 125 S. Main St., Lafayette 30728, 404-638-7042.

Committees: *Armed Services* (25th of 31 D). Subcommittees: Readiness; Research and Development. *Interior and Insular Affairs* (18d of 26 D). Subcommittees: Energy and the Environment; Insular and International Affairs; National Parks and Public Lands.

Group Ratings

	ADA	ACLU	COPE	CFA	LCV	ACU	NTU	NSI	COC	CEI
1986	10	10	39	33	42	79	32	100	82	28
1985	15	—	42	33	—	71	33	—	64	—

National Journal Ratings

	1986 LIB — 1986 CONS		1985 LIB — 1985 CONS	
Economic	37% —	62%	39% —	61%
Social	23% —	74%	34% —	64%
Foreign	16% —	79%	24% —	66%

Key Votes

1) Lmt Cln Water Act	FOR	5) Retain Gun Cont	AGN	9) Aid Angola Reb	FOR
2) Rpl Tobac Sub	AGN	6) Contra Aid	FOR	10) Tax Reform	AGN
3) Grm-Rdmn Def Red	FOR	7) Lmt Text Imp	FOR	11) S Africa Sanc	FOR
4) Ban Polygraph	AGN	8) Limit SDI	AGN	12) Immig Reform	FOR

Election Results

1986 general	George (Buddy) Darden (D)............	88,636	(66%)	($534,239)
	Joe Morecraft (R).....................	44,891	(34%)	($246,506)
1986 primary	George (Buddy) Darden (D)............	40,835	(100%)	
1984 general	George (Buddy) Darden (D)...........	106,586	(55%)	($544,598)
	Bill Bronson (R)	86,431	(45%)	

Campaign Contributions and Expenditures

1985-86		Direct Cont. 1985-86		PACS Breakdown 1985-86			
Receipts	$532,328	Indiv.	$244,667	Corp.	$94,125	T/M/H	$71,890
Expend.	$534,239	Party	$7,930	Labor	$54,962	Agr.	$3,250
Unspent	$49,834	PACS	$249,373	Ideo.	$21,058	CWOS	$88
		Cand.	$10,000				

EIGHTH DISTRICT

South Georgia—the part of the state with a large black population and thousands of poor white farmers, with a history that features Sherman's march through Georgia and remembers dimly better times—is not so much a geographical location as it is a state of mind. In that sense, the state's 8th Congressional District is very much a part of south Georgia, even though it reaches almost as far north as Atlanta and its portion of the southern edge of the state is only a few counties wide. The 8th District's northernmost counties are in fact part of Georgia's Black Belt: most of the population is black, as it has been since there were large plantations here in antebellum times. The black percentages are also high in and around Macon, the district's largest city, the home of music greats Otis Redding, Little Richard, and the Allman brothers—and also the proud possessor of 20 times as many Japanese cherry trees as Washington, D.C.

Historically, the 8th District was always Democratic. Now it is again, after two decades of turbulence in the civil rights revolution and after. Most of its blacks have been voting for Democrats since they got the vote after the Voting Rights Act of 1965. But whites, who voted heavily for George Wallace and Richard Nixon, came back to the Democrats when Jimmy Carter was nominated, and many of them have stayed. In 1984 the 8th District gave only 52% of its votes to Ronald Reagan; Macon, in a kind of country and rhythm and blues coalition, went for Walter Mondale. In 1986 the 8th District gave 57% of its votes to Atlanta Congressman Wyche Fowler over Senator Mack Mattingly; not only all blacks but more than 40% of whites here voted for Fowler. Here is one place in the South where Democrats have come up with a winning formula.

The congressman from this district is a Democrat elected in 1982 who has often, but by no means always, voted with his national party in the House. He is Dr. Roy Rowland, the only medical doctor, he likes to point out, in the 100th Congress. He won the seat by running against the incumbent, Billy Lee Evans, who had the double disadvantage of having been fined for accepting illegal campaign contributions and loans in the 1980 campaign and, in this national

Democratic district, of having voted for the Reagan budget and tax cuts in 1981. Rowland led in the primary 48%–42% and won the runoff 58%–42%.

In the House Rowland has concentrated on health issues, serving on the subcommittee with jurisdiction over veterans' hospitals, serving on the Select Committee on Children, Youth and Families and on national commissions on infant mortality and bioethics, and co-sponsoring with Republican John Paul Hammerschmidt benefits legislation for atomic veterans (those exposed to radiation). He sponsored a bill, adopted with changes, to outlaw the drug Quaalude. His efforts to get on the Energy and Commerce Committee have so far been unsuccessful. He has been renominated and reelected twice without significant opposition.

The People: Pop. 1980: 541,723, up 10.6% 1970–80. Households (1980): 78% family, 45% with children, 61% married couples; 31.9% housing units rented; median monthly rent: $94; median house value: $27,300. Voting age pop. (1980): 372,727; 32% Black, 1% Spanish origin.

1984 Presidential Vote:

Reagan (R)	89,777	(52%)
Mondale (D)	81,998	(48%)

Rep. J. Roy Rowland (D)

Elected 1982; b. Feb. 3, 1926, Wrightsville; home, Dublin; Emory U., S. GA Col., U. of GA, Medical Col. of GA, M.D. 1952; United Methodist; married (Luella).

Career: Army, WWII; Practicing physician 1953–82; GA House of Reps. 1976–82.

Offices: 423 CHOB 20515, 202-225-6531. Also 203 Fed. Bldg., Dublin 31021, 912-275-0024; P.O. Box 6258, Macon 31208, 912-743-0150; and Fed. Bldg., Rm. 116, Waycross 31601, 912-285-8420.

Committees: *Public Works and Transportation* (18th of 32 D). Subcommittees: Aviation; Investigations and Oversight; Surface Transportation. *Veterans' Affairs* (10th of 21 D). Subcommittees: Hospitals and Health Care; Housing and Memorial Affairs. *Select Committee on Children, Youth, and Families* (11th of 18 D). Task Force: Crisis Intervention; Prevention Strategies.

Group Ratings

	ADA	ACLU	COPE	CFA	LCV	ACU	NTU	NSI	COC	CEI
1986	40	25	45	50	42	55	25	90	56	26
1985	30	—	43	42	—	67	27	—	45	—

National Journal Ratings

	1986 LIB — 1986 CONS		1985 LIB — 1985 CONS	
Economic	62%	— 35%	46%	— 53%
Social	39%	— 59%	60%	— 38%
Foreign	39%	— 61%	24%	— 66%

Key Votes

1) Lmt Cln Water Act	AGN	5) Retain Gun Cont	AGN	9) Aid Angola Reb	FOR
2) Rpl Tobac Sub	AGN	6) Contra Aid	FOR	10) Tax Reform	AGN
3) Grm-Rdmn Def Red	FOR	7) Lmt Text Imp	FOR	11) S Africa Sanc	FOR
4) Ban Polygraph	AGN	8) Limit SDI	FOR	12) Immig Reform	AGN

Election Results

1986 general	J. Roy Rowland (D)	82,254	(86%)	($150,139)
	Eddie McDowell (R)...................	12,952	(14%)	
1986 primary	J. Roy Rowland (D)	57,204	(100%)	
1984 general	J. Roy Rowland (D)	100,936	(100%)	($134,916)

Campaign Contributions and Expenditures

1985-86		Direct Cont. 1985-86		PACS Breakdown 1985-86			
Receipts	$233,269	Indiv.	$126,903	Corp.	$47,498	T/M/H	$30,950
Expend.	$150,139	Party	$169	Labor	$7,250	Agr.	$2,500
Unspent	$142,306	PACS	$96,573	Ideo.	$5,025	CWOS	$3,350

NINTH DISTRICT

The 9th Congressional District of Georgia is the northeastern part of the state, where the rolling hills of the Piedmont meet the southernmost extension of the Appalachian chain. This was a backwater in the antebellum period, a part of the South never covered by large plantations and with very few slaves; it continues to have a low black percentage today. Indeed, some of the mountain counties here resisted secession in 1861 and supported the Union; for decades afterwards they regularly returned Republican majorities in heavily Democratic Georgia. Two waves of prosperity have swept over the 9th District in the last 40 years. The first was the growth of the textile industry along what is now Interstate 85, the highway which runs from Petersburg, Virginia, to Montgomery, Alabama, and along the way is within a few miles of perhaps half the textile producing capacity in the United States. There are no big textile cities in this part of Georgia; mills are strung out along the Interstate and main highways, within an hour's driving distance of the large supply of low-wage labor.

The second wave of prosperity comes from the outward expansion of metropolitan Atlanta, along the interstates and into the mountain country. The most striking example is in Gwinnett County, just outside Atlanta, where the population doubled in the 1970s and may have doubled again in the 1980s. The newcomers are young, affluent but not rich, almost all white and in many cases culturally traditional; they vote heavily Republican and in 1984 effected a political revolution by electing Republicans to most of the county offices long held by an old Democratic courthouse crowd. Even the mountain counties showed rates of increase not recorded since they were first settled. The reason: they have become the year-round home for retirees from Atlanta and the North or for people who have decided to forgo the high dollar incomes of the metropolitan area for the less obvious attractions of the mountains; the cool weather has also brought many summer home owners, including Jimmy and Rosalynn Carter. There is another, less pleasant factor: there are very few blacks in these hills. That was not always so; in Forsyth and Dawson Counties blacks were driven out in 1912 after a white woman was raped and a black accused of the crime lynched, and as late as 1981 a black Atlanta fireman was shot while picnicking in Forsyth; in January 1987 some 2,000 people came to Forsyth County to march in protest of the heritage of a county that has more than doubled in population since 1970, but still has no blacks.

The Dixie Democrats of the Piedmont and the foothills have been losing political ground to the remnants of the mountain Republicans in the 9th and the new Republicans of the expanding Atlanta area. The district as a whole still prefers Democrats in local and state contests, but it gave Republican Senator Mack Mattingly a solid margin in his losing race for reelection in 1986—and he carried it even outside of Gwinnett. Congressional elections in this district have mostly been uncontested, and the district has been represented for 30 years by congressmen closely attuned to the textile industry. One was Phil Landrum, whose name remains attached to the Landrum-Griffin Act of 1959, the last major piece of labor law Congress passed. The other is Ed Jenkins, the current congressman, who was elected when Landrum retired in 1976.

Jenkins, like Landrum, sits on the House Ways and Means Committee, and is regarded there as a leading champion of the textile industry. But he is a more important legislator than that, and his concerns are not just parochial, and if he has the appearance of a simple country lawyer he has, like so many other country lawyers, talents and shrewdness enough to do quite well, thank you, among the city slickers. His most visible legislative effort was the textile bill passed by both houses and, as expected, vetoed by President Reagan as protectionist. The bill was attacked as a cynical effort by Democrats to raise an issue, but it was also an attempt to show low-wage textile-producing countries the American determination to assert its interests. Jenkins is not in any way a naive man, and knows that on trade issues he is fighting a long-range, many-fronted battle, and he probably understands that protectionist measures, while they may protect jobs and investment in the short run give a long-run incentive to economic inefficiency. It will be interesting to see what role Jenkins plays on trade bills in the House. In 1986 he was cut out of some action when Chairman Dan Rostenkowski left him off Ways and Means's conferees on the tax bill; Jenkins, usually a Rostenkowski ally, will be working for a major role on the trade bill.

Jenkins has another, even more important role in the House, though an informal one: he is one of the chief links between northern and southern Democrats. He has always made it a point to maintain cordial relationships with his northern Democratic colleagues, whatever their disagreements on issues, and to work with them to achieve compromise; and on occasion he has voted with them on issues not popular in his or other southern constituencies. He is affable, reliable, and endowed with sensitive political antennae. His seat on the Budget Committee, which he obtained in 1985, is less an avenue to power for him than a recognition that he is one of the critical members of the House. Similarly his seat on the House Ethics Committee. His seat on the special committee investigating the Iran-Contra scandal is further evidence of the high regard he enjoys from Democratic leaders and rank-and-file: he is the only member whose choice was not suggested by his committee chairmanship or special experience in the field.

Jenkins had to fight hard to win the district in 1976, and he even had a significant primary in 1978. His major problem then was Gwinnett County, and his seat has been made safer by the removal of part of it from the 9th. In personal style and background, he seems much more at home among the older parts of the 9th than in what amounts to expanding metropolitan Atlanta. In 1984, against a weak Republican opponent, he carried most parts of the district easily, and won 67% of the vote, but lost the 9th District's portion of Gwinnett County. He was opposed only by a follower of Lyndon LaRouche in 1986, and can expect no real problems in the future, but he will probably be watching the redistricting process closely after the 1990 Census, as some of metropolitan Atlanta's most Republican voters move even farther out into hitherto Democratic territory.

The People: Pop. 1980: 551,782, up 35.1% 1970–80. Households (1980): 82% family, 47% with children, 71% married couples; 23.2% housing units rented; median monthly rent: $122; median house value: $36,400. Voting age pop. (1980): 384,588; 5% Black, 1% Spanish origin.

1984 Presidential Vote: Reagan (R) 119,570   (69%)
                               Mondale (D) 52,894   (31%)

Rep. Ed Jenkins (D)

Elected 1976; b. Jan. 4, 1933, Young Harris; home, Jasper; Young Harris Col., A.A. 1951, U. of GA, LL.B. 1959; Baptist; married (Jo).

Career: Coast Guard, 1952–55; A.A. to U.S. Rep. Phil Landrum, 1959–62; Asst. U.S. Atty., N. Dist. of GA., 1962–64; Practicing atty., 1965–76.

Offices: 203 CHOB 20515, 202-225-5211. Also P.O. Box 70, Jasper 30143, 404-692-2022; P.O. Box 1015, Gainesville 30503, 404-536-2531; and 307 Selvidge St., Dalton 30720, 404-226-5320.

Committees: *Budget* (11th of 21 D). Task Forces: Community and Natural Resources; State and Local Government. *Ways and Means* (8th of 23 D). Subcommittee: Trade.

Group Ratings

	ADA	ACLU	COPE	CFA	LCV	ACU	NTU	NSI	COC	CEI
1986	35	15	37	50	47	58	32	88	53	27
1985	25	—	37	42	—	55	37	—	50	—

National Journal Ratings

	1986 LIB — 1986 CONS			1985 LIB — 1985 CONS		
Economic	48%	—	52%	48%	—	50%
Social	30%	—	69%	51%	—	48%
Foreign	40%	—	60%	44%	—	56%

Key Votes

1) Lmt Cln Water Act	FOR	5) Retain Gun Cont	AGN	9) Aid Angola Reb	FOR
2) Rpl Tobac Sub	AGN	6) Contra Aid	FOR	10) Tax Reform	FOR
3) Grm-Rdmn Def Red	FOR	7) Lmt Text Imp	FOR	11) S Africa Sanc	FOR
4) Ban Polygraph	AGN	8) Limit SDI	—	12) Immig Reform	AGN

Election Results

1986 general	Ed Jenkins (D)	84,303	(100%)	($144,641)
1986 primary	Ed Jenkins (D)	70,484	(88%)	
	James K. Olson (D)	9,256	(12%)	
1984 general	Ed Jenkins (D)	109,422	(67%)	($116,485)
	Frank H. Cofer, Jr. (R)	52,731	(33%)	($58,230)

Campaign Contributions and Expenditures

1985-86		Direct Cont. 1985-86		PACS Breakdown 1985-86			
Receipts	$330,678	Indiv.	$66,025	Corp.	$103,700	T/M/H	$83,070
Expend.	$144,641	PACS	$225,670	Labor	$13,050	Agr.	$2,000
Unspent	$416,351			Ideo.	$18,750	CWOS	$5,100

TENTH DISTRICT

A slice of north Georgia, from the outskirts of Atlanta to the city of Augusta, forms the 10th Congressional District of Georgia. It is anchored by three urban areas. The first is around Augusta, the home of the Masters Golf Tournament, which no longer bars non-white players; Augusta, with a large black population, is very much a part of the Deep South. In the middle of the district is Athens, the home of the University of Georgia, famous for its football team and also as the retirement home of one-time Secretary of State and Georgia native Dean Rusk. At the western end of the district, added in the 1982 redistricting, is part of Gwinnett County, which is very much a part of the Atlanta metropolitan area. In the 1960s and 1970s, Augusta and Athens, with their black and university populations, were the liberal anchor of this area, with segregationist voting patterns in the smaller counties. Now the balance is different. The cutting edge of politics here is in the fast-growing areas at the edge of metropolitan areas, not only Gwinnett County, but Columbia County outside Augusta, where the young and somewhat affluent voters have proved to be heavily Republican; in the 1986 Senate race, for example, Columbia was first and Gwinnett third in percentage for Republican Mack Mattingly among Georgia's 159 counties. The opposite pole in the 10th District is in the black precincts in Augusta and in the heavily black and not much developed rural counties in between, all of which vote heavily Democratic.

The congressman from the 10th, Doug Barnard, was first elected in 1976 and, like his predecessor in the House, is a banker by trade; although why a place like this should favor bankers is unclear. In the politics of the early 1970s Barnard was counted a moderate, a one-time aide to Governor Carl Sanders, Jimmy Carter's opponent in the 1970 gubernatorial runoff, and victor himself in 1976 over a former aide to Governor Lester Maddox.

In the House, however, he is known primarily as a banker. He is a member of the House Banking Committee, and of all its leading Democrats probably the most sympathetic to banks, and he also heads a Government Operations subcommittee with jurisdiction over the Federal Reserve, FDIC, and Comptroller of the Currency—all three bank regulatory agenices. It should be added that the committee's work is complex: the banking and financial businesses are changing rapidly, and Congress has been caught in a stalemate between former Senate Banking Chairman Jake Garn's desire to deregulate and House Chairman Fernand St Germain's reluctance to go so far. Barnard is on the side of deregulation generally; he was the lead sponsor, for example, of the amendment to preserve banks' rights to stay in what amounts to the brokerage business—a matter of huge economic value to parties concerned, and on which he opposed not only committee Chairman Fernand St Germain but the ranking Republican, Chalmers Wylie (whose home town has a bank that is part of Merrill Lynch's money market account package). But Barnard approaches the issues independently and not as a tool of any lobby. He is not yet one of the most senior Democrats on Banking, but amid St Germain's ethics and electoral troubles he has been mentioned as a possible chairman; the consensus is that he is too conservative and considered too pro-bank to be elected by the Democratic Caucus and is in any case quite far down the seniority ladder.

On economic issues he is often the most conservative Democrat in the Georgia delegation (he supported the Reagan budget and tax cuts), and by no means is he liberal on cultural or foreign issues. He has been renominated and reelected since 1976 without serious opposition. If, as has been rumored, he retires in 1988, one candidate to succeed him might be John Russell, the distant relative of Richard Russell who ran for the Senate in 1986.

The People: Pop. 1980: 550,268, up 32.1% 1970–80. Households (1980): 76% family, 45% with children, 62% married couples; 34.1% housing units rented; median monthly rent: $153; median house value: $39,200. Voting age pop. (1980): 388,067; 23% Black, 1% Spanish origin, 1% Asian origin.

1984 Presidential Vote: Reagan (R) 116,188   (65%)
Mondale (D) 61,907   (35%)

Rep. Doug Barnard, Jr. (D)

Elected 1976; b. Mar. 20, 1922, Augusta; home, Augusta; Augusta Col., Mercer U., B.A. 1942, LL.B. 1948; Baptist; married (Naomi).

Career: Army, WWII; Banker, GA Railroad Bank and Trust, 1948–49, 1950–62, 1966–76; Fed. Reserve Bank of Atlanta, 1949–50; Exec. Secy. to the Gov. of GA, 1963–66.

Offices: 2227 RHOB, 202-225-4101. Also Stephens Fed. Bldg., Rm. 128, Athens 30601, 404-546-2194; 407 Telfair St., Augusta 30903, 404-724-0739.

Committees: *Banking, Finance and Urban Affairs* (10th of 31 D). Subcommittees: Domestic Monetary Policy; Economic Stabilization; Financial Institutions Supervision, Regulation and Insurance; General Oversight and Investigations. *Government Operations* (9th of 24 D). Subcommittee: Commerce, Consumer, and Monetary Affairs (Chairman).

Group Ratings

	ADA	ACLU	COPE	CFA	LCV	ACU	NTU	NSI	COC	CEI
1986	25	15	23	33	33	72	30	90	79	34
1985	15	—	23	50	—	71	38	—	50	—

National Journal Ratings

	1986 LIB — 1986 CONS	1985 LIB — 1985 CONS
Economic	41% — 58%	40% — 59%
Social	33% — 66%	44% — 56%
Foreign	33% — 67%	24% — 66%

Key Votes

1) Lmt Cln Water Act	FOR	5) Retain Gun Cont	AGN	9) Aid Angola Reb	FOR
2) Rpl Tobac Sub	AGN	6) Contra Aid	FOR	10) Tax Reform	FOR
3) Grm-Rdmn Def Red	FOR	7) Lmt Text Imp	FOR	11) S Africa Sanc	FOR
4) Ban Polygraph	AGN	8) Limit SDI	AGN	12) Immig Reform	AGN

Election Results

1986 general	Doug Barnard, Jr. (D)	79,548	(67%)	($210,274)
	Jim Hill (R)	38,714	(33%)	($117,315)
1986 primary	Doug Barnard, Jr. (D)	50,350	(100%)	
1984 general	Doug Barnard, Jr. (D)	116,364	(100%)	($73,527)

Campaign Contributions and Expenditures

1985-86		Direct Cont. 1985-86		PACS Breakdown 1985-86			
Receipts	$346,980	Indiv.	$98,777	Corp.	$91,725	T/M/H	$60,790
Expend.	$210,274	PACS	$170,465	Labor	$4,350	Agr.	$2,500
Unspent	$427,257			Ideo.	$7,500	CWOS	$3,600

HAWAII

Hawaii is a piece of America in the Pacific Ocean, the geographical center of the world region with the most explosive economic growth, the Pacific Rim. Of all the tropical islands acquired by western powers in the late 19th century, Hawaii is the only one which has become an integral part of the nation that acquired it. Yet its position in the Pacific gives it a special international significance, as was apparent in February 1986 when Governor George Ariyoshi at Hickam Air Force Base welcomed Ferdinand and Imelda Marcos after their flight acorss the ocean; they were still living in the land of Aloha more than a year later. That Hawaii would become America's 50th state was far from obvious in the 1890s, when the last Hawaiian monarch, Queen Liliuokalani, was ousted from power and the Islands were annexed by the United States. Yet Hawaii's ties with the United States dated back to the 1820s, when American missionary families landed in the islands to proselytize and incidentally to trade: as the saying goes, they came to do good and ended up doing well.

They made money from the incredibly rich and surprisingly extensive farmland of these volcanic islands. Well before annexation Hawaii was a major producer of sugar and later of pineapple for the American market. The missionary families built the big trading companies— the Big Five—that supplied capital and dominated shipping and commerce. But there were never enough native Hawaiians—particularly after their numbers were reduced by disease—to provide the hard labor these operations needed. So contract labor was imported. People were brought in systematically, first from China, then later from Japan, the Philippines, Korea, Spain, and Portugal. Native Hawaiians were outnumbered as early as the turn of the century (although their percentage of the Islands' population is increasing today because of their high birth rate). Like other Pacific islands, Hawaii developed its own pidgin, called da kine, based on English, with Japanese, Chinese, Portuguese, and Filipino influences. Unlike many other places on the Pacific Rim, from Malaya to pre-1945 California, Hawaii developed a tradition of tolerance (one meaning of the word aloha)—a tradition that delayed Hawaii's admission into the Union for some years; southern Democrats objected so much that Hawaii voted Republican for many years.

Yet the traditions of each group remain evident. The Japanese, the largest single migrant group after whites (who are sometimes called haoles), are by most measures the most successful, doing well in the professions and in organizations such as unions, government, and the Democratic Party. But they have not developed as many big entrepreneurs and businessmen as the Chinese community has. Whites still tend to have the highest incomes, many having come to Hawaii after they have been successful on the Mainland. Filipinos are more likely to be manual laborers. Native Hawaiians, from a culture that lived easily and well off a bounteous physical environment, also tend toward the lower end of the income scale. Hawaii's native and royal past have given it some unusual traditions, including large landholdings; homeowners typically hold their land on long-term (100 years or so) leases, though a state law, upheld by the U.S. Supreme Court in 1984, allows some to buy it outright. Much land is still held by estates, most notably the Bishop Estate (Mrs. Bishop was the last surviving member of the Hawaiian royal family) which owns about 10% of the state's land. Its five trustees, appointed by the state Supreme Court for life at $250,000 a year, are supposed to spend all the Estate's huge income on educating native Hawaiians; control of the Bishop Estate was finally cinched, after many years of waiting, by George Ariyoshi's allies in the 1980s. Land development generally has been closely controlled by the state—wisely to protect the environment, say some; foolishly to choke off economic growth with red tape, say others.

Hawaii has a standard of living today that matches the Mainland states. But there are reasons

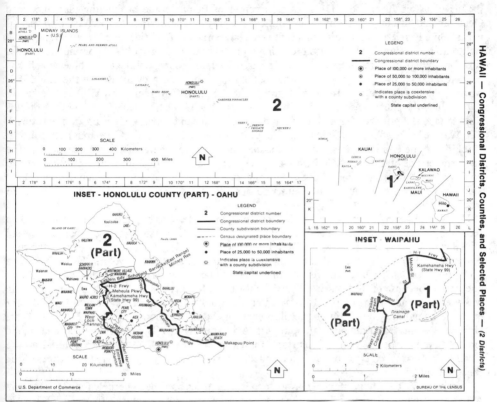

to worry about its economy. Even after three decades of explosive growth, Hawaii still has only one million people, not a big enough market to support its own industries, and none of its major industries is on solid footing. More than 5 million tourists in 1986—many from Japan and East Asia as well as the Mainland—account for one-third of Hawaii's jobs, but most are low-wage and menial. And the tourism business is subject to sudden contractions, when oil prices go up or recession strikes either side of the Pacific Rim. The military has been important since the Navy built fortifications and a huge drydock at Pearl Harbor in 1919; Hawaii is the center of American military power in the Pacific, and the Japanese attack on Pearl Harbor in 1941 struck not a peripheral outpost but the heart of the U.S. Navy, with Air Force and Army posts here as well. The 58,000 military personnel stationed in Hawaii bring in money. But to a considerable extent live separate and apart from most Hawaiians, and the big military buildup of the 1980s seems over. Then there is sugar, once the mainstay of the Hawaiian economy, but hard-stricken when quotas on sugar imports were removed between 1974 and 1981. Sugar plantations employed 56,000 Hawaiians in the 1920s and perhaps 25,000 in 1986, with the number falling. Even with quotas, the position of the industry is precarious: taxpayers may get tired of paying 20 cents a pound for a commodity which trades at a nickel on the world market. The docks, for years big employers, have been mostly containerized. The International Longshoremen's and Warehouseman's Union (ILWU) has long represented the sugar and dock workers and negotiated high wages for them, but its membership is down and its political clout vastly reduced.

One plausible future for Hawaii is as a center of Pacific trade, a meeting place between Occident and Orient: it has American political stability and is sensitive to East Asian ways, and it has a highly skilled labor force and first-rate transportation facilities. But it may not have the right habits of mind. Hawaii is used to being a producer of raw agricultural commodities and a site for tourism and military facilities; it has a well-developed political machine which has concentrated on propping up wages and modulating economic growth. But in the late 1980s wages are sagging and new sources of growth are needed. Governor John Waihee, elected in 1986, called the politicians who ran Hawaii since statehood "the first wave," and said, "Now it is time to take the gift they have given us and catch the second wave. Let us turn to the future." Yet Waihee is in effect the heir of the longest-entrenched and one of the toughest political machines in the United States. There are some who see echoes here, of the political style found on the other side of the East Asia Rim—tough, unsentimental, with a ruling group determined to hold power at almost any cost. That's an exaggeration: Hawaii's devotion to democracy and its aloha spirit are not in doubt. But there's no denying there was some rough play in the 1986 elections here.

Hawaii's Democratic machine had its beginning in the territorial politics of the 1950s, when returning World War II veterans like Daniel Inouye, Spark Matsunaga, and George Ariyoshi joined with former Mainlanders like Oren Long and John Burns, allied themselves with the then powerful ILWU, and cemented the allegiance of Japanese-American voters. For a few years after statehood, in 1959, Hawaii tended to vote Republican. Burns was elected governor in 1962 and retired because of illness in 1974; Ariyoshi won in 1974, 1978, and 1982, and retired as he was ineligible for a fourth term. In time Inouye, always interested in local issues (in 1986, for example, he put into the continuing resolution an amendment to build Interstate H-3 from Pearl Harbor over the Oahu mountains), split with Ariyoshi; the ILWU's clout declined and public employee unions became more important; increasingly, the machine became centered on the governor's office and the patronage it controlled, from every state judgeship to the trustees of the Bishop Estate.

Governor. With such big stakes, Hawaii's political battles have been fiercely fought. For years Ariyoshi's greatest rival was Frank Fasi, longtime mayor of Honolulu. Ariyoshi beat Fasi in primaries in 1974 (36%–31%) and 1978 (51%–49%) and in the 1982 general when Fasi ran as an Independent (45%–29%, with 26% for Republican Andy Anderson). Fasi was accused of bribery (the case was dropped), beaten in the 1980 mayoral primary by Ariyoshi protégée Eileen Anderson, and then, running as a Republican, beat her in 1984. In 1986 Fasi was backing his erstwhile Republican opponent, Andy Anderson, while the Ariyoshi forces, sustained in the past by big margins among Japanese-Americans, backed Lieutenant Governor John Waihee, a native Hawaiian, and, as his ticket-mate, Benjamin Cayetano, of Filipino extraction. The favorite in the September 20 primary—one of the nation's latest—was Honolulu Representative Cecil Heftel, a broadcasting millionaire free of ties to either City Hall or the Iolani Palace (the governor's residence). But a few days before the election, public employee and other unions and Fasi separately ran ad campaigns against Heftel, and someone—who?—released what purported to be a report of what an unidentified witness told state narcotics investigators suggesting that Heftel was a homosexual and had AIDS. Waihee claimed he had nothing to do with the "Heftel smear," as it quickly became known, but he was obviously helped, and he beat Heftel 46%–36%, with 16% for Patsy Mink. In the general election campaign Waihee was at pains to say he would name his own top appointees and was not part of an Ariyoshi machine. Waihee won a decisive but not impressive victory, and Hawaii had its first native Hawaiian governor. Unanswered questions in early 1987: Does a Waihee administration mean a continuation of America's longest-lived political machine? Will Waihee lead Hawaii to a stronger, more self-sufficient economy?

Senators. Daniel Inouye is now Hawaii's senior elected official, the only person who has held major statewide office throughout the three decades since statehood. Probably the most popular politician in Hawaii, he is routinely elected with huge margins. He has also achieved national prominence, as keynoter at the Democratic National Convention in 1968, as a dignified, low-key member of the Senate Watergate committee in 1973, and as chairman of the special Senate committee investigating the Iran-contra scandal in 1987. Inouye is one of those Japanese-Americans who served in the all-Nisei (segregated) 100th Battalion and 442d Regimental Combat Team, the most decorated and perhaps the most celebrated American military units in World War II. The fighting skill and courage of these Nisei, along with their mainland counterparts who volunteered out of the infamous Japanese-American internment camps set up by Franklin Roosevelt, produced acceptance of Japanese-Americans as part of the nation's mainstream. Also contributing here, but less heralded and publicized, were Japanese-American personnel out of the Military Intelligence Schools who very early in the Pacific war made it possible for MacArthur and Nimitz "to read Tojo's mail." Yet the U.S. Navy accepted no Japanese-Americans during World War II, and until 1952 Japanese immigrants to both Hawaii and the mainland were denied naturalization rights and American citizenship on the grounds they were "unassimilable."

Inouye owes much of his success to his reputation as a party loyalist and for being well prepared and intellectually rigorous. He supported Lyndon Johnson's Vietnam war policy steadfastly when it was most under attack in 1968 and in 1981 defended Senator Harrison Williams against expulsion for his part in Abscam; colleagues who disagreed with Inouye's positions still admire his determination to stick by his commitments and his colleagues. He has been known for years as a strong and steadfast believer in policies historically associated with Democratic presidents: in generous spending at home and a strong defense abroad. Yet beginning in 1983 he has opposed Reagan Administration policy in Central America, including military aid to El Salvador and aid to the Nicaraguan contras. He works hard at putting together the foreign aid bill, and is one of Israel's staunchest backers in the Senate (a Methodist, he says he once considered converting to Judaism). He is an important supporter also of federal maritime subsidy programs and is generally not eager to deregulate industries. Inouye believes instead in what the history of Hawaii teaches—the need for centralized control, planning, and funding. On spending issues, foreign and domestic, Inouye is one senator who consistently favors higher rather than lower figures.

On the Senate Watergate committee, Inouye was steely, self-contained, well prepared, and relentless in running down the details of the scandal. If he was partisan, as some Republicans thought, he was careful to stick to the facts and the law and never to engage in dramatics. He can be expected to proceed similarly in the Iran-Contra committee: cautiously but relentlessly, coolly and carefully.

Inouye's party loyalty and intellectual gifts have led Democrats to make him secretary of the Democratic Conference—the number three position in the leadership—and, long ago, gave him important committee assignments: Appropriations and Commerce. He is also widely thought to be in line to succeed Robert Byrd as Senate majority leader after the 1988 elections. Amid discontent with Byrd, there were rumors that Inouye might challenge him after first the 1984 and then the 1986 elections. Characteristically he didn't, but is said to have an understanding that his turn is next; if he is loyal publicly, it would not be out of character for him to drive a hard bargain behind the scenes. His interest in the leadership may be the greater because he is not in line to chair a major committee, standing behind John Stennis, Byrd, and William Proxmire on Appropriations and Ernest Hollings on Commerce. What kind of leader would he be? Well-organized and attentive to details, as Byrd is, and probably more concerned about how the Senate works internally than how Senate Democrats look to the country. Yet he must be aware that in a television age leaders give a party much of its images.

Hawaii's other senator, Spark Matsunaga, is less senior and less well known, although he is older than Inouye. He is a man of unusual interests. He writes haiku when inspiration strikes. His leading issues are peace and space. After 22 years of lobbying he got Congress to set up a U.S. Peace Institute. He has pushed a joint U.S.-Soviet exploration of Mars and he successfully proposed making Hawaii a center for the International Space Year of 1992. Matsunaga served in the House for 14 years, and then won his Senate seat in a 1976 primary fight with his House colleague Patsy Mink. Like Inouye, he is a party loyalist and, as deputy whip, a member of the Democratic leadership. In the House he sat on the Rules Committee, in the Senate on Finance though he was not a leader on tax reform on 1986, and Labor and Human Resources. Rating groups list him as one of the most liberal members of the Senate, but he is anything but a boat-rocker. Now Chairman of the Trade Subcommittee, he is basically a free trader and one who argues that a strong dollar and the cultural insensitivity of some U.S. exporters, and not simply Japanese non-tariff barriers, have exacerbated this country's trade deficit with Japan. At the same time, however, he is worried about protecting Hawaii's pineapple, macadamia nut and sugar industries. Finance Chairman Lloyd Bentsen, not Matsunaga, is likely to shepherd through any Senate trade bill.

In Washington, Matsunaga can be seen almost every day entertaining constituents at the large round table in the center of the Senate members' dining room; it is said that he has taken half of Hawaii to lunch, and he is miffed if the table is taken by someone else. He seems solidly popular at home. Reelected without serious opposition in 1982, he seems to be in excellent physical and political shape to win his third term in 1988 though he is past 70.

Both Matsunaga and Inouye are also strongly supporting the so-called "redress movement" among mainland Japanese-Americans. Legislation introduced calls for roughly $1.5 billion to be distributed through a trust fund, in parcels of $20,000, to each survivor of the World War II internment camps. Conventional Washington opinion has it that since the Treasury cannot afford the bill, Congress and the Reagan Administration will spurn it. Supporters, including some conservatives, say that, as a matter of principle, damages are in order whenever a specific federal administrative action grossly violates fundamental constitutional guarantees, as was surely the case here: expropriation and mass incarceration of 120,000 people by racial edict issued into more hysteria and longstanding envy and animosity.

Congressmen. Hawaii has two congressional districts: the 1st includes Honolulu within its old city limits (city elections now cover all of Oahu) and extends westward to Pearl Harbor; the 2d includes the rest of Oahu and the Neighbor Islands.

Of Honolulu, the tourist usually only sees the airport and adjacent Hickam Air Force Base, the Arizona monument in the harbor, and Waikiki, with its 40-story hotels rising within a few feet of one another, its restaurants and souvenir shops. But few voters live in any of these places. The neighborhoods around Honolulu's downtown and the university campus are ethnically diverse and usually Democratic; they are not slums, but they are low income. To the west, around the harbor, there are many military families; these modest neighborhoods may vote for Democrats but are sometimes attracted to Republicans. To the east, past Waikiki, around Diamond Head and out to the Kahala and Koko Head beach areas, is higher income territory; these places delivered the state's largest Reagan majorities in 1980 and 1984, and make the 1st the more Republican of Hawaii's two districts.

It is also the first Hawaii district to elect a Republican to the House, Representative Pat Saiki. For nearly 10 years it was represented by Cecil Heftel, who resigned during his gubernatorial campaign. The special election, called on the same day as the primary, was a first-past-the-post contest, won narrowly (by less than 1,000 votes) by state Senator Neil Abercrombie. But the Democratic primary for the full term was won by Ariyoshi aide Mufi Hannemann. They were both colorful candidates. Abercrombie often wears his 1960s-style long hair in a pony tail and drives an old taxicab; he was hurt by charges that he used marijuana, which were based on flimsy evidence (a 16-year-old article) and were unsupported (he was a probation officer and had a medical condition that precluded any drug-taking). Hannemann is a 6'7" Mormon native of Samoa and Harvard graduate who served as a White House fellow on George Bush's staff. The primary, with its "Heftel smear" and hardball tactics, left Abercrombie bitter and hurt Hannemann; Abercrombie continued to attack his opponent even after he told others he'd cool down, and may run again in 1988.

Saiki in the meantime was the perfect Republican candidate: experienced, of Asian descent competent and unconnected with political machines, and she won handily. Can she hold onto this seat? Abercrombie may try again, and some Democrat will surely contest it. But Republican strength has been growing in Hawaii, Saiki has a seat on the Banking Committee from which she can raise plenty of money, and Saiki has a good chance to make this a safe seat—or to win statewide in some future contest.

Three-quarters of Hawaii's population lives on Oahu, and so the 2d District includes not only the Neighbor Islands but the greater part, in area, of Oahu. It includes some of the middle-class area around Pearl Harbor, with many military families, and the farmlands further out the island, between the two jagged chains of mountains that lift it out of the sea. Over the mountains to the west is the Leeward Coast, calm, sultry, and lightly populated; over the mountains to the northeast is the Windward Coast, windy as its name implies, with many prosperous and Republican subdivisions. The Neighbor Islands have distinct personalities. Hawaii, the Big Island, is large enough to boast huge cattle ranches, the active volcano of Kilauea, and Mauna Kea, the highest mountain in the world if you count from its base far under the ocean to the peak, rising in a slow, endless slant from Hilo or the Kona (western) Coast. On the north shore, with heavy rainfall and tropical foliage, are the old port of Hilo and Hawaii's macadamia nut industry; this is a blue-collar Democratic area. On the Kona Coast, where there is little rainfall and the landscape is dominated by lava flows, there are retirement condominiums and a higher-income, more Republican population. Maui in the 1980s has been the fastest-developing island, with dozens of luxury condominiums and rapidly rising real estate prices. Kauai, west of Oahu, is the least-developed and most agricultural of the main islands; parts of it have the nation's highest rainfall, and it had serious floods in 1986. Its large farm work force makes it the most Democratic of the islands.

The congressman here, since he won a 1976 primary, is Democrat Daniel Akaka. A one-time Ariyoshi aide, Akaka serves quietly on Appropriations and its Agriculture Subcommittee—bodies with practical concerns that are especially important to Hawaii. His voting record on economic and cultural issues is generally liberal, but less so on foreign policy and defense. Akaka could run for the Senate if Matsunaga retires.

Presidential politics. Hawaii was one of only six states carried by President Carter in 1980, and the only one west of Minnesota; in 1984 it went for President Reagan, but was one of Walter Mondale's best states. Two factors seem to have combined to produce these results: a strong leaning toward Democrats generally, plus a strong inclination to support presidential candidates of the party in power. These two factors explain Hawaii's vote in every presidential election, its close elections when Republicans were in power (1984, 1976, 1960), its landslide margins for incumbents of different parties (1972, 1964), and its far higher than average percentages for Democrats when they were in power (1980, 1968). The Democratic bias can be explained by the state's big-government position on economic issues and tolerance of diversity on cultural issues. The pro-incumbent bias can be explained by the fact that this is a state that takes its patriotism very seriously, in part because the patriotism of so many of its citizens was, unjustly, doubted, and because, out here in the Pacific, foreign threats seem more menacing; in the only state whose population center has come under direct foreign attack since the War of 1812, America can seem dangerously vulnerable.

The People: Est. Pop. 1986: 1,062,000; Pop. 1980: 964,691, up 10.1% 1980–86 and 25.3% 1970–80; 0.44% of U.S. total, 39th largest. 18% with 1–3 yrs. col., 20% with 4+ yrs. col.; 9.9% below poverty level. Single ancestry: 3% Portuguese, English, 2% German, 1% Irish, Italian. Households (1980): 77% family, 45% with children, 63% married couples; 48.3% housing units rented; median monthly rent: $273; median house value: $119,400. Voting age pop. (1980): 689,108; 60% Asian origin, 6% Spanish origin, 2% Black. Registered voters (1986): 419,794; no party registration.

1986 Share of Federal Tax Burden: $3,158,000,000; 0.42% of U.S. total, 40th largest.

1986 Share of Federal Expenditures

	Total		Non-Defense		Defense	
Total Expend	$46432m	(0.56%)	$2,158m	(0.36%)	$2,486m	(1.08%)
St/Lcl Grants	473m	(0.42%)	472m	(0.42%)	1m	(0.90%)
Salary/Wages	1,961m	(1.63%)	192m	(0.33%)	1,768m	(2.86%)
Pymnts to Indiv	1,517m	(0.42%)	1,364m	(0.39%)	153m	(0.86%)
Procurement	619m	(0.30%)	56m	(0.10%)	563m	(0.38%)
Research/Other	73m	(0.27%)	73m	(0.27%)	0m	(0%)

Political Lineup: Governor, John D. Waihee III (D); Lt. Gov., Benjamin Cayetano (D); Atty, Gen., Warren Price (D); Comptroller, Russell Nagata (D). State Senate, 25 (20 D and 5 R); State House of Representatives, 51 (40 D and 11 R). Senators, Daniel K. Inouye (D) and Spark M. Matsunaga (D). Representatives, 1 D and 1 R.

1984 Presidential Vote

Reagan (R) 185,050 (55%)
Mondale (D) 147,154 (44%)

1980 Presidential Vote

Carter (D) 135,879 (45%)
Reagan (R) 130,112 (43%)
Anderson (I) 32,021 (11%)

GOVERNOR

Gov. John D. Waihee III (D)

Elected 1986, term expires Dec. 1990; b. Mar. 12, 1926, Honolulu; home, Honolulu; U. of HI, U. of MI, B.A. 1949, J.D. 1952; Protestant; married (Jean).

Career: Army, WWII; Practicing atty., 1953–70; HI Territorial House of Reps., 1954–58; HI Territorial Senate, 1958–59, HI Senate, 1959–70, Major. Ldr., 1965–66, Major. Flr. Ldr., 1969–70; Lt. Gov. of HI, 1970–73; Acting Gov. of HI, 1973–74.

Office: State Capitol, Executive Chambers, Honolulu 96813, 808-548-5420.

Election Results

1986 gen.	John D. Waihee (D)	173,655	(52%)
	D.G. Anderson (R)...........	160,460	(48%)
1986 prim.	John D. Waihee (D)	105,579	(46%)
	Cecil (Cec) Heftel (D)........	83,939	(36%)
	Patsy T. Mink (D)	37,998	(16%)
1982 gen.	George R. Ariyoshi (D)	141,043	(45%)
	D.G. Anderson (R)..........	81,507	(26%)
	Frank F. Fasi (I)	89,303	(29%)

SENATORS

Sen. Daniel K. Inouye (D)

Elected 1962, seat up 1992; b. Sept. 7, 1924, Honolulu; home, Honolulu; U. of HI, B.A. 1950, Geo. Wash. U., J.D. 1952; United Methodist; married (Margaret).

Career: Army, WWII; Honolulu Asst. Prosecuting Atty., 1953–54; Practicing atty., 1954–59; HI Territorial Senate, 1958–59; U.S. House of Reps., 1959–62.

Offices: 722 HSOB 20510, 202-224-3934. Also Prince Kuhio Fed. Bldg., Rm.7325, Honolulu 96850, 808-541-2542.

Committees: *Appropriations* (4th of 16 D). Subcommittees: Commerce, Justice, State, and Judiciary; Defense; Foreign Operations (Chairman); Labor, Health and Human Services, Education; Military Construction. *Commerce, Science, and Transportation* (2nd of 8 D). Subcommittees: Aviation; Communications (Chairman); Merchant Marine. *Rules and Administration* (4th of 9 D). *Select Committee on Indian Affairs* (Chairman of 5 D).

Group Ratings

	ADA	ACLU	COPE	CFA	LCV	ACU	NTU	NSI	COC	CEI
1986	90	100	89	53	38	6	34	10	29	27
1985	95	—	89	73	—	5	19	—	24	—

National Journal Ratings

	1986 LIB — 1986 CONS		1985 LIB — 1985 CONS	
Economic	94%	— 0%	95%	— 0%
Social	70%	— 29%	83%	— 16%
Foreign	75%	— 0%	88%	— 0%

Key Votes

1) Ease Gun Cont	AGN	5) Grm-Rdmn Def Red	—	9) Rehnquist Nom	AGN
2) Immig Reform	AGN	6) Contra Aid	AGN	10) Tax Reform	AGN
3) Lmt Text Imp	AGN	7) SDI Funding	AGN	11) Drug Death Pen	FOR
4) Aid Tobac Ind	FOR	8) Lmt PAC Contrib	FOR	12) S Africa Sanc	FOR

Election Results

1986 general	Daniel K. Inouye (D)	241,887	(74%)	($1,039,418)
	Frank Hutchinson (R)	86,910	(26%)	($31,843)
1986 primary	Daniel K. Inouye (D)	191,676	(100%)	
1980 general	Daniel K. Inouye (D)	224,485	(78%)	($480,113)
	Cooper Brown (R)	53,068	(18%)	($14,382)

Campaign Contributions and Expenditures

1985-86		Direct Cont. 1985-86		PACS Breakdown 1985-86			
Receipts	$1,173,721	Indiv.	$484,097	Corp.	$205,300	T/M/H	$143,022
Expend.	$1,039,418	Party	$17,500	Labor	$126,385	Agr.	$8,000
Unspent	$598,388	PACS	$573,277	Ideo.	$81,856	CWOS	$8,714

Sen. Spark M. Matsunaga (D)

Elected 1976, seat up 1988; b. Oct. 8, 1916, Kukuiula, Kauai; home, Honolulu; U. of HI, Ed.B. 1941, Harvard U., J.D. 1951; Episcopalian; married (Helene).

Career: Pub. sch. teacher, 1941; Army, WWII; Vet. Counselor, Surplus Prop. Ofc., U.S. Dept. of Interior, 1945–47; Chf., Priority Claimant's Div., War Assets Admin., 1947–48; Asst. Pub. Prosecutor, City and Cnty. of Honolulu, 1952–54; Practicing atty., 1954–63; HI Territorial House of Reps., 1954–59, Major. Ldr., 1959; U.S. House of Reps., 1962–76.

Offices: 109 HSOB 20510, 202-224-6361. Also 3104 Prince Kuhio Bldg., Honolulu 96850, 808-541-2534.

Committees: *Finance* (2nd of 11 D). Subcommittees: Energy and Agricultural Taxation; International Trade (Chairman); Taxation and Debt Management. *Labor and Human Resources* (4th of 9 D). Subcommittees: Aging (Chairman); Education, Arts, and Humanities; Labor. *Veterans' Affairs* (2d of 6 D). *Joint Committee on Taxation.*

Group Ratings

	ADA	ACLU	COPE	CFA	LCV	ACU	NTU	NSI	COC	CEI
1986	85	92	84	53	63	13	31	10	35	29
1985	95	—	85	80	—	4	21	—	29	—

National Journal Ratings

	1986 LIB — 1986 CONS		1985 LIB — 1985 CONS	
Economic	73% —	22%	84% —	14%
Social	74% —	24%	85% —	12%
Foreign	75% —	0%	67% —	0%

Key Votes

1) Ease Gun Cont	AGN	5) Grm-Rdmn Def Red	AGN	9) Rehnquist Nom	AGN
2) Immig Reform	FOR	6) Contra Aid	AGN	10) Tax Reform	FOR
3) Lmt Text Imp	AGN	7) SDI Funding	AGN	11) Drug Death Pen	FOR
4) Aid Tobac Ind	FOR	8) Lmt PAC Contrib	FOR	12) S Africa Sanc	FOR

Election Results

1982 general	Spark M. Matsunaga (D)	245,386	(80%)	($655,713)
	Clarence J. Brown (R)	52,071	(17%)	
	E. Bernier-Nachtwey (I)................	8,953	(3%)	
1982 primary	Spark M. Matsunaga (D)	187,708	(100%)	
1976 general	Spark M. Matsunaga (D)	162,305	(54%)	($435,130)
	William Quinn (R)	122,724	(41%)	($415,138)
	Tony Hodges (People's Party)...........	14,223	(5%)	

Campaign Contributions and Expenditures

1979-82		Direct Cont. 1979-82			PACS Breakdown			
Receipts	$969,999	Indiv.	$561,758	Agr	$9,525	Ideo	$16,300
Expend.	$655,713	Party	$17,500	Bus	$158,460	Lbr	$63,090
Unspent	$338,524	PACS	$289,770	Hlth	$28,800	Prof	$12,475

FIRST DISTRICT

The People: Pop. 1980: 482,321, up 16.0% 1970–80. Households (1980): 72% family, 39% with children, 59% married couples; 52.1% housing units rented; median monthly rent: $277; median house value: $139,800. Voting age pop. (1980): 362,478; 64% Asian origin, 5% Spanish origin, 1% Black.

1984 Presidential Vote:

Reagan (R) 112,138	(55%)
Mondale (D) 90,731	(44%)

Rep. Patricia Saiki (R)

Elected 1986; b. May 28, 1930, Hilo; home, Honolulu; U. of HI, B.S. 1952; Episcopalian; married (Stanley).

Career: School teacher, 1952–64; HI House of Reps., 1968–74; HI Senate, 1097–82; Chmn., HI Repub. Party, 1983–85.

Offices: 1407 LHOB 20515, 202-225-2726. Also 300 Ala Moana Blvd., Rm. 4104, Honolulu 96850, 808-546-8997.

Committees: *Banking, Finance and Urban Affairs* (19th of 20 R). Subcommittees: Economic Stabilization; Housing and Community Development; International Development Institutions and Finance; International Finance, Trade and Monetary Policy. *Merchant Marine* (15th of 17 R). Subcommittees: Coast Guard and Navigation; Fisheries and Wildlife Conservation and the Environment; Panama Canal and Outer Continental Shelf. *Select Committee on Aging* (26th of 26 R). Subcommittees: Housing and Consumer Interest; Human Services.

Group Ratings and Key Votes: Newly Elected

Election Results

1986 general	Patricia Saiki (R)	99,683	(60%)	($536,551)
	Mufi Hannemann (D)	63,061	(37%)	($500,716)
1986 primary	Patricia Saiki (R)	17,435	(100%)	
1986 special	Neil Abercrombie (D).	42,031	(30%)	
	Patricia Saiki (R)	41,067	(29%)	
	Mufi Hannemann (D)	39,800	(28%)	
	Steve Cobb (D)	16,721	(12%)	
1984 general	Cecil (Cec) Heftel (D)	114,884	(83%)	($260,014)
	Will Beard (R)	20,608	(15%)	($7,313)

Campaign Contributions and Expenditures

1985-86		Direct Cont. 1985-86			PACS Breakdown 1985-84			
Receipts	$545,260	Indiv.	$352,657	Corp.	$39,400	T/M/H	$56,674
Expend.	$536,551	Party	$31,064	Labor	$12,000	Agr.	$3,000
Unspent	$7,509	PACS	$161,549	Ideo.	$48,375	CWOS	$2,100

SECOND DISTRICT

The People: Pop. 1980: 482,370, up 36.2% 1970–80. Households (1980): 82% family, 53% with children, 68% married couples; 44.0% housing units rented; median monthly rent: $267; median house value: $102,300. Voting age pop. (1980): 326,630; 55% Asian origin, 7% Spanish origin, 2% Black.

1984 Presidential Vote:

Reagan (R)	72,912	(56%)
Mondale (D)	56,423	(43%)

Rep. Daniel K. Akaka (D)

Elected 1976; b. Sept. 11, 1924, Honolulu; home, Honolulu; U. of HI, B.Ed. 1952, M.Ed. 1966; Congregational; married (Mary Mildred).

Career: Welder, mechanic, and engineer, U.S. Army Corps of Engineers, WWII; Pub. sch. teacher and principal, 1953–71; Dir., HI Ofc. of Econ. Opp., 1971–74; Spec. Asst. to the Gov. of HI in Human Resources, 1975–76; Dir., Progressive Neighborhoods Program, 1975–76.

Offices: 2301 RHOB 20515, 202-225-4906. Also 5104 Prince Kuhio Federal Bldg., Honolulu 96850, 808-541-1986.

Committees: *Appropriations* (25th of 35 D). Subcommittees; Treasury–Postal Service–General Government; Rural Development, Agriculture and Related Agencies. *Select Committee on Narcotics Abuse and Control* (6th of 15 D).

Group Ratings

	ADA	ACLU	COPE	CFA	LCV	ACU	NTU	NSI	COC	CEI
1986	65	89	50	92	60	9	22	10	18	14
1985	90	—	75	75	—	14	28	—	22	—

National Journal Ratings

	1986 LIB — 1986 CONS		1985 LIB — 1985 CONS	
Economic	82% —	16%	72% —	27%
Social	85% —	14%	77% —	22%
Foreign	70% —	29%	62% —	37%

Key Votes

1) Lmt Cln Water Act	AGN	5) Retain Gun Cont	FOR	9) Aid Angola Reb	AGN
2) Rpl Tobac Sub	AGN	6) Contra Aid	AGN	10) Tax Reform	AGN
3) Grm-Rdmn Def Red	FOR	7) Lmt Text Imp	AGN	11) S Africa Sanc	FOR
4) Ban Polygraph	FOR	8) Limit SDI	FOR	12) Immig Reform	AGN

Election Results

1986 general	Daniel K. Akaka (D)	123,830	(76%)	($110,490)
	Maria M. Hustace (R)	35,371	(21%)	($32,339)
1986 primary	Daniel K. Akaka (D)	93,729	(100%)	
1984 general	Daniel K. Akaka (D)	112,377	(82%)	($121,914)
	A. D. Shipley (R)	20,000	(15%)	

Campaign Contributions and Expenditures

1985-86		Direct Cont. 1985-86		PACS Breakdown 1985-86			
Receipts	$132,196	Indiv.	$78,110	Corp.	$13,495	T/M/H	$12,400
Expend.	$110,490	PACS	$49,145	Labor	$16,750	Agr.	$1,750
Unspent	$54,791			Ideo.	$4,500	CWOS	$250

IDAHO

West of Wyoming's and Montana's Rocky Mountains, creeks and rivers run down into a giant valley, a narrow bowl 150 miles long and 50 miles wide, along the Snake River. Then the Snake plunges north through the mountains in the aptly named Hells Canyon and moves into the eastern edge of the Columbia River basin. The large Snake River valley and the eastern margin of the Columbia basin, edged by giant mountains, joined by only one highway and no railroads, together form the state of Idaho. Criss-crossed by mountains, it is the only state with three separate state fairs. Idaho's peculiar shape is the result of historical accident (Montana was split off from Idaho, leaving the panhandle isolated from the Snake River valley), and its development was similarly diverse. The first whites here were mountain men, trappers who rendezvoused once a year; they were followed by ministers heading west to Oregon and Mormons moving north from Utah. Gold was found here in 1860, and later silver in great abundance. Two transcontinental railroads crossed the state in the 1880s. But what really shaped Idaho's character was federal water reclamation projects, first authorized in 1894, using the Snake's water to transform its barren valley into some of the nation's best farmlands. Idaho's economy is still based largely on agriculture, especially the "famous potatoes" featured on its license plates until it was replaced with "centennial" in 1987, and Idaho today, with only one city over 100,000 and much of its population still on the farm, uses more water per capita than any other state.

This leaves Idaho much more like what its first settlers expected and wanted it to be than other Rocky Mountain states. Idaho has no giant urban concentrations like metropolitan Denver or Phoenix; people are spread fairly evenly from the Panhandle in the north, with its grimy mining towns and lumber mills, through the Snake River valley, from Boise and Nampa in the west through the Magic Valley around Twin Falls to the area around Pocatello and Idaho Falls in the east, directly north of Utah, where most residents are Mormons. Boise, which in 1980 for the first time reported a population over 100,000, is a city of some dynamism—the home of such important companies as Boise Cascade (lumber and paper) and Morrison Knudsen (construction). The city's several gleaming towers and its proud older high-rises shine against the backdrop of the mountains; its tree-shaded streets and Spanish-style railroad station bespeak a comfort that contrasts sharply with the arid expanse of plains beyond the city.

Idaho's economic growth and its physical attractions and lifestyle have made it one of the fastest-growing states in the nation. Its population has grown by about 50% since 1970, but with the exception of a few places, like the resort town of Sun Valley, the influx has not been of liberal-minded environmentalists but of family people interested in a less hurried but still comfortable way of life in a small-town atmosphere where traditional values are given more respect than they are in big metropolitan areas. There are few trendy singles here; among all states, Idaho has the second highest percentage of households occupied by married people. For every Carole King (the singer who moved to Idaho because she loves the physical environment) there are a dozen new Idahoans who left California because they thought Orange County was not conservative enough.

The great influx of the 1970s strengthened a political trend already under way when the decade began: a shift from the Democrats to the Republicans. Most Idaho farmers had a Republican heritage. But Idaho was for Bryan and free silver in 1896, was part of Woodrow Wilson's and Harry Truman's alliance of the colonial South and West against the rich East at the turn of the century, and was generally in favor of the New Deal. As late as 1960 John Kennedy was able to win 46% of the vote here. But in the 1960s Idahoans began to think of themselves less as downtrodden employees of absentee corporations in need of a protective federal government and more as pioneering entrepreneurs who need to get a bloated, bossy

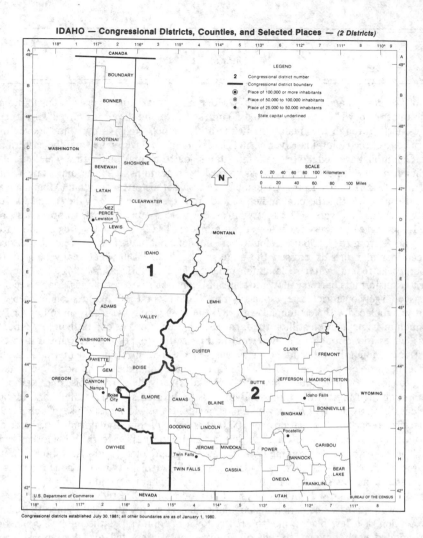

IDAHO — Congressional Districts, Counties, and Selected Places — *(2 Districts)*

Congressional districts established July 30, 1981; all other boundaries are as of January 1, 1980.

federal government off their backs. The federal government is a real presence here: it owns most of Idaho's land and when it blocks exploitation of local resources to protect the environment—when it vetoes a logging operation or prevents farmers from trapping coyotes, it arouses strong resentment. Voters tend to forget how Idaho has benefited over the years from railroad subsidies, government silver purchases, water reclamation projects, and federal maintenance of scenic lands. Yet Idahoans' hostility to environmentalists should not be overstated. Newcomers and old-timers alike appreciate their land's beauty and wildness and do not want it all gobbled up by development.

That is one reason why this very Republican state—Jimmy Carter got only 25% of the vote here in 1980, Walter Mondale 26% in 1984—has elected nothing but Democratic governors since 1970. Another is the tendency of even minority parties in every state to produce competition. A third is the tendency of Democrats, who after all are fond of government and politics, to field some of the ablest men in the state as their candidates while able men and women who are Republicans dislike government so much they shun politics and stick with entrepreneurship and making money. Idaho's best known politicians over the years were Democrat Frank Church and maverick Republican William Borah who, elected from this state of mountain-rimmed basins, both chaired the Senate Foreign Relations Committee. And in 1986 Democrats held the governorship and the 2d District House seat and nearly beat Senator Steven Symms.

Governor. The Republicans have not won a gubernatorial election here since 1966. The Democrats's secret has been good candidates—and weak opposition. Cecil Andrus beat an incumbent in 1970, won overwhelmingly in 1974, and went off to Washington to be Jimmy Carter's Secretary of the Interior. His successor as governor, John Evans, won two full terms on his own, in 1978 against a Mormon from the Mormon southeast who wanted to impose Mormon restrictions on the rest of the state and in 1982 against a lieutenant governor who campaigned against farm workers' unions and for a right-to-work law. Evans had a creditable record in hard times, negotiating a major water rights agreement with Idaho Power, and he was popular enough to overcome the handicaps of his party label and his several vetoes of right-to-work laws. Right-to-work was finally put on the ballot in 1986, and passed 54%–46%, despite spirited opposition from Idaho's small union movement. The label is appealing, and Idaho has an unusually large number of voters, notably farmers, who think of themselves as employers rather than employees. Andrus, who returned to Boise after Carter was beaten, remained widely popular, and against Republican Lieutenant Governor David Leroy was able to carry heavily the northern panhandle, hurt by layoffs in mining and timber, and blue-collar Pocatello, won a narrow edge in Boise, and won statewide 50%–49%. Andrus decries Republican legislators' opposition to spending on education and industrial development and characterizes himself as a problem-solver. With the economy ailing and, as ever, a heavily Republican legislature, he will have problems to solve.

Senators. The most powerful member of Idaho's congressional delegation these days is Senator James McClure, first elected to the House in 1966 and to the Senate in 1972. One of the most senior of conservative leaders, he has held important positions, yet he has not emerged, as he hoped, as a leader in the Republican Party. He was chairman for six years of the Energy and Natural Resources Committee and until 1984 was chairman of the Senate Republican Conference. But when he ran for Senate majority leader after the 1984 election, he won only 8 of the 53 votes, and was the first of the five candidates to be eliminated from the race. He lost even though he was the most conservative candidate and is a competent speaker, presentable on television. But as Energy chairman he had failed to push some conservative causes—notably deregulation of natural gas—as energetically or effectively as colleagues would have liked. Rather than aggressively representing the causes of western ranchers and developers, he wobbled and eventually promoted more wilderness areas in Idaho and elsewhere. And he had gained a reputation for unreliability in 1983 when he pushed through a significant change in nuclear power law after telling senators it was uncontroversial. Legislators necessarily depend on colleagues, and especially on leaders, to characterize the bills they are managing accurately and to inform them of their political significance, and evidently many Republicans were not confident that they could depend on McClure in their most important leadership post.

McClure's defeat and the Republicans' loss of control in 1986 has not been the end of his career. He won an important victory—and one likely to be appreciated by Idaho voters—when his McClure-Volkmer bill to relax federal gun control laws was passed into law. On Energy and on the Interior Appropriations subcommittee he used to chair he continues to do hard slogging detail work on important but unglamorous issues like liability for nuclear accidents, and hydropower, and also intervened on at least one occasion to get the government to pay several Idaho investors $3.9 million for property Uncle Sam said was worth no more than $321,000. McClure is nonetheless electorally strong in Idaho. He has not had serious opposition since his first election in 1972, when he accused his opponent, a backer of Cesar Chavez's lettuce boycott, of contemplating a boycott of potatoes; he won without strain in 1978 and 1984 and will likely win without difficulty in 1990 unless a popular Democrat like Governor Cecil Andrus opposes him.

Idaho's junior Senator, Steven Symms, is more controversial and flamboyant and, although he is considered a staunchly conservative in a staunch conservative state, he has been elected twice by only narrow margins. Admittedly he has had tough opponents both times. In 1980 he beat Frank Church, then Foreign Relations chairman and in his 24th year in the Senate; in 1986 he beat John Evans, a popular governor for 10 years and as steady and solid in his personal character as Symms sometimes seems flaky and half-cocked. Symms likes to portray himself as a simple apple-grower, determined to get big government out of everybody's hair; but he was also investing heavily in the silver futures market and at the same time sponsoring legislation that would have helped him and his friend and supporter Nelson Bunker Hunt. In heavily Mormon and tradition-minded Idaho, Symms campaigns as a backer of family values, yet he was dogged by rumors that he was a womanizer and showed up drunk on the floor of the Senate. There is something slapdash, almost whimsical, to Symms and his politics; he has not only a sense of humor, but a tendency to take his humor just a bit too far. Against the stolid, slow-speaking, steady small-town banker and devout Mormon, John Evans, Symms's qualities were in even bolder relief: if Symms was more in line with Idaho on issues, Evans was in character.

Yet Symms won 52%–48%. Evans carried the panhandle and Pocatello and ran almost even in the Magic Valley, despite Ronald Reagan's appearance there for Symms. But Symms carried the heavily Mormon areas around Idaho Falls nearly 2 to 1 and carried Boise as well—which was probably decisive. The right-to-work referendum may have helped him by emphasizing to voters their disagreement with Democrats on national issues, even with a moderate and cautious Democrat like Evans. And Symms's hard work, intensive and good-natured personal campaigning, and nitty-gritty Republican organizing (in contrast to the computerized phone messages Republicans used in other states) all made a difference, boosting Republican turnout and enthusiasm and enhancing Symms's attractive personal qualities and deemphasizing his negatives.

Symms has good committee assignments: Budget, Armed Services, Environment and Public Works. But he is usually not a leader on issues and, when he is, his reputation for slapdash work and oddball ideas makes it difficult for him to win much support. He led the fight on the Environment Committee to relax the terms of the Clean Air Act; the result was near-unanimous passage of a bill backed by Chairman Robert Stafford that not only reaffirmed the terms of the original law but strengthened them.

Congressmen. Idaho for some years has had one of the weakest House delegations. But by 1986 its quality had improved. First District Representative Larry Craig, first elected in 1980, made some early missteps, but seems to have gotten his footing. Craig sits on the Government Operations and Interior Committees. He is an active booster of the balanced budget amendment but, as a junior member of the minority party, has not been a major force as a legislator. The 1st District, which includes the Panhandle and Canyon County around Nampa, as well as most of Boise, is marginally the less Republican of the two districts. Craig won his first two elections by unimpressive margins; taking no chances, though he had weak opponents, he raised sizable sums and won handily in 1984 and 1986.

The 2d District, although in presidential elections it is one of the most Republican districts in the nation, has nevertheless had more spirited contests. The reason is George Hansen, 2d District congressman off and on for since 1964—more recently off, since he spent part of 1986 in jail after being convicted on income tax charges. It was not his first scrape with the law. In 1975 he pleaded guilty to violating the campaign finance laws and was sentenced to two months in jail—a sentence changed to a fine after his lawyer argued that Hansen had behaved stupidly rather than viciously. He also admitted filing late income tax returns. In 1984 he was convicted by a jury of filing false personal disclosure forms that omitted loans purportedly made to his wife, Connie, but in reality, the jury found, to Hansen himself from billionaire Nelson Bunker Hunt and a Virginia bank swindler. He was fined $40,000 and sentenced to 5 to 15 months in jail. Hansen argued that he was being persecuted for his opposition to big government. His 1975 lawyer seems closer to the truth. He appears to be a stupid man who expresses his hostility to government laws and regulations by disobeying them, and for that he has certainly paid a price.

The current congressman from the 2d District, Richard Stallings, has shown much greater political acumen. The loser to Hansen in 1982, he was fortunate that Hansen won, barely, the 1984 primary; even so he beat Hansen by only 133 votes. In 1986 he was probably sad to see Hansen's wife Connie lose the Republican primary to Idaho Falls broadcaster Mel Richardson. But by that time Stallings had political strength of his own. He is used to operating on Republican territory: he was a professor from Ricks College in Rexburg, where the county vote was Reagan 93%, Mondale 7%; he is a practicing Mormon who describes himself as "very, very conservative"; he sported one of the most conservative of voting records of non-southern Democrats. But more important may have been his constituency services and the work he did in the agricultural Magic Valley around Twin Falls. In 1986 Stallings lost his home area, carried Democratic Pocatello 2 to 1, and carried the district's portion of Boise. Most impressively, in the Magic Valley, which Reagan carried over Mondale 79%–20%, Stallings ran ahead 57%–43%. This is one of those races where the Democrats' ability to channel PAC money into close races made a difference. Richardson raised more non-PAC money than Stallings, but Stallings raised $300,000 from PACs and outspent the Republican $453,000 to $307,000.

In the House Stallings has seats on the Agriculture and Science, Space and Technology Committees, both parochially advantageous, and he has the sympathy of his fellow Democrats, who appreciate how tough a district this is for their party and are grateful for any votes he gives them.

Presidential politics. Idaho has a presidential primary late in the season, which both media and candidates tend to ignore. It is usually predictable, and the number of delegates elected is very small. In general elections, Idaho is just as predictable: next to neighboring Utah, in 1980 and 1984 it was the nation's most Republican state.

The People: Est. Pop. 1986: 1,003,000; Pop. 1980: 943,935, up 6.2% 1980–86 and 32.4% 1970–1980; 0.42% of U.S. total, 41st largest. 21% with 1–3 yrs. col., 16% with 4+ yrs. col.; 12.6% below poverty level. Single ancestry: 18% English, 10% German, 4% Irish, 2% Swedish, 1% French, Norwegian, Scottish, Dutch, Italian. Households (1980): 76% family, 44% with children, 67% married couples; 28.0% housing units rented; median monthly rent: $172; median house value: $45,900. Voting age pop. (1980): 637,270; 3% Spanish origin, 1% American Indian, 1% Asian origin. Registered voters (1986): 549,934; no party registration.

1986 Share of Federal Tax Burden: $2,308,000,000; 0.31% of U.S. total, 45th largest.

1986 Share of Federal Expenditures

	Total		Non-Defense		Defense	
Total Expend	$3,005m	(0.36%)	$2,698m	(0.45%)	$306m	(0.13%)
St/Lcl Grants	435m	(0.39%)	432m	(0.38%)	1m	(0.90%)
Salary/Wages	413m	(0.34%)	253m	(0.43%)	160m	(0.26%)
Pymnts to Indiv	1,331m	(0.36%)	1,248m	(0.36%)	83m	(0.47%)
Procurement	642m	(0.31%)	580m	(1.04%)	63m	(0.04%)
Research/Other	183m	(0.69%)	183m	(0.69%)	0m	(0%)

Political Lineup: Governor, Cecil D. Andrus (D); Lt. Gov., C. L. (Butch) Otter (R); Secy. of State, Pete T. Cenarrusa (R); Atty. Gen., Jim Jones (R); Treasurer, Lydia Justice Edwards (R); Auditor, Joe R. Williams (D). State Senate, 42 (28 R and 14 D); State House of Representatives, 84 (67 R and 17 D). Senators, James A. McClure (R) and Steven D. Symms (R). Representatives, 2 (1 D and 1 R).

1984 Presidential Vote

Reagan (R) 297,523 (72%)
Mondale (D) 108,510 (26%)

1980 Presidential Vote

Reagan (R) 290,699 (66%)
Carter (D) 110,192 (25%)
Anderson (I) 27,058 (6%)

1984 Democratic Presidential Primary

Hart 31,737 (58%)
Mondale 16,460 (30%)
Others 3,421 (6%)
Jackson 3,104 (6%)

1984 Republican Presidential Primary

Reagan 97,450 (92%)
Others 8,237 (8%)

GOVERNOR

Gov. Cecil D. Andrus (D)

Elected 1986, term expires Jan. 1991; b. Aug. 25, 1931, Hood River, OR; home, Boise; OR St. U., 1947–49; Lutheran; married (Carol).

Career: ID Senate, 1961–66, 1969–70; Gov. of ID, 1971–77; U.S. Secy. of Interior, 1977–81.

Office: State House, Boise 83720, 208-334-2100.

Election Results

1986 gen.	Cecil D. Andrus (D)	193,429	(50%)
	David Leroy (R)	189,794	(49%)
1986 prim.	Cecil D. Andrus (D)	49,663	(100%)
1982 gen.	John V. Evans (D)	165,365	(51%)
	Phil Batt (R)	161,157	(49%)

SENATORS

Sen. James A. McClure (R)

Elected 1972, seat up 1990; b. Dec. 27, 1924, Payette; home, McCall; U. of ID, J.D. 1950; United Methodist; married (Louise).

Career: Practicing atty., 1950–66; Payette Cnty. Prosecuting Atty., 1951–57; Payette City Atty., 1953–59, 1962–66; ID Senate, 1960–66; U.S. House of Reps., 1966–72.

Offices: 309 HSOB 20510, 202-224-2752. Also 149 Borah Station, Boise 83702, 208-334-1560; 305 Fed. Bldg., Coeur d'Alene 83814, 208-664-3086; 482 C St., Rm. 304, Idaho Falls 83401, 208-523-5541; FBUSCH, Rm. 210, 250 S. 4th Ave., Pocatello 833201, 208-236-6817; 401 2d St. N., Ste. 106, Twin Falls 83301, 208-734-6780; and 301 D St., Ste. 103, Lewiston 83501, 208-743-3578.

Committees: *Appropriations* (4th of 13 R). Subcommittees: Agriculture and Related Agencies; Defense; Energy and Water Development; Interior (Ranking Member); Labor, Health and Human Services, Education. *Energy and Natural Resources* (Ranking Member of 9 R). *Rules and Administration* (3d of 7 R).

Group Ratings

	ADA	ACLU	COPE	CFA	LCV	ACU	NTU	NSI	COC	CEI
1986	0	7	9	0	0	100	51	100	95	85
1985	0	—	9	0	—	100	67	—	93	—

National Journal Ratings

	1986 LIB — 1986 CONS		1985 LIB — 1985 CONS	
Economic	0%	84%	0%	86%
Social	0%	91%	0%	83%
Foreign	0%	86%	12%	80%

Key Votes

1) Ease Gun Cont	FOR	5) Grm-Rdmn Def Red	FOR	9) Rehnquist Nom	FOR
2) Immig Reform	AGN	6) Contra Aid	FOR	10) Tax Reform	FOR
3) Lmt Text Imp	FOR	7) SDI Funding	FOR	11) Drug Death Pen	AGN
4) Aid Tobac Ind	FOR	8) Lmt PAC Contrib	AGN	12) S Africa Sanc	AGN

Election Results

1984 general	James A. McClure (R)	293,193	(72%)	($1,016,944)
	Peter Martin Busch (D)	105,591	(26%)	($31,001)
1984 primary	James A. McClure (R)	102,125	(100%)	
1978 general	James A. McClure (R)	194,412	(68%)	($434,871)
	Dwight Jensen (D)	89,635	(32%)	($55,163)

Campaign Contributions and Expenditures

1979-84		Direct Cont. 1979-84		PACS Breakdown 1979-84			
Receipts	$1,310,902	Indiv.	$615,391	Corp.	$352,520	T/M/H	$132,650
Expend.	$1,016,944	Party	$16,072	Labor	$11,000	Agr.	$11,750
Unspent	$305,402	PACS	$599,928	Ideo.	$35,992	CWOS	$4,250

Sen. Steven D. Symms (R)

Elected 1980, seat up 1992; b. Apr. 23, 1938, Nampa; home, Caldwell; U. of ID, B.S. 1960; Free Methodist; married (Frances).

Career: USMC, 1960–63; Personnel and Production Mgr., V.P., Symms Fruit Ranch, Inc., 1963–72; U.S. House of Reps., 1972–80.

Offices: 509 HSOB 20510, 202-224-6142. Also P.O. Box 1190, Boise 83701, 208-334-1776; 207 Fed. Bldg., Pocatello 83201, 208-236-6775; 305 Fed. Bldg., Coeur d'Alene 83814, 208-664-5490; 105 Fed. Bldg., Moscow 83843, 208-882-5560; 301 D St., Ste. 103, Lewiston 83501, 208-743-1492; and 401 2d St., No. 106, Twin Falls 83301, 208-734-2515.

Committees: *Armed Services* (8th of 9 R). Subcommittees: Defense Industry and Technology; Manpower and Personnel; Projection Forces and Regional Defense. *Budget* (5th of 11 R). *Environment and Public Works* (4th of 7 R). Subcommittees: Hazardous Wastes and Toxic Substances; Nuclear Regulation; Water Resources; Transportation and Infrastructure (Ranking Member). *Joint Economic Committee.* Subcommittees: Economic Resources and Competitiveness; Fiscal and Monetary Policy; Investment, Jobs and Prices.

Group Ratings

	ADA	ACLU	COPE	CFA	LCV	ACU	NTU	NSI	COC	CEI
1986	0	7	2	7	0	100	50	100	100	87
1985	0	—	2	0	—	100	71	—	90	—

National Journal Ratings

	1986 LIB — 1986 CONS			1985 LIB — 1985 CONS		
Economic	0%	—	84%	0%	—	86%
Social	0%	—	91%	0%	—	83%
Foreign	14%	—	82%	12%	—	80%

Key Votes

1) Ease Gun Cont	FOR	5) Grm-Rdmn Def Red	FOR	9) Rehnquist Nom	FOR
2) Immig Reform	AGN	6) Contra Aid	FOR	10) Tax Reform	FOR
3) Lmt Text Imp	AGN	7) SDI Funding	FOR	11) Drug Death Pen	AGN
4) Aid Tobac Ind	FOR	8) Lmt PAC Contrib	AGN	12) S Africa Sanc	AGN

Election Results

1986 general	Steven D. Symms (R)	196,958	(52%)	($3,229,939)
	John V. Evans (D)	185,066	(48%)	($2,135,537)
1986 primary	Steven D. Symms (R)	90,508	(100%)	
1980 general	Steven D. Symms (R)	218,701	(50%)	($1,780,777)
	Frank Church (D)	214,439	(49%)	($1,931,487)

Campaign Contributions and Expenditures

1985-86		Direct Cont. 1985-86		PACS Breakdown 1985-86			
Receipts	$3,387,726	Indiv.	$1,860,953	Corp.	$829,091	T/M/H	$323,270
Expend.	$3,229,939	Party	$22,485	Labor	$11,500	Agr.	$3,750
Unspent	$157.787	PACS	$1,371,618	Ideo.	$163,290	CWOS	$40,717

FIRST DISTRICT

The People: Pop. 1980: 472,412, up 40.5% 1970–80. Households (1980): 77% family, 43% with children, 67% married couples; 26.7% housing units rented; median monthly rent: $173; median house value: $47,400. Voting age pop. (1980): 324,509; 3% Spanish origin, 1% American Indian, 1% Asian origin.

1984 Presidential Vote:	Reagan (R)	140,142	(68%)
	Mondale (D)	61,983	(30%)

Rep. Larry E. Craig (R)

Elected 1980; b. July 20, 1945, Council; home, Boise; U. of ID, B.S. 1969, Geo. Wash. U., M.A. 1971; United Methodist; married (Suzanne).

Career: Rancher/farmer; ID Senate, 1975–81.

Offices: 1318 LHOB 20515, 202-225-6611. Also 304 N. 8th St., Rm. 134, Boise 83701, 208-334-9046.

Committees: *Government Operations* (5th of 15 R). Subcommittee: Commerce, Consumer, and Monetary Affairs (Ranking Member). *Interior and Insular Affairs* (5th of 15 R). Subcommittees: Energy and the Environment; Mining and Natural Resources (Ranking Member); National Parks and Public Lands. *Standards of Official Conduct* (6th of 6 R).

Group Ratings

	ADA	ACLU	COPE	CFA	LCV	ACU	NTU	NSI	COC	CEI
1986	5	5	8	17	11	86	60	100	100	69
1985	0	—	16	17	—	90	91	—	91	—

National Journal Ratings

	1986 LIB — 1986 CONS	1985 LIB — 1985 CONS
Economic	21% — 77%	0% — 95%
Social	0% — 89%	0% — 76%
Foreign	14% — 84%	0% — 76%

Key Votes

1) Lmt Cln Water Act	FOR	5) Retain Gun Cont	AGN	9) Aid Angola Reb	FOR
2) Rpl Tobac Sub	FOR	6) Contra Aid	FOR	10) Tax Reform	AGN
3) Grm-Rdmn Def Red	FOR	7) Lmt Text Imp	AGN	11) S Africa Sanc	AGN
4) Ban Polygraph	AGN	8) Limit SDI	AGN	12) Immig Reform	AGN

Election Results

1986 general	Larry E. Craig (R)	120,553	(65%)	($310,471)
	William Currie (D)	59,723	(32%)	($12,507)
	David Shepherd (I).....................	4,848	(3%)	
1986 primary	Larry E. Craig (R)	40,045	(100%)	
1984 general	Larry E. Craig (R)	139,085	(69%)	($266,875)
	William R. (Bill) Hellar (D).............	63,591	(31%)	($33,992)

Campaign Contributions and Expenditures

1985-86		Direct Cont. 1985-86		PACS Breakdown 1985-86			
Receipts	$318,428	Indiv.	$177,852	Corp.	$59,900	T/M/H	$46,950
Expend.	$310,471	Party	$9,718	Labor	$750	Agr.	$4,925
Unspent	$14,829	PACS	$125,780	Ideo.	$12,049	Prof	$1,206

SECOND DISTRICT

The People: Pop. 1980: 471,523, up 25.1% 1970–80. Households (1980): 76% family, 44% with children, 67% married couples; 29.3% housing units rented; median monthly rent: $170; median house value: $44,300. Voting age pop. (1980): 312,761; 4% Spanish origin, 1% American Indian, 1% Asian origin.

1984 Presidential Vote:

	Reagan (R)	157,381	(76%)
	Mondale (D)	46,527	(23%)

Rep. Richard H. Stallings (D)

Elected 1984; b. Oct. 7, 1940, Ogden, UT; home, Rexburg; Weber St. Col., B.S. 1965, UT St. U., M.S. 1968; Mormon; married (Ranae).

Career: History Professor, Ricks Col., Rexburg, ID, 1969–84.

Offices: 1233 LHOB 20515, 202-225-5531. Also 304 N. 8th, Rm. 434, Boise 83702, 208-334-1953; and 250 S. 4th, Rm. 220, Pocatello 83201, 208-236-6734.

Committees: *Agriculture* (20th of 26 D). Subcommittees: Conservation, Credit, and Rural Development; Cotton, Rice, and Sugar; Forests, Family Farms, and Energy. *Science, Space and Technology* (17th of 27 D). Subcommittees: Energy Research and Development; International Scientific Cooperation. *Select Committee on Aging* (36th of 39 D). Subcommittees: Retirement Income and Employment.

Group Ratings

	ADA	ACLU	COPE	CFA	LCV	ACU	NTU	NSI	COC	CEI
1986	45	35	33	33	55	32	40	30	71	40
1985	35	—	58	58	—	40	46	—	55	—

National Journal Ratings

	1986 LIB — 1986 CONS		1985 LIB — 1985 CONS	
Economic	29%	— 71%	48%	— 50%
Social	31%	— 67%	36%	— 60%
Foreign	57%	— 41%	56%	— 43%

Key Votes

1) Lmt Cln Water Act	FOR	5) Retain Gun Cont	AGN	9) Aid Angola Reb	FOR
2) Rpl Tobac Sub	FOR	6) Contra Aid	AGN	10) Tax Reform	FOR
3) Grm-Rdmn Def Red	FOR	7) Lmt Text Imp	AGN	11) S Africa Sanc	FOR
4) Ban Polygraph	FOR	8) Limit SDI	FOR	12) Immig Reform	FOR

Election Results

1986 general	Richard H. Stallings (D)	103,035	(54%)	($470,363)
	Mel Richardson (R)	86,528	(46%)	($325,004)
1986 primary	Richard H. Stallings (D)	18,174	(100%)	
1984 general	Richard H. Stallings (D)	101,266	(50%)	($320,169)
	George Hansen (R)..................	101,133	(50%)	($327,285)

Campaign Contributions and Expenditures

1985-86		Direct Cont. 1985-86		PACS Breakdown 1985-86			
Receipts	$474,949	Indiv.	$142,622	Corp.	$33,650	T/M/H	$59,129
Expend.	$470,363	Party	$11,277	Labor	$119,600	Agr.	$13,300
Debts	$4,773	PACS	$293,899	Ideo.	$66,220	Prof	$2,000

ILLINOIS

Chicago, wrote a Scots traveler passing through in 1836, "is rather pleasantly situated. The streets are wide and the houses are all wooden, excepting two large stores, which are brick. Four years ago it did not contain more than a hundred inhabitants, and now it boasts of nearly five thousand." Just three years after it was incorporated the signs of growth were obvious: buying and selling of town lots, rumors that one speculator made $200,000, shiploads of goods and British immigrants arriving from New York, Irish workmen digging a canal to connect Lake Michigan and the Illinois River system. It was only four years after Black Hawk's war in northwest Illinois, but settlers from New England and Kentucky, coming overland on Great Lakes steamers and southern riverboats were filling up Illinois's prairies, the flat, treeless, deep-topsoiled land that started where the eastern forests ended near the Indiana border. Later, to Anthony Trollope in 1862, Chicago was America's "most remarkable" city. "Its growth has been the fastest and its success most assured." The 120,000 Chicagoans "do not mind failures, and when they have failed, instantly begin again." Illinois by then had a central place in the Republic: Abraham Lincoln of Springfield was President, Ulysses S. Grant from Galena was a leading general, and thousands of young Illinoisans were enlisting in the Union Army. By 1893, when Chicago hosted the world's fair, it had more than one million people and was clearly a world-class city; and Illinois, with four million people, was the third most populous state.

In the nearly 100 years since Illinois and Chicago, at the junction of the Great Lakes and Mississippi Valley, have maintained their central position as the focus of the American transportation and manufacturing. Chicago may no longer be the nation's second largest metropolitan area (Los Angeles, if defined properly, is larger), but O'Hare is the busiest airport. Chicago may no longer be the hog butcher of the world (big meatpacking operations are now located near feedlots), and the Chicago of Saul Bellow does not command the awe of the Chicago of Theodore Dreiser. But Chicago has become the center of the world's futures markets and Illinois is the nation's center for producing and processing soybeans—one crop in which the United States still dominates world markets. Manufacturing is declining in Illinois, as in other Great Lakes states, and the farm sector is ailing. But the white-collar economy is of greater mass here than anywhere else between the coasts, and incomes remain well above the national average.

This Illinois is not conducive to philosophical speculation or airy dreams; it is a land of concrete and topsoil, of steel and water, of railroads and grain elevators and factories: people are here to make and grow things and earn a living. The state's economic growth and prosperity are the result, not of political theory or bureaucratic agency, but almost entirely of the strength and growth of its private economy. Illinois likes to boast of Abraham Lincoln, the most important politician Illinois has produced; but Lincoln's greatest contribution to Illinois (dwarfed, to be sure, by his contributions to the nation), was his legal work for the east-west railroads. In this bustling and muscular Illinois, politicians have had the unglamorous job of managing the everyday government and keeping it from fouling up commerce and industry. The huge masses that thronged Chicago alarmed 19th century businessmen, who prompted the government to keep troops nearby in Fort Sheridan and to use force to quell protest in the Haymarket Massacre of 1886 and the Pullman strike of 1894. Chicago Mayor Carter Harrison was assassinated in 1893, and men of property feared revolution and anarchy. The elite was happy, despite the grumbling of a few progressives, to see the growth of Chicago's political machines, which brokered the demands of the city's ethnic groups and kept government operating at what most businessmen regarded as a reasonable price in corruption and honest graft.

Machine politics was bipartisan. Big Bill Thompson, the mayor in the 1920s who threatened to

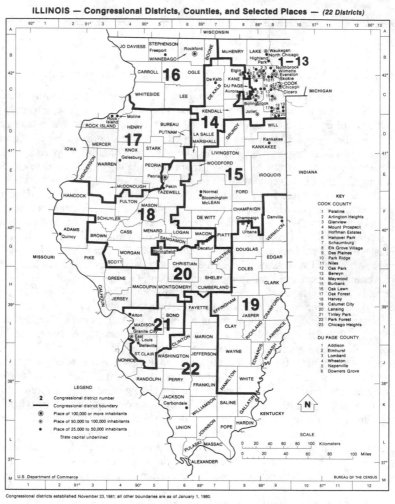

ILLINOIS — Congressional Districts, Counties, and Selected Places — *(22 Districts)*

KEY

COOK COUNTY
1 Palatine
2 Arlington Heights
3 Glenview
4 Mount Prospect
5 Hoffman Estates
6 Hanover Park
7 Schaumburg
8 Elk Grove Village
9 Des Plaines
10 Park Ridge
11 Niles
12 Oak Park
13 Berwyn
14 Maywood
15 Burbank
16 Oak Lawn
17 Oak Forest
18 Harvey
19 Calumet City
20 Lansing
21 Tinley Park
22 Park Forest
23 Chicago Heights

DU PAGE COUNTY
1 Addison
2 Elmhurst
3 Lombard
4 Wheaton
5 Naperville
6 Downers Grove

LEGEND
2 Congressional district number
— Congressional district boundary
◉ Place of 100,000 or more inhabitants
◉ Place of 50,000 to 100,000 inhabitants
• Place of 25,000 to 50,000 inhabitants
State capital underlined

SCALE
0 20 40 60 80 100 Kilometers
0 20 40 60 80 100 Miles

U.S. Department of Commerce   BUREAU OF THE CENSUS

Congressional districts established November 23, 1981; all other boundaries are as of January 1, 1980.

See pages 1369-1374 for additional metropolitan area maps.

"smash King George on the snoot" if he came to Chicago but opened up the city to Al Capone, was as staunch a Republican as Richard J. Daley was a Democrat. It was in a Republican primary in 1928 that a bomb was set off under the front porch of Thompson's party rival, Senator Charles Deneen, and someone—no one was saying who—shot and killed the challenger of Thompson's ally, 20th ward committeeman and city collector Morris Eller, just as someone—no one was saying who—pumped bullets into 24th ward Democratic Alderman Ben Lewis in 1964. Though Illinois state politics has spirited party competition, the New Deal made the city overwhelmingly Democratic and Anton Cermak's election as mayor in 1931 began a period of Democratic machine control of City Hall lasting till Jane Byrne beat Michael Bilandic after the snowstorm of 1979. By the time Daley became mayor in 1955, the machine had sunk roots deep in almost every neighborhood and had filled public payrolls with patronage employees required to produce votes on election day. Public office became almost hereditary: Representative Dan Rostenkowski, three-term Sheriff Richard Elrod, and of course State's Attorney Richard M. Daley are all sons of war committeemen. It lasted longer than other big city machines, because of Daley's personal probity, because of his efficiency and building of great structures like McCormick Place and O'Hare Airport, which helped keep Chicago a world-class city, because the reform element was small and business interests saw the Mayor as an ally not a rival.

Today the Chicago Democratic machine is in ruins, and Illinois politics has become a kind of spectator sport—raucous, sometimes bawdy, full of play-acting, on a level somewhere between the Chicago Cubs and professional wrestling. You hear with every election that this is the end for machine politics, but actually the Daley machine was done in around 1972, when Daley's delegation was thrown out of the McGovern-controlled Democratic national convention, the Better Government Association and the *Chicago Tribune* pretty well stamped out ballot-stuffing in the West Side wards, and James Thompson, then U.S. attorney and since 1976 governor, was bringing indictments and getting convictions of key machine politicians. Patronage jobs were becoming less attractive; who wants an $11,000 job that requires you to work nights and weekends and live in the city, when you can make two or three times the money in the private sector and live in the suburbs?

So now statewide campaigns in Illinois are fought out primarily on television, while the press, in the 1920s-style newspaper war between the *Tribune* and the *Sun-Times,* follows the blunders of the state's politicians and the dying twitches of machine politics with relish. The 1986 governor's race was a prime example. The central event was Democrat Adlai Stevenson's efforts to disengage himself from the follower of Lyndon LaRouche who was nominated to run for lieutenant governor with him in the March primary. Chicago Mayor Harold Washington and his bitter enemy Edward Vrdolyak, then Cook County Democratic chairman, blithely disclaimed responsibility for this absurd result, though nominating respectable candidates for minor office is a traditional responsibility of party leaders. So Stevenson had to form another party, get enough signatures to get it on the ballot, resign his Democratic nomination and select a slate of Solidarity candidates who everyone knew would lose. He had no choice, since voters were not going to put a LaRouchite fanatic a heartbeat away from the governor's office and command of the National Guard. But the interesting case Stevenson was prepared to make against Jim Thompson got lost in the shuffle. Thompson won with just 53% of the vote, midway between Ronald Reagan's 50% in 1980 and 56% in 1984. This seems to reflect the balance in a state where Democratic Chicago casts 25% of the votes but the heavily Republican suburbs cast 35%, where one-eighth of the voters are black, and where the Republican trend among white Chicago-area voters is balanced by a Democratic trend in ailing industrial and farm counties Downstate. But the Republican advantage is tenuous, and Democrats hold both Senate and most House seats and control the state legislature. Brawling is at least competition.

But even during the 1986 campaign, most observers were looking ahead to the spring 1987 contest for mayor. Harold Washington's surprise win over Jane Byrne and Richie Daley in the 1983 primary and his victory over Republican Bernard Epton gave Chicago its first black mayor, and one who promised to throw patronage hacks out of office; but Vrdolyak and his mostly white allies kept them in because they controlled the council 29–21 until court-mandated redistricting and new elections in 1986 gave Washington a 25–25 tie he could break with his own vote. Washington has made some high-quality appointments, but his administration has also been touched by scandal; the Mayor himself is bright and forthright, but sometimes sloppy and slapdash; he served time in jail years ago for not filing income tax returns. White voters hate and mistrust him, and with more than half the votes could beat him if they could unite on a single opponent. So the politicians maneuvered for advantage and even threatened in this most partisan of cities to hold a nonpartisan primary and runoff, to force Washington to face off against one white opponent. But Washington, particularly after he won council control, ran things with a steady enough hand—steadier than any of his opponents, anyway—to win over crucial votes from whites. Jane Byrne announced early for the Democratic primary, bluffing other Washington opponents out; but memories of her own tenure were not sweet, and Washington won 54%–46%, with about 20% of the white vote. In the April general election, three erstwhile Democrats maneuvered to become Washington's sole rival; Cook County Assessor and one-time Byrne aide, running as an Independent and Republican, essentially dropped out, leaving the standard to Vrdolyak, who was running as the candidate of Stevenson's Solidarity party (and was thrown out of his party chairmanship, logically enough, for doing so). But Washington won 53% of the vote to 42% for Vrdolyak. Washington had a minor advantage in facing two of the least attractive of his rivals; even so, he won absolute majorities both times, carrying essentially all the black votes (99% in 10 of the city's 50 wards), between 50% and 60% of the growing Hispanic vote, and perhaps 15% of the white vote, mostly in Jewish and liberal lakefront precincts; in six wards at the edge of the city he got between 3% and 7%. Washington's forces also got a solid margin on the Council, at which point former opponents came over to his side with Chicagoesque shamelessness and sang-froid.

What is at stake is control of Chicago's city government, of the police and the everyday bureaucracies; but its white-collar private economy continues to boom and its factories to close regardless of the tussling at City Hall. Whites are still leery of Washington, but no longer think his being mayor will destroy their city. Patronage jobs are getting scarcer, and the LaRouchite primary victories in 1986 showed how weak the party leaders really are. A great fuss was made in the 1984 primary over whether Gary Hart should attack Walter Mondale because he was endorsed by Vrdolyak. But Illinois voters, like those in the other 49 states, no longer look to political bosses for guidance but watch the skirmishing and make up their own minds. Or they simply stay home: turnout declined from 3.7 to 3.1 million from 1982 to 1986.

Governor. James Thompson is perhaps the last big state governor in the liberal Republican tradition of Thomas E. Dewey and Nelson Rockefeller: a scourge of Democratic machine politicians who governs by accommodating the major interests in the state. As a Republican he has the backing of most of business, and in 1986 he was endorsed by the state AFL-CIO. But this style of governing means concentrating on questions of distribution rather than production. Thompson has taken Illinois's economy for granted, at least until his Build Illinois infrastructure program was launched in 1985, and he won the governorship in 1976 by beating the machine politician Daley had used to defeat renegade Democratic Governor Daniel Walker in the primary. That was Thompson's biggest victory; his share of the vote has declined from 65% to 59% in 1978 and 49% in 1982, when he ran only 5,000 votes ahead of Stevenson. In 1986 Stevenson was preparing to argue that Thompson's formula buttresses dying industries rather than nurtures growth. Thompson was prepared to counter by discussing how he brought business and labor together to agree on tax reform, how he got striking Chicago teachers and the board of education together to reach a contract, how he froze spending and built new prisons and set up an in-home care program for the elderly. Then came the LaRouche business. Stevenson squirmed to get on the ballot and hobbled around when he broke his foot. Thompson was embarrassed when the Republican candidate for attorney general left the ticket because of charges of spouse abuse. Name-calling started: Stevenson, who said, "I am not a wimp" in 1982, lacked "the guts and brains" to be governor, Thompson said; Thompson, said Stevenson, is a "big, blubbering whale."

For years there has been talk that Thompson would run for president. But it's hard to see how his liberal reputation will help him win the Republican nomination or how his formula for governing will play nationally. Thompson beat Stevenson by a solid margin, but his 53% against fatally weakened opposition was not an overwhelming vote of confidence after 10 years in office. In March 1987 Thompson took himself out of the running for the national ticket.

Illinois's other statewide offices don't usually give their holders much power (attorney general is sometimes an exception), but they can give them good political reputations which enable them to move up. Both senators held such offices: Paul Simon was lieutenant governor in 1968–72 and Alan Dixon was treasurer in 1970–76 and secretary of state 1976–80. The best known today is Democrat Neil Hartigan, elected lieutenant governor in 1972 and attorney general in 1982 and 1986, a one-time machine ally who reluctantly left the governor's race in 1985 though polls showed him leading Stevenson for the nomination. But Republican Lieutenant Governor George Ryan and Secretary of State Jim Edgar and Democratic Comptroller Roland Burris and

Treasurer Jerry Cosentino all could conceivably move up.

Senators. Among the least known of all senators is Illinois's Alan Dixon. Dixon is one of several northern Democrats—Glenn of Ohio, Melcher of Montana, and Exon of Nebraska are others—who do not always vote the liberal or labor line. One of Dixon's pet causes is the line-item presidential veto; another is to get more federal dollars for Illinois (it gets little defense money and pays high taxes); a third is to stop military waste. In 1985 he won a seat on the Armed Services Committee; anxious to become an expert on the Army's controversial Sergeant York gun before a critical Senate vote, he traveled to Fort Bliss in Texas for a personal test only to have the weapon jam in his hands; the Sergeant York was finally abandoned and the taxpayers saved $3 billion. Friendly and open, he convened the first bipartisan Illinois delegation meetings. Serendipitous, he takes on causes like setting up a National Endowment for the Homeless and wants to limit state severance taxes. He would have been an odd man out in the Senate a dozen years ago, but is at the center of things in the late 1980s.

Dixon won his first office, police magistrate in Belleville near St. Louis, in 1949, served 20 years in the legislature, compiled an honest and efficient record, and got rid of patronage jobs as treasurer and secretary of state in the 1970s. He was elected by a solid margin in 1980 and reelected by an overwhelming margin in 1986 against weak opposition; his good name helps deter Republicans from raising the vast sums needed to run statewide TV ads in Illinois. Curiously, he is a longtime friend of his colleague, Paul Simon, and was once Simon's business partner when he owned a small chain of Downstate papers.

Paul Simon, with his glasses and bow tie, his extra-flat midwestern accent and his habit of writing his own newsletters and books (he has published 11), is more distinctive. The rating groups call him a more liberal Democrat than Dixon, but he shares many of the same impulses. In patronage-choked Illinois they are both reformers of the political process: Simon pioneered an open meetings law years ago. They are parsimonious: Simon favors a pay-as-you-go constitutional amendment, and nearly got his version of the balanced budget amendment through the Senate. They take on unusual causes: Simon has sponsored legislation on missing children, rewrote his state adoption law, has taken up the cause of spouses divided by the Iron Curtain, has tried to direct foreign aid to poor countries' poorest inhabitants, promotes water desalination projects, wants to do something to stop greenmail and golden parachutes. About his major projects he writes books. *The Tongue-Tied American* bemoaned our ignorance of foreign languages, and he got the State Department to require that every employee at several U.S. embassies speak the local language. His latest, written in 1986 on welfare, is called *Let's Put America Back to Work*.

Simon is loaded with committee assignments. In 1985 and 1986 he headed the Democrats' panel scrutinizing Reagan judicial nominees, and is still the only Democratic non-lawyer on the committee. He is also a member of the Labor Committee, and in 1987 joined both Budget and Foreign Relations, where he chairs the Africa Subcommittee.

Simon got his start in public life when he bought the *Troy Tribune,* a paper published 15 miles from Dixon's Belleville, at age 19, and crusaded against local gangsters and machine politicians; he was elected to the legislature in 1954 and married a colleague in 1960; eventually owned 14 newspapers and sold the chain in 1966. In 1968 he was elected lieutenant governor, and was prepared to take on politically ailing Republican Governor Richard Ogilvie when he lost the Democratic primary to anti-Daley, anti-spending Daniel Walker. But when Ken Gray retired from the farthest Downstate Illinois House district, Simon ran for the seat and won; and in 1984, he won a heavily contested Democratic primary and then went on to beat Senate Foreign Relations Chairman Charles Percy 50%–48%. The key was Downstate. Simon got the usual Democratic margin in Chicago, Percy got nearly the usual Republican margin in the suburbs. But Downstate was already beset by low farm prices and closing factories, and Simon had a home-town advantage south of Springfield, and while Reagan in 1984 and Thompson in 1986 carried Downstate by nearly 20%, Percy's edge there was only 50%–49%. It's possible that in 1990 Simon will draw a weak opponent as Dixon did, but he may have to fight hard too; one possible opponent is 16th District Representative Lynn Martin. In the meantime at least 15 of his former House colleagues urged him to run for president and in May 1987 he announced his candidacy.

Presidential politics. Illinois can be a pivotal political state. It is a bellwether, voting for the presidential winner in the 20th century except for southerners Jimmy Carter in 1976 and Woodrow Wilson in 1916. It is arguably a national microcosm: Cairo, at its southern tip, is closer to Mississippi than to Chicago; and Chicago itself has hundreds of thousands of black residents with roots in the South as well as the descendants of immigrants with roots in every part of Europe and now an increasing number from Latin America. A line across central Illinois marks the division between Democratic and Republican counties in Lincoln's day and almost exactly separates counties carried by Jimmy Carter and by Gerald Ford in the 1976 presidential election.

With its early primary, Illinois was decisive in getting nominations for Gerald Ford in 1976, Ronald Reagan and Jimmy Carter in 1980, and Walter Mondale in 1984. But in 1988 Illinois will be voting a week after the southern regional primary and on the same day as at least one other major midwestern state. It still bears close watching. The state is arguably typical and the electorate one of the nation's biggest; only California and sometimes Pennsylvania and Texas cast more presidential primary votes. But it is not likely that local Chicago politics will play the role it did in 1984, when Gary Hart was hurt after he promised to yank a TV spot criticizing Walter Mondale for being endorsed by Edward Vrdolyak and then was unable to do so.

Congressional districting. Illinois, for all its rough politics, has one of the most competent and distinguished House delegations—perhaps the most. It elects Republican House leader Robert Michel and two others in the Republican leadership, Lynn Martin and Edward Madigan. It sends Ways and Means Chairman Dan Rostenkowski to Washington and good senior legislators like Sidney Yates and Frank Annunzio. Current district lines were drawn by the Democrats (but adopted by a court that was 2 to 1 Republican!) and extend Chicago districts out into the suburbs; at least one Chicago district will have to vanish after the 1990 Census. This is one state in which Republican claims of unfair redistricting are justified, though the plan was adopted by Republicans and has ended up producing three House Republican leaders.

The People: Est. Pop. 1986: 11,553,000; Pop. 1980: 11,426,518, up 1.1% 1980–86 and 2.8% 1970–80; 4.79% of U.S. total, 6th largest. 15% with 1–3 yrs. col., 15% with 4+ yrs. col.; 11.0% below poverty level. Single ancestry: 10% German, 6% English, 4% Irish, Polish, 3% Italian, 1% Swedish, Russian, Dutch, French, Greek. Households (1980): 73% family, 39% with children, 59% married couples; 37.4% housing units rented; median monthly rent: $201; median house value: $53,900. Voting age pop. (1980): 8,183,481; 13% Black, 5% Spanish origin, 1% Asian origin. Registered voters (1986): 6,003,811; no party registration.

1986 Share of Federal Tax Burden: $40,746,000,000; 5.42% of U.S. total, 4th largest.

1986 Share of Federal Expenditures

	Total		Non-Defense		Defense	
Total Expend	$30,149m	(3.63%)	$26,640m	(4.44%)	$3,509m	(1.53%)
St/Lcl Grants	5,010m	(4.45%)	5,007m	(4.45%)	3m	(2.70%)
Salary/Wages	4,000m	(3.32%)	2,505m	(4.27%)	1,495m	(2.42%)
Pymnts to Indiv	16,751m	(4.59%)	16,476m	(4.75%)	275m	(1.55%)
Procurement	3,014m	(1.47%)	1,280m	(2.30%)	1,733m	(1.15%)
Research/Other	1,374m	(5.15%)	1,372m	(5.15%)	2m	(5.88%)

Political Lineup: Governor, James R. Thompson (R); Lt. Gov., George H. Ryan (R); Secy. of State, James Edgar (R); Atty. Gen., Neil F. Hartigan (D); Treasurer, Jerry Cosentino (D); Comptroller, Roland W. Burris (D). State Senate, 59 (33 D and 26 R); State House of Representatives, 118 (67 D and 51 R). Senators, Alan J. Dixon (D) and Paul Simon (D). Representatives, 22 (13 D and 9 R).

1984 Presidential Vote		
Reagan (R)	2,707,103	(56%)
Mondale (D)	2,086,499	(43%)

1980 Presidential Vote		
Reagan (R)	2,358,094	(50%)
Carter (D)	1,981,413	(42%)
Anderson (I)	346,754	(7%)

1984 Democratic Presidential Primary		
Mondale	670,951	(40%)
Hart	584,579	(35%)
Jackson	348,843	(21%)
Five others	54,901	(3%)

1984 Republican Presidential Primary		
Reagan	594,742	(100%)

GOVERNOR

Gov. James R. Thompson (R)

Elected 1976, term expires Jan. 1991; b. May 8, 1936, Chicago; home, Chicago; U. of IL, Chicago, B.A. 1956; Northwestern U., J.D. 1959; Presbyterian; married (Jayne).

Career: Prosecutor for Cook Cnty. States Atty., 1959–64; Assoc. Prof., Northwestern Law Sch., 1964–69; Chief, Dept. of Law Enforcement and Pub. Protection, IL Atty. Gen.'s Ofc., 1969–71; 1st Asst. U.S. Atty., N. Dist. of IL, 1970; U.S. Atty., 1971–75.

Office: State Capitol Bldg., Rm. 207, Springfield 62706, 217-782-6830.

Election Results

1986 gen.	James R. Thompson (R)	1,655,945	(53%)
	Adlai E. Stevenson III	1,296,725	(40%)
	(Solidarity Party)		
	No candidate (D)	208,841	(7%)
1986 prim.	James R. Thompson (R)	452,685	(91%)
	Peter Bowen (R)	45,236	(9%)
1982 gen.	James R. Thompson (R)	1,816,101	(49%)
	Adlai E. Stevenson III (D)	1,811,027	(49%)

SENATORS

Sen. Alan J. Dixon (D)

Elected 1980, seat up 1992; b. July 7, 1927, Belleville; home, Belleville; U. of IL, B.S. 1949, Washington U., St. Louis, LL.B. 1949; Presbyterian; married (Joan).

Career: Navy, 1945–46; Belleville Police Magistrate, 1949; IL House of Reps., 1951–63; IL Senate, 1963–71; Treas. of IL, 1971–77; Secy. of State of IL, 1977–81.

Offices: 331 HSOB 20510, 202-224-2854. Also 230 S. Dearborn St., Chicago 60604, 312-353-5420; 108 P.O. Bldg., Rm 177, Springfield 62701, 217-492-4126; 10 E. Washington, Belleville 62220, 618-235-0998; and 105 S. 6th St., Mt. Vernon 62864, 618-244-6703.

Committees: *Armed Services* (7th of 11 D). Subcmtes.: Conventional Forces and Alliance Defense; Defense Industry and Technology; Readiness, Sustainability and Support (Chairman). *Banking, Housing, and Urban Affairs* (6th of 11 D). Subcmtes.: Housing and Urban Affairs; Intl. Finance and Monetary Policy. *Small Business* (6th of 10 D). Subcmte.: Government Contracting and Paperwork Reduction (Chairman); Rural Economy and Family Farming.

Group Ratings

	ADA	ACLU	COPE	CFA	LCV	ACU	NTU	NSI	COC	CEI
1986	65	42	78	60	50	43	44	78	58	40
1985	60	—	77	53	—	41	32	—	43	—

National Journal Ratings

	1986 LIB — 1986 CONS		1985 LIB — 1985 CONS	
Economic	73% —	22%	62% —	36%
Social	58% —	40%	74% —	22%
Foreign	59% —	40%	57% —	41%

Key Votes

1) Ease Gun Cont	FOR	5) Grm-Rdmn Def Red	FOR	9) Rehnquist Nom	FOR
2) Immig Reform	AGN	6) Contra Aid	FOR	10) Tax Reform	FOR
3) Lmt Text Imp	FOR	7) SDI Funding	AGN	11) Drug Death Pen	AGN
4) Aid Tobac Ind	AGN	8) Lmt PAC Contrib	FOR	12) S Africa Sanc	FOR

Election Results

1986 general	Alan J. Dixon (D)	2,033,926	(65%)	($1,928,750)
	Judy Koehler (R)	1,053,793	(34%)	($851,305)
1986 primary	Alan J. Dixon (D)	750,571	(85%)	
	Sheila Jones (D)	129,474	(15%)	
1980 general	Alan J. Dixon (D)	2,565,302	(56%)	($2,346,897)
	David C. O'Neal (R)	1,946,296	(42%)	($1,293,991)

Campaign Contributions and Expenditures

1985-86		Direct Cont. 1985-86		PACS Breakdown 1985-86			
Receipts	$2,219,982	Indiv.	$1,172,681	Corp.	$422,828	T/M/H	$229,876
Expend.	$1,928,750	Party	$17,500	Labor	$177,450	Agr.	$10,300
Unspent	$408,427	PACS	$958,697	Ideo.	$101,443	CWOS	$16,800

Sen. Paul Simon (D)

Elected 1984, seat up 1990; b. Nov. 29, 1928, Eugene, OR; home, Makanda; U. of OR, Dana Col.; Lutheran; married (Jeanne).

Career: Editor-Publisher, *Troy Tribune*, and weekly newspaper chain owner 1948–66; Army, 1951–53; IL House of Reps., 1955–63; IL Senate, 1963–69; Lt. Gov. of IL, 1969–73; Instructor, Sangamon St. U., 1973–74; U.S. House of Reps., 1974–84.

Offices: 462 DSOB 20510, 202-224-2152. Also 230 S. Dearborn, Rm. 3892, Chicago 60604, 312-353-4952; 3 W. Old Capital Plaza, Ste. 1, Springfield 62701; 250 W. Cherry, Rm 115B, Carbondale 62910, 618-457-3653; and 8787 State St., Ste. 212, E. St. Louis 62201, 618-398-7407.

Committees: *Budget* (8th of 13 D). *Judiciary* (8th of 8 D). Subcommittees: Antitrust, Monopolies and Business Rights; Constitution (Chairman); Immigration and Refugee Affairs. *Foreign Relations* (7th of 11 D). Subcommittee: African Affairs (Chairman); European Affairs. *Labor and Human Services* (6th of 9 D). Subcommittees: Education, Arts and Humanities; Employment and Productivity (Chairman); Handicapped.

Group Ratings

	ADA	ACLU	COPE	CFA	LCV	ACU	NTU	NSI	COC	CEI
1986	89	100	89	93	83	9	50	0	32	20
1985	95	—	83	80	—	5	28	—	34	—

National Journal Ratings

	1986 LIB — 1986 CONS			1985 LIB — 1985 CONS		
Economic	85%	—	8%	86%	—	11%
Social	78%	—	21%	88%	—	0%
Foreign	75%	—	0%	85%	—	14%

Key Votes

1) Ease Gun Cont	—	5) Grm-Rdmn Def Red	FOR	9) Rehnquist Nom	AGN
2) Immig Reform	AGN	6) Contra Aid	AGN	10) Tax Reform	—
3) Lmt Text Imp	FOR	7) SDI Funding	AGN	11) Drug Death Pen	—
4) Aid Tobac Ind	AGN	8) Lmt PAC Contrib	FOR	12) S Africa Sanc	FOR

Election Results

1984 general	Paul Simon (D)	2,397,165	(50%)	($4,545,786)
	Charles H. Percy (R)	2,308,039	(48%)	($5,391,567)
1984 primary	Paul Simon (D)	556,757	(36%)	
	Roland W. Burris (D)	360,182	(23%)	
	Alex R. Seith (D)	327,125	(21%)	
	Philip J. Rock (D)	303,397	(19%)	
1978 general	Charles H. Percy (R)	1,698,711	(53%)	($2,417,155)
	Alex R. Seith (D)	1,448,187	(46%)	($1,371,478)

Campaign Contributions and Expenditures

1983-84		Direct Cont. 1983-84		PACS Breakdown 1983-84			
Receipts	$4,550,571	Indiv.	$3,436,607	Corp.	$40,625	T/M/H	$75,990
Expend.	$4,545,786	Party	$61,537	Labor	$357,217	Agr.	$16,500
Debts	$408,966	PACS	$905,054	Ideo.	$402,847	CWOS	$2,285
		Cand.	$50,000				

FIRST DISTRICT

America's first urban black community—first in size, first in many ways in importance, first in 20th century history—is the South Side of Chicago. Here, as long ago as 1900, was a black neighborhood centered on the corner of 63d and Cottage Grove. There have always been poor people in the South Side, but there have always been middle class and prosperous blacks as well: this is the home of the nation's first black bourgeoisie. The South Side has been a center of black culture since before the jazz age, and there are twice as many blacks here today—800,000—as in New York's Harlem.

The South Side has also furnished political leadership for blacks. Illinois's 1st Congressional District, more than 90% black today, includes the larger part of the South Side black community. It covers a wide sociological range, from the mansions of Kenwood, once the home of the city's Jewish aristocracy and more recently the headquarters of the Black Muslims, where the Doric temple on East 50th Street that once belonged to the first Jewish congregation in Chicago is now the headquarters of Jesse Jackson's Operation Push, to the high-rise housing projects that line the Dan Ryan Expressway for what seems like miles. The 1st also includes the University of Chicago and the intellectual Hyde Park neighborhood around it, but the typical neighborhood here is one where the straight streets are lined with modest well-kept houses built around the turn of the century, in neighborhoods which have been entirely black for decades.

The 1st District has the longest continuous tradition of black representation in the nation. It elected its first black congressman, Republican Oscar DePriest in 1928; blacks then were still faithful to the party of Lincoln, and voted for Herbert Hoover even in the depression year of 1932. But the New Deal and the racial liberalism of Eleanor Roosevelt attracted blacks to the Democratic Party in the 1930s. DePriest was beaten by a black Democrat, Arthur Mitchell, in 1934; Mitchell was succeeded in 1942 by another black Democrat, William Dawson.

Dawson was the first black political boss of the 20th century, a ward committeeman with his own patronage jobs, always consulted by Democratic leaders, a quiet congressman who became chairman of the Post Office and Civil Service Committee but seldom spoke out on issues; he died in office at age 84 in 1970. Dawson's successor in Congress, Ralph Metcalfe, broke with Mayor Daley in 1972 when the Mayor refused to come to Metcalfe's office to discuss the beating of two black dentists by a policeman. Later that year, half the South Side's votes went to Republicans, Senator Charles Percy and Cook County State's Attorney Bernard Carey; the South Side, where turnout has always been high and Democratic percentages usually the highest in the city, got a taste of independence.

The dominant political figure in the South Side and in the 1st Congressional District of Illinois which includes its heart, is Mayor Harold Washington. When he was elected to the House in 1980, he was little known citywide, though he had been in the legislature since 1964; he had run for mayor in 1979 and got only 11% of the vote. Washington spent most of his two-plus years in Congress running for mayor, and his victory over incumbent Jane Byrne and State's Attorney Richard M. Daley in the Democratic primary electrified Chicago's blacks; the bitter opposition he received from whites in the general election campaign shocked them. His strength was his intellect and opposition to patronage politics; he was a top law student at Northwestern and a competent bill-drafter in a legislature that has many hacks. But he also had the weaknesses you might expect in a man active in South Side and hence machine politics for many years before and after 1972: the sloppiness of a pol confident the machine will protect him, the pride of a black politician suddenly made independent because he has the support of an autonomous black constituency. When he refused after his primary victory to meet with Democratic ward leaders or take a call from Walter Mondale (who had endorsed Daley), he might have been remembering Metcalfe's refusal to go down to City Hall to meet Daley; but his bitter feuds with white politicians have made it hard for him to govern effectively. Of course they have been almost totally hostile to him.

Washington's seat in the House has been assumed by Charles Hayes, who was chosen in a 1983 special election. Hayes comes out of the labor movement, and from a part of it that has a heritage of old-time indigenous radicalism. He was a vice president of the United Food and Commercial Workers Union, and was an official in the Amalgamated Meatcutters and Packinghouse Workers before they merged; he has been a union official since the 1940s and has been lobbying Congress for more than 20 years. In campaigns he supported insurgents like Metcalfe and Washington over the Democratic machine. In the House he serves on the Education and Labor Committee, where he is an automatic vote for more generous federal programs and against efforts to cut racial quotas. He is a pro-union stalwart, opposing the subminimum wage, favoring programs to discourage school dropouts, seeking restrictions on textile and apparel imports. He has a bill to provide guaranteed jobs at decent wages and guaranteed incomes. Hayes has been fighting for what he regards as social justice for nearly 50 years, and if his views are unfashionable now he has seen them go out of fashion before and then return. In this, the most Democratic of congressional districts in national elections, he can be reelected with ease—unless the district's leading politician, Mayor Washington, should decide to back someone else.

The People: Pop. 1980: 519,045, dn. 18.9% 1970–80. Households (1980): 63% family, 39% with children, 32% married couples; 72.1% housing units rented; median monthly rent: $183; median house value: $37,300. Voting age pop. (1980): 358,925; 90% Black, 1% Spanish origin, 1% Asian origin.

1984 Presidential Vote: Mondale (D) 196,351   (95%)
                                Reagan (R) 10,153   (5%)

Rep. Charles A. Hayes (D)

Elected Aug. 23, 1983; b. Feb. 17, 1918, Cairo; home, Chicago; Baptist; married (Edna).

Career: Trade unionist; Intl. Vice Pres., Region 12, United Food and Commercial Workers Union, 1979–83.

Offices: 1028 LHOB 20515, 202-225-4372. Also 7801 S. Cottage Grove Ave., Chicago 60619, 312-783-6800.

Committees: *Education and Labor* (11th of 21 D). Subcommittees: Elementary, Secondary and Vocational Education; Labor—Management Relations; Postsecondary Education. *Small Business* (18th of 25 D). Subcommittee: Procurement, Innovation and Minority Enterprise Development.

Group Ratings

	ADA	ACLU	COPE	CFA	LCV	ACU	NTU	NSI	COC	CEI
1986	95	94	100	67	71	0	29	0	6	11
1985	100	—	100	75	—	0	19	—	14	—

National Journal Ratings

	1986 LIB — 1986 CONS		1985 LIB — 1985 CONS	
Economic	87%	— 0%	89%	— 0%
Social	78%	— 21%	85%	— 0%
Foreign	80%	— 0%	92%	— 0%

Key Votes

1) Lmt Cln Water Act	AGN	5) Retain Gun Cont	FOR	9) Aid Angola Reb	AGN
2) Rpl Tobac Sub	AGN	6) Contra Aid	AGN	10) Tax Reform	FOR
3) Grm-Rdmn Def Red	AGN	7) Lmt Text Imp	FOR	11) S Africa Sanc	FOR
4) Ban Polygraph	FOR	8) Limit SDI	FOR	12) Immig Reform	AGN

Election Results

1986 general	Charles A. Hayes (D)	122,376	(96%)	($136,347)
	Joseph C. Faulkner (R)	4,572	(3%)	
1986 primary	Charles A. Hayes (D)	79,356	(93%)	
	Melverlene Clark (D)	6,363	(7%)	
1984 general	Charles A. Hayes (D)	177,438	(96%)	($465,159)
	Eddie L. Warren (Soc.)	8,086	(4%)	

Campaign Contributions and Expenditures

1985-86		Direct Cont. 1985-86		PACS Breakdown 1985-86			
Receipts	$170,174	Indiv.	$43,219	Corp.	$5,000	T/M/H	$7,000
Expend.	$136,347	PACS	$87,575	Labor	$69,225	Agr.	$0
Debts	$35,507	Cand.	$23,061	Ideo.	$1,850	CWOS	$0

*Includes receipts and expenditures for the 1983 special election.

SECOND DISTRICT

Chicago's big steel plants are concentrated on the far south side of town, around the city's artificial port in Lake Calumet. Standing on the 92d Street bridge across the Calumet River, which connects Lake Calumet and Lake Michigan, you are within sight of the largest concentration of ailing steel plants in the United States. To this part of Chicago, late in the 19th century, immigrants began coming from economically backward parts of Europe—from Sicily and Galicia, Bohemia and Lithuania—to work in the steel mills and in George Pullman's model factory town. Some of their descendants live there still, in neighborhoods with names like Slag Valley and the Island, places described colorfully in Ron Grossman's *Guide to Chicago Neighborhoods*. In this area also is the home of Edward Vrdolyak, 10th Ward Alderman, longtime Cook County Democratic chairman, the leader of the anti-Harold Washington majority on the Chicago city council for three years, and unsuccessful candidate against Washington in 1987. In a modest working-class neighborhood, Vrdolyak lives in a lavish house— a kind of lord living in a castle among the people he rules.

Lake Calumet and the steel mills are the central focus of Illinois's 2d Congressional District. But despite the remaining pockets of white ethnics here, this is a black congressional district. The 2d forms a kind of U around the 1st District. The upper left hand side of the U is an almost entirely black neighborhood, mostly Irish at the beginning of the 1960s, and the scene of some of the most rapid neighborhood racial change in the nation during the 1960s and 1970s. The bottom left part of the U is almost entirely black now as well, the result of more recent neighborhood change. There has been some black movement southward as well, into the suburbs directly south of Lake Calumet; some of that has been into a well-established black community in Markham and Harvey, some is just scattered around into neighborhoods of the kind which, 20 years ago, always remained all white. The 2d District's boundaries extend down into these suburbs, crossing the city line but following the natural migration of its ethnic groups outward.

The 2d District is represented by Gus Savage, who has made a career as an opponent of Mayor Daley's Democratic machine. He ran against Representative Morgan Murphy in 1970, in a district whose white majority was just then vanishing; when Murphy retired in 1980, Savage ran again. For 25 years before that he ran a community newspaper and attacked the powers that be. Savage is a temperamental rebel, a politician who called Edward Vrdolyak a "Reaganite racist," a man whose reaction, when his son was stopped in Washington for driving an unregistered car without a license, was to call up the police chief and protest, a candidate who filed blatantly incomplete disclosure statements with the Federal Election Commission, and then said it was the fault of his campaign treasurer whom he couldn't find—although the treasurer was his son. Savage strikes his admirers as a fearless, independent fighter for the people. He strikes others as a rascal—unscrupulous but mostly harmless.

For the fact is that Savage does not cut an important—or often much of any—figure in the House. His absenteeism has been among the highest in the House, and he is anything but a legislative craftsman. Black Muslim leader Louis Farrakhan has extolled him as "our fighter in Congress," but any clout that Savage has he wields in Chicago. Even so, his political base in the 2d District is weak. He was saved from having his district abolished out from under him by a federal court decision. But he has turned in poor performances in primaries. In 1982 he won only 39%, against 35% and 20% for two rivals; in 1984 he had 45% to 22% for the strongest of four weak opponents; in 1986 he got 51% to 21% and 12% for the strongest contenders. He is improving but very slowly and remains vulnerable to challenge. Working for him is the widespread belief in Chicago that real politics takes place at home and that everything else is out of town.

The People: Pop. 1980: 518,931, dn. 1.9% 1970–80. Households (1980): 78% family, 50% with children, 50% married couples; 44.0% housing units rented; median monthly rent: $190; median house value: $37,700. Voting age pop. (1980): 340,827; 66% Black, 7% Spanish origin.

1984 Presidential Vote:	Mondale (D)	168,174	(84%)
	Reagan (R)	32,693	(16%)

Rep. Gus Savage (D)

Elected 1980; b. Oct. 30, 1925, Detroit, MI; home, Chicago; Roosevelt U., B.A. 1951; Kent Col. of Law, 1952–53; Baptist; widowed.

Career: Army, WWII; Journalist, 1954–79; Editor-Publisher, Citizen Commun. Newspapers, 1965–79.

Offices: 1121 LHOB 20515, 202-225-0773. Also 11434 S. Halsted St., Chicago 60628, 312-660-2000.

Committees: *Public Works and Transportation* (10th of 32 D). Subcommittees: Aviation; Economic Development (Chairman); Public Buildings and Grounds; Water Resources. *Small Business* (11th of 27 D). Subcommittees: SBA and the General Economy; Procurement, Innovation and Minority Enterprise Development.

Group Ratings

	ADA	ACLU	COPE	CFA	LCV	ACU	NTU	NSI	COC	CEI
1986	95	100	98	58	79	0	32	0	7	14
1985	100	—	97	75	—	5	35	—	18	—

National Journal Ratings

	1986 LIB — 1986 CONS			1985 LIB — 1985 CONS		
Economic	87%	—	0%	81%	—	17%
Social	83%	—	15%	85%	—	0%
Foreign	80%	—	0%	92%	—	0%

Key Votes

1) Lmt Cln Water Act	AGN	5) Retain Gun Cont	FOR	9) Aid Angola Reb	AGN
2) Rpl Tobac Sub	FOR	6) Contra Aid	AGN	10) Tax Reform	FOR
3) Grm-Rdmn Def Red	AGN	7) Lmt Text Imp	FOR	11) S Africa Sanc	FOR
4) Ban Polygraph	FOR	8) Limit SDI	FOR	12) Immig Reform	AGN

Election Results

1986 general	Gus Savage (D).	99,268	(84%)	($150,979)
	Ron Taylor (R)	19,146	(16%)	
1986 primary	Gus Savage (D).	37,751	(51%)	
	Raymond C. Arias (D)	15,513	(21%)	
	Al Sampson (D)	9,059	(12%)	
	Lawrence Ragland, Jr. (D)	4,333	(6%)	
	Four others (D)	6,700	(9%)	
1984 general	Gus Savage (D).	155,349	(83%)	($116,710)
	Dale F. Harman (R)	31,865	(17%)	($7,987)

Campaign Contributions and Expenditures

1985-86		Direct Cont. 1985-86		PACS Breakdown 1985-86			
Receipts	$153,332	Indiv.	$62,032	Corp.	$6,050	T/M/H	$4,518
Expend.	$150,979	Party	$177	Labor	$67,975	Agr.	$1,625
Debts	$2,452	PACS	$83,668	Ideo.	$3,250	CWOS	$250
		Cand.	$11,300				

THIRD DISTRICT

The 3d Congressional District of Illinois consists of the southwest edge of the city of Chicago and Cook County suburbs adjacent to the south and west. It is an artfully designed district, one intended to reelect the current congressman, Democrat Marty Russo. The Chicago portion of the district has 40% of its people and in 1980 was 96% white, although the area just to the east is heavily black; the district line, running near Western Avenue and the Rock Island tracks, was the 1980 boundary of westward black expansion. Most of the people here are of Irish or Eastern European descent, family-oriented but with their children grown up now in many cases; they cover a broad economic spectrum, from the gritty neighborhoods around Midway Airport to the mansions and Prairie architecture homes of Beverly Hills and Morgan Park, old rich neighborhoods that sit atop one of Chicago's few perceptible hills.

This part of Chicago is only marginally Democratic in close state elections; the old ancestral Democratic preference is balanced by a dislike of programs that seem overly generous to the poor and by fear of the heavily Democratic blacks. But these areas provide solid support for local Democrats, like Marty Russo, whose politics is geared to their attitudes. The district lines seem drawn adroitly enough that movement of blacks up through the 1990 election will only increase Democratic margins in the general election without adding enough black votes to provide a basis for a challenge of a white candidate like Russo in the primary.

The suburban part of the district can be divided into two sections. Running west along 95th Street are predominantly white-collar suburbs, centered on Oak Lawn, a comfortable but not lavish product of the 1950s populated mainly by descendants of the immigrants who lived on Chicago's South Side. To the south, from Blue Island to Markham, are suburbs with a little more of a working-class cast to them, and with significant black populations in some cases. The 3d also swings east to take in parts of the comfortable white-collar suburbs of Homewood and South Holland (Russo's district residence). The suburban territory goes Republican in close statewide elections. But Russo has represented much of this territory since 1974, and has worked it hard, and he seems in little jeopardy.

Russo, like many others in the 1974 class of Democrats, had only a brief professional career before being elected to Congress; but while many of his colleagues were collecting Ivy League credentials or serving as acolytes to powers in Washington, Russo was scrambling upward in the political world of Chicago. He graduated from DePaul, was a law clerk to a judge, and was an assistant state's attorney; he had a law practice which surely benefited from his political connections. He made a shrewd move in running for Congress in 1974, at age 30, in a district which almost everyone else assumed was safely Republican. His victory then, and his impressive consolidation of his position in the seat, has opened up to him a new world in which he has applied, on major national and international issues, the skills and talents he developed in the anything but innocent world of Chicago politics.

He has also made himself an important force in the not very innocent world of the House of Representatives. Early in his House career he became an ally of Dan Rostenkowski, who helped him get good committee assignments—he served first on Energy and Commerce and is now on Ways and Means—and to get leadership assignments—Steering and Policy Committee and deputy whip. He serves on the Budget Committee as well. Russo is a practical-minded legislator, and has been ready to respond to the pleas of well-positioned interests from funeral directors eager to avoid federal regulation to Chicago-based businesses in need of special tax treatment to hospitals opposed to cost-containment proposals. But he is also responsive to organized labor, voting generally on the liberal side of economic issues and taking a tough line on trade. And he is also close to other young and liberal members, like his Capitol Hill roommates George Miller, Leon Panetta, and Charles Schumer, and he tends to vote with them on foreign as well as economic, though less often on cultural issues. Tall, athletic, a scratch golfer whom Rostenkowski likes to team up with in best-ball games, Russo is an aggressive party whip.

Russo played a significant role on the tax reform bill of 1985 and 1986. Through most of the proceedings he was a capable lieutenant for Rostenkowski, who named him over 10 more senior members to the conference committee. Yet Russo says he wants now to make the tax rates more progressive. Generally Russo does not seem overencumbered with abstract principles, but he is able to hold up his part in debate on even complex issues without faltering and in fact with considerable force.

It is not totally unrewarding work. Russo is a close friend of Rostenkowski and a link between the Ways and Means chairman and many of the active younger members. Both maintain their roots in Chicago and maintain rather modest standards of living there, but even in comparatively humble surroundings they are treated in restaurants or convention halls or on the street with the deference and respect that dukes and earls received on campaign with medieval armies. As a political warrior, Russo has been impressively successful as to deter conflict: he has not had a serious opponent since 1976. He complained that his Republican opponent in 1986 waged a negative campaign, but he spent almost no money while Russo spent $483,000 and won with 66% of the vote. Russo seems likely to continue to be an important—for many, a strategic—congressman for many years to come.

The People: Pop. 1980: 519,040, dn. 2.0% 1970–80. Households (1980): 78% family, 39% with children, 65% married couples; 25.2% housing units rented; median monthly rent: $238; median house value: $55,600. Voting age pop. (1980): 379,396; 5% Black, 3% Spanish origin, 1% Asian origin.

1984 Presidential Vote:

Reagan (R)	158,281	(65%)
Mondale (D)	84,752	(35%)

Rep. Martin A. (Marty) Russo (D)

Elected 1974; b. Jan. 23, 1944, Chicago; home, S. Holland; De Paul U., B.A. 1965, J.D. 1967; Roman Catholic; married (Karen).

Career: Law Clerk for IL Appellate Ct. Judge John V. McCormack, 1967–68; Cook Cnty. Asst. State's Atty., 1971–73.

Offices: 2233 RHOB 20515, 202-225-5736. Also 10634 S. Cicero, Oak Lawn 60453, 312-353-8093.

Committees: *Budget* (10th of 21 D). Task Forces: Defense and International Affairs; Economic Policy; Income Security. *Ways and Means* (12th of 23 D). Subcommittee: Trade.

Group Ratings

	ADA	ACLU	COPE	CFA	LCV	ACU	NTU	NSI	COC	CEI
1986	65	43	78	92	66	9	41	0	38	20
1985	70	—	77	50	—	14	46	—	36	—

National Journal Ratings

	1986 LIB — 1986 CONS			1985 LIB — 1985 CONS		
Economic	54%	—	45%	61%	—	38%
Social	48%	—	51%	41%	—	56%
Foreign	61%	—	37%	75%	—	21%

Key Votes

1) Lmt Cln Water Act	AGN	5) Retain Gun Cont	FOR	9) Aid Angola Reb	AGN
2) Rpl Tobac Sub	AGN	6) Contra Aid	AGN	10) Tax Reform	FOR
3) Grm-Rdmn Def Red	FOR	7) Lmt Text Imp	FOR	11) S Africa Sanc	FOR
4) Ban Polygraph	FOR	8) Limit SDI	FOR	12) Immig Reform	AGN

Election Results

1986 general	Martin A. (Marty) Russo (D)...........	102,949	(66%)	($483,102)
	James M. Tierney (R).................	52,618	(34%)	($42,977)
1986 primary	Martin A. (Marty) Russo (D)............	66,325	(91%)	
	Maurice E. Johnson (D)	6,601	(9%)	
1984 general	Martin A. (Marty) Russo (D)..........	143,363	(64%)	($300,237)
	Richard D. Murphy (R)	79,218	(36%)	($6,309)

Campaign Contributions and Expenditures

1985-86		Direct Cont. 1985-86		PACS Breakdown 1985-86			
Receipts	$478,353	Indiv.	$175,546	Corp.	$101,300	T/M/H	$91,675
Expend.	$483,102	PACS	$289,452	Labor	$71,176	Agr.	$2,000
Debts	$2,105	Cand.	$5,000	Ideo.	$7,301	CWOS	$16,000

FOURTH DISTRICT

On the southern edge of metropolitan Chicago—where the suburbs generated by the growth of the great city begin to thin out and the vast prairies, punctuated by neat rectangular-block towns begin—is the 4th Congressional District of Illinois. Its eastern end is anchored in suburbs directly south of Chicago's Lake Calumet industrial district: Calumet City, Lansing, Chicago Heights. In the center, west and south of the Cook County line, is Joliet; in the northwest, Aurora. Joliet and Aurora are little cities with histories of their own: Downstate cities, really, factory towns and marketplaces for the surrounding rich farmland. Settled by Yankees and Germans, they are hard working and prosperous, orderly and pious. Historically they saw Chicago—with its rapid, disorderly growth, its tolerance of graft and vice, its vast peasant immigrant populations—as a cultural enemy; and, as solid Republicans, after the New Deal era they saw Democratic Chicago as a political enemy as well.

Joliet and Aurora are now part of the Chicago metropolitan area, as much as Chicago Heights. People commute back and forth from these towns to Cook County and even the Loop; they tune into Chicago radio and TV stations. Politically, they are part of a vast suburban belt which outvotes Democratic Chicago and almost always delivers solid Republican margins, enough for example to deliver the Chicago metropolitan area to Ronald Reagan by a 54%–45% margin in 1984. Demographically, the 4th is out on Chicago's frontier, a district where 46% of the households contain children (one of the highest figures in Illinois) and 66% contain married couples (ditto).

This 4th District, drawn by Democrats as a Republican district, has had a complex electoral history in the 1980s. The 1982 contest pitted two friendly incumbents against one another; George O'Brien, with less seniority but more of his old district's territory, prevailed over Edward Derwinski, who went on to the State Department. O'Brien was reelected in 1984 and renominated in March 1986, but in May he resigned the nomination because he had cancer and in July he died. His resignation left both parties in a quandary. The Democrats had nominated

Shawn Collins, a 28-year-old accountant from Joliet, for what seemed to be a hopeless race. Now party and union leaders called on Collins to resign in favor of state Senator George Sangmeister, who had lost the lieutenant governor nomination in March to a LaRouche candidate but still was well known and highly popular around Joliet. They persisted through June and July, but Collins, who had worked briefly for Sangmeister and had gotten publicity investigating cost overruns on the McCormick Place rebuilding, insisted on staying in the race.

The Republicans held a convention in July in which each township's party chairman cast votes in proportion to the Republican vote there. The clear winner was Joliet-area legislator Jack Davis, a conservative Reagan enthusiast, Will County Republican chairman, and former steel warehouse business owner. But he was vehemently opposed by the mayor of Chicago Heights who had an old score to settle with him, and it took another month for them to reach a truce. Meanwhile, Collins was appearing at one empty steel plant after another attacking Davis on economic issues and calling for trade restrictions. Davis responded by emphasizing the drug issue and hoping that voters would vote Republican as usual.

Just enough did. The two ran even in Joliet's Will County, but Davis had a 3,500-vote edge in the Cook County portion of the district and won with 52%. So Collins must, for a time anyway, stop daydreaming about going to the House and who knows where else. The word is that Sangmeister, who after all did not have a very good 1986, is thinking about running for the seat in 1988. But this is Republican territory, and Davis will have two years to use the powers of incumbency to make it as safe for him as it was for O'Brien.

The People: Pop. 1980: 519,049, up 13.9% 1970–80. Households (1980): 79% family, 46% with children, 66% married couples; 28.6% housing units rented; median monthly rent: $221; median house value: $54,400. Voting age pop. (1980): 356,524; 10% Black, 5% Spanish origin, 1% Asian origin.

1984 Presidential Vote:

Reagan (R)	....	99,161	(50%)
Mondale (D)	....	98,980	(50%)

Rep. Jack Davis (R)

Elected 1986; b. Sept. 6, 1935, Chicago; home, New Lenox; Southern IL U., B.S. 1956, London Acad. of Sciences, Ph.D.; Protestant; married (Virginia).

Career: Navy, 1956–59; businessman, 1959–78; IL House of Reps., 1976–86.

Offices: 2369 RHOB 20515, 202-225-3635. Also 101 N. Joliet St., Joliet 60431, 815-740-2040; and 100 First National Plaza, Ste. 415, Chicago Heights, 60411, 815-754-4111.

Committees: *Armed Services* (21 of 21 R). Subcommittees: Readiness; Military Personnel and Compensation. *Veterans Affairs* (13th of 13 R). Subcommittees: Housing and Memorial Affairs; Oversight and Investigations.

Group Ratings and Key Votes: Newly Elected

Election Results

1986 general	Jack Davis (R)	 61,633	(52%)	($272,420)
	Shawn Collins (D)	 57,925	(48%)	($203,760)
July 1986	Jack Davis (R) nominated by convention			
1986 primary	George M. O'Brien (R)	 18,903	(100%)	
1984 general	George M. O'Brien (R)	 121,744	(64%)	($141,383)
	Dennis E. Marlow (D)	 68,547	(36%)	

Campaign Contributions and Expenditures

1985-86		Direct Cont. 1985-86		PACS Breakdown 1985-86			
Receipts	$284,318	Indiv.	$135,550	Corp.	$41,770	T/M/H	$41,811
Expend.	$272,420	Party	$9,946	Labor	$1,000	Agr.	$1,000
Unspent	$1,895	PACS	$112,273	Ideo.	$22,742	CWOS	$3,950

FIFTH DISTRICT

The South Branch of the Chicago River is the site of one of western civilization's astonishing engineering feats: here in 1900 the course of the river was turned backward, so that sewage flowed downstate through a canal rather than out into Lake Michigan. The river wards—the old name for the neighborhoods along the river—performed an historic function as important for Chicago as the Sanitary and Ship Canal: they provided a home for successive waves of immigrants from almost every quarter of Europe, the Mediterranean, and, more recently, Latin America. Work could be found nearby on the docks, in warehouses and factories, on the railroads, or on the canal itself. So the Jews came to Maxwell Street, the Czechs to Pilsen, the Irish to Bridgeport, the Italians near Halsted Street, where Jane Addams built Hull House.

These neighborhoods were the real heart of the Chicago Democratic machine. Their residents needed the patronage jobs or even the buckets of coal and turkeys the precinct committeeman or ward leader would supply at Christmas; and in return they were happy to give the Democratic ticket their votes. And more—or so some people charged, since the river wards tended to report their vote totals late, and had a habit of supplying the Democratic ticket with almost exactly the margin it needed to prevail.

Now most of the old residents are gone, particularly on the north side of the river. On the south side Bridgeport and the Back of the Yards (the stockyards) area remain mostly white and Irish; they are still neighborhoods full of young families and freckle-faced kids. And of course Bridgeport's 11th ward was the home of Mayor Richard J. Daley and of a succession of mayors, from 1933 to 1979; part of Daley's strength was that he always remained in Bridgeport, living in a modest bungalow on South Lowe, three blocks from where he was born. Most of the 5th District south of the canal has a distinct Irish flavor; Archer Avenue, a diagonal that heads out toward Midway Airport, was historically the path of outward migration for Chicago's South Side Irish population.

The north side of the river has changed, however—or, rather, is serving again the function it did for so many years. This time the group being welcomed is Chicago's Mexican-Americans. The 5th Congressional District includes wards on both sides of the river and extends into suburban communities on both sides of the canal out to the Cook County line; 21% of its adult population was of Spanish origin in 1980. More strikingly, fully 40% of the children in the district are of Spanish origin; most of the non-Spanish population here is relatively old, and it is not hard to see who will inherit the future. The Mexican-Americans are not an important factor in the 5th District's politics today; the machine is not able to help them get ahead as it did their predecessors, nor do they seem convinced—as the Irish and blacks tended to be—that politics is the way up for them. But by the 1990s it seems clear the Mexican-Americans will transform the politics of the river wards, and no one is sure how.

It could be quite a change, however, since today the 5th District is Chicago's strongest machine area. The current congressman, William Lipinski, was slated by the Cook County Democratic Committee in 1982 and beat the incumbent, John Fary, by a 61%–36% margin in the primary. The surprise is that Fary bothered to run at all: the story goes that he got the seat when he was summoned into Mayor Daley's office, expecting to be told that he was retiring from the legislature, and instead was told he would replace a deceased congressman. Lipinski, a parks patronage employee who became an alderman, won easily.

The 5th District, extended into the suburbs in 1982, includes some Republican territory, notably the suburbs of Cicero and Berwyn. Cicero is an oddity, a Bohemian town with an old-fashioned Republican machine, famous for welcoming Al Capone's operations in the 1920s. In the 1960s it was still all-white and was the site of a march by Martin Luther King, Jr.; more recently, it has been embroiled in debate over whether to let its bars continue to stay open till 6 a.m. But most of the suburbs along the canal are modest, working-class places which do not cast large Republican majorities; and overall the district is safely Democratic. Certainly that is the case in congressional contests. Lipinski has won impressive margins in 1984 and 1986 elections.

In Washington, the 5th District's previous congressmen took little legislative initiative. One, John Kluczynski, rose in seniority to chair a highways subcommittee, but he was not an initiator of legislation; Fary was almost inert. Lipinski, younger, politically more adept, does more. He serves on nuts-and-bolts committees (Public Works, Merchant Marine) and has spent much effort getting a southwest Chicago rail transit line built and promoting Chicago's Midway Airport. He is proud of his position as co-chairman of the national Democrats' Council on Ethnic Americans, and makes speeches lauding family values, opposing Libyan terrorism, and noting the advance of democracy around the world. His record on foreign and cultural issues is rather conservative; on economics he is more inclined to go along with liberal Democrats, but not always.

The People: Pop. 1980: 518,971, dn. 2.7% 1970–80. Households (1980): 73% family, 37% with children, 56% married couples; 47.9% housing units rented; median monthly rent: $161; median house value: $52,600. Voting age pop. (1980): 377,195; 21% Spanish origin, 3% Black, 2% Asian origin.

1984 Presidential Vote:

Reagan (R)	107,199	(58%)
Mondale (D)	76,570	(42%)

Rep. William O. Lipinski (D)

Elected 1982; b. Dec. 22, 1937, Chicago; home, Chicago; Loras Col., 1956–57; Roman Catholic; married (Rose Marie).

Career: Chicago Parks and Recreation Dept., 1958–75; Chicago City Alderman, 1975–83.

Offices: 1222 LHOB 20515, 202-225-5701. Also 5832 Archer Ave., Chicago 60638, 312-886-0481.

Committees: *Merchant Marine and Fisheries* (14th of 25 D). Subcommittees: Coast Guard and Navigation; Merchant Marine. *Public Works and Transportation* (17th of 32 D). Subcommittees: Aviation; Economic Development; Surface Transportation.

Group Ratings

	ADA	ACLU	COPE	CFA	LCV	ACU	NTU	NSI	COC	CEI
1986	45	26	90	58	53	45	20	78	27	17
1985	55	—	89	83	—	33	26	—	14	—

National Journal Ratings

	1986 LIB — 1986 CONS			1985 LIB — 1985 CONS		
Economic	68%	—	31%	68%	—	30%
Social	63%	—	36%	44%	—	54%
Foreign	34%	—	64%	44%	—	56%

Key Votes

1) Lmt Cln Water Act	AGN	5) Retain Gun Cont	FOR	9) Aid Angola Reb	FOR
2) Rpl Tobac Sub	AGN	6) Contra Aid	FOR	10) Tax Reform	FOR
3) Grm-Rdmn Def Red	AGN	7) Lmt Text Imp	FOR	11) S Africa Sanc	FOR
4) Ban Polygraph	FOR	8) Limit SDI	AGN	12) Immig Reform	FOR

Election Results

1986 general	William O. Lipinski (D)	82,466	(70%)	($152,573)
	Daniel John Sobieski (R)	34,738	(30%)	($11,303)
1986 primary	William O. Lipinski (D)	54,791	(100%)	
1984 general	William O. Lipinski (D)	106,597	(64%)	($86,392)
	John M. Paczkowski (R).	61,109	(36%)	

Campaign Contributions and Expenditures

1985-86		Direct Cont. 1985-86		PACS Breakdown 1985-86			
Receipts	$150,297	Indiv.	$74,766	Corp.	$14,100	T/M/H	$17,700
Expend.	$152,573	PACS	$69,775	Labor	$31,225	Agr.	$1,250
Unspent	$18,225			Ideo.	$4,750	CWOS	$750

SIXTH DISTRICT

North and west of O'Hare Airport, one to two dozen miles away from Chicago's Loop, is the 6th Congressional District of Illinois. This is one of the newer parts of the Chicago metropolitan area. Back in the 1950s, when Mayor Richard J. Daley first got the idea of making O'Hare into one of the major transportation centers in the world, this land was mostly cornfields and apple orchards. There were strings of suburbs along railroad commuter lines: Park Ridge, Des Plaines, and Mount Prospect on the Chicago and Northwestern line running directly northwest from the Loop; Elmhurst, Villa Park, Lombard, and Glen Ellyn on the lines running directly west. In the last 30 years, the land in between has been filled in with one suburb and subdivision after another, and the result is the current 6th District.

This is high income, almost all white, mostly but by no means exclusively Wasp suburbia. Economically it is market-oriented; politically, hostile to the Chicago Democratic machine; culturally, tradition-minded but with some ambivalence: this district has one of the highest percentages of working women in the nation. In partisan terms, it is one of the most heavily Republican districts in the nation.

This is the district that elects Henry Hyde, one of the Republicans' most competent and motivated legislators. He may come from hard-bitten Illinois, but he acts from deep belief more than political calculation. In time that often proves to be good politics. In the 1970s, for example, when abortion was hailed as a form of personal liberation and as science's answer to overpopulation, Hyde began proposing his amendments prohibiting the use of federal funds to pay for abortions in various circumstances. Most congressmen regarded this as a time-wasting diversion; Hyde, who regards abortion as murder, thought the issue was central. He brought not only dedication to his task, but ingenuity, attaching his amendments to all manner of bills. By the early 1980s the House was routinely passing Hyde Amendments; and the number of federally-funded abortions was close to zero.

Since then, Hyde has made a difference on a variety of issues, and increasingly on foreign policy, from his seat on the Foreign Affairs Committee and on the Intelligence Committee, on which he is now the ranking Republican (and which he would like to see folded into a joint House–Senate committee). He brings to his work intellectual honesty: he changed his position on the Voting Rights Act in 1982 because hearings convinced him it needed reauthorization. He brings a gift for invective: he called the SALT II treaty a "paper pussycat" and to the opponents of aid to the Nicaraguan contras he said in 1986 that history "is going to assign to you Democrats the role of pallbearers at the funeral of democracy in Central America." He is politically fearless: he took on the nuclear freeze advocates in 1983, and by forcing them to defend in detail their attractive-sounding proposal derailed it. He gives his adversaries the compliment of taking them seriously, by going to the trouble of finding out what they've said on issues in the past and quoting it back to them: he cited Stephen Solarz's prediction 10 years before that the Soviets would leave Angola if we didn't support their opponents and quoted John Kennedy and Hubert Humphrey to Democrats arguing for a comprehensive test ban treaty. He has an aversion to the political cheap shot: he stands up and supports foreign aid, including money for international agencies, when members of right and left vote against it or encumber it with restrictions. He takes on tough chores: he was one of the House managers for the impeachment trial of Judge Harry Claiborne in 1986.

Hyde's actions seem to stem from deep religious beliefs combined with a trial lawyer's combative instincts, a respect for rules combined with a certain compassion. Touched, apparently, by Barney Frank's jab that right-to-lifers cared about a child's quality of life from conception to birth, Hyde has gone out of his way to support programs to improve children's nutrition and chances in life. He took the lead in pushing through a bill providing Medicaid for prenatal medical care and food stamps for pregnant women, and is co-sponsor with Henry Waxman of measures to reduce infant mortality. Congressmen who oppose abortion, Hyde says, should "consider whether we do not also have a positive obligation to protect a baby's life and health beyond the action of simply prohibiting abortion." Hyde is a co-sponsor of legislation to redress the grievances of Japanese–Americans sent to internment camps during World War II. He was convinced by the argument that if fetuses have constitutional rights, so too did the people who were interned. On every issue Hyde is sensitive to the burdens of obligation and responsibility: in 1984 he took the lead when Mario Cuomo argued at Notre Dame that in a pluralistic society Catholics should not seek to put their views on abortion into law. Hyde went to Notre Dame and argued that they have the obligation to do as much as they can within the limits of representative government.

Hyde's zeal is sometimes impolitic, and he has lost out on leadership positions in the past. But Republican leader Robert Michel did not hesitate to put him on the special panel investigating the Iran-contra scandal. Hyde said he found it "incredible" that Oliver North "could be the sole genesis of this operation," but no one doubted that he would listen to the evidence and weigh it on the merits.

The People: Pop. 1980: 519,015, up 19.4% 1970–80. Households (1980): 79% family, 44% with children, 70% married couples; 24.4% housing units rented; median monthly rent: $293; median house value: $76,000. Voting age pop. (1980): 367,916; 3% Spanish origin, 2% Asian origin, 1% Black.

1984 Presidential Vote: Reagan (R) 121,280   (56%)
Mondale (D) 96,517   (44%)

Rep. Henry J. Hyde (R)

Elected 1974; b. Apr. 18, 1924, Chicago; home, Bensenville; Georgetown U., B.S. 1947, Loyola U., J.D. 1949; Roman Catholic; married (Jeanne).

Career: Navy, WWII; Practicing atty., 1950–75; IL House of Reps., 1967–74, Major. Ldr., 1971–72.

Offices: 2104 RHOB 20515, 202-225-4561. Also 50 East Oak St., Addison 60101, 312-832-5950.

Committees: *Foreign Affairs* (7th of 18 R). Subcommittees: Arms Control, International Security and Science; Western Hemisphere Affairs. *Judiciary* (3d of 14 R). Subcommittees: Courts, Civil Liberties, and the Administration of Justice; Monopolies and Commercial Law. *Permanent Select Committee on Intelligence* (Ranking Member of 6 R). Subcommittees: Oversight and Evaluation; Program and Budget Authorization.

Group Ratings

	ADA	ACLU	COPE	CFA	LCV	ACU	NTU	NSI	COC	CEI
1986	5	5	16	17	27	90	53	100	75	79
1985	15	—	17	50	—	81	55	—	74	—

National Journal Ratings

	1986 LIB — 1986 CONS			1985 LIB — 1985 CONS		
Economic	10%	—	88%	26%	—	74%
Social	23%	—	74%	0%	—	76%
Foreign	16%	—	79%	0%	—	76%

Key Votes

1) Lmt Cln Water Act	FOR	5) Retain Gun Cont	FOR	9) Aid Angola Reb	FOR
2) Rpl Tobac Sub	FOR	6) Contra Aid	FOR	10) Tax Reform	FOR
3) Grm-Rdmn Def Red	AGN	7) Lmt Text Imp	AGN	11) S Africa Sanc	AGN
4) Ban Polygraph	AGN	8) Limit SDI	AGN	12) Immig Reform	AGN

Election Results

1986 general	Henry J. Hyde (R)	98,196	(75%)	($229,898)
	Robert H. Renshaw (D)	32,064	(25%)	($6,378)
1986 primary	Henry J. Hyde (R)	24,376	(100%)	
1984 general	Henry J. Hyde (R)	157,370	(75%)	($226,737)
	Robert H. Renshaw (D)	52,189	(25%)	($6,324)

Campaign Contributions and Expenditures

1985-86		Direct Cont. 1985-86		PACS Breakdown 1985-86			
Receipts	$241,958	Indiv.	$123,396	Corp.	$44,308	T/M/H	$42,100
Expend.	$229,898	Party	$3,451	Labor	$250	Agr.	$0
Unspent	$133,497	PACS	$95,605	Ideo.	$6,011	CWOS	$2,936

SEVENTH DISTRICT

The Loop is usually the first thing you think of when you think of Chicago. Here, where Louis Sullivan pioneered high-rise construction, stand the city's great skyscrapers, including the Sears Tower, the world's tallest building. Chicago also means the luxury shopping and office district along North Michigan Avenue, and the vast parks (including the railroad lines they all but conceal) along Lake Michigan. This is the face Chicago likes to present to the world: the giant buildings rising where the prairies meet the inland sea, a vast concentration of brains and muscle, the nerve center of the nation.

But not all of Chicago is so dazzling. Behind the lakefront, there is virtually every kind of neighborhood. Directly west of the Loop you find the nation's largest skid row on West Madison and, beyond that, the West Side black ghetto. This is much less organized, less of a community, than the South Side; blacks who do well may stay on the South Side, but West Side blacks, when they do well, tend to get out as fast as they can. Farther west, there are more contrasts: cross Austin Boulevard and you come to the suburb of Oak Park, middle class since Ernest Hemingway grew up there 80 years ago, and now integrated. Just beyond is River Forest, with grander streets and bigger lots; both Oak Park and River Forest contain a number of Frank Lloyd Wright houses. Still further are Maywood, a black-majority suburb, and the modest working-class suburb of Bellwood.

Taken together, these disparate areas make up Illinois's 7th Congressional District. Chicago accounts for three-fourths of its population, and the West Side ghetto for most of that. This is a black majority district, extended into the suburbs in 1982 so as to maximize the number of Democratic and black districts. But if the purpose was political it did have a demographic justification, for Chicagoland blacks are moving, slowly but in significant numbers, to the suburbs.

The 7th District is represented in the House by Cardiss Collins. She cuts a different figure than she did when she was first elected in 1973. She was elected to fill the seat vacated when her husband died in a plane crash; he had been a routine machine backer and she was expected to be the same. But on occasion Collins has become more independent and articulate. She chaired the Black Caucus creditably in 1979 and 1980; she now serves on Energy and Commerce, the most sought after assignment for House Democrats. While not a legislative powerhouse (one of her pet projects is a proposal to establish a $100 billion national lottery, the proceeds of which would be used to buttress social programs), she has proved to be more the cipher that some had expected.

She does have one serious political problem, however: she backed Jane Byrne over her then-House colleague Harold Washington in the 1983 mayoral primary. It was a plausible thing to do: Washington started off a weak candidate (he had gotten only 11% of the vote four years before) and Byrne had genuine black support (she ended up with 20% of the black votes). But the enthusiasm almost all Chicago blacks felt after Washington's victory spelled trouble for Collins. In the last two elections she has had primary opposition from Alderman Danny Davis, a Washington supporter. In 1984 she beat him 48%–39%; in 1986, 60%–40%. These are not impressive scores for an incumbent, and unless she ingratiates herself with Washington supporters in the 1987 campaign she could have serious problems again in 1988.

The People: Pop. 1980: 519,034, dn. 15.8% 1970–80. Households (1980): 65% family, 42% with children, 36% married couples; 67.0% housing units rented; median monthly rent: $184; median house value: $54,500. Voting age pop. (1980): 343,964; 60% Black, 4% Spanish origin, 2% Asian origin.

1984 Presidential Vote:

Mondale (D)	141,185	(75%)
Reagan (R)	47,301	(25%)

Rep. Cardiss Collins (D)

Elected June 5, 1973; b. Sept. 24, 1931, St. Louis, MO; home, Chicago; Northwestern U.; Baptist; widowed.

Career: Stenographer, IL Dept. of Labor; secy., accountant, and revenue auditor, IL Dept. of Revenue.

Offices: 2264 RHOB 20515, 202-225-5006. Also 230 S. Dearborn St., Ste. 3880, Chicago 60604, 312-353-5754; and 328 West Lake, Oak Park 60302, 312-383-1400.

Committees: *Energy and Commerce* (11th of 23 D). Subcommittees: Commerce, Consumer Protection and Competitiveness; Health and the Environment; Telecommunications and Finance. *Government Operations* (3d of 24 D). Subcommittee: Government Activities and Transportation (Chairman). *Sel. Comm. on Narcotics Abuse and Control* (5th of 15 D).

Group Ratings

	ADA	ACLU	COPE	CFA	LCV	ACU	NTU	NSI	COC	CEI
1986	95	94	95	67	82	0	28	0	13	17
1985	95	—	94	92	—	5	34	—	10	—

National Journal Ratings

	1986 LIB — 1986 CONS		1985 LIB — 1985 CONS	
Economic	87% —	0%	89% —	0%
Social	83% —	15%	85% —	0%
Foreign	80% —	0%	92% —	0%

Key Votes

1) Lmt Cln Water Act	AGN	5) Retain Gun Cont	FOR	9) Aid Angola Reb	AGN
2) Rpl Tobac Sub	FOR	6) Contra Aid	AGN	10) Tax Reform	FOR
3) Grm-Rdmn Def Red	AGN	7) Lmt Text Imp	FOR	11) S Africa Sanc	FOR
4) Ban Polygraph	–	8) Limit SDI	FOR	12) Immig Reform	FOR

Election Results

1986 general	Cardiss Collins (D)	90,761	(80%)	($233,583)
	Caroline K. Kallas (R)	21,055	(19%)	($9,302)
1986 primary	Cardiss Collins (D)	35,249	(60%)	
	Danny K. Davis (D)	23,938	(40%)	
1984 general	Cardiss Collins (D)	135,493	(78%)	($195,427)
	James L. Bevel (R)	37,411	(22%)	($10,427)

Campaign Contributions and Expenditures

1985-86		Direct Cont. 1985-86		PACS Breakdown 1985-86			
Receipts	$304,742	Indiv.	$32,073	Corp.	$32,408	T/M/H	$51,488
Expend.	$233,583	PACS	$246,524	Labor	$118,363	Agr.	$1,000
Unspent	$103,880	Cand.	$38,800	Ideo.	$38,565	CWOS	$4,700

EIGHTH DISTRICT

The 8th Congressional District of Illinois is a large chunk of the North Side of Chicago, with a couple of square miles of suburbs added to meet the one-person-one-vote standard. This is one of the most polyglot places in the nation, a part of Chicago which for more than 100 years has been home to immigrants and refugees from around the world. It is in particular a Polish-American district. As long ago as 1876, you could hear Polish spoken more often than English in the neighborhoods near Holy Trinity and St. Stanislaus Kostka—there are always two main Polish churches, it seems—and today you still can. In Chicago, ethnic groups tend to move out radial avenues, and the Polish have moved out along Milwaukee Avenue, which parallels the Kennedy Expressway and the North Branch of the Chicago River; Italians tended to move out along Grand Avenue, to the point that there are now more in the suburbs than in the city; Ukrainians have their main churches and community in between. Following roughly in the same footsteps have been Mexican-Americans and Puerto Ricans. The 8th District's adult population in 1980 was 25% of Spanish origin; its under 18 population was 48% of Spanish origin. There are, by the way, virtually no blacks here. The boundary between the 7th and 8th Districts pretty closely tracks neighborhood racial barriers, and Mexican-Americans, here as elsewhere, seem to seek out white working-class rather than black neighborhoods.

In a comfortable but modest house looking across Pulaski Park and at St. Stanislaus Kostka lives 32d ward committeeman Dan Rostenkowski, who has also served as the 8th District's congressman for three decades. And he really does live there: his father was ward committeeman, he has spent fewer than a dozen weekends in Washington since he was first elected to Congress in 1958, and he has been careful to stay ward committeeman in a city which considers sending an alderman to Congress a demotion. In the rest of the country Rostenkowski is known as chairman of the House Ways and Means Committee, one of the most powerful members of Congress, and the man who as much as anyone else (except perhaps Bill Bradley) put together and got enacted the Tax Reform Act of 1986.

This is a bill that no one thought could pass and a man no one thought would get it passed. After all through most of his career Rostenkowski, like most Chicago organization Democrats, has been anything but quixotic or ideological. He is quite undeceived by the way lobbyists operate, and he has been happy to cater to the needs of big Chicago interests. The idea of him passing a bill flattening tax rates and eliminating most preferences, a bill few other members or voters were enthusiastic about and which would reduce the institutional power of his committee, seemed preposterous up through summer 1985. Yet it happened. How? Why?

To get to the answers, go back and review his record as Chairman of Ways and Means. He started off badly. In 1981, his first year in the post, he seemed determined above all else to have his name on the tax bill that passed the House, and so he bid for the support of all manner of lobbies by letting them tack their favorite provisions on his bill—and lost anyway. For much of 1982 he lay low. Despite the constitutional requirement that revenue measures originate in the House—a provision that has been the source of much of Ways and Means's traditional power— he let the Senate pass the 1982 tax bill and then mostly went along with it. Then he emerged as an active leader. He managed the 1983 Social Security rescue measure and supported a bill to cap the third year of the Reagan tax cut for high-income taxpayers. He helped lead the House to its prompt passage of budget and tax bills in 1984. What tied together most of his stands is his institutional interest, as chairman, in supporting his subcommittee chairmen. On Social Security, for example, he backed subcommittee chairman Jake Pickle, and opposed his close friend Tip O'Neill and Claude Pepper, on raising the retirement age. He stood behind free trader Sam Gibbons on trade issues, tax reformer Pete Stark on Select Revenue Measures, and liberal Harold Ford on welfare and unemployment compensation. In the process, Rostenkowski got comfortable with his position, and with taking risks.

Along came tax reform, an idea promoted by Bill Bradley, a senator of the minority party, and Richard Gephardt, a junior Ways and Means member, and advanced by then Treasury Secretary Donald Regan, who was lukewarm if not hostile to it thereafter; and Rostenkowski decided to take the biggest risk of all. This was the chairman's issue, on which he expected support from his subcommittee chairmen in return for the support he gave them (when Gibbons, number two on the committee, didn't back him up reliably, Rostenkowski coolly kept him off the conference committee). He decided that the country was ripe for tax reform, that the Democratic Congress should get or share the credit, and—something entirely new for him—he went on TV in the spring of 1985 and asked voters to "write Rosty." Not a lawyer, not even a college graduate and certainly not previously considered a tax expert, he nonetheless brilliantly brokered the bill through his committee, recovered when the Republicans voted down the rule needed to get it on the floor, and got it passed by the House in December 1985. He stayed in touch with Bradley as the bill moved, stalled, then rushed through the Senate, and then in the conference committee had the upper hand. The House conferees were picked carefully so that Rostenkowski always could rely on every House Democrat; senior Ways and Means Republicans, none of them strong, he treated with contempt, and the word is that they learned what the conference decided by reading the papers next morning. Senate Finance Chairman Bob Packwood lacked similar assurance about his conferees, and so Rostenkowski carried most of the points.

Can he top this? Rostenkowski will doubtless play a role on trade legislation, though he may defer to others—perhaps to Gibbons, more likely, despite his own free trade leanings, to Ed Jenkins, whom he kept off the tax reform conference committee. There will be technical tax work to do surely. And Rostenkowski will probably make some speeches to trade groups and get in a few rounds of golf in Palm Springs and Boca Raton. He is not on the best of terms with Speaker Jim Wright, who helped defeat him when he sought reelection as caucus chairman in 1971, and he refuses to rule out running for speaker. He dabbles in fights for committee posts, and sometimes wins. But all this is just paw exercise for a powerful and agile cat.

Rostenkowski holds the safest of seats. The 8th District is understandably proud of its congressman; so are prominent members of the Polish-American community; so are businessmen in Chicago and leaders of industries all over America who have dealt with him. He keeps about $1 million in his campaign treasury, but he didn't bother to raise much more in 1985 and 1986; no one doubts he could quickly raise several million any time—and this is money he could, on retiring, convert to personal income. There is talk he will retire. But Rostenkowski seems to like being a legislator: he went to Springfield when he was 24 and persuaded Mayor Daley to send him to Congress at 30. He enjoys golf outings and steak dinners at Morton's of Chicago, but his children are grown and he seems to have no desire to get really rich. Why shouldn't he stay in the House where he is such an important member?

The People: Pop. 1980: 519,034, dn. 9.3% 1970–80. Households (1980): 68% family, 36% with children, 49% married couples; 61.3% housing units rented; median monthly rent: $174; median house value: $51,500. Voting age pop. (1980): 375,186; 25% Spanish origin, 3% Black, 2% Asian origin.

1984 Presidential Vote:

Reagan (R)	90,875	(51%)
Mondale (D)	85,928	(49%)

Rep. Dan Rostenkowski (D)

Elected 1958; b. Jan. 2, 1928, Chicago; home, Chicago; Loyola U., 1948–51; Roman Catholic; married (LaVerne).

Career: Army, Korea; IL House of Reps., 1953–55; IL Senate, 1955–59.

Offices: 2111 RHOB 20515, 202-225-4061. Also 2148 N. Damen Ave., Chicago 60647, 312-431-1111.

Committees: *Ways and Means* (Chairman of 23 D). Subcommittee: Trade. *Joint Committee on Taxation* (Chairman).

Group Ratings

	ADA	ACLU	COPE	CFA	LCV	ACU	NTU	NSI	COC	CEI
1986	65	63	87	42	95	15	25	0	35	21
1985	75	—	87	67	—	20	29	—	36	—

National Journal Ratings

	1986 LIB — 1986 CONS	1985 LIB — 1985 CONS
Economic	55% — 44%	79% — 21%
Social	60% — 39%	41% — 56%
Foreign	72% — 27%	79% — 20%

Key Votes

1) Lmt Cln Water Act	AGN	5) Retain Gun Cont	FOR	9) Aid Angola Reb	AGN
2) Rpl Tobac Sub	AGN	6) Contra Aid	AGN	10) Tax Reform	FOR
3) Grm-Rdmn Def Red	FOR	7) Lmt Text Imp	AGN	11) S Africa Sanc	—
4) Ban Polygraph	FOR	8) Limit SDI	FOR	12) Immig Reform	FOR

Election Results

1986 general	Dan Rostenkowski (D)	82,873	(79%)	($240,208)
	Thomas J. DeFazio (R)	22,383	(21%)	
1986 primary	Dan Rostenkowski (D)	114,385	(87%)	
	Gerald Pechenuk (D)	8,005	(13%)	
1984 general	Dan Rostenkowski (D)	114,385	(71%)	($370,916)
	Spiro F. Georgeson (R)	46,030	(29%)	

Campaign Contributions and Expenditures

1985-86		Direct Cont. 1985-86		PACS Breakdown 1985-86			
Receipts	$243,976	Indiv.	$17,377	Corp.	$111,333	T/M/H	$72,800
Expend.	$240,208	PACS	$212,883	Labor	$14,250	Agr.	$0
Unspent	$596,703			Ideo.	$10,000	CWOS	$4,500

NINTH DISTRICT

Along Chicago's Lake Shore Drive, overlooking Lake Michigan, are more classic buildings of the International School than are collected anywhere else in the world. Interspersed with older, more traditional and evocative buildings, they present to the world the face Chicago likes to show: affluent, elegant, massive. Behind the apartment towers, however, is another Chicago— messier, grimier, but also more vibrant and various. This is the Chicago of Studs Terkel's Division Street, a city full of life's losers and winners; the Chicago of Saul Bellow, a city of successful small businessmen and irrationally vengeful hoodlums; the Chicago of Nelson Algren, a city of drug addicts and drifters. You can find all these Chicagos just a few short blocks from each other, within a mile or so of the lakefront, where the only threat to this funkiness is the continued march north and west of young affluent Chicagoans renovating and restoring old houses.

This is the Chicago of Illinois's 9th Congressional District that begins at the Near North Side and follows the lakefront, and the varied neighborhoods just to the west, to Chicago's northern city limits and beyond. It is the one large part of the city where the dominant political tone is intellectual and where voters' gut preference, at least sometimes, is for reform over regular. Demographically, this is a singles district, more like Manhattan than most parts of the Chicago metropolitan area; fewer than one-fourth of the households contain children, and less than half house families. The dominant ethnic bloc is Jewish: affluent Jews in high-rises, older ethnic Jews in the Rogers Park neighborhood near the northern city limit.

They are joined by many Jewish voters in the suburban portions of the 9th District added in the 1980s. These include Evanston, which with Northwestern University and a large black community has forgotten its Republican heritage and now votes Democratic; most of Skokie, the most heavily Jewish of Chicago's suburbs, where a handful of Nazis got the ACLU to defend their right to stage a march; Glenview and Northbrook, more Protestant and Republican, but not enough to tip the district's balance. Altogether, about three-fifths of the district's votes are cast in the city, two-fifths in the suburbs.

The 9th District's congressman, Sidney Yates, has represented the Chicago lakefront wards a long time; only four members of the current Congress (Claude Pepper, Jamie Whitten, Melvin Price, John Stennis) were already serving when he was first elected in 1948. His seniority is not so great, however, because he ran for the Senate in 1962, nearly beating Everett Dirksen, and gave up his House seat for two years. Otherwise, he would be the number two Democrat on Appropriations today.

Yates nevertheless is an important and, in his area, powerful congressman. He chairs the Appropriations Interior Subcommittee, and is an active player on environmental issues and on federal support of the arts and humanities. He is a kind of federal Maecenas, and has nurtured the national endowments for arts, humanities, and historic preservation, not just by giving them money, but by breathing into them something more than bureaucratic life. He continues to be an aggressive fighter and well-informed detail man. He also takes care of local matters, working to get federal dollars to rehabilitate Chicago's Navy Pier, trying to save Chicago's shoreline parks and neighborhoods from the thundering waves and cakes of ice from Lake Michigan as lake levels reach historic highs. Only an appropriations subcommittee chairman would consider it part of his duty as well as clearly within his power to hold back the rising floods of one-quarter of the fresh water in the world.

Yates's political base has always been in Chicago's Jewish community, and he has been a spokesman for national Jewish causes; he is proud that he was one of the members of Congress (Henry Jackson was another) who took on the cause of promoting Hyman Rickover to Admiral, and won over those in the Navy who feared his unorthodox ideas and, perhaps, disliked his ethnic background. Chicago's Jewish voters have always had an uneasy accommodation with the Democratic machine: they vote Democratic and usually don't support party insurgents, but in return get to run their own neighborhoods and express their own views on national issues. This is the course Yates has taken as well. It has served him well in lakefront congressional races and nearly got him into the Senate. He was supposed to have had a hard race in 1982, when the district was extended into the suburbs and targeted by Republicans. But he was reelected with 67% then and has done better since. Approaching 80, he has a safe seat.

The People: Pop. 1980: 519,120, dn. 8.9% 1970–80. Households (1980): 48% family, 22% with children, 37% married couples; 65.3% housing units rented; median monthly rent: $251; median house value: $88,100. Voting age pop. (1980): 422,900; 9% Black, 8% Spanish origin, 5% Asian origin.

1984 Presidential Vote: Mondale (D) 129,644   (55%)
Reagan (R) 106,151   (45%)

Rep. Sidney R. Yates (D)

Elected 1964; b. Aug. 27, 1909, Chicago; home, Chicago; U. of Chicago, Ph.B. 1931, J.D. 1933; Jewish; married (Adeline).

Career: Practicing atty.; Asst. Atty. for IL St. Bank Receiver, 1935–37; Asst. Atty. Gen. attached to IL Commerce Comm., 1937–40; Navy, WWII; U.S. House of Reps., 1949–63; Dem. Nominee for U.S. Senate, 1962; U.N. Rep., Trusteeship Council, 1963–64.

Offices: 2234 RHOB 20515, 202-225-2111. Also 230 S. Dearborn St., Rm. 3920, Chicago 60604, 312-353-4596; and 2100 Ridge Ave., Rm. 2700, Evanston, 60204, 312-328-2610.

Committees: *Appropriations* (5th of 35 D). Subcommittees: Foreign Operations; Interior (Chairman); Treasury–Postal Service–General Government.

Group Ratings

	ADA	ACLU	COPE	CFA	LCV	ACU	NTU	NSI	COC	CEI
1986	90	94	92	92	95	0	34	0	12	26
1985	100	—	92	100	—	10	37	—	20	—

National Journal Ratings

	1986 LIB — 1986 CONS		1985 LIB — 1985 CONS	
Economic	80%	— 19%	85%	— 11%
Social	89%	— 0%	85%	— 0%
Foreign	80%	— 0%	92%	— 0%

Key Votes

1) Lmt Cln Water Act	AGN	5) Retain Gun Cont	FOR	9) Aid Angola Reb	AGN
2) Rpl Tobac Sub	FOR	6) Contra Aid	AGN	10) Tax Reform	FOR
3) Grm-Rdmn Def Red	AGN	7) Lmt Text Imp	FOR	11) S Africa Sanc	FOR
4) Ban Polygraph	FOR	8) Limit SDI	FOR	12) Immig Reform	FOR

Election Results

1986 general	Sidney R. Yates (D)	94,738	(72%)	($97,479)
	Herbert Sohn (R)	36,715	(28%)	($38,385)
1986 primary	Sidney R. Yates (D)	36,513	(84%)	
	Judith Acheson (D)...................	6,783	(16%)	
1984 general	Sidney R. Yates (D)	144,879	(68%)	($106,200)
	Herbert Sohn (R)	69,613	(32%)	($80,917)

Campaign Contributions and Expenditures

1985-86		Direct Cont. 1985-86		PACS Breakdown 1985-86			
Receipts	$149,145	Indiv.	$125,552	Corp.	$4,550	T/M/H	$5,500
Expend.	$97,479	PACS	$20,729	Labor	$6,000	Agr.	$0
Unspent	$110,010			Ideo.	$4,679	CWOS	$0

TENTH DISTRICT

The North Shore suburbs of Chicago are where the elite of this metropolitan area mostly live. Running north from Evanston, a whole series of towns along Lake Michigan—Wilmette, Winnetka, Glencoe, Highland Park, Lake Forest—each has a slightly different personality and character, but all are similar economically: rich—with the average per capita income over $44,000. Here is where you will find New Trier Township High School, which has long prided itself as the academically most distinguished public school in the nation. These suburbs were settled long ago, pioneered by riders on one of Chicago's commuter railroad lines. The large houses and shady streets have a comfortable, lived-in look, and not a trace of shabbiness. This is the land of the book and movie *Ordinary People,* a place where pleasant, affluent people live in an environment which seems a long way from the clamorous ethnic neighborhoods of Chicago.

The 10th Congressional District of Illinois covers the North Shore, starting above Evanston and reaching north, past the rich suburbs, to the industrial city of Waukegan (once famous as the home of Jack Benny) and the Wisconsin border beyond. The 10th District also goes inland. As you move away from the Lake, housing prices fall, but slowly. Northbrook and Deerfield, just west of Glencoe and Highland Park, are still among the most affluent Chicago suburbs. Politically they are if anything more Republican than the lakefront towns; there is less hint here of fashionable liberalism or radical chic, and more unalloyed devotion to the free-market system and opposition to the party of the Chicago machine. Farther inland you pass over land that was cornfields not long ago (some still is) to suburbs like Arlington Heights, developed in the 1950s and 1960s on the Northwestern railroad line, and Wheeling, developed in the 1960s and 1970s near Interstate 294 and now with one of the nation's most famed French restaurants. The 10th District is mostly urbanized now, and does not really reach out to the more modest, sparkling clean towns where you meet the mentality of Downstate Illinois; except for Waukegan and the towns around it, this district is very much within the Chicago orbit.

The congressman from the 10th District is John Porter, a Republican who seems to fit the district exactly. He is a North Shore native, a graduate of Northwestern, a Republican who is against tax increases and looks with favor on free markets, but who takes liberal stands on some foreign and cultural issues. Porter serves on the Appropriations Committee, and on the subcommittees handling labor, health, and foreign aid issues. Although he cultivates an anti-spending image, he does not inveigh against foreign aid or suggest that federal job training is an entering wedge to socialism. Like liberals of yore, he is ready to use federal power to encourage states to take action on economic issues, though not the kind of action the liberals want: Porter would like them to limit the liability for damages of people in voluntary organizations and to limit tort liability generally. On foreign matters, he is one of the organizers of the congressional group to monitor human rights violations in the Soviet Union.

For a congressman so well adapted to a district, Porter had a bit of a time winning it. He lost his first race, in 1978, to liberal Democrat Abner Mikva, by 650 votes; Mikva, one of the shrewdest and best-humored of House liberals, was appointed to a federal judgeship, and Porter won the ensuing special election. Reelected easily in 1980, he was faced with running against another incumbent in 1982 after redistricting. He chose to move out of Evanston where he would have had to face Chicago Democrat Sidney Yates and north into a district mostly represented by fellow Republican Robert McClory. It was a shrewd decision: Yates, who won with 67% that year against a well-financed opponent, probably would have won, and McClory decided to retire. This leaves Porter with a safe North Shore seat and at the beginning of what could be a long congressional career.

The People: Pop. 1980: 519,660, up 5.7% 1970–80. Households (1980): 79% family, 45% with children, 69% married couples; 26.6% housing units rented; median monthly rent: $275; median house value: $92,100. Voting age pop. (1980): 368,611; 5% Black, 4% Spanish origin, 2% Asian origin.

1984 Presidential Vote: Reagan (R) 153,888   (68%)
                              Mondale (D) 70,590   (31%)

Rep. John E. Porter (R)

Elected 1980; b. June 1, 1935, Evanston; home, Winnetka; MIT, Northwestern U., B.A., B.S. 1957, U. of MI, J.D. 1961; Presbyterian; married (Kathryn).

Career: Atty., U.S. Dept. of Justice, 1961–63; Practicing atty., 1963–80; IL House of Reps., 1973–79.

Offices: 1131 LHOB 20515, 202-225-4835. Also 104 Wilmot Rd., Ste. 410, Deerfield 60015, 312-940-0202; 1650 Arlington Hgts. Rd., Ste. 104, Arlington Hgts. 60004, 312-392-0303; and 18 N. County St., County Bldg., No. 601A Waukegan 60085, 312-662-0101.

Committees: *Appropriations* (15th of 22 R). Subcommittees: Foreign Operations; Labor–Health and Human Services–Education; Legislative.

Group Ratings

	ADA	ACLU	COPE	CFA	LCV	ACU	NTU	NSI	COC	CEI
1986	15	5	14	25	58	64	63	70	94	81
1985	20	—	15	50	—	71	66	—	82	—

National Journal Ratings

	1986 LIB — 1986 CONS		1985 LIB — 1985 CONS	
Economic	15%	— 54%	24%	— 74%
Social	11%	— 85%	54%	— 45%
Foreign	41%	— 57%	45%	— 54%

Key Votes

1) Lmt Cln Water Act	FOR	5) Retain Gun Cont	FOR	9) Aid Angola Reb	FOR
2) Rpl Tobac Sub	FOR	6) Contra Aid	FOR	10) Tax Reform	FOR
3) Grm-Rdmn Def Red	FOR	7) Lmt Text Imp	AGN	11) S Africa Sanc	AGN
4) Ban Polygraph	AGN	8) Limit SDI	FOR	12) Immig Reform	AGN

Election Results

1986 general	John E. Porter (R)	87,530	(75%)	($176,228)
	Robert A. Cleland (D)	28,990	(25%)	($103,817)
1986 primary	John E. Porter (R)	23,243	(100%)	
1984 general	John E. Porter (R)	153,330	(73%)	($141,964)
	Ruth C. Braver (D)...................	57,809	(27%)	($28,938)

Campaign Contributions and Expenditures

1985-86		Direct Cont. 1985-86		PACS Breakdown 1985-86			
Receipts	$188,340	Indiv.	$96,238	Corp.	$29,185	T/M/H	$33,600
Expend.	$176,228	Party	$2,164	Labor	$0	Agr.	$0
Unspent	$96,786	PACS	$75,035	Ideo.	$11,900	CWOS	$350

ELEVENTH DISTRICT

The 11th Congressional District of Illinois is the northwest corner of Chicago and adjacent suburban areas. Demographically, the 11th is a family district, but one without children; this is a part of the metropolitan area filled with older people, their children grown and gone. People here are in a sense in transit: from the old ethnic neighborhoods where so many of them grew up, halfway out the radial highways to the new suburban neighborhoods where so many of their children live. At its southeastern corner the 11th contains Chicago's Greek Town, where its

Greek community moved after its old neighborhood was torn down. The northern corner near the lake, around Rogers Park, is a mostly Jewish neighborhood, though its longtime ward committeeman is Illinois Attorney General Neil Hartigan, a machine politician of Irish descent

The 11th's northern suburbs, Lincolnwood and a part of Skokie, are mostly Jewish, and the highest income and most Democratic part of the district; to the west are Polish and Italian and Irish and German neighborhoods and suburbs. The half of the district west of North Cicero Avenue is no longer reliably Democratic in statewide contests, though all the wards here have gotten into the habit of electing Democratic aldermen. The western suburbs, regular rectangular-blocked old neighborhoods south of O'Hare Airport, interspersed with factories and warehouses, have an increasing Mexican-American population; the Mexicans are in effect following the footsteps of Italians and other earlier immigrant groups. These suburbs, historically Republican, have been trending Democratic.

Generally the political tradition in the 11th District is Democratic: many immigrants and their children bought houses in these modest but pleasant neighborhoods with their hard-won savings. Now, while they may find the Republicans more attractive in national and state contests, they stay Democratic when the issue is local and the real struggle is between yeasty Chicago and the flat plains beyond.

Frank Annunzio, congressman from the 11th District, is a veteran of Chicago politics who has found his way to the top of the House. He has the look of an old-time machine politico and the record of an independent-minded detail man. The political machine to which he had such loyalty has crumbled, and the labor movement which he worked for in the 1940s is in trouble. He charges on. Annunzio in all his years on the Banking Committee has never been cozy with the banking lobby, although he has always been a strong savings and loan man (old Chicago neighborhoods are strewn with ethnic-based S&Ls and small banks). Annunzio has also been aggressive in regulating debt-collection agencies, which are sometimes guilty of incredible abuses, and in making a federal crime of serious credit card fraud; he pushed the bill to prohibit surcharges for credit card customers. His Banking subcommittee chairmanship has made him the czar of the nation's coinage, and he has taken his duties seriously. His greatest moment in the limelight, so far, was when he killed a measure that would have allowed Armand Hammer's Occidental Petroleum to make money minting Olympic commemorative coins; and if that sounds like a trivial matter, the fact is that there are very few politicians in any country who have succeeded in frustrating one of Dr. Hammer's projects—and Annunzio won 302–84. Annunzio's government-managed coin program raised $70 million for the Olympics, more than the alternative even promised. The Statue of Liberty commemorative he pushed raised $74 million in only 14 months.

Annunzio has been chairman since 1984 of the House Administration Committee, an unpublicized hot seat. That tends to make him the partisan point man for Democrats on committee budgets, although in the 1985 dispute over whom to seat for the Indiana 8th District Speaker O'Neill assigned the toughest spot to Leon Panetta. House Administration also has jurisdiction over campaign finance laws. This issue could very well come to the fore in 1987 or 1988, putting Annunzio under great pressure. He is a product of an old politics, but he has adapted to the new, and he may end up setting some important rules for the even newer. He has not in the past favored public financing, nor has he voted down the line with Common Cause. But he is open to persuasion and aware that many members of both parties are disgusted with the influence of PACs and the constant need to angle members to angle for PAC support and vice versa. He could end up a chief architect or broker of reform of campaign finance, just as his 8th District neighbor Dan Rostenkowski became the chief architect and broker of tax reform.

Rough-hewn, an ally of Chicago's Democratic machine but with his own independence Annunzio has proved to be an adroit electoral politician as well as a skilled legislator. He was first elected to Congress in 1964 from a district centered in the Loop, then jumped after the post 1970 redistricting to the 11th, whose congressman, Roman Pucinski, was running for U.S. Senator and now holds the more powerful office, for Chicagoans, of alderman. Annunzio adapted comfortably after the district moved out partially into the suburbs in 1982. Years ago many observers figured he'd be retired by now, but he is more active and powerful than ever.

The People: Pop. 1980: 518,995, dn. 7.8% 1970–80. Households (1980): 72% family, 29% with children, 59% married couples; 40.6% housing units rented; median monthly rent: $239; median house value: $69,400. Voting age pop. (1980): 409,539; 5% Spanish origin, 4% Asian origin.

1984 Presidential Vote:

Reagan (R)	149,521	(59%)
Mondale (D)	102,584	(41%)

Rep. Frank Annunzio (D)

Elected 1964; b. Jan. 12, 1915, Chicago; home, Chicago; De Paul U., B.S. 1940, M.A. 1942; Roman Catholic; married (Angeline).

Career: Pub. sch. teacher, 1935–43; Legis. and Ed. Dir., United Steel Workers of Amer., Chicago, Calumet Region Dist. 31, 1943–49; Dir., IL Dept. of Labor, 1949–52; Priv. business, 1952–64.

Offices: 2303 RHOB 20515, 202-225-6661. Also 4747 W. Peterson Ave., Ste. 201, Chicago 60646, 312-736-0700; and Kluczynski Bldg., Ste. 3816, 230 S. Dearborn St., Chicago 60604, 312-353-2525.

Committees: *Banking, Finance and Urban Affairs* (3d of 31 D). Subcommittees: Consumer Affairs and Coinage (Chairman); Financial Institutions Supervision, Regulation and Insurance. *House Administration* (Chairman of 12 D). *Joint Committee on the Library* (Vice Chairman). *Joint Committee on Printing* (Chairman).

Group Ratings

	ADA	ACLU	COPE	CFA	LCV	ACU	NTU	NSI	COC	CEI
1986	70	66	92	83	68	5	23	10	39	19
1985	75	—	91	92	—	5	32	—	23	—

National Journal Ratings

	1986 LIB — 1986 CONS			1985 LIB — 1985 CONS		
Economic	62%	—	20%	75%	—	22%
Social	69%	—	28%	46%	—	53%
Foreign	75%	—	20%	64%	—	33%

Key Votes

1) Lmt Cln Water Act	AGN	5) Retain Gun Cont	FOR	9) Aid Angola Reb	AGN
2) Rpl Tobac Sub	FOR	6) Contra Aid	AGN	10) Tax Reform	FOR
3) Grm-Rdmn Def Red	AGN	7) Lmt Text Imp	FOR	11) S Africa Sanc	FOR
4) Ban Polygraph	FOR	8) Limit SDI	FOR	12) Immig Reform	FOR

Election Results

1986 general	Frank Annunzio (D)	106,970	(71%)	($171,298)
	George S. Gottlieb (R)	44,341	(29%)	($29,870)
1986 primary	Frank Annunzio (D)	138,171	(63%)	
	Terry E. Allen (D)	9,285	(15%)	
1984 general	Frank Annunzio (D)	138,171	(63%)	($206,706)
	Charles J. Theusch (R)	82,518	(37%)	($74,153)

Campaign Contributions and Expenditures

1985-86		Direct Cont. 1985-86		PACS Breakdown 1985-86			
Receipts	$225,627	Indiv.	$75,006	Corp.	$31,700	T/M/H	$48,650
Expend.	$171,298	Party	$269	Labor	$39,982	Agr.	$0
Unspent	$147,155	PACS	$134,782	Ideo.	$11,500	CWOS	$2,950

TWELFTH DISTRICT

Somewhere in the Chicago metropolitan area there is an invisible line, between the two different Chicagos. One is the Chicago dominated by blacks and the products of the vast immigration of 1840–1924, a Chicago where loyalties are taken for granted: loyalty to ethnic group, to church (usually the Catholic Church, but often with an ethnic prefix), and to party (almost always the Democratic Party, but occasionally, as in Cicero, the Republican). This Chicago is a gritty city, where occasional acts of cheerfulness and courtesy lighten up days otherwise as cold and behavior as impersonal as the Chicago sky is gray during most of the winter. This part of Chicago sees the city not only as the center of life, but as the whole of it; people for whom there is not much life outside of Chicago, except perhaps a little beach house on the Indiana shore of Lake Michigan.

The other Chicago is the Chicago of the Great Plains, a white Anglo-Saxon Protestant Chicago, a place whose residents are products of the first great wave of immigration to America. The tone of this Chicago is cheerier, its streets and highways cleaner and neater, its daily life somehow free from evidence of unpleasantness and deprivation. This is the Chicago of dozens of suburban and Downstate towns, all laid out on neat geometric grids on the flatness of the prairie, the Chicago which extends hundreds of miles out from the city and which seems separate from it. People in this Chicago think of themselves as the typical Americans, and their geographical vision takes in the vast plains. This is the Chicago of Colonel McCormick's *Chicago Tribune* and Don McNeill's *Breakfast Club* (the radio show, not the movie), of Paul Harvey and Sears catalogues. It is an optimistic world which knows personal, but not social, tragedy; a world in which all things are possible and most things are for the best. Ronald Reagan grew up in Downstate Illinois within the orbit of this kind of Chicago, and it can be seen in his optimism today. His migration to southern California, incidentally, is not atypical: you can see in the geometric grids and Republican voting patterns of Orange County or Phoenix almost precise replicas of the grids and patterns in Chicago's suburban "collar counties," transported out on the Atchison, Topeka & Santa Fe or U.S. 66 from their beginnings in Chicago's Loop to the vast and once empty southwest.

The line between these two Chicagos passes somewhere near the southern end of the 12th Congressional District of Illinois. This is part of metropolitan Chicago, beginning at the northwest corner of Cook County, taking in the western half of Lake County and most of McHenry County just to the west. And it contains many descendants of the second wave of immigrants, moved out from Chicago one or two generations ago. But the cultural style of this area is very much that of the second, Great Plains Chicago.

That is apparent from the 12th District's voting habits, which are very much Republican. This is not just a function of income, though this area does have one of the highest income levels of any district in the Midwest or the nation; the 10th District, along Lake Michigan, is richer and less Republican. The difference is cultural. The North Shore suburbanites are part of an urbane tradition, lineal descendants of the merchant princes who amassed great fortunes and patronized advanced arts and letters. The suburbanites inland are descendants of small town burghers, who uphold the traditions and observe the courtesies that are the fabric of life in cozy, affluent communities.

The 12th District is represented in Congress by a man who personifies many of the qualities of the kind of Chicago he represents. Philip Crane is the son of Dr. George Crane, who broadcast a medical advice radio program on Chicago's WGN for years and was a pillar of conservative thought; two of his sons have served as congressmen from Illinois and a third was a nearly successful candidate in Indiana. Phil Crane is handsome, congenial, loyal to his beliefs but full of good-hearted camaraderie.

Yet something vital seems missing. In an era when others of similar views, from Jack Kemp to Lewis Lehrman, from Henry Hyde to Robert Michel, have shaped national policies, he continues as a spokesman—to whom no one pays attention. He was one of the first announced presidential candidates for 1980, and one of the least successful; his strategy depended on picking up support when the Reagan candidacy faded, but even when it looked, after the Iowa caucuses, that that might happen, Crane made no headway. Today no one thinks of him as a presidential candidate. Nor do many colleagues think of him as an original thinker or as an active legislator. He is a member of the Ways and Means Committee, but if he shows up at meetings, it is a source for comment; he had no role in passing the 1981 tax cuts; his presence on the tax reform conference committee was a matter for laughter and he skipped the final conference. He looks and sounds like a vibrant leader, but isn't. In the 12th District, he is reelected by huge margins in what are for all practical purposes uncontested elections.

The People: Pop. 1980: 519,181, up 39.0% 1970–80. Households (1980): 79% family, 47% with children, 69% married couples; 25.7% housing units rented; median monthly rent: $300; median house value: $71,900. Voting age pop. (1980): 356,939; 3% Spanish origin, 1% Asian origin, 1% Black.

1984 Presidential Vote:

Reagan (R) 168,010	(77%)
Mondale (D) 50,512	(23%)

Rep. Philip M. Crane (R)

Elected Nov. 25, 1969; b. Nov. 3, 1930, Chicago; home, Mt. Prospect; DePauw U., Hillsdale Col., B.A. 1952, IN U., M.A. 1961, Ph.D. 1963; Protestant; married (Arlene).

Career: Instructor, IN U., 1960–63; Asst. Prof., Bradley U., 1963–67; Dir. of Schools, Westminster Acad., 1967–68.

Offices: 1035 LHOB 20515, 202-225-3711. Also 1450 S. New Wilke Rd., Arlington Heights 60005, 312-394-0790; and 56 N. Williams St., Crystal Lake 60014, 815-459-3399.

Committees: *Ways and Means* (4th of 13 R). Subcommittees: Social Security; Trade (Ranking Member).

Group Ratings

	ADA	ACLU	COPE	CFA	LCV	ACU	NTU	NSI	COC	CEI
1986	0	5	7	8	23	100	75	90	93	90
1985	5	—	7	25	—	95	76	—	82	—

National Journal Ratings

	1986 LIB — 1986 CONS			1985 LIB — 1985 CONS		
Economic	0%	—	94%	5%	—	92%
Social	0%	—	89%	0%	—	76%
Foreign	0%	—	86%	0%	—	76%

Key Votes

1) Lmt Cln Water Act	FOR	5) Retain Gun Cont	AGN	9) Aid Angola Reb	FOR
2) Rpl Tobac Sub	FOR	6) Contra Aid	FOR	10) Tax Reform	AGN
3) Grm-Rdmn Def Red	AGN	7) Lmt Text Imp	AGN	11) S Africa Sanc	AGN
4) Ban Polygraph	AGN	8) Limit SDI	AGN	12) Immig Reform	AGN

Election Results

1986 general	Philip M. Crane (R)	89,044	(78%)	($365,932)
	John A. Leonardi (D)	25,536	(22%)	($7,879)
1986 primary	Philip M. Crane (R)	32,515	(100%)	
1984 general	Philip M. Crane (R)	159,582	(78%)	($443,808)
	Edward J. La Flamme (D)	45,537	(22%)	

Campaign Contributions and Expenditures

1985-86		Direct Cont. 1985-86		PACS Breakdown 1985-86			
Receipts	$339,052	Indiv.	$300,766	Corp.	$4,840	T/M/H	$750
Expend.	$365,932	Party	$1,047	Labor	$0	Agr.	$0
Unspent	$129,371	PACS	$5,798	Ideo.	$0	CWOS	$208
		Cand.	$55,075				

THIRTEENTH DISTRICT

The radial avenues that fan out from Chicago's Loop are the routes taken by the city's various ethnic groups—immigrants who came to Chicago and their descendants who have moved up and out as they prospered over the years. One of these routes runs almost straight west from the Loop, and the group that has trod it include many of the Chicago area's white Anglo–Saxon Protestants. From anonymous clerks in Loop offices to the aristocratic Colonel Robert Rutherford McCormick, proprietor of the *Chicago Tribune,*they have made their way westward, past the Chicago city limits and the Bohemian suburbs of Cicero and Berwyn, to the westernmost suburbs of Cook County and farther to almost entirely affluent DuPage County.

This is the land of Illinois's 13th Congressional District. It begins, if you start nearest to Chicago, in the turn-of-the-century suburb of Riverside; with its curved streets and Frank Lloyd Wright houses, it was an elite place in the days of *art nouveau* and still is today. Farther west are affluent railroad commuter suburbs: the string of LaGrange, Western Springs, and Hinsdale, more middle-income Downers Grove, and the newer suburb of Oak Brook which is the headquarters of McDonald's, among other enterprises. The boundaries of the 13th District were carefully crafted to exclude Democratic suburbs (the Democrats who drew the plan wanted them to pad the Chicago-based Democratic districts); the district has a salient into southwest Cook County, in somewhat different socioeconomic country (affluent Irish), to meet the population standard. People from elsewhere may think of Chicago as Democratic, but this part of Chicagoland is almost unanimously hostile to the city's Democratic machine, both for its reputed corruption and for its support of big government programs over the years. The 13th is, election after election, one of the most Republican districts in the nation.

The congressman from the 13th, Harris Fawell, has deep roots in DuPage County and its politics. He was first elected to the Illinois Senate in 1962, after losing a race for state Supreme Court. He practiced law in the county, and was a key supporter of Representative John Erlenborn. When Erlenborn decided to retire in 1984, after some years of frustration as the ranking Republican on the liberal-dominated Education and Labor Committee, Fawell jumped into the race and got the local party endorsement. But he was attacked by his opponents as too liberal and won the four-way race 30%–23%–22%–12%.

So this pillar of the suburban establishment became a congressman at 53. He boasts of his opposition to increased federal spending and is, for the middle 1980s, unusually blunt about opposing protectionism. But he supports ample funding for Argonne National Laboratory, which is in the district, and his voting record on cultural issues is rather liberal. He serves on the Science and Education and Labor Committees—forums where he might find in practical instances more need for federal spending than he is inclined generally to support. No doubt this leaves movement conservatives furious, but Fawell probably represents the balance of opinion in the upscale 13th better than they do, and he had no primary opposition in 1986.

The People: Pop. 1980: 519,441, up 33.5% 1970–80. Households (1980): 79% family, 42% with children, 71% married couples; 24.0% housing units rented; median monthly rent: $291; median house value: $78,500. Voting age pop. (1980): 370,153; 2% Asian origin, 2% Spanish origin, 1% Black.

1984 Presidential Vote:

Reagan (R) 133,234	(54%)
Mondale (D) 112,891	(46%)

Rep. Harris W. Fawell (R)

Elected 1984; b. Mar. 25, 1929, West Chicago; home, Naperville; attended North Central Col., Chicago-Kent Col. of Law, J.D. 1953; United Methodist; married (Ruth).

Career: Practicing atty., 1953–84; IL Senate, 1963–77.

Offices: 318 CHOB 20515, 202-225-3515. Also 115 West 55th St., Ste. 100. Clarendon Hills 60514, 312-655-2052.

Committees: *Education and Labor* (10th of 13 R). Subcommittees: Elementary, Secondary, and Vocational Education; Labor-Management Relations. *Science, Space and Technology* (12th of 18 R). Subcommittees: Energy Research and Development; International Scientific Cooperation. *Select Committee on Aging* (17th of 26 R). Subcommittee: Retirement Income and Employment.

Group Ratings

	ADA	ACLU	COPE	CFA	LCV	ACU	NTU	NSI	COC	CEI
1986	20	20	10	42	68	73	65	90	89	88
1985	15	—	6	50	—	81	65	—	95	—

National Journal Ratings

	1986 LIB — 1986 CONS		1985 LIB — 1985 CONS	
Economic	19% —	79%	12% —	85%
Social	27% —	71%	63% —	33%
Foreign	41% —	57%	35% —	65%

Key Votes

1) Lmt Cln Water Act	FOR	5) Retain Gun Cont	FOR	9) Aid Angola Reb	FOR
2) Rpl Tobac Sub	FOR	6) Contra Aid	FOR	10) Tax Reform	FOR
3) Grm-Rdmn Def Red	FOR	7) Lmt Text Imp	AGN	11) S Africa Sanc	FOR
4) Ban Polygraph	AGN	8) Limit SDI	FOR	12) Immig Reform	AGN

Election Results

1986 general	Harris W. Fawell (R)	107,227	(73%)	($193,882)
	Dominick J. Jeffrey (D)	38,874	(27%)	
1986 primary	Harris W. Fawell (R)	28,160	(100%)	
1984 general	Harris W. Fawell (R)	157,603	(67%)	($176,693)
	Michael J. Donohue (D)	77,623	(33%)	($29,735)

Campaign Contributions and Expenditures

1985-86		Direct Cont. 1985-86		PACS Breakdown 1985-86			
Receipts	$194,887	Indiv.	$112,580	Corp.	$37,236	T/M/H	$29,05
Expend.	$193,882	Party	$5,030	Labor	$500	Agr.	$50
Unspent	$35,230	PACS	$73,546	Ideo.	$4,911	CWOS	$1,34

FOURTEENTH DISTRICT

The 14th Congressional District is, numerically, the first of the Downstate Illinois districts Technically, most of its people live in the metropolitan Chicago area, in some of the so-called "collar counties"; in the residents' own minds, however, they are very far indeed from Chicago in the clean—physically clean, politically clean—and neat towns of Downstate Illinois. The 14th District gets as close as 30 miles to Chicago's Loop, in western DuPage County, where the subdivisions now are almost as built up and densely populated as they are in Cook County. The 14th contains the industrial city of Elgin and part of Aurora, both on the Fox River that run parallel to Lake Michigan, 35 miles away. Past the Fox River, the subdivisions start thinning ou and you see more cornfields; soon the cornfields devoted to producing fresh corn for suburban ites in the summer give way to serious commercial farming operations. By the time you get as fa west as DeKalb, site of Northern Illinois University, or as far southwest as the industrial towns o Ottawa, LaSalle, and Peru on the Illinois River, you are unmistakably in the midst of some o the richest and most productively cultivated agricultural land in the world.

This is also one of the most heavily Republican belts of territory in the country. Northern Illinois was settled, when Chicago was just one of thousands of frontier villages, by Yankees from Ohio, Indiana, Upstate New York, and New England, by people who formed the heart o the Republican Party from the year it was founded, in 1854, just as they would form the core o the Grand Army of the Republic a few years later. Their descendants remain mostly loyal to the Republican Party today. That does not mean that there are not parts of Illinois, either firs settled by southerners or by immigrants from Europe, which are not Democratic; the majo example is of course Chicago, and there are much smaller examples, like the ailing industria towns of LaSalle and Ottawa, which went for Walter Mondale in 1984. But on the whole this i Republican territory that very seldom elects anyone but Republican congressmen.

The 14th District has been seriously contested in the last two elections, in 1984 in the Republican primary and in 1986 in the general election. The first contest was won by state Senator John Grotberg, from the Fox River town of St. Charles. Grotberg had had cancer fo years, but campaigned vigorously and served full-time; then after winning the 1986 primary, hi health deteriorated and he resigned the nomination; he went into a coma that spring and died That left the Republican Party here, as in the adjoining 4th District, with the duty to choose a new nominee, and it left the Democrat, here Kane County Coroner Mary Lou Kearns, with an unusual and probably never-to-be-repeated opportunity to capture an otherwise safe Republican district. The Republican choice, state Senator Dennis Hastert, was attacked by one 1984 Grotberg opponent as insufficiently conservative; like Grotberg, his devotion to abstrac conservative principle on some cultural issues was tempered by his practical experience and sympathies.

Ultimately the Republican Party label prevailed. Kearns held Hastert even in Kane County (Elgin, Aurora, Fox River Valley). But the remaining parts of the district in the Chicago orbit though they cast only 17% of its votes, went 2 to 1 for Hastert, enough to give him a 52%–48% victory. That will probably be enough to establish him as the congressman here for some years to come.

The People: Pop. 1980: 521,909, up 17.7% 1970–80. Households (1980): 77% family, 44% with children, 67% married couples; 28.9% housing units rented; median monthly rent: $220; median house value: $63,200; Voting age pop. (1980): 367,441; 3% Spanish origin, 2% Black, 1% Asian origin.

1984 Presidential Vote:

Reagan (R) 154,144   (69%)
Mondale (D) 68,645   (31%)

Rep. Dennis Hastert (R)

Elected 1986; b. Jan. 2, 1942, Aurora, IL; home, Yorkville; Wheaton Col., B.A. 1962, Northern IL U., M.S. 1967; Protestant; married (Jean).

Career: Teacher and coach, Yorkville H.S., 1964–80; IL House of Reps., 1980–86.

Offices: 515 CHOB 20515, 202-225-2976. Also 100 W. Lafayette, Ottawa 61350, 815-434-5666; 27 N. River, Batavia 60510, 312-406-1114.

Committees: *Government Operations* (12th of 15 R). Subcommittees: Government Activities and Transportation; Government Information, Justice and Agriculture. *Public Works and Transportation* (17th of 20 R). Subcommittees: Surface Transportation; Water Resources. *Select Committee on Children, Youth and Families* (10th of 12R). Task Force: Economic Security.

Group Ratings and Key Votes: Newly Elected

Election Results

1986 general	Dennis Hastert (R)	77,288	(52%)	($327,219)
	Mary Lou Kearns (D)	70,293	(48%)	($322,625)
June 1986	Dennis Hastert (R) nominated by convention			
1986 primary	John E. Grotberg (R)	37,451	(62%)	
	Mark Powell (R)	37,451	(99%)	
1984 general	John E. Grotberg (R)	135,967	(62%)	($430,461)
	Dan McGrath (D)	82,756	(38%)	($58,521)

Campaign Contributions and Expenditures

1985-86		Direct Cont. 1985-86		PACS Breakdown 1985-86			
Receipts	$342,005	Indiv.	$148,278	Corp.	$62,757	T/M/H	$58,860
Expend.	$327,219	Party	$15,503	Labor	$0	Agr.	$0
Debts	$15,521	PACS	$151,553	Ideo.	$27,883	CWOS	$2,053
		Cand.	$25,000				

FIFTEENTH DISTRICT

South from Chicago the Illinois Central Railroad heads, the roadbed elevating its tracks slightly above the level of some of the nation's richest farmland. If the IC tracks were to lie on the earth below the topsoil, they would be several feet—not inches—lower than they are; so deep is this marvelous black soil. This land was settled, 150 years ago, by Yankee farmers, but it is not family farm country any more. Cultivating this soil has become a big business: choosing the right crops (soybeans and corn are the current favorites), maximizing yields, selecting proper pesticides, making marketing decisions. Farm owners here typically hold thousands, not hundreds, of acres; while they may lease some to farmers who cannot afford to buy land, they of course keep close control over the major decisions. There is no room for sentimentality in these matters, not with land values first rising then sinking and interest rates still comparatively high; no room, either, for producing vegetables and fruits for the family to eat. The land is too valuable to be put to anything but its highest economic use.

Such a place is the 15th Congressional District of Illinois. It begins not quite 40 miles from Chicago, where the Illinois Central heads toward Kankakee and moves over 150 miles of prairie to the courthouse towns of Lincoln and Monticello. Its largest city is Bloomington, whose best-known citizen was the first Adlai Stevenson, grandfather of the presidential candidate and one-term vice president of the United States; he was a Democrat, but a *laissez faire* Cleveland Democrat, with a philosophy similar to those of the Republicans who have been the majority in this area since the Republican Party was created in 1854.

The congressman from the 15th is Edward Madigan, one of the Republican Party's leaders in the House and one of its best instinctive politicians, a successful businessman in Lincoln and one-time Republican state legislator. Madigan's father was an alderman in the small city of Lincoln, and Madigan, owner of a taxi company, was elected to the state legislature in 1966 and, after chairing the redistricting committee, to the U.S. House in 1972. Coming quietly into the then quiet ranks of House Republicans, he seemed indistinguishable from a dozen or so dull legislators. But he has made a vast difference.

One reason has been good committee positions. He got a seat on the Energy and Commerce Committee which by the middle 1970s became the cockpit for one important economic issue after another. Madigan specialized in transportation issues first and then, after becoming ranking Republican on Henry Waxman's subcommittee, on health and clean air. (Incidentally, Waxman also chaired his state house's redistricting committee.) Madigan's impulse usually is to reduce government regulation, but he is also interested in solving practical problems; and those two impulses put him at the fulcrum point in one policy-making decision after another. He wants, for example, to sell Conrail and he opposes acid rain bills that would put burdens on coal-burning midwestern utilities; but he also has originated successful organ transplant legislation, a nursing research center, an agriculture trade and export policy commission, a bill to increase the number of drugs that can be sold generically, a compromise natural gas deregulation measure, and a new version of the Safe Water Drinking Act.

Madigan's second important position is as ranking Republican on the Agriculture Committee. He was off the committee altogether in 1981 and 1982, while serving as chairman of the Republican Research Committee; but he reclaimed his seat on Agriculture in 1983, in part to prevent Vermont's liberal James Jeffords from getting the ranking position. Madigan, representing a relatively prosperous farming area, has been a staunch opponent of what he considers overgenerous farm bill provisions. He led the fight against the Democrats' proposal for farmers' referenda to limit grain production.

On both Agriculture and Energy and Commerce, Madigan has shown himself to be a cool operator, maintaining orderly working relationships with Democrats and keeping his lines clearly open with his fellow Republicans; he works hard, knows his details, and obviously is genuinely interested in the issues. He is the antithesis of the confrontationists of the Conservative Opportunity Society, but they are playing different games: Newt Gingrich and company want to change opinion in the country, confident that Congress will come to reflect it; Madigan wants to change policy in the House, confident that he can improve the way government serves the people. The COS group may get more publicity, but it was Madigan who was chosen after the 1986 election as the party's chief deputy whip. It is not inconceivable that he could become the House Republican leader, and maybe speaker, some day.

The voters of the 15th District, with their long Republican tradition, have reelected Madigan easily every two years; in 1986 he did not even have a Democratic opponent.

The People: Pop. 1980: 518,995, up 8.4% 1970–80. Households (1980): 75% family, 42% with children, 65% married couples; 31.6% housing units rented; median monthly rent: $182; median house value: $44,900. Voting age pop. (1980): 370,509; 5% Black, 1% Spanish origin.

1984 Presidential Vote:

Reagan (R)	140,972	(68%)
Mondale (D)	66,325	(32%)

Rep. Edward R. Madigan (R)

Elected 1972; b. Jan. 13, 1936, Lincoln; home, Lincoln; Lincoln Col., B.A. 1956; Roman Catholic; married (Evelyn).

Career: Owner, Yellow-Lincoln Taxi Co., 1956–74; IL House of Reps., 1966–72.

Offices: 2312 RHOB 20515, 202-225-2371. Also 2401 E. Washington, Bloomington 61701, 309-662-9371; 70 Meadowview Ctr., Kankakee 60901, 815-937-0875; and 219 S. Kickapoo, Lincoln 62656, 217-735-3521.

Committees: *Agriculture* (Ranking Member of 17 R). *Energy and Commerce* (2d of 17 R). Subcommittee: Health and the Environment (Ranking Member).

Group Ratings

	ADA	ACLU	COPE	CFA	LCV	ACU	NTU	NSI	COC	CEI
1986	0	16	29	17	27	76	49	100	79	50
1985	30	—	29	25	—	71	52	—	71	—

National Journal Ratings

	1986 LIB — 1986 CONS		1985 LIB — 1985 CONS	
Economic	34%	77%	34%	66%
Social	0%	89%	30%	69%
Foreign	21%	77%	37%	60%

Key Votes

1) Lmt Cln Water Act	AGN	5) Retain Gun Cont	AGN
2) Rpl Tobac Sub	AGN	6) Contra Aid	FOR
3) Grm-Rdmn Def Red	FOR	7) Lmt Text Imp	AGN
4) Ban Polygraph	—	8) Limit SDI	AGN

9) Aid Angola Reb	FOR
10) Tax Reform	AGN
11) S Africa Sanc	FOR
12) Immig Reform	AGN

Election Results

1986 general	Edward R. Madigan (R)...............	115,284	(100%)	($209,409)
1986 primary	Edward R. Madigan (R)...............	42,840	(100%)	
1984 general	Edward R. Madigan (R)...............	149,096	(73%)	($203,851)
	John M. Hoffmann (D)................	54,516	(27%)	($31,092)

Campaign Contributions and Expenditures

1985-86		Direct Cont. 1985-86		PACS Breakdown 1985-86			
Receipts	$334,872	Indiv.	$87,003	Corp.	$98,203	T/M/H	$70,800
Expend.	$209,409	Party	$2,222	Labor	$12,082	Agr.	$7,500
Unspent	$262,375	PACS	$200,350	Ideo.	$8,061	CWOS	$3,704

SIXTEENTH DISTRICT

When Abraham Lincoln arrived in his 12-car train on the morning of his debate in Freeport, it was cold and drizzling—summer already over in late August, 1858, in this northernmost part of Illinois. But there were 2,000 people on hand to greet him (in a town of 5,000); they gave him six deafening cheers and then escorted him around the streets to the "elegant hotel." Such was the enthusiasm for the standard-bearer of the then 4-year-old Republican Party in what has been ever since one of its heartlands, the northwestern corner of Illinois. Here in the old Mississippi River town of Galena was the home of one two-term Republican President, and here in rented apartments in Tampico, Dixon, and other small towns was born and raised another two-term Republican President, Ronald Reagan. The largest city in these parts, Rockford, was the home base of Representative John Anderson, Reagan's opponent first in the 1980 primaries and then, as a third-party candidate, in the general election—a rare instance of the same congressional district giving us two candidates for President.

This is the 16th Congressional District of Illinois, and if the style of politics has changed here since Lincoln and Douglas debated in Freeport, the party preference is the same: it is as Republican now that the party is 134 years old as it was when it was 4 years old. Lower farm prices have hurt the area's economy, and layoffs in Rockford's factories and the Chrysler plant in Belvidere gave it for a while one of the nation's highest unemployment rates. But in 1980 it gave its Republican presidential candidates 56% and 16% of the vote, and in 1984 it was 63% for Ronald Reagan.

The congresswoman from the 16th, Lynn Martin, has emerged as one of the national leaders of her party. In the 1960s she was a wife and teacher; in the 1970s she was elected to the county board and to the Illinois House and Senate from Rockford; in the 1980s she has been a member of the Budget Committee and vice-chairman of the House Republican Conference. At each step she has shown political acumen combined with a sharp sense of humor. She is a moderate on cultural issues (she supported the Equal Rights Amendment, for example, and sponsors the civil rights bill to repeal the *Grove City* decision) and sometimes on foreign policy, and solidly conservative and market-oriented on economics; she is, moreover, a sharp and aggressive partisan, always ready to point out weaknesses in the Democrats' arguments and always ready to raise a standard to which all Republicans can repair.

Martin has been in the national spotlight several times. In 1984 she was chosen to play the role of Geraldine Ferraro in mock-debates with George Bush prior to the 1984 vice presidential face-off in Philadelphia, and her aggressive style and close knowledge of Ferraro surely improved Bush's performance. In 1986, when ranking Republican Delbert Latta was recuperating from surgery, Martin was the party's leader on the Budget Committee, and put together the Republican alternative that got many more votes than those in the past. In 1987 she had to rotate off Budget, but she still has her leadership position and a seat on the Armed Services Committee as well. But she lost her fight for a seat on Appropriations, despite the support of Bob Michel, because of the opposition of Trent Lott and the small state coalition that dominated the Republican Committee on Committees.

Martin has not been able to take this very Republican district for granted. She won the seat in 1980 by beating 45%–26% the right-wing minister who had given John Anderson a primary scare; the Democrat was no threat. But in 1982 and 1984 Democrat Skip Schwerdtfeger ran aggressive campaigns that held Martin under 60%. In 1986 she was reelected easily and seems to have a safe seat, but she may decide to make a statewide race, most likely against Senator Paul Simon in 1990.

The People: Pop. 1980: 519,035, up 2.8% 1970–80. Households (1980): 76% family, 42% with children, 65% married couples; 29.8% housing units rented; median monthly rent: $175; median house value: $42,300. Voting age pop. (1980): 364,824; 4% Black, 2% Spanish origin.

1984 Presidential Vote: Reagan (R) 138,250   (63%)
Mondale (D) 80,648   (37%)

Rep. Lynn M. Martin (R)

Elected 1980; b. Dec. 26, 1939, Chicago; home, Loves Park; U. of IL, B.A. 1960; Roman Catholic; married (Harry Leineweber).

Career: High sch. teacher, 1960–69; Mbr., Winnebago Cnty. Bd., 1972–76; IL House of Reps., 1977–79; IL Senate, 1979–81.

Offices: 1208 LHOB 20515, 202-225-5676. Also 150 N. 4th St., Rockford 61104, 815-987-4326; and 420 Ave. A, Sterling 61081, 815-626-1616.

Committees: *Armed Services* (11th of 20 R). Subcommittees: Military Installations and Facilities; Research and Development.

Group Ratings

	ADA	ACLU	COPE	CFA	LCV	ACU	NTU	NSI	COC	CEI
1986	15	31	30	25	26	68	63	90	94	65
1985	20	—	28	42	—	67	65	—	81	—

National Journal Ratings

	1986 LIB — 1986 CONS			1985 LIB — 1985 CONS		
Economic	10%	—	88%	0%	—	95%
Social	39%	—	59%	63%	—	37%
Foreign	27%	—	70%	44%	—	55%

Key Votes

1) Lmt Cln Water Act	FOR	5) Retain Gun Cont	FOR	9) Aid Angola Reb	FOR
2) Rpl Tobac Sub	FOR	6) Contra Aid	FOR	10) Tax Reform	FOR
3) Grm-Rdmn Def Red	FOR	7) Lmt Text Imp	AGN	11) S Africa Sanc	FOR
4) Ban Polygraph	FOR	8) Limit SDI	AGN	12) Immig Reform	FOR

Election Results

1986 general	Lynn M. Martin (R)	92,982	(67%)	($239,059)
	Kenneth F. Bohnsack (D)	46,087	(33%)	($44,369)
1986 primary	Lynn M. Martin (R)	35,229	(100%)	
1984 general	Lynn M. Martin (R)	127,684	(58%)	($325,703)
	Carl R. (Skip) Schwerdtfeger (D)	90,850	(42%)	($196,277)

Campaign Contributions and Expenditures

1985-86		Direct Cont. 1985-86		PACS Breakdown 1985-86			
Receipts	$359,953	Indiv.	$197,660	Corp.	$78,875	T/M/H	$52,970
Expend.	$239,059	Party	$2,206	Labor	$1,300	Agr.	$2,800
Unspent	$145,740	PACS	$145,536	Ideo.	$8,761	CWOS	$830

SEVENTEENTH DISTRICT

The 17th Congressional District of Illinois is a part of Downstate Illinois that includes all the ingredients of Middle America. It has one major industrial center, around the cities of Rock Island and Moline on the Mississippi River. It has other, smaller industrial centers on the Illinois River, including some suburbs of Peoria, and the small city of Galesburg, the birthplace of Carl Sandburg. It has hundreds of square miles of Illinois prairie—the flat grasslands, which the white man found unforested and converted, after the difficult task of turning the soil, into some of the most productive farmland in the world. The 17th is an agricultural district; although only a handful of its residents are actually farmers, the economy of this part of Illinois depends almost entirely on agriculture. The main product of the industrial center is agricultural equipment: tractors and backhoes and plows and harrows; the main business of the white-collar sector is financing the production, storing, and transportation of agricultural commodities.

This land was first settled by Yankees coming overland from northern Indiana and Ohio and Upstate New York, and, after 1848, by Germans who left their homeland in search of better opportunities in a land that in so many ways resembles the flat, orderly plains of northern Germany. Their politics has been Republican since the 1850s. The only variation for many years, this far north in Illinois, is the Democratic leaning of the working-class, drawn primarily from a later wave of immigration; most are now members of the United Auto Workers employed by John Deere plants, in Rock Island and Moline. Yet in the 1980s, against the national trend, and despite the fact that Ronald Reagan is nearly a native son (he grew up in nearby Dixon, in the 16th District, and the road to Eureka College in the 18th passes through the 17th), this part of Illinois has been moving toward the Democrats. The farm country to the east has remained as solidly Republican as ever. But the 17th District, like Iowa just to the west, has seen its factories close down, its banks go under, and numerous small farmers lose their land. In 1984 Reagan almost lost this district, and in 1986 it gave less than a majority of its votes to Governor James Thompson—the only district outside Chicago to do so.

This Democratic trend came along at a good time for Democratic Congressman Lane Evans—though he may have helped it along. He was first elected in 1982, when incumbent Republican Tom Railsback, mentioned in the Paula Parkinson affair, was beaten by a conservative state Senator in the primary; in a recession year Evans won with 53% of the vote. He compiled one of the most anti-Reagan voting records in the House, but that didn't hurt in one of the few congressional districts in the nation where Reagan's percentage in the two-way race of 1984 was lower than in the three-way contest of 1980. In 1986, against another hard-charging conservative opponent, Evans won with 56% of the vote, including 59% in his opponent's (and his) home base, Rock Island County.

What enables a mild-mannered legal services attorney to win in an historically Republican district? The local economy, of course. Frequent trips back to the district (Evans, like so many hard-working young members of Congress, is unmarried). Good constituency services. A pleasant, almost boyish demeanor (Evans parts his hair down the center and will never be mistaken for a limousine liberal). His votes against aid to the Nicaraguan contras have probably helped, and when attacked on foreign policy he can always cite his service in the Vietnam-era Marine Corps. But the thing that is most distinctive about him is his populism. He is a co-founder of the New Populist Forum, and had the satisfaction of seeing other members (Harkin, Fowler, Conrad, Mikulski, Daschle) elected to the Senate. He summons memories of the Populism of the 1890s and says today's populism "is rooted in the realization that too few people control too much money and wealth, and this balance must be redressed.

So far at least this populism of the 1980s is not quite like that of the 1890s: there is no major push, for example, for steeply progressive income and estate taxes to redistribute income and wealth, and in fact Congress has moved in precisely the opposite direction. Evans seems more interested in letting grain farmers vote to limit production, reregulating railroads, subsidizing loans to farmers, and encouraging employee stock ownership plans. He holds annual forums on building the local economy and seeks to restore the local Hennepin Canal. He tries to bar defense contracts with foreign companies partially owned by Libya. Modest, polite, he was leader of the Vietnam Veterans Caucus in 1985 and 1986; he returns $20,000 of his salary to the Treasury. But he is not shy about raising campaign money: this liberal raised $632,000 for the 1986 race, more than half of it from PACs, and outspent the Republicans almost 2 to 1. He has not made himself politically invulnerable in the 17th District, and if the market economy here should suddenly become buoyant much of his appeal might be undercut and his stands on some other issues might cause him some problems. But local economic problems are likely to continue, and Evans seems by example and argument to have made headway in changing voters' views and so may only be at the beginning of a long congressional career.

The People: Pop. 1980: 519,333, up 4.0% 1970–80. Households (1980): 75% family, 40% with children, 65% married couples; 27.3% housing units rented; median monthly rent: $172; median house value: $42,500. Voting age pop. (1980): 372,502; 2% Black, 2% Spanish origin.

1984 Presidential Vote:

Reagan (R)	123,054	(54%)
Mondale (D)	103,528	(46%)

Rep. Lane Evans (D)

Elected 1982; b. Aug. 4, 1951, Rock Island; home, Rock Island; Augustana Col., B.A. 1974, Georgetown U. Law Sch., J.D. 1978; Roman Catholic; single.

Career: USMC, 1969–71; Practicing atty., 1978–82.

Offices: 328 CHOB 20515, 202-225-5905. Also 3919 16th St., Moline 61265, 309-793-5760; and 125 E. Main St., Galesburg 61401, 309-342-4411.

Committees: *Agriculture* (16th of 26 D). Subcommittees: Conservation, Credit, and Rural Development; Wheat, Soybeans, and Feed Grains. *Veterans' Affairs* (6th of 21 D). Subcommittees: Compensation, Pension, and Insurance; Education, Training, and Employment; Oversight and Investigation. *Select Committee on Children, Youth, and Families* (15th of 15 D). Task Forces: Economic Security.

Group Ratings

	ADA	ACLU	COPE	CFA	LCV	ACU	NTU	NSI	COC	CEI
1986	100	95	93	100	95	0	29	0	11	16
1985	100	—	94	92	—	5	36	—	18	—

National Journal Ratings

	1986 LIB — 1986 CONS			1985 LIB — 1985 CONS		
Economic	84%	—	13%	89%	—	0%
Social	86%	—	11%	85%	—	0%
Foreign	80%	—	0%	85%	—	8%

Key Votes

1) Lmt Cln Water Act	AGN	5) Retain Gun Cont	FOR	9) Aid Angola Reb	AGN
2) Rpl Tobac Sub	FOR	6) Contra Aid	AGN	10) Tax Reform	FOR
3) Grm-Rdmn Def Red	AGN	7) Lmt Text Imp	FOR	11) S Africa Sanc	FOR
4) Ban Polygraph	FOR	8) Limit SDI	FOR	12) Immig Reform	AGN

Election Results

1986 general	Lane Evans (D)	85,442	(56%)	($620,183)
	Sam McHard (R)	68,101	(44%)	($312,698)
1986 primary	Lane Evans (D)	22,761	(100%)	
1984 general	Lane Evans (D)	128,273	(57%)	($462,782)
	Kenneth G. McMillan (R)	98,069	(43%)	($435,184)

Campaign Contributions and Expenditures

	1985-86	Direct Cont. 1985-86			PACS Breakdown 1985-86			
Receipts	$632,359	Indiv.	$205,738	Corp.	$13,150	T/M/H	$55,564
Expend.	$620,183	PACS	$353,944	Labor	$186,498	Agr.	$19,750
Debts	$14,307	Cand.	$56,750	Ideo.	$72,932	CWOS	$6,050

EIGHTEENTH DISTRICT

"How will it play in Peoria?" is a question Washington insiders like to ask, using Peoria as a surrogate for every middle American small town. But Peoria, like most American small cities, is too distinctive to be a reliable national barometer. It is one of the heartlands of midwestern Republicanism, just across the river from Pekin, the home of Everett Dirksen, who represented Peoria in Congress for 32 years, and it is also Reagan country: the President grew up in Dixon some 85 miles away, and he graduated from Eureka College just across the Illinois River, and has visited the Peoria area twice as President. It is representecd now in Congress by Robert Michel, the House Republican Leader.

Yet in the Reagan years Peoria has moved perceptibly to the Democrats. The collapse of the farm economy and the federal trade deficit have had heavy impact here, partly because Peoria is a farming center, but more important because it is a manufacturing center of farm machinery and equipment. Peoria's biggest employer is Caterpillar, long the world's leading producer of earth-moving and construction equipment, whose export sales plunged in the 1980s, even as local farm machinery factories were laying off hundreds of workers. Peoria's recovery has lagged behind the nation's, and its Republican percentages have fallen. It voted for Senator Paul Simon in 1984 and gave Governor James Thompson less than a majority in 1986. In 1982 the 18th Congressional District, where Peoria is the largest city, gave Michel a scare, reelecting him over a young Democratic lawyer by only a 52%–48% margin. Even in 1986, Michel took the trouble to raise and spend over $600,000 though he had only nominal opposition.

Yet as House Republican Leader Michel has performed ably throughout the 1980s. In 1981 and 1982, when Republicans had enough votes to have a working majority in the House, he nurtured unprecedented party unanimity: there were virtually no dissenters from the Reagan budget or tax cuts of 1981. After the 1982 elections, he came under attack from the younger conservatives around Newt Gingrich for being insufficiently confrontational. Michel has served three decades in a Democratic-majority House, and he is a man of old-fashioned personal decency and good fellowship; he enjoys a golf game with Tip O'Neill and when miffed will break into cries of "gosh!" and "gee whillikers!" But he is also, as Gingrich and others found out, quite capable of being a tough partisan, at least where—and this is probably what he would emphasize—it gets results. Michel is a master of the metier of the House floor, the rousing extemperaneous five-minute or one-minute speech, at once full of vitriol at the majority's lack of fairness and full of exhortations to his copartisans and friends across the aisle to uphold the standards of sensible, decent America; and he is a master as well of the behind-the-scenes negotiation.

Sometimes he is more aggressive than others. In 1985 and 1986 he helped lead the Republicans' hopeless fight on the Indiana 8th challenge, helped put together a House Republican alternative budget that united much of the party, and argued strongly and finally effectively for aid to the Nicaraguan contras. But in 1987 he was antagonizing Republicans by predicting (accurately) that Republicans would lose a vote on the contras and by his vote to override the President's veto of the highway bill because it included a project in the 18th District ("The President doesn't see Route 121 as I do," Michel said.) Still, though there are more breaks from Republican ranks than there were in 1981, party unity is near the historic high, a considerable achievement considering the wide breadth of views. For Republicans disagree not just, as they did in the 1940s when Michel was on his predecessor's staff and in the 1950s when he was first elected, on how to respond to the Democrats' initiatives; they disagree on what their own initiatives should be. The 92 Group wants to see the party more liberal on cultural and sometimes on economic issues; cultural conservatives want to make abortion the leading issue; Gingrich's Conservative Opportunity Society has a startling new idea, it seems, every 6 months; senior Republicans on many committees are busy working with their Democratic chairmen to maintain programs they have nurtured for years.

Michel himself is from the midwestern Taft conservative wing of the party, and first came to Washington in 1948, when it was still a live question whether America would have an isolationist foreign policy and whether the New Deal would be repealed. Michel's father came to isolationist Peoria from Alsace-Lorraine, long fought over in European wars, and Michel himself was wounded in the Battle of the Bulge, not far away. His predecessor Richard Velde was chairman of the House Un-American Activities Committee; Michel himself, on the floor and in the Appropriations Committee, was a steady and unflagging but often unsuccessful opponent of federal spending. He chaired the Republicans' campaign committee in its tough years in the middle 1970s and was party whip in the late 1970s. After the 1980 election he beat Guy VanderJagt, then and now chairman of the Republican campaign committee, for the party leadership.

Michel has had more than his share of political disappointments through these years, but he has also had cause for satisfaction, and has almost always remained of good cheer. He must have been disappointed by his party's minor gains in the 1984 elections, but if so he could be cheered by the fact that the opposition made only minor gains in 1986. He must be pleased at the elevation to the leadership of two talented Illinois colleagues, Edward Madigan and Lynn Martin, although Martin's failure to win a seat on Appropriations, Michel's old committee, suggests that they may not be able to follow in his leadership footsteps. There is talk that he may retire from the House in 1988, and if he does he will have to tip his hand early; Illinois has a December filing deadline, the first in the nation. But after half a dozen years of battering and confrontation, inside his party and out, he has never been in a stronger position as leader, and those Republicans who are looking for an alternative might do better to appreciate now, as they probably will later, the leader they have.

The People: Pop. 1980: 519,026, up 8.3% 1970–80. Households (1980): 75% family, 41% with children, 65% married couples; 28.3% housing units rented; median monthly rent: $185; median house value: $44,400. Voting age pop. (1980): 368,659; 4% Black, 1% Spanish origin.

1984 Presidential Vote: Reagan (R) 107,217   (62%)
Mondale (D) 66,107   (38%)

Rep. Robert H. Michel (R)

Elected 1956; b. Mar. 2, 1923, Peoria; home, Peoria; Bradley U., B.S. 1948; Apostolic Christian; married (Corinne).

Career: Army, WWII; A.A., U.S. Rep. Harold Velde, 1949–56.

Offices: 2112 RHOB 20515, 202-225-6201. Also 100 N.E. Monroe, Rm. 107, Peoria 61602, 309-671-7027; and 236 W. State St., Jacksonville 62650, 217-245-1431.

Committees: *Minority Leader.*

Group Ratings

	ADA	ACLU	COPE	CFA	LCV	ACU	NTU	NSI	COC	CEI
1986	5	10	11	25	5	86	49	100	88	71
1985	5	—	12	33	—	86	54	—	81	—

National Journal Ratings

	1986 LIB — 1986 CONS		1985 LIB — 1985 CONS	
Economic	0% —	94%	22% —	77%
Social	34% —	65%	0% —	76%
Foreign	14% —	84%	0% —	76%

Key Votes

1) Lmt Cln Water Act	FOR	5) Retain Gun Cont	AGN	9) Aid Angola Reb	FOR
2) Rpl Tobac Sub	FOR	6) Contra Aid	FOR	10) Tax Reform	FOR
3) Grm-Rdmn Def Red	FOR	7) Lmt Text Imp	AGN	11) S Africa Sanc	AGN
4) Ban Polygraph	AGN	8) Limit SDI	AGN	12) Immig Reform	FOR

Election Results

1986 general	Robert H. Michel (R)	94,308	(63%)	($639,765)
	Jim Dawson (D)	56,331	(37%)	($11,949)
1986 primary	Robert H. Michel (R)	41,133	(100%)	
1984 general	Robert H. Michel (R)	136,183	(61%)	($702,567)
	Gerald A. Bradley (D)	86,884	(39%)	($59,997)

Campaign Contributions and Expenditures

1985-86		Direct Cont. 1985-86		PACS Breakdown 1985-86			
Receipts	$689,849	Indiv.	$199,614	Corp.	$258,735	T/M/H	$153,476
Expend.	$639,765	Party	$6,742	Labor	$23,750	Agr.	$1,000
Unspent	$100,315	PACS	$463,111	Ideo.	$16,932	CWOS	$9,218

NINETEENTH DISTRICT

For 200 years the Englishmen and their descendants who settled the eastern United States had to clear their land before they planted their crops. The Eastern Seaboard, the Appalachian Mountains, and the Ohio River Valley were all covered with forests. But when the first white settlers got as far west as the Wabash River, they suddenly encountered the prairie: a vast sea of flat, unforested land that stretched much farther than the eye could see, all the way to the

Mississippi River and beyond. It was hard land to tame at first: the soil resisted the plow and the old stump-clearing methods were inapplicable. But the settlers learned to make plows that would pierce the surface and bring up the wonderful topsoil.

White men came to the prairie of Illinois from two directions. The northern half of the state was settled originally by Yankees coming overland from Ohio, Upstate New York, and New England, people who soon formed the bedrock of the new Republican Party. The southern part was settled by people we would now call southerners, people born in Kentucky (like Abraham Lincoln) or Virginia or Tennessee. The rough boundary between these two migrations runs through the middle of the 19th Congressional District, along the old National Road—now U.S. 40, paralleled by Interstate 70. North of this the accents are hard and the politics traditionally Republican; Danville, in the northern end of the district, used to elect Joseph Cannon, the speaker of the House against whom the progressives rebelled in 1910. South of the National Road, the accents are softer and more drawling and the politics traditionally Democratic. Voters here have had little use for national Democrats, but as late as 1976 they regularly reelected a Democratic congressman.

In recent times this part of Illinois has gone back and forth between Republican and Democratic congressmen, but not necessarily for partisan reasons. The most recent change was in 1984, when Republican Daniel Crane was defeated. The year before Crane was censured by the House for having had sex with a female page, and despite repentance and a tearful appearance with his family back home, he was defeated by Democrat Terry Bruce. (Ironically, Massachusetts's Gerry Studds, censured the same year for having sex with a male page, was never contrite, yet was reelected.) The winner by a 52%–48% margin was the man Crane had beaten when the seat was open in 1978, state Senator Bruce.

Bruce is one of those younger Democrats who are professional politicians and whose instinct for the business enables them to win even in unlikely territory and to hold onto constituencies even in difficult years. After two years on the staff of the Illinois Senate president, he was elected senator himself in 1970 at age 26. He showed himself able to pass bills on everything from education to grain elevators and was reelected regularly. In the House he got seats on the Agriculture, Education and Labor, and Science, Space and Technology Committees, and got busy getting scientific grants for the University of Illinois, working on student loan programs, and encouraging ethanol production. He was a visible supporter of Gramm-Rudman ready to hide behind its seemingly automatic budget-cutting mechanism when tough questions arose; he made a point of promoting local economic development.

All this cemented Bruce's ties with the district. In 1986, against a young law school graduate who was poorly financed, he won reelection with 66% of the vote. Interestingly, his percentage in Champaign-Urbana, the home of the University of Illinois and the most Democratic area in this part of Downstate Illinois in the 1970s, actually went down. But Danville and the rural counties, which he narrowly lost to Crane in 1984, went better than 2 to 1 for Bruce in 1986. The 19th District still sits uneasily on a political borderland, tottering between the two parties. But Bruce seems to have done the lion's share of the work of making it a safe seat for him.

The People: Pop. 1980: 518,350, up 4.9% 1970–80. Households (1980): 70% family, 36% with children, 61% married couples; 30.3% housing units rented; median monthly rent: $161; median house value: $35,100. Voting age pop. (1980): 386,732; 3% Black, 1% Asian origin, 1% Spanish origin.

1984 Presidential Vote:

Reagan (R)	141,611	(62%)
Mondale (D)	85,323	(38%)

Rep. Terry L. Bruce (D)

Elected 1984; b. Mar. 25, 1944, Olney; home, Olney; U. of IL, B.S. 1966, J.D. 1969; United Methodist; married (Charlotte).

Career: U.S. Dept. of Labor, 1965; Staff asst., IL Senate Pres., 1969–70; Practicing atty., 1970–84; IL Senate, 1970–84.

Offices: 419 CHOB 20515, 202-225-5001. Also 202 E. Main St., P.O. Box 206, Olney 62450, 618-395-8585; 106 N. Vermillion St., Danville 61832, 217-446-7445; and 102 E. University Ave., Champaign 61820, 217-398-0020.

Committees: *Energy and Commerce* (25th of 25 D). Subcommittees: Energy and Power; Health and the Environment. *Science, Space and Technology* (16th of 27 D). Subcommittees: Energy Research and Development; Science, Research and Technology.

Group Ratings

	ADA	ACLU	COPE	CFA	LCV	ACU	NTU	NSI	COC	CEI
1986	80	70	87	83	74	9	35	0	33	14
1985	70	—	76	67	—	19	36	—	36	—

National Journal Ratings

	1986 LIB — 1986 CONS		1985 LIB — 1985 CONS	
Economic	58%	— 41%	57%	— 41%
Social	67%	— 32%	57%	— 42%
Foreign	80%	— 0%	75%	— 21%

Key Votes

1) Lmt Cln Water Act	FOR	5) Retain Gun Cont	AGN	9) Aid Angola Reb	AGN
2) Rpl Tobac Sub	AGN	6) Contra Aid	AGN	10) Tax Reform	AGN
3) Grm-Rdmn Def Red	FOR	7) Lmt Text Imp	FOR	11) S Africa Sanc	FOR
4) Ban Polygraph	FOR	8) Limit SDI	FOR	12) Immig Reform	FOR

Election Results

1986 general	Terry L. Bruce (D)	111,105	(66%)	($278,421)
	Al Salvi (R).........................	56,186	(34%)	($37,570)
1986 primary	Terry L. Bruce (D)	35,399	(100%)	
1984 general	Terry L. Bruce (D)	117,634	(52%)	($300,840)
	Daniel B. Crane (R)	107,463	(48%)	($389,043)

Campaign Contributions and Expenditures

1985-86		Direct Cont. 1985-86		PACS Breakdown 1985-86			
Receipts	$371,735	Indiv.	$82,509	Corp.	$30,750	T/M/H	$52,009
Expend.	$278,421	Party	$698	Labor	$105,850	Agr.	$12,500
Unspent	$96,020	PACS	$223,316	Ideo.	$17,757	CWOS	$4,450
		Cand.	$60,000				

TWENTIETH DISTRICT

The 20th District of Illinois is a descendant of the district that elected the 37-year-old Abraham Lincoln, railroad lawyer and Whig opponent of the Mexican War, to the House of Representatives in 1846. The western part of the district, to outward appearances, hasn't changed much since the 19th century. It remains a land of fertile prairies, the bottomlands of the Mississippi and Illinois Rivers, farm marketing towns and courthouse villages. The river port of Quincy on the Mississippi River looks pretty much the way it did at the turn of the century, as does the little village of Nauvoo, from which the Mormons were expelled in 1846 and led by Brigham Young to their promised land of Utah. Some of these counties are historically Democratic (one produced Henry Rainey, Speaker of the House during Franklin Roosevelt's first 100 days); others historically Republican.

The largest city in the district is Springfield, with 99,000 people. It must have been a bustling, perhaps even a gracious town in Abe Lincoln's and Mary Todd's time. Today it is a middle-sized state capital with an old capitol building, several not-so-elegant hotels, a small black ghetto, a little industry and a few shopping centers, but little of the gentrification and glitter that has made Albany and Sacramento and Austin into considerable cities in the last 10 years. Next to state government, the Lincoln tourist business seems to be the mainstay of the local economy. Still, Springfield survives recessions better than Decatur, the 20th's second largest city and headquarters of Dwayne Andreas's Archer-Daniels-Midland soybean and corn combine and of large Caterpillar plants.

The 20th District is now a solid political base for Democratic Representative Richard Durbin. He is another one of those workhorse younger members who, as the local Republican paper that carries Lincoln's picture on the masthead noted while endorsing him, has a 98% attendance record and yet came home 48 weekends a year. In Springfield he worked for Democrats in the state Senate and for Senator Paul Simon when he was lieutenant governor (1969–73); he lost two races for office in the 1970s, but developed an in-depth knowledge of parliamentary procedure and an instinctive understanding of the legislative process. In 1982 he was able to win the nomination to oppose a clearly vulnerable congressman and to raise and spend a large campaign budget intelligently. He won a seat on the Agriculture Committee and on Science and Technology as well; after the 1984 election he had the political savvy to win a seat on Appropriations over tough competition. He serves on the Agriculture and Transportation subcommittees, and is proud of his work funneling money to Springfield and Illinois. A reflector of contemporary opinion, he was proud of measures aimed at drug-exporting nations and to get states to raise the drinking age to 21. He is one of the proponents of the individual training account idea (analogous to IRAs), in which workers could defer tax on income set aside for future job training—one of Gary Hart's "new ideas" in 1984. For 1987 he says he wants to cut down on imports of fruits and vegetables from Latin American countries that don't have strong pesticide regulations. During the 1986 campaign, alarmed by the rise in Republican popularity among college students, he and other young Democrats set up a group to barnstorm campuses and give their pitch.

He won the district in 1982 by beating Republican Paul Findley, a 22-year House veteran; Findley won easily when he concentrated on farm issues, but as a senior Foreign Affairs Committee member in the late 1970s he met with Yasir Arafat and was happy to characterize himself as Arafat's best friend in Congress—thus generating plenty of campaign money to any serious opponent. In 1984 Durbin had serious opposition from a Sangamon County official, and won with 61%; in 1986, against a weaker opponent, he got 68%. This impressive showing is a good indication that Durbin's formula of hard work plus a moderate voting record has made this a safe seat for him.

The People: Pop. 1980: 519,015, up 3.2% 1970–80. Households (1980): 72% family, 38% with children, 61% married couples; 28.0% housing units rented; median monthly rent: $162; median house value: $37,200. Voting age pop. (1980): 375,764, 4% Black.

1984 Presidential Vote:

Reagan (R)	107,579	(58%)
Mondale (D)	77,720	(42%)

Rep. Richard J. Durbin (D)

Elected 1982; b. Nov. 21, 1944; East St. Louis; home, Springfield; Georgetown U., B.S. 1966, J.D. 1969; Roman Catholic; married (Loretta).

Career: Staff of Lt. Gov. Paul Simon, 1969–72; Legal counsel to IL Sen. Judiciary Cmtee., 1972–82; professor, Southern IL Sch. of Medicine, 1978–82.

Offices: 417 CHOB 20515, 202-225-5271. Also 1307 S. 7th St., Springfield 62703, 217-492-4062; 363 S. Main St., Rm. 110, Decatur 62523, 217-428-4745; and 531 Hampshire, Rm. 305, Quincy 62301, 217-228-1042.

Committees: *Appropriations* (33th of 35 D). Subcommittees: Rural Development, Agriculture and Related Agencies; Transportation. *Budget* (20th of 21 D). Task Forces: Community and Natural Resources; Human Resources. *Select Committee on Children, Youth and Families* (16th of 18 D). Task Force: Prevention Strategies.

Group Ratings

	ADA	ACLU	COPE	CFA	LCV	ACU	NTU	NSI	COC	CEI
1986	85	65	84	75	71	14	27	20	22	19
1985	65	—	81	83	—	19	34	—	36	—

National Journal Ratings

	1986 LIB — 1986 CONS			1985 LIB — 1985 CONS		
Economic	77%	—	22%	57%	—	41%
Social	57%	—	40%	60%	—	38%
Foreign	75%	—	20%	71%	—	26%

Key Votes

1) Lmt Cln Water Act	FOR	5) Retain Gun Cont	FOR	9) Aid Angola Reb	AGN
2) Rpl Tobac Sub	FOR	6) Contra Aid	AGN	10) Tax Reform	FOR
3) Grm-Rdmn Def Red	FOR	7) Lmt Text Imp	FOR	11) S Africa Sanc	FOR
4) Ban Polygraph	FOR	8) Limit SDI	FOR	12) Immig Reform	FOR

Election Results

1986 general	Richard J. Durbin (D)	126,556	(68%)	($289,085)
	Kevin B. McCarthy (R)	59,291	(32%)	($108,129)
1986 primary	Richard J. Durbin (D)	50,610	(100%)	
1984 general	Richard J. Durbin (D)	145,092	(61%)	($441,584)
	Richard G. Austin (R)	91,728	(39%)	($217,728)

Campaign Contributions and Expenditures

1985-86		Direct Cont. 1985-86		PACS Breakdown 1985-86			
Receipts	$343,599	Indiv.	$158,484	Corp.	$38,300	T/M/H	$48,820
Expend.	$289,085	Party	$180	Labor	$61,050	Agr.	$7,300
Unspent	$62,833	PACS	$175,727	Ideo.	$17,207	CWOS	$3,050

TWENTY-FIRST DISTRICT

The 21st Congressional District of Illinois is the area across from St. Louis's Gateway Arch where you can see East St. Louis, Belleville, and Granite City through the smoggy air across the Mississippi River. These are not the verdant St. Louis suburbs, but grimy industrial towns criss crossed by miles of railroad tracks. They have all the problems associated with core city areas air pollution, inadequate housing, crime, and a declining tax base. The Illinois side of the St. Louis metropolitan area has a disproportionate share of its poor and low-income working-class residents; the rich stay on the Missouri side of the river.

The 21st proceeds north and inland from the river enough to take in territory more typical of Downstate Illinois. There is Alton, home of the antislavery martyr Elijah Lovejoy and, later, of Robert Wadlow, at 8'11" the world's tallest man, and Phyllis Schlafly. And there are the flat farmlands of southern Illinois, alive with the latest miracle plant, soybeans, a crop exported in great quantities to Japan. Yet politically this district is different from others in this part of the state: it has long been a solidly Democratic constituency. In the close presidential elections of 1960, 1968, and 1976 it delivered Democratic majorities; it has not elected a Republican congressman since 1942. Yet it may be moving away from the Democratic column. The rural counties added after the 1980 Census attracted young, tradition-minded families from the St. Louis orbit and are heavily Republican. Meanwhile, Democratic turnout and enthusiasm are declining within view of the Gateway Arch. The 21st District went heavily for Senator Paul Simon, a native son, in 1984. But it delivered a majority just below his statewide average for Governor James Thompson in 1986.

The congressman from this district since 1944 has been Democrat Melvin Price. He has a past of some accomplishment and a forlorn present. A one-time newspaperman and congressional aide, Price became a pillar of the military and atomic energy establishments in the years after World War II. He served for years on the Joint Committee on Atomic Energy, working to develop nuclear weapons and nuclear power plants; he co-authored the Price–Anderson Act which, by limiting the liability of nuclear plant operators for accidents, helped encourage the development of nuclear power. For 10 years he was chairman of the House Armed Services Committee, from 1974 when Edward Hébert was ousted by the Democratic Caucus until 1984 when he himself was. One reason that happened was that Price, an old-fashioned New Deal Democrat, was too hawkish for many Democrats; he is as inclined to support the Pentagon as he is domestic branches of government. The other reason is that, sadly, by 1984 Price was simply too inattentive for the job. He was not an active chairman and certainly was in no shape to represent House Democrats on important issues on TV. Price, a pleasant and likeable man, gave a gracious speech when he was rejected in favor of Les Aspin. But he must have felt some momentary satisfaction when in early 1987 Aspin too was voted out by the caucus, though not when Aspin regained the chair weeks later.

Price's loss of the chairmanship also hurt him in the district. He had been fortunate in 1984 in keeping a strong primary opponent out of the race and then in defeating Republican Robert Gaffner 60%–40%. In 1986 he was opposed by 40-year-old Madison County Auditor Pete Fields in the primary; Fields carried the district outside St. Clair County, but Price's big margin among East St. Louis blacks was enough for a 52%–40% win. In the general election, the 53-year-old Gaffner again carried the district outside St. Clair County, but East St. Louis came through once more for Price, giving him a 50.4%–49.6%, 943-vote victory in a race in which neither candidate spent heavily. In the campaign Price promised that he would retire in 1988, and in early 1987 reaffirmed that promise. So there will probably be a serious contest again. The Democratic nomination will be seriously contested, but Republicans have a chance too: the district is trending Republican enough that Gaffner nearly won while running only a couple of points ahead of Thompson's showing in the district.

The People: Pop. 1980: 521,036, dn. 2.0% 1970–80. Households (1980): 76% family, 42% with children, 62% married couples; 29.1% housing units rented; median monthly rent: $155; median house value: $36,700. Voting age pop. (1980): 367,291; 12% Black, 1% Spanish origin.

1984 Presidential Vote:

Reagan (R)	114,814	(53%)
Mondale (D)	100,098	(47%)

Rep. Melvin Price (D)

Elected 1944; b. Jan. 1, 1905, East St. Louis; home, East St. Louis; St. Louis U., 1923–25; Roman Catholic; married (Garaldine).

Career: Reporter, *East St. Louis Journal*, 1925–1933; St. Clair Cnty. Bd. of Sprvsrs., 1929–31; Secy. to U.S. Rep. Edwin M. Schaefer, 1933–43; Reporter, *St. Louis Globe-Democrat*, 1943; Army, WWII.

Offices: 2110 RHOB 20515, 202-225-5661. Also Fed. Bldg., 650 Missouri Ave., East St. Louis 62201, 618-482-9420; and 1990 Troy Rd., Edwardsville 62025, 618-656-9575.

Committees: *Armed Services* (2d of 31 D). Subcommittees: Research and Development (Chairman).

Group Ratings

	ADA	ACLU	COPE	CFA	LCV	ACU	NTU	NSI	COC	CEI
1986	65	65	96	83	57	18	22	40	29	11
1985	40	—	96	71	—	29	23	—	29	—

National Journal Ratings

	1986 LIB — 1986 CONS		1985 LIB — 1985 CONS	
Economic	82%	— 16%	78%	— 21%
Social	64%	— 34%	46%	— 54%
Foreign	60%	— 39%	54%	— 45%

Key Votes

1) Lmt Cln Water Act	AGN	5) Retain Gun Cont	AGN	9) Aid Angola Reb	AGN
2) Rpl Tobac Sub	AGN	6) Contra Aid	AGN	10) Tax Reform	FOR
3) Grm-Rdmn Def Red	—	7) Lmt Text Imp	FOR	11) S Africa Sanc	FOR
4) Ban Polygraph	FOR	8) Limit SDI	FOR	12) Immig Reform	FOR

Election Results

1986 general	Melvin Price (D)	65,722	(50%)	($143,009)
	Robert H. Gaffner (R)	64,779	(50%)	($137,353)
1986 primary	Melvin Price (D)	25,660	(52%)	
	Pete Fields (D)	19,340	(40%)	
	Ronald (Rink) Lucas (D)	2,527	(5%)	
	Steve Maragides (D)	1,386	(3%)	
1984 general	Melvin Price (D)	127,046	(60%)	($93,283)
	Robert H. Gaffner (R)	84,148	(40%)	($2,605)

Campaign Contributions and Expenditures

1985-86		Direct Cont. 1985-86		PACS Breakdown 1985-86			
Receipts	$127,045	Indiv.	$13,570	Corp.	$32,950	T/M/H	$8,191
Expend.	$143,009	Party	$2,588	Labor	$62,450	Agr.	$0
Unspent	$3,094	PACS	$109,341	Ideo.	$5,750	CWOS	$0

TWENTY-SECOND DISTRICT

Little Egypt is the name given to the southernmost part of Illinois—the flat, fertile farmland where the Ohio River joins the Mississippi. This is low, alluvial land, subject to floods almost as often as ancient Egypt itself. The countryside is protected by giant levees that rise above the fields and hide any view of the waters. There is more than a touch of Dixie here: the southern tip of Illinois is closer to Jackson, Mississippi, than to Chicago. The unofficial capital of Little Egypt is Cairo (pronounced KAYroh), a declining town at the exact confluence of the two rivers; today there is some contact and reconciliation, some common feeling between the races, but also suspicion and hatred between two groups of people who mostly live separate lives in an economically declining community.

There are no official boundaries to Little Egypt, but it is safe to say that the 22d Congressional District goes north considerably beyond them. The district takes in the coal mining area around West Frankfort and Marion—one of the most heavily strip-mined areas in the United States— and it includes Carbondale, site of Southern Illinois University. Following the 1982 redistricting, it even has a salient that goes north on the Mississippi River to the city limits of heavily industrial, black-majority East St. Louis. Nearly all this territory is Democratic in most elections, because of ancestral southern preference (this is southern drawl, not midwestern hard R territory) or because of the Democratic leanings of coal miners and industrial workers. But it has not been reliably Democratic in national elections. The 21st went against the Catholic John Kennedy in 1960 and the Great Society's Hubert Humphrey in 1968; it gave southerner Jimmy Carter a majority in 1976 but turned sharply against him, as did many border areas, in 1980. A few counties went for Walter Mondale in 1984, but mostly this remained Reagan country.

The 22d District in 1984 also changed congressmen. The outgoing congressman was Paul Simon, who ran for and won Charles Percy's Senate seat; he won the district when Kenneth Gray retired after 20 years in office, allegedly for health reasons. The newcomer-oldtimer was Ken Gray, who came back from Florida, his health restored, to run for and win the seat once again. Gray will probably remain best known to history as the one-time employer of Elizabeth Ray and to Washingtonians as the Public Works Committee power who effected the gutting and near-destruction of Union Station. In Washington he traveled around in a white Cadillac limousine and partied on boats; in southern Illinois he was known as an auctioneer and magician. He made his political reputation as the Prince of Pork, for bringing dams, highways, and post offices to Little Egypt. Since his return he has achieved other fame. He still dresses distinctively, in pink coats and purple ties, and his hair is uniquely blow-dried. So dressed and coiffed, he presides often over the House and does what many consider a brilliant job: keeping track of the parliamentary procedure while maintaining a steady flow of quips, assessing the strength of the yeas and nays honestly and giving all sides their share of the debate.

At home, where that may not be appreciated, Gray has an insecure hold on the seat. In the 1984 primary against state Senator Kenneth Buzbee he won by only a 56%–44% margin; without his big margins in the coal-mining counties around West Frankfort and Marion and in the East St. Louis area he would have lost. In the general election, Republican Randy Patchett, a local prosecutor, ran an aggressive campaign and won such not-always-Republican areas as Carbondale. But West Frankfort and East St. Louis came through for the Prince of Pork. In 1986 Gray seemed on primary day to be home free: he had no primary opponent, and no Republican filed. But Patchett, encouraged by national Republican officials, got 938 write-in votes and the Republican nomination. He attacked pork barrel spending as a temporary expedient with no lasting benefits and blamed the closing of coal mines on deficits he in turn blamed on Gray. Gray told voters "I want to make you mad" about Ronald Reagan's deficits and MX missile. To dramatize his attacks on Gray for voting against aid to the Nicaraguan Contras, Patchett brought to his announcement ceremony one Leonel Teller who Patchett said was "now fighting in the jungles" to save Nicaragua; "that's the way I talk," Teller said, "with a machine gun." But campaign committee chairman Tony Coelho pointed out that Teller was the manager of an Adidas shoe shop in Georgetown and said, "The only jungle war he fights is Georgetown traffic." Patchett responded that Teller was more of a contra than Elizabeth Ray was a secretary.

It was a close contest, and Patchett got 47% of the vote, not far behind Governor James Thompson's run. Gray outspent Patchett thanks to his larger PAC contributions and won with 53% and has at least one more term ladeling out pork on the Public Works Committee and presiding over the House.

The People: Pop. 1980: 521,303, up 9.3% 1970–80. Households (1980): 73% family, 37% with children, 62% married couples; 25.6% housing units rented; median monthly rent: $131; median house value: $29,500. Voting age pop. (1980): 381,684; 6% Black, 1% Spanish origin.

1984 Presidential Vote:

Reagan (R)	131,531	(56%)
Mondale (D)	104,010	(42%)

Rep. Kenneth J. Gray (D)

Elected 1984; b. Nov. 14, 1924, West Frankfort; home, West Frankfort; Baptist; married (June).

Career: Air Force, 1943–46; Car dealer, 1946–54; U.S. House of Reps., 1954–74; Owner, Ken Gray's Antique Car Museum; Pres., business consulting firm.

Offices: 2109 RHOB 20515, 202-225-5201. Also 234 W. Main, West Frankfort 62896, 618-937-6402; Williamson Cnty Airport, P.O. Drawer 398, Herrin 62948, 618-997-3341; P.O. Bldg., 1500 Washington Ave., Rm. 319, Cairo 62914, 618-734-2617; and 418 S. Poplar, Centralia 62801, 618-532-5800; and 4831 Bond Ave., Alorton 62207, 618-874-2221.

Committees: *Public Works and Transportation* (20th of 32 D). Subcommittees: Economic Development; Investigations and Oversight; Surface Transportation. *Veterans' Affairs* (13th of 21 D). Subcommittees: Hospitals and Health Care.

Group Ratings

	ADA	ACLU	COPE	CFA	LCV	ACU	NTU	NSI	COC	CEI
1986	5	66	91	67	43	18	19	20	35	14
1985	5	—	90	50	—	26	28	—	37	—

National Journal Ratings

	1986 LIB — 1986 CONS		1985 LIB — 1985 CONS	
Economic	82% —	16%	70% —	29%
Social	64% —	34%	44% —	56%
Foreign	56% —	43%	60% —	40%

Key Votes

1) Lmt Cln Water Act	AGN	5) Retain Gun Cont	AGN	9) Aid Angola Reb	AGN
2) Rpl Tobac Sub	AGN	6) Contra Aid	AGN	10) Tax Reform	FOR
3) Grm-Rdmn Def Red	FOR	7) Lmt Text Imp	FOR	11) S Africa Sanc	FOR
4) Ban Polygraph	FOR	8) Limit SDI	AGN	12) Immig Reform	FOR

Election Results

1986 general	Kenneth J. Gray (D)...................	97,585	(53%)	($304,950)
	Randy Patchett (R)....................	85,733	(47%)	($220,564)
1986 primary	Kenneth J. Gray (D)...................	44,973	(100%)	
1984 general	Kenneth J. Gray (D).................	116,952	(50%)	($195,189)
	Randy Patchett (R).................	115,775	(49%)	($225,308)

Campaign Contributions and Expenditures

1985-86		Direct Cont. 1985-86		PACS Breakdown 1985-86			
Receipts	$316,379	Indiv.	$135,766	Corp.	$11,100	T/M/H	$17,350
Expend.	$304,950	Party	$7,400	Labor	$108,900	Agr.	$3,250
Debts	$15,001	PACS	$158,161	Ideo.	$15,811	CWOS	$1,750
		Cand.	$9,500				

INDIANA

If you want to see traditional American politics in action, with old-fashioned political machines and plenty of patronage jobs, with a Republican Party deeply rooted in blue-collar towns and rural counties whose allegiance to the Democratic Party was cemented during the Civil War, you'd better go to Indiana—and fast. For years Indiana has been a political museum piece, roped off from the rest of the continental 48 states by the invisible dotted lines and ancient river beds that mark one state from another. Traveling on interstates feeding into the state or staring across the Ohio River from Kentucky or across the industrial wastes of Lake Calumet from Chicago to Hammond and Gary, you don't see much difference between Indiana and the states around it. Physically, Indiana is just another slice of the limestone-bottomed plain that begins where the hills west of Pittsburgh subside and that moves west across the Mississippi River and ultimately to the Rocky Mountains—land that is well-watered and fertile and, lying astride the great east–west land and water routes, has been industrial for a century.

But Indiana's distinctiveness has always been obvious when you start talking politics. The Hoosier—no other state has a word like it—political tradition with its strong partisanship goes back to Civil War divisions. Into the 1980s it continued to require patronage employees (notably the license plate sellers) to contribute 2% of their salaries to their party organizations—a common practice once in all the older midwestern states, but in most phased out 40 or 50 years ago. Political machines have thrived well into the 1980s, while those in other states—even in Mayor Daley's Chicago—have crumbled. The Indiana Republican Party over the past 20 years has been the most successful political machine, holding onto power in recession years in an industrial state and by most accounts managing the state's affairs intelligently. Republicans currently remain in control of the governorship, which they have held since 1968, all the top state offices, both U.S. Senate seats and large majorities in the state legislature. They hold the mayoralty in Indianapolis, the state's largest city and capital, and patronage-rich county offices in most of the state's large counties.

Indiana's political distinctiveness has been not just a persistence of custom, but reflects the fact that life here has changed less than in other places. The cultural and ethnic patterns in

Indiana today are not much different from what they were in the 1920s. Ethnically, Indiana remains mostly the product of the first wave of American immigration, of people whose ancestors arrived in the New World between 1640 and 1720, and moved overland—down from New England, up from Kentucky and Virginia—to these plains. So today the basic political geography of the state remains much the same as it was just after the Civil War. South of the old National Road, or U.S. 40, people speak with something like a southern drawl and tend to vote Democratic. North of the National Road (which goes right through Indianapolis) people talk with midwestern hard Rs and flat As and vote heavily Republican. Except for the steel area around Gary—really an extension of the Chicago metropolitan area—Indiana has relatively few ethnics from the second wave (1840–1924) of immigration, and no major metropolitan areas. Technically, Greater Indianapolis now has a population over one million but no one would mistake it for a smaller Chicago or Cleveland. The Indiana city is much closer in spirit to the America of barbershop quartets and ice cream socials, a seemingly more innocent time.

Nor has Indiana undergone much change sociologically. Again, the absence of major metropolitan areas is the critical factor; nowhere in Indiana will you find large neighborhoods or significant political constituencies made up of young singles, not to speak of gays. The divorce rate here is lower than the American average, and the percentage of households occupied by families and married people higher. The percentage of households with children is also high and, if the population weren't a little older than the national average, would be among the highest in the United States. These patterns have important political consequences in a time when the old economic antagonisms between union members and management supporters seem to have dissipated. Ronald Reagan in 1984 carried almost every auto-worker town from Michigan and Ohio west through Indiana and Missouri; in 1982 Richard Lugar, always an adversary of unions and opponent of big government programs, carried the factory towns of Kokomo and Anderson, Muncie and Fort Wayne—despite the presence in them of some of the highest unemployment rates in the nation.

But even in Indiana the signs of change are beginning to appear. Republican Governor Robert Orr, after being challenged on the issue and being held by the Democrats to an unimpressive 52% of the vote in 1984, decided to outlaw the practice of earmarking license plate fees for the political parties—and just in time, for Democrat Evan Bayh captured the secretary of state's office, which issues the license plates, in 1986. The practice of requiring 2% contributions seems to be on the way out too. And in 1988 the Republican organization, monolithic through most of 20 years of Republican governorships, may be split over the succession. Lieutenant Governor John Mutz wants to succeed Orr, just as in 1980 Orr, as lieutenant governor, succeeded Governor Otis Bowen, but Indianapolis Mayor William Hudnut, with his own separate power bases and somewhat different views on issues, may be interested in the job too. A victory for the out party would not be out of line with Indiana tradition: for years politics here was competitive, and power roughly equally, if grudgingly, shared between the parties (there is little or no camaraderie between members of the two parties in Indiana). But it's possible that a Democratic governor might not stick with Indiana's tradition of relatively low levels of state taxation and services, and likely (because the Democrats would know they are not going to be in forever) that they would continue to abolish the state's antique political customs.

The Democrats already have made advances—in the governor's race in 1984, in the 1986 congressional races in which they picked up one seat and won a solid majority of the votes cast statewide, for the first time since 1978, and in the 1986 secretary of state's race, in which Democrat Evan Bayh, son of the former senator, beat Republican Rob Bowen, son of the former governor, by a 54%–46% margin. Indiana's industrial base has not done well in the 1980s, despite the efforts of state Republicans to use government to assist it; and the Democrats have moved ahead on economic issues. The national Republicans' emphasis on free markets and association with the Sun Belt do not play well here. Other issues matter less. The culturally traditional tone of daily life in Indiana has meant there has been little mileage for the Republicans in stressing culturally conservative values; they don't seem seriously threatened.

INDIANA — Congressional Districts, Counties, and Selected Places — *(10 Districts)*

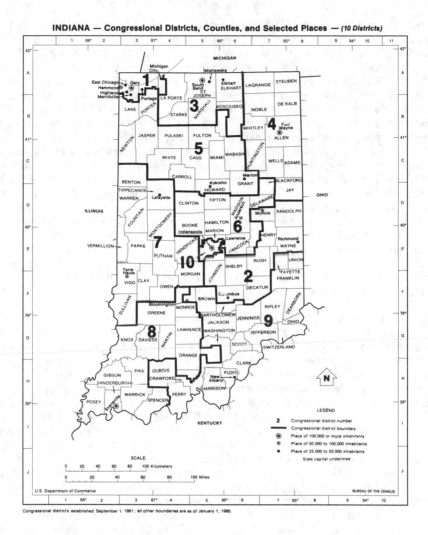

Foreign policy likewise does not play much role in electoral politics, even though Richard Lugar chaired the Senate Foreign Relations Committee for two years and exerted great influence on foreign issues; Indianapolis is the home of the American Legion, and support of an assertive foreign policy is not controversial.

Governor. Robert Orr is now the nation's oldest governor (though that did not stop him from running what was probably the nation's first MTV-type political spot in 1984) and was reelected in 1984 with only 52% of the vote, running at the bottom rather than the top of the Republican ticket. This was all the more striking because his opponent, former state Senator Wayne Townsend, was known mainly as a supporter of organized labor in a state where unions have conspicuously failed to deliver majorities even during a recession. Orr may suffer perhaps by comparison with his predecessor, Otis (Doc) Bowen, who was appointed Secretary of Health and Human Services in 1986 and who is still regarded as one of Indiana's most popular governors. The key question for 1988, when Orr is not eligible to run, is the succession. Indiana parties for years nominated their candidates in conventions, dominated by party officials and patronage employees. But there could be a primary here between John Mutz and William Hudnut. For the Democrats possible candidates include: Wayne Townsend, though his union ties might still hurt; Mayor Winfield Moses of Fort Wayne, though he was forced to resign from office for using Democratic funds to help defeat a strong Republican in his primary, and then was voted back into office by his county party; former U.S. Attorney Virginia Dill McCarthy, though it's not clear Indiana is ready for a woman governor; Kokomo Mayor Stephen Dailey; state Senator Frank O'Bannon; and Evan Bayh, who led in early polls though in 1988 he will be all of 30.

Senators. Indiana's two senators are two Republicans of similar voting records but different temperaments who have made important differences in national policy. Richard Lugar's success in politics seems a triumph of intellect: he is not gregarious, he has little sense of humor, his appearance is not striking. But he does have brains, works hard, and has shown a strength of character and quiet persistence that have stood him well. His brilliance led Republican Party leaders to slate him for mayor of Indianapolis in 1967, when he was 35; he won and made a record of some note, consolidating the city and county into Unigov, which added tax resources to the city and also had the happy effect of adding more Republican votes to city elections. Lugar bucked fashion among big-city mayors and called for fewer rather than more federal programs, and nonetheless upset the much-ballyhooed John Lindsay for the presidency of the National Council of Mayors in 1970. He became known as Richard Nixon's favorite mayor—not a political asset in 1974, when he ran against and lost narrowly to Senator Birch Bayh. But two years later, in a more favorable climate and against the weaker incumbent Vance Hartke, he won easily.

In the Senate Lugar continued to concentrate on domestic policy. Like most Indiana Republicans, he has always been an adversary of organized labor, and in 1978 he organized the filibuster that killed the AFL-CIO's labor law reform bill, of which nothing has been heard since. He provided key support in 1978 for the loan guarantees to Chrysler—a big employer in Indiana—but he also insisted on requiring bigger wage and benefit concessions than the UAW wanted. He generally favors market over government action, but running for reelection in the recession year of 1982 he produced with much fanfare a bill to lower interest rates for home-buyers. Lugar is also an advocate of free trade, but in early 1985 he supported an extension of the so-called "voluntary" limits on imports of Japanese automobiles. He became an admirer and close lieutenant of first Minority and then Majority Leader Howard Baker, and ran to succeed Baker after the 1984 election but ran behind Bob Dole and Ted Stevens.

Then Lugar became the chairman of the Senate Foreign Relations Committee, and became a major and positive force in American foreign policy. Lugar quickly took command over a committee sharply divided between Jesse Helms, who tends to conduct his own foreign policy, and liberal Democrats. Lugar supports the Reagan foreign policy generally and is a vigorous advocate of aid to the Nicaraguan contras. But on the Philippines he was ahead of the Administration: keeping in touch with Corazon Aquino as well as Ferdinand Marcos, and observing the elections. Lugar quickly concluded that Marcos's "victory" was fraudulent and at a decisive point called on him to leave office; the Administration followed. On South Africa Lugar backed the Senate bill that Reagan vetoed and then led the fight to override the veto. For all this he received some criticism on the right. But he had done much to forge a bipartisan consensus to advance democracy abroad and to oppose dictatorship, and Lugar is the first Foreign Relations chairman since William Fulbright to genuinely move the mind of the nation. He also seems to have moved Senate Republicans. Technically, Lugar's influence is reduced because Helms, based on his greater Senate though not committee seniority and in spite of his promise to North Carolina voters to take the lead seat on Agriculture, claimed the ranking minority position on Foreign Relations after the 1986 election. In early January 1987 committee Republicans voted 7–0 for Lugar, but that victory was overturned by the whole body of Republican senators, 24–17. Helms quickly threw out Lugar's staff and installed his own; Lugar, who got the ranking position on Agriculture Helms had vacated, did likewise. All this presumably diminishes Lugar's influence on foreign policy. But the committee vote, and the narrowness of the wider vote despite the seniority principle, shows that Lugar in the long run is in the stronger and more respected position.

Lugar remains, for all his foreign policy success and intellectual patina, a successful electoral politician. You don't rise in Indiana politics by being naive about how to win elections, and when an Indiana politician describes an election, as Lugar described Marcos's, as clearly fraudulent, you can be sure he knows whereof he speaks. Lugar was reelected with only 54% in the recession year of Indiana; but in this closely balanced state, any weaker Republican might well have lost in that recession year. He chaired the Republican Senate campaign committee in 1983 and 1984 and helped maintain the Republican majority. He seems strong heading into the 1988 election, and his work on foreign policy does not seem likely to be an electoral handicap.

Dan Quayle brings to the Senate sunny good looks, a cheerful temperament, and an inclination that many observers found surprising to dig into issues, do his homework, and come up with workmanlike legislative solutions to problems of government. He arrived in the Senate at 33, after two not especially distinguished terms in the House. He comes from a family prominent in publishing; his grandfather was Eugene Pulliam, proprietor of the *Indianapolis Star* and the *Arizona Republic*. Cheerful and articulate, he does not seem particularly cerebral. Yet Quayle has been smart enough to pick out political openings that have produced for him an apparently safe Senate seat. In 1976 he challenged a Democratic congressman everyone else considered unbeatable, and beat him by a solid margin. In 1979 he announced early that he'd run for the Senate if popular incumbent Governor Otis Bowen didn't; Bowen, for personal reasons, did not, and Quayle got the nomination without serious opposition. In the general election he ran against one of the nation's best instinctive political campaigners, Birch Bayh, in a year in which Bayh's views on issues, never an asset in Indiana, were a crushing liability.

In the Senate, Quayle has been one of the most active and successful members of the Republican class of 1980. With choice committee assignments—Budget, Armed Services, Labor and Human Resources—he has worked harder and accomplished more than almost anyone expected. He is a prime example of a Senate Republican becoming immersed in the details and discipline of running a large federal government much of which he had been running against not so long before. In 1981 he found himself chairing the subcommittee with jurisdiction over jobs programs, many of which the Administration wanted to zero out; he spent a year developing the Job Training Partnership Act, which sought to get private businesses involved in training, rather than the local governments used in the little-lamented CETA program; he continued to work on jobs programs in his second term. He supported the President's economic program stalwartly, but as time went on became concerned about deficits and stood behind Budget chairman Pete Domenici's efforts to force deficit cuts. On Armed Services, he has been skeptical about the need for defense spending increases as large as those proposed by Secretary Caspar Weinberger, and in 1985 he proposed changes in defense procurement to promote more competition between contractors and require more disclosure of the hiring of former Pentagon aides by them. Yet he is an aggressive supporter of the Strategic Defense Initiative and was one of four Budget Committee members (all Republicans) to vote against a freeze in the defense budget.

Usually Quayle is a team player, cooperating with Republican leaders, careful to get things for Indiana when he can. But he has been willing to roil some feathers on occasion. In 1984 he got himself appointed head of a committee studying Senate procedures, with which just about everyone seems discontented. After the elections, he unveiled his proposals to raise the votes necessary to cut off debate but make such votes effectively final and to decrease the number of committees each senator can serve on. In theory almost every Senator believes that these address genuine problems sensibly; in practice, many are unwilling to give away political advantages they enjoy or hope soon to enjoy. With Republicans back in the minority, he has a "porkbuster" proposal for a rules change to force up or down votes on presidential rescissions of congressional spending. It seems apparent by now that Quayle is not just a political accident, but a fortunate young man with good political instincts.

As Lugar has concentrated on foreign affairs and national issues, monitoring elections in the Philippines and commenting on the Reykjavik summit, Quayle has tended to Indiana matters, working with local congressmen on projects from the Indiana Dunes on Lake Michigan to the fate of shipping on the Ohio River. He took the lead in urging the confirmation of Indiana Republican Daniel Manion as a federal judge. His visibility in the state surely helped in the 1986 election. His Democratic opponent, Valparaiso council member Jill Long, was underfinanced and scarcely visible in the state; she got 38% of the vote, which many consider the Democratic minimum in this partisan state. Quayle's 61% is the highest percentage any Indiana senator has ever received. He seems to have a chance to beat another record, if Lugar doesn't beat him to it: no Indiana Senator has been elected to a fourth term. But that is looking ahead to 1994 and 1998, which may be too far even in tradition-minded Indiana.

Presidential politics. In presidential elections Indiana is, to paraphrase A. J. Liebling, more Republican than any state that is larger and larger than any state that is more Republican. It always goes Republican, except in landslide Democratic years when the Democrats don't need the votes anyway. Indiana has a presidential primary that was once one of the earlier contests: in May 1968, for example, it was the scene of an epic battle between Robert Kennedy, Eugene McCarthy, and Roger Branigin, the hapless governor who was a stand-in for President Johnson. In 1984 Indiana's primary was overshadowed by Ohio's the same day; the results, as it happened, were almost identical. Gary Hart actually carried old-fashioned Indiana, but his victory was little noticed and in the end availed him very little.

Congressional districting. Indiana's 1981 redistricting was the most partisan Republican plan in the nation. Passed early in 1981 by Indiana's organization-dominated legislature, it may have been counterproductive by convincing Democrats in other states to proceed accordingly. The Indiana plan was the subject of a 1986 Supreme Court decision that, with typical intellectual confusion, said that state legislatures can draw lines for partisan advantage but that courts can overturn them if they're egregious; it then went on to uphold Indiana's lines, although it's not likely that anyone could come up with a clearer case of partisan motivation. The better course would have been to uphold these lines and any that meet the equal-population standard, because the advantage any party can get from district-drawing is limited severely by the one-person-one-vote rule. Indiana is the best example of this. In 1982 Republicans won 51% of House votes and 5 of the 10 seats. In 1984 they won 53% of the House votes and 5 seats, counting the bitterly contested 8th District the way the House did, for Democrat Frank McCloskey. In 1986 they won 49% of House votes and 4 of the 10 seats. Altogether under their own plan Republicans have won 51% of the votes but only 13 of 30 seats; and even if you count the 8th District for them, as the Republican secretary of state did in 1984, and assume they would have held it in 1986, that's only a 15-15 split for the party that won the majority of the votes. And if the Democratic vote should climb much more, almost every Republican seat would be vulnerable: Secretary of State Evan Bayh, with a less-than-landslide statewide percentage of 54%, nonetheless carried 9 out of 10 of the Republican-designed districts. Some partisan bonanza.

The People: Est. Pop. 1986: 5,504,000; Pop. 1980: 5,490,224, up 0.2% 1980–86 and 5.7% 1970–80; 2.28% of U.S. total, 14th largest. 12% with 1–3 yrs. col., 12% with 4+ yrs. col.; 9.7% below poverty level. Single ancestry: 13% German, 12% English, 4% Irish, 1% Polish, French, Dutch, Italian. Households (1980): 76% family, 42% with children, 64% married couples; 28.3% housing units rented; median monthly rent: $166; median house value: $37,200. Voting age pop. (1980): 3,871,906; 7% Black, 1% Spanish origin. Registered voters (1986): 2,878,498; no party registration.

1986 Share of Federal Tax Burden: $15,822,200,000; 2.10% of U.S. total, 15th largest.

1986 Share of Federal Expenditures

	Total		Non-Defense		Defense	
Total Expend	$14,686m	(1.77%)	$11,373m	(1.89%)	$3,313m	(1.44%)
St/Lcl Grants	2,000m	(1.78%)	1,998m	(1.78%)	2m	(1.8%)
Salary/Wages	1,446m	(1.20%)	783m	(1.33%)	664m	(1.07%)
Pymnts to Indiv	7,732m	(2.12%)	7,565m	(2.18%)	167m	(.94%)
Procurement	2,997m	(1.46%)	517m	(0.93%)	2,480m	(1.65%)
Research/Other	511m	(1.92%)	511m	(1.92%)	(0m)	(0.42%)

Political Lineup: Governor, Robert D. Orr (R); Lt. Gov., John M. Mutz (R); Secy. of State, Evan Bayh (D); Atty. Gen., Linley E. Pearson (R); Treasurer, Marjorie H. O'Laughlin (R); Auditor, Ann DeVore (R). State Senate, 50 (30 R and 20 D); State House of Representatives, 100 (52 R and 48 D). Senators, Richard G. Lugar (R) and J. Danforth (Dan) Quayle (R). Representatives, 10 (6 D and 4 R).

1984 Presidential Vote

Reagan (R)	1,377,230	(62%)
Mondale (D)	841,481	(38%)

1980 Presidential Vote

Reagan (R)	1,255,656	(56%)
Carter (D)	844,197	(38%)
Anderson (I)	111,639	(5%)

1984 Democratic Presidential Primary

Hart	299,491	(42%)
Mondale	293,413	(41%)
Jackson	98,190	(14%)
Glenn	16,046	(2%)

1984 Republican Presidential Primary

Reagan	428,559	(100%)

GOVERNOR

Gov. Robert D. Orr (R)

Elected 1980, term expires Jan. 1989; b. Nov. 17, 1917, Ann Arbor, MI; home, Evansville; Yale U., B.A. 1940, Harvard U. Bus. Sch.; Presbyterian; married (Joanne).

Career: Army, WWII; Businessman, industrialist, 1957–1973; IN Senate, 1968–72; Lt. Gov., 1972–80; not included in other states.

Office: 206 State House, Indianapolis 46204, 317-232-4567.

Election Results

1984 gen.	Robert D. Orr (R)	1,146,497	(52%)
	W. Wayne Townsend (D)	1,036,832	(47%)
1984 prim.	Robert D. Orr (R)	319,879	(72%)
	John Snyder (R)	126,778	(28%)
1980 gen.	Robert D. Orr (R)	1,257,383	(58%)
	John A. Hillenbrand (D)	913,116	(42%)

SENATORS

Sen. Richard G. Lugar (R)

Elected 1976, seat up 1988; b. Apr. 4, 1932, Indianapolis; home, Indianapolis; Denison U., B.A. 1954; Rhodes Scholar, Oxford U., M.A. 1956; Methodist; married (Charlene).

Career: Navy, 1957–60; Vice Pres. and Treasurer, Thomas L. Green & Co., 1960–67; Indianapolis Bd. of Sch. Commissioners, 1964–67; Mayor of Indianapolis, 1968–75; Repub. Nominee for U.S. Senate, 1974; Visiting prof., U. of Indianapolis, 1975.

Offices: 306 HSOB 20510, 202-224-4814. Also 46 E. Ohio, Rm. 447, Indianapolis 46204, 317-269-5555; Fed. Bldg., 1300 S. Harrison St., Rm. 340, Fort Wayne 46802, 219-422-1505; 5530 Sohl Ave., Hammond 47320, 219-937-5380; Fed. Ctr., Rm. 103, 1201 E. 10th St., Jeffersonville 47132, 812-288-3377; and Fed. Bldg., 101 N.W. 7th St., Rm. 122, Evansville 47708, 812-465-6313.

Committees: *Agriculture, Nutrition, and Forestry* (Ranking Member of 9 R). *Foreign Relations* (2nd of 9 R). Subcommittees: East Asian and Pacific Affairs; International Economic Policy, Trade, Oceans and Environment; Western Hemisphere and Peace Corps Affairs (Ranking Member).

Group Ratings

	ADA	ACLU	COPE	CFA	LCV	ACU	NTU	NSI	COC	CEI
1986	10	21	10	7	50	78	56	100	89	76
1985	5	—	11	20	—	74	63	—	90	—

National Journal Ratings

	1986 LIB — 1986 CONS		1985 LIB — 1985 CONS	
Economic	0%	— 70%	21%	— 76%
Social	32%	— 66%	25%	— 72%
Foreign	27%	— 84%	22%	— 70%

Key Votes

1) Ease Gun Cont	FOR	5) Grm-Rdmn Def Red	FOR	9) Rehnquist Nom	FOR
2) Immig Reform	FOR	6) Contra Aid	FOR	10) Tax Reform	FOR
3) Lmt Text Imp	AGN	7) SDI Funding	FOR	11) Drug Death Pen	AGN
4) Aid Tobac Ind	FOR	8) Lmt PAC Contrib	AGN	12) S Africa Sanc	FOR

Election Results

1982 general	Richard G. Lugar (R)................	978,301	(54%)	($2,987,573)
	Floyd Fithian (D)	828,400	(46%)	($870,023)
1982 primary	Richard G. Lugar (R)................	404,050	(100%)	
1976 general	Richard G. Lugar (R)................	1,275,833	(59%)	($727,720)
	Vance Hartke (D)....................	868,522	(40%)	($654,729)

Campaign Contributions and Expenditure

1980-82		Direct Cont. 1981-82		PACS Breakdown			
Receipts	$3,041,685	Indiv.	$2,120,643	Agr	$33,400	Ideo	$32,100
Expend.	$2,987,573	Party	$55,457	Bus	$603,371	Lbr	$2,000
Unspent	$53,814	PACS	$715,139	Hlth	$26,960	Prof	$10,250

Sen. J. Danforth (Dan) Quayle (R)

Elected 1980, seat up 1992; b. Feb. 4, 1947, Indianapolis; home, Huntington; DePauw U., B.A. 1969, IN U., J.D. 1974; Protestant; married (Marilyn).

Career: Chief investigator, Consumer Protection Div., IN Atty. Gen. Ofc., 1970–71; A. A. to the Gov. of IN, 1971–73; Dir., IN Inheritance Tax Div., 1973–74; Practicing atty.; Assoc. Publ., *Huntington Herald-Press*, 1974–76; U.S. House of Reps., 1976–80.

Offices: 524 HSOB 20510, 202-224-5623. Also 46 E. Ohio, Rm. 447, Indianapolis 46204, 317-269-5555; Fed. Bldg., 1300 S. Harrison St., Rm. 340, Fort Wayne 46802, 219-422-1505; 5530 Sohl Ave., Hammond 47320, 219-937-5380; Fed. Ctr., Rm. 103, 1201 E. 10th St., Jeffersonville 47132, 812-288-3377; and Fed. Bldg., 101 N.W. 7th St., Rm. 122, Evansville 47708, 812-465-6313.

Committees: *Armed Services* (5th of 8 R). Subcommittees: Conventional Forces and Alliance Defense (Ranking Member); Defense Industry and Technology, Strategic Forces and Nuclear Defense. *Budget* (8th of 11 R). *Labor and Human Services* (3d of 7 R). Subcommittees: Education, Arts, and Humanities; Labor (Ranking Member); Employment and Productivity.

Group Ratings

	ADA	ACLU	COPE	CFA	LCV	ACU	NTU	NSI	COC	CEI
1986	5	7	8	7	25	82	48	100	89	77
1985	0	—	10	20	—	87	61	—	90	—

National Journal Ratings

	1986 LIB — 1986 CONS		1985 LIB — 1985 CONS	
Economic	0%	— 84%	39%	— 60%
Social	25%	— 74%	28%	— 68%
Foreign	27%	— 70%	41%	— 58%

Key Votes

1) Ease Gun Cont	FOR	5) Grm-Rdmn Def Red	FOR	9) Rehnquist Nom	FOR
2) Immig Reform	FOR	6) Contra Aid	FOR	10) Tax Reform	FOR
3) Lmt Text Imp	AGN	7) SDI Funding	FOR	11) Drug Death Pen	—
4) Aid Tobac Ind	FOR	8) Lmt PAC Contrib	AGN	12) S Africa Sanc	FOR

Election Results

1986 general	J. Danforth (Dan) Quayle (R)	936,143	(61%)	($1,979,561)
	Jill Long (D)	595,192	(38%)	($127,187)
1986 primary	J. Danforth (Dan) Quayle (R)	357,612	(100%)	
1980 general	J. Danforth (Dan) Quayle (R)	1,182,414	(54%)	($2,289,838)
	Birch E. Bayh, Jr. (D).	1,015,922	(46%)	($2,773,254)

Campaign Contributions and Expenditures

1985-86		Direct Cont. 1985-86		PACS Breakdown 1985-86			
Receipts	$2,300,828	Indiv.	$1,356,569	Corp.	$536,961	T/M/H	$241,077
Expend.	$1,979,561	Party	$16,720	Labor	$14,500	Agr.	$4,620
Unspent	$385,126	PACS	$850,849	Ideo.	$39,355	CWOS	$14,336

FIRST DISTRICT

The most impressive and these days some of the most depressing industrial landscape in the country can be seen, between the highway and the unseen shores of Lake Michigan, on the Indiana East–West Toll Road just before you get to Chicago. Here are some of the nation's largest steel mills. For years from their chimneys and smokestacks came sulphurous fumes by day and the flare of flames at night; now many furnaces are cold and nothing comes out of the smokestacks, monuments to silence and inactivity. This is the heart of the 1st Congressional District of Indiana, the northwest corner of Hoosier America.

This is a part of the Midwest created, literally, by steel. The district's largest city, Gary, was founded in 1906 on the sand dunes by the shores of Lake Michigan by J. P. Morgan's colossal United States Steel Corporation and named for one of Morgan's partners, Chicago Judge Elbert Gary. The site chosen seemed ideal. Iron ore from the Lake Superior ranges could be carried on Great Lakes freighters to the huge man-made port at the southern tip of Lake Michigan. Coal from West Virginia and Pennsylvania could be shipped in by rail on the great east–west rail lines that pass through Gary, Hammond, and East Chicago on their way to Chicago. The local political environment was favorable: Indiana has always been a low-tax state, and for years the Lake County Assessor was pleased to let the steel company's own auditors set their assessments. Now the mills no longer are worth much. U.S. Steel has changed its name to USX and gets its revenues mostly from oil; the Texas conglomerate LTV, which bought Jones & Laughlin and Republic, has been in Chapter 11 bankruptcy. Unemployment is high, and the geese which laid the golden (or soot-covered) eggs seem well-nigh extinct.

For nearly 70 years the steel mills attracted a diverse work force to this corner of Indiana— Irish, Poles, Czechs, Ukrainians, and blacks from the American South. These groups live today in uneasy proximity, and much of the politics in the area has reflected ethnic and racial rivalries. Blacks became the majority in Gary in the middle 1960s, and in 1967 Richard Hatcher became the first black mayor of a large American city; that infuriated other Lake County politicians who were used to having the city hall patronage to themselves and white homeowners who feared the consequences of black control. Hatcher was bright and competent, but he has found no way to avoid being a divisive figure in this environment, and had difficulty improving the quality of life in a city whose economic base has been disintegrating for reasons far out of his control. He was a vice-chairman of the Democratic National Committee until 1984, but was removed after the election, not because of his strong support for and from Jesse Jackson, but because he joined in Jackson's attacks on the party rules he himself had helped to adopt. At home his base was weakened, and some blacks started voting against him in primaries, and in 1987 he was defeated for the nomination.

Racial divisions and the decline of the steel industry have inevitably shaped congressional politics here. The current congressman, Pete Visclosky, was a staff member for six years to Representative Adam Benjamin, a savvy politico and hard-working legislator who collapsed and died while working late in 1982. That left the Democratic nomination vacant and it was filled by the district party chairman, none other than Richard Hatcher. He chose Katie Hall, a black state senator who was undergoing personal misfortunes of her own. She served one term and was the name sponsor of the Martin Luther King holiday, but in this racially polarized environment predictably lost two-thirds of the votes in the primary; she had 33% to Visclosky's 34% and another white candidate's 31%.

Visclosky's secret was assiduous door-to-door campaigning, and he seems to be a workhorse in Washington as well. His seats on the Public Works and Interior Committees are helpful here. As part of the Congressional Steel Caucus, he naturally lobbies for steel import restrictions, and for bills to protect benefits for employees and retired employees of bankrupt steel companies; but he also has started what he calls the Marquette Project, to stimulate growth along the lakeshore, and as part of that got a bill through in 1986 adding 900 acres to the Indiana Dunes National Lakeshore with $9 million for its development.

The People: Pop. 1980: 547,100, dn. 5.9% 1970–80. Households (1980): 77% family, 45% with children, 60% married couples; 32.7% housing units rented; median monthly rent: $170; median house value: $40,100. Voting age pop. (1980): 375,863; 22% Black, 7% Spanish origin.

1984 Presidential Vote:

Mondale (D)	124,834	(57%)
Reagan (R)	94,470	(43%)

Rep. Peter J. Visclosky (D)

Elected 1984; b. Aug. 13, 1949, Gary; home, Merrillville; IN U., B.S. 1970, U. of Notre Dame, J.D. 1973, Georgetown U., LL.M. 1982; Roman Catholic; married (Anne).

Career: Legal Asst., Ofc. of the Manhattan Dist. Atty., 1972; Practicing atty., 1973–76, 1983–84; Aide to U.S. Rep. Adam Benjamin, Jr., 1977–82.

Offices: 420 CHOB 20515, 202-225-2461. Also 215 W. 35th St., Gary 46408, 219-884-1177.

Committees: *Education and Labor* (19th of 21 D). Subcommittees: Elementary, Secondary and Vocational Education; Human Resources. *Interior and Insular Affairs* (19th of 26 D). Subcommittee: National Parks and Public Lands. *Public Works and Transportation* (21st of 32 D). Subcommittees: Aviation; Water Resources.

Group Ratings

	ADA	ACLU	COPE	CFA	LCV	ACU	NTU	NSI	COC	CEI
1986	90	90	81	92	63	0	27	0	33	25
1985	80	—	71	75	—	5	36	—	36	—

National Journal Ratings

	1986 LIB — 1986 CONS		1985 LIB — 1985 CONS	
Economic	84% —	13%	68% —	30%
Social	74% —	23%	81% —	15%
Foreign	75% —	20%	80% —	17%

Key Votes

1) Lmt Cln Water Act	AGN	5) Retain Gun Cont	FOR	9) Aid Angola Reb	AGN
2) Rpl Tobac Sub	FOR	6) Contra Aid	AGN	10) Tax Reform	FOR
3) Grm-Rdmn Def Red	AGN	7) Lmt Text Imp	FOR	11) S Africa Sanc	FOR
4) Ban Polygraph	FOR	8) Limit SDI	FOR	12) Immig Reform	AGN

Election Results

1986 general	Peter J. Visclosky (D).................	86,983	(73%)	($163,283)
	William Costas (R)....................	30,395	(26%)	($63,460)
1986 primary	Peter J. Visclosky (D).................	49,782	(57%)	
	Katie Hall (D)........................	30,964	(35%)	
	Sandra Kay Smith (D).................	3,116	(4%)	
	William M. Herber (D)	3,116	(4%)	
1984 general	Peter J. Visclosky (D)................	147,035	(71%)	($174,919)
	Joseph B. Grenchik (R)	59,986	(29%)	($46,469)

Campaign Contributions and Expenditures

1985-86		Direct Cont. 1985-86		PACS Breakdown 1985-86			
Receipts	$198,528	Indiv.	$58,632	Corp.	$16,350	T/M/H	$20,409
Expend.	$163,283	Party	$911	Labor	$53,000	Agr.	$3,750
Unspent	$14,301	PACS	$96,959	Ideo.	$3,450	CWOS	$0

SECOND DISTRICT

Muncie, Indiana, is perhaps the best-known community in the United States—best-known in the sense that it has been studied in great detail no less than three times by sociologists. Robert and Helen Lynd came here in 1924 and 1925, expecting to find a homogeneous midwestern city of shared values and beliefs; instead they presented in *Middletown* a picture of a culturally homogeneous but economically driven factory town, with hostilities seething below the surface. Certainly they were below the surface politically in the 1920s, when Indianans were voting along the same partisan lines forged during the Civil War and the major issues were cultural rather than economic. But the differences between the parties seemed minimal: they both celebrated free market capitalism, they both embraced traditional American cultural values, they both favored limited government.

The Lynds themselves were political radicals, but their analysis was not just wishful thinking. When they returned to Muncie in 1935, they found a political revolution taking place. The business elite—local bankers, merchants, executives at the Ball family's glass company and at the General Motors plants—who saw themselves as typical Muncie citizens and ran community affairs in what they believed was the common interest, were being fiercely opposed by the working class, which was voting Democratic and joining unions. Muncie, like most of the industrial Midwest, was unionized in what amounted sometimes to a violent uprising; partisan politics took on the sharp, bitter tone of a struggle for shares of the wealth between two rival classes whose claims seemed irreconcilable; the New Deal majority, which some Democrats are always trying to revive, was forged in an atmosphere of class hatred and mistrust.

Now the picture seems to have changed once more. A team of sociologists following the Lynds' footsteps in 1976–78 found both economic life and cultural values changed. As incomes tripled over 40 years, class antagonisms cooled; it turned out there was plenty for everyone. At the same time, increasing affluence and the waning of some traditions allowed for more variety in personal life. As cultural issues come to the fore, the cultural and family values shared by the majority of Middletowners of various income levels tended to bring them together. Politically, party labels are not so firmly fixed as they were in the 1930s. The Republicans' sleek party machine tends to carry most elections here as Republicans did in the 1920s. But they have been conspicuously unsuccessful in attempts to unseat Democratic Representative Philip Sharp, who has represented Muncie and the surrounding area now in the 2d Congressional District of Indiana since 1974.

Sharp's career illustrates the movement in Middle America from a class-conscious politics to something rather different. When Sharp first ran for Congress here, in 1970, it was assumed that, if elected, he would vote a straight liberal-labor line on economic issues, like almost every non-southern Democrat in the House. But Sharp, who lost that year and in 1972, ultimately won the seat on non-economic as much as economic issues. Republican economic policies were unpopular in 1974, when he beat Republican David Dennis, but as important a factor was Dennis's opposition, on the House Judiciary Committee, to the impeachment of Richard Nixon. Once in the House, he opposed the Democratic orthodoxy of oil and gas price controls and, as chairman of a special task force appointed by Speaker O'Neill, helped fashion a compromise energy program which phased out the price controls over several years. By 1981 he was well-placed on the Interior Committee and was one of the high-ranking members on the sought-after Energy and Commerce Committee and chairman of the subcommittee on Fossil and Synthetic Fuels.

This is not quite as hot a seat as it once was, now that the price controls issue has been mostly settled, but plenty of detail work and ancillary issues remain, on which Sharp is constantly making policy. He has been a strong backer of the strategic petroleum reserve, which has helped to protect the U.S. against abrupt oil price rises. He helped broker an attempt to get environmentalists, oil companies, and the Interior Department to agree on oil leasing policy in the Bering Sea. He got the amount of insurance for nuclear accidents in the Price–Anderson Act increased to $6.5 billion. He has helped block sale of the naval petroleum reserves. He opposed the oil import fee and suggested a broader energy tax instead. After supporting the Synfuels Corporation for years, he came out for abolishing it in 1985. Sharp remains one of the most important subcommittee chairmen in the House, and one who can carry his bills in full committee and on the floor. He is trusted by other members (even some from energy-producing states) as candid, thoughtful, and fair-minded.

At home, Sharp has been a target of the Republicans for years, but since 1974 has always gotten at least 53% of the vote. In the 1980s redistricting was supposed to hurt him, but his appeal went across old party lines and, spread by television, across county and old district boundaries. With better than 2 to 1 margins in Muncie's Delaware County and more than 60% in Wayne County, which centers on the heavily Republican old Quaker center of Richmond, he won with 56% and 53% in 1982 and 1984. In 1986 he had his easiest race ever, facing an inexperienced evangelical who won an upset victory in the Republican primary, campaigned against AIDS and abortion, and said he had an "invisible army" supporting him. It remained invisible on election day when Sharp won 62%–37%.

That does not mean he is forever safe from challenge. But it does give this young (and younger-looking) congressman more time to enjoy his work as an accomplished legislator and his minor celebrity as the spouse of Marilyn Sharp, whose mystery novels set in Washington (*Sunflower, Masterstroke, Falseface*) have been critical and commercial successes.

The People: Pop. 1980: 553,510, up 7.8% 1970–80. Households (1980): 77% family, 43% with children, 66% married couples; 28.0% housing units rented; median monthly rent: $165; median house value: $38,200. Voting age pop. (1980): 390,981; 2% Black, 1% Spanish origin.

1984 Presidential Vote: Reagan (R) 151,940   (68%)
                                 Mondale (D) 71,784   (32%)

Rep. Philip R. Sharp (D)

Elected 1974; b. July 15, 1942, Baltimore, MD; home, Muncie; Georgetown U., B.S. 1964, Oxford U., 1966, Georgetown U., Ph.D. 1974; United Methodist; married (Marilyn).

Career: Legis. Aide to U.S. Sen. Vance Hartke, 1964–69; Asst. and Assoc. Prof., Ball St. U., 1969–74.

Offices: 2452 RHOB 20515, 202-225-3021. Also 2900 W. Jackson, Ste. 101, Muncie 47304, 317-747-5566.

Committees: *Energy and Commerce* (4th of 25 D). Subcommittees: Commerce, Consumer Protection and Competitiveness; Energy and Power (Chairman). *Interior and Insular Affairs* (3d of 26 D). Subcommittees: Energy and the Environment; Water and Power Resources.

Group Ratings

	ADA	ACLU	COPE	CFA	LCV	ACU	NTU	NSI	COC	CEI
1986	65	80	72	67	84	10	33	20	41	32
1985	65	—	71	83	—	38	51	—	50	—

National Journal Ratings

	1986 LIB — 1986 CONS	1985 LIB — 1985 CONS
Economic	58% — 41%	51% — 48%
Social	69% — 28%	68% — 32%
Foreign	74% — 25%	63% — 37%

Key Votes

1) Lmt Cln Water Act	FOR	5) Retain Gun Cont	AGN	9) Aid Angola Reb	AGN
2) Rpl Tobac Sub	FOR	6) Contra Aid	AGN	10) Tax Reform	FOR
3) Grm-Rdmn Def Red	FOR	7) Lmt Text Imp	FOR	11) S Africa Sanc	FOR
4) Ban Polygraph	FOR	8) Limit SDI	FOR	12) Immig Reform	FOR

Election Results

1986 general	Philip R. Sharp (D).................	102,456	(62%)	($384,009)
	Don Lynch (R)	62,013	(37%)	($117,598)
1986 primary	Philip R. Sharp (D)..................	32,135	(94%)	
	Bruce D. Watts (D).................	1,954	(6%)	
1984 general	Philip R. Sharp (D)................	118,965	(53%)	($409,117)
	Ken MacKenzie (R)................	103,061	(46%)	($399,755)

Campaign Contributions and Expenditures

1985-86		Direct Cont. 1985-86		PACS Breakdown 1985-86			
Receipts	$403,720	Indiv.	$123,392	Corp.	$89,575	T/M/H	$72,350
Expend.	$384,009	Party	$5,960	Labor	$67,957	Agr.	$1,750
Unspent	$67,639	PACS	$260,557	Ideo.	$24,725	CWOS	$4,200

THIRD DISTRICT

South Bend is one of those industrial cities set incongruously into the flat landscape of the limestone-bottomed plains of the Midwest. Surrounded by farm counties whose origins—and Republican allegiance—go back to the days when they served as northern terminals on the Underground Railroad, South Bend has a different origin. It is mostly the creation of the early 20th century, when its factories attracted an ethnic population, which has always voted

Democratic. Sixty years ago South Bend was a boom town, like Silicon Valley in the late 1970s, but since World War II the place has frequently been in trouble. South Bend saw the collapse of a portion of the auto industry long before Detroit or Flint: in the 1960s Studebaker went out of business, and South Bend lost its largest employer. More recently its economy has suffered from other, less dramatic shutdowns and layoffs, to the point that its most vibrant economic institution is probably the University of Notre Dame. Interestingly, rural northern Indiana, which South Bend once threatened to overshadow, has done pretty well in recent decades. Its agricultural economy has generally been strong, and its small towns have attracted factories and mills even as those in cities like South Bend have been closing.

The 3d Congressional District of Indiana has centered for years on South Bend; but it has mattered a great deal what other territory is included, particularly as South Bend, stagnant in population, has comprised a smaller and smaller percentage of the total district. Democrats have joined South Bend with the similar industrial city of Michigan City, to the west; Republicans have joined it with Elkhart, a higher income and heavily Republican city to the east, and with the rural counties directly south (one of which, however, Starke, often votes Democratic). The current redistricting plan was designed by Republicans and follows predictable outlines.

It has been enough, though not by much, to reelect Republican Representative John Hiler in 1982, 1984 and 1986. Hiler had achieved one of the nation's notable upsets in 1980 when he beat John Brademas, for 22 years South Bend's congressman and then House Democratic Whip. Brademas's increasing prominence on national issues, and the unpopularity of the Carter Administration with which he was increasingly associated, worked to beat him. Elected at 27, Hiler was an especially pure Reagan Republican in the early 1980s. He made a point of not seeking federal money for the district—though by 1986 he was bragging about landing an Army contract to build the Hummer vehicle for a South Bend company. He prided himself in the early 1980s on his lockstep support of Reagan Administration programs, though by 1986 dissented occasionally, on Superfund and South Africa sanctions.

In 1986 Hiler faced his least-known opponent and had his toughest race. Thomas Ward was from a rural county, but did well in South Bend. The election night returns showed a Ward victory; Republican election officials in rural Kosciusko County then found some extra Hiler votes; the new Indiana secretary of state, Democrat Evan Bayh, took office in December and declined to certify Hiler as the winner. Hiler stood by and did not take the oath in January 1987, and many House Democrats and Republicans feared a reprise over the bitter and lengthy Indiana 8th fight of 1985. But on January 23 the state recount board certified Hiler the winner by 47 votes, and with the Democratic secretary of state not objecting the House Democrats went along. Ward said he will run again in 1988; Hiler said he would too, unless he decides instead to run for lieutenant governor. This would mean running for nomination at the state party convention and having his fate in the general election tied to that of the candidate for governor. Risky, but so is a district where you won by 47 votes.

The People: Pop. 1980: 558,100, up 5.5% 1970–80. Households (1980): 76% family, 41% with children, 65% married couples; 24.9% housing units rented; median monthly rent: $168; median house value: $35,600. Voting age pop. (1980): 395,121; 4% Black, 1% Spanish origin.

1984 Presidential Vote: Reagan (R) 136,450   (62%)
Mondale (D) 83,076   (38%)

Rep. John P. Hiler (R)

Elected 1980; b. Apr. 24, 1953, Chicago, IL; home, La Porte; Williams Col., B.A. 1975, U. of Chicago, M.B.A. 1977; Roman Catholic; married (Katherine).

Career: Marketing Dir., Charles O. Hiler and Sons, Accurate Castings, Inc., 1977–81; Delegate, White House Conf. on Small Business, 1980.

Offices: 407 CHOB 20515, 202-225-3915. Also 120 River Glenn Ofc. Plaza, 501 E. Monroe, South Bend 46601, 219-236-8282.

Committees: *Banking, Finance, and Urban Affairs* (11th of 20 R). Subcommittees: Consumer Affairs and Coinage (Ranking Member); Financial Institution Supervision, Regulation and Insurance; Housing and Community Development. *Small Business* (5th of 17 R). Subcommittee: Antitrust, Impact of Deregulation and Privatization (Ranking Member).

Group Ratings

	ADA	ACLU	COPE	CFA	LCV	ACU	NTU	NSI	COC	CEI
1986	0	0	5	16	32	86	59	100	94	86
1985	5	—	6	25	—	90	67	—	85	—

National Journal Ratings

	1986 LIB — 1986 CONS	1985 LIB — 1985 CONS
Economic	0% — 94%	0% — 95%
Social	0% — 89%	0% — 76%
Foreign	16% — 79%	24% — 66%

Key Votes

1) Lmt Cln Water Act	FOR	5) Retain Gun Cont	AGN	9) Aid Angola Reb	FOR
2) Rpl Tobac Sub	FOR	6) Contra Aid	FOR	10) Tax Reform	FOR
3) Grm-Rdmn Def Red	FOR	7) Lmt Text Imp	AGN	11) S Africa Sanc	FOR
4) Ban Polygraph	AGN	8) Limit SDI	AGN	12) Immig Reform	AGN

Election Results

1986 general	John P. Hiler (R)	75,979	(50%)	($336,768)
	Thomas W. Ward (D)	75,932	(50%)	($189,509)
1986 primary	John P. Hiler (R)	31,599	(100%)	
1984 general	John P. Hiler (R)	115,139	(52%)	($460,238)
	Michael P. Barnes (D)	103,961	(47%)	($260,517)

Campaign Contributions and Expenditures

1985-86		Direct Cont. 1985-86		PACS Breakdown 1983-84			
Receipts	$400,335	Indiv.	$235,837	Corp.	$64,650	T/M/H	$60,750
Expend.	$336,768	Party	$9,611	Labor	$0	Agr.	$3,000
Unspent	$115,830	PACS	$135,199	Ideo.	$5,500	CWOS	$1,299

FOURTH DISTRICT

The 4th Congressional District of Indiana centers on Fort Wayne, technically the state's second largest city, but actually just the largest of several small industrial towns; the metropolitan areas that rival Indianapolis are Indiana's portions of greater Chicago and Louisville. Fort Wayne cannot be mistaken for either big city, but is instead a typical medium-sized midwestern community, with a small black ghetto and nondescript frame houses that belong to people who work—or used to—in the factories and small businesses. Like many other such cities, Fort

Wayne faced rough times in the early 1980s: double-digit unemployment and plant closings like that at International Harvester which wiped out 4,500 jobs in one fell swoop. But as the decade went on, it kept a big General Electric plant that was threatening to move, attracted a new General Motors plant, and got unemployment down to 6%.

Yet then and in the less dramatic economic revival, voters here remained solidly Republican in national and congressional elections. Ancestrally, this part of northern Indiana is heavily Republican: people here speak with hard R accents, and their ancestors supported and fought for the Union in the Civil War. In the years following the New Deal and the unionization of many plants here, Fort Wayne and the surrounding area would turn to the Democrats in recession years like 1958 and 1970, and up to 1976 the 4th District was represented by a Democrat. But the Democrats' nomination of a southerner for President in 1976 seemed to stimulate a residual regional Republicanism here, and the increasing importance of cultural patterns in voting has helped the Republicans in this corner of America where traditional family patterns still prevail.

The current congressman, Dan Coats, served as an aide to Dan Quayle, the young newspaper scion who captured the district from the Democrats in 1976 and was elected to the Senate in 1980. Coats won the House seat that year easily, and had even less trouble winning reelection.

In the House Coats sits on the Energy and Commerce Committee, one of the most sought-after assignments because its jurisdiction includes most of the federal regulatory agencies and air pollution regulations. Coats is occasionally liberal on economic issues, but generally votes with the Republicans. Like other members from energy consuming states, Coats did not support energy industry efforts to have all sources of natural gas decontrolled (though he didn't side fully with consumer groups either). In 1985 he was distancing himself from Administration proposals to eliminate subsidies for Amtrak. But he usually takes the view that businesses have been overregulated, that the economy as a result has been hurt, and that consumers and the public would be better off with less onerous restriction of economic activity.

He is more distinctive as an advocate of cultural conservatism, an enthusiastic backer of school prayer and the ranking Republican on the Select Committee on Children, Youth, and Families. There he has worked with Chairman George Miller on reports about poverty among children, but he and other committee Republicans split sharply from Miller and the Democrats over the issue of teenage pregnancy; Coats believes that sex counseling in schools that includes dispensing of contraceptives encourages premarital sex, and believes the emphasis should be put on encouraging abstinence until marriage.

The People: Pop. 1980: 553,698, up 7.2% 1970–80. Households (1980): 76% family, 43% with children, 66% married couples; 24.4% housing units rented; median monthly rent: $168; median house value: $38,100. Voting age pop. (1980): 382,150; 4% Black, 1% Spanish origin.

1984 Presidential Vote:

Reagan (R)	144,009	(67%)
Mondale (D)	70,300	(33%)

Rep. Daniel R. Coats (R)

Elected 1980; b. May 16, 1943, Jackson, MI; home, Fort Wayne; Wheaton Col., B.A. 1965, IN U., J.D. 1971; Baptist; married (Marcia).

Career: Army, 1966–68; Econ. consulting firm, 1968–70; Legal Intern, American Fletcher Natl. Bank, 1970–72; Asst. Vice Pres. & Legal Counsel, Mutual Security Life Insur. Co., 1972–76; Dist. Rep. for U.S. Rep. J. Danforth (Dan) Quayle, 1976–80.

Offices: 1417 LHOB 20515, 202-225-4436. Also 326 Fed. Bldg., Fort Wayne 46802, 219-424-3041.

Committees: *Energy and Commerce* (9th of 17 R). Subcommittees: Health and the Environment; Oversight and Investigations; Telecommunications and Finance. *Select Committee on Children, Youth, and Families* (Ranking Member of 10 R).

Group Ratings

	ADA	ACLU	COPE	CFA	LCV	ACU	NTU	NSI	COC	CEI
1986	10	5	13	25	32	82	58	90	80	77
1985	20	—	12	33	—	86	65	—	85	—

National Journal Ratings

	1986 LIB — 1986 CONS	1985 LIB — 1985 CONS
Economic	6% — 90%	12% — 85%
Social	0% — 89%	0% — 76%
Foreign	25% — 74%	35% — 63%

Key Votes

1) Lmt Cln Water Act	FOR	5) Retain Gun Cont	AGN	9) Aid Angola Reb	FOR
2) Rpl Tobac Sub	FOR	6) Contra Aid	FOR	10) Tax Reform	FOR
3) Grm-Rdmn Def Red	FOR	7) Lmt Text Imp	AGN	11) S Africa Sanc	FOR
4) Ban Polygraph	AGN	8) Limit SDI	AGN	12) Immig Reform	AGN

Election Results

1986 general	Daniel R. Coats (R)	99,865	(70%)	($225,157)
	Greg Scher (D)	43,105	(30%)	($20,082)
1986 primary	Daniel R. Coats (R)	35,554	(100%)	
1984 general	Daniel R. Coats (R)	129,674	(61%)	($201,659)
	Michael H. Barnard (D)	82,053	(39%)	($35,267)

Campaign Contributions and Expenditures

1985-86		Direct Cont. 1985-86		PACS Breakdown 1985-86			
Receipts	$139,888	Indiv.	$139,888	Corp.	$72,920	T/M/H	$59,376
Expend.	$225,157	Party	$2,849	Labor	$1,275	Agr.	$0
Unspent	$147,443	PACS	$142,526	Ideo.	$7,785	CWOS	$1,170
		Cand.	$25,835				

FIFTH DISTRICT

People in the flatlands of northern Indiana think of themselves as living in the heartland of America, and for many good reasons. They live on the divide between the Great Lakes and Mississippi River systems, on the major east–west railroads and highways that connect the nation's largest cities and industrial areas. They also live in small cities and large towns whose geometric regularity and neatness bespeak the virtues we think of as peculiarly American; and if those same cities and towns contain a few criminals, or if they suffer now from layoffs and unemployment, people there remain confident that most Americans are competent, decent, sensible people who will do the right thing in time of crisis. This is a part of America with little immigrant heritage, with relatively few blacks, with only a handful of the Latin and Asian immigrants who are so prominent in other parts of the country.

This is the land of the 5th Congressional District of Indiana, which extends most of the way across northern Indiana from the suburbs of Gary to the factory town of Marion and the much smaller town of North Manchester, home of Thomas R. Marshall, Woodrow Wilson's vice president. There are notes of discord here and there: echoes in the northwest corner of the racial animosities that dominate Gary politics, very high unemployment rates in Kokomo, where the Chrysler plant nearly closed down. But basic values have not been shaken so much here as in many other parts of the nation: fully 79% of the households here contain families and 69% married couples—among the highest figures in the Midwest—and 45% have children, a high percentage given the rather old age structure.

In 1986 the 5th District was the scene of an open House race that pitted candidates who typified the most aggressive politicians of both parties and, in this historically Republican district, the Democrat won. The occasion was the retirement after 16 years of Republican Elwood Hillis, and the first headlines came when evangelical Christian Jim Butcher, after being endorsed by Pat Robertson, won an upset victory in the Republican primary over the party-endorsed state treasurer. Butcher was not an entirely unconventional candidate. He was a member of the state Senate, based in Kokomo, an industrial city that is about the most Democratic part of the district; he boasted about his sponsorship of a Chrysler Recovery Act that channeled state aid to the ailing automaker. Dedicated evangelicals provided the enthusiasm behind Butcher's primary win, but in the general he said, "I'm a politician who happens to be a Christian."

But it turned out he was not as active or aggressive a politician as Democrat Jim Jontz. A year out of school, at age 22, Jontz was elected to the Indiana House by beating its majority leader by two votes; this was in a Democratic year but in a very Republican part of rural northwestern Indiana. Single, interested almost exclusively in politics, he has been politically successful ever since. He has a flair for trademarks, riding his bicycle in parades and handing out potholders to voters. He has a flair as well for issues. In a district where General Motors moved Delco operations from Kokomo to Matamoros, Mexico, Jontz ran ads denouncing the "theft" of U.S. jobs through unfair foreign trade; he attacked Butcher, who said he would not vote to repeal the generous 1985 farm bill, as being satisfied with current agricultural policies; he accused Butcher of absenteeism and of changing positions on issues.

Republican strategists thought Butcher started with a big lead, but no one had strong support, and Jontz plain outcampaigned Butcher. Nor was this a return of blue-collar voters to some ancestral Democratic allegiance. Jontz got 52% in the counties containing Kokomo and Marion, but he also got 51% in the counties just south of Gary and 51% in the large rural area in between that casts most of the district's votes. Jontz actually spent more money than Butcher, though the difference was marginal; but this was one of many districts where the Democrat equalized the money factor or better thanks to heavy PAC contributions, orchestrated in part by Tony Coelho. Thus Jontz got $305,000 in PAC money to Butcher's $161,000, in a district not represented by a Democrat for decades. Jontz will probably have a serious challenge in 1988, but he has shown he has the know-how and energy to win. Republican strategists puzzled at why, during the Reagan years, the Democrats have continued to hold a majority in the House should come here, to the heartland of America, and look at the 5th District of Indiana and see the reason why: political talent.

The People: Pop. 1980: 548,257, up 13.2% 1970–80. Households (1980): 79% family, 45% with children, 69% married couples; 24.4% housing units rented; median monthly rent: $166; median house value: $40,300. Voting age pop. (1980): 380,248; 2% Black, 1% Spanish origin.

1984 Presidential Vote: Reagan (R) 150,354 (69%)

Mondale (D) 67,224 (31%)

Rep. James Jontz (D)

Elected 1986; b. Dec. 18, 1951, Indianapolis; home, Brookston; IN U., B.A. 1973; United Methodist; single.

Career: IN House of Reps., 1974–84; IN Senate, 1984–86.

Offices: 1005 LHOB 20515, 202-225-5037. Also 104 Walnut, Kokomo 46901, 317-459-4375; 302 Lincolnway, Valparaiso 46383, 219-462-6499.

Committees: *Agriculture* (22d of 26 D). Subcommittees: Conservation, Credit and Rural Development; Forests, Family Farms and Energy; Wheat, Soybeans and Feed Grains. *Education and Labor* (21st of 21 D). Subcommittees: Employment Opportunities; Labor-Management Relations. *Veterans' Affairs* (21st of 21 D). Subcommittee: Education, Training and Employment.

Group Ratings and Key Votes: Newly Elected

Election Results

1986 general	James Jontz (D)	80,772	(52%)	($462,970)
	James R. Butcher (R).................	75,507	(48%)	($424,538)
1986 primary	James Jontz (D)	22,009	(100%)	
1984 general	Elwood H. (Bud) Hillis (R)	143,560	(68%)	($123,630)
	Allen B. Maxwell (D).................	66,631	(32%)	($26,170)

Campaign Contributions and Expenditures

1985-86		Direct Cont. 1985-86		PACS Breakdown 1985-86			
Receipts	$463,733	Indiv.	$141,401	Corp.	$5,525	T/M/H	$34,872
Expend.	$462,970	Party	$9,999	Labor	$207,571	Agr.	$2,250
Unspent	$762	PACS	$305,635	Ideo.	$55,417	CWOS	$0
		Cand.	$7,333				

SIXTH DISTRICT

There are no more solid Republican suburbs in the United States than those that encircle Indianapolis. At the end of World War II, this was a compact city; most residents lived within four or five miles of the Soldiers' and Sailors' Monument downtown. The few rich neighborhoods were on the streets directly north of the city's core, beyond the home of Benjamin Harrison, Indiana's one president. But most of Indianapolis consisted of modest neighborhoods of frame houses with clapboard shutters where most people voted Republican in most elections. In the years since, real incomes have risen here as elsewhere, and people have moved farther and farther outward. The old central neighborhoods have populations more Democratic and sometimes more black. And the once vacant flat fields and low hills 10 to 20 miles from downtown have become filled with people seemingly self-selected as strong Republicans. Affluent young families and older couples have moved out past the extended Indianapolis city limits, which are coextensive with Marion County, and into the seven once rural and now increasingly suburban counties that surround it.

There is nothing in Indianapolis resembling radical chic. People who have made money pride themselves on being brighter than other people. To them it seems natural that those who have not done so well—people with low incomes, union members, and the like—will be Democrats and that intelligent people will usually be Republicans. After all, almost all the articulate sources of opinion in Indianapolis—the newspapers, the mayor and the governor, leading businessmen and civic leaders—are Republicans, and they are boosters of free enterprise and traditional values, of the flag and motherhood and the other institutions that bind the less successful to the more successful here. The 6th Congressional District of Indiana covers most of the Indianapolis suburbs, including some 120,000 people on the affluent north side of Indianapolis, going out into rural counties that gave Ronald Reagan as much as 82% of the vote in 1984, and taking in, incongruously, the industrial city of Anderson.

The congressman from the 6th District is Dan Burton, an active and enthusiastic Republican who has been running for office since he was in his 20s. With 28% of the vote he won the decisive Republican primary, beating among others the state Republican chairman who was endorsed by Indianapolis Mayor (and former congressman) William Hudnut and former Governor Otis Bowen. But Burton, a hearty, backslapping type of politician and an enthusiastic conservative on virtually all issues, had been running for office every two years, with one exception, since 1966. He was elected to the Indiana House in 1966, 1976, and 1978, and to the Indiana Senate in 1968 and 1980; he lost elections for the U.S. House in 1970 (to Democrat Andrew Jacobs) and 1972 (in the primary to Hudnut).

Burton is probably best known in the House as the Republicans' best golfer, who has taken on and beaten the Democrats' best, Marty Russo. But he has also used his seat on the Foreign Affairs Committee to become a notable spokesman on foreign policy. He is an enthusiastic supporter of aid to the Nicaraguan contras and to the El Salvador government of José Napoleon Duarte. On African policy he has attacked not only the Democrats, but also the Reagan Administration; he was saddened when the President met with the late Mozambique leader Samora Machel and has urged that the United States support those he considers freedom fighters in that country. He opposes sanctions against South Africa and made the strained argument that sanctions would hurt Indiana's economy. But on most foreign issues Burton has made the more solid and attractive argument that Americans should be backing freedom and, although Republicans don't like to use this Carteresque phrase, human rights; and he has a point that is more serious than it is usually taken when he points out that Democrats propitiating the Sandinistas and Reaganites negotiating with Machel are compromising with evil regimes. His aggressiveness reportedly carries over to his behavior in his office, and he has one of the higher staff turnover rates on the Hill.

Burton seems firmly entrenched in one of the nation's safest Republican districts.

The People: Pop. 1980: 540,939, up 16.1% 1970–80. Households (1980): 77% family, 42% with children, 67% married couples; 27.6% housing units rented; median monthly rent: $200; median house value: $45,600. Voting age pop. (1980): 381,833; 3% Black, 1% Spanish origin.

1984 Presidential Vote: Reagan (R) 179,556   (72%)
Mondale (D) 69,858   (28%)

Rep. Dan Burton (R)

Elected 1982; b. June 21, 1938, Indianapolis; home, Indianapolis; IN U., 1956–57, Cincinnati Bible Seminary, 1958–60; Protestant; married (Barbara).

Career: Army, 1956–57; Founder, Dan Burton Insur. Agency; IN House of Reps., 1967–68, 1977–80; IN Senate, 1969–70, 1981–82.

Offices: 120 CHOB 20515, 202-225-2276. Also 8900 Keystone at the Crossing, Ste. 1050, Indianapolis 46240, 317-848-0201; and 922 Meridian Plaza, Anderson 46016, 317-649-6887.

Committees: *Foreign Affairs* (14th of 18 R). Subcommittees: Africa (Ranking Member); Arms Control, International Security and Science. *Post Office and Civil Service* (7th of 8 R). Subcommittees: Census and Population; Human Resources (Ranking Member). *Veterans' Affairs* (7th of 13 R). Subcommittees: Housing and Memorial Affairs (Ranking Member); Oversight and Investigations.

Group Ratings

	ADA	ACLU	COPE	CFA	LCV	ACU	NTU	NSI	COC	CEI
1986	5	5	14	8	22	100	63	100	89	86
1985	5	—	11	25	—	100	66	—	30	—

National Journal Ratings

	1986 LIB —	1986 CONS	1985 LIB —	1985 CONS
Economic	21% —	77%	0% —	95%
Social	0% —	89%	0% —	76%
Foreign	0% —	86%	0% —	76%

Key Votes

1) Lmt Cln Water Act	AGN	5) Retain Gun Cont	AGN	9) Aid Angola Reb	FOR
2) Rpl Tobac Sub	—	6) Contra Aid	FOR	10) Tax Reform	AGN
3) Grm-Rdmn Def Red	FOR	7) Lmt Text Imp	AGN	11) S Africa Sanc	AGN
4) Ban Polygraph	AGN	8) Limit SDI	AGN	12) Immig Reform	AGN

Election Results

1986 general	Dan Burton (R).....................	118,363	(68%)	($216,290)
	Tom McKenna (D)	53,431	(31%)	($48,045)
1986 primary	Dan Burton (R).......................	47,672	(93%)	
	George Thomas Holland (R)	3,482	(7%)	
1984 general	Dan Burton (R).....................	178,814	(73%)	($236,210)
	Howard O. Campbell (D)..............	65,772	(27%)	($14,921)

Campaign Contributions and Expenditures

1985-86		Direct Cont. 1985-86		PACS Breakdown 1985-86			
Receipts	$325,163	Indiv.	$160,953	Corp.	$36,904	T/M/H	$61,145
Expend.	$216,290	Party	$3,265	Labor	$10,250	Agr.	$10,250
Unspent	$148,379	PACS	$142,323	Ideo.	$22,090	CWOS	$1,724

SEVENTH DISTRICT

Perhaps the most famous, or at least the most picturesquely named, of the fabled and now vanished passenger trains was the old Wabash Cannonball, the Detroit-to-St. Louis train that followed the Wabash River across the rolling farmland of northern Indiana. The railroad heads west and the river heads south, crossing the old National Road, now U.S. 40, which runs in a nearly straight line from Indianapolis to St. Louis, in Terre Haute, which with fewer than 100,000 people is still the largest city in Indiana's 7th Congressional District. Despite its elegant French name, Terre Haute is a rough and crude place, once known for its gambling and vice, and still known for having the look of a rundown factory town. Politically Terre Haute has long had a strong Democratic machine (although it was the home town of the great Socialist leader Eugene Debs), which more often than not has controlled the Vigo County Courthouse; it was strong enough recently to carry the county against incumbent Governor Robert Orr in 1984.

The Wabash Cannonball traversed, in its day, both Republican and Democratic territory. The dividing line, roughly, was Terre Haute and the National Road. To the north people speak with the hard-edged accent of the Midwest; to the south they drawl in a manner reminiscent of Dixie. The counties to the north are traditionally Republican, those to the south traditionally Democratic. You can see the demarcation in maps of voting behavior in the 1860s, and more than a century later, it surfaced again when Jimmy Carter, of Plains, Georgia, ran against Gerald Ford, of Grand Rapids, Michigan, in 1976. Carter carried the southern part of the district in 1976 and even in 1980.

The 7th District was created in something like its present form by a Democratic legislature in 1966 with the intention of electing a Democratic congressman. Instead it has elected Republican John Myers ever since. He has benefited from weak opposition and from the 1982 redistricting, which added two suburban Indianapolis counties, and substituted for Bloomington and liberal arts Indiana University engineering-oriented Purdue and the city of Lafayette which is eagerly welcoming an Isuzu assembly plant scheduled to open in 1989. Myers has not been seriously opposed and has won easily.

That makes Myers one of the more senior House Republicans. Like so many of the midwestern Republicans who served in the House for years, Myers is quiet and uncontroversial. Younger Republicans seek to expose Democratic wrongdoing and to throw the House into turmoil; Myers does his duty by opposing what the Democrats propose on issues generally and by working constructively and in a bipartisan manner on his major committee duties. He is third-ranking Republican on the Appropriations Committee, and ranking Republican on the Energy and Water Development Subcommittee, which parcels out money for rivers and harbor projects; he and Chairman Tom Bevill typically report out a bipartisan bill with projects for many districts. That once would have made Myers one of the more powerful members of the House, but in a Congress that cares less than it once did for pork barrel projects and is skeptical of their worth, it is considerably less important. That has been a winning formula anyway in the 7th District, and in 1984 and 1986 Myers was reelected by margins of 2 to 1, the largest in his House career.

The People: Pop. 1980: 555,192, up 9.2% 1970–80. Households (1980): 75% family, 40% with children, 66% married couples; 26.2% housing units rented; median monthly rent: $159; median house value: $36,400. Voting age pop. (1980): 403,139; 2% Black, 1% Spanish origin, 1% Asian origin.

1984 Presidential Vote: Reagan (R) 147,763   (66%)
Mondale (D) 73,751   (33%)

Rep. John T. Myers (R)

Elected 1966; b. Feb. 8, 1927, Covington; home, Covington; IN St. U., B.S. 1951; Episcopalian; married (Carol).

Career: Army, WWII; Cashier and Trust Officer, Foundation Trust Co., 1954–66.

Offices: 2372 RHOB 20515, 202-225-5805. Also 107 Fed. Bldg., Terre Haute 47808, 812-238-1619; and 107 Halleck Fed. Bldg., Lafayette 47901, 317-423-1661.

Committees: *Appropriations* (3d of 22 R). Subcommittees: Energy and Water Development (Ranking Member); Legislative; Rural Development, Agriculture and Related Agencies. *Post Office and Civil Service* (5th of 8 R). Subcommittees: Compensation and Employee Benefits (Ranking Member); Postal Personnel and Modernization. *Standards of Official Conduct* (2d of 6 R).

Group Ratings

	ADA	ACLU	COPE	CFA	LCV	ACU	NTU	NSI	COC	CEI
1986	20	20	16	0	10	91	30	90	50	43
1985	20	—	15	8	—	71	38	—	90	—

National Journal Ratings

	1986 LIB — 1986 CONS	1985 LIB — 1985 CONS
Economic	39% — 60%	31% — 67%
Social	35% — 64%	40% — 59%
Foreign	21% — 77%	0% — 76%

Key Votes

1) Lmt Cln Water Act	FOR	5) Retain Gun Cont	AGN	9) Aid Angola Reb	FOR
2) Rpl Tobac Sub	AGN	6) Contra Aid	FOR	10) Tax Reform	AGN
3) Grm-Rdmn Def Red	AGN	7) Lmt Text Imp	AGN	11) S Africa Sanc	AGN
4) Ban Polygraph	AGN	8) Limit SDI	AGN	12) Immig Reform	AGN

Election Results

1986 general	John T. Myers (R)...................	104,965	(67%)	($163,877)
	L. Eugene Smith (D)	49,675	(32%)	($27,139)
1986 primary	John T. Myers (R)...................	42,809	(88%)	
	Joseph J. Crugnal, Jr. (R)...............	5,669	(12%)	
1984 general	John T. Myers (R)...................	147,787	(67%)	($165,646)
	Arthur E. Smith (D).................	69,097	(31%)	($94,222)

Campaign Contributions and Expenditures

1985-86		Direct Cont. 1985-86		PACS Breakdown 1985-86			
Receipts	$181,484	Indiv.	$70,252	Corp.	$35,043	T/M/H	$31,626
Expend.	$163,877	Party	$1,033	Labor	$7,100	Agr.	$3,250
Unspent	$125,521	PACS	$86,613	Ideo.	$9,000	CWOS	$594
		Cand.	$2,600				

EIGHTH DISTRICT

The 8th Congressional District of Indiana covers the southwest portion of the state. Its boundaries are as irregular as pieces of a jigsaw puzzle, the result of a partisan redistricting by the Republican legislature. The district extends eastward to take in a hunk of Republican Washington County and has a piece taken out of it in the west to remove Democratic Dubois.

Only the more Republican parts of the university town of Bloomington are included. The largest city in the district remains Evansville; it would have been hard to remove the Democratic precincts of this usually closely divided industrial city, because it sits right on the Ohio River across from Kentucky. Oddly, this corner of Indiana was the first part of the state settled by white men. Vincennes, now a small town on the banks of the Wabash River, was once the metropolis of Indiana, and Robert Owen, the Scottish philanthropist and visionary, established the town of New Harmony downstream. Owen's son was the first congressman from the area, elected in 1842 and 1844.

Much of southwestern Indiana was settled by German Catholics, who have traditionally voted Democratic. During the Civil War most of this area was copperhead country, friendly to the South and hostile to Mr. Lincoln's war. Today, although the issues have changed, the 8th remains one part of Indiana within the Democrats' reach. It went for Jimmy Carter in 1976, and for Birch Bayh as late as 1980; even with its current borders, it came close to voting against Senator Richard Lugar in 1982 and Governor Robert Orr in 1984.

The clash of local Democratic heritage with state and national Republican trends has made the 8th one of the nation's premier marginal congressional districts. It elected four different congressmen in four election years in the 1970s—the only district in the nation to do so. It ousted incumbents of varying parties in 1958, 1966, 1974, 1978, and 1982. In 1984, this was the closest and most bitterly disputed congressional race in the nation. Incumbent Democrat Frank McCloskey, Mayor of Bloomington for 11 years, had won in 1982 after the incumbent was charged in October with drunk driving. He made a moderate record in his two years on the floor and in the Armed Services Committee, but was one of the clearest targets for Republicans. Their nominee, Richard McIntyre, had already served two terms in the state legislature at age 27 and seemed to be one of those natural politicians whom Republicans usually have a hard time locating.

In the first count, a week after the election, McCloskey led by 72 votes out of 233,000 cast. But after ballots were rechecked in one Democratic county, two precincts turned out to have been counted twice; that left a 34-vote McIntyre lead which Republican state officials quickly certified without checking anywhere else. Democrats charged foul, especially when a recanvass in another county put McCloskey ahead by 72 votes, and the House declined to seat either man. Republicans cried foul, arguing that state officials' certified results should determine which man gets seated initially, though they conceded that the House is the judge of its members' credentials. In April 1985, a special task force made its own count and, 2 to 1, concluded that McCloskey had won the election by four votes, and on May 1st the House voted to seat him. Republicans vowed revenge. Ironically, later that summer eight Democrats in Crawford County, partially in the district, were indicted for vote-buying; but no one knew that when the House debated.

But this time McCloskey clearly won. In his plodding, earnest way McCloskey kept working the district hard, jumping to stop the contracting out of jobs at Crane Army Ammunition Activity Plant. Republicans sent Gerald Ford, George Bush, and Ronald Reagan in for McIntyre—the only House candidate Reagan stumped for. But the key event in this "McRace" was when McIntyre put two Bloomington policemen on the platform and accused McCloskey of using opium while he was mayor. McCloskey had admitted using marijuana twice in 1972, but not opium; and the charge boomeranged, as the Republican county prosecutor taped a radio ad for McCloskey. The result was an unambiguous 53%–47% win for McCloskey and an end, for the moment, to controversy. But no one can guarantee that this district, in which more than $2 million has been spent in the last two campaigns, will not be seriously contested again.

The People: Pop. 1980: 546,744, up 9.3% 1970–80. Households (1980): 74% family, 39% with children, 64% married couples; 26.1% housing units rented; median monthly rent: $154; median house value: $34,700. Voting age pop. (1980): 395,151; 2% Black.

1984 Presidential Vote: Reagan (R) 142,987   (60%)
Mondale (D) 92,874   (39%)

Rep. Francis X. (Frank) McCloskey (D)

Elected 1982; b. June 12, 1939, Philadelphia, PA; home, Bloomington; IN U., B.A. 1968, J.D. 1971; Roman Catholic; married (Roberta).

Career: Air Force, 1957–61; Journalist; Mayor of Bloomington, 1971–82.

Offices: 127 CHOB 20515, 202-225-4636. Also 501 S. Madison, Bloomington 47401, 812-334-1111; 10 N.E. 4th St., Washington 47501, 812-254-6646; and Fed. Bldg., Rm. 124, 101 N.W. 7th St., Evansville 47701, 812-465-6484.

Committees: *Armed Services* (23d of 31 D). Subcommittees: Investigations; Research and Development. *Post Office and Civil Service* (10th of 14 D). Human Resources; Postal Personnel and Modernization (Chairman).

Group Ratings

	ADA	ACLU	COPE	CFA	LCV	ACU	NTU	NSI	COC	CEI
1986	55	57	85	67	63	18	30	22	50	28
1985	68	—	85	—	67	28	34	—	20	—

National Journal Ratings

	1986 LIB — 1986 CONS		1985 LIB — 1985 CONS	
Economic	62% —	35%	67% —	32%
Social	49% —	49%	56% —	43%
Foreign	64% —	34%	68% —	32%

Key Votes

1) Lmt Cln Water Act	AGN	5) Retain Gun Cont	AGN	9) Aid Angola Reb	AGN
2) Rpl Tobac Sub	AGN	6) Contra Aid	AGN	10) Tax Reform	FOR
3) Grm-Rdmn Def Red	FOR	7) Lmt Text Imp	FOR	11) S Africa Sanc	FOR
4) Ban Polygraph	FOR	8) Limit SDI	FOR	12) Immig Reform	FOR

Election Results

1986 general	Francis X. (Frank) McCloskey (D)	106,662	(53%)	($625,188)
	Richard D. McIntyre (R)	93,586	(47%)	($581,786)
1986 primary	Francis X. (Frank) McCloskey (D)	48,567	(89%)	
	John W. Taylor (D)	6,049	(11%)	
1984 general	Francis X. (Frank) McCloskey (D)	116,645	(50%)	($468,873)
	Richard D. McIntyre (R)	116,641	(50%)	($472,020)

Campaign Contributions and Expenditures

1985-86		Direct Cont. 1985-86		PACS Breakdown 1985-86			
Receipts	$622,667	Indiv.	$232,379	Corp.	$30,125	T/M/H	$34,018
Expend.	$625,188	Party	$13,788	Labor	$224,414	Agr.	$800
Unspent	$3,832	PACS	$333,788	Ideo.	$44,431	CWOS	$0
		Cand.	$14,350				

NINTH DISTRICT

The Ohio River Valley was the first part of Indiana settled by white men. Most of them were southerners, from across the river in Kentucky or over the mountains in Virginia. They came here during the first two decades of the 19th century and established a new state. Their old city of Madison, on the Ohio, still has many of its marvelous old buildings from the days when it was one of the busiest ports on the Ohio River; but it has been a backwater since the middle of the 19th century. Farther down the river is Corydon, from 1816 to 1825 the state capital. Many other towns have 19th century buildings, well preserved beacuse they were bypassed by railroads. The river is still an artery of commerce, but utilitarian barges have replaced the steamers, and even the barges have been overbuilt; the last Ohio River shipyard in Jeffersonville, across from Louisville, closed in 1986.

The settlers in this part of Indiana retained their affection for things southern into the Civil War and beyond; one of their number, Jesse Bright, was expelled from the Senate in 1862 because of his Confederate sympathies. The hills along the Ohio typically deliver Democratic majorities, as they did in the close gubernatorial election of 1984; Democratic as well are the working-class Indiana suburbs of Louisville.

Most of Indiana's Ohio River counties, and an oddly shaped collection of lightly populated counties inland form Indiana's 9th Congressional District. The boundaries are irregularity because Republican legislators wanted to pack as much Democratic territory as possible into the 9th. In effect, they were conceding it to Democratic Representative Lee Hamilton, as well they might.

First elected in the 1964 landslide, Hamilton has become one of the most respected members of the House. Second ranking Democrat on the Foreign Affairs Committee, he was chosen by Speaker Tip O'Neill to chair the House Intelligence Committee after the 1984 election, and after the 1986 election he was chosen by Speaker Jim Wright to chair the special committee investigating the Iran-contra scandal. When those choices were made, Hamilton was still little known outside the House. He seldom appeared on national news shows; he was not a regular at tweedy foreign affairs seminars; his name did not often get in the paper. But for years he has commanded vast respect in the House. Other members rise and talk and sway one or two votes. When Hamilton comes down on one side, he often persuades dozens of different members, of widely varying views, to support that position. Such influence is acquired painstakingly and slowly. Hamilton instinctively approaches difficult issues cautiously, hears out all sides, researches the facts personally, reaches decisions or makes recommendations judiciously and on the merits. He seems impervious to personal influence and the blandishments of friendship and camaraderie. His reluctance to take stands makes him all the more influential when he does so. As a result, on an area as controversial as the Middle East, he is one of the few members of Congress who is genuinely respected—and spoken of in hushed tones—on all sides. Even the most aggressive and contemptuous of the young House Republicans speak his name only in tones of respect.

The Middle East, where he is one Foreign Affairs member the Israel lobby cannot count on but can sometimes persuade, is not the only touchy issue Hamilton has played a major role on. He staunchly supported the Pershing II missile deployment in Europe. He works against trade barriers. He is one of the House's leading experts on international lending institutions. On all these matters he has helped to lead a Democratic House in the same direction as the Republican Administration. But he has differed with the Administration on other things. On intelligence matters, the House could not have chosen a more stern chairman, one less inclined to tolerate hanky-panky and coverups; he is serious, a bit uneasy with all the national attention, and seems to have a perpetually knitted brow. He has been the lead sponsor of House Democrats' efforts to block covert aid to Nicaragua's contras, and upon taking over the Intelligence Committee promised a wholesale review of the CIA's clandestine programs. His opposition to contra aid has played a major role in defeating it several times in the House and has made the vote exceedingly close when it did pass as in 1986. He was unsuccessful in 1986 in getting the House to pass a bill requiring periodic congressional approval of aid to rebels in Angola. The measure illustrates his approach, however: he believes in close congressional oversight of covert intelligence activities, and he is cautious about U.S. government involvement in hostilities abroad.

In investigating the Iran-contra scandal, Hamilton can be expected to be a stickler for correct procedure—for the Administration and for himself. His committee, made up mostly of chairmen senior to himself, is not as likely to leak evidence as the Senate Intelligence Committee is, and despite the fact that more of its members oppose Contra aid, it is not likely to take cheap shots at substantive Administration policy. Its decisions are likely to be accorded respect in the full House.

Hamilton's time in the national spotlight may not turn out to be brief. His special committee assignment will end, but he is almost sure to be chairman some day of Foreign Affairs, and his work and that of Dante Fascell have made this committee more influential and listened to than it has been in years. He can also have, if he chooses, influence on other issues in the House. He served on the ethics committee during the Koreagate and Abscam scandals and takes a stern tone and insists on harsh penalties for what he considers transgressions. He is a strong voice for a strong House ethics code.

Hamilton has had no difficulty winning reelection in the 9th District for many years, and although the Republican redistricters took his home town of Columbus out of the 9th, they otherwise gave him a seat as favorable as he has ever had. He seems certain to win reelection indefinitely here.

The People: Pop. 1980: 544,873, up 14.2% 1970–80. Households (1980): 77% family, 44% with children, 67% married couples; 25.2% housing units rented; median monthly rent: $158; median house value: $36,500. Voting age pop. (1980): 383,018; 2% Black, 1% Spanish origin.

1984 Presidential Vote: Reagan (R) 134,753   (60%)
Mondale (D) 86,932   (39%)

Rep. Lee H. Hamilton (D)

Elected 1964; b. Apr. 20, 1931, Daytona Beach, FL; home, Nashville; DePauw U., B.A. 1952, Goethe U., Frankfurt, Germany, 1952–53, IN U., J.D. 1956; United Methodist; married (Nancy).

Career: Practicing atty., 1956–64.

Offices: 2187 RHOB 20515, 202-225-5315. Also 107 Fed. Ctr., Bldg. 66, 1201 E. 10th St., Jeffersonville 47130, 812-288-3999.

Committees: *Foreign Affairs* (2d of 27 D). Subcommittees: Arms Control, International Security and Science; Europe and the Middle East (Chairman). *Science, Space and Technology* (20th of 27 D). Subcommittees: Science Research and Technology. *Joint Economic Committee* (Vice Chairman). Task Forces: Economic Goals and Intergovernmental Policy; Economic Growth, Trade and Taxes; International Economic Policy.

Group Ratings

	ADA	ACLU	COPE	CFA	LCV	ACU	NTU	NSI	COC	CEI
1986	55	75	67	67	60	23	37	30	56	30
1985	60	—	67	83	—	33	42	—	57	—

National Journal Ratings

	1986 LIB — 1986 CONS		1985 LIB — 1985 CONS	
Economic	37%	62%	48%	50%
Social	64%	34%	62%	38%
Foreign	67%	30%	64%	33%

Key Votes

1) Lmt Cln Water Act	AGN	5) Retain Gun Cont	AGN	9) Aid Angola Reb	AGN
2) Rpl Tobac Sub	AGN	6) Contra Aid	AGN	10) Tax Reform	FOR
3) Grm-Rdmn Def Red	FOR	7) Lmt Text Imp	AGN	11) S Africa Sanc	FOR
4) Ban Polygraph	FOR	8) Limit SDI	FOR	12) Immig Reform	FOR

Election Results

1986 general	Lee H. Hamilton (D)	120,586	(69%)	($306,485)
	Robert Kilroy (R)	46,398	(31%)	($16,610)
1986 primary	Lee H. Hamilton (D)	69,591	(92%)	
	Ronald R. Bettag (D)	2,848	(4%)	
	Robert L. Murphy (D)	3,248	(4%)	
1984 general	Lee H. Hamilton (D)	137,018	(65%)	($208,183)
	Floyd E. Coates (R)	72,652	(35%)	($11,702)

Campaign Contributions and Expenditures

1985-86		Direct Cont. 1985-86		PACS Breakdown 1985-86			
Receipts	$286,915	Indiv.	$143,448	Corp.	$35,100	T/M/H	$26,200
Expend.	$306,485	PACS	$124,749	Labor	$33,750	Agr.	$6,750
Unspent	$15,851			Ideo.	$22,549	CWOS	$400

TENTH DISTRICT

Situated precisely in the center of the state, with avenues radiating out in eight directions to all its ends and corners, Indianapolis is Indiana's largest city and its capital. It is one of the few cities that indisputably sets a distinctive tone for an entire state, a tone best described as businesslike. Indianapolis has its factories, but it is really an office town, with major banks, insurance companies, and state government. Nor does it have the yeasty ethnic mix of most midwestern cities. There are some blacks here and some identifiable ethnics, but the dominant tone is very much white Protestant. Indianapolis did not share in the dynamic growth of the industrial Great Lakes cities in the 1900–1930 period, and it is not today participating in their sharp and precipitous decline.

As in all of Indiana, politics is just one more everyday business here. Of the two major banks, for example, one is Republican and the other Democratic; both care which party will win the state treasurer's office. Patronage employees still "contribute" the traditional 2% of their paychecks to their political parties. The national headquarters of the American Legion stares down toward the federal building and the state capital; the Republican and Democratic banks glare at each other across the Soldiers' and Sailors' Monument. Indianapolis is proud that it spirited away the Colts from Baltimore and the Hudson Institute from Westchester County; it is proud that it is the host of the 1987 Pan American Games as well as the annual Indianapolis 500. Still, this is a serious town, without much sense of humor.

Yet stern, usually Republican Indianapolis is represented in Congress by a Democrat with a puckish sense of humor. Andrew Jacobs has been a member of Congress for all but two years since 1964, but he refuses to take things too seriously. He is fatalistic: in 1975 he refused to board a plane because only first class seats were available; it crashed, killing all aboard. He flouted tradition later that year when he married Representative Martha Keys of Kansas; they met in the House Ways and Means Committee. On weekends Jacobs flew to Indianapolis and Keys took the same plane on to Kansas City, until she was defeated for reelection in 1978. (They have since divorced).

Jacobs owed his initial election to the Democratic sweep in 1964 and his first reelections to Democratic redistricting in 1966 and 1968. Because 1970 was a recession year, it was a good Democratic year in Indiana; in 1972 he was defeated by William Hudnut, now Indianapolis's mayor. Returned to office in the Watergate year of 1974, Jacobs has developed a record that has made him close to unbeatable. He has grown less enthusiastic and more skeptical about federal spending programs over the years; he has been backing a constitutional amendment to require a balanced budget since 1979. He brought to the Reagan economic program the same bemused skepticism he brought to Democratic panaceas, pointing out that the 1981 tax cut would save Reagan $25,000 in taxes.

He opposed sending the Marines to Lebanon and, as a Marine veteran who sustained a disability in combat in Korea, he twitted young Republican hawks like Newt Gingrich and Vin Weber by calling them "war wimps." For months many of them were unaccustomedly silent on the issue. Then Jacobs asked former California Republican Representative Pete McCloskey about his recollections of presidential candidate Pat Robertson's service in the Marines during the Korean war; McCloskey replied that he had heard that Robertson was kept out of combat by his father, who was a Senator from Virginia at the time. Jacobs gave McCloskey's letter wide circulation, and Robertson, who admits that he was not under fire but claims that he served in a rear echelon in what was technically a combat zone, sued them both for libel. It's a lawsuit that could become a major event in the 1988 presidential campaign. McCloskey's story may be particularly interesting to Jacobs because like Robertson he had a father in Congress when the Korean war broke out, but served in combat anyway.

Jacobs also brings the same detachment to his own ambitions. He once chaired Ways and Means's Health Subcommittee, which has jurisdiction over Medicare. Characteristically, Jacobs announced he took that chairmanship only because a better one was not available. In 1985, Jacobs had to surrender control of the panel to Pete Stark in the reshuffle that followed Jim Jones's becoming chairman of the Social Security Subcommittee. But Jacobs gave up the Public Assistance and Unemployment Compensation Subcommittee that seniority entitled him to, and let Harold Ford keep it. He is not a favorite of Chairman Dan Rostenkowski and did not play a major role on the 1985–86 tax reform bill.

Jacobs's self-denial extends to campaigning. He accepts no PAC contributions, raises and spends little money even when seriously opposed, and wins anyway. In 1982 his Democratic colleague David Evans, redistricted into a heavily Republican seat, raised plenty of money and opposed Jacobs in the primary; he outspent Jacobs, but Jacobs won 60%–35%. In 1984, against black Republican Joseph Watkins, he won 59%–41%. In 1986 the American Medical Association was miffed when Jacobs moved successfully to limit doctors' fees ("Vote for the canes, not for the stethoscopes," he said) and went into Indianapolis and spent $300,000 on an independent expenditure campaign against him. He had an active Republican opponent again who outspent him by more than 10–1, and his percentage fell to 58%. This is not so comfortable for most longtime incumbents, particularly when you remember that the district, which includes almost all of Indianapolis inside the Interstate 465 loop, except for the rich precincts directly north of downtown, has many black and white working-class precincts, and had enough Democrats to go for Walter Mondale in 1984. But Jacobs, going his own way as always, seems entirely comfortable in this political situation, and seems likely to continue being himself in the House for some time to come.

The People: Pop. 1980: 541,811, dn. 12.4% 1970–80. Households (1980): 68% family, 39% with children, 51% married couples; 43.0% housing units rented; median monthly rent: $164; median house value: $28,400. Voting age pop. (1980): 384,402; 25% Black, 1% Spanish origin.

1984 Presidential Vote:	Mondale (D)	100,848	(51%)
	Reagan (R)	94,948	(48%)

Rep. Andrew Jacobs, Jr. (D)

Elected 1974; b. Feb. 24, 1932, Indianapolis; home, Indianapolis; IN U., B.S. 1955, LL.B. 1958; Roman Catholic; divorced.

Career: USMC, Korea; Practicing atty., 1958–65, 1973–74; IN House of Reps., 1959–60; U.S. House of Reps., 1965–73.

Offices: 1533 LHOB 20515, 202-225-4011. Also 441-A Fed. Bldg., 46 E. Ohio St., Indianapolis 46204, 317-269-7331.

Committees: *Ways and Means* (6th of 23 D). Subcommittees: Oversight and Investigations; Social Security (Chairman).

Group Ratings

	ADA	ACLU	COPE	CFA	LCV	ACU	NTU	NSI	COC	CEI
1986	85	80	71	67	60	0	48	10	50	36
1985	80	—	71	83	—	24	62	—	59	—

National Journal Ratings

	1986 LIB — 1986 CONS		1985 LIB — 1985 CONS	
Economic	48% —	52%	56% —	43%
Social	74% —	23%	85% —	0%
Foreign	61% —	37%	69% —	30%

Key Votes

1) Lmt Cln Water Act	FOR	5) Retain Gun Cont	FOR	9) Aid Angola Reb	AGN
2) Rpl Tobac Sub	FOR	6) Contra Aid	AGN	10) Tax Reform	AGN
3) Grm-Rdmn Def Red	FOR	7) Lmt Text Imp	FOR	11) S Africa Sanc	FOR
4) Ban Polygraph	FOR	8) Limit SDI	FOR	12) Immig Reform	AGN

Election Results

1986 general	Andrew Jacobs, Jr. (D)	68,817	(58%)	($40,577)
	Jim Eynon (R)	49,064	(41%)	($531,148)
1986 primary	Andrew Jacobs, Jr. (D)	24,223	(95%)	
	Benson D. Skelton (D)	1,233	(5%)	
1984 general	Andrew Jacobs, Jr. (D)	115,274	(59%)	($30,192)
	Joseph P. Watkins (R)	79,342	(41%)	($112,081)

Campaign Contributions and Expenditures

1985-86		Direct Cont. 1986-85		PACS Breakdown 1985-86			
Receipts	$52,005	Indiv.	$50,409	Corp.	$0	T/M/H	$0
Expend.	$40,577			Labor	$0	Agr.	$0
Unspent	$18,346			Ideo.	$0	CWOS	$0

IOWA

Iowa, where America's presidential campaigns begin, and where President Ronald Reagan's career in radio broadcasting took root, appears the all-American state. The landscape of rolling hills and regularly spaced furrows, small courthouse towns and tree-lined river bottoms seem the natural home of Norman Rockwell's freckle-faced boys and turkey-serving grandmothers. Iowa looks like the America many people who are now in their 50s and 60s grew up in, and it is: 53% of the housing stock here was built before 1950, a higher share than anywhere else except some northeastern states. If you want to see what old-time Middle America looked like, come to Iowa.

Yet economically, culturally, and politically Iowa, far from being a typical American state, is atypical almost to the point of being quirky and eccentric. Historically, this state was settled in a rush, in the generation following the Mexican War of 1846–48, mostly by yeomen of Yankee and German stock. The first Iowans raised large families, and many of their children moved farther west or to the big city of Chicago; Iowa has been exporting people, and has had an older-than-average population, since 1900. Ethnically, Iowa does not seem diverse today, with a handful of blacks and Hispanics and few descendants of the eastern and southern European migrants of the 1880-1924 period. But the ancient tension between German and British stock here has political reverberations even today (46% of Iowans in 1980 volunteered that they had German ancestry). German-Americans were pilloried for their opposition to American entry into World War I, and their skepticism about American involvement in a foreign war has been echoed by Iowa's isolationism in the 1930s and 1940s and dovishness in the 1970s and 1980s.

But if Iowa is out of step for being liberal on foreign policy in a conservative decade, it has also been out of step for its cultural conservatism in an age of liberation. Most Iowans still live in families and Iowa has one of the nation's lowest divorce rates. School attendance is high and Iowans are proud of having the nation's highest literacy rate.

Economically, this is a farm state, with more acreage under cultivation than any other and a harvest of greater value than any but California. People in other places may applaud when farm prices are low, and Americans may feel fitter from eating less red meat. But both trends spell trouble for Iowa. It is hurt also, ironically, by the vast growth in productivity of American agriculture since the turn of the century—one reason Iowa started exporting people, for it takes fewer and fewer people each decade to produce more and more food. In 1900, when the railroad network was complete and food processing was already a big industry, 30 million Americans lived on farms and grew enough among them to feed a nation of 76 million and export some besides. Today only 6 million Americans live on farms but produce more than enough to feed a nation of 226 million.

Iowa is responsible for much of that, not only because it has some of America's richest farmland, but also because it has developed some of the most important crop hybrids and has greatly improved agricultural management and marketing techniques. If Iowa's houses and its values seem old-fashioned, it is still completely open to scientific innovation. Far from being closed to the outside world, Iowans are more open to it than many residents of the insular urban villages which, together, make up most of New York City. And unlike most Americans, Iowans are export-conscious: they know that their prosperity depends in large part on exports and world markets and are uncomfortably aware that the major reason for the sagging farm economy of the 1980s is the steep drop in American agricultural exports. They are aware as well of the importance to their own lives of USDA regulations made in Washington and price fluctuations on the Chicago Board of Trade. In all this, Iowans are served by sophisticated newspapers, led by the *Des Moines Register & Tribune,* one of the few papers in the nation with genuine statewide circulation. Back in 1900 most Iowans seldom left their home counties and only on

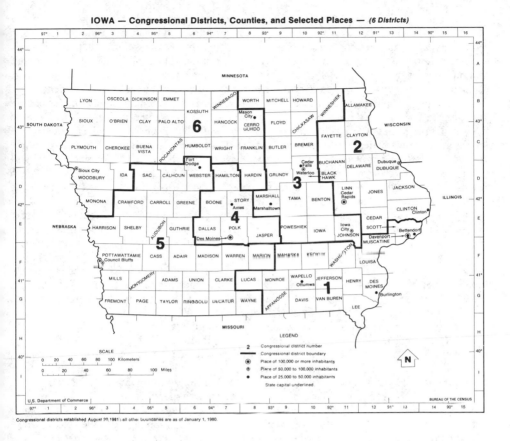

IOWA — Congressional Districts, Counties, and Selected Places — (6 Districts)

rare occasions left the state. Now the farthest reaches of the world are only a few hours' plane ride away through connections at O'Hare Airport.

Still, Iowa's economy remains dependent on agriculture— particularly corn, hogs, soybeans, wheat, dairy and beef cattle. Farmers who produce these commodities are the nation's largest class of entrepreneurs, and on their revenues—not their profits—depends not only the farmer himself but the small town banker and the worker in the ag-implement factory. A small drop in prices, a plausible miscalculation of market trends, a small increase in interest rates or fertilizer prices or pesticide requirements or simply a break in the weather can have huge effects on a farmer's income. In short, Iowa's entrepreneurial economy generates mass uncertainty, near-constant dissatisfaction, and continual demands for government action. When prices fall, Iowa demands that the government prop them up in various complicated ways; when interest rates rise, Iowa demands that they be forced back down; when presidential candidates come to Iowa's precinct caucuses in January, as they did in droves in 1980 and 1984, Iowa forces most of them to pledge that they will not embargo grain sales or interrupt the flow of grain to the Soviet Union whatever the foreign policy consequences. The high grain prices of the late 1970s generated complaints that land was becoming too expensive and that government must act to keep small farmers from being squeezed out. The lower grain prices of the 1980s generated demands for subsidizing farm credit and maintaining federal price support payments in some cases more than 100% of the world market price.

So the farm economy, and the demands it generates for government action, is one reason for

Iowa's political quirkiness. Another is the state's vested interest in inflation, which produces rising land values and commodity prices. Boom and bust down on the farm during the 1970s and 1980s and the loss of price competitiveness in world export markets have severely hurt this state.

In sum, Iowa has a certain orneriness, born perhaps in the vulnerability of its farm economy, and nurtured in the heritage of the Germans and Scandinavians and Yankees who came here often because they were unwilling to conform to the traditions of their native lands. Accordingly, Iowa runs counter politically to national cycles—sometimes in seemingly maddening fashion. In 1986, as the Democrats were making gains elsewhere, Iowa reelected its Republican Senator, Charles Grassley, and the Republican governor as well. But Democrats gained seats in the legislature and the parties traded two seats in the U.S. House. In prosperous 1984, this one-time Republican bastion was Walter Mondale's sixth best state and had the nation's second biggest swing toward Mondale and second smallest increase in the Reagan percentage (after North Dakota). This is not the first time Iowa has seemed to move against (or at least not toward) a popular administration and its party; that happened also in 1980, 1972 and 1956.

Iowa's counter-cyclical politics actually makes sense of the result of its combined proclivities on issues. First, this farm state is usually conservative on economic questions but used to relying on government assistance in agriculture. But, second, Iowa is otherwise stingy about other forms of spending, particularly if it spots waste. Some of the all-time congressional pinch-pennies come from Iowa. Third, it abhors corruption. Iowa gave Richard Nixon in 1972 a lower percentage than in 1968; Watergate was then only a minor issue elsewhere, but it cut in Iowa. Fourth, Iowa is tolerant generally but not particularly pleased with new cultural styles. This is family country. Finally, Iowa has been dovish at least since the first World War. It is wary of military involvements abroad now, and hostile to large defense budgets.

This is an unusual mix. You find something like it in adjacent parts of Wisconsin and Minnesota, and nowhere else—a product of Yankee settlement and Scandinavian leavening, moral uprightness and a penchant for reform; 1986, for example, was the first time it reelected a U.S. Senator in 20 years. That year Iowa returned to Washington Republican Charles Grassley, who shrewly combines a reputation as a tightwad on domestic spending and at the Pentagon with a willingness to use government to help farmers. Democrats may benefit from Iowa's dovishness but they have been hurt by its cultural conservatism, especially among Catholic voters (a bloc without which a Democrat can't win here) on the issue of abortion. The appeal of Walter Mondale—opponent of Star Wars, son of a minister, of Norwegian descent—makes sense in a dovish, church-going, German-Scandinavian state. So does the relative coolness of Iowa voters for a president who has been so popular elsewhere, and who is the only president in American history who spent part of his adult life in Iowa.

Presidential politics. Iowa does not have a presidential primary, but it does have what has been since 1976 the first real race in the primary season: the Democratic and Republican precinct caucuses. On frigid January nights Iowans gather in designated schools, public buildings, or just someone's house, and caucus. They divide themselves into groups according to presidential preference (or non-preference) and elect delegates to their county conventions; those delegates are entitled later in the season to elect delegates to the state convention in accordance with the presidential preference expressed at the county level, which is then finally translated into presidential convention delegates. So you can get a fair—not quite a precise—idea of the composition of Iowa's delegations from the initial caucus results, if you weigh each precinct's results by its contributions to the final state delegation (the parties try to do this, but the calculations take a while) and keep in mind that candidates' withdrawals can have varying effects.

But mathematics really isn't critical here. This is one of the few chances ordinary American voters—more than 100,000 Iowans vote in each party's precinct caucuses, and Governor Terry Branstad was predicting 200,000 for the Republicans in 1988—get a chance to watch candidates in person, assess their mettle, and decide among them whom to back. It is well-nigh impossible for a little-known candidate to make himself personally known to any appreciable number of voters in the larger states that choose later. But in Iowa a Gary Hart can come in and, by winning second place with 16% of the caucus vote make him a contender in New Hampshire and later contests. Just as important, Iowa winnows out candidates: in the 1984 Democratic contests the well-publicized John Glenn was a casualty, as were Alan Cranston and Reubin Askew and George McGovern who, had he won only a few more votes, might have edged Hart out as Walter Mondale's chief rival. In 1980 the Republican caucuses here filled a similar function, selecting a surprise winner, George Bush, and making him Ronald Reagan's chief rival, and giving a ticket to further contests to John Anderson, whose performance on a statewide televised debate helped him make contact with his constituency. On the Democratic side, the 1980 caucuses established Edward Kennedy's unpopularity; he had the support of labor leaders and many active Democrats, but thousands of Iowans left their homes on a cold night to vote for an incumbent president for whom, as it turned out in November, their enthusiasm was limited.

It is said that the caucuses place too much premium on organization and too much power in the hands of a few party activists. But the results seem to show that the candidates' own appeal is the critical factor. It is said that Iowa is too quirky a state to make such decisions for the whole nation. Iowa leads candidates to make commitments for too much in government farm subsidies, its NEA teachers union (which backed Carter in 1980 and Mondale in 1984) has too much clout, it is too dovish on foreign policy. Going into 1988 it was possibly the most anti-Reagan state in a nation where in the previous two presidential elections 93 of a possible 100 states had voted for Reagan. But in all these respects Iowa is probably counterbalanced by New Hampshire. If Iowa tilts toward government subsidy, New Hampshire tilts toward low taxes; if Iowa is culturally cautious and long-settled, New Hampshire has a certain New England trendiness and is full of new migrants; if Iowa depends on old-fashioned farming and manufacturing, New Hampshire is increasingly high tech; if Iowa is dovish, New Hampshire does not seem to mind hawkishness. The pair are not a perfect balance, to be sure, but a candidate must not tilt too far to one or the other if he is to run in both, unless he wants to risk bypassing one—a risk no nomination winner has taken in two decades.

In 1988 Iowa promises to be especially important, since none of the likely national candidates of either party will be known in depth nationally as were the nominees of the 1980s. Democrats Bruce Babbitt and Richard Gephardt criss-crossed Iowa in 1986 and 1987; Joseph Biden spoke widely and to great applause; Gary Hart appeared several times before his demise, though he was criticized for travelling abroad and around the country—to learn about governing, his backers said—rather than chatting with active Democrats in Iowa. Farm issues help some candidates and hurt others: Paul Simon in early 1987 hoped that his strong showings in adjacent regions of Downstate Illinois would carry over across the Mississippi River, while Michael Dukakis was widely ridiculed for urging Iowa farmers to produce the fancy vegetables that have been doing so well for New England farmers. Gephardt hopes his sponsorship of the Harkin–Gephardt production controls bill and his campaigners from next-door Missouri will help. On the Republican side, George Bush, winner of the 1980 Iowa caucuses, operates under the special handicap that Ronald Reagan is less popular here than in any other state, and Bob Dole has the special advantage of having represented a neighboring farm state in Congress for nearly 30 years. Pete du Pont and Jack Kemp have been in the state as well, though du Pont's proposal to phase out all federal farm supports seems risky and Kemp's career-long emphasis on low taxes seem likely to be more congenial in New Hampshire than here.

For the general election different rules apply. Historically Iowa was a Republican state for many years, but it trended Democratic in 1972 and 1984 when the Democrats nominated preacher's kids from neighboring farm states, although it ended up in the Republican column in both years. In the close election of 1976 it was seriously contested and with its strong anti-Reagan feelings may well lean toward the Democrats in 1988.

Governor. Governor Terry Branstad, as a conservative Republican elected in part because his 1982 opponent legally avoided paying state taxes, might have seemed headed for trouble in 1986. The farm economy was in dire straits, as he himself well knew: he owed more money on his own farm than its market value. But Branstad had no trouble criticizing the Reagan Administration or pushing programs to help farmers. He was proud of cutting business taxes. But he also pushed for a moratorium on farm foreclosures. The Democratic candidate, former state Senate leader Lowell Junkins, offered a plan to issue $400 million in bonds to stimulate new business and trade, to be paid back out of proceeds from the lottery. Against this Branstad made a blistering attack, and it seems likely that parsimonious Iowa voters were uncertain that government could allocate money intelligently and worried that lottery proceeds would, as they have in other states, drop after the novelty wears off. Branstad, a 53% winner in 1982, won with 52% in 1986.

For his second term, Branstad proposed big spending increases for teachers' salaries and education and more money for highways—an activist program for a man always labelled a conservative. For 1988, he appears likely to back Bob Dole; getting a farm state politician on the head of the ticket may be the only way to save the Republican Party in Iowa. Having run a close race, Branstad would presumably like a farm state native on the ticket. The lieutenant governor and attorney general are Democrats, as are large majorities in both houses of the legislature.

Senators. In 1986 Charles Grassley became the first Iowa Senator to win reelection in 20 years. He also set, early in the two-year cycle, the political strategy and tone for Republican senators in the 1986 elections. Grassley has been underestimated throughout his political career. He likes to point out that he is a simple farmer, that he worked as a machinist while serving the legislature; he talks and looks like an archetypical hayseed. But he is also a shrewd and successful politician, winning a seat in the Iowa legislature in the Democratic year of 1958, a House seat in the Democratic year of 1974, and a Senate seat by beating a strong incumbent, John Culver, in 1980. He began by sponsoring a budget freeze proposal, emphasizing the frugality and fairness Iowans have always sought; and he went on to attack the Pentagon for wasting money and made headlines when he asked Pentagon analyst Chuck Spinney to testify before Congress. The Pentagon ordered Spinney not to appear, at which point he suddenly made the cover of *Time;* then Spinney did appear and testified—a perfect episode for Iowa's dovish, pinch-penny voters. In 1985 someone in the White House said publicly that if Grassley did not vote for the MX missile, the President was not going to come in and campaign for him. Grassley, no doubt aware that Reagan had won only 53% in 1984 in Iowa, said that that was just fine with him. But Grassley was not just maneuvering. He is strong precisely because his popular stands reflect his genuine, long-held beliefs, and that he advances them as shrewdly as he has his own career.

From that point on other incumbent Republicans rushed forward to record their dissents from this or that item on the Administration's agenda and tailored their reelection campaigns closely to the views and priorities of their home states. Pretty much lost—and, anyway, not really sought by Reagan strategists—was the kind of national theme that accounted for so many Republican gains in 1980 and 1984 and minimized the number of Republican losses in 1982. Not all his colleagues were as successful as Grassley; but then he has been winning with this kind of formula for three decades. No serious candidate filed to run against him, and he was reelected with 66% of the vote—more than any other Iowa Senator has ever received.

Legislatively, Grassley is not likely to be a power in a Democratic Senate. Yet he has shown the capacity to change the terms of debate, and future historians may date the end of the Reagan Administration's huge increases in defense spending to Grassley's initiatives. He still has his seat on the Budget Committee and he has moved from Labor to Appropriations—a fine forum for his penny-pinching politics.

Iowa's other Senator, Tom Harkin, has a rather different formula, one that has played quite well with Iowa politics for nearly two decades now. He is one of the Democrats' Watergate babies, but he has a craggy and almost worn look; he grew up poor in a tiny rural town, worked his way through college and law school, spent five years in the 1960s in the Navy. He worked on Representative Neal Smith's staff. He was the man who exposed the South Vietnamese "tiger cage" prison. He ran for Congress in a Republican district in the Republican year of 1972 and nearly won: the incumbent wasn't working hard, and Iowa's countercyclical voting habits were working for him. In 1974 he ran again and invented a campaign technique widely imitated since: work days; he spent a day working at each of a dozen or two jobs. He won solidly and held the seat with good percentages. Well before the 1984 election, he cornered the Democratic nomination to run against Senator Roger Jepsen, who was gravely weakened by, among other things, insisting he was entitled to commute to work alone in the highway lane reserved for cars with four passengers and having visited years ago a massage parlor despite his campaigning for family values and against abortion. Representing dovish Iowa, Harkin served on Armed Services and supported the Weinberger defense budgets. Representing agricultural Iowa he chaired the Joint Economic Committee and put out studies advocating on theoretical grounds unfettered free markets. 1984 was a tough year for Democrats elsewhere, but a marvelous year for Harkin; he was elected to the Senate with 56% of the vote and carried all six congressional districts.

Harkin runs as a populist, has set up a New Populist Forum, argues that "too few people have too much money and too much power," and summons up memories of the Populist party of the 1890s. Harkin talks generally of redistributing wealth and power, but his specific proposals tend to hone in on redistributing certain kinds of wealth to certain kinds of people. He is the lead sponsor of the Harkin–Gephardt bill to let farmers vote on whether to have mandatory production controls—a proposal which admittedly would raise the price of crops and of food and which has almost no support on the congressional Agriculture committees and elicited a mixed response in farm district elections in 1986. He talks about the need for "economic justice" in the United States and abroad, and says in Central American countries it must come first, before freedom of the press and freedom of speech. He is an outspoken opponent of American military involvement in Central America and on most issues is one of the most liberal senators. Yet he is also practical-minded: as chairman of the House Agriculture subcommittee handling the dairy program, he tended one of the programs politically important to Democrats. He serves on the Appropriations, Agriculture, and Labor committees—nice posts for an Iowa Democrat.

It is too early now to say whether Harkin's populist formula will enable him in 1990 to become the first Iowa Democrat in history to win two six-year terms. But he has this in common with Grassley: he has deep convictions on important issues which are in line with basic Iowa values, and he has the political instinct to exploit them electorally. His abortion stand could be a problem, as it was for Democrats Dick Clark and John Culver in 1978 and 1980, and his production controls program is by no means universally popular.

Congressional districting. The redistricting process in Iowa was controlled by Republicans but, in line with state tradition, district lines were drawn disregarding partisan advantage. A state commission presented plans, which the legislature could vote up or down; the plan that was finally accepted seemed to weaken the state's one shaky Republican incumbent (though, as it turned out, not severely) and did not hurt any of the three Democrats.

The People: Est. Pop. 1986: 2,851,000; Pop. 1980: 2,913,808, dn. 2.2% 1980–86 and up 3.1% 1970–80; 1.18% of U.S. total, 29th largest. 15% with 1–3 yrs. col., 14% with 4+ yrs. col.; 10.1% below poverty level. Single ancestry: 21% German, 7% English, 4% Irish, 2% Dutch, Norwegian, 1% Swedish, French. Households (1980): 73% family, 39% with children, 64% married couples; 26% housing units rented; median monthly rent: $176; median house value: $40,600. Voting age pop. (1980): 2,087,935; 1% Black, 1% Spanish origin. Registered voters (1986): 1,611,438; 568,988 D (35%), 504,589 R (31%), 537,861 unaffiliated (34%).

1986 Share of Federal Tax Burden: $8,566,000,000; 1.14% of U.S. total, 28th largest.

1986 Share of Federal Expenditures

	Total		Non-Defense		Defense	
Total Expend	$8,345m	(1.01%)	$7,595m	(1.27%)	$751m	(0.33%)
St/Lcl Grants	1,158m	(1.03%)	1,157m	(1.03%)	2m	(1.80%)
Salary/Wages	603m	(0.50%)	506m	(0.86%)	96m	(0.16%)
Pymnts to Indiv	4,406m	(1.21%)	4,334m	(1.25%)	72m	(0.41%)
Procurement	882m	(0.40%)	242m	(0.44%)	580m	(0.39%)
Research/Other	1,356m	(5.08%)	1,356m	(5.09%)	(0m)	(0%)

Political Lineup: Governor, Terry E. Branstad (R); Lt. Gov., Jo Ann Zimmerman (D); Secy. of State, Elaine Baxter (D); Atty. Gen., Tom Miller (D); Treasurer, Michael L. Fitzgerald (D); Auditor, Richard D. Johnson (R). State Senate, 50 (30 D and 20 R); State House of Representatives, 100 (58 D and 42 R). Senators, Charles E. Grassley (R) and Tom Harkin (D). Representatives, 6 (4 R and 2 D).

1984 Presidential Vote

Reagan (R) 703,088 (53%)
Mondale (D) 605,620 (46%)

1980 Presidential Vote

Reagan (R) 676,026 (51%)
Carter (D) 508,672 (39%)
Anderson (I) 115,633 (9%)

GOVERNOR

Gov. Terry E. Branstad (R)

Elected 1982, term expires Jan. 1991; b. Nov. 17, 1946, Leland; home, Des Moines; U. of IA, B.A. 1969, Drake U. Law Sch., J.D. 1974; Roman Catholic; married (Christine).

Career: Army, 1969–71; Practicing atty., farmer; IA House of Reps., 1973–79; Lt. Gov., 1979–83.

Office: State Capitol, Des Moines 50319, 515-281-5211.

Election Results

1986 gen.	Terry E. Branstad (R)	....	472,712	(52%)
	Lowell L. Junkins (D)	....	436,924	(48%)
1986 prim.	Terry E. Branstad (R)	....	104,482	(100%)
1982 gen.	Terry E. Branstad (R)	....	548,313	(53%)
	Roxanne Conlin (D)	....	483,291	(47%)

SENATORS

Sen. Charles E. Grassley (R)

Elected 1980, seat up 1992; b. Sept. 17, 1933, New Hartford; home, New Hartford; U. of N. IA, B.A. 1955, M.A. 1956, U. of IA, 1957–58; Baptist; married (Barbara).

Career: Farmer, 1960–74; IA House of Reps., 1959–74; U.S. House of Reps., 1974–80.

Offices: 135 HSOB 20510, 202-224-3744. Also 721 Fed. Bldg., 210 Walnut St., Des Moines 50309, 515-284-4890; 210 Waterloo, 531 Commercial St., Waterloo 50701, 319-232-6657; 116 Fed. Bldg., 131 E. 4th St., Davenport 52801, 319-322-4331; 103 Fed. Courthouse, 320 6th St., Sioux City 51101, 712-233-3331; and 206 Fed. Bldg., 101 1st St., S.E., Cedar Rapids 52401, 319-399-2555.

Committees: *Appropriations* (12 of 13 R). Subcommittees: Agriculture, Rural Development and Related Agencies; District of Columbia; HUD-Independent Agencies; Legislative Branch (Ranking Member). *Budget* (6th of 11 R). *Judiciary* (4th of 6 R). Subcommittees: Courts and Administrative Practice (Ranking Member); Patents, Copyrights and Trademarks. *Special Committee on Aging* (4th of 9 R).

Group Ratings

	ADA	ACLU	COPE	CFA	LCV	ACU	NTU	NSI	COC	CEI
1986	18	7	11	47	33	70	64	70	74	51
1985	15	—	16	20	—	57	47	—	69	—

National Journal Ratings

	1986 LIB — 1986 CONS	1985 LIB — 1985 CONS
Economic	33% — 64%	41% — 56%
Social	17% — 80%	17% — 76%
Foreign	42% — 55%	51% — 46%

Key Votes

1) Ease Gun Cont	FOR	5) Grm-Rdmn Def Red	FOR	9) Rehnquist Nom	FOR
2) Immig Reform	FOR	6) Contra Aid	FOR	10) Tax Reform	FOR
3) Lmt Text Imp	AGN	7) SDI Funding	AGN	11) Drug Death Pen	AGN
4) Aid Tobac Ind	FOR	8) Lmt PAC Contrib	FOR	12) S Africa Sanc	FOR

Election Results

1986 general	Charles E. Grassley (R)	588,880	(66%)	($2,513,319)
	John P. Roehrick (D)	299,406	(34%)	($255,673)
1986 primary	Charles E. Grassley (R)	108,370	(100%)	
1980 general	Charles E. Grassley (R)	683,014	(53%)	($2,183,028)
	John C. Culver (D)	581,545	(46%)	($1,750,680)

Campaign Contributions and Expenditures

1985-86		Direct Cont. 1985-86		PACS Breakdown 1985-86			
Receipts	$2,749,564	Indiv.	$1,585,655	Corp.	$478,522	T/M/H	$304,348
Expend.	$2,513,319	Party	$15,642	Labor	$16,100	Agr.	$26,700
Unspent	$487,347	PACS	$959,431	Ideo.	$106,135	CWOS	$27,626

Sen. Tom Harkin (D)

Elected 1984, seat up 1990; b. Nov. 19, 1939, Cumming; home, Cumming; IA St. U., B.S. 1962, Catholic U., J.D. 1972; Roman Catholic; married (Ruth).

Career: Navy, 1962–67; Practicing atty., 1972–74; U.S. House of Reps., 1974–84.

Offices: 316 HSOB 20510, 202-224-3254. Also 733 Fed. Bldg., 210 Walnut St., Des Moines 50309, 515-284-4574. Box H, Fed. Bldg., Council Bluffs 51501, 712-325-5533. Lindale Mall, Ste. 101, 4444 1st Ave. N.E., Cedar Rapids 52402, 319-393-6374. 131 E. 4th St., 314B Fed. Bldg., Davenport, 52801, 319-322-1338.

Committees: *Agriculture, Nutrition, and Forestry* (6th of 10 D). Subcommittees: Agricultural Credit; Domestic and Foreign Marketing and Product Promotion; Nutrition and Investigations (Chairman). *Appropriations* (14th of 16 D). Subcommittees: Agriculture, Rural Development and Related Agencies; District of Columbia (Chairman); Foreign Operations; Labor, Health and Human Services, Education; Transportation. *Labor and Human Services* (7th of 9 D). Subcommittees: Children, Family, Drugs and Alcoholism; Labor; Handicapped (Chairman). *Small Business* (8th of 10 D). Subcommittees: Competition and Antitrust Enforcement (Chairman); Export and Expansion.

Group Ratings

	ADA	ACLU	COPE	CFA	LCV	ACU	NTU	NSI	COC	CEI
1986	90	92	92	87	90	20	32	11	28	17
1985	100	—	90	87	—	5	27	—	24	—

National Journal Ratings

	1986 LIB — 1986 CONS		1985 LIB — 1985 CONS	
Economic	92%	— 7%	92%	— 5%
Social	92%	— 0%	84%	— 15%
Foreign	75%	— 0%	88%	— 0%

Key Votes

1) Ease Gun Cont	FOR	5) Grm-Rdmn Def Red	AGN	9) Rehnquist Nom	AGN
2) Immig Reform	FOR	6) Contra Aid	AGN	10) Tax Reform	FOR
3) Lmt Text Imp	AGN	7) SDI Funding	AGN	11) Drug Death Pen	FOR
4) Aid Tobac Ind	FOR	8) Lmt PAC Contrib	FOR	12) S Africa Sanc	FOR

Election Results

1984 general	Tom Harkin (D)	716,883	(55%)	($2,838,277)
	Roger W. Jepsen (R)	564,381	(44%)	($3,420,153)
1984 primary	Tom Harkin (D)	106,005	(100%)	
1978 general	Roger W. Jepsen (R)	421,598	(51%)	($728,268)
	Dick Clark (D)	395,066	(48%)	($860,774)

Campaign Contributions and Expenditures

1983-84		Direct Cont. 1983-84		PACS Breakdown 1983-84			
Receipts	$2,842,333	Indiv.	$1,935,255	Corp.	$74,865	T/M/H	$118,483
Expend.	$2,838,277	Party	$52,054	Labor	$309,268	Agr.	$29,500
Debts	$1,537	PACS	$799,060	Ideo.	$219,586	CWOS	$18,500

FIRST DISTRICT

In downtown Davenport, Iowa, just across the Mississippi River from his native Illinois, Ronald Reagan first began performing for a living, as a radio announcer for WOC. The station was housed in the same building as the Palmer School of Chiropractic, and WOC stood for "world of chiropractic." Both were founded by B. J. Palmer, and while Reagan soon went on to other things, the Palmer School remains the leading chiropractic institution in the United States and one of the major civic institutions of Davenport. Davenport is also known as the largest of the Quad Cities, and the most affluent; Rock Island, Moline, and East Moline are on low land east of the Mississippi, while Davenport is backed up by hills where most of the area's affluent people live. This is the more Republican side of the river: in 1984 Rock Island County, Illinois, went for Walter Mondale, while Davenport's Scott County went for its old sportscaster.

Davenport is the largest city in the 1st Congressional District of Iowa, which covers roughly the southeast part of the state, including the Mississippi River towns to the south and the farmland stretching west almost to Des Moines. The river towns include Muscatine, heavily Protestant and Republican; Burlington, the namesake of the railroad which became the nucleus of today's giant Burlington Northern, and which tends to vote Democratic; Fort Madison and Keokuk in the south, where the influence of the early southern-accented settlers from Missouri is apparent in Democratic voting preferences. Inland are the heavily Republican farm counties and the Democratic factory town of Ottumwa.

The 1st District has been represented since 1976 by Republican Congressman Jim Leach. His positions on issues are well suited to the district. On economic issues, he is fairly frugal with the taxpayers' money, at about the midpoint of the House. But on cultural issues he is one of the chamber's more liberal members, and on foreign policy he votes more often on seriously contested issues with the Democrats than with his fellow Republicans. He has chosen an interesting set of issues to concentrate on. He is a staunch supporter of numerous programs, such as the National Endowment for the Arts, that the White House would like to cripple. He concentrates not on lifestyle issues, but on those relating to the political process: he is one of the leaders in the fight to reduce the importance of political action committees in financing campaigns and co-sponsors the bill supported by Common Cause. On foreign policy he has supported and occasionally has been one of the leaders of the fight against U.S. involvement in El Salvador and Nicaragua; in 1985 he co-sponsored legislation that would even prohibit private citizens from sending money to the contras. Leach is one of the highest ranking Republicans on the Foreign Affairs Committee, and if his vote is not often pivotal there, where liberal Democrats have a solid majority, his support is often sought to give a bipartisan appearance to causes which, at least at first, have little Republican support. A member of the Banking Committee, Leach is also ranking Republican on its International Finance, Trade and Monetary Policy Subcommittee and has become a spokesman against protectionism.

Most of these stands are thoroughly popular with his parsimonious, dovish constituents in the 1st District—and highly unpopular with the large majority of his fellow House Republicans. Leach, who accepted the presidency of the then moribund Ripon Society in 1981, enraged many Republicans when he set up in 1984 what he called the Republican Mainstream Committee. The name recalled Nelson Rockefeller's claim in the 1960s that his politics represented the mainstream of his party—a claim one should have thought had been refuted by the failure of anything like a Rockefeller-style Republican to win a Republican nomination in any of the next six presidential years. For years Ripon was a kind of Rockefeller government-in-exile whose central premise was that Republicans should nominate liberals because conservatives couldn't win elections; now the only Rockefeller on the scene is a Democrat, and conservative Republicans have won four of the last five presidential elections by running conservatives. Leach is also a member of the 92 Group, which has a broader base of Republicans, many of them active partisans.

Before Leach's first victory in 1976, this had been one of the most marginal and closely contested House seats in the nation for 12 years. Now, however much he is disliked by Republicans in Washington, Leach is nominated without serious opposition and reelected by overwhelming margins; though, should he not run, there would surely be a serious race here.

The People: Pop. 1980: 485,961, up 5.0% 1970–80. Households (1980): 74% family, 40% with children, 64% married couples; 25% housing units rented; median monthly rent: $178; median house value: $39,600. Voting age pop. (1980): 345,540; 2% Black, 1% Spanish origin.

1984 Presidential Vote:

Reagan (R)	110,057	(52%)
Mondale (D)	99,112	(47%)

Rep. James A. S. (Jim) Leach (R)

Elected 1976; b. Oct. 15, 1942, Davenport; home, Davenport; Princeton U., B.A. 1964, Johns Hopkins U., M.A. 1966, London Sch. of Econ., 1966–68; Episcopalian; married (Elisabeth).

Career: Staff Asst., U.S. Rep. Donald Rumsfeld, 1965–66; U.S. Foreign Svc., 1968–69; 1971–72; A.A. to Dir. of U.S. Office of Equal Opp., 1969–70; Pres., Flamegas Co., Inc., propane gas marketers, 1973–75; Dir., Fed. Home Loan Bank Bd., Midwest Region, 1975–76.

Offices: 1514 LHOB 20515, 202-225-6576. Also 322 W. 3d St., Davenport 52801, 319-326-1841; 306 F&M Bank Bldg., 3rd & Jefferson Sts., Burlington 52601, 319-752-4584; and Park View Plaza, Rm. 204, 107 E. 2nd St., Ottumwa 52501, 515-682-8549.

Committees: *Banking, Finance and Urban Affairs* (3d of 20 R). Subcommittees: Domestic Monetary Policy; Financial Institutions Supervision, Regulation and Insurance; International Finance, Trade, and Monetary Policy (Ranking Member). *Foreign Affairs* (4th of 18 R). Subcommittees: Arms Control, Asian and Pacific Affairs (Ranking Member).

Group Ratings

	ADA	ACLU	COPE	CFA	LCV	ACU	NTU	NSI	COC	CEI
1986	55	80	31	67	89	22	62	10	61	59
1985	60	—	32	75	—	33	66	—	50	—

National Journal Ratings

	1986 LIB — 1986 CONS		1985 LIB — 1985 CONS	
Economic	31% —	67%	45% —	55%
Social	69% —	28%	63% —	33%
Foreign	67% —	30%	85% —	8%

Key Votes

1) Lmt Cln Water Act	FOR	5) Retain Gun Cont	FOR	9) Aid Angola Reb	AGN
2) Rpl Tobac Sub	FOR	6) Contra Aid	AGN	10) Tax Reform	FOR
3) Grm-Rdmn Def Red	FOR	7) Lmt Text Imp	AGN	11) S Africa Sanc	FOR
4) Ban Polygraph	FOR	8) Limit SDI	FOR	12) Immig Reform	FOR

Election Results

1986 general	James A. S. (Jim) Leach (R)	86,834	(66%)	($231,937)
	John R. Whitaker (D)	43,985	(34%)	($23,526)
1986 primary	James A. S. (Jim) Leach (R)	15,523	(100%)	
1984 general	James A. S. (Jim) Leach (R)	131,182	(67%)	($197,589)
	Kevin Ready (D)	65,293	(33%)	($44,207)

Campaign Contributions and Expenditures

1985-86		Direct Cont. 1985-86		PACS Breakdown 1985-86			
Receipts	$229,607	Indiv.	$210,471	Corp.	$0	T/M/H	$0
Expend.	$231,937	Party	$9,848	Labor	$0	Agr.	$0
Unspent	$31,443			Ideo.	$0	CWOS	$0

SECOND DISTRICT

For those who suppose that the landscape of the American Midwest is monotonously flat, a trip to the Mississippi River comes as a pleasant surprise. Here the river's banks are hilly, to a midwesterner's eye mountainous: the most varied topography between Upstate New York and the Black Hills of South Dakota. From the bluffs you get views of miles of rolling landscape, of towns nestled on flat floodplain or rising along some crevice in a hill—landscape that must have reminded some of the early German settlers of the Rhineland. The German migrants left their imprint on northeastern Iowa's political geography. The river town of Clinton, settled by German Protestants, still tends to be Republican. Dubuque, farther upriver, is almost entirely German Catholic, and is heavily Democratic in most elections. (This city, made famous by Harold Ross's remark that his *New Yorker* was not edited for "the little old lady in Dubuque," voted as heavily as Manhattan for George McGovern in 1972.) The agriculture here is less intensive than on the flatter plains to the west; the towns somehow seem more isolated and separate. This part of Iowa forms half of the state's 2d Congressional District.

The other half is farther west of the Mississippi, on the plains, with most clustered in and around Cedar Rapids. This is Iowa's second largest city, and has one of its more diversified economies: its big employers include not only agricultural implement manufacturers, but Collins Radio, a high-tech firm. Politically, Cedar Rapids is very marginal, split closely between the parties, as it was in the 1984 general election. The surrounding rural counties usually go Republican.

The 2d District for two decades has voted close to national and state averages; it just missed going for Jimmy Carter in 1976 and was within 2% of the national percentages in the 1980 presidential election. In 1984, like most of Iowa, it was far more favorable to Walter Mondale than was the rest of the nation. In House elections this district has been contested seriously in almost half the elections of the last 20 years, and was held by Democrats for most of that period. But in the late 1970s it saw a Republican trend, particularly because of the abortion issue; Democrats cannot carry the 2d without a big vote in Dubuque, but Democratic Senator Dick Clark actually lost Dubuque in the 1978 election.

Also in 1978 the district's present congressman, Tom Tauke, was first elected. He was only 28 then, a veteran of four years in the Iowa legislature, a Republican elected from Democratic Dubuque, and one of those instinctive politicians who are found more often among the Democrats than the Republicans. Tauke spent some $250,000 in that election, and has not stinted since. He knows how to raise money, and has fundraisers who work political action committees so aggressively that he puts ceilings on the amounts they may raise. Tauke is well situated to raise that kind of money: he sits on the Energy and Commerce Committee, which handles most federal regulatory and air pollution laws; practically every business (and labor) interest in the country is affected, and they are all willing to contribute to ensure they get a hearing.

As a general rule Tauke favors reducing government regulation, but his votes on regulatory issues are not entirely predictable. He tends to favor deregulation of broadcasting and to be dubious about the Democrats' approach to the Superfund. On cultural issues, he seems in line with Iowa opinion: cautiously conservative on cultural issues, often liberal on foreign policy though he has supported the Strategic Defense Initiative and aid to the Nicaraguan contras. He is one of the leaders of the moderate Republican 92 Group, and took a major role in drafting its budget resolution in 1985—a resolution whose approach was closely followed, without much credit, by Budget Chairman William Gray and the Democrats.

Tauke has been reelected by substantial margins against creditable opponents. His 1986 challenger, Democrat Eric Tabor, raised impressive sums and hammered away at Tauke's opposition to Senator Tom Harkin's plan for production controls. But Tauke nonetheless dominated the campaign dialogue and won by a substantial margin.

The People: Pop. 1980: 485,708, up 2.9% 1970–80. Households (1980): 74% family, 41% with children, 65% married couples; 25% housing units rented; median monthly rent: $180; median house value: $43,200. Voting age pop. (1980): 338,272; 1% Black.

1984 Presidential Vote:

Reagan (R)	113,814	(53%)
Mondale (D)	100,647	(46%)

Rep. Thomas J. Tauke (R)

Elected 1978; b. Oct. 11, 1950, Dubuque; home, Dubuque; Loras Col., B.A. 1972, U. of IA, J.D. 1974; Roman Catholic; married (Beverly).

Career: Newspaper reporter, 1969–71; Editor, *The Daily Iowan*, 1973; Practicing atty, 1977–79; IA House of Reps., 1975–79.

Offices: 2244 RHOB 20515, 202-225-2911. Also 698 Central Ave., Dubuque 52001, 319-557-7740; 176 1st Ave., N.E., Cedar Rapids 52402, 319-366-8709; and 116 S. 2d St., Clinton 52732, 319-242-6180.

Committees: *Education and Labor* (8th of 13 R). Subcommittees: Human Resources (Ranking Member); Postsecondary Education. *Energy and Commerce* (7th of 17 R). Subcommittees: Health and the Environment; Telecommunications and Finance; Transportation, Tourism and Hazardous Materials. *Select Committee on Aging* (7th of 26 R). Subcommittee: Retirement Income and Employment (Ranking Member).

Group Ratings

	ADA	ACLU	COPE	CFA	LCV	ACU	NTU	NSI	COC	CEI
1986	30	37	18	25	47	50	62	20	88	72
1985	35	—	18	42	—	57	74	—	82	—

National Journal Ratings

	1986 LIB — 1986 CONS		1985 LIB — 1985 CONS	
Economic	6% —	90%	9% —	88%
Social	41% —	59%	24% —	72%
Foreign	57% —	41%	57% —	42%

Key Votes

1) Lmt Cln Water Act	FOR	5) Retain Gun Cont	FOR	9) Aid Angola Reb	FOR
2) Rpl Tobac Sub	FOR	6) Contra Aid	AGN	10) Tax Reform	FOR
3) Grm-Rdmn Def Red	FOR	7) Lmt Text Imp	AGN	11) S Africa Sanc	FOR
4) Ban Polygraph	FOR	8) Limit SDI	FOR	12) Immig Reform	FOR

Election Results

1986 general	Thomas J. Tauke (R)	88,708	(61%)	($387,840)
	Eric Tabor (D)	55,903	(39%)	($170,816)
1986 primary	Thomas J. Tauke (R)	11,216	(100%)	
1984 general	Thomas J. Tauke (R)	136,893	(64%)	($269,439)
	Joseph J. Welsh (D)	77,335	(36%)	($132,482)

Campaign Contributions and Expenditures

1985-86		Direct Cont. 1985-86		PACS Breakdown 1985-86			
Receipts	$392,207	Indiv.	$173,503	Corp.	$80,121	T/M/H	$64,095
Expend.	$387,840	Party	$9,803	Labor	$625	Agr.	$9,400
Unspent	$103,575	PACS	$173,733	Ideo.	$17,592	CWOS	$1,900

THIRD DISTRICT

Iowa's 3d Congressional District cuts a swath through the central part of the state, from the university town of Iowa City in the south all the way to the Minnesota border. This is prime agricultural land, but the population is not all rural. Iowa City, home of the State University of Iowa, is the liberal bastion of the state politically, a town that prides itself far more on its writers' workshop than on the fact that Herbert Hoover's birthplace is nearby. Waterloo, the district's largest city, is an industrial town, and ailing; the Rath meatpacking plant, taken over by the workers a few years ago when no one else was willing to keep it running, was at the mercy of creditors and has since been shut down by a federal bankruptcy court judge. Waterloo is not, however, a Democratic town; surrounded by heavily Republican rural counties, it is closely divided politically.

The rural counties have their touches of color, most notably the Amana Colonies, near Iowa City, with their old habits and new appliance factories. But mostly people here like to think of their Iowa as just plain farmland, a place as typically American as anywhere in the United States. But like most of Iowa, they often move in the opposite political direction from the rest of the country. In the Reagan years, for example, they have become more Democratic; and the 3d District, represented by Republicans since 1934, finally, after close races in 1974 and 1980, elected a Democratic congressman in 1986.

The occasion was the retirement of Republican Representative Cooper Evans, who had displayed both an impressive knowledge of farm issues and an impressive vote-getting ability. There were contests in both parties' primaries, won by two candidates from Waterloo. Democrat Dave Nagle, the party's state chairman during the 1984 Iowa presidential caucuses, and Republican legislator John McEntee disagreed on Gramm-Rudman, the Strategic Defense Initiative, and school prayer, but the key was probably farming. McEntee suggested that farmers tackle their storage problem by leaving crops in the fields over the winter; but of course most would be destroyed, and Nagle ran ads saying that at least he knows when to harvest corn. That gave him a solid victory. In Washington his fellow Democrats gave him a seat on the House Agriculture Committee, and he seems to have a chance to hold this district as his Republican predecessors have before him.

The People: Pop. 1980: 485,529, up 3.9% 1970–80. Households (1980): 72% family, 38% with children, 64% married couples; 28% housing units rented; median monthly rent: $185; median house value: $43,500. Voting age pop. (1980): 352,455; 2% Black.

1984 Presidential Vote:

	Reagan (R)	118,411	(52%)
	Mondale (D)	108,563	(47%)

Rep. David R. Nagle (D)

Elected 1986; b. Apr. 15, 1943, Grinnell; home, Cedar Falls; U. of Northern IA, 1961–65, U. of IA, LL.B. 1968; Roman Catholic; married (Diane).

Career: Asst. Black Hawk Cnty. Atty., 1969–70; Evansdale City Atty., 1971–74; Chmn., IA Dem. Party, 1982–85.

Offices: 214 CHOB 20515, 202-225-3301. Also 524 Washington St., Waterloo 50701, 319-234-3623; and 102 S. Clinton, Rm. 505, Iowa City 52240, 319-351-0789.

Committees: *Agriculture* (21st of 26 D). Subcommittees: Conservation, Credit, and Rural Development; Livestock, Dairy and Poultry; Wheat, Soybeans and Feed Grains. *Science, Space and Technology* (25th of 27 D). Subcommittees: Science, Research and Technology; Space Science and Applications.

Group Ratings and Key Votes: Newly Elected

Election Results

1986 general	David R. Nagle (D)	83,504	(55%)	($294,811)
	John McIntee (R)......................	69,386	(45%)	($418,486)
1986 primary	David R. Nagle (D)	10,787	(50%)	
	Lowell Norland (D)	9,123	(43%)	
	Anne Meskimen (D)....................	1,434	(7%)	
1984 general	Cooper Evans (R).....................	133,737	(61%)	($366,391)
	Joseph C. Johnston (D)................	86,574	(39%)	($107,462)

Campaign Contributions and Expenditures

1985-86		Direct Cont. 1985-86		PACS Breakdown 1985-86			
Receipts	$291,713	Indiv.	$87,658	Corp.	$9,300	T/M/H	$34,500
Expend.	$294,811	Party	$10,505	Labor	$104,250	Agr.	$2,500
Unspent	$1,618	PACS	$199,832	Ideo.	$49,032	CWOS	$250
		Cand.	$8,600				

FOURTH DISTRICT

The 4th Congressional District of Iowa is the geographical center of the state. It includes Ames, the home of Iowa State University, and the small manufacturing towns of Webster City, Boone, and Newton. But most of its votes are cast in and around Des Moines, Iowa's capital and largest city. Des Moines is the largest financial and commercial center of Iowa; it is a significant though currently depressed manufacturing center as well, whose main product is farm machinery. It is also the home of the *Des Moines Register & Tribune,* one of the nation's few newspapers with statewide circulation and one that is in many ways a leader of opinion in the state. Des Moines is a Democratic city in an historically Republican state, the most Democratic part of Iowa in most elections except for Dubuque and scattered Catholic rural counties.

Representing the 4th District in the House is Neal Smith, a Democrat first elected in 1958, and the senior member of the Iowa delegation. Smith is an old-fashioned farm belt Democrat, one whose liberalism is tempered by a moderate personal temperament and by a constituency which seems reluctant to go overboard in any direction. Caught on the wrong side of a generation gap, he began to enjoy significant seniority just as seniority was being devalued by, among other things, his own proposal to require committee chairmen to be elected. In 1975 he sought to be the first chairman of the Budget Committee; he lost that post to Brock Adams, who became Jimmy Carter's first Secretary of Transportation. In running, Smith may have recognized that the Appropriations Committee, on which he serves, would inevitably lose influence to Budget.

But he also had successes in the 1960s and 1970s on what seemed quixotic crusades when he began, getting tougher meat inspection laws and imposing an anti-nepotism rule on congressmen.

Now Smith is the number four Democrat on Appropriations, behind three other men a decade older. But he didn't get a subcommittee chairmanship until 1980, and the body he chairs—Commerce, Justice, State and Judiciary—was much more powerful in the hands of a ruthless chairman like John Rooney than it is in the hands of a man as scrupulous and fair-minded as Smith. The budgets it handles are not large, and a chairman not determined to interfere in operations will have relatively little influence in policymaking. Nonetheless, Smith manages to make a difference on policy both foreign and domestic. Incidentally, Smith gave up the chair of the Small Business Committee to take the Appropriations subcommittee chair. That's a good indication of the importance of Small Business, a committee with a very limited jurisdiction which maintains a separate existence only because so many members like to tell voters that they sit on it.

Smith has a fair chance of becoming chairman of the full Appropriations Committee some day, and his Democratic colleagues would probably be happy to see him in that position: he is hard-working and capable but not overbearing or dictatorial, and his views on issues are in line with those of most Democrats. His popularity at home seemed great for years, and he never attracted serious opposition. In the Republican year of 1980, however, he was held to 54% of the vote. Since then, former Des Moines broadcaster Ronald Reagan has become less popular in these parts, and Smith's winning percentages have again become very high.

The People: Pop. 1980: 485,480, up 6.6% 1970–80. Households (1980): 70% family, 37% with children, 60% married couples; 30% housing units rented; median monthly rent: $214; median house value: $46,900. Voting age pop. (1980): 356,227; 3% Black, 1% Spanish origin, 1% Asian origin.

1984 Presidential Vote:

Mondale (D)	118,092	(50%)
Reagan (R)	115,898	(49%)

Rep. Neal Smith (D)

Elected 1958; b. Mar. 23, 1920, Hedrick; home, Altoona; MO U. Col., B.A. 1946, Syracuse U., 1946–48, Drake U., LL.B. 1950; United Methodist; married (Beatrix).

Career: Farmer; Army Air Corps, WWII; Asst. Polk Cnty. Atty., 1950–52; Practicing atty., 1952–58; Chmn., Polk Cnty. Bd. of Social Welfare, 1956.

Offices: 2373 RHOB 20515, 202-225-4426. Also 544 Insurance Exchange Bldg., Des Moines 50309, 515-284-4634; and 215 P.O. Bldg., Ames 50010, 515-232-5221.

Committees: *Appropriations* (4th of 35 D). Subcommittees: Commerce, Justice, State and Judiciary (Chairman); Labor–Health and Human Services–Education; Rural Development, Agriculture and Related Agencies. *Small Business* (2d of 27 D). Subcommittee: SBA and the General Economy.

Group Ratings

	ADA	ACLU	COPE	CFA	LCV	ACU	NTU	NSI	COC	CEI
1986	70	75	79	58	47	30	24	4	22	20
1985	75	—	79	75	—	10	29	—	24	—

National Journal Ratings

	1986 LIB	—	1986 CONS	1985 LIB	—	1985 CONS
Economic	65%	—	35%	73%	—	26%
Social	61%	—	37%	81%	—	15%
Foreign	72%	—	27%	85%	—	8%

Key Votes

1) Lmt Cln Water Act	AGN	5) Retain Gun Cont	AGN	9) Aid Angola Reb	AGN
2) Rpl Tobac Sub	AGN	6) Contra Aid	AGN	10) Tax Reform	FOR
3) Grm-Rdmn Def Red	AGN	7) Lmt Text Imp	AGN	11) S Africa Sanc	FOR
4) Ban Polygraph	FOR	8) Limit SDI	FOR	12) Immig Reform	FOR

Election Results

1986 general	Neal Smith (D)	107,271	(68%)	($100,675)
	Robert R. Lockard (R)	49,641	(32%)	($65,866)
1986 primary	Neal Smith (D)	23,796	(89%)	
	Harry Clark (D)	2,964	(11%)	
1984 general	Neal Smith (D)	136,922	(61%)	($107,754)
	Robert R. Lockard (R)	88,717	(39%)	($73,075)

Campaign Contributions and Expenditures

1985-86		Direct Cont. 1985-86		PACS Breakdown 1985-86			
Receipts	$153,681	Indiv.	$29,024	Corp.	$21,550	T/M/H	$47,600
Expend.	$100,675	Party	$1,304	Labor	$31,170	Agr.	$4,250
Unspent	$143,017	PACS	$112,950	Ideo.	$7,500	CWOS	$880

FIFTH DISTRICT

On the ground, or even from the air, it's not clear—the line that passes north and south through the Great Plains separating the well-watered croplands of the east from the more arid grazing lands of the west. In fact, it's a highly irregular line, since most Plains farmers fatten hogs with their corn and most cattle raisers grow some of their own feed. But there is a difference. As you go farther west, from the Mississippi to the Missouri River, the plains grow browner and less green, the towns become less frequent and less thickly settled, and the spaces seem more wide open.

Across this invisible, irregular line lies the 5th Congressional District of Iowa. On the map it appears only mildly irregular in shape, the southeastern quadrant of the state, roughly, minus Des Moines. In fact there are significant economic and political differences. The counties south of Des Moines are classic corn and hog country, with a little metropolitan development; their politics is ancestrally Republican but in the 1980s—when corn and hog prices have not been propped up as much by the government as by wheat prices—they have voted for Democrats in some races. To the northwest of Des Moines, around the small farm machine manufacturing city of Fort Dodge, you are getting closer to wheat country, though crop patterns are mixed; Fort Dodge is usually Democratic, and so are some rural Catholic counties.

All these areas are within the radius of Des Moines television stations and the *Des Moines Register & Tribune,* relatively liberal media. The counties to the south and west, on the other side of the invisible line, are within reach of the Omaha television stations and the *Omaha World Herald,* more conservative in tone. These counties also raise more beef and fewer hogs. Nowhere were these differences more pronounced than in the closely contested 1984 race for Congress. The 5th District had been represented for ten years by Democrat Tom Harkin, who was running for the Senate; it was apparent that Harkin and Ronald Reagan would both carry the district. Both parties fielded strong candidates. Democrat Jerry Fitzgerald was once a leader in the legislature and ran two respectable races for governor. Republican Jim Ross Lightfoot was a farm broadcaster well known (as Jim Ross) in the counties around Omaha, which cast 40% of the district's votes. Fitzgerald was known as one of the rising young liberals in his party. Lightfoot was hailed as one of the Republicans' articulate and attractive new conservatives.

The race was one of the closest of any in the country. But it wasn't close in any of the three major parts of the district. The counties around Fort Dodge went 60% for Fitzgerald. The counties south of Des Moines were 56% for the Democrat. But in the 11 Omaha-area counties, Lightfoot ran virtually even with President Reagan and got 63% of the votes. This was enough for a 51% Lightfoot victory.

Lightfoot has turned out to be not only a folksy campaigner but a supple politician. He managed to put a relief provision for farmers forced out of business into the tax reform bill. He organized a plan to help drought-stricken southern farmers ship their cattle to winter in Iowa, which is cheaper than shipping hay south. He hustled to get more federal loan money for small businesses, to support the Job Corps because of local successes. On cultural issues he is the most conservative member of the Iowa delegation. But he was one of the few Republicans to oppose aid to the Nicaraguan contras. All this plus his folksy presence in the district made Lightfoot much stronger for 1986 than Democrats expected. His opponent pushed Tom Harkin's farm production controls referendum bill, but to no avail. Lightfoot won with 59%, carrying every county in the district—the first congressman to do so.

The People: Pop. 1980: 485,639, up 1.5% 1970–80. Households (1980): 75% family, 39% with children, 67% married couples; 24% housing units rented; median monthly rent: $144; median house value: $33,400. Voting age pop. (1980): 346,800; 1% Spanish origin.

1984 Presidential Vote:

Reagan (R)	122,424	(57%)
Mondale (D)	89,132	(42%)

Rep. Jim Ross Lightfoot (R)

Elected 1984; b. Sept. 27, 1938, Sioux City; home, Shenandoah; Roman Catholic; married (Nancy).

Career: Army, 1955–56; Mgr., farm equip. manufacturing facility; Owner, ice cream, lingerie stores; Farm editor, KMA Radio, 1971–84.

Offices: 1609 LHOB 20515, 202-225-3806. Also 501 W. Lowell, Shenandoah 51601, 712-246-1984; 105 Pearl, Council Bluffs 51501, 712-325-5572; 220 W. Salem, Indianola 50125, 515-961-0591; 908 1st Ave. S., Walden Plaza, Ste. 7, Ft. Dodge 50501, 515-955-5319.

Committees: *Government Operations* (8th of 15 R). Subcommittee: Human Resources and Intergovernmental Relations (Ranking Member). *Public Works and Transportation* (16th of 20 R). Subcommittees: Aviation; Surface Transportation; Water Resources. *Select Committee on Aging* (16th of 26 R). Subcommittee: Health and Long-Term Care.

Group Ratings

	ADA	ACLU	COPE	CFA	LCV	ACU	NTU	NSI	COC	CEI
1986	10	10	19	8	21	30	24	80	94	64
1985	10	—	24	42	—	81	63	—	82	—

National Journal Ratings

	1986 LIB — 1986 CONS		1985 LIB — 1985 CONS	
Economic	13% —	85%	29% —	70%
Social	11% —	85%	0% —	76%
Foreign	45% —	54%	37% —	60%

Key Votes

1) Lmt Cln Water Act	FOR	5) Retain Gun Cont	AGN	9) Aid Angola Reb	FOR
2) Rpl Tobac Sub	FOR	6) Contra Aid	AGN	10) Tax Reform	FOR
3) Grm-Rdmn Def Red	FOR	7) Lmt Text Imp	AGN	11) S Africa Sanc	FOR
4) Ban Polygraph	AGN	8) Limit SDI	AGN	12) Immig Reform	FOR

Election Results

1986 general	Jim Ross Lightfoot (R)	85,025	(59%)	($474,179)
	Scott Hughes (D)	58,552	(41%)	($250,384)
1986 primary	Jim Ross Lightfoot (R)	22,613	(100%)	
1984 general	Jim Ross Lightfoot (R)	104,632	(51%)	($404,128)
	Jerry Fitzgerald (D)	101,435	(49%)	($449,359)

Campaign Contributions and Expenditures

1985-86		Direct Cont. 1985-86		PACS Breakdown 1985-86			
Receipts	$464,116	Indiv.	$231,687	Corp.	$70,270	T/M/H	$68,328
Expend.	$474,179	Party	$9,156	Labor	$200	Agr.	$16,450
Unspent	$3,467	PACS	$202,635	Ideo.	$37,324	CWOS	$10,063

SIXTH DISTRICT

The fertile plains of northwestern Iowa make up the 6th Congressional District. Except for Sioux City, an old river city that is larger than its neighbor, Sioux Falls, South Dakota, and Mason City, a manufacturing town in the eastern end of the district, the 6th is almost entirely rural, with small farm market towns and grain elevators towering here and there over the flat or gently rolling landscape. The district has traditionally been Republican, as most of Iowa has been, but with notable exceptions—the kind of political divergences from the normal that dot the political maps of the Great Plains states. These arise from settlement by various ethnic groups. A colony of German Catholics or Norwegians, to name only one usually Democratic and one usually Republican group, would send encouraging letters back to the Old Country, and sometimes would forward steamship passage and railroad fare so that relatives and friends could make their way to new homes in Iowa or Kansas or the Dakotas. Such history makes sense of the Republican preference of Sioux County, Iowa (settled by Dutch Protestants and 82% for Ronald Reagan in 1984) or the Democratic leanings of nearby Palo Alto County (settled by German Catholics and 52% for Walter Mondale in 1984). Palo Alto had a further distinction: until 1984, it was one of two American bellwether counties that had always voted for the winner in presidential elections. The last one left is Crook County, Oregon.

The 6th District was the unlikely setting in 1986 for the election of a television actor to Congress. Fred Grandy is known to millions of Americans after 10 years of prime time (and will be known to millions more thanks to reruns) as Gopher, the purser on *The Love Boat*. Now he is a Republican congressman. He has genuine roots in the district, but he left to attend prep school, where he roomed with David Eisenhower, and then went on to Harvard. His Republican allegiance must have been cemented in fire then: those were years of students riots, but after college Grandy went to work for the 6th District's Republican congressman, Wiley Mayne. Mayne, hard pressed in the 1972 election, in an act of political courage which has not been appreciated, cast a damaging vote against the impeachment of Richard Nixon, and was beaten in 1974 by Democrat Berkley Bedell; it was Bedell's retirement, because of a chronic illness he got from a tick bite, that set off the 1986 race Grandy won.

Grandy's victory is the more impressive because he beat Bedell's chief district aide, Clayton Hodgson, at a time of farm distress, and against the strong opposition of the very popular Bedell. The millionaire inventor of monofilament fishing line, Bedell worked hard for high price supports in farm bills and against American military intervention abroad; Hodgson agreed and Grandy disagreed with these stands. But farm issues do not seem to have helped Democrats much in Iowa in 1986; voters recognize that subsidies are going down, not up, and seem to have an air of resignation about their problems. Moreover, Grandy seemed thoroughly up to speed and knowledgeable about farm issues. Early on in the campaign voters came out to see Gopher in person. But he seems to have convinced them that he was a genuine article. He won the June primary with 68% of the vote, and when the Democrats insisted he release a tape of an appearance on the Johnny Carson show, where he made some mildly disparaging remarks about Iowa, he balked for a week, then relented, and didn't seem to be hurt. The Democrats may have spent too much time bellyaching about Hollywood actors, while Grandy was airing endorsements from Iowa's favorite 1986 candidate, Senator Chuck Grassley.

In the end Grandy won with 51% of the vote, one of 1986's closest results. Given his background and party label, this represents a strong showing. He has a seat on the Agriculture Committee, and if he masters farm issues there as well as he did on the campaign trail, he may be able to turn this farm country into a safe Republican seat—a result which would be much to the chagrin of Bedell, who is surely regretting his decision to retire.

The People: Pop. 1980: 485,491, dn. 0.8% 1970–80. Households (1980): 74% family, 38% with children, 66% married couples; 25% housing units rented; median monthly rent: $152; median house value: $36,600. Voting age pop. (1980). 348,641; 1% Spanish origin.

1984 Presidential Vote:

Reagan (R)	122,484	(57%)
Mondale (D)	90,074	(42%)

Rep. Fred Grandy (R)

Elected 1986; b. June 29, 1948, Sioux City; home, Sioux City; Harvard Col., B.A. 1970; Episcopalian; married (Catherine).

Career: Asst. to U.S. Rep. Wiley Mayne, 1970–71; Professional actor, 1975–85.

Offices: 1711 LHOB 20515, 202-225-5476. Also 508 Pierce St., Sioux City 51101, 712-252-3733; and 211 N. Delaware, Rm. 307, Mason City, 50401, 515-424-0233.

Committees: *Agriculture* (15th of 17 R). Subcommittees: Conservation, Credit and Rural Development; Department Operations, Research and Foreign Agriculture; Wheat, Soybeans and Feed Grains. *Education and Labor* (12th of 13 R). Subcommittees: Elementary, Secondary and Vocational Education; Employment Opportunities; Human Resources. *Select Cmtee. on Children, Youth and Families* (12th of 12 R). Task Force: Crisis Intervention.

Group Ratings and Key Votes: Newly Elected

Election Results

1986 general	Fred Grandy (R)	81,861	(51%)	($677,082)
	Clayton Hodgson (D)	78,807	(49%)	($407,916)
1986 primary	Fred Grandy (R)	19,498	(68%)	
	George P. Moriarty (R)	5,248	(18%)	
	Terry Jobst (R)	4,028	(14%)	
1984 general	Berkley Bedell (D)	127,706	(62%)	($357,150)
	Darrel W. Rensink (R)	78,182	(38%)	($243,165)

Campaign Contributions and Expenditures

1985-86		Direct Cont. 1985-86		PACS Breakdown 1985-86			
Receipts	$680,193	Indiv.	$253,442	Corp.	$93,090	T/M/H	$77,219
Expend.	$677,082	Party	$16,254	Labor	$0	Agr.	$5,500
Debts	$3,111	PACS	$239,415	Ideo.	$61,606	CWOS	$2,000
		Cand.	$166,971				

KANSAS

"I have a feeling we're not in Kansas any more," Dorothy said to Toto, gazing at the wonders of the land of Oz. The line means something—it did in 1900, when L. Frank Baum wrote *The Wizard of Oz*, and in 1939, when MGM made the movie, and it does today—because Kansas is a symbol of what is ordinary about America. Smack in the center of the 48 contiguous states, about as far as you can get from either ocean, and hundreds of miles from the Rockies, which start rivers moving down over the slightly rolling plains that tilt imperceptibly toward the east, Kansas seems topographically and geographically unremarkable. Settled almost entirely by whites of Anglo-Saxon stock, full of small towns and farms and entirely lacking a big city, Kansas is demographically the picture of ordinary small town America.

Yet Kansas's very ordinariness makes it atypical. Kansas was born middle class and Middle American, and has remained both, while other states and regions go through crises and fads. It is a farming state in a country long since industrial and now struggling to find post-industrial labels to attach to itself. It seems (a little misleadingly) ethnically homogeneous in a nation whose very essence is ethnic diversity. Politically, its seeming ordinariness also sets it apart. This has long been one of the most Republican states in a nation that, from the 1930s to the 1970s and perhaps again, seemed mostly Democratic. While most states elected mostly Democrats to the U.S. Senate in the half-century after 1932, Kansas has elected nothing but Republicans. And despite Kansas's reputation as a conservative, well-ordered state, its political history has been punctuated with bitter controversy and even violence, of rebellion against society's established rules and fierce resentment of the powers that be.

Certainly Kansas's beginnings were anything but placid. The land here was almost vacant in 1850, when the Kansas–Nebraska Act of 1854 left the question of whether Kansas would be free or slave territory to its voters—at a time when it didn't yet have any. Almost immediately pro-slavery southerners and abolitionist New Englanders were financing like-minded settlers and moving them to Kansas. Soon armed fighting broke out between Democratic "bushwhackers" and free soil "jayhawkers." Pro-slavery raiders from Missouri rode into the territory, and John Brown massacred anti-abolitionists at Pottawatomie Creek. This was "Bleeding Kansas"—a major national issue and one of the direct causes of the Civil War. When the South seceded in 1861, Kansas was admitted to the Union as a free state, with a solid Republican majority. It has been a Republican state ever since.

But it has also been a farm state, with dozens of farm revolts, the greatest of which was the Populist uprising sparked by the depression of the 1890s. The 1880s were years of high rainfall on the plains, when Kansas attracted hundreds of thousands of new settlers. All at once the rainfall and world wheat prices plummeted; the Kansas plains seemed unable to support all who had come to depend on them. Kansas's boom went bust; some Kansas counties never again reached the population levels recorded in the 1890 Census. Suddenly Populists were winning Kansas elections, politicians like "Sockless Jerry" Simpson and Mary Ellen Lease ("What you farmers should do is to raise less corn and more hell"). Populists advocated arcane doctrines like free silver and commodity credit programs. William Jennings Bryan, the lion of the prairies, was their man, and he swept Kansas in 1896. But the revolt was soon over. Soon after 1896 the nation began to enjoy an extended period of agricultural prosperity so great that parity prices are still based on those years. Small town Republicans were back in the majority, and Bryan lost Kansas in 1900 and 1908.

Echoes of the Populist revolt have reverberated in Kansas every few years, with farm revolts against the Republicans in the early 1930s, the late 1950s, and the early 1970s, and farm revolts against the Democrats in the late 1960s and again in the late 1970s. Fewer Kansans than ever

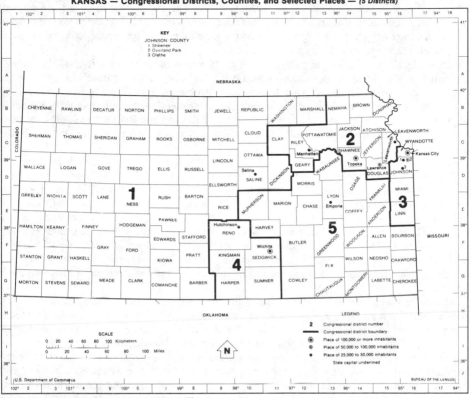

KANSAS — Congressional Districts, Counties, and Selected Places — (5 Districts)

Congressional districts established June 2, 1982; all other boundaries are as of January 1, 1980.

are actually farmers, but the state's economy still depends heavily on agriculture; and however much they may favor free enterprise in the abstract, Kansans believe that government is responsible for the condition of the farm economy. Farmers may be our largest class of entrepreneurs, but the existence of so many practitioners of free enterprise has spawned an irresistible political demand for government action.

Farmers, like all entrepreneurs, are always nervous. Plenteous crops may bring prices down or a poor crop may produce little income, rain can bring disaster and so can sunshine. Agricultural commodities are traded on the world market and their prices can be pulled downward by a green revolution in the Punjab or good weather in the wheatfields around Chartres. Farmers and those who depend on them crave reassurance and help, and they have received it from the federal government, in the form of subsidies, price supports, and technical assistance; and they argue, vigorously and vociferously, over the exact terms of these sometimes all-important government programs. No set of abstract principles justifies this jerry-built structure, but this can be said for it: it mostly works. American agriculture is incredibly productive, even if that productivity costs the taxpayers lots of money and often translates into losses rather than profits for many farmers.

But no farm revolt has materialized in Kansas in the 1980s. Just as voters in cities 15 years ago decided that the federal government couldn't do anything to stop crime, so voters in at least this part of the farm belt seem to have given up on the idea that the federal government can restore days of high crop prices amid plenteous harvests. Sharp drops in farm prices and land values, increasingly expensive farm programs which nonetheless leave farmers with lower incomes—

these have undercut faith that anything can be done by politicians, and have left elections to be settled on other issues. And if farmers' profits are down, and if Wichita's private aircraft business has been ailing, Kansas's economy has nevertheless been growing; unemployment is low and real incomes are up. Most Kansans' economic condition is far less precarious and far more comfortable than it was even a generation ago.

Meanwhile, Kansas has long been loyal to the party which, though a minority, has always been dominated by the white Anglo-Saxon Protestants who believed (inaccurately) they were the majority; and it has remained loyal, despite farm problems, as that party has proved itself capable of winning national majorities in election after election. For the moment, Kansas is happy with a party and its leading politicians—Ronald Reagan and Robert Dole—who for them symbolize the ordinariness that made Oz so easily distinguishable not only to Dorothy but to Toto, too.

Senators. Clearly the leading politician from Kansas, one of the towering political figures in Washington despite his switch from majority to minority leader after the 1986 elections, quite possibly the next President of the United States, is Robert Dole, from Russell, Kansas. He is also now one of the most experienced politicians in Washington: he was first elected to Congress in 1960, and has served longer than all but seven other senators (Inouye, Matsunaga, Stennis, Burdick, Thurmond, Byrd, Proxmire) and has been serving as a Republican in Congress longer than any of them. He is, after two years as Senate Majority Leader, now the Senate Minority Leader; he ranks just behind Bob Packwood on the Finance Committee and just behind Richard Lugar on Agriculture, and he has more seniority and would outrank them but for his leadership position.

Dole, as he himself insists, hasn't changed much at all—nor has his sharp, caustic wit. He remains, literally, a Kansas Republican, a man whose values and beliefs remain deeply rooted in Kansas and its traditional Republican Party, but who is also, by dint of a generation of experience, a Washington insider, a politician who knows the Senate, the lobbyists, the media— and has seen them all come and go. But remember that he comes from a state where Republicans are the majority, and where the party's base is broad. It includes not just rich people and country club members, but the mechanic at the garage and the clerk at the feed store; not just the banker and the lawyer, but the farmer and the minister. Kansas Republicanism believes in free enterprise, but after years of farm depressions it also understands that the untrammeled operation of the free market is going to hurt a lot of people. And, living in small towns where everyone knows everyone else, Kansans see the problems of the poor, not as theoretical, but as practical and personal.

Add to that background Bob Dole's grievous war injuries, and you can understand why he is one of the few Republicans who seems instinctively compassionate. Dole was seriously injured in World War II; his recovery was long and painful; he does not have use of his right hand, suffers considerable pain, and has difficulty dressing himself. The note of bitterness in his reference to "Democrat wars" in his 1976 debate with Walter Mondale comes from the same experiences that have made him one of the leading congressional advocates of the handicapped (well before his colleagues began putting sign language interpreters in the corners of their ads). A strain of compassion runs through his career. With George McGovern, he was the architect of the food stamp program—the one form of aid to the really poor that grew in the 1970s and which, thanks to Dole and the perception that it is a voucher system, was not much cut back in the 1980s. Operating from a seat on the Judiciary Committee, he rescued the Voting Rights Act from deadlock in 1982 and got it renewed.

Yet Dole remains a strong partisan. In his first Senate term, he was chosen in 1971 by the Nixon White House to be Republican national chairman because of his vehement and usually volunteered defenses of Administration policy. Relieved of that job in early 1973, he made some acerbic comments about Watergate, but was a faithful enough party man to be considered a conservative ticket-balancer when he was chosen as Gerald Ford's vice presidential candidate in 1976. In the first Reagan term, as chairman of the Senate Finance Committee, he aroused the ire of administration supply-siders by his lack of enthusiasm for their doctrine and his constant pushing, dazzlingly succcessful in 1982, for tax increases. But Dole was moved by nothing more than the longtime Republican belief in balanced budgets; as a young congressman in the 1960s he voted against the Keynesian tax cuts of the Kennedy-Johnson Administration, and so it's not surprising that he was skeptical about the Reagan cuts in the 1980s. And his tax increase passed almost exclusively with Republican votes.

Dole's victory as majority leader after the 1984 elections was a surprise, engineered in part with support from conservatives like Jesse Helms; also a surprise were the moves Dole made to please the Republican right. He stood up in 1985 against what he considered overgenerous farm bills, even though he was up for reelection in Kansas in 1986. He supported vigorously aid to the Nicaraguan contras and to Angola rebel Jonas Savimbi. He held back from sanctions on South Africa. He jumped ahead of the Administration in denouncing SALT II. Even more than Howard Baker, and more like Tip O'Neill in the House, Dole relied almost entirely on his own party to get his majorities, and didn't dicker with the opposition. With parliamentary legerdemain, he got Indiana Republican Daniel Manion confirmed as judge. Dole also hired prominent conservative staffers and kept his door open to conservative activists, and campaigned actively for Republicans of all stripes. The New Right's expectations, after losing on abortion constitutional amendments and other issues, have been diminished, and Dole, once labelled by Newt Gingrich as "the tax collector for the welfare state," had little trouble exceeding them.

Dole's exercise of responsibility under pressure, his opening to the right while maintaining his reputation as a moderate, left him surprisingly well positioned in early 1987 for his expected run for the presidency. Even his unwanted demotion to minority leader will presumably give him more time to campaign, and the Iran-contra scandal and his quick demands that the administration get out the truth propelled George Bush downward and Dole upward in the polls. He is, in short, acceptable to both the right and left of his party. His support in Kansas seems enthusiastic: the *Wichita Eagle-Beacon* endorsed him early in 1987, and 500 Kansans signed up to be a "sunflower army" to work for him in Iowa and adjoining states. But his earlier excursions into national politics have been disastrous: his partisanship as national chairman in 1971 and 1972 and vice presidential candidate in 1976 did little to help him. His hapless 1980 campaign, with little staff and less money, he must hope people have forgotten. Meanwhile, his sardonic wit continues to sparkle, and his performance on the job, under conflicting political pressures, within time limits, and in full public view has given the public a better sense of how he would perform in the White House than they have of any other presidential candidate. As of 1987 that was a pretty favorable impression overall.

In Kansas Dole's popularity has had its ups and downs. Elected to the House from western Kansas as a farm revolt was receding, he had a fairly safe seat, and moved to the Senate without much problem in the politically divisive year of 1968. But he was nearly beaten in 1974 by Representative Bill Roy, and had to resort to the abortion issue in the last weeks. He did not attract serious opposition in 1980 or 1986, and was reelected with large margins both times.

Kansas's other Senator, Nancy Landon Kassebaum, has a fine Kansas heritage, for she is the daughter of Alf Landon, one-time governor and the Republican nominee against FDR in 1936. Landon, more progressive than his 1930s reputation, had the pleasure of seeing his daughter elected and reelected to the Senate in his 90s, and stands to become on September 9, 1987, the first American presidential nominee to reach the age of 100. Kassebaum entered the Senate with less than dazzling credentials of her own (she had served on a local school board), and proceeded hesitatingly at first; but she has emerged as a thoughtful legislator whose lead is often followed by others.

On the Budget Committee, for example, she has worked to put together bipartisan budget resolutions. On Foreign Affairs, she has chaired the Africa subcommittee and took the lead in advocating limited economic sanctions. In both cases she broke somewhat from her party and her own previous positions, and with some reluctance. But she thought that events required positive action. She is generally less hawkish and less likely to back assertive policies than most other Republicans. In Central America, Kassebaum led the team monitoring El Salvador's elections and tends to favor negotiated rather than military solutions. She has been skeptical about weapons systems and Pentagon procurement policies, too: she became an MX opponent in 1985 and has been a leader of the congressional military reform caucus and efforts to create a weapons testing office. On economic issues, she is counted as somewhat more moderate than the median Senate Republicans; on cultural issues, she is near the midpoint of the Senate.

Kassebaum's key electoral victory was in the 1978 Republican primary, where she led eight other candidates with 31% of the vote. (One, Wayne Angell, is now on the Federal Reserve Board; another, Jan Meyers, is congresswoman from the 3d District.) In the general election she ran comfortably ahead of Dole's 1974 opponent, Bill Roy. She had little trouble winning reelection in 1984: no serious Democrat ran. Her 76% of the vote and 545,000-vote margin are records for Kansas Senate elections. She said when she first ran that she would retire after two terms, but Kansas Republican leaders want her to change her mind, especially if Bob Dole is elected president; then there might be two seats up with no elected incumbent, seats which popular Democratic congressmen like Dan Glickman and Jim Slattery could conceivably win.

Presidential politics. Kansas is so heavily Republican in presidential elections that it is left off the calculations: everyone knows where it will go. Its Republican national convention delegates surely will go in 1988 to Bob Dole; its Democratic delegation will be small and probably not influential.

Governor. Oddly, Kansas, which last elected a Democratic Senator in 1932, had Democratic governors for 20 of the 30 years leading up to 1986; two of them were named Docking. In 1986 the state nearly elected a third, 31-year-old lieutenant governor Tom Docking, grandson of Governor George (1957–61) and son of Governor Bob (1967–75); he won the primary to succeed Democratic Governor John Carlin, who over eight years got a severance tax imposed and made Kansas more export-conscious. But the winner instead was Mike Hayden, a Vietnam combat veteran, rough-hewn rancher, and speaker of the House, a tough negotiator and a biologist who says he entered politics because of "environmental concerns." He won a seven-candidate primary despite being far outspent. Docking criticized Hayden for urging an embargo on grain sales to South Africa but was put on the defensive when Hayden called on him to sell stocks in companies that do business there. Hayden's victory was not large; but it's interesting that he and other Republicans, despite farm troubles, won every 1986 gubernatorial election in Great Plains farm states. For presidential politics, Hayden's win means that if Dole is elected President, he can be sure a Republican, perhaps Representative Pat Roberts, will take his place in the Senate for two years; then that seat plus Kassebaum's would be up in 1990.

Congressional districting. Kansas redistricted its congressional seats, after some tussling between Carlin and the Republican legislature, with only a few significant changes. Democrats now hold two seats, both because of the personal popularity of the incumbents.

The People: Est. Pop. 1986: 2,461,000; Pop. 1980: 2,363,679, up 4.1% 1980–86 and 5.1% 1970–80; 1.02% of U.S. total, 32d largest. 17% with 1–3 yrs. col., 16% with 4+ yrs. col.; 10.1% below poverty level. Single ancestry: 15% German, 11% English, 4% Irish, 1% Swedish, French, Dutch. Households (1980): 73% family, 38% with children, 63% married couples; 29.8% housing units rented; median monthly rent: $168; median house value: $37,800. Voting age pop. (1980): 1,714,644; 5% Black, 2% Spanish origin, 1% Asian origin, 1% American Indian. Registered voters (1986): 1,172,670; 341,200 D (29%), 483,520 R (41%); 347,950 unaffiliated and minor parties (30%).

1986 Share of Federal Tax Burden: $7,936,000,000; 1.06% of U.S. total, 29th largest.

1986 Share of Federal Expenditures

	Total		Non-Defense		Defense	
Total Expend	$8,757m	(1.05%)	$5,913m	(0.98%)	$2,844m	(1.24%)
St/Lcl Grants	884m	(0.79%)	883m	(0.78%)	1m	(2.90%)
Salary/Wages	1,265m	(1.05%)	535m	(0.91%)	730m	(1.18%)
Pymnts to Indiv	3,769m	(1.03%)	3,605m	(1.04%)	164m	(0.92%)
Procurement	2,166m	(1.05%)	217m	(0.39%)	1,949m	(1.30%)
Research/Other	673m	(2.52%)	673m	(2.53%)	0m	(0%)

Political Lineup: Governor, Mike Hayden (R); Lt. Gov., Jack Walker (R); Secy. of State, Bill Graves (R); Atty. Gen., Robert T. Stephan (R); Treasurer, Joan Finney (D); Commissioner of Insurance, Fletcher Bell (R). State Senate, 40 (24 R and 16 D); State House of Representatives, 125 (74 R and 51 D). Senators, Robert Dole (R) and Nancy Landon Kassebaum (R). Representatives, 5 (3 R and 2 D).

1984 Presidential Vote

Reagan (R) 677,296 (66%)
Mondale (D) 333,149 (33%)

1980 Presidential Vote

Reagan (R) 566,812 (58%)
Carter (D) 326,150 (33%)
Anderson (I) 68,231   (7%)

GOVERNOR

Gov. Mike Hayden (R)

Elected 1986, term expires Jan. 1991; b. Mar. 16, 1944, Atwood; home, Atwood; KS St. U., B.S. 1966; Ft. Hayes U., M.S., 1974; United Methodist; married (Patti).

Career: Army, 1967–70; KS House of Reps., 1972–86, Speaker, 1983–86.

Office: State Capitol, 2d Flr., Topeka 66612, 913-296-3232.

Election Results

1986 gen.	Mike Hayden (R)		436,267	(52%)
	Tom Docking (D)		404,338	(48%)
1986 prim.	Mike Hayden (R)		99,669	(37%)
	Larry Jones (R)		85,989	(32%)
	Jack Brier (R)		37,410	(14%)
	Gene Bicknell (R)		25,733	(10%)
	Richard Peckham (R)		18,876	(7%)
1982 gen.	John W. Carlin (D)		405,309	(53%)
	Sam Hardage (R)		339,700	(44%)

SENATORS

Sen. Robert Dole (R)

Elected 1968, seat up 1992; b. July 22, 1923, Russell; home, Russell; U. of KS, Washburn Municipal U., A.B., LL.B. 1952; United Methodist; married (Mary Elizabeth).

Career: Army, WWII; KS House of Reps., 1951–53; Russell Cnty. Atty., 1953–61; U.S. House of Reps., 1961–69; Chmn., Repub. Natl. Cmtee., 1971–73; Repub. Nominee for Vice Pres., 1976.

Offices: 141 HSOB 20510, 202-224-6521. Also 636 Minnesota Ave., Kansas City 66101, 913-371-6108; 444 S.E. Quincy, Ste. 392, Topeka 66603, 913-295-2745; 100 N. Broadway, Wichita 67202, 316-263-4956; and 76 Parsons Plaza, Ste. 102, Parsons 67357, 316-421-5380.

Committees: *Minority Leader. Agriculture, Nutrition, and Forestry* (2d of 9 R). Subcommittees: Agricultural Production and Stabilization of Prices; Nutrition and Investigations (Ranking Member). *Finance* (2d of 9 R). Subcommittees: Health; International Debt; Social Security and Family Policy (Ranking Member). *Rules and Administration* (2nd of 7 R). *Joint Committee on Taxation.*

Group Ratings

	ADA	ACLU	COPE	CFA	LCV	ACU	NTU	NSI	COC	CEI
1986	0	7	16	13	35	91	53	100	89	77
1985	0	—	17	7	—	91	64	—	90	—

National Journal Ratings

	1986 LIB — 1986 CONS	1985 LIB — 1985 CONS
Economic	0% — 84%	0% — 86%
Social	21% — 77%	0% — 83%
Foreign	18% — 77%	22% — 70%

Key Votes

1) Ease Gun Cont	FOR	5) Grm-Rdmn Def Red	FOR	9) Rehnquist Nom	FOR
2) Immig Reform	FOR	6) Contra Aid	FOR	10) Tax Reform	FOR
3) Lmt Text Imp	FOR	7) SDI Funding	FOR	11) Drug Death Pen	AGN
4) Aid Tobac Ind	FOR	8) Lmt PAC Contrib	AGN	12) S Africa Sanc	AGN

Election Results

1986 general	Robert Dole (R)	576,902	(70%)	($1,517,585)
	Guy MacDonald (D)	246,664	(30%)	
1986 primary	Robert Dole (R)	228,301	(84%)	
	Shirley J. Ashley Landis (R)	42,237	(16%)	
1980 general	Robert Dole (R)	598,686	(64%)	($1,224,494)
	John Simpson (D)	340,271	(36%)	($323,792)

Campaign Contributions and Expenditures

1985-86		Direct Cont. 1985-86		PACS Breakdown 1985-86			
Receipts	$2,640,050	Indiv.	$1,298,106	Corp.	$627,264	T/M/H	$300,019
Expend.	$1,517,585	Party	$15,275	Labor	$22,000	Agr.	$27,000
Unspent	$2,166,732	PACS	$1,036,433	Ideo.	$48,900	CWOS	$11,250

Sen. Nancy Landon Kassebaum (R)

Elected 1978, seat up 1990; b. July 29, 1932, Topeka; home, Wichita; U. of KS, B.A. 1954, U. of MI, M.A. 1956; Episcopalian; divorced.

Career: Member, Maize Sch. Bd., 1972–75; Staff of U.S. Sen. James B. Pearson, 1975.

Offices: 302 RSOB 20510, 202-224-4774. Also 444 S.E. Quincy St., Topeka 66683, 913-295-2888; 8th and Grant, Garden City 67846, 316-276-3423; 4200 Somerset, Ste. 152, Prairie Village 66208, 913-648-3103; and 111 N. Market, Wichita 67202, 316-269-6251.

Committees: *Budget* (3rd of 11 R). *Commerce, Science, and Transportation* (3rd of 9 R). Subcommittees: Aviation (Chairman); Science, Technology, and Space; Surface Transportation. *Foreign Relations* (3rd of 9 R). Subcommittees: African Affairs (Ranking Member); Western Hemisphere and Peace Corps Affairs. *Select Committee on Ethics* (3rd of 3 R).

Group Ratings

	ADA	ACLU	COPE	CFA	LCV	ACU	NTU	NSI	COC	CEI
1986	45	28	21	33	8	45	57	70	58	59
1985	35	—	20	21	—	48	61	—	69	—

National Journal Ratings

	1986 LIB — 1986 CONS		1985 LIB — 1985 CONS	
Economic	29% —	70%	31% —	68%
Social	45% —	52%	56% —	38%
Foreign	51% —	47%	54% —	44%

Key Votes

1) Ease Gun Cont	FOR	5) Grm-Rdmn Def Red	AGN	9) Rehnquist Nom	FOR
2) Immig Reform	FOR	6) Contra Aid	FOR	10) Tax Reform	FOR
3) Lmt Text Imp	AGN	7) SDI Funding	AGN	11) Drug Death Pen	AGN
4) Aid Tobac Ind	FOR	8) Lmt PAC Contrib	FOR	12) S Africa Sanc	FOR

Election Results

1984 general	Nancy Landon Kassebaum (R)	757,402	(76%)	($355,077)
	James R. Maher (D)	211,664	(21%)	($30,444)
1984 primary	Nancy Landon Kassebaum (R)	214,664	(100%)	
1978 general	Nancy Landon Kassebaum (R)	405,354	(54%)	($856,644)
	Bill Roy (D)	317,602	(42%)	($813,754)

Campaign Contributions and Expenditures

1983-84		Direct Cont. 1983-84		PACS Breakdown 1983-84			
Receipts	$570,629	Indiv.	$288,952	Corp.	$157,930	T/M/H	$81,217
Expend.	$355,077	Party	$19,845	Labor	$9,068	Agr.	$2,000
Unspent	$217,804	PACS	$214,269	Ideo.	$23,445	CWOS	$4,050

FIRST DISTRICT

More than half of Kansas's land area lies in the 1st Congressional District, which contains more counties (58) than any other congressional district in the country except the three directly to the north, the 3d of Nebraska and the at-large districts of North and South Dakota. That fact is more than just a bit of trivia; it tells us a good deal about the expectations of the people who first settled this part of Kansas. Most came here in the 1880s from Illinois, Iowa, and Missouri. When they organized counties, as they quickly did, they made them 30 or 36 miles square, just as they had in the states of the old Northwest Territory. Misled by a few years of unusually high rainfall, the settlers expected the new counties would eventually contain as many people as the ones they came from; hence it made sense to make them the same size. Not only the small size of the counties, but the grandiose place names (Concordia, Minneapolis, Montezuma) testify to the settlers' hopes, dreams, and ambitions.

But they never materialized. Out here past 98° longitude, rainfall is normally half what it is in Illinois. In the early years of the 19th century, this part of the country was called the Great American Desert—a howling wilderness of arid, treeless land and blowing soil, harder to cross than a stormy ocean. The early settlers worked hard to prove this image wrong, but never entirely succeeded. There are prosperous towns out here on the plains, particularly where cattle are raised or oil is pumped, but making a living has proved difficult, and sometimes impossible. Since the 1890s, the population flow here has been out: tens of thousands of young people have left to seek their fortunes elsewhere. The thousands more who were expected by the early settlers never arrived; today the average population of the district's 58 counties is only a little over 8,000.

Most are far less populous because the average is inflated by the district's "urban" concentrations. The largest city, Salina, has only 41,000 people; Dodge City, terminus of the old cattle drives and once the home of Wyatt Earp, has 18,000 residents; Holcomb, made famous by Truman Capote's *In Cold Blood,* has exactly 816. Hays, a German Catholic town of 16,000, is the one part of the district that usually goes Democratic; so sometimes do counties along the Arkansas River first settled by southerners. But the real 1st District cannot be found in the towns. This is livestock and wheat country, one of the most agricultural districts in the nation. For miles on end you can see nothing but rolling brown fields, sectioned off here and there by barbed wire fence, and in the distance a grain elevator towering over a tiny town and its miniature railroad depot. The winds and rain and tornadoes that come suddenly out of the sky remind you that the original settlers likened this part of Kansas to an ocean and thought themselves in their wooden wagons almost as helpless as passengers at sea in a wooden rowboat. And you can see why Dorothy's flight to Oz did not seem so improbable to turn-of-the-century Kansans.

The 1st District is basically Republican; it used to vote for Democrats during years of farm distress, but the last time that happened was in 1960. The current congressman, Pat Roberts, is a solid Republican. His father served briefly as Republican national chairman during the Eisenhower years, and he was the top aide to 1st District Representative Keith Sebelius for his entire 12-year tenure. In 1980 Sebelius retired and Roberts, having moved from Topeka to Dodge City, ran and won the 1980 Republican primary (56%–36% over his nearest rival) to succeed him. The general election was not even close. Roberts continues to campaign over cups of coffee in small-town cafés and at barbecues and chili suppers; but he has not been hard-pressed in elections and, despite falling farm prices and land values, has won reelection easily. Roberts has been mentioned as a possible appointee to the Senate should Dole be elected president in 1988.

Representing this district is a specialized job. Roberts, like Sebelius and Bob Dole before him, serves on the House Agriculture Committee. He describes himself as "a nuts and bolts congressman," and has concentrated on shaping the quadrennial farm bills and on tending to the thousands of details—when the Agriculture Department makes its feed grain programs announcements, for example—that can make the difference between big profits and big losses for a Great Plains farmer. But with rising costs and falling prices, federal farm programs are under tremendous pressure, and even before the bargaining began on the 1985 farm bill it was obvious that subsidies would be reduced. Farmers seem to have given up on the hope that the federal government can maintain the high income levels of the 1970s, and Roberts by early 1986 was confessing that "our nuts and bolts were doing, at best, a temporary patch job for our family farms, our Main Street businesses, and our smaller communities." He sees the Great Plains as the victims in deregulation of airlines, railroads, and trucking, and calls for a government lending agency for rural areas. He draws the line against the mandatory production of Iowa's Democratic Senator Tom Harkin. But he's a good example of a faithful Republican who concentrates on agriculture and is temperamentally not at all uncomfortable with considering major extensions of government into the private economy.

The People: Pop. 1980: 472,139, up 0.2% 1970–80. Households (1980): 73% family, 36% with children, 66% married couples; 25.3% housing units rented; median monthly rent: $133; median house value: $31,300. Voting age pop. (1980): 342,439; 2% Spanish origin, 1% Black.

1984 Presidential Vote:	Reagan (R)	158,955	(74%)
	Mondale (D)	53,970	(25%)

Rep. Pat Roberts (R)

Elected 1980; b. Apr. 20, 1936, Topeka; home, Dodge City; KS St. U., B.A. 1958; United Methodist; married (Franki).

Career: USMC, 1958–62; Co-owner, editor, *The Westsider* (AZ Newspaper) 1962–67; A. A. to U.S. Sen. Frank Carlson, 1967–68; A.A. to U.S. Rep. Keith G. Sebelius, 1968–80.

Offices: 1314 LHOB 20515, 202-225-2715. Also P.O. Box 550, Dodge City 67801, 316-227-2244; P.O. Box 128, Norton 67654, 913-877-2454; and P.O. Box 1334, Salina 67402, 913-825-5409.

Committees: *Agriculture* (7th of 17 R). Subcommittees: Department Operations, Research and Foreign Agriculture (Ranking Member); Tobacco and Peanuts; Wheat, Soybeans, and Feed Grains. *House Administration* (7th of 7 R). Subcommittees: Accounts; Elections; Personnel and Police (Ranking Member). *Joint Committee on the Library. Joint Committee on Printing.*

Group Ratings

	ADA	ACLU	COPE	CFA	LCV	ACU	NTU	NSI	COC	CEI
1986	0	5	5	17	21	82	65	70	94	76
1985	15	—	5	8	—	71	68	—	95	—

National Journal Ratings

	1986 LIB — 1986 CONS		1985 LIB — 1985 CONS	
Economic	13% —	85%	22% —	77%
Social	0% —	89%	0% —	76%
Foreign	36% —	64%	40% —	59%

Key Votes

1) Lmt Cln Water Act	FOR	5) Retain Gun Cont	AGN	9) Aid Angola Reb	FOR
2) Rpl Tobac Sub	AGN	6) Contra Aid	FOR	10) Tax Reform	AGN
3) Grm-Rdmn Def Red	AGN	7) Lmt Text Imp	AGN	11) S Africa Sanc	FOR
4) Ban Polygraph	AGN	8) Limit SDI	FOR	12) Immig Reform	AGN

Election Results

1986 general	Pat Roberts (R)	141,297	(75%)	($87,221)
	Dale Lyon (D)	43,359	(25%)	($8,637)
1986 primary	Pat Roberts (R)	60,290	(100%)	
1984 general	Pat Roberts (R)	159,931	(76%)	($95,381)
	Darrell T. Ringer (D)	49,015	(23%)	($33,633)

Campaign Contributions and Expenditures

1985-86		Direct Cont. 1985-86		PACS Breakdown 1985-86			
Receipts	$181,783	Indiv.	$54,513	Corp.	$40,056	T/M/H	$49,400
Expend.	$87,221	Party	$2,000	Labor	$250	Agr.	$1,002
Unspent	$219,871	PACS	$96,958	Ideo.	$5,250	CWOS	$1,000

SECOND DISTRICT

Topeka, the capital of Kansas, is the last real city on the road west from Kansas City to Denver. Like many state capitals, it was a small town not so long ago, and has been quietly booming, helped along by the growth of local colleges and, in this case, the Menninger Psychiatric Clinic. The economy is based first on state government, but Topeka is also an important agricultural center. There are a few big new buildings downtown; clean-cut, pleasant neighborhoods in all directions. This is the home town of Alf Landon, the still vigorous and progressive Republican 50 years after he carried Maine and Vermont in the 1936 Roosevelt landslide. And although Topeka does not like to remember it, this is the city where the lawsuit *Brown v. Board of Education* was filed, the case in which the Supreme Court outlawed segregation in public schools in 1954—and where a case brought by one of the original schoolchildren-plaintiffs was dismissed in 1987 on the grounds that the public school system in Topeka was in compliance with the original court order barring separate but equal facilities.

The 2d Congressional District of Kansas is centered on Topeka, which with its surrounding county casts almost 40% of the district's votes. The district also contains the state's two major universities, Kansas State in Manhattan and the University of Kansas in Lawrence; two major military installations, Fort Riley near Manhattan and the Army's Leavenworth Prison, high on the bluffs overlooking the Missouri River; and even some Indian reservations. But otherwise the district is mostly agricultural. West of the Missouri the rolling hills flatten out to gently rolling, fertile plains. Rainfall here in the eastern part of the state is almost always sufficient to produce a good crop.

The 2d District has a Republican heritage and a Democratic congressman. Lawrence was the Republicans' capital in the Bleeding Kansas days, the rival to the pro-slavery forces' Lecompton; Topeka has produced the longest-lived Republican presidential candidate. But talented Democrats—Dr. Bill Roy in 1970 and 1972, Martha Keys in 1974 and 1976—have won the district in most recent elections. The current congressman is Jim Slattery, born and raised in Atchison County farmland, near where the bluffs drop down to the Missouri River, who won a state legislative seat in 1972 while still in law school in Topeka, and who was elected in the House to replace a weak Republican incumbent in 1982. Jim Slattery is one of those young Democrats who seems to have a knack for politics. He was speaker pro tem of the state House at age 28, after the Democrats won control in 1976. His timing has been good: he retired from the legislature, to make money in the real estate business, when the Democrats lost control in 1978; he passed up a chance to run for Congress in the Republican year of 1980 and chose 1982 instead. He won his first election in 1982 rather easily, with no primary opposition and 57% of the vote in the general election; in the Reagan reelection year he raised that to 60%.

Slattery's political acumen is also apparent from his work in the House. In his first term he won a seat on the the Energy and Commerce Committee—the most coveted committee in the House. In his second term he won a seat on Budget too. Slattery insists that he is a fiscal conservative, bringing "Kansas values" to the budget process, and, like the other Democrats who have represented the district, he doesn't support every big government measure. He is often anxious, as he demonstrated on natural gas decontrol, to carve out on issues a position that distinguishes him from either side. As a result, his is usually one of the last votes to be counted and gets ratings near 50% from almost every rating group. Yet he falls in line with the Democratic leadership on most Energy and Commerce and national issues. He works energetically as well on the little issues that still make a difference, like getting federal retirement credit to cadet nurses from World War II. At home he raised his percentage slightly in 1984 and got over 70% of the vote in 1986; he spent over $300,000 in each of those campaigns. He is mentioned occasionally as a candidate for Senator, but declined to run against Nancy Kassebaum in 1984 or Bob Dole in 1986; against another Republican, he might run and win. In the meantime he seems to have made the 2d District a safe seat.

The People: Pop. 1980: 472,988, up 5.8% 1970–80. Households (1980): 71% family, 38% with children, 61% married couples; 35.9% housing units rented; median monthly rent: $176; median house value: $40,600. Voting age pop. (1980): 348,994; 7% Black, 3% Spanish origin, 1% Asian origin, 1% American Indian.

1984 Presidential Vote:

Reagan (R)	120,455	(64%)
Mondale (D)	67,134	(35%)

Rep. Jim Slattery (D)

Elected 1982; b. Aug. 4, 1948, Atchison; home, Topeka; Washburn U., B.S. 1970, J.D. 1974, Netherlands Sch. of Intl. Econ. and Bus., 1969–70; Roman Catholic; married (Linda).

Career: KS House of Reps., 1972–78, Chmn. of Dem. Policy Group, 1975–79, Spkr. Pro Tem, 1977–79; KS Acting Secy. of Revenue, 1979; Real estate and develop., Brosius, Slattery and Meyer, Inc.

Offices: 1440 LHOB 20515, 202-225-6601. Also 444 S.E. Quincy, Ste. 280, Topeka 66684, 913-295-2811.

Committees: *Budget* (16th of 21 D). Task Forces: Community and Natural Resources; Defense and International Affairs; Economic Policy. *Energy and Commerce* (19th of 25 D). Subcommittees: Oversight and Investigations; Telecommunications and Finance; Transportation, Tourism and Hazardous Materials.

Group Ratings

	ADA	ACLU	COPE	CFA	LCV	ACU	NTU	NSI	COC	CEI
1986	45	60	56	58	53	27	44	30	56	40
1985	55	—	55	58	—	33	48	—	55	—

National Journal Ratings

	1986 LIB — 1986 CONS			1985 LIB — 1985 CONS		
Economic	37%	—	62%	50%	—	49%
Social	52%	—	46%	49%	—	49%
Foreign	57%	—	41%	54%	—	45%

Key Votes

1) Lmt Cln Water Act	FOR	5) Retain Gun Cont	AGN	9) Aid Angola Reb	AGN
2) Rpl Tobac Sub	FOR	6) Contra Aid	AGN	10) Tax Reform	FOR
3) Grm-Rdmn Def Red	FOR	7) Lmt Text Imp	AGN	11) S Africa Sanc	FOR
4) Ban Polygraph	FOR	8) Limit SDI	FOR	12) Immig Reform	FOR

Election Results

1986 general	Jim Slattery (D)	110,737	(71%)	($377,067)
	Phillip Kline (R)	46,029	(29%)	($20,414)
1986 primary	Jim Slattery (D)	25,169	(100%)	
1984 general	Jim Slattery (D)	112,263	(60%)	($311,477)
	Jim Van Slyke (R)	73,045	(39%)	($56,620)

Campaign Contributions and Expenditures

1985-86		Direct Cont. 1985-86		PACS Breakdown 1985-86			
Receipts	$380,857	Indiv.	$133,533	Corp.	$85,235	T/M/H	$93,265
Expend.	$377,067	Party	$512	Labor	$41,325	Agr.	$8,500
Unspent	$10,132	PACS	$240,825	Ideo.	$11,250	CWOS	$1,250

THIRD DISTRICT

Four of Kansas's five congressional districts lie beyond any major metropolitan area; the other is the 3d District, in metropolitan Kansas City. The big Kansas City, the one with the big office buildings, is in Missouri, separated from Kansas on the north by the Missouri River and on the south by only a rather minor residential street. Directly west of downtown Kansas City is Kansas City, Kansas, an industrial, meatpacking town. This is the Democratic bastion of Kansas: working class, middle income with a few slummy looking streets and the largest black neighborhood in the state.

To the south is Johnson County, adjoining high-income neighborhoods in Missouri. Johnson County is basically white-collar, middle to upper income; it contains some of metro Kansas City's newest and fastest-growing suburbs, with gleaming office parks and cul-de-sac streets; it is easily the highest-income county in Kansas. It is also one of the most Republican parts of a Republican state, and has helped make Kansas more Republican in statewide elections. Yet when an issue pits metropolitan areas against rural Kansas—as liquor by the drink did in 1970 or the oil severance tax did in 1982—Johnson County votes metropolitan, for bars and for taxing oilmen.

Suburban growth has changed politics here. In 1960 Johnson County cast only 65,000 votes to 76,000 in Kansas City's Wyandotte County. In 1984 Johnson cast 140,000 to Wyandotte's 64,000. Johnson's growth, more than anything else, accounts for the continued Republican success in the 3d District. For 18 years the district was represented by Republican Larry Winn, who achieved a high-ranking position but not great influence and occasionally had tough challenges at home. Now its representative is Jan Meyers, a Republican elected after a spirited primary and against serious general election competition in 1984.

Meyers is one of those candidates both parties would like to have more of: a woman with plenty of experience in state and local government and a set of issue positions of some attraction to the opposite party. She served five years on the city council of Overland Park, the largest suburb in Johnson County, and in 1972 was elected to the state Senate, where she ended up chairing the Public Health and Welfare Committee. The toughest hurdle in the congressional race was probably the Republican primary. Meyers supports the Supreme Court decision legalizing abortion, and has taken other positions considered relatively liberal by Republican activists. Although she began the race by far the best known of five Republicans, she ended up winning with just 35% of the vote. In the general election, against Mayor Jack Reardon of Kansas City, she did better. Meyers, perhaps singed by the primary, campaigned as a Reagan Republican, for the balanced budget amendment and a strong defense. Meyers had a solid 63%–32% lead in Johnson County; Reardon, who had taken his base pretty much for granted, got only 58% in Wyandotte County, just 2% ahead of Walter Mondale, whose campaign he pointedly shunned.

In office, Meyers has had a middle-of-the-road record on most issues, which seems to suit her constituents just fine. In this district which is not particularly used to a strong constituency-service representative, the opportunities that incumbency gives for helping voters could be particularly valuable. In two years Meyers solidified her position to the point that she had no opposition in the primary or the general election in 1986.

The People: Pop. 1980: 472,456, up 8.9% 1970–80. Households (1980): 76% family, 42% with children, 64% married couples; 29.0% housing units rented; median monthly rent: $216; median house value: $52,000. Voting age pop. (1980): 334,153; 8% Black, 2% Spanish origin, 1% Asian origin.

1984 Presidential Vote:

Reagan (R)	....	138,118	(63%)
Mondale (D)	....	78,289	(36%)

Rep. Jan Meyers (R)

Elected 1984; b. July 20, 1928, Lincoln, NE; home, Overland Park; Williams Wood Col., A.A. 1948, U. of NE, B.A. 1951; United Methodist; married (Louis).

Career: Member, Overland Park City Cncl., 1967–72; KS Senate, 1972–84.

Offices: 315 CHOB 20515, 202-225-2865. Also 204 Fed. Bldg., Kansas City 66101, 913-621-0832.

Committees: *Foreign Affairs* (15th of 18 R). Subcommittees: Europe and the Middle East; Human Rights and International Organizations. *Small Business* (8th of 17 R). Subcommittees: Regulation and Business Opportunities; SBA and the General Economy. *Select Committee on Aging* (18th of 26 R). Subcommittees: Health and Long-Term Care; Human Services.

Group Ratings

	ADA	ACLU	COPE	CFA	LCV	ACU	NTU	NSI	COC	CEI
1986	25	20	17	58	69	55	61	80	78	74
1985	15	—	19	58	—	71	59	—	86	—

National Journal Ratings

	1986 LIB — 1986 CONS		1985 LIB — 1985 CONS	
Economic	6% —	90%	34% —	66%
Social	42% —	57%	54% —	45%
Foreign	44% —	55%	40% —	60%

Key Votes

1) Lmt Cln Water Act	FOR	5) Retain Gun Cont	FOR	9) Aid Angola Reb	FOR
2) Rpl Tobac Sub	FOR	6) Contra Aid	FOR	10) Tax Reform	FOR
3) Grm-Rdmn Def Red	FOR	7) Lmt Text Imp	AGN	11) S Africa Sanc	FOR
4) Ban Polygraph	AGN	8) Limit SDI	FOR	12) Immig Reform	AGN

Election Results

1986 general	Jan Meyers (R)	109,266	(100%)	($139,791)
1986 primary	Jan Meyers (R)	33,948	(100%)	
1984 general	Jan Meyers (R)	117,159	(55%)	($442,459)
	John E. (Jack) Reardon (D)	85,441	(40%)	($273,950)
	John S. Ralph, Jr. (I)	11,302	(5%)	($29,387)

Campaign Contributions and Expenditures

1985-86		Direct Cont. 1985-86		PACS Breakdown 1985-86			
Receipts	$172,359	Indiv.	$54,205	Corp.	$49,961	T/M/H	$40,271
Expend.	$139,791	Party	$5,142	Labor	$3,800	Agr.	$1,000
Debts	$33,914	PACS	$102,482	Ideo.	$7,450	CWOS	$0
		Cand.	$1,500				

FOURTH DISTRICT

Before World War II, Wichita, Kansas, was a small city, a trading center for farm commodities, living off the agricultural yield of the surrounding counties. Today Wichita is a substantial medium-sized city, with a metropolitan population over 400,000, at the northern limit of the Sun Belt. Wichita owes much of its growth to the general aviation industry. During World War II and the years immediately after, aircraft factories sprouted up here, on the Kansas plains. Today Boeing has a major plant here, its only one outside Washington state; so do Cessna, Beechcraft, and Gates Learjet. Wichita is far and away the nation's leading center for producing small airplanes—everything short of jetliners. At times this has been a boom business, and at times a bust: the market for small planes depends on business profits, and when they are squeezed sales plummet. In the middle 1980s, general aviation was once again on hard times, as bankruptcy trustees sold off planes once owned by oil drillers and corporations pared down their fleets. During most of the 1970s Wichita did very well: the market for small planes was robust, and the rise in oil prices made the stripper wells around Wichita economically attractive once again. But in the 1980s low wheat prices, low oil prices, and the bust in general aviation left Wichita far short of its expectations.

Wichita's politics is the product of two conflicting tendencies. Its belief in free enterprise tilt it toward the Republicans in most elections. But the need for federal help and subsidy for wheat, oil, and general aviation, plus the southern origin of many residents, sometimes incline it to the Democrats.

The 4th Congressional District of Kansas includes all of Wichita and Sedgwick County; the much smaller city of Hutchinson to the northwest; and rural areas like Sumner County, usually the number one wheat-producing county in Kansas. Its congressman is Dan Glickman, a Democrat first elected in 1976, who combines political acumen with energy and an interest in a wide variety of policy areas. From the beginning, he was more skeptical about government programs than most Democrats and more inclined to hold down spending. Since the Carter years, when many of the creative ideas in politics came from Republicans, Glickman has been coming forth with many ideas on how government can be made to work better—or can be done without.

He has had useful committee assignments for the district: a seat on Agriculture, chairmanship (for over four years) of the Aviation subcommittee of Science, Space and Technology, plus a seat on Judiciary. On Agriculture he has not only worked on the wheat program but has been attentive to and an expert on regulation of the futures markets and pushed to passage a bill tightening up regulation of them. In early 1987 he announced he would become chairman of the Wheat Subcommittee. He is likely to continue spending time on aviation issues, however, on which he has provoked a flurry of activity: he is pushing a bill to limit liability for aircraft, he is calling for better airport weather information, he demands tighter airport security measures, he wants tougher antitrust review of airline mergers, he seeks relief for workers laid off by Cessna, he moves to suspend aviation fuel taxes. Glickman has also been a stickler on government ethics. But he is also popular with his colleagues and in 1987 got a seat on the Steering and Policy Committee that makes Democratic committee assignments.

In 1986 Glickman, after deciding not to run for senator or governor, faced the toughest opponent he's had in the 4th District since he beat incumbent Republican Garner Shriver in

1984. Wichita city commissioner Bob Knight started off well known and popular, raised some $231,000, and argued that Glickman was too soft on defense and generally too liberal. But Glickman spent $515,000 and won 65% of the vote—a high figure for a Democrat in this nationally Republican district, although the lowest figure Glickman has had since his first election. This test seems to show that Glickman has a safe seat and is still a prospect, as he has been in the past, for statewide office.

The People: Pop. 1980: 473,180, up 4.7% 1970–80. Households (1980): 72% family, 38% with children, 61% married couples; 33.9% housing units rented; median monthly rent: $192; median house value: $40,100. Voting age pop. (1980): 341,718; 6% Black, 2% Spanish origin, 1% Asian origin, 1% American Indian.

1984 Presidential Vote:

Reagan (R)	124,731	(63%)
Mondale (D)	70,140	(35%)

Rep. Dan Glickman (D)

Elected 1976; b. Nov. 24, 1944, Wichita; home, Wichita; U. of MI, B.A. 1966; Geo. Wash. U., J.D. 1969; Jewish; married (Rhoda).

Career: Trial atty., SEC, Washington, D.C., 1969–70; Practicing atty., 1971–76; Wichita Board of Ed., 1973–76, Pres., 1975–76.

Offices: 1212 LHOB 20515, 202-225-6216. Also U.S. Crthse., Rm. 224, P.O. Box 403, Wichita 67201, 316-262-8396; and 301 Wolcott Bldg., 201 N. Main, Hutchinson 67501, 316-669-9011.

Committees: *Agriculture* (9th of 26 D). Subcommittees: Department Operations, Research and Foreign Agriculture; Domestic Marketing, Consumer Relations, and Nutrition; Wheat, Soybeans, and Feed Grains (Chairman). *Judiciary* (10th of 21 D). Subcommittees: Administrative Law and Governmental Relations; Monopolies and Commercial Law. *Science, Space and Technology* (6th of 27 D). Subcmtee.: Transportation, Aviation and Materials.

Group Ratings

	ADA	ACLU	COPE	CFA	LCV	ACU	NTU	NSI	COC	CEI
1986	55	70	61	67	68	32	38	20	50	36
1985	55	—	64	58	—	35	43	—	41	—

National Journal Ratings

	1986 LIB — 1986 CONS		1985 LIB — 1985 CONS	
Economic	42% —	58%	55% —	45%
Social	57% —	40%	73% —	23%
Foreign	60% —	39%	58% —	40%

Key Votes

1) Lmt Cln Water Act	FOR	5) Retain Gun Cont	AGN	9) Aid Angola Reb	FOR
2) Rpl Tobac Sub	AGN	6) Contra Aid	AGN	10) Tax Reform	FOR
3) Grm-Rdmn Def Red	FOR	7) Lmt Text Imp	AGN	11) S Africa Sanc	FOR
4) Ban Polygraph	FOR	8) Limit SDI	FOR	12) Immig Reform	FOR

Election Results

1986 general	Dan Glickman (D)	111,164	(65%)	($523,533)
	Bob Knight (R)	61,178	(35%)	($227,587)
1986 primary	Dan Glickman (D)	27,705	(93%)	
	James M. Saiz (D)	1,954	(7%)	
1984 general	Dan Glickman (D)	138,917	(74%)	($162,320)
	William V. Krause (R)	47,776	(26%)	($17,908)

Campaign Contributions and Expenditures

1985-86		Direct Cont. 1985-86		PACS Breakdown 1985-86			
Receipts	$456,405	Party	$4,350	Corp.	$63,000	T/M/H	$59,100
Expend.	$523,533	PACS	$194,015	Labor	$34,927	Agr.	$2,500
Unspent	$10,391			Ideo.	$24,110	CWOS	$10,378

FIFTH DISTRICT

The 5th Congressional District of Kansas consists of two fairly heavily populated farming areas, separated by the sand hills that were such a barrier to the first westward-bound pioneers and which remain a lightly populated corridor running north and south about 100 miles west of the boundary with Missouri. One of those regions, in the southeastern corner of Kansas, was nicknamed "the Balkans"—a reference to the Eastern European origin of some of the residents and to its low hill country, the outer fringe of the Ozarks. The hills here contain some coal, and the main town was named Pittsburg—another example of the unrealistic optimism of the people who first settled Kansas. This part of the state never became a notable coal or manufacturing center, and for many years it was in unmistakable decline. Its population has increased slightly since. But it feels cut off from most of America because it has not only no interstate but no four-lane highway of any kind; one of the major political demands here is for a four-lane road to Wichita.

The other major part of the district, west of the sand hills, centers on the town of Emporia, the home of William Allen White, the newspaper editor whose name was a household word 40 years ago but draws blank stares today. White was the voice of progressive midwestern Republicanism. Horrified by the Populists of his youth, as were most townspeople in the Midwest, White was enchanted by Theodore Roosevelt and came to care about the plight of society's unfortunates. Although a native of one of the nation's most isolationist regions, White was a leading spokesman for American aid to the British during the ominous days before Pearl Harbor.

The 5th District's politics has been pretty consistently Republican, although the Balkans, near the borders of Missouri and Oklahoma, sometimes vote Democratic. The 5th has never had a congressman who attracted national attention. In 1978, when the incumbent retired, there was a spirited competition for the seat, with five Democrats and six Republicans running. The Republican primary was won by a dark horse, optometrist Robert Whittaker. A friendly man who served one term in the Kansas legislature, Whittaker went door to door talking with voters and worked at various jobs around the district for a day at a time. He won with 57% in the 1978 general election and has been reelected easily ever since.

Generally conservative on economic issues, moderate on cultural issues, very hawkish on foreign policy, he has a record reasonably well in line with his constituency. He devotes much of his energy to getting the four-lane road to Wichita built. He has become one of the senior Republicans on the Energy and Commerce Committee, where health issues have attracted most of his energies, and he generally supports easing regulations and reducing government interference in business. When Energy and Commerce ranking Republican James Broyhill moved to the Senate in July 1986, Whittaker became ranking Republican on the Commerce, Transportation, and Tourism Subcommittee that handles such issues as the Superfund, hazardous waste, railroads, and the Federal Trade Commission. In the past, the panel was dominated by its chairman, James Florio of New Jersey, but Whittaker is in a position to weld alliances with some subcommittee Democrats. But he will be handicapped because he was not serving on the panel immediately before getting the position and its subject matter is sometimes dauntingly technical.

The People: Pop. 1980: 472,916, up 6.2% 1970–80. Households (1980): 73% family, 36% with children, 65% married couples; 25.2% housing units rented; median monthly rent: $128; median house value: $28,600. Voting age pop. (1980): 347,340; 2% Black, 1% Spanish origin, 1% American Indian.

1984 Presidential Vote:
Reagan (R)	135,037	(67%)
Mondale (D)	63,616	(32%)

Rep. Robert (Bob) Whittaker (R)

Elected 1978; b. Sept. 18, 1939, Eureka; home, Augusta; IL Col. of Optometry, Doctor of Optometry 1962; Christian Church; married (Marlene).

Career: Optometrist, 1962–78; KS House of Reps., 1974–77.

Offices: 2436 RHOB 20515, 202-225-3911. Also P.O. Box 280, Augusta 67010, 316-775-1127 P.O. Box 1102, Emporia 66801, 316-342-6464; P.O. Box 1003, McPherson 67460, 316-241-5797; and P.O. Box 1111, Pittsburg 66762, 316-232-2320.

Committees: *Energy and Commerce* (6th of 17 R). Subcommittees: Health and the Environment; Transportation, Tourism and Hazardous Materials (Ranking Member).

Group Ratings

	ADA	ACLU	COPE	CFA	LCV	ACU	NTU	NSI	COC	CEI
1986	10	10	8	25	32	91	55	90	94	70
1985	10	—	5	17	—	81	61	—	86	—

National Journal Ratings

	1986 LIB — 1986 CONS		1985 LIB — 1985 CONS	
Economic	15% —	84%	24% —	74%
Social	18% —	78%	52% —	47%
Foreign	23% —	76%	0% —	76%

Key Votes

1) Lmt Cln Water Act	FOR	5) Retain Gun Cont	AGN	9) Aid Angola Reb	FOR
2) Rpl Tobac Sub	FOR	6) Contra Aid	FOR	10) Tax Reform	AGN
3) Grm-Rdmn Def Red	FOR	7) Lmt Text Imp	AGN	11) S Africa Sanc	AGN
4) Ban Polygraph	AGN	8) Limit SDI	AGN	12) Immig Reform	AGN

Election Results

1986 general	Robert (Bob) Whittaker (R)............	116,800	(71%)	($97,850)
	Kym E. Myers (D)	47,540	(29%)	
1986 primary	Robert (Bob) Whittaker (R)............	54,713	(100%)	
1984 general	Robert (Bob) Whittaker (R)............	144,075	(74%)	($78,687)
	John A. Barnes (D)..................	49,435	(25%)	

Campaign Contributions and Expenditures

1985-86		Direct Cont. 1985-86		PACS Breakdown 1985-86			
Receipts	$210,029	Indiv.	$33,900	Corp.	$50,002	T/M/H	$62,985
Expend.	$97,850	Party	$2,607	Labor	$2,250	Agr.	$1,750
Unspent	$341,269	PACS	$119,487	Ideo.	$1,500	CWOS	$1,000

KENTUCKY

In 1775 Daniel Boone made his way through the Cumberland Gap in the Appalachian Mountains and came upon what we now know as Kentucky—a fertile, virgin land of gently rolling hills. After the Revolutionary War, streams of people from Virginia traveled Boone's Wilderness Road and settled in the hills and countryside around Lexington. The exodus was the new nation's first frontier boom and, up to that time, one of the most extensive mass migrations in western history. No more than a few dozen whites lived in Kentucky before the war; the 1790 Census counted 73,000; by 1820 there were 564,000 Kentuckians, and the state was the sixth largest in the nation. In those days Kentucky was the frontier, its communities full of opportunity, free of the hierarchies that structured the societies of coastal America. Henry Clay, to take the most famous example, came to Kentucky from Virginia as a penniless youth. By the time he was 30 he had done well enough in law and land speculation to build a mansion with silver doorknobs and well enough in politics to become a United States Senator.

In some respects Kentucky has not changed much since Clay's time. The state is still largely non-urban: only 21% of its residents live in metropolitan Louisville and only 7% in the Kentucky suburbs of Cincinnati, the state's only major metropolitan areas. During the 1950s and 1960s thousands of young people left the state; Kentuckians looking for jobs left the hills for the industrial cities of the Midwest, California, and Texas. In the 1970s, when coal prices rose with oil, the rural areas boomed for a time, and many people returned; but the outmigration started again in the early 1980s. Even so, life in rural Kentucky today is far different from the 1930s, when central heating, indoor plumbing, and electricity were luxuries almost never seen. Cable TV and satellite dishes, four-lane highways and RVs have all become common as electricity and running water did decades ago; people no longer feel isolated by the mountains from the rest of the world. But there is, among Kentuckians who have stayed and those who have left, an attachment to roots, to place and family. Kentuckians remain very family-oriented: the percentage of households occupied by families and married couples are among the highest in the nation. But the percentage of households with children is not quite so far above average, because the population is older here.

Superficially, not even the local landscape has changed very much. The tobacco fields, the thoroughbred horse country of the Blue Grass region, and the flat fields of western Kentucky look the same as they have for years, though they are more likely to be planted in soybeans than cotton now. The small towns, with their 19th century courthouses, look mostly the same except for the fast food stands and small shopping centers grown up on the roads leading out. The coal industry, important 50 years ago, became important again in the 1970s, after two rough decades. Underground mining is, however, less common, and there is more strip mining than before. Coal towns are still isolated amid the mountains and the hills, but they are less grimy than they used to be and the work is less hazardous; more work is done by machines and less by union miners. Strip mining is far safer than underground mining, but it is also more damaging to the environment and generates fewer jobs.

Politics in Kentucky also seems, with some few exceptions, stuck in a kind of time warp. As in other border states, in Kentucky political divisions are still based on the splits caused by the Civil War. Kentucky was a slave state, but it voted to stay with the Union, and there were strong feelings on both sides. Most of the hill country was pro-Union and remains Republican today; the major exceptions are counties where coal miners joined the United Mine Workers in the 1930s and became Democrats. The Blue Grass region and the western part of the state, areas called the Jackson Purchase and the Pennyrile, were more likely to be slaveholding territory, and today remain mostly Democratic, except for the rapidly growing city of Lexington. Louisville,

KENTUCKY — Congressional Districts, Counties, and Selected Places — *(7 Districts)*

Congressional districts established March 10, 1982; all other boundaries are as of January 1, 1980.

influenced from its early days by German immigrants, was an anti-slavery river town, and for years supported a strong Republican organization. These patterns, which have prevailed now for more than 100 years, were as apparent as ever in the 1976 and 1980 elections, in which southern Democrat Jimmy Carter lost Louisville's Jefferson County and the Cincinnati suburbs and carried the mining counties in the east, the Blue Grass country around Lexington, and Jackson Purchase and the Pennyrile—patterns not all that much different from the patterns in the elections of 1950, 1920, or 1890. Ronald Reagan, running against a northern liberal Democrat, carried Kentucky as Republicans usually do, with big margins in the hills and the urban areas overshadowing narrow carries in many rural areas and losses in the coal country.

On balance Kentucky is a Democratic state, and often, especially in the gubernatorial elections that are always the focus of politics here, the Democratic primary is decisive. For more than 50 years now these have usually been struggles between two factions with remarkable continuity. The seminal contest was the 1938 Senate primary between Alben Barkley, then Senate majority leader and faithful New Deal supporter, and Governor Happy Chandler, whose politics was more conservative. Barkley won decisively, remained majority leader for 10 years, was elected vice president in 1948, and died, again a Senator, in mid-oration. Chandler became Senator, baseball commissioner, and governor again in 1947 and 1955, and was still attending political gatherings in late 1986 at age 89. The lineal descendant of the Barkley faction is the group around Governor Bert Combs, a mountain liberal elected in 1959, whose choices Edward Breathitt won in 1963 and Julian Carroll in 1975; descending from the Chandler faction is the group around Combs's one-time top assistant, Wendell Ford, who beat Combs for the gubernatorial nomination in 1971 and whose candidate Martha Layne Collins won the office in 1983 over Combs's candidate, Harvey Sloane. Collins is from Versailles (pronounced vursayles), which is also Happy Chandler's home town. Ford himself went to the Senate in 1974, not sure that giving up the governorship to Carroll for a year was worth what seems to have turned out to be a lifetime Senate seat. John Gunther quotes a story told by Fred Vinson (longtime congressman, Chief Justice of the Supreme Court 1946-53, Barkley faction) about a Kentucky politician who had not decided whom to support in a primary a few weeks away: "I don't know yet. I'm waiting to see what the opposition does, so I can take the other side."

But not all elections are won by Democrats. In the 1950s and 1960s, Kentucky slowly became more Republican, until during one four-year period (1967–71) Republicans held the governorship and both Senate seats. The first Republican victories were won by moderates from the Louisville area and the Cumberland Plateau, men like John Sherman Cooper and Thruston Morton, whose politics came out of the Civil War tradition (and included support of civil rights). The Democrats they beat were southern in style and usually well to the right of the party on national issues. Then, in the 1960s, Kentucky began to fit more into the national pattern. The Republicans, under Governor Louie Nunn, were conservative on economics and civil rights (a symbolic issue in Kentucky: only 7% of Kentuckians are black and most areas of the state are all white). The Democrats, under both Combs and Ford, put in programs to help the poor. The Democrats had a resurgence beginning with the 1971 gubernatorial election, and were winning statewide races by large margins until Ford's protégé and Senate colleague, Walter (Dee) Huddleston, was upset by Republican Mitch McConnell in 1984. But Republicans lost the 1986 race to Ford by a record margin, their 1983 governor candidate, Jim Bunning, settled for a suburban House seat which is safe Republican in 1986, and the party's best known candidate for governor, Larry Forgy, announced as he has in past years that he would not run in 1987.

Governor. There is no question who stands at the apex of Kentucky politics: the governor. The governor's appointment powers are wide; this is not a state with a vibrant civil service tradition. The legislature is allowed to meet only 60 days every two years; after that, the governor can shift around line items in the budget as he likes. The governor is also the undisputed leader of his state party. These are powers rooted in tradition and history, but so are the restrictions on governors: they cannot serve consecutive terms and they must swear that they have never participated in a duel.

The factions that have dominated Democratic politics for years may be fading. Martha Layne Collins, after a term distinguished by her role presiding over the 1984 Democratic National Convention and being summoned to North Oaks, Minnesota, as a vice presidential possibility, and by her landing a giant Toyota plant for the town Georgetown, near Lexington and Frankfort, is not trying to anoint a successor. The best known candidate to succeed her, Kentucky Fried Chicken millionaire and former Governor John Y. Brown, Jr., had enough money to run independently of factional support, as he did when he won the 1979 primary with 29% (Kentucky has no runoff). Brown has had his problems: voters in 1982 refused to change the constitution to allow governors a second term, it was revealed he indulged in heavy gambling, quit the Senate race after announcing a primary challenge to Dee Huddleston, and he never got much more than 40% in polls. He was battered by ads attacking him and his wife Phyllis George as the "fab couple" which were run by Lieutenant Governor Steven Beshear, who also had organization support. But Beshear opened the way not for himself, but for Wallace Wilkinson, a businessman who came from a small county, started out with a bookstore in Lexington, and by 1987 had done well enough to generate something like $4 million for a media campaign. He called for a lottery, opposed new taxes, promised that he could find jobs for Kentuckians, and combined denunciations of the state's current conditions and standard politicos with home-state boosterism. That enabled him to beat Brown in the May 26 primary by 35%–25%, with Beshear lagging far behind. Yet Wilkinson, for all his denunciations of standard politicians, made his own alliances, and his campaign brochure carried a picture of him embraced by Happy Chandler.

Perhaps faction endures. Republican primary winner John Harper promptly attacked Wilkinson and his lottery proposal. But the Democrat was a very heavy favorite to win in November.

Senators. Wendell Ford has not been a particularly visible Senator, but he has been an important insider. He looks like a weatherbeaten old pro, and he has risen from humble beginnings to positions of great power without seeming out of place. He is now third ranking Democrat on the Commerce Committee, third on Energy and Natural Resources, and chairman of Rules and Administration. On Commerce Committee, which handles many issues of federal regulation, Ford is often a swing vote. There and on the Energy Committee, he is an advocate of Kentucky's major industries: tobacco, coal, autos (there are assembly plants here), TVA. He also chairs the Aviation Subcommittee. On economic issues generally he usually votes with most other Democrats, but he is willing to listen to business lobbyists and to support them when persuaded. On foreign issues he usually is with other Democrats as well, but he is rather conservative on cultural matters.

Rules Committee has one important jurisdiction, over campaign finance reform. Other Senators, particularly David Boren, have taken the lead in seeking to decrease the power of PACs; Ford is likely to approach the issue from a partisan and practical standpoint. Chairing the Senate Democratic Campaign Committee from 1976 to 1982, he specialized in raising big contributions from business sources, but failed to build a base of thousands of direct mail contributors as the Republicans were doing. Ford does have convictions on issues, and he does seem to identify with the little guy and wants to help him; but like most Kentucky politicians he is a practical man whose idealism seldom gets in the way as he goes about his business from day to day.

Skill at inside maneuvering has not only characterized Ford's legislative career, but explains his success at the polls. He won his seat in 1974 by beating incumbent Republican Marlow Cook in a close and bitter race. But since then he has had only the weakest of opposition. In 1980 Kentucky still seemed heavily Democratic, and in fact nearly went for Jimmy Carter in the fall; Ford that year got 65%, setting a record for the highest percentage ever won by a candidate for senator in Kentucky. After Huddleston's defeat in 1984, Democrats looked more vulnerable. But Ford preempted all serious opposition and in 1986 was reelected with 75%, another record. Amazingly, in a state where partisan tradition is so strong that George McGovern carried 8 counties and Barry Goldwater 21, Ford carried all of Kentucky's 120 counties, the first opposed candidate ever to do so.

Kentucky's junior Senator, Mitch McConnell, had two major advantages in winning the biggest upset of 1984. One was his own ambition, and the other was Huddleston's low profile. McConnell has been aiming for the Senate over a long career. He served on the staff of Senator Marlow Cook during his single and often stormy term in office (1968–74), then moved back to Louisville and won, in an upset, the office that had been Cook's political stepping stone: Jefferson County judge. This is the executive position in the county that includes Louisville and most of its suburbs; it is the largest constituency in the state in which Republicans are usually competitive. It also, unlike the governorship or the mayoralty of Louisville, allows incumbents to run for a second consecutive term; McConnell won reelection in 1982, though by a lackluster margin. He passed up the governor's race in 1983, which he almost surely would have lost, in return for a promise of the senatorial nomination in 1984. That gave him a statewide race on national issues, in a year when Ronald Reagan was carrying Kentucky 3–2 and the Democrats' national positions were not popular in most parts of the state.

All that might not have availed him if Huddleston had had stronger ties with the voters of the state. But his basic non-election-year strategy seemed to be to stay off the front pages and stay out of trouble. So McConnell's ads showing bloodhounds sniffing for Huddleston in vacation locales where he had collected fees for speeches while the Senate was in session struck a chord for many voters. All they knew about Huddleston was that he was from the rural part of the state and was a moderate; they didn't know much about what he'd done; and the ad, by suggesting he'd been doing little but feathering his nest, cost him just enough votes to keep him from getting the 11% he needed to run ahead of Walter Mondale. McConnell ran unimpressively in Jefferson County, but ran strongly enough in rural counties to win.

In the Senate McConnell serves on the Agriculture Committee and in 1987 left Judiciary for Foreign Relations. In his two years in the majority he did not emerge into the front rank of legislators and will have a harder time doing so as a junior member of the minority, though he did manage to play a key role in fashioning the South Africa sanctions compromise that passed the Senate. He will probably have a serious opponent in 1990, possibly Harvey Sloane, the doctor who has been mayor of Louisville and took McConnell's old job of Jefferson County judge; possibly Martha Layne Collins, who leaves the governor's office in 1987; possibly any Democrat who is elected to succeed her or does well enough to almost win. But McConnell is as methodical as he is ambitious and prides himself on being a meticulous early planner. By early 1987 he was busy staking out issues like encouraging tobacco exports and uniform federal limits on tort liability to hold insurance costs down and, with $564,000 cash in hand for 1990, was arguing vehemently after public financing of Senate elections.

Presidential politics. Kentucky had a presidential primary, abolished it, and has now joined the southern regional primary scheduled for March 8, 1988. The delegation of the governor's party is typically dominated by the governor, then in his or her first and usually most powerful year in office; that was the case in San Francisco in 1984. In the general election, Kentucky could very well be a closely contested state if the Democratic nominee, as in 1976 and 1980, and in contrast to 1968, 1972, and 1984, has appeal to southern voters.

Congressional districting. Kentucky's Democrats typically redraw its congressional district lines without major change and without much controversy.

The People: Est. Pop. 1986: 3,728,000; Pop. 1980: 3,660,777, up 1.9% 1980–86 and 13.7% 1970–80; 1.55% of U.S. total, 23d largest. 11% with 1–3 yrs. col., 11% with 4+ yrs. col.; 17.6% below poverty level. Single ancestry: 25% English, 7% German, 6% Irish, 1% French. Households (1980): 78% family, 44% with children, 65% married couples; 30.0% housing units rented; median monthly rent: $151; median house value: $34,200. Voting age pop. (1980): 2,578,047; 7% Black, 1% Spanish origin. Registered voters (1986): 1,998,899; 1,360,728 D (68%), 572,767 R (29%), 63,024 unaffiliated (3%), 2,380 minor parties.

1986 Share of Federal Tax Burden: $9,004,000,000; 1.20% of U.S. total, 26th largest.

1986 Share of Federal Expenditures

	Total		Non-Defense		Defense	
Total Expend	$12,516m	(1.51%)	$10,730m	(1.79%)	$1,786m	(0.78%)
St/Lcl Grants	1,784m	(1.58%)	1,782m	(1.58%)	2m	(1.80%)
Salary/Wages	1,709m	(1.42%)	641m	(1.09%)	1,068m	(1.73%)
Pymnts to Indiv	5,576m	(1.53%)	5,397m	(1.56%)	180m	(1.01%)
Procurement	3,300m	(1.60%)	2,764m	(4.97%)	536m	(0.36%)
Research/Other	147m	(0.55%)	147m	(0.55%)	0m	(0.69%)

Political Lineup: Governor, Martha Layne Collins (D); Lt. Gov., Steven L. Beshear (D); Secy. of State, Drexell (Drex) Davis (D); Atty. Gen., Dave Armstrong (D); Treasurer, Frances Jones Mills (D); Auditor, Mary Ann Tobin (D). State Senate, 38 (29 D and 9 R); State House of Representatives, 100 (73 D and 27 R). Senators, Wendell H. Ford (D) and Mitch McConnell (R). Representatives, 7 (4 D and 3 R).

1984 Presidential Vote

Reagan (R) 821,702   (60%)
Mondale (D) 539,539   (39%)

1980 Presidential Vote

Reagan (R) 635,274   (49%)
Carter (D) 617,417   (48%)
Anderson (I) 31,127   (2%)

GOVERNOR

Gov. Martha Layne Collins (D)

Elected 1983, term expires Dec. 1987; b. Dec. 7, 1936, Bagdad; home, Versailles; U. of KY, B.S. 1959; Baptist; married (Bill).

Career: Teacher, 1959–70; Coord., Women's Activities, KY Dem. Hdqrtrs., 1972–75; Clerk, KY Supreme Crt., 1975–79; Lt. Gov. of KY, 1979–83; Chwmn., 1984 Dem. Natl. Convention.

Office: Office of the Governor, State Capitol, Frankfort 40601, 502-564-2611.

Election Results

1983 gen.	Martha Layne Collins (D)	561,674	(54%)
	Jim Bunning (R)	454,650	(44%)
1983 prim.	Martha Layne Collins (D)	223,692	(34%)
	Harvey Sloane (D)	219,160	(33%)
	Grady Stumbo (D)	199,795	(30%)
1979 gen.	John Young Brown, Jr. (D)	588,088	(59%)
	Louie B. Nunn (R)	381,278	(41%)

SENATORS

Sen. Wendell H. Ford (D)

Elected 1974, seat up 1992; b. Sept. 8, 1924, Daviess Cnty.; home, Owensboro; U. of KY, MD School of Insurance; Baptist; married (Jean).

Career: Army, WWII; Family insur. bus.; Chf. A.A. to Gov. Bert Combs; KY Senate, 1965–67; Lt. Gov., 1967–71; Gov., 1971–74.

Offices: 173A RSOB 20510, 202-224-4343. Also 172-C New Fed. Bldg., 600 Fed. Pl., Louisville 40202, 502-582-6251; 305 Fed. Bldg., Frederica St., Owensboro 42301, 502-685-5158; 343 Waller Ave., Ste. 204, Lexington 40504, 606-233-2484; 19 U.S. P.O. and Crthse., Covington 41011, 606-491-7929.

Committees: *Commerce, Science, and Transportation* (3rd of 11 D). Subcommittees: Aviation (Chairman); Communications; Consumer. *Energy and Natural Resources* (3rd of 10 D). Subcommittees: Energy, Research and Development (Chairman); Mineral Resources Development and Production; Water and Power. *Rules and Administration* (Chairman of 9 D). *Joint Committee on Printing* (Vice Chairman).

Group Ratings

	ADA	ACLU	COPE	CFA	LCV	ACU	NTU	NSI	COC	CEI
1986	55	21	73	60	42	35	40	50	53	30
1985	50	—	74	47	—	43	26	—	48	—

National Journal Ratings

	1986 LIB	—	1986 CONS		1985 LIB	—	1985 CONS
Economic	73%	—	22%		65%	—	31%
Social	41%	—	56%		28%	—	68%
Foreign	67%	—	30%		64%	—	38%

Key Votes

1) Ease Gun Cont	FOR	5) Grm-Rdmn Def Red	FOR	9) Rehnquist Nom	FOR
2) Immig Reform	FOR	6) Contra Aid	AGN	10) Tax Reform	FOR
3) Lmt Text Imp	FOR	7) SDI Funding	AGN	11) Drug Death Pen	AGN
4) Aid Tobac Ind	FOR	8) Lmt PAC Contrib	FOR	12) S Africa Sanc	FOR

Election Results

1986 general	Wendell H. Ford (D).................	503,755	(75%)	($1,201,624)
	Jackson M. Andrews (R)	173,330	(25%)	($58,572)
1986 primary	Wendell H. Ford (D) unopposed			
1980 general	Wendell H. Ford (D).................	720,891	(65%)	($491,522)
	Mary Louise Foust (R)...............	386,029	(35%)	($7,406)

Campaign Contributions and Expenditures

1985-86		Direct Cont. 1985-86		PACS Breakdown 1985-86			
Receipts	$1,519,672	Indiv.	$606,323	Corp.	$336,975	T/M/H	$219,847
Expend.	$1,201,624	Party	$1,146	Labor	$180,867	Agr.	$21,000
Unspent	$360,775	PACS	$831,618	Ideo.	$54,609	CWOS	$18,320

Sen. Mitch McConnell (R)

Elected 1984, seat up 1990; b. Feb. 20, 1942, Sheffield, AL; home, Louisville; U. of Louisville, B.A. 1964, U. of KY, J.D. 1967; Baptist; divorced.

Career: Chief Legis. Asst. to U.S. Sen. Marlow Cook, 1967–69; Dpty. Asst. Atty. Gen., 1974–76; Judge/Exec., Jefferson Cnty., KY, 1977–1985.

Offices: 120 RSOB 20510, 202-224-2541. Also 600 Federal Pl., Rm. 136-C, Louisville 40202, 502-582-6304; Fed. Bldg., Rm 307, Covington 41011, 606-261-6304; Irvin Cobb Bldg., 602 Broadway, Paducah 42001, 502-442-4554; 1501 S. Main St., Ste. N, London 40741, 606-864-2026; Fed. Bldg., 241 Main St., Rm. 305, Bowling Green 42101; and 155 E. Main St., Ste. 210, Lexington 40508, 606-252-1781.

Committees: *Agriculture, Nutrition, and Forestry* (9th of 9 R). Subcommittees: Agricultural Production and Stabilization of Prices; Agricultural Credit; Rural Development and Rural Electrification (Ranking Member). *Foreign Relations* (9th of 9 R). Subcommittees: East Asian and Pacific Affairs; Terrorism, Narcotics and International Communications; Western Hemisphere and Peace Corps Affairs.

Group Ratings

	ADA	ACLU	COPE	CFA	LCV	ACU	NTU	NSI	COC	CEI
1986	8	0	73	7	25	83	51	89	89	64
1985	10	—	73	0	—	78	57	—	79	—

National Journal Ratings

	1986 LIB — 1986 CONS			1985 LIB — 1985 CONS		
Economic	16%	—	76%	24%	—	73%
Social	9%	—	89%	0%	—	83%
Foreign	27%	—	70%	34%	—	63%

Key Votes

1) Ease Gun Cont	FOR	5) Grm-Rdmn Def Red	FOR	9) Rehnquist Nom	FOR
2) Immig Reform	FOR	6) Contra Aid	FOR	10) Tax Reform	FOR
3) Lmt Text Imp	FOR	7) SDI Funding	FOR	11) Drug Death Pen	AGN
4) Aid Tobac Ind	FOR	8) Lmt PAC Contrib	AGN	12) S Africa Sanc	FOR

Election Results

1984 general	Mitch McConnell (R).................	644,990	(50%)	($1,767,114)
	Walter D. (Dee) Huddleston (D)	639,721	(49%)	($2,444,091)
1984 primary	Mitch McConnell (R)..................	39,465	(79%)	
	Three others (R)......................	10,352	(21%)	
1978 general	Walter D. (Dee) Huddleston (D)	290,730	(61%)	($461,808)
	Louie Guenthner, Jr. (R)...............	175,766	(37%)	($76,445)

Campaign Contributions and Expenditures

1983-84		Direct Cont. 1983-84		PACS Breakdown 1983-84			
Receipts	$1,582,289	Indiv.	$1,257,157	Corp	$120,450	T/M/H	$70,522
Expend.	$1,767,114	Party	$23,934	Labor	$2,500	Agr.	$2,000
Debts	$8,935	PACS	$204,056	Ideo.	$85,274	CWOS	$2,750
		Cand.	$40,000				

FIRST DISTRICT

In 1818 General Andrew Jackson and Kentucky Governor Isaac Shelby agreed that the United States would pay the Chickasaw Indians $300,000 for more than 8,000 square miles of land between the Tennessee and Mississippi rivers, land that now makes up the western end of Kentucky and part of Tennessee. In Kentucky, it's still known as the Jackson Purchase, and almost seems part of another state—of west Tennessee or the lowlands of the bootheel of Missouri or even the Mississippi Delta. This is low-lying land, protected from the great muddy river by levees and cut off from the rest of Kentucky by the dammed-up Tennessee and Cumberland rivers. Economically and physically, it's like the low-lying cotton and now soybean and tobacco fields of west Tennessee or the bootheel of Missouri or Illinois's Little Egypt. The Jackson Purchase was first settled not long after Jackson and Shelby bought it, and people here today mostly come from families that have been here since the 19th century. They retain a living memory of the generations that came before, in family lore and in the annual Big Singing in the courthouse in Benton, on the fourth Sunday in May, in which perhaps 50 Jackson Purchase residents sing hymns in an old style called Southern Harmony.

Just to the east of the Tennessee and the Cumberland rivers is a region called the Pennyrile (after pennyroyal, a prevalent variety of wild mint). Here you find a land of low hills and small farms. It is also where you find the west Kentucky coal fields, the site of much strip mining in recent years. The Jackson Purchase and, to a lesser extent, the Pennyrile have a southern atmosphere: they grow southern crops, they speak in what sound to northerners like deep southern accents, they have a significant black population (whereas otherwise in Kentucky there are almost no blacks outside Louisville), and in most elections they vote Democratic.

This makes the 1st Congressional District of Kentucky, which is made up of the Jackson Purchase and much of the Pennyrile, one of the most Democratic parts of the state. Earlier in the century Paducah, the largest city here, produced one of the nation's most famous journalists, Irvin S. Cobb, and one of its most successful politicians, Representative (1913–27), Senator (1927–49, 1954–56), and Vice President (1949–53) Alben Barkley. It has elected Democrats to the House ever since. The current incumbent, Carroll Hubbard, was first elected in 1974 after he had the foresight to challenge a weak incumbent in the primary. On arrival in Washington, Hubbard was chosen chairman of the Freshman Caucus, the very existence of which was something of an innovation. Actually Hubbard turned out to be very far from typical of the Democrats first elected that year. His record on non-economic issues is mostly conservative; on economic issues he calls for a balanced budget and for lower interest rates. He lacks the fluency— some might call it glibness—that characterizes so many of the 1974 freshmen.

In 1985, Hubbard became chairman of the General Oversight and Investigations Subcommittee, a panel with jurisdiction to oversee the sensitive and difficult issues arising from changes in financial markets; there this congressman from the Jackson Purchase and Pennyrile questions the likes of Federal Reserve Chairman Paul Volcker and Federal Home Loan Bank Board Chairman Edwin Gray. He is a Democratic deputy whip and a favorite of Speaker Jim Wright. He has been a loyal Democrat, yet has been far enough apart from most other Democrats on major issues to feel a bit isolated. In Kentucky his one attempt for statewide office was unsuccessful. In 1979 he ran for governor, but after a fast start, finished with just 12% of the vote. He was not aligned with any of the state's major political factions, and he could not come close to matching the spending of Kentucky Fried Chicken millionaire John Y. Brown, Jr.; he carried the 1st District with a respectable but not overwhelming 33% of the vote. In 1983 he supported Martha Layne Collins, whose husband was Hubbard's college roommate, in her successful race for the office.

In congressional elections, on the other hand, Hubbard has had little opposition, and sometimes none at all.

The People: Pop. 1980: 525,844, up 12.3% 1970–80. Households (1980): 78% family, 42% with children, 68% married couples; 25.8% housing units rented; median monthly rent: $128; median house value: $29,900. Voting age pop. (1980): 379,011; 8% Black, 1% Spanish origin.

1984 Presidential Vote: Reagan (R) 104,613   (54%)
Mondale (D) 87,339   (45%)

Rep. Carroll Hubbard, Jr. (D)

Elected 1974; b. July 7, 1937, Murray; home, Mayfield; Georgetown Col., KY, B.A. 1959, U. of Louisville, J.D. 1962; Baptist; married (Carol).

Career: Practicing atty., 1962–74; KY Senate, 1967–75.

Offices: 2182 RHOB 20515, 202-225-3115. Also 145 E. Center St., Madisonville 42431, 502-825-1371 P.O. Box 1420, Paducah 42002-2450, 502-442-9804; P.O. Box 1457, Henderson 42420, 502-826-5776; and 100 Hammond Plaza, Ste. 1, Hopkinsville 42240, 502-885-2625.

Committees: *Banking, Finance and Urban Affairs* (6th of 31 D). Subcommittees: Domestic Monetary Policy; Financial Institutions Supervision, Regulation and Insurance; General Oversight and Investigations (Chairman); Housing and Community Development. *Merchant Marine and Fisheries* (5th of 25 D). Subcommittees: Merchant Marine; Panama Canal and Outer Continental Shelf.

Group Ratings

	ADA	ACLU	COPE	CFA	LCV	ACU	NTU	NSI	COC	CEI
1986	35	20	63	50	21	59	45	90	50	38
1985	20	—	61	17	—	63	49	—	68	—

National Journal Ratings

	1986 LIB — 1986 CONS		1985 LIB — 1985 CONS	
Economic	50%	— 50%	39%	— 60%
Social	39%	— 59%	0%	— 76%
Foreign	39%	— 60%	24%	— 66%

Key Votes

1) Lmt Cln Water Act	—	5) Retain Gun Cont	AGN	9) Aid Angola Reb	FOR
2) Rpl Tobac Sub	AGN	6) Contra Aid	AGN	10) Tax Reform	AGN
3) Grm-Rdmn Def Red	AGN	7) Lmt Text Imp	FOR	11) S Africa Sanc	FOR
4) Ban Polygraph	FOR	8) Limit SDI	FOR	12) Immig Reform	AGN

Election Results

1986 general	Carroll Hubbard, Jr. (D)...............	64,315	(100%)	($237,748)
1986 primary	Carroll Hubbard, Jr. (D)...............	63,141	(80%)	
	Tom Barlow (D)	15,088	(20%)	
1984 general	Carroll Hubbard, Jr. (D)...............	112,180	(100%)	($166,779)

Campaign Contributions and Expenditures

1985-86		Direct Cont. 1985-86		PACS Breakdown 1985-86			
Receipts	$288,918	Indiv.	$43,774	Corp.	$78,850	T/M/H	$72,225
Expend.	$237,748	PACS	$193,292	Labor	$26,267	Agr.	$5,550
Unspent	$291,699			Ideo.	$6,500	CWOS	$3,900

SECOND DISTRICT

The 2d Congressional District of Kentucky is a sprawling, largely rural area extending from the Blue Grass country to the hilly Pennyrile area around Bowling Green. Its largest city is the factory town of Owensboro on the Ohio River, which has only 54,000 people. The best-known features of the district are Fort Knox, where much of the nation's gold bullion is kept, and Bardstown, where you can find Stephen Collins Foster's "Old Kentucky Home." Also in the district is the birthplace and boyhood home of Abraham Lincoln. This is rural and small town country, and if people here have all of the conveniences and many of the luxuries that those in America's big metropolitan areas enjoy, they also have family roots that go down here for generations and a connection with the past that isn't often found in big cities.

Much of that past revolves around the Civil War. Kentucky was a slave state that was sharply divided when the South seceded; for a while it said that it was remaining neutral, but finally sided with the Union. But much of Kentucky was unenthusiastic for Mr. Lincoln's cause; Lincoln himself had negligible support in his native state in the 1860 election. The current 2d District was divided: the map shows splotches of counties pro-South and splotches pro-Union, but the bits of color only hint at the deep and often bitter feelings caused by the splits over the war and the losses people suffered. Of those splits and feelings current partisan preferences are a dim but persistent reflection.

William Natcher, one of the House's most hard-working and conscientious members, has represented this district since he won a special election in 1953. He is one of a kind—one of the men and women who makes the House work, and work much better than its detractors know. He is above all meticulous and attentive to detail; he abhors waste and disorder; he is appalled by anything that smacks of corruption. He insists on doing what he regards as his duty, even when it means staying in the chair for long, wearying days during the debate on immigration reform, or when it means responding to harassing quorum calls.

Natcher is often called on to take the chair when the House meets under the committee as a whole procedure. He is the ideal presiding officer: courteous, scrupulously fair, but determined to keep the proceedings moving along. In his middle 70s, he is an active committee member as well. He is the number three Democrat on the House Appropriations Committee, and chairs the Labor-HHS-Education Subcommittee. This is a position of great influence and potential power. The bill is the target for a wide variety of amendments, particularly those to limit abortions; it takes a long time to consider, and instead of passing it the Senate has been content to let these appropriations be taken care of by the continuing resolution, which essentially continues previous funding. That doesn't mean that Natcher cannot wield influence; a telephone call from him to the secretary of any of these departments would be returned speedily. And if he hints that a particular program should be conducted in a different way, his suggestion may very well be followed, regardless of administration or party. But Natcher, as a stickler for propriety, is not going to exert surreptitious influence. He does his work in full view, in committee and on the floor. His record—perhaps surprisingly, for one of his temperament and district, is similar on many though by no means all issues with those of most House Democrats.

Natcher's influence may also be limited, ironically, by his attention to duty. He prides himself on never having missed a roll call vote or quorum call since he was elected in 1953—by the end of the 1986 session he had responded to roll calls 14,926 times—the all-time record. Natcher also, in the old-fashioned manner, resists relying on staff; he does his own reading and research and prides himself on being well prepared. But a lot of the roll call votes on the House floor are on trivial matters or are delaying tactics. Natcher's presence on the floor cuts into his study time; and he has a jurisdiction which cannot be mastered by any single person anyway. Still, there is something awesome about his stubborn devotion to duty.

Natcher brings the same old-fashioned attitudes to elections in the 2d District. He refuses to spend any money but his own on campaigns and, in an age when voters will not pay attention to politicians unless they slip their messages into the middle of television shows, he may not be communicating very effectively with them. His attitude is like that of John Quincy Adams when he served in the House: he will do his duty, and people can vote for him if they want to. So far this has been a winning formula. Four primary opponents in 1982 held him to 60% of the vote, but Kentucky does not have runoffs and so this seems like a comfortable showing. In 1984 and 1986 he was returned to office with overwhelming support.

The People: Pop. 1980: 520,634, up 17.5% 1970–80. Households (1980): 80% family, 47% with children, 69% married couples; 28.0% housing units rented; median monthly rent: $150; median house value: $34,500. Voting age pop. (1980): 361,229; 6% Black, 1% Spanish origin.

1984 Presidential Vote:

Reagan (R)	112,019	(63%)
Mondale (D)	64,163	(36%)

Rep. William H. Natcher (D)

Elected Aug. 1, 1953; b. Sept. 11, 1909, Bowling Green; home, Bowling Green; W. KY St. Col., A.B. 1930, OH St. U., LL.B. 1933; Baptist; married (Virginia).

Career: Practicing atty., 1934–54; Fed. Conciliation Commissioner, W. Dist. of KY, 1936–37; Warren Cnty. Atty., 1937–49; Navy, WWII; Commonwealth Atty., 8th Judicial Dist. of KY, 1951–53.

Offices: 2333 RHOB, 202-225-3501. Also 414 E. 10th St., Bowling Green 42101, 502-842-7376; and #11, The Mall, 50 Public Square, Elizabethtown 42701, 502-765-4360.

Committees: *Appropriations* (3d of 35 D). Subcommittees: District of Columbia; Labor–Health and Human Services–Education (Chairman); Rural Development, Agriculture and Related Agencies.

Group Ratings

	ADA	ACLU	COPE	CFA	LCV	ACU	NTU	NSI	COC	CEI
1986	65	50	72	75	42	23	20	20	28	13
1985	60	—	71	67	—	24	26	—	25	—

National Journal Ratings

	1986 LIB —	1986 CONS	1985 LIB —	1985 CONS
Economic	62% —	35%	68% —	30%
Social	57% —	40%	36% —	60%
Foreign	57% —	41%	61% —	39%

Key Votes

1) Lmt Cln Water Act	AGN	5) Retain Gun Cont	AGN	9) Aid Angola Reb	FOR
2) Rpl Tobac Sub	AGN	6) Contra Aid	AGN	10) Tax Reform	FOR
3) Grm-Rdmn Def Red	FOR	7) Lmt Text Imp	FOR	11) S Africa Sanc	FOR
4) Ban Polygraph	FOR	8) Limit SDI	FOR	12) Immig Reform	FOR

Election Results

1986 general	William H. Natcher (D)................	57,644	(100%)	($5,717)
1986 primary	William H. Natcher (D)................	34,018	(79%)	
	Bob Evans (D)........................	9,317	(21%)	
1984 general	William H. Natcher (D)................	93,042	(62%)	($7,216)
	Timothy A. Morrison (R)...............	56,700	(38%)	

Campaign Contributions and Expenditures

1985-86		Direct Cont. 1985-86		PACS Breakdown 1985-86			
Receipts	$5,717	Cand.	$5,608	Corp.	$0	T/M/H	$0
Expend.	$5,714			Labor	$0	Agr.	$0
				Ideo.	$0	CWOS	$0

THIRD DISTRICT

The 3d Congressional District of Kentucky is made up of the city of Louisville and a few of its suburbs to the south and west. Despite the local pronunciation (LOOuhv'l) and southern traditions—Alistair Cooke calls Kentucky the most self-consciously southern of states, although it never secceded—Louisville is really less a southern town than it likes to think. It is closer in spirit to other old river ports, like Cincinnati and St. Louis, which though larger sprang up at about the same time in similar locations. All three cities, and particularly their large German communities, were hostile to the southern-leaning politics of their slaveholding rural neighbors at the time of the Civil War, and all three had long-standing Republican traditions, among blacks as well as whites. St. Louis turned Democratic in the 1930s, Cincinnati is still decidedly Republican, and Louisville moves back and forth.

Louisville is best known perhaps for its Kentucky Derby, its distilleries, and tobacco factories. Of late, it has probably gained as much global attention because of the mechanical hearts that have been implanted here by a $2 billion local company, Humana Inc., the nation's second-largest operator of for-profit hospitals. Humana's apparent success (though there has been great overcapacity and pervasive fear among the nation's public and private hospitals), and the 3,600 jobs the firm has generated locally, have given Louisville a boost at a time of uncertainty for the city's economy. Brown & Williamson Tobacco, Navistar, and Seagram have recently closed down facilities here; General Electric has laid off thousands of workers at their local plants. Louisville, like many other American cities, is busy replacing a manufacturing economy with a service economy—and experiencing some discomfort in the process.

Louisville candidates are at a disadvantage in Kentucky gubernatorial politics, but Louisville and adjoining Jefferson County have long had a vigorous two-party politics of their own. The office of Jefferson County judge, an administrative position, has become almost a stepping stone to the Senate. Republican Marlow Cook made that move in 1968 and his one-time staffer, Mitch McConnell, did the same in 1986. There is talk that the current county judge, Democrat and former Louisville Mayor Harvey Sloane, who has run for governor twice, may run against McConnell in 1990.

The congressman from the 3d District is Democrat Romano Mazzoli, who won the seat in 1970 by one of the nation's closest margins that year, beating a Republican incumbent who had been mayor of Louisville. Mazzoli has been one of the workhorses in Congress on the difficult issue of immigration reform. In 1981 he became chairman of the immigration subcommittee of Judiciary, and worked with Senator Alan Simpson to produce a reform bill that responded to the sharp increases in illegal immigration in the 1970s by promising, on one side, an amnesty for illegal migrants in the country for several years and, on the other, for employer sanctions to discourage future illegal migration. The Simpson-Mazzoli bill passed the Senate in 1982 and 1983 and the House in 1984 with some differences, but a 1984 conference committee failed to reach agreement. In 1985, after Mazzoli had voted with the Republicans rather than the Democrats on the Indiana 8th challenge, the word came down that he must cede his lead role on immigration to Judiciary Chairman Peter Rodino. After yeoman effort and many perils of Pauline, immigration reform finally became law at the end of the 1986 session. Mazzoli got little of the credit, yet undoubtedly his hard work over many long committee and floor sessions laid the groundwork for what may turn out to be one of the 1980s' most significant laws.

Mazzoli is active on other Judiciary issues as well, including antitrust, and he has served on the District of Columbia and Small Business Committees. His record on economic and foreign policy issues over the years has gotten less and less liberal—which has probably miffed the Democratic leadership, which figures that this urban district would support a more cooperative member—and his record on cultural issues is close to downright conservative. All this may have contributed to his popularity in Louisville, however. In the middle 1970s a local busing controversy caused him some rough going, especially when he refused to support certain anti-busing constitutional amendments. The addition in redistricting of new suburban territory, mostly in the moderate income south and west suburbs, did not hurt him in 1982 or, despite a ballyhooed Republican challenge, in 1984 when Republican Cissy Musselman was expected to make a strong race of it. But it was discovered that she had not earned two college degrees she claimed, and in July—as the immigration reform debate was looming—she withdrew from the race. In 1986 Mazzoli won with 73%, his largest percentage ever.

The People: Pop. 1980: 522,252, dn. 9.3% 1970–80. Households (1980): 70% family, 37% with children, 53% married couples; 38.1% housing units rented; median monthly rent: $162; median house value: $33,100. Voting age pop. (1980): 381,792; 18% Black, 1% Spanish origin.

1984 Presidential Vote:

Reagan (R)	....	109,042	(52%)
Mondale (D)	....	99,200	(48%)

Rep. Romano L. Mazzoli (D)

Elected 1970; b. Nov. 2, 1932, Louisville; home, Louisville; U. of Notre Dame, B.S. 1954, U. of Louisville, J.D. 1960; Roman Catholic; married (Helen).

Career: Army, 1954–56; Law Dept., L & N Railroad Co., 1960–62; Practicing atty., 1962–70; Lecturer, Bellarmine Col., 1963–67; KY Senate, 1968–70.

Offices: 2246 RHOB 20515, 202-225-5401. Also Fed. Bldg., 600 Fed. Pl., Louisville 40202, 502-582-5129.

Committees: *District of Columbia* (3d of 8 D). Subcommittee: Judiciary. *Judiciary* (6th of 21 D). Subcommittees: Crime; Immigration, Refugees and International Law (Chairman); Monopolies and Commercial Law. *Small Business* (11th of 25 D). Subcommittees: Regulation and Business Opportunities; SBA and the General Economy.

Group Ratings

	ADA	ACLU	COPE	CFA	LCV	ACU	NTU	NSI	COC	CEI
1986	50	50	66	67	32	32	29	30	24	41
1985	55	—	66	75	—	33	41	—	53	—

National Journal Ratings

	1986 LIB — 1986 CONS			1985 LIB — 1985 CONS		
Economic	57%	—	42%	57%	—	41%
Social	51%	—	48%	32%	—	67%
Foreign	60%	—	40%	56%	—	44%

Key Votes

1) Lmt Cln Water Act	FOR	5) Retain Gun Cont	FOR	9) Aid Angola Reb	AGN
2) Rpl Tobac Sub	AGN	6) Contra Aid	AGN	10) Tax Reform	FOR
3) Grm-Rdmn Def Red	FOR	7) Lmt Text Imp	AGN	11) S Africa Sanc	FOR
4) Ban Polygraph	FOR	8) Limit SDI	FOR	12) Immig Reform	FOR

Election Results

1986 general	Romano L. Mazzoli (D)	81,943	(73%)	($125,577)
	Lee Holmes (R)	29,348	(26%)	($169)
1986 primary	Romano L. Mazzoli (D) unopposed			
1984 general	Romano L. Mazzoli (D)	145,680	(68%)	($157,243)
	Suzanne M. Warner (R)...............	68,185	(32%)	($31,103)

Campaign Contributions and Expenditures

1985-86		Direct Cont. 1985-86		PACS Breakdown 1985-86			
Receipts	$146,795	Indiv.	$52,661	Corp.	$30,350	T/M/H	$31,600
Expend.	$125,577	PACS	$82,500	Labor	$9,200	Agr.	$350
Unspent	$23,680			Ideo.	$11,000	CWOS	$0

FOURTH DISTRICT

The 4th Congressional District of Kentucky is the state's only suburban district. It consists of two separate suburban areas, connected by a strip of rural Kentucky extending 120 miles along the Ohio River, combining some of the newest with some of the oldest parts of the state. About half its residents live in the suburban counties directly across the river from Cincinnati, Ohio. These are not necessarily bucolic: they include the gritty towns of Covington and Newport (once a noted sin city, but its nude-dancing bars closed down and its old housing gentrified in the 1980s) on the lowlands by the river, as well as old affluent suburbs like Fort Thomas and new middle-income suburbs like Florence and Erlanger on the heights which overlook Cincinnati. Historically these counties, like Cincinnati, have leaned Republican; and so they go in most Kentucky elections. But, with media oriented more to Ohio than Kentucky, people here seem to have political attitudes less anchored to a traditional party preference, and so they are often swing areas. The Louisville suburbs, on the other hand, which include about 40% of the 4th District's voters, are Republican both by heritage and current inclination. The 4th goes right up to the city limits on Louisville's more affluent east side; it includes the farther out, more Republican suburbs on the less affluent south and west sides.

The central, connecting corridor of the district is quite different. Here you find tobacco fields along the Ohio River bottomlands, small farms with wooden fences in the knobby hills a few miles inland, and the old river town of Carrollton near where the Kentucky River that winds through the Bluegrass country flows into the Ohio. This part of Kentucky was settled nearly 200 years ago, and it has been heavily—often almost unanimously—Democratic since the Civil War. It casts only 10% of the 4th district's votes, but those are heavily Democratic.

The 4th District has a freshman congressman who made headlines 30 years before he was elected, Republican Jim Bunning. Bunning was a major league baseball pitcher and a good one; he threw a no-hitter for the Detroit Tigers in 1958 and pitched a perfect game for the Philadelphia Phillies in 1964; he also played for the Pittsburgh Pirates, the Los Angeles Dodgers, and the Phillies again and retired in 1971 with a 224-184 record. He also had one of the highest totals in baseball history for hitting batters, 160, as compared to 18 for contemporary Sandy Koufax and 40 for Juan Marichal. Does he bring similar aggressiveness to politics?

Though he never played for the Cincinnati Reds just across the river, he got involved in Kentucky politics, was elected to the state Senate in 1979, and won a respectable 44% as the Republican nominee against Governor Martha Layne Collins in 1983. Bunning was mentioned briefly as a possible candidate against Senator Wendell Ford in 1986. But 4th district Congressman Gene Snyder, a Republican from the Louisville suburbs, had been hard pressed in 1982 and 1986 despite his status as ranking Republican on the Public Works Committee; and early in the season he called it quits. Bunning quickly sewed up the Republican nomination and, as it turned out, the election. Democratic legislator Terry Mann from the Cincinnati suburbs had run a strong race against Snyder in 1982. But he was fatally hurt in 1986 when it was revealed that he had jimmied his automatic voting device with a rubber band in Frankfort so that he would be recorded as present when he was not. Mann still carried the river counties. But Bunning, with 52% in the Cincinnati suburbs and 63% around Louisville, won with 55% of the vote.

That leaves this perfect game pitcher in a strong political position, with a reasonably safe Republican seat. Some will sniff at the idea of a professional athlete in such a position. But a nation which has chosen a peanut farmer and a movie actor for President, and whose leading political idea men include a football quarterback who majored in Phys Ed and a former New York Knick, is certainly ready to accept Bunning as a respectable practicing politician.

The People: Pop. 1980: 523,090, up 18.6% 1970–80. Households (1980): 79% family, 46% with children, 68% married couples; 26.6% housing units rented; median monthly rent: $175; median house value: $43,400. Voting age pop. (1980): 363,075; 2% Black.

1984 Presidential Vote: Reagan (R) 143,262   (70%)
Mondale (D) 62,253   (30%)

Rep. Jim Bunning (R)

Elected 1986; b. Oct 23, 1931, Campbell County; home, Ft. Thomas; Xavier U., B.S. 1953; Roman Catholic; married (Mary).

Career: Professional baseball player, 1950–71; investment broker and agent, 1960–86; Ft. Thomas City Cncl., 1977–79; KY Senate, 1979–83.

Offices: 1123 LHOB 20515, 202-225-3465. Also 1717 Dixie Hwy., Ste. 160, Fort Wright 41011, 606-341-2602; and 10301 Linn Station Rd., Ste. 105, Louisville 40223, 502-429-5588.

Committees: *Banking, Finance and Urban Affairs* (20th of 20 R). Subcommittees: General Oversight and Investigations; Housing and Community Development; International Development Institutions and Finance; International Finance, Trade and Monetary Policy. *Merchant Marine and Fisheries* (17th of 17 R). Subcommittees: Coast Guard and Navigation; Panama Canal and Outer Continental Shelf.

Group Ratings and Key Votes: **Newly Elected**

Election Results

1986 general	Jim Bunning (R)	67,626	(55%)	($895,709)
	Terry L. Mann (D)	53,906	(44%)	($332,845)
1986 primary	Jim Bunning (R) unopposed			
1984 general	Gene Snyder (R)	108,398	(54%)	($311,716)
	William Patrick Mulloy II (D)	93,640	(46%)	($280,298)

Campaign Contributions and Expenditures

1985-86		Direct Cont. 1985-86		PACS Breakdown 1985-86			
Receipts	$898,648	Indiv.	$555,199	Corp.	$109,622	T/M/H	$76,563
Expend.	$895,709	Party	$24,424	Labor	$11,337	Agr.	$4,000
Unspent	$2,937	PACS	$251,710	Ideo.	$46,194	CWOS	$3,994

FIFTH DISTRICT

If you wanted to find the congressional district most consistently and solidly Republican over the course of the 20th century, you would do well to look not in the high-income suburbs of Houston or in central Utah (both voted for Franklin Roosevelt and Harry Truman) nor in the high-income suburbs of Westchester County, New York, or the North Shore outside Chicago (which elected liberal Democratic Congressman Richard Ottinger and Abner Mikva in the 1970s). You would be well advised to avoid the Sun Belt and high-income areas altogether, and go to the Cumberland Plateau in the south central part of Kentucky. There, in an area with some of the lowest income levels in the United States, is the 5th Congressional District of Kentucky, one of the most Republican parts of the nation.

Roots run deep here. Most people in these hills are the descendants of people whose families had already been there two or three generations during the Civil War; and over the years, cousins have married so that it seems that practically everyone in a community is related to everyone else. Handed down are living memories of the old ways of doing things, when the only contact with the outside world was a steamboat coming up a narrow river, as one did as late as the 1930s, or a coal company owner's agent suddenly ordering the digging up of farmers' land. Harriet Arnow's *Seedtime in the Cumberland* relays the memories her parents relayed, that go back to the time when thousands of settlers were following Daniel Boone through the Cumberland Gap into Kentucky, and John Egerton's *Generations* tells the story of Burnam and Addie Ledford, born in 1876 and 1885, who remembered a great-grandparent who had come to Kentucky in the 1790s and who read the proofs of Egerton's book in 1982. In that perspective, the 1931 feud that divides the numerous Sizemores of Clay County is only yesterday, and the Civil War, which threatened people's lives and everything they had, is recent history. Here in the mountains of Kentucky people are still living in the same communities, attending the same churches, farming the same land, and voting the same party as their grandparents and great-great-grandparents did, and in most cases, in this pro-Union, anti-slaveholding area, it is the Republican Party. The major exception is Harlan County, known as Bloody Harlan during the union organizing days of the 1930s, where the influence of the United Mine Workers is evident in its Democratic voting habits.

The 5th District always goes Republican in presidential and congressional elections, and its congressman is an aggressive Republican, Hal Rogers. Rogers won the seat in the 1980 primary, an 11-candidate contest in which he played up his association with his predecessor, Dr. Tim Lee Carter. In the House Rogers served first on Energy and Commerce and then on the Appropriations Committee—plum assignments for this district. Rogers is a conservative on most issues, but not always on economic matters; politically, he was for Gerald Ford over Ronald Reagan in 1976. But clearly what is most important to him is serving the interests of his district. He is a tiger on coal and tobacco issues. He gets interested in broader issues when they affect folks back home: pipeline safety after several natural gas explosions in Kentucky, restricting textile imports because there are 13,000 textile workers in the district. He is a vociferous critic of any form of smoking ban and supporter of tobacco programs; they ban cigarette advertising in Poland, he says, and yet have the world's highest smoking rate. He is active in trying to promote coal exports and prohibit coal imports and opposes acid rain legislation that would discourage coal-burning.

With his record and the 5th District's strong Republican leanings, Rogers has a safe seat.

The People: Pop. 1980: 523,664, up 22.4% 1970–80. Households (1980): 82% family, 47% with children, 70% married couples; 26.2% housing units rented; median monthly rent: $100; median house value: $25,000. Voting age pop. (1980): 359,513; 2% Black, 1% Spanish origin.

1984 Presidential Vote:

Reagan (R) 133,941	(69%)
Mondale (D) 58,733	(30%)

Rep. Harold (Hal) Rogers (R)

Elected 1980; b. Dec. 31, 1937, Barrier; home, Somerset; U. of KY, B.A. 1962, J.D. 1964; Baptist; married (Shirley).

Career: Practicing atty., 1964–69; Pulaski-Rockcastle Commonwealth Atty., 1969–81; Repub. Nominee for Lt. Gov. of KY, 1979.

Offices: 206 CHOB 20515, 202-225-4601. Also 216 Poplar Ave., Somerset 42501, 606-679-8346.

Committees: *Appropriations* (16th of 22 R). Subcommittees: Commerce, Justice, State, and Judiciary (Ranking Member). *Budget* (9th of 14 R). Task Forces: Budget Process; Defense and International Affairs; Economic Policy.

Group Ratings

	ADA	ACLU	COPE	CFA	LCV	ACU	NTU	NSI	COC	CEI
1986	10	0	29	33	11	86	36	100	67	46
1985	10	—	27	8	—	76	41	—	76	—

National Journal Ratings

	1986 LIB — 1986 CONS		1985 LIB — 1985 CONS	
Economic	37% —	62%	27% —	73%
Social	18% —	78%	0% —	76%
Foreign	0% —	86%	0% —	76%

Key Votes

1) Lmt Cln Water Act	AGN	5) Retain Gun Cont	AGN	9) Aid Angola Reb	FOR
2) Rpl Tobac Sub	AGN	6) Contra Aid	FOR	10) Tax Reform	FOR
3) Grm-Rdmn Def Red	FOR	7) Lmt Text Imp	FOR	11) S Africa Sanc	AGN
4) Ban Polygraph	AGN	8) Limit SDI	AGN	12) Immig Reform	FOR

Election Results

1986 general	Harold (Hal) Rogers (R)	56,760	(100%)	($253,110)
1986 primary	Harold (Hal) Rogers (R) unopposed			
1984 general	Harold (Hal) Rogers (R)	125,164	(76%)	($188,495)
	Sherman Wilson McIntosh (D)	39,783	(24%)	($151)

Campaign Contributions and Expenditures

1985-86		Direct Cont. 1985-86		PACS Breakdown 1985-86			
Receipts	$253,110	Indiv.	$99,184	Corp.	$27,300	T/M/H	$26,162
Expend.	$172,875	Party	$2,750	Labor	$1,500	Agr.	$4,250
Unspent	$135,552	PACS	$62,056	Ideo.	$2,844	CWOS	$0

SIXTH DISTRICT

The 6th Congressional District of Kentucky is the heart of Kentucky's Bluegrass country. Here you find the rolling green meadows where, behind the white wooden fences, thoroughbreds graze; the stately white mansion on the hillock overlooking the fields; the colonel sitting on the mansion's front porch, dressed in a white suit and sipping a mint julep. There actually are places like this in the 6th District, for it contains most of the beautiful horse country around Lexington. It is here that Kentucky Derby winners traditionally are trained, where elegant parties are held during the Keeneland yearling sales, and here at Will Farish's Lane's End Farm that Queen Elizabeth II came to inspect horseflesh during her unofficial 1984 visit to the United States.

But there is history too. These fertile valleys and hills, where the grass seems to shine green in the spring, were the promised land that Daniel Boone and the thousands who came over the Cumberland Gap were seeking in the late 1700s and early 1800s. More typical of the Bluegrass country than the horse farms are the small towns with houses built as long ago as the 1810s—this part of Kentucky was the first part of America settled by migrants from across the Appalachians—or the small, poorer farms with their frame houses. The spiritual capital of this part of the 6th District is Frankfort, the small town where the state Capitol sits between the Kentucky River and hills and trees. Frankfort and Franklin County lead the district in Democratic allegiance; the town's usual preference is strengthened by the fact that Kentucky is a patronage state and the Democrats have held the governor's office for all but 8 of the last 50 years. Overall, the smaller Bluegrass counties in the 6th District almost always deliver Democratic majorities—enough to enable Jimmy Carter to carry this district in both 1976 and 1980.

But they are often offset by the fastest-growing part of the district, the city of Lexington. This is a far bigger town than the city Henry Clay knew, although it retains a few historic structures; much of its recent growth was sparked by the main IBM typewriter plant there, which has made Lexington a major center for high-technology industry and white-collar employment. The Lexington area's population grew 18% in the 1970s, and its unemployment rate was one of the lowest in the nation in the early 1980s recession. The city's new population has been filling up Fayette County (now consolidated with Lexington) with prosperous neighborhoods and spilling over into hitherto rural counties. These affluent, technology-minded voters find rural-oriented Democrats or the patronage politicians of Frankfort entirely uncongenial. While the 6th as a whole went for Carter in 1980, Lexington delivered a nearly 5,000-vote margin for Ronald Reagan.

The congressman from the 6th District is a Republican, Larry Hopkins, and he was elected two years before Reagan's first victory, in 1978. That was something of a fluke: Hopkins was not even the Republican nominee in 1978 when the incumbent, a Democrat with the fine old Kentucky name of John C. Breckinridge, was beaten in the primary. The Republicans dumped their nominee, 68-year-old Mary Louise Foust, and named Hopkins instead; gave him a $300,000 campaign budget; helped him campaign against the Democrat as a backer of big government, big labor, and big spending. That was enough to give him a 2 to 1 margin in Lexington and a 51%–46% districtwide victory. In 1980 and 1982 he won by solid margins; in 1984 and 1986 he won overwhelmingly.

Hopkins's major issue is tobacco, as Kentucky is the second largest tobacco state. He is ranking Republican on the Tobacco and Peanuts Subcommittee, and of course he opposes any changes in the small tobacco subsidy or cozy tobacco allotment programs. The 1982 tax bill, which included a doubling of the excise on tobacco, gave him a medium in which to trumpet his devotion to the crop; he was able to back tobacco and oppose a tax rise, all in one convenient vote which had no conceivable effect on the outcome.

But Hopkins has done more than tend tobacco. He has a seat on the Armed Services Committee and in 1985 and 1986, along with Democrat Bill Nichols, he was one of the sponsors of the Pentagon reorganization bill. This was one of the major legislative products of the 99th Congress, and may have had its genesis in trips Nichols and Hopkins took to Beirut when American Marines were stationed there: both warned that they were in danger and were appalled when 249 Marines were killed by an explosion. They were appalled also that the command structure of the military is so convoluted as to make it very difficult to take sensible precautions. Nichols, who was gravely wounded in World War II, and Hopkins, who served in the Marines in Korea, took the lead in fashioning a positive response, and pushed it through despite the opposition of Caspar Weinberger's Pentagon. Hopkins has also differed with the Administration on nerve gas and some other military and foreign issues; he cannot be stereotyped as a reflexive hawk. His performance on these issues indicates a thoughtfulness and attention to duty which helps to explain his strong electoral showings, well ahead of his party, in this previously Democratic district.

The People: Pop. 1980: 519,009, up 18.5% 1970–80. Households (1980): 74% family, 41% with children, 61% married couples; 38.7% housing units rented; median monthly rent: $174; median house value: $43,800. Voting age pop. (1980): 377,249; 9% Black, 1% Spanish origin.

1984 Presidential Vote: Reagan (R) 123,859   (62%)
Mondale (D) 72,942   (37%)

Rep. Larry J. Hopkins (R)

Elected 1978; b. Oct. 25, 1933, Detroit, MI; home, Lexington; Murray St. U.; United Methodist; married (Carolyn).

Career: USMC, Korea; stockbroker; Fayette Cnty. Clerk, 1969–72; KY House of Reps., 1972–78; KY Senate, 1978.

Offices: 2437 LHOB, 202-225-4706. Also Vine Ctr., 333 W. Vine St., Rm. 207, Lexington 40507, 606-233-2848.

Committees: *Agriculture* (5th of 17 R). Subcommittees: Livestock, Dairy and Poultry; Tobacco and Peanuts (Ranking Member). *Armed Services* (6th of 21 R). Subcommittees: Investigations (Ranking Member); Procurement and Military Nuclear Systems.

Group Ratings

	ADA	ACLU	COPE	CFA	LCV	ACU	NTU	NSI	COC	CEI
1986	10	15	27	8	21	73	54	90	94	71
1985	10	—	27	25	—	71	63	—	81	—

National Journal Ratings

	1986 LIB — 1986 CONS		1985 LIB — 1985 CONS	
Economic	13%	— 85%	23%	— 77%
Social	18%	— 78%	0%	— 76%
Foreign	36%	— 64%	42%	— 56%

Key Votes

1) Lmt Cln Water Act	FOR	5) Retain Gun Cont	AGN	9) Aid Angola Reb	FOR
2) Rpl Tobac Sub	AGN	6) Contra Aid	FOR	10) Tax Reform	FOR
3) Grm-Rdmn Def Red	FOR	7) Lmt Text Imp	FOR	11) S Africa Sanc	FOR
4) Ban Polygraph	AGN	8) Limit SDI	AGN	12) Immig Reform	AGN

Election Results

1986 general	Larry J. Hopkins (R)	75,906	(74%)	($160,669)
	Jerry W. Hammond (D)	26,315	(26%)	($10,141)
1986 primary	Larry J. Hopkins (R) unopposed			
1984 general	Larry J. Hopkins (R)	126,525	(71%)	($166,558)
	Jerry W. Hammond (D)	49,657	(28%)	($35,158)

Campaign Contributions and Expenditures

1985-86		Direct Cont. 1985-86		PACS Breakdown 1985-86			
Receipts	$409,277	Indiv.	$210,668	Corp.	$69,815	T/M/H	$34,583
Expend.	$160,669	Party	$2,354	Labor	$0	Agr.	$12,600
Unspent	$547,846	PACS	$128,548	Ideo.	$10,900	CWOS	$150

SEVENTH DISTRICT

The 7th Congressional District of Kentucky is part—perhaps the heart—of Appalachia. There is hardly a flat acre of land anywhere in this mountainous district, and no city of any size: the largest is Ashland, down on the Ohio River, with 27,000 people. Yet driving on the twisting roads, up and down hills and through hollows, you are never out of sight of a house: this is one of the most densely populated rural areas of the country. Many of the people here are descendants of original settlers, people who came here with or not long after Daniel Boone, in the years after the Revolution. But some came here much later, from other places in the hills or from the flatlands. They were attracted in the early 20th century by coal, the major energy source of its day; and many, though not all, of the counties that now make up the 7th District found that they were sitting on top of beds of coal.

Coal is a difficult mistress. Conditions in underground mines were usually dreadful; the old songs probably understate the miners' misery and dependence and isolation. Then, in the 1930s, the United Mine Workers moved in and organized most of eastern Kentucky's mines, but this was no easy task; there was violence, bloodshed, something approaching civil war. Mostly the union won, and in the short run raised wages and built hospitals for the miners and their families; in the longer run, the UMW planned to and did phase out jobs in the mines, in return for job security and health benefits, as coal was replaced by oil as our major fuel. There was a steady outflow of people from these hills in the 1940s, 1950s, and 1960s: the counties which made up the 7th District had 579,000 people, and people with large families, in 1940; by 1970 the population was down to 459,000. With rising coal prices, there was prosperity, and the population rose to 526,000 in 1980. But it probably has declined again in the 1980s.

Economic change was accompanied by political change. The hills had been solidly Republican since they supported the Union during the Civil War. But the UMW organizing drives and the New Deal converted many miners and their families to the Democratic Party, raising Democratic percentages as much as 40%—a vast change in Kentucky, where political allegiances otherwise have mostly stayed the same for a century. The 7th District went for Walter Mondale and Geraldine Ferraro in 1984.

The plight of the 7th District, and other parts of Appalachia like it, inspired in the 1960s many of the nation's antipoverty programs. One of the architects of those programs was Carl Perkins, the district's congressman from 1948 until his death in 1984. During the days when the Great Society laws were enacted, Perkins was the number two Democrat on the House Education and Labor Committee, which had jurisdiction over many of the bills; when Adam Clayton Powell was thrown out of the House in 1967, Perkins became chairman. He held that position for 17 years, tenaciously guarding his programs, fighting first to expand them and later against cuts. He was one of the last really strong committee chairmen, making sure that only sympathetic Democrats got on his committee, negotiating like a master poker player, and fighting for what he believed in. The Appalachia program, the various aid to education programs, the more generous welfare programs of the 1960s, have improved life in the 7th District and made it more prosperous and more comfortable.

Perkins ended his congressional career characteristically with a victory, though not with all his usual allies. He pushed through the House the so-called equal access bill, a measure to make schools open to religious groups by requiring that they enjoy the same use of school facilities as other extracurricular organizations. He died during the recess, and his son, Chris Perkins, a Kentucky legislator for four years, was given the Democratic nomination, the seat, and spots on the Education and Labor and Public Works and Transportation Committees. Perkins claims credit for passing vocational education and Kentucky wilderness bills, and seems to have succeeded in establishing himself in the district. In 1986 he had no primary opposition and won reelection with 80% of the vote, and he may have as safe a seat as his father did.

The People: Pop. 1980: 526,284, up 23.4% 1970–80. Households (1980): 83% family, 49% with children, 71% married couples; 25.1% housing units rented; median monthly rent: $113; median house value: $27,900. Voting age pop. (1980): 356,178; 1% Black, 1% Spanish origin.

1984 Presidential Vote:

Mondale (D)	92,010	(51%)
Reagan (R)	88,609	(49%)

Rep. Carl C. (Chris) Perkins (D)

Elected 1984; b. Aug. 6, 1954, Washington, D.C.; home, Leburn; Davidson Col., B.S. 1976, U. of Louisville, J.D. 1978; Baptist; married (Cathy).

Career: Practicing atty., 1979–84; law clerk and Asst. Commonwealth Atty., Jefferson Cnty., 1977–78; TV talk show host, 1980–87; KY House of Reps., 1981–84.

Offices: 1004 LHOB 20515, 202-225-4935. Also Fed. Bldg., Pikeville 41501, 606-432-4191; P.O. Box 127, Ashland 41105, 606-325-8530; P.O. Box 486, Morehead 40351, 606-784-1000.

Committees: *Education and Labor* (12th of 21 D). Subcommittees: Elementary, Secondary, and Vocational Education; Postsecondary Education. *Science, Space and Technology* (22d of 27 D). Subcommittees: Science, Research and Technology; Space Science and Applications. *Public Works and Transportation* (32d of 32 D). Subcommittee: Aviation.

Group Ratings

	ADA	ACLU	COPE	CFA	LCV	ACU	NTU	NSI	COC	CEI
1986	80	75	90	75	37	9	24	0	17	4
1985	85	00	88	50	—	10	27	—	23	—

National Journal Ratings

	1986 LIB — 1986 CONS			1985 LIB — 1985 CONS		
Economic	87%	—	0%	89%	—	0%
Social	61%	—	37%	52%	—	47%
Foreign	67%	—	30%	71%	—	26%

Key Votes

1) Lmt Cln Water Act	AGN	5) Retain Gun Cont	AGN	9) Aid Angola Reb	AGN
2) Rpl Tobac Sub	AGN	6) Contra Aid	AGN	10) Tax Reform	AGN
3) Grm-Rdmn Def Red	AGN	7) Lmt Text Imp	FOR	11) S Africa Sanc	FOR
4) Ban Polygraph	FOR	8) Limit SDI	FOR	12) Immig Reform	FOR

Election Results

1986 general	Carl C. (Chris) Perkins (D)	90,619	(80%)	($240,757)
	James T. (Jim) Polley (R)...............	23,209	(20%)	($57,712)
1986 primary	Carl C. (Chris) Perkins (D) unopposed			
1984 general	Carl C. (Chris) Perkins (D)	122,679	(74%)	($40,450)
	Aubrey (Aub) Russell (R)	43,890	(26%)	

Campaign Contributions and Expenditures

1985-86		Direct Cont. 1985-86		PACS Breakdown 1985-86			
Receipts	$217,949	Indiv.	$68,906	Corp.	$13,050	T/M/H	$27,200
Expend.	$240,757	PACS	$144,337	Labor	$91,587	Agr.	$3,250
Unspent	$12,226			Ideo.	$9,000	CWOS	$250

LOUISIANA

No state in recent times has shot up as fast or come down to earth with a more painful impact than Louisiana. It knew poverty, then prosperity, and now fears the prospect of poverty once again. Forty years ago the state's income level was about 60% of the national average; as late as 1970 it was about 75%. In 1982 it reached 90%, within distance, given the low local cost of living, of the national average; in 1984 it was back down to 85% and falling, and in 1986 Louisiana had 13% unemployment, the highest rate in the nation. Meanwhile, a state government with a $700 million surplus in 1982 was facing a $400 million deficit four years later. The sudden economic reversal here may later look like just a downtick in a long upward trend, but for many Louisianans—and perhaps for the state as a whole—it looks like catastrophe right now. Even as the 1984 Summer Olympics in sunny California became a symbol of the nation's mood of optimism and pride, New Orleans's World's Fair became a metaphor for Louisiana's troubles. Unrealistically planned, held outdoors during the steamy Louisiana summer, overpriced for tourists and of no interest to business travelers, sloppily and perhaps scandalously financed by the state government, the event ended up millions of dollars in debt—although you can be sure there are some people who did very well off it.

The reason for the violent ups and downs is that this state's prosperity depends, to a greater extent than any other, on oil. Louisianans grow sugar and rice; they manufacture various products; they practice law and buy and sell real estate and drive trucks and run hospitals. But oil has made the difference here between an economy that gets by and one that thrives. Money from oil helped to preserve Louisiana's traditional way of life, but those traditions often resemble those of a fairly sophisticated Third World country; and without the special income provided by oil Louisiana is in danger of having a Third World economy as well. Louisiana remains, as A. J. Liebling described it 25 years ago, an outpost of the Levant along the Gulf of Mexico. While most of the United States faces east toward the Atlantic Ocean or west toward the Pacific, Louisiana faces resolutely south, to the Gulf of Mexico and the steamy heat and volatile societies of Latin America beyond. Meanwhile, New Orleans is our one major city that preserves the look and feel it had as a French and Spanish outpost in the New World, and Louisiana is the only state whose legal system comes not from British common law but from the Napoleonic Code of continental Europe.

Louisiana was not easy land to settle. About half of it is delta land, soil deposits brought downstream by the Mississippi River and accumulated at its mouth. The Mississippi once emptied into the Gulf in what is now northern Louisiana; the land below that point is soggy, swampy delta, laced with tributaries and offshoots of the Mississippi, bayous and major rivers like the Atchafalaya. The Mississippi itself is held between giant levees, high above the surrounding land. While it is possible to farm some of this land, most is nearly under water, and from a distance it's hard to tell where the land ends and water begins. At the edge of settlement of New Orleans, the swamp abruptly begins; people in nearby subdivisions sometimes find alligators in their back yards. Houses here can't have basements, and in New Orleans even the cemeteries, with their ornate 19th century headstones, are above ground.

Louisiana was the site of an advanced civilization when almost all the rest of the South was still Indian territory (although some of the Indians were pretty advanced too). When the Civil War broke out, New Orleans was one of the nation's five largest cities and the only significant urban center in the Confederacy. Yet in the years after the Civil War Louisiana became one of the poorest of states. There was always a large black population here, because the sugar, rice, and cotton plantations required many slaves. War and emancipation destroyed the wealth of the plantations, and while New Orleans remained a great port—its position at the mouth of the Mississippi and as the terminus of the Illinois Central Railroad guaranteed that—it was also very much a low-wage labor town. In its rickety frame houses, not always strong enough to keep the rain out and never tight enough to keep out the summer humidity or the damp winter chill, lived New Orleans's working class, blacks often living close by whites. New Orleans was one of the most corrupt of American cities in the years of Reconstruction and after, when its votes were regularly bid for and bought; and like other southern cities it became rigidly segregated after 1890.

The Louisiana of the 1920s had enough vitality to give jazz to America and the world, but it also remained desperately poor: a kind of underdeveloped nation, with an impoverished rural hinterland and a single metropolis, where a small number of people managed to become (or remain) very rich and the large majority scratched out a living in low-wage jobs. As in underdeveloped countries, public spending was negligible and public services very limited. One out of four Louisianans was illiterate, and most were poorly educated; while there were streetcar scandals in New Orleans, most of the parishes (the Louisiana name for counties) of the state had not a single paved road. That was the situation when Huey P. Long became governor in 1928. So you can see why no other politician has had as great and enduring an effect on the life of the state as the Kingfish, as he was called: he is still regarded with the kind of awe and affection that underdeveloped countries reserve for their national liberators and caudillos.

Long was governor for only four years and Senator for three more. But in that time he ruled Louisiana with an iron hand. If his political enemies were willing to bribe and cheat, so would he—and he beat them at their own game. Long built Louisiana's skyscraper Capitol and Louisiana State University; he built a network of concrete roads; he passed an old age pension program. He was a serious national figure as well. His nebulous "share the wealth" program became popular enough to pressure Franklin Roosevelt to support Social Security and the National Labor Relations Act in 1935. Roosevelt believed that Long would have been his most dangerous opponent in 1936, and many Americans believed it was only a matter of time before Long would become President. Instead he was assassinated in the halls of the Capitol in Baton Rouge in 1935 at age 42.

For the next half-century, until Senator Russell Long's retirement in 1986, protégés of Huey and members of the Long family have held high political office in Louisiana; elections for 30 years split on pro- and anti-Long lines. Huey Long built a coalition of the poor, including some blacks, against the rich and better off; he never, however, did well in New Orleans, even in its poor neighborhoods. What is so amazing is that this structure of politics was superimposed on a state already divided in two other ways. First was division by race. Although Louisiana has

always had a large black population (in 1980 the third highest black percentage among states), many blacks, especially in New Orleans, were always allowed to vote.

The other division was between Catholic and Protestant, Cajun and Baptist. The Cajun population of Louisiana is descended from the Acadians, French settlers of Nova Scotia driven out when the British took over the territory in 1755. The Cajuns settled in Louisiana, and, except for some New England textile mill towns, they are the only major settlements of French-speaking people in the United States. In any case, about one in every six Louisianans today speaks French as his native tongue, and at least as many more have French names or (as in the case of Governor Edwin Edwards) French blood. And more than one-third of Louisianans are Catholic; Catholicism is the prevalent religion in the New Orleans area, but the real Cajun country is farther west, among the bayous and crawfish-laden swamps of southern Louisiana. The culture is different here, valued more since the Cajun revival of the 1970s than it was in the past. French is used widely and English is spoken with a peculiar accent; the cuisine, spicy and laden with shellfish, is unique, and so is the music and humor. In short, there are many cultural differences between the teetotaling Baptists of northern Louisiana and the beer-drinking Cajuns of the south, and those differences emerge from time to time in politics, usually in no more threatening form than a preference for a candidate of one religious background or another.

Louisiana's rapid economic growth for a time smoothed over some of these old divisions: elections are not referenda on the Longs any more, racism is deeply enough submerged that a Republican drive in 1986 to challenge black voters' eligibility hurt Republicans rather than

Democrats, and cultural rivalry between Cajuns and Baptists is more friendly than bitter. During the 1970s and early 1980s this was one state which did not see itself as a victim of economic trends and in which big economic institutions were regarded with respect rather than mistrust. As for politicians and businessmen, they were judged by results, not procedure: the ends justify the means. Louisiana politics combines a Levantine tolerance of the means by which the world's business must be done with a Latin American gaudiness and fondness for display. That lay behind the buoyant mood when Edwin Edwards, the Cajun governor who presided over the state during the oil boom of the 1970s, was returned to office by a wide margin in 1983 amid the cry of "Laisser les bons temps rouler!"

But the times that rolled ahead were not good. With the collapse of oil prices, Louisiana's affection for free enterprise and opposition to government regulation, never based on principle but on self-interest, vanished, to be replaced by a corrosive suspicion of institutions. That suspicion was strengthened by the trials of Edwin Edwards in 1985 and 1986, on federal charges of steering to his brother profits that he and others made by obtaining approval certificates for hospitals from state government officials who in exchange were promised promotions when Edwards returned to office. Edwards admitted—bragged—that he made $2 million on the deal, but said it was entirely legal and he earned the money while out of office. In December 1985 a jury voted 11–1 for acquittal; in May 1986 the vote was 12–0. But politically Edwards's ratings plummeted while he went off during recesses in the trial to pay telephones to confer with appointees and legislators about the state's burgeoning deficits. Within two years of returning to office as the most popular and commanding politician Louisiana had seen since Huey Long, Edwards had ratings lower than Richard Nixon's during his last days in office, and he had no success in persuading the legislature to institute a state lottery or to license 13 casinos in New Orleans or to turn over to him power to rearrange the state budget single-handed. Louisiana, it was becoming apparent, had emerged from the oil boom with little but a hangover and some hazardous waste sites to show for it.

But revulsion against Edwards was overshadowed by a turn toward economic class politics not seen in most parts of the United States in the 1980s. In the 1986 Senate race Republican candidate Henson Moore ran an ad saying "the party is over, it's morning in Louisiana," but despite a huge financial edge and national party support he was unable to win. The new senator, replacing the retiring Russell Long, was John Breaux, a congressman who gingerly campaigned on traditional Democratic themes and amassed a majority coalition of blacks, Cajuns, and about half the non-Cajun white working-class vote—enough to overcome Moore's majorities in affluent white precincts. It's worth remembering that the big increases in Democratic support in the New Deal came in places like the steel-autos-coal belt from Pennsylvania to Lake Michigan where rapid economic growth and personal upward mobility had been halted suddenly by economic collapse—which is approximately what happened to so many in Louisiana in the 1980s.

The focus for 1987 is on the governor's race when Louisiana, Venezuela-style, will have a half dozen candidates spending millions apiece, with none likely to get the 50% in the primary that, under Louisiana's unique law, gives you victory right there, and with the top two finishers, regardless of party label, heading into a runoff. There will be flamboyant personalities worth watching, but also the possibility of the emergence of a different kind of economic politics, tinged with the procedural irregularity and gaudiness of the Third World, in this unique periphery of the United States.

Governor. The dominant figure in every Louisiana governor's race in the 1970s and 1980s has been Edwin Edwards and, for all his problems, that is true again in 1987. Just after his one-time staffer John Breaux was elected to the Senate in 1986, less than six months after his own acquittal, Edwards announced he was running again; and if his vote-getting prowess turns out to be as gravely impaired as it has seemed to be since 1985 he still has the gift for the pithy phrase and the sense of command to make himself a central figure in any drama. Edwards's problem is not so much the suspicion that his administration is corrupt—Louisianans still don't care much about that. His problem is that the "bons temps" did not "rouler" once he got back in office. Edwards has not found a way to continue the spending on education and welfare programs he says he wants to preserve without raising taxes that he is reluctant to press for and the legislature has refused to raise. But he hopes that his base among blacks, Cajuns, and union members is enough to get him into the runoff, and that there his sharp wit and air of command will enable him to win this election as he has won every election he has been in before.

As usual, Edwards does not lack for opposition. A serious Republican, Representative Bob Livingston, is running, and doesn't have to give up his House seat to do so; the possessor of an old aristocratic name, he also has a common touch, a prosecutor's temperament, and a solid base among New Orleans area whites, which is probably enough to assure him a spot in the runoff. Representative Billy Tauzin comes from the Cajun country and has a record of getting things done and knowing how to raise money, but his base overlaps with Edwards's, and he'll have a hard time getting into the runoff. Two other candidates seem likely to run well in Protestant northern Louisiana, Shreveport's congressman, Buddy Roemer, who is running as a kind of inspirational reformer, though his father, Charles Roemer, was once a top Edwards appointee and went to jail in the Brilab scandal, and Secretary of State Jim Brown. The first election is October 25 (Louisiana state elections are held on Saturday); if, as seems likely, no one gets 50%, the top two finishers run on November 21.

Senators. Russell Long was thinking of running for the office his father won 60 years before; Long himself was first elected to the Senate in 1948 and could have stayed for life. He has his considerable achievements, including encouragement of employee stock ownership plans, the dollar-checkoff campaign financing system, and his stewardship of the tax code as chairman of the Senate Finance Committee from 1965 to 1980. But Long ended his career with far from the power he once enjoyed: in the 1970s he was like an inspired maestro orchestrating tax preferences to perfect the harmony and rhythm of the economy. But in his last year in the Senate Congress abolished most tax preferences and lowered rates, so that even if Long had returned to the Senate and become chairman again he could not have performed as he did.

Louisiana's new senior senator is Bennett Johnston, one of the new generation of powerful southerners now that the Democrats have regained control of the Senate. Johnston is chairman of the Energy and Natural Resources Committee (it was called Interior before the energy crisis), a quiet place indeed under the stewardship of Republican James McClure, which may become more active under Johnston. Energy is of course an important committee for the oil industry, and Johnston is both knowledgeable and a good negotiator; he is an advocate of oil and gas producers, of course, but insists is less sympathetic to the big oil companies than to smaller producers (who are inclined to be very rich individuals, and ready to contribute to political candidates); and he also has an eye on less parochial interests. Johnston earned his knowledge the hard way, hammering out the incredibly complex provisions of the oil and gas deregulation bills under great pressure; he performed so well that even adversaries had to ask him to tell them what was going on. He is also chairman of the Energy and Water Development Appropriations Subcommittee, which together with the Energy chair gives him as much to say on a wide range of environmental issues as any senator. Like most Louisianans, he is alert to the need for economic growth and not interested in curtailing development, but is also aware that some development really can ruin things worth keeping.

Johnston is on the outs with Senate Majority Leader Robert Byrd. He openly backed Lawton Chiles in his unsuccessful challenge of Byrd late in 1984, and in 1986 was himself a declared candidate for the Democratic leadership; he took himself out of the race before the election, presumably because it was clear that Byrd had the votes. This helped to cost him a return stint chairing the Democrats' Senate campaign committee, and may reduce his clout on Appropriations, where Byrd could become chairman if he relinquishes the chairmanship in 1989.

Over the years, Johnston has led a charmed electoral life. He ran for governor in 1972, and just barely lost the Democratic runoff to Edwin Edwards. Months later, he became the only major challenger to Senator Allen Ellender, a Huey Long protégé who had held the seat since

1936; Ellender died between the filing deadline and the primary, and Johnston won the seat easily. In 1978 he was held to 59% by Woody Jenkins, a conservative legislator who ran a race with similar results against Long in 1980. But in 1984 Johnston drew only nuisance opposition (one candidate appeared on the ballot as Larry Napoleon "Boo-Ga-Loo" Cooper) and won 86% of the vote in the September 29 primary. So now he seems to hold one of the safest seats in the Senate.

Louisiana's junior Senator is John Breaux, elected in 1986. He is from Crowley, the same small Cajun town as Edwin Edwards, and for four years he served as the congressman's district aide. When Edwards was elected governor, Breaux ran for the seat and was elected in 1972, the youngest man then in Congress. Practical-minded, he served on the Public Works and Merchant Marine Committee, worked to get federal money for the Cajun country, aggressively promoted the oil business, and helped torpedo the Law of the Sea treaty. His moment of note in the House came when President Reagan invited him to the White House to seek his support for his 1981 budget, and Breaux got him to agree to reinstate sugar price supports. "Does that mean your vote is for sale?" he was asked. "No," he replied, "but it is available for rent."

In most years, Breaux's record would have been an asset; in 1986 it seemed a liability. Republican Representative Henson Moore began the campaign with an overwhelming money advantage; as a member of Ways and Means with little recent opposition, he had $722,000 in his treasury when Russell Long surprised everyone by announcing his retirement in 1985. Edwards was on trial through May 1986, and Moore's "morning in Louisiana" message was intended to associate Breaux with his former employer and political ally; practices that before seemed shrewd now seemed to many voters unacceptably shady. When several other Democrats entered the race over the summer, and Breaux went off the TV for a month, it looked like Moore might win it all in the September primary.

But he fell short, leading Breaux just 44%–37%, and then went dead in the water. Moore was hurt when national Republicans targeted a "ballot security" drive at Louisiana and Moore money, despite initial denials, went into it; this was a thinly disguised attempt to intimidate black voters, but succeeded only in infuriating blacks and increasing their turnout while—no one would have believed this two decades ago—making no favorable impression on whites. Breaux in the meantime began campaigning more and more as an aggressive Democrat on economic issues and, in Louisiana after the collapse of the oil industry, this proved good politics. Black voters gave Breaux margins as large as anyone has ever won in Louisiana; the Cajun parishes came in for him at better than 2 to 1; he carried or ran about even in white Baptist parishes and blue collar neighborhoods. Moore carried all affluent suburbs, the growing cities of Baton Rouge, Shreveport, Monroe, and Alexandria, his own congressional district (though only barely), and— despite appearances by Ronald Reagan and George Bush and plenty of money—not much else. Moore was not able to improve much on his September showing, and in New Orleans, some Cajun parishes, and his home district even fell behind it. It was one example of Democrats winning a seat on economics and party label in a part of the country where in the early 1980s those things seemed to be working against them.

In the Senate Breaux has seats on the Environment and Public Works and the Commerce Committees—expanded versions of his House assignments. He begins his term disposed by his 1986 success and the camaraderie of the last Democratic freshman class to be a party man; but he also is attentive to the economic interests of his state. In the longer run, he is likely to go as Louisiana does: toward a politics of economic classes, if times stay bad and incomes recede below national averages; toward a politics of incentives and minimal government, if the palmy days of oil patch prosperity return.

Presidential politics. Louisiana has been a closely divided state in two of the last three presidential elections: Jimmy Carter won by a small margin in 1976 and lost by a small margin in 1980. Even in 1984 Ronald Reagan ran only slightly ahead of his national average here, and that is thanks to his overwhelming support in the New Orleans suburbs and affluent precincts in Shreveport and other smaller cities. There is a large black vote here, and the Cajun vote has gone

Democratic in national contests. Two developments have made the national Democrats' stands on oil issues not much of a handicap here: first, decontrol of oil prices is now a *fait accompli*, not a live issue; second, the oil industry itself is doing less for Louisianans than they had come to expect. To be sure, Louisiana still seems pretty Republican in national contests. But it has the makings, more than most southern states, of a political turnaround depending on the turn of events and the economy.

Congressional districting. Louisiana's congressional redistricting occupied quite a bit of the legislators' and courts' time but ended up strengthening at least seven of the eight House incumbents. The exception is the 2nd, where after a court-ordered change in the 1982 plan Lindy Boggs ended up in 1984 with a black-majority district and a black opponent; thanks to her solid record on issues, she won decisively and has not attracted serious opposition again. Louisiana's unique all-party primary means that the critical congressional election here for incumbents is in September, for if they win 50% then they are reelected; so far in the 1980s every incumbent who has run has been. That record may be tested in 1988 in the 8th District, where Republican Clyde Holloway, elected in a fluke in 1986, will have a hard time retaining a district that tends to favor national, not to mention local, Democrats.

The People: Est. Pop. 1986: 4,501,000; Pop. 1980: 4,205,900, up 7.0% 1980–86 and 15.4% 1970–80; 1.87% of U.S. total, 18th largest. 13% with 1–3 yrs. col., 13% with 4+ yrs. col.; 18.6% below poverty level. Single ancestry: 11% French, 10% English, 3% Irish, German, 2% Italian. Households (1980): 76% family, 45% with children, 60% married couples; 34.5% housing units rented; median monthly rent: $156; median house value: $43,000. Voting age pop. (1980): 2,875,432; 27% Black, 2% Spanish origin, 1% Asian origin. Registered voters (1986): 2,179,317; 1,704,570 D (78%), 293,990 R (14%), 180,757 unaffiliated and minor parties (8%).

1986 Share of Federal Tax Burden: $12,199,000,000; 1.62% of U.S. total, 22d largest.

1986 Share of Federal Expenditures

	Total		Non-Defense		Defense	
Total Expend	$12,372m	(1.49%)	$9,825m	(1.64%)	$2,547m	(1.11%)
St/Lcl Grants	2,039m	(1.81%)	2,038m	(1.81%)	1m	(0.90%)
Salary/Wages	1,479m	(1.23%)	717m	(1.22%)	762m	(1.23%)
Pymnts to Indiv	5,856m	(1.61%)	5,571m	(1.61%)	285m	(1.60%)
Procurement	2,562m	(1.25%)	436m	(1.64%)	1,498m	(1.00%)
Research/Other	436m	(1.63%)	436m	(1.64%)	0m	(0.69%)

Political Lineup: Governor, Edwin W. Edwards (D); Lt. Gov., Robert L. Freeman (D); Secy. of State, James H.(Jim) Brown (D); Atty. Gen., William J. Guste, Jr. (D); Treasurer, Mary Evelyn Parker (D). State Senate, 39 (36 D and 3 R); State House of Representatives, 105 (83 D and 22 R). Senators, J. Bennett Johnston, Jr. (D) and John B. Breaux (D). Representatives, 8 (5 D and 3 R).

1984 Presidential Vote

Reagan (R)	1,037,299	(61%)
Mondale (D)	651,586	(38%)

1980 Presidential Vote

Reagan (R)	792,853	(51%)
Carter (D)	708,453	(46%)
Anderson (I)	26,345	(2%)

1984 Democratic Presidential Primary

Jackson	136,707	(43%)
Hart	79,593	(25%)
Mondale	71,162	(22%)
Five others, uncomm.	31,348	(10%)

1984 Republican Presidential Primary

Reagan	14,964	(90%)
Uncommitted	1,723	(10%)

GOVERNOR

Gov. Edwin W. Edwards (D)

Elected 1983, term expires Mar. 1988; b. Aug. 7, 1927, Marksville; home, Baton Rouge; LA State U., LL.B. 1949, J.D. 1967; Roman Catholic; married (Elaine).

Career: Practicing atty., 1949–64; Crowley City Cncl., 1954–64; LA Senate, 1964–65; U.S. House of Reps., 1965–71; Gov. of LA, 1971–1980.

Office: P.O. Box 94004, Baton Rouge 70804, 504-342-7015.

Election Results

1983 prim.	Edwin W. Edwards (D)	1,006,561	(62%)
	David C. Treen (R)	588,508	(36%)
1979 gen.	David C. Treen (R)	690,691	(50%)
	Louis Lambert (D)...........	681,134	(50%)

SENATORS

Sen. J. Bennett Johnston, Jr. (D)

Elected 1972, seat up 1990; b. June 10, 1932, Shreveport; home, Shreveport; Wash. & Lee U., 1950–51, 1952–53, U.S. Military Academy, 1951–52, LA St. U., LL.B. 1956; Baptist; married (Mary).

Career: Army, 1956–59; Practicing atty., 1959–72; LA House of Reps., 1964–68; LA Senate, 1968–72.

Offices: 136 HSOB 20510, 202-224-5824. Also Hale Boggs Fed. Bldg., 500 Camp St., Rm. 1010, New Orleans 70130, 504-589-2427; and Joe D. Waggoner, Jr., Fed. Bldg., 500 Fannin St., Ste. 7A12, Shreveport 71161, 318-226-5085; and 1 American Pl., Ste. 1510, Baton Rouge 70825, 504-389-0395.

Committees: *Appropriations* (7th of 16 D). Subcommittees: Defense; Energy and Water Development (Chairman); Foreign Operations; HUD–Independent Agencies; Interior. *Budget* (3d of 13 D). *Energy and Natural Resources* (Chairman of 10 D). *Special Committee on Aging* (7th of 10 D).

Group Ratings

	ADA	ACLU	COPE	CFA	LCV	ACU	NTU	NSI	COC	CEI
1986	50	23	47	33	17	35	29	75	44	30
1985	60	—	45	53	—	45	27	—	28	—

National Journal Ratings

	1986 LIB — 1986 CONS			1985 LIB — 1985 CONS		
Economic	47%	—	48%	70%	—	0%
Social	50%	—	48%	32%	—	16%
Foreign	56%	—	41%	59%	—	0%

Key Votes

1) Ease Gun Cont	FOR	5) Grm-Rdmn Def Red	AGN	9) Rehnquist Nom	FOR
2) Immig Reform	FOR	6) Contra Aid	FOR	10) Tax Reform	FOR
3) Lmt Text Imp	FOR	7) SDI Funding	AGN	11) Drug Death Pen	AGN
4) Aid Tobac Ind	FOR	8) Lmt PAC Contrib	FOR	12) S Africa Sanc	FOR

Election Results

1984 primary	J. Bennett Johnston, Jr. (D)	838,181	(86%)	($1,046,293)
	Robert M. Ross (R)	86,546	(9%)	
	Larry Napoleon Cooper (R)	52,746	(5%)	
1978 primary	J. Bennett Johnston, Jr. (D)	498,773	(59%)	($857,860)
	Louis (Woody) Jenkins (D).	340,896	(41%)	($327,340)

Campaign Contributions and Expenditures

1979-84		Direct Cont. 1979-84		PACS Breakdown 1979-84			
Receipts	$2,312,701	Indiv.	$1,298,263	Corp.	$412,056	T/M/H	$140,155
Expend.	$1,046,293	Party	$4,300	Labor	$36,500	Agr.	$6,000
Unspent	$1,387,880	PACS	$645,358	Ideo.	$35,850	CWOS	$14,000

Sen. John B. Breaux (D)

Elected 1986, seat up 1992; b. Mar. 1, 1944, Crowley; home, Crowley; U. of S.W. LA, B.A. 1964, LA St. U., J.D. 1967; Roman Catholic; married (Lois).

Career: Practicing atty., 1967–68; Legis. Asst., Dist. Mgr. to U.S. Rep. Edwin W. Edwards, 1968–72.

Offices: 516 HSOB 20510, 202-224-4623. Also 705 Jefferson, Rm. 301, Lafayette 70503, 318-264-6071; 500 Camp St., Ste. 1005, New Orleans 70130, 504-589-2531.

Committees: *Agriculture* (10th of 10 D). Subcommittees not available. *Commerce, Science and Transportation* (10th of 11 D). Subcommittees: Aviation; Consumer; Merchant Marine (Chairman). *Environment and Public Works* (6th of 9 D). Subcommittees: Environmental Protection; Nuclear Regulation (Chairman); Water Resources, Transportation and Infrastructure. *Special Committee on Aging* (8th of 10 D).

Group Ratings (as Member of U.S. House of Representatives)

	ADA	ACLU	COPE	CFA	LCV	ACU	NTU	NSI	COC	CEI
1986	30	20	37	25	32	63	47	100	25	33
1985	35	—	35	50	—	62	37	—	62	—

National Journal Ratings (as Member of U.S. House of Representatives)

	1986 LIB — 1986 CONS			1985 LIB — 1985 CONS		
Economic	*	—	*	44%	—	55%
Social	*	—	*	28%	—	72%
Foreign	*	—	*	24%	—	66%

Key Votes (as Member of U.S. House of Representatives)

1) Lmt Cln Water Act	AGN	5) Retain Gun Cont	AGN	9) Aid Angola Reb	—
2) Rpl Tobac Sub	FOR	6) Contra Aid	FOR	10) Tax Reform	FOR
3) Grm-Rdmn Def Red	FOR	7) Lmt Text Imp	FOR	11) S Africa Sanc	—
4) Ban Polygraph	FOR	8) Lmt SDI	—	12) Immig Reform	—

Election Results

1986 general	John B. Breaux (D).................	723,586	(53%)	($2,958,313)
	W. Henson Moore (R)...............	646,311	(47%)	($5,986,460)
1986 primary	John B. Breaux (D).................	447,328	(37%)	
	W. Henson Moore (R)...............	529,433	(44%)	
	Samuel B. Nunez (D)...............	73,505	(6%)	
	J.E. Jumonville (D)................	53,394	(5%)	
	Sherman A. Bernard (D)	52,479	(5%)	
1980 primary	Russell B. Long (D)	484,770	(58%)	($2,166,838)
	Louis (Woody) Jenkins (D).........	325,922	(39%)	($237,242)
	Three others (D, R, No party)	30,321	(4%)	

Campaign Contributions and Expenditures

1985-86		Direct Cont. 1985-86		PACS Breakdown 1985-86			
Receipts	$3,000,614	Indiv.	$1,752,188	Corp.	$317,847	T/M/H	$165,588
Expend.	$2,958,313	Party	$20,502	Labor	$238,568	Agr.	$9,250
Unspent	$42,301	PACS	$875,717	Ideo.	$122,587	CWOS	$22,237

FIRST DISTRICT

The 1st District of Louisiana includes most of the white, upper income, affluent parts of the New Orleans metropolitan area, places most tourists never see—but where they would feel most at home in if they had to live here. Only about 5% of the district is in New Orleans itself, and that is the neat, all-white, 1950s neighborhoods on straight streets headed out to Lake Pontchartrain west of City Park. Just to the west is Metairie, the suburb that is home to more of the city middle- and upper-income whites than is the city itself; stretching farther out, along canals and just south of Lake Pontchartrain, is the more modest suburb of Kenner; and below the railroad lines, beneath the levees on the west and east banks of the Mississippi River, lined with docks and grain elevators and the Avondale Shipyard, are working-class suburbs. All this land is Jefferson Parish, which still has the politics of a rural satrapy, with a fine cast of Louisiana characters, from District Attorney John Mamoulides, who was hovering behind the candidacy of Senator John Breaux, to Assessor Lawrence Chehardy, who despite his Democratic label appeared with his father, a judge, beside President Reagan at an appearance for Republican Senate candidate Henson Moore.

The 1st District extends to the edges of the New Orleans metropolitan area, from the new Jefferson Parish subdivisions along Interstate 10, just reclaimed from swamp, to St. Tammany Parish north and east of Lake Pontchartrain, where people commute to New Orleans from Covington, 30 miles out on the Lake Pontchartrain Causeway, or Slidell, 25 miles east on Interstate 10. The district owes its present shape to the Voting Rights Act, as interpreted by a local federal judge, which required packing almost all of black-majority New Orleans into a single district. That left the 1st District, which once had a demographic cross-section of the metropolitan area, with a 9% black population. It also left the 1st, which until 1976 elected a chairman of the House Armed Services Committee, F. Edward Hébert, and after his death was furiously contested between the parties, a solidly Republican district. The richest people in New Orleans have a reputation for exclusivity, staying off by themselves, uninterested in anything but making comfortable business deals with each other and participating in the right krewe in Mardi Gras. To the extent these people, and those several echelons below them on the socioeconomic scale, do have political opinions, they are solidly conservative. The elite here grew up, as rich people do in underdeveloped countries, in a society where it seemed inconceivable that the large majority of people could become financially comfortable or could handle anything more demanding than menial jobs. They are quite unsentimental about maintaining their privilege and position, and completely unapologetic: since it is inconceivable that others could obtain or even manage such riches, why should they give anything away? That kind of thinking, which you would encounter inside the houses in Caracas, Venezuela, where the tops of the surrounding walls are studded with broken glass, you will find in the neater and more gracious looking homes of outer New Orleans, Metairie or St. Tammany Parish.

Representative Bob Livingston has had no difficulty getting elected in this district or in its more heterogeneous predecessor. He is one Louisiana Republican who has a positive appeal to black and blue collar voters. He bears a proud old New Orleans name; his family were Hudson Valley aristocrats from New York, who settled in New Orleans after Mr. Jefferson purchased Louisiana. But this Livingston grew up in modest circumstances, worked six summers in the shipyards, enlisted in the Navy after high school, and approaches voters without any hint of condescension. He was once a federal prosecutor and approaches politics with a prosecutorial frame of mind; he won the seat in a 1977 special after the Democrat who won it in 1976 was forced to resign due to fraud and eventually went to jail. Livingston was a stern judge of colleagues on the House Ethics Committee and seems to consider issues on their merits and is open to persuasion. He has been given sensitive assignments by the Republican leadership—the Defense Appropriations Subcommittee, the House Intelligence Committee—and has generally taken hawkish positions, strongly supporting aid to the Nicaraguan contras, for example.

With a firm base in the 1st District and important assignments in the House, Livingston has achieved considerable success. But in January 1987 he announced that he was running for governor of Louisiana. With his reputation for probity, he begins with an important asset in a contest whose issues are framed by the conduct—and misconduct—of incumbent Governor Edwin Edwards. It is possible that Livingston could begin 1988 as the central political figure in Louisiana—or remain an important secondary figure in the House in Washington.

The People: Pop. 1980: 525,883, up 35.2% 1970–80. Households (1980): 76% family, 44% with children, 64% married couples; 33.2% housing units rented; median monthly rent: $243; median house value: $59,100. Voting age pop. (1980): 367,724; 9% Black, 4% Spanish origin, 1% Asian origin.

1984 Presidential Vote:

Reagan (R)	. . . .	164,183	(77%)
Mondale (D)	. . . .	47,092	(22%)

Rep. Robert L. (Bob) Livingston (R)

Elected Aug. 27, 1977; b. Apr. 30, 1943, Colorado Springs, CO; home, Metairie; Tulane U., B.A. 1967, J.D. 1968; Episcopalian; married (Bonnie).

Career: Navy, 1961–63; Practicing atty., 1959–72; Asst. U.S. Atty., 1970–73; Chf. Spec. Prosecutor, Orleans Parish Dist. Atty.'s Ofc., 1974–75; Chf. Prosecutor, LA Atty. Gen.'s Ofc., Organized Crime Unit, 1975–76.

Offices: 2412 RHOB 20515, 202-225-3015. Also 111 Veterans Blvd., Ste. 700, Metairie 70005, 504-589-2753.

Committees: *Appropriations* (12th of 22 R). Subcommittee: Defense. *Permanent Select Committee on Intelligence* (3d of 6 R). Subcommittees: Legislation (Ranking Member).

Group Ratings

	ADA	ACLU	COPE	CFA	LCV	ACU	NTU	NSI	COC	CEI
1986	0	0	11	25	11	82	41	100	78	63
1985	0	—	10	33	—	86	49	—	86	—

National Journal Ratings

	1986 LIB — 1986 CONS	1985 LIB — 1985 CONS
Economic	21% — 77%	5% — 92%
Social	11% — 85%	0% — 76%
Foreign	0% — 86%	24% — 66%

Key Votes

1) Lmt Cln Water Act	FOR	5) Retain Gun Cont	AGN	9) Aid Angola Reb	FOR
2) Rpl Tobac Sub	FOR	6) Contra Aid	FOR	10) Tax Reform	FOR
3) Grm-Rdmn Def Red	FOR	7) Lmt Text Imp	AGN	11) S Africa Sanc	AGN
4) Ban Polygraph	AGN	8) Limit SDI	AGN	12) Immig Reform	FOR

Election Results

1986 primary	Robert L. (Bob) Livingston (R) unopposed			($201,033)
1984 primary	Robert L. (Bob) Livingston (R)	86,466	(88%)	($214,072)
	John B. Levy (D)	7,800	(8%)	
	Kevin Curley (D)	4,257	(4%)	

Campaign Contributions and Expenditures

1985-86		Direct Cont. 1985-86		PACS Breakdown 1985-86			
Receipts	$236,023	Indiv.	$130,570	Corp.	$28,675	T/M/H	$13,150
Expend.	$201,033	Party	$104	Labor	$1,500	Agr.	$0
Unspent	$403,766	PACS	$45,963	Ideo.	$2,500	CWOS	$138

SECOND DISTRICT

Since New Orleans came into American hands with the Louisiana Purchase of 1803, it has been one of the nation's most distinctive cities. The heritage of the city's French and Spanish past can still be seen in the French Quarter, where carefully preserved old houses with their iron balconies stand amid the squalor of tourist-packed bars and some of the nation's finest restaurants. New Orleans is our second busiest port, adding the new functions of shipping out Louisiana's oil and petroleum products in huge tankers to its historic role as the outlet of the Mississippi Valley's agriculture and the entrepot of Latin American trade.

Louisiana's 2d Congressional District is made up of almost all the city of New Orleans, including all its older, more distinctive neighborhoods. It includes all of the French Quarter, its 19th century homes still intact because the Americans who moved here after 1803 wanted to stay away from the snobbish creoles and built a new downtown west of Canal Street. Just above the Quarter is the site of Storyville, where prostitution was legal before 1918 and where jazz was probably first played; the old frame houses have long since been torn down, and replaced by housing projects. But many similar neighborhoods remain, inhabited mostly but not always by blacks, in the vividly named streets that go north from the river wharves east of the Quarter. In the other direction, you go through the downtown—full of particularly cold and severe skyscrapers—past the old slum known as the Irish Channel—a reminder that New Orleans had more foreign immigrants than any other part of the South—to the Garden District. This was the home of the rich early American settlers, and its antebellum homes are still covered with vines and Spanish moss. Quaintly named trolley cars still roll out St. Charles Avenue, passing out of the 2d District in the affluent uptown area and back into it when they reach a poor black neighborhood beyond.

Going out east and north from the French Quarter, you find another New Orleans. Past the old frame houses, off Interstate 10, are garden apartment complexes and shopping centers, built on recently reclaimed swampland; just beyond it still is swamp, and you find yourself on a causeway, heading to the Mississippi border. This current 2d District was drawn after the 1982 election and was intended to meet the requirements of the Voting Rights Act by maximizing the number of blacks within its borders (thereby minimizing the number of blacks, and the influence of black voters, in the neighboring 1st and 3d Districts). It has created a black-majority district whose voters seem pleased to continue electing their now long-time Representative, congresswoman Lindy Boggs.

Boggs was first elected to the House, as many women are, as a widow replacing her husband; she has been more than the typical widow just as her husband, Hale Boggs, was more than the typical congressman. He was House majority leader when he was lost in a plane crash in 1972 while campaigning in Alaska; he had a congressional career that went back to 1940, which was distinguished by his courageous, and nearly politically fatal, support of the Civil Rights Acts of 1965 and 1968. Had he lived, Boggs would have been Speaker of the House.

Lindy Boggs will not be speaker, but she has achieved distinction on her own. For years she was considered one of the most knowledgeable of congressional wives and she managed her husband's campaigns in New Orleans—not a job for a political innocent. She has the manners of a girl raised on a plantation (which she was), the panache of someone with an elegant old house in the French Quarter (which she has), and the political savvy of one who has managed tough campaigns and moved in the highest circles of Washington for years (which she has). Her talents were on view to the nation when she served as permanent chairwoman of th000023 Democratic National Convention. She was mentioned occasionally as a possible vice presidential candidate in 1984, although she was not given the consideration younger women like Dianne Feinstein and Geraldine Ferraro received. In the House she serves on the Appropriations Committee and on the HUD-Independent Agencies and Energy and Water Development Subcommittees. On major issues she is inclined to support the House Democratic leadership: she tends to be somewhat generous on economic issues, cautious on cultural issues, and supportive of defense spending (though not the MX). She spends great effort getting Navy contracts for the Avondale Shipyard, getting the Mississippi River dredged 45 feet up to Mile 181, getting $33 million for restoring New Orleans's streetcars—local projects on which she is increasingly well-positioned to help.

No one doubts that Boggs played an important role in persuading her husband to vote for civil rights legislation, and that—plus her current voting record and constituency services—enabled her to overcome a challenge in 1984 from a serious black candidate, Judge Israel Augustine. He got an impressive vote, but Boggs did better: in a district where 55% of the voters are black, she got 60% of the votes. There were predictions that Boggs would step down in 1986 or that outgoing Mayor Dutch Morial would run against her. But Morial's candidate lost the mayoral office to Sidney Barthelemy, a black less given to racial confrontation, and Morial himself lost a race for city council. Boggs had only token opposition in 1986, and the signs—the mayoral race, her 1984 showing, the lack of 1986 opposition—suggest that New Orleans's black majority is not interested in electing a new black congressman and rejecting a congresswoman they believe has served them well.

The People: Pop. 1980: 525,331, dn. 5.3% 1970–80. Households (1980): 64% family, 37% with children, 41% married couples; 62.0% housing units rented; median monthly rent: $151; median house value: $48,500. Voting age pop. (1980): 370,324; 52% Black, 3% Spanish origin, 1% Asian origin.

1984 Presidential Vote:

Mondale (D)	116,480	(62%)
Reagan (R)	70,452	(37%)

Rep. Lindy (Mrs. Hale) Boggs (D)

Elected Mar. 20, 1973; b. Mar. 13, 1916, Brunswick Plantation; home, New Orleans; Newcomb Col. of Tulane U., B.A. 1935; Roman Catholic; widowed.

Career: Pub. sch. teacher, 1936-37; Gen. Mgr., campaigns of U.S. Rep. Hale Boggs; Co-chwmn., Presidential Inaugural Balls, 1961, 1965; Chwmn., 1976 Dem. Natl. Convention.

Offices: 2353 RHOB 20515, 202-225-6636. Also Hale Boggs Fed. Bldg., Ste. 1012, 500 Camp St., New Orleans 70130, 504-589-2274.

Committees: *Appropriations* (16th of 35 D). Subcommittees: Energy and Water Development; HUD–Independent Agencies; Legislative. *Select Committee on Children, Youth, and Families* (4th of 18 D). Task Forces: Crisis Intervention (Chairman).

Group Ratings

	ADA	ACLU	COPE	CFA	LCV	ACU	NTU	NSI	COC	CEI
1986	80	64	74	83	55	18	16	30	25	11
1985	65	—	73	50	—	19	24	—	29	—

National Journal Ratings

	1986 LIB — 1986 CONS		1985 LIB — 1985 CONS	
Economic	87%	0%	74%	25%
Social	79%	19%	40%	60%
Foreign	55%	44%	64%	33%

Key Votes

1) Lmt Cln Water Act	AGN	5) Retain Gun Cont	AGN	9) Aid Angola Reb	FOR
2) Rpl Tobac Sub	AGN	6) Contra Aid	AGN	10) Tax Reform	FOR
3) Grm-Rdmn Def Red	AGN	7) Lmt Text Imp	FOR	11) S Africa Sanc	FOR
4) Ban Polygraph	FOR	8) Limit SDI	FOR	12) Immig Reform	AGN

Election Results

1986 primary	Lindy (Mrs. Hale) Boggs (D)	105,661	(91%)	($261,984)
	Roger C. Johnson (R)	8,474	(7%)	
1984 primary	Lindy (Mrs. Hale) Boggs (D)	76,272	(60%)	($802,065)
	Israel M. Augustine (D)	48,976	(39%)	($81,866)

Campaign Contributions and Expenditures

1985-86		Direct Cont. 1985-86		PACS Breakdown 1985-86			
Receipts	$318,411	Indiv.	$139,776	Corp.	$55,700	T/M/H	$47,500
Expend.	$261,984	PACS	$151,350	Labor	$36,000	Agr.	$2,000
Debts	$60,219	Cand.	$15,000	Ideo.	$8,650	CWOS	$1,500

THIRD DISTRICT

The 3d Congressional District is made up of two quite different parts of southern Louisiana. Most of the physical expanse of the district, and 70% of its population, is part of Louisiana's Cajun country—miles of bayou and swamp giving way to little ribbons of highway pavement and crossroads towns where French remains the first language and roadside diners feature crawfish étouffé. But Cajun country looks not just to tradition. It has become one of the nation's major oil-producing areas, and many of the people here work in local oil production or on offshore rigs. The oil industry indirectly and inadvertently may be responsible for preserving

Cajun culture, for people here, unlike those in many southern rural areas, for years did not have to move out to find well-paying jobs and opportunities for advancement.

The other part of the district consists of geographically disparate and jaggedly-bounded parts of the New Orleans suburbs. It includes parts of the working-class towns of Jefferson Parish along the Mississippi River, hemmed in by swamps and the river (elevated behind levees above street level) and the grain elevators that flank it. Then, on the other side of industrial New Orleans, the 3d crosses over swampland to include St. Bernard and Plaquemines Parishes. St. Bernard was once a tightly controlled fiefdom but is now increasingly white working-class suburbia. Closer in, as you get near the Gulf, is Plaquemines Parish, where the Perez family held sway for decades. The late Leander Perez, Sr., once a Huey Long lieutenant, was excommunicated from the Catholic Church for opposing desegregation, but was still able to deliver a virtually unanimous vote for any candidate he chose. He also managed to make vast sums—no one knows how much—off the oil and sulfur deposits here; no one else seemed interested in extracting them so long as his family controlled local government.

These two disparate parts of the state were thrown together by the one-person-one-vote doctrine. Its current congressman, Billy Tauzin, a Democrat from Thibodaux in Lafourche Parish, was potentially vulnerable when the 3d had suburban territory more upper-income and Republican. But the current district suits him quite nicely. Tauzin first won in a 1980 special election with the support of Governor Edwin Edwards (a Cajun himself); he won that contest narrowly and has not been seriously challenged since.

Tauzin serves on the Merchant Marine and Fisheries Committee, where he can protect local interests; they include wildlife preservation, since the Cajun country is full of sportsmen. He is also a member of the Energy and Commerce Committee. That is the body with jurisdiction over oil and gas price controls, and Tauzin has of course opposed them; but more than that, he has been an active, competent, and aggressive advocate of what he considers to be Louisiana's interest on oil and gas issues. Sometimes combative, Tauzin is not afraid to oppose Energy and Commerce's imposing chairman John Dingell, but he also specializes in biding his time on many issues, establishing himself as a key deciding vote, and then dickering with both sides for an agreement that is most favorable to his position.

Tauzin was a member of the state House and state Senate staffer before going to Washington; he has been in politics essentially all his adult life, and most of that in Baton Rouge. In 1987 he announced he will try to go back, this time as governor. He began the year as probably the candidate most closely associated with Edwin Edwards: although he has never worked for him directly, he did support him in the legislature and was supported by him in turn; both men are proud of their Cajun backgrounds and of their ability to get things done. But in November 1986 Edwards declared that he himself was running again—threatening Tauzin's base. The governor's race is one of those titanic struggles of talented politicians with an uncertain outcome—except that in Tauzin's case it is clear that this wily, knowledgeable politician will be wielding power in 1988 either in Baton Rouge or Washington.

The People: Pop. 1980: 527,280, up 19.5% 1970–80. Households (1980): 82% family, 52% with children, 69% married couples; 28.9% housing units rented; median monthly rent: $168; median house value: $46,100. Voting age pop. (1980): 346,013; 18% Black, 3% Spanish origin, 1% American Indian, 1% Asian origin.

1984 Presidential Vote: Reagan (R) 139,964   (65%)
Mondale (D) 71,187   (33%)

Rep. W. J. (Billy) Tauzin (D)

Elected May 22, 1980; b. June 14, 1943, Chackbay; home, Thibodaux; Nicholls St. U., B.A. 1964, LA St. U., J.D. 1967; Roman Catholic; married (Gayle).

Career: Legis. Aide, LA Senate, 1964–68; Practicing atty., 1968–80; LA House of Reps., 1971–79.

Offices: 222 CHOB 20515, 202-225-4031. Also 2439 Manhattan Blvd., Ste. 304, Harvey 70058, 504-361-1892; 107 Fed. Bldg., Houma 700360, 504-876-3033; and 210 E. Main St., New Iberia 70560, 301-367-8231.

Committees: *Energy and Commerce* (13th of 25 D). Subcommittees: Energy and Power; Telecommunications and Finance; Transportation, Tourism and Hazardous Materials. *Merchant Marine and Fisheries* (10th of 25 D). Subcommittees: Coast Guard and Navigation; Fisheries and Wildlife Conservation and the Environment; Panama Canal and Outer Continental Shelf.

Group Ratings

	ADA	ACLU	COPE	CFA	LCV	ACU	NTU	NSI	COC	CEI
1986	20	10	35	58	33	64	35	90	72	38
1985	25	—	33	33	—	65	38	—	65	—

National Journal Ratings

	1986 LIB — 1986 CONS	1985 LIB — 1985 CONS
Economic	44% — 55%	42% — 57%
Social	27% — 71%	30% — 70%
Foreign	34% — 64%	24% — 66%

Key Votes

1) Lmt Cln Water Act	FOR	5) Retain Gun Cont	AGN	9) Aid Angola Reb	FOR
2) Rpl Tobac Sub	AGN	6) Contra Aid	FOR	10) Tax Reform	FOR
3) Grm-Rdmn Def Red	FOR	7) Lmt Text Imp	FOR	11) S Africa Sanc	FOR
4) Ban Polygraph	FOR	8) Limit SDI	AGN	12) Immig Reform	AGN

Election Results

1986 primary	W. J. (Billy) Tauzin (D) unopposed	($329,823)
1984 primary	W. J. (Billy) Tauzin (D) unopposed	($202,540)

Campaign Contributions and Expenditures

1985-86		Direct Cont. 1985-86		PACS Breakdown 1985-86			
Receipts	$378,802	Indiv.	$180,745	Corp.	$84,450	T/M/H	$52,200
Expend.	$329,823	Party	$700	Labor	$7,400	Agr.	$2,500
Unspent	$421,002	PACS	$150,882	Ideo.	$4,000	CWOS	$332

FOURTH DISTRICT

Northern Louisiana is part of the Deep South, with none of the Creole ambience of New Orleans or the French accents of the Cajun country. For 150 years Baptist farmers have worked the upcountry hills around Shreveport, the commercial center of northwestern Louisiana and the adjacent part of Texas and the largest city in Louisiana's 4th Congressional District. Shreveport and the adjacent suburban areas in Caddo and Bossier (pronounced bohzh-yer) Parishes form about half the district, but in recent years these two segments have diverged in political attitude. The rural parishes seemed to remain wedded—with spats and splits sometimes—with the traditional Deep South attachment to the Democratic Party. They supported George Wallace in

1968 and Richard Nixon in 1972, went back to Jimmy Carter in both 1976 and 1980, gave Ronald Reagan less than overwhelming margins in 1984, and favored John Breaux over Henson Moore in the 1986 Senate race.

Shreveport started off with the same tradition; it was just another market town for the surrounding agricultural parishes. But in the 1940s oil was found in the area, and Shreveport's population grew rapidly. Now Shreveport is more like the small oil cities of east Texas than the rural territory that surrounds it. The newly rich are closely acquainted with the virtues of the free enterprise system (and give little attention to the ways the government subsidized the oil business for years), and they bring doctrinaire free-market ideas to politics. Traditional Democratic allegiance means nothing to them, though they are willing to support likeminded Democrats. Just as they are economically more conservative than their neighbors they are culturally more advanced and urbane. They wait not only for the latest edition of *Human Events* but for the current Neiman Marcus catalogue. So in recent years Caddo and Bossier Parish have gone Republican in most presidential elections.

The congressman from the district, Buddy Roemer, illustrates its leading cultural and political tendencies. He looks like the Louisiana version of a city slicker—young, Harvard-educated, and well-connected. His father was a leading operative for Governor Edwin Edwards (and was convicted of bribery and conspiracy in federal court along with reputed Mafia boss Carlos Marcello). Buddy Roemer is emotional, an inspirational speaker, intense and hard-driving, an instinctive salesman who always believes the pitch he is making. Roemer had to fight hard for his House seat, which he won in 1980 by beating another Democrat who was under indictment on vote fraud charges. He fought in the House, where he threatened to vote against Tip O'Neill for speaker in 1981 (he didn't follow through on that) and voted for the Reagan budget and tax cuts. In 1987 he is fighting for the governorship, insisting that he won't take contributions over $5,000 but still hopes to raise the $4 million that seems to be necessary in a statewide race in Louisiana these days.

Admirers see Roemer as a fiercely independent politician; detractors see him as a grandstanding blowhard. His defiance of the House leadership cost him a chance for a Budget Committee seat; his vote against Louisiana public works projects which lost 203–202 helped fray his already tattered relations with his Louisiana colleagues. Not all his positions are daring: his advocacy as a candidate for governor of more accountability for teachers and campaign finance reform just bring to Louisiana politics ideas that have been common for 10 years in most southern states, and his support of the Martin Luther King holiday and sanctions on South Africa are not uncommon among southern Democrats. But Roemer's brashness makes it difficult for him to get colleagues to go along with even his most sensible and elaborately supported proposals.

Roemer was unopposed in 1982, 1984, and 1986; the 4th District got a breather from fiercely contested elections in which $2.6 million was spent in 1978 and 1980. He seems to have a solid hold on the 4th District, and the question is whether he can convert this strength in a comparatively small media market into a first- or second-place finish in a statewide primary for governor. And there is another question: whether this talented and effervescent politician can, in Washington or in Baton Rouge, settle down to the sometimes unflamboyant business of persuading his colleagues to join him in common action, or whether his major contribution to government will continue to be advocacy and oratory.

The People: Pop. 1980: 525,194, up 11.3% 1970–80. Households (1980): 76% family, 44% with children, 60% married couples; 31.6% housing units rented; median monthly rent: $139; median house value: $34,900. Voting age pop. (1980): 363,684; 29% Black, 2% Spanish origin.

1984 Presidential Vote:

Reagan (R)	130,580	(65%)
Mondale (D)	67,840	(34%)

Rep. Buddy Roemer (D)

Elected 1980; b. Oct. 4, 1943, Shreveport; home, Bossier City; Harvard U., B.A. 1964, M.B.A. 1967; United Methodist; married (Patti).

Career: Businessman, farmer, banker, 1967–80; Delegate, LA Constitutional Convention, 1972.

Offices: 103 CHOB 20515, 202-225-2777. Also 228 Spring St., Ste. 100, Shreveport 71101, 318-226-5080; and 203 E. Texas St., Leesville 71446, 318-239-9916.

Committees: *Banking, Finance and Urban Affairs* (14th of 31 D). Subcommittees: Financial Institutions Supervision, Regulation and Insurance; General Oversight and Investigations; Housing and Community Development; International Development Institutions and Finance. *Small Business* (12th of 25 D). Subcommittees: Energy and Agriculture; SBA and the General Economy.

Group Ratings

	ADA	ACLU	COPE	CFA	LCV	ACU	NTU	NSI	COC	CEI
1986	35	21	25	58	71	60	42	90	61	54
1985	25	—	22	58	—	81	61	—	77	—

National Journal Ratings

	1986 LIB — 1986 CONS		1985 LIB — 1985 CONS	
Economic	42%	— 58%	30%	— 69%
Social	42%	— 57%	40%	— 59%
Foreign	41%	— 57%	24%	— 66%

Key Votes

1) Lmt Cln Water Act	FOR	5) Retain Gun Cont	AGN	9) Aid Angola Reb	AGN
2) Rpl Tobac Sub	FOR	6) Contra Aid	FOR	10) Tax Reform	FOR
3) Grm-Rdmn Def Red	FOR	7) Lmt Text Imp	FOR	11) S Africa Sanc	FOR
4) Ban Polygraph	FOR	8) Limit SDI	AGN	12) Immig Reform	AGN

Election Results

1986 primary	Buddy Roemer (D) unopposed	($197,235)
1984 primary	Buddy Roemer (D) unopposed	($176,796)

Campaign Contributions and Expenditures

1985-86		Direct Cont. 1985-86		PACS Breakdown 1985-86			
Receipts	$190,084	Indiv.	$179,115	Corp.	$1,500	T/M/H	$2,000
Expend.	$197,235	PACS	$500	Labor	$0	Agr.	$0
Unspent	$54,322			Ideo.	$0	CWOS	$0

FIFTH DISTRICT

The upcountry 5th Congressional District of Louisiana, the state's most rural, is part of the Deep South. Aside from the small city of Monroe, the 5th has no urban center of any note. The agricultural establishments in this cotton and piney woods country range from large plantations along the Mississippi River to small, poor hill farms in places like Winn Parish, the boyhood home of Huey P. Long. Politics here was all white as recently as 25 years ago, and some figures suggest that blacks are still excluded today: but today 27% of the district's registered voters are black—virtually the same as the 28% of voting age population that are black. At the same time, fully 38% of the district's children are black. At a time when black outmigration from the South seems to have ended, that is the statistic that matters most to the future: black voters will almost certainly be more numerous and more powerful in districts like this 20 years from now than they are today.

The congressman from the 5th District is Jerry Huckaby, a dairy farmer and former Western Electric management employee, who had the shrewdness to challenge 30-year incumbent Otto Passman in 1976 and the attractiveness to beat him. Huckaby has held the district ever since, and had serious competition only in 1978; in the September 1986 primary he won 68% of the vote and under Louisiana's unique all-party-primary law, was declared elected. Huckaby has good prospects for holding the seat as long as Passman did.

The reason: In 1983 he succeeded to the chairmanship of the Agriculture Committee's Subcommittee on Cotton, Rice, and Sugar. Those are Louisiana's three main crops, and historically producers of all three have depended on heavy subsidies, support programs, or import restrictions. The care and maintenance of such programs will be Huckaby's main work, and he can be counted on to further the interests of Louisiana farmers and middlemen. On other issues he will take a quieter role. His instincts are to the political right; he was one of the Boll Weevil Democrats who supported the Reagan budget and tax cut bills in 1981, and he seems to feel no particular obligation to go along with the Democratic leadership. But as the 1980s have gone on, he has begun to go along with other Democrats more often. That probably reflects the changing nature of congressional issues, the changing views of many northern Democrats, and, not least, the fact that full committee chairmanships are voted by the Democratic Caucus. That means Huckaby has a long-term incentive to keep his record not too far out of line with those of most of his fellow Democrats.

The People: Pop. 1980: 527,220, up 12.6% 1970–80. Households (1980): 76% family, 44% with children, 61% married couples; 26.7% housing units rented; median monthly rent: $96; median house value: $29,400. Voting age pop. (1980): 360,687; 28% Black, 1% Spanish origin.

1984 Presidential Vote: Reagan (R) 140,228   (66%)
Mondale (D) 69,083   (32%)

Rep. Jerry Huckaby (D)

Elected 1976; b. July 19, 1941, Hodge; home, Ringgold; LA St. U., B.S. 1963, GA St. U., M.B.A. 1968; United Methodist; married (Suzanna).

Career: Mgmt. position, Western Electric, 1963–73; farmer, businessman, 1973–76.

Offices: 2421 RHOB 20515, 202-225-2376. Also 211 N. 3rd St., Monroe 71201, 318-387-2244; P.O. Box 34, Old Court House Bldg., Natchitoches 71458, 318-352-9000.

Committees: *Agriculture* (8th of 26 D). Subcommittees: Cotton, Rice, and Sugar (Chairman); Domestic Marketing, Consumer Relations, and Nutrition; Wheat, Soybeans and Feed Grain. *Interior and Insular Affairs* (8th of 26 D). Subcommittees: Energy and the Environment; National Parks and Public Lands.

Group Ratings

	ADA	ACLU	COPE	CFA	LCV	ACU	NTU	NSI	COC	CEI
1986	20	12	28	67	47	65	33	60	73	39
1985	35	—	28	50	—	57	39	—	71	—

National Journal Ratings

	1986 LIB — 1986 CONS		1985 LIB — 1985 CONS	
Economic	41% —	58%	44% —	55%
Social	37% —	63%	34% —	64%
Foreign	43% —	57%	35% —	63%

Key Votes

1) Lmt Cln Water Act	FOR	5) Retain Gun Cont	AGN	9) Aid Angola Reb	FOR
2) Rpl Tobac Sub	AGN	6) Contra Aid	FOR	10) Tax Reform	FOR
3) Grm-Rdmn Def Red	FOR	7) Lmt Text Imp	FOR	11) S Africa Sanc	—
4) Ban Polygraph	AGN	8) Limit SDI	AGN	12) Immig Reform	FOR

Election Results

1986 primary	Jerry Huckaby (D)	96,200	(68%)	($326,332)
	Thomas (Bud) Brady (D)	32,284	(23%)	($41,293)
	Fred Huenefeld (D)	11,966	(9%)	($25,634)
1984 primary	Jerry Huckaby (D) unopposed			($112,825)

Campaign Contributions and Expenditures

1985-86		Direct Cont. 1985-86		PACS Breakdown 1985-86			
Receipts	$234,409	Indiv.	$69,565	Corp.	$47,900	T/M/H	$36,890
Expend.	$326,332	PACS	$111,040	Labor	$2,350	Agr.	$14,100
Unspent	$222,559			Ideo.	$9,550	CWOS	$250

SIXTH DISTRICT

When Huey P. Long came to Baton Rouge as governor-elect in 1928, Louisiana's capital was a small, sleepy southern town of 30,000 people. Today Baton Rouge is a bustling city of 219,000, with a population up 32% in the 1970s. The change has been brought about by both the Kingfish and his bitterest political enemies. Long built a major university in Baton Rouge (Louisiana State) and vastly increased the size and scope of state government. His old enemies, the oil companies, primarily Standard Oil of New Jersey (now Exxon), built the big refineries and petrochemical plants that are the other basis of Baton Rouge's prosperity. For Exxon, long the nation's number one or two industrial corporation, Baton Rouge is especially important; managing the big refinery here is a key job at Exxon, an important step up the ladder for several Exxon CEOs.

Baton Rouge (except for a few black precincts) and its suburban fringe make up about two-thirds of Louisiana's 6th Congressional District. The remainder of the district is to the east, in farming and piney woods country, stretching northeast to the Mississippi border. This area is known as the Florida Parishes, because it was acquired by the United States when West Florida was annexed in 1810. Ancestral politics here is Democratic, but both Baton Rouge and the Florida parishes have been supporting many Republicans for 20 years. In congressional politics, the 6th District has been a Republican district since 1975 and perhaps 1974: the 1974 election had to be rerun, because the machines in one heavily Democratic precinct did not work; the winner of the runoff was Republican Henson Moore, congressman for 11 years, member of the House Ways and Means Committee, and nearly successful candidate for the U.S. Senate in 1986.

Moore's successor in Congress is another Republican, Richard Baker. Politics in Louisiana sometimes sounds mixed-up, and nowhere more than in the 1986 House race here. Baker was a Democratic legislator first elected in 1972 at age 24, and chairman of the roads committee for years; he represented a blue collar Baton Rouge district; but he became a Republican in 1985. His opponent, state Senator Tommy Hudson, once served on Senator Bennett Johnston's staff; he represented a Baton Rouge country club district; but he stayed a Democrat. In the

September primary Baker managed to make more inroads into Hudson's territory than Hudson did into Baker's; high income voters showed more party loyalty than low. The district's overall vote for Henson Moore the same day was reflected in the result here: 51% for Baker, 45% for Hudson, which under Louisiana's all-party primary law meant Baker was elected. This was good news for Republicans—they held an endangered seat—and bad. For in the Senate runoff Moore had no local race to boost turnout while there was a runoff between two Democrats in John Breaux's 7th District.

In Washington Baker got assigned to the Interior Committee, which has jurisdiction over some oil and environmental issues but is usually dominated by Democrats. It will be interesting to see how a southern Republican who started off from a working-class base will deal with national issues—and whether he can make this a safe Republican seat as Moore did.

The People: Pop. 1980: 524,770, up 29.5% 1970–80. Households (1980): 75% family, 45% with children, 61% married couples; 32.6% housing units rented; median monthly rent: $194; median house value: $50,800. Voting age pop. (1980): 362,252; 23% Black, 1% Spanish origin.

1984 Presidential Vote:

Reagan (R)	143,578	(64%)
Mondale (D)	78,263	(35%)

Rep. Richard H. Baker (R)

Elected 1986; b. May 22, 1948, New Orleans; home, Baton Rouge; LA St. U., B.S. 1971; United Methodist; married (Karen).

Career: Real estate developer, 1972–86; LA House of Reps., 1972–86.

Offices: 506 CHOB 20515, 202-225-3901. Also 5200 Corporate Blvd., Ste. B, Baton Rouge 70806, 504-389-0324; 105 S. Cherry, Hammond 70403, 504-345-4845.

Committees: *Interior and Insular Affairs* (15th of 26 D). Subcommittees: Energy and the Environment; Insular and International Affairs; Water and Power Resources. *Small Business* (13th of 17 R). Subcommittees: Regulation and Business Opportunities; SBA and the General Economy.

Group Ratings and Key Votes: Newly Elected

Election Results

1986 primary	Richard Baker (R)	76,833	(51%)	($433,281)
	Thomas H. Hudson (D)	67,774	(45%)	($712,083)
	Willis E. Blackwell (D)	6,120	(4%)	
1984 primary	W. Henson Moore (R)	119,548	(78%)	($274,942)
	Herb Rothschild (D)	33,501	(22%)	($233,096)

Campaign Contributions and Expenditures

1985-86		Direct Cont. 1985-86		PACS Breakdown 1985-86			
Receipts	$434,290	Indiv.	$307,378	Corp.	$25,700	T/M/H	$30,800
Expend.	$433,281	Party	$21,895	Labor	$0	Agr.	$2,250
Unspent	$1,009	PACS	$86,600	Ideo.	$27,850	CWOS	$0
		Cand.	$22,852				

SEVENTH DISTRICT

The 7th Congressional District of Louisiana is one of the very few in the nation where nearly half the population grew up speaking a language other than English. Here the language is French, Cajun style, and it is the mother tongue of more than 40% of the 7th District's residents. This district covers the southwestern part of Louisiana, hugging the Gulf Coast, from the swamps along the Atchafalaya River west to Lake Charles and the Texas border. In the middle is the city of Lafayette, unofficial capital of the Cajun country, and the center of oil exploration in the Tuscaloosa Trend, which in the late 1970s and early 1980s may have produced more millionaires in Lafayette than any other small city in the country.

Many rural backwaters like this have died in the years since World War II; not so the Cajun country of Louisiana. What has kept people here is petroleum, in plentiful quantities under the swampy soil and in even greater amounts below the Gulf of Mexico a few miles out to sea. Oil and attendant industries have generated money to keep Cajuns who wish to stay in their homeland and to attract others as well. Cajun culture—language, music, cuisine—remains healthy as well. For years the use of French was discouraged, and seemed to be dying out; but in the 1970s, people here worked to keep the language alive—even while making sure, sensibly, that their children learned to become completely proficient in English.

But in the middle 1980s the Cajun country seemed caught in a crisis of rising expectations. Rising, because the giddy growth of the oil industry in the late 1970s seemed to promise ever-rising prosperity here—and then, in the early 1980s, it stopped rising. That left borrowers overextended, plungers ruined, and ordinary homeowners unable to maintain a standard of living they expected to achieve. The Cajun country has always been less unfavorable to the national Democratic party than other parts of the South, and in 1984 it gave the Mondale–Ferraro ticket a respectable percentage. Underlying those numbers is the possibility of a liberal movement on economic issues in an area which seemed, a few years ago, a stronghold of confidence in untramelled free enterprise. Was it such a movement, or was it just local pride, that led the 7th District to give its incumbent congressman, John Breaux, more than 60% of the vote in his successful race for the Senate in 1986?

And what is to account for the fact that here in the oil patch, which has been trending Republican since the early 1970s, along the Gulf of Mexico, which has become a Republican stronghold from Gulfport, Mississippi, to Naples, Florida, the Republican party did not even field a serious candidate here in the race to replace Breaux? The contest was all among Democrats, and none of the top three contenders had a Cajun name. In September the most liberal candidate, James David Cain, got just 24% and was eliminated. The American Medical Association and other conservative PACs made independent expenditures on behalf of state Senator Margaret Lowenthal for November, but they were unavailing against Jimmy Hayes, a businessman and formerly Governor Edwin Edwards's commissioner of financial institutions, who raised and spent over $800,000. His ideological and issues appeal seemed to matter more than home town strength: Hayes carried his home area around Lafayette heavily, while Lowenthal won only a small majority in her Lake Charles base. Hayes succeeds to the Public Works chair and presumably to the same practical-minded style of representation as Breaux and has a seat on Science, Space, and Technology as well.

The People: Pop. 1980: 525,361, up 19.6% 1970–80. Households (1980): 78% family, 47% with children, 66% married couples; 28.5% housing units rented; median monthly rent: $154; median house value: $41,500. Voting age pop. (1980): 355,571; 18% Black, 2% Spanish origin.

1984 Presidential Vote:

Reagan (R)	133,221	(59%)
Mondale (D)	91,268	(40%)

Rep. James A. Hayes (D)

Elected 1986; b. Dec. 21, 1946, Lafayette; home, Lafayette; U. of S.W. LA, B.A. 1967, Tulane U., J.D. 1970; United Methodist; married (Leslie).

Career: Asst. City Atty., Lafayette, 1971–72; Asst. Dist. Atty., Lafayette Parish, 1974–83; LA Commissioner of Financial Institutions, 1983–85.

Offices: 503 CHOB, 202-225-2031. Also 109 E. Vermillion, Lafayette 70501, 318-233-4773; 901 Lake Shore Dr., Ste. 402, Lake Charles 70601, 318-433-1613.

Committees: *Public Works and Transportation* (31st of 32 D). Subcommittees: Economic Development, Water Resources. *Science, Space and Technology* (26th of 27 D). Subcommittees: Aviation; Natural Resources, Agriculture Research and Environment; Space Science and Applications.

Group Ratings and Key Votes: Newly Elected

Election Results

1986 general	James A. Hayes (D)	109,205	(57%)	($846,953)
	Margaret Lowenthal (D)	82,293	(43%)	($350,505)
1986 primary	James A. Hayes (D)	51,136	(30%)	
	Margaret Lowenthal (D)	41,938	(25%)	
	James David Cain (D)	40,407	(24%)	
	David Thibodaux (R)	21,082	(13%)	
	Phil Bell (D)	7,479	(4%)	
1984 primary	John B. Breaux (D)	98,674	(86%)	($234,123)
	Johnny Myers (D)	15,752	(14%)	

Campaign Contributions and Expenditures

1985-86		Direct Cont. 1985-86		PACS Breakdown 1985-86			
Receipts	$850,942	Indiv.	$337,230	Corp.	$13,600	T/M/H	$20,950
Expend.	$846,953	Party	$177	Labor	$6,750	Agr.	$500
Unspent	$3,987	PACS	$68,355	Ideo.	$26,555	CWOS	$0
		Cand.	$464,126				

EIGHTH DISTRICT

The 8th Congressional District is in the center of Louisiana, on the cusp between Cajun and Baptist country; most of its residents are blacks or Cajuns. The district begins about where the real delta lands—the silting up of the Gulf of Mexico—begin, about 150 miles inland from the current Gulf coast. Here the Red River joins the Mississippi and, almost immediately, the Mississippi's waters run into dozens of channels, from small bayous to the Atchafalaya and the lower Mississippi River itself. The Mississippi is enclosed by levees here and its flow carefully restricted; it is dredged up to 40 feet all the way to Baton Rouge and will be deepened to 45 feet thanks to the clout of the Louisiana delegation: this is an avenue of commerce, not just a pathway of nature. There are large black populations in the parishes along the river, vestiges of the days when this was Louisiana's great plantation country, and the planters walked down the lane from the mansion and supervised the loading of sugar and rice onto river ships for the trip to New Orleans and the world. Inland you find a large Cajun population: the 8th District includes the northern part of Louisiana's Cajun country.

The presence of the blacks and Cajuns makes this an atypical Louisiana district politically; aside from the 2d District in the New Orleans area, this is the closest thing in the state to a constituency which supports national Democratic policies. It went for Jimmy Carter in both his elections and nearly for Walter Mondale in 1984. Oil is less important here than it is in other districts (though the 8th includes a small part, almost all black, of Baton Rouge), and the civil rights revolution seems to have met less resistance here than elsewhere in the state. Yet in 1986 the district elected a Republican congressman, Clyde Holloway.

Holloway's victory came in unusual circumstances. The long-time (1963–65, 1973–85) congressman from the 8th, Democrat Gillis Long, died in January 1985, after serving usefully as a promoter of ideas in his position as chairman of the House Democratic Caucus; his seat was won in a special election by his widow Cathy later that year. But she decided to retire in 1986. In the old days that would have triggered a battle of white Democrats. But under Louisiana's all-party primary, three white Democrats were eliminated in the September primary, and the candidates who made it into the November runoff were black Democrat Faye Williams, with 25% of the vote, and white Republican Clyde Holloway, with 23%. Neither quite fit the district's profile of an ideal congressman. Williams is bright and articulate and knowledgeable, but she had left Louisiana after graduating from college in 1962 and made her career as an NEA and Democratic staffer in Michigan, California, and Capitol Hill. Holloway raised a family and built a successful nursery business in the district, but his political strength seemed minimal: he got 25% of the vote against Gillis Long in September 1980 and 16% against Cathy Long in March 1985.

Then the race heated up when it was revealed that in 1971 Williams's estranged husband broke into her house, beat her, and shot to death the college professor, who Holloway said was a Communist, she had been dating. Williams, as she pointed out, was the victim (the husband went to jail) and had made no effort to conceal it, but the incident raised a lurid specter of a side of life that many voters prefer not to think about. Surely it must have dominated conversations over coffee or backyard fences more than the candidates' opposite positions on aid to the contras, gay rights, abortion, and gun control. Yet those who wish to ascribe Williams's defeat to racism will have a hard time doing so: with all her handicaps she still managed to carry industrial parishes along the river and to run nearly even in Cajun areas, as well as to win almost unanimously in black precincts. The 8th District showed again its national Democratic leanings when Williams lost by the same margin Walter Mondale lost the district to Ronald Reagan, 51%–49%.

Can Holloway keep this seat? House Republicans gave him a chair on the Agriculture Committee and are hopeful. But it will be uphill going. He is sure to have serious opposition, and it's theoretically possible, though it seems highly unlikely, he could even finish third in the September primary; his chances hinge on whether he ends up with an opponent with liabilities as great as Williams's.

The People: Pop. 1980: 524,861, up 10.4% 1970–80. Households (1980): 80% family, 49% with children, 63% married couples; 29.0% housing units rented; median monthly rent: $93; median house value: $32,600. Voting age pop. (1980): 349,177; 36% Black, 1% Spanish origin.

1984 Presidential Vote: Reagan (R) 115,095   (51%)
                              Mondale (D) 110,380   (49%)

Rep. Clyde Holloway (R)

Elected 1986; b. Nov. 28, 1943, Lecompte, LA; home, Forest Hill; Baptist; married (Cathy).

Career: Owner and operator, wholesale nursery, 1969–86.

Offices: 1207 LHOB 20515, 202-225-4926. Also 515 Murray St., P.O. Box 410, Alexandria 71309, 318-473-7430; City Hall Bldg., 120 S. Erma Blvd., Gonzales 70737, 504-647-2000; and P.O. Box 907, Opelousas 70570, 318-942-1115.

Committees: *Agriculture* (17th of 17 R). Subcommittees: Cotton, Rice and Sugar; Forests, Family Farms and Energy; Tobacco and Peanuts. *Select Committee on Children, Youth and Families* (11th of 18 R). Task Force: Prevention Strategies.

Group Ratings and Key Votes: Newly Elected

Election Results

1986 general	Clyde Holloway (R)	102,276	(51%)	($454,661)
	Faye Williams (D)	96,864	(49%)	($403,804)
1986 primary	Clyde C. Holloway (R)	41,618	(23%)	
	Faye Williams (D)	46,025	(26%)	
	Morgan Goodeau (D)	36,338	(20%)	
	Joe Sevario (D)	34,847	(19%)	
	Carson K. Killen (D)	21,116	(12%)	
1985 special	Cathy Long (D)	61,791	(56%)	($638,675)
	John (Jock) Scott (D)	27,138	(25%)	
	Clyde Holloway (R)	18,013	(16%)	
	Two others (D)	3,808	(3%)	

Campaign Contributions and Expenditures

1985-86		Direct Cont. 1985-86		PACS Breakdown 1985-86			
Receipts	$452,410	Indiv.	$112,429	Corp.	$14,389	T/M/H	$37,974
Expend.	$454,661	Party	$17,955	Labor	$0	Agr.	$1,000
Unspent	$4,157	PACS	$83,148	Ideo.	$29,785	CWOS	$0
		Cand.	$183,917				

MAINE

By road it should not be far from the L. L. Bean store in Freeport, Maine, to Carolyn Chute's *The Beans of Egypt, Maine*. But the distance between the two Maines—the bustling, sensible, and fashionable store which is always open and whose catalogue is well enough known to be lampooned, and the dirt poor, ignorant, ill-clothed, seemingly hopeless family of Chute's novel—captures the extremes of life in Maine today. Here are the resorts, pristine in their unpretentiousness, where Walter Lippmann and Nelson Rockefeller used to summer (the latter used to heat the ocean water near his beach). Here are also farms where the descendants of Yankee pioneers and French Canadian immigrants try to scratch potatoes out of the hard earth in the short months when it's not frozen. Maine's coastal scenery and unfeigned simplicity have a hold on the national imagination, but Maine has also become one of the poorest of states, the far northeastern corner of the United States, bypassed in our *drang nach* west and south.

Maine, frontier when the rest of the East was settled, was not admitted to the Union until 1820, and young families sought their fortunes here up to the Civil War. Like the midwestern states settled at the same time, Maine has been a significant agricultural state; although the land to the south is stony and not very productive, Aroostook County in northern Maine is still one of our major producers of potatoes—a crop which lately could almost be given away. But nature also imposed limits. The growing season is too short, the climate too cold, and the products Maine can easily produce—lumber and potatoes—do not require large settlements of people. Maine had 600,000 people by 1860, 700,000 about 1905, 800,000 in the 1930s, and topped one million in 1971—extraordinarily low population growth that resulted from the outmigration of people and a steady aging of a once young population.

Politically, Maine was famous for the adage, "as Maine goes, so goes the nation." But people watched Maine not because it was a good barometer—it has been more Republican than the rest of the country since the 1850s—but because it voted early, holding its state elections in September, when the weather is still mild and there is daylight after 5:00. The adage was definitively debunked in 1936, when James A. Farley proclaimed after the 1936 Roosevelt landslide, "As Maine goes, so goes Vermont," and more recently Maine's political behavior has been almost perfectly contrarian. It is the only state to have voted for the losers in the last four close presidential elections: for Dewey in 1948, Nixon in 1960, Humphrey in 1968, Ford in 1976. In 1980 it came within 4% of going for Jimmy Carter. In local elections as well, Maine has produced contrarian results. Democrats captured the governorship and both the state's House seats in 1966, a Republican year elsewhere; in Democratic 1974 Maine elected two Republican congressmen and the Democrats lost the governorship to a Republican running as an Independent. In Republican 1978 Maine elected a Democratic governor; in Democratic 1986 Maine elected a Republican governor. This low-income Yankee and French Canadian commonwealth is not a reliable national indicator.

Since 1970 Maine has had its highest rate of population growth since the 1840s. But not all this growth has resulted in—or reflected—a buoyant local economy. Portland, with its late 19th century waterfront gussied up, is now partaking of New England's high tech boom and low unemployment rates. But farther north the migrants tend to be retirees and younger people willing to settle for low dollar incomes in what used to be resort and vacation areas. They are less interested in money than in a particular physical and psyhic environment, and wages in most of the state have not caught up with the local cost of living (including those winter oil heating bills and high taxes) which leaves Maine with what is arguably the lowest level of disposable income of any state.

In its frontier days, Maine was settled mostly by Yankees from farther south in New England,

MAINE 505

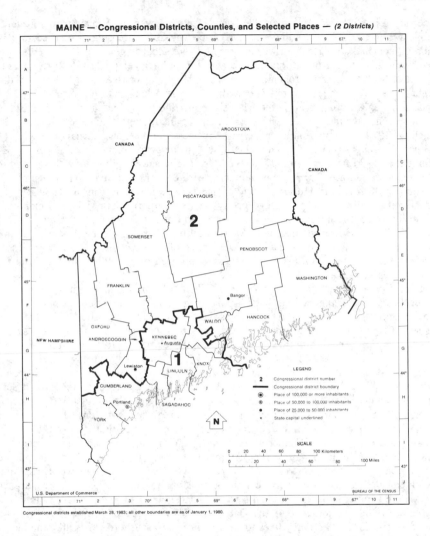

MAINE — Congressional Districts, Counties, and Selected Places — *(2 Districts)*

and that accounts for the Republican preference that has characterized most of the state's political history. Later, in the 20th century, as the Yankee stock aged, Maine had other immigrants: French Canadians from Quebec especially, Irish from Ireland and Boston, Greeks attracted perhaps from their own rocky coasts to the much colder rocky coasts of Maine. As the years went by, Maine became increasingly less Protestant and less Republican, until finally the Democrats became competitive here. That time was reached when Edmund Muskie was elected Governor in 1954 and Senator in 1958—the first time Maine voters ever elected a Democratic Senator. Muskie probably accelerated the process by which Maine became a two-party state: his craggy honesty, his braininess, his national celebrity as vice presidential nominee in 1968 and presidential candidate in 1972 made him something considerably more than the run-of-the-mill ethnic politician, and he proved attractive to Yankee as well as non-Yankee voters.

Since that time Maine voters have gotten into the habit of splitting their tickets, electing an independent candidate as governor in 1974 and giving 30% of their votes to two independent candidates for governor in 1986, meanwhile sending their Democratic governor to the House to replace the Republican congressman they were electing governor. Yankees are still generally Republican, and Catholics are still generally Democratic. But increasingly voters seem to weigh candidates' personal strengths and weaknesses and vote accordingly.

Governor. Maine's governor is John McKernan, a Republican elected in 1986 after two terms in Congress. McKernan is photogenic and a star athlete, personable and good-humored. As a teenager he helped manage his family's Bangor newspaper when his father died; in 1972 he was elected to the legislature and authored Maine's returnable bottle law; he left the legislature in 1976, practiced law, and ran for Congress when the incumbent challenged Senator George Mitchell in 1982. An environmentalist with business support, McKernan was clearly the Republicans' strongest contender since they last won the governorship in 1962, by a 483-vote margin. Yet in 1986 he only won 40% of the vote. The rest was split among three candidates. Attorney General James Tierney, the Democrat with consumerist and environmental credentials, won just 30%; Sherry Huber, a critic of nuclear power who lost in the 1982 Republican gubernatorial primary, won 15% spread pretty evenly across the state, while former Portland city manager John Menario, a conservative, won 15% centered around Portland. Taking up residence in Blaine House (named after Maine's 19th century presidential paladin, James G. Blaine), McKernan talked about leading Maine into a high tech, prosperous, and environment-conscious future; his views on taxes and services appeared only mildly different from former Governor Joseph Brennan's views.

Senators. Maine's senior Senator is William Cohen, a Republican, who has emerged in less than a decade as one of the leading Senate spokesmen on military and defense policy. That was not how he started off in politics: when he was first elected to the House in 1972, he seemed a liberal sort of Republican, supporting the Democratic position on some economic issues and, as a member of the Judiciary Committee, voting for the impeachment of Richard Nixon. But in 1978 he not only took on Senator William Hathaway, and beat him by a wide margin, but he also took on the generally dovish views which Democrats like Hathaway espoused and which seemed at the time to be politically obligatory in Maine. He immediately got a seat on the Armed Services Committee, opposed the SALT II treaty, and supported defense buildups. He has not been, however, a rubber stamp for the Pentagon. He favors more money for defense, but he wants to be clear on what that *more* is going to be spent on. He was one of the originators of the build-down proposal, an alternative to the nuclear freeze and unilateral disarmament approaches, and working with others in the Senate got the Administration to agree to a build-down approach in return for congressional support of the MX missile. He chaired the Seapower Subcommittee and, with Gary Hart of Colorado (his co-author on a spy novel published in 1985), argued for building more smaller ships rather than fewer big ones. He is also concerned, as any Senator from Maine would be, to see that the Bath Iron Works in Bath, Maine, gets its share of shipbuilding contracts. The Navy likes to shift contracts to southern yards, like the inefficient Litton Shipyards in Pascagoula, Mississippi; Cohen insists on pointing out that Bath does better work.

Cohen's combination of military expertise and intellectual independence helped give him a spotlight assignment after the 1986 elections. One was the ranking Republican position on the Senate Intelligence Committee. His Republican predecessor, Dave Durenberger, took the assignment while having troubles in his personal life and operated like a loose cannon, leaking information right and left; Cohen, moving up from a lower spot on the committee, is likely to be more circumspect. Cohen was also chosen to serve on the special Senate committee investigating the Iran-contra scandal. Here his concentration on detail and his nonconfrontational demeanor, already proven on Armed Services and in the Nixon impeachment hearings, is likely to push toward consensus and agreement.

On other issues Cohen has usually not taken a leading role. On economic issues, he shares with most Republicans a faith in the free-market mechanism, but his experience growing up in a family that owned a bakery and then serving as mayor in Bangor inclines him to believe that government should help people out. He pushed, for example, for a measure easing up on the

Reagan Administration's tightening of Social Security disability requirements. On cultural issues, he is one of those East Coast Republicans who take positions which are generally considered liberal. But not always. Consider the Lincoln-Dickey Dam, a local issue of great controversy in Maine for more than 30 years. Democrats and unions want to build the dam, to generate cheap hydroelectric power and provide jobs. Most Republicans, including Cohen, tend to oppose it, to keep government out of the utility business and to protect the environment. Cohen also serves on the Governmental Affairs Committee, and from 1981–84 chaired the Select Committee on Indian Affairs. Indian issues are important in Maine, where a small local tribe sued, claiming they still owned most of the state, and held out for large payments in return for relinquishing their claims; Cohen made a point in 1978 of opposing the Carter Administration's offer as too generous.

Cohen writes and has published poetry, and also a journal of a year in the Senate. He is so pleasant that he seems to lack the aggressiveness needed to get ahead in politics; but get ahead he has. He beat an incumbent Senator 57%–37% in 1978, then was reelected with 73% in 1984 over a Democratic legislator who campaigned on the then withering issue of the nuclear freeze. His prospects for 1990 are excellent, and probably enhanced rather than diminished by the fact that this sometimes liberal, not always predictable Republican from this contrarian corner of the country has not been considered a likely candidate for national office.

Maine's other Senator, Democrat George Mitchell, has also distinguished himself in a short time. When Edmund Muskie was named Secretary of State in May 1980, Mitchell was appointed to replace him. At the time, he looked like a lame duck; he had never won an election (he was the Democrat who lost the governorship to Longley in 1974), and he would face in 1982 a proven vote-getter, former 1st District Congressman David Emery. But in the campaign Mitchell showed steadiness and good humor, while Emery made mistakes; and in a recession year the Democrat won with 61% of the vote. Mitchell was underestimated again when he got himself selected chairman of the Democratic Senatorial Campaign Committee after the 1984 election. For most of the biennium it seemed possible the Republicans would hold the Senate, but Mitchell plugged on, raising money, monitoring the races closely, encouraging strong candidates to run, and the Democrats ended up winning control of 55 seats, more than almost anyone thought possible. Suddenly Mitchell was mentioned as a candidate for a Democratic leadership position, and he began to look like a possible Senate Democratic leader some day.

Mitchell also had a good season on the Senate Finance Committee. Here his basic sympathies were with the Bradley-Gephardt approach of cutting tax rates and eliminating preferences and, aside from Bill Bradley, he was one of the committee Democrats most ready to work with Chairman Bob Packwood to this end. He decided, however, that Packwood's plan was flattening the rates too much, and put forward his own amendment to make them somewhat more progressive. It failed, but Mitchell staked out a position consistent with his party's history and at the same time not inconsistent with the basic thrust of the reform. On Finance and on Environment (where Edmund Muskie made his early mark) Mitchell's detailed approach to issues and political know-how have made him effective. He seems to approach 1990 in solid political shape.

Congressional districting. Maine's current redistricting is a slight modification, made in 1983, of a 20-year-old Republican plan intended to split Democratic strength between the two districts; the modification is that part of Waldo County was added to the population-shy 2d District. Given the ticket-splitting propensity of Maine voters, it hasn't much mattered how the lines are drawn: the districts have sometimes elected two Democrats, sometimes two Republicans, and in 1986 one of each. In modifying the lines in 1983, the Democratic legislature made no attempt to win partisan advantage, nor is it clear how it could have done so.

1st Congressional District. This district stretches from Democratic York County and the area around Portland, the state's largest city, to the craggy-shored ancestrally Republican counties farther east. When the 1st's John McKernan ran for governor in 1986, the governor, Democrat Joseph Brennan, barred from seeking a third term, ran for the House. He is generally counted as a liberal Democrat; he was the only governor to back Edward Kennedy in 1980, and is likely to favor more generous government spending. But the issue which first brought him to voters' attention was Indian claims; as the state's attorney general, he resolutely opposed them and was against a compromise. He is, in whatever direction, a pugnacious man who has made some enemies—but, apparently, more friends.

2nd Congressional District. Republican Olympia Snowe, elected in 1978 to replace Bill Cohen in the 2d District, is now one of the more senior Republicans in the House, and one of the more aggressive and conspicuous. She is one of the founders of the 92 Group, the cluster of somewhat more liberal but still usually partisan Republicans who are working for their party to become the majority by 1992. She is also one of two deputy minority whips in the House, and her voting record reflects considerable fidelity to the Reagan economic programs. On cultural issues, she is more to the center; on foreign and defense issues, cautiously conservative. It is in the last that her committee work, as a member of the Foreign Affairs Committee and ranking Republican on the International Operations Subcommittee, is concentrated. She is a key vote on many issues, giving Republican support to the committee Democrats' approach on South Africa, for instance, or opposing in March 1986 and then favoring in June 1986 Reagan Administration proposals for aid to the Nicaraguan Contras. She is of Greek descent, and is one of the Congress's leading advocates of cutting military aid to Turkey. Geographically her district covers the northern three-quarters of the state; in the more thickly populated part of Maine, however, the boundary line is actually rather jagged, and it takes in the heavily Democratic mill town of Lewiston as well as some more Republican coastal area down east. Snowe has not had strong competition in the last three elections, but her margins are impressive nonetheless: 76% in 1984, 77% in 1986. She would be a strong opponent for Senator George Mitchell, though she does not seem likely to run.

Presidential politics. Maine has no presidential primary and casts four electoral votes. But in 1984 it had a Democratic caucus the week after the New Hampshire primary. Some tried to make this a major event, and Ernest Hollings, backed by a couple of savvy local politicos, took his South Carolina accent Down East and campaigned intensively among the several thousand party activists eligible to vote. It was to little avail. The enthusiasm for New Hampshire winner Gary Hart swept all before it, including a long-standing advantage for Walter Mondale. As for the Republicans, George Bush (who has a summer home in Kennebunkport, which he claimed as his chief residence for tax purposes) won an upset victory in their convention procedure in 1980, presumably making him a favorite here in 1988. For 1988 its Republican caucus may be held in January, before Iowa and New Hampshire, and its Democratic caucuses are scheduled for the Sunday 11 days after New Hampshire. But Maine may well be discounted in all the speculation about what happens to the Iowa and New Hampshire leaders in the huge southern regional primary. Maine's four electoral votes, however unpredictable and counter-cyclical, do not attract much attention in the general election period.

The People: Est. Pop. 1986: 1,174,000; Pop. 1980: 1,124,660, up 4.3% 1980–86 and 13.2% 1970–80; 0.49% of U.S. total, 37th largest. 15% with 1–3 yrs. col., 14% with 4+ yrs. col.; 13.0% below poverty level. Single ancestry: 23% English, 13% French, 5% Irish, 2% German, Scottish, 1% Italian, Polish, Swedish. Households (1980): 74% family, 41% with children, 63% married couples; 29.1% housing units rented; median monthly rent: $173; median house value: $37,900. Voting age pop. (1980): 803,273. Registered voters (1986): 773,944; 263,031 D (34%), 235,122 R (30%), 275,791 unaffiliated and minor parties (36%).

1986 Share of Federal Tax Burden: $2,916,000,000; 0.39% of U.S. total, 42d largest.

1986 Share of Federal Expenditures

	Total		Non-Defense		Defense	
Total Expend	$3,742m	(0.45%)	$2,824m	(0.47%)	$918m	(0.40%)
St/Lcl Grants	672m	(0.60%)	672m	(0.60%)	1m	(.90%)
Salary/Wages	455m	(0.38%)	222m	(0.38%)	233m	(0.38%)
Pymnts to Indiv	1,924m	(0.53%)	1,825m	(0.53%)	99m	(0.56%)
Procurement	645m	(0.31%)	60m	(0.11%)	585m	(0.39%)
Research/Other	448m	(1.68%)	45m	(0.17%)	0m	(0.01%)

Political Lineup: Governor, John R. McKernan (R); Sec. of State, Rodney S. Quinn (D); Atty. Gen., James Tierney (D); Treasurer, Samuel Shapiro (D). State Senate, 35 (20 D and 15 R); State House of Representatives, 151 (86 D and 65 R). Senators, William S. Cohen (R) and George J. Mitchell (D). Representatives, 2 (1 D and 1 R).

1984 Presidential Vote

Reagan (R) 336,500 (61%)
Mondale (D) 214,515 (39%)

1980 Presidential Vote

Reagan (R) 238,522 (46%)
Carter (D) 220,974 (42%)
Anderson (I) 53,450 (10%)

GOVERNOR

Gov. John R. McKernan, Jr. (R)

Elected 1986, term expires Jan. 1991; b. May 2, 1948, Bangor; home, Cumberland Foreside; Dartmouth Col., B.A. 1970, U. of ME, J.D. 1974; Protestant; divorced.

Career: Practicing atty.; ME House of Reps., 1973–77; Asst. House Minor. Ldr., 1975–76; U.S. House of Reps., 1982–86.

Office: State House, Station 1, Augusta 04333, 207-289-3531.

Election Results

1986 gen.	John R. McKernan, Jr. (R)	170,312	(40%)
	James Tierney (D)	128,744	(30%)
	Sherry F. Huber (I)	64,317	(15%)
	John E. Menario (I)	63,474	(15%)
1986 prim.	John R. McKernan, Jr. (R)	79,393	(68%)
	Porter D. Leighton (R).	36,705	(32%)
1982 gen.	Joseph E. Brennan (D).	281,066	(61%)
	Charles L. Cragin (R)	172,949	(38%)

SENATORS

Sen. William S. Cohen (R)

Elected 1978, seat up 1990; b. Aug. 28, 1940, Bangor; home, Bangor; Bowdoin Col., B.A. 1962, Boston U., LL.B. 1965; Unitarian Universalist; divorced.

Career: Practicing atty., 1965–72; Asst. Penobscot Cnty. Atty., 1968; Instructor, Husson Col., 1968, U. of ME, 1968–72; Bangor City Cncl., 1969–72, Mayor of Bangor, 1971–72; U.S. House of Reps., 1973–79.

Offices: 322 HSOB 20510, 202-224-2523. Also 154 State St., Augusta 04330, 207-622-8414; Fed. Bldg., Rm. 204, 202 Harlow St., Bangor 04401, 207-945-0417; 2 Adams St., Biddeford 04005, 207-283-1101; 11 Lisbon St., Lewiston 04240, 207-784-6969; 15 Monument Sq., Portland 04104, 207-780-3575; and 523 Main St., Presque Isle 04769, 207-764-3266.

Committees: *Armed Services* (4th of 9 R). Subcommittees: Conventional Forces and Alliance Defense; Strategic Forces and Nuclear Defense; Projection Forces and Regional Defense (Ranking Member). *Governmental Affairs* (3d of 6 R). Subcommittees: District of Columbia; Investigations (Ranking Member); Oversight of Government Management (Ranking Member). *Select Committee on Intelligence* (Ranking Member of 7 R). *Special Committee on Aging* (2d of 9 R).

Group Ratings

	ADA	ACLU	COPE	CFA	LCV	ACU	NTU	NSI	COC	CEI
1986	50	64	37	60	83	52	51	88	63	56
1985	65	—	39	73	—	55	48	—	68	—

National Journal Ratings

	1986 LIB	—	1986 CONS	1985 LIB	—	1985 CONS
Economic	40%	—	55%	46%	—	52%
Social	53%	—	46%	64%	—	32%
Foreign	35%	—	62%	44%	—	55%

Key Votes

1) Ease Gun Cont	FOR	5) Grm-Rdmn Def Red	FOR	9) Rehnquist Nom	FOR
2) Immig Reform	AGN	6) Contra Aid	FOR	10) Tax Reform	FOR
3) Lmt Text Imp	FOR	7) SDI Funding	FOR	11) Drug Death Pen	FOR
4) Aid Tobac Ind	AGN	8) Lmt PAC Contrib	FOR	12) S Africa Sanc	FOR

Election Results

1984 general	William S. Cohen (R)	404,414	(73%)	($1,063,188)
	Elizabeth H. Mitchell (D)	142,626	(26%)	($410,611)
1984 primary	William S. Cohen (R)	36,606	(100%)	
1978 general	William S. Cohen (R)	212,294	(57%)	($648,739)
	William D. Hathaway (D)	127,327	(37%)	($423,027)
	Hayes Gahagan (I)	27,824	(7%)	($115,901)

Campaign Contributions and Expenditures

1979-84		Direct Cont. 1979-84		PACS Breakdown 1979-84			
Receipts	$1,193,674	Indiv.	$687,793	Corp.	$198,488	T/M/H	$109,470
Expend.	$1,063,188	Party	$19,402	Labor	$14,000	Agr.	$13,250
Unspent	$139,971	PACS	$419,637	Ideo.	$78,217	CWOS	$6,700

Sen. George J. Mitchell (D)

Appointed May 17, 1980, elected 1982, seat up 1988; b. Aug. 20, 1933, Waterville; home, South Portland; Bowdoin Col., B.A. 1954, Georgetown U., J.D. 1960; Roman Catholic; divorced.

Career: Army Counter-intelligence, 1954–56; U.S. Dept. of Justice, 1960–62; Exec. Asst. to U.S. Senator Edmund S. Muskie, 1962–65; Practicing atty., 1965–77; Asst. Atty., Cumberland Cnty., 1971; U.S. Atty. for ME, 1977–79; U.S. Dist. Judge for ME, 1979–80.

Offices: 176 RSOB 20510, 202-224-5344. Also 151 Forest Ave., P.O. Box 8300, Portland 01401, 207-780-3561; Fed. Bldg., 40 Western Ave., Rm. 101C, Augusta 04330, 207-622-8292; 231 Main St., Biddeford 04005, 207-282-4144; 387 Main St., Rockland 04841, 207-596-0311; Fed. Bldg., 202 Harlow St., P.O. Box 1237, Bangor 04401, 207-945-0451; 11 Lisbon St., Lewiston 04240, 207-784-0163; 33 College Ave., P.O. Box 786, Waterville 04901, 207-873-3361; and 6 Church St., Presque Isle 04769, 207-764-5601.

Committees: *Environment and Public Works* (3d of 9 D). Subcommittees: Environmental Protection (Chairman); Nuclear Regulation; Water Resources, Transportation, and Infrastructure. *Finance* (7th of 11 D). Subcommittees: Health (Chairman); International Trade; Social Security and Family Policy. *Governmental Affairs* (7th of 8 D). Governmental Efficiency, Federalism and the District of Columbia; Oversight of Government Management; Investigations. *Veterans' Affairs* (4th of 6 D).

Group Ratings

	ADA	ACLU	COPE	CFA	LCV	ACU	NTU	NSI	COC	CEI
1986	85	78	86	87	92	14	49	20	32	35
1985	65	—	85	87	—	17	34	—	31	—

National Journal Ratings

	1986 LIB	—	1986 CONS	1985 LIB	—	1985 CONS
Economic	72%	—	27%	70%	—	26%
Social	89%	—	10%	68%	—	28%
Foreign	75%	—	0%	78%	—	19%

Key Votes

1) Ease Gun Cont	FOR	5) Grm-Rdmn Def Red	FOR	9) Rehnquist Nom	AGN
2) Immig Reform	AGN	6) Contra Aid	AGN	10) Tax Reform	FOR
3) Lmt Text Imp	FOR	7) SDI Funding	AGN	11) Drug Death Pen	FOR
4) Aid Tobac Ind	AGN	8) Lmt PAC Contrib	FOR	12) S Africa Sanc	FOR

Election Results

1982 general	George J. Mitchell (D)	279,819	(61%)	($1,209,599)
	David F. Emery (R)	179,882	(39%)	($1,081,122)
1982 primary	George J. Mitchell (D)	68,169	(100%)	
1976 general	Edmund S. Muskie (D)	199,954	(60%)	($320,427)
	Robert A.G. Monks (R)	193,489	(40%)	($598,490)

Campaign Contributions and Expenditures

1981-82		Direct Cont. 1981-82		PACS Breakdown			
Receipts	$1,218,350	Indiv.	$619,439	Agr	$7,350	Ideo	$117,050
Expend.	$1,209,599	Party	$20,134	Bus	$164,620	Lbr	$209,547
Unspent	$8,523	PACS	$563,836	Hlth	$16,100	Prof	$21,280

FIRST DISTRICT

The People: Pop. 1980: 563,073, up 17.2% 1970–80. Households (1980): 73% family, 39% with children, 62% married couples; 30.4% housing units rented; median monthly rent: $186; median house value: $42,000. Voting age pop. (1980): 405,831.

1984 Presidential Vote:
Reagan (R)	175,472	(60%)
Mondale (D)	117,450	(40%)

Rep. Joseph E. Brennan (D)

Elected 1986; b. Nov. 2, 1934, Portland; home, Portland; Boston Col., A.B. 1958, U. of ME, J.D. 1963; Roman Catholic; divorced.

Career: Practicing atty.; ME House of Reps., 1965–71; Cumberland Cnty. Atty., 1971–73; ME Senate, 1973–75, Dem. Flr. Ldr.; Atty. Gen. of ME, 1975–78.

Offices: 1428 LHOB 20515, 202-225-6116. Also P.O. Box 10240, Portland 04104, 207-780-3381; 154 State St., Augusta 04330, 207-622-8303; 118 Main St., Sanford 04073, 207-324-2911; and P.O. Box 469, Fed. Bldg., 21 Limerock St., Rockland 04841, 207-594-7285; 111 Commercial St., Portland 04101; 207-772-8240; and 128 State St., Ste. 102, Augusta 04330, 207-623-2883, 207-623-3175.

Committees: *Armed Services* (30th of 31 D). Subcommittees: Research and Development; Seapower and Strategic and Critical Materials. *Merchant Marine and Fisheries* (24th of 25 D). Subcommittees: Coast Guard and Navigation; Merchant Marine; Panama Canal and Outer Continental Shelf.

Group Ratings and Key Votes: Newly Elected

Election Results

1986 general	Joseph E. Brennan (D)	121,848	(53%)	($287,695)
	H. Rollin Ives (R)	100,260	(44%)	($261,403)
1986 primary	Joseph E. Brennan (D)	54,088	(100%)	
1984 general	John R. McKernan, Jr. (R)	182,785	(64%)	($411,575)
	Barry J. Hobbins (D)	104,972	(36%)	($195,285)

Campaign Contributions and Expenditures

1985-86		Direct Cont. 1985-86		PACS Breakdown 1985-86			
Receipts	$287,821	Indiv.	$154,652	Corp.	$21,850	T/M/H	$23,200
Expend.	$287,695	Party	$915	Labor	$61,037	Agr.	$3,350
Unspent	$124	PACS	$137,617	Ideo.	$23,680	CWOS	$4,500

SECOND DISTRICT

The People: Pop. 1980: 561,587, up 9.4% 1970–80. Households (1980): 76% family, 42% with children, 64% married couples; 27.7% housing units rented; median monthly rent: $161; median house value: $33,600. Voting age pop. (1980): 397,442.

1984 Presidential Vote:
Reagan (R)	161,028	(62%)
Mondale (D)	97,065	(37%)

Rep. Olympia J. Snowe (R)

Elected 1978; b. Feb. 21, 1947, Augusta; home, Auburn; U. of ME, B.A. 1969; Greek Orthodox; widowed.

Career: Dir., Superior Concrete Co.; Member, Bd. of Voter Regis., Auburn, ME, 1971–73; ME House of Reps., 1973–76; ME Senate, 1976–78.

Offices: 2464 LHOB 20515, 202-225-6306. Also 202 Harlow St., Room 209, Bangor 04401, 207-945-0432; 197 State St., P.O. Box 722, Presque Isle 04769, 207-764-5124; and 2 Great Falls Plaza, Ste. 7B, Auburn 04210, 207-786-2451.

Committees: *Foreign Affairs* (6th of 18 R). Subcommittees: Arms Control, International Security and Science; International Operations (Ranking Member). *Select Committee on Aging* (5th of 26 R). Subcommittee: Human Services (Ranking Member). *Joint Economic Committee.* Task Forces: Education and Health; Fiscal and Monetary Policy; International Economic Policy.

Group Ratings

	ADA	ACLU	COPE	CFA	LCV	ACU	NTU	NSI	COC	CEI
1986	50	50	44	58	68	48	46	60	61	46
1985	35	—	42	83	—	48	52	—	69	—

National Journal Ratings

	1986 LIB — 1986 CONS	1985 LIB — 1985 CONS
Economic	29% — 70%	36% — 63%
Social	52% — 46%	69% — 28%
Foreign	52% — 47%	48% — 51%

Key Votes

1) Lmt Cln Water Act	FOR	5) Retain Gun Cont	AGN	9) Aid Angola Reb	FOR
2) Rpl Tobac Sub	FOR	6) Contra Aid	AGN	10) Tax Reform	FOR
3) Grm-Rdmn Def Red	FOR	7) Lmt Text Imp	FOR	11) S Africa Sanc	FOR
4) Ban Polygraph	FOR	8) Limit SDI	FOR	12) Immig Reform	FOR

Election Results

1986 general	Olympia J. Snowe (R)	148,770	(77%)	($215,659)
	Richard R. Charette (D)...............	43,614	(23%)	($23,779)
1986 primary	Olympia J. Snowe (R) unopposed			
1984 general	Olympia J. Snowe (R)	192,166	(76%)	($236,791)
	Chipman C. Bull (D)	57,347	(23%)	($44,868)

Campaign Contributions and Expenditures

1985-86		Direct Cont. 1985-86		PACS Breakdown 1985-86			
Receipts	$216,402	Indiv.	$126,418	Corp.	$31,900	T/M/H	$23,950
Expend.	$215,659	Party	$2,744	Labor	$44750	Agr.	$2,750
Unspent	$4,375	PACS	$76,425	Ideo.	$12,200	CWOS	$1,250

MARYLAND

Maryland suddenly found itself bursting with local pride in 1986. Like so many states with boundaries set years ago in ways that seem to make no sense today, Maryland went years with no identity and—with its burgeoning suburbs, decaying old cities, its hidden-away rural areas with their molasses-thick accents—was often an object of derision. No more. The 1986 election year saw local patriotism and local pride come forward in political races around the country. But nowhere was it more vibrant and more determinative of the results, and nowhere did it have more gaps to bridge, than in Maryland.

For within the convoluted limits of this state you can find a working example of practically every stage of American history. You can start on the Eastern Shore, where the 18th and 19th century houses of tiny Oxford overlook a small harbor where, 300 years ago, wooden ships were loaded with the fabulously lucrative crop of tobacco—the crop that made Maryland a commercially workable and successful colony. Or consider the watermen of the Eastern Shore town of Crisfield, still rising before dawn and coaxing from Chesapeake Bay the crabs and fish (but not rockfish: the legislature has banned the catch so the fish population can recover) that make Maryland cuisine distinctive. First settled when people and goods traveled whenever possible by water, not land, the colony first and then state included both sides of the Chesapeake and the broad tidal rivers that flow into it, plus the land north of the largest of those rivers, the Potomac, west to its headwaters in the mountains.

If it's easy to visualize the colonial economy of Maryland, or the days of slavery and racial segregation, on the Eastern Shore, it's also easy to recall later phases of American life from other parts of Maryland. From Baltimore's gleaming Inner Harbor development it's only a few blocks to older docks and to the rowhouse neighborhoods, where native-born and immigrant Americans jostled against each other in the 19th and early 20th centuries. To the west, you can see wheatfields and Appalachian uplands where the huge armies of the Civil War marched back and forth and waged bloody battles. Around the beltways that gird Baltimore and Washington are the new glass-and-steel, condominium-and-treeless-subdivision suburbs that show the vibrancy of the growth of America over the last 30 years: the Sun Belt starts here. Tiny Maryland has just about every kind of people—northerners and southerners, blacks and ethnics, civil servants and Chesapeake Bay watermen—almost all the diversity of the United States compressed into one historical and sociological microchip.

Maryland enjoyed an earlier period of secure identity half-a-century ago, when H. L. Mencken was extolling the virtues of the pleasant life of his native city in the *Baltimore Sun*. Maryland was then a kind of city-state: 49% of its residents lived in the closely packed, rowhouse-lined streets of Baltimore, with most of the rest spread in distinct hinterlands: the southern-oriented counties of both shores of the Chesapeake, the northern-accented wheat-growing country around the antique small cities of Frederick and Hagerstown, and the mountain-bound industrial city of Cumberland. In Mencken's time Maryland was tolerant of regional eccentricities: Prohibition was enforced only laxly in Baltimore; slot machines were legal in the rural counties of the Western Shore; the state's old law guaranteeing blacks equal access to public accommodations specifically excluded the Eastern Shore. But that notion Maryland had of itself couldn't be sustained after years of change. Only 19% of Marylanders live in Baltimore City now, and the Eastern Shore and western counties have a much smaller share of the state's population than they did 50 years ago. Most Marylanders now live in the suburbs, 52% in suburban counties around Baltimore and 29% in the two suburban counties around Washington, D.C. Just 40 miles apart, these two big metropolitan areas are in many ways different. Baltimore is a major port with big shipbuilding companies and the nation's largest

MARYLAND — Congressional Districts, Counties, Independent City, and Other Selected Places — *(8 Districts)*

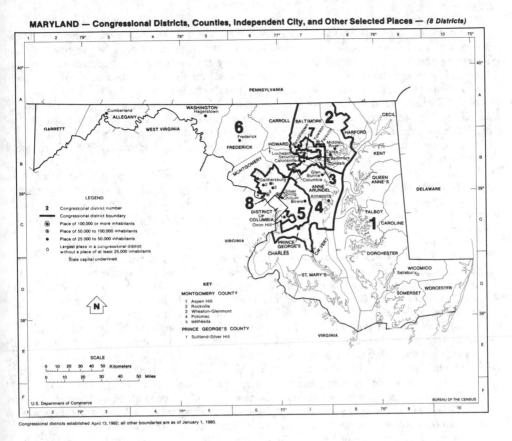

Congressional districts established April 13, 1982; all other boundaries are as of January 1, 1980.

steel mill. Its heavy industries attracted a large number of America's second wave (1840–1924) immigrants like other big East Coast cities, as well as a large black migration from southern states and rural Maryland; Washington, whose economy has always been based on government, was a sleepy town until the 1930s, and since has boomed, in war or peace, boom or bust. Both have done well in the 1980s. Washington's Maryland suburbs have grown impressively: Montgomery County continues to have the highest median income in the nation, while Prince George's County, long a stepchild, with nearly half its population black, has visibly surged with the Capital Centre, commercial development topped by the proposed PortAmerica tower on the Potomac, and a public school system with magnet schools and rising test scores that set an example for the nation.

As for Baltimore, what was once a bottleneck on the road to New Jersey is now recognized as one of America's most charming and vibrant cities. Much of the credit goes to William Donald Schaefer, Mayor from 1971 to 1987, who not only got the Inner Harbor restored and Harborplace built and strengthened the city's diversified local economy, but insisted on delivery of services to neighborhoods and bridged the gap between black and white. Schaefer is a shrewd inside negotiator with a flare for capturing the public's imagination, and he has made his Baltimore the center of Maryland and the focus of its sense of itself as a state has not been since Mencken's time. Schaefer is not photogenic, squirms when interviewed, dislikes confrontation— is in other words something like the opposite of the ideal candidate. Yet he dominated Maryland's politics in 1986, winning the Democratic gubernatorial nomination over strong opposition, winning the largest percentage in a contested governor or senator race in the nation in November, and setting policy even before he took office. At the same time Congresswoman Barbara Mikulski, whose Baltimore accent is as distinctive as Schaefer's, was elected to the Senate against impressive competition in the primary and despite a negative campaign in the general. She won with overwhelming support in the Baltimore area and because Maryland has one of the largest (a little over 21%) black electorates outside the Deep South.

Nicely forgotten in this burst of local pride and good feeling is the reputation Maryland had a dozen years ago for corruption and the nasty savings and loan scandal of 1985, when inactivity by state regulators allowed greedy S&L proprietors to plunder depositors. Now Maryland and Baltimore seem to have politicians they can be proud of and leaders who typify and trumpet their homegrown virtues.

Governor. Harry Hughes, governor for eight years, left a deeper imprint on the state than may be realized. Although he was pilloried for inaction on the S&L fiasco, he had two impressive achievements—cleaning up Chesapeake Bay and banishing scandal from the quaint 18th century capital of Annapolis. It is on these achievements that Donald Schaefer can build. Schaefer wants to attract industry and build Maryland's economic base, which is already pretty strong; though he seems conservative in temperament, he is an activist at governing. In Baltimore he would cruise down alleys, give roses to neighbors whose yards were clean and send blistering memos to city bureaucrats demanding that uncollected garbage be picked up within hours. In Annapolis he must share power with legislators and serve the Washington suburbs as well as the Baltimore area he knows so well and the rural areas he has been cultivating for several years. Elected with 82% of the vote, it was hard to see how he could go anywhere but down.

Yet after starting off raggedly with the legislature, arguing his plan to hold onto the state's windfall from federal tax reform, he won victory after victory—an increased gas tax, changes in workmen's compensation and medical malpractice, and construction of two new stadiums—one for football, one for baseball—in the Camden Yards near Harborplace. On pure efficiency grounds, the cost of the stadiums makes no sense, but Schaefer is a leader who believes that symbolism, ritual, and ceremony build civic pride and bring out people's best efforts and better selves. This is after all a man who, when introduced as Mayor an Orioles' World Series game—usually an occasion for booing politicians—was instead given a standing ovation.

Senators. Maryland's senior Senator, Paul Sarbanes, is a Democrat who has a conventional voting record, but who is careful and cautious and never eager to commit himself. A hard worker in the Senate, Sarbanes has disdain for using the advantages of incumbency to get favorable publicity. He declines to introduce bills with attractive titles which will never get anywhere; nor does he send videotape cassettes of his comments on the issues of the day to all local television stations. Although Sarbanes prides himself on continuing to live in Baltimore, where he served three terms as congressman, and to which he commutes every day, he does not have a high profile in the city.

Sarbanes is nonetheless a hearty and intense partisan, and as pleased as any Democrat that his party is back in the majority in the Senate. He can be expected to devote much of his attention to the Foreign Relations Committee, where he is third ranking Democrat, behind the self-effacing Claiborne Pell and the brash Joseph Biden. Of Greek descent, he was the leader within the committee in the mid-1970s of the successful effort to impose an arms embargo on Turkey because of its invasion of Cyprus. He is wary of American military involvement abroad, and particularly in Central America; yet he is not disposed to demagogue the issue or to speak with the certitude and flashiness of a Christopher Dodd. His instinct instead is to study the details and be ready to back up any stand he takes—an instinct that makes him in the long run a more effective adversary of Administration policies he chooses to oppose. That was certainly the case when he served on the House Judiciary Committee during the hearings on the impeachment of Richard Nixon and presented the case for impeaching him for obstruction of justice.

Besides Foreign Relations he is Chairman of the Joint Economic Committee, a post which predecessors Democratic and Republican have used as an opportunity to promote their own views of where the economy is going and, sometimes, their view of what government should do about it. Sarbanes's impulses here are similar to those of outgoing Chairman David Obey, to look to see if some haven't been left behind in the middle 1980s' recovery. Sarbanes also has a seat on the Banking Committee, which may be more active under William Proxmire and which has jurisdiction over the housing programs which Baltimore under Donald Schaefer made such creative use of.

Politically, Sarbanes has been a cautious rebel, a carefully aggressive candidate who has never lost an election. He was a reformer in the Maryland House of Delegates, and no ally of Marvin Mandel, who was elected governor by the legislature when Spiro Agnew became vice president. In 1970, when Baltimore had three House committee chairmen, he challenged one of them, George Fallon of Public Works, and beat him (the same year Parren Mitchell beat Samuel Friedel of House Administration); in 1972 Sarbanes was thrown into the same district as Edward Garmatz of Merchant Marine, but was so strong Garmatz retired. In 1976 Sarbanes decided to challenge Republican Senator J. Glenn Beall, Jr., a surprise winner six years before, and proceeded methodically to win the primary over Joseph Tydings, the man Beall beat, and then to beat Beall. In 1982 Sarbanes faced voluble opposition when he was targeted by NCPAC, which hoped to impress all of political Washington by running negative ads on local TV. But they also infuriated and energized Sarbanes, who raised more money than he had wanted to and easily beat the hapless Republican nominee, his former Judiciary Committee colleague Lawrence Hogan. Sarbanes approaches 1988, despite his aversion to publicity, with great strengths. He has deep roots in Baltimore and shares its local pride; he grew up on the Eastern Shore and has always run well there; he and Governor Schaefer admire each other; plus, he is a Democrat in a state that is now one of the most Democratic in the nation.

Maryland's junior Senator is the shortest and probably the most distinctive member of the Senate, Barbara Mikulski. She has deep roots in east Baltimore and a rapport with Baltimoreans that is unshakeable. She got her start in politics as a social worker organizing Highlandtown (where her parents ran a bakery) to stop a highway from going through; she won, and in the process was elected to the Baltimore Council in 1971, in time to serve (and spar) with the then incoming mayor, Donald Schaefer. As a local official with genuine ethnic roots and a woman with genuine liberal impulses, she was chosen head of the national Democratic Party's commission on delegate selection in 1973, and avoided the pitfalls on either side. She ran for the Senate in 1974, and got a respectable percentage (43%) against Charles Mathias; when Paul Sarbanes ran for the other Senate seat in 1976, Mikulski ran for his 3d District seat and won.

Mikulski is loud and brash, humorous and warm, brusque and aggressive when she feels she should be, curious and thoughtful when she encounters another new part of the world. She knows Baltimore warp and woof—its neighborhoods and government agencies, charitable institutions and ethnic politicians—and she still lives there, in the Fells Point neighborhood being restored on the waterfront: Fells Point and Don Schaefer's Harborplace, she points out, stand where the highway she opposed was supposed to go through. She is liberal on economic issues, a feminist, pro-choice on abortions; but she also is fascinated with high tech businesses, is not an automatic liberal vote on foreign policy, and spent much of her time in the House on local issues, like dredging Baltimore harbor. In the Senate she quickly got a seat on Appropriations and is likely to follow the same course.

Mikulski gave up her safe House seat to run for the Senate in 1986. In the Democratic primary she had strong competition from Montgomery County Representative Michael Barnes and Governor Harry Hughes. But Hughes was weakened by the S&L failures and Barnes could not loosen Mikulski's hold on Baltimore voters. Nearly 60% of the votes were cast in the Baltimore metropolitan area, and Mikulski got 63% there to 19% for Barnes and 13% for Hughes. Barnes's 62% in the Washington suburbs was not nearly enough to prevent her from winning 50%–31%–14%.

In the general election, Mikulski had a well-informed and well-connected opponent in former White House aide Linda Chavez. But she had only recently moved over the D.C. line into

Maryland, established rapport with neither ethnics nor Republican contributors, and in a year in which local pride was sweeping Maryland, you could not imagine that Chavez, with her cool demeanor, had ever had Maryland crab seasonings caked under her fingernails. Chavez tried to attack Mikulski by innuendo, citing her hiring in 1981 of an Australian feminist and requiring her staff to read the woman's graduate thesis on "The Age of Megalomania." But, as Schaefer pointed out to Mikulski, most Maryland voters knew her and liked her the way she is. One Mikulski ad showed a shopper in Baltimore's Lexington Market compliment her on losing weight, to which Mikulski replied, spontaneously, "I'm counting my calories, I'm counting my votes, and I'm counting my blessings." And so this 4'11" Polish American woman from Highlandtown was elected to the U.S. Senate with 61% of the vote.

Presidential politics. Maryland has a May presidential primary which in past years has been important. George Wallace was campaigning in Prince George's County a day before the 1972 contest when he was shot; he swept the race. Jerry Brown, running as the candidate of outsiders, got the support of most of the political insiders and beat Jimmy Carter here in 1976. In 1984 Gary Hart finished third, behind Jesse Jackson (who carried Baltimore City and Prince George's County) and Walter Mondale (who carried just about everything else). When the outcome is already determined, Maryland is happy to flirt with oddball candidates; when the race is still undecided, Maryland Democrats tend to go where their political organizations and officeholders lead, and in 1984 most were lined up for Mondale. The Republican primary electorate is small and conservative, and the Republican presidential primary seldom attracts much notice.

For years Maryland was a close November battleground in presidential elections, and with its regional diversity was from 1960 to 1976 a good indicator of national results. Then in 1980 it was one of only six states to go for Jimmy Carter and in 1984 it was Walter Mondale's fourth best state. The reason: Maryland's black population is increasing rapidly (it was 23% in 1980), as many Washington area blacks move out from the District to Prince George's County which, in the middle 1980s, had the nation's highest concentration of affluent suburban blacks. The black percentage will likely increase, even if that migration slows down, because 27% of Maryland's under-18 population in 1980 was black.

Congressional districting. For the 1980s Maryland's Democratic legislature extended the two Baltimore districts, which had lost population out into the suburbs, leaving them with convoluted but sharply defined boundaries. The one incumbent really hurt was Democrat Clarence Long of Baltimore County, who was beaten in 1984 by Helen Bentley. Incidentally, in 1978 and 1984 four of Maryland's eight districts elected women to the House; in 1986 three did, with Mikulski beating Linda Chavez in the Senate race.

The People: Est. Pop. 1984: 4,463,000; Pop. 1980: 4,216,975, up 5.8% 1980–86 and 7.5% 1970–80; 1.85% of U.S. total, 19th largest. 15% with 1–3 yrs. col., 20% with 4+ yrs. col.; 9.8% below poverty level. Single ancestry: 10% English, 9% German, 4% Irish, 2% Italian, Polish, 1% Russian, French. Households (1980): 75% family, 42% with children, 59% married couples; 38% housing units rented; median monthly rent: $222; median house value: $59,200. Voting age pop. (1980): 3,049,445; 21% Black, 1% Asian origin, 1% Spanish origin. Registered voters (1986): 2,139,690; 1,443,183 D (67%); 536,138 R (25%); 160,369 declined to state and minor parties (8%).

1986 Share of Federal Tax Burden: $16,119,100,000; 2.14% of U.S. total; 14th largest.

1986 Share of Federal Expenditures

	Total		Non-Defense		Defense	
Total Expend	$21,686m	(2.61%)	$14,592m	(2.43%)	$7,094m	(3.09%)
St/Lcl Grants	1,959m	(1.74%)	1,958m	(1.74%)	2m	(1.80%)
Salary/Wages	4,988m	(4.14%)	2,890m	(4.92%)	2,096m	(3.39%)
Pymnts to Indiv	7,326m	(2.01%)	6,863m	(1.98%)	463m	(2.61%)
Procurement	6,776m	(2.39%)	2,243m	(4.03%)	4,534m	(3.02%)
Research/Other	638m	(2.39%)	638m	(2.39%)	0m	(0.18%)

Political Lineup: Governor, William Donald Schaefer (D); Lt. Gov., Melvin A. Steinberg, Jr. (D); Atty. Gen., J. Joseph Curran, Jr. (D); Comptroller of Treasury, Louis L. Goldstein (D). State Senate, 47 (40 D and 7 R); State House of Delegates, 141 (122 D and 25 R). Senators, Paul S. Sarbanes (D) and Barbara A. Mikulski (D). Representatives, 8 (6 D and 2 R).

1984 Presidential Vote

Reagan (R)	879,918	(53%)
Mondale (D)	787,935	(47%)

1980 Presidential Vote

Carter (D)	726,161	(47%)
Reagan (R)	680,606	(44%)
Anderson (I)	119,537	(8%)

1984 Democratic Presidential Primary

Mondale	215,222	(42%)
Jackson	129,387	(26%)
Hart	123,365	(24%)
Five others, uncomm.	38,192	(8%)

1984 Republican Presidential Primary

Reagan	73,663	(100%)

GOVERNOR

Gov. William Donald Schaefer (D)

Elected 1986, term expires Jan. 1991; b. Nov. 2, 1921, Baltimore; home, Baltimore; Baltimore City Col., B.A. 1939, U. of Baltimore, LL.B., 1942; Episcopalian; single.

Career: Baltimore City Cncl., 1955–67, President 1967–71; Mayor of Baltimore, 1971–86.

Offices: State House, Annapolis 21404, 301-269-3901.

Election Results

1986 gen.	William Donald Schaefer (D)	907,291	(82%)
	Thomas J. Mooney (R)	194,185	(18%)
1986 prim.	William Donald Schaefer (D)	395,170	(62%)
	Stephen H. Sachs (D)	224,755	(35%)
1982 gen.	Harry R. Hughes (D)	705,910	(62%)
	Robert A. Pascal (R)	432,826	(38%)

SENATORS

Sen. Paul S. Sarbanes (D)

Elected 1976, seat up 1988; b. Feb. 3, 1933, Salisbury; home, Baltimore; Princeton U., A.B. 1954, Rhodes Scholar, Oxford U., B.A. 1957, Harvard U., LL.B. 1960; Greek Orthodox; married (Christine).

Career: Law Clerk to Judge Morris A. Soper, U.S. 4th Circuit Crt. of Appeals, 1960–61; Practicing atty., 1961–62, 1965–70; A. A. to Chmn. Walter W. Heller of the Pres. Cncl. of Econ. Advisers, 1962–63; Exec. Dir., Baltimore Charter Revision Comm., 1963–64; MD House of Delegates, 1969–70; U.S. House of Reps., 1971–77.

Offices: 332 DSOB 20510, 202-224-4524. Also 1518 Fed. Ofc. Bldg., 31 Hopkins Plaza, Baltimore 21201, 301-962-4436; 1110 Fidler Lane, Silver Spring, 301-589-8800; 1906 Fredrick St., Cumberland 21502; 87 Bondhill Dr., Salisbury 21801, 301-546-4988.

Committees: *Banking, Housing and Urban Affairs* (4th of 11 D). Subcmtees: Housing and Urban Affairs; International Finance and Monetary Policy (Chairman). *Foreign Relations* (3d of 11 D). Subcmtees: Near Eastern and South Asian Affairs (Chairman); European Affairs. *Joint Economic Committee* (Chairman). Subcmtees: Intl. Economic Policy (Chairman); National Security Economics; Investment, Jobs and Prices.

Group Ratings

	ADA	ACLU	COPE	CFA	LCV	ACU	NTU	NSI	COC	CEI
1986	100	92	98	93	92	0	33	0	16	14
1985	100	—	98	100	—	0	23	—	25	—

National Journal Ratings

	1986 LIB — 1986 CONS			1985 LIB — 1985 CONS		
Economic	94%	—	0%	95%	—	0%
Social	92%	—	0%	88%	—	0%
Foreign	75%	—	0%	77%	—	22%

Key Votes

1) Ease Gun Cont	AGN	5) Grm-Rdmn Def Red	AGN	9) Rehnquist Nom	AGN
2) Immig Reform	FOR	6) Contra Aid	AGN	10) Tax Reform	FOR
3) Lmt Text Imp	FOR	7) SDI Funding	AGN	11) Drug Death Pen	FOR
4) Aid Tobac Ind	AGN	8) Lmt PAC Contrib	FOR	12) S Africa Sanc	FOR

Election Results

1982 general	Paul S. Sarbanes (D)	707,356	(63%)	($1,623,533)
	Lawrence J. Hogan (R)	407,334	(37%)	($90,976)
1982 primary	Paul S. Sarbanes (D)	432,931	(81%)	
	Eight others (D)	100,985	(19%)	
1976 general	Paul S. Sarbanes (D)	772,101	(57%)	($891,533)
	J. Glenn Beall, Jr. (R)	530,439	(39%)	($572,016)
	Bruce Bradley (I)	62,750	(5%)	

Campaign Contributions and Expenditures

1979-82		Direct Cont. 1981-82		PACS Breakdown			
Receipts	$1,632,112	Indiv.	$1,089,539	Agr	$16,275	Ideo	$64,383
Expend.	$1,623,533	Party	$17,500	Bus	$80,590	Lbr	$274,906
Unspent	$8,637	PACS	$463,287	Hlth	$4,700	Prof	$5,600

Sen. Barbara A. Mikulski (D)

Elected 1986, seat up 1992; b. July 20, 1936, Baltimore; home, Baltimore; Mt. St. Agnes Col., B.A. 1958, U. of MD, M.S.W., 1965; Roman Catholic; single.

Career: Admin., Baltimore Dept. of Soc. Svs.; caseworker; Baltimore City Cncl., 1971–76; Adjunct prof., Loyola Col., 1972–76; Chwmn., Dem. Natl. Comm. on Delegate Selection and Party Structure; Dem. Nominee for U.S. Senate, 1974; U.S. House of Reps., 1976–86.

Offices: 320 HSOB 20510, 202-224-4654. Also World Trade Center, Ste. 253, Baltimore 21202-3041, 301-962-4510; 419 S. Highland Ave., Baltimore 21224, 301-363-4000; and 3 Church Circle, Annapolis 21401, 301-263-1805.

Committees: *Appropriations* (15th of 16 D). Subcommittees: Foreign Operations; HUD-Independent Agencies; Legislative Branch; Treasury, Postal Service, General Government. *Environment and Public Works* (7th of 9 D). Subcommittees: Superfund and Environmental Oversight; Hazardous Wastes and Toxic Substances; Water Resources, Transportation and Infrastructure. *Labor and Human Services* (9th of 9 D). Subcommittees: Education, Arts and Humanities; Labor; Employment and Productivity. *Small Business* (10th of 10 D). Subcommittees: Government Contracting and Paperwork; Urban and Minority-owned Business Development.

Group Ratings (as Member of U.S. House of Representatives)

	ADA	ACLU	COPE	CFA	LCV	ACU	NTU	NSI	COC	CEI
1986	90	85	91	67	69	5	44	0	25	16
1985	80	—	91	92	—	10	30	—	32	—

National Journal Ratings (as Member of U.S. House of Representatives)

	1986 LIB — 1986 CONS		1985 LIB — 1985 CONS	
Economic	87%	— 0%	71%	— 28%
Social	73%	— 26%	85%	— 0%
Foreign	80%	— 0%	71%	— 26%

Key Votes (as Member of U.S. House of Representatives)

1) Lmt Cln Water Act	AGN	5) Retain Gun Cont	FOR	9) Aid Angola Reb	AGN
2) Rpl Tobac Sub	AGN	6) Contra Aid	AGN	10) Tax Reform	FOR
3) Grm-Rdmn Def Red	AGN	7) Lmt Text Imp	FOR	11) S Africa Sanc	FOR
4) Ban Polygraph	FOR	8) Lmt SDI	—	12) Immig Reform	FOR

Election Results

1986 general	Barbara A. Mikulski (D)	675,225	(61%)	($2,097,216)
	Linda Chavez (R)	437,411	(39%)	($1,699,175)
1986 primary	Barbara A. Mikulski (D)	307,876	(50%)	
	Michael D. Barnes (D)	195,086	(31%)	
	Harry Hughes (D)	88,908	(14%)	
1980 general	Charles McC. Mathias, Jr. (R)	850,970	(66%)	($841,446)
	Edward T. Conroy (D)	435,118	(34%)	($46,456)

Campaign Contributions and Expenditures

1985-86		Direct Cont. 1985-86		PACS Breakdown 1985-86			
Receipts	$2,160,812	Indiv.	$1,251,938	Corp.	$119,395	T/M/H	$115,104
Expend.	$2,097,216	Party	$1,000	Labor	$293,705	Agr.	$5,750
Unspent	$103,596	PACS	$651,818	Ideo.	$112,314	CWOS	$5,550
		Cand.	$204,146				

FIRST DISTRICT

The Chesapeake is not really a bay, but a flooded river valley—the submerged lower Susquehanna River with tidal waters turning small streams like the Patuxent and the Choptank into wide estuaries and making offshoots like the Potomac navigable to ocean-going boats as far upriver as Georgetown. The rivers leading off from the Chesapeake, on either side, were the most thickly settled part of the American colonies in the 17th century; the Bay was the avenue by which the rich tobacco crops of Maryland and Virginia reached the world. On the Western Shore of the Chesapeake and its branch river the Potomac have grown two of America's metropolises, Baltimore and Washington. But on the lower part of the Western Shore, and on the whole Eastern Shore, life in many respects has not changed for many years.

There are a surprisingly small number of family names here, and population growth was low, scarcely more than doubling on the Eastern Shore between 1790 and 1970. The Western Shore was first settled by the Catholics for whom Maryland was founded as a religious haven, and there still is a Catholic influence here; also, the area has its own peculiarities, such as the slot machines which were legal for many years. The Eastern Shore was southern segregationist country and still has many blacks. It remains a region of southern drowsiness, chicken farms, fishing villages, and, on the necks of land that jut into the bay, big estates of some of the nation's richest families. It is also an area that has produced more than its share of Maryland's politicians, including Governor Harry Hughes and Senator Paul Sarbanes.

The 1st Congressional District of Maryland includes the whole Eastern Shore, the Western Shore counties below Annapolis and the Washington suburbs, and part of suburban Baltimore's Harford County. These areas have a reputation for being Democratic; actually, in congressional and national elections, they have been voting mostly Republican since the 1950s. In the 1970s and 1980s the 1st District has been the scene of bizarre episodes in congressional politics. One congressman killed himself amid charges of financial improprieties. Another, Robert Bauman, a brilliant parliamentarian and acerbic critic of the House Democratic leadership, in 1980 was charged in Washington with soliciting sex from a 16-year-old boy in circumstances suggesting he was courting discovery; Bauman's quandary split conservative activists and cost him enough votes to elect Roy Dyson, a Maryland legislator who had run for the seat before with poor results.

Dyson is a pretty conservative Democrat, especially on foreign and cultural issues, and does not seem temperamentally inclined to be a risk-taker or rock-thrower. Dyson's record on cultural and foreign issues has been conservative enough to suit the district, and his record on economic issues is barely liberal enough to keep him in good standing with his fellow Democrats. Yet Dyson has a satisfactory relationship with the Democratic leadership, which seems to understand his need to propitiate his constituency. Dyson sits on two committees where his views are in line with those of solid majorities: Armed Services, where he tends to support the higher of defense spending alternatives, and Merchant Marine and Fisheries, where he supports maritime subsidies as well as measures that serve the environmental interests of Chesapeake Bay.

Dyson now seems to have made this a safe seat. Bauman tried for a comeback in 1982, but after some vicious attacks from a Republican rival left the race; no Republican candidate since has seemed very strong. Dyson was held to 58% in 1984 when Ronald Reagan was carrying 65% of the votes in the district, but he snapped back to 67% in 1986.

The People: Pop. 1980: 526,206, up 21.7% 1970–80. Households (1980): 78% family, 45% with

children, 65% married couples; 28.1% housing units rented; median monthly rent: $159; median house value: $49,500. Voting age pop. (1980): 369,721; 17% Black, 1% Spanish origin, 1% Asian origin.

1984 Presidential Vote:

Reagan (R)	121,294	(65%)
Mondale (D)	64,381	(35%)

Rep. Roy Dyson (D)

Elected 1980; b. Nov. 15, 1948, Great Mills; home, Great Mills; U. of Baltimore, 1970, U. of MD, 1971; Roman Catholic; single.

Career: Legis. Asst., Agr. Labor Subcmtee., U.S. House of Reps., 1973–74; MD House of Delegates, 1974–80.

Offices: 224 CHOB 20515, 202-225-5311. Also 1 Plaza E., Salisbury 21801, 301-742-9070; P.O. Box 742, Waldorf 20601, 301-645-4844; and 20 W. Bel Air Ave., Aberdeen 21001, 301-272-7070.

Committees: *Armed Services* (17th of 31 D). Subcommittees: Military Personnel and Compensation; Procurement and Military Nuclear Systems; Seapower and Strategic and Critical Materials. *Merchant Marine and Fisheries* (13th of 25 D). Subcommittees: Fisheries and Wildlife Conservation and the Environment; Merchant Marine.

Group Ratings

	ADA	ACLU	COPE	CFA	LCV	ACU	NTU	NSI	COC	CEI
1986	30	10	72	8	47	64	33	100	50	29
1985	30	—	72	58	—	65	33	—	50	—

National Journal Ratings

	1986 LIB — 1986 CONS		1985 LIB — 1985 CONS	
Economic	46% —	54%	45% —	55%
Social	27% —	71%	32% —	67%
Foreign	27% —	70%	34% —	66%

Key Votes

1) Lmt Cln Water Act	AGN	5) Retain Gun Cont	AGN	9) Aid Angola Reb	FOR
2) Rpl Tobac Sub	AGN	6) Contra Aid	FOR	10) Tax Reform	AGN
3) Grm-Rdmn Def Red	FOR	7) Lmt Text Imp	FOR	11) S Africa Sanc	FOR
4) Ban Polygraph	FOR	8) Limit SDI	FOR	12) Immig Reform	AGN

Election Results

1986 general	Roy Dyson (D)	88,113	(67%)	($354,240)
	Harlan C. Williams (R)	43,764	(33%)	($171,876)
1986 primary	Roy Dyson (D)	58,909	(100%)	
1984 general	Roy Dyson (D)	96,683	(58%)	($273,655)
	Harlan C. Williams (R)	68,865	(42%)	($199,429)

Campaign Contributions and Expenditures

1985-86		Direct Cont. 1985-86		PACS Breakdown 1985-86			
Receipts	$356,603	Indiv.	$104,701	Corp.	$78,630	T/M/H	$51,120
Expend.	$354,240	Party	$106	Labor	$103,621	Agr.	$5,500
Debts	$6,821	PACS	$250,371	Ideo.	$11,500	CWOS	$0

SECOND DISTRICT

Baltimore as a state of mind doesn't end at the boundary between Baltimore City and Baltimore County: the County may be almost entirely white and uninterested in assuming the City's fiscal burdens, but the "Bawlmer" accent is unmistakable in every corner of the suburban jurisdiction that almost encircles the central city, and the pride in Baltimore's civic achievements radiates well beyond the city line. Most people here grew up in Baltimore; they remember when the St. Louis Browns moved to Baltimore in 1954 and the glory days of Johnny Unitas's Baltimore Colts; they may recall when a Towson lawyer named Spiro Agnew won an upset victory in the race for county executive in 1962. County residents today may work in gleaming new office buildings and seldom get down to Harborplace or Memorial Stadium, but their picture of local government is more likely to be Baltimore's ornate jewel of a city hall than the old-fashioned county courthouse building in a park a few blocks off the six-lane highways in Towson.

The 2d Congressional District of Maryland includes almost three-quarters of Baltimore County, plus some of Harford County just beyond. On the soggy low-lying peninsulas jutting into Chesapeake Bay are the working class communities of Dundalk and Essex, extensions of east Baltimore where many residents worked for years at Bethlehem Steel's Sparrows Point mill. The political tradition here is Democratic. Directly north of Baltimore are Towson, Lutherville, Timonium—relatively high income suburbs situated, geographically and sociologically, between the more modest suburbs to the east and the green horse country to the west. This is solidly Republican territory. In the western part of the district Baltimoreans are moving out from older Jewish neighborhoods and in the eastern part they are moving out from older Catholic neighborhoods to the countryside.

The congresswoman from the 2d District is Helen Delich Bentley, a Republican who beat an incumbent in her third try in 1984 and beat a Kennedy in 1986. Her secret both times was dedication to local issues. The daughter of an immigrant from Yugoslavia to Nevada, Bentley was for 24 years a reporter for the *Baltimore Sun*, specializing in maritime news; for six years she was chairman of the Federal Maritime Commission. Her major issue, when she first challenged Representative Clarence (Doc) Long in 1980, was dredging the harbor of Baltimore, which Long opposed on environmental grounds; in 1982, her main issue was dredging the harbor; in 1984, her main issue again was dredging the harbor, which by this time Long favored. But Long was 75, had concentrated for years on his work as chairman of the appropriations subcommittee handling the foreign aid bill, and did not seem likely to pursue the dredging issue vigorously. Bentley, a tough-talking, often profane woman, did.

She won with 51% of the vote and, in her first term, she delivered. She got federal money for the dredging. She got funding for the Brewerton Channel extension and Chesapeake and Delaware Canal improvements. She got Baltimore declared an extension of the Norfolk Navy home port, bringing Baltimore shipyards big repair contracts. She got an aircraft carrier superstructure ship contract shifted from Canada to Sparrows Point. In an election in which the Baltimore area was concentrating on local issues and bursting with local pride, Bentley was headed for reelection by a wide margin.

Enter Kathleen Kennedy Townsend, daughter of the late Robert Kennedy, a lawyer in Attorney General Stephen Sachs's office, a resident of Baltimore County where her husband grew up. When she decided to run for Congress in 1986, the national press, following the lead of *People*, flooded into the district, and found not only (wow!) a Kennedy, but also a thoughtful and original thinker. Townsend had written articles for the *Washington Monthly*— ignored in the Collier and Horowitz *Kennedys* book, evidently because it didn't reflect badly on the family— arguing that liberals should think not only about how society should serve the helpless, but how those who are not helpless should serve society. So in the campaign she not only proposed extending Medicare to geriatric nursing, but also called for a national police corps and supported the draft.

But all this was beside the point in the Baltimore area in 1986. Bentley, who will never be accused of being a philosopher, has roots in Baltimore going back 40 years and genuine achievements for the area's economy. She carried not only the Republican areas but also Dundalk and Essex, the kind of places which supposedly have a sentimental attachment to the Kennedys, and won with a resounding 59% of the vote. Townsend would probably have done just as well with the same ideas and campaign budget if she were not a Kennedy; but this was not her year or her district. She said after the election that she would run again and seems determined to show her commitment to the area; yet it is difficult to see how she can beat Bentley unless the pride in things local that was so evident in Baltimore and Maryland in 1986 somehow vanishes by 1988. Both candidates, incidentally, spent more than $1 million—the only House race in 1986 in which this was so.

The People: Pop. 1980: 526,354, up 13.6% 1970–80. Households (1980): 78% family, 41% with children, 66% married couples; 34.7% housing units rented; median monthly rent: $227; median house value: $57,100. Voting age pop. (1980): 388,788; 5% Black, 1% Asian origin, 1% Spanish origin.

1984 Presidential Vote:

Reagan (R)	145,320	(66%)
Mondale (D)	74,102	(34%)

Rep. Helen Delich Bentley (R)

Elected 1984; b. Nov. 28, 1923, Ely, NV; home, Lutherville; U. of MO, B.A. 1944, U. of NV, Geo. Wash. U.; Greek Orthodox; married (William).

Career: Reporter and Maritime Ed., *The Sun*, Baltimore, 1945–69; Chmn., Fed. Maritime Comm., 1969–75; Businesswoman, 1975–85; Columnist and Ed., *World Ports Magazine*, 1981–85.

Offices: 1610 LHOB 20515, 202-225-3061. Also 200 E. Joppa Rd., Shell Bldg., Ste. 400, Towson 21204, 301-337-7222; and 7458 German Hill Rd., Dundalk 21222, 301-285-2726.

Committees: *Merchant Marine and Fisheries* (10th of 17 R). Subcommittees: Coast Guard and Navigation; Merchant Marine; Oversight and Investigations; Panama Canal and Outer Continental Shelf. *Public Works and Transportation* (15th of 20 R). Subcommittees: Economic Development; Investigations and Oversight; Water Resources. *Select Committee on Aging* (15th of 26 R). Subcommittee: Health and Long-Term Care.

Group Ratings

	ADA	ACLU	COPE	CFA	LCV	ACU	NTU	NSI	COC	CEI
1986	20	10	41	25	21	62	33	90	63	40
1985	15	—	24	25	—	76	41	—	73	—

National Journal Ratings

	1986 LIB — 1986 CONS		1985 LIB — 1985 CONS	
Economic	43% —	57%	31% —	55%
Social	31% —	67%	0% —	67%
Foreign	30% —	69%	0% —	66%

Key Votes

1) Lmt Cln Water Act	AGN	5) Retain Gun Cont	AGN	9) Aid Angola Reb	FOR
2) Rpl Tobac Sub	AGN	6) Contra Aid	FOR	10) Tax Reform	AGN
3) Grm-Rdmn Def Red	AGN	7) Lmt Text Imp	FOR	11) S Africa Sanc	FOR
4) Ban Polygraph	FOR	8) Limit SDI	AGN	12) Immig Reform	AGN

Election Results

1986 general	Helen Delich Bentley (R)............... 96,745	(59%)	($1,070,161)
	Kathleen Kennedy Townsend (D)......... 68,200	(41%)	($1,071,713)
1986 primary	Helen Delich Bentley (R) unopposed		
1984 general	Helen Delich Bentley (R).............. 111,517	(51%)	($598,181)
	Clarence D. Long (D)................ 105,571	(49%)	($808,710)

Campaign Contributions and Expenditures

1985-86		Direct Cont. 1985-86		PACS Breakdown 1985-86			
Receipts	$1,076,329	Indiv.	$609,209	Corp.	$158,494	T/M/H	$88,002
Expend.	$1,070,161	Party	$11,494	Labor	$73,544	Agr.	$1,800
Debts	$13,577	PACS	$361,282	Ideo.	$36,768	CWOS	$2,674
		Cand.	$23,312				

THIRD DISTRICT

Twenty years ago, Baltimore seemed to be a city in trouble. Like other big cities farther up the East Coast, its housing was aging, its population declining, and its economy seemed to be sagging. But the last two decades have turned out to be better ones for Baltimore than almost anyone predicted. Rather than collapsing, its diversified economy kept up with inflation and stayed at least even with the rest of the nation during recession. Both high- and low-wage jobs have been generated, and the city's downtown and some of its neighborhoods have been revitalized with new building that is also respectful of the old. The city government led for 15 years by Mayor Donald Schaefer not only improved services but captured the imagination of Baltimoreans, suburbanites, and ultimately the whole nation with projects like Harborplace and the Aquarium. Baltimore also avoided the racial divisiveness of many cities. It has had a black majority since the 1970s. But Schaefer was reelected in 1975, 1979, and 1983 with majorities from black as well as white voters.

The 3d Congressional District of Maryland is centered on Baltimore, though you would hardly know it to look at its convoluted boundaries. Actually there is a very easy explanation for them: the district includes most of the white majority precincts in the city, plus adjacent parts of Baltimore County, plus—added on to meet the population standard—most of the planned town of Columbia, 15 miles from downtown Baltimore. The central focus is Harborplace, overlooking the city's busy harbor; across the bay, not far away, is Fort McHenry, where Francis Scott Key stood and watched the star-spangled banner yet wave. Going counterclockwise from downtown, the district moves east to include the mostly Polish Highlandtown neighborhood, the original political base of Senator Barbara Mikulski; the middle-class northeastern corner of the city; upper-income WASPy neighborhoods north of Johns Hopkins University and in the Baltimore County suburb of Towson; and the mostly Jewish area around the Pimlico Race Track and the suburb of Pikesville. West of downtown, this time clockwise, the 3d takes in the old ethnic neighborhoods overlooking the harbor, the modest suburbs of Arbutus and Catonsville, and goes out to Howard County and Columbia. Now 15 years old, this was a much heralded "new town" whose architecture is less distinctive than one might think, but which has attracted a population of nearly 40,000 which is by suburban standards unusually well integrated (20% black) and politically liberal.

One of the reasons Baltimore has so visibly been bursting with pride is that this city, once depicted as the home of political hacks and crooks, has been producing outstanding politicians. They include Schaefer, now governor, and Senators Paul Sarbanes and Mikulski, who both represented the 3d District in the House; and they include the 3d District's new congressman, Ben Cardin. Though just 43 when he ran, he had a political career running back 20 years and impressive political strength. He was elected to the Maryland House of Delegates from a Jewish district in northwest Baltimore, an area full of political talent, as long ago as 1966; he chaired the

Ways and Means Committee by 1975; he served as Speaker from 1979 to 1986. The Maryland legislature is a fast track with a dizzying pace, where Cardin demonstrated great finesse and skill as well as complete honesty. It was logical that he was thinking about running for governor in 1986, and logical that he was deterred by Donald Schaefer's strength; logical as well that when Mikulski ran for the Senate, he ran for her seat and won the Democratic primary—tantamount to election—with 82% of the vote.

Cardin's first months in the House must have been disappointing. He sought seats on the Ways and Means and Budget Committees, which freshmen usually don't get, and settled for Public Works instead. Tip O'Neill, a former Massachusetts speaker, had a soft spot for former speakers when it came to committee assignments; Jim Wright, who served one term in the Texas House and was defeated for reelection, evidently doesn't. Cardin, accustomed to being a central figure in Annapolis, is bound to be peripheral for a while in Washington. But he has impressive talents and a safe seat in Baltimore, and will surely make his mark.

The People: Pop. 1980: 527,699, dn. 3.3% 1970–80. Households (1980): 71% family, 35% with children, 54% married couples; 38.9% housing units rented; median monthly rent: $197; median house value: $43,500. Voting age pop. (1980): 399,019; 14% Black, 1% Spanish origin, 1% Asian origin.

1984 Presidential Vote:

Reagan (R) 110,231	(50%)
Mondale (D) 108,399	(49%)

Rep. Benjamin L. Cardin (D)

Elected 1986; b. Oct. 5, 1943, Baltimore; home, Baltimore; U. of Pittsburgh, B.A. 1964, U. of MD, LL.B., J.D. 1967; Jewish; married (Myrna).

Career: MD House of Delegates, 1966–86, Speaker, 1979–86; practicing atty., 1967–86.

Offices: 507 CHOB 20515, 202-225-4016. Also 540 E. Belvedere Rd., Ste. 201, Baltimore 21212, 301-443-8886.

Committees: *Judiciary* (21st of 21 D). Subcommittees: Administrative Law and Government Relations; Courts, Civil Liberties and the Administration of Justice. *Public Works* (28th of 32 D). Subcommittees: Aviation; Public Buildings and Grounds; Water Resources.

Group Ratings and Key Votes: Newly Elected

Election Results

1986 general	Benjamin L. Cardin (D)	100,161	(79%)	($487,797)
	Ross Z. Pierpont (R)..................	26,452	(21%)	($46,542)
1986 primary	Benjamin I. Cardin (D)................	69,980	(82%)	
	Edward A. Ellison (D)	4,422	(5%)	
	John B. Ascher (D).....................	4,085	(4%)	
	Earl Koger, Sr. (D)	3,714	(4%)	
	Robert B. Lewis (D)...................	2,968	(3%)	
1984 general	Barbara A. Mikulski (D)	133,189	(68%)	($259,880)
	Ross Z. Pierpont (R).................	59,493	(30%)	($113,726)

Campaign Contributions and Expenditures

1985-86		Direct Cont. 1985-86		PACS Breakdown 1985-86			
Receipts	$518,530	Indiv.	$359,587	Corp.	$39,370	T/M/H	$48,134
Expend.	$487,797	Party	$287	Labor	$38,000	Agr.	$800
Unspent	$30,731	PACS	$156,195	Ideo.	$25,691	CWOS	$4,200

FOURTH DISTRICT

America's oldest capitol building still used for its original purpose can be found in a circle—a real one, not a misnamed rectangular block—in Annapolis, Maryland. For blocks around this old State House, down to the waterfront and the United States Naval Academy, Annapolis is an 18th century town—not preserved under glass, but a working city, a waterman's as well as a yachtist's port, a market town as much as a lobbying emporium, a little bit gritty under the fingernails even as another coat of white enamel is applied to its Georgian woodwork.

Annapolis is the center and focal point of Maryland's 4th Congressional District, most of which is thoroughly unquaint, unhistorical suburban territory, stretching from the Baltimore city limits to the District of Columbia line. The constituency includes all of Anne Arundel County (Annapolis and Baltimore suburbs) and part of Prince George's County (near Washington). Between Annapolis and Baltimore are a series of not-so-fashionable suburbs of Baltimore where about half the 4th District's residents live: Linthicum, Glen Burnie, Severna Park. The Prince George's County portion is shaped oddly, like a fishhook, and includes, in addition to Andrews Air Force Base, several mostly black suburbs.

The 4th District was the scene of one of America's closest congressional elections in 1986. The only representative the district had since its creation, Republican Marjorie Holt, decided to retire after 14 years of steady conservative service. The partisan balance was close. Republicans carry the district in national elections by hefty margins. But Democrats have a strong base in the growing black precincts in southern Prince George's, and in 1986 their statewide candidates Donald Schaefer and Barbara Mikulski, well known in Anne Arundel from their continual exposure on Baltimore TV, were headed for massive wins. Democrats had a strong candidate in basketball player Tom McMillen, who played for the University of Maryland in nearby College Park and for the Washington Bullets in Prince George's County's Capital Centre; a native of New York, he had settled in the new suburb of Crofton. Republicans also had a strong candidate, urged into the race by Holt, in Robert Neall, who was not only the leader of the small Republican minority in the House of Delegates but also a genuine player in the high-level game of politics played in the State House.

At first, McMillen's greater celebrity was expected to give him an easy win. But he proved stiff on the stump and was far less assured and supple in handling issues than his fellow basketball pro and Rhodes Scholar, Bill Bradley. Neall, in contrast, showed both an infectious good humor and an instinctive feel for the legislative process seldom seen in Republican candidates these days, and by the end of the campaign he was visibly gaining. But not quite enough. Neall won 55% of the vote in Anne Arundel County. McMillen had 56% in the district's small portion of Howard County and 71% in Prince George's. That was enough for a 428-vote victory.

At 6'11"—exactly two feet taller than Senator Barbara Mikulski—McMillen will in one sense be a prominent House member. He has a good chance to make this a safe district, particularly since there are never very many well-known Republicans in Maryland politics in a position to challenge him. The interesting question is whether he can sharpen his political skills as other athletes in politics have.

The People: Pop. 1980: 525,453, up 17.7% 1970–80. Households (1980): 78% family, 47% with children, 64% married couples; 35.3% housing units rented; median monthly rent: $261; median house value: $66,200. Voting age pop. (1980): 372,900; 19% Black, 1% Asian origin, 1% Spanish origin.

1984 Presidential Vote: Reagan (R) 115,669   (59%)
Mondale (D) 79,144   (40%)

Rep. Thomas McMillen (D)

Elected 1986; b. May 26, 1952, Elmira, NY; home, Crofton; U. of MD, B.S., 1974; Rhodes Scholar, Oxford U., M.A., 1978; Roman Catholic; single.

Career: Professional basketball player, 1974–86; founder, McMillen Communications, regional paging network.

Offices: 1508 LHOB 20515, 202-225-8090. Also Arundel Center N., 101 Crain Hwy. N.W., Ste. 509, Glen Burnie 21061, 301-767-8050; 132 Holiday Ct., Ste. 207, Annapolis 21403, 301-841-5392; and 6188 Oxon Hill Rd., Ste. 501, Oxon Hill 20745, 301-567-9212.

Committees: *Banking, Finance and Urban Affairs* (26th of 31 D). Subcommittees: Economic Stabilization; Financial Institution Supervision, Regulation and Insurance. *Science, Space and Technology* (23d of 27 D). Subcommittees: Natural Resources, Agriculture Research and Environment; Space Science and Applications; Transportation, Aviation and Materials.

Group Ratings and Key Votes: Newly Elected

Election Results

1986 general	Thomas McMillen (D)	65,071	(50%)	($796,344)
	Robert R. Neall (R)	64,643	(50%)	($640,939)
1986 primary	Thomas McMillen (D)	36,980	(66%)	
	John S. Pantelides (D)	15,682	(28%)	
	Susan Zurkowski (D)	3,727	(7%)	
1984 general	Marjorie S. Holt (R).	114,430	(66%)	($260,487)
	Howard M. Greenebaum (D)	58,312	(34%)	($79,385)

Campaign Contributions and Expenditures

1985-86		Direct Cont. 1985-86		PACS Breakdown 1985-86			
Receipts	$796,615	Indiv.	$373,006	Corp.	$31,708	T/M/H	$53,731
Expend.	$796,344	Party	$1,557	Labor	$181,922	Agr.	$2,250
Unspent	$1,281	PACS	$316,465	Ideo.	$44,854	CWOS	$2,000
		Cand.	$112,715				

FIFTH DISTRICT

Two generations ago, Prince George's County, Maryland, just north and east of Washington, D.C., was mostly low-lying farmland, with a few suburbs strung out along U.S. 1 from Washington toward Baltimore. Today Prince George's is home to nearly 700,000 people, and is one of the nation's most important counties— and a place that gives us a hopeful glimpse of a possible future. This is not conventional wisdom in official Washington, where Prince George's is seen as a working class haven, overshadowed by Montgomery County to the west, which has the nation's highest income levels, and Virginia's Fairfax County, whose growth is so rapid the roads are clogged all day. But Prince George's is by national standards affluent, and it has its own impressive and accelerating growth. All this is especially interesting, because Prince George's is the nation's biggest black suburban community. The black percentage here increased from 14% in 1970 to 37% in 1980; by 1990 it will probably be close to 50%. Through all that change, levels of achievement have remained high. Prince George's 5th Congressional District ranked 36th out of 435 in 1979 median family income; in black family income it ranked 13th, behind 12 suburban districts with far smaller black populations. For some years Prince George's was buoyed upward by the high level of federal wages. In 1970, when federal salaries were quite generous, 38% of the 5th District's work force here was employed by Uncle Sam—the highest figure in the nation. But by 1980, when federal pay was starting to fall behind the private sector, the federal share was down to 25%; more Prince George's residents were moving into the private sector. And make no mistake about it, this is a hard-working community. Fully 65% of women age 16 and over in the 5th District were in the work force in 1980—the highest figure for any congressional district in the nation.

The racial change in Prince George's has occasioned some strain—but less than might be thought. The county was riven by a school busing case in the 1970s and early 1980s. But in the middle 1980s, school superintendent John Murphy instituted a set of magnet schools and promised to raise black students' test scores to the level of whites—and by 1986 had made impressive progress. Local politics in the 1970s and early 1980s was filled with bickering. But by the middle 1980s Prince George's was attracting major developments like the PortAmerica project on the Potomac (scaled down from a proposed 53 stories) to accompany the Capital Centre as a generator of business. In the 1970s and early 1980s blacks complained about police conduct. But under County Executive Parris Glendenning, product of a competent and biracial Democratic organization, such complaints appear to have tapered off. Prince George's seems to be giving the nation lesson after lesson in how successful, hard-working blacks can work with whites to build a productive, tolerant, attractive community.

Maryland's 5th Congressional District includes most of Prince George's County, all but the close-in suburb of Oxon Hill and a strip of land to the south. Its congressman is Steny Hoyer, one of those instinctive politicians who seem to rise out of the Maryland soil and flourish in Annapolis and Washington. He was elected to the Maryland Senate at age 27 and was Senate president from 1974 to 1978; he made a misstep running for lieutenant governor on a losing ticket in 1978. But when the 5th District was declared vacant in 1981, when Representative Gladys Spellman went into an irreversible coma, Hoyer edged out Spellman's husband and several other Democrats in the primary and beat a well financed, competent Republican candidate in the general.

Hoyer has followed the usual Washington suburban pattern of providing extensive constituency services, especially to federal employees, but as federal payrolls become less important here he has pioneered another pattern (which also had been followed by Montgomery's Michael Barnes) in becoming a national party leader. He left the Post Office and Civil Service Committee in 1983 for a seat on Appropriations, where he serves on subcommittees that have jurisdiction over the Treasury, Postal Service, General Government; Labor, HHS, Education; and District of Columbia.

Hoyer is part of the Democratic leadership as an at-large whip, and is on the Democratic Steering and Policy Committee that makes committee assignments. He hoped for more, and sought the job of chief deputy whip after the 1986 elections. But Speaker Jim Wright chose David Bonior instead and offered Hoyer the chairmanship of the Democrats' campaign committee, which he declined. He remains busy; he is chosen for leadership trips to the Soviet Union, and uses his Appropriations chair for, among other things, local projects like completing the mass transit Metro Green Line to serve Prince George's. Hoyer occasionally breaks with the leadership, as when he supported the MX missile in 1985. But with a solid base in his Democratic biracial constituency, he seems likely to continue to be an important politician on Capitol Hill, two miles from the edge of his district, for many years to come. The only threat to his tenure would be primary opposition from a black, but he comes from a county with an increasingly biracial political tradition, and he himself has endorsed black politicians like the county's District Attorney, Alex Williams, who beat a white incumbent in the 1986 primary. That record is likely to give him continued support from black voters.

The People: Pop. 1980: 527,469, up 0.5% 1970–80. Households (1980): 74% family, 45% with children, 56% married couples; 44.1% housing units rented; median monthly rent: $282; median house value: $64,100. Voting age pop. (1980): 374,737; 31% Black, 2% Asian origin, 2% Spanish origin.

1984 Presidential Vote:

Mondale (D)	108,074	(57%)
Reagan (R)	79,134	(42%)

Rep. Steny H. Hoyer (D)

Elected May 19, 1981; b. June 14, 1939, New York City; home, Forestville; U. of MD, B.S. 1963, Georgetown U., J.D. 1966; Baptist; married (Judith).

Career: Practicing atty., 1966–80; MD Senate, 1967–78, Pres., 1975–78; Mbr., MD Bd. for Higher Education, 1978–81.

Offices: 1513 LHOB 20515, 202-225-4131. Also 4351 Garden City Dr., Ste. 625, Landover 20785, 301-436-5510.

Committees: *Appropriations* (30th of 35 D). Subcommittees: District of Columbia; Labor–Health and Human Services–Education; Treasury–Postal Service–General Government.

Group Ratings

	ADA	ACLU	COPE	CFA	LCV	ACU	NTU	NSI	COC	CEI
1986	75	95	92	83	58	5	21	20	22	13
1985	95	—	92	67	—	14	22	—	32	—

National Journal Ratings

	1986 LIB — 1986 CONS			1985 LIB — 1985 CONS		
Economic	84%	—	13%	75%	—	22%
Social	89%	—	0%	73%	—	23%
Foreign	64%	—	34%	58%	—	40%

Key Votes

1) Lmt Cln Water Act	AGN	5) Retain Gun Cont	FOR	9) Aid Angola Reb	AGN
2) Rpl Tobac Sub	AGN	6) Contra Aid	AGN	10) Tax Reform	AGN
3) Grm-Rdmn Def Red	AGN	7) Lmt Text Imp	FOR	11) S Africa Sanc	FOR
4) Ban Polygraph	FOR	8) Limit SDI	FOR	12) Immig Reform	FOR

Election Results

1986 general	Steny H. Hoyer (D)	82,098	(82%)	($368,388)
	John Eugene Sellner (R).	18,102	(18%)	
1986 primary	Steny H. Hoyer (D)	45,545	(91%)	
	George W. Benns (D)	1,918	(3%)	
	Charles Dean Ingram (D).	1,260	(3%)	
	Leighton D. Williams (D).	1,208	(3%)	
1984 general	Steny H. Hoyer (D)	116,310	(72%)	($213,480)
	John E. Ritchie (R).	44,839	(28%)	($11,666)

Campaign Contributions and Expenditures

1985-86		Direct Cont. 1985-86		PACS Breakdown 1985-86			
Receipts	$382,725	Indiv.	$184,255	Corp.	$47,987	T/M/H	$55,000
Expend.	$368,388	Party	$395	Labor	$68,265	Agr.	$3,650
Unspent	$237,908	PACS	$190,502	Ideo.	$14,350	CWOS	$1,250
		Cand.	$1,750				

SIXTH DISTRICT

West of Baltimore and Washington a series of gentle Maryland hills rise to the low mountains of the Catoctins and the Appalachian ridges. Here is a land known for its fertile valleys and its antique cities, like Frederick, where Barbara Fritchie supposedly reared her old gray head. Also here are the small industrial cities of Hagerstown and, nestled in the mountains, Cumberland. This is, traditionally, the most Republican part of Maryland. Some of the mountain folk and Pennsylvania Dutch who settled western Maryland have a long Republican tradition. Thus western Maryland went solidly for Ronald Reagan in 1980, when he lost the state, as well as in 1984, when he won it; western Maryland even went Republican in the 1982 and 1986 Senate races, when Democrat Paul Sarbanes and Barbara Mikulski easily won statewide.

The 6th Congressional District of Maryland takes in all of western Maryland and touches on Washington and Baltimore suburbs besides. In the Washington area, it takes in very high income Potomac all the way to the Capital Beltway; in the Baltimore area it reaches the edge of the planned town of Columbia. For the most part, however, this is a rural not a cosmopolitan district, a place where family patterns are traditional and patriotism is never scoffed at.

Beverly Byron, the representative from the 6th District, is the fourth Byron elected to Congress in western Maryland. Her husband's father and mother served in the 1940s, and her husband, Goodloe Byron, was elected in 1970 and served until he died while jogging in October 1978. Mrs. Byron, who had no political record of her own, got the nomination then. Some might have expected her to be a caretaker congresswoman. But she seems comfortably ensconced. She continues her husband's general voting pattern: conservative on most issues, little different really from many Republicans elected from similar districts. Her pro-environment record on the Interior Committee—including support of the Alaska Lands Act of 1980—helped her avoid the primary opposition which gave her husband close races in the 1976 and 1978 primaries.

Byron married into a political family, but her family background is career military; her father, Harry Butcher, was an important aide to Dwight Eisenhower in World War II, and she grew up in Washington. She does much of her work on Armed Services where she is part of the solid committee majority sympathetic to requests for military spending; she enjoys examining military equipment first hand on inspection trips. Occasionally Byron has dissented from Pentagon positions and has not been shy about championing the interests of western Maryland defense contractors. In 1985 new Armed Services Chairman Les Aspin wanted to give the chair of his Personnel Subcommittee to Patricia Schroeder, but couldn't because Byron had the votes for it, and kept it himself; in 1987 Byron backed Marvin Leath against Aspin. Approaching her 10th year in Congress, she is dean of the Maryland House delegation, and a more active member than many thought she would be.

The People: Pop. 1980: 528,168, up 24.3% 1970–80. Households (1980): 80% family, 45% with children, 70% married couples; 27.4% housing units rented; median monthly rent: $167; median house value: $58,100. Voting age pop. (1980): 376,405; 4% Black, 1% Spanish origin, 1% Asian origin.

1984 Presidential Vote: Reagan (R) 146,543   (69%)
Mondale (D) 66,062   (31%)

Rep. Beverly B. Byron (D)

Elected 1978; b. July 27, 1932, Baltimore; home, Frederick; Hood Col., 1963–64; Episcopalian; married (Kirk Walsh).

Career: Campaign Asst., U.S. Rep. Goodloe E. Byron.

Offices: 1216 LHOB 20515, 202-225-2721. Also 10 E. Church St., Frederick 21701, 301-662-8622; 100 W. Franklin St., #110, Hagerstown 21700, 301-797-6043; P.O. Box 3275, Cumberland 21504, 301-729-0300; 6 N. Court St., Westminster 21157, 301-848-5366.

Committees: *Armed Services* (10th of 31 D). Subcommittees: Investigations; Military Personnel and Compensation (Chairman). *Interior and Insular Affairs* (11th of 26 D). Subcommittees: National Parks and Public Lands; Water and Power Resources. *Select Committee on Aging* (12th of 39 D). Subcommittee: Housing and Consumer Interests.

Group Ratings

	ADA	ACLU	COPE	CFA	LCV	ACU	NTU	NSI	COC	CEI
1986	10	16	46	42	37	71	32	90	63	42
1985	20	—	46	42	—	65	34	—	59	—

National Journal Ratings

	1986 LIB — 1986 CONS	1985 LIB — 1985 CONS
Economic	38% — 61%	40% — 59%
Social	48% — 52%	34% — 64%
Foreign	33% — 66%	40% — 60%

Key Votes

1) Lmt Cln Water Act	FOR	5) Retain Gun Cont	AGN	9) Aid Angola Reb	FOR
2) Rpl Tobac Sub	AGN	6) Contra Aid	FOR	10) Tax Reform	FOR
3) Grm-Rdmn Def Rcd	FOR	7) Lmt Text Imp	FOR	11) S Africa Sanc	FOR
4) Ban Polygraph	FOR	8) Limit SDI	FOR	12) Immig Reform	FOR

Election Results

1986 general	Beverly B. Byron (D)	102,975	(72%)	($206,120)
	John Vandenberge (R)	39,600	(28%)	($137,069)
1986 primary	Beverly B. Byron (D)	42,847	(98%)	
	Charles J. Walters (D)	8,228	(2%)	
1984 general	Beverly B. Byron (D)	123,383	(65%)	($188,978)
	Robin Ficker (R)	66,056	(35%)	($65,137)

Campaign Contributions and Expenditures

1985-86		Direct Cont. 1985-86		PACS Breakdown 1985-86			
Receipts	$213,159	Indiv.	$73,056	Corp.	$75,110	T/M/H	$35,700
Expend.	$206,120	Party	$601	Labor	$6,200	Agr.	$3,300
Unspent	$72,853	PACS	$128,052	Ideo.	$7,242	CWOS	$500

SEVENTH DISTRICT

Baltimore is one of the few American cities which has always had large numbers of white immigrants and blacks. Maryland was a slave state decidedly unsympathetic to the cause of the Union: Abraham Lincoln had to sneak through on his way to his first inauguration, and "the patriotic gore that flecked the streets of Baltimore" in the state song "Maryland, My Maryland" was the blood of pro-Confederate rioters suppressed by Union troops under martial law.

Segregation was the rule, if not the law, in Baltimore until the early 1960s, and the city's large black population lived in well-defined communities, one on the east side and one on the west. Baltimore blacks always had the vote, however; and they were courted by pro-civil rights Republicans like Theodore McKeldin as well as urban Democrats. "Walking around money" was always floating around in black precincts on election day, but Baltimore's black community also produced strong institutions and political leaders, the most brilliant of whom was Clarence Mitchell, for many years the NAACP's lobbyist in Washington.

Since the late 1970s Baltimore has had a black majority, but only with the election of Donald Schaefer as governor has there been a black mayor; Schaefer, who stayed in the house he grew up in on the now all-black west side, won majorities from black as well as white voters in 1971, 1975, 1979, and 1983. His successor, Council President Clarence (Du) Burns, is not as commanding a figure; he was a locker room attendant who served 15 years on the Council where he loyally supported Schaefer. Yet under his leadership Baltimore kept its streets clear in the January 1987 blizzard when Washington, led by a mayor who completed all the course requirements for a Ph.D., was snowed in. In early 1987 Burns seemed likely to be challenged later in the year by State's Attorney Kurt Schmoke, a young, Yale-educated black who won his office by overwhelming margins. Black politics below the mayoral level in Baltimore is a series of alliances, feuds, personal loyalties, and decade-long hatreds. The most prominent black politician, at least until 1986, was Representative Parren Mitchell, elected in 1970 when he upset a Jewish incumbent in the primary when the district still had a white majority, for six years chairman of the House Small Business Committee, and, after he decided to retire from the House, Attorney General Stephen Sachs's running mate in the 1986 gubernatorial primary. Despite Schaefer's popularity, the Sachs-Mitchell ticket carried most black precincts in Baltimore and Prince George's County.

In the meantime a primary fight was raging in the 7th District, which includes almost all of the mostly black neighborhoods and, aside from most of Johns Hopkins and the old patrician neighborhood of Bolton Hill, very few white areas; it also extends out directly west into the Baltimore County suburbs of Lochearn and Milford Mill, both of which have black majorities. The most familiar name in the race was Clarence Mitchell III, the congressman's nephew, a veteran of 24 years in the state Senate. But this Mitchell seems deeply flawed: in 1964 he pleaded no contest to charges of failing to file income taxes for several years, in 1983 he was charged with carrying a weapon on a plane, in 1981 he was reported under investigation for real estate dealings with a convicted drug dealer, and in 1987 he and his brother were indicted for conspiring to block an investigation into the Bronx's Wedtech. In 1986 he won an embarrassing 16% of the primary vote. Another well-known candidate was Wendell Phillips, a minister and head of the city's House of Delegates delegation; he was attacked for being too close to Donald Schaefer. The winner was Kweisi Mfume, city council member since 1979, talk show host on the Morgan State radio station, supporter of Jesse Jackson in 1984. He won a resounding 44% of the vote. In the general election it was revealed that Mfume, formerly named Frizzell Gray, fathered five sons by four different women while a young man; he admitted that he had done so after his own family disintegrated and said he supported them. His story was given credence by his reserved demeanor and his oft-voiced disapproval of drug use and immoral conduct. He won the general election, and a safe seat in Congress, with 87% of the vote. He has seats on the two committees, Banking and Small Business, on which Parren Mitchell served.

The People: Pop. 1980: 527,590, dn. 11.2% 1970–80. Households (1980): 67% family, 40% with children, 37% married couples; 58.1% housing units rented; median monthly rent: $158; median house value: $28,300. Voting age pop. (1980): 376,566; 70% Black, 1% Spanish origin, 1% Asian origin.

1984 Presidential Vote:

Mondale (D)	151,669	(82%)
Reagan (R)	32,980	(18%)

Rep. Kweisi Mfume (D)

Elected 1986; b. Oct. 24, 1948, Baltimore; home, Baltimore; Morgan St. U., B.S. 1976, Johns Hokins U., M.A. 1984; Baptist; divorced.

Career: Baltimore City Cncl., 1979–87.

Offices: 1107 LHOB 20515, 202-225-4741. Also 3000 Druid Park Drive, Baltimore 21205, 301-367-1900; and 2203 N. Charles St., Baltimore 21218, 301-235-2700.

Committees: *Banking, Finance and Urban Affairs* (29th of 31 D). Subcommittees: Economic Stabilization; Housing and Community Development; International Development Institutions and Finance. *Small Business* (21st of 27 D). Subcommittees: Exports, Tourism and Special Problems; Procurement, Innovation and Minority Enterprise Development. *Select Committee on Hunger* (15th of 16 D). Task Force: Domestic Task Force.

Group Ratings and Key Votes: Newly Elected

Election Results

1986 general	Kweisi Mfume (D)	79,226	(87%)	($104,550)
	St. George I.B. Crosse, III (R)	12,170	(11%)	($52,593)
1986 primary	Kweisi Mfume (D)	38,357	(44%)	
	Wendell H. Phillips (D)	20,318	(12%)	
	Clarence M. Mitchell (D)	13,783	(16%)	
	Edward Jack Makowski (D)	4,348	(5%)	
	Three others (D)	7,029	(8%)	
1984 general	Parren J. Mitchell (D) unopposed			($133,159)

Campaign Contributions and Expenditures

1985-86		Direct Cont. 1985-86		PACS Breakdown 1985-86				
Receipts	$149,882	Indiv.	$87,065	Corp.	$2,890	T/M/H	$9,000
Expend.	$104,550	Party	$500	Labor	$24,500	Agr.	$0
Unspent	$45,331	PACS	$52,590	Ideo.	$15,200	CWOS	$1,000
		Cand.	$23				

EIGHTH DISTRICT

Montgomery County, Maryland, by most measures is the richest county in the United States. Out in what was once rolling Maryland farmland, affluent Washingtonians and newcomers from all over the country have built a set of communities with private spaces and public amenities which, taken together, are not equalled by any place of similar size in the United States. Montgomery County experienced a vast population increase in the 1950s and 1960s, from 164,000 to 522,000 in those 20 years. The increase continued, much less rapidly, to 579,000 in 1980, then spurted ahead to well over 600,000 in the middle 1980s: the most explosive recent growth has been along the I-270 corridor out to Gaithersburg and beyond. The migrants are almost all affluent, highly educated, upscale in demographers' language.

The typical resident of Montgomery County, and of the 8th Congressional District of Maryland, which includes well over half its land area and 90% of its people, is a high-ranking civil servant, a lawyer in private practice, or, increasingly, a professional employee of a firm that does consulting for the government. He (or she) is as likely as not to have a graduate degree and to belong to a liberal-oriented Protestant church or a Reform Jewish temple. He is sympathetic to the striving nations of the Third World, to efforts to clean up political campaigns, to environmentalists. On his coffee table you will find *Smithsonian* rather than *National*

Geographic, the *New Yorker* rather than *People*. He professes a vaguely liberal sort of politics. Montgomery County voters are usually willing to support Democrats, and the 8th District, in a nice refutation of the theory that Americans always vote their pocketbooks, favored Walter Mondale over Ronald Reagan. But for years their favorite kind of candidate was the liberal Republican who cares deeply about the political process, like former Senator Charles Mathias.

Mathias himself represented a House district that included Montgomery, and he was succeeded by liberal Republicans Gilbert Gude and Newton Steers. But the mold was broken in 1978 by Democrat Michael Barnes, who defeated Steers and, two years later, became one of the most prominent Democrats in the House when despite his lack of seniority he was elected chairman of the subcommittee handling Latin American policy. Barnes was a strong opponent of Reagan Administration policy in El Salvador and Nicaragua, yet even while emphasizing national issues also kept in constant touch with a district that is always just a local phone call away from Capitol Hill and provided the kind of constituency service suburban Washington voters expect. Barnes was not successful when he ran for the Senate in 1986, losing the primary to Baltimore's Barbara Mikulski. But in a nice testimonial to his work, he carried 75% of the vote in Montgomery County.

The current representative from the 8th District is not a Barnes Democrat but a Mathias liberal. Or, rather, she is a Connie Morella liberal, for personal character and background played an important role in her victory. Her opponent, state Senator Stewart Bainum, had a maverick but effective record in the state Senate, leading the fight to deny a tax break to Burning Tree Country Club because it doesn't admit women and to require chemical firms to disclose toxic waste they use; he also had plenty of money, thanks to building up his family's nursing home business to a huge conglomerate, and spent almost $1.5 million—the third highest figure in the nation in 1986. But Morella had her own record in the House of Delegates, plus her experience raising nine children (including six of her late sister's), and she had a warm, articulate demeanor, while Bainum often seemed stiff and ill-at-ease; and she raised and spent a very hefty $640,000 herself. Bainum won a riproaring Democratic primary. But after Morella was endorsed by *The Washington Post,* she took the lead and won 53%–47%.

In the House, where the Republicans of all stripes have shown impressive unity, she will likely fit in well; in vivid contrast to Barnes, she backs at least some aid to Nicaragua's contras and Angola's UNITA, supports the B-1 bomber and the Strategic Defense Initiative. She has seats on the Post Office and Civil Service and Science, Space and Technology Committees—useful positions in this district in which federal employees are still a major presence and high tech industry a growing one.

The People: Pop. 1980: 528,036, up 7.3% 1970–80. Households (1980): 72% family, 38% with children, 60% married couples; 37.1% housing units rented; median monthly rent: $332; median house value: $96,900. Voting age pop. (1980): 391,309; 8% Black, 4% Spanish origin, 4% Asian origin.

1984 Presidential Vote: Mondale (D) 136,104   (51%)
Reagan (R) 128,747   (48%)

Rep. Constance A. Morella (R)

Elected 1986; b. Feb. 12, 1931, Somerville, MA; home, Bethesda; Boston U., A.B. 1954; American U., M.A. 1967; Roman Catholic; married (Anthony).

Career: MD House of Delegates, 1979–86.

Offices: 1024 CHOB 20515, 202-225-5341. Also 11141 Georgia Ave., Ste. 302, Wheaton 20902, 301-946-6801.

Committees: *Science, Space and Technology* (18th of 18 R). Subcommittees: Energy Research and Development; Space Science and Applications. *Post Office and Civil Service* (8th of 8 R). Subcommittees: Census and Population; Compensation and Employee Benefits. *Select Committee on Aging* (25th of 26 R). Subcommittee: Human Services.

Group Ratings and Key Votes: Newly Elected

Election Results

1986 general	Constance A. Morella (R)	92,917	(53%)	($640,270)
	Stewart Bainum, Jr. (D)	82,825	(47%)	($1,500,531)
1986 primary	Constance A. Morella (R)	17,817	(68%)	
	William Shepard (R)	6,788	(26%)	
	Philip N. Buford (R)	1,638	(6%)	
1984 general	Michael D. Barnes (D)	181,947	(71%)	($198,749)
	Albert Ceccone (R)	70,715	(28%)	($12,923)

Campaign Contributions and Expenditures

1985-86		Direct Cont. 1985-86		PACS Breakdown 1985-86			
Receipts	$633,909	Indiv.	$414,010	Corp.	$62,500	T/M/H	$59,920
Expend.	$640,270	Party	$14,180	Labor	$6,600	Agr.	$0
Unspent	$3,592	PACS	$164,610	Ideo.	$35,090	CWOS	$500
		Cand.	$1,000				

MASSACHUSETTS

After the first Pilgrims and Puritans sloshed through the cold waters of Massachusetts Bay and reached the shore, they looked upon a forbidding land: Massachusetts, stony and infertile, with a short growing season, no ores precious or otherwise, and a population of furry animals rapidly depleted by trappers. Its rivers trailed into quiet hills or led into the mountain fastness of New Hampshire and Vermont. Its bays made treacherous by shoals and riptides, Massachusetts has the physical characteristics of the west coast of Ireland or the Highlands of Scotland, the ragged edges of Europe which have always been among the poorest lands of Christendom. Yet Massachusetts over most of the last 350 years has been rich, one of the richest lands in the world. The commonwealth has fished cod from the Grand Banks of Newfoundland and stole the designs for textile factories from the English Midlands. It built railroads to the Pacific Ocean, marketed bananas from Central America, and mined coal in West Virginia. It invented the go-go mutual fund and wired together microchips manufactured in Texas and California into computer systems. Massachusetts is where the descendants of Puritans from East Anglia and Wessex find themselves living with the offspring of Catholics from Ireland and Italy, even while in its most recent gubernatorial election both major parties ran candidates whose ancestors came from Greece.

Massachusetts's economic success comes from ingenuity. The commonwealth that the theocratic John Winthrop wanted to make "a city on a hill" has been careful to keep a cold eye on the rest of the world below for products and ideas from which to make money. In politics, meanwhile, Massachusetts has been characterized not by ingenuity and curiosity about the world beyond, but by insecurity and a desire to huddle inside the world within. But the world within has been anything but serene, and much of the political struggle over the years reflects a clash of different cultures, arguments not so much over the distribution of income or wealth but over whose vision of Massachusetts should be honored, whose mores regarded as the norm.

Two events in history have made Massachusetts politics what it is today: the Irish potato famine of the 1840s and the development of the digital computer in the 1970s. Taken together, they explain why Massachusetts is one of the most Democratic states and also one of the most prosperous, with low unemployment and rapid economic growth; why the only state to reject Richard Nixon in 1972 has voted twice (albeit by narrow margins) for Ronald Reagan; why a state that seemed uncritically accepting of big government in the middle 1970s has by the middle 1980s cut its taxes—and services—several times; and even why a state which has been consistently skeptical of American foreign and military policy also has one of the nation's highest levels of defense spending—spending which in turn has stimulated much of the technological innovation which is the key ingredient of its economic growth.

Much Massachusetts history started with the blight that destroyed Ireland's potato crop and cut its population from 8 million in 1840 to 4 million a few decades later. Irish immigrants came flooding into Boston, the nearest American port, and began settling in alarmingly large numbers in a commonwealth that for 200 years was homogeneously Yankee. Once hemmed in by French Catholics in Quebec and Dutch in the Hudson Valley, New England Yankees in the 1800s were now expanding rapidly westward, along the Erie Canal, the Great Lakes, into the Mississippi Valley and California. But at home they saw themselves threatened by the Irish, rough, rowdy, and most disturbingly of all Catholic: for New England Protestants, from the 17th century, had seen the Catholic Church as a foreign power, an aggressive militant enemy, with no scruples against untruth or torture—as subversive a force as 20th century Communism. The English had thrown out a Catholic king in 1689, and New England Yankees did not want to see their land in the new world dominated by Catholics again. As for the Irish, they remembered 100 years later the "No Irish need apply" signs; the reception they got was as hostile as any group of immigrants have received in this country.

Ever since, politics in Massachusetts has usually been a struggle between Yankee and Irish. Sometimes the stakes have been concrete—control of patronage jobs, command of the Boston Police Department—and sometimes they have just been symbolic. Whatever, party politics became centered on ethnic conflict. The Yankees of the 1840s, not long removed from Federalism, were solid Whigs and would become one of the bulwarks of the Republican Party when it was formed a decade later. The Whigs and Republicans backed policies that appealed to Yankees: promoting public works and protective tariffs to help business, and sympathy for suitably distant oppressed people like the blacks of the South, and for uplifting (and productivity-enhancing) social movements like temperance.

The Irish knew from the beginning that they were not going to get very far in the party of the Yankees, and they found the Democrats of the 19th century more congenial. We now think of the Democrats as a party promoting government action, but in those days the Democrats represented laissez-faire. That was fine with the Irish. They came from a place where the government was the enemy; they didn't want government spending money to help the rich or to stimulate commerce (with which they had little acquaintance in agricultural Ireland); they didn't want government to restrict immigration; they didn't want it to advance the blacks who might compete with them in the labor market; and they didn't want it to prohibit the consumption of liquor. They were people familiar with competing hierarchies—the hierarchy of

MASSACHUSETTS — Congressional Districts, Counties, County Subdivisions (Towns), and Places — *(11 Districts)*

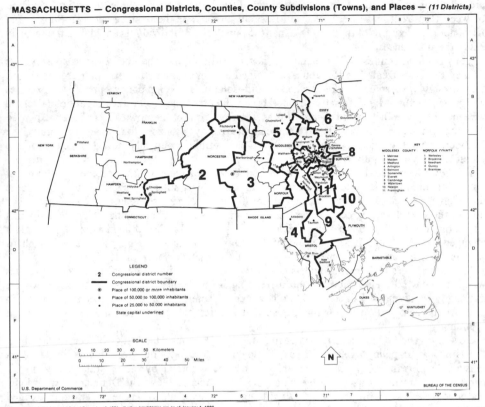

Congressional districts established December 3, 1981; all other boundaries are as of January 1, 1980.

the hated English lords and the hierarchy of their own, often suppressed, Roman Catholic Church. The Democratic Party, with its ward organization and rituals, seemed like a sympathetic hierarchy. So the Irish went into politics, determined to beat the Protestants.

Over the years the percentage of Irish and Catholics slowly rose. Yankees had smaller families, they moved out west, they intermarried with people of immigrant stock and lost their Yankee identity. The Irish mostly stayed put, raised large families, and eventually ruled as Massachusetts very slowly moved from being one of our most Republican states to becoming one of the most Democratic. The state's economy waxed and waned several times, thriving in the early 19th century as the leading maritime center of a trading nation and then falling as the country turned inward to the frontier; thriving again later in the 19th century and in the early 20th as a manufacturing center, then lapsing as employers sought lower wage workers elsewhere; thriving now in the late 20th century as a center of high technology.

But politics followed its own rhythms. Massachusetts gave Republicans majorities in every presidential election from the Civil War to 1924, when the last New England Yankee, Calvin Coolidge, was elected. Since 1928, when the Democrats nominated the Catholic Al Smith, Massachusetts has gone Democratic in all but the two Eisenhower elections. In the 1920s, 1930s, 1940s, and 1950s, the parties were closely balanced statewide, but Republicans won in most congressional districts; Irish Democrats were heavily concentrated in a few cities, as black Democrats are in many states today. An Irish Democrat was elected Senator as long ago as 1918, but Republicans did better at fielding attractive candidates. Throughout, the state's preference in presidential elections shifted very little in this period. While the nation oscillated between Roosevelt and Eisenhower, in Massachusetts it was the balance between Yankee and Irish, not the programs of the New Deal nor the popularity of individual candidates, that usually made the difference.

Thus political conflict in Massachusetts never really fell into the liberal-versus-conservative lines of the New Deal. The Republicans retained a Yankee interventionism, an urge to tinker: they strongly favored civil rights, pushed an anti-isolationist foreign policy, opposed the excesses of Joe McCarthy. Massachusetts Democrats, on the other hand, like the Republic of Ireland were hostile to the British and cheered Joe McCarthy as one of their own. (Joseph Kennedy used to invite him to Hyannisport.) The Republicans also always promised to root out corruption. The Democrats had the complacent attitude typical of an ethnic group only recently able to aspire to public office and the public payroll.

For a while in the 1960s and 1970s, when Edward Kennedy had become the dominant political figure in the state, Irish Democrats and Yankee Republicans began moving in the same direction for the first time in Massachusetts history. Kennedy's support of civil rights even during the Boston busing controversy, his opposition to the war in Vietnam, his stand against corruption during Watergate—all appealed to Yankee sensibilities while his appeal to the Irish changed their attitudes. It was no accident that Massachusetts—upper-crust Yankee Lincoln as well as lower-income Irish Somerville—voted for George McGovern in 1972.

Massachusetts's high tech boom has now moved its politics in a different direction. Catholics who are ancestral Democrats have been trending Republican in Massachusetts as they have nationally, while many Yankees and highly-educated voters generally have been moving, as in other high tech parts of the nation, toward a politics of lower taxes and less government spending.

Governor. The key figure here has been Governor Michael Dukakis. Cool, cerebral, talking the language of policy experts, he has the loyalty of college-educated liberals and appears reasonable to Yankee Republicans. Dukakis has been forced by circumstances beyond his control and contrary to his choosing to adopt policies acceptable to the Democrats' traditional Catholic base. The instrument was Edward King, who beat Dukakis in the 1978 primary, called for lower taxes, and then in fact lowered them, and saw them lowered again—property tax rates were cut 40%—by voters in 1980's Proposition 2½. The *Boston Globe,* as bossy a voice of orthodox liberalism as Colonel McCormick's *Chicago Tribune* was of conservatism, insisted this would devastate revenues and damage the state; as it has since conceded, exactly the contrary happened. Lower property tax rates generated more revenue as Massachusetts property values and construction boomed. Personal income, which grew at the nation's slowest rate during the first Dukakis term, was growing at one of the nation's fastest rates during his second term after the four years of Ed King. The unemployment rate, in Dukakis's first term among the highest in the country, was one of the lowest shortly after he defeated King in 1982 and returned, more or less permanently it seems, to office.

Dukakis took advantage of the state's newly booming economy to push policies widely hailed as innovative and effective; politically, he has been an innovator since, as a state legislator, he sponsored in the 1960s what became the nation's first no-fault auto insurance bill. He initiated the first major state tax amnesty, which brought lots of new revenue without any new taxes, and which may have changed basic attitudes in what, when it had such high tax rates, was becoming a cynical scofflaw state. His Employment and Training Program, widely known as ET, had placed 23,000 welfare recipients into paying jobs, as he proclaimed far and wide. The achievement was probably overstated; some—no one knows how many, because there was no control group study—would have gotten jobs anyway, and it's easier to find jobs when you have 3% unemployment than when it's 13%. Yet even with these cavils, it seems that Dukakis has changed the operation and the goals of the state's welfare bureaucracy—no small task. These programs may or may not be models for the nation: a federal tax amnesty might only undermine the IRS's tough enforcement, and it's not clear that ET would work very well in, say, Louisiana with its 13% unemployment. Dukakis is attacked by the *Boston Herald* and the right for expanding government too fast, while the left took his welfare program to court and got a judge to issue a crackpot order requiring the state to pony up $500 million so that all welfare recipients would get $11,000 incomes.

Dukakis talks again and again about state government cooperating with business to produce more jobs, but he has done something a bit more subtle: he has used the instrumentality of activist government, which his liberal, well-educated core constituency has a philosophic preference for, to help increase the already buoyant growth of a private sector economy, which that constituency in practice has tied its personal hopes to. In campaigns in the old days the Kennedys—John Kennedy in 1952, Edward Kennedy in 1962—used to promise to "do more for Massachusetts." The appeal was to a lower-income Catholic constituency that thought government aid could compensate for a stagnant local economy. Under Michael Dukakis the argument is almost turned upside down: the booming private sector is doing more for Massachusetts, and government is helping out some here and a bit there.

In the process Dukakis has left mostly behind the liberalism on cultural issues which was represented most vividly in the state by court-ordered busing in Boston schools in the 1970s; as Anthony Lukas's *Common Ground* suggests, busing at best failed to achieve many of its goals and at worst ripped apart much of the city for little positive gain. Massachusetts liberals no longer feel they must tell lower-income whites how to live; and in fact the state's economic development has been accompanied by an outmigration of low-skill people that until about 1985 was larger than the in-migration of high-skill newcomers.

Dukakis's successes, his air of command, and the state's booming economy have impressed the voters: Dukakis was reelected essentially without opposition in 1986. The Republican party became a joke. Former Governor King switched his registration, then declined to run. Raymond Shamie, who made respectable showings against Senators Kennedy and Kerry and in 1987 became Republican state chairman, decided not to run. One Republican candidate, legislator Royall Switzler, bowed out of the race after falsely claiming to have served in the Army Special Forces in Vietnam. Another, Proposition 2½ leader Gregory Hyatt, left the field after it was revealed that he was found twice in his office with no clothes on. Hyatt won the primary but renounced the nomination, which was given to businessman George Kariotis, who predictably lost. The Republicans looked like a party in terminal decline. But we may be looking at the thrashings of a party whose candidates are inexperienced and unpolished, often the children of immigrant families, but whose ideas and programs have appeal—like the Democrats of 50 years ago.

Dukakis remains strong not only in Massachusetts, but even in New Hampshire, where a *Globe* poll showed him competitive with Republican Governor John Sununu, and where he attracted attention by opposing the controversial Seabrook nuclear plant. Early 1987 polls showing Dukakis running even with or ahead of Gary Hart in New Hampshire helped to stimulate his presidential candidacy, announced in April 1987. Some considered him a substitute for Mario Cuomo as a representative of big-government Democrats, though this misses the point of much of Dukakis's record (and Cuomo's too, for that matter). The better claim for his candidacy is that he has shown that he can make government make a fast-growing economy grow even faster and provide a leg up for those not doing so well besides.

Senators. Edward Kennedy, after a quarter-century in the Senate, is Massachusetts's most enduring politician. With Tip O'Neill retiring and the Democrats back in the majority in the Senate, Kennedy is also the state's most powerful member of Congress. Yet he is also a less imposing figure on the national scene: nearly 30 years after his brother's victory in 1960, it is clear that this Kennedy will never be President. In the 1970s the rumor mills buzzed with speculation over whether Kennedy would run. But in 1980, he did run—and lost decisively to a weak incumbent. When he announced he wouldn't run in 1984 and 1988, there was no draft movement to change his mind, no sense that the Democrats were doomed without a candidate from this one family. Most voters can't remember, or never knew, what made the Kennedys so exciting.

All of which has enabled Kennedy to do what he evidently wants, to work conscientiously for what he considers the interests of the poorest and most helpless in our society. For this he had little preparation and no firsthand knowledge: he spent his first three decades as a rich playboy and his next three as a celebrity who could not walk down a street without being mobbed. He came from a political family whose concern for the poor was limited, until about 1963, to how many votes the poor would cast for them and, in some places, how much those votes would cost. In his early years in the Senate Edward Kennedy was quiet, listened respectfully to his elders, learned the rules written and unwritten, and prepared himself to be the legislator his brothers never were. After the deaths of his brothers John and Robert, after the awful year of urban riots and antiwar demonstrations and the murder of Martin Luther King, Edward Kennedy evidently decided he had a mission to help the helpless; and ever since he has been America's most conspicuous supporter of greater government spending on programs aimed at helping the poor.

In the process he assembled a crackerjack staff (many members of which had daydreams about their White House offices) that became a model for other Democrats, generating one big-government bill after another, working as part of iron triangles with agency bureaucrats and think tank professionals to create and nurture new government programs, under the sometimes loose supervision of the Senator. Kennedy himself worked hard to master details and shepherded to passage such diverse measures as immigration reform (the 1965 bill; he opposed the thrust of the 1986 reform), criminal code revision, and airline deregulation. He became chairman of the Judiciary Committee in 1979, on the retirement of James Eastland, and undertook the burden of upholding liberal positions on issues like abortion, capital punishment, busing, and the balanced budget constitutional amendment; in the minority, he relinquished the ranking chair on Judiciary for Labor, but worked with Strom Thurmond on writing a new federal criminal code. In the first six Reagan years, in the minority, he had a far smaller staff, few likeminded colleagues, and much less influence. He got a seat on Armed Services, where he tended to oppose Caspar Weinberger's Pentagon.

When the Democrats won control in 1986, Kennedy decided to chair Labor and Public Welfare rather than Judiciary, looking forward again to doing something for the poor. Possibilities included raising the minimum wage (though in prosperous states like Massachusetts the market has already raised wages above the minimum), requiring advance notice of plant closings (but that only tries to freeze in place yesterday's economy at some cost to building tomorrow's), improving infant nutrition, restricting employers' use of lie detectors and drug tests, prohibiting companies from setting up non-union affiliates, requiring all employers to offer health insurance and to pay for health insurance for laid-off employees. He is busy trying to get federal bonuses for states that target job training programs on hard-core welfare parents. He might also be one of the leaders of the Senate's workfare package. But Kennedy seems unlikely, at least in the short term, to resurrect the proposals which he and other liberals seemed almost on the verge of enacting in the 1970s: national health insurance, forms of which Kennedy proposed; a strengthened union movement enrolling a larger rather than smaller number of workers; welfare payments that guarantee an above-poverty income to everyone. These are things Americans, even in rich states like Massachusetts, have decided they cannot afford. His proposals instead are an ambitious and creative effort to provide more security and help for ordinary citizens and the poor without taking much money from the federal treasury (or adding to the federal deficit).

Kennedy remains politically strong in Massachusetts, though in a different way than he was 15 or 20 years ago. Then he was revered by Irish voters who remembered discrimination and loved him as a member of the family that had brought them all into the American mainstream; now he is more likely to be respected as a hardworking, competent, earnest public official. His conduct at Chappaquiddick in 1969 still causes some voters problems, as it did when he ran for President in 1980, and probably always will; and he stirs Republican as well as Democratic partisan juices, both among Massachusetts voters and among recipients of Republican and New

Right direct mail. After a spirited challenge from Republican high tech entrepreneur Raymond Shamie, he was reelected with 61% of the vote in 1982—less than the 69% he had against weaker opposition in 1976 or the 62% he won in 1970 just after Chappaquiddick. No one expects Kennedy to have political trouble in 1988. But he is not likely to be reelected with a near-unanimous vote.

Massachusetts's junior Senator, John F. Kerry, is a less well-known new face, elected in 1984 after the surprise retirement of incumbent Paul Tsongas. Kerry had already had a long political career, however. He served in the Navy in Vietnam and was one of the organizers of Vietnam Veterans Against the War. He ran for Congress in 1972, and though George McGovern was carrying the district, he lost. He was hurt by several things, including blatant district-shopping—he bought a house in Worcester and when an incumbent retired moved to Lowell, by the vitriolic opposition of the *Lowell Sun*, and because he tossed a set of medals over a fence in an anti-war rally. There had been talk of Kerry as a presidential candidate some day; chastened by his loss, he went to law school, worked for a prosecutor, was elected lieutenant governor on the Dukakis ticket in 1982, and squeaked to a narrow victory in the 1984 Senate primary over Representative (and since 1986 Attorney General) James Shannon, who made the mistake of attacking him for serving in the military at all. In the meantime, Republican primary voters were surprising observers across the nation by rejecting the candidacy of Elliot Richardson—former holder of several Cabinet offices, as well as lieutenant governor and attorney general of Massachusetts—and selecting instead Raymond Shamie. The once Yankee and socially interventionist ranks of the Republican party have been so thinned that the children of immigrants who believe in Ronald Reagan's politics now are a majority in primaries here as elsewhere, and naturally they preferred Shamie to Richardson. But newly rising groups make mistakes in politics: Shamie, it seems, used to be involved with the John Birch Society and kept Birch literature around his office; this is pretty weird stuff, and the *Globe* had a lot of fun with it. Kerry won with 55%—a good share for a freshman Senator, but also a sign that Massachusetts is not so one-sidedly Democratic on national issues as it once was.

In his first two years Kerry attracted little attention in the Senate; now he seems sure to attract more. He is part of the dovish Democratic majority on the Senate Foreign Relations Committee and spent time observing the 1986 elections in the Philippines and trying to find out what happened to Contra aid on the ground in Honduras. He seems to infuriate conservative activists, who have been enraged by the uses to which he has put his combat record in Vietnam from the time he returned medals (another man's, he later admitted) in a public ceremony. They see him as a "radical leftist," charge that he and Iowa's Tom Harkin let themselves be used as Daniel Ortega's couriers after a visit to Nicaragua in 1985, and that he has used his committee position to cover up evidence that the Sandinistas are involved in the drug trade.

Kerry seems puzzled by this animosity and evidently does not understand how the course of his career seems contrived to many and evil to conservatives. He sees himself as concentrating on practical issues. After two years he rotated off Labor and Public Welfare, where he would have been inevitably in Kennedy's shadow, and got onto Commerce, which under regulation-minded Ernest Hollings is likely to be a battleground between all kinds of economic interests. That is also a good place from which to raise political contributions, a subject Kerry is bound to be interested in, since he fought for and won the chairmanship of the Senate Democratic Campaign Committee. A good performance there built great respect for George Mitchell in 1986, and might do the same for Kerry in 1988. Democrats start off with the odds in their favor: they have 54 seats, and probably fewer vulnerable incumbents than Republicans. But the lesson of the Republican capture of the Senate in 1980 and the Democratic recapture in 1986 is that almost all the close races can go one way, and that every detail that can make the difference in one race can make the difference in control.

Presidential politics. Massachusetts remains one of the most Democratic states in national elections, but the movement of high-tech voters to Ronald Reagan's Republicans has reduced the Democrats' advantage. The state was 17% more Democratic than the national average in

1972, and only 8% more Democratic than average in 1984. Ronald Reagan won here in 1980 because the anti-Reagan vote was split between Jimmy Carter (42%) and John Anderson (15%), and won only barely in 1984. His percentage here in 1980 was his lowest in any state except Rhode Island and Georgia, and his percentage in 1984 was his lowest in any state but Minnesota. Massachusetts is not a state where either party tends to campaign much, although in late 1984 they did, as President Reagan sought a 50-state sweep and Walter Mondale tried to prevent it. Perhaps the less than spectacular showings of both parties shows a lack of faith in politics in a state which the private economy has done more for than government ever did.

Massachusetts has one of the earliest primaries, on Super Tuesday in mid-March; and since most of New Hampshire is covered by Boston TV, campaigning for Massachusetts goes on well before. It has produced some surprise winners, from Henry Jackson in 1976 to Gary Hart in 1984. On the Republican side, this is the only state where George Bush and John Anderson finished ahead of Ronald Reagan in 1980—although the Republican electorate seems to have moved right since then. But the 1988 primary, coming on the same day as the southern regional primary, is likely to be ignored by candidates and media alike. Who wants to risk having your plane snowed in at Logan when it could be hip-hopping across the sunny South?

Congressional districting. Massachusetts's congressional district lines look almost as grotesque as the original Gerrymander, drawn after the 1810 Census in what is now the 6th Congressional District. But there is little partisan controversy here, since Republicans hold only one seat, and in the one district where two incumbents were thrown together after the 1980 Census, it was Republican Margaret Heckler rather than Democrat Barney Frank who had the advantage; Frank won anyway. With only one Republican, the House delegation is essentially divided between old pols, liberal on everything but some cultural issues, with bases in traditional Democratic constituencies (Boland, Early, Mavroules, Moakley, Donnelly); and young pols, liberal on just about everything, elected from historically Republican areas (Frank, Atkins, Markey, Studds).

The People: Est. Pop 1986: 5,832,000; Pop. 1980: 5,737,037, up 1.7% 1980–86 and 0.8% 1970–80; 2.42% of U.S. total, 12th largest. 16% with 1–3 yrs. col., 20% with 4+ yrs. col.; 9.8% below poverty level. Single ancestry: 12% Irish, 8% English, Italian, 5% French, 3% Portuguese, Polish, 2% German, 1% Russian, Swedish, Greek, Scottish. Households (1980): 71% family, 36% with children, 57% married couples; 42.5% housing units rented; median monthly rent: $197; median house value: $48,500. Voting age pop. (1980): 4,246,648; 3% Black, 2% Spanish origin, 1% Asian origin. Registered voters (1986): 2,933,364; 1,3678692 D (47%); 389,839 R (13%); 1,175,656 unaffiliated (40%).

1986 Share of Federal Tax Burden $21,690,000,000; 2.88% of U.S. total, 10th largest.

1986 Share of Federal Expenditures

	Total		Non-Defense		Defense	
Total Expend	$24,937m	(3.00%)	$15,300m	(2.55%)	$9,637m	(4.19%)
St/Lcl Grants	3,082m	(2.74%)	3,078m	(2.74%)	3m	(2.70%)
Salary/Wages	2,079m	(1.72%)	1,405m	(2.39%)	675m	(1.09%)
Pymnts to Indiv	9,521m	(2.61%)	9,300m	(2.68%)	222m	(1.25%)
Procurement	9,461m	(4.60%)	725m	(1.30%)	8,736m	(5.82%)
Loan/Insurance	793m	(2.97%)	789m	(2.96%)	4m	(11.76%)

Political Lineup: Governor, Michael S. Dukakis (D); Lt. Gov., Evelyn F. Murphy (D); Secy. of Commonwealth, Michael Joseph (D); Atty. Gen., James Shannon (D); Treasurer, Robert Q. Crane (D); Auditor, Joseph DeNucci (D). State Senate, 40 (32 D and 8 R); State House of Representatives, 160 (133 D and 27 R). Senators, Edward M. Kennedy (D) and John F. Kerry (D). Representatives, 11 (10 D and 1 R).

1984 Presidential Vote

Reagan (R)	1,310,936	(51%)
Mondale (D)	1,239,606	(48%)

1980 Presidential Vote

Reagan (R)	1,056,223	(42%)
Carter (D)	1,053,802	(42%)
Anderson (I)	382,539	(15%)

1984 Democratic Presidential Primary

Hart	245,943	(39%)
Mondale	160,893	(25%)
McGovern	134,341	(21%)
Glenn	45,456	(7%)
Jackson	31,824	(5%)
Five others, no pref.	12,505	(2%)

1984 Republican Presidential Primary

Reagan	58,996	(89%)
Others	6,941	(11%)

GOVERNOR

Gov. Michael S. Dukakis (D)

Elected 1982, term expires Jan. 1991; b. Nov. 3, 1933, Brookline; home, Brookline; Swarthmore Col., B.A. 1955, Harvard U., LL.B. 1960; Greek Orthodox; married (Katharine).

Career: Army, Korea; Practicing atty., 1960–74; MA House of Reps., 1963–70; Dem. Nominee for Lt. Gov., 1970; Moderator, "The Advocates," Natl. TV show, 1970–73; Gov. of MA, 1974–79; Dir., Intergovernmental Studies, Harvard U., appointed 1979.

Office: State House, Rm. 360, Boston 02133, 617-727-3600.

Election Results

1986 gen.	Michael S. Dukakis (D)	1,157,786	(69%)
	George S. Kariotis (R)	525,364	(31%)
1986 prim.	Michael S. Dukakis (D)	499,572	(100%)
1982 gen.	Michael S. Dukakis (D)	1,219,109	(59%)
	John W. Sears (R)	749,679	(37%)

SENATORS

Sen. Edward M. Kennedy (D)

Elected 1962, seat up 1988; b. Feb. 22, 1932, Boston; home, Boston; Harvard U., B.A. 1956, Acad. of Intl. Law, The Hague, The Netherlands, 1958, U. of VA, LL.B. 1959; Roman Catholic; divorced.

Career: Army, 1951–53; Asst. Dist. Atty., Suffolk Cnty., 1961–62.

Offices: 315 RSOB 20510, 202-224-4543. Also JFK Fed. Bldg., Rm. 2400A, Boston 02203, 617-565-3170.

Committees: *Armed Services* (5th of 11 D). Subcommittees: Manpower and Personnel; Strategic Forces and Nuclear Defense; Projection Forces and Regional Defense (Chairman). *Judiciary* (2d of 8 D). Subcommittees: Antitrust, Monopolies and Business Rights; Constitution; Immigration and Refugee Affairs (Chairman); Patents, Copyrights and Trademarks. *Labor and Human Resources* (Chairman of 9 D). *Joint Economic Committee.* Subcommittees: Investment, Jobs and Prices; International Economic Policy; Fiscal and Monetary Policy (Chairman).

Group Ratings

	ADA	ACLU	COPE	CFA	LCV	ACU	NTU	NSI	COC	CEI
1986	80	100	93	80	78	10	45	0	47	31
1985	85	—	93	93	—	9	29	—	39	—

National Journal Ratings

	1986 LIB — 1986 CONS		1985 LIB — 1985 CONS	
Economic	70% —	29%	70% —	26%
Social	84% —	15%	88% —	0%
Foreign	75% —	0%	88% —	0%

Key Votes

1) Ease Gun Cont	AGN	5) Grm-Rdmn Def Red	FOR	9) Rehnquist Nom	AGN
2) Immig Reform	AGN	6) Contra Aid	AGN	10) Tax Reform	FOR
3) Lmt Text Imp	FOR	7) SDI Funding	AGN	11) Drug Death Pen	—
4) Aid Tobac Ind	FOR	8) Lmt PAC Contrib	FOR	12) S Africa Sanc	FOR

Election Results

1982 general	Edward M. Kennedy (D)	1,247,084	(61%)	($2,470,473)
	Raymond Shamie (R).................	784,602	(38%)	($2,305,996)
1982 primary	Edward M. Kennedy (D)	869,985	(100%)	
1976 general	Edward M. Kennedy (D)	1,726,657	(69%)	($896,196)
	Michael S. Robertson (R).............	722,641	(29%)	($168,854)

Campaign Contributions and Expenditures

1981-82		Direct Cont. 1981-82		PACS Breakdown			
Receipts	$2,609,514	Indiv.	$2,149,499	Agr	$2,200	Ideo	$27,612
Expend.	$2,470,473	Party	$19,000	Bus	$35,675	Lbr	$225,150
Unspent	$139,041	PACS	$305,082	Hlth	$6,500	Prof	$2,250

Sen. John F. Kerry (D)

Elected 1984, seat up 1990; b. Dec. 11, 1943, Denver, CO; home, Boston; Yale U., A.B. 1966, Boston Col. of Law, LL.B. 1976; Roman Catholic; separated.

Career: Navy, Vietnam; Organizer, Vietnam Veterans Against the War; Asst. Dist. Atty., Middlesex Cnty., 1976–81; Practicing atty., 1981–82; Lt. Gov. of MA, 1982–84.

Offices: 166 RSOB 20510, 202-224-2742. Also Transportation Bldg., 10 Park Plaza, Rm. 3220, Boston 02216, 617-565-8519.

Committees: *Commerce, Science and Transportation* (9th of 11 D). Subcommittees: Aviation; Communications; Science, Technology and Space. *Foreign Relations* (6th of 11 D). Subcommittees: East Asian and Pacific Affairs; International Economic Policy, Trade, Oceans and Environment (Chairman); Western Hemisphere and Peace Corps Affairs. *Small Business* (9th of 10 D). Subcommittee: Innovation, Technology and Productivity; Urban and Minority-Owned Business Development (Chairman).

Group Ratings

	ADA	ACLU	COPE	CFA	LCV	ACU	NTU	NSI	COC	CEI
1986	85	100	94	80	92	9	37	0	32	30
1985	90	—	95	93	—	5	29	—	38	—

National Journal Ratings

	1986 LIB — 1986 CONS			1985 LIB — 1985 CONS		
Economic	94%	—	0%	86%	—	11%
Social	92%	—	0%	88%	—	0%
Foreign	75%	—	0%	88%	—	0%

Key Votes

1) Ease Gun Cont	AGN	5) Grm-Rdmn Def Red	FOR	9) Rehnquist Nom	AGN
2) Immig Reform	AGN	6) Contra Aid	AGN	10) Tax Reform	FOR
3) Lmt Text Imp	FOR	7) SDI Funding	AGN	11) Drug Death Pen	—
4) Aid Tobac Ind	AGN	8) Lmt PAC Contrib	FOR	12) S Africa Sanc	FOR

Election Results

1984 general	John F. Kerry (D)	1,393,150	(55%)	($2,070,004)
	Raymond Shamie (R)	1,139,913	(45%)	($4,180,961)
1984 primary	John F. Kerry (D)	322,470	(41%)	
	James M. Shannon (D).............	297,941	(38%)	
	David M. Bartley (D)	85,910	(11%)	
	Michael Joseph Connolly (D)...........	82,999	(11%)	
1978 general	Paul E. Tsongas (D)	1,093,283	(55%)	($768,383)
	Edward W. Brooke (R)	890,584	(45%)	($1,284,855)

Campaign Contributions and Expenditures

1984		Direct Cont. 1984		PACS Breakdown 1984			
Receipts	$2,169,775	Indiv.	$1,826,936	Corp.	$,500	T/M/H	$766
Expend.	$2,070,004	Party	$17,500	Labor	$3,600	Agr.	$0
Debts	$367,994	Cand.	$309,000	Ideo.	$404	CWOS	$0

FIRST DISTRICT

Far west of Massachusetts Bay, sealing off the Commonwealth from almost everywhere else, are the Berkshires—the rubbed-down remains of what once was a string of peaks like the Rockies. But they were rugged enough to keep the aggressive colonial Puritans out of the Iroquois empire in what is now Upstate New York and to thwart early Boston canal- and railroad-builders, thus giving the advantage in westbound trade to New York City. This part of Massachusetts has the look of a wilderness about it, but if you walk in the twice-grown woods here, you will come on stone walls, running up and down the hills. These walls, celebrated by Robert Frost, were built by Yankee farmers 150 and even 200 years ago. But the glacier-rubbed land that produced so many stones, picked, hauled, and piled up to mark one field or one farmer from another never yielded much to the plow, and the farms were abandoned, their owners moving west or to the new factory towns in the valleys. This was the second, industrial, transformation of western Massachusetts. Waterpower was the chief energy source of the day, and the fast-flowing streams of the Berkshires were harnessed to waterwheels and millraces. Railroads wended their way through the hills to the factory towns of Pittsfield and North Adams, and this became a prosperous high-wage area. It also became a resort: the Berkshires, near the big eastern cities but definitely rural, have always been a favorite of artists, from Edith Wharton to Arlo Guthrie, and each summer members of the Boston Symphony Orchestra relax, perform and teach at the Tanglewood Music Festival.

The Berkshires form the spine of the 1st Congressional District of Massachusetts. To the west are the valleys with the factory towns of Pittsfield, North Adams, and Great Barrington, now with increasingly upscale economies and, in the case of smaller towns like Stockbridge, a culture built around the now aging veterans of the 1960s counterculture. To the east is the Pioneer Valley (the Massachusetts name for the Connecticut River valley). The portion of it in the 1st District, north of Springfield, is now one of the nation's prime college and private school areas, and the area around Amherst, home of Amherst College and the University of Massachusetts, with Smith and Mt. Holyoke has become the western Massachusetts stronghold of liberal and leftish politics. Just to the south is the old industrial town of Holyoke and the middle-class suburbs of Westfield and West Springfield, across the Connecticut River from Springfield.

For generations the Berkshires were a heartland of Yankee Republicanism. But as the Protestants in the hills came to be outnumbered by the Catholics in the mill towns, not to mention the students on campus, this 1st District has become mostly Democratic. It went for George McGovern in 1972 and nearly for Walter Mondale in 1984. But in congressional races this is still a Republican—a very Republican—district. That is because of the popularity of Representative Silvio Conte, one of the most senior of House Republicans.

Conte is an old-fashioned politician who can play any fashion of politics you like, and play it well. His recipe for political success was once common in the East: the Republican label to attract old-line Yankee votes, liberal votes on issues to attract the Democrats, and he adds to this deep roots in the Italian community in Pittsfield. But he adds to each of the ingredients a special flair. Conte can be among the most partisan of Republicans when the issue, for example, is committee ratios: his friendship with Tip O'Neill didn't prevent him from taking on the Democrats for packing committees in 1985, and winning: the Democrats agreed earlier on fairer ratios for 1987. And for years he was one of the leaders on the Republicans' great softball team. He stood up for the Reagan budget cuts of 1981.

But he can bellow with rage at White House budget cutting for programs for the poor. On the Labor-HHS-Education Subcommittee and elsewhere he is loath to cut programs that help feed the poor and elderly, put students through college and underwrite scientific research, especially in the bio-medical area. A leader on acid rain and hazardous waste legislation, Conte is also one of the environmentalist community's most reliable Republican allies. Although he has fine political instincts, he flares up at programs that he thinks waste the taxpayers' money on the well-positioned: he is an opponent of subsidies to big farmers, for example, of politically targeted water projects, of the Synfuels Corporation. Self-righteous, but in the hearty, competitive way of most politicians, he can roar in indignation with the best of them. But he is not offended when others, of different views, do the same. He is shrewd enough to advance his views and his district's interests with considerable success, but he is not at all devious or underhanded. He is on excellent terms with Minority Leader Robert Michel as he was with Tip O'Neill.

In fact Michel, who served with him on the Appropriations Committee for years, supported him in 1979 when some conservatives wanted to deny him the position to which the seniority principle entitled him of ranking Republican on the committee. Seniority was not the only reason; Michel seems to feel that Conte does real service to his party, and probably most House Republicans agree.

Conte won the seat in the Democratic year of 1958, when he faced Williams College political scientist James MacGregor Burns. The professor got the national publicity but Conte, who had represented Berkshire County in the state Senate for eight years, got the local votes. So Burns went on to finish his Roosevelt biography and Conte remained a legislator. And just as Burns, in his recent book, *The Vineyard of Democracy,* shows himself at the top of his profession, so Conte is at the top of his. He is reelected easily. His 1986 Democratic opponent, Robert Weiner, a former Claude Pepper aide, peppered Conte with criticism. But his campaign was undercut at the end when he forwarded some charges against Conte to the FBI and the Democratic state chairman, 5th District Representative Chester Atkins, wrote him a letter calling on him to stop. Conte won with 78% of the vote. It is possible that Conte, who had reportedly successful cancer surgery in February 1987, may decide to retire, in which case a plethora of local pols would be interested in running; but otherwise he has a safe seat.

The People: Pop. 1980: 522,540, up 4.1% 1970–80. Households (1980): 71% family, 36% with children, 58% married couples; 37.5% housing units rented; median monthly rent: $176; median house value: $38,600. Voting age pop. (1980): 391,008; 1% Spanish origin, 1% Black.

Rep. Silvio O. Conte (R)

Elected 1958; b. Nov. 9, 1921, Pittsfield; home, Pittsfield; Boston Col., Boston Col. Law Sch., LL.B. 1949; Roman Catholic; married (Corinne).

Career: Seabees, SW Pacific, WWII; Practicing atty., 1949–58; MA Senate, 1951–59.

Offices: 2300 RHOB 20515, 202-225-5335. Also 78 Center Arterial, Pittsfield 01201, 413-442-0946; and 187 High St., #202, Holyoke 01040, 413-532-7010.

Committees: *Appropriations* (Ranking Member of 22 R). Subcommittees: Labor–Health and Human Services–Education (Ranking Member); Legislative; Transportation. *Small Business* (2d of 17 R). Subcommittee: Procurement, Innovation and Minority Enterprise Development (Ranking Member).

Group Ratings

	ADA	ACLU	COPE	CFA	LCV	ACU	NTU	NSI	COC	CEI
1986	75	65	64	83	84	14	26	0	22	28
1985	75	—	63	100	—	14	41	—	32	—

National Journal Ratings

	1986 LIB — 1986 CONS		1985 LIB — 1985 CONS	
Economic	81% —	18%	65% —	33%
Social	69% —	28%	47% —	52%
Foreign	80% —	0%	69% —	30%

Key Votes

1) Lmt Cln Water Act	FOR	5) Retain Gun Cont	FOR	9) Aid Angola Reb	AGN
2) Rpl Tobac Sub	FOR	6) Contra Aid	AGN	10) Tax Reform	FOR
3) Grm-Rdmn Def Red	AGN	7) Lmt Text Imp	FOR	11) S Africa Sanc	FOR
4) Ban Polygraph	FOR	8) Limit SDI	FOR	12) Immig Reform	FOR

Election Results

1986 general	Silvio O. Conte (R).....................113,653	(78%)	($204,921)
	Robert S. Weiner (D)..................32,396	(22%)	($123,426)
1986 primary	Silvio O. Conte (R).....................4,972	(100%)	
1984 general	Silvio O. Conte (R)..................162,646	(73%)	($91,890)
	Mary L. Wentworth (D)...............60,372	(27%)	($10,409)

Campaign Contributions and Expenditures

1985-86		Direct Cont. 1985-86		PACS Breakdown 1985-86			
Receipts	$255,921	Indiv.	$77,738	Corp.	$42,500	T/M/H	$41,852
Expend.	$204,921	Party	$2,000	Labor	$31,347	Agr.	$0
Unspent	$268,326	PACS	$130,249	Ideo.	$13,250	CWOS	$1,300

SECOND DISTRICT

Springfield, Massachusetts, a metropolis that has given the nation its unabridged dictionaries (2d and 3d editions) and the game of basketball (invented at a YMCA here in 1891), has also produced more than its share of canny politicians. Stuck out in the far western part of the state, with far fewer people than Boston, Springfield does not have the heft in its state politics as similar-sized Hartford, down the river in Connecticut, has in its. Springfield must make up in nimbleness and cunning what it does not get by numbers and clout. Thus Springfield and its surrounding towns have produced over the years such political pros as Lawrence O'Brien, the Kennedy campaign manager and Democratic national chairman; Joseph Napolitan, long one of the leading national and international political consultants; and James B. King, the first chief of personnel in the Carter White House and known by insiders for years as the best advance man in the business.

Springfield and the surrounding towns on the east bank of the Connecticut River form the heart of Massachusetts's 2d Congressional District, which has been represented in the House for more than three decades by a politician every bit as skillful as any Springfield has ever produced. From Springfield, Chicopee, Ludlow, and Longmeadow the district proceeds north and east. Springfield and Chicopee, which together have about half the district's population, are its Democratic bastions; the rest of the district, although often Democratic, went for Ronald Reagan in 1980 and 1984. The image of the small New England town is of a clapboard village peopled by taciturn Yankees. But in fact many of the old Protestants have died off, moved west, or married into immigrant families, and in the towns they once lived in most people consider themselves to be of Irish, Italian, or Polish background. The storefronts may have New England Yankee facades, but hanging above are signs with names of Italian or Polish proprietors. You will see them not only in the industrial towns of Fitchburg, Leominster, and Gardner, at the northeast corner of the district, but also in the smaller towns that dot the stony hillsides of central Massachusetts between Fitchburg and Springfield.

Edward Boland is the 2d District's congressman, a quiet political pro who looks far younger than his years and remains effective in a youth-oriented House. For many years Boland, long a bachelor, roomed with Tip O'Neill, whose wife remained in Cambridge; the two pols were close, although Boland married in 1973 (and has four children) and O'Neill's wife came to Washington when he became speaker in 1977. Like O'Neill, Boland was for many years a politician who could bridge the gap between the senior big-city politicians—a group to which he temperamentally belonged—and the younger, more ideological liberals in the Democratic Caucus. Now the bridge spans a different gap, between young post-Watergate Democrats skeptical about big government programs and old-time Democrats who still itch to support them. But Boland, careful of his facts and utterly reliable when he makes commitments, continues to link together various kinds of Democrats and almost invariably carries his bills when he brings them to the floor.

Boland is the second-ranking Democrat on the Appropriations Committee, and chairman of its HUD–Independent Agencies Subcommittee—not the most important appropriations unit, perhaps, but one which does its work in orderly fashion and, unlike many of its counterparts, gets a new bill through just about every session. Boland had an even more sensitive assignment in the first Reagan term: he was chairman of the Permanent Select Committee on Intelligence in the House. Boland has supported some defense budget cuts and questioned some intelligence practices, but he did not begin by sharing the suspicion of national security bureaucracies which is endemic among many younger Vietnam-era Democrats. But after four years of dealing with William Casey's CIA, he ended up authoring the various Boland Amendments which have prohibited or limited to humanitarian purposes U.S. government aid to the Nicaraguan contras. The 1985 amendment, ultimately repealed in 1986, may have been violated by Oliver North and perhaps others at the White House in their eagerness to funnel aid to the contras, though it's not clear that exceeding the limits in an appropriations bill is or should be a violation of criminal law.

In accordance with House rules, Boland gave up the Intelligence chairmanship in 1985; he was naturally appointed to the committee to investigate the Iran-contra affair. He could probably be chairman of Appropriations if he wanted to; in 1979 there was a move to make him that, and in the Democratic Caucus he got 88 votes to 157 for Jamie Whitten of Mississippi—a smaller margin than it looks, because only 35 switches would have changed the result. But Boland did not challenge Whitten: he instinctively backs the seniority system, and he recognizes in Whitten another able politician who, since committee chairmen started being elected and not selected automatically, has supported most national Democratic policies and obstructed none. Whitten and Boland are both temperamentally team players, and though their records look different to ratings groups they seldom work at cross purposes.

Since they're both the same age—a year older than Ronald Reagan—it's quite possible that Boland will never be chairman. But he is under no constituency pressure to do so, however; his percentages in the 1980s have been lower than any since the 1950s, when this was still counted as a marginal seat, but he won with a solid 66% in 1986.

The People: Pop. 1980: 521,949, dn. 2.2% 1970–80. Households (1980): 74% family, 39% with children, 60% married couples; 38.5% housing units rented; median monthly rent: $158; median house value: $37,100. Voting age pop. (1980): 377,798; 4% Black, 3% Spanish origin.

1984 Presidential Vote:

Reagan (R) 113,384	(53%)
Mondale (D) 98,340	(46%)

Rep. Edward P. Boland (D)

Elected 1952; b. Oct. 1, 1911, Springfield; home, Springfield; Boston Col. Law Sch.; Roman Catholic; married (Mary).

Career: MA House of Reps., 1935–41; Hampton Cnty. Registrar of Deeds, 1941–42, 1946–49; Army, WWII; Military Aide to Gov. Paul A. Dever, 1949–52.

Offices: 2426 RHOB 20515, 202-225-5601. Also Fed. Office Bldg., Rm. 309, 1550 Main St., Springfield 01103, 413-785-0325; and 881 Main St., Philbin Bldg., Fitchburg 01420, 617-342-8722.

Committees: *Appropriations* (2d of 35 D). Subcommittees: HUD–Independent Agencies (Chairman); Interior; Treasury–Postal Service–General Government.

Group Ratings

	ADA	ACLU	COPE	CFA	LCV	ACU	NTU	NSI	COC	CEI
1986	70	57	90	58	69	5	24	0	17	22
1985	75	—	89	83	—	10	31	—	27	—

National Journal Ratings

	1986 LIB	—	1986 CONS	1985 LIB	—	1985 CONS
Economic	87%	—	0%	85%	—	11%
Social	72%	—	27%	44%	—	54%
Foreign	73%	—	26%	70%	—	29%

Key Votes

1) Lmt Cln Water Act	AGN	5) Retain Gun Cont	FOR	9) Aid Angola Reb	—
2) Rpl Tobac Sub	FOR	6) Contra Aid	AGN	10) Tax Reform	FOR
3) Grm-Rdmn Def Red	AGN	7) Lmt Text Imp	FOR	11) S Africa Sanc	FOR
4) Ban Polygraph	FOR	8) Limit SDI	FOR	12) Immig Reform	FOR

Election Results

1986 general	Edward P. Boland (D).................	91,033	(66%)	($281,963)
	Brian P. Lees (R)......................	47,022	(34%)	($100,628)
1986 primary	Edward P. Boland (D).................	40,899	(100%)	
1984 general	Edward P. Boland (D).................	132,693	(69%)	($51,502)
	Thomas P. Swank (R).................	60,463	(31%)	

Campaign Contributions and Expenditures

1985-86		Direct Cont. 1985-86		PACS Breakdown 1985-86			
Receipts	$206,524	Indiv.	$93,735	Corp.	$28,700	T/M/H	$26,420
Expend.	$281,963	PACS	$86,170	Labor	$27,300	Agr.	$250
Unspent	$24,157	Cand.	$10,000	Ideo.	$500	CWOS	$3,000

THIRD DISTRICT

Worcester, pronounced locally as if it had no Rs, is the second largest city in Massachusetts and is roughly in the geographical center of the state. But it is far smaller than Boston and bulks much smaller in Bay Staters' consciousness. It is basically a small manufacturing city which has maintained reasonable prosperity over the years; it has always had a high-skill, high-wage labor market, and was not one of those New England cities that was devastated by the flight of the textile mills decades ago. Now metropolitan Boston has been growing out toward Worcester, and the computer and electronics industries are beginning to concentrate now along Interstate 495, some 20 miles east of Worcester, as they did around the circumferential highway closer to Boston, Route 128, 20 years ago. The biggest such company is Digital, the giant of the mini-computer industry—a company recently troubled but now so successful it has begun to challenge IBM in the mainframe business. The movement of high tech industry into the district has brought with it prosperity, new residents, and higher housing prices to the towns and suburbs along I–495 and toward Worcester itself.

The Worcester area, and the 3d Congressional District with which it is roughly coincident, have been Democratic strongholds politically as long as anyone can remember. The older, nitty gritty New England is where political attitudes are bred into people and remain almost as rock-solid as the stony terrain in these parts. The 3d District spreads north from Worcester to the mill town of Lunenburg, south to the Rhode Island border, east to Interstate 95, and west just beyond Worcester.

The congressman from this district is Joseph Early, a Democrat first elected in 1974. Unlike many other members of that freshman Democratic class, Early did not get his political start canvassing against the Vietnam war or trying to save sea birds from an oil spill. His district is a town, not a gown, district, and he is very much a product of town politics: a teacher and coach who won a seat in the Great and General Court (that is, the legislature) in 1962, at age 29, and was strong enough after 12 years to win the House seat in a seriously contested primary and against a serious Republican in a general election complicated by an independent candidate. Early's voting record looks a lot like those of his Massachusetts colleagues on most issues, but on cultural issues he tends to vote like the Catholic father of eight he is. He is, rather, an insider, a member of the Appropriations Committee who seldom gets publicity but has a chance to make policy. That seems to suit his constituents fine: since 1974, he has had no difficulty winning reelection, and seems unlikely to have any in the near future.

The People: Pop. 1980: 521,354, up 2.2% 1970–80. Households (1980): 75% family, 40% with children, 62% married couples; 38.5% housing units rented; median monthly rent: $175; median house value: $46,800. Voting age pop. (1980): 376,641; 2% Spanish origin, 1% Black.

1984 Presidential Vote:

Reagan (R)	131,134	(57%)
Mondale (D)	100,152	(43%)

Rep. Joseph D. Early (D)

Elected 1974; b. Jan. 31, 1933, Worcester; home, Worcester; Col. of the Holy Cross, B.S. 1955; Roman Catholic; married (Marilyn).

Career: Navy, 1955–57; High sch. teacher and coach, 1957–63; MA House of Reps., 1963–74.

Offices: 2349 RHOB, 202-225-6101. Also 34 Mechanic St., Rm. 203, Worcester 01608, 617-752-6718.

Committees: *Appropriations* (14th of 35 D). Subcommittees: Commerce, Justice, State, and Judiciary; Labor–Health and Human Services–Education; Military Construction.

Group Ratings

	ADA	ACLU	COPE	CFA	LCV	ACU	NTU	NSI	COC	CEI
1986	85	68	85	50	77	14	29	0	20	25
1985	80	—	84	83	—	10	34	—	21	—

National Journal Ratings

	1986 LIB — 1986 CONS			1985 LIB — 1985 CONS		
Economic	71%	—	28%	83%	—	15%
Social	79%	—	19%	52%	—	48%
Foreign	67%	—	30%	85%	—	8%

Key Votes

1) Lmt Cln Water Act	AGN	5) Retain Gun Cont	FOR	9) Aid Angola Reb	AGN
2) Rpl Tobac Sub	FOR	6) Contra Aid	AGN	10) Tax Reform	FOR
3) Grm-Rdmn Def Red	AGN	7) Lmt Text Imp	FOR	11) S Africa Sanc	FOR
4) Ban Polygraph	FOR	8) Limit SDI	FOR	12) Immig Reform	FOR

Election Results

1986 general	Joseph D. Early (D)	120,222	(100%)	($186,651)
1986 primary	Joseph D. Early (D)	47,429	(100%)	
1984 general	Joseph D. Early (D)	148,461	(67%)	($168,851)
	Kenneth J. Redding (R)	71,765	(33%)	($44,447)

Campaign Contributions and Expenditures

1985-86		Direct Cont. 1985-86		PACS Breakdown 1985-86			
Receipts	$243,369	Indiv.	$153,500	Corp.	$24,400	T/M/H	$19,950
Expend.	$186,651	Party	$189	Labor	$25,750	Agr.	$250
Unspent	$95,439	PACS	$83,200	Ideo.	$5,100	CWOS	$7,750

FOURTH DISTRICT

The 4th Congressional District of Massachusetts is a slice of the commonwealth beginning at the Boston city limit, across the street from Boston University and a block or two from Kenmore Square, and proceeding west and south through leafy suburbs to newly settled subdivisions and finally ending in the old textile mill town of Fall River and the shores of Rhode Island Sound just beyond. These could hardly be more diverse. About one-third of the 4th's residents live in the old, close-in Boston suburbs of Brookline and Newton, places with comfortable old houses, intersections with shops built in the 1920s but stocked and decorated in the most chic 1980s styles. They are mostly (but not entirely) high income, with large numbers of Jews and students. Politically, they are self-consciously liberal, particularly on cultural issues; heavily Democratic in most elections.

Just beyond the old Route 128 (the number has now been suppressed and it's just part of Interstate 95) are the rich Waspy suburbs of Wellesley and Dover, where some of Boston's most affluent and oldest families live. If you want to find the pure preppy style—from Weejuns to a bird watcher's life list—these are the places to visit. The suburbs are Republican strongholds, but Massachusetts Waspy Republican, with roots in the old Yankee interventionist tradition; voters look to the League of Women Voters and Common Cause for advice and look askance at anything that reminds them of bigotry. This was the political base of Margaret Heckler, congresswoman from one of the two districts that was folded into the current 4th, from 1966 to 1982; she was later Secretary of Health and Human Services and then Ambassador to Ireland.

Then there is the newer middle class belt of towns, from almost working class Natick in the north to newly built and upper middle-income Medfield, Sharon with its large Jewish population; Foxboro, the home of the New England Patriots; to Attleboro and Norton, pleasant old New England towns of mixed ethnic background, all with relatively large family populations: within range of Boston TV but outside its trendy cultural orbit. This is marginal country politically. Finally there is Fall River, once a textile center, that like so much of Massachusetts has adapted to the late 20th century. Once full of Yankee farm girls (and the home of Lizzie Borden) and Irish immigrants, it now has a population with many Portuguese. Fall River is ancestrally very Democratic, but is culturally conservative.

The congressman from this district is Barney Frank, one of the most talented liberal Democrats in the House, a man with a mind so fast that he sometimes can change the outcome of a vote in a single extemporized one-minute speech. Frank did not have an easy time getting to the House or staying there. He moved from graduate school to work for Boston Mayor Kevin White, one of the canniest politicians of our time, and then as a congressional aide, he was elected to the Massachusetts legislature in 1972. In 1980 he won the old 4th District, which veered westward from Brookline and Newton, after Father Robert Drinan was forced by the Vatican to retire, but only with 52% in both primary and general. In 1982, he ran against Heckler in territory most of which was hers, but he raised $1 million and capitalized on her mistakes to win with 60%. Now it's a safe seat.

Frank's record is one of the most liberal in Congress, but it is seldom reflexive. He opposed the Democrats' drug bill in 1986 because he thought it "the legislative equivalent of crack," but he actively backed the immigration reform measure that most liberals shunned. He wants to get rid of the silly anti-subversive law that lets the State Department bar visitors whose politics it doesn't like, but he strenuously opposes the dairy subsidies which help to hold House Democrats together. He pushed a bill through the House allowing servicemen to sue the military for negligence, fought unsuccessfully to avoid cuts in public housing,and got the House to vote momentarily to build only 40 rather than 50 MX missiles, wants to spend more on the elderly. He may very well have the deadliest—and politically most effective—wit in Congress: commenting on the New Right's opposition to abortion and to child-feeding programs, he said "Sure, they're pro-life. They believe that life begins at conception and ends at birth." A lot of self-styled pro-lifers were stung by that comment, and started to back nutrition and child-care programs which they had reflexively opposed in the past.

Frank has accumulated a fair amount of seniority now, but his real power in the House comes not from specialization and seniority, but from his knowledge of a wide range of issues and skill at argumentation. After his 1982 victory, Frank lost 70 pounds, shed glasses for contact lenses, began to exercise regularly, bought nice-looking suits. He says he has a job he has a good chance of keeping till he is 75, and he looks in shape—politically, legislatively, and otherwise—to do it.

The People: Pop. 1980: 521,995, up 1.8% 1970–80. Households (1980): 74% family, 38% with children, 61% married couples; 39.2% housing units rented; median monthly rent: $202; median house value: $58,900. Voting age pop. (1980): 386,245; 1% Spanish origin, 1% Asian origin, 1% Black.

1984 Presidential Vote:

Mondale (D) 123,489	(51%)
Reagan (R) 115,692	(48%)

Rep. Barney Frank (D)

Elected 1980; b. Mar. 31, 1940, Bayonne, NJ; home, Newton; Harvard Col., B.A. 1962; Harvard U., 1962–67, J.D. 1977; Jewish; single.

Career: Chf. of Staff to Boston Mayor Kevin White, 1968–71; A. A. to U.S. Rep. Michael Harrington, 1971–72; MA House of Reps., 1973–80; Lecturer on Pub. Policy, Harvard JFK Sch. of Gov., 1979–80.

Offices: 1030 LHOB 20515, 202-225-5931. Also 437 Cherry St., West Newton 02165, 617-332-3920; 10 Purchase St., Fall River 02722, 617-674-3551; and 8 N. Main St., Attleboro 02703, 617-226-4723.

Committees: *Banking, Finance and Urban Affairs* (13th of 31 D). Subcommittees: Financial Institutions Supervision, Regulation and Insurance; Housing and Community Development. *Government Operations* (10th of 24 D). Subcommittees: Legislation and National Security; Human Resources and Intergovernmental Relations. *Judiciary* (11th of 21 D). Subcommittees: Administrative Law and Governmental Relations; Immigration, Refugees and International Law. *Select Committee on Aging* (18th of 39 D). Subcommittees: Health and Long-Term Care.

Group Ratings

	ADA	ACLU	COPE	CFA	LCV	ACU	NTU	NSI	COC	CEI
1986	100	95	91	67	100	0	32	0	17	28
1985	100	—	91	100	—	10	42	—	23	—

National Journal Ratings

	1986 LIB — 1986 CONS		1985 LIB — 1985 CONS	
Economic	69% —	30%	85% —	11%
Social	86% —	11%	85% —	0%
Foreign	80% —	0%	80% —	17%

Key Votes

1) Lmt Cln Water Act	AGN	5) Retain Gun Cont	FOR	9) Aid Angola Reb	AGN
2) Rpl Tobac Sub	FOR	6) Contra Aid	AGN	10) Tax Reform	FOR
3) Grm-Rdmn Def Red	AGN	7) Lmt Text Imp	FOR	11) S Africa Sanc	FOR
4) Ban Polygraph	FOR	8) Limit SDI	FOR	12) Immig Reform	FOR

Election Results

1986 general	Barney Frank (D)	134,387	(89%)	($213,909)
	Thomas D. DeVisscher (R).	16,857	(11%)	($1,017)
1986 primary	Barney Frank (D)	46,336	(90%)	
	William F. Rosa (D)	5,382	(10%)	
1984 general	Barney Frank (D)	172,903	(74%)	($370,174)
	Jim Forte (R)	60,121	(26%)	($16,736)

Campaign Contributions and Expenditures

1985-86		Direct Cont. 1985-86		PACS Breakdown 1985-86			
Receipts	$208,533	Indiv.	$123,793	Corp.	$26,025	T/M/H	$29,349
Expend.	$213,909	Party	$195	Labor	$18,750	Agr.	$0
Unspent	$37,478	PACS	$80,924	Ideo.	$3,475	CWOS	$3,325

FIFTH DISTRICT

The 5th Congressional District, northwest of Boston, is probably the commonwealth's number one high-tech district. This is not the first time this part of the state has been the engine for more than one of Massachusetts's spurts of economic growth. In the early 19th century, when Massachusetts was a kind of maritime republic, with a few farmers struggling to scratch a living from the stony soil, a few ingenious Yankees decided to tame the rapidly flowing Merrimack River and build cotton spinning mills. They created the cities of Lowell and Lawrence, built model housing for the local farm girls and, later, the Irish and French Canadian immigrants they used as their work force. When the maritime trading business faded, Massachusetts continued to grow because of the textile industry; it lasted here for nearly 100 years. Then, in the 1920s, the price of labor rose in New England and newly built mills in the Carolinas, nearer the cotton supply, essentially ended the businesses Lawrence and Lowell built. Yet many in the work force, by then rather elderly, waited forlornly for some upturn in the local economy.

It came from an unexpected source. Starting in the 1960s in Cambridge, around MIT, moving out to the old Route 128 circumferential highway, and more recently locating also along Interstate 495, which passes through Lowell and Lawrence, high tech has powered growth for Massachusetts. The computer, software, and defense industries here have had their ups and downs; but in the early 1980s, when the rest of the country was in recession, Massachusetts had one of the nation's lowest unemployment rates and continued to enjoy strong economic growth.

The 5th Congressional District's main urban centers are Lowell and Lawrence, which with surrounding suburbs account for about half its population. Since the 1950s they have been transformed by high tech: Wang Laboratories, for example, is headquartered in Lowell, which also, thanks to former Senator and Representative Paul Tsongas, has a national historical restoration project in its old mill area. Like Tsongas, who shocked liberals by questioning many of their dogmas in his book *The Road From Here*, they have lost their faith in government spending programs, and see free markets and new technology as the means to economic growth and a better life. Lowell, long a Democratic bastion, went for Ronald Reagan over Walter Mondale in 1984, and the suburbs next door were more than 60% for Reagan.

A similar trend in the same direction is apparent in the white-collar towns in the southern part of the district, in modest-income Framingham, and in old New England towns like Concord, Lincoln, Littleton, and Harvard, which have become high income Waspy suburbs. Their old New England houses and stone walls recall earlier times, but residents make their livings in the latest high tech industries, and pride themselves on their contemporary attitudes. Culturally liberal, they are economically Republican, in the old Yankee interventionist tradition. Lincoln, for example, voted for McGovern in 1972 and Ford in 1976; it gave John Anderson 28% of its votes in 1980 and went, very narrowly, for Mondale in 1984 while all the surrounding towns went for Reagan.

Congressional races in the 5th District have been a kind of lagging political indicator for years now. This ancestrally Republican area, which voted for many Democrats in the 1950s and 1960s, nonetheless elected Republican congressmen up through and including 1972 (when John Kerry, now a U.S. Senator, lost here); now the district has trended Republican in national and statewide contests (it preferred high tech entrepreneur Ray Shamie over Kerry in 1984), but has remained Democratic in congressional races. This, despite a considerable turnover. Paul Tsongas, who beat the last Republican congressman in 1974, went on to be elected to the Senate in 1978; James Shannon, the talented young legislator from Lawrence who succeeded him in the House, lost the Senate primary to Kerry in 1984 but was elected attorney general in 1986.

The current congressman from the 5th, Chester Atkins, is a talented politician who spans the gap between Yankee and immigrant, Democratic millhand and Republican high tech entrepreneur. He comes from a rich family in Concord, but speaks with a broad Massachusetts accent out of a George V. Higgins novel; he got elected to the state Senate from a Republican district and became a trusted Ways and Means chairman for Senate President Billy Bulger of South Boston. He has been chairman since 1977 of what may be the nation's most fractious Democratic party. Atkins had a tough primary against a Lowell legislator in 1984, and had to beat Greg Hyatt, an organizer of 1980's Proposition 2½ tax cut, in the general.

In the House during the last term of Speaker Tip O'Neill, Atkins became the only freshman Democrat on the Budget Committee, where his positions on proposed cuts in domestic programs may prove somewhat more conservative than the leadership's; he questions, for example, the need for continuing federal revenue sharing at its present levels. He also got a temporary seat on Education and Labor and on its Higher Education Subcommittee, a panel of particular importance to the Boston area. He served his first term on Public Works, reportedly to maintain pressure for Tip O'Neill's pet project, another tunnel in Boston Harbor; in 1986 he moved onto Foreign Affairs, a good outlet for his district. At every step Atkins has shown unerring political instincts and the ability to become an influential congressman over the long term. He had no Republican opposition at all in 1986.

The People: Pop. 1980: 518,313, up 3.3% 1970–80. Households (1980): 75% family, 42% with children, 62% married couples; 40.0% housing units rented; median monthly rent: $207; median house value: $61,100. Voting age pop. (1980): 368,925; 3% Spanish origin, 1% Black, 1% Asian origin.

1984 Presidential Vote:

Reagan (R)	130,968	(57%)
Mondale (D)	98,649	(43%)

Rep. Chester G. Atkins (D)

Elected 1984; b. Apr. 14, 1948, Geneva, Switzerland; home, Concord; Antioch Col., B.A. 1970; Unitarian; married (Corinne).

Career: MA House of Reps., 1970–72; MA Senate, 1972–84; Chmn., MA State Dem. Cmtee.

Offices: 504 CHOB 20515, 202-225-3411. Also 134 Middle St., Ste. 301, Lowell 01852, 617-459-0101.

Committees: *Budget* (17th of 21 D). Task Forces: Budget Process; Community and Natural Resources; Human Resources; Defense and International Affairs. *Education and Labor* (20th of 21 D). Subcommittees: Elementary, Secondary and Vocational Education; Employment Opportunities; Postsecondary Education. *Foreign Affairs* (22d of 27 D). Subcommittee: Asian and Pacific Affairs. *Standards of Official Conduct* (6th of 6 D).

Group Ratings

	ADA	ACLU	COPE	CFA	LCV	ACU	NTU	NSI	COC	CEI
1986	90	89	86	83	79	0	35	0	25	29
1985	90	—	81	83	—	5	33	—	33	—

National Journal Ratings

	1986 LIB — 1986 CONS		1985 LIB — 1985 CONS	
Economic	74%	23%	73%	26%
Social	89%	0%	85%	0%
Foreign	80%	0%	85%	8%

Key Votes

1) Lmt Cln Water Act	AGN	5) Retain Gun Cont	FOR	9) Aid Angola Reb	AGN
2) Rpl Tobac Sub	FOR	6) Contra Aid	AGN	10) Tax Reform	FOR
3) Grm-Rdmn Def Red	FOR	7) Lmt Text Imp	FOR	11) S Africa Sanc	FOR
4) Ban Polygraph	FOR	8) Limit SDI	FOR	12) Immig Reform	FOR

Election Results

1986 general	Chester G. Atkins (D)................	113,690	(100%)	($563,019)
1986 primary	Chester G. Atkins (D).................	38,751	(100%)	
1984 general	Chester G. Atkins (D)...............	120,008	(53%)	($854,403)
	Gregory S. Hyatt (R)................	104,912	(47%)	($484,780)

Campaign Contributions and Expenditures

1985-86		Direct Cont. 1985-86		PACS Breakdown 1985-86			
Receipts	$564,489	Indiv.	$456,600	Corp.	$1,300	T/M/H	$563
Expend.	$563,019	PACS	$3,338	Labor	$2,000	Agr.	$0
Debts	$13,845	Cand.	$98,412	Ideo.	$0	CWOS	$0

SIXTH DISTRICT

The rocky coast running north of Boston in the 18th and early 19th century was the mercantile center of the United States, home of daring merchant plungers who sailed sloops and flew on clipper ships from the then small ports of Salem, Boston's rival as the Bay State metropolis, Marblehead, Gloucester, and Newburyport, to the West Indies and Africa and, most glamorously, to China. The ships were gone often for a year, sometimes forever; if and when they returned, their owners could make profits in the hundreds of percents. Their descendants, ironically, have been known for decades as investors who sought the safest harbors for their money, putting them in low interest railroad bonds and blue chip stocks. But some of them are risk takers still. The Boston area is full of management consultants and venture capitalists who have organized and financed many of the high tech companies that have contributed so much to the growth of Massachusetts; quietly, behind their estate walls on the North Shore or in their colonial era houses in Lincoln or Dover, they have profited as greatly from their foresight as did their ancestors.

But the North Shore is not just estate country. It includes the old fishing village of Gloucester, whose atmosphere is probably closer to the Salem of the clipper ships than are the manicured estates of today. Salem itself, Nathaniel Hawthorne's old town, is now a place filled mostly with people of immigrant stock, as is the newer suburb of Peabody next door. Nearby are the boating suburbs of Marblehead and Swampscott, and Lynn, whose troubled shoe industry pressed for years for protection against imports. The Merrimack River flows through the northern edge of the district, just below New Hampshire, past the old mill towns of Haverhill, John Greenleaf Whittier's town, and Newburyport.

The North Shore from Lynn onward, plus towns and cities several miles inland, form

Massachusetts's 6th Congressional District. This is a varied area demographically and politically. High-income Wasps tend to be Republicans, but self-consciously liberal ones; Lynn, Salem, and Peabody are basically Irish working-class Democratic, as are the Merrimack mill towns. On balance it is a Democratic district, but Republicans have a base here; they represented the district in Congress until 1969 and made serious attempts to win it in 1969, 1976, 1978, 1980, and 1982. This is, by the way, the site of the original gerrymander, named because its architect, Elbridge Gerry, a Jeffersonian, wanted to corral all the area's Federalist towns into one grotesquely shaped district. Ironically, the current 6th District's boundaries are about as regular and politically unobjectionable as those of any district in the country.

The district's current congressman, Nicholas Mavroules, has deep roots in local politics, and was mayor of Peabody for 11 years; he planned in 1978 to challenge liberal incumbent Michael Harrington in the Democratic primary and then got the nomination when Harrington retired. Ironically, Mavroules, who came to office as a critic of Harrington's preoccupation with the Vietnam war and the ouster of Salvador Allende in Chile, has been distinguished in the House primarily by his liberal positions on foreign and defense policy. Mavroules inherited Harrington's seat on the Armed Services Committee, probably intending to concentrate on keeping defense business in General Electric's jet engine plant in Lynn. But in 1981 he became the body's leading supporter of the nuclear freeze resolution. Then in 1983 he became the House's leading spokesman in the fight against the MX missile. He has been one of the leaders of that fight, with varying levels of success, sometimes pitted against Armed Services chairman Les Aspin. In early 1987 Mavroules became one of several challengers for Aspin's chair; but he got just 35 votes and was eliminated on the first ballot, as Aspin ultimately won. Some might take that as a humiliating defeat. But for a member whose credentials on major national issues were not taken seriously a few years ago it can also be seen as an impressive achievement.

Mavroules's prominence on the nuclear freeze and the MX have vastly strengthened him in the 6th District, although it doesn't hurt that he is prepared to argue in the same breath for GE jet engines and other local defense contractors. With his solid roots in Peabody, he now has enthusiastic support from the district's antiwar activists, most of whom come from a far different social background and speak with different accents. He overcame his last tough challenge, in 1982, with 58% of the vote; he had no Republican opposition at all in 1986 in a district that 20 years before was one of the premier Republican congressional seats in the country.

The People: Pop. 1980: 518,841, dn. 0.8% 1970–80. Households (1980): 72% family, 37% with children, 59% married couples; 38.5% housing units rented; median monthly rent: $216; median house value: $55,000. Voting age pop. (1980): 383,191; 1% Spanish origin, 1% Black.

1984 Presidential Vote:

Reagan (R)	137,258	(55%)
Mondale (D)	110,771	(44%)

Rep. Nicholas Mavroules (D)

Elected 1978; b. Nov. 1, 1929, Peabody; home, Peabody; Greek Orthodox; married (Mary).

Career: Sprvsr. of Personnel, Sylvania Electronics Corp., 1949–67; Peabody Ward Cncl., 1958–61, Councillor-at-Large, 1964–65; Mayor of Peabody, 1967–78.

Offices: 2432 RHOB, 202-225-8020. Also 70 Washington St., Salem 01970, 617-745-5800; 140 Union St., Lynn 01902, 617-599-7105; and 10 Welcome St., Haverhill, 01830, 617-372-3461.

Committees: *Armed Services* (11th of 31 D). Subcommittees: Investigations; Procurement and Military Nuclear Systems. *Small Business* (7th of 27 D). Subcommittee: Procurement, Innovation and Minority Enterprise Development (Chairman).

Group Ratings

	ADA	ACLU	COPE	CFA	LCV	ACU	NTU	NSI	COC	CEI
1986	85	55	92	67	71	5	27	0	24	18
1985	85	—	92	75	—	10	32	—	27	—

National Journal Ratings

	1986 LIB — 1986 CONS		1985 LIB — 1985 CONS	
Economic	65%	— 34%	83%	— 15%
Social	69%	— 28%	44%	— 54%
Foreign	80%	— 0%	75%	— 21%

Key Votes

1) Lmt Cln Water Act	AGN	5) Retain Gun Cont	FOR	9) Aid Angola Reb	AGN
2) Rpl Tobac Sub	FOR	6) Contra Aid	AGN	10) Tax Reform	FOR
3) Grm-Rdmn Def Red	FOR	7) Lmt Text Imp	FOR	11) S Africa Sanc	FOR
4) Ban Polygraph	FOR	8) Limit SDI	FOR	12) Immig Reform	FOR

Election Results

1986 general	Nicholas Mavroules (D)	131,051	(100%)	($184,485)
1986 primary	Nicholas Mavroules (D)	39,630	(100%)	
1984 general	Nicholas Mavroules (D)	168,662	(70%)	($242,844)
	Frederick S. Leber (R)	63,363	(26%)	($10,897)

Campaign Contributions and Expenditures

1985-86		Direct Cont. 1985-86		PACS Breakdown 1985-86			
Receipts	$235,761	Indiv.	$137,463	Corp.	$41,125	T/M/H	$10,550
Expend.	$184,485	Party	$101	Labor	$36,472	Agr.	$300
Unspent	$94,283	PACS	$100,447	Ideo.	$10,000	CWOS	$2,000

SEVENTH DISTRICT

The history of many Boston area families is the story of movement inland from Boston harbor, from a dockside where bewildered immigrants landed, seasick perhaps and squinting to find friends and relatives or anyone who spoke their language or in their brogue, to a comfortable suburb, with a New England white frame house with red or bright blue shutters, furnished in Early American, with a view out the paned windows of a large tree in the side or back yard. You can see this kind of history just by traveling through the 7th Congressional District of

Massachusetts, just north of downtown Boston.

A good place to start is Chelsea, long a disembarkation point for immigrants, a grim industrial place now with some of the lowest income levels in Massachusetts. It is host now to the newest immigrants, Puerto Ricans; with Boston and Lawrence, it is the only part of the state with a significant Hispanic population. Next you come to Everett, still a working-class town; then out to Malden and Medford, which still have the look they did when they were inhabited mostly by ethnic-conscious Yankees in the 1920s. About here the streetcars stop and bus lines thin out. Some of the towns farther out remain Yankee strongholds, like Melrose; others are solidly high income, like Winchester; but just beyond is working-class Woburn (pronounced as if it had two Os); and to the side the high tech suburb of Lexington, with its proud revolutionary heritage. Added to the 7th District in 1981, to meet the population standard, are Billerica (from an old English name that has a Celtic ring) and Tewksbury, which are part of the high tech country around Lowell.

Political attitudes have changed as families have moved up from the dockside and fanned out through this area. Up through the 1950s, this was a Republican district; only Chelsea and Everett were dependably Democratic. By the 1960s it had become so solidly Democratic that House races were never seriously contested by Republicans. In 1976, when the district's congressman died, 12 Democrats filed to run in the primary—and no Republican. Now it may be trending back mildly to the Republicans; it has voted twice, though by narrow margins, for Ronald Reagan.

The winner of the 1976 free-for-all was Edward Markey, a young state legislator (30 then) who like Jimmy Stewart in *Mr. Smith Goes to Washington* had never been in the nation's capital. Now Markey is among the more senior House members, chairman of an important subcommittee, but he still has the look of the young liberal, with no doubts about the wisdom of traditional Democratic economic programs and a Vietnam-bred mistrust of American military adventures abroad. He was one of the leaders—and perhaps the most fervent of the leaders—in the battle for the nuclear freeze resolution in the House in 1983 and a backer of the comprehensive test ban treaty in 1986. He is also one of the House's most vociferous opponents of nuclear power. He brings to the causes on which he is liberal a devotion that amounts almost to zealotry, and not a hint of self-deprecating humor or irony. He is not a congressman who evokes lukewarm opinions. His admirers consider him one of their greatest heroes in politics, a man whom they can trust to fight for their deepest beliefs. His detractors consider him naive at best and an unscrupulous cheap shot artist at worst.

Markey's prominence in the House arises partly from accident: he inherited, perhaps with a boost from fellow Boston College alumnus Tip O'Neill, his predecessor's seat on Energy and Commerce, which soon became one of the most sought-after committees in the House; he is now the 6th ranking Democrat there as well as 4th ranking Democrat on Interior. When he came to Congress, oil price controls were still in effect and were highly popular in Massachusetts; he has always steadfastly backed them. He has inherited important subcommittee slots which have given him important leverage to hobble the already troubled nuclear power industry. The course of events over 10 years has not shaken Markey's faith. The fall in oil prices after decontrol has not convinced him that markets regulate supply better than bureaucrats, nor has the growth of Massachusetts's private economy when taxes were lowered, shaken his belief that more rather than less domestic spending is needed. The withering attacks by Henry Hyde on his nuclear freeze proposal did not shake the faith he expressed again and again in direct mail.

There are in fact cynics who see Markey more as a direct mail entrepreneur than as a legislator. In the early 1980s Markey raised vast sums which did nothing more than build up a mailing list for his own causes; then in 1984 he announced he was running for the Senate seat Paul Tsongas was vacating. Evidently the direct mail response was not strong enough, or his support otherwise was too weak; for whatever reason, he left the race at the last minute, after dozens of local politicians had filed for higher office assuming he would too. One contender for the 7th District seat, Winchester legislator Sam Rotondi, held Markey to an embarrassingly small 54%–41% margin in the primary. Unanswered is the question why he even made the race when he was so well positioned on House committees to further his causes; did he, like so many young politicians, see a future president in the mirror when he shaved in the morning?

Markey was in any case legislatively more productive in 1985 and 1986 than he had been. He was busy as chairman of the Energy Conservation and Power Subcommittee of Energy and Commerce, working on prosaic issues like extending daylight savings time and relicensing hydroelectric power plants, keeping a close eye on the fine print in U.S.–China agreements so they won't allow nuclear proliferation and urging a 12-month moratorium on nuclear tests. He was busy discovering in Energy Department files recommendations that the government found Hanford, Washington, to be one of the worst nuclear dump sites rather than the best as it said— information that may have swung the Washington Senate race to Democrat Brock Adams. In 1987 he replaced Tim Wirth as chairman of the Telecommunications and Finance Subcommittee, which has jurisdiction over the communications industry and the securities business. Doubtless many people in these industries are afraid of what Markey will do on issues like hostile takeovers and Wall Street insider trading, though the most intensive investigations will probably be conducted by the Investigations Subcommittee chaired by full committee chairman John Dingell. Markey himself seems to oscillate between the workmanlike and procedurally correct professional legislator and the impassioned prophet of nuclear disaster and doom. Others will be wondering whether Markey will concentrate on becoming one of the direct mail politicians of the left or will focus on his work as a legislator.

The People: Pop. 1980: 523,982, dn. 3.7% 1970–80. Households (1980): 75% family, 38% with children, 61% married couples; 38.9% housing units rented; median monthly rent: $220; median house value: $58,100. Voting age pop. (1980): 387,217; 1% Spanish origin, 1% Black, 1% Asian origin.

1984 Presidential Vote:

Reagan (R)	123,559	(50%)
Mondale (D)	121,018	(49%)

Rep. Edward J. Markey (D)

Elected 1976; b. July 11, 1946, Malden; home, Malden; Boston Col., B.A. 1968, J.D. 1972; Roman Catholic; single.

Career: Practicing atty.; MA House of Reps., 1973–76.

Offices: 2133 RHOB 20515, 202-225-2836. Also JFK Fed. Bldg., Rm. 2100A, Boston 02203, 617-565-2900.

Committees: *Energy and Commerce* (6th of 27 D). Subcommittees: Energy and Power; Telecommunications and Finance (Chairman). *Interior and Insular Affairs* (4th of 26 D). Subcommittees: Energy and the Environment; National Parks and Public Lands; Water and Power Resources.

Group Ratings

	ADA	ACLU	COPE	CFA	LCV	ACU	NTU	NSI	COC	CEI
1986	95	93	89	67	100	0	33	0	13	24
1985	100	—	89	100	—	10	40	—	29	—

National Journal Ratings

	1986 LIB — 1986 CONS			1985 LIB — 1985 CONS		
Economic	66%	—	32%	85%	—	15%
Social	89%	—	0%	85%	—	0%
Foreign	80%	—	0%	92%	—	0%

Key Votes

1) Lmt Cln Water Act	AGN	5) Retain Gun Cont	FOR	9) Aid Angola Reb	AGN
2) Rpl Tobac Sub	FOR	6) Contra Aid	AGN	10) Tax Reform	FOR
3) Grm-Rdmn Def Red	AGN	7) Lmt Text Imp	FOR	11) S Africa Sanc	FOR
4) Ban Polygraph	FOR	8) Limit SDI	FOR	12) Immig Reform	FOR

Election Results

1986 general	Edward J. Markey (D)	124,183	(100%)	($314,410)
1986 primary	Edward J. Markey (D)	57,567	(100%)	
1984 general	Edward J. Markey (D)	167,211	(71%)	($520,629)
	S. Lester Ralph (R)	66,930	(29%)	($11,065)

Campaign Contributions and Expenditures

1985-86		Direct Cont. 1985-86		PACS Breakdown 1985-86			
Receipts	$412,155	Indiv.	$388,588	Corp.	$500	T/M/H	$550
Expend.	$314,410	PACS	$9,825	Labor	$5,250	Agr.	$0
Debts	$101,126	Cand.	$11,954	Ideo.	$3,275	CWOS	$250

EIGHTH DISTRICT

The 8th Congressional District of Massachusetts is a district with a number of distinctions. It is the home of no less than two national universities—Harvard and MIT—and of dozens of other universities and colleges; altogether, about 15% of its adults are students, one of the two or three highest proportions in congressional districts nationwide. It is the home of some of the nation's greatest historic sites: Bunker Hill and the frigate *Constitution* in the Charlestown section of Boston, the gold-domed State House overlooking the Boston Common and, on the side, townhouse-bedecked Beacon Hill. The district contains literally dozens of distinctive neighborhoods, from the stately grandeur of Boston's Back Bay, built in high Victorian times, to the insular Irish community in Charlestown, the Portuguese in East Cambridge and the Armenians in Watertown, the elderly Jews in Brighton, and the upper-income Yankees and professors in Belmont. It is one of the centers and progenitors of high tech industry in the United States, from Lechmere Square in Cambridge, thronged with software manufacturers, through the high-rises of downtown Boston, with their venture capitalists and investors, and out Route 2 toward the technological promised land of Route 128.

It is also the district which has over the past 40 years elected as its congressmen a President of the United States and a speaker of the House—and, a few years before that, a brilliant scamp of a politician who was five times mayor of Boston and twice went to jail. This was John F. Kennedy's district, when he came home from the war; and it was Tip O'Neill's district since 1952, when Kennedy ran for the Senate and O'Neill was the first Irish Catholic Democrat to be speaker of the Great and General Court of the Commonwealth of Massachusetts. Kennedy was a rich man who had only a nominal residence in the district and spent his six years in the House waiting to run for the Senate. O'Neill (who was born five years before Kennedy) is a product of local politics, with deep roots in North Cambridge—not Harvard Square—and local politics, who still enjoyed coming back and talking to the barber and the drugstore clerk and the old lady down the street. Tip O'Neill served ten consecutive years as speaker, the longest term in history, and vastly strengthened the office; an instinctive politician, he was sympathetic to reforms, chose carefully the issues on which he took a stand, and fought for what he believed in without flinching when he lost. In the early 1980s Republicans were licking their chops at the prospect of campaigning against this man that looked like an old-time political hack. But as the public got to know him, as they saw him stand up for what he believed under pressure, he became the most widely respected national legislator in 20th century history. When he left office, voluntarily and still at the peak of his powers, he had a positive job rating of 67%—higher than his old adversary Ronald Reagan's. He left behind a stronger House and a stronger Democratic party, firmly based on traditional values but adapted to the 1980s, and he left a stronger country too.

Politics in the 8th District has changed vastly since Tip O'Neill and John Kennedy won the Democratic primaries of 1952 and 1946; most notably, many of the working class children that packed the three-deckers in those days have long since moved out to middle and upper income suburbs to raise families of their own, and university students and post-students have formed an increasing, though still not dominant, percentage of Cambridge, Somerville, and the 8th's wards of Boston. When O'Neill announced his retirement, it looked like half a dozen candidates, all of them leftish and with various local bases, would split the district's votes. But all that changed when Joseph Kennedy II, the oldest son of the late Robert Kennedy, moved from the South Shore town of Marshfield into the district and entered the race in January 1986. Two years before he had told the *Boston Globe*, "It's just not in me to do it. It's such a crummy system. It's just a bog. I really wonder whether it's better to go out and do something than fight this ball of molasses. Every time I get near government, it strikes me that it just doesn't work. I hate things that don't work." Evidently he was able to overcome this distaste. Other candidates began to withdraw, photographers from *People* began thronging in, and what had been a battle of lefties ended up a battle between a Kennedy capitalizing on the sentimental attachments of older, culturally conservative voters, versus a left-leaning, neighborhood-based Cambridge state Senator George Bachrach.

All this was a bit odd: at the 1979 dedication of the Kennedy Library, in front of President Carter, Joseph Kennedy had made a strident speech criticizing Carter from the left. That same year, he established a community presence with the Citizens Energy Corporation, using family money to buy oil in bulk and distribute it to low-income citizens; it looked both compassionate and hardheaded, although it has been criticized for getting more publicity for Kennedy than savings for the poor. In 1986 Kennedy was positioning himself on the right, advocating capital punishment and arguing that more federal money is not the solution to everything; but that may have been a handicap in the 8th, and in the last weeks he was running only even with Bachrach. Then Tip O'Neill endorsed Kennedy and Bachrach made a terrible mistake, implying in debate that Kennedy's company had ties with Qaddafi's Libya; Kennedy said it was "totally off base" to suggest that he was tied to a country that offered asylum to his father's assassin. He won the primary with a not overwhelming 52% of the vote and beat think-tank founder Clark Abt in the general 72%–28%, while spending some $1.7 million—more than any other House candidate in the country but Jack Kemp.

Kennedy comes to Washington regarded as a kind of infant Kennedy; he looks young, talks hesitatingly and makes arguments only with some effort, grinning when he gets it right; he has leaped from one philosophy to another with all the appearance of a young man looking for something plausible. Yet, elected at 34, he is older than many young congressmen are when first elected and is pretty far along by the standards of his family. At his age, his father was managing a successful presidential campaign and his uncle Edward had been elected to the Senate and had successfully floor-managed a major piece of legislation. No one can imagine Joseph Kennedy doing anything like those things any time soon. He arouses in some a strong dislike: the *New Republic,* whose editor-in-chief Martin Peretz lives in Cambridge, called him a "lout"; some criticize him for dropping out of college for a time, or for being the driver in an accident which left a girl passenger paralyzed. But surely some sympathy is due a man who saw his father murdered when he was 15. The election of Joseph Kennedy is hailed or cursed as the coming to power of a third generation of the Kennedy family. But Joseph Kennedy's small majority in his family's political heartland and the defeat in the Maryland 2d District of his more articulate sister, Kathleen Kennedy Townsend, suggest that enthusiasm for the Kennedys, the uncritical desire to elect them to whatever office they seek, has died down, and that what we are looking at is the embers rather than a new surge of flame. The 8th District will probably reelect its new congressman without difficulty. But there's little reason to believe that he will come anywhere near to matching the eminence of the two who came before him.

The People: Pop. 1980: 521,548, dn. 7.1% 1970–80. Households (1980): 50% family, 22% with children, 37% married couples; 69.1% housing units rented; median monthly rent: $236; median house value: $60,600. Voting age pop. (1980): 434,109; 4% Black, 3% Asian origin, 3% Spanish origin.

1984 Presidential Vote:

Mondale (D)	....	142,158	(64%)
Reagan (R)	....	80,756	(36%)

Rep. Joseph P. Kennedy II (D)

Elected 1986; b. Sept. 4, 1952, Brighton; home, Brighton; U. of MA., B.A. 1976; Roman Catholic; married (Sheila).

Career: Peace Corps, 1974; Community Services Admin., 1977–79; Founder and Pres., Citizens Energy Corp., 1979-86; Founder, Citizens Conservation Corp., 1981.

Offices: 1631 LHOB 20515, 202-225-5111. Also JFK Fed. Bldg., Rm. 2007, Boston 02203, 617-367-0288.

Committees: *Banking, Finance and Urban Affairs* (27th of 31 D). Subcommittees: Financial Institutions Supervision, Regulation and Insurance; Housing and Community Development; International Development Institutions and Finance. *Veterans' Affairs* (18th of 21 D). Subcommittees: Education, Training and Employment; Hospitals and Health Care. *Select Committee on Aging* (38th of 39 D). Subcommittee: Human Services.

Group Ratings and Key Votes: Newly Elected

Election Results

1986 general	Joseph P. Kennedy II (D)	....	104,651 (72%)	($1,800,781)
	Clark C. Abt (R).	....	40,259 (28%)	($591,652)
1986 primary	Joseph P. Kennedy II (D)	....	59,192 (52%)	
	George Bachrach	....	34,021 (30%)	
	Melvin H. King.	....	10,700 (9%)	
	Seven others	....	8,719 (4%)	
1984 general	Thomas P. O'Neill, Jr. (D)	....	179,617 (92%)	($208,271)
	Laura Ross (Communist)	....	15,810 (8%)	

Campaign Contributions and Expenditures

1985-86		Direct Cont. 1985-86		PACS Breakdown 1985-86			
Receipts	$1,822,025	Indiv.	$1,462,656	Corp.	$8,850	T/M/H	$18,000
Expend.	$1,800,781	PACS	$96,356	Labor	$41,325	Agr.	$0
Unspent	$21,244	Cand.	$250,000	Ideo.	$27,231	CWOS	$950

NINTH DISTRICT

Boston is the most political of cities. In a conversation in a working class bar, even over lunch at the Somerset Club, there is a shared assumption that people use government to shape political ends, as well as the other way around; that politics pervades everything. And so it may, in a city where building contractors and Ph.D. candidates for years looked to government to enrich them, in the knowledge that political connections will determine whether they succeed or fail.

Politics has been very much a part of the fabric of Boston life throughout the city's history. Boston malcontents were starting the American revolution when the burghers of Philadelphia and New York still thought mostly about making money. Later, Boston was the hotbed for the abolitionist movement that had much to do with igniting the Civil War. Boston is also, and this is no coincidence, the nation's most Irish city; for the Irish seem to have some magical aptitude for politics. The Irish have been here a long time now—since the 1840s in many families—but they retain their ethnic consciousness. You can still find little ladies in Boston who will tell you that they don't know much about the candidates but "I always vote for all the good Irish names"; and you will find people who, when asked about discrimination, say, "Oh, yes. You mean 'No Irish need apply.'" Even in the majority, in a city governed by a series of Irish mayors since 1906, the Irish still feel beleaguered and put down, resentful of the privileges and connections Boston's Brahmins seem to enjoy, disdainful of what they consider the disrespectful behavior of many blacks, confused by the denunciations of their neighborhoods during the busing crisis by intellectuals from Boston's universities and writers for the *Boston Globe*.

Once you get outside the northern edge of Boston, away from the downtown skyscrapers, Back Bay and Beacon Hill, you are likely to be in an Irish neighborhood, or in a black neighborhood which was, not too many years ago, mostly Irish. Most of these neighborhoods—the geographic heart of Boston—are part of the 9th Congressional District of Massachusetts. It stretches from the Italian North End and the refurbished Quincy Market, near Faneuil Hall and the modern City Hall, out Washington Street, past mostly black Roxbury and mostly white South Boston— the political base of Mayor Raymond Flynn, elected in 1983 and getting along well with blacks and intellectuals despite his base in Southie—to the rolling hills lined with three-decker houses of Jamaica Plain, Forest Hills, Roslindale, and West Roxbury. Once this area formed all of a district. But over the years, Boston's population has been declining: young people move out to newer neighborhoods with their families, houses which once held half a dozen families now hold just a few old people, some neighborhoods decay and are filled with empty houses.

So the 9th District, to meet the one-person-one-vote standard without robbing the neighboring 11th District of Democratic votes in the Dorchester section of Boston, moves out in Massachusetts far beyond where most of the people who grew up in Boston went. It includes the well-to-do suburbs of Needham and Westwood, more modest towns like Stoughton, the small industrial city of Taunton, far south of Boston, and several small rural towns roundabout. Less than half the district's population is now in Boston.

This is the district that since 1972 has elected Representative Joe Moakley. he has the appearance and demeanor of an old Boston Irish pol, and the pedigree as well: he holds the 9th District seat represented from 1925 to 1970 by Speaker John McCormack and the Rules Committee seat held from 1954 to 1972 by Speaker Tip O'Neill of the 8th district. Moakley is a solid party man, a deputy majority whip, who was always responsive on Rules to O'Neill (although, sitting in the chair, he was forced to rule O'Neill in violation of House rules when the Speaker attacked Newt Gingrich in the spring of 1984) and presumably will be to Speaker Jim Wright as well. He is solidly liberal on economic and foreign issues, but not on cultural ones—an attractive combination in Boston and many of the 9th District suburbs. As a Rules member, he is well positioned to get things done as an insider, and doesn't speak out often on substantive issues. But he has led the fight to allow more Central American immigrants to stay in this country as refugees, and he was an early and has been a consistent critic of anti-satellite weapons tests and the Reagan Administration's Strategic Defense Initiative.

Curiously, considering his party regularity, Moakley was first elected, in· 1972, as an Independent; he was running against Louise Day Hicks, the busing opponent who had won the Democratic nomination over Moakley and the seat in 1970 with minority votes. But Moakley was an experienced legislator (he served in both houses in Massachusetts and on the Boston Council) and competent parliamentarian who was not going to give up his political career, so he used the Independent candidacy to beat Hicks in 1972 and got the Rules Committee seat shortly thereafter. He is now the number two Democrat on Rules, behind Claude Pepper, a good bet to be chairman of that committee someday soon. In the 9th District Moakley has not had serious competition for a dozen years; he is surely not vulnerable in a primary and the district, even with all the suburbs, is still Democratic enough to have gone for Walter Mondale over Ronald Reagan in 1984.

The People: Pop. 1980: 519,226, dn. 5.2% 1970–80. Households (1980): 68% family, 36% with children, 49% married couples; 51.5% housing units rented; median monthly rent: $172; median house value: $49,400. Voting age pop. (1980): 380,987; 14% Black, 4% Spanish origin, 1% Asian origin.

1984 Presidential Vote:

Mondale (D)	111,765	(51%)
Reagan (R)	104,484	(48%)

Rep. John Joseph (Joe) Moakley (D)

Elected 1972; b. Apr. 27, 1927, Boston; home, Boston; U. of Miami, Suffolk U., LL.B. 1956; Roman Catholic; married (Evelyn).

Career: Navy, WWII; MA House of Reps., 1953–65, Major. Whip, 1957; Practicing atty., 1957–72; MA Senate, 1965–69; Boston City Cncl., 1971.

Offices: 221 CHOB 20515, 202-225-8273. Also 4 Court St., Taunton 02780, 617-824-6676; and World Trade Ctr., Ste. 220, Boston 02210, 617-565-2920.

Committees: *Rules* (2d of 9 D). Subcommittee: Rules of the House (Chairman).

Group Ratings

	ADA	ACLU	COPE	CFA	LCV	ACU	NTU	NSI	COC	CEI
1986	95	65	92	75	79	5	25	0	18	17
1985	90	—	92	75	—	5	34	—	23	—

National Journal Ratings

	1986 LIB — 1986 CONS		1985 LIB — 1985 CONS	
Economic	87% —	0%	89% —	0%
Social	69% —	28%	49% —	49%
Foreign	80% —	0%	85% —	8%

Key Votes

1) Lmt Cln Water Act	AGN	5) Retain Gun Cont	FOR	9) Aid Angola Reb	AGN
2) Rpl Tobac Sub	FOR	6) Contra Aid	AGN	10) Tax Reform	FOR
3) Grm-Rdmn Def Red	AGN	7) Lmt Text Imp	FOR	11) S Africa Sanc	FOR
4) Ban Polygraph	FOR	8) Limit SDI	FOR	12) Immig Reform	FOR

Election Results

1986 general	John Joseph (Joe) Moakley (D)	110,026	(84%)	($314,452)
	Robert W. Horan (I)	21,292	(16%)	
1986 primary	John Joseph (Joe) Moakley (D)	48,429	(90%)	
	David T. Kenner (D)	5,475	(10%)	
1984 general	John Joseph (Joe) Moakley (D) unopposed			($228,957)

Campaign Contributions and Expenditures

1985-86		Direct Cont. 1985-86		PACS Breakdown 1985-86			
Receipts	$403,732	Indiv.	$244,677	Corp.	$68,975	T/M/H	$42,720
Expend.	$314,452	Party	$225	Labor	$47,875	Agr.	$200
Unspent	$178,641	PACS	$173,520	Ideo.	$6,950	CWOS	$8,600

TENTH DISTRICT

Like an outstretched arm into the Atlantic, Cape Cod beckons to visitors; it is here that the Pilgrims first put ashore, before scuttling across Cape Cod Bay and settling in Plymouth. The Cape, like much of Massachusetts, has a bustling past which is long forgotten: the picturesque towns here and on the islands of Nantucket and Martha's Vineyard were once whaling and China trade ports; a railroad steamed up the spine of the Cape; lumber was harvested here as in northern Maine or the Pacific Northwest. The biggest city in these parts was New Bedford, also once a whaling port. Then, around the turn of the 20th century, quiet set in in this southeastern corner of Massachusetts. New Bedford continued as a port and factory town; though its population has stayed at around 100,000 for seven decades, there was considerable turnover, as the Yankees died out, moved west, or intermarried, and were replaced by the nation's largest Portuguese-American (actually, mostly Azorean-American) community. As for the Cape and the area around Plymouth, its industry withered away, it became vacation and poor farming country. But as metropolitan Boston grew down the South Shore, and as rising affluence enabled more and more people to buy second homes or to retire in comfortable circumstances, the Cape became one of the boom areas of New England, sprouting new subdivisions every year.

This is the land of the 10th Congressional District of Massachusetts, starting at the beach suburb of Hull on Boston's South Shore and proceeding down through Plymouth and the towns on Buzzards Bay to the Cape and New Bedford. Historically this whole area, except for New Bedford and a few smaller mill towns, were heavily Republican. By the late 1960s, however, it was trending Democratic on cultural issues: the 10th went for Richard Nixon over George McGovern, but only narrowly—a striking result in an area that was always heavily against Franklin D. Roosevelt. With economic issues becoming more important, the 10th is now somewhat more Republican, and in most elections the most Republican district in Massachusetts: it has given Ronald Reagan substantial margins twice. The Cape continues to vote Republican in most elections, as it has for years; the South Shore is mostly Republican; the New Bedford area ordinarily is not heavily enough Democratic to counterbalance them.

The congressman here, however, is a Democrat, Gerry (pronounced "Gary") Studds, whose political career began in the late 1960s and has flourished ever since even under the most bizarre of circumstances. He became nationally known in 1983 when it was revealed that he had had sex with a young man who was serving as a congressional page. The House quite properly censured Studds and Daniel Crane of Illinois, who had sex with a female page; under House rules, that meant Studds also lost his subcommittee chairmanship. He did not deign to show much contrition, though the page in question was a minor when the incident occurred, and as a page was under the protection and supervision of the House. It apparently did not matter to Studds that he had violated a trust and had used a position of power to get an adolescent to have sex with him. But what some saw as effrontery others considered courage; after all, Studds chose to continue serving in the House and to stand for reelection after so much of his personal life suddenly became open to view.

But Studds was already well known in the 10th District, and he had several assets there that enabled him to overcome serious challenges in the primary and general elections in the 1984 elections. One was his identification as a foreign policy dove, always helpful in dovish Massachusetts. Studds serves on the Foreign Affairs Committee, where he opposes U.S. support for the Nicaraguan contras. He was one of Eugene McCarthy's key organizers in 1968; when he first ran for Congress in 1970 and lost, and then when he ran again in 1972 and won, he had the support of the usually diffident McCarthy. His dovishness probably helped most in the traditionally Republican Cape, which he carried with more than 80% of the vote in the 1984 primary and by a solid margin in the general. His next asset is his knowledge of Portuguese. He took the trouble to learn the language (not an easy one) between his first and second campaigns, and has kept in close and constant touch with the Portuguese communities in New Bedford and elsewhere. As a result, even after his censure he was able to march in the annual New Bedford parade and be greeted with dozens of cheers and only a few catcalls. He got two-thirds of the votes in the New Bedford area both in the primary and general elections in 1984.

His third asset is his support of the fishing industry. The 10th District may be the single district most dependent on commercial fishing. He sits on the Merchant Marine and Fisheries Committee and, after losing it under the terms of his censure, has regained the chairmanship of the Coast Guard subcommittee. In his first term he succeeded in pushing through to passage a bill extending the territorial waters of the United States to 200 miles off the shoreline; since then he has been looking out for the interests of small fishermen, and trying to keep their waters free from foreign trawlers and oil spills. This may seem humdrum work, but surely it has some fascination, and it helped Studds politically when he really needed it. He was deprived of his subcommittee chair when he was censured in 1983, but it was restored after he was reelected the next year.

Studds is, in other words, one of those congressmen who never forgets his principles or his district. After his censure, he attended briskly and effectively to his legislative duties, faithfully supporting the Coast Guard, winning passage of the Striped Bass Conservation bill, working on a variety of maritime, environmental, and foreign policy bills. In 1987 he chose to take over the chairmanship of the Fisheries, Wildlife Conservation and Environment Subcommittee of Merchant Marine, rather than seek the chair of the Western Hemisphere Subcommittee of Foreign Affairs, as many other Democrats would. Studds pointed out that the Merchant Marine panel would give him more opportunity for legislating and less to appeal to national public opinion; considering his legislative skills and personal background, he surely made the correct choice: he has been effective legislatively, and he is probably not the man national Democratic leaders would choose as their party's point man on an issue that makes the television screens almost daily.

The People: Pop. 1980: 522,200, up 26.6% 1970–80. Households (1980): 75% family, 38% with children, 62% married couples; 29.5% housing units rented; median monthly rent: $161; median house value: $48,800. Voting age pop. (1980): 377,639; 1% Black, 1% Spanish origin.

1984 Presidential Vote: Reagan (R) 142,887   (55%)
                                Mondale (D) 116,933   (45%)

Rep. Gerry E. Studds (D)

Elected 1972; b. May 12, 1937, Mineola, NY; home, Cohasset; Yale U., B.A. 1959, M.A.T. 1961; Episcopalian; single.

Career: U.S. Foreign Svc., 1961–63; Exec. Asst. to William R. Anderson, Pres. Consultant for a Domestic Peace Corps, 1963; Legis. Asst. to U.S. Sen. Harrison J. Williams, 1964; Prep. sch. teacher, 1965–69.

Offices: 1501 LHOB 20515, 202-225-3111. Also P.O. Bldg., New Bedford 02740, 617-999-1251; Barston's Landing, Ste. 6, 2 Columbia Rd., Pembroke 02359, 617-826-3866; and 146 Main St., Hyannis 02601, 617-771-0666.

Committees: *Foreign Affairs* (6th of 27 D). Subcommittees: Arms Control, International Security and Science; Western Hemisphere Affairs. *Merchant Marine and Fisheries* (4th of 25 D). Subcommittees: Coast Guard and Navigation; Fisheries and Wildlife Conservation and the Environment (Chairman); Oceanography; Panama Canal and Outer Continental Shelf.

Group Ratings

	ADA	ACLU	COPE	CFA	LCV	ACU	NTU	NSI	COC	CEI
1986	95	95	89	75	100	0	32	0	19	23
1985	100	—	90	100	—	10	43	—	27	—

National Journal Ratings

	1986 LIB — 1986 CONS			1985 LIB — 1985 CONS		
Economic	80%	—	19%	85%	—	11%
Social	89%	—	0%	85%	—	0%
Foreign	80%	—	0%	92%	—	0%

Key Votes

1) Lmt Cln Water Act	AGN	5) Retain Gun Cont	FOR	9) Aid Angola Reb	AGN
2) Rpl Tobac Sub	FOR	6) Contra Aid	AGN	10) Tax Reform	FOR
3) Grm-Rdmn Def Red	AGN	7) Lmt Text Imp	FOR	11) S Africa Sanc	FOR
4) Ban Polygraph	FOR	8) Limit SDI	FOR	12) Immig Reform	FOR

Election Results

1986 general	Gerry E. Studds (D).................	121,578	(65%)	($396,216)
	Ricardo M. Barros (R)................	49,451	(26%)	($97,191)
	Alexander Byron (I)................	15,687	(8%)	
1986 primary	Gerry E. Studds (D).................	34,339	(81%)	
	Norman J. Livergood (D).............	8,228	(19%)	
1984 general	Gerry E. Studds (D).................	143,062	(56%)	($565,479)
	Lewis S. W. Crampton (R)............	113,745	(44%)	($194,582)

Campaign Contributions and Expenditures

1985-86		Direct Cont. 1985-86		PACS Breakdown 1985-86			
Receipts	$384,646	Indiv.	$293,179	Corp.	$1,200	T/M/H	$20,500
Expend.	$396,216	PACS	$86,025	Labor	$49,975	Agr.	$0
Unspent	$34,826			Ideo.	$13,850	CWOS	$500

ELEVENTH DISTRICT

The 11th Congressional District of Massachusetts includes the southern third of Boston, most of the city's South Shore suburbs, and more suburban territory stretching to the shoe manufacturing city of Brockton and the towns just beyond. This is the lineal descendant of the district whose Yankee voters elected John Quincy Adams to the House for the last years of his life (1831–48), despite his refusal to campaign; but it is not a district Yankee in tone today. With few exceptions, the 11th District's suburban cities and towns—Quincy, Braintree, and the newer Holbrook, Stoughton, and Randolph, away from the Shore—are filled with the grandsons and granddaughters of Irish, Italian, and Jewish immigrants; the Hyde Park and Dorchester wards of Boston are a mixture of old Irish and younger blacks. These are not grand places; except for Milton, housing values here are below the metropolitan average. Politically, this is Democratic country—much as that might surprise the staunchly anti-Jacksonian John Quincy Adams.

The congressman from the 11th is Brian Donnelly, a man with political roots in Boston. He won the seat in 1978, when James Burke retired; Burke and other local politicos backed him, in pique over a challenger who opposed and nearly beat Burke in 1976 when he was sick. Donnelly has a moderate attitude on cultural issues; on economic and foreign issues, he is solidly liberal. He served during the first Reagan term on the Budget Committee and in 1985 he won a seat on the Ways and Means Committee, which Burke had served on; he had Tip O'Neill's active support in both cases and has generally supported Democratic leadership positions. He has been reelected easily since he first won, and he can hold this seat for years, as Burke did, unless he should run for and win another office; with his Ways and Means seat in hand, that is unlikely.

The People: Pop. 1980: 525,089, dn. 2.8% 1970–80. Households (1980): 73% family, 38% with children, 56% married couples; 42.2% housing units rented; median monthly rent: $211; median house value: $42,600. Voting age pop. (1980): 382,888; 7% Black, 1% Spanish origin, 1% Asian origin.

1984 Presidential Vote:

Reagan (R)	114,122	(52%)
Mondale (D)	104,938	(48%)

Rep. Brian J. Donnelly (D)

Elected 1978; b. Mar. 2, 1946, Dorchester; home, Dorchester; Boston U., B.S. 1970; Roman Catholic; married (Virginia).

Career: Dir. of Youth Activities, Dorchester YMCA, 1968–70; High sch. and trade sch. teacher and coach, 1969–72; MA House of Reps., 1973–78.

Offices: 438 CHOB, 202-225-3215. Also 47 Washington St., Quincy 02169, 617-472-1800; JFK Fed. Bldg., Rm. 2307, Boston 02203, 617-565-2910; and 61 Main St., Brockton 02401, 617-583-6300.

Committees: *Ways and Means* (19th of 23 D). Subcommittees: Health; Public Assistance.

Group Ratings

	ADA	ACLU	COPE	CFA	LCV	ACU	NTU	NSI	COC	CEI
1986	75	60	88	75	71	14	24	0	29	17
1985	80	—	87	92	—	5	31	—	23	—

National Journal Ratings

	1986 LIB — 1986 CONS		1985 LIB — 1985 CONS	
Economic	71% —	29%	81% —	26%
Social	69% —	28%	49% —	49%
Foreign	63% —	36%	71% —	26%

Key Votes

1) Lmt Cln Water Act	AGN	5) Retain Gun Cont	FOR	9) Aid Angola Reb	AGN
2) Rpl Tobac Sub	FOR	6) Contra Aid	AGN	10) Tax Reform	FOR
3) Grm-Rdmn Def Red	AGN	7) Lmt Text Imp	FOR	11) S Africa Sanc	FOR
4) Ban Polygraph	FOR	8) Limit SDI	FOR	12) Immig Reform	FOR

Election Results

1986 general	Brian J. Donnelly (D)	114,926	(100%)	($46,171)
1986 primary	Brian J. Donnelly (D)	46,571	(88%)	
	David J. Peterson (D)	6,272	(12%)	
1984 general	Brian J. Donnelly (D) unopposed			($49,077)

Campaign Contributions and Expenditures

1985-86		Direct Cont. 1985-86		PACS Breakdown 1985-86			
Receipts	$253,794	Indiv.	$77,322	Corp.	$41,550	T/M/H	$53,550
Expend.	$46,171	PACS	$143,850	Labor	$29,350	Agr.	$0
Unspent	$365,379			Ideo.	$12,250	CWOS	$7,150

MICHIGAN

From an orbiting satellite, on a cloudless day, you could make out the shapes of only four of the 50 American states: Alaska and Hawaii, Florida and Michigan. Most states' boundaries are dotted lines drawn by treaty negotiators or government officials. Michigan is defined by nature: two peninsulas surrounded on three sides by the Great Lakes, the inland oceans that contain one-fifth of all the fresh water in the world. Michigan has always had a distinctive history, never precisely mirroring the states around it. No other state (except Alaska, Hawaii, and Maine) has so small a portion of its boundaries directly touching other states. People in Michigan live in their own state of mind, with the rest of the country a great out-there, which they suppose in most ways resembles Michigan—though (as employees of the Big Three automakers, commuting to work on freeways full of new, full-sized American cars, learned) that is sometimes not the case.

But suddenly in the middle 1980s there are hopeful signs that Michigan is becoming less distinctive in one important way—in the dependence of its economy on a single industry. This is land with every potential for a diversified economy, yet at different stages in its history it has prospered mightily, then sagged agonizingly, with the rise and fall of single dominating industries. The first was furs: the French *courreurs du bois* of the 17th century sailed up the Great Lakes and the icy rivers of Ontario to what is now Michigan, set up fur trading posts there that are still commemorated in names (Mackinac, Sault Ste. Marie, Detroit, and Michigan itself), and left after the British won the Battle of Quebec in 1759 and expelled France from North America. Then came lumber: Michigan was the nation's leading lumber state in the late 19th century, until it was lumbered or burned out. Then came the iron and copper ores from the mines of the Upper Peninsula, the biggest producers in the nation in the early 20th century.

Finally, starting around 1900, came autos. That this industry came to be centered in Michigan was an accident; Ohio or Chicago, on the major east–west transportation routes, were likelier sites. But several of the early entrepreneurs came from Michigan (Henry Ford, W.C. Durant, R.E. Olds) and Detroit bankers were more willing to provide venture capital than bankers in the bigger, more established cities of Cleveland and Chicago. From 1905 to 1930 (as the perception of the auto shifted from being a novelty to a necessity) and then again from 1940 to 1965 (as the one-car family became the two-car family) the auto industry enabled Michigan to grow more rapidly than the national average (gaining congressional seats in the 1930, 1940, 1950, and 1960 censuses). Income levels grew even faster. In the process, Michigan became dependent on this most cyclical of industries —which in turn produced a transformation of its politics. Then as the basic assumptions of the industry collapsed—as the auto makers and workers found, to their surprise, that most Americans did not *have* to buy a new full-sized American-made car every two or three years—Michigan politics was transformed once again. In the 1980s the auto industry recovered, with record profits in the middle 1980s and reasonably steady sales thereafter. But auto employment, in Michigan and elsewhere, is way below pre-1980 levels, and unlikely ever to rise again; auto wages are, in real dollars, no higher, and seem unlikely to race ahead of inflation and productivity again as they did in the 1970s; the auto companies' tie-ins with Japanese manufacturers cut the risks for their shareholders, but do very little for Michigan's economy.

The story of Michigan politics begins long before anyone heard of automobiles, in the 1830s and 1840s, when settlers poured into the empty forests of southern Michigan. Most of them were from Upstate New York, part of the vast Yankee migration westward, which transferred the values of the Puritans west from New England (where they were about to become a minority) through Upstate New York, lower Michigan, northern Illinois, Iowa, and Kansas to southern California. They brought with them the Yankee urge for improvement. Not only were they successful farmers and good businessmen, they were also lovers of learning, setting up plenty of public schools and colleges (some of which made a point of accepting women and blacks), and instinctive reformers. Michigan by the 1850s had a large temperance movement, it was the first state to prohibit capital punishment, it had active supporters of the underground railway, and it became one of the birthplaces of the Republican Party, which was founded in Jackson in 1854 and swept the state in the elections later that year.

In those days the Democrats were the party of laissez faire, in both economics and on issues like slavery; the Republicans were the busybodies who wanted government to act to improve society. And in Michigan they were generally successful. As the 19th century wore on, Michigan was a successful commonwealth. Still mainly a farm state, it also had a major lumber industry (until the forests were clear-cut or swept by fires like the 1881 blaze that turned skies dark with ashes and burned half the Thumb) and several of its cities became significant manufacturing centers. Its civic institutions were of high quality—its higher education system was already one of the nation's best—and its quality of life high.

But until the development of the automobile industry in the 30 years after 1900, Michigan remained something of a backwater. Suddenly it became one of the world's leading immigrant destinations. The three-county area around Detroit had 426,000 people in 1900; in 1930, it had 2,177,000. Detroit was like Houston as oil prices shot up, the nation's fastest-growing major metropolitan area in 1900–30 except for Los Angeles. A few outstate cities—Flint, Lansing— with auto factories grew at similar rates, though on a much smaller scale. The auto industry drew immigrants into Detroit and Michigan from all over: from rural Michigan and southern Ontario, from the farms of Ohio and Indiana, whites from the mountains of Kentucky and Tennessee and (mostly after 1940) blacks from Alabama and Mississippi. Michigan had had relatively few European immigrants before this: some Germans in the southwestern part of the state, a Dutch colony (the nation's largest) around Grand Rapids and Holland, Finns in the mining towns of the Upper Peninsula. But Detroit attracted Poles and Italians, Hungarians and Serbs, Greeks and Jews.

This sudden influx of a polyglot proletariat also changed Michigan's politics in time. The catalyst was the great depression of the 1930s, but the impetus came not so much from actual

MICHIGAN — Congressional Districts, Counties, and Selected Places — *(18 Districts)*

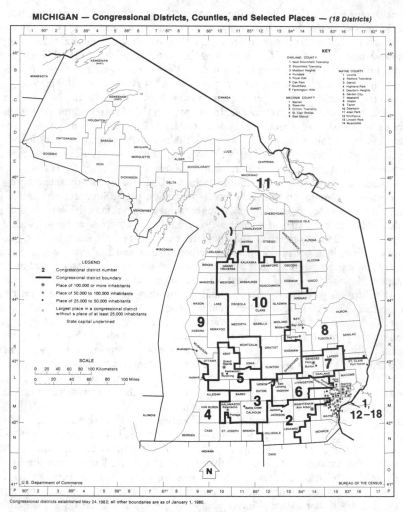

See pages 1369-1374 for additional metropolitan area maps.

privation, as from the fact that the auto companies paid relatively good wages but treated their employees mechanically and with great distrust. Henry Ford and other assembly line pioneers had made production very efficient, but they also made the factory a place of adversary confrontation. So in 1937, when it began to appear that the economy wouldn't grow much any more, the workers supported the sit-in strikes organized by the new United Auto Workers; in effect, management and labor were fighting, sometimes in the literal sense of the word, for shares of what both sides thought was a static-sized pie. The UAW won those strikes and organized the companies, in large part because Governor Frank Murphy, a Democrat, declined to send in troops to break them, even though they were clearly illegal.

The success of the union organizing drives set the tone of Michigan politics for at least 25 years. The union won, but it did not carry all before it; much of the rest of the state resented its tactics and feared they would be the losers. As evidence, consider that Murphy's Democrats lost the 1938 elections, not only statewide but in factory towns like Flint; and Republicans won most contests for a decade-and-a-half afterwards. Demographics finally worked for the Democrats:

the auto workers and post-1900 immigrants were producing more children than outstate Yankees and management personnel. Following Walter Reuther's election as UAW president in 1947, they elected G. Mennen Williams, then a young liberal, governor in 1948 (he retired from service on the state Supreme Court in 1986), and by 1954 the Democrats, closely allied to and heavily supported by the UAW, seemed to have become the natural majority in the state. The class-warfare atmosphere of Michigan politics continued up through 1962, when Republican George Romney only barely was elected governor. But, in office, Romney and his successor William Milliken made it clear that they accepted the welfare state policies which were the goal of the UAW leadership and the liberal Democrats. In the 1970s, as auto wages rose to levels unsurpassed by those in any other industry but steel, and as Michigan's standard of living surged ahead of those of other states, this seemed to be a state that had built an exemplary standard of living and had reached a solid political consensus.

The collapse of the auto industry in 1979–82 changed all that. As late as 1979, Michigan had income levels at least 10% above the national average, it had the nation's highest blue-collar wages, its residents had one of the highest rates of ownership of second homes and pleasure boats. The state government was one of the nation's most generous, to the poor and the unemployed and to others as well: it supported one of the nation's most distinguished and extensive systems of higher education; it had a fine system of state parks and recreation areas; it had been a pioneer in many efforts to end racial discrimination. Yet suddenly a state which seemed admirably governed by talented and enlightened moderates found itself suddenly faced with a crisis it seemed unable to handle. Chrysler nearly went bankrupt, Ford was in financial difficulty, and even General Motors had its first losses in years. The auto industry, which had grown faster than the economy for most of the 20th century, now seemed certain to grow more slowly; significantly for Michigan, its labor force, even given a recovery, seemed likely to grow not at all, after shrinking in 1979–82 by nearly half.

It took a few years to convince people that Michigan's golden years of auto-propelled prosperity would never return again. But by the middle 1980s they seemed to understand that and to realize that their problem was no longer how to divide up an automatically growing pie, but to bake an entirely new pie from scratch. The state's politics and its public life were knocked akilter by the suddenness of Michigan's economic crisis: the state's major institutions no longer work as they used to; the rules of the game seem permanently changed. The assumption in Michigan for 30 years has been that the way to handle recessions and spur economic growth is to increase government spending and stimulate the economy to spur auto sales. Now that assumption has been abandoned, in fact if not entirely in rhetoric. Now government is considered part of the problem rather than the solution.

Oddly, it has been a Democratic governor who has done most to help people reach those conclusions and put the state on the road to developing a more diversified private sector economy. James Blanchard was elected governor in 1982 largely because of his record, as a young congressman, of getting the Chrysler bailout passed in the House, and because of the mistakes of his opponent, Richard Headlee. His margin was an unspectacular 51%–45%, and the next year, after Democrats in the legislature passed a temporary tax increase, two state senators were recalled and the Republicans won control of the Senate. In 1984 Michigan, for 30 years one of the most Democratic states in national elections, went for Ronald Reagan by a 59%–40% margin, almost precisely the national average. Senator Carl Levin won reelection with only 53% (although one of his ads showed a videotape of the Republican candidate, former astronaut Jack Lousma, telling Japanese auto executives how pleased he was with his Toyota). Republicans who had gotten 40% of the vote for state House of Representatives in 1982 got 52% in 1984. All that seemed to indicate a Republican trend, a desire for lower taxes dominating politics just as the state's private economy was beginning to diversify and revive.

The diversification and revival continued through 1986. Michigan's population dropped 2.3% in 1980–83, the sharpest drop of any state, but in 1983–86 it was up 1%, more than any other Great Lakes industrial state. Unemployment was 15% at the trough of the recession in 1982–83, the nation's highest; it dropped sharply—by 1.9% in the single month of August 1986 alone—and was no worse than in Ohio or Illinois. More important, the revival was not just an uptick in the payrolls of the Big Three. Manufacturing jobs in 1986 were still more than 200,000 below the 1979 level of 1.2 million, but other work was up. Blanchard, an inveterate Michigan booster, sought out not just a new Mazda plant but smaller, more diverse new businesses; the state's strategy was to use Michigan's manufacturing expertise and specialize in high-skill, capital-intensive, flexible manufacturing, and it seemed to be working. Michigan's work force, unable to extract high wages from Americans who refused to buy poorly-designed, poorly-assembled cars, were now determined and apparently able to get high wages the old-fashioned way—to earn them. As the state's economy picked up, Blanchard was able to get rid of the temporary tax hike, thus depriving Republicans of their major issue, and to identify himself with the pride that was bursting out in almost every quarter of Michigan. In the process, his Democratic party seems to have become identified with the revival of the state's economy and to be reaping the political benefits.

That was frustrating for Republicans who believed, with some justice, that they had moved the state away from high taxes and big government and toward the policies for which Blanchard and the Democrats were receiving credit. But the Republicans were hampered by their own mistakes. Republican voters in the August 1986 primary chose precinct delegates who would end up determining the party's presidential preference in 1988; this was the first presidential contest in the nation, and backers of George Bush, Jack Kemp, and Pat Robertson were visible in the state. Robertson's appearances and the antics of the evangelicals (they wanted to nominate for attorney general a state senator who had called for the execution of a judge) made the Republicans look ridiculous to voters, as did the primary contest between Wayne County Executive William Lucas and auto customizer Dick Chrysler, when Chrysler was accused of a scheme for his employees to collect unemployment compensation while working. Lucas attracted national attention because he switched from the Democratic party in 1985 and because he is black; a former FBI agent and Wayne County Sheriff with a stern attitude toward crime and government spending, he provided a vivid contrast with Detroit Mayor Coleman Young, who is highly unpopular in the suburbs and outstate. But while the evidence suggests that Lucas lost few votes because of race (black secretary of state Richard Austin was reelected with 70% of the vote), the Lucas candidacy did not capture the imagination of most black voters. Voters were simply not in the market for a new governor. Suspense was minimal, turnout was low, and Blanchard won 68%–31%, the highest percentage since Fred Green won in 1928 and the best Democratic percentage since Stevens T. Mason won in 1835. Democrats captured 55% of the vote for state legislators, though Republicans still control the state Senate 20–18, and rebounded especially well in ancestrally Democratic Macomb County and Wayne County outside Detroit.

All this suggests that voters are confident Michigan is on the way to a sounder economy and are pleased with the leadership of Blanchard's Democrats. That does not mean that they have returned to the class-conscious politics of the Walter Reuther era when, for example, the Detroit metropolitan area delivered a 62%–38%, 379,000-vote margin for John Kennedy over Richard Nixon; metropolitan Detroit now casts a smaller share of the state's votes and has been more evenly divided between the parties: 49%–44% for Carter over Reagan in 1980, for example, and 54%–46% for Reagan in 1984. Michigan moved only hesitatingly to the Democrats in the recession year of 1982, but overwhelmingly to them in the revival year of 1986—one more reversal of the old rules.

Governor. The 1980s in Michigan saw the failure of the old politics of the middle, the politics of seeking a boardroom-like consensus among the enlightened, well-intentioned half a dozen men who ran Michigan's big institutions, the Big Three, the UAW, the utilities. It seems to be seeing the success of a new politics of the middle—of encouraging small business units and of lowering taxes and refraining from intervening in the economy to maintain everyone at their status quo. Ironically, it was the Democrats who created the old politics but a Republican, William Milliken

(Governor from 1969–82), was its most skilled practitioner. Republicans, on the other hand, did much to invent the new politics, but its best-known practitioner is the Democratic Governor, James Blanchard. With his huge margin in 1986, and no competitors of stature on the scene, Blanchard is the commanding figure of Michigan politics and a governor who, if the economic revival of the state continues, could remain in office as long as his predecessor—or more.

Senators. Michigan has two Democratic Senators, both strong opponents of the Reagan Administration, but with different backgrounds and personalities. Donald Riegle, while still in his 40s, has served more than 20 years in Congress, chastened a bit in his ambitions but not cynical, a little mellower than he used to be but scarcely less energetic. Riegle was first elected to Congress in 1966 as a Republican from Flint; he won UAW support for his record, supported Pete McCloskey against Richard Nixon in 1972, and became a Democrat in 1973. He won a close race in 1976 distinguished by a particularly nasty story in the *Detroit News,* featuring extracts from tapes of Riegle and a woman he had an affair with; a backlash against the often harshly partisan *News* probably helped elect Riegle. He spent most of his years in the House and has spent most of his years in the Senate as part of the minority party, critical of those in power, sometimes caustically and bitterly so; yet he does have some accomplishments of his own.

Riegle has spent most of his Senate career on money committees: Commerce, Banking, Budget, and, in 1987, as one of three new Democrats on Finance tilting it away from the Oil Patch predilections of its new chairman Lloyd Bentsen. One highlight of his service was the Chrysler loan guarantee law, which, as a member of the Banking Committee from Michigan, it fell on him to manage; but his was a heartfelt, not a perfunctory approach. He has spent much time hustling UDAG (Urban Development Action) grants for Michigan cities. His voting record is among the most liberal of Senators on economic and on other issues as well; he is a reliable ally of the United Auto Workers and organized labor generally. Riegle voted for most of the Reagan economic plan, but he soon became one of the harshest critics of Reaganomics, appearing sometimes on national newscasts excoriating Administration witnesses. Critics of Riegle see him as a grandstander or even a demagogue, a Senator whose denunciations, as one source told the *Washington Post,* routinely empty out the Senate chamber. His defenders see him as a principled advocate of policies to help the ordinary citizen, particularly in Michigan as economic disaster struck. Some would argue that his responsiveness to the UAW and the Big Three auto companies contributed more to Michigan's problems than its solutions. But as a hard-working advocate of what are generally seen as the economic interests of the state, he is in a good position to benefit politically if the state's economic revival is sustained.

Riegle was notorious when he was in the House for his national ambitions. Now his record is so heavily tailored to his state that he seems to have none, although he could get some attention as chairman of the Senate's space subcommittee; he has been ripping into NASA since the *Challenger* disaster. He won his seat against tough competition in the 1976 primary (Representative James O'Hara, Secretary of State Richard Austin) and has beaten two competent moderate Republican congressmen (Marvin Esch in 1976, Philip Ruppe in 1982). He seems now to have as safe a seat as most Senators from large states ever get, which is not very safe; but he has gone some way to persuading constituents that he is a workhorse with real accomplishments as well as an articulate rhetorical tribune of the people. Possible Republican challengers in 1988 include Levin's 1984 opponent, astronaut Jack Lousma, unsuccessful 1986 governor candidate Dick Chrysler (no relation to the auto company), state Senate Majority Leader John Engler, and GOP State Chairman Spencer Abraham.

Michigan's junior Senator, Carl Levin, is now the third ranking Democrat on the Armed Services Committee, behind only Sam Nunn and John Stennis. He is the highest ranking Armed Services member in many years with a generally dovish approach to foreign and defense policy. Levin has been an opponent of the MX missile and a voice of caution on the Strategic Defense Initiative; he has led criticism of the Administration's interpretation of the ABM treaty which would permit it to do more SDI testing than Levin thinks is allowed or wise. He takes sides sometimes with the military reform group led by William Cohen and others, who emphasize the need for creative strategy and simple, reliable weapons, but he seems generally more interested in furthering arms control and less eager to build weapons systems.

Levin is smart and dogged, a stickler for detail and willing to stick his neck out. He was one of three Senators who voted against the 1986 tax reform bill on final passage—a vote that will likely look either very good or very bad in a few years. He was particularly incensed with the provision allowing homeowners to deduct interest when they remortgage their houses but was unable to come up with a way to give renters a corresponding advantage. His record on domestic issues is, according to the ratings groups, one of the most liberal in the Senate. He supports relatively generous funding of most domestic programs, but is also receptive to arguments that things need to be done differently. He is a man of passionate convictions who is also capable of understanding the passions of others—which is to say a naturally effective legislator.

Levin came to the Senate with a background mostly in local, not national, politics; not often given to grandstanding, he is more self-effacing than ambitious. In racially torn Detroit in the years just after the 1967 riots, he won elections to the City Council—and led the field in 1973— with support from both black and white voters. He is anything but a perfectly packaged candidate—rumpled, balding, inclined to speak his mind when it might be more prudent to be silent. In elections he has benefited twice from opponents' mistakes. In 1978 incumbent Robert Griffin announced his retirement, proceeded to miss dozens of roll call votes, and then reentered the race. Levin attacked him for absenteeism as much for his Republican stands on issues; and Griffin, who through most of his career was a hard-working advocate and an effective partisan, lost. In 1984, he was helped by the praise for Toyota from his opponent, former astronaut Jack Lousma. It helped too that Lousma had not lived in the state most of his adult life, and that the space program is not a particular favorite of Michigan. Yet even so Levin won only a narrow victory in a year when Republicans generally did well in Michigan. Their weaker performance may augur well for his reelection chances in 1990, but he is not likely to trim many sails even if that is not the case.

Presidential politics. Michigan, which seemed in the 1960s to be one of the most Democratic states, hasn't voted for a Democratic presidential candidate since. It has delivered solid majorities not just to native son Gerald Ford (who would surely have lost the state if he were from Ohio) but twice for Ronald Reagan. The state's movement away from its traditional labor-versus-management politics and its preference for big-government solutions are evident perhaps in the 1980 and certainly in the 1984 results. James Blanchard's victory and the Democrats' general success suggests that Democrats, at least the right kind of Democrats, will enjoy a natural advantage in Michigan again in 1988. But no one can be sure.

In the 1980s Michigan is attracting attention as a battleground for the Republican nomination. Under an old state law that the Democrats can't use because of their party rules but which Republicans do follow, the Republican precinct delegates elected in August 1986 are to choose county convention delegates in mid-January 1988, who in turn will elect delegates to a state convention expected to be scheduled for January 29 and 30 in Grand Rapids. That is where national convention delegates will be chosen: your last chance to be guaranteed a vote in the county conventions has passed unless you were elected precinct delegate in August 1986. George Bush's PAC spent more than $1 million on this contest; Jack Kemp was highly active and visible in a state which resembles his own Buffalo area congressional district; Pat Robertson, not officially a candidate, saw his Freedom Council, a non-profit organization which according to IRS rules is not supposed to take part in elections, encourage evangelical-minded voters to run for precinct delegate. But no one knows who won. Precinct delegates' preferences aren't listed on the ballot and there is nothing to stop them from changing their minds many times before 1988. The results were not easy to tally, because precincts are of many different sizes and in different counties elect different numbers of delegates; each of the 18 Congressional Districts, no matter how many Republican voters it has or (as in the majority-black 1st and 13th Districts) how few, elects the same two national convention delegates. So Michigan's Republican contest will be the first early test in either party with significant numbers of black voters. On election night in

August 1986 many of the pro-Robertson delegate candidates who had opposition on the ballot were beaten, and Bush spokesmen were claiming just under 50% of the precinct delegates, but at the February 1987 state convention they seemed well short of that, and control seemed to be in the hands of a coalition of supporters of Robertson, who had more of the delegates, and Kemp, who had a disproportionate number of the leaders. Bush supporters point out that nothing presidential was at stake in this convention and that turnout of delegates may be different in 1988. But it seems likely that Bush will have to make inroads into the opposition if he is to duplicate in 1988 the victory he won in Michigan in 1980.

Michigan Democrats, who are prevented by party rules from having precinct delegates elected before 1988 to choose their national convention delegations, have chosen them in almost every possible way, from the presidential primary which George Wallace won in 1972 to the firehouse primary of 1984, in which anyone could show up at one of several hundred designated sites around the state and declare, publicly, his or her preference—publicly, because technically this was a caucus and caucus participants, who theoretically represent others, aren't supposed to vote in secret. But operationally it resembled a primary, and Gary Hart's supporters cried foul: some caucus sites were union halls, and the UAW was very much in Walter Mondale's corner. Not surprisingly, Mondale won solidly—and got big majorities in the black districts, thanks in large part to the anything-but-shy support of Detroit Mayor Coleman Young. For 1988 the state party has modified the system only slightly, reducing from 20% to 15% the percentage of the vote a candidate needs to qualify for delegates in a congressional district caucus. This responds to one of Jesse Jackson's 1984 criticisms but is likely to only marginally increase the splintering of the vote.

Congressional districting. Michigan lost a seat in the 1980 Census, and everyone decided it would be Blanchard's when he decided to run for governor. The adjustments made to other district lines were not especially elegant but mostly protected incumbents. Michigan now has several closely contested seats, but also elects some senior and powerful members of both parties: Democratic committee chairmen John Dingell and William Ford, from Detroit's southwestern industrial suburbs, and Republicans William Broomfield, ranking member of Foreign Affairs, and Guy Vander Jagt, head of his party's campaign committee. Two of the leading debaters on aid to the Nicaraguan contras, Broomfield, who favors it, and Democrat David Bonior, who is opposed, come from adjoining districts in the suburbs north of Detroit.

The People: Est. Pop. 1986: 9,145,000; Pop. 1980: 9,262,078, dn. 1.3% 1980–86 and up 4.3% 1970–80; 3.79% of U.S. total, 8th largest. 16% with 1–3 yrs. col., 15% with 4+ yrs. col.; 10.4% below poverty level. Single ancestry: 8% German, English, 4% Polish, 3% Irish, 2% Dutch, Italian, French, 1% Scottish, Swedish, Hungarian. Households (1980): 75% family, 42% with children, 61% married couples; 27.3% housing units rented; median monthly rent: $197; median house value: $39,000. Voting age pop. (1980): 6,510,092; 12% Black, 1% Spanish origin, 1% Asian origin. Registered voters (1986): 5,790,753; no party registration.

1986 Share of Federal Tax Burden: $27,728,000,000; 3.69% of U.S. total, 9th largest.

1986 Share of Federal Expenditures

	Total		Non-Defense		Defense	
Total Expend	$23,402m	(2.82%)	$20,232m	(3.37%)	$3,170m	(1.38%)
St/Lcl Grants	4,354m	(3.87%)	4,351m	(3.87%)	2m	(1.80%)
Salary/Wages	1,959m	(1.62%)	1,337m	(2.28%)	622m	(1.00%)
Pymnts to Indiv	13,491m	(3.70%)	13,301m	(3.83%)	190m	(1.07%)
Procurement	3,101m	(1.51%)	749m	(1.35%)	2,352m	(1.57%)
Research/Other	498m	(1.87%)	496m	(1.86%)	2m	(5.31%)

Political Lineup: Governor, James J. (Jim) Blanchard (D); Lt. Gov., Martha W. Griffiths (D); Secy. of State, Richard H. Austin (D); Atty. Gen., Frank J. Kelley (D). State Senate, 38 (20 R and 18 D); State House of Representatives, 110 (64 D and 46 R). Senators, Donald W. Riegle, Jr. (D) and Carl Levin (D). Representatives, 18 (11 D and 7 R).

1984 Presidential Vote

Reagan (R) 2,251,571 (59%)
Mondale (D) 1,529,638 (40%)

1980 Presidential Vote

Reagan (R) 1,915,225 (49%)
Carter (D) 1,661,532 (42%)
Anderson (I) 275,223 (7%)

GOVERNOR

Gov. James J. (Jim) Blanchard (D)

Elected 1982, term expires Jan. 1991; b. Aug. 8, 1942, Detroit; home, Pleasant Ridge; MI St. U., B.A. 1964, M.B.A. 1965, U. of MN, J.D. 1968; Unitarian; married (Paula).

Career: Legal Aide, MI Secy. of State, 1968; Asst. Atty. Gen. of MI, 1969–73; U.S. House of Reps., 1974–1982.

Office: Capitol Bldg., Lansing 48909, 517-373-3400.

Election Results

1986 gen.	James J. (Jim) Blanchard (D) . .	1,632,138	(68%)
	William Lucas (R)	753,647	(31%)
1986 prim.	James J. (Jim) Blanchard (D) . .	428,125	(93%)
	Henry Wilson (D).	28,940	(3%)
1982 gen.	James J. (Jim) Blanchard (D) . .	1,561,291	(51%)
	Richard H. Headlee (R).	1,369,582	(45%)

SENATORS

Sen. Donald W. Riegle, Jr. (D)

Elected 1976, seat up 1988; b. Feb. 4, 1938, Flint; home, Flint; Flint Jr. Col., W. MI U., U. of MI, B.A. 1960, MI St. U., M.B.A. 1961, Harvard U. Grad. Sch., 1964–66; United Methodist; married (Lori).

Career: Consultant, IBM Corp., 1961–64; Faculty Mbr., MI St. U., Boston U., Harvard U., U. of Southern CA; U.S. House of Reps., 1967–77.

Offices: 105 DSOB 20510, 202-224-4822. Also 1850 McNamara Bldg., Detroit 48226, 313-226-3188; 30800 Van Dyke, 3d floor, Warren 48093, 313-573-9017; Sabuco Bldg., Ste. 910, 352 Saginaw St., Flint 48502, 313-234-5621; Washington Sq. Bldg., Ste. 705, 109 W. Michigan Ave., Lansing 48933, 517-377-1713; Fed. Bldg., Rm. 716, Grand Rapids 49503, 616-456-2592; 309 E. Front St., Traverse City 49685, 616-946-1300; and 200 W. Washington, Ste. 31, Marquette 49855, 906-228-7457.

Committees: *Banking, Housing and Urban Affairs* (3d of 11 D). Subcommittees: Housing and Urban Affairs; Securities (Chairman). *Budget* (5th of 13 D). *Commerce, Science, and Transportation* (4th of 11 D). Subcommittees: Foreign Commerce and Tourism; Science, Technology and Space (Chairman); Surface Transportation. *Finance* (9th of 11 D). Subcommittees: Health; International Debt; International Trade.

Group Ratings

	ADA	ACLU	COPE	CFA	LCV	ACU	NTU	NSI	COC	CEI
1986	95	85	94	81	90	9	32	10	26	22
1985	95	—	94	73	—	4	25	—	24	—

National Journal Ratings

	1986 LIB — 1986 CONS			1985 LIB — 1985 CONS		
Economic	94%	—	0%	95%	—	0%
Social	79%	—	16%	82%	—	17%
Foreign	75%	—	0%	81%	—	18%

Key Votes

1) Ease Gun Cont	FOR	5) Grm-Rdmn Def Red	AGN	9) Rehnquist Nom	AGN
2) Immig Reform	AGN	6) Contra Aid	AGN	10) Tax Reform	FOR
3) Lmt Text Imp	FOR	7) SDI Funding	AGN	11) Drug Death Pen	AGN
4) Aid Tobac Ind	AGN	8) Lmt PAC Contrib	FOR	12) S Africa Sanc	FOR

Election Results

1982 general	Donald W. Riegle, Jr. (D).............	1,728,793	(58%)	($1,583,439)
	Philip E. Ruppe (R).................	1,223,286	(41%)	($1,045,545)
1982 primary	Donald W. Riegle, Jr. (D).............	633,028	(100%)	
1976 general	Donald W. Riegle, Jr. (D).............	1,831,031	(52%)	($795,821)
	Marvin L. Esch (R)	1,635,087	(47%)	($909,564)

Campaign Contributions and Expenditures

1978-82		Direct Cont. 1981-82		PACS Breakdown			
Receipts	$1,845,680	Indiv.	$1,044,110	Agr	$48,600	Ideo	$56,701
Expend.	$1,585,439	Party	$37,005	Bus	$220,853	Lbr	$240,621
Unspent	$274,240	PACS	$610,646	Hlth	$9,030	Prof	$14,950

Sen. Carl Levin (D)

Elected 1978, seat up 1990; b. June 28, 1934, Detroit; home, Detroit; Swarthmore Col., B.A. 1956, Harvard U., LL.B. 1959; Jewish; married (Barbara).

Career: Practicing atty.; Asst. Atty. Gen. of MI and Gen. Counsel for the MI Civil Rights Comm., 1964–67; Spec. Asst. Atty. Gen. of MI and Chief Appellate Defender for the City of Detroit, 1967–69; Detroit City Cncl., 1969–78, Pres., 1973–78.

Offices: 459 RSOB 20510, 202-224-6221. Also 1860 McNamara Bldg., 477 Michigan Ave., Detroit 48226, 313-226-6020; Fed. Bldg., 145 Water St., Rm. 102, Alpena 49707, 517-354-5520; 2409 1st Ave., Escanaba 49829, 517-789-0052; Gerald R. Ford Fed. Bldg., 110 Michigan Ave. N.W., Rm. 134, Grand Rapids 49503, 616-456-2531; 124 W. Michigan Ave., Rm. G30, Lansing 48933, 517-377-1508; P.O. Box 817, Saginaw 48606, 517-754-4562; 24580 Cunningham, Rm. 110, Warren 48091, 313-759-0477.

Committees: *Armed Services* (4th of 11 D). Subcommittees: Conventional Forces and Alliance Defense (Chairman); Stategic Forces and Nuclear Defense; Readiness, Sustainability and Support. *Governmental Affairs* (4th of 8 D). Subcommittees: Federal Spending, Budget and Accounting; Government Efficiency, Federalism and the District of Columbia; Oversight of Government Management (Chairman); Investigations. *Small Business* (5th of 10 D). Subcommittees: Innovation, Technology and Productivity (Chairman); Rural Economy and Family Farming.

Group Ratings

	ADA	ACLU	COPE	CFA	LCV	ACU	NTU	NSI	COC	CEI
1986	90	100	94	93	81	9	45	10	26	26
1985	85	—	95	80	—	4	27	—	31	—

National Journal Ratings

	1986 LIB — 1986 CONS		1985 LIB — 1985 CONS	
Economic	82% —	16%	89% —	8%
Social	90% —	8%	88% —	0%
Foreign	70% —	29%	82% —	15%

Key Votes

1) Ease Gun Cont	AGN	5) Grm-Rdmn Def Red	FOR	9) Rehnquist Nom	AGN
2) Immig Reform	AGN	6) Contra Aid	AGN	10) Tax Reform	AGN
3) Lmt Text Imp	FOR	7) SDI Funding	AGN	11) Drug Death Pen	AGN
4) Aid Tobac Ind	AGN	8) Lmt PAC Contrib	FOR	12) S Africa Sanc	FOR

Election Results

1984 general	Carl Levin (D) 1,915,831	(52%)	($3,569,330)
	Jack Lousma (R). 1,745,302	(47%)	($1,765,786)
1984 primary	Carl Levin (D) unopposed		
1978 general	Carl Levin (D) 1,484,193	(52%)	($971,775)
	Robert P. Griffin (R) 1,362,165	(48%)	($1,681,550)

Campaign Contributions and Expenditures

1983-84		Direct Cont. 1983-84		PACS Breakdown 1983-84			
Receipts	$3,646,298	Indiv.	$2,734,684	Corp.	$70,665	T/M/H	$82,812
Expend.	$3,569,330	Party	$32,545	Labor	$274,879	Agr.	$15,350
Unspent	$55,177	PACS	$719,154	Ideo.	$270,901	CWOS	$4,850

FIRST DISTRICT

If you want to see, in steel and concrete, factory and house, the rise and the fall of Michigan's auto industry over the last 80 years, one place to come is the north central portion of the city of Detroit and the close-in suburb of Highland Park, which comprises Michigan's 1st Congressional District. In 1903 when Henry Ford set up his company—and there were as many fledgling auto companies as there are computer chip companies today—this whole area was vacant, flat farmland and scrubby swamp on the northern and western edges of urban settlement. There the young automakers decided to build their first big factories, like the huge Ford Highland Park plant, on cheap land at the city's outskirts. Railroad tracks were laid, to bring in steel and coal, and neighborhoods were laid out, on straight streets.

The houses sprang up rapidly, with whole square miles being built up within a single year: workingmen's cottages for the Polish and other immigrants on the city's east side, larger and more comfortable houses for the rapidly growing middle class on the northwest side as one got farther away from the factories themselves. These factories today still form a kind of ring about five miles from downtown Detroit—a line that coincides with the southern limits of the 1st District. But the plants are mostly vacant now. Most of the Highland Park plant—where Ford offered to pay workers $5 a day in 1914—has been torn down; the old DeSoto assembly plant is long gone; even the Cadillac plant is due to be phased out, to be replaced by a new facility out near today's edge of urban settlement. GM built a new plant in an area called Poletown, but only after great civic controversy—a reminder of why managements instinctively prefer vacant, cheap, unoccupied lands for new plants.

Just as the auto industry and the neighborhoods were built quickly, so they changed quickly, and each time the change surprised people. The most noticeable movement was racial change. At the end of World War II, the area that is now the 1st District, extending westward almost all the way to Detroit's city limits, was almost fully built up, with a population somewhat larger than today's—and virtually all white. That changed rapidly. Thousands of blacks who came to Detroit during the war left the small ghettos where they had been confined, while whites fled to the outer limits of the city or the FHA-financed suburbs. Whole square miles of Detroit changed racial composition within a year or two—just as rapidly as they had been built. That process continued into the 1960s and was accelerated by the riots of 1967; that was when most of Detroit's Jewish population moved to the suburbs. Even the city's most affluent areas, just north of Highland Park, were opened up to blacks; today some of the most elegant housing in the Detroit area—the kind they don't build any more—can be found in black or integrated neighborhoods.

The 1st district is now the home of most of Detroit's successful black middle and upper classes, although some are moving on to suburbs like Southfield. Evidence of social disorganization—depopulation, high crime, lack of voter participation—are lower here than in the neighboring 13th District; this is an area with many stable households and families with children. Even so, there is still an unsettling amount of crime, and an unwillingness, based partly on fear, among law-abiding citizens to do much about it.

The 1st District is one of the most heavily Democratic districts in the country—almost a unanimously Democratic district in national elections. Its voters are articulate, active in civic and political affairs, upwardly mobile—but none of these qualities has tended to make them, as some conservatives hoped, more Republican. On the contrary, they seem more fiercely anti-Republican than the blacks, many of them members of tradition-minded churches, who are the only voters in less pleasant neighborhoods.

The 1st District's congressman is John Conyers, a Democrat who was only the fifth black in the House when he was first elected at age 34 in 1964. Conyers's father was an activist in the United Auto Workers, allied with the group ousted by Walter Reuther in 1947 and attacked by some Reuther supporters as allies of the Communists. He was from his first years in the House the most militant, an opponent from the beginning of the Vietnam war, a critic of every Administration for spending too little on the poor. He was instrumental in setting up the Congressional Black Caucus, in part to get around the mellow ways of the older black members; now it is some of the younger blacks who are more inclined to work quietly within the system while Conyers seems more interested in denouncing and expressing his disgust. For a while he seemed to be an operator within the system in the 1960s; but, jeered by Detroit blacks when he tried to calm the 1967 riot, rebuffed totally when he tried to get a high guaranteed annual income for the poor, and disgusted when white Democratic colleagues opposed busing in 1972 (although they would have been defeated if they had not), he seems to have soured on everything but his own principles; he often appears more a disgusted observer than an involved participant in the House.

That has not prevented him from some workmanlike efforts as chairman of the Judiciary subcommittees first on Crime and then Criminal Justice. He opposes anything he regards as an infringement on civil liberties, and is not afraid to stand against a tide of opinion, opposing capital punishment on the drug bill in 1986 or opposing what he considered the abolition of the insanity defense after the Reagan assassination attempt in 1981. He has helped to stop revision of the federal criminal code, and in 1984 conducted hearings on police brutality in New York City heavily tilted against Mayor Edward Koch and the city's black police commissioner. After 20 years Conyers is still only the fifth-ranking Democrat on the Judiciary Committee, but he is considerably younger than all but one of the others (Robert Kastenmeier of Wisconsin) and could some day be chairman; while he might be as effective as Chairman Peter Rodino in bottling up legislation he doesn't like, it's not clear that he'd be as effective in advancing what he does. He is also second-ranking on Government Operations, behind the canny and anything-but-retiring Jack Brooks. So it is possible that Conyers could be a much more visible representative of the national Democratic party in the 1990s.

At home, Conyers does not always get along with local politicos; while his old ally Mayor Coleman Young and the UAW backed Walter Mondale in 1984, for example, he was backing Jesse Jackson. Not to great effect: in Michigan's unique "firehouse primary," Mondale beat Jackson in the two black-majority districts. Still, no one thinks Conyers is under any threat at home. He has not had significant opposition since he beat Richard Austin, now Michigan's secretary of state, by 108 votes out of 60,000 cast. He often wins with more than 90% of the vote.

The People: Pop. 1980: 514,560, dn. 10.0% 1970–80. Households (1980): 73% family, 44% with children, 44% married couples; 33.0% housing units rented; median monthly rent: $166; median house value: $21,400. Voting age pop. (1980): 349,182; 66% Black, 2% Spanish origin.

1984 Presidential Vote: Mondale (D) 151,800   (86%)
Reagan (R) 24,697   (14%)

Rep. John Conyers, Jr. (D)

Elected 1964; b. May 16, 1929, Detroit; home, Detroit; Wayne St. U., B.A. 1957, LL.B. 1958; Baptist; single.

Career: Army, Korea; Legis. Asst. to U.S. Rep. John D. Dingell, 1958–61; Practicing atty., 1959–61; Referee, MI Workmen's Compensation Dept., 1961–63.

Offices: 2313 RHOB 20515, 202-225-5126. Also 669 Fed. Bldg., 231 W. Lafayette St., Detroit 48226, 313-961-5670.

Committees: *Government Operations* (2d of 24 D). Subcommittees: Human Resources and Intergovernment Relations; Legislation and National Security. *Judiciary* (5th of 21 D). Subcommittees: Civil and Constitutional Rights; Criminal Justice (Chairman). *Small Business* (19th of 27 D). Subcommittee: Procurement, Innovation and Minority Enterprise Development (Chairman).

Group Ratings

	ADA	ACLU	COPE	CFA	LCV	ACU	NTU	NSI	COC	CEI
1986	85	100	91	83	97	0	34	11	9	13
1985	75	—	91	92	—	12	42	—	28	—

National Journal Ratings

	1986 LIB — 1986 CONS		1985 LIB — 1985 CONS	
Economic	71%	— 28%	67%	— 33%
Social	89%	— 0%	85%	— 0%
Foreign	80%	— 20%	75%	— 21%

Key Votes

1) Lmt Cln Water Act	AGN	5) Retain Gun Cont	FOR	9) Aid Angola Reb	AGN
2) Rpl Tobac Sub	FOR	6) Contra Aid	AGN	10) Tax Reform	AGN
3) Grm-Rdmn Def Red	AGN	7) Lmt Text Imp	FOR	11) S Africa Sanc	FOR
4) Ban Polygraph	FOR	8) Limit SDI	FOR	12) Immig Reform	—

Election Results

1986 general	John Conyers, Jr. (D)	94,307	(89%)	($163,360)
	Bill Ashe (R).	10,407	(10%)	
1986 primary	John Conyers, Jr. (D)	35,461	(89%)	
	Patricia Noble (D)	4,178	(11%)	
1984 general	John Conyers, Jr. (D)	152,432	(89%)	($34,451)
	Edward J. Mack (R).	17,393	(10%)	

Campaign Contributions and Expenditures

1985-86		Direct Cont. 1985-86		PACS Breakdown 1985-86			
Receipts	$132,208	Indiv.	$54,710	Corp.	$12,050	T/M/H	$15,325
Expend.	$163,360	Party	$187	Labor	$45,325	Agr.	$1,250
Unspent	$8,352	PACS	$75,450	Ideo.	$1,500	CWOS	$0

SECOND DISTRICT

Each spring in the 1840s, settlers fresh from steamer rides across Lake Erie trudged over the hills of southern Michigan, still wet with thawing snows, and founded the new communities that today dot the lower part of Michigan's Lower Peninsula. They were mostly New Englanders and Upstate New Yorkers of Yankee stock, and they brought with them their habits of literacy, community self-improvement, and strict morality. As the years went on, they led the nation on issues like women's rights, temperance, opposition to capital punishment, and resistance to the extension of slavery, and support of the new Republican party. Joined by German refugees from the failed revolutions of 1848, they formed prosperous farming and industrial communities, governed for years by folksy members of the local elite—the kind of men who, in Congress and the state legislature, formed the core of opposition to New Deal measures during Franklin D. Roosevelt's four terms and for years after.

The 2d Congressional District of Michigan includes much of this historic terrritory: Ann Arbor, where the University of Michigan was established in 1817; Jackson, where the Republican Party was founded in 1854; Hillsdale, a picturebook old town and home of E. Harold Munn, longtime Prohibition Party presidential candidate. Hillsdale College, founded in the 1850s, has always admitted women and blacks but has refused federal money because it doesn't want equal opportunity investigators around; its students never stopped wearing traditional clothes, always sported short hair, and never protested against the Vietnam war. The 2d District's eastern extremity also verges into the Detroit metropolitan area. It includes half of Livonia, which was farmland in 1950 and filled up with more than 100,000 people 20 years later, and the affluent suburban territory around the old town, redolent of its New England namesake, of Plymouth. On balance this is a Republican district, though parts of it have gone Democratic: Livonia, when economic issues recall residents' working-class origins and loyalties; Ann Arbor, when cultural or war issues turn out a leftish student vote. This made it a seriously contested seat in the 1970s, though no Democrat was able to combine the trends and win. Since the 1970s Ann Arbor was almost perfectly countercyclical, an indicator of the way the nation is not going: it went for George McGovern in 1972, U of M alumnus Gerald Ford in 1976, gave John Anderson a big vote in 1980, and voted twice against Ronald Reagan.

This rather disparate district was assembled to suit the political needs of Representative Carl Pursell and has done so. Pursell is a Republican, a rumpled and comfortable man who has been a professional legislator for almost 20 years. Elected to the House in 1976, he got a seat on the Appropriations Committee in his second term, and there has been a quiet but often effective legislator. He is one of those Republicans known briefly in the early 1980s as Gypsy Moths, who were uncomfortable with many of the Reagan budget cuts; he is also a leader of the 92 Group—moderate Republicans whose goal is to make their party a majority in the House by 1992. Pursell is not flashy or voluble on the floor, but works on the Labor-HHS-Education Subcommittee to preserve many programs that some Republicans would like to zero out, and he has been particularly assiduous on health issues and higher education. He organized a group of Northeast and Midwest Republicans to protect their regional interests; for much of the detail work on Capitol Hill comes in writing the formulas for federal disbursements that can make vast differences for local communities.

Nevertheless, Pursell's overall record on economic issues is more Republican than Democratic; on cultural and foreign policy issues, he is somewhat more liberal. This helps him in Ann

Arbor, the base for the liberal Democrat who nearly beat him in his first race in 1976; even so, against an Ann Arbor-based opponent he lost the city in 1986. However, he cleared more than 60% in each of the other outstate counties, with their long Republican traditions, and in his home base of Livonia and Plymouth he won 70% of the vote, for an overall showing of 59%. That is not quite overwhelming for a House veteran, but enough to indicate that he has a solid seat.

The People: Pop. 1980: 514,560, up 10.1% 1970–80. Households (1980): 73% family, 40% with children, 62% married couples; 30.7% housing units rented; median monthly rent: $251; median house value: $52,200. Voting age pop. (1980): 375,911; 5% Black, 1% Asian origin, 1% Spanish origin.

1984 Presidential Vote:
Reagan (R)	142,572	(64%)
Mondale (D)	79,004	(35%)

Rep. Carl D. Pursell (R)

Elected 1976; b. Dec. 19, 1932, Imlay City; home, Plymouth; E. MI U., B.A. 1957, M.A. 1962; Protestant; married (Peggy).

Career: Army, 1957–59; Educator; Businessman; Mbr., Wayne Cnty. Bd. of Commissioners, 1969–70; MI Senate, 1971–76.

Offices: 1414 LHOB 20515, 202-225-4401. Also 361 W. Eisenhower, Ann Arbor 48104, 313-761-7727; 134 N. Main, Plymouth 48170, 313-455-8830; and 111 N. West Ave., Jackson 49201, 517-787-0552.

Committees: *Appropriations* (10th of 22 R). Subcommittees: Energy and Water Development; Labor–Health and Human Services–Education.

Group Ratings

	ADA	ACLU	COPE	CFA	LCV	ACU	NTU	NSI	COC	CEI
1986	45	30	45	33	36	55	51	60	76	61
1985	15	—	45	33	—	71	54	—	75	—

National Journal Ratings

	1986 LIB — 1986 CONS			1985 LIB — 1985 CONS		
Economic	27%	—	72%	22%	—	78%
Social	44%	—	54%	53%	—	46%
Foreign	48%	—	52%	41%	—	59%

Key Votes

1) Lmt Cln Water Act	FOR	5) Retain Gun Cont	FOR	9) Aid Angola Reb	FOR
2) Rpl Tobac Sub	FOR	6) Contra Aid	FOR	10) Tax Reform	FOR
3) Grm-Rdmn Def Red	FOR	7) Lmt Text Imp	AGN	11) S Africa Sanc	FOR
4) Ban Polygraph	AGN	8) Limit SDI	FOR	12) Immig Reform	AGN

Election Results

1986 general	Carl D. Pursell (R)	79,567	(59%)	($140,396)
	Dean Baker (D)	55,204	(41%)	($32,181)
1986 primary	Carl D. Pursell (R)	25,995	(100%)	
1984 general	Carl D. Pursell (R)	140,688	(69%)	($124,941)
	Mike McCauley (D)	62,374	(30%)	($31,031)

Campaign Contributions and Expenditures

1985-86		Direct Cont. 1985-86		PACS Breakdown 1985-86			
Receipts	$231,209	Indiv.	$145,507	Corp.	$24,425	T/M/H	$25,700
Expend.	$140,396	Party	$6,440	Labor	$6,600	Agr.	$1,800
Unspent	$155,432	PACS	$66,515	Ideo.	$6,940	CWOS	$1,050

THIRD DISTRICT

The 3d Congressional District of Michigan is in the south central part of the state—a place first settled by migrants from New England and Upstate New York in the 1830s and a quiet, prosperous part of the nation ever since. The local economy has been in better shape than in many parts of Michigan. Battle Creek's largest industry is not autos, but cereal: it was at a sanitarium there that W. K. Kellogg invented corn flakes as a health food. Kalamazoo, the largest city, has a diversified industrial base; pharmaceuticals are a major employer as well as autos. Courthouse towns like Marshall and Charlotte look like museum pieces, with early Victorian homes and old-fashioned miniature downtowns. But these are not economically somnolent communities: people here have started small businesses, built them up, and made them significant employers for miles around. It's money from these innovations which has enabled people to keep the old building preserved; it would have been cheaper, after all, to tear them down or put aluminum siding all over them. And Lansing (whose west side is in the 3d), ailing in the early 1980s as state revenues and Oldsmobile sales went down, has had an economic revival in the middle 1980s.

Historically, this is all Republican territory, and has been since the party was founded nearby in Jackson in 1854. It was the kind of place where America seemed to work just fine, with no New Deal tinkering needed, thank you: people took care of each other, economic innovation and growth seemed to happen every generation, traditional morals and community institutions continued strong. The Republican Party represented all these things to the mostly Yankee stock people here (with some even more conservative Dutch in Kalamazoo); the Democrats represented the kind of corruption, ethnic discord, labor unrest, and exotic socialistic theories you got in Detroit or Chicago. But in the early 1970s, as metro Detroit trended Republican, outstate Michigan moved the other way. Culturally, people became more open to variety and tolerant of change; the old racially liberal traditions of outstate Republicanism, dating from Underground Railroad days, may have played a role here. On economic issues, the makeshift American welfare state came to be taken for granted, and even welcomed. State government and education were big employers in this part of Michigan, and people who believed in them found the Democrats more generous and more likeminded.

These changes paved the way for the House career of Democratic Congressman, Howard Wolpe. He came to the district from the West Coast and Washington as a teacher at Western Michigan University in Kalamazoo; he was elected to the city council and the state legislature; and he ran for Congress in 1976. He barely lost that year, but worked the next two years as a staffer for Senator Donald Riegle in Lansing, and then ran again and won in 1978. In his first term he got a seat on the Foreign Affairs Committee. In his second term, he became chairman of the Africa Subcommittee—an appropriate assignment: he lived for two years in Nigeria and later taught African political systems at Western Michigan University. In his third term he got a seat on the Budget Committee.

With all these assignments he has been busy in Washington—and in the 3d District as well. On African issues, he has generally been a leader, though he deferred somewhat to Congressional Black Caucus members in the successful drive for sanctions legislation against South Africa; he has been bitterly critical of the Reagan Administration's "constructive engagement" policy toward the South African regime. He has always been sympathetic to the leaders of African nations who wish to remain unaligned, away from the two superpowers, and has called on Americans to look at issues there more from these Africans' point of view; he has been slow to criticize African dictators like Ethiopia's Mengistu even when their policies have led to famine and deliberate starvation. He has urged the United States to spend more on famine relief and seems to see more aid, rather than a turn to free enterprise, as providing the best chance for economic growth. He has been the lead opponent of American aid to Jonas Savimbi and his UNITA group that seeks to overthrow the Cuban-supported Angolan government; he has pushed too for a policy to get South Africa to withdraw from Namibia.

On the budget, Wolpe has worked with other Democrats across a broad spectrum, including Chairman William Gray and Texan Marvin Leath, to come up with party alternatives; he ardently supported Leath's challenge to Armed Services Committee Chairman Les Aspin. He believes strongly in government acting to boost economic development, and strongly supports programs like UDAG (Urban Development Action) and EDA (Economic Development Action) grants which are supposed to give seed money to development. He has worked hard to get such money into the 3d district, and maintains excellent relations with officials of both parties; in Michigan, during its economic downturn and in revival as well, such federal programs have become part of the fabric of local life and Wolpe in working on them is a kind of Burkean conservative, busy with the practical business of everyday life.

His opponents, in contrast, though their Republican Party was stitched for so many years within the local fabric, have sounded a shrill and theoretical note. Jackie McGregor, the Republican who ran against him in 1984 and 1986, called him "the liberal, far left radical puppet of the anti-American Third World," and was the intended beneficiary of a 1984 letter from then 4th district Republican Mark Siljander—a student to whom Wolpe gave a C at Western Michigan—urging ministers to "send another Christian to Congress"; to that Wolpe, who is Jewish, and quite a lot of other 3d district voters took umbrage. In this basically Republican district, he won with only 53% in 1984; he rose to 60%, as turnout fell, in 1986, running not too far behind Governor James Blanchard's record-breaking percentages. It probably helped that he raised and spent a phenomenal $852,000—evidence that he has plenty of support from both idealists and practical-minded people too. This is a seat Wolpe will probably always have to fight for, but he has certainly shown the energy and ingenuity to win.

The People: Pop. 1980: 514,560, up 3.7% 1970–80. Households (1980): 71% family, 40% with children, 58% married couples; 32.0% housing units rented; median monthly rent: $199; median house value: $35,800. Voting age pop. (1980): 367,512; 8% Black, 2% Spanish origin.

1984 Presidential Vote:
Reagan (R)	131,761	(63%)
Mondale (D)	75,868	(36%)

Rep. Howard E. Wolpe (D)

Elected 1978; b. Nov. 2, 1939, Los Angeles, CA; home, Lansing; Reed Col., B.A. 1960, M.I.T., Ph.D., 1967; Jewish; divorced.

Career: Prof., W. MI U., 1967–72; Kalamazoo City Cncl., 1969–72; MI House of Reps., 1972–76; Regional Rep. to U.S. Sen. Donald W. Riegle, Jr., 1976–78.

Offices: 1535 LHOB 20515, 202-225-5011. Also 938 W. Columbia Ave., Ste. B, Battle Creek 49015, 616-961-4576; 610 S. Burdick, Ste. 608, Kalamazoo 49007, 616-385-0039; and 316 N. Capitol, Lansing 48933, 517-482-9386.

Committees: *Budget* (7th of 21 D). Task Forces: Community and Natural Resources (Chairman); Defense and International Affairs. *Foreign Affairs* (8th of 27 D). Subcommittees: Africa (Chairman); International Economic Policy and Trade.

Group Ratings

	ADA	ACLU	COPE	CFA	LCV	ACU	NTU	NSI	COC	CEI
1986	90	95	90	75	89	5	32	0	33	23
1985	85	—	90	92	—	10	37	—	20	—

National Journal Ratings

	1986 LIB — 1986 CONS		1985 LIB — 1985 CONS	
Economic	66%	— 32%	71%	— 28%
Social	89%	— 0%	85%	— 0%
Foreign	80%	— 0%	85%	— 8%

Key Votes

1) Lmt Cln Water Act	FOR	5) Retain Gun Cont	FOR	9) Aid Angola Reb	AGN
2) Rpl Tobac Sub	FOR	6) Contra Aid	AGN	10) Tax Reform	FOR
3) Grm-Rdmn Def Red	FOR	7) Lmt Text Imp	FOR	11) S Africa Sanc	FOR
4) Ban Polygraph	FOR	8) Limit SDI	FOR	12) Immig Reform	FOR

Election Results

1986 general	Howard E. Wolpe (D)	78,720	(60%)	($852,746)
	Jackie McGregor (R)	51,678	(40%)	($223,082)
1986 primary	Howard E. Wolpe (D)	11,970	(100%)	
1984 general	Howard E. Wolpe (D)	106,505	(53%)	($393,790)
	Jackie McGregor (R)	94,714	(47%)	($231,307)

Campaign Contributions and Expenditures

1985-86		Direct Cont. 1985-86		PACS Breakdown 1985-86			
Receipts	$878,634	Indiv.	$545,619	Corp.	$16,540	T/M/H	$23,664
Expend.	$852,746	Party	$24,750	Labor	$140,254	Agr.	$6,750
Unspent	$107,429	PACS	$275,134	Ideo.	$87,726	CWOS	$200

FOURTH DISTRICT

The 4th Congressional District of Michigan is the southwest corner of the state, an area that, more than any other part of Michigan, gets its politics from other states. The Benton Harbor–St. Joseph area, the largest urban center in the district, is part of the Chicago media market, while Niles, just to the south, is within the orbit of South Bend, Indiana. The northern part of the district goes up to the city of Holland, in the center of the nation's premier Dutch-American community. The Dutch brought with them tulip bulbs, wooden shoes, native costumes and a determination to preserve their rigorous Christian Reformed religion; they have built small businesses and prospered, but have kept their mores very much the same, and their politics very conservative and Republican. Holland is in the only county of Michigan's 83 that went for Republican William Lucas over Governor James Blanchard in 1986. The southern part of the 4th District, along the Indiana border, was settled like most of southern Michigan by settlers of Yankee stock from Upstate New York and New England in the 1830s and 1840s. Its towns like to recall their heritage as stations on the Underground Railroad, and there is even a small rural black community in Cass County, dating from those days; these areas have stayed pretty solidly Republican over the years.

The 4th District has always been represented by Republicans who have no use for the welfare state. They include the crusty anti-New Dealer Clare Hoffman (1935–63); Edward Hutchinson (1963–77), the ranking Republican on the Judiciary Committee who defended Richard Nixon in the impeachment hearings; and David Stockman (1977–81), who as a provocative back-bencher in the House spent the Carter years learning the details of the federal budget that would serve him so well as President Reagan's OMB Director.

Stockman has been followed by a protégé in the seat—but not after a five-year hiatus in which the 4th District was represented by one of the wackiest and least effective congressmen on the right. That was Mark Siljander, who beat a Stockman choice in the 1981 special primary by 38%–36% and won the 1982 and 1984 with weak showings of 56% and 58% of the vote. His problem was not his opposition to the welfare state, but his evangelical religion and the way he inserted it into politics. In 1984 he urged ministers in the adjoining 3d District to "send another Christian to Congress" to replace a Jewish incumbent; in 1986, in a tape he sent out to 4th District ministers, he said, "We need to break the back of Satan and the lies that are coming our way." The comments not only sounded nutty to most voters, but made it clear that Siljander's definition of "Christian" excludes most of them. Siljander proved he had a significant core of support, but the very things that mobilized the core turned off most of the rest of the voters.

The winner, by a 55%–45% margin, was Fred Upton, a former aide to Stockman at OMB and grandson of the founder of Whirlpool, a big employer in St. Joseph. His voting record will probably not be much different from Siljander's, and he is likely to be no friend of the welfare state; but he is also likely to be more effective and to last longer in the House.

The People: Pop. 1980: 514,560, up 12.8% 1970–80. Households (1980): 77% family, 43% with children, 66% married couples; 24.4% housing units rented; median monthly rent: $178; median house value: $35,600. Voting age pop. (1980): 355,746; 6% Black, 1% Spanish origin.

1984 Presidential Vote:

Reagan (R)	140,832	(69%)
Mondale (D)	61,564	(30%)

Rep. Frederick S. Upton (R)

Elected 1986; b. Apr. 23, 1953, St. Joseph; home, St. Joseph; U. of MI, B.A. 1973, M.A. 1975; Protestant; married (Amey).

Career: Asst. Dir. for Legislative Affairs, U.S. Office of Mgt. and Budget, 1975–85.

Offices: 1607 LHOB 20515, 202-225-3761. Also 421 Main St., St. Joseph 49085, 616-982-1986; 225 W. 30th St., Holland 49423, 616-394-4900; .

Committees: *Public Works and Transportation* (20th of 20 R). Subcommittees: Surface Transportation; Water Resources. *Small Business* (16th of 17 R). Subcommittees: Exports, Tourism and Special Problems; Procurement, Innovation and Minority Enterprise Development. *Select Committee on Hunger* (7th of 10 R). Task Force: Domestic Task Force.

Group Ratings and Key Votes: Newly Elected

Election Results

1986 general	Frederick S. Upton (R)	70,331	(62%)	($382,663)
	Daniel Roche (D)	41,624	(37%)	($15,314)
1986 primary	Frederick S. Upton (R)	31,800	(55%)	
	Mark D. Siljander (R)	26,487	(45%)	
1984 general	Mark D. Siljander (R)	127,907	(67%)	($222,395)
	Charles S. Rodebaugh (D)	63,159	(33%)	($21,209)

Campaign Contributions and Expenditures

1985-86		Direct Cont. 1985-86		PACS Breakdown 1985-86			
Receipts	$383,071	Indiv.	$234,435	Corp.	$19,557	T/M/H	$24,422
Expend.	$382,663	Party	$10,370	Labor	$0	Agr.	$2,500
Unspent	$377	PACS	$53,154	Ideo.	$6,675	CWOS	$0
		Cand.	$95,002				

FIFTH DISTRICT

Grand Rapids, the second largest city in Michigan, though it is far smaller than Detroit, has bulked large in the politics of the state and, on occasion, the nation. Settled by Upstate New York Yankees, populated in large part by the descendants of Dutch immigrants, with a steadily growing economy based on such solid foundations as the furniture industry (rather than volatile automobiles), Grand Rapids has always been Michigan's premier Republican city. It was the home of Michigan's Republican boss in the 1920s and 1930s, Frank McKay, and of Arthur Vandenberg, the newspaper editor McKay helped to make U.S. Senator. Vandenberg survived the New Deal in office to become chairman of the Foreign Relations Committee in 1947, the man who made Harry Truman's postwar foreign policy truly bipartisan.

Vandenberg hoped to become president himself and never made it, but unknowingly (he died in 1951), he launched another president on his political career when he decided to beat Grand Rapids's isolationist congressman in the 1948 primary and backed a young lawyer and former University of Michigan football player, Gerald Ford. Congenial, hard-working, faithful to party and principle, Ford became House minority leader after the Republicans' 1964 debacle and Vice President in 1973, when Richard Nixon needed someone the Democratic Congress would confirm. The 5th District in turn helped to make Ford President, by electing (much to his surprise and shock) a Democrat as his successor in the House. That was one of the four Democratic victories in Republican districts, two of them in Michigan, that convinced many Republicans in 1974 that Nixon had to go. In fact, there had been a minor Democratic trend in Grand Rapids for several years, and Democrat Richard VanderVeen held the district in November 1974 and lost it only narrowly to Republican Harold Sawyer in 1976. Sawyer, thanks to his stormy temperament, nearly lost a couple of times later and retired in 1984.

Now the 5th District has, for the first time since Ford, a congressman it seems entirely comfortable with. He is Paul Henry, a former state senator, a former aide to John Anderson (before David Stockman was), a professor at Calvin College who was singled out for praise by no less than David Broder of the *Washington Post*. Henry won his primary easily against Sawyer's son, and then got the best percentage in the general election since Ford. In 1986, a good year for Democrats in Michigan, he raised that to 71%—better than Ford ever got.

In the House, Henry is a member of the Education and Labor and Science, Space and Technology Committees, and has been working to fashion government programs to achieve what he wants, rather than trying to abolish them altogether. He is a strong opponent of abortion, and not especially liberal on most cultural issues, has a mixed record on foreign policy, and sticks pretty close to Republican and free market principles on economics, apart from trade. He is a member of the House Wednesday Group, a moderate organization which has advanced some constructive proposals with success far disporportionate to its small numbers and unpivotal place in the balance of the House. He got a little publicity in 1987 when he opened up his family's finances to show how they did not live lavishly on the $77,400 congressional salary, although Henry promised to vote against increasing it.

The People: Pop. 1980: 514,560, up 9.5% 1970–80. Households (1980): 75% family, 43% with children, 63% married couples; 26.8% housing units rented; median monthly rent: $188; median house value: $38,400. Voting age pop. (1980): 359,611; 5% Black, 2% Spanish origin.

1984 Presidential Vote:

Reagan (R)	159,335	(68%)
Mondale (D)	73,908	(31%)

Rep. Paul B. Henry (R)

Elected 1984; b. July, 9, 1942, Chicago, IL; home, Grand Rapids; Wheaton Col., B.A. 1963, Duke U., M.A. 1968, Ph.D. 1970; Christian Reformed; married (Karen).

Career: Peace Corps, 1963–65; Legis. Asst. to U.S. Rep. John B. Anderson, 1968–69; Instructor, Duke U., 1969–70; Prof., Calvin Col., 1970–78; Mbr., MI Bd. of Ed., 1975–78; MI House of Reps., 1979–82; MI Sen., 1983–84.

Offices: 215 CHOB 20515, 202-225-3831. Also 166 Federal Bldg., Grand Rapids 49503, 616-451-8383.

Committees: *Education and Labor* (11th of 13 R). Subcommittees: Elementary, Secondary and Vocational Education; Employment Opportunities; Health and the Environment. *Science, Space and Technology* (11th of 27 R). Subcommittees: Natural Resources, Agriculture Research and Environment; Science, Research and Technology. *Select Committee on Aging* (21st of 26 R). Subcommittee: Retirement Income and Employment.

Group Ratings

	ADA	ACLU	COPE	CFA	LCV	ACU	NTU	NSI	COC	CEI
1986	40	20	32	50	63	45	59	50	89	54
1985	25	00	24	50	—	67	63	—	68	—

National Journal Ratings

	1986 LIB — 1986 CONS	1985 LIB — 1985 CONS
Economic	30% — 69%	27% — 71%
Social	35% — 64%	30% — 69%
Foreign	48% — 52%	41% — 58%

Key Votes

1) Lmt Cln Water Act	FOR	5) Retain Gun Cont	FOR	9) Aid Angola Reb	FOR
2) Rpl Tobac Sub	FOR	6) Contra Aid	FOR	10) Tax Reform	FOR
3) Grm-Rdmn Def Red	FOR	7) Lmt Text Imp	FOR	11) S Africa Sanc	FOR
4) Ban Polygraph	AGN	8) Limit SDI	FOR	12) Immig Reform	FOR

Election Results

1986 general	Paul B. Henry (R)	100,577	(71%)	($304,765)
	Teresa Decker (D)	40,608	(29%)	($17,074)
1986 primary	Paul B. Henry (R)	36,490	(100%)	
1984 general	Paul B. Henry (R)	140,131	(62%)	($450,266)
	Gary J. McInerney (D)	85,232	(38%)	($361,990)

Campaign Contributions and Expenditures

1985-86		Direct Cont. 1985-86		PACS Breakdown 1985-86			
Receipts	$344,221	Indiv.	$236,118	Corp.	$43,845	T/M/H	$45,018
Expend.	$304,765	Party	$3,368	Labor	$7,500	Agr.	$4,250
Unspent	$39,583	PACS	$107,193	Ideo.	$6,080	CWOS	$500

SIXTH DISTRICT

Centuries ago Ice Age glaciers scooped out tons of earth from the path before them and deposited them where they stopped, along a diagonal line in what now is the Lower Peninsula of Michigan. They left behind a row of lakes and hills through the otherwise flat—often monotonously flat—landscape. Through one of these belts of hills, and over rolling land to the north and west, lies the 6th Congressional District of Michigan. It is anchored, on either end, by giant auto plants, the main factories that produce Oldsmobiles (in Lansing) and Pontiacs (in Pontiac). The land in between is marginal farmland and was sparsely settled for years; in the last two decades, it has sprouted subdivisions, trailer parks, and rows of lakeside cottages for new residents who have left the Detroit metropolitan area. These are people who left the city to seek a more rural, culturally traditional environment in which to live and raise their children, and who in the prosperous Michigan of the 1960s and 1970s were able to do so and now with Michigan's economic revival can once again. Even Pontiac, though part of affluent suburban Oakland County, is outside the Detroit orbit, with its own newspaper and radio station, and its own population mix of blacks from the Black Belt of Alabama and whites from Appalachian Kentucky and Tennessee; it was the site of one of the nation's bitterest busing disputes in the early 1970s, with many of the whites leaving for its lake-studded suburb of Waterford Township.

The congressman from the 6th District is Democrat Bob Carr, at this point a battle-scarred but victorious veteran of congressional politics. He first ran for Congress in 1972, and as a 29-year-old Mark Spitz look-alike nearly beat a 16-year Republican incumbent. Two years later the man retired, and Carr won, and became one of the most outspoken of Watergate babies; it was he who in 1975 got the Democratic Caucus to vote against military aid to Cambodia as the Khmer Rouge were closing in on Phnom Penh; he served on the Armed Services Committee and opposed its hawkish majority often. On economics he started off a conventional pro-labor Democrat for years, but since the late 1970s, when he supported the Kemp–Roth tax cut, has been more cautious on economic issues. His foreign policy stands helped him in the 1970s, and like almost all of the Watergate class, he was reelected in 1976 and 1978. But in 1980, after Iran and Afghanistan, his dovish stands were a liability and he lost to Republican Jim Dunn. State Democrats pretty much gave up on him and took away some of his most Democratic precincts to help Howard Wolpe in the 3d District.

But Carr ran against Dunn in 1982 and, in the trough of the recession, won 51%–48%. He then got a seat on the Appropriations Committee, but not on its Defense Subcommittee, steered clear of most defense issues (though he calls on his expertise as a pilot sometimes) and concentrated on arranging federal aid programs for local areas, boosting the Pontiac Fiero, and raising plenty of campaign dollars. He also showed himself a more adroit campaigner than his opponent. In 1984 Republican Tom Ritter, with deep roots in Waterford, campaigned as a supporter of "family values," but Carr was able to attack him in ads for being late in child support payments. That enabled him to carry Oakland County when it was still rebelling against Governor James Blanchard's 1983 tax hike. In 1986 he faced Dunn (who lost a Senate primary in 1984) and charged him with supporting the (bipartisan) 1982 tax increase and turned aside criticism of his early 1970s support of liberalization of marijuana laws by saying that he (like many voters) had changed his mind. That, plus spending of $692,000, was enough to carry both Lansing and Pontiac areas and run almost even on the land in between, for a 57% win—his best percentage in what is now an 8–2 win-loss record. But he's likely to face serious challenges again, possibly from former state legislator Colleen Engler, the Republican lieutenant governor candidate in 1986.

The People: Pop. 1980: 514,559, up 19.0% 1970–80. Households (1980): 74% family, 45% with children, 62% married couples; 30.0% housing units rented; median monthly rent: $234; median house value: $46,700. Voting age pop. (1980): 360,961; 6% Black, 2% Spanish origin, 1% Asian origin.

1984 Presidential Vote: Reagan (R) 119,396   (63%)
Mondale (D) 68,578   (36%)

Rep. Robert (Bob) Carr (D)

Elected 1982; b. Mar. 27, 1943, Janesville, WI; home, Okemos; U. of WI, B.S. 1965, J.D. 1968, MI State U., 1968–69; Baptist; divorced.

Career: Staff Mbr., MI Senate Minor. Ldr.'s Ofc., 1968–69; A.A. to Atty. Gen. of MI, 1969–70; Asst. Atty. Gen. of MI, 1970–72; Counsel to MI Legislature Special Comm. on Legal Educ., 1972; Dem. Nominee for U.S. House of Reps., 1972, 1980; U.S. House of Reps., 1975–81.

Offices: 2439 RHOB 20515, 202-225-4872. Also 2848 E. Grand River, Ste. 1, E. Lansing 48823, 517-351-7203; and 91 N. Saginaw, Pontiac 48058, 313-332-2510.

Committees: *Appropriations* (31st of 35 D). Subcommittees: Commerce, Justice, State, and the Judiciary; Transportation. *Select Committee on Hunger* (9th of 16 D). Task Force: International Task Force.

Group Ratings

	ADA	ACLU	COPE	CFA	LCV	ACU	NTU	NSI	COC	CEI
1986	70	60	83	42	42	24	34	10	33	25
1985	65	—	82	33	—	15	39	—	50	—

National Journal Ratings

	1986 LIB — 1986 CONS		1985 LIB — 1985 CONS	
Economic	50%	— 48%	47%	— 53%
Social	44%	— 54%	60%	— 38%
Foreign	61%	— 37%	64%	— 33%

Key Votes

1) Lmt Cln Water Act	FOR	5) Retain Gun Cont	AGN	9) Aid Angola Reb	AGN
2) Rpl Tobac Sub	AGN	6) Contra Aid	AGN	10) Tax Reform	AGN
3) Grm-Rdmn Def Red	AGN	7) Lmt Text Imp	FOR	11) S Africa Sanc	FOR
4) Ban Polygraph	FOR	8) Limit SDI	FOR	12) Immig Reform	AGN

Election Results

1986 general	Robert (Bob) Carr (D)	74,927	(57%)	($692,787)
	Jim Dunn (R)	57,283	(43%)	($244,913)
1986 primary	Robert (Bob) Carr (D)	15,945	(94%)	
	Steven Carr (D)	1,043	(6%)	
1984 general	Robert (Bob) Carr (D)	106,705	(52%)	($569,900)
	Tom Ritter (R)	95,113	(47%)	($481,938)

Campaign Contributions and Expenditures

1985-86		Direct Cont. 1985-86		PACS Breakdown 1985-86			
Receipts	$734,919	Indiv.	$237,546	Corp.	$75,646	T/M/H	$76,139
Expend.	$692,787	Party	$25,937	Labor	$195,941	Agr.	$12,170
Debts	$52,534	PACS	$444,603	Ideo.	$73,572	CWOS	$11,135
		Cand.	$3,000				

SEVENTH DISTRICT

Flint, Michigan, with a metropolitan population of 500,000 and five major General Motors plants, for 60 years has been the nation's largest company town. For years 60% of Flint's wage earners were on the GM payroll; traffic jams came not after five, but at 3:30 when the shifts break. Even management is factory-oriented: the plushest residential district here has a panoramic view of a Chevrolet plant. For years civic life in Flint was dominated by Charles Stewart Mott, a member of the General Motors board of directors for 60 years and for most of that time the largest individual shareholder in the corporation; as a very old man he continued to run the Mott Foundation, one of the nation's largest, out of Flint and concentrated on local projects until his death at age 97.

For much of the early 1980s Flint seemed about to become an ex-company town. Flint was settled, mostly between 1910 and 1930, by migrants, from local rural areas, the American South, and Eastern Europe; the basic facts of life were set by the GM plants built by the 1920s and by the recognition, after turbulent sitdown strikes, of the UAW as the workers' bargaining agent in 1937. Layoffs were a fact of life for years, but the union and the company built the nation's most generous unemployment benefits, providing 95% of weekly non-overtime pay for 65 weeks. But they failed to plan for one contingency, the total collapse of American car sales following the 1979 oil shock. Suddenly, as they approached their 65th week, thousands of Flint workers were stunned to find that they were falling through the safety net, with nothing below to catch them. With unemployment rates up toward 20% in 1981 and 1982, the whole city withered: stores were forced to close, local businesses went bankrupt, and in most neighborhoods the bidding price for houses fell to zero.

Now Flint has come back, but in not quite the same form. There are fewer jobs at Buick, Chevrolet, and Fisher Body, and more of the GM payroll is working for the EDS computer processing subsidiary purchased from H. Ross Perot. Flint's downtown is spruced up with new (federally aided) projects, its shopping malls are humming, and real estate is worth something again. Politically, the conventional wisdom was always that recession turns Flint to the Democrats, inflation or racial problems to the Republicans. But in the middle 1980s Flint, like most of Michigan, responded positively to the leaders who took charge during the period of economic revival. Usually Democratic Flint and Genesee County gave Ronald Reagan a majority of its votes in 1984, after three years of recession, and it gave an overwhelming margin to Democratic Governor James Blanchard in 1986.

In House races there has been nothing like this partisan instability in the 7th Congressional District, which includes Flint, most of its suburbs, and the formerly rural and now growing county of Lapeer to the east, thanks largely to the popularity of Democratic Representative Dale Kildee. He was first elected when Donald Riegle ran for Senator in 1976 and he has been reelected easily, sometimes without Republican opposition, ever since. Kildee's strength is based on personal contact—he served 12 years in the legislature and in a 1974 Senate race had campaigned through most of Flint door to door—and on familiarity. This is one of the few congressional districts which coincides almost precisely with a television media market; so Kildee, as congressman and even as state senator, got plenty of free air time.

Kildee was once a seminarian, and his views on issues stem from deep moral beliefs. He comes out of the liberal Catholic tradition that recognizes a need to provide social services and help for the poor and disadvantaged, and he applies this approach to his work on the Education and Labor Committee. On foreign policy he is skeptical of American military involvement abroad; on cultural issues, he is an opponent of abortion and cautious about some other items on the standard liberal agenda. He has chaired the Human Resources Subcommittee of Education and Labor at a time when many of its programs have been under attack or subjected to cuts when his own predilections run in the other direction; he also serves on Interior where he has tended to support chairman Morris Udall. His efforts to change committees in 1983 were reportedly nixed by the Democratic leadership because—an example of his personal austerity—he opposed the congressional pay raise the year before.

The People: Pop. 1980: 514,560, up 5.0% 1970–80. Households (1980): 77% family, 47% with children, 61% married couples; 24.4% housing units rented; median monthly rent: $209; median house value: $36,800. Voting age pop. (1980): 346,868; 14% Black, 1% Spanish origin.

1984 Presidential Vote: Reagan (R) 112,880   (54%)
Mondale (D) 94,963   (45%)

Rep. Dale E. Kildee (D)

Elected 1976; b. Sept. 16, 1929, Flint; home, Flint; Sacred Heart Seminary, Detroit, B.A. 1952, U. of MI, M.A. 1961, Rotary Fellow, U. of Peshawar, Pakistan; Roman Catholic; married (Gayle).

Career: High sch. teacher, 1954–64; MI House of Reps., 1965–75; MI Senate, 1975–77.

Offices: 2432 RHOB 20515, 202-225-3611. Also 1176 Robert L. Longway Blvd., Flint 48503, 313-239-1437.

Committees: *Education and Labor* (7th of 21 D). Subcommittees: Elementary, Secondary, and Vocational Education; Human Resources (Chairman); Labor-Management Relations. *Interior and Insular Affairs* (9th of 26 D). Subcommittees: National Parks and Public Lands; Water and Power Resources.

Group Ratings

	ADA	ACLU	COPE	CFA	LCV	ACU	NTU	NSI	COC	CEI
1986	95	89	94	100	84	0	26	0	17	9
1985	85	—	93	82	—	5	33	—	25	—

National Journal Ratings

	1986 LIB — 1986 CONS	1985 LIB — 1985 CONS
Economic	87% — 0%	74% — 25%
Social	81% — 17%	54% — 45%
Foreign	80% — 0%	92% — 0%

Key Votes

1) Lmt Cln Water Act	AGN	5) Retain Gun Cont	FOR	9) Aid Angola Reb	AGN
2) Rpl Tobac Sub	—	6) Contra Aid	AGN	10) Tax Reform	FOR
3) Grm-Rdmn Def Red	AGN	7) Lmt Text Imp	FOR	11) S Africa Sanc	FOR
4) Ban Polygraph	FOR	8) Limit SDI	FOR	12) Immig Reform	FOR

Election Results

1986 general	Dale E. Kildee (D)	101,225	(80%)	($101,545)
	Trudie Callihan (R).	24,848	(19%)	
1986 primary	Dale E. Kildee (D)	25,180	(94%)	
	Samuel Johnson, Jr. (D)	1,511	(6%)	
1984 general	Dale E. Kildee (D)	145,070	(93%)	($59,927)
	Samuel Johnson, Jr. (I).	10,663	(7%)	

Campaign Contributions and Expenditures

1985-86		Direct Cont. 1985-86		PACS Breakdown 1985-86			
Receipts	$96,112	Indiv.	$13,728	Corp.	$8,800	T/M/H	$16,720
Expend.	$101,545	Party	$171	Labor	$51,490	Agr.	$1,050
Unspent	$984	PACS	$83,060	Ideo.	$5,000	CWOS	$0

EIGHTH DISTRICT

To understand the geography of the 8th Congressional District of Michigan, remember that Michigan's Lower Peninsula is shaped like the back of a mittened left hand. The 8th District includes most of the Thumb (as it actually is called locally) and the bottom part of the index finger. The Thumb is almost entirely agricultural, tilled by descendants of the Yankee, German, and Canadian farmers who settled it a little more than a century ago. Life's rhythms have changed little since then, although agriculture has become immensely more productive; the area's chief products are navy beans (used in Senate bean soup) and sugar beets. At the base of the index finger (this is not local nomenclature) are the old industrial cities of Saginaw and Bay City. Both have been important since the 19th century when Michigan was the nation's leading lumber producer and these cities were, briefly, its major lumber ports. Today their economy is based in large part on the auto industry; Saginaw remains the biggest producer of power steering equipment in the world.

For many years, both the Thumb and the Saginaw area were mainstays of the Republican Party. Their impact on national politics, however, was slight, except for the time a Saginaw congressman co-authored the Fordney–McCumber tariff, until 1974. Representative James Harvey was appointed a federal judge, and a special election was held in which Richard Nixon became the central issue. Nixon even campaigned in the Thumb, but for the second time, a longtime Republican outstate Michigan district rejected the President and voted Democratic.

The victor in that race, Bob Traxler, is still congressman today. His local political base is Bay City, the one traditionally Democratic part of the district. But in recent years, even before the collapse of the auto industry, he carried Saginaw easily, and he has run well in the Thumb also. Traxler has specialized in agriculture issues, and he is now second-ranking Democrat on two Appropriations subcommittees, Agriculture and HUD-Independent Agencies. Since the chairmen of these were born in 1910 and 1911 respectively, Traxler's chance of joining the "college of cardinals"—the old name for the chairmen of the Appropriations subcommittees—is excellent. Of the two posts, the more powerful is probably Agriculture, through which Jamie Whitten has had a major hand in shaping American farm and food policy for more than 30 years; on that subcommittee Traxler has been a major supporter of providing food for the poor—and for maintaining U.S. sugar prices at well above world levels. Traxler attached a rider giving $400 million in PIK certificates to farmers who lost their crops in 1986. Jovial and a seasoned legislator—he was first elected to the Michigan House in 1962—Traxler is effective at getting things done in Washington and remains popular at home where he has had no serious competition since 1976.

The People: Pop. 1980: 514,560, up 8.3% 1970–80. Households (1980): 78% family, 45% with children, 65% married couples; 22.0% housing units rented; median monthly rent: $189; median house value: $35,600. Voting age pop. (1980): 350,577; 6% Black, 3% Spanish origin.

1984 Presidential Vote:

Reagan (R)	122,705	(60%)
Mondale (D)	79,934	(39%)

Rep. Bob Traxler (D)

Elected Apr. 16, 1974; b. July 21, 1931, Kawkawlin; home, Bay City; MI St. U., B.A. 1952, Detroit Col. of Law, LL.B. 1959; Episcopalian; divorced.

Career: Army, 1953–55; Asst. Bay Cnty. Prosecutor, 1960–62; MI House of Reps., 1962–74, Major. Flr. Ldr., 1965–66.

Offices: 2336 RHOB 20515, 202-225-2806. Also New Fed. Bldg., Rm. 1051, 100 S. Warren St., Saginaw 48606, 517-754-4226; and Fed. Bldg., Rm. 317, 1000 Washington Ave., Bay City 48708, 517-894-2906.

Committees: *Appropriations* (13th of 35 D). Subcommittees: HUD–Independent Agencies; Legislative; Rural Development, Agriculture and Related Agencies. *Select Committee on Hunger* (3d of 16 D). Task Force: Domestic Task Force.

Group Ratings

	ADA	ACLU	COPE	CFA	LCV	ACU	NTU	NSI	COC	CEI
1986	80	73	86	83	43	9	25	0	29	14
1985	80	—	85	67	—	5	29	—	27	—

National Journal Ratings

	1986 LIB — 1986 CONS		1985 LIB — 1985 CONS	
Economic	82%	— 16%	85%	— 11%
Social	67%	— 33%	48%	— 52%
Foreign	67%	— 30%	85%	— 8%

Key Votes

1) Lmt Cln Water Act	FOR	5) Retain Gun Cont	AGN	9) Aid Angola Reb	AGN
2) Rpl Tobac Sub	AGN	6) Contra Aid	AGN	10) Tax Reform	FOR
3) Grm-Rdmn Def Red	AGN	7) Lmt Text Imp	FOR	11) S Africa Sanc	FOR
4) Ban Polygraph	FOR	8) Limit SDI	FOR	12) Immig Reform	FOR

Election Results

1986 general	Bob Traxler (D)......................	97,406	(73%)	($98,670)
	John Levi (R)	36,695	(27%)	($31,955)
1986 primary	Bob Traxler (D)......................	23,066	(64%)	
	Larry Samuelson (D)	1,632	(7%)	
1984 general	Bob Traxler (D)......................	126,161	(64%)	($123,732)
	John Heussner (R)	69,683	(36%)	($19,567)

Campaign Contributions and Expenditures

1985-86		Direct Cont. 1985-86		PACS Breakdown 1985-86			
Receipts	$149,142	Indiv.	$47,932	Corp.	$23,795	T/M/H	$26,599
Expend.	$98,670	Party	$106	Labor	$21,810	Agr.	$10,000
Unspent	$130,143	PACS	$88,264	Ideo.	$6,060	CWOS	$0

NINTH DISTRICT

Michigan's 9th Congressional District consists of the little finger of the hand that, on the map, forms Michigan's Lower Peninsula, extending upward from where it joins the palm around Grand Rapids up to the slightly cocked pinkie of the Leelenau Peninsula. This whole eastern shore of Lake Michigan is flanked by sand dunes, which have kept this side of Lake Michigan free of the heavy industrialization found on the Wisconsin, Illinois, and Indiana shores. It was not always so: its small industrial towns got their starts as lumber ports, when Michigan was the number-one lumber state in the country; and until several disastrous fires in the late 19th century, huge numbers of logs were floated down the rivers to Muskegon, Ludington, and Manistee. Each of these harbors lies at a river mouth; some have been sealed off by the dunes, while at others the lake waters, at record high levels, are lapping menacingly far up the docks. The dunes, and the peculiar climatic conditions produced by the Lake, have made this northern part of the country one of its major fruit and vegetable producers, specializing particularly in the tart cherries for which Traverse City, just below the Leelenau Peninsula, holds a festival every year. The 9th District also extends inland, to lake and resort country in the northern end and to farm country settled by Dutch immigrants in the southern end, around Grand Rapids.

This is one of the nation's most solidly Republican districts, despite some Democratic precincts in the small industrial city of Muskegon and a couple of the lumber towns, and it elects one of the nation's most prominent Republican congressmen, Guy Vander Jagt. He has a diverse background: he was a television newscaster and a state senator, and is both an attorney and an ordained minister. He prides himself on his speaking ability, and he is not one of those new-fashioned orators who speaks conversationally to the television camera. Vander Jagt thunders out his speeches, which he likes to practice while walking through the woods, and which he insists on delivering extemporaneously. He is cited by speech professors as an exemplary orator, though his style seems suited not to the television age, but to some earlier America, where eloquent phrases, heart-warming stories, and homey similes had the capacity to send chills up and down listeners' spines.

Vander Jagt's major job in the House has been as chairman of the House Republican Campaign Committee since 1975. He can claim credit for much of the Republican gains in 1978 and 1980, and for holding the party's losses in 1982 to 26 seats in a recession year. During Vander Jagt's tenure, the committee built up huge mailing lists and developed sophisticated media and polling techniques which enable it to step in and put massive resources—including prepared TV ads—into any campaign which shows signs of needing them, literally within 24 hours. Yet in the 1980s the yield from all this apparatus has been disappointing. His staff is competent and professional, but his credibility among PAC operatives, so critical to the funding of Republican candidacies, was injured by his predictions in 1981 that the Republicans would capture control of the House in 1982, and in 1983 and 1984 that the Republicans would make major gains as President Reagan won reelection. He was more cautious for 1986, and justifiably as it turned out; but the minimal net loss the Republicans achieved left them well short of a working, much less an actual, majority. Not all the blame can be laid at Vander Jagt's doorstep. Candidate recruiters cannot force talented politicians to run or prevent hamhanded candidates from making blunders. But Vander Jagt's committee inevitably lost some of its fundraising edge over the Democrats as Tony Coelho frankly copied its tactics, and the Republican did not match Coelho's strategic sense.

From time to time Vander Jagt has sought other positions, but his lack of legislative effort has been a handicap. He ran for House Republican leader after 1980, with support from many of the freshmen his committee had helped; but Robert Michel, more experienced on the floor and more knowledgeable about substance, won. In 1985 Vander Jagt thought momentarily about running for governor of Michigan—almost as preposterous an idea as the rumor someone spread that he was thinking of running for President. He is the number three Republican on the Ways and Means Committee, but he was not a force on the tax bill, and Dan Rostenkowski was able to treat him and the other Republican conferees with contempt. He still has skill at painting the broad picture in bright colors and vivid contrasts. But it is not clear now that that skill is being put to much practical use.

The People: Pop. 1980: 514,560, up 13.9% 1970–80. Households (1980): 77% family, 43% with children, 67% married couples; 20.9% housing units rented; median monthly rent: $163; median house value: $33,500. Voting age pop. (1980): 356,896; 4% Black, 1% Spanish origin.

1984 Presidential Vote: Reagan (R) 155,242   (69%)
Mondale (D) 69,276   (31%)

Rep. Guy Vander Jagt (R)

Elected 1966; b. Aug. 26, 1931, Cadillac; home, Luther; Hope Col., B.A. 1953, Yale U., B.D. 1955, Rotary Fellow, Bonn U., Germany, 1956, U. of MI, LL.B. 1960; Presbyterian; married (Carol).

Career: Practicing atty., 1960–64; MI Senate, 1965–66.

Offices: 2409 RHOB 20515, 202-225-3511. Also Roosevelt Park, 950 W. Norton Ave., Muskegon 49441, 616-733-3131; 31 W. E St., Holland 49423; 124 N. Division St., Traverse City 49684, 616-946-3832.

Committees: *Ways and Means* (3d of 13 R). Subcommittees: Select Revenue Measures (Ranking Member); Trade.

Group Ratings

	ADA	ACLU	COPE	CFA	LCV	ACU	NTU	NSI	COC	CEI
1986	0	5	16	17	32	79	52	90	89	73
1985	5	—	16	25	—	79	53	—	89	—

National Journal Ratings

	1986 LIB — 1986 CONS		1985 LIB — 1985 CONS	
Economic	12%	— 88%	15%	— 85%
Social	0%	— 89%	0%	— 76%
Foreign	24%	— 75%	0%	— 76%

Key Votes

1) Lmt Cln Water Act	FOR	5) Retain Gun Cont	AGN	9) Aid Angola Reb	FOR
2) Rpl Tobac Sub	AGN	6) Contra Aid	FOR	10) Tax Reform	FOR
3) Grm-Rdmn Def Red	—	7) Lmt Text Imp	AGN	11) S Africa Sanc	—
4) Ban Polygraph	AGN	8) Limit SDI	AGN	12) Immig Reform	AGN

Election Results

1986 general	Guy Vander Jagt (R)	89,991	(64%)	($398,996)
	Richard Anderson (D)	49,702	(36%)	($18,006)
1986 primary	Guy Vander Jagt (R)	38,079	(100%)	
1984 general	Guy Vander Jagt (R)	150,885	(71%)	($347,748)
	John M. Senger (D)	61,233	(29%)	($56,148)

Campaign Contributions and Expenditures

1985-86		Direct Cont. 1985-86		PACS Breakdown 1985-86			
Receipts	$428,048	Indiv.	$205,369	Corp.	$99,600	T/M/H	$86,830
Expend.	$398,996	Party	$7,391	Labor	$13,900	Agr.	$3,100
Unspent	$102,356	PACS	$228,809	Ideo.	$20,999	CWOS	$4,380

TENTH DISTRICT

The Yankee farmers who first settled Michigan's Lower Peninsula never moved north of Grand Rapids or Saginaw: the land thawed too late in the spring to plow and the frost came too soon in the fall for you to harvest your crops. So they left the forests of the northern half of the Lower Peninsula in place, and moved west, leaving lands here for the lumber barons to clear-cut later in the 19th century, leaving behind sawdust and stumps that caused huge forest fires. To this day, the timber growth along the inland lakes of the northern Lower Peninsula is new forest, only barely regenerated since that terrific pillage.

On both sides of the boundary of these forest lands and the farmland just to the south is the 10th Congressional District of Michigan, for many years one of the forgotten parts of America. It contains no great cities, although it has some small towns like Owosso, the boyhood home of Thomas E. Dewey, which once had reason to think they might turn into a Lansing or a Grand Rapids; it has college towns like Alma and Mount Pleasant and Big Rapids, where parka-clad students stomp to class through snow and under winter grey skies; it has Midland, home of Dow Chemical, a company that inspires almost unanimous loyalty here and bitter ostracism of any critic; it has also many of Michigan's ski resorts and some of its inland lakes. Here thousands of midwesterners spent summers, sleeping four to a room in log cabins or knotty pine cottages tightly spaced around the lakes, getting up at dawn to fish or, after sleeping late, watching the children swim in the icy green waters. In the fall there are traffic jams as thousands of men drive up north to hunt; in the winter thousands of young people come north to ski. Rapidly rising incomes in auto-affluent Michigan made this resort country accessible not just to white-collar and professional families, but increasingly to blue-collar families as well. And, as everyone got even more affluent and economically secure in the 1970s, they began moving up here as well: retirees, planning to spend the worst of the winter in Florida; young parents willing to give up larger paychecks to raise their families in a natural environment free from the social problems (drugs, crime, large numbers of blacks) they felt existed in Detroit. Since 1970 this part of Michigan has had the state's most rapid population growth.

That growth has made for political change. Ancestrally these were all Republican counties, suspicious of big cities and labor unions; many of their new residents come from Democratic families. It has been the scene of close congressional elections in 1978, 1980, 1984, and 1986, all of them involving Democrat Donald Albosta. A successful farmer, he made a name protesting the state's handling of PBB contamination; that helped him unseat a longtime Republican incumbent in 1978. He survived a tough challenge in 1980, but was beaten in 1984 after chairing the subcommittee investigating the Carter briefing books brouhaha; he argued, unconvincingly, that for the Reagan campaign to get a copy of these campaign documents amounted to theft of government property. This may have been one of those times when national fame is a political detriment; or the election may have been swung by Schuette's attack on Albosta for not seeking a seat on the Agriculture Committee.

Representative Schuette is young (30 when first elected), handsome, the stepson of the chairman of Dow Chemical, the chief (and virtually only) employer in Midland and a company which inspires among many local residents feelings of great warmth and allegiance. He has spent vast sums (over $1.5 million in two elections), run well-organized computerized campaigns, and benefited not only from issues but from the underlying mood of affirmation which worked against a protest candidate like Albosta. Schuette took a seat on Agriculture and promised to keep it, sought government aid for local bean farmers while voting conservative on virtually all other issues, and went about methodically raising money and priming the computers for a second race against Albosta, which he again won by the narrowest of margins. Against any candidate but Albosta, he would probably do better. But in this district, with its constant flow of new residents, any political rule of thumb may prove wrong and this could be the scene of yet another serious race in 1988.

The People: Pop. 1980: 514,560, up 23.5% 1970–80. Households (1980): 78% family, 44% with children, 68% married couples; 20.1% housing units rented; median monthly rent: $170; median house value: $34,400. Voting age pop. (1980): 357,369; 1% Spanish origin, 1% Black.

1984 Presidential Vote:

Reagan (R)	145,480	(67%)
Mondale (D)	69,170	(32%)

Rep. Bill Schuette (R)

Elected 1984; b. Oct. 13, 1953, Midland; home, Sanford; Georgetown U., B.S. 1976, U. of San Francisco, J.D. 1979; Episcopalian; single.

Career: Practicing atty.

Offices: 415 CHOB 20515, 202-225-3561. Also 304 E. Main St., P.O. Box 631, Midland 48640, 517-631-2552; 300 W. Main St., Owosso 48867, 517-723-6759; 120 W. Harris St., Parkview Plaza N., Cadillac 49601, 616-775-2722.

Committees: *Agriculture* (14th of 17 R). Subcommittees: Domestic Marketing, Consumer Relations and Nutrition; Wheat, Soybeans and Feed Grains. *Select Committee on Aging* (22d of 26 R). Subcommittees: Housing and Consumer Interests; Retirement Income and Employment.

Group Ratings

	ADA	ACLU	COPE	CFA	LCV	ACU	NTU	NSI	COC	CEI
1986	10	5	13	25	21	76	47	100	73	58
1985	5	—	6	25	—	81	51	—	68	—

National Journal Ratings

	1986 LIB — 1986 CONS		1985 LIB — 1985 CONS	
Economic	35% —	64%	24% —	74%
Social	18% —	82%	0% —	76%
Foreign	27% —	70%	0% —	76%

Key Votes

1) Lmt Cln Water Act	FOR	5) Retain Gun Cont	AGN	9) Aid Angola Reb	FOR
2) Rpl Tobac Sub	AGN	6) Contra Aid	FOR	10) Tax Reform	FOR
3) Grm-Rdmn Def Red	FOR	7) Lmt Text Imp	FOR	11) S Africa Sanc	FOR
4) Ban Polygraph	AGN	8) Limit SDI	AGN	12) Immig Reform	AGN

Election Results

1986 general	Bill Schuette (R)	78,475	(51%)	($897,825)
	Donald Joseph (Don) Albosta (D)	74,941	(49%)	($405,971)
1986 primary	Bill Schuette (R)	34,966	(100%)	
1984 general	Bill Schuette (R)	104,950	(50%)	($726,134)
	Donald Joseph (Don) Albosta (D)	103,636	(49%)	($476,285)

Campaign Contributions and Expenditures

1985-86		Direct Cont. 1985-86		PACS Breakdown 1985-86			
Receipts	$891,901	Indiv.	$464,150	Corp.	$147,817	T/M/H	$129,725
Expend.	$897,825	Party	$14,829	Labor	$0	Agr.	$23,000
Debts	$17,657	PACS	$344,475	Ideo.	$36,629	CWOS	$7,304
		Cand.	$32,000				

ELEVENTH DISTRICT

Michigan's Upper Peninsula (or the UP, as it is called here) is a world unto itself. It is isolated most of the year from the rest of the world by the elements, and for years travel here was discouraged by the high tolls ($3.75, since lowered to $1.50) on the Mackinac Straits Bridge. Sault Ste. Marie was founded as early as 1668, but the UP didn't undergo major settlement until the turn of the 20th century, when the iron and copper mines were booming, and the place had a Wild West air about it. The population influx was polyglot: Irish, Italians, Swedes, Norwegians, and Finns. The Finns remain the largest ethnic group here, and this land, so reminiscent of Finland with its lakes and its cold, has the largest concentration of Finnish-Americans. Some of the mine workers picked up radical or even socialist ideas, and many developed Democratic voting habits; their descendants, those who are left, retain the latter.

A major strike in 1913-14, falling ore prices after World War I—events that would be long forgotten elsewhere—are remembered in the UP as the beginning of its decline: the UP's population peaked at 332,000 in 1920. The fabulous copper and iron ores simply were exhausted in many mines, or became too expensive to extract, and nothing else could hold so many people up here. There is some agriculture, but the growing season is too short for most crops. Lumber and paper and pulp mills employ many UPers too, and are still humming. But in the 40-plus years since World War II, most young people have left the Upper Peninsula for Detroit, Chicago, and the West Coast. From 1940 to 1970, the UP's population hovered around 300,000; in 1980, after some increase, though nothing like the substantial migration from metropolitan areas to the northern part of the Lower Peninsula, the UP was up to 318,000. The closest thing here to a city is Marquette, with 23,000 people.

The Upper Peninsula forms about 60% of Michigan's 11th Congressional District, which has 40% of Michigan's land but only 6% of its people and extends 477 miles from one end to the other. In the Lower Peninsula, it includes the upper-income resort towns of Petoskey and Charlevoix on the Lake Michigan side, the factory town of Alpena on Lake Huron, and the Tawas-Oscoda resort area, an area favored by Flint residents. The Lower Peninsula portion of the 11th is more prosperous than the UP; its Lake Michigan side remains Republican, but the central and Lake Huron counties have been trending Democratic. Overall, this is an evenly divided district; but since 1966 it has elected nothing but Republican congressmen.

This reflects the strength of successive incumbents: Philip Ruppe, scion of an Upper Peninsula brewing family, and the current congressman, Robert Davis, a mortician and former state legislator who became something of a national figure in 1985 when newspapers and magazines around the world published a revealing photograph of his attractive wife Marty; she attracted more, and less favorable, attention in the Upper Peninsula in 1987 when she wrote an article arguing that the $77,400 congressional salary didn't amount to much in Washington. Davis won a closely contested race here in 1978, to hold the seat for the Republicans; he has won by solid margins ever since. Davis serves on the Armed Services Committee (there are a couple of Air Force bases in frozen UP forests protecting our northern borders) and is also ranking Republican on Merchant Marine and Fisheries and on the Coast Guard Subcommittee. You won't find him debating philosophical points there or elsewhere, however: his interests lie in finding money for Great Lakes ports (and some way to hold down rising lake levels), seeking trade protection for a district that is or would like to be part of the steel-and-autos economy, and trying to prop up the price of copper. Ideologically, his voting record looks all over the lot; it makes better sense when you look at the district.

For Davis this has proved to be a winning formula. He is not regarded as a legislative heavyweight in Washington, but he is seen back home as a fighter for UP and northern Michigan interests. He has had several competent Democratic opponents and has beaten them all handily, never running less than even in the Upper Peninsula and in the Democratic year of 1986 carrying every county there.

The People: Pop. 1980: 514,560, up 10.9% 1970–80. Households (1980): 75% family, 40% with children, 65% married couples; 22.8% housing units rented; median monthly rent: $160; median house value: $30,800. Voting age pop. (1980): 367,779; 1% American Indian, 1% Black.

1984 Presidential Vote: Reagan (R) 135,537   (59%)
                                 Mondale (D) 93,600   (41%)

Rep. Robert W. (Bob) Davis (R)

Elected 1978; b. July 31, 1932, Marquette; home, Gaylord; N. MI U., 1950, 1952, Hillsdale Col., 1951–52, Wayne St. U., B.S. 1954; Episcopalian; married (Marty).

Career: Mortician, 1954–66; St. Ignace City Cncl., 1964–66; MI House of Reps., 1966–70; MI Senate, 1970–78, Major. Whip, 1970–74, Minor. Ldr., 1974–78.

Offices: 1124 LHOB 20515, 202-225-4735. Also 215 W. Washington St., Marquette 49855, 906-228-3700; 145 Main St., Ste. 103B, Gaylord, 49735, 517-732-3151; City-County Bldg., Sault Ste. Marie 49783, 906-635-5261; 144 S. 2d St., Alpena 49707, 517-356-2028; 18 N. 22d St., Escanaba 49829, 906-786-4504; 100 Portage, Haughton 49931, 906-482-2464; 200 E. Ayer St., Ironwood 49983; 410 N. Main St., Cheboygan 49721, 616-627-4603; 207 E. Mitchell St., Petoskey 49770, 616-347-4960.

Committees: *Armed Services* (7th of 21 R). Subcommittees: Procurement and Military Nuclear Systems; Research and Development. *Merchant Marine and Fisheries* (Ranking Member of 17 R). Subcommittees: Coast Guard and Navigation (Ranking Member).

Group Ratings

	ADA	ACLU	COPE	CFA	LCV	ACU	NTU	NSI	COC	CEI
1986	35	30	58	25	45	60	26	89	57	36
1985	35	—	54	75	—	62	37	—	55	—

National Journal Ratings

	1986 LIB — 1986 CONS	1985 LIB — 1985 CONS
Economic	47% — 52%	47% — 52%
Social	31% — 67%	40% — 59%
Foreign	41% — 57%	37% — 60%

Key Votes

1) Lmt Cln Water Act	AGN	5) Retain Gun Cont	AGN	9) Aid Angola Reb	FOR
2) Rpl Tobac Sub	FOR	6) Contra Aid	FOR	10) Tax Reform	FOR
3) Grm-Rdmn Def Red	FOR	7) Lmt Text Imp	FOR	11) S Africa Sanc	FOR
4) Ban Polygraph	FOR	8) Limit SDI	AGN	12) Immig Reform	FOR

Election Results

1986 general	Robert W. (Bob) Davis (R).	91,575	(63%)	($207,080)
	Robert Anderson (D)	53,180	(37%)	($58,826)
1986 primary	Robert W. (Bob) Davis (R).	28,351	(100%)	
1984 general	Robert W. (Bob) Davis (R).	126,992	(59%)	($220,520)
	Tom Stewart (D).	89,640	(41%)	($241,122)

Campaign Contributions and Expenditures

1985-86		Direct Cont. 1985-86		PACS Breakdown 1985-86			
Receipts	$396,340	Indiv.	$208,686	Corp.	$77,100	T/M/H	$36,500
Expend.	$207,080	Party	$7,736	Labor	$26,000	Agr.	$2,750
Unspent	$197,990	PACS	$147,672	Ideo.	$5,322	CWOS	$0

TWELFTH DISTRICT

East and northeast of Detroit, just beyond the city limits, is Lake St. Clair, the smallest and shallowest of the Great Lakes. It is really just a place where the huge volume of water in the Great Lakes—one-quarter of the fresh water in the world—funneled through the St. Clair River, spreads out over the extremely flat, swampy lands of southern Michigan and Ontario before being channeled once again in the Detroit River. Few major cities have a recreational facility as useful as Lake St. Clair: it is large enough to accommodate many boats, but not so large as to be very dangerous; its waters are warm enough for swimming in the summer (and have been cleaned up greatly in recent years); it provides fishing in the summer and ice fishing in the winter.

Forty years ago, there was little settlement along Lake St. Clair. Between the Grosse Pointes, still Detroit's most exclusive high-income suburbs, and the old industrial city of Port Huron, where Lake Huron empties into the St. Clair River, the only urban settlement was the old spa town of Mount Clemens. Otherwise the roads stretched out on empty flat farmland, with an occasional rustic lakeshore restaurant or beach shack. In the years since, this part of Michigan has filled up with people moving out of Detroit. It was a migration seen only in post-1945 America: predominantly blue-collar and relatively affluent. High auto wages helped families finance large homes in the new subdivisions which sprouted in Macomb County, in suburbs along Lake St. Clair (St. Clair Shores, Harrison Township) and a little inland (East Detroit, Roseville, Warren, Clinton Township). Commercial strips went up, followed by shopping malls, and even by some office buildings, in land which just a few years before had been farmfields.

This is the heart of Michigan's 12th Congressional District, which continues along Lake St. Clair from St. Clair Shores and Roseville in the south on past Port Huron in the north. It goes inland to include the working-class suburb of Roseville and part of Warren. In the process, it moves inland as much as 25 miles, but most of the population is concentrated along the lake. Before 1950, this was mostly Republican country; the new migrants made it, for a while, heavily Democratic; now they have moved more toward the Republicans, and it is politically marginal. President Kennedy won 63% of the vote in Macomb County in 1960, when it was the most Democratic major suburban county in the United States. But it moved against the Democrats on a number of issues: busing in the early 1970s (Macomb County was spiritedly against a busing decision which would have sent many of its children to dangerous schools in Detroit 25 miles away), aid to parochial schools and tuition tax credits later in the decade (Macomb was 48% Catholic in 1971), and high taxes late in the 1970s (high wages and upward social mobility made Macomb one of the highest-income counties in the nation for a while). From being a Democratic stronghold, Macomb has become a kind of fulcrum in state politics. In 1983 northern Macomb voters recalled a Democratic state senator who voted for a tax increase and replaced him with a Republican, and the next year elected three Republicans to the state House. But with the economic recovery of the state, Macomb elected all Democrats to the state House again, nearly ousted its Republican state senator, and voted 68%–31% for Governor James Blanchard—exactly his statewide margin. That looks like Macomb's Democratic roots reasserting themselves. But its class-consciousness seems clearly to have receded: Macomb was 17% more Democratic than next-door, more upscale Oakland County in 1960, only 1% more Democratic in the 1984 presidential election, and only 6% more Democratic in 1986.

The congressman from the 12th District is David Bonior, a Democrat who stylistically seems a little out of place for Macomb—he wears a beard and suspenders, is concerned about environmental issues, and seems earnest in the manner of the liberal activists of the 1970s. But he has demonstrated considerable political popularity and talent. In the 100th Congress, he was selected by Speaker Jim Wright to be chief deputy democratic whip, one of the top four or five positions in the Democratic leadership. And just before, in 1986, he was reelected with 66% of the vote—his best showing to date.

Bonior is the first member of the Democratic leadership to come from the ranks of Vietnam veterans and from the ranks of anti-Vietnam war politicians. He was elected to the state legislature in 1972 and, after a tough primary and general election, to the House in 1976; running after an ice storm had killed many Macomb County trees, he gave out thousands of pine seedlings as a campaign gimmick. He formed the Vietnam Veterans caucus and wrote a book called *The Vietnam Veteran: A History of Neglect*. As an environmentalist he oppposed not only water projects in other states, but also the Army Corps of Engingeers' proposal for year-round navigation on the Great Lakes, which he knew would be expensive and believed would damage fish and lakefront property. Early on, Bonior became known as a close student of House procedures, and he won a seat—a sure sign of leadership favor—on the House Rules Committee. He became one of seven Democratic deputy whips in 1985. One of the best House athletes, he became known as a team player and a leader: he was drafted in 1983 to be the Democrats' lead opponent of aid to the Nicaraguan contras. From his days in Catholic school and college, Bonior had heard of the evils of the Somoza regime; he traveled to Nicaragua in 1985 and talked with President Daniel Ortega; he argued his case passionately, suggesting Nicaragua could be another Vietnam, and was successful for several years until his side lost narrowly to the Reagan Administration position in 1986.

Wright's selection of Bonior as a chief deputy whip was something of a surprise, and Bonior is notably to the left of Wright and other Democratic leaders on some issues. "I have to temper myself in order to be an effective leader in the House," he said, but in fact his unassuming temperament and capacity for hard work seems to suit his duties quite well. He also seems to suit the 12th District, winning reelection with comfortable though not always overwhelming margins in the 1980s. The Republicans attack him as too liberal, but he keeps giving away the pine seedlings many of which are, now that he is a power in Washington, tall "Bonior pines" back on the flatlands along Lake St. Clair.

The People: Pop. 1980: 514,560, up 9.4% 1970–80. Households (1980): 78% family, 44% with children, 66% married couples; 22.1% housing units rented; median monthly rent: $243; median house value: $47,200. Voting age pop. (1980): 362,035; 2% Black, 1% Spanish origin.

1984 Presidential Vote:

Reagan (R)	121,510	(66%)
Mondale (D)	61,591	(33%)

Rep. David E. Bonior (D)

Elected 1976; b. June 6, 1945, Hamtramck; home, Mt. Clemens; U. of IA, B.A. 1967, Chapman Col., M.A. 1972; Roman Catholic; divorced.

Career: Probation officer and adoption caseworker, 1967–68; Air Force, 1968–72; MI House of Reps., 1973–77.

Offices: 2242 RHOB 20515, 202-225-2106. Also 82 Macomb Pl., Mt. Clemens 48043, 313-469-3232; and 526 Water St., Port Huron 48060, 313-987-8889.

Committees: *Rules* (6th of 9 D). Subcommittee: Rules of the House.

Group Ratings

	ADA	ACLU	COPE	CFA	LCV	ACU	NTU	NSI	COC	CEI
1986	95	84	92	67	83	0	29	0	6	9
1985	90	—	92	75	—	5	33	—	25	—

National Journal Ratings

	1986 LIB — 1986 CONS		1985 LIB — 1985 CONS	
Economic	77%	22%	89%	0%
Social	89%	0%	55%	44%
Foreign	80%	0%	85%	8%

Key Votes

1) Lmt Cln Water Act	AGN	5) Retain Gun Cont	FOR	9) Aid Angola Reb	AGN
2) Rpl Tobac Sub	AGN	6) Contra Aid	AGN	10) Tax Reform	FOR
3) Grm-Rdmn Def Red	AGN	7) Lmt Text Imp	FOR	11) S Africa Sanc	FOR
4) Ban Polygraph	FOR	8) Limit SDI	FOR	12) Immig Reform	FOR

Election Results

1986 general	David E. Bonior (D)	87,643	(66%)	($283,904)
	Candice Miller (R)	44,442	(34%)	($62,244)
1986 primary	David E. Bonior (D)	25,694	(90%)	
	Gary Genazzio (D)	2,786	(10%)	
1984 general	David E. Bonior (D)	113,772	(58%)	($135,098)
	Eugene J. Tyza (R)	79,824	(41%)	($962)

Campaign Contributions and Expenditures

1985-86		Direct Cont. 1985-86		PACS Breakdown 1985-86			
Receipts	$315,545	Indiv.	$101,541	Corp.	$37,800	T/M/H	$37,810
Expend.	$283,904	Party	$5,945	Labor	$82,215	Agr.	$17,280
Unspent	$48,366	PACS	$201,087	Ideo.	$25,482	CWOS	$500

THIRTEENTH DISTRICT

When Henry Ford's company built its first automobile in 1903, Detroit was an old but still second-rank industrial city, no larger than Milwaukee, smaller than Cincinnati or Cleveland, with three-story brick factories and on straight blocks running inland from the Detroit River several miles of neat frame and brick houses, sturdy enough to stand the cold winters. There were less than half a million people here, all within a five-mile radius of where the French built

Fort Pontchartrain in 1701; just beyond were fields and farms like the one where Ford, the son of Irish immigrants, grew up. In the next quarter century, as the auto industry boomed, Detroit grew outward in every direction, along giant radial avenues paved nine lanes wide; and the downtown, filling up in the 1920s with exuberant skyscrapers and anchored by Hudson's, one of the nation's large department stores, looked to bustling Detroiters to be the nucleus of a world-city. Yet in many ways the center of the city was elsewhere. The new auto factories were all built on what was the edge of urban settlement, where there was plenty of cheap empty land; then the city grew rapidly, in tight rows of working class houses within walking distance of the plants (for who thought the workers would ever be able to afford cars?) and middle class neighborhoods running outward into farmland. The auto companies built their headquarters away from downtown, near their factories, and though no one knew it at the time, the basic pattern of Detroit's urban growth was set: rapid outward growth, unfocused on a single center, leaving behind every generation the previous generation's neighborhoods and civic institutions.

Today metropolitan Detroit has a population of 4 million, but there are fewer people within the 1903 boundaries than there were then: the 13th Congressional District includes all of that older city plus several miles of what was then still farmland. The depredations of continual outward migration show everywhere: on the radial avenues, with their boarded-up stores and hulks of movie palaces; on side streets, with abandoned houses, many of them burned by arsonists, perhaps on Halloween, some occupied by squatters; in downtown, where Hudson's Department Store has closed, the 70-story Renaissance Center has seen its retail stores fail (one of its office towers has remained empty for years) and is designed so that you can only get there from the rest of Detroit by car and after passing through easily guarded entrances. The 13th District still has some viable middle-class neighborhoods on its edge, and even includes two of the exclusive Grosse Pointe suburbs. But altogether it has seen the biggest population loss in the United States over the last-quarter century, from about 800,000 in 1960 to about 680,000 in 1970 to around 400,000 in the middle 1980s.

The main reason for this depopulation is crime. There has always been a hard-edged tone to life in Detroit, the clang of steel on steel: see Elmore Leonard's *City Primeval*. And moving farther out, as far as your car can carry you, is very much in the Detroit tradition; so is white flight away from what rapidly became all-black neighborhoods. Traditionally, people moving outward have been replaced by new, lower-wage residents. But by the 1970s, as auto wages rose, low-wage jobs tended to disappear; and after the riot of 1967, almost everyone decided they needed a gun. Inner city neighborhoods lost their natural leaders, the kind of people who nurture and maintain community institutions; left in charge were people who made their livings by crime. By the middle 1980s Detroit had a murder rate twice as high as any other major city, and more murders a year than all of Canada. The *Detroit Free Press* ran a series on children who had been killed in 1986 by gunfire, murdered for a stylish shirt or struck by randomly fired bullets; in 1986, 365 Detroit children under 17 were shot, and 43 died. By April 1987, 102 children under age 16 had been shot, and 10 died. "Everybody in Detroit is scared," writes columnist William Raspberry. "The city is going to hell, and nobody has the faintest idea what to do about it."

Politically, the reflexive cry in Detroit has been for more federal aid, government jobs, guaranteed incomes, more social programs; that has been the theme, for example, of Detroit's longtime (since 1973) Mayor Coleman Young, whose political base is in the 13th District. Young has had some successes, helping to revive the warehouse district on the river east of the Renaissance Center, getting government money to finance General Motors's controversial Poletown plant. But Young's main response to proposals for gun control was to say, "I'll be damned if I'm going to collect guns in the city of Detroit while we're surrounded by hostile suburbs and the whole rest of the state who have guns." But as one black councilman pointed out, the problem is not white suburbanites killing city blacks, it is city blacks killing city blacks; and the reflex that blames any problem on white racism is not responsive to the lawlessness that plagues a city which has had a black mayor and black police commissioner for 15 years. The white suburbs are hostile—the all-white city of Dearborn in 1985 passed an ordinance aimed at

Detroit blacks barring city parks to non-residents—but quite uninterested in physically invading Detroit. What is needed is a civic resolve not to tolerate armed violence; but Young, a politician of great skill who has spent a long career making government more generous and more tolerant, seems unable to express the same more indignation at violent individual rule-breaking that he has so eloquently expressed at unfair group rule-making.

The congressman from the 13th District is George Crockett, a longtime political ally of Young and a major figure in Detroit's public life for decades himself. Crockett was general counsel of the United Auto Workers in 1946 and 1947, part of the left-wing group sometimes allied with Communists which was thrown out by Walter Reuther's liberal anti-Communist group in 1947. Crockett became a left winger when only a few people on the fringes of American politics, some of them followers of Soviet Russia, even thought of backing national civil rights laws; he served on the wartime Fair Employment Practices bureaucracy that was created only when A. Philip Randolph threatened to disrupt the war effort if it was not: he has reason to believe that progress toward equality and fairness sometimes requires acting against American traditions and asserted American interests in the direst circumstances. As a judge on Detroit's criminal court in the 1960s, Crockett aroused great controversy when, prompted only by his own ideas of justice, he went down to the courthouse in the middle of the night, held hearings, and released on bail men arrested for killing a policeman. Whites launched a movement to recall him; but he had solid black support and was never defeated. Forced to retire as a judge after age 70, he ran for the 13th District seat from which Charles Diggs, convicted of payroll-padding, was forced to retire, and was easily elected in 1980 at age 71. Routinely reelected, he does not seem to address the appalling reign of crime in his district; implicit in his voting record is a conviction it should be addressed by more government aid to the poor.

Crockett has now succeeded to a position of prominence in the House, as chairman of the Foreign Affairs subcommittee handling Latin America; in that capacity he will be a lead spokesman against Administration policy in Central America. He brings to foreign policy the suspicions of one who sees the United States as too often the supporter of right-wing dictatorships and racist regimes, and which sees Soviet-allied states like Nicaragua and Cuba as progressive to the extent they redistribute income, provide welfare state services, and stamp out racism. He serves on the Africa subcommittee, and he was among the first congressmen arrested at the South African Embassy in Washington during the recent protests there. It was not the first time: he was jailed also while serving as counsel to a witness before the old House Un-American Activities Committee. Crockett was attacked by a conservative group in early 1987 as "a threat to national security," and argued that he has consistently supported pro-Soviet positions, to the point of abstaining on the resolution passed 416–0 criticizing the Soviet Union for the shooting down of Korean Air Lines 007. The critics surely overshot the mark and damaged their case by arguing that Crockett's service as an attorney for Communists in the 1950s justifies an inference that he is a security risk today. Yet they have a point when they argue that Crockett's views seem consistently over the years to have followed something like a pro-Soviet line, one that few Democratic congressmen share and most would be uncomfortable defending to their constituents. The argument is probably moot, since the Democrats have no intention of depriving a black colleague of a subcommittee chair, and since Crockett continues to perform his duties with the courtesy and serenity that has marked his public career for nearly 50 years, and in times of controversy much more bitter than these. But he seems deterred not at all by his isolation on some issues. As subcommittee chairman he is likely to perform his duties calmly and fairly, without either violating his trust or swaying many of his colleagues one way or the other.

The People: Pop. 1980: 514,560, dn. 30.8% 1970–80. Households (1980): 60% family, 36% with children, 31% married couples; 59.1% housing units rented; median monthly rent: $143; median house value: $17,900. Voting age pop. (1980): 360,241; 67% Black, 3% Spanish origin, 1% Asian origin.

1984 Presidential Vote: Mondale (D) 136,251   (85%)
                            Reagan (R) 23,926   (15%)

Rep. George W. Crockett, Jr. (D)

Elected 1980; b. Aug. 10, 1909, Jacksonville, FL; home, Detroit; Morehouse Col., A.B. 1931, U. of MI, J.D. 1934; Baptist; married (Harriette).

Career: Practicing atty., 1934–39, 1946–66; Sr. Atty., U.S. Dept. of Labor, 1939–43; Founder-Dir., UAW Fair Practices Dept., 1944–46; Judge, Recorder's Crt., 1966–78; Visiting Judge, MI Crt. of Appeals, 1979; Acting Corp. Counsel, Detroit, 1980.

Offices: 1531 LHOB 20515, 202-225-2261. Also 8401 Woodward Ave., Detroit 48202, 313-874-4900.

Committees: *Foreign Affairs* (9th of 27 D). Subcommittees: Africa; Western Hemisphere Affairs (Chairman). *Judiciary* (12th of 21 D). Subcommittees: Crime; Courts, Civil Liberties and the Administration of Justice. *Select Committee on Aging* (21st of 39 D). Subcommittee: Retirement Income and Employment.

Group Ratings

	ADA	ACLU	COPE	CFA	LCV	ACU	NTU	NSI	COC	CEI
1986	95	100	93	67	69	0	33	0	15	16
1985	80	—	94	75	—	10	39	—	18	—

National Journal Ratings

	1986 LIB — 1986 CONS		1985 LIB — 1985 CONS	
Economic	66%	— 34%	70%	— 30%
Social	77%	— 22%	78%	— 21%
Foreign	80%	— 0%	74%	— 25%

Key Votes

1) Lmt Cln Water Act	AGN	5) Retain Gun Cont	FOR	9) Aid Angola Reb	AGN
2) Rpl Tobac Sub	FOR	6) Contra Aid	AGN	10) Tax Reform	FOR
3) Grm-Rdmn Def Red	—	7) Lmt Text Imp	FOR	11) S Africa Sanc	FOR
4) Ban Polygraph	FOR	8) Limit SDI	FOR	12) Immig Reform	AGN

Election Results

1986 general	George W. Crockett, Jr. (D)	76,435	(85%)	($56,271)
	Mary Griffin (R)	12,395	(14%)	($13,663)
1986 primary	George W. Crockett, Jr. (D)	26,784	(75%)	
	Alonzo Bates (D)	4,746	(13%)	
	Lucy Randolph (D)	2,079	(6%)	
1984 general	George W. Crockett, Jr. (D)	132,222	(87%)	($53,400)
	Robert Murphy (R)	20,416	(13%)	

Campaign Contributions and Expenditures

1985-86		Direct Cont. 1985-86		PACS Breakdown 1985-86			
Receipts	$71,784	Indiv.	$27,188	Corp.	$7,150	T/M/H	$4,970
Expend.	$56,271	PACS	$39,095	Labor	$24,675	Agr.	$500
Unspent	$50,359	Cand.	$1,200	Ideo.	$1,500	CWOS	$300

FOURTEENTH DISTRICT

You could almost call Michigan's 14th Congressional District the Polish Corridor—a ring around the inner city of Detroit where the grandchildren of the Polish immigrants who came to work in the auto plants now live. Not everyone in the district is Polish, of course; there are also plenty of Americans of Italian, German, British, Irish, and Belgian stock (the largest concentration of Flemish-Americans). Nor is every neighborhood particularly ethnic. The 14th extends east to include most of the Grosse Pointes, the posh and exclusive suburbs on Lake St. Clair; it extends as far north as suburban Sterling Heights, indistinguishable physically from any one of a hundred shopping center suburbs which went up in the 1960s and 1970s; it includes East Detroit, where residents were trying in 1987 to change the name to East Pointe, out of displeasure from being confused with Coleman Young's Detroit; it extends as far west as the suburbs of Hazel Park and Madison Heights, where most people speak in the accent of Appalachian Kentucky and Tennessee.

The Polish heart of the district is Hamtramck, a tiny industrial town surrounded by Detroit. Here thousands of immigrants flocked to get jobs in the Dodge Main, Plymouth, and Packard auto plants; during the 1910s Hamtramck was the fastest growing city in the nation. As many as 56,000 people—mostly young parents and their large families—lived there in 1930. Today the population is down to 21,000, mostly old people, and Dodge Main has been torn down. Hamtramck has been the butt of dozens of Polish jokes, but anybody who takes the trouble to visit the town will find freshly painted houses and carefully tended lawns—evidence of the pride of ownership that still flourishes here and in neighborhoods where younger Polish-Americans live.

The congressman from the 14th is Dennis Hertel, a Democrat whose two brothers are also in politics. Hertel's record is liberal on economic and foreign policy issues, moderate on cultural issues; this district may be aging, but it is still definitely family, not singles, country, and traditional on many cultural matters. Hertel serves on the Armed Services Committee, where he is one of the members more skeptical about military projects; Michigan, after its economic woes of the early 1980s, has become conscious that it receives very little defense spending (though much of what there is goes to plants in this district). He also has a seat on the Fisheries and Wildlife Conservation Subcommittee of Merchant Marine, which has jurisdiction over a number of issues of importance to environmentalists.

Hertel's critical election was in 1980, when his popularity as a state legislator enabled him to win an eight-candidate primary with 62% of the vote and his hard work enabled him to beat a Republican and former anchor on Channel 2. His next hurdle, redistricting, turned out to be easy when James Blanchard gave up his House seat to run for governor; Hertel got some of Blanchard's old territory in Oakland County, and seems to have a safe seat now.

The People: Pop. 1980: 514,559, dn. 1.2% 1970–80. Households (1980): 76% family, 39% with children, 62% married couples; 20.8% housing units rented; median monthly rent: $223; median house value: $39,000. Voting age pop. (1980): 372,422; 4% Black, 1% Asian origin, 1% Spanish origin.

1984 Presidential Vote:

Reagan (R)	156,332	(63%)
Mondale (D)	90,562	(37%)

Rep. Dennis M. Hertel (D)

Elected 1980; b. Dec. 7, 1948, Detroit; home, Harper Woods; E. MI U., B.S. 1971, Wayne St. U., J.D. 1974; Roman Catholic; married (Cynthia).

Career: Practicing atty.; MI House of Reps., 1974–80.

Offices: 218 CHOB 20515, 202-225-6276. Also 28221 Mound Rd., Warren 48092, 313-574-9420; and 18927 Kelly Rd., Detroit 48224, 313-526-5900.

Committees: *Armed Services* (18th of 31 D). Subcommittees: Military Installations and Facilities; Research and Development. *Merchant Marine and Fisheries* (12th of 25 D). Subcommittees: Coast Guard and Navigation; Fisheries and Wildlife Conservation and the Environment; Merchant Marine. *Select Committee on Aging* (24th of 39 D). Subcommittee: Health and Long-Term Care.

Group Ratings

	ADA	ACLU	COPE	CFA	LCV	ACU	NTU	NSI	COC	CEI
1986	85	83	92	83	84	9	38	0	19	23
1985	80	—	92	92	—	14	52	—	27	—

National Journal Ratings

	1986 LIB — 1986 CONS			1985 LIB — 1985 CONS		
Economic	60%	—	38%	81%	—	17%
Social	86%	—	11%	48%	—	51%
Foreign	71%	—	28%	85%	—	8%

Key Votes

1) Lmt Cln Water Act	FOR	5) Retain Gun Cont	FOR	9) Aid Angola Reb	AGN
2) Rpl Tobac Sub	FOR	6) Contra Aid	AGN	10) Tax Reform	AGN
3) Grm-Rdmn Def Red	FOR	7) Lmt Text Imp	FOR	11) S Africa Sanc	FOR
4) Ban Polygraph	FOR	8) Limit SDI	FOR	12) Immig Reform	AGN

Election Results

1986 general	Dennis M. Hertel (D)	92,328	(73%)	($172,835)
	Stanley Grot (R)	33,831	(27%)	($73,988)
1986 primary	Dennis M. Hertel (D)	31,898	(96%)	
	William Osipoff (D)	1,357	(4%)	
1984 general	Dennis M. Hertel (D)	113,610	(59%)	($162,051)
	John Lauve (R)	77,427	(40%)	

Campaign Contributions and Expenditures

1985-86		Direct Cont. 1985-86		PACS Breakdown 1985-86			
Receipts	$199,966	Indiv.	$62,910	Corp.	$25,105	T/M/H	$20,790
Expend.	$172,835	Party	$22,037	Labor	$67,684	Agr.	$2,000
Unspent	$48,563	PACS	$122,604	Ideo.	$7,025	CWOS	$0

FIFTEENTH DISTRICT

Coming in from the airport on I-94, you see it: the giant tire over the billboard with the digital counter showing America's car production so far this year. It's a monument to and symbol of one of what was once and what bids fair to be again one of America's major manufacturing centers: the flat lands southwest of Detroit. When Henry Ford built the Ford Rouge plant just east of here in Dearborn in 1920, this land was a flat, swampy expanse stretching farther than the eye could see west almost to the college town of Ann Arbor. Crisscrossed early on by railroads and later by freeways, this is industrial land, a natural site for many of the auto factories built in the 1940s and 1950s; the most famous in its time was Willow Run, at the western end of Wayne County, which Henry Ford made into the nation's biggest aircraft factory during World War II. The area was so empty then that the government built an expressway so that workers from Detroit could drive (with extra gas rations) the 35 miles to Willow Run in reasonable time. The expressway still stands, pockmarked with potholes, the giant meter under the tire recording, most years in the last decade, disappointly low levels of auto production.

Yet there are also signs of revival. In the early 1980s workers here were biding their time on supplemental unemployment benefits that gave them 90% of non-overtime pay for 65 weeks—and then discovered that they weren't going to be called back by the big employers. Now many are back working again, for smaller employers and sometimes at lower wages, but in enterprises that are growing through their own efforts rather than begging government to keep them from closing down. The area along I-94 has become known as Automation Alley and seems to be the center of America's robotics business. This part of Michigan has taken its historical strength in manufacturing and converted it into an asset for the future.

This is the land of the 15th Congressional District of Michigan, staring not far west of the Rouge and the Downriver steel and chemical factories and continuing westward almost to Ann Arbor. In the 45 years since the Willow Run expressway was built, the area around it has filled up with working-class suburbs and some that are more upscale. Some are gleaming and carefully trimmed, like Westland (named after a shopping center) and Canton Township (one of the few parts of the district with rapid population growth in the 1970s). Others like Romulus have the look of places where people with not much money worked a little at a time to build their own houses, on land so flat that the ground oozes with water after it rains. Historically, this has been Democratic country since the UAW forced an unwilling Henry Ford to sign a collective bargaining contract. But as working-class wages went up and working-class consciousness went down, the Democratic margins here have diminished, and the 15th District voted twice for Ronald Reagan.

The congressman from the 15th District is William Ford, a Democrat first elected in 1964 (and no relation to Henry or Gerald Ford). Although he is not well known in many parts of Washington, he is chairman of the Post Office and Civil Service Committee and second ranking Democrat, behind octogenarian Chairman Augustus Hawkins, in Education and Labor. Ford has a political faith considered a little old-fashioned in some quarters: he is a believer in labor unions, and in strengthening them; he believes in the Great Society programs he voted for as a freshman; he believes in a generous, active federal government, helping people who cannot help themselves. He believes in higher pay for federal employees and for congressmen. On cultural and foreign issues he also has a liberal voting record. But his real fervor and energy seems concentrated on economic issues, in the broad sense of the term.

The Post Office chair is an often thankless job. Ford is a strong supporter of unions for government workers, but he is not about to change the federal government's longstanding and successful refusal to tolerate strikes. He is more concerned to protect the ordinary employee's rights more than most Democrats are these days. But he was willing to compromise on the civil service reform bill in the Carter years. Education and Labor, in contrast, was the glamor committee of the House when Ford came to Washington, with jurisdiction over the new and exciting antipoverty programs. Now it is a very practical body, on which organized labor and education lobbies are counting to protect the gains they have won in the past and which are threatened by the Reagan budget cuts. It took a beating in the first year of Reagan budget cuts, but Ford and some other canny politicians, like the late Chairman Carl Perkins, have managed to save programs and preserve benefits more than almost anyone thought possible. On the committee Ford has specialized in the big money education bills (such as ESEA—the Elementary and Secondary Education Act) and chairs the Post Secondary Education Subcommittee.

Ford usually wins reelection easily in Michigan, but in 1984 his percentage fell sharply against a nuisance candidate; Republicans also came surprisingly close in legislative races in southwest Wayne County. But with the state's economic revival, Democrats led by Governor James Blanchard rallied in 1986, and Ford was reelected with 75% of the vote. He is likely, unless Republicans surge to control the House, to be one of the most important legislators of the 1990s.

The People: Pop. 1980: 514,560, up 11.1% 1970–80. Households (1980): 78% family, 48% with children, 65% married couples; 28.6% housing units rented; median monthly rent: $258; median house value: $46,400. Voting age pop. (1980): 356,253; 5% Black, 1% Spanish origin, 1% Asian origin.

1984 Presidential Vote:

Reagan (R)	112,238	(61%)
Mondale (D)	71,126	(39%)

Rep. William D. Ford (D)

Elected 1964; b. Aug. 6, 1927, Detroit; home, Taylor; Wayne St. U., 1947–48, U. of Denver, B.S. 1949, J.D. 1951; United Church of Christ; divorced.

Career: Navy, 1944–46; Practicing atty., 1951–60; Taylor Township Justice of the Peace, 1955–57; Melvindale City Atty., 1957–59; MI Senate, 1962–64.

Offices: 239 CHOB 20515, 202-225-6261. Also Federal Bldg., Wayne 48184, 313-722-1411; and 31 S. Huron St., Ypsilanti 48197, 313-482-6636.

Committees: *Education and Labor* (2d of 21 D). Subcommittees: Elementary, Secondary, and Vocational Education; Health and Safety; Labor-Management Relations; Postsecondary Education. *Post Office and Civil Service* (Chairman of 14 D). Subcommittee: Investigations (Chairman).

Group Ratings

	ADA	ACLU	COPE	CFA	LCV	ACU	NTU	NSI	COC	CEI
1986	80	88	97	83	75	5	27	0	6	8
1985	80	—	97	67	—	5	32	—	20	—

National Journal Ratings

	1986 LIB — 1986 CONS		1985 LIB — 1985 CONS	
Economic	87% —	0%	89% —	0%
Social	83% —	15%	79% —	19%
Foreign	80% —	0%	85% —	15%

Key Votes

1) Lmt Cln Water Act	AGN	5) Retain Gun Cont	AGN	9) Aid Angola Reb	AGN
2) Rpl Tobac Sub	AGN	6) Contra Aid	AGN	10) Tax Reform	AGN
3) Grm-Rdmn Def Red	AGN	7) Lmt Text Imp	FOR	11) S Africa Sanc	FOR
4) Ban Polygraph	FOR	8) Limit SDI	FOR	12) Immig Reform	FOR

Election Results

1986 general	William D. Ford (D)....................	77,950	(75%)	($306,543)
	Glenn Kassel (R)......................	25,078	(24%)	($5,600)
1986 primary	William D. Ford (D)....................	20,039	(91%)	
	Three others (D)	2,073	(9%)	
1984 general	William D. Ford (D)....................	98,973	(60%)	($244,963)
	Gerald R. Carlson (R)	66,172	(40%)	

Campaign Contributions and Expenditures

1985-86		Direct Cont. 1985-86		PACS Breakdown 1985-86			
Receipts	$331,369	Indiv.	$108,278	Corp.	$40,565	T/M/H	$53,165
Expend.	$306,543	Party	$10,040	Labor	$108,723	Agr.	$1,650
Unspent	$55,943	PACS	$213,893	Ideo.	$9,540	CWOS	$250

SIXTEENTH DISTRICT

The 16th Congressional District of Michigan is one of the nation's most heavily industrial areas. From the Interstate 75 bridge over the Rouge River, the 16th spreads out before you: on the right you can see the Ford Rouge plant, built in Dearborn by Henry Ford, on what amounts to an inlet off the Detroit River, as a single unit in which he could convert iron ore, coal, and other raw materials into an automobile within 48 hours; on the left, stretching out to the horizon are the steel mills, chemical plants, stamping plants, and auto assembly plants of the downriver suburbs. It is one of the premier industrial landscapes in America, ranking with the view of the Gary and Chicago steel mills from the Indiana Turnpike and the spectacle of northern New Jersey from the Pulaski Skyway. This is a natural location for industry: the Detroit River, flowing into Lake Erie, provides a natural avenue for bulky raw materials like iron ore and limestone; the railroad lines along the flat, originally swampy shores, bring in coal and ship out finished products, connecting easily with the nation's main east–west rail lines, a few miles to the south.

Almost flush up against the older factories and well within range of their sulphurous odors are the neat, tightly packed houses of the old ethnic neighborhoods—some still mostly Polish, Hungarian, and Italian, some now black, Mexican, or Arab (the 16th District probably has the nation's largest proportion of Arab-Americans). There are a few high-income enclaves, in west Dearborn and on Grosse Ile in the Detroit River. And the 16th extends not only south across the industrial flatlands to Toledo, Ohio, but also west into the old Yankee town of Adrian. For years most of it was working-class, vintage Democratic country, although in the desperate 1980s it thrashed around for a while, giving Ronald Reagan a large majority and electing some Republican legislators in 1984, giving Democratic Governor James Blanchard a bigger margin in 1986.

Representing the 16th District in the House is John Dingell, chairman since 1981 of the House Energy and Commerce Committee, named in 1984 as "the best congressman" by *Washington Monthly* magazine. A *National Journal* poll of lobbyists voted him "the most effective House member." These are judgments few would quibble with. The House Energy and Commerce Committee, "claims jurisdiction over anything that moves, burns or is sold," according to *National Journal's* Richard E. Cohen and Burt Solomon; in the 1980s it has been the most sought-after committee assignment for Democrats; it handles up to 40% of all House bills and has the largest budget and staff of any House committee. But his power comes not just from that. It comes from John Dingell's aggressiveness, his ability, his hard work, and his determination to do his duty, and to see that others do theirs. He has assembled a top-notch staff that is solidly loyal to him—and never condescends to him or smirks about him behind his back, as so many staffers do. He insists that facts be solidly documented. He gives leeway—and often valuable publicity—to subcommittee chairmen and to junior members, particularly on the Oversight and Investigations Subcommittee he chairs. But only to those he respects and believes have played fair with him; others get nothing—like James Scheuer, who is number two Democrat on the committee but chairs none of its subcommittees. Dingell knows the rules, and is willing to use them to the utmost in his own interest; he swings a very fast gavel indeed when he wants to. But it's hard to find anyone who will say he is unfair.

Dingell's committee and subcommittee have made news and law again and again in the Reagan years. It was a Dingell request for information from the General Accounting Office that triggered the investigation of Michael Deaver for lobbying the White House before he'd been out of office the requisite time; Dingell's curiosity was piqued when he read that Deaver, ordinarily uninterested in policy, worked to shape an agreement with Canadians on acid rain which Dingell, who thinks the acid rain problem is overstated and many proposed remedies unwarranted, opposed. It was Dingell's demands for subpoenas that drove Ann Burford out as head of the Environmental Protection Agency and led to the conviction of EPA official Rita Lavelle. It was Dingell's subcommittee that found out that the Pentagon had paid $640 for a toilet seat and that General Dynamics had billed the Pentagon for country-club dues and dog-kennel boarding. It was Dingell's committee that held up the sale of Conrail to the Norfolk Southern, and resulted in its sale by public offering instead. It is Dingell's committee which superintends the communications industry, handling issues like the AT&T breakup and its consequences. It has jurisdiction over the securities industry, and in 1987 Dingell was planning an investigation of Ivan Boesky, pushing a bill to outlaw greenmail, arguing for Ron Wyden's bill to require accountants to report fraud to the SEC. It has jurisdiction over health (Dingell wants to stop drug companies from giving doctors free samples of prescription medicines), energy (Dingell has resisted proposals to complete the deregulation of natural gas), and the environment.

Dingell has not been successful on every issue. Representing a Detroit area district, he sought to relax clean air standards in the early 1980s, and was blocked by subcommittee chairman Henry Waxman, usually an ally, who is also ready to use the rules to the utmost. Like most northern Democrats, he opposed deregulation of oil in the 1970s, and lost both legislatively and intellectually. He has opposed the Superfund legislation drafted by subcommittee chairman James Florio, with more success. In general, Dingell supports government regulation, but he is open to the argument, and not only when the auto and steel industries are involved, that regulation is strangling an enterprise. On trade, he strongly favors retaliating against Japan and other countries whose practices he considers unfair; and though Ways and Means tends to have jurisdiction here, he is a force to be reckoned with on the issue. He has a reputation, earned over many years, as a conservationist; he is an enthusiastic hunter (and opponent of gun controls) and an avid outdoorsman, and he fought to maintain natural habitats and environments long before it was fashionable. For years he stayed on the Merchant Marine and Fisheries Committee not, as most members do, to funnel subsidies to the maritime industry, but to advance conservation.

Dingell's seat is safe. His father was elected to Congress in 1932, one of the first Polish-Americans in the House and a sponsor of the Social Security Act and the Truman-supported national health insurance. John Dingell, Jr., was a House page from 1938 to 1943—starting out before any current member was serving there—and he was elected after his father's death in 1955 from a district with large Polish, black, and Jewish minorities (Ivan Boesky's family's delicatessen, probably the biggest in Detroit, was a block outside his district's boundary). He had one serious fight, because of redistricting, in 1964, beating a fellow Democrat who opposed the Civil Rights Act, even though most of the district was new to Dingell; he has been reelected easily since. He has had an interesting personal life, raising his children after his divorce (one son was elected to the Michigan Senate in 1986) and marrying in 1981 a granddaughter of one of General Motors's Fisher brothers. He is the most powerful and formidable member of the Michigan delegation, and the heavily industrial 16th District surely would not want to be represented by anyone else.

The People: Pop. 1980: 514,560, dn. 0.7% 1970–80. Households (1980): 77% family, 41% with children, 65% married couples; 24.0% housing units rented; median monthly rent: $208; median house value: $44,000. Voting age pop. (1980): 367,589; 3% Black, 2% Spanish origin.

1984 Presidential Vote:

Reagan (R)	125,502	(60%)
Mondale (D)	83,958	(40%)

Rep. John D. Dingell (D)

Elected Dec. 13, 1955; b. July 8, 1926, Colorado Springs, CO; home, Trenton; Georgetown U., B.S. 1949, J.D. 1952; Roman Catholic; married (Deborah).

Career: Army, WWII; Practicing atty., 1952–55; Wayne Cnty. Asst. Prosecuting Atty., 1953–55.

Offices: 2221 RHOB 20515, 202-225-4071. Also 5461 Schaefer Rd., Dearborn 48126, 313-846-1276; and 241 E. Elm, Ste. 105, Monroe 48161, 313-243-1849.

Committees: *Energy and Commerce* (Chairman of 25 D). Subcommittee: Oversight and Investigations (Chairman).

Group Ratings

	ADA	ACLU	COPE	CFA	LCV	ACU	NTU	NSI	COC	CEI
1986	75	75	92	92	60	19	23	10	6	12
1985	85	—	92	50	—	14	29	—	25	—

National Journal Ratings

	1986 LIB — 1986 CONS		1985 LIB — 1985 CONS	
Economic	87%	— 0%	89%	— 0%
Social	74%	— 23%	67%	— 33%
Foreign	67%	— 30%	64%	— 36%

Key Votes

1) Lmt Cln Water Act	AGN	5) Retain Gun Cont	AGN	9) Aid Angola Reb	AGN
2) Rpl Tobac Sub	AGN	6) Contra Aid	AGN	10) Tax Reform	AGN
3) Grm-Rdmn Def Red	AGN	7) Lmt Text Imp	FOR	11) S Africa Sanc	FOR
4) Ban Polygraph	FOR	8) Limit SDI	FOR	12) Immig Reform	FOR

Election Results

1986 general	John D. Dingell (D)	101,659	(78%)	($510,044)
	Frank W. Grzywacki (R)	28,971	(22%)	
1986 primary	John D. Dingell (D)	33,903	(92%)	
	Thomas McLenaghan (D)................	2,940	(8%)	
1984 general	John D. Dingell (D)	121,463	(64%)	($335,826)
	Frank W. Grzywacki (R)	68,116	(36%)	($160)

Campaign Contributions and Expenditures

1985-86		Direct Cont. 1985-86		PACS Breakdown 1985-86			
Receipts	$522,685	Indiv.	$102,146	Corp.	$177,130	T/M/H	$92,935
Expend.	$510,044	Party	$981	Labor	$84,800	Agr.	$4,500
Unspent	$100,677	PACS	$371,815	Ideo.	$10,450	CWOS	$2,000
		Cand.	$27,025				

SEVENTEENTH DISTRICT

The 17th Congressional District of Michigan forms almost a semicircle around the city of Detroit—at a point just beyond, in most cases, where significant numbers of blacks live. Most of Detroit's blacks are in the 1st and 13th Districts, whose boundaries were drawn to make safe black constituencies; what is left over, on the far northwest side of Detroit, and in its near western and northwestern suburbs, is the 17th. That means that the 17th has plenty of variety. Some of its suburbs, like Ferndale and Royal Oak, along Woodward Avenue in Oakland County, or Redford Township just west of Detroit, are aging now: originally mixed Protestant and Catholic, and leaning Republican, Royal Oak has become more Democratic and older, as young families move farther out. Southfield, once empty swampland, has now become the main high-rise office center in Michigan, with more square footage than downtown Detroit. The 17th's portion of Detroit includes what was once one of the metropolitan area's high-income neighbor-hoods, Rosedale Park, as well as miles of straight streets lined by frame and white aluminum siding workingmen's houses from the 1940s. Blacks have been moving westward in Detroit, and the 17th's portion of the city is already one-third black; there are also a significant number of blacks in the mostly Jewish suburbs of Oak Park and Southfield. To the south the 17th takes in white working-class Dearborn Heights and, just next door, the mostly black suburb of Inkster.

The 17th District's congressman, Sander Levin, has a wealth of political experience. Twice he came within a hairsbreadth of beating William Milliken and becoming Michigan's governor, in 1970 and 1974; before that he was an important state legislator and Michigan's Democratic chairman in the turbulent year of 1968. In the Carter Administration he was in charge of population control programs in AID—not a noncontroversial job. He is the older brother of Senator Carl Levin, and came to Congress later; but he was the first in his family to run for office, and the two brothers seem to have an entirely comfortable relationship. Sander Levin had not been expecting to run for Congress at all in 1982, but 18th District incumbent James Blanchard (who worked in Levin's gubernatorial campaigns) ran for governor, and 17th District incumbent William Brodhead retired at age 40; their districts were collapsed and included Levin's home base; so he ran and after a spirited primary won.

Representative Levin is a natural legislator: a hard worker, a detail man, a strong partisan who is less interested in trumpeting his own opinions than he is in working out compromise and agreement among everyone involved in an issue—and who is willing to spend endless hours doing so. In his first term he was a member of the Freshman Budget Group which was more willing than the Democratic leadership to come out openly with plans to close the budget deficit. In his second term he chaired the House Democrats' task force on what could emerge as the hottest domestic issue—or the biggest domestic policy accomplishment—of the 100th Congress, workfare. Levin's task force recommended increased help for the working poor, but shifted the historical focus of many Democrats on benefit levels by urging greater education and training to enable welfare recipients to get into the work force. He co-sponsored with Senator Daniel Patrick Moynihan a workfare bill requiring states to provide job training, child care, and transportation to welfare recipients, holding states accountable for placing them in decent jobs, and providing incentives for states that do well.

At the beginning of the 100th Congress Levin also gained one of two open seats on the Ways and Means Committee, which will be handling important parts of the workfare and trade issues. At home he has had no trouble since his first election: he had no Republican opposition in 1984 and won with 76% of the vote in 1986.

The People: Pop. 1980: 514,560, dn. 11.7% 1970–80. Households (1980): 73% family, 36% with children, 60% married couples; 25.4% housing units rented; median monthly rent: $268; median house value: $41,200. Voting age pop. (1980): 382,414; 10% Black, 1% Spanish origin, 1% Asian origin.

1984 Presidential Vote: Reagan (R) 119,118   (54%)
Mondale (D) 101,902   (46%)

Rep. Sander M. Levin (D)

Elected 1982; b. Sept. 6, 1931, Detroit; home, Southfield; U. of Chicago, B.A. 1952, Columbia U., M.A. 1954, Harvard U. Law Sch., LL.B. 1957; Jewish; married (Victoria).

Career: Practicing atty.; Oakland Bd. of Sprvrs., 1961–64; MI Senate, 1965–70; Fellow, Harvard U., Kennedy Sch. of Govt., 1975; Asst. Admin., Agency for Intl. Develop., 1977–81.

Offices: 323 CHOB 20515, 202-225-4961. Also 17117 West Nine Mile Rd., Ste. 1120, Southfield 48075, 313-559-4444.

Committees: *Ways and Means* (22d of 23 D). Subcommittees: Health; Social Security. *Select Committee on Children, Youth, and Families* (9th of 18 D). Task Force: Crisis Intervention.

Group Ratings

	ADA	ACLU	COPE	CFA	LCV	ACU	NTU	NSI	COC	CEI
1986	85	85	92	92	79	0	25	0	33	20
1985	95	—	89	75	—	10	34	—	32	—

National Journal Ratings

	1986 LIB — 1986 CONS		1985 LIB — 1985 CONS	
Economic	74%	— 23%	81%	— 17%
Social	89%	— 0%	73%	— 23%
Foreign	73%	— 26%	75%	— 21%

Key Votes

1) Lmt Cln Water Act	FOR	5) Retain Gun Cont	FOR	9) Aid Angola Rcb	AGN
2) Rpl Tobac Sub	AGN	6) Contra Aid	AGN	10) Tax Reform	FOR
3) Grm-Rdmn Def Red	FOR	7) Lmt Text Imp	FOR	11) S Africa Sanc	FOR
4) Ban Polygraph	FOR	8) Limit SDI	FOR	12) Immig Reform	FOR

Election Results

1986 general	Sander M. Levin (D)	105,031	(76%)	($134,327)
	Calvin Williams (R)	30,897	(22%)	
1986 primary	Sander M. Levin (D)	31,869	(94%)	
	Robert Bell (D).....................	2,097	(6%)	
1984 general	Sander M. Levin (D)unopposed			($154,724)

Campaign Contributions and Expenditures

1985-86		Direct Cont. 1985-86		PACS Breakdown 1985-86			
Receipts	$221,609	Indiv.	$91,149	Corp.	$32,253	T/M/H	$37,274
Expend.	$134,327	Party	$525	Labor	$43,125	Agr.	$2,100
Unspent	$102,814	PACS	$118,002	Ideo.	$2,500	CWOS	$750

EIGHTEENTH DISTRICT

Northwest of Detroit, which is situated on some of the flattest land in the nation, is a line of hills and lakes, beginning about 20 miles from downtown. This line runs from northeast to southwest, from northern Macomb County, down toward Ann Arbor. It marks the southernmost advance of an Ice Age glacier, which dug up the hills and valleys here and deposited unusual soil and moraine. The advance of the glacier also marks the beginning, roughly, of Detroit's affluent suburbs. Since World War II, Detroiters with money have sought this hillier, more picturesque part of the metropolitan area in preference to the flat, more cramped affluent areas closer in; they didn't mind the long commutes, and by the 1970s many of the offices and most of the fancy shops had moved northwest anyway.

This affluent belt is approximately coincident with the 18th Congressional District of Michigan. In the center are Birmingham and Bloomfield Hills, the former once a small outstate Michigan town and now a major shopping and office center, the latter the highest income suburb in the Detroit area. To the northeast are the affluent parts of Troy, Rochester, and, across the Macomb County line, Shelby Township. Southwest of Birmingham are Farmington Hills and the suburb of Novi; the 18th proceeds west, across hilly country almost all the way to Ann Arbor. This is not only the most affluent, but also the most heavily Republican district in Michigan; it was designed to take in the most heavily Republican parts of the metropolitan area, leaving safe Democratic constituencies for its other congressmen.

The congressman here is William Broomfield, one of the senior Republicans in the House. First elected in 1956, he is not a man who seeks the spotlight or looks particularly comfortable in it. Nonetheless, he is a professional politician, first elected to the Michigan legislature in 1948, and a solid party man, who wants never to embarrass his party or its administration. He is the ranking Republican on the Foreign Affairs Committee, and in that capacity acts as the Administration's spokesman on such unpopular issues as aid to El Salvador. Broomfield is old enough to remember when the phrase "bipartisan foreign policy" was more than a cliché, and his instinct is to cooperate with administrations of either party, to present a united front abroad. Often quiet and pro forma in his support of measures his committee position gives him the lead on, he was a vigorous, heartfelt, and effective—in 1986 anyway—supporter of the Reagan Administration policy of aid to the Nicaraguan Contras; he surprised some of the younger Republicans who did not suspect him of such fervor. They should have remembered that there are plenty of precedents in the bipartisan foreign policy of the Eisenhower years, when Broomfield came to Congress, of American support for military action against Communist-allied regimes.

Broomfield has been a major player on the Iran-Contra investigation, as one of the members of the special committee investigating it; he called early for a fast investigation and for granting immunity to Oliver North and John Poindexter to get down to the facts. Broomfield has become a foreign policy player off Capitol Hill too, meeting with Soviet leader Gorbachev in 1986 and presenting a list of Jewish refusniks to him; Broomfield has always been a strong supporter of aid to Israel and the rights of Soviet Jews, and arms sales to Arab states are one issue on which he has opposed the Reagan Administration. He fought to get Macomb County resident Peter Ivezaj released from a Yugoslav prison and won after threatening to withdraw Yugoslavia's most favored nation status.

Broomfield once had to fight hotly contested general elections, when his district included the tough working-class town of Pontiac and the affluent suburbs were not so populous. He survived the Democratic year of 1958 nimbly and beat another Republican incumbent in the 1972 primary when they were redistricted together. Now he has a safe seat for as long as he wants: he is regularly reelected with more than 70% of the vote.

The People: Pop. 1980: 514,560, up 31.4% 1970–80. Households (1980): 79% family, 45% with children, 70% married couples; 22.0% housing units rented; median monthly rent: $314; median house value: $80,500. Voting age pop. (1980): 360,726; 1% Asian origin, 1% Spanish origin, 1% Black.

1984 Presidential Vote:

Reagan (R)	202,418	(75%)
Mondale (D)	66,683	(25%)

Rep. William S. Broomfield (R)

Elected 1956; b. Apr. 28, 1922, Royal Oak; home, Birmingham; MI St. U.; Presbyterian; married (Jane).

Career: MI House of Reps., 1949–55, Spkr. Pro Tem, 1953; MI Senate, 1955–57; Amb.to Gen. Assembly of U.N., 1967.

Offices: 2306 RHOB 20515, 202-225-6135. Also 430 N. Woodward, Birmingham 48011, 313-642-3800; and 371 N. Main, Milford 48042, 313-685-2640.

Committees: *Foreign Affairs* (Ranking Member of 18 R). Subcommittee: Arms Control, International Security and Science (Ranking Member). *Small Business* (3d of 17 R). Subcommittee: Regulation and Business Opportunity (Ranking Member).

Group Ratings

	ADA	ACLU	COPE	CFA	LCV	ACU	NTU	NSI	COC	CEI
1986	5	0	19	17	38	73	55	100	100	75
1985	5	—	20	50	—	85	59	—	71	—

National Journal Ratings

	1986 LIB — 1986 CONS		1985 LIB — 1985 CONS	
Economic	12% —	88%	27% —	73%
Social	18% —	78%	0% —	76%
Foreign	16% —	79%	0% —	76%

Key Votes

1) Lmt Cln Water Act	FOR	5) Retain Gun Cont	FOR	9) Aid Angola Reb	FOR
2) Rpl Tobac Sub	FOR	6) Contra Aid	FOR	10) Tax Reform	FOR
3) Grm-Rdmn Def Red	FOR	7) Lmt Text Imp	AGN	11) S Africa Sanc	AGN
4) Ban Polygraph	AGN	8) Limit SDI	AGN	12) Immig Reform	AGN

Election Results

1986 general	William S. Broomfield (R)	110,099	(74%)	($68,497)
	Gary Kohut (D)	39,144	(26%)	($5,929)
1986 primary	William S. Broomfield (R)	47,524	(100%)	
1984 general	William S. Broomfield (R)	186,505	(79%)	($102,270)
	Vivian H. Smargon (D)................	46,191	(20%)	($13,481)

Campaign Contributions and Expenditures

1985-86		Direct Cont. 1985-86		PACS Breakdown 1985-86			
Receipts	$179,403	Indiv.	$85,023	Corp.	$11,735	T/M/H	$14,250
Expend.	$68,497	Party	$2,421	Labor	$0	Agr.	$0
Unspent	$430,594	PACS	$35,335	Ideo.	$9,350	CWOS	$0

MINNESOTA

It is a small commonwealth set far to the north, where farmers until the early 20th century scratched out a living on land frozen over much of the year. Here also politicians beginning in the 1930s developed a vibrant tradition of clean politics and a generous welfare state. Yet by the middle 1980s Minnesota, like so much of the nation, is pruning back its government, aggressively going after new business, and wobbling erratically between its two major parties as cultural as well as economic issues help determine election outcomes. The commonwealth is Minnesota, but it could just as easily be Norway: for in the eerie way in which Europe seems to reflect mirror-like the American regions, with the British Isles and France taking the role of the East Coast, Germany and Poland the industrial Midwest, the Mediterranean countries an until-recently-impoverished South, there can be no doubt that the Upper Midwest states of Minnesota, Wisconsin, and North Dakota are reflections of Scandinavia. And like Scandinavia, which pioneered the post-1945 European welfare state, these states have had an effect on continental politics out of proportion to the number of their voters. Just as Wisconsin's LaFollette Progressives pioneered many reforms instituted by the New Deal, so Minnesota's Democratic-Farmer-Labor party, through its leaders (especially Hubert Humphrey) and by example, has shaped the post-1945 Democrats; the only other American party so influential has been the Tammany Democrats of New Yorkers Al Smith and Robert Wagner.

Yet the signs are that Minnesota's DFL is on the wane. It still wins its share of elections: it holds the governor's office and both houses of the state legislature, plus five of the state's eight House seats. But it also loses some too: Republicans (known since 1975 as Independent Republicans or IRs) have held both Senate seats since 1978 and surprised just about everyone by winning control of the state House, thanks mostly to anti-abortion activists, in 1984. Minnesota DFLers have been on five of the last six national Democratic tickets, and Democrats have carried Minnesota five of those six times; it was even George McGovern's third best state (46%), after Massachusetts and Rhode Island, in 1972. But no one expects a DFLer to be on the national Democratic ticket again any time soon, and Minnesota's Walter Mondale was able to carry the state only by the narrowest of margins in 1984. Governor Rudy Perpich was reelected by a large margin in 1986. But his first acts were to promise tax reform and to make Minnesota "the brainpower state," so it would be more attractive to business. As Norway, Sweden, and Denmark debate cutting back on welfare state measures, so do Minnesota and Wisconsin. So the question becomes, how did the welfare state idea grow here, and why isn't it growing any more?

Start with the beginning, which in Minnesota's case goes back not to the Vikings but to 1850, when the state was still wilderness, far north of the nation's great paths of east–west migration; Minneapolis and St. Paul are as far north as Bangor, Maine, or Vancouver, Washington. The Yankee immigrants who were pushing on the great east–west railroads into Iowa, Nebraska, and Kansas shunned Minnesota's icy lakes and ferocious winters. So the builders of the Great Northern and Northern Pacific and the developers of Minneapolis and St. Paul—already twin cities by 1860—concentrated on attracting Norwegian, Swedish, and German migrants who would find the terrain and climate unexceptional. Within two decades the Twin Cities were the nerve center of a sprawling and rich agricultural empire stretching west from Minnesota through the Dakotas and eventually into Montana and beyond; Minneapolis and St. Paul became the termini of its rail lines and the site of its grain-milling companies.

Thus was a wilderness converted quickly into one of the most productive parts of the world. But the Scandinavians and Germans were alarmed by the unprecedented concentration of economic power and wealth into the hands of just a few identifiable millionaires on Minneapolis's and St. Paul's Summit Avenue. The immigrants had brought to Minnesota traditions of

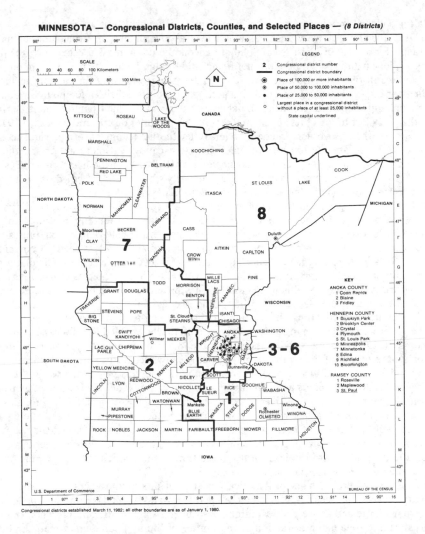

MINNESOTA — Congressional Districts, Counties, and Selected Places — *(8 Districts)*

Congressional districts established March 11, 1982; all other boundaries are as of January 1, 1980.

cooperative activity and bureaucratic socialism, and their rebellion against market capitalism and the magnates' dominance gave the politics of Minnesota from the turn of the 20th century a Scandinavian flavor. As in Wisconsin and North Dakota, a strong third party developed here in the years after the Populist era; and this Farmer-Labor Party elected Senators in the 1920s and dominated state politics in the 1930s. The Farmer-Laborites, hurt by their ties to Communists, were beaten by Harold Stassen's Republicans in 1938, but this was still a New Deal state; the logical thing, the merger that created the DFL, was negotiated by Hubert Humphrey, the young mayor of Minneapolis, in the wartime 1940s. Humphrey's DFL—clean, idealistic, closely tied to labor, backed by many farmers—attracted dozens of talented politicians, including Eugene McCarthy, Orville Freeman, Walter Mondale, and Minneapolis's current mayor, Donald Fraser. In 1948 Mayor Humphrey's speech calling on the Democrats to support civil rights changed his party; he himself was elected Senator that year, carrying even the traditionally Republican 2d District where his coordinator was a 20-year-old student named Walter Mondale. For 30 years the DFL dominated Minnesota politics, winning most elections and setting the agenda for policy even when, usually because of internal feuds, it lost an election.

The DFL stood for a generous, compassionate federal government, for strong labor unions and high wages, for an expansionist fiscal policy to encourage consumer-led economic growth, for civil rights, for an anti-Communist but not bombastic foreign policy. Its base was among blue-collar workers in the Twin Cities and in Duluth and the Iron Range and among farmers of Scandinavian origin. The party succeeded in getting most of its policies adopted in St. Paul and Washington, and helped its constituents achieve affluence. At which point, some time in the 1970s, the party lost much of its appeal and saw its base splinter on cultural issues. In 1978 the DFL was hurt when Governor Wendell Anderson let the lieutenant governor who succeeded him, Rudy Perpich, appoint him to Mondale's Senate vacancy. But more important, the once dominant party was split by issues like abortion and whether part of the northern woods should be sealed off from development; in other words, the party's liberal wing seemed oblivious to the moral concerns and economic needs of its core constituency.

Nor did increasingly affluent Minnesotans believe that ever-increasing public spending was in their interest any more. The Twin Cities, which with the surrounding metropolitan area accounted for half the state's population, was developing a white-collar, high tech, professional-based economy which had greater respect for market forces and saw less need for government assistance. What's surprising here is not that the DFL has lost some elections, but that a party which initially saw itself as the protectors of the downtrodden has adapted as well as it has to the task of representing a mostly affluent electorate. They have been aided by the inexperience and gaffes of the Republicans. Governor Albert Quie, elected in 1978, was embarrassed as his revenue estimates proved wrong, and again and again he had to come forward to ask for more taxes; he declined to run again in 1982. The right-to-lifers who enabled Republicans to carry the state House in 1984 ended up giving their party the image of a one-issue pressure group, with views on that issue out of line with the majority's. Meanwhile, Rudy Perpich, returned to the governor's office after four years in 1982, spent much time flying around the world promoting Minnesota as a site for business and denying that he wanted any federal government help at all.

Culturally, Minnesota remains riven: most of it tolerant of new mores, the Twin Cities with one of the largest percentages of working women in the country, yet still anchored to old mores. On foreign policy, it retains tinges of the isolationism and aversion to American risk-taking which Samuel Lubell 40 years ago found rooted in its German and Scandinavian heritage. So on balance it leans a bit toward the DFL. But the economic issues, which once tipped the balance solidly to the DFL, no longer do so.

Governor. Rudy Perpich is one of America's most colorful and idiosyncratic governors—and also an experienced survivor now of Minnesota's political wars. Perpich is from the Iron Range, a dentist from a large and active political family descended from Croatian immigrants, and there is in his style and tone much of the rough-and-tumble of life in a community made up almost entirely of people with working class roots living in a forbidding and unforgiving physical environment. That must strike a chord: his support in the Iron Range and outside the Twin Cities generally was critical in enabling him to beat the party-convention-endorsed candidate in the 1982 primary and to whip, by a 57%–41% margin, St. Paul Mayor George Latimer in the 1986 primary. In the 1986 general, Perpich's politics of wooing business and disciplining but not dismantling Minnesota's welfare state helped him win by a 56%–43% margin. That was a solid enough victory, but it was less than he won by in 1982, and suggests that the DFL no longer has an automatic majority in Minnesota.

Senators. Minnesota's two Republican Senators both have held nationally important and sometimes visible positions, and have wielded more responsibility than almost anyone expected when they both were first elected in 1978. The best known certainly is David Durenberger, who was chairman of the Senate Intelligence Committee in 1985 and 1986. He came to the post after six years of legislative busy-ness, on the Finance Committee working on health measures, and promoting various forms of "new federalism"; suddenly he was a major foreign policy actor.

And not a shy one. Durenberger began by opposing the Reagan Administration's policy of aid to the Nicaraguan Contras, and he attacked then CIA director William Casey for lacking "a sense of direction"—though it often seemed his real problem was that he didn't like the direction Casey was assiduously taking, and telling Congress little about. Durenberger and ranking Democrat Patrick Leahy succeeded Barry Goldwater and Daniel Patrick Moynihan, both of whose views were formed in the Cold War period and who favored active, even aggressive, intelligence operations, though they bridled when misled by Casey; Durenberger and Leahy, whose attitudes were formed in the Vietnam era, were inclined not just to be skeptical, but to be scathingly critical—and to go public with their criticisms. Leaks became so common on the Senate side that House Intelligence Committee members—by no means hawks—requested a meeting with Durenberger and a few days later House Intelligence Chairman Edward Boland told the House, "I do not believe that it is helpful or appropriate for members of Congress who sit on oversight committees to regularly or recklessly comment on intelligence matters, either critically or favorably." In context, that was a scathing criticism of Durenberger.

Durenberger's leaks and outbursts may have been related to turbulence in his personal life. Just as he was taking the chairmanship, he separated from his second wife, who had just finished raising his four children after his first wife died; he moved to a nondenominational Christian retreat house amid rumors that he had had an affair with a staffer and was drinking too much. He talked about his personal life with *Minneapolis Star and Tribune* reporter Steve Berg; "maybe one of my problems," he said in the argot of a situation comedy supporting actress being interviewed on *Entertainment Tonight,* "was that I didn't love myself well enough to be a good lover or neighbor." But intelligence officials must consider it bizarre that a Republican Senate entrusted to a man in these straits the responsibilities of the Intelligence chair and access to secrets it grants. In 1986 he moved back home. But he was also under fire for divulging what some thought was classified information in a speech to a Jewish group in Florida. "People have begun to develop deep questions about him," Berg reported a Minnesota Republican as saying, and what had looked for years like independence started to look more like a lack of compass or even flakiness.

It was not clear early in 1987, however, that Durenberger was suffering with the voters. In the past he has shown great electoral strength, beating two millionaires who self-financed their campaigns: Bob Short, who antagonized many liberals by the way he beat Donald Fraser in the 1978 primary; and Mark Dayton, the department store heir whose wife is Jay Rockefeller's sister, and who spent $7 million of his (not her) money on his 1982 race. But Durenberger, fortified by his seat on Finance, is no slouch at all in raising money: he raised nearly $4 million for that race and will probably spend more in 1988. He is likely to have serious opposition, however, quite possibly from Hubert Humphrey III, better known as Skip, the state attorney general, who has his father's good humor and ebullience without all of his intensity. In early 1987 Humphrey, with heavy support from rural farm areas, was running behind by only a 44%–40% margin.

Rudy Boschwitz, Minnesota's junior Senator, may play a role in this; after the 1986 election he got himself elected chairman of the Republicans' Senate campaign committee. Boschwitz also is one of a kind. He was born in Germany, and came to the United States as a child; he moved to Minnesota and made his fortune in the plywood business. Boschwitz is a booster of free-market principles in economics, on agricultural and trade as well as budget and pork-barrel issues; he is also one of the Senate's most passionate opponents of nuclear power. On foreign policy he tends to be hawkish, and used to chair the Near Eastern and South Asian Subcommittee of Foreign Affairs; throughout he has been a strong and passionate supporter of Israel. He also serves on the Budget Committee and on Agriculture, where he believes that federal policy should be more market-oriented. He has spent considerable time crafting newer, less expensive dairy programs and tending to the details of wheat. On campaign finance, he was careful, when the Boren bill to limit PACs and reform the finance laws came up in 1986, to look out for Republican party interests; the result was his successful amendment to stop PAC contributions to parties, on which the Democrats are much more dependent.

He has also shown considerable talent as a candidate. In 1978 he took on Wendell Anderson, who as governor had gotten himself appointed to fill Walter Mondale's seat; this is always an unpopular tactic (only one such governor-turned-senator has won in 50 years) and Boschwitz, drawing on his TV exposure in ads for his plywood business, won 57%–40%. In 1984 several potentially strong opponents dropped out—Mark Dayton, capable of spending unlimited funds, became a state department head; Representative James Oberstar ran for reelection after losing in the DFL endorsement convention. Boschwitz ran well ahead of President Reagan, who nearly carried the state anyway, and won 58%–41%. As campaign committee chairman, Boschwitz has a tough job. He is a good fundraiser, but must cope with dissatisfaction by big givers and direct mail recipients with the committee's giving bonuses of up to $50,000 to employees after the party lost eight seats and control of the Senate; the Republicans took in a lot of money but too much went to pay the cost of direct mailings and to political consultants and purveyors of services like computerized phone calls. Peppery, unembarrassable, Boschwitz seems determined to shake things up and get more for his contributors' money. Although the Democrats have more seats up than Republicans, they did not in early 1987 seem to have appreciably more at risk. Boschwitz might be doing well if Republicans make a net gain, putting themselves in position to win a majority in 1990 or 1992.

Presidential politics. Will Minnesota remain one of the most Democratic states in the nation in presidential elections? Probably yes: but not for sure. With no Minnesota nominee on the national ticket, with a certain strength to its free market, high tech economy at least in the Twin Cities, and with its large right-to-life movement, Minnesota could be seriously contested and might wind up in the Republican column.

Minnesota's DFLers and IRs both pride themselves on strong party organizations, based on volunteers, which endorse state candidate and select presidential delegates in caucuses and conventions, not primaries. In 1988 Minnesota's caucuses were scheduled as of early 1987 to be held the week of March 15, 1988, to coincide with other Midwest contests. It seems unlikely, however, that candidates after weeks of courting Iowans will want to come back up to the still frozen Midwest to court activists many of whose attitudes will strike most ordinary voters as unpalatable or bizarre.

Congressional districting. Minnesota's House districts were redrawn by a federal court, which adopted a Democratic plan. The Twin Cities metropolitan area now has four complete districts, and none of the four outstate districts now reaches far into metropolitan territory. Four of Minnesota's eight districts were seriously contested in 1982, three in 1984, two in 1986— evidence of how closely divided most of the state is outside the Twin Cities metro area and the Iron Range.

The People: Est. Pop. 1986: 4,214,000; Pop. 1980: 4,075,970, up 3.4% 1980–86 and 7.1% 1970–80; 1.75% of U.S. total, 21st largest. 17% with 1–3 yrs. col., 17% with 4+ yrs. col.; 9.5% below poverty level. Single ancestry: 17% German, 7% Norwegian, 4% Swedish, 3% English, 2% Irish, Polish, 1% French, Dutch, Italian. Households (1980): 72% family, 40% with children, 62% married couples; 28.3% housing units rented; median monthly rent: $212; median house value: $54,300. Voting age pop. (1980): 2,904,162; 1% Black, 1% American Indian, 1% Spanish origin, 1% Asian origin. Registered voters (1986): 2,655,650; no party registration.

1986 Share of Federal Tax Burden: $13,249,000,000; 1.76% of U.S. total, 20th largest.

1986 Share of Federal Expenditures

	Total		Non-Defense		Defense	
Total Expend	$12,431m	(1.50%)	$9,836m	(1.64%)	$2,595m	(1.13%)
St/Lcl Grants	2,110m	(1.87%)	2,109m	(1.87%)	1m	(0.90%)
Salary/Wages	1,019m	(0.84%)	340m	(0.58%)	180m	(0.29%)
Pymnts to Indiv	5,470m	(1.50%)	5,357m	(1.54%)	113m	(.64%)
Procurement	2,674m	(1.30%)	374m	(0.67%)	2,300m	(1.53%)
Research/Other	1,158m	(4.43%)	1,158m	(4.35%)	0m	(0.04%)

Political Lineup: Governor, Rudy Perpich (DFL); Lt. Gov., Marlene Johnson (DFL); Secy. of State, Joan Anderson Growe (DFL); Atty. Gen., Hubert H. Humphrey III (DFL); Treasurer, Michael McGrath (DFL); Auditor, Arne Carlson (IR). State Senate, 67 (47 DFL and 20 IR); State House of Representatives, 134 (81 DFL and 51 IR). Senators, David Durenberger (IR) and Rudy Boschwitz (IR). Representatives, 8 (5 DFL and 3 IR).

1984 Presidential Vote		
Mondale (D)	1,036,364	(50%)
Reagan (R)	1,032,603	(50%)

1980 Presidential Vote		
Carter (D)	954,173	(47%)
Reagan (R)	873,268	(43%)
Anderson (I)	174,997	(9%)

GOVERNOR

Gov. Rudy Perpich (DFL)

Elected 1982, term expires Jan. 1991; b. June 27, 1928, Carson Lake; home, Hibbing; Hibbing Jr. Col., A.A. 1950, Marquette U., D.D.S. 1954; Roman Catholic; married (Lola).

Career: Army, 1946–48; Dentist; Hibbings Bd. of Ed., 1952–62; MN Senate, 1963–71; Lt. Gov., 1971–76; Gov., 1976–79; Vice Pres., World Tech, Inc., 1979–82.

Office: 130 State Capitol Bldg., Aurora Ave., St. Paul 55155, 612-296-3391.

Election Results

1986 gen.	Rudy Perpich (DFL)	790,138	(56%)
	Cal R. Ludeman (IR)	606,755	(43%)
1986 prim.	Rudy Perpich (DFL)	293,426	(57%)
	George Latimer (DFL)	207,198	(41%)
1982 gen.	Rudy Perpich (DFL)	1,049,104	(59%)
	Wheelock Whitney (IR)	711,796	(40%)

SENATORS

Sen. David Durenberger (IR)

Elected 1978, seat up 1988; b. Aug. 19, 1934, St. Cloud; home, Minneapolis; St. John's U., B.A. 1955, U. of MN, J.D. 1959; Roman Catholic; married (Penny).

Career: Army, 1955–57; Practicing atty., 1959–66; Exec. Secy. to Gov. Harold LeVander, 1967–71; Counsel for Legal & Commun. Affairs, Corporate Secy., Mgr., Intl. Licensing Div., H.B. Fuller Co., 1971–78.

Offices: 154 RSOB 20510, 202-224-3244. Also 1020 Plymouth Bldg., 12 S. 6th St., Minneapolis 55402, 612-349-5111.

Committees: *Environment and Public Works* (5th of 7 R). Subcommittees: Environmental Protection; Hazardous Wastes and Toxic Substances (Ranking Member); Water Resources, Transportation and Infrastructure. *Finance* (8th of 9 R). Subcommittees: Health (Ranking Member); International Trade; Social Security and Family Policy. *Special Committee on Aging* (8th of 9 R).

Group Ratings

	ADA	ACLU	COPE	CFA	LCV	ACU	NTU	NSI	COC	CEI
1986	40	38	40	42	92	43	46	70	58	55
1985	30	—	41	25	—	48	44	—	54	—

National Journal Ratings

	1986 LIB — 1986 CONS	1985 LIB — 1985 CONS
Economic	55% — 43%	44% — 55%
Social	41% — 56%	40% — 58%
Foreign	45% — 54%	45% — 52%

Key Votes

1) Ease Gun Cont	FOR	5) Grm-Rdmn Def Red	FOR	9) Rehnquist Nom	FOR
2) Immig Reform	FOR	6) Contra Aid	AGN	10) Tax Reform	FOR
3) Lmt Text Imp	AGN	7) SDI Funding	FOR	11) Drug Death Pen	FOR
4) Aid Tobac Ind	AGN	8) Lmt PAC Contrib	AGN	12) S Africa Sanc	FOR

Election Results

1982 general	David Durenberger (IR)...............	949,207	(53%)	($4,189,619)
	Mark Dayton (DFL)..................	840,401	(47%)	($7,172,312)
1982 primary	David Durenberger (IR)...............	287,651	(93%)	
	Mary Jane Rachner (IR)	20,401	(7%)	
1978 general	David Durenberger (IR)...............	957,908	(61%)	($1,062,271)
	Robert E. Short (DFL)...............	538,675	(35%)	($1,972,060)

Campaign Contributions and Expenditures

1981-82		Direct Cont. 1981-82		PACS Breakdown			
Receipts	$4,268,602	Indiv.	$3,093,425	Agr	$54,100	Ideo	$100,100
Expend.	$4,189,619	Party	$27,861	Bus	$748,725	Lbr	$17,250
Unspent	$89,846	PACS	$1,078,954	Hlth	$67,675	Prof	$12,275
		Cand.	$50,000				

Sen. Rudy Boschwitz (IR)

Elected 1978, seat up 1990; b. Nov. 7, 1930, Berlin, Germany; home, Plymouth; Johns Hopkins U., N.Y.U., B.S. 1950, LL.B. 1953; Jewish; married (Ellen).

Career: Army, 1953–55; Founder and Pres., Plywood Minnesota, Inc., 1963–78.

Offices: 506 HSOB 20510, 202-224-5641. Also 210 Bremer Bldg., 419 N. Robert St., St. Paul 55101, 612-221-0904.

Committees: *Agriculture, Nutrition, and Forestry* (5th of 9 R). Subcommittees: Agricultural Credit (Ranking Member); Domestic and Foreign Marketing and Product Promotion; Nutrition and Investigations. *Budget* (4th of 11 R). *Foreign Relations* (4th of 9 R). Subcommittees: European Affairs; Near Eastern and South Asian Affairs (Ranking Member). *Small Business* (2d of 9 R). Subcommittees: Export Expansion (Ranking Member); Rural Economy and Family Farming.

Group Ratings

	ADA	ACLU	COPE	CFA	LCV	ACU	NTU	NSI	COC	CEI
1986	15	21	17	67	50	57	50	90	74	66
1985	5	—	16	17	—	78	60	—	79	—

National Journal Ratings

	1986 LIB	—	1986 CONS	1985 LIB	—	1985 CONS
Economic	16%	—	76%	36%	—	62%
Social	41%	—	56%	25%	—	72%
Foreign	30%	—	65%	12%	—	80%

Key Votes

1) Ease Gun Cont	FOR	5) Grm-Rdmn Def Red	FOR	9) Rehnquist Nom	FOR
2) Immig Reform	FOR	6) Contra Aid	FOR	10) Tax Reform	FOR
3) Lmt Text Imp	AGN	7) SDI Funding	FOR	11) Drug Death Pen	FOR
4) Aid Tobac Ind	FOR	8) Lmt PAC Contrib	AGN	12) S Africa Sanc	FOR

Election Results

1984 general	Rudy Boschwitz (IR)	1,119,926	(56%)	($6,657,484)
	Joan Anderson Growe (DFL)	852,844	(43%)	($1,592,885)
1984 primary	Rudy Boschwitz (IR)	162,555	(97%)	
	Two others (IR).......................	5,739	(3%)	
1978 general	Rudy Boschwitz (IR)	894,092	(57%)	($1,872,443)
	Wendell Anderson (DFL)	638,375	(40%)	($1,154,351)

Campaign Contributions and Expenditures

1979-84		Direct Cont. 1979-84		PACS Breakdown 1979-84			
Receipts	$6,843,489	Indiv.	$5,314,501	Corp.	$560,592	T/M/H	$282,498
Expend.	$6,657,484	Party	$24,030	Labor	$1,975	Agr.	$55,500
Unspent	$207,032	PACS	$1,099,767	Ideo.	$199,197	CWOS	$13,000
		Cand.	$3,989				

FIRST DISTRICT

The northwestern salient of the Yankee migration across the Great Plains of America nears its end in the southern reaches of Minnesota. As you move west toward the gorges of the Mississippi River between the hills of Wisconsin and Minnesota, the Yankee stock begins to thin out, and you move into country where more and more of the original settlers were Germans and Scandinavians. It seems little different today from the Yankee country to the south and east, but once—before the German-bashing of World War I—this Germano-America was a distinctive place, with its own cultural institutions and ways. The German language and German turnvereins were wiped out in a sudden frenzy in 1917, but resentment lingered on long afterward, showing up politically as isolationist sentiment in the 1930s and 1940s and McCarthyism in the early 1950s.

Today this heritage shows up in the readiness of voters here to switch parties, unlike Yankee and southern voters farther south who seem to vote forever as they did during the Civil War. There is also some class-consciousness here. In blue-collar Austin, whose county went 61% for Walter Mondale in 1984, Local P-9 of the United Food and Commercial Workers conducted a bitter strike against the Hormel meatpacking firm, protesting concessions agreed to by the international union; but the company prevailed in 1986. In Rochester, whose county gave Ronald Reagan 64% in 1984, you find the prosperous Mayo Clinic with its teams of expert physicians and well-paid professional staff. In congressional elections, however, the area is ready to vote heavily for a congenial representative of either party. For 20 years it was happy to be represented by Republican Albert Quie. Now it seems at least as happy with Democrat Timothy Penny.

Penny is one of those young Democrats who startles everyone with his political acumen and energy—and who are so numerous as to account for most of the Democratic majority in the House. He was elected to the state Senate in 1976 at age 24, after visiting every home in the district; he won in a Republican district, and when (to judge from his current young appearance) he must have looked scarcely old enough to vote. Six years later, at age 30, he used the same door-to-door, personal campaigning tactics, plus $182,000, to win in a seat into which two Republicans had been redistricted. He campaigned personally throughout the district, and has done so ever since. He also proceeded immediately to follow a political course that has proved exceedingly popular. He became chairman of the Freshman Budget Group in 1983 and called himself a "compassionate conservative," and he compiled a more conservative record on economic issues than any DFL congressman has for years. He got a seat on the Agriculture Committee. A family man with four children, he kept a middle-of-the-road profile on cultural issues. On foreign affairs he was more liberal, like most Upper Midwest Democrats.

In 1984 there was much speculation about whether a moderate or a right-to-life Republican would get to take Penny on. The right-to-lifer won, in a district that was once the home of Harry Blackmun, then counsel to the Mayo Clinic, and author of the 1973 *Roe v. Wade* decision. But Penny won with a solid 57% while Walter Mondale was losing the district. Two years later, Penny won reelection with a phenomenal 72%; he carried Rochester's Olmsted County with 65%. There is every indication that Penny has made southeast Minnesota into a safe Democratic district.

The People: Pop. 1980: 509,460, up 5.2% 1970–80. Households (1980): 74% family, 40% with children, 66% married couples; 24.7% housing units rented; median monthly rent: $180; median house value: $45,800. Voting age pop. (1980): 362,626; 1% Spanish origin.

1984 Presidential Vote:

Reagan (R) 137,333	(55%)
Mondale (D) 109,652	(44%)

Rep. Timothy J. Penny (DFL)

Elected 1982; b. Nov. 19, 1951, Albert Lea; home, New Richland; Winona St. U., B.A. 1974; U. of MN; Lutheran; married (Barbara).

Career: MN Senate, 1976–82.

Offices: 436 CHOB 20515, 202-225-2472. Also Park Towers, 22 N. Broadway, Rochester 55904, 507-281-6053; and 410 S. 5th St., Mankato 56001, 507-625-6921.

Committees: *Agriculture* (19th of 26 D). Subcommittees: Conservation, Credit and Rural Development; Wheat, Soybeans, and Feed Grains. *Education and Labor* (16th of 21 D). Subcommittee: Labor Standards. *Veterans' Affairs* (8th of 21 D). Subcommittees: Compensation, Pension and Insurance; Hospitals and Health Care. *Select Committee on Hunger* (10th of 16 D).

Group Ratings

	ADA	ACLU	COPE	CFA	LCV	ACU	NTU	NSI	COC	CEI
1986	75	65	55	58	68	18	48	0	50	39
1985	60	—	57	58	—	24	58	—	50	—

National Journal Ratings

	1986 LIB — 1986 CONS			1985 LIB — 1985 CONS		
Economic	43%	—	56%	44%	—	56%
Social	57%	—	40%	52%	—	47%
Foreign	80%	—	0%	75%	—	21%

Key Votes

1) Lmt Cln Water Act	FOR	5) Retain Gun Cont	AGN	9) Aid Angola Reb	AGN
2) Rpl Tobac Sub	AGN	6) Contra Aid	AGN	10) Tax Reform	FOR
3) Grm-Rdmn Def Red	FOR	7) Lmt Text Imp	AGN	11) S Africa Sanc	FOR
4) Ban Polygraph	FOR	8) Limit SDI	FOR	12) Immig Reform	FOR

Election Results

1986 general	Timothy J. Penny (DFL)	125,115	(72%)	($334,484)
	Paul H. Grawe (IR)	47,750	(27%)	($44,112)
1986 primary	Timothy J. Penny (DFL)	42,896	(93%)	
	Gare LeGare (DFL)....................	3,416	(7%)	
1984 general	Timothy J. Penny (DFL)	140,095	(57%)	($424,313)
	Keith Spicer (IR)	105,723	(43%)	($338,338)

Campaign Contributions and Expenditures

1985-86		Direct Cont. 1985-86		PACS Breakdown 1985-86			
Receipts	$375,626	Indiv.	$197,613	Corp.	$20,900	T/M/H	$36,350
Expend.	$334,484	PACS	$146,425	Labor	$46,875	Agr.	$21,750
Unspent	$104,056			Ideo.	$18,983	CWOS	$1,650

SECOND DISTRICT

The southwest quarter of Minnesota, approximately, forms the state's 2d Congressional District. Most of this land is drained by the Minnesota River. In the eastern part of the district, the land is relatively green during the warm months; it was once heavily forested, and is still verdant, especially in the hilly land near the river banks. This area was settled by German Lutherans and Scandinavians, no-nonsense folk who farmed its land profitably. Farther west, there were fewer trees and less rainfall. This is part of the vast grain-growing Great Plains. Politically, the difference can be summed up thus: the eastern counties are Republican, in some cases very heavily Republican, a preference dating back to their first settlement; the western counties are politically volatile, swinging usually away from the party in power in protest against any depression or threatened depression of the farm economy.

The 2d District is represented by one of the Republican party's best instinctive politicians and most resourceful strategists—but also one who nearly got caught off political base in 1986. Vin Weber, like Democrats Tim Penny of the 1st and Gerry Sikorski of the 6th Districts, has been running for office since he was in his 20s; he had his first big success managing Senator Rudy Boschwitz's 1978 campaign, at age 26. Unlike most political children of the 1970s, however, Weber has always had a conservative tilt, a respect for free markets, a belief in conservative cultural values, an opposition to the dovish foreign policy views that became orthodoxy in the Upper Midwest in the late 1970s. In 1980, Democrat Rick Nolan of the 6th District became one of the first Watergate babies to retire from office, and Weber ran for the seat and won it. In 1982, the Democratic redistricting plan placed much of Weber's old territory in Tom Hagedorn's 2d District, but Weber persuaded Hagedorn, on whose staff he once worked, to run in the 1st; Hagedorn, who had other problems, lost, and Weber won. In the more Republican year of 1984 Weber won easily, by almost a 2 to 1 margin.

By that time he had emerged as a national figure. With Newt Gingrich of Georgia, he led the Conservative Opportunity Society, a group with a small membership, loose (or nonexistent) organization, and great impact. They used the House's special orders procedure to appeal to a C-SPAN cable audience; they commissioned thoughtful papers; they needled the Democrats for the intellectual weakness of some of their positions and demagogued them on others. At its best, their movement is thought provoking. Weber, for example, on economic issues tends to be against government regulation and involvement, and on cultural issues usually favors endorsement of traditional values. But on foreign policy he has opposed the Reagan Administration on the South Africa (though COS skinned back a bit on sanctions), the MX missile, chemical warfare, and the AWACS sale to Saudi Arabia. He was the leader on the Science, Space and Technology Committee of the ultimately successful fight to stop the Clinch River Breeder Reactor, which he opposed as a waste of money and as a threat to the environment. As a member of the minority, he was not an active legislator, even while he served on the Budget Committee; but he was making an impact.

Which was one of the things that prompted the tough challenge he faced in 1986. While Weber was provoking thought on issues national and global, farm owners and local businessmen were going bankrupt in agricultural Minnesota, losing their equity and their dreams. The fact that he didn't serve on the Agriculture Committee and was not highly visible on farm policy hurt him—though farm issues were the one set of economic issues where he left behind his free market principles. Opposition surfaced in the person of Dave Johnson, a successful farmer himself, and a Reagan delegate to the 1984 Dallas convention where Weber was busy working on platform planks; Johnson ran against the trends that "threaten to change what I grew up in. Our small towns are being turned into old age homes." Weber resisted any temptation to reply that this is always what happens when businesses become more efficient, require less labor, and lower prices to consumers. Weber was one of the few Republican incumbents with a huge fundraising advantage; he spent $909,000 and was confident enough to leave $165,000 in the bank afterwards—perhaps a little too confident, since his margin was only 52%–48%.

He returned to the House with his political instincts still sharp, giving up his seat on Budget where William Gray's Democrats have the initiative anyway and getting one of the Republicans' rare seats on Appropriations, where he can both tend to things that matter to the district and make a national record. He may run for statewide office some day, though both Senate seats are held by Republicans; in the meantime, he remains an important and interesting politician.

The People: Pop. 1980: 509,500, up 2.1% 1970–80. Households (1980): 74% family, 38% with children, 67% married couples; 23.4% housing units rented; median monthly rent: $142; median house value: $37,300. Voting age pop. (1980): 363,087.

1984 Presidential Vote:

Reagan (R)	....	139,872	(57%)
Mondale (D)	....	105,227	(43%)

Rep. Vin Weber (IR)

Elected 1980; b. July 24, 1952, Slayton; home, North Mankato; U. of MN, 1970–73; Roman Catholic; divorced.

Career: Press Secy./Researcher for U.S. Rep. Tom Hagedorn, 1974–76; Co-publisher, *The Murray County Herald*, 1976–78; Campaign Mgr., Chief MN Aide, Sen. Rudy Boschwitz, 1978–80.

Offices: 106 CHOB 20515, 202-225-2331. Also P.O. Box 279, New Ulm 56073, 507-354-6400; 919 S. 1st St., Willmar 56201, 612-235-6820; and P.O. Box 1214, Marshall 56258, 507-532-9611.

Committees: *Appropriations* (20th of 22 R). Subcommittees: Labor–Health and Human Services–Education; Rural Development, Agriculture and Related Agencies.

Group Ratings

	ADA	ACLU	COPE	CFA	LCV	ACU	NTU	NSI	COC	CEI
1986	15	20	9	25	60	73	58	90	67	62
1985	15	—	11	25	—	85	65	—	76	—

National Journal Ratings

	1986 LIB — 1986 CONS		1985 LIB — 1985 CONS	
Economic	15% —	84%	21% —	78%
Social	39% —	59%	0% —	76%
Foreign	33% —	66%	35% —	63%

Key Votes

1) Lmt Cln Water Act	FOR	5) Retain Gun Cont	AGN	9) Aid Angola Reb	FOR
2) Rpl Tobac Sub	AGN	6) Contra Aid	FOR	10) Tax Reform	FOR
3) Grm-Rdmn Def Red	FOR	7) Lmt Text Imp	AGN	11) S Africa Sanc	FOR
4) Ban Polygraph	FOR	8) Limit SDI	AGN	12) Immig Reform	FOR

Election Results

1986 general	Vin Weber (IR)	100,249	(52%)	($909,607)
	Dave Johnson (DFL)	94,048	(48%)	($296,080)
1986 primary	Vin Weber (IR)	36,648	(100%)	
1984 general	Vin Weber (IR)	153,308	(63%)	($565,465)
	Todd Lundquist (DFL)	89,770	(37%)	($63,753)

Campaign Contributions and Expenditures

1985-86		Direct Cont. 1985-86		PACS Breakdown 1985-86			
Receipts	$942,499	Indiv.	$560,801	Corp.	$98,017	T/M/H	$101,449
Expend.	$909,607	Party	$10,515	Labor	$0	Agr.	$30,150
Unspent	$165,880	PACS	$312,483	Ideo.	$78,103	CWOS	$4,764
		Cand.	$18,478				

THIRD DISTRICT

The Twin Cities of Minneapolis and St. Paul are ringed by suburbs, and the two central city congressional districts, which once contained most of the metropolitan area's population, are surrounded by two suburban seats, which move out toward, but no longer quite up to, the current limits of suburban expansion. The southern of these two suburban seats is the 3d Congressional District of Minnesota. This is the most affluent, most highly educated, most Republican district in Minnesota. You get little sense, though, as you drive around these suburbs that they are the home of an elite. Even in Edina, the highest income town in the district, the houses, streets, and cars do not proclaim themselves as extraordinary; there is nothing showy or extravagant about these neighborhoods. They are places where people can enjoy their success without bragging about it, where they can savor the pleasure (and endure the pain) of Minnesota's environment without ostentation. The 3d includes high-income Protestant suburbs like Edina, predominantly Jewish St. Louis Park, and the younger suburbs of Burnsville, Eagan, and Inver Grove Heights. To the south and west the suburbs thin out, and you come to farmlands; the district extends as far as 30 miles outward from the Twin Cities. In the Twin Cities, political preference correlates highly with economic status, and this affluent district votes Republican in most elections.

The 3d District's congressman, Bill Frenzel, is now the senior member of the Minnesota delegation and one of the hardest working and most influential Republicans in the House. First elected by a narrow margin in 1970, Frenzel has won big ever since. Loud and brainy, partisan and thoughtful, he puts his stamp on every debate he participates in. He also has important committee assignments: Ways and Means and House Administration. With long experience in a family-owned business, he is a strong supporter of free enterprise, and looks with suspicion on government interference in the marketplace. On the Ways and Means Committee, he was one of the leaders in efforts to cut taxes. He is perhaps the premier free trade advocate on both sides of the aisle in the House: knowledgeable about the arcana of trade law, ready to pounce upon any hint of protectionism in any bill. His importance comes not from committee position, but from a combination of convictions and expertise.

On other Ways and Means matters, he is also important, although on tax reform his partisan instincts seem to have outweighed his desire for lower rates. He was one of the Republicans—and an instrumental one, for without his prestigious support it would not have worked—behind the vote to beat the rule on Dan Rostenkowski's tax bill in December 1985; he said he wanted more incentives for business, but it's hard to escape the conclusion that he was bridling at supporting a measure concocted by the other side. He did end up supporting the 1986 bill, grudgingly, but he must be frustrated because the four Republicans who rank ahead of him on Ways and Means are very much his inferiors in either intellect or energy or both.

Frenzel is the rankling Republican on House Administration, where he is a vigorous, even vitriolic, opponent of public financing of campaigns—to the point of cheering proposals to abolish the presidential fund check-off on tax returns—and of limitations on political action committees. He is in effect the Republican Party's lead player on these issues, which are of such great personal importance to so many of his colleagues.

Over the years Frenzel has become more partisan and increasingly hostile to government interference in business. He retains, however, a reputation as a moderate Republican, justified because of some of his stands on many cultural and foreign policy issues, and a political asset in a district of this nature, where even strong Republican voters like to think of themselves as moderate and thoughtful. But he seems more frustrated than fulfilled. His ideas have made great progress since he came to Congress, but his party has not, and he is held back from the leadership role he has reason to believe himself entitled by the numeric and intellectual weaknesses of his colleagues. He is reelected by very wide margins in an appreciative 3d District, and he performs ably. But his judgment is too often tilted askew by his anger and partisanship; he is a talented man who has not quite found an institutional fit.

The People: Pop. 1980: 509,499, up 25.3% 1970–80. Households (1980): 77% family, 46% with children, 67% married couples; 24.9% housing units rented; median monthly rent: $289; median house value: $73,900. Voting age pop. (1980): 352,682; 1% Asian origin, 1% Black.

1984 Presidential Vote:

Reagan (R) 172,921	(59%)
Mondale (D) 120,020	(41%)

Rep. Bill Frenzel (IR)

Elected 1970; b. July 31, 1928, St. Paul; home, Golden Valley; Dartmouth Col., B.A. 1950, M.B.A. 1951; No religious affiliation; married (Ruth).

Career: Navy, Korea; Pres., MN Terminal Warehouse Co., 1960–71; MN House of Reps., 1962–70.

Offices: 1026 LHOB 20515, 202-225-2871. Also 8120 Penn Ave., S., Bloomington 55431, 612-881-4600.

Committees: *House Administration* (Ranking Member of 7 R). Subcommittees: Elections; Libraries and Memorials. *Ways and Means* (5th of 13 R). Subcommittees: Oversight; Public Assistance and Unemployment Compensation; Trade.

Group Ratings

	ADA	ACLU	COPE	CFA	LCV	ACU	NTU	NSI	COC	CEI
1986	25	35	16	33	47	64	71	70	81	74
1985	20	—	15	33	—	67	71	—	90	—

National Journal Ratings

	1986 LIB — 1986 CONS			1985 LIB — 1985 CONS		
Economic	10%	—	88%	12%	—	88%
Social	49%	—	49%	60%	—	38%
Foreign	50%	—	49%	45%	—	54%

Key Votes

1) Lmt Cln Water Act	FOR	5) Retain Gun Cont	FOR	9) Aid Angola Reb	FOR
2) Rpl Tobac Sub	FOR	6) Contra Aid	AGN	10) Tax Reform	AGN
3) Grm-Rdmn Def Red	FOR	7) Lmt Text Imp	AGN	11) S Africa Sanc	FOR
4) Ban Polygraph	AGN	8) Limit SDI	FOR	12) Immig Reform	FOR

Election Results

1986 general	Bill Frenzel (IR)	127,434	(70%)	($323,232)
	Ray Stock (DFL)	54,261	(30%)	($52,716)
1986 primary	Bill Frenzel (IR)	26,669	(100%)	
1984 general	Bill Frenzel (IR)	207,819	(73%)	($475,273)
	Dave Peterson (DFL)	76,132	(27%)	($14,419)

Campaign Contributions and Expenditures

1985-86		Direct Cont. 1985-86		PACS Breakdown 1985-86			
Receipts	$493,504	Indiv.	$174,038	Corp.	$150,840	T/M/H	$101,478
Expend.	$323,232	Party	$2,090	Labor	$500	Agr.	$9,700
Unspent	$313,940	PACS	$296,493	Ideo.	$23,375	CWOS	$10,350

FOURTH DISTRICT

On top of the hills, above the Mississippi River, on what must have been forested bluffs when the first settlers came here in the 1850s, stand the two edifices which stamp the character of St. Paul: the state Capitol and Archbishop Ireland's Cathedral. This is the older and smaller of Minnesota's Twin Cities, an old river town picked early to be the state capital. It was settled mainly by Catholic Irish and German immigrants, while Minneapolis was attracting Protestant Swedes and Yankees; its lands sloping down to the river became a major transportation hub, a railroad center and river port, while Minneapolis, farther upriver at the falls of St. Anthony, became the nation's largest grain milling center. Long before the Democratic-Farmer-Labor Party was formed, St. Paul was one of the few places in Minnesota where Democrats sometimes won elections, and through all the changes that have occurred since, the city and its suburbs have remained staunchly Democratic. Walter Mondale, who spent much of the campaign year in his house in the exclusive St. Paul suburb of North Oaks, announced his candidacy in St. Paul, claimed the nomination there after the California primary, and conceded defeat there, got 60% of the vote in St. Paul's Ramsey County, one of his best performances among white voters anywhere.

St. Paul and its close-in suburbs make up Minnesota's 4th Congressional District. It includes the working class, DFL suburbs south, east, and northeast of the city, as well as the richer suburbs to the north and the old-fashioned rich neighborhood along Summit Avenue, where F. Scott Fitzgerald grew up in a neighborhood of sturdy mansions west of where the Cathedral overlooks the Capitol, the river, and St. Paul's now sparkling new downtown.

The 4th District has been held by the DFL since 1948, when Eugene McCarthy won it. McCarthy, incidentally, was a fine congressman: a hardworking member of Ways and Means who was both a favorite of Speaker Sam Rayburn and one of the founders of the liberal Democratic Study Group. The current congressman, Bruce Vento, was first elected in 1976; he was a successful state legislator who won the party endorsement at the district DFL convention, and then won the primary easily.

Vento is one of those Democratic subcommittee chairmen who sometimes make policy but seldom break into the national consciousness. He chairs an important Interior subcommittee handling public lands, historic preservation, and forest reserves; it was split off from John Seiberling's subcommittee which was handling most of Interior's business, and after Seiberling retired in 1986, Vento, who was next in line on that subcommittee anyway, moved to gain more jurisdiction. He is counted as a supporter of the environmental movement, though not always a successful one; he promoted state cost sharing of federal water projects in the early 1980s, but pork-minded colleagues balked at this obviously sensible idea. He has been busy in other areas as well, pushing his pipeline safety bill and putting together the package House Democrats passed in early 1987 to help the homeless. Generally his voting record is among the more liberal of younger Democrats, though a tad more moderate on cultural issues: in St. Paul the Archbishop still keeps his eye on the Capitol.

Vento ordinarily has uninteresting IR opposition, but in 1986 he faced Harold Stassen, wildly popular as Minnesota's governor in 1939–43, now returned to the state after years of presidential campaigns and Pennsylvania residency at age 79. Faced is perhaps not the right word. Stassen, an erudite man whose good judgment on politics was apparent when he tried to dump Richard Nixon from the Republican ticket in 1956, decided this time to make drugs the main issue and made quite a point of submitting to urinalysis. Vento, unphased, won with 73%.

The People: Pop. 1980: 509,532, dn. 3.4% 1970–80. Households (1980): 67% family, 36% with children, 55% married couples; 37.5% housing units rented; median monthly rent: $226; median house value: $60,700. Voting age pop. (1980): 375,922; 2% Black, 2% Spanish origin, 1% Asian origin.

1984 Presidential Vote:

Mondale (D) 157,060	(59%)
Reagan (R) 107,329	(40%)

Rep. Bruce F. Vento (DFL)

Elected 1976; b. Oct. 7, 1940, St. Paul; home, St. Paul; U. of MN, A.A. 1961; WI St. U., B.S. 1965; Roman Catholic; married (Mary Jean).

Career: Teacher, 1965–76; MN House of Reps., 1971–77, Asst. Major. Ldr., 1974–76.

Offices: 2304 RHOB 20515, 202-225-6631. Also 5th & Minnesota Ave., Ste. 905, St. Paul 55101, 612-290-3724.

Committees: *Banking, Finance and Urban Affairs* (9th of 31 D). Subcommittees: Economic Stabilization; Financial Institutions Supervision, Regulation and Insurance; Housing and Community Development. *Interior and Insular Affairs* (7th of 26 D). Subcommittees: National Parks and Public Lands (Chairman); Insular and International Affairs. *Select Committee on Aging* (17th of 39 D). Subcommittee: Health and Long-Term Care.

Group Ratings

	ADA	ACLU	COPE	CFA	LCV	ACU	NTU	NSI	COC	CEI
1986	90	84	92	100	99	0	31	0	28	20
1985	95	—	92	92	—	5	38	—	18	—

National Journal Ratings

	1986 LIB — 1986 CONS			1985 LIB — 1985 CONS		
Economic	84%	—	13%	89%	—	0%
Social	81%	—	17%	72%	—	28%
Foreign	80%	—	0%	85%	—	8%

Key Votes

1) Lmt Cln Water Act	AGN	5) Retain Gun Cont	FOR	9) Aid Angola Reb	AGN
2) Rpl Tobac Sub	FOR	6) Contra Aid	AGN	10) Tax Reform	FOR
3) Grm-Rdmn Def Red	AGN	7) Lmt Text Imp	FOR	11) S Africa Sanc	FOR
4) Ban Polygraph	FOR	8) Limit SDI	FOR	12) Immig Reform	FOR

Election Results

1986 general	Bruce F. Vento (DFL)................	112,662	(73%)	($197,906)
	Harold Stassen (IR)	41,926	(27%)	($76,954)
1986 primary	Bruce F. Vento (DFL).................	61,269	(89%)	
	Kent S. Herschback (IR)	7,362	(11%)	
1984 general	Bruce F. Vento (DFL)...............	167,678	(74%)	($120,369)
	Mary Jane Rachner (IR)	57,450	(25%)	($8,462)

Campaign Contributions and Expenditures

1985-86		Direct Cont. 1985-86		PACS Breakdown 1985-86			
Receipts	$219,213	Indiv.	$59,413	Corp.	$21,625	T/M/H	$29,254
Expend.	$197,906	Party	$299	Labor	$72,446	Agr.	$8,125
Unspent	$110,355	PACS	$141,395	Ideo.	$8,920	CWOS	$1,025

FIFTH DISTRICT

At the Falls of St. Anthony, at the head of navigation of the Mississippi River, has grown up one of America's largest metropolitan areas, Minneapolis-St. Paul. The falls which gave birth to Minneapolis and powered its early grain mills are all but invisible now, sealed off below bridges and beneath a downtown where people walk from building to building much of the year through enclosed skyways, preferring the weather man has made to the winter blasts nature provides outside. Today's Minneapolis is much more than just a grain milling center, though it still is that; it is a center of high tech industry, and of banking and finance; it is a regional railroad center, and the headquarters of one of the nation's largest airlines, Northwest; it is also the nerve center of an economic area that extends almost 1,000 miles west to the Rocky Mountains in Montana.

The city of Minneapolis itself, together with some working-class suburbs just to the northwest and some middle-income suburbs directly to the south, make up Minnesota's 5th Congressional District. The city itself has been declining in population—521,000 in 1950, 370,000 in 1980— but increasing in vigor. Small frame houses on grid streets in the old working-class neighborhoods which once held large families now typically hold an elderly couple or widow; the children are out in bigger houses on larger lots in the suburbs. The large old houses along the chain of lakes in western and southern Minneapolis, which once held the families of some of the city's richest citizens, now hold young professional couples who like being close to the still vital downtown. In northeastern Minneapolis, behind the railroad and warehouse district along the Mississippi, is an old working-class neighborhood which has become the new home of many Hmongs from the mountains of Laos.

Minneapolis has a political liberalism drawn from its Scandinavian and Yankee heritage, given to extremes in clean government, original reforms (like the law requiring no-smoking sections), and cultural tolerance—extremes that are usually tolerable even for those who don't like them. Its mayor, Donald Fraser, was the DFL congressman from the 5th District from 1962 till he ran unsuccessfully for the Senate in 1978; quiet, seemingly dull, he is one of the most dedicated and intellectually honest liberal politicians in America. His wife is also a politician: Arvonne Fraser was St. Paul Mayor George Latimer's running mate in his strong race against Governor Rudy Perpich in the 1986 primary.

Fraser's successor in the House is a political savvy DFL politician, Martin Olav Sabo. In 1960 he was elected to the Minnesota House of Representatives at age 22; at 30 he was the minority leader (members were elected without party labels then, putting the DFL at a disadvantage); at 34 speaker. Sabo won the House seat easily in 1978, though it was a Republican year in Minnesota, and got a seat on the Appropriations Committee in his first year; Tip O'Neill, who was speaker of the Massachusetts House before he came to Congress, had a soft spot in his heart for former speakers.

Sabo is not a particularly voluble legislator, but he doesn't have to be: he has an important committee position, he has the trust of his party's leadership, and he has a safe seat and an appreciative constituency back home in Minneapolis. His record on all issues is one of the most liberal in the House, and he's a competent behind-the-scenes worker; he chaired the caucus committee that drew up a blueprint for the national party's platform in San Francisco. He's also willing to be an insurgent on occasion; he supported Les Aspin for the Armed Services Committee chairmanship in the caucus after the 1984 election. He himself in 1985 was running for party whip, but in May 1986 left the race before the election; "I think I know how to count," Sabo said, and he knew that campaign chairman Tony Coelho had too many votes to be stopped. As a sort of consolation prize he got the seat on the Defense Appropriations Subcommittee vacated when Chairman Joseph Addabbo died in 1986. Here he can provide some balance to the much more conservative new chairman, Bill Chappell of Florida.

At home he is reelected routinely and without difficulty.

The People: Pop. 1980: 509,506, dn. 15.3% 1970–80. Households (1980): 56% family, 27% with children, 44% married couples; 45.8% housing units rented; median monthly rent: $220; median house value: $57,800. Voting age pop. (1980): 401,381; 5% Black, 1% American Indian, 1% Asian origin, 1% Spanish origin.

1984 Presidential Vote:

Mondale (D)	168,686	(62%)
Reagan (R)	103,103	(38%)

Rep. Martin Olav Sabo (DFL)

Elected 1978; b. Feb. 28, 1938, Crosby, ND; home, Minneapolis; Augsburg Col., B.A. 1959, U. of MN; Lutheran; married (Sylvia).

Career: MN House of Reps., 1961–79, Minor. Ldr., 1969–73, Spkr., 1973–79.

Offices: 2201 RHOB 20515, 202-225-4755. Also 462 Fed. Courts Bldg., 110 S. 4th St., Minneapolis 55401, 612-349-5110.

Committees: *Appropriations* (20th of 35 D). Subcommittees: Defense, District of Columbia; Transportation.

Group Ratings

	ADA	ACLU	COPE	CFA	LCV	ACU	NTU	NSI	COC	CEI
1986	95	95	90	83	68	0	27	0	11	13
1985	95	—	90	75	—	5	30	—	18	—

National Journal Ratings

	1986 LIB — 1986 CONS			1985 LIB — 1985 CONS		
Economic	87%	—	0%	89%	—	0%
Social	89%	—	0%	85%	—	0%
Foreign	80%	—	0%	85%	—	8%

Key Votes

1) Lmt Cln Water Act	AGN	5) Retain Gun Cont	FOR	9) Aid Angola Reb	AGN
2) Rpl Tobac Sub	AGN	6) Contra Aid	AGN	10) Tax Reform	FOR
3) Grm-Rdmn Def Red	AGN	7) Lmt Text Imp	FOR	11) S Africa Sanc	FOR
4) Ban Polygraph	FOR	8) Limit SDI	FOR	12) Immig Reform	FOR

Election Results

1986 general	Martin Olav Sabo (DFL)	105,410	(73%)	($208,403)
	Rick Serra (IR).	37,583	(26%)	($22,088)
1986 primary	Martin Olav Sabo (DFL) unopposed			
1984 general	Martin Olav Sabo (DFL)	165,075	(70%)	($129,245)
	Richard D. Weiblen (IR)	62,642	(27%)	

Campaign Contributions and Expenditures

1985-86		Direct Cont. 1985-86		PACS Breakdown 1985-86			
Receipts	$237,778	Indiv.	$71,828	Corp.	$39,290	T/M/H	$23,786
Expend.	$208,043	PACS	$140,501	Labor	$59,825	Agr.	$6,250
Unspent	$99,669	Cand.	$53,300	Ideo.	$8,200	CWOS	$3,150

SIXTH DISTRICT

The 6th Congressional District of Minnesota, forming a semi-circle around Minneapolis and St. Paul, is the less upscale of the two suburban Twin Cities districts. Its oldest part is the town of Stillwater, facing Wisconsin on hills above the St. Croix River, which nearly became Minnesota's capital and is full of Midwest Victoriana from its days as a lumber port. But just outside Stillwater, on the road to St. Paul, is a more typical example of the architecture of this district: a new shopping center. The most thickly populated part of the 6th District are the suburbs just north of Minneapolis: Brooklyn Park, Fridley, Blaine, Coon Rapids—blue-collar suburbs, affluent by any historic standard, though pinched during the 1979–83 recession. You can tell a lot about people's tastes here by looking in the shopping centers: you won't find much gourmet cooking equipment or designer clothes, but you will find elaborate tools, camping gear, and comfortable, inexpensive clothes for small children. The 6th District has Minnesota's—and one of the nation's—highest percentages of households with families, married couples, children, and working women. To the west the 6th extends almost all the way to St. Cloud and to Hubert Humphrey's lakeside home in Waverly. Closer to Minneapolis, it includes the very high-income Minneapolis suburbs around Lake Minnetonka.

The congressman here is one of the DFL's sharp young politicos, Gerry Sikorski. When current 6th District lines were drawn in 1982, Sikorski had already served in the legislature for six years and run for Congress once; this time he got into a rematch with Republican incumbent Arlen Erdahl. But aside from Stillwater's Washington County, the district was new to Erdahl and well-suited to Sikorski, and he won 51%–49%.

In the House Sikorski had enough savvy to win a seat on the much coveted Energy and Commerce Committee; he worked with Henry Waxman on acid rain legislation (which can do no political harm in a state with 10,000 lakes); he served on John Dingell's Oversight and Investigations Subcommittee and took part in the investigations of General Dynamics (which billed the Pentagon for kennel fees) and EPA official Rita Lavelle. He got himself appointed a deputy whip. In all this he showed impressive legislative expertise, and none of it did him any political harm back home.

In 1984 an avid right-to-lifer and Reagan supporter got the Republican nomination; his only problems were, Sikorski has always opposed abortion himself and Reagan ran not much better than even in the district. In 1986 his opponent was Barb Sykora, daughter of Representative John Zwach who represented from 1966 to 1974 a 6th District with considerably different boundaries. But Sikorski got 66% of the vote. He is one reason why the Democrats have kept control of the House in a Republican era.

The People: Pop. 1980: 509,446, up 38.8% 1970–80. Households (1980): 81% family, 54% with children, 72% married couples; 20.6% housing units rented; median monthly rent: $249; median house value: $65,000. Voting age pop. (1980): 332,303; 1% Asian origin, 1% Spanish origin.

1984 Presidential Vote:

Reagan (R)	135,232	(52%)
Mondale (D)	123,181	(47%)

Rep. Gerry Sikorski (DFL)

Elected 1982; b. Apr. 26, 1948, Breckenridge; home, Stillwater; U. of MN, B.A. 1970, J.D. 1973; Roman Catholic; married (Susan).

Career: Practicing atty.; MN Senate, 1976–82, Major. Whip, 1980–82.

Offices: 414 CHOB 20515, 202-225-2271. Also 8060 University Ave., N.E., Fridley 55432, 612-780-5801.

Committees: *Energy and Commerce* (20th of 25 D). Subcommittees: Health and the Environment; Oversight and Investigations; Transportation, Tourism and Hazardous Materials. *Post Office and Civil Service* (9th of 14 D). Subcommittees: Census and Population; Human Resources (Chairman). *Select Committee on Children, Youth, and Families* (12th of 18 D). Task Force: Crisis Intervention.

Group Ratings

	ADA	ACLU	COPE	CFA	LCV	ACU	NTU	NSI	COC	CEI
1986	85	73	94	100	84	5	33	0	33	19
1985	75	—	95	83	—	14	39	—	27	—

National Journal Ratings

	1986 LIB — 1986 CONS		1985 LIB — 1985 CONS	
Economic	84% —	13%	71% —	28%
Social	74% —	23%	48% —	51%
Foreign	80% —	0%	71% —	26%

Key Votes

1) Lmt Cln Water Act	FOR	5) Retain Gun Cont	AGN	9) Aid Angola Reb	AGN
2) Rpl Tobac Sub	AGN	6) Contra Aid	AGN	10) Tax Reform	FOR
3) Grm-Rdmn Def Red	FOR	7) Lmt Text Imp	FOR	11) S Africa Sanc	FOR
4) Ban Polygraph	FOR	8) Limit SDI	FOR	12) Immig Reform	FOR

Election Results

1986 general	Gerry Sikorski (DFL)	110,598	(66%)	($492,385)
	Barbara Zwach Sykora (IR)	57,460	(34%)	($154,337)
1986 primary	Gerry Sikorski (DFL)	45,987	(100%)	
1984 general	Gerry Sikorski (DFL)	154,603	(60%)	($689,233)
	Patrick A. Trueman (IR)	101,058	(40%)	($540,709)

Campaign Contributions and Expenditures

1985-86		Direct Cont. 1985-86		PACS Breakdown 1985-86			
Receipts	$506,995	Indiv.	$116,270	Corp.	$49,050	T/M/H	$79,800
Expend.	$492,385	PACS	$306,792	Labor	$116,714	Agr.	$12,200
Debts	$16,421	Cand.	$70,000	Ideo.	$45,864	CWOS	$3,164

SEVENTH DISTRICT

The 7th Congressional District of Minnesota is farming country, stretched out along the highways and rail lines that extend northwest from Minneapolis and St. Paul toward North Dakota and the Pacific Northwest. Nearer Minneapolis is the country on both sides of the Mississippi River around St. Cloud, settled by German Catholics and dotted with farm villages with saints' names; it is densely populated, productive farmland. This was the boyhood home of Sinclair Lewis, and his *Main Street* is set in a thinly disguised Sauk Centre. This was one of the most isolationist parts of Minnesota in both world wars—and one of the most politically volatile. Among these German-Americans there was an underlying sympathy for Germany, which most were reluctant to admit, but which, as Samuel Lubell found, was expressed in huge margins against the Democrats associated with those wars. Yet later it swung heavily to Democrats in times of agrarian distress.

Farther northwest, along the Red River of the North, which separates Minnesota from North Dakota, are vast fields of wheat and sugar beets; the farmers here are primarily of Norwegian descent. To the east are acres of forests, lakes, and occasional resort areas. This is the country of the legendary Paul Bunyan and his blue ox, Babe, whose statues stand together in Bemidji, a small town on the shores of one of Minnesota's 10,000 lakes. The lake country tends to be Democratic, the wheat country marginal and responsive to discontent on the farms.

The 7th has a colorful political history full of close elections. It made national headlines in 1958, when Coya Knutson was congresswoman here; her husband Andy issued a plaintive statement urging her to come home and make his breakfast again. Knutson was the only Democratic incumbent to lose in the heavily Democratic year of 1958. Since then, the district has been represented mostly by conservative Republicans, who have been close pressed in most of their elections. Odin Langen, who beat Knutson, was finally beaten by Democrat Bob Bergland in 1970. Bergland became very popular in the district and was appointed Jimmy Carter's Secretary of Agriculture in 1977; in the special election to fill it the winner was Republican Arlan Stangeland.

Despite marvelous credentials—he is a bona fide farmer, of Norwegian descent—Stangeland has a history of close elections and a political life no one would write an insurance policy on. His record is conservative on just about every issue except pork barrel projects and, of course, agriculture. On the Agriculture Committee he boasts of getting sugar price supports up and in 1985 just barely failed in getting the committee to adopt a new system of supports through a marketing loan aimed at cutting costs and moving U.S. grain into world markets while holding up farm income. He said the final 1985 farm bill was "the best we could get." On Public Works he tends to go along with the committee's pro-pork majority and to be dubious about spending too much to clean up rivers and lakes. After winning the seat in a special election, Stangeland got no more than 52% in successive races against the same DFL opponent. In 1984 he won with 57%—about even with Reagan's showing in the district, but in 1986 against the same opponent he won by only 121 votes. Finance records show the escalation of campaign costs and spending: the same two candidates spent a total of $701,000 in 1984 and $1,013,000 in 1986.

With this record Stangeland is almost sure to have a tough race again in 1988. He may be comforted by the fact that his national party ticket is no drag on his fortunes, and it may be that in a year of genuine agricultural distress—land prices were down more than 25% in the early 1980s—voters may be concluding that the federal government can no more maintain the value of farmowners' equity than it can prevent muggings on big city streets. But in a close race do those things help or hurt? No one can be sure.

The People: Pop. 1980: 509,521, up 10.8% 1970–80. Households (1980): 75% family, 42% with children, 66% married couples; 22.7% housing units rented; median monthly rent: $168; median house value: $39,300. Voting age pop. (1980): 355,632; 1% American Indian.

1984 Presidential Vote:	Reagan (R)	135,320	(57%)
	Mondale (D)	102,240	(43%)

Rep. Arlan Stangeland (IR)

Elected Feb. 22, 1977; b. Feb. 8, 1930, Fargo, ND; home, Barnesville; Lutheran; married (Virginia).

Career: Farmer; MN House of Reps., 1966–74.

Offices: 2245 RHOB 20515, 202-225-2165. Also M-F Bldg., 403 Center Ave., Moorhead 56560, 218-233-8631; and Fed. Bldg., 720 Mall Germain, St. Cloud 56301, 612-251-0740.

Committees: *Agriculture* (6th of 17 R). Subcommittees: Cotton, Rice and Sugar (Ranking Member); Livestock, Dairy, and Poultry; Wheat, Soybeans and Feed Grains. *Public Works and Transportation* (3d of 19 R). Subcommittees: Aviation; Public Buildings and Grounds; Water Resources (Ranking Member).

Group Ratings

	ADA	ACLU	COPE	CFA	LCV	ACU	NTU	NSI	COC	CEI
1986	10	15	10	17	21	80	42	100	59	56
1985	15	—	11	17	—	81	44	—	67	—

National Journal Ratings

	1986 LIB — 1986 CONS			1985 LIB — 1985 CONS		
Economic	25%	—	75%	37%	—	63%
Social	37%	—	61%	0%	—	76%
Foreign	30%	—	70%	0%	—	76%

Key Votes

1) Lmt Cln Water Act	AGN	5) Retain Gun Cont	AGN	9) Aid Angola Reb	FOR
2) Rpl Tobac Sub	AGN	6) Contra Aid	FOR	10) Tax Reform	FOR
3) Grm-Rdmn Def Red	FOR	7) Lmt Text Imp	AGN	11) S Africa Sanc	—
4) Ban Polygraph	FOR	8) Limit SDI	AGN	12) Immig Reform	FOR

Election Results

1986 general	Arlan Stangeland (IR)	94,024	(50%)	($547,810)
	Collin C. Peterson (DFL)	93,903	(50%)	($465,898)
1986 primary	Arlan Stangeland (IR)	30,651	(100%)	
1984 general	Arlan Stangeland (IR)	135,087	(57%)	($434,655)
	Collin C. Peterson (DFL)	101,720	(43%)	($266,954)

Campaign Contributions and Expenditures

1985-86		Direct Cont. 1985-86		PACS Breakdown 1985-86			
Receipts	$578,421	Indiv.	$289,568	Corp.	$84,266	T/M/H	$109,720
Expend.	$547,810	Party	$8,562	Labor	$6,000	Agr.	$37,300
Unspent	$49,377	PACS	$275,200	Ideo.	$33,214	CWOS	$4,700

EIGHTH DISTRICT

The lifeline of America's heavy industry begins in the Iron Range of Minnesota, where the Arctic winds that blow down over the Canadian Shield's thousands of inland lakes often make nearby International Falls the nation's coldest town, and then runs south along railroad lines to the port of Duluth, nestled beneath bluffs near the always cold and every winter frozen waters of Lake Superior. The Iron Range has been America's biggest source of iron ore for more than 60 years, and over that time millions of tons have been dug out and shipped into rail cars for the ride down to Duluth, where the ore is loaded into Great Lakes freighters for shipment to Cleveland, Gary, Detroit, Chicago, Pittsburgh, and Buffalo. Since the turn of the century, about 100,000 people have lived on the Iron Range and another 100,000 in Duluth, most of them the products of America's 1880–1924 wave of immigration—Italians, Poles, Serbs and Croats, Jews, Swedes, Finns. In this punishing environment, they worked to the point of exhaustion, built solid houses with staunch central heating, and bought layers of warm clothing to survive the winter.

These were rough-and-ready communities, with little local elite: the men who owned the mines and the freighters were having lunch in their clubs in Chicago or Detroit while the miners stopped briefly for a bite out of their lunchpails. Life was rough: the work was hard, the hours long, pay low. There was little time and few facilities for recreation back in those days when working people couldn't afford special winter sports clothes or summer gear; the churches, a separate one for each ethnic group, were the main community institution. Living conditions improved vastly in the decades of great economic growth after World War II, but there is a rough-hewn tone to life here today. And there has also been economic distress. As the iron and steel industry got more efficient, they needed fewer workers; as the American steel industry collapsed after 1959, they needed even fewer, or none at all. Mining employment dropped from 15,000 to 6,500 in 1980–85; unemployment reached 21% in 1981. Now the Iron Range and Duluth seem to be diversifying. They are hoping that tourism, UDAG grants, and an enterprise zone will provide growth and jobs. They are proud of the new chopsticks factory in Hibbing that hopes to produce a billion chopsticks for export to Japan.

The Iron Range and Duluth have always been Democratic, and so is the 8th Congressional District of which they are the largest part. As unemployment rose and population declined, voter turnout zoomed up to record levels in 1982 and 1984, helping the Iron Range's Rudy Perpich recapture the governorship and Walter Mondale carry Minnesota. But in 1986 turnout fell back again, from 229,000 in 1982 to 187,000 in 1986. In the early 1980s the 8th District seemed to be looking for government to revive its economy. In the middle 1980s, as signs of revival began to appear, it seemed less interested in politics.

The congressman from the 8th, Democrat James Oberstar, has long experience working for the district; before he was first elected in 1974, he worked for John Blatnik, who represented the 8th for 28 years starting in 1946. Oberstar is the product of a Catholic education, and his views seem to reflect the social gospel side of Catholicism. He believes government has an obligation to help the poor and disadvantaged and to stimulate economic growth; he is dubious about American military involvement abroad, especially in Central America; he is also culturally traditional and an opponent of abortion. Oberstar chaired the Economic Development Subcommittee of Public Works and Transportation, and helped to save the EDA program from complete destruction by the Reagan Administration. Oberstar was a leading backer of the move to extend supplemental unemployment benefits in 1985 when President Reagan, citing nationwide job growth, wanted to zero them out. He has broader interests as well, as indicated by his proposal to allow tax deductions for expenses in adopting a child.

Oberstar inherited not only Blatnik's seat but also his feuds. Politics in the Iron Range and Duluth is a personal business, one of the few ways to move up in the world. Oberstar first won the seat in 1974 with a narrow victory in the primary over Rudy Perpich's brother Tony; he had close primaries over Duluth council member Thomas Dougherty in 1980 and 1984, the latter after he returned to the House race after failing to win endorsement for the Senate race at the DFL state convention. Republicans are never any problem in this heavily Democratic district.

The People: Pop. 1980: 509,506, up 10.7% 1970–80. Households (1980): 74% family, 40% with children, 65% married couples; 22.0% housing units rented; median monthly rent: $166; median house value: $38,100. Voting age pop. (1980): 360,529; 1% American Indian.

1984 Presidential Vote:

Mondale (D)	....	150,038	(59%)
Reagan (R)	....	101,068	(40%)

Rep. James L. Oberstar (DFL)

Elected 1974; b. Sept. 10, 1934, Chisholm; home, Chisholm; St. Thomas Col., B.A. 1956, Col. of Europe, Bruges, Belgium, M.A. 1957; Roman Catholic; married (Jo).

Career: A. A. to U.S. Rep. John A. Blatnik, 1963–74; Administrator, U.S. House of Reps. Cmtee. on Pub. Works, 1971–74.

Offices: 2351 RHOB 20515, 202-225-6211. Also 231 Fed. Bldg., Duluth 55802, 218-727-7474; Chisolm Fed. Bldg., 316 W. Lake St., Chisholm 55719, 218-254-5761; and Brainerd City Hall, 501 Laurel St., Brainerd 56401.

Committees: *Budget* (8th of 21 D). Task Forces: Budget Process; Community and Natural Resources; Defense and International Affairs. *Public Works and Transportation* (5th of 32 D). Subcommittees: Economic Development; Investigations and Oversight (Chairman); Water Resources.

Group Ratings

	ADA	ACLU	COPE	CFA	LCV	ACU	NTU	NSI	COC	CEI
1986	85	75	93	92	74	5	24	0	6	12
1985	95	—	93	75	—	5	33	—	18	—

National Journal Ratings

	1986 LIB — 1986 CONS		1985 LIB — 1985 CONS	
Economic	87% —	0%	89% —	0%
Social	74% —	23%	48% —	51%
Foreign	80% —	0%	92% —	0%

Key Votes

1) Lmt Cln Water Act	AGN	5) Retain Gun Cont	AGN	9) Aid Angola Reb	AGN
2) Rpl Tobac Sub	—	6) Contra Aid	AGN	10) Tax Reform	FOR
3) Grm-Rdmn Def Red	AGN	7) Lmt Text Imp	FOR	11) S Africa Sanc	FOR
4) Ban Polygraph	FOR	8) Limit SDI	FOR	12) Immig Reform	FOR

Election Results

1986 general	James L. Oberstar (DFL)	135,718	(73%)	($163,619)
	Dave Rued (IR)	51,315	(27%)	($68,931)
1986 primary	James L. Oberstar (DFL)	84,505	(100%)	
1984 general	James L. Oberstar (DFL)	165,727	(67%)	($286,810)
	Dave Rued (IR)	79,181	(32%)	($53,911)

Campaign Contributions and Expenditures

1985-86		Direct Cont. 1985-86		PACS Breakdown 1985-86			
Receipts	$297,056	Indiv.	$71,858	Corp.	$54,120	T/M/H	$43,509
Expend.	$163,619	PACS	$235,754	Labor	$107,225	Agr.	$10,200
Debts	$134,706	Cand.	$8,692	Ideo.	$17,950	CWOS	$2,750

MISSISSIPPI

Few states have made such progress over the past 25 years, and few states feel they still have so far to go, as Mississippi. In 1964 civil rights workers were murdered for encouraging blacks to register and vote; in 1986 Mississippi had a black congressman and black Supreme Court justice, and its secretary of state in a glossy brochure recalled the "oppression of the black population of the state," and says, "a change from the old racial status quo was necessary and morally correct." Yet black voter turnout has lagged in many rural counties, and voting has often been polarized: in 1984 more than 80% of Mississippi blacks voted for Walter Mondale and more than 80% of Mississippi whites voted for Ronald Reagan. In other elections, for governor in 1983 and Senator in 1984, there has been less polarization, but few Republicans aside from Senator Thad Cochran have won many black votes. Economically, Mississippi has grown along with the rest of the nation, and faster—Mississippi incomes were 70% of the national average in 1984, up from 65% in 1970. But even accounting for Mississippi's lower cost of living, that still is perceptibly lower than the norm, and here, as on so many other indexes, Mississippi is uncomfortably aware of the fact that it ranks number 50 among the states.

That rankles in a state which takes pride in being the quintessential southern state, the place you think of when you come across southern clichés, from the magnolia blossom-strewn lawn of the antebellum mansion to the southern belle dressed in all her petticoats and finery. But behind that image always were the tarpaper shacks of black sharecroppers. In the 1940s Mississippi seemed like another country to most Americans. Along its dusty roads leading from market towns were loose-jointed frame farmhouses, where people, white as well as black, lived without automobiles and farmed without machines; they had no electricity and no leisure time to speak of; their isolation was more like the life of farmers in the age of Andrew Jackson than like the life of Americans about to enter the freeway age. Many Mississippians were still sharecroppers, living outside the money economy; and many others considered themselves lucky to make $100 a month. Mississippi's per capita income was just 36% of the national average. There were successful businesses and plantations in Mississippi, but somehow the wealth here never seemed to trickle down. The families who had money had mostly had it for generations; they considered it inconceivable that most other Mississippians could make much money or, if they did, would know how to spend it. Mississippi was more like what we now call an underdeveloped country than it was like most of the rest of the United States.

In that era, Mississippi politics had no match in the nation for crudity and, on occasion, savagery. There was always an economic division, between the rich white planters of the Delta and the River valley and the poor white farmers of the hillier north and east. But even more important was the division between the races. In 1940, 49% of Mississippians were black, and white supremacy was maintained by a system as rigid and severe as South Africa's is today. Blacks were not allowed to vote; they could not mingle with whites in schools or public accommodations; they had to address whites with particular phrases. Infractions were sometimes punished with death; lynchings were not uncommon in the 1940s and occurred up through the 1950s and early 1960s.

With this grim background, Mississippi's economy languished and its politics attracted few topnotch people. The state elected politicians like Governor and Senator Theodore Bilbo, who liked to compare blacks with monkeys, and Ross Barnett, the buffoonish governor who served when the University of Mississippi was integrated by federal troops in 1963. In national politics, Mississippi increasingly diverged from the rest of the country. In 1960, it backed an independent slate of electors—the only state to do so—and in 1964, when virtually no blacks voted, it went 87% for Goldwater. In 1968, with many blacks voting, it was still 63% for Wallace, and in 1972 it

MISSISSIPPI — Congressional Districts, Counties, and Selected Places — (5 Districts)

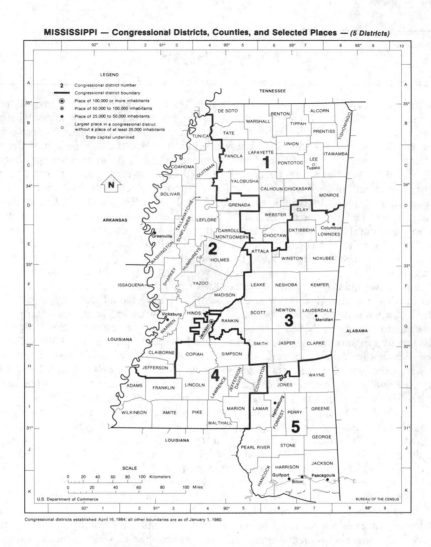

Congressional districts established April 16, 1984; all other boundaries are as of January 1, 1980.

went for the winner, Richard Nixon, but gave him a larger percentage than any other state.

But in the 1970s, as desegregation was accepted so much more readily than almost anyone imagined, Mississippi's politics moved back into the national mainstream. In national elections it voted much like the rest of the country: narrowly for Jimmy Carter in 1976, against him in 1980. In county seats and in the state capital, blacks were gaining political influence. Black support was no longer the kiss of death for a white politician; it was for William Winter, for example, in the gubernatorial races of 1967 and 1975, but not by 1979. In these circumstances, a state legislator or city council member with a 10% or 20% or 30% black constituency is likely to be interested in what black voters want; no sensible politician likes to write off permanently a constituency that large. Mississippi blacks became more adroit at exerting political pressure and have, quietly and out of the national spotlight, been getting more of what they want out of government.

There was another reason for the change: the state's economy, long 50th in the nation, took off. State per capita income, 36% of the national average in 1940 and 54% in 1960, was 65% in

1970 and 70% in 1984. This growth may be one result of integration: the economy got a boost just as Mississippi was forced to get rid of segregation. That makes sense: investors are more willing to put up money in a state with no racial strife; integration helped improve Mississippians' education and skills, even while wages and tax levels in many northern states were soaring to uncompetitive levels. Another reason—not mentioned by those who focus only on the motives of white businessmen and the performance of politicians—is that Mississippi's blacks themselves, finally free to express themselves and to make their livings as they wish, have been more likely, if they are skilled, to stay in Mississippi and more likely, whether skilled or not, to work harder and put out more effort than they were in the days when it seemed that anything they might gain could be taken away by whites.

Mississippi's top offices are held today by men who, in their most recent elections at least, have won votes from both blacks and whites: Senators John Stennis and Thad Cochran and Governor Bill Allain. National politics, particularly if Jesse Jackson is again prominently on the scene, may polarize state politics, but within the single marketplace of Mississippi there are few politicians who care to concede all the votes of one race to the opposition and little penalty to be paid for seeking black support. Mississippi still has a ways to go. But this is progress.

Governor. Mississippi's dominant governor in recent times has been William Winter, elected in 1979 and confined to a single four-year term. His major achievement was an education package with the potential to change the state—and help the 50% of Mississippi public schoolchildren who are black. Some changes would seem unremarkable in other states—state-supported kindergartens, raising the school leaving age to 14. To do this the legislature agreed to raise taxes specifically for education. So Mississippi is moving, as others have, from a state whose low taxes are its greatest attraction to one which is concentrating on raising the skills and abilities of its work force. This is a key step in development—and a repudiation of those who don't want to improve blacks' skills, in order to maintain traditional cultural patterns. Winter's second major achievement was political: taking major steps to bring blacks into the Democratic party and thereby reducing to nil the impact of independent black candidacies which in the 1970s cost Democrats one Senate and one House seat.

Governor Bill Allain, elected in 1983, was dogged for years after he came to office by charges advanced by Republican Leon Bramlett that he used the services of black transvestite prostitutes in Jackson. Allain denied it heatedly, and voters gave him a solid majority. But his powers as governor are limited; semi-permanent legislative leaders have more say over the budget than the governor does. Allain got a constitutional amendment passed allowing governors to run for a second consecutive term, but early in the year he seemed disinclined to make the 1987 race. So did Lieutenant Governor Brad Dye, whose mind could be changed if the state Supreme Court upholds a ruling stripping him of his powers over the state Senate. The most aggressive candidate seems to be state Auditor Ray Mabus, whose investigations into courthouse payrolls have given him plenty of publicity and a reputation as a reformer; Mabus is close to Winter and backs a tax hike which Allain has opposed. Other Democratic contenders include former Governor Bill Waller, Attorney General Ed Pittman, 1978 Senate candidate Maurice Dantin, 1979 third-place finisher Mike Sturdivant, and populist John Arthur Eaves. The choice of the Republican establishment seems to be businessman Jack Reed, but he may have competition from Pat Robertson follower Doug Lemon, former Democrat Jim Herring, or the party's 1975 and 1979 nominee, Gil Carmichael.

Senators. Mississippi is represented by the nation's oldest and most senior Senator, John Stennis. He is a tough old bird: he was shot by a burglar in 1973, and he had his leg amputated in 1984. But he has insisted on remaining in office and returned to work after the shooting much sooner than anyone expected. For the six years the Republicans controlled the Senate, Stennis wielded less power than he once did as Armed Services and then Appropriations chairman; now, back as Appropriations chairman and second on Armed Services, he has important positions again but, in his middle 80s, probably less energy and enterprise than he once did. Appropriations subcommittee chairmen in any case have often acted autonomously, and in Sam Nunn,

Stennis has a successor on Armed Services who is congenial personally and on policy.

But he still may be looked to for his wisdom. Stennis has seen a lot of history now from the Senate; he has seen Presidents come and go, wars fought and forgotten, new ideas advanced and implemented and then brought back as the next generation's new ideas again. His longtime backing of a strong defense and his tendency to defer to incumbent Presidents come from the experiences of the 1940s and his sense of the flow of history; but he comes also from a congressional tradition of expressing dissenting judgments quietly and in private. He does not like to attack as foolish a policy which sends men out under the flag, but he does not like men to be sent out under the flag, sometimes to die, to advance foolish policies either. His judgments can't be categorized as hawkish or dovish: he opposed President Reagan on Lebanon and condemned as too moderate his response to the attack on the Korean airliner.

Stennis has remained interested in local issues as well, notably the Tennessee–Tombigbee Waterway, which he has pushed through despite the major argument against it (nature has already provided a connection betwen the Tennessee Valley and the Gulf: the Mississippi River) and its great cost. For a long time the assumption has been that Stennis will retire when his seat is up in 1988, when he will be 87. But he has made no move to do so yet, seems to have the stamina to perform his duties, and has the precedent of his 1982 campaign to show how he can win in his 80s. Republican Haley Barbour even staged a birthday party to highlight Stennis's age, but Stennis campaigned actively among blacks and whites, raised $1 million and ran a media campaign, and carried all but two counties in the state. Should Stennis retire, possible Democratic candidates include former Governors Winter and Waller and Representative Wayne Dowdy. Squaring up to seek the Republican nomination are Barbour, who left a political post in the White House to return to Yazoo City, and 5th District congressman, Trent Lott, the House Minority Whip who shows up very well in statewide polls. Lott as a young graduate of Ole Miss ran the alumni affairs office there and has accumulated a stateful of good contacts; Barbour is a loyal alumnus of Mississippi State, and much of his backing comes from the heated longtime rivalry between the two state universities.

Thad Cochran, Mississippi's Republican Senator, is a pleasant man who has proved his political mettle again and again. He was elected to fill James Eastland's seat in 1978 with a minority of the vote in a three-sided race; he was reelected with 58%, against William Winter, in 1984. In personal demeanor though not always in political attitudes, Cochran personifies the upwardly mobile urban elite—found in Jackson, along the Gulf Coast, and in some smaller Mississippi cities—which has sometimes seemed the dominant force in Mississippi's politics. Cochran is less doctrinaire than many well-off Mississippians, however, and more inclined to accommodate his own views to the system. On any ideological scale Cochran is a solid conservative and supporter of the Reagan Administration. But in terms of basic political instincts, as well as personal style, he has seemed closer to leaders like Robert Dole and Howard Baker; and on some cultural issues his record is not conservative. He serves as secretary of the Republican Policy Committee, a leadership post that has given him some national visibility. He also has seats on the Agriculture, Appropriations, and Labor and Human Resources Committees. He works without much fanfare, pushing amendments to end government purchases of honey, pushing to prohibit the use of imported cement in federal highways, switching toward support of Israel.

Cochran positioned himself well for the 1984 election. He benefited from the racially polarized voting patterns in the state that year, but in all likelihood he would have won comfortably in any case. His record on issues was in line with the views of the majority, and his pleasant personal qualities are widely appreciated. Cochran profited from William Winter's indecision about making the race, particularly when Winter announced he would become chancellor of Ole Miss and then declined the position weeks later to make the Senate race. Mississippi has a gubernatorial and senatorial election to go through before thinking about whether Cochran will win again. But no one doubts that he has been thinking about it.

Presidential politics. So long as Mississippi's electorate is racially polarized, its seven electoral votes will go to the Republican candidate. But it has been a close state: in 1980 it went for Ronald Reagan over Jimmy Carter by only a 49%–48% margin. Success of an economic liberal like Ray Mabus in a state election might signal that Mississippi is ready to divide more on economic than racial lines, and be competitive again. Mississippi Democrats have agreed to hold a presidential primary on the southern Super Tuesday date, but as the second smallest of the southern states Mississippi is not likely to get much attention.

Congressional districting. Mississippi's congressional districting plans have been changed twice to comply with the Voting Rights Act, in each case to increase the black percentage in the 2d Congressional District. In 1986 that finally resulted in the election of Democrat Mike Espy, the first black to represent Mississippi in Congress since Reconstruction.

The People: Est. Pop. 1986: 2,625,000; Pop. 1980: 2,520,638, up 3.1% 1980–86 and 13.7% 1970–80; 1.09% of U.S. total, 31st largest. 14% with 1–3 yrs. col., 13% with 4+ yrs. col.; 23.9% below poverty level. Single ancestry: 20% English, 6% Irish, 2% German, 1% French. Households (1980): 78% family, 46% with children, 62% married couples; 29.0% housing units rented; median monthly rent: $113; median house value: $31,400. Voting age pop. (1980): 1,706,441; 31% Black, 1% Spanish origin. Registered voters (1986): 1,643,191; no party registration.

1986 Share of Federal Tax Burden $5,243,000,000; 0.70% of U.S. total, 33d largest.

1986 Share of Federal Expenditures

	Total		Non-Defense		Defense	
Total Expend	$8,475m	(1.02%)	$5,876m	(0.98%)	$3,599m	(1.13%)
St/Lcl Grants	1,344m	(1.19%)	1,338m	(1.19%)	7m	(1.80%)
Salary/Wages	1,145m	(.95%)	399m	(0.68%)	746m	(1.201)
Pymnts to Indiv	3,928m	(1.08%)	3,719m	(1.07%)	209m	(1.18%)
Procurement	1,835m	(0.89%)	221m	(0.36%)	1,637m	(1.09%)
Research/Other	222m	(0.83%)	222m	(0.86%)	0m	(0.06%)

Political Lineup: Governor, William A. (Bill) Allain (D); Lt. Gov., Brad Dye (D); Secy. of State, Dick Molpus (D); Atty. Gen., Ed Pittman (D); Treasurer, Bill Cole (D); Auditor, Ray Mabus (D). State Senate, 52 (49 D and 3 R); State House of Representatives, 122 (116 D and 6 R). Senators, John C. Stennis (D) and Thad Cochran (R). Representatives, 5 (3 D and 2 R).

1984 Presidential Vote

Reagan (R)	582,377	(62%)
Mondale (D)	352,192	(37%)

1980 Presidential Vote

Reagan (R)	441,089	(49%)
Carter (D)	429,281	(48%)
Anderson (I)	12,036	(1%)

GOVERNOR

Gov. William A. (Bill) Allain (D)

Elected 1983, term expires Jan. 1988; b. Feb. 14, 1928, Washington; home, Jackson; U. of Notre Dame, U. of MS, LL.B. 1950; Roman Catholic; divorced.

Career: Army, Korea; Practicing atty., 1953–62; MS Asst. Atty. Gen., 1962–75; MS Atty. Gen., 1979–83.

Office: P.O. Box 139, Jackson 39205, 601-359-3100.

Election Results

1983 gen.	William A. (Bill) Allain (D)....	409,209	(55%)
	Leon Bramlett (R)	288,764	(39%)
1983 runoff	William A. (Bill) Allain (D)....	405,348	(52%)
	Evelyn Gandy (D)	367,953	(48%)
1983 prim.	Evelyn Gandy (D)	316,304	(38%)
	William A. (Bill) Allain (D)....	293,348	(35%)
	Michael Sturdivant (D)	172,526	(21%)
	Two others (D)	46,033	(6%)
1979 gen.	William F. Winter (D)	413,620	(61%)
	Gil Carmichael (R)	263,702	(39%)

SENATORS

Sen. John C. Stennis (D)

Elected 1947, seat up 1988; b. Aug. 3, 1901, Kemper Cnty.; home, DeKalb; MS St. U., B.S. 1923, U. of VA, LL.B. 1928; Presbyterian; widowed.

Career: MS House of Reps., 1928–32; Dist. Prosecuting Atty., 16th Judicial Dist., 1931–37; Circuit Judge, 1937–47.

Offices: 205 RSOB 20510, 202-224-6253. Also 303 P.O. Bldg., Jackson 39205, 601-353-5494; DeKalb 39328; 601-743-2631.

Committees: *Appropriations* (Chairman of 16 D). Subcommittees: Agriculture and Related Agencies; Defense (Chairman); Energy and Water Development; HUD–Independent Agencies; Transportation. *Armed Services* (2d of 11 D). Subcommittees: Projection Forces and Regional Defense; Readiness, Sustainability and Support; Strategic Forces and Nuclear Defense.

Group Ratings

	ADA	ACLU	COPE	CFA	LCV	ACU	NTU	NSI	COC	CEI
1986	35	41	30	27	0	40	43	100	56	43
1985	25	—	29	40	—	67	29	—	50	—

National Journal Ratings

	1986 LIB — 1986 CONS			1985 LIB — 1985 CONS		
Economic	40%	—	55%	54%	—	45%
Social	64%	—	34%	32%	—	65%
Foreign	23%	—	76%	37%	—	62%

Key Votes

1) Ease Gun Cont	—	5) Grm-Rdmn Def Red	FOR	9) Rehnquist Nom	FOR
2) Immig Reform	FOR	6) Contra Aid	FOR	10) Tax Reform	FOR
3) Lmt Text Imp	FOR	7) SDI Funding	FOR	11) Drug Death Pen	FOR
4) Aid Tobac Ind	FOR	8) Lmt PAC Contrib	FOR	12) S Africa Sanc	FOR

Election Results

1982 general	John C. Stennis (D)	414,099	(64%)	($944,054)
	Haley Barbour (R)	230,927	(36%)	($1,133,384)
1982 primary	John C. Stennis (D)	145,817	(75%)	
	Charles Pittman (D)	33,651	(17%)	
	Colon Johnson (D)	14,696	(6%)	
1976 general	John C. Stennis (D)	554,433	(100%)	($119,852)

Campaign Contributions and Expenditures

1981-82		Direct Cont. 1981-82		PACS Breakdown			
Receipts	$949,213	Indiv.	$584,834	Agr	$14,000	Ideo	$8,800
Expend.	$944,054	Party	$37,500	Bus	$188,550	Lbr	$6,500
Unspent	$5,156	PACS	$232,300	Hlth	$12,350	Prof	$1,750
		Cand.	$50,000				

Sen. Thad Cochran (R)

Elected 1978, seat up 1990; b. Dec. 7, 1937, Pontotoc; home, Jackson; U. of MS, B.A. 1959, J.D. 1965, Rotary Fellow, Trinity Col., Dublin, Ireland, 1963–64; Baptist; married (Rose).

Career: Navy, 1959–61; Practicing atty., 1965–72; U.S. House of Reps., 1973–78.

Offices: 326 RSOB 20510, 202-224-5054. Also P.O. Box 22581, Jackson 39205, 601-965-4499.

Committees: *Agriculture, Nutrition, and Forestry* (4th of 9 R). Subcommittees: Agricultural Credit; Agricultural Production and Stabilization of Prices; Domestic and Foreign Marketing and Product Promotion (Ranking Member). *Appropriations* (6th of 13 R). Subcommittees: Agriculture and Related Agencies (Ranking Member); Defense; Energy and Water Development; Interior; Transportation. *Labor and Human Resources* (6th of 7 R). Subcommittees: Aging (Ranking Member); Children, Family, Drugs and Alcoholism; Handicapped.

Group Ratings

	ADA	ACLU	COPE	CFA	LCV	ACU	NTU	NSI	COC	CEI
1986	5	21	13	20	33	78	49	100	89	64
1985	5	—	15	13	—	74	55	—	81	—

National Journal Ratings

	1986 LIB — 1986 CONS			1985 LIB — 1985 CONS		
Economic	0%	—	84%	14%	—	83%
Social	30%	—	69%	40%	—	58%
Foreign	18%	—	77%	22%	—	70%

Key Votes

1) Ease Gun Cont	FOR	5) Grm-Rdmn Def Red	FOR	9) Rehnquist Nom	FOR
2) Immig Reform	FOR	6) Contra Aid	FOR	10) Tax Reform	FOR
3) Lmt Text Imp	FOR	7) SDI Funding	FOR	11) Drug Death Pen	—
4) Aid Tobac Ind	FOR	8) Lmt PAC Contrib	AGN	12) S Africa Sanc	AGN

Election Results

1984 general	Thad Cochran (R)...................	508,314	(58%)	($2,870,894)
	William Winter (D)	371,926	(42%)	($738,739)
1984 primary	Thad Cochran (R) unopposed			
1978 general	Thad Cochran (R)...................	263,089	(45%)	($1,052,303)
	Maurice Danton (D).................	185,454	(32%)	($873,518)
	Charles Evers (I)...................	133,646	(23%)	($135,119)

Campaign Contributions and Expenditures

1979-84		Direct Cont. 1979-84		PACS Breakdown 1979-84			
Receipts	$2,860,815	Indiv.	$1,664,711	Corp.	$532,780	T/M/H	$281,000
Expend.	$2,870,894	Party	$12,917	Labor	$18,750	Agr.	$42,750
Unspent	$138,875	PACS	$998,918	Ideo.	$91,914	CWOS	$23,250

FIRST DISTRICT

The keystone of William Faulkner's fictional universe, the university town of Oxford in northern Mississippi, sits on a divide between two parts of the state. To the east are the mostly white hill counties, going all the way up to the northeast corner, where Mississippi's Tishomingo County meets the Tennesse River. The Tennessee Valley Authority brought electricity here, and the Tennessee-Tombigbee Waterway provided construction jobs for years and a new shipping canal when it was completed in 1985: this is one part of Mississippi where the federal government is regarded as a helper and not a meddling intruder by articulate white opinion. West of Oxford is Mississippi's Delta, the swampy land pioneered by large planters around the turn of the century, with large black work forces little removed, in the conditions of their daily lives or long-term economic chances, from slavery. In the center is Oxford, the home of Ole Miss and the town that was the inspiration for Faulkner's mythical Jefferson. All this land is included in Mississippi's 1st Congressional District, which also includes the Mississippi suburbs of Memphis, Tennessee, touches on the river itself, and goes as far west as Tallahatchie County, home of Representative Jamie Whitten.

Whitten is the dean of the House and chairman of the Appropriations Committee. He was first elected in 1941, a month before Pearl Harbor. Since 1949 (except for 1953–55, when Republicans had control) he has chaired the Agriculture Subcommittee of Appropriations—the longest service of any House subcommittee chairman in history. This has enabled him to become a kind of permanent secretary of agriculture; the top bureaucrats in the department believe that Whitten will be around a lot longer than the current official secretary; and so far they have been right. Whitten is not afraid to use his influence. He was a strong force for large subsidy payments to cotton farmers; for years the cotton program was the most costly of Agriculture's crop subsidy operations. He has strongly backed attempts to kill vermin with pesticides, and is unsympathetic to critics who claim they are harmful or in the long run self-defeating: he wants to protect farmers from sudden and potentially catastrophic crop failures and drops in prices. Whitten has developed a network of friends in state agriculture departments and among county agricultural agents all over the country. A Secretary of Agriculture who ignores him is a fool.

But Whitten's mastery of politics goes beyond farm issues. He is one of the few southern politicians from the pre-civil rights days who has made the transition to today's House, and made it skillfully, gracefully, and with powers enhanced. Though he is from a Delta county, almost all of his constituency from 1941 to 1962 was in hill counties, and like many hill county southerners he supported some New Deal economic programs, including generous spending for farmers, and of course absolutely opposed any change in the system of racial segregation. In 1962 he was placed in the same district with a colleague reputed to be a moderate and given many Delta counties, where of course no blacks were then voting; Whitten ran as the more conservative candidate and won. For a dozen years, as issues changed and Mississippi whites seethed with anger at Washington liberals, Whitten concentrated on agriculture and compiled a conservative voting record on other issues. Then in 1974 the Democratic Caucus began to elect all committee chairmen by secret ballot, and Whitten, by this time the second ranking member of Appropriations behind 74-year-old George Mahon, took note. On the Agriculture Subcommittee he fought attempts to kill the food stamp program—not a Whitten favorite before 1975, but well-loved by most House Democrats and by the increasing number of black voters in his district. On other issues, his rating from organized labor jumped from the 10% level to about 40%. In effect he rejoined the national Democratic party, compiling a liberal voting record on economic issues and sometimes agreeing with most other Democrats on cultural and foreign issues. When Mahon retired in 1978 and it came time to elect a new Appropriations chairman, Edward Boland, popular, respected, liberal, and one notch below Whitten, decided not to run, and Whitten won the secret ballot 157–88. Those 88 votes represented the minimum opposition then, a strong base for any challenge. Whitten is pleased to point out that after six years as chairman the secret ballot vote was 224–14.

Whitten has not just voted with the Democrats; he has been one of the leaders of the party, helping younger members with their projects, carrying the party flag on major issues, accumulating favors. He opposes the Reagan economic programs, fights Reagan cutbacks in the Appropriations Committee, and uses his parliamentary skills (despite an accent unintelligible to many members) to good advantage. For a time it seemed his power as Appropriations chairman was diminished by the congressional budget process, which sets limits on spending which are supposed to and often do bind the Appropriations subcommittees. But there remains plenty of room for subcommittee chairmen—known collectively as the College of Cardinals—to steer federal programs in the direction they want. Moreover, as Congress has missed its budget deadlines, and as the Gramm-Rudman law squeezes spending down further, every subcommittee's bill has been rolled into a single continuing resolution which is considered, under pressure of one deadline after another, in the fall. Getting your pet provision in or out of the CR, as it is called, can be critical to your whole congressional career; deciding which parts of the House version of the CR to insist on in conference with the Senate can determine the direction of national policy; fending off pesky amendments can make the difference between a functioning and a shut-down federal government. The floor manager and the chairman of the House conferees on the CR is Jamie Whitten (the Senate conferees will be led by Mississippian John Stennis). Somewhat defensively, he points out that 11 of the 13 House Appropriations subcommittees got their bills passed by the full House in 1986, and typically with his support of the subcommittee chairman, but that they had to be rolled into the continuing resolution because of the Senate's inaction. In the process Jamie Whitten has become a more powerful congressman than ever.

Whitten has never been inattentive to things in Mississippi. He got the Tennessee-Tombigbee built by arranging to have worked started at both ends and then in the middle; when the crunch came, he could argue that it made no sense not to connect the parts already completed. The waterway cost $2 billion and was projected to carry 27 to 40 million tons of cargo a year; in its first 20 months it carried 5 million, plus a lot of pleasure craft. But Whitten is still enthusiastic about its prospects, and proud as well of the $11 million acoustics lab the Congress told the Agriculture Department to build at Ole Miss, or the watershed protection and flood control project for the foothills of the Delta, or money to build Route 302 to connect I-55 and U.S. 72. "My district is a part of the nation," he has said, "and if you handle a national program and leave out your district, you would not want to go home." Whitten is not afraid to go home, and the same geniality and marbles-in-the-mouth diction that works for him in Washington works in

Mississippi. Redistricting in the 1980s has pared away the Delta counties and black Democratic voters, leaving him with a whiter and more Republican district, but he wins by at least 2 to 1 margins. Whitten, one year older than Ronald Reagan, is as politically wily as ever and has plenty of energy; so it is likely he will continue as Appropriations Chairman for some time to come.

The People: Pop. 1980: 504,136, up 18.2% 1970–80. Households (1980): 80% family, 46% with children, 67% married couples; 24.2% housing units rented; median monthly rent: $98; median house value: $30,000. Voting age pop. (1980): 345,943; 21% Black, 1% Spanish origin.

1984 Presidential Vote:

Reagan (R)	111,501	(63%)
Mondale (D)	66,722	(37%)

Rep. Jamie L. Whitten (D)

Elected 1941; b. Apr. 18, 1910, Cascilla; home, Charleston; U. of MS; Presbyterian; married (Rebecca).

Career: Practicing atty.; School principal; MS House of Reps., 1932–33; Dist. Prosecuting Atty., 17th Judicial Dist., 1933–41.

Offices: 2314 RHOB 20515, 202-225-4306. Also P.O. Bldg., Charleston 38921, 601-647-2413; P.O. Box 667, Oxford 38655, 601-234-9064; and P.O. Box 1482, Tupelo 38801.

Committees: *Appropriations* (Chairman of 35 D). Subcommittee: Rural Development, Agriculture and Related Agencies (Chairman).

Group Ratings

	ADA	ACLU	COPE	CFA	LCV	ACU	NTU	NSI	COC	CEI
1986	55	62	40	58	22	16	24	50	31	23
1985	55	—	39	50	—	26	26	—	20	—

National Journal Ratings

	1986 LIB — 1986 CONS		1985 LIB — 1985 CONS	
Economic	53% —	47%	71% —	28%
Social	60% —	39%	46% —	54%
Foreign	51% —	48%	55% —	44%

Key Votes

1) Lmt Cln Water Act	AGN	5) Retain Gun Cont	AGN	9) Aid Angola Reb	FOR
2) Rpl Tobac Sub	AGN	6) Contra Aid	AGN	10) Tax Reform	FOR
3) Grm-Rdmn Def Red	AGN	7) Lmt Text Imp	FOR	11) S Africa Sanc	FOR
4) Ban Polygraph	AGN	8) Limit SDI	FOR	12) Immig Reform	AGN

Election Results

1986 general	Jamie L. Whitten (D)	59,870	(66%)	($170,878)
	Larry Cobb (R)	30,267	(34%)	($112,195)
1986 primary	Jamie L. Whitten (D)	26,310	(77%)	
	Jim Bush (D)	7,796	(23%)	
1984 general	Jamie L. Whitten (D)	136,530	(88%)	($45,373)
	John Hargett (I)	17,991	(12%)	

Campaign Contributions and Expenditures

1985-86		Direct Cont. 1985-86		PACS Breakdown 1985-86			
Receipts	$253,863	Indiv.	$37,129	Corp.	$68,600	T/M/H	$71,395
Expend.	$170,878	PACS	$186,290	Labor	$34,550	Agr.	$8,000
Unspent	$230,809			Ideo.	$2,250	CWOS	$1,500

SECOND DISTRICT

The Mississippi Delta, the flat, incredibly fertile land between the Mississippi and the Yazoo, criss-crossed and refertilized by tributaries, is a fabled land, a source of great wealth and a scene of great misery. It was swampy land, often flooded, until well after the Civil War; but wanderers through the Delta wilderness discovered that the topsoil here, accumulated over centuries of Mississippi spring floods, reached depths of 25 feet. To nature late 19th century entrepreneurs applied technology: the Delta was drained by great machines, the river was lined with levees, and the Illinois Central tracks were laid down on elevated tracks from Memphis to New Orleans, labor was attracted from the older black belts of the Deep South, and the Delta became America's richest cotton country.

This was a kind of industrial revolution in agriculture, and the workers were treated with the same indifference and callousness that northern factory owners treated the immigrants and farmboys who worked their machines. The patina of graciousness which often covered the brutality of slavery was not often seen in the Delta. Most new planters didn't bother to build beautiful antebellum-type mansions, but lived in more functional, austere houses. They were capitalists, not cavaliers, and when they replaced labor with capital by bringing in cotton-picking machines in the 1940s, they did everything they could (perhaps in anticipation of the day when blacks would get the vote) to encourage local blacks to move north to Chicago or Memphis. Welfare payments and aid to the poor are as stingy—or nonexistent—in the Delta as anywhere in the United States.

This was the land that produced some of the most obdurate segregationists in American politics, like Delta planter James Eastland, U.S. Senator from 1941 to 1979, chairman of the Judiciary Committee from 1955 to 1979, unrelenting opponent of civil rights laws. But it is also the land that has produced, for the first time here since Reconstruction, and 20 years after the Voting Rights Act first gave black Mississippians the vote, a black congressman. He is Mike Espy, and is a political beneficiary of the sections of the Voting Rights Act that have been interpreted as requiring a maximization of black percentages in a few congressional districts. Twice in the 1980s, Mississippi's district lines have been drawn, leaving all of the Delta plus a few of the foothills to the east, a small part of the city of Jackson, and the Mississippi Valley just below Vicksburg, into a new black-majority 2d Congressional District.

Espy had several assets unsuccessful black candidate Robert Clark did not have in 1982 and 1984. One was district lines: Clark would have won in 1982 with the 1984 district lines. Another was his background: his grandfather decided to build a hospital and asked every black in audiences around the state to contribute $1 for a brick; he also built 28 funeral homes and became one of the biggest landowners in the state. A third advantage was articulateness: Espy, a lawyer, educated in northern schools, experienced after several years in state government enforcing land laws over recalcitrant locals, was at ease on the stump attacking Republican Webb Franklin's record. And there was sheer luck: in the low-turnout primary Espy beat a nephew of former Governor Paul Johnson and a cousin of James Eastland with 50.1% of the vote—just 79 more votes than he needed to avoid a runoff. Final reasons were the saliency of farm issues and the strong support Espy received from other Democrats. Espy campaigned against the Republican farm programs Franklin supported on the Agriculture Committee and carried around in his pocket a promise from Speaker-to-be Jim Wright that if elected he would get a seat on the Agriculture Committee himself. This combination was enough for Espy to carry the Delta with enough votes to spare to overcome Franklin's edge in Vicksburg and one mostly-white rural county.

Most young congressmen follow a simple formula to make their seats safe: deluge constituents with mail, smother them with constituency service, avoid unpopular stands on issues voters care about, and return home every week. Espy has a harder job. Racially polarized voting has kept each party's percentage within an exceedingly narrow range—Democrats have varied from 48% to 52% in the 1980s—and so long as polarization continues a slight advantage for the Republicans can beat Espy. He needs to solidify some significant share of white support. He may have made a beginning by stressing the agriculture issues so strongly. In the past there has been almost entirely missing in Delta politics any sense that blacks and whites have interests in common. To blacks and whites alike, the economy in this resource-rich and enterprise-poor area seems a zero-sum game: the only question is who gets how much from the bounty of the soil. Espy seems to want to bolster farm income and to stimulate economic development for everyone. His seats on the Agriculture and Budget Committees show the help the Democratic leadership has given him, and Appropriations Chairman Jamie Whitten of the 1st District seems willing to help. But Espy probably needs to do something more than bring in pork; he has to break the hold of segregationist politics where it grew so efficiently in Mississippi Delta soil.

The People: Pop. 1980: 503,935, up 0.4% 1970–80. Households (1980): 76% family, 47% with children, 56% married couples; 37.3% housing units rented; median monthly rent: $78; median house value: $26,800. Voting age pop. (1980): 323,647; 53% Black, 1% Spanish origin.

1984 Presidential Vote:

Reagan (R)	86,648	(50%)
Mondale (D)	84,965	(50%)

Rep. Mike Espy (D)

Elected 1986; b. Nov. 30, 1953, Yazoo City; home, Yazoo City; Howard U., B.A. 1975, U. of Santa Clara, J.D. 1978; Baptist; married (Sheila).

Career: Asst. Secy. of State, MS., 1980–84; Asst. Atty. Gen., Dir. of MS Consumer Protection, 1984–85.

Offices: 216 CHOB 20515, 202-225-5876. Also 300 S. Main St., Yazoo City 39194, 1-800-746-247-9395, 601-746-1400; Vicksburg City Hall, Rm. 302, 1401 Walnut St., Vicksburg 39180, 601-638-3779; Clarksdale City Hall, 1st floor, 420 3d St., Clarksdale 38614, 601-624-9929; Greenville City Hall, City Hall Annex, 340 Main St., Greenville 38701, 601-334-3779; and 118 Kings St., Granada 38901, 601-226-1436.

Committees: *Agriculture* (26th of 26 D). Subcommittees: Conservation, Credit, and Rural Development; Department Operations, Research and Foreign Agriculture; Domestic Marketing, Consumer Relations and Nutrition; Wheat, Soybeans and Feed Grains. *Budget* (21st of 21 D). Task Forces: Community and Natural Resources; Economic Policy; Human Resources. *Select Committee on Hunger* (12th of 16 D). Task Force: Domestic Task Force.

Group Ratings and Key Votes: **Newly Elected**

Election Results

1986 general	Mike Espy (D)	73,119	(52%)	($591,002)
	Webb Franklin (D)	68,292	(48%)	($574,120)
1986 primary	Mike Espy (D)	29,724	(50%)	
	Pete Johnson (D)	15,335	(26%)	
	Hiram Eastland (D)	14,229	(24%)	
1984 general	Webb Franklin (R)	92,392	(51%)	($607,258)
	Robert Clark (D)	89,154	(49%)	($381,495)

Campaign Contributions and Expenditures

1985-86		Direct Cont. 1985-86		PACS Breakdown 1985-86			
Receipts	$600,375	Indiv.	$240,103	Corp.	$21,975	T/M/H	$20,900
Expend.	$591,002	Party	$13,574	Labor	$176,993	Agr.	$3,750
Unspent	$9,373	PACS	$311,510	Ideo.	$87,392	CWOS	$500
		Cand.	$36,207				

THIRD DISTRICT

The 3d Congressional District of Mississippi is the east central part of the state, a mostly rural area studded with small cities. Blacks are not in the majority today, but some day they may be a much larger percentage than they are today: 27% of this district's adult population and 40% of its children are black. The 3d stretches from Columbus and Starkville, home of Mississippi State University, in the north, to Laurel in the south. Its largest city is Meridian, near the Alabama border, but the district also includes most of the Rankin County suburbs of Jackson, a relatively high-income area and one of the most Republican counties in the state.

The congressman from the 3d District is Sonny Montgomery. He is an exemplar of the traditional southern Democrat: devoted to his work, a delightful companion, dedicated to his principles, possessed of a fine sense of humor. A veteran of both World War II and Korea, Montgomery serves on the Armed Services and Veterans' Affairs Committee. In 1981 he became chairman of Veterans' Affairs, a body led for years by conservative southerners. Veterans' Affairs bills are traditionally considered on the floor of the House under a closed rule, which means that no amendments are allowed; that means that the bill Montgomery and his allies on the committee report out is the one that passes.

On some issues Montgomey has represented the traditional views of older veterans' organizations against those of younger veterans. He has tended to be skeptical about the claims that Agent Orange caused injuries which should be compensated, and he resisted a proposal by Don Edwards to allow veterans to hire lawyers to make claims on the Veterans' Administration rather than rely on traditional veterans' organizations to pursue them. But his biggest achievemnt as chairman is the new G.I. education bill, which allows servicemen to put aside $100 a month of their first 12 months pay and receive $300 a month for 36 months in education aid. He argues that this will help recruitment in the all-volunteer military and provide thousands of servicemen and women with a chance to improve their skills and earnings.

On the Armed Services Committee Montgomery is Capitol Hill's strongest champion of the Reserves and National Guard, which do not boast as many members of Congress in their ranks as they used to; he sponsored the successful amendment to take away governors' powers to veto assignment of their states' guards to overseas training exercises (some have been held in Honduras). He has not been successful in his effort to require doctors and nurses to register for a possible draft. On military issues Montgomery is invariably hawkish, on cultural matters traditional, on economic issues sometimes willing to spend money domestically. Over the years he has usually voted with Republican administrations. But he remains on friendly terms with the Democratic leadership, seldom opposes them volubly, and is sometimes available to help—a party loyalist, in his own way. He is regularly reelected by huge margins.

The People: Pop. 1980: 505,169, up 16.5% 1970–80. Households (1980): 78% family, 45% with children, 64% married couples; 26.1% housing units rented; median monthly rent: $114; median house value: $31,800. Voting age pop. (1980): 348,335; 28% Black, 1% Spanish origin, 1% American Indian.

1984 Presidential Vote: Reagan (R) 133,167   (65%)
                                  Mondale (D) 70,385   (35%)

Rep. G. V. (Sonny) Montgomery (D)

Elected 1966; b. Aug. 5, 1920, Meridian; home, Meridian; MS St. U., B.S. 1943; Episcopalian; single.

Career: Army, WWII and Korea; Owner, Montgomery Insur. Agcy.; MS Senate, 1956–66.

Offices: 2184 RHOB 20515, 202-225-5031. Also Fed. Bldg., Meridian 39701, 601-693-6681; Fed. Bldg., Laurel 39440, 601-649-1231; Golden Triangle Airport, Columbus 39701, 601-327-2766; and 110-D Airport Rd., Pearl 39208, 601-932-2410.

Committees: *Armed Services* (7th of 31 D). Subcommittees: Military Installations and Facilities; Military Personnel and Compensation. *Veterans' Affairs* (Chairman of 21 D). Subcommittees: Hospitals and Health Care (Chairman).

Group Ratings

	ADA	ACLU	COPE	CFA	LCV	ACU	NTU	NSI	COC	CEI
1986	5	5	13	33	21	86	34	100	76	46
1985	15	—	12	8	—	76	41	—	82	—

National Journal Ratings

	1986 LIB — 1986 CONS	1985 LIB — 1985 CONS
Economic	30% — 69%	34% — 65%
Social	18% — 78%	0% — 76%
Foreign	0% — 86%	0% — 76%

Key Votes

1) Lmt Cln Water Act	AGN	5) Retain Gun Cont	AGN	9) Aid Angola Reb	FOR
2) Rpl Tobac Sub	AGN	6) Contra Aid	FOR	10) Tax Reform	AGN
3) Grm-Rdmn Def Red	FOR	7) Lmt Text Imp	FOR	11) S Africa Sanc	AGN
4) Ban Polygraph	AGN	8) Limit SDI	AGN	12) Immig Reform	FOR

Election Results

1986 general	G. V. (Sonny) Montgomery (D)	80,575	(100%)	($70,580)
1986 primary	G. V. (Sonny) Montgomery (D) unopposed			
1984 general	G. V. (Sonny) Montgomery (D)	158,002	(100%)	($62,603)

Campaign Contributions and Expenditures

1985-86		Direct Cont. 1985-86		PACS Breakdown 1985-86			
Receipts	$50,708	Indiv.	$3,005	Corp.	$23,324	T/M/H	$9,600
Expend.	$70,580	PACS	$34,174	Labor	$0	Agr.	$0
Unspent	$98,995	Cand.	$750	Ideo.	$1,250	CWOS	$0

FOURTH DISTRICT

A generation ago, Jackson, Mississippi, was a sleepy small town, proud of its state capital, but defensive about its state's national reputation as a stronghold of bigotry and poverty. In the decades since, life in Mississippi has changed, and a new spirit—and new vibrancy—has been apparent in Jackson. Like the state's other significant urban center on the Gulf Coast, it has grown rapidly, generated new businesses, attracted people from outside the state. On the north side of town, in new subdivisions of pleasant, large colonial houses under huge, overhanging trees, you can get a sense of what growth has meant to Jackson—especially when you consider that at least some of the people in these neighborhoods came from humble houses in rural Mississippi. Even the less well-to-do—people who grew up poor and now make $40,000 a year, more than they ever dreamed of—tend to think of themselves as the new rich, and in fact money goes a good deal further in Jackson than in a large metropolitan area.

This kind of economic growth has made white Jackson one of the Republican strongholds of Mississippi. Evidently these white voters have not paused to ask whether the civil rights revolution, which coincides with the beginnings of boom times for Jackson and the Sun Belt, had anything to do with the economic explosion from which they have benefited. Yet surely it has, if only to make places like Jackson more attractive to investors and to the talented blacks who used to migrate en masse to northern cities. The other side of this paradox is that black Jackson, almost unanimously Democratic, does not have much appreciation for what free markets and gutsy entrepreneurs have done to raise living standards for everyone in Jackson. Central to their political experience has been the fact that civil rights were won only by an activist, even meddlesome federal government, and reflexively they see big government as their ally and even savior generally. Between these points of view there is little room for accommodation. When William Winter was governor the Democrats here made progress toward building a biracial party; it helped that Winter himself was an integral and unthreatening part of the state's economic elite. Even so, the affluent and near-affluent neighborhoods of Jackson have continued to vote almost as overwhelmingly Republican in most elections as the black neighborhoods vote Democratic.

Jackson and most of its affluent suburban fringe form half of Mississippi's 4th Congressional District. The rest consists of the rural areas and small towns of south central and southwestern Mississippi, from the antebellum mansions of Natchez to small cities like Brookhaven, McComb, and Columbia. These are mini-Jacksons: they have growing white affluent populations plus black near-majorities. Nationally they have been trending Republican, but there are still many rural white Democratic votes in congressional elections. They tend to balance off Jackson, and to make this one of the more spiritedly contested congressional districts in the South.

The 4th District's congressman, Democrat Wayne Dowdy, is like so many of his constituents a product of small town Mississippi with a thick accent and a country manner who has moved up a long way in the world. Tall, gangly, Dowdy started off as a country lawyer in McComb, bought himself a couple of radio stations and got mildly rich, and then ran for Congress in 1981 when 4th District Republican Jon Hinson resigned after being arrested in a House office building men's room and charged with a sexual offense. To the surprise of just about everyone, Dowdy beat a better-financed Republican and, in the first Reagan year, recaptured a southern district from the Republicans. He forged a biracial coalition by, among other things, backing the Voting Rights Act—which showed southern politicians that there were lots of votes in being for Voting Rights and none in being against it—which may have helped the act get renewed in 1982. He did even better, as far as Speaker Tip O'Neill was concerned, by voting against the Reagan tax cut; O'Neill promised him a seat on the much-coveted Energy and Commerce Committee, and delivered after the 1982 election.

On Energy and Commerce, he has not always joined John Dingell's Democrats, but that was not to be expected of a Mississippi Democrat; what is interesting is that he joins most other Democrats very often indeed on both economic and cultural issues. He is an especially insistent supporter of trade restriction legislation—which politically gives him a chance to be a macho opponent of foreigners who are hurting America, even while Japanese direct investment in Mississippi is courted and grows. After his 1986 reelection victory, he was promised (and given) a Veterans' Affairs subcommittee chair by full committee Chairman Sonny Montgomery, his neighbor in the 3d District.

Dowdy won reelection in 1982 and 1984 with just 53% and 55% of the vote. He showed his mettle by winning enough black support to forestall any independent black candidacies, like those that sunk several Mississippi Democrats in the 1970s, and by using his Energy and Commerce seat to raise lots of campaign money. By 1986, against weaker opposition, he won with a very impressive 72% of the vote, carrying Jackson handily, running even in even the most affluent precincts. These upwardly mobile voters seem to recognize one of their kind. Dowdy has expressed interest in running for Senate if John Stennis doesn't run in 1988, and with his base in Jackson, whose TV stations hit a large percentage of state households, his black support and country manners, he could be a strong competitor, even against so formidable an opponent as his 5th District Republican colleague Trent Lott. If he does run, look for a seriously contested race in the 4th.

The People: Pop. 1980: 503,297, up 12.5% 1970–80. Households (1980): 76% family, 44% with children, 59% married couples; 29.4% housing units rented; median monthly rent: $129; median house value: $34,200. Voting age pop. (1980): 345,335; 37% Black, 1% Spanish origin.

1984 Presidential Vote:

Reagan (R)	122,823	(59%)
Mondale (D)	85,513	(41%)

Rep. Wayne Dowdy (D)

Elected July 7, 1981; b. July 27, 1943, Fitzgerald, GA; home, Macomb; Millsaps Col., B.A. 1965, Jackson School of Law, LL.B. 1968; United Methodist; married (Susan).

Career: Practicing atty., 1969–1981; City Judge, McComb, 1970–74, Mayor 1978–81.

Offices: 240 CHOB 20515, 202-225-5865. Also P.O. Box 569, Jackson 39205, 601-969-3300; 703 Franklin St., Natchez 39120, 601-446-8628; and Marion Cnty. Courthouse Annex, Columbia 39429, 601-731-1029.

Committees: *Energy and Commerce* (17th of 25 D). Subcommittees: Energy and Power; Health and the Environment; Telecommunications and Finance. *Veterans' Affairs* (5th of 21 D). Subcommittees: Education, Training and Employment (Chairman); Oversight and Investigations.

Group Ratings

	ADA	ACLU	COPE	CFA	LCV	ACU	NTU	NSI	COC	CEI
1986	45	16	78	58	45	32	22	50	29	16
1985	40	—	78	42	—	48	23	—	45	—

National Journal Ratings

	1986 LIB — 1986 CONS			1985 LIB — 1985 CONS		
Economic	71%	—	29%	51%	—	49%
Social	43%	—	57%	34%	—	66%
Foreign	49%	—	50%	46%	—	52%

Key Votes

1) Lmt Cln Water Act	AGN	5) Retain Gun Cont	AGN	9) Aid Angola Reb	AGN
2) Rpl Tobac Sub	AGN	6) Contra Aid	FOR	10) Tax Reform	AGN
3) Grm-Rdmn Def Red	AGN	7) Lmt Text Imp	FOR	11) S Africa Sanc	FOR
4) Ban Polygraph	AGN	8) Limit SDI	FOR	12) Immig Reform	FOR

Election Results

1986 general	Wayne Dowdy (D)	85,819	(72%)	($325,665)
	Gail Healy (R)	34,190	(28%)	($62,347)
1986 primary	Wayne Dowdy (D)	42,192	(86%)	
	Emily Carter (D)	6,648	(14%)	
1984 general	Wayne Dowdy (D)	113,635	(55%)	($412,196)
	David Armstrong (R)	91,797	(45%)	($164,600)

Campaign Contributions and Expenditures

1985-86		Direct Cont. 1985-86		PACS Breakdown 1985-86			
Receipts	$407,099	Indiv.	$113,200	Corp.	$99,900	T/M/H	$81,200
Expend.	$325,665	PACS	$285,900	Labor	$87,000	Agr.	$2,750
Unspent	$173,731			Ideo.	$12,650	CWOS	$2,400

FIFTH DISTRICT

The fastest growing and economically most vibrant part of Mississippi is the state's Gulf Coast. Here, on the strand where Jefferson Davis built his mansion, Beauvoir, are the cities of Biloxi and Gulfport, greatly enlarged in recent years after a nasty hurricane. To the east are Pascagoula and Moss Point, beneficiaries of the giant Litton shipyard often favored with military contracts; to the west are smaller resort towns frequented by the rich and not-so-rich of nearby New Orleans. The Gulf Coast includes about 60% of the people of the 5th Congressional District of Mississippi. The remainder live inland, in farm counties or in the medium-sized cities of Hattiesburg and Laurel. Much of this land is piney woods and paper mill country—scrubby land that was not good enough for antebellum plantations. As a result there are relatively few blacks here: only one in six of the district's adults are black, the lowest percentage in Mississippi. With its low black percentage and booming economy, the 5th District, like most of the Gulf Coast, has become prime Republican territory. It went Republican twice against fellow southerner Jimmy Carter, and in 1972 it gave Richard Nixon his highest percentage in any of the 435 congressional districts, a whopping 87%. In the House it is represented by one of the leading Republicans on Capitol Hill, Trent Lott.

Lott inherited the seat, in a way: he was a staffer for 5th District Democrat William Colmer, chairman of the House Rules Committee and solid conservative, and when Colmer retired in 1972 ran for the seat with Colmer's encouragement and endorsement. In his first term he served on the Judiciary Committee, where he defended Richard Nixon in the impeachment hearings. In 1975 he got a seat on the Rules Committee. In 1980 he was elected Republican whip, the number two position in the leadership. In 1980 and 1984 he has headed or dominated the Republican national convention's platform committees.

Lott has accomplished all this without quite being anyone's protégé. On the surface his views seem conventional. He has the instinctive conservatism of a small town poor boy who worked his way up through college and law school during the civil rights revolution without being affected by it much one way or the other. He still has trouble understanding how others will perceive racial issues: he was the man who kept urging the Reagan Administration to grant a tax exemption to Bob Jones University. He sees himself as representing the little guy fed up with paying high taxes, and of the American who is proud of his country and wants to see its interests advanced abroad. He is instinctively a loyal party man who does not want to make waves— which is one reason he got the whip post. Yet he is also articulate, quick on his feet, well up on his facts and procedure, and aggressively partisan.

But he does want to change America in some important ways. He wants to permanently hold down taxes and spending; he is a close ally of Jack Kemp, and agrees with Kemp that the beginning of wisdom on economics is to keep tax rates low. He wants to strengthen belief in traditional moral values and in the rightness of the economic order: wants people to believe that America is good to the core, not riddled with rottenness. In a Republican Conference seething with ideas and blessed with at least three separate—and not necessarily friendly—brands of conservatives, Lott is on good terms with and is generally trusted by all sides. To his fellow party members, though less often to Democrats, he is personable, pleasant, cooperative. But he can be sharp in debate, and exceedingly combative, so much so that his judgment can be warped: he was one of those Republicans who was gleeful in December 1985 when his party almost killed the lower tax rates it has long sought.

Lott passed up a race for the Senate in 1982, but is obviously considering it if Stennis should not run in 1988 or if there is a special election (in which case he wouldn't have to give up his House seat). He has built a network of friends and supporters across the state from his days working in the Ole Miss alumni office, and he is a good campaigner—charming when he wants to be, peppery, always ready with an answer or a quip. Probably he considers the Senate a better bet than the House to have a Republican majority one day, yet if he stays in the House (and he is overwhelmingly reelected every two years in the 5th) there is also the not negligible chance that he could be speaker. Or is he thinking of things beyond that? He will probably dominate the platform proceedings at the 1988 Republican convention in New Orleans, just an hour's drive from his political base.

The People: Pop. 1980: 504,101, up 23.7% 1970–80. Households (1980): 78% family, 47% with children, 65% married couples; 28.3% housing units rented; median monthly rent: $156; median house value: $33,500. Voting age pop. (1980): 343,181; 17% Black, 1% Spanish origin, 1% Asian origin.

1984 Presidential Vote: Reagan (R) 128,188   (74%)
Mondale (D) 45,663   (26%)

Rep. Trent Lott (R)

Elected 1972; b. Oct. 9, 1941, Grenada; home, Pascagoula; U. of MS, B.A. 1963, J.D. 1967; Baptist; married (Patricia).

Career: Practicing atty., 1967–68; A. A. to U.S. Rep. William M. Colmer, 1968–72.

Offices: 2185 RHOB 20515, 202-225-5772. Also 1 Govt. Plaza, P.O. Box 1557, Gulfport 39501, 601-864-7670; 215 Fed. Bldg., Hattiesburg 39401, 601-582-3246; and 3100 S. Pascagoula St., Pascagoula 39567, 601-762-6435.

Committees: *Minority Whip. Rules* (3d of 4 R). Subcommittees: Rules of the House; The Legislative Process (Ranking Member).

Group Ratings

	ADA	ACLU	COPE	CFA	LCV	ACU	NTU	NSI	COC	CEI
1986	5	0	14	17	10	95	54	100	86	65
1985	0	—	14	17	—	90	58	—	95	—

National Journal Ratings

	1986 LIB — 1986 CONS			1985 LIB — 1985 CONS		
Economic	18%	—	82%	5%	—	92%
Social	18%	—	82%	0%	—	76%
Foreign	0%	—	86%	0%	—	76%

Key Votes

1) Lmt Cln Water Act	FOR	5) Retain Gun Cont	AGN	9) Aid Angola Reb	FOR
2) Rpl Tobac Sub	AGN	6) Contra Aid	FOR	10) Tax Reform	FOR
3) Grm-Rdmn Def Red	FOR	7) Lmt Text Imp	FOR	11) S Africa Sanc	AGN
4) Ban Polygraph	AGN	8) Limit SDI	AGN	12) Immig Reform	FOR

Election Results

1986 general	Trent Lott (R).......................	75,288	(82%)	($264,822)
	Larry L. Albritton (D)	16,143	(18%)	($531)
1986 primary	Trent Lott (R) unopposed			
1984 general	Trent Lott (R).......................	142,637	(85%)	($199,040)
	Arlan (Blackie) Coate (D)	25,840	(15%)	($1,461)

Campaign Contributions and Expenditures

1985-86		Direct Cont. 1985-86		PACS Breakdown 1985-86			
Receipts	$374,246	Indiv.	$95,430	Corp.	$104,918	T/M/H	$89,632
Expend.	$264,822	Party	$3,263	Labor	$15,000	Agr.	$7,000
Unspent	$441,592	PACS	$229,050	Ideo.	$12,000	CWOS	$500

MISSOURI

At the center of Middle America, at one and the same time southern and northern, eastern and western, containing the geographical center of the nation's population and not far from the geographic midpoint of the 48 continental states, at the confluence of the continent's two greatest rivers, Missouri is a central, *the* central American state. Yet as we approach the end of the century it does not bulk very large in the national consciousness. At the beginning of the century, it did. Kansas City was on its way to becoming an "up-to-date" major metropolitan area, and St. Louis, its street grid curving back from the Mississippi levees, was the nation's fourth largest city. It was the site of the 1904 World's Fair and one of the few cities with two major league baseball teams. Missouri was one of the hubs of the nation's railroad network, one of its major farm as well as manufacturing states, and in the 1890s America's leading producer of mules. In those pre-tractor days, the mule was the farmer's most efficient energy source, and Missouri mules were bred in record numbers and sent out over the rail lines to states from Mississippi to Nebraska, Ohio and Texas.

Turn-of-the-century Missouri had been, within living memory, the frontier—the first state created entirely out of territory west of the Mississippi River, jutting far out past white settlement. St. Louis had been just a trading post when Lewis and Clark passed through, and the site of Kansas City was just another point on the bluffs that overlooked the Missouri River moving from the northwest to the southeast. Missouri, the northernmost slave state, sent proslavery raiders over the border into the Kansas Territory in the 1850s to fight settlers sent in by abolitionists, and in the 1860s it had its own civil war in the hilly counties along the Missouri River. But Missouri's most important historical role was that of a gateway to the West, an avenue for the great Yankee migrations west from Ohio, Indiana, and Illinois and the southern migration west from Kentucky (Missouri is where Daniel Boone finally stopped looking for elbow room), the eastern terminus of the Pony Express and the Transcontinental Railroad.

Missouri in the 20th century has not entirely realized its once glowing promise. It has had below-average population growth since 1900, as its rural residents leave for big cities and suburbs and its cities grow at no more than ordinary rates. Neither St. Louis nor Kansas City has grabbed hold of the national imagination, like Chicago or San Francisco. And since 1945, population growth has been at the periphery of the nation, on the West Coast, in Texas, in Florida and the coastal South, and (though not lately) in the Great Lakes. As a result, inland states like Missouri have become demographically old. But having continuity, Missouri retains a civic life and politics akin to what it had when mules were an industry here. As in other border states, political divisions split along Civil War lines, but the geographical pattern is not what you might expect. Little Dixie, first settled by Virginians, lies in the northeast part of the state; the southwest, in the Ozarks, was Union and is Republican country. Meanwhile, St. Louis, once a German-Republican island in a southern Democratic sea, became heavily Democratic in the 1930s, though now metropolitan St. Louis seems to be trending Republican. The Kansas City area, less anchored to the state, is the most volatile part politically. So political preference is still a matter of economic divisions only lightly superimposed on Civil War regional allegiances. On cultural and foreign controversies as defined nationally, there is in Missouri the sort of consensus that the nation had 30 years ago.

For years Missouri's political inclinations were personified by its most famous politician, Harry Truman—partisan Democrat, the son of a mule trader and a Confederate sympathizer who became an urban machine politician and integrated the armed services. Yet today Missouri has trended distinctly Republican; not only are its governor and Senators all Republicans, but so are all statewide officials except the lieutenant governor. For years it favored rough-hewn politicos, but Governor John Ashcroft and Senators John Danforth and Christopher Bond are all Ivy League graduates and reformers who have made their political careers exposing scandal and running against old boy networks. Missouri has not voted Democratic for president since Jimmy Carter carried its rural areas in 1976, and has not elected a Democratic governor since that year. Metropolitan St. Louis, heavily Democratic in the Truman years, is about evenly split now. The rural counties have gone Democratic only in the recessions of the mid-1970s and 1982. Their traditional attitudes on cultural issues, never undermined by the kind of explosive economic growth that has taken wives out of kitchens and put them into offices, have helped the Republicans. So has the propensity of the Democrats to nominate St. Louis-based candidates who call the state Missour*ee*—a distinct handicap against outstate candidates who say, as Truman did and most Missourians do, Missour*ah*. This may be the number one success story for the Republican Party in the nation, a state where they have run better candidates and run government better than the Democrats, and have outpoliticked them at every turn.

Governor. Missouri, once almost as reliable a Democratic state as Mississippi, has now elected Republican governors in three out of the last four elections. It also has elected lieutenant governors, attorneys general, and other minor statewide officials—a performance indicating that this has become a Republican state. If so, credit is due to two rich, eastern-educated young men who, rather than make their way up in Wall Street or Washington law firms, decided to return to Missouri and run for office. One was John Danforth, whose election as attorney general in 1968 was the Republicans' first statewide win in a generation. He didn't meet the eligibility requirement for the governorship, however, and went on, after losing in 1970, to the Senate in 1976. The other young Republican was Christopher Bond, elected state auditor in 1970 and governor in 1972, at age 33. He was upset by Democrat Joseph Teasdale in 1976, but Teasdale's deficiencies as a politician and administrator helped Bond win a second term—the maximum allowed in Missouri—in 1980. He left office in 1984 running for the Senate and was elected in 1986.

Bond's successor, John Ashcroft, is a different kind of Republican. The son of a fundamentalist minister, a gospel singer and songwriter from the southwest part of the state, his base is rural and culturally conservative. But he is also a graduate of Yale and the University of Chicago Law

MISSOURI — Congressional Districts, Counties, Independent City, and Other Selected Places — (9 Districts)

Congressional districts established January 7, 1982; all other boundaries are as of January 1, 1980.

School and he and his wife, also a lawyer, have co-authored two legal textbooks. His positions on issues—against new taxes, for higher educational achievement—are both conservative and popular; if he emphasizes attracting new business, he can also point to aggressive cases he brought against big businesses during his two terms as attorney general. Ashcroft won two solid margins against St. Louis area opponents: in the primary against the St. Louis County Executive and in the general against the Democratic lieutenant governor, a veteran legislator from the St. Louis area. He barely carried the metro areas but got 63% in the rest of the state. The main threat to Ashcroft for 1988 comes from Lieutenant Governor Harriett Woods, who won 49% against John Danforth in 1982 and 47% against Christopher Bond in 1986. She may want to wait, however, to run against Danforth again in 1990, or she might be deterred by the fact that she lost twice in Democratic years.

Senators. Missouri's two Senators are political allies whose careers have run in tandem: both are Republicans who first ran for office in 1968, both have suffered defeats, both have made it occasionally into the national spotlight, and both won close races against Harriett Woods. Their philosophies seem similar as well.

John Danforth has had the advantage of serving in the majority in the Senate for six years. He is one of the wealthiest Senators, from the family that started Ralston Purina, and is also the only ordained minister in the Senate: he was at the Yale Law and Divinity Schools at the same time as Gary Hart. Danforth brings a certain moral intensity to politics: he is rumpled, informal, and candid, but not a natural horse-trader or storyteller. He tends to arrive at positions after a moral inventory rather than a political calculus; he is unusual in the Senate because he opposes both abortion and capital punishment. Danforth was elected attorney general of Missouri at age 32, in 1968—the breakthrough victory for Republicans in Missouri—but he lost narrowly to Senator Stuart Symington in 1970 and was not the favorite six years later when Symington retired. But the Democratic nominee, Representative Jerry Litton, died in a plane crash on primary night, and in November Danforth easily beat the substitute candidate, former Governor Warren Hearnes.

Danforth's moments in the spotlight have come on the Senate Finance Committee. There he was one of the players on the tax reform bill of 1986. He originally was more sympathetic than Chairman Bob Packwood to the idea of rate-lowering in return for preference-cutting—the essence of the reform. But when Packwood emerged from conference committee in 1986 with a bill that raised taxes on corporations, particularly the heavy industry corporations and big defense contractors (McDonnell-Douglas, General Dynamics) headquartered in Missouri, Danforth had qualms; and eventually ended up opposing the whole package. The bill was going through anyhow, but Danforth's actions illustrates his awkwardness as a legislator: he backed an idea initially but then opposed it when the legislative process turned it into something that could have been predicted at the beginning.

Danforth has been, and even in a Democratic Senate could continue to be, a major legislator on trade. He is now ranking Republican on the trade subcommittee and lead co-sponsor with Finance Chairman Lloyd Bentsen on the trade bill introduced with 54 Senate sponsors that would require the presidential retaliation against countries found to commit unfair labor practices. Danforth is generally a free trader, but he is alert to the possibility of unfair competition especially to Missouri industries (including shoes and autos: there are big assembly plants here), and in such cases his concern for the plight of particular individuals and principles of fairness outweighs his commitment to free market economics. Similarly in his Commerce Committee assignment, where he is not an all-out backer of deregulation, and on Budget.

Such concerns about suffering individuals help explain his work on hunger and famine. He made a trip to a number of Sub-Saharan countries in 1984 well before their starving children began appearing on televison screens and newsmagazine covers, and in 1985 he led the Senate to pass a major relief bill for famine victims throughout Africa. If his interest in alleviating hunger and his devotion to market economics, tempered by the political process, seem inconsistent to some, he can argue that free markets are the best—perhaps the only—way to produce the kind of massive economic growth that has abolished famine in most of the world. He might go on to argue that the Democrats' excessive welfare state policies of the past choked off growth here and hence elsewhere. At the same time, he is concerned about federal budget deficits and wants to explore means—even raising taxes—to close them. Deficits are why he was a principle advocate of increasing the excise tax on tobacco and keeping intact the since-repealed withholding requirement for interest on dividend income.

So for a man of rather unconventional temperament, Danforth ends up with a fairly conventional, old-fashioned Republican voting record. He is temperamentally disposed to cooperate with Presidents of his own party, especially on foreign policy; he seems to believe that at least some of the economic discomfort of the early 1980s was necessary to improve the economy in the long run. If he is not exactly a team player and certainly not a vote-trader, he is not a boat-rocker either.

Danforth started off in 1982 wanting to run a positive campaign and expecting routine reelection; he did not figure on Harriett Woods. Then a St. Louis County state senator, she has a natural aptitude for sympathizing with any popular discontent without always offering a solution for it and a former TV producer's aptitude for speaking to the camera. In 1986, for example, her campaign emphasized the woes of farmers and she said "we have to restore the capability of farmers to get a price in the market," but at the same time attacked mounting surpluses, the huge price of subsidies, and rising food costs for consumers: all problem and no solution. In 1982 Woods peppered Danforth with criticisms for supporting Reaganomics, and arguing that she knew what it was like to live on an ordinary income, while Danforth is one of the richest men in the Senate. By mid-October Woods was running even with the much better known Danforth, but her campaign ran out of money and pulled its ads for a week; Danforth's well-financed campaign, tipped off by Republican tracking polls, was able to counter attack effectively. Danforth went negative, accusing Woods of demagoguery and distortion. The result: a 51%-49% Danforth victory that was one of the closest in the nation. Interestingly, Woods's strength came from good showings in rural Missouri, which she almost carried; Danforth's media helped him carry the once heavily Democratic St. Louis area, even though it was Woods's base. For 1988, Woods may run once again, and would have a good chance if Danforth has the bad luck to be running in the trough of an economic cycle for the second straight election.

Woods was also the opponent Senator Christopher Bond had to beat in 1986, and he ran a little better than Danforth. Bond started with the asset of a popular record as governor and with the advantage of being, as governor for most of the last 14 years, the best-known public figure in Missouri. He played smartly on the home state pride that was as evident in Missouri as in so many other states in 1986. Woods's campaign tried to run on farm belt discontent, running in late spring a three-part ad showing a farmer breaking into tears as he and his wife tell Woods how they were foreclosed on, and then identifying Bond as a member of the board of the insurance company that foreclosed. Furor. Bond forces screamed foul; Woods fired admaker Bob Squier (although she had approved the ad); Woods went down in the polls. Woods may have been helped a bit among farmers; she ended up running ahead of her 1982 showing in some northern wheat and corn-growing counties. But she ran behind in the rest of the rural counties, which don't depend so heavily on federally-assisted commodities, and in Kansas City. The ad seemed an invasion of privacy, an exploitation of personal misery; many viewers must have felt, and there was a question from Woods responding to such feelings, that the people on the screen had just made a bad business decision—and that Kit Bond wasn't bent on destroying them. Bond carried rural Missouri handily and the St. Louis area as well and won 53%-47%.

In the Senate Bond has seats on the Agriculture and Banking Committees, bodies more specifically appropriate to Missouri's economic problems than Danforth's assignments. He is the only freshman Republican Senator, elected after all in a Democratic year; but if more senior Republicans are winnowed out as rapidly as they were in 1986, he will be one of the more senior Republicans in the 1990s.

Presidential politics. Near the center of the nation geographically, Missouri is also near the center in partisan preference. Missouri is a good presidential bellwether; the only time in the last century it hasn't supported the winning presidential candidate was in 1956, when it went for Adlai Stevenson. In four of the last nine elections, the winning candidate has carried the state by less than 30,000 votes; Ronald Reagan carried Missouri with almost precisely his national percentage in 1984.

Missouri's old-fashioned parties choose their national convention delegates through the party machinery. Missouri Democrats charged the timing has been changed so that Missouri will be part of the southern regional bloc choosing delegates the week of March 8. This was done to help Richard Gephardt, although presumably his candidacy will rise or fall on what happens elsewhere, particularly in Iowa just to the north.

Congressional districting. Missouri has nine congressional districts now, one less than in the 1970s. The legislature joined two districts represented by Democrat Ike Skelton and Republican Wendell Bailey. With a Democratic legislature, Skelton had the advantage and won.

The People: Est. Pop. 1986: 5,066,000; Pop. 1980: 4,916,686, up 3.0% 1980–86 and 5.1% 1970–80; 2.1% of U.S. total, 15th largest. 14% with 1-3 yrs. col., 14% with 4+ yrs. col.; 12.2% below poverty level. Single ancestry: 13% German, 11% English, 5% Irish, 1% Italian, French, Polish, Dutch. Households (1980): 73% family, 39% with children, 62% married couples; 30.4% housing units rented; median monthly rent: $153; median house value: $36,700. Voting age pop. (1980): 3,554,203; 9% Black, 1% Spanish origin. Registered voters (1986): 2,769,184; no party registration.

1986 Share of Federal Tax Burden $14,988,000,000; 1.99% of U.S. total, 16th largest.

1986 Share of Federal Expenditures

	Total		Non-Defense		Defense	
Total Expend	$20,894m	(2.52%)	$14,092m	(2.35%)	$6,801m	(2.96%)
St/Lcl Grants	1,982m	(1.76%)	1,981m	(1.76%)	1m	(0.90%)
Salary/Wages	2,342m	(1.94%)	1,366m	(2.33%)	976m	(1.58%)
Pymnts to Indiv	8,314m	(2.23%)	7,857m	(1.95%)	5,547m	(3.70%)
Procurement	6,633m	(3.23%)	1,086m	(1.95%)	5,547m	(3.70%)
Research/Other	1,803m	(6.76%)	1,803m	(6.77%)	0m	(0.58%)

Political Lineup: Governor, John Ashcroft (R); Lt. Gov., Harriett Woods (D); Secy. of State, Roy D. Blunt (R); Atty. Gen., William Webster (R); Treasurer, Wendell Bailey (R); Auditor, Margaret Kelly (R). State Senate, 34 (21 D and 13 R); State House of Representatives, 163 (108 D and 55 R). Senators, John C. Danforth (R) and Christopher S. Bond (R). Representatives, 9 (5 D and 4 R).

1984 Presidential Vote

Reagan (R)	1,274,188	(60%)
Mondale (D)	848,583	(40%)

1980 Presidential Vote

Reagan (R)	1,074,181	(51%)
Carter (D)	931,182	(44%)
Anderson (I)	77,920	(4%)

GOVERNOR

Gov. John Ashcroft (R)

Elected 1984, term expires Jan. 1989; b. May 9, 1942, Chicago; home, Jefferson City; Yale U., B.A. 1964, U. of Chicago, J.D. 1967; Assembly of God; married (Janet).

Career: Practicing atty.; Professor, 1968–1973; MO Auditor, 1973–75; Asst. Atty. Gen. of MO, 1975–76, Atty. Gen. of MO, 1976–84.

Office: P.O. Box 720, Jefferson City 65102, 314-751-3222.

Election Results

1984 gen.	John Ashcroft (R)	1,194,506	(57%)
	Kenneth J. Rothman (D)	913,700	(43%)
1984 prim.	John Ashcroft (R)	245,308	(67%)
	Gene McNary (R)	115,516	(32%)
1980 gen.	Christopher S. Bond (R)	1,098,950	(53%)
	Joseph P. Teasdale (D)	981,884	(47%)

SENATORS

Sen. John C. Danforth (R)

Elected 1976, seat up 1988; b. Sept. 5, 1936, St. Louis; home, Newburg; Princeton U., A.B. 1958, Yale U., B.D., LL.B. 1963; Episcopalian; married (Sally).

Career: Practicing atty., 1963–69; Ordained Clergyman; Atty. Gen. of MO, 1969–77; .

Offices: 497 RSOB 20510, 202-224-6154. Also 1795 E. Sunshine, Plaza Towers, Ste. 705, Springfield 65804; 417-881-7068; 1815 Olive St., St. Louis 63101, 314-425-6381; 1233 Jefferson St., Jefferson City 65101; 314-635-7292; and 811 Grand Ave., 943 U.S. Courthouse, Kansas City 64106, 816-374-6101.

Committees: *Budget* (9th of 11 R). *Commerce, Science, and Transportation* (Ranking Member of 9 R). *Finance* (4th of 9 R). Subcommittees: International Debt; International Trade (Ranking Member); Taxation and Debt Management.

Group Ratings

	ADA	ACLU	COPE	CFA	LCV	ACU	NTU	NSI	COC	CEI
1986	30	23	28	27	63	57	51	75	61	62
1985	40	—	27	47	—	65	56	—	75	—

National Journal Ratings

	1986 LIB — 1986 CONS	1985 LIB — 1985 CONS
Economic	55% — 43%	39% — 60%
Social	21% — 77%	28% — 68%
Foreign	41% — 58%	41% — 58%

Key Votes

1) Ease Gun Cont	FOR	5) Grm-Rdmn Def Red	FOR	9) Rehnquist Nom	FOR
2) Immig Reform	FOR	6) Contra Aid	FOR	10) Tax Reform	AGN
3) Lmt Text Imp	AGN	7) SDI Funding	FOR	11) Drug Death Pen	FOR
4) Aid Tobac Ind	FOR	8) Lmt PAC Contrib	AGN	12) S Africa Sanc	FOR

Election Results

1982 general	John C. Danforth (R)	784,876	(51%)	($1,849,025)
	Harriett Woods (D)....................	758,629	(49%)	($1,193,966)
1982 primary	John C. Danforth (R)	217,162	(74%)	
	Mel Hancock (R)	61,378	(21%)	
	Two others (R)	15,289	(5%)	
1976 general	John C. Danforth (R)	1,090,067	(57%)	($741,465)
	Warren E. Hearnes (D)...............	813,571	(42%)	($660,953)

Campaign Contributions and Expenditures

1979-82		Direct Cont. 1979-82		PACS Breakdown	
Receipts	$1,829,501	Indiv.	$1,138,122	Corp. $323,293	T/M/H $167,641
Expend.	$1,849,025	Party	$16,368	Lbr. $5,325	Agr. $11,600
Unspent	$9,069	PACS	$572,658	Ideo. $58,449	CWOS $6,350

Sen. Christopher S. (Kit) Bond (R)

Elected 1986, seat up 1992; b. Mar. 6, 1939, St. Louis; home, Kansas City; Princeton U., B.A. 1960, U. of VA, LL.B. 1963; Presbyterian; married (Carolyn).

Career: Practicing atty., 1964–69; MO Asst. Atty. Gen., 1969–70; MO Auditor, 1971–72; Gov. of MO, 1973–85.

Offices: 293 RSOB 20510, 202-224-5721. Also 811 Grand Ave., Rm. 911, Kansas City 64106, 816-374-2748; 320 Jackson St., Jefferson City 65101, 314-634-2488; and Old Post Office Bldg., 815 Olive St., Rm. 224, St. Louis 63101, 314-425-5067.

Committees: *Agriculture, Nutrition and Forestry* (7th of 9 R). Subcommittees: Agicultural Production and Stabilization of Prices; Agricultural Research, Conservation, Forestry and General Legislation (Ranking Member); Domestic and Foreign Marketing and Product Promotion. *Banking, Housing and Urban Affairs* (7th of 9 R). Subcommittees: Housing and Urban Affairs; Securities. *Small Business* (8th of 9 R). Subcommittees: Innovation, Technology and Productivity; Urban and Minority-Owned Business Development (Ranking Member).

Group Ratings and Key Votes: Newly Elected
Election Results

1986 general	Christopher S. (Kit) Bond (R)	777,612	(53%)	($5,376,255)
	Harriet Woods (D)	699,624	(47%)	($4,397,780)
1986 primary	Christopher S. (Kit) Bond (R)	239,961	(89%)	
	Richard J. Gimpelson (R).	10,471	(4%)	
	David A. Brown (R)	10,407	(4%)	
	Joyce Padgett Lea (R)	9,407	(3%)	
1980 general	Thomas F. Eagleton (D)	1,074,859	(52%)	($1,272,272)
	Gene McNary (R)	985,399	(48%)	($1,173,161)

Campaign Contributions and Expenditures

1985-86		Direct Cont. 1985-86		PACS Breakdown 1985-86			
Receipts	$5,444,030	Indiv.	$3,969,756	Corp.	$843,731	T/M/H	$273,456
Expend.	$5,376,255	Party	$31,615	Labor	$7,200	Agr.	$21,250
Unspent	$67,773	PACS	$1,334,222	Ideo.	$165,773	CWOS	$22,812
		Cand.	$41,589				

FIRST DISTRICT

At the turn of the century St. Louis was the nation's fourth largest city, still rivaling Chicago as the transportation hub of America, the gateway to the west since the expedition of Lewis and Clark. The street grids radiating from downtown were already filled with densely-packed brick houses in those pre-autombile days when people lived within walking distance of work. When the World's Fair (officially the Louisiana Purchase Exposition) was held here in 1904, St. Louis was considered one of the nation's most modern cities. Now it has a different image. Its solidly built neighborhoods have little appeal to Americans who want large lots and two-car garages, and the fear of crime has kept homeowners seething indoors till they can buy housing elsewhere. St. Louis, more than any other American city, has become depopulated over the past several decades. In 1930, 821,000 people lived within its city limits; in 1950, 856,000. By 1980 the figure was down to 453,000—about the same as its population in 1890. Some of the change is accounted for by the aging of its white population and smaller household sizes generally. But some of it represents the abandonment and disappearance of housing units, even public housing projects like Pruitt-Igoe which was demolished in spectacular fashion in the 1970s.

In this process of change, St. Louis has become a black-majority city. The north side of the city, north of the expressways that feed into downtown, has essentially become all black; the south side has remained all white. Blacks live in suburbs north and west of the city; virtually none have chosen to live on the south side. There is a tendency to ascribe St. Louis's problems to its black majority; but the same demographic and sociological trends are apparent, though less pronounced, on the south side as well as the north.

Missouri's 1st Congressional District includes the north side of St. Louis and adjacent parts of all-suburban St. Louis County. It is a measure of the depopulation of St. Louis that this district, once entirely within the city limits, now has 60% of its voters in the suburbs. Its suburbs include the mostly black towns along St. Charles Rock and Natural Bridge Roads, northwest of the city; high-income Clayton, with its office building developments, and the white-collar suburbs of University City (once mostly Jewish, by 1980, 43% black), Richmond Heights, and Maplewood, directly west; and virtually all-white Bellefontaine Neighbors, Spanish Lake, and Black Jack, directly north. The 1st District is the most heavily Democratic in Missouri, by a considerable margin.

Since 1968 this district has been represented by Bill Clay, who got his political start as a union staffer and civil rights activist. When he was first elected, he was considered one of the more militant black members; only five years before, he had served 105 days in jail for participating in a civil rights demonstration. By the middle 1980s, things seemed to come full circle: Clay was arrested again, as one of several congressmen demonstrating before the South African embassy.

In between Clay's career has had its ups and downs. For a time it appeared he might be brought down by charges of scandal. In 1976 it was revealed that he had been billing the government for numerous auto trips home, although he was actually purchasing less expensive airline tickets and, presumably, pocketing the difference. The next year he was under investigation for tax fraud. His administrative assistant was sent to jail for falsification of payroll records. All that helped inspire opposition in the Democratic primary, and in four primaries in a row, from 1976 to 1982, he won by relatively small margins, and either lost or barely carried the St. Louis County portion of the district. In Washington he did not seem highly respected, either. His efforts to repeal the Hatch Act's limitations on the political activities of federal employees during the Carter years were unsuccessful. He also worked with public employee unions to defeat the Carter Administration's civil service reforms—and again lost. Despite his pro-labor record he was passed over for a labor subcommittee chairmanship.

Now Clay seems in better shape. He has his subcommittee chair, and has even done something with it: he got a bill through the House in 1986 to stop construction firms from setting up non-union subsidiaries, and it may even become law now that there is a Democratic Senate. He has been working with Senator John Heinz on pension reform legislation. He is reaching high committee positions just as changes in the political climate may give one of his views majorities again. He is fourth ranking Democrat on Education and Labor and second ranking on Post Office and Civil Service; he is likely to succeed William Ford as chairman of the latter if Ford succeeds Augustus Hawkins, who turns 81 in 1988, as chairman of Education and Labor. On Post Office his stands in favor of allowing federal employees to engage in political activity and his desire to make the Postal Service more directly responsive to Congress could have important ramifications.

At home Clay has consolidated his position in the 1st District. He won his 1982 primary with just 61%, with voters divided on racial lines; but in 1984 he had no primary opposition and in 1986 he won 80% against two minor candidates. His problem may be redistricting. The 1st District is still losing population rapidly, and Missouri legislators, who had to be persuaded not to eliminate Clay's District in redistricting for 1982, are probably even less favorably disposed toward him now. But he seems to have a knack for political survival.

The People: Pop. 1980: 546,208, dn. 20.7% 1970–80. Households (1980): 66% family, 36% with children, 45% married couples; 45.6% housing units rented; median monthly rent: $145; median house value: $31,800. Voting age pop. (1980): 393,146; 46% Black, 1% Spanish origin, 1% Asian origin.

1984 Presidential Vote:

Mondale (D)	130,288	(63%)
Reagan (R)	76,256	(37%)

Rep. William (Bill) Clay (D)

Elected 1968; b. Apr. 30, 1931, St. Louis; home, St. Louis; St. Louis U., B.S. 1953; Roman Catholic; married (Carol).

Career: Real estate broker; Life insur. business, 1959–61; St. Louis City Alderman, 1959–64.

Offices: 2470 RHOB 20515, 202-225-2406. Also 6197 Delmar Blvd., St. Louis 63112, 314-725-5770; and 12263 Bellefontaine Rd., St. Louis 63138, 314-355-6811.

Committees: *Education and Labor* (4th of 21 D). Subcommittees: Health and Safety; Labor-Management Relations (Chairman). *House Administration* (10th of 12 D). Subcommittees: Accounts; Elections; Office Systems. *Post Office and Civil Service* (2d of 14 D). Subcommittees: Civil Service; Postal Operations and Services.

Group Ratings

	ADA	ACLU	COPE	CFA	LCV	ACU	NTU	NSI	COC	CEI
1986	75	100	95	75	91	0	25	0	15	6
1985	100	—	95	75	—	5	34	—	24	—

National Journal Ratings

	1986 LIB — 1986 CONS		1985 LIB — 1985 CONS	
Economic	87% —	0%	72% —	27%
Social	89% —	0%	85% —	0%
Foreign	80% —	0%	92% —	0%

Key Votes

1) Lmt Cln Water Act	AGN	5) Retain Gun Cont	FOR	9) Aid Angola Reb	—
2) Rpl Tobac Sub	AGN	6) Contra Aid	AGN	10) Tax Reform	AGN
3) Grm-Rdmn Def Red	AGN	7) Lmt Text Imp	FOR	11) S Africa Sanc	FOR
4) Ban Polygraph	FOR	8) Limit SDI	—	12) Immig Reform	FOR

Election Results

1986 general	William (Bill) Clay (D)	91,044	(66%)	($217,113)
	Robert J. Wittman (R)	46,599	(34%)	($28,414)
1986 primary	William (Bill) Clay (D)	46,266	(80%)	
	Clifford Wilson, Sr. (D)	7,865	(14%)	
	Elsa Debra Hill (D)	3,753	(6%)	
1984 general	William (Bill) Clay (D)	147,436	(68%)	($142,556)
	Eric Rathbone (R)	68,538	(32%)	

Campaign Contributions and Expenditures

1985-86		Direct Cont. 1985-86		PACS Breakdown 1985-86			
Receipts	$230,437	Indiv.	$26,009	Corp.	$17,256	T/M/H	$20,932
Expend.	$217,113	PACS	$156,538	Labor	$111,500	Agr.	$1,600
Unspent	$58,734	Cand.	$33,500	Ideo.	$2,250	CWOS	$3,000

SECOND DISTRICT

St. Louis County, once separated from the city because it was regarded as a useless agricultural backwater, has now grown so much that it has more than twice as many people, and casts three times as many votes, as the city. In effect most of St. Louis has moved out here. The 2d Congressional District of Missouri is the heart of St. Louis County, and runs the political gamut of suburbs. On its north side, north of Interstate 70, centered on the big McDonnell–Douglas Aircraft plants near the airport, are blue-collar suburbs: Hazelwood, Berkley, St. John, St. Ann, Overland. These are mostly white, filled with people who grew up on the north side of St. Louis, but most of the towns have black residents too, some in large numbers (like Berkley); no one is quite sure whether this represents stable integration or rapid neighborhood change, though it is probably the latter. In the south end of the district are comfortable white-collar suburbs like Kirkwood and Webster Groves, pleasant but not really rich places which remain mostly white but with older populations than they used to have. In the center of the county are high-income Ladue, the home of most of St. Louis's elite, Creve Coeur, and the more Jewish suburb of Olivette. Farther west, you come to new subdivisions, with large, air-conditioned houses which keep their storm doors up all year, and with few trees; they are interspersed among a few crumbling remains of rural houses built higgledy-piggledy by their owners years ago. Out here also is Times Beach, the bedraggled subdivision near a toxic waste dump which was a center of national attention in 1983, and whose population increased substantially in the 1970s, even as the dumping was going on.

Politically, the 2d is a very mixed bag. The working-class suburbs are Democratic, especially on economic issues, but sometimes leave the party on cultural isssues; the southern suburbs and most of the new subdivisions are pretty solidly Republican, though they look at the world from quite different perspectives; the rich Protestants are heavily Republican, the Jews more Democratic, and both can be attracted to Democrats on liberal cultural issues. The history of congressional politics here has been a story of shifting electoral proportions. In the 1970s the demographic balance favored the northern, working class suburbs and the Democrats. But by the 1980s the working class areas had grown little or saw their residents move to semi-rural surroundings far beyond the county line, while the affluent suburbs in the west were the fastest growing part of the metropolitan area. This hurt the Democrats and helped the Republicans, and the predictable result was the defeat of Democratic Representative Bob Young by Republican John Buechner in 1986.

It was a classic confrontation of political types. Young is a pipefitter who represented St. Ann for 20 years in the legislature, is an old political pro who prided himself on a perfect AFL–CIO voting record, a member of the Public Works Committee who prided himself on getting money for projects for the districts. Buechner (pronounced Beek-ner), a middle-class lawyer from Kirkwood, was a state legislator for 10 years who was fiscally conservative and open to supporting measures like the Equal Rights Amendment. Buechner turned Young's pork barrel prowess against him, not just by getting the Sierra Club endorsement, but by calling him in 1986 a "back-scratching, back room deal maker"—part of the problem rather than the solution, a slavish follower of organized labor rather than a leader. Buechner's campaign was outspent and Young raised much more PAC money. But Buechner's message, delivered via an exceedingly effective TV ad, was enough to make him the one Republican who beat an incumbent Democratic congressman in 1986.

This message went over well in an increasingly affluent district accustomed, before Young, to electing erudite congressmen like Republican Thomas Curtis and Democrat James Symington. Buechner got 48% of the vote in 1984 and, after mollifying some of the cultural right groups here, he won with 52% in 1986. That went against the national trend, but in line with long-run trends in the 2d District. So Buechner, with his quick sense of humor and a total absence of self-importance, went off to Washington, with the plums of seats on the Budget Committee and

Science, the latter of importance to big district employer McDonnell–Douglas. Young, a pleasant and mellow man, moved back to the northern St. Louis suburbs with contracts to lobby for the airport and other local interests he had supported as a congressman. In effect Young's pork barrel projects had been privatized by a market-minded electorate, and Buechner's market politics has, at not the most favorable time in the 1980s, been conscripted into the public sector.

The People: Pop. 1980: 546,039, up 11.4% 1970–80. Households (1980): 79% family, 44% with children, 68% married couples; 24.3% housing units rented; median monthly rent: $232; median house value: $53,700. Voting age pop. (1980): 386,511; 5% Black, 1% Asian origin, 1% Spanish origin.

1984 Presidential Vote:			
	Reagan (R)	189,802	(66%)
	Mondale (D)	96,557	(34%)

Rep. Jack Buechner (R)

Elected 1986; b. June 6, 1940, Kirkwood; home, Kirkwood; Benedictine Col., B.A. 1962, St. Louis U., J.D. 1965; Roman Catholic; married (Marietta).

Career: Practicing atty.; MO House of Reps., 1972–82.

Offices: 502 CHOB 20515, 202-225-2561. Also 13545 Barrett Pkwy. Dr., Ste. 5, Ballwin 63021, 314-965-1101.

Committees: *Budget* (13th of 14 R). Task Forces: Defense and International Affairs; Economic Policy. *Science, Space and Technology* (16th of 18 R). Subcommittees: Science, Research and Technology; Space Science and Applications.

Group Ratings and Key Votes: Newly Elected
Election Results

1986 general	Jack Buechner (R)	101,010	(52%)	($326,375)
	Robert A. Young (D)	93,538	(48%)	($528,101)
1986 primary	Jack Buechner (R)	24,217	(72%)	
	Hugh V. Murray (R)	7,016	(21%)	
	Charles A. Van Esler (R)	2,455	(7%)	
1984 general	Robert A. Young (D)	139,123	(52%)	($368,595)
	Jack Buechner (R)	127,710	(48%)	($309,410)

Campaign Contributions and Expenditures

1985-86		Direct Cont. 1985-86		PACS Breakdown 1985-86			
Receipts	$326,579	Indiv.	$213,736	Corp.	$28,907	T/M/H	$32,959
Expend.	$326,375	Party	$18,152	Labor	$500	Agr.	$300
Unspent	$3,409	PACS	$80,760	Ideo.	$17,400	CWOS	$694
		Cand.	$9,240				

THIRD DISTRICT

Represented by one of the national leaders of the Democratic party, the 3d Congressional District of Missouri is one of the nation's older districts in one of its most settled areas. The district is essentially the south side of the St. Louis metropolitan area—a slice of pie with its apex in downtown St. Louis, extending outward and getting wider in suburban St. Louis County and finally ending in Jefferson County, once a rural area alongside the turbulently flowing Mississippi River, now a suburban extension of St. Louis. The south side of St. Louis is almost entirely white, and there are still signs there of the German immigrants who helped make St. Louis one of the nation's most bustling and progressive cities in the late 19th century; the most famous St. Louis German was Carl Schurz, a friend of Lincoln, a Union Army officer in the Civil War, Secretary of the Interior, and Senator from Missouri. St. Louis's south side, like the north, has lost about half its population in the last 40 years, much of it moving directly out to St. Louis County, where the solid middle class of St. Louis lives, people who keep its offices humming, its stores and warehouses bustling, its schoolchildren instructed and disciplined. And others have been moving farther out, to Jefferson County, where old towns sitting near the banks of the Mississippi are now receiving an infusion of shopping centers, spanking new subdivisions, and apartment complexes, and even a few office buildings.

Carl Schurz was a Republican, and for years St. Louis was a Republican island in Missouri's Southern Democratic sea. In the New Deal years, St. Louis became heavily Democratic, and this older district remains Democratic in local, though not in national, contests.

The congressman from this district, first elected in 1976, is Democrat Richard Gephardt. He is now chairman of the House Democratic Caucus, a high-ranking member of the Ways and Means Committee, and a presidential candidate. He was co-sponsor of the Bradley–Gephardt tax bill, the proposal that became the 1986 tax reform law; he is one of the leaders of the Democratic Leadership Council, the group of mainly southern Democrats who want the Democrats to stand for innovation and compassion but not a reflexive and never-ending expansion of government to solve all problems. Although he was first elected as recently as 1976, Gephardt became by the early 1980s a major force in the House, a constructive legislator who seems genuinely respected and liked by almost all his colleagues.

He did this not just by adroit politicking or by taking advantage of committee positions or internal workings of the House—though he knows how to do these things—but because of his work on substantive issues. He was noticed back in the Carter years for his work on the complex and knotty issue of hospital cost control, helping to scuttle a Carter Administration initiative to increase government control and coming up with an alternative (with David Stockman) relying on competition by offering employees choices between different medical insurance plans. That is the general direction in which policy has moved since. Similarly, on taxes he unlike most Democrats was open to arguments that taxes should be lowered to encourage investment and recognized that nominal high rates were actually unsustainable and could be sacrificed to get rid of preferences. He was one of those younger Democrats exploring issues like industrial policy; he is interested less in questions of economic distribution than in ways to increase total wealth. And he has been exploring issues, it seems, because of genuine intellectual curiosity and a desire to solve problems—not in response to a political imperative to get himself named a candidate of "new ideas."

Gephardt combines this originality of mind with great legislative skill. He is able to get colleagues to work with him on measures he sponsors, and to garner support; success in this pursuit is possible only when you're obviously prepared and your position is defensible. He talks with the flat midwestern accent and sincere tones of the Eagle Scout he was, and convinces colleagues to support him in face-to-face conversations much as he did constituents in his race for the St. Louis Council and Congress. Gephardt, coming to Washington from the old-fashioned ward politics of an aging central city, seems to be the personification of a new age Democrat. He was able to sew up a year ahead of time the post of caucus chairman in 1984, and stumbled only when he was linked in October 1984 to members discontented with the party leadership.

But by that time, or not long after, Gephardt seems to have decided to leave the House. He spurned two chances to run for the Senate, in 1982 and 1986, when in retrospect though not in prospect it seems likely he could have won, and by 1986 he was appearing regularly in Iowa and New Hampshire. Despite his moderate reputation, his voting record is pretty close to what is now the Democratic center. His major assets are his rare ability to come up with original and defensible solutions to complex and seemingly insoluble problems and his openness and intellectual honesty. His liabilities include his youthful appearance, and his issue-spotting ability seems sometimes to have been impaired by a tendency to let constituency pressures determine his course: in 1985 he left the tax issue largely to Rostenkowski, Bradley, and others (though, in fairness, Rostenkowski was not going to let him have the spotlight in Ways and Means) and instead stressed the need for trade protections so long sought by organized labor; in 1986, he abandoned his long-time support of anti-abortion measures in a bow to the power of feminists in the Democratic nominating process; in 1987 he was advocating a referendum to let farmers authorize the government to impose production controls, a step that would probably be impracticable and certainly would be costly to consumers. Characteristically Gephardt produced not just speeches but legislation: on trade he co-sponsored the Democrats' major measure with Lloyd Bentsen; on farm production controls he was the lead co-sponsor of legislation with Senator Tom Harkin of—yes—Iowa.

Gephardt's presidential campaign began against long odds, but he starts not just with an attractive line of patter but with a record of knowing how to govern. If he should do as well as he hopes in Iowa and New Hampshire, he will be one of the major Democratic contenders and perhaps President. The central tension in his campaign is between the record he made in his first eight years in Congress, when he questioned standard Democratic programs, challenged entrenched lobbies, and came up with his own creative solutions, and his platform for 1988, which seems to stress aggressive trade legislation to please organized labor, the production controls act to appeal to Iowa farmers, and his change of position on abortion, to avoid antagonizing feminists. Gephardt seems to be reckoning, as Walter Mondale did, that the Democratic party is a collection of interests each of which must be attracted or at least propitiated on their own special issue.

It is nonetheless impressive that Gephardt has wholehearted support from many of his colleagues—and many of the most talented of them. Of course they all know the election calendar: Missouri's filing deadline for Congress is March 29, so that if Gephardt fails to emerge from Super Tuesday as a serious candidate he can run for reelection to the House, and surely will win. Or, far less likely, he could pursue both races, resigning the House nomination if he is chosen by the Democratic convention in August, in which case the place on the Missouri ticket would be filled by the 3d District Democratic committee.

The People: Pop. 1980: 546,102, up 0.3% 1970–80. Households (1980): 72% family, 36% with children, 61% married couples; 31.2% housing units rented; median monthly rent: $151; median house value: $43,900. Voting age pop. (1980): 403,646; 1% Black, 1% Spanish origin.

1984 Presidential Vote:

Reagan (R)	158,483	(65%)
Mondale (D)	86,792	(35%)

Rep. Richard A. Gephardt (D)

Elected 1976; b. Jan. 31, 1941, St. Louis; home, St. Louis; Northwestern U., B.S. 1962, U. of MI, J.D., 1965; Baptist; married (Jane).

Career: Practicing atty., 1965–76; St. Louis City Alderman, 1971–76.

Offices: 1432 LHOB 20515, 202-225-2671. Also 9959 Gravois, St. Louis 63123, 314-631-9959.

Committees: *Ways and Means* (9th of 23 D). Subcommittees: Social Security; Trade.

Group Ratings

	ADA	ACLU	COPE	CFA	LCV	ACU	NTU	NSI	COC	CEI
1986	70	64	80	67	74	0	26	22	18	17
1985	60	—	79	75	—	19	27	—	19	—

National Journal Ratings

	1986 LIB — 1986 CONS		1985 LIB — 1985 CONS	
Economic	87%	— 0%	75%	— 22%
Social	89%	— 0%	56%	— 43%
Foreign	74%	— 25%	62%	— 37%

Key Votes

1) Lmt Cln Water Act	AGN	5) Retain Gun Cont	FOR	9) Aid Angola Reb	AGN
2) Rpl Tobac Sub	AGN	6) Contra Aid	AGN	10) Tax Reform	FOR
3) Grm-Rdmn Def Red	FOR	7) Lmt Text Imp	FOR	11) S Africa Sanc	FOR
4) Ban Polygraph	—	8) Limit SDI	FOR	12) Immig Reform	FOR

Election Results

1986 general	Richard A. Gephardt (D)..............	116,403	(69%)	($881,325)
	Roy Amelung (R).....................	52,382	(31%)	
1986 primary	Richard A. Gephardt (D)..............	53,061	(100%)	
1984 general	Richard A. Gephardt (D)..............	193,537	(100%)	($379,308)

Campaign Contributions and Expenditures

1985-86		Direct Cont. 1985-86		PACS Breakdown 1985-86			
Receipts	$830,682	Indiv.	$336,276	Corp.	$196,050	T/M/H	$124,450
Expend.	$881,325	Party	$100	Labor	$83,919	Agr.	$6,500
Unspent	$178	PACS	$455,073	Ideo.	$34,500	CWOS	$9,654
		Cand.	$61,100				

FOURTH DISTRICT

The 4th Congressional District of Missouri is a slice of basically rural and small-town Missouri, extending from Jefferson City, the state capital, at the center of the state, all the way to Kansas City. Its political attitudes are a vestige of its early responses to the Civil War. There are battle sites here, remembrances that the war was fought in Missouri (though it never formally left the Union) as well as in Virginia and Georgia. The district's most famous son, Harry Truman, was born in the town of Lamar, in the southern end of the district, near the Arkansas and Oklahoma borders. The 4th includes a part of Independence (though not the old Truman home) and some of the fringe of Kansas City; the rest is thoroughly nonmetropolitan. And it is by no means all Democratic. Jefferson City, for example, was a solid Union town, and remains very heavily Republican today.

The congressman from this district, Ike Skelton, looks and talks like an old-fashioned Missouri Democrat. He has been chairman of the Congressional Rural Caucus. On economic issues, he often but not always joins most other Democrats; on cultural and foreign issues he is more conservative. His most important work comes on the Armed Services Committee. That body has been dominated for years by representatives of rural southern constituencies, men who are resolutely patriotic, convinced that the greatest risk in defense is to spend too little, generally trustful of the Pentagon, versed in detail but not overall strategists. Skelton is a little different. Unlike most committee southerners, he supported Les Aspin over the elderly Mel Prince after the 1984 election. He was a strong proponent of reorganizing the Pentagon command structure, unifying the service commands and strengthening the chairman of the Joint Chiefs of Staff, and played a key role in passing the reorganization law of 1986. He was also a lead sponsor of the successful move to fund the Nicaraguan contras in 1986. Skelton generally favors large defense spending and an assertive foreign policy. But he insists on making his own independent judgments of how the money should be spent and what risks should be taken,

Skelton has been given leave to do this work by his constituency. The current 4th District lines put Skelton in with another incumbent, Republican Wendell Bailey, in 1982, but Skelton had represented 64% of the new district and that year his party label was a distinct advantage. He won with 55% and Bailey in 1984 was elected state treasurer. Since then Skelton's reelection has been routine and in 1986 unanimous: he had no opponents in the primary or the general election. He has been mentioned as a possible candidate against Senator John Danforth in 1988, although he does not seem eager to leave the House.

The People: Pop. 1980: 546,637, up 19.7% 1970–80. Households (1980): 77% family, 42% with children, 69% married couples; 25.5% housing units rented; median monthly rent: $141; median house value: $35,600. Voting age pop. (1980): 390,415; 3% Black, 1% Spanish origin.

1984 Presidential Vote:

Reagan (R)	156,449	(67%)
Mondale (D)	76,523	(33%)

Rep. Ike Skelton (D)

Elected 1976; b. Dec. 20, 1931, Lexington; home, Lexington; Wentworth Military Acad., U. of MO, B.A. 1953, LL.B. 1956; Disciples of Christ; married (Susan).

Career: Lafayette Cnty. Prosecuting Atty., 1957–60; Spec. Asst. Atty. Gen. of MO, 1961–63; Practicing atty., 1957–76; MO Senate, 1971–76.

Offices: 2453 RHOB 20515, 202-225-2876. Also 314 Jackson St., Jefferson City 65101, 314-635-3499; 1700 W. 40 Hwy., Blue Springs 64015, 816-228-4242; and 319 S. Lamine, Sedalia 65301, 816-826-2675.

Committees: *Armed Services* (13th of 31 D). Subcommittees: Military Installations and Facilities; Military Personnel and Compensation; Procurement and Military Nuclear Systems. *Small Business* (5th of 27 D). Subcommittee: Export, Tourism and Special Problems (Chairman). *Select Committee on Aging* (23d of 39 D). Subcommittee: Health and Long-Term Care.

Group Ratings

	ADA	ACLU	COPE	CFA	LCV	ACU	NTU	NSI	COC	CEI
1986	35	20	66	67	32	55	24	90	47	20
1985	40	—	65	33	—	50	27	—	33	—

National Journal Ratings

	1986 LIB — 1986 CONS		1985 LIB — 1985 CONS	
Economic	74% —	23%	59% —	41%
Social	39% —	59%	32% —	67%
Foreign	24% —	76%	42% —	56%

Key Votes

1) Lmt Cln Water Act	AGN	5) Retain Gun Cont	AGN	9) Aid Angola Reb	FOR
2) Rpl Tobac Sub	AGN	6) Contra Aid	FOR	10) Tax Reform	FOR
3) Grm-Rdmn Def Red	FOR	7) Lmt Text Imp	FOR	11) S Africa Sanc	—
4) Ban Polygraph	FOR	8) Limit SDI	AGN	12) Immig Reform	AGN

Election Results

1986 general	Ike Skelton (D)	129,471	(100%)	($183,973)
1986 primary	Ike Skelton (D)	55,958	(100%)	
1984 general	Ike Skelton (D)	150,624	(67%)	($214,496)
	Carl D. Russell (R)	74,434	(33%)	

Campaign Contributions and Expenditures

1985-86		Direct Cont. 1985-86		PACS Breakdown 1985-86			
Receipts	$300,019	Indiv.	$145,483	Corp.	$60,300	T/M/H	$45,228
Expend.	$183,973	Party	$847	Labor	$32,300	Agr.	$6,100
Unspent	$187,017	PACS	$150,178	Ideo.	$5,750	CWOS	$500

FIFTH DISTRICT

"Everything's up-to-date in Kansas City," goes the song from *Oklahoma!*, which was set in 1907, when Kansas City then had all the modern accoutrements. It still does today. The 5th Congressional District of Missouri includes the heart of Kansas City—downtown and Hallmark's Crown Center and Country Club Plaza, one of the first shopping centers in America, built in the 1920s, and flooded badly by nearby Brush Creek in the 1970s, and the adjacent high-income neighborhood; the city's black neighborhood, including Arthur Bryant's barbecue restaurant; the industrial areas below the bluffs down by the river and the Kansas City stockyards. The district goes as far east as Independence, including the old white Truman home on Truman Road.

This is a pretty solidly Democratic district, and getting more so, as some of its middle-class Republican voters, or their children, move to farther-out suburban areas. It was represented for 34 years by Richard Bolling, one of the truly creative critics and effective leaders of the House. As the initiator of reforms including the election of committee chairmen and the congressional budget process, he is probably more responsible than anyone else for the way the House works—and it does work—today. Bolling capped his career as chairman of the House Rules Committee and leading lieutenant of Speaker O'Neill, and retired in 1982, still in the prime of life.

The career of the current congressman, Alan Wheat, may turn out to be as significant as Bolling's, for different reasons. For Wheat is that political oddity: a black office-holder representing a mostly white district. Wheat is the son of an Air Force colonel, and grew up all over the world: one of the few members of Congress from a career military family, and the only black congressman who grew up in what has been for 40 years the most thoroughly integrated sector of American life. He was a state legislator from a mostly black district when he ran for Bolling's seat in 1982, and his base helped him win the Democratic primary with 32% of the vote. It's possible that he would not have won if Missouri, like most southern states, had a runoff law. But Wheat understood that he could not win any further elections in an 80% non-black district with only black votes, and he made sure to appeal to whites. With solid support from Bolling, he won the 1982 general election with with 58% of the vote—below the normal Democratic share, but still comfortable. Then he used his two years of incumbency shrewdly. Against two opponents he won 82% in the 1984 Democratic primary, and won with 66% in the general election. In 1986 he had no primary opposition and won the general with 71%. By all standard criteria Wheat has made this a safe seat.

Wheat has done this without compromising his positions on issues of special concern to blacks, and even while emphasizing one, urban enterprise zones, on which he has his own particular angle: he wants to use tax credits for health and child care to encourage residents to continue living in the zones. But he has avoided emphasizing stands which most whites oppose, and has not made a point of calling for vast government expenditures for the poor. Wheat has worked not so much to increase the fervor with which blacks support him as to convince voters of all races that he is actively representing them; he works attentively with community leaders and is proud of getting federal funds for Brush Creek flood control. It doesn't hurt that he has inherited Bolling's seat on the Rules Committee; he can argue to his constituents that he already has clout in the House—and the prospects of being a major national leader some day.

Wheat's career has national significance. If there are to be more blacks in the House, they will have to be elected, as Wheat was, in mostly white districts; the number of black-majority districts has already been maximized by the Voting Rights Act, and almost all of them already elect blacks. The relevant models for the successful black politicians of the future are not Jesse Jackson and Chicago Mayor Harold Washington, who have concentrated on making emotional appeals to blacks, but Los Angeles Mayor Thomas Bradley and Representative Alan Wheat, who have done the hard work of convincing white voters they'll do a good job for them.

The People: Pop. 1980: 546,882, dn. 10.3% 1970–80. Households (1980): 65% family, 34% with children, 51% married couples; 40.2% housing units rented; median monthly rent: $167; median house value: $35,100. Voting age pop. (1980): 405,263; 20% Black, 2% Spanish origin, 1% Asian origin.

1984 Presidential Vote:

Mondale (D)	122,535	(54%)
Reagan (R)	106,239	(46%)

Rep. Alan Wheat (D)

Elected 1982; b. Oct. 16, 1951, San Antonio, TX; home, Kansas City; Grinnell Col., B.A. 1972; Church of Christ; single.

Career: Economist, Dept. of HUD, Kansas City and Mid-America Regional Cncl., 1972–74; Aide to Jackson Cnty. Exec., Mike White, 1974–75; MO House of Reps., 1977–82.

Offices: 1204 LHOB 20515, 202-225-4535. Also 811 Grand Ave., Rm. 935, Kansas City 64106, 816-842-4545; and 301 W. Lexington, Rm. 221, Independence 64050, 816-833-4545.

Committees: *District of Columbia* (7th of 8 D). Subcommittee: Government Operations and Metropolitan Affairs (Chairman); Judiciary and Education. *Rules* (8th of 9 D). Subcommittee: The Legislative Process. *Select Committee on Children, Youth, and Families* (13th of 18 D). Task Forces: Crisis Intervention; Economic Security.

Group Ratings

	ADA	ACLU	COPE	CFA	LCV	ACU	NTU	NSI	COC	CEI
1986	95	100	95	92	79	0	28	0	22	13
1985	100	—	98	75	—	0	30	—	14	—

National Journal Ratings

	1986 LIB — 1986 CONS		1985 LIB — 1985 CONS	
Economic	69% —	30%	89% —	0%
Social	89% —	0%	85% —	0%
Foreign	80% —	0%	92% —	0%

Key Votes

1) Lmt Cln Water Act	AGN	5) Retain Gun Cont	FOR	9) Aid Angola Reb	AGN
2) Rpl Tobac Sub	AGN	6) Contra Aid	AGN	10) Tax Reform	FOR
3) Grm-Rdmn Def Red	AGN	7) Lmt Text Imp	FOR	11) S Africa Sanc	FOR
4) Ban Polygraph	FOR	8) Limit SDI	FOR	12) Immig Reform	FOR

Election Results

1986 general	Alan Wheat (D)	101,030	(71%)	($192,612)
	Greg Fisher (R)	39,340	(28%)	
1986 primary	Alan Wheat (D)	51,333	(100%)	
1984 general	Alan Wheat (D)	150,675	(66%)	($411,215)
	Jim Kenworthy (R)	72,477	(32%)	($398)

Campaign Contributions and Expenditures

1985-86		Direct Cont. 1985-86		PACS Breakdown 1985-86			
Receipts	$268,786	Indiv.	$58,493	Corp.	$46,480	T/M/H	$32,134
Expend.	$192,612	PACS	$189,784	Labor	$81,408	Agr.	$4,950
Unspent	$136,934	Cand.	$32,710	Ideo.	$21,062	CWOS	$3,750

SIXTH DISTRICT

If you want to see the originals of Thomas Hart Benton's rolling, surging farmlands, one place to go is the farm country of northwest Missouri, above the bluffs that line the Missouri River and the smaller rivers that feed into it. In some ways this is a place left behind by the 20th century. The mechanization of the family farm has thinned out the population here, as young people seek a better—or easier—way to make a living elsewhere. All the counties of northwest Missouri, except those in the Kansas City metropolitan area, had more people in 1900 than they do today; in 1900 they had a total population of 508,000 and in 1980, 301,000. Perhaps the most poignant story belongs to St. Joseph, once one of the leading ports of entry to the American West: it was here that the Pony Express rider first saddled up for his transcontinental sprint to Sacramento. In 1900 St. Joseph was a solid commercial competitor of Kansas City, with 102,000 people compared to Kansas City's 163,000. Today metropolitan Kansas City has more than a million people, while St. Joseph's population has dwindled to 72,000 and is diminishing still.

The 6th Congressional District covers almost precisely the northwest corner of Missouri, the land north and east of the Missouri River, west of a north-south line drawn through the middle of the state. It is split about equally between farm counties and urban areas around St. Joseph and that part of Kansas City north of the Missouri River. To give itself space to grow, Kansas City has been systematically annexing land for 25 years; much of it has been bulldozed for subdivisions or to accommodate Kansas City's giant new airport. This part of Kansas City looks suburban and ranges politically from Democratic working-class areas down near the river to culturally and economically conservative new subdivisions off the Interstate on the way to Kansas City International.

In the 1960s and 1970s the 6th District didn't like Kennedy's Catholicism, Johnson's Great Society, or Humphrey's or McGovern's liberalism, and trended Republican. Falling crop and collapsing land prices in the 1980s have made it Democratic again. Even as far-off a candidate as Harriett Woods from the St. Louis suburbs was able to play on farm discontent and win 54% here in 1984 for lieutenant governor and 49% in 1986 for Senator. In congressional representation the 6th has moved from Democrat to Republican, though as much by accident as anything else. Republican Tom Coleman was elected in 1976 when the *Kansas City Star* revealed that Democratic nominee Morgan Maxfield was bragging about fraudulent credentials.

Coleman is now one of the more senior Republicans in the House, ranking third on both the Agriculture and Education and Labor Committees. Yet farm revolts, more similar to Iowa than to the rest of Missouri, have given him scares. In 1982 he won with just 55% and in 1986 with 57%; in the latter year he won by virtue of a thumping 62% in the urban areas, while getting a bare 53% majority in the rural counties. This is not because of lack of attention to farm problems. On Agriculture Coleman sided with South Dakota Democrat Tom Daschle against the Reagan administration on the 1985 farm bill. Since then Coleman has done a good job of keeping in touch with constituents and handling farm issues on the Agriculture Committee. But with the cost of farm programs rising and farm profits and land values falling, Coleman like all farm belt representatives cannot plausibly promise to restore the equity in land and equipment which farm entrepreneurs have lost.

Apart from farm issues, Coleman is a generally conservative Republican, tending to favor the lower of any two domestic spending alternatives and cautious about opposing conservative positions on cultural and foreign policy issues. As a member of the Education and Labor Committee, he has focused his energies on highlighting illiteracy in America and providing financial incentives for would-be teachers. His interests have not been limited to domestic issues: he chaired a Republican task force on foreign policy in the 98th Congress, and was one of Minority Leader Bob Michel's choices to represent the House as an observer to the Geneva arms talks (the trip was scrapped amid controversy).

Coleman considered running for the Senate in 1986, but deferred to the better-known and better-financed Christopher Bond, who only barely carried the 6th District. That leaves him as a senior Republican in the House—provided he can avoid becoming the target of farm belt discontent.

The People: Pop. 1980: 546,614, up 7.2% 1970–80. Households (1980): 74% family, 38% with children, 65% married couples; 27.2% housing units rented; median monthly rent: $151; median house value: $34,800. Voting age pop. (1980): 396,507; 2% Black, 1% Spanish origin.

1984 Presidential Vote:

Reagan (R) 144,857	(61%)
Mondale (D) 94,371	(39%)

Rep. E. Thomas (Tom) Coleman (R)

Elected 1976; b. May 29, 1943, Kansas City; home, N. Kansas City; Wm. Jewell Col., B.A. 1965, N.Y.U., M.P.A. 1969, Washington U., St. Louis, J.D. 1969; Protestant; married (Marilyn).

Career: Asst. Atty. Gen. of MO, 1969–72; MO House of Reps., 1973–76.

Offices: 2344 RHOB 20515, 202-225-7041. Also 5950 N. Oak, Kansas City 64118, 816-454-7117; 851 N.W. 45th St., Kansas City 64116, 816-454-7117; 8th and Edmond, St. Joseph 64501, 816-364-3900.

Committees: *Agriculture* (3d of 17 R). Subcommittees: Conservation, Credit and Rural Development (Ranking Member); Domestic Operations, Research and Foreign Agriculture. *Education and Labor* (3d of 13 R). Subcommittees: Human Resources; Postsecondary Education (Ranking Member).

Group Ratings

	ADA	ACLU	COPE	CFA	LCV	ACU	NTU	NSI	COC	CEI
1986	5	10	19	25	11	75	42	100	75	44
1985	10	—	19	42	—	67	44	—	75	—

National Journal Ratings

	1986 LIB — 1986 CONS			1985 LIB — 1985 CONS		
Economic	27%	—	72%	29%	—	71%
Social	18%	—	78%	24%	—	72%
Foreign	16%	—	84%	24%	—	66%

Key Votes

1) Lmt Cln Water Act	FOR	5) Retain Gun Cont	FOR	9) Aid Angola Reb	FOR
2) Rpl Tobac Sub	AGN	6) Contra Aid	FOR	10) Tax Reform	AGN
3) Grm-Rdmn Def Red	FOR	7) Lmt Text Imp	FOR	11) S Africa Sanc	—
4) Ban Polygraph	AGN	8) Limit SDI	AGN	12) Immig Reform	FOR

Election Results

1986 general	E. Thomas (Tom) Coleman (R)	95,865	(57%)	($250,606)
	Doug R. Hughes (D)...................	73,155	(43%)	($134,325)
1986 primary	E. Thomas (Tom) Coleman (R)	27,588	(100%)	
1984 general	E. Thomas (Tom) Coleman (R)	150,996	(65%)	($148,335)
	Kenneth C. Hensley (D)...............	81,917	(35%)	($52,034)

Campaign Contributions and Expenditures

1985-86		Direct Cont. 1985-86		PACS Breakdown 1985-86			
Receipts	$241,448	Indiv.	$92,200	Corp.	$47,820	T/M/H	$55,817
Expend.	$250,606	Party	$5,269	Labor	$3,780	Agr.	$10,534
Unspent	$102,879	PACS	$129,174	Ideo.	$6,600	CWOS	$4,623

SEVENTH DISTRICT

"Ozark" is one of those regional names that conjures up an image to most Americans, in this case a picture of a sort of Dogpatch, of people with quaint accents living in hillside shacks, cut off from the life of 20th-century America. That picture has long been inaccurate. Today the Ozark region of southwest Missouri is in the mainstream of American life and is the only part of Missouri to show much growth in recent years. Folks from sophisticated big cities and middle-income suburbs have been moving to the hills and mountains of southern Missouri; migrants from St. Louis and Kansas City and even Chicago build vacation houses or year-round homes in the pleasant green hills, along the large man-made lakes, or on the outskirts of the pleasant middle-sized cities of Springfield and Joplin. The climate here is relatively temperate, and the Ozarks are free from many of the stresses of metropolitan life that so many Americans find unpleasant. The Ozarks, long a backwater, are now one of the faster-growing parts of the country.

They are also no longer isolated from the political mainstream. For years this part of Missouri has been heavily Republican. Most people in these hills in the 1860s did not share the slaveholding habits or Confederate sympathies of central Missourians, and during the Civil War they became staunch Republicans—and for years stayed that way. Its conservative responses to the big-spending government of the 1960s and cultural liberalism of the 1970s reinforced its partisanship, although in recessionary 1982 it trended for a moment sharply to the Democrats: the 7th District gave Harriett Woods 46% of the vote against Senator John Danforth. But in prosperous 1984 it swung heavily Republican, solidly supporting the Ozark region's first governor in some time, Republican John Ashcroft, and in 1986 it was 61% for Republican Senate candidate Christopher Bond.

The 7th District's congressman, Gene Taylor, is now a veteran of the House, one of its more senior Republicans. He is an aggressive, gruff partisan and a solid supporter of the Republican leadership. A former car dealer, an outgoing raconteur with an earthy sense of humor, he is the kind of personable, good-humored, conventional-minded Republican who was once the only member of his party in the Missouri delegation. He is not much interested in the theoretical debates that rage between various factions of House conservatives; you will not hear him discussing heatedly the latest misdeeds of the Federal Reserve or describing lyrically the scientific spinoffs of manned space travel. Nor is he temperamentally inclined to go out of his way to harrass the Democrats; he opposes them, squarely and solidly, does his duty, sees his side win or lose, and that is that. Taylor is a member of the Rules Committee, a post that is mostly perfunctory since it is controlled by a 9–4 Democratic majority. He is also is ranking Republican on the Post Office and Civil Service Committee, where decisions tend to be made by Democratic Chairman William Ford.

The People: Pop. 1980: 545,921, up 22.2% 1970–80. Households (1980): 75% family, 37% with children, 66% married couples; 25.7% housing units rented; median monthly rent: $135; median house value: $31,100. Voting age pop. (1980): 399,610; 1% Black, 1% American Indian, 1% Spanish origin.

1984 Presidential Vote:

Reagan (R)	164,696	(69%)
Mondale (D)	74,275	(31%)

Rep. Gene Taylor (R)

Elected 1972; b. Feb. 10, 1928, near Sarcoxie; home, Sarcoxie; S.W. MO St. U.; United Methodist; married (Dorothy).

Career: Pub. sch. teacher, 1948–49; Mayor of Sarcoxie, 1954–60; Pres., Gene Taylor Ford Sales, Inc. (auto dealership), 1960–72.

Offices: 2134 RHOB 20515, 202-225-6536. Also 300 Sherman Pkwy., Ste. 101, Springfield 65806, 417-862-4317; and 302 Fed. Bldg., Joplin 64801, 417-781-1041.

Committees: *Post Office and Civil Service* (Ranking Member of 8 R). Subcommittee: Investigations (Ranking Member). *Rules* (4th of 4 R). Subcommittees: Rules of the House (Ranking Member); The Legislative Process.

Group Ratings

	ADA	ACLU	COPE	CFA	LCV	ACU	NTU	NSI	COC	CEI
1986	5	5	12	25	16	90	43	100	71	59
1985	10	—	12	25	—	81	52	—	76	—

National Journal Ratings

	1986 LIB — 1986 CONS			1985 LIB — 1985 CONS		
Economic	26%	—	73%	26%	—	74%
Social	11%	—	85%	0%	—	76%
Foreign	0%	—	86%	0%	—	76%

Key Votes

1) Lmt Cln Water Act	AGN	5) Retain Gun Cont	AGN	9) Aid Angola Reb	FOR
2) Rpl Tobac Sub	AGN	6) Contra Aid	FOR	10) Tax Reform	AGN
3) Grm-Rdmn Def Red	FOR	7) Lmt Text Imp	FOR	11) S Africa Sanc	AGN
4) Ban Polygraph	—	8) Limit SDI	AGN	12) Immig Reform	AGN

Election Results

1986 general	Gene Taylor (R)	114,210	(67%)	($143,284)
	Ken Young (D)	56,291	(33%)	
1986 primary	Gene Taylor (R)	55,973	(100%)	
1984 general	Gene Taylor (R)	164,586	(70%)	($173,861)
	Ken Young (D)	71,867	(30%)	

Campaign Contributions and Expenditures

1985-86		Direct Cont. 1985-86		PACS Breakdown 1985-86			
Receipts	$269,948	Indiv.	$60,435	Corp.	$43,550	T/M/H	$51,950
Expend.	$143,284	Party	$2,252	Labor	$27,250	Agr.	$10,050
Unspent	$411,650	PACS	$138,268	Ideo.	$2,968	CWOS	$2,500

EIGHTH DISTRICT

The Bootheel of Missouri, the far southeast corner of the state that dips down into Arkansas and faces Tennessee across the Mississippi River, is topographically and sociologically part of the South. Like the Mississippi Delta, this alluvial land was not thickly settled till the late 19th and early 20th century when engineers and levee-builders came in and using industrial methods protected it from constant flooding. Southerners looking for fertile, moist, level cotton lands came up with some of their black field hands; more recently farmers here have been switching from cotton to soybeans. The Bootheel, with a Democratic heritage that echoes the Deep South (one county went for George Wallace in 1968), is the most thickly settled part and political center of the 8th Congressional District of Missouri.

There are other parts, however. The 8th goes westward to the Ozarks, although it does not reach the usually Republican counties there; the names of the counties recall prophecies of mineral riches (Iron), Gaelic provenance (Shannon), and westward ambitions (Oregon). The river counties' names recall the French settlers of the 1700s, although the pronunciations neither 17th nor 20th century Frenchmen would recognize. They vary politically. Cape Girardeau is the one solidly Republican part of the district, St. Francois and Ste. Genevieve are more evenly divided. Over the years the 8th has been Democratic in state and local politics. But it trended Republican in the middle 1980s: after voting for Democrat Harriett Woods in 1982 and 1984, it went 55% for Christopher Bond in 1986.

The 8th District is one of the few which Republicans wrested from Democrats in 1980 and have managed to hold onto ever since. Representative Bill Emerson was a Washington lobbyist with roots in the district when he spotted the vulnerability, on personal grounds, of Democratic Representative Bill Burlison and went back to run in 1980 and won with 55%. He has made the right moves to hold the district in the 1980s. He moved his residence when redistricting removed his home county from the 8th in 1982. He got a seat on the Agriculture Committee and became an active legislator. He worked the district hard, sending his mobile office around to 40 stops each month.

And he championed the cause of embattled farmers, notably that of Puxico farmer Wayne Cryts, who removed from a bankrupt grain elevator 30,000 bushels of soybeans he had pledged on a loan he had never repaid; Cryts became a national folk hero, perhaps on the theory that the whole economy could be revived if folks could sell their collateral and pocket the proceeds without paying off their loans. Emerson's sympathy for Cryts helped him beat a serious challenge in Democratic 1982; he won easily in Republican 1984. In 1986 Cryts himself became the Democratic nominee, but the district was not in as great distress as the corn and wheat country in northern Missouri, and the Republican trend here helped Emerson squeeze out a 53%–47% victory. That was close enough that he may face another serious challenge in 1988, and Cryts promises to run again.

The People: Pop. 1980: 546,112, up 14.3% 1970–80. Households (1980): 76% family, 41% with children, 66% married couples; 26.3% housing units rented; median monthly rent: $105; median house value: $26,500. Voting age pop. (1980): 387,786; 3% Black.

1984 Presidential Vote:

Reagan (R)	126,547	(61%)
Mondale (D)	82,559	(39%)

Rep. Bill Emerson (R)

Elected 1980; b. Jan. 1, 1938, St. Louis; home, Cape Girardeau; Westminster Col., B.A. 1959, U. of Baltimore, LL.B. 1964; Presbyterian; married (Jo Ann).

Career: Spec. Asst. to U.S. Rep. Bob Ellsworth, 1961–65; A. A. to U.S. Rep. Charles Mathias, 1965–70; Dir. of Govt. Relations, Fairchild Indus., 1970–73; Dir. of Public Affairs, Interstate Natural Gas Assn., 1974–75; Exec. Asst. to Chmn, Fed. Election Comm., 1975; Dir., Fed. Relations, TRW, Inc., 1975–79; Govt. relations consultant, 1979–80.

Offices: 418 CHOB, 202-225-4404. Also Fed. Bldg., 339 Broadway, Cape Girardeau 63701, 314-335-0101.

Committees: *Agriculture* (8th of 17 R). Subcommittees: Cotton, Rice, and Sugar; Domestic Marketing, Consumer Relations, and Nutrition (Ranking Member); Wheat, Soybeans and Feed Grains. *Interior and Insular Affairs* (10th of 15 R). Subcommittees: Mining and Natural Resources; National Parks and Public Lands; General Oversight and Investigations. *Select Committee on Hunger* (2d of 10 R). Task Force: Domestic Task Force (Ranking Member).

Group Ratings

	ADA	ACLU	COPE	CFA	LCV	ACU	NTU	NSI	COC	CEI
1986	10	5	21	17	5	77	38	100	72	47
1985	10	—	20	8	—	80	42	—	81	—

National Journal Ratings

	1986 LIB — 1986 CONS		1985 LIB — 1985 CONS	
Economic	31%	— 67%	38%	— 61%
Social	0%	— 89%	0%	— 76%
Foreign	0%	— 86%	0%	— 76%

Key Votes

1) Lmt Cln Water Act	FOR	5) Retain Gun Cont	AGN	9) Aid Angola Reb	FOR
2) Rpl Tobac Sub	AGN	6) Contra Aid	FOR	10) Tax Reform	FOR
3) Grm-Rdmn Def Red	FOR	7) Lmt Text Imp	FOR	11) S Africa Sanc	AGN
4) Ban Polygraph	AGN	8) Limit SDI	AGN	12) Immig Reform	AGN

Election Results

1986 general	Bill Emerson (R).....................	79,142	(53%)	($598,090)
	Wayne Cryts (D).....................	71,532	(47%)	($309,504)
1986 primary	Bill Emerson (R).....................	19,653	(100%)	
1984 general	Bill Emerson (R).....................	134,186	(65%)	($507,466)
	Bill Blue (D)	70,922	(35%)	($43,225)

Campaign Contributions and Expenditures

1985-86		Direct Cont. 1985-86		PACS Breakdown 1985-86			
Receipts	$595,182	Indiv.	$280,419	Corp.	$135,118	T/M/H	$106,565
Expend.	$598,090	Party	$10,971	Labor	$3,750	Agr.	$23,000
Debts	$5,548	PACS	$300,778	Ideo.	$29,359	CWOS	$2,986
		Cand.	$5,093				

NINTH DISTRICT

Little Dixie, in the northeastern part of the state, has given the nation perhaps its greatest writer, Mark Twain, and has given the Congress a Speaker, Champ Clark, who came very close to becoming President of the United States. Both Twain and Clark drew some of their strengths from the southern heritage of Little Dixie, north of the Missouri River and across the Mississippi from Yankee-settled Illinois, which was settled early in the 19th century mainly by migrants from Kentucky, Tennessee, and Virginia. During the Civil War, some citizens of Little Dixie fought on the Confederate side, and at least one county declared itself independent of the unionist state of Missouri. Going with this southern heritage is a Democratic tradition which is more pronounced here than in any other part of non-metropolitan Missouri. Since then, not much urbanization has come to this part of the state—so little that Mark Twain would probably recognize his native Hannibal, one of Little Dixie's largest towns, were it not for the tourist traps that use Twain himself for bait. Nor have voting habits changed much in these still Democratic rural counties.

Little Dixie was once a congressional district unto itself, represented for 40 years by Clarence Cannon, one-time parliamentarian of the House and the long-time crusty chairman of the Appropriations Committee. Now, because of the one-person-one-vote requirement, it dips down into St. Charles County, full of conservative-minded young parents moving far out from St. Louis; Columbia, home of the University of Missouri; and the old German counties along the Missouri River, like Gasconade, overwhelmingly Republican since the Civil War.

Representative Harold Volkmer's Democratic affiliation and Germanic name summon up the heritages of the 9th District; and his attitudes on major issues—notably, his hostility to gun control—express some of its deep-felt attitudes. Yet his hold on the district is not entirely solid. He is not far out of line with most northern Democrats on economic issues, but his record is conservative on cultural issues and mixed on foreign policy. A man of some temper, he is a strong opponent of abortion and gun control; he is the chief House sponsor of the law passed in the 99th Congress easing restrictions on the purchase and transport of firearms. Characteristically that was something outside his committees' jurisdiction and opposed by the committee chairman in question, but Volkmer is not one to respect these lines and is unafraid of nettling turf-minded colleagues. That helps explain why, despite this accomplishment, he has not otherwise been a very effective legislator. He chaired the Space subcommittee for a term, but was pushed aside by Cape Canaveral's Bill Nelson in 1985. He is 12th ranking Democrat on Agriculture, and now chairs the Subcommittee on Forests, Family Farms and Energy.

Little Dixie has elected nothing but Democratic congressmen since the irascible Cannon was elected in 1922, but Volkmer has had some serious opposition, in his first election in 1976, and in 1980, 1984, and 1986 as well. The additions to the district have not seemed his kind of territory. He won only 53% against Republican Carrie Francke in 1984, a former John Danforth staffer, losing Columbia for the second time in a row; she was hurt when it was revealed that she had not yet won a masters degree cited in her campaign literature. In 1986 Francke ran again, but was beaten by abortion opponent state Senator John Uthlaut in the primary; in a less Republican year he was not as strong a candidate, but held Volkmer to 57%. This is a low showing for a veteran congressman who had just gotten a popular law passed. Volkmer's support in Little Dixie remains high, and his support from the National Rifle Association remains strong, but he may find himself on the Republican target list again.

The People: Pop. 1980: 546,171, up 20.6% 1970–80. Households (1980): 75% family, 41% with children, 66% married couples; 25.8% housing units rented; median monthly rent: $143; median house value: $35,700. Voting age pop. (1980): 391,319; 3% Black, 1% Spanish origin.

1984 Presidential Vote: Reagan (R) 150,859   (64%)
Mondale (D) 84,683   (36%)

Rep. Harold L. Volkmer (D)

Elected 1976; b. Apr. 4, 1931, Jefferson City; home, Hannibal; Jefferson City Jr. Col., St. Louis U., U. of MO, LL.B. 1955; Roman Catholic; married (Shirley).

Career: Army, 1955–57; Practicing atty.; Marion Cnty. Prosecuting Atty., 1960–66; MO House of Reps., 1967–77.

Offices: 2411 RHOB 20515, 202-225-2956. Also 370 Fed. Bldg., Hannibal 63401, 314-221-1200.

Committees: *Agriculture* (12th of 26 D). Subcommittees: Forests, Family Farms and Energy (Chairman); Livestock, Dairy and Poultry; Wheat, Soybeans, and Feed Grains. *Science, Space and Technology* (7th of 27 D). Subcommittees: Investigations and Oversight; Space Science and Applications. *Select Committee on Aging* (32d of 39 D). Subcommittees: Housing and Consumer Interests; Retirement Income and Employment.

Group Ratings

	ADA	ACLU	COPE	CFA	LCV	ACU	NTU	NSI	COC	CEI
1986	55	30	68	75	37	32	28	20	33	22
1985	80	—	67	50	—	33	38	—	36	—

National Journal Ratings

	1986 LIB — 1986 CONS		1985 LIB — 1985 CONS	
Economic	50%	— 48%	55%	— 44%
Social	44%	— 54%	36%	— 60%
Foreign	53%	— 47%	58%	— 40%

Key Votes

1) Lmt Cln Water Act	FOR	5) Retain Gun Cont	AGN	9) Aid Angola Reb	FOR
2) Rpl Tobac Sub	AGN	6) Contra Aid	AGN	10) Tax Reform	FOR
3) Grm-Rdmn Def Red	FOR	7) Lmt Text Imp	FOR	11) S Africa Sanc	FOR
4) Ban Polygraph	FOR	8) Limit SDI	FOR	12) Immig Reform	FOR

Election Results

1986 general	Harold L. Volkmer (D)	95,939	(57%)	($383,791)
	Ralph Uthlaut, Jr. (R)	70,972	(43%)	($147,986)
1986 primary	Harold L. Volkmer (D)	54,869	(100%)	
1984 general	Harold L. Volkmer (D)	123,588	(53%)	($314,540)
	Carrie Francke (R)	110,100	(47%)	($407,207)

Campaign Contributions and Expenditures

1985-86		Direct Cont. 1985-86		PACS Breakdown 1985-86			
Receipts	$373,872	Indiv.	$104,011	Corp.	$35,675	T/M/H	$68,636
Expend.	$383,791	PACS	$243,233	Labor	$92,850	Agr.	$24,500
Unspent	$462	Cand.	$10,200	Ideo.	$20,372	CWOS	$1,200

MONTANA

Big sky, everywhere. Montana is a place of distances and vistas, of mountains and deserted vast plains—a large hunk of North America which looks scarcely more thickly settled than it did when Lewis and Clark paddled up the Missouri in the cold and still ice-white spring, the herds of buffalo and elk strung out over the shimmering distance beyond the brown bluffs. Montana, the nation's fourth largest state in area and 44th in population, is less mountainous than flat, a vast plain tilted away from the Rockies and toward the east where the Missouri, foaming with brown water in spring, a trickle in summer, frozen in winter, goes. Montana epitomizes the small-town America so many Americans in franchise-studded suburbs think ideal: there are no big cities here, and the largest metropolitan area, pleasant Billings, has little more than 100,000 people. You can go hunting, fishing, camping, and boating in unspoiled surroundings and wide open spaces close to home. The famous big sky is everywhere.

The terrain is surreal, the tone of life is brashly American. Cowboy hats and blue jeans are worn everywhere; there is little trace of a regional accent; ethnic differences (aside from Indians) are not prominent. The establishment of these outposts of western civilization, so far from the big cities and in a difficult if beautiful physical environment, is a considerable achievement. For life in Montana can be harsh. During the winter, winds sweep down mostly unimpeded from the Arctic, and snow is feet thick in the mountains; during the summer, the plains are often baked in heat unrelieved by rain.

After Lewis and Clark came the mountain men, fur traders who rendezvoused every year at a prearranged location; after the mounatin men came miners. Montana's first white settlers were after gold, silver, copper—sudden riches that would make them kings not of this barren land but of the metropole back East, and some of them found them. Raucous mining towns sprang up, complete with outlaws and vigilantes. Butte, sitting on "the richest hill on earth," was for many years the state's largest city—and, aside from Denver, the only recognizably urban center in the Rockies, known all over the country as a wild place, full of company goons and IWW organizers, a city with a Socialist mayor and with millionaires who bought seats in the U.S. Senate. The early "copper kings," Marcus Daly, William A. Clark, and Augustus Heinze, made millions and feuded with each other. Clark got himself elected to the Senate in 1899 and, after he resigned because of fraud charges, again in 1901, and ended up in a 130-room Parisian baroque mansion at 77th Street and Fifth Avenue; Daly's interests were acquired by the Rockefellers for a time and became the Anaconda Company.

Beginning in the early 20th century, Anaconda exerted unparalleled control over the public life of the state. It created the Montana Power Company to suit its needs. It bought up all of Montana's newspapers except the *Great Falls Tribune*. Even so, it did not win all its political battles. Montana elected many notable progressives, even in Anaconda's heyday, Republicans such as Joseph Dixon, Democrats such as Thomas Walsh (who exposed the Teapot Dome scandal), and the young progressive Democrat Burton K. Wheeler. But Anaconda did make sure it escaped significant state taxation and regulation. That increased Anaconda's profits or, as the company might have said, it helped make its metals competitive in world markets and thus created more jobs and prosperity in Montana and the United States.

The old fights between Anaconda and the progressives cut across party lines, but the New Deal tended to organize the state's politics in a partisan manner. On the Republican side were Anaconda (although it became less interested in state politics when it bought copper mines in Chile), Montana Power, the Stockmen's Association of the eastern plains, and the successful farmers of the Farm Bureau. On the Democratic side were most of the old progressives, labor unions (Montana has never passed a right-to-work law and is the most pro-union state in the

MONTANA — Congressional Districts, Counties, National Park, and Selected Places — *(2 Districts)*

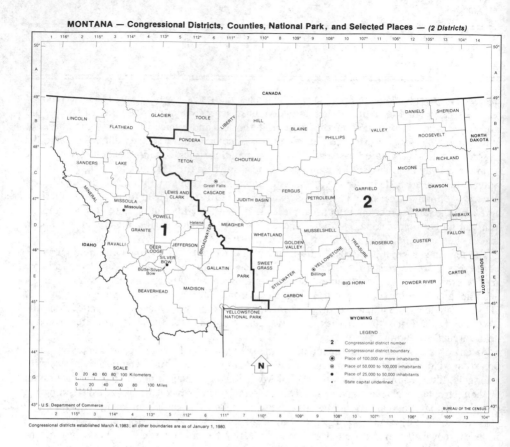

Congressional districts established March 4, 1983; all other boundaries are as of January 1, 1980.

Rockies), small farmers' groups such as the National Farmers Union, and backers of New Deal programs (for a while in the 1930s Montana received more federal money per capita than almost any other state). Geographically, the eastern plains and Billings typically go Republican, and the western mountains and Butte, Great Falls, and Missoula usually go Democratic. The echoes of class warfare have grown dimmer over the years. The federal and state governments are now Montana's biggest employers. Anaconda sold its newspapers in 1959, and after it was acquired by Arco in the 1970s it closed its big smelter in Montana, though many of its old enemies would like to have it back. The mines are still worked, though they're now run by a Japanese concern that pellitizes low-grade ore and hauls its off to the Far East.

But the divisions in politics here remain primarily economic. Butte, now with less than half its 1920 population, and the town of Anaconda about to become a ghost town like so many mining towns before it, are still heavily Democratic, as are some of the Indian reservations. The mining community has produced such important leftish figures as Seattle's Catholic Archbishop Raymond Hunthausen and MIT economist Lester Thurow. Great Falls, with an Air Force base and not mines to defend, is more placid; Billings, riding a local boom based on coal, is heavily Republican and went 63% for Reagan.

Governor. Few people think that the actions of Montana state government or the policies of the governor of Montana are of much importance to the nation, and in most respects they are not. But sometimes they are. During the energy crisis of the 1970s, Montana imposed a 30% severance tax on coal, the highest in the country, and got it sustained in the Supreme Court. It has been scaled back in the 1980s, however, by Governor Ted Schwinden, a Democrat who evidently fears that it could price Montana's plenteous and strip-minable coal out of the market. Similarly, union men were smarting in 1986 because one of Butte's mines reopened—without any union this time—and the operators of Montana's new platinum mine in Stillwater County are quick to cite the much lower wage levels of platinum miners in the other leading source, South Africa. Montana's economy remains centered around basic commodities—minerals, coal, wheat—whose prices have mostly (platinum is an exception) been plummeting in the 1980s and Montanans remain aware that except for a few resort areas they have nothing but these industries to keep people up here.

The current governor, Ted Schwinden, is a pleasant and low-key politician who, as lieutenant governor, beat his more abrasive predecessor in the 1980 primary and has dominated state politics ever since. Like a number of other Rocky Mountain Democratic governors, Schwinden has worn well with the voters after years in a constant spotlight. He may have won praise in some quarters for his "Build Montana" program, but he appears to have captured voters' hearts with his accessibility and such gestures as listing his home telephone number in the Helena-area directory. He has irritated some Democrats by relaxing the severance tax and not backing unions strongly, but voters generally seem to approve: in 1984 he was reelected by a 70%–26% margin—the largest in Montana history.

Senators. Democrats have won every Montana Senate election but one, but seldom by huge margins. Montana elected its only a Republican Senator in 1946 but came within a few percentage points of doing so half a dozen times. Its most notable Senator was Mike Mansfield, the Senate majority leader from 1961 to 1977 and ambassador to Japan since then. The current Democratic Senators, John Melcher and Max Baucus, have won two impressive election victories each. But in the conservative climate of the Rockies—even in this closest thing to an old-fashioned liberal Rocky Mountain state—both have benefited from their opponents' weaknesses.

The senior Senator, John Melcher, has been winning Montana elections since 1969, when he won a special election to the House in the 2d District (the eastern, plains part of the state, including Billings and Great Falls). This is a vast expanse—the fourth largest district in the nation in area—where cattle ranches stretch as far as the eye can see and towering buttes rise over the magnificently eroded High Plains. It is the agricultural part of the state and the part that has Montana's strip mines; but almost half of its votes are cast in the two urban areas. Melcher became a strong vote-getter in this usually Republican half of Montana, and when Mansfield retired Melcher had no serious opposition for the seat and won with 64%. In the Senate, Melcher seems to have committee assignments well geared to the state. One is Agriculture, Nutrition and Forestry; the other is Energy and Natural Resources—the old Interior Committee. This has jurisdiction over the federal government's vast landholdings in the West, over grazing and hunting rights, national parks and wilderness areas, Indian tribes and strip mining. Melcher is somewhere between the environmentalists and James Watt; he has sympathy with development interests, and is not particularly interested in having more of Montana fenced off as wilderness areas.

In the Senate he has been known for his obstructive tactics, holding up farm bills to criticize support levels as too low while denouncing the idea of supports generally, pushing favorite causes like animal research (he is a veterinarian). Senate rules indulge such protests, even from a Senator with few allies and views regarded by some as unsophisticated. But Melcher's populist streak has not stopped him from having some trouble in Montana. In 1982, he had some flak from Democrats and labor leaders for supporting some Reagan economic programs and opposing the Panama Canal treaties, while Republican candidate Larry Williams, who had run against Baucus in 1978, argued that Melcher backed too much federal spending. He counterattacked Williams, who had problems of his own. An investment counselor and author of *How to Prosper in the Coming Good Years*, Williams had gone through a number of transformations. Baucus in 1978 used a picture Williams once circulated showing him with long hair and a gold chain; Melcher's backers cited a section of Williams's book where he advised investors to buy old people's property with bonds that could be bought heavily discounted from their face value. In a negative year, those attacks, plus Melcher's old home district strength, were enough to give him a 54%–42% victory.

In the years since, Melcher has concentrated especially on farm legislation, seeking higher price supports, and has opposed Reagan economic programs. He certainly approaches 1988 as a favorite for reelection, and the cantankerousness that bothers some colleagues probably delights many more constituents. Yet he cannot be regarded as totally safe, particularly if Montana Republicans break their string and come up with a competent challenger.

Max Baucus, who as recently as 1984 seemed legislatively junior and politically vulnerable, now is in a strong position, with high seniority on key committees and demonstrated vote-getting ability. Before the 1984 election, he was a natural target for Republican strategists: a Watergate era Democrat, elected to the House in the 1st District in 1974 and to the Senate in 1978, just as the kind of national Democrats who are his natural allies were running out of steam and about to lose their majority. As a junior member of the minority who concentrated on Montana issues, he had not made a major splash. His strong personal campaigning in 1978 helped him to a primary win over Paul Hatfield, appointed by Governor Thomas Judge to fill a vacancy that spring, and in the general he won after the picture of Williams in love beads was widely circulated. In 1984 Secretary of State Jim Waltermire ducked out of the race and Republican nominee Chuck Cozzens, after stressing abstract issues like abortion and balancing the budget, called Baucus a "wimp" who "talks out of both sides of his mouth and lives in fear that we'll get wise to his games." That wasn't credible in a state where voters are used to chatting with their Senators over coffee in the local café.

Baucus's approach on issues has generally been in line with other Democrats—liberal on economic policy (but somewhat parsimonious on the budget), somewhat liberal on foreign policy and cultural issues (he was a leader in the move to prevent federal courts from being stripped of jurisdiction over certain constitutional issues). He won a seat on the Finance Committee in his first term and specialized in health care issues there, trying to expand coverage under Medicare. He played a part in the tax reform bill of 1986. From an export-dependent state many of whose potential markets are over the Rockies and across the Pacific, Baucus tends to oppose trade barriers, and in 1986 became one of the heads of a congressional Competitive Caucus; the "competitiveness" push may have become a cliché, but the problem it addresses is genuine and its approach constructive.

Baucus seems to be trying to follow Mansfield's course of maintaining Montana roots but working on national and international issues. He has not attained Mansfield's popularity, but he did win smartly in Republican 1984, with 57% of the vote, losing only 11 scattered counties. He is up for reelection in 1990: no telling if Montana Republicans will produce serious competition by then.

Presidential politics. Montana is arguably the most marginal of the Rocky Mountain states, yet it never sees much of presidential candidates. Even in the airplane age, it takes most of the day just to get up to Montana and touch down, and all for only four electoral votes. For similar reasons, Montana's presidential primary has attracted few campaigners here.

Congressional districting. Montana redistricted for the 1984 election, switching a couple of counties from the 1st to the 2d District.

1st Congressional District. The 1st District seat that Baucus held is basically Democratic; Republicans have won it only four times since the 1920s. There are strong Democratic voting blocs: Butte, Anaconda, and the miners have been 2 to 1 Democratic for more than 50 years (but their influence is diminishing: they had 27% of the state's population in 1900 and 6% in 1980); Missoula has been usually Democratic since the students at the University of Montana got the vote; mining and Indian counties in various parts of the district produce Democratic margins. The Republican strongholds—the new-rich city of Kalispell, the state capital of Helena, the southwestern corner of the state near Yellowstone National Park and the Big Sky development—are usually not enough to overcome the Democrats.

The congressman in the 1st is Pat Williams, a teacher and former legislator and Melcher aide. He is an old-fashioned liberal Democrat, close enough to organized labor that the state AFL–CIO director is godfather to one of his children. Williams has a seat on the Budget Committee and chairs the Human Resources Task Force. He also serves on Education and Labor—a solid pro-labor, pro-teacher vote—and in 1987 became chairman of the Postsecondary Education Subcommittee. In 1985, Williams became one of seven deputy majority whips. He is pleasant, affable, dedicated—one of *National Journal*'s "rising stars" in 1987. He lost a 1974 primary to Baucus but has won easily since 1978 and got 62% against better-than-usual competition in 1986.

2d Congressional District. When Melcher ran for the Senate, the 2d District reverted to the normalcy of a Republican congressman, Ron Marlenee. Marlenee's record seems more directed toward his home district rather than national issues. He is a senior member of the Agriculture and Interior and Insular Affairs Committees—the same assignments Melcher has in the Senate—and holds the ranking minority seat on the Wheat, Soybeans, and Feed Grains Subcommittee, which gave him say in fashioning the 1985 farm bill. Conservative on other economic issues, he is understandably generous when it comes to farm programs. On Interior he is ranking minority member on the Public Lands Subcommittee—a valuable assignment in a state where so much of the land, including much valuable grazing and timber land, is owned by the federal government, and he shares many Montanans' resentment with federal restrictions. He is a Montana version of the old-fashioned Main Street Republican, not a theoretician, but unlike some older Republicans not accommodation-minded; his style is one of vehement denunciations, not bipartisan back-patting.

In 1986 Marlenee was held to a 53%–47% win by Democrat Buck O'Brien, who accused him of not doing enough for farmers; in 1982 he was held to a 54%–44% win even after his Democratic opponent's creditors foreclosed on his ranch and feedlot to secure $2 million in debts. This suggests his seat could be in jeopardy in some farm rebellion year.

The People: Est. Pop. 1986: 819,000; Pop. 1980: 786,690, up 4.1% 1980–86 and 13.3% 1970–80; 0.34% of U.S. total, 44th largest. 20% with 1–3 yrs. col., 17% with 4+ yrs. col.; 12.3% below poverty level. Single ancestry: 14% German, 7% English, 5% Irish, Norwegian, 2% Swedish, 1% French, Scottish, Dutch, Italian, Polish. Households (1980): 72% family, 40% with children, 63% married couples; 31.4% housing units rented; median monthly rent: $165; median house value: $46,400. Voting age pop. (1980): 554,795; 4% American Indian, 1% Spanish origin. Registered voters (1986): 443,935; no party registration.

1986 Share of Federal Tax Burden: $2,171,000,000; 0.29% of U.S. total, 46th largest.

1986 Share of Federal Expenditures

	Total		Non-Defense		Defense	
Total Expend	$2,821m	(0.34%)	$2,583m	(0.43%)	$238m	(0.10%)
St/Lcl Grants	592m	(0.53%)	591m	(0.53%)	1m	(0.90%)
Salary/Wages	413m	(0.34%)	290m	(0.49%)	123m	(0.20%)
Pymnts to Indiv	1,231m	(0.34%)	1,179m	(0.34%)	52m	(0.29%)
Procurement	158m	(0.08%)	96m	(0.17%)	62m	(0.04%)
Research/Other	427m	(1.60%)	427m	(1.60%)	0m	(0%)

Political Lineup: Governor, Ted Schwinden (D); Lt. Gov., George Turman (D); Secy. of State, Jim Waltermire (R); Atty. Gen., Mike Greely (D); Auditor, Andrea (Andy) Hemstad (R). State Senate, 50 (25 D and 25 R); State House of Representatives, 100 (49 D and 51 R). Senators, John Melcher (D) and Max Baucus (D). Representatives, 2 (1 D and 1 R).

1984 Presidential Vote

Reagan (R) 232,450 (60%)
Mondale (D) 146,742 (38%)

1980 Presidential Vote

Reagan (R) 206,814 (57%)
Carter (D) 18,132 (32%)
Anderson (I) 29,281 (8%)

1984 Democratic Presidential Primary
No preference 28,385 (100%)

1984 Republican Presidential Primary
Reagan 66,432 (93%)
Others 5,378 (7%)

GOVERNOR

Gov. Ted Schwinden (D)

Elected 1980, term expires Jan. 1989; b. Aug. 31, 1925, Wolf Point; home, Helena; U. of MT, B.A. 1949, M.A. 1950, U. of MN, 1950–54; Lutheran; married (Jean).

Career: Army, WWII; Grain farmer 1954–80; MT House of Reps., 1958; MT Legis. Cncl., 1959–61; Commissioner of State Lands, 1969–76; Lt. Gov. of MT, 1976–80.

Office: Office of the Governor, Helena 59620, 406-444-3111.

Election Results

1984 gen.	Ted Schwinden (D)	266,578	(70%)
	Pat M. Goodover (R)	100,070	(26%)
1984 prim.	Ted Schwinden (D)	80,633	(81%)
	Robert Carlson Kelleher (D) ...	18,423	(19%)
1980 gen.	Ted Schwinden (D)	199,574	(55%)
	Jack Ramirez (R)	160,892	(45%)

SENATORS

Sen. John Melcher (D)

Elected 1976, seat up 1988; b. Sept. 6, 1924, Sioux City, IA; home, Forsyth; U. of MN, 1942–43, IA St. U., D.V.M. 1950; Roman Catholic; married (Ruth).

Career: Army, WWII; Veterinarian, 1950–69; Forsyth City Cncl., 1953–55, Mayor, 1955–61; MT House of Reps., 1961–63, 1969; MT Senate, 1963–67; U.S. House of Reps., 1969–77.

Offices: 730 HSOB 20510, 202-224-2644. Also 23 S. Last Chance Gulch, Helena 59601, 406-449-5251; 1016 Fed. Bldg., Billings 59101, 406-657-6644; 106 Fed. Bldg., Bozeman 59715, 406-586-7718; 104 4th St. N., Great Falls 59041, 406-452-9585; 575 Sunset Blvd., Ste. 101, Kalispell 59901, 406-752-6612; P.O. Box 8568; Missoula 59807, 406-329-3528; and 55 W. Granite, Butte 59710, 406-723-8211.

Committees: *Agriculture, Nutrition, and Forestry* (2d of 10 D). Subcommittees: Agricultural Research, Conservation, Forestry, and General Legislation (Chairman); Domestic and Foreign Marketing and Product Promotion; Nutrition and Investigations. *Energy and Natural Resources* (5th of 10 D). Subcommittees: Energy Research and Development; Mineral Resources, Development and Production (Chairman); Public Lands, Natural Parks and Forests. *Joint Economic Committee.* Subcommittees: Economic Growth and Taxes; Economic Goals and Intergovernmental Policy; Economic Resources and Competitiveness. *Select Cmtee. on Indian Affairs* (2d of 5 D). *Special Cmtee. on Aging* (Chairman of 10 D).

Group Ratings

	ADA	ACLU	COPE	CFA	LCV	ACU	NTU	NSI	COC	CEI
1986	90	71	82	60	63	17	42	0	26	21
1985	85	—	82	80	—	9	28	—	29	—

National Journal Ratings

	1986 LIB — 1986 CONS	1985 LIB — 1985 CONS
Economic	81% — 18%	92% — 5%
Social	60% — 36%	48% — 50%
Foreign	75% — 0%	88% — 0%

Key Votes

1) Ease Gun Cont	FOR	5) Grm-Rdmn Def Red	AGN	9) Rehnquist Nom	AGN
2) Immig Reform	FOR	6) Contra Aid	AGN	10) Tax Reform	AGN
3) Lmt Text Imp	FOR	7) SDI Funding	AGN	11) Drug Death Pen	FOR
4) Aid Tobac Ind	FOR	8) Lmt PAC Contrib	FOR	12) S Africa Sanc	FOR

Election Results

1982 general	John Melcher (D)	174,861	(54%)	($830,892)
	Larry Williams (R)	133,789	(42%)	($708,286)
1982 primary	John Melcher (D)	83,539	(68%)	
	Mike Bond (D)	33,565	(27%)	($67,182)
1976 general	John Melcher (D)	206,861	(64%)	($311,101)
	Stanley C. Burger (R)	115,213	(36%)	($563,543)

Campaign Contributions and Expenditures

1979-82		Direct Cont. 1979-82		PACS Breakdown			
Receipts	$829,938	Indiv.	$313,631	Corp.	$43,950	T/M/H	$24,300
Expend.	$830,892	Party	$17,500	Labor	$164,560	Agr.	$225,975
Unspent	$3,059	PACS	$481,474	Ideo.	$18,400	CWOS	$25,650

Sen. Max Baucus (D)

Elected 1978, seat up 1990; b. Dec. 11, 1941, Helena; home, Missoula; Stanford U., B.A. 1964, LL.B. 1967; Protestant; married (Wanda).

Career: Staff Atty., Civil Aeronautics Bd., 1967–69; Legal Staff, Securities and Exchange Comm., 1969–71, Legal Asst. to the Chmn., 1970–71; Practicing atty., 1971–75; MT House of Reps., 1973–75; U.S. House of Reps., 1975–78.

Offices: 706 HSOB 20510, 202-224-2651. Also Granite Bldg., 32 N. Last Chance Gulch, Helena 59601, 406-449-5480; 202 Fratt Bldg., 2817 2d Ave., N., Billings 59101, 406-657-6970; Fed. Bldg., 32 E. Babcock, Rm. 114, P.O. Box 1689, Bozeman 59715, 406-586-6104; Fed. Bldg., Rm. 256, Butte 59701, 406-782-8700; 107 5th St. N., Great Falls 59401, 406-761-1574; and 211 N. Higgins, No. 102, Missoula 59802, 406-329-3123.

Committees: *Environment and Public Works* (4th of 9 D). Subcommittees: Environmental Protection; Hazardous Wastes and Toxic Substances (Chairman); Superfund and Environmental Oversight. *Finance* (4th of 11 D). Subcommittees: Health; International Trade; Taxation and Debt Management (Chairman). *Small Business* (4th of 10 D). Subcommittees: Innovation, Technology and Productivity; Rural Economy and Family Farming (Chairman).

Group Ratings

	ADA	ACLU	COPE	CFA	LCV	ACU	NTU	NSI	COC	CEI
1986	80	78	74	53	81	13	43	10	37	38
1985	65	—	76	60	—	9	34	—	37	—

National Journal Ratings

	1986 LIB — 1986 CONS	1985 LIB — 1985 CONS
Economic	66% — 32%	65% — 31%
Social	74% — 24%	78% — 21%
Foreign	71% — 25%	88% — 0%

Key Votes

1) Ease Gun Cont	FOR	5) Grm-Rdmn Def Red	FOR	9) Rehnquist Nom	AGN
2) Immig Reform	FOR	6) Contra Aid	AGN	10) Tax Reform	FOR
3) Lmt Text Imp	AGN	7) SDI Funding	AGN	11) Drug Death Pen	AGN
4) Aid Tobac Ind	AGN	8) Lmt PAC Contrib	FOR	12) S Africa Sanc	FOR

Election Results

1984 general	Max Baucus (D)	215,704	(57%)	($1,386,561)
	Chuck Cozzens (R)	154,308	(41%)	($492,391)
1984 primary	Max Baucus (D)	80,726	(79%)	
	Bob Ripley (D)	20,979	(21%)	($233,018)
1978 general	Max Baucus (D)	160,353	(56%)	($653,756)
	Larry Williams (R)	127,589	(44%)	($346,721)

Campaign Contributions and Expenditures

1979-84		Direct Cont. 1979-84		PACS Breakdown 1979-84			
Receipts	$1,418,534	Indiv.	$599,890	Corp.	$187,248	T/M/H	$226,628
Expend.	$1,386,561	Party	$17,845	Labor	$188,815	Agr.	$7,300
Unspent	$29,910	PACS	$775,794	Ideo.	$131,328	CWOS	$18,250

FIRST DISTRICT

The People: Pop. 1980: 393,298, up 19.0% 1970–80. Households (1980): 71% family, 40% with children, 62% married couples; 31.3% housing units rented; median monthly rent: $163; median house value: $46,900. Voting age pop. (1980): 280,180; 3% American Indian, 1% Spanish origin.

1984 Presidential Vote:

Reagan (R)	113,967	(58%)
Mondale (D)	78,513	(40%)

Rep. Pat Williams (D)

Elected 1978; b. Oct. 30, 1937, Helena; home, Helena; U. of MT, U. of Denver, B.A. 1961; Roman Catholic; married (Carol).

Career: Pub. sch. teacher; MT House of Reps., 1967, 1969; Humphrey Presidential Campaign, 1968; Exec. Asst. to U.S. Rep. John Melcher, 1969–71; MT State Coord., Family Ed. Prog., 1971–78.

Offices: 2457 RHOB 20515, 202-225-3211. Also 32 N. Last Chance Gulch, Helena 59601, 406-443-7878; Finlen Complex, Butte 59701, 406-723-4404; and 302 W. Broadway, Missoula 59802, 406-549-5550.

Committees: *Budget* (6th of 21 D). Task Forces: Community and Natural Resources; Economic Policy; Human Resources (Chairman). *Education and Labor* (8th of 21 D). Subcommittees: Elementary, Secondary, and Vocational Education; Employment Opportunities; Labor Standards; Postsecondary Education (Chairman); Select Education.

Group Ratings

	ADA	ACLU	COPE	CFA	LCV	ACU	NTU	NSI	COC	CEI
1986	85	95	88	67	63	5	27	10	20	9
1985	95	—	87	67	—	10	31	—	23	—

National Journal Ratings

	1986 LIB — 1986 CONS		1985 LIB — 1985 CONS	
Economic	74%	— 26%	89%	— 0%
Social	69%	— 28%	72%	— 28%
Foreign	80%	— 0%	75%	— 21%

Key Votes

1) Lmt Cln Water Act	AGN	5) Retain Gun Cont	AGN	9) Aid Angola Reb	AGN
2) Rpl Tobac Sub	AGN	6) Contra Aid	AGN	10) Tax Reform	FOR
3) Grm-Rdmn Def Red	AGN	7) Lmt Text Imp	FOR	11) S Africa Sanc	FOR
4) Ban Polygraph	FOR	8) Limit SDI	FOR	12) Immig Reform	FOR

Election Results

1986 general	Pat Williams (D).....................	98,501	(62%)	($252,708)
	Don Allen (R)........................	61,230	(38%)	($154,551)
1986 primary	Pat Williams (D).....................	39,224	(100%)	
1984 general	Pat Williams (D).....................	126,998	(66%)	($140,925)
	Gary K. Carlson (R).................	61,794	(32%)	($13,112)

Campaign Contributions and Expenditures

1985-86		Direct Cont. 1985-86		PACS Breakdown 1985-86			
Receipts	$301,149	Indiv.	$72,590	Corp.	$18,200	T/M/H	$34,138
Expend.	$252,708	Party	$1,000	Labor	$112,365	Agr.	$1,500
Unspent	$74,863	PACS	$175,910	Ideo.	$9,707	CWOS	$0
		Cand.	$23,852				

SECOND DISTRICT

The People: Pop. 1980: 393,392, up 8.1% 1970–80. Households (1980): 73% family, 41% with children, 64% married couples; 31.6% housing units rented; median monthly rent: $167; median house value: $46,100. Voting age pop. (1980): 274,615; 5% American Indian, 1% Spanish origin.

1984 Presidential Vote: Reagan (R) 118,483   (63%)
Mondale (D) 68,229   (36%)

Rep. Ron Marlenee (R)

Elected 1976; b. Aug. 8, 1935, Scobey; home, Scobey; MT St. U., U. of MT, Reisch Sch. of Auctioneering; Lutheran; married (Cynthia).

Career: Farmer, rancher, and businessman, 1953–76.

Offices: 409 CHOB, 202-225-1555. Also 2717 1st Ave., N., Billings 59101, 406-657-6753; and 312 9th St., S., Great Falls 59405, 406-453-3264.

Committees: *Agriculture* (4th of 17 R). Subcommittees: Forests, Family Farms and Energy; Wheat, Soybeans, and Feed Grains (Ranking Member). *Interior and Insular Affairs* (4th of 15 R). Subcommittees: Energy and the Environment; Mining and Natural Resources; National Parks and Public Lands (Ranking Member).

Group Ratings

	ADA	ACLU	COPE	CFA	LCV	ACU	NTU	NSI	COC	CEI
1986	0	10	20	0	16	95	61	100	82	71
1985	10	—	21	8	—	95	51	—	71	—

National Journal Ratings

	1986 LIB — 1986 CONS		1985 LIB — 1985 CONS	
Economic	25%	— 74%	33%	— 67%
Social	18%	— 78%	28%	— 71%
Foreign	24%	— 76%	0%	— 76%

Key Votes

1) Lmt Cln Water Act	FOR	5) Retain Gun Cont	AGN	9) Aid Angola Reb	FOR
2) Rpl Tobac Sub	AGN	6) Contra Aid	FOR	10) Tax Reform	AGN
3) Grm-Rdmn Def Red	AGN	7) Lmt Text Imp	AGN	11) S Africa Sanc	AGN
4) Ban Polygraph	AGN	8) Limit SDI	FOR	12) Immig Reform	AGN

Election Results

1986 general	Ron Marlenee (R)	84,548	(53%)	($251,163)
	Buck O'Brien (D)	73,583	(47%)	($223,231)
1986 primary	Ron Marlenee (R)	32,013	(100%)	
1984 general	Ron Marlenee (R)	116,932	(66%)	($332,572)
	Chet Blaylock (D)	60,445	(34%)	($168,433)

Campaign Contributions and Expenditures

1985-86		Direct Cont. 1985-86		PACS Breakdown 1985-86			
Receipts	$265,900	Indiv.	$138,418	Corp.	$46,920	T/M/H	$46,621
Expend.	$251,163	Party	$7,394	Labor	$500	Agr.	$8,700
Unspent	$51,639	PACS	$113,065	Ideo.	$8,500	CWOS	$1,824

NEBRASKA

"The little town behind them had vanished as if it had never been, had fallen behind the swell of the prairie, and the stern frozen country received them into its bosom. The homesteads were few and far apart; here and there a windmill gaunt against the sky, a sod house crouching in a hollow." This is Willa Cather in *O Pioneers!* telling how she saw Nebraska settled in the 1880s— that single decade when Anglo-Saxon Protestant civilization, fortified by the immigrants Cather describes as well, fastened its hold on a land of grassy plains and sand hills that had been the preserve of the Indians and the buffalo for time immemorial. In 1880 Nebraska had a population of 452,000; in 1890, 1,062,000—not far below the 1980 figure of 1,570,000. Within a single decade Nebraska became a corn and hog and dry-land wheat state, Omaha became a major regional center, and Lincoln became a state capital; Nebraska is still utterly dependent on farming, and Omaha and Lincoln are its only significant cities still. This is a state that sprang suddenly into existence and has changed strikingly little in the years since.

That is not exactly what its founders intended: they hoped Nebraska would develop just as the states to the immediate east—Missouri, Illinois, Iowa—did. After all, Chicago itself had grown from nothing to become one of the largest cities in the world in just 30 years. But while the 1880s were a time of plentiful rain here, the 1890s were a decade of drought, and Nebraska stopped growing: many rural counties and even Omaha lost population—and have been exporting people ever since. Most of Nebraska's settlers, like most migrants, were young people, optimistic and motivated, in search of opportunity, with families full of children. Fully 48% of the one million Nebraskans of 1890 were children, and a very large percentage of them moved elsewhere when they grew up. Since 1890 Nebraska has exported people to the West, the great metropolitan areas of the Midwest, and to Texas and the Southwest. Only 28% of Nebraska's 1.6 million residents today are children, meaning that there are actually 60,000 fewer children here than there were 90 years ago. So for years Nebraska's population has been elderly (a happier reason: people live longer here than in any other state).

The sudden boom of the 1880s and the bust of the 1890s produced the most colorful—and atypical—politics of Nebraska's history, the populist movement and William Jennings Bryan, "the silver-tongued orator of the Platte." Bryan was only 36 when he delivered the famous Cross of Gold speech at the 1896 Democratic National Convention and was swept to the Democratic nomination; he was thought so radical that Democratic President Grover Cleveland wouldn't support him, but he won 47% of the vote. Nebraskans supported Bryan, whose program may have been forward-looking, but whose purpose was essentially retrograde: to restore Nebraska to the prosperity and hopes it had enjoyed a few years before. Bryan won the Democratic nomination again in 1900 and 1908 but never came as close to winning as he did the first time. By then Nebraska had already gone back to the Republicans, and Bryan himself eventually moved to Florida. Since Bryan's time, Nebraska's most notable politician has been George Norris, Representative (1909–13) and Senator (1913–43). During the progressive era Norris led the House rebellion against Speaker Joseph Cannon; during the 1930s he pushed through the Norris-LaGuardia Anti-Injunction Act, the first national pro-union legislation, and the Tennessee Valley Authority.

Presidential politics. Since 1900, 92% of Nebraska's population growth has been in and around Omaha and Lincoln; these cities and their suburbs now contain 43% of the state's people. There is a sizable Czech community on the south side of Omaha which, like the city's small black neighborhood, usually votes Democratic; so too do a few isolated rural counties. But as a whole Nebraska, city and farm, is almost always solidly Republican in national elections. In the close elections of 1960, 1968, and 1976, Republicans carried both big cities and lost only three or

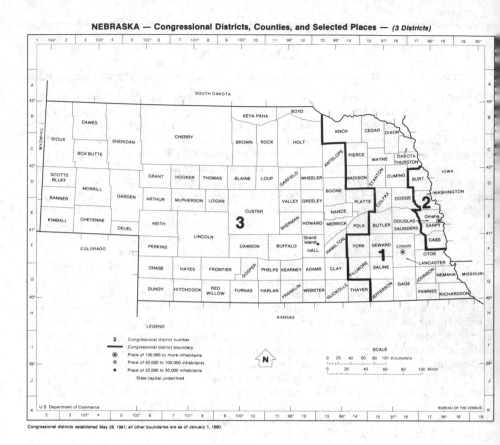

NEBRASKA — Congressional Districts, Counties, and Selected Places — (3 Districts)

Congressional districts established May 28, 1981; all other boundaries are as of January 1, 1980.

four counties out of 93. In 1984, this was Reagan's fourth best state, in 1980 his second best.

Nebraska has a presidential primary which, in the middle of the season, used to attract a lot of attention; the whole national press followed Robert Kennedy and Eugene McCarthy out here in 1968 and took note when Frank Church won in 1976. No more. There are too many other primaries, and Nebraska's delegations are small.

Governor. Nebraska may be conservative, but it has also been a social pathfinder: the pioneer women who built sod houses, raised children, and kept up cultural standards on the side would be less surprised than many easterners would today that Nebraska turned out to be the first state whose two major parties both nominated women for governor. They were Kay Orr, Republican state treasurer, and Helen Boosalis, Democratic mayor of Lincoln; both won 1986 primaries against two well-known male candidates; both ran creditable races. Orr, an opponent of sales tax increases, beat Boosalis, who said they might be necessary. Oddly, Orr is one of the few Republicans elected governor in recent history: Democrats held the office for 20 of the 28 years up to 1986. Orr's predecessor, Robert Kerrey, was the most distinctive of the lot, a restaurant owner who won the Congressional Medal of Honor in Vietnam, later went around the country denouncing the war, runs marathons although he lost his right leg below the knee, and while in office dated sultry movie star Debra Winger. Nebraskans, incidentally, were charmed, and pleased that Hollywood was coming to Nebraska rather than vice versa. But Winger and Kerrey split up and Kerrey, after only one term, decided not to seek reelection despite 70% job ratings. He may be back.

In the meantime, Orr must deal with a state whose agriculture-based economy is in trouble. Kerrey was trying to figure out how to funnel public money to family farms, and voters in 1982 passed a referendum purporting to bar corporations and tax shelters from buying farms. But it is hard to see how the latter will bring land prices up or the former compensate for crop price drops. Yet the crisis may be less severe than it seems. There was little evidence here that Republicans were suffering from the farm revolt apparent in Iowa or the Dakotas. Orr won while proclaiming her support for Ronald Reagan and all three Republican House members were easily reelected.

Senators. Nebraska's senior Senator is James Exon, who served eight years as a popular, pennypinching governor in the 1970s and was elected to the Senate in 1978. Exon is a team player in the Senate, instinctively cooperating with other Democrats and working amiably sometimes with Republicans to get legislative solutions—which gives him a record that is a little hard to characterize as staunchly conservative. On the Budget Committee he can be a key vote, usually for maximum reduction of the deficit. On the Armed Services Committee he is sometimes skeptical of weapons projects, but not nearly so often as some other Democrats; like most Nebraskans he is concerned about the big SAC base near Omaha. A member of the minority during most of his Senate service, Exon does not have any major achievements, but he has his accomplishments: the minting of the American eagle gold coin and an odometer fraud bill, for instance; and he backs causes popular in Nebraska, like the 65 mile per hour speed limit and restrictions on Canadian pork imports.

Running for reelection in 1984, Exon found himself under surprisingly harsh attack from Republican Nancy Hoch, who not only made the not very credible claim that he was too liberal but also advanced the more telling argument that he was a backbencher. This made Exon, unaccustomed to harsh criticism, furious, and he cited all manner of bills he helped pass and various work he did on the Armed Services, Commerce, and Budget Committees. But the fact is that Exon could not credibly portray himself as a national leader. Hoch nearly pulled the upset of the year; morning exit polling showed her ahead, and she ended up holding Exon to 52% of the vote. Interestingly, the PACs, so often attacked by Democrats and liberals, may have made the difference in this race. They gave Exon about $500,000 but, up to mid-October, had only contributed about $57,000 to Hoch's campaign. Exon's near defeat puts him under more political pressure in the future—pressure not just to keep in touch with Nebraska voters but to establish himself as a visible national leader.

Nebraska's junior Senator, David Karnes, was appointed to fill the vacancy caused by the sudden death in March 1987 of Edward Zorinsky. It came just after he appeared in an Omaha Press Club skit singing, "The party that I choose can never lose, and I'll be its favorite son." The line came close to characterizing Zorinsky's career, just as his good-humored willingness to zing himself epitomized his character. Zorinsky was a Republican who, as Mayor of Omaha in 1976, was passed over for the Senate nomination to replace Roman Hruska, and so ran as a Democrat and won. Before the 1986 election, he was threatening to switch parties again if his votes should prove decisive in determining party control; he was miffed that Vermont's Patrick Leahy had indicated he would take the chair of the Agriculture Committee if the Democrats won, and wanted to see if the Republicans could do better for Nebraska and for him. His leverage gone when the Democrats won 55 seats, he remained brash and unpredictable, and a favorite, on whatever party ticket he chose, for reelection in 1988.

David Karnes, vice president of an Omaha agribusiness firm, an assistant to HUD Secretary Samuel Pierce as a White House Fellow in 1981, a board of education member in Omaha, was also, more pertinently, Governor Kay Orr's 2d Congressional District chairman in the 1986 campaign. She evidently was impressed with his work and his judgment and chose him over several better-known Nebraska Republicans who were not entirely happy to have been passed over. Karnes is the youngest Senator, six days younger than Oklahoma's Don Nickles; he is the first Senator in a long time with a mustache. Karnes took Zorinsky's seat on the Agriculture Committee, an assignment which is of paramount importance to his constituency.

Karnes's mettle will be tested in the next 18 months. Omaha congressman Hal Daub and former Republican chairman and 1986 runner-up to Orr, Kermit Brashear, both wanted the appointment, and both may run in the primary for what could be a lifetime seat. Another possible candidate is Bob Kerrey, who is said to have regretted leaving public office and who would surely be the Democrats' strongest candidate in a general election.

Congressional districting. Nebraska revised its congressional district lines very slightly after the 1980 Census, with no political effect on any of its three Republican congressmen.

The People: Est. Pop. 1986: 1,598,000; Pop. 1980: 1,569,825, up 1.8% 1980–86 and 5.7% 1970–80; 0.66% of U.S. total, 36th largest. 17% with 1–3 yrs. col., 16% with 4+ yrs. col.; 10.7% below poverty level. Single ancestry: 22% German, 6% English, 4% Irish, 2% Swedish, Polish, 1% French, Italian, Dutch, Norwegian. Households (1980): 72% family, 38% with children, 63% married couples; 31.6% housing units rented; median monthly rent: $170; median house value: $38,000. Voting age pop. (1980); 1,122,655; 3% Black, 1% Spanish origin. Registered voters (1986): 849,762; 359,281 D (42%), 435,289 R (51%), 55,192 I (7%).

1986 Share of Federal Tax Burden: $4,711,000,000; 0.63% of U.S. total, 34th largest.

1986 Share of Federal Expenditures

	Total		Non-Defense		Defense	
Total Expend	$5,211m	(0.63%)	$4,444m	(0.74%)	$767m	(0.33%)
St/Lcl Grants	661m	(0.59%)	661m	(0.59%)	1m	(0.90%)
Salary/Wages	773m	(0.64%)	343m	(0.58%)	430m	(0.69%)
Pymnts of Indiv	2,421m	(0.66%)	2,310m	(0.67%)	111m	(0.62%)
Procurement	507m	(0.25%)	282m	(0.51%)	226m	(0.15%)
Research/Other	849m	(3.18%)	849m	(3.19%)	0m	(0%)

Political Lineup: Governor, Kay A. Orr (R); Lt. Gov., Bill Nichol (R); Secy. of State, Allen J. Beermann (R); Atty. Gen., Robert Spire (R); Treasurer, Frank Marsh (R); Auditor, Ray A. C. Johnson (R). Unicameral legislature, 49 (23 D, 25 R, 1 I). Senators, David K. Karnes (R) and J. James Exon (D). Representatives, 3 R.

1984 Presidential Vote

Reagan (R)	460,054	(71%)
Mondale (D)	187,866	(29%)

1980 Presidential Vote

Reagan (R)	419,214	(66%)
Carter (D)	166,424	(26%)
Anderson (I)	44,854	(7%)

1984 Democratic Presidential Primary

Hart	86,582	(58%)
Mondale	39,635	(27%)
Jackson	13,495	(9%)
Four others, uncomm.	9,143	(6%)

1984 Republican Presidential Primary

Reagan	145,245	(99%)

From the publishers of
The 1988 Almanac
of American Politics:

What the Leaders Read.

Week after week, NATIONAL JOURNAL brings you the most complete, accurate, non-partisan coverage of national politics available... from weekly updates on Congressional activity to in-depth, behind-the-scenes analyses of the workings of the federal government.

If you need to stay up-to-date on the national policy-making process... if you need to know about decisions *before* they happen... return the subscription card below to make sure you get NATIONAL JOURNAL every week. (over, please...)

DETACH HERE AND MAIL

National Journal Subscription Order Form
Special Introductory Offer! New Subscribers Only...

☐ Yes, I would like a trial subscription to NATIONAL JOURNAL... 20 weeks for only $199.

☐ Please send me a full year's subscription for $498 (a savings of $66 off the regular price).

☐ Payment enclosed.   ☐ Bill me.

☐ Charge my: ☐ Visa   ☐ MasterCard   ☐ American Express

Acct. # ☐☐☐☐☐☐☐☐☐☐☐☐☐☐☐☐☐☐☐☐   Exp. Date ☐☐☐☐

Signature _____

Name _____ Phone _____

Organization _____ Title _____

Address _____

City _____ State _____ Zip _____

1730 M Street, N.W. • Washington, D.C. 20036   ALM88

National Journal What the Leaders Read.

❝Until a public policy controversy has been put under NATIONAL JOURNAL'S high-powered microscope, the controversy has not been fully considered. Fortunately, NATIONAL JOURNAL is never late, and usually is prescient, in identifying the controversies that matter most.**❞**

George F. Will,
Syndicated Columnist

❝NATIONAL JOURNAL I find indispensable for behind-the-scenes knowledge of events.**❞**

John Glenn,
U.S. Senator, Ohio

❝Yours is the first-read, best-read publication among Washington insiders…There isn't a Member of Congress who doesn't check your index for his or her name. Your stories are thorough, accurate and timely. What more can a reader ask for?**❞**

Heather J. Gradison
Chairman, Interstate Commerce Commission

1988 Almanac Extra Copy Order Form

	QUANTITY	ITEM	AMOUNT
YES! Send me:	_____	Hardcover ALMANAC(s) @ $42.95	_____
	_____	Softcover ALMANAC(s) @ $39.95	_____
		D.C. orders add 6% sales tax	_____
		Shipping & Handling @ $2.00 per book	_____
		TOTAL	_____

☐ I enclose a check (payable to National Journal)

☐ Charge my: ☐ Visa ☐ MasterCard ☐ American Express

Acct. # ☐☐☐☐☐☐☐☐☐☐☐☐☐☐☐☐ Exp. Date ☐☐☐☐

Signature _____

Name _____ Phone_____

Organization _____ Title_____

Address_____

City_____ State_____ Zip_____

Discounts begin with 2 copies! For more information call 1-800-424-2921. (In D.C. call 857-1491.)
MAIL TO: ALMANAC 1988 • 1730 M Street, N.W. • Washington, D.C. 20036   ALM88

- -
DETACH HERE AND MAIL

DETACH HERE AND MAIL
- -

Free Information Request Card

National Journal
What the Leaders Read.

government EXECUTIVE

THE CAPITAL SOURCE

The only weekly magazine
devoted exclusively
to coverage of politics
and government.

The U.S. Government's
business magazine.

The most comprehensive,
most useful
Washington phone directory
ever published.

☐ Please send me more information about these and other NATIONAL JOURNAL publications.

Name _____ Phone_____

Organization _____ Title_____

Address_____

City_____ State_____ Zip_____

ALM88

BUSINESS REPLY MAIL

FIRST CLASS   PERMIT NO. 10574   WASHINGTON, D.C.

POSTAGE WILL BE PAID BY ADDRESSEE

ALMANAC 1988
1730 M Street, N.W.
Washington, D.C. 20036

BUSINESS REPLY MAIL

FIRST CLASS   PERMIT NO. 10574   WASHINGTON, D.C.

POSTAGE WILL BE PAID BY ADDRESSEE

NATIONAL JOURNAL
1730 M Street, N.W.
Washington, D.C. 20036

GOVERNOR

Gov. Kay A. Orr (R)

Elected 1986, term expires Jan. 1991; b. Jan. 2, 1939, Burlington, IA; home, Lincoln; U. of IA; Protestant; married (William).

Career: Exec. Asst. to NE Gov. Charles Thone, 1979–81; NE Treasurer, 1981–86.

Office: State Capitol Bldg., Rm. 2316, Lincoln 68509, 402-471-2244.

Election Results

1986 gen.	Kay A. Orr (R)	298,325	(53%)
	Helen Boosalis (D)	265,156	(47%)
1986 prim.	Kay A. Orr (R)	75,914	(39%)
	Kermit Brashear (R)	60,308	(31%)
	Nancy Hoch (R)	42,649	(22%)
1982 gen.	Robert Kerrey (D)	277,436	(51%)
	Charles Thone (R)	270,203	(49%)

SENATORS

Sen. J. James Exon (D)

Elected 1978, seat up 1990; b. Aug. 9, 1921, Geddes, SD; home, Lincoln; U. of Omaha; Episcopalian; married (Patricia).

Career: Army, WWII; Branch Mgr., Universal Finance Co., 1946–54; Pres., Exon's Inc., office equip. business, 1954–70; Gov. of NE, 1970–78.

Offices: 330 HSOB 20510, 202-224-4224. Also 8305 New Fed. Bldg., 215 N. 17th St., Omaha 68102, 402-221-4665; 287 Fed. Bldg., 100 Centennial Mall N., Lincoln 68508, 402-471-5591; and 275 Fed. Bldg., North Platte 69101, 308-534-2006.

Committees: *Armed Services* (3d of 11 D). Subcommittees: Manpower and Personnel; Strategic Forces and Nuclear Defense (Chairman); Projection Forces and Regional Defense. *Budget* (6th of 13 D). *Commerce, Science, and Transportation* (6th of 8 D). Subcommittees: Aviation; Communications; Surface Transportation (Chairman).

Group Ratings

	ADA	ACLU	COPE	CFA	LCV	ACU	NTU	NSI	COC	CEI
1986	35	35	40	53	50	48	46	60	32	38
1985	25	—	39	30	—	64	34	—	46	—

National Journal Ratings

	1986 LIB — 1986 CONS		1985 LIB — 1985 CONS	
Economic	47% —	48%	* —	*
Social	60% —	36%	28% —	68%
Foreign	55% —	44%	60% —	38%

Key Votes

1) Ease Gun Cont	FOR	5) Grm-Rdmn Def Red	AGN	9) Rehnquist Nom	AGN
2) Immig Reform	FOR	6) Contra Aid	AGN	10) Tax Reform	AGN
3) Lmt Text Imp	AGN	7) SDI Funding	FOR	11) Drug Death Pen	AGN
4) Aid Tobac Ind	FOR	8) Lmt PAC Contrib	FOR	12) S Africa Sanc	FOR

Election Results

1984 general	J. James Exon (D)...................	332,217	(52%)	($866,760)
	Nancy Hoch (R)....................	307,147	(48%)	($583,632)
1984 primary	J. James Exon (D) unopposed			
1978 general	J. James Exon (D)...................	334,096	(68%)	($234,862)
	Don Shasteen (R)..................	159,706	(32%)	($218,148)

Campaign Contributions and Expenditures

1979-84		Direct Cont. 1979-84		PACS Breakdown 1979-84			
Receipts	$893,539	Indiv.	$325,745	Corp.	$206,245	T/M/H	$159,851
Expend.	$866,760	Party	$23,391	Labor	$58,500	Agr.	$19,800
Unspent	$51,762	PACS	$519,307	Ideo.	$47,317	CWOS	$18,400

Sen. David K. Karnes (R)

Appointed Mar. 11, 1987, to fill the unexpired term of Sen. Edward Zorinsky, seat up 1988; b. Dec. 12, 1948, Omaha; home, Omaha; U. of NE, B.A. 1971, J.D. 1974; United Methodist; married (Elizabeth).

Career: White House Fellow, U.S. Dept. of HUD, 1981; Asst. Undersecretary of HUD, 1982; Special Cnsl., Fed. Home Loan Bank Bd., 1983; Sr. Vice Pres. & Gen. Coun., Scoular Co., agric., grain-handling & merchandising business, 1983–86.

Offices: 107 DSOB 20510, 202-224-6551. Also 8311 Fed. Bldg., 215 N. 17th St., Omaha 68102, 402-221-4381; 100 Centennial Mall N., Lincoln 68508, 402-471-5246; and 1811 W. 2d St., Grand Island 68801, 308-381-5552.

Committees: *Agriculture, Nutrition, and Forestry* (9th of 9 R). *Banking, Housing, and Urban Affairs* (9th of 9 R). *Small Business* (9th of 9 R). Subcommittees not available.

Group Ratings and Key Votes: Newly Appointed

Election Results

1982 general	Edward Zorinsky (D)................	363,350	(67%)	($523,141)
	Jim Keck (R)	155,760	(29%)	($489,186)
1982 primary	Edward Zorinsky (D)................	124,288	(100%)	
1976 general	Edward Zorinsky (D)................	313,805	(53%)	($237,613)
	John Y. McCollister (R)..............	279,284	(47%)	($319,287)

FIRST DISTRICT

The 1st Congressional District of Nebraska is a band of 26 counties covering most of the eastern part of the state from South Dakota down to Kansas, except for the Omaha area. Outside of Lincoln, the district's largest city, the economy of the 1st is based almost entirely on agriculture. The political inclination of the region is Republican, but there are a couple of rural Catholic Democratic counties and plenty of ticket-splitting in state races. Lincoln, the capital and—more important to people here—home of the University of Nebraska Cornhuskers, is traditionally

Republican, but state employees and university voters sometimes put it in the Democratic column; Lincoln Mayor Helen Boosalis got 61% here in 1986, though she lost statewide to Republican Governor Kay Orr.

The congressman from the 1st District is Douglas Bereuter, a Republican who began as a city-planner, was once a top aide to a Republican governor defeated in 1970 for raising taxes, and worked on a committee of the National Council of State Legislators. He seems disposed not so much to denounce government as to study it and try to make it work better. He is a bit more willing to spend than other Nebraska Republicans and is fairly spending-minded on farm programs.

Bereuter is one of the Farm Belt members who has shown a special interest in trade issues, and like other Nebraskans of both parties he has been a solid free trader, searching for export markets for American agricultural products (including behind the Iron Curtain) and opposing import restrictions. On the Banking Committee he co-sponsored with Richard Lehman of California a "Farmer Mac" bill to create a second market for agricultural mortgages. As ranking member of a Banking subcommittee he has provided bipartisan support for international lending institutions. On foreign policy he sometimes takes liberal positions but tends to be solidly conservative on cultural issues—not unpopular stands in tradition-minded, once isolationist Nebraska.

This was a fiercely contested district from 1964 to 1976, but Bereuter won the seat in 1978 against a strong opponent, and has held it easily ever since. Against the strongest candidate he has faced in eight years, he won in 1986 with 64%, carrying every county.

The People: Pop. 1980: 523,079, up 6.6% 1970–80. Households (1980): 71% family, 36% with children, 63% married couples; 31.1% housing units rented; median monthly rent: $167; median house value: $38,300. Voting age pop. (1980): 383,987; 1% Spanish origin, 1% Black, 1% American Indian.

1984 Presidential Vote:

Reagan (R) 144,198	(67%)
Mondale (D) 69,923	(32%)

Rep. Douglas K. (Doug) Bereuter (R)

Elected 1978; b. Oct. 6, 1939, York; home, Utica; U. of NE, B.A. 1961, Harvard U., M.C.P. 1966, M.P.A. 1973; Lutheran; married (Louise).

Career: Army, 1963–65; Residential/commercial dev. consultant; Urban Planner, U.S. Dept. of HUD., 1965–66; Asst. Dir. of Planning, NE Div. of Resources, 1966–67; Dir., St. and Urban Affairs, NE Econ. Dev. Dept., 1967–68; Dir., NE St. Plng. Office, 1969–71; NE Senate, 1975–78.

Offices: 2446 RHOB 20515, 202-225-4806. Also P.O. Box 82887, Lincoln 68501, 402-471-5400.

Committees: *Banking, Finance and Urban Affairs* (9th of 20 R). Subcommittees: Financial Institutions Supervision, Regulation and Insurance; Housing and Community Development; International Development Institutions and Finance (Ranking Member). *Foreign Affairs* (9th of 18 R). Subcommittees: Europe and the Middle East; International Economic Policy and Trade. *Select Committee on Hunger* (6th of 10 R). Task Force: International Task Force.

Group Ratings

	ADA	ACLU	COPE	CFA	LCV	ACU	NTU	NSI	COC	CEI
1986	15	20	18	58	26	59	52	80	72	65
1985	15	—	17	42	—	67	57	—	82	—

National Journal Ratings

	1986 LIB — 1986 CONS			1985 LIB — 1985 CONS		
Economic	16%	—	82%	38%	—	62%
Social	31%	—	67%	0%	—	76%
Foreign	41%	—	57%	44%	—	55%

Key Votes

1) Lmt Cln Water Act	FOR	5) Retain Gun Cont	AGN	9) Aid Angola Reb	FOR
2) Rpl Tobac Sub	FOR	6) Contra Aid	FOR	10) Tax Reform	FOR
3) Grm-Rdmn Def Red	FOR	7) Lmt Text Imp	AGN	11) S Africa Sanc	FOR
4) Ban Polygraph	FOR	8) Limit SDI	FOR	12) Immig Reform	FOR

Election Results

1986 general	Douglas K. (Doug) Bereuter (R)	121,772	(64%)	($227,910)
	Steve Burns (D)	67,137	(36%)	($92,746)
1986 primary	Douglas K. (Doug) Bereuter (R)	56,367	(91%)	
	Jim Lessman (R)	5,626	(9%)	
1984 general	Douglas K. (Doug) Bereuter (R)	158,836	(74%)	($163,916)
	Monica E. Bauer (D)	55,508	(26%)	($50,995)

Campaign Contributions and Expenditures

1985-86		Direct Cont. 1985-86		PACS Breakdown 1985-86			
Receipts	$200,466	Indiv.	$83,681	Corp.	$40,300	T/M/H	$51,275
Expend.	$227,910	Party	$4,470	Labor	$0	Agr.	$5,950
Unspent	$24,901	PACS	$102,325	Ideo.	$3,750	CWOS	$1,050

SECOND DISTRICT

Omaha more than any other American city is the creation of Abraham Lincoln; it was Lincoln, the old railroad lawyer from Illinois, who chose Omaha to be the eastern terminus of the first transcontinental railroad. From that beginning it grew explosively in the 1880s to become suddenly one of the great railroad and meatpacking centers of the Great Plains; and that it still is, though its economy is more diversified today. It has never spread out as far on the plains as Kansas City or Denver, but it is still the biggest city west of Chicago on the direct route to the Rockies, a still family-oriented city with its own proud civic traditions and institutions. Yet it remains a small enough city—famous on Wall Street as the place where Warren Buffett lives and works—to be readily comprehensible; you don't feel distant, physically or psychologically, from neighborhoods on the other side of town, and you usually know people from a broader range of backgrounds than you would in a large homogeneous neighborhood in a big metropolitan area. Leaders here are known personally, and politics can become personal: Omaha went through something of a trauma in January 1987 when it recalled its mayor, Michael Boyle, after five years for firing the police chief after police staked out and arrested his brother-in-law for drunk driving.

Metropolitan Omaha (the Nebraska side of the Missouri River, that is; not Council Bluffs, Iowa) is more or less coextensive with the 2d Congressional District of Nebraska. On balance it is Republican, but with ethnic and black communities, some union members, and talented Democratic politicos, it sometimes goes Democratic. Representative Hal Daub is a market-oriented small businessman and a Republican first elected in 1980 and now a member of the Ways and Means Committee. Daub's political debut came before the Reagan Administration: he challenged the Democratic congressman here in 1978 only to see him retire in 1980, and he sets to some extent his own course, though on economic issues he has been pretty loyal to the Administration. His major achievement so far has been to win after the 1984 election a seat on the Ways and Means Committee, beating out Hank Brown of Colorado, who has since gotten one himself. On Ways and Means Daub supported the 1986 tax reform even when most Republicans were voting against it. He has moved to restore income averaging for farmers, and wants catastrophic health care coverage to concentrate on long-term and nursing home care.

Daub has a somewhat more acerbic personality than many politicians, but he has managed to win some impressive victories. He held his seat in 1982, won big in 1984, and in 1986 got a pretty solid though not overwhelming 59% against a Democratic lawyer who advocated government production controls for farmers—the pet remedy of Senator Tom Harkin, a familiar figure in Omaha because he represented the Iowa 5th District just across the river for 10 years before going to the Senate in 1984. In most circumstances, Daub could be expected to hold onto this seat for years. But he had hopes of being appointed to the Senate vacancy caused by Edward Zorinsky's death, and deliberately saved the option of running against Governor Kay Orr's appointee David Karnes in the 1988 primary. This has traditionally been regarded as Omaha's Senate seat, and Daub has had his eyes on it for years; since the other competitors are about his age, this may be his last chance to win it in his political lifetime.

The People: Pop. 1980: 522,919, up 6.2% 1970–80. Households (1980): 72% family, 42% with children, 60% married couples; 35.7% housing units rented; median monthly rent: $190; median house value: $40,500. Voting age pop. (1980): 364,998; 7% Black, 2% Spanish origin, 1% Asian origin.

1984 Presidential Vote:

Reagan (R) 144,901	(67%)
Mondale (D) 70,238	(32%)

Rep. Harold J. (Hal) Daub (R)

Elected 1980; b. Apr. 23, 1941, Fort Bragg, NC; home, Omaha; Washington U., St. Louis, B.S. 1963, U. of NE, Lincoln, J.D. 1966; Presbyterian; married (Cindy).

Career: Army, 1966–68; Practicing atty., 1968–71; Vice Pres., Gen. Counsel, Standard Chemical Mfg. Co., 1971–81.

Offices: 1019 LHOB 20515, 202-225-4155. Also 8424 Fed. Bldg., 215 N. 17th St., Omaha 68102, 402-221-4216.

Committees: *Ways and Means* (10th of 13 R). Subcommittees: Health; Social Security.

Group Ratings

	ADA	ACLU	COPE	CFA	LCV	ACU	NTU	NSI	COC	CEI
1986	5	10	14	17	32	86	59	90	78	75
1985	5	—	15	25	—	81	58	—	73	—

National Journal Ratings

	1986 LIB — 1986 CONS		1985 LIB — 1985 CONS	
Economic	19% —	79%	27% —	71%
Social	18% —	78%	0% —	76%
Foreign	16% —	79%	37% —	60%

Key Votes

1) Lmt Cln Water Act	FOR	5) Retain Gun Cont	AGN	9) Aid Angola Reb	FOR
2) Rpl Tobac Sub	FOR	6) Contra Aid	FOR	10) Tax Reform	FOR
3) Grm-Rdmn Def Red	FOR	7) Lmt Text Imp	AGN	11) S Africa Sanc	FOR
4) Ban Polygraph	AGN	8) Limit SDI	AGN	12) Immig Reform	AGN

Election Results

1986 general	Harold J. (Hal) Daub (R)...............	99,569	(59%)	($509,019)
	Walter M. Calinger (D)	70,372	(41%)	($57,627)
1986 primary	Harold J. (Hal) Daub (R)...............	38,762	(100%)	
1984 general	Harold J. (Hal) Daub (R)..............	139,384	(65%)	($414,409)
	Thomas F. Cavanaugh (D)	75,210	(35%)	($73,959)

Campaign Contributions and Expenditures

1985-86		Direct Cont. 1985-86		PACS Breakdown 1985-86			
Receipts	$568,197	Indiv.	$262,627	Corp.	$108,375	T/M/H	$126,600
Expend.	$509,019	Party	$3,838	Labor	$6,950	Agr.	$6,200
Unspent	$116,402	PACS	$276,981	Ideo.	$19,100	CWOS	$11,006

THIRD DISTRICT

One-third of Nebraska's population is spread out over the western three-fourths of its land area—the 3d Congressional District. As you drive west here, the rolling fields of corn and wheat give way to the sand hills and cattle country, much of it devoid of signs of human habitation for miles on end; the main streets of the small towns grow shorter, and the towns themselves become fewer. This is where settlers thronged in the unusually moist 1880s, and from which their descendants for years have been leaving, often reluctantly, ever since. Today most of the people here live along the Platte River or near such towns as Grand Island, Hastings, Kearney, and Scottsbluff—none with more than 35,000 people.

When people divide the country into regions, they always put Nebraska in the Midwest. But the part of the state that is the 3d Congressional District is in many ways more similar to Wyoming, just to the west, than it is to Iowa on the east. Economically, the cowman is more important than the corn or wheat farmer here; physically, the rainfall is usually low, not much more than on the High Plains of Wyoming or Colorado. Politically, this region seems more western than midwestern as well. Thirty years ago western Nebraska was the scene of farm rebellions against Ezra Taft Benson, and Democrats even won House seats in this area. Now western Nebraska is as heavily Republican as the Rocky Mountain states. The 3d District went 74% for Ronald Reagan in 1980 and 81% in 1984; it went Republican in the close 1982 and 1986 gubernatorial race and was the only one of the three districts to vote against Democratic Senator James Exon in 1984. It has also become one of the safest Republican seats in the House of Representatives.

It is especially safe for Representative Virginia Smith, a chipper and enthusiastic Republican first elected, narrowly, in Democratic 1974. In 1984 she won with 83% of the vote—one of the strongest showings in the nation—and in 1982 she had been unopposed. For 20 years Smith chaired the American Farm Bureau Women, one of the free enterprise pillars of Republican strength in the Farm Belt for many years; she was an active Republican as well. Now she has a seat on the Appropriations Committee and is a vote for frugality, even sometimes on defense issues. She was the lead opponent of the proposed congressional pay raise in 1987. But she does favor spending on almost all farm programs, which is important since she is ranking Republican on Jamie Whitten's Agriculture Subcommittee; and she has been known to lobby for millions of tax dollars for dams that would benefit just a few families in her district. In western Nebraska she is overwhelmingly popular, running unopposed in 1982, winning 83% in 1984, and against a respectable opponent in a Democratic year getting 70% in 1986.

The People: Pop. 1980: 523,827, up 4.2% 1970–80. Households (1980): 73% family, 38% with children, 66% married couples; 28.1% housing units rented; median monthly rent: $142; median house value: $34,700. Voting age pop. (1980): 373,670; 2% Spanish origin.

Rep. Virginia Smith (R)

Elected 1974; b. June 30, 1911, Randolph, IA; home, Chappell; U. of NE, B.A. 1936; United Methodist; married (Haven).

Career: Natl. Chwmn., Amer. Farm Bureau Women, 1955–74; Chwmn. and Pres., Task Force on Rural Development, 1971–72.

Offices: 2202 RHOB 20515, 202-225-6435. Also 312 W. 3d St., P.O. Box 2146, Grand Island 68802, 308-381-5555; and 1502 2d Ave., Scotts Bluff 69361, 307-622-3333.

Committees: *Appropriations* (9th of 22 R). Subcommittees: Rural Development, Agriculture and Related Agencies (Ranking Member); Energy and Water Development.

Group Ratings

	ADA	ACLU	COPE	CFA	LCV	ACU	NTU	NSI	COC	CEI
1986	10	11	10	25	16	71	51	80	81	68
1985	10	—	10	25	—	62	51	—	73	—

National Journal Ratings

	1986 LIB — 1986 CONS			1985 LIB — 1985 CONS		
Economic	26%	—	73%	29%	—	70%
Social	29%	—	70%	24%	—	72%
Foreign	37%	—	62%	44%	—	55%

Key Votes

1) Lmt Cln Water Act	FOR	5) Retain Gun Cont	AGN	9) Aid Angola Reb	FOR
2) Rpl Tobac Sub	AGN	6) Contra Aid	FOR	10) Tax Reform	FOR
3) Grm-Rdmn Def Red	FOR	7) Lmt Text Imp	AGN	11) S Africa Sanc	FOR
4) Ban Polygraph	AGN	8) Limit SDI	FOR	12) Immig Reform	FOR

Election Results

1986 general	Virginia Smith (R) 136,985	(70%)	($253,292)
	Scott E. Sidwell (D) 59,182	(30%)	($74,227)
1986 primary	Virginia Smith (R) 73,734	(100%)	
1984 general	Virginia Smith (R) 183,901	(83%)	($144,746)
	Tom Vickers (D) 36,899	(17%)	($56,827)

Campaign Contributions and Expenditures

1985-86		Direct Cont. 1985-86		PACS Breakdown 1985-86			
Receipts	$219,973	Indiv.	$94,427	Corp.	$37,800	T/M/H	$67,608
Expend.	$253,292	Party	$10,532	Labor	$0	Agr.	$1,700
Unspent	$11,108	PACS	$112,958	Ideo.	$4,350	CWOS	$1,500

NEVADA

Nevada is a state that gambled—and hit the jackpot. Or at least the great bulk of Nevadans, most of whom came from somewhere else to Nevada, think so, and so do the hordes of tourists who still come (their numbers diminished by competition from Atlantic City, but still awesome) to the garish casinos that line Las Vegas's Strip, Reno's downtown, and the shores of Lake Tahoe. Without gambling, which was legalized in the 1930s, there probably wouldn't be much of anything in Nevada, and the state government itself might have gone bankrupt.

By most rules of common sense, in fact, Nevada never had much reason to exist as a separate state at all. Its history began in 1859 with the discovery of the Comstock Lode—one of those huge mineral finds that triggers a rush of prospectors, speculators, and the usual hangers-on. Suddenly there was a boom town, Virginia City, in empty territory and soon a territorial government in Carson City. There were opera houses, saloons, brothels, and even a United States Mint, to coin some of the silver from the mines. But such booms are ephemeral, as even the Comstock Lode millionaires seemed to realize (they lived in San Francisco). But if there were no good economic reasons then there were compelling political ones to make Nevada a state. Civil War Republicans thought (mistakenly, it turned out) they needed a few more electoral votes to reelect Lincoln in 1864, so they created some by admitting as the state of Nevada these two towns, plus tens of thousands of square miles of the vacant, arid Great Basin to the north, east, and southeast. The motif runs through Nevada's history: the search for riches, the twist of fortune, the creation of an unexpected new reality.

Soon the veins of gold and silver petered out. The opera houses closed and the prospectors scattered—to Lead, South Dakota; Bisbee, Arizona; and the Klondike River in the Yukon Territory. Nevada had only 42,000 residents in 1900, 91,000 in 1930, idling in desert towns. Facing the depression, the legislature liberalized its divorce laws and legalized gambling at just about the same time the federal government was building Hoover Dam near the little crossroads of Las Vegas. Without exactly realizing it, Nevada had tied its economy to what would be one of the leading growth industries 50 years hence: tourism.

During that time, Nevada's population has increased explosively, and now there are almost one million Nevadans. Naturally the state bears little resemblance to its impermanent origins. Up to the end of World War II, Nevada's population was almost all concentrated around Reno and Carson City. That changed in 1947, when Bugsy Siegel opened the Flamingo, the first big casino hotel on the Las Vegas Strip. Las Vegas has since become the state's largest city, and more than half of Nevada's residents today live there or in surrounding Clark County. Reno has also grown rapidly, and in the first six years of the 1980s Nevada's population increased by more than 20%—the highest percentage growth rate in the nation except for Alaska's—with the fastest growth now in and around Reno. Yet outside the gleaming new cities, in the vast expanse of the Cow Counties, Nevada remains as empty as it always has been, or in ghost towns even emptier.

Politically, Nevada is a state that seems uncomfortable with what it has become. Like most of the Rocky Mountain states, Nevada has voted heavily Republican in recent national elections. It has supported candidates backed by the Moral Majority and in the late 1970s gave birth to the Sagebrush Rebellion, the move to force the federal government to give federal lands to the states. Yet Nevada is probably the least family-oriented state: 32% of its households do not contain families (the highest percentage in the nation), while 64% don't have children (a proportion exceeded only in Florida) and 44% aren't occupied by married couples (exceeded only by California and New York). Nevada is filled now with people who came here thinking they were sharper than others, that they had a special angle, that they are a step ahead of the

NEVADA — Congressional Districts, Counties, Independent City, and Other Selected Places — *(2 Districts)*

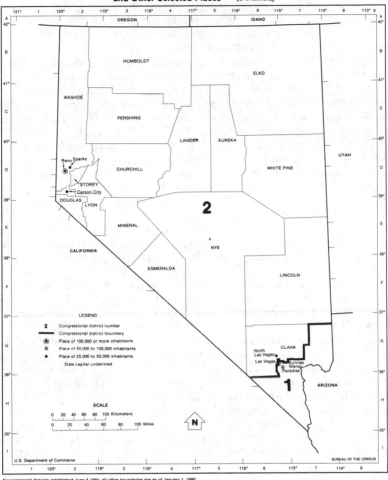

Congressional districts established June 4, 1981; all other boundaries are as of January 1, 1980.

market, that they would and could beat the odds—not the steady virtues we associate with traditional morality.

And Nevada's economy is based on two industries the New Right tends to disapprove of—gambling and government (not to mention prostitution, which is legal in some of the Cow Counties and is said to exist in Las Vegas and Reno as well). The big casinos and the government's atomic proving grounds remain the state's two biggest employers, and the federal government retains title to 87% of Nevada's land. On this base, Nevada has built a buoyant private economy; but underneath, it is based on money that outsiders—gamblers, federal taxpayers—bring in.

Governor. Nevada has a popular Democratic governor, Richard Bryan. Elected in 1982 when Republican Robert List's switch to reliance on the sales tax was not bringing in the predicted revenue, he like many governors of larger states and in both parties has become a kind of consensus choice as revenues increased and growth continued. He was reelected almost by acclamation, with 72% of the vote; his unfortunate opponent was a daughter of Representative

Barbara Vucanovich. The hard question for Bryan—and for Nevada—is whether the state's economy is being diversified and moving toward self-sufficiency. The gaming industry remains vulnerable to competition, and the federal government doesn't look like much of a growth industry these days. Nevada's gamble has paid off for more than 50 years now, but a prudent plunger always likes to hedge when circumstances call for it.

Senators. Until 1986, Nevada's dominant political figure was Paul Laxalt, President Reagan's best friend on Capitol Hill, senior Senator, general chairman of the Republican Party, governor during the four exciting years (1967–70) when Howard Hughes bought most of Las Vegas's casinos from reputedly mob-connected owners—without talking to anyone in the state except Paul Laxalt. But Laxalt shocked everyone by not seeking what would have been sure reelection in 1986 and then by seeing his seat go to the same Democrat he beat in 1974, Harry Reid. It was not the first time Laxalt has bowed out of politics: he left the governorship after one term in 1970, to run a casino in Carson City which didn't make as much money as he hoped. This Ormsby House was the subject of the story in the *Sacramento Bee* which alleged that substantial sums of money had been "skimmed"; although Laxalt himself was not charged with any wrongdoing, he filed a $250 million suit in September 1984 against the *Bee*. His lawyers successfully discouraged CBS and ABC from broadcasting stories on the subject, and *Newsweek*, which had repeated some of the *Bee's* charges, was prompted to run a correction asserting that the magazine had not meant "to impugn the Senator's reputation," but the lawsuit was cited in 1986 as something Laxalt decided he wanted settled before he decided on running for President.

Before the election Laxalt admitted that "a Santini loss, coupled with a loss of the Senate, would be very damaging to a Laxalt candidacy"; after the election he signed on with the nation's largest law firm for something like $1 million a year. Laxalt's assets are similar to Ronald Reagan's: he is a fervent believer in a mostly popular political philosophy, yet remains affable and civil with opponents as well as allies. But he has some of the same liabilities—he is not a workaholic—and he does not have the steely ambition which prompted began to challenge an incumbent Republican President. He stepped back twice from running in elections he would have won, did not advance himself as a vice presidential candidate in 1980 (though he was pointedly absent from the hall when Bush's selection was announced), and did not try to elbow Howard Baker aside after the Republicans unexpectedly won their Senate majority in 1980. Laxalt was a nationally and internationally important politician, letting Ferdinand Marcos know that Reagan thought he must go in 1986, but he let his stands on national issues be influenced by parochial Nevada concerns, as when he helped kill the mobile basing mode for the MX missile in 1981.

One of Nevada's two Senators is a Laxalt protégé, the other a Laxalt opponent. The protégé is Chic Hecht, a Las Vegas clothing store owner who was a Republican legislative leader during Laxalt's governorship; he was Laxalt's choice to run for the seat of Senator Howard Cannon in 1982. Cannon, who had beaten Laxalt by 64 votes in 1964, had severe liabilities: he had lost the chairmanships that helped him serve Nevada interests; he was named in the indictment of Teamsters president Roy Lee Williams and mob figure Allen Dorfman and testified extensively in their trial a month before the election; he was nearly beaten in the Democratic primary by congressman-at-large Jim Santini. Everything had to click to produce a Hecht victory: he won his primary with only 42% of the vote while Cannon edged Santini, whose conservative record would have enabled him to easily beat Hecht; the Williams-Dorfman trial got Cannon devastating free media. With all that, Hecht won by a 50%–48% margin.

Hecht is probably the least prepossessing member of the Senate. He is short, speaks with a squeaky voice and a lisp, and is anything but a brilliant phrasemaker. He has seats on the Energy and Banking Committees. One of his main projects in the Senate has been to allow states to set 65 mile per hour speed limits on all federally assisted roads (before 1974, Nevada had no speed limit); the Senate voted to do so, but then President Reagan vetoed the bill, giving Hecht the choice of 65 or Reagan. He chose 65. Hecht appears to be inclined toward national security affairs. Asserting that he had been an Army counter-intelligence official in Berlin during his years in the Korean War-era Army, he received one of the Intelligence Committee seats that opened after the 1984 election. His major asset for reelection is a sincere conservatism on almost all issues which is not far out of line with most Nevadans' beliefs. But with Laxalt practicing law in Washington and contemplating a presidential candidacy, with Reagan weakened and about to retire, with a popular Democratic governor and other potential opponents who are well known, this is one seat national Republican strategists must consider in jeopardy. Early 1987 polls showed Hecht trailing Attorney General Brian McKay by almost 2 to 1 in a Republican primary and trailing Governor Richard Bryan and former Governor Mike O'Callaghan by similar or greater margins in the general elections—astonishingly weak showings for an incumbent. But Hecht seems determined not to step aside.

Nevada's junior Senator is Harry Reid, who while still in his 40s has had what amounts to two political careers in Nevada. He went to the legislature back in 1968 and was elected lieutenant governor in 1970; from there he challenged and nearly beat Laxalt when he was just 35. He lost a race for mayor of Las Vegas in 1976, and then became head of the Gaming Commission from 1977 to 1981—a position than which there is none more sensitive in Nevada. When Santini ran for the Senate in 1982, Reid ran for the new 1st District seat that covers most of Las Vegas and suburbs—the 1980 Census gave Nevada for the first time a second House member—and won. Reelected in 1984, he had no serious competition for the Democratic nomination for the Laxalt seat.

In contrast, Santini entered the race under circumstances which fatally compromised his campaign. Days after Laxalt's announcement, hours before the state law's deadline, he switched to the Republican Party and filed for Laxalt's seat. Voters who themselves are not at all averse from switching parties and splitting their tickets nonetheless resent it when a politician does so for reasons reeking of opportunism and without some compulsion from principle; and they could not help but regard the switch by Santini, who had been quite comfortable running for the Senate as a Democrat just four years before, as nothing but opportunism. It also made Santini less than plausible as a clone of Laxalt or as a favorite of Ronald Reagan, who came in and spoke for him no less than three times. Reid ran devastating ads, crafted by Michael Kaye, which used Santini quotes to tweak him about his party switch, his 1982 absenteeism record, and his vote to save Tip O'Neill's limousine, and painted Reid as David to the Republicans' Goliath.

The ads worked also because they emphasized Reid's own strengths. He is a quiet, almost mousy man, a religious Mormon and straight arrow, but he also has a quiet sense of humor and a considerable ambition. His voting record is somewhat conservative, especially on cultural issues, and did not differ much with Santini in debates. In the Senate he has seats on the Appropriations and Environment Committees—both of local importance to Nevada.

Presidential politics. In the 1940s, Nevada was a Democratic state; in the 1960s, it was divided much as the nation was, voting narrowly for John Kennedy in 1960 and Richard Nixon in 1968. Now it is heavily Republican. Ronald Reagan carried the state 63%–27% over Jimmy Carter and 66%–32% over Walter Mondale; there is simply not much backing for national Democrats here any more. New residents, attracted by Nevada's glitz and sure they're smarter than the rubes, have been heavily Republican. Nevada at one time had a presidential primary, predictably ignored by the candidates.

1st Congressional District. Nevada's congressional districts are of vastly different physical size; the 1st consists of the southern half, roughly, of Clark County, and the 2d is the whole rest of the state. The 1st includes almost all of Las Vegas, the Strip (actually in a suburban area called Paradise Valley), North Las Vegas with its large black population, and the Hoover Dam area. It is a solidly Democratic constituency in state elections, but seriously contested in congressional elections; after all, Nevada has few voters who like the Democrats' national politics. When Reid ran for the Senate in 1986, the district was seriously contested. Bob Ryan, a blind state Senator, won the Republican primary and ran a game campaign, but lost by a narrow margin to Democratic state Senator James Bilbray, 54%–44%; this was one of many districts which were seriously contested in which the Democrat significantly outspent the Republican. This was not Bilbray's first brush with congressional politics: he spent four years in his 20s on Cannon's staff, and at age 34 beat conservative congressman-at-large Walter Baring in the 1972 Democratic primary. But he couldn't win statewide in that Republican year, and lost to a Republican who lost two years later to Santini. Bilbray has seats on the Foreign Affairs and Small Business Committees.

2d Congressional District. This is the more Republican district. The 2d's portion of Clark County—about one-sixth of the whole district—is heavily Democratic; most of the Cow Counties and Reno's Washoe County are heavily Republican. The 1982 election went to Paul Laxalt's candidate, Barbara Vucanovich. A longtime Republican worker, she managed Laxalt's Reno office after he went to the Senate. He urged her to get into the race, appeared on TV spots for her in the primary, helped her to raise money in the general. A strong Reagan supporter, Vucanovich has seats on the Interior and House Administration Committees. She sits on the Public Lands Subcommittee, where the Democrats tried to get her to support more wilderness land in Nevada; she is temperamentally more inclined to the Sagebrush Rebellion point of view. When Laxalt announced his retirement from the Senate, she was brushed aside as a possible candidate—something which many Nevadans resented, and she had a right to resent too; she certainly would have entered the race with fewer handicaps than Jim Santini. Against a well-known opponent, Reno Mayor and state Democratic chairman Pete Sferrazza, she won 58% of the vote in 1986—not overwhelming, but an indication that this is a safe seat for her.

The People: Est. Pop. 1986: 963,000; Pop. 1980: 800,493, up 20.3% 1980–86 and 63.8% 1970–80; 0.40% of U.S. total, 43d largest. 20% with 1–3 yrs. col., 15% with 4+ yrs. col.; 8.7% below poverty level. Single ancestry: 10% English, 7% German, 4% Irish, Italian, 1% French, Polish, Swedish, Scottish, Norwegian, Dutch, Russian. Households (1980): 68% family, 36% with children, 56% married couples; 40.4% housing units rented; median monthly rent: $268; median house value: $69,200. Voting age pop. (1980): 584,694; 6% Spanish origin, 5% Black, 2% Asian origin, 1% American Indian. Registered voters (1986): 367,596; 183,971 D (50%), 157,700 R (43%), 25,233 unaffiliated (7%), 692 minor parties.

1986 Share of Federal Tax Burden: $3,180,100,000; 0.42% of U.S. total, 39th largest.

1986 Share of Federal Expenditures

	Total		Non-Defense		Defense	
Total Expend	$3,723m	(0.45%)	$3,172m	(0.53%)	$552m	(0.24%)
St/Lcl Grants	418m	(0.37%)	418m	(0.37%)	0m	(0%)
Salary/Wages	476m	(0.39%)	233m	(0.40%)	243m	(0.69%)
Pymnts to Indiv	1,378m	(0.38%)	1,210m	(0.35%)	168m	(0.62%)
Procurement	1,426m	(0.69%)	1285m	(2.31%)	141m	(0.15%)
Research/Other	25m	(0.09%)	25m	(0.09%)	0m	(0.18%)

Political Lineup: Governor, Richard H. Bryan (D); Lt. Gov., Bob Miller (D); Secy. of State, Frankie Sue Del Papa (D); Atty. Gen., Brian McKay (R); Treasurer, Ken Santor (R); Controller, Darrel R. Daines (R). State Senate, 21 (12 R and 9 R); State Assembly, 42 (29 R and 13 D). Senators, Jacob (Chic) Hecht (R) and Harry Reid (D). Representatives, 2 (1 D and 1 R).

1984 Presidential Vote

Reagan (R) . . . . 188,770　(66%)
Mondale (D) . . . . 91,655　(32%)

1980 Presidential Vote

Reagan (R) . . . . 155,017　(63%)
Carter (D) . . . . 66,666　(27%)
Anderson (I) . . . . 17,651　(7%)
Others . . . . 8,551　(3%)

GOVERNOR
Gov. Richard H. Bryan (D)

Elected 1982, term expires Jan. 1991; b. July 16, 1937, Washington D.C.; home, Carson City; U. of NV, B.A. 1959, U. of CA, Hastings Col. of Law, LL.B. 1963; Episcopalian; married (Bonnie).

Career: Dpty. Dist. Atty., Clark Cnty., 1964–66; Clark Cnty. Public Defender, 1966–68; Counsel to the Clark Cnty. Juv. Crt., 1968–69; NV Assembly, 1969–73; NV Senate, 1973–79; Atty. Gen. of NV, 1978–83.

Office: Executive Chambers, Capitol Bldg., Carson City 89710, 702-885-5670.

Election Results

1986 gen.	Richard H. Bryan (D)	187,268	(72%)
	Patty Cafferata (R)	65,081	(25%)
1986 prim.	Richard H. Bryan (D)	71,920	(80%)
	Herb Tobman (D)	13,776	(15%)
1982 gen.	Richard H. Bryan (D)	128,132	(53%)
	Robert F. List (R)	100,104	(42%)

SENATORS
Sen. Jacob (Chic) Hecht (R)

Elected 1982, seat up 1988; b. Nov. 30, 1928, Cape Girardeau, MO; home, Las Vegas; Washington U., St. Louis, B.S. 1949; Jewish; married (Gail).

Career: Army Counter-intelligence, 1951–53; Owner, clothing store, 1954–82; NV Senate, 1967–75, Minor. Ldr., 1968; S. NV Chmn. of Reagan for Pres., 1976; NV Dpty. Dir., Reagan for Pres., 1980.

Offices: 420 HSOB 20510, 202-224-6244. Also 300 Las Vegas Blvd. S., Las Vegas 89101, 702-388-6605; 300 Booth St., Ste. 2014, Reno 89509, 702-784-5007; and 308 N. Curry St., Rm. 201, Carson City 89701, 702-885-9111.

Committees: *Banking, Housing, and Urban Affairs* (5th of 9 R). Subcommittees: Housing and Urban Affairs; Securities. *Energy and Natural Resources* (8th of 9 R). Subcommittees: Energy Research and Development; Mineral Resources Development and Production (Ranking Member); Public Lands, National Parks and Forests. *Select Committee on Intelligence* (6th of 7 R).

Group Ratings

	ADA	ACLU	COPE	CFA	LCV	ACU	NTU	NSI	COC	CEI
1986	0	0	3	0	8	96	58	100	100	84
1985	0	—	4	7	—	100	67	—	93	—

National Journal Ratings

	1986 LIB — 1986 CONS		1985 LIB — 1985 CONS	
Economic	16%	— 76%	0%	— 86%
Social	0%	— 91%	17%	— 76%
Foreign	0%	— 86%	0%	— 88%

Key Votes

1) Ease Gun Cont	FOR	5) Grm-Rdmn Def Red	FOR	9) Rehnquist Nom	FOR
2) Immig Reform	FOR	6) Contra Aid	FOR	10) Tax Reform	FOR
3) Lmt Text Imp	AGN	7) SDI Funding	FOR	11) Drug Death Pen	AGN
4) Aid Tobac Ind	FOR	8) Lmt PAC Contrib	AGN	12) S Africa Sanc	AGN

Election Results

1982 general	Jacob (Chic) Hecht (R)	120,377	(50%)	($1,657,070)
	Howard W. Cannon (D)	114,720	(48%)	($1,592,094)
1982 primary	Jacob (Chic) Hecht (R)	26,940	(39%)	
	R. Fore (R)	17,065	(25%)	
	J. Kenney (R)	12,191	(18%)	
	Two others (R)	7,291	(11%)	
	Others	5,411	(8%)	
1976 general	Howard W. Cannon (D)	127,214	(63%)	($405,380)
	David Towell (R).....................	63,471	(31%)	($54,842)

Campaign Contributions and Expenditures

1982		Direct Cont. 1982		PACS Breakdown			
Receipts	$1,025,847	Indiv.	$398,655	Agr	$2,000	Ideo	$92,000
Expend.	$1,657,070	Party	$26,040	Bus	$110,752	Lbr	$0
Unspent	$44,648	PACS	$250,010	Hlth	$1,300	Prof	$1,000
		Cand.	$370,000				

Sen. Harry Reid (D)

Elected 1986, seat up 1992; b. Dec. 2, 1922, Searchlight; home, Searchlight; UT St. U., B.S. 1961, Geo. Wash. Sch. of Law, J.D. 1964; Mormon; married (Landra).

Career: Practicing atty.; City Atty., Henderson, 1964–66; NV Assembly, 1969–70; Lt. Gov. of NV, 1970–74; Chmn., NV Gaming Comm., 1977–81; U.S. House of Reps., 1982–86.

Offices: 702 HSOB 20510, 202-224-3542. Also 300 Booth St., Reno 89509, 702-784-5568; 701 Bridger Rd., 7th floor, Las Vegas 89101, 702-388-6547; and 705 N. Plaza St., Carson City 89701, 702-883-1930.

Committees: *Appropriations* (10th of 16 D). Subcommittees: District of Columbia; Interior; Legislative Branch; Military Construction. *Environment and Public Works* (8th of 9 D). Subcommittees: Hazardous Wastes and Toxic Substances; Water Resources, Transportation and Infrastructure. *Select Committee on Aging* (10th of 10 D).

Group Ratings (as Member of U.S. House of Representatives)

	ADA	ACLU	COPE	CFA	LCV	ACU	NTU	NSI	COC	CEI
1986	60	45	89	92	60	89	46	20	44	29
1985	55	—	87	83	—	58	27	—	32	—

National Journal Ratings (as Member of U.S. House of Representatives)

	1986 LIB — 1986 CONS			1985 LIB — 1985 CONS		
Economic	62%	—	35%	65%	—	33%
Social	49%	—	49%	44%	—	54%
Foreign	51%	—	48%	57%	—	42%

Key Votes (as Member of U.S. House of Representatives)

1) Lmt Cln Water Act	AGN	5) Retain Gun Cont	AGN	9) Aid Angola Reb	AGN
2) Rpl Tobac Sub	FOR	6) Contra Aid	AGN	10) Tax Reform	FOR
3) Grm-Rdmn Def Red	FOR	7) Lmt Text Imp	FOR	11) S Africa Sanc	FOR
4) Ban Polygraph	FOR	8) Lmt SDI	AGN	12) Immig Reform	AGN

Election Results

1986 general	Harry Reid (D)	130,955	(50%)	($2,055,756)
	Jim Santini (R)	116,606	(45%)	($2,656,747)
	Others	14,271	(5%)	
1986 primary	Harry Reid (D)	74,275	(83%)	
	Manny Beals (D)	7,039	(8%)	
	Others	8,486	(9%)	
1980 general	Paul Laxalt (R)	144,224	(59%)	($1,126,826)
	Mary Gojack (D)	92,129	(37%)	($285,619)
	Others	3,163	(4%)	

Campaign Contributions and Expenditures

1985-86		Direct Cont. 1985-86		PACS Breakdown 1985-86			
Receipts	$2,089,246	Indiv.	$1,084,711	Corp.	$153,754	T/M/H	$104,716
Expend.	$2,055,756	Party	$40,000	Labor	$253,000	Agr.	$12,500
Unspent	$33,490	PACS	$796,742	Ideo.	$263,422	CWOS	$9,350
		Cand.	$30,000				

FIRST DISTRICT

The People: Pop. 1980: 400,636, up 69.5% 1970–80. Households (1980): 67% family, 36% with children, 54% married couples; 42.3% housing units rented; median monthly rent: $267; median house value: $68,400. Voting age pop. (1980): 292,870; 8% Black, 7% Spanish origin, 2% Asian origin, 1% American Indian.

1984 Presidential Vote:			
	Reagan (R)	82,265	(62%)
	Mondale (D)	47,156	(36%)

Rep. James Bilbray (D)

Elected 1986; b. May 19, 1938, Las Vegas; home, Las Vegas; U. of NV, American U., B.A. 1962, J.D. 1964; Roman Catholic; married (Michaelene).

Career: Alt. Municipal Judge, Las Vegas 1978–80; NV Senate, 1980–86; U. Regent, U. of NV, 1968–72.

Offices: 1431 LHOB 20515, 202-225-5965. Also 1701 W. Charleston, Ste. 300, Las Vegas 89101, 702-477-7000; and 201 Lead St., Rm. 26, Henderson 89015, 702-565-4788.

Committees: *Foreign Affairs* (25th of 27 D). Subcommittees: Africa; International Economic Policy and Trade. *Small Business* (20th of 27 D). Subcommittees: Energy and Agriculture; Exports, Tourism and Special Problems. *Select Committeee on Hunger* (14th of 16 D). Task Force: Domestic Task Force.

Group Ratings and Key Votes: Newly Elected

Election Results

1986 general	James Bilbray (D)..................... 61,830	(54%)	($387,717)
	Bob Ryan (R)....................... 50,342	(44%)	($276,138)
1986 primary	James Bilbray (D)................... 16,181	(36%)	
	Helen A. Foley (D)................... 15,045	(34%)	
	Paul Fisher (D)..................... 12,950	(29%)	
1984 general	Harry M. Reid (D)................... 73,242	(56%)	($387,717)
	Peggy Cavnar (R)................... 55,391	(42%)	($366,438)

Campaign Contributions and Expenditures

1985-86		Direct Cont. 1985-86		PACS Breakdown 1985-86			
Receipts	$391,041	Indiv.	$113,574	Corp.	$18,300	T/M/H	$21,650
Expend.	$387,717	Party	$10,000	Labor	$101,125	Agr.	$250
Unspent	$3,324	PACS	$180,524	Ideo.	$37,699	CWOS	$1,500
		Cand.	$94,500				

SECOND DISTRICT

The People: Pop. 1980: 399,857, up 58.5% 1970–80. Households (1980): 69% family, 37% with children, 58% married couples; 38.5% housing units rented; median monthly rent: $269; median house value: $70,200. Voting age pop. (1980): 291,824; 5% Spanish origin, 2% Black, 2% American Indian, 2% Asian origin.

1984 Presidential Vote:

Reagan (R)....................... 106,505	(69%)
Mondale (D)..................... 44,499	(29%)

Rep. Barbara F. Vucanovich (R)

Elected 1982; b. June 22, 1921, Camp Dix, NJ; home, Reno; Manhattanville Col., 1938–39; Roman Catholic; married (George).

Career: Owner, NV franchise of Evelyn Wood Speed Reading Co., 1964–68; Owner, travel agcy., 1968–74; Campaign staffer for U.S. Sen. Paul Laxalt, 1974, 1980; Dist. Rep. for U.S. Sen. Paul Laxalt, 1974–81.

Offices: 312 CHOB 20515, 202-225-6155. Also 300 Booth St., Reno 89509, 702-784-5003; P.O. Box A, 2200 Civic Ctr. Dr., N. Las Vegas 89030, 702-399-3555.

Committees: *House Administration* (4th of 7 R). Subcommittees: Accounts; Elections. *Interior and Insular Affairs* (11th of 15 R). Subcommittees: Energy and the Environment; Mining and Natural Resources; National Parks and Public Lands. *Select Committee on Children, Youth, and Families* (5th of 10 R). Task Force: Crisis Intervention.

Group Ratings

	ADA	ACLU	COPE	CFA	LCV	ACU	NTU	NSI	COC	CEI
1986	0	0	7	17	10	86	53	100	89	65
1985	10	—	7	42	—	86	61	—	95	—

National Journal Ratings

	1986 LIB — 1986 CONS			1985 LIB — 1985 CONS		
Economic	6%	—	90%	15%	—	84%
Social	11%	—	85%	0%	—	76%
Foreign	0%	—	86%	0%	—	76%

Key Votes

1) Lmt Cln Water Act	FOR	5) Retain Gun Cont	AGN	9) Aid Angola Reb	FOR
2) Rpl Tobac Sub	FOR	6) Contra Aid	FOR	10) Tax Reform	AGN
3) Grm-Rdmn Def Red	FOR	7) Lmt Text Imp	AGN	11) S Africa Sanc	AGN
4) Ban Polygraph	AGN	8) Limit SDI	AGN	12) Immig Reform	FOR

Election Results

1986 general	Barbara F. Vucanovich (R)	83,479	(58%)	($367,044)
	Pete Sferrazza (D)	59,433	(42%)	($69,777)
1986 primary	Barbara F. Vucanovich (R) unopposed			
1984 general	Barbara F. Vucanovich (R)	99,775	(71%)	($398,177)
	Andrew L. Barbano (D)	36,130	(26%)	($13,390)

Campaign Contributions and Expenditures

1985-86		Direct Cont. 1985-86		PACS Breakdown 1985-86			
Receipts	$328,346	Indiv.	$194,423	Corp.	$63,800	T/M/H	$39,274
Expend.	$367,044	Party	$27,560	Labor	$3,750	Agr.	$500
Unspent	$8,158	PACS	$118,972	Ideo.	$7,450	CWOS	$3,648

NEW HAMPSHIRE

There are worse ways to choose a leader—hereditary monarchy, for example, or by consensus within an aged Politburo—but one wonders what history's verdict will be as it records how the 240 million people of the greatest nation in the free world allowed some 250,000 voters off in one odd corner of the country to winnow down, from a field of dozens of candidates trudging through the melting snow and gooey mud of small industrial cities and tiny New England towns, the list of three or four serious competitors for the preeminent position in American government and American life. Yet that is what the New Hampshire primary, along with the Iowa precinct caucuses held eight days before, amounts to. New Hampshire has had the nation's first presidential primary since 1920 and has passed a law setting its primary a week before anyone else's in order to keep it first (no one knows what would happen if another state passed a law setting its primary for the same day as New Hampshire's). For three decades New Hampshire selected slates of unpledged delegates; then in 1952 it figured out that its leverage would be vastly increased by having contests, and no general election winner since has come in anywhere but first in the New Hampshire primary. New Hampshire is less likely to forecast the nominee of the losing party, and has done so only in picking an incumbent vice president in 1960 and incumbent Presidents in 1976 and 1980. But by giving front-runners fewer votes than expected (Barry Goldwater in 1964, Lyndon Johnson in 1968, Edmund Muskie in 1972, Walter Mondale in 1984) it has helped determine the course of the race for what turned out to be the losing party's nomination, in the process propelling candidates who did better than expected (Henry Cabot Lodge in 1964, Eugene McCarthy in 1968, George McGovern in 1972, Gary Hart in 1984) to national attention.

Yet the presidential primary takes place in a state whose politics otherwise can lay no claim to being typical. Nor would New Hampshire voters claim it is: most are proud of their state's distinctiveness and success. New Hampshire is one of the nation's fastest-growing states, with the nation's lowest unemployment rate during much of the 1980s. It is also one of the few with no sales or income tax, and that is no coincidence, say many New Hampshirites: from the early 1960s, when other states were scrambling to adopt one broad-based tax or another so they could increase spending, through the middle 1980s, New Hampshire's population rose from 600,000 to over 1 million. It is a spot of the Sun Belt far off in the Northeast.

If New Hampshire's economy is atypical, so is its electorate. In a nation where for years more voters have said they were Democrats than Republicans, New Hampshire has been one of the most Republican states. Its Democratic electorate, heavy with mill workers of French-Canadian descent who vote Republican in every general election, is different from that in any other state. Its Republicans are more numerous and, arguably, more representative, but they are an odd mixture of back-country Yankees and high tech engineers. The primary gives undue prominence to what seems an unusually large number of living former Republican governors, whose support is avidly sought and whose pronouncements on the merits of the contenders are taken with utmost seriousness. The best that can be said for the New Hampshire primaries is that they are the main arena for what columnist Mark Shields calls retail politics: a candidate here can actually talk to voters personally, and is expected to do so. It is just about the only place in the nation that presidential candidates listen to—and seek to impress—ordinary citizens. Retail campaigning is possible, and expected, because the electorate is small and the state is a geographically manageable size; more than two-thirds of its citizens live clustered in the southern half of the state, not much more than 90 minutes from Boston's Logan Airport. But it's not clear that the skills at a premium in retail politics are what the nation always needs in the White House.

Further, a case can be made that the emphasis on retail politics may have a perverse impact on the political process. It works against front-runners, who are burdened with large entourages and great expectations; it gives a premium to candidates unencumbered by the duties of public office, and able, because of their extreme or simple views on issues, to mobilize volunteers. There is also a premium on novelty. New Hampshire voters are aware that they are the first to vote in the process, and they seem eager to give little-known candidates a chance, on the theory that if they don't turn out to be up to the job voters in other states can reject them later. So they cast votes which they do not intend to be taken entirely seriously. A week before the 1984 primary only a handful of voters knew anything at all about Gary Hart. It stretches credulity to say that the 37,702 (37% of the total) who voted for him a week later were sure they wanted him in the White House; at most they wanted him winnowed in, rather than winnowed out of, the field. Similarly with Jimmy Carter in 1976 (who won with 28%, exactly 23,733 votes), George McGovern in 1972 (second with 37%), Eugene McCarthy in 1968 (second to a write-in with 42%), Henry Cabot Lodge (who won with 36% as a write-in while he was ambassador in Saigon) in 1964, and Estes Kefauver in 1952 (55% against Harry Truman). None carried New Hampshire in November, or would have if nominated.

One argument often made against the New Hampshire primary is the prominence it gave to the *Manchester Union Leader* and its late publisher William Loeb. Actually Loeb, who died in 1981, never swayed that many votes in presidential primaries. His real clout lay in state politics. In the early 1960s New Hampshire was only one of several states without a state income or sales tax. Many politicians here as elsewhere thought state government could use more revenue, but Loeb disagreed, and called on all candidates for governor to "take the pledge"—not to sign a sales or income tax bill. Some declined and were defeated: Republican Walter Peterson in 1972, Democrat Hugh Gallen in 1982. The result is lots of economic growth and low levels of public services. New Hampshire's taxes look nice, Massachusetts Governor Michael Dukakis has said, but you wouldn't want to live there if you have a child with a serious handicap. You might not like either the ticky-tack subdivisions and storefronts that have spoiled much of the woodsy environment. Yet you have to concede that a policy that has helped New Hampshire grow nearly 40% since 1970 (while Massachusetts has grown just 3%) and still to have a labor shortage is a success. Businesses came across the New Hampshire line or started up there; wages and salaries increased and the old, long-abandoned textile mills of Manchester and Nashua were occupied by high-tech firms. Now New Hampshire is being flattered by imitation: high tax states, including Massachusetts, have been forced to lower their tax rates, and have ended up the more prosperous for it.

NEW HAMPSHIRE — Congressional Districts, Counties,
County Subdivisions, and Places — *(2 Districts)*

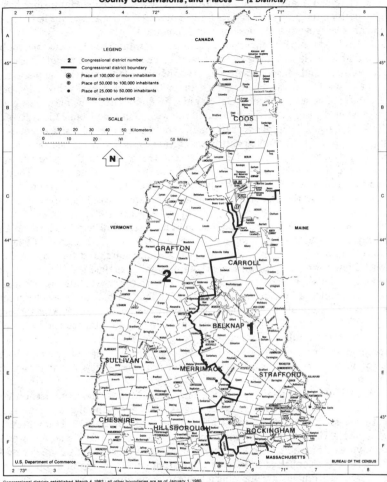

Congressional districts established March 4, 1982 ; all other boundaries are as of January 1, 1980.

The success of New Hampshire's low-tax policy has had a limited effect on its other politics: Democratic primary voters still seem interested mainly in novelty and giving an outsider a shot, while Republicans here, who have always been conservative, have a large enough electorate that they are not narrow in any noteworthy way. In general elections, New Hampshire, which voted 20 years ago close to the national average, is now one of the most Republican states; after all, it's been attracting enthusiasts for low taxes by the tens of thousands for two decades now. But that's part of the state's local, not presidential, politics. In late February or early March, within 24 hours after the primary returns are in, the politicians, their camp followers, and the media are gone. New Hampshire, with its four safe Republican electoral votes, seldom sees a national candidate again.

Governor. The key issues in state politics have been "the pledge" and the Seabrook nuclear plant. The pledge has helped elect Republican governors; opposition to Seabrook, or more specifically, to the utility's desire to bill customers for the huge costs of construction work in progress, helps Democrats. Republican Governor John Sununu is a firm believer in both the pledge and Seabrook. As an engineer and a professor at Tufts, he is familiar with Taxachusetts, as many folks here call it, and is proud of cutting the few taxes New Hampshire has; he thinks the state gets better education and services for less money if cities and towns have to pony up the money and can keep government close-by and accountable.

His problem is Seabrook: he believes in nuclear power, wants the plant completed, but by now it is going to cost at least $5 billion and will raise electricity rates in a high energy cost state. Anti-nuclear activists and Massachusetts Governor Michael Dukakis fear the plant might not be safe. Sununu upset Democrat Hugh Gallen in 1982 and won easily in 1984, but in 1986 Democrat Paul McEachern, a former Gallen aide, made Seabrook his major issue and carried the eastern edge of the state near Seabrook and the west along the Connecticut River, losing by only a 54%–46% margin. That means that Sununu could be on the defensive again in 1988. New Hampshire, by the way, has antique political institutions: it is one of the last three states to elect governors every two years, it has an executive council to advise the governor and rule on appointments, and it has a House with 400 members, the most in the nation. They are paid a pittance, and a great many are retirees, students, housewives, and others who aren't tied to regular jobs. Sununu was the first of New Hampshire's statewide officials to endorse in the 1988 presidential contest, coming out for George Bush in February 1987.

Senators. New Hampshire has two Republican Senators, of different background and impact. Gordon Humphrey, the senior Senator, used to be an Allegheny Airlines pilot who, like many pilots, moved to low-tax, pleasant-environment New Hampshire, and then became involved in politics. With New Right fundraising support, campaigning against the Panama Canal treaties and abortion, he blindsided Senator Thomas McIntyre in the most stunning upset of 1978. At first Humphrey seemed an exotic, maladroit and ineffective; and he has not authored major legislation. But after Republicans got their majority in 1980, he began working on some smaller issues and in 1983 joined the Environment and Public Works Committee and became an ardent supporter of the Superfund and proponent of tough measures to curb acid rain. These were popular stands in environment-conscious New Hampshire, with the additional advantage that most of the costs would be paid by others (chemical companies, high-sulphur coal users in states like Ohio).

These helped Humphrey against a strong opponent, Manchester Representative Norman D'Amours, and it helped also that he was running as a Reagan Republican in a prosperous, less-government state about to give Reagan a better than 2 to 1 margin. A Humphrey ad showed D'Amours saying, "The federal government makes our country work," and followed it up with Humphrey saying, "It is the people who make the country work." He was reelected by a solid 59%–41% margin. He continues to take on interesting causes, chairing a bipartisan Congressional Task Force on Afghanistan, opposing a nuclear waste dump in New Hampshire, starting a bipartisan Congressional Coalition on Adoption. His presidential politics is unconventional too: in 1986 he was urging Colorado Senator Bill Armstrong to run, and then cast around for another candidate to support when he didn't.

The name of New Hampshire's junior Senator has now gone into the political thesaurus as the second, though not necessarily the less influential half, of Gramm–Rudman. Not less influential because Warren Rudman, after five years in the Senate, had impressed his colleagues with his seriousness and his perseverance, beginning in 1982 when he took on and licked the AMA while defending the Federal Trade Commission's regulation of doctors' fees, continuing after the 1984 election when he took the unpleasant assignment of chairing the Ethics Committee. In 1985, dismayed by the deficit, he joined forces with Texas's Phil Gramm in support of what purported to be a mechanism to automatically reduce it to zero by 1990; Rudman, however, said he doubted that the mechanism would be triggered and trusted that it would spur Congress to make tough decisions instead. History will judge whether it succeeds, but Rudman's prestige and persistence helped win it unanimous support from Senate Republicans and then widespread support from Democrats as well.

Rudman says he almost didn't run for reelection, discouraged by the ways of Washington. It was generally conceded he could win: in 1980, four years after he quit being state attorney general, he beat former Governor Wesley Powell and John Sununu in the Republican primary and then beat longtime adversary Senator John Durkin in the general 52%–48%. After Gramm–Rudman passed he decided to run and won 64%–32% over former Massachusetts Governor Endicott Peabody, a recent migrant to New Hampshire who volunteered to run when no one but a LaRouchie would. Rudman quickly picked up important assignments, including a seat on the Budget Committee which, together with his seat on Appropriations, makes him an important fiscal power even in a Democratic Senate, and a seat on the special committee investigating the Iran-contra scandal. He was close to Howard Baker in the Senate and promised to support him if he ran for President; when Baker became White House chief of staff, Rudman was thought likely to support Bob Dole. Rudman's support confers little organizational help, but considerable prestige among Republicans of all stripes.

Congressional districting. With only slight changes, New Hampshire's two congressional districts have had the same boundaries since 1881, neatly separating the Merrimack River mill towns of Manchester and Nashua, the state's largest cities. That was done to split the Catholic Democratic vote; but both cities are now high tech havens and usually go Republican.

1st Congressional District. Manchester and its suburbs cast nearly half of the 1st District's votes, and the *Manchester Union-Leader* tends to set the tone here. Manchester, nominally Democratic, votes heavily against high-tax candidates, and thus mostly for Republicans. For 10 years this district was represented by Democrat Norman D'Amours, who made bows to the *Union Leader* philosophy in his voting record, and had a strong personal base in Manchester. But when D'Amours ran for the Senate in 1984, the 1st District reverted to form and elected conservative Republican Bob Smith. A real estate agent who came from New Jersey, Smith had run twice before, running a respectable race against D'Amours in 1982; a firm opponent of taxes, he carried the small towns by margins large enough to beat former Assistant Commerce Secretary Larry Brady in the primary and then carried almost everything against liberal Executive Councillor Dudley Dudley. In 1986 he had no trouble whalloping Executive Councillor Louis Georgopoulos in the primary, but slipped a little against Democrat James Demers who raised some money and carried Portsmouth and the industrial towns on the Maine border and ran about even in the Seabrook area as well. In the House Smith is as solid an economic and foreign policy conservative as there is; his conservatism on cultural issues is tempered by bit of libertarianism. He is an early and strong supporter of Jack Kemp for President. He has not established a high profile at home or in the House, where some may still confuse him with the Bob Smith from Oregon, also a conservative Republican.

2d Congressional District. The 2d District is somewhat less urban and more Yankee than the 1st. It does include Nashua, the state's second city, the capital of Concord, and the fast-growing region around Salem on the Massachusetts border. It is a mistake, incidentally, to think that voters who live near Massachusetts share that commonwealth's views on issues. On the contrary: the reason they came to New Hampshire was to get away from Massachusetts's high taxes and cultural liberalness.

The 2d District's congressman is Judd Gregg, who was first elected in 1980. He is the son of Hugh Gregg, a former Republican governor whose support was anxiously sought by Republican presidential candidates, though his most recent choices lost (Reagan in 1976, Bush in 1980). The younger Gregg outcampaigned ten other Republicans in the 1980 primary and in the general beat the mayor of Nashua, who carried only his home city and the mill town of Berlin in the far north. Gregg won by an even wider margin in 1982. In the House he is an aggressive, partisan Republican, conservative on most issues, particularly on economics, as is appropriate in a state where the free market has done so well by people. It was Gregg who protested loud and long (and with excellent cause) when a Democratic Government Operations Subcommittee staffer (a protégé of Connecticut's Toby Moffett) altered Republican members' statements and testimony gathered during joint House committee hearings on alleged misconduct at the Environmental Protection Agency. He won a seat on the Ways and Means Committee after the 1984 election—

the first New Hampshire man there since 1853, just in time to serve during the tax reform fight; a free market advocate on most issues but not always on trade, he has worked with California Democrat Robert Matsui on a bill to pry open foreign markets to American high tech exports. He has been reelected three times with more than 70% of the vote.

The People: Est. Pop. 1986: 1,027,000; Pop. 1980: 920,610, up 11.5% 1980–86 and 24.8% 1970–80; 0.43% of U.S. total, 40th largest. 17% with 1–3 yrs. col., 18% with 4+ yrs. col.; 8.5% below poverty level. Single ancestry: 14% English, 12% French, 6% Irish, 2% German, Italian, Polish, 1% Scottish, Greek, Swedish. Households (1980): 74% family, 40% with children, 63% married couples; 32.4% housing units rented; median monthly rent: $206; median house value: $48,000. Voting age pop. (1980): 662,528; 1% Spanish origin. Registered voters (1986): 551,297; 169,371 D (30%), 202,119 R (37%), 181,767 unaffiliated (33%).

1986 Share of Federal Tax Burden: $3,338,000,000; 0.44% of U.S. total, 38th largest.

1986 Share of Federal Expenditures

	Total		Non-Defense		Defense	
Total Expend	$2,973m	(0.36%)	$2,028m	(0.34%)	$945m	(0.41%)
St/Lcl Grants	404m	(0.36%)	404m	(0.36%)	0m	(0%)
Salary/Wages	557m	(0.46%)	182m	(0.31%)	375m	(0.39%)
Pymnts to Indiv	1,447m	(0.40%)	1,349m	(0.39%)	98m	(0.95%)
Procurement	518m	(0.25%)	47m	(0.08%)	471m	(0.09%)
Research/Other	48m	(0.18%)	47m	(0.18%)	0m	(1.49%)

Political Lineup: Governor, John H. Sununu (R); Secy. of State, William Gardner (D); Treasurer, Georgie Thomas (R); Atty. Gen., Steven Merrill (R). State Senate, 24 (16 R, 2 R&D, 3 D, and 3 D&R); State House of Representatives, 400 (260 R, 36 R&D, 84 D, 20 D&R). Senators, Gordon J. Humphrey (R) and Warren Rudman (R). Representatives, 2 R.

1984 Presidential Vote:

Reagan (R)	267,051	(69%)
Mondale (D)	120,377	(31%)

1984 Democratic Presidential Primary

Hart	37,702	(37%)
Mondale	28,173	(28%)
Glenn	12,088	(12%)
Others	7,582	(7%)
Jackson	5,311	(5%)
McGovern	5,217	(5%)
Reagan	5,058	(5%)

1980 Presidential Vote:

Reagan (R)	221,705	(58%)
Carter (D)	108,864	(28%)
Anderson (I)	49,693	(13%)

1984 Republican Presidential Primary

Reagan	65,033	(86%)
Others	6,569	(9%)
Hart	3,968	(5%)

GOVERNOR

Gov. John H. Sununu (R)

Elected 1982, term expires Jan. 1989; b. July 2, 1939, Havana, Cuba; home, Salem; MIT, B.S. 1961, M.S. 1962, Ph.D. 1966; Roman Catholic; married (Nancy).

Career: Cofounder, chief engineer, Astro Dynamics, Inc., 1960–65; Tufts U., Assoc. Dean, 1968–73; Engineering consultant, 1965–82; NH House of Reps., 1973–74; Pres., JHS Engineering, 1965–82.

Office: State House, Concord 03301, 603-271-2121.

Election Results

1986 gen.	John H. Sununu (R).	134,824	(54%)
	Paul McEachern (D)	116,142	(46%)
1986 prim.	John H. Sununu (R).	44,906	(77%)
	Rodger Easton (R). . . . . , ,	12,702	(22%)
1984 gen	John H. Sununu (R).	256,571	(67%)
	Chris Spirou (D).	127,156	(33%)

SENATORS

Sen. Gordon J. Humphrey (R)

Elected 1978, seat up 1990; b. Oct. 9, 1940, Bristol, CT; home, Chichester; Geo. Wash. U., U. of MD, Burnside-Ott Aviation Inst.; Baptist; married (Patricia).

Career: Air Force, 1958–62; Pilot, 1965–78.

Offices: 531 HSOB 20510, 202-224-2841. Also One Eagle Sq., Concord 03301, 603-228-0453; 157 Main St., Berlin 03570, 603-752-2600.

Committees: *Armed Services* (3d of 9 R). Subcommittees: Strategic Forces and Nuclear Defense; Projection Forces and Regional Defense; Readiness, Sustainability and Support (Ranking Member). *Judiciary* (6th of 6 R). Subcommittees: Antitrust, Monopolies and Business Rights; Technology and the Law (Ranking Member). *Labor and Human Services* (7th of 7 R). Subcommittees: Employment and Productivity (Ranking Member); Labor.

Group Ratings

	ADA	ACLU	COPE	CFA	LCV	ACU	NTU	NSI	COC	CEI
1986	0	14	6	20	83	86	73	100	89	89
1985	5	—	6	40	—	90	73	—	83	—

National Journal Ratings

	1986 LIB — 1986 CONS			1985 LIB — 1985 CONS		
Economic	16%	—	76%	0%	—	86%
Social	20%	—	79%	24%	—	75%
Foreign	0%	—	86%	12%	—	80%

Key Votes

1) Ease Gun Cont	FOR	5) Grm-Rdmn Def Red	FOR	9) Rehnquist Nom	FOR
2) Immig Reform	AGN	6) Contra Aid	FOR	10) Tax Reform	FOR
3) Lmt Text Imp	AGN	7) SDI Funding	FOR	11) Drug Death Pen	AGN
4) Aid Tobac Ind	FOR	8) Lmt PAC Contrib	AGN	12) S Africa Sanc	AGN

Election Results

1984 general	Gordon J. Humphrey (R)	225,828	(59%)	($1,806,653)
	Norman E. D'Amours (D)	157,447	(41%)	($1,066,485)
1984 primary	Gordon J. Humphrey (R)	57,763	(100%)	
1978 general	Gordon J. Humphrey (R)	133,745	(51%)	($357,107)
	Thomas J. McIntyre (D).	127,945	(49%)	($289,628)

Campaign Contributions and Expenditures

1979-84		Direct Cont. 1979-84		PACS Breakdown 1979-84			
Receipts	$1,825,940	Indiv.	$906,761	Corp.	$436,566	T/M/H	$203,644
Expend.	$1,806,653	Party	$35,874	Labor	$13,650	Agr.	$1,500
Debts	$36,272	PACS	$742,004	Ideo.	$120,664	CWOS	$9,889
		Cand.	$50,000				

Sen. Warren Rudman (R)

Elected 1980, seat up 1992; b. May 18, 1930, Boston, MA; home, Nashua; Syracuse U., B.S. 1952, Boston Col., LL.B. 1960; Jewish; married (Shirley).

Career: Army, Korea; Practicing atty.; Atty. Gen. of NH, 1970–76; Pres., Natl. Assn. of Attys. Gen., 1975.

Offices: 530 HSOB 20510, 202-224-3324. Also Thomas J. McIntyre Fed. Bldg., 80 Daniel St., Portsmouth 03801, 603-431-5900; 125 N. Main St., Concord 03301, 603-225-7115; Norris Cotton Fed. Bldg., 275 Chestnut St., Manchester 03103, 603-666-7591; and 157 Main St., Berlin 03570, 603-752-2604.

Committees: *Appropriations* (9th of 13 R). Subcommittees: Commerce, Justice, State and Judiciary (Ranking Member); Defense; Foreign Operations; Interior; Labor, Health and Human Services, Education. *Budget* (11th of 11 R). *Governmental Affairs* (4th of 6 R). Subcommittees: Federal Spending, Budget and Accounting (Ranking Member); Government Management; Investigations. *Small Business* (3d of 9 R). Subcommittees: Innovation, Technology, and Productivity (Ranking Member); Government Contracting and Paperwork Reduction. *Select Committee on Ethics* (Ranking Member of 3 R).

Group Ratings

	ADA	ACLU	COPE	CFA	LCV	ACU	NTU	NSI	COC	CEI
1986	10	35	17	33	75	83	63	100	84	79
1985	10	—	20	47	—	68	66	—	86	—

National Journal Ratings

	1986 LIB — 1986 CONS			1985 LIB — 1985 CONS		
Economic	16%	—	76%	14%	—	83%
Social	45%	—	52%	50%	—	46%
Foreign	14%	—	82%	30%	—	69%

Key Votes

1) Ease Gun Cont	FOR	5) Grm-Rdmn Def Red	FOR	9) Rehnquist Nom	FOR
2) Immig Reform	FOR	6) Contra Aid	FOR	10) Tax Reform	FOR
3) Lmt Text Imp	FOR	7) SDI Funding	FOR	11) Drug Death Pen	AGN
4) Aid Tobac Ind	FOR	8) Lmt PAC Contrib	FOR	12) S Africa Sanc	AGN

Election Results

1986 general	Warren Rudman (R).................	154,090	(63%)	($831,098)
	Endicott Peabody (D).................	79,222	(32%)	($307,760)
1986 primary	Warren Rudman (R)..................	52,003	(98%)	
1980 general	Warren Rudman (R).................	195,559	(52%)	($634,264)
	John A. Durkin (D).................	179,455	(48%)	($676,150)

Campaign Contributions and Expenditures

1985-86		Direct Cont. 1985-86		PACS Breakdown 1985-86			
Receipts	$852,877	Indiv.	$803,674	Corp.	$8,800	T/M/H	$6,300
Expend.	$831,098	Party	$15,970	Labor	$0	Agr.	$0
Unspent	$57,085	PACS	$15,662	Ideo.	$0	CWOS	$562

FIRST DISTRICT

The People: Pop. 1980: 460,863, up 27.4% 1970–80. Households (1980): 73% family, 40% with children, 62% married couples; 33.8% housing units rented; median monthly rent: $205; median house value: $49,000. Voting age pop. (1980): 332,498; 1% Spanish origin.

1984 Presidential Vote:

	Reagan (R)	98,523	(70%)
	Mondale (D)	41,234	(29%)

Rep. Robert C. Smith (R)

Elected 1984; b. Mar. 30, 1941, Allentown, NJ; home, Tuftonboro; Lafayette Col., B.A. 1965; United Church of Christ; married (Mary Jo).

Career: Navy, Vietnam; Teacher, 1975–85; Businessman (real estate); Chmn., Gov. Wentworth Reg. Sch. Bd., 1978–83.

Offices: 506 CHOB 20515, 202-225-5456. Also Technology Center, 340 Commercial St., 2d Fl., Manchester 03101, 603-644-3387; 90 Washington St., Ste. 303, Dover 03820, 603-742-0404; and P.O. Box 737, Wolfeboro 03894, 603-569-4993.

Committees: *Science, Space and Technology* (10th of 18 R). Subcommittees: Natural Resources, Agriculture Research and Environment; Space Science and Applications. *Veterans' Affairs* (12th of 13 R). Subcommittees: Compensation, Pension and Insurance; Housing and Memorial Affairs.

Group Ratings

	ADA	ACLU	COPE	CFA	LCV	ACU	NTU	NSI	COC	CEI
1986	5	0	16	17	58	91	71	100	100	86
1985	5	—	18	50	—	90	76	—	95	—

National Journal Ratings

	1986 LIB — 1986 CONS		1985 LIB — 1985 CONS	
Economic	6% —	90%	0% —	95%
Social	18% —	78%	24% —	72%
Foreign	0% —	86%	0% —	76%

Key Votes

1) Lmt Cln Water Act	FOR	5) Retain Gun Cont	AGN	9) Aid Angola Reb	FOR
2) Rpl Tobac Sub	FOR	6) Contra Aid	FOR	10) Tax Reform	FOR
3) Grm-Rdmn Def Red	FOR	7) Lmt Text Imp	FOR	11) S Africa Sanc	AGN
4) Ban Polygraph	AGN	8) Limit SDI	AGN	12) Immig Reform	AGN

Election Results

1986 general	Robert C. Smith (R).................	70,739	(56%)	($409,068)
	James Demers (D)	54,787	(44%)	($242,845)
1986 primary	Robert C. Smith (R).................	23,899	(77%)	
	Louis Georgopoulos (R)	7,207	(23%)	
1984 general	Robert C. Smith (R).................	111,627	(59%)	($333,891)
	Dudley Dudley (D)...................	76,854	(40%)	($363,747)

Campaign Contributions and Expenditures

1985-86		Direct Cont. 1985-86		PACS Breakdown 1985-86			
Receipts	$407,080	Indiv.	$196,860	Corp.	$50,825	T/M/H	$44,530
Expend.	$409,068	Party	$12,330	Labor	$2,000	Agr.	$2,250
Unspent	$10,412	PACS	$130,501	Ideo.	$29,759	CWOS	$1,137
		Cand.	$21,536				

SECOND DISTRICT

The People: Pop. 1980: 459,747, up 22.3% 1970–80. Households (1980): 74% family, 41% with children, 64% married couples; 30.9% housing units rented; median monthly rent: $208; median house value: $46,900. Voting age pop. (1980): 330,030.

1984 Presidential Vote:

Reagan (R)	168,528	(68%)
Mondale (D)	79,143	(32%)

Rep. Judd Gregg (R)

Elected 1980; b. Feb. 14, 1947, Nashua; home, Greenfield; Columbia U., A.B. 1969, Boston U., J.D. 1972; Congregational; married (Kathleen).

Career: Practicing atty., 1976–80; Chmn., Nashua Repub. Cmtee., 1976; NH St. Exec. Cncl., 1979–80.

Offices: 308 CHOB 20515, 202-225-5206. Also NH Hwy. Hotel, Ft. Eddy Rd., Concord 03301, 603-228-0315; 1 Spring St., Nashua 03060, 603-883-0800; and 157 Main St., Berlin 03570, 603-752-5358.

Committees: *Ways and Means* (11th of 13 R). Subcommittees: Health; Select Revenue Measures.

Group Ratings

	ADA	ACLU	COPE	CFA	LCV	ACU	NTU	NSI	COC	CEI
1986	20	20	15	17	71	80	76	80	88	83
1985	10	—	13	42	—	76	72	—	86	

National Journal Ratings

	1986 LIB — 1986 CONS		1985 LIB — 1985 CONS	
Economic	10% —	88%	9% —	88%
Social	30% —	70%	41% —	56%
Foreign	36% —	64%	41% —	58%

Key Votes

1) Lmt Cln Water Act	FOR	5) Retain Gun Cont	AGN	9) Aid Angola Reb	FOR
2) Rpl Tobac Sub	FOR	6) Contra Aid	FOR	10) Tax Reform	FOR
3) Grm-Rdmn Def Red	FOR	7) Lmt Text Imp	FOR	11) S Africa Sanc	—
4) Ban Polygraph	FOR	8) Limit SDI	AGN	12) Immig Reform	AGN

Election Results

1986 general	Judd Gregg (R).......................	85,479	(74%)	($138,713)
	Laurence Craig-Green (D)..............	29,688	(26%)	($5,309)
1986 primary	Judd Gregg (R) unopposed			
1984 general	Judd Gregg (R).......................	138,975	(76%)	($86,387)
	Larry Converse (D)...................	42,257	(23%)	

Campaign Contributions and Expenditures

1985-86		Direct Cont. 1985-86		PACS Breakdown 1985-86			
Receipts	$239,333	Indiv.	$96,284	Corp.	$42,425	T/M/H	$56,225
Expend.	$138,713	Party	$3,118	Labor	$4,250	Agr.	$0
Unspent	$182,310	PACS	$120,367	Ideo.	$12,900	CWOS	$4,567

NEW JERSEY

No longer is New Jersey "a valley of humility between two mountains of conceit," as one observer called it in colonial times, when Philadelphia and New York City were no bigger than a New Jersey suburb today. New Jersey in the middle 1980s, like so many other states, has a new-found identity and a newly bursting pride. It is the home of Bruce Springsteen and of the 1987 Super Bowl-winning New York Giants; it has spawned at least two politicians of national—maybe presidential—stature, Senator Bill Bradley and Governor Thomas Kean (pronounced cane). Its Atlantic City has America's only gambling casinos outside Nevada. It is seeing its manufacturing base being overshadowed by high tech growth that builds on a large existing base, such as Bell Labs. Long overshadowed by New York and Pennsylvania, it is now growing faster than both of them, and in March 1987 surpassed Massachusetts and had the lowest unemployment rate of any of the major industrial states: 3.7%. Most Americans are becoming aware that there is more to New Jersey than the swamps of the Meadowlands and the grimy New Jersey Turnpike corridor. To the west are rolling countryside and mountains of surprising height; to the east are the mysterious Pine Barrens, still as virgin as they were in colonial times, and the kaleidoscopic variety of the resort towns of the Jersey Shore.

New Jersey's new prominence and pride have resulted partly from the fact that American urban centers increasingly are centered not in a single downtown, but on "urban villages" scattered throughout metropolitan areas. New Jersey's downtowns historically have been on the wrong side of the river, Manhattan across the Hudson and Center City Philadelphia across the Delaware. Downtown Newark, the preserve of insurance companies who have been gradually moving their major operations elsewhere, has never been a rival; certainly Trenton and Camden weren't. But the buoyant growth that produced subdivisions and shopping centers in the 1950s and 1960s suddenly in the 1980s was producing office and even entertainment centers. Private companies are making the urban corridor around Princeton into the state's biggest office center. Freeway interchanges in northern New Jersey are sprouting office buildings, corporate headquarters, and luxury hotels. State government has played an important role here. The Meadowlands complex, first developed during Brendan Byrne's terms as governor in the 1970s, has taken land once used only for truck terminals and oil tank farms and turned it into the prime real estate its proximity to Manhattan suggests it should have been all along; in the process, New Jersey has gotten its own sports teams. The legalization of casino gambling in Atlantic City, also during the Byrne years, has not only spruced up that bedraggled resort, but has made New Jersey a national entertainment center. New Jersey now has its own VHF television station, but the big network affiliates in New York and Philadelphia still give it less attention than their home states receive.

Even politics has helped New Jersey establish its identity. Public financing of gubernatorial campaigns has, at last, made New Jersey politicians personally known statewide through their TV ads, and a succession of strong governors, first Democrat Byrne and then Republican Kean, has made a genuine impact on people's lives. For years New Jersey's politics was shaped by the lack of interest in the state among its own citizens, and by its social and economic variegation. They left New Jersey vulnerable to control by a few county political bosses, to corruption, to fits of sudden enthusiasm for politicians who inevitably disappointed, and with a congressional delegation mostly ineffective in Washington and at home. Now all that is no more.

All of which makes a certain sense: for New Jersey has had all along most of the ingredients of a separate American commonwealth. The outsider's image of New Jersey is of the industrial turnpike corridor and the soot-blackened row houses that you can see before entering the Lincoln or Holland Tunnel on the way to New York. But you can find practically any kind of neighborhood you want in New Jersey. Especially in northern New Jersey, within 60 miles of New York, there are many high-income suburbs, as well as the horse farm country around Far Hills and the university town of Princeton. There are old row-house communities in Hudson County as well—but they are being changed and often renovated by new immigrants, Cubans and other Latins, who have been thronging to these once stagnant entrepôts in the 1970s and 1980s. There are old industrial towns, like Paterson with its factories on the old millrace of the Passaic River, and 1950s working-class suburbs, like those south of Elizabeth that line both sides of the Turnpike. There are retirement villages and old beach resorts and in south Jersey even a few towns that have the southern atmosphere of Delaware or the Eastern Shore of Maryland.

Governor. Thomas Kean has proved to be New Jersey's most popular governor since his ancestor William Livingston was elected to the office in 1776. While Byrne had to struggle for reelection after getting New Jersey to adopt an income tax, Kean was reelected overwhelmingly, carrying every county and winning 70% of the vote. Four years before he had not seemed so formidable: an aristocrat who speaks with an accent like that of Yankee Boston, he won a multi-candidate Republican primary with 31% of the vote and beat Representative James Florio by exactly 1,797 votes of 2.3 million cast. Moreover, though he is usually pigeonholed as a moderate to liberal Republican, he was preaching the supply-side gospel—tax cuts, enterprise zones, more market and less government—in country where that was supposed to be anathema.

But as governor, Kean took command in a state where the governor dominates government: he is the only official elected statewide, he appoints the attorney general and all county prosecutors, he can fiddle with the budget even after the legislature passes it. Kean cut at least some taxes (though he had to raise others), spent $8 million yearly on TV ads to attract tourists and build Jerseyites' morale, built highways and started a clean water environmental trust fund, taking state money out of companies with investments in South Africa. He carried the black vote against Peter Shapiro who as Essex County Executive represented half the blacks in the state; his well-organized campaign captured critical seats in the Assembly, mostly in blue-collar districts, and gave Republicans a majority. In his second term Kean has been even more venturesome, launching an education reform package and proposing in 1987 increases in state spending that leave some Republicans queasy, proposing greater aid to cities and a Clean Ocean

NEW JERSEY — Congressional Districts, Counties, and Selected Places — *(14 Districts)*

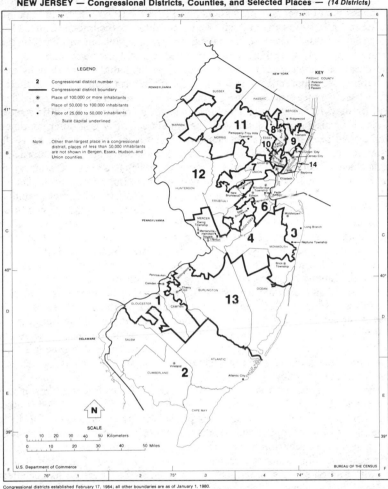

Congressional districts established February 17, 1984; all other boundaries are as of January 1, 1980.

Authority, and seeking welfare reform. But his overall vision remains one of a buoyant and growing private sector, with government providing infrastructure, a highly qualified work force, and a clean environment, but which it must not overtax or overregulate.

It is a vision with considerable appeal, and by 1987 Kean was travelling around the country to good notices, and being mentioned as a possible national candidate. It would be a little hard for him to find an opening: his reputation is similar to George Bush's, his record is in many regards similar to Pete du Pont's, and he would not balance a ticket with either one. It would help him also, in New Jersey and nationally, to elect a Republican state Senate in 1987; New Jersey has no lieutenant governor, and the state senate president—in 1987, Democrat John Russo— succeeds if the governor leaves office.

Senators. New Jersey has two Democratic Senators, one whose name is a household word, the other little known outside the state. The more famous is the younger and, in Senate terms, the more senior: Bill Bradley. He is still known to many as the basketball star at Princeton and for the New York Knicks, and for taking two years off in between on a Rhodes Scholarship. During his athletic career, he refused to make commercial endorsements and wrote *Life on the Run,* a thoughtful book about his years in professional basketball. Always interested in politics, he ran for the Senate in 1978. It was an aggressive and shrewd move. Incumbent Clifford Case looked invulnerable, but he was 74 and so liberal he lost the Republican primary. In the general, Bradley beat early supply-sider Jeffrey Bell by a decisive, but not huge, margin.

Aggressiveness and shrewdness have continued to be the hallmarks of Bradley's career, and they were never more apparent than in his fight for tax reform, a fight that resulted in the tax reform act of 1986—a measure that surely would not have gotten anywhere near becoming law without Bill Bradley. It was a stunning achievement for a politician with little seniority on the minority side of the aisle and freighted with the kind of celebrity that other politicians usually resent. Bradley had been thinking about economic issues since the campaign of 1978, the year when anti-tax sentiment was surging to the surface from Howard Jarvis's California to Edward King's Massachusetts. Unlike most other Democrats, Bradley had to face the supply-side theory and Kemp–Roth early, and he attacked them both head-on. But he wasn't satisfied either with traditional Democratic economics. Government spending was growing more rapidly than the private economy, revenues were ballooning because of inflation, and the Democratic Congress was adjusting tax rates to help the well-placed while the economy as a whole was winding down.

Bradley, joining Russell Long's Finance Committee in 1979, began a search for another way. He proceeded cautiously and quietly. He was careful to defer to committee chairmen, volunteer for housekeeping tasks, and learn the rules. Then he came forward with a proposal to require a reluctant Carter Administration to stock the nation's strategic oil reserve—and won. During the first months of the Reagan Administration, Bradley again showed himself to be an independent economic thinker by voting for Reagan budget cuts but against the Reagan supply-side tax cuts. He was one of three Senators to take this position (the others were Dale Bumpers and Ernest Hollings), which, if it had prevailed, would have reduced the deficit nearly to zero at a time of still sharp inflation. Bradley worked closely with Finance Chairman Bob Dole in 1982 on Dole's tax package; although he, like all other Democrats, voted against the bill as a whole, he provided key support for important reforms.

By this time it was apparent that Bradley was taking a far different approach to economic issues than Russell Long and other Finance Committee Democrats who used to fine-tune the economy a loophole at a time. Then he went public with the Bradley–Gephardt "fair tax," reducing the 11 tax brackets to 3, abolishing most deductions except for those most commonly used (mortgage interest, charitable contributions), and cutting tax rates sharply with the revenue gained from eliminating tax preferences. It was a proposal that repelled traditional Democrats who wanted sharply progressive rates, even if they were no longer effective, and traditional Republicans who liked tax preferences for business, even if they weren't stimulating much investment. In 1984 Jack Kemp unveiled a tax simplification program which he admitted was modeled on Bradley–Gephardt, and President Reagan, fearing that Walter Mondale would embrace it, announced in his 1984 State of the Union that Treasury Secretary Donald Regan would study the issue and recommend a reform package after the election. But Mondale plunged for a deficit-cutting tax increase instead, and Regan's Treasury I plan seemed too theoretical to ever be adopted. But these were only the first of the perils of Pauline that the Bradley tax reform always seemed to overcome. Quietly, without any publicity at all, Bradley met constantly with House members, starting with Ways and Means Chairman Dan Rostenkowski; he even played basketball (which he has otherwise given up) with younger House members.

Bradley played a key role in getting the bill through Ways and Means and the House, as Rostenkowski handsomely acknowledged. And when the bill got stalled in Senate Finance, as first one and then another Senator saved his pet preference, it was Bradley and his ideas that inspired Chairman Bob Packwood, over a pitcher of beer, to come up with the sharply lower rates that eventually produced a bill.

What is next for Bradley? Even as the tax reform bill was pending, he was already coming forward with a proposal to reduce Third World debt (by having banks scale down interest and principal on loans by 3%), by co-sponsoring with Kemp an international monetary conference, by proposing to deny business deductions for the cost of cigarette advertising. He quietly but firmly backed aid to the Nicaraguan Contras in 1986, a vote anathema to most northern Democratic activists. He chooses his issues carefully, masters them intellectually and politically, and has the discipline to prevent himself from being distracted by other matters. It has been suggested often that Bradley run for President; and if the Democrats could somehow revive the method by which Adlai Stevenson was selected in 1952, by party bosses at a deadlocked convention, the candidate they would probably choose is Bill Bradley. But he has insisted steadily that he is doing nothing to run and is not interested; the implication is that he does not feel as well prepared as he likes to be. Yet Bradley has declined to run before in what looked to be a Democratic year, turning down offers to run for Congress in 1974, and he has seen his turn come in times that to others seemed less propitious. Reelected with a solid 64% of the vote, Bradley has a safe Senate seat that does not come up again until the offyear of 1990 and the presidential year of 1996. He has a platform from which to address the most difficult of issues, his views are taken with the utmost seriousness, and he has proved he can make a major change in American government. That is not a bad position to be in seven or eight years after you enter politics.

New Jersey's other Senator, Frank Lautenberg is a Democrat who has not made as big a splash in politics. But he has his claims to distinction as a successful businessman and an upset winner in one of the nation's largest states in 1982. Back in 1952, he started a company called Automatic Data Processing, which by 1982 employed 16,000 people and processed the payroll for 1 of every 14 non-government workers in the entire country; and it also made Lautenberg, an active Democratic money-giver, able to afford spending $5 million on his own Senate campaign. Lautenberg's high tech experience also gave him an important political asset. He was seeking the seat from which Democrat Harrison Williams, after 23 years in the Senate, was expelled after his Abscam conviction, and which was being filled temporarily by Wall Street investment banker and George Bush confidant Nicholas Brady. Lautenberg won a nine-candidate Democratic primary, but was an underdog to Republican Representative Millicent Fenwick—a septuagenarian with a winning personality, known for smoking her pipe and lampooned in *Doonesbury*. But Fenwick nearly lost her primary to Jeff Bell, then awkwardly praised President Reagan when more conservative Republicans were shunning him, and never raised enough money for the nation's second most expensive media state (because you have to buy New York and Philadelphia TV, reaching nearly 20 million viewers, to reach the 7 million people of New Jersey). As a computer entrepreneur Lautenberg could argue that he could provide jobs and improve the economy at a time when practically the whole nation was convinced that the computer was the wave of the future. He won with 51% of the vote.

In the Senate he has been on the Environment and Public Works Committee, working on the Superfund and other environmental issues important to New Jersey; he has backed increased patent protection, got one of the nation's four supercomputers installed in Princeton, has a bill to strengthen U.S. inventors' patent and copyright protection abroad. He was a staunch backer of the national 21-year-old drinking age, popular in New Jersey which had a 21 drinking age while the drinking age in neighboring New York was 18 for 40 years after Repeal. He has seats on the Appropriations and Budget Committees, and a voting record among the more liberal in the Senate. Republicans have been thinking about targeting Lautenberg's seat for years. But Thomas Kean doesn't seem interested in running, and Representative Jim Courter, who had been eyeing the race for years, pulled out in 1987. Former Army general, football player, and Wall Streeter Pete Dawkins was mentioned as a possible candidate in 1987, although his connection with New Jersey is brief. But almost any candidate will start off behind Lautenberg in funds, publicity, and political astuteness.

Presidential politics. New Jersey has been a Republican state presidentially for years, although it's not always thought of as such. Its humming cities as well as its prosperous suburbs kept it Republican through much of the 1930s and 1940s; with its large Catholic population, it still went only narrowly to John Kennedy in 1960. In the close elections of 1968 and 1976 it went

Republican. No wonder Richard Nixon, now a resident of the expensive suburb of Saddle River, feels at home here.

New Jersey has a presidential primary, which has always been scheduled late in the season, and in fact elects rather sizable delegations. But turnout has always been low and it has usually been overshadowed by California. The 1984 primary was an exception. Gary Hart was hurt here when he joked to a Beverly Hills fundraiser about his bad luck in having to campaign in New Jersey while his wife got to stump in California. In a state just beginning to enjoy its identity and pride, this hurt, and Hart lost 45%–30%. That gave Walter Mondale enough delegates to clinch the nomination. The legislature voted in 1987 to move the June primary date back to late May, to take it out of California's shadow. Both Thomas Kean and Bill Bradley were mentioned early as possible presidential candidates, but by early 1987 both seemed to have taken themselves conclusively out of their parties' races.

Congressional districting. New Jersey has redistricted twice now for the 1980s—the only state to do so. Its first plan was a Democratic gerrymander passed in Brendan Byrne's last year as governor; it was thrown out by the courts. The second plan helped the Republicans win one extra seat; it was only slightly modified for 1986. The surprising thing, for all the whoop-de-doo about redistricting, is that most incumbents, even in a state weak in local media, were able to win regardless of who was drawing the lines.

The People: Est. Pop. 1986: 7,620,000; Pop. 1980: 7,364,823, up 3.5% 1980–86 and 2.7% 1970–80; 3.16% of U.S. total, 9th largest. 13% with 1–3 yrs. col., 19% with 4+ yrs. col.; 9.5% below poverty level. Single ancestry: 11% Italian, 6% Irish, German, 4% English, Polish, 1% Russian, Hungarian, Dutch, Ukrainian, Scottish, Portuguese, Greek. Households (1980): 76% family, 39% with children, 61% married couples; 38.0% housing units rented; median monthly rent: $228; median house value: $61,400. Voting age pop. (1980): 5,373,962; 11% Black, 6% Spanish origin, 1% Asian origin. Registered voters (1986): 3,773,260 (June), 3,777,278 (Nov.); 1,295,218 D (34%), 768,785 R (21%), 1,709,263 unaffiliated and minor parties (45%).

1986 Share of Federal Tax Burden: $31,583,000,000; 4.20% of U.S. total, 8th largest.

1986 Share of Federal Expenditures

	Total		Non-Defense		Defense	
Total Expend	$22,302m	(2.69%)	$17,583m	(2.93%)	$4,718m	(2.05%)
St/Lcl Grants	3,354m	(2.98%)	3,350m	(2.98%)	4m	(3.60%)
Salary/Wages	2,737m	(2.27%)	1,507m	(2.57%)	1,230m	(1.99%)
Pymnts to Indiv	11,768m	(3.23%)	11,510m	(3.32%)	258m	(1.45%)
Procurement	4,124m	(2.01%)	898m	(1.61%)	3,226m	(2.15%)
Research/Other	319m	(1.20%)	318m	(1.19%)	1m	(1.59%)

Political Lineup: Governor, Thomas H. Kean (R); Secy. of State, Jane Burgio (R); Atty. Gen., W. Cary Edwards (R); Treasurer, Feather O'Connor (R). State Senate, 40 (23 D and 17 R); State Assembly, 80 (30 D and 49 R, 1 vacancy). Senators, Bill Bradley (D) and Frank R. Lautenberg (D). Representatives, 14 (8 D and 6 R).

1984 Presidential Vote

Reagan (R) 1,933,630 (60%)
Mondale (D) 1,261,323 (39%)

1980 Presidential Vote

Reagan (R) 1,546,557 (52%)
Carter (D)............... 1,147,364 (39%)
Anderson (I) 234,632   (8%)

1984 Democratic Presidential Primary

Mondale 305,516 (45%)
Hart..................... 200,948 (30%)
Jackson 159,788 (24%)

1984 Republican Presidential Primary

Reagan 240,054 (100%)

GOVERNOR
Gov. Thomas H. Kean (R)

Elected 1981, term expires Jan. 1990; b. Apr. 21, 1935, New York City; home, Livingston; Princeton U., B.A. 1957, Columbia U., M.A. 1963; Episcopalian; married (Deborah).

Career: Educator; TV news commentator; NJ Assembly, 1968–77, Speaker, 1972–74; Chmn. and Pres., Realty Transfer Co., 1977–81.

Office: State House, 125 W. State St., CN–001, Trenton 08625, 609-292-6000.

Election Results

1985 gen.	Thomas H. Kean (R)	1,372,631	(70%)
	Peter Shapiro (D)	578,402	(30%)
1985 prim.	Thomas H. Kean (R)	151,259	(100%)
1981 gen.	Thomas H. Kean (R)	1,145,999	(45%)
	James J. Florio (D)	1,144,202	(45%)
	Eleven others	269,380	(11%)

SENATORS
Sen. Bill Bradley (D)

Elected 1978, seat up 1990; b. July 28, 1943, Crystal City, MO; home, Denville; Princeton U., B.A. 1965, Rhodes Scholar, Oxford U., M.A. 1968; Protestant; married (Ernestine).

Career: U.S. Olympic Team, 1964; Pro basketball player, New York Knicks, 1967–77.

Offices: 731 HSOB, 202-224-3224. Also P.O. Box 1720, 1609 Vauxhall Rd., Union 07083, 201-688-0960; 1 Greentree Ctr., Ste. 303, Rte. 73, Marlton 08053, 609-983-4143.

Committee: *Energy and Natural Resources* (6th of 10 D). Subcommittees: Energy Regulation and Conservation; Public Lands, National Parks and Forests; Water and Power (Chairman). *Finance* (6th of 11 D). Subcommittees: International Debt (Chairman); International Trade; Health. *Select Committee on Intelligence* (6th of 8 D). *Special Committee on Aging* (5th of 10 D).

Group Ratings

	ADA	ACLU	COPE	CFA	LCV	ACU	NTU	NSI	COC	CEI
1986	85	78	86	80	90	23	37	33	31	42
1985	90	—	86	73	—	9	30	—	28	—

National Journal Ratings

	1986 LIB	—	1986 CONS		1985 LIB	—	1985 CONS
Economic	80%	—	19%		77%	—	19%
Social	90%	—	8%		88%	—	0%
Foreign	67%	—	30%		66%	—	33%

Key Votes

1) Ease Gun Cont	—	5) Grm-Rdmn Def Red	AGN	9) Rehnquist Nom	AGN
2) Immig Reform	AGN	6) Contra Aid	FOR	10) Tax Reform	FOR
3) Lmt Text Imp	AGN	7) SDI Funding	AGN	11) Drug Death Pen	AGN
4) Aid Tobac Ind	AGN	8) Lmt PAC Contrib	FOR	12) S Africa Sanc	FOR

Election Results

1984 general	Bill Bradley (D)	1,986,644	(64%)	($5,142,316)
	Mary V. Mochary (R)...............	1,080,100	(35%)	($956,398)
1984 primary	Bill Bradley (D)	404,301	(93%)	
	Elliot Greenspan (D).................	30,680	(7%)	
1978 general	Bill Bradley (D)	1,082,960	(56%)	($1,688,499)
	Jeffrey Bell (R).....................	844,200	(43%)	($1,418,931)

Campaign Contributions and Expenditures

1979-84		Direct Cont. 1979-84		PACS Breakdown 1979-84			
Receipts	$5,497,613	Indiv.	$4,276,333	Corp.	$319,508	T/M/H	$217,020
Expend.	$5,142,316*	Party	$5,480	Labor	$173,639	Agr.	$4,500
Unspent	$283,675	PACS	$869,400	Ideo.	$121,796	CWOS	$20,700
		Cand.	$2,526				

*Includes $175,000 debt retirement from 1978 campaign.

Sen. Frank R. Lautenberg (D)

Elected 1982, seat up 1988; b. Jan. 23, 1924, Paterson; home, Montclair; Columbia U., B.S. 1949; Jewish; married (Lois).

Career: Army, WWII; Cofounder, Automatic Data Processing, 1952–82; Commissioner, Port Authority of NY and NJ, 1978–82.

Offices: 717 HSOB 20510, 202-224-4744. Also Gateway 1, Gateway Ctr., Newark 07102, 201-645-3030; Court Plaza N., 25 Main St., Hackensack 07601, 201-342-0610, 201-342-0610; Parkade Bldg., Ste. 225, 518 Market St., Camden 08102, 609-757-5353.

Committees: *Appropriations* (13th of 16 D). Subcommittees: Commerce, Justice, State, and Judiciary; District of Columbia; Foreign Operations; HUD–Independent Agencies; Transportation (Chairman). *Budget* (7th of 13 D). *Environment and Public Works* (5th of 7 D). Subcommittees: Environmental Protection; Hazardous Wastes and Toxic Substances; Superfund and Environmental Oversight (Chairman).

Group Ratings

	ADA	ACLU	COPE	CFA	LCV	ACU	NTU	NSI	COC	CEI
1986	85	92	95	87	99	17	41	10	22	27
1985	85	—	94	93	—	4	30	—	32	—

National Journal Ratings

	1986 LIB — 1986 CONS			1985 LIB — 1985 CONS		
Economic	94%	—	0%	83%	—	16%
Social	92%	—	0%	88%	—	0%
Foreign	75%	—	0%	74%	—	23%

Key Votes

1) Ease Gun Cont	AGN	5) Grm-Rdmn Def Red	AGN	9) Rehnquist Nom	AGN
2) Immig Reform	AGN	6) Contra Aid	AGN	10) Tax Reform	FOR
3) Lmt Text Imp	FOR	7) SDI Funding	AGN	11) Drug Death Pen	—
4) Aid Tobac Ind	AGN	8) Lmt PAC Contrib	FOR	12) S Africa Sanc	FOR

Election Results

1982 general	Frank R. Lautenberg (D)	1,117,549	(51%)	($6,435,743)
	Millicent Fenwick (R).	1,047,626	(48%)	($2,606,633)
1982 primary	Frank R. Lautenberg (D)	104,666	(26%)	
	Andy Maguire (D)	92,878	(23%)	
	Joseph A. LeFante (D)	81,440	(20%)	
	Barbara Boggs Sigmund (D)	45,708	(11%)	
	Howard Rosen (D)	28,427	(7%)	
	Five others (D)	49,840	(12%)	
1976 general	Harrison A. Williams, Jr. (D).	1,681,140	(61%)	($610,090)
	David F. Norcross (R).	1,054,508	(38%)	($73,499)

Campaign Contributions and Expenditures

	1982		Direct Cont. 1982		PACS Breakdown			
Receipts	$6,496,088	Indiv.	$1,150,766	Agr	$0	Ideo	$13,000
Expend.	$6,435,743	Party	$25,227	Bus	$23,950	Lbr	$91,800
Unspent	$60,343	PACS	$143,899	Hlth	$250	Prof	$0
		Cand.	$5,142,812				

FIRST DISTRICT

William Penn's colonists, sailing up the Delaware River looking for a site for their settlement, didn't give much thought to the east bank, the land that is now southern New Jersey. And little wonder. Almost perfectly flat, occasionally marshy, it is punctuated every few miles by a slow-moving stream quietly snaking sluggishly through the cattails on its way from the Pine Barrens of central New Jersey to the Delaware. Philadelphia was built on the other bank of the river, and farmers seeking fertile land moved west toward the Pennsylvania Dutch country. As late as 1900, southern New Jersey was a backwater: the small industrial city of Camden, across the river from Philadelphia, once the home of Walt Whitman and later of Campbell soups and RCA records; miles of vegetable fields, producing for the huge canneries then coming on line; quiet small towns which seem even today far from any metropolis.

The great industries of the turn of the century—railroads, steel—had been moving west, to the natural place to process the great product of the first industrial revolution, steel, where the transportation lines for iron ore and coal intersected—Pittsburgh, Cleveland, Chicago. The natural place to process the great products of the second industrial revolution—organic chemicals, formed mainly of hydrocarbons—was anywhere you could ship oil cheaply and could find a skilled labor supply. One such place was along the wide, deep Delaware River, a still lightly populated area then but close to the huge city of Philadelphia. And so vast chemical complexes were built south on the Pennsylvania shore, in Delaware, and across the river in southern New Jersey. In no part of the country will you find such an intensive concentration of the petrochemical industry, and nowhere will you find such a high concentration of toxic waste, such malodorous smells, such high cancer rates as in southern New Jersey opposite Philadelphia, much of which forms the 1st Congressional District of New Jersey.

The 1st District is concentrated on the urbanized industrial riverfront, from Riverton and Palmyra, connected by bridge with northeast Philadelphia, through Camden and down to a point opposite Delaware. It proceeds inland as well, out the Lindenwold commuter line to thinly settled barren land halfway to Atlantic City. Settled first by Swedes and Dutch, it was one of the polyglot middle colonies; its 20th century industrialization brought in Irish and Italians from across the river and elsewhere. Petrochemicals provided these people with well-paying jobs, houses in the suburbs in stable communities, a level of affluence most of their parents never dreamed of. But levels of pollution and threats to health once considered tolerable or just ignored are today a major political issue. This is an area with a Democratic heritage, and a tendency to vote for the candidate who promises to do the most to clean up toxic wastes.

In House elections that is Representative James Florio, the father of the Superfund, congressional impresario of federal toxic waste legislation. This match of congressman and district came about serendipitously. Florio, a young Camden legislator, won the seat in 1974 away from a hardline Republican who had won it at the height of ethnic resentment at the trends of the 1960s. Florio got a seat on Interstate and Foreign Commerce, as it then was, not nearly so sought after as a seat on Energy and Commerce (its current name) is now. In 1978 he succeeded to the chairmanship of the subcommittee that handled railroad bills—not a terribly important post at the time: one of the two previous chairmen switched to become a Republican, and the other was defeated in a traditionally Democratic District in 1978. However, that subcommittee also had jurisdiction over the Superfund.

The idea was to accumulate money for cleaning up toxic wastes by assessing major chemical companies and other polluters; naturally, great sums of money were at stake in the details, and the bills were heavily lobbied. It was aimed at just the kind of pollution that was becoming obvious in places like the 1st district of New Jersey in the 1970s, where chemical waste dumps turned out, against everyone's expectations, to be poisoning the soil and groundwater. Florio is one of the fathers of the Superfund, and one of the members of Congress who knows the critical details of the legislation best; he is a key figure in attempts to rewrite the law, and is a force to be reckoned with by anyone who administers it. He is not always successful: his most recent bills would have provided a vast fund from a tax on industry and would have given huge fees to lawyers who brought suits; that last provision smelled like a rat to many otherwise sympathetic members. Florio was opposed by Energy and Commerce Chairman John Dingell, and stymied. It did not help Florio that he is something of a loner, a rather private man who is not always closely in touch with his Democratic colleagues.

Florio is active on other matters as well, denouncing federal aid to the maquiladoria program in which manufactured goods are assembled duty-free in border plants in Mexico, calling for tougher inspection for asbestos in New Jersey schools, and urging an investigation of the stability of insurance companies. He was unsuccessful in getting a unisex insurance bill. But he worked on the bill deregulating railroads, helped to block the sale of Conrail to the Norfolk Southern and force a public stock offering instead, and will be a key member on any efforts to reregulate railroad rates.

Through all this he has retained an interest in New Jersey politics. In 1981 he ran for governor, won the 13-candidate Democratic primary with 26%, and came within 1,797 votes of winning the general election against Thomas Kean. His electoral base is southern New Jersey, which gave him 56% of the votes he won in the primary. He was a loner here, raising his own money for the primary and relying on New Jersey's generous public financing of state campaigns for the general. But he passed up the 1982 Senate race, which Democrat Frank Lautenberg ended up winning, and decided against running for governor in 1985, when Democrat Peter Shapiro was trounced. New Jersey, with a large Italian–American population, has never had an Italian governor or Senator, and Florio, for all his aloofness and intensity, benefits from a large Italian vote as well as his south Jersey base. But he has a safe seat and an important position in the House, and it will be interesting to see if he runs for governor in 1989, when Kean's term expires.

The People: Pop. 1980: 526,069, up 6.0% 1970–80. Households (1980): 75% family, 42% with children, 59% married couples; 31.7% housing units rented; median monthly rent: $211; median house value: $39,600. Voting age pop. (1980): 370,997; 13% Black, 3% Spanish origin, 1% Asian origin.

Reagan (R)	118,015	(55%)
Mondale (D)	96,877	(45%)

Rep. James J. Florio (D)

Elected 1974; b. Aug. 29, 1937, Brooklyn, NY; home, Gloucester; Trenton St. Col., B.A. 1962, Columbia U., 1962–63, Rutgers U., J.D. 1967; Roman Catholic; divorced.

Career: Navy, 1955–58; Practicing atty., 1967–74; NJ Gen. Assembly, 1970–74.

Offices: 2162 RHOB 20515, 202-225-6501. Also 208 White Horse Pike, Ste. 5, Barrington 08007, 609-546-0888.

Committees: *Energy and Commerce* (5th of 25 D). Subcommittees: Commerce, Consumer Protection and Competitiveness (Chairman); Transportation, Tourism and Hazardous Materials. *Veterans' Affairs* (12th of 21 D). Subcommittees: Hospitals and Health Care; Housing and Memorial Affairs; Oversight and Investigations. *Select Committee on Aging* (6th of 39 D). Subcommittees: Health and Long-Term Care; Human Services.

Group Ratings

	ADA	ACLU	COPE	CFA	LCV	ACU	NTU	NSI	COC	CEI
1986	70	68	92	83	79	10	24	0	15	22
1985	85	—	91	100	—	10	32	—	14	—

National Journal Ratings

	1986 LIB — 1986 CONS			1985 LIB — 1985 CONS		
Economic	87%	—	0%	85%	—	11%
Social	78%	—	21%	62%	—	37%
Foreign	75%	—	0%	69%	—	30%

Key Votes

1) Lmt Cln Water Act	AGN	5) Retain Gun Cont	FOR	9) Aid Angola Reb	AGN
2) Rpl Tobac Sub	FOR	6) Contra Aid	AGN	10) Tax Reform	FOR
3) Grm-Rdmn Def Red	AGN	7) Lmt Text Imp	FOR	11) S Africa Sanc	FOR
4) Ban Polygraph	FOR	8) Limit SDI	FOR	12) Immig Reform	FOR

Election Results

1986 general	James J. Florio (D)	93,497	(76%)	($322,534)
	Frederick A. Busch, Jr. (R)	29,173	(24%)	($9,719)
1986 primary	James J. Florio (D)	22,581	(100%)	
1984 general	James J. Florio (D)	152,125	(72%)	($648,833)
	Frederick A. Busch, Jr. (R)	58,800	(28%)	($6,526)

Campaign Contributions and Expenditures

1985–86		Direct Cont. 1985–86		PACS Breakdown 1985–86			
Receipts	$475,582	Indiv.	$175,353	Corp.	$87,083	T/M/H	$85,295
Expend.	$322,534	Party	$847	Labor	$104,907	Agr.	$2,000
Debts	$156,949	PACS	$290,082	Ideo.	$10,297	CWOS	$500

SECOND DISTRICT

Miss America, the Boardwalk, Donald Trump—what could be more American than Atlantic City? But though it is right on the ocean, Atlantic City has been inhabited for scarcely one of the four centuries of American settlement—a product of industrialization and affluence, a resort made possible by the railroad era and by the conquest of diseases which used to make summer a time of terror for parents and doctors. The oceanfront strand from Brigantine to Cape May was America's first seaside resort, made accessible by railroad from Philadelphia in 1852; the first Boardwalk was built in 1870. This was nature for the masses, though nature was increasingly crowded out by ferris wheels and rolling chairs and crowds as dense and less orderly than those back home. Atlantic City was never elite and in the early 1970s was grim and bedraggled. But New Jersey voters legalized casino gambling for Atlantic City in 1977, and gleaming new hotels sprang up and rotting hulks were revived.

Behind the beach is swamp and flatland, the pine barrens and vegetable fields that gave New Jersey the name of Garden State. Here and there amidst this flatness are small towns and gas station intersections, communities in whose eerie calmness in the summer you can hear the mosquitoes whining. In the flatness you can also find factory towns, clustered around low-wage apparel factories or petrochemical plants on the Delaware estuary: the high tech service economy of the northeast has not reached this far in south Jersey yet. This is the land that makes up New Jersey's 2d Congressional District.

The congressman from the district, William Hughes, is a Democrat first elected in 1974. That year he beat Charles Sandman, the most vitriolic defender of Richard Nixon in the House Judiciary Committee impeachment hearings; since then he has held the district by his own talents. Hughes has always been notably more middle-of-the-road than most northern Democrats, especially on economic issues, and is something of a workhorse in the House. He chairs the Crime Subcommittee of Judiciary, and he has authored a number of measures to tighten drug laws. He was one of the prime backers of the law to keep government appointees from moving directly into jobs in industries they used to oversee. Another of his concerns is computer crime; he is the author of a new law that provides criminal penalties for unauthorized use of a computer, public or private. He has worked to ban cop-killer bullets, child pornography, product tampering, and money laundering. One of his most frustrating tasks has been to assemble big omnibus anti-crime bills, and then to see them attacked as Republicans seize on one or another controversial subsection. But he saw his Comprehensive Crime Control Act pass the Congress in 1984, and put his imprint on the drug bill Congress enacted in 1986.

Hughes tends carefully to district matters, from the Pinelands bill to ocean dumping, and has remained highly popular in this varied district. The 2d has been closely divided in close state elections, but Hughes has won reelection by wide margins. His toughest challenge was in 1980, when he won with 57% of the vote.

The People: Pop. 1980: 526,070, up 13.5% 1970–80. Households (1980): 73% family, 38% with children, 57% married couples; 31.8% housing units rented; median monthly rent: $201; median house value: $42,300. Voting age pop. (1980): 381,227; 12% Black, 3% Spanish origin.

1984 Presidential Vote:

Reagan (R)	138,241	(62%)
Mondale (D)	84,704	(38%)

Rep. William J. Hughes (D)

Elected 1974; b. Oct. 17, 1932, Salem; home, Ocean City; Rutgers U., A.B. 1955, J.D. 1958; Episcopalian; married (Nancy).

Career: Practicing atty., 1959–74; Cape May Cnty. Asst. Prosecutor, 1960–70.

Offices: 341 CHOB 20515, 202-225-6572. Also 2307 New Rd., Northfield 08225, 609-645-7957; 151 N. Broadway, P.O. Box 248, Pennsville 08070, 609-678-3333.

Committees: *Judiciary* (7th of 21 D). Subcommittees: Crime (Chairman); Monopolies and Commercial Law. *Merchant Marine and Fisheries* (7th of 25 D). Subcommittees: Coast Guard and Navigation; Fisheries and Wildlife Conservation and the Environment; Oceanography. *Select Committee on Aging* (8th of 39 D). Subcommittee: Human Services. *Select Committee on Narcotics Abuse and Control* (11th of 15 D).

Group Ratings

	ADA	ACLU	COPE	CFA	LCV	ACU	NTU	NSI	COC	CEI
1986	75	75	73	83	79	9	43	20	22	30
1985	75	—	73	83	—	19	52	—	41	—

National Journal Ratings

	1986 LIB — 1986 CONS	1985 LIB — 1985 CONS
Economic	44% — 55%	52% — 47%
Social	64% — 34%	73% — 23%
Foreign	75% — 20%	62% — 37%

Key Votes

1) Lmt Cln Water Act	AGN	5) Retain Gun Cont	FOR	9) Aid Angola Reb	AGN
2) Rpl Tobac Sub	FOR	6) Contra Aid	AGN	10) Tax Reform	FOR
3) Grm-Rdmn Def Red	AGN	7) Lmt Text Imp	FOR	11) S Africa Sanc	FOR
4) Ban Polygraph	FOR	8) Limit SDI	FOR	12) Immig Reform	AGN

Election Results

1986 general	William J. Hughes (D)	83,821	(68%)	($241,948)
	Alfred J. Bennington (R)	35,167	(29%)	($138,115)
	Len Smith	3,812	(3%)	
1986 primary	William J. Hughes (D)	12,113	(95%)	
	Robert Wesser (D)	623	(5%)	
1984 general	William J. Hughes (D)	132,841	(63%)	($147,239)
	Raymond G. Massie (R)	77,231	(37%)	($33,756)

Campaign Contributions and Expenditures

1985-86		Direct Cont. 1985-86		PACS Breakdown 1985-86			
Receipts	$247,513	Indiv.	$129,170	Corp.	$27,750	T/M/H	$35,630
Expend.	$241,948	PACS	$99,915	Labor	$30,785	Agr.	$0
Unspent	$89,313			Ideo.	$5,000	CWOS	$750

THIRD DISTRICT

The ocean is not always clean enough to swim in now, the ferris wheels and carnival rides may have chipped paint and gnashing gears, the old brick hotels lording it over the boardwalks may have no lights in their windows after the sun sets over the lagoons behind the beach—the Jersey Shore may be tattered and bedraggled, but it is still one of America's favorite resort areas, just as surely as it was one of the first. The northern section of the Jersey Shore, from Long Branch down to Point Pleasant, was connected by rail to New York early on, and by 1881 Long Branch was well enough known for its clean ocean air that President James Garfield came here to convalesce after he was shot. Today the Jersey Shore is better known to millions as the home of Bruce Springsteen, and his music comes to life when you see teenagers accelerate from a side street onto one of the four-lane highways that leads from one Shore adventure to another.

There was not much settlement here before the Shore towns were built; the dunes were bypassed by the original colonial settlers and by the Americans who continually moved west in later years. And so the beach towns took the form most desired by the kinds of people who came there, and each one is somewhat different from the others. You can find grand and rather forbidding houses in Deal, clapboard Victorians in Allenhurst, slummy neighborhoods in parts of Long Branch, stucco contemporary condominiums, freshly built to attract retiring New Yorkers afraid to remain in the city, farther south in Ocean County or a few miles back of the beach.

The northern Jersey Shore, from Sandy Hook south to Seaside Heights and some of the cities and townships inland, form the 3d Congressional District of New Jersey. In the middle the district goes inland only about a mile from the beach; politically, the district stitches together the more Democratic areas in this part of New Jersey. That's not always easy. Many newcomers to the Shore in recent years have been relatively affluent retirees leaving behind in New York things they disliked—crime, high taxes, minorities, liberal politicians.

This is the district that elects, though not always by large margins, James Howard, chairman of the House Public Works and Transportation Committee. A teacher, elected to Congress from a Republican district in the 1964 Democratic landslide, Howard has specialized in highway legislation ever since. He has been chairman of Public Works since 1980 and an important force on highway bills throughout the 1970s. For much of that time his specialty has been out of style. Environmentalists have attacked the highways and dams that traditionally have been the currency of Public Works, and voters in an affluent America tend to be less impressed by projects that provide a few temporary jobs than they used to. Still, Howard has had major successes. He brought around many big city colleagues suspicious of highways by including mass transit in the highway bill, but not so generously as to antagonize congressmen with no subways in their districts. He marshals support for pork barrel projects and has literally kept a list of those who oppose any of them, presumably to make sure they get nothing for their districts. He got a Shore Protection Act passed in 1986, and he shepherded through the Water Projects bill which, vetoed in 1986, was passed overwhelmingly and over President Reagan's veto in the first weeks of the 100th Congress in 1987. His most notable success was the roads-and-gas-tax bill he passed, in cooperation with Transportation Secretary Drew Lewis, in the 1982 lame duck session; after two years of orchestrated worrying about crumbling bridges and the nation's rotting infrastructure, Howard helped pass the gasoline tax increase that everyone not so long before considered a political impossibility. It provides continuing funds for the highway projects of the 1980s and 1990s.

It should surprise no one that Howard has channeled highway funds to his district; if he believes that highways stimulate economic growth and improve the quality of people's lives, and he does, then how could he justify denying such benefits to the people who elect him? There is already a project named after Howard in Asbury Park. Even so, Howard is not reelected automatically. His voting record is generally liberal, especially on economic issues, and he has had strong Republican opponents who held him to 50% in 1980 and 53% in 1984. In Democratic 1986, against weaker opposition, he got 59%—a comfortable win, but far short of what most committee chairmen routinely get. But he can raise vast sums operating from his chairmanship, and is resourceful enough to do things like get Drew Lewis to come to the Shore and appear with him during the campaign. But the question remains: how long can he continue to exercise great responsibilities on issues and tend to the needs of a marginal district?

The People: Pop. 1980: 526,074, up 15.4% 1970–80. Households (1980): 74% family, 38% with

children, 61% married couples; 30.8% housing units rented; median monthly rent: $243; median house value: $57,700. Voting age pop. (1980): 382,244; 7% Black, 2% Spanish origin, 1% Asian origin.

1984 Presidential Vote:

Reagan (R)	161,447	(67%)
Mondale (D)	79,811	(33%)

Rep. James J. Howard (D)

Elected 1964; b. July 24, 1927, Irvington; home, Spring Lake Heights; St. Bonaventure U., B.A. 1952, Rutgers U., M.Ed. 1958; Roman Catholic; married (Marlene).

Career: Navy, WWII; Teacher and Acting Principal, Wall Township Sch. Dist., 1952–64.

Offices: 2188 RHOB 20515, 202-225-4671. Also 808 Belmar Plaza, Belmar 07719, 201-681-3321; and 1174 Fischer Blvd., Toms River 08753, 201-929-1400.

Committees: *Public Works and Transportation* (Chairman of 32 D).

Group Ratings

	ADA	ACLU	COPE	CFA	LCV	ACU	NTU	NSI	COC	CEI
1986	85	75	94	83	68	5	19	0	18	15
1985	90	—	94	83	—	0	27	—	23	—

National Journal Ratings

	1986 LIB — 1986 CONS		1985 LIB — 1985 CONS	
Economic	87% —	0%	89% —	0%
Social	81% —	17%	73% —	23%
Foreign	75% —	20%	80% —	17%

Key Votes

1) Lmt Cln Water Act	AGN	5) Retain Gun Cont	FOR	9) Aid Angola Reb	AGN
2) Rpl Tobac Sub	AGN	6) Contra Aid	AGN	10) Tax Reform	FOR
3) Grm-Rdmn Def Red	AGN	7) Lmt Text Imp	FOR	11) S Africa Sanc	FOR
4) Ban Polygraph	FOR	8) Limit SDI	FOR	12) Immig Reform	FOR

Election Results

1986 general	James J. Howard (D)	73,743	(59%)	($540,240)
	Brian T. Kennedy (R)	51,882	(41%)	($202,242)
1986 primary	James J. Howard (D)	11,684	(95%)	
	Jeanne Martines (D)	586	(5%)	
1984 general	James J. Howard (D)	122,291	(53%)	($529,480)
	Brian T. Kennedy (R)	105,028	(46%)	($87,641)

Campaign Contributions and Expenditures

1985-86		Direct Cont. 1985-86		PACS Breakdown 1985-86			
Receipts	$600,469	Indiv.	$228,399	Corp.	$115,463	T/M/H	$82,930
Expend.	$540,240	PACS	$338,343	Labor	$123,450	Agr.	$1,000
Unspent	$79,531			Ideo.	$15,500	CWOS	$0

FOURTH DISTRICT

The 4th Congressional District of New Jersey sprawls across the middle of New Jersey, on the boundary of both New York and Philadelphia TV markets, stretching to within 5 miles of the Philadelphia city limits and within 10 miles across Raritan Bay to New York's Staten Island. The heart of the district, however, is the little industrial city of Trenton ("Trenton makes, the world takes," a large neon sign proclaims), where New Jersey's State House perches overlooking the Delaware River. The district includes the rolling hill country, suburban and rural, north of Trenton and the old industrial towns south along the Delaware. It also stretches far inland, through the northern part of the Pine Barrens, and gets within a mile of the Jersey Shore.

Trenton, like other small industrial cities on the fast-flowing rivers of the northeast, has a Democratic past—but not necessarily a Democratic present. Its Irish and Italian voters went almost unanimously for John Kennedy in 1960, but they have been displeased and even puzzled by many of the things the Democrats have done since. The 4th District has not voted for a Democratic presidential candidate for more than 20 years now, and when its Democratic congressman, Frank Thompson, was implicated in the Abscam scandal, it threw him out of office after 26 years in 1980.

The beneficiary was Republican Representative Christopher Smith, who at the time looked like one of his party's weakest candidates but now seems to be one of the strongest. He was a 27-year-old anti-abortion activist who in 1978 spent only $15,000 and got just 37% of the vote against Thompson. But Smith won easily in 1980 and has proved to be no political fluke. He has worked hard, on the floor of the House and on the Foreign Affairs Committee, to discourage abortions; he worked to get abortions excluded from federal employees' insurance coverage, and has sponsored amendments to bar foreign aid funds to organizations that encourage abortion. But his interest in human life doesn't end when the child is born. He is proud of sponsoring the Child Survival Fund, a foreign aid program designed to prevent infant deaths from diarrhea and dehydration; he worked on the bill to promote adoption of Amerasian children; he has supported spending on domestic programs to help the poor more than almost any other House Republican.

Smith has also worked the district hard. He has used his seat on the Veterans' Affairs Committee to expand veterans' services, he has struck out against toxic waste, he has gotten federal dollars for housing projects in Trenton, and he has kept in close touch with voters. His middle-of-the-road voting record and his legislative activity have refuted the idea that he is a single-issue anti-abortion politician, and in fact his record seems very close to district opinion. Serious Democrats have failed three times to beat him. Longtime Trenton state Senator Joseph Merlino was too much the old pol in 1982; the head of New Jersey's AFSCME could not carry the Trenton area with its many state employees in 1984, and a young (but older than Smith) and experienced liberal who raised plenty of money still could not prevent Smith from winning the AFL–CIO endorsement and 61% of the vote in 1986. Smith remains a sincere and dedicated opponent of abortion, and concentrates on that issue more than any other; but he is also an active congressman who has made a safe seat out of a district filled with people who grew up in working-class Democratic homes.

The People: Pop. 1980: 526,080, up 10.6% 1970–80. Households (1980): 77% family, 42% with children, 63% married couples; 29.3% housing units rented; median monthly rent: $234; median house value: $54,700. Voting age pop. (1980): 379,038; 12% Black, 2% Spanish origin, 1% Asian origin.

1984 Presidential Vote:

Reagan (R)	141,308	(59%)
Mondale (D)	98,386	(41%)

Rep. Christopher H. Smith (R)

Elected 1980; b. Mar. 4, 1953, Rahway; home, Trenton; Worcester Col., England, 1974, Trenton St. Col., B.S. 1975; Roman Catholic; married (Marie).

Career: Sales exec., family-owned sporting goods business, 1975–78; Exec. Dir., NJ Right to Life, 1976–78; Legis. Agent, NJ Senate and Assembly, 1979.

Offices: 422 CHOB 20515, 202-225-3765. Also 1720 Greenwood, Trenton 08609, 609-890-2800; 427 High St., Rm. 1, Burlington City 08016, 609-386-5534; and 655 Park Ave., Rte. 33, Freehold 07734, 201-780-0707.

Committees: *Foreign Affairs* (11th of 18 R). Subcommittees: Europe and the Middle East; Human Rights and International Organizations. *Veterans' Affairs* (6th of 13 R). Subcommittees: Education, Training and Employment (Ranking Member); Hospitals and Health Care. *Select Committee on Aging* (11th of 26 R). Subcommittee: Health and Long-Term Care.

Group Ratings

	ADA	ACLU	COPE	CFA	LCV	ACU	NTU	NSI	COC	CEI
1986	45	35	60	67	74	45	27	60	33	29
1985	65	—	58	100	—	52	39	—	41	—

National Journal Ratings

	1986 LIB — 1986 CONS	1985 LIB — 1985 CONS
Economic	50% — 48%	55% — 45%
Social	61% — 37%	36% — 60%
Foreign	44% — 55%	45% — 54%

Key Votes

1) Lmt Cln Water Act	AGN	5) Retain Gun Cont	FOR	9) Aid Angola Reb	FOR
2) Rpl Tobac Sub	FOR	6) Contra Aid	FOR	10) Tax Reform	FOR
3) Grm-Rdmn Def Red	FOR	7) Lmt Text Imp	FOR	11) S Africa Sanc	FOR
4) Ban Polygraph	FOR	8) Limit SDI	AGN	12) Immig Reform	FOR

Election Results

1986 general	Christopher H. Smith (R)	78,699	(61%)	($338,244)
	Jeffrey Laurenti (D)	49,290	(38%)	($304,077)
1986 primary	Christopher H. Smith (R)	8,008	(100%)	
1984 general	Christopher H. Smith (R)	139,295	(61%)	($289,953)
	James C. Hedden (D)	87,908	(39%)	($294,611)

Campaign Contributions and Expenditures

1985-86		Direct Cont. 1985-86		PACS Breakdown 1985-86			
Receipts	$324,732	Indiv.	$202,595	Corp.	$14,305	T/M/H	$38,900
Expend.	$338,244	Party	$12,323	Labor	$13,250	Agr.	$0
Unspent	$628	PACS	$97,051	Ideo.	$30,346	CWOS	$250

FIFTH DISTRICT

Most Americans don't think of New Jersey as a mountainous state. But if you're running for Congress in the state's 5th District, you will find yourself crossing one mountain ridge after another. The 5th sweeps across the northern edge of New Jersey, separated from New York State by one of those arrow-straight lines that make it easy to make jigsaw puzzles out of the map of the United States. It starts at the Palisades that overlook the glorious Hudson, includes the affluent suburbs built along the old Dutch farm communities of northern Bergen County, climbs over the mountains and spans the lakes of northern Passaic County, passes through old rural townships with little subdivisions filling up with young families, and finally stops at the Delaware River. At one end of the district you can look down the Hudson at the George Washington Bridge and at the other you can see through the defile of the mountains the turn-of-the-century railroad junction town of Port Jervis, New York.

About two-thirds of the 5th's residents live in the suburbs of Bergen County, most of them long-established, almost all of them very affluent, in what is officially part of the New York City metropolitan area; the city is easily reachable over the G.W. Bridge or the tunnels from these generally well-settled suburbs. The district includes most of the suburbs north of Routes 4 and, west of Paterson, 208. Paramus, at the intersection of three major highways, is known for its concentration of shopping centers; Saddle River, with beautiful houses sprawling over several-acre lots, is known now as the home of Richard Nixon. As you go west, and especially when you get over the mountains, the orientation is less to New York City and more to New Jersey; increasingly people work out here and want little or nothing to do with the City.

These are all Republican areas, and this is a safe Republican district. The congresswoman since 1980 has been Marge Roukema, who has always been well positioned on issues for this affluent constituency. Her committee assignments (Banking, Education and Labor) echo some of her community activities before she became a political candidate—founding a senior citizens' housing corporation, serving on a local school board; like some other Republican women, she brings to politics maturity and wide experience in the actual workings of civic institutions. She has expended some effort on a special committee to get the government further involved in feeding the hungry, and she is sponsoring a bill to require companies that employee more than 50 people to provide unpaid family leave of 8 weeks and 13 weeks' medical leave. But generally speaking she is a conservative on economic issues, preferring to rely on markets rather than regulation. On cultural issues her record is more varied, and she has moved to lower defense spending well below the levels requested by the Reagan Administration.

Roukema first won the seat by beating liberal Democrat Andy Maguire in 1980 when the district was entirely within Bergen County. But since redistricting her only conceivable problem has been in the Republican primary. In 1982 that was obviated when Matthew Rinaldo decided to run in the 7th District and Millicent Fenwick ran for the Senate, leaving the 12th District open for Jim Courter and the 5th for Roukema. In 1986 she had opposition from a Republican angry because of her opposition to some Reagan defense policies, but she won 75% of the vote. That indicates that this is a pretty safe seat for her.

The People: Pop. 1980: 526,075, up 3.8% 1970–80. Households (1980): 84% family, 46% with children, 72% married couples; 17.3% housing units rented; median monthly rent: $306; median house value: $78,600. Voting age pop. (1980): 377,765; 2% Spanish origin, 1% Asian origin, 1% Black.

1984 Presidential Vote: Reagan (R) 182,030   (71%)
Mondale (D) 75,000   (29%)

Rep. Margaret S. (Marge) Roukema (R)

Elected 1980; b. Sept. 19, 1929, Newark; home, Ridgewood; Montclair St. Col., B.A. 1951, Rutgers U.; Protestant; married (Richard).

Career: High sch. teacher, 1951–55; Ridgewood Bd. of Educ., 1970–73; Cofounder, Ridgewood Sr. Citizens Housing Corp., 1973; Repub. Nominee for U.S. House of Reps., 1978.

Offices: 303 CHOB 20515, 202-225-4465. Also 58 Trinity St., Newton 07860, 201-579-3039; and 555 Rte. 17 S., Ridgewood 07450, 201-447-3900.

Committees: *Banking, Finance and Urban Affairs* (8th of 20 R). Subcommittees: Financial Institutions Supervision, Regulation and Insurance; Housing and Community Development; International Development Institutions and Finance. *Education and Labor* (5th of 13 R). Subcommittees: Elementary, Secondary and Vocational Education; Labor–Management Relations (Ranking Member); Postsecondary Education. *Select Committee on Hunger* (Ranking Member of 7 R) Task Force: Domestic Task Force.

Group Ratings

	ADA	ACLU	COPE	CFA	LCV	ACU	NTU	NSI	COC	CEI
1986	30	40	27	50	58	36	53	60	78	53
1985	45	—	24	75	—	40	57	—	68	—

National Journal Ratings

	1986 LIB — 1986 CONS		1985 LIB — 1985 CONS	
Economic	23%	— 76%	31%	— 67%
Social	42%	— 57%	63%	— 33%
Foreign	41%	— 57%	63%	— 37%

Key Votes

1) Lmt Cln Water Act	AGN	5) Retain Gun Cont	FOR	9) Aid Angola Reb	FOR
2) Rpl Tobac Sub	FOR	6) Contra Aid	FOR	10) Tax Reform	FOR
3) Grm-Rdmn Def Red	FOR	7) Lmt Text Imp	FOR	11) S Africa Sanc	FOR
4) Ban Polygraph	AGN	8) Limit SDI	FOR	12) Immig Reform	AGN

Election Results

1986 general	Margaret S. (Marge) Roukema (R)	94,253	(75%)	($304,786)
	H. Vernon Jolley (D)	32,145	(25%)	($23,139)
1986 primary	Margaret S. (Marge) Roukema (R)	15,048	(75%)	
	William B. Grant (R)	5,023	(25%)	
1984 general	Margaret S. (Marge) Roukema (R)	171,979	(71%)	($296,159)
	Rose Brunetto (D)	69,666	(29%)	($69,866)

Campaign Contributions and Expenditures

1985-86		Direct Cont. 1985-86		PACS Breakdown 1985-86			
Receipts	$357,780	Indiv.	$177,060	Corp.	$67,835	T/M/H	$74,775
Expend.	$304,786	Party	$6,694	Labor	$6,800	Agr.	$0
Unspent	$89,326	PACS	$156,735	Ideo.	$5,225	CWOS	$2,100
		Cand.	$2,000				

SIXTH DISTRICT

Through the sluggish oily waters of Raritan Bay and Kill Van Kull, on either side of Staten Island, inch giant tankers filled with crude oil and feedstock for the refineries and chemical plants of New Jersey; just inland, locomotives on the Conrail main line and trucks roaring along the 12-lane-wide New Jersey Turnpike are ready to ship refined oil and chemicals to the rest of the country. This stretch of New Jersey, from Newark south to Perth Amboy, is one of the most heavily industrialized areas in America, the product of the second oil-and-chemicals, industrial revolution earlier in this century. Much of it, from Linden in Union County to south of Perth Amboy in Middlesex, and going inland to New Brunswick, forms the 6th Congressional District of New Jersey.

Here Thomas Edison came and set up his laboratory in Menlo Park, when it was still surrounded by fields but accessible to New York; and in the neighborhoods here thousands of ethnic Americans moved when they got decent jobs and could afford something better than the old row houses of Jersey City or New York. This 6th District has the largest concentration of Hungarian-Americans in the nation, in and around New Brunswick; it also has sizeable neighborhoods of Polish-Americans in Woodbridge and Italian-Americans in Perth Amboy. The children of the original immigrants have moved out into such places as Edison Township, Piscataway Township, and Sayreville, where they live in pleasant subdivisions. Middlesex County had its fastest growth in the 1950s, when New Jersey had a rising number of manufacturing jobs and the second generation of immigrants were having large numbers of babies themselves.

These suburban voters are in the process of sloughing off their Democratic heritage. John Kennedy got 58% in Middlesex County, well above his national average; Jimmy Carter did no better than average here when he ran in 1976 and 1980; Walter Mondale lost Middlesex by almost as wide a margin as he lost the next-door Monmouth. As life here has become less distinctive and less visibly different from the experiences of other Americans, its political behavior has been, in the language of political scientists, regressing toward the mean. Middlesex County had a well-known Democratic machine, run for years by David Willentz, who first gained fame in the 1930s as the prosecutor of accused Lindbergh kidnapper Bruno Hauptmann and whose Perth Amboy law office in later years somehow seemed to attract some of the nation's largest corporations as clients; his son Robert is New Jersey's Chief Justice, reappointed in 1986 by Republican Governor Kean and confirmed despite some opposition from Republicans.

The Willentz machine has pretty well determined who holds the Middlesex County congressional district since the first one was created in 1962. It has favored experienced and loyal political veterans: in 1962 it picked 57-year-old Edward Patten, then the appointive Secretary of State; in 1980 it favored 59-year-old state Senator Bernard Dwyer. His voting record is on the liberal side of the spectrum, and not only on economic issues. He is a solid leadership man, and has won important committee assignments as a result. He got a seat on Appropriations his first term, and works hard and concentrates on details: he is busy getting reimbursement for the cost of holding Mariel Cubans in state prisons, extending the dredging of Kill Van Kull, getting more money in the continuing resolution for the homeless of Middlesex County, getting more research money for basic research on fuel cells conducted by New Jersey's Engelhard Corporation. He was tapped by Speaker O'Neill for a seat on the Intelligence Committee and on the five-member delegation to observe the elections in the Philippines.

Dwyer depends on the Democratic organization to deliver votes for him, although that is a bit risky these days: in 1980 and 1984 he won only 53% and 56% of the vote. But in his mid-60s, after a political career that began on the Edison Township Council in 1958 and led to the presidency of the New Jersey Senate and membership in the U.S. Congress, Dwyer evidently prefers to continue with what has been for him a winning formula.

The People: Pop. 1980: 526,075, dn. 3.1% 1970–80. Households (1980): 77% family, 39% with children, 63% married couples; 36.9% housing units rented; median monthly rent: $259; median house value: $59,600. Voting age pop. (1980): 394,413; 8% Black, 5% Spanish origin, 1% Asian origin.

1984 Presidential Vote:	Reagan (R) 135,654	(59%)
	Mondale (D) 94,024	(41%)

Rep. Bernard J. Dwyer (D)

Elected 1980; b. Jan. 24, 1921, Perth Amboy; home, Edison; Roman Catholic; married (Lilyan).

Career: Navy, WWII; Insur. exec., 1945–80; Edison Township Cncl., 1958–70; Mayor, 1970–74; NJ Senate, 1974–80.

Offices: 404 CHOB 20515, 202-225-6301. Also 214 Smith St., Perth Amboy 08861, 201-826-4610; 86 Bayard St., New Brunswick 08901, 201-545-5655; and 628 Wood Ave., N., Linden 07036, 201-486-4600.

Committees: *Appropriations* (28th of 35 D). Subcommittees: Commerce, Justice, State, and Judiciary; Labor–Health and Human Services–Education. *Standards of Official Conduct* (3d of 6 D). *Permanent Select Committee on Intelligence* (9th of 10 D). Subcommittees: Legislative; Oversight and Evaluation.

Group Ratings

	ADA	ACLU	COPE	CFA	LCV	ACU	NTU	NSI	COC	CEI
1986	80	66	96	75	68	9	21	0	22	15
1985	80	—	95	92	—	0	29	—	23	—

National Journal Ratings

	1986 LIB — 1986 CONS		1985 LIB — 1985 CONS	
Economic	87% —	0%	89% —	0%
Social	81% —	17%	73% —	23%
Foreign	71% —	28%	80% —	17%

Key Votes

1) Lmt Cln Water Act	AGN	5) Retain Gun Cont	FOR	9) Aid Angola Reb	AGN
2) Rpl Tobac Sub	FOR	6) Contra Aid	AGN	10) Tax Reform	FOR
3) Grm-Rdmn Def Red	AGN	7) Lmt Text Imp	FOR	11) S Africa Sanc	FOR
4) Ban Polygraph	FOR	8) Limit SDI	FOR	12) Immig Reform	FOR

Election Results

1986 general	Bernard J. Dwyer (D).................. 67,460	(69%)	($115,192)
	John D. Scalamonti (R) 28,286	(29%)	($18,461)
1986 primary	Bernard J. Dwyer (D).................. 20,918	(88%)	
	Anne DeGennaro (D) 2,981	(12%)	
1984 general	Bernard J. Dwyer (D)............... 118,532	(56%)	($114,649)
	Dennis Adams (R) 90,862	(43%)	($98,826)

Campaign Contributions and Expenditures

1985-86		Direct Cont. 1985-86		PACS Breakdown 1985-86			
Receipts	$144,564	Indiv.	$32,393	Corp.	$21,300	T/M/H	$35,450
Expend.	$115,192	PACS	$104,475	Labor	$41,725	Agr.	$500
Unspent	$58,750			Ideo.	$4,500	CWOS	$1,000

SEVENTH DISTRICT

From the old industrial city of Elizabeth on Newark Bay, to its close-in suburb of Union, then out on U.S. 22, maybe the archetypical American strip highway, through the valley of the Raritan River between corduroy-like mountain ridges, stretches the 7th Congressional District of New Jersey. The district offers a nice picture of American upward mobility. Elizabeth, its largest city, now has a large Cuban and Puerto Rican population, poised it seems to move upward and out as generations of ethnics did before them. Out U.S. 22, once the main highway into New York, you pass through suburbs which once considered themselves Waspy, and are now a little more ethnic in flavor, with Italian and Spanish names and black faces now quite common (a solid majority in Plainfield) where they were seldom seen a generation ago. Out past Plainfield, you are in newer suburbs, places where young couples are starting new households and singles live in garden apartment complexes adjacent to the horse farm country of Somerset County.

The congressman from this district is a highly popular Republican, Matthew Rinaldo. He has been winning elections in the Union County suburbs since 1963. He was popular enough to win a marginal congressional seat by an overwhelming margin in 1972, and to hold on to it after an unfavorable redistricting and against a candidate, shopping center heir Adam Levin, who spent $2.3 million against him in the Democratic year of 1982. Rinaldo, who spent $719,000 himself, won 56%–43%. He has had no serious competition since.

One reason Rinaldo could raise so much money is that he is a high-ranking member of the Energy and Commerce Committee and ranking Republican on the Telecommunications Subcommittee, which has jurisdiction as well over the securities industry. It's hard to overestimate the power a man like Rinaldo, in the middle of the political spectrum, has in such a spot. The committee decides issues which can make entrepreneurs tens of millions of dollars and which may have much more effect on life in America 50 years from now than anything you see in today's headlines. Issues don't always cut on partisan lines; and on a whole series of issues the more important question is whether a member joins the younger liberals and theoretical conservatives who favor deregulation to spur competition or the older liberals and close-to-business conservatives who often favor regulation to provide stability. Rinaldo is often found with both groups because, some critics say, he has no consistent philosophy—a claim that is buttressed by the wildly different ratings he has gotten from both liberal and conservative groups in different years. He supports deregulation of AT&T but always favored oil price regulation. He is a water-carrier for certain unions and for many business interests. Rinaldo's view is that he decides particular issues on their merits and with regard to the public's views—and is rewarded by being reelected overwhelmingly every two years. He has "transcended traditional party lines," said the *Elizabeth Daily Journal* in an editorial entitled "Rinaldo, of course."

With his seniority, Rinaldo is more highly placed than highly thought of in the House. But he has come up with a winning political formula. His seat on Energy and Commerce and his often critical vote make it easy for him to raise campaign funds; he ended the 1986 campaign with $508,000 cash-on-hand. His reputation as a moderate and middle-of-the-roader make it easy for him to win elections in the 7th district, even against a free-spending opponent as in 1982. Few vested or activist interest groups have any incentive to try to beat him. So he is likely to remain in his present enviable position for some time.

The People: Pop. 1980: 526,076, dn. 6.8% 1970–80. Households (1980): 78% family, 38% with children, 64% married couples; 35.1% housing units rented; median monthly rent: $248; median house value: $73,300. Voting age pop. (1980): 393,910; 10% Black, 7% Spanish origin, 1% Asian origin.

1984 Presidential Vote:

Reagan (R)	151,973	(63%)	
Mondale (D)	88,874	(37%)	

Rep. Matthew J. Rinaldo (R)

Elected 1972; b. Sept. 1, 1931, Elizabeth; home, Union; Rutgers U., B.S. 1953, Seton Hall U., M.B.A. 1959, NYU, D.P.A. 1979; Roman Catholic; single.

Career: Pres., Union Township Zoning Bd. of Adjustment, 1962–63; Union Cnty. Bd. of Freeholders, 1963–64; NJ Senate, 1967–72.

Offices: 2469 RHOB 20515, 202-225-5361. Also 1961 Morris Ave., Union 07083, 201-687-4235; and 290 Rte. 22, Green Brook 08812, 201-981-9090.

Committees: *Energy and Commerce* (4th of 17 R). Subcommittees: Commerce, Consumer Protection and Competitiveness; Telecommunications and Finance (Ranking Member). *Select Committee on Aging* (Ranking Member of 26 R). Subcommittee: Health and Long-Term Care.

Group Ratings

	ADA	ACLU	COPE	CFA	LCV	ACU	NTU	NSI	COC	CEI
1986	45	30	82	83	68	55	27	70	28	27
1985	55	—	80	67	—	52	34	—	41	—

National Journal Ratings

	1986 LIB — 1986 CONS		1985 LIB — 1985 CONS	
Economic	60%	— 38%	59%	— 41%
Social	52%	— 46%	36%	— 60%
Foreign	41%	— 57%	41%	— 58%

Key Votes

1) Lmt Cln Water Act	AGN	5) Retain Gun Cont	FOR	9) Aid Angola Reb	FOR
2) Rpl Tobac Sub	FOR	6) Contra Aid	FOR	10) Tax Reform	—
3) Grm-Rdmn Def Red	FOR	7) Lmt Text Imp	FOR	11) S Africa Sanc	FOR
4) Ban Polygraph	FOR	8) Limit SDI	AGN	12) Immig Reform	AGN

Election Results

1986 general	Matthew J. Rinaldo (R)	92,254	(79%)	($387,616)
	June S. Fischer (D)	24,462	(21%)	($7,644)
1986 primary	Matthew J. Rinaldo (R)	10,541	(100%)	
1984 general	Matthew J. Rinaldo (R)	165,685	(74%)	($370,981)
	John F. Feeley (D)	56,798	(25%)	

Campaign Contributions and Expenditures

1985-86		Direct Cont. 1985-86		PACS Breakdown 1985-86			
Receipts	$630,990	Indiv.	$353,651	Corp.	$84,885	T/M/H	$73,365
Expend.	$387,616	Party	$2,167	Labor	$49,645	Agr.	$250
Unspent	$508,842	PACS	$224,561	Ideo.	$10,750	CWOS	$5,666

EIGHTH DISTRICT

Twenty miles was a long way to travel in the 1790s, but Alexander Hamilton journeyed the distance from his home in Manhattan into the vastness of New Jersey to see the Great Falls of the Passaic River. Watching the water surge down 72 feet—the highest falls along the East Coast—he predicted that an industrial city would rise at this place. And so it did. A century later Paterson, founded here at the Great Falls, was one of the major manufacturing cities in the United States. It developed major locomotive factories and silk mills and attracted immigrants from England, Ireland, and, after the turn of the century, Italy and Poland. Paterson was a tough town, and even as its fathers were erecting imposing public buildings, its narrow streets were buzzing with rumors of anarchist plots. The great silk strike of 1913 here was led by the revolution-minded Industrial Workers of the World.

Today Paterson is a kind of misfit in its time and place: still a manufacturing center (although neither silk nor locomotives are its mainstay) at a time when manufacturing is no longer considered the nation's prime work, still an old-fashioned central city, though it is surrounded by suburbs of New York and Newark and is an easy freeway ride away from the George Washington Bridge. Paterson is the center of New Jersey's 8th Congressional District, which includes most of the surrounding Passaic County communities and, to the south, working-class Nutley and Belleville, white collar Bloomfield, and, up on the ridge with views of New York City, the mixed-rich-and-black Montclair. To the north and west are the higher-income suburbs of Passaic County, notably Wayne Township. The political heritage of the 8th District is Democratic, less because of its radical past than because of the allegiances of its immigrant groups. But in the cultural politics of recent years, the district has moved to the right. When economic issues come to the fore, the area can go Democratic, as it did in the 1982 Senate race for Frank Lautenberg (who was a home town candidate here: his ADP computer company is headquartered in Clifton, just south of Paterson, and he lives in Montclair). But it can also go Republican, as it did twice for Ronald Reagan, and by solid margins.

The 8th District's congressman, Robert Roe, is now one of the most senior Democrats in the New Jersey delegation; he first won in a special election in 1969. Appropriately for a congressman from a district whose economy was first built on water power, the centerpiece of his whole congressional career is water. He is the third ranking member of the Public Works Committee, and it was the Water Resources Subcommittee that he chaired that fashioned the water projects bill on which President Reagan's veto was overridden in early 1987, the first major water projects bill to pass in 10 years. The bill had near-unanimous support on Capitol Hill—testimony to Roe's hard work and knowledge of detail or to his willingness to lace the bill with projects for almost every member's district, take your pick. Roe is an engineer, experienced in local government, a workaholic who is familiar with every detail in his bill. Not afraid of the charge of pork barrel politics, he has been willing to take on Presidents and beat them—as he took on Jimmy Carter in 1977 and now Reagan 10 years later.

Roe is now chairman of the Science Committee, on which he was less active until 1986. But after the space shuttle *Challenger* blew up, and with the retirement of Chairman Don Fuqua, Roe became instantly more active and brought his habit of insisting on details into play. But Science handles more than just the space program, and Roe has an exceptional opportunity here. Americans in the 1980s have recovered some of their respect and awe for what science and technology have accomplished and can do in the future; they are ready to commit the nation to more basic research and the right kind of development. But there can be too much enthusiasm too; in early 1987 Roe was urging caution in the development of the multi-billion dollar supercollider atom smasher. Knowledgeable, respected on both sides of Capitol Hill, Roe could steer the national effort in a useful direction.

Roe seems less interested than he once was in New Jersey state government. He ran a strong race for governor in 1977, running second to Brendan Byrne (and 86% in Passaic County); in 1981, he ran again but made the mistake of turning down New Jersey's public financing, and finished a distant second to colleague James Florio with 16% of the vote. But he got 86% and 71% in those races in Passaic County—strong showings which, together with his solid reelection percentages, suggest that this water specialist from the Great Falls of the Passaic has a safe seat.

The People: Pop. 1980: 526,087, dn. 6.4% 1970–80. Households (1980): 74% family, 37% with children, 57% married couples; 48.8% housing units rented; median monthly rent: $219; median house value: $66,900. Voting age pop. (1980): 390,558; 12% Black, 10% Spanish origin, 1% Asian origin.

1984 Presidential Vote:

Reagan (R)	121,422	(58%)
Mondale (D)	89,625	(42%)

Rep. Robert A. Roe (D)

Elected 1969; b. Feb. 28, 1924, Wayne; home, Wayne; OR St. U., WA St. U.; Roman Catholic; single.

Career: Army, WWII; Wayne Township Committeeman, 1955–56; Mayor, 1956–61; Passaic Cnty. Bd. of Freeholders, 1959–63, Dir., 1962–63; Commissioner, NJ Dept. of Conservation and Econ. Develop., 1963–69.

Offices: 2243 RHOB 20515, 202-225-5751. Also 158 Boonton Rd., Wayne 07470, 201-696-2077; 102 Law Bldg., 66 Hamilton St., Paterson 07505, 201-523-5152; and U.S. Post Office Bldg., Bloomfield Ave., Bloomfield 07003, 201-645-6299.

Committees: *Public Works and Transportation* (3d of 32 D). Subcommittees: Investigations and Oversight; Surface Transportation; Water Resources. *Science, Space and Technology* (Chairman). Subcommittees: Investigations and Oversight (Chairman). *Permanent Select Committee on Intelligence* (6th of 11 D). Subcommittee: Program and Budget Authorization.

Group Ratings

	ADA	ACLU	COPE	CFA	LCV	ACU	NTU	NSI	COC	CEI
1986	75	50	91	83	63	10	20	0	18	14
1985	75	—	90	67	—	11	26	—	29	—

National Journal Ratings

	1986 LIB — 1986 CONS		1985 LIB — 1985 CONS	
Economic	87% —	0%	75% —	22%
Social	61% —	37%	49% —	51%
Foreign	73% —	26%	63% —	36%

Key Votes

1) Lmt Cln Water Act	AGN	5) Retain Gun Cont	FOR	9) Aid Angola Reb	—
2) Rpl Tobac Sub	AGN	6) Contra Aid	AGN	10) Tax Reform	FOR
3) Grm-Rdmn Def Red	AGN	7) Lmt Text Imp	FOR	11) S Africa Sanc	FOR
4) Ban Polygraph	FOR	8) Limit SDI	FOR	12) Immig Reform	FOR

Election Results

1986 general	Robert A. Roe (D)	57,820	(63%)	($298,400)
	Thomas P. Zampino (R)	14,699	(37%)	($14,848)
1986 primary	Robert A. Roe (D)	13,782	(96%)	
	Arthur Fairchild (D)	610	(4%)	
1984 general	Robert A. Roe (D)	118,793	(63%)	($165,875)
	Marguerite A. Page (R)	69,973	(37%)	($2,287)

Campaign Contributions and Expenditures

1985-86		Direct Cont. 1985-86		PACS Breakdown 1985-86			
Receipts	$450,486	Indiv.	$139,908	Corp.	$80,208	T/M/H	$53,750
Expend.	$298,400	PACS	$207,807	Labor	$65,149	Agr.	$1,000
Unspent	$257,388	Cand.	$87,165	Ideo.	$6,950	CWOS	$750

NINTH DISTRICT

Few parts of New Jersey are better known to outsiders than the Meadowlands. Until the middle 1970s this was a giant swamp on both sides of the Hackensack River before it emptied into Newark Bay. For many years when you drove in on Route 3 to the Lincoln Tunnel, you would pass straight through these Jersey meadows, pocked with gas stations and their giant signs, oil tank farms, truck terminals, and 12 lanes of New Jersey Turnpike. They symbolized to many Americans the whole state of New Jersey—a smelly, ugly mess that meant that you were still not where you wanted to go.

But today the Meadowlands present a different picture and symbolize a more vibrant New Jersey. In retrospect what is astonishing is that so much prime real estate, so close to Manhattan, went undeveloped so long; were the engineering problems really so great? Finally during Brendan Byrne's term as governor, the state built the Meadowlands stadium and sports complex—including Giants Stadium (Giants and Jets), the Meadowlands Racetrack, and the Meadowlands (formerly Brendan Byrne) Arena (Nets and Devils)—at the intersection of the Turnpike and Route 3. Private construction—hotels, offices—followed. At last northern New Jersey has a focus of its own, something to point to beyond industrial waste smoldering within view of the towers of Manhattan.

The Meadowlands are the focus also of New Jersey's 9th Congressional District, made up of cities, towns, and boroughs around and north of the Meadows complexes. Huddled to the west, on high land overlooking the Passaic River, are towns like Rutherford and Carlstadt, peopled with Polish- and Italian-Americans who usually vote Democratic, extensions really of ethnic communities once rooted in Newark. In the heart of the Meadows area is Secaucus, in Hudson County.

Another major part of the 9th District, with almost half its population, is a series of towns running along the spine of land which forms the Palisades along the Hudson River. This area, psychologically and almost physically, is part of New York City. The giant apartment complexes in Fort Lee and Cliffside Park advertise what a good view of New York they have and how easy it is to get into the city on an express bus; these are renter and condominium towns where people have only the vaguest sense that they are in New Jersey. Farther north and west are the leafy and pleasantly aged suburbs of Englewood; Alpine; Teaneck, a predominantly Jewish suburb of somewhat more recent vintage; Hackensack, an old industrial town that is the Bergen County seat; and Fair Lawn, a planned town with a large Jewish population.

All these areas, in their different ways, are excellent examples of the aging of close-in suburbs in the 1970s. There was rapid population growth in most of this area in the 1950s and mild growth in the 1960s; in the 1970s the 9th District's population declined 6%. The reason was not decay—you would have a hard time finding an abandoned house or a dilapidated neighborhood here—but empty-nest syndrome. Blocks once thronged with children running out of houses to play now are eerily quiet; the parents now live alone, and keep the windows and doors closed to hold in the air conditioning. Young families are moving farther and farther out in New Jersey, to Morris County and beyond; the 9th District increasingly is the home of grandparents.

It is also increasingly Democratic. Bergen County, like Westchester in New York, has a reputation for being Republican which was, in national elections at least, exaggerated. There have always been large Democratic pockets here, in the Meadowlands towns and in Jewish neighborhoods in particular, and Democrats have often carried Bergen. They have carried this part of Bergen County off and on in congressional elections since 1964, and the 9th District has had a Democratic congressman since 1982, Robert Torricelli.

Torricelli is an example of the aide-turned-candidate: he worked for Brendan Byrne and for Walter Mondale; he was politically able enough to have been the resident director of the Carter–Mondale campaign in Illinois six months before the 1980 primary—Carter's crucial victory over Edward Kennedy—and to have been its leading spokesman on the rules at the 1980 Democratic

National Convention. In 1982 he returned to his native New Jersey, amassed a substantial campaign treasury, and took on Republican Representative Harold Hollenbeck, who had a generally liberal record but had voted for the Reagan economic program and against gun control. Torricelli won 53%–46%.

Torricelli took seats on the Foreign Affairs and Science and Technology Committees, bodies seemingly removed from local concerns. But many of his constituents have strong interests in American policy toward particular countries—Israel, Greece, even Korea. And on occasion Torricelli was capable of direct action, as when he went down to El Salvador and personally recovered the body of a Bergen County journalist killed there. As for Science, northern New Jersey, though not so glamorous in this respect as Massachusetts or California, remains an important research and development center for the rest of the country; it is the home, most notably, of Bell Labs, perhaps the single most consistently productive research facility in history. Toricelli also ventured into other areas, getting the federal government to clean up toxic thorium in Maywood, getting an amendment through to ban the sale of submachine guns, urging a new space shuttle after the *Challenger* blew up.

Torricelli has been easily reelected, with 63% in 1984 and 69% in 1986, despite slightly less favorable district lines. Hard-charging and aggressive, he seems interested in statewide office; he was sharply critical of Peter Shapiro's losing gubernatorial campaign in 1985, and may run himself in 1989.

The People: Pop. 1980: 526,066, dn. 6.0% 1970–80. Households (1980): 72% family, 31% with children, 60% married couples; 45.9% housing units rented; median monthly rent: $270; median house value: $67,800. Voting age pop. (1980): 415,175; 5% Black, 4% Spanish origin, 2% Asian origin.

1984 Presidential Vote:	Reagan (R) 150,514	(59%)
	Mondale (D) 103,831	(41%)

Rep. Robert G. Torricelli (D)

Elected 1982; b. Aug. 26, 1951, Paterson; home, New Milford; Rutgers U., B.A. 1974, J.D., 1977, Kennedy Sch. of Govt., Harvard U., M.P.A. 1980; United Methodist; married (Susan).

Career: Asst. to NJ Gov. Brendan Byrne, 1975–77; Counsel to Vice Pres. Walter Mondale, 1978–81; Practicing atty., 1981–82.

Offices: 317 CHOB 20515, 202-225-5061. Also 25 Main St., Court Plaza, Hackensack 07601, 201-646-1111.

Committees: *Foreign Affairs* (14th of 27 D). Subcommittees: Asian and Pacific Affairs; Europe and the Middle East. *Science, Space and Technology* (18th of 27 D). Subcommittees: Investigations and Oversight; Space Science and Applications.

Group Ratings

	ADA	ACLU	COPE	CFA	LCV	ACU	NTU	NSI	COC	CEI
1986	70	61	93	67	79	9	24	0	13	21
1985	80	—	91	100	—	5	36	—	19	—

National Journal Ratings

	1986 LIB — 1986 CONS		1985 LIB — 1985 CONS	
Economic	87% —	0%	74% —	25%
Social	78% —	21%	73% —	23%
Foreign	75% —	20%	71% —	26%

Key Votes

1) Lmt Cln Water Act	AGN	5) Retain Gun Cont	FOR	9) Aid Angola Reb	AGN
2) Rpl Tobac Sub	FOR	6) Contra Aid	AGN	10) Tax Reform	FOR
3) Grm-Rdmn Def Red	AGN	7) Lmt Text Imp	FOR	11) S Africa Sanc	FOR
4) Ban Polygraph	FOR	8) Limit SDI	FOR	12) Immig Reform	FOR

Election Results

1986 general	Robert G. Torricelli (D)	89,634	(69%)	($408,779)
	Arthur F. Jones (R)	40,226	(31%)	($64,091)
1986 primary	Robert G. Torricelli (D)	14,201	(96%)	
	Elliot Greenspan (D)	520	(4%)	
1984 general	Robert G. Torricelli (D)	149,493	(63%)	($518,869)
	Neil Romano (R)	89,166	(37%)	($90,499)

Campaign Contributions and Expenditures

1985-86		Direct Cont. 1985-86		PACS Breakdown 1985-86			
Receipts	$579,688	Indiv.	$334,857	Corp.	$39,575	T/M/H	$25,900
Expend.	$408,779	PACS	$170,019	Labor	$70,622	Agr.	$3,500
Unspent	$256,355	Cand.	$39,405	Ideo.	$26,922	CWOS	$3,500

TENTH DISTRICT

As World War II ended, Newark, New Jersey, was one of America's major office centers, a white-collar city with thriving neighborhoods, beautiful parks, and ready access to New York City and to the green mountainsides nearby in New Jersey. Similar in ethnic composition to New York, it was a place apart politically: a Republican city surrounded by heavily Republican suburbs in a Republican state, facing the Tammany Democratic colossus across the Hudson. Today the downtown remains, although the big insurance companies have been siting most of their jobs elsewhere, but much of the rest of Newark seems in ruins. With one major exception, the city's middle-class—including middle-class blacks—have left Newark in search of nicer lawns and safer streets in the suburbs; houses and apartments have been abandoned, commercial property boarded up or vandalized; most of the people remaining are here because they cannot get out. This is not just a matter of racial change: in fact, the proportion of blacks in Newark in the 1970s barely changed, increasing only from 56% to 58%, because of the rapid abandonment of inner-city neighborhoods by middle-income and working-class blacks. Newark suffered through organized crime control of its city government in the 1960s and a major riot in 1967; it saw its population decrease from 438,000 in 1950 to 329,000 in 1980.

The major exception to that pattern is the Italian-American community in Newark's North Ward. The Jews who once lived in Philip Roth's Weequahic Park have long since moved to places like Maplewood and Short Hills; the Irish have vanished far beyond the city limits into Livingston or West Orange; the Yankees are now even farther away in Morris or Somerset Counties. But many Italians remain, in close-knit neighborhoods where everyone knows everyone else, there is little crime or violence, and people still speak Italian in the streets and shops. The North Ward has steadily resisted integration, but it is a mistake to see it as a peculiarly racist place; there is something positive here people want to protect and something negative, wholly apart from the race of the people involved, which has happened to other parts of Newark, and which North Ward residents sensibly want to avoid. Blacks have been moving west and south instead of north: to East Orange (83% black in 1980), Orange (57%), Irvington (38%), Hillside (30%), and high-income South Orange (10%).

All these suburbs except the last plus Newark and a few precincts in Belleville just above the North Ward make up the 10th Congressional District of New Jersey. One thing has remained the same about the Newark area since the postwar years: it has been represented in Congress by Peter Rodino. He was first elected in 1948, replacing Fred Hartley, the Republican co-author of the Taft-Hartley Act so bitterly fought by the unions. Rodino then was a young Roosevelt Democrat, a lawyer who had risen to colonel during World War II, a blue-ribbon candidate and the first Italian-American to rise so high in New Jersey politics. Now he is one of the most senior and on key issues one of the most powerful members of Congress, representing a black-majority constituency that is easily the most Democratic in New Jersey. His standing remains as strong as ever.

Rodino's place in history has been clear since he chaired the Judiciary Committee that voted in 1974 to impeach Richard Nixon. His performance exceeded many people's expectations. Rodino had been chairman of the Judiciary Committee for only a year, following the primary defeat of New York's Emanuel Celler; and Celler, though 86 when he lost, had been an assertive chairman who let Rodino take little responsibility. But these apprehensions proved unfounded. Relying on the Judiciary staff assembled by Celler as well as on the more publicized services of impeachment counsel John Doar, Rodino was able to master the factual and legal case against Nixon and to get smoothly past the parliamentary difficulties as well. His chairing of the hearings was even-handed and fair; he was careful to give the minority every opportunity to advance its views. But there could be little doubt of where Rodino stood in the face of the massive evidence and, to be a bit cynical about it, in light of the overwhelming sentiments of his constituency; he came out solemnly for impeaching the President.

One strength of the American political system is that it has produced people of extraordinary talent who have happened to find their way into crucial positions at critical times and who have performed far better than their records gave anyone the right to expect. Such leaders have come from the most unlikely places: a Lincoln from the midwestern hick town of Springfield, Illinois; a Franklin Roosevelt from the aristocratic patroon families of the Hudson Valley. Peter Rodino, from Newark, New Jersey, proved himself in 1974 to be very much in that tradition.

In the 1980s, Rodino, as chairman of the Judiciary Committee, has been the key man on all sorts of legislation—determining the contents of some measures, and killing others. He has spent considerable time and effort obstructing what he considers bad legislation, bottling up proposed constitutional amendments to ban abortions, allow school prayer, and ban school busing, and when the balanced budget and school prayer measures finally got to the floor, managing to keep them from passing with the required vote. But he has also been a positive legislator. He became the lead sponsor of the immigration bill in 1983 and saw it through to passage in 1986. He is the House's leading legislator on the important, though largely unheralded, area of bankruptcy, and the main force resisting attempts by big retail creditors to make filing individual bankruptcies more difficult; he resists such attractive-sounding but unwise measures as allowing farmers to reclaim their grain from bankrupt grain elevators ahead of other unsecured creditors. He was a major actor in efforts to reform the bankruptcy court system. Naturally he was appointed to the special committee investigating the Iran-contra scandal. Peter Rodino is a man of resolute and usually liberal views; he knows the legislative process and how to steer it in the direction he wants; he is widely respected in the House and personally well liked.

There was some thought when the district first got a black majority, in 1972, that Rodino would be vulnerable in the Democratic primary. But he won 57% against strong black opposition that year, 62% in the 1980 primary, a stunning 76% in 1984, and 60% against a strong opponent in 1986. He obviously has the respect and affections of many Newark-area black voters; they understand not only that he is a well-placed, effective advocate of positions which they believe in, but also that he was working for black causes and helping black constituents (and their families down South, at a time when southern congressmen would do nothing for them) years before anyone imagined he would have a a black-majority constituency. His 1986 primary opponent, Donald Payne, had backing from Newark's new Mayor Sharpe James, who had just beaten Kenneth Gibson, a longtime Rodino supporter, and the benefit of four days of campaigning from Jesse Jackson as well. The argument was that only a black could represent blacks, an argument that if applied to whites elsewhere would bar blacks from winning in all but one other congressional district not currently represented by a black; but Newark-area voters would have none of it, and Rodino won 60%–36%. Rodino may choose to retire in 1988, when he turns 79; but he remains in good health and seems happy spending full days on the floor managing legislation and returning to Newark each weekend, and having won eight elections in a majority-black district could probably win a ninth and tenth.

The People: Pop. 1980: 525,886, dn. 8.8% 1970–80. Households (1980): 69% family, 42% with children, 39% married couples; 74.6% housing units rented; median monthly rent: $197; median house value: $37,000. Voting age pop. (1980): 360,309; 54% Black, 12% Spanish origin, 1% Asian origin.

1984 Presidential Vote:

Mondale (D)	110,470	(75%)
Reagan (R)	36,554	(25%)

Rep. Peter W. Rodino, Jr. (D)

Elected 1948; b. June 7, 1909, Newark; home, Newark; NJ Sch. of Law, LL.B. 1937; Roman Catholic; widowed.

Career: Army, WWII; Practicing atty.

Offices: 2462 RHOB 20515, 202-225-3436. Also Fed. Bldg., 970 Broad St., Ste. 1435A, Newark 07102, 201-645-3213.

Committees: *Judiciary* (Chairman of 21 D). Subcommittee: Monopolies and Commercial Law (Chairman). *Select Committee on Narcotics Abuse and Control* (2d of 15 D).

Group Ratings

	ADA	ACLU	COPE	CFA	LCV	ACU	NTU	NSI	COC	CEI
1986	100	100	95	100	74	0	24	0	19	19
1985	100	—	95	100	—	5	36	—	19	—

National Journal Ratings

	1986 LIB — 1986 CONS			1985 LIB — 1985 CONS		
Economic	87%	—	0%	89%	—	0%
Social	89%	—	0%	79%	—	19%
Foreign	80%	—	0%	92%	—	0%

Key Votes

1) Lmt Cln Water Act	AGN	5) Retain Gun Cont	FOR	9) Aid Angola Reb	AGN
2) Rpl Tobac Sub	FOR	6) Contra Aid	AGN	10) Tax Reform	FOR
3) Grm-Rdmn Def Red	AGN	7) Lmt Text Imp	FOR	11) S Africa Sanc	FOR
4) Ban Polygraph	FOR	8) Limit SDI	FOR	12) Immig Reform	FOR

Election Results

1986 general	Peter W. Rodino, Jr. (D)................	46,666	(96%)	($407,220)
	Chris Brandlon (R).....................	1,977	(4%)	
1986 primary	Peter W. Rodino, Jr. (D)................	25,138	(60%)	
	Donald M. Payne (D)	15,216	(36%)	
	Two others (D)	1,898	(4%)	
1984 general	Peter W. Rodino, Jr. (D)................	111,244	(84%)	($200,525)
	Howard E. Berkeley (R)................	21,712	(16%)	($1,338)

Campaign Contributions and Expenditures

1985-86		Direct Cont. 1985-86		PACS Breakdown 1985-86			
Receipts	$394,739	Indiv.	$107,452	Corp.	$65,699	T/M/H	$53,502
Expend.	$407,220	Party	$3,416	Labor	$88,749	Agr.	$4,500
Unspent	$22,176	PACS	$230,875	Ideo.	$14,425	CWOS	$4,000
		Cand.	$50,000				

ELEVENTH DISTRICT

For millions of American families, the story of urban life is a story of moves upward and outward, up on the social ladder and out away from the central city. You can plot those moves over time on a map, and one good place to do so is in northern New Jersey. Follow the wide swath of Interstate 280 west from downtown Newark across heavily built-up East Orange and Orange, into West Orange where Llewellyn Park was one of the first planned suburbs of the 19th century (Thomas A. Edison and his bride moved there) and Livingston where Governor Kean's family has had an estate for generations, then across the swamps along the Passaic River into Morris County, once countryside and now suburbia. This is the route traveled by tens of thousands of Jerseyites, and helps to explain what happened to the 400,000 whites who lived in Newark right after World War II when there are only 75,000 whites left there today. So Newark, once a Republican-leaning city, has become heavily Democratic, but a new, bigger-than-Newark constituency has come into existence which is more Republican than the city ever was.

This is the 11th Congressional District of New Jersey, which was anchored in Newark up through the 1960s but begins now in West Orange and Maplewood and extends west to include most of Morris County and to go into the rural counties beyond. Its largest community is not Newark any more or West Orange, but the Morris County township with the ungainly name of Parsippany-Troy Hills. It is overall a very Republican district, with only speckles of Democratic territory here and there. Outsiders may assume that people here feel they are part of metropolitan New York. But they tend to identify more with Newark or with New Jersey generally. Most people here work in New Jersey rather than commute to the city; they enjoy entertainment and cultural events more often at home than in New York; they share much more of the traditional cultural outlook you would find in a suburb of Chicago or even Indianapolis rather than the one that might embrace the latest fashion or intellectual trend found in Manhattan. Some people here grew up in New York City, but a great many are from Newark or close-in towns nearby and their heritage in many cases is working class and Democratic. But their present economic condition is affluent and their politics are usually Republican.

The congressman from this territory is Dean Gallo, a Republican who grew up in the mill town of Boonton, where iron ore once came down from the Delaware River in canals, and who served on the Parsippany-Troy Hills Council, on the Morris County Board of Freeholders, and in the New Jersey Assembly. There he was a Republican leader working closely with Kean, and he shares Kean's liking for positive governmental action and low tax rates. In the House Gallo has worked closely with Democrats, including Robert Roe from the next-door 8th District. That makes good sense since Roe is a high-ranking Democrat on Public Works and the packager of the water projects bill President Reagan tried to kill, and Gallo by working with him has been able to get through amendments he wants—stricter landfill standards for aquifers, for example. He backs catastrophic health insurance and takes an interest in home health care. On cultural issues he is fairly liberal, but even on economics and foreign policy, he is not always supportive of market principles or Reagan Administration initiatives.

Gallo won the district after a court-ordered redistricting plan removed several Democratic-leaning suburbs from Newark from the 11th and thrust it far out into Morris County, in the process representing fairly accurately the outward population movement from Newark. The hapless incumbent, Joseph Minish, had been a low-key Democrat with few achievements who had always relied on old organization retainers and the Democratic label to reelect him; but neither the retainers nor the label were any help in Morris County. Gallo won 56% of the vote then; in 1986 he spent liberally and won by more than 2 to 1. He seems to have a safe seat.

The People: Pop. 1980: 526,078, up 2.6% 1970–80. Households (1980): 82% family, 44% with children, 71% married couples; 24.5% housing units rented; median monthly rent: $299; median house value: $78,300. Voting age pop. (1980): 381,844; 2% Spanish origin, 2% Black, 2% Asian origin.

1984 Presidential Vote:

Reagan (R)	171,632	(69%)
Mondale (D)	78,701	(31%)

Rep. Dean A. Gallo (R)

Elected 1984; b. Nov. 23, 1935, Boonton; home, Parsippany; United Methodist; divorced.

Career: Parsippany-Troy Hills Cncl., 1968–71, Pres., 1970–71; Morris Cnty. Bd. of Freeholders, 1971–1975, Dir., 1973–75; NJ House of Reps., 1975–84.

Offices: 1318 LHOB 20515, 202-225-5035. Also 22 N. Sussex St., Dover 07801, 201-328-7413; 140 Littleton Rd., Parsippany 07054; and 3 Fairfield Ave., W. Caldwell 07006, 201-228-9262.

Committees: *Public Works and Transportation* (14th of 20 R). Subcommittees: Public Buildings and Grounds; Surface Transportation; Water Resources. *Small Business* (9th of 17 R). Subcommittee: Exports, Tourism and Special Problems; Procurement, Innovation and Minority Enterprise Development.

Group Ratings

	ADA	ACLU	COPE	CFA	LCV	ACU	NTU	NSI	COC	CEI
1986	35	25	42	50	58	68	44	90	61	50
1985	20	—	29	58	—	81	46	—	68	—

National Journal Ratings

	1986 LIB — 1986 CONS			1985 LIB — 1985 CONS		
Economic	40%	—	60%	31%	—	67%
Social	55%	—	44%	63%	—	33%
Foreign	32%	—	67%	24%	—	66%

Key Votes

1) Lmt Cln Water Act	AGN	5) Retain Gun Cont	AGN	9) Aid Angola Reb	FOR
2) Rpl Tobac Sub	AGN	6) Contra Aid	FOR	10) Tax Reform	FOR
3) Grm-Rdmn Def Red	FOR	7) Lmt Text Imp	AGN	11) S Africa Sanc	FOR
4) Ban Polygraph	FOR	8) Limit SDI	AGN	12) Immig Reform	AGN

Election Results

1986 general	Dean A. Gallo (R)	75,037	(68%)	($660,059)
	Frank Askin (D)	35,280	(32%)	($167,857)
1986 primary	Dean A. Gallo (R)	14,806	(87%)	
	Kevin E. Reid (R)	2,266	(13%)	
1984 general	Dean A. Gallo (R)	133,662	(56%)	($735,394)
	Joseph G. Minish (D)	106,038	(44%)	($407,772)

Campaign Contributions and Expenditures

1985-86		Direct Cont. 1985-86		PACS Breakdown 1985-86			
Receipts	$713,273	Indiv.	$501,776	Corp.	$77,557	T/M/H	$51,970
Expend.	$660,059	Party	$5,007	Labor	$29,000	Agr.	$5,500
Unspent	$73,445	PACS	$178,005	Ideo.	$13,334	CWOS	$644
		Cand.	$20,000				

TWELFTH DISTRICT

The newest part of New Jersey, and the part least typical of the increasingly inaccurate stereotypes of the state, is growing up between the hills and ridges in what is the 12th Congressional District of New Jersey. This irregularly shaped portion of northwest and north central New Jersey takes in the campus of Princeton University and the horse farm country around Far Hills and Bernardsville; it fronts on the Delaware Water Gap and includes all of the Great Swamp National Wildlife Refuge near Morristown. But more typical of the district are spacious suburban townships like East Brunswick and Morris or the area around Princeton, where office complexes are springing up near Interstate interchanges and prosperous subdivisions are being carved carefully from the wooded New Jersey hills. This is white-collar, high tech, affluent New Jersey, solidly Republican in politics (except for trendy Princeton). Twenty-five years ago there were only about half as many people within the current 12th District's limits as were needed for a congressional district, and old-time politicos looking at its boundaries may scratch their heads and wonder where the city is with enough people to entitle this countryside to its own representative. But there are plenty of people and plenty of Republican voters.

The 12th District's congressman, Jim Courter, is one of the Republican party's most interesting young House members. He was once a Peace Corps volunteer and a legal services lawyer—the sort of background you expect to produce liberal Democrats—but is instead classed as a solid conservative. He was a leading supporter of Ronald Reagan's 1980 campaign when you didn't find many in New Jersey, and an early backer of Governor Thomas Kean in 1981. He is a member of the Armed Services Committee and one of the leading Republicans in the loosely organized military reform caucus; he favors more defense spending, but is more interested in where it's going. He is an enthusiastic backer of the Strategic Defense Initiative, an advocate of abrogating the ABM treaty, a supporter of the reform strengthening the chairman of the Joint Chiefs of Staff, a strong advocate of building the MX missile and giving military aid to the Nicaraguan Contras; on SDI he has been particularly effective, prodding even President Reagan to move ahead more aggressively on the program. Coming from a state in which most candidates stress environmentalist sympathies, Courter is also proud of an amendment prohibiting offshore oil and gas drilling in 60 tracts off New Jersey. He is a close ally of Jack Kemp and shares many of his approaches. He is also well thought of by the House leadership and was appointed to the committee investigating the Iran-contra scandal.

Courter was first elected to the House in 1978, beating Democrat Helen Meyner in a victory that presaged the Republican gains of 1980. A Democratic redistricting plan threatened to pit him against another incumbent in 1982, but Millicent Fenwick ran for the Senate, Matthew Rinaldo ran in the 7th District, and Marge Roukema was in the 5th. So Courter ran in the 12th, where he had to face Rodney Frelinghuysen, son of a 22-year Morris County congressman and scion of one of New Jersey's most distinguished families; Courter got President Reagan's endorsement, won 63%–27%, and has had little trouble holding the district since. For some time rumor had it that Courter would run against Senator Frank Lautenberg in 1988 but, busy spotting issues and making policy in the House, he has decided not to make the race.

The People: Pop. 1980: 526,063, up 11.8% 1970–80. Households (1980): 80% family, 43% with children, 69% married couples; 26.5% housing units rented; median monthly rent: $275; median house value: $74,000. Voting age pop. (1980): 380,628; 5% Black, 2% Asian origin, 2% Spanish origin.

1984 Presidential Vote   Reagan (R) 160,027   (65%)
Mondale (D) 84,541   (35%)

Rep. James A. (Jim) Courter (R)

Elected 1978; b. Oct. 14, 1941, Montclair; home, Hackettstown; Colgate U., B.A. 1963, Duke U., J.D. 1966; United Methodist; married (Carmen).

Career: Peace Corps, Venezuela, 1967–69; Practicing atty., 1969–70; Atty., Union Cnty. Legal Svcs., 1970–71; 1st Asst. Warren Cnty. Prosecutor, 1973–77.

Offices: 2422 RHOB, 202-225-5801. Also P.O. Bldg., 1 Morris St., Morristown 07960, 201-538-7267; and 3084 Rte. 27, Ste. 12, Kendall Park 08824, 201-297-1550.

Committees: *Armed Services* (5th of 21 R). Subcommittees: Procurement and Military Nuclear Systems; Research and Development. *Select Committee on Aging* (9th of 26 R). Subcommittee: Health and Long-Term Care.

Group Ratings

	ADA	ACLU	COPE	CFA	LCV	ACU	NTU	NSI	COC	CEI
1986	25	15	26	50	42	64	46	100	61	54
1985	15	—	22	75	—	86	63	—	57	—

National Journal Ratings

	1986 LIB — 1986 CONS	1985 LIB — 1985 CONS
Economic	39% — 60%	31% — 67%
Social	52% — 46%	33% — 66%
Foreign	16% — 79%	24% — 66%

Key Votes

1) Lmt Cln Water Act	AGN	5) Retain Gun Cont	FOR	9) Aid Angola Reb	FOR
2) Rpl Tobac Sub	FOR	6) Contra Aid	FOR	10) Tax Reform	FOR
3) Grm-Rdmn Def Red	FOR	7) Lmt Text Imp	AGN	11) S Africa Sanc	FOR
4) Ban Polygraph	FOR	8) Limit SDI	AGN	12) Immig Reform	AGN

Election Results

1986 general	James A. (Jim) Courter (R)	72,966	(63%)	($779,078)
	David B. Crabiel (D)	41,967	(37%)	($318,869)
1986 primary	James A. (Jim) Courter (R)	15,037	(100%)	
1984 general	James A. (Jim) Courter (R)	148,042	(65%)	($406,116)
	Peter J. Bearse (D)	78,167	(34%)	($90,759)

Campaign Contributions and Expenditures

1985-86		Direct Cont. 1985-86		PACS Breakdown 1985-86			
Receipts	$730,514	Indiv.	$580,161	Corp.	$62,565	T/M/H	$20,950
Expend.	$779,078	Party	$2,208	Labor	$14,750	Agr.	$0
Unspent	$123,793	PACS	$113,648	Ideo.	$11,750	CWOS	$3,633

THIRTEENTH DISTRICT

The Pine Barrens of New Jersey are the largest area on the East Coast that has not been changed since the first white settlers came here in the 17th century. They found the Barrens forbidding, an unchasmable barrier between the long-undeveloped Jersey Shore and the valley opened up by the Delaware River; and it is not hard to see why. The Barrens are low-lying swampy land, thick with trees and rich with small game, and even today they are crossed for most of their length only by two-lane roads hemmed by trees—a convenient place for military bases like Fort Dix, theme parks like Great Adventure, and, where the ground is not too swampy, vegetable gardens. Only in recent years has government considered the Pine Barrens worth preserving.

The Pine Barrens are, geographically, the heart of New Jersey's 13th Congressional District. It starts out—starts, because this is the older and more thickly settled part of the district—in the more affluent of the south Jersey suburbs of Philadelphia, close-in enclaves like Collingswood and the newer, more spread out Cherry Hill. On the other side of the Pine Barrens is Ocean County, most of it in the 13th, which includes the barrier islands from Seaside Park south to Little Egg Inlet, and includes the inland townships with their new apartment complexes and the beachfront communities on the Long Beach sand spit facing the ocean. Politically both the Philadelphia suburbs and Ocean County are solidly Republican, and this is a safe Republican seat.

The congressman from the 13th, James Saxton, was elected in 1984 after the death of 14-year incumbent Edwin Forsythe. The decisive contest was the Republican primary, which was a regional contest: Saxton, a state senator, carried his home county of Burlington with 85% and lost Camden only narrowly to a Cherry Hill candidate; his main opponent, Dean Haines, won 84% in Ocean County. The Democrat, the Mayor of Mount Holly, never had much of a chance and didn't do much campaigning; Saxton won with 61%. Saxton acted as Governor Thomas Kean's point man in the New Jersey legislature (where his accomplishments included a reduction in state insurance rates) and has a generally conservative voting record in the House. Like many junior Republicans, he was not satisfied with his initial committee assignments, and switched from Government Operations in his first term to Banking in his second. He has voted to hold down government spending—and to get the federal government to pay 65% of the cost of jetty construction in Barnegat Inlet. He was reelected easily.

The People: Pop. 1980: 526,062, up 29.0% 1970–80. Households (1980): 81% family, 42% with children, 70% married couples; 18.8% housing units rented; median monthly rent: $244; median house value: $50,100. Voting age pop. (1980): 377,446; 7% Black, 2% Spanish origin, 1% Asian origin.

1984 Presidential Vote: Reagan (R) 161,435   (65%)
                                 Mondale (D) 86,540   (35%)

Rep. H. James Saxton (R)

Elected 1984; b. Jan. 22, 1943, Scranton, PA; home, Vincentown; East Stroudsburg St. Col., B.A. 1965, Temple U., 1967–68; United Methodist; married (Helen).

Career: Teacher, 1965–68; Real estate broker, 1968–84, NJ House of Reps., 1975–81; NJ Senate, 1981–84.

Offices: 324 CHOB 20515, 202-225-4765. Also P.O. Box 38., Mt. Holly 08060, 609-261-5800; 1 Main Ave., Cherry Hill 08002, 609-428-0520; and 23 Crestwood Village Shopping Ctr., Schoolhouse Rd., Whiting 08759, 201-350-3535.

Committees: *Banking, Finance and Urban Affairs* (17th of 20 R). Subcommittees: Domestic Monetary Policy; Economic Stabilization; Financial Institutions Supervision, Regulation and Insurance; Housing and Community Development. *Merchant Marine and Fisheries* (8th of 17 R). Subcommittees: Fisheries and Wildlife Conservation and the Environment; Merchant Marine; Oceanography. *Select Committee on Aging* (14th of 26 R). Subcommittee: Health and Long-Term Care.

Group Ratings

	ADA	ACLU	COPE	CFA	LCV	ACU	NTU	NSI	COC	CEI
1986	30	15	32	42	53	64	46	80	56	54
1985	15	—	12	50	—	81	52	—	82	—

National Journal Ratings

	1986 LIB — 1986 CONS	1985 LIB — 1985 CONS
Economic	39% — 60%	16% — 81%
Social	42% — 57%	24% — 72%
Foreign	34% — 64%	24% — 66%

Key Votes

1) Lmt Cln Water Act	AGN	5) Retain Gun Cont	FOR	9) Aid Angola Reb	FOR
2) Rpl Tobac Sub	FOR	6) Contra Aid	FOR	10) Tax Reform	FOR
3) Grm-Rdmn Def Red	FOR	7) Lmt Text Imp	AGN	11) S Africa Sanc	FOR
4) Ban Polygraph	FOR	8) Limit SDI	AGN	12) Immig Reform	AGN

Election Results

1986 general	H. James Saxton (R)	82,866	(65%)	($331,286)
	John Wydra (D)	43,920	(35%)	($60,843)
1986 primary	H. James Saxton (R)	16,928	(100%)	
1984 general	H. James Saxton (R)	141,136	(61%)	($514,179)
	James B. Smith (D)	89,307	(38%)	($48,830)

Campaign Contributions and Expenditures

1985–86		Direct Cont. 1985–86		PACS Breakdown 1983–84			
Receipts	$401,064	Indiv.	$219,680	Corp.	$50,790	T/M/H	$60,620
Expend.	$331,286	Party	$12,029	Labor	$31,122	Agr.	$1,500
Unspent	$72,292	PACS	$154,260	Ideo.	$10,100	CWOS	$128
		Cand.	$6,359				

FOURTEENTH DISTRICT

On a spit of land that juts into New York Harbor, you can see her—the Statue of Liberty, with Ellis Island to one side, the towers of Lower Manhattan behind, the Verrazano Narrows Bridge off to the other. Behind you, as you stand in New Jersey's Liberty Park, along a ridge of hard granite and gneiss that rises up between the deep waters of the Hudson River and the swamp of the Jersey Meadowlands, is Hudson County, New Jersey, a place that has been home to generations of immigrants to these shores. The docks here are the busiest in New York Harbor; railroads headed into and back from the continent load and unload their freight; Hudson County is a natural industrial and warehousing site. Here generation after generation of immigrants have gathered in ethnic neighborhoods that remind them of home, building churches and civic institutions in the few hours left over after their usually backbreaking work. Hudson County's function throughout its history has been to house some of America's millions of immigrants, to provide them with jobs, on the waterfront or in the great factories or on the railroads or in Jersey City's huge City Hall. Physically, it is a kind of island, cut off from New York (some Hudson Countians have never set foot in the city whose skyline they see every day, and which is a short ride away on the PATH tubes) and separated from the rest of New Jersey. It stands apart not only from the bucolic suburbs but, separated by the Meadowlands, also from industrial Newark, which has had a quite different ethnic and political history. Yet it is not a slum. The five-story Victorian apartment buildings of Hoboken, unshaded by trees, sparkle in light that takes on tone from the River, and the substantial 1920s houses in Weehawken stare across from the skyscrapers of Manhattan, guarding middle-class values against the sophistication of the city.

Through all this history, Hudson County has been known as an insular community, peculiarly resistant to change and impervious to the forces that control life in the outside world. From the 1920s to the 1970s, it didn't seem to be changing much—ethnically, economically, politically—but that was just because of the unusually long interval between America's most recent waves of immigration. For five decades it was mostly white Catholic, Irish and Italian, blue collar, ruled over absolutely by a political machine the likes of which few places in America has ever seen. "I am the law," the most famous of its bosses, Frank Hague used to say in the 1930s and 1940s; and he was: his Hudson County Democratic machine chose governors and U.S. Senators, prosecutors and judges, and even had some influence in the White House of Franklin D. Roosevelt. In Jersey City and other Hudson County towns—then and now the most densely populated part of the United States outside Manhattan—Hague controlled almost every facet of life. He determined who would stay in business and who would fail; he controlled tax assessments and the issuance of parking tickets; he had the support of the workingman and kept the CIO out of town for years (resulting in a major Supreme Court case). Hague's power was firmly anchored in votes. Jersey City and Hudson County had huge payrolls, and every jobholder was expected to produce a certain number of votes on election day. So statewide Democratic candidates could expect a 100,000-vote margin in Hudson County and since they often lost the rest of the state by less than that, they were indebted indeed.

Hague's power lasted into the 1940s, until some of his former allies turned on him and captured the machine. The next 25 years of Hudson County politics was a history of entangling alliances, occasional betrayals, indictments, and reform movements whose leaders quickly became the heads of the new machines. Physically, Hudson County still consisted of the same series of towns on the granite Palisades ridge between New York Harbor and the Jersey Meadowlands: Jersey City, Bayonne, Weehawken, Union City, and (below the ridge, entirely on the waterfront) Hoboken. For a generation most of them had dwindling populations. Hudson County reached its peak population of 690,000 in 1930, just a few years after most immigration was cut off, when its row houses and apartments were filled with young foreigners who spoke English in broken phrases or with a thick brogue, and raised large families full of children who spoke with the distinctive Jersey City accent. As the children grew up, some stayed in Hudson

County, but many moved away, to less distinctive suburban communities, to blend in with the great middle class. By 1980 Hudson County's population had fallen to 555,000.

But now immigration and economic growth have got Hudson County growing and changing again. The more visible change, though probably less important in the long run, was the building of new high-rise buildings—and self-enclosed communities—on the Hudson County spine overlooking Manhattan. Particularly in the northern end of the county, just below the George Washington Bridge, Hudson County suddenly found itself with thousands of middle- and upper-income residents. At the same time, young professionals and the like were taking the PATH tubes from Manhattan to Hoboken and Jersey City, rehabilitating the rowhouses which had been the homes of generations of immigrants, and spreading Manhattan-style gentrification to the ridge west of the Hudson. Another change was the development of the Meadowlands complex, which is just outside Hudson's limits but has brought economic growth, jobs, and new buildings to land that formerly was dotted with nothing more than diners and oil tank farms. Going up in Jersey City, in the bedraggled area near the docks and the railroad tracks, but only 2,000 feet from the World Trade Center, is the 40,000-unit Newport City development of Samuel LeFrak, who boasts of building units where 1 out of 16 New York City residents live but is now only interested in building where there is no rent control.

And—the final change—once again, beginning about 50 years after the restrictive immigration laws of 1921 and 1924, Hudson County is filling up with immigrants, particularly of Spanish-speaking people from Latin America. Union City has become predominantly Cuban (64% Spanish origin in 1980, according to the Census Bureau), while there are mixed Latin-American communities in West New York (63%), Hoboken (40%), and Jersey City itself (19%). The new migrants, like those of the earlier 20th century, tend to be young people with many children; if they entered the country illegally, as some have, they are still paying U.S. taxes (through wage withholding) and are raising children who will be U.S. citizens paying taxes to support the native 1947–62 baby boomers, who have had small families, when they become Social Security recipients. Altogether 27% of the total population, and 35% of the children, in the 14th District are of Spanish origin.

The Latin migration is having more impact on Hudson County politics each year. Most of the voters here are elderly people from earlier migrations. In Hague's day they almost always voted Democratic (except when Hague was punishing some Democrat); so important was the machine in people's lives that they were happy to help out on election day. By the 1960s the machine had become less important. Prosperity had come to Hudson County; at least people no longer depended on the machine for jobs or coal; service in the machine's cadres came to be more of a burden with fewer rewards; people whose relatives had moved elsewhere no longer felt so confined or helpless. Tussles between local politicos continued, and were written up by outsiders as titanic battles for control of an all-powerful machine. But if the machine could still pick judges and state legislators, and if it still had influence in Democratic gubernatorial primaries, its power to affect votes in general elections became very limited. Meanwhile, Hudson County trended Republican. Its traditional Democratic voters, with their faith in church and family, had little use for McGovernish Democrats; terrified of street crime, they were ready to vote for politicians who seemed tough on crime.

Now the politics of the new Spanish residents are becoming more important. The Cubans evidently see their values reflected much more accurately in the Republican than in the Democratic Party; others are more inclined to the Democrats—or up for grabs. The assumption that some Democratic strategists carry in their heads, that people with low incomes will vote Democratic in order to get more government help, doesn't necessarily follow: most of them came here not to seek government help but to work their own way up. So the 100,000-plus Democratic margins in Hudson County have vanished. Jimmy Carter carried the county by only 4,000 votes in 1980, and Walter Mondale lost it to Ronald Reagan in 1984. Governor Thomas Kean helped Republican candidates win in two of the three Hudson legislative districts in 1985. When Democrats do win statewide, as Senators Frank Lautenberg and Bill Bradley have in the 1980s, they carry Hudson handsomely—but both would have won without it.

New Jersey's 14th Congressional District includes almost all of Hudson County—a change from Hague's day when there were two Hudson seats. The congressman is Frank Guarini, a sure-footed lawyer who served in the state Senate and was county Democratic chairman before he won the crucial 1978 primary. Guarini appears to be a polished, knowledgeable man with important political credentials, and he obviously has clout in Hudson County. Nationally as well: he played a key role in Walter Mondale's campaign in 1984, helping him to win what turned out to be the crucial New Jersey primary and then at the San Francisco convention casting the ballots that put Mondale over the top. Yet he is not a particular glad-hander among his colleagues and not widely known outside the House and Hudson County.

In the House, Guarini has a pretty solid Democratic voting record. He got a seat on the Ways and Means Committee in his first term and so played some role in the tax reform legislation of 1986; he was not, however, on the conference committee. He is on the Trade Subcommittee, and has one of the least protectionist records of northeastern Democrats. Although he is known to spend some of his time on New York's plush Central Park South, he remains politically very strong in Hudson County. He retains support from the vestiges of the Hudson County machine, but has the polish to appeal to Hudson County's new upscale voters and the adaptability to win votes among its latest immigrants; he got 71% against a Cuban–American Republican in 1986.

The People: Pop. 1980: 526,062, dn. 8.7% 1970–80. Households (1980): 69% family, 35% with children, 48% married couples; 71.8% housing units rented; median monthly rent: $186; median house value: $40,100. Voting age pop. (1980): 388,408; 24% Spanish origin, 11% Black, 3% Asian origin.

1984 Presidential Vote:

Reagan (R)	102,475	(53%)
Mondale (D)	89,414	(47%)

Rep. Frank J. Guarini (D)

Elected 1978; b. Aug. 20, 1924, Jersey City; home, Jersey City; Columbia U., Dartmouth Col., B.A. 1947, NYU, J.D. 1950, LL.M. 1955, Acad. of Intl. Law, The Hague, Holland; Roman Catholic; single.

Career: Navy, WWII; Practicing atty.; NJ Senate, 1965–72.

Offices: 2458 RHOB 20515, 202-225-2765. Also 15 PATH Plaza, Jersey City 07306, 201-659-7700; 654 Ave. C, Bayonne 07002, 201-823-2900; and 428 60th St., West New York 07093, 201-868-0325.

Committees: *Budget* (19th of 21 D). Task Forces: Budget Process; Economic Policy. *Ways and Means* (11th of 23 D). Subcommittee: Trade. *Select Committee on Narcotics Abuse and Control* (7th of 15 D).

Group Ratings

	ADA	ACLU	COPE	CFA	LCV	ACU	NTU	NSI	COC	CEI
1986	80	65	91	75	74	14	21	0	17	26
1985	85	—	91	83	—	5	32	—	20	—

National Journal Ratings

	1986 LIB — 1986 CONS			1985 LIB — 1985 CONS		
Economic	84%	—	13%	89%	—	0%
Social	64%	—	34%	69%	—	28%
Foreign	64%	—	34%	80%	—	17%

Key Votes

1) Lmt Cln Water Act	AGN	5) Retain Gun Cont	FOR	9) Aid Angola Reb	AGN
2) Rpl Tobac Sub	FOR	6) Contra Aid	AGN	10) Tax Reform	FOR
3) Grm-Rdmn Def Red	AGN	7) Lmt Text Imp	FOR	11) S Africa Sanc	FOR
4) Ban Polygraph	FOR	8) Limit SDI	FOR	12) Immig Reform	AGN

Election Results

1986 general	Frank J. Guarini (D)	63,057	(71%)	($407,120)
	Albio Sires (R)	23,822	(27%)	($62,073)
1986 primary	Frank J. Guarini (D)	30,043	(87%)	
	Marie R. Vaughan (D)	3,844	(11%)	
	Herbert D. Smith (D)	479	(2%)	
1984 general	Frank J. Guarini (D)	115,117	(66%)	($380,350)
	Edward T. Magee (R)	58,265	(33%)	($1,569)

Campaign Contributions and Expenditures

1985-86		Direct Cont. 1985-86		PACS Breakdown 1985-86			
Receipts	$556,150	Indiv.	$138,744	Corp.	$78,400	T/M/H	$86,540
Expend.	$407,120	PACS	$288,063	Labor	$86,374	Agr.	$2,000
Unspent	$79,729	Cand.	$94,867	Ideo.	$21,249	CWOS	$13,500

NEW MEXICO

Before the Mayflower dropped anchor, New Mexico was already New Mexico—something you can say of no other American state except perhaps Hawaii. When the Pilgrims were building flimsy wood houses, the Indians in New Mexico were living in pueblos hundreds of years old, made with the adobe that is New Mexico's characteristic building material and which lasts so long that you can't tell a 1680 building from its 1980 neighbor. Every other state's culture is based on what its early white settlers brought to the land; natives except in Hawaii have mostly disappeared. Not so in much of New Mexico. The English-speaking culture here is superimposed, rather lightly it sometimes seems, on a society whose written history dates back to 1609, when the Spaniards first established a settlement in Santa Fe, and to centuries long past when the pueblo Indians set up stable agricultural societies on the sandy, rocky lands of northern New Mexico. A very substantial minority of New Mexicans are descendants of these Indians or the Spanish, or both. Nearly one-third of the people in this state speak Spanish in ordinary everyday life, and only a few of them are recent migrants from Mexico. This is the northernmost salient of the great Indian civilizations of the Cordillera, which extend along the mountain chain through Mexico, Central America, to South America as far away as Chile and Argentina.

The Hispanic-Indian culture dominates most of northern and western New Mexico, except for enclaves—usually related to mining or, in the case of Los Alamos, nuclear research—where Anglos have settled. In vivid contrast to the Hispanic part of New Mexico is the area called Little Texas. With small cities, plenty of oil wells, vast cattle ranches, and desolate military bases, this region resembles, economically and culturally, the adjacent High Plains of west Texas. Oil is important here but not as vital as the military presence: a couple of Air Force bases and the Army's White Sands Missile Range, near Alamogordo, where the first atomic bomb was detonated.

In the middle of the state is Albuquerque which, with the coming of the air conditioner, grew from a small desert town into a booming Sun Belt city. Here you get glimpses of the national future. Albuquerque has a large Hispanic minority, as many of our fastest-growing cities do; its economy is based heavily on high technology, particularly the nuclear variety. The military is a major presence: there are two bases within the city limits; its largest employer is a nuclear contractor, Western Electric's Sandia Laboratories. Metropolitan Albuquerque now has almost precisely one-third of the state's population—about the same percentage as the Hispanic areas and Little Texas. By fortunate coincidence, the three regions also coincide quite closely with the state's three congressional districts.

For many years New Mexico politics was a somnolent business. Local bosses—first Republican, later Democratic—controlled the large Hispanic vote. Elections in many counties featured irregularities that would have made a Chicago ward committeeman blush. New Mexico also had for years another evidence of boss-controlled politics, the balanced ticket: one Spanish and one Anglo Senator, with the offices of governor and lieutenant governor split between the groups.

Now all that has changed. In national politics, New Mexico has had a distinct Republican trend, enough to make a bellwether state that never voted for a losing presidential candidate until 1976 into a Republican stronghold. But in local and state politics Democrats—sometimes even liberal Democrats—can win elections. There is some ethnic voting, and the Democrats usually have a solid base in the Hispanic areas, but one finds there is no extreme polarization.

The most prominent politician in the state is a Republican, Peter Domenici, who is the son of an Italian immigrant; and large enough minorities in Albuquerque and Little Texas voted for him to elect an outspokenly liberal Hispanic governor, though he was so unpopular in office that the leftward trend, apparent in the early 1980s in what is after all the bargain basement of the Sun Belt, now seems clearly to have been reversed. New Mexico tends to attract the least affluent of the migrants, low-skill laborers and retirees who can afford a trailer but not a Scottsdale condominium. But any desire for a more active government or for boosting local wages or redistributing income may be diminished by the unseen but always remembered proximity of Mexico. There are more than one million Mexicans in Juarez and the state of Chihuahua just across the border from El Paso and New Mexico—more people than in all of New Mexico today. New Mexico has not seen all that much migration from Mexico; its Hispanic population is growing rapidly because of high birth and low death rates. But Mexicans could start coming here, and that possibility must exert some discipline over wage levels.

Governor. New Mexico's Republican Governor, Garrey Carruthers, elected in 1986, was an assistant secretary of the Interior under James Watt; he was also a professor of agricultural economics at New Mexico State in Las Cruces. In his campaign he made much of the fact that he was not a legislator; he won with 53% over a Democrat who was assistant head of the Sandia Laboratories. The selection of technocrats by both parties was not an accident, for New Mexico was disgusted with its politicians, and particularly with its liberal Democratic Governor, Toney Anaya. He was ineligible to seek a second consecutive term, but no one thinks he could have won.

In office Anaya feuded constantly with the legislature, particularly with a bipartisan conservative coalition that took control after 1984, eventually vetoing the bill funding the legislature and his own office; he failed to get his education and tax increase proposal through even before that; he tried to appoint his nephew to the State Fair Board and his barber to a $30,000 sinecure, hired ostentatiously liberal women, Hispanics, and blacks, then fired officials abruptly; he told a magazine interviewer about his loneliness, and the magazine published his words and three psychologists' analyses. At the beginning of his term he was attacked for traveling around the country boosting liberal candidates and promoting voter registration; at the end he evoked fury when the day before Thanksgiving he commuted the death sentences of the five men on death row.

Anaya's election in 1982 shows that New Mexico voters have no overriding prejudice against Hispanics; the reaction to his governorship shows that the large majority of voters don't want a liberal politician using what is after all the rather fragile lever of the governor's office to try to move the world that is inertia-bound New Mexico. Carruthers, who came in promising to streamline government and attract economic development, will presumably be a governor more to New Mexico's liking.

NEW MEXICO — **Congressional Districts, Counties, and Selected Places** — *(3 Districts)*

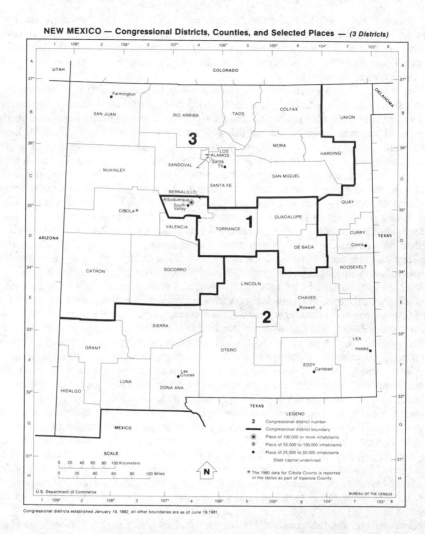

Congressional districts established January 19, 1982; all other boundaries are as of June 19, 1981.

Senators. New Mexico's most prominent politician is Senator Pete Domenici, chairman of the Senate Budget Committee for six years, now ranking minority member of Budget. He was largely unknown when the Republicans' capture of the Senate in 1980 put him in his high post, and not long removed from the time when his major governmental responsibility was superintending the budget of the city of Albuquerque. Only one of the other Republicans on Budget had any experience on the committee, and none had both the knowledge and the tenacity to compete with Domenici as the Republicans' driving force. For his first months as Budget chairman, Domenici worked closely with OMB Director David Stockman and the Reagan Administration, cutting domestic programs and boosting defense. But by the beginning of 1982 he had embarked on the constantly frustrating course he followed for five long years: trying to get the deficit down with the President digging in his heels against tax increases, the Administration and Congress insisting, through 1984 anyway, on large defense increases, and all politicians recognizing that almost all the politically palatable domestic cuts had already been made. Hard-working, intense, frank often to the point of belligerence, genuinely worried about the deficit, but reluctant to set an entirely separate course from his fellow Republicans in the Administration, Domenici found himself again and again in the midst of grinding negotiations unable to accomplish what he wanted.

As the ranking Republican on Budget, Domenici will not have all that responsibility, and he can watch his friend Lawton Chiles try to hold the heretofore fractious Senate Democrats together and deal with the Administration. But Domenici, like most legislators who used to be in the majority, will still miss the chair and the gavel. He will have plenty of work to do anyway. He is a member of Appropriations; of Energy and Natural Resources, the old Interior Committee which is so important in western states. He is not a favorite of the New Right, whose approach he dislikes, although his voting record comes out looking pretty conservative; many self-identified conservatives frowned on his emphasis on cutting budget deficits and his concentration on budget issues rather than on the cultural or foreign policy causes that energize them. Although he may not talk much about family values, he practices them: in 1986 he had seven children in college or law school.

Domenici's political position in New Mexico seems very strong. He won his first election narrowly in 1972 and was reelected in 1978 by an unimpressive margin over the then much less well-known Toney Anaya. But in 1984 he got 72% of the vote—the highest percentage any New Mexico Senator has ever won. This is one case where a Senator's national stature has been a political asset, and not just because New Mexico depends in important ways on federal spending. New Mexico voters saw Domenici being subjected to some very demanding circumstances, and he was not found wanting. No one doubts that he can win reelection easily in 1990.

New Mexico's junior Senator, Jeff Bingaman, is a largely unknown quantity in Washington. Young, handsome, rich enough to self-finance half his campaign, he served four years as New Mexico's attorney general. Bingaman serves on two committees—Armed Services and Energy and Natural Resources—of vast importance to his state. On economic issues, he joins his fellow Democrats pretty faithfully. On military matters he has generally lined up with Democrats skeptical of higher defense spending and younger members in the military reform movement, questioning traditional assumptions; legislatively he came forward as the leading opponent of Navy Secretary John Lehman's homeporting plan to assign ships to various ports rather than a few (a position that may come easily to a Senator from a state whose largest body of water is the trickle that is the Rio Grande) and he moved unsuccessfully to bar arms export loans from being converted to grants. As Chairman of the Armed Services Subcommittee on Defense, Industry, and Technology, Bingaman is in an excellent position to tend to the needs of his state, with its scientific/military facilities. On Energy and Natural Resources, Bingaman's interests are likely to involve not only oil but also such issues as ground water development and air pollution caused by plants in Mexico.

But Bingaman may end up known less for his legislative detail work than for his promotion of physical fitness. He is a seasoned jogger, who started a Senate Health Promotion Program in 1986. In 1985 he got Domenici to agree to set up a HealthNet New Mexico organization, which in the winter of 1986–87 got 7,000 New Mexicans, including the two Senators, to sign up to abide by an "Eat Right New Mexico" regimen, and they lost a total of 34,000 pounds. On schedule for the spring was "Get Fit New Mexico" and in the fall "Tobacco Free New Mexico."

Will Bingaman be reelected in 1988? In 1982 he won the Democratic primary over former Governor Jerry Apodaca, who was reputed to have ties to organized crime figures, by carrying everything but the heavily Hispanic rural counties. He won the general election over incumbent Republican Harrison Schmitt, the former astronaut, partly because it was a recession year, but also because of Schmitt's own negative TV spots, which made damaging and, it quickly became apparent, misleading charges against Bingaman. Bingaman's election demonstrates that he can win in the right circumstances. But he had only 54% of the vote, and the last time a Democratic Senator was reelected here was in 1970. It's not apparent who will be the Republican nominee, and Representative Joe Skeen, who twice got 49% in statewide races for governor, took himself out of the race in the spring of 1987. But this is one seat the Republicans will be targeting.

Congressional districting. New Mexico got a third congressional district out of the 1980 Census and created a new, heavily Hispanic and Democratic district in the northern part of the state. The others are competitive. They correspond quite closely to the major demographic regions of the state: the 1st is the Albuquerque area; the 2d mostly Little Texas; the 3d mostly Hispanic counties.

Presidential politics. New Mexico has voted for the loser only once in presidential elections since it was admitted to the Union in 1912. But its five electoral votes are not a major prize, and its presidential primary has never attracted more than a quick visit from a major candidate. This was the most Democratic of the Rocky Mountain states in the 1984 election, but that's not very Democratic; no one expects it to be furiously, if obscurely, contested again any time soon, as it was in 1960 when John Kennedy carried it by some 2,294 votes.

The People: Est. Pop. 1984: 1,479,000; Pop. 1980: 1,302,894, up 13.5% 1980–86 and 28.1% 1970–80; 0.61% of U.S. total, 37th largest. 17% with 1–3 yrs. col., 17% with 4+ yrs. col.; 17.6% below poverty level. Single ancestry: 9% English, 5% German, 3% Irish, 1% Italian, French, Scottish. Households (1980): 75% family, 45% with children, 62% married couples; 31.9% housing units rented; median monthly rent: $178; median house value: $45,400. Voting age pop. (1980): 884,987; 33% Spanish origin, 7% American Indian, 2% Black, 1% Asian origin. Registered voters (1986): 632,787; 380,193 D (60%), 214,977 R (34%), 33,459 unaffiliated (5%), 4,158 minor parties (1%).

1986 Share of Federal Tax Burden: $3,617,100,000; 0.48% of U.S. total, 37th largest.

1986 Share of Federal Expenditures

	Total		Non-Defense		Defense	
Total Expend	$7,092m	(0.85%)	$5,692m	(0.95%)	$1,400m	(0.61%)
St/Lcl Grants	857m	(0.76%)	857m	(0.76%)	0m	(0%)
Salary/Wages	1,103m	(.91%)	466m	(0.79%)	638m	(1.03%)
Pymnts to Indiv	2,029m	(0.56%)	1,831m	(0.53%)	198m	(1.11%)
Procurement	2,984m	(1.45%)	2,421m	(4.35%)	564m	(0.38%)
Research/Other	118m	(0.44%)	118m	(0.44%)	0m	(0.26%)

Political Lineup: Governor, Garrey E. Carruthers (R); Lt. Gov., Jack L. Stahl (R); Secy. of State, Rebecca D. Vigil (D); Atty. Gen., Hal Stratton (R); Treasurer, James B. Lewis (D); Auditor, Haroll H. Adams (D). State Senate, 42 (20 D and 22 R); State House of Representatives, 70 (43 D and 27 R). Senators, Peter V. (Pete) Domenici (R) and Jeff Bingaman (D). Representatives, 3 (2 R and 1 D).

1984 Presidential Vote

Reagan (R)	307,101	(60%)
Mondale (D)	201,769	(39%)

1980 Presidential Vote

Reagan (R)	250,779	(55%)
Carter (D)	167,832	(37%)
Anderson (I)	29,459	(6%)

1984 Democratic Presidential Primary

Hart	87,610	(47%)
Mondale	67,675	(36%)
Jackson	22,168	(12%)
Two others, uncomm.	9,950	(5%)

1984 Republican Presidential Primary

Reagan	40,805	(95%)
Uncommitted	2,189	(5%)

GOVERNOR

Gov. Garrey Carruthers (R)

Elected 1986, term expires Jan. 1991; b. Aug. 29, 1939, Alamosa, CO; home, Las Cruces; NM State U., B.S., 1964, M.S. 1965, IA St. U., Ph.D. 1968; United Methodist; married (Katherine).

Career: Asst. Secy., U.S. Dept. of Int., 1981–84; Dir., NM Water Resources Research Inst., 1976–78; Prof., NM State U., 1968–85.

Office: State Capitol, Rm. 417, Santa Fe 87503, 505-827-3000.

Election Results

1986 gen.	Garrey E. Carruthers (R)......	209,455	(53%)
	Ray B. Powell (D)	185,378	(47%)
1986 prim.	Garrey E. Carruthers (R)......	27,671	(31%)
	Joseph H. Mercer (R)	23,560	(26%)
	Colin R. McMillan (R)	19,807	(22%)
	Frank M. Bond (R)	10,619	(12%)
	Paul F. Becht (R)	6,566	(7%)
1982 gen.	Toney Anaya (D)	215,840	(53%)
	John Irick (R)...............	190,626	(47%)

SENATORS

Sen. Peter V. (Pete) Domenici (R)

Elected 1972, seat up 1990; b. May 7, 1932, Albuquerque; home, Albuquerque; St. Joseph's Col., 1950–52, U. of NM, B.S. 1954, Denver U., LL.B. 1958; Roman Catholic; married (Nancy).

Career: Practicing atty., 1958–72; Albuquerque City Comm., 1966–70, Mayor Ex-Officio, 1967–70.

Offices: 434 DSOB 20510, 202-224-6621. Also Fed. Bldg. and U.S. Crthse., Rm. 10013, Albuquerque 87102, 505-766-3481; New Postal Bldg., Rm. 3004, Santa Fe 87501, 505-988-6511; 202 E. New Fed. Bldg., Las Cruces 88001, 505-523-8150; and Fed. Bldg. and U.S. Crthse., Rm. 140, Roswell 88201, 505-623-6130.

Committees: *Appropriations* (11th of 13 R). Subcommittees: Energy and Water Development; HUD–Independent Agencies; Labor, Health and Human Services, Education; Treasury, Postal Service, General Government (Ranking Member). *Budget* (Ranking Member of 11 R). *Energy and Natural Resources* (4th of 9 R).

Subcommittees: Energy Research and Development (Ranking Member); Public Lands, National Parks and Forests. *Special Committee on Aging* (6th of 9 R).

Group Ratings

	ADA	ACLU	COPE	CFA	LCV	ACU	NTU	NSI	COC	CEI
1986	5	21	22	7	17	83	50	100	79	67
1985	15	—	22	13	—	82	62	—	83	—

National Journal Ratings

	1986 LIB — 1986 CONS			1985 LIB — 1985 CONS		
Economic	16%	—	76%	0%	—	86%
Social	17%	—	80%	25%	—	72%
Foreign	18%	—	77%	20%	—	79%

Key Votes

1) Ease Gun Cont	FOR	5) Grm-Rdmn Def Red	FOR	9) Rehnquist Nom	FOR
2) Immig Reform	AGN	6) Contra Aid	FOR	10) Tax Reform	FOR
3) Lmt Text Imp	FOR	7) SDI Funding	FOR	11) Drug Death Pen	AGN
4) Aid Tobac Ind	FOR	8) Lmt PAC Contrib	AGN	12) S Africa Sanc	FOR

Election Results

1984 general	Peter V. (Pete) Domenici (R)	361,371	(72%)	($2,658,008)
	Judith A. Pratt (D)	141,253	(28%)	($301,661)
1984 primary	Peter V. (Pete) Domenici (R)	42,760	(100%)	
1978 general	Peter V. (Pete) Domenici (R)	183,442	(53%)	($914,634)
	Toney Anaya (D).	160,045	(47%)	($175,633)

Campaign Contributions and Expenditures

1979-84		Direct Cont. 1979-84		PACS Breakdown 1979-84			
Receipts	$2,675,819	Indiv.	$1,669,980	Corp.	$489,402	T/M/H	$196,593
Expend.	$2,658,008	Party	$21,579	Labor	$27,950	Agr.	$6,500
Debts	$88,215	PACS	$825,368	Ideo.	$67,389	CWOS	$8,500

Sen. Jeff Bingaman (D)

Elected 1982, seat up 1988; b. Oct. 3, 1943, El Paso, TX; home, Santa Fe; Harvard Col., B.A. 1965, Stanford Law Sch., LL.B. 1968; United Methodist; married (Anne).

Career: NM Asst. Atty. Gen., 1969; Practicing atty., 1970–78; NM Atty. Gen., 1979–82.

Offices: 502 HSOB 20510, 202-224-5521. Also 231 Washington Ave., Santa Fe 87501, 505-988-6647; Dennis Chavez Fed. Bldg., Rm. 9017, 500 Gold Ave. S.W., Albuquerque 87102, 505-766-3636; U.S. Crthse, Ste. 201-B, Las Cruces 88001, 505-523-8237; and Fed. Bldg., Ste. 175, Roswell 88201, 505-622-7113.

Committees: *Armed Services* (6th of 11 D). Subcommittees: Defense Industry and Technology (Chairman); Readiness, Sustainability and Support; Strategic Forces and Nuclear Deterrence. *Energy and Natural Resources* (7th of 10 D). Subcommittees: Energy, Regulation, and Conservation; Mineral Resources Development and Production; Public Lands, National Parks and Forests. *Governmental Affairs* (8th of 8 D). Subcommittees: Federal Services, Post Office and Civil Service; Federal Spending, Budget and Accounting; Oversight of Government Management. *Joint Economic Committee.* Subcommittees: Economic Resources and Competitiveness; Education and Health; National Security Economics.

Group Ratings

	ADA	ACLU	COPE	CFA	LCV	ACU	NTU	NSI	COC	CEI
1986	65	92	84	67	63	35	41	30	26	41
1985	90	—	88	67	—	13	34	—	34	—

National Journal Ratings

	1986 LIB — 1986 CONS			1985 LIB — 1985 CONS		
Economic	68%	—	30%	70%	—	26%
Social	79%	—	16%	74%	—	22%
Foreign	62%	—	37%	67%	—	31%

Key Votes

1) Ease Gun Cont	FOR	5) Grm-Rdmn Def Red	AGN	9) Rehnquist Nom	AGN
2) Immig Reform	AGN	6) Contra Aid	AGN	10) Tax Reform	FOR
3) Lmt Text Imp	FOR	7) SDI Funding	FOR	11) Drug Death Pen	AGN
4) Aid Tobac Ind	AGN	8) Lmt PAC Contrib	FOR	12) S Africa Sanc	FOR

Election Results

1982 general	Jeff Bingaman (D)	217,682	(54%)	($1,586,245)
	Harrison H. (Jack) Schmitt (R)	187,682	(46%)	($1,692,204)
1982 primary	Jeff Bingaman (D)	91,780	(54%)	
	Jerry Apodaca (D)	66,598	(39%)	
	Virginia R. Keehan (D)	10,466	(6%)	
1976 general	Harrison H. (Jack) Schmitt (R)	234,681	(57%)	($441,309)
	Joseph M. Montoya (D)	176,382	(43%)	($451,111)

Campaign Contributions and Expenditures

1981-82		Direct Cont. 1981-82		PACS Breakdown			
Receipts	$1,606,965	Indiv.	$480,776	Agr	$8,900	Ideo	$61,725
Expend.	$1,586,245	Party	$17,500	Bus	$15,180	Lbr	$157,250
Unspent	$20,719	PACS	$308,917	Hlth	$6,500	Prof	$7,250
		Cand.	$790,941				

FIRST DISTRICT

At the junction of a river that is just a trickle most of the year and a road which was nothing more than a line on a surveyor's map when the Santa Fe Railroad was built a century ago is the metropolis of New Mexico, Albuquerque. Named for a Spanish grandee, it was in the 1940s still a small city of 35,000 huddled in the blocks around the Old Town and the Indian School, just above the Rio Grande, a place you could pass through quickly on the Santa Fe or U.S. 66. In the 1980s you see a city of 350,000, with another of 90,000 close by: with its prosperous neighborhoods climbing the gently rising heights to the east, and its poorer people concentrated north and south of downtown in the Rio Grande valley. Albuquerque is counted as part of the Sun Belt, but its climate is closer to that of the High Plains of west Texas: hot in the summer, sometimes very cold in the winter, with high winds most of the time. Unlike most other Sun Belt cities, it owes its growth more to the public than the private sector: its biggest employers include the Sandia Labs, military bases, and defense contractors.

The 1st Congressional District of New Mexico is, for all practical purposes, the city of Albuquerque and its suburbs. Albuquerque itself accounts for 76% of the district's population, with 21% more in the suburban fringe; that leaves just 3% in the three desert counties which have most of the district's land area. In the 1960s it trended Republican but, almost uniquely among Sun Belt cities, it moved toward the Democrats in the late 1970s and early 1980s, partly because of its large Hispanic community, partly perhaps because of its dependence on government, mostly probably because it is not as affluent and self-assured as Phoenix or Orange County.

The congressman from the 1st District is a product of the 1960s Republican upsurge. Manuel Lujan, Jr., is part of a politically prominent Republican family. He was first elected in 1968 and for years won reelection easily. He was prized by national Republicans as their most visible Hispanic elected official. At the same time, he was a reliable party man. Lujan is a pretty solid free enterpriser on economic issues, and pretty solidly conservative on cultural and foreign issues as well. From 1981 to 1985 he was ranking Republican on the Interior Committee, a particularly fractious place in those days of confrontation between environmentalists and James Watt. In 1985, after a retirement opened up the slot, he switched to become ranking Republican on the Science Committee. This committee has concentrated on the space program, but under incoming chairman Robert Roe may go farther afield; and science in any case is of great local interest in Albuquerque and New Mexico.

Lujan seemed averse to confrontation on Interior; he was mentioned as a possible Interior Secretary twice, when James Watt and William Clark quit, but in neither case did he get the job or seem much to want it. He was sidelined for much of 1986 with a heart attack. Nevertheless, he seems to have recovered from the political troubles he suffered earlier in the 1980s. In 1980 he was almost beaten by Bill Richardson, now his colleague in the new 3d District; in 1982 he won with only 52% against a son of former Indiana Senator Vance Hartke. In 1984 and 1986 he did much better against weaker opponents at a time when the performance of Governor Toney Anaya was souring voters on liberal Democrats. Lujan remains an important legislator, but one whose energy level is uncertain and who still may have some problems back home.

The People: Pop. 1980: 434,141, up 32.1% 1970–80. Households (1980): 72% family, 41% with children, 58% married couples; 36.3% housing units rented; median monthly rent: $202; median house value: $55,000. Voting age pop. (1980): 307,647; 33% Spanish origin, 2% American Indian, 2% Black, 1% Asian origin.

1984 Presidential Vote:

Reagan (R)	. . . .	108,766	(60%)
Mondale (D)	. . . .	70,395	(39%)

Rep. Manuel Lujan, Jr. (R)

Elected 1968; b. May 12, 1928, San Ildefonso; home, Albuquerque; St. Mary's Col., San Francisco, CA, Col. of Santa Fe., B.A. 1950; Roman Catholic; married (Jean).

Career: Insurance exec., Manuel Lujan Agencies; Vice Chmn., NM Repub. Party.

Offices: 1323 LHOB, 202-225-6316. Also 500 Gold Ave., S.W., Ste. 10001, Albuquerque 87102, 505-766-2538.

Committees: *Interior and Insular Affairs* (2d of 15 R). Subcommittee: Energy and the Environment (Ranking Member); Water and Power Resources. *Science, Space and Technology* (Ranking Member of 17 R).

Group Ratings

	ADA	ACLU	COPE	CFA	LCV	ACU	NTU	NSI	COC	CEI
1986	5	10	22	17	16	68	`51	100	80	54
1985	15	—	22	17	—	67	52	—	77	—

National Journal Ratings

	1986 LIB — 1986 CONS		1985 LIB — 1985 CONS	
Economic	12% —	87%	27% —	71%
Social	22% —	78%	0% —	76%
Foreign	27% —	73%	0% —	76%

Key Votes

1) Lmt Cln Water Act	FOR	5) Retain Gun Cont	—	9) Aid Angola Reb	FOR
2) Rpl Tobac Sub	AGN	6) Contra Aid	FOR	10) Tax Reform	FOR
3) Grm-Rdmn Def Red	FOR	7) Lmt Text Imp	AGN	11) S Africa Sanc	FOR
4) Ban Polygraph	AGN	8) Limit SDI	AGN	12) Immig Reform	AGN

Election Results

1986 general	Manuel Lujan, Jr. (R)	90,476	(71%)	($243,795)
	Manny Garcia (D)	37,138	(29%)	($71,407)
1986 primary	Manuel Lujan, Jr. (R)	23,975	(100%)	
1984 general	Manuel Lujan, Jr. (R)	115,808	(65%)	($497,504)
	Charles Ted Asbury (D)	60,598	(34%)	($217,640)

Campaign Contributions and Expenditures

1985-86		Direct Cont. 1985-86		PACS Breakdown 1985-86			
Receipts	$336,142	Indiv.	$185,708	Corp.	$71,050	T/M/H	$49,395
Expend.	$243,795	Party	$5,912	Labor	$4,500	Agr.	$750
Unspent	$119,598	PACS	$128,756	Ideo.	$2,875	CWOS	$186

SECOND DISTRICT

The Little Texas region of New Mexico is just what it says: an extension of the High Plains of west Texas over the invisible New Mexico state border. Oil is the mainstay of the economy here; cattle ranching is common; cotton is grown on irrigated land. There is a considerable Hispanic population—at least 19% in each county—and yet the regional accent is the twang of west Texas, not the lilt of northern New Mexico. As you move west from the towns near the Texas border—Clovis, Portales, Lovington, Hobbs—the towns become fewer and agricultural settlement sparser. Around Carlsbad and Roswell the landscape looks to an outsider like desert, with 9,000 foot peaks rising in the crystalline distance.

The 2d Congressional District of New Mexico is roughly coincident with Little Texas. The southwestern corner of the district, though still near Texas, is a little different in tone. Las Cruces, one of New Mexico's largest towns, is also a majority Spanish community; so are the mining towns in the hills above Silver City and the tiny border town of Columbus, which was raided by Pancho Villa's revolutionary army in 1916.

The 2d District is represented by a Republican who seems to personify the views and values of Little Texas accurately. Joe Skeen is a sheep rancher who chaired the state Republican party in the 1960s, when it won few elections, and was the party's nominee for governor twice in the 1970s, losing both times by narrow margins. His record in the House is solidly conservative, in a rough-and-ready rather than intellectual way. Generally opposed to high government spending, he is happy to make exceptions for defense, science, and agriculture. After the 1984 election he switched off two good committees for a congressman from his district, Agriculture and Science and Technology, for an even better one, Appropriations; he serves on Jamie Whitten's Agriculture Subcommittee and is ranking Republican on the panel that handles funding for the Treasury Department and Postal Service, among other agencies.

In 1986 Skeen won an impressive victory running against a well-known name. His opponent was Mike Runnels, son of the 2d District's former Representative Harold Runnels. He was a conservative Democrat, and his death after winning the 1980 primary set off a wild-and-woolly race: Governor Bruce King got his nephew named Democratic nominee, Runnels's widow, Dorothy, ran as a write-in, and so did Skeen. Skeen won with 38% to 34% for King and 28% for Mrs. Runnels. Mike Runnels was running after a four-year stint as lieutenant governor though outgoing Governor Toney Anaya was highly unpopular in Little Texas; he carried only one county and Skeen won with 63% of the vote. Many Republicans hoped Skeen, with his solid base and proven statewide vote-getting ability would run against Senator Jeff Bingaman in 1988. But he declined in early 1987 to make the race and presumably will stay in the House.

The People: Pop. 1980: 436,261, up 17.9% 1970–80. Households (1980): 77% family, 45% with children, 66% married couples; 31.7% housing units rented; median monthly rent: $154; median house value: $33,400. Voting age pop. (1980): 297,158; 29% Spanish origin, 3% Black, 1% American Indian, 1% Asian origin.

1984 Presidential Vote: Reagan (R) 108,723   (66%)
Mondale (D) 53,600   (33%)

Rep. Joseph R. (Joe) Skeen (R)

Elected 1980; b. June 30, 1927, Roswell; home, Picacho; TX A&M U., B.S. 1950; Roman Catholic; married (Mary).

Career: Navy, WWII; Engineer, Navajo Reservation, 1950–51; Sheep rancher, 1951–80; NM Senate, 1960–70, Minor. Ldr., 1965–70; Repub. Nominee for Gov. of NM, 1974, 1978.

Offices: 1007 LHOB 20515, 202-225-2365. Also Fed. Bldg., A-206, Las Cruces 88001, 505-523-8245; and Fed. Bldg., Rm. 127, Roswell 88201, 505-622-0055.

Committees: *Appropriations* (17th of 22 R). Subcommittees: Rural Development, Agriculture and Related Agencies; Treasury–Postal Service–General Government (Ranking Member).

Group Ratings

	ADA	ACLU	COPE	CFA	LCV	ACU	NTU	NSI	COC	CEI
1986	10	10	8	8	5	82	44	100	69	61
1985	0	—	9	8	—	76	41	—	86	—

National Journal Ratings

	1986 LIB — 1986 CONS		1985 LIB — 1985 CONS	
Economic	16% —	82%	22% —	77%
Social	18% —	78%	0% —	76%
Foreign	0% —	86%	0% —	76%

Key Votes

1) Lmt Cln Water Act	FOR	5) Retain Gun Cont	AGN
2) Rpl Tobac Sub	AGN	6) Contra Aid	FOR
3) Grm-Rdmn Def Red	FOR	7) Lmt Text Imp	FOR
4) Ban Polygraph	AGN	8) Limit SDI	AGN

9) Aid Angola Reb   FOR
10) Tax Reform   FOR
11) S Africa Sanc   AGN
12) Immig Reform   AGN

Election Results

1986 general	Joseph R. (Joe) Skeen (R) 77,787	(63%)	($293,428)
	Mike Runnels (D)...................... 45,924	(37%)	($48,409)
1986 primary	Joseph R. (Joe) Skeen (R) 19,902	(100%)	
1984 general	Joseph R. (Joe) Skeen (R) 116,006	(74%)	($328,159)
	Peter R. York (D) 40,063	(26%)	($26,012)

Campaign Contributions and Expenditures

1985-86		Direct Cont. 1985-86		PACS Breakdown 1985-86			
Receipts	$287,216	Indiv.	$150,541	Corp.	$50,757	T/M/H	$48,745
Expend.	$293,428	Party	$6,443	Labor	$2,750	Agr.	$5,900
Unspent	$3,598	PACS	$119,792	Ideo.	$10,000	CWOS	$1,640
		Cand.	$1,000				

THIRD DISTRICT

Artists like Georgia O'Keeffe, novelists like D. H. Lawrence, rich cultivators of artists and writers like Mabel Dodge Luhan—they have been coming to northern New Mexico for almost 100 years. They have been attracted by the clear air, the massive mountains, the long, cold, empty vistas in which physical detail stands out with pinpoint clarity; but they have been attracted most by the unique civilization here—part Indian, part Spanish, only a little Mexican (for northern New Mexico was Mexican only briefly, from 1810 to 1848), part Anglo-American. The Spanish language, Indian pottery and dances, the adobe pueblos, and most of all a sense that here was a civilization rooted in the unlikeliest of desert soil and rock outcroppings, a place not settled a few decades or generations ago like most of the United States, but where life had gone on for centuries under these same skies in much the same way.

Actually, life here has not been so stable: the pueblos were built in sudden spurts; the Spanish conquistadors and priests brought the Catholic religion, the baroque accents of the adobe buildings, and the Spanish language in a rush; successive waves of American settlement have changed New Mexico. The Indian crafts which are thriving in the 1980s today nearly died out in the 1880s, and the Palace of the Governors, built in 1610, had its Victorian balustrade torn off and its original appearance restored in 1913. The unchanged look must be carefully maintained. Yet up the back roads in Rio Arriba or Taos Counties, you can find the religion an admixture of Catholicism with adaptations of Indian festivals and old superstitions and the buildings not that much different after all from the old pueblos. Politics here, too, is a unique blend. Debate is conducted and votes are bartered often in Spanish, but the Republican and Democratic parties have been firmly established here for a century, and there has been nothing smacking of cultural revolution or massive income redistribution coming from any politician. Quite the contrary: politics here tends to be a cynical, sometimes corrupt, business; loyalties run to families and communities more than to principles or parties. In the back country, you can still find more than vestiges of the old communities and the old politics—though no one is going to let you in on them much, even if you speak good Spanish.

The 3d Congressional District of New Mexico contains most of the Spanish-speaking and Indian parts of the state. The district covers most of the northern part of New Mexico, from the High Plains as they rise to the haunting Sangre de Cristo Mountains in the east, through the vast ridges and isolated buttes in the center, to the windy and dusty desert-like plains, dotted occasionally by mountains, with their Indian reservations in the west. It is centered on Santa Fe and Taos and includes traditional Indian villages and the isolated mountaintop scientific village of Los Alamos. The population is 39% Spanish origin and 21% Indian (there is some overlap between the categories). In recent decades television has brought the Anglo world into the mountains, and Santa Fe and Taos have become year-round resorts for affluent young Texans and easterners attracted by ski slopes, summer coolness, and Indian culture. But the future belongs to the products of the old culture: 44% of the children in this district are Hispanic and 27% are Indian.

The creation of the new 3d District in 1982 led to the election of an Hispanic Congressman who has an Anglo name and shallow roots in the district. He is Bill Richardson, born in California of a Mexican mother, raised in Mexico City, fluent in Spanish. He came to New Mexico in 1978 after holding staff jobs on Capitol Hill (the importance of which he exaggerated in 1980 campaign literature). And he worked not in the Hispanic community but as executive director of the state Democratic Party. Richardson lost no time running for office. He won what most observers thought was a worthless nomination to run against Representative Manuel Lujan, raised over $200,000, and won 49% of the vote. (Only afterward was a $100,000 loan investigated by the Federal Election Commission; Richardson was cleared of wrongdoing.) He did have serious competition in the new 3d District primary, from former Lieutenant Governor Roberto Mondragon, and he lost the counties in the heart of the Hispanic area; but he won enough other territory over the much less well-financed Mondragon to win the nomination with 36% of the vote. In the general election he was subject to some criticism, but won easily with 64% of the vote.

Richardson is obviously a young man in a hurry, whose political strategy has gotten him at least part way to where he wants to go. He has done just about everything he would need to to win a Senate seat in New Mexico some day. But for 1984 he decided not to make the race against Pete Domenici, and given Domenici's high popularity and the fact that the other seat is held by a Democrat, Richardson may not find an opening until at least 1994. In the meantime Richardson has made some adroit moves on Capitol Hill. He made a good start in 1983 by winning a much coveted seat on the House Energy and Commerce Committee as well as one on Veterans' Affairs; in 1985, he switched off the latter panel for a seat on Interior. He serves on subcommittees which handle hot issues like toxic waste and, especially in his state, water and public lands. He has been a changeable vote on some important issues, opposing immigration reform hotly in 1984 but switching toward a less hostile attitude in 1986; he voted for aid to the Nicaraguan contras in 1985 but against in 1986, winding up on the losing side both times. These switches by a politician with sensitive antennas suggests that opinion on these issues is not one-sided among Hispanic voters: they may be afraid of anti-Hispanic discrimination, but they also fear job competition from illegal immigrants; they may be wary as most Americans are of military involvement abroad, but they may also see the Sandinistas not as social democratic good guys but as thugs whose rule they wouldn't like to live under.

But none of these currents of opinion have affected many votes in the 3d District lately. In 1982 and 1984 Richardson easily beat Hispanic opponents; in 1986 he similarly dispatched former Governor David Cargo. Cargo put on a game campaign, highlighted by his correspondence with a government agency that told him he lived in a foreign country because his address was New Mexico; but he had been living in Oregon most of the time and had even run for office there after serving as governor of New Mexico from 1966 to 1970, and his name has not been a household word in New Mexico for some time. Richardson won with 71% in this safe Democratic seat.

The People: Pop. 1980: 432,492, up 35.8% 1970–80. Households (1980): 77% family, 50% with children, 63% married couples; 27.2% housing units rented; median monthly rent: $166; median house value: $47,900. Voting age pop. (1980): 280,182; 37% Spanish origin, 17% American Indian, 1% Black.

1984 Presidential Vote: Reagan (R) 89,612   (53%)
                               Mondale (D) 77,774   (46%)

Rep. Bill Richardson (D)

Elected 1982; b. Nov. 15, 1947, Pasadena, CA; home, Santa Fe; Tufts U., B.A. 1970, Fletcher Sch. of Law and Diplomacy, M.A. 1971; Roman Catholic; married (Barbara).

Career: Staff, NM House of Reps., 1981–72; State Dept., Ofc. of Congressional Relations, 1973–75; Staff, Sen. Subcmtee. on Foreign Relations Assistance, 1975–78; Businessman, 1978–82.

Offices: 325 CHOB 20515, 202-225-6190. Also U.S. Crthse. Bldg., Rm. B26, Santa Fe 87501, 505-988-6177; Gallup City Hall, 2d and Aztec, Gallup 87301, 505-722-6522; San Miguel Cnty. Cthse., P.O. Box 1805, Las Vegas 87701, 505-425-7270; and The Harvey House, 104 N. 1st St., Belen 87003, 505-864-1419.

Committees: *Energy and Commerce* (18th of 25 D). Subcommittees: Commerce, Consumer Protection and Competitiveness; Energy and Power; Telecommunications and Finance. *Interior and Insular Affairs* (16th of 26 D). Subcommittees: National Parks and Public Lands; Water and Power Resources. *Education and Labor* (17th of 21 D). Subcommittees. Elementary, Secondary and Vocational Education. *Select Committee on Aging* (31st of 39 D). Subcommittees: Housing and Consumer Interests; Human Services.

Group Ratings

	ADA	ACLU	COPE	CFA	LCV	ACU	NTU	NSI	COC	CEI
1986	75	75	90	75	82	18	21	20	41	20
1985	70	—	87	67	—	14	30	—	32	—

National Journal Ratings

	1986 LIB — 1986 CONS		1985 LIB — 1985 CONS	
Economic	62%	35%	68%	32%
Social	60%	39%	81%	15%
Foreign	64%	34%	64%	33%

Key Votes

1) Lmt Cln Water Act	AGN	5) Retain Gun Cont	AGN	9) Aid Angola Reb	AGN
2) Rpl Tobac Sub	AGN	6) Contra Aid	AGN	10) Tax Reform	FOR
3) Grm-Rdmn Def Red	FOR	7) Lmt Text Imp	FOR	11) S Africa Sanc	FOR
4) Ban Polygraph	FOR	8) Limit SDI	AGN	12) Immig Reform	FOR

Election Results

1986 general	Bill Richardson (D)	95,760	(71%)	($354,849)
	David F. Cargo (R)	38,552	(29%)	($86,865)
1986 primary	Bill Richardson (D)	50,858	(100%)	
1984 general	Bill Richardson (D)	100,470	(61%)	($425,939)
	Louis H. Gallegos (R)	62,351	(38%)	($201,909)

Campaign Contributions and Expenditures

1985-86		Direct Cont. 1985-86		PACS Breakdown 1985-86			
Receipts	$370,329	Indiv.	$118,261	Corp.	$54,750	T/M/H	$66,604
Expend.	$354,849	Party	$1,269	Labor	$69,793	Agr.	$6,500
Debts	$30,556	PACS	$233,597	Ideo.	$35,200	CWOS	$750

NEW YORK

The clatter of trucks rocking over the metal plates that cover potholes, the screech of brakes and steel wheels grinding to a halt on the subway rails, the anrgy shouts from taxi drivers, the newsboys crying at the long lines in front of the toll booths, the high whine of construction cranes, the whooshes of buses accelerating just before the light turns green, the clashing and gnashing of arguments and insults and the occasional showing of kindness to a stranger, the never-ending blare of car horns—all make up the cacophony that makes New York the noisiest city in the world. As early as the 1830s visitors noted the extraordinary bustle and busy-ness of New York, as the Erie Canal and then the water-line railroad was changing a claustrophobic Dutch colonial town, clustered at the foot of Manhattan, into the greatest American commercial city. By the early 20th century, when more than one million immigrants some years disembarked beneath the Statue of Liberty onto Ellis Island to become Americans, New York had already acquired the grittiness of tone, the contentiousness and argumentativeness which has seemed as much a part of its nature this century as the soot that once turned white shirt cuffs black by early afternoon and the crisp division between edifice and air that still marks the boundary between the countless interior rooms where the lives and business of New Yorkers take place and the daunting exterior vistas that always astonish the visitor.

Behind the clangor and the rudeness is an assumption—sometimes warranted, sometimes not—that New Yorkers are just a bit smarter than, just a step ahead of, their countrymen. Nature endowed New York with a good harbor, but during the Revolution it was only America's third city. Not until the 19th century did the descendants of Dutch patroons, Huguenot refugees, English West Indies traders, and Yankee farmers in New York become the nation's most successful merchants and capitalists, forging the first routes to the great American interior through the valleys of the Hudson and the Mohawk over the Finger Lakes and the Great Lakes, and building the grand brownstone mansions on broad avenues in midtown Manhattan. By the beginning of the 20th century, New York was a rival to London as a center of world capitalism, but peered over its shoulder at Chicago's rise as a transportation and manufacturing center; but by 1920, the World War had helped New York eclipse London in finance and the vast immigration of the early 20th century enabled it to stay well ahead of Chicago in manufacturing, transportation, and communications. New York was helped by geography and circumstance. But the key to its preeminence has always been talented people.

New York's success has been a triumph of the market, but government—and politics—have always played an important part. The Iroquois, perhaps the most deep-rooted and militarily strong native Americans, kept in place for 100 years by an alliance with British troops, were driven out by Revolutionary troops; the Erie Canal was the project of Governor DeWitt Clinton and the state of New York; the railroads were subsidized by land grants and favorable laws. New York led the nation in political invention: Martin Van Buren's Albany Regency was the first state political machine, an ally of New York City's Tammany Hall, and Van Buren himself invented the Democratic party and the national political convention. In response, adept politicians like Thurlow Weed and William Seward invented the Whig party and ultimately became Republicans; noting that Van Buren's Democrats were winning large margins from Irish Catholics and other immigrants, they too made bids for the newcomers' votes. Both parties served the function of mediating between the divergent interests of the masses in New York City and the farmers and burghers of Upstate New York, making bearable the conflict you can still see in New York between city and country, immigrant versus native, Big Apple versus appleknockers.

Sitting astride a cultural chasm almost as wide as those that spawned the trenches of World

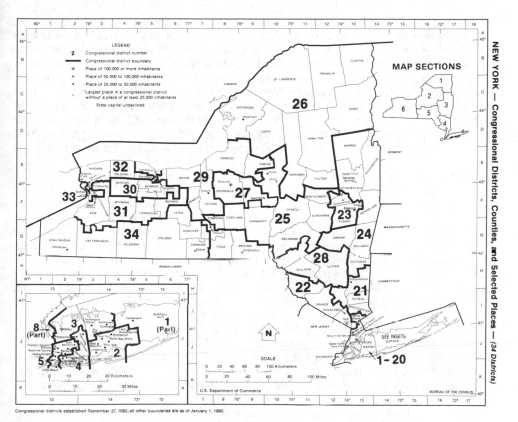

Congressional districts established September 27, 1983; all other boundaries are as of January 1, 1980.

See pages 1369-1374 for additional metropolitan area maps.

War I in Europe, New York built one of the world's most productive and rapidly growing economies, one of its most progressive and tolerant communities, and the prototype of the American welfare state. The key event was the fire in the Triangle Shirtwaist factory, just off Washington Square in 1911, when hundreds of women died, many jumping 11 stories, because fire escapes had not been installed and exits had been blocked off. To the investigative committee headed by young Tammany Democrats Robert F. Wagner and Alfred E. Smith it was obvious that government had to step in to regulate business and use some of the great wealth produced in New York to protect the 2.3 million New Yorkers then packed into Manhattan (there were only 1.4 million there in 1980) and the hundreds of thousands of immigrants and others working in tiny factories in thousands of loft buildings all around the city. The canny Democrat who headed Tammany Hall, Charles F. Murphy, noticed that there were votes in these measures, and he knew that he faced competition for the votes of the Jews in the Lower East Side and in the new neighborhoods developing around subway stops in the Bronx and Brooklyn from Socialists (who were winning some congressional elections then) and for the votes of Italians from progressive Republicans like Fiorello LaGuardia. Tammany Democrats, disciplined by Murphy and led by Smith and Wagner, wrote wage and working conditions laws, passed a minimum wage, got New York state into the electric power business, and built the nation's best system of paved roads.

So New York was a forerunner of the New Deal, and New York politics in the 1920s was a foretaste of the American politics of the 1930s and 1940s. In the 40 years following the first

World War, New York produced perhaps half of the leading politicians: Smith, Roosevelt, Wagner, Averell Harriman among the Democrats, Thomas E. Dewey, Wendell Willkie, Dwight Eisenhower (a New York resident as president of Columbia in 1952), Nelson Rockefeller among Republicans. New York pioneered public housing and fair housing laws, industrywide unions (in the garment trades) and high minimum wages, residential rent control and dairy price fixing (to help Upstate farmers). It took largely for granted the productivity of Wall Street and New York City's thousands of small entrepreneurs, the factories of the Upstate industrial corridor and the affluence of its growing suburbs. Just as it led the nation in the canal and railroad eras, so in the 20th century it spawned high tech companies sometimes with headquarters in the New York City area and their biggest factories Upstate: General Electric and IBM, Eastman Kodak and Xerox.

Smith and his Democratic successors carried New York by amassing margins in New York City overwhelming enough to overcome the margins the Republicans almost always had Upstate. Often their margins were small: it is forgotten now, but Franklin Roosevelt carried New York by only small margins in 1940 and 1944, Truman lost it in 1948, and Stevenson ran a strong race in New York in 1952. In New York the key swing voters were the Jews, then as now about one-fourth of New York City's population. Their aversion for Tammany and their affection for vaguely socialist ideas was reflected in the creation of separate American Labor and Liberal Parties, so that Jewish immigrants who didn't read much English could vote for Roosevelt and Mayor LaGuardia's candidates on the same party lever. The welfare state policies of Smith, Roosevelt, and Governor Herbert Lehman attracted these votes and the Democrats held the governorship for 22 of 24 years; the liberal Republican policies—which is to say, acceptance and enlargement of the welfare state—by Thomas Dewey and Nelson Rockefeller helped them win enough of these crucial votes to give their party control of state government for 28 of the next 32 years. Oddly, national strategists took the peculiarities of New York—particularly the presence of a large, leftish Jewish population—as a model for the nation, and built political strategies based on the theory that Republicans couldn't win without appealing to big liberal independent blocs.

By the 1960s New York's welfare state garments were beginning to fray. Immigration pretty much stopped after the Immigration Act of 1924; and the post-1945 immigrants, southern blacks and Puerto Ricans, did not move as rapidly up the ladder as their pre-1924 counterparts. New York's incomes were rising, but not as rapidly as the nation's; some of the most affluent moved to low-tax New Jersey or Connecticut or retired to low-tax Florida. Then in the middle 1970s New York's welfare state politics collapsed. Overgenerous spenders—ironically, they were mostly Republicans, Rockefeller and Mayor John Lindsay—spent the city almost to the point of bankruptcy in 1975; the state government nearly tumbled in after; retrenchment followed, supervised not only by Governor Hugh Carey, but by private leaders heading ad hoc public organizations, like Felix Rohatyn. Public employees unions had to accept cutbacks in jobs and salaries; citizens had to endure loss of services and deterioration of streets, bridges, subways; even renters lost some of their advantages after rent control had helped devastate vast city neighborhoods by forcing landlords to abandon buildings and leaving them open to arsonists and looters. In the 1970s the population of New York, city and state, dropped by one million—a hemorrhage of the talented and the productive, a flight of the middle-class away from a system that seemed to be shrivelling and dying.

But by the middle 1980s New York was once again brimming with confidence, and the buzzing of economic growth and cultural innovation could be heard again over the honking of horns. Its economy was growing, its population was rising, it was attracting immigrants once again. Manhattan was booming as an office center; it remained the center of the financial, clothing, entertainment, media, and publishing industries. Meanwhile, the outlying boroughs have attracted a significant migration from Latin America, the eastern Mediterranean, Asia, and even Russia—Colombians and Salvadorians, Koreans and Chinese, Greeks and Russian Jews—injecting vitality and a younger generation into what were aging, listless communities. It had two leaders of genuine intellectual distinction, capable even of writing bestsellers, Governor Mario Cuomo and Mayor Edward Koch, New York has balanced its budgets and paid off its debts, cut its taxes and seen enough revenue come in to permit at least some experiments and exercises of compassion. The clash between trendy Manhattan and tradition-minded outer boroughs, so vast in John Linsday's day, has narrowed as both these two executives, whose strength is in the outer boroughs, have proved to all but the most Manhattan-bound that they have the capacity to govern. They have done it the New York way—both men are as argumentative as anyone in American public life; they are ready to pounce, Cuomo more often with righteous anger, Koch sometimes ponderously and sometimes with sarcastic wit, on those they think mistaken. And they have been bitter rivals themselves, in the 1977 mayor's and 1982 governor's race, debating dozens of times and not at ease with each other still. They differ with each other on issues: Cuomo is against capital punishment, Koch for; Koch denounces racial quota, while Cuomo is quieter on the subject; as representatives of the huge city and state governments, they have different and sometimes conflicting institutional interests.

But, like their core constituencies in the outer boroughs, their basic approach to government is similar. Neither is much of an enthusiast for the old New York ideas that the government should hold down the price of housing through rent control and the price of transportation through cheap subway fares; the idea has taken hold that the apartment dweller and the subway rider should pay his or her way. Yet neither Cuomo nor Koch has jettisoned the welfare state entirely, and in the national perspective both men are, in different ways, among its greatest champions— Cuomo as the nation's most articulate defender of welfare state values, Koch as the mayor of the nation's biggest city. Even as they have kept New York's welfare and transfer payments from shooting up wildly out of line with those in the rest of the nation, they have criticized the Reagan Administration and Congress for cuts that have been made. If they have lowered expectations for New Yorkers, making it clear that the vast increases in government benefits and government salaries of the 1965–75 period could not go on forever, the programs they back go considerably farther than voters in most states have supported so far.

The New York of the middle 1980s had its problems. Koch was surprised in early 1986 by a series of scandals centering around Queens Borough President Donald Manes, who killed himself with a butcher knife as associates of his were indicted. *Village Voice* writers and others who praised Lindsay as he bankrupted the city and hated Koch for puncturing liberal dogmas pounced on Koch. It was clear he was guilty of nothing more than bad judgment in appointing people recommended by corrupt borough leaders who had done nothing to get him elected. Koch and Cuomo were both appalled by the killing in late 1986 of a black who was chased by white youths and run over by a passing car in Queens's Howard Beach neighborhood; both appointed special committees and questioned whether there was more racism in New York than they thought. Also in late 1986 and early 1987 New York's vibrant economic growth was cast under a cloud by the insider trading scandal centering on abritrager Ivan Boesky; breaking the rules and cheating the public seemed to be common practice in the most visible part of New York's market economy, Wall Street. There is always the danger in a city centered on commerce that the desire for gain will turn into a greed that oversteps all moral bounds.

If New York's private markets seemed to be functioning all too vigorously, New York's public sector sometimes seemed incapable of functioning. It spent hundreds of millions building a 63d Street subway tunnel that was flooded with water and even if it ever opened would end in a vacant industrial lot in Queens. It kept dozens of infants untended in nurseries—the boarder babies—because it could not find the black and Hispanic adoptive parents that black social workers insisted could be the only ones to adopt them—though others were eager to provide them homes. The public sector that built bridges and tunnels over terrifying heights and under terrifying depths took three years to resurface Wollman Rink in Central Park, and failed—at which point developer Donald Trump came in and did it at his own expense in weeks. Why can't a public sector staffed by bright people get anything done? Because it is tied down by a million requirements to make it responsive to different constituencies and to prevent anyone from stealing anything. And neither reason can be waved away: the body politick must have its say in a democracy, and in a commercial city-state like New York with so much conspicuous wealth, there are always tremendous pressures tending to cause corruption—as the scandals of 1986 and 1987 show. The answer for New Yorkers has not been to abandon the public sector altogether—it is too late for that. But the answer of many has been to distrust it more, to rely on it less than people used to, to scale it back rather than let it grow bigger.

New York was once far and away the most liberal as well as the most affluent part of America: in both respects it is now less distinctive. New York now has a significant leftish vote in Democratic primaries—a vote that enabled onetime Ralph Nader associate Mark Green to beat millionaire businessman John Dyson in 1986 for the nomination to oppose Senator Alfonse D'Amato. But in the general elections its left-wing vote is no larger than those in many other states: D'Amato was easily reelected, the first time a Republican generally considered conservative has won a majority in a major New York race since 1920. In 1984 Walter Mondale won just 46% of New York's votes; in 1980 Jimmy Carter won only 44% of the vote, and John Anderson's independent candidacy (even with the once much-valued Liberal line on the New York ballot) took only 8%. New York City, which gave 14% of its votes to Communist-supported Henry Wallace in 1948, gave only 6% to the *Doonesbury*-celebrated Anderson in 1980. The children and grandchildren of the immigrants who made New York a self-consciously liberal state, now dispersed to outer boroughs and suburbs, on many issues embrace the politics of Ronald Reagan.

Upstate New York, like other old industrial areas, has not had substantial population growth, but has not been plunged into a depression as Detroit and Cleveland were in the early 1980s. Geographically, it has become a kind of backwater: passenger trains seldom or no longer run, its freight lines are bankrupt and poorly maintained, and its airports are not very busy. In an air-conditioned age people seek the warmer environment of the Sun Belt and shun Upstate. Its largest city, Buffalo, is one of those Great Lakes metropolises whose economy is visibly sagging; old steel mills are being closed and there is little new investment. But Upstate has its assets. It has high tech industries and a highly skilled labor force. It has a fine physical environment—green hills, majestic mountains, glistening lakes, a plentiful water supply—and its winters are no colder than those in booming Minnesota. For all the talk about this part of the country being doomed to economic stagnation, it sits on Lake Ontario just opposite the most economically productive part of Canada. Rochester has always had high tech industries; Albany's capital area has been booming in the 1980s. Upstate's biggest problem may be that it gets little attention: in the state it is overshadowed by New York City; it is not considered an integral part of either the East Coast or the Great Lakes Midwest; its cities do not loom large in the national consciousness. Its history—it was one of America's first frontiers, one of its first industrial workshops—does not fascinate us as much as it should; its fine colleges and cultural institutions do not command national attention.

But most New York politicians do. Robert Kennedy and Nelson Rockefeller used to bring national reporters to Rochester and Watertown, and now Mario Cuomo and Senator Daniel Patrick Moynihan—one of the most original and consistently interesting thinkers in American political history—do. New York's current leaders have come to power seemingly accidentally, by winning tiny margins in crucial elections: Moynihan in the 1976 Senate primary over Bella Abzug, Koch in the 1977 mayoral primary over Cuomo, and Cuomo in the close 1982 general election race against drugstore millionaire and free-market advocate Lewis Lehrman. But once in office these leaders have helped to make the state and city once again a lesson to all Americans in how things can work and how government can help make a better life for people. That may not be as great an achievement as the creation of New York's productive economy and the building of its generous welfare state. But it is no small achievement in a time when many had given up on government and politics and in a state where any voice has a hard time being heard over the noise and clangor that are part—perhaps the heart—of everyday life.

Presidential politics. The basic constituencies in the New York electorate are now quite different from those in the 1940s which still shape much journalism and analysis. Instead of machine Democrats in New York City, we have their children and grandchildren in the outer boroughs and suburbs—Catholic or Jewish, middle-income, with a Democratic heritage, always pressed for money in this high-priced metropolis, distrustful of culturally liberal trendy Manhattan, interested in preserving but disciplining the welfare state that was established for their forebears. In place of Yankee Upstate Republicans, we have an Upstate electorate that is heavily Catholic, that is heavily Republican out of suspicion of the Democratic City, but is also temperamentally inclined to support incumbents of either party. Instead of a large leftish bloc of Jewish voters, we have very much smaller and dispirited blocs of blacks and Puerto Ricans, while the most recent immigrants who have not yet started to vote much may turn out to be as conservative as Italian-Americans. In the 1940s, most of New York's votes were cast in New York City, which cast 7% of the votes in the entire nation. In the 1980s, about one-quarter of New York state's votes were cast in the city, with almost as many in the suburbs, and nearly half Upstate.

That basic mix adds up to a state that is closer to being, in a close national election, the exceedingly marginal constituency that Roosevelt and Dewey strategists considered it in the 1940s than the safe Democratic state that analysts in the 1960s and 1970s supposed. It is a couple of points more Democratic than the national average, barring special circumstances. In 1976, the aid to New York City issue boosted the vote here for south Georgia peanut farmer Jimmy Carter, who got a higher percentage in the New York metropolitan area than liberal Hubert Humphrey in 1968, Catholic John Kennedy in 1960, or New Yorker Franklin Roosevelt in 1940 and 1944. Balancing that is Upstate's predilection to rally to incumbent presidents of whatever party. Upstate gave above-national-average landslide percentages to Reagan in 1984, Nixon in 1972, Johnson in 1964, and Eisenhower in 1956. Its percentage for Reagan rose 12% between 1980 and 1984, one of his biggest rises outside the South; the Upstate percentage for Carter declined only from 44% in 1976 to 42% in 1980, one of the lowest drops in the nation.

If New York's general electorate is closer to the national average than is generally supposed, its primary electorates are very odd indeed. This is a state without primary traditions: Nelson Rockefeller vetoed state primary laws in the 1960s, because he feared that his kind of Republican would lose in primaries (he was right: in 1980 Jacob Javits lost to Al D'Amato), and because a convention system allowed Republicans to depict Democratic candidates as the choice of nefarious political bosses. Democratic primary turnout in 1984 was about 1.4 million in a state which cast nearly seven million votes in the general election; probably one-fourth of Democratic primary voters are Jewish, and about 70% live in the New York metropolitan area.

New York's results turn out to be unusual, too, and unequivocal. In 1984 this looked to be a closely contested primary. Gary Hart made a point of calling for moving the American embassy from Tel Aviv to Jerusalem—a sensible proposal but one which, in this context, was interpreted, not least by Jewish voters, as a blatant appeal for the Jewish vote. But Jewish votes went heavily to Walter Mondale, because of his longstanding views on Middle Eastern issues: many Jewish voters in New York see the Democratic primary as the single opportunity for American Jews to exert electoral pressure in American politics. Another reason may have been to present a united front against the visible threat of Jesse Jackson's candidacy. Black turnout was up sharply in 1984, out of enthusiasm for Jesse Jackson's candidacy and because many black leaders were eager to beat Mayor Koch the next year; and this at a time when Jackson had been referring to New York as "Hymietown" and featuring the anti-Jewish bigot Louis Farrakhan as warmup speaker at his rallies. In any case Mondale, who carried Upstate by the same kind of small margins he won in Pennsylvania and Illinois, led Hart overwhelmingly in New York City, enough to generate a 45%–27% statewide victory, with 26% for Jackson.

Republican primaries are as heavily tilted toward Upstate as Democratic contests are toward the city. They seem dominated not by laconic Yankees or upscale Wasps, but by Italian-Americans, who indeed form practically the entire Republican primary electorate in New York City. They are not averse to a little government interference in the economy, but on cultural issues their approach is traditional and even on economic issues like rent control they see themselves as adversaries of the great Democratic majority in New York City. In presidential contests, the Republicans elect delegates whose presidential preference is not identified on the ballot; there is no direct vote on the candidates themselves. But no one should have been surprised when Ronald Reagan ended up dominating the 1980 New York delegation. This was no more surprising than Lewis Lehrman's landslide victory in 1982 over a candidate supported by heirs of the old Dewey-Rockefeller organizations or Alfonse D'Amato's defeat of Jacob Javits in 1980.

Any observer of New York politics should resist the temptation to focus on the machinations of New York City's Democratic bosses, the county chairmen in each of the four biggest boroughs—just as Edward Koch should have resisted the temptation to heed their recommendations for appointments. It should be apparent to anyone by now that they have little to do with the outcome of statewide or national elections. They are in a different business, the brokering of patronage; for higher office, a county chairman's endorsement is more often a liability than an asset. The only genuine boss in New York, in the old sense of the word, has been Joseph Margiotta, longtime head of Nassau County's Republican Party, but he was convicted of the seemingly harmless offense of steering insurance business to politically favored firms (who should get it: the losers?) and is no longer a power. As for the state's minor parties, they have some potential influence because they can threaten to run separate candidates, but they no longer seem to move state politics in the direction they want, as the Liberals did in the 1950s and early 1960s and the Conservatives in the late 1960s and 1970s. Both suffered from supporting mayoral candidates their constituents came to consider unsatisfactory: the Liberals for backing John Lindsay in 1965 and 1969, the Conservatives for backing Mario Biaggi in 1973. Even the big fundraisers are no longer necessarily powers here: Mario Cuomo was far outspent by Edward Koch and Lewis Lehrman in 1982, and won anyway; Lehrman spent his own money, and Koch won the mayoralty in the first place without much in the way of smart money contributions. The real power brokers may be the media consultants who prepare TV ads and the news directors of New York TV stations who determine who gets on the air.

Governor. For the first time in nearly a generation, New York has a governor who is taken seriously as a presidential candidate. By force of intellect and character, he has made himself a major force in American politics, a national leader of the Democratic party. Yet just a few years ago, when he was running for governor in 1982, his resume was not impressive and his victory margin was only just sufficient. Elected lieutenant governor in 1978, he entered the 1982 governor's race the underdog in the primary to Edward Koch, who had beaten him for mayor in 1977, and with the prospect of lagging financially far behind Republican Lewis Lehrman, the Rite-Aid drug entrepreneur who was spending liberally of his own fortune to highlight his popular stands for capital punishment and big tax cuts. But Cuomo upset Koch in the primary, partly because many New Yorkers wanted to keep Koch as mayor, and he managed to raise enough money and win enough votes to beat Lehrman 51%–47%—not a huge margin in historically Democratic New York.

Once elected, Cuomo dominated public life. He lowered taxes and vetoed capital punishment bills, thus addressing issues raised by others, but he also made clear his own priorities. Education spending was raised and more money budgeted for new prisons, while new projects to help the poor were deferred; he opposed the Shoreham nuclear power plant on Long Island and got a toxic waste cleanup bill through in 1986, but was faulted by environmental lobbyists for not doing more; he pushed to raise New York's drinking age from 18, which it had been for more than 50 years, to 21; he got through bills on enterprise zones and $400 million for low and moderate income housing. Nationally, Cuomo was known for lashing out at the Reagan Administration for neglecting the needy and for being complacent as America was increasingly divided between the affluent and the poor. But as governor he has insisted that the private sector be nurtured by lower taxes and that the public sector be limited from spending money on programs he would like. The emphasis sounds different, but the positions are consistent when you put New York in context. It has been for 50 or 60 years America's most generous welfare state. The same policy preferences which lead Cuomo to cut taxes and limit spending in New York could lead him to raise taxes (to cut the the federal deficit he often decries) and raise spending in Washington.

In 1986 Cuomo's reelection was certain and his Republican opponent, Westchester County Executive Andrew O'Rourke, a humorous man who had just written his first mystery novel, could do little more than get in a few quips. But Cuomo's testiness and contentiousness prevented him from showcasing his record and his philosophy as much as he might have liked. Early in the year he defensively claimed there was no such thing as the Mafia and took umbrage at a remark that there were "not many Marios" in the South; he got into an imbroglio when George Bush distorted some of his remarks and attacked him for granting clemency to a prisoner. In the fall campaign he was criticized for going to court to get a rival to his choice for lieutenant governor off the primary ballot; he got into a shouting match with O'Rourke on the radio and agreed only at the last minute to debate; he criticized O'Rourke harshly for not disclosing his legal clients and responded angrily to criticism of his top aide and 28-year-old son, Andrew Cuomo. He won the election by a 65%–32% margin in a low turnout—a record percentage for New York: in fact, he would have won a record percentage for any New York governor even if not a single person had voted in New York City. It was another of the consensus victories seen in so many states in 1986, but came after more rancor and clash between candidate and, if not his opponent, then the press. In all this you could hear the feisty clamor you hear every day on the often very parochial streets of New York, and you could perhaps see a competitive athlete compelled to intimidate the opposition, an ace pitcher dusting even weak hitters away from the plate.

But you could also see, in Cuomo's larger record, the temperament of a mediator—which is how he began in politics, when Mayor Lindsay in 1972 asked him to mediate between advocates and opponents of a low-income housing project in middle-income Forest Hills. Cuomo prides himself on making judicial appointments on the basis of merit and without regard for party lines or legal ideology for New York's highest court, one of whose judges he had once served as a law clerk—a policy in vivid contrast to the determination of national liberals and conservatives to pack the courts with judges who will bend the law their way. His insistence in his 1984 Notre Dame speech that Catholics who believe abortion is murder should nonetheless refrain from trying to outlaw it in a society where most of their fellow citizens behave differently again shows a deference to the views of others. For New York he was willing to insist that any tax reform still allow state and local taxes to be deductible and with firm support from Daniel Patrick Moynihan, the first New Yorker on the Senate Finance Committee in this century, he prevailed.

But even as Cuomo directs attention at the poor, he also insists, as he did most vividly in his 1984 Democratic convention keynote, on how all Americans are descended from immigrants and poor people who have moved up in the world. That message reminds Americans of their nation's successes as well as its shortcomings. Cuomo's use of the metaphor of the family is not idle: he believes he has a responsibility to protect others from the harm that can come of liberation (hence the 21-year-old drinking age); his instinctive argument for gay rights and AIDS research is not an appeal for liberation but a call for parental compassion: how would you feel, he asks, if your child were gay? But his recurrent metaphor of society as a family is not an image that would spring to the lips of those liberals who seek various forms of liberation from traditional moral values, nor does it have much room for the notion that all the ills people may suffer from are the fault of society. Responsibility, yes; fault, no—it is a recipe for a politics of compassion that nevertheless embraces traditional standards of personal morality. Cuomo's is the kind of politics that naturally comes from the product of a hard-working family in a tight-knit neighborhood in Queens. His rhetoric can sound as divisive as a Bronx cheer, but he responds to issues as hard-bitten New Yorkers responded to the woman who was trapped under a construction crane, with skill and compassion. He is contentious almost always, but underneath he wants unity: "as I grow older, I am more eager to find a solution where we all can win."

In early 1987 Cuomo stunned everyone, including his staff and the interviewer on the radio call-in show he was with, when he announced that he would not run for President in 1988. Cynical observers had taken his statements that he wasn't at all sure he wanted to run lightly; evidently he meant them. Speculation about why he bowed out was rife: was he unhappy about criticism of his son, was he wary of the treatment an Italian–American would receive, did he think he was too liberal for his party or the people? Better to take him at his word: he saw some of the Democratic candidates in forums he set up in 1986, he decided they were up to the job, and he didn't especially want it himself. Everyone assumes every politician wants to be President, but it's not clear the job is so attractive to a man of Cuomo's temperament. He does seem pleased to be governor and probably will be for a long time—although it's just barely possible that his party will come to him in 1988, hat in hand, and ask whether he wouldn't like to rethink that decision and seek a place on the national ticket.

Senators. Every year a tall, gray-haired former Harvard professor spends several weeks in an old one-room schoolhouse in Pindar's Corners, deep in the hills of Upstate New York, writing in distinctive prose another book filled with original thought about—oh, almost anything: arms control or the Constitution and deficits, the tendency of opposing organizations to resemble each other or the rising proportion of children raised in single-parent homes. He is Senator Daniel Patrick Moynihan, the kind of philosopher-politician who would fill the ranks of the Senate in many people's ideal republic. Yet for all his academic credentials, Moynihan has had a range of experience in American government as broad as any Senator. He worked for Governor Averell Harriman in the 1950s, served as Assistant Secretary of Labor in the Kennedy and Johnson Administrations, was chief domestic advisor to President Nixon and his ambassador to India, and was ambassador to the United Nations under President Ford.

In all these jobs he displayed his penchant for original thinking and his taste for controversy. For years he was regarded with hostility by black political activists because of his warning about the breakup of black families in the middle 1960s, though they are now concerned about the same trend, much worsened, and by foreign policy doves for his assertive beliefs in American principles, though they now realize that those principles provide the strongest basis for their own beliefs. He crafted the Nixon Administration's Family Assistance Program and saw it savaged by the left and scuttled by the right in the Senate Finance Committee, on which he now has a seat. At the United Nations he spoke out against Russia and for Israel and ignored the conventional wisdom that policymakers should accept the premises of Third World and Soviet demands and negotiate quietly for small concessions; his policy is now approaching consensus status, as the Third World itself has been forced by events and stands like Moynihan's to turn away from anti-American rhetoric. Moynihan's prescience, his ability to spot rising issues is almost eerie. In the early 1960s, to cite just one example, before Ralph Nader, he was writing about auto safety.

Moynihan showed the same uncanny instinct for spotting issues throughout the 1980s. In the spring of 1981, when he pounced on Reagan Administration proposals to cut scheduled future Social Security benefits, striding forward with a resolution denouncing any benefit cuts which was beaten only by a 49–48 vote; promptly the Senate adopted a resolution by Bob Dole, that said much the same thing, by 96–0. In his 1985 Godkin Lectures at Harvard, published as *Family and Nation*, Moynihan returned 20 years after his family report on the Negro (as it then was) family to the subject of society's treatment of children and found it wanting. We have eliminated poverty for the elderly, he said in essence, only to see it burgeon for children.

Legislatively in 1985 and 1986 he concentrated on his duties as vice-chairman of the Intelligence Committee, resigning momentarily after CIA Director William Casey withheld required information, and returning again to cooperate with chairman Barry Goldwater. He sharply attacked Gramm-Rudman on constitutional and institutional grounds. And on the Finance Committee he worked on the tax reform bill, insisting early on maintaining deductions for state and local taxes (worth more in New York than anywhere else) and supporting steadfastly thereafter the kind of reform that passed. In early 1987 he returned to the problem of poor children, advancing his own outlines for a welfare reform package scrapping AFDC, encouraging mothers to work, and underlining the obligations of parents—fathers as well as mothers—to support their children.

A conventional politician Moynihan is not. Yet he has had great success in New York politics. His hardest race so far was the 1976 primary in which he beat Bella Abzug by only 10,000 votes of 916,000 cast; he was fresh from denouncing the Soviets and Third World bloc in the U.N. and she fresh from denouncing the United States over Vietnam. In the general election he won routinely over incumbent James Buckley, who improved on the percentage with which he won the three-way race of 1970 but not enough to win a two-way battle. For 1982 Moynihan underplayed his support of higher defense budgets and emphasized his disagreement with the Reagan Administration on issues like Social Security, the Equal Rights Amendment, and aid to cities, and had no primary opposition on the left or right; Republican Representative Bruce Caputo left the race in the spring when it was learned that he had a falsified military record. That fall Moynihan won with the largest percentage and the largest plurality of any Senator in New York's history.

Moynihan enters 1988 a solid favorite for reelection. In early 1987 prominent Republicans were rumored to be interested: Lew Lehrman, Ambassador to Austria and cosmetics heir Ronald Lauder, and U.S. Attorney Rudolph Giuliani, the prosecutor of Ivan Boesky and other inside traders. But it's not clear that any will run or can beat an incumbent who has not only a party advantage but also a record that is attuned to local needs and distinguished by the leadership on national issues New York has usually expected in its politicians. There is grumbling among New York's neoconservative intellectuals, whom Moynihan did not follow into Ronald Reagan's Republican Party, that he has deserted their principles, and he has; but he hasn't deserted his own, which were rather different, even idiosyncratic, all along. It is sometimes asked whether Moynihan has national ambitions. But to a considerable extent, he has already realized them. He has been a figure of national importance for two decades, and not just because of the offices he has held, but because of the ideas he has generated and the policies he has advocated.

New York's other Senator, Alfonse D'Amato, cuts less of a national figure, concentrating almost entirely on local matters; where Moynihan articulates original principles, D'Amato has been the most slavish follower of the conventional wisdom of New York politics. And with considerable success: a seeming political fluke when he won the Senate seat in 1980, with 45% of the vote in a three-way race, he won reelection comfortably with 57% in 1986. Nonetheless, he has made progress in persuading observers that he should be regarded as more than a fluke and has succeeded in establishing himself as a formidable politician in his own right. D'Amato may or may not be wise, but he is certainly shrewd—shrewd in challenging Jacob Javits in the Republican primary, whose voters considered him far too liberal, for all his brilliant achievements; shrewd, in attacking Javits as too old and infirm; shrewd, in running hard against liberal Democrat Elizabeth Holtzman, now the district attorney in Brooklyn, and in not shunning Ronald Reagan, who carried New York comfortably.

As a Senator, D'Amato has also been shrewd to the point of shamelessness in taking practically any position, espousing any cause, and lobbying for any project or program that could be popular with even the smallest segment of the New York electorate, while turning his back without a moment's hesitation on those who helped him get where he is (like his longtime patron, former Nassau County Republican boss Joseph Margiotta). All the while he remains jovial and good-humored—as if he were elbowing erstwhile opponents in the ribs and saying, it's only a game, right? "O.K., I love ya, babes," he signs off his phone conversations. Shamelessly he fastens on the sudden popularity of a Bernhard Goetz or proposes to give terrorist victim Leon Klinghoffer the Congressional Medal of Honor. Elected on the Reagan ticket, he has had no problems voting often against the Administration, particularly on economic issues where its position is unpopular in New York.

Before 1980 D'Amato was an upper-operative in a patronage-oriented machine, the presiding supervisor of the town of Hempstead (a big town, with 800,000 people, but a post of limited powers) in a county where employees had to give 1% of their salaries to the Republican Party. Suddenly he had a say over all federal patronage in New York—federal judges, U.S. attorneys, federal marshals, the heads of the New York regional offices of the various federal bureaucracies. Yet he has used that power hesitantly and carefully. He has been more brazen in using his committee assignments to bring pork to New York—he likes to be called "the pothole Senator"—and to raise money for his own campaign. In particular, his chairmanship of the subcommittee with jurisdiction over the SEC helped him raise at least $500,000 in contributions from New York's financial district; on the Banking Committee he invariably backs Wall Street firms in their fights against the big banks. He was able to amass some $5 million by June 1986, while his seemingly strongest opponent, former congresswoman and vice presidential nominee Geraldine Ferraro, was appearing in Pepsi ads and confronting the legal problems of her husband and son.

Leading Democrats finally got businessman John Dyson, who as commerce commissioner inspired the "I Love New York" promotion, to run against D'Amato. But Dyson was upset in the primary by Mark Green, a longtime associate of Ralph Nader, who carried the New York City area after charging that the maladroit but heavy-spending Dyson was too conservative and promising himself to run without any PAC contributions. Vastly outspent, scorned by Mayor Koch, supported formally by Cuomo, Green got 41% in the general election. D'Amato is in the minority now, but doubtless will be hustling for local interests as much as ever.

Mayor. For many years the budget of New York City was bigger than the budget of New York state, and in many ways the mayor of New York sets the tone for public life in the city. Edward Koch, elected in 1977, 1981, and 1985, has been wildly popular with most voters in the outer boroughs, whose views he tends to express volubly and often at length and whose gritty style he personifies. He has made a success of city government in New York, restoring its finances, raising slowly the quality of public services, forestalling the excesses of racial quotas while appointing the city's first black police commissioner. He stumbled when he ran for governor in 1982: book smart and street smart, capable of dazzling urban ethnologists and of giving a heckler the raspberry, Koch is a quintessential mayor, and belongs in Albany no more than Jimmy Carter belongs in the Bronx. Blacks and liberals summoned up much outrage but few votes against him in 1985, when he carried almost every assembly district in the city against council president Carol Bellamy and Assemblyman Herman Farrell. The next year was tougher, with the Queens and Bronx scandals and the Howard Beach incident, but in 1987 most voters continued to respect Koch's honesty and competence. He could turn out to be the first New York mayor to win a fourth 4-year term.

Congressional districting. Every 10 years the New York legislature is faced with the unhappy task of reducing the number of New York's congressional districts—from 39 to 34 most recently, in 1982. As usual, the losers were mostly political mavericks with limited clout. Altogether the New York delegation is not as powerful as its numbers might suggest, though it is less fractious today than in the early 1970s. It was successful, however, in insisting on keeping deductions for state and local taxes in the 1986 reform law.

The People: Est. Pop. 1986: 17,772,000; Pop. 1980: 17,558,072, up 1.2% 1980–86 and dn. 3.7% 1970–80; 7.37% of U.S. total, 2d largest. 14% with 1–3 yrs. col., 19% with 4+ yrs. col.; 13.4% below poverty level. Single ancestry: 11% Italian, 6% Irish, 5% German, English, 3% Polish, 2% Russian, 1% French, Greek, Hungarian. Households (1980): 70% family, 37% with children, 54% married couples; 51.4% housing units rented; median monthly rent: $211; median house value: $45,900. Voting age pop. (1980): 12,870,209; 12% Black, 8% Spanish origin, 2% Asian origin. Registered voters (1986): 8,078,779; 3,820,085 D (47%); 2,602,782 (R); 1,461,281 unaffiliated (18%); 194,631 minor parties (3%).

1986 Share of Federal Tax Burden: $62,877,000,000; 8.36% of U.S. total, 2d largest.

1986 Share of Federal Expenditures

	Total		Non-Defense		Defense	
Total Expend	$59,448m	(7.16%)	$48,169m	(8.02%)	$11,279m	(4.19%)
St/Lcl Grants	12,380m	(11.00%)	12,374m	(11.00%)	2m	(5.41%)
Salary/Wages	5,217m	(4.32%)	4,144m	(7.06%)	1,072m	(1.73%)
Pymnts to Indiv	28,554m	(7.83%)	28,259m	(8.15%)	295m	(1.66%)
Procurement	11,679m	(5.68%)	1,779m	(3.20%)	9,900m	(6.60%)
Research/Other	1,618m	(6.07%)	1,613m	(6.05%)	6m	(17.13%)

Political Lineup: Governor, Mario Cuomo (D); Lt. Gov., Stanley N. Lundine (D); Atty. Gen., Robert Abrams (D); Comptroller, Edward V. Regan (R). State Senate, 61 (35 R and 26 D); State Assembly, 150 (93 D and 56 R, 1 vacancy). Senators, Daniel Patrick Moynihan (D) and Alfonse M. D'Amato (R). Representatives, 34 (21 D and 13 R).

1984 Presidential Vote

Reagan (R) 3,664,763 (54%)
Mondale (D) 3,119,609 (46%)

1984 Democratic Presidential Primary

Mondale 621,581 (45%)
Hart. 380,564 (27%)
Jackson 355,541 (26%)
Four others 30,180 (2%)

1980 Presidential Vote

Reagan (R) 2,893,831 (47%)
Carter (D) 2,728,372 (44%)
Anderson (I) 467,801 (8%)

GOVERNOR

Gov. Mario M. Cuomo (D)

Elected 1982, term expires Jan. 1991; b. June 15, 1932, Queens; home, Queens; St. John's U., B.A. 1953, LL.B. 1956; Roman Catholic; married (Matilda).

Career: Confidential Legal Asst. to Judge Adrian T. Burke, NY State Crt. of Appeals, 1956–58; Practicing atty., 1958–74; Prof., St. John's U. Sch. of Law, 1958–74; Secy. of State of NY, 1975–78, Lt. Gov., 1978–82.

Office: Executive Chamber, State Capitol, Albany 12224, 518-474-8390.

Election Results

1986 gen.	Mario M. Cuomo (D).	2,775,229	(65%)
	Andrew J. O'Rourke (R)	1,363,810	(32%)
	Dillon Droseskey (RTL).	130,802	(3%)
1986 prim.	Mario M. Cuomo (D) unopposed		
1982 gen.	Mario M. Cuomo (D–L)	2,675,213	(51%)
	Lewis E. Lehrman (R–C–SI). . .	2,494,827	(47%)

SENATORS

Sen. Daniel Patrick Moynihan (D)

Elected 1976, seat up 1988; b. Mar. 16, 1927, Tulsa, OK; home, W. Davenport; CCNY, 1943, Tufts U., B.A. 1948, M.A. 1949, Ph.D. 1961, LL.D. 1968; Roman Catholic; married (Elizabeth).

Career: Navy, 1944–47; University professor; Aide to Gov. Averell Harriman, 1955–58; U.S. Asst. Secy. of Labor, 1963–65; Dir., Joint Ctr. for Urban Studies, MIT and Harvard, 1966–69; Asst. to the Pres. for Urban Affairs, 1969–70; Ambassador to India, 1973–75; Ambassador to the U.N., 1975–76.

Offices: 464 RSOB 20510, 202-224-4451. Also 733 3d Ave., New York 10017, 212-661-5150; Guaranty Bldg., 28 Church St., Buffalo 14202, 716-846-4097; and 214 Main St., Oneonta 13820, 607-433-2310.

Committees: *Environment and Public Works* (2d of 9 D). Subcommittees: Environmental Protection; Nuclear Regulation; Water Resources, Transportation and Infrastructure (Chairman). *Finance* (3d of 11 D). Subcommittees: International Trade; Social Security and Family Policy (Chairman); Taxation and Debt Management. *Foreign Relations* (10th of 11 D). Subcommittees: African Affairs; Near Eastern and South Asian Affairs; Terrorism, Narcotics and International Communications. *Rules and Administration* (7th of 9D). *Joint Committee on the Library. Joint Committee on Taxation.*

Group Ratings

	ADA	ACLU	COPE	CFA	LCV	ACU	NTU	NSI	COC	CEI
1986	85	85	91	73	64	13	36	10	39	27
1985	90	—	93	93	—	4	28	—	33	—

National Journal Ratings

	1986 LIB — 1986 CONS		1985 LIB — 1985 CONS	
Economic	73% —	22%	89% —	8%
Social	86% —	11%	88% —	0%
Foreign	71% —	25%	70% —	28%

Key Votes

1) Ease Gun Cont	AGN	5) Grm-Rdmn Def Red	AGN	9) Rehnquist Nom	AGN
2) Immig Reform	FOR	6) Contra Aid	AGN	10) Tax Reform	FOR
3) Lmt Text Imp	FOR	7) SDI Funding	AGN	11) Drug Death Pen	AGN
4) Aid Tobac Ind	AGN	8) Lmt PAC Contrib	FOR	12) S Africa Sanc	FOR

Election Results

1982 general	Daniel Patrick Moynihan (D–L)	3,232,146	(65%)	($2,708,660)
	Florence Sullivan (R–C–RTL)	1,696,766	(34%)	($117,875)
1982 primary	Daniel Patrick Moynihan (D)	922,059	(85%)	
	Melvin Klenetsky (D)	161,012	(15%)	
1976 general	Daniel Patrick Moynihan (D)	3,422,594	(54%)	($1,210,796)
	James L. Buckley (R)	2,836,633	(45%)	($2,101,424)

Campaign Contributions and Expenditures

1979-82		Direct Cont. 1979-82		PACS Breakdown			
Receipts	$3,093,286	Indiv.	$2,415,198	Agr	$3,000	Ideo	$29,450
Expend.	$2,708,660	Party	$18,600	Bus	$160,490	Lbr	$145,370
Unspent	$116,647	PACS	$481,861	Hlth	$13,100	Prof	$12,000

Sen. Alfonse M. D'Amato (R)

Elected 1980, seat up 1992; b. Aug. 1, 1937, Brooklyn; home, Island Park; Syracuse U., B.S. 1959, J.D. 1961; Roman Catholic; separated.

Career: Nassau Cnty. Public Admin., 1965–68; Hempstead Town Receiver of Taxes, 1969, Sprvsr., 1971–77, Presiding Sprvsr., Vice Chmn. Nassau Cnty. Bd. of Sprvsrs., 1977–80.

Offices: 520 HSOB 20510, 202-224-6542. Also 420 Leo O'Brian Fed. Bldg., Albany 12207, 518-463-2244; Fed. Bldg., 111 W. Huron, Rm. 620, Buffalo 14202, 716-846-4111; 1 Penn Plaza, Ste. 1635, New York 10001, 212-947-7390; 1259 Fed. Bldg., 100 S. Clinton St., Syracuse 13260, 315-423-5471; and 100 State St., 304 Fed. Bldg., Rochester 14614, 716-263-5866.

Committees: *Appropriations* (8th of 13 R). Subcommittees: Defense; Foreign Operations; HUD–Independent Agencies; Treasury, Postal Service, General Government; Transportation and Related Agencies (Ranking Member). *Banking, Housing, and Urban Affairs* (4th of 9 R). Subcommittees: Housing and Urban Affairs; Securities (Ranking Member). *Small Business* (4th of 9 R). Subcommittees: Export and Expansion, Rural Economy and Family Farming (Ranking Member). *Joint Economic Committee.* Subcommittees: Economic Growth Trade and Taxes; Education and Health; Investment, Jobs and Prices.

Group Ratings

	ADA	ACLU	COPE	CFA	LCV	ACU	NTU	NSI	COC	CEI
1986	35	7	42	53	54	70	36	100	56	48
1985	20	—	41	47	—	65	41	—	62	—

National Journal Ratings

	1986 LIB — 1986 CONS	1985 LIB — 1985 CONS
Economic	59% — 39%	51% — 47%
Social	26% — 73%	35% — 62%
Foreign	49% — 49%	31% — 66%

Key Votes

1) Ease Gun Cont	FOR	5) Grm-Rdmn Def Red	FOR	9) Rehnquist Nom	FOR
2) Immig Reform	FOR	6) Contra Aid	FOR	10) Tax Reform	FOR
3) Lmt Text Imp	FOR	7) SDI Funding	FOR	11) Drug Death Pen	AGN
4) Aid Tobac Ind	FOR	8) Lmt PAC Contrib	FOR	12) S Africa Sanc	FOR

Election Results

1986 general	Alfonse M. D'Amato (R-C-RTL)	2,378,197	(57%)	($12,914,822)
	Mark Green (D)	1,723,216	(41%)	($1,635,676)
1986 primary	Alfonse M. D'Amato (R) unopposed			
1980 general	Alfonse M. D'Amato (R–C–RTL)	2,699,965	(45%)	($1,699,709)
	Elizabeth Holtzman (D)	2,618,661	(44%)	($2,173,056)
	Jacob K. Javits (L)	664,544	(11%)	($1,846,313)

Campaign Contributions and Expenditures

1985-86		Direct Cont. 1985-86		PACS Breakdown 1985-86			
Receipts	$11,333,629	Indiv.	$4,825,412	Corp.	$466,365	T/M/H	$191,206
Expend.	$12,914,822	Party	$18,113	Labor	$83,272	Agr.	$8,500
Unspent	$456,293	PACS	$885,668	Ideo.	$102,507	CWOS	$33,818
		Cand.	$885,668				

FIRST DISTRICT

The Montauk Lighthouse, the old fishing ports of Sag Harbor and Shelter Island, the beach at Southampton lined with grand mansions behind the dunes, the potato fields near Riverhead—these are all sights you might see approaching the eastern end of Long Island, America's largest island, from the sea. But the most important place politically on eastern Long Island is Shoreham, an old town on the north shore, where the local utility Lilco has been trying to build a nuclear power plant since the 1970s. In a familiar pattern, costs have skyrocketed while safety concerns have grown; a federal regulatory official was fired because he would not say Lilco's evacuation procedures were satisfactory; electricity users find themselves paying vastly higher rates to finance a plant that isn't yet operating and which most of them hope never will be. It got to the point that in 1986 Governor Mario Cuomo and other Democrats were urging, in the free enterprise 1980s, a state takeover of all of Lilco.

Ironically, all of this happened in one of the most self-consciously conservative parts of the Northeast. The resort area around the Hamptons may be trendily leftish in the summer when it is thronged with New York writers and artists, but the bulk of the people here are conservative-minded New Yorkers and Long Islanders, moving eastward and filling up Long Island to the point where the pine barrens in the town of Brookhaven begin, some 45 miles east of Manhattan. Culturally conservative family people, economically upwardly mobile private sector employees, they were James Buckley Conservatives before becoming Ronald Reagan Republicans. Yet the sheer incompetence of Lilco's Shoreham enterprise repulsed them, to the point that Representative Robert Carney, representing the 1st District that stretches from the shopping centers of Brookhaven to the New Englandish farmhouses of the Hamptons, was nearly defeated in both the primary (he won with 52%) and the general (53%) election in 1984 because he stoutly supported Shoreham. When the Chernobyl accident of April 1986 made Long Islanders even more apprehensive and angry, Carney announced suddenly in May 1986 that he was retiring at age 44.

The contest in 1986 was between the two men who nearly beat Carney two years before, and the winner was Democrat George Hochbrueckner. Republican Gregory Blass had an advantage in having opposed Shoreham first, but he alienated some Republicans by winning the presiding officer of the Suffolk legislature with mostly Democratic votes. Hochbrueckner had the advantage of solid popularity in the Brookhaven area district he represented in the New York Assembly for 10 years until his 1984 race against Carney and membership in the majority party in the House which he promised to use to foil Lilco and stop Shoreham. He had the advantage as well of a sizable edge in PAC funds—even so that this Democrat could outspend the Republican in a Republican-held seat. Hochbrueckner won with 51% of the vote. A former Grumman engineer, he was given a seat on the Armed Services Committe—important on Long Island, with all its defense contractors—and on Merchant Marine and Fisheries. Other Democrats have held Long Island seats using the power of incumbency, notably Otis Pike who represented eastern Long Island from 1960 until he retired in 1978. Hochbrueckner will have a chance in 1988 to see if he can too.

The People: Pop. 1980: 516,407, up 36.7% 1970–80. Households (1980): 81% family, 49% with children, 69% married couples; 21.5% housing units rented; median monthly rent: $281; median house value: $43,700. Voting age pop. (1980): 350,987; 4% Black, 3% Spanish origin, 1% Asian origin.

1984 Presidential Vote:

Reagan (R)	137,855	(66%)
Mondale (D)	70,592	(34%)

Rep. George Hochbrueckner (D)

Elected 1986; b. Sept. 20, 1938, Jamaica, Queens; home, Coram; St. U. of NY, Stonybrook, Hofstra U.; Roman Catholic; married (Carol Ann).

Career: Navy, 1956–59; Engineer, 1961–75; NY Assembly, 1975–84.

Offices: 1008 LHOB 20515, 202-225-3826. Also 3771 Nesconset Hwy., Ste. 213, Centereach 11720, 516-689-6767; and Bagshaw Office Bldg., 437 E. Main, Riverhead 11901, 516-727-2152.

Committees: *Armed Services* (29th of 31 D). Subcommittees: Readiness; Research and Development; Seapower and Strategic and Critical Materials. *Merchant Marine and Fisheries* (25th of 25 D). Subcommittees: Coast Guard and Navigation; Merchant Marine; Panama Canal and Outer Continental Shelf.

Group Ratings and Key Votes: Newly Elected

Election Results

1986 general	George J. Hochbrueckner (D)	67,139	(51%)	($416,332)
	Gregory J. Blass (R–CAL).	55,413	(42%)	($277,947)
	Dominic J. Santoro (C).	4,345	(3%)	
	William J. Doyle (RTL)	4,134	(3%)	
1986 primary	George J. Hochbrueckner (D) unopposed			
1984 general	William Carney (R–C–RTL)	107,029	(53%)	($353,433)
	George J. Hochbrueckner (D–RAL)	94,551	(47%)	($191,966)

Campaign Contributions and Expenditures

1985-86		Direct Cont. 1985-86		PACS Breakdown 1985-86			
Receipts	$416,038	Indiv.	$154,412	Corp.	$7,950	T/M/H	$32,000
Expend.	$416,332	Party	$6,557	Labor	$148,790	Agr.	$2,500
Unspent	$467	PACS	$243,006	Ideo.	$51,266	CWOS	$500
		Cand.	$5,500				

SECOND DISTRICT

Into the potato fields of central Long Island, in the 20 booming years after World War II, poured hundreds of thousands of New Yorkers—mostly people who thought they would always live within the boundaries of the City and never imagined that they would find their way—except for Sunday outings—this far out on the Island. The highways that Robert Moses built to connect Jones Beach with the masses of Queens and Brooklyn suddenly became routes of migration, commuter paths, as young veterans and their families found they could afford to leave the row-house neighborhoods where they had grown up for the comparatively spacious lots and single-family houses of Levittown and other Long Island subdivisions. The first wave of postwar migration moved into Nassau County, and it was a pretty accurate cross-section of all but the poorest New Yorkers: almost half Catholic, about one-fourth Jewish and one-fourth Protestant. Then, as Long Island developed an employment base of its own, the next wave of migration started, this time far out into Suffolk County. This second wave was more Catholic and less Jewish, more blue collar (aircraft manufacturers are Suffolk County's biggest employers) and less white collar, more Democratic perhaps in ancestral politics but culturally more firmly traditional and conservative in their approach to life.

The 2d Congressional District of New York covers a large part of Suffolk County—essentially the South Shore towns of Babylon and Islip, which within them contain dozens of suburbs with different names—one community after another strung out along the Sunrise

Highway. With a few exceptions (notably Dix Hills in the north) this is the lowest income part of Long Island, out past the fashionable and expensive suburbs with their minimum acreage zoning, far from the picturesque North Shore and separated by the Great South Bay from the beaches of Fire Island. The area filled up with people in the 1950s and 1960s and has had little population change since; the modest homes are being upgraded by their owners or sometimes left with chipped paint and cracked shingle siding.

Yet there has been change: the district has one of the highest percentages of households with children in New York, and one reason is that young families have been buying here, where decent houses can still be bought for under $100,000, and planning to move up to better neighborhoods later. Nor are all these people white. There are black concentrations in North Amityville and Wyandanch, and substantial numbers of blacks and Latin Americans scattered elsewhere to make the district 9% black and 7% Spanish origin.

Thomas Downey, the congressman from the 2d District, is still one of the youngest members of Congress and sometimes the brashest; he was definitely the youngest and quite possibly the brashest when he was first elected as part of the Watergate class of 1974. In that race Downey showed the kind of political acumen he has demonstrated since in the House. He was smart enough to spot the weaknesses in an incumbent who had gotten 66% two years before; he was energetic enough to promise credibly that he would give the district more active representation; and he was experienced enough to be able to cite three years' service in the Suffolk County legislature.

In the House Downey has been aggressive, active, a strong partisan, ready to debate big issues. In his first two terms, he was a member of the Armed Services Committee, dovish on policy generally but eager to promote the programs of Long Island's aircraft manufacturers. In 1979 he switched to Ways and Means, and from 1981 to 1987 he had a seat on Budget. Throughout the 1980s he has been one of the House's voluble and sarcastic critics of the Reagan Administration, regularly denouncing it for stinginess on domestic programs and profligacy on defense. He attacked in particular the MX missile, criticized the Strategic Defense Initiative, and called for a nuclear test moratorium. Often he speaks in tones of sarcasm, but he is also able to summon up facts and figures and master arguments: he usually has done his homework.

These qualities which endear Downey to many of his fellow Democrats tend to infuriate many conservative Republicans. In 1985 he was attacked as a "draft-dodging wimp" by California Republican Robert Dornan, whose nomination to an arms control agency post Downey had helped to kill two years before. Dornan went beyond insults and grabbed Downey's necktie in a confrontation between the two in the Capitol. Downey coolly walked away in an exercise of admirable self-control.

On Ways and Means, he supported the 1986 tax reform bill but, with other New Yorkers, insisted on that state and local income taxes remain deductible, as they have. He staunchly opposes any value added tax ("the devil's work," as he puts it), whether used for revenues generally or for the Superfund program. He has a seat on the Trade Subcommittee, and like other Long Island Democrats—perhaps because of the prominence of the export-hungry aircraft industry there—he has been considerably more faithful to free trade principles than most northeastern Democrats.

This is not a Democratic district in most elections, though it certainly went for Governor Mario Cuomo and Senator Daniel Patrick Moynihan in their most recent contests. But Downey has been almost the paradigmatic constituency service congressman since he was elected in 1974. He is a harsh critic of Lilco's Shoreham nuclear plant and criticized the Reagan Administration's firing of a FEMA official critical of its evacuation plan as "bizarre." He works to maintain Section 8 housing in Babylon and Islip and to maintain funding for T-46 trainer jets built by Fairchild in Farmingdale just over the Nassau County line. All this has helped him win reelection, though usually with less than 60%; against a spirited challenge from an even younger conservative in 1984 he won 55%. He rebounded to 64%—his highest percentage—in 1986. Downey has the potential to be an able and effective legislator for many, many years, but he will always have to closely tend this marginal district. There has been talk that he would run for statewide office, but he has not yet taken that plunge.

The People: Pop. 1980: 515,595, up 5.1% 1970–80. Households (1980): 85% family, 53% with children, 71% married couples; 21.4% housing units rented; median monthly rent: $314; median house value: $41,700. Voting age pop. (1980): 351,055; 8% Black, 6% Spanish origin, 1% Asian origin.

1984 Presidential Vote:

Reagan (R)	123,453	(66%)
Mondale (D)	62,326	(33%)

Rep. Thomas J. Downey (D)

Elected 1974; b. Jan. 28, 1949, Ozone Park; home, Amityville; Cornell U., B.S. 1970, St. John's U. Sch. of Law, 1972–74; American U., J.D. 1978; United Methodist; married (Chris).

Career: Personnel mgmt. and labor relations, Macy's Dept. Store, 1970; Suffolk Cnty. Legislature, 1971–74.

Offices: 2232 RHOB 20515, 202-225-3335. Also 4 Udall Rd., West Islip 11795, 516-661-8777.

Committees: *Ways and Means* (10th of 23 D). Subcommittees: Public Assistance and Unemployment Compensation; Trade. *Select Committee on Aging* (5th of 39 D). Subcommittees: Human Services; Retirement Income and Employment.

Group Ratings

	ADA	ACLU	COPE	CFA	LCV	ACU	NTU	NSI	COC	CEI
1986	95	94	87	92	85	5	28	0	17	19
1985	85	—	88	93	—	5	35	—	26	—

National Journal Ratings

	1986 LIB — 1986 CONS			1985 LIB — 1985 CONS		
Economic	69%	—	30%	89%	—	0%
Social	89%	—	0%	85%	—	0%
Foreign	80%	—	0%	85%	—	8%

Key Votes

1) Lmt Cln Water Act	—	5) Retain Gun Cont	FOR	9) Aid Angola Reb	AGN
2) Rpl Tobac Sub	FOR	6) Contra Aid	AGN	10) Tax Reform	FOR
3) Grm-Rdmn Def Red	AGN	7) Lmt Text Imp	AGN	11) S Africa Sanc	FOR
4) Ban Polygraph	FOR	8) Limit SDI	FOR	12) Immig Reform	FOR

Election Results

1986 general	Thomas J. Downey (D–RAL)	69,771	(64%)	($739,062)
	Jeffrey A. Butzke (R–CAL–RTL)	35,132	(33%)	($30,153)
	Veronica Windishman (RTL)	3,651	(3%)	
1986 primary	Thomas J. Downey (D) unopposed			
1984 general	Thomas J. Downey (D–I)	97,648	(55%)	($491,483)
	Paul Aniboli (R–C–RTL)	80,855	(45%)	($149,131)

Campaign Contributions and Expenditures

1985-86		Direct Cont. 1985-86		PACS Breakdown 1985-86			
Receipts	$823,272	Indiv.	$470,803	Corp.	$77,192	T/M/H	$83,750
Expend.	$739,062	Party	$370	Labor	$58,811	Agr.	$0
Unspent	$239,970	PACS	$249,651	Ideo.	$28,498	CWOS	$1,400

THIRD DISTRICT

A yatch cruising the inlets off Long Island Sound in the 1920s would sail beneath the great mansions of Vincent Astor and the Guggenheims, Teddy Roosevelt's Sagamore Hill and the grand houses occupied by Eddie Cantor and F. Scott Fitzgerald. This was the original Gatsby country, where the richest people in business and show business took their leisure and watched as their servants unloaded the bootleggers' boats at their docks. Inland, behind the bright green lawns, Long Island was then still mostly farm country, with little villages clustered at railroad stations, occasional colonial era houses, and acres of billboard-strewn wasteland on the main highways to New York City. Only in the years after World War II did settlers stream in from the City. The North Shore suburbs, hilly and green, attracted many of the better educated and higher income migrants in the 1940s and 1950s; by the 1960s, they were pretty well built up through Syosset in Nassau County and into Huntington in Suffolk County. Since then their population has not changed much. Households have lost people as children have grown up and moved away; new housing units, mostly apartments and condominiums, have been added.

New York's 3d Congressional District consists of the North Shore suburbs from Manhasset, Port Washington, and the New York City line in the west, all the way through Nassau and into Suffolk County, to Smithtown in the east. The southern boundary throughout runs near the Long Island Expressway. This is almost entirely affluent country, with the highest housing prices of any New York suburban district, except for the 20th in Westchester County. It tends to go Republican in national and state elections, although its Jewish voters provide a solid liberal base for a Democratic candidate.

The congressman from the 3d is Robert Mrazek, a Democrat who has skillfully extracted every bit of political advantage from an unusual set of circumstances. He won the seat as a Suffolk County legislator in 1982 by beating Republican John LeBoutillier, the brash freshman descendant of Vanderbilts and Whitneys who called Speaker Tip O'Neill "fat, bloated, and out of control—just like the federal budget." O'Neill made sure Mrazek's campaign was well funded, and Mrazek used the money ably, charging that LeBoutillier was ineffective and uninterested in the practical problems of Long Island. Mrazek has spent his own congressional career trying to prove that he is the opposite on both counts, and with considerable success.

He began by becoming the only freshman on the House Appropriations Committee, thanks again to the speaker. He authored a successful amendment barring U.S. troops from training Nicaraguan contras within 20 miles of the Nicaragua–Honduras border and another cutting $112 million from the Strategic Defense Initiative. On the Transportation Subcommittee he has pushed for electrification of the Long Island Railroad's Port Jefferson line. He sponsored an amendment to help the local firm that imports Riunite wine by requiring labelling of ingredients on imported wine. He presented a letter signed by 257 House members to the West German government asking it to call off President Reagan's 1985 visit to Bitburg. He introduced legislation outlawing plastic guns that can't be detected in airport security machines. He introduced a law banning the use of pound animals for scientific research.

All of these positions, plus his local base in Suffolk County, have helped him win reelection in the Republican-leaning 3d. In 1984 he beat a retired investment banker who spent liberally on a campaign stressing his Reagan conservatism; in 1986 he vastly outspent and beat a local Nassau County official who tried to make garbage the top issue. None of the results says that Mrazek has a safe seat, but he has certainly showed the political skill to hold it for some time.

The People: Pop. 1980: 516,610, dn. 3.3% 1970–80. Households (1980): 83% family, 44% with children, 73% married couples; 20.1% housing units rented; median monthly rent: $325; median house value: $70,500. Voting age pop. (1980): 378,027; 3% Black, 2% Spanish origin, 1% Asian origin.

1984 Presidential Vote:

Reagan (R)	159,039	(64%)
Mondale (D)	87,624	(35%)

Rep. Robert J. Mrazek (D)

Elected 1982; b. Nov. 6, 1945, Newport, RI; home, Centerport; Cornell U., B.A. 1967; United Methodist; married (Catherine).

Career: Navy, 1967–68; Staff, U.S. Sen. Vance Hartke, 1969–71; Owner, small business, 1971–75; Suffolk Cnty. Legislature, 1975–82, Minor. Ldr., 1979–82.

Offices: 306 CHOB 20515, 202-225-5956. Also 143 Main St., Huntington 11743, 516-673-6500; and 80 Forest Ave., Glen Cove 11542, 516-671-8300.

Committees: *Appropriations* (32d of 35 D). Subcommittees: Foreign Operations; Transportation.

Group Ratings

	ADA	ACLU	COPE	CFA	LCV	ACU	NTU	NSI	COC	CEI
1986	80	95	86	67	80	5	29	0	31	28
1985	90	—	87	75	—	19	43	—	43	—

National Journal Ratings

	1986 LIB — 1986 CONS		1985 LIB — 1985 CONS	
Economic	60% —	38%	64% —	35%
Social	85% —	14%	79% —	19%
Foreign	64% —	34%	85% —	8%

Key Votes

1) Lmt Cln Water Act	FOR	5) Retain Gun Cont	FOR	9) Aid Angola Reb	AGN
2) Rpl Tobac Sub	FOR	6) Contra Aid	AGN	10) Tax Reform	AGN
3) Grm-Rdmn Def Red	FOR	7) Lmt Text Imp	FOR	11) S Africa Sanc	FOR
4) Ban Polygraph	FOR	8) Limit SDI	FOR	12) Immig Reform	FOR

Election Results

1986 general	Robert J. Mrazek (D)..................	83,985	(56%)	($646,610)
	Joseph A. Guarino (R–C)..............	60,367	(41%)	($200,651)
	Charles W. Welch (RTL)	4,440	(3%)	
1986 primary	Robert J. Mrazek (D) unopposed			
1984 general	Robert J. Mrazek (D).................	120,191	(51%)	($706,247)
	Robert P. Quinn (R–C)................	112,909	(48%)	($738,118)

Campaign Contributions and Expenditures

1985-86		Direct Cont. 1985-86		PACS Breakdown 1985-86			
Receipts	$726,814	Indiv.	$461,968	Corp.	$25,825	T/M/H	$40,602
Expend.	$646,610	PACS	$229,949	Labor	$113,516	Agr.	$0
Unspent	$123,517			Ideo.	$48,106	CWOS	$1,900

FOURTH DISTRICT

In 1945 Nassau County, just beyond the New York City limits, was mostly empty land, with 450,000 people in one or another of its little suburban towns. Then came William Levitt, a young builder who bought a potato field and built a town full of mass-produced, identical, tiny tract houses and named it for himself. Levittown soon became the home of young New York families who loved the (comparatively) open spaces and over the years improved and individualized their homes. All around similar communities were built and marketed, lived in and improved, so by 1960 there were 1.3 million New Yorkers in Nassau County and by 1970 1.4 million; by 1980, as children moved out and homeowners aged, the population was back to 1.3 million.

Nassau County was also the scene in these years of the growth of America's premier suburban political machine. It was the creation of Nassau Republican Chairman J. Russel Sprague, who managed to carry the county for Alf Landon in 1936 and that same year persuade the voters to adopt a county executive form of government, in which control of political patronage would center in one man responsible to the Nassau County Republican chairman. That is more or less how it has worked out since. In the post-1945 years Nassau tended to attract Republican-leaning young migrants, and in the Eisenhower years the County shared in the national trend toward the Republicans; in the 1960s, when Catholics and Jews swung heavily to the party of John F. Kennedy, Nassau elected a Democrat as county executive for several terms. But for most of the 1970s and the early 1980s political power in Nassau was wielded mostly by Republican Chairman Joseph Margiotta. He chose Republican nominees, enforced the practice of 1% contributions by public employees to the party and oversaw the spending, and as chairman of the county casting more votes than any other in New York, wielded statewide power. Margiotta was brought down when he was convicted of diverting public business to favored insurance brokers and went to jail in 1983; he fell out with his hand-picked successor Joseph Mondello when Mondello would not appoint him executive director of the party when he was released. But the system goes on. Nassau's Republican machine is attacked by many. But it has this to say for itself: it has provided competent local government and candidates returned to office by an intelligent and well-informed electorate.

The 4th Congressional District of New York, wholly within Nassau County and including most of the original Levittown, was one of the political units once within the gift of Joseph Margiotta. It includes much of central Nassau around Levittown plus a string of suburbs along the South Shore of Long Island (actually along the shore of the bay that separates the sand spits of Long Beach and Jones Beach from the main part of the Island) that were tiny separate towns in 1945 but that have long since grown together, from East Rockaway to Massapequa)—places where you find Nassau County zoning lawyers and New York City policemen, owners of small businesses and stores, and engineers at Long Island's big aircraft factories. When it came time for the county Republican organization to find a candidate to run against anti-Vietnam war activist Allard Lowenstein, who had won a 1968 race in a House seat then mostly on the south shore, it picked a lawyer still in his 30s who had served in the state Senate for eight years and who had made a name as an opponent of a local busing plan, Norman Lent.

Lent won and has been the congressman from this district ever since. Now he is one of the most senior Republicans in the House and ranking minority member on the House Energy and Commerce Committee—one of the busiest and most powerful committees in Congress, which handles a host of regulatory and environmental matters. Lent has not been particularly voluble or visible on national issues, but can claim to have made significant contributions—to the original Superfund law and to the update he co-sponsored with Ohio's Dennis Eckart and which prevailed over James Florio's version, to an insurance liability risk retention act he co-sponsored with Oregon's Ron Wyden, to a bill allowing Conrail to be sold on the open market. Lent's voting record generally is conservative, favoring alternatives that tend to minimize government spending and regulation. But on Energy and Commerce and on Merchant Marine and Fisheries, where he used to be ranking minority member, he has often been willing to work with Democrats to fashion practical government solutions to problems experienced by Americans in Long Island and elsewhere.

This approach seems to suit the 4th District. Lent had some close races in the middle 1970s, but has been reelected easily ever since.

The People: Pop. 1980: 516,641, dn. 8.9% 1970–80. Households (1980): 88% family, 46% with children, 77% married couples; 14.3% housing units rented; median monthly rent: $321; median house value: $55,800. Voting age pop. (1980): 376,675; 3% Black, 3% Spanish origin, 1% Asian origin.

1984 Presidential Vote:

Reagan (R)	155,268	(64%)
Mondale (D)	88,668	(36%)

Rep. Norman F. Lent (R)

Elected 1970; b. Mar. 23, 1931, Oceanside; home, E. Rockaway; Hofstra U., B.A. 1952, Cornell U., LL.B. 1957; United Methodist; married (Barbara).

Career: Navy, Korea; Practicing atty., 1957–70, Asst. E. Rockaway Police Justice, 1960–62; NY Senate, 1962–70.

Offices: 2408 RHOB 20515, 202-225-7896. Also 2280 Grand Ave., Ste. 300, Baldwin 11510, 516-223-1616.

Committees: *Energy and Commerce* (Ranking Member of 17 R). Subcommittee: Oversight and Investigations (Ranking Member). *Merchant Marine and Fisheries* (3d of 17 R). Subcommittee: Merchant Marine (Ranking Member).

Group Ratings

	ADA	ACLU	COPE	CFA	LCV	ACU	NTU	NSI	COC	CEI
1986	20	5	30	42	28	64	45	100	64	43
1985	10	—	30	42	—	75	44	—	57	—

National Journal Ratings

	1986 LIB — 1986 CONS			1985 LIB — 1985 CONS		
Economic	31%	—	67%	35%	—	65%
Social	0%	—	76%	34%	—	66%
Foreign	24%	—	66%	31%	—	68%

Key Votes

1) Lmt Cln Water Act	AGN	5) Retain Gun Cont	FOR	9) Aid Angola Reb	FOR
2) Rpl Tobac Sub	AGN	6) Contra Aid	FOR	10) Tax Reform	AGN
3) Grm-Rdmn Def Red	FOR	7) Lmt Text Imp	AGN	11) S Africa Sanc	FOR
4) Ban Polygraph	—	8) Limit SDI	AGN	12) Immig Reform	AGN

Election Results

1986 general	Norman F. Lent (R–C)	92,214	(65%)	($337,118)
	Patricia Sullivan (D–L)	43,581	(31%)	($11,829)
	George F. Patterson (RTL)	6,493	(4%)	
1986 primary	Norman F. Lent (R) unopposed			
1984 general	Norman F. Lent (R–C)	154,875	(69%)	($260,233)
	Sheldon Englehard (D–L)	65,678	(29%)	($53,167)

Campaign Contributions and Expenditures

1985-86		Direct Cont. 1985-86		PACS Breakdown 1985-86			
Receipts	$492,418	Indiv.	$184,818	Corp.	$146,567	T/M/H	$94,700
Expend.	$337,118	Party	$2,020	Labor	$25,750	Agr.	$0
Unspent	$336,403	PACS	$279,982	Ideo.	$7,375	CWOS	$5,590

FIFTH DISTRICT

Just beyond the New York City limits on Long Island, where Nassau County begins, you can see on any map that charts election results the shift from Democratic to Republican territory. Most of eastern Queens, with many black and Jewish residents, is heavily Democratic; most of western Nassau County, with only a few blacks and spread out in neighborhoods of single family homes rather than in blocks of apartments, is heavily Republican. Some towns here date back from before World War II: Garden City, the model suburb in the 1920s, and the Five Towns of Lawrence, Inwood, Cedarhurst, Hewlett, and Woodmere between Kennedy Airport and the ocean. These two communities are quite different politically: Garden City is mostly Protestant and heavily Republican, the Five Towns are mostly Jewish and heavily Democratic. The 5th District has its pockets of black neighborhoods, in Hempstead and Roosevelt. But more typical of the district are postwar suburbs like Valley Stream, or East Meadow and Uniondale, east of Hempstead. These are the homes of typical Long Islanders: homeowners (unlike the renters in the City), parents (unlike the singles of Manhattan), people of above-average education and talents who are struggling to live comfortable, affluent lives in the most expensive, demanding, and exasperating of our metropolitan areas.

The 5th District was marginal political territory in the middle 1970s, solidly Republican in the 1980s. Its congressman, Raymond McGrath, has thinner credentials than any other Long Island member and no particular reputation for hard work, but he seems to have made the seat entirely safe. A former teacher, deputy parks commissioner, and state legislator, an "ordinary guy" in his own words, McGrath was tapped for the seat by Nassau County Republican boss Joseph Margiotta in 1980, and beat tough Democrats that year and in 1982. He tended to mix in well with most Republicans, though his stands on various issues—Superfund and foreign policy—were sometimes more liberal.

In 1985 he got a much-coveted seat on the Ways and Means Committee, just in time for the tax reform issue. He announced that the only issue he was interested in was the deductibility of state and local taxes, that he'd vote for any bill that made them deductible and against any that wouldn't. And so he did, arguing with President Reagan in the White House, becoming one of the (at times) very lonely Republicans in support of Dan Rostenkowski's bill. McGrath ended up standing behind the President when he signed the bill and the recipient of special benefits—tax breaks for the towns of Hempstead and Oyster Bay, for a Garden City firm, for Merrill Lynch, 19 of the 21 transition rules he sought—from Chairman Rostenkowski.

After all that, McGrath's reelection was never in doubt. But his campaign did heat up when it was revealed that Democrat Michael Sullivan had spent $18,000 on hiring four women to meet McGrath in a bar and tape what he said. Governor Mario Cuomo and Democratic Representative Thomas Downey denounced Sullivan's move, and the voters gave McGrath a 65%–35% victory, his biggest yet.

The People: Pop. 1980: 516,712, dn. 7.6% 1970–80. Households (1980): 81% family, 39% with children, 68% married couples; 25.5% housing units rented; median monthly rent: $300; median house value: $56,900. Voting age pop. (1980): 386,288; 10% Black, 3% Spanish origin, 1% Asian origin.

1984 Presidential Vote:

Reagan (R)	146,746	(60%)
Mondale (D)	95,862	(39%)

Rep. Raymond J. McGrath (R)

Elected 1980; b. Mar. 27, 1942, Valley Stream; home, Valley Stream; St. U. of NY, Brockport, B.S. 1963, N.Y.U., M.A. 1968; Roman Catholic; married (Joanne).

Career: High sch. phys. ed. teacher, 1963–65; Hempstead Dpty. Commissioner of Parks and Recreation, 1969–76; NY Assembly, 1976–80.

Offices: 205 CHOB 20515, 202-225-5516. Also 203 Rockaway Ave., Valley Stream 11580, 516-872-9550.

Committees: *Ways and Means* (9th of 13 R). Subcommittees: Oversight; Select Revenue Measures.

Group Ratings

	ADA	ACLU	COPE	CFA	LCV	ACU	NTU	NSI	COC	CEI
1986	20	10	32	58	38	55	45	80	69	45
1985	20	—	30	67	—	71	43	—	52	—

National Journal Ratings

	1986 LIB — 1986 CONS		1985 LIB — 1985 CONS	
Economic	38%	— 61%	37%	— 62%
Social	18%	— 78%	33%	— 66%
Foreign	36%	— 63%	24%	— 66%

Key Votes

1) Lmt Cln Water Act	AGN	5) Retain Gun Cont	FOR	9) Aid Angola Reb	FOR
2) Rpl Tobac Sub	AGN	6) Contra Aid	FOR	10) Tax Reform	FOR
3) Grm-Rdmn Def Red	FOR	7) Lmt Text Imp	FOR	11) S Africa Sanc	FOR
4) Ban Polygraph	AGN	8) Limit SDI	FOR	12) Immig Reform	AGN

Election Results

1986 general	Raymond J. McGrath (R–C)	93,473	(65%)	($294,365)
	Michael T. Sullivan (D–L–RTL)	49,728	(35%)	($66,389)
1986 primary	Raymond J. McGrath (R) unopposed			
1984 general	Raymond J. McGrath (R–C)	138,560	(62%)	($238,483)
	Michael D'Innocenzo (D)	78,429	(35%)	($83,929)

Campaign Contributions and Expenditures

1985-86		Direct Cont. 1985-86		PACS Breakdown 1985-86			
Receipts	$439,322	Indiv.	$178,188	Corp.	$114,514	T/M/H	$81,252
Expend.	$294,365	Party	$2,588	Labor	$20,300	Agr.	$250
Unspent	$152,017	PACS	$236,908	Ideo.	$14,000	CWOS	$6,592

SIXTH DISTRICT

In the early 19th century, coaches clattered along the turnpike road from Brooklyn through Jamaica to Hempstead, along the spine of Long Island and passed north of empty fields and marshlands that, depending on the tides and precipitation, were mud flats or islands or the waters of Jamaica Bay. A century later southern Queens was still mostly vacant land, but as the

20th century progressed subway lines and the railroad brought out migrants from Brooklyn and Manhattan who built, between the old community of Jamaica and the uncleared swamp out near what became Kennedy Airport, tightly-packed, close-knit neighborhoods; far across the bay was the Rockaway peninsula, once a summer resort for high society and now given over to high rises and a few slums.

Every section of Queens is divided into neighborhoods and sub-neighborhoods and sub-subneighborhoods, as reporters discovered in late 1986 and early 1987 when they went out to Howard Beach, a late development on flatlands just west of JFK, where three blacks were beaten by a gang of teenagers and one, fleeing, was run over by a car on Belt Parkway. "The most horrendous incident of violence in the nine years since I've been mayor," said Edward Koch, who was booed when he came to speak at Catholic services there. "We are NOT a racist community," Howard Beach residents replied; "an American tragedy," a local Republican said. Each one had a point. Howard Beach, like the black middle-class neighborhoods that developed in the 1960s and 1970s off avenues fanning eastward from the south Jamaica ghetto neighborhood (where Governor Mario Cuomo grew up), is an enclave of families who are leaving behind unsafe streets, who believe in work and duty and standard morality, of adults who are ready to recognize the personal worth of those of different backgrounds and races and who would recoil at being rude to someone because of race. Yet there are negative feelings here too: fear, distrust, distaste, feelings expressed by few responsible adults, but by many of the excited adolescents— the teenagers who chased Michael Griffith out onto the Belt Parkway, the black youths who pummeled whites at Jamaica bus stops in response.

The Howard Beach incident stirs the emotion not because Howard Beach is a specially evil place—it isn't—but because it reminds us of the potential in all of us for hatred and aggression; the exaggeration and parody of adults' emotions seen in adolescents' actions suggests how in even a decent society like the United States there exists at least the kernel of the potential for racial persecution or even genocide.

Politically, southern Queens from Jamaica southward across the bay to the Rockaways, with Howard Beach and the solidly middle-class black neighborhoods of St. Albans, Laurelton, Springfield Gardens, Rosedale, and Cambria Heights, form the 6th Congressional District of New York. It is a district where, within the past four years, most black voters have felt comfortable voting for a white congressman and most white voters have felt comfortable voting for a black. The white was Joseph Addabbo, who first won the district in 1960 when Catholic Democrats began outnumbering white Protestant Republicans in southern Queens; he rose to become chairman of the Defense Appropriations Subcommittee, an opponent of indiscriminant Pentagon spending whose amendments shut off the bombing of Cambodia in 1973 and slowed down spending on the MX missile in 1982. All the while, he was careful to use his chair to help Long Island's big defense contractors and get defense installations into New York. When white Democrats were outnumbered by black Democrats, Addabbo kept on winning: he beat Simeon Golar, a former city commissioner, in the 1982 and 1984 primaries, with 59% and 68% of the vote, winning more black votes each time.

What neither Addabbo's admirers or opponents knew at the time was that he was suffering from cancer; he collapsed and went into a coma in March 1986 and died a month later. In the June special election both major contenders were black. Minister Floyd Flake led by 167 votes at the polls, but Assemblyman Alton Waldon was declared the winner by 276 votes when absentee ballots were counted. Flake complained that his name wasn't printed on absentees, but the courts said he should have objected earlier. The September primary for the full term— tantamount to election in the heavily Democratic 6th—amounted to a rematch and this time, despite Waldon's two months of incumbency, Flake won. Waldon is a former housing policeman who rose up through the ranks, went to school, won appointive city jobs, and was the choice of the weakened (by the Donald Manes scandal) Queens Democratic organization. Flake is a minister of a 4,000-member church that built a big senior citizens' homes and runs small businesses; he has a big following in the middle class communities along the Nassau County line.

He has seats on the Banking and Small Business Committees, arguably important for this constituency, and will undoubtedly be working hard to forestall yet another seriously contested primary in this diverse middle-class district.

The People: Pop. 1980: 516,312, dn. 5.7% 1970–80. Households (1980): 77% family, 43% with children, 55% married couples; 44.7% housing units rented; median monthly rent: $222; median house value: $42,800. Voting age pop. (1980): 368,500; 47% Black, 8% Spanish origin, 1% Asian origin.

1984 Presidential Vote:

Mondale (D)	111,850	(67%)
Reagan (R)	54,867	(33%)

Rep. Floyd H. Flake (D)

Elected 1986; b. Jan. 30, 1945, Los Angeles, CA; home, Queens; Wilberforce U., B.A., 1967; Payne Theological Seminary, 1968–70, Northeastern U., 1974–75; St. John's U., 1982–85; African Methodist Episcopal; married (Margaret).

Career: Minister; Founder of Allen Christian School, Allen Home Care Agency.

Offices: 1427 LHOB, 202-225-3461. Also 114-60 Merrick Blvd., Jamaica 11434, 718-657-2968.

Committees: *Banking, Finance and Urban Affairs* (28th of 31 D). Subcommittees: Economic Stabilization; General Oversight and Investigation; Housing and Community Development. *Small Business* (22d of 27 D). Subcommittees: Procurement, Innovation and Minority Enterprise Development; Regulation and Business Opportunities. *Select Committee on Hunger* (13th of 16 D). Task Force: Domestic Task Force.

Group Ratings and Key Votes: Newly Elected

Election Results

1986 general	Floyd Flake (D)	58,317	(68%)	($359,382)
	Richard Dietl (R–C)	27,773	(32%)	($55,318)
1986 primary	Floyd Flake (D)	22,328	(48%)	
	Alton R. Waldon, Jr. (D)	18,968	(41%)	
	Simeon Golar (D)	3,387	(7%)	
	Hubert H. James (D	3,387	(7%)	
1986 spec.	Alton R. Waldon, Jr. (D)	12,654	(51%)	
	Floyd Flake (D)	12,378	(49%)	
1984 general	Joseph P. Addabbo (D–L)	120,098	(83%)	($934,263)
	Philip J. Veltre (R–C–RTL)	25,040	(17%)	

Campaign Contributions and Expenditures

1985-86		Direct Cont. 1985-86		PACS Breakdown 1985-86			
Receipts	$401,263	Indiv.	$313,059	Corp.	$4,500	T/M/H	$14,200
Expend.	$359,382	PACS	$87,550	Labor	$49,300	Agr.	$0
Unspent	$41,879	Cand.	$17,500	Ideo.	$19,550	CWOS	$0

SEVENTH DISTRICT

The scene of America's juiciest local political scandal of 1986 was not some slum-ridden central city neighborhood or a quaint rural backwater; it was the borough of Queens, the home of Mario Cuomo and Geraldine Ferraro, the political base of Borough President Donald Manes, who killed himself as the New York parking meter bribery scandal started to unravel. Its focus was the unimpressive brick Borough Hall, on eight-lane Queens Boulevard just after it passes over the Grand Central Parkway, across from the Pastrami King and Crossroads Drugs. This is the geographical center of a borough of nearly two million people which casts more votes than Manhattan or Brooklyn or the Bronx; yet it is not usually the focus of anyone's attention—like Queens itself. Queens has no long urban past: much of it was still countryside before World War II, and longtime residents still talk of going into "the city" when they mean Manhattan.

In those days the built-up parts of Queens consisted mostly of modest one- and two-family houses, inhabited by Irish, Italian, and German immigrants as well as a considerable number of people of Yankee stock. It was a Republican stronghold that happened, technically, to be part of a much larger Democratic city. Since World War II, most of the new housing units in Queens have been in apartment houses, many of them giant, like the units in Lefrak City. Added to its older residents have been a large number of Jews, mostly from Manhattan and Brooklyn. It is an airier place to live and raise a family than Manhattan; there are good public schools; rents are lower, and on the subway Manhattan offices are not so far away. It was here, on 64th Road in Rego Park a couple of blocks off Queens Boulevard, that the first condominium conversion in New York took place in 1966: an opportunity for the owners to get out from under rent control and the tenants to convert their low rental into a capital asset.

The 7th Congressional District of New York takes in the heart of Queens: Borough Hall and most of the length of Queens Boulevard, plus the mostly Latin Corona neighborhood up to LaGuardia Airport; and it runs eastward toward Long Island on both sides of the Grand Central Parkway, taking in single-family neighborhoods that might be somewhere in the suburbs and high-rise developments filled with New Yorkers affluent enough to afford big houses in almost any other American city. Cuomo lives here on a curving street in Hollis Wood, in a house behind a tall pine tree his father worked all night to replant when it was uprooted in a storm; Ferraro lives a block outside the district on Deepdene Drive in Forest Hills. But they are exceptions: most Queens residents live on streets and avenues whose names were changed to numbers by efficiency-minded city planners much earlier in this century. This is an affluent district, although seldom rich and including some slummy neighborhoods; it includes some Republican areas, but overall is solidly Democratic.

The congressman here is Gary Ackerman, a Democrat elected in March 1983 after Benjamin Rosenthal, an idealistic yet good-humored product of Queens politics, died after 20 years of service. Ackerman's background is also in local politics; a former teacher who served four years in the state Senate. He serves on the Foreign Affairs Committee and its Subcommittee on Europe and the Middle East, on which, not surprisingly, he is a staunch supporter of Israel. He also has a seat on the Post Office and Civil Service Committee, where he has been one of the few congressmen willing to stand up during the almost hysterical drive against drugs in 1986 to argue that drug tests are unreliable, and he authored legislation to prevent indiscriminate drug testing of federal employees. He has endeared himself as well to the civil service unions for his opposition to privatization and contracting out of government jobs. Bearded, shaggy, large, and often sporting a white carnation, living on a houseboat in Washington, Ackerman is a distinctive congressman in the capital, and evidently a popular one at home: he was reelected with 77% of the vote in 1986.

The People: Pop. 1980: 516,544, dn. 2.5% 1970–80. Households (1980): 67% family, 29% with children, 52% married couples; 70.4% housing units rented; median monthly rent: $266; median house value: $56,300. Voting age pop. (1980): 407,309; 17% Spanish origin, 11% Black, 6% Asian origin.

1984 Presidential Vote:

Mondale (D)	87,366	(53%)
Reagan (R)	75,972	(46%)

Rep. Gary L. Ackerman (D)

Elected Mar. 1, 1983; b. Nov. 19, 1942, Brooklyn; home, Flushing; Queens Col., B.A. 1965; Jewish; married (Rita).

Career: Pub. sch. teacher, 1966–72; Newspaper ed. and publisher; Adv. agcy. owner; NY Senate, 1979–83.

Offices: 1725 LHOB, 202-225-2601. Also 118–35 Queens Blvd., Forest Hills 11375, 718-263-1525.

Committees: *Foreign Affairs* (20th of 27 D). Subcommitees: Asian and Pacific Affairs; Europe and the Middle East; Human Rights and International Organizations. *Post Office and Civil Service* (11th of 14 D). Subcommittees: Compensation and Employee Benefits (Chairman); Postal Personnel and Modernization. *Select Committee on Hunger* (11th of 16 D). Task Force: Domestic Task Force.

Group Ratings

	ADA	ACLU	COPE	CFA	LCV	ACU	NTU	NSI	COC	CEI
1986	85	94	98	83	89	0	25	0	13	11
1985	100	—	98	75	—	10	35	—	20	—

National Journal Ratings

	1986 LIB — 1986 CONS		1985 LIB — 1985 CONS	
Economic	87% —	0%	83% —	15%
Social	89% —	0%	85% —	0%
Foreign	75% —	20%	80% —	17%

Key Votes

1) Lmt Cln Water Act	AGN	5) Retain Gun Cont	FOR	9) Aid Angola Reb	AGN
2) Rpl Tobac Sub	—	6) Contra Aid	AGN	10) Tax Reform	AGN
3) Grm-Rdmn Def Red	AGN	7) Lmt Text Imp	FOR	11) S Africa Sanc	FOR
4) Ban Polygraph	FOR	8) Limit SDI	FOR	12) Immig Reform	FOR

Election Results

1986 general	Gary L. Ackerman (D).................	62,836	(77%)	($116,950)
	Edward Nelson Rodriguez (R–C)	18,384	(23%)	($8,456)
1986 primary	Gary L. Ackerman (D) unopposed			
1984 general	Gary L. Ackerman (D–L)..............	97,674	(69%)	($343,959)
	Gustave A. Reifenkugel (R–C)	43,370	(31%)	

Campaign Contributions and Expenditures

1985-86		Direct Cont. 1985-86		PACS Breakdown 1985-86			
Receipts	$181,226	Indiv.	$72,674	Corp.	$8,450	T/M/H	$25,940
Expend.	$116,950	Party	$576	Labor	$66,982	Agr.	$0
Unspent	$114,070	PACS	$110,622	Ideo.	$8,750	CWOS	$500

EIGHTH DISTRICT

The 1939–40 and 1964–65 New York World's Fairs were held in Flushing Meadow, a reclaimed creek bottom a mile or so from the site of one of New York's oldest villages, Flushing. It was named by Dutch settlers after their town of Vlissingen and anglicized when the British took Nieuw Amsterdam in 1664; the best evidence of old Flushing today are a couple of old buildings and the crooked street pattern, on which Queens's scheme of numbered names is awkwardly superimposed. Flushing is the heart of the 8th Congressional District of New York, which includes most of northern Queens plus small parts of the Bronx and suburban Nassau County. The Queens portion includes the working-class neighborhoods of Whitestone and College Point, the more affluent double-house neighborhood of Bayside, and higher-income Douglaston, right next to the rich, mostly Jewish suburb of Great Neck in Nassau County, most of which is in the 8th also. In Queens the district goes south, below the Long Island Expressway, to pleasant home-owner neighborhoods with names like Utopia, Fresh Meadows, and Oakland Gardens. But even here, far from Manhattan and in relatively affluent areas, there are plenty of high-rises, the population density not approached, except for a few odd neighborhoods, in other metropolitan areas.

The population in this part of the district includes few blacks or Puerto Ricans; there are more in the Bronx portion of the 8th. This area is a little misleading: it looks like a sliver on the map, but it has 29% of the district's population; its statistics make it sound mostly black (24%) and Spanish origin (30%), but most of the voters here are Jewish. The district's rather jagged boundaries take in several of the Bronx's longstanding Jewish neighborhoods and shopping districts, at least as of 1982, including the Parkchester apartment project, which houses some 40,000 people.

For Representative James Scheuer, representing this district means he has come full circle: he was first elected to the House in 1964, when he lived in Manhattan, from a Bronx district that included some of his present territory; he was beaten for reelection in redistricting in 1972; he was elected again in 1974 from a district that included southern portions of Queens and Brooklyn, around Jamaica Bay, and even bought a house there; he lost that district in 1982, but with the help of Queens Borough President Donald Manes cinched the nomination in the new incumbentless 8th. He is thus the Flying Dutchman of New York congressmen, or the stormy termagant: he has represented parts of four different counties (while coming originally from another) and has run against two other Democratic incumbents (beating Jacob Gilbert in 1964, losing to Jonathan Bingham in 1972). This is a heavily Democratic district and will likely provide a base to keep Scheuer in Congress another decade; how he will handle the 1990 redistricting heaven knows.

Scheuer's good fortune is all the more remarkable because he is not particularly popular with his fellow politicians or congressmen. He suffered the indignity of seeing Energy and Commerce Committee Chairman John Dingell abolish his subcommittee out from under him in 1981, even though he is the second-ranking Democrat on the full committee; he has not been active since on the committee and he seems likely to be passed over for the chair in favor of third-ranking Henry Waxman—though it should be added that Dingell is not likely to step down. Scheuer now chairs a Science, Space and Technology subcommittee of considerably less legislative importance, although it did give him a piece of the action in investigating former EPA Administrator Anne McGill Burford and her subordinates in 1982 and 1983.

But Scheuer's problems should not be overstated. He is an active, aggressive legislator who works hard at his job, takes it seriously, and does his homework. He was one of the Science Committee members who sternly admonished NASA and its officials after the *Challenger* accident. He wants to ban smoking in all federal offices. He tends local problems, trying to keep the noisy Concorde out of Kennedy Airport in the 1970s and trying to get better wind shear radar for Kennedy and LaGuardia in the 1980s. Once he had other ambitions: he ran for mayor in 1969 and finished fifth among five candidates, behind Mario Procaccino, Robert Wagner, Herman Badillo, and novelist Norman Mailer; perhaps he even dreamed of statewide office as well. Now he has to work hard and fight as contentiously as ever to remain an important congressman after more than 20 years in the House. But he hasn't quit fighting.

The People: Pop. 1980: 516,165, dn. 6.5% 1970–80. Households (1980): 73% family, 32% with children, 57% married couples; 62.5% housing units rented; median monthly rent: $246; median house value: $68,400. Voting age pop. (1980): 402,776; 12% Spanish origin, 9% Black, 4% Asian origin.

1984 Presidential Vote:

Mondale (D)	102,439	(53%)
Reagan (R)	92,013	(47%)

Rep. James H. Scheuer (D)

Elected 1974; b. Feb. 6, 1920, New York City; home, Douglaston; Swarthmore Col., A.B. 1945; Harvard Business Sch., 1946; Columbia U., LL.B. 1948; Jewish; married (Emily).

Career: Army Air Corps, WWII; Economist, U.S. Foreign Econ. Admin., 1945–46; Mbr., Legal Staff, U.S. Ofc. of Price Stabilization, 1951–52; U.S. House of Reps., 1965–72; Pres., NY City Citizens Housing and Planning Cncl., 1972–74; Pres., Natl. Housing Conf., 1972–74.

Offices: 2466 RHOB 20515, 202-225-5471. Also 13708 Northern Blvd., Flushing 11354, 718-445-8770.

Committees: *Energy and Commerce* (2d of 25 D). Subcommittees: Commerce, Consumer Protection and Competitiveness; Health and the Environment; Oversight and Investigations. *Science, Space and Technology* (3d of 27 D). Subcommittees: International Scientific Cooperation; Natural Resources, Agriculture Research and Environment (Chairman); Space Science and Applications. *Select Committee on Narcotics Abuse and Control* (4th of 15 D). *Joint Economic Committee.* Task Forces: Economic Resources and Competitiveness; Education and Health (Chairman); National Security Economics.

Group Ratings

	ADA	ACLU	COPE	CFA	LCV	ACU	NTU	NSI	COC	CEI
1986	95	85	92	92	74	0	30	0	18	20
1985	90	—	92	92	—	0	33	—	23	—

National Journal Ratings

	1986 LIB	—	1986 CONS	1985 LIB	—	1985 CONS
Economic	87%	—	0%	89%	—	0%
Social	89%	—	0%	85%	—	0%
Foreign	80%	—	0%	75%	—	25%

Key Votes

1) Lmt Cln Water Act	AGN	5) Retain Gun Cont	FOR	9) Aid Angola Reb	AGN
2) Rpl Tobac Sub	FOR	6) Contra Aid	AGN	10) Tax Reform	FOR
3) Grm-Rdmn Def Red	AGN	7) Lmt Text Imp	FOR	11) S Africa Sanc	FOR
4) Ban Polygraph	FOR	8) Limit SDI	FOR	12) Immig Reform	FOR

Election Results

1986 general	James H. Scheuer (D–L)	70,605	(90%)	($65,543)
	Gustave Reifenkugel (C-RTL)	7,679	(10%)	
1986 primary	James H. Scheuer (D) unopposed			
1984 general	James H. Scheuer (D–L)	104,558	(63%)	($67,591)
	Robert L. Brandofino (R–C)	62,015	(37%)	($1,290)

Campaign Contributions and Expenditures

1985-86		Direct Cont. 1985-86		PACS Breakdown 1985-86			
Receipts	$81,374	Indiv.	$16,952	Corp.	$12,300	T/M/H	$21,450
Expend.	$65,543	Party	$392	Labor	$11,332	Agr.	$0
Unspent	$22,526	PACS	$48,032	Ideo.	$2,450	CWOS	$500
		Cand.	$18,000				

NINTH DISTRICT

All over America, in late afternoon or on independent stations in the evening, you can see the credits for *All in the Family* roll on and get a TV camera's eye view of the 9th Congressional District of New York. This is where Archie and Edith Bunker live, in one of the aging, but still neatly maintained, one- and two-family houses that line the streets of Jackson Heights, Astoria, Long Island City, Ridgewood, and Glendale. Yet as the Bunkers go deep into syndication, the picture is getting a little out of date. Many of these Queens neighborhoods still are filled with older couples of Yankee, Dutch, Irish, or German stock, still raging at John Lindsay's Manhattan and fearful of the blacks that live not too far away in Brooklyn's Bedford-Stuyvesant or Queens's South Jamaica. But the function of these modest neighborhoods of tightly-packed brick and frame houses is changing. From the 1920s to the 1950s they were one step up, the place children of immigrants moved when they got steady jobs and wanted to raise their children in tradition-minded neighborhoods. With little immigration and few blacks moving here, many of those children stayed when they grew up, and Woodhaven and Ridgewood seemed totally unchanging.

But immigration to New York slowly increased, starting in the late 1960s, and almost all of Manhattan was turned over to the affluent, the trendy, and the well-positioned who held on forever to rent controlled apartments and highly valued places in elderly housing projects, the neighborhoods of western Queens thus became one of the major immigrant destinations in America. Greeks came into Astoria, not far from the Astoria Studios where silent films were once made and independent producers now shoot interiors for talkies; Colombians and other Latin Americans moved in large numbers to Jackson Heights; nearby you can find the homes of many of the Koreans that seem to run all the green groceries of New York.

There is visible change also in commercial construction. Near the covered tennis courts where Upper East Side Manhattanites come to play, a huge Merchandise Mart has opened up near the Queensborough Bridge in Long Island City and Citicorp is planning a giant office building there. It has finally occurred to New Yorkers that this is a great place for back office operations, just a quick subway ride from Manhattan, but much, much cheaper.

The political story from the middle 1960s in the 9th District was cultural conservatism; the political story from the middle 1970s was Geraldine Ferraro. Facing the East Side across the River, Western Queens, more than any other part of New York, seemed to hate John Lindsay; while the rich East Side was voting for George McGovern, the modest 9th district was favoring Richard Nixon. Ferraro, running in 1978 when incumbent James Delaney, chairman of the Rules Committee, retired, campaigned as a former prosecutor with roots deep in Queens, an Italian-American sympathetic both to feminist causes and traditional family values. She found her way into the House leadership and then onto the 1984 Democratic national ticket for similar reasons: she had a record that appealed to national Democrats, a biography that appealed to almost everyone (until the attacks on her husband's business dealings, anyway), and a manner that personified the fast-talking, wise-cracking New Yorker without really antagonizing those from out of town. Ferraro's political strengths enabled her to win this seat and to make it safe; they probably would have enabled her to be a tough, maybe a successful, challenger to Senator Alfonse D'Amato in 1986, the race she was aiming for all along; they were enough to make her a creditable, if not towering, Democratic vice presidential nominee; they were not enough to enable her to overcome her liabilities and remain a major political figure after the 1984 campaign.

The current congressman from the 9th is Thomas Manton, a former policeman who served on the City Council from 1969 to 1984; he ran against Delaney in 1972 as the tribune of anti-Vietnam war liberals and as the organization choice against Ferraro in 1978, losing both times. He is the son of Irish immigrants—a personal link between the older stock second- and third-generation residents of the district and the newer residents who are immigrants themselves. His critical race was the 1984 primary, which he won 30%–27%–22%–21%. Serphin Maltese, the longtime Conservative party leader who was the Republican nominee in the general, simply did not have the political moves to take advantage of the issues and the year, and Manton won 53%–47%. Now he seems firmly ensconced. His voting record is pretty liberal on economic and foreign issues, rather conservative on cultural matters—well suited to the district. He has seats on the Banking Committee, which handles housing and covers financial institutions, and Merchant Marine and Fisheries, which handles the maritime subsidies that are still important to at least a few voters here. The 9th District, having been represented by a Rules chairman and a VP nominee, now seems content to be represented by a man with local roots and local interests.

The People: Pop. 1980: 516,143, dn. 4.5% 1970–80. Households (1980): 66% family, 29% with children, 50% married couples; 72.0% housing units rented; median monthly rent: $206; median house value: $57,600. Voting age pop. (1980): 407,420; 15% Spanish origin, 5% Asian origin, 3% Black.

1984 Presidential Vote:

Reagan (R)	84,812	(57%)
Mondale (D)	64,701	(43%)

Rep. Thomas J. Manton (D)

Elected 1984; b. Nov. 3, 1932, New York City; home, Sunnyside; St. John's U., B.B.A. 1958, LL.B. 1962; Roman Catholic; married (Diane).

Career: USMC, 1951–53; New York City Police Dept., 1955–60; IBM Salesman, 1960–64; Practicing atty., 1964–84; New York City Council, 1969–84.

Offices: 327 CHOB 20515, 202-225-3965. Also 46–12 Queens Blvd., Sunnyside 11104, 718-706-1400.

Committees: *Banking, Finance and Urban Affairs* (24th of 31 D). Subcommittees: Financial Institutions Supervision, Regulation and Insurance; Housing and Community Development; International Finance, Trade, and Monetary Policy. *Merchant Marine and Fisheries* (22d of 25 D). Subcommittees: Fisheries and Wildlife Conservation and the Environment; Oceanography; Panama Canal and Outer Continental Shelf. *Select Committee on Aging* (34th of 39 D). Subcommittee: Retirement Income and Employment.

Group Ratings

	ADA	ACLU	COPE	CFA	LCV	ACU	NTU	NSI	COC	CEI
1986	75	65	90	83	49	9	19	0	29	15
1985	70	—	81	58	—	10	25	—	27	—

National Journal Ratings

	1986 LIB — 1986 CONS			1985 LIB — 1985 CONS		
Economic	87%	—	0%	75%	—	22%
Social	55%	—	44%	49%	—	49%
Foreign	75%	—	20%	70%	—	29%

Key Votes

1) Lmt Cln Water Act	AGN	5) Retain Gun Cont	FOR	9) Aid Angola Reb	AGN
2) Rpl Tobac Sub	AGN	6) Contra Aid	—	10) Tax Reform	AGN
3) Grm-Rdmn Def Red	FOR	7) Lmt Text Imp	FOR	11) S Africa Sanc	FOR
4) Ban Polygraph	FOR	8) Limit SDI	FOR	12) Immig Reform	FOR

Election Results

1986 general	Thomas J. Manton (D)	50,738	(69%)	($416,151)
	Salvatore J. Calise (R)	18,040	(25%)	
	Thomas V. Ognibene (C)	4,348	(6%)	
1986 primary	Thomas J. Manton (D) unopposed			
1984 general	Thomas J. Manton (D)	71,420	(53%)	($262,590)
	Serphin R. Maltese (R–C–RTL)	63,910	(47%)	($116,782)

Campaign Contributions and Expenditures

1985-86		Direct Cont. 1985-86		PACS Breakdown 1985-86			
Receipts	$415,865	Indiv.	$63,391	Corp.	$73,771	T/M/H	$77,578
Expend.	$416,151	PACS	$271,048	Labor	$101,549	Agr.	$3,500
Unspent	$6,924	Cand.	$100,000	Ideo.	$12,100	CWOS	$2,550

TENTH DISTRICT

From the green rises of Prospect Park to the marshy flats of Canarsie, from the Lefferts homestead built by 17th century Dutch settlers to the new shopping center and high-rises along Sheepshead Bay, the 10th Congressional District of New York includes most of the heart of Brooklyn, from the borough's old downtown to the Atlantic Ocean. This is the part of Brooklyn which most often comes to mind when the borough is mentioned, mile after mile of grid streets, built up with solid brick houses and three- and four-story apartment buildings: the Brooklyn that grew up along the subway lines in the 1910s and 1920s. Its population is mostly Jewish: this and the next-door 13th District may be the only majority-Jewish congressional districts in the whole United States. In the 1970s blacks began moving in large numbers into Flatbush, formerly a mostly Jewish neighborhood, but most of the Flatbush blacks are in the neighboring 12th District. And the Jewish neighborhoods along Ocean Parkway and Coney Island Avenue seem likely to remain mostly Jewish in the future. There is a renaissance of Orthodox Judaism here, and to some extent a turning away from the goals of secular education and advancement; the Jews here are, in many cases, not tremendously affluent, and they seem more interested in celebrating their traditions than in trying to emulate the dazzling successes of Jews who have long since moved on to Great Neck or Beverly Hills. Similar attitudes, on the part of both Jews and Gentiles, seem to prevail in the two-family house neighborhoods farther out, from Sheepshead Bay near Coney Island to Flatlands and Canarsie.

The 10th District is heavily Democratic country in partisan terms; but not in quite the way it used to be. In the 1930s it was enthusiastic for liberal Democrats at the top of the ticket like Franklin D. Roosevelt but suspicious of the Irish politicians and, sometimes, Italian gangsters who dominated the local Democratic machine. Now, increasingly conservative on many cultural issues, hostile to racial quotas and suspicious that dovish politicians may abandon Israel, it votes overwhelmingly for local Democratic candidates but gives national Democrats only small margins. Jimmy Carter lost many Jewish neighborhoods here to Ronald Reagan in 1980, and Walter Mondale, the heavy choice over Gary Hart in the 1984 primaries, nonetheless ran only about 60%–40% in Jewish precincts in the general.

In congressional elections, this heart of Brooklyn has been represented by liberal Democrats for longer than anyone can remember. Emanuel Celler, first elected in 1922, was chairman of the Judiciary Committee for many years; in 1972 he was upset in the primary by Elizabeth Holtzman, a rather solemn lawyer who won the 1980 Democratic Senate primary but lost the general election to Alfonse D'Amato; in 1982 she was elected Brooklyn's district attorney.

The current congressman is Charles Schumer, who in just a few terms has become one of the real movers in the House. He has done so through energy, imagination, and a certain amount of chutzpah. He comes forward with interesting and imaginative ideas and works and lobbies and nags until they are adopted. In his second term, operating from the Banking Committee, he got through a low- and middle-income housing program in place of the faltering Section 8: a Nehemiah program, proposed by east Brooklyn churches, with government providing land and mortgage subsidies, churches or other sponsors providing a revolving fund of capital, and building whole blocks of homes to be bought rather than rented by residents. This is the only new housing program of the 1980s, and one with the additional advantage, from Schumer's point of view, of being able to rehabilitate the vast acres of abandoned housing in Brownsville and East New York just at the edge of his district. This safeguards the neighborhoods and housing values of his political base.

Politically, Schumer in 1983 was the leader in getting the House Democratic Caucus to sponsor presidential debates, and devised a unique question-and-cross-examination format— unique enough that Walter Mondale balked before agreeing to appear at the Dartmouth debate. Schumer later became Gary Hart's prime backer in New York—with results that prove his political clout goes only so far. Then in his third term, he came up with proposals to scale back Third World debt, criticized banks for never lowering their credit card interest rates, and came forward with a key compromise on the farm labor provisions of the long-deadlocked immigration reform bill. Constantly advancing his own proposals, keeping his lines out to others, unburdened by any stake in his district, schmoozing on the floor of the House and in the coatrooms, he played a key role in getting the immigration bill passed in October 1986.

On many issues Schumer is political allies with three other members with whom he shares a Capitol Hill townhouse, Californians George Miller and Leon Panetta and Illinois's Marty Russo. This gives him lines to the big California delegation and to Ways and Means Chairman Dan Rostenkowski; he was campaign manager for Charles Rangel's unsuccessful bid for House majority whip. Bubbling over with ideas, Schumer seems ready to join every debate, armed with his latest proposal for a national presidential primary (preceded by regional non-binding contests) or for a federal law limiting plaintiffs' rights in libel cases. He has also started Talmudic classes for congressmen.

At home, after winning the 1980 primary with 59% of the vote, he has had little trouble. His biggest problem was the charge that he violated election laws by using his employees in that campaign; but nothing came of that. Schumer, temperamentally a legislator, found his metier early: he was elected to the New York Assembly at 23, just after finishing law school, and is now a prominent congressman while still under 40. His only political problem is redistricting. Both he and Stephen Solarz, anticipating a primary together, amassed huge campaign war chests for 1982, but both found safe districts; Schumer after the 1986 election had $503,000 in his treasury. They and others are nervously hoping that Brooklyn doesn't lose another seat in 1990.

The People: Pop. 1980: 516,471, dn. 6.9% 1970–80. Households (1980): 71% family, 30% with children, 56% married couples; 66.2% housing units rented; median monthly rent: $228; median house value: $53,600. Voting age pop. (1980): 401,703; 7% Spanish origin, 4% Black, 2% Asian origin.

1984 Presidential Vote:			
	Mondale (D)	93,499	(51%)
	Reagan (R)	90,357	(49%)

Rep. Charles E. Schumer (D)

Elected 1980; b. Nov. 23, 1950, Brooklyn; home, Brooklyn; Harvard Col., B.A. 1971, Harvard Law Sch., J.D. 1974; Jewish; married (Iris).

Career: Practicing atty.; NY Assembly, 1974–80.

Offices: 126 CHOB 20515, 202-225-6616. Also 1628 Kings Hwy., Brooklyn 11229, 718-965-5400.

Committees: *Banking, Finance and Urban Affairs* (8th of 31 D). Subcommittees: Consumer Affairs and Coinage; Financial Institutions Supervision, Regulation and Insurance; General Oversight and Investigations; Housing and Community Development; International Finance, Trade, and Monetary Policy. *Budget* (13th of 21 D). Task Forces: Health; State and Local Government. *Judiciary* (13th of 21 D). Subcommittees: Civil and Constitutional Rights; Immigration, Refugees, and International Law.

Group Ratings

	ADA	ACLU	COPE	CFA	LCV	ACU	NTU	NSI	COC	CEI
1986	85	90	93	100	88	5	26	0	29	22
1985	90	—	95	83	—	14	33	—	32	—

National Journal Ratings

	1986 LIB — 1986 CONS		1985 LIB — 1985 CONS	
Economic	68%	— 31%	79%	— 21%
Social	89%	— 0%	85%	— 0%
Foreign	80%	— 0%	85%	— 8%

Key Votes

1) Lmt Cln Water Act	FOR	5) Retain Gun Cont	FOR	9) Aid Angola Reb	AGN
2) Rpl Tobac Sub	FOR	6) Contra Aid	AGN	10) Tax Reform	FOR
3) Grm-Rdmn Def Red	AGN	7) Lmt Text Imp	AGN	11) S Africa Sanc	FOR
4) Ban Polygraph	FOR	8) Limit SDI	FOR	12) Immig Reform	FOR

Election Results

1986 general	Charles E. Schumer (D–L)............. 76,318	(93%)	($65,543)
	Alice Gaffney (C)...................... 5,472	(7%)	
1986 primary	Charles E. Schumer (D) unopposed		
1984 general	Charles E. Schumer (D–L)............ 115,867	(72%)	($82,417)
	John H. Fox (R–C)................... 42,009	(26%)	

Campaign Contributions and Expenditures

1985-86		Direct Cont. 1985-86		PACS Breakdown 1985-86			
Receipts	$81,374	Indiv.	$16,952	Corp.	$12,300	T/M/H	$21,450
Expend.	$65,543	PACS	$48,032	Labor	$11,332	Agr.	$0
Unspent	$22,526	Cand.	$18,000	Ideo.	$2,450	CWOS	$500

ELEVENTH DISTRICT

The 11th Congressional District of New York includes most of the northern and eastern parts of the borough of Brooklyn, an area which, taken together, has no single personality of its own. It includes most of downtown Brooklyn, with a skyline and a set of civic institutions that would be impressive in most American metropolitan areas but that tend to get lost in New York. It also has the row houses—some of them splendid solid stone houses, many pleasant, some still wretched slums—of the neighborhoods that fan out in every direction: South Brooklyn and

Carroll Gardens to the south, Fort Greene and Clinton Hill to the east. To the north is the center of the old working-class neighborhood of Williamsburg; fanning out southeast are the grid streets of Bushwick. These were old manufacturing areas, where 19th-century Brooklynites produced the most prosaic of commodities—rope, glue, ships, and beer—now made in places like Mexico, the Philippines, and Korea. Almost detached from the rest of the district is the East New York neighborhood at the edge of Queens. Once it was mostly Italian; now it has many black and Puerto Rican inhabitants.

The 11th District has a long and varied ethnic history. Its early patricians were Dutchmen and Yankees; its mid-20th century residents were mostly Italian and other Catholics. It still includes some of Brooklyn's Hasidic Jewish community. But it is now what lawyers call a majority minority district. Some 47% of its residents are black and 34% Hispanic; there is, it should be noted, some overlap between these categories. In the process it has not developed much of a civic culture. Part of the reason may be that the civic loyalties of many residents remain elsewhere. Blacks and the Hispanics from the Caribbean often move to Brooklyn intending to stay only a while, to make enough money to set themselves up in a good situation back home. They continue to read newspapers from San Juan or Barbados; they pay U.S. taxes and even become U.S. citizens (if they are not already), but their country is elsewhere.

The congressman from the 11th District is Ed Towns, a black Democrat from East New York more experienced in government than politics and used to serving members of all races. Towns has been a teacher, social worker, and hospital administrator and active in the civic affairs of a racially changing community. He served as Brooklyn's deputy borough president for six years. That is an office with duties more mundane than it sounds, but is nonetheless one which keeps a conscientious incumbent in close touch with organized communities across Brooklyn. Towns evidently succeeded in making himself both popular and non-controversial, and keeping himself from becoming involved in the political feuds that have captivated Bedford-Stuyvesant, a part of which he represents. In Washington, Towns is a member of the Government Operations and Public Works and Transportation Committees; he serves on the latter committee's Aviation and Surface Transportation panels, workaday assignments in which he can serve local interests. He maintains a solidly liberal voting record on most issues.

Throughout his career Towns has been the opposite of controversial. When the 11th District was drawn in 1982 to satisfy the Voting Rights Act, it seemed at first as if white incumbent Frederick Richmond would win. But Richmond, a rich businessman who had been pouring political and charitable money into Brooklyn for years was forced to retire after it was revealed, four years after his arrest on homosexual charges, that he had gotten an ex-convict a job in the House under a false name. Towns won easily and now seems to have a safe seat, at least till the next redistricting in 1992.

The People: Pop. 1980: 516,554, dn. 26.6% 1970–80. Households (1980): 70% family, 47% with children, 35% married couples; 83.4% housing units rented; median monthly rent: $174; median house value: $33,700. Voting age pop. (1980): 331,181; 47% Black, 34% Spanish origin, 1% Asian origin.

1984 Presidential Vote: Mondale (D) 94,574 (78%)
Reagan (R) 25,558 (21%)

Rep. Edolphus Towns (D)

Elected 1982; b. July 21, 1934, Chadbourn, NC; home, Brooklyn; NC A&T U., B.S. 1956, Adelphi U., M.S.W. 1973; Presbyterian; married (Gwendolyn).

Career: Army, 1956–58; Prof., Medgar Evers Col.; Dpty. hospital administrator, 1965–71; Dpty. Borough Pres. of Brooklyn, 1976–82.

Offices: 1726 LHOB 20515, 202-225-5936. Also 93 Prospect Pl., Brooklyn 11217, 718-622-5700.

Committees: *Government Operations.* (14th of 24 D). Subcommittees: Environment, Energy, and Natural Resources; Government Information, Justice, and Agriculture. *Public Works and Transportation* (16th of 32 D). Subcommittees: Aviation; Surface Transportation; Investigations and Oversight. *Select Committee on Narcotics Abuse and Control* (15th of 15 D).

Group Ratings

	ADA	ACLU	COPE	CFA	LCV	ACU	NTU	NSI	COC	CEI
1986	95	94	98	83	69	0	26	0	15	16
1985	95	—	98	67	—	5	29	—	32	—

National Journal Ratings

	1986 LIB — 1986 CONS		1985 LIB — 1985 CONS	
Economic	87%	— 0%	89%	— 0%
Social	83%	— 17%	81%	— 15%
Foreign	80%	— 0%	92%	— 0%

Key Votes

1) Lmt Cln Water Act	AGN	5) Retain Gun Cont	FOR	9) Aid Angola Reb	AGN
2) Rpl Tobac Sub	AGN	6) Contra Aid	AGN	10) Tax Reform	FOR
3) Grm-Rdmn Def Red	AGN	7) Lmt Text Imp	FOR	11) S Africa Sanc	FOR
4) Ban Polygraph	—	8) Limit SDI	FOR	12) Immig Reform	AGN

Election Results

1986 general	Edolphus Towns (D–L).................	41,689	(89%)	($185,565)
	Nathaniel Hendricks (R)	4,053	(9%)	($543)
1986 primary	Edolphus Towns (D) unopposed			
1984 general	Edolphus Towns (D–L).................	81,002	(85%)	($278,064)
	Nathaniel Hendricks (R)	12,494	(13%)	($1,670)

Campaign Contributions and Expenditures

1985-86		Direct Cont. 1985-86		PACS Breakdown 1985-86			
Receipts	$224,253	Indiv.	$99,957	Corp.	$25,100	T/M/H	$20,830
Expend.	$185,565	PACS	$132,740	Labor	$73,310	Agr.	$2,000
Unspent	$39,036			Ideo.	$9,750	CWOS	$1,750

TWELFTH DISTRICT

Bedford–Stuyvesant is the largest, yet not the best-known of America's large black urban neighborhoods. While Harlem, a focus of attention since the 1920s, has been depopulated, and large parts of the South Bronx have become vacant as landlords abandon rent controlled apartments and young thugs burn them up, Bed–Stuy has grown and, to some extent, prospered. By 1980 Harlem had withered so much that there were more blacks in Queens and in the Bronx than in Manhattan. Nearly twice as many, 722,000, lived in Brooklyn, most in the few square miles of Bedford–Stuyvesant and the adjoining communities of Crown Heights, Brownsville, and East Flatbush.

Together these areas form New York's 12th Congressional District, a more varied area than appears on the surface to many outsiders. The solid stone row houses of Bedford–Stuyvesant, many of them renovated or sparkling with new paint, house many upwardly mobile families, some of them straight from the West Indies; the blacks who have moved recently into once all-white East Flatbush are by no means impoverished. Brownsville, on the other hand, is about as wretched and disorganized a place as there is in America. Once Brooklyn's premier Jewish neighborhood, where young immigrants moved from the Lower East Side and debated socialism and labor unions in streets dense with peddlers and children, Brownsville became all black in the 1950s, and is now a desert of abandoned buildings; vacant lots with hints of the outlines of the houses that once stood there; uncontrolled youth gangs, drugs, and frequent arson. It is the sort of place anybody with an ability to make his own way will get out of, and so it is the province of the helpess and the vicious, the crippled and the criminal.

The 12th District is 80% black, heavily Democratic, and possessed of a lively political culture which, however, seems to directly touch very few of its citizens. Voter turnout for years was about as low here as any place in the United States; elections were decided by small groups of hardy civic activists. Turnout rose suddenly in 1984 in the spring presidential primary, thanks almost entirely to Jesse Jackson; while Manhattan's leading black politician, Representative Charles Rangel, was uncomfortably keeping his word and supporting Walter Mondale, Bedford–Stuyvesant Assemblyman Albert Vann, with more than an eye on the 1985 race against Mayor Edward Koch, was leading Jackson's campaign. Jackson did indeed sweep the district, and won 38% of the vote in Brooklyn, an impressive showing; but Vann and other anti-Koch politicians were unable to agree on a single opponent for the Mayor in 1985 and were routed. Vann himself was embarrassed when he was knocked off the Democratic primary ballot for technical reasons, but he and Roger Green in an adjoining district were both returned to the Assembly as the Liberal nominees.

The congressman from the 12th District, Major Owens, has had a long career in New York politics and government. He started out as a librarian, worked in the Brownsville Community Council, was commissioner of New York City's Community Development Agency under Mayor John Lindsay from 1968 to 1972, and was called by critic Charles Morris "the most capable and canny" of New York's anti-poverty program directors. That was a high-pressure job, with few guidelines to draw on; Owens may have been relieved when he was elected to serve in the antique chamber of the New York Senate in 1974. In 1982, when Representative Shirley Chisholm, immigrant from Barbados and presidential candidate in 1972, announced her retirement, Owens got into the primary to succeed her. Chisholm backed another state Senator, Vander Beatty, who also had support from the Brooklyn organization; but Owens won. A Brooklyn court, responsive presumably to an organization that does little but determine judicial nominations, ordered a rerun of the primary after Owens was counted the winner by a margin of some 2,400 votes—more than enough to survive a recount in most states, let alone a congressional district with low turnout. That decision was overturned, however, and Owens became congressman.

He sits on two committees—Education and Labor and Government Operations—that have less clout than they used to but which are of obvious relevance to this district and on which Owens can usefully draw on his experience. He can be counted to look after the interests of libraries; as he likes to point out, he is the only librarian in the House. On national issues, Owens can be counted on as a solid liberal Democratic vote. General elections are, of course, no problem for him, but he must always be wary of the primary: even Chisholm, after years of incumbency and national fame, had to worry about primary opposition.

The People: Pop. 1980: 516,983, dn. 12.5% 1970–80. Households (1980): 70% family, 46% with children, 37% married couples; 83.2% housing units rented; median monthly rent: $203; median house value: $46,200. Voting age pop. (1980): 348,549; 78% Black, 9% Spanish origin, 2% Asian origin.

1984 Presidential Vote: Mondale (D) 91,344   (85%)
                                Reagan (R) 15,414   (14%)

Rep. Major R. Owens (D)

Elected 1982; b. June 28, 1936, Memphis, TN; home, Brooklyn; Morehouse Col., B.A. 1956, Atlanta U., M.S. 1957; Baptist; divorced.

Career: Vice Pres., Metropolitan Cncl. of Housing, 1964; Commun. Coord., Brooklyn Pub. Library, 1964–65; Exec. Dir., Brownsville Commun. Cncl., 1966–68; Commissioner, NYC Commun. Develop. Agcy., 1968–73; Dir., Commun. Media Library Prog., Columbia U., 1974; NY Senate, 1974–82.

Offices: 114 CHOB 20515, 202-225-6231. Also 289 Utica Ave., Brooklyn 11213, 718-773-3100.

Committees: *Education and Labor* (10th of 21 D). Subcommittees: Employment Opportunities; Labor Management Relations; Postsecondary Education; Select Education (Chairman). *Government Operations* (13th of 24 D). Subcommittees: Employment and Housing; Government Activities and Transportation.

Group Ratings

	ADA	ACLU	COPE	CFA	LCV	ACU	NTU	NSI	COC	CEI
1986	95	88	98	100	77	0	29	0	20	12
1985	95	—	100	83	—	0	30	—	14	—

National Journal Ratings

	1986 LIB — 1986 CONS	1985 LIB — 1985 CONS
Economic	81% — 18%	89% — 0%
Social	89% — 0%	85% — 0%
Foreign	80% — 0%	75% — 25%

Key Votes

1) Lmt Cln Water Act	AGN	5) Retain Gun Cont	FOR	9) Aid Angola Reb	AGN
2) Rpl Tobac Sub	FOR	6) Contra Aid	AGN	10) Tax Reform	FOR
3) Grm-Rdmn Def Red	AGN	7) Lmt Text Imp	FOR	11) S Africa Sanc	FOR
4) Ban Polygraph	FOR	8) Limit SDI	FOR	12) Immig Reform	FOR

Election Results

1986 general	Major R. Owens (D–L).................	42,138	(91%)	($167,617)
	Owen Augustin (R)......................	2,752	(6%)	($24,506)
	Joseph N.O. Caesar (C)	1,168	(3%)	($1,895)
1986 primary	Major R. Owens (D)....................	14,892	(78%)	
	Roy Innis (D)	4,165	(22%)	
1984 general	Major R. Owens (D–L).................	82,047	(91%)	($187,585)
	Joseph N. Caesar (R–C–RTL)...........	8,609	(9%)	($3,127)

Campaign Contributions and Expenditures

1985-86		Direct Cont. 1985-86		PACS Breakdown 1985-86			
Receipts	$169,403	Indiv.	$76,770	Corp.	$3,775	T/M/H	$14,097
Expend.	$167,617	PACS	$95,136	Labor	$62,264	Agr.	$500
Unspent	$1,053	Cand.	$600	Ideo.	$14,250	CWOS	$250

THIRTEENTH DISTRICT

Along the Brooklyn waterfront, from Williamsburg with its Hasidic Jewish community and its single skyscraper, past downtown Brooklyn and the old Brooklyn Heights neighborhood overlooking downtown Manhattan and Wall Street from Columbia Heights, past the old and often abandoned docks of South Brooklyn, Red Hook, and the Bush Terminal, dodging inland to avoid middle-class Bay Ridge and then facing the ocean, stretches the 13th Congressional District of New York. Seldom more than a mile wide, it extends far enough that it would take you most of a working day to drive through it. It has high-income pockets, like trendy Brooklyn Heights, and some poverty-stricken slums here and there; it has Hasidic neighborhoods in the north, burgeoning Orthodox communities in Borough Park and along Ocean Parkway, and neighborhoods brimming with new Jewish emigrants from Soviet Russia in Brighton Beach and Coney Island on the ocean. The 13th is basically the poor Jewish district, one of the few majority-Jewish districts in the nation and the home of many of the nation's least affluent Jewish communities.

It is a district with mixed political leanings. On economic issues the tradition here is liberal, even socialistic: government should act to help the ordinary person. On civil liberties, of course the tradition is for tolerance—though some of the Orthodox would just as soon not tolerate practices other than their own. On cultural issues, there is fear of crime, dislike of racial quotas, overwhelming support of Mayor Edward Koch. On foreign policy, the trend has been conservative. Brooklyn was ready early on to support candidates who didn't favor the Vietnam war. But this part of Brooklyn is always worried about the survival of Israel and has come to believe that an assertive, maybe even aggressive American approach is needed toward the Soviets and unfriendly Third World nations.

The congressman from the 13th District is Stephen Solarz, an able, ambitious, and powerful member of the large Democratic class of 1974. Solarz is a Brooklyn politician and a foreign policy scholar, an elected official who has been supple in adapting to the changing views and priorities of his constituency and a leader on foreign policy who has had a major effect on American actions and who is a player in NATO meetings and Philippine showdowns. Solarz has roots in Brooklyn, but he was also a graduate student studying under Zbigniew Brzezinski at Columbia in the 1960s; he was opposed to the Vietnam war, but he also believes that the United States must assert leadership and not simply accept whatever Soviet and Third World leaders decide to do. He has been a political insurgent, beating the rotted old Brooklyn machine in a race for the New York Assembly in 1968 and beating a scandal-tarred incumbent congressman in the Democratic primary in 1974. But he is by now a member of the establishment, fourth ranking Democrat on the Foreign Affairs Committee, chairman of a major subcommittee, a widely respected participant in foreign policy debate.

The critical period in his career came after the 1980 election, after the Republicans' surprising victory. Solarz had been chairman for two years of the subcommittee covering Africa, an area on which there was predictably going to be a clash between Democratic liberals and Reagan Republicans. But there was an opening on the Asian and Pacific Affairs Subcommittee, on which issues were not so polarized, and on which, given the fate of Cambodia and Vietnam, it was hard for Democratic liberals to wax as self-righteous as they could on South Africa. Solarz chose the Asia chair. It has given him an opportunity to be a leader, but not always in a confrontational way. To be sure, he has criticized East Asian countries for their lack of democracy, in contrast to a Jesse Helms protégé who was ambassador to South Korea, for instance. But on the Philippines he turned out to be a pioneer and maker, rather than an opponent, of American policy. Travelling often to Manila, keeping up a barrage of criticism of Ferdinand Marcos since before Benigno Aquino was murdered in 1983, he was harshly critical of the elections Marcos held in 1986; joined by Republicans like Senate Foreign Relations Chairman Richard Lugar, he helped create a climate in which the Administration tilted sharply toward Corazon Aquino and signalled Marcos into exile without bloodshed. He deserves much of the credit for the revolution that put Aquino into office, and he was even with her in the Malacanang Palace when he discovered the closet with Imela Marcos's 3,000 pairs of shoes.

Asia has been a good place to forge American consensus because the limits of both liberal and conservative policies are apparent there. It is clear that Vietnam and Cambodia are worse off than they would have been if U.S.-backed forces had won there (though not clear whether or not they could have), but clear also that Communist victories there have not proved an attractive example for the rest of East Asia, as many conservatives feared they would. Solarz, backing military aid for the non-communist faction of the Cambodian resistance movement, inferentially at least recognizes this. It is apparent that authoritarian East Asia countries like South Korea have produced much greater economic growth and more tolerable living conditions than Communist alternatives, but clear also that human rights there could be improved.

But Solarz is involved in issues outside Asia too. He helps to shepherd foreign aid bills through, making sure they contain plenty for Israel. He keeps a hand in arms control, calling for a willingness to trade the Strategic Defense Initiative for Soviet concessions. He criticizes unilateral disarmers abroad, like the British Labor party. He issues his own conclusions on the Iran-contra scandal. He calls for a peaceful settlement in Nicaragua, and is willing to correspond directly with the Sandinistas just as he was willing to visit North Korea, against Administration wishes. Solarz sometimes talks as if he were bucking constituency pressures. But his views seem to fit 13th District preferences pretty closely.

He is active sometimes on domestic issues, as well, calling for example for fast food restaurants to list the ingredients of their fare. At home he has essentially a safe seat. During the redistricting process after the 1980 Census it looked as though Solarz and the 10th District's Charles Schumer would be put in the same seat, and both accumulated huge campaign treasuries in anticipation of that, but they both got safe, separate districts and no electoral problems until 1992 at the earliest. Solarz accumulated enough money so that after the 1986 election he had $812,000 in his campaign treasury. But not all his ambitions are electoral. Many think he would like to be secretary of state in a Democratic administration, and it's just possible he could.

The People: Pop. 1980: 516,512, dn. 9.8% 1970–80. Households (1980): 67% family, 31% with children, 51% married couples; 77.5% housing units rented; median monthly rent: $195; median house value: $53,600. Voting age pop. (1980): 387,947; 13% Spanish origin, 6% Black, 2% Asian origin.

1984 Presidential Vote:

Mondale (D)	71,441	(53%)
Reagan (R)	64,033	(47%)

Rep. Stephen J. Solarz (D)

Elected 1974; b. Sept. 12, 1940, New York City; home, Brooklyn; Brandeis U., A.B. 1962, Columbia U., M.A. 1967; Jewish; married (Nina).

Career: NY Assembly, 1968–74.

Offices: 1536 LHOB 20515, 202-225-2361. Also 532 Neptune Ave., Brooklyn, 11224, 718-372-8600.

Committees: *Education and Labor* (14th of 21 D). Subcommittees: Elementary, Secondary, and Vocational Education; Human Resources. *Foreign Affairs* (4th of 27 D). Subcommittees: Asian and Pacific Affairs (Chairman); Western Hemisphere Affairs. *Post Office and Civil Service* (4th of 14 D). Subcommittee: Civil Service. *Joint Economic Committee.* Task Forces: Fiscal and Monetary Policy; International Economic Policy; Investment, Jobs and Prices.

Group Ratings

	ADA	ACLU	COPE	CFA	LCV	ACU	NTU	NSI	COC	CEI
1986	90	87	89	100	88	5	27	0	20	27
1985	90	—	89	100	—	14	33	—	20	—

National Journal Ratings

	1986 LIB — 1986 CONS			1985 LIB — 1985 CONS		
Economic	74%	—	23%	85%	—	11%
Social	89%	—	0%	79%	—	19%
Foreign	80%	—	0%	75%	—	21%

Key Votes

1) Lmt Cln Water Act	AGN	5) Retain Gun Cont	FOR	9) Aid Angola Reb	AGN
2) Rpl Tobac Sub	FOR	6) Contra Aid	AGN	10) Tax Reform	FOR
3) Grm-Rdmn Def Red	AGN	7) Lmt Text Imp	AGN	11) S Africa Sanc	FOR
4) Ban Polygraph	FOR	8) Limit SDI	FOR	12) Immig Reform	FOR

Election Results

1986 general	Stephen J. Solarz (D–L)................	61,089	(82%)	($417,975)
	Leon Nadrowski (R).................	10,941	(15%)	($294,811)
	Samuel Roth (C).....................	2,106	(3%)	
1986 primary	Stephen J. Solarz (D) unopposed			
1984 general	Stephen J. Solarz (D–L).............	82,610	(66%)	($174,183)
	Lew Y. Levin (R–C–RTL)	42,737	(34%)	($41,926)

Campaign Contributions and Expenditures

1985-86		Direct Cont. 1985-86		PACS Breakdown 1985-86			
Receipts	$608,701	Indiv.	$434,527	Corp.	$4,250	T/M/H	$13,027
Expend.	$417,975	PACS	$39,977	Labor	$17,200	Agr.	$0
Unspent	$812,706			Ideo.	$5,000	CWOS	$500

FOURTEENTH DISTRICT

Still connected to Manhattan by the ferry that is the best bargain in New York (25 cents), Staten Island is the smallest (pop. 352,000) and by far the least densely populated of the five boroughs of New York City (6,000 people per square mile versus 27,000 for the rest of the city). Geographically, it is off to the side; you could make a good case that it should have been part of New Jersey. Physically, some of it is still rural: cows still graze in the nation's largest city. Before 1965, when the Verrazano Narrows Bridge was completed, the only land route from the rest of New York to Staten Island was through New Jersey, and the New York connection was by ferry. Since then Staten Island's population has increased by more than 50%. Yet it still has an unsettled atmosphere, a disorganized, random air, as subdivisions do when they are not oriented to a particular center or situated in a recognizable grid.

Most Staten Islanders are quite happy with their comparative isolation. They are in many ways more suburban than real suburbanites. Many are middle-income Italian and Irish Catholics, brought up in Brooklyn and happy to leave the City (as they call it) behind. Politically, Staten Islanders are conservative; Conservative Party candidates have occasionally outpolled Democrats. They are home-owners, not renters; family people, not singles; religious people, not skeptics. They have little in common with Manhattan. Yet while many people here think of themselves as Democrats, they don't have much in common with Upstaters either.

Staten Island forms two-thirds of New York's 14th Congressional District. The other one-third is the part of New York City which may be closest to Staten Island in attitudes, as well as in proximity: the Bay Ridge section of Brooklyn. At the eastern terminus of the Verrazano Narrows Bridge, Bay Ridge is mostly Catholic, mostly middle-class; there are some large apartment buildings and even high-rises, but 30% of the housing units are owner-occupied, and there are even some large single-family homes overlooking New York Harbor. In heavily Democratic Brooklyn, Bay Ridge consistently votes Republican.

The congressman from the 14th District is Staten Islander Guy Molinari, a Republican first elected in 1980. But he owed his victory less to the Reagan landslide than to local circumstances: other Republicans were beaten by Democratic Representative John Murphy before in Republican presidential years, but in 1980 Murphy ran after having been convicted in the Abscam scandal, and lost. Since then, Molinari has remained in office more by tending local interests than by following national conservative agendas. He first got notice in 1981 when he threatened to retire unless President Reagan paid more attention to him on a trip to New York; Reagan did, and Molinari ended his pout. Since then, he has championed the Navy's homeporting plan, dispersing ships from Norfolk and San Diego; one result of the 1986 decision is that Staten Island will become a Navy port. Like many northeastern Republicans, he is as eager as his Democratic neighbors to be seen cleaning up the environment, and was quick to sponsor amendments to the Clean Water Act to help Staten Island.

On the Public Works Committee he has specialized in air safety issues, calling unsuccessfully for the rehiring of some of the air traffic controllers fired by President Reagan for striking in 1981 and opposing the transfer of controllers from the New York to the Boston sector. Here as elsewhere Molinari is a kind of Burkean conservative in a mature welfare state, ready to use existing institutions including government to help his local constituents, willing to serve the interests of ongoing lobbies (like the labor unions, which were hurt by the controller firings) and to subordinate legal or free market principles. Nor is he attracted to theoretical conservatives in the presidential race. He was the leader of nine New York Republican congressmen who made a show in 1986 of endorsing George Bush over their New York colleague Jack Kemp.

Molinari has had his reverses, and was disappointed when Newt Gingrich took away (as he was entitled to by seniority) his ranking position on a Public Works subcommittee in 1985—although he is now ranking member on the Public Buildings and Grounds Subcommittee. But by concentrating his efforts on a small number of issues, most of which have clear local impact, he has made a difference on policy and helped establish himself in a strong political position. In 1982 redistricting put him in a race against Bay Ridge Democratic incumbent Leo Zeferetti, but Molinari won with a big margin in Staten Island. He has been reelected easily twice since.

The People: Pop. 1980: 516,537, up 8.7% 1970–80. Households (1980): 75% family, 38% with children, 60% married couples; 50.5% housing units rented; median monthly rent: $217; median house value: $62,000. Voting age pop. (1980): 379,638; 6% Spanish origin, 4% Black, 2% Asian origin.

1984 Presidential Vote: Reagan (R) 118,383   (66%)
Mondale (D) 61,868   (34%)

Rep. Guy V. Molinari (R)

Elected 1980; b. Nov. 23, 1928, New York City; home, Staten Island; Wagner Col., B.A. 1949, NY Law Sch., LL.B. 1951; Roman Catholic; married (Marguerite).

Career: USMC, Korea; Practicing atty., 1953–74; NY Assembly, 1974–80.

Offices: 208 CHOB 20515, 202-225-3371. Also Ft. Wadsworth, Bldg. 203, Staten Island 10305, 718-981-9800; and 1305 73d St., Brooklyn 11228, 718-236-9292.

Committees: *Public Works and Transportation* (6th of 20 R). Subcommittees: Investigations and Oversight; Public Buildings and Grounds (Ranking Member); Water Resources.

Group Ratings

	ADA	ACLU	COPE	CFA	LCV	ACU	NTU	NSI	COC	CEI
1986	15	5	24	33	42	59	49	90	72	49
1985	30	—	22	67	—	67	45	—	64	—

National Journal Ratings

	1986 LIB — 1986 CONS		1985 LIB — 1985 CONS	
Economic	31% —	67%	36% —	63%
Social	27% —	71%	41% —	56%
Foreign	25% —	74%	35% —	63%

Key Votes

1) Lmt Cln Water Act	AGN	5) Retain Gun Cont	FOR	9) Aid Angola Reb	FOR
2) Rpl Tobac Sub	FOR	6) Contra Aid	FOR	10) Tax Reform	AGN
3) Grm-Rdmn Def Red	FOR	7) Lmt Text Imp	FOR	11) S Africa Sanc	FOR
4) Ban Polygraph	AGN	8) Limit SDI	AGN	12) Immig Reform	AGN

Election Results

1986 general	Guy V. Molinari (R–C–RTL)	64,647	(69%)	($152,312)
	Barbara Walla (D)	27,950	(30%)	($41,310)
1986 primary	Guy V. Molinari (R) unopposed			
1984 general	Guy V. Molinari (R–C–RTL)	117,041	(70%)	($174,443)
	Kevin L. Sheehy (D)	49,776	(30%)	($42,724)

Campaign Contributions and Expenditures

1985-86		Direct Cont. 1985-86		PACS Breakdown 1985-86			
Receipts	$200,527	Indiv.	$99,351	Corp.	$14,425	T/M/H	$21,600
Expend.	$152,312	Party	$6,556	Labor	$14,950	Agr.	$0
Unspent	$137,333	PACS	$56,781	Ideo.	$5,230	CWOS	$576

FIFTEENTH DISTRICT

The 15th Congressional District of New York is the latest version of a district first created in 1918 and known since at least the 1930s as the Silk Stocking District. It includes most of the skyscrapers of midtown Manhattan and the lights of Times Square; it goes as far south now as City Hall and as far north as 98th Street and Central Park. It includes the Lower East Side, with its high-rise housing for elderly Jews, a reminder of the days, 70 years ago, when these neighborhoods were packed full of young immigrants and their large families. The Silk Stocking

District includes almost everything—the glitzy stores and apartment towers, restaurants and grand hotels and private clubs—that make New York a world-class city, whose only rivals are Paris and London. But many of the residents here are Brazilians and French fleeing high taxes and expropriation; there are probably more New York voters in middle-income housing developments like Stuyvesant Town, Peter Cooper Village and the quaint old square of Gramercy Park.

The 15th District is where, more than anywhere else in the country, the American establishment lives, works, and plays. Yet most of the voters here are people with shallow roots in New York or anywhere else: young singles from somewhere else, in search of a spouse and an eventual suburban house; older people whose interest in local affairs is limited mostly to who will be allowed to live in the swanky Park Avenue cooperative or super-low-priced public housing development they are fortunate enough to get. Most of the voters in this district live on the Upper East Side, from the East 50s to the East 90s, between Central Park and the East River. But the very rich huddle, along Fifth, Madison, Park, and Sutton Place, just as they did 70 years ago, when the rest of the East Side was filled with factories, breweries, and the German immigrants of Yorkville. Now the factories are torn down and the row houses increasingly replaced with high-rises, faced in that ugly pale grey brick which must be New York's cheapest building material, and filled with highly educated, usually single young professionals and white-collar workers.

This is the largest concentration of singles in America. These are the people who make Manhattan the center of the nation's securities, publishing, advertising, entertainment, broadcasting, and communications industries. And these are the people who fill Bloomingdale's every Saturday, in ever-hot pursuit of the latest style and fashion. They are people who love the struggle of New York life—the struggle to keep clean and well dressed in the dirty, gritty New York air, to maintain fashionable hairstyles in the New York wind, to keep themselves going to fashionable vacation places and the latest little restaurants.

The Silk Stocking District, in the 1950s when it was one of six Manhattan districts and today when it is one of three, has been both more Republican and more liberal than the rest of New York. Its liberalism is particularly notable on cultural and foreign policy issues, and is less pronounced on economics. Its politics in the 1950s came from the old *New York Herald-Tribune* and from the *Time* magazine of Henry Luce. They represented a Republican elite used to running major financial and governmental institutions in line with old rules, and sought to protect them against Democrats who represented lawless immigrant masses or socialistic labor unions. Silk Stocking Republicans were internationalists, in the sense that they wanted to help Britain in World War II, and liberal in their support of civil rights for blacks. They were the prime force behind the Dewey and Eisenhower candidacies. One of the last *Herald-Tribune* Republicans to win office was John Lindsay, when he was elected to Congress in 1958.

Lindsay compiled a liberal Republican record in office, then ran for mayor and won in 1965. The *Herald-Tribune* was going out of business, and Lindsay embraced the growing Manhattan liberalism, eventually ending up running a hapless race for President as a Democrat in 1972. He never carried New York City outside Manhattan, and his policies, based on an assumption that affluence of the society at large was unlimited and an adolescent rebellion against the very system that produced the wealth—proved wildly unpopular in the outer boroughs. But he could have gone on winning in Manhattan forever—or at least until his fiscal policies sent the city to the brink of bankruptcy in 1975.

The Silk Stocking District preceded Lindsay into the Democratic party, electing as congressman in 1968 Edward Koch, then a veteran of Greenwich Village reform politics. The 1970s changed Koch, who became more sympathetic to the outer boroughs, and came to oppose racial quotas, educational policies that stressed liberation from norms rather than learning basics, the fashionable liberal isolationism in foreign policy. The 1970s also changed the Silk Stocking District, turning its focus increasingly inward—away from poverty programs and toward exercise programs. The affluence that was taken for granted in the late 1960s suddenly seemed threatened, and East Siders began to appreciate a little more the market economics that produces so much of their wealth. When Koch was elected mayor in 1977 and the district elected a replacement, it chose not a rich Democrat like Carter Burden nor an ultraliberal like Bella Abzug, but Republican Bill Green.

Green is smart and rich, and was the last Republican elected to the New York Assembly from Manhattan. He has a voting record more liberal than most Democrats on cultural issues; he is an ardent backer of the Equal Rights Amendment and of feminist and gay rights measures. On foreign policy he is a bit more cautious, and his record is mixed on economic matters. He is a spokesman for old-fashioned liberal Republicanism, maintaining against the weight of the evidence that his party has won four of the last five presidential elections and much else besides with conservative nominees. He has a seat on the Appropriations Committee and is ranking Republican on the housing subcommittee; he is hard-working and knowledgeable, and manages to channel a lot of money to New York housing programs. The Republican leadership probably does not much mind: they understand that without a record like this, Green would have no chance of surviving in this district. Careful, diffident, almost shy, possessed of a quiet sense of humor, Green is not a natural gladhander or spellbinder and does not personify the glitzy and trendy qualities so often seen in his district.

Even so, he does not have complete security electorally. This was a Mondale, not a Reagan, district in 1984; Green is one of the few Republicans who has had to run ahead of Reagan to win. In that cause he has spent from his own considerable fortune and has raised much from others. After beating Burden and Abzug in 1977 and 1978, he beat Nader's raider (and 1986 Senate nominee) Mark Green in 1980, Betty Lall in 1982, then Manhattan Borough President (and now City Council President) Andrew Stein in 1984, and George Hirsch, one of the originators of *New York* magazine, in 1986. A creditable opponent each time, and against none of them has Green won as much as 60% of the vote. He has done enough to make most congressional seats safe, but he continues to have to work hard to hold the Silk Stocking District.

The People: Pop. 1980: 516,409, dn. 3.2% 1970–80. Households (1980): 37% family, 14% with children, 28% married couples; 89.3% housing units rented; median monthly rent: $317; median house value: $185,800. Voting age pop. (1980): 444,395; 12% Spanish origin, 9% Asian origin, 5% Black.

1984 Presidential Vote:

Mondale (D)	118,791	(60%)
Reagan (R)	77,670	(39%)

Rep. Bill Green (R)

Elected Feb. 14, 1978; b. Oct. 16, 1929, New York City; home, New York City; Harvard U., B.A. 1950, J.D. 1953; Jewish; married (Patricia).

Career: Army, 1953–55; Law Secy., U.S. Court of Appeals for DC Circuit, 1955–56; Practicing atty., 1956–70; NY Assembly, 1965–70; NY Regional Administrator, HUD, 1970–77.

Offices: 1110 LHOB 20515, 202-225-2436. Also 110 E. 45th St., New York 10017, 212-826-4466.

Committees: *Appropriations* (13th of 22 R). Subcommittees: District of Columbia; HUD–Independent Agencies (Ranking Member).

Group Ratings

	ADA	ACLU	COPE	CFA	LCV	ACU	NTU	NSI	COC	CEI
1986	70	63	56	75	89	18	39	10	39	41
1985	60	—	55	83	—	35	45	—	57	—

National Journal Ratings

	1986 LIB — 1986 CONS	1985 LIB — 1985 CONS
Economic	44% — 55%	48% — 50%
Social	81% — 17%	85% — 0%
Foreign	61% — 37%	69% — 30%

Key Votes

1) Lmt Cln Water Act	AGN	5) Retain Gun Cont	FOR	9) Aid Angola Reb	FOR
2) Rpl Tobac Sub	FOR	6) Contra Aid	AGN	10) Tax Reform	AGN
3) Grm-Rdmn Def Red	FOR	7) Lmt Text Imp	AGN	11) S Africa Sanc	FOR
4) Ban Polygraph	FOR	8) Limit SDI	FOR	12) Immig Reform	FOR

Election Results

1986 general	Bill Green (R–IN)	58,214	(58%)	($709,384)
	George A. Hirsch (D–L).	42,147	(42%)	($395,185)
1986 primary	Bill Green (R) unopposed			
1984 general	Bill Green (R–IN)	107,644	(56%)	($1,120,783)
	Andrew J. Stein (D–L).	84,404	(44%)	($1,779,281)

Campaign Contributions and Expenditures

1985-86		Direct Cont. 1985-86		PACS Breakdown 1985-86			
Receipts	$696,203	Indiv.	$475,627	Corp.	$53,932	T/M/H	$39,232
Expend.	$709,384	Party	$19,571	Labor	$13,477	Agr.	$0
Unspent	$9,863	PACS	$125,991	Ideo.	$16,600	CWOS	$2,750
		Cand.	$10,000				

SIXTEENTH DISTRICT

Harlem has been on America's mind since the 1920s, when this street-grid filled with five-story tenements built for white working-class families became America's most famous black neighborhood, attracting white jazz-lovers to its clubs, nurturing writers and performers, and becoming the undisputed center of black American culture. These were good years for Harlem, when New York seemed a land of opportunity and tolerance—no one then expected integration—for blacks. But the Depression of the 1930s hit Harlem hard, and in many ways it never recovered. A few middle-class pockets are still left here, in the apartment complexes built along the Harlem River or at the edge of Morningside Heights. But most of Harlem is very poor and culturally disorganized, plagued by crime and drugs, the kind of place people leave if they get a chance. For all the concentration on Harlem's problems, many of its one-time residents have figured out how to solve them, at least for their families—they got out and moved to more comfortable, spread-out, safer, and socially less disorganized neighborhoods in the outer boroughs or the suburbs. And so there are 200,000 fewer people in Harlem than there were 20 years ago. There are now more blacks in southeast Queens than there are in Harlem, and many more in Brooklyn's large black neighborhoods; nor have Harlem's cultural institutions or places of entertainment retained their central role in black life. Harlem is a place American blacks have outgrown, without entirely replacing.

Harlem has had its own congressional district since 1944—a district whose size has had to expand every 10 years because it has been losing population. The present 16th District, centered on Harlem, includes, on the east, the Puerto Rican (once Italian) neighborhood of East Harlem and, on the west, dips down into the Upper West Side almost as far as Zabar's delicatessen at

80th Street and includes Columbia University, most of Morningside Heights (an academic neighborhood), virtually all of Washington Heights (once Jewish, now mostly Puerto Rican), and the Inwood neighborhood at the northern tip of Manhattan (still mostly Irish). Less than a majority, 49%, of its residents are black; they are almost outnumbered by the 38% who are of Spanish origin (though many fall into both categories); given turnout rates, probably a significant majority of voters here are white, though like the blacks they are heavily Democratic.

In the 40 years it has formed the nucleus of a congressional district, Harlem has had only two congressmen: Adam Clayton Powell and Charles Rangel. Powell was an accomplished legislator, an able chairman of the Education and Labor Committee during the years the Great Society and antipoverty laws were passed through it; he was one of the most eloquent, gifted—and most flawed—black leaders of his generation. He was ousted from the House in 1967—the Supreme Court later ruled the procedure illegal—because of outrage over payroll-padding charges. Powell believed, with some justice, that voters were far more outraged when he did such things than when white congressmen did them; still, why did he have to? Powell won two elections afterwards but never really returned to Congress. He lost the 1970 primary to 40-year-old Charles Rangel, a four-year veteran of the New York Assembly.

Rangel is now one of the most powerful of New York House members and one of the most widely respected. He ran second in his race for majority whip after the 1986 election, but still garnered support well beyond the Black Caucus and the New York delegations. He is the fourth-ranking Democrat on the House Ways and Means Committee, a supporter generally of Chairman Dan Rostenkowski and a key player on the 1986 tax reform—and on the retention of deductibility for state and local taxes, which are higher in New York City than anywhere else. He chairs the Select Revenues Subcommittee, which has jurisdiction over a lot of tricky and complex tax measures. He is also chairman of the Select Committee on Narcotics Abuse and Control, and a firm believer in suppressing drug use by almost any means—by taking action against Latin drug-producing countries, for example, or by refusing to let doctors prescribe heroin for terminal cancer patients, a measure he makes a point of speaking out and rallying support against.

Rangel has had to work hard and pass some difficult tests to get where he is. He served two terms in the New York Assembly, a pretty fast track, and then beat Powell, reeling but still a dangerous opponent, in the 1970 primary. Serving on the usually obscure Judiciary Committee, he found himself in the national spotlight during the hearings on the impeachment of Richard Nixon, and, with his New York accent and sense of humor, performed ably. The next year, in what is usually a struggle, he won the fight for Hugh Carey's seat on Ways and Means when Carey became governor.

Rangel has also been a player in New York politics. He was friendly with Ed Koch when they were in Congress together—a friendship which did not survive Koch's opposition to racial quotas as mayor. But when Koch was denouncing the beating and death of blacks in Howard Beach, Rangel came forward and urged the black witnesses to testify when their lawyers said they would not. He endorsed Walter Mondale for president in 1984, a move which put him on the same side as most Democratic House members, and with Governor Mario Cuomo and Mayor Koch—but on the opposite side from many vociferous black politicians and most black New York voters. His own district was split nastily in the 1985 mayoral race, the black assembly districts tending to favor Koch's two opponents,with the white portions a little warily but still decisively backing Koch.

Through all these vicissitudes and under the spotlight Rangel retains the good humor, ebullience, and friendliness which have served him well in his political career. He is a firm believer in enough causes which seem to give him varying groups of allies—in civil rights, but also in sternly suppressing the drug trade, for example—that he seems to have a wide range of sympathies and a broad-gauged view of society. He is regularly reelected without serious opposition or difficulty.

The People: Pop. 1980: 516,405, dn. 16.7% 1970–80. Households (1980): 58% family, 34% with children, 29% married couples; 96.0% housing units rented; median monthly rent: $169; median house value: $37,800. Voting age pop. (1980): 381,724; 49% Black, 35% Spanish origin, 1% Asian origin.

1984 Presidential Vote:

Mondale (D)	126,326	(84%)
Reagan (R)	23,403	(16%)

Rep. Charles B. Rangel (D)

Elected 1970; b. June 11, 1930, New York City; home, New York City; N.Y.U., B.S. 1957, St. John's U. Sch. of Law, LL.B. 1960; Roman Catholic; married (Alma).

Career: Army, Korea; Asst. U.S. Atty., S. Dist. of NY, 1961; Legal Counsel, NYC Housing and Redevelopment Bd., Neighborhood Conservation Bureau; Gen. Counsel, Natl. Advisory Comm. on Selective Svc., 1966; NY Assembly, 1966–70.

Offices: 2330 RHOB 20515, 202-225-4365. Also 163 W. 125 St., Rm. 730, New York 10027, 212-663-3900; 656 W. 181st St., New York 10033, 212-927-5333; and 2112 2d Ave., New York 10029, 212-348-9630.

Committees: *Ways and Means* (4th of 23 D). Subcommittees: Oversight; Select Revenue Measures (Chairman). *Select Committee on Narcotics Abuse and Control* (Chairman of 15 D).

Group Ratings

	ADA	ACLU	COPE	CFA	LCV	ACU	NTU	NSI	COC	CEI
1986	100	94	91	100	74	0	26	0	11	11
1985	90	—	92	75	—	0	32	—	10	—

National Journal Ratings

	1986 LIB — 1986 CONS			1985 LIB — 1985 CONS		
Economic	87%	—	0%	89%	—	0%
Social	86%	—	11%	85%	—	0%
Foreign	80%	—	0%	92%	—	0%

Key Votes

1) Lmt Cln Water Act	AGN	5) Retain Gun Cont	FOR	9) Aid Angola Reb	AGN
2) Rpl Tobac Sub	AGN	6) Contra Aid	AGN	10) Tax Reform	FOR
3) Grm-Rdmn Def Red	AGN	7) Lmt Text Imp	FOR	11) S Africa Sanc	FOR
4) Ban Polygraph	FOR	8) Limit SDI	FOR	12) Immig Reform	AGN

Election Results

1986 general	Charles B. Rangel (D–R–L)	61,262	(96%)	($375,344)
	Two others	2,283	(2%)	
1986 primary	Charles B. Rangel (D) unopposed			
1984 general	Charles B. Rangel (D–R)	117,759	(97%)	($182,838)
	Two others	3,639	(3%)	

Campaign Contributions and Expenditures

1985-86		Direct Cont. 1985-86		PACS Breakdown 1985-86			
Receipts	$480,918	Indiv.	$161,196	Corp.	$135,451	T/M/H	$78,995
Expend.	$375,344	Party	$250	Labor	$62,874	Agr.	$500
Unspent	$259,760	PACS	$310,578	Ideo.	$17,800	CWOS	$14,958

SEVENTEENTH DISTRICT

The West Side of Manhattan was not always one of America's most left-wing political constituencies. In the early 1900s, it was split between Tammany slums in the blocks back of the docks, loyal to a Democratic machine that was culturally conservative and anything but a threat to the economic status quo, and the middle-class brownstone neighborhoods between the rows of elegant houses on Central Park West and Riverside Drive. Greenwich Village was already a cultural haven for artists, writers, and bohemians before World War 1, but they were insignificant politically, heavily outvoted by the Irish machine stalwarts and new Italian immigrants who occupied most of the Village's buildings and helped make it picturesque. What happened to the West Side over the last 70 years was what has happened to much of urban America, only more so: the affluent middle-class mostly moved out to the suburbs. The people who stayed behind tend to share attitudes which correlate with political liberalism: they are more likely than average to be single, or gay; more likely to make their living in a job that requires verbal or artistic skills, but doesn't pay them especially well; more likely than most Americans to be hostile to the middle class values that are seen as pervading the rest of the country, to traditional cultural institutions and norms, and to the assertion of American interests overseas.

That is what has happened on Manhattan's West Side, not only on the Upper West Side west of Central Park and Greenwich Village, but in the adjacent and neighborhoods of Chelsea and Soho, Morningside Heights and Tribeca. It may be happening again in Washington Heights, at the end of the George Washington Bridge, where low-income Puerto Ricans are being replaced by somewhat higher-income young liberal professionals. This is the land of New York's 17th Congressional District, which starts at the lower tip of Manhattan (and thus, ironically, takes in Wall Street), includes the huge new Battery Park City project built on river fill, goes north through Tribeca and Soho (once industrial areas now being colonized, with renovated lofts and kicky restaurants, by artists and gays), the Village, and Chelsea to the wastes west of midtown, then includes most of the Upper West Side and Morningside Heights and a thin strip along the Hudson all the way up past the Cloisters to Spuyten Duyvil at the northern tip of Manhattan. To meet the population requirement the 17th also includes two neighborhoods in the Bronx: high-income Riverdale, with its estates, apartments and big houses, and, across two golf courses and a cemetery, the middle income interracial community of Williamsbridge.

You can get a good idea of the political attitudes and tone that prevail in the 17th District by reading the *Village Voice*. The relatively affluent voters of the West Side pride themselves on their liberalism, or even radicalism; they seem fond of seeing themselves as part of an oppressed proletariat, exploited by greedy corporations, mad generals, rapacious landlords, and vicious gentrifiers. Given their obvious affluence, this view is a little difficult to maintain; but in the 1970s their focus shifted from broad cultural to personal issues, from the nation to New York and finally to themselves. Even as the nation became culturally more heterogeneous and tolerant, many voters here kept a stake in viewing themselves as beleaguered because of their sexual preference or life-style. Their demands escalated from tolerance to validation and endorsement in the 1970s; but the discrimination and harassment they complained about was negligible next to the hideous tragedy of AIDS which in the 1980s has killed so many talented men and filled the lives of so many others with fears which the long delayed passage of New York City's anti-sexual discrimination ordinance in 1986 can do nothing to assuage.

The result is lack of morale in an electorate which once confidently thought it had answers for all of society and looked out with contempt at the yahoos west of the Hudson. The Manhattan and West Side votes, once solidly mobilized in behalf of candidates like John Lindsay and George McGovern, is a bit more fragmented. In the 1984 presidential race, for example, it wasn't clear to West Siders whether Mondale, Hart, or Jackson was the most progressive candidate; in the 1985 mayor's race, Edward Koch carried much of the West Side, despite the weekly denunciations of the *Village Voice*. It is against the background of this often frenzied liberalism that you need to read exhortationists like Norman Podhoretz: they argue so strenuously for Ronald Reagan's policies because they, unlike almost everyone else in America, live in neighborhoods where they're uncomfortably aware that almost everyone else would never vote for Reagan in a million years. Or, as Betty Friedan reportedly put it, "I can't understand how Reagan got elected. I don't know anyone who voted for him."

Once upon a time West Side congressional politics featured primary fights that broke up friendships and dominated dinner party conversations and delicatessen encounters for months. But the current congressman from the 17th, Ted Weiss, was first elected in 1976 without a primary at all and has had only nominal opposition from Republicans since. Weiss is a veteran of the reform movement—that political rebellion of gentrifying professionals against the often corrupt hacks who, with the aid of immigrant and stew-bum votes, controlled Manhattan's Democratic Party for years—and was elected to the City Council as long ago as 1961. He ran two unsuccessful House races against Leonard Farbstein in 1966 and 1968, and by the time Bella Abzug retired from the House to run for the Senate in 1976, he was well established as the West Side's tribune.

Weiss has a solid liberal—some on the right would prefer you to say leftish—voting record. He is a member of the Foreign Affairs and Government Operations Committees; he chairs the latter panel's Human Resources and Intergovernmental Subcommittee. Weiss is a competent congressman who has done craftsmanlike work on oversight of the Food and Drug Administration. He was an original sponsor of Africa famine relief. On foreign policy generally his sympathies are often with those most congressmen regard as the adversaries of America. Like some other Democrats he calls for normalization of relations with Cuba and like many others he criticized the invasion of Grenada; unlike most of them he seems not embarrassed about the latter, but still to think that ousting a murderous pro-Communist government and helping to install one that is democratically elected is anti-progressive. It would be a mistake to call Weiss pro-Communist: he came to this country a refugee one step ahead of the Nazis in 1938 and appreciates its civil liberties more vividly than most of his countrymen. But it does not seem a mistake to call him, in West Side parlance, anti-anti-Communist.

Weiss's stands on these issues are probably an asset rather than a liability in the 17th District. He has endeared himself to constituents in other ways, pressing hard for more research on AIDS and against automatic expulsion from the military of those who test positive for the AIDS virus; he strongly opposed the Westway highway-cum-real-estate project; he works hard on constituency service. Challenged for renomination in 1986 by a Democrat whose views are well to his right, especially on foreign policy, Weiss won an overwhelming victory which dispells any doubt that he is in line with thinking at home. So Weiss seems likely to have a safe seat through 1992. Then comes redistricting, in which this seat will be vulnerable: it is at the edge of the state, can easily be split among its members, and is a more likely candidate for dismemberment than the black-represented 16th and Puerto Rican-represented 18th. But Weiss has strong enough support that he could beat another incumbent, such as the 15th district Republican Bill Green, if they are thrown into the same district together.

The People: Pop. 1980: 516,239, up 0.3% 1970–80. Households (1980): 39% family, 16% with children, 28% married couples; 89.8% housing units rented; median monthly rent: $271; median house value: $51,800. Voting age pop. (1980): 442,060; 14% Black, 13% Spanish origin, 3% Asian origin.

1984 Presidential Vote:

Mondale (D)	164,511	(74%)
Reagan (R)	55,449	(25%)

Rep. Theodore S. (Ted) Weiss (D)

Elected 1976; b. Sept. 17, 1927, Gava, Hungary; home, New York City; Syracuse U., B.A. 1951, LL.B. 1952; Jewish; married (Sonya).

Career: Army, 1946–47; Practicing atty., 1953–76; Asst. Dist. Atty., NY Cnty., 1955–59; NYC Cncl., 1961–77.

Offices: 2442 RHOB 20515, 202-225-5635. Also 252 7th Ave., New York 10001, 212-620-3970; 4060 Broadway, New York 10032, 212-927-7726; 131 Waverly Pl., New York 10011, 212-420-9393; 490 W. 238th St., Bronx 10463, 212-884-0441; and 655 E. 233d St., Bronx 10466, 212-652-0400.

Committees: *Foreign Affairs* (19th of 27 D). Subcommittees: Arms Control, International Security and Science; Human Rights and International Organizations; Western Hemisphere Affairs. *Government Operations* (6th of 24 D). Subcommittees: Employment and Housing; Human Resources and Intergovernmental Relations (Chairman). *Select Committee on Children, Youth, and Families* (6th of 18 D). Task Forces: Crisis Intervention; Prevention Strategies.

Group Ratings

	ADA	ACLU	COPE	CFA	LCV	ACU	NTU	NSI	COC	CEI
1986	95	93	91	82	99	0	32	0	25	19
1985	100	—	92	100	—	5	38	—	18	—

National Journal Ratings

	1986 LIB — 1986 CONS		1985 LIB — 1985 CONS	
Economic	84% —	16%	89% —	0%
Social	77% —	23%	85% —	0%
Foreign	80% —	0%	92% —	0%

Key Votes

1) Lmt Cln Water Act	AGN	5) Retain Gun Cont	FOR	9) Aid Angola Reb	AGN
2) Rpl Tobac Sub	FOR	6) Contra Aid	AGN	10) Tax Reform	AGN
3) Grm-Rdmn Def Red	AGN	7) Lmt Text Imp	FOR	11) S Africa Sanc	FOR
4) Ban Polygraph	AGN	8) Limit SDI	FOR	12) Immig Reform	—

Election Results

1986 general	Theodore S. (Ted) Weiss (D)	95,094	(85%)	($242,860)
	Thomas A. Chorba (R)	15,587	(14%)	($13,305)
1986 primary	Theodore S. (Ted) Weiss (D)	37,824	(83%)	
	Julian Schroeder (D)	7,604	(17%)	
1984 general	Theodore S. (Ted) Weiss (D–L)	162,489	(81%)	($147,091)
	Kenneth Katzman (R)	33,316	(17%)	

Campaign Contributions and Expenditures

1985-86		Direct Cont. 1985-86		PACS Breakdown 1985-86			
Receipts	$277,935	Indiv.	$175,191	Corp.	$1,403	T/M/H	$12,750
Expend.	$242,860	PACS	$94,916	Labor	$68,561	Agr.	$0
Unspent	$46,952	Cand.	$4,238	Ideo.	$11,202	CWOS	$1,000

EIGHTEENTH DISTRICT

The South Bronx became in the 1970s the nation's most famous slum. Presidential candidates trudged through here every four years, their mouths agape as they looked at the destroyed buildings and mouthed the inevitable comparison with Berlin after the war. The evidence of the arson that has become widespread in the South Bronx was there for all to see; so were abandoned buildings; so were boarded up or vandalized stores. Yet the South Bronx was not anything like the nation's worst slum as late as the middle 1960s. The suddenness of the change can be gauged by looking at the population within the boundaries of the 21st Congressional District as it was defined in the 1970s. In 1960 there were 476,000 people there. In 1970 the population was down slightly, to 460,000. In 1980, it was half that, 233,000. A very large part of urban New York, built up on the Manhattan schist ridges through which the first subway tubes were drilled in the first decade of the century, was simply depopulated in just a few years. It was a few years, moreover, when politicians were promising to do things to alleviate poverty and spending considerably more on them than they do now in the 1980s, when population loss in the South Bronx seems to be much slower.

One thing that happened here in the 1970s was mass turnover as one generation of settlers replaced another. The South Bronx was settled in a rush. Most of its housing was built in the years between 1906 and 1917, when the newly built subways opened up the Bronx to settlement by the hundreds of thousands of immigrants then jammed into Lower Manhattan. By the late 1960s most of these original Italian, Irish, and Jewish settlers were elderly; their children had long since been dispersed, and they were dying or moving out. Moving in—again in a rush—were blacks and Puerto Ricans who could not find housing in the more stable communities of Harlem or Upper Manhattan.

But that movement had one bad effect: a huge rise in crime. With no community institutions and little parental supervision, the black and Puerto Rican teenagers here committed hundreds of crimes every day, with seeming impunity. Arson became an increasingly common crime, committed by kids for kicks or on behalf of landlords who decided to get insurance money for their rent-controlled buildings. The rise in crime helped drive away businesses that provided low-wage jobs—historically the mainstay of the local economy that helped so many immigrants move upward in the years from 1906 to the 1960s. Union demands, high minimum wages, the high cost of doing business generally in New York also got low-wage employers to take their businesses to the places where their most recent workers came from, the southeastern states and Puerto Rico. The migrants who had stayed in the South Bronx were left to welfare, which tends to split families. In no other part of America have so many low-wage jobs been lost so fast; and nowhere else is there a community as large that was as suddenly depopulated as the South Bronx was in the 1970s.

Antipoverty programs do not seem to have helped, and may have hurt by anchoring people to a place where there was little opportunity for them; welfare certainly hurt; the attitude toward crime reflected in the statistic that from 1964 to 1976 the prison population was constant while crime rates soared helped to make the South Bronx a place anyone would flee from if he could. So the elderly moved out, either farther in the Bronx, to the suburbs, or to Florida; middle class residents, including blacks and Puerto Ricans who worked at steady jobs, moved out too, to the Bronx or other boroughs or even the suburbs. The programs for revitalizing the South Bronx didn't work because they ignored the fact that most of the people who could help with revitalization have already left the area for safer and more stable neighborhoods elsewhere and because they tended to reinforce rather than discourage socially destructive behavior.

Now there are signs that things are getting better. Community institutions have taken hold in many parts of the South Bronx, more criminals are sent to jail for longer terms, and the freezing of welfare payments for a decade after 1981 (which meant a drop in real dollars) discouraged low-skill people from moving to New York. Many poor people seem to have left as well. New

York's welfare payments were frozen for seven years after 1974, and it must have occurred to even the most sluggish welfare recipient after a while that they might be better off back in North Carolina or Puerto Rico, where there are more jobs and better living conditions for low-income people. Puerto Ricans, in particular, seem to have moved back to Puerto Rico, easily accessible on inexpensive midnight 747s; Puerto Ricans in the Bronx have always retained their interest in and identification with Puerto Rican culture. The San Juan newspapers have much higher circulation here than do New York's Spanish language newspapers; Puerto Ricans on the mainland follow Puerto Rico politics closely and with considerable fervor, but seldom vote in New York elections. As a result, the 18th District has the lowest voter turnout in the United States—even though the turnout of Puerto Ricans in Puerto Rico is higher than turnout in any American state. Finally, the city government in the 1980s found some programs that would work: a few isolated housing units in the midst of cleared land, and commercial property for light industry and warehousing. The South Bronx is actually well located: right on main trucking lines, with access to rail spurs, not far from airports and port facilities.

The current congressman from the 18th is Robert Garcia, a Democrat first elected in a 1978 special election. Garcia is an articulate, fast-talking, enthusiastic legislator who has been active on a number of fronts. He is, with Jack Kemp, the House's leading proponent of enterprise zones, a proposal of obvious appeal in the South Bronx. It has not gotten anywhere in Congress because of the opposition of Ways and Means Chairman Dan Rostenkowski, but it has spawned a number of state enterprise zones programs, including one in New York. He was an active opponent of immigration reform, arguing that employer sanctions would lead to discrimination against Hispanics. He has worked hard to maintain federal housing programs and even to encourage some innovations.

Garcia seemed to have a solid hold on the South Bronx district and on the respect of his colleagues until rumors began circulating in 1987 that he would be indicted in the Wedtech case. Wedtech is a South Bronx contractor that got federal business under the clauses reserving some contracts for minority-owned businesses; it is alleged to have been bribing Bronx and other politicians right and left. Other Bronx politicians—notably Borough President Stanley Simon—have been sentenced to jail, and the New York Times reported in February 1987 that a San Juan lawyer said he funneled some $4,000 a month to Garcia's wife. But by the end of May 1987 there was no indictment. If Garcia is indicted, he will probably attract opposition in 1988, probably from Assemblyman Jose Serrano, who was passed over in favor of another Hispanic for the vacant borough presidency. But it is also possible Garcia will be exonerated and reelected.

The People: Pop. 1980: 517,278, dn. 37.0% 1970–80. Households (1980): 70% family, 50% with children, 31% married couples; 94.4% housing units rented; median monthly rent: $177; median house value: $35,200. Voting age pop. (1980): 327,637; 49% Spanish origin, 44% Black, 1% Asian origin.

1984 Presidential Vote: Mondale (D) 94,844   (81%)

Reagan (R) 22,258   (19%)

Rep. Robert Garcia (D)

Elected Feb. 14, 1978; b. Jan. 9, 1933, New York City; home, Bronx; CCNY; Pentecostal; married (Jane).

Career: Army, Korea; Computer engineer, 1957–65; NY Assembly, 1965–67; NY Senate, 1967–78.

Offices: 2338 RHOB 20515, 202-225-4361. Also 890 Grand Concourse, Bronx 10451, 212-860-6200.

Committees: *Banking, Finance and Urban Affairs* (11th of 31 D). Subcommittees: Economic Stabilization; Housing and Community Development; International Finance, Trade and Monetary Policy (Chairman). *Post Office and Civil Service* (5th of 14 D). Subcommittees: Census and Population; Postal Operations and Services.

Group Ratings

	ADA	ACLU	COPE	CFA	LCV	ACU	NTU	NSI	COC	CEI
1986	95	94	96	75	77	0	26	0	17	16
1985	95	—	95	92	—	0	32	—	19	—

National Journal Ratings

	1986 LIB — 1986 CONS		1985 LIB — 1985 CONS	
Economic	87%	— 0%	89%	— 0%
Social	83%	— 15%	85%	— 0%
Foreign	80%	— 0%	92%	— 0%

Key Votes

1) Lmt Cln Water Act	AGN	5) Retain Gun Cont	FOR	9) Aid Angola Reb	AGN
2) Rpl Tobac Sub	FOR	6) Contra Aid	AGN	10) Tax Reform	FOR
3) Grm-Rdmn Def Red	AGN	7) Lmt Text Imp	FOR	11) S Africa Sanc	FOR
4) Ban Polygraph	FOR	8) Limit SDI	FOR	12) Immig Reform	AGN

Election Results

1986 general	Robert Garcia (D–L)	43,343	(94%)	($314,485)
	Melanie Chase (R)	2,479	(5%)	
1986 primary	Robert Garcia (D) unopposed			
1984 general	Robert Garcia (D–L)	85,960	(89%)	($227,049)
	Curtis Johnson (R)	8,970	(9%)	

Campaign Contributions and Expenditures

1985–86		Direct Cont. 1985–86		PACS Breakdown 1985–86			
Receipts	$409,702	Indiv.	$248,745	Corp.	$62,250	T/M/H	$22,775
Expend.	$314,485	PACS	$145,649	Labor	$50,524	Agr.	$0
Unspent	$146,449			Ideo.	$8,000	CWOS	$2,100

NINETEENTH DISTRICT

The 19th Congressional District of New York is a collection of middle class, mostly Catholic neighborhoods in the Bronx, from the ridge that overlooks the Harlem River in the west to the flatlands at the edge of Long Island Sound in the east, plus most of the suburb of Yonkers to the north. It may surprise some people to hear that there are middle class areas in the Bronx; but when most of the borough was built up, from the advent of the subway in 1906 to the 1920s, very little of the Bronx was anything else. This is what remains. It is not a poverty-stricken area, but it is not rich either; about one-quarter of its residents are homeowners, but even renters in two-family houses and small apartments have a kind of pride of ownership which is apparent in the way they maintain their homes. Yet the buildings themselves are, like so many buildings in New York, built in the cheapest way with the cheapest materials possible, occupying the maximum space allowed by the zoning code. The 19th also includes Co-op City, where 35 35-story towers (that's not a misprint) were erected on landfill surrounded by two limited access highways; the rents are low (and naturally tenants yelped and staged a rent strike when asked to pay for the rise in maintenance costs), the crime of the South Bronx seems far away, and, eventually, the whole area was connected to New York's transportation system. Here came many of the old residents of the Grand Concourse and other parts of the Bronx.

The congressman from the 19th District is, by now, a veteran of the House: Mario Biaggi. He personifies and exaggerates the strengths and, perhaps, the weaknesses of the constituency he represents. He has made his career almost entirely in New York City's public sector: he was a police officer for 23 years, and when he retired he was the most decorated officer in the New York police force. He become an attorney—he finished law school at night, like so many ambitious city employees in New York—but his real interest was politics. When a Republican congressman from the East Bronx retired in 1968, Biaggi was easily elected to succeed him. As a kind of urban populist with a law and order accent, he was the favorite in the 1973 mayor race; he had the Conservative nomination and seemed likely to win the Democratic. But in April 1973 newspapers charged that Biaggi had lied when he said he had not taken the Fifth Amendment before a grand jury. Brazenly Biaggi sued to get some, but not all, of the grand jury records made public; the judge, not to be toyed with, revealed them all. They showed that Biaggi was lying, and his law-and-order candidacy collapsed.

That did not end his congressional career, but it does characterize it: it has been a combination of useful public service and unfortunate lapses. Biaggi has spent much effort in recent years leading the fight to ban the "cop-killer" bullets which can penetrate bullet-proof vests, and has taken flak from the National Rifle Association for that. But he is also Congress's most vocal supporter of groups sympathetic to the terrorist Irish Republican Army—groups that have been repudiated sternly by Irish-American politicians Tip O'Neill, Edward Kennedy, Daniel Patrick Moynihan, and Hugh Carey. He is the second-ranking Democrat on the Merchant Marine and Fisheries, and has spent much time supporting and perpetuating the system of maritime subsidies that benefits a handful of shipowners and union members. On the Education and Labor Committee, and on economic issues generally, Biaggi has voted generally against the Reagan Administration and on occasion has sternly denounced it. On cultural and foreign policy issues his record is mixed, not wildly out of line with those of other New York City representatives. Is this the record of an independent-minded tribune of the middle-class people of the outer boroughs? Or is it the record of a showboater who picks up any cause that he thinks might advance his career? Or both?

Biaggi's bid to be mayor was frustrated by a touch of scandal in 1973; his career in Congress seems threatened by scandal in 1987. In March 1987 he was indicted for bribery, fraud, and conspiracy, together with former Brooklyn Democratic leader Meade Esposito; it was alleged that Esposito had paid for Florida vacation trips for Biaggi, and that Biaggi had tried to get new contracts and speedier payment on old ones for Coastal Dry Dock and Repair Corporation, a Brooklyn Navy Yard contractor. He was also subpoenaed to testify before a grand jury investigating charges relating to Wedtech, a Bronx defense contractor which had gotten under clauses encouraging minority-owned businesses and which has been accused of widespread bribery of public officials. Biaggi was not indicted by the end of May 1987 in the Wedtech case. Biaggi represents a hard-working constituency which gets ahead through brains, effort, and cutting corners, by working extra jobs off the books and subletting rent controlled apartments; in his career he has shown more than average brains, more than average effort, and, perhaps, more than permissible corner-cutting.

Up until his indictment, he was exceedingly popular in the 19th District, winning reelection without serious opposition since 1968, although the Conservatives, who bent their principles to endorse him in 1973 and then were stuck with him as their candidate in the general election, have not endorsed him since. But a conviction will probably end his congressional career and begin one for one of the Bronx's remaining unindicted and unconvicted politicians.

The People: Pop. 1980: 516,498, up 1.2% 1970–80. Households (1980): 69% family, 32% with children, 51% married couples; 73.4% housing units rented; median monthly rent: $219; median house value: $58,000. Voting age pop. (1980): 398,578; 11% Black, 13% Spanish origin, 1% Asian origin.

1984 Presidential Vote:

Reagan (R)	93,925	(52%)
Mondale (D)	85,898	(48%)

Rep. Mario Biaggi (D)

Elected 1968; b. Oct. 26, 1917, New York City; home, Bronx; NY Law Sch., LL.B. 1963; Roman Catholic; married (Marie).

Career: NY City Police Dept., 1942–65; Commun. Relations Specialist, NY Div. of Housing; Asst. to the NY Secy. of State, 1961–65; Practicing atty., 1966–68; Pres., Natl. Police Officers Assn., 1967.

Offices: 2428 RHOB 20515, 202-225-2464. Also 3255 Westchester Ave., Bronx 10461, 212-931-0100; and 5 Seminary Ave., Yonkers 10704, 914-375-0500.

Committees: *Education and Labor* (5th of 21 D). Subcommittees: Elementary, Secondary and Vocational Education; Human Resources; Labor-Management Relations; Select Education. *Merchant Marine and Fisheries* (2d of 25 D). Subcommittees: Merchant Marine; Panama Canal and Outer Continental Shelf. *Select Committee on Aging* (3d of 39 D). Subcommittee: Human Services.

Group Ratings

	ADA	ACLU	COPE	CFA	LCV	ACU	NTU	NSI	COC	CEI
1986	65	52	88	67	66	18	21	40	21	15
1985	55	—	87	92	—	25	26	—	28	—

National Journal Ratings

	1986 LIB — 1986 CONS			1985 LIB — 1985 CONS		
Economic	87%	—	0%	79%	—	19%
Social	68%	—	31%	49%	—	49%
Foreign	57%	—	41%	49%	—	50%

Key Votes

1) Lmt Cln Water Act	FOR	5) Retain Gun Cont	FOR	9) Aid Angola Reb	FOR
2) Rpl Tobac Sub	AGN	6) Contra Aid	AGN	10) Tax Reform	FOR
3) Grm-Rdmn Def Red	AGN	7) Lmt Text Imp	FOR	11) S Africa Sanc	FOR
4) Ban Polygraph	FOR	8) Limit SDI	FOR	12) Immig Reform	AGN

Election Results

1986 general	Mario Biaggi (D–R–L).................	87,774	(90%)	($252,790)
	Alice Farrell (C).......................	6,906	(7%)	
	John J. Barry (RTL)....................	2,669	(3%)	
1986 primary	Mario Biaggi (D) unopposed			
1984 general	Mario Biaggi (D–R–L)................	155,067	(95%)	($206,834)
	Alice Farrell (C).......................	8,472	(5%)	

Campaign Contributions and Expenditures

1985-86		Direct Cont. 1985-86		PACS Breakdown 1985-86			
Receipts	$356,455	Indiv.	$208,678	Corp.	$19,926	T/M/H	$21,033
Expend.	$252,790	PACS	$105,892	Labor	$61,933	Agr.	$0
Unspent	$316,084			Ideo.	$2,000	CWOS	$1,000

TWENTIETH DISTRICT

Westchester County, New York, has long been considered the quintessential American suburb, the home of the super-rich like the Rockefellers of Pocantico Hills and of the ordinary rich like the business executives and doctors and ad men in big, comfortable houses in Scarsdale and White Plains, with their gently sloping lawns shaded by towering trees. But Westchester is, when you look closely at it, not a typical World War II suburb at all. The densely populated part of the county, south of the old county seat of White Plains and the Cross–Westchester Expressway, was all laid out and almost as thickly settled as it is today before World War II; it is really urban territory, similar to expensive and moderate neighborhoods of many cities, which happens to lie just north of the New York City line. Politically, it was always Republican while the city was Democratic, but when you look a little more closely you'll see that at least historically the similar neighborhoods inside the New York City limits—Riverdale in the Bronx, Forest Hills in Queens—were Republican too. The difference was that Westchester had no tenements. More recently, this part of Westchester has trended Democratic, between blacks moving into Mount Vernon and liberal chic spreading from Scarsdale to adjacent towns; it is now competitive between the parties.

Then there is the second Westchester north of White Plains. Here the hills get more rugged: this is the closest that the chains paralleling the Appalachians get to the Atlantic Ocean. Nestled beneath the hills are tiny old towns like Pleasantville, full of Italian-American craftsmen with houses that would look right in place in Upstate New York; all around, shaded from view by trees, are the houses of the affluent on their one- to four-acre lots. On expressways or near intersections are giant corporate headquarters, typically moved near the house of the current CEO: the Platinum Mile near the Cross–Westchester where General Foods, Texaco, and Pepsi are located, or the campus farther out in Armonk which is the nerve center of IBM. Politically this area is distinctly Republican, though not as overwhelmingly so as most affluent suburban areas.

The 20th Congressional District of New York includes most of Westchester, all of the county facing Long Island Sound on the east, from the ethnic neighborhoods of Mount Vernon, through the rich, Catholic, and very conservative suburbs of Pelham, Eastchester, and Bronxville, up through rich, Jewish, and liberal Scarsdale, and the New Haven Railroad commuter towns of New Rochelle, Larchmont, Mamaroneck, and Rye. Just above them is White Plains, the county seat/corporate headquarters/shopping mall center; the 20th also includes part of the city of Yonkers, on the Hudson. North of White Plains are the tiny villages and the little cities on the Hudson, Washington Irving's Tarrytown and John Cheever's Ossining, and the woodsy surrounding suburbs like Briarcliff Manor and Chappaqua. Everywhere residential real estate values, fed by the local and Manhattan boom, have skyrocketed, and the once small village of Mount Kisco in northern Westchester is plagued by traffic jams, as residents call for a lid on future development.

The 20th District is thought of as liberal Republican, but it hasn't been represented by a liberal Republican since Ogden Reid, heir to the *New York Herald-Tribune*, switched to the Democratic party in 1972 and Peter Peyser left the House to run against Senator James Buckley in the 1976 primary, only to return to the House in 1978 as a Democrat. Liberal Democrat Richard Ottinger had served 16 years (1964–70, 1974–84) when he retired in 1984. But the congressman now is Joseph DioGuardi, a Republican who is proud of his support of Ronald

Reagan. DioGuardi is even prouder, it seems, that he is a certified public accountant, one of the few CPAs in Congress, and he is constantly making statements about how government should be run like a business—the kind of talk most Republican political consultants despair of hearing in their clients. For DioGuardi nothing is so appealing as a column of figures, and in 1986 he took over the House Republicans' Baltimore conference, once a lively forum of ideas, and turned it into a session on how to pare the budget down to meet the Gramm–Rudman targets.

DioGuardi has been fortunate in electoral politics. Ottinger chose to retire in what turned out to be a Republican year, and in November DioGuardi barely edged former Ottinger staffer Oren Teicher. In 1986 Teicher was the favorite to win the nomination, when all of a sudden Bella Abzug, a veteran of Manhattan politics, announced she had moved to White Plains and was running. As Abzug pointed out, she had lived in Westchester for years, raising her daughters there; and she was the object of sympathy when her husband suddenly died two months before the primary which she ended up barely winning. Abzug campaigned for an end to the nuclear arms race and urged that something be done to provide more lower-cost housing in places like Westchester; her longtime leftish ties were not much mentioned in the race, nor were her glory days as a strident but often effective congresswoman denouncing the Vietnam war and the Nixon Administration. DioGuardi emphasized his support of budget-cutting and, in the end, resurrected for TV ads some old negative quotes from Mario Cuomo ("Bella, you're lying . . . and you're good at it") and Ottinger; when the Iran-contra scandal broke after the election DioGuardi, ever the numbers man, proposed just subtracting whatever the contras got from the arms sale from the $100 million Congress voted them in 1986.

Many will interpret DioGuardi's second victory in a row as an indication that Westchester and the 20th have returned to their longtime Republican ways. But DioGuardi's unimpressive percentages in a Republican year and against an opponent with severe negatives of her own suggest that this seat may still be seriously contested before district lines are redrawn for 1992.

The People: Pop. 1980: 516,507, dn. 4.9% 1970–80. Households (1980): 73% family, 36% with children, 59% married couples; 49.5% housing units rented; median monthly rent: $272; median house value: $92,400. Voting age pop. (1980): 388,570; 14% Black, 5% Spanish origin, 2% Asian origin.

1984 Presidential Vote:	Reagan (R) 129,284	(56%)
	Mondale (D) 100,394	(44%)

Rep. Joseph J. DioGuardi (R)

Elected 1984; b. Sept. 20, 1940, New York City; home, Scarsdale; Fordham U., B.S. 1962; Roman Catholic; married (Carol).

Career: Accountant, Arthur Andersen and Co., 1962–84.

Offices: 325 CHOB 20515, 202-225-6506. Also 1 N. Broadway, Ste. 901, White Plains 10601, 914-997-6440.

Committees: *Government Operations* (7th of 15 R). Subcommittees: Employment and Housing (Ranking Member). *Merchant Marine and Fisheries* (13th of 17 R). Subcommittees: Coast Guard and Navigation; Fisheries and Wildlife Conservation and the Economy; Oceanography. *Select Committee on Narcotics Abuse and Control* (7th of 10 R).

Group Ratings

	ADA	ACLU	COPE	CFA	LCV	ACU	NTU	NSI	COC	CEI
1986	35	10	48	50	37	55	44	70	78	51
1985	10	—	35	58	—	67	54	—	76	—

National Journal Ratings

	1986 LIB — 1986 CONS		1985 LIB — 1985 CONS	
Economic	40%	— 59%	24%	— 74%
Social	27%	— 71%	40%	— 59%
Foreign	44%	— 56%	42%	— 56%

Key Votes

1) Lmt Cln Water Act	FOR	5) Retain Gun Cont	AGN	9) Aid Angola Reb	FOR
2) Rpl Tobac Sub	FOR	6) Contra Aid	FOR	10) Tax Reform	FOR
3) Grm-Rdmn Def Red	FOR	7) Lmt Text Imp	FOR	11) S Africa Sanc	FOR
4) Ban Polygraph	AGN	8) Limit SDI	AGN	12) Immig Reform	FOR

Election Results

1986 general	Joseph J. DioGuardi (R)................	80,220	(54%)	($1,264,167)
	Bella A. Abzug (D)....................	66,359	(45%)	($902,535)
1986 primary	Joseph J. DioGuardi (R) unopposed			
1984 general	Joseph J. DioGuardi (R–C)	106,958	(50%)	($644,128)
	Oren J. Teicher (D).................	102,842	(48%)	($433,059)

Campaign Contributions and Expenditures

1985-86		Direct Cont. 1985-86		PACS Breakdown 1985-86			
Receipts	$1,280,057	Indiv.	$839,101	Corp.	$158,049	T/M/H	$82,901
Expend.	$1,264,167	Party	$18,805	Labor	$21,300	Agr.	$0
Unspent	$16,722	PACS	$294,981	Ideo.	$31,551	CWOS	$1,180
		Cand.	$85,000				

TWENTY-FIRST DISTRICT

The Hudson River is an arm of the sea, with detectable tides all the way north to Albany and a sluggish current; but the force of its waters, draining half of Upstate New York, is enough to carve a channel through the Appalachian chains and form some of the most spectacular scenery in the United States. Coming up the Metro North rail line at water level, you can see the river twist and then plunge between the Hudson Highlands, with West Point clinging to the rock on one side, where the Revolutionary Army built a chain across the river. They recognized, as did the builders of the Erie Canal and the New York Central Railroad after them, that the Hudson is the best natural route from the seacoast to the interior of America. Yet so imposing is its scenery, especially where it passes through the mountains, that the Hudson has been little spoiled in the three centuries it has served as an avenue inland. You can still see pretty much what the first Dutch patroons saw as they sailed to claim their huge land grants farther up the Hudson Valley.

The 21st Congressional District of New York covers most of the lower Hudson, starting in northern Westchester County, occupying both sides of the rivers through most of the Highlands, and proceeding as far north on the east bank as Poughkeepsie, just a few miles short of Franklin Roosevelt's house at Hyde Park. It includes northern Westchester County, with its estates and the much more modest subdivisions-cum-shopping centers that have sprung up around express-way interchanges there and just to the north, in Putnam County and across the Hudson in Orange County as well. You can find some of New York's richest and most prominent people here—the disgraced inside trader Ivan Boesky for one, who bought Charles Revson's old estate—but they are outnumbered increasingly by the offspring of early 20th-century immigrants—white-collar workers in Westchester office headquarters, policemen and firemen in New York City—who have been fleeing the outer borough neighborhoods in which they grew up, seeking a quieter place to raise their families, one where their children will be educated in schools where tradition is respected and prohibitions against drug use firmly enforced. These new residents, far from bringing Democratic voting habits from the city, have made the Lower Hudson area one of the most Republican parts of New York state; Mario Cuomo, while winning the state 2 to 1 in 1986, ran no better than even here.

Amid these new migrants from New York City you can find descendants of the Dutch settlers 300 years ago and of the Yankees that came over the hills from New England a century or so later. The rich here prospered in the 19th century by pursuing their business investments in the city on weekdays and steaming up the Hudson to their estates on weekends. But the large majority worked in the old river town that became small industrial cities in the 19th century—Newburgh, Beacon, Poughkeepsie—or in modest farming communities where they filed in for church services each Sunday with scions of the great families of the Hudson valley like the Roosevelts or the Fishes. For years this was a heavily Republican area—the Hudson valley never voted for FDR for President—and while it trended Democratic in the 1960s when the Kennedys appealed to many of the newer Catholic voters here, it has become increasingly Republican in the 1980s, because of the cultural and economic conservatism of the newer residents.

The 21st District is represented in the House by the holder of a distinguished Hudson Valley name, Hamilton Fish. Hamilton Fishes have been representing New York in Congress since 1842, and one Hamilton Fish was Secretary of State under President Grant. The current Hamilton Fish's father served in the House for 24 years, and was one of the most acerbic critics of his longtime constituent, Franklin D. Roosevelt; Fish, Sr., was finally defeated, with the help of redistricting, in 1944.

The current Hamilton Fish fits into a different place on our political spectrum (although both he and his father, still alive and writing letters to the editor in 1987, were skeptical of U.S. Vietnam policy). Representative Fish tends to take conservative views on economic issues, though not invariably; he tends to be somewhat liberal on cultural issues. He is the ranking Republican on the House Judiciary Committee, a body which handles—or refuses to act on—some of the most controversial issues of the 1980s. Undoubtedly many on the New Right dislike the part Fish often takes, for he agrees and cooperates with Chairman Peter Rodino on some of these issues, and sometimes provides Democrats with bipartisan sponsorship for legislation strongly opposed by most Republicans. He is nonetheless an opponent of abortion, and has introduced his own legislation against it. He also quietly supported the immigration reform bill during its various travails in the 1980s, and was one of those who helped it win passage late in 1986.

Fish was first elected in 1968, after a career in the Foreign Service and service in Dutchess County civic affairs. One of his opponents in the Republican primary, incidentally, was then local Assistant District Attorney G. Gordon Liddy, Jr., later of Watergate fame; Fish was one of the House Judiciary Committee Republicans who voted to impeach Richard Nixon. Fish had serious opposition in the 1968 general election and, through two redistrictings, has held onto the seat easily ever since.

The People: Pop. 1980: 516,778, up 11.3% 1970–80. Households (1980): 78% family, 45% with children, 66% married couples; 31.4% housing units rented; median monthly rent: $234; median house value: $56,600. Voting age pop. (1980): 365,060; 6% Black, 3% Spanish origin, 1% Asian origin.

1984 Presidential Vote: Reagan (R) 150,345   (68%)
Mondale (D) 70,809   (32%)

Rep. Hamilton Fish, Jr. (R)

Elected 1968; b. June 3, 1926, Washington, D.C.; home, Millbrook; Harvard Col., A.B. 1949, N.Y.U., LL.B. 1957; Episcopalian; widowed.

Career: Navy, WWII; Vice Consul, U.S. Foreign Svc., Ireland, 1951–53; Practicing atty. 1957–68; Counsel, NY Assembly Judiciary Cmtee., 1961; Dutchess Cnty. Civil Defense Dir., 1967–68.

Offices: 2269 RHOB 20515, 202-225-5441. Also 82 Washington St., Poughkeepsie 12601, 914-452-4220; 36 Gleneida Ave., Carmel 10512, 914-225-5200; and Bldg. 710, Stewart Intl. Airport, Newburgh 12550, 914-564-4302.

Committees: *Judiciary* (Ranking Member of 14 R). Subcommittees: Criminal Justice; Immigration, Refugees, and International Law; Monopolies and Commercial Law (Ranking Member). *Joint Economic Committee.* Task Forces: Economic Growth, Trade and Taxes; Investment, Jobs and Prices; National Security Economics.

Group Ratings

	ADA	ACLU	COPE	CFA	LCV	ACU	NTU	NSI	COC	CEI
1986	45	42	46	58	74	32	36	50	44	34
1985	35	—	45	58	—	40	39	—	55	—

National Journal Ratings

	1986 LIB — 1986 CONS		1985 LIB — 1985 CONS	
Economic	47% —	52%	45% —	54%
Social	46% —	53%	62% —	38%
Foreign	52% —	47%	51% —	48%

Key Votes

1) Lmt Cln Water Act	FOR	5) Retain Gun Cont	AGN	9) Aid Angola Reb	AGN
2) Rpl Tobac Sub	FOR	6) Contra Aid	FOR	10) Tax Reform	FOR
3) Grm-Rdmn Def Red	FOR	7) Lmt Text Imp	FOR	11) S Africa Sanc	FOR
4) Ban Polygraph	AGN	8) Limit SDI	FOR	12) Immig Reform	FOR

Election Results

1986 general	Hamilton Fish, Jr. (R–C)	102,070	(77%)	($217,637)
	Lawrence W. Grunberger (D)	28,339	(21%)	($6,340)
1986 primary	Hamilton Fish, Jr. (R) unopposed			
1984 general	Hamilton Fish, Jr. (R–C)	160,053	(78%)	($173,523)
	Lawrence W. Grunberger (D)	44,274	(22%)	

Campaign Contributions and Expenditures

1985-86		Direct Cont. 1985-86		PACS Breakdown 1985-86			
Receipts	$246,927	Indiv.	$97,753	Corp.	$58,055	T/M/H	$52,150
Expend.	$217,637	Party	$2,476	Labor	$19,275	Agr.	$800
Unspent	$88,093	PACS	$137,780	Ideo.	$6,250	CWOS	$1,250

TWENTY-SECOND DISTRICT

Tappan Zee, the Dutch called it: the widest part of the Hudson River, where the waters that have drained half of Upstate New York have plunged through the mountain ridges around West Point and spread out over flattish land. On the east side is Washington Irving country—the old towns of Tarrytown, Irvington, Dobbs Ferry, and Hastings-on-Hudson, around the Sunnyside mansion where Irving returned to the Hudson he had immortalized after decades in Europe;

these are now comfortable affluent suburbs. On the west side of the river is Rockland County, full of little towns with Dutch names long since surrounded by suburban developments. When James A. Farley grew up here nearly 100 years ago, this was Upstate, but now it is an extension of the New York metropolitan area. Politically, it is mildly Republican, as most affluent New York suburbs are, but its large number of Jewish residents help to make it a bit more liberal on cultural and economic issues than many other suburbs.

The 22d Congressional District of New York spans the Tappan Zee, connecting most of the Irving suburbs with Rockland County and proceeding over the Ramapos some 120 miles inland to the state's borders with New Jersey and Pennsylvania. Past the Ramapos is Orange County—a part of Upstate whose population has been swelled for 20 years by people from New York City, many of them policemen, firemen, teachers, and other civil servants; they talk of wanting to protect their children from contact with the horrors of the city even as they congratulate themselves quietly for dealing with them. Farther out, past the Shawangunk Mountains, is Sullivan County, the heart of the Catskills Borscht Belt resort district, part of which is in the 22d District. This is one of the few predominantly Jewish non-metropolitan areas in the United States, and has been a Jewish resort area, with huge kosher hotels, since before the turn of the century. Politically, this is a district that usually goes Republican, but not always by huge margins. Westchester has been trending mildly toward the Democrats, but the farther out areas, with their many new residents fleeing the city, have tilted them farther toward the Republicans.

The 22d's congressman is Benjamin Gilman, a moderate Republican first elected in 1972. Gilman often votes with the Democrats on economic issues, is quite liberal on cultural issues, but less so on foreign policy. This is important, since he is the second ranking Republican on the Foreign Affairs Committee. Like ranking member William Broomfield, he is a strong supporter of Israel, and a co-sponsor of the bill to move the U.S. embassy in Israel from Tel Aviv to Jerusalem; he has been a crusader against the international narcotics trade for some time, and seems to have a hand in all manner of anti-drug legislation; he has worked too on hunger relief and child immunization abroad.

Gilman first won the seat in 1972, beating ulrtaliberal John Dow who had won in unusual circumstances (the LBJ landslide of 1964, a scandal affecting the Republican incumbent in 1970), and his most difficult race came in 1982, when he was placed in the same district with Democrat Peter Peyser. Peyser too had gone to the House as a Republican in the early 1970s, but their careers took different courses, as much from temperament as differences on issues. Peyser left his House seat to run a quixotic primary campaign against Senator James Buckley in 1976 and after he lost was elected to the House as a Democrat, while Gilman remained quietly working within Republican ranks. In the faceoff, Gilman had the clear advantage in redistrict-ing: only 18% of the votes in the new 22d were cast in Westchester. Peyser won 65% in Westchester, but Gilman won 70% of the vote in Orange County and carried Sullivan and Rockland as well. He won handily in 1984 and 1986, though he does not seem to have sewed up the Westchester vote: in 1986 he carried it by only 52%–45% while winning districtwide by 69%–27%.

The People: Pop. 1980: 516,625, up 14.4% 1970–80. Households (1980): 79% family, 45% with children, 68% married couples; 31.5% housing units rented; median monthly rent: $267; median house value: $63,000. Voting age pop. (1980): 363,184; 6% Black, 4% Spanish origin, 1% Asian origin.

1984 Presidential Vote: Reagan (R) 141,052   (61%)
Mondale (D) 88,027   (38%)

Rep. Benjamin A. Gilman (R)

Elected 1972; b. Dec. 6, 1922, Poughkeepsie; home, Middletown; U. of PA, B.S. 1946, NY Law Sch., LL.B. 1950; Jewish; married (Rita).

Career: Army Air Corps, WWII; Asst. Atty. Gen. of NY State, 1953–55; Practicing atty., 1955–72; Atty., NY Temp. Comm. on the Courts; NY Assembly, 1967–72.

Offices: 2160 RHOB 20515, 202-225-3776. Also 44 E. Ave., P.O. Box 358, Middletown 10940, 914-343-6666; 223 Rte. 59, Monsey 10952, 914-357-9000; and 32 Main St., Hastings-on-Hudson 10706, 914-478-5550.

Committees: *Foreign Affairs* (2d of 18 R). Subcommittees: Europe and the Middle East (Ranking Member); International Operations. *Post Office and Civil Service* (2d of 8 R). Subcommittees: Human Resources; Investigations. *Select Committee on Hunger* (4th of 10 R). Task Force: International Task Force. *Select Committee on Narcotics Abuse and Control* (Ranking Member of 10 R).

Group Ratings

	ADA	ACLU	COPE	CFA	LCV	ACU	NTU	NSI	COC	CEI
1986	40	45	72	67	74	55	19	90	28	15
1985	45	—	71	67	—	43	27	—	27	—

National Journal Ratings

	1986 LIB — 1986 CONS	1985 LIB — 1985 CONS
Economic	57% — 42%	53% — 46%
Social	49% — 49%	73% — 23%
Foreign	39% — 61%	37% — 60%

Key Votes

1) Lmt Cln Water Act	AGN	5) Retain Gun Cont	AGN	9) Aid Angola Reb	FOR
2) Rpl Tobac Sub	FOR	6) Contra Aid	FOR	10) Tax Reform	AGN
3) Grm-Rdmn Def Red	AGN	7) Lmt Text Imp	FOR	11) S Africa Sanc	FOR
4) Ban Polygraph	FOR	8) Limit SDI	AGN	12) Immig Reform	FOR

Election Results

1986 general	Benjamin A. Gilman (R)	94,244	(69%)	($305,258)
	Eleanor Burlingham (D)	36,852	(27%)	($16,066)
	Richard Bruno (RTL)	4,560	(4%)	
1986 primary	Benjamin A. Gilman (R) unopposed			
1984 general	Benjamin A. Gilman (R)	144,278	(69%)	($280,131)
	Bruce M. Levine (D–L)	57,934	(28%)	($154,974)

Campaign Contributions and Expenditures

1985-86		Direct Cont. 1985-86		PACS Breakdown 1985-86			
Receipts	$345,314	Indiv.	$201,690	Corp.	$28,481	T/M/H	$29,405
Expend.	$305,258	PACS	$129,059	Labor	$59,185	Agr.	$6,800
Unspent	$103,292			Ideo.	$5,100	CWOS	$88

TWENTY-THIRD DISTRICT

Founded by the Dutch in 1624 as Fort Orange, on the banks of the Hudson where seagoing ships could dock, at the edge of the great gloomy forests teeming with beaver and Iroquois, renamed after one of the titles of King James II when the British took the colony in 1664, Albany has been an important American city for 300 years. This is the natural crossroads of Upstate New York, a port for sailing ships and an important junction for boat traffic on the Erie Canal and railroad traffic on the water-level New York Central route. The building of the canal made William and Henry James's father a rich man, which allowed the grandsons to do pretty much what they wanted. Troy, up the river just a few miles on the other bank, was a steel manufacturing center rivaling Pittsburgh in the 1840s, and later becoming America's leading producer of detachable collars; the town of Cohoes at the junction of the Hudson and the Mohawk became one of America's leading textile producers. Schenectady a few miles up the Mohawk was the site of Charles Steinmetz's fabled General Electric laboratories and GE is still a major employer there. Albany was a burly lumber mill and factory town as well.

For much of the 20th century Albany has been a kind of antique: its stolid rowhouses showed its 19th century prosperity, its once teeming lumberyards and railroad car shops, its old restaurants and hotels carried the patina of age and the accumulated soot and grime of decades of coal smoke rising in its six-month-long winters. It also had an antique political machine, headed since 1921 by Democratic boss Daniel O'Connell, who died in 1977 at age 91, and by Erastus Corning II, mayor from 1942 to his death in 1983; it was sustained by rafts of city and county employees, by a certain creativity when it came to counting votes, by the raffish atmosphere that you found in the speakeasies of so many cities during Prohibition and which lingered in Albany for decades after.

Yet Albany now has a shining new face, as its bard William Kennedy makes clear in O Albany! Mayor Corning provided the creative financing for Governor Nelson Rockefeller's monumental South Mall, yuppies began buying up and renovating old townhouses, expressways were built, and even the old Union Station was spruced up. The capital area around Albany is now one of the faster-growing parts of Upstate New York, not quite a high tech boom area like Boston or New Hampshire, but doing much better than almost anyone expected. The Albany Democratic machine still seems to be in power in the H. H. Richardson City Hall that faces up to the gaudy State House, but slowly the bulk of voters in the capital region have moved to the suburbs, and while they tend to favor Democrats, they have to be persuaded just as voters anywhere else do to support them.

The 23d Congressional District of New York includes Albany, Troy, Schenectady, the old carpet manufacturing town of Amsterdam on the Mohawk, and the old industrial towns, suburban subdivisions, and rural land in between. Oddly enough it has not been represented by a product of the Albany machine since 1966. Its current congressman, Samuel Stratton, is a Democrat whose original base was in Schenectady, and was first elected to the House in 1958. Republicans tried to redistrict him out, and his district once stretched halfway across Upstate New York; but in 1970 they gave up and gave him Albany and Troy, which they expected would elect a Democrat anyway. Since then he has been routinely reelected by margins of 3 to 1 or better.

Stratton's major interest today is in defense issues. His experience on Capitol Hill goes back to 1940, when he served as a young aide to Massachusetts Representative Thomas Eliot, a supporter of FDR's military preparedness program. Those were the days when aid to Britain was highly controversial, when even Britain seemed likely to be conquered by Hitler, and when the draft passed the House a month before Pearl Harbor by just one vote. Roosevelt himself resorted to underhanded tactics to get aid to Britain and to get the United States more involved in the fight against Hitler than most Americans wanted. Those times made a deep impression on many young men in Congress then, including Lyndon Johnson and Henry Jackson, and they seem to have made a lasting impression on Sam Stratton as well.

Stratton sees himself as a Roosevelt and Truman Democrat, reasonably liberal on economic issues, and resolutely in favor of a strong defense and a foreign policy supportive of freedom abroad. He strongly backed the Vietnam war and believes the United States should have made a stronger commitment there. He favors most proposed increases in defense spending and new weapons systems. He is wary of arms control agreements and proposals. He is one of Congress's leading opponents of the nuclear freeze proposal. He is chairman of the Armed Services Subcommittee on Procurement and Military Nuclear Systems, which guarantees him a major voice in most House weapons policy debates.

But he is a disappointed man in one respect: he has been passed over, apparently permanently, for the chairmanship of the House Armed Services Committee. In 1984, after the Democratic Caucus voted out elderly Mel Price, they voted in the much younger and less senior Les Aspin; in 1986, Stratton was one of those who opposed Aspin as the Caucus voted not to confirm him as chairman again, but then he was disappointed again as Aspin won the chair back in January 1987. In any case, Stratton was not his main opponent; that was Marvin Leath of Texas, who is less senior than Aspin.

But Stratton temperamentally is more of an iconoclast than a consensus leader. He is justly proud of his many years' fight to prevent the destruction of the West Front of the Capitol and to have it restored instead; that meant bucking every Democratic leader for years, but Stratton seemed to enjoy it. Similarly, he has no compunction in moving to ban tobacco advertising— though that costs him valuable allies in the Carolinas and elsewhere. Stratton fights for what he believes, and seems to take particular relish when he takes on an unfashionable cause; and if that means that some of the younger Democrats regard him as a predictable scold while a few of the oldtimers left still regard him as an uppity troublemaker, so be it: he has the comfort of feeling that he is taking a long view of history and has stayed true to his principles. He has the comfort also of remaining exceedingly popular in the capital area, and politically untouchable. Whatever disappointments he has suffered in Washington, he can be reelected in the 23d District as long as he likes.

The People: Pop. 1980: 516,943, dn. 4.0% 1970–80. Households (1980): 67% family, 33% with children, 54% married couples; 42.3% housing units rented; median monthly rent: $169; median house value: $38,900. Voting age pop. (1980): 389,983; 4% Black, 1% Spanish origin, 1% Asian origin.

1984 Presidential Vote: Reagan (R) 135,744   (53%)
                              Mondale (D) 120,950   (47%)

Rep. Samuel S. Stratton (D)

Elected 1958; b. Sept. 27, 1916, Yonkers; home, Schenectady; U. of Rochester, A.B. 1937, Haverford Col., M.A. 1938, Harvard U., M.A. 1940; Presbyterian; married (Joan).

Career: Secy. to U.S. Rep. Thomas H. Eliot, 1940–42; Navy, WWII and Korea; Dpty. Secy. Gen., Far Eastern Comm., U.S. Dept. of State, 1946–48; Radio and TV news commentator; College lecturer; Schenectady City Cncl., 1950–56, Mayor, 1956–59.

Offices: 2205 RHOB 20515, 202-225-5076. Also P.O. Bldg., Jay St., Schenectady 12305, 518-374-4547; Leo O'Brien Fed. Bldg., Albany 12207, 518-465-0700; P.O. Bldg., Amsterdam 12010, 518-843-3400; and P.O. Bldg., Troy 12180, 518-271-0822.

Committees: *Armed Services* (4th of 31 D). Subcommittees: Investigations; Procurement and Military Nuclear Systems (Chairman).

Group Ratings

	ADA	ACLU	COPE	CFA	LCV	ACU	NTU	NSI	COC	CEI
1986	45	31	78	73	39	42	20	100	29	22
1985	40	—	78	67	—	55	24	—	30	—

National Journal Ratings

	1986 LIB — 1986 CONS	1985 LIB — 1985 CONS
Economic	87% — 0%	57% — 41%
Social	66% — 34%	60% — 40%
Foreign	23% — 76%	24% — 66%

Key Votes

1) Lmt Cln Water Act	AGN	5) Retain Gun Cont	FOR	9) Aid Angola Reb	FOR
2) Rpl Tobac Sub	FOR	6) Contra Aid	FOR	10) Tax Reform	FOR
3) Grm-Rdmn Def Red	AGN	7) Lmt Text Imp	FOR	11) S Africa Sanc	FOR
4) Ban Polygraph	FOR	8) Limit SDI	AGN	12) Immig Reform	AGN

Election Results

1986 general	Samuel S. Stratton (D)................	140,759	(96%)	($38,035)
	James Joseph Callahan (SW).............	5,279	(4%)	
1986 primary	Samuel S. Stratton (D) unopposed			
1984 general	Samuel S. Stratton (D)................	188,144	(78%)	($51,729)
	Frank Wicks (R–NF)	53,060	(22%)	

Campaign Contributions and Expenditures

1985-86		Direct Cont. 1985-86		PACS Breakdown 1985-86			
Receipts	$77,124	Indiv.	$4,304	Corp.	$40,550	T/M/H	$6,520
Expend.	$38,035	PACS	$54,674	Labor	$7,750	Agr.	$0
Unspent	$117,714			Ideo.	$0	CWOS	$104

TWENTY-FOURTH DISTRICT

Climb to Olana, the artist Frederick Church's bizarre Moorish house on top of a hill, and you can see the landscape that inspired the generation of Hudson River painters. A major artery of commerce for 300 years, the Hudson and the hills and mountains around it still look wild: nature writes in bigger letters than the canal and railroad giants of the 19th century. The Hudson Valley has also been one of the nation's centers of political innovation. It was on a trip up the Hudson in the 1790s that James Madison and Aaron Burr welded the Virginia–New York alliance that made possible Jeffersonian Democracy. And two descendants of Dutch settlers on the Hudson helped create the Democratic party as we know it. Martin Van Buren, an innkeeper's son from Kinderhook, created the first Democratic organizations—the Albany Regency in New York, Andrew Jackson's Democracy in Washington—and invented the national convention in 1832. Franklin Roosevelt, an aristocratic businessman's son from Hyde Park, forged the New Deal Democratic coalition which seems to have lasted longer and won more elections than Van Buren's and Jackson's.

Yet ironically the Hudson Valley is not at all Democratic these days, and hasn't been for about 100 years. The 24th Congressional District, which includes most of the river valley from Roosevelt's Hyde Park north through Van Buren's Kinderhook and, skipping the cities of Albany and Troy, goes up through the old battlefield, spa, and racetrack town of Saratoga to the mountains around the headwaters of the Hudson, is one of the most Republican districts in New York; the town-by-town voting figures may show it to be the only district that went for Republican Andrew O'Rourke over Democrat Mario Cuomo in the 1986 gubernatorial race.

The 24th District has a congressman, Gerald Solomon, who is one of the staunchest and most forthright of Republicans, with probably the most conservative record of any New York member. He also has his name on significant legislation: the Solomon Amendment, to bar young men who have not registered for the draft from receiving federal scholarship or college loan aid. This was initially a matter of some controversy, with Democrats professing to see it as a violation of freedoms of expression and charging that it was punitive; but as time went on, and as it has been upheld by the courts, it has come to be seen as a rather unremarkable piece of legislation. Why should people who violate a federal law be entitled to collect federal money? If there is fault to be found, it is with the registration law, which has no real effect on our adversaries but which gives conscientious and other opponents of current American policies something to object to.

Solomon is a member of the Foreign Affairs Committee, where he is a staunch, even fierce, backer of conservative policies. He is also ranking Republican on the Veterans' Affairs Committee and a strong supporter of making permanent the 1984 G.I. Bill, which seems to have been a remarkable and, in most quarters in Washington, remarkably unheralded success. His positions seem to be popular in the 24th District. He first won the seat in 1978, defeating a Democrat elected in 1974 who held on, barely, in 1976 and then confessed he had once smoked marijuana. Solomon has been reelected easily since and seems likely to be for some time to come.

The People: Pop. 1980: 515,614, up 15.8% 1970–80. Households (1980): 76% family, 42% with children, 65% married couples; 26.9% housing units rented; median monthly rent: $174; median house value: $38,500. Voting age pop. (1980): 364,047; 1% Black, 1% Spanish origin.

1984 Presidential Vote:

Reagan (R)	162,977	(69%)
Mondale (D)	73,186	(31%)

Rep. Gerald B. H. Solomon (R)

Elected 1978; b. Aug. 14, 1930, Okeechobee, FL; home, Glens Falls; Siena Col., St. Lawrence U.; Presbyterian; married (Freda).

Career: USMC, Korea; Queensbury Town Sprvsr. and Warren Cnty. Legis., 1968–72; NY Assembly, 1973–78.

Offices: 2342 RHOB 20515, 202-225-5614. Also Gaslight Square, Saratoga Springs 12866, 518-587-9800; and 568 Columbia Turnpike, East Greenbush 12061, 518-477-2703; 419 Warren St., Hudson 12534, 518-828-0181; and 21 Bay St., Glens Falls 12801, 518-792-3013.

Committees: *Foreign Affairs* (8th of 18 R). Subcommittees: International Economic Policy; Human Rights and International Organizations (Ranking Member). *Veterans' Affairs* (Ranking Member of 13 R).

Group Ratings

	ADA	ACLU	COPE	CFA	LCV	ACU	NTU	NSI	COC	CEI
1986	0	0	20	17	37	81	56	100	83	64
1985	15	—	20	42	—	84	69	—	86	—

National Journal Ratings

	1986 LIB — 1986 CONS			1985 LIB — 1985 CONS		
Economic	21%	—	77%	12%	—	85%
Social	0%	—	89%	0%	—	76%
Foreign	14%	—	84%	0%	—	76%

Key Votes

1) Lmt Cln Water Act	AGN	5) Retain Gun Cont	AGN	9) Aid Angola Reb	FOR
2) Rpl Tobac Sub	FOR	6) Contra Aid	FOR	10) Tax Reform	FOR
3) Grm-Rdmn Def Red	FOR	7) Lmt Text Imp	FOR	11) S Africa Sanc	AGN
4) Ban Polygraph	AGN	8) Limit SDI	AGN	12) Immig Reform	AGN

Election Results

1986 general	Gerald B. H. Solomon (R–C–RTL)	117,285	(70%)	($153,651)
	Edward James Bloch (D)	49,225	(30%)	($79,334)
1986 general	Gerald B. H. Solomon (R) unopposed			
1984 general	Gerald B. H. Solomon (R–C–RTL)	164,019	(73%)	($152,451)
	Edward James Bloch (D)	60,188	(27%)	($72,959)

Campaign Contributions and Expenditures

1985-86		Direct Cont. 1985-86		PACS Breakdown 1985-86			
Receipts	$162,192	Indiv.	$87,260	Corp.	$23,760	T/M/H	$25,670
Expend.	$153,651	Party	$6,538	Labor	$6,400	Agr.	$1,000
Unspent	$54,018	PACS	$63,438	Ideo.	$5,500	CWOS	$1,108

TWENTY-FIFTH DISTRICT

For 150 years, from the establishment of Fort Orange in what now is Albany until the Revolutionary War, the Mohawk Valley of Upstate New York was the frontier. The six nations of the Iroquois, the fiercest of Indians, were allied with the British; the Iroquois would provide a buffer against the French, and the British would keep Yankees from New England from settling west of Albany. This alliance was a victim of success: after the French were driven from North America in 1759, the pressures for westward settlement were huge; the British tried to keep their word and the Iroquois attacked the rebellious colonists in the Revolution; but when the rebels won, the Indian society was doomed, and the Yankees, held back for 150 years, pressed westward and reached the Pacific coast two generations later.

This is the background of *Drums Along the Mohawk*, and there is little in these rolling hills today to give any hint of the shrieks of war whoops or the bloody violence whose conclusion made possible the digging of the Erie Canal, the building of the New York Central, the forging of the great path westward into the interior of America. This route accounted for much of the phenomenal growth in the 19th century of New York City and its port; Boston and Philadelphia, with no similar access inland, were left behind. As migration slowed and trade increased, the Mohawk Valley became one of the early industrial centers of the nation. The little Oneida County hamlets of Utica and Rome grew to become sizable factory towns. First settled by New England Yankees, these towns attracted a new wave of immigration from the Atlantic coast in the early 20th century. Today they are the most heavily Italian- and Polish-American communities between Albany and Buffalo.

The 25th Congressional District of New York consists of most of the Mohawk Valley, from Amsterdam (but not including Herkimer) through Utica and Rome, where the canal-builders had to dig through the route's highest ground. It also includes a row of counties to the south which are more sparsely settled. These are hilly areas are not along any major east–west route; the population here remains more Yankee, the area less industrial. The most famous town here is Cooperstown, with 19th-century houses and commercial buildings maintained in better-than-pristine condition, thanks in large part to the money brought in by the Baseball Hall of Fame. Politically, these counties are heavily Republican, under practically all circumstances; they gave Mario Cuomo only a bare margin when he was winning overwhelmingly in 1986. The Mohawk Valley, on the other hand, is more marginal: it almost went for Cuomo in 1982 when he barely won, and it supported Robert Kennedy heavily in 1964; evidently the key factor is the presence of a Democrat with appeal to Italian and other ethnic voters.

The congressional representation of this district is regularly settled in the Republican primary. The winner in 1982 was Sherwood Boehlert, who had been familiar with the job of representing this district for nearly 20 years. He served as an aide to Representative Alexander Pirnie, who retired in 1972, and to Representative Donald Mitchell, after Mitchell beat him in the primary. The difficulties of running for Congress from Washington may have persuaded him to move back to Utica, where he was elected Oneida County Executive in 1979. His local strength persuaded incumbent Gary Lee not to run in this district in 1982, though it contained his legal residence. Boehlert won both the Republican primary and general election by respectable, though not overwhelming, margins.

Boehlert has put his own particular stamp on the job of representing the district. Pirnie and Mitchell voted pretty much along orthodox Republican lines; Boehlert has had the support of the state AFL-CIO in since 1982, and has been notably more liberal on economic issues, and has often opposed the Reagan Administration and the Republican leadership. Pirnie and Mitchell both served on the Armed Services Committee, in part to protect Rome's Griffiss Air Force Base. Boehlert serves on Science, Space and Technology and in 1985 got a seat on Public Works, and appears more interested in building a stronger, new economy in this region which has experienced relatively little economic growth than he does in just protecting what the district already has. As ranking Republican on a Science subcommittee, he has been pushing for more government aid in developing robotics, and he has introduced, with Richard Durbin of Illinois, legislation to create "individual training accounts"; Gary Hart, who sponsored a similar measure in the Senate, offered this as one of his "new ideas" during the 1984 presidential campaign. With other Republicans in the '92 Group, he worked to come up with a new proposal to deal with acid rain, and ended up getting the support of leading Democrat Henry Waxman.

Boehlert has been an active, thoughtful, innovative legislator whose basic views are well in line with a district historically Republican and inclined to favor government action to help the economy. He beat a conservative 2 to 1 in the 1986 Republican primary and has won general elections easily.

The People: Pop. 1980: 516,201, dn. 0.4% 1970–80. Households (1980): 73% family, 39% with children, 61% married couples; 32.5% housing units rented; median monthly rent: $155; median house value: $32,400. Voting age pop. (1980): 374,606; 2% Black, 1% Spanish origin.

1984 Presidential Vote:

Reagan (R)	137,582	(63%)
Mondale (D)	81,369	(37%)

Rep. Sherwood L. Boehlert (R)

Elected 1982; b. Sept. 28, 1936, Utica; home, New Hartford; Utica Col., B.A. 1961; Roman Catholic; married (Marianne).

Career: Army, 1956–58; Mgr., pub. relations, Wyandotte Chemicals Corp., 1961–64; A.A. to Rep. Alexander Pirnie, 1964–72; A.A. to Rep. Donald Mitchell, 1972–79; Cnty. Exec., Oneida Cnty., 1979–82.

Offices: 1641 LHOB, 202-225-3665. Also 200 Fed. Bldg., 10 Broad St., Utica 13501, 315-793-8146; Rome City Hall, Rome 13440, 315-339-0013; 125 Main Street, Rm. 203, Oneonta 13820, 315-793-8146; 42 S. Broad St., Norwich 13815, 607-336-7130; and 17 Main St., Cortland 13045, 607-753-9324.

Committees: *Public Works and Transportation* (13th of 20 R). Subcommittees: Aviation; Economic Development. *Science, Space and Technology* (5th of 18 R). Subcommittees: Science, Research and Technology (Ranking Member); Intl. Scientific Cooperation. *Select Committee on Aging* (13th of 26 R). Subcommittees: Health and Long-Term Care; Housing and Consumer Interests.

Group Ratings

	ADA	ACLU	COPE	CFA	LCV	ACU	NTU	NSI	COC	CEI
1986	50	50	66	67	79	41	37	40	56	38
1985	45	—	57	75	—	52	40	—	57	—

National Journal Ratings

	1986 LIB — 1986 CONS	1985 LIB — 1985 CONS
Economic	49% — 50%	42% — 58%
Social	57% — 40%	69% — 28%
Foreign	48% — 51%	46% — 52%

Key Votes

1) Lmt Cln Water Act	AGN	5) Retain Gun Cont	AGN	9) Aid Angola Reb	FOR
2) Rpl Tobac Sub	FOR	6) Contra Aid	AGN	10) Tax Reform	FOR
3) Grm-Rdmn Def Red	FOR	7) Lmt Text Imp	FOR	11) S Africa Sanc	FOR
4) Ban Polygraph	FOR	8) Limit SDI	AGN	12) Immig Reform	FOR

Election Results

1986 general	Sherwood L. Boehlert (R).............	104,216	(69%)	($268,122)
	Kevin J. Conway (D)	33,864	(22%)	($2,660)
	Robert S. Barstow (C–RTL)............	12,999	(9%)	($31,567)
1986 primary	Sherwood L. Boehlert (R).............	17,842	(67%)	
	Robert S. Barstow (R)	8,808	(33%)	
1984 general	Sherwood L. Boehlert (R).............	140,256	(73%)	($146,546)
	James J. Ball (D)	52,434	(27%)	

Campaign Contributions and Expenditures

1985-86		Direct Cont. 1985-86		PACS Breakdown 1985-86			
Receipts	$293,347	Indiv.	$150,900	Corp.	$35,801	T/M/H	$24,067
Expend.	$268,122	Party	$2,343	Labor	$49,849	Agr.	$5,000
Unspent	$68,810	PACS	$122,217	Ideo.	$6,000	CWOS	$1,500
		Cand.	$32,175				

TWENTY-SIXTH DISTRICT

The far frozen north of Upstate—this is the 26th Congressional District of New York. Most of its people live in the counties across the St. Lawrence River from Canada or at the eastern end of Lake Ontario. It dips down as far south as Herkimer, on the Mohawk River. Geographically, much of the 26th is taken up with the Adirondack Forest Preserve, a giant state park that the New York Constitution stipulates must remain "forever wild." This includes Lake Placid, site of the 1980 Winter Olympics. North of the Forest Preserve is Massena, on the St. Lawrence River, which has been blessed with the administrative headquarters of the St. Lawrence Seaway. This project was supposed to give the north country an economic boost. But there have been continual problems: the Seaway freezes over three months a year, yet icebreaking would harm the shore land; its locks are too small for the large containerized ships that have become the rule in most kinds of trade; and the time it takes to negotiate the locks is longer than most shippers want to wait. So despite the Seaway the economy of this part of New York has not grown spectacularly since the days in the early 19th century when it was settled by farmers moving west from northern New England to seek their own farms in this agriculturally marginal land.

The large French Canadian population in Clinton and Franklin Counties, just 60 miles south of Montreal, forms the only Democratic voting bloc in the district; as one moves south and west there are fewer French and more Yankees, fewer Democrats and more Republicans. Here in the farm country of the St. Lawrence and in the Adirondacks, where it gets bitterly cold in the winter and not very warm in the summer, the voting preference is decidedly Republican—

enough so to make the 26th District Republican in almost every election.

That has been true since the Republican Party began. The prime political celebrity up here was William Wheeler, vice president under Rutherford B. Hayes, who left office in 1881. The 26th District does not bulk large in the affairs of New York state, and it has elected quiet Republican congressmen. The current incumbent, David Martin, has been a faithful Republican who seems to avoid the spotlight and who makes a point of keeping his family in the district and returning there every weekend. He reacted to a flurry of speculation about his seeking statewide office with intelligent modesty. First elected in 1980, he was a solid supporter of the Reagan Administration in his first two years, but he is occasionally liberal on economics. He is not one of the more prominent members of the Armed Services Committee, his only assignment, but is a reliable supporter of increased defense spending. As the ranking member of the subcommittee handling military construction, he is in a good position to keep bolstering Watertown's Fort Drum. A veteran of the New York Assembly, with a base in the north country, he won his 1980 primary with 70% of the vote and has been easily reelected, with no opposition at all in 1986.

The People: Pop. 1980: 516,196, up 3.1% 1970–80. Households (1980): 74% family, 42% with children, 63% married couples; 29.5% housing units rented; median monthly rent: $144; median house value: $29,200. Voting age pop. (1980): 364,170; 1% Black, 1% Spanish origin, 1% American Indian.

1984 Presidential Vote:

Reagan (R)	135,207	(65%)
Mondale (D)	70,730	(34%)

Rep. David O'B. Martin (R)

Elected 1980; b. Apr. 26, 1944, Ogdensburg; home, Canton; U. of Notre Dame, B.B.A. 1966, Albany Law Sch., J.D. 1973; Roman Catholic; married (DeeAnn).

Career: USMC, 1966–70; Practicing atty., 1973–80; St. Lawrence Cnty. Legislature, 1973–77; NY Assembly, 1977–80.

Offices: 442 CHOB 20515, 202-225-4611. Also E.J. Noble Med. Ctr. Bldg., Main St., Canton 13617, 315-379-9611.

Committees: *Armed Services* (9th of 20 R). Subcommittees: Military Installations and Facilities (Ranking Member); Readiness.

Group Ratings

	ADA	ACLU	COPE	CFA	LCV	ACU	NTU	NSI	COC	CEI
1986	15	0	27	27	21	74	34	100	79	38
1985	15	—	24	33	—	71	39	—	71	—

National Journal Ratings

	1986 LIB — 1986 CONS		1985 LIB — 1985 CONS	
Economic	40% —	60%	35% —	65%
Social	0% —	89%	0% —	76%
Foreign	0% —	86%	24% —	66%

Key Votes

1) Lmt Cln Water Act	FOR	5) Retain Gun Cont	AGN	9) Aid Angola Reb	FOR
2) Rpl Tobac Sub	AGN	6) Contra Aid	FOR	10) Tax Reform	AGN
3) Grm-Rdmn Def Red	AGN	7) Lmt Text Imp	FOR	11) S Africa Sanc	—
4) Ban Polygraph	AGN	8) Limit SDI	AGN	12) Immig Reform	AGN

Election Results

1986 general	David O'B. Martin (R–C)...............	94,840	(100%)	($76,301)
1986 primary	David O'B. Martin (R) unopposed			
1984 general	David O'B. Martin (R–C)...............	131,257	(71%)	($125,395)
	Bernard J. Lammers (D)................	54,663	(29%)	($31,375)

Campaign Contributions and Expenditures

1985-86		Direct Cont. 1985-86		PACS Breakdown 1985-86			
Receipts	$123,746	Indiv.	$45,105	Corp.	$45,500	T/M/H	$16,250
Expend.	$76,301	Party	$2,187	Labor	$4,900	Agr.	$250
Unspent	$55,729	PACS	$71,734	Ideo.	$4,750	CWOS	$84

TWENTY-SEVENTH DISTRICT

Smack in the middle of Upstate New York, halfway between Albany and Buffalo on the Erie Canal and the New York Central water line, for years the nation's major east–west transportation routes, Syracuse is a manufacturing city that is sufficiently diversified to weather some highly-publicized plant closings while retaining an unemployment rate below the national average, and sufficiently middle American that for many years it was a favorite test marketing site. Syracuse invented the dental chair, Stickley mission furniture, the drive-in bank teller, and the foot measuring devices used in shoe stores; it is a big manufacturing city still, one of the nation's largest salt producers, the site of the New York State Fair. Its agricultural hinterland is rich (with specialty crops like wine grapes), its industrial jobs mostly high skill. The weather may have helped to motivate its achievements. Syracuse gets as much snow as any city in the United States, and if you are going to live up here you are going to have to earn enough money to build a solid, well-insulated house to protect you through the winter.

In another state, where it would have been the center of one of the major metropolitan areas, Syracuse might have been a Democratic city; in New York, where it is vastly overshadowed by the masses of New York City, it is heavily Republican. This partisan preference has survived the glacial ethnic change which has transformed Syracuse from a mostly Protestant Yankee city in 1880 to a mostly Catholic and heavily Italian city in 1980. There is a feeling —reinforced by the 1975 fiscal crisis, and still lively despite the recovery—that New York City, if it ever got the chance, would tax honest, hardworking Upstaters to bankruptcy to support the welfare cheaters and civil service loafers who, in this view, dominate New York City politics. Also contributing to Syracuse's Republicanism are the views of its longtime biggest employer, General Electric— propagated in the 1950s and early 1960s by Ronald Reagan.

But in 1986 Syracuse, like almost all of New York state, went solidly for Governor Mario Cuomo, and the 27th Congressional District, which is made up of Syracuse, surrounding Onondaga County, and most of Madison County to the east, nearly elected a Democratic congressman. Cuomo's strength was based on his commanding leadership and consensus record; the close congressional race resulted mainly from the weakness of the local congressman, Republican George Wortley, and the superior aggressiveness of his challenger, Public Service Commissioner Rosemary Pooler. Wortley is the sort of Republican many Upstate districts have elected over the years: a local businessman (he owns a chain of newspapers in suburban Syracuse) with a record of civic involvement but no great flair for electoral politics. He ran in 1980, and won his primary 40%–30%; in 1982, pitted against fellow Representative Gary Lee by redistricting he won by 354 votes out of 39,000 cast. He won the general election in 1982 with 53% and in 1984 with 57%—not stunning scores for this strongly Republican area.

Wortley had additional problems in 1986. In May he fired the director of his Syracuse office who then threatened to sue him. He asked Democrat Fernand St Germain, chairman of the Banking Committee he serves on, to attend one of his fundraisers, though Wortley also served on the ethics committee that was then investigating St Germain. In addition, the Democrat who had tapes made of Washington bar conversations of Long Island's Raymond McGrath had said that he could "definitely raise George a hundred grand" from a Syracuse businessman and "99 friends." Pooler, arguing that Wortley was too much of a free trader and that he hadn't done enough for economic development in the district, was actually ahead of the incumbent in early October polls. But then she had problems of her own. She was charged with accepting a campaign contribution from a director of New York Telephone while still serving on the PSC and then approving a phone rate increase. Wortley went ahead in the polls and ended up winning one of 1986's narrower victories, 50%–49%.

But he lost in Syracuse and Onondaga County and cannot be counted as secure. He has been emphasizing his work on banking bills to shorten the time for check clearing and to choke off money laundering and his support of the big water projects bill President Reagan vetoed. But he may have to hustle hard to avoid another tough challenge.

The People: Pop. 1980: 516,364, dn. 1.1% 1970–80. Households (1980): 71% family, 39% with children, 58% married couples; 36.8% housing units rented; median monthly rent: $186; median house value: $38,100. Voting age pop. (1980): 372,785; 5% Black, 1% Spanish origin, 1% American Indian, 1% Asian origin.

1984 Presidential Vote:

Reagan (R)	136,687	(60%)
Mondale (D)	88,959	(39%)

Rep. George C. Wortley (R)

Elected 1980; b. Dec. 8, 1926, Syracuse; home, Fayetteville; Syracuse U., B.S. 1948; Roman Catholic; married (Barbara).

Career: Navy, WWII; Newspaper publisher, 1949–80.

Offices: 229 CHOB 20515, 202-225-3701. Also 1269 Fed. Bldg., Clinton Sq., Syracuse 13260, 315-423-5657.

Committees: *Banking, Finance and Urban Affairs* (7th of 20 R). Subcommittees: Economic Stabilization; Financial Institutions Supervision, Regulation and Insurance; Housing and Community Development. *Select Committee on Aging* (8th of 26 R). Subcommittees: Health and Long-Term Care; Housing and Consumer Interests. *Select Committee on Children, Youth and Families* (7th of 12 R). Task Force: Prevention Strategies.

Group Ratings

	ADA	ACLU	COPE	CFA	LCV	ACU	NTU	NSI	COC	CEI
1986	20	12	26	33	42	60	36	80	65	44
1985	15	—	21	42	—	80	43	—	82	—

National Journal Ratings

	1986 LIB — 1986 CONS		1985 LIB — 1985 CONS	
Economic	33% —	66%	27% —	71%
Social	31% —	69%	0% —	76%
Foreign	30% —	69%	35% —	63%

Key Votes

1) Lmt Cln Water Act	FOR	5) Retain Gun Cont	AGN	9) Aid Angola Reb	FOR
2) Rpl Tobac Sub	AGN	6) Contra Aid	FOR	10) Tax Reform	FOR
3) Grm-Rdmn Def Red	FOR	7) Lmt Text Imp	AGN	11) S Africa Sanc	FOR
4) Ban Polygraph	AGN	8) Limit SDI	AGN	12) Immig Reform	FOR

Election Results

1986 general	George C. Wortley (R–C).............. 83,430	(50%)	($697,045)
	Rosemary S. Pooler (D–ECP) 82,491	(49%)	($505,254)
1986 primary	George C. Wortley (R) unopposed		
1984 general	George C. Wortley (R–C)............. 122,215	(57%)	($353,778)
	Thomas C. Buckel, Jr. (D–L) 93,601	(43%)	($49,987)

Campaign Contributions and Expenditures

1985-86		Direct Cont. 1985-86		PACS Breakdown 1985-86			
Receipts	$706,272	Indiv.	$354,825	Corp.	$132,460	T/M/H	$85,301
Expend.	$697,045	Party	$16,185	Labor	$18,300	Agr.	$0
Unspent	$12,653	PACS	$290,513	Ideo.	$52,552	CWOS	$1,900

TWENTY-EIGHTH DISTRICT

New York's 28th Congressional District is a swath along the state's southern border from the Hudson River to the shores of Lake Cayuga. This spans several parts of Upstate New York. Ulster County, along the Hudson, was first settled by Dutch patroons and their retainers; just above the river are the Catskill Mountains: Rip Van Winkle country. On the other side of the Catskills is the Borscht Belt resort district, part of which is in this district; here a predominantly Jewish clientele has been summering for nearly 100 years. Westward into the vastness of Upstate New York is the Delaware River, the source of much of New York City's excellent water supply. Farther west you come to the beginning of what is called the Southern Tier, along the Pennsylvania border. Here, nestled along a river valley circled by rising hills, are towns like Binghamton, old manufacturing centers with IBM plants nearby. Off to the north, in the beginning of the Finger Lakes region, Ithaca and Cornell.

This whole area has had little population growth in the past several decades, but it would be a mistake to see it as economically stagnant. In fact, old industries have been replaced rather steadily by new; low-wage jobs have been replaced by high-wage jobs. Some children choose to leave, to seek opportunities elsewhere; but this part of Upstate New York continues to provide good livings for its frugal, industrious citizens. Politically, they, like most Upstaters, consider themselves Republicans. They are sympathetic to civil rights and arms control; but on economic issues they do not see themselves, as residents of New York City do, as the main beneficiaries of generous federal programs.

Nonetheless, this district has a Democratic congressman, former Ithaca area District Attorney Matthew McHugh. He was first elected in 1974, due to a combination of favorable circumstances: the retirement of a popular Republican congressman, a recession, Watergate. He was reelected easily in 1976, but had tough races in the next four elections. In the first three his Republican opponents spent liberally, and McHugh raised and spent even more; in each case he won with 55% or 56% of the vote. In 1984 he and his opponent, former Assemblywoman Constance Cook, agreed on a media spending limit, which probably helped the better-known incumbent; McHugh got 57%. This was an interesting and by no means typical race. Cook, who once worked for Governor Thomas E. Dewey, represented Ithaca in the Assembly from 1966 to 1976; she was proud of her work in building the huge state university system and attacked McHugh for his opposition to abortion. But she could not overcome the advantages of eight years of incumbency in the rest of the district.

In the House McHugh has been a member of the Appropriations Committee since 1978 and of two subcommittees with a tradition of overseeing closely the operations of the programs they fund. One is Agriculture, ruled for years by Jamie Whitten of Mississippi; Whitten was born in 1910, and McHugh ranks behind only him and Bob Traxler of Michigan. On that McHugh is a key supporter of nutrition programs. He also serves on Foreign Operations, chaired by David Obey of Wisconsin; this has supervision over the foreign aid program and funding for international agencies. It considers dozens of amendments designed to change U.S. policy in various directions, and is the critical forum often in determining levels of American aid to Israel. McHugh is a supporter of aid to Israel and of assistance to the international lending agencies.

He has taken on other chores as well. As head of the Democratic Study Group in 1983 and 1984 he helped to put together an alternative budget resolution that got a respectable vote. In 1985 he became a member of the Intelligence Committee. Pleasant, hard-working, not given to cheap shots, he is called on for a number of difficult and testing assignments.

All these activities, plus his need to tend to his district, which is hard to reach from Washington—thanks in part to airline deregulation championed by Alfred Kahn, who is now back in Ithaca again as a Cornell professor—gives him one of the heavier workloads in the Congress. He won by better than 2 to 1 in 1986, but previous elections have shown that this is not a district that even this Democrat can take for granted.

The People: Pop. 1980: 516,402, up 4.1% 1970–80. Households (1980): 71% family, 37% with children, 59% married couples; 33.8% housing units rented; median monthly rent: $185; median house value: $39,400. Voting age pop. (1980): 382,338; 3% Black, 2% Spanish origin, 1% Asian origin.

1984 Presidential Vote:

Reagan (R) 140,748	(61%)
Mondale (D) 89,680	(39%)

Rep. Matthew F. (Matt) McHugh (D)

Elected 1974; b. Dec. 6, 1938, Philadelphia, PA; home, Ithaca; Mt. St. Mary's Col., Emmitsburg, MD, B.S. 1960, Villanova U., J.D. 1963; Roman Catholic; married (Eileen).

Career: Practicing atty., 1964–68, 1972–74; Ithaca City Prosecutor, 1968; Tompkins Cnty. Dist. Atty., 1969–72.

Offices: 2335 RHOB 20515, 202-225-6335. Also 201 Fed. Bldg., Binghamton 13902, 607-773-2768; Terrace Hill-Babcock Hall, Ithaca 14850, 607-273-1388; and 292 Fair St., Kingston 12401, 914-331-4466.

Committees: *Appropriations* (18th of 35 D). Subcommittees: Foreign Operations; Rural Development, Agriculture and Related Agencies. *Select Committee on Children, Youth, and Families* (5th of 18 D). Task Forces: Economic Security; Prevention Strategies. *Permanent Select Committee on Intelligence* (8th of 11 D). Subcommittee: Legislative (Chairman).

Group Ratings

	ADA	ACLU	COPE	CFA	LCV	ACU	NTU	NSI	COC	CEI
1986	80	75	81	100	74	9	23	0	17	24
1985	85	—	82	92	—	10	30	—	18	—

National Journal Ratings

	1986 LIB — 1986 CONS		1985 LIB — 1985 CONS	
Economic	62% —	35%	89% —	0%
Social	81% —	17%	81% —	15%
Foreign	80% —	0%	85% —	8%

Key Votes

1) Lmt Cln Water Act	AGN	5) Retain Gun Cont	FOR	9) Aid Angola Reb	AGN
2) Rpl Tobac Sub	FOR	6) Contra Aid	AGN	10) Tax Reform	FOR
3) Grm-Rdmn Def Red	AGN	7) Lmt Text Imp	AGN	11) S Africa Sanc	FOR
4) Ban Polygraph	FOR	8) Limit SDI	FOR	12) Immig Reform	FOR

Election Results

1986 general	Matthew F. (Matt) McHugh (D) 103,908	(68%)	($287,642)
	Mark R. Masterson (R–C–RTL) 48,213	(32%)	($7,218)
1986 primary	Matthew F. (Matt) McHugh (D) unopposed		
1984 general	Matthew F. (Matt) McHugh (D–L)...... 123,334	(57%)	($381,060)
	Constance E. Cook (R)................ 90,324	(41%)	($136,255)

Campaign Contributions and Expenditures

1985-86		Direct Cont. 1985-86		PACS Breakdown 1985-86			
Receipts	$279,797	Indiv.	$184,179	Corp.	$9,790	T/M/H	$13,100
Expend.	$287,642	Party	$187	Labor	$32,743	Agr.	$2,750
Unspent	$6,161	PACS	$83,979	Ideo.	$25,096	CWOS	$500

TWENTY-NINTH DISTRICT

It's hard to believe when you see the autumn leaves of the rolling hillsides above the long, thin deep-blue lakes, but the Finger Lakes of Upstate New York were once one of America's most dynamic places. The lakes themselves are deep folds in a gentle landscape, whose shores provide shelter for New York's wine grapes. In the old town squares are monuments to the enthusiasms of the 1830s and 1840s, a time when these communities were almost brand new, full of young families on the move and on the rise. In this threshold of the American interior, the religious revivals were so fervent that the area was known as the Burnt-Over district. Here in the village of Palmyra, near the Erie Canal, Joseph Smith had his vision of the angel Moroni and saw the golden tablets which led him to found the Mormon Church. Here preachers fanned the local enthusiasm for abolition of slavery, greater here than anywhere else in the country. It was the birthplace of the women's suffrage movement; the great 1848 women's convention was held in Seneca Falls, at the head of one of the Finger Lakes. It was the birthplace as well of the temperance movement—and, hard as it may be for the liberated women of today to believe, the two causes were often linked in those days. This part of Upstate New York has always had a taste for learning. It is full of small colleges, and some anonymous scholar gave many of its towns classical names: Scipio, Marcellus, Cicero, Ovid, Romulus, Hannibal.

The Finger Lakes region forms about half of New York's 29th Congressional District; the other half is on the east side of Rochester and includes some of its eastern suburbs. Here are the mansions on East Avenue of Kodak's George Eastman and other inventors who have made Rochester for a century a high tech city, and also some of its cultural institutions. Follwers of the progressive historians might ask why, after all its initial cultural ferment, this part of Upstate New York has been so somnolently Republican ever since. But Upstaters don't consider themselves somnolent, and the reformers of the Burnt-Over District, like the New Dealers whom the progressives admire, saw their ardor cool not so much because of failure but because of success. Women did get liberated, temperance did cut down drinking, slavery was abolished, new churches were built, and the personal and moral lives of these communities were put on a solid footing where they have remained ever since.

The Republican Party, which believed in restricting slavery in territories and building land-grant schools in colleges, was an activist party which helped to achieve these goals and then to consolidate them. Well into the 20th century, Upstate Republicans saw themselves as the upholders of standards and learning against the immigrant mobs of New York City, and as the conservers of an economic system, which proved vastly productive, against the importers of foreign socialism. And so it does today, as the welfare state has stopped short of socialism but embedded itself in the lives of local communities, and as traditional morality has again asserted its claims against those who denigrated it.

The congressman from this district is Frank Horton, one of the more senior Republicans in the House and one of the more liberal, particularly on cultural issues. Horton was first elected in

1962, one of a long line of liberal Republicans from the east side of Rochester, which included former Senator Kenneth Keating. Horton is now the ranking Republican on the Government Operations Committee. This is an odd legislative body: it produces little ongoing legislation, and has a power to investigate that in practice is difficult to focus. Horton is proudest of the work he has done on the Paperwork Reduction Act, which he got through in 1980 and which seems to have counteracted some of the natural tendency of government forms to multiply in the night. Horton was also a lead sponsor of revenue sharing, which has now been phased out, and a founder and co-chairman of the Northeast-Midwest Coalition, which focused attention on the distribution of federal funds and aid through the nation and lobbied for the older industrial areas. Its creation signalled the first time this hitherto richest part of the nation considered itself in need of federal dollars, and showed how deeply intermeshed federal programs have become in local communities' lives.

Horton was also a mover behind the establishment of Inspectors General in federal departments; some cynics argue that they have not had much impact, but the very existence of such monitoring must affect those potentially monitorable. Horton is the New York representative on the Republican Committee on Committees, and it was he who decided that Raymond McGrath would get the vacant New York Ways and Means seat in 1985—useful for New York, since McGrath was the most obdurate proponent of maintaining state and local tax deductibility in the tax reform bill.

To many House Republicans Horton must seem an anachronism. His generally liberal voting record (though not always on foreign or even economic policy), and his amiable relations with Government Operations Chairman Jack Brooks of Texas (which is also where Horton hails from: both sides of Rochester are represented now by native southerners) infuriate many young Republicans, who remember how a Democratic staffer on Government Operations altered Republican committee members' remarks in transcripts of hearings, a despicable offense which Horton did not seem very upset about.

Horton does, however, seem to remain popular in his district which in its current boundaries would surely support a Republican congressman of whatever stripe. His potential problems are in the Republican primary; a little-known candidate in the 1984 primary got 38% of the vote, carrying Monroe and Seneca Counties. That was in a light turnout, but there is no tradition of heavy primary voting in New York, and so Horton—though unopposed in the 1986 primary— could be vulnerable in the future to a candidate with conservative activist support, particularly in the Finger Lakes and Oswego County, which he has represented for only two years.

The People: Pop. 1980: 515,404, up 2.1% 1970–80. Households (1980): 72% family, 40% with children, 60% married couples; 31.7% housing units rented; median monthly rent: $190; median house value: $36,600. Voting age pop. (1980): 365,972; 4% Black, 1% Spanish origin.

1984 Presidential Vote: Reagan (R) 187,701   (61%)
Mondale (D) 118,461   (39%)

Rep. Frank J. Horton (R)

Elected 1962; b. Dec. 12, 1919, Cuero, TX; home, Rochester; LA St. U., B.A. 1941, Cornell U., LL.B. 1947; Presbyterian; (Nancy).

Career: Army, WWII; Practicing atty., 1947–62; Rochester City Cncl., 1955–61.

Offices: 2229 RHOB 20515, 202-225-4916. Also 314 Kenneth B. Keating Bldg., 100 State St., Rochester 14614, 716-263-6270; 304 Metcalf Plaza, 144 Genesee St., Auburn 13021, 315-255-1125; and Riverfront Office Bldg., Oswego 13126, 315-342-4688.

Committees: *Government Operations* (Ranking Member of 15 R). Subcommittee: Legislation and National Security (Ranking Member). *Post Office and Civil Service* (4th of 8 R). Subcommittees: Civil Service; Postal Operations and Services (Ranking Member).

Group Ratings

	ADA	ACLU	COPE	CFA	LCV	ACU	NTU	NSI	COC	CEI
1986	75	73	67	50	55	10	25	40	31	18
1985	50	—	66	58	—	30	28	—	35	—

National Journal Ratings

	1986 LIB — 1986 CONS		1985 LIB — 1985 CONS	
Economic	56%	— 43%	53%	— 46%
Social	55%	— 44%	85%	— 0%
Foreign	70%	— 30%	48%	— 51%

Key Votes

1) Lmt Cln Water Act	AGN	5) Retain Gun Cont	AGN	9) Aid Angola Reb	AGN
2) Rpl Tobac Sub	AGN	6) Contra Aid	AGN	10) Tax Reform	AGN
3) Grm-Rdmn Def Red	FOR	7) Lmt Text Imp	FOR	11) S Africa Sanc	FOR
4) Ban Polygraph	FOR	8) Limit SDI	FOR	12) Immig Reform	AGN

Election Results

1986 general	Frank J. Horton (R)	99,704	(71%)	($96,489)
	James R. Vogel (D)	34,194	(24%)	($20,893)
	Two others (C–RTL)	7,110	(5%)	
1986 primary	Frank J. Horton (R) unopposed			
1984 general	Frank J. Horton (R)	138,362	(70%)	($79,014)
	James R. Toole (D)	48,301	(24%)	
	Two others (C–RTL)	11,999	(6%)	

Campaign Contributions and Expenditures

1985-86		Direct Cont. 1985-86		PACS Breakdown 1985-86			
Receipts	$134,984	Indiv.	$19,030	Corp.	$27,000	T/M/H	$29,650
Expend.	$96,489	Party	$2,179	Labor	$32,260	Agr.	$6,750
Unspent	$109,567	PACS	$105,160	Ideo.	$9,000	CWOS	$500

THIRTIETH DISTRICT

Rochester was one of America's first high tech cities. New York's third largest metropolitan area, vastly overshadowed by New York City and—even in its corner in western New York, smaller than Buffalo—is nonetheless the home of great enterprises. Its great industries include Bausch & Lomb, the lensmakers; Eastman Kodak, a company that has thrived for years thanks to technological breakthroughs and good management; and Xerox, which started here as Haloid though its headquarters is now in Stamford, Connecticut. Technical innovation, precision workmanship, high reliability, customer service—these are the qualities that have made Rochester a prosperous and pleasant city.

The 30th Congressional District of New York includes most of the Rochester metropolitan area plus a swath of rural and small-town Upstate New York to the south along the New York Thruway. It is shaped oddly, with one wide end along Lake Ontario, a narrow pinched waist through downtown Rochester, and then a vast base running along the Thruway. It includes Rochester's highest-income suburb, Pittsford, in hilly country southeast of the city; and it also includes the lakefront suburbs, where working people move out when they move up: Irondequoit, Greece, and Parma. Its southern portion contains the kind of small towns, originally settled by Yankees from New England, which for so many years in Upstate New York and through the Midwest produced the leaders of the Republican Party in the House.

But the 30th District is represented now not by a Republican man with roots deep in Upstate New York, but by a Democratic woman whose accent reflects her origins in eastern Kentucky. She is Louise Slaughter, who like many women first ran for office in her 40s and became an experienced and popular Monroe County legislator and New York Assemblywoman. Slaughter's predecessor-but-one was a prototypical Upstater, Barber Conable, a lover of ancient rolltop desks and Upstate history, thoughtful and moderate in temperament but capable of partisan crusading on occasion: as ranking Republican on the Ways and Means Committee he was an enthusiast for the 10-5-3 depreciation proposal that became part of the 1981 Reagan tax cut. (Conable was unenthusiastic about the other part, the 5-10-10 income tax rate cut championed by his Upstate neighbor Jack Kemp.) Conable retired in 1984, and after a year was tapped to be president of the World Bank; his successor, for one term, was Republican Fred Eckert.

By all the standard rules Eckert as an incumbent Republican should have been able to hold this seat, but he lost it to Slaughter. Why? Personality was an important factor: Eckert is variously described as arrogant, blunt, abrasive, and, by his friends, shy. An outspoken conservative in a district used to being represented by conciliatory-sounding moderates, he had detractors even among his fellow conservatives. In a year in which Americans were voting heavily for leaders with positive records, Eckert could be attacked by Slaughter as "Congressman No" for his blunt opposition to programs from revenue sharing to abortion. Slaughter even ran TV ads showing a Rochester area woman accusing Eckert of refusing to do anything to help her brother, a hostage held in Lebanon (this was before the Iran-contra revelations, of course). Slaughter in the meantime raised as much money as Eckert—one of many examples of Democratic challengers matching Republican incumbents—and with her pleasant personality scored one media coup after another. This was one House race that was closely watched by voters. Slaughter won 51%–49%, carrying Rochester and Monroe County with 53% and getting at least 44% in the smaller counties.

Slaughter, who seems to have all the political skills Eckert lacks, has seats on the Public Works and Government Operations Committees. She will have to work hard to hold this heretofore Republican seat, but if she does make it through 1988 and 1990, the odds are that the legislature, divided between Democrats and Republicans, will redistrict the Rochester area seats to provide a safe Democratic constituency for her.

The People: Pop. 1980: 516,819, up 3.5% 1970–80. Households (1980): 74% family, 41% with children, 62% married couples; 31.4% housing units rented; median monthly rent: $211; median house value: $44,100. Voting age pop. (1980): 371,098; 4% Black, 1% Spanish origin, 1% Asian origin.

1984 Presidential Vote:

Reagan (R)	146,995	(63%)
Mondale (D)	86,565	(37%)

Rep. Louise M. Slaughter (D)

Elected 1986; b. Aug. 14, 1929, Harlan Cnty., KY; home, Fairport; U. of KY, B.A. 1951, M.S. 1953; Episcopalian; married (Robert).

Career: Monroe Cnty. Leg., 1976–79; Regional Coord., Lt. Gov. Mario Cuomo, 1976–79; NY Assembly, 1983–86.

Offices: 1313 LHOB 20515, 202-225-3615. Also 311 Fed. Bldg., 100 State St., Rochester 14614, 716-232-4850; and 216 Main St., 3d floor, Batavia 14020, 716-343-2524.

Committees: *Government Operations* (22d of 24 D). Subcommittees: Employment and Housing; Government Information, Justice and Agriculture. *Public Works and Transportation* (25th of 32 D). Subcommittees: Investigations and Oversight; Surface Transportation; Water Resources. *Select Committee on Aging* (39th of 39 D). Subcommittee: Human Services.

Group Ratings and Key Votes: Newly Elected
Election Results

1986 general	Louise M. Slaughter (D)...............	86,777	(51%)	($558,744)
	Fred J. Eckert (R–C))	83,402	(49%)	($565,374)
1986 primary	Louise M. Slaughter (D)...............	9,335	(81%)	
	William Bastuk (D)....................	1,614	(14%)	
	Keith Perez (D).......................	582	(5%)	
1984 general	Fred J. Eckert (R–C)	119,844	(54%)	($231,795)
	W. Douglas Call (D).................	100,066	(45%)	($111,641)

Campaign Contributions and Expenditures

1985-86		Direct Cont. 1985-86		PACS Breakdown 1985-86			
Receipts	$587,731	Indiv.	$266,313	Corp.	$6,325	T/M/H	$19,244
Expend.	$558,744	Party	$5,175	Labor	$165,223	Agr.	$0
Unspent	$28,792	PACS	$282,988	Ideo.	$92,096	CWOS	$100
		Cand.	$15,984				

THIRTY-FIRST DISTRICT

It has already produced two presidents; it is the industrial metropolis of Upstate New York and long the biggest grain port on the Great Lakes; it is the nearest big city to what was long North America's biggest tourist attraction, Niagara Falls—yet, for all this, Buffalo weighs light on the national consciousness. In state politics it is eclipsed by New York City, economically it is eclipsed by the bigger Great Lakes industrial cities of Cleveland and Detroit and Chicago, architecturally its bold City Hall and downtown skyscrapers are now far overshadowed by the high-rise horizon of Toronto, not so many miles away across Lake Ontario. Buffalo has become known nationally for its snowfall, which is especially heavy because it sits just at the eastern apex of Lake Erie; and for some it is a metaphor, with its cold steel furnaces and weed-choked waterfront, of a failed industrial city. Yet Buffalo has its strengths as well, from the sturdiness of its buildings to a new vigor in its white-collar economy to the close ties of its ethnic neighborhoods and lack of racial animosity in its politics.

Buffalo has also produced a politician who seeks to follow Buffalonians Grover Cleveland and Millard Fillmore into the White House, Representative Jack Kemp. Actually, his district no longer includes any part of the city of Buffalo: he was originally elected, as long ago as 1970, in a district almost entirely in the Buffalo suburbs, but the 31st District he currently represents begins in suburban Erie County and includes a swath of Upstate New York stretching east to the Finger Lakes. That area, of course, is heavily Republican, but Buffalo and Erie County have long been the most Democratic parts of the state north of the New York City line, the home of an often formidable Democratic organization, and filled with voters whose politics dates back to the time when their immigrant grandparents faced ruin when they were laid off from their jobs or were injured in an industrial accident and were shunned by the Yankee Protestants who regarded themselves as the only real Americans. The policies of the Democratic party from the New Deal to the Great Society responded to this constituency, understood its demands, and helped it rise each generation higher than it ever hoped. The politics of Jack Kemp has been a response to what he sees as the excesses and defects of welfare state politics, and it has grown into more of a national force—and has had more success in Buffalo—than practically anyone foresaw when the former Buffalo Bills quarterback, who grew up in sunny southern California, was elected to Congress in 1970, mostly as the result of a split among the Democrats.

Kemp's role in politics is much like that of Ronald Reagan—or Hubert Humphrey. Each came to politics from an unusual profession; each is a natural optimist; each won his first victories in a constituency that belonged for years to the political opposition. Each, in different ways, has been an entrepreneur of ideas. Reagan in a sense is the transition figure: he started off as a believer in the welfare state and civil rights liberalism of Hubert Humphrey (and both were small town midwesterners born in 1911); he won the presidency in 1980 as the supporter of the supply-side tax cuts championed by Jack Kemp (who worked briefly on his staff in 1967). Like Reagan the actor, Kemp the football player was a competent and dependable but not quite top-rank star, who persevered through years of obscurity and was always prepared and easy to work with; like Reagan, he became head of his fellow workers' union. Like Reagan, he went through a period where his political ideas changed; unlike Reagan, that change did not lead him to change parties, since he had been a Republican all along.

In his first years in Congress Kemp was a conventional, little-noticed Republican. But Kemp, a physical education major in college, began to study economics—and leavened his studies with reflections on the America he knew in Los Angeles and Buffalo. He grew up in an area that had one of the highest economic growth rates in American history, and he represented an area with very little economic growth. He grew up in an environment where government was not a looming presence (though tax rates were not low, and government spent lots of money on schools, freeways, and water) and represented an area more highly taxed than almost any other part of the nation. While Democratic economists seemed concerned about the distribution of wealth, Kemp was concerned about the creation of wealth. He came to believe that government was overtaxing productive (i.e., rich) people—killing the geese that laid the golden eggs. He was the politician who popularized the term supply-side economics and who advanced, and convinced virtually every Republican officeholder to support, the Kemp–Roth plan to cut taxes 10% a year for three years. It had this additional advantage, from the point of view of a representative from the Buffalo area: it would not, in Kemp's view, require cutting many federal programs, for greater economic growth would generate revenues to pay for them.

So to a considerable extent Kemp wrote the agenda and the program for the Reagan economic policy. Kemp–Roth, in modified form, passed the Congress in 1981; Kemp's friend David Stockman became head of the Office of Management and Budget. And if Kemp's supply-side policies have not seemed entirely successful, if they produced for a while far more unemployment than he predicted and far less revenue, they can also be plausibly credited with the extended economic recovery of 1982–87 which, among other things, helped to reelect Ronald Reagan. Just as important, Kemp put the focus of the national debate on how to stimulate economic growth, not on how to redistribute the wealth. Kemp's ideas differ in important respects not only from those of conventional Democrats but from those of conventional Republicans. He championed the 30% tax rate cut and got almost all Republicans to endorse it by 1978, despite their misgivings; and he saw 25% of it enacted in 1981. In response to the Bradley–Gephardt tax plan, he came up with his own Kemp–Kasten proposal to cut tax rates and eliminate most tax preferences; thus he was one of the politicians who produced the Tax Reform Act of 1986. He has established himself again and again as one of the genuine intellectual leaders of his party and as a politician who has moved history in unanticipated directions.

Unlike many other Republicans, Kemp is not much concerned about the size of deficits, nor is he particularly unfriendly to federal spending programs; he opposed the constitutional amendment purporting to require balanced budgets and voted against Gramm–Rudman. Nor is he much concerned about cutting business taxes; Kemp was caught out on a limb in December 1985 when his fellow House Republicans gleefully pounced on Dan Rostenkowski's tax bill on the grounds that it raised business taxes, for he has long felt that low personal income tax rates are the key to economic growth. Unlike many traditional conservatives, he is genuinely interested in improving the lot of the poor, and is proud to be the sponsor of the urban enterprise zones proposal, which has gone nowhere in Congress but has been adopted successfully in many states and cities. He has stoutly opposed protectionism; he takes the politically risky course of talking about gold standards and proposing, more vaguely, that the value of the dollar be tied to some steady commodity index. He gets arguments from standard economists, but he is ready to argue back at them in their own lingo. He did not start out in politics as an orator. But he is now one of America's most forceful and persuasive politicians when he presents his vision of vibrant economic growth and how it can improve the lives of ordinary people.

Despite his intensity and challenges to the old Republican orthodoxy, Kemp has become one of the leading Republicans in the House. He has been chairman of the House Republican Conference, although he is expected to give that post up in the summer of 1987, and he is a close ally of Republican Whip Trent Lott. He was until 1987 the second-ranking Republican on the House Budget Committee. He also has experience in non-economic issues. He used to serve on the Defense Appropriations Subcommittee and chaired the committee drafting the Republicans' defense platform at the 1980 National Convention. He now serves on the Foreign Operations Appropriations Subcommittee, which has jurisdiction over the foreign aid appropriation which so many of his colleagues have prided themselves on always voting against and now, with a Republican administration in office, must support. On that body he tends to support aid to Israel and to criticize the International Monetary Fund for what he considers austerity. Despite—or perhaps because of—Kemp's originality and intellectual integrity, he has raised hackles at the Reagan White House, and his fervor on economic issues has led some cultural conservatives to mistrust him. But he is a longstanding and articulate opponent of abortion and champion of the conservatives' family values.

Through early 1987 Kemp's support in presidential polls stayed in single digits. He seemed to be trying to corral the support of movement conservatives, though it's not clear that they are in charge of the troops in the field any more, and to establish himself as the clearest proponent of Ronald Reagan's ideas—just as they seemed to be muddled by the Iran-contra affair. House Democrats tried to give him a tough time in 1986 by ballyhooing the candidacy of James Keane, member of a Buffalo political family, who held him to only 51% of the vote in Erie County and 57% district-wide; Kemp, who geared so much of his economic platform to Buffalo for so many years, has been looking at things from a national perspective and has found himself vulnerable locally on issues like trade. But these developments may help Kemp by liberating him from his former political constraints and giving him an opportunity to present his view of the future. He is disadvantaged, at a time when voters seem to want competence at governing, to be part of the minority in the House, and he could be hurt further if he shows the tendency to flinch when under opposition from his own party as he was briefly in 1985 on tax reform. It may be that most Americans believe that all the work of limiting government they want done has been done, and that they want practical-minded men with hands-on experience, not inspirational idea men, in the White House; if so, the Kemp candidacy will come to nothing.

But Kemp's political career, win or lose in 1988, has already come to a great deal. This one-time quarterback has demonstrated, over what is now a long political career, what one-time pharmacist Hubert Humphrey also showed: that a political party's chief producer and purveyor of ideas can come from the most unlikely of quarters; and that the politician who makes the biggest contribution to his party and his nation is not always he who wins the nominations or holds the most prestigious posts but he who, at an auspicious moment, injects into the political dialogue the ideas that can change government and change a nation.

The People: Pop. 1980: 516,271, up 9.0% 1970–80. Households (1980): 78% family, 42% with children, 68% married couples; 25.3% housing units rented; median monthly rent: $201; median house value: $45,300. Voting age pop. (1980): 369,104; 1% Black, 1% Spanish origin, 1% Asian origin.

1984 Presidential Vote:

Reagan (R)	142,852	(62%)
Mondale (D)	88,264	(38%)

Rep. Jack F. Kemp (R)

Elected 1970; b. July 13, 1935, Los Angeles, CA; home, Hamburg; Occidental Col., B.A. 1957, Long Beach St. U., CA Western U.; Presbyterian; married (Joanne).

Career: Pro football quarterback, San Diego Chargers and Buffalo Bills, 1957–70; Cofounder and Pres., AFL Players Assn., 1965–70; Army, 1958; Radio and TV commentator; Special Asst. to Gov. Ronald Reagan, 1967; Special Asst. to Chmn. of Repub. Natl. Cmtee., 1969.

Offices: 2252 RHOB 20515, 202-225-5265. Also 1101 Fed. Bldg., 111 W. Huron St., Buffalo 14202, 716-846-4123; and 484 S. Main St., Geneva 14456, 315-789-3360.

Committee: *Appropriations* (7th of 22 R). Subcommittee: Foreign Operations. *Select Committee on Children, Youth and Families* (6th of 12 R). Task Force: Economic Security.

Group Ratings

	ADA	ACLU	COPE	CFA	LCV	ACU	NTU	NSI	COC	CEI
1986	15	21	18	25	3	89	44	100	58	74
1985	10	—	18	25	—	81	54	—	79	—

National Journal Ratings

	1986 LIB — 1986 CONS		1985 LIB — 1985 CONS	
Economic	29% —	71%	27% —	73%
Social	43% —	56%	0% —	76%
Foreign	0% —	86%	0% —	76%

Key Votes

1) Lmt Cln Water Act	FOR	5) Retain Gun Cont	AGN	9) Aid Angola Reb	FOR
2) Rpl Tobac Sub	—	6) Contra Aid	FOR	10) Tax Reform	FOR
3) Grm-Rdmn Def Red	AGN	7) Lmt Text Imp	AGN	11) S Africa Sanc	AGN
4) Ban Polygraph	FOR	8) Limit SDI	AGN	12) Immig Reform	AGN

Election Results

1986 general	Jack F. Kemp (R–C–RTL)	92,508	(57%)	($2,613,605)
	James P. Keane (D–FTP)	67,574	(42%)	($234,487)
1986 primary	Jack F. Kemp (R) unopposed			
1984 general	Jack F. Kemp (R–C)	168,332	(75%)	($530,585)
	Peter J. Martinelli (D–L)	56,156	(25%)	($7,361)

Campaign Contributions and Expenditures

1985-86		Direct Cont. 1985-86		PACS Breakdown 1985-86			
Receipts	$2,530,981	Indiv.	$2,094,201	Corp.	$173,365	T/M/H	$83,200
Expend.	$2,613,605	Party	$3,717	Labor	$26,000	Agr.	$0
Unspent	$52,018	PACS	$320,115	Ideo.	$34,750	CWOS	$2,800

THIRTY-SECOND DISTRICT

The Niagara Frontier, once bristling with guns, when it was the site of skirmishes in the War of 1812, is now bristling with other things: tourist attractions, to snare the millions who still come to see Niagara Falls, power lines strung out on giant pylons fanning out in every direction to provide cheap electric power to the industrial heartland, and industrial plants and dumps, some idle, like the Hooker Chemical facility that poisoned the Love Canal area. That is the other side of the tourist city: the gritty little frame houses, built where Hooker warned the city that no one should live, sitting abandoned near piles of dirt-covered hard late-season ice.

The 32d Congressional District of New York includes the heart of the Niagara Frontier: the Falls; the Buffalo suburbs of Tonawanda, Kenmore, and Amherst, with its big new state university campus and more new office buildings than downtown Buffalo; the towns and farm country along the south shore of Lake Ontario to the Rochester suburbs; and a salient of low income black neighborhoods in Rochester itself. Like most of Upstate New York this was once Republican territory. But as its industrial base has declined, it has become less interested in the production of wealth and more in its distribution, and has trended Democratic. The area that from 1950 to 1962 elected William Miller, Republican national chairman in the early 1960s and Barry Goldwater's running mate in 1964, now routinely reelects a Democratic congressman.

He is John LaFalce, who as a young state legislator became part of the large Watergate congressional class of 1974. His career presents an interesting counterpoint to the other representative of suburban Buffalo, Jack Kemp, who was first elected in 1970. When they entered Congress, the Democrats still seemed the party of ideas, full of initiatives for government, while the Republicans, at best, seemed to be the voices of small town burghers who maintained local institutions and mistrusted national change. Now the positions seem to be reversed. Kemp has become an entrepreneur of ideas, and has seen his tax cut iniative result in lowering top income tax rates from 70% to 28%—an achievement no one thought possible when he started—and has become a candidate for President. LaFalce, while interested in ideas of national scope, has been tending to the practical business of bolstering the economies of local areas like the Niagara Frontier.

For that he has used his forums on the Banking and Small Business Committees. On Banking in the 1970s he helped establish the UDAG program, a favorite of mayors across the country because it provides government financing of private projects which might otherwise not be built and which become tangible evidence of accomplishment in reelection campaigns. LaFalce used a subcommittee chairmanship in the early 1980s to try to formulate a national industrial policy for the Democrats, and was one of the first to urge that government try to make American industry more competitive in markets abroad. He has not been reflexively protectionist, perhaps because he represents a border constituency. He came up with his own proposal for Third World debt in 1987, calling for an intermediary agency to buy up the debt with backing from the IMF's gold fund. But most of LaFalce's initiatives, including a Bank for Induistrial Competitiveness, have not gone anywhere, and the industrial policy idea failed to surface in the 1984 presidential campaign or later. They have gone the way of the wages and price controls which LaFalce's subcommittee handled in the 1970s. Few even among Democrats have confidence that government can usefully pick winners and avoid losers and invest money in a way that will stimulate growth.

Now LaFalce has another assignment, as chairman of the Small Business Committee. He has used his seat there previously to come forward with constructive proposals, shunned by insurers and trial lawyers, to handle the alleged liability crisis, and he evidently hopes to affect many issues. The problem is that the committee's jurisdiction is mostly limited to the Small Business Administration, an agency that hands out small amounts of money under limited programs requiring lots of paperwork—the antithesis of useful capital formation.

The 32d is not a heavily Democratic district in national terms, but it is close enough to one that LaFalce has been able to win reelection by large margins; essentially he has had no serious opposition. If anything, the new territory added in the 1982 redistricting made the district more Democratic and LaFalce has won there easily. The prospect is for him to continue winning throughout the 1980s.

The People: Pop. 1980: 516,387, dn. 6.6% 1970–80. Households (1980): 74% family, 39% with children, 61% married couples; 32.5% housing units rented; median monthly rent: $174; median house value: $37,600. Voting age pop. (1980): 375,165; 7% Black, 1% Spanish origin, 1% American Indian.

1984 Presidential Vote:

Reagan (R)	119,656	(55%)
Mondale (D)	98,874	(45%)

Rep. John J. LaFalce (D)

Elected 1974; b. Oct. 6, 1939, Buffalo; home, Tonawanda; Canisius Col., B.S. 1961, Villanova U., J.D. 1964; Roman Catholic; married (Patricia).

Career: Law Clerk, Ofc. of Gen. Counsel, U.S. Dept. of the Navy, 1963; Lecturer, Geo. Wash. U., 1965–66; Practicing atty.; Army, 1965–67; NY Senate, 1971–72; NY Assembly, 1973–74.

Offices: 2367 RHOB 20515, 202-225-3231. Also Fed. Bldg., Buffalo 14202, 716-846-4056; Main P.O. Bldg., Niagara Falls 14302, 716-284-9976; and Fed. Bldg., Rochester 14614, 716-263-6424.

Committees: *Banking, Finance and Urban Affairs* (7th of 31 D). Subcommittees: Economic Stabilization; Financial Institutions Supervision, Regulation and Insurance; International Development Institutions and Finance; International Finance, Trade, and Monetary Policy. *Small Business* (Chairman of 27 D). Subcommittee: SBA and the General Economy (Chairman).

Group Ratings

	ADA	ACLU	COPE	CFA	LCV	ACU	NTU	NSI	COC	CEI
1986	85	63	83	83	55	10	25	10	25	25
1985	70	—	83	75	—	14	40	—	38	—

National Journal Ratings

	1986 LIB — 1986 CONS			1985 LIB — 1985 CONS		
Economic	57%	—	42%	70%	—	29%
Social	66%	—	33%	46%	—	53%
Foreign	70%	—	30%	75%	—	21%

Key Votes

1) Lmt Cln Water Act	FOR	5) Retain Gun Cont	FOR	9) Aid Angola Reb	AGN
2) Rpl Tobac Sub	FOR	6) Contra Aid	AGN	10) Tax Reform	FOR
3) Grm-Rdmn Def Red	AGN	7) Lmt Text Imp	AGN	11) S Africa Sanc	FOR
4) Ban Polygraph	FOR	8) Limit SDI	FOR	12) Immig Reform	FOR

Election Results

1986 general	John J. LaFalce (D–L) 99,745	(91%)	($108,258)
	Dean L. Walker (C) 6,234	(6%)	
	Anthony M. Murty (RTL) 3,678	(3%)	
1986 primary	John J. LaFalce (D) 12,486	(91%)	
	Elizabeth Spiro-Carman (D). 1,167	(9%)	
1984 general	John J. LaFalce (D–L) 139,979	(69%)	($104,231)
	Anthony J. Murty (R–C–RTL) 61,797	(31%)	

Campaign Contributions and Expenditures

1985-86		Direct Cont. 1985-86		PACS Breakdown 1985-86			
Receipts	$151,800	Indiv.	$23,621	Corp.	$31,750	T/M/H	$21,350
Expend.	$108,258	Party	$167	Labor	$21,750	Agr.	$250
Unspent	$342,253	PACS	$78,500	Ideo.	$2,750	CWOS	$650

THIRTY-THIRD DISTRICT

At the far eastern end of Lake Erie, in position to receive Great Lakes freighters full of iron ore and grain in the summer and some of the nation's biggest snowfalls in the winter, is Buffalo, the second largest city in New York and one of the important industrial centers on the Great Lakes. Huge steel mills, rusted and often closed down, line the shores of Lake Erie, as the principal east–west rail lines feed into downtown Buffalo and the industrial areas that circle it. The skyscrapers downtown rise bravely, but have a forlorn look about them: Buffalo has not continued to grow as its city fathers a half-century ago, when it was America's biggest grain port, thought it would.

Back in those flush days, when Buffalo's basic industries were the fastest-growing, most dynamic sector of the economy, and the city sat on the nation's leading transportation arteries, tens of thousands of Italian and Polish immigrants moved here, eager to work in its factories. Now their descendants have mostly moved to the suburbs, leaving behind the sturdy frame and solid brick houses they raised their families in; the economy is changing, and slowly diversifying, but not growing anywhere near as fast as it once did. Buffalo's basic industries have stopped growing and, in some cases, have shut down. The major transportation routes have shifted to the south, and the great new mode of transportation, the airplane, scarcely touches down in Buffalo at all. Earlier in the century, when the great threat in cities was summer's heat and the diseases and discomfort it brought, Buffalo's climate was no disadvantage; today, when Americans get antsy when the temperature varies more than 10 degrees from 70, Buffalo's snowfall has become a national joke. All of this does not mean that Buffalo is moribund as a city. In the end its economic troubles may help: the price of housing and the cost of labor are now much lower here than in many Sun Belt cities, and it has a vast supply of fresh water. But its economy is not generating enough jobs for its current residents' children—much less any new migrants. The downtown is in trouble, and even the Buffalo branch of the State University of New York has moved to the suburbs.

Virtually all of Buffalo, with the steel-mill town of Lackawanna just to the south, the white-collar suburb of Grand Island in the Niagara River to the north, and the blue-collar suburbs of Cheektowaga, Depew, and Lancaster directly to the east, make up the 33d Congressional District of New York. This is a very heavily Democratic district—the most Democratic of any in Upstate New York. Republican voters have died or moved to the suburbs, and Buffalo's relatively depressed economy has increased the demand for various kinds of federal aid.

Representative Henry Nowak has represented the Buffalo district since 1974, when he was tapped by Erie County Chairman Joseph Crangle's organization to succeed the retiring Thaddeus Dulski. Nowak was then County Controller, an amiable organization Democrat, and he is that still. Nowak is a member of the Public Works and Transportation Committee, and now chairs the Water Resources subcommittee, in which capacity he will no doubt concentrate on such regional priorities as reducing shore erosion in the Great Lakes and sprucing up the Buffalo waterfront. Buffalo, in its days of flushness, sent lots of money to the treasury and did not get much back; now, though incomes are still above the national average, it seems to think it should.

If anyone in Congress has a safe seat, Henry Nowak does. He is a practical politician, one adept at persuading his colleagues to help him on a project, but quiet almost to the point of silence in debate. He wins reelection easily every two years.

The People: Pop. 1980: 516,392, dn. 17.4% 1970–80. Households (1980): 67% family, 34% with children, 48% married couples; 47.5% housing units rented; median monthly rent: $138; median house value: $32,400. Voting age pop. (1980): 383,256; 17% Black, 2% Spanish origin.

1984 Presidential Vote:

Mondale (D)	138,687	(63%)
Reagan (R)	82,638	(37%)

Rep. Henry J. Nowak (D)

Elected 1974; b. Feb. 21, 1935, Buffalo; home, Buffalo; Canisius Col., B.B.A. 1957, U. of Buffalo, J.D. 1961; Roman Catholic; married (Rose).

Career: Army, 1957–58, 1961–62; Practicing atty.; Erie Cnty. Asst. Dist. Atty., 1964; Confidential Secy. to NY Supreme Ct. Justice Arthur J. Cosgrove, 1965; Erie Cnty. Comptroller, 1966–75.

Offices: 2240 RHOB 20515, 202-225-3306. Also U.S. Crthse., 68 Court St., Rm. 212, Buffalo 14212, 716-853-4131.

Committees: *Public Works and Transportation* (6th of 32 D). Subcommittees: Investigations and Oversight; Surface Transportation; Water Resources (Chairman). *Science, Space and Technology* (21 of 27 D). Subcommittees: Natural Resources, Agriculture Research and Environment; Science, Research and Technology.

Group Ratings

	ADA	ACLU	COPE	CFA	LCV	ACU	NTU	NSI	COC	CEI
1986	95	75	91	92	63	5	25	0	28	19
1985	80	—	90	92	—	10	33	—	27	—

National Journal Ratings

	1986 LIB — 1986 CONS			1985 LIB — 1985 CONS		
Economic	81%	—	18%	75%	—	22%
Social	89%	—	0%	54%	—	45%
Foreign	75%	—	20%	71%	—	26%

Key Votes

1) Lmt Cln Water Act	AGN	5) Retain Gun Cont	FOR	9) Aid Angola Reb	AGN
2) Rpl Tobac Sub	FOR	6) Contra Aid	AGN	10) Tax Reform	FOR
3) Grm-Rdmn Def Red	AGN	7) Lmt Text Imp	FOR	11) S Africa Sanc	FOR
4) Ban Polygraph	FOR	8) Limit SDI	FOR	12) Immig Reform	FOR

Election Results

1986 general	Henry J. Nowak (D–L)	109,256	(85%)	($76,902)
	Charles A. Walker (R–C)	19,147	(15%)	($8,432)
1986 primary	Henry J. Nowak (D) unopposed			
1984 general	Henry J. Nowak (D–L)	155,198	(78%)	($79,146)
	David S. Lewandowski (R–C–RTL)	44,880	(22%)	($3,522)

Campaign Contributions and Expenditures

1985-86		Direct Cont. 1985-86		PACS Breakdown 1985-86			
Receipts	$110,284	Indiv.	$57,585	Corp.	$18,200	T/M/H	$15,020
Expend.	$76,902	Party	$246	Labor	$31,600	Agr.	$0
Unspent	$152,256	PACS	$68,145	Ideo.	$2,600	CWOS	$725

THIRTY-FOURTH DISTRICT

The 34th Congressional District of New York is the western half of the Southern Tier—the local name for the counties on the northern side of the border between Upstate New York and Pennsylvania. Extending from the small city of Elmira to Lake Erie, the district contains the Corning Glass Works in Steuben County, two small Indian reservations, miles and miles of dairy farms, and most of New York's wine country. Near the western end, not far from Lake Erie, is Lake Chautauqua, where the Chautauqua gatherings of the late 19th century were held: in the summer, down by the lake, on wide green lawns and on porches and in gazebos decorated with ornate white Victorian gingerbread, whole families came and listened to educational talks and inspirational lectures from the likes of William Jennings Bryan.

The small cities scattered among the district's valleys—Jamestown, Olean, Hornell, Corning—and on the shores of Lake Erie—Dunkirk, Fredonia—tend to be Democratic or politically marginal, reflecting the preference of the Irish and Italian Catholics who came to this part of Upstate New York after it had first been settled by New England Yankees. Outside the towns the Yankee Republicans still predominate and overall this is usually a Republican district.

The current congressman won the seat almost by inheritance—yet he was also the beneficiary of political accidents. He is Amory Houghton, Jr., scion of the exceedingly wealthy family that owns the Corning Glass Works, and a top executive at Corning for 25 years who was considering retiring and becoming a missionary in Africa as he approached age 60. The Houghtons, moreover, are not just rich folks in a small town, they are charter members of the American establishment: Houghton's father was ambassador to France, his grandfather while congressman in the 1920s built one of the biggest mansions on Washington's Embassy Row, his family endowed the rare books library at Harvard, and this latest Houghton sat on boards of companies like IBM, Citicorp, and Procter and Gamble. But Amory Houghton's missionary plans were changed when Representative Stan Lundine, a Democrat who captured the district in a 1976 special election and held it ever since, was tapped by Mario Cuomo to be his lieutenant governor candidate. Suddenly Houghton decided to run for Congress, at which point the other Republicans in the race dropped out. He had a serious Democratic opponent, a young district attorney who carried the eastern part of the district. But Houghton got 77% in his home county of Steuben and won with a comfortable 60%.

Houghton is not the typical freshman congressman, but he may well be more what the Founding Fathers had in mind than the politically adept youngsters with few local ties who win in so many districts. He seems to have the cheerful unassuming nature of one to whom much is given who has been busy most of his life living up to his responsibilities and has enjoyed himself in the process. He said during the campaign that he understood how to create jobs, though he may find it was easier to do that as CEO at Corning than in the Democratic House. But who knows? Surely it is useful for the House to have a member with his level of experience and contacts. It seems likely that Houghton will be able to serve the 34th District as long as he chooses.

The People: Pop. 1980: 516,154, up 1.3% 1970–80. Households (1980): 74% family, 40% with children, 63% married couples; 27.3% housing units rented; median monthly rent: $152; median house value: $30,600. Voting age pop. (1980): 368,422; 1% Black, 1% Spanish origin.

1984 Presidential Vote: Reagan (R) 142,401   (68%)
Mondale (D) 67,870   (32%)

Rep. Amory Houghton, Jr. (R)

Elected 1986; b. Aug. 7, 1926, Corning; home, Corning; Harvard, B.A. 1950, M.B.A. 1952; Episcopalian; married (Ruth).

Career: USMC, WWII; Corning Glass Works, 1951–86, Chmn. of the Bd., C.E.O., 1964–83.

Offices: 1217 LHOB 20515, 202-225-3161. Also 700 W. Gate Plaza, W. State St., Olean 14760, 716-372-2127; 203 Lake St., Hazlett Bldg., Ste. 411, Elmira 14902, 607-734-8580; 32 Denison Pkwy. W., Corning 14830, 607-937-3333; and Fed. Bldg., Rm. 122, Prendergast & 3d Sts., Jamestown 14701, 716-484-0252.

Committees: *Budget* (14th of 14 R). Task Forces: Economic Policy; Income Security. *Government Operations* (11th of 15 R). Subcommittees: Commerce, Consumer and Monetary Affairs; Government Information, Justice and Agriculture.

Group Ratings and Key Votes: Newly Elected

Election Results

1986 general	Amory Houghton, Jr. (R–C).............	85,856	(60%)	($465,710)
	Larry M. Himelein (D).................	56,898	(40%)	($107,100)
1986 primary	Amory Houghton, Jr. (R) unopposed			
1984 general	Stanley N. Lundine (D)	110,902	(54%)	($465,710)
	Jill Houghton Emery (R–C).............	91,016	(45%)	($288,526)

Campaign Contributions and Expenditures

1985-86		Direct Cont. 1985-86		PACS Breakdown 1985-86			
Receipts	$466,016	Indiv.	$175,565	Corp.	$53,800	T/M/H	$52,004
Expend.	$465,710	Party	$14,239	Labor	$112,188	Agr.	$10,800
Unspent	$28,660	PACS	$262,136	Ideo.	$32,894	CWOS	$1,300

NORTH CAROLINA

North Carolina is "the prototype of America's future" John Herbers writes in *The New American Heartland*. Long in the shadow of its less populous but better known neighbors, Virginia and South Carolina and Tennessee; ignored by national media except by that unusually large number who have roots themselves in the state's first-rate journalistic tradition; undistinctive and largely unknown to foreigners, North Carolina officially became one of America's megastates when the 1980 Census recorded it as the nation's tenth largest. North Carolina is not noticed much because it has no large metropolis, in fact no very large city at all; Charlotte, with less than 300,000 is the biggest. Instead North Carolina has, in Herbers's words, "pioneered scattered growth away from its cities and suburbs. A "countrified city" one expert has called it, and Herbers describes how that state policy of encouraging dispersed growth has created a new pattern in which new housing is bunched together not in or on the edge of towns, but on land surrounded by forests and farms and at least several miles drive away from shopping centers and workplaces.

This growth comes in a state whose vitality has often surprised outsiders. North Carolina was settled mostly by poor colonists, many of whose offspring (including Presidents Jackson, Polk, and Johnson) moved west; it contributed more troops to the Confederacy than any other state but not many leaders. It won a progressive reputation in the century after the Civil War for its emphasis on education—and particularly for the University of North Carolina at Chapel Hill and Duke University at Durham—and for its progressive politicians and journalists as well (sometimes they were the same people: Josephus Daniels, publisher of the *Raleigh News & Observer,* was Woodrow Wilson's Secretary of the Navy and hence Franklin Roosevelt's boss in World War I). In the years after World War II, it has had sterling leadership from governors like Luther Hodges, who started the Research Triangle Park between Raleigh, Durham, and Chapel Hill, and Terry Sanford, who cooperated with integration orders rather than resisting them like most other southern governors.

When industrialization was seen as the hallmark of economic progress, North Carolina industrialized: by the 1960s it had the highest percentage of employees in manufacturing in the nation. Textiles was the biggest industry here, with mills scattered around on railroad sidings, highway interchanges, and just country crossroads; they sopped up the extra labor force in rural areas and gave North Carolina for years one of the highest percentages of working women in the country. But of course textile wages have always been low, working conditions usually poor, and unions always discouraged. *Norma Rae* was no exaggeration: North Carolina has the lowest percentage of unionization in the United States. The state's two other big industries, furniture and tobacco, have paid somewhat better. But in the 1970s and 1980s wage levels were rising, the unemployment trend line went lower; the rest of America moved away from urbanization and unionization, in the same direction North Carolina had been going all along.

Is North Carolina the prototype of America's political future as well? Maybe so: the tenth largest state has developed its own brand of politics, in which elections are fiercely fought between politicians who represent not just different stands on issues, but utterly different views of what government should be used for. This politics is personified by the state's two leading political figures, Senator Jesse Helms and former Governor Jim Hunt, whose 1984 Senate race was the most expensive in the nation's history and quite possibly the most bitterly contested—a battle between the forces of light and darkness most North Carolinians would agree, though not on which was which.

It's important to understand what the fight between these two sides was not about. It was not a battle over redistribution of income or major expansion of the public sector or unionization—the essence of Humphrey-Mondale Democratic politics—because neither side favors them. It was not a battle to endorse ideas of cultural liberation: Jim Hunt is as much a scourge of criminals, as fierce an advocate of capital punishment, as determined a proponent of basics in education as anyone in American politics. It was more a battle over the posture of government and attitudes toward cultural tradition. Hunt stands for an active government working with local business leaders to encourage economic growth; Helms stands for a tradition of government standing aloof from such matters and leaving the low-wage economy alone. Hunt stands for abandoning the old southern tradition of racial segregation and for a certain open-mindedness toward different cultural attitudes in other parts of the nation and the world; Helms stands for steadfast belief in traditional religious fundamentals, in the clear, stark rules that have structured the lives of millions of Americans, and in a certain lingering affection or at least an unwillingness to repudiate the rules of segregation and ethnocentrism which have had to be left behind. Hunt's side approaches issues with ebullience, confident that they can make a difference, looking forward to the future. Helms, for all his political successes, looks ahead with a sour expression, fearful that things are not going his way, hopeful of staving off disaster for just a few more years. Hunt tends to be a doer; Helms tends to be an attitudinizer. Hunt's backers are knitted together by long involvement together in civic and business activities; Helms's backers are tied together sometimes by their church ties but mostly because they are on the same mailing lists.

Although Hunt lost that election, 52%–48%, his ideas have mostly prevailed in the governance of the state and have done more to affect its daily life than anything Helms has done in

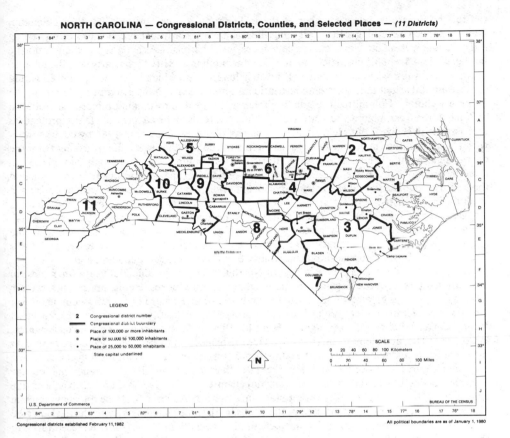

NORTH CAROLINA — Congressional Districts, Counties, and Selected Places — *(11 Districts)*

LEGEND

2 Congressional district number
Congressional district boundary
Place of 100,000 or more inhabitants
Place of 50,000 to 100,000 inhabitants
Place of 25,000 to 50,000 inhabitants
State capital underlined

SCALE

U.S. Department of Commerce

BUREAU OF THE CENSUS

Congressional districts established February 11, 1982

All political boundaries are as of January 1, 1980

government. In the early 1970s Hunt recognized that North Carolina needed to upgrade its work force if it wanted to move beyond a low-wage, textile-based economy. In his 1976 campaign for governor he raised issues which swept first the South and later the rest of the nation ever since: competency tests in education to make sure students were learning the basics, a stern approach to crime including more prisons and capital punishment, affirmative government action to encourage economic development and bring in high-wage, high-skill jobs, the preservation and marketing of a pleasant physical environment. Hunt built on earlier governors' strategies of scattering state institutions—universities, the School for the Arts, the state symphony—around the state, put into practice his own platform, and helped North Carolina achieve sustained economic growth with higher wage levels and one of the nation's lowest unemployment rates by the middle 1980s. At the same time, North Carolina's pleasant physical environment and high tech strength has brought talented migrants in. It had reason to believe it was a prototype for what the rest of the nation would—or might hope to—become. As David Broder has pointed out, if Hunt had won in 1984, he would have become a presidential candidate by 1986—and might very well have ended up the Democratic nominee and the next chief executive.

Helms's record, in contrast, has been one of opposition. Helms began his political career in the 1950 race against Senator Frank Graham, the longtime president of the University of North Carolina, and made his name with voters as a Raleigh television and Tobacco Radio Network commentator denouncing Richard Nixon's recognition of Communist China and the latest civil rights legislation. He has never held or sought executive office: his only political office before he ran for the Senate was as a member of the Raleigh city council in the 1950s. As a Senator, Helms has been a scathing critic of all things liberal and legislatively has concentrated on getting roll calls that will enable him to charge colleagues with liberalism. As a manager of legislation he has been a flop, from his mismanagement of the farm bill in 1981 (which nearly cost the tobacco growers their subsidy) to his bungling of the abortion issue (in which he ended up himself voting against an embattled anti-abortion constitutional amendment) to his attempt to dominate the Foreign Relations Committee (he got Republicans to make him ranking minority member in 1987, but the year before the committee pointedly refused to confirm a Helms protégé as ambassador to Belize). But Helms made his clarity on issues an asset in 1984 by contrasting it with Hunt's positions in between extremes; Helms the complainer was tellingly asking Hunt the doer in ad after ad, "Where do you stand, Jim?" Helms's politics is one of despair that this nation is on the brink of irreversible disaster and of a conviction that the only thing left to do is to sound the alarm as loudly as possible. He is the perfect politician in an age of direct mail fundraising, a medium in which the shrillest apocalyptic appeal always nets the most money; and Helms's Congressional Club, based in Raleigh, has become one of the nation's largest direct-mail fundraisers. The Club not only gives contributions as a PAC but provides at low cost (some argue, at illegally low cost) campaign services to Helms-backed candidates; in early 1987 it was even bruiting about the preposterous possibility of a Helms presidential campaign.

Helms's politics has always played best in North Carolina in presidential years when most of the state's voters have been against the national Democratic ticket. Helms himself first won in 1972, against a young, faintly liberal congressman and while Richard Nixon was winning 69% of the state's votes; his protégé, John East, won 50%–49% in 1980 when Ronald Reagan upset Jimmy Carter here; he won 52% against Hunt in 1984 while Reagan was winning 62% against Walter Mondale, and Republican (but not a Helmsish one) Jim Martin was elected governor. At the same time, it's unfair to say that Helms benefits passively from coattails. On the contrary, dominant figures like Helms and Hunt create their own coattails, beginning not on the presidential line but at the top of the state ticket: in the 1980s North Carolina has been the closest thing to a straight-ticket voting state in America. At least 8 of the 11 congressional districts have been seriously contested in the 1980s, with three changing hands, one of them (the 11th) four times in four elections. Helms benefited, especially in 1984, from increased turnout; that year, some 150,000 voters were registered by the American Coalition For Traditional Values, far outnumbering those registered by black organizations (and some blacks from tradition-minded churches voted for Helms). The Democrats, in contrast, do better in the low-turnout off-years, though they did not recoup all their 1984 losses in 1986.

The big event of 1986, the election of Democratic Senator Terry Sanford, seemed to reverse the result of 1984. But surely it is just one more battle in a long war. Politicians on all sides, except perhaps Helms himself, were weary after the 1984 Senate campaign, with its constant barrage of negative ads, and when Senator John East announced his retirement for health reasons (the same reasons that evidently prompted his tragic suicide in 1986), few candidates were eager to run. Hunt, who could probably have won fairly easily, refused to run. The Helms organization's candidate turned out to be David Funderburk, a former college professor and ambassador to Romania who resigned on principle against the Reagan Administration's favorable relations with its brutal and corrupt regime; but he was beaten 67%–30% in the Republican primary by longtime Representative James Broyhill, a stunning defeat for the Congressional Club whose candidates have been winning Republican primaries since 1972. But Helms backers could argue that Broyhill lost the general election to Democrat Terry Sanford precisely because he failed to mobilize the fundamentalist, evangelical vote, the North Carolinians eager to affirm in their politics, as they do in their daily lives by staying in their home counties and old churches, their traditional root. In east Carolina, the sun-baked tobacco counties, Helms has always eaten heavily into the ancestrally Democratic vote here, but Broyhill, a congressional insider from the western mountains ran 10% to 20% behind Helms's showings in most of these counties, while the numbers were almost precisely the same in the state's urban areas.

North Carolina politics is a struggle of Democrats ready to use government to bolster traditional values and stimulate economic growth and Helms Republicans eager to denounce government in defense of traditional values with little concern about economic growth; and more moderate Republicans, unwilling to make such denunciations, have a hard time winning unless the Democrats' nomination fight results in a weakened candidate, as it did in the 1984 governor's race. So the key part of Helms's political base, it would puzzle a Marxist to learn, is North Carolina's rural industrial proletariat and small tobacco farmers, working to scratch a living off 15 or 20 acres of land. On top of the Civil War alignments which still are apparent in North Carolina's election returns has been superimposed a contest for the votes of a tradition-minded, lower- and middle-income, rural-based, low-informational segment which has become the key voting bloc in North Carolina.

Whether this is the prototype for political alignments in other states is not clear. As David Broder has argued, the Democrats in 1987 were looking for just the kind of candidate Jim Hunt would have been if he had beaten Helms in 1984—a progressive, but not income-redistributing southerner with a record of accomplishment. And the Republicans in many states—witness Pat Robertson's strong showing in the Michigan Republican precinct delegate elections in August 1986—have a strong predilection for cultural conservatives who preach a politics of protest. So it may turn out that North Carolina in the 1970s and 1980s provided a preview of America in the 1990s.

Meanwhile, it is clear that the techniques used in the 1984 Helms–Hunt race have been a prototype for other Senate contests. The huge sums of money raised enabled both candidates to poll constantly on the issues and to prepare instant rebuttals and response ads for broadcasting across the 100 counties of the state. Those who yearn for the revival of old-fashioned political debate have decried such back-and-forth ads, and yet they serve the same function as protracted debate did in the days of Lincoln and Douglas. Then the candidates would come to town and provide entertainment, speaking for hours amid crowds that included romping children and dogs, gossiping wives and spirited—sometimes drunken—hecklers. Now the candidates must bring their messages and make their debating points in the forum where voters seek entertainment, on television, and so make their cases amid episodes of *Dallas* and *Dynasty* to an audience many of whose members are also reading the paper or are out in the kitchen breaking open a bag of potato chips.

Governor. Jim Martin, chemistry professor at Davidson College, congressman and member of the Ways and Means Committee, was elected in 1984 because of his own strengths and his opponents' weaknesses. The Democrats' 1984 primary was a bitter battle between former Charlotte Mayor Eddie Knox and Attorney General Rufus Edmisten, known nationally from his time as Senator Sam Ervin's counsel in the Watergate hearings. Edmisten won but Knox, miffed because he had not gotten Jim Hunt's support, reacted bitterly, with members of his family pointedly endorsing Martin. In office, Martin has pushed through a reduction in business taxes, a road improvement program, and more spending on schools plus an accelerated merit pay system for teachers—logical extensions of Hunt's program. He did clash bitterly with the Democratic legislature and campaigned against them in 1986; both Martin and the Democrats must have been disappointed when the Democrats made gains, but only minor ones, in the 1986 legislative elections. Martin has shown a mastery of his own party, despite the fundraising prowess of the Congressional Club, overpowering the Helms followers in the 1987 county conventions. He is eligible for a second four-year term in 1988; speculation about his opposition includes Lieutenant Governor Robert Jordan, son of Senator (1958–72) B. Everett Jordan, and Attorney General Lacy Thornburg.

Senators. Jesse Helms in the Senate is now where he promised North Carolina voters in 1984 he wouldn't be: at the head of the Republicans on the Foreign Relations Committee. It is also where Foreign Relations Republicans don't want him: they voted 7–0 for Richard Lugar, the outgoing chairman, for the post. But Helms, declining to lobby, made it an issue of seniority; he came to the Senate four years ahead of Lugar though they got on Foreign Relations at the same time. "I am sorry to disappoint you folks," Helms told the press as he emerged from the closed session, "but you lost"—that is, Helms won 24–17. Crucial were the votes of quite different Republicans, like Lowell Weicker, who feared rightly that their own committee posts might be endangered if seniority wasn't rigorously followed.

Did Helms dishonor his pledge to the voters? He can argue that he didn't: he promised not to become chairman, and kept that promise, gritting his teeth while Lugar supported sanctions and exerted crucial pressure for Corazon Aquino and against Ferdinand Marcos in 1986. Now that he can't chair Agriculture any more, and after presiding over the writing of a new farm bill that didn't gut tobacco programs, he may feel he has fulfilled his promise. In any case, the Foreign Affairs position, with the staff it confers, gives Helms great leverage to run the kind of alternative foreign policy he has been pushing since Ronald Reagan was elected. He insists that he is only trying to see that a careerist State Department and public-relations-minded White House advisers don't prevent Reagan from being Reagan, that the appointments he is forcing through, the holds he puts on other appointments, the questions he asks and policies he pushes are just an attempt to make sure the Administration is true to the policies for which it was elected.

Ronald Reagan might not always agree. He is known to have little use for Helms personally, even though Helms played a vital role in the 1976 campaign, keeping Reagan's candidacy alive after five straight primary defeats and then helping him win the North Carolina primary; otherwise his candidacy would not have gone on to the Kansas City convention, and he might have been a 69-year-old has-been rather than a frontrunner for the 1980 nomination. But Reagan dislikes Helms for the same reasons so many Senators do: he is truer to his principles than to his allies, and he insists on making his points in ways that make it harder rather than easier to achieve their mutual goals.

Thus Helms has been almost continuously frustrated on cultural issues: abortion is still allowed, state-written prayers are forbidden in public schools, practices Helms regards as immoral are condoned and sometimes even approved all across the country, the Martin Luther King holiday Helms inveighed against (and won some votes on in 1984) is established. But this may not bother him as much as you might think. For Helms, the bearing of witness against evil seems more important, or at least more feasible, than the extirpation thereof. And if things he doesn't like suddenly disappeared, what would he attack? He is a genuine political innovator, the man who has knitted together a national constituency by direct mail, and has used Senate rules to create threats—through contrived roll call votes on issues that make no practical difference— that his followers can then respond to.

It has been successful politics in many ways, not the least of which is keeping in office for a third term a Senator with a strong negative core of voters in his home state almost amounting to a majority. But its positive effects on American life—positive as measured by Helms's own criteria—seem puny compared to the noise and furor and fuss being kicked up. Ironically, the 1988 presidential election may separate Helms from the constituency he has helped to create. Movement conservatives, frustrated by their failure to get all they want in the Reagan years, have been thrashing about against Republican frontrunner, Senator Robert Dole. But Helms has high regard and warm feelings for Bob Dole, whose close ally he has been in the Senate and who has helped him mightily on the Agriculture Committee. So Helms might support or be soft on a candidate many conservatives consider a moderate. As for 1990, Helms certainly cannot be counted out as a candidate for reelection. But he cannot be considered a shoo-in either.

Helms no longer has a sympathetic colleague—and would not have had one even if Republican James Broyhill rather than Democrat Terry Sanford had been elected in 1986. This was one of the year's close elections, with a result most observers didn't anticipate. Broyhill became an incumbent when Martin appointed him to the seat after John East's death, but he campaigned woodenly and talked mechanically about supporting President Reagan. Sanford hadn't won an election since 1960; he was considered too liberal; his unsuccessful presidential candidacy in 1976 did not add to his luster. But he campaigned with vigor and skill, attacking Broyhill for failing to persuade Reagan not to veto the protectionist textile bill the Democrats rammed through. Broyhill attacked Sanford for the sales tax on food he had passed as governor; Sanford turned that around by arguing that it was the only way the state could spend what it needed to on education. Sanford racked up the big majorities in east Carolina that Hunt had been unable to amass against Helms, ran even in the urban counties and the west as Hunt did, and won despite Broyhill's home district strength.

As governor during the testing civil rights years, and as president of Duke, one of the nation's great universities, Sanford brings to the Senate an unusual depth and range of experience. He snared seats on the Budget and Foreign Relations Committees, and on Banking and Ethics as well. Yet in his first outing in the national spotlight he showed unsureness. He was one of the few Democrats opposed to the highway bill President Reagan vetoed in 1987, and when it became apparent that he was the crucial vote on overriding, he hesitated, voted "present," switched two minutes later to sustain Reagan's veto, then on reconsideration changed his mind again and voted to override. Sanford explained that he wanted to give a "victory" to a beleaguered President and then to support his party, but he showed peculiar indecisiveness for such a seasoned politician.

Presidential politics. North Carolina has a relatively early presidential primary. It played a key role in 1976, keeping Ronald Reagan in the race; it has never had much impact on the Democratic side.

In the general election, North Carolina has been winnable for the Democrats when they nominate a southerner for president and well out of reach when they do not.

Congressional districting. North Carolina's congressional districting, modified by a federal court to meet the requirements of the Voting Rights Act, has produced some of the closest results of the 1980s in election after election. This is straight-ticket country now, and seriously contested races usually don't vary by much more than a couple of points from the top of the state ticket (Helms–Hunt in 1984, Sanford–Broyhill in 1986). In 1982 the 2d, 3d, 4th, 6th, 8th, and 11th Districts were seriously contested; in 1984 the 4th, 5th, 6th, 8th, 9th, and 11th; in 1986, the 4th, 5th, 6th, 9th, and 11th were. Most of them probably will be again in 1988 and 1990. Plenty of money is spent in these races: the major party candidates spent a total of $5.8 million in 1982, $6.0 million in 1984, and $8.9 million in 1986.

This has an effect in the House. North Carolina Democrats have become party loyalists, sticking together to get favors—like support of their tobacco positions and for trade restrictions on textiles—from other Democrats and to exert leverage to keep the caucus from getting too liberal. The Democratic leadership in turn has helped the North Carolinians all it can. As for the Republicans, their most important member was Broyhill, as ranking Republican on John Dingell's Energy and Commerce Committee. None of the rest can come close to matching his seniority, proven competence, or clout.

The People: Est. Pop. 1986: 6,331,000; Pop. 1980: 5,881,766, up 7.7% 1980–86 and 15.7% 1970–80; 2.63% of U.S. total, 10th largest. 14% with 1–3 yrs. col., 13% with 4+ yrs. col.; 14.8% below poverty level. Single ancestry: 23% English, 5% German, 4% Irish, 1% Scottish, French. Households (1980): 77% family, 43% with children, 63% married couples; 31.6% housing units rented; median monthly rent: $135; median house value: $36,000. Voting age pop. (1980): 4,224,031; 20% Black, 1% American Indian, 1% Spanish origin. Registered voters (1986): 3,080,990; 2,114,536 D (69%), 836,726 R (27%), 129,728 unaffiliated (4%).

1986 Share of Federal Tax Burden: $16,138,000,000; 2.15% of U.S. total, 13th largest.

1986 Share of Federal Expenditures

	Total		Non-Defense		Defense	
Total Expend	$15,746m	(1.90%)	$11,910m	(1.98%)	$3,836m	(1.67%)
St/Lcl Grants	2,281m	(2.03%)	2,279m	(2.03%)	2m	(1.80%)
Salary/Wages	3,163m	(2.62%)	932m	(1.59%)	2,231m	(3.60%)
Pymnts to Indiv	8,421m	(2.31%)	7,866m	(2.27%)	555m	(3.12%)
Procurement	1,530m	(0.74%)	483m	(0.87%)	1,047m	(0.70%)
Research/Other	352m	(1.32%)	350m	(1.31%)	1m	(4.17%)

Political Lineup: Governor, James G. (Jim) Martin (R); Lt. Gov., Robert B. (Bob) Jordan III (D); Secy. of State, Thad Eure (D); Atty. Gen., Lacy H. Thornburg (D); Treasurer, Harlan Boyles (D); Auditor, Edward Renfrow (D). State Senate, 50 (40 D and 10 R); State House of Representatives, 120 (84 D and 36 R). Senators, Jesse A. Helms (R) and Terry Sanford (D). Representatives, 11 (4 D and 7 R).

1984 Presidential Vote

Reagan (R) 1,346,481 (62%)
Mondale (D) 824,287 (38%)

1984 Democratic Presidential Primary

Mondale 342,324 (36%)
Hart. 289,877 (30%)
Jackson 243,945 (25%)
Five others, no pref. 84,711 (9%)

1980 Presidential Vote

Reagan (R) 915,018 (49%)
Carter (D). 873,635 (47%)
Anderson (I) 52,800 (3%)

GOVERNOR

Gov. James G. (Jim) Martin (R)

Elected 1984, term expires Jan. 1989; b. Dec. 11, 1935, Savannah, GA; home, Lake Norman; Davidson Col., B.S. 1957, Princeton U., Ph.D. 1960; Presbyterian; married (Dorothy).

Career: Prof., Davidson Col., 1960–72; Mecklenberg Cnty. Bd. of Commissioners, 1966–72, Chmn., 1967–68, 1970–71; U.S. House of Reps., 1972–84.

Office: State Capitol, Raleigh 27611, 919-733-4240.

Election Results

1984 gen.	James G. (Jim) Martin (R)	1,208,167	(54%)
	Rufus Edmisten (D)	1,011,209	(45%)
1984 prim.	James G. (Jim) Martin (R)	128,714	(92%)
	Ruby T. Hooper (R)	11,640	(8%)
1980 gen.	James B. Hunt, Jr. (D)	1,143,145	(62%)
	Beverly Lake (R)	691,449	(37%)

SENATORS

Sen. Jesse A. Helms (R)

Elected 1972, seat up 1990; b. Oct. 18, 1921, Monroe; home, Raleigh; Wingate Col., Wake Forest U.; Baptist; married (Dorothy).

Career: Navy, WWII; City Ed., *Raleigh Times*; A. A. to U.S. Sens. Willis Smith, 1951–53 and Alton Lennon, 1953; Exec. Dir., NC Bankers Assn., 1953–60; Raleigh City Cncl., 1957–61; Exec. V.P., WRAL-TV and Tobacco Radio Network, 1960–72.

Office: 402 DSOB 20510, 202-224-6342. Also P.O. Box 2888, Raleigh 27602, 919-856-4630; and P.O. Box 2944, Hickory 28603, 704-322-5170.

Committees: *Agriculture, Nutrition, and Forestry* (3d of 9 R). Subcommittees: Agricultural Production and Stabilization of Prices (Ranking Member); Domestic and Foreign Marketing and Product Promotion; Nutrition and Investigation. *Foreign Relations* (Ranking Member of 9 R). Subcommittee: African Affairs. *Rules and Administration* (4th of 7 R). *Select Committee on Ethics* (2d of 3 R).

Group Ratings

	ADA	ACLU	COPE	CFA	LCV	ACU	NTU	NSI	COC	CEI
1986	0	7	7	7	17	100	65	100	95	88
1985	0	—	7	7	—	100	76	—	93	—

National Journal Ratings

	1986 LIB — 1986 CONS	1985 LIB — 1985 CONS
Economic	0% — 84%	0% — 86%
Social	0% — 91%	0% — 83%
Foreign	0% — 86%	12% — 80%

Key Votes

1) Ease Gun Cont	FOR	5) Grm-Rdmn Def Red	FOR	9) Rehnquist Nom	FOR
2) Immig Reform	AGN	6) Contra Aid	FOR	10) Tax Reform	AGN
3) Lmt Text Imp	FOR	7) SDI Funding	FOR	11) Drug Death Pen	AGN
4) Aid Tobac Ind	FOR	8) Lmt PAC Contrib	AGN	12) S Africa Sanc	AGN

Election Results

1984 general	Jesse A. Helms (R).................	1,156,768	(52%)	($16,917,559)
	James B. (Jim) Hunt, Jr. (D)	1,070,488	(48%)	($9,461,924)
1984 primary	Jesse A. Helms (R)...................	134,675	(91%)	
	George Wimbish (R)...................	13,899	(9%)	
1978 general	Jesse A. Helms (R)...................	619,151	(55%)	($8,123,205)
	John R. Ingram (D)	516,663	(45%)	($264,088)

Campaign Contributions and Expenditures

1979-84		Direct Cont. 1979-84		PACS Breakdown 1979-84			
Receipts	$17,180,720	Indiv.	$16,200,119	Corp.	$377,630	T/M/H	$214,535
Expend.	$16,917,559	Party	$20,517	Labor	$0	Agr.	$56,197
Debt	$429,549	PACS	$865,528	Ideo.	$178,110	CWOS	$22,027

Sen. Terry Sanford (D)

Elected 1986, seat up 1992; b. Aug. 20, 1917, Laurinburg, IL; home, Durham; U. of NC, B.A. 1939, J.D. 1946; United Methodist; married (Margaret).

Career: FBI Agent, 1941–42; Army, WWII; Asst. Dir., U. of NC Inst. of Govt., 1946–48; Practicing atty., 1948–60; Gov. of NC, 1961–65; Pres., Duke U., 1969–85.

Offices: 716 HSOB 20510, 202-224-3154. Also P.O. Box 25009, Raleigh 27661, 919-856-4401; and P.O. Box 2137, Asheville 28802, 704-254-3099; and 401 W. Trade St., Rm. 212, Charlotte 28202, 704-371-6800.

Committees: *Banking, Housing and Urban Affairs* (8th of 11 D). Subcommittees: International Finance and Monetary Policy; Securities. *Budget* (9th of 13 D). *Foreign Relations* (8th of 11 D). Subcommittees: African Affairs; Near Eastern and South Asian Affairs; Western Hemisphere and Peace Corps Affairs. *Select Committee on Ethics* (3d of 3 D).

Group Ratings and Key Votes: Newly Elected

Election Results

1986 general	Terry Sanford (D)	823,662	(52%)	($4,168,509)
	James T. Broyhill (R)	767,668	(48%)	($5,188,244)
1986 primary	Terry Sanford (D)	409,394	(60%)	
	John Ingram (D)	111,557	(16%)	
	Fountain Odom (D)	49,689	(7%)	
	William Irwin Belk (D)	33,821	(5%)	
1980 general	John P. East (R)	898,064	(50%)	($1,175,875)
	Robert Morgan (D)	887,653	(49%)	($948,209)

Campaign Contributions and Expenditures

1985-86		Direct Cont. 1985-86		PACS Breakdown 1985-86			
Receipts	$4,181,701	Indiv.	$2,478,344	Corp.	$149,503	T/M/H	$130,550
Expend.	$4,168,509	Party	$22,300	Labor	$245,250	Agr.	$3,000
Unspent	$13,190	PACS	$658,632	Ideo.	$149,329	CWOS	$8,000
		Cand.	$1,082,000				

FIRST DISTRICT

The word "Croatoan" carved on a tree was the only record left by the first English settlement in North America, the lost colony of Roanoke. The settlers had unknowingly found their way to a part of the continent that even 400 years later would be only lightly settled: the Outer Banks and Pamlico Sounds of North Carolina. The open beaches and strong ocean currents that made this eastern extremity of North Carolina attractive to early settlers impeded later ones: there is no really good port here, and Cape Hatteras, where the warm Gulf Stream meets the colder currents, creates seas that have sunk countless ships. The constant winds brought the Wright brothers here in 1903 to fly the first airplane, and they bring tourists to the beaches of Nags Head and Duck every summer now. But most of the people in east Carolina live inland, on the densely settled tobacco farm land and in little towns and cities. The largest, with 35,000 people, is Greenville, home of East Carolina University; smaller towns, like Edenton and New Bern, still boast colonial houses and buildings which have survived out of pride and because it never paid here, as it did in New York or Boston, to tear them down and build something else.

This has always been Democratic country, and still is: even Walter Mondale got a respectable vote in the 1st District. Jesse Helms has cut into the Democratic vote sharply, but even so this was a Hunt district in 1984 and overwhelmingly for Terry Sanford in 1986. National Democratic politicians now come from the required-to-be-smoke-free rooms of Minnesota, New York, and San Francisco. But they cannot forget, if they count their votes, that it's awfully hard for them to win 270 electoral votes without carrying a big margin in east Carolina.

The 1st Congressional District of North Carolina includes much of the east Carolina plain and waterways. Its congressman is Walter Jones, a Democrat first chosen in a 1966 special election. Well past 70, representative of a Deep South district heavily dependent on tobacco, Jones must be, many observers would think, an old-fashioned Dixiecrat uninterested in anything but local issues. Not exactly. He used to hold the Tobacco and Peanuts Subcommittee chair on Agriculture, a post of obvious importance to this district. But he gave it up in 1980 to take over the chairmanship of the Merchant Marine and Fisheries Committee. To be sure, he can assure constituents that it's still in the good hands of Charles Rose, from North Carolina's 7th District, a canny political operator with lots of friends in all parts of the Democratic party; and he can assure them also—and at the drop of a hat will—that Merchant Marine is important to them too.

For this aging and often ill congressman has taken an aging and often ailing committee and subject matter and pumped life and verve into them. He is working to patch up the tattered system of maritime subsidies and exemptions, and has adeptly attached his cause to every topical issue that comes along. If you are worried about our trade deficit, here is Chairman Jones with a bill to require Japanese cars to be transported in U.S. ships. If you are worried about the drug traffic, here he is with a plan to expand the Coast Guard. Just when you're reading about the divers who found the wreck of the Titanic, here he is with a bill to prevent commercial exploitation of it. And if you're not worried now about the Navy's sealift capacity in time of war, here is Chairman Jones with facts and figures and arguments about why we must subsidize and protect high-wage U.S. flag ships in order to have the sealift capacity when we need it.

Of course there are local interests at stake. Jones is pushing a five-year Albemarle-Pamlico Estuary study and is urging stabilization of the oft-wandering Oregon Inlet between the barrier isles. Fishermen and those who are concerned about coastal environments are surely grateful for some of his other efforts. It begins to look as if Jones has been aiming through his long congressional career at holding this chairmanship, which was also held by his 1st District predecessor Herbert Bonner. One tipoff is this: he votes a solid national Democratic line on most issues. Committee chairmen are elected by the Democratic Caucus, and Jones has obviously been taking care for years, long before most members thought he wanted the post, to make sure that most northern liberal Democrats would have no reason to vote reflexively against him for this chairmanship he dearly wants. At the same time he has taken care to keep his standing high at home. In 1984 a high-spending primary opponent held him to 61% of the vote, but he had no primary opponent in 1986, and seems determined to convince voters that he is an active and useful representative. In early 1987 some conservatives were talking about running William Keyes, a black conservative from the district who is a lobbyist for South Africa, but it seems unlikely he could seriously threaten Jones.

The People: Pop. 1980: 536,219, up 13.2% 1970–80. Households (1980): 77% family, 43% with children, 61% married couples; 32.4% housing units rented; median monthly rent: $111; median house value: $33,600. Voting age pop. (1980): 382,422; 32% Black, 1% Spanish origin.

1984 Presidential Vote: Reagan (R) 109,441   (57%)
                                Mondale (D) 82,194   (43%)

Rep. Walter B. Jones (D)

Elected Feb. 5, 1966; b. Aug. 19, 1913, Fayetteville; home, Farmville; NC St. U., B.S. 1934; Baptist; married (Elizabeth).

Career: Office supply business, 1934–49; Mayor of Farmville, 1949–53; NC Gen. Assembly, 1955–59; NC Senate, 1965–66.

Offices: 241 CHOB 20515, 202-225-3101. Also 108 E. Wilson St., P.O. Drawer 90, Farmville 27828, 919-753-3082.

Committees: *Agriculture* (2d of 26 D). Subcommittees: Tobacco and Peanuts; Wheat, Soybeans and Feed Grains. *Merchant Marine and Fisheries* (Chairman of 25 D). Subcommittee: Oversight and Investigations (Chairman).

Group Ratings

	ADA	ACLU	COPE	CFA	LCV	ACU	NTU	NSI	COC	CEI
1986	55	61	47	67	43	22	27	10	40	17
1985	70	—	46	42	—	5	27	—	25	—

National Journal Ratings

	1986 LIB — 1986 CONS		1985 LIB — 1985 CONS	
Economic	66% —	32%	61% —	38%
Social	44% —	56%	69% —	31%
Foreign	63% —	37%	80% —	17%

Key Votes

1) Lmt Cln Water Act	AGN	5) Retain Gun Cont	AGN	9) Aid Angola Reb	AGN
2) Rpl Tobac Sub	AGN	6) Contra Aid	AGN	10) Tax Reform	FOR
3) Grm-Rdmn Def Red	AGN	7) Lmt Text Imp	FOR	11) S Africa Sanc	—
4) Ban Polygraph	AGN	8) Limit SDI	FOR	12) Immig Reform	AGN

Election Results

1986 general	Walter B. Jones (D)	91,122	(70%)	($87,114)
	Howard Moye (R).....................	39,912	(30%)	($47,184)
1986 primary	Walter B. Jones (D) unopposed			
1984 general	Walter B. Jones (D)	122,815	(67%)	($164,033)
	Herbert W. Lee (R)...................	60,153	(33%)	($30,185)

Campaign Contributions and Expenditures

1985-86		Direct Cont. 1985-86		PACS Breakdown 1985-86			
Receipts	$196,760	Indiv.	$25,004	Corp.	$55,050	T/M/H	$37,900
Expend.	$87,114	Party	$5,000	Labor	$31,350	Agr.	$3,000
Unspent	$253,016	PACS	$131,550	Ideo.	$4,250	CWOS	$0

SECOND DISTRICT

After the Civil War, as thousands of soldiers slogged back home, a young Confederate veteran returned to his family's farm near where Durham is today. This part of the coastal plain had been tobacco growing country since it was settled in the 18th century, but tobacco was not the bonanza crop it had been in colonial Virginia; it was sold mainly as chewing tobacco, and the market was limited. This young farmer, James B. Duke, had another idea: he invented the cigarette and started a company that became the American Tobacco Trust; he established

Durham as it now is as the site for his early cigarette families and near the end of his life, from his mansion in New York City, he endowed Durham's Duke University, now one of the great institutions in the land.

Duke's story illustrates, among other things, the centrality of tobacco to the economy and, more important, to the life of coastal North Carolina: this is a labor-intensive crop, and all the networks of life here depend on it. North Carolina's 2d Congressional District occupies a major portion of its tobacco lands north of Raleigh and south of the Virginia line. Durham is its largest city, though its boundary wiggles around and doesn't include Raleigh just to the east; on the other side of Raleigh it includes the town of Rocky Mount. You can still find tobacco marketed here in the old courthouse towns, and there are textiles produced in mills scattered here and there, usually near rivers or main highways; new subdivisions are being built on farm and forest land out in the country. Historically, textile mills didn't hire blacks, but Duke's and the other tobacco factories did, and many black farmers grow tobacco as well (and today a higher proportion of blacks than whites smoke cigarettes). The 2d District has more blacks than any other House seat in North Carolina, 36% of the population in 1980, 28% of the registered voters in 1981 and 37% in 1986.

The 2d District was represented by a black in Congress—but not since the last century. George White, a Republican and a contemporary of James B. Duke, won the seat in 1896 and 1898; the Democrats, running on a platform of education and segregation, won it in 1900 and have held it ever since. For 30 years it was held by a conservative, white-linen-suited Democrat, L. H. Fountain; when he retired in 1982, he was succeeded by a Democrat of similar ilk, Tim Valentine. Yet Valentine has had serious competition from talented black candidates for the post, and was nearly defeated.

Both challengers came from Durham, which has long had a sophisticated black political and business community. H. M. (Mickey) Michaux, who ran in 1982, had been U.S. attorney in the Carter years. He sparked a large black turnout—109,000 people voted in the 1982 runoff, as against 93,000 in the general election, and got 46% of the vote; he got 14% as a write-in in the general election that year, though he repudiated the effort. His defeat was cited constantly by Jesse Jackson in 1984 as one reason for abolishing runoff primaries. In 1984 the challenger was Ken Spaulding, a state legislator and member of the family that owns a big insurance company in Durham. In a turnout of 125,000, Spaulding won 48% of the vote.

In 1986, however, no primary opposition surfaced, and nothing came of the idea, bruited in some quarters, of an independent black candidacy. Established local politicians like Michaux and Spaulding have a stake in the Democratic party and while they lost by tantalizingly narrow margins they have a stake too in the principle of majority rule. The independent candidacy, like Jackson's idea of no-runoff primaries, are strategies based on minority-rule, strategies that are ultimately unsustainable in a single-member-district democracy like ours: for if you can't win a majority, sooner or later the voters will coalesce around one opponent and beat you. Now that the Mississippi 2d District has elected Mike Espy, the North Carolina 2d will not be the first non-metropolitan southern district to elect a black; but it could do so some election soon.

In the meantime, Valentine has an obvious political incentive to provide services to black constituents and vote their way on major issues; for a black-based candidacy is the only way he could lose. He serves now on the Public Works and Transportation and Science, Space and Technology committees; he has a seat on the latter's Science Research and Technology Subcommittee, a politically useful post for a congressman whose district takes in part of the Research Triangle high tech park between Raleigh, Durham and Chapel Hill. His instincts and background are those of a Boll Weevil Democrat, but his voting record is well in the mainstream of North Carolina Democrats these days, which is to say often in line with those of the Democratic majority.

The People: Pop. 1980: 536,210, up 10.4% 1970–80. Households (1980): 76% family, 43% with children, 59% married couples; 39.0% housing units rented; median monthly rent: $119; median house

value: $34,700. Voting age pop. (1980): 382,220; 36% Black, 1% Spanish origin.

1984 Presidential Vote: Reagan (R) 103,780   (53%)
                               Mondale (D) 92,146   (47%)

Rep. Tim Valentine (D)

Elected 1982; b. Mar. 15, 1926, Nash County; home, Nashville; The Citadel, A.B. 1948, U. of NC, LL.B., 1952; Baptist; married (Barbara).

Career: Air Force, WWII; NC House of Reps., 1955–60; Legal Advisor to the Gov., 1965, Counsel to the Gov., 1967; Chmn., NC Dem. Exec. Cmtee., 1966–68; Practicing atty., 1952–82.

Offices: 1510 LHOB 20515, 202-225-4531. Also 121 E. Parrish St., Durham 27701, 919-683-1495; and 124 Station Sq., Rocky Mount 27804, 919-446-1147.

Committees: *Public Works and Transportation* (15th of 32 D). Subcommittees: Aviation; Water Resources. *Science, Space and Technology* (13th of 27 D). Subcommittees: Energy Research and Development; Natural Resources, Agriculture Research and Environment; Science, Research and Technology.

Group Ratings

	ADA	ACLU	COPE	CFA	LCV	ACU	NTU	NSI	COC	CEI
1986	30	25	39	50	37	55	31	70	65	28
1985	35	—	38	58	—	48	28	—	59	—

National Journal Ratings

	1986 LIB	—	1986 CONS	1985 LIB	—	1985 CONS
Economic	45%	—	54%	48%	—	50%
Social	23%	—	74%	57%	—	42%
Foreign	44%	—	55%	42%	—	56%

Key Votes

1) Lmt Cln Water Act	AGN	5) Retain Gun Cont	AGN	9) Aid Angola Reb	FOR
2) Rpl Tobac Sub	AGN	6) Contra Aid	AGN	10) Tax Reform	FOR
3) Grm-Rdmn Def Red	FOR	7) Lmt Text Imp	FOR	11) S Africa Sanc	FOR
4) Ban Polygraph	AGN	8) Limit SDI	FOR	12) Immig Reform	AGN

Election Results

1986 general	Tim Valentine (D)...................	95,320	(75%)	($164,680)
	Bud McElhaney (R)..................	32,515	(25%)	($69,193)
1986 primary	Tim Valentine (D) unopposed			
1984 general	Tim Valentine (D)...................	122,292	(68%)	($348,207)
	Frank H. Hill (R)	58,312	(32%)	($38,557)

Campaign Contributions and Expenditures

1985-86		Direct Cont. 1985-86		PACS Breakdown 1985-86			
Receipts	$178,317	Indiv.	$59,845	Corp.	$43,100	T/M/H	$40,955
Expend.	$164,680	Party	$5,000	Labor	$15,350	Agr.	$3,250
Unspent	$51,098	PACS	$108,945	Ideo.	$6,200	CWOS	$90

THIRD DISTRICT

The flat coastal plain of eastern North Carolina, with its small farms and little cities, its roadside textile mills and subdivisions cropping up on ten acres of farmland, is part of the historical Democratic bedrock of the United States. Yet it seems to have little in common with the Democracy that gathered in San Francisco in 1984 or in the three conventions before that. Those Democrats believe in liberating people from cultural restraints, they mistrust the American military, and they see government control and guidance of the economy as the means to their end of economic equality. On all those points almost everyone—at least almost everyone in the large white majority here—disagrees. Traditional religion remains strong here, may well be getting stronger; and as the rest of America moves from liberation to restraint, confidence here in traditional morality grows rather than wanes. Respect for the military remains strong in a part of the country bristling with military bases—Seymour Johnson Air Force Base near Goldsboro, the Marine Corps's Camp Lejeune on the swampy coast, the Army's Fort Bragg near Fayetteville; the sight of servicemen with their short haircuts cruising on one of the garish strip highways outside the base is not an exotic one here.

Otherwise, government seems remote, and while people here usually have no principled objection to government action, they are suspicious of programs that spend vast sums in decaying northern slums even as they take for granted the programs—farm subsidies and aid, dams and highways and harbor improvements—that affect their own community. In local and state elections the 3d Congressional District, which includes much of the coastal plain of North Carolina from Camp Lejeune inland past Goldsboro all the way to the golf course country around Southern Pines, remains steadfastly Democratic. In presidential elections it voted twice for Jimmy Carter but is otherwise Republican; it has voted three times for Senator Jesse Helms.

For 52 years this district was down in a kind of succession from one congressman to the next; but no more. From 1934 to 1960 the seat was held by Graham Barden, a stuffy and bigoted conservative, who as chairman of the Education and Labor Committee refused to call on the number two Democrat, Adam Clayton Powell, to ask questions, because he was black. When Barden retired in in 1960 he was succeeded by David Henderson, who had served on his staff. When Henderson, who became chairman of the Post Office and Civil Service Committee, retired in 1976, he was succeeded by a member of his staff, Charles Whitley. When Whitley decided to retire in 1986, the first candidate to announce was his staffer Lewis Renn. But this time Renn was beaten in the Democratic primary.

The winner was Martin Lancaster, an experienced state legislator from Goldsboro. Lancaster grew up on a tobacco farm, served in the Navy in the Vietnam war, served since 1978 in the legislature and in his third session was voted the fifth most effective legislator of 120 by the state Center for Public Policy Research. He was an ally of Governor Jim Hunt and shepherded major bills, like a tough drunk driving measure, through the legislature. The primary contest turned out to be a classic friends-and-neighbors contest; Lancaster got 85% in a big turnout in his home county and only 13% in Renn's. But Lancaster did best where no other candidate was strong and led 44%–26% in the first primary and Renn declined to call for a runoff. Lancaster seems to share the basic values of the large majority here; and if that seems contradictory with his identification with the more liberal of the parties and with politicians like Hunt, it makes more sense when you ponder Whitley's description of him as "caring and civic-minded." For this tradition-minded Democratic constituency's values are based not on abstract principles of laissez-faire market economics or cultural conservatism, but are anchored in the facts of everyday experience and a lifetime of exposure to community institutions.

The People: Pop. 1980: 535,906, up 13.2% 1970–80. Households (1980): 80% family, 47% with children, 65% married couples; 33.2% housing units rented; median monthly rent: $123; median house value: $31,500. Voting age pop. (1980): 379,853; 25% Black, 2% Spanish origin, 1% American Indian.

1984 Presidential Vote: Reagan (R) 98,076   (61%)
                              Mondale (D) 63,862   (39%)

Rep. H. Martin Lancaster (D)

Elected 1976; b. Mar. 24, 1943, Wayne Cnty.; home, Goldsboro; U. of NC, Chapel Hill, A.B. 1965, J.D. 1967; Presbyterian; married (Alice).

Career: Research Asst., U.S. Senate Subcommittee on Constitutional Rights, 1964–67; Navy, 1967–70; NC House of Reps., 1978–86; Practicing atty.

Offices: 1408 LHOB 20515, 202-225-3415. Also Fed. Bldg., Goldsboro 27530, 919-736-1844.

Committees: *Public Works and Transportation* (24th of 32 D). Subcommittees: Investigations and Oversight; Public Buildings and Grounds; Surface Transportation. *Small Business* (23d of 27 D). Subcommittees: Exports, Tourism and Special Problems; Procurement, Innovation and Minority Enterprise Development.

Group Ratings and Key Votes: Newly Elected

Election Results

1986 general	H. Martin Lancaster (D)	71,460	(64%)	($439,725)
	Gerald B. Hurst (R)	39,408	(36%)	($61,265)
1986 primary	H. Martin Lancaster (D)	31,971	(44%)	
	Lewis W. Renn (D)	18,668	(26%)	
	Walter P. Henderson (D).	13,323	(18%)	
	Nurham O. Warwick (D)	9,049	(12%)	
1984 general	Charles O. Whitley (D)	100,185	(64%)	($36,293)
	Danny G. Moody (R)	56,096	(36%)	

Campaign Contributions and Expenditures

1985-86		Direct Cont. 1985-86		PACS Breakdown 1985-86			
Receipts	$439,428	Indiv.	$265,301	Corp.	$30,350	T/M/H	$6,584
Expend.	$439,725	Party	$9,999	Labor	$11,850	Agr.	$2,000
Unspent	$1,702	PACS	$140,097	Ideo.	$28,806	CWOS	$1,250
		Cand.	$20,166				

FOURTH DISTRICT

How many futurologists, asked 20 or 30 years ago to name the boom metropolitan areas of the 1980s, would have picked Raleigh-Durham, North Carolina? Not many. Raleigh was a sleepy state capital, with aging downtown buildings in the middle 1950s; Durham was a cigarette factory town, with a university off to the side; Chapel Hill was a jewel, but a tiny one, of a university town nearby. But in the middle 1950s Governor Luther Hodges opened Research Triangle Park between the three towns, as an attempt to get high tech business into North Carolina's low-wage environment before anyone heard the term high tech. After 30 years, it is plain it succeeded. By the middle 1980s the Raleigh-Durham area had one of the nation's lowest unemployment rates and wage levels and economic growth which North Carolinians of Hodges's era would have found unbelievable. There are still some poor neighborhoods here, and the downtowns are not glittering; but evidence of the growth is apparent in the shopping centers and pine-shaded neighborhoods of colonial houses farther out.

The 4th Congressional District of North Carolina includes Raleigh, Chapel Hill, and three rural counties, one north of Raleigh and two to the west (Durham is in the 2d District). The politics in the rural counties is typical of old North Carolina: two are conservative Democratic, the farthest west, which has a Quaker tradition, is solidly Republican. But Chapel Hill and surrounding Orange County vote almost like a university town in California or the Midwest; Raleigh and Wake County, the home base of Jesse Helms and Jim Hunt, of Terry Sanford's law firm and Tom Ellis's Congressional Club, is much fought-over territory. In the late 1970s it became increasingly Republican as it grew more affluent.

Congressional elections in the 1980s have been turbulent. For some time district and congressman were mismatched: Ike Andrews was a rural Democrat first elected in 1972 who was content to run on his party label when it no longer guaranteed him a win; the surprising thing, and an example of the swing that year against Helms and his allies, was that Andrews held on in 1982 after he was arrested a month before the election and charged with drunk driving, in a state that did not allow liquor by the drink until 1978. He lost in 1984 to Republican Bill Cobey, the former University of North Carolina athletic director and a strong Helms man. But Cobey proved to be mismatched too. He is strongly religious, and in September 1984 sent out a "dear Christian friend" letter pleading to potential direct mail contributors, "Will you help me so our voice will not be silenced and then replaced by someone who is not willing to take a strong stand for the principles outlined in the Word of God?"

This was too much for Cobey's Democratic opponent David Price and too much for the 4th District. Price, who was a political science professor at Duke, and headed the state Democratic party and the staff of the national Democrats' 1982 delegate selection reform commission for Jim Hunt, also has a divinity degree (he was a contemporary of Gary Hart and John Danforth at Yale) and is active in the Southern Baptist Church; he demanded and got an apology from Cobey. As for the 4th District, it has tended to be a little less culturally conservative than the rest of North Carolina and, though Cobey liked to attack Price as a Hunt clone, went for Hunt over Helms in the 1984 election. In 1986 the result was not much in doubt: Price, who had won a solid primary victory over state Senator Wilma Woodard, pummeled Cobey as a man isolated from mainstream thinking in both parties, and won the general election with 56%. He may have competition from Congressional Club operative Tom Fetzer in 1988, but in this district he would be the clear favorite to win.

The 4th is one of several North Carolina districts that have seen close contests throughout the 1980s; will it change hands again soon? Possibly, but Price seems better matched to the district than any of his predecessors. His academic background commands a certain respect, yet at the same time he has none of the obtuseness of so many academics and has proved himself in the very practical world of North Carolina politics. He has seats on the Banking and Science Committees.

The People: Pop. 1980: 533,580, up 27.3% 1970–80. Households (1980): 73% family, 40% with children, 60% married couples; 35.0% housing units rented; median monthly rent: $182; median house value: $47,000. Voting age pop. (1980): 395,635; 18% Black, 1% Spanish origin, 1% Asian origin.

1984 Presidential Vote: Reagan (R) 137,174   (60%)
Mondale (D) 90,622   (40%)

Rep. David E. Price (D)

Elected 1986; b. Aug. 17, 1940, Johnson City, TN; home, Chapel Hill; U. of NC, Chapel Hill, B.A. 1961, Yale U., B.D. 1964, Ph.D. 1969; Baptist; married (Lisa).

Career: Leg. Aide, Sen. E.L. Bartlett, 1963–67; Pol. Sci. Prof., Duke U., 1973–86.

Offices: 1223 LHOB 20515, 202-225-1784. Also 225 Hillsborough St., Ste, 330 Raleigh 27603, 919-857-8611; 1777 Chapel Hill-Durham Blvd., Ste. 100, Chapel Hill 27514, 919-967-8500; 101 Fed. Bldg., Sunset Ave., Asheboro 27203, 919-625-3060.

Committees: *Banking, Finance and Urban Affairs* (30th of 31 D). Subcommittees: Economic Stabilization; Financial Institutions Supervision, Regulation and Insurance. *Science, Space and Technology* (25th of 27 D). Subcommittees: Investigations and Oversight; Science, Research and Technology.

Group Ratings and Key Votes: Newly Elected

Election Results

1986 general	David E. Price (D)	92,216	(56%)	($854,616)
	William W. Cobey (D)	73,469	(44%)	($792,031)
1986 primary	David E. Price (D)	32,098	(48%)	
	Wilma Woodard (D)	21,422	(32%)	
	William W. Webb (D)	6,488	(10%)	
	Kirsten Nyrop (D)	6,450	(10%)	
1984 general	William W. (Bill) Cobey, Jr. (R)	117,436	(51%)	($514,538)
	Ike F. Andrews (D)	114,462	(49%)	($276,263)

Campaign Contributions and Expenditures

1985-86		Direct Cont. 1985-86		PACS Breakdown 1985-86			
Receipts	$863,825	Indiv.	$426,388	Corp.	$21,650	T/M/H	$38,200
Expend.	$854,616	Party	$15,423	Labor	$156,900	Agr.	$500
Debts	$9,207	PACS	$272,778	Ideo.	$55,028	CWOS	$500
		Cand.	$87,259				

FIFTH DISTRICT

The most thickly settled part of America's Piedmont—the rolling land east of the first Appalachian chain, the Blue Ridge—is in North Carolina. It is attractive land, well watered and green, the weather pleasant much of the year, escaping the extremes of the snowbound winters of the mountains or the humid, muggy summers of the swampy flatlands to the east. Before the Revolution a group of Mennonites, a religious sect from Pennsylvania and, earlier, from Germany, made a settlement here and called it Salem. Later it joined with the Southern Presbyterian settlement of Winston, and together they became one of North Carolina's largest cities, Winston-Salem. The city's name has been memorialized in two popular cigarette brands. For years it has been the headquarters of the R. J. Reynolds Company, and the Reynolds family has been among its grand benefactors; but RJR (as it was renamed) merged with Nabisco whose hotshot young president decided to move the headquarters to Atlanta. This slight to Winston-Salem's pride came a decade or so after the huge home town Wachovia Bank was eclipsed by Charlotte's NCNB.

Winston-Salem shares to some extent the political habits of the hills to the north and west. Here in hollows surrounded by ridges, there lives a Republicanism that grew up in opposition to the domination of the wealthy tobacco farmers on the coastal plain. While most recent

Republicans in the state, notably Senator Jesse Helms, have styled themselves as conservatives, mountain Republicans have been more insurgent in mood. When coastal Republicans talk about law and order, mountain Republicans are likely to think—not entirely with approval—of revenuers driving up into the hills and smashing moonshine stills.

The 5th Congressional District of North Carolina extends from Winston-Salem and the industrial town of Eden in the east to the mountains on both sides of the Blue Ridge in the west. The mountain Republican tradition lives on here, particularly in Wilkes County, home of the Holly Farms chicken operation, which only on the most unusual occasions votes Democratic. Winston-Salem shows signs of mountain influence as well. It has never showed much enthusiasm for Helms; in 1984 the city and surrounding Forsyth County voted against him and in favor of Governor Jim Hunt.

The pleasant landscape of the 5th District has been the scene in the 1970s and 1980s of one pitched political battle after another. Congressman Stephen Neal, a Democrat who beat Republican Wilmer "Vinegar Bend" Mizell in the Democratic year of 1974, has always looked precarious. Yet he has always won, and over various kinds of Republicans. In the 1980s he has faced two opponents, former state legislator Ann Bagnall and religious broadcaster Stuart Epperson, and beaten them both twice, the second time by a bigger margin than the first. But that may only be due to the fact that each ran first in a presidential year, when Republicans almost always do better in North Carolina. Only once, in 1982, has Neal gotten as much as 60% of the vote, and his most recent victory, over the eccentric Epperson, was with 54%. He may have another kind of Republican in 1988: Epperson was nearly beaten in the party's primary by Lyons Gray, a member of one of Winston-Salem's richest families, who could conceivably run again in 1988.

For all this turbulence Neal does not cut a commanding figure in the House. He is a member of the Banking Committee, and has worked hard to support ongoing funding of the International Monetary Fund and the Export-Import Bank—not things a political consultant would advise him to concentrate on. His votes on issues generally are similar to those of other North Carolina Democrats, which is to say not too far away from the Democratic norm in the House. He has had his successes on locally important issues, blocking the building of a dam on the scenic New River a decade ago and more recently opposing the placement of a high-level nuclear waste repository anywhere in the eastern United States.

The People: Pop. 1980: 535,212, up 16.5% 1970–80. Households (1980): 77% family, 42% with children, 64% married couples; 27.8% housing units rented; median monthly rent: $136; median house value: $36,500. Voting age pop. (1980): 388,006; 15% Black, 1% Spanish origin.

1984 Presidential Vote:

Reagan (R)	136,330	(64%)
Mondale (D)	76,012	(36%)

Rep. Stephen L. Neal (D)

Elected 1974; b. Nov. 7, 1934, Winston-Salem; home, Winston-Salem; U. of CA at Santa Barbara, U. of HI, A.B. 1959; Presbyterian; married (Landis).

Career: Bank executive, 1959–66; Newspaper business, 1966–74; Pres., Community Press, Inc., Suburban Newspapers, Inc., King Publishing Co., and Yadkin Printing Co., Inc.

Offices: 2463 RHOB 20515, 202-225-2071. Also 421 Fed. Bldg., Winston-Salem 27101, 919-761-3125.

Committees: *Banking, Finance and Urban Affairs* (5th of 31 D). Subcommittees: Domestic Monetary Policy (Chairman); Financial Institutions Supervision, Regulation and Insurance; Housing and Community Development; International Finance, Trade, and Monetary Policy. *Government Operations* (8th of 24 D). Subcommittee: Legislation and National Security.

Group Ratings

	ADA	ACLU	COPE	CFA	LCV	ACU	NTU	NSI	COC	CEI
1986	65	78	51	83	77	29	33	40	50	33
1985	50	—	50	67	—	33	41	—	48	—

National Journal Ratings

	1986 LIB — 1986 CONS		1985 LIB — 1985 CONS	
Economic	43%	— 56%	59%	— 41%
Social	57%	— 43%	73%	— 23%
Foreign	53%	— 46%	54%	— 45%

Key Votes

1) Lmt Cln Water Act	FOR	5) Retain Gun Cont	AGN	9) Aid Angola Reb	AGN
2) Rpl Tobac Sub	AGN	6) Contra Aid	AGN	10) Tax Reform	FOR
3) Grm-Rdmn Def Red	FOR	7) Lmt Text Imp	FOR	11) S Africa Sanc	FOR
4) Ban Polygraph	FOR	8) Limit SDI	FOR	12) Immig Reform	AGN

Election Results

1986 general	Stephen L. Neal (D)	86,410	(54%)	($494,014)
	Stuart Epperson (R)	73,261	(46%)	($939,377)
1986 primary	Stephen L. Neal (D) unopposed			
1984 general	Stephen L. Neal (D)	109,831	(51%)	($255,987)
	Stuart Epperson (R)	106,599	(49%)	($317,773)

Campaign Contributions and Expenditures

1985-86		Direct Cont. 85-86		PACS Breakdown 1985-86			
Receipts	$493,483	Indiv.	$178,772	Corp.	$116,300	T/M/H	$65,550
Expend.	$494,014	Party	$9,599	Labor	$50,325	Agr.	$5,950
Unspent	$43,650	PACS	$285,135	Ideo.	$41,610	CWOS	$5,400

SIXTH DISTRICT

Every year furniture store managers and owners from all over the country gather in the huge furniture mart in High Point, the center of the U.S. furniture business, for a giant trade show put on by manufacturers. The business grew here early in the 20th century because of the proximity of hardwoods in the mountains not far west and the abundance of low-wage labor in the flatlands not far east. This was the big era of industrialization of North Carolina's Piedmont, with textile and hosiery factories also built in High Point and in the much bigger town of Greensboro nearby.

Once this had been rolling farmland, settled by Quakers, site of the Battle of Guilford Courthouse in the Revolutionary War. But by the 1920s, smokestacks were puffing smoke at all hours and the local saying was that "only a wise man knows his own factory whistle."

The 6th Congressional District of North Carolina includes Greensboro and High Point, Lexington, another furniture town to the west, and Burlington and Alamance County, big textile producers just to the east. Its economy in recent decades has diversified and income levels have risen vastly; but it still feels dependent on textiles, and threatened by cheap imports abroad. The district is closely matched between the parties, and has been fiercely contested throughout the 1980s, but on one thing you won't find disagreement, and that is that the textile industry should be protected.

The politics of the 6th District, like much of North Carolina, has been transformed by the aggressiveness of Jesse Helms's Republicans. In the 1970s it was happy to be represented by Richardson Preyer, a moderate and respected Democrat who was scion of one of Greensboro's leading families. But he was beaten in 1980 by Republican Eugene Johnston, a Helms protégé; and Johnston was beaten in 1982 by Robin Britt, a moderate Democrat in the Jim Hunt mold; and Britt was beaten in 1984 by Howard Coble, an experienced legislator who barely beat a candidate supported by Helms and the Congressional Club in the Republican primary. In 1986 the revolving door finally stopped. Britt ran against Coble and tried to reverse the 1984 result, but missed—by one of the narrowest margins in the country. Every likelihood is that this will be a seriously contested district again in 1988.

Coble is a hard-working, intense legislator who has emphasized textile protection more than abortion in his campaigns; but his voting record is almost uniformly conservative. He serves on the Judiciary Committee—which can be a frustrating assignment for a man of his views—and in 1987 switched from the frying pan of Small Business to the fire of Merchant Marine and Fisheries. But he has had some accomplishments, like a bill making criminal interference with communication satellite signals, and he does occasionally surprise, as when he cast the decisive vote against a chemical warfare measure.

The People: Pop. 1980: 529,635, up 10.2% 1970–80. Households (1980): 76% family, 41% with children, 62% married couples; 32.9% housing units rented; median monthly rent: $144; median house value: $38,900. Voting age pop. (1980): 386,301; 19% Black, 1% Spanish origin.

1984 Presidential Vote:

Reagan (R)	129,630	(65%)
Mondale (D)	68,726	(35%)

Rep. Howard Coble (R)

Elected 1984; b. Mar. 18, 1931, Greensboro; home, Greensboro; Guilford Col., A.B. 1958, U. of NC, Chapel Hill, J.D. 1962; Presbyterian; single.

Career: State Farm Insur., 1961–67; NC House of Reps., 1969, 1979–83; Asst. U.S. Atty., Middle Dist. of NC, 1969–73; Commissioner, NC Dept. of Revenue, 1973–77; Practicing atty., 1979–84.

Offices: 430 LHOB 20515, 202-225-3065. Also P.O. Box 299, 324 W. Market St., Greensboro 27402, 919-333-5005; P.O. Box 1813, 116A W. 2d St., Lexington 27293, 704-246-8230; P.O. Box 814, 124 W. Elm St., Graham 27253, 919-229-0159; and 510 Ferndale Blvd., High Point 27260, 919-886-5106.

Committees: *Judiciary* (12th of 14 R). Subcommittees: Administrative Law and Governmental Relations; Courts, Civil Liberties, and the Administration of Justice. *Merchant Marine and Fisheries* (11th of 17 R). Subcommittees: Coast Guard and Navigation; Merchant Marine; Panama Canal and Outer Continental Shelf.

Group Ratings

	ADA	ACLU	COPE	CFA	LCV	ACU	NTU	NSI	COC	CEI
1986	10	5	23	25	21	81	54	100	89	66
1985	0	—	12	17	—	81	63	—	91	—

National Journal Ratings

	1986 LIB — 1986 CONS	1985 LIB — 1985 CONS
Economic	27% — 72%	12% — 85%
Social	18% — 78%	0% — 76%
Foreign	27% — 70%	0% — 76%

Key Votes

1) Lmt Cln Water Act	FOR	5) Retain Gun Cont	AGN	9) Aid Angola Reb	FOR
2) Rpl Tobac Sub	AGN	6) Contra Aid	FOR	10) Tax Reform	FOR
3) Grm-Rdmn Def Red	FOR	7) Lmt Text Imp	FOR	11) S Africa Sanc	AGN
4) Ban Polygraph	AGN	8) Limit SDI	FOR	12) Immig Reform	AGN

Election Results

1986 general	Howard Coble (R)	72,329	(50%)	($585,703)
	Charles Robin Britt (D)	72,250	(50%)	($562,711)
1986 primary	Howard Coble (R) unopposed			
1984 general	Howard Coble (R)	102,925	(51%)	($369,280)
	Charles Robin Britt (D)	100,263	(49%)	($384,541)

Campaign Contributions and Expenditures

1985-86		Direct Cont. 1985-86		PACS Breakdown 1985-86			
Receipts	$595,301	Indiv.	$236,014	Corp.	$103,608	T/M/H	$97,588
Expend.	$585,703	Party	$16,690	Labor	$1,500	Agr.	$9,250
Debts	$18,486	PACS	$247,846	Ideo.	$35,900	CWOS	$0
		Cand.	$72,859				

SEVENTH DISTRICT

As the Constitution turns 200, it is worth remembering—if you have a taste for irony, anyway—that the crop that made the largest of the 13 colonies economically viable, the product that was the mainstay of the economy that sustained Washington and Jefferson and Madison, was none other than tobacco, which is really a drug. Indigenous to the North American soil, tobacco can still be produced in only a few places in the world, one of which is the coastal plain of North Carolina, just south of its where the colonists first raised it in Tidewater Virginia. Tobacco was then and is now a labor-intensive crop, requiring close tending and serial picking (one leaf on a stalk matures before the one above it), and it was then and is now a valuable one. Colonial farmers could make a living off 10 or 15 acres of tobacco, and today North Carolina farmers, if they have one of the tobacco allotments handed out in the 1930s or have bought the rights to one, can too.

The tobacco colonies were the most populous part of colonial America, and the tobacco lands of east Carolina are some of the most densely populated rural areas in the United States. Or, to look at it from a political point of view, there are more voters per federally assisted acre for tobacco than for any other crop. If you want to know why tobacco farming is still subsidized and encouraged by a federal government that also seeks to discourage smoking, you only have to come to the eastern coastal plain of North Carolina, and reflect on what would happen to the communities here if the tobacco economy were vastly changed; and then you would see why there is such strong political pressure coming from representatives of this area to maintain tobacco's privileged position.

For many years tobacco was the only real mainstay of the economy in eastern North Carolina.

Job opportunities were so scarce that eastern North Carolina produced thousands of migrants north; it has always produced high percentages of volunteers for the military services, from the Civil War to the post-Vietnam era. More recently, there have been more jobs: new textile and apparel mills, factories built by European and Japanese companies. But there are virtually no unions here, and wages are still low. So tobacco retains its symbolic and most of its economic importance.

Nowhere more so than in the 7th Congressional District of North Carolina, in the southern portion of the state's coastal plain. Between its two cities—Wilmington, an old port now in the center of growing beach communities, and Fayetteville, next door to the Army's Fort Bragg— are miles of flat land, much of it used for tobacco. Also there is Robeson County, with a population that is 40% white, 35% black, and 25% Lumbees Indian; altogether the Lumbees, whose ethnic origin is shrouded in history, make up 8% of the district, making the 7th the most Indian district east of the Mississippi.

This is one of the most Democratic parts of North Carolina, and elects a Democratic congressman, Charlie Rose. He first won the seat in 1972 and has built quite a power base in the House since then. He has a seat on the House Administration Committee, and is the resident expert on the House's computer systems; he helped computerize the House in the 1970s and has continued to refine the systems which help congressmen and their staffs in many unanticipated ways. He has also worked on the problem of protecting individual privacy in an age of computerized records.

But much of Rose's work—and surely the most important part from his constituents' point of view—he does as chairman of Agriculture's Tobacco and Peanuts Subcommittee. Since 1981, when he took the chair, he has been striving to preserve the tobacco and peanut allotment systems, invented in the 1930s and 1940s to control production, which give only allotment owners the right to produce those crops and be eligible for federal assistance. Rose is of course a strong backer of subsidies and price supports for tobacco and peanuts, and has used his standing and alliances within the Democratic party to push his position. He has long been interested in inside politics, and was a leading backer of Phil Burton for majority leader in 1976; Burton lost by one vote, but Rose got in the habit of working with northern Democrats, though not always successfully: he backed Charles Rangel's losing 1986 race to be party whip. He has helped to hold the North Carolina Democrats together as a delegation loyal to the party's leadership in return for the leadership's support or benevolent neutrality on tobacco and peanut issues. Sometimes the pressure for tougher cigarette warning labels or for cutting the burgeoning cost of the tobacco program is too much. But Rose has won important victories for his cause and gained it votes it could not otherwise have hoped for in the House of the 1980s. And he has had the additional disadvantage of having as the leading spokesman for tobacco in the Senate Jesse Helms, whose unpopularity among colleagues is such that he probably costs his side votes.

Rose's seat in the House seems to be safe. He won the seat in 1972 by elbowing aside an aging incumbent whom he nearly beat two years before. He has not had significant primary opposition since 1974 and Republicans are not likely to be a serious threat in this Democratic territory.

The People: Pop. 1980: 539,055, up 19.5% 1970–80. Households (1980): 79% family, 49% with children, 63% married couples; 35.4% housing units rented; median monthly rent: $148; median house value: $33,500. Voting age pop. (1980): 371,808; 25% Black, 7% American Indian, 2% Spanish origin, 1% Asian origin.

1984 Presidential Vote: Reagan (R) 87,143   (57%)
Mondale (D) 65,964   (43%)

Rep. Charles G. (Charlie) Rose (D)

Elected 1972; b. Aug. 10, 1939, Fayetteville; home, Fayetteville; Davidson Col., A.B. 1961, U. of NC, LL.B. 1964; Presbyterian; married (Joan).

Career: Practicing atty., 1964–72; Chf. Dist. Crt. Prosecutor, 12th Judicial Dist., 1967–70.

Offices: 2230 RHOB 20515, 202-225-2731. Also P.O. Bldg., Rm. 208, Wilmington 28401, 919-343-4959; 218 Fed. Bldg., Fayetteville 28301, 919-323-0260.

Committees: *Agriculture* (5th of 26 D). Subcommittees: Cotton, Rice, and Sugar; Department Operations, Research and Foreign Agriculture; Livestock, Dairy and Poultry; Tobacco and Peanuts (Chairman). *House Administration* (4th of 12 D). Subcommittees: Elections; Office Systems (Chairman).

Group Ratings

	ADA	ACLU	COPE	CFA	LCV	ACU	NTU	NSI	COC	CEI
1986	55	66	62	50	42	37	26	22	44	16
1985	60	—	61	50	—	17	25	—	25	—

National Journal Ratings

	1986 LIB — 1986 CONS		1985 LIB — 1985 CONS	
Economic	70%	— 29%	70%	— 29%
Social	51%	— 48%	63%	— 33%
Foreign	57%	— 43%	57%	— 43%

Key Votes

1) Lmt Cln Water Act	AGN	5) Retain Gun Cont	AGN	9) Aid Angola Reb	AGN
2) Rpl Tobac Sub	AGN	6) Contra Aid	AGN	10) Tax Reform	FOR
3) Grm-Rdmn Def Red	AGN	7) Lmt Text Imp	FOR	11) S Africa Sanc	—
4) Ban Polygraph	AGN	8) Limit SDI	FOR	12) Immig Reform	FOR

Election Results

1986 general	Charles G. (Charlie) Rose (D)	70,471	(64%)	($302,654)
	Thomas J. Harrelson (R)	39,289	(36%)	($403,005)
1986 primary	Charles G. (Charlie) Rose (D) unopposed			
1984 general	Charles G. (Charlie) Rose (D)	92,157	(59%)	($202,189)
	S. Thomas Rhodes (R)	63,625	(41%)	($127,731)

Campaign Contributions and Expenditures

1985-86		Direct Cont. 1985-86		PACS Breakdown 1985-86			
Receipts	$403,808	Indiv.	$121,788	Corp.	$55,250	T/M/H	$73,374
Expend.	$302,654	PACS	$205,949	Labor	$35,550	Agr.	$21,775
Unspent	$257,769	Cand.	$11,895	Ideo.	$15,250	CWOS	$4,750

EIGHTH DISTRICT

Along Interstate 85 on North Carolina's Piedmont you can almost see the textile lint. The highway here passes through the nation's leading textile-producing area, past Salisbury, Concord, and Kannapolis, a company town for years owned by Cannon Mills, but whose houses new owner David Murdock was selling to workers even as he was fighting a union organizing drive as hard as Uncle Charlie Cannon would have. Eastern North Carolina was settled by English settlers coming up the rivers or overland from the coast, and as far west as the Sand Hills counties, not far east of Interstate 85. But the Piedmont land along Interstate 85 was settled by diverse groups, by Quakers and Scotsmen and German sects like the Moravians, coming down along the valleys and hills just east of the Blue Ridge from Pennsylvania through Virginia to North Carolina. These migratory patterns were reflected in Civil War divisions and in current voting habits. The coastal counties all the way up through the Sand Hills (except for the rich golfing condominium country around Southern Pines) were Confederate and are Democratic. The textile mill towns along 85 were anti-secession and are Republican.

The 8th Congressional District of North Carolina combines many of the textile mill counties with several Sand Hill counties. The textile counties have more people, but even so the district has been electing a Democratic congressman since Bill Hefner first won in 1974. Hefner used to be a country music disc jockey and radio station owner in Kannapolis, and his campaigns typically have featured a little Democratic oratory and a lot of country music. His politics, however, has been an adroit mix of Democratic principle and southern sentiment. Adroit, because he has used his support and that of his fellow North Carolina Democrats for many Democratic programs to win crucial victories for their causes, like textile restrictions and tobacco subsidies. Hefner and others from the state stuck with the Democrats on the tough Reagan budget votes in 1981, and have been reaping the benefits ever since.

Defense is Hefner's major preoccupation. He serves on the Defense Appropriations Subcommittee and, after only eight years in the House, became Chairman of the Military Construction Appropriations Subcommittee. This is a key pork barrel committee, which determines, among other things, spending on military bases including the Army's Fort Bragg, partly in the 8th District, and other North Carolina bases. Hefner must balance his desire for frugality on the one hand with the institutional bias of his chairmanship toward heavy military construction spending on the other. Hefner has been less successful in his own leadership aspirations. In 1986 he ran for whip, the number three position in the leadership, but was unable to win much support beyond his North Carolina base. He wound up with only 15 votes in the Democratic Caucus, far behind winner Tony Coelho and runner-up Charles Rangel. He was appointed a deputy whip afterwards.

Hefner has done better against the Republicans in the 1980s. He won reelection easily in the 1970s, but faced tough competition from Jesse Helms protégé Harris Blake in 1982 and 1984. Blake got 42% of the vote the first time, then 49% in the presidential year, when North Carolina Republicans run best; but Hefner hung on with 51%. His percentage rose, against weaker opposition, to 58% in 1986. But given the Republican leanings of the textile counties, the aggressiveness of the Republicans, and their likely advantage in the presidential year, he could very well have serious opposition again in 1988.

The People: Pop. 1980: 535,526, up 17.6% 1970–80. Households (1980): 79% family, 43% with children, 66% married couples; 24.9% housing units rented; median monthly rent: $106; median house value: $32,400. Voting age pop. (1980): 381,299; 18% Black, 1% American Indian, 1% Spanish origin.

1984 Presidential Vote:

Reagan (R)	128,219	(66%)
Mondale (D)	65,912	(34%)

Rep. W. G. (Bill) Hefner (D)

Elected 1974; b. Apr. 11, 1930, Elora, TN; home, Concord; Baptist; married (Nancy).

Career: Mbr., Harvesters Quartet, with weekly TV show on WXII, Winston-Salem; Promoter, "Carolina Sings," gospel music entertainment; Owner, WRKB Radio, Kannapolis.

Offices: 2161 RHOB 20515, 202-225-3715. Also 101 Union St., S., Concord 28025, 704-933-1615, 704-786-1612; 507 W. Innes St., Salisbury 28144, 704-636-0635; and 202 E. Franklin St., Rockingham 28379, 919-997-2070.

Committees: *Appropriations* (23d of 35 D). Subcommittees: Defense; Military Construction (Chairman).

Group Ratings

	ADA	ACLU	COPE	CFA	LCV	ACU	NTU	NSI	COC	CEI
1986	50	58	51	67	31	36	22	63	40	24
1985	25	—	51	50	—	46	26	—	37	—

National Journal Ratings

	1986 LIB — 1986 CONS		1985 LIB — 1985 CONS	
Economic	60% —	38%	65% —	35%
Social	52% —	48%	% —	%
Foreign	53% —	47%	48% —	52%

Key Votes

1) Lmt Cln Water Act	—	5) Retain Gun Cont	AGN	9) Aid Angola Reb	FOR
2) Rpl Tobac Sub	AGN	6) Contra Aid	AGN	10) Tax Reform	FOR
3) Grm-Rdmn Def Red	FOR	7) Lmt Text Imp	FOR	11) S Africa Sanc	FOR
4) Ban Polygraph	AGN	8) Limit SDI	FOR	12) Immig Reform	FOR

Election Results

1986 general	W. G. (Bill) Hefner (D)	80,959	(58%)	($157,576)
	William G. Hamby (R).	58,941	(42%)	($50,554)
1986 primary	W. G. (Bill) Hefner (D) unopposed			
1984 general	W. G. (Bill) Hefner (D)	99,731	(51%)	($263,869)
	Harris D. Blake (R)	96,354	(49%)	($273,400)

Campaign Contributions and Expenditures

1985-86		Direct Cont. 1985-86		PACS Breakdown 1985-86			
Receipts	$356,337	Indiv.	$103,912	Corp.	$108,391	T/M/H	$60,850
Expend.	$157,576	Party	$15,010	Labor	$40,050	Agr.	$6,550
Unspent	$256,999	PACS	$231,441	Ideo.	$15,600	CWOS	$0

NINTH DISTRICT

Charlotte is the biggest city in a big state that doesn't have big cities, a comfortable and growing commercial metropolis that sits off to one side of North Carolina and has never succeeded in dominating the state's consciousness. It is a southern city with a large white majority that has elected and reelected a black mayor, Harvey Gantt, who was one of those pioneers who integrated southern schools in the 1950s and 1960s; it is known as the subject of a landmark 1971 busing order which has been so widely accepted that when President Reagan came down and attacked it he was tellingly rebuked by the *Charlotte Observer*. Charlotte has no particular geographical reason for being: it is on no major river, it stands astride no historically important artery of transportation, although Interstate 85, the spinal column of the supposedly ailing (actually pretty healthy) American textile industry, now runs through it. It was not a significant city in colonial times nor even in the period following the Civil War.

Yet in the 1980s Charlotte has been one of the boom towns of the South, a medium-sized metropolitan area that is fast becoming a large one. Charlotte was once described as a town from which traveling salesmen empty out every Monday morning and return every Friday afternoon, and over the years its seems simply to have outhustled the competition. In blue-collar North Carolina this is a city with a substantial white-collar job base; it provides banking, insurance, and marketing services for many of the textile, furniture, and tobacco factories scattered around North Carolina and much of South Carolina as well. Charlotte sometimes thinks of itself, not a little defensively, as a smaller Atlanta, but in some ways it has done Atlanta one better. The Atlanta which once prided itself as the southern city too busy too hate is now increasingly spread out over a dozen different counties, with its citizens separated from each other increasingly by race. Charlotte, in contrast, seems to have maintained a common community spirit better than most places in our culturally varied country.

Historically, Charlotte is Republican, part of the belt in the western Piedmont settled overland by Scots and Quakers and German sects from Virginia and Pennsylvania; and on economic issues it is pretty devoted to market economics. Culturally it is more split, torn between the traditions to which Jesse Helms makes some reference but more taken with the spirit of community involvement and cooperation exemplified in North Carolina by Helms's 1984 opponent Jim Hunt, who carried Charlotte and Mecklenburg County in that race. The 9th Congressional District, which includes Charlotte and all of Mecklenburg, plus the textile county of Iredell to the north and rural Lincoln County to the northwest, has elected nothing but Republican congressmen since 1952, including Jim Martin, who left the seat in 1984 and was elected governor. Yet the last two races have been exceedingly close, and this is one part of the state that is trending Democratic.

The congressman is Republican Alex McMillan, member of a Charlotte family prominent in local business, a longtime civic activist, a moderate in North Carolina Republican terms who beat a candidate supported by Helms's Congressional Club 58%–42% in the 1984 primary. McMillan's political problem has been the strength of his 1984 and 1986 opponent, Democrat D. G. Martin. His personal character, his local civic activities and connections, his good speaking style, and his independent stands on issues all made him a strong contender; he emphasized that he was accepting no PAC money and raised a considerable war chest nonetheless. Martin lost by only 321 votes in 1984 and won 49% of the vote in 1986; both times he carried Charlotte and Mecklenburg counties, but lost in the smaller counties. His refusal of PAC contributions surely hurt him in 1986, when he raised almost as much as McMillan from non-PAC sources, but was outspent heavily because McMillan raised $316,000 from PACs.

In the House, McMillan is a member of the Banking and Small Business Committees, good enough assignments for a member who wants to help a growing metropolitan area, and of the Joint Economic Committee. His record, moderate in North Carolina Republican circles, is one of the most conservative in the House of Representatives. Naturally he favors any law that purports to help textiles—though Charlotte's unemployment rate is one of the lowest in the country. Against a lesser candidate than D. G. Martin he can probably be reelected easily, but Martin could make another serious race of it if he ran again.

The People: Pop. 1980: 536,325, up 15.3% 1970–80. Households (1980): 74% family, 42% with children, 60% married couples; 35.7% housing units rented; median monthly rent: $164; median house value: $44,800. Voting age pop. (1980): 385,849; 21% Black, 1% Spanish origin, 1% Asian origin.

1984 Presidential Vote: Reagan (R) 144,258   (64%)
Mondale (D) 79,612   (36%)

Rep. J. Alex McMillan, III (R)

Elected 1984; b. May 9, 1932, Charlotte; home, Charlotte; U. of NC, B.A. 1954, U. of VA, M.B.A. 1958; Presbyterian; married (Caroline).

Career: Army Intelligence, 1954–56; Businessman, Harris-Teeter Super Markets, Ruddick Corp., R.S. Dickson and Co., Carolina Paper Board Co., 1958–83; Mecklenburg Cnty. Bd. of Commissioners, 1973.

Offices: 401 CHOB 20515, 202-225-1976. Also 401 W. Trade St., Charlotte 28202, 704-372-1976; 207 W. Broad St., Statesville 28677, 704-872-7331; Municipal Bldg., Mooresville, 28115, 704-663-1976; P.O. Bldg., Rm. B-01, Lincolnton 28092, 704-735-1976.

Committees: *Banking, Finance and Urban Affairs* (16th of 20 R). Subcommittees: Economic Stabilization; Financial Institutions Supervision, Regulation and Insurance; General Oversight and Investigation; International Finance, Trade, and Monetary Policy. *Small Business* (10th of 17 R). Subcommittee: SBA and the General Economy; Regulation and Business Opportunity. *Joint Economic Committee.* Task Forces: National Security Economics; Fiscal and Monetary Policy.

Group Ratings

	ADA	ACLU	COPE	CFA	LCV	ACU	NTU	NSI	COC	CEI
1986	10	0	19	25	21	82	46	100	100	67
1985	5	—	6	8	—	81	59	—	91	—

National Journal Ratings

	1986 LIB — 1986 CONS		1985 LIB — 1985 CONS	
Economic	24%	— 76%	16%	— 81%
Social	15%	— 84%	0%	— 76%
Foreign	0%	— 86%	0%	— 76%

Key Votes

1) Lmt Cln Water Act	FOR	5) Retain Gun Cont	AGN	9) Aid Angola Reb	FOR
2) Rpl Tobac Sub	AGN	6) Contra Aid	FOR	10) Tax Reform	FOR
3) Grm-Rdmn Def Red	FOR	7) Lmt Text Imp	FOR	11) S Africa Sanc	AGN
4) Ban Polygraph	AGN	8) Limit SDI	AGN	12) Immig Reform	FOR

Election Results

1986 general	J. Alex McMillan, III (R)	80,352	(51%)	($884,385)
	D.G. Martin (D)	76,240	(49%)	($475,545)
1986 primary	J. Alex McMillan, III (R) unopposed			
1984 general	J. Alex McMillan, III (R)	109,420	(50%)	($683,535)
	D.G. Martin (D)	109,099	(50%)	($686,495)

Campaign Contributions and Expenditures

1985-86		Direct Cont. 1985-86		PACS Breakdown 1985-86			
Receipts	$894,034	Indiv.	$448,139	Corp.	$163,985	T/M/H	$101,478
Expend.	$884,385	Party	$16,111	Labor	$9,700	Agr.	$2,000
Unspent	$19,099	PACS	$315,847	Ideo.	$35,576	CWOS	$3,102
		Cand.	$6,888				

TENTH DISTRICT

The mountains of North Carolina, smooth and rounded, heavily wooded and wreathed with the haze that makes them called Smokies, are some of the oldest ranges in the world, mellow after eons of wear. Running right up toward the mountains, and in some of the valleys between them, is the manufacturing belt of North Carolina's Piedmont, with its textile mills and furniture factories. The 10th Congressional District of North Carolina includes six counties, plus part of another, in the western Piedmont, just where the mountains begin. The southern part of the district, on the South Carolina border, is textile country; Gaston County here may have more textile workers than any other single American county. North of Gastonia, the hills rise to mountains around such towns as Morganton, the home of former Senator Sam Ervin, who died in 1985 at age 88. The nearby hardwood forests provide some of the raw materials for the big furniture factories here, like the Broyhill establishment in the town of Lenoir. Farther north, you reach some of North Carolina's most pleasant vacation country, around Grandfather Mountain.

This district, running from Piedmont to mountains, also spans the gamut of political preferences which date back to the Civil War. Even though there were not many slaves this far west, the lowland areas were pro-Confederate then and are Democratic now, though with a distinct Dixie accent. Gaston County was once a George Wallace stronghold; Cleveland County next door years ago produced a string of Democratic governors. In the northern part of the district, you come to some of North Carolina's most heavily Republican counties; Democrats are as scarce here as big plantation owners were before the war. The counties in the middle are split between the parties; on balance, however, the district has been Republican.

And very steadily so in congressional elections. James Broyhill, scion of the furniture-making family, was elected to the House in 1962 and was reelected by wide margins except in 1968 when he beat another incumbent, and he could be there still. An economic conservative who tended to oppose government regulation in business and who was little interested in the cultural issues championed by Jesse Helms, he was the ranking Republican on the House Energy and Commerce Committee from 1981 to 1986, and by virtue of that position and of his own talent and knowledge one of the most active and effective legislators in the House. But when Helms's protégé John East decided to retire from the Senate, Broyhill decided to run, and in the Republican primary he won an overwhelming 67%–30% victory over a candidate backed by Helms's Congressional Club (although Helms himself kept mum). After East's suicide, Governor Jim Martin appointed Broyhill to fill out the vacancy. In the fall Senator Broyhill was beaten by Democrat Terry Sanford. But he got a nice testimonial from his old constituents: 65% of the vote in November and a whopping 91% in the primary.

It was generally assumed that the new congressman would be chosen in the Republican primary, and he was. He is Cass Ballenger, a man very much like Broyhill: from a prominent local family, a successful businessman, a civic leader and active legislator who chaired an education committee in the Democratic-controlled North Carolina Senate. He was elected to the Catawba County Board of Commissioners in 1966 and to the legislature in 1974. Ballenger won the primary against a younger opponent whom he accused of the sin (in these parts) of association with Helms's Congressional Club by carrying 80% of the vote in his home county and carrying majorities in the southern part of the district. In the general election, against the former mayor of Shelby, he lost the Democrat's home county but won comfortably elsewhere. He sits on the Education and Labor and Public Works Committees—good assignments for a freshman Republican. Like most Republicans who are counted as moderates in North Carolina he will probably have a solidly conservative record in Washington. It's hard to see why he should have any trouble winning reelection.

The People: Pop. 1980: 532,954, up 15.6% 1970–80. Households (1980): 80% family, 44% with children, 66% married couples; 27.6% housing units rented; median monthly rent: $125; median house value: $33,400. Voting age pop. (1980): 379,876; 9% Black, 1% Spanish origin.

1984 Presidential Vote: Reagan (R) 136,320   (70%)
                             Mondale (D) 59,796   (30%)

Rep. Cass Ballenger (R)

Elected 1986; b. Dec. 6, 1926, Hickory; home, Hickory; U. of NC, Amherst Col., B.A. 1948; Episcopalian; married (Donna).

Career: Catawba Cnty. Bd. of Commissioners, 1966-74, Chmn. 1970–74; NC House of Reps., 1974–76; NC Senate, 1976–86.

Offices: 116 CHOB 20515, 202-225-2576. Also P.O. Box 1830, Hickory 28603, 704-327-6100; and 832 E. Garrison Blvd., Gastonia 28054, 704-864-9922.

Committees: *Education and Labor* (13th of 13 R). Subcommittee: Health and Safety; Labor–Management Relations. *Public Works and Transportation* (19th of 20 R). Subcommittees: Aviation; Economic Development.

Group Ratings and Key Votes: Newly Elected

Election Results

1986 general	Cass Ballenger (R)	83,902	(57%)	($463,830)
	Lester D. Roark (D)	62,035	(43%)	($196,438)
1986 primary	Cass Ballenger (R)	14,703	(53%)	
	George S. Robinson (R)	11,654	(42%)	
	Wood H. Young (R)	1,228	(5%)	
1986 special	Cass Ballenger.......................	82,973	(58%)	
	Lester D. Roark	61,205	(42%)	
1984 general	James T. Broyhill (R)	142,873	(73%)	($263,636)
	Ted A. Poovey (D)	51,860	(27%)	

Campaign Contributions and Expenditures

1985-86		Direct Cont. 1985-86		PACS Breakdown 1985-86			
Receipts	$469,277	Indiv.	$232,553	Corp.	$51,904	T/M/H	$42,564
Expend.	$463,830	Party	$9,842	Labor	$1,500	Agr.	$1,000
Unspent	$5,447	PACS	$116,830	Ideo.	$18,228	CWOS	$1,634
		Cand.	$118,342				

ELEVENTH DISTRICT

Western North Carolina, the protrusion of the Tarheel state deep into the fastness of the eastern United States' highest and oldest mountains, is a land of long and ornery traditions. First settled by whites not long after Independence, it still has its tiny Indian communities, and has also hollow towns where people are descended from the first white settlers. Its biggest city, Asheville, is memorialized in Thomas Wolfe's novels, a home for lung patients in the early 20th century, it was the home also of the eccentric Vanderbilt who built the Gothic Biltmore mansion, now a tourist attraction, and who started the scientific study of forestry by hiring Gifford Pinchot to oversee the forests on the property. Over a ridge is the Smoky Mountains National Park, the nation's most heavily visited, with enough traffic to require a stoplight. During the summer it is 20° cooler in the mountains than in the lowland towns not far away; the climate and the forested, green, fog-wisped mountains attract some seven million people to the Smokies each year.

The orneriness of the mountains has come out in its politics. During the Civil War, it was the part of the state most reluctant to secede. With few slaves (only 5% of the people here today are black), many of the small farmers in the hollows remained loyal to the Union, and those who took up the Confederate cause did so largely because of the efforts of Governor Zebulon Vance, an Asheville native and reluctant secessionist himself. Ancestral party loyalties are strong, and evenly balanced between the parties; the retirees who have come to Asheville and pleasant places like Hendersonville and Rutherford County haven't tipped things much. The western end of the state makes up the 11th Congressional District of North Carolina, which, over the past dozen years, may very well have been the most closely contested district in the entire nation.

It is also the only district which in every election in the 1980s has thrown out its incumbent congressman. It did so in 1980 when Lamar Gudger, a Democrat who benefited from the coattails of Jimmy Carter in 1976 and the popularity of Governor Jim Hunt in 1978, was beaten in the Reagan tide by 36-year-old Republican Bill Hendon. Then in 1982 Hendon was upset by 65-year-old Democrat James Clarke. Clarke and Hendon have run against each other twice again: Hendon won with 51% of the vote in 1984, and Clarke won with 51% in 1986. After that election Hendon said he wasn't going to try again. But someone surely will, and Clarke, who turns 71 in 1988, will probably have a tough and quite possibly losing race again.

In the meantime Clarke seems to enjoy serving in the House. Hendon was an enthusiastic Reagan backer, while Clarke is a loyal North Carolina Democrat; Clarke wants to create more wilderness areas, while Hendon wanted to free up more land for development. Clarke has a seat on the Interior Committee, an important post here where there is so much federal land; the last congressman with secure tenure here, Democrat Roy Taylor, was chairman of Interior when he retired in 1976. Clarke also serves on Foreign Affairs, where it will be interesting to see if he follows other Democrats in opposing American aid to the Nicaraguan contras. Clarke has the gentleness of a gentleman farmer who has worked for years for charitable foundations in western North Carolina; and he has shown a willingness to vote his conscience and beliefs without too great a regard for its effects on his prospects in the next election. Sensibly so: for in this age when incumbents are routinely reelected in most districts across the country, no one can guarantee the tenure of a congressman from the North Carolina 11th.

The People: Pop. 1980: 531,144, up 15.6% 1970–80. Households (1980): 78% family, 39% with children, 66% married couples; 24.5% housing units rented; median monthly rent: $126; median house value: $34,300. Voting age pop. (1980): 390,762; 5% Black, 1% American Indian, 1% Spanish origin.

1984 Presidential Vote:

Reagan (R)	135,124	(63%)
Mondale (D)	79,149	(37%)

Rep. James McClure Clarke (D)

Elected 1986; b. June 12, 1917, Manchester, VT; home, Fairview; Princeton U., A.B., 1939; Presbyterian; married (Elspeth).

Career: USN, 1942–45; Farmers Fed. Coop., 1939–59; Assoc. Editor, *Asheville Citizen Times*, 1961–69; Asst. to Pres., Warren Wilson Col., 1970–82; Chmn., Buncombe Cnty. Bd. of Ed., 1969–76; NC House of Reps., 1977–80; NC Senate, 1981–82; U.S. House of Reps., 1983–84; Dairy Farmer and Orchard Operator.

Offices: 217 CHOB 20515, 202-225-6401. Also 1 N. Pack Sq., Ste. 434, Asheville 28801, 704-254-1747; 301 W. Main St., Spindale 28160, 704-286-4890; and 319 W. Main St., Sylva 28779, 704-586-6631.

Committees: *Interior and Insular Affairs* (12th of 26 D). Subcommittees: Energy and the Environment; Insular and International Affairs; National Parks and Public Lands. *Foreign Affairs* (23d of 27 D). Subcommittees: Africa; Arms Control, International Security and Science. *Select Committee on Aging* (37th of 39 D). Subcommittee: Human Services.

Election Results

1986 general	James McClure Clarke (D) 91,575	(51%)	($435,435)
	William M. Hendon (R)................ 89,069	(49%)	($474,166)
1986 primary	James McClure Clarke (D) 50,787	(75%)	
	Ralph Ledford (D) 17,108	(25%)	
1984 general	William M. Hendon (R)............... 112,598	(51%)	($448,494)
	James McClure Clarke (D) 108,284	(49%)	($393,878)

Campaign Contributions and Expenditures

1985-86		Direct Cont. 1985-86		PACS Breakdown 1985-86			
Receipts	$427,321	Indiv.	$221,169	Corp.	$5,500	T/M/H	$24,363
Expend.	$435,435	Party	$10,165	Labor	$88,300	Agr.	$0
		PACS	$168,848	Ideo.	$50,185	CWOS	$500
		Cand.	$8,000				

NORTH DAKOTA

In the winter of 1804-05 the Lewis and Clark expedition wintered among 4,400 Indians, building Fort Mandan—the first men from the United States to set foot in what is now North Dakota. In the 1830s the German painter Karl Bodmer wintered at Fort Mandan with another expedition, and painted watercolors of the Indians he lived among—paintings all the more poignant because most of the Indians died in an epidemic a few years later. The history of North Dakota has a melancholy undertone: Theodore Roosevelt came here in the 1880s after his first wife died and rode about furiously trying to find a buffalo to shoot—almost all of them had been wiped out a few years before. The settlers who began moving on to the plains from the east, brought thither on the railroads that crossed the blank territory on their way from Minneapolis and St. Paul to the Rockies and the Pacific, were mostly those who had missed out on the lands with an easier climate: Norwegians, Germans, Swedes, Volga Germans from Tsarist Russia.

What they found was a vast, treeless expanse of the North American steppe always at the mercy of the wind, freezing cold much of the year, but swept by tornadoes and blazing hot in July and August. But it was also, once the soil was broken, some of the best wheat land in the world, empty now of Indians and buffalo, connected to markets by the rails, ready to become a cog in the industrial world which was being created by entrepreneurs and raising living standards to unparalleled heights. In a sudden rush of settlement during the 20 years before World War I, North Dakota filled up with pretty much its present population; there were 632,000 people here in 1920 and the number has fluctuated in the 600,000s ever since. Wheat is not the only crop; as the plains become more arid in the west, ranching and livestock grazing— along with strip mining and oil production—become more important than wheat, and other hardy root crops like potatoes and sugar beets are grown as well. But there is no question that wheat is North Dakota's premier crop. Typically the state produces about one-tenth of the nation's crop; only Kansas grows more.

Few other states have an economy that serves the same functions as it did 90 years ago; North Dakota does. It has the nation's largest share of population—about 25%—still living on farms and ranches. Naturally this affects people's politics. In most states, prosperity depends on the level of wages; but in North Dakota, where farmers are really small businessmen, prosperity depends on the level of profits. This is inherently volatile and uncertain: the demand for food, as food processors know, is always there, but commodity prices in any market system are unstable—they have to be, if the market is to keep suppliers informed about demand—just as the weather is undependable. So entrepreneurs, who must make their plans on worst-case analyses, try to minimize their risks by calling on government, and in a democracy government usually complies. But the resulting farm programs are so complicated, and the circumstances of the business so uncertain that there is almost always some sort of raging dissatisfaction with the federal government's farm programs. This has made North Dakota temperamentally inclined to vote against all incumbent administrations, and was the driving force behind the most interesting episode in the state's politics: its spell of radicalism in the years around World War I.

North Dakota's politics has also been colored by the fact that many of its settlers, during its years of surging growth, were of immigrant stock: Norwegians in the eastern part of the state, Canadians along the northern border, Volga Germans in the west, and native Germans throughout the state. (Volga Germans were people who had migrated to Russia from Germany in the early 19th century, but who retained their German language and character. They are recorded in census figures as Russian stock.) The new North Dakotans lived on lonely, often marginal farms, cut off in many cases from the wider American culture by the barrier of language. Their economic fate seemed to be at the mercy of the grain millers of Minneapolis, the railroads, the banks, and the commodity traders.

These circumstances led A. C. Townley and William Lemke to organize the North Dakota Non-Partisan League (NPL) in 1915. Its program was frankly socialistic government owner- ship of the railroads and grain elevators—and, like many North Dakota ethnics, the League opposed going to war with Germany. The positions taken by the NPL won it many adherents in North Dakota, and the League spread to neighboring states. But North Dakota was its bastion. The NPL often determined the outcome of the usually decisive Republican primary and sometimes swung its support to the otherwise heavily outnumbered Democrats. It achieved some of its goals in North Dakota, such as establishing a state-owned bank. A particular favorite of the NPL was "Wild Bill" Langer, who served intermittently as governor during the 1930s. He was elected to the Senate in 1940 but was allowed to take his seat only after a lengthy investigation of campaign irregularities. His subsequent career was fully as controversial; one of his pet projects was to get a North Dakotan on the Supreme Court, and he filibustered every nomination from 1954 on in an unsuccessful attempt to seat a Justice.

Another NPL favorite was Representative Usher Burdick, who served from 1935 to 1945 and then again from 1949 to 1959. Burdick, like Langer, was a nominal Republican, but usually voted with the Democrats on economic issues. Burdick's son Quentin, a Democrat, was a member of the House when Langer died. Young Burdick, as some North Dakotans still call him though he turns 80 in 1988, won a special election to fill the Senate seat after waging a campaign against the inequities of Agriculture Secretary Ezra Taft Benson. The Non-Partisan League of course supported Burdick, and by the 1960s its name had become misleading; it supported Democrats in almost every election.

Governor. The governor of North Dakota, George Sinner, a prosperous sugar beet farmer who served many years in the legislature, beat incumbent Republican Allen Olson in 1984 after Olson made several gaffes. Sinner took office only after a panel of judges ruled that he was entitled to do so before two Supreme Court seats became vacant rather than, as Olson claimed, after. Sinner has been frustrated that he can't persuade voters a tax increase is necessary, but he remains popular and well ahead in polls against possible opponents Public Service Commissioner Leo Reinbold and legislative leader Earl Strinden. This is a small state where all public figures are well known, and judgments are made mostly on character; people trust each other implicitly, so much in fact that North Dakota is the only American state without voter registration: you just show up at the polls and vote.

Senators. It is becoming a recurrent motif in North Dakota politics: the old Senator, jealous and mistrustful of a popular young politician in his own party, is reluctant to retire and hangs on, working all the harder as the years go on. Back in 1974 Republican Milton Young, at 77 and a veteran of 29 years in the Senate, ran again partly to preempt Representative Mark Andrews, whom he disliked; Young, who had a speech impediment, ran an ad showing him splitting a block of wood with a karate crop and that evidence of his vigor, plus his reputation as "Mr.

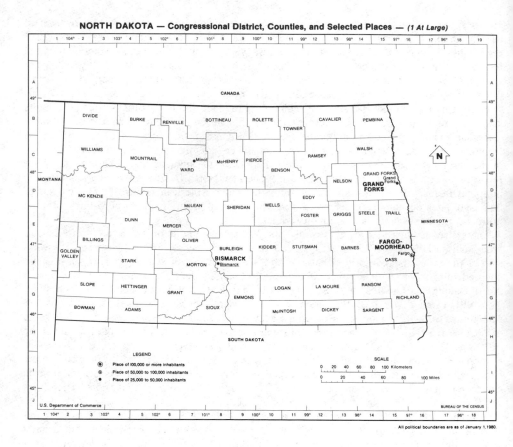

NORTH DAKOTA — Congresssional District, Counties, and Selected Places — (1 At Large)

All political boundaries are as of January 1, 1980.

Wheat," gave him six more years. Even so, at 83 he was still trying to manuever Andrews out of running, unsuccessfully: Andrews won and lost. But Young, though he had moved on to another constituency, may have had the last laugh in 1986, when Andrews was upset by Democrat Kent Conrad in an election in which character factors played an important part.

Now Senator Quentin Burdick is working vigorously to win another term in 1988, when he turns 80—and in the process frustrate the ambitions of Congressman Byron Dorgan whom he regards, as Young did Andrews, with the distaste so many kings of England showed for their princes of Wales. For years Burdick has been quiet in Washington; with his rumpled clothes, aw shucks manner, and beat-up old car, he cut a modest social figure indeed. He managed deftly to avoid the high responsibilities that usually come to veteran Senators, and for 26 years was not a committee chairman: he left Judiciary (which has had two Democratic chairmen with less seniority than he has) and saw Post Office and Civil Service abolished out from under him in 1977 just as he was about to take the chair. But one effect of the Democratic capture of the Senate in 1986 is that Burdick, the second ranking minority member on Environment and Public Works in 1986, suddenly became chairman in 1987 (he actually ranks behind Lloyd Bentsen on the committee, though Bentsen came to the Senate 10 years later, but Bentsen chose to be chairman of Finance). He also became chairman of the Appropriations Committee's Agriculture Subcommittee.

In the first weeks of 1987 he pushed the clean water bill President Reagan vetoed through the Senate and spent a much-publicized night with the homeless in Fargo; he began running "public service announcements" (paid for out of campaign funds) on North Dakota TV showing him as chairman; he announced that his major legislative priority was getting a highway bill; he stepped up and challenged the congressional pay raise; he started billing himself as "one of the most powerful people in Washington." Whether this burst of activity will enable Burdick to win in 1988 remains to be seen. In spring 1987 Dorgan was leading Burdick 67%–23% among Democrats in one poll, and in a three-way general election matchup Dorgan had 51% to 17% for Burdick and 24% for Mark Andrews. But voters have positive feelings about all three, and it's not unknown for small events to tip a large number of votes one way or the other in such contests.

North Dakota's junior Senator, Kent Conrad, was elected in what would have been one of the big upsets of 1986—except that political reporters and pollsters watch the races so closely now that every upset is anticipated months in advance. Conrad was running against Mark Andrews, who in six years in the Senate and 17 in the House never hesitated to bellow out in support of wheat and against the farm policies of the President in power at the time; and he did in 1986 as well. But Andrews had some personal weaknesses in a state where politicians are closely watched: some voters resented a medical malpractice suit he filed on behalf of his wife, others bridled when a close Andrews friend in Washington hired a private detective to monitor the personal life of Representative Byron Dorgan, who as state tax commissioner was Conrad's boss and then saw Conrad succeed him when he was elected to the House in 1980. Andrews, with his penchant for loud denunciations, seemed something of a blowhard, while Conrad quietly and methodically talked about what could be done about low wheat prices and his own record of squeezing more money from out-of-state corporations. Drawing on North Dakota's longtime mistrust of outside corporations and market forces and its affection for those who would use government to help the small farmer-entrepreneur, he carried most of the rural counties while Andrews carried most of North Dakota's small cities. But nowhere was the vote lopsided, as Conrad won 50%–49%.

Congressman. Byron Dorgan wins reelection by the largest margins of any North Dakota politician, yet he is in the House, and two of his fellow Democrats are in the Senate. Dorgan's political career was hatched in the unlikely precincts of the office in Bismarck's 19-story state capital of the state tax commissioner, an elective office to which he was appointed in 1969 and elected and reelected in the 1970s. By 1980 he was an easy winner in the House race. Dorgan started by getting out-of-state corporations to pay more taxes in North Dakota. Then he emerged as the champion of the embattled farmer. That was a technical, legalistic battle, the kind of battle prairie farmers are accustomed to losing to big-city lawyers, but Dorgan won victories that brought back memories of the old Non-Partisan League struggles.

Dorgan harks back to North Dakota's prairie populism, its distrust of big institutions (especially banks and grain companies) and its solicitude for the individual family farmer. An opponent of the Vietnam war when that was an issue, he remains a skeptic about defense spending increases. (North Dakota, as it happens, is loaded with missile silos; some residents are a little worried about that, since it never occurred to them before that they would be a target in a nuclear war.) Like his fellow North Dakotans, he is an unyielding supporter of the state's wheat growing interests. He is a low-interest-rate man and a denouncer of Paul Volcker and the big bankers. But he was sophisticated enough in the ways of the House to win a seat on the Ways and Means Committee in his second term. He approaches issues with a zest and the kind of cornball good humor that New Deal enthusiasts liked to summon up when liberals thought they represented the ordinary, inarticulate little guy, and saw the conservatives as representing the stuck-up old stuffed shirts.

Dorgan's problem for 1988 is that his successes may hold him back. Burdick argues that voters should keep him in the Senate where he has clout and keep Dorgan on Ways and Means. Conrad's election suggests that Republicans have no strong chance for the Burdick seat and so there is no need for the younger man to run now; the fact that the governor is a Democrat means that if there is a vacancy, Dorgan or another Democrat could be appointed to fill it. In early 1987 he was facing a hard choice: run for the Senate seat he has been aiming for for years, or let the newly invigorated Burdick have the Democratic nomination and keep waiting for his turn.

Presidential politics. North Dakota is historically Republican, but it is competitive in many elections. Currently its three-member congressional delegation is all Democratic, but in the Carter years it was 2 to 1 Republican (note the countercyclical pattern). Republicans hold most of the statewide offices, but not the governorship, but it has had Democratic governors for all but four years since 1960. In presidential politics North Dakota is usually Republican but has a tendency to move away from the party in power. In 1976 Gerald Ford won by only a 52%–46% margin. In the next four years wheat prices did pretty well and the state's economy was in pretty good shape. But wheat-producing counties across the nation reacted angrily to President Carter's embargo on wheat sales to Russia, and in North Dakota most counties are wheat counties. Ronald Reagan carried North Dakota by a 64%–26% margin. That was the third biggest Republican gain in the nation. In 1984 Reagan carried North Dakota again without trouble. But his 65% of the vote represents one of his smallest percentage gains in the nation, and North Dakota had the biggest increase in the nation in the Democrats' percentage from 1980 to 1984—evidence of a continuing anti-incumbent bias which, if muted in the presidential race, came out in the 1984 governor and 1986 Senator races.

The People: Est. Pop. 1984: 679,000; Pop. 1980: 652,717, up 4.1% 1980–86 and 5.7% 1970–80; 0.29% of U.S. total, 45th largest. 20% with 1–3 yrs. col., 15% with 4+ yrs. col.; 12.6% below poverty level. Single ancestry: 26% German, 15% Norwegian, 2% English, Irish, Swedish, 1% French, Polish. Households (1980): 73% family, 40% with children, 65% married couples; 31.3% housing units rented; median monthly rent: $175; median house value: $43,800. Voting age pop. (1980): 461,726; 2% American Indian. No state registration of voters.

1986 Share of Federal Tax Burden: $2,001,000,000; 0.27% of U.S. total, 48th largest.

1986 Share of Federal Expenditures

	Total		Non-Defense		Defense	
Total Expend	$2,818m	(0.31%)	$1,820m	(0.35%)	$456m	(0.22%)
St/Lcl Grants	433m	(0.38%)	433m	(0.38%)	0m	(0.00%)
Salary/Wages	440m	(0.36%)	176m	(0.30%)	264m	(0.43%)
Pymnts to Indiv	967m	(0.27%)	944m	(0.27%)	23m	(0.13%)
Procurement	314m	(0.15%)	85m	(0.15%)	229m	(0.15%)
Research/Other	664m	(2.49%)	664m	(2.49%)	0m	(0%)

Political Lineup: Governor, George A. Sinner (D); Lt. Gov., Lloyd Omdahl (D); Secy. of State, Ben Meier (R); Atty. Gen., Nicholas Spaeth (D); Treasurer, Robert Hanson (D); Auditor, Robert W. Peterson (R). State Senate, 53 (26 R and 27 D); State House of Representatives, 106 (61 R and 45 D). Senators, Quentin N. Burdick (D) and Kent Conrad (D). Representatives, 1 D at large.

1984 Presidential Vote

Reagan (R)	200,336	(65%)
Mondale (D)	104,429	(34%)

1980 Presidential Vote

Reagan (R)	193,695	(64%)
Carter (D)	79,189	(26%)
Anderson (I)	23,640	(8%)

1984 Democratic Presidential Primary

Hart	28,603	(85%)
LaRouche	4,018	(12%)
Mondale	943	(3%)

1984 Republican Presidential Primary

Reagan	44,109	(100%)

GOVERNOR

Gov. George A. Sinner (D)

Elected 1984, term expires Jan. 1989; b. May 29, 1928, Fargo; home, Casselton; St. John's U., B.A. 1950; Roman Catholic; married (Jane).

Career: Partner, Sinner Bros. & Bresnahan (Farming partnership); ND Senate, 1962–66; ND House of Reps., 1982–84.

Office: State Capitol, Bismarck 58505, 701-224-2200.

Election Results

1984 gen.	George A. Sinner (D).........	173,992	(55%)
	Allen I. Olson (R)............	140,460	(45%)
1984 prim.	George A. Sinner (D).........	36,461	(88%)
	Anna Belle Bourgois (D)	5,180	(12%)
1980 gen.	Allen I. Olson (R)............	162,230	(54%)
	Arthur A. Link (D)	140,391	(46%)

SENATORS

Sen. Quentin N. Burdick (D)

Elected June 28, 1960, seat up 1988; b. June 19, 1908, Munich; home, Fargo; U. of MN, B.A. 1931, LL.B. 1932; Congregationalist; married (Jocelyn).

Career: Practicing atty., 1932–58; Dem. Nominee for Gov., 1946; U.S. House of Reps., 1959–60.

Offices: 511 HSOB, 202-224-2551. Also Fed. Bldg., Fargo 58102, 701-237-4000; Fed. Bldg., Bismarck 58501, 701-255-2553; Fed. Bldg., Minot 58701, 701-852-4503; 108 Fed. Bldg., Grand Forks 58201, 701-746-1014.

Committees: *Appropriations* (8th of 16 D). Subcommittees: Agriculture and Related Agencies (Chairman); Energy and Water Development; Interior; Labor, Health and Human Services, Education. *Environment and Public Works* (Chairman of 9 D). Subcommittees: Water Resources; Transportation. *Select Committee on Indian Affairs* (4th of 5 D). *Special Committee on Aging* (6th of 10 D).

Group Ratings

	ADA	ACLU	COPE	CFA	LCV	ACU	NTU	NSI	COC	CEI
1986	100	92	85	73	58	4	42	10	21	22
1985	85	—	84	80	—	9	27	—	21	—

National Journal Ratings

	1986 LIB — 1986 CONS		1985 LIB — 1985 CONS	
Economic	85% —	8%	92% —	5%
Social	92% —	0%	62% —	36%
Foreign	75% —	0%	88% —	0%

Key Votes

1) Ease Gun Cont	FOR	5) Grm-Rdmn Def Red	AGN	9) Rehnquist Nom	AGN
2) Immig Reform	AGN	6) Contra Aid	AGN	10) Tax Reform	FOR
3) Lmt Text Imp	AGN	7) SDI Funding	AGN	11) Drug Death Pen	FOR
4) Aid Tobac Ind	AGN	8) Lmt PAC Contrib	AGN	12) S Africa Sanc	FOR

Election Results

1982 general	Quentin N. Burdick (D)	164,873	(62%)	($783,020)
	Gene Knorr (R)	89,304	(34%)	($406,601)
1982 primary	Quentin N. Burdick (D)	44,835	(100%)	
1976 primary	Quentin N. Burdick (D)	175,772	(62%)	($117,514)
	Robert Stroup (R)	103,466	(37%)	($136,748)

Campaign Contributions and Expenditures

1978-82		Direct Cont. 1981-82		PACS Breakdown			
Receipts	$912,059	Indiv.	$309,160	Corp.	$34,850	T/M/H	$72,975
Expend.	$783,020	Party	$17,500	Labor	$137,592	Agr.	$214,150
Unspent	$129,142	PACS	$489,919	Ideo.	$12,300	CWOS	$7,374

Sen. Kent Conrad (D)

Elected 1986, seat up 1992; b. May 12, 1948, Bismarck.; home, Bismarck; U. of MO, Stanford U., B.A. 1971, George Washington U., M.B.A. 1975; Unitarian; married (Lucy).

Career: Asst. to ND Tax Commissioner, 1974–80; Dir., Mgt. Planning & Personnel, ND Tax Dept., 1980; ND Tax Commissioner, 1981–86.

Offices: 361 DSOB 20510, 202-224-2043. Also Fed. Bldg., Rm. 232, 3d & Roffer Ave., Bismarck 58501, 701-258-4648; 657 2d Ave. N., Fed. Bldg., Rm. 306, Fargo 58102, 701-232-8030; 100 1st St. S.W., Minot 58701, 701-852-0703; and 102 N. 4th St., Ste. 106, Grand Forks 58201, 701-775-9601.

Committees: *Agriculture, Nutrition, and Forestry* (7th of 10 D). Subcommittees: Agricultural Production and Stabilization of Prices; Domestic and Foreign Marketing and Product Promotion; Nutrition and Investigations. *Budget* (12th of 11 D). *Energy and Natural Resources* (10th of 10 D) Subcommittees: Mineral Resources Development and Production; Public Lands, National Parks and Forests; Water and Power.

Group Ratings and Key Votes: Newly Elected

Election Results

1986 general	Kent Conrad (D)	143,932	(50%)	($908,374)
	Mark Andrews (R)	141,797	(49%)	($2,270,557)
1986 primary	Kent Conrad (D)	58,213	(100%)	
1980 general	Mark Andrews (R)	210,347	(70%)	($402,129)
	Kent Johanneson (D)	86,658	(29%)	($139,203)

Campaign Contributions and Expenditures

	1985-86	Direct Cont. 1985-86		PACS Breakdown 1985-86			
Receipts	$993,040	Indiv.	$507,904	Corp.	$46,800	T/M/H	$94,148
Expend.	$908,374	Party	$16,500	Labor	$232,200	Agr.	$15,350
Unspent	$85,667	PACS	$500,387	Ideo.	$107,889	CWOS	$4,000
		Cand.	$2,196				

REPRESENTATIVE

Rep. Byron L. Dorgan (D)

Elected 1980; b. May 14, 1942, Dickinson; home, Bismarck; U. of ND, B.S. 1964, U. of Denver, M.B.A. 1966; Lutheran; married (Kimberly).

Career: Martin-Marietta Exec. Develop. Prog., 1966-67; ND Dpty. Tax Commissioner, 1967–68, Tax Commissioner, 1969–80.

Offices: 238 CHOB 20515, 202-225-2611. Also 358 Fed. Bldg., Bismarck 58502, 701-255-4011; and 112 Robert St., Fargo 58107, 701-237-5771.

Committees: *Ways and Means* (17th of 23 D). Subcommittees: Oversight; Select Revenue Measures. *Select Committee on Hunger* (8th of 16 D). Task Force: International Task Force.

Group Ratings

	ADA	ACLU	COPE	CFA	LCV	ACU	NTU	NSI	COC	CEI
1986	70	70	72	75	58	27	42	10	29	30
1985	65	—	73	58	—	10	43	—	31	—

National Journal Ratings

	1986 LIB — 1986 CONS			1985 LIB — 1985 CONS		
Economic	53%	—	47%	55%	—	44%
Social	55%	—	44%	57%	—	42%
Foreign	61%	—	37%	92%	—	0%

Key Votes

1) Lmt Cln Water Act	FOR	5) Retain Gun Cont	AGN	9) Aid Angola Reb	AGN
2) Rpl Tobac Sub	AGN	6) Contra Aid	AGN	10) Tax Reform	FOR
3) Grm-Rdmn Def Red	AGN	7) Lmt Text Imp	AGN	11) S Africa Sanc	FOR
4) Ban Polygraph	FOR	8) Lmt SDI	FOR	12) Immig Reform	FOR

Election Results

1986 general	Byron L. Dorgan (D)	216,258	(76%)	($391,909)
	Syver Vinje (R).......................	66,989	(23%)	($73,278)
1986 primary	Byron L. Dorgan (D)	62,700	(100%)	
1984 general	Byron L. Dorgan (D)	242,968	(79%)	($279,687)
	Lois Ivers Altenburg (R)	65,761	(21%)	($128,238)

Campaign Contributions and Expenditures

	1985-86	Direct Cont. 1985-86		PACS Breakdown 1985-86			
Receipts	$458,532	Indiv.	$100,983	Corp.	$75,125	T/M/H	$117,410
Expend.	$391,909	Party	$850	Labor	$61,050	Agr.	$12,000
Unspent	$203,570	PACS	$314,628	Ideo.	$37,543	CWOS	$11,500

OHIO

Scattering apple seeds across the rolling land, a half-crazed New Englander named Jonathan Chapman—known in folklore as Johnny Appleseed—helped create the landscape we know as Ohio. We would not recognize the Ohio of the Indians that existed even after the Revolutionary War, a land covered almost entirely with trees where the untrained eye could not see much further than the next trunk and the crackle of branches and hoots of animals were ominous and indecipherable. But by 1847, when Chapman died, a civilization had been created here that we could discern as Ohio. There were no huge factories yet, though there were forges and foundries almost everywhere; and no looming skyscrapers, though every town had a hotel. Almost every town, it seemed, had a college too, and several churches, reflecting the origins of its settlers— Congregationalist for the New Englanders in the northeast, Connecticut's old Western Reserve; Baptists in the hills of the south, where descendants of slaveholders lived, though Ohio, under the Northwest Ordinance of 1787, was free soil; Presbyterians scattered about, the descendants of the Scots who came from the hills of Pennsylvania and Virginia; sects of Mennonites from the Pennsylvania Dutch country, clinging to their old ways.

On this stable but yeasty base was built the manufacturing empire of Ohio. Yeasty, because in 19th century America, nothing mattered so much as cultural differences, especially the divide between north and south; and Ohio was sitting right on top of it. It connected the farm states where Lincoln drew so many of his Union troops with the eastern states laden with heavy industry; it had long been the third largest state in the Union, and yet during much of the war it was governed by Copperheads whose loyalty was so dubious that Lincoln had some of them imprisoned. Civil War divisions persisted for years afterwards, structuring the otherwise humdrum politics of a state with prosperous farms and a rapidly growing manufacturing sector. Cincinnati, the fourth largest city in the nation in Lincoln's day, continued growing, but the fastest growth came in the Western Reserve of northeast Ohio. From the 1880s immigrants from the rural hinterlands of the United States and of central, eastern, and southern Europe poured into Cleveland, the Mahoning Valley, and Toledo to form the gritty ethnic cities which were the most dynamic part of Ohio at the turn of the century. By 1910 Cleveland was larger than Cincinnati and was, momentarily, the nation's fourth largest city. Cleveland dreamed then, as Houston did in the early 1980s, of becoming a world-class city; instead, it lost the auto industry to the more venturesome bankers of Detroit and became merely a regional industrial center, thriving through the 1950s, in trouble later as its industries declined.

Ohio's industrialization brought a new politics. From 1896, when Ohio's William McKinley beat William Jennings Bryan of Nebraska, Ohio was Republican: it supported McKinley's high-tariff and gold-standard policies which were intended to and, until the 1930s, did prop up America's manufacturing wages, even then the nation's highest, and provide a stable currency and hence an environment conducive to long-term investment. To that the Republicans added railroad regulation and antitrust, to prevent big units from exercising too much economic power. Democrats were competitive, but their strength was mostly in rural and southern-oriented areas. Then came the Great Depression, and the politics of economic warfare. In the industrial centers of northern Ohio, labor union members sat down in plants and refused to let their owners throw them out; a Democratic governor declined to evict them.

The result was the unionization, in the late 1930s, of the steel, rubber, and auto industries. Workers and management alike assumed that the economy had stopped growing; they were fighting—sometimes in bloody battles in the streets—for bigger shares of the same pie. Conservatives like Ohio's Senator Robert Taft feared that unions would organize most of the work force and would, through their support of New Deal Democrats, control government and

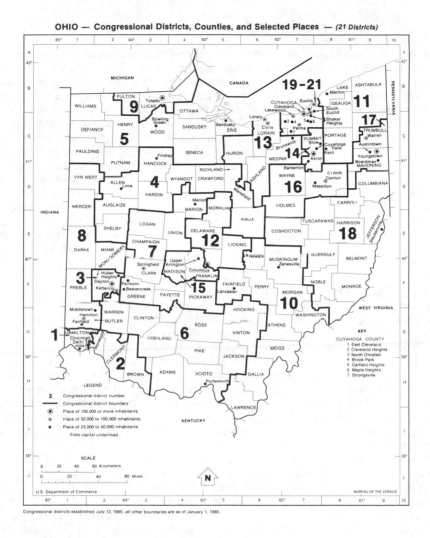

OHIO — Congressional Districts, Counties, and Selected Places — *(21 Districts)*

Congressional districts established July 12, 1985; all other boundaries are as of January 1, 1980.

institute something like Marxist Socialism in the United States. He counterattacked with the Taft–Hartley Act, passed in 1947, which was intended to and did end the wave of union organization. It was obviously difficult for Republicans to win elections in a mostly blue-collar state while pursuing such policies. But with the aid of political strategists like Ray Bliss, longtime Ohio Republican chairman, they kept control of the state's congressional delegation; and malapportionment, which swelled the power of the old small towns where McKinley politics was alive, helped them keep control of the legislature. Careful organization helped the part of the state that was declining demographically to maintain political control.

Ohio still leads the nation in some respects, ranking third in value added by manufacturing, not far behind California and New York, and well ahead of Illinois and Texas. And Ohio comes very close to ranking third in the number of full-time students in institutions of higher education. But what had been strengths in the 1950s and early 1960s had become weaknesses by the early 1980s. For this is a state whose number of young people shrunk even faster than the nation's, and many of its colleges—and its public universities as well—were facing severe fiscal problems.

And this is a state whose manufacturing base, all of a sudden, seemed to be obsolete and whose factories all seemed to be closing.

The apparent suddenness of these problems made Ohioans almost panicky about their future. They survived depression and recession before, but they were panicky, not sure they would do it again, or how. Actually, the problems had been building for a long time. The last decade in which Ohio grew rapidly enough to win rather than lose congressional districts was the 1950s (Michigan and New Jersey, two other manufacturing states, gained seats then as well). That was also the last decade in which Ohio's number of young people increased significantly. Since then, its economy, despite publicized attempts by former Governor James Rhodes to attract jobs, has grown more slowly than the national average; it has had steady, though slow, outmigration. Moreover, it has failed to do what Ohio did for many Americans and immigrants in the 1830s and in the 1890s—to capture their imagination, to attract them with a vision of a better tomorrow. Ohio is basically a manufacturing state, without the huge white-collar and managerial classes you find in New York City or Chicago or Los Angeles or San Francisco; and in decades when paper-shuffling rather than tinkering with machines has seized the nation's imagination—when the national hero is merger artist Felix Rohatyn rather than mechanical genius Henry Ford—manufacturing has failed to attract the brightest minds and has quietly declined.

On top of this, Ohio has the additional embarrassment in March 1985 of the Home State Savings & Loan scandal: this Cincinnati S&L, the largest insured by the state, owned by Democratic campaign contributor Marvin Warner, had not been properly regulated; Governor Richard Celeste, who had received crucial financial support from Warner in 1982, seemed to be reeling. But by 1986 all the savings and loans were reopened and no depositors had lost their funds; more important, the indicators seemed to be saying that Ohio's economy was coming to. The big steel mills along Cleveland's Cuyahoga River were still cold, but the number of jobs was on the rise again, increasing more rapidly in small businesses than they were decreasing in the more visible big units. Americans were beginning to realize that the nation's economic future depended on making products others will buy, and manufacturing which will remain Ohio's strong suit inched closer to being in fashion again. There are signs of turnaround. Unemployment is down, and Ohio's Thomas Edison state investment program is helping to stimulate innovation and to build on Ohio's industrial strengths.

For years Ohio's political leanings came pretty close to reflecting the nation's, though sometimes in exaggerated form; and they have followed national trends in presidential contests in the 1980s. But in state elections Ohio sets its own course. In the 1960s, when the nation was Democratic, Ohio was electing Republican James Rhodes to the first and second of his four terms as governor; his platform was low taxes, low spending, all to bring in jobs, jobs, jobs. In the 1970s and 1980s, when the nation moved toward the Republicans, Ohio moved toward Democrats: it hasn't elected a Republican U.S. Senator since 1970, and while it did elect Rhodes governor again, in 1974 and 1978, he won by only the narrowest of margins and voters gave him Democratic legislatures to deal with. When the two-consecutive-term limit required Rhodes to retire again in the recession year of 1982, Democrat Richard Celeste was easily elected governor, and he won easily again in 1986 when Rhodes ran again at age 76 for the job he won four times. In the 1980s, when the state was facing economic disaster, turnout rose to historic highs, with off-year turnout up from 2.8 to 3.3 million between 1978 and 1982 and presidential turnout up from 4.3 to 4.6 million between 1980 and 1984. But as the economy improved, turnout sank back to 3.1 million.

But it may be useful to look at two halves (roughly) of Ohio: the northeast industrial rim, from Cleveland west to Toledo and south through Canton and Youngstown to the strip-mining coal fields near the Ohio River—coal, steel, and auto country—and the rest of the state. Northeast industrial Ohio has become heavily Democratic: it came within a hair of going for Walter Mondale in 1984 (he did about as well here as in Minnesota, and this is bigger), and it has given Richard Celeste 68% and 70% of its votes—the sort of near-unanimous response you usually don't get outside city-states like Massachusetts, Rhode Island, and Maryland. The rest of the state is different, but not overwhelmingly Republican: Reagan carried it 2 to 1 in 1984, but it has also given majorities to Celeste, Senator Howard Metzenbaum, and, without difficulty, Senator John Glenn. This is manufacturing country, some of it (like Cincinnati) with a Republican tradition, and it seems to be voting these days much like Indiana.

Governor. Elected twice by large margins, with policies that meet general approval, Governor Richard Celeste nonetheless lacks a firm hold on the electorate. The savings and loan failures were just one problem; the *Cleveland Plain Dealer,* while supporting Celeste, complained that the "breaches of public confidence were legion—favoritism in contracts, appointments of cronies, lapses in sound judgment and hiring or association with numerous people who were subsequently indicted." Celeste is quick to explain away each instance, but the overall impression is of a governor with a flair for politics that degenerates too often into a weakness for rogues and corner-cutters.

Otherwise Celeste has worked successfully to change the focus of Ohio's public life. He has talked since 1982 about improving the state's economy, not by reviving old big units but by encouraging new small ones; he has been willing to spend more on public education than Ohio in Rhodes's tradition has been inclined to do, and was able to take the heat for a temporary tax increase, beating a 1983 referendum that would have overturned it. In 1986 Rhodes tried to use scandals and Celeste's support of gay rights to beat him, but aside from getting off a few good quips (he said he'd debate Celeste on Marvin Warner's farm) he made no headway and was unable to persuade voters that a 77-year-old politician could do better. Celeste, in contrast, stuck with his own positive economic themes. Celeste's large majorities and policy successes entitle him to national attention, but unless the weaknesses so apparent in his first term are visibly corrected in his second, he will not be a competitor for the position in national politics which, since his election as lieutenant governor in 1974 and his days as head of the Peace Corps in 1979 and 1980, it has been apparent he was aiming for.

Celeste was reelected by one of those surges of near-unanimous support that were seldom seen in the negative 1973-83 period but which several incumbents of both parties were beneficiaries of in 1986: in Massachusetts and California, New York and Georgia, Michigan and Arkansas. What's striking is the extent to which support for at least the Democratic tickets ran in tandem with those of the ticket leaders. Celeste's 61% (70% in northeast industrial Ohio, 53% in the other half of the state) was matched by the 55% to 65% showings of Democrats for lower state offices and was almost exactly equal to the 62% won by Senator John Glenn. In the past, Glenn had won by carrying almost every county, running far ahead of normal Democratic showings in the rural areas; this time, he was not much ahead of Celeste, with 71% in the industrial northeast and 56% in the rest of the state. As Democrats have become more popular, Glenn has come to be seen more as a Democrat.

Senators. Ohio's best known politician in the 1980s has been Senator John Glenn. Since his moment in the spotlight when he became the first American to orbit the earth in 1962, Glenn has been a personification of the small town virtues of family, God-fearing religion, duty, patriotism, and hard work. He actually is from the small town of New Concord, right on the National Road divide, and he really does believe in its values. Yet he also has the aggressiveness needed to be a brilliant fighter pilot in World War II and Korea, to have gotten himself into the astronaut program, to have been a successful businessman afterwards, and to have succeeded in being elected, after a couple of missteps, to the Senate.

Yet he was not a success as a presidential candidate. In critical debates in the winter of 1983-84 he did not seem to have the suppleness of mind of some of his competitors and failed to give a sense of command over them. He was hurt as well, as he has been in Democratic primaries in Ohio, because the same wholesomeness which makes him so appealing to the general electorate tends to turn off the party activists and self-conscious minorities who are disproportionately influential in Democratic politics: remember how his keynote speech at the 1976 national convention was overshadowed by Barbara Jordan's. There was lots of talk in Iowa and New

Hampshire about organizational deficiencies in Glenn's campaign. But the greater problem was that this competent and engaging Senator was not able to convince many party activists and voters that he had the stuff it takes to be President. Hanging over from the 1984 campaign was a $2 million-plus debt, most of it accumulated in the two weeks after New Hampshire when Glenn struggled to win a primary in the South; and although other candidates, notably Alan Cranston, paid their debts off, Glenn had been unable to do so as of early 1987. The Federal Election Commission did rule that he could transfer $800,000 left over from his Senate campaign treasury, but that would still leave $1.2 million unpaid. An additional problem was that much of the money was advanced by Ohio banks which received "letters of comfort" from several rich Ohioans (including Marvin Warner) not guaranteeing the debt, which would be illegal, but saying they would try to get it paid off. Glenn's 1986 opponent Thomas Kindness attacked this arrangement with cause; it's a bit jarring to see a man whose integrity no one doubts skate so close to, if not over, the edge of what the campaign finance laws allow.

Glenn has been criticized as a man who gets too involved in the minutiae of issues and lacks a broad perspective. But in the Senate that has enabled him to make useful contributions on sticky issues most Senators avoid. The prime example is nuclear proliferation, on which he has been vigilant about transfers of nuclear technology and materials to countries like India and Pakistan. On this critical issue he knows the details, masters the arguments, and never quits fighting his good fight, towering over everyone else in American government. Naturally Glenn is interested in military matters—so much so, in fact, that after the 1984 election he gave up a high-ranking seat on Foreign Relations to serve on Armed Services. On Foreign Relations, he followed the SALT talks very closely and, despite an obvious desire to support the treaty, hesitated because of concerns about verification (later resolved, he said, by technical innovations). As a military man who advanced through channels, Glenn is not especially sympathetic to the new breed of Pentagon critics, and he tends to support weapons systems recommended by the services. When Glenn came to the Senate, he seemed notably less liberal than most northern Democrats. Now the gap is much narrower, but more because the others—and the issues—have changed than because Glenn has. He was never enthusiastic about income redistribution schemes, but he is not an enthusiast for market economics either: he has spent his life in the public sector and represents a state which feels that the market—and particularly foreign trade—doesn't treat it fairly. On cultural issues this son of middle America has always been willing to vote against abortion restrictions and school prayer amendments; who is going to say he is insufficiently patriotic or pious?

In the 100th Congress, Glenn chairs the Governmental Affairs Committee, sometimes described as a hunting license to get involved on any issue you want and sometimes as a committee in search of a role. Glenn will probably use it to spotlight the nuclear proliferation issue and to look into the issues of nuclear waste disposal, sunset and zero-based budgeting legislation, and airline safety.

Glenn's senatorial career had two false starts: he began running in 1964, then left the race when he injured himself in a household accident; he ran again in 1970, but was upset in the primary by Howard Metzenbaum, who in turn lost the general election narrowly to Robert Taft, Jr. In 1974 Glenn and Metzenbaum ran against each other again, in one of the most bitter primaries of recent times; this time Glenn won. He won the general election easily that year and has had no trouble at all holding the seat. (Metzenbaum won the other Ohio seat in 1976 and he and Glenn are now on friendly terms.) He won reelection with a record-breaking 69% of the vote in 1980, even while Reagan was carrying the state; he was cut back to 62% in 1986, when he had a serious opponent in Representative Thomas Kindness. Kindness cut Glenn's inroads into the normal Republican vote, but in a very Democratic year in Ohio that still left Glenn with an overwhelming majority.

Senator Howard Metzenbaum has a background almost entirely different from Glenn's. Metzenbaum is from Cleveland; spent most of his life in business, making his fortune in airport parking lots (not a business one enters for love). He had been politically active for years. He was campaign manager for Senator Stephen Young's surprise victories in 1958 against John Bricker at age 74, and against Robert Taft, Jr., in 1964. Then he ran himself, beat Glenn and almost beat Taft in 1970; lost to Glenn in the primary in 1974, after having been appointed to fill a vacancy by Governor John Gilligan; then ran again in 1976, and beat Cleveland Congressman William Stanton in the primary and Taft in the general.

Metzenbaum has fought his way upward in business, in elections, and now in the Senate. His record on issues is one of the most liberal in the Senate. But more distinctive and important has been his role as a watchdog for legislation that in his view benefits special interests. On the floor of the Senate, he is a kind of Horatius at the bridge, putting holds near the end of the session on dozens of pieces of what he considers special interest legislation and then filibustering them if they came up. In effect Metzenbaum forces Senators backing these bills to negotiate with him, even if they had a large majority and he represented only himself. He first got interested in the possibilities for delay in the Senate rules when he and James Abourezk of South Dakota staged a two-man filibuster against deregulation of oil and gas prices; that failed, but Metzenbaum saw that the possibilities for delay were tremendous, and that at the end of the session delay means death for a bill. So he is ready with amendments (as many as 100 to a single bill) and with extended comment. Metzenbaum himself has proposed changing the rules that allow him to do this; but in the meantime he proposes to take advantage of them. Colleagues get infuriated with Metzenbaum; they vow to deny him any special breaks he might seek; but they cannot get around him and so, grumbling, make their plans with him in mind and seek to get his approval for legislation that, before he was in the Senate, would probably pass through easily.

Metzenbaum takes on big issues and small. He held up passage of a bill giving the Alaska Railroad to the state until an infuriated Ted Stevens persuaded the state to pay something for it. He almost singlehandedly forced Judiciary Committee Chairman Strom Thurmond to put an indefinite hold on the nomination of presidential counselor Edwin Meese as Attorney General in 1984 while an independent counsel investigated charges that Meese had used his White House office for personal gain; when the nomination was resubmitted in 1985, Metzenbaum again led the campaign against it—even though the independent counsel had cleared Meese of criminal wrong doing and the appointment was headed for confirmation. Nonetheless, he wasn't immune himself to charges of ethical improprieties: he was criticized in 1984 for accepting a $250,000 "finder's fee" for making a phone call putting a buyer in touch with the owner of Washington's Hay-Adams hotel, and returned the money when that was revealed. Metzenbaum is proud of delaying natural gas price decontrol, of hounding the Synfuels Corporation to its death, of delaying and ultimately blocking the sale of Conrail to the Norfolk Southern, and of blocking what he considered bad transition rules in the 1986 tax reform.

All these are negative achievements. Metzenbaum has his positive causes as well—banning bullet-piercing bullets, to name one—but in the Reagan years his posture has inevitably been defensive. With the Democrats' recapture of the Senate, he now chairs three subcommittees; Edward Kennedy's decision to take the Labor and Public Welfare chair keeps Metzenbaum out of it. But it's not clear that Ohio voters want a big expansion of the federal government, and Metzenbaum is certainly conscious of what Ohio voters want as his seat is up in 1988. Metzenbaum's fighting style and opposition to powers perceived as entrenched helped him win reelection against a weak opponent with a solid 57% in the recession year of 1982; he got 68% in industrial northeast Ohio and carried the rest of the state with 52%. He is likely to have stronger opposition—from Cleveland Mayor George Voinovich or 6th District Representative Bob McEwen—in what may not be as favorable a year. For a while there was speculation that Metzenbaum would retire at 71, perhaps in favor of his son-in-law, Hyatt Legal Services entrepreneur Joel Hyatt. But Metzenbaum could have had a more-than-comfortable retirement long ago and has opted instead for the rigors of end-of-the-session midnight quorum calls and campaigning in Cleveland and Chillicothe. He and the man whose campaigns he managed have held Ohio Senate seats for 25 of the last 30 years; that suggests he's unlikely to quit and will be difficult to defeat.

Presidential politics. Ohio is one of those states that is always a major prize in presidential elections, and always seriously contested. Its 23 electoral votes are less than it used to have, but are still too many to be ignored, and in any close race the result here is likely to be close. Remembering the old saying that no Republican candidate can win without Ohio, and with the knowledge that there was no way Walter Mondale could put together an electoral college majority without this state, Reagan campaign manager Ed Rollins put extra money into Ohio, and ran specially crafted ads comparing Mondale's tax position to Celeste. This effort seems to have put Ohio out of reach for Mondale early, and in effect to have doomed his campaign even before his victory in the first debate.

In 1987 Ohio switched its primary from May, when it has generally had little effect on nominations, to March 15, a week after the southern megaprimary. The idea was to create a Great Lakes regional contest, with the Illinois primary, the Michigan Democratic primary, and the Minnesota caucuses; but as 1987 went on it was not clear whether these races together would be enough to spotlight the region, and there was some talk the Ohio primary might be rescheduled for May. If it does come off, the interesting thing will be to see whether candidates focus on the ailing steel and auto industries and call for trade barriers to protect them, or whether they look at the growing parts of the Great Lakes economies—a more difficult task, because growing businesses are smaller and less visible than those which are declining, and don't have entrenched political constituencies. But it's worth noting that the governors who won big victories in this region in 1986—Celeste and Michigan's Jim Blanchard—accentuated the positive and emphasized the new growth rather than the old decline in their campaigns. And it's worth remembering that Gary Hart, quite against the odds and prognostication, beat Walter Mondale by a 42%–40% margin here (and by nearly identical percentages in the less-noticed contest next door in Indiana the same day). Hart ran even or only barely behind in most of Ohio's cities and carried Youngstown with a set of ads hand-crafted to its problems; his biggest margins, however, were in the smaller areas which have had a disproportionate share of Ohio's growth.

Congressional redistricting. Congressional redistricting was a bipartisan exercise in Ohio in 1982, not because its politicians are altruistic, but because the Democrats controlled the state House of Representatives and Republicans, the state Senate and governorship. The bipartisanship is apparent in the Cincinnati and Columbus areas, where partisans of either side would have drawn the lines differently. The court-ordered redistricting of 1985 turned out to be virtually identical, since the Democrats picked up the governorship in 1982 but lost control of the state Senate in 1984.

The People: Est. Pop. 1986: 10,752,000; Pop. 1980: 10,797,630, dn. 0.4% 1980–86 and up 1.3% 1970–80; 4.46% of U.S. total, 7th largest. 13% with 1–3 yrs. col., 15% with 4+ yrs. col.; 10.3% below poverty level. Single ancestry: 13% German, 9% English, 4% Irish, 2% Italian, Polish, 1% Hungarian, French. Households (1980): 74% family, 41% with children, 62% married couples; 31.6% housing units rented; median monthly rent: $167; median house value: $45,100. Voting age pop. (1980): 7,703,310; 9% Black, 1% Spanish origin. Registered voters (1986): 5,938,889; 1,869,124 D (32%), 1,148,286 R (19%); 2,921,479 unaffiliated (49%).

1986 Share of Federal Tax Burden: $32,466,000,000; 4.32% of U.S. total, 7th largest.

1986 Share of Federal Expenditures

	Total		Non-Defense		Defense	
Total Expend	$31,823m	(3.83%)	$24,894m	(4.15%)	$6,929m	(3.01%)
St/Lcl Grants	4,764m	(4.23%)	4,759m	(4.23%)	5m	(4.50%)
Salary/Wages	3,175m	(2.63%)	1,775m	(3.02%)	1,400m	(2.26%)
Pymts to Indiv	15,880m	(4.35%)	15,555m	(4.48%)	325m	(1.83%)
Procurement	7,452m	(3.62%)	2,251m	(4.05%)	5,201m	(3.47%)
Research/Other	553m	(2.07%)	553m	(2.08%)	0m	(0.17%)

Political Lineup: Governor, Richard F. Celeste (D); Lt. Gov., Paul R. Leonard (D); Secy. of State, Sherrod Brown (D); Atty. Gen., Anthony J. Celebrezze, Jr. (D); Treasurer, Mary Ellen Withrow (D); Auditor, Thomas E. Ferguson (D). State Senate, 33 (18 R and 15 D); State House of Representatives, 99 (60 D and 39 R). Senators, John H. Glenn, Jr. (D) and Howard M. Metzenbaum (D). Representatives, 21 (11 D and 10 R).

1984 Presidential Vote:

Reagan (R)	2,678,559 (59%)	Reagan (R)	2,206,545 (52%)
Mondale (D)	1,825,440 (40%)	Carter (D)	1,752,414 (41%)
		Anderson (I)	254,472 (6%)

1984 Democratic Presidential Primary		**1980 Republican Presidential Primary**	
Hart	608,528 (42%)	Reagan	unopposed
Mondale	583,595 (40%)		
Jackson	237,133 (16%)		
Three others	17,980 (1%)		

GOVERNOR

Gov. Richard F. Celeste (D)

Elected 1982, term expires Jan. 1991; b. Nov. 11, 1937, Lakewood; home, Columbus; Yale U., B.A. 1959; Rhodes Scholar, Oxford U., 1960-62; United Methodist; married (Dagmar).

Career: Exec. Asst. to U.S. Ambassador to India, 1963–67; Real estate developer, Natl. Housing Corp., 1967–75; OH House of Reps., 1971–75; Lt. Gov. of OH, 1975–79; Dir., Peace Corps., 1979–81.

Office: State House, Columbus 43266-0601, 614-466-3555.

Election Results

1986 gen.	Richard F. Celeste (D)	1,858,372	(61%)
	James A. Rhodes (R)	1,207,264	(39%)
1986 prim.	Richard F. Celeste (D)	684,206	(100%)
1982 gen.	Richard F. Celeste (D)	1,981,882	(59%)
	Clarence J. Brown (R)	1,303,962	(39%)

SENATORS

Sen. John H. Glenn Jr. (D)

Elected 1974, seat up 1986; b. July 18, 1921, Cambridge; home, Columbus; Muskingum Col., B.S. 1943; Presbyterian; married (Annie).

Career: USMC, 1942–65; NASA Astronaut, 1959–65, First American to orbit the Earth, 1962; Vice Pres., Royal Crown Cola Co., 1966–68, Pres., Royal Crown Intl., 1967–69.

Offices: 503 HSOB 20510, 202-224-3353. Also 200 N. High St., Rm. 400, Columbus 43215, 614-469-6697; and 201 Superior Ave., Cleveland 44114, 216-522-7095.

Committees: *Armed Services* (8th of 11 D). Subcommittees: Conventional Forces and Alliance Defense; Manpower and Personnel (Chairman); Projection Forces and Regional Defense. *Governmental Affairs* (Chairman of 8 D). Subcommittee: Investigations. *Special Committee on Aging* (2d of 10 D).

Group Ratings

	ADA	ACLU	COPE	CFA	LCV	ACU	NTU	NSI	COC	CEI
1986	65	78	80	73	50	30	30	60	44	27
1985	75	—	79	67	—	27	22	—	34	—

National Journal Ratings

	1986 LIB — 1986 CONS	1985 LIB — 1985 CONS
Economic	78% — 20%	65% — 31%
Social	73% — 26%	74% — 22%
Foreign	53% — 45%	62% — 37%

Key Votes

1) Ease Gun Cont	FOR	5) Grm-Rdmn Def Red	AGN	9) Rehnquist Nom	AGN
2) Immig Reform	FOR	6) Contra Aid	AGN	10) Tax Reform	FOR
3) Lmt Text Imp	FOR	7) SDI Funding	FOR	11) Drug Death Pen	FOR
4) Aid Tobac Ind	AGN	8) Lmt PAC Contrib	FOR	12) S Africa Sanc	FOR

Election Results

1986 general	John H. Glenn Jr. (D)	1,949,208	(62%)	($1,319,026)
	Thomas N. Kindness (R)	1,171,893	(38%)	($657,908)
1986 primary	John H. Glenn Jr. (D)	678,171	(88%)	
	Don Scott (R)	96,309	(12%)	
1980 general	John H. Glenn Jr. (D)	2,770,786	(69%)	($1,157,965)
	James E. Betts (R)	1,137,695	(28%)	($423,060)

Campaign Contributions and Expenditures

1985-86		Direct Cont. 1985-86		PACS Breakdown 1985-86			
Receipts	$2,088,191	Indiv.	$1,345,763	Corp.	$220,633	T/M/H	$83,896
Expend.	$1,319,026	Party	$17,749	Labor	$233,100	Agr.	$4,250
Unspent	$818,910	PACS	$625,803	Ideo.	$71,704	CWOS	$12,220
		Cand.	$47,872				

Sen. Howard M. Metzenbaum (D)

Elected 1976, seat up 1988; b. June 4, 1917, Cleveland; home, Shaker Heights; OH State U., B.A. 1939, LL.D. 1941; Jewish; married (Shirley).

Career: Practicing atty.; Cofounder, Airport Parking Co. of America, ComCorp Communications Corp.; Chmn. of the Bd., ITT Consumer Services Corp., 1966–68; OH House of Reps., 1943–46; OH Senate, 1947–50; Campaign Mgr. for Sen. Stephen M. Young, 1958, 1964.

Offices: 140 RSOB 20510, 202-224-2315. Also 200 N. High St., Rm. 405, Columbus 43215, 614-469-6774; 1240 E. 9th St., Rm. 2919, Cleveland 44114, 216-544-7272; City Ctr. One, Ltd., 100 Fed. Plaza E., Ste. 510, Youngstown 44503, 216-746-1132; 10411 Fed. Bldg., Cincinnati 45202, 513-684-3894; and 234 Summit St., Toledo 43603, 419-259-7536.

Committees: *Energy and Natural Resources* (4th of 10 D). Subcommittees: Energy Regulation and Conservation (Chairman); Energy Research and Development; Water and Power. *Judiciary* (4th of 8 D). Subcommittees: Antitrust, Monopolies and Business Rights (Chairman); Constitution; Courts and Administrative Practice. *Labor and Human Resources* (3d of 9 D). Subcommittees: Aging; Education, Arts and Humanities; Handicapped; Labor (Chairman).

Group Ratings

	ADA	ACLU	COPE	CFA	LCV	ACU	NTU	NSI	COC	CEI
1986	100	92	94	93	83	4	41	10	21	22
1985	100	—	94	100	—	0	31	—	29	—

National Journal Ratings

	1986 LIB — 1986 CONS		1985 LIB — 1985 CONS	
Economic	85%	8%	89%	8%
Social	92%	0%	88%	0%
Foreign	75%	0%	86%	12%

Key Votes

1) Ease Gun Cont	AGN	5) Grm-Rdmn Def Red	AGN	9) Rehnquist Nom	AGN
2) Immig Reform	FOR	6) Contra Aid	AGN	10) Tax Reform	FOR
3) Lmt Text Imp	FOR	7) SDI Funding	AGN	11) Drug Death Pen	FOR
4) Aid Tobac Ind	AGN	8) Lmt PAC Contrib	FOR	12) S Africa Sanc	FOR

Election Results

1982 general	Howard M Metzenbaum (D)	1,923,767	(57%)	($2,794,172)
	Paul E. Pfeifer (R)	1,396,790	(41%)	($1,025,595)
1982 primary	Howard M. Metzenbaum (D)	810,785	(83%)	
	Norbert G. Dennerll, Jr. (D)	167,778	(17%)	
1976 general	Howard M. Metzenbaum (D)	1,941,113	(50%)	($1,092,053)
	Robert A. Taft, Jr. (R)	1,823,774	(47%)	($1,304,207)

Campaign Contributions and Expenditures

1979-82		Direct Cont. 1981-82		PACS Breakdown			
Receipts	$3,767,625	Indiv.	$3,065,814	Agr	$21,600	Ideo	$68,925
Expend.	$2,794,172	Party	$17,500	Bus	$57,844	Lbr	$227,723
Unspent	$970,455	PACS	$404,182	Hlth	$10,500	Prof	$17,050

FIRST DISTRICT

One of the leading industrial waterways in America is the trickle of Mill Creek as it runs past steep slopes toward the Ohio River down the center of Cincinnati. This is Cincinnati's industrial corridor: here are the great Procter & Gamble detergent factories and many of the city's machine tool makers; not far to the north is the General Electric jet engine plant. Just about all of Cincinnati and suburban Hamilton County west of Mill Creek forms Ohio's 1st Congressional District. The 1st includes some of the oldest and poorest parts of the city, like the Over-the-Rhine area (a name that recalls Cincinnati's German heritage) and some of the city's black slums (though only 16% of its residents are black). More typical are the old neighborhoods, some dating back more than 100 years, of wooden houses tucked in the valleys or ravines between Cincinnati's many hills. Here immigrant Germans moved, commuting to work in the factories on foot or downtown by the horsecar; in such neighborhoods today you could easily imagine yourself in the America of 50 or even 80 years ago. Cincinnati was one of America's largest cities at the turn of the century, and the comfortable urbanity of that period is still apparent in many of its streets and neighborhoods.

Cincinnati's main ethnic group is German, and its ancestral politics is Republican. As its more prosperous offspring have moved off to the suburbs, the city of Cincinnati itself has become more Democratic; the suburbs in most elections are overwhelmingly Republican. Nevertheless, this is a district which elects a Democratic congressman. He is Thomas Luken, and by now he is a House veteran and chairman of a subcommittee of the powerful Energy and Commerce Committee. Yet in Cincinnati he is remembered by many from his days on the Cincinnati Council—a body with limited jurisdiction these days, but which gets enough publicity to make its members the strongest candidates in the whole metropolitan area, even though they represent only a fraction of it. In some ways he resembles his district: he is an old-fashioned, not especially articulate congressman, one who reflects old values and has plodded on with considerable success.

Luken was elevated to a chairmanship in 1987, and to his own surprise. When Chairman John Dingell reshuffled the jurisdiction of Energy and Commerce subcommittees, everyone expected James Florio of New Jersey to take the panel handling transportation and the Superfund which is so popular in his New Jersey district. But Florio opted for the subcommittee with jurisdiction over trade and consumer affairs instead, which gave Luken transportation. That has important policy implications. Luken has backed measures to reregulate railroad rates in response to complaints from shippers. And he has been somewhat less eager to impose restrictions on industry for the sake of cleaning up the environment than many Democrats in response to the calls from industry groups and unions.

In fact the major complaint about Luken is that he seems to make most of his decisions on Energy and Commerce in response to pressure from well-organized groups. He has supported measures to relax the Clean Air Act, arguing that its present terms unduly restrict industry; he was the leader in the effort to overturn the Federal Trade Commission's regulations on funeral homes. He is known, and was attacked in the 1984 election, for being one of the committee members most responsive to the appeals of PACs, and most assiduous in seeking political contributions from them; against nuisance opposition he collected $225,000 from PACs for 1986. He was named in 1984 as one of the 10 worst congressmen by *Washington Monthly*, which criticized his performance on PAC issues and his temper (also on the list were Dan Rostenkowski and Pat Moynihan). His record is notably less liberal on economic issues than those of most northern Democrats, and his approach to cultural issues reflects traditional Catholic attitudes; he is a fervent opponent of abortion, for example, though an equally fervent backer of a national lottery.

Luken may or may not be overly responsive to lobbyists' pressures, but he is certainly aware that well-positioned Energy and Commerce members can easily raise hundreds of thousands of dollars of campaign money, money that can be very useful for a congressman who started off without a firm hold on his seat. Luken was first elected from the east side district in the spring of 1974, in one of those contests that helped end Richard Nixon's career. But Willis Gradison, the loser in the spring, came back in the fall and beat Luken. Two years later Luken ran in the west Cincinnati district against an incumbent who spent most of his time in Florida. He won that race, and beat a strong opponent again in 1978.

Fortified with big campaign treasuries, he has only had tough opposition once since, in 1984. It might have been more interesting if Cincinnati Councilman Kenneth Blackwell had won the nomination—Blackwell is one of the few black Republican politicians with a genuine local base in the nation. But Blackwell lost the primary 52%–48%, and Luken rather easily beat a more conventional Republican. He was reelected without serious opposition in 1986, and with his subcommittee chair, his capacity to raise funds, and his local popularity, he seems capable of continuing to win for some time.

The People: Pop. 1980: 514,190, dn. 2.2% 1970–80. Households (1980): 72% family, 40% with children, 57% married couples; 40.2% housing units rented; median monthly rent: $171; median house value: $47,900. Voting age pop. (1980): 364,014; 14% Black, 1% Spanish origin.

1984 Presidential Vote: Reagan (R) 144,629   (65%)
Mondale (D) 77,558   (35%)

Rep. Thomas A. Luken (D)

Elected 1976; b. July 9, 1925, Cincinnati; home, Cincinnati; Bowling Green U., 1943–44, Xavier U., A.B. 1947, Salmon P. Chase Law Sch., LL.B. 1950; Roman Catholic; married (Shirley).

Career: USMC, WWII; Practicing atty.; Deer Park City Solicitor, 1955–61; U.S. Dist. Atty. for S. Dist. of OH, 1961–64; Cincinnati City Cncl., 1964–67, 1969–71, 1973; Mayor, 1972–73; U.S. House of Reps., 1973–74.

Offices: 2368 RHOB 20515, 202-225-2216. Also Gwynne Bldg., Ste. 712, 602 Main St., Cincinnati 45202, 513-684-2723.

Committees: *Energy and Commerce* (7th of 25 D). Subcommittees: Oversight and Investigations; Transportation, Tourism and Hazardous Materials (Chairman). *Small Business* (4th of 25 D). Subcommittees: Antitrust, Impact of Deregulation and Privatization; Regulation and Business Opportunities. *Select Committee on Aging* (11th of 39 D). Subcommittee: Health and Long-Term Care.

Group Ratings

	ADA	ACLU	COPE	CFA	LCV	ACU	NTU	NSI	COC	CEI
1986	80	68	77	75	42	19	29	0	25	33
1985	65	—	76	83	—	32	45	—	41	—

National Journal Ratings

	1986 LIB — 1986 CONS	1985 LIB — 1985 CONS
Economic	72% — 27%	59% — 39%
Social	55% — 44%	28% — 72%
Foreign	80% — 0%	68% — 32%

Key Votes

1) Lmt Cln Water Act	AGN	5) Retain Gun Cont	AGN	9) Aid Angola Reb	AGN
2) Rpl Tobac Sub	FOR	6) Contra Aid	AGN	10) Tax Reform	FOR
3) Grm-Rdmn Def Red	FOR	7) Lmt Text Imp	AGN	11) S Africa Sanc	FOR
4) Ban Polygraph	FOR	8) Limit SDI	FOR	12) Immig Reform	FOR

Election Results

1986 general	Thomas A. Luken (D)	90,477	(62%)	($261,455)
	Fred E. Morr (R)	56,100	(38%)	($127,653)
1986 primary	Thomas A. Luken (D)	18,903	(88%)	
	David McArthur Douglas (D)	2,699	(22)	
1984 general	Thomas A. Luken (D)	121,392	(55%)	($563,003)
	Norman A. Murdock (R)	88,713	(40%)	($309,768)

Campaign Contributions and Expenditures

1985-86		Direct Cont. 1985-86		PACS Breakdown 1985-86			
Receipts	$392,054	Indiv.	$153,233	Corp.	$86,904	T/M/H	$87,323
Expend.	$261,455	Party	$127	Labor	$39,650	Agr.	$1,250
Unspent	$135,628	PACS	$224,896	Ideo.	$8,233	CWOS	$1,536
		Cand.	$23,600				

SECOND DISTRICT

The east side of Cincinnati and its eastern Hamilton County suburbs, plus two counties along the Ohio River, make up the 2d Congressional District of Ohio. Since 1852, Cincinnati and Hamilton County have been divided, by a vertical line, into two congressional districts; in the 1980 Census, they lacked enough population for two districts by themselves, so more territory was added to this district. Sensible, because Clermont County, just to the east, has been filling up with people who have moved out from Cincinnati and its close-in suburbs, doubling its population in the last 20 years. The district goes as far as Brown County, farther up the Ohio River—at the spot where Liza crossed the ice in *Uncle Tom's Cabin*—is still almost entirely rural, but may be in line for some development as well.

The east side of Cincinnati is, by and large, the more prosperous and fashionable side of the city, which was the cultural and commercial capital of the Midwest even before the Tafts arrived. In some neighborhoods within Cincinnati and in suburbs like Indian Hill are the fashionable estates of the city's elite. But in the interstices of the hills are warehouses and factories, some of them the machine tool shops which make Cincinnati one of the nation's leaders in this now beleaguered industry. The northern suburbs are a mix of shopping centers and high-income subdivisions; within the city itself are the formerly Jewish sections of Avondale and Walnut Hills, now mostly black. Many neighborhoods, such as Norwood, a suburban enclave surrounded by Cincinnati, are inhabited mainly by migrants from the hills of Kentucky and Tennessee. The 2d has most of the city's Jewish population; from its early days as a German river town, Cincinnati has had an important German-Jewish community. Politically, it is more conservative and Republican than Jewish communities in other major cities.

Cincinnati has a well-deserved reputation for being a Republican city. Of the nation's 25 largest metropolitan areas, only Dallas–Fort Worth and San Diego turn in Republican margins with greater regularity. That has been the case since before the Civil War, when Cincinnati was a German, pro-Union, and Republican island in a sea of southern Democratic sentiment; it was the home then of Harriet Beecher Stowe, the author of *Uncle Tom's Cabin,* and of other antislavery agitators. In later years Cincinnati did not attract as many southern and eastern European immigrants as did Great Lakes industrial cities like Cleveland, Detroit, and Chicago; its ethnic character (like its physical appearance) and its political preference have remained pretty well fixed. Even many of the Appalachians here are Republicans, from Civil War Republican counties in the hills. Culturally, it is the home of one of the most successful anti-pornography drives of any city in the nation.

Out of Cincinnati have come several prominent Republicans, including Salmon P. Chase (the dithering Treasury Secretary in Gore Vidal's *Lincoln,* later Chief Justice), President and Chief Justice William Howard Taft, Speaker of the House Nicholas Longworth (who married Teddy Roosevelt's daughter Alice), and the late Senator Robert Taft. All were men of urbanity and learning, conservatives who sought to maintain the values and the political system which had allowed the growth and prosperity of ordered communities like Cincinnati, the articulate advocates of a system that worked. In the 1960s this district has had a series of prominent congressmen: John Gilligan, later governor of Ohio, and Robert Taft Jr., later U.S. Senator.

The current congressman from the district, Willis Gradison, is in Cincinnati's tradition of urbane conservatives. He is a believer in free market economics and shares the traditional Republican belief that business should be taxed lightly if you want investment and economic growth. As second ranking Republican on the Budget Committee, he is potentially one of his party's lead spokesmen on macroeconomic issues, particularly since ranking member Delbert Latta was ailing in the last Congress and tends toward partisan sarcasm rather than dispassionate analysis. Gradison is the opposite, though capable of sarcasm too ("I have questioned whether meeting the $108 billion target is possible, even if we were to draw liberally from our arsenal of blue smoke and mirrors, as we did last year"—but note that "we" is the whole

Congress). At the beginning of 1987, for example, he was proposed to his fellow Republicans to scale upward the Gramm-Rudman deficit targets but to insist on a genuine sequestration threat: an attempt to make Gramm-Rudman work as intended rather than to paper over the fact that no one has a realistic way to get anywhere close to its current targets.

On Ways and Means he proceeded similarly, questioning in 1985 and 1986 whether Dan Rostenkowski's tax reform bill would eliminate too many advantages for business. Yet Gradison did not join in the glee with which other, more partisan Republicans temporarily derailed Rostenkowski's bill in December 1985. On the Health subcommittee where he is ranking minority member, he was working with Chairman Pete Stark in early 1987 on their own version of a catastrophic health care program, essentially extending Medicare coverage to longer illnesses. Gradison is willing to consider even outlandish ideas on their merits, but usually he ends up seeing little merit in them; he is no enthusiast of Jack Kemp's supply-side economics, for example, or of Milton Friedman's monetarism. His approach is to ask basic questions about program and to find long-range solutions that make sense; not just to patch things up for the short term. He is a clear-sighted and fair-minded analyst of what is going on, the kind of man members of both parties go to to find out what is happening and what is at stake.

Gradison had to try twice to win this district: he lost to Thomas Luken in a 1974 special election, in which the main issue was Richard Nixon and Watergate; then, with Nixon gone, he beat Luken in November. (Luken went on to win the west Cincinnati district in 1976.) Since his first victory, Gradison has been elected by very large margins and has not attracted serious opposition; the extension of the district out into Clermont County has strengthened him. His policics and temperament seem to suit the district well, and there is no reason he cannot go on representing it for some time.

The People: Pop. 1980: 514,168, dn. 0.8% 1970–80. Households (1980): 70% family, 39% with children, 57% married couples; 39.4% housing units rented; median monthly rent: $168; median house value: $49,500. Voting age pop. (1980): 370,100 16% Black, 1% Spanish origin; 1% Asian origin.

1984 Presidential Vote:

Reagan (R)	144,299	(64%)
Mondale (D)	78,294	(35%)

Rep. Willis D. (Bill) Gradison, Jr. (R)

Elected 1974; b. Dec. 28, 1928, Cincinnati; home, Cincinnati; Yale U., B.A. 1948, Harvard U., M.B.A. 1951, D.C.S. 1954; Jewish; married (Heather).

Career: Investment broker; Asst. to U.S. Undersecy. of the Treasury, 1953–55; Asst. to U.S. Secy. of HEW, 1955–57; Cincinnati City Cncl., 1961–74, Vice-Mayor, 1967–71, Mayor, 1971.

Offices: 2311 RHOB 20515, 202-225-3164. Also 8008 Fed. Bldg., 550 Main St., Cincinnati 45202, 513-684-2456.

Committees: *Budget* (2d of 14 R). Task Forces: Budget Process (Ranking Member); Economic Policy; Health; Income Security. *Ways and Means* (7th of 13 R). Subcommittee: Health (Ranking Member); Public Assistance and Unemployment Compensation.

Group Ratings

	ADA	ACLU	COPE	CFA	LCV	ACU	NTU	NSI	COC	CEI
1986	15	10	14	42	32	59	61	60	94	79
1985	20	—	15	50	—	60	65	—	85	—

National Journal Ratings

	1986 LIB — 1986 CONS		1985 LIB — 1985 CONS	
Economic	10% —	88%	24% —	76%
Social	37% —	61%	0% —	76%
Foreign	37% —	62%	50% —	49%

Key Votes

1) Lmt Cln Water Act	FOR	5) Retain Gun Cont	FOR	9) Aid Angola Reb	FOR
2) Rpl Tobac Sub	AGN	6) Contra Aid	FOR	10) Tax Reform	FOR
3) Grm-Rdmn Def Red	FOR	7) Lmt Text Imp	AGN	11) S Africa Sanc	FOR
4) Ban Polygraph	AGN	8) Limit SDI	AGN	12) Immig Reform	AGN

Election Results

1986 general	Willis D. (Bill) Gradison, Jr. (R)	105,061	(70%)	($68,473)
	William F. Stineman (D).	43,448	(30%)	($1,474)
1986 primary	Willis D. (Bill) Gradison, Jr. (R)	33,207	(100%)	
1984 general	Willis D. (Bill) Gradison, Jr. (R)	149,603	(69%)	($88,702)
	Thomas J. Porter (D)	68,425	(31%)	($20,354)

Campaign Contributions and Expenditures

1985-86		Direct Cont. 1985-86		PACS Breakdown 1985-86			
Receipts	$197,857	Indiv.	$163,538	Corp.	$2,550	T/M/H	$950
Expend.	$68,473	Party	$2,006	Labor	$0	Agr.	$0
Unspent	$292,762	PACS	$3,600	Ideo.	$100	CWOS	$0

THIRD DISTRICT

Dayton, Ohio, just below the old National Road that spans the Midwest, at a point which was once the center of U.S. population, not far from the divide between northern and southern accents, has long been hailed as the typical American city. Yet when you look closely at Dayton or any other city hailed as typical, what is most interesting is what is distinctive. For one thing, Dayton is not a small town; it has a metropolitan population over 900,000, which puts it in the same league with nearby Columbus, Cincinnati, and Indianapolis; it boasts that it ranks 8th among cities in population within a 90-minute drive.

Moreover, Dayton has a proud history as the home of some of America's most inspired mechanics and tinkerers. It was here, for example, that Wilbur and Orville Wright designed their airplane and manufactured it; they took it down to Kitty Hawk to fly only because of the steady high winds there. It was the home of James Ritty, who invented the cash register—that indispensable instrument for large retail trade—and of John Henry Patterson, who made a success of the company that is now National Cash Register. It was home for a while of a trusted Patterson subordinate who feuded with him, Tom Watson, Sr., the founder of IBM. It was the hometown of Charles Kettering, who invented the automatic starters and several other innovations which revolutionized the automobile from a plaything to a practical form of everyday transportation. Dayton at the turn of the century was a town buzzing with mechanical innovations, and with inventors practical enough to turn them into profitable businesses.

In the early 1980s the atmosphere was different. Dayton's major businesses seem beleaguered: NCR by the volatility of the office and personal computer markets; Mead Paper by a huge antitrust verdict; companies supplying the Big Three auto firms by the collapse of auto sales. Dayton's population started to decline as young people left to find jobs elsewhere. Had the spirit of tinkering and innovation, of practical organization and mechanical dreaming entirely vanished? The experience of the early 1980s showed Dayton it could no longer coast on the achievements of its old inventors. It got Piedmont Airlines and Emery Air Freight to make Dayton a major air hub, built on the aerospace base it got from Wright-Patterson, and sought to build on its engineering and manufacturing expertise. The unemployment rate was down by 1987, but the verdict was still out on whether Dayton was going to create again its old spirit.

Dayton's economic troubles were accompanied by political volatility in a city which has never had really strong political machines or politically domineering business establishments or unions. In the early 1980s Dayton and Montgomery County trended sharply Democratic; in 1984 they trended toward Ronald Reagan and other Republicans; in 1986 they gave large margins to Richard Celeste and the Democrats, though not as large as they received in northeast industrial Ohio. The apparent conclusion is that the Dayton area and the 3d Congressional District of Ohio, which includes almost all of Montgomery County, was not clear whether the Democrats' active-government or the Republicans' less-government approach was the best for Dayton's ills—or maybe they just voted for whomever seemed best at the moment.

Any upsurge in Republican fortunes in the Dayton area has not been reflected in 3d Congressional District elections: the incumbent Democratic congressman, Tony Hall, unburdened with Republican opposition in 1982 or 1984, beat a black conservative Republican in 1986 with 74% of the vote. Hall has deep roots in Dayton, where his father was once mayor; like many younger members, most of them liberal Democrats, Hall served in the Peace Corps in the 1960s; he went on to be a real estate broker and to serve in the Ohio legislature for 10 years. It was a bit jarring to learn that he has a brother who has been a kind of soldier of fortune and was arrested by the Sandinistas in late 1986. But perhaps we should just take this as an example of the picturesque variety you can find in almost any American extended family.

In the House Hall has shown a certain moderation, especially on cultural issues and on economics seems interested in providing incentives for the kinds of businesses Dayton once developed and now needs again. He keeps up on local issues, insisting that a fighter plane whose pilots shot down six MIGs in Vietnam be sent to the U.S. Air Force Museum at nearby Wright-Patterson Air Force Base (though voting against Wright-Pat money when aid to the Nicaraguan contras was attached to it) and doing something for the problems of Mead and NCR. But he says he became a born-again Christian in the early 1980s and has increasingly concentrated on problems of hunger and human rights: he calls for more World Bank aid to the very poor and for attention to genocide in East Timor; he was an early critic of Ferdinand Marcos, he is a promoter of worldwide childhood immunizations. Hall is a member of the Rules Committee, and a loyal follower of the Democratic leadership when it comes to procedural matters. Once Rules concentrated on bottling up liberal legislation; now Rules Democrats concentrate on advancing pet projects and causes, usually with success.

The People: Pop. 1980: 514,173, dn. 7.6% 1970–80. Households (1980): 72% family, 39% with children, 57% married couples; 37.0% housing units rented; median monthly rent: $159; median house value: $39,500. Voting age pop. (1980): 370,952; 16% Black, 1% Spanish origin.

1984 Presidential Vote: Reagan (R) 113,499   (56%)
Mondale (D) 87,666   (43%)

Rep. Tony P. Hall (D)

Elected 1978; b. Jan. 16, 1942, Dayton; home, Dayton; Denison U., A.B. 1964; Presbyterian; married (Janet).

Career: Peace Corps, Thailand, 1966–67; Real estate broker, 1968–78; OH House of Reps., 1969–73; OH Senate, 1973–79.

Offices: 2448 RHOB 20515, 202-225-6465. Also 501 Fed. Bldg., 200 W. 2d St., Dayton 45402, 513-225-2843.

Committees: *Rules* (7th of 9 D). Subcommittee: Rules of the House. *Select Committee on Hunger* (2d of 16 D). Task Force: International Task Force (Chairman).

Group Ratings

	ADA	ACLU	COPE	CFA	LCV	ACU	NTU	NSI	COC	CEI
1986	65	50	79	50	74	9	38	11	44	21
1985	65	—	81	75	—	11	40	—	41	—

National Journal Ratings

	1986 LIB — 1986 CONS		1985 LIB — 1985 CONS	
Economic	52%	— 48%	63%	— 36%
Social	47%	— 52%	52%	— 47%
Foreign	64%	— 34%	79%	— 20%

Key Votes

1) Lmt Cln Water Act	FOR	5) Retain Gun Cont	FOR	9) Aid Angola Reb	AGN
2) Rpl Tobac Sub	FOR	6) Contra Aid	AGN	10) Tax Reform	AGN
3) Grm-Rdmn Def Red	FOR	7) Lmt Text Imp	FOR	11) S Africa Sanc	FOR
4) Ban Polygraph	AGN	8) Limit SDI	FOR	12) Immig Reform	AGN

Election Results

1986 general	Tony P. Hall (D)	98,311	(74%)	($76,558)
	Ron Crutcher (R)	35,167	(26%)	($48,368)
1986 primary	Tony P. Hall (D)	25,490	(92%)	
	Juanita Ratliff (D)	1,215	(4%)	
	Henry D. Wilson (D)	1,096	(4%)	
1984 general	Tony P. Hall (D)	151,333	(100%)	($63,997)

Campaign Contributions and Expenditures

1985-86		Direct Cont. 1985-86		PACS Breakdown 1985-86			
Receipts	$181,650	Indiv.	$39,310	Corp.	$31,836	T/M/H	$49,350
Expend.	$76,558	PACS	$116,456	Labor	$30,670	Agr.	$0
Unspent	$239,470			Ideo.	$4,350	CWOS	$250

FOURTH DISTRICT

Northern Ohio, where the rail lines criss-cross on the flat, limestone-based plains, is one of the Republican heartlands of the United States. When Ronald Reagan's campaign managers wanted to stage an old-fashioned whistle stop tour in October 1984, they chose the B&O tracks running north from Dayton to Toledo, the same line Richard Nixon used in 1968. So Reagan, like Nixon, was seen on TV in Wapakoneta, the typically modest home town of the first man on the moon, Neil Armstrong, and Lima, an old industrial city that is in the largest county east of Chicago and north of Richmond to have voted for Barry Goldwater in 1964. As it passed through the increasingly flatter plains of northern Ohio, the Reagan train crossed the great transcontinental highways and railroads; in small towns like Deshler, where a little girl had held up a sign in 1968 saying "Bring us together," it attracted enthusiastic, telegenic crowds, reminiscent of the politics of an earlier, seemingly simpler day.

Much of this territory is in the 4th Congressional District of Ohio. This is a shallow, upside-down U-shaped group of counties, rural in appearance but with most of its people in small cities and towns, in western and central Ohio. It includes Wapakoneta, Lima, Findlay, the prosperous home of Marathon Oil (acquired by U.S. Steel after some brouhaha), Bucyrus, which gave its name to a company producing giant earth-moving equipment, and Mansfield, home of John Sherman, one of Ohio's great Republican statesmen of the 19th century. This has been a Republican stronghold since the Civil War, yet it has also been subject to, and momentarily shaken by, the woes of Ohio's manufacturing economy. For the chief economic activity here is not farming—most of its fields are pretty marginal operations—but manufacturing; this is one of the most gadget-prone, mechanically inclined parts of the country.

The congressman from the 4th is Michael Oxley, a Republican chosen by the surprisingly narrow margin of 378 votes in a special election in the recession year of 1981. The Ohio Republican delegation was long dominated by men of the World War II generation; now it is increasingly made up of men like Oxley, 20 and even 30 years younger. Their politics is a bit less orthodox; in this decade of Republican deficits they don't have a religious fervor for balancing the budget, but they are as aggressively partisan as any Republican generation Ohio has elected. Oxley was called a moderate when he ran because he supported George Bush in 1980; but just as Bush has done, he has backed conservative positions with vigor and consistency.

Oxley has a seat on one of the key committees in Congress, Energy and Commerce, where he has been a consistent vote to reduce federal regulation; and of course he is sympathetic to the problems of midwestern industries. That leaves him mostly against, but sometimes allied, to the committee's aggressive chairman John Dingell. Energy and Commerce is a marvelous base from which to raise campaign contributions, but since his narrow victory in the special election, Oxley does not seem to need much; he has won easily and by overwhelming margins.

The People: Pop. 1980: 514,172, up 5.1% 1970–80. Households (1980): 77% family, 42% with children, 67% married couples; 26.1% housing units rented; median monthly rent: $153; median house value: $39,600. Voting age pop. (1980): 360,450; 3% Black, 1% Spanish origin.

1984 Presidential Vote:
Reagan (R)	158,640	(74%)
Mondale (D)	54,963	(26%)

Rep. Michael G. Oxley (R)

Elected June 25, 1981; b. Feb. 11, 1944, Findlay; home, Findlay; Miami U. of OH, B.A. 1966, OH State U., J.D. 1969; Lutheran; married (Patricia).

Career: FBI Spec. Agent, 1969–72; OH House of Reps., 1972–81; Practicing atty., 1972–1981.

Offices: 1108 LHOB 20515, 202-225-2676. Also 3121 W. Elm Plaza, Lima 45805, 419-999-6455; 24 W. 3d St., Rm. 314, Mansfield 44902, 419-522-5757; and 110 W. Main Cross, Rm. 206, Findlay 45840, 419-423-3210.

Committees: *Energy and Commerce* (12th of 17 R). Subcommittees: Energy and Power; Oversight and Investigations; Telecommunications and Finance. *Select Committee on Narcotics Abuse and Control* (4th of 10 R).

Group Ratings

	ADA	ACLU	COPE	CFA	LCV	ACU	NTU	NSI	COC	CEI
1986	0	10	7	25	21	95	61	100	100	78
1985	10	—	7	17	—	86	62	—	91	—

National Journal Ratings

	1986 LIB — 1986 CONS			1985 LIB — 1985 CONS		
Economic	6%	—	90%	5%	—	92%
Social	27%	—	71%	24%	—	72%
Foreign	0%	—	86%	0%	—	76%

Key Votes

1) Lmt Cln Water Act	FOR	5) Retain Gun Cont	FOR	9) Aid Angola Reb	FOR
2) Rpl Tobac Sub	AGN	6) Contra Aid	FOR	10) Tax Reform	FOR
3) Grm-Rdmn Def Red	FOR	7) Lmt Text Imp	AGN	11) S Africa Sanc	—
4) Ban Polygraph	AGN	8) Limit SDI	AGN	12) Immig Reform	FOR

Election Results

1986 general	Michael G. Oxley (R)................	115,751	(75%)	($215,276)
	Clem T. Cratty (D).....................	26,320	(17%)	
1986 primary	Michael G. Oxley (R).................	46,227	(100%)	
1984 general	Michael G. Oxley (R)................	162,024	(77%)	($106,984)
	William O. Sutton (D)	47,042	(23%)	

Campaign Contributions and Expenditures

1985-86		Direct Cont. 1985-86		PACS Breakdown 1985-86			
Receipts	$215,841	Indiv.	$35,841	Corp.	$98,052	T/M/H	$47,460
Expend.	$184,379	Party	$2,318	Labor	$850	Agr.	$4,500
Unspent	$176,024	PACS	$156,076	Ideo.	$4,750	CWOS	$464

FIFTH DISTRICT

A century and a half ago, New England Yankees began to settle the flat lands in the northwestern corner of Ohio, to be joined by German Protestants. The land here is more fertile and easier to work than the knobby hills of southern Ohio. Northwest Ohio is the beginning of the great corn and hog belt that stretches into Illinois and Iowa, and has also been one of the heartlands of the Republican Party since it was founded in 1854. It is also prime industrial country: all this farmland is undergirded by limestone, needed in heavy industry, it lies on the great east–west rail lines, and it is accessible via nearby Lake Erie with the great iron ore deposits of Lake Superior. So by the early 20th century, what had been a farm economy changed almost invisibly to a factory economy; and this has been one part of rural America that has never been drained of people. Even in the 1970s and early 1980s, when the economies of the big industrial cities were in trouble, the economic base here continued to be relatively strong. Labor costs were lower than in the big metropolitan areas, labor unions less obdurate, taxes lower, and racial tensions largely nonexistent.

The 5th Congressional District covers most of northwestern Ohio, except for Toledo and most of its suburbs, which make up the 9th District. The 5th has been one of the most solidly Republican districts in the nation over the years, and since 1958 has elected and reelected Representative Delbert Latta (the name, incidentally, is Welsh, not Italian). Latta is one of those congressmen who has labored for years with only occasional public notice. As a member of the Rules Committee he was often part, or even the architect, of the coalition of conservative Republicans and southern Democrats who would kill liberal legislation by refusing to schedule it for debate or by allowing crippling amendments. Always a fierce and aggressive partisan, Latta could be trusted to follow the wishes of the Republican leadership; and within the leadership he usually has been an advocate of hard-line opposition to the Democrats.

For a moment in 1974, Latta became much more prominent, and his approach remained much the same. His well-deserved reputation for partisanship got him a seat on the Judiciary Committee in 1974; he filled a vacancy just for the impeachment hearings, in which he provided a no-holds-barred defense of Richard Nixon. When the congressional budget process was established in 1975, Latta again got a key role. He was named the ranking Republican on the Budget Committee, a position he still holds. On the Senate committee in the 1970s there was bipartisan cooperation; on the House there was—and is—partisan struggle. Latta fought for lower domestic spending in the 1970s, and then had the satisfaction after the 1980 election of seeing his Gramm–Latta substitute pass the House in 1981. In 1982 he continued to work against higher taxes, and opposed the 1982 tax increase even after President Reagan endorsed it. Yet he is also a balanced budget man, and must be discomfited—though he is not a man who, when pleading a partisan case, likes to show discomfiture—by the whopping deficits the policies he has backed so effectively have produced.

So Latta has often been frustrated in recent years. House Republicans have had little taste for administration budgets and little success brokering one of their own. Meanwhile, Latta is also in a small minority on the House Rules Committee; the nine Democrats, all loyal to the speaker, can easily outvote the four Republicans. That leaves this partisan bulldog in an uncomfortable position: he is unlikely to prevail often in the House, and yet he can be thrown on the defensive when attacks are made on the apparent imperfections in Reagan policies. Interestingly, he has not been part of the group of younger conservative Republicans who have been harassing the Democrats in innovative ways. As newcomers to the House, the younger Republicans are more willing to flout tradition; and as, in some cases, intellectuals they are interested in exploring and advancing genuinely new ideas. Latta, operating from a base in northwestern Ohio where Republican bankers, lawyers, businessmen, and landowners have run things—and pretty ably too, for generations—is not much for intellectual debate; his style is just to attack the bad guys with the familiar arguments he has been using for a generation.

Meanwhile, the 5th District has been trending Democratic in the 1980s, particularly in the counties along Lake Erie. Governor Richard Celeste has carried the district handily twice, and Latta himself had a scare in 1982 when he got an unaccustomedly low 55% of its vote. He rebounded smartly to 63% in 1984 and did as well in 1986, though he had been absent due to illness for some time; but he seems to have recovered, and to be returning to his strong and sometimes bitterly abrasive partisanship.

The People: Pop. 1980: 514,173, up 7.7% 1970–80. Households (1980): 77% family, 44% with children, 67% married couples; 24.4% housing units rented; median monthly rent: $165; median house

value: $43,200. Voting age pop. (1980): 358,616; 2% Spanish origin, 2% Black.

1984 Presidential Vote: Reagan (R) 145,121   (67%)
                           Mondale (D) 68,285   (32%)

Rep. Delbert L. Latta (R)

Elected 1958; b. Mar. 5, 1920, Weston; home, Bowling Green; OH Northern U., A.B. 1943, LL.B. 1946; Churches of Christ; married (Rose Mary).

Career: Practicing atty.; OH Senate, 1952–58.

Offices: 2309 RHOB 20515, 202-225-6405. Also 100 Fed. Bldg., 280 S. Main St., Bowling Green 43402, 419-353-8871; and 157 Columbus, Sandusky 44870, 419-625-0052.

Committees: *Budget* (Ranking Member of 14 R). Task Force: Defense and International Affairs. *Rules* (2d of 4 R).

Group Ratings

	ADA	ACLU	COPE	CFA	LCV	ACU	NTU	NSI	COC	CEI
1986	5	5	13	33	16	91	60	100	86	73
1985	5	—	12	25	—	90	65	—	86	—

National Journal Ratings

	1986 LIB — 1986 CONS	1985 LIB — 1985 CONS
Economic	19% — 79%	16% — 81%
Social	17% — 82%	0% — 76%
Foreign	0% — 86%	0% — 76%

Key Votes

1) Lmt Cln Water Act	FOR	5) Retain Gun Cont	AGN	9) Aid Angola Reb	FOR
2) Rpl Tobac Sub	AGN	6) Contra Aid	FOR	10) Tax Reform	FOR
3) Grm-Rdmn Def Red	FOR	7) Lmt Text Imp	AGN	11) S Africa Sanc	AGN
4) Ban Polygraph	—	8) Limit SDI	AGN	12) Immig Reform	—

Election Results

1986 general	Delbert L. Latta (R)	102,016	(65%)	($268,667)
	Tom Murray (D)	54,864	(35%)	($146,492)
1986 primary	Delbert L. Latta (R)	39,974	(85%)	
	Mark J. McGory (R)	3,636	(8%)	
	Gerald F. Buchman (R)	3,418	(7%)	
1984 general	Delbert L. Latta (R)	126,322	(63%)	($185,106)
	James R. Sherck (D)	75,534	(37%)	($152,552)

Campaign Contributions and Expenditures

1985-86		Direct Cont. 1985-86		PACS Breakdown 1985-86			
Receipts	$305,439	Indiv.	$135,382	Corp.	$65,955	T/M/H	$65,499
Expend.	$268,667	Party	$8,076	Labor	$500	Agr.	$850
Unspent	$157,952	PACS	$142,251	Ideo.	$8,753	CWOS	$694

SIXTH DISTRICT

After the Revolutionary War, George Washington procured for his Virginia veterans bounty grants of land in what was then called the Virginia Military District of Ohio. This region, between the Scioto and Miami Rivers, stretching north from the Ohio River to what would become Columbus, has retained more than a touch of a southern accent, in speech and in politics, to this day. Much of the old Virginia Military District makes up today's 6th Congressional District of Ohio. It touches the metropolitan areas of Cincinnati, Dayton, and Columbus, and includes the gritty industrial city of Portsmouth on the Ohio River. But nothing in it partakes of metropolitan ambience; this is still small-town America. The rolling hill country of the valley of the Scioto River, which runs through Columbus, Chillicothe, and Portsmouth, is laid out in irregular-shaped parcels as in Virginia, not in the checkerboard grid of most of the Midwest; and politically this was once Democratic rather than Republican terrain. But in the 1950s and 1960s this part of Ohio, like much of the South, became more conservative and Republican. It still elects some notable Democrats, like Ohio House Speaker Vern Riffe, a power in Columbus and the senior House speaker in the nation. But it has been solidly Republican in congressional elections since 1960.

The current congressman, Bob McEwen, came to office in 1980 after serving in the legislature and working for his predecessor William Harsha, and at first he, like Harsha, seemed to concentrate on bringing public works projects to the district. But by the middle 1980s McEwen, still in his middle 30s, was aiming for the United States Senate. In his third term, he began staking out some interesting positions on issues, becoming lead sponsor of measures to require the President to state a national strategy statement with each military budget, to target the about-to-be-phased-out revenue sharing funds to poorer cities and towns, and to put the highway trust funds off budget so no one can use their surpluses to balance the overall budget. At the same time he got a seat on the House Intelligence Committee. He began speaking around the state to good reviews and contributed half of his campaign fund to other Ohio Republicans.

McEwen's path to the Senate is not clear. Cleveland Mayor George Voinovich, a Republican with a proven ability to carry big city votes, seems to be running too, and begins better-known and many Republicans assume he's a stronger candidate. Nor is anyone belittling the electoral prowess or political cunning of Democratic Senator Howard Metzenbaum. McEwen's reputation as a spirited backer of President Reagan and supply-side economics seemed an advantage in late 1986; it's not clear whether it will be in the 1988 primary. Still, most Republican legislators, some angry because Voinovich passed up the 1986 governor's race, said in early 1987 they favored McEwen. So this congressman from a lightly populated corner of the state with the youngish good looks that lead many Washington observers to assume there's nothing underneath his seemingly blow-dried hair has gone a considerable distance toward making himself a plausible Senate candidate, and against tough competition.

The People: Pop. 1980: 514,173, up 13.0% 1970–80. Households (1980): 79% family, 45% with children, 69% married couples; 26.1% housing units rented; median monthly rent: $143; median house value: $39,800. Voting age pop. (1980): 359,077; 2% Black.

1984 Presidential Vote:

Reagan (R)	142,779	(68%)
Mondale (D)	65,522	(31%)

Rep. Bob McEwen (R)

Elected 1980; b. Jan. 12, 1950, Hillsboro; home, Hillsboro; U. of Miami (FL), B.B.A. 1972; Protestant; married (Liz).

Career: Real estate developer; OH House of Reps., 1974–80.

Offices: 329 CHOB 20515, 202-225-5705. Also P.O. Bldg., Portsmouth 45662, 614-353-5171; and P.O. Bldg., Rm. 202, Hillsboro 45133, 513-393-4223.

Committees: *Public Works and Transportation* (8th of 20 R). Subcommittees: Investigations and Oversight; Surface Transportation. *Veterans' Affairs* (5th of 13 R). Subcommittees: Compensation, Pension and Insurance (Ranking Member); Hospitals and Health Care. *Permanent Select Committee on Intelligence* (4th of 6 R). Subcommittee: Oversight and Evaluation.

Group Ratings

	ADA	ACLU	COPE	CFA	LCV	ACU	NTU	NSI	COC	CEI
1986	5	6	19	8	27	86	42	100	79	55
1985	15	—	17	33	—	85	57	—	79	—

National Journal Ratings

	1986 LIB — 1986 CONS		1985 LIB — 1985 CONS	
Economic	27%	— 72%	21%	— 78%
Social	0%	— 89%	0%	— 76%
Foreign	0%	— 86%	0%	— 76%

Key Votes

1) Lmt Cln Water Act	AGN	5) Retain Gun Cont	AGN	9) Aid Angola Reb	FOR
2) Rpl Tobac Sub	AGN	6) Contra Aid	FOR	10) Tax Reform	FOR
3) Grm-Rdmn Def Red	FOR	7) Lmt Text Imp	AGN	11) S Africa Sanc	AGN
4) Ban Polygraph	AGN	8) Limit SDI	AGN	12) Immig Reform	—

Election Results

1986 general	Bob McEwen (R)	106,354	(70%)	($248,157)
	Gordon Roberts (D)	42,155	(28%)	($21,324)
1986 primary	Bob McEwen (R)	39,410	(100%)	
1984 general	Bob McEwen (R)	150,852	(74%)	($143,829)
	Bob Smith (D)	52,679	(26%)	($3,208)

Campaign Contributions and Expenditures

1985-86		Direct Cont. 1985-86		PACS Breakdown 1985-86			
Receipts	$360,154	Indiv.	$203,340	Corp.	$73,379	T/M/H	$48,650
Expend.	$248,157	Party	$2,221	Labor	$12,000	Agr.	$5,500
Unspent	$5,657	PACS	$146,385	Ideo.	$5,575	CWOS	$1,281

SEVENTH DISTRICT

Springfield, Ohio, "a town of tinkerers and inventors, of farmers and their ties to the land, of immigrants and black Americans with their visions of a better life, of entrepreneurs and executives and union men," was was the choice of the editors of *Newsweek* when they were looking in the early 1980s for a typical American community—"every American town"—to profile for their 50th anniversary issue. It was a good choice, not only to show how America has changed, but also to show how the nation has remained stable and steady, even as it has experienced vast economic growth. Springfield is a small industrial city, one which physically resembles the Springfield of the 1920s. Its major industries got their impetus from the various electrical and mechanical innovations brought to market during the first decades of the 20th century. Yet for all its appearance of having stayed the same, Springfield has in fact enjoyed vast economic growth. The working men who exhausted themselves working 60-hour weeks now take home much higher real wages working 40 hours; without much notice, factories that once existed have been torn down and others erected in their place.

In the dozen years beginning with the 1973 oil embargo Springfield was buffeted by economic shock waves, and has yet to entirely recover. Unemployment rose to the highest percentages since the days of Franklin Roosevelt. This manufacturing state no longer seemed a beehive of economic innovation; the glamour industries of the present and projected future were not locating here. The way of life—vastly improved over 50 years time—which people worked so hard to build seemed suddenly in jeopardy. Yet politically the result has not been upheaval, though there were some thrashings back and forth between the parties, as it has been a search for leaders who can impose a certain order. Long divided almost equally between the parties, Springfield has given large margins to Republican President Ronald Reagan and Democratic Governor Richard Celeste. In congressional elections, it has given large margins to one of the young Republican leaders of the House, Michael DeWine.

Springfield is part of the 7th Congressional District of Ohio, an odd-shaped unit which forms a sort of horseshoe some 20 to 50 miles around Columbus. It includes such notable places as Bellefontaine, site of the first concrete street in America; Marion, where young Socialist-to-be Norman Thomas delivered newspapers edited by President-to-be Warren Harding; and Marysville, site of Honda's new U.S. plant. Historically, this is Republican territory. The policies of the party of William McKinley—tariff protection, railroad regulation, antitrust suits against monopolies, discouragement of labor unions—seemed to work very well to produce economic growth in the years 1900–30; the low tax Republican policies of the 1950s also seemed to work; this was the last decade in which Ohio had a significant increase in the number of manufacturing jobs. From the 1980s a new consensus has only begun to emerge, supporting not only bedrock welfare state protections and an activist government, especially at the state and local level, but also a government respectful of and reinforcing traditional cultural values and arrangements.

Michael DeWine, elected when Clarence (Bud) Brown ran for governor in 1982, has distinguished himself throughout his career as an aggressive young prosecutor. He started off in the prosecutor's office in Greene County, just south of Springfield, which covers Dayton suburbs, farming countryside, and the small town of Xenia made famous by the octogenarian Helen Hooven Santmyer's . . . *And Ladies of the Club*. On Capitol Hill DeWine is one of the group of pugnacious young Republicans who delights in harassing the Democrats, supporting aid to the Nicaraguan contras on the Foreign Affairs Committee and tussling with liberals on Judiciary. He was one of the active managers for the House in the impeachment of Judge Harry Claiborne, and in 1986 he was appointed to serve on the special committee investigating the Iran-contra scandal.

DeWine is reelected easily in the 7th District, and in 1986 had no opposition at all.

The People: Pop. 1980: 514,170, up 3.7% 1970–80. Households (1980): 78% family, 44% with children, 67% married couples; 28.2% housing units rented; median monthly rent: $153; median house value: $41,500. Voting age pop. (1980): 362,126; 5% Black, 1% Spanish origin.

1984 Presidential Vote:

Reagan (R)	135,554	(68%)
Mondale (D)	62,431	(31%)

Rep. Michael DeWine (R)

Elected 1982; b. Jan. 5, 1947, Springfield; home, Cedarville; Miami U. of OH, B.S. 1969, OH Northern U., J.D. 1972; Roman Catholic; married (Frances).

Career: Practicing atty.; Asst. Prosecuting Atty., Greene Cnty., 1973–75, Prosecuting Atty., 1977–81; OH Senate, 1981–82.

Offices: 1519 LHOB 20515, 202-225-4324. Also 150 N. Limestone St., Rm. 220, Springfield 45501, 513-325-0474; and 399 E. Church St., Marion 43302, 614-387-5300.

Committees: *Foreign Affairs* (13th of 18 R). Subcommittees: International Operations; Western Hemisphere Affairs. *Judiciary* (9th of 14 R). Subcommittees: Civil and Constitutional Rights; Courts, Civil Liberties, and the Administration of Justice.

Group Ratings

	ADA	ACLU	COPE	CFA	LCV	ACU	NTU	NSI	COC	CEI
1986	0	5	13	33	38	91	53	100	94	73
1985	10	—	13	50	—	86	60	—	64	—

National Journal Ratings

	1986 LIB — 1986 CONS		1985 LIB — 1985 CONS	
Economic	23%	— 76%	24%	— 74%
Social	31%	— 67%	24%	— 72%
Foreign	23%	— 77%	0%	— 76%

Key Votes

1) Lmt Cln Water Act	FOR	5) Retain Gun Cont	FOR	9) Aid Angola Reb	FOR
2) Rpl Tobac Sub	FOR	6) Contra Aid	FOR	10) Tax Reform	FOR
3) Grm-Rdmn Def Red	AGN	7) Lmt Text Imp	AGN	11) S Africa Sanc	AGN
4) Ban Polygraph	AGN	8) Limit SDI	AGN	12) Immig Reform	FOR

Election Results

1986 general	Michael DeWine (R)	119,238	(100%)	($142,205)
1986 primary	Michael DeWine (R)	45,245	(100%)	
1984 general	Michael DeWine (R)	141,678	(74%)	($194,367)
	Donald E. Scott (D)	45,908	(24%)	($8,038)

Campaign Contributions and Expenditures

1985-86		Direct Cont. 1985-86		PACS Breakdown 1985-86			
Receipts	$186,105	Indiv.	$87,158	Corp.	$36,189	T/M/H	$42,450
Expend.	$142,205	Party	$2,581	Labor	$0	Agr.	$3,500
Unspent	$51,838	PACS	$88,339	Ideo.	$5,250	CWOS	$950

EIGHTH DISTRICT

At the crossroads of the nation, or so you could argue, is the 8th Congressional District of the United States. In the 19th century, when economic growth in the South was sluggish and there was little migration across the Mason-Dixon line and the Ohio River, this western end of Ohio was at the chokepoint of national commerce as it moved over the National Road, later U.S. 40, and the east–west railroads running across the occasionally swelling, often flat plains of the Midwest. In these counties, between Columbus and Indianapolis, near Cincinnati and Dayton, grew small manufacturing cities like Middletown and Hamilton! (city fathers added the exclamation point in 1986) amid rich farmland.

The southern end of the 8th District, around these two cities, had many settlers from around the Ohio River and farther south and still has a trace of southern accent and Dixiecrat politics; George Wallace got 18% of the vote here in the 1968 general election, his highest percentage in any district of a state that barred slavery at the time of the Civil War. The northern counties were settled overland and have little southern accent or heritage. People here rooted for the Union in the Civil War, and most of their descendants have voted for the Republicans ever since, except for some Catholic communities and except in deep recession years.

The congressman from this district is Donald "Buz" Lukens, who has had a long career as a conservative enfant terrible but enters the 100th Congress, technically, as a freshman at age 55. But he has been in the House before. In the early 1960s, when it was widely assumed that the future of the Republican party lay with its liberal wing, Lukens was an activist conservative who won attention as head of the Young Republicans in 1963; in 1966 he was elected to the House from a district anchored in Hamilton and Middletown (ironically, it was created by the one-person-one-vote decisions so many conservatives abhorred). Lukens was always pushing for higher office, but in 1970 was defeated for the governor's nomination by the organization choice, Roger Cloud; in 1971 he won the state Senate seat vacated by the man who replaced him in Congress. For 15 years he labored in Columbus, running once unsuccessfully for state auditor; in 1985 and 1986 he was chairing the banking committee charged with cleaning up the savings and loan scandal.

Then the congressional seat opened up again when 12-year veteran Thomas Kindness ran against Senator John Glenn. Lukens was strong enough to win the seat without primary opposition and with only weak general election opposition. Two decades after first coming to Congress, he has junior seats on Foreign Affairs and Government Operations—not the seats of power; he remains more the activist and orator rather than the doer, a spectator of the national conservative revival he was so lonely in calling for 25 years ago. There is a certain gallantry to his career. He can claim to have been the first House member to endorse Ronald Reagan for President, back in 1968, and has fought steadfastly for his beliefs; and he ran and won in 1986 after suffering through bouts of skin and throat cancer. He began his second House career characteristically, casting one of the votes against the Clean Water Act that passed 406–8.

The People: Pop. 1980: 514,171, up 11.3% 1970–80. Households (1980): 78% family, 44% with children, 68% married couples; 26.5% housing units rented; median monthly rent: $164; median house value: $44,800. Voting age pop. (1980): 361,343; 3% Black, 1% Spanish origin.

| **1984 Presidential Vote:** | Reagan (R) . . . . 151,663 | (73%) |
| | Mondale (D) . . . . 55,471 | (27%) |

Rep. Donald E. (Buz) Lukens (R)

Elected 1986; b. Feb. 11, 1931, Harveysburg; home, Middletown; OH State U., B.A. 1951; Quaker; single.

Career: USAF, 1954–60; U.S. House of Reps., 1967–71; OH House of Reps., 1971–86.

Offices: 2417 RHOB 20515, 202-225-6205. Also 646 High St., Hamilton 45011, 513-895-5656; 101 E. Main St., Greenville 45331, 513-548-8817; and 1345 Central Ave., Middletown 45044, 513-423-2100.

Committees: *Government Operations* (10th of 15 R). Subcommittees: Government Activities and Transportation; Legislation and National Security. *Foreign Affairs* (17th of 18 R). Subcommittees: Africa; Europe and the Middle East.

Group Ratings and Key Votes: Newly Elected
Election Results

1986 general	Donald (Buz) Lukens (R)...............	98,475	(68%)	($218,387)
	John W. Griffin (D).....................	46,195	(32%)	($3,814)
1986 primary	Donald (Buz) Lukens (R)...............	30,377	(100%)	
1984 general	Thomas N. Kindness (R)	155,155	(77%)	($102,279)
	John T. Francis (D)....................	46,663	(23%)	($21,405)

Campaign Contributions and Expenditures

1985-86		Direct Cont. 1985-86		PACS Breakdown 1985-86			
Receipts	$223,679	Indiv.	$65,955	Corp.	$39,057	T/M/H	$60,478
Expend.	$218,387	Party	$11,103	Labor	$7,650	Agr.	$1,500
Unspent	$5,272	PACS	$131,740	Ideo.	$19,487	CWOS	$3,568
		Cand.	$10,098				

NINTH DISTRICT

At the mouth of the Maumee, the largest river to flow into Lake Erie, is Toledo—port, factory town, an ethnically diverse city sitting amid the rich agricultural country and Anglo-Saxon and German farmers and small-towners of northern Ohio. Toledo is one of those industrial cities especially hard hit by the collapse of the automobile industry in the late 1970s; its leading products for years were Jeeps (now the mainstay of American Motors) and automobile safety glass. Like Detroit, just 60 miles to the north, Toledo grew explosively between 1910 and 1930, during the initial expansion of the auto industry, and in the 20 years after 1945, as America moved from the one- to the two-car family.

Now Toledo is being reshaped by the economic changes of the 1970s and 1980s. In 1978, just before the second oil shock, there were 79,000 manufacturing and 185,000 non-manufacturing employees in the Toledo metropolitan area. By the 1982 trough, manufacturing employment was off to 60,000 while non-manufacturing held steady at 184,000. After four years of recovery, in 1986 manufacturing bounced back only to 62,000, but non-manufacturing was up to 219,000. Toledo's economy has been remolded by events mostly beyond its control and by initiatives sometimes highly visible—like big companies' layoffs and plant closings—but often quite unnoticed, like small businesses' decisions to hire a few workers or start a new line of products.

In the process, Toledo's politics has gone through a bit of upheaval. This has been a Democratic city since the CIO unions organized the plants in the late 1930s; it was the only Ohio city carried by George McGovern in 1972. But in 1980, the 9th Congressional District, which includes Toledo and most of its suburbs, threw out its 26-year Democratic congressman, Thomas Ashley, for local businessman Ed Weber, a backer of Reaganomics. Two years later, at the trough of the recession, Weber too was upset, by Democrat Marcy Kaptur, who remains 9th District congresswoman today.

Kaptur is a classic example of a Washington staffer who has made a congressional career on her own. Not an especially well known Carter White House aide, she was shrewd enough to return home to Toledo in 1982 when no one else wanted to make the race. Naturally she has concentrated on initiatives to rebuild Toledo's economy. She calls for measures to get the Japanese to buy their fair share of American auto parts and to bar American officials from lobbying for foreign clients after they left government service. She voted for Gramm-Rudman but has tried to keep senior citizen housing funding up. At the beginning of the 1980s the Democrats were yearning to rebuild the high-wage, big-company, big-union environment that was so comfortable for them politically in the 1970s. Now Democrats like Kaptur seem to have given up on that and to be trying to adapt their records as their constituencies adapt their economies to the new world of the 1980s.

For the moment at least Kaptur has done well politically. After a tough challenge in 1984 from a local newscaster which held her below her 1982 percentage, she won overwhelmingly in

1986. After the election she got a seat on the Democratic Steering and Policy Committee. But no one can be completely certain what will happen in Toledo's volatile political environment.

The People: Pop. 1980: 514,174, up 1.0% 1970–80. Households (1980): 71% family, 39% with children, 57% married couples; 32.4% housing units rented; median monthly rent: $179; median house value: $42,600. Voting age pop. (1980): 364,640; 11% Black, 2% Spanish origin.

1984 Presidential Vote:

Reagan (R)	110,570	(51%)
Mondale (D)	104,597	(48%)

Rep. Marcy Kaptur (D)

Elected 1982; b. June 17, 1946, Toledo; home, Toledo; U. of WI, B.A. 1968, U. of MI, M.A.U.P. 1974; Roman Catholic; single.

Career: Urban planner, Toledo–Lucus Cnty. Planning Comm., 1969–75; Development and Urban Planning Consultant, 1975–77; Asst. Dir. for Urban Affairs, Domestic Policy Staff, White House, 1977–80; Dpty. Secy., National Consumer Coop. Bank, 1980–81.

Offices: 1228 LHOB 20515, 202-225-4146. Also Fed. Bldg., 234 Summitt St., Rm. 719, Toledo 43604, 419-259-7500.

Committees: *Banking, Finance and Urban Affairs* (17th of 31 D). Subcommittees: Economic Stabilization; Financial Institutions Supervision, Regulation and Insurance; Housing and Community Development. *Veterans' Affairs* (7th of 21 D). Subcommittees: Education, Training and Employment; Housing and Memorial Affairs (Chairman).

Group Ratings

	ADA	ACLU	COPE	CFA	LCV	ACU	NTU	NSI	COC	CEI
1986	75	68	90	83	63	5	24	0	33	20
1985	60	—	89	92	—	14	40	—	41	—

National Journal Ratings

	1986 LIB — 1986 CONS			1985 LIB — 1985 CONS		
Economic	80%	—	19%	59%	—	39%
Social	64%	—	36%	62%	—	37%
Foreign	75%	—	20%	80%	—	17%

Key Votes

1) Lmt Cln Water Act	FOR	5) Retain Gun Cont	FOR	9) Aid Angola Reb	AGN
2) Rpl Tobac Sub	FOR	6) Contra Aid	AGN	10) Tax Reform	AGN
3) Grm-Rdmn Def Red	FOR	7) Lmt Text Imp	FOR	11) S Africa Sanc	FOR
4) Ban Polygraph	FOR	8) Limit SDI	FOR	12) Immig Reform	AGN

Election Results

1986 general	Marcy Kaptur (D)	105,646	(78%)	($317,798)
	Mike Shufeldt (R)	30,643	(22%)	($47,514)
1986 primary	Marcy Kaptur (D)	27,382	(100%)	
1984 general	Marcy Kaptur (D)	117,536	(55%)	($333,078)
	Frank Venner (R)	92,605	(43%)	($459,852)

Campaign Contributions and Expenditures

1985-86		Direct Cont. 1985-86		PACS Breakdown 1985-86			
Receipts	$283,989	Indiv.	$88,156	Corp.	$15,540	T/M/H	$35,958
Expend.	$317,798	Party	$1,099	Labor	$116,052	Agr.	$3,500
Unspent	$2,139	PACS	$182,845	Ideo.	$10,845	CWOS	$950

TENTH DISTRICT

Below U.S. 40, the old National Road, in the hilly lands north of the Ohio River and southeast of Columbus, is the 10th Congressional District of Ohio. This is part of southern-accented Ohio, and the part of the state first settled by whites: Marietta, on the Ohio River, was the site of the first permanent American settlement, in 1788, in the old Northwest Territory, the land north and west of the Ohio River ceded to the new nation by the British after the Revolutionary War. For years it remained one of the least industrialized and least thickly populated parts of Ohio, a part of America seemingly left behind by progress. Yet in the 1980s, some of the hilly counties here have been among the few parts of Ohio showing evidence of population growth.

Politically the heritage here is mixed, between the Democratic tendencies of some of the areas settled by Virginians and the Republican leanings of parts settled by Yankees. In many places the voters since the 1960s have tended to call themselves Democrats and to vote for Republicans, except when a particularly congenial Democrat comes along, like John Glenn or the Jimmy Carter of 1976. Those contrary leanings made this a marginal area in congressional elections in the 1950s and 1960s; party control changed in 1958, 1962, 1964, and 1966. But the 10th District has stayed solidly Republican since then.

Representative Clarence Miller, elected that year, is an engineer and seems to approach politics seeking precision and orderliness. He established a record of never missing a House roll call vote since he was elected—an example of stern discipline, particularly since many roll calls are demanded for dilatory or mischievous reasons. As a member of the Appropriations Committee he has introduced numerous amendments to require across-the-board cuts of specific percentages in departmental spending. At the hard work of actually paring down appropriations, he like so many other critics of big government, has been less successful than he would like; it must be frustrating for him to see huge deficits piled up under a Republican President who styles himself a conservative. But Miller perseveres. His old-fashioned brand of politics remains hugely popular in the 10th District, and he is routinely reelected by large margins.

The People: Pop. 1980: 514,173, up 12.7% 1970–80. Households (1980): 77% family, 43% with children, 67% married couples; 26.0% housing units rented; median monthly rent: $150; median house value: $37,700. Voting age pop. (1980): 362,509; 2% Black.

1984 Presidential Vote: Reagan (R) 139,324   (66%)
Mondale (D) 68,985   (33%)

Rep. Clarence E. Miller (R)

Elected 1966; b. Nov. 1, 1917, Lancaster; home, Lancaster; United Methodist; married (Helen).

Career: Electrician; Lancaster City Cncl., 1957–63; Mayor of Lancaster, 1964–66.

Offices: 2208 RHOB 20515, 202-225-5131. Also 212 S. Broad St., Lancaster 43130, 614-654-5149; and 27 S. Park Pl., Newark 43055, 614-349-8279.

Committees: *Appropriations* (4th of 22 R). Subcommittee: Defense.

Group Ratings

	ADA	ACLU	COPE	CFA	LCV	ACU	NTU	NSI	COC	CEI
1986	5	0	12	0	16	86	53	100	78	66
1985	0	—	12	17	—	89	53	—	85	—

National Journal Ratings

	1986 LIB — 1986 CONS	1985 LIB — 1985 CONS
Economic	18% — 82%	12% — 88%
Social	0% — 89%	0% — 76%
Foreign	0% — 86%	0% — 76%

Key Votes

1) Lmt Cln Water Act	FOR	5) Retain Gun Cont	AGN	9) Aid Angola Reb	FOR
2) Rpl Tobac Sub	AGN	6) Contra Aid	FOR	10) Tax Reform	AGN
3) Grm-Rdmn Def Red	FOR	7) Lmt Text Imp	FOR	11) S Africa Sanc	AGN
4) Ban Polygraph	AGN	8) Limit SDI	AGN	12) Immig Reform	AGN

Election Results

1986 general	Clarence E. Miller (R)	106,870	(70%)	($67,073)
	John M. Buchanan (D)	44,847	(30%)	($1,023)
1986 primary	Clarence E. Miller (R)	43,980	(100%)	
1984 general	Clarence E. Miller (R)	149,286	(73%)	($70,378)
	John M. Buchanan (D)	55,276	(27%)	($6,813)

Campaign Contributions and Expenditures

1985-86		Direct Cont. 1985-86		PACS Breakdown 1985-86			
Receipts	$85,899	Indiv.	$5,730	Corp.	$37,699	T/M/H	$27,600
Expend.	$67,073	Party	$2,285	Labor	$500	Agr.	$2,500
Unspent	$71,615	PACS	$69,499	Ideo.	$1,050	CWOS	$150

ELEVENTH DISTRICT

The Western Reserve—it is a name you still hear in northeast Ohio, the land set aside after the Revolution for Connecticut, which was blocked from expanding by Upstate New York. Well into the 20th century, the New England Yankee imprint was strong here. The Western Reserve was one of the nation's strongest antislavery constituencies before the Civil War and one of its most heavily Republican areas afterwards. Its thrifty, hard-working, well-educated citizens built communities with fine schools and with their accumulated savings invested in what became some of the nation's leading industries. That brought in great masses of immigrants to Cleveland and the other cities of northeast Ohio, but they remained solidly Republican until the Great Depression and the bloody CIO organizing drives of the late 1930s; then, for 30 years, the Western Reserve was Democratic in Ohio's class warfare politics.

Now the Western Reserve may be moving toward a post-industrial economy similar to that of Connecticut or Massachusetts. Factory employment has been falling, but total jobs are rising again; small, adaptive business units and highly skilled work are the growth sectors. In politics, the Western Reserve now seems to prefer Democrats as overwhelmingly as it once did Republicans, with only a few Republicans with liberal reputations, like Cleveland Mayor George Voinovich, surviving. Yet the Democrats are careful to promise lower rather than higher taxes and to sketch out a future in which entrepreneurs play a bigger role than union leaders.

The 11th Congressional District of Ohio takes in most of the geographical expanse of the Western Reserve, the northeast corner of Ohio. But it skirts the central cities. Cleveland and Akron are just to the west, Canton and Youngstown to the south. The 11th does include the Cleveland suburbs strung out along Lake Erie, in Lake County; it includes Ashtabula, also on the lake; it includes Kent, site of Kent State University, where students were shot and killed by

National Guardsmen in 1970; and it still includes some rural areas in between the industrial cities, like Hiram, the home of James Garfield, who once (1863–81) represented a very similarly shaped district (then numbered the 19th) when it was the most Republican part of Ohio, and was the last President elected directly from the House, in 1880.

The current congressman from the Western Reserve district, Dennis Eckart, does not seem likely to be elected President from the House, but otherwise he has done pretty well. First elected in 1980, he has become an important congressman in the 1980s, one of the leaders of the younger Democrats and a crucial swing vote on some issues. Eckart came to the House after six successful years in the Ohio legislature, with a reputation for competence as a legislator and the ability to express his own views yet go along generally with the leadership. In his second term he got the plum committee assignment of Energy and Commerce; he serves on subcommittees that handle toxic waste, air pollution and nuclear power issues. In his fourth term he was named a Democratic deputy whip.

On Energy and Commerce Eckart finds himself continually drawn between environment-minded Democrats who want to toughen anti-pollution laws and regulations on business and industry and (often more vocal) labor unions which want to relax them. There are usually strong arguments on either side, forcefully made, and both with political supporters in the 11th District. Eckart keeps in touch with both sides, but when he has been forced to choose on tough issues like clean air and acid rain, he has usually come out on the side of the more relaxed standards. He favors higher nuclear accident liability, which helps the nuclear industry. He is proud of his work on reauthorizing the Superfund, on which he opposed the stringent version backed by James Florio; on reauthorization of the safe drinking water act; and on blocking the sale of Conrail to the Norfolk Southern.

That has hurt him with Health Subcommittee Chairman Henry Waxman, but helped him with full committee Chairman John Dingell, to whom Eckart has become very close. They have much in common: both are of Eastern European descent (though neither has a distinctively ethnic name), both had fathers in politics (Dingell's was congressman, Eckart's a Euclid city councilman), both represent suburban districts of industrial cities where most voters have working-class roots, and both have shown great skill at handling the details of complex legislation. They hunt and socialize together on off hours, and then legislate together at work—though occasionally Eckart will dissent from even a chairman as strong-minded as Dingell.

Eckart has shown skill on the campaign trail as well. He won a Democratic primary against a senior legislator in 1980 to represent the 22d District in the close-in Cleveland suburbs. Then, after redistricting carved up this seat, he moved outward to the 11th District being vacated by moderate Republican William Stanton and won there as well. He was reelected by overwhelming margins in 1984 and 1986, and has become an important congressman with a safe seat while still in his middle 30s.

The People: Pop. 1980: 514,173, up 10.1% 1970–80. Households (1980): 80% family, 46% with children, 70% married couples; 23.6% housing units rented; median monthly rent: $208; median house value: $55,700. Voting age pop. (1980): 355,787; 2% Black.

1984 Presidential Vote:

Reagan (R)	124,751	(59%)
Mondale (D)	83,671	(40%)

Rep. Dennis E. Eckart (D)

Elected 1980; b. Apr. 6, 1950, Euclid; home, Mentor; Xavier U., B.A. 1971, Cleveland State U., J.D. 1974; Roman Catholic; married (Sandra).

Career: Practicing atty.; OH House of Reps., 1975–80.

Offices: 1221 LHOB, 202-225-6331. Also 5970 Heisley Rd., Mentor 44060, 216-522-2056.

Committees: *Energy and Commerce* (16th of 25 D). Subcommittees: Commerce, Consumer Protection and Competitiveness; Oversight and Investigations; Telecommunications and Finance. *Small Business* (10th of 27 D). Subcommittees: Antitrust, Impact of Deregulation and Privatization (Chairman); Procurement, Innovation and Minority Enterprise Development.

Group Ratings

	ADA	ACLU	COPE	CFA	LCV	ACU	NTU	NSI	COC	CEI
1986	65	75	86	83	74	14	31	0	22	23
1985	70	—	87	75	—	19	40	—	36	—

National Journal Ratings

	1986 LIB — 1986 CONS		1985 LIB — 1985 CONS	
Economic	62%	— 35%	61%	— 38%
Social	69%	— 28%	63%	— 33%
Foreign	64%	— 34%	64%	— 33%

Key Votes

1) Lmt Cln Water Act	AGN	5) Retain Gun Cont	FOR	9) Aid Angola Reb	AGN
2) Rpl Tobac Sub	FOR	6) Contra Aid	AGN	10) Tax Reform	FOR
3) Grm-Rdmn Def Red	FOR	7) Lmt Text Imp	FOR	11) S Africa Sanc	FOR
4) Ban Polygraph	FOR	8) Limit SDI	FOR	12) Immig Reform	FOR

Election Results

1986 general	Dennis E. Eckart (D)	104,740	(70%)	($348,852)
	Margaret R. Mueller (R)	39,944	(29%)	($275,584)
1986 primary	Dennis E. Eckart (D)	33,162	(92%)	
	Alan T. Arthur (D)	2,785	(8%)	
1984 general	Dennis E. Eckart (D)	133,019	(67%)	($248,568)
	Dean Beagle (R)	66,240	(33%)	($45,779)

Campaign Contributions and Expenditures

1985-86		Direct Cont. 1985-86		PACS Breakdown 1985-86			
Receipts	$403,429	Indiv.	$142,449	Corp.	$77,133	T/M/H	$58,050
Expend.	$348,852	PACS	$228,854	Labor	$70,070	Agr.	$6,620
Unspent	$11,933			Ideo.	$10,981	CWOS	$6,000

TWELFTH DISTRICT

The third largest repository of data in the world, after Washington and Moscow, is Columbus, Ohio. That may sound preposterous, but Columbus boosters are prepared to document it: between Ohio State University, Bell Labs, Chemical Abstracts Service, Online Computer Library, and the Battelle Memorial Institute, Columbus is evidently just crammed with data. That is not a result far out of line with the history of this city. It is the largest Ohio city not built on a navigable river, which means that for years it didn't get the factories that built the economies of Cincinnati and Cleveland. Accordingly, it has fewer of their problems in an era of industrial decline. Columbus's first big industry was state government; its second was Ohio State University; and it has insurance companies and banks. Politically and culturally conservative, it prides itself on its economic innovativeness: Columbus had the first 24-hour automated bank teller in 1973; it had the first two-way cable TV system, QUBE, in 1977; it has all that data. It has also grown smartly in the 1970s and 1980s while much of Ohio has sent its young people elsewhere.

If its economy is up-to-date, sometimes its local politics seems old-fashioned, with a Republican organization that wins most local elections and with politicians possessed of the common touch of longtime Governor James Rhodes, who was elected auditor of Columbus in 1939 and mayor in 1943. Yet the congressman from the 12th District of Ohio, which includes the east side of Columbus and its suburbs plus two adjacent rural counties, is a very up-to-date Republican who rose through his own efforts. This should be a heavily Republican district. Though it includes more than half of Columbus's blacks, most of its wards in Columbus and all of the affluent suburbs of Bexley and Gahanna are heavily Republican, and it includes none of the academic community aound Ohio State University. Yet the last time an old-style Republican won the seat comfortably was in 1968.

In that year the current congressman, Republican John Kasich, was a 14-year-old high school student living with his parents in McKees Rocks, Pennsylvania. Kasich got to Columbus by attending Ohio State; in 1978, at age 24, he ran a strenuous door-to-door campaign and beat an incumbent Democratic state Senator. Four years later, in the second election in which he was constitutionally eligible, he ran for the House and won. With the help of favorable redistricting, he beat Bob Shamansky, a Democrat who had beaten veteran Republican Samuel Devine in 1980; Kasich was the only Republican to beat an incumbent Democrat in 1982, and the 12th was the only district to oust a Republican incumbent in the Republican year of 1980 and then oust a Democratic incumbent in the Democratic year of 1982.

Kasich is brash, publicity-minded, and sometimes effective in the House. On issues Kasich is rated a strong conservative, an opponent of almost every form of government spending (except defense) and of abortion; he backed Philip Crane in the 1980 presidential election. He serves on the Armed Services Committee—the only member from Ohio—and worked with subcommittee chairman Bill Nichols on the military reorganization bill. He tends to favor increased defense spending, but he insists he wants the money spent effectively, and co-sponsored with Massachusetts dove Nicholas Mavroules a measure to require the baseline weapons procurement system recommended by the Packard commission.

His approach seems popular, and the 12th District's years of countercyclical politics seem to be over: Kasich was reelected by huge margins in 1984 and 1986.

The People: Pop. 1980: 514,173, up 14.1% 1970–80. Households (1980): 72% family, 41% with children, 58% married couples; 37.7% housing units rented; median monthly rent: $179; median house value: $47,100. Voting age pop. (1980): 366,117; 14% Black, 1% Spanish origin.

1984 Presidential Vote:

Reagan (R)	151,294	(65%)
Mondale (D)	76,873	(33%)

Rep. John R. Kasich (R)

Elected 1982; b. May 13, 1952, McKees Rocks, PA; home, Westerville; OH State U., B.S. 1974; Roman Catholic; single.

Career: A. A. to State Sen. Donald Lukens, 1975–77; OH Senate, 1979–82.

Offices: 1133 LHOB 20515, 202-225-5355. Also Fed. Bldg., 200 N. High St., Columbus 43215, 614-469-7318.

Committees: *Armed Services* (10th of 21 R). Subcommittees: Investigations; Readiness (Ranking Member).

Group Ratings

	ADA	ACLU	COPE	CFA	LCV	ACU	NTU	NSI	COC	CEI
1986	10	0	16	33	21	82	56	100	89	68
1985	5	—	13	33	—	90	56	—	86	—

National Journal Ratings

	1986 LIB — 1986 CONS	1985 LIB — 1985 CONS
Economic	19% — 79%	16% — 81%
Social	11% — 85%	0% — 76%
Foreign	16% — 79%	24% — 66%

Key Votes

1) Lmt Cln Water Act	FOR	5) Retain Gun Cont	AGN	9) Aid Angola Reb	FOR
2) Rpl Tobac Sub	FOR	6) Contra Aid	FOR	10) Tax Reform	FOR
3) Grm-Rdmn Def Red	FOR	7) Lmt Text Imp	AGN	11) S Africa Sanc	FOR
4) Ban Polygraph	AGN	8) Limit SDI	AGN	12) Immig Reform	FOR

Election Results

1986 general	John R. Kasich (R)	117,905	(73%)	($424,678)
	Timothy C. Jochim (D)	42,727	(27%)	($22,945)
1986 primary	John R. Kasich (R)	48,386	(100%)	
1984 general	John R. Kasich (R)	148,083	(69%)	($405,810)
	Richard S. Sloan (D)	65,105	(31%)	($264,399)

Campaign Contributions and Expenditures

1985-86		Direct Cont. 1985-86		PACS Breakdown 1985-86			
Receipts	$348,000	Indiv.	$190,179	Corp.	$37,699	T/M/H	$27,600
Expend.	$424,678	Party	$2,285	Labor	$500	Agr.	$2,500
Unspent	$24,835	PACS	$69,499	Ideo.	$1,050	CWOS	$150

THIRTEENTH DISTRICT

The south shore of Lake Erie, sweeping westward toward Chicago, is one of the great paths of migration that took Yankees from New England, where they had been living for 200 years, in a rush westward to California in less than two generations. The Yankee influence still lingers here, notably in higher education: this district includes Oberlin College, one of Ohio's oldest schools, and numerous other small colleges. The New Englanders also brought the reformist impulse that produced the abolitionist and women's suffrage movements: Oberlin was the first American college to admit blacks and women. In partisan terms, the area was naturally Republican territory. The Yankees, with their reformist ideas and dislike of slavery and the South, were the natural Republican base wherever they moved in the young nation, and this was a heavily Republican area for years.

But now northern Ohio, like most areas of early Yankee settlement, is inclined away from the Republicans and toward the Democrats. The industrial development which changed the face of Cleveland also affected the shoreline of Lake Erie to the west. Here are some pleasant suburbs on the lake, but also electric generating plants and giant factories. This is the land of Ohio's 13th Congressional District, which includes the factory towns of Lorain and Elyria which have become part of the Cleveland metropolitan area and the shoreline west to the picturesque town of Vermillion, and goes inland to include Medina County, filling up in the 1970s and 1980s with outmigrants from Cleveland, and the once rural area around Ashland and Mansfield.

Yet the switch from a Republican to a Democratic congressman did not come until 1976. You could say, however, that it happened in stages: Republican Charles Mosher, of Oberlin, first elected in 1960, had a voting record that increasingly resembled that of a Democrat, especially on cultural issues; it was a metamorphosis typical of that going on at the same time among many New England Yankees. His successor in Congress is Donald Pease, also of Oberlin, who followed Mosher on the *Oberlin News-Tribune,* in the Ohio Senate, and in basic political leanings—although Pease is a Democrat.

Pease is now a member of the House Ways and Means Committee. On economic issues he, like other Ohio Democrats, is inclined toward generosity—an inclination that becomes focused when the issue is trade adjustment assistance or unemployment benefits in the high-unemployment atmosphere of the early 1980s. His instincts on foreign policy are for international amity and cooperation, for arms control and multilateral development agencies. On taxes he supported the rate-lowering, preference-eliminating tax reform of 1986, and was one of the Democrats Dan Rostenkowski hand-picked to serve on the conference committee.

But increasingly he has concentrated on trade issues. As one of the leading Ways and Means Democrats from a constituency that feels beleaguered by foreign imports, Pease supported the Democrats' 1986 initiative on trade and came forward with his own proposal to set up labor standards stipulating that any country that doesn't pay its workers enough and provide them with good enough working conditions has violated U.S. trade laws and can't get its products into the U.S. market. That position doesn't seem to have much support on Ways and Means, but it obviously has an appeal to labor union leaders and members who have seen their high wages and benefits undermined by low-wage competition from abroad. In effect Pease is trying to reinvent the policy followed by Republicans for 70 years after the Civil War, to protect high American wages (and they, like Pease's Democrats, represented most of the high-wage working-class areas) by building barriers against low-wage imports from abroad. A little of this may be a useful thing, but if the barriers get too high the danger is that international trade will be choked off altogether, as it was by the Republicans' Smoot-Hawley tariff of 1930.

Pease is certainly aware of the dangers, and seems genuinely to want to gain access to foreign markets, not to shut off access to America. But more than most congressmen he is made aware of the problem every time he returns home. So far his stand seems to have pleased his constituents; he has won each of his five congressional elections with more than 60% of the vote, and seems unlikely to encounter a serious Republican challenge soon.

The People: Pop. 1980: 514,176, up 11.9% 1970–80. Households (1980): 80% family, 47% with children, 69% married couples; 25.0% housing units rented; median monthly rent: $181; median house value: $50,600. Voting age pop. (1980): 350,858; 5% Black, 2% Spanish origin.

1984 Presidential Vote: Reagan (R) 121,812   (58%)
Mondale (D) 84,648   (40%)

Rep. Donald J. (Don) Pease (D)

Elected 1976; b. Sept. 26, 1931, Toledo; home, Oberlin; OH U., B.S. 1953, M.A. 1955, Fulbright Scholar, U. of Durham, England, 1954–55; United Methodist; married (Jeanne).

Career: Army, 1955–57; Co-editor and publisher, *Oberlin News-Tribune*, 1957–68, Ed., 1968–77; Oberlin City Cncl., 1961–64; OH Senate, 1965–67, 1975–77; OH House of Reps., 1969–75.

Offices: 1127 LHOB 20515, 202-225-3401. Also 1936 Cooper-Foster Park Rd., Lorain 44053, 216-282-5003; Cnty. Admin. Bldg., Medina 22456, 216-725-6120; The Center, Ste. 101, 42 E. Main St., Ashland 44805, 419-325-4148; and 180 Milan Ave., Norwalk 44857, 419-668-0206.

Committees: *Ways and Means* (13th of 23 D). Subcommittees: Public Assistance and Unemployment Compensation; Trade.

Group Ratings

	ADA	ACLU	COPE	CFA	LCV	ACU	NTU	NSI	COC	CEI
1986	75	80	82	83	68	18	33	0	17	28
1985	70	—	89	83	—	14	40	—	38	—

National Journal Ratings

	1986 LIB — 1986 CONS		1985 LIB — 1985 CONS	
Economic	62%	35%	61%	38%
Social	81%	17%	73%	23%
Foreign	67%	30%	80%	17%

Key Votes

1) Lmt Cln Water Act	AGN	5) Retain Gun Cont	FOR
2) Rpl Tobac Sub	FOR	6) Contra Aid	AGN
3) Grm-Rdmn Def Red	FOR	7) Lmt Text Imp	AGN
4) Ban Polygraph	FOR	8) Limit SDI	FOR

9) Aid Angola Reb	AGN
10) Tax Reform	FOR
11) S Africa Sanc	FOR
12) Immig Reform	FOR

Election Results

1986 general	Donald J. (Don) Pease (D)	88,612	(63%)	($415,486)
	William D. Nielsen, Jr. (R)	52,452	(37%)	($256,604)
1986 primary	Donald J. (Don) Pease (D)	25,892	(77%)	
	Michael Ryan (D)	5,302	(16%)	
	Robert W. Stewart, Jr. (D)	2,554	(7%)	
1984 general	Donald J. (Don) Pease (D)	130,867	(66%)	($103,754)
	William G. Schaffner (R)	59,014	(30%)	($123)

Campaign Contributions and Expenditures

1985-86		Direct Cont. 1985-86		PACS Breakdown 1985-86			
Receipts	$483,277	Indiv.	$153,973	Corp.	$65,045	T/M/H	$61,308
Expend.	$415,486	Party	$7,030	Labor	$91,850	Agr.	$5,250
Unspent	$118,167	PACS	$254,001	Ideo.	$23,598	CWOS	$6,950

FOURTEENTH DISTRICT

Akron is one of America's premier factory towns which in the 1980s is turning into something else. For many years the word Akron was synonymous with tires, and five leading tire companies had their headquarters and major plants here. The headquarters are still there (though, in May 1987, Firestone announced it was moving its corporate headquarters to Chicago) but the last

Akron tire plant was closed by General Tire in 1983, and the companies have been busy diversifying (General Tire is now GenCorp). Akron has been busy diversifying too. It was once the world's biggest rubber manufacturer, the city that produced virtually all the tires for America's cars and trucks.

From all over unskilled laborers came to work in the rubber plants, many from eastern and southern Europe, whole towns from the hills of West Virginia—the sense of uprootedness formed certain themes in the old hillbilly songs composed by the famed Carter family. In the 1930s and 1940s, when the United Rubber Workers organized the tire companies, there was something like class warfare politics here; management and labor alike doubted the future would bring significant economic growth, and both fought hard for bigger slices of the existing pie. The 1950s became more placid: the economy boomed, American families increasingly bought two cars and a great amount of original equipment and replacement tires. Akron experienced its last spurt of growth. Its politics modulated: Akron and Ohio Republican boss Ray Bliss shrewdly decided that workers would always outvote managers, and so recruited candidates (James Rhodes at the statewide level, Representative William Ayres in Akron) with appeal to blue-collar voters.

All of Akron's calculations were based on the assumption that the rubber business would go on forever as it did here; and of course it didn't. The companies started decentralizing their plants, looking for cheaper labor; the European competitors they scorned started making money on radials; the auto market sagged. Then in the late 1970s it collapsed, and so did Akron's economy. The grandchildren of the migrants attracted here from Eastern Europe and West Virginia in the 1910–30 period, when Akron like Detroit grew explosively, were drifting away in the early 1980s or wandering dazedly in a city where the unemployment benefits which they always assumed would tide them over forever had run out.

By this time Ray Bliss had retired, and Akron had long since become one of the most Democratic cities in America. Its first political response was to vote for labor/liberal Democrats who emphasized maintaining the economic positions people have achieved, supporting public spending programs even at the cost of raising taxes, and encouraging economic development while maintaining environmental protections and anti-pollution programs, the prime local example being Representative John Seiberling, the Democrat who beat Ayres in 1970 and was unbeatable thereafter. But there was also an economic response: Akron, like the tire companies, diversified. It built new hotels and meeting centers downtown even as its tire factories were closing; its small businesses added white-collar jobs as its big businesses cut their blue-collar payrolls. It got out of tires and into polymers—plastics and other such materials that can be formed or shaped (like rubber!) into useful industrial products. "The Pontiac Fiero should be a symbol for Akron," Mayor Tom Sawyer said in 1986, because its outer skin is made of polymers; "our goal should be nothing less than making this region the Polymer Capital of the World." All this is part of the so-called materials revolution in high tech.

Ohio's 14th Congressional District, which includes Akron and most of suburban Summit County, is one of the state's most heavily Democratic districts, and Seiberling could have gone on representing it as long as he liked. Chairman of the Interior Public Lands Subcommittee, he had started off creating a Cuyahoga Valley National Recreation Area north of Akron, had managed the Alaska Lands Act in the late 1970s, and had passed more than a dozen wilderness bills in the 1980s.

But Seiberling surprised everyone by quitting in 1986, and the politics he represented did not achieve an easy triumph in the race to replace him. In the Democratic primary Seiberling endorsed Mayor Sawyer, whom another Democrat called "a shining star," over state Senator Oliver Ocasek, an old-time legislator first elected in 1958. Sawyer won but only by a 49%–39% margin. In the general Sawyer had serious opposition from Republican county prosecutor Lynn Slaby, who attacked Sawyer in ads on Cleveland TV for being too liberal. Sawyer campaigned on his record of solving the problems of the city's troubled Recycle Energy System and of being the only mayor in Ohio not to raise taxes. But all that was only enough for a 54% win in a district where Richard Celeste was winning over 70% of the vote. It will be interesting to see whether Sawyer is able to make the new 14th as safe as Seiberling did the old one.

The People: Pop. 1980: 514,172, dn. 5.6% 1970–80. Households (1980): 74% family, 38% with children, 60% married couples; 30.4% housing units rented; median monthly rent: $180; median house value: $44,700. Voting age pop. (1980): 373,433; 10% Black.

1984 Presidential Vote: Reagan (R) 112,676 (51%)
Mondale (D) 107,638 (49%)

Rep. Thomas C. Sawyer (D)

Elected 1986; b. Aug. 15, 1945, Akron; home, Akron; U. of Akron, B.A. 1968, M.A. 1970; Presbyterian; married (Joyce).

Career: OH House of Reps., 1977–83; Mayor of Akron, 1983–86.

Offices: 1225 LHOB 20515, 202-225-5231. Also Fed. Bldg., 2 S. Main St., Akron 44308, 216-375-5710.

Committees: *Education and Labor* (13th of 21 D). Subcommittees: Elementary, Secondary and Vocational legislation; Labor Standards; Human Resources. *Government Operations* (21st of 24 D). Subcommittees: Government Activities and Transportation; Human Resources and Intergovernmental Relations.

Group Ratings and Key Votes: Newly Elected

Election Results

1986 general	Thomas C. Sawyer (D).................	83,257	(54%)	($546,302)
	Lynn Slaby (R)......................	71,713	(46%)	($411,539)
1986 primary	Thomas C. Sawyer (D).................	24,132	(50%)	
	Oliver Ocasek (D)....................	19,206	(40%)	
	Mark T. Ravenscraft (D)	3,091	(6%)	
	Four others (D)......................	2,168	(4%)	
1984 general	John F. Seiberling (D)................	153,350	(71%)	($91,098)
	Jean E. Bender (R)...................	61,562	(29%)	($5,247)

Campaign Contributions and Expenditures

1985–86		Direct Cont. 1985–86		PACS Breakdown 1985–86			
Receipts	$565,591	Indiv.	$218,872	Corp.	$16,035	T/M/H	$42,010
Expend.	$546,302	Party	$14.892	Labor	$140,089	Agr.	$3,000
Unspent	$19,288	PACS	$259,084	Ideo.	$56,950	CWOS	$1,000
		Cand.	$85,142				

FIFTEENTH DISTRICT

In American literature Columbus serves as a symbol of Middle America: the place where James Thurber grew up, the town My Sister Eileen left behind for New York, the college town where Philip Roth's Newark-born hero was finally able to say Goodbye, Columbus. Yet today Columbus is growing and thriving, the center of a metropolitan area that, 1980s-style, is spreading out into the countryside with one little subdivision here and another there, separated by farm fields or river bottoms. Nor can you dismiss as hicksville a city that is the home of Leslie Wexner's fabulously successful The Limited and is home base of the Lazarus family who started Federated Department Stores. Columbus (sometimes pronounced with two syllables: C'lumbus), more than many modish cities, is in touch with what's latest in America.

The 15th Congressional District of Ohio is made up of the west and south sides of Columbus and suburban Franklin County, plus most of rural Madison County directly to the west. The 15th includes some (but not most) of Columbus's black population, some white working-class areas on the south side of the city, and the Ohio State University campus area. These are more than balanced by the heavily Republican suburb of Upper Arlington, across the Olentangy River from Ohio State, and by the Republican subdivisions that seem to be sprouting in the rural land and in between the old villages to the west.

Representative Chalmers Wylie is an old-school Columbus Republican, who worked himself up the political ladder and was able to claim the 15th when redistricting produced a second district in the Columbus area in 1966. Wylie is now the ranking Republican on the House Banking, Finance and Urban Affairs Committee. He is a pleasant man who must work with the hard-driving and abrasive chairman, Fernand St Germain. Wylie's impulses seem standard Republican: he tends to want to minimize federal regulation and big government. But he is an incrementalist rather than a revolutionary. He is ready to strengthen interest rate disclosure, for example, but not as stringently as the Democrats would like; he is for extending federal housing programs, but favors smaller authorizations than the Democrats do. Wylie does embrace some new ideas, like tenant management for public housing projects, and he is ready to respond flexibly to meet crises, like the Ohio savings and loan scandal. But he dismays some of the younger, brasher Republicans by his refusal to tackle the Democrats head on and his lack of interest in their favorite new conservative theories.

But this is a man whose career has been entirely practical, not theoretical; whose impetus to get into politics does not come from immersion in the finery of microeconomics; and whose constituency, while containing many affluent precincts, also contains almost the whole range of society. He is dealing, moreover, on Banking with an industry that almost everyone since the days of the Founding Fathers has realized needs close regulation. So it should not be surprising that Wylie favors things like check-hold legislation, interest rate disclosure, anti-money laundering bills, emergency grants for the homeless, and continuation of International Monetary Fund programs.

Banking is a good committee from which to raise money, but for many years he didn't need much; the hot races in Columbus always seemed to be in the 12th District. But in 1986 Wylie got a well-regarded opponent, Dr. David Jackson, former head of the state health department. Jackson raised money and seemed to be a threat, but Wylie won reelection with 64% of the vote. That's an impressive total for a Democratic year, and indicates that he has a safer seat than some Democratic strategists hoped.

The People: Pop. 1980: 514,176, up 0.8% 1970–80. Households (1980): 68% family, 37% with children, 54% married couples; 42.6% housing units rented; median monthly rent: $168; median house value: $47,500. Voting age pop. (1980): 377,458; 10% Black, 1% Asian origin, 1% Spanish origin.

1984 Presidential Vote: Reagan (R) 150,714   (66%)
Mondale (D) 71,086   (31%)

Rep. Chalmers P. Wylie (R)

Elected 1966; b. Nov. 23, 1920, Norwich; home, Worthington; Otterbein Col., OH State U., Harvard U., J.D. 1948; United Methodist; married (Marjorie).

Career: Army, WWII; Asst. Atty. Gen. of OH, 1948, 1951–53; Asst. Columbus City Atty., 1949–50, City Atty., 1954–57; Admin., OH Bureau of Workmen's Comp., 1957; First Asst. to the Gov. of OH, 1957; Practicing atty.; OH House of Reps., 1961–66.

Offices: 2310 RHOB 20515, 202-225-2015. Also 200 N. High St., Rm. 500, Columbus 43215, 614-469-5614.

Committees: *Banking, Finance and Urban Affairs* (Ranking Member of 20 R). Subcommittees: Consumer Affairs and Coinage; Financial Institutions Supervision, Regulation and Insurance (Ranking Member); Housing and Community Development. *Veterans' Affairs* (3d of 13 R). Subcommittees: Compensation, Pension, and Insurance; Education, Training and Employment. *Joint Economic Committee.* Task Forces: Fiscal and Monetary Affairs; National Security Economics; International Economic Policy.

Group Ratings

	ADA	ACLU	COPE	CFA	LCV	ACU	NTU	NSI	COC	CEI
1986	15	5	23	58	16	64	51	100	71	61
1985	10	—	23	33	—	76	51	—	73	—

National Journal Ratings

	1986 LIB	—	1986 CONS	1985 LIB	—	1985 CONS
Economic	31%	—	67%	38%	—	61%
Social	26%	—	74%	0%	—	76%
Foreign	33%	—	66%	24%	—	66%

Key Votes

1) Lmt Cln Water Act	FOR	5) Retain Gun Cont	FOR	9) Aid Angola Reb	FOR
2) Rpl Tobac Sub	FOR	6) Contra Aid	AGN	10) Tax Reform	FOR
3) Grm-Rdmn Def Red	FOR	7) Lmt Text Imp	AGN	11) S Africa Sanc	FOR
4) Ban Polygraph	—	8) Limit SDI	AGN	12) Immig Reform	FOR

Election Results

1986 general	Chalmers P. Wylie (R)	97,745	(64%)	($338,230)
	David L. Jackson (D)	55,750	(36%)	($319,640)
1986 primary	Chalmers P. Wylie (R)	51,837	(100%)	
1984 general	Chalmers P. Wylie (R)	147,647	(71%)	($181,503)
	Duane Jager (D)	59,180	(29%)	($66,534)

Campaign Contributions and Expenditures

1985-86		Direct Cont. 1985-86		PACS Breakdown 1985-86			
Receipts	$305,756	Indiv.	$102,698	Corp.	$69,333	T/M/H	$102,499
Expend.	$338,230	Party	$9,690	Labor	$250	Agr.	$2,500
Unspent	$13,813	PACS	$185,808	Ideo.	$8,750	CWOS	$2,476

SIXTEENTH DISTRICT

William McKinley is not remembered today as a master politician—but maybe he should be. He won two elections by decisive margins and began a period of three decades in which the Republican Party, with scarcely a bit of support in the one-third of the nation that was the South, was nonetheless the clear majority party in the United States—the only time it has been so. The policies he championed stood the test of the political market over that long period of time: the protective tariff, the gold standard, the enforcement of law and order in labor relations. McKinley talked of a "full dinner pail" and meant that government should foster high wages and a safe investment climate, and he made the Republican Party for the first time, as it was a generation after, the clear choice of most American blue-collar workers. McKinley has been painted as a mindless reactionary, as a pawn of the millionaire Mark Hanna, as an overcautious bumbler who was pushed into the Spanish-American War by Theodore Roosevelt. A better view is that this martyred President was a decent man and a competent politician who did his duty and turned out to be in sync with his time.

Some of McKinley's politics remains alive in his home town of Canton, Ohio. It was here that McKinley sat on his front porch and received delegations of thousands of voters carefully selected by Republican organizations around the country—and heard that he had been elected President over William Jennings Bryan. Unlike Cleveland and Akron, Canton has had no decades of explosive growth, and perhaps correspondingly its downturns have been relatively mild. Canton, plus the nearby towns of Massillon and Alliance, where some of our current National Football League teams were first organized, still retain a basic preference for the Republican Party; in 1984 the cities were more solidly for Ronald Reagan than the nation as a whole. Taken together, they form the nucleus of the 16th Congressional District of Ohio, which also includes the smaller counties of Wayne and Holmes to the west.

McKinley was elected to the House six times from the Canton area and served as chairman of the Ways and Means Committee. Thus the 16th District's current congressman, Republican Ralph Regula, is one of the few House members who can claim to represent a district formerly represented by a President of the United States. Regula is in the McKinley mold—a principled, yet practical and adaptable professional politician of good personal character. He is, appropriately, a graduate of the William McKinley School of Law, and in the 1970s he worked to retain the name Mount McKinley for the highest mountain in North America (although Alaska natives did get the surrounding area named Denali National Park).

Regula is considered a moderate, a man with an instinct to be a party regular but also one who works amicably and constructively with those across the aisle. He is a member of the Appropriations Committee, and, since 1985, ranking Republican on the Interior Subcommittee. There he works with Chairman Sidney Yates on most but not all issues; Regula is a bit more inclined to favor economic development over protecting the environment than Yates is on these balancing issues. But their differences are limited and cooperation is usually the order of the day. Regula spent much time, for example, negotiating an agreement on offshore oil drilling in California. Once a teacher, Regula is often favorable to claims for more domestic spending. He has a moderate record on cultural and foreign policy issues.

Regula has held the 16th District with ease. The economy of the Canton area in the early 1980s was not in such visible trouble as many parts of Ohio, and he was able to win reelection easily, against a weak opponent, even in the trough year of 1982.

The People: Pop. 1980: 514,171, up 5.2% 1970–80. Households (1980): 78% family, 42% with children, 67% married couples; 27.3% housing units rented; median monthly rent: $167; median house value: $45,600. Voting age pop. (1980): 363,139; 4% Black, 1% Spanish origin.

1984 Presidential Vote:

Reagan (R)	129,748	(62%)
Mondale (D)	79,292	(38%)

Rep. Ralph S. Regula (R)

Elected 1972; b. Dec. 3, 1924, Beach City; home, Navarre; Mt. Union Col., B.A. 1948, Wm. McKinley Sch. of Law, LL.B. 1952; Episcopalian; married (Mary).

Career: Navy, WWII; Teacher and school principal, 1948–55; Practicing atty., 1952–73; OH Bd. of Educ., 1960–64; OH House of Reps., 1965–66; OH Senate, 1967–72.

Offices: 2209 RHOB 20515, 202-225-3876. Also 4150 Belden Village Ave., N.W., Canton 44718, 216-489-4414.

Committees: *Appropriations* (8th of 22 R). Subcommittees: Commerce, Justice, State, and Judiciary; District of Columbia; Interior (Ranking Member). *Select Committee on Aging* (3d of 26 R). Subcommittee: Health and Long-Term Care (Ranking Member).

Group Ratings

	ADA	ACLU	COPE	CFA	LCV	ACU	NTU	NSI	COC	CEI
1986	15	20	34	42	32	45	41	80	61	42
1985	25	—	32	50	—	52	43	—	59	—

National Journal Ratings

	1986 LIB — 1986 CONS		1985 LIB — 1985 CONS	
Economic	38%	61%	40%	59%
Social	23%	74%	32%	67%
Foreign	37%	62%	42%	56%

Key Votes

1) Lmt Cln Water Act	FOR	5) Retain Gun Cont	AGN	9) Aid Angola Reb	FOR
2) Rpl Tobac Sub	FOR	6) Contra Aid	FOR	10) Tax Reform	AGN
3) Grm-Rdmn Def Red	FOR	7) Lmt Text Imp	FOR	11) S Africa Sanc	FOR
4) Ban Polygraph	FOR	8) Limit SDI	FOR	12) Immig Reform	AGN

Election Results

1986 general	Ralph S. Regula (R)	118,206	(76%)	($103,471)
	William J. Kennick (D)	36,639	(24%)	
1986 primary	Ralph S. Regula (R)	40,102	(100%)	
1984 general	Ralph S. Regula (R)	152,134	(72%)	($113,337)
	James S. Gwin (D)	58,149	(28%)	($30,624)

Campaign Contributions and Expenditures

1985-86		Direct Cont. 1985-86		PACS Breakdown 1985-86			
Receipts	$128,324	Indiv.	$113,452	Corp.	$839	T/M/H	$0
Expend.	$103,471	Party	$5,802	Labor	$0	Agr.	$0
Unspent	$84,348	PACS	$839	Ideo.	$0	CWOS	$0

SEVENTEENTH DISTRICT

The Mahoning Valley, the part of easternmost Ohio area around Youngstown and Warren, where the bumpy hills of western Pennsylvania give way, almost with the suddenness suggested by the dotted line found on a topographical map to the flat plains of northern Ohio, is—or was— one of the leading steel-producing regions of the United States. The Valley seemed marked for steel: it is halfway between the Lake Erie docks that unload iron ore from Great Lakes freighters, and the coalfields of western Pennsylvania and West Virginia. After the turn of the century, the capitalists from downtown Pittsburgh and Cleveland put immense amounts of money into building giant steel mills here, huge industrial hulks that must have taken people's breath away then—and do now, as they stand empty and smokeless and silent. The first steel-mill builders were ahead of the technological curve, anticipating correctly the gigantic demand for steel the 20th century would bring—automobiles, skyscrapers, airplanes.

But American steel has been in trouble for the last 25 years. Foreign producers gained a technological edge of American companies in the 1950s and 1960s, and overcapacity was built into the industry when practically every nation decided that, to show it was an advanced industrial power, it must have its own steel mill. Foreign producers had cost advantages not only from efficiency, but because of lower wage costs. The steel industry and the United Steel Workers, after the long strike which held the nation's attention through much of 1959, decided to avoid strikes and grant large wage and benefit increases which, they were confident, could be passed along to consumers who would always need a lot of steel; if there were problems with imports, they could be barred. This strategy worked in the short run but in the long run it failed to preserve the industry; foreign steel made its way in, and users found lower-priced substitutes.

The result was economic disaster for the Mahoning Valley. Most of its steel mills have been shut down; some have even been dynamited. During the early 1980s metropolitan Youngstown had one of the nation's highest unemployment rates—in some months the highest. The high-wage standard of living that was maintained through the late 1970s has vanished, and here, in contrast to other industrial areas in Ohio, it does not seem likely to return soon. Young people have been leaving since at least 1960, looking for new opportunities; those who have remained seem anchored here by community ties or by an inertia that seems to have been at least partly encouraged by safety nets like unemployment compensation and welfare. Unlike their immigrant grandparents, who came thousands of miles from southern Italy and southern Poland, with no hope of ever returning, today's Mahoning Valley residents are waiting for something to turn up locally. People watch as their friends leave, the equity in their houses is wiped out, the community institutions they have relied on dissolve.

The events, of course, have shaken basic political values and preferences. The Mahoning Valley has been a solidly Democratic area since the United Steelworkers organized the plants after sometimes bloody skirmishes in the late 1930s, and in the past they have responded to hard times by voting even more heavily Democratic. Their responses have been more volatile in the 1980s. In 1978 the voters of the 17th Congressional District, which includes Youngstown, Warren, and most of the Mahoning Valley, actually elected a Republican congressman, and reelected him in 1980 and 1982. They gave Jimmy Carter in 1980 no higher a percentage of their votes than they had given George McGovern eight years before. In the 1982 and 1986 state elections and in the 1984 and 1986 congressional races they have switched back to the Republicans, and they gave Walter Mondale a good majority in 1984 against Ronald Reagan. But in the 1984 primary they surprised almost everyone by voting for Gary Hart over Mondale.

The congressman here is James Traficant, former Mahoning County Sheriff, a politician whose style is redolent of the high times when the steel mill smokestacks were pouring out soot, the bars across from the plant gates were thronged at shift break, and mobsters prowled the streets in shiny black Cadillacs. Traficant once admitted in court that he took $55,000 in bribes from mobsters to overlook gambling, loan-sharking, drug trafficking, and prostitution in Mahoning County; his excuse was that this was part of his own sting operation—although the man he said he returned the money to had disappeared. The jury found Traficant innocent, and helped make him a local hero. Also helping was his championing of the death penalty for drug smugglers. Two years before the Mahoning County Democratic chairman called him "a nitwit, a lunatic, a raving maniac." But in 1984 he won a seven-candidate Democratic congressional primary with 56% of the vote, an election in which the astonishing total of 120,000 votes were cast.

That contest and the general election proved Traficant a gifted demagogue, capable of articulating the discontents of people who feel suddenly cheated by history. In Congress he has inevitably calmed down. He was head of the small class of 1984 freshmen, got on the Public Works and Science Committees, started voting a liberal line on most issues. He jumped in with other steel district representatives to protect benefits of LTV workers and retirees when the company went bankrupt, he pushed a bill to stop foreclosures (as sheriff he refused to foreclose on workingmen, but the lenders cannot have been too miffed, for some of the houses were worth little or nothing on the market), he pushed for the canal sought by longtime Mahoning Valley Representative Michael Kirwan from Lake Erie to the Ohio, he pressed "buy American" bills and a revival of the investment tax credit on projects with 65% or more domestic content. On all these issues Traficant is surely speaking his district's views. Yet none of these items seems likely to pass, and the Mahoning Valley's problems seem likely to continue. Traficant, however, seems sure to be reelected easily, as he was in 1986.

The People: Pop. 1980: 514,172, dn. 1.6% 1970–80. Households (1980): 77% family, 40% with children, 64% married couples; 26.7% housing units rented; median monthly rent: $168; median house value: $39,300. Voting age pop. (1980): 372,108; 10% Black, 1% Spanish origin.

1984 Presidential Vote:

Mondale (D)	129,930	(57%)
Reagan (R)	95,840	(42%)

Rep. James A. Traficant, Jr. (D)

Elected 1984; b. May 8, 1941, Youngstown; home, Poland; U. of Pittsburgh, B.S. 1963; Youngstown State U., M.S. 1973, M.S. 1976; Roman Catholic; married (Patricia).

Career: Dir., Mahoning Cnty. Drug Program, 1971–81; Sheriff, 1981–85.

Offices: 128 CHOB 20515, 202-225-5261. Also 11 Overhill Rd., Boardman 44512, 216-788-2414; and City Hall, 319 Mahoning Ave., Warren 44483, 216-399-3513.

Committees: *Public Works and Transportation* (22d of 32 D). Subcommittees: Economic Development; Surface Transportation; Water Resources. *Science, Space and Technology* (18th of 27 D). Subcommittees: Energy Research and Development; Investigations and Oversight; Space Science and Applications.

Group Ratings

	ADA	ACLU	COPE	CFA	LCV	ACU	NTU	NSI	COC	CEI
1986	95	65	100	83	63	9	30	0	28	13
1985	95	—	100	83	—	0	34	—	27	—

National Journal Ratings

	1986 LIB — 1986 CONS		1985 LIB — 1985 CONS	
Economic	87% —	0%	75% —	22%
Social	57% —	40%	81% —	15%
Foreign	71% —	28%	92% —	0%

Key Votes

1) Lmt Cln Water Act	AGN	5) Retain Gun Cont	FOR	9) Aid Angola Reb	AGN
2) Rpl Tobac Sub	AGN	6) Contra Aid	AGN	10) Tax Reform	FOR
3) Grm-Rdmn Def Red	AGN	7) Lmt Text Imp	FOR	11) S Africa Sanc	FOR
4) Ban Polygraph	FOR	8) Limit SDI	FOR	12) Immig Reform	AGN

Election Results

1986 general	James A. Traficant, Jr. (D)	112,855	(72%)	($91,338)
	James H. Fulks (R)	43,334	(28%)	($91,035)
1986 primary	James A. Traficant, Jr. (D)	64,733	(76%)	
	Michael R. Antonoff (D)	17,260	(20%)	
	Frank E. Haney (D)	3,698	(4%)	
1984 general	James A. Traficant, Jr. (D)	123,026	(53%)	($99,270)
	Lyle Williams (R)	104,861	(46%)	($411,145)

Campaign Contributions and Expenditures

1985-86		Direct Cont. 1985-86		PACS Breakdown 1985-86			
Receipts	$139,761	Indiv.	$47,029	Corp.	$4,350	T/M/H	$9,700
Expend.	$91,338	Party	$210	Labor	$71,680	Agr.	$800
Unspent	$51,577	PACS	$104,480	Ideo.	$17,500	CWOS	$450

EIGHTEENTH DISTRICT

The 18th Congressional District of Ohio, just across the Ohio River from West Virginia, is a land of marginal farms and hills pockmarked by strip mines. The area is part of the great coal and steel belt that stretches from the coal mines of West Virginia to Lake Erie, the destination of the once common freighters filled with iron ore from Minnesota's Mesabi Range. This area is filled with small cities, each with their little steel mill or factory, most of them old towns whose storefronts and wooden, working-class houses, with hills rising behind them, bear the unmistakable imprint of the early 20th century. There is nothing chic or fashionable here: these are gritty places where working people have long toiled long hours at physically demanding work for whatever pay might be available. For a time the pay was good. But in the late 1970s the coal and steel economy, long in trouble, seemed about to collapse. The impact here was cushioned by continuing demand for coal from electric utilities; but with even union steel wages falling in real dollars, the impact on ordinary people's lives here has been substantial.

The 18th District lies along the Ohio River, beginning in the north just below Youngstown and proceeding almost all the way to Marietta, Ohio, and Parkersburg, West Virginia. Some of the people here are from the Scotch-Irish stock, part of the first wave of migration over the Appalachians. But more are descended from later immigrants: Italians, Poles, Czechs, Germans. The 18th District, sociologically and politically, is a kind of ethnic working-class neighborhood. Politically, the district is heavily Democratic; it voted for Ronald Reagan in 1984, but only barely, and in 1986 returned Governor Richard Celeste to office with 62% of the vote. Culturally, this is still a place where people believe in, and usually live according to, traditional values, where church, family, home, and hometown are more important than notions about escape from restraint. Economically, the area has prospered only occasionally in the last few decades but its lack of really large factories has made it less vulnerable to the sudden economic dislocation caused by the unexpected closing of a huge factory, which has been so common in much of Ohio.

The congressman from this district is Douglas Applegate, a veteran state legislator who was elected in 1976 after Wayne Hays, chairman of the House Administration Committee and tyrant of the House, was forced to leave office by the Elizabeth Ray scandal.

Applegate is a member of the kind of practical committees—Public Works and Transportation and Veterans' Affairs—that help him do something concrete for his district. He chairs the Veterans' Affairs subcommittee that handles military pensions—a hot issue—and he sits on the Surface Transportation Subcommittee of Public Works, where the sale of Conrail was debated. He has a moderate voting record on most issues, and interestingly enough, in a district considered hawkish in the 1960s, votes often with the liberals on foreign policy. He is routinely reelected with little or no opposition.

The People: Pop. 1980: 514,173, up 4.1% 1970–80. Households (1980): 77% family, 41% with children, 67% married couples; 24.0% housing units rented; median monthly rent: $132; median house value: $34,200. Voting age pop. (1980): 367,705; 2% Black.

1984 Presidential Vote: Reagan (R) 111,625   (53%)

Mondale (D) 96,643   (46%)

Rep. Douglas Applegate (D)

Elected 1976; b. Mar. 27, 1928, Steubenville; home, Steubenville; Presbyterian; married (Betty).

Career: Real estate salesman, 1950–56, broker, 1956–76; OH House of Reps., 1961–69; OH Senate, 1969–77.

Offices: 2464 RHOB 20515, 202-225-6265. Also Scott Complex, Ste. 2, St. Clairsville 43950, 614-695-4600; Ohio Valley Tower, Rm. 610, Steubenville 43952, 614-283-3716; 109 W. 3d St., E. Liverpool 43920, 216-385-5921; and 1330 4th St., N.W., New Philadelphia 44663, 216-343-9112.

Committees: *Public Works and Transportation* (8th of 32 D). Subcommittees: Economic Development; Surface Transportation; Water Resources. *Veterans' Affairs* (5th of 20 D). Subcommittees: Compensation, Pension, and Insurance (Chairman); Oversight and Investigations.

Group Ratings

	ADA	ACLU	COPE	CFA	LCV	ACU	NTU	NSI	COC	CEI
1986	65	40	73	25	49	23	28	0	35	22
1985	55	—	72	50	—	19	45	—	50	—

National Journal Ratings

	1986 LIB — 1986 CONS		1985 LIB — 1985 CONS	
Economic	65%	35%	47% —	53%
Social	42% —	57%	36% —	60%
Foreign	57% —	41%	64% —	33%

Key Votes

1) Lmt Cln Water Act	AGN	5) Retain Gun Cont	FOR	9) Aid Angola Reb	AGN
2) Rpl Tobac Sub	FOR	6) Contra Aid	AGN	10) Tax Reform	AGN
3) Grm-Rdmn Def Red	FOR	7) Lmt Text Imp	FOR	11) S Africa Sanc	FOR
4) Ban Polygraph	FOR	8) Limit SDI	FOR	12) Immig Reform	AGN

Election Results

1986 general	Douglas Applegate (D).	126,526	(100%)	($83,591)
1986 primary	Douglas Applegate (D).	52,743	(91%)	
	Michael Anthony Palmer (D).	5,520	(9%)	
1984 general	Douglas Applegate (D).	155,173	(76%)	($59,276)
	Kenneth P. Burt, Jr. (R)	49,338	(24%)	($1,894)

Campaign Contributions and Expenditures

1985-86		Direct Cont. 1985-86		PACS Breakdown 1985-86			
Receipts	$104,752	Indiv.	$33,181	Corp.	$12,000	T/M/H	$21,300
Expend.	$83,591	Party	$165	Labor	$21,500	Agr.	$500
Unspent	$96,185	PACS	$56,650	Ideo.	$1,300	CWOS	$0

NINETEENTH DISTRICT

As Cleveland emerges from the recession of the early 1980s, it is a metropolis more white-collar than blue, one where health services and government payrolls account for more jobs than steel mills and auto assembly plants. The change has been a wrenching process for tens of thousands of wage-earners who had been going about their personal lives, confident that they could count on a good paycheck and generous fringe benefits; some have had to move away, and others have had to take jobs with lower pay and smaller benefits. Yet in the longer run, the economic change may come to be seen as part of a natural progression—painfully and perhaps unnecessarily concentrated in just a few years, perhaps—a progression upward that began when poor immigrants from Eastern and Southern Europe arrived at Cleveland's railroad terminal and which has ended, for the moment anyway, somewhere in the comfortable ring of suburbs around the city.

Much of this suburban ring makes up Ohio's 19th Congressional District. It forms a kind of convoluted U around Cleveland and some of its close-in suburbs, encircling the 20th and 21st Districts. The 19th can be divided into three distinct sections. One is the southern blue-collar suburbs. Parma is the largest town here, a working-class suburb that grew rapidly in the 1950s; it is reputed to have the nation's largest concentration of bowling alleys, and accordingly draws more than its share of the nation's political reporters looking for opinion in blue-collar America. The suburbs south of Parma enjoy higher real estate values, largely because their houses and condominiums are newer. This is the home of comfortable blue-collar families, those with skilled workers and two paychecks, prime beneficiaries of the rises in real income in metropolitan Cleveland over the past three decades.

Quite different are the white-collar suburbs running west from Cleveland along Lake Erie and south along the Rocky River, whose ravine is lined with parks, not factories. They have the comfortable look of places long settled; their populations tend to be older, more Protestant, and more Republican. The eastern suburbs are in many cases even better off, but they are also more ethnic, with many Italians and Jews; the Jewish suburbs in particular vote Democratic. Throughout the district, however, there is a sort of warfare going on in voters' hearts, between the Democratic leanings of most of their forebears and the Republican preference they have had on many issues since the middle 1960s. This is the most affluent congressional district in Ohio, yet it tends to vote right along the statewide average, as it did for President in 1984 and governor in 1986. This leaves it a seriously contested district in House elections.

The winner of all those contests so far in the 1980s has been Democrat Edward Feighan. Feighan, a former state legislator, county commissioner, and candidate for mayor of Cleveland in 1977, has won three serious contests here. The first was against Representative Ron Mottl, a Democrat from Parma who backed the Reagan budget and tax cuts in 1981—the only Boll Weevil this far north of the Mason-Dixon line. Feighan won 49%–47%. His second battle was in the 1984 general election against the well-financed challenge of Republican Matt Hatchadorian. Feighan had compiled a liberal record in the House, notable especially for his opposition to Reagan Administration policies in El Salvador and Nicaragua, and Hatchadorian attacked him for opposing President Reagan. Feighan, in contrast, stressed his work in solving constituents' problems and ministering to the needs of suburban governments, and won 55%–43%. Feighan's third battle came in 1986, when Republican state Senator Gary Suhadolnick, a movement conservative with a base in Parma, and a strong personal campaigner, again challenged his record as too liberal. This time Feighan won 56%–45%. These past two races have been serious battles: Feighan and his opponents spent $1.1 million in each.

It's easy to see why Feighan's record enrages Republicans; he generally votes with liberals, though he supported Gramm-Rudman, and he is especially impassioned opponent of the Administration's often unpopular Central American policies. But like other Democrats on Foreign Affairs, he finds that his support for Israel and advocacy of human rights—he had the distinction of being one of the Americans who received a cool welcome from South Korean police as they accompanied dissident Kim Dae Jung on his return to Seoul in early 1985—can be an asset at home.

Feighan may have other serious challenges in 1988 and 1990, and he is one member who must be worried about the 1992 redistricting; geographically, it would be easy to divide the U-shaped 19th among its neighbors. But Feighan may be politically adroit enough to overcome this obstacle too.

The People: Pop. 1980: 514,174, dn. 1.4% 1970–80. Households (1980): 76% family, 35% with children, 66% married couples; 25.7% housing units rented; median monthly rent: $257; median house value: $67,300. Voting age pop. (1980): 386,888; 1% Black, 1% Asian origin.

1984 Presidential Vote:

Reagan (R)	152,025	(59%)
Mondale (D)	103,904	(40%)

Rep. Edward F. Feighan (D)

Elected 1982; b. Oct. 22, 1947, Lakewood; home, Lakewood; Loyola U., B.A. 1969, Cleveland State U., J.D. 1977; Roman Catholic; married (Nadine).

Career: High sch. teacher, 1969–72; OH House of Reps., 1973–79; Cuyahoga Cnty. Commissioner, 1979–82; Practicing atty., 1978–82.

Offices: 1124 LHOB 20515, 202-225-5731. Also 2951 Fed. Office Bldg., Cleveland 44199, 216-522-4382.

Committees: *Foreign Affairs* (18th of 27 D). Subcommittees: Europe and the Middle East; Human Rights and International Organizations; International Economic Policy and Trade. *Judiciary* (15th of 21 D). Subcommittees: Crime; Monopolies and Commercial Law.

Group Ratings

	ADA	ACLU	COPE	CFA	LCV	ACU	NTU	NSI	COC	CEI
1986	95	90	89	92	74	0	28	0	33	18
1985	70	—	85	83	—	10	38	—	32	—

National Journal Ratings

	1986 LIB — 1986 CONS			1985 LIB — 1985 CONS		
Economic	60%	—	38%	68%	—	30%
Social	89%	—	0%	73%	—	23%
Foreign	80%	—	0%	71%	—	26%

Key Votes

1) Lmt Cln Water Act	FOR	5) Retain Gun Cont	FOR	9) Aid Angola Reb	AGN
2) Rpl Tobac Sub	FOR	6) Contra Aid	AGN	10) Tax Reform	FOR
3) Grm-Rdmn Def Red	FOR	7) Lmt Text Imp	FOR	11) S Africa Sanc	FOR
4) Ban Polygraph	FOR	8) Limit SDI	FOR	12) Immig Reform	FOR

Election Results

1986 general	Edward F. Feighan (D)	97,814	(55%)	($630,626)
	Gary Suhadolnik (R)	80,743	(45%)	($524,243)
1986 primary	Edward F. Feighan (D)	37,216	(87%)	
	Norbert G. Dennerll, Jr. (D)	3,971	(9%)	
	George Barabas (D)	1,682	(4%)	
1984 general	Edward F. Feighan (D)	139,413	(55%)	($541,431)
	Matthew J. Hatchadorian (R)	107,844	(43%)	($583,639)

Campaign Contributions and Expenditures

1985–86		Direct Cont. 1985–86		PACS Breakdown 1985–86			
Receipts	$660,275	Indiv.	$296,992	Corp.	$23,500	T/M/H	$57,643
Expend.	$630,626	Party	$8,767	Labor	$167,267	Agr.	$4,000
Unspent	$33,115	PACS	$338,359	Ideo.	$83,449	CWOS	$2,500
		Cand.	$329				

TWENTIETH DISTRICT

Has Cleveland reached a turning point? For much of the 1970s and well into the 1980s it has been America's most maligned major city, a synonym for a crumbling industrial city, the belt buckle of the Rust Belt. There was some truth behind the caricature: yes, the Cuyahoga River, lined by steel mills, once did catch fire; yes, many of Cleveland's steel mills and other old factories shut down; yes, Cleveland has some poor black neighborhoods and has a mostly black east side and almost white west side; yes, Cleveland did have a series of weak mayors climaxed by Dennis Kucinich, a sort of Willie Stark à la Saturday Night Live, who shouted that he was going to redistribute the wealth and left the city unable to pay the bills. But the picture of Cleveland's decrepitude was always overdrawn and often downright inaccurate, and the scoffers have missed the city's enduring strengths and its turnaround.

For Cleveland was always more than just a factory town. True, the Cuyahoga, winding beneath limestone walls toward Lake Erie, has been lined with factories for nearly 100 years; it's one of the few places on shallow Lake Erie where the giant Great Lakes freighters can unload their iron ore so it can be smelted by West Virginia coal. But as long as there have been steel mills along the Cuyahoga, there have been skyscrapers in downtown Cleveland, and a thriving business district; and if Cleveland is no longer America's fourth largest city, as it was in 1910, it has consistently been a national leader in symphony and surgery, the home of some of the nation's largest law firms, a city whose spacious downtown parks are thronged on festival days. It has gone through a painful economic adjustment in the 1980s in which many individuals have been hurt; city government has been cleaned up and cut back by Republican Mayor George Voinovich. But it remains a city where hundreds of thousands of immigrants from Eastern and Southern Europe and from the American South have moved upward in a community originally built by New England Yankees.

The 20th Congressional District of Ohio includes the west side of Cleveland and adjacent suburbs. It spans both sides of the Cuyahoga to include the ethnic (in Cleveland, cosmo) wards east of the river, along Broadway and in the suburb of Garfield Heights; and it includes most of downtown. Technically it is not a pure big city district: half its residents live in suburbs. But these are mostly modest, working-class suburbs: the northern half of Parma (once famed for having the nation's largest number of bowling alleys), the factory suburbs around the airport. The 20th is almost entirely white, with lower incomes than the other white suburban district; one reason is high unemployment, another is that these are older neighborhoods.

This has been a heavily Democratic district since Franklin Roosevelt first fired the enthusiasm of the ethnic residents of industrial Cleveland in the 1930s. The current representative, Mary Rose Oakar, is an important member of the House with deep roots in her district and a background that would have been unusual in politics not so long ago. She comes from a modest ethnic (Arab-American) family, and worked her way through college as a telephone operator. She was elected to the Cleveland City Council while the city was in the midst of racial and fiscal turmoil, and was one west side Representative who maintained good relations with blacks. She was popular enough to have won a 12-candidate primary with 24% of the vote in 1976, and has not been seriously challenged since. She is an ardent Cleveland booster and Cleveland, or at least the 20th District, seems an ardent booster of hers.

Oakar has a solidly liberal record on economic issues but is somewhat more conservative on cultural issues. An active member of various women's movements, she is also an opponent of abortion. One of her pet causes is comparable worth, the idea that courts or government employees should determine what wages and salaries people in the private sector receive; she got a bill through the House calling for a study of existing pay and job classification systems, but might have more trouble if there was a chance the Senate would approve it. She serves on three committees—Banking, Finance and Urban Affairs, Post Office and Civil Service, and House Administration—which are workmanlike assignments. On Banking, she has been an advocate of requiring banks to provide services like checking at less than exorbitant rates; on Post Office, she favors generous treatment of federal employees; everywhere, she argues for fairer and more favorable treatment for women.

She is also ambitious, and not only for herself: she was a staunch advocate of the nomination of Geraldine Ferraro, and made sure that she and not Governor Richard Celeste introduced Ferraro when she spoke in Cleveland. After the 1984 election she was chosen secretary of the House Democratic Caucus, the leadership position Ferraro had held. In 1987 Oakar was the subject of a spate of articles in the Cleveland press about her staff: how she paid one staffer a high salary though she lived and worked in New York (she began repaying the money out of personal funds) and how she promoted another woman with whom she shares a house and mortgage payments. Whether these stories will erode any of her political strength remains to be seen.

The People: Pop. 1980: 514,164, dn. 14.7% 1970–80. Households (1980): 70% family, 34% with children, 56% married couples; 36.6% housing units rented; median monthly rent: $167; median house value: $45,700. Voting age pop. (1980): 383,041; 2% Spanish origin, 2% Black, 1% Asian origin.

1984 Presidential Vote: Mondale (D) 103,715   (51%)
Reagan (R) 98,665   (48%)

Rep. Mary Rose Oakar (D)

Elected 1976; b. Mar. 5, 1940, Cleveland; home, Cleveland; Ursuline Col., B.A. 1962, John Carroll U., M.A. 1966; Roman Catholic; single.

Career: Clerk, Higbee Co., 1956–58; Operator, OH Bell Telephone Co., 1957–62; Instructor, Lourdes Acad., 1963–70; Asst. Prof., Cuyahoga Commun. Col., 1968–75; Cleveland City Cncl., 1973–77.

Offices: 2231 RHOB, 202-225-5871. Also 523 Fed. Court Bldg., 215 Superior Ave., Cleveland 44114, 216-522-4927.

Committees: *Banking, Finance and Urban Affairs* (8th of 31 D). Subcommittees: Economic Stabilization (Chairman); Financial Institutions Supervision, Regulation and Insurance; Housing and Community Development; International Development Institutions and Finance; International Finance, Trade and Monetary Policy. *House Administration* (7th of 12 D). Subcommittees: Accounts; Elections; Libraries and Memorials (Chairman). *Post Office and Civil Service* (8th of 14 D). Subcommittees: Compensation and Employee Benefits (Chairman); Investigations. *Select Committee on Aging* (10th of 39 D). Subcommittees: Health and Long-Term Care; Retirement Income and Employment. *Joint Committee on the Library.*

Group Ratings

	ADA	ACLU	COPE	CFA	LCV	ACU	NTU	NSI	COC	CEI
1986	95	80	93	75	71	5	24	0	12	10
1985	80	—	93	67	—	5	20	—	23	—

National Journal Ratings

	1986 LIB — 1986 CONS		1985 LIB — 1985 CONS	
Economic	87%	— 0%	85%	— 15%
Social	74%	— 26%	63%	— 33%
Foreign	80%	— 0%	80%	— 17%

Key Votes

1) Lmt Cln Water Act	AGN	5) Retain Gun Cont	FOR	9) Aid Angola Reb	AGN
2) Rpl Tobac Sub	AGN	6) Contra Aid	AGN	10) Tax Reform	FOR
3) Grm-Rdmn Def Red	AGN	7) Lmt Text Imp	FOR	11) S Africa Sanc	FOR
4) Ban Polygraph	FOR	8) Limit SDI	FOR	12) Immig Reform	AGN

Election Results

1986 general	Mary Rose Oakar (D).	110,976	(85%)	($378,170)
	William Smith (R)	19,794	(15%)	
1986 primary	Mary Rose Oakar (D).	40,465	(94%)	
	Leslie W. Polgar (D)	2,574	(6%)	
1984 general	Mary Rose Oakar (D).	11,059	(100%)	($115,188)

Campaign Contributions and Expenditures

1985–86		Direct Cont. 1985–86		PACS Breakdown 1985–86			
Receipts	$409,025	Indiv.	$128,065	Corp.	$15,540	T/M/H	$35,958
Expend.	$378,170	Party	$1,099	Labor	$116,052	Agr.	$3,500
Unspent	$95,567	PACS	$182,845	Ideo.	$10,845	CWOS	$950
		Cand.	$28,000				

TWENTY-FIRST DISTRICT

The 21st Congressional District of Ohio is the east side of Cleveland, plus several adjacent suburbs to the east and southeast. This area was once a checkerboard of Polish, Czech, Hungarian, Italian, and Jewish neighborhoods, but today most of their descendants have moved to the suburbs, and the 21st has a large black majority. Media attention usually focuses on the grim suburbs of Hough and other areas not far from Cleveland's downtown; they are especially visible because they lie on the commuting line from the elite suburbs of Shaker Heights and Pepper Pike. But these form only a part of Cleveland's black community. Farther out, blacks live in comfortable working-class neighborhoods, and they have moved out in large numbers to pleasant eastern and southeastern suburbs; in small, but quite significant numbers, they live in the high-income suburbs of Shaker Heights (24% black in 1980) and Cleveland Heights (25%). The boundaries of the 21st District, over successive redistrictings, have followed them.

The congressman from the 21st District is the most enduring member of the first family of Cleveland black politics, Louis Stokes. His younger brother Carl Stokes made headlines when he was elected the first black mayor of a city with over 200,000 people in 1967, but he left office in 1971, and white-majority Cleveland has not elected a black mayor since; Louis Stokes, elected to the House in 1968, goes on. The Stokes brothers have a rags-to-riches family history; able and successful, they changed the course of Cleveland politics. Before they became powerful, Cleveland's blacks felt excluded from high civic positions and were unhappy particularly with the city's police department. Now they are integrated into city politics. Blacks and whites combined to get rid of wacko Mayor Dennis Kucinich and blacks as well as whites have supported the Republican Mayor, George Voinovich; controversies over the school board or city council members have split the city not on racial lines but on other divides. For black political strategists, that is a good thing; the city does not have a black majority and does not seem likely to have one soon, since black population movement is toward the suburbs to the east.

Louis Stokes is now a senior congressman of recognized abilities who has been called on for one difficulty assignment after another. One was the chairmanship on the Select Committee on Presidential Assassinations, which he assumed after Henry Gonzalez resigned in 1977. Stokes supervised responsible hearings and the production of a report which has held up as the last word on the subject. In 1981, in the wake of the Abscam scandal, Stokes was called on to chair the Committee on Standards of Official Conduct—the official name of the House Ethics Committee. This he did for four years, despite the embarrassment of having drunk driving charges brought against him. Stokes's fairness was shown when the committee took action on Republican charges against Geraldine Ferraro in 1984; a more partisan chairman might have refused to take the case. Stokes was relieved of that assignment after the 1984 election.

Now, beginning in 1987, he is Chairman of the House Intelligence Committee and a member of the special committee investigating the Iran-contra scandal. Stokes seems profoundly mistrustful of the CIA after the revelations of late 1986, and in early 1987 proposed legislation reducing to zero the Executive Branch's discretion about when to notify Congress of covert activities. Stokes is also a high-ranking member of the Appropriations Committee, generally inclined to favor generous federal domestic spending. He has done yeoman work on producing the Congressional Black Caucus budget resolution alternatives which, while attracting relatively few votes, provide a useful look at what a more generous government would look like. He is routinely reelected every two years.

The People: Pop. 1980: 514,169, dn. 19.7% 1970–80. Households (1980): 66% family, 36% with children, 43% married couples; 52.1% housing units rented; median monthly rent: $143; median house value: $38,000. Voting age pop. (1980): 372,949; 58% Black, 1% Spanish origin, 1% Asian origin.

1984 Presidential Vote: Mondale (D) 164,178   (78%)
Reagan (R) 43,331   (21%)

Rep. Louis Stokes (D)

Elected 1968; b. Feb. 23, 1925, Cleveland; home, Cleveland; Western Reserve U., 1946–48, Cleveland Marshall Law Sch., J.D. 1953; United Methodist; married (Jeanette).

Career: Army, 1943–46; Practicing atty., 1954–68.

Offices: 2365 RHOB 20515, 202-225-7032. Also New Fed. Ofc. Bldg., 1240 E. 9th St., Rm. 2947, Cleveland 44199, 216-522-4900; and 2140 Lee Rd., Cleveland Hgts. 44118, 216-522-4907.

Committees: *Appropriations* (8th of 35 D). Subcommittees: District of Columbia; HUD–Independent Agencies; Labor–Health and Human Services–Education. *Permanent Select Committee on Intelligence* (Chairman of 11 D). Subcommittees: Legislation; Program and Budget Authorization (Chairman).

Group Ratings

	ADA	ACLU	COPE	CFA	LCV	ACU	NTU	NSI	COC	CEI
1986	100	100	94	83	74	0	24	0	12	3
1985	95	—	94	58	—	0	31	—	24	—

National Journal Ratings

	1986 LIB — 1986 CONS		1985 LIB — 1985 CONS	
Economic	87%	— 0%	73%	— 26%
Social	89%	— 0%	85%	— 0%
Foreign	80%	— 0%	92%	— 0%

Key Votes

1) Lmt Cln Water Act	AGN	5) Retain Gun Cont	—	9) Aid Angola Reb	AGN
2) Rpl Tobac Sub	AGN	6) Contra Aid	AGN	10) Tax Reform	—
3) Grm-Rdmn Def Red	AGN	7) Lmt Text Imp	FOR	11) S Africa Sanc	FOR
4) Ban Polygraph	FOR	8) Limit SDI	FOR	12) Immig Reform	FOR

Election Results

1986 general	Louis Stokes (D)	99,878	(82%)	($164,171)
	Franklin H. Roski (R)	22,594	(18%)	
1986 primary	Louis Stokes (D)	41,503	(100%)	
1984 general	Louis Stokes (D)	164,844	(82%)	($113,546)
	Robert L. Woodall (R)	29,444	(15%)	

Campaign Contributions and Expenditures

1985-86		Direct Cont. 1985-86		PACS Breakdown 1985-86			
Receipts	$225,810	Indiv.	$80,426	Corp.	$17,150	T/M/H	$26,168
Expend.	$164,171	Party	$1,005	Labor	$44,150	Agr.	$500
Unspent	$122,718	PACS	$99,264	Ideo.	$10,446	CWOS	$850
		Cand.	$11,850				

OKLAHOMA

Boom and bust: that is the history of Oklahoma, over and over again. This is a state with a history as short as any, and as tragic. It was home first to the Cherokee and other Civilized Tribes driven here by Andrew Jackson's troops over the Trail of Tears. Not until 1889 was even part of Oklahoma opened up to white settlement; then, on the morning of the great land rush memorialized in the Rodgers and Hammerstein musical, an Edna Ferber novel, and half a dozen Hollywood movies, thousands of would-be homesteaders drove their wagons across the territorial line, the most adventurous or unscrupulous of them jumping the gun—the Sooners. Of course, it wasn't such attractive land in the first place, or Jackson wouldn't have given it to the Indians. Interestingly, there are many Indians left: Oklahoma has the second largest Indian population of any state, not on reservations but assimilated into the rest of the population.

Oklahoma's first bust came within a generation of statehood, in the 1930s. The first settlers were modest people from the South, eager for a second chance on these wide open plains. But then came the great bust of the 1930s. Not only did the economy of Oklahoma collapse, but the land itself vanished from under people's feet: poor soil conservation methods and drought produced the great black clouds that roared across the plains, and thousands of Okies fled the Dust Bowl of Oklahoma for the greener fields of California.

Oklahoma took some time recovering. There were 1.5 million Oklahomans at statehood in 1907 and 2.4 million in 1930. Then with outmigration, and later with movement out of the rural counties in Oklahoma City and Tulsa, population was stable: 2.5 million in 1970. Then, with the oil shocks of the 1970s, Oklahoma took off, to 3 million in 1980 and 3.3 million in 1983. Now, with the collapse of oil prices and the collapse of Oklahoma's farm economy as well, the movement is in the other direction. Just as the dust cloud was the symbol of Oklahoma's 1930s bust, so the auction of oil drilling equipment might be the symbol of the 1980s blowout. Alongside Oklahoma highways in the middle 1980s you could see rows of drill rigs and tractors, their still bright paint flecked with rust; in muddy lots, you could see bidders watch as yet another oil man's derrick trailers, rig-up trucks, cranes, compressors, and Mercedes were auctioned off.

To understand how sickening Oklahoma's fall has been, you need to understand how giddy was its rise. In January 1982 the rig count was 882; in February 1983, 232, and by 1986, 128. Between 1980 and 1983, 186,000 people moved into the state; between 1983 and 1986, more than that moved out. In the early 1980s it was the scene of feverish oil drilling in established fields and of deep-well gas exploration in the Anadarko Basin which promised to take care of America's energy needs for years. By the middle 1980s one bank after another followed Penn Square, the Oklahoma City shopping center bank whose oil lending officer, who reportedly sipped champagne from a cowboy boot, made $2.5 billion in energy loans and sold them to banks like Continental Illinois and Seattle First—and was shut down in July 1982 when the FDIC found out that almost none of the loans were any good. In the midst of national recession, Oklahoma had the nation's lowest unemployment rate, below 4%, in 1982; by 1986, it was above 8%, after the state lost 59,000 oil and gas jobs. Historians may record that Oklahoma ended up after the oil bust pretty much where it was headed before the oil boom, but that ignores the human cost. Thousands of Oklahomans, many from dirt-poor backgrounds, for a fleeting moment struck it rich—and then found themselves shorn of their money and their dreams.

Presidential politics. Curiously, the collapse of Oklahoma's oil economy has not much changed its politics. Historically, party preference was determined by where you came from: southern Oklahoma's Little Dixie was Democratic; the wheat country in the northwest, settled from Kansas, was Republican. Southerners and Democrats were more numerous, and Okla-

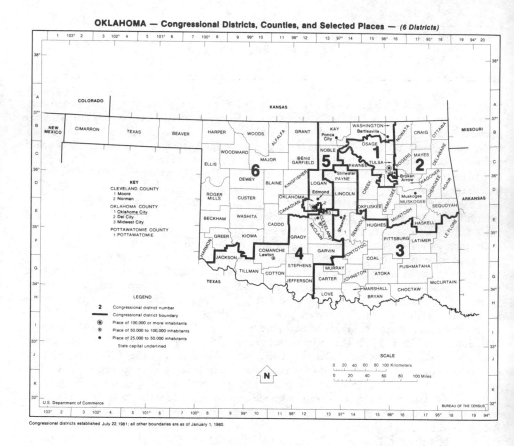

OKLAHOMA — Congressional Districts, Counties, and Selected Places — *(6 Districts)*

homa was mostly Democratic, and became more so in the bust of the 1930s. The same split remains today, in different proportions. In the close gubernatorial race of 1986, Republican Henry Bellmon carried almost every county north of Interstate 40 and west of Tulsa and lost almost every one on the other side of that line. The balance favors the Republicans, however, because of their strength in the two big cities, Oklahoma City and Tulsa, which have long been Republican, and among people in the oil business, who believe they prosper from free markets and were hurt by regulation, except for regulations and tax preferences that helped them, of course.

The Republican trend continues through the 1980s bust. George Bush with flawless timing came to Oklahoma City the day after Penn Square Bank was closed and proclaimed that "the recession is over," that it "has bottomed out, economic recovery is under way and gaining momentum." Not exactly so, here. Yet Oklahoma went overwhelmingly for Ronald Reagan, and in 1986, when most of the country trended mildly Democratic, Oklahoma reelected a Republican Senator who had a strong opponent and, like its Oil Patch neighbor Texas (known here sometimes as Baja Oklahoma), replaced a Democratic governor with a Republican. It seems the Oil Patch turns to Republicans in hard times about as reliably as the industrial states of the Great Lakes used to turn to Democrats. Also interestingly, in a low turnout year and after several years of outmigration, voter turnout in Oklahoma was up from 1982, up particularly in the counties which have been getting an affluent overflow from the two cities, in the Anadarko Basin, and in the hills of Little Dixie. Some people have given up on Oklahoma; many have not.

Governor. When Governor George Nigh retired in 1986, it was expected that former Governor (1962–66) and Senator (1969–81) Henry Bellmon would be elected to succeed him. He was, but only narrowly. Bellmon is a tactiturn wheat farmer who disliked Washington life and refuses to serve liquor in the governor's mansion, and an old-fashioned Republican who dislikes supply-side deficits and New Right cultural conservatives. The surprise winner of the Democratic primary was David Walters, a 34-year-old businessman who campaigned as a "greenhorn" in electoral politics, but his momentum was slowed by a mid-October court case in which he was accused of violating the campaign finance law by accepting $162,000 in loans from four supporters. Majorities rejected both major party nominees: there were two minor candidates, and Bellmon won 47%–45%. Perhaps voters were afraid of the austerity ahead. In his first months in office, Bellmon proposed a six-cent rise in the gas tax, across-the-board cuts in all spending but education, and abolition of the pension reserve funds: real austerity.

Senators. Oklahoma's Senator David Boren has become, in the middle of his second term, an important national figure. When he entered the Senate he seemed to be one of its most conservative young Democrats, a supporter of the Kemp-Roth tax cut before 1980 and a resolute backer of decontrol of oil and gas prices. He snagged a seat on the Senate Finance Committee, where Oklahoma's Robert Kerr once reigned, and he had considerable success in these original objectives: taxes have been cut and energy prices mostly decontrolled. But in the process of achieving these objectives, Boren has become popular with his fellow Democrats, partly because he has voted with them more often than they anticipated, partly because he is pleasant and competent. He is capable of sharp partisan maneuver: he led a filibuster of Edwin Meese's nomination as attorney general in early 1985 until Republican leaders agreed to consideration of his farm credit proposals. But he doesn't seem to alienate Republicans much in the process.

In the middle 1980s he has been concentrating on two new issues. One is campaign finance reform. He has never accepted PAC contributions himself, and the Boren bill which he introduced with Barry Goldwater in 1985 would limit the total amount of PAC money candidates could receive and provide the option of federal financing which would be conditioned on accepting limits on campaign and personal spending. Boren had to struggle to get a vote on it, but finally succeeded and saw 69 senators agree—the number might have been inflated because it was clear it would not pass the House. As 1987 began, there was increasing pressure for campaign finance reform, and Boren's bill could very well end up as the centerpiece of changing a system even the Senators who use it most adeptly have come to dislike.

The other major area for Boren's attention is foreign policy, now that he is chairman of the Senate Intelligence Committee. Boren seems likely to be a quieter chairman than David Durenberger was, less prone to go to the press with complaints and disclosures, more willing to work with the CIA which, under its new leadership in 1987, seemed itself more willing to work with Congress.

Boren has been the most popular politician in recent Oklahoma history. He has long experience in politics: his father was a congressman, and after Yale and a Rhodes scholarship he returned to Oklahoma for law school, was elected to the legislature, and was elected to be governor in 1974. In the Democratic primary he beat an incumbent who later went to jail; Boren's symbol was a broom. Boren was an early Carter supporter, but was disappointed when he didn't back total decontrol of energy prices. He ran for the Senate when Republican Dewey Bartlett retired in 1978 and won easily; the major event of the campaign was Boren swearing on a Bible that he was not, as some were charging, a homosexual. He won reelection easily in 1984, carrying every county in both primary and general elections; he did lose in a few *precincts*. He has been mentioned locally as a possible favorite son candidate for President; when Oklahoma's Robert Kerr ran as a favorite son at the 1952 national convention, Boren, then 11, was a page for him.

Oklahoma's other Senator, Don Nickles, turns out to have a safer seat than many Washington observers thought. Nickles was one of the real surprise winners in 1980, a 31-year-old state Senator with little command of national issues, a Catholic whose strongest support came from

Protestant fundamentalists. But that is an asset here: if polls could measure intensity of religious feeling, Oklahoma would probably rank near the top of the nation. This is Southern Baptist and evangelical country: Oklahoma still does not allow liquor by the drink, and Tulsa is the headquarters of evangelist and Pentacostal faith healer Oral Roberts. With that support, Nickles won typically light-turnout Republican primary and runoff contests and prevailed over a not very well-known Democrat in the general. In Washington, Nickles was one of the least visible of the Republican freshmen, not coming forward with venturesome legislation or constitutional amendments, not denouncing colleagues for backing conventional policy.

This may have been shrewder than it looked. Certainly the Democrats seemed to underestimate Nickles going into 1986. His opponent was Tulsa Representative Jim Jones, chairman for the first four Reagan years of the House Budget Committee, 14-year-House incumbent from a basically Republican district, an aide when a very young man to President Lyndon Johnson. By any measure of legislative competence or raw ability, Jones was the superior candidate. But he had some liabilities which Nickles shrewdly exploited. His ability to rally all House Democrats around a single budget package also gave Nickles an opening to charge him with being a liberal—a charge repeated over and over, most tellingly by a farmer in an ad who says, "You know, Jim, if you talk like a liberal and act like a liberal and vote like a liberal, you're a liberal." It got to the point that Jones's wife appeared in a spot to refute this canard, but to no great avail.

Jones may have been undercut by one of his own TV spots, in which he appeared before the cameras with a blow-dryer and said he doesn't need that. This might have worked in a coastal state, but not in the heartland. To smart, smirky coastal voters, a deeply religious young man with neat clothes and hair perfectly combed in place is some kind of fraud, a con man trying to fleece the rubes, a Bob Forehead (in Mark Stamaty's *Washingtoon*, which appears in the *Village Voice* and the *Washington Post*) full of empty phrases out to help the rich. But to Oklahomans Nickles seemed a patently sincere and plausible man; the suggestion in Jones's ad that his appearance showed his insincerity was utterly implausible and the tone of the ad off-putting. For heartland voters it proved not that Nickles was a fake but that Jones was a liberal. Jones could not exploit Nickles's vote—you could call it courageous or foolhardy—against a Democratic farm-credit measure or his support of Reagan economic programs generally. The Democrats' hopes of forging a majority coalition of the poor and those hurt by the drops in farm and oil prices utterly failed, as Jones, clearly the more qualified candidate, lost by a 55%–45% margin.

Nickles, not very visible in a Republican Senate, will probably be well-nigh invisible in a Democratic one. He can be counted as a solid vote for conservative causes and, on the Energy and Natural Resources Committee, for oil producers.

Congressional districting. Oklahoma's congressional districting plan is, to put it bluntly, a Democratic gerrymander. It was designed to safeguard the seats of the state's five Democratic congressmen and to place the maximum number of Republican voters in the seat of its one Republican House member. It succeeded up through 1986, when Jim Jones's decision to run for the Senate enabled the Republicans to take the Tulsa-based 1st District that always seemed likely to be theirs if Jones were not a candidate.

The People: Est. Pop. 1986: 3,305,000; Pop. 1980: 3,025,290, up 9.2% 1980–86 and 18.2% 1970–80; 1.37% of U.S. total, 26th largest. 16% with 1–3 yrs. col., 16% with 4+ yrs. col.; 13.4% below poverty level. Single ancestry: 13% English, 6% German, 5% Irish, 1% French, Dutch. Households (1980): 74% family, 40% with children, 63% married couples; 29.3% housing units rented; median monthly rent: $164; median house value: $35,600. Voting age pop. (1980): 2,170,406; 6% Black, 5% American Indian, 2% Spanish origin, 1% Asian origin. Registered voters (1986): 2,018,401; 1,354,313 D (67%), 610,891 R (30%), 53,197 unaffiliated and minor parties (3%).

1986 Share of Federal Tax Burden: $8,657,000,000; 1.28% of U.S. total, 24th largest.

1986 Share of Federal Expenditures

	Total		Non-Defense		Defense	
Total Expend	$9,750m	(1.17%)	$7,351m	(1.22%)	$2,400m	(1.04%)
St/Lcl Grants	1,400m	(1.24%)	1,397m	(1.24%)	3m	(2.70%)
Salary/Wages	1,990m	(1.65%)	669m	(1.14%)	1,321m	(2.13%)
Pymts to Indiv	4,902m	(1.34%)	4,602m	(1.33%)	300m	(1.69%)
Procurement	973m	(0.47%)	198m	(0.36%)	775m	(0.52%)
Research/Other	485m	(1.82%)	485m	(1.82%)	0m	(0%)

Political Lineup: Governor, Henry Bellmon (R); Lt. Gov., Robert S. Kerr, II (D); Secy. of State, Jeannette B. Edmondson (D); Atty. Gen., Robert Henry (D); Treasurer, Ellis Edwards (D). State Senate, 48 (31 D and 17 R); State House of Representatives, 101 (70 D and 31 R). Senators, David Lyle Boren (D) and Don Nickles (R). Representatives, 6 (4 D and 2 R).

1984 Presidential Vote

Reagan (R) 861,530 (69%)
Mondale (D) 385,080 (31%)

1980 Presidential Vote

Reagan (R) 695,570 (60%)
Carter (D) 402,026 (35%)
Anderson (I) 38,284 (3%)

GOVERNOR

Gov. Henry Bellmon (R)

Elected 1986, term expires Jan. 1991; b. Sept. 3, 1921, Tonkawa; home, Billings; OK State U., B.S. 1942; Presbyterian; married (Shirley).

Career: USMC, WWII; Farmer; OK House of Reps., 1946–62; Gov. of OK, 1962–66; U.S. Senate, 1968–80.

Office: State Capitol Bldg., Rm. 212, Oklahoma City 73105, 405-521-2342.

Election Results

1986 gen.	Henry Bellmon (R).	431,762	(47%)
	David Walters (D)	405,295	(45%)
	Jerry Brown (I).	60,115	(7%)
1982 prim.	Henry Bellmon (R).	111,665	(70%)
	Mike Fair (R).	33,266	(21%)
	Three othes (R)	13,968	(7%)
1982 gen.	George P. Nigh (D)	548,159	(62%)
	Tom Daxon (R).	332,207	(38%)

SENATORS

Sen. David Lyle Boren (D)

Elected 1978, seat up 1990; b. Apr. 21, 1941, Washington, DC; home, Seminole; Yale U., B.A. 1963, Rhodes Scholar, Oxford U., 1965, U. of OK, J.D. 1968; United Methodist; married (Molly).

Career: OK House of Reps., 1968–74; Prof. and Chmn., Dept. of Govt., OK Baptist U., 1968–74; Practicing atty.; Gov. of OK, 1975–79.

Offices: 453 RSOB 20510, 202-224-4721. Also 621 N. Robinson, Rm. 350, Oklahoma City 73102, 405-231-4381; 440 S. Houston, Tulsa 74127, 918-581-7785; and Municipal Bldg., Seminole 74868, 405-382-6480.

Committees: *Agriculture, Nutrition, and Forestry* (4th of 8 D). Subcommittees: Agricultural Production and Stabilization of Prices; Agricultural Credit (Chairman). *Finance* (5th of 11 D). Subcommittees: Energy and Agricultural Taxation (Chairman); International Trade; Social Security and Family Policy. *Small Business* (7th of 9 D). Subcommittees: Innovation, Technology and Productivity; Rural Economy and Family Farming. *Select Committee on Intelligence* (Chairman of 8 D).

Group Ratings

	ADA	ACLU	COPE	CFA	LCV	ACU	NTU	NSI	COC	CEI
1986	35	35	38	20	33	65	38	67	65	54
1985	45	—	40	40	—	55	39	—	54	—

National Journal Ratings

	1986 LIB — 1986 CONS		1985 LIB — 1985 CONS	
Economic	33% —	64%	60% —	39%
Social	44% —	55%	62% —	36%
Foreign	47% —	51%	48% —	51%

Key Votes

1) Ease Gun Cont	FOR	5) Grm-Rdmn Def Red	FOR	9) Rehnquist Nom	FOR
2) Immig Reform	FOR	6) Contra Aid	FOR	10) Tax Reform	AGN
3) Lmt Text Imp	AGN	7) SDI Funding	AGN	11) Drug Death Pen	—
4) Aid Tobac Ind	FOR	8) Lmt PAC Contrib	FOR	12) S Africa Sanc	FOR

Election Results

1984 general	David Lyle Boren (D)	906,131	(76%)	($1,192,026)
	William E. (Bill) Crozier (R)	280,638	(23%)	($6,925)
1984 primary	David Lyle Boren (D)	432,534	(90%)	
	Marshall Luse (D)	48,761	(10%)	
1978 general	David Lyle Boren (D)	493,953	(65%)	($751,286)
	Robert B. Kamm (R)	247,857	(33%)	($443,712)

Campaign Contributions and Expenditures

1979-84		Direct Cont. 1979-84		PACS Breakdown 1979-84			
Receipts	$1,218,068	Indiv.	$1,139,519	Corp.	$5,200	T/M/H	$0
Expend.	$1,192,026	Party	$12,803	Labor	$0	Agr.	$0
Unspent	$52,468	PACS	$5,700	Ideo.	$500	CWOS	$0

Sen. Don Nickles (R)

Elected 1980, seat up 1992; b. Dec. 6, 1948, Ponca City; home, Ponca City; OK St. U., B.A. 1971; Roman Catholic; married (Linda).

Career: Natl. Guard, 1970–76; Vice Pres. and Gen. Mgr., Nickles Machine Corp., 1976–80; OK Senate, 1979–80.

Offices: 713 HSOB, 202-224-5754. Also 215 Dean McGee Ave., Rm. 820, Oklahoma City 73102, 405-231-4941; 3310 Mid-Continent Tower, 401 S. Boston, Tulsa 74103, 918-581-7651; 1916 Lake Rd., Ponca City 74601, 405-767-1270; and 106 Fed. Bldg., 5th and E Ave., Rm. 115, Lawton 73501, 405-357-9878.

Committees: *Appropriations* (13th of 13 R). Subcommittees: District of Columbia (Ranking Member); Foreign Operations; HUD-Independent Agencies; Interior. *Budget* (10th of 11 R). *Energy and Natural Resources* (7th of 9 R). Subcommittees: Energy Regulation and Conservation (Ranking Member); Mineral Resources Development and Production; Water and Power.

Group Ratings

	ADA	ACLU	COPE	CFA	LCV	ACU	NTU	NSI	COC	CEI
1986	0	0	2	13	39	91	48	90	79	76
1985	0	—	2	20	—	87	65	—	90	—

National Journal Ratings

	1986 LIB — 1986 CONS		1985 LIB — 1985 CONS	
Economic	0%	— 84%	35%	— 64%
Social	9%	— 89%	0%	— 83%
Foreign	14%	— 82%	22%	— 70%

Key Votes

1) Ease Gun Cont	FOR	5) Grm-Rdmn Def Red	FOR	9) Rehnquist Nom	FOR
2) Immig Reform	FOR	6) Contra Aid	FOR	10) Tax Reform	AGN
3) Lmt Text Imp	AGN	7) SDI Funding	FOR	11) Drug Death Pen	AGN
4) Aid Tobac Ind	FOR	8) Lmt PAC Contrib	FOR	12) S Africa Sanc	AGN

Election Results

1986 general	Don Nickles (R)	493,436	(55%)	($3,252,965)
	James R. Jones (D)	400,230	(45%)	($2,564,982)
1986 primary	Don Nickles (R) unopposed			
1980 general	Don Nickles (R)	587,252	(53%)	($828,346)
	Andy Coats (D)	478,283	(44%)	($996,447)

Campaign Contributions and Expenditures

1985-86		Direct Cont. 1985-86		PACS Breakdown 1985-86			
Receipts	$2,995,708	Indiv.	$1,866,044	Corp.	$526,082	T/M/H	$224,779
Expend.	$3,252,964	Party	$17,153	Labor	$0	Agr.	$900
Unspent	$375,674	PACS	$859,335	Ideo.	$80,930	CWOS	$26,644
		Cand.	$16,616				

FIRST DISTRICT

Tulsa is a major city built by oil, inspired by religion, and eager to be uplifted by culture. It is Oklahoma's second city in population, though in its residents' view, first in many other respects. Oil derricks were pumping here and skyscrapers going up in the early 1920s when every hole drilled in Oklahoma City was still dry. Today, Tulsa's economy continues to depend heavily on oil, and despite the collapse of oil prices in the 1980s, Tulsa is still full of a contagious enthusiasm for new business enterprises and innovations. Ordinary people here do not resent or attack the oil companies or the new rich; they identify with them. They see not class conflict, but a coincidence of economic interests. They see government as interfering with efforts to produce goods and services people want and are ready to pay for—although Tulsans are pleased that the federal government built the McClellan-Kerr Waterway that has made the Tulsa suburb of Catoosa a seaport. Tulsa residents view the liberal cultural values and toleration of diversity they see in government and the media as literally subversive of decent moral values; this is a center not only of the oil business but the home of Oral Roberts University. It has impressive cultural institutions and an evangelist who declared that "God would call him home" unless he raised $4.5 million by April 1, 1987 for his medical programs; he was saved at the last minute when a Florida dog track owner gave him $1.3 million.

Politically, Tulsa is Republican. It has gone Republican in every presidential election since 1940, giving 73% of its votes to Ronald Reagan in 1984, 79% to Richard Nixon in 1972. Tulsa forms most of Oklahoma's 1st Congressional District; all of the city except for an affluent corner on the south side around Oral Roberts University are in the 1st. The district also includes some adjacent rural territory, in Osage County, which was once an Indian reservation, in the flat plains north of Tulsa, and in the more heavily settled rural area to the south.

Despite its Republican leanings, the 1st District elected a Democratic congressman for 14 years until 1986 and probably would have elected him again. He was Jim Jones, one time assistant to Lyndon Johnson, Chairman of the House Budget Committee in the first Reagan term and member of the Ways and Means Committee. Jones was a savvy legislator, a free-market, pro-oil Democrat who thought he could be elected to the Senate in 1986 after fighting years of close House races in Tulsa. But he was defeated by Don Nickles and Republicans, as generally assumed, won the seat.

The new congressman is James Inhofe, a Republican, who emerged the victor from a weak field of candidates. One Republican primary opponent, energy company executive Bill Calvert, was indicted in Chicago on charges relating to kickbacks on a natural gas pipeline; the indictment, however, was dropped. Another Republican, the Tulsa County Clerk, raised only $31,000 by the end of June for her August primary campaign. The primary winner, James Inhofe, had political experience, but not all of it favorable. He had been elected to the legislature in the 1970s but lost the 1976 race to Jones 54%–46%. He was elected mayor of Tulsa in 1978 but defeated for reelection in 1983. His campaign raised only $23,000 by June 30 and in July a bank called a $200,000 note against Inhofe and a business partner.

He nevertheless won the nomination with 54% of the vote. His Democratic opponent, a law professor, attacked him for allowing Pat Robertson to appear at one of his fundraisers and attacked groups that "are trying to control our personal lives through government"; even in Oral Roberts's home town, Inhofe fell in the polls and the Democrat rose. Not enough, however, to win in this very Republican town. Inhofe had an unimpressive 55%–43% victory. He serves on the Public Works Committee and says his goal is to get the Administration to put a "floating floor" under oil prices—which seems highly unlikely in a country where maybe only 35 of the 435 congressional districts are, as the 1st of Oklahoma is, dependent on the oil industry.

The People: Pop. 1980: 503,739, up 14.1% 1970–80. Households (1980): 71% family, 38% with children, 59% married couples; 34.3% housing units rented; median monthly rent: $204; median house value: $42,500. Voting age pop. (1980): 365,006; 8% Black, 4% American Indian, 1% Spanish origin, 1% Asian origin.

1984 Presidential Vote:

Reagan (R)	158,304	(70%)
Mondale (D)	65,241	(29%)

Rep. James M. Inhofe (R)

Elected 1986; b. Nov. 17, 1934, Des Moines, IA; home, Tulsa; U. of Tulsa, B.A. 1961; Presbyterian; married (Kay).

Career: OK House of Reps., 1968–69; OK Senate, 1969–77, Repub. Ldr., 1975–77; Mayor of Tulsa, 1968–84.

Offices: 1017 LHOB 20515, 202-225-2211. Also 201 W. 5th St., Tulsa 74103, 918-581-7111.

Committees: *Government Operations* (15th of 15 R). Subcommittees: Commerce, Consumer and Monetary Affairs; Human Resources and Intergovernmental Relations. *Public Works and Transportation* (18th of 20 R). Subcommittees: Aviation; Water Resources.

Group Ratings and Key Votes: Newly Elected

Election Results

1986 general	James M. Inhofe (R)	78,919	(55%)	($410,286)
	Gary D. Allison (D)	61,663	(43%)	($119,550)
1986 primary	James M. Inhofe (R)	19,575	(54%)	
	Bill Calvert (R)	10,577	(29%)	
	Joan Hasting (R)	5,956	(17%)	
1984 general	James R. Jones (D)	113,919	(52%)	($1,433,794)
	Frank Keating (R)	103,098	(47%)	($700,066)

Campaign Contributions and Expenditures

1985-86		Direct Cont. 1985-86		PACS Breakdown 1985-86			
Receipts	$415,771	Indiv.	$189,616	Corp.	$43,100	T/M/H	$54,371
Expend.	$410,286	Party	$19,780	Labor	$1,000	Agr.	$1,000
Unspent	$5,486	PACS	$130,108	Ideo.	$25,550	CWOS	$5,087
		Cand.	$68,000				

SECOND DISTRICT

The largest concentration of Indians in any congressional district in the United States is in the 2d District of Oklahoma. This covers much of the northeast quadrant of the state, which was Indian Territory from the time in the 1830s the Five Civilized Tribes were driven here from Georgia and Alabama over the Trail of Tears. The Indian Territory was open to white settlement in 1889, and today 12% of the people in this part of Oklahoma report their race as American Indian; many more claim some percentage of Indian blood. The Indian percentage is highest in the hilly counties just west of the Ozarks of Arkansas, where the county names—Cherokee, Delaware, Sequoyah—recall what were called the Civilized Tribes. Much attention nationally is focused on the problems of Indians in states where there are large reservations. But no one seems to be asking whether the experience of the Indians in Oklahoma—where they are now relatively prosperous, assimilated, and living comfortably with the white population—has any useful lessons for Indians and whites in other parts of the country.

Perhaps one reason they don't ask is that the cultural tone of this part of Oklahoma otherwise is very much southwestern—the sort of Okie spirit articulated in Merle Haggard's "Okie From Muskogee," a song about attitudes in one of the biggest towns here. Oklahoma was settled too late for a Populist movement, and it never had much of an establishment for ordinary people to rebel against (although there was a big Socialist vote in the 1910s, reflecting hatred of eastern financial interests), and people here have been very positive about traditional cultural values and patriotism, the more so as they see them questioned elsewhere. Those who want to think of Indians as a rebellious minority must be puzzled to find so many of them out here in Middle America.

Most of northeastern Oklahoma, minus most of Tulsa and its immediate surroundings, makes up the 2d Congressional District of Oklahoma. It is represented by a man from Muskogee, Mike Synar, who is not an ordinary Oklahoma politician. Synar is aggressive, pushy, independent to the point of cussedness, yet possessed of a sense of humor that keeps him in most colleagues'— and most constituents'—good graces. His record on the issues is about as liberal as that of any Oklahoma congressman, and his energy is not concentrated on parochial issues. He made headlines in 1985 when he brought a lawsuit challenging the constitutionality of Gramm-Rudman—after several colleagues who said they'd join him ducked out—and more headlines in 1986 when the Supreme Court ruled that Gramm-Rudman's trigger mechanism was indeed unconstitutional.

Synar sometimes seems to be a fly in every well-entrenched group's ointment. Although he like virtually all Oklahomans supports deregulation of energy prices, he was one of the most vitriolic and assiduous opponents of the Synthetic Fuels Corporation ("corporate welfare"), for which such leading Democrats as Speaker Jim Wright are enthusiasts. He bellowed in protest when the Energy Department guaranteed a loan for a troubled company owned by Saudi financier Adnan Khashoggi. In his first term, as a young member of the Judiciary Committee, he sponsored a key amendment strengthening the fair housing law the House passed in 1980, which passed by a 205–204 vote. He is sponsoring a bill to ban all forms of tobacco promotion. In his current term he promises to try to track down the cost of the Stealth bomber program and complains that the Pentagon won't give members of Congress enough information about it. But Synar is not just a gadfly. He has a seat on Energy and Commerce, the busiest legislating committee in the 1980s. He has worked out compromises on such sticky issues as who should pay for state and local costs imposed by the immigration reform bill and family farm bankruptcy procedures. He worked with Henry Waxman on a compromise generic drug bill and with David Boren and David Obey on various measures to limit total PAC contributions to any congressional candidate. He himself takes no money from out-of-state PACs. Attentive to local matters, he criticized the Pentagon for not monitoring shipping of munitions after a truck carrying Air Force bombs exploded in Oklahoma, injuring 42 people and causing $3.5 million worth of damage. In 1985 he seemed poised to concentrate on the evils of big mergers and hostile takeovers—a familiar and congenial subject in this part of Oklahoma because of the foiled attempt by T. Boone Pickens to take over Phillips Petroleum of nearby Bartlesville.

To his work he brings a certain irreverence and a gift for phrases with a certain Oklahoma twang. He first won the seat in a fluke, beating an incumbent who had recently been divorced and was rumored to have a heart-shaped waterbed in the 1978 Democratic primary and winning reelection by a lesser margin in 1980. But he comes from a prominent ranching family in Muskogee County and has been reelected with more than 70% of the vote in the last three elections. He is one example of a politician who has taken risks on issue after issue and has made them pay off. Synar was mentioned as a possible Senate candidate for 1986, but did not run and presumably will not have another chance until Don Nickles's seat comes up again in 1992. In the meantime he seems sure to keep busy and to keep raising hackles in the House.

The People: Pop. 1980: 505,149, up 33.6% 1970–80. Households (1980): 78% family, 42% with children, 68% married couples; 23.0% housing units rented; median monthly rent: $118; median house value: $31,500. Voting age pop. (1980): 353,938; 10% American Indian, 4% Black, 1% Spanish origin.

| **1984 Presidential Vote:** | Reagan (R) . . . . 139,721 | (64%) |
| | Mondale (D) . . . . 77,923 | (35%) |

Rep. Michael L. (Mike) Synar (D)

Elected 1978; b. Oct. 17, 1950, Vinita; home, Muskogee; U. of OK, B.A. 1972, J.D. 1977, Northwestern U., M.S. 1973, U. of Edinburgh, Rotary International Scholar, 1974; Episcopalian; single.

Career: Rancher, practicing atty., real estate broker.

Offices: 2441 RHOB 20515, 202-225-2701. Also Fed. Bldg., 125 S. Main, Rm. 2B22, Muskogee 74401, 918-687-2533.

Committees: *Energy and Commerce* (12th of 25 D). Subcommittees: Energy and Power; Telecommunications and Finance. *Government Operations* (7th of 24 D). Subcommittee: Environment, Energy, and Natural Resources (Chairman). *Judiciary* (8th of 21 D). Subcommittees: Courts, Civil Liberties, and the Administration of Justice; Criminal Justice. *Select Committee on Aging* (15th of 39 D). Subcommittees: Health and Long-Term Care; Retirement Income and Employment.

Group Ratings

	ADA	ACLU	COPE	CFA	LCV	ACU	NTU	NSI	COC	CEI
1986	70	88	58	75	79	15	32	0	22	29
1985	75	—	58	58	—	14	33	—	36	—

National Journal Ratings

	1986 LIB — 1986 CONS			1985 LIB — 1985 CONS		
Economic	52%	—	48%	59%	—	39%
Social	89%	—	0%	81%	—	15%
Foreign	75%	—	20%	71%	—	26%

Key Votes

1) Lmt Cln Water Act	AGN	5) Retain Gun Cont	FOR	9) Aid Angola Reb	AGN
2) Rpl Tobac Sub	AGN	6) Contra Aid	AGN	10) Tax Reform	AGN
3) Grm-Rdmn Def Red	AGN	7) Lmt Text Imp	FOR	11) S Africa Sanc	FOR
4) Ban Polygraph	FOR	8) Limit SDI	FOR	12) Immig Reform	FOR

Election Results

1986 general	Michael L. (Mike) Synar (D) 114,543	(73%)	($268,187)
	Gary K. Rice (R) 41,795	(27%)	($11,276)
1986 primary	Michael L. (Mike) Synar (D) 89,145	(84%)	
	Richard DeHay (D) 16,623	(16%)	
1984 general	Michael L. (Mike) Synar (D) 148,124	(74%)	($265,815)
	Gary K. Rice (R) 51,889	(26%)	($17,998)

Campaign Contributions and Expenditures

1985-86		Direct Cont. 1985-86		PACS Breakdown 1985-86			
Receipts	$269,885	Indiv.	$250,702	Corp.	$0	T/M/H	$0
Expend.	$268,187	Party	$1,413	Labor	$0	Agr.	$0
Unspent	$82,108			Ideo.	$0	CWOS	$0

THIRD DISTRICT

Little Dixie has been the name for the southeastern part of Oklahoma since it was first settled between 1889 and 1907 by white southerners, most of them dirt poor; some of the county names here (Leflore, Pontotoc) were taken directly from Mississippi. Ever since statehood Little Dixie has been the most Democratic part of Oklahoma. The 3d Congressional District of Oklahoma includes most of the Little Dixie counties, and juts up into the center of the state, into the old university town of Stillwater, to include enough people to meet the population standard.

This is the district that for 30 years elected Carl Albert to the House of Representatives. Albert was part of the class of World War II veterans first elected in 1946. Others include John Kennedy and Richard Nixon; only two current House members, Jamie Whitten and Mel Price, were there when these veterans came in. Albert was an example of the way leaders were selected in the old days: he was chosen early in his career, in 1955, by Speaker Sam Rayburn to be majority whip, and he was advanced automatically to majority leader after Rayburn died in 1961 and speaker after John McCormack retired in 1970. Albert's performance as speaker from 1971 to 1977 was a disappointment to those who remembered him as a hard-fighting vote counter in the 1950s and 1960s. He deferred to committee chairmen and to hoary tradition; he had little to say about scheduling and did not establish legislative priorities. He never got close to the younger members who were potential allies for a strong speaker. Albert had been in the leadership for so long, at a time when it was difficult to lead, that he had a hard time taking advantages of opportunities when they did seem to appear.

Little Dixie was always proud of Carl Albert and reelected him without difficulty. But he proved unable to hand the 3d District seat on to his administrative assistant. Instead state Senator Wes Watkins won the Democratic primary and captured the district. In his first four years in the House, Watkins had one of the most conservative voting records of any young Democrat. Since 1980, he has joined his fellow Democrats more often, particularly on economic issues. This apparent change, which took place before the Reagan economic program became unpopular in 1982, may have something to do with his political ambitions. Before 1980, Watkins considered running for the Senate that year, and in Oklahoma, a Republican state in presidential elections, a conservative record is an asset. But he decided not to make that race. Now he wants to stay in the 3d District, which is the most Democratic district in the state in most elections, and to advance to a position of power in the House, where chairmanships are determined by votes of mostly northern Democrats. So increasingly he has had a record unlikely to cause them offense.

So far this strategy, if that is what it is, seems to be successful. Watkins is a member of the Appropriations Committee, and of two subcommittees which can do his district a lot of good: Agriculture and Energy and Water Development. He devotes much time, energy, and ingenuity in snaring more water projects for Little Dixie; and he has been active as a promoter of rural areas generally, and was for three Congresses chairman of a Rural Caucus. He pushed projects like a federal-state agricultural research center in Atoka County, a wildlife refuge in one of the last bottomlands left in the state, an Oklahoma State center for international trade development, and a bill to develop rural technology transfer to stimulate new jobs in rural areas.

In every election, Watkins is reelected routinely in the 3d District. He is not likely to be speaker or anything close to that, but he seems to have forged a successful congressional career.

The People: Pop. 1980: 504,268, up 20.1% 1970–80. Households (1980): 74% family, 39% with children, 64% married couples; 27.6% housing units rented; median monthly rent: $113; median house

value: $25,100. Voting age pop. (1980): 365,865; 6% American Indian, 4% Black, 1% Spanish origin.

1984 Presidential Vote:

Reagan (R)	124,798	(62%)
Mondale (D)	75,671	(38%)

Rep. Wes Watkins (D)

Elected 1976; b. Dec. 15, 1938, DeQueen, AR; home, Ada; OK St. U., B.S. 1960, M.S. 1961, U. of MD, 1961; Presbyterian; married (Elizabeth).

Career: USDA, 1963; Asst. Dir. of Admissions, OK St. U., 1963–66; Exec. Dir., Kiamichi Econ. Develop. Dist. of OK, 1966–68; Realtor and homebuilder, 1968–76; OK Senate, 1975–76.

Offices: 2348 RHOB 20515, 202-225-4565. Also 232 P. O. Bldg., Ada 74820, 405-436-1980; 118 Fed. Bldg., McAlester 74501, 918-423-5951; and 720 S. Husband, Stillwater 74074, 405-743-1400.

Committees: *Appropriations* (26th of 35 D). Subcommittees: Energy and Water Development; Rural Development, Agriculture and Related Agencies.

Group Ratings

	ADA	ACLU	COPE	CFA	LCV	ACU	NTU	NSI	COC	CEI
1986	40	40	41	50	27	41	28	60	29	27
1985	50	—	39	42	—	48	31	—	45	—

National Journal Ratings

	1986 LIB — 1986 CONS		1985 LIB — 1985 CONS	
Economic	44% —	55%	53% —	46%
Social	49% —	49%	44% —	54%
Foreign	47% —	53%	45% —	54%

Key Votes

1) Lmt Cln Water Act	AGN	5) Retain Gun Cont	AGN	9) Aid Angola Reb	FOR
2) Rpl Tobac Sub	AGN	6) Contra Aid	FOR	10) Tax Reform	AGN
3) Grm-Rdmn Def Red	FOR	7) Lmt Text Imp	FOR	11) S Africa Sanc	FOR
4) Ban Polygraph	FOR	8) Limit SDI	FOR	12) Immig Reform	AGN

Election Results

1986 general	Wes Watkins (D)	114,008	(78%)	($210,936)
	Patrick K. Miller (R)	31,913	(22%)	
1986 primary	Wes Watkins (D)	111,203	(85%)	
	Eugene Victor Poling (D)	19,506	(15%)	
1984 general	Wes Watkins (D)	137,964	(78%)	($193,451)
	Patrick K. Miller (R)	39,454	(22%)	($6,505)

Campaign Contributions and Expenditures

1985-86		Direct Cont. 1985-86		PACS Breakdown 1985-86			
Receipts	$209,653	Indiv.	$113,330	Corp.	$27,800	T/M/H	$39,480
Expend.	$210,936	PACS	$81,030	Labor	$5,750	Agr.	$4,000
Unspent	$117,836			Ideo.	$3,750	CWOS	$250

FOURTH DISTRICT

The 4th Congressional District of Oklahoma starts out within a few miles of the oil-derrick-surrounded state Capitol in Oklahoma City, smack dab in the middle of the state, and proceeds south and west to cover half of Oklahoma's Red River Valley. It includes Lawton, a small city whose major industries are Goodyear and the Army's Fort Sill; Norman, home of the University of Oklahoma; and some mostly blue-collar parts of Oklahoma City itself and its suburbs of Midwest City and Moore. But the predominant tone, demographically and politically, is rural. Even in the cities and towns the red or brown dust gets tracked indoors by your boots, and the entrée of choice is still chicken-fried steak. Politically, this country is ancestrally Democratic, although Republicans have carried it in recent national elections. The counties down along the Red River border with Texas are one of the Democratic heartlands of America, producing not only Democratic majorities in almost every election but some of the party's great leaders: House Speakers Sam Rayburn, Carl Albert, and Jim Wright also come from within 50 miles of the river.

The congressman from the 4th District, Dave McCurdy, has emerged as one of the national leaders of his party on several defense and foreign policy issues, even though he was first elected only in 1980, and then by a narrow margin. In his first term he got a seat on the Armed Services Committee, which could only help him in his hawkish district laden with military bases (Fort Sill, Oklahoma City's Tinker Air Force Base, Altus Air Force Base). There he generally supported increased military spending, but he also responded to the concerns of some of his fellow Democrats. He was sympathetic early on with the military reform movement, but he also supported embattled weapons systems like the MX missile. With John Spratt of South Carolina, he was one of the early supporters of Les Aspin for chairman of Armed Services, feeling that chairman Mel Price was too elderly and infirm to lead.

And on Central America, the most divisive foreign policy issue of the middle 1980s, he has become one of the point men for the Democratic party. His instinct has been for compromise. In May 1983 he voted to cut off aid to the contras in Nicaragua. But he feels the Sandinista regime is dangerous and threatens fragile democracies elsewhere in Central America. So in July 1985 he was the lead sponsor of the proposal to give the contras $27 million in "humanitarian" aid, but no military aid. In March 1986 he came forward with another proposal for $100 million more in humanitarian aid, but spaced out and premised on progress in negotiations and continuing review by Congress. House Republicans were convinced that this half-a-loaf was worse than no loaf at all, because congressional meddling and dithering would dissipate the worth of any aid and give adversaries an incentive not to negotiate, and managed to deep-six McCurdy's amendment, but in June 1986 the House, faced with the choice of $100 million in unrestricted contra aid or none at all, opted for the aid. But McCurdy and many other Democrats would clearly prefer the classic politician's solution of splitting the difference down the middle.

McCurdy's views continue to be important because he is the second ranking Democrat on the House Intelligence Committee, behind Louis Stokes of Ohio, and the highest-ranking of the southern Democrats who on this issue are likely to be key votes. He also had headed a Coalition for a Democratic Majority panel that called for a form of alternative national service and wants to encourage more ordinary citizens to serve limited periods in the currently pretty much career military. McCurdy does more mundane things as well. He got himself a seat in 1987 on an Armed Services subcommittee handling military bases—obviously of importance in the 4th district. And he chairs a Science, Space and Technology subcommittee on Transportation, Aviation, and Materials—important again in the 4th District, which has the big FAA Aeronautical Center in Oklahoma City and a weather research project at O.U. in Norman.

In the midst of all this involvement in foreign and defense policy, McCurdy has transformed the 4th District from the most marginal of districts to a safe seat. McCurdy got the seat initially only after winning a series of cliffhanger elections, trailing in the Democratic primary, 40%–

34%, winning the runoff with 51%, then beating former prisoner of war Howard Rutledge with 51% again. Against Rutledge in 1982 and a weaker opponent in 1984 he won by nearly 2 to 1; in 1986 he got a whopping 76%. He has been mentioned as a possible Senate candidate, but having let 1986 go by the next opening would not seem to be until Don Nickles's seat comes up in 1992.

The People: Pop. 1980: 505,869, up 24.3% 1970–80. Households (1980): 77% family, 44% with children, 67% married couples; 30.6% housing units rented; median monthly rent: $181; median house value: $37,200. Voting age pop. (1980): 356,658; 6% Black, 3% Spanish origin, 3% American Indian, 1% Asian origin.

1984 Presidential Vote:			
	Reagan (R)	131,690	(69%)
	Mondale (D)	57,118	(30%)

Rep. Dave McCurdy (D)

Elected 1980; b. Mar. 30, 1950, Canadian, TX, home, Norman; U. of OK, B.A. 1972, J.D. 1975; Lutheran; married (Pam).

Career: OK Asst. Atty. Gen., 1975–77; Practicing atty., 1977–80.

Offices: 409 CHOB 20515, 202-225-6165. Also P.O. Box 1265, Norman 73070, 405-329-6500; 103 Fed. Bldg., Lawton 73501, 405-357-2131; and P.O. Box 1051, Duncan 73534, 405-252-1434.

Committees: *Armed Services* (15th of 31 D). Subcommittees: Military Installations and Facilities; Research and Development. *Science, Space and Technology* (10th of 27 D). Subcommittees: Transportation, Aviation and Materials (Chairman); Natural Resources, Agriculture Research and Environment. *Permanent Select Committee on Intelligence* (2d of 10 D). Subcommittees: Oversight and Evaluation; Program and Budget Authorization.

Group Ratings

	ADA	ACLU	COPE	CFA	LCV	ACU	NTU	NSI	COC	CEI
1986	35	40	42	58	47	38	30	50	80	28
1985	30	—	42	50	—	52	35	—	64	—

National Journal Ratings

	1986 LIB — 1986 CONS			1985 LIB — 1985 CONS		
Economic	35%	—	65%	40%	—	59%
Social	48%	—	52%	69%	—	28%
Foreign	52%	—	47%	46%	—	52%

Key Votes

1) Lmt Cln Water Act	FOR	5) Retain Gun Cont	AGN	9) Aid Angola Reb	FOR
2) Rpl Tobac Sub	AGN	6) Contra Aid	FOR	10) Tax Reform	AGN
3) Grm-Rdmn Def Red	FOR	7) Lmt Text Imp	FOR	11) S Africa Sanc	FOR
4) Ban Polygraph	–	8) Limit SDI	FOR	12) Immig Reform	FOR

Election Results

1986 general	Dave McCurdy (D)	94,984	(76%)	($176,096)
	Larry Humphreys (R)	29,697	(24%)	
1986 primary	Dave McCurdy (D)	71,876	(81%)	
	Howard Bell (D)	16,744	(19%)	
1984 general	Dave McCurdy (D)	109,447	(64%)	($263,278)
	Jerry F. Smith (R)	60,844	(35%)	($206,051)

Campaign Contributions and Expenditures

1985-86		Direct Cont. 1985-86		PACS Breakdown 1985-86			
Receipts	$247,408	Indiv.	$107,386	Corp.	$71,050	T/M/H	$31,875
Expend.	$176,096	PACS	$130,475	Labor	$14,350	Agr.	$3,500
Debts	$75,721			Ideo.	$9,700	CWOS	$0

FIFTH DISTRICT

With a half a million people, situated almost precisely at midcontinent and in the middle of the state, with the oil derrick outside the state Capitol still pumping some oil, Oklahoma City is the metropolis of Oklahoma. Like many state capitals, it is not the spontaneous creation of commerce but the deliberate creation of government, built on land that is browner and more eroded by creeks than the greener, rolling Oklahoma farther east. During the 1960s the city fathers decided that they would not let the old city limits fence them in, so Oklahoma City, unlike most American central cities, started annexing land all around, so that it now spills over into five counties and four congressional districts, and includes hundreds of acres which even today are farms or grazing land.

By the early 1980s, the oil boom here transformed much of Oklahoma City. Its once small downtown is now replete with numerous towering high-rises, and the city's parking lots are full of the luxury cars of its dozens of new—and sometimes temporary—millionaires. Oklahoma City was the scene in 1982 of the collapse of the Penn Square Bank—whose story tells a lot about the boom here. The bank itself was headquartered (and named after) a shopping center; yet a vice president in his early 30s managed to make $2.5 billion in loans to oil drillers, many of them of dubious creditworthiness, and the bank then sold the loans to some of the nation's largest financial institutions, including Continental Illinois. He was helped by eccentric habits—he was reputed to drink champagne out of one of his boots—that evidently convinced the city slickers that they had stumbled onto the real thing. So for awhile you could find in Oklahoma City the atmosphere you always find on a frontier when it seems suddenly very easy to become very rich.

The 5th Congressional District of Oklahoma includes most of Oklahoma City, but it is a carefully chosen part: the most Democratic sections of the city, including its black areas, are chopped off and included in Democratic districts. The 5th is intended to be Republican. Besides the prosperous parts of Oklahoma City, which are heavily Republican as only prosperous parts of oil cities are, it includes wheat-growing counties to the north, and the market town of Ponca City, which is as Republican as any similar-sized town in nearby Kansas. Connected by a strip of mostly uninhabited Osage County is the well-to-do oil town of Bartlesville, headquarters of Phillips Petroleum, whose management, allied with the equally worried townspeople-employees, succeeded in warding off T. Boone Pickens, but only after saddling the firm with huge debt. The 5th is a collection of urban Republican voting precincts stitched together by swaths of thinly populated rural territory.

The direct beneficiary of this is Representative Mickey Edwards. When he was first elected in 1976, he was conspicuous as one of the few conservatives in Congress or in Washington for that matter. He denounced federal spending programs and during the dark days of the Carter years insisted on the importance of traditional moral and family values. In the 1980s his emphasis has become a little different. He is still one of the most market-oriented of congressmen, with a record on foreign and cultural issues which is second to none in conservatism. For the first four years he chaired the American Conservative Union. But he has been busy during the Reagan years working on the Appropriations Committee, where he serves on the Military Construction Subcommittee. He became a member of the Budget Committee in 1987 and could be a leader when the more senior Republicans there rotate off. And he has extended his conservatism to the institution where he serves.

This has raised some hackles from the likes of Newt Gingrich and company, who have used the House mainly as a sounding board for their ideas and have shown little interest in what kind of legislation is passed—on everyday matters or even on big things like the tax bill. Edwards, in contrast, wrote in early 1987 that "The Congress simply doesn't work any more," and advanced his own virtually ideology-free solutions. He wants time to review amendments and bills. He wants the House to meet five days a week. He wants fewer overlapping subcommittee meetings. He is opposed to the line-item veto, though it is a Reagan cause, because it concentrates power in one man. He wants to consider two-year budgets and appropriations. He wants recorded votes on all appropriations.

Much of this is the natural response of an Appropriations member who has watched most of the government's money be appropriated each year in a catchall continuing resolution, of a man who wants work done in an orderly and careful manner; and many of his reforms seem unexceptionable. Yet surely Edwards is wrong when he says that nothing had been done: the 99th Congress reformed the tax system, voted aid to the Nicaraguan contras, made momentous arms decisions, and passed the first water projects bill in 10 years (vetoed, but repassed immmediately over the veto in 1987). Congress has acted, though sloppily. The problem for Edwards may be that as a thoughtful man given to contrary thoughts he is without many allies— a minority of the minority of the minority. That is an uncomfortable position for a man who remains a firebrand on the substance of issues but wants to meet his institutional responsibilities.

Also, Edwards is becoming something of an oldtimer: he turns 50 in 1987, but is serving his sixth term in the House and is the oldest and second most senior member of the startlingly young Oklahoma delegation. He had a chance to run for the Senate in 1980 and passed it by, only to see Don Nickles, a politician of similar views but much less articulate and experienced, win the seat. He has seen, in the years since, others win the headlines and plaudits of the Washington press. But he seems determined to make some headlines and some laws and, with an important committee assignment and a safe seat, perhaps he will do so.

The People: Pop. 1980: 502,974, up 17.1% 1970–80. Households (1980): 71% family, 37% with children, 61% married couples; 30.8% housing units rented; median monthly rent: $199; median house value: $43,600. Voting age pop. (1980): 367,630; 5% Black, 3% American Indian, 2% Spanish origin, 1% Asian origin.

1984 Presidential Vote:

Reagan (R)	170,703	(76%)
Mondale (D)	50,701	(23%)

Rep. Mickey Edwards (R)

Elected 1976; b. July 12, 1937, Cleveland, OH; home, Oklahoma City; U. of OK, B.A. 1958, OK City U., J.D. 1969; Presbyterian; married (Lisa).

Career: Practicing atty.; Editor, *Private Practice* magazine; Asst. City Editor, *Oklahoma City Times*; Instructor (law and journalism), OK City U.

Offices: 2434 RHOB 20515, 202-225-2132. Also 900 N.W. 63rd St., Ste. 105, Oklahoma City 73116, 405-231-4541; 1200 SE Frank Phillips Blvd., Ste. 102, Bartlesville 74003, 918-336-5436; and 114 N. 4th, Ste. 105, Ponca City 74601, 405-762-8121.

Committees: *Appropriations* (11th of 22 R). Subcommittees: Foreign Operations; Military Construction. *Budget* (7th of 14 D). Task Forces: Budget Process; Community and Natural Resources (Ranking Member); Defense and International Affairs; Defense and International Affairs; Economic Policy.

Group Ratings

	ADA	ACLU	COPE	CFA	LCV	ACU	NTU	NSI	COC	CEI
1986	5	0	8	17	11	85	48	100	81	65
1985	5	—	8	25	—	90	53	—	85	—

National Journal Ratings

	1986 LIB — 1986 CONS		1985 LIB — 1985 CONS	
Economic	6% —	90%	12% —	85%
Social	0% —	89%	0% —	76%
Foreign	0% —	86%	0% —	76%

Key Votes

1) Lmt Cln Water Act	FOR	5) Retain Gun Cont	—	9) Aid Angola Reb	FOR
2) Rpl Tobac Sub	FOR	6) Contra Aid	FOR	10) Tax Reform	AGN
3) Grm-Rdmn Def Red	FOR	7) Lmt Text Imp	AGN	11) S Africa Sanc	—
4) Ban Polygraph	AGN	8) Limit SDI	AGN	12) Immig Reform	AGN

Election Results

1986 general	Mickey Edwards (R).................	108,774	(71%)	($289,552)
	Donna Compton (D)..................	45,256	(29%)	($16,217)
1986 primary	Mickey Edwards (R) unopposed			
1984 general	Mickey Edwards (R).................	135,167	(76%)	($274,655)
	Allen Greeson (D)....................	39,089	(22%)	($15,285)

Campaign Contributions and Expenditures

1985-86		Direct Cont. 1985-86		PACS Breakdown 1985-86			
Receipts	$308,740	Indiv.	$204,703	Corp.	$44,870	T/M/H	$25,400
Expend.	$289,552	Party	$6,548	Labor	$1,000	Agr.	$0
Unspent	$39,285	PACS	$87,991	Ideo.	$13,750	CWOS	$2,971
		Cand.	$5,079				

SIXTH DISTRICT

One of the most exciting parts of the United States in the late 1970s and early 1980s was the Anadarko Basin of western Oklahoma. There was one of the major natural gas and oil finds of the great mineral exploration that followed OPEC's raising of oil prices in 1973 and 1979. This boom created almost a mining camp atmosphere in some small towns of this region, like Elk City and Hammon, with drilling workers living in trailers; now the trailers are gone or empty, the drilling equipment has been auctioned off, and the wells have been capped and thus destroyed.

The Anadarko Basin, plus the wheat and grazing lands to the north, northeast, and, in Oklahoma's panhandle, the northwest, plus the blue-collar and black neighborhoods in Oklahoma City form Oklahoma's 6th Congressional District. Most of this land has long been Republican: it was settled by farmers moving south from Kansas, starting when (or a little before) the gun went off that morning in 1889. They came with large families and high hopes, but the Dust Bowl of the 1930s swept their topsoil into the air and led many families and children to move elsewhere to make a living. From 1907 to 1970, the population of the counties wholly included in the 6th District declined from 360,000 to 282,000. The gas and oil boom has turned that around; in the 1970s there was in-migration and their population was raised to 308,000. But with the oil price collapse beginning in 1982, that number seemed headed back down again. Curiously, the oil and gas boom doesn't seem to have affected the political leanings of the 6th. A few of its counties in the south are heavily Democratic, and always have been; most of the rest are heavily Republican, and always have been: these divisions are as permanent as if Oklahoma had been split down the middle in the Civil War, except that of course there were no white people settled in the state at all at that time.

Yet the 6th District elects and reelects a Democratic congressman, Glenn English. He was helped in the 1980s by redistricting, which carefully included a part of Oklahoma City which is 25% black and contains most of the city's white working-class areas; but he is by no means dependent on these votes. English was once an aide to liberal Democrats in the California Assembly, but you wouldn't know it from his voting record, which is one of the most conservative in the Democratic Caucus. His Oklahoma credentials are in order: he grew up here and served as executive director of the state Democratic Party before he ran for Congress in 1974. Perhaps his greatest political achievement so far was to seize a propitious moment—just four days before the showdown on the 1981 Reagan tax cut—and extract from Ronald Reagan, in a letter in his own handwriting, a commitment to veto "with pleasure" any windfall profits tax on natural gas. That promise effectively protected that otherwise vulnerable revenue source in 1982, when Republicans were scrambling around looking for politically painless ways to, in the phrase of the day, enhance revenues.

English serves on the Agriculture Committee, which of course is of great interest to this wheat-growing district. A fiscal conservative on most issues, he makes exceptions for local pork barrel projects and especially for wheat programs; a free trader generally, he is a hawk when it comes to restricting meat imports. He wants to stimulate U.S. farm exports and advocates an oil import fee. He also serves on Government Operations, and chairs a subcommittee on Government Information, Justice, and [sic] Agriculture.

The addition of the "Agriculture" may be an attempt to conceal from his constituents the fact that he has spent considerable time on the difficult and important, but not at all parochial, problems of government computers, individual privacy, and the Freedom of Information Act; he has been, to the surprise and delight of many of his fellow Democrats, a tiger in preventing relaxation of the FOIA. He is one of several congressmen who have tried to reduce the federal expenditure on presidential libraries, and has authored legislation that would require private endowments to pay for their upkeep (in early 1985 he discovered that the Administration supported his initiative, but only if it exempted the Reagan library). National Republicans, apparently respectful of English's strength, have never targeted him, and he has won reelection by huge margins most years; in 1986 he had no opposition at all.

The People: Pop. 1980: 503,291, up 4.1% 1970–80. Households (1980): 73% family, 38% with children, 62% married couples; 29.1% housing units rented; median monthly rent: $152; median house value: $32,500. Voting age pop. (1980): 361,309; 9% Black, 3% American Indian, 2% Spanish origin.

1984 Presidential Vote:

Reagan (R)	136,314	(69%)
Mondale (D)	58,246	(30%)

Rep. Glenn English (D)

Elected 1974; b. Nov. 30, 1940, Cordell; home, Cordell; Southwestern St. Col., B.A. 1964; United Methodist; married (Jan).

Career: Chf. Asst., Major. Caucus, CA Assembly; Exec. Dir., OK Dem. Party, 1969–73; Petroleum leasing business.

Offices: 2235 RHOB 20515, 202-225-5565. Also 264 Old P.O. Bldg., 215 Dean A. McGee Ave., Oklahoma City 73102, 405-231-5511; Fed. Bldg., P.O. Box 3612, Enid 73702, 405-233-9224; and 1120 9th St., Woodward 73801, 405-256-5752.

Committees: *Agriculture* (6th of 26 D). Subcommittees: Conservation, Credit and Rural Development; Cotton, Rice, and Sugar; Tobacco and Peanuts; Wheat, Soybeans, and Feed Grains. *Government Operations* (4th of 24 D). Subcommittee: Government Information, Justice, and Agriculture (Chairman).

Group Ratings

	ADA	ACLU	COPE	CFA	LCV	ACU	NTU	NSI	COC	CEI
1986	35	20	29	50	32	48	39	100	61	41
1985	15	—	28	33	—	76	46	—	82	—

National Journal Ratings

	1986 LIB — 1986 CONS	1985 LIB — 1985 CONS
Economic	29% — 70%	27% — 71%
Social	44% — 54%	0% — 76%
Foreign	40% — 60%	24% — 66%

Key Votes

1) Lmt Cln Water Act	FOR	5) Retain Gun Cont	AGN
2) Rpl Tobac Sub	AGN	6) Contra Aid	FOR
3) Grm-Rdmn Def Red	FOR	7) Lmt Text Imp	FOR
4) Ban Polygraph	FOR	8) Limit SDI	FOR

9) Aid Angola Reb	FOR
10) Tax Reform	AGN
11) S Africa Sanc	FOR
12) Immig Reform	AGN

Election Results

1986 general	Glenn English (D) unopposed			($149,998)
1986 primary	Glenn English (D) unopposed			
1984 general	Glenn English (D)	96,994	(59%)	($209,080)
	Craig Dodd (R)	67,601	(41%)	($229,632)

Campaign Contributions and Expenditures

1985-86		Direct Cont. 1985-86		PACS Breakdown 1985-86			
Receipts	$248,458	Indiv.	$105,609	Corp.	$51,950	T/M/H	$44,557
Expend.	$149,998	Party	$3,239	Labor	$8,600	Agr.	$12,900
Unspent	$164,549	PACS	$129,007	Ideo.	$5,050	CWOS	$5,950

OREGON

Lewis and Clark made their way over the Rockies, "those tremendous mountains," and reached the mouth of the Columbia in 1805, but failed to see much of the Pacific because it rained all but 12 days that winter, and six of those were overcast. John Jacob Astor's fur traders set up Astoria in 1811 less with an eye to the U.S. market—after all, they had had to go around Cape Horn to get there—than to China. The first settlers traipsing west on the Oregon Trail had to go the last 60 miles over the rapids of the Columbia Gorge, or else climb many more miles over the Cascades in the shadow of 11,000-foot Mount Hood. They were going to Oregon, the green, moist Willamette Valley between the Cascades and the Coast Range, which by 1843 had become an outpost of Yankee civilization, complete with county seats and temperance society. Oregon was a hot issue in American politics then: James K. Polk won the 1844 election on the cry of "54'–40' or fight!" although in 1846 he settled with the British for the 49th parallel, gaining Oregon and Washington peacefully and declining to fight for British Columbia. But it was as if we were arguing with another power who should have which slice of the moon: Oregon's tiny Yankee civilization was nearly 2,000 miles and weeks of travel away from the American frontier along the Mississippi River and at least 700 miles from the equally small settlements in California.

Oregon still is remote. Its people, 80% of whom live between the Cascades and the Coast Range, are still hundreds or thousands of miles from any similarly concentrated population except the one up on Puget Sound. Culturally it is quintessentially American, but geographically it looks out across the Pacific Rim to the Orient: most of the Japanese cars sold in the United States are unloaded in Portland, and this is one state which resolutely backs free trade. Oregon's culture still bears the imprint of its early New England Yankee settlers, and its farms in the Willamette Valley continue to thrive. Its major product for many years was—in good years, still is—lumber, but there is less of the raucousness of the lumber camp to its history and more of the decorum of the small town with its library and literary society. When the West was the stronghold of populism, Oregon was different; and it was the most Republican of the western states as late as 1948, when it favored Thomas E. Dewey over Harry Truman. It was a well-ordered little commonwealth, affluent without being showy, so far away from most of the rest of the United States that very few people learned of its charms.

That changed in the 1960s. As Americans became aware of the drawbacks of affluence, of pollution of air and water and crowding in bursting metropolitan areas, they began to seek out places like Oregon, with its small cities (even metropolitan Portland is only a little over one million) and nearby wilderness, its pristine mountains, seacoast, and desert. Oregonians, however, did not want to see their state follow the same path as the big metro areas in California. Its attitude was summed up by Governor Tom McCall (1966–74), who urged people to visit Oregon, "but for heaven's sake don't come to live here."

By the late 1970s, Oregon shifted attitudes once again—and once again ahead of the rest of the nation. Four years of recession made environment-conscious Oregon yearn for a little more of the economic growth it had been taking for granted. For a time migration into the state—long heavy, despite McCall's admonition—stopped, and unemployment rates zoomed up to some of the nation's highest levels. The problem was the vulnerability of the lumber industry: demand for lumber depends on the level of new construction, which in turn depends on interest rates; the combination of high interest rates and recession during the first Reagan term hit Oregon especially hard.

Their goal was to stimulate economic growth, and the solution ultimately arrived at was not big, but active government. In 1978 it elected a conservative Republican governor, Vic Atiyeh, who beat both his predecessors, McCall in the Republican primary and Robert Straub in the general election. In 1982 he beat a liberal Democrat by the biggest margin in 30 years. But as time went on, Atiyeh seemed too passive, and in 1986 both parties' candidates campaigned as activists. The winner, Democrat Neil Goldschmidt, based his campaign on a blueprint for Oregon's future and stressed his role as an innovator as mayor of Portland in the 1970s—"a public-sector risk-taker in the entrepreneurial mold," the *Portland Oregonian* called him. Goldschmidt is identified as a liberal because of his attitudes on cultural issues, and Oregon remains a culturally liberal state on many issues; there are a relatively large number of young and single voters here, and Oregon is still proud of being the first state to ban throwaway bottles and one of the first to allow abortions (though it may be a little sheepish about having decriminalized marijuana in the early 1970s; in 1986 it rejected an initiative to completely legalize marijuana by the overwhelming margin of 74%–26%. But what worked more for Goldschmidt was his support from many businessmen and his own business experience: after serving as mayor and for two years as Jimmy Carter's secretary of transportation, he worked for five years for the Nike running shoe company based in the Portland area. Oregon voters now seem to value highly the economic growth they once took for granted—or regarded as a foreboding of incipient Californiazation. They want to place more emphasis on economic growth and a little less to the environment.

Oregon seems to have reached these conclusions not after dialectical struggle, but through the emergence of a consensus. Unlike most states, it does not have long-standing political differences between different regions. The coastal areas and the lower Columbia River valley are marginally more Democratic than the rest of the state, and Salem, the state capital, is usually more Republican than Eugene, the site of the University of Oregon; the low-lying, less affluent sections of Portland east of the Willamette River are usually Democratic, while the more affluent city neighborhoods and suburbs in the hills in the west tend to be Republican. But the

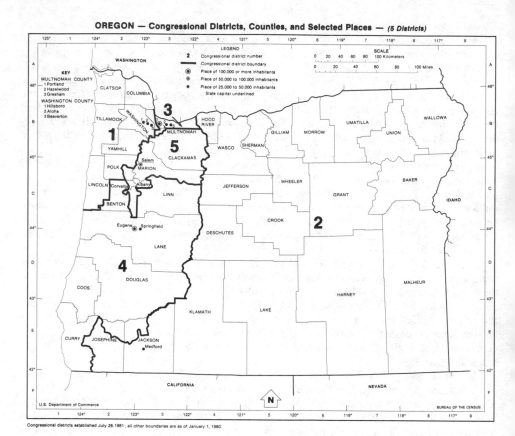

OREGON — Congressional Districts, Counties, and Selected Places — (5 Districts)

differences are small, and there is not the vast gap between lifestyles you find in California. The longhaired young here like to backpack and think of themselves as middle-class; so do blue-collar workers and affluent people in the high-income suburbs.

Governor. Neil Goldschmidt talks so fast that the best courtroom reporters can't keep up with him. To many he seems the city slicker, and when in the summer of 1985 he refused to debate his Republican opponent, Norma Paulus, in the town of Bend, because it was "the middle of nowhere," he had to apologize; he wound up carrying only two counties west of the Cascades. For much of 1986 he trailed Paulus, a steady moderate Republican who had served two creditable terms as secretary of state. But in the fall Goldschmidt shot ahead on his economic program and his record of cutting crime as mayor—a contrast with Portland in 1986, when police chief Penny Harrington was forced to resign for mismanagement and favoring her relatives and there was a move on to recall Mayor Bud Clark, a tavern owner who once posed for a photo showing him wearing only a raincoat.

In contrast, Goldschmidt's activism is directed to goals that are original but not wacky, like Portland's newly opened light rail line. He carried the Portland area, where he is best known, and also won the Willamette Valley counties as far south as Eugene. He entered office crackling with energy, calling for "an activist state role on the economy." So now Oregon, like Washington next door, has a Democratic governor, fresh from the private sector rather than government, whose politics are a contrast not only to Reagan Republicanism, but to the labor liberalism of Democrats past. It will be interesting to see what comes of these laboratories of reform out on

America's Pacific Rim.

Senators. Oregon has two of the senior Republicans in the Senate, the chairmen of the Appropriations and Finance Committees when their party was in control, and important legislators now when it is in the minority. Both are men of considerable intellect and character and of distinctive views. And, as so often is the case when a state is represented by two Senators of the same party, considered to be in the same place on the ideological scale, and roughly the same age, they have not always been the closest of friends or political allies.

The senior Senator is Mark Hatfield, Ranking Member of the Senate Appropriations Committee, and holder of statewide office in Oregon since 1956, when he was elected secretary of state at 34. In 1958 he was elected governor, and served for eight years; in 1966 he was elected to the Senate, and has been there ever since. The issue that Hatfield has always cared most about is peace. He is a deeply religious man, and as a young serviceman was one of the first Americans to see Hiroshima after it was bombed. That experience—and deep convictions—have left him a strong proponent of disarmament and of understanding with our adversaries. He was the cosponsor of the McGovern–Hatfield amendment to end the Vietnam war in the early 1970s; he was an enthusiastic backer of the nuclear freeze in the 1980s; he regularly votes against defense appropriations. As Appropriations chairman, when the Republicans controlled the Senate, he used what leverage he had to hold down defense spending increases, but could not really prevent the round of sharp increases of 1979–84. He is no unilateral disarmer, but he is skeptical about the worth of weapons systems and fearful that stockpiles of arms or large conscript armies will be used to make war. Hatfield is not the kind of Senator who will use every trick in the book to get his way, and he will let his fellow Republicans have their chance to vote increases he thinks unwise. But he will not be working with the Administration on the defense spending increases it believes are so important.

On other issues Hatfield is not so far from the Reagan Administration as many believe. He is not an unqualified believer in free-market economics, but he has—long before the current slump in the lumber industry—favored measures to give the lumber companies more access to Oregon's forests than many environmentalists would like. He is not an enthusiast for most domestic spending programs. On cultural issues, his strong religious beliefs usually do not make him join forces usually with the New Right. But neither is he an enthusiast for the latest form of cultural liberation, and in vivid contrast to Packwood he opposes abortion. He has been willing to use his seat on Appropriations to funnel money to Oregon, especially for water projects and dams. Appropriations has been a frustrating committee in the 1980s, its powers reined in by the Budget Committee and by Gramm-Rudman, yet more powerful than ever late in the session when few of the appropriations bills have been passed, all are behind schedule, and most are wrapped together in a single continuing resolution. Hatfield is not a cynical horse-trader at such times, but he is willing to take on some fights and able to win some. Now that he is not chairman, his clout is reduced. But since he never relied on slick use of the gavel and maintains the closest of relationships with the chairman, John Stennis, who turns 87 in 1988, he should continue to be an important player in government spending decisions—which sooner or later means almost all government policies.

If there were any doubts about Hatfield's popularity in Oregon, and there were in the late 1970s when he did not run particularly well in statewide polls, they were dispelled by his performance in the 1984 election. His major problem was not his opponent, a state Senator whose consistently liberal views on foreign policy and the environment were probably a little too liberal for Oregon, but the fact that he was, for the first time in his career, tinged with scandal. Hatfield began public life as a young academic with no money, but his wife has become a successful Washington real estate broker. Then it was revealed that Mrs. Hatfield had received a $40,000 fee in return for little or no services from one Basil Tsakos, and that Hatfield had been soliciting support on official stationary for Tsakos's proposal to build a $15 billion oil pipeline across Africa. To some it seemed a pretty clear case of influence-buying. The Hatfields changed their story of what Mrs. Hatfield had done to earn the fee several times. Finally they appeared together in Portland, confessed an error in judgment, promised to donate the money to charity, and asked the voters' forgiveness. They got it. One reason, surely, is that it seemed so totally out of character for Mark Hatfield to do anything untoward. Hatfield comes up for reelection in 1990, when he will be 68. Some of the state's young congressmen, like Les AuCoin and Ron Wyden, and perhaps Governor Neil Goldschmidt, may be eyeing the seat. But Hatfield, if he runs, will have considerable strength.

Oregon's junior Senator, Bob Packwood, made history in 1986 as the Chairman of the Senate Finance Committee who played a major role in producing America's most sweeping tax reform act in 45 years. His role was all the more surprising, since it was such a departure from his previous posture. Packwood spent most of his years on the Finance Committee when Russell Long was chairman, and for years he shared Long's view that government should use the tax code—granting tax credits, accelerated depreciation, allowing deductions and tax shelters—to achieve policy goals; and he also seemed to share Long's unspoken view that a Finance chairman maximizes his power by keeping tax rates high and then doling out exemptions and favors and lower rates to his colleagues and constituents. Far from sharing Jimmy Carter's view that the tax code was a disgrace to the human race, he stated openly that it was pretty good as it was. In the first months of 1986, after Dan Rostenkowski's Ways and Means Committee passed its tax reform bill lowering rates and eliminating preferences, Packwood followed his old approach. He announced early on that he would insist on favorable treatment for the timber industry—a maladroit move that gave others leverage over him—and watched as fellow Finance members piled preference after preference into the bill.

By mid-April 1986 enough preferences had been voted to boost the deficit by $100 billion— and kill the bill. Packwood was being lampooned in the *Portland Oregonian* as "H & R Packwood with another of my 17 versions of tax reform," and he was facing opposition in the May 20 primary from a charismatic young conservative named Joe Lutz. Packwood had amassed some $4 million in campaign contributions (not difficult when you're Finance chairman doling out tax preferences) but Lutz was attacking him with style and humor, and was drawing on the anti-Packwood base among registered Republicans that had held him to 62% against weak opposition in the 1980 primary. A fiasco on tax reform would undercut Packwood's greatest strength with Republican primary voters, his reputation for competence and his ability as a committee chairman to get things done.

So in late April Packwood repaired to a Capitol Hill bar with an aide and over a pitcher of beer started pencilling out some figures—and came up with a bill that stripped away far more preferences than the House or Reagan version and that would lower rates far more, to a high of 27%. "I came around full circle to think [Bill] Bradley was right," Packwood said. "We ought to get the rates as low as we can, [and] let economic efficiency guide decisions." Packwood's turnaround stunned Washington, which had been writing off tax reform for 18 months, and carried the day in early May on the Finance Committee and in the Senate. There was almost an audible sigh of relief from the politicians at the prospect of getting out of the business of doling out preferences to favored causes and lobbyists.

Packwood was banged around somewhat later by Dan Rostenkowski in the conference committee, where Rostenkowski controlled his conferees while Packwood didn't control his. But the bill finally passed into law. In the meantime, Packwood won renomination over Joe Lutz May 20 by the none too huge margin, for a primary, of 58%–42%. That was the contest for him: the Democratic nominee, Representative James Weaver, withdrew from the race in August while he was being investigated by the House ethics committee, and the Democrats nominated a young man who had won 14% in their primary. Packwood, with millions left in campaign funds and his reputation for competence and clout restored, won easily.

Packwood is no longer chairman of Finance, since the Republicans lost their majority, but he still has plenty to keep him busy in the Senate. He remains ranking minority member on Finance, and quite possibly a key player on the trade issue; coming from Oregon he has a vested interest in exports (most Oregon timber goes across the Pacific) and a good record as a free trader. He is also a high ranking member of the Commerce Committee, which he chaired for the first four Reagan years; this has jurisdiction over most federal regulatory agencies and is of surpassing interest to many regulated industries. Packwood's general thrust on Commerce was towards deregulation. He is inclined to think that government regulation has perverse results, unintended consequences that make things worse; he has been a major force in favor of deregulating broadcasting, for example, and trucking.

Packwood has causes as well as committees. In the early 1970s he was the Senate's leading advocate of zero population growth, and in the late 1970s he became its leading opponent of bans on abortion. The Senate still, despite New Right gains, is the branch of government least inclined to restrict abortions; Packwood has proven skillful at using parliamentary devices to rally the majority he has on this issue in the face of attacks from Jesse Helms and others. That issue has also been a major electoral asset to Packwood. Women's rights advocates made his reelection their number one priority in 1980, and they in turn were the single biggest bloc of contributors to his campaign that year, and they even provided a substantial share of his funds in 1986, though most of course could be attributed to his Finance chair.

Another Packwood cause is electing Republicans. He is proud that as a young Oregon legislator he helped his party gain legislative seats in the Goldwater year of 1964, and has been chairman several times of the National Republican Senatorial Committee, most recently for the 1982 elections, in which the party did not, as many expected it would, lose control of the Senate in a recession year. He is one of those who put together the fundraising capability and technical services which have been crucial in giving the Republicans control of the Senate. He was miffed when he didn't get another term as chairman in 1983, but not with good reason: consecutive terms aren't customary and Packwood had been blasting the Reagan Administration and hinting that he would go up to New Hampshire and test the waters. Still, conservative Republicans have never given him enough credit (nor his feminist allies enough blame) for the seats he has helped many conservative Republicans win. Packwood was also the originator of the yearly Tidewater talks, when Republican officeholders from around the country, wearing sweaters and using first names, meet on Maryland's Eastern Shore and try to share the new ideas they have had about policy. There is no doubt about his commitment to the Republican Party, nor to free-market economics; he seems eager to lead the party rather than ready to leave it.

Packwood, like many prominent Senators, first won office in an upset: he was a surprise winner when he ran, at age 36, against four-term incumbent Wayne Morse in 1968. He won reelection in 1974 and 1980 by margins that have to be considered unimpressive, and despite the fact that he heavily outspent his opponents both times. In 1986 his real challenge was in the primary, and it looks as if the religious right will always oppose him (but not Hatfield, because of his well-known deep religious beliefs). The distance factor may be playing a part here. Much of Oregon is nine flying hours from Washington, D.C., and it's hard for any of Oregon's members of Congress to keep in close touch with their constituents. Packwood is a man of calculation more than passion, an experienced observer now of the game who still plays it to win. Those who see him as a cynical man who believes in nothing have got it wrong; he does believe in things—encouraging free enterprise, women's rights, the Republican party to name three—but he is also interested in surviving, and other things—tax preferences, for example—may become negotiable. His strategy for 1992, as it has been for previous races, is to raise plenty of money and try to avoid serious competition; and the surprise of previous elections is not that he has won but that some of his margins have been as close as they have.

Presidential politics. Oregon, with seven electoral votes, and geographically closer to Vancouver, British Columbia, than it is to any population concentration in any state but neighboring Washington, does not see much of presidential candidates in general elections. Looking at Oregon's election figures over the last 20 years—since the beginning of the McCall era—what is uncanny is how stable they are at a time when the nation generally, and many states even more so, have oscillated wildly in their preferences between the parties. This once Republican state shifted leftward on the non-economic issues of the Vietnam war and the environment: it was one of George McGovern's best states and came within 2,000 votes of going for Jimmy Carter in 1976. In 1984 Oregon, like Washington, gave Walter Mondale a better-than-average vote, despite the practically complete absence here of the black voters who provided such a large part of the Mondale vote elsewhere. So it's possible that Oregon and Washington could be trending Democratic for 1988—a possibility enhanced by the popularity, at least in early 1987, of their Democratic governors.

The halcyon days of Oregon's presidential primary are probably over. This late May contest ended Harold Stassen's career as a serious presidential candidate in 1948, when he lost 52%–48% to Thomas Dewey, and it gave Robert Kennedy his only defeat in 1968. Oregon in those days was part of a West Coast swing, since it came just before the California primary; at a time when campaigners were not yet used to flying all over the country they, like National Football League teams in the 1950s, scheduled West Coast contests together, to minimize travel time. By the 1980s Oregon seemed to come too late in the season and to have too few delegates at stake to earn much attention. The Republican primary electorate, incidentally, though far more conservative than it used to be, gave Ronald Reagan one of his lowest percentages in western primaries in 1980.

Congressional districts. Oregon gained a fifth congressional district in 1982; it was one of two districts carried by Republicans. Oregon House races have a certain volatility: the distance factor makes it hard for even the most conscientious and attractive congressman to keep winning by the kinds of percentages that members whose districts are within two hours of Washington National Airport can count on.

The People: Est. Pop. 1986: 2,698,000; Pop. 1980: 2,633,105, up 2.5% 1980–86 and 25.9% 1970–80; 1.12% of U.S. total, 30th largest. 20% with 1–3 yrs. col., 17% with 4+ yrs. col.; 10.7% below poverty level. Single ancestry: 10% English, 9% German, 4% Irish, 2% Norwegian, 1% Swedish, French, Scottish, Italian, Dutch. Households (1980): 70% family, 37% with children, 60% married couples; 34.9% housing units rented; median monthly rent: $212; median house value: $59,000. Voting age pop. (1980): 1,910,048; 2% Spanish origin, 1% Asian origin, 1% Black, 1% American Indian. Registered voters (1986): 1,502,244; 728,177 D (48%); 587,154 R (39%); 186,913 unaffiliated and minor parties (12%).

1986 Share of Federal Tax Burden: $7,466,000,000; .99% of U.S. total, 31st largest.

1986 Share of Federal Expenditures

	Total		Non-Defense		Defense	
Total Expend	$7,409m	(0.89%)	$6,720m	(1.12%)	$689m	(0.30%)
St/Lcl Grants	1,340m	(1.19%)	1,339m	(1.19%)	1m	(0.90%)
Salary/Wages	915m	(0.76%)	750m	(1.28%)	165m	(0.27%)
Pymts to Indiv	4,356m	(1.19%)	4,172m	(1.20%)	183m	(1.03%)
Procurement	593m	(0.29%)	253m	(0.45%)	340m	(0.23%)
Research/Other	206m	(0.77%)	206m	(0.77%)	0m	(0%)

Political Lineup: Governor, Neil Goldschmidt (R); Secy. of State, Barbara Roberts (D); Atty. Gen., Dave Frohnmayer (R); Treasurer, Bill Rutherford (R). State Senate, 30 (17 D and 30 R); State House of Representatives, 60 (31 D and 29 R). Senators, Mark O. Hatfield (R) and Robert W. Packwood (R). Representatives, 5 (3 D and 2 R).

1984 Presidential Vote

Reagan (R)	685,700	(56%)
Mondale (D)	536,479	(44%)

1980 Presidential Vote

Reagan (R)	571,044	(48%)
Carter (D)	456,890	(39%)
Anderson (I)	112,389	(10%)

1984 Democratic Presidential Primary

Hart	233,638	(59%)
Mondale	110,374	(28%)
Jackson	37,106	(9%)
Two others	16,774	(4%)

1984 Republican Presidential Primary

Reagan	238,594	(100%)

GOVERNOR

Gov. Neil Goldschmidt (D)

Elected 1986, term expires Jan. 1991; b. June 16, 1940, Eugene; home, Portland; U. of OR, B.A., 1963, U. of CA at Berkeley, J.D. 1967; Jewish; married (Margie).

Career: Legal Aide, Portland City Commission, 1971–73; Practicing atty., 1967–70; Mayor of Portland, 1973–73; U.S. Secy. of Transportation, 1979–81; Vice Pres., Nike, Inc., 1981–85.

Office: State Capitol, Rm. 254, Salem 97310, 503-378-3111.

Election Results

1986 gen.	Neil Goldschmidt (D)	549,456	(52%)
	Norma Paulus (R)	506,989	(48%)
1986 prim.	Neil Goldschmidt (D)	214,148	(68%)
	Edward N. Fadeley (D)	81,300	(26%)
1982 gen.	Victor G. Atiyeh (R)	639,841	(61%)
	Ted Kulongoski (D)	374,316	(36%)

SENATORS

Sen. Mark O. Hatfield (R)

Elected 1966, seat up 1990; b. July 12, 1922, Dallas; home, Tigard; Willamette U., B.A. 1943, Stanford U., M.A. 1948; Baptist; married (Antoinette).

Career: Navy, WWII; Assoc. Prof. of Pol. Sci., Dean of Students, Willamette U., 1949–57; OR House of Reps., 1951–55; OR Senate, 1955–57; Secy. of State of OR, 1957–59; Gov. of OR, 1959–67.

Offices: 711 HSOB 20510, 202-224-3753. Also 475 Cottage St. N.E., Salem 97301, 503-363-1629; and 114 Pioneer Courthouse, 555 S.W. Yamhill, Portland 97204, 503-221-3380.

Committees: *Appropriations* (Ranking Member of 13 R). Subcommittees: Commerce, Justice, State, and Judiciary; Energy and Water Development (Ranking Member); Foreign Operations; Labor, Health and Human Services, Education and Related Agencies; Legislative Branch. *Energy and Natural Resources* (2d of 9 R). Subcommittees: Public Lands, National Parks and Forests; Water and Power. *Rules and Administration* (2d of 7 R). *Joint Committee on the Library. Joint Committee on Printing.*

Group Ratings

	ADA	ACLU	COPE	CFA	LCV	ACU	NTU	NSI	COC	CEI
1986	75	75	50	47	26	30	50	10	39	47
1985	45	—	50	67	—	18	57	—	70	—

National Journal Ratings

	1986 LIB	—	1986 CONS	1985 LIB	—	1985 CONS
Economic	40%	—	55%	45%	—	54%
Social	50%	—	48%	43%	—	55%
Foreign	75%	—	0%	86%	—	12%

Key Votes

1) Ease Gun Cont	—	5) Grm-Rdmn Def Red	AGN	9) Rehnquist Nom	FOR
2) Immig Reform	FOR	6) Contra Aid	AGN	10) Tax Reform	FOR
3) Lmt Text Imp	AGN	7) SDI Funding	AGN	11) Drug Death Pen	FOR
4) Aid Tobac Ind	AGN	8) Lmt PAC Contrib	FOR	12) S Africa Sanc	FOR

Election Results

1984 general	Mark O. Hatfield (R)................	808,152	(67%)	($671,167)
	Margie Hendriksen (D)...............	406,122	(33%)	($257,512)
1984 primary	Mark O. Hatfield (R)................	214,114	(79%)	
	John T. Scheiss (R)...................	26,848	(10%)	
	Sherry Reynolds (R)...................	18,590	(7%)	
	Ralph H. Preston (R).................	12,662	(5%)	
1978 general	Mark O. Hatfield (R)...............	550,165	(62%)	($223,874)
	Vernon Cook (D)....................	341,616	(38%)	($38,976)

Campaign Contributions and Expenditures

1979-84		Direct Cont. 1979-84		PACS Breakdown 1979-84			
Receipts	$860,361	Indiv.	$400,173	Corp.	$185,476	T/M/H	$102,831
Expend.	$671,167	Party	$23,235	Labor	$39,018	Agr.	$1,300
Unspent	$243,511	PACS	$376,194	Ideo.	$50,874	CWOS	$2,000

Sen. Robert W. (Bob) Packwood (R)

Elected 1968, seat up 1992; b. Sept. 11, 1932, Portland; home, Aloha; Willamette U., B.S. 1954, N.Y.U., LL.B. 1957; Unitarian; married (Georgie).

Career: Law clerk, OR Supreme Crt., 1957–58; Practicing atty., 1958–68; OR House of Reps., 1963–69.

Offices: 259 RSOB 20510, 202-224-5244. Also 101 S.W. Main St., Ste. 240, Portland 97204-3210, 503-294-3448.

Committees: *Commerce, Science, and Transportation* (2d of 9 R). Subcommittees: Communications (Ranking Member); Foreign Commerce and Tourism; Surface Transportation. *Finance* (Ranking Member of 9 R). Subcommittees: Health; International Trade. *Joint Committee on Taxation.*

Group Ratings

	ADA	ACLU	COPE	CFA	LCV	ACU	NTU	NSI	COC	CEI
1986	60	69	44	47	81	37	54	63	58	59
1985	35	—	44	47	—	40	51	—	66	—

National Journal Ratings

	1986 LIB — 1986 CONS			1985 LIB — 1985 CONS		
Economic	40%	—	55%	32%	—	65%
Social	67%	—	32%	64%	—	32%
Foreign	67%	—	30%	56%	—	43%

Key Votes

1) Ease Gun Cont	FOR	5) Grm-Rdmn Def Red	FOR	9) Rehnquist Nom	FOR
2) Immig Reform	FOR	6) Contra Aid	AGN	10) Tax Reform	FOR
3) Lmt Text Imp	AGN	7) SDI Funding	AGN	11) Drug Death Pen	AGN
4) Aid Tobac Ind	FOR	8) Lmt PAC Contrib	FOR	12) S Africa Sanc	FOR

Election Results

1986 general	Robert W. (Bob) Packwood (R)	656,317	(63%)	($6,523,492)
	Rick Bauman (D)	375,735	(36%)	($64,139)
1986 primary	Robert W. (Bob) Packwood (R)	171,985	(58%)	
	Joe P. Lutz, Sr. (R)	126,315	(42%)	
1980 general	Robert W. (Bob) Packwood (R)	594,290	(52%)	($1,534,607)
	Ted Kulongoski (D)	501,963	(44%)	($190,047)

Campaign Contributions and Expenditures

1985-86		Direct Cont. 1985-86		PACS Breakdown 1985-86			
Receipts	$6,725,027	Indiv.	$5,194,632	Corp.	$579,350	T/M/H	$166,500
Expend.	$6,523,492	Party	$16,282	Labor	$101,045	Agr.	$4,500
Unspent	$692,290	PACS	$936,759	Ideo.	$71,514	CWOS	$40,850

FIRST DISTRICT

In the northwest corner of Oregon, near the antique town of Astoria, where John Jacob Astor's fur traders were the state's first white settlers, around the mouth of the Columbia River, and in the coastal counties of Clatsop, Tillamook, and Lincoln, the countryside still has a frontier ambience to it: rain falls constantly on the weathered frame houses, and men in plaid flannel jackets work in lumber mills and on docks. The towns have an unfinished look to them, as if they were villages in the late 19th century, waiting for a railroad hookup or a new factory to make one of them into one of Oregon's major cities. This land is part of the 1st Congressional District of Oregon. The 1st also includes part of the Willamette Valley south of Portland, which has long been farmland, the most fertile land in the state, settled by Yankees in the middle 19th century. But in recent years, areas close to Portland have had an influx of settlers from the metropolitan area, people looking for wider spaces, closer access to the countryside, and a more traditional atmosphere in which to raise their families.

That is the historical 1st District, the descendant of a congressional district first established in 1892. But there is also a newer 1st District, which was largely unsettled then; this is in the Portland metropolitan area, and it includes most of the current 1st District's population. The district includes the part of the city of Portland west of the Willamette River. Geographically it is the smaller part of the city; there is only a little flat land before the hills start to rise. But the district includes both the downtown business section and the affluent neighborhoods in the hills overlooking it.

Nearly half the district's population is in Washington County, once a valley full of farms, separated from Portland by the hills west of the Willamette. In the years since 1945 it has been filling up with comfortable subdivisions and grew rapidly all through the 1970s. This is an affluent, but not an exclusive area; a home for engineers rather than top executives, for middle managers rather than civic leaders. Computer and high tech companies have been flocking here, attracted by the environment—at the foot of mountains, woodsy and even rustic, but outfitted with all the comforts and services of modern civilization—that attracts a high-skill work force, so that Washington County is now known as the Silicon Forest.

The congressman from this district that elected Republicans for 82 years is Les AuCoin, one of the leaders of, and perhaps the archetypical member of, the Watergate class of Democrats. His approach to issues is as different from that of typical labor-liberal Democrats as the 1st District is different from typical big city Democratic districts, and he has shown the capacity to win elections in difficult territory and bad years for his party. He typifies the Watergate class also in legislative skill; he had served in the Oregon state legislature and after one term became House Majority Leader. His base was not on the Democratic coast, but in high-income Washington County; his primary emphasis was not on economic issues but on non-economic matters like Vietnam, Watergate, and the environment.

In the 1980s he has emerged, from his seat on the Appropriations Committee, as one of the most visible and fervent opponents of the Reagan Administration's foreign and defense policy. He is one of only two doves on the Defense Appropriations Subcommittee, and has taken the lead role opposing the MX missile, for example; he is strongly opposed to aiding the Nicaraguan contras; he has argued against the loose interpretation of the 1972 ABM treaty and opposes the Strategic Defense Initiative as "a first-strike capable offensive technology"; he has criticized the Administration bitterly for doing nothing on arms control. He has also taken a lead role on some environmental issues, working with Senator Mark Hatfield to pass the Columbia River Gorge bill in 1986, for example, and helping to put together the 1984 Oregon Wilderness bill and getting it passed over the objections of the two Oregon House Republicans.

On economic issues, in contrast, AuCoin's views are not reflexively pro-spending. He does, however, tend to district needs, putting in a Job Corps Center or taking care of the Coast Guard station in Astoria. Representing a port that unloads a lot of cars from Japan and ships a lot of lumber to the Far East, he is inclined to be a free trader. He is ready to hear arguments why business needs incentives, and has cultivated many of the business interests in his district.

Yet AuCoin has never had a free ride in a general election. The Silicon Forest, trending Republican in national elections, provides a base for opposition, and he doesn't run much better than even in the Willamette Valley counties. Moreover, AuCoin with his cheeriness and his burning opposition to many of their favorite causes is just the kind of Democrat that enrages many conservative Republicans. In 1982 and 1984 Republican Bill Moshofsky, former governmental affairs director for Georgia-Pacific, raised plenty of money and argued that AuCoin's policies were stifling economic growth; that was a theme that resonates in Oregon in the 1980s, and AuCoin was held to 54% and 53% of the vote. In 1986 Republican legislator Tony Meeker from the Willamette Valley argued that AuCoin had not done enough for the district; the argument evidently fell flat as AuCoin won 62% of the vote.

That doesn't mean that AuCoin will have an easy time of it in 1988, but it does suggest the odds will be in his favor. These have all been tough races, fought out with budgets as big as those for many Senate contests: AuCoin spent over $870,000 in 1984 and 1986, and in the last three elections House candidates have spent more than $3.4 million here. With such exposure in the media market that reaches three-quarters of the state, and a proven record of success, AuCoin has long eyed the Senate seats held by Oregon's two Republicans; and it's possible he will run for Mark Hatfield's seat in 1990 or Bob Packwood's in 1992.

The People: Pop. 1980: 526,840, up 32.4% 1970–80. Households (1980): 67% family, 35% with children, 58% married couples; 38.1% housing units rented; median monthly rent: $226; median house value: $68,100. Voting age pop. (1980): 387,395; 2% Spanish origin, 2% Asian origin, 1% American Indian, 1% Black.

1984 Presidential Vote: Reagan (R) 147,889   (57%)
Mondale (D) 112,844   (43%)

Rep. Les AuCoin (D)

Elected 1974; b. Oct. 21, 1942, Portland; home, Forest Grove; Pacific U., B.A. 1969; Protestant; married (Susan).

Career: Army, 1961–64; Reporter, *Portland Oregonian*, 1965–66; Dir. of Pub. Info., Pacific U., 1966–73; OR House of Reps., 1971–75, Major. Ldr., 1973–75; Admin., Skidmore, Owings, and Merrill, architectural firm, 1973–74.

Offices: 2159 RHOB 20515, 202-225-0855. Also 1716 Fed. Bldg., 1220 S.W. 3d Ave., Portland 97204, 503-221-2901.

Committees: *Appropriations* (24th of 35 D). Subcommittees: Defense; District of Columbia; Interior.

Group Ratings

	ADA	ACLU	COPE	CFA	LCV	ACU	NTU	NSI	COC	CEI
1986 90	89	71	75	71	9	37	0	33	31	
1985	65	—	70	67	—	29	50	—	64	—

National Journal Ratings

	1986 LIB	—	1986 CONS		1985 LIB	—	1985 CONS
Economic	50%	—	50%		46%	—	53%
Social	86%	—	11%		78%	—	21%
Foreign	80%	—	0%		71%	—	26%

Key Votes

1) Lmt Cln Water Act	AGN	5) Retain Gun Cont	AGN	9) Aid Angola Reb	AGN
2) Rpl Tobac Sub	FOR	6) Contra Aid	AGN	10) Tax Reform	FOR
3) Grm-Rdmn Def Red	FOR	7) Lmt Text Imp	AGN	11) S Africa Sanc	FOR
4) Ban Polygraph	FOR	8) Limit SDI	FOR	12) Immig Reform	FOR

Election Results

1986 general	Les AuCoin (D)	141,585	(62%)	($946,767)
	Anthony Meeker (R)	87,874	(38%)	($492,655)
1986 primary	Les AuCoin (D)	56,196	(88%)	
	Thomas H. Repasky (D)	7,577	(12%)	
1984 general	Les AuCoin (D)	138,393	(53%)	($875,059)
	Bill Moshofsky (R)	122,247	(47%)	($664,011)

Campaign Contributions and Expenditures

1985-86		Direct Cont. 1985-86		PACS Breakdown 1985-86			
Receipts	$958,023	Indiv.	$403,537	Corp.	$76,850	T/M/H	$91,230
Expend.	$946,767	Party	$10,798	Labor	$144,300	Agr.	$5,200
Unspent	$25,698	PACS	$436,028	Ideo.	$115,648	CWOS	$2,800
		Cand.	$93,650				

SECOND DISTRICT

"The middle of nowhere" is what Neil Goldschmidt, former mayor of Portland, called the town of Bend during his ultimately successful campaign for governor. He apologized and should have, for Bend is the middle, geographically anyway, of Oregon's 2d Congressional District. This vast expanse covers all of the state east of the Cascades and the southernmost valley between the

Cascades and the Coast Range: 73% of Oregon's land area and 20% of its population. This is the barren land that some of the first settlers of the Willamette Valley came from—and many died on the way. To the south, the terrain is desertlike, and mostly uninhabited. To the east, along the Idaho border, are the irrigated farmlands along the Snake River as it flows northwest to the Columbia. The northern part of eastern Oregon is forested land, with occasional lumber mill towns; settlements are sparse and separated by many miles. There are a few larger towns here—Pendleton in the northeastern wheat fields, La Grande in the rich Grande Ronde Valley, The Dalles where the Columbia River Gorge begins, and Bend, the largest town here, whose location even Governor Goldschmidt now knows.

So sparsely populated is this area that almost half the district's population is clustered in the southwestern corner, in an area separated from the rest by the Cascades and the once huge volcano whose blown-off cone is now 2,000-foot deep Crater Lake. This is lumbering country. Medford, Ashland, Klamath Falls, and Grants Pass are pleasant towns whose ornate Victorian houses remind you of the past.

Historically this is a politically marginal area. It includes Crook County, a lumbering area east of the Cascades, which has the distinction of being the last remaining bellwether county in the United States: it has always voted for the winning candidate for President. (Its last rival as a bellwether, Palo Alto County, Iowa, went for its Minnesota neighbor Walter Mondale in 1984.) The old lumber camps sprouted a radical tradition, one often forcibly squelched by management. But in recent years the area east of the mountains has been voting like most of the Rocky Mountain states—heavily Republican in national elections. Democrat Al Ullman represented this area for 24 years and became chairman of the House Ways and Means Committee in 1974; despite that—or perhaps because his national duties kept him out of Oregon most of the time, and identified him with national Democratic policies—he was defeated in 1980. The victor in that race, Denny Smith, had the choice of running here or in the more compact 5th, where his legal residence was; he chose the 5th. That in effect made the 2d Oregon's new district, and set up a hotly contested race with no incumbent.

The winner and still congressman is Bob Smith, a onetime speaker of the Oregon House and a rancher from the southeastern part of the state. He won the 1982 primary with 63% and has won with fairly solid margins in three general elections. Smith is a quiet member of the minority; he was disappointed when the 1984 Oregon Wilderness Act was passed despite his opposition. After the 1984 election he switched from the Public Works Committee to Agriculture, where he worked aggressively to gain White House support for a tariff on cheap Canadian timber. He is one of two Bob Smiths in the House; the other is a similarly rough-hewn and conservative Republican from New Hampshire first elected in 1984.

The People: Pop. 1980: 526,968, up 34.2% 1970–80. Households (1980): 75% family, 39% with children, 65% married couples; 30.5% housing units rented; median monthly rent: $186; median house value: $49,900. Voting age pop. (1980): 374,066; 3% Spanish origin, 1% American Indian, 1% Asian origin.

1984 Presidential Vote:

Reagan (R)	155,530	(64%)
Mondale (D)	85,806	(36%)

Rep. Robert F. (Bob) Smith (R)

Elected 1982; b. June 16, 1931, Portland; home, Burns; Willamette U., B.A. 1953; Presbyterian; married (Kaye).

Career: Cattle rancher; OR House of Reps., 1960–72, Spkr. 1968–72; OR Senate, 1972-82.

Offices: 118 CHOB 20515, 202-225-6730. Also 1150 Crater Lake Ave., Ste. K, Medford 97504, 503-776-4646.

Committees: *Agriculture* (12th of 17 R). Subcommittees: Forests, Family Farms, and Energy; Livestock, Dairy, and Poultry; Wheat, Soybeans, and Feed Grains. *Select Committee On Hunger* (5th of 10 R). Task Force: International Task Force.

Group Ratings

	ADA	ACLU	COPE	CFA	LCV	ACU	NTU	NSI	COC	CEI
1986	5	15	11	17	16	82	58	89	100	65
1985	20	—	11	8	—	75	57	—	90	—

National Journal Ratings

	1986 LIB — 1986 CONS		1985 LIB — 1985 CONS	
Economic	10%	— 88%	34%	— 65%
Social	0%	— 89%	30%	— 69%
Foreign	33%	— 67%	37%	— 60%

Key Votes

1) Lmt Cln Water Act	FOR	5) Retain Gun Cont	AGN	9) Aid Angola Reb	FOR
2) Rpl Tobac Sub	AGN	6) Contra Aid	FOR	10) Tax Reform	FOR
3) Grm-Rdmn Def Red	FOR	7) Lmt Text Imp	AGN	11) S Africa Sanc	AGN
4) Ban Polygraph	AGN	8) Limit SDI	FOR	12) Immig Reform	AGN

Election Results

1986 general	Robert F. (Bob) Smith (R)	113,566	(60%)	($323,210)
	Larry Tuttle (D)	75,124	(40%)	($104,266)
1986 primary	Robert F. (Bob) Smith (R)	54,602	(100%)	
1984 general	Robert F. (Bob) Smith (R)	132,649	(57%)	($417,447)
	Larryann C. Willis (D)	100,152	(43%)	($281,726)

Campaign Contributions and Expenditures

1985-86		Direct Cont. 1985-86		PACS Breakdown 1985-86			
Receipts	$333,973	Indiv.	$191,917	Corp.	$44,359	T/M/H	$41,265
Expend.	$323,210	Party	$8,228	Labor	$2,500	Agr.	$4,500
Unspent	$49,601	PACS	$97,924	Ideo.	$4,100	CWOS	$1,200

THIRD DISTRICT

Below snow-topped Mount Hood, the rose city of Portland is Oregon's metropolis. About 40% of Oregonians live in its metropolitan area, and more than half live within 60 miles of its downtown. Portland was founded by New England Yankees (had a coin toss come up heads, it would be called Boston) and started off as a muscular blue-collar town—the place where Oregon unloaded its supplies from the east, on the docks or in the railroad yards, and where it shipped out Oregon's products, mainly lumber and fruit. Portland has gained the reputation lately of being a culturally advanced city, where ecology-minded young marrieds jog together in the mornings, eat health food for dinner, and pray at night that no one else moves here. Indeed, its Yuppies were a key constituency in the election of its new mayor, Bud Clark, a popular tavern owner who posed in an open trench coat for the best-selling poster, "Expose Yourself to Art," and who has continued to liven things up by doing things like firing three police chiefs within two years.

But the Yuppies are concentrated in the hills that rise just west of the Willamette River and in some of the more expensive suburbs; on the flat plains east of the Willamette, which slope exceedingly gradually into the distance and seem unconnected with the looming presence of Mount Hood, Portland has a great many residents and voters who are just plain folks. True, there are more singles here and this is the most Democratic part of Oregon. But many of those singles are elderly people, and much of that Democratic support comes from blue-collar workers who, if they like to fish and hunt in Oregon's wilderness, are still not vastly different in attitudes from their counterparts back east. Portland may not be Pittsburgh, but it is not a college town like Eugene either.

The 3d Congressional District of Oregon takes in all of Portland and Multnomah County east of the Willamette River, plus a couple of suburbs along the Willamette just to the south. These are mostly modest-looking areas, with small houses and rows of commercial buildings on the main streets built in the 1950s. The population begins to thin out as you go east, toward Mount Hood; there is even a little agricultural land there.

The congressman from the 3d District is Ron Wyden, who started off in the 1970s as director of the Oregon Gray Panthers, a militant organization for the elderly; he was, among other things, the spark behind the successful statewide referendum to reduce the price of dentures. In 1980 he ran against the incumbent congressman, Bob Duncan, who evidently had not kept in touch with Portland—which has no non-stop flights to Washington, D.C.—and won with a solid 60%.

Wyden has a pleasant personality and a low-key style which contrasts with his aggressiveness and creativity as a legislator. He was a freshman Democrat in a Republican year, but won easily; he got a seat on the Energy and Commerce Committee, which has jurisdiction over almost everything that moves, just when the aggressive and competent John Dingell became chairman; he serves on Henry Waxman's Health Subcommittee and Dingell's Investigations panel and has remained on excellent terms with both even when they were fighting fiercely over the Clean Air Act. Wyden has used his committee slots creatively, developing new lab reimbursement rules that saved the government some $1 billion, encouraging competition among health care providers, honing in on witnesses like Anne Burford and the General Dynamics executives who billed the Pentagon for dogs' kennel fees. He is likely to be at Dingell's side in his investigation of Ivan Boesky and insider trading. He has used his seat on the usually inactive Small Business Committee to pass a bill delaying access charges on single business phones and a bill imposing severe penalties for computer crime.

But Wyden gets involved in all kinds of issues beyond his committees' purviews. A law he sponsored set up college scholarships for students who want to go into teaching. With Richard Gephardt, whose presidential candidacy he supports, he authored bills that would provide a carefully screened number of unemployed workers with an advance on benefits, as a form of seed capital to start their own businesses and that would encourage private pension plans to invest in housing. Wyden is always looking for issues on which he can make common cause with conservatives and Republicans as well as younger and older Democrats. He approaches issues with almost a child-like wonder but works out solutions that are politically shrewd and make sense as policy.

Wyden's performance at the polls has been superlative. The 3d is a Democratic district; it went for Walter Mondale in 1984; but Wyden surpassed all records when he received 86% of the vote here in 1986—the highest percentage ever won by a congressional candidate with major party opposition in Oregon's history. Well-positioned in the House, he decided after some thought not to run for the Senate in 1986. But he might be tempted to run for Mark Hatfield's seat in 1990 or Bob Packwood's in 1992.

The People: Pop. 1980: 526,715, up 2.6% 1970–80. Households (1980): 65% family, 33% with children, 51% married couples; 39.8% housing units rented; median monthly rent: $220; median house value: $56,400. Voting age pop. (1980): 394,345; 5% Black, 2% Asian origin, 2% Spanish origin, 1% American Indian.

1984 Presidential Vote:

Mondale (D)	....	127,984	(53%)
Reagan (R)	....	111,509	(47%)

Rep. Ron Wyden (D)

Elected 1980; b. May 3, 1949, Wichita, KS; home, Portland; Stanford U., B.A. 1971, U. of OR, J.D. 1974; Jewish; married (Laurie).

Career: Campaign aide to Sen. Wayne Morse, 1972, 1974; Practicing atty., 1974–80; Codir. and Cofounder, OR Gray Panthers, 1974–80; Dir., OR Legal Svcs. for the Elderly, 1977–79; Prof. of Gerontology, U. of OR, 1976, Portland St. U., 1979, U. of Portland, 1980.

Offices: 1406 LHOB 20515, 202-225-4811. Also 500 N.E. Multnomah, Ste. 250, Portland 97232, 503-231-2300.

Committees: *Energy and Commerce* (14th of 25 D). Subcommittees: Energy Conservation and Power; Health and the Environment; Oversight and Investigations. *Small Business* (9th of 27 D). Subcommittees: Regulation and Business Opportunities (Chairman). *Select Committee on Aging* (20th of 39 D). Subcommittees: Health and Long-Term Care.

Group Ratings

	ADA	ACLU	COPE	CFA	LCV	ACU	NTU	NSI	COC	CEI
1986	80	75	80	92	79	14	35	0	28	30
1985	60	—	80	83	—	29	43	—	59	—

National Journal Ratings

	1986 LIB — 1986 CONS		1985 LIB — 1985 CONS	
Economic	53% —	46%	55% —	45%
Social	69% —	28%	73% —	23%
Foreign	67% —	30%	64% —	33%

Key Votes

1) Lmt Cln Water Act	FOR	5) Retain Gun Cont	AGN	9) Aid Angola Reb	AGN
2) Rpl Tobac Sub	FOR	6) Contra Aid	AGN	10) Tax Reform	FOR
3) Grm-Rdmn Def Red	FOR	7) Lmt Text Imp	AGN	11) S Africa Sanc	FOR
4) Ban Polygraph	FOR	8) Limit SDI	FOR	12) Immig Reform	FOR

Election Results

1986 general	Ron Wyden (D)......................	180,067	(86%)	($242,600)
	Thomas Phelan (R).....................	29,321	(14%)	
1986 primary	Ron Wyden (D).......................	65,416	(95%)	
	Sam Kahl (D).......................	3,591	(5%)	
1984 general	Ron Wyden (D)......................	173,438	(72%)	($307,330)
	Drew Davis (R)......................	66,394	(28%)	($84,925)

Campaign Contributions and Expenditures

1985-86		Direct Cont. 1985-86		PACS Breakdown 1985-86			
Receipts	$269,263	Indiv.	$96,798	Corp.	$44,975	T/M/H	$60,673
Expend.	$242,600	Party	$5,791	Labor	$25,800	Agr.	$750
Unspent	$128,785	PACS	$151,448	Ideo.	$15,750	CWOS	$3,500

FOURTH DISTRICT

Eugene, at the head of the Willamette Valley, set between two buttes, is Oregon's second city. White settlers first arrived in 1846, and in 1876 the University of Oregon was set up here—a symbol of Oregon's Yankee cultural ethic and of how sparsely inhabited Oregon was: there were just five students in the first graduating class. The University is much bigger now, and so is Eugene, though not nearly so big as Portland; and the university population gives the city and adjacent Springfield much of their tone. There are bicycle paths along the river banks and on main streets, and Eugene likes to bill itself as the Running Capital of the Universe; the annual Bach Festival includes a Bach Run, a one-to-five kilometer dash through downtown.

Yet Eugene's economy and that of the smaller towns amid the hills to the south and on the Pacific Coast to the southwest, depend on that most prosaic of commodities, lumber. This area makes up Oregon's 4th Congressional District—one of the premier lumber districts in the nation. The prevailing winds from the Pacific bring moist air over the mountains, and it is deposited on the hillsides here in the form of almost constant rain. The year-round cool temperatures are conducive to the growth of Douglas firs and other large trees, and they are thick enough in many places that not a ray of sunshine seems to reach the ground. The lumber companies, spurred by government, conservationists, and self-interest, have taken care to restrain their harvests and keep a steady supply of lumber. But society, alas, does not generate a steady demand: the high interest rates of 1979–83 dried up the housing market and devastated the lumber industry; mills were shut down, workers laid off, whole communities seemed to be waiting in line for unemployment checks—and wondering what would happen next.

Politically, Eugene and the surrounding area are strongly Democratic—for Mondale and McGovern though a bit lukewarm about Jimmy Carter—while the area around Roseburg and the coasts are more Republican. For some years this was one of the key marginal districts in the country, switching parties in House races in 1956, 1960, 1962, 1966, and 1974. But it has been Democratic ever since. It has had an interesting political history nonetheless, thanks to the personality of Representative James Weaver. Iconoclastic, irascible, stubborn, a steady opponent of the lumber companies, Weaver rose to the third-ranking position on the Interior Committee and to the chair of the subcommittee on forests. He was an arch foe of the Northwest Power bill backed by most Oregon and Washington representatives. But in 1986, with the chairmanship of Interior in sight, his congressional career evaporated. He decided early on to run against Senator Bob Packwood, though the Republican had far more money. Then he was charged with losing $80,000 in campaign funds in commodities speculation; he admitted losing the money, but said that it was personal funds, because his 1974 campaign owed him money which, compounded at 15% interest, amounted to more than the $80,000. In August he left the Senate race, when campaign finance reports showed he had $2,124 in his treasury to Packwood's $2.16 million; in October the House ethics committee decided he had violated the law barring personal use of campaign money.

In the meantime a serious race was going in the 4th District between former Weaver staffer Peter DeFazio, who had returned to Springfield and won a seat on the county commission, and Weaver's 1984 opponent, Bruce Long, a county commissioner from Roseburg. Both had depended heavily on hometown support to win primaries, DeFazio against a Eugene liberal who lost to Senator Mark Hatfield in 1984 and a state Senator from the coast, Long against a Eugene moderate. DeFazio stressed environmental issues, called for export of processed rather than unprocessed logs to Japan, and talked about his opposition to a city income tax in Eugene. Long, with less money and apparently weaker political instincts, said DeFazio's environmentalism had reduced the district's log output and attacked him as another Weaver. Each carried his home areas again, which was enough to produce a 54% win for DeFazio.

DeFazio has Weaver's old seat on Interior (minus the seniority, of course) and one on Public Works, and will probably have a similar voting record. But he is not likely to be as much of a loner or an irritant to his colleagues. His challenge is to consolidate his position in a district which gives Republicans a solid base on which to run and a chance to win on election day—and which is nine hours' flying time from Washington, D.C.

The People: Pop. 1980: 526,462, up 26.9% 1970–80. Households (1980): 73% family, 39% with children, 63% married couples; 33.0% housing units rented; median monthly rent: $208; median house value: $57,100. Voting age pop. (1980): 378,675; 2% Spanish origin, 1% American Indian, 1% Asian origin.

1984 Presidential Vote:

Reagan (R)	126,393	(54%)
Mondale (D)	109,603	(46%)

Rep. Peter A. DeFazio (D)

Elected 1974; b. May 27, 1947, Needham, MA; home, Springfield; Tufts U, B.A. 1969, U. of OR, M.S. 1977; Roman Catholic; married (Myrnie).

Career: District Office Dir., Rep. James Weaver, 1977–82; Lane Cnty. Bd. of Commissioners, 1982–86, chmn., 1984–86.

Offices: 1729 LHOB 20515, 202-225-6416. Also 215 S. 2d, Coos Bay 97420, 503-269-2609; and P.O. Box 123, Fed. Bldg., 211 E. 7th Ave., Eugene 97401, 503-687-6732.

Committees: *Interior* (26th of 26 D). Subcommittees: National Parks and Public Lands; Water and Power Resources. *Public Works and Transportation* (27th of 32 D). Subcommittees: Aviation; Water Resources. *Small Business* (25th of 27 D). Subcommittee: Regulation and Business Opportunities.

Group Ratings and Key Votes: Newly Elected

Election Results

1986 general	Peter A. DeFazio (D)	105,697	(54%)	($295,654)
	Bruce Long (R)	89,795	(46%)	($333,647)
1986 primary	Peter A. DeFazio (D)	22,530	(34%)	
	Bill Bradbury (D)	21,693	(33%)	
	Margie Hendriksen (D)	20,795	(31%)	
1984 general	James (Jim) Weaver (D)	134,190	(58%)	($96,333)
	Bruce Long (R)	96,487	(42%)	($26,945)

Campaign Contributions and Expenditures

1985-86		Direct Cont. 1985-86		PACS Breakdown 1985-86			
Receipts	$303,328	Indiv.	$101,344	Corp.	$6,638	T/M/H	$17,167
Expend.	$295,654	Party	$2,287	Labor	$100,425	Agr.	$1,500
Unspent	$7,945	PACS	$177,630	Ideo.	$50,900	CWOS	$1,000

FIFTH DISTRICT

The 5th Congressional District of Oregon occupies the heart of the Willamette Valley, south of Portland, where the first farming communities in Oregon were established. It was one of the few valleys which settlers to the West found that nature had already made suitable for agriculture. California's great valleys depend on irrigation; so does the cultivation of wheat in eastern Washington. But things grow in the Willamette Valley without much man-made help. The soil is fertile, the plain created by the waters of the Willamette sweeping down from the Cascades and the Coast Range are broad, and the rains everyone hears about in Oregon seem pretty much constant. Add to those natural endowments some Yankee ingenuity and ambition, and you have a prosperous agricultural commonwealth—the Willamette Valley from the 1850s to the present day.

The 5th District begins, in the north, where metropolitan Portland starts to thin out. It includes the old pioneer town of Oregon City, and part of the high-income suburb of Lake Oswego. In the south it includes Corvallis, home of Oregon State University. In the center of the district is the state capital of Salem—note the old New England name. This is a district drawn by a Democratic legislature, but which everyone knew would lean Republican. Salem has always been a Republican town, the high-income Portland suburbs here tend to outweigh the more modest Democratic ones, and the student vote in Corvallis is no longer a dependable source of large Democratic majorities.

The congressman from this district, Denny Smith, has a political pedigree: his father, Elmo Smith, was governor in 1956 and 1957. Smith was a Air Force and commercial pilot and Vietnam veteran who headed his family's newspaper chain and then ran against and upset House Ways and Means Committee Chairman Al Ullman in 1980. He ran as a Reagan conservative and attacked Ullman for not owning a home in the district and for backing a value-added tax when Oregon has always refused to have a sales tax (as it did again by a 4 to 1 margin in a 1985 referendum).

Smith has devoted much of his attention to military issues, though he doesn't serve on the Armed Services Committee. On most issues he is among the most hawkish of congressmen. But when he sets his pilot's eye on some projects, he doesn't like what he sees. Armed with test results and testimony from military men, he launched a non-stop attack on the Army's Sergeant York anti-aircraft gun, and in August 1985 Defense Secretary Caspar Weinberger scrapped it after the Pentagon spent $1.8 billion—the first time a weapons system in production had been scrapped in 20 years. Smith drew a bead as well at the Navy's Aegis antiaircraft missile. At the same time, he has moved on the Budget Committee, without success, to cut money from domestic programs to apply it to defense. Smith has been frustrated in Oregon matters as well: he opposed the Oregon Wilderness and Columbia River Gorge bills, but they were passed anyway with the support of the state's House Democrats and its two Republican Senators. Nor is this solid conservative pleased with the Reagan Administration's huge budget deficits.

Smith is not afraid to take political risks—some would even say he was politically reckless. In 1982 he had the choice of running in the new 2d District, most of it east of the Cascades, which was solidly Republican, or the new 5th District, in the Willamette Valley, which was more closely divided. He chose the 5th, because he lives in Salem, though he could easily have moved. That year he was almost beaten by state Senator Ruth McFarland, a liberal who held him to 51% of the vote; in 1984, McFarland held him to 54%. In 1986, fortified by his victory over the Sergeant York—remember that Oregon has virtually no defense industry and tends to have dovish attitudes—he did much better, beating a lesser known liberal woman, 60%–40%. Smith may not turn out to be politically invulnerable. But he seems sure to continue to work for what he believes with zest and with more success than most insiders expect as long as he keeps winning in the 5th District.

The People: Pop. 1980: 526,120, up 41.1% 1970–80. Households (1980): 74% family, 40% with children, 63% married couples; 32.4% housing units rented; median monthly rent: $207; median house value: $62,100. Voting age pop. (1980): 375,567; 2% Spanish origin, 1% Asian origin, 1% American Indian.

1984 Presidential Vote:

Reagan (R) 144,219	(59%)
Mondale (D) 100,146	(41%)

Rep. Denny Smith (R)

Elected 1980; b. Jan. 19, 1938, Ontario; home, Salem; Willamette U., B.A. 1961; Baptist; divorced.

Career: Air Force, 1958–67; Pilot/Flight Engineer, Pan-Am Airways, 1967–76; Chmn., family newspaper chain.

Offices: 1213 LHOB 20515, 202-225-5711. Also P.O. Box 13089, 4035 12th St. S.E., Ste. 40, Salem 97309, 503-399-5756.

Committees: *Budget* (5th of 14 R). Task Forces: Budget Process; Defense and International Affairs; State and Local Government. *Interior and Insular Affairs* (8th of 15 R). Subcommittees: General Oversight and Investigations; Water and Power Resources.

Group Ratings

	ADA	ACLU	COPE	CFA	LCV	ACU	NTU	NSI	COC	CEI
1986	0	5	8	0	16	95	72	100	88	86
1985	10	—	6	25	6	95	73	—	95	—

National Journal Ratings

	1986 LIB — 1986 CONS		1985 LIB — 1985 CONS	
Economic	16% —	84%	9% —	88%
Social	0% —	89%	0% —	76%
Foreign	0% —	86%	0% —	76%

Key Votes

1) Lmt Cln Water Act	FOR	5) Retain Gun Cont	AGN	9) Aid Angola Reb	FOR
2) Rpl Tobac Sub	FOR	6) Contra Aid	FOR	10) Tax Reform	AGN
3) Grm-Rdmn Def Red	FOR	7) Lmt Text Imp	FOR	11) S Africa Sanc	AGN
4) Ban Polygraph	AGN	8) Limit SDI	AGN	12) Immig Reform	AGN

Election Results

1986 general	Denny Smith (R)	125,906	(60%)	($312,236)
	Barbara Ross (D)	82,290	(40%)	($87,129)
1986 primary	Denny Smith (R)	53,238	(89%)	
	Gary Corgan (R)......................	4,287	(7%)	
	Duane Fulmer (R)	2,395	(4%)	
1984 general	Denny Smith (R)	130,424	(54%)	($609,655)
	Ruth McFarland (D)	108,919	(45%)	($394,732)

Campaign Contributions and Expenditures

1985-86		Direct Cont. 1985-86		PACS Breakdown 1985-86			
Receipts	$416,407	Indiv.	$280,002	Corp.	$58,000	T/M/H	$64,751
Expend.	$312,236	Party	$13,737	Labor	$5,000	Agr.	$1,450
Unspent	$131,965	PACS	$165,327	Ideo.	$30,000	CWOS	$6,126
		Cand.	$250				

PENNSYLVANIA

When the delegates assembled in that stifling summer of 1787 to meet in the Pennsylvania State House, keeping the windows closed so no one among the thick crowds on Chestnut Street could overhear their secret deliberations, Philadelphia—ocean port on the Delaware River, home of 43,000 people, with its wide streets and charitable and educational institutions, its Quakers and its Dr. Franklin—was unquestionably America's first city; and Pennsylvania had a fair claim to being its first state. Pennsylvania was a new colony, founded 50 years after the Puritans established New England and 70 years after the settlement of the first of the Chesapeake tobacco colonies, Virginia. Pennsylvania, under the benevolent rule of the Penns and with its Quaker traditions, soon became the major settlement in the Middle Colony: its tolerance attracted Englishmen of all sects and Germans as well; its vast and available farmlands west to the first Appalachian ridge attracted thousands of yeoman farmers while the patroons of the Hudson Valley could not attract tenants for all their land; even as the Constitution-writers were meeting, poor Scotch-Irish farmers were crossing the corduroy-like ridges and settling the mountainous interior where Braddock had been beaten by the French and Indians only three decades before, and where George Washington would ride again when the Whiskey Rebellion flared up a decade later. On the banks of a wide estuary, with its thriving commerce and rich hinterland, Philadelphia seemed destined to be the London of America, the capital and metropolis and academy all rolled into one.

But history took a few unexpected turns. Philadelphia and Pennsylvania have remained among the most important American cities and states, but they have not occupied the central position the Founding Fathers expected. The capital went to the Potomac, as part of a political deal, rather than to the Delaware. The Appalachian chains stalled the early development of transportation arteries west from Philadelphia, while New Yorkers were building the Erie Canal and the water-level railroad line which became the New York Central. By 1830 Philadelphia was eclipsed by Washington in government and New York in commerce, and rivaled by Boston in culture.

What Pennsylvania became instead in the 19th century was the energy and heavy industry capital of America. The key was coal: northeast Pennsylvania was the nation's primary source of anthracite, the hard coal used for home heating; western Pennsylvania was the major source of bituminous coal, the soft coal used in producing steel and other industrial products. As a result, the area around Pittsburgh, where the Allegheny and Monongahela rivers join to become the Ohio, became the center of the nation's steel industry by 1890. Immigrants poured in from Europe and from the surrounding hills to work in the mines and the factories; and Pittsburgh became synonymous with industrial prosperity and was the inspiration behind the civic pride that celebrated chuffing smokestacks. In 1900 Pennsylvania was the nation's second largest state and growing rapidly.

The boom ended conclusively with the Depression of the 1930s, and in parts of Pennsylvania good times have never really returned. The coal industry collapsed after World War II, as both home heating and industry switched out of coal; John L. Lewis's United Mine Workers decided to seek higher pay and benefits for fewer workers, and cooperated in sharply cutting the coal work force. Even when coal use rose sharply in the 1970s, the emphasis was on capital-intensive means of extraction, such as strip mines, and there are still far fewer jobs than in the 1940s; the anthracite country now lives on the apparel industry, and has had almost constant outmigration over the past 40 years. Most important, Pennsylvania steel has long since ceased to be a growth industry. American steel companies dispersed their operations, made bad guesses about new technology, and suffered from low-wage competition in a world in which almost every nation

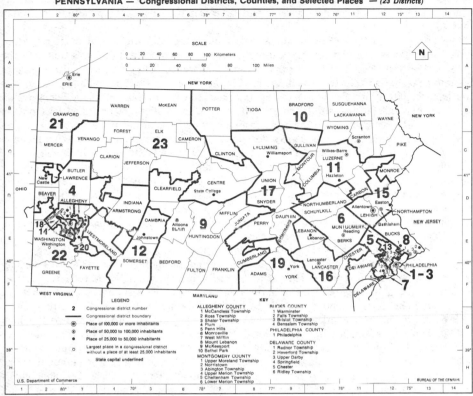

PENNSYLVANIA — Congressional Districts, Counties, and Selected Places — (23 Districts)

Congressional districts established March 3, 1982; all other boundaries are as of January 1, 1980.

thinks it must have the prestige of having its own steel industry. By 1969, the steel manufacturers and the United Steelworkers—after a series of amicable agreements for ever higher wages—persuaded the federal government to limit steel imports. Predictably that stimulated rather than assuaged demands for protection, which in the late 1980s are fiercer than ever. A century ago the steel producers made Pennsylvania the classic high-tariff state, when they sought protection for what they called infant industries. Now, in the late 20th century, Pennsylvania seems to be seeking protection for industries which have grown senile.

These economic developments for a long time left Pennsylvania in sorry shape. People growing up here were as likely to leave the state as stay, and out-of-staters showed no interest in moving in. Compared to the growth areas of the Sun Belt, with their garden condominiums and shopping malls, the cities and small towns of Pennsylvania give the traveler a sense of being 40 or 50 years back in time; to judge just from the structure, you would conclude you are in another country altogether. You can see, little changed, the suburb where John Updike lived as a boy and the gritty coal town where John O'Hara grew up. Sometimes the trip is pleasant, as in the spanking clean 1920s downtown of Lancaster, surrounded by early 19th century row houses. Sometimes it is grim, as in the coal towns where houses stand unoccupied and the woods and brush creep up to the edge of neighborhoods built 60 years ago. In 1930, after its last decade of above-national-average economic growth, Pennsylvania had 9.5 million people. In 1986 the number stood at 11.9 million—by far the smallest long-term growth among the nation's biggest states. By the 1980 Census Pennsylvania had slipped behind not only New York and California

but also the nation's new energy capital of Texas. This sluggish growth has political consequences. As recently as 1950, Pennsylvania had 32 seats in the House of Representatives. Today
it has 23.

Now there seem to be two Pennsylvanias, separated by the same first Appalachian ridge that
marked the edge of well-ordered English and German settlement in Franklin's time and the
ragged and lawless Scotch-Irish settlements in the mountains. Today the same ridge separates
the state's population into two equal halves. Southeast of the ridge is Philadelphia and its
suburban fringe reaching almost to Reading and Lancaster County, as well as the Pennsylvania
Dutch country and the industrial Lehigh Valley. Here in what might be called Cismontane
Pennsylvania the economy is shifting away from heavy manufacturing and toward services, an
economic gentrification lagging perhaps a decade behind what you see around New York and in
New England to the north and around Washington and Baltimore to the south. In Transmontane
Pennsylvania, the land beyond that first ridge, the economy has always been more dependent on
coal and steel, and the pains of contraction are still apparent. Population continues to decline,
wage levels are depressed, traditional cultural patterns remain unchallenged in places where
there is not enough work for men much less women. Yet there are signs of a turnaround here.
Pittsburgh, the center of Transmontane Pennsylvania, seems to be expanding its high-tech,
white-collar economy even as the steel furnaces go cold.

Traditionally Pennsylvania was heavily Republican, the most Republican of all the big states.
It was for Lincoln and the Union, for the steel industry and the high tariff; in 1932 it was the only
big state that stuck with Herbert Hoover and voted against Franklin Roosevelt. Yet it never
produced any Republican Presidents or national leaders. This was a state where the important
people were in business, and politics was left to faintly disreputable leaders like Matthew Quay
or the eccentric and cynical aristocrat Boies Penrose. Their job was not to build a party which
would mobilize one segment of the state enough to make a possible majority (as Tammany Hall
mobilized the Irish in New York), but to create an organization that would have a place for just
about everyone. Back in the days before the New Deal, working-class communities like
Pittsburgh and the anthracite country were overwhelmingly Republican, and Philadelphia's
City Hall remained in the control of the local Republican machine until 1951. There was a
consensus on policy here—the whole state was for the tariff—and the ethnic tensions were not so
great. A high proportion of Pennsylvania's immigrants were Welsh, Scottish, Scotch-Irish, and
English workingmen, who assimilated fairly easily; also, most of Pennsylvania's immigrants were
dispersed into hundreds of little mining and factory towns, almost inaccessibly set into narrow
valleys and in clefts between hills; they were not concentrated, as almost all of New York's
immigrants were concentrated, into one huge city. Political patronage, similarly, was not
concentrated in a single big city, but scattered in jobs in every county of the state.

The men who ran this system believed there was no conflict between the interests of the
millionaires who financed this party and the workingmen who voted for it. They had all come to
Pennsylvania, after all, to better their economic condition and together were succeeding—some,
admittedly, much more than others. Pennsylvania Republicans included within their ranks
progressives like Gifford Pinchot (one-time Interior Department official, early conservationist,
and later governor) and authentic representatives of the working class like James J. Davis
(Senator and Secretary of Labor). There was not much idealism, however; politics was a
practical business, as indeed it is in Pennsylvania today.

The New Deal undermined the Republican hegemony. In partisan terms, it made Pennsylvania one of the most marginal of states. The northern tier of counties along the border with
Upstate New York and the central part of the state—the Welsh railroad workers in Altoona and
the Pennsylvania Dutch farmers around Lancaster—remained the strongest Republican voting
bloc in the East. But Philadelphia became a Democratic city, and Pennsylvania's great blue-
collar enclaves—greater Pittsburgh and the whole western end of the state, the northeastern
anthracite country—became Democratic bulwarks. Life in these areas changed markedly in the
1930s, when the United Steelworkers organized the mills, against sometimes violent opposition;

the old Republican voting habits disappeared quite abruptly.

Now Pennsylvania seems to be changing again. Cismontane Pennsylvania, with its slowly gentrifying economy and lacking the culturally liberal elite you find in New England, seems to be trending Republican. This was the more Democratic half of the state in the early 1960s, when there was a strong Philadelphia Democratic machine; now the machine is in tatters, Philadelphia casts a smaller proportion of the vote, and the suburban counties which were closely contested in the 1960 and 1968 presidential races went heavily Republican in 1980 and 1984. Ronald Reagan carried the Cismontane region by a comfortable 10% both times. Transmontane Pennsylvania, on the other hand, is trending Democratic. In the 1960s and 1970s it grew lukewarm about the party of the New Deal when cultural issues came to the fore. But by the early 1980s the collapse of the steel industry completely overshadowed cultural issues. A Republican with a strong base here, like Senator John Heinz, can carry Transmontane Pennsylvania strongly, and a hard-working Republican like Senator Arlen Specter can outpoll an underfinanced Democrat like Bob Edgar. But in other races the trend is clear. Walter Mondale got 48% in Transmontane Pennsylvania and 55% in the Pittsburgh metropolitan area—the one major metro area where Reagan's percentage declined between 1980 and 1984. Governor Richard Thornburgh, who was supposed to win easy reelection in 1982, was nearly upset when his little-known Democratic rival got 51% here, and the 1986 governor's race was determined here. Republican William Scranton, whose father was elected governor in 1962, got 54% of the vote in Cismontane Pennsylvania. But Democrat Robert Casey, who had run unsuccessfully for the office three times before, got 56% in Transmontane Pennsylvania, enough for a 51%–48% victory.

Governor. Pennsylvania's new governor, Robert Casey, is the son of a coal miner from Scranton who finally won the governorship on his fourth try; he lost Democratic primaries in 1966, 1970, and 1978. He ran with a 76-page blueprint for developing the state's economy, but his campaigns relied heavily on precisely targeted negative ads in the hardball accents of Transmontane Pennsylvania. He lanced primary opponent Edward Rendell, the Philadelphia D.A., for accumulating 96 parking tickets. He attacked Republican William Scranton for neglecting meetings of boards he belonged to as lieutenant governor: "They gave him the job because of his father's name. The least he could do is show up to work." Scranton attacked Casey as a product of the old system who would keep the state liquor stores staffed with patronage employees and who earned $100,000 practicing law while state auditor general. Then in late October Scranton pulled his negative ads ("mudslinging is not leadership"), while Casey kept his barrage coming ("he's like a kid who picked a fight with somebody and got tagged on the chin a few times"), running the last week except in the Philadelphia market an ad featuring sitar music, a picture of the Maharishi Mahesh Yogi, and a picture of Scranton 15 years ago with long hair and a beard. Scranton, who admitted using marijuana recreationally as "my generation" did, was cast as the candidate of cultural liberalism, while in the older Casey the Democrats had for once a convincing representative of traditional values.

As governor, Casey is scrapping the commerce department used by his predecessor Richard Thornburgh to stimulate the economy and is setting up a partnership of government, business, and labor for that purpose. Its task is difficult, for it's probably not possible to duplicate beyond the mountains what seems to be the success of the white-collar Cismontane economy. As in so many things, Pennsylvania remains two rather different, sometimes hostile, never entirely congenial states.

Senators. Both of Pennsylvania's Senators are Republicans, both with unusual backgrounds: one is the scion of one of Pittsburgh's great industrial empire, the other a former Democrat scarred in the political battles of Philadelphia. Both have showed the political skill that has enabled Republicans to monopolize Senators in this Democratic state; Democrats have not won one since Joseph Clark squeaked through to a second term in 1962.

John Heinz, as he approaches 50, is now Pennsylvania's longest surviving top officeholder. Heir to the H. J. Heinz food fortune, he is one of the richest members of the Senate. He was elected to the House from the Pittsburgh suburbs in 1972 and became very popular in western Pennsylvania. His 1976 Senate race against William Green, then congressman and later mayor of Philadelphia, was a kind of Pirates versus Phillies contest, between two young politicians very popular in the two major parts of the state. The difference was money: Heinz spent $2.9 million of his own money, and won. Now he seems to hold one of the very few safe seats that either party can count on in a major state.

For that credit must go not only to his money, which does tend to intimidate opponents, but also to his political skill. Even when he was in the House, Heinz had already identified trade as an issue that resonated in western Pennsylvania, and he has been one of the Congress's most assiduous practitioners of what he might call a retaliatory and others would call a protectionist trade policy ever since. In those days liberal Republicans wooed union leaders and blue-collar voters with pro-union voting records generally; Heinz estbalished a linkage with the voters pretty much independently of the leaders with trade. On the Senate Finance Committee, he has pushed for aggressive enforcement of antidumping laws and has worked to deny administrations discretion in granting relief from injury due to imports. He was not a major player on the tax bill early on, but supported Finance Chairman Bob Packwood's stringent low-rate, preference-cutting approach at a critical point in late spring 1986, and apparently in return was able to get provisions helping the steel companies, notably a carryback procedure that let money-losing companies get refunds on taxes they paid on profits as long as 15 years ago. Under its new chairman Lloyd Bentsen, Finance does not have a particularly protectionist tilt, but Heinz may find allies in two new Democratic members, Riegle of Michigan and Rockefeller of West Virginia.

Heinz has a couple of other important committee niches. He is ranking Republican and formerly was chairman of the Special Committee on Aging; he has used that platform to help put together the 1983 Social Security rescue bill and to prevent Medicare cost-cutting reforms from hurting the quality of medical care for the elderly; he pushed for eliminating mandatory retirement ages; he tries to continue to spotlight problems faced by the elderly (like the cost of care for catastrophic illness) which might be forgotten as attention shifts to poor children. None of this hurts in Pennsylvania, which has one of the oldest populations of any states and thousands of voters heavily dependent on Social Security and Medicare. He is also one of a "gang of four" Senators trying to get the Reagan Administration to adhere to the unratified SALT II treaty.

Heinz's popularity in Pennsylvania is not always matched in the Senate, where he seems to have few close friends. He chaired the Republican Senate campaign committee in 1979 and 1980, helping it not only to raise huge sums but to spend them shrewdly and give good advice, and he is entitled to some of the credit for the Republican capture of the Senate in 1980. Yet right afterwards he lost the chairmanship of the Senate Republican Conference to James McClure of Idaho. He did win the campaign committee chairmanship again after the 1984 elections, but by only one vote over Malcolm Wallop of Wyoming; and then he was given much of the blame for the Republicans' loss of the Senate. In the longer run the verdict may be that the campaign committee did much to shore up incumbents who had done nothing to add to their 1980 totals and in the absence of any overall campaign theme from the Reagan White House. But it seems highly unlikely that Heinz will win a leadership position, as he once wanted to.

Reelection is another matter. Running in 1982, in a Democratic year in a Democratic state, he attracted only weak opposition from Cyril Wecht, a local Pittsburgh politico, and won with 59% of the vote, and without spending any of his own money. His base in Transmontane Pennsylvania was solid: Ronald Reagan got only 49% and 51% there, but Heinz won 59%. By early 1987 Heinz had not attracted any serious Democratic opponent. His willingness to spend of his own considerable wealth, presumably augmented since the death of his father in 1987, deters many potential opponents: who wants to run against a candidate who can, by writing one check, raise the same amount of money it will take you all year to raise? Especially when that candidate is generally popular and is especially strong in the part of the state which Democrats must now regard as their political base.

Pennsylvania's other Senator is Arlen Specter. A one-time Democrat, and a top staffer for the Warren Commission, Specter was a kind of boy wonder when, as a Republican, he was elected district attorney in Philadelphia in 1965. He won again in 1969, but didn't win another election for 11 years. He lost reelection in an increasingly Democratic city in 1973; he lost the 1976 Senate primary to Heinz; he lost the 1978 gubernatorial nomination to Richard Thornburgh. Finally, he beat former Republican state chairman Bud Haabestad 36%–33% in the 1980 Senate primary and then beat former Pittsburgh Mayor Peter Flaherty, who refused to spend much money, 50%–48% in the general. Not an awe-inspiring record. Yet in 1986, when the Democrats were recapturing the Senate, Specter won reelection in Pennsylvania by a 56%–43% margin.

His secrets are brains and hard work—and not much else. By other Senators Specter is respected (though, perhaps because he is a Kansas native, he gets on well with Majority Leader Robert Dole), but not well-liked; he is seen as calculating and self-serving. "They can't say I'm dumb or crooked," he once said, "so what do they say? That I'm calculating or ambitious? I have always thought those were good qualities, to think about what you want to do and to seek achievement." He managed not to dissent heavily from Reagan economic policies early in his first term, yet to compile a record that seems to reflect the views of a state that sees itself in need of federal help. He has taken his prosecutorial background to the Judiciary Committee, where he sponsored the 1984 law to give career criminals 15-year-to-life sentences; but he also cast the critical vote against the promotion of Assistant Attorney General William Bradford Reynolds. He will continue to be a crucial vote on Judiciary; without his support it will be hard for any controversial Reagan judicial appointee to be confirmed. In general, Specter sees himself as a kind of bridge between the parties. But his usefulness in that role is limited by the general perception, fostered for example by his emergence as one of the chief congressional cheerers-on of Bernhard Hugo Goetz or the hearings he held on Nazi war criminal Josef Mengele, that he is a master of the cheap shot. He flip-flops on issues like South Africa sanctions. Active, energetic, sometimes frenetic, Specter leaves no locally crucial issue unmined for votes.

While Washington rests, however, Specter criss-crosses Pennsylvania, in Philadelphia (where his wife Joan is a city councilwoman) and Pittsburgh and in little planes lighting down on small airstrips sandwiched in between two mountain ridges. Specter also worked hard, with help from his one-time opponent Heinz, to raise a large campaign treasury. These proved to be unbeatable assets in 1986. The Democrats had a riproaring primary between two candidates who represented, in exaggerated form, their party's activists in the two major regions of the state. Auditor general and former Representative Don Bailey, a Vietnam veteran from a county outside Pittsburgh, was pugnacious, traditional on cultural issues like abortion, still bitter against opponents of the Vietnam war; but he relied on support from Democratic organizations that were paper tigers and raised relatively little money. Representative Bob Edgar, a Methodist minister from suburban Philadelphia was a longtime opponent of the war, a congressional critic of pork barrel politics, an unbending liberal with enough political savvy to put together a large volunteer organization, win the endorsement of the state AFL-CIO, and raise far more money than Bailey (though far less than Specter). Edgar won 47%–45% in a fascinating regional battle: he rolled up a 68%–25% edge in Cismontane Pennsylvania, while losing to Bailey 58%–33% in Transmontane Pennsylvania.

But Edgar, who had won six House elections by narrow margins, did not pull off another miracle in the general election. He tried to argue that Specter was not for Social Security or unemployment benefits and was overly political, with ads showing a bust of Specter crumbling as his contradictory votes are ticked off: "Arlen Specter is just not what he is cracked up to be." Edgar attracted enthusiastic activists from Citizens Action and other groups determined to show that a leftish candidate can win in an industrial state. This is one race where money made a difference: if Edgar had had as much as Specter, he might have made the race closer and could conceivably have won. Yet the results must be disappointing for those who think the American working class is ready to vote for a principled backer of bigger government and liberal cultural values. Edgar ran no better than even in the Pittsburgh metro area and won only 44% of the vote in Transmontane Pennsylvania—12% behind Bob Casey. He ran close to even in his old congressional district, but otherwise in Cismontane Pennsylvania took only about one-third of the vote except among Philadelphia blacks. Specter's ultra-adaptable politics and frenetic activity seem to be more what the voters want.

Presidential politics. One of these days Pennsylvania may vote Democratic for President again, as it did in 1976 and 1968 and 1960; it came the closest of the biggest eight states to doing so in 1984. But there is a problem for the Democrats here. They like to campaign as the party of change. But their support comes from Transmontane Pennsylvania from people who want to keep things as they are—or, rather, restore them as they think they used to be. If the state as a whole does succeed in turning its economy around as most of Cismontane Pennsylvania has, then credit will go to any party associated with that effort; but it will not necessarily rub off on national Democrats who argue that they can move things back to what they used to be.

Pennsylvania's presidential primary, scheduled for years in late April, has occasionally been crucial, most recently in the 1976 Democratic race, when Jimmy Carter cinched the Democratic nomination by beating Henry Jackson and Morris Udall here. In 1980 it was anticlimactic; Ronald Reagan was essentially unopposed on one side and Edward Kennedy won a narrow and clearly indecisive victory, based on a big margin in the Philadelphia area. By 1984, after four more years of misery for the steel industry, it was Transmontane Pennsylvania that backed the candidate of bigger government, Walter Mondale, while Gary Hart carried Cismontane Pennsylvania. The Democratic primary remains heavily blue-collar, with few voters in the Philadelphia suburbs where registration remains, anachronistically, overwhelmingly Republican; the Republican primary is fairly representative of the state, except for the big cities and some industrial areas.

Congressional districting. Pennsylvania lost three congressional districts in the 1950 Census, two in 1960, two more in 1970, and two in 1980, reducing its delegation from 32 to 23; it may lose two more in 1990. With the legislature divided between the parties, and the House controlled for several years now by the Democrats by the narrowest of margins, it is likely that redistricting will probably be a compromise, dictated as much by the demographics of population loss as anything else. Pennsylvania's House delegation, not to put too fine a point on it, has long been considered a collection of political hacks, with not much talent for self-advancement. But John Murtha, an youngish old-time politician who likes to operate out of the limelight, helped put together the Pennsylvania big cities Black Caucus coalition that elected Philadelphia's William Gray chairman of the House Budget Committee, and Pennsylvania has emerged as one of the power blocs among House Democrats.

The People: Est. Pop. 1986: 11,889,000; Pop. 1980: 11,863,895, up 0.2% 1980–86 and 0.5% 1970–80; 5.93% of U.S. total, 4th largest. 11% with 1–3 yrs. col., 14% with 4+ yrs. col.; 10.5% below poverty level. Single ancestry: 15% German, 6% English, Italian, 5% Irish, 3% Polish, 1% Russian, Dutch, Hungarian, Ukrainian. Households (1980): 74% family, 38% with children, 61% married couples; 30.1% housing units rented; median monthly rent: $174; median house value: $39,100. Voting age pop. (1980): 8,740,599; 8% Black, 1% Spanish origin. Registered voters (1986): 5,846,975; 3,128,265 D (53%), 2,422,358 R (41%), 296,325 unaffiliated and minor parties (6%).

1986 Share of Federal Tax Burden: $36,283,000,000; 4.82% of U.S. total, 5th largest.

1986 Share of Federal Expenditures

	Total		Non-Defense		Defense	
Total Expend	$37,453m	(4.51%)	$30,941m	(5.15%)	$6,512m	(2.83%)
St/Lcl Grants	5,718m	(5.08%)	5,712m	(5.08%)	6m	(5.41%)
Salary/Wages	4,187m	(3.47%)	2,314m	(3.94%)	1,873m	(3.03%)
Pymts to Indiv	21,217m	(5.82%)	20,823m	(6.00%)	394m	(2.22%)
Procurement	5,581m	(2.71%)	1,340m	(2.41%)	4,241m	(2.83%)
Research/Other	750m	(2.81%)	749m	(2.81%)	0m	(0.85%)

Political Lineup: Governor, Robert Casey (D); Lt. Gov., Mark Singel (D); Secy. of Commonwealth, James Haggarty (D); Atty. Gen., LeRoy S. Zimmerman (R); Treasurer, R. Davis Greene (D). State Senate, 50 (26 R and 24 D); State House of Representatives, 203 (103 D and 100 R). Senators, H. John Heinz, III (R) and Arlen Specter (R). Representatives, 23 (12 D and 11 R).

1984 Presidential Vote

Reagan (R) 2,584,323 (53%)
Mondale (D) 2,228,131 (46%)

1984 Democratic Presidential Primary

Mondale. 747,267 (45%)
Hart. 551,335 (33%)
Jackson 264,463 (16%)
Seven others 91,886 (6%)

1980 Presidential Vote

Reagan (R) 2,261,872 (50%)
Carter (D). 1,937,540 (42%)
Anderson (I) 292,921 (6%)

1984 Republican Presidential Primary

Reagan. 616,916 (100%)

GOVERNOR

Gov. Robert Casey (D)

Elected 1986, term expires Jan. 1991; b. Jan. 9, 1932, Jackson Heights, NY; home, Scranton; Holy Cross Col., A.B. 1953 ; George Washington U., J.D. 1956; Roman Catholic; married (Ellen).

Career: Atty. and advisor, ALCOA, 1957–59; Practicing atty., 1959–69; U.S. Atty. for W. PA, 1969–75; Asst. U.S. Atty. Gen., U.S. Dept. of Justice, 1975–77.

Office: 225 Main Capitol Bldg., Harrisburg 17120, 717-787-2500.

Election Results

1986 gen.	Robert Casey (D).	1,717,484	(51%)
	William W. Scranton (R)	1,638,268	(48%)
1986 prim.	Robert Casey (D).	549,376	(51%)
	Edward G. Rendell (D)	385,539	(40%)
	Steve Douglas (D)	38,295	(4%)
1982 gen.	Richard L. Thornburgh (R). . . .	1,872,784	(51%)
	Allen E. Ertel (D).	1,772,353	(48%)

SENATORS
Sen. H. John Heinz III (R)

Elected 1976, seat up 1988; b. Oct. 23, 1938, Pittsburgh; home, Pittsburgh; Yale U., B.A. 1960, Harvard U., M.B.A. 1963; Episcopalian; married (Teresa).

Career: Special Asst. to U.S. Sen. Hugh Scott, 1964; Marketing, H.J. Heinz Co., 1965–70; U.S. House of Reps., 1971–77.

Offices: 227 RSOB 20510, 202-224-6324. Also 6th and Arch Sts., Philadelphia 19106, 215-925-8750; 2031 Fed. Bldg., Pittsburgh 15222, 412-562-0533; P.O. Box 55, Harrisburg 17108, 717-233-5849; 130 Fed. Sq., Perry Sq., Erie 16501, 814-454-7114; and Scranton Electric Bldg., 507 Linden St., Scranton 18503, 717-347-2341.

Committees: *Banking, Housing, and Urban Affairs* (2d of 9 R). Subcommittees: Housing and Urban Affairs; International Finance and Monetary Policy (Ranking Member). *Finance* (6th of 9 R). Subcommittees: Health; International Trade; Private Retirement and Oversight of IRS (Ranking Member). *Governmental Affairs* (5th of 6 R) Subcommittees: Federal Spending, Budget and Accounting; Governmental Efficiency, Federalism and the District of Columbia (Ranking Member); Oversight of Government Management. *Special Committee on Aging* (Ranking Member of 9 R).

Group Ratings

	ADA	ACLU	COPE	CFA	LCV	ACU	NTU	NSI	COC	CEI
1986	55	38	63	47	90	43	46	78	59	45
1985	35	—	64	57	—	55	40	—	59	—

National Journal Ratings

	1986 LIB — 1986 CONS	1985 LIB — 1985 CONS
Economic	59% — 39%	53% — 46%
Social	55% — 43%	55% — 44%
Foreign	49% — 49%	45% — 52%

Key Votes

1) Ease Gun Cont	FOR	5) Grm-Rdmn Def Red	—	9) Rehnquist Nom	FOR
2) Immig Reform	FOR	6) Contra Aid	FOR	10) Tax Reform	FOR
3) Lmt Text Imp	FOR	7) SDI Funding	FOR	11) Drug Death Pen	AGN
4) Aid Tobac Ind	FOR	8) Lmt PAC Contrib	AGN	12) S Africa Sanc	FOR

Election Results

1982 general	H. John Heinz III (R)	2,136,418	(59%)	($2,952,829)
	Cyril H. Wecht (D).................	1,412,965	(39%)	($424,507)
1982 primary	H. John Heinz III (R)	560,102	(100%)	
1976 general	H. John Heinz III (R)	2,318,891	(52%)	($3,004,814)
	William Green (D)	2,216,977	(47%)	($1,269,409)

Campaign Contributions and Expenditures

1979-82		Direct Cont. 1979-82		PACS Breakdown			
Receipts	$3,238,861	Indiv.	$2,389,821	Agr	$10,000	Ideo	$41,850
Expend.	$2,952,829	Party	$22,145	Bus	$416,107	Lbr	$72,200
Unspent	$524,957	PACS	$589,001	Hlth	$31,600	Prof	$20,900

Sen. Arlen Specter (R)

Elected 1980, seat up 1992; b. Feb. 12, 1930, Wichita, KS; home, Philadelphia; U. of PA, B.A. 1951, Yale U., LL.B. 1956; Jewish; married (Joan).

Career: Air Force, 1951–53; Practicing atty.; Asst. Counsel, Warren Comm., 1964; PA Asst. Atty. Gen., 1964–65; Philadelphia Dist. Atty., 1966–74, City Cncl., 1979.

Offices: 331 HSOB, 202-224-4254. Also Fed. Bldg., 600 Arch Street, Ste. 9400, Philadelphia 19106, 215-597-7200; 2017 Fed. Bldg., Pittsburgh 15222, 412-644-3400; and 118 Fed. Bldg., Erie 16501, 814-453-3010; Fed. Bldg, 228 Walnut St., Rm. 1159, Harrisburg 17101, 717-782-3951; P.O. Bldg., 5th & Hamilton Sts., Rm. 201, Allentown 18101, 215-434-1444; Park Plaza, 225 N. Washington Ave., Ste. 501, Scranton 18503, 717-346-2006; and 116 S. Main St., Main Towers, Wilkes-Barre 18701, 717-826-6265.

Committees: *Appropriations* (10th of 13 R). Subcommittees: Agriculture and Related Agencies; Energy and Water Development; Foreign Operations; Labor, Health and Human Services, Education; Military Construction (Ranking Member). *Judiciary* (5th of 6 R). Subcommittees: Antitrust, Monopolies and Business Rights; Constitution (Ranking Member). *Veterans' Affairs* (5th of 5 R). *Select Committee on Intelligence* (5th of 7 R).

Group Ratings

	ADA	ACLU	COPE	CFA	LCV	ACU	NTU	NSI	COC	CEI
1986	75	64	67	80	75	33	43	44	44	38
1985	55	—	63	33	—	32	38	—	55	—

National Journal Ratings

	1986 LIB — 1986 CONS	1985 LIB — 1985 CONS
Economic	85% — 8%	55% — 44%
Social	68% — 31%	56% — 38%
Foreign	75% — 0%	60% — 38%

Key Votes

1) Ease Gun Cont	FOR	5) Grm-Rdmn Def Red	FOR	9) Rehnquist Nom	FOR
2) Immig Reform	FOR	6) Contra Aid	AGN	10) Tax Reform	FOR
3) Lmt Text Imp	FOR	7) SDI Funding	AGN	11) Drug Death Pen	AGN
4) Aid Tobac Ind	AGN	8) Lmt PAC Contrib	FOR	12) S Africa Sanc	FOR

Election Results

1986 general	Arlen Specter (R)	1,906,537	(56%)	($5,993,230)
	Robert W. Edgar (D)	1,448,219	(43%)	($3,968,994)
1986 primary	Arlen Specter (R)	434,623	(76%)	
	Richard A. Stokes (R)	135,673	(24%)	
1980 general	Arlen Specter (R)	2,230,404	(50%)	($1,488,588)
	Peter Flaherty (D)	2,122,391	(48%)	($633,861)

Campaign Contributions and Expenditures

1985-86		Direct Cont. 1985-86		PACS Breakdown 1985-86			
Receipts	$5,450,763	Indiv.	$3,909,191	Corp.	$648,555	T/M/H	$249,753
Expend.	$5,993,230	Party	$20,464	Labor	$132,507	Agr.	$12,500
Unspent	$64,461	PACS	$1,313,401	Ideo.	$216,194	CWOS	$53,892
		Cand.	$29,741				

FIRST DISTRICT

William Penn, 37 feet high, stands atop the 548-foot tower of City Hall at Market and Broad, surveying the city he founded, Philadelphia. Actually, the real William Penn never saw North America, but he and his descendants exerted close, sometimes minute control over the colony that was established in 1682. Penn meant from the first to build a city; not content with the cowpath street patterns in other North American cities, his agents designed a grid of numbered and named streets which was replicated in dozens of American cities for more than 200 years afterwards. The grid proceeded several miles north and south along the Delaware River, and inland several miles to the Schuylkill; it was interrupted occasionally by the open squares which still grace Center City Philadelphia.

Today not many of the structures the Quakers built endure, but there are plenty of buildings here from which you can read more than 200 years of history: in the restored townhouses of Society Hill and the tree-shaded public buildings around Independence Hall, and, on the way to the ornate City Hall, the Federal and Greek Revival buildings, little temples of commerce, built when Philadelphia was the nation's largest city, and left standing because later big buildings—1920s masonry-faced skyscrapers and 1970s glass-and-steel towers—were built around City Hall and in Center City farther west. Then there are Philadelphia's residential districts, spread out like London's over a vast and mostly hilly countryside.

Some of the oldest parts of that expansion, plus the older part of Center City, form the 1st Congressional District of Pennsylvania. It has all of South Philadelphia, where Italian families, groceries, and restaurants have been pressed tightly into narrow streets with English and Indian names under a tangle of overhead wires; it has the neighborhood around the University of Pennsylvania. North of Center City it stays east of Broad Street, taking in some black wards but, as you get closer to the river, suddenly you find the closely packed 19th century houses are inhabited not by blacks but whites. Here is the old Kensington neighborhood, a place along the Delaware River where people of Irish and Italian descent live in rude frame houses, and income levels are lower than in most black neighborhoods. Walking around, you could easily imagine yourself (if you could blot out the cars) back in the 1930s. Overall, the 1st is about one-third black; blacks are just one more minority in the ethnic mix here.

The 1st District is a heavily Democratic district in national elections, although South Philly and Kensington voted for Ronald Reagan. The congressman from the 1st, Thomas Foglietta, is an Italian-American who represented South Philadelphia on the City Council for 20 years as a Republican; but he has one of the more liberal records in a Democratic Congress. He is a man with deep roots in his district but who concentrates heavily on national issues. He first won the seat in 1980 as an Independent, running against convicted Abscam defendant Ozzie Myers (one of former Mayor Frank Rizzo's gifts to Congress), 38%–34%; he held it in 1982 against another incumbent, Joseph Smith, when they were thrown together by redistricting, by 52%–48%. In 1982 and 1984 he was challenged in the Democratic primary by South Philadelphia politico James Tayoun, who criticized Foglietta for not coming back to the district every night and listening to constituents' problems as longtime representative(1945–47, 1949–76) William Barrett did; Tayoun held Foglietta to 52%–45% and 62%–38% margins.

These close victories don't seem to phase Foglietta. He has spent large amounts of his time on foreign affairs; he was one of the two congressmen who accompanied Kim Dae Jung in 1985 on the South Korean dissident's return to Seoul, and were roughed up at the Seoul airport. He is a member of the Armed Services Committee and a staunch supporter of chairman Les Aspin; and the committee does help him to channel business to the Philadelphia Navy Yard. His record on issues remains staunchly liberal with a few exceptions such as abortion.

Given his past record and modus operandi, Foglietta may have serious opposition in 1988. But after the 1986 primary he had a bit of a respite, as Philadelphia focused on former District Attorney Ed Rendell's primary challenge of Mayor Wilson Goode and on Frank Rizzo's candidacy as a Republican for mayor (ironically, Foglietta was the Republican candidate against Rizzo, the Democrat, in 1975). Politics here continues to be as spicy as the peppers on a cheese steak or the mustard on a hot pretzel.

The People: Pop. 1980: 515,145, dn. 16.6% 1970–80. Households (1980): 65% family, 35% with children, 40% married couples; 43.4% housing units rented; median monthly rent: $148; median house value: $26,000. Voting age pop. (1980): 374,046; 29% Black, 7% Spanish origin, 2% Asian origin.

1984 Presidential Vote:

Mondale (D)	140,556	(65%)
Reagan (R)	75,134	(35%)

Rep. Thomas M. Foglietta (D)

Elected 1980; b. Dec. 3, 1928, Philadelphia; home, Philadelphia; St. Joseph's Col., B.A. 1949, Temple U., J.D. 1952; Catholic; single.

Career: Practicing atty., 1952–80; Philadelphia City Cncl., 1955–75; Regional Dir., U.S. Dept. of Labor, 1976.

Offices: 1217 LHOB 20515, 202-225-4731. Also Wm. J. Green Fed. Bldg., 6th and Arch Sts., Rm. 10402, Philadelphia 19106, 215-925-6840.

Committees: *Armed Services* (16th of 31 D). Subcommittees: Military Installations and Facilities; Seapower and Strategic and Critical Materials. *Merchant Marine and Fisheries* (11th of 25 D). Subcommittees: Merchant Marine; Oceanography; Panama Canal and Outer Continental Shelf.

Group Ratings

	ADA	ACLU	COPE	CFA	LCV	ACU	NTU	NSI	COC	CEI
1986	90	84	97	83	88	5	27	0	14	17
1985	90	—	96	83	—	5	29	—	14	—

National Journal Ratings

	1986 LIB — 1986 CONS		1985 LIB — 1985 CONS	
Economic	87% —	0%	89% —	0%
Social	78% —	21%	81% —	15%
Foreign	80% —	0%	80% —	20%

Key Votes

1) Lmt Cln Water Act	AGN	5) Retain Gun Cont	FOR	9) Aid Angola Reb	AGN
2) Rpl Tobac Sub	FOR	6) Contra Aid	AGN	10) Tax Reform	FOR
3) Grm-Rdmn Def Red	AGN	7) Lmt Text Imp	FOR	11) S Africa Sanc	FOR
4) Ban Polygraph	FOR	8) Limit SDI	FOR	12) Immig Reform	FOR

Election Results

1986 general	Thomas M. Foglietta (D)	88,224	(75%)	($399,872)
	Anthony J. Mucciolo (R)	29,811	(25%)	($1,991)
1986 primary	Thomas M. Foglietta (D)	40,443	(62%)	
	James J. Tayoun (D)	25,253	(38%)	
1984 general	Thomas M. Foglietta (D)	148,123	(75%)	($444,101)
	Carmine Di Biase (R)	49,559	(25%)	

Campaign Contributions and Expenditures

1985-86		Direct Cont. 1985-86		PACS Breakdown 1985-86			
Receipts	$436,206	Indiv.	$218,956	Corp.	$27,075	T/M/H	$28,050
Expend.	$399,872	Party	$278	Labor	$118,325	Agr.	$750
Unspent	$36,332	PACS	$196,654	Ideo.	$20,954	CWOS	$1,500
		Cand.	$7,546				

SECOND DISTRICT

Running up and down along the spine of Philadelphia is the 2d Congressional District of Pennsylvania. It ranges from City Hall and Center City to the office centers on City Line Avenue, where the Main Line suburbs begin; it runs up and down the Schuylkill River, with Fairmount Park on both sides, from the 30th Street Railroad Station all the way north to the city limits. The 2d District includes North Philadelphia and West Philadelphia, where the MOVE rowhouse was firebombed by the city in May 1985; it also includes the 18th century stone houses and 19th century rowhouses of Germantown, farther out from Center City, and even farther are the postwar Jewish subdivisions just below the city line. All these are black neighborhoods now, and 80% of the 2d District's residents are black: this is Philadelphia's black district.

There was a day when Philadelphia's black community—a large and well-established one, even before the Civil War—often voted Republican. Even recently large numbers of blacks have voted Republican, against Mayor Frank Rizzo in 1971 and 1975, for example, for District Attorney and Senator Arlen Specter in 1965, 1969, and 1980, for Governor Richard Thornburgh in 1978. Blacks are still a minority of the city's electorate, 46% even of registered Democrats going into the 1987 mayoral election. But black Philadelphians, more perhaps than blacks in most cities and states, are used to being courted and able often to exert important leverage over elections. In the 1987 mayoral race, they seemed to be in that position once again. Mayor Wilson Goode, elected in 1983, had campaigned as a competent, apolitical, conciliatory city administrator; the MOVE bombing and the scathing report of the committee investigating it tarnished his reputation for competence and helped to inspire former District Attorney Ed Rendell to run in the primary and Frank Rizzo to switch parties. But Goode retained enough white support to beat Rendell and went into the general as a favorite against Rizzo, whom he had beaten in the 1983 primary. Blacks in many other cities call for power, and when they win the office find the city in decline. Blacks in Philadelphia exert power, and are in control of a city that is vital.

The 2d District's congressman, William Gray, is a man to whom the exercise of power seems to come naturally: parishioners walking out of the Bright Hope Baptist Church, at 12th Street and Columbia Avenue, where he preaches every Sunday as his father did before him, are aware that they have also been listening to the chairman of the Budget Committee of the U.S. House of Representatives.

Gray is not a veteran of the House, but he is one of its leaders. He was first elected in 1978, the second time he ran against an inept and over-age incumbent, Robert Nix. In the House Gray showed acumen by winning a seat on the Appropriations Committee his second term. By 1984 he was running for the Budget chairmanship, and with adroit politicking won. He got Speaker O'Neill to oppose any waiver of the three-term limit on Budget membership; that eliminated the outgoing chairman, James Jones, and Californian Leon Panetta, both of whom O'Neill mistrusted. Then he worked with fellow Pennsylvanian John Murtha to round up votes from old-line Democrats, even as he got the support of younger members. His election was an even more considerable achievement than first appears. The Pennsylvania delegation hasn't shown such clout in recent years; quite the contrary. And House Democrats were in no mood to elect a black as chairman at a time when most voters associated blacks with unpopular big-spending programs.

As chairman, Gray has worked hard and successfully to unite the Democrats around their own budget resolutions. This is not easy: there is almost as wide a range of views among Democrats as there is among House members generally. But Gray, as a black member from a central city district, can operate from one end of the spectrum, while making compromises with a Marvin Leath, the one-time Boll Weevil from Waco, Texas, who is at the other; this is perhaps easier than for someone in the middle, a Jones or a Panetta, to try to tie them both down at the same time. Gray may be assisted as well by circumstance. The budget process, for all the criticism of it, tends to narrow down choices: you can't credibly propose vast new domestic spending unless you're prepared to support some hefty new taxes which Gray, like most other Democrats, is not ready to do. You can get members from hawkish districts to agree to some defense cuts, but not huge ones. Gray as chairman ends up supporting budgets that he as a single congressman might not prefer. But, unlike some of the older blacks in Congress, he seems to find the work of coalition-building and compromising congenial, and he is very good at it. He has done such an excellent job of holding almost all House Democrats together on budget issues, that almost everyone has forgotten that only a few years ago almost nobody thought it could be done. And he provided some impassioned leadership, together with tactical surefootedness, on the issue of South African sanctions, helping to frame the House's and ultimately the nation's position on that difficult issue. The results are there to see: budget resolutions supported by virtually all Democrats and passed early, in 1985 and 1986 and 1987, and the South Africa bill passed in 1986.

Gray is on a workaday basis one of the leaders of the national Democratic party. He defers to Mayor Goode in city politics, though rather gingerly and did not endorse him for 1987 with enthusiasm; he did nothing to take the spotlight away from Charles Rangel's unsuccessful bid to become majority whip in 1986. He does not set himself up as a rival or alternative to Jesse Jackson. His term as Budget chairman comes to an end after the 1988 election, unless House Democrats waive their rules as they refused to do in 1984. But Gray is not likely to sink back into the quiet precincts of the Appropriations Committee without notice. Articulate and well-informed, armed with formidable political intuition, liked and respected by his colleagues, deeply rooted in his own constituency yet able to understand and empathize with others, he has the potential to be a national leader, and not just in the House: this is one House member who could end up on the national Democratic ticket, on either spot.

Gray's position in the 2d District is solid. His only noteworthy challenge came in 1982, from state Senator Milton Street, a militant who switched to the Republicans to give them control of the state Senate and ran as an Independent against Gray in 1982; he got 22% of the vote and Gray got 76%.

The People: Pop. 1980: 517,215, dn. 17.5% 1970–80. Households (1980): 61% family, 35% with children, 32% married couples; 48.4% housing units rented; median monthly rent: $157; median house value: $25,700. Voting age pop. (1980): 378,182; 76% Black, 1% Spanish origin, 1% Asian origin.

1984 Presidential Vote:

Mondale (D)	211,734	(90%)
Reagan (R)	24,593	(10%)

Rep. William H. Gray III (D)

Elected 1978; b. Aug. 20, 1941, Baton Rouge, LA; home, Philadelphia; Franklin and Marshall Col., B.A. 1963, Drew Theological Seminary, M. Div. 1966, Princeton Theological School, Th.M. 1970; Baptist; married (Andrea).

Career: Minister; Church history professor, Jersey City State Col., Montclair State Col., Rutgers U., 1968–74.

Offices: 204 CHOB 20515, 202-225-4001. Also 6753 Germantown Ave., Philadelphia 19119, 215-951-5388; 2316 W. Columbia Ave., Philadelphia 19121, 215-232-2770; and 22 N. 52d St., Philadelphia 19139, 215-476-8725.

Committees: *Appropriations* (27th of 35 D). Subcommittees: Foreign Operations; Transportation. *Budget* (Chairman of 21 D). *District of Columbia* (5th of 8 D). Subcommittees: Fiscal Affairs and Health; Government Operations and Metropolitan Affairs.

Group Ratings

	ADA	ACLU	COPE	CFA	LCV	ACU	NTU	NSI	COC	CEI
1986	80	90	96	83	80	5	26	0	33	13
1985	95	—	97	67	—	0	29	—	15	—

National Journal Ratings

	1986 LIB — 1986 CONS		1985 LIB — 1985 CONS	
Economic	74% —	23%	89% —	0%
Social	79% —	19%	85% —	0%
Foreign	80% —	0%	84% —	15%

Key Votes

1) Lmt Cln Water Act	AGN	5) Retain Gun Cont	FOR	9) Aid Angola Reb	AGN
2) Rpl Tobac Sub	AGN	6) Contra Aid	AGN	10) Tax Reform	FOR
3) Grm-Rdmn Def Red	AGN	7) Lmt Text Imp	FOR	11) S Africa Sanc	FOR
4) Ban Polygraph	FOR	8) Limit SDI	FOR	12) Immig Reform	FOR

Election Results

1986 general	William H. Gray III (D)	128,399	(98%)	($551,836)
1986 primary	William H. Gray III (D)	75,829	(97%)	
1984 general	William H. Gray III (D)	200,484	(91%)	($159,919)
	Ronald J. Sharper (R)	18,224	(8%)	($2,878)

Campaign Contributions and Expenditures

1985-86		Direct Cont. 1985-86		PACS Breakdown 1985-86			
Receipts	$663,653	Indiv.	$200,875	Corp.	$120,875	T/M/H	$124,402
Expend.	$551,836	Party	$372	Labor	$163,849	Agr.	$9,500
Unspent	$156,747	PACS	$457,131	Ideo.	$29,755	CWOS	$8,750

THIRD DISTRICT

The 3d Congressional District of Pennsylvania is northeast Philadelphia, an area with no exact counterpart in any of our other great cities. It includes now almost one-third of the city's population, and in its farther reaches its population is still growing. Along the Delaware River with blocks of closely packed brick row houses and neighborhood bars with neon lights, with mostly Irish and Italian residents and their pungent accents—you expect to see a Democratic (except that in Philadelphia it would often have been a Republican) ward leader knocking on the doors and distributing coal for the winter. Away from these old neighborhoods, 10 to 20 miles from Independence Hall, middle-income tract housing was still going up in the 1960s; more than half the housing units here, in fact, were built after 1950 (as compared to 20% in the rest of the city).

A sizable percentage of northeast Philadelphia's population is Jewish, in neighborhoods that are like neither Brooklyn nor Scarsdale. The houses are pleasant, but modest; the politics Democratic, but not always liberal. Many of these Jews are part of the hard-pressed lower middle-class, and can no more afford radical chic than designer clothes. Many voted for Frank Rizzo in his heyday, and many live in fear that blacks will move into their neighborhoods (as they did into Jewish neighborhoods farther west). Northeast Philadelphia also has a sizable Catholic population, which is still pretty conservative on cultural issues. In many ways this is a district out of the 1950s.

The congressman from the 3d District is Robert Borski, a young former stockbroker and state legislator from the older part of the district who got the 1982 nomination when other Democrats failed to see how Democratic a year it would be. To everyone's surprise, Borski beat Republican Charles Dougherty, who had gotten in himself in 1978 when Democrat Joshua Eilberg was indicted for accepting $100,000 to help a Philadelphia hospital get a federal grant. Borski has won reelection easily twice; the one highlight came in 1986 when Dougherty, who had switched to become a Democrat, switched back to run as a Republican the day of the filing deadline. But Dougherty lost that primary 2 to 1 to a more constant Republican who in turn lost to Borski by almost as great a margin. Borski makes few waves in the House, where he votes a generally liberal line except on cultural issues like abortion; he is a member of the Public Works Committee and is one of two Philadelphia Democrats on Merchant Marine and Fisheries. He is friendly to groups which support the Irish Republican Army. He stays close to local issues and, like most of his constituents, backed Ed Rendell against Mayor Wilson Goode in the May 1987 mayoral primary.

The People: Pop. 1980: 516,154, dn. 6.6% 1970–80. Households (1980): 74% family, 34% with children, 59% married couples; 26.6% housing units rented; median monthly rent: $201; median house value: $32,700. Voting age pop. (1980): 391,605; 7% Black, 1% Spanish origin, 1% Asian origin.

1984 Presidential Vote:

Reagan (R)	136,416	(54%)
Mondale (D)	116,335	(46%)

Rep. Robert A. Borski (D)

Elected 1982; b. Oct. 20, 1948, Philadelphia; home, Philadelphia; U. of Baltimore, B.A. 1971; Catholic; married (Barbara).

Career: Stockbroker, Philadelphia Stock Exchange, 1972–76; PA House of Reps., 1976–82.

Offices: 314 CHOB 20515, 202-225-8251. Also 7137 Frankford Ave., Philadelphia 19135, 215-335-3355.

Committees: *Merchant Marine and Fisheries* (15th of 25 D). Subcommittees: Merchant Marine; Oceanography; Panama Canal and Outer Continental Shelf. *Public Works and Transportation* (13th of 32 D). Subcommittees: Investigations; Surface Transportation; Water Resources. *Select Committee on Aging* (25th of 39 D). Subcommittee: Health and Long-Term Care.

Group Ratings

	ADA	ACLU	COPE	CFA	LCV	ACU	NTU	NSI	COC	CEI
1986	75	60	97	83	69	10	24	0	33	15
1985	80	—	96	67	—	5	27	—	23	—

National Journal Ratings

	1986 LIB — 1986 CONS	1985 LIB — 1985 CONS
Economic	77% — 22%	89% — 0%
Social	61% — 37%	47% — 52%
Foreign	75% — 20%	71% — 26%

Key Votes

1) Lmt Cln Water Act	AGN	5) Retain Gun Cont	FOR	9) Aid Angola Reb	AGN
2) Rpl Tobac Sub	AGN	6) Contra Aid	AGN	10) Tax Reform	FOR
3) Grm-Rdmn Def Red	AGN	7) Lmt Text Imp	FOR	11) S Africa Sanc	FOR
4) Ban Polygraph	FOR	8) Limit SDI	FOR	12) Immig Reform	FOR

Election Results

1986 general	Robert A. Borski (D)	107,804	(62%)	($391,980)
	Robert A. Rovner (R)	66,693	(38%)	($446,282)
1986 primary	Robert A. Borski (D)	58,902	(96%)	
	Jack C. Holton (D)	2,198	(4%)	
1984 general	Robert A. Borski (D)	152,598	(64%)	($310,421)
	Flora L. Becker (R)	85,358	(36%)	($73,252)

Campaign Contributions and Expenditures

1985-86		Direct Cont. 1985-86		PACS Breakdown 1985-86			
Receipts	$409,799	Indiv.	$133,879	Corp.	$28,285	T/M/H	$41,861
Expend.	$391,980	Party	$4,998	Labor	$157,282	Agr.	$3,000
Unspent	$19,781	PACS	$254,683	Ideo.	$23,255	CWOS	$1,000

FOURTH DISTRICT

The steel country of western Pennsylvania, within a 100-mile radius of Pittsburgh's Golden Triangle, was one of the economically most vibrant, if not picturesque, parts of the nation at the turn of the century. In the 1980s, after a long slow decline, it has now plunged precipitously downhill, and nowhere more disastrously than in Beaver County on the Ohio River northwest of Pittsburgh. Now the mills—especially those decades-old mills in the clefts between the hills of western Pennsylvania and the Allegheny and Monongahela, the Ohio and Beaver rivers—are cold and silent, with one of the big steel companies (LTV) bankrupt and others losing money, and the people and communities who had counted on them for a good living are now looking desperately for a solution which can restore what seemed so long to be rightfully theirs.

The western Pennsylvania steel country has seven congressional districts today; 35 years ago, before the decline of the steel industry and the outmigration that has accompanied it, the same area had 11 districts. Most of Beaver County forms about half of the 4th Congressional District of Pennsylvania, which travels east across the hills north of Pittsburgh to take in the mountainous country around the towns of Indiana and Ligonier. The erose boundaries were drawn by a Republican legislature in a vain attempt to preserve in 1982 the seat of one of the Reagan Administration's prized Democrats-turned-Republicans; the attempt failed, but the lines remain. The 4th and its predecessor districts, which have produced football players of the caliber of Joe Namath, have produced a melancholy string of incompetent congressmen. For 20 years Beaver County and the surrounding area were represented by Frank Clark, a Democrat who managed to lose his seat in the ultra-Democratic Watergate year of 1974 (he was held in such low regard by his colleagues that after losing he was able to win only 34 of 244 votes for the post of Clerk of the House). His conqueror was Gary Myers, a Republican who decided after two terms to return to his post as a foreman in a steel mill. The next congressman, Democrat Eugene Atkinson, had lost to Myers in 1976, won unimpressively in 1978, backed Edward Kennedy in the 1980 primary in which he lost western Pennsylvania, and then switched to the Republican Party just as the steel industry was going into its worst tailspin and the steel country was about to be the one part of the country trending Democratic: bad political moves every step of the way.

The craziest district lines in the world couldn't save a politician like this, and didn't. The new congressman, Joe Kolter, has not made any top 10 lists in the House, but he is far and away the most competent congressman this district has had in 30 years, and he beat Atkinson (who nearly lost his Republican primary!) by a 60%–39% margin. Kolter was a 14-year veteran of the legislature, with solid labor support. He serves on the Government Operations and Public Works Committees. He has a record pretty liberal on economics and foreign policy and traditional on cultural issues. He pitched the 4th District to General Motors for its Saturn plant and to Chrysler's Lee Iacocca. He was busy helping victims of a May 1985 tornado and pushed through a law restoring unemployment benefits to those who had lost them by pitching in and helping victims. He brought Lane Kirkland and Steelworkers' President Lynn Williams to Aliquippa to a hearing on how to stop imported steel. He has been pushing a high-speed rail transit line for Pennsylvania. He is a competent, active, pleasant congressman who, in a district designed to elect a member of the other party, has been reelected with 57% and 60% of the votes.

The People: Pop. 1980: 515,572, up 6.1% 1970–80. Households (1980): 78% family, 40% with children, 68% married couples; 24.1% housing units rented; median monthly rent: $155; median house value: $39,400. Voting age pop. (1980): 375,245; 2% Black.

1984 Presidential Vote:

Mondale (D)	104,970	(52%)
Reagan (R)	96,942	(48%)

Rep. Joseph P. Kolter (D)

Elected 1982; b. Sept. 3, 1926, McDonald; home, New Brighton; Geneva Col., B.S. 1950, Duquesne U., U. of Pittsburgh; Roman Catholic; married (Dorothy).

Career: Army, 1944–47; Accountant, 1950–67; High sch. teacher, 1950, 1965–67; New Brighton Borough Cncl., 1961–65; PA House of Reps., 1969–82.

Offices: 212 CHOB 20515, 202-225-2565. Also 1322 7th Ave., Beaver Falls 15010, 412-846-3600; 20 S. Mercer St., New Castle 16101, 412-658-4525; 104 P.O. Bldg., Butler 16001, 412-282-8081; and 7 N. 6th St., Indiana 15701, 412-349-3755.

Committees: *Government Operations* (19th of 23 D). Subcommittees: Commerce, Consumer, and Monetary Affairs; Environment, Energy, and Natural Resources. *Public Works and Transportation* (18th of 29 D). Subcommittees: Economic Development; Surface Transportation; Water Resources.

Group Ratings

	ADA	ACLU	COPE	CFA	LCV	ACU	NTU	NSI	COC	CEI
1986	70	45	90	50	38	14	26	0	33	12
1985	65	—	87	58	—	10	31	—	23	—

National Journal Ratings

	1986 LIB — 1986 CONS			1985 LIB — 1985 CONS		
Economic	58%	—	41%	63%	—	37%
Social	47%	—	52%	36%	—	60%
Foreign	75%	—	20%	69%	—	31%

Key Votes

1) Lmt Cln Water Act	AGN	5) Retain Gun Cont	AGN	9) Aid Angola Reb	AGN
2) Rpl Tobac Sub	AGN	6) Contra Aid	AGN	10) Tax Reform	AGN
3) Grm-Rdmn Def Red	AGN	7) Lmt Text Imp	FOR	11) S Africa Sanc	FOR
4) Ban Polygraph	FOR	8) Limit SDI	FOR	12) Immig Reform	AGN

Election Results

1986 general	Joseph P. Kolter (D)	86,133	(60%)	($249,885)
	Al Lindsay (R)	55,165	(39%)	($9,029)
1986 primary	Joseph P. Kolter (D)	33,599	(81%)	
	Frank M. Clark (D)	4,632	(11%)	
	Sam Blancato (D)	3,208	(8%)	
1984 general	Joseph P. Kolter (D)	114,040	(57%)	($201,910)
	Jim Kunder (R)	86,769	(43%)	($112,273)

Campaign Contributions and Expenditures

1985-86		Direct Cont. 1985-86		PACS Breakdown 1985-86			
Receipts	$280,062	Indiv.	$59,660	Corp.	$21,665	T/M/H	$48,967
Expend.	$249,885	PACS	$215,748	Labor	$119,119	Agr.	$6,000
Unspent	$63,815			Ideo.	$19,997	CWOS	$0

FIFTH DISTRICT

On the outer edges of the Philadelphia metropolitan area—technically in western Montgomery and Delaware counties, plus most of Chester County farther out—is the 5th Congressional District of Pennsylvania. This is country studded with separate settlements with histories and personalities which date back to the times when Philadelphia was a day or so's horse ride away. Chester, a small industrial town on the Delaware River, is really an old city which for years had its own Republican machine; most of its residents are black now. The Chadds Ford area, where the Wyeth family lives and paints, is peaceful countryside far from the brawling tone of Philadelphia public life. Kennett Square nearby is the center of the nation's mushroom industry. Coatesville, at the western edge of the district, is really part of the Pennsylvania Dutch country, although no one is sure just where the boundary is. Not far away is Oxford, home of Lincoln University, one of the nation's oldest black colleges—a symbol of the area's Lincoln Republican heritage and a reminder that there are many blacks scattered over this area. About 5% of the population of all the boroughs and townships is black.

The 5th District is one of the premier Republican congressional districts in the nation. Its Main Line commuters at the Paoli station, its Pennsylvania Dutch country, even the area around Chester—all are heavily Republican. This is one of those heartland Republican districts which for decades has supplied the House Republican Conference with its backbenchers and its most reliable supporters.

The current congressman, Richard Schulze, is a Republican Party loyalist with roots in the richest part of the district. He has taken jobs of sufficient modesty—Chester County register of wills, state representative—to suggest that he was seen as the kind of faithful local functionary who is allowed, by men of great power who commute to offices in the big city, to handle affairs in their small local community.

Schulze has greater responsibilities now, of course, but may still be similarly regarded. He easily won the Republican primary for this seat in 1974 and has been reelected without perceptible difficulty since. His record on major issues is solidly Republican. He serves on the Ways and Means Committee and is now ranking member on its Oversight Subcommittee. Schulze also has a seat on the Trade Subcommittee, and has concentrated on trade issues. Here he is true to Pennsylvania's century-old protectionist tradition, introducing bills calling for reciprocity and fairness and mandating vigorous retaliation against countries that do not comply. In 1986 he was an early sponsor of the steel-textiles-apparel-telecommunications trade bill that passed the House in May. By early 1987 he was appearing with "trade competitiveness" bills giving small businesses tax breaks and reinstating the investment tax credit for "productive equipment and machinery." He is particularly vigilant against imports of cheap Chinese mushrooms.

Schulze, who tends so carefully the traditional economic interests of this district, is reelected easily every two years.

The People: Pop. 1980: 515,528, up 9.8% 1970–80. Households (1980): 77% family, 42% with children, 64% married couples; 31.1% housing units rented; median monthly rent: $225; median house value: $57,300. Voting age pop. (1980): 370,556; 10% Black, 1% Spanish origin, 1% Asian origin.

1984 Presidential Vote:

Reagan (R)	134,101	(66%)
Mondale (D)	66,408	(33%)

Rep. Richard T. Schulze (R)

Elected 1974; b. Aug. 7, 1929, Philadelphia; home, Berwyn; U. of Houston, 1949, Villanova U., 1952, Temple U., 1968; Presbyterian; married (Nancy).

Career: Army, 1951–53; Businessman, appliances; Committeeman, Tredyffrin Township, 1960–67; Chester Cnty. Register of Wills and Clerk of Orphans Crt., 1967–69; PA House of Reps., 1969–74.

Offices: 2201 RHOB 20515, 202-225-5761. Also 2 E. Lancaster Ave., Paoli 19301, 215-648-0555.

Committees: *Ways and Means* (6th of 13 R). Subcommittees: Oversight (Ranking Member); Trade.

Group Ratings

	ADA	ACLU	COPE	CFA	LCV	ACU	NTU	NSI	COC	CEI
1986	15	0	20	33	10	58	47	100	81	54
1985	10	—	19	25	—	71	52	—	82	—

National Journal Ratings

	1986 LIB — 1986 CONS			1985 LIB — 1985 CONS		
Economic	33%	—	67%	26%	—	74%
Social	27%	—	73%	0%	—	76%
Foreign	27%	—	70%	34%	—	66%

Key Votes

1) Lmt Cln Water Act	FOR	5) Retain Gun Cont	AGN	9) Aid Angola Reb	FOR
2) Rpl Tobac Sub	AGN	6) Contra Aid	FOR	10) Tax Reform	FOR
3) Grm-Rdmn Def Red	FOR	7) Lmt Text Imp	FOR	11) S Africa Sanc	FOR
4) Ban Polygraph	AGN	8) Limit SDI	AGN	12) Immig Reform	FOR

Election Results

1986 general	Richard T. Schulze (R). 87,593	(66%)	($320,232)
	Tim Ringgold (D) 45,648	(34%)	($115,056)
1986 primary	Richard T. Schulze (R). 27,632	(100%)	
1984 general	Richard T. Schulze (R). 141,965	(73%)	($216,919)
	Louis J. Fanti (D) 53,586	(27%)	($8,035)

Campaign Contributions and Expenditures

1985-86		Direct Cont. 1985-86		PACS Breakdown 1985-86			
Receipts	$376,549	Indiv.	$137,968	Corp.	$100,700	T/M/H	$68,398
Expend.	$320,232	Party	$2,854	Labor	$4,000	Agr.	$0
Unspent	$291,355	PACS	$204,063	Ideo.	$15,915	CWOS	$15,050

SIXTH DISTRICT

The 6th Congressional District of Pennsylvania is betwixt and between—a part of eastern Pennsylvania beyond the Philadelphia orbit, south of the center of the anthracite area of northeastern Pennsylvania, and northeast of the Pennsylvania Dutch country. The terrain crosses the barrier between the fertile, rolling plains of southeastern Pennsylvania, and the ridges of mountains which run like corduroy, on a curved diagonal, across the northeastern and central parts of the state. About 60% of the district's population is south of Blue Mountain, on the hilly land around Reading. This is a factory town, famous in the 19th century for its black broad-brimmed hats and in the early 20th century for its ironware manufactures. The Reading Railroad once made this one of the leading railroad centers of the country. It is now a center of light, not heavy, industry, and its old brick factories are used for factory outlet stores that attract bargain hunters from all over the East. The Dutch country is not far away, and the 6th District now includes a small sliver of heavily Dutch Lancaster County.

North of Blue Mountain is the beginning of the anthracite country. Here in Schuylkill County you find the hard-bitten towns that John O'Hara described in so many of his novels, places where the rich people schemed with bootleggers to get a supply of the best smuggled liquor, where people of more modest background tried and usually failed to imitate upper-class manners, and where tough-talking miners and factory workers stayed menacingly in the background unless a character stumbled into the wrong roadhouse at night or diner at dawn. The anthracite mines were humming and the freight cars constantly loaded up in the small, grimy towns of Schuylkill County 50 years ago, when O'Hara's *Appointment in Samarra* shocked people here; there were 235,000 people living here then. Today, with the mines almost entirely closed, and the economy based on wages relatively lower than the national average, there are 160,000.

The 6th District, in national elections, is not as Democratic as you might expect. A lot of the working-class people who would have been good Democratic voters here moved away long since looking for jobs. And in Berks County there is a strong Pennsylvania Dutch population, which has been heavily Republican since it split over the slavery issue with local Democrats James Buchanan of Lancaster and his lieutenant, J. Glancy Jones of Reading, chairman of the House Ways and Means Committee, in the 1858 election.

Nevertheless, the congressional representation here has been Democratic since 1948. The current incumbent, Gus Yatron, has been elected since 1968, and continues to win by overwhelming margins. His general voting record in the House is liberal on economic issues, somewhat conservative on cultural matters—which seems very much in line with his district. His chief focus, however, has been on foreign policy, and he is now, nearing the end of his second decade in Congress, the third ranking Democrat on the House Foreign Affairs Committee. He has not been entirely unbruised in his service there. In 1981, after four years in the job, he was ousted from the chairmanship of the Inter-American Affairs Subcommittee by a 10–9 vote of Foreign Affairs Committee Democrats, in favor of Michael Barnes of Maryland. His opponents thought that Barnes would be a more articulate and more dependable critic of the Reagan Administration policy in Central America.

That loss must have been quite an indignity to Yatron, just as it was a good example of the accountability of committee and subcommittee chairmen, but he did not quit or walk away; perhaps his experience as a professional heavyweight boxer kept him in this political ring. After the 1982 election, he took over the chair of the Human Rights and International Organizations Subcommittee from Don Bonker of Washington, who relinquished it for another chair. There he has attended to his duties in a more than perfunctory way. He has risen with other committee Democrats to oppose aid to the Nicaraguan contras, but he has also pointed out, as some of them have been reluctant to do, that the Sandinistas in charge in Managua have been some pretty nasty human rights violators themselves. He has criticized Chile's General Pinochet and the Philippines' Ferdinand Marcos, but he has not overlooked the violations of Communists in other countries. Yatron is of Greek descent, and remains interested in and sympathetic to Greece, although that is sometimes difficult given the shenanigans of the Papandreou government.

So generally Yatron has been in line with his fellow Democrats; it is not likely he will be voted out of a chairmanship again, although he hasn't gone out to pick fights with the committee's other, more liberal subcommittee chairmen. Perhaps he hopes to succeed to the full committee chairmanship some day. That's unlikely, but it is possible; Yatron has proved to be a more enduring member in the House than many expected a few years ago.

The People: Pop. 1980: 515,952, up 3.9% 1970–80. Households (1980): 75% family, 36% with children, 63% married couples; 25.5% housing units rented; median monthly rent: $154; median house value: $32,400. Voting age pop. (1980): 384,537; 1% Black, 1% Spanish origin.

1984 Presidential Vote:

Reagan (R) 121,264	(64%)
Mondale (D) 68,281	(36%)

Rep. Gus Yatron (D)

Elected 1968; b. Oct. 16, 1927, Reading; home, Reading; Kutztown St. Teachers Col., 1950; Greek Orthodox; married (Millie).

Career: Pro heavyweight boxer, 1947–50; Proprietor, Yatron's Ice Cream, 1950–69; Mbr., Reading Sch. Bd., 1955–60; PA House of Reps., 1956–60; PA Senate, 1960–68.

Offices: 2267 RHOB 20515, 202-225-5546. Also P.O. Box 776, Reading 19603, 215-375-4573; and Meridian Bank Bldg., Pottsville 17901, 717-622-4212.

Committees: *Foreign Affairs* (3d of 27 D). Subcommittees: Human Rights and International Organizations (Chairman); International Operations. *Post Office and Civil Service* (7th of 14 D). Subcommittees: Human Resources; Investigations.

Group Ratings

	ADA	ACLU	COPE	CFA	LCV	ACU	NTU	NSI	COC	CEI
1986	65	36	82	67	64	27	27	20	38	24
1985	50	—	81	75	—	33	36	—	36	—

National Journal Ratings

	1986 LIB — 1986 CONS			1985 LIB — 1985 CONS		
Economic	66%	—	32%	54%	—	46%
Social	49%	—	51%	36%	—	60%
Foreign	56%	—	43%	57%	—	42%

Key Votes

1) Lmt Cln Water Act	AGN	5) Retain Gun Cont	AGN	9) Aid Angola Reb	FOR
2) Rpl Tobac Sub	AGN	6) Contra Aid	AGN	10) Tax Reform	FOR
3) Grm-Rdmn Def Red	FOR	7) Lmt Text Imp	FOR	11) S Africa Sanc	FOR
4) Ban Polygraph	FOR	8) Limit SDI	FOR	12) Immig Reform	AGN

Election Results

1986 general	Gus Yatron (D)	98,142	(69%)	($97,114)
	Norm Bertasavage (R)	43,858	(31%)	($18,211)
1986 primary	Gus Yatron (D)	27,249	(100%)	
1984 general	Gus Yatron (D)	181,165	(100%)	($66,824)

Campaign Contributions and Expenditures

1985-86		Direct Cont. 1985-86		PACS Breakdown 1985-86			
Receipts	$128,397	Indiv.	$35,066	Corp.	$12,250	T/M/H	$24,900
Expend.	$97,114	Party	$162	Labor	$35,350	Agr.	$250
Unspent	$111,244	PACS	$84,000	Ideo.	$10,750	CWOS	$500

SEVENTH DISTRICT

Delaware County, just outside Philadelphia, was once one of the most distinctive of American political constituencies, the home of one of the premier Republican political machines in the country. This was the old Delaware War Board, which still has some say in local elections here. The county itself is suburban, of course, but not uniformly affluent. You might not notice the difference if you drove over Cobbs or Darby Creeks, which separate the county from Philadelphia: the mostly white working-class neighborhood in Philadelphia looks a lot like the modest, long-settled close-in suburbs nearby, in Upper Darby Township and a dozen or so small incorporated boroughs. They are all, increasingly, the homes of older people whose families are grown, who still treasure traditional cultural values but also felt pinched during the recession and worried about how they would fare in retirement. Farther out, the houses spread out, and real estate values rise, in leafy suburbs like Swarthmore; these also are old, but the people are more secure and less anxious. To the north are some of the suburbs of the Main Line—the highest income and highest status communities in the Philadelphia area. Given the fact that many of the suburbs are inhabited by people who grew up in the closely packed neighborhoods of West and South Philadelphia, you might expect most of these to be Democratic suburbs.

Politically, the War Board is one of the last of the Republican machines which dominated so much of the middle-class American North in the 1920s, when Republicanism was the norm from which few decent-minded Protestant voters in such neighborhoods deviated, and political machines were as much a part of the urban landscape as trolley lines or overhead electrical wires. Philadelphia, after all, kept electing machine Republican mayors until 1951 and the War Board provided stable and reliable, if undistinguished and dull, local government and representation in Washington and Harrisburg. And if that era seems long gone, it may have returned: the entire Philadelphia metropolitan area, its economy reviving, gave majorities to Ronald Reagan in 1980 and 1984.

The one major exception to this organization's success has been in elections in the 7th Congressional District, which contains most of Delaware County plus one ward of Philadelphia. The 7th District was captured in 1974 by Bob Edgar, a Methodist minister from a working-class background and an opponent of the Vietnam war and Richard Nixon; whereupon Edgar compiled an almost unfailing liberal record, outraged colleagues in the Pennsylvania delegation and elsewhere by leading fights to defund pork barrel projects, and surprised everyone (probably including himself) by winning reelection five times, always by narrow margins. In 1986 he ran for the Senate, won the Democratic primary narrowly, but lost the general election to Arlen

Specter by a solid margin.

In the meantime the 7th District reverted to type by electing Representative Curt Weldon, a Republican supported by the War Board. Weldon is a former teacher and served five years as mayor of the borough of Marcus Hook, site of a big steel mill and oil tank farms on the Delaware River; he has genuine roots in the modest communities here. He showed less than great political acumen in 1984 when he declined to run TV ads, ending his campaign with a surplus in the treasury but a 412-vote deficit at the ballot box. This time he had no opposition in the Republican primary, while the Democrats had a battle between former Delaware County Commissioner Bill Spingler and former Gary Hart campaign aide David Landau. Spingler won that race narrowly but was wiped out by Weldon in November. In the House Weldon is a member of the Armed Services and Merchant Marine Committees—bread and butter assignment for a member many of whose constituents work in the Philadelphia Navy Yard or on the docks.

The People: Pop. 1980: 515,766, dn. 8.3% 1970–80. Households (1980): 75% family, 36% with children, 62% married couples; 26.3% housing units rented; median monthly rent: $233; median house value: $45,600. Voting age pop. (1980): 387,309; 5% Black, 1% Asian origin, 1% Spanish origin.

1984 Presidential Vote:

Reagan (R)	155,576	(62%)
Mondale (D)	94,017	(37%)

Rep. Curt Weldon (R)

Elected 1986; b. July 22, 1947, Marcus Hook; home, Aston; West Chester State Col., B.A. 1969; Protestant; married (Mary).

Career: Teacher, Vice Principal, 1969–76; Dir. Training and Manpower Dev., INA Corp., 1976–81; Mayor, Marcus Hook, 1977–82; Delaware Cnty. Cncl., 1984–86, Chmn. 1985–86.

Offices: 2352 RHOB 20515, 202-225-2011. Also 1554 Garrett Rd., Upper Darby 19082, 215-259-0700.

Committees: *Armed Services* (18th of 21 R). Subcommittees: Military Installations and Facilities; Military Personnel and Compensation; Seapower and Strategic and Critical Materials. *Merchant Marine and Fisheries* (14th of 17 R). Subcommittees: Coast Guard and Navigation; Fisheries, Wildlife Conservation and the Environment; Panama Canal and Outer Continental Shelf.

Group Ratings and Key Votes: Newly Elected

Election Results

1986 general	Curt Weldon (R)	110,118	(61%)	($617,063)
	Bill Spingler (D)	69,557	(39%)	($166,612)
1986 primary	Curt Weldon (R)	40,156	(100%)	
1984 general	Robert W. (Bob) Edgar (D)	124,458	(50%)	($625,252)
	Curt Weldon (R)	124,046	(50%)	($434,420)

Campaign Contributions and Expenditures

1985-86		Direct Cont. 1985-86		PACS Breakdown 1985-86			
Receipts	$641,985	Indiv.	$419,505	Corp.	$76,058	T/M/H	$56,607
Expend.	$617,063	Party	$15,775	Labor	$11,910	Agr.	$1,000
Unspent	$54,187	PACS	$178,526	Ideo.	$26,251	CWOS	$6,700

EIGHTH DISTRICT

Bucks County is one of those place names that have entered our literary imagination. The northwestern or upper part of the county is rolling farmland, easily reached by train from New York as well as Philadelphia. It has long been the residence of well-known writers and artists, who live in stone Quaker farmhouses near such villages as New Hope and Lumberville. Their neighbors are sometimes Pennsylvania Dutch farmers, or more often, comfortably-off people with jobs somewhere closer to the Philadelphia area.

But this is not the whole story of Bucks County; Upper Bucks has only about half the county's population. Lower Bucks County is an entirely different place—predominantly industrial and blue-collar. Here is U.S. Steel's giant Fairless Works; here also is one of the original Levittowns. In the other suburban Philadelphia counties, most of the blue-collar immigration took place a long time ago, when Philadelphia itself was solidly Republican and the suburban county machines ready to enroll new residents in their party. But in Bucks the blue-collar migration came late, in the 1950s and 1960s, and there is a strong Democratic voting base around Levittown and Bristol in the lower county.

The 8th Congressional District of Pennsylvania includes all of Bucks County plus a small slice of Montgomery County directly north of Philadelphia's Center City. Historically, this is Republican territory, and Republicans carry it most of the time, as they did for example in 1960, when the then Bucks County Democratic chairman described the race in Report of the County Chairman. But in the late 1970s and throughout the 1980s the 8th District has been the scene of close congressional elections, all but one of them won by Democrat Peter Kostmayer.

Kostmayer's political formula has been to emphasize his liberal stands on environmental and foreign issues, to vote somewhat more conservatively on economic issues, and to work hard on constituency services. He was a product of the Democratic politics of the middle 1970s: a press aide to Governor Milton Shapp who in 1976, at age 30, won a seat in Congress with some help from national trends, Republican feuds, and hard campaigning. Vigorous opposition to corruption—he urged early investigations of Korea-gate and of his fellow Pennsylvania Democrats Daniel Flood and Joshua Eilberg—and emphasis on environmental issues (he helped kill the Tocks Island Dam on the Delaware) helped Kostmayer to solidify support in Upper Bucks; he easily won reelection in 1978. But in 1980 the district went Republican, in a year in which economic issues were the center of attention, and elected James Coyne. Coyne in turn stumbled when he showed a lack of feel for the political process, attacking Kostmayer for continuing to help 8th District residents with problems and flip-flopping in public view on the nuclear freeze. Kostmayer won a 50%-49% victory in 1982.

In his second stint in Congress, Kostmayer has been less likely to publicly attack his colleagues, perhaps because they're less deserving of it; three of the four members from neighboring Philadelphia at one point in the late 1970s were convicted of crimes. Kostmayer has worked hard to defeat the MX missile, and as a member of the Foreign Affairs Committee has taken a front-row position opposing aid to the Nicaraguan contras. But he has been flexible enough to invite House Armed Services Chairman Les Aspin, who took the opposite view on both issues, into the 8th District to persuade him to save the Naval Air Defense Command in Warminster, the second biggest employer in the district. Similarly, on environmental matters, instead of protecting lands in Alaska, he has worked with other Pennsylvanians to protect wilderness areas in the state and the Gettysburg National Military Park.

Moreover, representing a steel district, Kostmayer has been willing to back protectionist measures and has scurried to bring UDAG grants and federal development money into the district. All of these things helped him to beat Republican David Christian in 1984 and 1986. On paper Christian is the perfect challenger: a Vietnam war hero brought up in Lower Bucks. But Christian evidently lacked Kostmayer's suppleness and ease with the issues, could not match his energy and attention to local matters, and—interestingly, considering the national Republican

Party's fund-raising abilities—raised considerably less money. Even in 1984, when Ronald Reagan was carrying the district with 64% of the vote, Kostmayer won with 51% of the vote. In 1986, Kostmayer won with 55%. Kostmayer may not hold this seat forever. But he has held it a long time already, and anyone interested in why the Republicans have failed to win working majorities in the House in most of the Reagan years could do worse than look at the 8th District of Pennsylvania.

The People: Pop. 1980: 516,902, up 14.1% 1970–80. Households (1980): 80% family, 45% with children, 70% married couples; 25.9% housing units rented; median monthly rent: $255; median house value: $57,100. Voting age pop. (1980): 364,239; 2% Black, 1% Spanish origin, 1% Asian origin.

1984 Presidential Vote:	Reagan (R)	142,572	(64%)
	Mondale (D)	79,464	(36%)

Rep. Peter H. Kostmayer (D)

Elected 1982; b. Sept. 27, 1946, New York, NY; home, Solebury; Columbia U., B.A. 1971; Episcopalian; married (Pamela).

Career: Reporter, *The Trentonian,* 1971–72; Press Secy. to Atty. Gen. of PA, 1972–73; Dpty. Press Secy. to PA Gov. Milton Shapp, 1973–76; U.S. House of Reps., 1977–81; Pub. relations consultant, 1981–82.

Offices: 123 CHOB 20515, 202-225-4276. Also 100 S. Main St., Doylestown 18901, 215-345-8543; 1 Oxford Valley, Ste. 700, Langhorne 19047, 215-757-8181; and 515 S. West End Blvd., Quakertown 18951, 215-538-2222.

Committees: *Foreign Affairs* (13th of 27 D). Subcommittees: International Operations; Western Hemisphere Affairs. *Interior and Insular Affairs* (14th of 26 D). Subcommittees: Mining and Natural Resources; National Parks and Public Lands; Water and Power Resources. *Select Committee on Hunger* (7th of 16 D). Task Force: International Task Force.

Group Ratings

	ADA	ACLU	COPE	CFA	LCV	ACU	NTU	NSI	COC	CEI
1986	90	95	87	92	100	5	32	0	39	31
1985	90	—	85	83	—	19	40	—	36	—

National Journal Ratings

	1986 LIB — 1986 CONS			1985 LIB — 1985 CONS		
Economic	62%	—	35%	65%	—	33%
Social	89%	—	0%	85%	—	0%
Foreign	80%	—	0%	75%	—	21%

Key Votes

1) Lmt Cln Water Act	AGN	5) Retain Gun Cont	FOR	9) Aid Angola Reb	AGN
2) Rpl Tobac Sub	FOR	6) Contra Aid	AGN	10) Tax Reform	FOR
3) Grm-Rdmn Def Red	FOR	7) Lmt Text Imp	FOR	11) S Africa Sanc	FOR
4) Ban Polygraph	FOR	8) Limit SDI	FOR	12) Immig Reform	FOR

Election Results

1986 general	Peter H. Kostmayer (D)............... 85,731	(55%)	($682,526)
	David A. Christian (R)................ 70,047	(45%)	($353,180)
1986 primary	Peter H. Kostmayer (D)............... 26,861	(91%)	
	Beth Biancosino (D).................... 1,789	(6%)	
	Richard M. Barnes (D).................... 990	(3%)	
1984 general	Peter H. Kostmayer (D).............. 112,648	(51%)	($656,765)
	David A. Christian (R)............... 108,696	(49%)	($387,928)

Campaign Contributions and Expenditures

1985-86		Direct Cont. 1985-86		PACS Breakdown 1985-86			
Receipts	$693,578	Indiv.	$318,329	Corp.	$32,599	T/M/H	$47,347
Expend.	$682,526	Party	$5,000	Labor	$160,425	Agr.	$1,250
Unspent	$20,905	PACS	$338,850	Ideo.	$95,429	CWOS	$1,800
		Cand.	$31,000				

NINTH DISTRICT

The Appalachian mountain chain, running like a series of vertebrae through central Pennsylvania, has been a formidable barrier through most of Pennsylvania's history. Up close the mountains look tantalizingly low: you imagine that you could hike over them in an hour or so. Wrong. These mountains are much more formidable than they seem. The colonials and British regulars led by General Braddock to his defeat near Pittsburgh in 1754 found it hard going, despite their guidance from George Washington; Scotch-Irish settlers and 19th century pioneers in Conestoga wagons found it not much easier, for there are few gaps in the ridges and unless you can build a tunnel you have to climb over the top. During the 18th century, the mountains provided Quaker Pennsylvania with a rampart against Indian attacks, and allowed the commonwealth to become the richest and most populous of the colonies. But in the 19th century, when people wanted to open up and trade with the vast interior, the mountains stopped them, and they went over New York's Erie Canal and New York Central Railroad instead. It took the aggressive capitalists who built the Pennsylvania Railroad to get trains over these ridges, and a nation at war in the 1940s to build the first road, the Pennsylvania Turnpike, that could dependably get trucks over them. Today the old towns look much as they did 60 years ago, and the farmhouses and red barns still sit on rolling hills in the shadow of one or another of the ridges, isolated and out of touch with the pulsing rhythms of the America of the 1980s.

The 9th is the only one of Pennsylvania's congressional districts to lie wholly within these mountains. This part of the Alleghenies (the term is often used interchangeably with Appalachians in Pennsylvania) was first settled by poor Scottish and Ulster Irish farmers just after the Revolutionary War. They were a people of fierce independence and pride, as the Whiskey Rebellion demonstrated—corn was not an article of commerce out here unless distilled into easily portable alcohol. The settlers worked their hardscrabble farms and built their little towns. Sometimes coal was found nearby, and their communities changed. But for the most part the 9th is not really coal country, and the area was denied—or spared—the boom-bust cycles of northeastern Pennsylvania and West Virginia. This was an important area for the Pennsylvania Railroad, however. Near Altoona was the railroad's famous Horseshoe Curve, and in Altoona itself the railroad built the nation's largest car yards. As rail transportation became less important, and the Pennsylvania moved from prosperity to merger to bankruptcy, Altoona's population declined from 82,000 at the end of the 1920s to 57,000 in 1980.

This part of Pennsylvania has been solidly Republican since the election of 1860, and it has not come close to electing a Democrat to Congress for years. The current incumbent, E. G. (Bud) Shuster, is an entrepreneur who made a fortune building up a business and selling it to IBM. He decided to settle in the southern Pennsylvania mountains, became interested in local affairs, decided to run for Congress, and beat the favorite, a local state Senator, in the 1972 Republican primary. Shuster has won easily since.

He has had essentially two careers in the House. In the 1970s he was a hard-driving partisan, the House's most vociferous opponent of the air bag, and chairman of the Republican Policy Committee until the 1980 election. Then he ran for minority whip against Trent Lott and lost. Since then he has concentrated on his work on the Public Works Committee, working with Democrats including Chairman James Howard to raise the gasoline tax and build more highways. One of the most vocal sounders of conservative themes in the late 1970s, by the late 1980s his main work was getting the water and highway bills passed over President Reagan's veto. The largest single "demonstration project" by far was the $9 million project to close a gap in the U.S. 220 freeway between Altoona and the borough of Tyrone "for the purpose of demonstrating state of the art delineation technology." All of which is ironic in terms of 1980s politics, but makes more sense when you think in terms of the 1780s or 1880s: for the conquest of these Appalachian ridges by western civilization, now as then, depends critically on support and subsidy from government, and a congressman from these parts, unless perhaps he has a national leadership role, is not in any position to forget that.

The People: Pop. 1980: 515,430, up 8.5% 1970–80. Households (1980): 78% family, 41% with children, 67% married couples; 24.6% housing units rented; median monthly rent: $137; median house value: $32,600. Voting age pop. (1980): 368,331; 1% Black.

1984 Presidential Vote:

Reagan (R)	118,517	(66%)
Mondale (D)	59,149	(33%)

Rep. E. G. (Bud) Shuster (R)

Elected 1972; b. Jan. 23, 1932, Glassport; home, Everett; U. of Pittsburgh, B.S. 1954, Duquesne U., M.B.A. 1960, American U., Ph.D. 1967; United Church of Christ; married (Patricia).

Career: Army, 1954–56; Vice Pres., Radio Corp. of Amer.; Operator, Shuster Farms.

Offices: 2268 RHOB 20515, 202-225-2431. Also RD 2, Box 711, Altoona 16601, 814-946-1653, 179 E. Queen St., Chambersburg 17201, 717-264-8308.

Committees: *Public Works and Transportation* (2d of 20 R). Subcommittees: Aviation; Investigations and Oversight; Surface Transportation (Ranking Member). *Select Committee on Intelligence* (6th of 6 R). Subcommittees: Legislation; Oversight and Evaluation.

Group Ratings

	ADA	ACLU	COPE	CFA	LCV	ACU	NTU	NSI	COC	CEI
1986	5	0	16	8	11	90	58	100	94	61
1985	10	—	17	25	—	81	59	—	86	—

National Journal Ratings

	1986 LIB — 1986 CONS			1985 LIB — 1985 CONS		
Economic	30%	—	0%	20%	—	79%
Social	11%	—	85%	24%	—	72%
Foreign	0%	—	86%	0%	—	76%

Key Votes

1) Lmt Cln Water Act	AGN	5) Retain Gun Cont	AGN	9) Aid Angola Reb	FOR
2) Rpl Tobac Sub	FOR	6) Contra Aid	FOR	10) Tax Reform	AGN
3) Grm-Rdmn Def Red	FOR	7) Lmt Text Imp	FOR	11) S Africa Sanc	AGN
4) Ban Polygraph	AGN	8) Limit SDI	AGN	12) Immig Reform	AGN

Election Results

1986 general	E. G. (Bud) Shuster (R)	120,890	(100%)	($276,463)
1986 primary	E. G. (Bud) Shuster (R)	28,368	(100%)	
1984 general	E. G. (Bud) Shuster (R)	118,437	(67%)	($498,847)
	Nancy Kulp (D)	59,549	(33%)	($85,848)

Campaign Contributions and Expenditures

1985-86		Direct Cont. 1985-86		PACS Breakdown 1985-86			
Receipts	$299,910	Indiv.	$120,915	Corp.	$58,837	T/M/H	$67,517
Expend.	$276,463	Party	$2,214	Labor	$27,250	Agr.	$2,000
Unspent	$44,821	PACS	$160,710	Ideo.	$3,450	CWOS	$1,656
		Cand.	$20,000				

TENTH DISTRICT

Scranton is the largest city in Pennsylvania's anthracite country. Back around the turn of the century, anthracite or hard coal was much in demand: it was the fuel used to heat most homes, in furnaces or pot-bellied stoves. Because the only major deposits of anthracite in the United States lie in the Scranton/Wilkes-Barre region of northeastern Pennsylvania, these two cities suddenly came on flush times. Immigrants from Italy, Poland, Austria-Hungary, and Ireland poured in to join the Scots and Welsh already working the mines. Scranton became the third largest city in Pennsylvania, and the region around Scranton and Wilkes-Barre held more than 750,000 people by the end of the 1920s.

Then came the Depression of the 1930s. Scranton and the anthracite region never really recovered. As the economy began to grow again, especially after the war, Americans switched from coal to oil or gas furnaces. Demand for anthracite dropped precipitously, and the number of jobs in the mines, and in ancillary businesses, plummeted. In the 1960s and the 1970s there was an influx of textile and apparel mills, bringing low-wage jobs to what had once been a relatively high-wage area. But many people in this area seemed just to be waiting forlornly for the old boom days to return—and many others have simply left. Scranton, which held 143,000 people in 1930, had 87,000 in 1980; the population of all of Lackawanna County fell from 310,000 to 227,000 in the same period. Just a look at the edges of Scranton shows what happened. Out past the downtown, with its beautifully restored old solid buildings, stand large houses, maintained with care, and obviously built in the 1920s—the city's last prosperous decade. In the next you find no new suburban housing tract or shopping center, only trees and hills. In few parts of the country can you see such a sudden halt in urban development.

Scranton and Lackawanna County make up almost half of Pennsylvania's 10th Congressional District. The rest of it is made up of the kind of territory Scranton was before the anthracite boom: Scotch-Irish mountain counties in the Poconos (a favorite resort of many middle-class New Yorkers) and the northern tier of counties just below Upstate New York. The railroads on which Scranton was a major switching point and roundhouse stop plow through here, often on high viaducts, occasionally through tunnels. But they have few reasons to stop in these small towns and quiet hills. The politics of the 10th District can be easily summarized: Scranton is Democratic, the rest of the district Republican; Scranton has been contracting and the hinterland slowly growing, so the district has been getting more Republican. And Scranton may make up in political acumen what it has lacked in economic growth: both candidates for governor in 1986 had roots here, with Scranton and the 10th District going strongly for

Democrat William Casey over Republican Lieutenant Governor William Scranton.

The congressman from this district, Joseph McDade, is the senior member of the Pennsylvania delegation, a Republican who seems to have the natural knack for politics so often seen in his fellow Irish Catholics. McDade was first elected in 1962, when one-term Representative William Scranton, father of the 1986 candidate, was elected governor. McDade was identified then with the same progressive wing of the Republican Party as Scranton, and for many years voted about half the time with Democrats on economic and other issues; he got support often from labor unions, and his lowest percentage since 1964 was the 63% he got against Democrat Edward Mitchell in 1976.

In the House he is the second-ranking Republican on the Appropriations Committee, behind Massachusetts's Silvio Conte, and although his record is often considered liberal he is also a stalwart upholder of the rights of the minority party. As ranking Republican on the Interior Subcommittee until 1985, he tended to cooperate with chairman Sidney Yates, and was generally considered sympathetic to environmental arguments, although he always fought for the interests of coal.

In 1985 he became ranking Republican on the Defense Subcommittee. There some expected—or feared—that he would oppose Reagan Administration policies. In fact he seems to be making a conscientious effort to support them. But at the same time he does not conceal his lack of enthusiasm for many Pentagon spending increases and some weapons systems. In 1985 and early 1986, when New York's Joseph Addabbo chaired the subcommittee, McDade may have felt an obligation to represent Republican views in counterpoint to the dovish chairman. But with much more hawkish and nuts-and-bolts minded Bill Chappell of Florida succeeding to the chair after Addabbo's death, McDade may feel himself freer to take different stands. Or perhaps, as he has on other subcommittees, he will find it more congenial to work toward common ground with a Democratic chairman.

In the meantime, McDade is too sharp a politician to neglect the 10th District. Like the late Daniel Flood of the 11th District, with whom he often worked, McDade was not shy about shovelling federal money into the anthracite country or protecting the interests of coal. At the end of the 1986 session, for example, he popped into a bill national historic site designation for a collection of mostly mid-20th century Canadian locomotives in Steamtown USA near Scranton. Most voters in the 10th District seem to feel they would be foolish to get rid of him.

The People: Pop. 1980: 515,442, up 7.1% 1970–80. Households (1980): 76% family, 38% with children, 64% married couples; 28.4% housing units rented; median monthly rent: $140; median house value: $34,400. Voting age pop. (1980): 376,348.

1984 Presidential Vote:			
	Reagan (R)	123,789	(61%)
	Mondale (D)	76,046	(38%)

Rep. Joseph M. McDade (R)

Elected 1962; b. Sept. 29, 1931, Scranton; home, Clarks Summit; U. of Notre Dame, B.A. 1953, U. of PA, LL.B. 1956; Roman Catholic; married (Mary).

Career: Clerk to Chf. Fed. Judge John W. Murphy, 1956–57; Practicing atty., 1957–62; Scranton City Solicitor, 1962.

Offices: 2370 RHOB 20515, 202-225-3731. Also 514 Scranton Life Bldg., Scranton 18503, 717-346-3834.

Committees: *Appropriations* (2d of 22 R). Subcommittees: Defense (Ranking Member); Interior. *Small Business* (Ranking Member of 17 R). Subcommittee: SBA and the General Economy (Ranking Member).

Group Ratings

	ADA	ACLU	COPE	CFA	LCV	ACU	NTU	NSI	COC	CEI
1986	45	18	68	67	43	63	25	80	35	28
1985	20	—	67	92	—	57	36	—	38	—

National Journal Ratings

	1986 LIB — 1986 CONS		1985 LIB — 1985 CONS	
Economic	73%	26%	20%	79%
Social	52%	48%	24%	72%
Foreign	38%	61%	0%	76%

Key Votes

1) Lmt Cln Water Act	FOR	5) Retain Gun Cont	AGN	9) Aid Angola Reb	FOR
2) Rpl Tobac Sub	FOR	6) Contra Aid	FOR	10) Tax Reform	FOR
3) Grm-Rdmn Def Red	FOR	7) Lmt Text Imp	FOR	11) S Africa Sanc	—
4) Ban Polygraph	FOR	8) Limit SDI	AGN	12) Immig Reform	FOR

Election Results

1986 general	Joseph M. McDade (R)	118,603	(75%)	($291,757)
	Robert C. Bolus (D)	40,248	(25%)	($10,195)
1986 primary	Joseph M. McDade (R)	30,632	(100%)	
1984 general	Joseph M. McDade (R)	150,166	(77%)	($146,337)
	Gene Basalyga (D)	44,571	(23%)	

Campaign Contributions and Expenditures

1985-86		Direct Cont. 1985-86		PACS Breakdown 1985-86			
Receipts	$394,141	Indiv.	$154,215	Corp.	$116,375	T/M/H	$53,320
Expend.	$291,757	Party	$3,067	Labor	$33,500	Agr.	$4,500
Unspent	$313,730	PACS	$216,570	Ideo.	$8,375	CWOS	$500

ELEVENTH DISTRICT

Some of the richest seams of coal in the world run under the corrugated mountain ridges of northeastern Pennsylvania drained by the Susquehanna River. This was the great anthracite coal region where, in the valley where Revolutionary-era pioneers established Wilkes-Barre (named after two Englishmen who supported their cause), thousands of immigrants came in the late 19th century, attracted by the high wages they were paid to scrape out the coal needed to heat the houses and smudge the skies of New York and Boston and Philadelphia. The high point of this industry came just before the crash of 1929, when there were almost half a million people in Wilkes-Barre and the coal towns in the rest of Luzerne County. The anthracite country has never totally recovered. Prosperity returned briefly in World War II, but in the years after homes switched from coal to oil and natural gas, the United Mine Workers cooperated with the phaseout of mining jobs, and the anthracite country languished. Population has declined (Luzerne County had 343,000 people in 1980), as young people have left to make their livings elsewhere; new industries that have come in, textile and apparel, pay low wages. In places like the town of Centralia, the only reminder of the boom days is the smoke seeping out of underground mine fires which have been burning for years and will burn for years more; the state has moved in to buy up the houses, and the town has had to be abandoned.

This is the land of Pennsylvania's 11th Congressional District, which includes all of Luzerne County and similar territory to the east and west. The miners have been a Democratic voting bloc since the 1930s, but there were also a lot of Republicans here, people in white-collar occupations and ancestral Pennsylvania Republicans of all walks of life. For more than 30 years the district was represented by Daniel Flood, a mustachioed Democrat who from his perch on the Appropriations Committee brought in millions of federal dollars to the anthracite country. But in 1978 he was charged with wrongly accepting money, was stripped of his subcommittee chairmanship, and resigned. Since then the 11th District has had a series of bizarre elections and no less than four different congressmen.

The first was Democratic legislator Ray Musto, who won the April 1980 special election to fill the rest of Flood's term and probably expected to stay in Congress the rest of his life. But he lost in the November 1980 landslide to Republican James Nelligan. Nelligan in turn lost the 1982 election to Democrat Frank Harrison. Harrison, in his turn, was beaten 47%–43% in the 1984 primary by Paul Kanjorski after Harrison was caught travelling in Central America while Wilkes-Barre area residents had to boil their tap water because it was contaminated. This succession, curiously, exactly matches the order of finish in the 1980 special election: Musto (with 27%), Nelligan (23%), Harrison (17%), Kanjorski (16%).

The 1986 election was the most bizarre of all. The Republican candidate was Marc Holtzman, 25-year-old son of a Wilkes-Barre jewelry manufacturer. At 16 Holtzman wrote a fan letter to candidate Ronald Reagan, who was soon chartering the family company's airplane and Marc would tag along. During the 1980 campaign shared an apartment with Edwin Meese, William Casey, and Drew Lewis. After the election he headed Lewis Lehrman's Citizens For America and started a "consulting" business that grossed $380,000 in 1984. In 1985 he began running for Congress in the 11th District, raising ultimately $1,353,000 from the likes of Cabinet members and White House staffers. "The textbook candidate," one Republican consultant called him, "you suggest that he do this, and he's already done it." Short, youthful-looking, with thick glasses, he was photographed smiling with Washington biggies and, back in Pennsylvania, emerging from a bathroom with his urine specimen.

The only problem is that Holtzman never gave 11th District voters much reason to vote for him. True, they had voted for Reagan in 1984, but not by a wide margin, and they wanted a congressman more to check Reagan than to support him reflexively. A much-publicized Holtzman trip to Taiwan to spotlight shoe imports fizzled when Reagan decided not to impose quotas on them. Holtzman's appearance and, more important, his résumé made him look like a mascot rather than a leader, and most voters would rather have a grown-up than a kid for their congressman. Kanjorski just plodded on, returning to the district and serving constituents and, for all of Holtzman's hoopla, raising enough money to spend an entirely respectable $713,000 himself. Outspent by more than 2 to 1, Kanjorski won 71% of the votes.

Kanjorski's victory was the first time an incumbent won in the 11th District since Flood was reelected in 1978. But having survived, Kanjorski will probably start to be routinely reelected as Flood was for so many years. The 11th District has probably had enough zany congressional politics for the time being.

The People: Pop. 1980: 515,729, up 2.7% 1970–80. Households (1980): 74% family, 34% with children, 61% married couples; 29.0% housing units rented; median monthly rent: $136; median house value: $30,100. Voting age pop. (1980): 388,822; 1% Black.

1984 Presidential Vote:

Reagan (R) 107,374	(55%)
Mondale (D) 84,245	(44%)

Rep. Paul E. Kanjorski (D)

Elected 1984; b. April 2, 1937, Nanticoke; home, Nanticoke; Temple U., Dickinson U.; Roman Catholic; married (Nancy).

Career: Practicing atty., 1966–84; Nanticoke City Solicitor, 1969–81; Admin. Law Judge, 1972–80.

Offices: 1518 LHOB 20515, 202-225-6511. Also 10 E. South St., Wilkes-Barre 18701, 717-825-2200, 9th and Spruce Sts., Kulpmont 17834, 717-373-1541.

Committees: *Banking, Finance and Urban Affairs* (23d of 31 D). Subcommittees: Economic Stabilization; Financial Institutions Supervision, Regulation and Insurance; General Oversight and Investigations; Housing and Community Development. *Veterans' Affairs* (14th of 20 D). Subcommittee: Hospitals and Health Care.

Group Ratings

	ADA	ACLU	COPE	CFA	LCV	ACU	NTU	NSI	COC	CEI
1986	65	40	84	67	53	32	24	20	28	16
1985	55	—	76	83	—	19	40	—	32	—

National Journal Ratings

	1986 LIB — 1986 CONS	1985 LIB — 1985 CONS
Economic	87% — 0%	57% — 41%
Social	47% — 52%	36% — 60%
Foreign	57% — 41%	61% — 39%

Key Votes

1) Lmt Cln Water Act	AGN	5) Retain Gun Cont	AGN	9) Aid Angola Reb	FOR
2) Rpl Tobac Sub	FOR	6) Contra Aid	AGN	10) Tax Reform	FOR
3) Grm-Rdmn Def Red	AGN	7) Lmt Text Imp	FOR	11) S Africa Sanc	FOR
4) Ban Polygraph	FOR	8) Limit SDI	FOR	12) Immig Reform	FOR

Election Results

1986 general	Paul E. Kanjorski (D)................. 112,405	(71%)	($713,740)
	Marc Holtzman (R) 46,785	(29%)	($1,353,170)
1986 primary	Paul E. Kanjorski (D)................. 49,726	(94%)	
	Daniel Russell Fisher (D) 3,013	(6%)	
1984 general	Paul E. Kanjorski (D)................. 108,430	(59%)	($318,963)
	Robert P. Hudock (R)................. 76,692	(41%)	($13,721)

Campaign Contributions and Expenditures

1985-86		Direct Cont. 1985-86		PACS Breakdown 1985-86			
Receipts	$778,137	Indiv.	$263,810	Corp.	$53,509	T/M/H	$108,940
Expend.	$713,740	Party	$18,879	Labor	$195,300	Agr.	$11,250
Unspent	$72,470	PACS	$415,829	Ideo.	$37,683	CWOS	$9,147
		Cand.	$65,200				

TWELFTH DISTRICT

The hills of western Pennsylvania, eastern Ohio, and northern West Virginia, which encircle the Pittsburgh metropolitan area, form the largest industrial section of the country without a major city. The urban focus here is Pittsburgh, though it may be 100 miles away; the economy throughout is based largely on steel and coal. Once upon a time, up through the 1920s, this was one of the most Republican parts of America, and Republican policies—the high tariff, discouragement of labor unions—were thought to have contributed greatly to steel's growth. Now, in the middle 1980s, people in these parts seem to see the Democrats—with their support for unions, for trade restrictions, perhaps for industrial policy—as the only possible savior of steel; and the steel country has been one of the few parts of America to trend away from the Republicans during the 1980s.

Much of the easternmost part of Pennsylvania's steel country, north of West Virginia and east of Pittsburgh, forms Pennsylvania's 12th Congressional District. It consists of two distinct areas. The largest city in the first is Johnstown, a steel town known best for its disastrous flood; it had 67,000 people in 1920, 35,000 in 1980. This area was first settled by Scotch-Irish farmers when it was still the frontier in the 1790s; in the 19th century bituminous coal was discovered here, and immigrants from other parts of Europe were attracted to work the mines and the blast furnaces. The other part of the district, containing about half its population, is almost all of Westmoreland County, just east of Pittsburgh's Allegheny County. Technically, this is a suburban county, which means that many people commute to jobs in Allegheny. Nevertheless, Westmoreland is large—40 miles east to west—and full of separate little industrial communities established on their own long before Pittsburgh's influence reached out this far. Both parts of the district are Democratic in local and congressional elections, and somewhat less reliably in presidential contests. Both, in the politics of the 1980s, are liberal on economic and conservative on cultural and foreign issues.

This 12th District is represented by John Murtha, the undisputed power broker of the Pennsylvania and steel country delegations and a major power among House Democrats generally as well. Murtha is an old-fashioned Democrat, with no prejudice against supporting big-government programs but no abstract yearning to do so either; his decision will likely depend on how it will help areas like the 12th District or whether it is a quid that he can trade for someone else's quo. On foreign policy he is strongly hawkish, a supporter of major defense systems and of U.S. aid to the Nicaraguan contras. His rare floor speeches are mostly on foreign policy and sometimes fervent: he was a Marine veteran of the Korean era who reenlisted in his middle 30s to serve in Vietnam, and was the first Vietnam veteran to be elected to the House. His foreign policy views are important partly because he serves on the Defense Appropriations Subcommittee, and could easily become its chairman in a few years, but more because he is, on his own and without much publicity, a power in the House.

He does it the old-fashioned way, standing in the back of the House with his fellow Pennsylvanians, watching what's going on on the floor; or marching down the aisles and demanding that his fellow Democrats support the amendment he has slipped in that allows them to earn more outside income. He has "the rounded face of an aging altar boy and the instincts of an enforcer" says reporter David Rogers. "He can bully and plead, connive and cajole." Murtha was always a close friend and confident of Speaker Tip O'Neill, and showed his clout after the 1984 election when he managed the campaign of William Gray to become chairman of the House Budget Committee; not only did he help Gray line up Pennsylvanians, oldtime big-city pols, and southerners, but he got the Speaker himself to come out publicly for Gray. At the same time he was helping Pittsburgh's Bill Coyne beat Houston's Mike Andrews for a seat on the Ways and Means Committee—even though Majority Leader Jim Wright was backing Andrews. Was he sending a message to the Speaker-to-be that Jack Murtha was an independent power he'd always have to deal with? Wright must have thought so.

Murtha shuns publicity as almost no 1980s politican does, to the point of refusing to be interviewed by reporters writing a story on him; you will not find him at a fashionable gathering of any kind. He has one political disability that may increase his shyness: he was mentioned on some of the Abscam tapes and one prosecutor wanted to indict him, although the tape clearly shows him refusing any money. But Murtha depends on fellow members, not only national reports, to transmit his messages; his audience is the House Democratic Caucus, nothing wider, though he will work with Administration lobbyists from time to time; evidently he has enough pride in his own work not to need the praise of others.

As for the 12th District, he seems confident he can win reelection. He first won the district in a 1974 special election to replace a Republican who had died, and he has not had serious Republican competition since; this has become a safe district as the steel country has trended Democratic. His one problem came in 1982, when he was placed in the same district with likeminded Democrat Don Bailey, also a Vietnam veteran; Murtha won 52%-38%, mostly because he had represented most of the new district. His prospects are for continued reelection and continued power in the House.

The People: Pop. 1980: 515,915, up 4.7% 1970–80. Households (1980): 78% family, 40% with children, 68% married couples; 24.9% housing units rented; median monthly rent: $153; median house value: $38,400. Voting age pop. (1980): 374,878; 1% Black.

1984 Presidential Vote:

Reagan (R) 101,621	(50%)
Mondale (D) 98,424	(50%)

Rep. John P. Murtha (D)

Elected Feb. 5, 1974; b. June 17, 1932, New Martinsville, WV; home, Johnstown; U. of Pitt., B.A. 1962, Indiana U. of PA; Roman Catholic; (Joyce).

Career: USMC, Korea, Vietnam; Owner, Johnstown Minute Car Wash; PA House of Reps., 1969–74.

Offices: 2423 RHOB 20515, 202-225-2065. Also Vine and Walnut Sts., 2d Floor, Centre Town Mall, Johnstown 15907, 814-535-2642; P.O. Bldg., 201 N. Center St., Somerset 15501, 814-445-6041; and 206 N. Main St., Greenburg 15601, 412-832-3088.

Committees: *Appropriations* (12th of 35 D). Subcommittees: Defense; Interior; Legislative.

Group Ratings

	ADA	ACLU	COPE	CFA	LCV	ACU	NTU	NSI	COC	CEI
1986	40	42	84	58	33	52	14	90	25	9
1985	45	—	83	33	—	50	18	—	14	—

National Journal Ratings

	1986 LIB — 1986 CONS			1985 LIB — 1985 CONS		
Economic	62%	—	35%	81%	—	17%
Social	74%	—	26%	36%	—	60%
Foreign	34%	—	64%	34%	—	66%

Key Votes

1) Lmt Cln Water Act	AGN	5) Retain Gun Cont	AGN	9) Aid Angola Reb	FOR
2) Rpl Tobac Sub	AGN	6) Contra Aid	FOR	10) Tax Reform	FOR
3) Grm-Rdmn Def Red	AGN	7) Lmt Text Imp	FOR	11) S Africa Sanc	FOR
4) Ban Polygraph	FOR	8) Limit SDI	AGN	12) Immig Reform	FOR

Election Results

1986 general	John P. Murtha (D)	97,135	(67%)	($272,436)
	Kathy Holtzman (R)	46,937	(33%)	
1986 primary	John P. Murtha (D)	44,280	(81%)	
	Christopher G. Lewis (D)	10,412	(19%)	
1984 general	John P. Murtha (D)	134,384	(69%)	($194,111)
	Thomas J. Fullard III (R)	57,446	(30%)	($2,322)

Campaign Contributions and Expenditures

1985-86		Direct Cont. 1985-86		PACS Breakdown 1985-86			
Receipts	$371,308	Indiv.	$97,822	Corp.	$141,850	T/M/H	$40,750
Expend.	$272,436	Party	$352	Labor	$47,875	Agr.	$5,250
Unspent	$206,198	PACS	$247,583	Ideo.	$10,250	CWOS	$1,608

THIRTEENTH DISTRICT

The Main Line—it's been a synonym for lush, rich suburbia for most of the 20th century. The towns strung out along the Main Line of the old Pennsylvania Railroad today look better than ever, their vast comfortable houses are now coming back into fashion, and their huge overhanging trees are as verdant as ever. On the Main Line and behind it, in suburbs like Gladwynne back toward the Schuylkill River, live most of greater Philadelphia's richest and most influential people. The Main Line forms part, but only part, of the 13th Congressional District of Pennsylvania; in fact, the Main Line past Bryn Mawr is outside the district, in the 7th and 5th. This is nonetheless the highest income district in Pennsylvania and one of the most affluent in the nation. But it has its patches of variety.

Out past the Main Line, for example, you come to the old Schuylkill factory towns of Conshohocken and Norristown and then to the shopping mall and high-rise office center at King of Prussia, just short of Valley Forge. On the eastern side of the 13th District are some of Philadelphia's more Jewish suburbs, just north of the city. Farther out in Montgomery County are small towns surrounded now by subdivisions where many of the residents are still members of the old German sects which settled these rolling hills in the 18th century; among their members are Richard Schweiker who was the 13th's congressman for eight years before he was elected to the Senate in 1968 and then served as Secretary of Health and Human Services in the first Reagan term. The 13th also includes two wards in Philadelphia: the old Chestnut Hill neighborhood, a posh area with grass tennis courts, and funkier, more working-class Manayunk, perched on hills above the Schuylkill River.

The congressman from this district is Lawrence Coughlin, a Republican first elected in 1968, a Yale contemporary of George Bush and graduate of Harvard Business School, who with his ever-present bow-tie looks the picture of comfortable Main Line chic. Coughlin is the fifth-ranking Republican on the Appropriations Committee, a supporter of aid to cities and particularly to Philadelphia, an opponent from his seat on the Transportation Subcommittee of New York's Westway and of Tennessee's Clinch River breeder reactor; he played a key role in killing both of these multi-billion dollar projects. Coughlin has also been a lead sponsor of amendments to prohibit testing the anti-satellite weapons that are connected with the Reagan Administration's Strategic Defense Initiative, so long as the Russians don't test theirs. Yet on most other issues, Coughlin tends to go along with most of his fellow Republicans; he supports aid to the Nicaraguan contras, for example. Overall, Coughlin's voting record can be described as conservative on economic issues, mildly liberal on cultural and foreign issues—which probably matches opinion in the district pretty well.

Yet in what is ordinarily a solidly Republican district Coughlin came under serious challenge from Democrat Joseph Hoeffel in 1984 and 1986. A state legislator in his 30s, Hoeffel campaigned with a vigor and visibility that contrasted sharply with Coughlin's rather laid-back posture in the district in 1984. The challenger raised money from unions and nuclear freeze advocates; he targeted the Philadelphia precincts and his own suburban legislative district. Coughlin did not awake to the challenge till rather late in the game; but in this Republican district in a Republican year he won with 56% of the vote. Two years later Hoeffel was just as vigorous, but by this time Coughlin had been working the district hard, raising lots of money, and was vigorous too. In a less Republican year he nonetheless raised his percentage to 59%. It's possible that Coughlin will attract a serious challenge from Hoeffel or someone else in 1988. But more likely the 1986 result will deter serious opponents and Coughlin, having proved his strength, will go back to winning without much trouble.

The People: Pop. 1980: 514,346, dn. 2.9% 1970–80. Households (1980): 74% family, 34% with children, 62% married couples; 30.9% housing units rented; median monthly rent: $269; median house value: $58,000. Voting age pop. (1980): 392,167; 6% Black, 1% Asian origin, 1% Spanish origin.

1984 Presidential Vote:

Reagan (R)	146,396	(60%)
Mondale (D)	97,418	(40%)

Rep. Lawrence Coughlin (R)

Elected 1968; b. Apr. 11, 1929, Wilkes-Barre; home, Villanova; Yale U., A.B. 1950, Harvard U., M.B.A. 1954, Temple U., LL.B. 1958; Episcopalian; married (Susan).

Career: USMC, Korea; Practicing atty., 1958–69; PA House of Reps., 1965–67; PA Senate, 1967–69.

Offices: 2467 RHOB 20515, 202-225-6111. Also 2 Stony Creek Office Ctr., 151 W. Marshall St., Norristown 19401, 215-277-4040. 4390 Main St., Philadelphia 19127, 215-482-3672.

Committees: *Appropriations* (5th of 22 R). Subcommittees: District of Columbia (Ranking Member); HUD–Independent Agencies; Transportation (Ranking Member). *Select Committee on Narcotics Abuse and Control* (2d of 10 R).

Group Ratings

	ADA	ACLU	COPE	CFA	LCV	ACU	NTU	NSI	COC	CEI
1986	45	35	36	50	84	41	46	30	61	44
1985	50	—	34	67	—	43	55	—	57	—

National Journal Ratings

	1986 LIB — 1986 CONS		1985 LIB — 1985 CONS	
Economic	40% —	59%	41% —	58%
Social	61% —	37%	59% —	40%
Foreign	48% —	51%	53% —	46%

Key Votes

1) Lmt Cln Water Act	AGN	5) Retain Gun Cont	FOR	9) Aid Angola Reb	FOR
2) Rpl Tobac Sub	FOR	6) Contra Aid	FOR	10) Tax Reform	FOR
3) Grm-Rdmn Def Red	FOR	7) Lmt Text Imp	FOR	11) S Africa Sanc	FOR
4) Ban Polygraph	FOR	8) Limit SDI	FOR	12) Immig Reform	FOR

Election Results

1986 general	Lawrence Coughlin (R)	100,701	(59%)	($702,834)
	Joseph M. Hoeffel (D)	71,381	(41%)	($455,101)
1986 primary	Lawrence Coughlin (R)	29,275	(100%)	
1984 general	Lawrence Coughlin (R)	133,948	(56%)	($463,344)
	Joseph M. Hoeffel (D)	104,756	(44%)	($341,471)

Campaign Contributions and Expenditures

1985-86		Direct Cont. 1985-86		PACS Breakdown 1985-86			
Receipts	$705,258	Indiv.	$443,148	Corp.	$97,795	T/M/H	$70,341
Expend.	$702,834	Party	$13,504	Labor	$21,600	Agr.	$0
Unspent	$48,228	PACS	$217,036	Ideo.	$26,300	CWOS	$1,000

FOURTEENTH DISTRICT

Pittsburgh, the center of America's steel industry from the time Andrew Carnegie built his first furnace, was a strategic site long before that: it was toward Fort Duquesne, where the Allegheny and Monongahela rivers join to form the Ohio, that Braddock's army was headed (with George Washington helping to lead the way) when it was ambushed and defeated in 1754. Not so many years later, trees were felled and a city was carved out of the wilderness here and named after the English statesman Pitt—the first urban center in the American interior. Pittsburgh grew rapidly in those days when most of the nation's commerce moved over water; when traffic switched to railroads, Pittsburgh also did nicely, since they had to run at riverside rather than scale the mountains. Soon Pittsburgh became the leading producer of one commodity the railroads needed, steel. With large deposits of coal nearby and ready access to iron ore from across the Great Lakes, Pittsburgh firmly established itself by 1890 as the nation's leading steel producer.

Today Pittsburgh wants to be known not as the steel city, but as a major white-collar center, a city most of whose jobs are in services, government, research and development; a city whose future is pegged not to a declining industry, but to rising businesses. There are signs that this is true. The Pittsburgh metropolitan area continues to have high unemployment; but in Allegheny County, which includes all of Pittsburgh and almost all its white-collar suburbs, unemployment in early 1987 was around 5%, well below the national average and not much above those of thriving New England states. For years Allegheny County's blue-collar boroughs have been exporting young people as the steel industry languished, while its white-collar areas have grown; now the central part of the metropolitan area almost seems to be a white-collar hole in a blue-collar donut.

Pittsburgh has always been a major headquarters city, and is today, with USX (formerly U.S. Steel), Rockwell International, Westinghouse, Alcoa, PPG, Heinz, and the Mellon Bank, the nation's 11th largest (but no longer, to Pittsburgh's sorrow, is Gulf Oil here: it was bought by Chevron, headquartered in San Francisco). It is a major research center for Westinghouse and other companies. It has good air service, now that it has become the main hub for USAir. It is even, people are discovering, a pleasant place to live: in 1985 Rand McNally even named it the best place to live in the country. The air pollution which plagued it was cured in the 1950s, long before most of the steel mills went cold. The hilly terrain—not just punctuated by hills like cities in California but so continuously hilly that it's hard to find a level city block—may have been a drawback in the days of stick shifts and streetcars, but to some it now seems charming. At the same time, Pittsburgh's slower economic development has meant that traditional family patterns, and the attitudes which accompany them, remain more entrenched here, among the rather old population with its large number of housewives and low number of divorcees, than in most other metropolitan areas; and for many Americans in the late 1980s that is an attraction too. All of which is not to say that Pittsburgh now has booming growth. But it may have turned a corner.

The 14th Congressional District of Pennsylvania includes all of the city of Pittsburgh plus a few adjacent suburbs. It takes in most of the Pittsburgh area's landmarks: the Golden Triangle; the University of Pittsburgh and its skyscraper campus; Carnegie–Mellon University, a center of artifical intelligence research. Not that many of the Pittsburgh area's steel mills lay in the 14th, but some present and former steelworkers do live here, mostly in ethnic neighborhoods nestled in the Pittsburgh hills. But the 14th also includes some of the metropolitan area's higher income areas, at a time when they seem to have new vitality: Shadyside, with newly renovated shops near some of Pittsburgh's old mansions, and the predominantly Jewish Squirrel Hill. neighborhood. About 24% of Pittsburgh's residents are black, a smaller figure than in most industrial cities because employment opportunities here peaked before the big wave of black migration from the South. Before the 1930s, in the heyday of Henry Clay Frick and Andrew Mellon, Pittsburgh was a solidly Republican town. Since the New Deal the 14th District has been solidly Democratic, in every election. In 1984 it was, aside from mostly black districts, one of the strongest Mondale districts in the country.

The congressman from the 14th District, first elected in 1980, is William Coyne. With a background in local politics, he is one of those Catholic bachelors who seem to have a quiet knack for the business. He was an ally of Pittsburgh Mayor Richard Caliguiri on the City Council, and demonstrated a strong base by beating the son of his predecessor, William Moorhead, in the 1980 Democratic primary by a 65%–35% margin. In Washington Coyne has made a record in line with those of representatives of safe Democratic districts in other states, and he seems to be well respected and well liked by other Democrats. After the 1984 election, in a campaign managed by the 12th District's Jack Murtha, he won a seat on the Ways and Means Committee, just in time to look after the needs of the steel industry. But if Pittsburgh continues to grow economically, Coyne will have room to expand his concerns. He is reelected without difficulty.

The People: Pop. 1980: 516,629, dn. 17.6% 1970–80. Households (1980): 63% family, 28% with children, 45% married couples; 47.7% housing units rented; median monthly rent: $174; median house value: $32,500. Voting age pop. (1980): 405,532; 19% Black, 1% Spanish origin, 1% Asian origin.

1984 Presidential Vote:

Mondale (D)	157,625	(68%)
Reagan (R)	69,649	(30%)

Rep. William J. Coyne (D)

Elected 1980; b. Aug. 24, 1936, Pittsburgh; home, Pittsburgh; Robert Morris Col., B.S. 1965; Roman Catholic; single.

Career: Army, Korea; Corporate accountant; PA House of Reps., 1970–72; Pittsburgh City Cncl., 1974–80.

Offices: 424 CHOB 20515, 202-225-2301. Also 2009 Fed. Bldg., 1000 Liberty Ave., Pittsburgh 15222, 412-644-2870.

Committees: *Ways and Means* (20th of 23 D). Subcommittees: Health; Select Revenue Measures.

Group Ratings

	ADA	ACLU	COPE	CFA	LCV	ACU	NTU	NSI	COC	CEI
1986	100	90	95	92	58	0	23	0	22	11
1985	95	—	94	83	—	0	28	—	19	—

National Journal Ratings

	1986 LIB — 1986 CONS	1985 LIB — 1985 CONS
Economic	87% — 0%	89% — 0%
Social	89% — 0%	63% — 33%
Foreign	80% — 0%	85% — 8%

Key Votes

1) Lmt Cln Water Act	AGN	5) Retain Gun Cont	FOR	9) Aid Angola Reb	AGN
2) Rpl Tobac Sub	FOR	6) Contra Aid	AGN	10) Tax Reform	FOR
3) Grm-Rdmn Def Red	AGN	7) Lmt Text Imp	FOR	11) S Africa Sanc	FOR
4) Ban Polygraph	FOR	8) Limit SDI	FOR	12) Immig Reform	FOR

Election Results

1986 general	William J. Coyne (D)	104,726	(90%)	($60,903)
	Richard E. Caligiuri (Libert.).............	6,058	(5%)	
	Mark Weddleton (SW)...................	3,120	(3%)	
	Two others...........................	2,955	(2%)	
1986 primary	William J. Coyne (D)	56,581	(86%)	
	Gary T. Forest (D)	9,429	(14%)	
1984 general	William J. Coyne (D)	163,818	(77%)	($56,263)
	John R. Clark (R)......................	42,616	(20%)	

Campaign Contributions and Expenditures

1985-86		Direct Cont. 1985-86		PACS Breakdown 1985-86			
Receipts	$110,445	Indiv.	$7,970	Corp.	$23,483	T/M/H	$34,300
Expend.	$60,903	Party	$272	Labor	$30,275	Agr.	$0
Unspent	$103,535	PACS	$97,158	Ideo.	$6,250	CWOS	$2,850

FIFTEENTH DISTRICT

Tucked in among the rolling hills of eastern Pennsylvania, little known to the rest of America, is Lehigh Valley, long one of America's heaviest industrial areas, now apparently on its way to becoming something else. Much of the Valley was settled by Pennsylvania Dutch, notably the Moravian sect who founded Bethlehem in 1741 (they are the same people who started the Salem in Winston-Salem, North Carolina); a farm area in the early 1800s, its dependable labor force and its location on a river emptying into the Delaware made it a natural location for early industries. As recently as the early 1980s, the Lehigh Valley was known for producing some of America's best-known products: Easton produced Crayola crayons and Dixie cups, Allentown was the home of the Mack Truck factory, and Bethlehem was the home base of the number two steelmaker, Bethlehem Steel. By early 1987, the Valley was still producing crayons and cups, but Mack Truck had moved one plant to Winnsboro, South Carolina, and was threatening to move another out when UAW headquarters in Detroit refused to approve concessions agreed to by the Mack Truck local, and Bethlehem's furnaces were mostly cold and the company tottering on the brink of bankruptcy.

Yet the Lehigh Valley does not seem to be sinking into permanent decrepitude. It retains important appliance factories, cement operations, and a big AT&T facility in Allentown. The completion of Interstate 78 across New Jersey means that the Lehigh Valley is just 1½ hours straight west from New York City. Its lower cost of living is attracting new residents, and its low wage costs have inspired insurance companies to move some of their office jobs here. New office buildings and shopping centers are springing up. Together with a small portion of an adjacent rural county, the Lehigh Valley forms Pennsylvania's 15th Congressional District. It is a seat which was Democratic for five decades until the late 1970s, but now seems to be safe Republican territory.

That political change and the evident economic growth here are both vindications of the political views of the 15th District's unusual congressman, Republican Don Ritter. He is unusual for the Congress because he is an engineer, and he spent a year in the Soviet Union and speaks Russian. He is unusual for Pennsylvania industrial districts because he is a devotee of free-market economics, with little interest in wooing union leaders or suburban liberals. He is unusual among market-oriented conservative Republicans, because he seems to have a flair for politics which has translated consistently into winning margins in this district. Ritter does fall away from the free-market crowd on trade issues. But otherwise he has preached the gospel that free enterprise will provide jobs and economic growth better than government can, and he and his constituents have seen it happen, evidently, in the Lehigh Valley.

Ritter serves on the Energy and Commerce Committee, perhaps the single most important committee when it comes to government regulation of business. In general, he supports deregulation and relaxation of rigid government regulations, as on clean air. He is on the Science, Space and Technology Committee and is ranking Republican on the Investigations and Oversight Subcommittee. His record on cultural and foreign issues, as well as economics, is solidly conservative. He is an especially strong—and well-informed—critic of Soviet internal repression. He is one of the few House members who by early 1987 endorsed Jack Kemp for President.

Ritter has perhaps been fortunate in his opposition. He won the seat in 1978 by upsetting Democrat Fred Rooney, who had not been spending much time in the district; Ritter's family still lives there, and he returns every weekend. In 1980 Ritter beat 65-year-old state Senator Jeanette Reibman; in 1982 his Democratic opponent spent all of $81,000 while Ritter, who as an Energy and Commerce member can raise much money, spent $339,000; in 1984 his highly touted opponent, Jane Wells-Schooley had as her main credential the former vice presidency of NOW, not an asset in a district which has seen its belief in traditional cultural values vindicated by the results of the liberations of the 1970s. In 1986 Ritter beat Democrat Joseph Simonetta 57%–43%. That was, marginally, the closest result here in the 1980s, but that probably indicates that only a very strong Democratic candidate, and one in better sync with the economic and cultural trends in the district, can give Ritter a serious challenge.

The People: Pop. 1980: 515,259, up 7.7% 1970–80. Households (1980): 75% family, 37% with children, 64% married couples; 28.8% housing units rented; median monthly rent: $189; median house value: $44,600. Voting age pop. (1980): 385,814; 2% Spanish origin, 1% Black.

1984 Presidential Vote: Reagan (R) 110,142   (57%)
                              Mondale (D) 81,072   (42%)

Rep. Donald L. (Don) Ritter (R)

Elected 1978; b. Oct. 21, 1940, New York, NY; home, Coopersburg; Lehigh U., B.S. 1961, M.I.T., M.S. 1963, Sc.D. 1966; Unitarian; married (Edith).

Career: Scientific Exchange Fellow, Moscow, USSR, 1967–68; Asst. Prof., CA St. Poly. U., 1968–69; Prof. and Asst. to Vice Pres. for Research, Lehigh U., 1969–76; Mgr., Research Develop. Program, Lehigh U., 1976–79.

Offices: 2447 RHOB 20515, 202-225-6411. Also 2 Bethlehem Plaza, Ste. 300, Bethlehem 18018, 215-866-0916; 1444 Hamilton St., Hotel Traylor, Ste. 206, Allentown 18102, 215-439-8861; and Alpha Bldg., Rm. 705, Easton 18042, 215-258-8383.

Committees: *Energy and Commerce* (8th of 17 R). Subcommittees: Commerce, Consumer Protection and Competitiveness; Telecommunications and Finance. *Science, Space and Technology* (7th of 18 R). Subcommittees: Investigations and Oversight (Ranking Member); Science, Research and Technology.

Group Ratings

	ADA	ACLU	COPE	CFA	LCV	ACU	NTU	NSI	COC	CEI
1986	15	10	34	25	49	90	54	100	94	64
1985	10	—	31	33	—	86	62	—	82	—

National Journal Ratings

	1986 LIB — 1986 CONS		1985 LIB — 1985 CONS	
Economic	25%	— 75%	23%	— 76%
Social	18%	— 78%	0%	— 76%
Foreign	21%	— 77%	0%	— 76%

Key Votes

1) Lmt Cln Water Act	FOR	5) Retain Gun Cont	AGN	9) Aid Angola Reb	FOR
2) Rpl Tobac Sub	FOR	6) Contra Aid	FOR	10) Tax Reform	FOR
3) Grm-Rdmn Def Red	FOR	7) Lmt Text Imp	FOR	11) S Africa Sanc	AGN
4) Ban Polygraph	FOR	8) Limit SDI	AGN	12) Immig Reform	AGN

Election Results

1986 general	Donald L. (Don) Ritter (R)	74,829	(57%)	($440,370)
	Joe Simonetta (D).....................	56,972	(43%)	($51,639)
1986 primary	Donald L. (Don) Ritter (R)	13,485	(100%)	
1984 general	Donald L. (Don) Ritter (R)	110,338	(58%)	($535,059)
	Jane Wells-Schooley (D)................	79,490	(42%)	($482,892)

Campaign Contributions and Expenditures

1985-86		Direct Cont. 1985-86		PACS Breakdown 1985-86			
Receipts	$439,700	Indiv.	$241,654	Corp.	$102,090	T/M/H	$71,625
Expend.	$440,370	PACS	$190,115	Labor	$9,500	Agr.	$500
Unspent	$35,501			Ideo.	$4,108	CWOS	$2,292

SIXTEENTH DISTRICT

Amish families clad in black, clattering over the back roads in horse-drawn carriages, scrupulously tended farms set amid rolling hills, barns decorated with hex signs: this is what millions of Americans know about the Pennsylvania Dutch country. Fewer people know that the Pennsylvania Dutch are actually German in origin ("Dutch" comes from Deutsch), descended from members of Amish, Mennonite, and other pietistic sects who left the principalities of 18th-century Germany for the religious freedom of the Quaker-dominated colony of Pennsylvania. The Quakers were happy to welcome the Germans, but not so eager to have them in Philadelphia. So they were sent to Germantown, a few miles away, until they could move out to what was then the frontier, where they could protect the pacifist Quakers against the Indians. Thus the Dutch came to the rolling green hills of the part of Pennsylvania centered on Lancaster County. The land was naturally fertile, and careful cultivation by the Dutch increased its productivity. Today the small farms in Lancaster County continue to produce some of the highest per-acre yields on earth.

There is no sign in the Pennsylvania Dutch country of the farm crisis you hear so much of on the Great Plains. Farms here are small, equipment simple, chemical fertilizer use very limited, cultivation intensive, with all the children in the usually large Amish families pitching in. The commercial ethos of farming on the prairies and Great Plains has always been tempered here by communal values and family responsibility. In the Sun Belt and on the Great Plains Americans seek the reassurance of cultural continuity in the midst of the economic change inevitably produced by market capitalism. In the Pennsylvania Dutch country cultural continuity is a fact and helps to sustain what other Americans might regard as an unduly modest standard of living. Most of the Pennsylvania Dutch, it should be added, are not plain people. But the heritage is important: most people here are of German descent and have a strong work ethic. Small industries have settled in the Lancaster area because of the skills and work habits of the labor force, and agriculture continues to be important economically. The brick townhouses of Lancaster, like the frame farmhouses of the Amish, are sparkingly well kept and seem little different from what they must have looked like 50 years ago.

The Pennsylvania Dutch country has produced one President, James Buchanan, and housed another in his retirement, Dwight Eisenhower, who was himself of Pennsylvania Dutch descent. For most of Buchanan's career the politics of this area was Jeffersonian Democratic. But in the 1850s the Pennsylvania Dutch country, antagonistic to the spread of slavery, became Republican; Lancaster County, once represented by Buchanan, elected as its congressman Thaddeus Stevens, the driving force behind thorough-going Reconstruction of the South after the Civil War. Today Lancaster County returns 3 to 1 Republican margins—the largest of any similar-sized area in the East.

The 16th Congressional District of Pennsylvania includes almost all of Lancaster County, mostly Dutch Lebanon County to the north and part of Chester County to the east. Of all eastern congressional districts, it consistently casts the highest Republican percentages in presidential elections. For years the Pennsylvania Dutch area was represented by Republican congressmen who were as languid in their demeanor as they were conservative on substantive issues.

The current incumbent, Robert Walker, is different. He is fully as conservative as any Republican—and eager to proclaim himself so. He is one of the leaders of the group of young Republicans who took advantage of the "special orders" procedure, which allows speechmaking after the legislative business of the day is completed, to present on the C-SPAN cable network—which broadcasts congressional proceedings—extensive denunciations of all things Democratic. Walker helped Newt Gingrich read into the record the paper documenting Democratic congressmen's congenital opposition to intervention abroad. Speaker Tip O'Neill was so enraged by this that he retaliated by ordering the C-SPAN cameras to show that the Republicans were speaking to an empty House during the special orders period. Walker was caught at the podium, gesturing at and asking rhetorical questions of an audience that was not there. O'Neill's act was within House rules (which give the Speaker complete control over the cameras), and Walker looked faintly ridiculous; but the Republicans have surely had the last laugh. They have found a forum in which to attract attention for their cases, substantive and procedural, against the Democrats, and they have goaded the majority into acting in an overbearing manner that suggests they are abridging the minority's rights.

Moreover, Walker and company have made their fellow Republicans much more likely—and eager—to challenge the Democrats, rather than to thank them meekly for the minor favors they grant from time to time. They've also irritated a lot of Republicans in the process, particularly the senior members used to long years of cooperation with their Democratic counterparts. But even those Republicans who consider Walker a blowhard and airhead have, to an extent they would be uncomfortable to admit, followed his lead. So have Minority Leader Robert Michel and Whip Trent Lott. Few people would have predicted such an influential career for Walker, who is gifted neither with the intellectual adverturousness of Gingrich or the oratorical virtuosity of Michel. He is, however, a hard worker, a plugger, a believer, and one whose views are thought through rather than reflexive: he was one of those conservatives, for example, who rather than defend South Africa in late 1984 and early 1985 instead organized a letter of protest to its government. He belongs to a group that also advocates a vast expansion of the space program, and as ranking Republican on the Space Subcommittee of Science, Space and Technology is in a good position to promote that goal.

Many of the young Republicans Walker has worked with have marginal or iffy districts, or ambitions for statewide office. Walker's seat is safe as safe can be, and no one has noted yet the glint of senatorial or gubernatorial ambition in his eye.

The People: Pop. 1980: 514,585, up 12.9% 1970–80. Households (1980): 77% family, 41% with children, 67% married couples; 30.4% housing units rented; median monthly rent: $179; median house value: $46,400. Voting age pop. (1980): 369,823; 2% Black, 2% Spanish origin.

1984 Presidential Vote:

Reagan (R) 137,697	(74%)
Mondale (D) 47,829	(26%)

Rep. Robert S. Walker (R)

Elected 1976; b. Dec. 23, 1942, Bradford; home, East Petersburg; Millersville St. Col., B.S. 1964, U. of DE, M.A. 1968; Presbyterian; married (Sue).

Career: Teacher, 1964–67; A. A. to U.S. Rep. Edwin D. Eshleman, 1967–77.

Offices: 2445 RHOB 20515, 202-225-2411. Also Lancaster Cnty. Crthse., 50 N. Duke St., Lancaster 17603, 717-393-0666; 307 Municipal Bldg., 400 S. 8th St., Lebanon 17402, 717-274-1641; and P.O. Box 69, Cochranville 19330, 215-593-2155.

Committees: *Government Operations* (2d of 16 R). Subcommittee: Legislation and National Security. *Science, Space and Technology* (2d of 17 R). Subcommittee: Space Science and Applications (Ranking Member); Transportation, Aviation and Materials.

Group Ratings

	ADA	ACLU	COPE	CFA	LCV	ACU	NTU	NSI	COC	CEI
1986	0	5	16	17	37	86	71	90	94	85
1985	15	—	17	33	—	86	74	—	91	—

National Journal Ratings

	1986 LIB — 1986 CONS		1985 LIB — 1985 CONS	
Economic	6% —	90%	9% —	88%
Social	11% —	85%	0% —	76%
Foreign	16% —	79%	24% —	66%

Key Votes

1) Lmt Cln Water Act	FOR	5) Retain Gun Cont	AGN	9) Aid Angola Reb	FOR
2) Rpl Tobac Sub	AGN	6) Contra Aid	FOR	10) Tax Reform	FOR
3) Grm-Rdmn Def Red	FOR	7) Lmt Text Imp	AGN	11) S Africa Sanc	FOR
4) Ban Polygraph	AGN	8) Limit SDI	AGN	12) Immig Reform	FOR

Election Results

1986 general	Robert S. Walker (R)................	100,784	(75%)	($75,730)
	James D. Hagelgans (D)...............	34,399	(25%)	
1986 primary	Robert S. Walker (R)................	26,902	(100%)	
1984 general	Robert S. Walker (R)................	138,477	(78%)	($55,373)
	Martin L. Bard (D).................	39,515	(22%)	($14,110)

Campaign Contributions and Expenditures

1985-86		Direct Cont. 1985-86		PACS Breakdown 1985-86			
Receipts	$79,700	Indiv.	$43,592	Corp.	$22,567	T/M/H	$8,550
Expend.	$75,730	Party	$3,864	Labor	$0	Agr.	$0
Unspent	$22,586	PACS	$32,611	Ideo.	$1,250	CWOS	$244
		Cand.	$623				

SEVENTEENTH DISTRICT

The Susquehanna is one of America's largest, and yet most obscure rivers—the longest river in the East, if you include the Chesapeake Bay, which is really the flooded lower Susquehanna valley. The Susquehanna is the one river strong enough to break through the mountain chains that run, like rugged corduroy, through central Pennsylvania. But few songs are written to celebrate the Susquehanna, it occupies nothing like the place of the Hudson or even the Schuylkill in our art, it has not given a name to a fever (Potomac), a school of painting (Hudson) or economics (Charles), or to a state (Ohio, Mississippi, Alabama, Missouri, Colorado).

The 17th Congressional District of Pennsylvania is a string of counties along the Susquehanna River, from Harrisburg in the south to Williamsport, up almost to the New York state border in the north. Cut diagonally by dozens of mountain ridges, the 17th includes several very different areas. About half its population is in and around the state capital of Harrisburg, an old city with a declining population and a large black community, not far upstream from the Three Mile Island nuclear plant. Several hours' drive north is Williamsport, a small manufacturing town that hosts the Little League World Series and has been the home for years of *Grit*, the world's largest family weekly newspaper. In the middle of the district, on the east shore of the Susquehanna, is Northumberland County, a one-time anthracite mining area. On the west shore are three counties reaching inland between the mountain chains, containing small manufacturing firms and such diverse institutions as Bucknell University and the cushiest of federal penitentiaries, Allenwood.

In most elections this is a solidly Republican district. Harrisburg seems to retain, from the 1860–1930 era of Republican dominance in Pennsylvania, a Republican preference that survives all ethnic and racial change; Williamsport is quintessential Republican country. Northumberland is sometimes Democratic, but the west shore counties are among the most Republican in the nation; two of the three went for Barry Goldwater in 1964. The district did elect a Democratic congressman, Allan Ertel, in 1976, 1978, and 1980; he went on to close defeats in the 1982 race for governor and 1984 race for attorney general.

The congressman now is George Gekas, former state Senator from Harrisburg who helped to design the district boundaries and, when Ertel ran for governor, won the primary with 60% and the general election with 58%. Gekas specialized in crime legislation as a member of the Pennsylvania legislature, and is proud of sponsoring the state's mandatory sentencing and child abuse laws. In the House he is ranking Republican on the Judiciary Subcommittee on Criminal

Justice, and although he often lacks the votes there to prevail he can often prevail on the floor. This is what happened on the insanity defense in the first Reagan term, and in the second term Gekas was heavily involved in the antidrug package, although he was disappointed when the Senate would not go along after he got the House to put the death penalty in the bill. His record on other cultural issues is mixed. His brand of politics seems very popular along the Susquehanna, and he has been reelected twice by overwhelming margins.

The People: Pop. 1980: 515,900, up 7.2% 1970–80. Households (1980): 74% family, 38% with children, 62% married couples; 31.4% housing units rented; median monthly rent: $164; median house value: $37,800. Voting age pop. (1980): 376,440; 6% Black, 1% Spanish origin.

1984 Presidential Vote:

Reagan (R)	123,660	(66%)
Mondale (D)	61,213	(33%)

Rep. George W. Gekas (R)

Elected 1982; b. April 14, 1930, Harrisburg; home, Harrisburg; Dickinson Col., B.A. 1952, Dickinson Law Sch., J.D. 1958; Greek Orthodox; married (Evangeline).

Career: Asst. Dist. Atty., Dauphin Cnty., 1960–66; PA House of Reps., 1967–75; PA Senate, 1977–83.

Offices: 1008 LHOB 20515, 202-225-4315. Also 1 Riverside Office Center, Ste. 301, 2101 N. Front St., Harrisburg 17110, 717-232-5123; Herman Schneebeli Fed. Bldg., P.O. Box 606, Williamsport 17703, 717-327-8161; and 25 N. Front St., Sunbury 17801, 717-286-6417.

Committees: *Judiciary* (8th of 14 R). Subcommittees: Crime; Criminal Justice (Ranking Member).

Group Ratings

	ADA	ACLU	COPE	CFA	LCV	ACU	NTU	NSI	COC	CEI
1986	10	15	21	42	21	73	53	100	83	56
1985	15	—	17	42	—	76	55	—	73	—

National Journal Ratings

	1986 LIB — 1986 CONS			1985 LIB — 1985 CONS		
Economic	39%	—	60%	29%	—	70%
Social	31%	—	67%	52%	—	47%
Foreign	16%	—	79%	24%	—	66%

Key Votes

1) Lmt Cln Water Act	AGN	5) Retain Gun Cont	AGN	9) Aid Angola Reb	FOR
2) Rpl Tobac Sub	FOR	6) Contra Aid	FOR	10) Tax Reform	AGN
3) Grm-Rdmn Def Red	FOR	7) Lmt Text Imp	AGN	11) S Africa Sanc	FOR
4) Ban Polygraph	FOR	8) Limit SDI	AGN	12) Immig Reform	AGN

Election Results

1986 general	George W. Gekas (R)	101,027	(74%)	($90,963)
	Michael S. Ogden (D)	36,157	(26%)	($3,335)
1986 primary	George W. Gekas (R)	28,669	(100%)	
1984 general	George W. Gekas (R)	129,716	(80%)	($138,512)
	Stephen A. Anderson (D)	31,770	(20%)	($5,714)

Campaign Contributions and Expenditures

1985-86		Direct Cont. 1985-86		PACS Breakdown 1985-86			
Receipts	$149,086	Indiv.	$87,582	Corp.	$17,284	T/M/H	$23,975
Expend.	$90,963	Party	$1,951	Labor	$1,700	Agr.	$500
Unspent	$108,171	PACS	$48,865	Ideo.	$5,250	CWOS	$156
		Cand.	$150				

EIGHTEENTH DISTRICT

Surrounding Pittsburgh like a thick but irregularly shaped doughnut with one bite taken out of it is the 18th Congressional District of Pennsylvania. The Republican legislature packed into this single seat just about all the strong Republican suburbs it could find, and connected them using as few Democratic areas as possible. So within the 18th you will find the residences of most of Pittsburgh's elite, in leafy, secluded suburbs like Fox Chapel and Sewickley. The district also includes solid high income, but not elite, suburbs like Mount Lebanon and Upper St. Clair Township, south of the Golden Triangle. But when you go down to the flood plain or over the next hill from these places, you run into much more modest suburban territory, from pleasant tract housing from the 1950s to gritty little factory towns built in a hurry 80 or 100 years ago.

This makes the 18th District a mixed bag politically—the most Republican constituency possible in metropolitan Pittsburgh, but still not Republican by any margin in most races. It elected John Heinz to Congress in 1972 and 1974, but when he ran for the Senate in 1976, the 18th elected Democrat Doug Walgren and has reelected him ever since. Walgren has had some good luck: he had a weak opponent in his first election and in the 1980 and 1984 presidential years.

Walgren is blessed with committee assignments which did not look interesting when he got them but do now. He has a seat on the Science, Space and Technology Committee and chairs a subcommittee on Science, Research and Technology at just the time when voters want more and better research—and nowhere more so than in the Pittsburgh area, where Walgren can argue that he has bills to spur steel technology, make Pittsburgh the nation's supercomputer center, invest in clean coal technology, and promote cogeneration from coal. He has pushed to give inventors more patent rights and to have Japanese technical literature translated. He also sits on the Energy and Commerce Committee—the most sought-after committee assignment in the 1980s, because it covers so much federal regulatory law. On this body he has been less active. Walgren is a bit out of place in the Pennsylvania delegation, a bit less liberal on economics and more so on non-economic issues than most of his colleagues; he voted for Gramm-Rudman, supported John Glenn in 1984 and was the only Pennsylvanian not to back the measure that allowed William Gray to win the Budget chairmanship.

Walgren's visibility on the technology issues increased greatly in the middle 1980's, just in time for the 1986 election, in which he faced a well-financed challenge from businessman Ernie Buckman. With this new record he could point to, and a voting record well-tailored to the most affluent part of the steel belt, Walgren won reelection with 63% of the vote and convinced skeptics he has a good hold on this seat.

The People: Pop. 1980: 516,050, dn. 0.8% 1970–80. Households (1980): 78% family, 38% with children, 68% married couples; 24.2% housing units rented; median monthly rent: $237; median house value: $57,300. Voting age pop. (1980): 382,408; 2% Black, 1% Asian origin.

1984 Presidential Vote:

Reagan (R)	144,507	(58%)
Mondale (D)	103,639	(41%)

Rep. Douglas (Doug) Walgren (D)

Elected 1976; b. Dec. 28, 1940, Rochester, NY; home, Mt. Lebanon; Dartmouth Col., B.A. 1963, Stanford U., LL.B. 1966; Roman Catholic; married (Carmala).

Career: Staff atty., Neighborhood Legal Services, 1967–68; Asst. Solicitor, Allegheny Cnty., 1967–69; Practicing atty., 1969–72; Corp. Counsel, Behavioral Research Lab., 1973–75.

Offices: 2441 RHOB 20515, 202-225-2135. Also 2117 Fed. Bldg., 1000 Liberty Ave., Pittsburgh 15222, 412-391-4016.

Committees: *Energy and Commerce* (8th of 25 D). Subcommittees: Energy and Power; Health and the Environment; Oversight and Investigations. *Science, Space and Technology* (5th of 27 D). Subcommittees: Energy Research and Development; Science, Research and Technology (Chairman).

Group Ratings

	ADA	ACLU	COPE	CFA	LCV	ACU	NTU	NSI	COC	CEI
1986	85	73	83	67	80	14	33	10	41	19
1985	70	—	83	50	—	10	37	—	29	—

National Journal Ratings

	1986 LIB — 1986 CONS		1985 LIB — 1985 CONS	
Economic	49%	— 50%	65%	— 33%
Social	67%	— 32%	72%	— 28%
Foreign	67%	— 30%	75%	— 21%

Key Votes

1) Lmt Cln Water Act	FOR	5) Retain Gun Cont	FOR	9) Aid Angola Reb	AGN
2) Rpl Tobac Sub	FOR	6) Contra Aid	AGN	10) Tax Reform	FOR
3) Grm-Rdmn Def Red	FOR	7) Lmt Text Imp	FOR	11) S Africa Sanc	FOR
4) Ban Polygraph	FOR	8) Limit SDI	FOR	12) Immig Reform	FOR

Election Results

1986 general	Douglas (Doug) Walgren (D)	104,164	(63%)	($557,031)
	Ernie Buckman (R)...................	61,164	(37%)	($983,798)
1986 primary	Douglas (Doug) Walgren (D)	40,314	(100%)	
1984 general	Douglas (Doug) Walgren (D)	149,628	(63%)	($193,540)
	John G. Maxwell (R)	87,521	(37%)	($6,923)

Campaign Contributions and Expenditures

1985-86		Direct Cont. 1985-86		PACS Breakdown 1985-86			
Receipts	$576,915	Indiv.	$190,915	Corp.	$61,200	T/M/H	$103,100
Expend.	$557,031	Party	$4,998	Labor	$144,070	Agr.	$2,350
Unspent	$51,795	PACS	$349,312	Ideo.	$35,667	CWOS	$2,925

NINETEENTH DISTRICT

The 19th Congressional District of Pennsylvania—Adams and York counties and half of Cumberland—sits at the western edge of the deeply conservative Pennsylvania Dutch country. This is a land of rolling green farmland extending up to the base of the Appalachian chains that rise at the district's western and northernmost boundaries. The most famous part of this district—Gettysburg, the tourist-thronged site of the Civil War's northernmost battle—is also the most sparsely populated, at least by permanent residents. Outside the town is the retirement home of President Eisenhower, who was of Pennsylvania Dutch stock himself; his father migrated in the late 19th century with a group of Mennonite brethren out into Kansas and Texas.

The largest city here is York, which from September 1777 to June 1778 was the capital of the young nation. When the Continental Congress met at York, it passed the Articles of Confederation, received word from Benjamin Franklin in Paris that the French would help with money and ships, and issued the first proclamation calling for a national day of thanksgiving. The other large population center of the 19th District encompasses the west shore suburbs of Harrisburg, opposite the state capital on the other side of the Susquehanna River. During the past two decades, the west shore has absorbed a considerable white flight away from Harrisburg and has been growing more Republican. Farther west is the town of Carlisle, home of Dickinson College, one of the nation's oldest, and the Army's Carlisle Barracks.

York for some years was more Democratic than other Pennsylvania Dutch areas, and this district was hotly contested by the two major parties for some time; Democrats actually won it in 1954, 1958, and 1964. Except for two years, it has been held by members of the Goodling family since 1961. The current congressman, William Goodling, started off as one of the most conservative members of the Pennsylvania delegation after he was first elected in 1974. But in the ensuing years Goodling, who was a teacher and principal, has risen to second-ranking position on the Education and Labor Committee and has supported, sometimes vehemently, education and school lunch programs slated for extinction or cuts by the Reagan Administration. Working closely with chairman Carl Perkins, he helped to save Chapters 1 and 2 of the basic education act from inclusion in block grants to the states; he has gotten through initiatives on technical assistance centers for teachers, vocational education, and the Talented Teacher Act; with the practical sense of a teacher, he pushed a policy that children be offered different foods but not served what they won't eat.

In addition, he seems considerably more liberal than most Republicans on foreign issues; he asked to be rotated off the Intelligence Committee after one term there, and has served since 1984 on Budget. On other issues, his record is in line with standard Republican doctrines. In any case, Goodling has become exceedingly popular in this district, and consistently runs well ahead of what have become solid Republican majorities here.

The People Pop. 1980: 516,605, up 14.4% 1970–80. Households (1980): 77% family, 40% with children, 67% married couples; 26.9% housing units rented; median monthly rent: $180; median house value: $46,500. Voting age pop. (1980): 376,801; 2% Black, 1% Spanish origin.

1984 Presidential Vote: Reagan (R) 131,292   (67%)
                            Mondale (D) 62,016   (32%)

Rep. William F. (Bill) Goodling (R)

Elected 1974; b. Dec. 5, 1927, Loganville; home, Jacobus; U. of MD, B.S. 1953, Western MD Col., M.Ed. 1956; United Methodist; married (Hilda).

Career: Army, 1946–48; Pub. sch. teacher and admin., 1952–74.

Offices: 2263 RHOB 20515, 202-225-5836. Also Fed. Bldg, 200 S. George St., York 17405, 717-843-8887.

Committees: *Budget* (4th of 14 R). Task Forces: Health; Human Resources (Ranking Member); Income Security. *Education and Labor* (2d of 13 R). Subcommittees: Elementary, Secondary, and Vocational Education (Ranking Member); Post secondary Education.

Group Ratings

	ADA	ACLU	COPE	CFA	LCV	ACU	NTU	NSI	COC	CEI
1986	25	20	26	33	37	55	49	80	88	53
1985	25	—	25	58	—	57	65	—	77	—

National Journal Ratings

	1986 LIB — 1986 CONS	1985 LIB — 1985 CONS
Economic	31% — 67%	27% — 71%
Social	39% — 59%	24% — 72%
Foreign	39% — 60%	49% — 50%

Key Votes

1) Lmt Cln Water Act	FOR	5) Retain Gun Cont	AGN	9) Aid Angola Reb	FOR
2) Rpl Tobac Sub	FOR	6) Contra Aid	FOR	10) Tax Reform	FOR
3) Grm-Rdmn Def Red	FOR	7) Lmt Text Imp	FOR	11) S Africa Sanc	FOR
4) Ban Polygraph	AGN	8) Limit SDI	AGN	12) Immig Reform	FOR

Election Results

1986 general	William F. (Bill) Goodling (R)	100,055	(73%)	($49,648)
	Richard F. Thornton (D)	37,223	(27%)	($19,535)
1986 primary	William F. (Bill) Goodling (R)	34,215	(100%)	
1984 general	William F. (Bill) Goodling (R)	141,196	(76%)	($58,225)
	John Rarig (D)	44,117	(24%)	($9,018)

Campaign Contributions and Expenditures

1985-86		Direct Cont. 1985-86		PACS Breakdown 1985-86			
Receipts	$49,648	Indiv.	$46,234	Corp.	$1,680	T/M/H	$6,000
Expend.	$46,812	Party	$2,441	Labor	$0	Agr.	$0
Unspent	$9,007	PACS	$7,681	Ideo.	$0	CWOS	$0

TWENTIETH DISTRICT

It's hard to understand the steel country of western Pennsylvania without understanding the topography. Pittsburgh is the center of one of the nation's hilliest metropolitan areas; if you saw it in unsettled form, as General Braddock did briefly in 1754, you would doubt that a city could be built there. Almost the only level spots are on the flood plains, along the rivers; above them banks rise steeply, to the hilly interior land. The great steel mills were all built along the rivers, mainly on the Monongahela from Pittsburgh southeast to Monessen, and the working-class towns or neighborhoods were built on higher land nearby, where frame houses were crowded into narrow streets and almost piled one on top of another. Then, over the next hill, an entirely different, white-collar community might develop, connected to the city by entirely different streets. It is in the blue-collar neighborhoods near the mills, places once prosperous due to high steel wages and now seeing most of their residents on unemployment or moving out, where ministers have barricaded themselves in their churches, preaching against the executives of the big companies—really, against the economies that no longer need the high-price steel produced by the high-wage, high-skill workers that used to man these steel mills, now sitting cold and black, brooding and unavoidable presences beside the rivers that all the houses look down on.

This is the land of the 20th Congressional District of Pennsylvania, most of whose residents are strung out in the towns along the Monongahela. There is a similar population concentration to the north, on the Allegheny, of similar makeup. Connecting them are modest working-class suburbs, interspersed with a few of higher status, just outside of Pittsburgh itself. Almost all of this district is heavily Democratic. It is populated by people of almost every ethnic background; the politics of Franklin D. Roosevelt not only gave them hope of economic recovery, but assured them that they were included and valued in America. That Democratic allegiance is sometimes strained by the party's cultural liberalism; this is a place where the population is old and the old patterns remain very much the rule. But in the 1980s this has been one of the most solidly Democratic parts of the country in presidential as well as House elections.

The 20th District's congressman is Joseph Gaydos, a former state Senator and attorney for United Mine Workers District 5. He had Democratic organization and union backing when he first won the seat, in 1968; in Washington he has been a reliable vote for organized labor and, usually, the Democratic leadership. There is no doubt where his loyalties lie as a member of the Education and Labor Committee. He has chaired the Subcommittee on Health and Safety, which has had jurisdiction over the Occupational Safety and Health Administration, since 1977. During that time, there have been all manner of controversies over OSHA; the burden of regulations was reduced by Carter-appointed Commissioner Eula Bingham as well as her Reaganite successor Thorne Auchter. Gaydos has seen his job as defending the agency from attack and preventing any relaxation of enforcement. Cost-cutting here, as he argues, can cost lives.

By all odds Gaydos should have a safe seat. But politics along the Monongahela can be turbulent; he won primaries in 1982 and 1984 with 67% and 73%—not quite the unanimous suport some congressmen get. In general elections he is reelected overwhelmingly. The serious threat to him is the redistricting that will follow the 1990 Census. The steel towns have been losing population rapidly, and the 20th District, elongated in shape and sandwiched between other Democratic districts, could easily get sliced up, putting him in a primary battle with another incumbent.

The People: Pop. 1980: 516,028, dn. 8.0% 1970–80. Households (1980): 76% family, 35% with children, 62% married couples; 28.9% housing units rented; median monthly rent: $157; median house value: $37,800. Voting age pop. (1980): 390,171; 5% Black.

1984 Presidential Vote:

Mondale (D)	137,742	(61%)
Reagan (R)	83,901	(37%)

Rep. Joseph M. Gaydos (D)

Elected 1968; b. July 3, 1926, Braddock; home, McKeesport; Duquesne U., U. of Notre Dame, LL.B. 1951; Roman Catholic; married (Alice).

Career: Navy, WWII; Dpty. Atty. Gen. of PA; Asst. Allegheny Cnty. Solicitor; Gen. Counsel, United Mine Workers of Amer., Dist. 5; PA Senate, 1967–68.

Offices: 2186 RHOB 20515, 202-225-4631. Also 318 5th Ave., McKeesport 15132, 412-673-7756; and Crown Bldg., 979 4th Ave., Rm. 217, New Kensington 15068, 412-339-7070.

Committees: *Education and Labor* (3d of 21 D). Subcommittees: Health and Safety (Chairman); Postsecondary Education. *House Administration* (2d of 12 D). Subcommittees: Accounts (Chairman); Procurement and Printing. *Standards of Official Conduct* (5th of 6 D). *Joint Committee on Printing.*

Group Ratings

	ADA	ACLU	COPE	CFA	LCV	ACU	NTU	NSI	COC	CEI
1986	55	47	90	67	53	44	20	25	31	20
1985	70	—	90	50	—	15	28	—	32	—

National Journal Ratings

	1986 LIB — 1986 CONS		1985 LIB — 1985 CONS	
Economic	74%	— 23%	63%	— 36%
Social	60%	— 39%	41%	— 56%
Foreign	48%	— 52%	60%	— 39%

Key Votes

1) Lmt Cln Water Act	AGN	5) Retain Gun Cont	AGN
2) Rpl Tobac Sub	AGN	6) Contra Aid	FOR
3) Grm-Rdmn Def Red	AGN	7) Lmt Text Imp	FOR
4) Ban Polygraph	FOR	8) Limit SDI	AGN

9) Aid Angola Reb	FOR
10) Tax Reform	FOR
11) S Africa Sanc	—
12) Immig Reform	AGN

Election Results

1986 general	Joseph M. Gaydos (D)	136,638	(98%)	($119,321)
1986 primary	Joseph M. Gaydos (D)	58,198	(87%)	
	Constance Brown Komm (D)	8,955	(13%)	
1984 general	Joseph M. Gaydos (D)	158,751	(76%)	($151,105)
	Daniel Lloyd (R).	50,247	(24%)	($8,318)

Campaign Contributions and Expenditures

1985-86		Direct Cont. 1985-86		PACS Breakdown 1985-86			
Receipts	$159,109	Indiv.	$33,355	Corp.	$30,750	T/M/H	$19,900
Expend.	$119,321	Party	$238	Labor	$54,275	Agr.	$4,800
Unspent	$42,798	PACS	$120,225	Ideo.	$9,500	CWOS	$1,000
		Cand.	$4,050				

TWENTY-FIRST DISTRICT

Situated in the northwestern corner of the state, Pennsylvania's 21st Congressional District is part of the industrial Great Lakes region. It's a long way overland to the East Coast, and the district has none of metropolitan Philadelphia's eastern ambiance. Erie, with 119,000 people, is the largest city in the district, but not the only urban center. In the southern part of the district Sharon, right on the Ohio border and part of the Youngstown–Warren area, is a major steel-producing town, and so is New Castle, whose suburbs are also part of the district. But there are rural areas, too. Crawford County, between Sharon and Erie, is mostly farming country.

This combination produces a pretty even political balance, with the Democratic majorities of Erie and the steel towns balanced off by the Republican majorities of Crawford County and other rural areas. In the last three presidential elections, the 21st District has come close to mirroring the state's results—and reflecting the swing of the western Pennsylvania steel country toward the Democrats in 1984. In congressional elections, this was for years one of the classic marginal districts in the nation, but now seems very happy with its Republican congressman, Tom Ridge.

Ridge has the perfect background for such a seat. He is from a Catholic Slovak-and-Irish working-class family in Erie, who lived once in a housing project; he went to Harvard and—unusual combination—served in Vietnam. On the Banking Committee he has worked with Democrats on some issues and has worked to further local projects. He has paid particular attention to local issues and local angles. He spent much effort trying to help constituents after the May 1985 hurricane that swept the area, and he worked afterwards with the 23d District's Bill Clinger on getting better federal disaster procedures. He called for action against foreign imports and he points out that Erie, on the St. Lawrence Seaway, is an international seaport. He profits by comparison with his predecessors: Republican Marc Marks left office with vehement blasts against Ronald Reagan's policies, but had supported its budget and tax cuts himself in 1981; Democrat Joseph Vigorito, the incumbent for 12 years after 1964, was named by reporter Nina Totenberg as one of the ten dumbest members of Congress.

Ridge won the seat in the recession year of 1982 by only 729 votes against an abrasive and overconfident Democrat, state Senator Anthony "Buzz" Andrezeski. Ridge, a Bush supporter in 1980, stressed his independence and his background. In a district where Democrats usually vote in lockstep with union leaders and where Republicans are usually lackluster choices of local country club denizens or eccentric loners, Ridge seemed earnest, hardworking, and thoughtful. His personal touch has helped him to reelection with 65% in 1984 and an astounding 81% in 1986.

The People: Pop. 1980: 516,645, up 5.5% 1970–80. Households (1980): 76% family, 40% with children, 64% married couples; 27.1% housing units rented; median monthly rent: $156; median house value: $37,600. Voting age pop. (1980): 370,614; 3% Black.

1984 Presidential Vote: Reagan (R) 105,513   (53%)
Mondale (D) 92,940   (46%)

Rep. Thomas J. Ridge (R)

Elected 1982; b. Aug. 26, 1945, Munhall; home, Erie; Harvard Col., B.A. 1967, Dickinson Sch. of Law, J.D. 1972; Roman Catholic; married (Michele).

Career: Army, 1968–70; Practicing atty., 1972–82.

Offices: 1714 LHOB 20515, 202-225-5406. Also 108 Fed. Bldg., Erie 16501, 814-456-2038; 305 Chestnut St., Meadville 16335, 814-724-8414; and 91 E. State St., Sharon 16146, 412-981-8440.

Committees: *Banking, Finance and Urban Affairs* (12th of 31 R). Subcommittees: Consumer Affairs and Coinage; Financial Institutions Supervision, Regulation and Insurance; Housing and Community Development. *Veterans' Affairs* (9th of 13 R). Subcommittees: Education, Training and Employment; Hospitals and Health Care. *Select Committee on Aging* (11th of 26 R). Subcommittees: Health and Long-Term Care; Housing and Consumer Interests.

Group Ratings

	ADA	ACLU	COPE	CFA	LCV	ACU	NTU	NSI	COC	CEI
1986	35	35	49	58	53	41	49	40	61	51
1985	30	—	45	67	—	48	51	—	73	—

National Journal Ratings

	1986 LIB — 1986 CONS		1985 LIB — 1985 CONS	
Economic	37%	— 62%	38%	— 61%
Social	44%	— 54%	44%	— 54%
Foreign	51%	— 48%	51%	— 49%

Key Votes

1) Lmt Cln Water Act	FOR	5) Retain Gun Cont	AGN	9) Aid Angola Reb	FOR
2) Rpl Tobac Sub	FOR	6) Contra Aid	AGN	10) Tax Reform	FOR
3) Grm-Rdmn Def Red	FOR	7) Lmt Text Imp	FOR	11) S Africa Sanc	FOR
4) Ban Polygraph	FOR	8) Limit SDI	FOR	12) Immig Reform	FOR

Election Results

1986 general	Thomas J. Ridge (R)	111,148	(81%)	($267,525)
	Joylyn Blackwell (D)	26,324	(19%)	
1986 primary	Thomas J. Ridge (R)	24,953	(100%)	
1984 general	Thomas J. Ridge (R)	125,730	(65%)	($421,282)
	James A. Young (D)	65,594	(34%)	($147,265)

Campaign Contributions and Expenditures

1985-86		Direct Cont. 1985-86		PACS Breakdown 1985-86			
Receipts	$298,273	Indiv.	$146,277	Corp.	$61,800	T/M/H	$51,600
Expend.	$267,525	Party	$5,770	Labor	$9,300	Agr.	$4,200
Unspent	$84,931	PACS	$132,900	Ideo.	$4,500	CWOS	$1,500

TWENTY-SECOND DISTRICT

Somewhere south of Pittsburgh, before you get to the West Virginia line, is an invisible line that separates people who think of themselves as part of one of the nation's largest metropolitan areas and those who think of themselves as part of the depressed part of America sometimes referred to as Appalachia. Straddling this line is the 22d Congressional District of Pennsylvania—the southwestern corner of the state between West Virginia and the Pittsburgh suburbs. This is a region of rugged hills and polluted rivers, lined with steel mills and smaller factories. Industrial towns are huddled around each factory, with frame houses built 70 years ago to house the immigrants from Italy, Poland, Scotland, and what later became Czechoslovakia. There is a small aristocracy here of top management and factory owners, but it lives in the kind of isolation and paranoia you find among the rich in a small Latin American city. This is rough country: it was in a small town here that Joseph Yablonski, the insurgent candidate for president of the United Mine Workers, was found shot to death with his wife and daughters in 1969.

The 22d is one of Pennsylvania's—and the nation's—most blue-collar and most Democratic districts. The long slide of the steel industry has made this a depressed area for going on two decades now. Its ethnic composition, its high union membership, its depressed economy, its appetite for federal help—all these make this a heavily Democratic district. In 1984 it was one of the few congressional districts with almost no blacks to give Walter Mondale a large majority.

The 22d District's congressman, Austin Murphy, is a native of the Monongahela Valley, a veteran of the Marine Corps, a supporter of organized labor, and a Democrat. Murphy's voting record is solidly Democratic and pro-labor; on cultural issues he is a moderate conservative, while on foreign policy his record is mixed. Murphy sits on the Interior Committee, where he naturally supports the interests of coal, and on Education and Labor, on which he spends most of his time. Beginning in 1985 he has chaired the Labor Standards Subcommittee, where he supports a higher minimum wage, a stronger Davis-Bacon Act (requiring high construction wages on government projects), and tougher occupational disease legislation. Yet when it comes to protecting local governments, he may be willing to subordinate the interests of their employees; in the 99th Congress he moved successfully to allow cities to set retirement ages for police and fire officers and to give employees compensatory time rather than overtime pay. He has fought to protect the black lung compensation program against cuts and to make it more generous. Like all western Pennsylvanians, he clamors for a tougher trade policy. On the subcommittee he chaired before 1985, he handled problems of the handicapped and still remains interested in them, and he proceeded sensitively and intelligently on inexpensive programs—special education, alcohol and drug abuse prevention, and adoption are a few—that can improve many people's lives, but where thoughtless federal action could disrupt personal and institutional relationships that have served people's needs for years. Murphy has ostensibly not dropped his interest in perpetuating these programs. He has even proposed creating a national lottery to ensure their funding.

Murphy effectively won the 22d District seat when he won 29% of the vote in a 12-candidate primary in 1976, when 32-year incumbent Thomas Morgan, Chairman of the House Foreign Affairs Committee, retired. He won the general election that year with 55% of the vote, and has not had a serious challenge since.

The People: Pop. 1980: 515,122, up 2.4% 1970–80. Households (1980): 78% family, 38% with children, 65% married couples; 26.0% housing units rented; median monthly rent: $136; median house value: $35,500. Voting age pop. (1980): 378,475; 3% Black.

1984 Presidential Vote:

Mondale (D) 102,681	(57%)
Reagan (R) 77,235	(43%)

Rep. Austin J. Murphy (D)

Elected 1976; b. June 17, 1927, North Charleroi; home, Mononga-hela; Duquesne U., B.A. 1949, U. of Pittsburgh, LL.B. 1952; Roman Catholic; married (Mona).

Career: USMC, WWII; Practicing atty.; Washington Cnty. Asst. Dist. Atty., 1956–57; PA House of Reps., 1959–71; PA Senate, 1971–77.

Offices: 2210 RHOB 20515, 202-225-4665. Also 306 Fallowfield Ave., Charleroi 15022, 412-489-4217; 70 E. Beau St., Washington 15301, 412-228-2777; 365 McClellandtown Rd., Uniontown 15401, 412-438-1490; and Hopewell Mncpl. Bldg., Clark Blvd., Aliquippa 15001, 412-372-1199.

Committees: *Education and Labor* (6th of 21 D). Subcommittees: Labor–Management Relations; Labor Standards (Chairman); Health and Safety. *Interior and Insular Affairs* (5th of 26 D). Subcommittees: Energy and the Environment; Insular and International Affairs; Mining and Natural Resources.

Group Ratings

	ADA	ACLU	COPE	CFA	LCV	ACU	NTU	NSI	COC	CEI
1986	70	50	80	67	58	19	31	10	33	18
1985	60	—	79	50	—	19	40	—	36	—

National Journal Ratings

	1986 LIB	—	1986 CONS	1985 LIB	—	1985 CONS
Economic	57%	—	42%	65%	—	33%
Social	57%	—	40%	36%	—	60%
Foreign	61%	—	39%	58%	—	40%

Key Votes

1) Lmt Cln Water Act	AGN	5) Retain Gun Cont	AGN	9) Aid Angola Reb	AGN
2) Rpl Tobac Sub	AGN	6) Contra Aid	AGN	10) Tax Reform	AGN
3) Grm-Rdmn Def Red	FOR	7) Lmt Text Imp	FOR	11) S Africa Sanc	FOR
4) Ban Polygraph	FOR	8) Limit SDI	FOR	12) Immig Reform	AGN

Election Results

1986 general	Austin J. Murphy (D)	131,650	(100%)	($118,557)
1986 primary	Austin J. Murphy (D)	57,312	(88%)	
	Donald A. Shapira (D)	7,858	(12%)	
1984 general	Austin J. Murphy (D)	153,514	(79%)	($91,922)
	Nancy S. Pryor (R)	39,752	(20%)	($11,423)

Campaign Contributions and Expenditures

1985-86		Direct Cont. 1985-86		PACS Breakdown 1985-86			
Receipts	$134,081	Indiv.	$15,599	Corp.	$26,175	T/M/H	$21,896
Expend.	$118,557	Party	$106	Labor	$44,265	Agr.	$2,100
Unspent	$103,364	PACS	$97,386	Ideo.	$2,950	CWOS	$0
		Cand.	$500				

TWENTY-THIRD DISTRICT

The 23d Congressional District of Pennsylvania is the rural north central part of the state. The region is the most sparsely populated part of Pennsylvania, and of the entire East. The district's terrain is mountainous, and its valleys have only a few towns here and there; this was a route ignored in the great migrations west, and it contains none of the great historical east–west transportation routes. The only significant concentrations of people are found in the Nittany Valley in the southern part of the district and around Oil City in the extreme west. The Nittany Valley is the home of Pennsylvania State University, commonly called Penn State, long known for the powerful football teams coached by Joe Paterno. Oil City is near the site of the nation's first oil well, sunk in 1859. Today Pennsylvania crude—a relatively scarce oil but of higher quality than that found in the Southwest—continues to occupy an important place in the area's economy.

North central Pennsylvania now has easy connections with the rest of the country through Interstate 80, the shortest main road from New York to Chicago, and through commuter airlines; yet the air of isolation persists. The solidly built courthouses and banks in the center of each county seat testify to the long prosperity of this part of the country; yet unemployment rates are high in most counties. The 23d remains a rural and small-town district, populated mainly by descendants of the English stock farmers who moved here in the early 19th century; it is one part of America where no further wave of immigration has reached.

Pennsylvania has a long Republican tradition going back to the years just before the Civil War, and no part of Pennsylvania more so than this. Yet the 23d District's Republican congressman, Bill Clinger, had to fight hard to win the district in 1978 over a one-term Democratic incumbent, and he has had to fight hard to hold it in the middle 1980s. This is all the more striking because Clinger is the kind of moderate Republican who presumably appeals across party lines. He chaired the House Wednesday Group, made up mostly of moderate and liberal Republicans, which under his leadership generated some actual legislation. As a member of the Public Works Committee, he has worked to refashion the Economic Development Administration in the hopes that it can generate more jobs in woebegone parts of the country, while the Reagan administration has been trying to zero it out. He is one of the congressional promoters of a federal capital budget, to set capital spending apart from current operations, and presumably to generate more of it. He helped to originate the individual training account idea popularized in the 1984 presidential campaign by Gary Hart.

But none of this prevented Democratic legislator Bill Wachob from running strong races in 1984 and 1986. A liberal from College Station, Wachob caught Clinger unawares in 1984, attacking him for his support of Ronald Reagan as if this was not a Reagan district, and actually making some gains thereby; for this, like many districts, as much as it wanted Reagan in the White House was wary of giving him compliant Republican majorities and carte blanche on Capitol Hill. Wachob managed to win 48% of the vote in 1984 and never stopped running. But Clinger started running hard too. For a moment in 1986 the race in the remote 23d looked like Star Wars: Ed Asner came in to campaign for Wachob and his rival in the Screen Actors Guild Charlton Heston came in to campaign for Clinger. It's not clear how much either knew about the candidates; Heston took potshots at Asner for working with Communist-connected supporters of the Sandinista regime. In the end, with both candidates campaigning hard, the district's native Republicanism asserted itself, and Clinger won with 55%, running slightly ahead of losing gubernatorial candidate William Scranton and well behind winning Senator Arlen Specter. It will be interesting to see whether Clinger gets another serious challenge in 1988.

The People: Pop. 1980: 515,976, up 6.1% 1970–80. Households (1980): 74% family, 39% with children, 64% married couples; 27.3% housing units rented; median monthly rent: $154; median house value: $34,100. Voting age pop. (1980): 378,256; 1% Black.

1984 Presidential Vote:

Reagan (R)	116,398	(63%)
Mondale (D)	68,729	(37%)

Rep. William F. (Bill) Clinger, Jr. (R)

Elected 1978; b. Apr. 4, 1929, Warren; home, Warren; Johns Hopkins U., B.A. 1951, U. of VA, LL.B. 1965; Presbyterian; married (Julia).

Career: Navy, 1951–55; Adv. Dept., New Process Co., 1955–62; Practicing atty., 1965–75, 1977–78; Chf. Counsel, U.S. Dept. of Commerce, Econ. Develop. Admin., 1975–77.

Offices: 1122 LHOB 20515, 202-225-5121. Also 315 S. Allen St., Ste. 219, State College 16801, 814-238-1776; and 805 Pennbank Bldg., Warren 16365, 814-726-3910.

Committees: *Government Operations* (3d of 15 R). Subcommittee: Environment, Energy, and Natural Resources (Ranking Member). *Public Works and Transportation* (5th of 20 R). Subcommittees: Economic Development; Investigations and Oversight (Ranking Member); Surface Transportation. *Select Committee on Aging* (24th of 26 R). Subcommittees: Housing and Consumer Interests; Human Services.

Group Ratings

	ADA	ACLU	COPE	CFA	LCV	ACU	NTU	NSI	COC	CEI
1986	50	40	40	50	32	45	34	70	44	33
1985	35	—	35	58	—	48	36	—	57	—

National Journal Ratings

	1986 LIB — 1986 CONS			1985 LIB — 1985 CONS		
Economic	47%	—	53%	45%	—	55%
Social	52%	—	46%	36%	—	60%
Foreign	41%	—	57%	48%	—	51%

Key Votes

1) Lmt Cln Water Act	AGN	5) Retain Gun Cont	AGN	9) Aid Angola Reb	FOR
2) Rpl Tobac Sub	FOR	6) Contra Aid	FOR	10) Tax Reform	FOR
3) Grm-Rdmn Def Red	FOR	7) Lmt Text Imp	FOR	11) S Africa Sanc	FOR
4) Ban Polygraph	FOR	8) Limit SDI	AGN	12) Immig Reform	FOR

Election Results

1986 general	William F. (Bill) Clinger, Jr. (R).........	79,595	(55%)	($695,266)
	Bill Wachob (D)	63,875	(45%)	($577,853)
1986 primary	William F. (Bill) Clinger, Jr. (R).........	29,676	(100%)	
1984 general	William F. (Bill) Clinger, Jr. (R).........	94,952	(52%)	($346,871)
	Bill Wachob (D)	88,957	(48%)	($241,903)

Campaign Contributions and Expenditures

1985-86		Direct Cont. 1985-86		PACS Breakdown 1985-86			
Receipts	$702,712	Indiv.	$361,562	Corp.	$122,117	T/M/H	$99,896
Expend.	$695,266	Party	$16,599	Labor	$23,250	Agr.	$2,250
		PACS	$292,403	Ideo.	$41,140	CWOS	$3,750
		Cand.	$22,225				

RHODE ISLAND

"Rhode Island," wrote George Washington from the Constitutional Convention to which Rhode Island refused to send a delegate, "still perseveres in that impolitic—unjust—and one might add without much impropriety scandalous conduct, which seems to have marked all her public counsels of late." One might add without much impropriety that scandalous conduct has marked the public life of the colony and state of Rhode Island and Providence Plantation—the official name—from beginning to end. Created by Roger Williams in 1636 as a haven for religious heretics, it also became a haven for wrongdoers; other colonies called it "Rogues' Island." Its Yankee merchants were sharp traders and unscrupulous ones, happy to profit from the triangle trade of rum, slaves, and sugar.

Its politics has been marked by bitter conflict, in the 1780s between hard money merchants and soft money farmers (it was they who refused to send delegates to Philadelphia), in the 1840s between large property owners who refused to give others the vote, in the 1930s between Republicans allied with the state's business interests and supported mostly by Protestants and Democrats allied with union leaders and supported mostly by Catholics. Sometimes things got violent. Argument over the franchise led to the Dorr War of the 1840s, during which Rhode Island had two separate state governments, each claiming sovereignty. In 1935, when Democrats under Governor Theodore Green—as blueblooded a Yankee as you could find—won only 20 of the 42 state Senate seats, they refused to seat two Republicans, voted Democrats into the seats, and then proceeded, within 15 minutes, to declare the state Supreme Court seats vacant, to abolish state boards that controlled Democratic cities, to strengthen the power of the governor, and to reorganize state government so as to get rid of Republicans.

Rhode Island's scandalous conduct continues today. This is a state where the chief justice of the state Supreme Court was suspended for four months, then impeached, and finally moved to resign in 1986 after it was revealed that he wrote a letter to the parole board for mob boss Raymond Patriarca, officiated at a Patriarca lieutenant's wedding, and had liaisons with women in a motel owned by men with links to mobsters. The same year a bank and three vice presidents were indicted for manipulating the state mortgage fund, and the governor's former chief of staff was convicted on similar charges; the governor attended the World Series in the bank's suite. Three parish priests were charged with sexual misconduct with children, and the Bishop of Providence went on television to deny he had been arrested. A heart surgeon was sentenced to 10 years for taking kickbacks to implant pacemakers in patients who didn't need them. A senior at prestigious Brown University was indicted on prostitution charges. Former Providence Mayor Buddy Cianci, who pled no contest to charges of assaulting his wife's lover, became a radio talk show host. The state's senior congressman, Fernand St Germain, was under investigation by the House Ethics Committee. Attorney General Arlene Violet, a Republican and a former nun, who won in 1984 largely because her opponent failed to convict Newport millionaire Claus von Bulow, was voted out in 1986 after dismissal of a fraud case four days before the election because of an altered transcript.

But public life in Rhode Island is not confined to circuses; there is also bread. Rhode Island was transformed from a merchant state to an industrial beehive beginning in 1793, when Samuel Slater, a British emigré, memorized the secret plans of an English mill, then regarded as ultra-high technology, and built America's first water-powered cotton mill in Pawtucket. So began America's industrial revolution. During the 19th century the textile industry in Rhode Island boomed, and the tiny state attracted immigrants eager to work the looms and toil on the cutting floor. They came from French Canada, Ireland, and especially from Italy. By the early 1900s this erstwhile colony of dissident Protestants had become the most heavily Catholic state in the nation; today about 65% of Rhode Island's citizens are Catholic. For years Protestant-Catholic rivalries structured politics, with shrewd Republicans trying to capture the French Canadian vote, but mostly failing after the Democrats nominated the Catholic Al Smith for President in 1928 and Theodore Green revolutionized state politics in 1935. Ever since Rhode Island has been one of our most Democratic states. It has gone Republican for President only four times in 60 years; it has elected only one Republican to the U.S. Senate since 1930; it elected not a single Republican to the House of Representatives between 1940 and 1978. In 1980 Rhode Island gave Ronald Reagan only 37% of its votes, his worst percentage outside Washington, D.C., and in 1984 Rhode Island was Reagan's worst state (52%) after Minnesota and Massachusetts.

But by the early 1980s the economic underpinnings of this politics had changed. Unions were still politically powerful, but they represented fewer and fewer workers; the state's economy was quietly, below the scandalous surface, being upgraded from blue-collar to white-collar, from textiles to high tech; the electorate, instead of being a mass of Catholic factory workers pressed into neighborhoods of three-story three-family houses, was becoming comfortably affluent and suburban. There was a pause in growth when the Newport Navy base closed in 1973, and for a while that attracted everyone's attention. But by the early 1980s both parties were ready with their ways to adapt to change and build for the future.

The response of Governor Joseph Garrahy, a popular Democrat elected in 1976, agreed with the widespread criticism that Rhode Island's high taxes and pro-labor laws (since the 1930s union members could collect unemployment benefits while on strike) was stifling Rhode Island's economy. With business and civic leaders and the guidance of Ira Magaziner, who had helped restructure Brown University in the 1970s, Garrahy proposed what they called the Greenhouse Compact, a kind of state industrial policy that would use government to encourage and incubate industry. But the voters, perhaps concerned that the $250 million package would lead to higher taxes, perhaps skeptical of government's ability to produce economic growth, rejected the Greenhouse Compact by almost an 80%–20% margin in a 1984 referendum.

Governor. The rejection of the Greenhouse Compact and the retirement of Governor Garrahy turned the state's politics in a new direction. The Democrats had an old-fashioned primary fight,

**RHODE ISLAND — Congressional Districts, Counties,
County Subdivisions (Towns), and Places — *(2 Districts)***

Congressional districts established April 9, 1982 ; all other boundaries are as of January 1, 1980.

which used to be determined by the state party endorsement, but isn't any more; but the result didn't matter; Republican Edward DiPrete, mayor of Cranston, was elected, as were two Republican women on the statewide ticket. He got the legislature (where Democrats gained seats in 1984 after losing many in 1983) to pass a 16% cut in the state income tax. He got the strikers' benefits statute repealed. He also repealed the state gift and estate tax. He restructured the state unemployment compensation system. He established a state Partnership for Science and Technology and increased funding for education, Head Start, and other children's programs. He ran ads in national newspapers saying "If you want to talk business in Rhode Island, talk to a businessman. The Governor."

DiPrete himself is a modest man, seen shopping weekly in supermarkets in this little city-state, a real estate firm owner with seven kids and a house full of pets. A *Providence Journal* reporter wrote that in his ceremonial office sometimes "he looks like a tourist who strayed in off a State House tour." But with Rhode Island's economy growing and an unemployment rate well under the national average, DiPrete's politics seemed to be working. His Democratic opponent in

1986—Rhode Island is one of only three states that still elect governors every two years—was Bruce Sundlun, a rich businessman who spent liberally on his campaign. But DiPrete won reelection by a 65%–32% margin—one of those consensus results seen in so many states in 1986. In early 1987 his program—more money for school texts, encouraging small business, workfare incentives—was meeting approval from Democrats as well as Republicans.

Senators. It must strike anyone as odd that heavily Catholic and ethnic Rhode Island has two blue-blooded Protestant Senators. Both of them, Democrat Claiborne Pell and Republican John Chafee, have had unusual careers. Pell, first elected in 1960, is now the state's senior politician. His father was congressman from New York for a term, a friend of Franklin Roosevelt, and minister to Portugal and Hungary during the outbreak of World War II. Pell himself served as a foreign service officer for several years, then settled back on Bellevue Avenue in Newport, where you find the Vanderbilt and Auchincloss "cottages." He is now what he always wanted to be, chairman of the Senate Foreign Relations Committee.

It is obligatory in Washington to deprecate Pell's political skills. He has an old-fashioned aristocratic accent, seems remote and diffident, uses corny old phrases, seems unable to rally his colleagues around his standard. Yet there is evidence that if he wears a velvet glove there is an iron fist inside. He has gotten everything he wanted in politics, and by beating the toughest competition this tough little state could offer. In the 1960 Democratic primary he beat former Governor Dennis Roberts and former Governor, Senator, and U.S. Attorney General J. Howard McGrath; this was the first time since Green's governorship that a candidate endorsed by the Democratic organization was beaten. One opponent in that race called Pell a "cream puff"; he promptly ran out and got the endorsement of the bakers' union. In 1972, when Rhode Island was going Republican for President, Pell faced John Chafee, then a popular former governor and Secretary of the Navy. Although Chafee began ahead, Pell turned the campaign around and won again. It is worth noting that Pell has the seat won by Theodore Green in 1936 when he was 69, a seat that a generation of Rhode Island politicians assumed would soon become open; Green, who chaired Foreign Relations himself, retired in 1960 at aged 93. Pell has now been elected to serve 30 years in that seat, longer than Green, and he will be 71 when it comes up again in November 1990.

How will Pell perform as chairman of Foreign Relations? His instincts are dovish, as are those of other committee Democrats; that will put him at odds on many issues with former Chairman Richard Lugar and on virtually all issues with the committee's new ranking Republican, Jesse Helms. Pell's personal approach is conciliatory, which is definitely not true of some committee Democrats and certainly not of Helms. His instinct is to push for arms control agreements of the type usually favored by Democrats; in early 1987 he was trying to get the Senate to ratify arms control pacts left over from the Carter years. But the Administration seemed able to frustrate him, and it's not clear how far he can push it; Senate hawks can get leverage by threatening to oppose treaties, but it's unlikely Pell would oppose any treaty Reagan would sign. On Central America, he and other Democrats oppose aid to the Nicaraguan contras. That leaves them for the moment on the popular and apparently winning side of the issue, though vulnerable in the long run if the Sandinistas prove as expansionist as the Reagan Administration suggests.

Pell's other major legislative interest is education. He is the second ranking Democrat on Labor and Human Resources and for years chaired the subcommittee in charge of education programs. He made a particular mark in setting up a grant program for needy college and university students; these Pell grants, as they are now officially called, were attacked unsuccessfully by the Reagan Administration. Those who disdain Pell's political talents should ask how many other Senators have their name on a program that sends money to tens of thousands of families in their states every year. He has also been one of the main promoters of federal aid to the arts and a promoter of ocean research (Rhode Island's license plates call it the "Ocean State").

After Chafee's challenge, Pell has been reelected with 75% and 73% in 1978 and 1984. Serious Republicans like Claudine Schneider have declined to take him on. Perhaps one will in

1990. But just as it doesn't seem likely that Pell will step down from a chairmanship he has wanted all his life, so it seems far from certain that Schneider or any other Republican, even given Rhode Island's recent Republican trend, will find Pell a "cream puff" when the election comes round.

Senator John Chafee is Rhode Island's most successful Republican politician in the last 50 years. Even so, he has had his setbacks: he was defeated when he sought a fourth term as governor in 1968, and he lost to Pell in 1972. He came back, however, in 1976 when Senator John Pastore retired, profiting when then-Governor Philip Noel was defeated in the Democratic primary by a Cadillac dealer who ran a self-financed campaign but exhausted most of his resources in the primary.

Chafee's popularity comes from a solid, pleasant personality and from his liberal stands on many issues. On economics, while he is not always a solid conservative, he cannot be mistaken for a Democrat either. He supported the Reagan budget and tax cuts in 1981, for example, and he has been lead sponsor of the measure to reduce American regulation of bribery of foreign officials (an absurd law, when you think about it: we don't try to enforce ordinary criminal laws against Americans who violate them abroad). But by 1983 Chafee broke rather conclusively with the Reagan Administration, calling for revision of some of its tax cuts; he is one of those Republicans who wouldn't mind seeing the deficit cut with a tax rise. As a New Englander, he has not supported price controls that remain on domestic oil production. On the Finance Committee he is a critic of greenmail, hostile takeovers, and "golden parachutes"—all populist stands, though some vulnerable to the charge that they entrench incompetent managements. On trade issues, he has been inclined toward free trade positions.

Chafee is most active on environmental issues. He was the chief packager in the Senate of the Water Projects bill that President Reagan vetoed in 1986, and cooperated with the Democrats in bringing it forward and get it passed over Reagan's veto in early 1987. On Environment and Public Works, he worked with his fellow New England Republican Robert Stafford to get a stronger Superfund and to reauthorize the Clean Air Act; the committee is likely to take some different tacks now that North Dakotan Quentin Burdick and not Stafford is chairman. In return, environmentalists provided critical support, both in money and volunteers, for Chafee in his tough reelection fight in 1982.

Chafee tends to be rather liberal on cultural and foreign policy issues and is anything but a favorite of the New Right. Yet, easy-going and popular, he won a leadership post, chairman of the Republican Conference, after the 1984 elections over the sometimes intense and abrasive Jake Garn of Utah, 28–25.

For all his popularity in Rhode Island, where he won his first statewide election in 1962, Chafee was nearly defeated for reelection in the recession year of 1982. The Democrat, former attorney general and state AFL–CIO counsel Julius Michaelson, denounced Reaganomics as heartless and disastrous, and got 49% of the votes. In early 1987 Democrats were already peppering Chafee with complaints about losing federal facilities, and Attorney General Richard Licht among others was eyeing the race. Their problem may be that Rhode Island is closer to being Chafee's kind of state—white collar, worried about the environment, convinced that free markets produce economic growth—than it was in 1976 when he won his first term in the Senate or in 1982. Still, this could be one of the seriously contested races of 1988, and one of the Democrats' not-too-numerous chances for a pickup in a year when most of the seats up are theirs.

Presidential politics. Rhode Island remains one of the most Democratic states in an increasingly less Democratic nation. It remains also the most Catholic state, but it should be added that the heavy Catholic population here is not invariably swayed by the Church. This is one of the states more tolerant of abortion, for example. One reason is that Catholics, like members of any other group, don't feel beleaguered and forced to stick to all the group's rules when they form a majority. Another is that most of the Catholics have ethnic backgrounds not in Ireland, where the Church was the defender of the people against an alien regime, but in Italy, Portugal, and French Canada, where the Church's dominance of civic as well as religious life made many people, especially men, strong anticlericals; men still call themselves Catholics in many parts of Italy and Rhode Island, yet have no intention of attending Mass regularly or letting a priest tell them what to do.

Rhode Island has had presidential primaries with the lowest rate of turnout of any state in the nation. In a state of nearly a million people, only 44,000 voted in the Democratic primary and a pathetic 2,235 in the Republican primary in 1984—far fewer than turn-out in the Iowa precinct caucuses. The main reason is probably habit, of the voters and the candidates. The candidates aren't used to Rhode Island being important, even though the primary was moved up to March in 1984; it's still overshadowed by Massachusetts and, two weeks earlier, New Hampshire. Anyway, people here are used to having the party organizations decide these things. The reality that the organizations can't deliver any more—Gary Hart, who won in 1984, wasn't exactly the old-timers' favorite—apparently has not caught up yet with the perception that they can.

The People: Est. Pop. 1986: 975,000; Pop. 1980: 947,154, up 2.9% 1980–86 and dn. 0.3% 1970–80; 0.40% of U.S. total, 42d largest. 13% with 1–3 yrs. col., 15% with 4+ yrs. col.; 10.3% below poverty level. Single ancestry: 13% Italian, 8% French, English, Irish, 7% Portuguese, 2% Polish, 1% German, Scottish, Swedish, Russian. Households (1980): 72% family, 37% with children, 59% married couples; 41.2% housing units rented; median monthly rent: $158; median house value: $47,000. Voting age pop. (1980): 704,303; 2% Black, 2% Spanish origin, 1% Asian origin. Registered voters (1986): 524,664; no party registration.

1986 Share of Federal Tax Burden: $3,067,000,000; 0.41% of U.S. total, 41st largest.

1986 Share of Federal Expenditures

	Total		Non-Defense		Defense	
Total Expend	$3,223m	(0.39%)	$2,478m	(0.41%)	$745m	(0.32%)
St/Lcl Grants	570m	(0.51%)	570m	(0.51%)	0m	(0%)
Salary/Wages	440m	(0.36%)	159m	(0.27%)	284m	(0.46%)
Pymts to Indiv	1,698m	(0.47%)	1,631m	(0.47%)	67m	(0.38%)
Procurement	448m	(0.22%)	55m	(0.10%)	393m	(0.26%)
Research/Other	66m	(0.25%)	66m	(0.25%)	0m	(0.85%)

Political Lineup: Governor, Edward D. DiPrete (R); Richard A. Licht (D); Secy. of State, Kathleen S. Connell (D); Atty. Gen., James E. O'Neil (D); Treasurer, Roger Begin (D). State Senate, 50 (38 D and 12 R); State House of Representatives, 100 (80 D, 20 R). Senators, Claiborne Pell (D) and John H. Chafee (R). Representatives, 2 (1 D and 1 R).

1984 Presidential Vote

Reagan (R)	208,513	(52%)
Mondale (D)	194,292	(48%)

1980 Presidential Vote

Carter (D)	198,342	(48%)
Reagan (R)	154,793	(37%)
Anderson (I)	59,814	(14%)

1984 Democratic Presidential Primary

Hart	20,011	(45%)
Mondale	15,338	(34%)
Jackson	3,875	(9%)
Glenn	2,249	(5%)
McGovern	2,146	(5%)
Three others, uncomm.	892	(2%)

1984 Republican Presidential Primary

Reagan	2,028	(91%)
Uncommitted	207	(9%)

GOVERNOR

Gov. Edward D. DiPrete (R)

Elected 1984, term expires Jan. 1989; b. July 8, 1934, Cranston; home, Cranston; Col. of the Holy Cross, B.S. 1955; Roman Catholic; married (Patricia)

Career: Cranston School Comm., 1970–74, Chmn., 1972–74; Cranston City Cncl., 1974–78; Mayor of Cranston, 1978–84; Pres., DiPrete Realty Co.

Office: 222 State House, Providence 02903, 401-277-2080.

Election Results

1986 gen.	Edward D. DiPrete (R)	203,203	(65%)
	Bruce G. Sundlun (D)	101,437	(32%)
	Two others (D)	9,382	(3%)
1986 prim.	Edward D. DiPrete (R) unopposed		
1984 gen.	Edward D. DiPrete (R)	245,059	(60%)
	Anthony J. Solomon (D)	163,311	(40%)

SENATORS

Sen. Claiborne Pell (D)

Elected 1960, seat up 1990; b. Nov. 22, 1918, New York, NY; home, Newport; Princeton U., A.B. 1940, Columbia U., A.M. 1946; Episcopalian; married (Nuala).

Career: Coast Guard, WWII; U.S. Foreign Svc. and State Dept., Czechoslovakia and Italy, 1945–52; Exec. Asst. to RI Dem. St. Chmn., 1952, 1954; Consultant, Dem. Natl. Cmtee., 1953–60.

Offices: 335 RSOB 20510, 202-224-4642. Also 418 Fed. Bldg., Providence 02903, 401-528-5456.

Committees: *Foreign Relations* (Chairman of 11 D) Subcommittee: Western Hemisphere and Peace Corps Affairs. *Labor and Human Resources* (2d of 9 D). Subcommittees: Aging; Children, Family, Drugs and Alcoholism; Education, Arts, and Humanities (Chairman). *Rules and Administration* (2d of 9 D). *Joint Committee on the Library* (Chairman).

Group Ratings

	ADA	ACLU	COPE	CFA	LCV	ACU	NTU	NSI	COC	CEI
1986	80	85	92	87	83	17	46	0	42	23
1985	95	—	93	87	—	9	33	—	29	—

National Journal Ratings

	1986 LIB — 1986 CONS			1985 LIB — 1985 CONS		
Economic	62%	—	35%	77%	—	19%
Social	71%	—	27%	85%	—	12%
Foreign	75%	—	0%	82%	—	15%

Key Votes

1) Ease Gun Cont	AGN	5) Grm-Rdmn Def Red	AGN	9) Rehnquist Nom	AGN
2) Immig Reform	FOR	6) Contra Aid	AGN	10) Tax Reform	FOR
3) Lmt Text Imp	FOR	7) SDI Funding	AGN	11) Drug Death Pen	FOR
4) Aid Tobac Ind	AGN	8) Lmt PAC Contrib	FOR	12) S Africa Sanc	FOR

Election Results

1984 general	Claiborne Pell (D).....................	286,780	(73%)	($430,739)
	Barbara M. Leonard (R)...............	108,492	(27%)	($143,842)
1984 primary	Claiborne Pell (D) unopposed			
1978 general	Claiborne Pell (D)...................	229,557	(75%)	($373,077)
	James G. Reynolds (R)................	76,061	(25%)	($85,614)

Campaign Contributions and Expenditures

1979-84		Direct Cont. 1979-84		PACS Breakdown 1979-84			
Receipts	$740,729	Indiv.	$464,835	Corp.	$29,525	T/M/H	$42,756
Expend.	$444,283	PACS	$213,030	Labor	$73,633	Agr.	$0
Unspent	$338,004			Ideo.	$61,868	CWOS	$2,100

Sen. John H. Chafee (R)

Elected 1976, seat up 1988; b. Oct. 22, 1922, Providence; home, Warwick; Yale U., B.A. 1947, Harvard U., LL.B. 1950; Episcopalian; married (Virginia).

Career: USMC, WWII, Korea; Practicing atty., 1952–63; RI House of Reps., 1957–63, Minor. Ldr., 1959–63; Gov. of RI, 1963–69; Secy. of the Navy, 1969–72.

Offices: 567 DSOB 20510, 202-224-2921. Also 301 John O. Pastore Bldg., Kennedy Plaza, Providence 02903, 401-528-5294.

Committees: *Banking, Housing and Urban Affairs* (8th of 9 R). Subcommittees: Consumer Affairs; Securities. *Environment and Public Works* (2d of 8 R). Subcommittees: Environmental Protection (Ranking Member); Hazardous Wastes and Toxic Substances; Water Resources, Transportation and Infrastructure. *Finance* (5th of 9 R). Subcommittees: Health; International Trade; Taxation and Debt Management (Ranking Member). *Special Committee on Aging* (7th of 9 R).

Group Ratings

	ADA	ACLU	COPE	CFA	LCV	ACU	NTU	NSI	COC	CEI
1986	60	71	45	67	75	35	51	30	63	62
1985	35	—	46	73	—	39	59	—	76	—

National Journal Ratings

	1986 LIB — 1986 CONS			1985 LIB — 1985 CONS		
Economic	47%	—	48%	36%	—	62%
Social	54%	—	45%	80%	—	18%
Foreign	64%	—	33%	63%	—	36%

Key Votes

1) Ease Gun Cont	AGN	5) Grm-Rdmn Def Red	FOR	9) Rehnquist Nom	FOR
2) Immig Reform	FOR	6) Contra Aid	AGN	10) Tax Reform	FOR
3) Lmt Text Imp	AGN	7) SDI Funding	AGN	11) Drug Death Pen	FOR
4) Aid Tobac Ind	AGN	8) Lmt PAC Contrib	FOR	12) S Africa Sanc	FOR

Election Results

1982 general	John H. Chafee (R)	175,248	(51%)	($1,065,627)
	Julius C. Michaelson (D)	167,283	(49%)	($438,630)
1982 primary	John H. Chafee (R) unopposed			
1976 general	John H. Chafee (R)	230,329	(58%)	($415,651)
	Richard Lorber (D)...................	167,665	(42%)	($782,931)

Campaign Contributions and Expenditures

1979-82		Direct Cont. 1979-82			PACS Breakdown			
Receipts	$1,117,187	Indiv.	$600,799	Agr	$7,500	Ideo	$20,150
Expend.	$1,065,627	Party	$15,838	Bus	$352,950	Lbr	$20,000
Unspent	$53,687	PACS	$421,203	Hlth	$28,500	Prof	$5,850

FIRST DISTRICT

The 1st Congressional District is the eastern half of Rhode Island, east of Narragansett Bay, a line that cuts through Providence and then proceeds west and north to the Massachusetts border. There are several Democratic strongholds here: Providence (although this is the more prosperous side of Rhode Island's capital and largest city) and next-door Pawtucket; the onetime textile mill towns of the Blackstone Valley, Woonsocket and Central Falls; and, south on the ocean, the old city of Newport, with its restored 18th-century houses, its so-called cottages that are really palaces, and an economy shattered when the Navy base was closed in 1973 but which seems to have been revived by the von Bulow trials of the 1980s. Most the rest of the district is Democratic by national standards, except for the high-income suburb of Barrington and the old Yankee beach town of Little Compton. Ethnically, this is the more French Canadian and less Italian of the two Rhode Island districts.

The congressman from the 1st District is Fernand St Germain, chairman of the House Banking, Finance and Urban Affairs Committee, one of the politically sharpest but ethically most dubious members of the House of Representatives. St Germain is an activist chairman of a committee charged with superintendency of a banking system threatened in the 1980s by big bank failures, by the collapse of much of the savings and loan industry, by the overexposure of major American banks on foreign debt, and by vast and rapid changes in financial institutions which politicians have a hard time keeping up with. He tends to favor savings institutions over the banks, and is skeptical about banking deregulation; his disagreements with Senate Banking Chairman Jake Garn over six years kept legislation from passing. Yet the deadlock has also allowed big banks to position themselves in ways that St Germain presumably does not like.

The committee has other jurisdiction as well. St Germain concentrated for years on housing programs, and had the happy opportunity to site much of the nation's supply of federally assisted senior citizen housing in eastern Rhode Island. In the 1980s the government has essentially been moving out of the housing business, but not without some opposition from St Germain. He protects. And in 1983 and 1984 he held hostage an International Monetary Fund bill that the Administration wanted (though they allowed it to be attacked by right-wing Republicans) and got a housing bill, that otherwise would have failed, passed. Other parts of the committee's jurisdiction are moribund. No one even talks about wage and price controls any more, and no big city or corporation at this writing is seeking a loan guarantee as New York did in 1975 and Chrysler in 1979.

But St Germain's biggest problem in 1985 and 1986 was not legislation but scandal. In 1985 the *Wall Street Journal* charged: that a top St Germain aide called a federal regulator agency on behalf of a Florida savings and loan in which St Germain, if an application were approved, would be enabled to buy stock; that St Germain obtained better than 100% financing from a bank to purchase International House of Pancakes restaurants (this may be the elixir: everyone could get rich if they could get 100% financing to buy an IHOP or two); and that he had accumulated $2 million in assets while on the public payroll for 25 years. That triggered an investigation by the House ethics committee and an appearance by St Germain at a fundraiser for one of the Republicans on that committee, George Wortley. In April 1987 the ethics committee finally reported, finding that St Germain had made minor errors in filing disclosure forms and accepting one too many rides on an S&L plane, but declining to draw inferences from the phone calls from his aide to the regulators that he was using his public office to enrich his private purse, and recommending that no disciplinary action be taken against him. It did, however, add that it would be a real good idea if members didn't make such calls or give anything like an appearance of impropriety in the future.

With all that hanging over the incumbent in 1986 Republican state chairman John Holmes, an architect of his party's early 1980s victories, got into the race. St Germain, never bashful about using his chairmanship, raised much more money, but in early fall Holmes seemed to have him on the run. National Republicans sent out letters attacking St Germain, but Democrats argued successfully that those should be counted toward the limit on party spending for Holmes. St Germain declined to release his income tax returns, campaigned as a consumer champion for getting interest paid on checking accounts, conversed with constituents in Canadian French and Ukrainian. He attacked Holmes for flip-flopping on contra aid, but most of his TV spots were positive, emphasizing his roots and what he had done for senior citizens and veterans. Starting off with money in the bank, he raised plenty more, and was able to spend $848,000, almost exactly double Holmes's total, and still end the campaign with $376,000 in the bank. St Germain ended up winning with 58%, with big margins in the Blackstone Valley and smaller ones in Providence and Newport.

If as seems likely the House does not differ from the ethics committee's recommendation that no action be taken against St Germain, he seems sure to remain a powerful and competent committee chairman. One factor that works for him, at least among Democrats, is the lineup on the committee. Banking is a committee whose strongest members aside from St Germain are in the middle in seniority, not at the top. The next ranking Democrat is the erratic Henry Gonzalez of Texas, indisputably honest, but never much involved in the minutiae of financial regulation and prone to anguished controversies with other members and staff. It's unthinkable that the Democrats would deny a chair to an Hispanic member with seniority and of patent good will and decency. But there is also a case to be made for not accelerating St Germain's departure from the chairmanship of a committee with jurisdiction over such a delicate part of our economy.

The People: Pop. 1980: 474,429, dn. 2.8% 1970–80. Households (1980): 71% family, 35% with children, 58% married couples; 45.3% housing units rented; median monthly rent: $157; median house value: $48,600. Voting age pop. (1980): 357,096; 2% Black, 2% Spanish origin, 1% Asian origin.

1984 Presidential Vote: Reagan (R) 101,628   (50%)
Mondale (D) 99,060   (49%)

Rep. Fernand J. St Germain (D)

Elected 1960; b. Jan. 9, 1928, Blackstone, MA; home, Woonsocket; Providence Col., Ph.B. 1948, Boston U., LL.B. 1955; Roman Catholic; married (Rachel).

Career: Army, 1949–52; RI House of Reps., 1952–60; Practicing atty.

Offices: 2108 RHOB 20515, 202-225-4911. Also 204 Fogarty Fed. Bldg., Providence 02903, 401-528-5050; and 206 P.O. Bldg., Newport 02840, 401-846-7511.

Committees: *Banking, Finance and Urban Affairs* (Chairman of 31 D). Subcommittees: Consumer Affairs and Coinage; Financial Institutions Supervision, Regulation and Insurance (Chairman); Housing and Community Development.

Group Ratings

	ADA	ACLU	COPE	CFA	LCV	ACU	NTU	NSI	COC	CEI
1986	80	55	90	75	78	5	28	0	35	22
1985	70	—	89	83	—	10	36	—	20	—

National Journal Ratings

	1986 LIB — 1986 CONS		1985 LIB — 1985 CONS	
Economic	58%	41%	89%	0%
Social	69%	31%	49%	49%
Foreign	75%	20%	85%	8%

Key Votes

1) Lmt Cln Water Act	AGN	5) Retain Gun Cont	FOR	9) Aid Angola Reb	AGN
2) Rpl Tobac Sub	FOR	6) Contra Aid	AGN	10) Tax Reform	FOR
3) Grm-Rdmn Def Red	—	7) Lmt Text Imp	FOR	11) S Africa Sanc	FOR
4) Ban Polygraph	FOR	8) Limit SDI	FOR	12) Immig Reform	—

Election Results

1986 general	Fernand J. St Germain (D)	85,077	(58%)	($848,082)
	John A. Holmes Jr. (R)	62,397	(42%)	($340,458)
1986 primary	Fernand J. St Germain (D)	22,873	(100%)	
1984 general	Fernand J. St Germain (D)	130,585	(69%)	($150,407)
	Alfredo R. Rego (R)	59,926	(31%)	($30,267)

Campaign Contributions and Expenditures

1985-86		Direct Cont. 1985-86		PACS Breakdown 1985-86			
Receipts	$686,929	Indiv.	$215,964	Corp.	$137,300	T/M/H	$103,153
Expend.	$848,082	PACS	$4,923	Labor	$30,700	Agr.	$500
Unspent	$376,962	PACS	$301,353	Ideo.	$12,700	CWOS	$17,000
		Cand.	$49,382				

SECOND DISTRICT

The 2d Congressional District is the western half of Rhode Island. While the 1st includes many mill towns, the 2d has most of its population in working- and middle-class suburbs like Cranston and Warwick, which despite their Anglo–Saxon names are inhabited mostly by people with Irish, Italian, French, and Portuguese surnames. Some of Providence's rich suburbs are also here, and to a very marginal degree this is Rhode Island's more Republican district.

This is a Democratic district, but since 1980 it has elected Republican Claudine Schneider. She got her start in politics by opposing a nuclear plant and running a losing race against Edward Beard, house-painter-turned-congressman, in 1978; she came back and won in 1980. That victory she may owe to Beard's weaknesses; her three reelection wins, by increasing margins, she owes to her own strengths. In her first term she voted against Reagan budget cuts and sponsored a law to prohibit construction of Navy ships abroad. She was one of the leaders in the fight, successful finally in 1983, to kill the Clinch River breeder reactor. She was less successful on the issue of sex discrimination in education; she and her civil rights group allies have been unable to obtain passage of a bill overturning the Supreme Court's *Grove City* decision; the hangup has been the controversy surrounding Title IX—non-discrimination in education—regulations and abortion. Another major cause is the waste-end tax she has co-sponsored with Ron Wyden of Oregon, which would seek to discourage hazardous waste by taxing its disposal.

National Republicans are quite ready to tolerate Schneider's apostasy on some or even many issues because they know she is the only kind of Republican that could be elected from the district. She votes with them quite often on economic issues; it is on cultural issues that she is most liberal. She passed up the chance to run against Senator Claiborne Pell in 1984, when she could have made a strong race; will she try in 1990? In the meantime she remains a pivotal and interesting Republican in the House.

The People: Pop. 1980: 472,725, up 2.4% 1970–80. Households (1980): 74% family, 38% with children, 60% married couples; 37.0% housing units rented; median monthly rent: $159; median house value: $45,700. Voting age pop. (1980): 347,207; 3% Black, 2% Spanish origin, 1% Asian origin.

1984 Presidential Vote:

Reagan (R)	110,452	(53%)
Mondale (D)	98,046	(47%)

Rep. Claudine Schneider (R)

Elected 1980; b. Mar. 25, 1947, Clairton, PA; home, Narragansett; Rosemont Col., U. of Barcelona, Spain, Windham Col., B.A. 1969; Roman Catholic; divorced.

Career: Founder, RI Cmtee. on Energy, 1973; Exec. Dir., Conservation Law Foundation, 1973–78; Producer, pub. affairs prog. on Providence TV, 1979–80.

Offices: 1512 LHOB 20515, 202-225-2735. Also 30 Rolfe Sq., Cranston 02910, 401-528-5020.

Committees: *Merchant Marine and Fisheries* (6th of 17 R). Subcommittees: Fisheries and Wildlife Conservation and the Environment; Oceanography; Oversight and Investigations (Ranking Member). *Science, Space and Technology* (4th of 17 R). Subcommittees: Natural Resources, Agriculture Research and Environment (Ranking Member); Science, Research and Technology. *Select Committee on Aging* (10th of 26 R). Subcommittee: Health and Long-Term Care.

Group Ratings

	ADA	ACLU	COPE	CFA	LCV	ACU	NTU	NSI	COC	CEI
1986	80	78	71	75	86	5	42	10	47	38
1985	55	—	67	100	—	26	56	—	44	—

National Journal Ratings

	1986 LIB — 1986 CONS			1985 LIB — 1985 CONS		
Economic	52%	—	48%	42%	—	58%
Social	89%	—	0%	78%	—	22%
Foreign	80%	—	0%	71%	—	26%

Key Votes

1) Lmt Cln Water Act	—	5) Retain Gun Cont	FOR	9) Aid Angola Reb	AGN
2) Rpl Tobac Sub	FOR	6) Contra Aid	AGN	10) Tax Reform	FOR
3) Grm-Rdmn Def Red	—	7) Lmt Text Imp	FOR	11) S Africa Sanc	—
4) Ban Polygraph	FOR	8) Limit SDI	FOR	12) Immig Reform	FOR

Election Results

1986 general	Claudine Schneider (R)	110,524	(72%)	($325,052)
	Donald J. Ferry (D)	43,149	(28%)	($67,685)
1986 primary	Claudine Schneider (R) unopposed			
1984 general	Claudine Schneider (R)	135,151	(68%)	($236,111)
	Richard Sinapi (D)	64,357	(32%)	($44,184)

Campaign Contributions and Expenditures

1985-86		**Direct Cont. 1985-86**		**PACS Breakdown 1985-86**			
Receipts	$365,759	Indiv.	$175,403	Corp.	$38,825	T/M/H	$32,005
Expend.	$325,052	Party	$9,326	Labor	$62,295	Agr.	$250
Unspent	$123,222	PACS	$157,612	Ideo.	$20,287	CWOS	$3,950

SOUTH CAROLINA

Settled by slave-driving sugar planters from Barbados, ruled by a handful of large landholders with hair-trigger tempers always jealous of their honor, South Carolina has been most of its history an oligarchy on the democratic North American continent. Its leading political theorist, John C. Calhoun, distilled his principles rigorously and came up with a philosophy more akin to steely capitalism than agrarian communalism; his followers, in their fierce opposition to any act that restricted or reflected negatively on slavery, were manuevered into firing on Fort Sumter and starting the Civil War. After the war many were ruined and South Carolina's economy was in tatters. Yet the community leaders reasserted their control over the black majority and were firmly back in power by the 1870s.

Through most of South Carolina's history there is an eerie continuity, of control by a very small number of its richest citizens. This was the only state in which presidential electors were still chosen by the state legislature as late as 1860, and as late as 1948 only 142,000 South Carolinians voted for President in a state of more than two million people. This was a state and a colony of a very few rich people and of a much larger mass—at some points in history, mostly black—without very much to show for their labors at all. Behind the fierceness of the oligarchy was of course fear. The planters of Barbados and early South Carolina were outnumbered 100 to 1 by their slaves, and through the antebellum period a frisson of fear ran up South Carolinians' spines when they recalled the Denmark Vesey slave rebellion of 1822. A century later white supremacists felt queasy when they remembered the time during the 1870s when South Carolina's blacks controlled the state legislature and the congressional delegation. The blacks did nothing more to oppress the whites than insist on being treated equally. But slavery and then segregation, based on force, would always raise the specter that force would be used in return, for liberation or just revenge.

After 280 years of oligarchy, South Carolina has had 40 years of democracy, as the franchise was extended, first to poor whites starting in the late 1940s, then to blacks after the Voting Rights Act of 1965. Interestingly, this coincides with a period of rapid economic growth. As late as World War II South Carolina's income, education, and health statistics were among the worst in the nation, more typical of a banana republic—or of its original West Indian model—than of most American states. Today South Carolina's income levels, discounted for a somewhat lower cost of living, are close to national levels; health standards are similar to the rest of the nation; education levels, though low, are now not far from the national average.

The South Carolina that emerged from World War II is today scarcely recognizable. That was a state where hundreds of thousands lived off subsistence agriculture and many up through the 1960s—when Ernest Hollings discovered them and made a federal case of it—were malnourished or even starved. For some years South Carolina saw as its economic salvations the naval bases that clustered around Charleston (helped along by Mendel Rivers, chairman of the House Armed Services Committee) and the textile mills that dotted the hilly upcountry landscape around Greenville and Spartanburg. More important, South Carolina by the 1970s had become perhaps the most aggressive state in the South in attracting new industry. It has gone over to Europe and enticed French and German firms to set up major operations in the Piedmont and the Lowlands. It advertised its business climate (translation: one of the lowest rates of unionization), its taxes (very low), and its willingness to meet local employers' needs (very high). Gradually, it saw its standard of living moved up toward the national average, even as that average was itself rising rapidly. And it has used some of that increase in affluence to upgrade the quality of its local work force, through public expenditures on schools as well as highways, teachers as well as policemen.

This dramatic change occurred gradually as another, more dramatic change occurred, suddenly: the end of racial segregation. The massive outmigration of blacks from the lowlands in the years after World War II stopped around the time civil rights were established and the state's economy took off. South Carolina long since has had a white majority: 30% of its residents were black in 1980; and it has long since stopped practicing white supremacy: 28% of its registered voters were black in 1986. Now, since these blacks are younger than whites and tend to have more children, the long-term prospect is for the black percentage to increase.

The old South Carolina was solidly Democratic for years: 88% for Franklin Roosevelt in 1944. But it was also the leading Dixiecrat state: Strom Thurmond, then South Carolina's governor, was the Dixiecrat ticket-bearer against Truman in 1948, and he carried his own state easily. The civil rights revolution; the expansion of the electorate to include first lower income whites and, after the Voting Rights Act of 1965, blacks; the increased prosperity of the state—all these changed the tone and substance of South Carolina politics. For a time it seemed the state might be going Republican: its newly prosperous and anti-civil rights whites went heavily Republican in state as well as national races in the 1960s, and Strom Thurmond became a Republican in 1964. But that Republican surge peaked as long ago as 1966. Discontented whites went for George Wallace in 1968, and blacks provided a large vote base for national and state Democrats.

By the early 1970s South Carolina had the politics it has today, with an electorate split almost precisely equally between three groups. One are the blacks, who remain heavily Democratic. The second are the country-club whites, who are solidly Republican in national and most state contests. The third are what used to be called textile-mill whites. They are the swing vote in South Carolina, the bloc that determines the outcome of just about every election. They are people at one and the same time exhilarated and terrified by the changes they have seen around them, and in their own lives, in South Carolina in the last generation. They live in affluence beyond their dreams, and if their pleasant subdivisions and small houses amid strip-development highways look quite ordinary to visiting intellectuals and journalists, they represent an undreamed-of comfort for many South Carolinians who grew up without indoor plumbing or electricity or, often enough that they can remember it, enough to eat. They are leery of policies—and institutions, like labor unions—that seem to threaten the economic order which has proved so bountiful. At the same time, there is an underlying appreciation among textile-mill whites, as there is not among country-club whites, that government has made some contribution to this bounty and to their affluence. Social Security is seen not just as a drain on one's paycheck or an added cost of household help, but as a vital supplement to income for old age.

But like most people who move upward, they also have a nostalgia for—and tend to

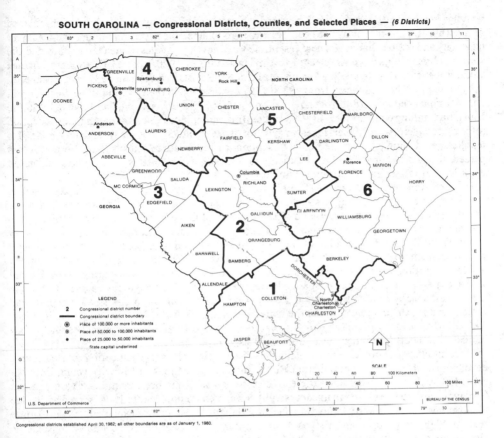

Congressional districts established April 30, 1982; all other boundaries are as of January 1, 1980.

sentimentalize—what they left behind. There is little yearning left to return to racial segregation, though there are nasty incidents occasionally like the hazing of black cadet at The Citadel in Charleston in 1986. Many others surely have an uneasy sense that old rules—however unjust they now seem—are no longer in force. More disturbingly, the affluent South Carolina they inhabit, so different from the underdeveloped country they grew up in, also is a land of divorce and abortion, of places where traditional moral values are flouted and even patriotism seems to be mocked. South Carolina, hotblooded enough to have started our only civil war, is perhaps the most bellicose of states, the least inclined to support a conciliatory foreign policy. The textile-mill whites' political legacy is Democratic, and for a time in the 1970s their concern for economic security and the attractiveness of candidates like Jimmy Carter moved them away from the Republicans they had flirted with after the civil rights revolution and toward the Democrats. When Carter appeared at the Firecracker 400 stock car race in 1976, he seemed to be speaking their language. But once in Washington, he seemed to be talking the language of public policy entrepreneurs and malaise merchants, and textile-mill whites began moving back to the Republicans. That movement has continued in the 1980s, as the textile-mill whites move into better jobs and more pleasant subdivisions. They will still vote for Democrats like Senator Ernest Hollings and Governor Richard Riley. But they will also vote for Republicans like Ronald Reagan, Strom Thurmond, and the Republican governor they helped to elect in 1986, Carroll Campbell.

Governor. South Carolina elected a Democratic governor, Richard Riley, in 1978 and 1982, who has been hailed as the nation's best and who retired with great popularity. Yet it replaced him with a Republican. Why? It becomes easier to understand if you remember the legacy of oligarchy and realize that voters here resent the way that tiny gaggles of men have controlled the state's politics. Edgar Brown, elected to the legislature in 1920, chaired the Senate Finance Committee from 1942 to 1972, when he retired at 84; Sol Blatt, elected in 1932, was Speaker of the House for all but four years from 1937 to 1972 and served in the House until he died in 1986. Riley campaigned in 1978 to "declare war on the Good Old Boy system," and bucked it in the legislature, failing on tax reform in 1983 but putting through in 1984 a thoroughgoing education reform, complete with higher taxes to pay for it. It included merit pay and pay raises for teachers, a building program, remedial education, cash bonuses to schools that improve; it was passed after Riley convinced businessmen and voters that the state needed a better educated work force if it is to enjoy further economic growth.

In 1986 Republican Representative Carroll Campbell, like Riley before him, promised to throw out the "good ol' boy system" of the entrenched politicians. The theme had some credibility because the Democratic nominee, Lieutenant Governor Mike Daniel, was a Columbia veteran who had beaten outsider Phil Lader in the primary (Lader, for the sake of party unity, declined a runoff which he was entitled to) and was quick to get defensive about Riley's record and Campbell's charges that the state was not doing well. During the campaign Campbell called for cutting insurance rates, reorganizing state government, and lowering taxes. He did well against the folksy Daniel in debates. In September he volunteered to take a urine test, while Daniel emotionally refused to do so; in the last week he charged that prominent Democrats had gotten "sweetheart contracts" from the state, and won 51%–49%. His margins came in urban and suburban areas, especially in his home base of Greenville, and he may have been helped by increased turnout upcountry; most rural counties went for Daniel.

Once in office, Campbell took the high road, stressing the same education and economic development themes Riley did. Campbell has the blow-dried look of so many young Republicans, but is an experienced and aggressive politician who has been mentioned as a possible Senator or maybe more. He ran unsuccessfully for lieutenant governor in 1974, served as an aide to Governor James Edwards, who did a better job than almost anyone expected, won his House seat in 1978, and won seats first on Appropriations and then on Ways and Means. Some Democrats claim that in the 1978 race Campbell encouraged a minor candidate to attack the Democrat Max Heller on the ground that, as a Jew, he did not believe in Jesus, and noted that a Campbell poll asked two questions about religion; Campbell denied that he had anything to do with the third candidate and and said the questions were asking voters which descriptions would best describe each candidate ("a Christian man," "Jewish," among others) and which qualities would make them more or less likely to vote for a candidate ("a Jewish immigrant," "a native South Carolinian," among others). In 1986 he not only showed talent but enjoyed good fortune: his House colleague Tom Hartnett bowed out of the race for governor and ran for lieutenant governor as part of a team with Campbell. But they were on separate lines and Hartnett lost 50%–49% to Democrat Nick Theodore. Campbell owes him one.

Unlike Edwards and so many other Republicans who by good fortune stumble into governorships, Campbell had to work hard to win his and seems to be building an effective Republican party. South Carolina had four special elections in early 1987 to fill vacancies in the state legislature; Republicans won four of four, including the seat formerly held by Democratic Representative Liz Patterson and one in rural and heavily black Edgefield County. "We're cutting them off at the grass roots," one Republican exulted, perhaps prematurely; but Republicans here are doing a better job than in most southern states of generating candidates able to win local elections in all kinds of constituencies.

Senators. For a long time South Carolina's Senate seats have in effect been the political reward of the most politically formidable of its governors: Burnet Maybank (first elected governor in 1938 and Senator in 1940), Olin Johnston (1934, 1944), Thurmond (1946, 1954), and Hollings (1958, 1966). The current Senators are formidable men who rose from humble beginnings, made their careers in the courtrooms, and ran unsuccessfully for President of the United States. They have proved to be two of the most durable and forceful members of the Senate today—or maybe ever. Strom Thurmond's career goes back more than 50 years now: he was first elected to the legislature at 29, in 1932, and was reelected senator at 81 in 1984. Hollings won his first election at 26, in 1948.

Thurmond has combined a reputation for firmness and steadfastness with a flexibility and adroitness that has enabled this onetime symbol of racial segregation to prosper politically in an era of integration. Thurmond was elected governor in 1946 and won 39 electoral votes as the States' Rights—*i.e.,* anti-civil rights—Democratic candidate for President in 1948. In 1954 he was elected to the Senate, stunningly, as a write-in candidate; he promised the voters that if he won he would resign and seek election in the ordinary manner, and in 1956 he did. During the 1964 campaign he switched to the Republican Party and supported Barry Goldwater for President; in 1968 he was the key power broker at the Republican National Convention, when he held the South for Richard Nixon.

This was his peak of national influence, but it was also a moment of peril: South Carolina's blacks were getting the vote, and for a moment Thurmond seemed to be in trouble. But he reacted to the enfranchisement of South Carolina's blacks by working as doggedly for them as he had for others: he hired black staffers in the early 1970s, pushed through the appointment of black federal judges, helped black local officials and citizens' groups with federal projects. He has ended up voting for renewal of the Voting Rights Act and the Martin Luther King holiday. He probably gets few black votes, but he has softened black voters' hostility; they don't turn out in large numbers to vote against him or form a strong political base for a possible opponent.

Thurmond as the senior Republican Senator was president pro tempore of the Senate for six years, a ceremonial post he enjoyed, and which put him in the theoretical line of succession to the Presidency. He also served as chairman of the Judiciary Committee, having taken care in the 1970s to use his seniority to outrank the liberal Charles Mathias. As chairman Thurmond was courteous, cooperative, conciliatory, but ready to move fast when he had the votes. He seems to have a pleasant working relationship with Joseph Biden. In his middle 80s, he remains in excellent health, though his hearing isn't good, and if he doesn't seem attentive to detail to some observers, those who think he might overlook some legislative detail or particle of procedure may find him alert and ready if the matter is something he cares about.

Thurmond is a retired Army general, an unabashed enthusiast for things military, and a supporter of an aggressive and assertive foreign policy. But in 1987 he did not exercise his option of becoming ranking Republican on the Armed Services Committee, declining to elbow aside Virginia's John Warner as he had Mathias. He is also a member of Veterans' Affairs and, as of 1985, Labor and Human Resources Committees. Thurmond has surprised some observers by not aggressively pursuing conservative causes. Instead he has worked on consensus measures like stopping cop-killer bullets, reforming the antitrust laws, outlawing designer drugs, and keeping South Carolina from getting more nuclear waste. He wants to bar former federal officials from lobbying for foreign countries. He did push the death penalty when he could and stoutly backed all Reagan judicial nominations. But one gets the impression that some time around 1970 Thurmond got tired of being a controversial figure widely hated, and decided to seek maximum acceptance and to make himself a consensus national leader instead. Not many then would have guessed he could do it, but he has.

Thurmond's seat came up in 1984, and he was reelected with scarcely any fuss. He has a solid bedrock of support in South Carolina that is well over 50%; he showed that in 1978 when he beat back a strong challenge by Democrat Charles Ravenel. There's been speculation about a possible Thurmond successor for nearly 20 years now. Should the seat become vacant, Governor Carroll Campbell might appoint Nancy Thurmond, whom the Senator married in 1968 when he was in his late 60s and she in her early 20s; she and their four children are a feature of every Thurmond campaign. But Thurmond shows no sign of retiring: in March 1985 he registered with the Federal Election Commission as a candidate for reelection in 1990. The span of his career is awesome; Thurmond knew Pitchfork Ben Tillman, the South Carolina governor and Senator who was born in 1847, and his children have a good chance of living into the 2050s.

South Carolina's other Senator, Ernest Hollings, ran for President in 1984 and made less impact than he wished—and less than his talents and program might seem to have warranted. Then in 1985 on the same issue he had emphasized in his campaign for the Presidency with such dismal results he made a great impact indeed. The issue was the federal deficit, and while he won few votes with the budget freeze he proposed on the stump and on the Senate Budget Committee, he was successful in proposing the Gramm-Rudman-Hollings deficit-cutting bill. Hollings has been tussling with budgets for a long time, as chairman of the Senate Budget Committee in 1980 after Edmund Muskie resigned to become Secretary of State, and as ranking Democrat on the committee in 1981 and 1982, when the groundwork for the deficits was laid by the Reagan budget and tax cuts.

Now, however, Hollings is devoting much attention to his duties as chairman of the Senate Commerce Committee. He was careful to relinquish the ranking seat on Budget and take it on Commerce in 1983; for Commerce, which has jurisdiction over most federal regulation, is much the better place from which to raise funds for campaigns, presidential or otherwise. As chairman, Hollings is well-informed and aggressive. He is dubious about some deregulation of communications, and backs the fairness doctrine in broadcasting. As a young lawyer he made his living as a plaintiffs' lawyer in negligence cases (he looks like a Charleston aristocrat, but has a modest background) and is not likely to back federal law limiting tort claims. He is skeptical about airline deregulation. For the first time in the 1980s Commerce seems to have a regulator as chairman.

Why did Hollings fall flat as a presidential candidate? One reason is the times: appeals for shared sacrifice fall flat in a peaceful, prosperous America. Another reason is the constituency. The Democrats' selection process is geared to mostly liberal party activists, and Hollings failed some of their litmus tests. He may have been the Senate's leading opponent of the MX missile in 1983, for example, but they recognized, accurately, that on most military and foreign issues he is an unreconstructed hawk. He may have been the Senate's most effective fighter against hunger in the 1960s and 1970s, when he was spurred to action by discovering how poorly many people were eating in South Carolina, but he expressed a not-at-all-veiled scorn for schemes of income redistribution and job guarantee programs.

But Hollings, like many politicians, was the victim of his successes. Successful in getting himself elected governor at age 36 in 1958, steering this bellicose state calmly toward complying with court desegregation orders, Hollings had faced his most difficult tests years before in an utterly different political world. This man who beat an incumbent Senator in 1966 and then established himself as a Senate insider betrayed on the campaign trail what he has shown in the committee room: a tendency to speak too quickly and too cruelly, a tendency to pounce on the weaknesses of others in a way that ends up hurting him. He won only 11% of the votes of the relatively few Maine Democrats eligible to vote after criss crossing their state; his weak showing days later in New Hampshire was anticlimactic.

Not that any of this hurt much when Hollings came up for reelection in 1986. There was a primary between two serious Republicans, but both had liabilities; the nominee, U.S. Attorney Henry McMaster, was stiff and lifeless;hHe emphasized drugs. Hollings worked hard in Washington and campaigned hard in South Carolina and won 63%–36%.

Presidential politics. South Carolina, more than most southern states, has been tilting Republican in presidential contests—more than can just be explained by the Reaganward movement of textile-mill whites. One explanation is changing demography: the growth of Hilton Head-like developments up and down the coast and even inland has brought Republican voters here from the suburbs of the Midwest and South. There is also evidence, in sharply rising turnout in Greenville and surrounding upcountry counties in 1984 and 1986, of a successful effort to register and turn out evangelical and fundamentalist Christians in the homeland of Bob Jones University. In contrast, there is little evidence of an increase in black turnout, despite the much publicized efforts of South Carolina native son Jesse Jackson, who took the trouble of registering to vote in Greenville in 1984 and then has played no role in the state's public life. South Carolina, with its oligarchic traditions, has not been particularly hospitable to presidential primaries. Oddly enough, the Republicans had one in 1980, and it turned out to be notable, if only as the endpoint of John Connally's electoral career. Even though Connally had the strong support of Senator Strom Thurmond, faithful even when it was apparent that the cause was lost, and even though it was a manageable country-club electorate (only 145,000 votes cast), Connally still got only 30% of the votes to Ronald Reagan's 55%. The Republican contest in 1988 could be very important: the party is caucusing the weekend before most of the other southern states vote in primaries. Evangelicals turned out in force for the 1987 Republican county conventions (there's no party registration to prevent former Democrats from doing so) and were expected to have a near-majority of the state convention; it's not clear whether this can be duplicated and whether such votes would go to Pat Robertson. George Bush strategist and South Carolina native Lee Atwater surely hopes that South Carolina will give his man a boost, and may have the inside track here.

Congressional districting. South Carolina's congressional districts were changed only slightly in redistricting; the Democratic legislature gave only minor help to Democrats. Two districts, the 4th and the 6th, have changed partisan hands in the 1980s, and the 1st and the 2d have seen close races.

The People: Est. Pop. 1986: 3,378,000; Pop. 1980: 3,121,820, up 8.2% 1980–86 and 20.5% 1970–80; 1.40% of U.S. total, 24th largest. 13% with 1–3 yrs. col., 14% with 4+ yrs. col.; 16.6% below poverty level. Single ancestry: 19% English, 5% Irish, 4% German, 1% French, Scottish. Households (1980): 78% family, 46% with children, 63% married couples; 29.8% housing units rented; median monthly rent: $133; median house value: $35,100. Voting age pop. (1980): 2,179,854; 27% Black, 1% Spanish origin. Registered voters (1986): 1,305,330; no party registration.

1986 Share of Federal Tax Burden: $7,842,000,000; 1.04% of U.S. total, 30th largest.

1986 Share of Federal Expenditures

	Total		Non-Defense		Defense	
Total Expend	$9,944m	(1.20%)	$7,208m	(1.20%)	$2,736m	(1.19%)
St/Lcl Grants	1,322m	(1.17%)	1,319m	(1.17%)	3m	(2.70%)
Salary/Wages	2,170m	(1.80%)	400m	(0.68%)	1,770m	(2.86%)
Pymnts to Indiv	4,552m	(1.25%)	4,108m	(1.18%)	443m	(2.49%)
Procurement	1,784m	(0.87%)	1,263m	(2.27%)	521m	(0.35%)
Research/Other	117m	(0.44%)	116m	(0.44%)	0m	(0.38%)

Political Lineup: Governor, Carroll A. Campbell, Jr. (R); Lt. Gov., Nick A. Theodore (D); Secy. of State, John T. Campbell (D); Atty. Gen., Travis Medlock (D); Treasurer, Grady L. Patterson, Jr. (D); Comptroller General, Earle E. Morris, Jr. (D). State Senate, 46 (35 D and 9 R); State House of Representatives, 124 (91 D and 33 R). Senators, Strom Thurmond (R) and Ernest F. Hollings (D). Representatives, 6 (4 D and 2 R).

1984 Presidential Vote

Reagan (R)	615,539	(64%)
Mondale (D)	344,459	(36%)

1980 Presidential Vote

Reagan (R)	441,841	(49%)
Carter (D)	430,385	(48%)
Anderson (I)	14,071	(2%)

GOVERNOR

Gov. Carroll A. Campbell, Jr. (R)

Elected 1986, term expires Jan. 1991; b. July 24, 1940, Greenville; home, Greenville; U. of SC, American U., M.A. 1985; Episcopalian; married (Iris).

Career: Real estate and farming; SC House of Reps., 1970–74; Exec. Asst. to Gov. James B. Edwards, 1975–76; SC Senate, 1976–78; U.S. House of Reps., 1978–86.

Office: P.O. Box 11369, The State House, Columbia 29211, 803-734-9818.

Election Results

1986 gen.	Carroll A. Campbell, Jr. (R) ...	384,565	(51%)
	Mike Daniel (D).............	361,325	(49%)
1986 prim.	Carroll A. Campbell, Jr. (R) unopposed		
1982 gen.	Richard W. Riley (D)........	468,819	(70%)
	William D. Workman, Jr......	202,806	(30%)

SENATORS

Sen. Strom Thurmond (R)

Elected 1956, seat up 1990; b. Dec. 5, 1902, Edgefield; home, Aiken; Clemson Col., B.S. 1923; Baptist; married (Nancy).

Career: Teacher and coach, 1923–29; Edgefield Cnty. Supt. of Educ., 1929–33; Practicing atty., 1930–38, 1951–55; SC Senate, 1933–38; Circuit Judge, 1938–42; Army, WWII; Gov. of SC, 1947–51; States Rights candidate for Pres. of U.S., 1948; U.S. Senate, 1954–56.

Offices: 218 RSOB 20510, 202-224-5972. Also 1835 Assembly St., Ste. 1558, Columbia 29201, 803-765-5496; 334 Meeting St., Rm. 600, Charleston 29493, 803-724-4282; 211 York St., N.E., Ste. 29, Aiken 29801, 803-649-2591; and 401 W. Evans St., Florence 29501, 803-662-8873.

Committees: *Armed Services* (2d of 9 R). Subcommittees: Conventional Forces and Alliance Defense; Readiness, Sustainability and Support; Strategic Forces and Nuclear Defense (Ranking Member). *Judiciary* (Ranking Member of 6 R). Subcommittees: Antitrust, Monopolies and Business Rights (Ranking Member); Courts and Administrative Practice. *Labor and Human Resources* (4th of 7 R). Subcommittees: Aging; Children, Family, Drugs, and Alcohol (Ranking Member); Education, Arts, and Humanities. *Veterans' Affairs* (3d of 5 R).

Group Ratings

	ADA	ACLU	COPE	CFA	LCV	ACU	NTU	NSI	COC	CEI
1986	5	0	10	27	8	91	46	100	78	71
1985	0	—	11	0	—	91	61	—	97	—

National Journal Ratings

	1986 LIB — 1986 CONS			1985 LIB — 1985 CONS		
Economic	0%	—	84%	0%	—	86%
Social	13%	—	85%	0%	—	83%
Foreign	0%	—	86%	0%	—	88%

Key Votes

1) Ease Gun Cont	FOR	5) Grm-Rdmn Def Red	FOR	9) Rehnquist Nom	FOR
2) Immig Reform	FOR	6) Contra Aid	FOR	10) Tax Reform	FOR
3) Lmt Text Imp	FOR	7) SDI Funding	FOR	11) Drug Death Pen	AGN
4) Aid Tobac Ind	FOR	8) Lmt PAC Contrib	FOR	12) S Africa Sanc	AGN

Election Results

1984 general	Strom Thurmond (R)	644,815	(67%)	($1,682,962)
	Melvin Purvis (D)....................	306,982	(32%)	($9,023)
1984 primary	Strom Thurmond (R)	44,662	(94%)	
	Robert H. Cunningham (R)	2,693	(6%)	
1978 general	Strom Thurmond (R)	351,733	(56%)	($2,013,431)
	Charles D. Ravenel (D)	281,119	(44%)	($1,134,168)

Campaign Contributions and Expenditures

1979-84		Direct Cont. 1983-84		PACS Breakdown 1979-84			
Receipts	$2,038,457	Indiv.	$1,346,556	Corp.	$373,374	T/M/H	$157,940
Expend.	$1,682,962	Party	$15,457	Labor	$5,000	Agr.	$1,000
Unspent	$364,686	PACS	$596,785	Ideo.	$22,973	CWOS	$9,250

Sen. Ernest F. (Fritz) Hollings (D)

Elected 1966, seat up 1992; b. Jan. 1, 1922, Charleston; home, Charleston; The Citadel, B.A. 1942, U. of SC, LL.B. 1947; Lutheran; married (Peatsy).

Career: Army, WWII; Practicing atty.; SC House of Reps., 1949–54, Speaker Pro Tem, 1951–54; Lt. Gov. of SC, 1955–59; Gov. of SC, 1959–63.

Offices: 125 RSOB 20510, 202-224-6121. Also 1835 Assembly St., Columbia 29201, 803-765-5731; and 112 Custom House, 200 E. Bay St., Charleston 29401, 803-724-4525; 126 Fed. Bldg., Greenville 29304, 803-585-3702; 233 Fed. Bldg., Florence 29503, 803-662-8135.

Committees: *Appropriations* (5th of 16 D). Subcommittees: Commerce, Justice, State, and Judiciary (Ranking Member); Defense; Energy and Water Development; Interior; Labor, Health and Human Services, Education. *Budget* (2d of 13 D). *Commerce, Science, and Transportation* (Chairman of 11 D). Subcommittees: Communications; Foreign Commerce and Tourism; Surface Transportation. *Select Committee on Intelligence* (5th of 8 D).

Group Ratings

	ADA	ACLU	COPE	CFA	LCV	ACU	NTU	NSI	COC	CEI
1986	35	28	56	67	67	52	48	80	32	40
1985	45	—	55	60	—	52	37	—	55	—

National Journal Ratings

	1986 LIB — 1986 CONS	1985 LIB — 1985 CONS
Economic	57% — 41%	57% — 42%
Social	66% — 33%	50% — 46%
Foreign	42% — 55%	51% — 46%

Key Votes

1) Ease Gun Cont	FOR	5) Grm-Rdmn Def Red	FOR	9) Rehnquist Nom	FOR
2) Immig Reform	FOR	6) Contra Aid	FOR	10) Tax Reform	FOR
3) Lmt Text Imp	FOR	7) SDI Funding	FOR	11) Drug Death Pen	AGN
4) Aid Tobac Ind	FOR	8) Lmt PAC Contrib	FOR	12) S Africa Sanc	FOR

Election Results

1986 general	Ernest F. (Fritz) Hollings (D)	456,500	(63%)	($2,233,843)
	Henry D. McMaster (R)	262,886	(36%)	($584,288)
1986 primary	Ernest F. (Fritz) Hollings (D) unopposed			
1980 general	Ernest F. (Fritz) Hollings (D)	612,554	(70%)	($723,427)
	Marshall Mays (R)	257,946	(30%)	($62,472)

Campaign Contributions and Expenditures

1985-86		Direct Cont. 1985-86		PACS Breakdown 1985-86			
Receipts	$2,395,632	Indiv.	$1,329,904	Corp.	$466,924	T/M/H	$264,933
Expend.	$2,233,843	Party	$17,223	Labor	$96,000	Agr.	$2,575
Unspent	$197,854	PACS	$913,697	Ideo.	$62,765	CWOS	$20,500

FIRST DISTRICT

There are few, if any, more beautiful urban scenes in America than the pastel row houses of Charleston wreathed with the springtime flowers of blossoming trees. Charleston, founded in 1670 and blessed with one of the finest harbors on the Atlantic, was one of the South's two leading cities up to the Civil War. Across its docks went cargoes of rice, indigo, cotton—all cultivated by black slaves and enriching the white planters and merchants who dominated the state's economic and political life. In the years that followed the Civil War, Charleston became an economic backwater. Today the old part of the city, beautifully preserved and still the home of the city's elite, houses fewer people than it did when it rained out shots on Fort Sumter in 1861.

This is an old society. The old South Carolina aristocracy, very private today, was once a leading force in American political life. The Democrats held their national convention in Charleston in 1860, and the hotheaded dandies in the galleries hooted down the northerners and so disrupted the proceedings that the northerners adjourned and reconvened in Baltimore while the southerners nominated a separate ticket that enabled Lincoln to be elected with 38% of the popular vote. South Carolina's blacks also have a colorful history. There were free blacks here before the Civil War (some even owned slaves themselves), and Charleston's blacks have been memorialized in *Porgy and Bess*. The local accent, which seems to outsiders to have a touch of New Jersey and which, rapidly spoken, can be incomprehensible, is best appreciated in the speech of Charleston native Ernest Hollings.

Since World War II, Charleston has been growing again, for two reasons. The first is military. The Navy established big bases here during the war and, with the help of Representative Mendel Rivers, chairman of the House Armed Services Committee from 1965 until his death in 1971, the bases grew to the point that they accounted for one-third of the payrolls in the Charleston area. The white working class area around the port and the bases in North Charleston remembers: its main street is Rivers Avenue. The military continues to be important here: every congressman since Rivers has taken care to serve on Armed Services. Another reason for Charleston's growth is that the economy has become more diversified and has prospered by the influx of Yankees and southerners to the condominium communities on the barrier islands. The first of these, Hilton Head, was started by Charles Fraser in 1957; it was an untested, risky concept at the time. Nearby were some of the poorest areas in the United States, where lowland blacks lived in poverty and malnutrition; many spoke a distinct dialect called Gullah. Now the blacks are much better off, and practically the entire coast is covered with developments inspired, in varying degrees, by the original.

The 1st Congressional District of South Carolina includes Charleston and its suburbs, the Low Country south and west of Charleston, and a couple of black-majority counties inland. Historically this was one of the most Democratic of constituencies in Franklin Roosevelt's time; now it leans Republican in Ronald Reagan's. High-income whites in these new areas, and in the affluent areas of Charleston, both in the old downtown and in new neighborhoods east of the Ashley River and out in the suburbs, have proved to be heavily Republican; blacks, who did not vote in most of this area until after 1965, are even more heavily Democratic. With a small white working-class, there is only a small margin of voters who are switchable.

The congressman from this district is a Republican freshman, Arthur Ravenel, who is an experienced Charleston politician. With a fine old South Carolina Huguenot name, he is a cousin of Charles Ravenel, the young Democrat and 1950s Harvard football hero, who was about to be elected governor in 1974 until his name was yanked off the ballot for failure to meet a residency requirement; he ran against Strom Thurmond in 1978 and in the 1st District in 1980, and lost both times. The Republican Ravenel is folksy ("Hi, I'm your cousin Arthur," he greets passers-by), worked hard on constituency service as a state legislator, and has, unusually for a Republican, significant support from black voters. The seat was up in 1986 because Republican Tom Hartnett, who showed a flip contempt for the business of legislating, left the House to run for lieutennat governor (an office he narrowly lost); the expected winner of the Democratic nomination was Hartnett's predecessor, Mendel Davis, who won the seat in 1971 as Mendel Davis's godson but retired at age 38 because of a bad back. But Davis lost to Charleston lawyer Jim Stuckey, who was able to carry a couple of inland counties, but lost in Charleston and its suburbs and on the coast.

In the House Arthur Ravenel got Hartnett's seat on Armed Services. Assuming he continues to work the district hard, he has a good chance to make it a safe seat.

The People: Pop. 1980: 520,338, up 25.3% 1970–80. Households (1980): 77% family, 47% with children, 61% married couples; 36.1% housing units rented; median monthly rent: $174; median house value: $41,400. Voting age pop. (1980): 362,866; 29% Black, 2% Spanish origin, 1% Asian origin.

1984 Presidential Vote:	Reagan (R)	106,107	(64%)
	Mondale (D)	58,243	(35%)

Rep. Arthur Ravenel, Jr. (R)

Elected 1986; b. Mar. 29, 1927, St. Andrews Parish; home, Mount Pleasant; Col. of Charleston, B.A. 1950; French Huguenot; married (Jean).

Career: USMC, 1945–46; Realtor, general contractor, cattleman; SC House of Reps., 1952–58; SC Senate, 1980–86.

Offices: 1730 LHOB 20515, 202-225-3176. Also 640 Fed. Bldg., Rm., 640, Charleston 29403, 803-724-4175; 263 Hampton St., Walterboro 29488, 803-549-5395; and P.O. Box 1538, Beaufort 29902, 803-524-2166.

Committees: *Armed Services* (20th of 20 R). Subcommittees: Military Installations and Facilities; Military Personnel and Compensation.

Group Ratings and Key Votes: Newly Elected

Election Results

1986 general	Arthur Ravenel, Jr. (R).	59,965	(52%)	($265,574)
	Jimmy Stuckey (D).	55,262	(48%)	($457,810)
1986 primary	Arthur Ravenel, Jr. (R).	8,487	(57%)	
	Steve Jones (R).	4,964	(33%)	
	Pat Vanderhoof (R).	1,561	(10%)	
1984 general	Thomas F. Hartnett (R)	103,288	(62%)	($339,508)
	Ed Pendarvis (D)	64,022	(38%)	($61,098)

Campaign Contributions and Expenditures

1985-86		Direct Cont. 1985-86		PACS Breakdown 1985-86			
Receipts	$272,559	Indiv.	$192,305	Corp.	$32,850	T/M/H	$34,419
Expend.	$265,574	Party	$8,636	Labor	$3,000	Agr.	$2,000
Unspent	$6,984	PACS	$83,052	Ideo.	$9,911	CWOS	$872
		Cand.	$5,000				

SECOND DISTRICT

In 1786, just after the Revolution, the South Carolina legislature decided to move the state's capital away from the aristocrats of Charleston and into the upcountry interior, away from a city named after a king to a new city they created smack dab in the middle of the state and named after a discoverer of America. So began Columbia. The State House was built on high ground above the Congaree River, amid a town of Columbia cottages—1½ story houses with first floor porticos, dormers, and raised brick basements. Columbia has kept on growing pretty steadily ever since, pausing only as General Sherman came through, ever since. State government and the university, the Army's Fort Jackson and local insurance companies have proved steady employers, and in the years since 1945 Columbia has attracted plants from Michelin and Allied Chemical, United Technologies and FN of Belgium, Du Pont and Square D. The Columbia metropolitan area on both sides of the Congaree is the largest and most prosperous in South Carolina, and some are projecting it as one of the fastest-growing U.S. metro areas of the 1990s.

Columbia is one of those southern metropolitan areas that has been trending Republican for at least 30 years. Post-1945 economic growth and Strom Thurmond's Dixiecrat tendency enlarged South Carolina's electorate and yanked it away from its Democratic roots. Upwardly mobile South Carolinians, transplanted from rural areas with no electricity to comfortable subdivisions with two-car garages, preferred Republicans first in national and then in state and local elections. The Columbia area went for Eisenhower in the 1950s; even when blacks got the vote in 1965, they were outnumbered usually by the increasingly Republican whites—particularly if you count not just Columbia's Richland County, but also the once rural and now suburban Lexington County across the river. South Carolina's 2d Congressional District is made up of those two counties, plus part of the South Carolina lowland country around Orangeburg. This was plantation country before 1865, and most of the people who live here now are black, and politics follows racial lines. Orangeburg is the site of South Carolina's main black state college and of a massacre of black students by white state highway patrolmen in 1968.

The congressman from the 2d District is Republican Floyd Spence, who once wowed Columbia as a University of South Carolina football player and has been running for office in the Columbia area since 1956. Spence became a Republican in 1962, two years before Strom Thurmond, and that year narrowly lost a House race to Albert Watson (a Democrat who supported Barry Goldwater in 1964, and was kicked out of the Democratic Caucus for it), and became a Republican in 1965. When he ran for governor in 1970, Spence ran for the seat and won it.

Spence is now one of the most senior Republicans in the House, a high-ranking member of the Armed Services Committee, and ranking Republican on the Seapower Subcommittee (although the district's parochial military interest is the Army's Fort Jackson). He is a solid hawk on military affairs, as well as a dependable conservative on all issues. He has another, thankless, assignment—ranking Republican on the House Ethics Committee. There he has generally let Democratic chairmen—Charles Bennett, Louis Stokes, Julian Dixon—take the lead, but he deserves credit for subordinating his natural camaraderie and supporting rigorous investigations of fellow members and, sometimes, stern punishment. He votes with many of the the newer, abrasive, intellectually adventurous House Republicans, but temperamentally he is part of the good-old-boy southern tradition.

For years the Republican trend among Columbia area whites combined with blacks' support of the Democrats has produced small but reliable majorities for Spence, even over such outstanding opponents as Matthew Perry, a black later made a federal judge by Strom Thurmond, and Jack Bass, a top newspaper reporter and the writer of the definitive work on the Orangeburg massacre. From 1974 to 1982 Spence's percentage was constant between 56% and 59%. Then in 1984 he won with 62%—his best percentage yet in this polarized district and precisely the same as President Reagan's share of the vote—and may have gotten overconfident. Democrat Fred Zeigler ran a vigorous campaign in 1986, arguing that Spence had accomplished little; to point up Spence's alleged health problems, Zeigler ads showed the Democrat running up the Capitol steps. Zeigler carried not only the Orangeburg area but Richland County. Spence carried just Lexington County, the most Republican in the state—with 71%, enough for a 54% showing district-wide. That apparently is a little too close for comfort. In early 1987 Spence was out declaring his candidacy, opposing the congressional pay raise, moving his district office to an accessible suburban location—signs that he is trying to forestall or at least be prepared for another tough challenge in 1988. But rumors circulate that he will retire, in which case Republican state Senator Addison Wilson of Lexington County and possibly Zeigler would be the favorites to succeed him.

The People: Pop. 1980: 522,688, up 24.6% 1970–80. Households (1980): 76% family, 45% with children, 60% married couples; 32.7% housing units rented; median monthly rent: $160; median house value: $40,800. Voting age pop. (1980): 372,290; 32% Black, 1% Spanish origin, 1% Asian origin.

1984 Presidential Vote: Reagan (R) 105,337   (62%)
                               Mondale (D) 61,368   (36%)

Rep. Floyd D. Spence (R)

Elected 1970; b. Apr. 9, 1928, Columbia; home, Lexington; U. of SC, A.B. 1952, LL.B. 1956; Lutheran; widowed.

Career: Navy, 1952–54; Practicing atty.; SC House of Reps., 1956–62; SC Senate, 1966–70, Minor. Ldr., 1966–70.

Offices: 2113 RHOB 20515, 202-225-2452. Also 140 Stone Ridge Dr., Ste. 104, Columbia 29201, 803-254-5120; 1681 Chestnut St., N.E., P.O. Box 1609, Orangeburg 29116-1609, 803-536-4641.

Committees: *Armed Services* (2d of 20 R). Subcommittees: Military Installations and Facilities; Seapower and Strategic and Critical Materials (Ranking Member). *Standards of Official Conduct* (Ranking Member of 6 R). *Select Committee on Aging* (23d of 26 R). Subcommittees: Human Services; Retirement Income and Employment.

Group Ratings

	ADA	ACLU	COPE	CFA	LCV	ACU	NTU	NSI	COC	CEI
1986	0	0	14	8	24	77	46	100	76	51
1985	10	—	13	17	—	81	52	—	95	—

National Journal Ratings

	1986 LIB — 1986 CONS		1985 LIB — 1985 CONS	
Economic	31%	— 67%	0%	— 95%
Social	0%	— 89%	0%	— 76%
Foreign	0%	— 86%	0%	— 76%

Key Votes

1) Lmt Cln Water Act	FOR	5) Retain Gun Cont	AGN	9) Aid Angola Reb	FOR
2) Rpl Tobac Sub	AGN	6) Contra Aid	FOR	10) Tax Reform	AGN
3) Grm-Rdmn Def Red	FOR	7) Lmt Text Imp	FOR	11) S Africa Sanc	AGN
4) Ban Polygraph	AGN	8) Limit SDI	AGN	12) Immig Reform	AGN

Election Results

1986 general	Floyd D. Spence (R)..................	73,455	(54%)	($294,665)
	Fred Zeigler (D)......................	63,592	(46%)	($179,860)
1986 primary	Floyd D. Spence (R) unopposed			
1984 general	Floyd D. Spence (R).................	108,085	(62%)	($240,229)
	Ken Mosely (D)	63,932	(37%)	($74,450)

Campaign Contributions and Expenditures

1985-86		Direct Cont. 1985-86		PACS Breakdown 1985-86			
Receipts	$277,527	Indiv.	$113,288	Corp.	$84,526	T/M/H	$46,980
Expend.	$294,665	Party	$9,908	Labor	$6,500	Agr.	$1,000
Unspent	$9,912	PACS	$148,199	Ideo.	$8,915	CWOS	$278

THIRD DISTRICT

As you move inland from the South Carolina coast, from the plantations owned by Charleston aristocrats, you find the upcountry lands pioneered by the likes of John C. Calhoun in the early 19th century. The pioneers wanted to make big plantations of these forests, but the land did not always cooperate: it was too hilly for the labor-intensive rice crop grown in the lowlands and sometimes too cold for cotton. So while the coastal plantations were tended by thousands of slaves, relatively few were brought here, and the land went mostly to smaller white farmers. That history has consequences today. The 3d Congressional District of South Carolina, which follows the Savannah River border with Georgia for most of its length, starts in the lowlands in Allendale County, which is 62% black, and proceeds north to 3,500-foot Sassafras Mountain, in Pickens County, which is 7% black.

The southern part of this district is Strom Thurmond country. He grew up in Edgefield and as county judge there in the 1930s maintained stern white control of the black majority. He maintains his residence now in Aiken, a prosperous town which has long been a winter haven for New York huntsmen, and which became solidly Republican—as Thurmond did— in the middle 1960s. The northern part of the district is Piedmont upcountry, with almost an Appalachian air. The largest city here is Anderson, a mostly white textile-mill town; a strong city for George Wallace in the 1960s, it moved strongly toward the Democrats in the middle 1970s and strongly away from them in the 1980s. This was the part of the state with the biggest swing against the national Democratic ticket between 1980 and 1984.

The congressman from the 3d District is Butler Derrick, a Democrat who won the seat in 1974 and is second in seniority in the oft-changing South Carolina House delegation. He attracted notice in his early years for defying old shibboleths. In 1977 he was a leader in stripping Florida's 37-year veteran Bob Sikes of his chairmanship for financial improprieties; about the same time he supported Jimmy Carter's move to cancel a dam in the 3d District. Derrick has been consistently more favorable to environmental claims than most southern congressmen of either party, and more inclined to support procedural reforms.

More recently he has won less notice, in part because he serves on the Rules Committee, the body which for the most part controls the flow of legislation to the House floor. When he was given that post in 1979, Derrick was expected to be loyal to the Democratic leadership, and he generally has been; in turn he was expected to express within inner Democratic councils the point of view of southern Democrats. His role is similar on the Budget Committee, of which Derrick became a member in 1983—his second rotation on the committee. The spotlight on budget issues goes to chairman William Gray and to the Speaker and Majority Leader. But junior members like Derrick, by helping to set parameters and to determine what the Democratic compromise position will be, help to make the decisions.

These are not terribly visible roles. But in the hands of a bright legislator, process issues can drive policy choices, and Derrick like other talented Rules members is in a position of considerable leverage. He can use it for causes important to the district, like the textile and apparel protection bill that Derrick, as chairman of the Textile Caucus, will be championing in this Congress. He can use it also as he did in 1986 to smooth the way for floor consideration and therefore passage of the McClure–Volkmer bill to relax federal gun control laws; South Carolina has one of the laxest attitudes towards guns in the nation, and its roadsides are festooned with gun shops. He can exert pressure to get the federal government to sell surplus property for a lakeside development in impoverished McCormick County. He can push also for development of more advanced nuclear reactors in the big Savannah River nuclear plant at the southern end of the district, which is also the place where nearly half the nation's nuclear wastes are now deposited.

Derrick proved himself popular in the district, despite a rather liberal voting record on many issues. He got his lowest percentage ever, 58%, in 1984, but immediately afterwards rejected all plans to run for statewide office and concentrated on his work in the House; he won with 68% in 1986. He may get a tough race in 1988 from Henry Jordan, the surgeon who with evangelical backing nearly won the 1986 Senate primary. Derrick is now the third ranking Democrat on Rules, 36 years younger than Chairman Claude Pepper and nine years younger than Joe Moakley of Massachusetts, the next man in line. So he has a good chance of being chairman of Rules some day.

The People: Pop. 1980: 519,280, up 20.2% 1970–80. Households (1980): 79% family, 44% with children, 65% married couples; 25.3% housing units rented; median monthly rent: $104; median house

value: $32,000. Voting age pop. (1980): 366,318; 20% Black, 1% Spanish origin.

1984 Presidential Vote:

Reagan (R) 102,301	(67%)
Mondale (D) 49,116	(32%)

Rep. Butler Derrick (D)

Elected 1974; b. Sept. 30, 1936, Springfield, MA; home, Edgefield; U. of SC, U. of GA, LL.B. 1965; Episcopalian; divorced.

Career: Practicing atty., 1965–74; SC House of Reps., 1969–74.

Offices: 201 CHOB 20515, 202-225-5301. Also P.O. Box 4126, Anderson 29622, 803-224-7401; 211 York St., N.E., Rm. 5, Aiken 29801, 803-649-5571; and 129 Fed. Bldg., Greenwood 29622, 803-223-8251.

Committees: *Budget* (4th of 21 D). Task Forces: Budget Process (Chairman); Economic Policy. *Rules* (3d of 9 D). Subcommittee: The Legislative Process (Chairman). *Select Committee on Aging* (16th of 39 D). Subcommittee: Health and Long-Term Care.

Group Ratings

	ADA	ACLU	COPE	CFA	LCV	ACU	NTU	NSI	COC	CEI
1986	55	70	54	75	75	26	27	22	44	23
1985	60	—	54	42	—	10	29	—	36	—

National Journal Ratings

	1986 LIB — 1986 CONS		1985 LIB — 1985 CONS	
Economic	69% —	30%	57% —	41%
Social	52% —	46%	58% —	41%
Foreign	63% —	37%	63% —	37%

Key Votes

1) Lmt Cln Water Act	AGN	5) Retain Gun Cont	AGN	9) Aid Angola Reb	AGN
2) Rpl Tobac Sub	AGN	6) Contra Aid	AGN	10) Tax Reform	FOR
3) Grm-Rdmn Def Red	AGN	7) Lmt Text Imp	FOR	11) S Africa Sanc	—
4) Ban Polygraph	AGN	8) Limit SDI	FOR	12) Immig Reform	FOR

Election Results

1986 general	Butler Derrick (D)	79,109	(68%)	($177,714)
	Richard Dickison (R)	36,495	(32%)	($4,261)
1986 primary	Butler Derrick (D) unopposed			
1984 general	Butler Derrick (D)	88,917	(58%)	($184,251)
	Clarence E. Taylor (R)	61,739	(41%)	($84,795)

Campaign Contributions and Expenditures

1985-86		Direct Cont. 1985-86		PACS Breakdown 1985-86			
Receipts	$282,849	Indiv.	$93,815	Corp.	$30,750	T/M/H	$52,009
Expend.	$177,714	Party	$698	Labor	$105,850	Agr.	$12,500
Unspent	$227,992	PACS	$223,316	Ideo.	$17,757	CWOS	$4,450

FOURTH DISTRICT

When textile manufacturers were looking for places to move their mills out of New England early in this century, one place they found was the land along the Southern Railway tracks between Charlotte and Atlanta. Cotton could be shipped in and finished products out over the railroad, and there was a plentiful supply of low wage white labor (for the mills didn't hire blacks in those days) in the hills of upcountry South Carolina. Today, this same stretch of land along South Carolina's Interstate 85, which parallels the Southern, remains the number one textile-producing area in the United States. But it is more than that. Greenville and Spartanburg, the biggest cities in a region where population is scattered in small towns and along major and minor highways, have attracted new businesses producing Michelin tires and Stouffer's Lean Cuisine and Digital Computer, most of them requiring higher skills and paying higher wages than the mills. This has long been one of the most industrialized and blue-collar parts of the nation, because of textiles; now with diversification it is becoming one of the economic growth centers of the South or, for that matter, the western world. It stages the largest balloon race east of the Mississippi, with some 200 balloons competing.

Northern observers have always thought that textiles and the textile belt would go the way of big northern industries like steel and autos: that the manufacturers would be concentrated into a few big companies, operating huge factories, and that the workers would join unions who would bargain for high wages and fringe benefits. But history has taken a different course. There are big textile companies, like Roger Millken's operation which is headquartered in Greenville. But there are lots of small producers as well, and the concentration of textile companies has not squeezed other businesses out as autos squeezed others out of Michigan. The plants have become not more concentrated, but more scattered—in some large mills and small, not usually in cities (which aren't very large here anyway) but at the edge of small towns or in the middle of heavily settled rural landscapes, near an interchange or on a side highway. Wages have not risen, and workers who want more go to the newer industries; and unions, despite a few publicized exceptions, have made almost no headway at all. Yet the textile country is thriving and diversification is more than compensating for jobs lost because of cheap foreign competition. And the industrial North which set itself up as a model is now—with smaller companies growing, and unions' power eroding—coming to resemble the textile country rather than vice versa.

The textile mill country has its own sets of civic institutions: business leaders and their allies in press and politics and religious fundamentalists and evangelicals like the proprietors of Greenville's Bob Jones University. The two biggest towns here have divergent political traditions. Spartanburg has been more Democratic and was the home base of politicians like James Byrnes when he was Senator (he was also congressman, Supreme Court Justice, Secretary of State, and finally governor in the early 1950s) and Olin Johnston (governor 1935–39 and 1943–45 and Senator 1945–65), who tended to support their party on economic issues. Greenville has been more likely to produce Republicans and very conservative Democrats, like Judge and defeated Supreme Court nominee Clement Haynsworth, Representative (1969–79) James Mann, and Representative (1979–87) and now Governor Carroll Campbell.

The 1986 race for Congress in the 4th District, which includes Greenville, Spartanburg, and the much smaller Union County, was a contest between these three forces. There was a Republican primary behind William Workman III, newspaper editor and scion of an established South Carolina Republican family with many ties to the business community, and two candidates with strong religious backing: Richard Rigdon, who was associated with funda-mentalists, and Thomas Marchant, associated with charismatics. Workman won, but got just 49% in the first primary and was hurt by attacks on his business ties, and because he had to spend more than $200,000 on the primary. In the first months of the general, he campaigned less actively than the Democrat, Elizabeth Patterson, a state Senator and former council member from Spartanburg, and the daughter of Olin Johnston. Patterson has a history of government service in the Peace Corps and Vista, civic involvement on college and agency boards, Sunday school teaching; she was attacked as a liberal but campaigned convincingly as a fiscal conservative concerned about human needs. Workman won 56% of the votes in Greenville County, but she won 60% in Spartanburg and 63% in Union, for a 52% victory. Given two years of incumbency, she has a chance to consolidate her hold on this district and may be helped if the Republicans continue to be split.

The People: Pop. 1980: 520,525, up 17.3% 1970–80. Households (1980): 78% family, 43% with children, 63% married couples; 30.4% housing units rented; median monthly rent: $132; median house value: $34,300. Voting age pop. (1980): 373,015; 17% Black, 1% Spanish origin.

1984 Presidential Vote:

Reagan (R)	....	114,650	(70%)
Mondale (D)	....	48,691	(30%)

Rep. Elizabeth J. Patterson (D)

Elected 1986; b. Nov. 18, 1939, Columbia; home, Spartanburg; Columbia Col., B.A. 1961; United Methodist; married (Dwight).

Career: Recruiting office, Peace Corps, 1962–64, VISTA, 1965–66; VISTA SC Coordinator, 1966–67; Head Start Coordinator, SC Offic of Econ. Opp., 1967–68; Aide to Rep. James R. Mann, 1969–70; Mbr., Spartanburg City Cncl., 1975–76; SC Senate, 1979–86.

Offices: 106 CHOB 20515, 202-225-6030. Also P.O. Box 10408, Fed. Station, Greenville 29603, 803-232-1141; P.O. Box 1330, Spartanburg 29304, 803-582-6422; and P.O. Box 904, Union 29379, 803-427-2205.

Committees: *Banking, Housing and Urban Affairs* (25th of 31 D). Subcommittees: Economic Stabilization; Financial Institutions Supervision, Regulation and Insurance; General Oversight and Investigations. *Veterans' Affairs* (19th of 21 D). Subcommittees: Education, Training and Employment; Housing and Memorial Affairs. *Select Committee on Hunger* (16th of 16 D). Task Force: Domestic Task Force.

Group Ratings and Key Votes: Newly Elected

Election Results

1986 general	Elizabeth J. Patterson (D)	67,012	(52%)	($594,026)
	Bill Workman (R).....................	61,648	(47%)	($639,859)
1986 primary	Elizabeth J. Patterson (D) unopposed			
1984 general	Carroll A. Campbell, Jr. (R)...........	105,139	(64%)	($690,962)
	Jeff Smith (D).......................	57,854	(35%)	($348,669)

Campaign Contributions and Expenditures

	1985-86	Direct Cont. 1985-86		PACS Breakdown 1985-86			
Receipts	$619,226	Indiv.	$93,815	Corp.	$17,802	T/M/H	$40,698
Expend.	$594,026	Party	$10,000	Labor	$72,700	Agr.	$2,500
Unspent	$25,202	PACS	$177,080	Ideo.	$40,180	CWOS	$3,200

FIFTH DISTRICT

In the years just before the American Revolution, Scotch and Scotch-Irish farmers, fleeing from the lands where they lived as impoverished tenants, moved up the valleys of the sluggish rivers of South Carolina and settled for the first time the uplands of the colony. Here they could farm their own land, away from the landlords and slaveholders of the big coastal plantations, and here they built rural communities which exist, much changed, today. This was fiercely contested country in the Revolutionary War—the battles of Kings Mountain and brilliantly executed Cowpens were fought here, and Andrew Jackson as a boy was scarred when he defied a British soldier—and the fighting spirit has never entirely subsided.

Such is the 5th Congressional District of South Carolina, an odd-shaped collection of rural counties between Columbia, Spartanburg, and Charlotte, North Carolina. It still looks like farming country, and many residents still cultivate their property, and even make a fair amount of money off it if they have a tobacco allotment. But it is really a part of industrial America: textile mills have long been the biggest employers, and there has been an influx since the 1970s of new plants as well; many people here routinely commute as much as 50 miles. The rigorous Calvinist religion which the earliest settlers brought with them lives on in various forms of Protestantism today. The 5th District is the home base of ousted PTL televangelist Jim Bakker and his wife Tammy Faye; here in Fort Mill, just south of the North Carolina line, they built the Heritage USA Christian vacation retreat, complete with luxury hotel and campsites, Heritage Island water park and a daily Passion Play. The fundamentalist spirit does not mean that this is a Republican area. In state and congressional elections South Carolina outside the major cities—which includes all the 5th District—remains solidly Democratic.

The congressman from the 5th District is John Spratt. To some he may seem an odd representative for such a district. He has degrees from Davidson, Yale Law, and Oxford and is part of the small group of wealthy lawyers, bankers, and businessmen who run economic life in small cities and towns in every county of South Carolina. Most such people are very conservative. But those who stuck with the Democratic Party during the difficult years of desegregation and of the national party's unpopularity here were often motivated by a real commitment to at least some of the party's liberal views. And some, like Spratt, were involved in the 1974 gubernatorial campaign of Charles Ravenel, an enterprise unsuccessful in its original intention but successful in involving a large number of highly motivated young people in Democratic politics in this state. The people who run things in places like York and Rock Hill understand that not everybody in these communities is capable of managing civic affairs. But those who are Fritz Hollings–Charles Ravenel Democrats hope and believe they are representing the interests of those ordinary citizens faithfully, however inarticulate they may be and however contrary-minded they may sometimes seem.

Spratt has made a name for himself in the House as a smart and hard-working member whose knowledge and judgments can be relied on. As a freshman he failed to get a seat on Energy and Commerce and went to Armed Services instead. There he became an expert on the issue of procurement, mastering the details while others were making headlines, with an understanding of the hard choices and tradeoffs that must be made in any procurement reform. After the 1984 election he was a leading backer of Les Aspin for the Armed Services chairmanship, and spoke for him in the Democratic Caucus just after Speaker Tip O'Neill made an impassioned plea for the aging Mel Price; when Aspin was under challenge after the 1986 election he stuck with him and helped him turn around the first caucus vote and keep his chairmanship. He has used his seat on the Government Operations Committee to build up expertise on trade issues and work for protection for the Carolinas' textile industry. On issues generally he has taken a mixed position, voting often but not always with the Democratic leadership.

Spratt was first elected in 1982, when incumbent Ken Holland announced his retirement a week before the filing deadline; involved in politics and civic affairs, Spratt was able to put a campaign together readily and won 38% in the primary, 55% in the runoff against a candidate who spent nearly $1 million, and 68% in the general election. He was reelected without Democratic or Republican opposition in 1984 and 1986. He has the capacity to be a strong statewide candidate but for the moment anyway seems more interested in working in the House.

The People: Pop. 1980: 519,716, up 12.9% 1970–80. Households (1980): 80% family, 47% with children, 64% married couples; 26.5% housing units rented; median monthly rent: $104; median house value: $31,000. Voting age pop. (1980): 357,907, 29% Black, 1% Spanish origin.

1984 Presidential Vote:

Reagan (R)	94,269	(62%)
Mondale (D)	58,350	(38%)

Rep. John M. Spratt, Jr. (D)

Elected 1982; b. Nov. 1, 1942, Charlotte, NC; home, York; Davidson Col., A.B. 1964, M.A., Oxford U., 1966, Yale U., LL.B. 1969; Presbyterian; married (Jane).

Career: Operations Ofc. of Asst. Secy. of Defense, 1969–71; Practicing atty., 1971–82; Pres., Bank of Ft. Mill, 1973–82; Pres., Spratt Insur. Agcy., 1973–82.

Offices: 1118 LHOB 20515, 202-225-5501. Also Box 350, Rock Hill 29731, 803-327-1114; 39 E. Calhoun St., Sumter 29150, 803-773-3362; and 214 W. Laurens St., Box 964, Laurens 29360, 803-984-5323.

Committees: *Armed Services* (22d of 31 D). Subcommittees: Investigations; Procurement and Military Nuclear Systems. *Government Operations* (15th of 24 D). Subcommittees: Commerce, Consumer, and Monetary Affairs; Government Information, Justice, and Agriculture.

Group Ratings

	ADA	ACLU	COPE	CFA	LCV	ACU	NTU	NSI	COC	CEI
1986	60	70	54	75	71	33	27	50	59	31
1985	35	—	51	67	—	38	36	—	57	—

National Journal Ratings

	1986 LIB — 1986 CONS		1985 LIB — 1985 CONS	
Economic	50% —	50%	48% —	50%
Social	67% —	32%	63% —	33%
Foreign	55% —	44%	54% —	46%

Key Votes

1) Lmt Cln Water Act	FOR	5) Retain Gun Cont	AGN	9) Aid Angola Reb	AGN
2) Rpl Tobac Sub	AGN	6) Contra Aid	AGN	10) Tax Reform	FOR
3) Grm-Rdmn Def Red	FOR	7) Lmt Text Imp	FOR	11) S Africa Sanc	FOR
4) Ban Polygraph	AGN	8) Limit SDI	FOR	12) Immig Reform	FOR

Election Results

1986 general	John M. Spratt, Jr. (D) unopposed			($66,944)
1986 primary	John M. Spratt, Jr. (D) unopposed			
1984 general	John M. Spratt, Jr. (D)	98,513	(92%)	($58,272)
	Two others	8,778	(8%)	

Campaign Contributions and Expenditures

1985-86		Direct Cont. 1985-86		PACS Breakdown 1985-86			
Receipts	$156,055	Indiv.	$75,873	Corp.	$32,100	T/M/H	$19,950
Expend.	$66,944	PACS	$65,550	Labor	$9,250	Agr.	$500
Unspent	$118,089			Ideo.	$3,750	CWOS	$0

SIXTH DISTRICT

The 6th Congressional District of South Carolina is part of the state's lowlands, north and east of Charleston, up to the North Carolina border. This is low-lying land; the rivers wind lazily toward the shoreline, where they come upon the barrier islands now developed as South Carolina's Grand Strand. Inland you find tobacco fields; 15 acres can support a family, though not very well, which helps to explain why tobacco district politicians defend its interests so assiduously. This was once plantation country, and a large percentage of the people here are black; three of the counties have black majorities, and overall the district is 41% black. This is the highest percentage in a South Carolina district, and the percentage of blacks is no longer declining as it was before 1970. For years blacks from this area lined up after high school graduation and got on the bus to New York (called the chicken bone special, because they packed chicken dinners) to make their livings. Now they remain in South Carolina, and over the long run the black percentage here is likely to rise.

The two places in the district with the lowest black percentages are also those with above-average economic growth that attracted people from outside the area (though usually from the South). One is Florence, the district's largest city; the other is the Grand Strand area in Horry County, which is only 22% black.

Nonetheless this is a district where black voters have had the satisfaction of influencing congressional politics greatly since the Voting Rights Act of 1965. In 1972 they ousted the chairman of the House District of Columbia Committee, John McMillan, who was often accused of being a racist. In 1974 and 1982 they ousted Republican congressmen who had gotten in under special circumstances. In the latter case, Republican John Napier beat incumbent Democrat John Jenrette in 1980 after Jenrette's Abscam conviction. Even so, most blacks stayed with him and he came close to winning.

Napier had a near-impossible assignment in trying to hold onto the district in 1982. He had a near-perfect Reagan voting record and suffered from the recession and from the President's perceived attitude on civil rights issues. He was also hurt when Democratic legislator and clothing chain store owner Robin Tallon finished far ahead in the Democratic primary and won the runoff. Tallon had the same kind of support among blacks that Jenrette did, and concentrated his campaign efforts on turning out the black vote. He ran close to racial percentages in most counties, but won enough white votes in Horry County to win districtwide with 52%. Napier's advantages of incumbency and money were not telling in a district in which most of the votes are committed and Democrats begin with the bigger base.

No one has ever accused Tallon of being an intellectual. He has a good old boy style, as you might expect of a small city clothing store owner, that goes over well at Rotary Club meetings and in black churches. His record is fairly liberal on economic and foreign policy, solidly conservative on cultural issues. In the House he is a member of the Agriculture Committee, and spent much of 1986 seeking aid for the drought-stricken farmers of his area; he also wants to change the farm credit system to make more money available to farmers. On the Tobacco and Peanuts Subcommittee he has been a solid vote for the chairman, North Carolina's Charlie Rose.

Back home Tallon has now what Jenrette had until he got into trouble: a district he seems likely to hold in fair partisan weather or foul. This is one southern district where the Democratic national ticket is not too much of a drag: Walter Mondale got 42% of the vote here, and a congressman who can't run 8% ahead of his presidential nominee doesn't deserve to win. Tallon got 60% of the vote in 1984 and 76% in 1986; the latter showing represents his first serious inroad into the Republican base.

The People: Pop. 1980: 519,273, up 23.6% 1970–80. Households (1980): 80% family, 49% with children, 63% married couples; 28.4% housing units rented; median monthly rent: $104; median house value: $33,100. Voting age pop. (1980): 347,458; 37% Black, 1% Spanish origin.

1984 Presidential Vote: Reagan (R)   92,875   (57%)
                              Mondale (D)   68,691   (42%)

Rep. Robin M. Tallon, Jr. (D)

Elected 1982; b. Aug. 8, 1946, Hemingway; home, Florence; U. of SC, 1964–65; United Methodist; married (Amy).

Career: Owner, Tallon Sales; SC House of Reps., 1980–82.

Offices: 432 CHOB 20515, 202-225-3315. Also P.O. Box 6286, Florence 29502, 803-669-9084; and Horry Cnty. Cthse., Conway 29526, 803-248-6256.

Committees: *Agriculture* (14th of 26 D). Subcommittees: Conservation, Credit, and Rural Development; Cotton, Rice, and Sugar; Tobacco and Peanuts. *Merchant Marine and Fisheries* (18th of 25 D). Subcommittees: Merchant Marine; Oceanography; Panama Canal and Outer Continental Shelf.

Group Ratings

	ADA	ACLU	COPE	CFA	LCV	ACU	NTU	NSI	COC	CEI
1986	40	0	63	25	49	57	31	60	44	25
1985	45	—	61	42	—	48	32	—	50	—

National Journal Ratings

	1986 LIB — 1986 CONS			1985 LIB — 1985 CONS		
Economic	54%	—	46%	52%	—	47%
Social	22%	—	77%	0%	—	76%
Foreign	44%	—	56%	46%	—	52%

Key Votes

1) Lmt Cln Water Act	FOR	5) Retain Gun Cont	AGN	9) Aid Angola Reb	FOR
2) Rpl Tobac Sub	AGN	6) Contra Aid	FOR	10) Tax Reform	AGN
3) Grm-Rdmn Def Red	AGN	7) Lmt Text Imp	FOR	11) S Africa Sanc	FOR
4) Ban Polygraph	AGN	8) Limit SDI	FOR	12) Immig Reform	AGN

Election Results

1986 general	Robin M. Tallon, Jr. (D).	92,398	(76%)	($269,708)
	Robert Cunningham (R).	29,922	(24%)	($61,949)
1986 primary	Robin M. Tallon, Jr. (D).	61,924	(90%)	
	Luther Lighty (D).	7,066	(10%)	
1984 general	Robin M. Tallon, Jr. (D).	97,329	(60%)	($422,256)
	Lois Eargle (R).	63,005	(39%)	($177,517)

Campaign Contributions and Expenditures

1985-86		Direct Cont. 1985-86		PACS Breakdown 1985-86			
Receipts	$344,115	Indiv.	$146,582	Corp.	$47,955	T/M/H	$61,550
Expend.	$269,708	PACS	$182,060	Labor	$47,305	Agr.	$6,800
Unspent	$76,934			Ideo.	$13,800	CWOS	$4,650

SOUTH DAKOTA

Almost everything started—or ended—in South Dakota in 1876. That year, General George Custer suited up in the Dakota Territory on his way to meet Crazy Horse's Sioux at Little Big Horn. But 1876 also marked the end for the Indians and their buffalo, as the discovery of gold in South Dakota's Black Hills brought prospectors into land that treaties had reserved for the Indians. It was the year Calamity Jane ruled in the saloons of Deadwood, and Wild Bill Hickock was shot in the back there while holding up two pairs of aces. It was a year when hunters started slaughtering the buffalo, who could not be contained by fences and barbed wire, so thoroughly that by the time Teddy Roosevelt got to the Dakota Territory in 1885 he had a hard time finding one to shoot. The mining towns flared brightly and then went dim or flickered out, though they're still taking gold out of one mine in Lead. But their fame attracted settlers, already headed west, to the plains of the Dakota Territory. It was not long before the railroad came through, before the Indians were massacred in 1890 at Wounded Knee, before enough settlers, many of them German and Scandinavian immigrants recruited by the railroads and land speculators, had built sodhouses and broken the land and set down roots to justify admitting both Dakotas to the Union in 1889.

That was just the moment that the Census Bureau and historian Frederick Jackson Turner proclaimed the closing of the American frontier. But bits and pieces of frontier, of marchland between the English-speaking American civilization and the civilizations that preceded it, remained then and remain now around the country. You can still see them in South Dakota. In the 25 years between statehood and World War I, the eastern third of the state, sectioned off Midwestern style into 640 acre square miles, filled up with farmers. But before you get to the Missouri River in the middle of the state, green turns to brown, cultivation grows sparser and then stops, the land is punctuated not by roads meeting every mile at precise angles but by buttes and gullies and grasslands sweeping all the way to the horizon with no sign of human habitation. These are the plains where the Sioux once built a civilization based on hunting the buffalo, and where the Sioux live today, on or just off reservations; currently, 7% of South Dakotans are Indians, the highest percentage in the nation. This is not an entirely peaceful frontier even yet: in 1973 Wounded Knee was occupied by Indian militants, and not until 1984 did Indian leader Dennis Banks return to serve his sentence for riot and assault. Echoes from this episode reverberated in the state's politics: the chief prosecutor in those trials, William Janklow, served two terms as governor; and the Republican Party, on the defensive before Wounded Knee, regained its position of political dominance afterwards.

By 1910 South Dakota's settlement patterns were established—with patches of frontier left here and there—and the state's political character had been pretty well set. During the 1890s voters here flirted briefly with the Populists and William Jennings Bryan; but by the 1920s, South Dakota had become almost as monolithically Republican as Nebraska. Voters in South Dakota never had much use for the socialistic ideas of the Non-Partisan League, which caught on in the more Scandinavian soil of North Dakota, and there was never anything here comparable to the Farmer-Labor Party of Minnesota. As in most other Great Plains states, there have been periodic farm revolts against incumbent administrations. Nearly one-fourth of the state's residents live on farms, and its day-to-day economy depends on farmers' profits, not revenues, and hence is subject to wide fluctuations. But South Dakota began with a large enough Republican base that, despite such revolts, the state between 1936 and 1970 had a Democratic governor for only two years and elected only one Democrat to the Senate, George McGovern.

The last two decades, in contrast, have seen sharp political fluctuations in South Dakota. For a while McGovern's Democrats were on the rise, capturing at various times the governorship, the

SOUTH DAKOTA — Congressional District, Counties, and Selected Places — (1 At Large)

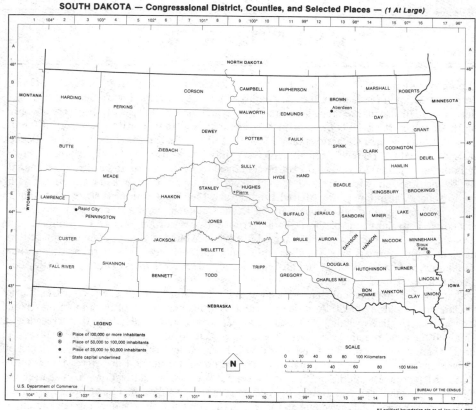

legislature, both Senate seats, and both House seats, and nearly carrying the state for McGovern's presidential campaign in 1972. This trend owed something to McGovern's personal popularity and something to South Dakotans' revulsion at Vietnam and Watergate. Like other Upper Midwest states, South Dakota tends to be dovish on foreign policy (as it was isolationist before Pearl Harbor) and sternly intolerant of corruption.

Then, around the time of the American Indian Movement's occupation of Wounded Knee, South Dakota shifted sharply to the right. Republicans picked up one House seat in 1972 and the other in 1974; they won one Senate seat in 1978 and soundly beat McGovern, the symbol of the state's Democratic Party, in 1980. In the early 1970s one house of the legislature went Democratic; since 1976 Republicans have had big majorities in both houses.

Then in the middle 1980s another shift, to the Democrats, evidently on the farm issue. Democrat Thomas Daschle was elected to the Senate and Democrat Tim Johnson to the House in 1986, and a Democrat was nearly elected governor to follow Janklow. Yet it's not clear that the farm issue has swept all before it. Farm prices and farm land values have fallen abruptly, local banks have been endangered, and local businessmen are squeezed. But South Dakota has also attracted, partly by changing its banking laws, new white-collar jobs in numbers which wouldn't make a ripple in other states but which in a state of only 700,000, whose economy hasn't generated enough jobs to employ all its young people since 1914, make a major difference. The state's unemployment rate is well under the national average; its income levels are pulled down by the Indians, but are otherwise well above the poverty range. The race between Daschle and Senator James Abdnor could easily have gone the other way. It may be that South Dakota is approaching a time, 100 years after the farmers started coming in, when farming won't be the be-all and end-all of the economy here.

Governor. Governor Bill Janklow is a hard, perhaps impossible, act to follow, a man whose feisty and uninhibited personality may put a stamp on the state after his term of office. Elected in 1978 largely because of his opposition to Indian militants, he made a great noise attracting jobs by deregulating banking and enticing Citicorp and other big banks to set up their credit card and other operations in Sioux Falls and Rapid City. He made a big show of attracting businesses from high-tax Minnesota over the line to low-tax South Dakota. He got the state to buy 936 miles of Milwaukee Road railroad tracks and lease them to the Burlington Northern, to hold down farmers' freight rates; he launched a state hail insurance program, coal operation, gas station chain, and cement plant. He was reelected by a huge margin in 1982, but was barred by a third term and unable to beat Abdnor in the 1986 Senate primary.

The two major parties' nominees to succeed him were both quieter and more conventional. Both were sons of former governors, with experience in state government. The winner, with 52% of the vote, was Republican George Mickelson. He got his winning margin in the state's two biggest cities, Sioux Falls and Rapid City, where Janklow's banking programs had created hundreds of jobs and stronger economies than in most similar-sized Farm Belt towns. In office he is stressing the need for more economic development and proposed increasing the sales tax.

Senators. South Dakota's senior Senator is Republican Larry Pressler. He has demonstrated his vote-getting prowess over and over again: he beat an incumbent Democratic congressman in the Democratic year of 1974; he beat a respectable opponent 2 to 1 in the 1978 Senate race; and he won the largest vote total, largest percentage, and by the largest margin in South Dakota history when he won his second term in 1984. He is one of those politicians who came of age in the early 1970s who seems to have an instinct for capitalizing on the latest turn in public opinion. He has a reputation as a liberal Republican; actually, his record shows adroit shifts at politically useful times. He shifted away from liberal economic policies in the late 1970s and back toward them in the middle 1980s—just as the voters have.

Pressler spent most of his four years in the House running for the Senate and his first months in the Senate launching a preposterous presidential candidacy. He was named by Albert Hunt of the *Wall Street Journal* as a prime example of a congressional show horse (as opposed to workhorse). He has not yet overcome his reputation as a dilettante. During the Republicans' six years in the Senate he held important committee positions but did not sponsor major legislation. He did prove to be unreliable as far as the Reagan Administration was concerned; he was the only Republican to vote against arms control nominee Kenneth Adelman in 1983 (who was, however, confirmed). He has opposed the MX missile and the Strategic Defense Initiative. But he has been unreliable for others too. Opponents of those measures don't count on him to be with them in the clutch.

He seems to specialize in a potpourri of different issues, many though not all of which have a local South Dakota angle. Some are useful, if arguably minor: he sponsored a successful measure to encourage shelter belts, the rows of trees which helped stop erosion on the Great Plains in the 1930s and could be useful again. Others are just demagoguery: he got an amendment recommending the appointment of a small business owner or farmer to the Federal Reserve Board through the Senate. He has worked to stop railroads from abandoning track on the Great Plains and helped stimulate development of a regional line in South Dakota. He is one of the advocates of in effect federalizing tort reform, to prevent absurdly high verdicts and cut the cost of insurance. This has not gotten very far; he has done better on opening up Mexico to wool imports and widening the road to Mount Rushmore. The picture you get is of a Senator who has taken up national issues that come across his committees' desks and done a workmanlike job on them, but who reserves his greatest efforts and gets his greatest success on issues which are primarily local and who on broader national issues is exquisitely sensitive to changes in the climate of opinion. So far that record has made him a champion vote-getter in South Dakota but not an influential member of the Senate. But one wonders what it will add up to when he seeks reelection in 1990 after 12 years in the Senate.

South Dakota had a riproaring contest for its other Senate seat in 1986, between some of the state's most popular politicians, and the winner was Democrat Thomas Daschle. The Republicans' problem was that their incumbent, James Abdnor, while personally popular, was not the strongest possible candidate. First elected from the western congressional district in 1972, he agreed to take on George McGovern in 1980 when both national issues and local trends worked against the Democrat, and when McGovern seemed plainly tired of returning to the state, and won an easy victory. But his rather conservative record in the Senate and lack of spectacular accomplishments were a handicap going into 1986. Abdnor managed to turn them into assets by shrewd campaign tactics. Governor William Janklow, widely and deeply popular, ran against him in the Republican primary. Abdnor's campaign focused on the question, Do you want to fire Jim Abdnor? In a state where most voters actually meet candidates, and in which few people had anything against a pleasant and hard-working incumbent, that was enough to give Abdnor a 55%–45% victory. Janklow carried Sioux Falls and the northeastern counties, where his policies had brought jobs; Abdnor carried his home area west of the Missouri River overwhelmingly.

Against Daschle, Abdnor also made assets out of his liabilities. He ran an ad attacking Daschle for, among other things, inviting Jane Fonda to testify before a congressional hearing, even though "Jane Fonda has been identified with more radical causes than practically anyone in America, including warning people against eating red meat." Then Daschle showed Abdnor, with his slight speech impediment, saying "God didn't make me a great speaker. Heck, God didn't make me a great dancer either. But I'm a great fighter for South Dakota." By early October Daschle was leading in the polls—stressing farm woes, attacking the 1985 farm bill, and arguing for continued high price subsidies, some form of production controls, and government encouragement (subsidy?) of exports. In the end this was enough. Daschle carried almost every county in the eastern end of the state, the congressional district (when the state had two) where he was first elected in 1978 by 139 votes after a door-to-door campaign. Abdnor carried most of the counties in the western district he represented during the 1970s, except for the heavily Indian areas. The result was a 52% Daschle victory; Abdnor ended up as head of the Small Business Administration, an agency the President wanted to but hasn't been able to abolish.

In the House Daschle was an active legislator. He was the chief promoter of compensation to Vietnam veterans who believe they have been hurt by Agent Orange, and in the farm credit crisis of 1985, he got his bill for restructuring farm debt and advancing loans through the House. Serious, a dogged hard worker, Daschle seems to personify the personal virtues South Dakota values. His record on economic issues is muted enough for the state, and on many of the non-economic issues on which he has liberal opinions he is not out of line with what is, in some respects, a culturally tolerant and liberal state. In the Senate he has seats on the Agriculture and Finance Committee and will inevitably spend much of his energy on farm programs.

Congressman. Until the 1980 Census results came in, South Dakota elected two congressmen; now it has one. He is Tim Johnson, a Democrat who, beneath the noise and furor of a multimillion dollar Senate contest, won two seriously contested elections in 1986. He beat fellow state Senator Jim Burg in the Democratic primary 48%–45%; Burg carried most of the counties in the state, but Johnson piled up big majorities in his home area in the southeast and in Sioux Falls and Rapid City. In the general election his opponent was Dale Bell, a Republican much touted by conservative strategists who had run against Daschle in 1984. But Bell proved to be a weak candidate, carrying only a scattering of counties, and Johnson won with a thumping 59%. House Democrats, happy to retain this seat, gave Johnson a seat on the Agriculture Committee. He may have another serious challenge, but he starts from a position of strength.

Presidential politics. South Dakota came close to going Democratic in the 1972 and 1976 presidential elections. In 1980 and 1984 it was one of the most heavily Republican states, as it was during most of its history. The farm crisis has moved it toward the Democrats, though it seems unlikely to be seriously contested in 1988. With only three electoral votes, it gets little attention.

That has been true, too, of its presidential primary, long held in June and always overshadowed by California and other states. Now it has been moved up to February 23, one week after New Hampshire. That may violate Democratic party rules, and few candidates relish campaigning up here in deep winter. But by late 1986 candidates were already paying visits. Bob Dole had the best line: he quipped that he was going to Mount Rushmore "for a fitting"; certainly as a farm state Senator, who quickly snared endorsements from Larry Pressler and Jim Abdnor, he starts off with an advantage on the Republican side.

The People: Est. Pop. 1986: 708,000; Pop. 1980: 690,768, up 2.5% 1980–86 and 3.7% 1970–80; 0.29% of U.S. total, 45th largest. 18% with 1–3 yrs. col., 14% with 4+ yrs. col.; 16.9% below poverty level. Single ancestry: 26% German, 7% Norwegian, 4% English, 3% Irish, 2% Dutch, Swedish, 1% French. Households (1980): 73% family, 40% with children, 64% married couples; 30.7% housing units rented; median monthly rent: $148; median house value: $36,600. Voting age pop. (1980): 485,162; 5% American Indian. Registered voters (1986): 428,097; 184,720 D (43%); 208,935 R (49%); 34,442 unaffiliated and minor parties (8%).

1986 Share of Federal Tax Burden: $1,745,000,000; 0.23% of U.S. total, 49th largest.

1986 Share of Federal Expenditures

	Total		Non-Defense		Defense	
Total Expend	$2,454m	(0.30%)	$2,216m	(0.35%)	$328m	(0.14%)
St/Lcl Grants	457m	(0.41%)	456m	(0.41%)	1m	(0.90%)
Salary/Wages	385m	(0.32%)	221m	(0.38%)	164m	(0.26%)
Ind Payments	1,066m	(0.29%)	1,032m	(0.30%)	35m	(0.20%)
Procurement	213m	(0.10%)	85m	(0.15%)	128m	(0.09%)
Loan/Insurance	332m	(1.24%)	332m	(1.25%)	0m	(0%)

Political Lineup: Governor, George S. Mickelson (R); Lt. Gov., Walter D. Miller (R); Secy. of State, Joyce Hazeltine (R); Atty. Gen., Roger Tellinghuisen (R); Treasurer, David L. Volk (R); Auditor, Vernon L. Larson (R). State Senate, 35 (24 R and 11 D); State House of Representatives, 70 (48 R and 22 D). Senators, Larry Pressler (R) and Thomas A. Daschle (D). Representatives, 1 D at large.

1984 Presidential Vote

Reagan (R)	200,267	(63%)
Mondale (D)	116,113	(37%)

1980 Presidential Vote

Reagan (R)	198,343	(61%)
Carter (D)	103,855	(32%)
Anderson (I)	21,431	(7%)

1984 Democratic Presidential Primary

Hart	26,641	(51%)
Mondale	20,495	(39%)
Jackson	2,738	(5%)
One other, uncomm.	2,687	(5%)

GOVERNOR

Gov. George S. Mickelson (R)

Elected 1986, term expires Jan. 1991; b. Jan. 31, 1941, Mobridge; home, Brookings; U. of SD, B.S. 1963, J.D. 1965; United Methodist; married (Linda).

Career: Brookings Cnty. States Atty., 1970–74; SD House of Reps., 1975–80, Speaker, 1977–80.

Office: State Capitol Bldg., Pierre 57501, 605-773-3212.

Election Results

1986 gen.	George S. Mickelson (R)	......	152,543	(52%)
	R. Lars Herseth (D)	....	141,898	(48%)
1986 prim.	George S. Mickelson (R)	......	49,979	(43%)
	Clint Roberts (D)	....	37,250	(40%)
	Lowell Hanson (D)	....	21,884	(23%)
	Alice Kundert (D)	....	15,985	(17%)
1982 gen.	William J. Janklow (R)	....	197,426	(71%)
	Michael O'Connor (D)	....	81,136	(29%)

SENATORS

Sen. Larry Pressler (R)

Elected 1978, seat up 1990; b. Mar. 29, 1942, Humboldt; home, Humboldt; U. of SD, B.A. 1964, Rhodes Scholar, Oxford U., 1966, Harvard U., M.A., J.D. 1971; Roman Catholic; married (Harriet).

Career: Army, Vietnam; U.S. House of Reps., 1975–79.

Offices: 411 RSOB 20510, 202-224-5842. Also 520 S. Main, Aberdeen 57401, 605-225-0250, ext. 471; Rushmore Mall, Rm. 105, Rapid City 57701, 605-341-1185, 1-800-952-3591; Empire Mall, 4001 W. 41st St., Sioux Falls 57106, 605-336-2980; and 221 S. Central, Pierre 57501, 605-224-9552.

Committees: *Commerce, Science, and Transportation* (4th of 9 R). Subcommittees: Communications; Science, Technology and Space (Ranking Member); Surface Transportation. *Environment and Public Works* (7th of 7 R). Subcommittees: Environmental Protection; Superfund and Environmental Oversight; Water Resources, Transportation and Infrastructure. *Foreign Relations* (5th of 9 R). Subcommittees: European Affairs (Ranking Member); Near Eastern and South Asian Affairs. *Small Business* (6th of 9 R). Subcommittee: Rural Economy and Family Farming. *Special Committee on Aging* (3d of 9 R).

Group Ratings

	ADA	ACLU	COPE	CFA	LCV	ACU	NTU	NSI	COC	CEI
1986	10	7	34	33	25	86	44	80	68	54
1985	10	—	34	0	—	74	48	—	71	—

National Journal Ratings

	1986 LIB — 1986 CONS			1985 LIB — 1985 CONS		
Economic	36%	—	60%	38%	—	61%
Social	11%	—	87%	17%	—	76%
Foreign	14%	—	82%	40%	—	59%

Key Votes

1) Ease Gun Cont	FOR	5) Grm-Rdmn Def Red	AGN	9) Rehnquist Nom	FOR
2) Immig Reform	FOR	6) Contra Aid	FOR	10) Tax Reform	AGN
3) Lmt Text Imp	AGN	7) SDI Funding	FOR	11) Drug Death Pen	—
4) Aid Tobac Ind	FOR	8) Lmt PAC Contrib	FOR	12) S Africa Sanc	AGN

Election Results

1984 general	Larry Pressler (R).....................	235,176	(74%)	($1,155,683)
	George V. Cunningham (D)	80,537	(26%)	($166,426)
1984 primary	Larry Pressler (R) unopposed			
1978 general	Larry Pressler (R).....................	170,832	(67%)	($449,541)
	Don Barnett (D)	84,767	(33%)	($152,006)

Campaign Contributions and Expenditures

1979-84		Direct Cont. 1979-84		PACS Breakdown 1979-84			
Receipts	$1,440,880	Indiv.	$671,725	Corp.	$253,695	T/M/H	$206,278
Expend.	$1,155,683	Party	$29,376	Labor	$36,500	Agr.	$31,600
Unspent	$325,441	PACS	$610,476	Ideo.	$61,300	CWOS	$7,856
		Cand.	$30,000				

Sen. Thomas A. Daschle (D)

Elected 1986, seat up 1992; b. Dec. 9, 1947, Aberdeen; home, Aberdeen; SD St. U., B.A. 1969; Roman Catholic; married (Linda).

Career: Air Force, 1969–72; Legis. Asst. to U.S. Sen. James Abourezk, 1972–77; U.S. House of Reps., 1978–86.

Offices: 317 HSOB 20510, 202-224-2321. P.O. Box 1274, Sioux Falls 57101, 605-334-9596; P.O. Box 1536, Aberdeen 57401, 605-225-8823; and P.O. Box 8168, Rapid City 57709, 605-348-3551.

Committees: *Agriculture, Nutrition and Forestry* (9th of 10 D). Subcommittees: Agricultural Production and Stabilization of Prices; Agricultural Research, Conservation, Forestry and General Legislation; Rural Development and Rural Electrification. *Finance* (9th of 11 D). Subcommittees: Energy and Agricultural Taxation; International Debt; Social Security and Family Policy. *Select Committee on Indians* (5th of 5 D).

Group Ratings (as Member of U.S. House of Representatives)

	ADA	ACLU	COPE	CFA	LCV	ACU	NTU	NSI	COC	CEI
1986	80	75	72	75	71	80	43	0	22	23
1985	70	—	73	58	—	63	34	—	38	—

National Journal Ratings (as Member of U.S. House of Representatives)

	1986 LIB — 1986 CONS			1985 LIB — 1985 CONS		
Economic	46%	—	53%	64%	—	36%
Social	55%	—	44%	69%	—	28%
Foreign	71%	—	28%	70%	—	29%

Key Votes (as Member of U.S. House of Representatives)

1) Ease Gun Cont	AGN	5) Grm-Rdmn Def Red	AGN	9) Rehnquist Nom	AGN
2) Immig Reform	AGN	6) Contra Aid	AGN	10) Tax Reform	AGN
3) Lmt Text Imp	FOR	7) SDI Funding	AGN	11) Drug Death Pen	FOR
4) Aid Tobac Ind	FOR	8) Lmt PAC Contrib	FOR	12) S Africa Sanc	FOR

Election Results

1986 general	Thomas A. Daschle (D)	152,657	(52%)	($3,485,870)
	James Abdnor (R).	143,173	(48%)	($3,410,387)
1986 primary	Thomas A. Daschle (D) unopposed			
1980 general	James Abdnor (R).	190,594	(58%)	($1,801,653)
	George McGovern (D)	129,018	(39%)	($3,237,669)

Campaign Contributions and Expenditures

1985-86		Direct Cont. 1985-86		PACS Breakdown 1985-86			
Receipts	$3,515,482	Indiv.	$2,241,772	Corp.	$151,850	T/M/H	$214,142
Expend.	$3,485,870	Party	$19,724	Labor	$378,899	Agr.	$26,035
Unspent	$40,245	PACS	$1,205,400	Ideo.	$400,364	CWOS	$34,110
		Cand.	$72,740				

REPRESENTATIVE

Rep. Tim Johnson (D)

Elected 1986; b. Dec. 28, 1946, Canton; home, Vermillion; U. of SD, B.A. 1969, M.A. 1970, J.D. 1975; Lutheran; married (Barbara).

Career: Practicing atty.; SD House of Reps., 1978–82; SD Senate, 1982–86.

Offices: 513 CHOB 20515, 202-225-2801. Also 1610 S. Minnesota Ave., P.O. Box 57101, Sioux Falls, 605-332-8896; 429 Kansas City St., P.O. Box 1098, Rapid City 57709, 605-341-3990; and 615 S. Main, P.O. Box 1554, Aberdeen 57401, 605-226-3440.

Committees: *Agriculture* (23d of 26 D). Subcommittees: Forests, Family Farms and Energy; Livestock, Dairy, and Poultry; Wheat, Soybeans, and Feed Grains. *Veterans' Affairs* (20th of 21 D). Subcommittees: Compensation, Pension and Insurance; Oversight and Investigations.

Group Ratings and Key Votes: Newly Elected

Election Results

1986 general	Tim Johnson (D).....................	171,462	(59%)	($430,806)
	Dale Bell (R).	118,261	(41%)	($483,394)
1986 primary	Tim Johnson (D).....................	33,503	(45%)	
	Jim Burg (D)........................	31,503	(45%)	
	Dean L. Sinclair (D)..................	4,830	(7%)	
1984 general	Thomas A. Daschle (D)	181,401	(57%)	($700,211)
	Dale Bell (R).	134,821	(43%)	($318,396)

Campaign Contributions and Expenditures

1985-86		Direct Cont. 1985-86		PACS Breakdown 1985-86			
Receipts	$438,138	Indiv.	$141,243	Corp.	$13,750	T/M/H	$45,600
Expend.	$430,806	Party	$9,999	Labor	$128,350	Agr.	$11,700
		PACS	$265,389	Ideo.	$65,989	CWOS	$0
		Cand.	$31,400				

TENNESSEE

The frontier was always a place of opportunity for young men, and nowhere more so than the frontier that became Tennessee in the 1790s. As settlers poured in through the narrow finger-like valleys of the Clinch and Holston Rivers, over the mountains from Virginia and the Carolinas, they found themselves suddenly in the vast expanse of the Cumberland Plateau: rolling hills, occasional rivers, mild climate, fertile farmland. Andrew Jackson, a poor boy in the Carolinas during the Revolution, moved to Nashville in his 20s and was elected a United States Senator at 30, in 1797; William Claiborne, a lawyer from Virginia, was elected to the House from the Upper Holston country at 21 and served two terms in contravention of the 25-year age limit. Tens of thousands of farmers and yeomen, men who had started out as indentured servants and men who had managed to become lawyers, came over the mountains and brought with them the accents and tones, the songs and fiddle music that all still find echoes in Tennessee today.

They also created political divisions which endure. Andrew Jackson was the first President who called himself a Democrat, and Tennessee supported him near-unanimously, just as next-door Kentucky supported its champion, the Whig Henry Clay; and middle Tennessee around Jackson's Hermitage in Nashville has remained heavily Democratic ever since. But the mountains in the east, which had never seen many slaves, split with middle Tennessee and the cotton-growing Mississippi bottomlands in the west over the Civil War; the mountains, the home of Lincoln's vice president and successor, Andrew Johnson, favored the Union and have remained Republican ever since, sometimes the most Republican part of the nation. Yet though it was Confederate, Tennessee did not have many slaves, and suffered less destruction during the war than other states (Sherman was still getting his provisions from the North by rail when he was here, before he started his scorched-earth march to the sea across Georgia). Later, Tennessee was never strong for segregation; this was the only southern state whose Senators refused to sign the Southern Manifesto in the 1950s. Today only 16% of its people are blacks, almost half of them concentrated in Memphis and Shelby County.

Tennessee's basic divisions are still in place. East Tennessee still remains a distinctive region politically, as do middle Tennessee and west Tennessee. Their political personalities—the east has been feisty and Republican, middle Tennessee has been devoutly Democratic since the days of Nashville's Andrew Jackson, the west has long been racially polarized—are well known even to ordinary Tennesseeans. Their persistence is matched, and their particular personalities analogous, to the musical traditions which have made Tennessee for many Americans the music capital of the nation. Tennessee is associated with country music, but there are several strains of it. That of east Tennessee has been influenced by the bluegrass music and fiddling tradition of the mountains. The country music of Nashville, in contrast, seems to have roots in the gospel music which is also centered in that city—which, as it happens, is also the nation's leading center of religious publishing. Nashville's Grand Ole Opry, broadcast since 1925, and Knoxville's Tennessee Barn Dance, broadcast since 1942, have names that suggest the differences between them.

As for west Tennessee, the lowlands along the Mississippi River, in and around Memphis, are economically and culturally part of a unit that includes the Mississippi Delta. This is the part of America that gave birth to blues music in the 1890–1920 period. Memphis produced many blues musicians, and others who drew on their tradition, from the jazz musicians of Beale Street in the 1920s to Elvis Presley of Graceland mansion in the 1950s and 1960s. Blues is a product of black American culture, and west Tennessee remains a heavily black part of the South; it was the one part of Tennessee that heavily favored segregation (at one time many rural blacks couldn't vote here, and what there was of the black vote in Memphis was deliverable by the

1102   TENNESSEE

TENNESSEE — Congressional Districts, Counties, and Selected Places — *(9 Districts)*

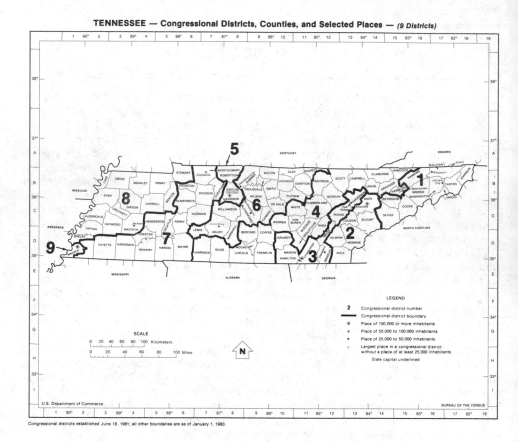

Congressional districts established June 18, 1981; all other boundaries are as of January 1, 1980.

Crump machine until 1948). But Memphis whites have an attraction to, and have been influenced by, black culture, even as they proclaim their superiority to it.

Both the musical traditions and the partisan patterns of the three regions in Tennessee have shown remarkable staying power. So long as middle and west Tennessee remained strongly Democratic, the Republicans could not win a statewide election, no matter how many votes they won in east Tennessee. But when there were defections in the west and middle, Republicans could win: in 1920 Harding carried Tennessee, and the state elected a Republican governor; in 1928 Hoover beat Al Smith here; in 1966 Howard Baker was elected Senator, to be followed by Bill Brock and Governor Winfield Dunn in 1970. In 1968 the Republicans even won half the seats in the Tennessee House.

But now the Democrats have come back, dominating top offices as they did in the days when Estes Kefauver and Albert Gore were the state's Senators and Frank Clement and Buford Ellington alternated as governor. Yet there is less harshness to Tennesseeans' partisanship than there was when the Civil War was a living memory to many voters or when differences over the Vietnam war embittered voters and politicians alike. Senators Jim Sasser and Albert Gore, Jr., elected in 1976 and 1984 to seats formerly held by Republicans, now seem politically safe, and Governor Ned Ray McWherter, after 14 years as Speaker, captured the governorship for the Democrats in 1986. But Gore and McWherter were more inclined to praise their Republican predecessors than damn them, and vice versa.

Governor. For the happy condition of Tennessee in the middle 1980s former Governor Lamar

Alexander deserves much of the credit. He came to office in 1978 following a Democrat later convicted of selling pardons and by beating another that went to jail for violating the banking laws; the state's economy was lagging and its morale was low. In eight years Alexander changed all that. His major achievement was his Better Schools program, including a master teacher plan, an early effort—predating the national commissions on education that issued their reports in 1983—to reward outstanding teachers with additional pay and recognition, and inferentially to advertise that teaching is more than a matter of putting in the hours for a paycheck and that learning is more than just attendance in what may or may not be an orderly classroom. Against the opposition of the teachers' unions, he got the $1.2 billion package through the legislature. Another Alexander success was winning the competition to get General Motors's Saturn plant, and without the hype and high pressure used by other governors. Alexander won in 1978 after walking across the state, and he made his last year in office, 1986, a Tennessee Festival time, celebrating the state's traditions, highlighting its achievements, building its pride.

Tennessee's new governor, Ned Ray McWherter, saluted Alexander for these achievements even as he beat his candidate, former Governor Winfield Dunn. McWherter looks like an old-fashioned political hack: he is tall and overweight, with white hair, he was never elected by a larger constituency than his state legislative district and his colleagues in Nashville. But he proved himself adept at winning votes. In the primary he beat two serious candidates, Public Service Commissioner Jane Eskind, the Democratic nominee against Howard Baker in 1978, who spent liberally on her campaign, and Richard Fulton, the mayor for 11 years of Nashville and, as such, regularly featured on the TV stations that reach most Democratic primary voters. Fulton carried Nashville and Eskind Memphis and Chattanooga, but McWherter carried almost all the rural areas and won with 42% to Eskind's 30% and Fulton's 26%. In the general election, McWherter and Dunn traded charges about conflicts of interest, but none really stuck. Instead, the same rural-urban split applied: McWherter ran behind usual Democratic showings in the four big cities, but ran ahead in the rural areas and carried the far tip of eastern Tennessee; voters still remembered that Dunn vetoed a medical school there. That gave McWherter a 54% victory. He had a setback in 1987 as the state Senate voted as lieutenant governor the choice of a coalition of conservative Democrats and Republicans. But increasingly the issues seem less partisan, and McWherter seemed determined to continue the state in the direction Alexander steered it.

Senators. Tennessee is now represented in the Senate, as it was from 1952 to 1963, by two generally liberal Democrats, both with pretty safe seats.

Tennessee's senior Senator, James Sasser, is now in his second decade in the Senate, without being as well known as many less senior colleagues. He has been a legislator at a time when Democrats have sponsored few new laws, and sits on nut-and-bolts committees—Appropriations, Banking—on which it is hard to change policy visibly. His politics owes something to an agrarian liberal tradition: his father was an agriculture official who moved all over rural Tennessee, one of those men who make government programs work to help people. Sasser has not voted for all big government programs, but on balance he seems to see government as a friend, not an enemy.

Much of Sasser's substantive work has been getting down to the details of how government actually operates. He has prowled around Honduras and cross-examined Pentagon witnesses to find out exactly how much U.S. military construction has really been going on in Central America; that exercise got him skeptical of Administration policy there, though he is no fan of the Sandinista regime, and wary of building more big American installations in Honduras. He attacked the Tennessee Valley Authority for withdrawing its nuclear program from public scrutiny and for raising rates to pay for nuclear plant construction, but argues strongly against privatizing it. He was an originator of sunset, grant reform, and grant consolidation legislation, which was never passed but which may be influencing legislation covering particular programs. He wants to allow military personnel to sue the government for malpractice (which you could say was just giving them a right everyone else has or was sending a windfall to plaintiffs' negligence lawyers). He makes a point of visiting each of Tennessee's 95 counties once a year, hiking through the Cherokee National Forest in Tennessee to see how much timber is harvested, boating over Kentucky Lake to see how the fish are affected by water pollution.

Sasser has won some tough political battles, beating Senator Bill Brock, now Labor Secretary, in 1976, then beating Representative Robin Beard, who ran an ad with a Castro lookalike taking a puff on a cigar and saying, "Muchas gracias, Señor Sasser," with 62% of the vote. He seems to enter 1988 in strong political shape, with no well-known candidates preparing to run against him. But Lamar Alexander, who left the state after being governor to spend six months in Australia, could be a formidable opponent if he decides to run.

Tennessee's junior Senator has a familiar name in Tennessee politics and in Washington policy-making circles; it could become much more familiar if he is successful in the presidential campaign he launched suddenly in April 1987. Albert Gore, Jr., probably owes his initial election to the House, in 1976, to his name: his father (still active in the middle 1980s as vice president of a big coal company) represented much the same middle Tennessee district from 1938 to 1952 before going on to the Senate for 18 years. But in the House Gore made an impressive name for himself. He became one of the most thoughtful members of the Science Committee, and conducted useful hearings on difficult issues like organ transplants. He was a member of the Select Committee on Intelligence. He was a leading member of the increasingly important Energy and Commerce Committee. And in areas not covered by his committees he also made a contribution. He studied arms control issues intensively for months, and came forward with a proposal—to de-MIRV missiles, that is, remove their multiple warheads—which was echoed by no one less than Henry Kissinger, who had backed MIRVing in the first place, and which soon became arms control conventional wisdom on both left and right. He played a key role in fashioning a compromise that saved the MX missile in 1983 and 1984.

When, in early 1983, Howard Baker stunned almost everyone by announcing that he wouldn't run for reelection in 1984, Gore was the obvious favorite to succeed him. He had no opponents in the Democratic primary—quite a startling situation in an open-seat race—and won 61% of the vote in the general election against a presentable and experienced, if slightly eccentric, Republican state legislator. Everyone thinks Gore has a safe seat.

In the Senate, Gore seems equally active. After the *Challenger* blowup, he ferreted up proof that NASA had cut back on quality monitoring. He continued to work on defense issues though he doesn't serve on Armed Services. To all his work he brings a seriousness, a determination to study the facts more closely than most members can find time to do, and an originality of thought that make him a natural leader and yet one that is not resented greatly by his colleagues. He is not the only member of the family that makes headlines, by the way: his wife Tipper together with James Baker's wife Susan lobbied the record industry to voluntarily rate and label obscene and violent lyrics.

Gore's presidential candidacy was launched after his fellow southerners Sam Nunn and Dale Bumpers announced they weren't running and after Gore himself got pledges of support from a group of Democratic fundraisers led by Nathan Landow. Some of the impetus for his candidacy comes from the calculation that the early southern regional primary could prove decisive, but no one seriously thinks southern Democrats will vote reflexively for someone just because he comes from Tennessee, as opposed to Missouri or Arkansas or Delaware; Gore must demonstrate he is presidential. He seems to be emphasizing his expertise in arms control and, to distinguish himself from the rest of the field, his concern that depletion of the ozone layer could be disastrous to the environment. As the youngest candidate in the field, and one who has never held executive office, he seems determined to present himself in a careful, austere manner, although occasional glints of humor shine through.

Presidential politics. The eerie continuity in Tennessee politics comes out in presidential elections: Tennessee went for Ronald Reagan over Jimmy Carter in 1980 by almost exactly the same small margin—not just statewide, but in almost every county—that it went for Dwight Eisenhower over Adlai Stevenson in 1952 and 1956. It went Republican again in 1984, but produced the highest percentage for the Mondale–Ferraro ticket in the South (unless you count as southern the hard-to-define state of West Virginia). Tennessee, for all its sunny optimism and pride in 1986, has not partaken so much of the Sun Belt boom as have the southern states on the Atlantic Coast; in the early 1980s it was part of the central belt from the Great Lakes down through the Mississippi Valley which has had higher-than-average unemployment for most of the 1980s. Nashville is now the center of a boom area, with lots of Japanese investment and white-collar employment; but other parts of the state lag behind; and Democratic preference seems to survive prosperity, as it has in middle Tennessee. So Tennessee could be the most Democratic southern state in the next few presidential elections, and an indicator of whether the Democrats have any chance in the region.

Tennessee's presidential primary has been switched to the southern regional primary date of March 8, so it will be lost sight of in the regional returns. Albert Gore, Jr., seems to have solid support from Democratic voters—testimony worth respect of his abilities and character. Its Republican primary voters are drawn from a broader socioeconomical spectrum than most southern Republican electorates, including many blue-collar as well as white-collar Tennessee-ans; but they're concentrated geographically in east Tennessee and in the white areas of Memphis.

Congressional districting. Tennessee gained one House seat from the 1980 Census, the same one it lost in 1970. The Democratic legislature tried to gain two seats, and got one.

The People: Est. Pop. 1986: 4,803,000; Pop. 1980: 4,591,120, up 4.6% 1980–86 and 16.9% 1970–80; 1.99% of U.S. total, 16th largest. 12% with 1–3 yrs. col., 12% with 4+ yrs. col.; 16.5% below poverty level. Single ancestry: 23% English, 5% Irish, 4% German, 1% French, Scottish. Households (1980): 77% family, 42% with children, 63% married couples; 31.4% housing units rented; median monthly rent: $148; median house value: $35,600. Voting age pop. (1980): 3,292,560; 14% Black, 1% Spanish origin. Registered voters (1986): 2,543,597; no party registration.

1986 Share of Federal Tax Burden: $12,294,000,000; 1.63% of U.S. total, 21d largest.

1986 Share of Federal Expenditures

	Total		Non-Defense		Defense	
Total Expend	$15,917m	(1.92%)	$13,980m	(2.33%)	$1,937m	(0.84%)
St/Lcl Grants	2,128m	(1.89%)	2,124m	(1.89%)	4m	(3.60%)
Salary/Wages	2,036m	(1.69%)	1.579m	(2.69%)	457m	(0.74%)
Pymts to Indiv	6,968m	(1.91%)	6,632m	(1.91%)	337m	(1.90%)
Procurement	4,550m	(2.21%)	3,411m	(6.13%)	1,140m	(0.76%)
Research/Other	235m	(.88%)	235m	(.88%)	0m	(0%)

Political Lineup: Governor, Ned McWherter (R); Lt. Gov., John Wilder (D); Secy. of State, Gentry Crowell (D); Atty. Gen., Mike Cody (D); Treasurer, Harlan Mathews (D). State Senate, 33 (24 D and 9 R); State House of Representatives, 99 (61 D and 38 R). Senators, James R. Sasser (D) and Albert Gore, Jr. (D). Representatives, 9 (6 D and 3 R).

1984 Presidential Vote

Reagan (R)	990,212	(58%)
Mondale (D)	711,714	(42%)

1980 Presidential Vote

Reagan (R)	787,761	(49%)
Carter (D)	783,051	(48%)
Anderson (I)	35,991	(2%)

1984 Democratic Presidential Primary

Mondale	132,201	(41%)
Hart	93,710	(29%)
Jackson	81,418	(25%)
Two others, uncomm.	14,704	(5%)

1984 Republican Presidential Primary

Reagan	75,367	(91%)
Uncommitted	7,546	(9%)

GOVERNOR

Gov. Ned McWherter (D)

Elected 1986, term expires Jan. 1991; b. Oct. 15, 1930, Palmersville; home, Dresden; United Methodist; widowed.

Career: Farmer, small businessman; TN House of Reps., 1969–86, Speaker, 1983–86.

Office: State Capitol, Nashville 37219, 615-741-2001.

Election Results

1986 gen.	Ned McWherter (D)	656,602	(54%)
	Winfield Dunn (R)	553,449	(46%)
1986 prim.	Ned McWherter (D6	314,449	(42%)
	Jane Eskind (D)	225,551	(30%)
	Richard H. Fulton (D)	190,016	(26%)
1982 gen.	Lamar Alexander (R)	737,963	(60%)
	Randall Tyree (D)	500,937	(40%)

SENATORS

Sen. James R. (Jim) Sasser (D)

Elected 1976, seat up 1988; b. Sept. 30, 1936, Memphis; home, Nashville; U. of TN, Vanderbilt U., B.A. 1958, J.D. 1961; United Methodist; married (Mary).

Career: Practicing atty., 1961–76; Chmn., TN State Dem. Cmtee., 1973–76.

Offices: 363 RSOB 20510, 202-224-3344. Also 569 U.S. Crthse., Nashville 37203, 615-736-7353; 239 Fed. Bldg., Chattanooga 37402, 615-756-8836; 320 P.O. Bldg., Knoxville 37902, 615-673-4204; 390 Fed. Bldg., 167 N. Main, Memphis 38103, 901-521-4187; B-8 U.S.P.O. Bldg., Jackson 38301, 901-424-6600; and Tri-City Airport, Blountville 37617, 615-323-6207.

Committees: *Appropriations* (10th of 16 D). Subcommittees: Agriculture and Related Agencies; Commerce, Justice, State and Judiciary; Defense; Energy and Water Development; Military Construction (Chairman). *Banking, Housing, and Urban Affairs* (7th of 11 D). Subcommittees: Housing and Urban Affairs; Securities. *Budget* (4th of 13 D). *Governmental Affairs* (5th of 8 D). Subcommittees: Government Efficiency, Federalism and the District of Columbia (Chairman); Federal Services, Post Office and Civil Service; Investigations. *Small Business* (3d of 10 D). Subcommittees: Export and Expansion (Chairman); Government Contracting and Paperwork Reduction.

Group Ratings

	ADA	ACLU	COPE	CFA	LCV	ACU	NTU	NSI	COC	CEI
1986	70	57	79	73	50	17	33	20	32	28
1985	60	—	78	60	—	26	26	—	38	—

National Journal Ratings

	1986 LIB — 1986 CONS		1985 LIB — 1985 CONS	
Economic	85% —	8%	84% —	14%
Social	71% —	27%	56% —	38%
Foreign	75% —	0%	70% —	28%

Key Votes

1) Ease Gun Cont	FOR	5) Grm-Rdmn Def Red	FOR	9) Rehnquist Nom	AGN
2) Immig Reform	FOR	6) Contra Aid	AGN	10) Tax Reform	AGN
3) Lmt Text Imp	FOR	7) SDI Funding	AGN	11) Drug Death Pen	AGN
4) Aid Tobac Ind	FOR	8) Lmt PAC Contrib	FOR	12) S Africa Sanc	FOR

Election Results

1982 general	James R. (Jim) Sasser (D)	780,113	(62%)	($2,091,872)
	Robin L. Beard (R)...................	479,642	(38%)	($1,639,858)
1982 primary	James R. (Jim) Sasser (D)	511,059	(89%)	
	Charles Gordon Vick (D) ....,....	63,488	(11%)	
1976 general	James R. (Jim) Sasser (D)	751,180	(52%)	($839,379)
	Bill Brock (R)	673,231	(47%)	($1,301,033)

Campaign Contributions and Expenditures

1979-82		Direct Cont. 1979-82		PACS Breakdown					
Receipts	$2,174,839	Indiv.	$1,263,033	Agr	$46,350	Ideo	$75,100		
Expend.	$2,091,872	Party	$25,033	Bus	$217,669	Lbr	$241,411		
Unspent	$58,064	PACS	$639,720	Hlth	$15,600	Prof	$26,000		
		Cand.	$40,417						

Sen. Albert Gore, Jr. (D)

Elected 1984, seat up 1990; b. Mar. 31, 1948, Washington, DC; home, Carthage; Harvard U., B.A. 1969, Vanderbilt U.; Baptist; married (Tipper).

Career: Army, Vietnam; Homebuilding business; Reporter, *Nashville Tennessean*, 1971–76; U.S. House of Reps., 1976–84.

Offices: 393 RSOB 20510, 202-224-4944. Also 530 Church St., Nashville 37219, 615-736-5129; 313 P.O. Bldg., Knoxville 37901, 615-673-4595; 9 E. Broad St., Cookeville 38501, 615-528-6475; Smith Cnty. Crthse., Carthage 37030, 615-735-0173; 403 Fed. Bldg., Memphis 38103, 901-521-4224; and 256 Fed. Bldg., Chattanooga 37402, 615-756-1328.

Committees: *Armed Services* (9th of 11 D). Subcommittees: Conventional Forces and Alliance Defense; Defense Industry and Technology; Projection Forces and Regional Defense. *Commerce, Science, and Transportation* (6th of 11 D). Subcommittees: Communications; Consumer (Chairman); Science, Technology, and Space. *Rules and Administration* (6th of 9 D). *Joint Committee on Printing.*

Group Ratings

	ADA	ACLU	COPE	CFA	LCV	ACU	NTU	NSI	COC	CEI
1986	70	78	86	80	67	9	36	20	32	27
1985	65	—	86	53	—	17	25	—	41	—

National Journal Ratings

	1986 LIB — 1986 CONS			1985 LIB — 1985 CONS		
Economic	85%	—	8%	77%	—	19%
Social	79%	—	16%	68%	—	28%
Foreign	71%	—	25%	69%	—	30%

Key Votes

1) Ease Gun Cont	FOR	5) Grm-Rdmn Def Red	FOR	9) Rehnquist Nom	AGN
2) Immig Reform	FOR	6) Contra Aid	AGN	10) Tax Reform	FOR
3) Lmt Text Imp	FOR	7) SDI Funding	AGN	11) Drug Death Pen	AGN
4) Aid Tobac Ind	FOR	8) Lmt PAC Contrib	FOR	12) S Africa Sanc	FOR

Election Results

1984 general	Albert Gore, Jr. (D)	1,000,607	(61%)	($3,035,498)
	Victor Ashe (R).	557,016	(34%)	($1,777,581)
	Ed McAteer (I).	87,234	(5%)	($382,364)
1984 primary	Albert Gore, Jr. (D)	345,527	(100%)	
1978 general	Howard H. Baker, Jr. (R).	642,644	(56%)	($1,922,945)
	Jane Eskind (D)	466,228	(42%)	($1,903,532)

Campaign Contributions and Expenditures

1983-84		Direct Cont. 1983-84		PACS Breakdown 1983-84			
Receipts	$3,101,546	Indiv.	$2,082,417	Corp.	$193,346	T/M/H	$179,577
Expend.	$3,035,498	Party	$29,927	Labor	$258,017	Agr.	$28,995
Debts	$19,335	PACS	$843,026	Ideo.	$114,805	CWOS	$8,700

FIRST DISTRICT

The far northeastern tip of Tennessee is an extension of the great valley of Virginia between the first ridges of the Appalachians. Two great movements have made its history. The first was the rush right after the Revolution of settlers over the mountains and through these valleys; this is where early settlers momentarily established the free state of Franklin and where Tennessee's first capital was, and you can still see some 18th and early 19th century buildings here. The second movement was the building of the railroads through these valleys in the 1850s. Other Appalachian areas are cut off from the rest of America, and if they have railroads they are only branch lines to coal mines. But the little industrial cities that have grown up here—Johnson City, Kingsport, Bristol—are on the main lines of national commerce, and have been since before the Civil War. The war itself was not as formative an event here as in the rest of the South, or not in the same way. With few slaves, connected to northern industry, this was Union territory, heavily Republican, and it has remained heavily Republican to this day.

The continuity in politics is all the more surprising, because this area has had continuous economic growth and has developed the sort of industrial economy which produced unions and Democrats in the North. Its growth has been helped by modest wage levels, a skilled and hard-working labor force, low electric power rates (because of TVA), and good transportation routes (it's on major rail lines); its small cities boast major paper and printing plants, and have the look of comfortable, clean 1920s factory towns. This is a part of America where things seem to work, and where the cultural trends of the 1960s and 1970s seem far away or altogether alien.

The far northeastern end of the state forms the 1st Congressional District of Tennessee, a district so heavily Republican that when it went for Democratic Governor Ned Ray McWherter in 1986 it was a matter for shocked comment. The reason he won is instructive. Republican candidate Winfield Dunn, as governor in the early 1970s, vetoed a proposed medical school in Johnson City—something people still remembered and resented. This part of Tennessee is far from the center of the state—closer to Richmond, Virginia, than to Memphis—and sensitive about its isolation. It managed to get the medical school built despite Dunn, and named it for a local contributor and for James Quillen, who was congressman since before Dunn came along.

Quillen won the seat in 1962, after the death of B. Carroll Reece, a Republican who represented the district for most of the time between 1921 and 1961 and once served as Republican national chairman. Quillen is one of those locally-rooted Burkean conservatives—a poor boy from a family of 10 who made money publishing weekly newspapers and running an insurance business—who for years provided the backbone for the outnumbered Republicans in the House. Quillen is one of the ranking Republican on the House Rules Committee, but since the Democrats have a 9–4 majority, and all of their nine members are loyal to the leadership, Republicans don't have much leverage; and lower-ranking members Delbert Latta and Trent Lott are more aggressive and legislatively creative respectively. Quillen devotes most of his attention to local issues, such as getting a Tennessee wilderness act passed in 1986 and persuading EPA to approve a sewage treatment plant for Bristol, and he has a more liberal voting record on economic issues than many Republicans; this is a working class district and it has some use for federal money. His takes great pride in the establishment of what now is the Quillen–Dishner Medical School in Johnson City, where a chair has been endowed in honor of his wife. He has little in common with the aggressive, brash crackling-with-ideas young Republicans who have dominated their party's ranks in the 1980s.

Quillen is routinely reelected by large margins and without significant opposition. Kingsport attorney Bill Anderson in early 1987 raised $100,000 and hired consultant Doug Bailey, who helped put together Lamar Alexander's campaigns, in anticipation of Quillen's retirement; but it's not at all clear that Quillen will quit or that he is vulnerable if he chooses to run again.

The People: Pop. 1980: 512,702, up 18.9% 1970–80. Households (1980): 80% family, 43% with children, 68% married couples; 24.8% housing units rented; median monthly rent: $128; median house value: $33,300. Voting age pop. (1980): 371,177; 2% Black.

1984 Presidential Vote:

Reagan (R)	129,514	(71%)
Mondale (D)	51,916	(28%)

Rep. James H. (Jimmy) Quillen (R)

Elected 1962; b. Jan. 11, 1916, Scott County, VA; home, Kingsport; United Methodist; married (Cecile).

Career: Founder and Pub., *Kingsport Mirror*, 1936–39, *Johnson City Times*, 1939–44; Navy, WWII; Pres. and Bd. Chmn., real estate and insur. business; Dir., 1st TN Bank, Kingsport; TN House of Reps., 1955–62, Minor. Ldr., 1959–60.

Offices: 102 CHOB 20515, 202-225-6356. Also Fed. P.O. Bldg., Rm. 157, Kingsport 37662, 615-247-8161.

Committees: *Rules* (Ranking Member of 4 R).

Group Ratings

	ADA	ACLU	COPE	CFA	LCV	ACU	NTU	NSI	COC	CEI
1986	20	10	16	33	10	77	36	90	60	47
1985	15	—	15	33	—	81	34	—	67	—

National Journal Ratings

	1986 LIB — 1986 CONS			1985 LIB — 1985 CONS		
Economic	30%	—	69%	40%	—	60%
Social	41%	—	59%	28%	—	71%
Foreign	21%	—	77%	0%	—	76%

Key Votes

1) Lmt Cln Water Act	AGN	5) Retain Gun Cont	AGN	9) Aid Angola Reb	FOR
2) Rpl Tobac Sub	AGN	6) Contra Aid	FOR	10) Tax Reform	FOR
3) Grm-Rdmn Def Red	FOR	7) Lmt Text Imp	FOR	11) S Africa Sanc	AGN
4) Ban Polygraph	FOR	8) Limit SDI	AGN	12) Immig Reform	FOR

Election Results

1986 general	James H. (Jimmy) Quillen (R)...........	80,289	(69%)	($459,119)
	John B. Russell (D)....................	36,278	(31%)	($8,044)
1986 primary	James H. (Jimmy) Quillen (R)...........	47,985	(88%)	
	Frank Ransom (R)	6,307	(22%)	
1984 general	James H. (Jimmy) Quillen (R) unopposed			($100,553)

Campaign Contributions and Expenditures

1985-86		Direct Cont. 1985-86		PACS Breakdown 1985-86			
Receipts	$472,262	Indiv.	$40,060	Corp.	$148,050	T/M/H	$122,000
Expend.	$459,119	Party	$2,135	Labor	$49,250	Agr.	$20,250
Unspent	$321,484	PACS	$359,050	Ideo.	$14,750	CWOS	$4,750

SECOND DISTRICT

Knoxville, Tennessee, established not long after the first wave of pioneers came through the gaps and down between the mountains of the Appalachian chain, named after the 300-pound Revolutionary War general, looks like an ordinary middle-sized industrial American city. Yet it has its distinctions. It is the home, for example, of the University of Tennessee. It is the headquarters of the Tennessee Valley Authority, a venture in government enterprise which has proved remarkably durable for more than 50 years now. It was host to a World's Fair in 1982, a financially successful enterprise promoted by the likes of Jake Butcher, 1978 Democratic candidate for governor whose own banking business came unravelled the next year and who went to prison not long after. Knoxville has come a long way since John Gunther called it "the ugliest city I ever saw in America." If it is not more beautiful, it is at least much more proserous than when Gunther saw it in the 1940s; it has higher wages and a better standard of living. People here no longer work six days a week and slave over housework; they have plenty of leisure time to enjoy the lakes TVA dams have created in the mountains or even, if they want to brave the crowds, the Great Smokies National Park.

One thing that has not changed in Knoxville, however, and in the nearby counties that make up Tennessee's 2d Congressional District, is their lopsided preference for the Republican Party. This has been the tradition here since before the Civil War, and it is still honored with religious fervor. The 2d District was represented for years by Howard Baker's father and, on his death, by his widow; Baker could have had it in 1964, but decided to run for the Senate instead. That left the job to then-Knoxville Mayor John Duncan. He won by a comfortable margin in that Democratic year and has represented the district ever since.

After 20 years of service, Duncan became ranking Republican on the House Ways and Means Committee in 1985—just in time for the tax reform bill. Yet he played at most a minor role in writing or passing it. His committee position is one to which he did not aspire and for which he never claimed vast expertise; he got it only on the surprise retirement of Upstate New York's Barber Conable. For many years House Republicans chose as their Ways and Means members reliable men from reliable districts, small city squires of decency and honor but little imagination or expertise, men who would not surprise. Duncan is such a man, and he has not. His legislative output for years was been limited to technical matters and local issues; he has never been accused of being a theorist of any economic school. His attitude on rate-lowering, preference-cutting tax reform was almost noncommittal: he said he thought it might be a good idea if it didn't hurt middle class taxpayers. But of course the House was not about to pass a bill that did.

In general, Duncan was ignored by Chairman Dan Rostenkowski as the bill was written, although he did get in a provision helping depositors in an insolvent Tennessee S&L. He stood by as House Republicans whooped it up when they defeated, momentarily, the rule bringing the bill to the floor and thus seemed about to derail the major cause of their party and President; he led the fight for the doomed Republican alternative to Rostenkowski's bill. In the conference committee, Duncan seems to have been ignored; Rostenkowski's Democrats were more knowledgeable than Duncan's Republicans and, more importantly, completely loyal to the chairman. An unkind person said that Duncan and other Republicans learned what the conference decided by reading the papers the next morning.

But this embarrassing lack of clout does not seem to have embarrassed this decent and honorable man before his constituents. Duncan was reelected easily in 1986 and surely can continue to be so long as he desires to run.

The People: Pop. 1980: 510,197, up 17.3% 1970 80. Households (1980): 75% family, 39% with children, 63% married couples; 31.8% housing units rented; median monthly rent: $152; median house value: $37,000. Voting age pop. (1980): 375,709; 6% Black, 1% Spanish origin.

1984 Presidential Vote:

Reagan (R)	....	123,657	(64%)
Mondale (D)	....	67,339	(35%)

Rep. John J. Duncan (R)

Elected 1964; b. Mar. 24, 1919, Scott County; home, Knoxville; U. of TN, B.S. 1942, Cumberland U., J.D. 1948; Presbyterian; married (Lois).

Career: Army, WWII; Asst. Atty. Gen. of TN, 1947–56; Dir., Knoxville Legal Dept., 1956–59; Pres., Knoxville Pro Baseball Club, 1956–59; Mayor of Knoxville, 1959–64.

Offices: 2206 RHOB 20515, 202-225-5435. Also 318 P. O. Bldg., Knoxville 37902, 615-673-4282, McMinn Cnty. Crthse., Athens 37303, 615-745-4671; Rm. 419 1st Amer. Bank Bldg., Maryville 37801, 615-984-5464.

Committees: *Ways and Means* (Ranking Member of 13 R). *Joint Committee on Taxation.*

Group Ratings

	ADA	ACLU	COPE	CFA	LCV	ACU	NTU	NSI	COC	CEI
1986	10	0	19	33	11	62	39	100	72	49
1985	15	—	19	17	—	71	41	—	68	—

National Journal Ratings

	1986 LIB — 1986 CONS			1985 LIB — 1985 CONS		
Economic	19%	—	79%	41%	—	58%
Social	23%	—	74%	0%	—	76%
Foreign	16%	—	79%	24%	—	66%

Key Votes

1) Lmt Cln Water Act	FOR	5) Retain Gun Cont	AGN	9) Aid Angola Reb	FOR
2) Rpl Tobac Sub	AGN	6) Contra Aid	FOR	10) Tax Reform	FOR
3) Grm-Rdmn Def Red	FOR	7) Lmt Text Imp	FOR	11) S Africa Sanc	FOR
4) Ban Polygraph	AGN	8) Limit SDI	AGN	12) Immig Reform	AGN

Election Results

1986 general	John J. Duncan (R)...................	96,396	(76%)	($408,092)
	John F. Bowen (D)	30,088	(24%)	
1986 primary	John J. Duncan (R)...................	39,934	(100%)	
1984 general	John J. Duncan (R)..................	132,604	(77%)	($185,668)
	John F. Bowen (D)	38,846	(23%)	

Campaign Contributions and Expenditures

1985-86		Direct Cont. 1985-86		PACS Breakdown 1985-86			
Receipts	$613,089	Indiv.	$74,626	Corp.	$198,100	T/M/H	$155,951
Expend.	$408,092	Party	$2,045	Labor	$18,000	Agr.	$5,000
Unspent	$512,878	PACS	$405,551	Ideo.	$19,000	CWOS	$9,500
		Cand.	$79,679				

THIRD DISTRICT

Etching its way through the serrated ridges of east Tennessee is the river that gave the state—and the Tennessee Valley Authority—their names. From Knoxville, where the Tennessee is formed by the confluence of the Holston and French Broad Rivers, the river cuts through a ridge and then plunges down a long valley to the city of Chattanooga. There it switches course again, winding around the table-top Lookout Mountain and then moving into northern Alabama. This is the land of the 3d Congressional District of Tennessee. Chattanooga, the largest city, was a village when it was a Civil War battlefield; it grew into an industrial city during the New South years after the Civil War. The 3d District, spreading out on either side of the city, is split between Civil War Democrats and Republicans. Democratic for years, it was marginal enough to elect Bill Brock, a fire-breathing conservative then, in 1962; for most of the 1970s and 1980s it has elected Democrat Marilyn Lloyd. Yet in national and even state elections it has been trending Republican; it was one of two districts that went for Republican Winfield Dunn in the 1986 governor's race. And in House elections, the trend has been Republican as well, for a rather specific reason.

This is a part of Tennessee and a district which has been profoundly affected by the federal government. First by the TVA, which dammed the river, controlled its flooding, generated cheap electricity, and attracted high-energy-consuming industry to the area; and then by the atomic energy laboratories at the Oak Ridge, built in secrecy during World War II, which have been promoting nuclear power ever since, including the controversial Clinch River breeder reactor; Oak Ridge may be the one place in the country that *wants* a nuclear waste dump. The care and tending of these federal facilities has been the main work of Representative Marilyn Lloyd. She is on the Science, Space and Technology Committee and chairs the Energy Research and Production Subcommittee; interestingly, she opposed the nuclear dump for Oak Ridge, which other communities in the area are against. For years she defended the breeder reactor every year against its critics, who included environmentalist opponents of nuclear power and fiscal conservatives who argued that the project would never pay off. Despite her efforts, support dwindled and opposition grew. By 1982 the House voted 217–196 to kill the Clinch River breeder reactor; it survived a little longer thanks to Howard Baker. By 1984 it was gone. Since then Lloyd's margins have shrunk to nearly nothing. In 1984, she won only 52% of the vote against little-known John Davis, a Howard Baker Republican. In 1986, though she prepared much better for the campaign, she won only 54%.

This race was also interesting because of her opposition. Davis ran again, with more support from established Republicans, but he had primary opposition from James Golden, who had strong support from the religious right. Golden is a graduate of a Christian college and member of the Christian Legal Foundation; he invited Pat Robertson in to speak for him at a 1985 fundraiser. Golden trailed far behind Davis in all the pre-primary polls, but he won 59%–41%, and not with just backwoods support: he got 68% of the primary vote in Chattanooga's Hamilton County. In the general election, Golden in a less Republican year against a forewarned incumbent ran almost as well as Davis had, carrying 49% of the vote in Hamilton County. Only Lloyd's big margins in Oak Ridge and a couple of rural counties carried her through. Financially, this was a battle between Washington-wise PACs, which gave Lloyd $324,000, more than half of her total budget, and individual evangelicals, who enabled Golden to raise and spend an impressive $445,000. Lloyd has followed a standard southern Democratic formula, supporting House Democrats often but not always, switching on some tough issues like the MX missile and contra aid, and tending closely to local issues. But her failure to keep the Clinch River breeder reactor alive has undercut her and left her vulnerable to Republicans of various styles to attack her general voting record.

The People: Pop. 1980: 516,692, up 17.1% 1970–80. Households (1980): 78% family, 42% with children, 64% married couples; 31.3% housing units rented; median monthly rent: $149; median house value: $35,400. Voting age pop. (1980): 370,457; 11% Black, 1% Spanish origin.

1984 Presidential Vote:

Reagan (R)	121,921	(63%)
Mondale (D)	72,122	(37%)

Rep. Marilyn Lloyd (D)

Elected 1974; b. Jan. 3, 1929, Ft. Smith, AR; home, Chattanooga; Shorter Col., 1967–70; Church of Christ; divorced.

Career: Co-owner and Mgr., WTTI Radio, Dalton, GA.

Offices: 2266 RHOB 20515, 202-225-3271. Also 253 Jay Solomon Fed. Bldg., Chattanooga 37401, 615-267-9108; and 1211 Joe L. Evins Fed. Bldg., Oak Ridge 37830, 615-576-1977.

Committees: *Armed Services* (19th of 31 D). Subcommittees: Procurement and Military Nuclear Systems. *Science, Space and Technology* (4th of 24 D). Subcommittees: Energy Research and Production (Chairman); International Scientific Cooperation. *Select Committee on Aging* (9th of 39 D). Subcommittees: Housing and Consumer Interests; Retirement Income and Employment.

Group Ratings

	ADA	ACLU	COPE	CFA	LCV	ACU	NTU	NSI	COC	CEI
1986	20	30	56	25	22	62	34	100	53	31
1985	35	—	57	42	—	48	30	—	45	—

National Journal Ratings

	1986 LIB — 1986 CONS			1985 LIB — 1985 CONS		
Economic	45%	—	54%	51%	—	49%
Social	31%	—	67%	34%	—	64%
Foreign	33%	—	67%	37%	—	60%

Key Votes

1) Lmt Cln Water Act	AGN	5) Retain Gun Cont	AGN	9) Aid Angola Reb	FOR
2) Rpl Tobac Sub	AGN	6) Contra Aid	AGN	10) Tax Reform	FOR
3) Grm-Rdmn Def Red	FOR	7) Lmt Text Imp	FOR	11) S Africa Sanc	FOR
4) Ban Polygraph	AGN	8) Limit SDI	AGN	12) Immig Reform	AGN

Election Results

1986 general	Marilyn Lloyd (D)	75,034	(54%)	($637,887)
	Jim Golden (R)........................	64,084	(46%)	($455,298)
1986 primary	Marilyn Lloyd (D)	49,326	(100%)	
1984 general	Marilyn Lloyd (D)	99,465	(52%)	($264,049)
	John Davis (R)	90,216	(48%)	($144,042)

Campaign Contributions and Expenditures

1985-86		Direct Cont. 1985-86		PACS Breakdown 1985-86			
Receipts	$636,851	Indiv.	$225,271	Corp.	$109,250	T/M/H	$88,824
Expend.	$637,887	PACS	$328,128	Labor	$90,950	Agr.	$5,850
		Cand.	$25,000	Ideo.	$32,754	CWOS	$500

FOURTH DISTRICT

Criss-crossing Tennessee from northeast to southwest, following roughly the corduroy-like lines of the western Appalachian ridges and spilling over onto the verdant Cumberland Plateau, is the 4th Congressional District of Tennessee. This is a seat newly created after the 1980 Census, the first new district entirely in rural Tennessee in many years (and a symbol therefore of renewed population growth outside metropolitan areas). It reaches from Virginia almost all the way to Mississippi: it is more than 250 miles long, yet seldom more than 20 miles wide. If you guess that its peculiar boundaries had their birth in politics, you are right.

The congressman here, Jim Cooper, is one of several Tennessee politicians who come from successful political families. His father, Prentice Cooper, was elected governor of Tennessee in 1938, 1940, and 1942. But such lineage gives a candidate only a mild head start. It's a long time since 1942, after all, and Jim Cooper was born 10 years after his father left the governor's office. Not every famous child wins. For every Albert Gore, Jr., who built on his father's name to become first a congressman and then U.S. Senator, there is a Bob Clement, son of a famous governor, who has now lost races for governor and congressman. Cooper won the seat in 1982 by beating Cissy Baker, daughter of Howard Baker and granddaughter of Everett Dirksen, even running ahead of party lines to win by a stunning 66%–34% margin.

Cooper has quietly shown a certain political acumen since in the House. He began quietly; he was after all the youngest person in Congress in 1983 and 1984. But he has shown an ability to take on well-entrenched interests and to advance his own prospects anyway. Coming from a district with tobacco growers, he told the Tobacco Institute, "Tobacco smoke is obnoxious; it's like body odor." Coming from a district with lots of gunowners and hunters, he opposed the National Rifle Association by refusing to vote its bill relaxing gun controls out of the Judiciary Committee and onto the floor. Coming from a hawkish rural district—albeit an area that has happily voted for the Albert Gores, Sr. and Jr.—he said of one Reagan speech on contra aid, "I wouldn't fault his communication skills, I would fault the product he was selling."

He comes up with clever ideas like requiring nutrition labels on lite and lean food products and requiring teenagers to show they are literate before they can get their driver's licenses. He managed, running against the daughter of the Senate Majority Leader, to raise $905,000 for his 1982 campaign, he managed to win in a rural district despite out-of-state schooling (University of North Carolina, Harvard Law, Rhodes Scholar at Oxford) and a Nashville law practice, and he managed in 1987 to get on the most sought-after committee in the House, Energy and Commerce. The quid for the quo, he told Tennessee voters, was support of the congressional pay raise—thus giving himself an excuse for one of the most unpopular votes a congressman can make. All of this is an impressive political performance. Cooper won reelection easily in 1984 and without opposition in 1986. He is barred from statewide contention because Tennessee has two popular Democratic Senators and an incoming Democratic governor. But he has the capacity to be an important member of the House.

The People: Pop. 1980: 510,732, up 22.2% 1970–80. Households (1980): 81% family, 45% with children, 70% married couples; 24.5% housing units rented; median monthly rent: $109; median house value: $29,000. Voting age pop. (1980): 359,160; 4% Black, 1% Spanish origin.

1984 Presidential Vote:

Reagan (R)	95,172	(57%)
Mondale (D)	69,685	(42%)

Rep. Jim Cooper (D)

Elected 1982; b. June 19, 1954, Nashville; home, Shelbyville; U. of NC, B.A. 1975, Rhodes Scholar, Oxford U., B.A., M.A. 1977, Harvard Law School, J.D. 1980; Episcopalian; married (Martha).

Career: Practicing atty., 1980–82.

Offices: 125 CHOB 20515, 202-225-6831. Also 116 Depot St., P.O. Box 725, Shelbyville 37160, 615-684-1114; City Hall, 7 S. High St., Winchester 37398, 615-967-4150; 208 E. 1st North St., Ste. 1, Morristown 37814, 615-587-9000; and 311 S. Main St., P.O. Box 845, Crossville 38555, 615-484-1864.

Committees: *Energy and Commerce* (24th of 25 D). Subcommittees: Oversight and Investigations; Telecommunications and Finance. *Small Business* (15th of 27 D). Subcommittees: Regulation and Business Opportunities; SBA and the General Economy.

Group Ratings

	ADA	ACLU	COPE	CFA	LCV	ACU	NTU	NSI	COC	CEI
1986	70	75	65	75	69	14	30	30	53	34
1985	55	—	65	75	—	24	37	—	45	—

National Journal Ratings

	1986 LIB — 1986 CONS		1985 LIB — 1985 CONS	
Economic	50% —	48%	57% —	41%
Social	79% —	19%	68% —	32%
Foreign	66% —	33%	56% —	44%

Key Votes

1) Lmt Cln Water Act	FOR	5) Retain Gun Cont	AGN
2) Rpl Tobac Sub	AGN	6) Contra Aid	AGN
3) Grm-Rdmn Def Red	FOR	7) Lmt Text Imp	FOR
4) Ban Polygraph	FOR	8) Limit SDI	FOR

9) Aid Angola Reb	AGN
10) Tax Reform	FOR
11) S Africa Sanc	FOR
12) Immig Reform	FOR

Election Results

1986 general	Jim Cooper (D)	86,997	(100%)	($128,007)
1986 primary	Jim Cooper (D)	71,646	(100%)	
1984 general	Jim Cooper (D)	93,848	(75%)	($426,824)
	James Beau Seigneur (R)	31,011	(25%)	($2,868)

Campaign Contributions and Expenditures

1985–86		Direct Cont. 1985–86		PACS Breakdown 1985–86			
Receipts	$147,613	Indiv.	$55,219	Corp.	$34,006	T/M/H	$34,435
Expend.	$128,007	PACS	$87,659	Labor	$9,479	Agr.	$4,000
Unspent	$20,648	Cand.	$899	Ideo.	$4,989	CWOS	$750

FIFTH DISTRICT

Nashville, in the middle of middle Tennessee, is also in this middle of Middle America. This was one of the first American cities established west of the Appalachians, and in the middle 1980s is one of the fastest-growing and economically most vibrant metropolitan areas in the interior of the country. It sits on the undulating hills of the Cumberland Plateau, within 600 miles—a day's drive on the interstates—of half the nation's population; in Tennessee, it is eclipsing Memphis, which technically has more people within its city limits, as the state's premier economic and cultural city. Nashville TV reaches most of Tennessee, Nashville newspapers—the Republican *Banner* and the Democratic *Tennesseean*—set the political tone, and Nashville musicmakers of course set the standard for American country music in this home of the Grand Ole Opry.

But country music is not an all-pervading cultural influence here: Nashville is thriving partly because it, like America, has room for cultural diversity. It has been called the buckle on the Bible Belt, and is the home of the nation's leading publisher of Bibles and religious books. But it is also the home of Ingram, America's leading and most innovative wholesaler of trade books. It has its own version of the Parthenon (featured in Robert Altman's movie *Nashville*), Vanderbilt University, major black institutions like Fisk University and Meharry Medical College, and several religious schools. M.I.T. has ranked Nashville as one of the best places to start a business, and some of the world's biggest companies—AT&T, J.C. Penney, Northern Telecom—are making their home or building facilities here. Nissan has chosen to build a big plant in Smyrna and General Motors sited its Saturn plant in Spring Hill, both within 30 miles of the Nashville skyline.

Nashville was also the home of Andrew Jackson, the first President to call himself a Democrat and the founder of what has been called continuously since the Democratic Party. Nashville's favorite shrine is still the Hermitage, Jackson's mansion. Old Hickory moved to Nashville from the Carolinas when Tennessee was still very much the frontier. He made a small fortune, won election to the House when George Washington was still President, and was elected to the Senate, where he served briefly just after he turned 30. It was only after this youthful political career, and after some financial setbacks, that Jackson made his national reputation as a merciless Indian fighter, the scourge of the British at the Battle of New Orleans, and the common man's candidate for President. Jackson was a Democrat, and Nashville has remained a Democratic city in most of the years since; it dallied with the Whig Party in the 1850s but, occupied by Union troops, it became Democratic again in the 1860s and has remained that way ever since.

The 5th Congressional District of Tennessee includes all of Nashville and Davidson County and one rural and partly suburban county to the north—but only part of the Nashville metropolitan area now that development is spreading into the once rural countryside. The 5th is usually a reliable Democratic district in statewide elections, and it has long elected pretty liberal Democrats, who vote with most of their copartisans from the North on most issues. Racial divisions have played less of a part in voting here than in most southern cities; blacks are 22% of the population, but even in the 1960s Nashville's congressman (and now Mayor), Richard Fulton, voted for civil rights laws and had no trouble winning votes from Nashville whites.

The current congressman from Nashville is Bill Boner, whose record does not measure up to Nashville's achievements. He won the seat by a fluke in 1978, when he was the only serious candidate to file in the primary against incumbent Clifford Allen, who died before primary day;

and he held it in 1986 despite revelations of acts that, if they did not constitute misconduct, certainly did amount to sleaziness. Boner's wife, a lawyer, received $50,000 from a defense contractor found guilty of selling inferior products to the government for legal work she could never describe in detail and public relations assistance; he was alleged to have used campaign funds for a car, furniture, and entertainment; a member of the Banking Committee until 1983, he obtained interests in a hotel and two Shoney's Inns with token investments. The House ethics committee suspended its investigation in the spring of 1986 while federal prosecutors looked into the case; the U.S. attorney decided in March 1987 not to prosecute; the ethics committee may look into Boner's affairs again.

But in the meantime he had won reelection and eight days after the U.S. attorney made his decision announced he was running for mayor of Nashville. Boner had a serious primary opponent in 1986, state legislator Steve Cobb, who had sponsored Lamar Alexander's Better Schools program among other things. But Boner parlayed his generally liberal voting record, the two nights he spent in 1984 on the street dressed as a homeless man, his constituency service operation, and fundraising that ultimately enabled him to spend $909,000 into a 58%–42% victory. His margin in the general election was similar, 58%–40%. The representation of this seat will depend on the disposition of the ethics charges and the outcome of the mayor's race; if Boner gets censured or if he is elected mayor, Cobb will presumably run again. In the meantime Boner continues as a not very influential member of the Appropriations Committee.

The People: Pop. 1980: 514,832, up 7.9% 1970–80. Households (1980): 71% family, 37% with children, 56% married couples; 41.5% housing units rented; median monthly rent: $193; median house value: $44,300. Voting age pop. (1980): 384,057; 20% Black, 1% Spanish origin.

1984 Presidential Vote:	Reagan (R)	103,600	(52%)
	Mondale (D)	95,254	(48%)

Rep. William Hill (Bill) Boner (D)

Elected 1978; b. Feb. 14, 1945, Nashville; home, Nashville; Middle TN St. U., B.S. 1967, Peabody Col., M.A. 1969, YMCA Night Law Sch., Nashville, J.D. 1978; United Methodist; married (Betty).

Career: College basketball coach, 1969–71; TN House of Reps., 1970–72, 1974–76; Sr. Staff Asst., Nashville Mayor's Ofc., 1971–72; Asst. Vice Pres. and Dir. of Pub. Rel., 1st Amer. Natl. Bank, Nashville, 1972–76; Law Clerk, 1976–77; TN Senate, 1976–78.

Offices: 107 CHOB 20515, 202-225-4311. Also 552 U.S. Crthse., 801 Broadway, Nashville 37203, 615-736-5295.

Committees: *Appropriations* (29th of 35 D). Subcommittees: Energy and Water Development; HUD–Independent Agencies. *Select Committee on Aging* (22d of 39 D). Subcommittee: Housing and Consumer Interests.

Group Ratings

	ADA	ACLU	COPE	CFA	LCV	ACU	NTU	NSI	COC	CEI
1986	50	42	84	50	51	30	26	30	18	23
1985	40	—	82	67	—	33	27	—	41	—

National Journal Ratings

	1986 LIB — 1986 CONS		1985 LIB — 1985 CONS	
Economic	87% —	0%	55% —	44%
Social	43% —	56%	52% —	47%
Foreign	55% —	45%	52% —	48%

Key Votes

1) Lmt Cln Water Act	FOR	5) Retain Gun Cont	AGN	9) Aid Angola Reb	AGN
2) Rpl Tobac Sub	AGN	6) Contra Aid	AGN	10) Tax Reform	FOR
3) Grm-Rdmn Def Red	FOR	7) Lmt Text Imp	FOR	11) S Africa Sanc	FOR
4) Ban Polygraph	FOR	8) Limit SDI	AGN	12) Immig Reform	AGN

Election Results

1986 general	William Hill (Bill) Boner (D)	78,658	(58%)	($909,521)
	Terry Holcomb (R)	58,701	(40%)	($189,566)
1986 primary	William Hill (Bill) Boner (D)	58,922	(58%)	
	Steve Cobb (D)	42,695	(42%)	
1984 general	William Hill (Bill) Boner (D) unopposed			($345,087)

Campaign Contributions and Expenditures

1985-86		Direct Cont. 1985-86		PACS Breakdown 1985-86			
Receipts	$881,787	Indiv.	$327,132	Corp.	$77,800	T/M/H	$63,550
Expend.	$909,521	Party	$500	Labor	$145,258	Agr.	$8,500
Unspent	$76,591	PACS	$314,100	Ideo.	$19,000	CWOS	$0
		Cand.	$134,550				

SIXTH DISTRICT

The 6th Congressional District of Tennessee is part of the Cumberland Plateau, the hilly and fertile land just west of the Appalachian chains, inside the U formed by the Tennessee River as it begins in the mountains, flows through northern Alabama, and then goes back up north again through Tennessee to meet the Ohio River near Paducah, Kentucky. Middle Tennessee, as this area is called, is one of the heartlands of the Democratic Party. It was the political home base of Andrew Jackson and supported him nearly unanimously; during the Civil War, though it had precious few slaves, it resented the invading Union armies, and has voted solidly Democratic ever since. It is neither particularly rich nor particularly poor; its farmers suffered during the Depression and saw their land values rise in some cases as people fanned out from Nashville and were attracted by new businesses like General Motors's Saturn plant in Spring Hill. Through all this, the Democratic allegiance has remained, almost magically, intact. In the 17 counties here east and south of Nashville that make up Tennessee's 6th Congressional District, Jimmy Carter got 65% of the vote in 1976 and won again easily in 1980. In 1984, Walter Mondale fell back and got 41%, the same as his national average; but in a district where only 7% of the voters are black, that means he did better than his national average with whites.

In congressional elections, middle Tennessee has produced national Democratic leaders from James K. Polk (1825–39), speaker of the House and later President, and Cordell Hull (1907–21, 1923–31), later Senator and Secretary of State, to Albert Gore, Sr., (1939–53), later Senator. Its most recent ex-congressman, Albert Gore, Jr. (1977–85), is now also Senator.

The current congressman, Bart Gordon, is an ambitious young man who won a multicandidate primary with 28% of the vote—there is no runoff in Tennessee—in 1984. Traditionally in this district, voters in the dusty courthouse towns of middle Tennessee expected to meet and talk several minutes with their political candidates. But new forms of campaigning are more important in the shopping center crossroads that are springing up in the countryside 50 miles from Nashville. Gordon ran a computerized fundraising operation and voter contact system, and a sophisticated ad campaign; he boasted that, as state Democratic chairman, he had put the state party back in the black. He talked convincingly of aiding local development and spoke out against unfair tax loopholes and for a verifiable arms control agreement.

This enabled him to overcome disadvantages that included relative youth, a Nashville image, and a pending paternity suit, and to carry not only his base, as most candidates do in old-fashioned friends-and-neighbors contests, but also to carry one-fifth to one-third of the vote in most of the rest of the district—enough to win the primary. In the general election Joe Simpkins, whose brother is publisher of the *Nashville Banner*, carried his home area of Williamson County, which is fast filling up with affluent suburbanites from Nashville and has been trending heavily Republican; but he lost all but one other county in the district.

In the House Gordon compiled a generally pro-leadership record, which paid off in early 1987 when he was chosen to fill the late Sala Burton's seat on the House Rules Committee. This is a good platform for a member from a safe district to undertake a variety of projects, and one the leadership fills with members it is sure will be faithful. Gordon evidently qualifies. He was reelected easily and surely has a safe seat.

The People: Pop. 1980: 511,805, up 37.0% 1970 80. Households (1980): 81% family, 46% with children, 70% married couples; 25.1% housing units rented; median monthly rent: $151; median house value: $40,400. Voting age pop. (1980): 362,322; 7% Black, 1% Spanish origin.

1984 Presidential Vote:

Reagan (R)	....	108,626	(59%)
Mondale (D)	....	75,667	(41%)

Rep. Bart Gordon (D)

Elected 1984; b. Jan. 24, 1949, Murfreesboro; home, Murfreesboro; Middle TN St. U., B.S. 1971, U. of TN Law Sch., J.D. 1973; United Methodist; single.

Career: Practicing atty., 1974–84; Chmn., TN Dem. Party, 1981–83.

Offices: 1517 LHOB 20515, 202-225-4231. Also P.O. Box 1986, Murfreesboro 37133, 615-896-1986; 102 W. 7th St., Columbia 38401, 615-388-8808; and P.O. Box 1140, Cookeville, 38503, 615-528-5907.

Committees: *Rules* (9th of 9 D). Subcommittee: The Legislative Process. *Select Committee on Aging* (32d of 39 D). Subcommittee: Housing and Consumer Interests.

Group Ratings

	ADA	ACLU	COPE	CFA	LCV	ACU	NTU	NSI	COC	CEI
1986	75	68	73	50	43	9	31	20	39	27
1985	55	—	63	67	—	20	35	—	45	—

National Journal Ratings

	1986 LIB — 1986 CONS		1985 LIB — 1985 CONS	
Economic	54% —	46%	48% —	50%
Social	61% —	37%	63% —	37%
Foreign	66% —	33%	53% —	46%

Key Votes

1) Lmt Cln Water Act	FOR	5) Retain Gun Cont	AGN	9) Aid Angola Reb	AGN
2) Rpl Tobac Sub	AGN	6) Contra Aid	AGN	10) Tax Reform	AGN
3) Grm-Rdmn Def Red	FOR	7) Lmt Text Imp	FOR	11) S Africa Sanc	FOR
4) Ban Polygraph	FOR	8) Limit SDI	FOR	12) Immig Reform	AGN

Election Results

1986 general	Bart Gordon (D)	102,180	(77%)	($253,689)
	Fred Vail (R)	30,823	(23%)	($3,382)
1986 primary	Bart Gordon (D)	82,359	(100%)	
1984 general	Bart Gordon (D)	103,989	(63%)	($656,222)
	Joe Simpkins (R)	61,559	(37%)	($355,364)

Campaign Contributions and Expenditures

1985-86		Direct Cont. 1985-86		PACS Breakdown 1985-86			
Receipts	$399,027	Indiv.	$178,272	Corp.	$61,950	T/M/H	$56,018
Expend.	$253,689	Party	$344	Labor	$51,150	Agr.	$5,500
Debts	$151,940	PACS	$193,716	Ideo.	$17,098	CWOS	$2,000
		Cand.	$3,979				

SEVENTH DISTRICT

The 7th Congressional District of Tennessee stretches from the heart of middle Tennessee to the heart of west Tennessee, from the city limits of Nashville to inside the city limits of Memphis. Politically, it contains several distinct areas. The counties nearest Nashville and along the lower Tennessee River are part of the heavily Democratic bloc which has existed in this part of the state in almost uninterrupted fashion since the time of Andrew Jackson. In the southern part of the district, just across the Tennessee River, are several rural counties which have been mostly Republican since the Civil War. Farther west are two counties just north of Mississippi with black majorities—just about the only heavily black rural part of Tennessee. The district also includes some 171,000 people in Memphis's Shelby County, 92% of them white, the large majority of them affluent.

In political analysis the sections of the district are usually collapsed into two: the rural counties, with about 60% of the population, generally preferring country-based Democratic candidates; and Shelby County, with about 40% and growing, strongly preferring conservative Republicans. Voting in the Memphis area is heavily polarized by race: blacks are almost unanimously Democratic; whites, especially affluent whites, go Republican by percentages nearly as high. In 1984 the Shelby County portion went 81% for Ronald Reagan; the rural counties went 45% for Mondale.

The congressman from the 7th District is Republican Don Sundquist, a businessman and former Howard Baker aide. As a member of the Public Works and Veterans' Affairs Committees, he does not have much seniority, but he seems poised to make a difference in the House. He has a solidly conservative record and has emerged as a Republican leader on some issues, heading up a party task force on trade (he has worked to protect the local footwear industry) and sponsoring an amendment that cut $15 million from the United Nations budget and prevents U.S. money from being used to pay salaries to Soviets on the UN payroll when they turn their money back over to their government. He criticized TVA officials harshly and saw some of his criticisms vindicated as TVA's nuclear program has gotten into more and more trouble. After making a skilled feint at Guy VanderJagt's job as campaign committee chairman, Sundquist won a seat on the Budget Committee after the 1986 elections and one on the ethics committee as well. Aggressive, competent, acceptable to most factions, he could be a party leader in the future.

Like most congressmen he also tends to local issues, getting a Doppler radar warning system for the Memphis airport and widening the road from Clarksville to Fort Campbell, Kentucky. When Republican Robin Beard left this seat to run against Senator Jim Sasser in 1982, there was a close race here: Sundquist beat Democrat Bob Clement, son of a former governor, narrowly by winning 75% in Shelby County and 35% in the rural counties, for a 51% win. But he seems to have a safe seat now: he had no opposition in 1984 and won with 72% in 1986, carrying not only Shelby County with 87% but the rural counties with 61%. He is now one of Tennessee's leading Republican officeholders and could conceivably run against Sasser in 1988.

The People: Pop. 1980: 503,611, up 47.4% 1970–80. Households (1980): 81% family, 47% with children, 70% married couples; 26.4% housing units rented; median monthly rent: $184; median house value: $42,200. Voting age pop. (1980): 351,201; 11% Black, 1% Spanish origin, 1% Asian origin.

1984 Presidential Vote:

Reagan (R) 130,862	(66%)
Mondale (D) 67,173	(34%)

Rep. Don Sundquist (R)

Elected 1982; b. Mar. 15, 1936, Moline, IL; home, Memphis; Augustana Col., B.A. 1957; Lutheran; married (Martha).

Career: Navy, 1957–59; Josten's Inc., 1961–72; Partner, Graphic Sales of Amer., 1972, Pres., 1973–82.

Offices: 230 CHOB 20515, 202-225-2811. Also 5909 Shelby Oaks Dr., Ste. 112, Memphis 38134, 901-382-5811; and 117 S. 2d St., Clarksville 37040, 615-552-4406.

Committees: *Budget* (10th of 14 R). Task Forces: Budget Process; Defense and International Affairs; Economic Policy. *Public Works and Transportation* (10th of 20 R). Subcommittees: Aviation; Public Buildings and Grounds; Water Resources.

Group Ratings

	ADA	ACLU	COPE	CFA	LCV	ACU	NTU	NSI	COC	CEI
1986	5	0	17	33	26	82	50	100	72	64
1985	15	—	17	17	—	81	51	—	91	—

National Journal Ratings

	1986 LIB — 1986 CONS			1985 LIB — 1985 CONS		
Economic	23%	—	76%	24%	—	74%
Social	11%	—	85%	0%	—	76%
Foreign	0%	—	86%	24%	—	66%

Key Votes

1) Lmt Cln Water Act	AGN	5) Retain Gun Cont	AGN	9) Aid Angola Reb	FOR
2) Rpl Tobac Sub	AGN	6) Contra Aid	FOR	10) Tax Reform	AGN
3) Grm-Rdmn Def Red	FOR	7) Lmt Text Imp	FOR	11) S Africa Sanc	AGN
4) Ban Polygraph	AGN	8) Limit SDI	AGN	12) Immig Reform	AGN

Election Results

1986 general	Don Sundquist (R)	93,902	(72%)	($281,817)
	M. Lloyd Hiler (D)	35,966	(28%)	($4,183)
1986 primary	Don Sundquist (R)	26,007	(100%)	
1984 general	Don Sundquist (R) unopposed			($511,053)

Campaign Contributions and Expenditures

1985-86		Direct Cont. 1985-86		PACS Breakdown 1985-86			
Receipts	$409,651	Indiv.	$230,380	Corp.	$83,850	T/M/H	$53,424
Expend.	$281,817	Party	$2,101	Labor	$11,550	Agr.	$2,300
Unspent	$189,861	PACS	$160,905	Ideo.	$5,800	CWOS	$3,981

EIGHTH DISTRICT

North of Memphis and west of Nashville and the TVA lakes on the lower Tennessee and Cumberland Rivers lies the 8th Congressional District of Tennessee. This is the land the rivers have flowed down from the mountains to; once roaring and frothing, they now lazily roll through the flat or only gently rolling land in the Mississippi Valley. This looks like eastern Arkansas or even the Delta of Mississippi; cotton and, increasingly, soybeans are the main crops; many of the blacks who worked these fields before mechanization have long since left, but enough remain to give this district the highest black percentage of any rural district in Tennessee. Outside of Memphis and Shelby County, the district's largest city is Jackson, with a population of 49,000.

Most of the counties here are traditionally Democratic, but they trended sharply to the Republicans starting in the late 1960s; now they seem to have trended back to the Democrats. Governor Ned Ray McWherter, who is from Dresden in Weakley County in the 8th, not only carried the 8th District but brought out a record off-year turnout here. Political preference again follows Civil War lines: the 8th has one Republican county here, and Jackson sometimes goes Republican, but the other rural counties are Democratic. Shelby County is another matter. The 8th includes the northern fringes of Memphis and its suburbs, a not particularly elite or affluent area where 22% of the residents are black. But partisan preferences in the Memphis area are so polarized on racial lines that this area goes Republican in most national and statewide elections.

The congressman from the 8th District, Ed Jones, is an old-fashioned Tennessee Democrat who spends most of his time on agricultural issues. He is the third-ranking Democrat on the Agriculture Committee (behind Chairman Kika de la Garza and Walter Jones) and has chaired the Conservation, Credit, and Rural Development Subcommittee, which governs all sorts of programs. Most urban Americans have little idea of how many safety nets and assistance programs there are for farmers, and how many ways the federal government regulates farming and the food business. Farmers, of course, like to think of themselves as lonely entrepreneurs, yeomen providers for their families; but of course they like any sensible people want the government to protect them against downside risks and looming disaster. Markets, after all, have no mercy.

Practical politicians like Ed Jones try to provide that help, but it becomes more difficult all the time as the cost of farm programs increases even as their effectiveness seems to diminish. He has worked hard over the years to put more federal dollars into the farm credit system and to get the government to be more liberal in extending credit and less aggressive in demanding repayment. He has also spent time on soil conservation, and pushed through the "sodbuster" and "swampbuster" laws encouraging farmers not to cultivate easily erodible land and putting a "conservation reserve" provision into the 1985 farm bill, to encourage farmers to take erodible land out of production. He got into trouble as chairman of a housekeeping subsidy for dismissing a restaurant employee because her $45,000 salary was "ridiculous for a woman"; the House counsel is defending him in the sex discrimination case she brought.

Jones first won this seat in what may have been the most difficult year for his kind of old-fashioned rural Democrat, 1969. The incumbent had died, and in the special election Richard Nixon's Republicans campaigned heavily for their candidate, and George Wallace came in and supported an American Party nominee. Jones, who had served as state agriculture commissioner, campaigned for himself and won the three-way race with 48%. He has had only one significant electoral challenge in his years in the House, in the 1976 primary. The Democratic trend in west Tennessee makes his seat even safer, but it is possible that he will choose one of these election years to retire.

The People: Pop. 1980: 504,957, up 12.2% 1970–80. Households (1980): 78% family, 43% with children, 65% married couples; 30.2% housing units rented; median monthly rent: $119; median house value: $30,400. Voting age pop. (1980): 358,805; 18% Black, 1% Spanish origin.

1984 Presidential Vote:

Reagan (R)	98,966	(57%)
Mondale (D)	74,732	(43%)

Rep. Ed Jones (D)

Elected Mar. 25, 1969; b. Apr. 20, 1912, Yorkville; home, Yorkville; U. of TN, B.S. 1934; Presbyterian; married (Llewellyn).

Career: Inspector, TN Dept. of Agric., 1934–41; Sprvsr., TN Dairy Products Assn., 1941–43; Agric. Rep., IL Central R.R., 1943–49, 1952–69; TN Commissioner of Agric., 1949–52; Chmn., TN Agric. Stablization and Conservation Comm., 1961–69.

Offices: 108 CHOB 20515, 202-225-4714. Also 3179 N. Watkins, Memphis 38127, 901-358-4094; P.O. Box 128, Yorkville 38389, 901-643-6123; and P.O. Bldg., Rm. B-7, Jackson 38301, 901-423-4848.

Committees: *Agriculture* (3d of 26 D). Subcommittees: Conservation, Credit, and Rural Development (Chairman); Cotton, Rice, and Sugar; Livestock, Dairy, and Poultry. *House Administration* (3d of 12 D). Subcommittees: Libraries and Memorials; Personnel and Police; Procurement and Printing (Chairman). *Joint Committee on Library.*

Group Ratings

	ADA	ACLU	COPE	CFA	LCV	ACU	NTU	NSI	COC	CEI
1986	45	65	62	50	29	29	28	40	40	27
1985	35	—	62	67	—	43	28	—	35	—

National Journal Ratings

	1986 LIB — 1986 CONS			1985 LIB — 1985 CONS		
Economic	68%	—	31%	51%	—	48%
Social	30%	—	70%	48%	—	51%
Foreign	54%	—	46%	51%	—	48%

Key Votes

1) Lmt Cln Water Act	AGN	5) Retain Gun Cont	AGN	9) Aid Angola Reb	AGN
2) Rpl Tobac Sub	AGN	6) Contra Aid	AGN	10) Tax Reform	FOR
3) Grm-Rdmn Def Red	FOR	7) Lmt Text Imp	FOR	11) S Africa Sanc	FOR
4) Ban Polygraph	AGN	8) Limit SDI	AGN	12) Immig Reform	AGN

Election Results

1986 general	Ed Jones (D)	101,699	(80%)	($108,957)
	Dan H. Campbell (R)	24,792	(20%)	
1986 primary	Ed Jones (D)	82,391	(100%)	
1984 general	Ed Jones (D) unopposed			($36,264)

Campaign Contributions and Expenditures

1985-86		Direct Cont. 1985-86		PACS Breakdown 1985-86			
Receipts	$124,341	Indiv.	$16,400	Corp.	$20,550	T/M/H	$36,950
Expend.	$108,957	Party	$100	Labor	$10,050	Agr.	$11,500
Unspent	$148,059	PACS	$86,800	Ideo.	$3,500	CWOS	$4,250

NINTH DISTRICT

On the muddy banks of the Mississippi River, in the far southwestern corner of Tennessee, is Memphis, largest city in the state, and financial and commercial center of much of the lower Mississippi Valley. Memphis looks south to Mississippi and west to Arkansas more than it does to the Appalachians far to the east. That separateness is symbolized by its musical tradition: Beale Street, near downtown Memphis, gave birth to jazz in the 1920s; and jazz, in turn, came from the blues music which is the product of the lower Mississippi Valley, particularly the Delta. Memphis and New Orleans were the natural conduits of the Delta's music, as they were of its cotton, to the outside world. Elvis Presley, Memphis's late musical hero, was born in Mississippi and drew much of his inspiration from black music.

Memphis was the site of one of the largest cotton markets in the United States for many years, and a look at the courtyard of the Peabody Hotel can bring back the days when big Mississippi planters came north to sell their one season's crop and make their financial arrangements for the next. Soybeans and rice have replaced cotton as the staple crop in the levee-protected lowlands here, and Memphis itself has a diversified economy. But demographically and politically it still bears the imprint of the cotton culture. Black slaves and field hands were used to pick cotton, and Memphis, like eastern Arkansas and the Mississippi Delta, has always had a large black population. Segregation was tradition and law here, and Memphis remained an obdurately segregationist city when other parts of the South were adapting to new ways. Voting patterns in Memphis, even today, in both nonpartisan and partisan elections, are firmly polarized on racial lines. Forty-eight percent of Memphis's residents, and 42% of the residents of Shelby County, are black, and nearly all black voters support Democrats. The white majority, in contrast, almost exclusively supports Republicans. This is particularly true in the affluent suburban tracts east and south of downtown Memphis, but even in white working-class areas you typically will find large Republican majorities in elections. Memphis sees itself as an all-American town, the site of the first supermarket (a Piggly Wiggly) in the 1920s, the first Holiday Inn in the 1950s, Federal Express in the 1970s—each on the leading edge of American commercial innovation. But it has also been the scene of the American tragedy of the murder of Martin Luther King in 1968.

That separatism coexists with a tradition of almost authoritarian bossism. For 39 years, the political machine run by Ed Crump ran the city government and could deliver Memphis's votes *en bloc,* particularly in the Democratic primary, making Crump the effective political boss of the state and a master of invective. In 1948, he attacked Estes Kefauver as "a pet coon that puts its foot in an open drawer in your room, but invariably turns its head while its foot is feeling around in the drawer. The coon hopes, through its cunning by turning its head, he will deceive any onlookers as to where his foot is and what it is into." Kefauver donned a coonskin cap, saying "At least I'm not Mr. Crump's pet coon," won the primary and ended Crump's control. But Crump governed efficiently, honestly, and with the support of blacks who were allowed to vote in Memphis unlike most southern cities—and voted almost unanimously for Mr. Crump's candidates.

The 9th Congressional District of Tennessee consists of most of the city of Memphis; most of its residents are black, and the district is solidly Democratic. Its congressman, Harold Ford, first elected in 1974, has gained more substantive power over major legislation than Crump ever did, but he appears also to have gotten into more trouble than Memphis's old boss ever experienced.

Ford sits on the Ways and Means Committee, and his power comes on the the Public Assistance and Unemployment Compensation Subcommittee which he chairs. This governs the rules of the basic welfare programs, and so touches on one of the most sensitive and hottest issues in this district and most others. Ford, who played a relatively minor role on the tax reform law of 1986, arguing most strongly for the exemption for charitable contributions, was concentrating on welfare reform instead, and with results. In 1985 he was advancing a far-ranging child care bill; in 1986 he got through the House a bill to allow welfare payments to go to eligible families with an unemployed father at home, in order to keep families together. In April 1987 the subcommittee reported out a welfare reform bill, authorizing and paying 60% of the cost for new state job-training, education, and work programs for welfare recipients; requiring welfare mothers with children over 3 to participate in them; adding the 1986 welfare-for-unemployed-fathers provision (already the law in half the states); and encouraging higher benefits in low-benefit states. Republicans opposed it as too costly (perhaps $5.5 billion a year) and on other grounds, but it looked like a good first step toward the workfare bill that members of both parties are longing to pass.

Then, less than a month later, Ford was indicted by a federal grand jury on charges of bank and tax fraud stemming from moneys he received from C. H. Butcher, Jr., a Tennessee banker and brother and partner of Jake Butcher, the 1982 Democratic candidate for governor whose banking empire collapsed in 1983 and who was sentenced to 20 years in jail in 1985 for defrauding depositors of $20 million. The indictment said that a $350,000 "loan" from one of C. H. Butcher's firms to a corporation controlled by Ford was used by Ford, not for his family funeral home business, but to pay personal debts and buy personal belongings. A spokesman for Ford said he did not know all the details and that he had loaned the funeral home personal funds so that any moneys advanced were repayments; Ford charged that the U.S. attorney bringing the case was politically motivated. Whatever the outcome of the case, the involvement of Ford with the Butcher interests does not improve his reputation or make it easier for him to advance the welfare legislation. The subcommittee's other members are all competent, but the Ford indictment, whatever else it does, may end the chances for welfare reform in the 100th Congress.

Ford, who first won this seat by the narrowest of margins in 1974 when most of its voters were still white, had a safe seat until his indictment. Probably his political standing depends on the outcome of the legal case. This is a safe Democratic district now, and any successor will be chosen in the Democratic primary.

The People: Pop. 1980: 505,592, dn. 9.4% 1970–80. Households (1980): 69% family, 38% with children, 46% married couples; 46.0% housing units rented; median monthly rent: $136; median house value: $32,300. Voting age pop. (1980): 359,672; 51% Black, 1% Spanish origin.

1984 Presidential Vote:
Mondale (D) 137,826 (64%)
Reagan (R) 77,894 (36%)

Rep. Harold E. Ford (D)

Elected 1974; b. May 20, 1945, Memphis; home, Memphis; TN St. U., B.S. 1967, John Gupten Col., A.A. 1969; Howard U., M.B.A. 1981; Baptist; married (Dorothy).

Career: Mortician, 1969–75; TN House of Reps., 1971–75.

Offices: 2305 RHOB 20515, 202-225-3265. Also Fed. Office Bldg., Ste. 369, 167 N. Main St., Memphis 38103, 901-521-4131.

Committees: *Ways and Means* (7th of 23 D). Subcommittees: Oversight; Public Assistance and Unemployment Compensation (Chairman). *Select Committee on Aging* (7th of 39 D). Subcommittee: Health and Long-Term Care.

Group Ratings

	ADA	ACLU	COPE	CFA	LCV	ACU	NTU	NSI	COC	CEI
1986	100	94	91	67	72	0	22	0	8	18
1985	90	—	92	75	—	0	27	—	14	—

National Journal Ratings

	1986 LIB — 1986 CONS		1985 LIB — 1985 CONS	
Economic	87% —	0%	89% —	0%
Social	89% —	0%	79% —	19%
Foreign	80% —	0%	80% —	17%

Key Votes

1) Lmt Cln Water Act	AGN	5) Retain Gun Cont	FOR	9) Aid Angola Reb	—
2) Rpl Tobac Sub	FOR	6) Contra Aid	AGN	10) Tax Reform	FOR
3) Grm-Rdmn Def Red	AGN	7) Lmt Text Imp	FOR	11) S Africa Sanc	FOR
4) Ban Polygraph	FOR	8) Limit SDI	FOR	12) Immig Reform	FOR

Election Results

1986 general	Harold E. Ford (D)...................	83,006	(83%)	($320,227)
	Isaac Richmond (R)..................	16,221	(16%)	
1986 primary	Harold E. Ford (D)...................	62,037	(73%)	
	Walton L. Evans (D).................	18,304	(22%)	
	Mark Flanigan (D)	4,620	(5%)	
1984 general	Harold E. Ford (D)..................	133,428	(72%)	($194,700)
	William B. Thompson, Jr. (R)	53,064	(28%)	

Campaign Contributions and Expenditures

1985-86		Direct Cont. 1985-86		PACS Breakdown 1985-86			
Receipts	$326,829	Indiv.	$88,280	Corp.	$79,556	T/M/H	$69,550
Expend.	$320,227	Party	$100	Labor	$48,990	Agr.	$5,000
Unspent	$68,059	PACS	$222,877	Ideo.	$10,000	CWOS	$9,781

TEXAS

For Texas, the 1980s have been a roller coaster decade—exhilarating climbs up, excruciating hurtles down, and some swings around in circles—all out of sync with similar but mostly milder movements in the rest of the United States. Yet it has been clear throughout that when Texans stepped off the ride, they'd be in a different place from where they started. For Texas, a nation-state that was only recently a kind of underdeveloped country, is now one of the high tech centers of the world; and if parts of Texas were economically advanced years ago, much of the state still looks underdeveloped today. There were 7 million Texans when World War II ended and 14 million when the oil shock of 1979 hit; by the middle 1980s there were 16 million and there could easily be 21 million by 2000. This was the largest state in size but only the sixth in population in 1945; now it is second in area to Alaska, but third in population, and pressing New York for second place. In many ways the center of gravity of the United States seems to be moving to Texas which was at the turn of the century a sun-parched, wind-blown, dirt-poor frontier. Yet Texas's advances should not be overstated. The state sits on the only land border between the First and Third Worlds, and Texas's income levels, despite all the millionaires and the growth during the years of high oil prices, have still not managed to climb above the national average.

Texas's history is a story of geography, geology, and technology. Geographically, this remote province of Mexico was the natural extension of the slaveholding South: the Texans who won independence in 1836 wanted to legalize their slaves, and Texas was a most enthusiastic Confederate state. Geology here means oil, starting with the Spindletop field in east Texas in 1901. Settled almost entirely by poor dirt farmers, Texas baked in the hot sun; in those days long before air conditioning, it had no industry and little commerce, some of the nation's lowest income levels and highest levels on endemic disease. Oil changed all that. But oil was not just a windfall: finding it and getting it out of the ground is high-skill work. Oil made instant millionaires out of some lucky Texas farmers, but more important it created a business which rewarded sophistication and placed a premium on knowledge. The men you'll see over scotch and steaks at the Petroleum Club in Fort Worth or Tyler or Midland may not look sophisticated to habitués of Ivy League faculty clubs, but beneath their bravado are plenty of brains. By the 1980s Texas was not so much the place where oil was found as the place where you found people who could find and drill and store and refine oil and natural gas. These skills led Texas naturally into technology. And starting in the 1960s Texas was building the critical mass of knowledge and financing to produce firms like Texas Instruments and H. Ross Perot's EDS. Oil by some measures accounts for only one-eighth of Texas's economy, but it is a volatile eighth, and one deeply implanted in the local consciousness, and the roller coaster of Texas's economy in the 1980s has been powered largely by the rise and fall in oil prices.

Local pride, the hallmark of so many states' politics in the middle 1980s, has never been lacking in Texas; but even in the Sesquicentennial year of 1986—that's 150 years from Texas's independence, not statehood, pardner—there was a certain unevenness to Texans' perceptions of where their state stood and ideas about where it should go. The benefits of a developing economy are never evenly distributed, and much of the tension in Texas politics comes from the wide disparities in wealth and the vast cultural variety in this huge state. Its politics, like its economy, has had its roller-coaster ride ups and downs over the last decade: Republican William Clements's surprise election as governor in 1978, his surprise defeat by Democrat Mark White in 1982, and then his not unexpected but nevertheless stunning victory over White in 1986. Meanwhile, Texas has given Ronald Reagan two big statewide victories, and in the second of them elected Senator Phil Gramm, the eponymous author of the measure that changed the federal budget process in 1985; yet it also elects Lloyd Bentsen, the new chairman of the Senate Finance Committee, and the latest in a line of Texas Democrats who have wielded great power in Washington. The state's congressional delegation has more Republicans than ever before, yet it is still a Democratic majority, and includes none less than Speaker of the House Jim Wright. In all this you can see Texas torn between faith in the free market and a desire for government safety nets, between the traditional culture of the rural South and the self-consciously modern culture of the rapidly growing cities, between Texas's traditional image of ethnic uniformity and suspicion of outsiders and its increasingly heterogeneous population and its natural friendliness.

In Texas's growing cities—in the Dallas–Fort Worth Metroplex, in greater Houston, in San Antonio and the once tiny capital, Austin, now spreading out into the hill country—politics tends to divide people along income lines. The divisions can be stark: you can drive just a few minutes on the freeway from the west side of Houston or north Dallas, where house sales of $750,000 are routine, and find neighborhoods of tiny, drafty frame houses which are little better than tarpaper shacks. Texas, for all its millionaires, has a substantial low-wage economy and, as the largest state with a right-to-work law, almost no union members; most of its blacks (12% of the population) and Hispanics (21%) are part of this low-wage economy, as are many whites of rural origin. All tend to vote Democratic, but they are not a homogeneous proletariat, and are seldom found together: there are few Mexicans in Dallas and almost no blacks in San Antonio or west of Fort Worth. Hispanics are sliding away from the Democrats in some elections, while blacks cast almost no Republican votes at all. The affluent neighborhoods, by contrast, are politically homogeneous, as heavily Republican as any in the United States. There is no apology or guilt about wealth; people here, like the rich in developing countries, do not feel defensive because others are still poor; they have grown up in a society in which most people are poor, and they realize that not everyone can get rich all at once. All this leaves the metropolitan areas more divided than tradition would have it. The biggest cities have mayors who are Democrats and don't fit Texas stereotypes: Houston's Kathy Whitmire, Dallas's Annette Strauss, San Antonio's Henry Cisneros. Dallas is well known as one of America's most Republican cities, and Fort Worth has been trending Republican too; yet in the 1986 governor's race Bill Clements carried

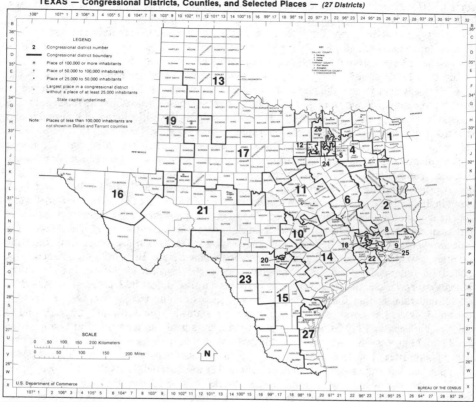

TEXAS — Congressional Districts, Counties, and Selected Places — *(27 Districts)*

Congressional districts established June 19, 1983; all other boundaries are as of January 1, 1980.

the Metroplex by the solid but not overwhelming margin of 57%–42%. Greater Houston, always a little more Democratic, went for Mark White, as did the combined San Antonio–Austin areas. The heavily Mexican–American border counties were a shade less Democratic than usual, 59%–39%.

The balance politically was in the rest of Texas, the smaller counties away from the Border where, after decades of metropolitan growth, nearly 40% of the state's votes are still cast. For decades this nonmetropolitan Texas was exporting young people to the cities, and some counties still are; around Lubbock, where the aquifers are giving out and irrigated cotton fields are going back to desert, or in the wheat-growing country of the High Plains, where people are still moving. But there has been enough job growth in east, central, and south Texas to hold people here and attract more, like the Vietnamese fishermen who are sometimes harassed in Gulf Coast ports. And just as Texas itself has not, as many easterners predicted, moved to the heavy-industry-and-big-unions economy of the Great Lakes (in fact, the movement has been in the other direction), so the small town values and cultural conservatism of the countryside has not withered away any more than the towns have died. Some things have changed: county option liquor by the drink came in in 1970, divorce has grown more common. But there is still a vivid contrast between the big metropolitan areas, where the percentage of women working out of the home is among the highest in the country, and the smaller counties, where it is among the lowest. Ancestrally almost all of these counties are heavily Democratic, though there are interesting exceptions, as in the Texas German country around San Antonio and up in the Panhandle not far from Kansas.

But increasingly in the 1980s rural Texas has been moving toward the Republicans. Jimmy Carter carried the state in 1976 when he won the rural counties with 53%; Democrats lost in 1978 when they took 51% in them. By 1980 Carter was down to 42% in rural Texas, and lost the state by a wide margin; in 1984 Walter Mondale, having conspicuously rejected Lloyd Bentsen for Geraldine Ferraro, got only 34% in rural Texas. Mark White rallied rural Texas to his side for a 56% showing there and victory in 1982; he got only 41% in rural Texas in 1986 when he lost. White's policies of more taxes for education, his steadfast support of Ross Perot's no-pass-no-play rule (which means that high school football players who flunk one course can't play: revolutionary in Texas), his embrace of his considerably more liberal ticketmates all seem to have played poorly in the rural areas. White ran behind his 1982 showing by just 3% in the metropolitan and Border counties—a showing that if sustained statewide would have reelected him. But his percentage in rural Texas fell 15%. In the Democratic primary, against unknown candidates, he won only 43% in rural Texas, and only 33% of all votes. True, Lieutenant Governor Bill Hobby won with 62%, the kind of showing moderate Democrats used to always make. But scandal-tarred Attorney General Jim Mattox, who went on trial and was acquitted during his first term, managed to win only 52% of the vote against Republican Roy Barrerra, Jr., a San Antonio judge recruited by the Republicans but whom they unaccountably failed to raise enough money for. And Senator Phil Gramm's crazy-brave initiative of forcing a special congressional election in the 1st District in 1985 and trying for a Republican breakthrough in the most Democratic of the rural counties was foiled, but by the smallest of margins. But the corner seems to have been turned in 1984, when for the first time Republicans did better in rural than in metropolitan Texas. Republicans picked up five House seats they had lost in 1982; they also picked up enough seats in the legislature to maintain their largest presence there ever; they even captured county-wide offices in such unlikely places as Tarrant County (Fort Worth) and Bexar County (San Antonio). The pattern held in 1985 and 1986, and if it holds in 1988 it could be ominous for the Democrats, who have never won a presidential election without Texas and have never carried Texas without carrying the rural counties.

Another index of Republican strength is the increasing number of Texans who choose, in a state without party registration, to vote in its primary. In 1978, when Clements first ran, 1.8 million Texans voted in the Democratic primary and only 158,000 in the Republican contest. In 1982 some 1.3 million Democratic votes were cast and 265,000 Republican. In 1986 the Democratic vote was down to 1.1 million and the Republican vote up to 544,000. In greater Houston nearly half the primary votes cast were Republican; in the Dallas-Fort Worth Metroplex 61% were. Even in rural Texas nearly one-quarter of the primary voters chose Republican ballots—even though Democrats have almost always won legislative and local offices in these counties.

Yet this trend toward the Republicans occurred in a disastrous year economically for much of Texas, a time when unemployment in half the state was rising, not falling. The Oil Patch in the Reagan years seems to have developed political reflexes the opposite of those the industrial belt developed in the Roosevelt years. In those days industrial voters called in theory-minded Democrats to stimulate the economy in hard times, but otherwise were pleased to let experienced and practical-minded Republicans deal with the nuts and bolts of everyday government. In Texas in the 1980s the voters have tended to call the Republicans in to deal with a weak economy; they see the free market, not government intervention, as more likely to produce economic growth. In other times, or when they are looking for practical men of action to run the everyday business of government, they might very well indulge their historic preferences and call in the Democrats. These tendencies were apparent in the metropolitan half of the state in the 1970s. The difference in the 1980s is that they are apparent in rural Texas as well.

All of which threatens, though it has not yet destroyed, the political base of the men who have run Texas's politics for most of the last 40 years, the Tory Democrats. The irony is that they can claim credit for much of the economic growth that has undermined their political base. Their philosophic impulse was laissez faire, but they felt obliged as representatives of a poor state to use government to foster and protect Texas's agriculture and oil. In the 1930s Texans like Jesse Jones got Franklin Roosevelt to prop up prices through the hot oil act, which gave control of world oil prices to the Texas Railroad Commission, which limited production, while federal law prohibited shipment of oil for sale at lower prices. Speaker Sam Rayburn saw that there was always a pro-oil majority on the House Ways and Means Committee; Senate Majority Leader and President Lyndon Johnson always kept sight of Texas's interests. Tory Democrats were always ready to raise huge sums for their candidates, and Texas's open primary let Republican voters in national elections help nominate Tory Democrats for state and congressional office. The incendiary approach of Texas liberals, their association with the national Democratic Party on issues like civil rights, and their inability to raise money made them easy to beat.

Today Texas still has its Tory Democrats, but they have to survive on their wits—or fall by the wayside, as Mark White did. The most prominent is Senator Lloyd Bentsen, seemingly fortified in his position by the Finance chairmanship. But Bentsen depends heavily on rural Texas, which gave him over 60% in his last two elections; if he had done as poorly there as White did in 1986, his 59%–41% margin of 1982 would have been 50%–49% instead. Yet Bentsen of all Democrats seems strongest in the rural base, and took special pains to shore it up by helping to engineer, behind the scenes, his party's upset win in the 1st District special election in 1985. Another Democrat with roots in the old tradition is Bill Hobby, son of a 1920s governor, lieutenant governor since 1972, possible candidate for governor in 1990 when Clements says he will not run again. Texas is one state where the lieutenant governor has power—he runs the state Senate— and Hobby played a key role in getting tax increases through the special session in summer 1986. But he could have primary opposition from the likes of Jim Mattox or Agriculture Commissioner Jim Hightower, a populist with a gift for vivid vernacular, and for a candidate like Hobby the decline in Democratic primary voting is not a good portent. Nor is the precedent of the 1984 Senate primary auspicious: conservative Democrat Bob Krueger got squeezed out by Kent Hance, who demagogued the immigration issue (and ultimately ran as a Republican for governor in 1986), and liberal Lloyd Doggett; Doggett, a talented and careful state Senator, barely won the runoff and then was wiped out 59%–41% by Phil Gramm in the general election.

Not everything is working for the Republicans, of course. The unexpected economic downturn of 1982 hurt Republican élan and turnout, and Democrats won a big statewide victory. And the market-generated economic growth which is the Republicans' biggest asset can be a liability as it uproots communities, changes traditional arrangements and ways of life. Growth means change, change hurts people sometimes, and people who are hurt usually vote. Remember that in Latin America the Catholic Church—with its historic prejudice against the free market and economic mechanisms like interest—is the strongest opponent of economic conservatives who believe free markets generate growth. The alliance of north Dallas entrepreneurs like Bill Clements (much less a laissez-faire theorist like Phil Gramm) with rural Texas Baptists and fundamentalists has not always been a natural one and may be threatened as much by continuing growth as by sudden halts. In Texas the Democrats, traditionally the party of the small farmer and the small town, may again gain appeal as the modulators of economic change, whether through environmental protection, regulation of wages and working conditions, or the erection of trade barriers. The Republicans in their Gallerias can seem contemptuous of traditional values and of the ordinary people who still cherish them. Men who have achieved great economic success in the ethnically stratified Northeast have been persuaded that many others would have done as well with similar advantages. But men who become very rich in the ethnically homogeneous and egalitarian climate of Texas often assume that anyone who doesn't is just stupid.

So there is every reason to believe that Texas's politics, like its economy, is still developing— and may provide a few surprises for the nation in the 1990s or perhaps as early as 1988.

Governor. The future of Texas politics may be foretold by the terms of Governor William Clements's victory. Just as Mark White abandoned his Tory Democratic roots to support education reform, higher taxes, and deemphasized football in favor of academics, so Bill

Clements left behind his conservative Republican roots to accept most of that legacy, going so far as to criticize White for not spending enough on education. The difference between the two governors is as much in temperament and background as in ideas. White is an instinctive politician, prone to smooth over disagreements, sloppily leaving loose ends hanging, avoiding tough and unpopular remedies until he is finally forced to embrace them—only to find that his popularity was greater when he bit bullets than when he dodged them. Clements is a gruff and hardnosed businessman, with the angry streak apparent for years among Dallas Republicans, instinctively impolitic though well-disciplined enough to keep himself looking almost avuncular during the campaign. He left the tough decisions of 1986 for White and pledged vaguely to hold down taxes while raising education spending. But as the 1987 legislative session began he was distracted by revelations that, as chairman of the SMU board of trustees, he approved payments to football players. And he seemed to be in a showdown with Bill Hobby, who was insisting that more taxes were necessary to maintain quality Texas education while Clements seemed determined to keep taxes down to stimulate the economy and that education can take some further cuts. Ironically, it is Hobby the Democrat who is basing his plan on the conservative, worst-case assumption that oil prices will stay low; Clements seems to be banking on rising oil prices. History will show who is right.

Clements's victory was evidence of Republican strength in Texas in 1986; so was the Democrats' failure to gain back legislative seats in the off year. When Clements was first elected Democrats had a 130–20 edge in the House; for the 1987 session it was 94–56. That means Republicans can sustain a gubernatorial veto, and it is also beginning to mean that Republican legislators are players rather than just spectators in the pink granite Capitol in Austin. But while Clements and the legislature make important decisions, many eyes will be on the 1990 elections. Redistricting will be unusually important in Texas, and Republicans will want to hold the governorship; possible candidates include Tom Loeffler, who lost the 1986 primary to Clements, and possibly Kent Hance, though his party-switching seems to have hurt him; he got 49% in the 1984 Democratic Senate runoff but only 20% in the 1986 Republican primary. Bill Hobby, Jim Mattox, and Jim Hightower are all statewide Democrats who might run; another is San Antonio Mayor Henry Cisneros. Cisneros is a Mexican–American who carries Anglo as well as Hispanic precincts in San Antonio, a graduate of Texas A&M and Harvard, who is not a stereotypical liberal and could just end up as the Democrats' dream candidate in some future election. But with his aggressive, take-charge leadership of the Democrats' cause in 1987, Hobby starts out as a clear favorite for the nomination and the election.

Senators. Texas has two of the most powerful and effective Senators in Washington. But they are powerful and effective in entirely different ways and are certainly not friends; in fact Phil Gramm ran in the Democratic primary against Lloyd Bentsen in 1976. Gramm won 28% of the vote to Bentsen's 64%, but don't think that either of them has forgotten. Their most recent struggle was in the 1985 1st District special election. Gramm set up the contest by getting Representative Sam Hall appointed a federal judge and recruiting former Texas A&M quarterback Edd Hargett to run in the hopes of producing a victory that would undermine Democrats in rural Texas and the whole rural South; his goal was nothing less than to pull the electoral rug out from under Democrats like Bentsen and overturn Democratic control of the House. Bentsen raised money for the Democrats well before it was clear who their candidate would be and brought forward the trade issue he had been raising in Washington. Eventually it proved decisive in Democrat Jim Chapman's hairsbreadth victory. This prevented a Republican breakthrough in the rural South, at least for the time being. These are tough politicians, betting big stakes and playing for keeps.

Lloyd Bentsen is now chairman of the Senate Finance Committee, one of the most powerful Democrats in Washington, and beautifully placed to help Texas's oil industry. He already has, in the 1986 tax reform battle. As the leader of the oil state bloc on Finance, he insisted on retaining the intangible drilling allowance and other favorable tax treatment in the bill as his price for supporting Chairman Bob Packwood's reform package; Packwood and reform author Bill

Bradley had to go along. And when it came time to write transition rules, Bentsen's knowledge of detail and tough bargaining skills conferred plenty of benefits on Texas. Ditto on the Superfund legislation. Yet the conventional wisdom in Washington is that he is a dull politician. Certainly he is not a spellbinder, but he is operating in an era when voters are not looking for oratory; and he is anything but self-revealing in the manner of the Hollywood starlets or minor politicos who babble on about how they got in touch with themselves last week.

Actually Bentsen comes from a background that can only be called romantic and has shown aggressiveness to the point of daring in his career. His father moved from the Dakotas to the Lower Rio Grande Valley in 1921 with $5 in his pocket and became one of the great Texas landowners. Back in the days when he started, the border was not patrolled, most of the people spoke Spanish, and business was done with people who toted guns. Bentsen grew up in a bungalow on a dirt road, speaking Spanish as fluently as English; he went off to war and came back and was elected to Congress in 1948 at age 27. After six years he left to start an insurance business in Houston and make his millions; then in 1970 he ran for the Senate. In the primary against liberal incumbent Ralph Yarborough, he raised Tory money and ran ads featuring footage of the riots outside the Democratic National Convention in Chicago in 1968; in the general election he ran with labor and black endorsements and many white rural votes and beat a Houston congressman named George Bush.

Bentsen has shown the same adroitness in the Senate, establishing himself clearly as a national Democrat, yet not getting out of line with Texas opinion. This has been helped by the fact that the Democratic liberalism of the early 1970s has moved closer to the traditional Texas Tory variety: government should help business be productive and maintain a safety net for the poor, but should not aggressively redistribute income or regulate businesses. His penchant for detail has enabled him to play major roles on pension reform as well as tax legislation; his free market ideas he aired in the Carter years as chairman of the Joint Economic Committee, calling for lower taxes on capital gains and greater incentives for investment.

As Finance Committee chairman, he will play a major role on issues from technical changes to the tax reform act to catastrophic health insurance. But his major issue in the middle 1980s has been trade. In 1985 he came forward with a tough retaliatory trade bill, co-sponsored with Dan Rostenkowski and Richard Gephardt, which became the cornerstone of the Democrats' political thrust on the issue. In 1987 his bill was distinctly more cautious than the House Democrats' approach. Was this evidence of philosophic confusion or political manuevering? The better explanation is that Bentsen sees himself as a player in a complex game, threatening Japan and other trading partners but not really wanting to be protectionist, staking out an issue for his Democrats but not boxing them in a corner; hence his greater caution when in the majority than when the Republicans had the votes to keep his bill from moving in the Senate. There remains some question exactly what Bentsen will do on trade, but little question that he will be the key player in the Senate on the issue, where the stakes are global stability and domestic political advantage.

Bentsen was embarrassed in early 1987 by one of his campaign tactics, a breakfast with Bentsen program, for $10,000 a head: Eggs McBentsen, it was called, and the furor helped spur demands for campaign finance reform. But it was just Bentsen operating with typical efficiency; and with typical astuteness, he quickly disbanded the breakfasts and returned the money. But no one doubts he will raise enough to put together a solid campaign for 1988. No serious Texas Democrat will oppose him; his job raising money and using his own treasury to finance voter registration in 1982 gave Texas Democrats their one successful election in the 1980s. For Republicans, demographic and electoral trends are auspicious, and early polls showed Bentsen hovering around the 50% mark against several lesser-known opponents. But few candidates seem interested. It's hard to come up with a rationale for dumping a Texan as chairman of the Senate Finance Committee (the next in line is Spark Matsunaga of Hawaii). If Bentsen retains his appeal to voters in rural Texas, where he has won more than 60% against three different Republicans, he is likely to win a fourth term. There was some talk before the Democrats won the Senate that he would retire. But it's not likely that a man whose father has remained active in his highly successful business in his 90s is going to hang up his hat while still in his 60s. Lloyd Bentsen may not be a presidential candidate, as he was unsuccessfully in 1976, when Democrats picked another moderate southerner instead, nor a vice presidential hopeful, as he was in 1984; but he is likely to remain a major national politician through the 1990s.

Phil Gramm, in Congress less than 10 years, has already changed the American fiscal firmament twice. A decade ago he was a Democrat in College Station, Texas, an economics professor at Texas A&M, which was founded as a military school and about whose students Aggie jokes are told, but whose academic achievements rival those of the vastly rich and much more famous University of Texas. Until his unsuccessful race against Bentsen, he was politically unknown, unconnected to the great wealth and power brokers of Texas (he is a native of Georgia), armed with little but his belief in free market economics, a gift for making his political case pithily, and plenty of nerve. These have taken him a long way. He was elected to Congress in 1978 after squeaking into the Democratic runoff by 115 votes out of 81,000 votes cast (just ahead of Chet Edwards, now one of the smartest Texas state Senators) and winning the runoff 53%–47%. In his second term, after Jim Wright helped him onto the House Budget Committee, he was happy to be the Democratic co-sponsor of the 1981 Reagan budget cuts, attending Democrats' strategy meetings and then reporting the results to Republican strategists; and so made the biggest dents in the domestic budget since the 1940s. Expelled from the Democratic Caucus after the 1982 election, he resigned, switched parties, and ran as a Republican in a special election quickly called by outgoing Governor Clements. It was both an honorable move (voters should be able to say whether they want a congressman of a different party) and a shrewd one (his district ran from the Houston to the Fort Worth suburbs, allowing him to campaign heavily in media markets covering almost half the state). His gift for aphorism did not fail him ("I had to choose between Tip O'Neill and y'all, and I decided to stand with y'all") and he won with 55% against nine Democrats and a Libertarian.

That set the stage for his 1984 Senate race. When John Tower surprised everyone by announcing his retirement in 1983, just after a big fundraiser, Gramm immediately jumped in. His Republican rivals had little chance; the Democrats were caught in an epic three-way race between Bob Krueger, the Shakespeare-quoting former congressman who nearly beat Tower in 1978; Kent Hance, a west Texas congressman who had sponsored the Reagan tax cut but then had gone back over to the House Democrats, unlike Gramm; and Lloyd Doggett, a highly competent and liberal state Senator from Austin. Krueger or Hance might have won a general election but Doggett, too close on the issues to Walter Mondale, couldn't. It didn't help that Gramm kept attacking Doggett for receiving some $500 raised at a gay male strip joint in San Antonio.

Then in his first year in the Senate, two bold initiatives: the 1st District special election and, the week after that came up short, Gramm–Rudman. The idea—an orderly ratcheting down of the federal deficit—had appeal on all sides: conservatives thought it would force down domestic spending, liberals hoped it would squeeze defense, deficit-cutters of both parties figured it might force Ronald Reagan to allow a tax increase. Gramm surely hoped it would forestall any new spending initiatives—as through early 1987 it mostly has. It passed, it should be added, despite and not because of Phil Gramm's personal appeal. He is among the least popular of Senators. Colleagues will admit that he is true to his principles, but add that in their behalf he is ready to be untrue to his colleagues or his word. Some think he has his eye on the presidency, and he does not deny that he might some day be interested. In the meantime, he has been the subject of some grumbling in Texas for his willingness to let the market drive down oil prices, his opposition to pork barrel projects, and his lack of interest in local issues: principle over politics again. He is a breathtakingly bold politician who is out to change government and politics, and fast, and he has already had more success than anyone expected of an economics professor from A&M. But he might end up vulnerable to a challenge in 1990 from an unusual quarter—perhaps from San Antonio Mayor Henry Cisneros, an A&M graduate and trustee himself.

Presidential politics. Texas is now the nation's third biggest prize in presidential elections, with 29 electoral votes. It is also a major source of funds and at least has been a major source of candidates, from Lyndon Johnson to John Connally and Lloyd Bentsen and George Bush, though all have been embarrassed on their home turf from time to time (Bush lost two Senate races, in 1964 and 1970, and narrowly lost the 1980 presidential primary to Ronald Reagan). It is part, the biggest single part, of the southern regional primary March 8, 1988, and the state primary will be held the same day, which Democrats hope will boost their turnout and hold down that of the Republicans; but 1986 suggests that it may not, particularly if Lloyd Bentsen has no serious competition.

The Democrats' bigger problem here is the general election. They have never won the presidency without Texas since it was admitted to the Union, and they have never won Texas without carrying the rural counties. Yet what reason is there to think that any of the party's likely candidates as of 1987 can carry rural Texas in November 1988? That question may have prompted the decision of Bill Hobby and Railroad Commissioner Mack Wallace to endorse Gary Hart in early 1987, at a time when seasoned practical politicians in other states were shunning his candidacy. What initially attracted them to Hart was his support of an oil import fee—a talking point in his favor, at least, in rural as well as metropolitan Texas, and an indication that he was one Democrat who would not write off Texas from the beginning. They must recognize that Texas has actually been moving away from the national Democrats for years: the last election in which it went unanimously Democratic was 1940, and as early as 1952 it voted Republican for Eisenhower over Stevenson. But they know special advantages—ties with LBJ, a rural Dixie background—enabled John Kennedy, Hubert Humphrey, and Jimmy Carter to win enough votes in rural Texas to carry the state; and they are quick to seize on any hope that it can happen again.

Congressional districting. Texas's House delegation, with 27 members, is its largest in history, but Democratic by the narrowest margin in history, 17 to 10. The Republicans have gained seats before in presidential years, and picked up five in 1984; in 1986, unlike past offyears, they held them all. Still, the leading congressman from Texas, by far, is Jim Wright of Fort Worth, Speaker of the House; the delegation also includes two committee chairmen (Jack Brooks of Government Operations, Kika de la Garza of Agriculture). Delegation solidarity is not what it was when Sam Rayburn was Speaker, but is greater than it was in 1981, when Phil Gramm led the Boll Weevils off the reservation; now Texas Democrats cooperate, and sometimes even with Texas Republicans. Texas will probably gain a couple seats in the 1990 Census; demography and (if a Republican is elected governor in 1990) politics will probably give them to the Republicans.

The People: Est. Pop. 1986: 16,682,000; Pop. 1980: 14,229,191, up 17.3% 1980–86 and 27.1% 1970–80; 6.92% of U.S. total, 3d largest. 17% with 1–3 yrs. col., 16% with 4+ yrs. col.; 14.7% below poverty level. Single ancestry: 12% English, 5% German, 4% Irish, 1% French, Italian. Households (1980): 75% family, 43% with children, 63% married couples; 35.7% housing units rented; median monthly rent: $213; median house value: $39,100. Voting age pop. (1980): 9,923,085; 18% Spanish origin, 11% Black, 1% Asian origin. Registered voters (1986): 7,287,173; no party registration.

1986 Share of Federal Tax Burden: $53,626,000,000; 7.13% of U.S. total, 3d largest.

1986 Share of Federal Expenditures

	Total		Non-Defense		Defense	
Total Expend	$47,343m	(5.70%)	$30,438m	(5.07%)	$16,904m	(7.35%)
St/Lcl Grants	5,225m	(4.64%)	5,219m	(4.64%)	6m	(5.41%)
Salary/Wages	7,524m	(6.24%)	3,248m	(5.53%)	4,276m	(6.91%)
Pymts to Indiv	20,473m	(5.61%)	18,684m	(5.39%)	1,789m	(10.07%)
Procurement	12,692m	(6.17%)	1,858m	(3.34%)	10,834m	(7.22%)
Research/Other	1,429m	(5.36%)	14,428m	(5.36%)	1m	(2.94%)

Political Lineup: Governor, Bill Clements (R); Lt. Gov., Bill Hobby (D); Atty. Gen., Jim Mattox (D); Treasurer, Ann Richards (D); Comptroller of Public Accounts, Bob Bullock (D). State Senate, 31 (25 D and 6 R); State House of Representatives, 150 (94 D and 56 R). Senators, Lloyd Bentsen (D) and Phil Gramm (R). Representatives, 27 (17 D and 10 R).

1984 Presidential Vote		
Reagan (R)	3,433,428	(64%)
Mondale (D)	1,949,276	(36%)

1980 Presidential Vote		
Reagan (R)	2,510,705	(55%)
Carter (D)	1,881,417	(41%)
Anderson (I)	111,613	(2%)

GOVERNOR

Gov. William (Bill) Clements (R)

Elected 1986, term expires Jan. 1991; b. Apr. 13, 1917, Dallas; home, Dallas; Southern Methodist U., B.A. 1939; Episcopalian; married (Rita).

Career: Founder and Chmn. of the Bd. of SEDCO, Inc.; Deputy Secy., U.S. Dept. of Defense, 1973–77; Gov. of TX, 1979–83.

Office: State Capitol, P.O. Box 12428, Austin 78711, 512-463-2000.

Election Results

1986 gen.	William (Bill) Clements (R)	1,813,779	(53%)
	Mark White (D)	1,584,515	(46%)
1986 prim.	William (Bill) Clements (R)	318,808	(58%)
	Kent Hance (R)	108,238	(20%)
	Tom Loeffler (R)	117,673	(22%)
1982 gen.	Mark W. White, Jr. (D)	1,697,527	(53%)
	William (Bill) Clements (R)	1,465,952	(46%)

SENATORS

Sen. Lloyd Bentsen (D)

Elected 1970, seat up 1988; b. Feb. 11, 1921, Mission; home, Houston; U. of TX, LL.B. 1942; Presbyterian; married (Beryl Ann).

Career: Army Air Corps, WWII; Practicing atty., 1945–46, Judge, Hidalgo Cnty., 1946–48; U.S. House of Reps., 1949–55; Pres., Lincoln Consolidated, Inc., 1955–71.

Offices: 703 HSOB 20510, 202-224-5922. Also Fed. Office Bldg., Austin 78701, 512-482-5834; 515 Rusk, Ste. 4026, Houston 77002, 713-229-2595; and Earle Cabell Bldg., Rm. 7C14, Dallas 75242, 214-767-0577.

Committees: *Commerce, Science and Transportation* (8th of 11 D). Subcommittees: Foreign Commerce and Tourism; Merchant Marine; Science, Technology and Space. *Finance* (Chairman of 11 D). Subcommittees: Health; International Trade; Private Retirement and Oversight of the IRS. *Select Committee on Intelligence* (3d of 7 D). *Joint Economic Committee* (3d of 6 D) Subcommittees: Economic Growth Trade and Taxes (Chairman); Economic Goals and Intergovernmental Policy; Education and Health. *Joint Committee on Taxation* (Vice Chairman).

Group Ratings

	ADA	ACLU	COPE	CFA	LCV	ACU	NTU	NSI	COC	CEI
1986	45	30	50	33	50	50	46	78	68	46
1985	35	—	51	53	—	62	36	—	46	—

National Journal Ratings

	1986 LIB — 1986 CONS	1985 LIB — 1985 CONS
Economic	25% — 71%	59% — 40%
Social	57% — 42%	42% — 57%
Foreign	56% — 41%	39% — 60%

Key Votes

1) Ease Gun Cont	FOR	5) Grm-Rdmn Def Red	FOR	9) Rehnquist Nom	FOR
2) Immig Reform	FOR	6) Contra Aid	FOR	10) Tax Reform	FOR
3) Lmt Text Imp	FOR	7) SDI Funding	AGN	11) Drug Death Pen	—
4) Aid Tobac Ind	FOR	8) Lmt PAC Contrib	FOR	12) S Africa Sanc	FOR

Election Results

1982 general	Lloyd Bentsen (D)	1,818,223	(59%)	($5,097,445)
	James M. Collins (R)	1,256,759	(40%)	($4,285,377)
1982 primary	Lloyd Bentsen (D)	987,967	(78%)	
	Joe Sullivan (D)	276,453	(22%)	
1976 general	Lloyd Bentsen (D)	2,199,956	(57%)	($1,237,910)
	Alan Steelman (R)	1,636,370	(42%)	($665,058)

Campaign Contributions and Expenditures

1979-82		Direct Cont. 1979-82		PACS Breakdown			
Receipts	$5,083,557	Indiv.	$3,679,289	Agr	$27,907	Ideo	$38,250
Expend.	$5,097,445	Party	$17,500	Bus	$604,220	Lbr	$47,250
Unspent	$12,801	PACS	$826,593	Hlth	$37,300	Prof	$65,400
		Cand.	$75,000				

Sen. Phil Gramm (R)

Elected 1984, seat up 1990; b. July 8, 1942, Ft. Benning, GA; home, College Station; U. of GA, B.A. 1964, Ph.D. 1967; Episcopalian; married (Wendy).

Career: Professor, TX A&M U., 1967–78; U.S. House of Reps., 1978–84.

Offices: 370 RSOB 20510, 202-224-2934. Also 900 Jackson, Ste. 570, Dallas 75202, 214-767-3000; 222 E. Van Buren., Ste. 404, Harlingen 78550, 512-423-6118; 515 Rusk, Houston 77002, 713-229-2766; 113 Fed. Bldg., 1205 Texas Ave., Lubbock 79401, 806-743-7533; 123 Pioneer Plaza, 6th Flr., Rm. 665, El Paso 79901, 915-534-6896; and InterFirst Plaza, 102 N. College St., 201, Tyler 75701, 214-593-0902.

Committees: *Armed Services* (7th of 9 R). Subcommittees: Conventional Forces and Alliance Defense; Defense Industry and Technology (Ranking Member); Readiness, Sustainability and Support. *Banking, Housing, and Urban Affairs* (6th of 9 R). Subcommittees: Consumer Affairs (Ranking Member); International Finance and Monetary Policy.

Group Ratings

	ADA	ACLU	COPE	CFA	LCV	ACU	NTU	NSI	COC	CEI
1986	0	7	0	7	17	100	70	100	89	95
1985	0	—	0	7	—	95	72	—	86	—

National Journal Ratings

	1986 LIB — 1986 CONS			1985 LIB — 1985 CONS		
Economic	0%	—	84%	0%	—	86%
Social	0%	—	91%	0%	—	83%
Foreign	0%	—	86%	0%	—	88%

Key Votes

1) Ease Gun Cont	FOR	5) Grm-Rdmn Def Red	FOR	9) Rehnquist Nom	FOR
2) Immig Reform	AGN	6) Contra Aid	FOR	10) Tax Reform	FOR
3) Lmt Text Imp	AGN	7) SDI Funding	FOR	11) Drug Death Pen	AGN
4) Aid Tobac Ind	FOR	8) Lmt PAC Contrib	AGN	12) S Africa Sanc	AGN

Election Results

1984 general	Phil Gramm (R) 3,111,348	(59%)	($9,452,360)
	Lloyd Doggett (D) 2,202,557	(41%)	($5,887,858)
1984 primary	Phil Gramm (R) 246,716	(73%)	
	Ron Paul (R)........................ 55,431	(16%)	
	Rob Mosbacher (R) 26,279	(8%)	
1978 general	John G. Tower (R) 1,151,376	(50%)	($4,359,365)
	Robert Krueger (D) 1,139 149	(49%)	($2,428,666)

Campaign Contributions and Expenditures

1983–84		Direct Cont. 1983–84		PACS Breakdown 1983–84			
Receipts	$9,785,936	Indiv.	$7,947,011	Corp.	$888,430	T/M/H	$245,843
Expend.	$9,452,360	Party	$30,180	Labor	$12,500	Agr.	$1,550
Unspent	$250,355	PACS	$1,397,224	Ideo.	$159,902	CWOS	$17,150

FIRST DISTRICT

A stranger might think, if he was plunked down in one of the counties near the Arkansas or Louisiana borders, that he was in the separate and distinct state of East Texas: for that is how many people here respond when they talk about where they live. The distinction is made to mean that this is not the Dallas–Fort Worth Metroplex or some other big metropolitan part of Texas; east Texas is small town and rural, incomes are relatively low and wives seldom work, where you find more churches and Wal-Marts than fern-clad restaurants and Gallerias. No barren plains here; the land is green and only mildly undulating, overrun it seems with vegetation, swampy down by the rivers; the towns are no longer the dusty crossroads they were in the days before roads were paved, and some old buildings have been carefully preserved, but they are pretty plain places still. East Texas is clearly part of the Deep South, with almost no Mexican–Americans and more blacks than any part of America farther west.

About half of east Texas—the northeastern corner of the state, but with jagged boundaries to exclude the oil towns of Tyler and Longview—forms the 1st Congressional District of Texas. The largest city here is Texarkana, with its city hall so squarely on the Texas–Arkansas line that different wings serve Texarkana, Texas, and Texarkana, Arkansas. This is part of the historic Democratic heartland: Bonham, the home of Speaker Sam Rayburn, is just one county west of the district; the district that elected Speaker Carl Albert is just across the Red River in Oklahoma. The 1st District was represented for nearly 50 years by Wright Patman, an old-fashioned populist, who began his career by moving the impeachment of Treasury Secretary Andrew Mellon (forcing him to resign to become Ambassador to Britain) and who ultimately became Chairman of the Banking Committee; a gentle and good-humored man, he was voted out of his chairmanship at 81 in 1974, died in 1976, and was replaced by a much more conservative Democrat, Sam Hall.

The 1st District was the scene in summer 1985 of what could have been the pivotal political battle of the middle 1980s in Texas—but wasn't. Senator Phil Gramm had long wanted to undermine the Democrats' hold on rural Texas, and pounced on the 1st District as a battleground; he caused Sam Hall, a judicious man with few enemies, to be appointed a federal judge, and recruited Edd Hargett, a former Texas A&M and pro quarterback who lived in one of the poorer towns in the 1st District, to be the Republican candidate. Money and topflight consultants poured in, while the Democrats were handicapped because they had more than one serious candidate. Gramm claimed, plausibly, that if a Republican could win in the 1st in a nonpresidential year, Republicans could win in any southern district.

But this particular Republican didn't win. Even before the primary, Senator Lloyd Bentsen and Campaign Committee Chairman Tony Coelho were raising money to oppose Hargett. He fell short of the 50% needed to win without a runoff, and Democrat Jim Chapman, a former district attorney, proved to be an adept candidate. Hargett stumbled on the trade issue, saying "I don't know what trade policies have to do with bringing jobs to east Texas"—despite the recent closing of the Lone Star Steel plant in Morris County. That and a relentless emphasis on Social Security helped Chapman to a 51%–49% win.

Democrats naturally exulted, the more so when it became clear that Gramm's attempt to stimulate Republican challengers in rural southern districts for 1986 would come to nothing; Hargett himself declined to run again, and Chapman was reelected unopposed. Yet it was a close thing; this is one of the strongest yellow dog Democratic districts left in the country, and it nearly fell. The elderly voted heavily for Chapman, young voters heavily for Hargett—not a good harbinger for the Democrats either. They will probably hold onto the 1st now; Hargett passed up the 1986 House race, lost a race for state Senate, and seems unlikely to run for anything again. But Democrats remain vulnerable in similar districts in the future.

The People: Pop. 1980: 527,016, up 20.4% 1970–80. Households (1980): 76% family, 39% with children, 65% married couples; 24.9% housing units rented; median monthly rent: $123; median house value: $26,300. Voting age pop. (1980): 376,964; 17% Black, 1% Spanish origin.

1984 Presidential Vote:

Reagan (R)	126,587	(61%)
Mondale (D)	79,104	(38%)

Rep. Jim Chapman, Jr. (D)

Elected Aug. 3, 1985; b. Mar. 8, 1945, Washington, DC; home, Sulphur Springs; U. of TX, B.A. 1968, Southern Methodist U., J.D. 1970; United Methodist; married (Betty).

Career: Practicing atty.; D.A., 8th Judicial Dist. of TX, 1976–84.

Offices: 429 CHOB, 202-225-3035. Also P.O. Box 538, Sulphur Springs 75482, 214-885-8682; Fed. Bldg., G-15, 100 E. Houston, Marshall 75670, 214-938-8386; 210 U.S.P.O. & Fed. Bldg., Paris 75460, 214-785-0723; and 401 U.S.P.O. & Fed. Bldg., Texarkana 75504, 214-793-6728.

Committees: *Public Works* (23d of 32 D). Subcommittees: Aviation; Water Resources. *Science, Space and Technology* (19th of 27 D). Subcommittees: Energy Research and Development; Science, Research and Technology; Space Science and Applications.

Group Ratings

	ADA	ACLU	COPE	CFA	LCV	ACU	NTU	NSI	COC	CEI
1986	40	16	48	58	54	38	29	0	50	27
1985	—	—	20	40	—	71	36	—	92	—

National Journal Ratings

	1986 LIB — 1986 CONS		1985 LIB — 1985 CONS	
Economic	54% —	45%	35% —	64%
Social	37% —	63%	* —	*
Foreign	48% —	52%	* —	*

Key Votes

1) Lmt Cln Water Act	—	5) Retain Gun Cont	AGN	9) Aid Angola Reb	FOR
2) Rpl Tobac Sub	AGN	6) Contra Aid	FOR	10) Tax Reform	AGN
3) Grm-Rdmn Def Red	FOR	7) Lmt Text Imp	FOR	11) S Africa Sanc	FOR
4) Ban Polygraph	AGN	8) Limit SDI	FOR	12) Immig Reform	AGN

Election Results

1986 general	Jim Chapman (D)	84,445	(100%)	($894,772)
1986 primary	Jim Chapman (D)	56,004	(100%)	
1985 special	Jim Chapman (D)	52,665	(51%)	
	Edd Hargett (R)	50,741	(49%)	
1984 general	Sam B. Hall, Jr. (D)	139,829	(100%)	($88,426)

Campaign Contributions and Expenditures

1985-86		Direct Cont. 1985-86		PACS Breakdown 1985-86			
Receipts	$915,098	Indiv.	$444,403	Corp.	$66,350	T/M/H	$76,936
Expend.	$894,772	Party	$22,242	Labor	$35,500	Agr.	$22,750
Unspent	$20,282	PACS	$234,773	Ideo.	$26,000	CWOS	$7,237
		Cand.	$252,105				

SECOND DISTRICT

In east Texas you can see many landmarks of Lone Star history. There's still an Indian reservation in Polk County, and the Big Thicket National Preserve, to remind you of what this land looked like when the first Texans came through. Over near Beaumont is the site of Spindletop, the world's first gusher that was also the first major oil find in the state in 1901; not far away is the huge oil field that wildcatter H. L. Hunt found in 1931 and made the foundation of his billion dollar fortune. To the uneducated eye, east Texas looks little different from the wildcat days of 50 years ago: the town squares with courthouses and churches, the stands of cheap, quick-growing pine are still there, plus the strip highway culture of the 1950s and 1980s. Yet in many ways things have changed. Real incomes have tripled since the 1930s, endemic diseases have been wiped out, racial segregation has been abolished, and the isolation of the small town has been ended by television and the interstate highway.

The 2d Congressional District of Texas includes all or part of 16 counties in east Texas, most of them still seemingly rural, all of them more imbued with traditional values than most parts of America these days. It includes the oil port of Orange (but not nearby Beaumont or Port Arthur), the Big Thicket and the Indian reservation, and goes past Lufkin and Nacogodoches to Palestine. Politically, it remains one of the most Democratic parts of rural Texas; it almost went for Democrat Mark White in 1986 as he was losing rural Texas nearly 60%–40%. There was even a mild trend toward Walter Mondale in high-unemployment Orange in 1984.

The 2d District's congressman, Charles Wilson, is a distinctive figure in Congress: tall, almost spectrally thin, flamboyant. He is always ready with a wisecrack or quip; after President Carter fired HEW Secretary Joseph Califano and others in 1979 he said, "Good grief! He's cut down the tall trees and left the monkeys." He once invested ostentatiously in a chic Washington club called Élan, he escorts gorgeous women to parties, and in 1983 was dogged by an investigation of charges that he had used cocaine—charges made by an old political enemy which never seemed credible and seemed clearly unsubstantiated. But behind the glitter there seems to be some substance. He has represented east Texas in Austin and Washington since 1960, and with a voting record that got him classified with the liberals in the Texas Senate and a record in the House that could easily be called liberal today. And he has committee positions that confer on him important national responsibilities.

The common thread in all this is aggressiveness. Wilson is a graduate of the Naval Academy and served four years in the Navy. He got himself elected to the legislature the year he returned to east Texas. He won the House seat of a scandal-plagued conservative in the 1972 Democratic primary; a term later he shoved aside a fellow Texan for a seat on Appropriations. Always a feisty liberal on economic issues, he is a hawk on matters military. He now sits on the Defense Appropriations Subcommittee, the small and mostly hawkish panel that gives the defense budget as close a combing as it usually gets on Capitol Hill; he also sits on the subcommittee that handles foreign aid, which gives him a potentially broad view of the whole range of foreign policy.

For some time Wilson seemed to spend most of his time promoting, aggressively, the interests of Texas defense contractors. But he also has broader interests. He has been the Congress's most effective advocate of American support for the Afghan rebels; in secret Appropriations hearings, he made sure to put lots of money into the cause. In 1977 Speaker Tip O'Neill put him on his special energy committee, where he could look after the interests of oil producers. In 1987 Speaker Jim Wright put him on the Intelligence Committee, where he could look at all manner of foreign policy and derring-do. He would not have gotten that assignment if Wright had any doubts about his integrity.

Wilson's voting record has never been a great problem for him in his district, and his wise guy reputation in Washington is belied back home by the fact that he sends out one of Congress's more literate and thoughtful newsletters. The rumors about drug use caused him problems in 1984, when he was held to 55% of the vote by four primary opponents (though the strongest got only 29% himself) and 59% in the general election. But redistricting helped him for the 1980s by removing most of Montgomery County, once a rural area but now an affluent, and Republican, part of greater Houston. But in 1986 he was back to his customary reelection without serious opposition.

The People: Pop. 1980: 526,772, up 35.4% 1970–80. Households (1980): 78% family, 43% with children, 67% married couples; 25.3% housing units rented; median monthly rent: $155; median house value: $31,300. Voting age pop. (1980): 372,792; 14% Black, 3% Spanish origin.

1984 Presidential Vote:

Reagan (R)	115,240	(58%)
Mondale (D)	81,216	(41%)

Rep. Charles Wilson (D)

Elected 1972; b. June 1, 1933, Trinity; home, Lufkin; U.S. Naval Acad., B.S. 1956; United Methodist; divorced.

Career: Navy, 1956–60; Mgr., retail lumber store, 1961–72; TX House of Reps., 1960–66; TX Senate, 1966–72.

Offices: 2265 RHOB 20515, 202-225-2401. Also 701 N. 1st St., Rm. 201, Lufkin 75901, 409-637-1770.

Committees: *Appropriations* (15th of 35 D). Subcommittees: Defense; Foreign Operations; Military Construction. *Permanent Select Committee on Intelligence* (10th of 11 D). Subcommittees: Legislative; Oversight and Evaluation.

Group Ratings

	ADA	ACLU	COPE	CFA	LCV	ACU	NTU	NSI	COC	CEI
1986	35	23	65	42	46	50	15	67	27	16
1985	40	—	64	33	—	55	18	—	44	—

National Journal Ratings

	1986 LIB — 1986 CONS		1985 LIB — 1985 CONS	
Economic	66%	32%	55%	45%
Social	64%	36%	67%	32%
Foreign	37%	62%	0%	76%

Key Votes

1) Lmt Cln Water Act	AGN	5) Retain Gun Cont	AGN	9) Aid Angola Reb	FOR
2) Rpl Tobac Sub	AGN	6) Contra Aid	FOR	10) Tax Reform	FOR
3) Grm-Rdmn Def Red	FOR	7) Lmt Text Imp	FOR	11) S Africa Sanc	FOR
4) Ban Polygraph	FOR	8) Limit SDI	AGN	12) Immig Reform	FOR

Election Results

1986 general	Charles Wilson (D)	78,529	(57%)	($339,873)
	Julian Gordon (R)	55,986	(40%)	($47,660)
1986 primary	Charles Wilson (D)	53,856	(100%)	
1984 general	Charles Wilson (D)	113,225	(59%)	($597,333)
	Louis Dugas, Jr. (R)	77,842	(41%)	($25,966)

Campaign Contributions and Expenditures

1985–86		Direct Cont. 1985–86		PACS Breakdown 1985–86			
Receipts	$367,600	Indiv.	$96,278	Corp.	$128,850	T/M/H	$42,005
Expend.	$339,873	PACS	$273,093	Labor	$80,600	Agr.	$4,050
Unspent	$48,222			Ideo.	$10,500	CWOS	$7,088

THIRD DISTRICT

North Dallas is a fabled part of America, part of the title of a bestselling novel about football players, the locus of one of the world's most popular TV shows of the 1980s, the place where J. R. Ewing lives on South Fork and H. L. Hunt lived in a replica of Mount Vernon and where insurance heir John Post bought a new $3 million 19,000-square foot mansion and, saying it had structural flaws, tore it down because he didn't like it. In new cities like Dallas, affluent people live in huge solidly affluent neighborhoods, and the 3d Congressional District, which is basically coincident with north Dallas, is one of the nation's most affluent, best educated, and most Republican congressional districts in the nation. It begins, as affluent Dallas does, in the old suburbs of University Park and Highland Park, where most of the houses date back to the 1950s and where many of the elite elite, like Governor Bill Clements, still live, north through dozens of different half and million dollar neighborhoods, north through rich suburbs like Farmers Branch, Addison, Carrollton and Richardson—which together call themselves the Metrocrest— into the Collin County suburb of Plano. Four decades ago you would have found here little but mildly rolling hillsides with occasional trees and a little scrub; today you see huge office buildings and glittering shopping malls, high-walled condominiums and sprawling singles apartment complexes, neighborhoods full of schoolchildren farther out, neighborhoods for affluent empty nesters closer in.

Where does all of Dallas's wealth come from? And why is this city so especially strongly Republican? To the first question, the answer is that the wealth comes from a lot of things; that is why when drooping oil prices choked off growth in Houston, Dallas still grew. Dallas was where the first railroad in Texas stopped at the three forks of the Trinity river; Dallas became the great shipping point for Texas cotton, and by 1900 it was the banking, finance, and insurance center for Texas. It has its share, perhaps more, of oil wealth, but also plenty of high tech and defense industries.

As to its Republicanism, affluent Dallas had soured on national Democrats by the 1940s, and by the 1950s there was a bitter, angry tone to its conservative politics seldom heard elsewhere, a tone that reverberated across the nation in the 1960 campaign when Republican Representative Bruce Alger led a group that shoved Lyndon and Lady Bird Johnson in the Adolphus Hotel lobby and was echoed sickeningly three years later when John Kennedy was murdered in Dallas, even though the killer was evidently a left-wing fanatic. Dallas has sobered up since 1963, but the faith of affluent Dallas in free enterprise has grown, if anything, stronger. Unlike many rich people back East, they don't feel that they have done something evil by getting rich; they have the 1950s optimisim that technology and free enterprise can produce a better life for all, and they have transformed the small provincial Dallas of the 1950s into the world capital of industry and finance of the 1980s. The role government has played in this—by providing education, infrastructure, defense contracts, a secure world market, and a very large consumer class—is largely invisible from their perspective; what they have seen instead is entrepreneurs going out and fighting against the forces of inertia and mishap and regulation and bureaucracy which keep most enterprises from succeeding. Dallas was a fitting site for the 1984 Republican national convention (though the hall itself is downtown, north Dallas was clearly the host)—especially fitting because Dallas's own conquest of the elements was symbolized by the Texas-cold-air-conditioning weather in which Reagan delivered his speeches while it was a scorching 106 degrees outside.

The 3d District is represented in the House by one of its smarter and harder-working young Republicans, Steve Bartlett. He will take second place to no one as a champion of conservative principles, and as a former head of a company building custom knobs and molded plastic gears he personifies the entrepreneurial ethic which is strong in Dallas. But unlike many other young conservatives, he is a busy and successful legislator. Operating from the unlikely precincts of the Banking Committee, he got the House to shift public housing programs from new construction to repair of existing units; from the even more liberal precincts of Education and Labor, he beat back a labor-backed plant closing law. Yet he has also cooperated with Democrats in making changes on Medicaid law and repealing a law interpreted by the Supreme Court as requiring overtime for state and local employees, and he played key roles on the "equal access" bill allowing religious groups in public schools and in creating bigger secondary mortgage markets. He has something unusual for a free market conservative: an interest in how government works.

Bartlett won the seat in the 1982 Republican primary, when he was a 35-year-old Dallas councilman, beating former state legislator Kay Hutchinson by emphasizing gun control and abortion. There is no conceivable threat to his tenure in the House except an ambition to run for statewide office; he has been mentioned as a possible candidate against Lloyd Bentsen in 1988, but the odds seem too long for this politician who obviously enjoys legislating.

The People: Pop. 1980: 527,023, up 66.5% 1970–80. Households (1980): 66% family, 36% with children, 57% married couples; 40.4% housing units rented; median monthly rent: $296; median house value: $82,100. Voting age pop. (1980): 389,627; 3% Black, 3% Spanish origin, 1% Asian origin.

1984 Presidential Vote:

Reagan (R)	235,644	(82%)
Mondale (D)	52,426	(18%)

Rep. Steve Bartlett (R)

Elected 1982; b. Sept. 19, 1947, Los Angeles, CA; home, Dallas; U. of TX, B.A. 1971; Presbyterian; married (Gail).

Career: Real estate broker, 1971–76; Pres. and Founder, Meridian Products Corp., 1976–82; Dallas City Council, 1977–81.

Offices: 1709 LHOB 20515, 202-225-4201. Also 6600 LBJ Freeway, Ste. 4190, Dallas 75240, 214-767-4848.

Committees: *Banking, Finance and Urban Affairs* (13th of 20 R). Subcommittees: Financial Institutions Supervision, Regulation and Insurance; General Oversight and Investigations; Housing and Community Development. *Education and Labor* (7th of 13 R). Subcommittees: Elementary, Secondary and Vocational Education; Labor Standards; Select Education (Ranking Member).

Group Ratings

	ADA	ACLU	COPE	CFA	LCV	ACU	NTU	NSI	COC	CEI
1986	5	10	5	17	43	95	70	90	94	86
1985	5	—	4	25	—	95	68	—	100	—

National Journal Ratings

	1986 LIB — 1986 CONS		1985 LIB — 1985 CONS	
Economic	6% —	90%	0% —	95%
Social	18% —	78%	0% —	76%
Foreign	25% —	74%	0% —	76%

Key Votes

1) Lmt Cln Water Act	FOR	5) Retain Gun Cont	AGN	9) Aid Angola Reb	FOR
2) Rpl Tobac Sub	FOR	6) Contra Aid	FOR	10) Tax Reform	AGN
3) Grm-Rdmn Def Red	FOR	7) Lmt Text Imp	AGN	11) S Africa Sanc	AGN
4) Ban Polygraph	AGN	8) Limit SDI	AGN	12) Immig Reform	AGN

Election Results

1986 general	Steve Bartlett (R)	143,381	(94%)	($592,304)
	Brent Barnes (I)	6,268	(4%)	
	Don Gough (Libert.)	2,736	(2%)	
1986 primary	Steve Bartlett (R)	42,668	(100%)	
1984 general	Steve Bartlett (R)	228,819	(83%)	($410,666)
	Jim Westbrook (D)	46,890	(17%)	($3,481)

Campaign Contributions and Expenditures

1985-86		Direct Cont. 1985-86		PACS Breakdown 1985-86			
Receipts	$810,359	Indiv.	$582,326	Corp.	$102,528	T/M/H	$54,032
Expend.	$592,304	Party	$2,097	Labor	$0	Agr.	$0
Unspent	$438,405	PACS	$171,029	Ideo.	$9,450	CWOS	$5,019

FOURTH DISTRICT

Each year the Dallas–Fort Worth Metroplex, as it is called here, marches another mile or so farther out into rural north Texas. Hops rather than marches, actually, for the new subdivisions which are housing people working in downtown Dallas and around the LBJ Freeway are not built next to each other, but separately on patches of farmland or near the edge of an old crossroads town on land bought cheap by developers and sold somewhat dearer to young parents who want a country atmosphere to raise their kids but still within reach of their jobs. This steady march also means a conflict between political views about as sharp as that between General Sherman and the southerners whose plantations his troops commandeered. For the rural area north and east of Dallas, the counties of the Red River Valley settled 10 years ago, are one of the most heavily Democratic parts of the nation, while Dallas is one of our most heavily Republican cities.

The political results are apparent in the 4th Congressional District of Texas, which sits along the cusp between the Red River Valley and the Metroplex and includes the two conservative oil towns of Tyler and Longview as well. It was represented for almost 50 years by Sam Rayburn, leader of the Democrats in the House from 1940 till 1961 and Speaker all that time except for four years when the Republicans had the majority. When Rayburn was speaker of the Texas House in 1911 and first elected to the U.S. House in 1912, this was dirt-poor farmland, settled by Confederate veterans, and loyal to the Democrats unto death. But rural population was peaking about then, as young people moved elsewhere, and the future of north Texas lay with Dallas. The change was not much to Rayburn's liking, but he managed to serve the interests of Texas and of the national Democratic Party at one and the same time: he never allowed the oil depletion allowance to be tampered with, but his last great victory was the packing of the Rules Committee to allow Kennedy Administration legislation to come to the floor.

Now the 4th District is enough within the Dallas orbit to vote Republican in most elections and elects a Democratic congressman who declined to vote for Tip O'Neill for Speaker. Representative Ralph Hall, was first elected in 1980 after a long career in business and state and local politics. He got good committee assignments in his first term—Energy and Commerce and Science and Technology—and promptly proceeded to vote with the Republicans on the budget and tax cuts. He and most House Democrats don't think much of each other, but he stays in the party he grew up in and the Democratic leaders evidently don't think he's troublesome or powerful enough to punish. Presumably they think he will retire before he reaches the subcommittee chairman level, and in the meantime holds a district that would otherwise go Republican. Hall has won by wide margins in offyears, but in presidential years his percentages have been lower: 52% in 1980, 58% against a not-heavy-spending Republican in 1984.

The People: Pop. 1980: 526,991, up 25.8% 1970–80. Households (1980): 76% family, 40% with children, 66% married couples; 28.0% housing units rented; median monthly rent: $159; median house value: $32,500. Voting age pop. (1980): 377,899; 13% Black, 2% Spanish origin.

1984 Presidential Vote:

Reagan (R)	150,182	(69%)
Mondale (D)	66,550	(31%)

Rep. Ralph M. Hall (D)

Elected 1980; b. May 3, 1923, Fate; home, Rockwall; U. of TX, TX Christian U., Southern Methodist U., LL.B. 1951; United Methodist; married (Mary Ellen).

Career: Navy, WWII; Rockwall Cnty. Judge, 1950–62; TX Senate, 1962–72; Pres. and CEO, Texas Aluminum Corp.; Gen. Counsel, Texas Extrusion Co., Inc.; Practicing atty.

Offices: 236 CHOB 20515, 202-225-6673. Also 104 N. San Jacinto St., Rockwall 75087, 214-722-9118; 122 N. Fed. Bldg., Sherman 75090, 214-892-1112; and 122 Fed. Bldg., Tyler 75702, 214-597-3729.

Committees: *Energy and Commerce* (15th of 25 D). Subcommittees: Energy and Power; Health and the Environment; Telecommunications and Finance. *Science, Space and Technology* (9th of 27 D). Subcommittees: International Scientific Cooperation (Ranking Member); Space Science and Applications.

Group Ratings

	ADA	ACLU	COPE	CFA	LCV	ACU	NTU	NSI	COC	CEI
1986	10	11	37	50	22	80	48	90	80	41
1985	15	—	38	33	—	70	38	—	67	—

National Journal Ratings

	1986 LIB — 1986 CONS		1985 LIB — 1985 CONS	
Economic	41%	— 58%	37%	— 62%
Social	0%	— 89%	30%	— 70%
Foreign	27%	— 73%	0%	— 76%

Key Votes

1) Lmt Cln Water Act	AGN	5) Retain Gun Cont	AGN
2) Rpl Tobac Sub	AGN	6) Contra Aid	FOR
3) Grm-Rdmn Def Red	FOR	7) Lmt Text Imp	FOR
4) Ban Polygraph	—	8) Limit SDI	AGN

9) Aid Angola Reb	FOR
10) Tax Reform	AGN
11) S Africa Sanc	—
12) Immig Reform	AGN

Election Results

1986 general	Ralph M. Hall (D)	97,540	(72%)	($269,235)
	Thomas Blow (R)	38,578	(28%)	($20,000)
1986 primary	Ralph M. Hall (D)	32,441	(100%)	
1984 general	Ralph M. Hall (D)	120,749	(58%)	($214,335)
	Thomas Blow (R)	87,553	(42%)	($100,058)

Campaign Contributions and Expenditures

1985–86		Direct Cont. 1985–86		PACS Breakdown 1985–86			
Receipts	$276,235	Indiv.	$69,980	Corp.	$114,541	T/M/H	$59,310
Expend.	$269,676	PACS	$183,155	Labor	$0	Agr.	$1,500
Unspent	$128,654			Ideo.	$5,800	CWOS	$2,004

FIFTH DISTRICT

Not all of Dallas is rich and glitzy and affluent. Some of it is funky and musty-old or filled with fresh-faced 1950s style middle class families or just plain poor. Nor is all of this city, which includes almost one million people within its limits, heavily committed to the Republican party; there are enough others to have elected Annette Strauss, a Democrat and sister-in-law of Democratic megapolitico Robert Strauss, mayor over Republican Fred Meyer in April 1987.

Most of these humbler parts of Dallas form Texas's 5th Congressional District. It takes in Dallas's booming downtown, the singles and apartment Oak Lawn neighborhood just to the north, and the Trinity River bottomlands to the northwest, which developer Trammell Crow has converted from marshland to prime commercial property, with not only warehouses and factories, but Dallas's huge furniture and apparel marts and the cathedral-like Anatole Hotel. It takes in the south Dallas black ghetto around the State Fair grounds. And it includes most of east Dallas, with its renovated prairie houses near downtown and the middle-class neighborhoods farther out and in the modest suburbs of Garland and Mesquite. Here people live in small frame houses, commute to unexciting office and factory jobs, try to make ends meet and keep their neighborhoods up. About one-fifth of the people here are black and one-eighth Mexican-American; but, as Representative John Bryant puts it, "Generally speaking, what you have in the 5th District are regular, red-blooded working Americans."

"Working" is the clue that this is an old-fashioned Democratic District in newly glitzy Republican Dallas. The 5th District went for Reagan over Mondale, but it almost always votes Democratic in Texas elections, and its boundaries were drawn by a Democratic legislature determined to put as many Republican precincts as possible into the north Dallas 3d District and to leave just enough Democrats to keep the 5th and the next-door 24th safely Democratic. There is enough resentment of north Dallas here for Bryant to denounce "Republican moneybags in north Dallas who want to have two congressmen and to control this district also." But it should be added that most east Dallas residents are upwardly mobile and hoping to be more so.

Bryant is one of the most politically talented of the young Democratic congressman. He won this district in 1982; after the district lines were set, Republican Steve Bartlett left the race here and ran in the 3d—a gain for the republic since both these young men, born the same year but of very different views, have proved to be skilled legislators. Bryant, a minister's son and a rebellious liberal in high school, was elected to the Texas legislature in 1974, a year after finishing SMU Law School; he performed skillfully in Austin and won the endorsement of his predecessor, Jim Mattox (now Texas's scandal-beleaguered attorney general) and 65% of the vote against a well-known opponent in the Democratic primary; he won the general election by a 2 to 1 margin.

In his first term, after narrowly losing a Texas–California fight for a seat on the Steering and Policy Committee, he got a seat on the most coveted legislative committee, Energy and Commerce. There he has worked ably to represent oil interests, but he has been busy on other matters as well: an odometer-tampering bill, the end user-access fees legislation (to prevent phone companies from charging users of long distance services other than AT&T), and a Texas wilderness bill that passed in his first term. He has a fairly solid liberal voting record, but is ready to cite votes to protect business interests and limit regulation, against rent control and part of the bank secrecy act for example. He is something of a workhorse, serving on Judiciary and Veterans' Affairs as well as Energy and Commerce, where he is one of John Dingell's aggressive interrogators on the Oversight and Investigations Subcommittee.

Bryant has not been shy in using his Energy and Commerce seat to collect campaign contributions and is one of the leading PAC recipients in the House. Dallas area Republicans would love to beat him, and though he was unopposed in 1984 he had an aggressive opponent, a former oil company lobbyist, in 1986. But Bryant outraised and outargued him, spending $806,000 and winning 59% of the vote. He seems to have a sparkling legislative career ahead of him, provided he can keep winning as he did in 1986 and get a good break from the post-1990 redistricting.

The People: Pop. 1980: 526,633, up 0.8% 1970–80. Households (1980): 68% family, 39% with children, 53% married couples; 46.8% housing units rented; median monthly rent: $222; median house value: $35,500. Voting age pop. (1980): 374,926; 18% Black, 10% Spanish origin, 1% Asian origin.

1984 Presidential Vote:

Reagan (R)	100,261	(59%)
Mondale (D)	68,926	(41%)

Rep. John Bryant (D)

Elected 1982; b. Feb. 22, 1947, Lake Jackson; home, Dallas; Southern Methodist U., B.A. 1969, J.D. 1972; United Methodist; married (Janet).

Career: Practicing atty., 1972–82; Chief counsel, TX Senate Subcommittee on Consumer Affairs, 1973; TX House of Reps., 1974–83.

Offices: 412 CHOB 20515, 202-225-2231. Also 8035 East R. L. Thornton Freeway, Ste. 518, Dallas 75228, 214-767-6554.

Committees: *Energy and Commerce* (21st of of 25 D). Subcommittees: Energy and Power; Telecommunications and Finance; Transportation and Hazardous Materials. *Judiciary* (20th of 21 D). Subcommittees: Courts, Civil Liberties and the Administration of Justice; Criminal Justice; Immigration, Refugees and International Law. *Veterans' Affairs* (11th of 21 D). Subcommittee: Hospitals and Health Care; Oversight and Investigations.

Group Ratings

	ADA	ACLU	COPE	CFA	LCV	ACU	NTU	NSI	COC	CEI
1986	65	55	92	67	84	23	25	20	44	10
1985	55	—	91	67	—	10	30	—	41	—

National Journal Ratings

	1986 LIB — 1986 CONS		1985 LIB — 1985 CONS	
Economic	62%	35%	55%	44%
Social	52%	46%	85%	0%
Foreign	61%	37%	68%	31%

Key Votes

1) Lmt Cln Water Act	FOR	5) Retain Gun Cont	AGN	9) Aid Angola Reb	FOR
2) Rpl Tobac Sub	FOR	6) Contra Aid	AGN	10) Tax Reform	AGN
3) Grm-Rdmn Def Red	FOR	7) Lmt Text Imp	FOR	11) S Africa Sanc	FOR
4) Ban Polygraph	FOR	8) Limit SDI	FOR	12) Immig Reform	FOR

Election Results

1986 general	John Bryant (D)	57,410	(59%)	($994,285)
	Tom Carter (R)......................	39,945	(41%)	($349,937)
1986 primary	John Bryant (D)	12,715	(93%)	
	Gregory Witherspoon (D).................	912	(7%)	
1984 general	John Bryant (D)	94,391	(100%)	($310,485)

Campaign Contributions and Expenditures

1985-86		Direct Cont. 1985-86		PACS Breakdown 1985-86			
Receipts	$1,016,970	Indiv.	$468,015	Corp.	$98,407	T/M/H	$107,023
Expend.	$994,285	Party	$9,999	Labor	$106,975	Agr.	$6,850
Unspent	$109,738	PACS	$371,347	Ideo.	$45,702	CWOS	$6,390
		Cand.	$150,000				

SIXTH DISTRICT

From the Trinity River in Fort Worth to the city limits of Houston, across Texas farmland and College Station, the home of Texas A&M University, stretches the 6th Congressional District of Texas. On the map it looks like the sort of a rural and small town district that has always elected conservative Democrats to Congress, where they accumulated seniority and became committee chairmen. Until the 1980s that is pretty much what it was. Then along came Phil Gramm, the economics professor elected to replace Veterans Committee Chairman Tiger Teague in 1978. In his second term Gramm sponsored the biggest domestic budget cuts in American history, got thrown off the Budget Committee, resigned his seat, became a Republican, won triumphant reelection, and the next year was elected Senator from the third largest state in the nation.

Gramm is certainly evidence for the proposition that individuals matter in history, and yet you can see him also as the product of social forces. For the district that elected him had ceased some time in the 1970s to be a rural constituency. By the late 1970s almost 40% of its people lived within 40 miles of downtown Fort Worth or Dallas, in rich neighborhoods in Fort Worth or in spacious subdivisions out in what had once been vacant countryside; another 20% lived in Montgomery County, a similar area just north of Houston; another 15% or so were in Brazos County, around A&M, an institution whose emphasis on engineering, high tech, and the military has infected its home town with conservatism as much as UT (the University of Texas) has infected its home town of Austin with liberalism. That leaves only about one-third of the district as old-fashioned rural Texas, and even this was trending Republican by the middle 1980s.

This changing demography was apparent in the 1986 reelection victory of Representative Joe Barton. On the surface, he had not been the ideal candidate in 1984: he had spent the past few years as a Reagan Administration appointee and oil company operative, he won the Republican runoff by only 10 votes, and his opponent was a well-known Democratic legislator from College Station. But Barton won with 57%—2% better than Gramm himself got as a Republican in the 1983 special. In 1986, against Pete Geren, a wealthy lawyer from Fort Worth, Barton got 56%. The two major party nominees spent $1.1 million in 1984 and $1.9 million in 1986; in both elections Barton carried all the counties touching the Dallas–Fort Worth Metroplex plus Montgomery and Brazos County, while losing all the Democratic counties. There seems to be a pattern.

In his first term Barton got seats on the Interior and Science and Technology Committees; in his second, as a beneficiary of an alliance between Texas and small states on the Republican Committee on Committees, he got a seat on Energy and Commerce. That makes him the second young Texas Republican there (Jack Fields from greater Houston is the other) and one of five Texans on the 42-member committee. This assignment should strengthen his already strong position in the new 6th District.

The People: Pop. 1980: 526,765, up 48.1% 1970–80. Households (1980): 75% family, 40% with children, 65% married couples; 28.4% housing units rented; median monthly rent: $192; median house value: $42,500. Voting age pop. (1980): 379,330; 10% Black, 5% Spanish origin.

1984 Presidential Vote:

Reagan (R)	166,428	(70%)
Mondale (D)	72,109	(30%)

Rep. Joe L. Barton (R)

Elected 1984; b. Sept. 15, 1949, Waco; home, Ennis; Texas A & M U., B.S. 1972, Purdue U., M.S. 1973; United Methodist; married (Janet).

Career: Asst. to Vice Pres., Ennis Business Forms, 1973–81; White House Fellow, U.S. Dept. of Energy, 1981–82; Consultant, Atlantic Richfield Co., 1982–84.

Offices: 1225 LHOB 20515, 202-225-2002. Also InterFirst Tower, Ste. 507, Conroe 77301, 409-760-2291; 809 University Ave., Rm. 222, Creekwide Plaza, Bryan 77840, 409-846-9791; InterFirst Bank Bldg., Ste. 101, Ennis 75119, 214-875-8488; and 3509 Hulen, Ste. 110, Ft. Worth 76107, 817-737-7737.

Committees: *Energy and Commerce* (16th of 17 R). Subcommittees: Commerce, Consumer Protection and Competitiveness; Energy and Power.

Group Ratings

	ADA	ACLU	COPE	CFA	LCV	ACU	NTU	NSI	COC	CEI
1986	0	0	3	17	39	95	61	100	94	87
1985	5	—	0	17	—	100	70	—	95	—

National Journal Ratings

	1986 LIB — 1986 CONS		1985 LIB — 1985 CONS	
Economic	13%	— 85%	0%	— 95%
Social	0%	— 89%	0%	— 76%
Foreign	0%	— 86%	0%	— 76%

Key Votes

1) Lmt Cln Water Act	FOR	5) Retain Gun Cont	AGN	9) Aid Angola Reb	FOR
2) Rpl Tobac Sub	FOR	6) Contra Aid	FOR	10) Tax Reform	FOR
3) Grm-Rdmn Def Red	FOR	7) Lmt Text Imp	AGN	11) S Africa Sanc	AGN
4) Ban Polygraph	AGN	8) Limit SDI	AGN	12) Immig Reform	AGN

Election Results

1986 general	Joe L. Barton (R)	86,190	(56%)	($1,034,515)
	Preston Geren (D)	68,270	(44%)	($895,746)
1986 primary	Joe L. Barton (R)	17,890	(100%)	
1984 general	Joe L. Barton (R)	131,482	(57%)	($480,021)
	Dan Kubiak (D)	100,799	(43%)	($665,537)

Campaign Contributions and Expenditures

1985-86		Direct Cont. 1985-86		PACS Breakdown 1985-86			
Receipts	$1,024,246	Indiv.	$633,196	Corp.	$209,407	T/M/H	$87,112
Expend.	$1,034,515	Party	$14,659	Labor	$500	Agr.	$1,500
		PACS	$344,687	Ideo:	$42,472	CWOS	$3,696
		Cand.	$12,083				

SEVENTH DISTRICT

What happens when a boom goes bust? For the answer, come to Houston. In the years after the 1970s oil shocks, Houston was the biggest boom city of the United States, its skylines full of postmodernist silhouettes, its gallery/shopping malls full of Swiss chocolates and French furs and Italian jewels, its glittering subdivisions rising from swamplike land off main streets with a jumble of gas stations and U-Tote-Ms in America's largest city without zoning. By the middle

1980s Houston had gone bust. It is still the center of the world's oil industry, but with the American rig count down to a new low, with drilling equipment rusting away, with banks holding loans made on the assumption that oil prices would reach $50 a barrel now hoping for $20, with the nation's biggest glut of unrented office space and with newly sold houses abandoned and deteriorated—Houston has its problems.

Yet Houston still has formidable assets and not everyone is hurting. Its expertise in the oil business may prove an asset again. Its huge petrochemical complexes are breeding ever higher technology. It has the Johnson Space Center (saved from cuts by the area's congressional delegation). It has a highly skilled, ambitious, resourceful work force. And the traffic congestion, probably the worst in the country, which Houstonians have been complaining bitterly about, may be a harbinger of better times. The key question is whether Houston, with a metropolitan population approaching three million, can diversify its economy, as Los Angeles did in the 1950s and Chicago in the 1880s, or whether it will stay tied to oil as Detroit was to the automobile or Pittsburgh to steel, remaining vulnerable to the declines that will come sooner or later. One good sign: bad times have spurred tens of thousands of Houstonians, who were once happy to rise upward on oil prices and regular corporate paychecks and bonuses, to go out and start their own businesses.

Most of the visible growth in Houston occurred on the west side of the city. The downtown sits separately, between a marginal residential area and slums; and to the east are the great refineries and the Houston Ship Channel. The west, the southwest, and most recently the far north sides are where most of the city's high-income people live. The commercial streets here do not look special, but the neighborhoods behind the main streets preserve their character through protective covenants, and use the lush greenery that thrives in humid Houston to compensate for the less than interesting flatness of the landscape. The growth of the west side of Houston mirrors the growth of Houston's entrepreneurial and professional sectors. There were about 150,000 people living on the west side in 1960; by 1980 there were 900,000 in the same area. About half this area forms the present-day 7th Congressional District of Texas—a constituency that did not exist 20 years ago. The 7th District covers the area west of Memorial Park, on both sides of the Katy Freeway; generally it stays north of Westheimer, one of the main business streets here. It takes in the vast, flat, still empty expanse of the western part of Harris County, a place once dotted with tiny towns amid a part of Texas with a high proportion of blacks. The affluent part of Houston has been advancing relentlessly into this empty quarter, conquering new square miles every year.

The 7th District is one of the two or three most Republican congressional districts in the United States. People here believe strongly in free enterprise; they see the federal government as an impediment to salutary business and economic growth. You can attack this position as selfish, and it does serve people's short-term interests. But people here can see in Houston in their own lifetimes how capitalism has transformed a sleepy, backward community into a busy, productive metropolis whose goods and services have improved the lives of people around the world. The conservatism here is more economic than cultural; many of these people, after all, have moved far from their original roots and they are not particularly interested in influencing other people's lifestyles. But few voters here are aggressive liberals on cultural issues, and very few dissent from the hawkish consensus on foreign policy. You won't find many Democrats in these precincts; at least three-fourths of the votes here regularly go to Republican presidential candidates.

The 7th District produced two Republican presidential candidates in 1980: John Connally, who lives in River Oaks and practiced law in downtown Houston; and George Bush, who lived off Woodway Drive, and was elected the 7th District's congressman in 1966 and 1968. Bush's later successes have come more in Washington and various primary states than in Texas; he lost two Senate races here, in 1964 and 1970, and he failed, barely, to win the 1980 Texas presidential primary.

The district's current congressman is Bill Archer, Bush's successor and one of the senior Republicans in the House. Born and brought up in Texas—as are most people here, despite the talk of northern migrants and Bush's example—Archer was elected to the legislature as a Democrat and then became a Republican. He has been a member of the Ways and Means Committee for ten years, and there he has been an articulate spokesman for positions backed by the oil industry, especially independent producers.

But Archer is more a spokesman than a legislator. He spent several years with Jake Pickle trying to reach a compromise on Social Security refinancing, and then opposed the measure that went through in 1983. He has favored lower tax rates for years, but is proud of having opposed the 1986 tax reform and was one of the House Republicans who came close to scuttling it in December 1985. With the Democrats firmly in control of the House, Archer evidently feels that he has the luxury of opposing grand compromises on principle and can leave to others, including Republicans in the Administration and the Senate, the messy business of putting them through. Archer stands in line to succeed Tennessee's John Duncan as ranking Republican on Ways and Means and could conceivably be chairman some day. But through most of the 1980s he seems more interested in being a critic than a doer.

The People: Pop. 1980: 527,083, up 103.6% 1970–80. Households (1980): 72% family, 42% with children, 62% married couples; 37.9% housing units rented; median monthly rent: $302; median house value: $79,200. Voting age pop. (1980): 375,483; 6% Spanish origin, 3% Black, 2% Asian origin.

1984 Presidential Vote:

Reagan (R) 207,297	(83%)
Mondale (D) 42,452	(17%)

Rep. Bill Archer (R)

Elected 1970; b. Mar. 22, 1928, Houston; home, Houston; Rice U., 1945–46, U. of TX, B.B.A. 1949, LL.B. 1951; Roman Catholic; married (Sharon).

Career: Air Force, 1951–53; Pres., Uncle Johnny Mills, Inc., 1953–61; Hunters Creek Village Cncl. and Mayor Pro Tem, 1955–62; TX House of Reps., 1966–70; Dir., Heights State Bank, Houston, 1967–70; Practicing atty., 1968–71.

Offices: 1135 LHOB 20515, 202-225-2571. Also 7501 Fed. Bldg., 515 Rusk St., Houston 77002, 713-229-2763.

Committees: *Ways and Means* (2d of 13 R). Subcommittees: Social Security (Ranking Member); Trade. *Joint Committee on Taxation.*

Group Ratings

	ADA	ACLU	COPE	CFA	LCV	ACU	NTU	NSI	COC	CEI
1986	0	5	5	0	38	95	72	100	94	92
1985	5	—	5	25	—	100	74	—	100	—

National Journal Ratings

	1986 LIB — 1986 CONS		1985 LIB — 1985 CONS	
Economic	0% —	94%	5% —	92%
Social	0% —	89%	0% —	76%
Foreign	14% —	84%	0% —	76%

Key Votes

1) Lmt Cln Water Act	FOR	5) Retain Gun Cont	AGN	9) Aid Angola Reb	FOR
2) Rpl Tobac Sub	FOR	6) Contra Aid	FOR	10) Tax Reform	AGN
3) Grm-Rdmn Def Red	FOR	7) Lmt Text Imp	AGN	11) S Africa Sanc	AGN
4) Ban Polygraph	AGN	8) Limit SDI	AGN	12) Immig Reform	AGN

Election Results

1986 general	Bill Archer (R)	129,673	(87%)	($152,779)
	Harry Kniffen (D)	17,635	(12%)	
1986 primary	Bill Archer (R)	24,362	(100%)	
1984 general	Bill Archer (R)	213,480	(87%)	($102,745)
	Billy Willibey (D)	32,835	(13%)	

Campaign Contributions and Expenditures

1985-86		Direct Cont. 1985-86		PACS Breakdown 1985-86			
Receipts	$281,736	Indiv.	$210,269	Corp.	$-775	T/M/H	$500
Expend.	$152,779	Party	$2,086	Labor	$0	Agr.	$0
Unspent	$540,472	PACS	$7,734	Ideo.	$8,009	CWOS	$0

EIGHTH DISTRICT

The west side of Houston, where fancy subdivisions fill in the flat land through which the Katy and Southern Pacific Railroads head toward California, is the white-collar side of town; the east side, where the Houston Ship Channel murkily flows past factories and petrochemical plants and docks out to Galveston Bay and the Gulf of Mexico, is the blue-collar side. The glitter on the west side and in the mirrored surface of the downtown skyscrapers is what attracts the eye of the visitor, but Houston is also heavily a factory town, with large numbers of blacks and Mexican-Americans and large numbers of whites from the rural South and even from Michigan and California who came here to move up in the world. Politically, Houston is one of the most divided cities in America: the west side 7th Congressional District went 83% for Ronald Reagan in 1984, while the next-door inner city 18th District was 72% for Walter Mondale. They were all watching the same TV ads and news from the same city, they depend on the same economy— but they vote as if they lived in different countries.

In between—politically, not geographically—is the 8th District on the north and east side of town. About one-third of the people here live within the city of Houston, and about a third of them are black; there are modest working-class precincts on the city's east side. To the north, the district includes what was once countryside, dotted by roadside stores and jerry-built houses, and what is now the home of Houston's Intercontinental Airport, and the glass high-rise office buildings and glittery subdivisions that were built nearby. At the far eastern end of the district is Baytown, an industrial refinery town where the Ship Channel empties out into the bay. People here believe in traditional cultural values, perhaps a little more fervently than their neighbors on the west side; they believe also in free enterprise, though their faith has been tested as the 1980s have gone on, and they are not averse to some government intervention here and there and a little tighter mesh in the safety net. This is the swing district in the Houston area. It went for Ronald Reagan in 1984, enabling him to carry greater Houston; but it also seems to have gone for Governor Mark White in his losing campaign for reelection in 1986 in which he still managed to carry greater Houston, and the portion of Houston here seems to have given Mayor Kathy Whitmire a margin in 1985 despite the shrill anti-gay campaign of her opponent, former Mayor Louie Welch. For many years Houston was a Republican city in a Democratic state; if in the 1990s it becomes a Democratic city in a Republican state, the place to look for the reasons why is here.

But it should be added that the 8th is not Democratic in every race; it has elected and smartly reelected Republican Representative Jack Fields. In Washington Fields has been seen as a blow-dried Reagan robot swept into office in 1980 and swept to reelection on billows of PAC money. The reality seems a little different. Fields won in 1980 in a district closer-in to the central city and more Democratic, and he beat a veteran and accomplished liberal, incumbent Bob Eckhardt—even while Jimmy Carter was beating Ronald Reagan in the district. Fields was helped by redistricting, but not overwhelmingly: the 8th is no more Republican than the 5th

District in Dallas that elects Democrat John Bryant or the 12th in Fort Worth that elects Speaker Jim Wright. Fields won with 57% in 1982 against a weak opponent; he raised that percentage to 65% in 1984 and 68% in 1986.

His political assets seem to be these. He has genuine roots in the district, in the old Exxon company town of Humble out near Intercontinental Airport. He won a seat on the Energy and Commerce Committee in his second term—a valuable political asset in energy-dependent Houston. He is not enough of a free market ideologue to pass up chances to help the district, fighting efforts to move space station work away from the nearby Johnson Space Center, getting $38 million for flood control on White Oak Bayou and $3.3 million to clean up toxic wastes in the Highlands Acid Pit, nor is he so staunch a cold warrior as to cavil at selling oil field equipment to the Soviet Union ("the largest market in the world"). All these have helped Fields gain a solid hold on what might otherwise be a Democratic district—a formidable political achievement for someone the Democrats have tried to dismiss as just another pretty face.

The People: Pop. 1980: 527,531, up 65.7% 1970–80. Households (1980): 81% family, 52% with children, 69% married couples; 30.4% housing units rented; median monthly rent: $256; median house value: $46,700. Voting age pop. (1980): 347,798; 15% Black, 11% Spanish origin, 1% Asian origin.

1984 Presidential Vote:

Reagan (R)	109,321	(60%)
Mondale (D)	71,779	(40%)

Rep. Jack Fields (R)

Elected 1980; b. Feb. 3, 1952, Humble; home, Humble; Baylor U., B.A. 1974, J.D. 1977; Baptist; divorced.

Career: Practicing atty.; Vice Pres., Rosewood Memorial Funeral Home and Cemetery. 1977–80.

Offices: 413 CHOB 20515, 202-225-4901. Also 12605 E. Freeway, Ste. 320, InterFirst Bank Bldg., Houston 77015, 713-451-6334.

Committees: *Energy and Commerce* (11th of 13 R). Subcommittees: Energy and Power; Health and the Environment; Telecommunications and Finance. *Merchant Marine and Fisheries* (5th of 17 R). Subcommittees: Merchant Marine; Panama Canal and Outer Continental Shelf (Ranking Member).

Group Ratings

	ADA	ACLU	COPE	CFA	LCV	ACU	NTU	NSI	COC	CEI
1986	5	5	6	17	28	95	67	90	94	78
1985	10	—	7	33	—	90	67	—	91	—

National Journal Ratings

	1986 LIB — 1986 CONS			1985 LIB — 1985 CONS		
Economic	0%	—	94%	5%	—	92%
Social	0%	—	89%	0%	—	76%
Foreign	14%	—	84%	0%	—	76%

Key Votes

1) Lmt Cln Water Act	AGN	5) Retain Gun Cont	AGN	9) Aid Angola Reb	FOR
2) Rpl Tobac Sub	FOR	6) Contra Aid	FOR	10) Tax Reform	AGN
3) Grm-Rdmn Def Red	FOR	7) Lmt Text Imp	AGN	11) S Africa Sanc	AGN
4) Ban Polygraph	AGN	8) Limit SDI	AGN	12) Immig Reform	AGN

Election Results

1986 general	Jack Fields (R)	66,280	(68%)	($574,657)
	Blaine Mann (D)	30,617	(32%)	($19,666)
1986 primary	Jack Fields (R)	9,635	(100%)	
1984 general	Jack Fields (R)	113,031	(65%)	($934,914)
	Don Buford (D)	62,072	(35%)	($357,653)

Campaign Contributions and Expenditures

1985-86		Direct Cont. 1985-86		PACS Breakdown 1985-86			
Receipts	$590,309	Indiv.	$304,962	Corp.	$158,083	T/M/H	$68,960
Expend.	$574,657	Party	$6,199	Labor	$22,750	Agr.	$0
Unspent	$42,055	PACS	$263,499	Ideo.	$10,000	CWOS	$3,706

NINTH DISTRICT

From Spindletop park in Beaumont, where Texas's oil industry began, to the Lyndon B. Johnson Space Center south of Houston, where America's probes into space are planned, stretches the 9th Congressional District of Texas. It has two concentrations of population. One is around Beaumont and Port Arthur, near the border with Cajun Louisiana, an area of refineries, petrochemical plants, and other big processing operations. Heavily blue-collar and dependent on oil, this area had one of the highest levels of unemployment in Texas in the middle 1980s. The other populated area is around Galveston, built on a sand spit and rebuilt after 6,000 died in the devastating hurricane of 1900 (at which point even venturesome Texans decided it was better to build the big city which became Houston on swamps inland rather than on sand scarcely above sea level) and Texas City, just inland where more than 500 perished in a huge liquified natural gas tanker explosion in 1947: this is not gentle country. Nonetheless the Space Center was located here, under pressure from Vice President Johnson and longtime Houston Representative Albert Thomas; and when NASA threatened to move space station operations out, they were stymied by the area delegation led by 9th District Representative Jack Brooks.

They could hardly have picked a more aggressive or astute champion. Brooks worked his way through school as a reporter, was a Marine in the South Pacific in World War II, was elected to the legislature from the Beaumont area at age 23 (the same day as Speaker Jim Wright, who is exactly four days younger), politicked astutely enough to chair the Banks and Banking Committee in his mid-20s, and was elected to Congress in 1952, just before turning 30. He is undeniably brainy and even more undeniably forceful; an old-fashioned man's man who likes to hunt and fish with no evident interest in introspection but an impressive ability to figure out how to get things done and then the temperament to see that they are. He is probably the current member of Congress who most closely resembles Lyndon Johnson, in both his virtues and his faults, in his accent and even a bit in his craggy appearance. Brooks is extremely partisan, profane, knowledgeable, witty, effective. A story that may be apocryphal has it that he was charged with being pro-Communist in his 1952 House campaign. "I fought the fascists for five years in World War II," he is supposed to have told a political meeting; "I own an eight-inch revolver back at home and I'll *shoot* any man who calls me a Communist."

Brooks is generally a liberal on economic issues, out of conviction but also because he believes in going along with the Democratic leadership on important matters; he is no maverick. He has supported civil rights bills since he came to Congress, which may not sound especially noteworthy today, but which took real guts in east Texas in the 1950s and 1960s. His positions recently on foreign issues have been more liberal than they were when he supported Johnson on the Vietnam war; on cultural issues his record is mixed.

Brooks is the number two Democrat on Judiciary, and will be chairman if Peter Rodino retires; he serves now as chairman of the Government Operations Committee and chairman of its Legislative and National Security Subcommittee. On Judiciary he has been active on some technical matters with economic consequences, not always in tandem with Rodino; he was the main sponsor of the bill to exempt beer distributors from antitrust laws, for example. Government Operations has a charter which allows it to investigate most government agencies. But it passes relatively little legislation, and much of it deals with government reorganization, the Paper Reduction Act, inspectors general of various sorts—useful stuff surely, but seldom as important as its advocates claim. Brooks, in a move which looks better and better as the years go by, was skeptical of the worth of the Carter Administration's reorganization proposals and fought them on constitutional grounds. More recently Government Operations discovered that well-over two thirds of all federal contracts were doled out without competitive bidding—a revelation that led to specific remedies in the Deficit Reduction Act of 1984 which the Reagan Administration has tried to ignore.

Brooks also serves on the special committee investigating the Iran-contra scandal, just as he served on Judiciary's impeachment hearings a dozen years ago. He can be expected to be a tough partisan who will look hard at the facts, bearing down on witnesses as much as possible, but never getting himself out on a limb. Richard Nixon called Brooks "the executioner" after Brooks tracked down all the public money spent on Nixon's San Clemente house. Brooks himself says, "I never thought being a congressman was supposed to be an easy job, and it doesn't bother me a bit to be in a good fight."

Brooks had some electoral problems in the early 1980s, in 1980 edging a challenger by an uncomfortably narrow 50%–43% margin and beating him two years later, after spending over $700,000, with just 53%. He has not had primary opposition since, but has won general elections with 59% and 62%—a little lower than most congressmen with his seniority usually get, but not in the danger zone. The 9th District, with its blacks and Cajuns, union members and unemployed oil workers, is in any case pretty solidly Democratic; it nearly voted against Ronald Reagan in 1984 and went solidly for Governor Mark White in 1986. Brooks seems likely to be an even more important congressman as the 1980s turn into 1990s.

The People: Pop. 1980: 526,443, up 17.5% 1970–80. Households (1980): 76% family, 43% with children, 63% married couples; 32.0% housing units rented; median monthly rent: $209; median house value: $39,300. Voting age pop. (1980): 370,362; 20% Black, 7% Spanish origin, 1% Asian origin.

1984 Presidential Vote:

Reagan (R)	110,918	(52%)
Mondale (D)	99,905	(47%)

Rep. Jack Brooks (D)

Elected 1952; b. Dec. 18, 1922, Crowley, LA; home, Beaumont; Lamar Col., 1939–41, U. of TX, B.J. 1943, J.D. 1949; United Methodist; married (Charlotte).

Career: USMC, WWII; TX House of Reps., 1946–50; Practicing atty., 1949–52.

Offices: 2449 RHOB 20515, 202-225-6565. Also 230 Jack Brooks Fed. Bldg., Beaumont 77701, 409-839-2508; 601 25th St., Galveston 77550, 409-766-3608.

Committees: *Government Operations* (Chairman of 24 D). Subcommittee: Legislation and National Security (Chairman). *Judiciary* (2d of 21 D). Subcommittees: Administrative Law and Government Procedure; Monopolies and Commercial Law.

Group Ratings

	ADA	ACLU	COPE	CFA	LCV	ACU	NTU	NSI	COC	CEI
1986	70	81	75	58	56	9	29	10	33	12
1985	70	—	74	33	—	11	24	—	28	—

National Journal Ratings

	1986 LIB — 1986 CONS		1985 LIB — 1985 CONS	
Economic	80%	— 19%	74%	— 25%
Social	72%	— 27%	85%	— 0%
Foreign	67%	— 30%	64%	— 33%

Key Votes

1) Lmt Cln Water Act	AGN	5) Retain Gun Cont	AGN	9) Aid Angola Reb	FOR
2) Rpl Tobac Sub	FOR	6) Contra Aid	FOR	10) Tax Reform	AGN
3) Grm-Rdmn Def Red	FOR	7) Lmt Text Imp	AGN	11) S Africa Sanc	AGN
4) Ban Polygraph	AGN	8) Limit SDI	AGN	12) Immig Reform	AGN

Election Results

1986 general	Jack Brooks (D)	73,285	(62%)	($400,038)
	Lisa D. Duperier (R)	45,834	(38%)	($237,179)
1986 primary	Jack Brooks (D)	32,728	(100%)	
1984 general	Jack Brooks (D)	120,559	(59%)	($244,695)
	Jim Mahan (R)	84,306	(41%)	($96,444)

Campaign Contributions and Expenditures

1985-86		Direct Cont. 1985-86		PACS Breakdown 1985-86			
Receipts	$447,111	Indiv.	$180,518	Corp.	$101,930	T/M/H	$94,139
Expend.	$400,038	Party	$188	Labor	$44,450	Agr.	$4,000
Unspent	$242,155	PACS	$259,669	Ideo.	$10,250	CWOS	$4,900

TENTH DISTRICT

Austin, the southernmost state capital in the continental 48 states, is also one of the boom towns of America—and by the middle 1980s it seemed the only boom town left in Texas. There is an irony here, for Austin was not established for an economic reason, it has been through most of its history a city with only a limited interest in commerce, its skies almost totally untainted with the smoke of industry, its ground not pocked with pumping oil rigs. Nor has state government been a major employer during most of Austin's history: the dome on the pink granite Capitol is just a tad higher than its counterpart in Washington, but Texas has always believed in minimalist government. The real secret behind Austin's growth and vitality is the University of Texas. Endowed with thousands of west Texas acres that turned out to sit on top of oil, it has the nation's largest single university campus here in Austin and has become one of the great institutions of higher learning in America.

For years the University gave an easygoing and tolerant liberal tone to life in the capital of an uptight and angrily conservative state; there were a few places—the old Driskill Hotel, the mansion of former Governor Allan Shivers, an early Democrat-who-endorsed-Republicans—where the rich hung out, but much of this small sleepy city lived a beer-and-blue-jeans lifestyle, with attitudes typified by the peskily liberal and perpetually broke *Texas Observer*. This made Austin and the surrounding 10th Congressional District liberal Democratic bastions, tempered by the more conservative attitudes in the German counties to the east and the hill country counties to the west.

But since the middle 1970s Austin has changed, almost doubling in size, bursting with outsiders, spreading shopping centers and condominiums willynilly into the surrounding hills. The catalyst again is the University, plus Austin's selection in 1983 as the site of the

Microelectronics and Computer Technology Corporation research consortium headed by Admiral Bobby Inman. Austin seems to be on its way to becoming one of the high tech centers of America, imperilled only if state government cuts back too vigorously at the University. Austin in the 1980s has become not exactly yuppified, but more affluent, less of a college town and more a place where families with technical-minded breadwinners live ordered and disciplined lives. Its attitudes are now more those of the *Texas Monthly,* probably the most successful—editorially and financially—of the nation's regional magazines, which eyes Texas critically but sometimes affectionately, less the adolescent eager to overthrow all the older generation's pieties and more the adult interested in understanding and appreciating the interesting society around him.

Politically, Austin has become more Republican. Austin and the 10th District have voted for Ronald Reagan now twice; they gave only a puny margin to liberal Democrat Lloyd Doggett, Austin's own state Senator, in his losing race against Phil Gramm in 1984; they voted only narrowly for Mark White over Bill Clements in 1986. The city's blacks remain unanimously Democratic, and Democrats' percentages among Mexican-Americans and students have not fallen too much (conservative young people in Texas today tend to choose A&M or SMU or Baylor over UT). But the new affluent neighborhoods spreading all over the countryside are Republican. Not quite so heavily as affluent neighborhoods in Dallas or Houston, of course; no place else in America is that Republican. But Republican enough to give a different tilt to Austin politics.

But not, so far, to the congressional politics of the 10th. There is an old tradition here, going back to Lyndon Johnson's victory in the 1937 special election, of fairly liberal Democratic congressmen, fairly generous with public funds (especially for central Texas), tolerant on civil rights, hawkish on military affairs, and politically able, a tradition upheld by LBJ ("the best congressman ever," in the words of his unadmiring biographer Robert Caro), his successor Homer Thornberry, and the man who succeeded Thornberry when Johnson made him a federal judge in 1963, the current congressman, Jake Pickle. All three were contemporaries, born between 1908 and 1913; the 10th has been represented by politicians of the same generation for more than 50 years. It must have occurred to many in Austin that a pleasant, 70-ish man like Jake Pickle is not the kind of congressman a city full of newcomers wants.

Something like that certainly occurred to Carole Keeton Rylander, who served as mayor of Austin in the 1970s. She is the daughter of a dean of UT Law School, a family friend of Pickle's, and a longtime Democrat who switched to the Republican party after the 1984 campaign, lost 80 pounds and wrote a book about her diet, then announced she was opposing Pickle because he was too big a spender and too liberal. If she expected him to bow out or roll over, she was mistaken. Jake Pickle showed energy, aggressiveness, tenacity, and skill of which Lyndon Johnson would have been proud. He raised more than $1.1 million—not impossible if you're number three on Ways and Means and Congress is considering tax reform—and spent it shrewdly, starting TV ads in late spring, but husbanding plenty for the fall. He was attentive to local interest: paw through the tax reform bill's transition rules carefully and you'll find plenty that are helpful to Austin. He campaigned at state office buildings at 6 a.m. and at closing hour at 6th Street nightspots. He cut the ribbon at new high tech building openings and emphasized his national work on Social Security, the environment, the tax bill, and encouraging high tech. "Jake Pickle. Unique. Ours," his ads said. He affected to be hurt that Rylander was running and portrayed her as motivated only by ambition: "I've been challenged by someone who was part of our team. I value her family's friendship very highly, and then to be challenged by someone whose only motivation is to take my seat . . ."

Pickle removed any doubts about his hold on the 10th District by winning reelection with 72% of the vote. He returns to Washington as the architect of the Social Security rescue of 1983, when benefits were in effect cut by raising the normal retirement age over the years to 67; he now chairs the Oversight Subcommittee. Should Social Security become a major issue again, he may be called on to shape another compromise. He was a serious player on tax reform and will likely be a serious player on any trade bill that comes through Ways and Means; he is not the kind to challenge Chairman Dan Rostenkowski idly, but he also knows how to get what he wants. Pickle, seemingly threatened on the left when college students got the vote in the early 1970s, then seemingly threatened on the right when all the high tech engineers moved to town, has shown that he knows how to play politics and to govern with the best of them, in the 10th District tradition, and he has served notice that he intends to remain in the House for some time to come.

The People: Pop. 1980: 527,181, up 41.0% 1970–80. Households (1980): 65% family, 35% with children, 53% married couples; 45.4% housing units rented; median monthly rent: $222; median house value: $47,800. Voting age pop. (1980): 390,909; 15% Spanish origin, 9% Black, 1% Asian origin.

1984 Presidential Vote:

Reagan (R) 154,846	(58%)
Mondale (D) 111,902	(42%)

Rep. J. J. (Jake) Pickle (D)

Elected Dec. 17, 1963; b. Oct. 11, 1913, Roscoe; home, Austin; U. of TX, B.A. 1938; United Methodist; married (Beryl).

Career: Area Dir., Natl. Youth Admin., 1938–41; Navy, WWII; Coorganizer, KVET Radio, Austin; Adv. and pub. rel. business; Dir., TX State Dem. Exec. Cmtee., 1957–60; Mbr., TX Employment Comm., 1961–63.

Offices: 242 CHOB 20515, 202-225-4865. Also 763 Fed. Bldg., Austin 78701, 512-482-5921.

Committees: *Ways and Means* (3d of 23 D). Subcommittees: Health; Oversight (Chairman). *Joint Committee on Taxation.*

Group Ratings

	ADA	ACLU	COPE	CFA	LCV	ACU	NTU	NSI	COC	CEI
1986	40	65	52	33	57	38	31	40	44	32
1985	50	—	52	58	—	38	31	—	43	—

National Journal Ratings

	1986 LIB — 1986 CONS		1985 LIB — 1985 CONS	
Economic	45% —	54%	63% —	37%
Social	49% —	49%	85% —	0%
Foreign	48% —	51%	51% —	48%

Key Votes

1) Lmt Cln Water Act	FOR	5) Retain Gun Cont	AGN	9) Aid Angola Reb	FOR
2) Rpl Tobac Sub	AGN	6) Contra Aid	FOR	10) Tax Reform	FOR
3) Grm-Rdmn Def Red	FOR	7) Lmt Text Imp	AGN	11) S Africa Sanc	FOR
4) Ban Polygraph	FOR	8) Limit SDI	AGN	12) Immig Reform	FOR

Election Results

1986 general	J. J. (Jake) Pickle (D) 135,863	(72%)	($1,369,912)
	Carole Rylander (R) 52,000	(28%)	($316,175)
1986 primary	J. J. (Jake) Pickle (D) 49,101	(81%)	
	Nina Butts (D) 11,502	(19%)	
1984 general	J. J. (Jake) Pickle (D) 186,447	(100%)	($162,970)

Campaign Contributions and Expenditures

	1985-86	Direct Cont. 1985-86		PACS Breakdown 1985-86			
Receipts	$1,151,264	Indiv.	$666,380	Corp.	$188,583	T/M/H	$141,065
Expend.	$1,369,912	Party	$5,187	Labor	$19,500	Agr.	$7,000
Unspent	$137,936	PACS	$404,198	Ideo.	$30,050	CWOS	$18,000

ELEVENTH DISTRICT

The heart of Texas, just off the geographic center of the state, but the heart of its traditional rural culture, is not in greater Houston or the Dallas–Fort Worth Metroplex, or even in the state capital of Austin. It is betwixt and between, a part of Texas whose farm fields and small towns recall the state as it was half a century ago, before the growth of the oil industry transformed Texas, once a rural backwater, into one of the centers of western capitalism. This is the Texas around Waco, home of Baptist Baylor University, and of the Army's huge Fort Hood, which occupies most of one of the counties next door, and of the 11 still mostly small town and rural counties around that make up Texas's 11th Congressional District.

This part of Texas has been changed, too, of course. It is much more affluent than it was even 15 years ago, and less insular. But some things have remained the same. Cotton is a major crop here; in fact, Texas is one of the largest cotton producers. The Army's giant Fort Hood continues not only to be a mainstay of the area, but its presence seems to bolster the hawkish instincts of Texans. Politically, this part of Texas is filled with ancestral Democrats. There are not all that many blacks here and not many Mexican-Americans, not many labor unions or universities. But Waco, the largest city here, Killeen, near Fort Hood, and the other parts of the district have been solidly Democratic since the Civil War. They were not deterred by the national Democrats' support of civil rights: they gave Hubert Humphrey an absolute majority of their votes in 1968. In 1980 the 11th District did shift and give Ronald Reagan a slight plurality. But by 1982 it was roaring back Democratic. By 1984 it was for Reagan again, and in 1986 it went for Bill Clements over Mark White. You can bet Lloyd Bentsen is watching it closely for 1988.

For more than 50 years the 11th District has elected Democrats who have been leaders of the bipartisan conservative bloc. One was Bob Poage, longtime House Agriculture Committee chairman who pushed early in his career for rural electrification but had a conservative record on most issues that got him ousted from his chairmanship in 1974; he retired in 1978 after 42 years in the House and died at 87 in early 1987. He was succeeded by a small town banker who had worked several years on Poage's staff, Marvin Leath, a conservative Democrat who, quite against the odds, has ended up one of the pivotal figures in the House. This bona fide hawk was almost elected chairman of the House Armed Services Committee by the dovish Democratic Caucus in early 1987.

Character rather than issues explains Leath's ascent. With his deep drawl, his tanned weatherbeaten look, the cigarette in his hand, he looks like the kind of Texan who keeps a shotgun mounted on his pickup truck; he plays guitar and sings country music to great acclaim from Democrats for whom this is not a familiar idiom. Leath was one of the Boll Weevils who supported the Reagan budget and tax programs in 1981, but he has made a specialty of working since then with his fellow Democrats, even while bemoaning their liberalism. He worked on the veterans' training and G.I. bills in 1983 and 1984—which have turned out to be one of the unsung public policy successes of the 1980s. He championed military spending and protected Fort Hood from his seat on Armed Services. But he also listened to his colleagues, pondered the issues coolly and objectively, and looked for common ground. He has "infinite patience in pulling people together," says Caucus Chairman Richard Gephardt, and in 1985 and 1986 he found his forum when he got a seat on the Budget Committee.

Unlike the Boll Weevils of 1981 who worked, sometimes surreptitiously, with the Republicans, Leath has always caucused with Democrats. He has advanced his own budget alternatives which have been rejected by other Democrats (though they have gotten more votes than you might think) and then he has gone on to support the alternative other Democrats have embraced with force and vigor as the best available. When you start counting votes in the House, and realize that Leath carries with him many former Boll Weevils from Texas and other parts of the South, you realize that he makes the difference between Democrats having sure control of the budget process in the House and always being about to be undercut. So it's easy to understand why he's a special favorite of Budget Chairman William Gray and Speaker Jim Wright.

When liberals were casting around for alternatives to Armed Services Chairman Les Aspin after he supported the MX missile in 1985 and voted for contra aid in 1986, they went down the committee list to number 14 in seniority and came to Leath. By any measure, he's more hawkish than Aspin, but they thought him more reliable, more open, more candid, and a nicer guy: thus he ran with support from Ron Dellums and Sonny Montgomery. Eventually the move failed: Aspin was rejected in caucus in late 1986, but in January the Leath forces came up short after leading liberals passed a letter backing Aspin and pointing to Leath's defense record. But the Leath candidacy—all those doves supporting such a strong hawk, no matter how fine his personal qualities—was an implausible thing all along: too cute by half. Leath took his defeat with characteristic good grace and seems not at all inclined to quit looking for common ground with all kinds of Democrats. And so not as chairman, but as the kind of member who could get such diverse support for chairman, he is likely to continue to be a key policymaker in the House.

Leath had to beat a liberal in the 1978 primary and a well-financed Republican in the general that year, both tough races. He has not had a serious opponent since, nor is he likely to in a district he fits like a glove.

The People: Pop. 1980: 527,382, up 25.3% 1970–80. Households (1980): 75% family, 41% with children, 65% married couples; 36.6% housing units rented; median monthly rent: $162; median house value: $30,400. Voting age pop. (1980): 381,013; 13% Black, 8% Spanish origin, 1% Asian origin.

1984 Presidential Vote:

Reagan (R) 118,091	(66%)
Mondale (D) 60,086	(34%)

Rep. J. Marvin Leath (D)

Elected 1978; b. May 6, 1931, Henderson; home, Waco; U. of TX, B.B.A. 1954; Presbyterian; married (Alta).

Career: Army, 1954–56; High sch. teacher and coach, 1957–59; Salesman, 1959–62; Banker; Spec. Asst. to U.S. Rep. Bob Poage, 1972–74.

Offices: 336 CHOB 20515, 202-225-6105. Also 206 Fed. Bldg., Waco 76701, 817-752-9600.

Committees: *Armed Services* (14th of 31 D). Subcommittees: Military Installations and Facilities; Procurement and Military Nuclear Systems; Readiness. *Budget* (12th of 21 D). Task Force: Defense and International Affairs.

Group Ratings

	ADA	ACLU	COPE	CFA	LCV	ACU	NTU	NSI	COC	CEI
1986	40	26	26	75	10	57	35	100	50	36
1985	10	—	23	33	—	76	43	—	77	—

National Journal Ratings

	1986 LIB — 1986 CONS			1985 LIB — 1985 CONS		
Economic	46%	—	54%	31%	—	67%
Social	35%	—	64%	34%	—	64%
Foreign	46%	—	54%	0%	—	76%

Key Votes

1) Lmt Cln Water Act	FOR	5) Retain Gun Cont	AGN	9) Aid Angola Reb	AGN
2) Rpl Tobac Sub	AGN	6) Contra Aid	FOR	10) Tax Reform	AGN
3) Grm-Rdmn Def Red	FOR	7) Lmt Text Imp	FOR	11) S Africa Sanc	FOR
4) Ban Polygraph	AGN	8) Limit SDI	FOR	12) Immig Reform	AGN

Election Results

1986 general	J. Marvin Leath (D)	84,201	(100%)	($83,069)
1986 primary	J. Marvin Leath (D)	42,486	(100%)	
1984 general	J. Marvin Leath (D)	112,940	(100%)	($126,544)

Campaign Contributions and Expenditures

1985-86		Direct Cont. 1985-86		PACS Breakdown 1985-86			
Receipts	$157,069	Indiv.	$14,915	Corp.	$65,535	T/M/H	$26,250
Expend.	$83,996	Party	$0	Labor	$0	Agr.	$1,000
Unspent	$397,935	PACS	$95,685	Ideo.	$1,750	CWOS	$1,150

TWELFTH DISTRICT

Fort Worth, Texas, has a fair claim to being the quintessential mid-American city. Halfway across the continent, midway between the oceans, it is where the West begins and the East ends, just west of the Balcones Escarpment that divides the dry treeless grazing lands of west Texas from the humid green croplands of east Texas. It is southern in its hell-of-a-fellow heritage and northern in its advanced post-industrial economy. It has the nation's biggest row of Western wear shops and in the redeveloped Stockyards the nation's largest honkytonk, Billy Bob's Texas; it has the nation's richest family, the Basses, who have put up the steel-sheen skyscrapers that dominate the skyline from hills miles away and at whose base is the Sundance Square dream-world built by the eccentric Bass brother. Fort Worth is the place where an eight-engine B-1 bomber rolled off the runway and, circling lazily in the sky, broke the United States out of the SALT II treaty in 1986; it took off from Carswell Air Force Base, right across the street from where General Dynamics built it in the nation's largest defense plant. Fort Worth has some of the nation's premier small museums (better, it likes to tell you, than Dallas's) and the definitive museum of Western art; it will also be the site of the second Bureau of Engraving and Printing plant to make paper money. Fort Worth had its beginning as a cow town, where stockmen drove their herds to the railhead, when it pushed west from Dallas; today it has a high tech economy, with big employers like General Dynamics and Texas Instruments and Tandy Radio Shack. It has long been seen as a defensive rival looking over its shoulder at Dallas; now it is entitled to stand up on its own. Other cities have their claims, but the visitor from abroad who wants to see as much as possible of what is quintessentially American would be well advised to fly to the Dallas–Fort Worth Regional Airport and head west to Fort Worth.

Fort Worth also has its political distinction: it is the home of the Speaker of the United States House of Representatives, Jim Wright, and as Fort Worth residents like to tell you of the Speaker of the Texas House of Representatives as well, Gib Lewis: this is the first time in American history that a federal and state speaker come from the same town. After years of being hidden or sulking in the shadow of Dallas, Fort Worth has finally come into its own.

Fort Worth's political heritage is Democratic. In 1954, when Wright was first elected to Congress after beating an anti-labor Democrat in the primary, this was still a dusty blue-collar town, in contrast to white-collar Dallas, which was electing its first Republican congressman the same year. But like the rural Texas where many Fort Worth citizens come from, Fort Worth has been shifting towards Republicans in the 1980s: Fort Worth's Tarrant County was actually 1% more for Ronald Reagan than Dallas County in 1984, and that same year Tarrant joined Dallas in electing the Republican slate to county-wide offices—a revolution in local politics. In 1986 Tarrant was only 2% less for Republican Governor Bill Clements than Dallas. Wright himself had a tough race in 1980, when then Fort Worth Mayor Jim Bradshaw ran against him; but Wright raised $1.2 million and won with 60%. Over the years sympathetic legislatures have shorn some of the more Republican parts of Tarrant County away from Wright's 12th District; currently Arlington and other affluent suburbs to the north are in the 26th district, and some of the heavily Republican neighborhoods in southwest Fort Worth are in the 6th District which stretches south all the way to Houston. That leaves the 12th District with almost all of Fort Worth's blacks and Hispanics, with most of its blue-collar voters, with ordinary white Texans living in neighborhoods sprinkled with shopping centers, small Mexican and barbecue restaurants, and Southern Baptist and fundamentalist churches. But Wright takes no chances. For 1986 he raised more than $1.2 million and spent nearly $1.1 million.

Wright is a man of tense ambition and mellifluous charm, a politician of remarkably unchanging principles over a 40-year public career but with a tendency sometimes to flinch under pressure. For years he seemed to change because the world changed around him: in the 1950s this admirer of Franklin Roosevelt was the most liberal member of the Texas delegation, a young national Democrat among a group of old and mostly conservative nominal members of the party; by the late 1960s he was being scorned by party liberals for his support of public works projects and the Vietnam war. But public works and an interventionist foreign policy had been the heart of Roosevelt's policies. Wright has had severe political setbacks. He lost renomination to the legislature in 1948 when his opponent was murdered days before the primary. He ran for Lyndon Johnson's Senate seat in 1961 and ran third—tantalyzingly close to the second place which would have put him in a runoff with John Tower he probably would have won. He tried for the Senate again in 1966, going on television to ask for $10 contributions, but he didn't get enough to make a statewide race. By the early 1970s this Texan who surely hoped he might follow Lyndon Johnson to the White House some day was reduced to hoping that he might eradicate his 1961 campaign debt and succeed some day to the chairmanship of the House Public Works Committee.

Then in 1976 he ran for House majority leader. He began the race with support from the Texas delegation and many but not all southerners. On the second of the secret ballots he edged out Richard Bolling by two votes; on the third he beat Phillip Burton 148–147. A reform-minded group of Democrats elected the one candidate without distinguished reform credentials. Suddenly Wright was a national leader, spokesman for the Democratic party, in line for the speakership. His relationship with O'Neill turned out to be good; he made peace eventually with his 1976 opponents; he worked hard and often effectively though to find common ground with the majority of House Democrats on issues like energy and foreign policy that tended to separate them. He made his share of missteps along the way, championing and spotlighting the synfuels program which most Democrats eventually voted to kill, switching positions on the MX missile, putting Phil Gramm on the Budget Committee where he ended up sponsoring the Reagan budget cuts. But steadily he consolidated his position until by the middle 1980s it seemed highly unlikely that anyone else would succeed O'Neill. By 1985, when O'Neill announced his retirement, Wright was able to announce that he had a majority of votes; Dan Rostenkowski and John Dingell, aggressive and ambitious men who admitted they'd like the job themselves, declined to run, knowing the vote count.

Wright's major problem as Speaker is that he has big shoes to fill. Tip O'Neill, content to pass a Democratic President's program in the 1970s, found that he had to make Democratic policy in the 1980s—and did it so effectively that Democrats gained rather than lost House seats in the Reagan era. Wright is probably as good as anyone could be in putting together issue positions that can command 218 Democratic votes in the House—like O'Neill, he is not much interested in depending on Republican votes to pass his program. He knows the substance of the issues better than O'Neill and the politics probably as well. He has forged a good relationship with Senate Majority Leader Robert Byrd, who came to the House two years before he did from a district also at the edge of the South; and in their joint appearance in response to the 1987 State of the Union speech Wright showed that he can mold his old-fashioned oratorical style to the medium of television. There were some signs of unsteadiness: his snap decision to allow a roll call on the congressional pay raise, his failure to either prevent or make successful the candidacy of Texan Marvin Leath for the Armed Services chairmanship, his proposal for a tax rate increase which he then skinned back on a bit. But there were also signs—in his leadership on taxes and trade especially—that the new Speaker, a little less visibly than the old because the Senate is now Democratic too, was leading his party toward policies in which he has had long and deep-seated beliefs. Wright's performance as Speaker cannot yet be gauged. But he has begun by setting a demanding and interesting course.

The People: Pop. 1980: 527,715, up 4.7% 1970–80. Households (1980): 73% family, 41% with children, 59% married couples; 36.0% housing units rented; median monthly rent: $204; median house value: $33,500. Voting age pop. (1980): 374,842; 15% Black, 9% Spanish origin.

1984 Presidential Vote:

Reagan (R)	113,047	(58%)
Mondale (D)	80,077	(41%)

Rep. Jim Wright (D)

Elected 1954; b. Dec. 22, 1922, Ft. Worth; home, Ft. Worth; Weatherford Col., U. of TX; Presbyterian; married (Betty).

Career: Army Air Corps, WWII; Partner, trade extension and adv. firm; TX House of Reps., 1947–49; Mayor of Weatherford, 1950–54; Pres., TX League of Municipalities, 1953.

Offices: 1236 LHOB 20515, 202-225-5071. Also 9A10 Lanham Fed. Bldg, 819 Taylor St., Ft. Worth 76102, 817-334-3212; and 536 B Seminary Dr., Ft. Worth 76115, 817-334-4845.

Committees: *The Speaker of the House.*

Group Ratings

	ADA	ACLU	COPE	CFA	LCV	ACU	NTU	NSI	COC	CEI
1986	80	81	76	75	35	14	18	13	31	10
1985	50	—	75	33	—	13	25	—	37	—

National Journal Ratings

	1986 LIB — 1986 CONS			1985 LIB — 1985 CONS		
Economic	87%	—	0%	73%	—	26%
Social	69%	—	31%	68%	—	32%
Foreign	57%	—	43%	61%	—	38%

Key Votes

1) Lmt Cln Water Act	—	5) Retain Gun Cont	FOR	9) Aid Angola Reb	AGN
2) Rpl Tobac Sub	AGN	6) Contra Aid	AGN	10) Tax Reform	AGN
3) Grm-Rdmn Def Red	FOR	7) Lmt Text Imp	FOR	11) S Africa Sanc	FOR
4) Ban Polygraph	—	8) Limit SDI	FOR	12) Immig Reform	FOR

Election Results

1986 general	Jim Wright (D)	84,831	(69%)	($1,098,252)
	Don McNiel (R)	38,620	(31%)	($269,946)
1986 primary	Jim Wright (D)	18,135	(91%)	
	Elizabeth Arnold (D)	1,869	(9%)	
1984 general	Jim Wright (D)	106,299	(100%)	($321,723)

Campaign Contributions and Expenditures

1985-86		Direct Cont. 1985-86		PACS Breakdown 1985-86			
Receipts	$1,237,895	Indiv.	$199,035	Corp.	$324,366	T/M/H	$167,744
Expend.	$1,098,252	PACS	$667,620	Labor	$122,870	Agr.	$7,250
Unspent	$248,314	Cand.	$831,297	Ideo.	$37,790	CWOS	$7,600

THIRTEENTH DISTRICT

As you head west in Texas, the population thins out, the land becomes browner, till you can travel through a whole county where only a few hundred people—plus quite a few more head of cattle—live. And then you go up nearly 1,000 feet of elevation, up the steep gulleys that surround the rivers which are most of the year just a tiny trickle, till you come to the tilted tableland that is the High Plains of west Texas. The winds here sweep down from the Rockies, the land is barren except where it is irrigated, often with the now dangerously depleted waters of the Ogallala Aquifer, but here and there in this demanding environment—sticky-hot in the summer, swept by north winds from Canada in much of the winter—comfortable cities have been built to house the people and businesses that bring forth oil and natural gas and helium and other elements from the earth.

The 13th Congressional District of Texas, the northernmost district in the state, spans all this territory. Its easternmost part, around Wichita Falls, is part of the agricultural land of the Red River Valley. It is dusty land, with empty skylines, afflicted with the woes—low crop and land prices, worse export markets, banks failing because of bad loans—characteristic in the middle 1980s of the Farm Belt. This is white Anglo Texas: few blacks got this far west and few Mexican-Americans go this far north. Population has been declining here not only in the rural counties, but also in the district's second largest city, Wichita Falls, whose population fell below 100,000 in 1980. Wichita Falls is the home of former Senator John Tower, but historically this area, like the entire Red River Valley, has been one of the heartlands of the Democratic party, and some of the sparsely populated counties to the west vote heavily Democratic still.

Up on the High Plains, the economy is different: the economy here is based on minerals. The 13th District's largest city is Amarillo, the home of former oilman and now corporate raider T. Boone Pickens, the helium capital of the world, just 15 miles west of the Pantex plant that builds America's nuclear bombs. It has churches whose members believe that the end of the world is near and nuclear destruction will come soon, and Stanley Marsh 3d who planted a row of 10 Cadillacs nose down in his "Cadillac ranch." Settled partly by people from neighboring northwest Oklahoma and western Kansas, the Panhandle has always been one of the most Republican parts of Texas. Opposition to energy price regulation has strengthened this area's Republicanism, and in national elections it almost seethes hostility toward the Democrats.

The congressman from the 13th District is Beau Boulter, an Amarillo lawyer whose political ambition seems to come from strong religious convictions; he believes in a literal interpretation of the Bible and absolute rights and wrongs. He lost the Republican primary in 1982, but started campaigning against Wichita Falls-based Democrat Jack Hightower (no relation to flamboyant state Agriculture Commissioner Jim Hightower) early, and, blessed with a big Panhandle turnout, won a 53%–47% upset victory. In the House Boulter got a seat on the Budget Committee, an unusual assignment for a freshman; he headed a predictably ineffective Grace Commission Caucus; he sponsored a bill to stop the U.S. from subsidizing foreign agricultural production because it harms American exports.

In many ways he seems politically maladroit, yet usually in ways that help him in the 13th, and especially in traditionally Democratic Wichita Falls. His biggest triumph—"my happiest day was when I was sworn in, but this might be second"—came in October 1986 when the House passed the $560 billion continuing resolution that included $700,000 for the Lake Wichita-Holliday Creek flood control project. Of all the five Republicans who captured Democratic seats in Texas in 1984, Boulter had the weakest opposition in 1986, but this bit of pork, plus his fundraising prowess, probably cinched the election. He lost some of the sparsely-populated counties in the middle of the district, while carrying heavily the rural counties in the northern end of the Panhandle; but what was critical was that he added to the 71% he won in the two counties which contain Amarillo a 64% showing in the county that contains Wichita Falls. That added up to a 65% victory and what looks like a safe seat for this Republican of the religious right—unless a higher wind comes off the High Plains or down the Red River Valley than anyone has seen since the Watergate year of 1974 when Democrat Hightower first won the district.

The People: Pop. 1980: 526,840, up 7.7% 1970–80. Households (1980): 75% family, 39% with children, 66% married couples; 30.0% housing units rented; median monthly rent: $166; median house value: $28,800. Voting age pop. (1980): 376,878; 7% Spanish origin, 5% Black, 1% Asian origin.

1984 Presidential Vote:

Reagan (R)	....	145,536	(72%)
Mondale (D)	....	56,686	(28%)

Rep. Beau Boulter (R)

Elected 1984; b. Feb. 23, 1942, El Paso; home, Amarillo; U. of TX, B.A. 1965, Baylor U., J.D. 1968; Bible Church; married (Rosemary).

Career: Briefing atty., TX Supreme Crt., 1968–69; Amarillo City Commissioner, 1981–83; Practicing atty., 1969–84.

Offices: 124 CHOB 20515, 202-225-3706. Also 205 E. 5th, Amarillo 79101, 806-376-2381; Fed. Bldg., 1000 Lamar, Ste. 208, Wichita Falls 76301, 817-767-0541.

Committees: *Budget* (6th of 14 R). Task Forces: Budget Process; Defense and International Affairs; Economic Policy (Ranking Member). *Government Operations* (9th of 15 R). Subcommittees: Environment, Energy and Natural Resources; Legislation and National Security. *Select Committee on Children, Youth and Families* (10th of 12 R). Task Force: Economic Security.

Group Ratings

	ADA	ACLU	COPE	CFA	LCV	ACU	NTU	NSI	COC	CEI
1986	5	5	7	17	11	90	54	100	89	79
1985	0	—	0	25	—	100	63	—	95	—

National Journal Ratings

	1986 LIB — 1986 CONS			1985 LIB — 1985 CONS		
Economic	19%	—	79%	0%	—	95%
Social	0%	—	89%	0%	—	76%
Foreign	0%	—	86%	0%	—	76%

Key Votes

1) Lmt Cln Water Act	FOR	5) Retain Gun Cont	AGN	9) Aid Angola Reb	FOR
2) Rpl Tobac Sub	FOR	6) Contra Aid	FOR	10) Tax Reform	FOR
3) Grm-Rdmn Def Red	FOR	7) Lmt Text Imp	AGN	11) S Africa Sanc	AGN
4) Ban Polygraph	AGN	8) Limit SDI	AGN	12) Immig Reform	AGN

Election Results

1986 general	Beau Boulter (R)...................... 84,980	(65%)	($744,332)
	Doug Seal (D)........................ 45,907	(35%)	($52,914)
1986 primary	Beau Boulter (R)...................... 17,488	(100%)	
1984 general	Beau Boulter (R)................... 107,600	(53%)	($417,842)
	Jack Hightower (D) 95,367	(47%)	($423,857)

Campaign Contributions and Expenditures

1985-86		Direct Cont. 1985-86		PACS Breakdown 1985-86			
Receipts	$753,243	Indiv.	$499,452	Corp.	$105,047	T/M/H	$71,550
Expend.	$744,332	Party	$15,701	Labor	$250	Agr.	$1,500
		PACS	$202,528	Ideo.	$23,609	CWOS	$572
		Cand.	$500				

FOURTEENTH DISTRICT

Going south from Houston, on the flat coastal plains along the Gulf of Mexico, you come to some of the hottest and most humid places in the United States. These cottonlands were settled well after the more temperate-climated northeast Texas, and they have always been dedicated to market-oriented rather than subsistence farming; the lifeline here is the railroad, with the cotton gin beside it. The coastline, though it has plenty of inlets, never had any important ports in the stretch between Houston and Corpus Christi, until the discovery of oil in this part of Texas made it worthwhile to build channels to ship the oil out.

This is the land of the 14th Congressional District of Texas, an area made up of rural areas, small towns, and a couple of small cities, along the Gulf coast and inland toward the old Texas German country, between Houston and Austin and San Antonio and Corpus Christi. These cotton lands, settled well after the Civil War, don't have very many blacks (11% districtwide); the percentage of Mexican-Americans (20% districtwide) is only average for Texas. You don't find many Mexicans until you get down to Victoria and to the south. This is mostly white Anglo country, ancestrally Democratic except for a couple of counties settled by Texas Germans, who were pro-Union in the Civil War and have remained Republican ever since.

The 14th District has been represented by some odd congressmen: one was beaten in 1978 after a woman staffer charged him with sexual improprieties; his conservative successor retired after he was arrested on homosexual charges in 1979. But it may turn out than none of them was odder than the current incumbent, Republican Mac Sweeney, though no charges of sexual wrongdoing have been made against him. From the outside Sweeney looks like a standard successful young Republican politician. He is young—the second youngest member of Congress, he kept pointing out in his first term—handsome, experienced in Washington, the winner of two campaigns. He beat incumbent Democrat William Patman in 1984 in the ancestrally Democratic 14th; he won over a well financed and nationally promoted challenger in Democratic 1986 in a district with some of the highest unemployment rates in the nation. He won a seat on Armed Services by sitting on colleagues' doorsteps at 6 a.m. to lobby for it.

So far so good. But when you start looking at Sweeney's career, it starts looking peculiar. His 1984 campaign literature highlighted his time at the University of Texas Law School and said his work had been published in the Texas Law Review. But according to *Texas Monthly* he dropped out of law school and never had anything published in the review. The *El Campo Leader-News* charged that he misrepresented his Republican primary opponent's platform in the campaign; he declined to respond. His late fall campaign literature charged that Patman voted for busing. But as Patman pointed out, on the votes Sweeney cited Patman voted against busing. Sweeney criticized Patman for using the congressional frank for a mailing that "thinly disguises his campaign activities." But in February 1986 he sent out a franked mailing that included, as he admitted after a complaint was filed, a campaign picture of him with Vice President Bush and two girls in Sweeney T-shirts. In that same newsletter he admitted that his staff was behind in answering mail, but added, "after some rocky starts and bumps along the way, my staff is driving in high gear now and on smooth roads. The strong and capable people who shape my staff will do good work for the people of South Texas over the next year." Yet in June 1986, when a staffer charged that she had been told to work on his campaign or lose her job—it's a federal criminal offense to force a government employee to perform campaign work—he said, "Most of what we're talking about here is junior staff indiscretions by a young staff." In September he sent out a franked mailer claiming to have co-sponsored five measures, including Jim Wright's major trade bill, that he didn't sign up to co-sponsor until after the piece was submitted to House mailers.

It makes you wonder about just what Sweeney did at the Reagan White House, where he claims to have been director of administrative operations and to have managed a staff of 140 people and a budget of $8 million. He may have benefited in 1984 from a perception that he was an experienced manager and budget-cutter. But his management of campaign finances certainly leaves something to be desired. He had troubles paying back $66,000 in unsecured personal bank loans connected with his first campaign. He raised some $465,000 in the first 18 months of the 1985–86 campaign cycle, but had no campaign headquarters, had $5,400 in cash and debts of $86,000; he raised more than $400,000 more, but that left him not much better than even with his Democratic opponent. He spent $46,000 in campaign funds on a one-day trip by Jack Kemp into the district and raised considerably less. Bad staff work again, presumably.

There is a saying among political consultants that the campaign always reflects the candidate. William Patman, who has every reason to dislike Sweeney, says of him: "He's very flexible. I think he'd be a Chinese Communist if it would further his cause. I don't think you can be in politics long without some measure of integrity, and I think he has none." Sweeney's conduct, or what is known of it so far, raises the serious possibility that this admittedly partisan assessment is accurate. Sweeney's 1986 opponent, attorney Greg Laughlin, was able to win 48% of the vote here even though he had little experience in bigtime campaigns; confronted with charges that he hadn't been working hard, he responded by citing the number of miles he'd put on his car. Sweeney most likely will have serious competition in 1988.

The People: Pop. 1980: 526,920, up 26.0% 1970–80. Households (1980): 77% family, 42% with children, 67% married couples; 28.0% housing units rented; median monthly rent: $153; median house value: $34,900. Voting age pop. (1980): 368,619; 17% Spanish origin, 11% Black.

1984 Presidential Vote: Reagan (R) 139,706   (67%)
                               Mondale (D) 67,157   (32%)

Rep. Mac Sweeney (R)

Elected 1984; b. Sept. 15, 1955, Wharton; home, Wharton; U. of TX, B.A. 1978, U. of TX Sch. of Law, 1979–81; United Methodist; married (Cathy).

Career: Staff asst. to Sen. John Tower, 1977–78; Campaign staff, Connally for President, 1979–80; Dir. of Admin. Operations, White House, 1981–83.

Offices: 1713 LHOB 20515, 202-225-2831. Also 1908 N. Laurent, Ste. 580, Victoria 77901, 512-576-6001.

Committees: *Armed Services* (13th of 21 R). Subcommittees: Investigations; Research and Development. *Merchant Marine and Fisheries* (12th of 17 R). Subcommittees: Fisheries and Wildlife Conservation and the Environment; Merchant Marine; Panama Canal and Outer Continental Shelf.

Group Ratings

	ADA	ACLU	COPE	CFA	LCV	ACU	NTU	NSI	COC	CEI
1986	5	5	10	17	32	86	54	100	94	71
1985	10	—	0	17	—	90	59	—	95	—

National Journal Ratings

	1986 LIB — 1986 CONS	1985 LIB — 1985 CONS
Economic	34% — 66%	5% — 92%
Social	0% — 89%	0% — 76%
Foreign	0% — 86%	0% — 76%

Key Votes

1) Lmt Cln Water Act	FOR	5) Retain Gun Cont	AGN	9) Aid Angola Reb	FOR
2) Rpl Tobac Sub	FOR	6) Contra Aid	FOR	10) Tax Reform	AGN
3) Grm-Rdmn Def Red	FOR	7) Lmt Text Imp	FOR	11) S Africa Sanc	AGN
4) Ban Polygraph	AGN	8) Limit SDI	AGN	12) Immig Reform	AGN

Election Results

1986 general	Mac Sweeney (R)	74,471	(52%)	($883,081)
	Greg Laughlin (D)	67,852	(48%)	($429,672)
1986 primary	Mac Sweeney (R)	13,733	(100%)	
1984 general	Mac Sweeney (R)	104,181	(51%)	($651,532)
	William N. (Bill) Patman (D)	98,885	(49%)	($310,793)

Campaign Contributions and Expenditures

1985–86		Direct Cont. 1985–86		PACS Breakdown 1985–86			
Receipts	$901,176	Indiv.	$499,769	Corp.	$135,280	T/M/H	$76,447
Expend.	$883,081	Party	$13,378	Labor	$7,000	Agr.	$0
Unspent	$23,794	PACS	$273,441	Ideo.	$48,898	CWOS	$5,816
		Cand.	$106,952				

FIFTEENTH DISTRICT

When you get down near the border between the United States and Mexico in the Lower Rio Grande Valley, many of the rules of thumb and statistics that are used to gauge life in the rest of the United States do not apply. The Census Bureau tells us, for example, that the Lower Valley lost population in the 1960s but gained in the 1970s and has lost in some of the 1980s. But those numbers may only mean that at the arbitrary dates the censuses are taken more people found it advantageous to live on this or that side of the border. Oldtimers will tell you that in the 1920s people went back and forth without any official notice at all, and of course today the border remains as easily permeable as the Rio Grande is, in most seasons, fordable.

What about the economy? The Bureau of Labor Statistics says the Lower Valley has some of the nation's highest unemployment—even in years when bank deposits are sharply up. Other sources say incomes are low here. And wages are, compared to the rest of the United States; but compared to most of Mexico, they're generous, and a worker can live quite well on off-the-books money and lavishly from smuggling drugs and other goods—a major industry in some of the smaller counties. Retail sales per capita in the early 1980s were the highest in the country here, but Mexicans flush with oil earnings were shopping in shopping centers in McAllen and the string of towns just north of the river. When the peso started being devalued in 1982, retail sales plummeted; but bank deposits went way up. The valley has had its other woes. An unprecedented freeze in 1983 destroyed many of its citrus trees. But in the middle 1980s it was gaining more and more Winter Texans, retirees and RV owners coming down here to enjoy warm weather (it's as far south as Miami) and lower prices; McAllen calls itself the RV capital of the world.

The border is a place apart; but this side of the border is distinctly American, not Mexican, in its politics and government—even though the large majority of border voters are of Mexican heritage. The pattern of big landowners casting their workers' votes is coming to an end; the most celebrated instance of that was the Parr family holding out the Duval County returns in the 1948 Senate runoff and then reporting 4,622 votes for Lyndon Johnson and 40 for his opponent—enough to give Johnson an 87-vote win statewide. More typical now in the increasingly urban are local Mexican–American political operators and an electorate which, in statewide elections, is willing to consider Republicans as well as Democrats.

The 15th Congressional District of Texas includes much of the Lower Rio Grande Valley, including McAllen and Harlingen, and Hidalgo, Starr, and Zapata Counties along the river. It also goes north, almost as far as San Antonio, although 60% of its population in the 1980 Census was along the border. This is the descendant of a district that in 1948 elected Lloyd Bentsen to the House; his father, Lloyd Bentsen, Sr., came to the valley after World War I with $5 in his pocket and became one of its biggest landowners, remaining active in the business into his 90s.

The current congressman from the 15th District is Eligio (Kika) de la Garza. He came up from poverty, served 12 years in the legislature, was a favorite of the big landowners who was sometimes attacked by Austin-based liberals and militants. His voting record for years was rather conserative; he is somewhat liberal on economic issues and always supported civil rights, but he may be hawkish on foreign policy and rather conservative on cultural issues. This is out of line with many professional Hispanics but meshes well with the views of Mexican-American voters, who tend to be pro-military and culturally traditional. Generally de la Garza is an earnest, pleasant man, who takes the trouble constantly to learn new languages and to surprise foreign visitors by speaking to them in their native tongue.

De la Garza has been chairman of the House Agriculture Committee since 1981—a troubled time for that assignment. He got the chair when Thomas Foley moved up in the leadership and Foley, now Majority Leader, is now off the committee altogether; he may still try to keep an eye on things, however. As chairman, de la Garza has superintended the committee's work on two major farm bills, in 1981 and 1985. These have been melancholy duties: even as spending on farm programs goes up to unprecedented heights, crop prices, land values, and farm exports have been declining disastrously. For years the Democratic party has knitted together Farm Belt politicians who want to use government to bolster the family farmer and urban politicians who want to use government for other purposes, and who have voted for each others' programs. Now on both sides they know that government must pay less. The 1981 farm bill, in a way quite unanticipated by anyone, boosted costs enormously, so much so that de la Garza and everyone else knew that the 1985 bill would have to skin them back, and they did.

De la Garza is not the House's most adept legislative craftsman, but he is not the clumsiest either. He has worked satisfactorily with his subcommittee chairmen, who handle different commodities and problems, and he has done adquately in conference with the Senate (it helps that for four years his Senate counterpart was Jesse Helms, who knows little of the detail in farm programs). To some he seems prone to malapropisms, but there are signs that a shrewd political intelligence is at work beneath—and that Kika, as he is widely called, tends to get what he wants. Results say something, and the 1981 and 1985 farm bills are far better than some things that might have been produced—or the nothing that might have been produced—with other leadership. No opposition has arisen to his chairmanship, and he has been reelected by overwhelming margins in the 15th District.

The People: Pop. 1980: 527,203, up 38.4% 1970–80. Households (1980): 84% family, 54% with children, 71% married couples; 27.8% housing units rented; median monthly rent: $126; median house value: $23,100. Voting age pop. (1980): 329,023; 66% Spanish origin, 1% Black.

1984 Presidential Vote:

Mondale (D)	90,082	(54%)
Reagan (R)	77,846	(46%)

Rep. E (Kika) de la Garza (D)

Elected 1964; b. Sept. 22, 1927, Mercedes; home, Mission; Edinburg Jr. Col., St. Mary's U., San Antonio, LL.B. 1952; Roman Catholic; married (Lucille).

Career: Navy, WWII, Army, Korea; Practicing atty., 1952–64; TX House of Reps., 1952–64.

Offices: 1401 LHOB 20515, 202-225-2531. Also 1418 Beech St., McAllen 78501, 512-682-5545; and Alice Fed. Bldg., Rm. 210, 401 E. 2d St., Alice 78332, 512-664-2215.

Committees: *Agriculture* (Chairman of 26 D).

Group Ratings

	ADA	ACLU	COPE	CFA	LCV	ACU	NTU	NSI	COC	CEI
1986	55	50	60	42	49	27	20	33	39	15
1985	60	—	58	50	—	24	25	—	20	—

National Journal Ratings

	1986 LIB — 1986 CONS		1985 LIB — 1985 CONS	
Economic	87% —	0%	71% —	29%
Social	35% —	64%	53% —	46%
Foreign	51% —	49%	49% —	50%

Key Votes

1) Lmt Cln Water Act	AGN	5) Retain Gun Cont	AGN	9) Aid Angola Reb	AGN
2) Rpl Tobac Sub	AGN	6) Contra Aid	AGN	10) Tax Reform	AGN
3) Grm-Rdmn Def Red	AGN	7) Lmt Text Imp	FOR	11) S Africa Sanc	FOR
4) Ban Polygraph	AGN	8) Limit SDI	FOR	12) Immig Reform	AGN

Election Results

1986 general	E (Kika) de la Garza (D)	70,777	(100%)	($141,973)
1986 primary	E (Kika) de la Garza (D)	52,354	(100%)	
1984 general	E (Kika) de la Garza (D)	104,863	(100%)	($126,004)

Campaign Contributions and Expenditures

1985-86		Direct Cont. 1985-86		PACS Breakdown 1985-86			
Receipts	$169,003	Indiv.	$32,385	Corp.	$36,000	T/M/H	$56,050
Expend.	$141,973	PACS	$131,900	Labor	$7,950	Agr.	$19,950
Unspent	$127,733			Ideo.	$3,450	CWOS	$8,500

SIXTEENTH DISTRICT

North America's largest border city, perhaps the largest border city in the world, is the city known as El Paso in Texas and Juarez in Mexico. Other American border cities owe their prominence to other factors: San Diego to the Navy, Detroit to autos, Buffalo to grain-shipping and steel. El Paso and Juarez would be little more than crossroads without the border. The Spaniards started a town here because this is where the Rio Grande comes through big mountains on either side—hence El Paso Del Norte—but as late as the end of World War II there were only a little more than 100,000 people on the U.S. side of the border and fewer on the Mexican. Not so any more. For 1986 El Paso County is estimated to have some 525,000 residents and Juarez 838,000.

They live in physical isolation—a kind of heavily populated island in the midst of a vast sea of sand. From El Paso it is more than 600 miles east to Dallas–Fort Worth and 400 west to Phoenix; the smaller urban centers of Albuquerque and Chihuahua are 260 miles north and 230 miles south. El Paso's economy depends on government —there are big military bases here—and low-wage labor; it manufactures a lot of apparel for people hundreds and thousands of miles distant. In the 1970s there was a much publicized strike against the Farah slacks company, and it was supported by the Catholic archbishop. Juarez's economy increasingly depends on the maquiladoria plants which enable U.S. and foreign (especially Japanese) firms to assemble products in Mexico but sell them duty-free in the U.S. market: even lower wage labor than in El Paso. To a north-of-the-border eye, life for most people in El Paso and Juarez looks pretty mean. Yet the huge migration from other parts of Mexico is mute evidence that this represents a significant improvement for most of the people here.

The 16th Congressional District of Texas is made up of El Paso and several desert counties to the east; 91% of the 16th's votes are in El Paso County and Loving County, out in the desert, is America's lowest-population county with only 91 people in 1980 (but 113 registered voters in 1986: it's growing), and the town of Langtry, where Judge Roy Bean once held court as the only law west of the Pecos. Politics here is very much divided on ethnic lines: most Anglos vote Republican in any contested race, almost all Mexican-Americans Democratic. The census-takers say there is an Hispanic majority here, but many are not citizens. For years the border has been porous, and many workers cross it every day to go to work, in both directions. But the employer sanctions in the 1986 immigration reform law, plus the record high levels of the Rio Grande in early 1987 may cut immigration down to a trickle in the part of the continent where the term "wetback" originated.

The congressman from the 16th District is Ron Coleman, a Democrat with an aggressive personality, an old-fashioned Texas Anglo personal style and a voting record which means that most of his votes are cast by Hispanics. In a House where members try to please everyone in their districts, Coleman is not afraid to antagonize some in his—which may just be good politics, since the district is polarized anyway. He was the attorney for the Farah strikers, and he served 10 years in the legislature, where he didn't mind tangling with the conservative House speaker. He gets along better with the Democratic leadership in Washington, though he's not always a reliable vote for them. In his first term Coleman had a seat on the Armed Services Committee—a local asset, since the Fort Bliss Military Reservation is one of the mainstays of El Paso's economy. He competed with Mike Andrews of Houston to be the Texas candidate for a vacant Democratic seat on Ways and Means after the 1984 election, but the seat ultimately went to someone else. But Coleman converted the loss to a victory, by getting a seat on Appropriations instead; his first subcommittee assignment there was Military Construction, whose potential for district service need not be explained.

With his rather controversial politics, Coleman had some difficulty winning this seat when conservative Democrat Richard White retired in 1982; his task was complicated by the presence of a Mexican-American candidate in the initial Democratic primary. But Coleman had a strong enough base to lead with 33% in the first primary, and he had enough Mexican-American turnout to beat a conservative Democrat in the runoff, and to get 54% against a Republican heavily supported by the national party in the general. In 1984 he was reelected with 57% of the vote; Ronald Reagan, with some appeal to Hispanics was carrying El Paso comfortably, but Republican Senate candidate Phil Gramm lost it to liberal Democrat Lloyd Doggett. In 1986 Coleman again had vociferous Republican opposition, but in a more Democratic year got 66%, for the first time breaking heavily, perhaps with the help of his Appropriations seat, into the Anglo Republican base.

The People: Pop. 1980: 527,401, up 29.9% 1970–80. Households (1980): 81% family, 53% with children, 66% married couples; 39.3% housing units rented; median monthly rent: $158; median house value: $36,800. Voting age pop. (1980): 341,560; 55% Spanish origin, 4% Black, 1% Asian origin.

1984 Presidential Vote:

Reagan (R)	75,896	(57%)
Mondale (D)	57,337	(43%)

Rep. Ronald D. Coleman (D)

Elected 1982; b. Nov. 29, 1941, El Paso; home, El Paso; U. of TX, B.A. 1963, J.D. 1967; U. of Kent, England, 1981; Presbyterian; married (Tammy).

Career: Army, 1967–69; Teacher, El Paso public schools, TX Schl. for the Deaf; Asst. El Paso Cnty. Atty., 1969; First Asst. El Paso Cnty. Atty., 1971; TX House of Reps., 1973–82.

Offices: 416 CHOB 20515, 202-225-4831. Also 146 U.S. Crthse., El Paso 79901, 915-541-7650; and U.S.P.O. Bldg., Rm. 304, Pecos 79772, 915-445-6218.

Committees: *Appropriations* (34th of 35 D). Subcommittees: Military Construction; Treasury–Postal Service–General Government.

Group Ratings

	ADA	ACLU	COPE	CFA	LCV	ACU	NTU	NSI	COC	CEI
1986	70	65	83	67	68	35	23	40	56	21
1985	60	—	83	58	—	19	25	—	33	—

National Journal Ratings

	1986 LIB — 1986 CONS		1985 LIB — 1985 CONS	
Economic	58% —	41%	65% —	33%
Social	49% —	49%	81% —	15%
Foreign	51% —	48%	54% —	45%

Key Votes

1) Lmt Cln Water Act	AGN	5) Retain Gun Cont	AGN	9) Aid Angola Reb	AGN
2) Rpl Tobac Sub	AGN	6) Contra Aid	AGN	10) Tax Reform	AGN
3) Grm-Rdmn Def Red	FOR	7) Lmt Text Imp	FOR	11) S Africa Sanc	FOR
4) Ban Polygraph	AGN	8) Limit SDI	AGN	12) Immig Reform	AGN

Election Results

1986 general	Ronald D. Coleman (D)	50,590	(66%)	($511,094)
	Roy Gillia (R)	26,421	(34%)	($538,622)
1986 primary	Ronald D. Coleman (D)	26,722	(100%)	
1984 general	Ronald D. Coleman (D)	76,375	(57%)	($421,140)
	Jack Hammond (R)	56,589	(43%)	($212,892)

Campaign Contributions and Expenditures

1985-86		Direct Cont. 1985-86		PACS Breakdown 1985-86			
Receipts	$518,723	Indiv.	$202,911	Corp.	$62,227	T/M/H	$59,624
Expend.	$511,094	Party	$9,999	Labor	$118,100	Agr.	$5,100
Unspent	$11,123	PACS	$298,801	Ideo.	$49,750	CWOS	$4,000
		Cand.	$56,300				

SEVENTEENTH DISTRICT

From Fort Worth west to the horizon and past stretches the 17th Congressional District of Texas. Here are thousands and thousands of acres of arid farming and grazing land punctuated occasionally by oases of irrigated farmland (often in those circles that show the reach of the sprinklers). The 17th is primarily cattle country, although there is some oil here and some raising of cotton and grain. Its largest city is Abilene, with 98,000 people. As is usually the case in Texas, the town is more conservative than the countryside; all the bankers, lawyers, and professionals are concentrated in the town, as well as all the men who congregate in the local Petroleum Club, where they discuss the state of the world while watching the sunset out the window of one of Abilene's few several-storied buildings. Like most of central Texas, this area was settled originally by southerners who brought their Democratic politics with them, and it remained pretty solidly Democratic up through 1978. In 1980 it shifted sharply to the Republicans, back to the Democrats in 1982, then back to the Republicans in 1984 and 1986 when Governor Mark White carried only two sparsely populated counties in the western edge of the 17th and lost 33.

The congressman from the 17th is Charles Stenholm, a conservative Democrat who became one of the more prominent members of his party in the early 1980s even though he was first elected only in 1978 and has no penchant for self-promotion in Washington. This was a seat the Republicans had hoped to get when ultraconservative Democrat Omar Burleson retired after serving 32 years. But Stenholm, active in Democratic party affairs and in the Rolling Plains Cotton Growers Association, won the seat handily. As soon as he hit Washington, where Democrats think a lot different from those in Abilene or his home town of Stamford (also the home town of Democratic megaleader Robert Strauss), he started complaining. He complained, correctly, that southern conservatives were not getting good committee assignments in 1978 and that Democratic leaders, used to 2 to 1 majorities, didn't care much about them. But when the Democrats lost badly in 1980 Stenholm and those like him got more leverage. They got Jim Wright to put Phil Gramm on the Budget Committee, they supported Gramm and voted for the Reagan budget and tax cuts, they became known as the Boll Weevils and formed a group called the Conservative Democratic Forum, for which Stenholm served as spokesman.

After the Democrats gained seats in the 1982 election, Stenholm and his friends on one side and the Democratic leaders on the other grew more conciliatory. But in 1984 he was visibly discontented with the national party's direction, and after the election he threatened momentarily to run against Speaker O'Neill—and got O'Neill to promise to give Democrats like him full representation in the Caucus. Yet over what is getting to be a long congressional career, he finds himself pretty much committed to remaining a Democrat. It makes great political sense in this district: as a Republican Stenholm could win a general election here, but he would have in most years what he doesn't have now, serious political opposition. In the House, he is advancing in seniority on the Agriculture Committee, which is his chief substantive legislative interest, and he has managed to avoid alienating other Democrats by working with them often and by never going behind their backs to deal surreptitiously with the Republicans as Gramm did.

The People: Pop. 1980: 526,913, up 9.3% 1970–80. Households (1980): 76% family, 38% with children, 67% married couples; 27.3% housing units rented; median monthly rent: $144; median house value: $25,900. Voting age pop. (1980): 380,499; 9% Spanish origin, 3% Black.

1984 Presidential Vote:

Reagan (R) 141,365	(68%)
Mondale (D) 65,558	(32%)

Rep. Charles W. Stenholm (D)

Elected 1978; b. Oct. 26, 1938, Stamford; home, Avoca; Tarleton St. Jr. Col., 1959, TX Tech. U., B.S. 1961; M.S. 1962; Lutheran; married (Cynthia).

Career: Teacher, vocational agriculture, 1962–65; Exec. Vice Pres., Rolling Plaines Cotton Growers, 1965–68; Mgr., Stamford Electric Coop., 1968–76; Farmer, 1976–78.

Offices: 1226 LHOB 20515, 202-225-6605. Also 903 E. Hamilton St., Stamford 79553, 915-773-3623; and 341 Pine St., Abilene 79604, 915-673-7221.

Committees: *Agriculture* (11th of 26 D). Subcommittees: Cotton, Rice, and Sugar; Department Operations, Research and Foreign Agriculture; Livestock, Dairy and Poultry (Chairman); Tobacco and Peanuts. *Veterans Affairs* (16th of 21 D). Subcommittees: Education, Training and Employment; Hospitals and Health Care.

Group Ratings

	ADA	ACLU	COPE	CFA	LCV	ACU	NTU	NSI	COC	CEI
1986	5	5	16	17	21	81	57	100	78	63
1985	20	—	15	0	—	90	60	—	86	—

National Journal Ratings

	1986 LIB — 1986 CONS		1985 LIB — 1985 CONS	
Economic	34% —	66%	29% —	70%
Social	11% —	85%	0% —	76%
Foreign	27% —	70%	24% —	66%

Key Votes

1) Lmt Cln Water Act	FOR	5) Retain Gun Cont	FOR	9) Aid Angola Reb	FOR
2) Rpl Tobac Sub	AGN	6) Contra Aid	FOR	10) Tax Reform	AGN
3) Grm-Rdmn Def Red	FOR	7) Lmt Text Imp	FOR	11) S Africa Sanc	AGN
4) Ban Polygraph	AGN	8) Limit SDI	FOR	12) Immig Reform	AGN

Election Results

1986 general	Charles W. Stenholm (D) 97,791	(100%)	($217,744)
1986 primary	Charles W. Stenholm (D) 44,490	(100%)	
1984 general	Charles W. Stenholm (D) 143,012	(100%)	($207,943)

Campaign Contributions and Expenditures

1985-86		Direct Cont. 1985-86		PACS Breakdown 1985-64			
Receipts	$225,411	Indiv.	$101,973	Corp.	$41,000	T/M/H	$43,890
Expend.	$217,744	Party	$155	Labor	$0	Agr.	$7,000
Unspent	$200,152	PACS	$9,190	Ideo.	$1,800	CWOS	$1,500

EIGHTEENTH DISTRICT

Radiating outward in every direction from the off-of-compass grid of Houston's downtown is the 18th Congressional District of Texas. Like most American downtowns, Houston's is only lightly populated; the affluent people who make their livings here escape home each night out Memorial Drive or the always-clogged Katy or Southwest Freeways. The 18th District, which goes east beyond the Houston Ship Channel's Turning Basin, south to Loop 610, west to the edge of ultrarich River Oaks and Memorial Park and far north, in some places past the city limits, toward Houston Intercontinental Airport, is Houston's minority district. It was created after the 1970 Census for then state Senator Barbara Jordan, famed later for her performance in the House Judiciary Committee impeachment hearings and as one of the Democrats' 1976 keynoters; within its current boundaries, in 1980 41% of its residents were black and 31% of Spanish origin, with very little overlap. The number of Mexican-Americans has been rising in the inner-city neighborhoods, as a result of heavy immigration in the 1970s; blacks have been moving outward, mostly to the north.

This is a very different part of Houston from the gleaming west side, although the districts are right next to each other. Like many rapidly growing cities in developing countries, Houston seems to have great disparities of income and wealth. While entrepreneurs were getting rich in the oil business and buying $750,000 houses off Westheimer and Memorial Drive, many black and Mexican-American residents live east and south of downtown in unpainted frame houses full of cracks wide enough to let in Houston's humid, smoggy air. The Houston slums look like something out of the sharecropper 1930s, and they remind us that although this was until recently one of our fastest-growing cities, its growth is based in large part on the availability of cheap labor. Yet there has been plenty of upward mobility here. Moving north in the 18th District, you find solid working- and middle-class neighborhoods, some even with a touch of grandeur from when their houses were built many years ago. Politically, Houston's black neighborhoods may be the most Democratic territory in the entire United States, just as the west side neighborhoods are among the most Republican. Election results depend on who outvotes whom. In 1978, 1980, and 1984 the rich turned out in large numbers and with great enthusiasm and swept Texas for the Republicans. In mayor's races in the 1980s blacks and Mexican-Americans have turned out and helped elect liberal Kathy Whitmire; in 1982 they turned out heavily enough to elect Democrats Mark White and Lloyd Bentsen, and in 1986 they turned out heavily for White again; if his showing statewide had sagged as little as it did in greater Houston, he would have been reelected.

The congressman from the 18th District since 1978 has been Mickey Leland, who has turned out, contrary to expectations, to be an active legislator. Leland started off in politics as a dashiki-clad militant; now he is a Giorgio Armani-clad committee chairman. In his first term he snagged a seat on the Energy and Commerce Committee, the hot committee in most of the 1980s because of all the regulatory work it handles. He serves on the Telecommunications and Health subcommittees, where he has pushed for pet causes like getting more blacks on TV programs and lifeline phone rates for senior citizens. Leland also serves on the Post Office and Civil Service Committee, where he chairs a subcommittee. He served during the 99th Congress as chairman of the Congressional Black Caucus. Yet he was one of the few black politicians with the inclination and nerve to have backed Walter Mondale over Jesse Jackson in the 1984 presidential primaries.

His most visible assignment in this and the last Congress was as chairman of the Select Committee on Hunger he helped set up. He got it in place just as Americans began focusing on famine in Ethiopia and other African countries, and got Congress to spend $800 million for aid to sub-Saharan nations. But like most congressmen he has been slow to criticize the Marxist government of Ethiopia whose policies helped create the famine and exacerbated it; maybe he remained silent prudently, to get as much food as possible to the starving. Leland has also criticized the Reagan Administration for not doing enough for the hungry and homeless in the United States and wants to spend $4 billion on health care and housing for the latter. Some see him as a grandstander: he was one of the congressmen who spent a night outside in winter 1987 to show their sympathy for the homeless. But he can also provide vivid testimony of what is happening in the world outside the committee room, as when he describes how he saw a starved 14-year-old Ethiopian girl die before his eyes.

Leland is an individual, even an eccentric, Congress's closest personal acquaintance of Fidel Castro and a booster of the Houston economy. As a young man he ran into the barriers of segregation, now he not only serves but also exercises power in Congress. Incidentally, he is a licensed pharmacist, the most prominent in American politics since Hubert Humphrey.

The People: Pop. 1980: 527,393, dn. 5.9% 1970–80. Households (1980): 65% family, 39% with children, 46% married couples; 57.2% housing units rented; median monthly rent: $185; median house value: $31,900. Voting age pop. (1980): 366,424; 39% Black, 27% Spanish origin, 1% Asian origin.

1984 Presidential Vote: Mondale (D) 103,082   (72%)
                              Reagan (R) 39,242   (28%)

Rep. Mickey Leland (D)

Elected 1978; b. Nov. 27, 1944, Lubbock; home, Houston; TX Southern U., B.S. 1970; Roman Catholic; married (Alison).

Career: Instructor, TX St. U., 1970–71; Dir. of Spec. Development Projects, Hermann Hosp., 1971–78; TX House of Reps., 1973–78.

Offices: 2236 RHOB 20515, 202-225-3816. Also 1919 Smith, Ste. 820, Houston 77002, 713-739-7339.

Committees: *Energy and Commerce* (10th of 25 D). Subcommittees: Energy and Power; Health and the Environment; Telecommunications and Finance. *Post Office and Civil Service* (6th of 14 D). Subcommittees: Compensation and Employee Benefits; Postal Operations and Services (Chairman). *Select Committee on Hunger* (Chairman of 16 D). Task Forces: Domestic Task Force; International Task Force.

Group Ratings

	ADA	ACLU	COPE	CFA	LCV	ACU	NTU	NSI	COC	CEI
1986	100	95	94	67	79	0	27	0	12	9
1985	100	—	95	75	—	0	31	—	10	—

National Journal Ratings

	1986 LIB — 1986 CONS	1985 LIB — 1985 CONS
Economic	87% — 0%	89% — 0%
Social	81% — 17%	85% — 0%
Foreign	80% — 0%	92% — 0%

Key Votes

1) Lmt Cln Water Act	AGN	5) Retain Gun Cont	FOR	9) Aid Angola Reb	AGN
2) Rpl Tobac Sub	AGN	6) Contra Aid	AGN	10) Tax Reform	AGN
3) Grm-Rdmn Def Red	AGN	7) Lmt Text Imp	FOR	11) S Africa Sanc	FOR
4) Ban Polygraph	FOR	8) Limit SDI	FOR	12) Immig Reform	AGN

Election Results

1986 general	Mickey Leland (D)	63,335	(90%)	($207,419)
	Joanne Kuniansky (I)	6,884	(10%)	
1986 primary	Mickey Leland (D)	17,895	(91%)	
	Dorothy K. Stephans (D)	1,706	(9%)	
1984 general	Mickey Leland (D)	109,626	(79%)	($207,947)
	Glen E. Beaman (R)	26,400	(19%)	

Campaign Contributions and Expenditures

1985-86		Direct Cont. 1985-86		PACS Breakdown 1985-86			
Receipts	$217,214	Indiv.	$49,619	Corp.	$49,612	T/M/H	$45,750
Expend.	$207,419	Party	$102	Labor	$45,239	Agr.	$2,300
Unspent	$20,407	PACS	$157,318	Ideo.	$10,517	CWOS	$3,900
		Cand.	$700				

NINETEENTH DISTRICT

Up on the High Plains of Texas, on land separated from the dusty cattlelands further east by rising gullies astride wide river courses, is some of the most productive cotton and wheat land in the United States, centered around the city of Lubbock. This fertility is a triumphant work of man: for this is irrigated land, which gets its water from the giant Ogallala Aquifer that undergirds so much of the western Great Plains, making this part of Texas a sort of green island in a vast brown sea of arid grazing land, to the east, west, north, and south. It was settled relatively late, with most of the growth after World War II; Lubbock grew from 31,000 in 1940 to 128,000 in 1960 and 173,000 in 1980. But in the 1980s the growth seems to have stopped. There are signs the aquifer is going dry, and some irrigated land has had to be abandoned to sagebrush. Low crop and cattle prices have made the area part of ailing agricultural America.

The 19th Congressional District of Texas includes Lubbock and most of the agricultural counties around it, just east of the New Mexican border. It also stretches north to Deaf Smith County, where the government wants to dispose of nuclear waste in a cavern 2,600 feet deep in the Palo Duro Basin, and south to the Permian Basin, where oil and gas reserves were first developed in the 1950s. The 19th includes Odessa, more roughneck of the two main Permian Basin towns, which houses many of the technically skilled men who do the gritty, sweaty work of making the oil rigs work and getting the oil to the surface; just over the line in the 21st District is Midland, more white-collar, a kind of rich suburb in the midst of the desert.

In almost every kind of politics, this is Republican territory. People here may not be rich—in the middle 1980s, many of them were hurting economically—but they still prefer the risks of the free enterprise system (modulated by a little help for oil and irrigation, to be sure) to a fully articulated welfare state, and the traditional values of Bible-reading Christianity are still the guideposts for most people here. Even so, the 19th District has had a Republican congressman only since 1984. For 44 years it was represented by Democrat George Mahon, who chaired the Appropriations Committee his last 14 years in the House. In 1978 it was won by Kent Hance, a Democrat adept enough to beat Midland oilman George W. Bush, son of the Vice President. Too adept, as it turned out: Hance co-sponsored the Reagan tax cut in 1981, then begged to be let back in the Democrats' good graces after they gained seats in 1982, lost the 1984 Democratic Senate runoff by a 51%–49% margin, and then switched parties and running for governor got only 20% in the Republican primary.

The current congressman, Larry Combest, had to win a tough primary, runoff, and general election to get to Congress, but now seems as safely ensconced there as a Republican in an economically ailing district can be. Combest's specialty is agriculture (though professionally he was an electronics distributor rather than a farmer). He worked on agriculture issues for seven years on Senator John Tower's staff (whose alumni seem to include most of the Texas

Republican delegation) and got a seat on the Agriculture Committee his first term. There he started off with a good knowledge of farm programs and opposed Reagan Administration policy on occasion; otherwise he voted a pretty straight conservative line. In 1986 despite opposition from a veteran of the 1970s farmers' tractorcade to Washington, queasiness about the proposed nuclear dump in Deaf Smith County, and the general nationwide Democratic trend, Combest increased his percentage from 1984's 58% to 1986's 62%. Oddly, for all his emphasis on agricultural issues, he ran even or behind in the agricultural counties around Lubbock; but he won in Lubbock with 69% and Odessa with 70%, and between them that's where most (63%) of the district's votes are. So in all likelihood Combest has a safe seat.

The People: Pop. 1980: 527,805, up 15.2% 1970–80. Households (1980): 77% family, 45% with children, 68% married couples; 34.7% housing units rented; median monthly rent: $191; median house value: $33,200. Voting age pop. (1980): 360,942; 20% Spanish origin, 5% Black.

1984 Presidential Vote:

Reagan (R)	133,422	(75%)
Mondale (D)	44,562	(25%)

Rep. Larry Combest (R)

Elected 1984; b. Mar. 20, 1945, Memphis; home, Lubbock; West TX St. U., B.B.A. 1969; United Methodist; married (Sharon).

Career: Farmer; teacher, 1970–71; Dir., U.S. Agric. Stabilization and Conserv. Svc., Graham, TX, 1971; Aide to U.S. Sen. John Tower, 1971–78; Founder and Pres., Combest Distributing Co., 1978–1985.

Offices: 1529 LHOB 20515, 202-225-4005. Also 613 Fed. Bldg., 1205 Texas Ave., Lubbock 79401, 806-763-1611; and 3419 W. 4th St., Rm. 601, Odessa 79761, 915-337-1669.

Committees: *Agriculture* (13th of 17 R). Subcommittees: Conservation, Credit and Rural Development; Cotton, Rice and Sugar; Tobacco and Peanuts. *District of Columbia* (4th of 4 R). Subcommittees: Government Operations and Metropolitan Affairs (Ranking Member); Judiciary. *Small Business* (12th of 17 R). Subcommittees: Energy and Agriculture; Regulation and Business Opportunities.

Group Ratings

	ADA	ACLU	COPE	CFA	LCV	ACU	NTU	NSI	COC	CEI
1986	5	5	10	8	26	91	59	100	94	79
1985	5	—	0	8	—	100	62	—	91	—

National Journal Ratings

	1986 LIB — 1986 CONS		1985 LIB — 1985 CONS	
Economic	19% —	79%	5% —	92%
Social	0% —	89%	0% —	76%
Foreign	14% —	84%	0% —	76%

Key Votes

1) Lmt Cln Water Act	FOR	5) Retain Gun Cont	AGN	9) Aid Angola Reb	FOR
2) Rpl Tobac Sub	AGN	6) Contra Aid	FOR	10) Tax Reform	AGN
3) Grm-Rdmn Def Red	FOR	7) Lmt Text Imp	FOR	11) S Africa Sanc	AGN
4) Ban Polygraph	AGN	8) Limit SDI	AGN	12) Immig Reform	AGN

Election Results

1986 general	Larry Combest (R)	68,695	(62%)	($317,265)
	Gerald McCathern (D)	42,129	(38%)	($112,732)
1986 primary	Larry Combest (R)	26,735	(100%)	
1984 general	Larry Combest (R)	102,805	(58%)	($428,247)
	Don R. Richards (D)	74,044	(42%)	($237,022)
	Tom Schaefer (R)	1,624	(14%)	

Campaign Contributions and Expenditures

1985-86		Direct Cont. 1985-86		PACS Breakdown 1985-86			
Receipts	$318,347	Indiv.	$155,357	Corp.	$70,119	T/M/H	$52,550
Expend.	$317,265	Party	$6,671	Labor	$0	Agr.	$9,297
		PACS	$140,136	Ideo.	$7,250	CWOS	$920
		Cand.	$1,055				

TWENTIETH DISTRICT

San Antonio sits at the frontier: not on the banks of the Rio Grande, but on that invisible line separating territory that is on the one side mostly Hispanic and on the other mostly Anglo. It has been at the frontier for a long time: San Antonio was the most important town in Texas when it was part of Mexico, and it was here that Santa Ana and his troops wiped out Davy Crockett, Jim Bowie, and 184 others at the Alamo in 1836. (Crockett was a Tennessee congressman from 1827–31 and 1833–35; if he had not lost his bid for reelection in 1835, he never would have left Tennessee for Texas.) Today San Antonio is Texas's third largest city, with 842,000 people and a metropolitan population over one million. That's only one-third the size of metropolitan Dallas–Fort Worth or Houston; but San Antonio in the 1980s has been a boom town in its own right. The local economy has been based not on oil but on government: this is one of America's prime military towns, with Fort Sam Houston, Brooks Aero Medical Center, and three Air Force bases, with tens of thousands of military personnel and employees. Mayor Henry Cisneros has built on that base by linking San Antonio with Austin, 70 miles north, and promoting them together as high tech centers; at the same time San Antonio has the advantages of the low wages of a border city.

It also has the advantage of having its own special atmosphere. A block from the Alamo the Riverway along the little San Antonio River is lined with overhanging trees and with pleasant shops and restaurants below street traffic. Nearby is the Hemisfair, preserved from the 1972 World's Fair here. San Antonio has ancient buildings from its Spanish days and old neighborhoods redolent of the Texas Germans who were its chief Anglo citizens for many years. On the west side, beginning with the bare-tabled Mexican restaurants in the market area, San Antonio is a Mexican-American city, with an Hispanic majority. There is all the potential here for angry clashes between Hispanics and Anglos, and in partisan elections they vote quite differently.

But Cisneros, since his first election in 1981, has declined to engage in confrontational politics, and has instead emphasized economic growth and planning together. He has helped spearhead the Westover Hills development where Pope John Paul II agreed to appear in September 1987 and which will get a new Sea World the next year—which will help make San Antonio Texas's top tourist destination. Cisneros's success has given him such strong support all over town that he was reelected in 1987 with 67% of the vote. Cisneros is one of the brightest young Democrats in the country, and was on the short list of possible Democratic vice-presidential candidates in 1984; he served on the Kissinger Commission on Central America that recommended against American withdrawal there; in a 1987 statewide poll he received more favorable ratings than any other Texas politician tested. He seems to reflect the interests of Hispanic-Americans better than the leaders of many of the more militant organizations; he sees that Hispanics in the U.S. are upwardly mobile and will benefit from economic growth, and he understands, too, that Latin

Americans will in the long run be better off with governments the United States can support than with the kind of regime Fidel Castro has imposed on Cuba.

The 20th Congressional District of Texas includes the central part of San Antonio, leaving the mostly Anglo northern fringes and suburbs as part of the 21st District and the southern fringes and suburbs on three sides as part of the 23d. More than 60% of the residents of the current 20th, according to the 1980 Census, are Mexican-American, and so the 20th is a national Democratic district in every election.

The congressman here is Henry B. Gonzalez, first elected in 1961, when Mexican-American politicians were far less common than they are now; in those days he was the patron saint of Texas liberalism. Later in the late 1960s and early 1970s he alienated liberals by supporting the Vietnam war effort and Hispanic activists by heaping scorn on them. His stubbornness—or adherence to principle—seems vindicated now: our abandonment of the Vietnam war produced a result few of its opponents are proud of, and Gonzalez's policies, rather than the separatist impulses of the activists of the 1960s, assimilation rather than polarization, seem to be the wave of the future. Mexican-Americans are rapidly becoming a part—and a successful part—of the larger American society, bringing some of their traditions with them but embracing the wider culture. People from other parts of the country find it odd, but most Mexican-Americans here speak English with a Texas accent.

Gonzalez's course in Congress has been erratic. He is prickly and quick to take offense, as he showed in the fight he got into when he quit as chairman of the House committee investigating the Kennedy and King assassinations; he does not find it easy to compromise or wheel and deal. He has had his successes: the poll tax, which he opposed early, is long gone. He is the second-ranking Democrat on the Banking, Finance and Urban Affairs Committee, but has never gotten comfortable dealing with the international lending agencies, though he chaired a subcommittee on their programs for years, and has not gotten much involved in banking problems. In his sixth year chairing the Housing subcommittee, he did get a housing bill in 1986, but it contained measures—like spending all public housing money on renovation, not new construction—that infuriated him. There was some talk about ousting Chairman Fernand St Germain who has been the subject of charges before the ethics committee, but few Democrats were eager either to promote or to pass over Gonzalez. His temper still comes out: he took a swing in 1963 at Texas Republican Ed Foreman when he accused him of being a Communist; in 1986 he punched a 40-year-old man in a San Antonio restaurant for the same offense—one which must particularly rankle a man who has served his country loyally and long.

Gonzalez has become something of a civic institution in San Antonio and has no trouble winning reelection.

The People: Pop. 1980: 526,333, dn. 5.8% 1970–80. Households (1980): 75% family, 45% with children, 56% married couples; 42.5% housing units rented; median monthly rent: $142; median house value: $23,500. Voting age pop. (1980): 358,798; 56% Spanish origin, 9% Black, 1% Asian origin.

1984 Presidential Vote: Mondale (D) 83,214   (59%)
                                  Reagan (R) 58,751   (41%)

Rep. Henry B. Gonzalez (D)

Elected Nov. 4, 1961; b. May 3, 1916, San Antonio; home, San Antonio; San Antonio Col., U. of TX, St. Mary's U., San Antonio, LL.B. 1943; Roman Catholic; married (Bertha).

Career: Bexar Cnty. Chf. Probation Officer, 1946; Dpty. Dir., San Antonio Housing Authority, 1950–51; San Antonio City Cncl., 1953–56, Mayor Pro Tem, 1955–56; TX Senate, 1956–61.

Offices: 2413 RHOB 20515, 202-225-3236. Also B-124 Fed. Bldg., 727 E. Durango St., San Antonio 78206, 512-229-6195.

Committees: *Banking, Finance and Urban Affairs* (2d of 31 D). Subcommittees: Consumer Affairs and Coinage; Financial Institutions Supervision, Regulation and Insurance; General Oversight and Investigations; Housing and Community Development (Chairman). *Small Business* (3d of 27 D). Subcommittees: Antitrust, Impact of Deregulation and Privatization; Regulation and Business Opportunities.

Group Ratings

	ADA	ACLU	COPE	CFA	LCV	ACU	NTU	NSI	COC	CEI
1986	95	100	90	75	74	0	20	0	17	10
1985	85	—	90	58	—	0	24	—	14	—

National Journal Ratings

	1986 LIB — 1986 CONS	1985 LIB — 1985 CONS
Economic	84% — 13%	75% — 22%
Social	86% — 11%	81% — 15%
Foreign	71% — 28%	79% — 20%

Key Votes

1) Lmt Cln Water Act	AGN	5) Retain Gun Cont	FOR	9) Aid Angola Reb	AGN
2) Rpl Tobac Sub	AGN	6) Contra Aid	AGN	10) Tax Reform	AGN
3) Grm-Rdmn Def Red	AGN	7) Lmt Text Imp	FOR	11) S Africa Sanc	FOR
4) Ban Polygraph	FOR	8) Limit SDI	FOR	12) Immig Reform	AGN

Election Results

1986 general	Henry B. Gonzalez (D).................	55,363	(100%)	($142,694)
1986 primary	Henry B. Gonzalez (D).................	26,936	(100%)	
1984 general	Henry B. Gonzalez (D)...............	100,443	(100%)	($67,191)

Campaign Contributions and Expenditures

1985-86		Direct Cont. 1985-86		PACS Breakdown 1985-86			
Receipts	$142,694	Indiv.	$112,307	Corp.	$4,800	T/M/H	$5,250
Expend.	$133,055	PACS	$30,346	Labor	$15,996	Agr.	$3,000
Unspent	$11,329	Cand.	$500	Ideo.	$1,300	CWOS	$0

TWENTY-FIRST DISTRICT

Slightly larger than Ohio, with a single county that is larger than Connecticut, 500 miles from end to end, the 21st Congressional District of Texas is a Texas-sized chunk of the Texas landscape, geographically the largest district in the state. Demographically, it is a series of modern urban settlements across ranges of arid hills and miles of rugged desert. It begins in the Anglo neighborhoods on the north side of San Antonio and goes all the way to the Big Bend territory, where 7,000-foot peaks tower up over stony desert where the Rio Grande makes a big bend. The largest part of the district in population is in and around San Antonio: the 21st has the north side, where few Mexican-Americans and most of the city's affluent Anglos live. Voters here in Bexar County (pronounced as a drawn-out bear) cast 35% of the district's votes in 1984. Affluent Anglos in San Antonio have voted heavily Republican since 1961, when Representative Henry Gonzalez was elected to replace Paul Kilday, the conservative Democrat whose machine controlled city politics. Then Bexar was Democratic; now the impact of the north side is great enough that the county often goes Republican in statewide races and even elected a Republican sheriff in 1984. Mayor Henry Cisneros, however, remains trusted and popular here, and was able to defeat a spending cap referendum in 1986.

Just north and west of San Antonio you get into the Texas hill country, much of it first settled by refugees from the failed German revolutions of 1848. They made good livings, even off barren soil, but they disliked slavery, instinctively favored the Union, and when Texas became one of the most heavily Democratic states in the Union after the Civil War they insisted on voting Republican in every election. They still do. The hill country around Fredericksburg and Kerrville got electricity back in the 1930s, thanks to Lyndon Johnson, whose LBJ Ranch is just at the edge of German country; the hill country now is the site of condominium developments for prosperous Texans who want a second home in a pleasant, quiet environment.

Beyond the hill country is flat plateau: ranch lands, oil fields, blank desert. Actually few people live out on the land, and their cities are distinctive. The most distinctive is Midland, the headquarters of the people who run the Permian Basin, the rich oil and gas terrain where George Bush made his fortune in the 1950s and which till the crash in oil prices gave Midland one of the highest income levels in the country. Now you can get a lot of good buys on used drilling equipment and Mercedes there. Midland remains one of the most Republican cities in America. More typical is San Angelo, a center of cattle ranching as well as oil, which is ancestrally Democratic, but in current practice Republican.

The 21st District in 1986 elected its second Republican congressman, Lamar Smith. His predecessor, Tom Loeffler, was first elected in 1978, held seats on three plum committees (Energy and Commerce, Appropriations, Budget), and became chief deputy whip under Minority Leader Robert Michel and Whip Trent Lott. But Loeffler said he wanted to return to Texas and in 1986 he decided to run for governor. He got only 22% of the vote, a distant second behind 69-year-old William Clements. But he still has his options open: he quickly made peace with Clements, who won't run again in 1990.

There were six candidates for the Republican nomination, and the top three all had Bexar County bases: Jeff Wentworth, who ran in the 23d district in 1982, got 20%; Van Archer, former Bexar County Commissioner, got 25%; Lamar Smith, Bexar County Commissioner and former legislator, got 31%. Archer claimed to be the most conservative, but many back home regarded him as flaky. Senator Phil Gramm took the unusual step of endorsing Smith in the runoff and Smith won 54%–46%. The Democrats had about as strong a candidate as they could have in the general: Pete Snelson, an 18-year state Senator from Midland, and in fact he won a solid margin west of the German counties. But Smith won 67% in the German counties and 74% in Bexar County for a convincing 61% win.

Smith is a member of the family that owns the Seeligson Ranch in Jim Wells County in south Texas, one of the biggest oil-producing ranches in Texas; his grandmother, Ramona Frates Seeligson, has been described as "one of Texas's great *grandes dames*." He was able to spend liberally on his own campaign and now seems to have a safe House seat for as long as he wants. He serves on the Science, Space, and Technology and Judiciary Committees, and was elected freshman whip.

The People: Pop. 1980: 526,846, up 38.0% 1970–80. Households (1980): 74% family, 39% with children, 65% married couples; 31.1% housing units rented; median monthly rent: $221; median house value: $47,700. Voting age pop. (1980): 381,130; 16% Spanish origin, 3% Black, 1% Asian origin.

1984 Presidential Vote:

Reagan (R)	200,152	(78%)
Mondale (D)	56,786	(22%)

Rep. Lamar S. Smith (R)

Elected 1986; b. Nov. 1, 1947, San Antonio; home, San Antonio; Yale Col., B.A., 1968, Southern Methodist U., J.D., 1975; Christian Scientist; married (Jane).

Career: Small Bus. Admin. official, 1969–70; Bus. & Fin. Reporter, *Christian Science Monitor*, 1971–72; Practicing atty., 1975–76; TX House of Reps., 1981–82; Bexar Cnty. Commissioner, 1982–85.

Offices: 509 CHOB 20515, 202-225-4236. Also 10010 San Pedro, Ste. 530, San Antonio 78216, 512-229-5880; 201 W. Wall St., Ste. 104, Midland 79701, 915-687-5232; 1006 Junction Hwy., Kerrville 78028, 512-895-1414; and 33 E. Twohig, Ste. 302, San Angelo 76903, 915-653-3971.

Committees: *Judiciary* (14th of 14 R). Subcommittees: Administrative Law and Governmental Relations; Crime. *Science, Space and Technology* (14th of 18 R). Subcommittees: Energy Research and Development; Science, Research and Technology.

Group Ratings and Key Votes: Newly Elected

Election Results

1986 general	Lamar Smith (R)	100,346	(61%)	($1,062,154)
	Pete Snelson (D)	63,779	(39%)	($345,117)
1986 runoff	Lamar Smith (R)	18,140	(54%)	
	Van Archer (R)......................	15,714	(46%)	
1986 primary	Lamar Smith (R)	18,390	(31%)	
	Van Archer (R)......................	14,616	(25%)	
	Jeff Wentworth (R)...................	11,781	(20%)	
	G. Thome Akins (R)...................	8,103	(14%)	
	Henry Gandy (R)	5,809	(10%)	
1984 general	Thomas G. (Tom) Loeffler (R)	199,909	(81%)	($228,062)
	Joe Sullivan (D)	48,039	(19%)	($4,245)

Campaign Contributions and Expenditures

1985-86		Direct Cont. 1985-86		PACS Breakdown 1985-86			
Receipts	$1,066,535	Indiv.	$733,282	Corp.	$44,595	T/M/H	$43,900
Expend.	$1,062,154	Party	$9,296	Labor	$1,000	Agr.	$0
Unspent	$4,379	PACS	$110,654	Ideo.	$17,041	CWOS	$4,118
		Cand.	$164,102				

TWENTY-SECOND DISTRICT

Forty years ago, you didn't have to get very far southwest of downtown Houston to get to the cotton fields. Treasury Secretary James Baker can remember when his grandfather used to hunt on his property, a few miles from downtown. Out as far as Post Oak and Westheimer—now with glitzy shopping centers, the Fifth Avenue and 57th Street of the oil kingdom—there were fields planted in the staple which made the fortunes of the great Houston cotton traders and political operators Jesse Jones and Will Clayton. Going farther out what is now the perpetually traffic-jammed Southwest Freeway, you would quickly find yourself in utterly rural territory as you left Harris County and traveled through Fort Bend County and then down to the coastal flatness of Brazoria County. Most times of the year the sun would beat down mercilessly, the humidity would be fierce, the ground would be thick with bugs.

On this unforgiving environment was built an urban civilization that includes what is now the 22d Congressional District of Texas. It includes monuments of greater Houston's development:

the high-rises airily flanking the Southwest Freeway near the Galleria, the Sharpstown shopping center and subdivision put up by a local wheeler-dealer whose financial collapse and political dealings brought down a governor in 1972, the newly-sprouted suburban towns of Sugar Land and Missouri City in Fort Bend County, the steamy Brazosport oil shipping complex around Freeport and Lake Jackson on the Gulf of Mexico. Air conditioning—in malls, cars, homes— has made this civilization possible; insecticides have helped; the automobile ties it together (if the traffic would ever clear up). There were fewer than 100,000 people in what now is the 22d District as World War II ended, less than 200,000 in 1960; as the Sharpstown scandal was breaking there were 300,000 and 526,000 when oil prices went over $30 a barrel in the early 1980s.

This is a heavily Republican district: you will be hard put to find many national Democrats among the people who have come from other parts of Houston and Texas, the South and North and even foreign countries, and live now in the new and affluent subdivisions of Houston or Sugar Land or in the more widely-spaced subdivisions scattered farther out in Fort Bend and Brazoria; and even in local elections the historic Democratic leanings of the rural areas are usually overwhelmed by the strong Republican allegiance of the newcomers. In the 1970s the 22d, then mostly in Houston and with more black neighborhoods, had a series of turbulent elections, in large part because of Republican Representative Ron Paul, a libertarian so pure that he was an isolationist abroad and Congress's foremost champion of the gold standard. But Paul ran for the Senate in 1984, running second behind Phil Gramm in the Republican primary, and the current congressman, Republican Tom DeLay, fits the preferences of the newcomer majority here more easily.

Even so, DeLay has an interesting background. He was born in the border town of Laredo and spent much of his childhood in Venezuela, where his father drilled oil wells. In Sugar Land the son built a pest control business—environmentalists might not like that, but in Houston people would rather control the bugs than preserve them—and was elected to the state legislature in 1978, the first Republican from Fort Bend County. When Paul retired, he easily won the Republican primary and the general election: this is a safe seat for him. DeLay's voting record is solidly conservative on practically every issue, but he seems also to have traditional political instincts. In his first term he was the freshman representative on the Republican Committee on Committees, and in his second term he got a seat on the Appropriations Committee. He is proud of helping Houston get $64 million to build a busway on the Southwest Freeway, Rice University get $1.6 million to study how to improve mass transit, and Freeport $15 million for harbor development. Libertarianism may be fine as a general principle, but he is ready to use government to, in his phrase, "conquer traffic problems."

The People: Pop. 1980: 526,602, up 76.9% 1970–80. Households (1980): 67% family, 38% with children, 57% married couples; 46.8% housing units rented; median monthly rent: $271; median house value: $64,200. Voting age pop. (1980): 381,492; 12% Spanish origin, 9% Black, 3% Asian origin.

1984 Presidential Vote: Reagan (R) 138,662   (70%)
Mondale (D) 58,984   (30%)

Rep. Thomas D. (Tom) DeLay (R)

Elected 1984; b. Apr. 8, 1947, Laredo; home, Sugar Land; U. of Houston, B.S. 1970; Baptist; married (Christine).

Career: Owner, Albo Pest Control; TX House of Reps., 1979–85.

Offices: 1039 LHOB 20515, 202-225-5951. Also 9000 S.W. Freeway, Ste. 205, Houston, 77074, 713-270-4000; and 500 N. Shenango, Ste. 310, Angleton 77515, 409-849-4446.

Committees: *Appropriations* (21st of 22 R). Subcommittees: Military Construction; Transportation.

Group Ratings

	ADA	ACLU	COPE	CFA	LCV	ACU	NTU	NSI	COC	CEI
1986	0	5	3	0	5	100	68	100	94	90
1985	5	—	0	25	—	100	72	—	95	—

National Journal Ratings

	1986 LIB — 1986 CONS		1985 LIB — 1985 CONS	
Economic	0%	— 94%	0%	— 95%
Social	0%	— 89%	0%	— 76%
Foreign	0%	— 86%	0%	— 76%

Key Votes

1) Lmt Cln Water Act	FOR	5) Retain Gun Cont	AGN	9) Aid Angola Reb	FOR
2) Rpl Tobac Sub	FOR	6) Contra Aid	FOR	10) Tax Reform	AGN
3) Grm-Rdmn Def Red	FOR	7) Lmt Text Imp	AGN	11) S Africa Sanc	AGN
4) Ban Polygraph	AGN	8) Limit SDI	AGN	12) Immlg Reform	AGN

Election Results

1986 general	Thomas D. (Tom) DeLay (R)............	76,459	(72%)	($294,850)
	Susan Director (D)....................	30,079	(28%)	
1986 primary	Thomas D. (Tom) DeLay (R)............	17,524	(100%)	
1984 general	Thomas D. (Tom) DeLay (R)...........	125,225	(65%)	($527,850)
	Doug Williams (D)....................	66,495	(35%)	($82,087)

Campaign Contributions and Expenditures

1985-86		Direct Cont. 1985-86		PACS Breakdown 1985-86			
Receipts	$316,191	Indiv.	$103,779	Corp.	$90,098	T/M/H	$48,901
Expend.	$294,850	Party	$2,746	Labor	$0	Agr.	$2,000
Unspent	$45,652	PACS	$156,547	Ideo.	$13,600	CWOS	$1,948

TWENTY-THIRD DISTRICT

From San Antonio south, you are in the border country: a part of the United States which is neither entirely American nor entirely Mexican, but a mixture—a volatile and constantly changing mixture—of the two. Historically the picture here has been of desert-like rural counties where big landowners rule the lives—and cast the votes—of their Mexican-American field hands. But these small counties have no economic future and few resources, as the "brown power" militants found out when they took over over local government. The real economic growth comes from the contrast between the two sides of the border, the balance of wages and exchange rates and the flow of immigration. These things change constantly. Laredo, down on the border, had chain stores with some of the highest sales in the U.S. before the peso devaluation of 1982; now many have closed and others are quiet. But those developments also made U.S. wages all the more attractive to residents of Mexico, stimulating twin-plant development here and there.

The 23d Congressional District of Texas extends from the south side of San Antonio south to Laredo and west to Eagle Pass, both on the Rio Grande. Most of the land area is in the border counties, which in most elections are among the most heavily Democratic counties in the nation. But some 62% of the population is in San Antonio and surrounding Bexar County (pronounced with something like the soft Spanish X, which sounds like an H to English-speakers). The district includes the southern fringes of San Antonio, working-class neighborhoods near big military bases where nearly half the residents are Mexican-Americans. But the district also includes suburban territory east, west, and north of the city. This takes in some of the most affluent precincts in Bexar County, where, historically, mistrust of Mexicans and Democrats is high.

The congressman from the 23d grew up in a small Mexican-American town, but he has made his political career in San Antonio. He is Albert Bustamente, who served a few years on Representative Henry B. Gonzalez's staff and then returned home to make his political fortune. He was elected to the Bexar County Commission in 1972 and was elected County Judge in 1978. In 1984 he decided to run for Congress in the 23d, and challenged the incumbent, Abraham Kazen, who had served quietly and unobtrusively for 18 years. Kazen, who is Lebanese-American, had his base in Laredo, and had compiled a generally liberal voting record. But after 18 years in Congress, and with enough seniority to be number two on the Interior Committee, he was still hard put to recite accomplishments or to show that he was much more than a nice guy. He survived the 1982 challenge of Republican Jeff Wentworth by an unimpressive 54%–46% margin, but lost the 1984 Democratic primary to Bustamante by a 59%–37% margin.

Bustamante was elected president of the Democratic freshman class—a small one, since 1984 was a Republican year—but has otherwise been almost as quiet as Kazen, with a similar voting record. He has a seat on the Armed Services Committee, the second south Texas Hispanic on that body; presumably he will look after San Antonio's military personnel and retirees. He has been a key vote on contra aid, opposing it in 1985 and voting for it in 1986, and he supported the immigration reform bill—not the votes of the stereotypical liberal many in Washington expect a Mexican-American to be. But he represents a military city and a district where citizens and voters don't want low-wage competitors to freely cross the border. Given the political leanings of his district, Bustamante should be able to make this a safe seat.

The People: Pop. 1980: 526,746, up 50.0% 1970–80. Households (1980): 84% family, 56% with children, 70% married couples; 30.2% housing units rented; median monthly rent: $163; median house value: $33,100. Voting age pop. (1980): 332,851; 51% Spanish origin, 4% Black, 1% Asian origin.

1984 Presidential Vote:

Reagan (R)	95,995	(59%)
Mondale (D)	66,186	(41%)

Rep. Albert G. Bustamante (D)

Elected 1984; b. Apr. 8, 1935, Asherton; home, San Antonio; San Antonio Col., Sul Ross St. Col., B.A. 1961; Roman Catholic; married (Rebecca).

Career: Army, 1954–56; High school teacher & coach, 1961–68; Cong. Dist. Asst., U.S. Rep. Henry B. Gonzalez, 1968–71; Bexar Cnty. Commissioner, 1973–78, Judge, 1979–83.

Offices: 1116 LHOB 20515, 202-225-4511. Also Fed. Bldg., 727 E. Durango St., Rm. B-146, San Antonio 78206, 512-229-6191; 1300 Matamoros St., Rm. 115, Laredo 78040, 512-724-7774; Uvalde Cnty. Crthse., Uvalde 78801, 512-278-5021; Fed. Crthse. Bldg., Rm. 103, 100 E. Broadway, Del Rio 78841, 512-774-6549; 101 E. Dimmit, W. Annex, Crystal City 78839, 512-374-5200; Dimmit Cnty. Cthse., Carrizo Springs 78834, 512-876-2323; and Maverick Cnty. Cthse., P.O. Box 995, Eagle Pass 78852, 512-773-4110.

Committees: *Armed Services* (27th of 31 D). Subcommittees: Military Personnel and Compensation; Procurement and Military Nuclear Systems. *Government Operations* (19th of 24 D). Subcommittees: Commerce, Consumer, and Monetary Affairs; Environment, Energy, and Natural Resources.

Group Ratings

	ADA	ACLU	COPE	CFA	LCV	ACU	NTU	NSI	COC	CEI
1986	50	72	93	50	55	33	21	50	10	0
1985	65	—	88	58	—	19	19	—	24	—

National Journal Ratings

	1986 LIB — 1986 CONS		1985 LIB — 1985 CONS	
Economic	87% —	0%	85% —	11%
Social	66% —	34%	73% —	23%
Foreign	50% —	49%	53% —	47%

Key Votes

1) Lmt Cln Water Act	AGN	5) Retain Gun Cont	AGN	9) Aid Angola Reb	FOR
2) Rpl Tobac Sub	AGN	6) Contra Aid	AGN	10) Tax Reform	AGN
3) Grm-Rdmn Def Red	AGN	7) Lmt Text Imp	FOR	11) S Africa Sanc	FOR
4) Ban Polygraph	FOR	8) Limit SDI	FOR	12) Immig Reform	FOR

Election Results

1986 general	Albert G. Bustamante (D)	68,131	(91%)	($199,090)
	Ken Hendrix (L).......................	7,001	(9%)	
1986 primary	Albert G. Bustamante (D)	40,170	(100%)	
1984 general	Albert G. Bustamante (D)	95,721	(100%)	($584,425)

Campaign Contributions and Expenditures

1985-86		Direct Cont. 1985-86		PACS Breakdown 1985-86			
Receipts	$258,156	Indiv.	$148,778	Corp.	$36,000	T/M/H	$15,100
Expend.	$199,090	PACS	$99,100	Labor	$32,500	Agr.	$5,000
Unspent	$62,616	Cand.	$12,374	Ideo.	$10,250	CWOS	$250

TWENTY-FOURTH DISTRICT

Overlooking downtown Dallas, across the cement-lined bed of the Trinity River, is Oak Cliff. The river forms a clean dividing line; because of floods, the bottomlands are maintained as parkland, and there are not many bridges across; Oak Cliff, on the south side, is a kind of alternative Dallas—a road the larger part of the city has not taken. Traveling Oak Cliff's back streets, you can find old Victorian gingerbread houses; there is more evidence here than on the other side of the river of the kind of city Dallas was before steel-and-glass skyscrapers towered over downtown and were scattered around freeway interchanges on the north side of the city. The south side of Dallas, from Oak Cliff on, is where most of the city's black residents live and almost half of its much smaller number of Mexican-Americans.

This is the heart of the 24th Congressional District of Texas, the strongest national Democratic district in the Dallas–Fort Worth Metroplex, though it did prefer Reagan to Mondale, barely, in 1984. Its population is 32% black and 13% Spanish origin, according to the 1980 Census, and its housing prices are relatively inexpensive. It does include some suburban territory, however: the modest suburb of Grand Prairie and somewhat higher-income Irving. The 24th District's boundaries were the key issue in the partisan fights over Texas's redistricting; the current lines were drawn by Democrats in 1983 after a federal court intervened.

The congressman from the 24th District is Martin Frost, who started his political career by challenging an incumbent congressman and is now one of the young congressmen in tightest with the Democratic leadership of the House. The incumbent was conservative Democrat Dale Milford, the only former television weathercaster to have served in Congress; campaigning door-to-door and in snappy TV ads, Frost came close to beating Milford in 1974 and polished him off, with the help of large majorities from blacks, in 1978. His rapport with black voters helped him again in 1982, enabling him to face down black primary opposition when it looked like the district would have a black majority and then beating a black Dallas councilwoman running as a Republican by a 73%–26% margin. Against white Republicans he won 59% in 1984 and 67% in 1986.

Frost's House career took off when then Majority Leader Jim Wright got him a seat on the Rules Committee in 1979, making him only the second Democratic freshman in the 20th century to get a seat on Rules. Frost has generally not disappointed the Democratic leadership, voting often but not always on the liberal side. He was disappointed, however, in his run for the chairmanship of the Budget Committee after the 1984 elections. He led the move to deny waivers of the three-term rule to Jim Jones and Leon Panetta, thus barring them from the leadership; on this he was serving not just himself, but also Tip O'Neill and Jim Wright, who mistrusted both men. But it was apparent that William Gray of Pennsylvania had the votes sewn up to be chairman, and so Frost withdrew. Nevertheless, he remains an important congressman, and is probably the Rules member closest to the Speaker; and, so long as he is not imperilled by redistricting, he seems to have a safe seat.

The People: Pop. 1980: 527,267, up 14.2% 1970–80. Households (1980): 77% family, 48% with children, 60% married couples; 40.9% housing units rented; median monthly rent: $217; median house value: $37,900. Voting age pop. (1980): 352,993; 29% Black, 11% Spanish origin, 1% Asian origin, 1% American Indian.

1984 Presidential Vote:

Reagan (R)	96,596	(53%)
Mondale (D)	85,078	(47%)

Rep. Martin Frost (D)

Elected 1978; b. Jan. 1, 1942, Glendale, CA; home, Dallas; U. of MO, B.A., B.J. 1964, Georgetown U., J.D. 1970; Jewish; married (Valerie).

Career: Practicing atty., 1970–78.

Offices: 2459 RHOB 20515, 202-225-3605. Also Republic Bank Tower, Ste. 1319, 400 S. Zang Blvd., Dallas 75208, 214-767-2816; and Republic Bank Tower, Ste. 720, 801 West Freeway, Grand Prairie 75051, 214-262-1503.

Committees: *Budget* (8th of 21 D). Task Forces: Budget Process; Defense and International Affairs; Health (Chairman). *Rules* (5th of 9 D). Subcommittee: The Legislative Process.

Group Ratings

	ADA	ACLU	COPE	CFA	LCV	ACU	NTU	NSI	COC	CEI
1986	45	55	76	58	49	26	23	40	43	14
1985	55	—	77	50	—	24	20	—	35	—

National Journal Ratings

	1986 LIB — 1986 CONS		1985 LIB — 1985 CONS	
Economic	54%	— 45%	67%	— 33%
Social	51%	— 49%	81%	— 15%
Foreign	54%	— 45%	54%	— 45%

Key Votes

1) Lmt Cln Water Act	FOR	5) Retain Gun Cont	FOR	9) Aid Angola Reb	FOR
2) Rpl Tobac Sub	AGN	6) Contra Aid	AGN	10) Tax Reform	AGN
3) Grm-Rdmn Def Red	FOR	7) Lmt Text Imp	FOR	11) S Africa Sanc	FOR
4) Ban Polygraph	—	8) Limit SDI	FOR	12) Immig Reform	AGN

Election Results

1986 general	Martin Frost (D)	69,368	(67%)	($709,864)
	Bob Burk (R)	33,819	(33%)	($23,676)
1986 primary	Martin Frost (D)	19,701	(100%)	
1984 general	Martin Frost (D)	105,210	(59%)	($640,083)
	Bob Burk (R)	71,703	(41%)	($25,061)

Campaign Contributions and Expenditures

1985-86		Direct Cont. 1985-86		PACS Breakdown 1985-86			
Receipts	$775,479	Indiv.	$362,595	Corp.	$145,007	T/M/H	$84,550
Expend.	$709,864	PACS	$345	Labor	$83,875	Agr.	$9,700
Unspent	$81,566	Party	$345,339	Ideo.	$17,257	CWOS	$4,950

TWENTY-FIFTH DISTRICT

Working class Houston, west from the scruffy towns where the Houston Ship Channel empties out into the bay, through Pasadena where country music honkytonk Gilley's, with its mechanical bulls still sits on Spencer Highway, out past the black neighborhoods near Houston's (comparatively) close-in Hobby Airport to the Astrodome and up to a mile or so just west of Main, where the neighborhoods are suddenly affluent rather than working-class, with Rice University and some of Houston's Jewish neighborhoods—this is Texas's 25th Congressional District. The number tells you that this is one of the three new districts created after the 1980 Census, a kind of political bonus to the Houston area for the demographic gains it made from the oil price rises of the 1970s. The political benefit has gone, as the Texas legislature hoped it would, to the Democrats: working-class Houston, not only in black and Mexican neighborhoods but in white as well, votes pretty faithfully Democratic, and if one of the effects of the new district lines was to strengthen Republican Jack Fields in the 8th District and make the 22d District safely Republican, the other was to open up the 25th to an ambitious young Democrat like Mike Andrews.

Andrews had already run for Congress once, in the 22d District against libertarian and gold bug Ron Paul, where he won 49% of the vote after spending $750,000. But he didn't capture the 22d without a fight. He was challenged by a former Pasadena mayor in the primary who charged he was too liberal and then by a Republican in the general who said he'd be a better supporter of President Reagan; Andrews spent $647,000 and won those races with 58% and 60%. As the size of his campaign treasury suggests, Andrews knows how to raise money from Houston's downtown business community even as he was winning the primary endorsement of the 18th district's black congressman Mickey Leland.

In Congress Andrews has worked hard to justify this support. His voting record has not always been as liberal as blacks and labor leaders might like, and he has not always gone along with the Democratic leadership. But he had two signal successes in the summer of 1986 which show he has learned how to do business in Washington. The first was winning the Ways and Means seat he tried for after the 1984 election and lost to Pennsylvania's William Coyne by one vote. This time Andrews got it easily when Hawaii's Cecil Heftel resigned from Congress to run for governor of Hawaii. The other was the fight he led with Republican Jack Fields and expert advice from old pro Jack Brooks against NASA's plan to transfer several thousand jobs in the space station program from the Johnson Space Center south of Houston to Huntsville, Alabama. Andrews used his leverage and knowledge from serving on the Science and Technology subcommittee on space to help organize the Texans' lobbying which, after a two-month battle, proved successful in getting NASA to revoke its plans in September 1986.

The fall campaign was anticlimactic for Andrews. He had only desultory opposition in 1984 and his only opponent in 1986 was a Lyndon LaRouche follower he dispatched in the spring primary. Now ensconced on Ways and Means, this pleasant-looking and articulate politician now seems well launched on a long House career.

The People: Pop. 1980: 526,801, up 20.4% 1970–80. Households (1980): 74% family, 44% with children, 60% married couples; 41.6% housing units rented; median monthly rent: $261; median house value: $46,700. Voting age pop. (1980): 366,175; 23% Black, 12% Spanish origin, 1% Asian origin.

1984 Presidential Vote: Reagan (R) 97,381   (53%)
Mondale (D) 86,808   (47%)

Rep. Michael A. (Mike) Andrews (D)

Elected 1982; b. Feb. 7, 1944, Houston; home, Houston; U. of TX, B.A. 1967, Southern Methodist U., J.D. 1970; United Methodist; married (Ann).

Career: Law clerk, U.S. Dist. Judge for Southern Dist. of Texas, 1970–72; Asst. D.A., Harris Cnty., TX, 1972–76; Practicing atty., 1976–82.

Offices: 322 CHOB 20515, 202-225-7508. Also 1001 E. Southmore, Ste. 810, Pasadena 77503, 713-473-4334; and Fed. Bldg., 515 Rusk, Houston 77002, 713-229-2244.

Committees: *Ways and Means* (21st of 23 D). Subcommittees: Public Assistance; Select Revenue Measures.

Group Ratings

	ADA	ACLU	COPE	CFA	LCV	ACU	NTU	NSI	COC	CEI
1986	50	55	60	58	60	45	34	60	61	32
1985	55	—	59	42	—	57	35	—	71	—

National Journal Ratings

	1986 LIB	—	1986 CONS		1985 LIB	—	1985 CONS
Economic	42%	—	57%		37%	—	62%
Social	44%	—	54%		63%	—	33%
Foreign	48%	—	51%		46%	—	52%

Key Votes

1) Lmt Cln Water Act	FOR	5) Retain Gun Cont	AGN	9) Aid Angola Reb	FOR
2) Rpl Tobac Sub	AGN	6) Contra Aid	AGN	10) Tax Reform	FOR
3) Grm-Rdmn Def Red	FOR	7) Lmt Text Imp	FOR	11) S Africa Sanc	FOR
4) Ban Polygraph	FOR	8) Limit SDI	AGN	12) Immig Reform	AGN

Election Results

1986 general	Michael A. (Mike) Andrews (D)	67,435	(100%)	($133,817)
1986 primary	Michael A. (Mike) Andrews (D)	16,678	(100%)	
1984 general	Michael A. (Mike) Andrews (D)	113,946	(64%)	($249,973)
	Jerry Patterson (R)	63,974	(36%)	($16,660)

Campaign Contributions and Expenditures

1985-86		Direct Cont. 1985-86		PACS Breakdown 1985-86			
Receipts	$300,074	Indiv.	$143,817	Corp.	$55,032	T/M/H	$41,125
Expend.	$133,817	PACS	$117,522	Labor	$11,300	Agr.	$2,000
Unspent	$246,561			Ideo.	$5,565	CWOS	$2,500

TWENTY-SIXTH DISTRICT

Almost invisible from the freeways crossing the open-skied Texas landscape, it was one of the major geographical barriers in our history—the Balcones Escarpment, the rim of higher west Texas land that passes between Dallas and Fort Worth and extends southwest to Waco and Austin. East of the escarpment the land is low and green, often forested and sometimes swampy; west it is high and brown, with little water and few trees. This is the boundary between East and West, the reason why the first railroads here stopped at Dallas. It is still crucial territory today, just west of the huge Dallas–Fort Worth Regional Airport, running down the midst of once rural and now almost fully developed Arlington.

Arlington is one of the extraordinary cities of Texas, a symbol of its growth and prosperity over the last 20 years—the more so, because little of that growth and prosperity has come from oil. Thirty years ago Arlington was almost entirely vacant land: rolling hills with scrubby vegetation, and long views from the escarpment over the plains to the skyscrapers of Fort Worth and Dallas. Now it is a city of more than 200,000 people, and not just a bedroom suburb of Fort Worth: it is the home, thanks to the enterprise of its mayor for 26 years, of Chevrolet dealer Tom Vandergriff, of the Texas Rangers, of Six Flags Over Texas, of a branch of the University of Texas. Arlington is full of the people whose talents and skills have made the Dallas–Fort Worth Metroplex a ranking center of high tech and defense industries; it is progressive, with clean new streets and commodious public services; it seems safe and secure against the urban ills that afflict so many neighborhoods in so many of America's other major metropolitan areas. In national politics, Arlington is heavily Republican, receptive to the message of free enterprise and traditional moral values transmitted by Ronald Reagan. It seems difficult, in this pleasant, hard-working America, to understand that there are other parts of the country (though not many whole states) which disagree.

Arlington forms almost half of Texas's 26th Congressional District, a new seat created after the 1980 Census and made up of incipient or quasi-Arlingtons to the north, including several suburbs of north Dallas and going up through formerly rural territory and the county seat of Denton almost to the Red River. Its first congressman, fittingly, was Tom Vandergriff, running as a conservative Democrat. But even with his local fame and in a Democratic year it took him $700,000 of his own money to win a 344-vote victory; and it is not too surprising that he lost in the Republican year of 1984.

The congressman now is Dick Armey, former professor of economics at North Texas State in Denton, a Republican who plunged into the race when more experienced and better known politicians hesitated and who has now reaped the reward of a safe seat in Congress. Armey seems a spirited eccentric: he campaigned in 1984 with a comic book linking Vandergriff and Tip O'Neill and enunciating his own free-market views; he talked about phasing out Social Security; he lapses into the arcane language of microeconomics. In his first term he was assigned to two liberal-dominated committees, Education and Labor and Government Operations.

Yet Armey has proved to be surprisingly effective. He has championed such causes as selling public housing to tenants and has opposed parental leave bills as "yuppie welfare." Armey has been busy proposing privatization of Amtrak's Northeast Corridor, of catastrophic health insurance, the sale of government loan assets. He has opposed protectionism and has tried to encourage exports. None of Armey's initiatives has been entirely successful. But his aggressiveness has changed the terms of the discussion on many issues in the House, and his political success—he was reelected in a district which considers itself Middle-American with 68% of the vote—suggests that his views may not be so outlandish as conventional wisdom assumes. After the 1986 election he won a seat on the Budget Committee, and he is likely to be heard from loud and clear in the 100th Congress.

The People: Pop. 1980: 526,598, up 62.2% 1970–80. Households (1980): 76% family, 45% with children, 67% married couples; 33.7% housing units rented; median monthly rent: $251; median house value: $57,400. Voting age pop. (1980): 372,244; 4% Spanish origin, 3% Black, 1% Asian origin.

1984 Presidential Vote: Reagan (R) 194,141   (76%)
                                  Mondale (D) 59,341   (23%)

Rep. Richard K. (Dick) Armey (R)

Elected 1984; b. July 7, 1940, Cando, ND; home, Denton; Jamestown Col., B.A. 1963, U. of ND, M.A. 1964, U. of OK, Ph.D. 1969; Presbyterian; married (Susan).

Career: Prof., West TX St. U., 1967–68, Austin Col., 1968–72, North TX St. U., 1972–77; Chmn., Dept. of Economics, North TX St. U., 1977–83.

Offices: 514 CHOB 20515, 202-225-7772. Also 1301 S. Bowen Rd., Ste. 422, Arlington 76013, 817-461-2556; and 250 S. Stemmons, Ste. 210, Lewisville 75067, 214-221-4527.

Committees: *Budget* (12th of 14 R). Task Forces: Budget Process; Community and Natural Resources; Economic Policy. *Education and Labor* (9th of 12 R). Subcommittees: Labor-Management Relations; Postsecondary Education.

Group Ratings

	ADA	ACLU	COPE	CFA	LCV	ACU	NTU	NSI	COC	CEI
1986	0	5	3	0	37	100	75	90	100	96
1985	15	—	0	33	—	95	72	—	95	—

National Journal Ratings

	1986 LIB — 1986 CONS			1985 LIB — 1985 CONS		
Economic	0%	—	94%	0%	—	95%
Social	0%	—	89%	0%	—	76%
Foreign	16%	—	79%	24%	—	66%

Key Votes

1) Lmt Cln Water Act	FOR	5) Retain Gun Cont	AGN	9) Aid Angola Reb	FOR
2) Rpl Tobac Sub	FOR	6) Contra Aid	FOR	10) Tax Reform	FOR
3) Grm-Rdmn Def Red	FOR	7) Lmt Text Imp	AGN	11) S Africa Sanc	AGN
4) Ban Polygraph	AGN	8) Limit SDI	AGN	12) Immig Reform	AGN

Election Results

1986 general	Richard K. (Dick) Armey (R)	101,735	(68%)	($541,542)
	George Richardson (D).................	47,651	(32%)	($133,785)
1986 primary	Richard K. (Dick) Armey (R)	26,545	(100%)	
1984 general	Richard K. (Dick) Armey (R)	126,641	(51%)	($333,184)
	Tom Vandergriff (D).................	120,451	(49%)	($382,139)

Campaign Contributions and Expenditures

1985-86		Direct Cont. 1985-86		PACS Breakdown 1985-86			
Receipts	$548,668	Indiv.	$325,018	Corp.	$99,850	T/M/H	$69,452
Expend.	$541,542	PACS	$194,082	Labor	$0	Agr.	$0
Unspent	$31,220	Cand.	$79,014	Ideo.	$26,500	CWOS	$2,280

TWENTY-SEVENTH DISTRICT

Following the Gulf of Mexico from the port and industrial city of Corpus Christi down past the King Ranch and along Padre Island to the Mexican border is the 27th Congressional District of Texas. This is one of three new districts created after the 1980 Census, and it has, as planned, an Hispanic majority. It contains more variety than you might think. Corpus, as it is called locally, is an oil port, the most important one south of Houston; it has big petrochemical plants. About half its citizens are Mexican-American, but they are less segregated and set apart than was once the case. Overall they may be fitting into the city's blue-collar, roughneck tone. Half the 27th's people live in and around Corpus Christi.

Most of the other half live in and around Brownsville and Harlingen in the Lower Rio Grande Valley. Harlingen became a figure of fun for many when backers of Ronald Reagan's Central American policy suggested it would be the next place to be invaded. But the fun is less apparent when you're there: Harlingen is not about to be overrun by Nicaraguans, of course, but its position down on the border could be an uncomfortable one if a government hostile to the United States should come to power in Mexico. Any Mexican development—the devaluation of the peso, unemployment in the northern Mexico states, the success or failure of maquiladoria plants—changes life on the border, and a hostile Mexico could do more to damage the quality of American life, especially here, than any other foreign development short of war.

In between these two nodes are Texan versions of dreamland. Fronting the Gulf is the sandspit of Padre Island, for most of its length a national seashore, where the hot sands meet the almost steamy waters of the summertime Gulf. At its south end, there are extensive high-rise developments, where residents can sit high in air conditioning and watch the beach shimmer in the heat. Inland are the vast grazing and oil lands of the King Ranch, long America's largest, and other big properties, like that of Texas Republican leader Anne Armstrong.

This is an overwhelmingly Democratic district, and the congressman, Solomon Ortiz, was chosen in the Democratic primary in 1982. There were five main candidates, and in the first primary their votes fell in the narrow range between 14% and 26%. The high figure was won by Solomon Ortiz, the sheriff of Nueces County, known as a tough law enforcer. His major opponent was former Corpus Christi legislator Joe Salem. But Ortiz outmaneuvered him for support in the Brownsville area; by making a local alliance there he cinched the runoff. The general election was anticlimactic: the Republican candidate had the impressive-sounding credential of having been mayor of Corpus Christi, but he had not been active recently and his party label was a handicap impossible to overcome.

Ortiz has a safe seat. His voting record is liberal on economics, moderate on cultural and military issues—like Kika de la Garza's in the 15th. Many in Washington assume that a Mexican-American will vote on the left wing of the Democratic party, but Mexican-American voters are vociferously patriotic and culturally traditional; and Ortiz seems to share their attitudes. He is a member of Merchant Marine and Fisheries and the Armed Services Committee, where he seems to fit in well with the generally hawkish majority.

The People: Pop. 1980: 526,988, up 23.7% 1970–80. Households (1980): 80% family, 50% with children, 66% married couples; 37.8% housing units rented; median monthly rent: $171; median house value: $31,000. Voting age pop. (1980): 341,512; 55% Spanish origin, 3% Black.

1984 Presidential Vote: Reagan (R)   91,382   (53%)
                                               Mondale (D)   80,883   (47%)

Rep. Solomon P. Ortiz (D)

Elected 1982; b. June 3, 1937, Robstown; home, Corpus Christi; Del Mar Col., Natl. Sheriffs' Training Inst., 1977; United Methodist; divorced.

Career: Army, 1960–62; Nueces Cnty. Constable, 1965–68, Commissioner, 1969–76, Sheriff, 1977–82.

Offices: 1524 LHOB 20515, 202-225-7742. Also 3649 Leopard, Ste. 510, Corpus Christi 78408, 512-883-5868; and 3505 Boca Chica Blvd., Ste. 438, Brownsville 78521, 512-541-1242.

Committees: *Armed Services* (24th of 31 D). Subcommittees: Investigations; Military Installations and Facilities; Seapower and Strategic and Critical Materials. *Merchant Marine and Fisheries* (20th of 25 D). Subcommittees: Coast Guard and Navigation; Fisheries and Wildlife Conservation and the Environment; Panama Canal and Outer Continental Shelf. *Select Committee on Narcotics Abuse and Control* (13th of 15 D).

Group Ratings

	ADA	ACLU	COPE	CFA	LCV	ACU	NTU	NSI	COC	CEI
1986	45	42	87	42	45	40	18	60	29	9
1985	60	—	87	58	—	33	20	—	16	—

National Journal Ratings

	1986 LIB — 1986 CONS		1985 LIB — 1985 CONS	
Economic	87%	— 0%	75%	— 22%
Social	56%	— 43%	49%	— 49%
Foreign	44%	— 55%	46%	— 52%

Key Votes

1) Lmt Cln Water Act	AGN	5) Retain Gun Cont	AGN	9) Aid Angola Reb	FOR
2) Rpl Tobac Sub	AGN	6) Contra Aid	FOR	10) Tax Reform	AGN
3) Grm-Rdmn Def Red	AGN	7) Lmt Text Imp	FOR	11) S Africa Sanc	FOR
4) Ban Polygraph	AGN	8) Limit SDI	FOR	12) Immig Reform	FOR

Election Results

1986 general	Solomon P. Ortiz (D).................	64,165	(100%)	($138,793)
1986 primary	Solomon P. Ortiz (D).................	44,709	(85%)	
	Ken Rich (R)	8,013	(15%)	
1984 general	Solomon P. Ortiz (D)................	105,516	(64%)	($309,617)
	Richard Moore (R)..................	60,283	(36%)	

Campaign Contributions and Expenditures

1985-86		Direct Cont. 1985-86		PACS Breakdown 1985-86			
Receipts	$191,246	Indiv.	$67,969	Corp.	$38,050	T/M/H	$26,200
Expend.	$138,793	PACS	$100,300	Labor	$35,800	Agr.	$0
Unspent	$94,577	Cand.	$11,000	Ideo.	$250	CWOS	$0

UTAH

In October 1985 three pipe-bombs exploded in Salt Lake City, killing a successful businessman and the wife of a business associate and seriously wounding Mark Hofmann, a 30-year-old bespectacled documents dealer. In February 1987 Hofmann pled guilty to setting off the bombs as part of an plot to extort money through selling forged documents. In any other state this would have been the lead for a couple of days' evening newscasts. In Utah it was, literally, a bombshell, a threat to the very basis of the community. For the documents that Hofmann was peddling purported to show that Joseph Smith, the founder of the Church of Jesus Christ of the Latter Day Saints was directed not by the Angel Moroni but by a "white salamander" to the golden tablets inscribed with hieroglyphic writings that, with the aid of special spectacles, Smith translated and published as the Book of Mormon in 1831. Little wonder that the businessman who was killed and the Church itself paid what amounted to hush money to Hofmann: his brilliantly executed forgeries thus seemed to undermine the most basic tenets of the Mormon religion.

For the Church of the Latter Day Saints (LDS) cares passionately about its history and is defensive about the skepticism many gentiles—non-Mormons—express toward its deepest beliefs. In caves in the mountains of Utah the Church preserves America's most complete genealogical records, which have great religious significance for Mormons, and its own vitality and success in today's Utah and around the nation and the world where every good Mormon spends a year proselytizing, is a link with the wave of religious enthusiasm, prophecy, and utopianism that swept across the "burnt-over district" of Upstate New York in the 1820s and 1830s, of which Joseph Smith, the Book of Mormon, and the LDS Church are the most enduring products. The Mormons attracted thousands of converts and created their own communities; persecuted for their beliefs, they moved west to Ohio, Missouri, and then Illinois. In 1844 the Mormon colony at Nauvoo, Illinois, had some 15,000 members, all living under the strict theocratic rule of Joseph Smith. In secular Illinois politics Nauvoo—then the largest city in the state—held the balance of power between contending Democrats and Whigs. It was here that Smith received a revelation sanctioning the practice of polygamy, which led to his death at the hands of a mob in 1844.

After the murder, the new president of the church, Brigham Young, decided to move the faithful, "the saints," farther west into territory that was still part of Mexico and far beyond the pale of white settlement. Young led a well-organized march across the Great Plains and into the Rocky Mountains. In 1847 the prophet and his followers stopped on the western slope of the Wasatch Range and, as Brigham Young gazed over the valley of the Great Salt Lake spread out below, he uttered the now famous words, "This is the place."

The place was Utah. It is today the only state that continues to live by the teachings of the church responsible for its founding. Throughout the 19th century and even today "Zion" has attracted thousands of converts from the Midwest, the north of England, and Scandinavia. The object of religious fear, prejudice, and perhaps some repressed envy, Utah was not granted statehood until 1896, after the church renounced polygamy. Today about 70% of all Utah citizens are members of the Latter Day Saints Church. And while American mainline denominations are losing members, the Mormon Church is growing. Its faith prohibits tobacco, alcohol, caffeine; it encourages large families and hard work; its members are healthier than the average American, better educated and more affluent. Mormons tend to be conservative voters, and the Church has taken conservative positions on public issues from abortion to right-to-work laws. Its current president, Ezra Taft Benson, was President Eisenhower's Secretary of Agriculture and later an enthusiast for the Republican right and the John Birch Society.

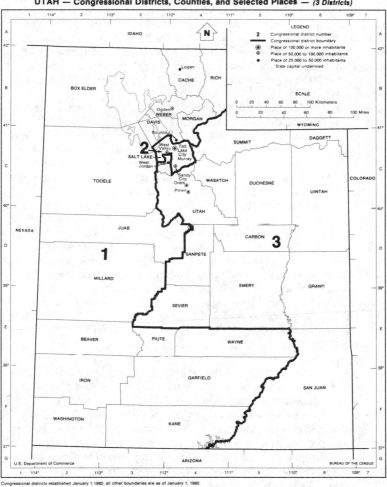

UTAH — Congressional Districts, Counties, and Selected Places — *(3 Districts)*

But the Church's bar against blacks becoming full members was overturned in a revelation to LDS President Spencer Kimball in 1978. In the early 1980s the Church opposed the racetrack basing mode for the MX missile which would have required laying tracks down over much of Utah and Nevada. And the Church itself, financed by the tradition of tithing, runs its own high-quality welfare programs: this is a society that favors market economics and free enterprise, but also has a lively tradition of communal effort and responsibility. The Church's influence in Utah is great—it owns the two leading Salt Lake City newspapers and a TV station, it has holdings in an insurance company, several banks, and real estate, and owns ZCMI, the largest department store in Salt Lake City—and it is often resented. But Mormons, long derided by coastal sophisticates as old-fashioned, have the satisfaction in the late 1980s of seeing their respect for tradition and discipline accepted more and more in an America grown weary and wary of liberation from traditional cultural standards. The moral code of the Mormons has proved a good basis for building a productive and confident society; in Utah, at least, the Mormon way of life works.

Utah in the 1980s is a thriving, prosperous, decent society. It has risen from a state that saw itself as a colonial victim of East Coast plutocrats to a state that sees itself as a busy—beehive, in the Mormon image—generator of wealth. It remains self-conscious: Utah stands out in 1980s America as the most family-style state, the state with the highest birth rates and the heaviest internal population growth. Utah's population shot up 38% in the 1970s and 14% more in 1980–86. Economically it is doing better than national statistics—per capita statistics particularly—indicate, for so many Utahans are children, and there are fewer two-paycheck families here than in big metropolitan areas.

So the conviction of Mark Hofmann removed a threat to a system of beliefs which has produced a successful way of life. In Utah the 1950s American ideal is still alive—and thriving, with as many intact families and a much higher income level than America at the height of the baby boom. That America was a nation (and the Utah of the time was a state) which was Democratic in its political preference, welcoming government intervention in the economy; the Utah of today (and the nation which has given Ronald Reagan 93 of a possible 100 states in two elections) observes the workings of the welfare state and likes not what it sees. Utah a generation or two ago had income levels below the national average, and considered itself a logical recipient of federal assistance; now it is probably above the national average and sees itself as successful and self-reliant. For some years now Utah has been uncomfortably aware of living in a nation where the lessons its own experience seems so vividly to teach and confirm are increasingly ignored. As a result, Utah changed from being a mildly Democratic state in the Roosevelt–Truman years to a pretty solidly Republican one by the middle 1960s. Now Utah has become the most Republican of states—sticking out of the national statistics politically just as it does demographically. In 1960 Richard Nixon carried Utah with 55% of the vote; by 1972 he won with 72%. In 1980 Ronald Reagan won 73% of Utah's votes and in 1984, 75%. These results are almost as one-sided as the Democrats' leads in the District of Columbia.

Governor. Utah's Governor Norman Bangerter is one of those western politicians with experience in government and a liking for it: what makes him surprising is that he's a Republican. For Utah is the paradigm of the western state with many smart Republicans who hate the public sector and refuse to run for office and a few smart Democrats who like government and run. Bangerter's predecessor, Scott Matheson, was that kind of Democrat: elected in 1976, he could have been returned to office indefinitely, but decided to go back to law practice in 1984. Bangerter, the speaker of the state House, beat Republican Representative Dan Marriott in the primary and then former and now again current Representative Wayne Owens in the general. In office he has not proved to be a supporter of minimalist government. On the contrary, he proposed that the state absorb the windfall revenue from the 1986 tax reform law, and in early 1987 was urging the biggest tax increase in Utah's history, to replace revenue lost from slowdowns in Utah's mineral economy. "Conservatism, in my definition," he explained, "is facing up to our responsibilities and paying our bills. Increased taxes will go for the most important and basic functions of government: education and infrastructure." He comes up for reelection in 1988.

Senators. Utah has two Republican Senators who both chaired important committees for six years and who are both back, but not necessarily quiet, on the minority bench. Senior Senator Jake Garn has made more news in space and on the operating table than in the Senate in the past few years. In April 1985 he went up in the space shuttle *Discovery* and was monitored for seven days for, among other things, motion sickness. Garn was a Navy pilot and as chairman of the Senate's Space Subcommittee was an enthusiast for the space shuttle program before the *Challenger* explosion and has remained one since. Garn's interest in the space program is not out of character. Like many other political conservatives, he is an aficionado of high technology, in part perhaps because it enhances American military capabilities. He showed his personal courage and his willingness to submit to the risks imposed by the latest technology when in 1986 he donated one of his kidneys to one of his daughters.

If Garn is known outside the Senate for his courage, he is known inside for his temper. He exploded at Ralph Nader in a 1979 hearing when Nader suggested that a safety regulation Garn opposed would have saved the life of his late wife who had died in a 1976 accident. He has exploded frequently when legislation he backed deregulating various financial services was stymied in the Banking Committee, on the Senate floor, or by inaction in the House. Garn was successful, during his six years as chairman (and while chairing the Appropriations subcommittee on housing), in cutting back on federal housing programs, but he was not able to make as much progress as he wanted in the complex business of adjusting banking laws to the realities of the financial business in the electronic age; and by 1986 he had pretty much given up trying.

Garn started off in municipal politics in Salt Lake City and ran for the Senate in 1974 as a mayor who was frequently and vocally fed up with federal regulations. His conservatism and his temper have endeared him to Utahans ever since. He had to fight hard in that first election in 1974, eventually beating Wayne Owens, who was serving on the House Judiciary Committee as it voted to impeach Richard Nixon, by a 50%–44% margin. In the Carter years he was a vocal hawk, denouncing SALT II and the Panama Canal Treaties; he began the Reagan years by helping to kill the racetrack basing mode for the MX missile, which would have required tearing up a considerable part of Utah's and Nevada's desert; the missile program has never fully recovered. Garn's career has thrived, however. He won reelection with 74% in 1980 and 72% in 1986.

Orrin Hatch is also classed as a conservative, but with a different temperament and different career. In 1981, after only four years in the Senate, he became chairman of the Labor and Human Resources Committee, the spawning ground of a great many Great Society measures, and the place where Hatch was expected to bury them again. But that is not exactly what happened. One reason was that Hatch never had a reliable conservative majority on the committee: Republicans Robert Stafford and Lowell Weicker often voted with the Democrats. The second is that some of Hatch's anti-labor causes got overtaken by events. He gained fame in the Carter years by filibustering the AFL–CIO's labor law reform, and for the 1980s his agenda included the subminimum wage and repeal of the Davis–Bacon Act. But as the real worth of the minimum wage declined and the work force expanded to include record numbers of teenagers and housewives, the minimum wage started doing what advocates said the subminimum would do; meanwhile, the position of the construction unions which are the beneficiaries of Davis–Bacon was undermined by the high interest rates and deunionization of the early 1980s.

The final reason Hatch did not prove the Attila the Hun of the Great Society is that he took seriously his responsibilities of superintending these programs and worked hard to get the details right. He did push the Reagan Administration's block grants early on. But he approached the remaining programs as you might expect of a bishop in a church which runs a wide array of social welfare programs itself: he looked to see who was helped or hurt, if money was spent efficiently, if there were better ways to do it, or if more federal help was needed. Hatch became a work horse, and if he was an opponent of federal funding of abortion, he became one of the biggest boosters of the Job Corps. Hatch takes his committee's work seriously and doesn't intend to be caught unprepared; he takes his position in the Senate seriously too, and wants to be respected. Somewhat grudgingly, he is.

All this irritated some of New Right Republicans who remember how Hatch first won in 1976. He had only gotten into the 1976 Senate race at the last minute, when as a Reagan backer and a newcomer to the state he felt the other Republicans running for liberal Democrat Frank Moss's seat were too moderate; he ran a tough negative issues campaign against Moss and won an upset victory. But Hatch's position with Utah voters has never been as solid as Garn's. In 1982 he was closely pressed by Ted Wilson, then the mayor of Salt Lake City, a man with moderate views and a pleasant, modest personality. Eventually Hatch was able to capitalize on Utah's Republicanness and win a 58%–41% victory. In 1988 he could have a tougher opponent if former Governor Scott Matheson runs; Matheson may be the most popular man in the state and led Hatch in early 1987 polls. Other opponents may be a threat too, but this remains a Republican state; except for Matheson, no Democrat has won a major race except against an opponent with some serious weakness since 1982. Another possibility: there are rumors that President Reagan might appoint Hatch, a hard-working Judiciary Committee member, to the Supreme Court if there is a vacancy; Hatch seems to fancy himself something of a constitutional scholar, though his efforts to show himself a master of that increasingly idiosyncratic discipline have not been entirely convincing. Generally Senators will confirm one of their own, though some Democrats might want to make an exception in Hatch's case.

Presidential politics. Utah is not likely to see many presidential candidates any time soon. It has been the most Republican state in the nation now for three presidential elections in a row, and for the national conventions its relatively few delegates are chosen by party officials.

Congressional districting. In 1982 Utah got its third congressional district; the lines were drawn by the Republican legislature pretty much as predicted. The 2d District, which includes most of Salt Lake County, is the least Republican of the three, and actually went Democratic in 1986, when Wayne Owens won it—the first Democratic victory in a federal election here since 1978 when Gunn McKay, nephew of a former president of the LDS Church, won his fifth term in the 1st District. But when McKay tried again in 1986 he lost. The 3d District, whose big population center is around Provo and Brigham Young University, may very well be the most Republican congressional district in the nation.

The People: Est. Pop. 1986: 1,665,000; Pop. 1980: 1,461,037, up 13.0% 1980–86 and 37.9% 1970–80; 0.69% of U.S. total, 35th largest. 24% with 1–3 yrs. col., 20% with 4+ yrs. col.; 10.3% below poverty level. Single ancestry: 28% English, 4% German, 2% Irish, 1% Swedish, Scottish, Dutch, Italian, French, Norwegian. Households (1980): 78% family, 50% with children, 69% married couples; 29.3% housing units rented; median monthly rent: $190; median house value: $60,000. Voting age pop. (1980): 920,932; 4% Spanish origin, 1% Asian origin, 1% American Indian, 1% Black. Registered voters (1986): 770,000; no party registration.

1986 Share of Federal Tax Burden: $3,886,000,000; 0.52% of U.S. total, 36th largest.

1986 Share of Federal Expenditures

	Total		Non-Defense		Defense	
Total Expend	$5,501m	(0.66%)	$3,816m	(0.64%)	$1,685m	(0.73%)
St/Lcl Grants	807m	(0.72%)	807m	(0.72%)	0m	(0%)
Salary/Wages	1,176m	(0.97%)	391m	(0.67%)	785m	(1.27%)
Pymts to Indiv	1,757m	(0.48%)	1,663m	(0.48%)	95m	(0.53%)
Procurement	1,624m	(0.79%)	818m	(1.47%)	806m	(0.54%)
Research/Other	137m	(0.51%)	137m	(0.51%)	0m	(0%)

Political Lineup: Governor, Norman H. Bangerter (R); Lt. Gov., W. Val Oveson (R); Atty. Gen., David L. Wilkinson (R); Treasurer, Edward T. Alter (R); Auditor, Tom L. Allen (R). State Senate, 29 (21 R and 8 D); State House of Representatives, 75 (48 R and 27 D). Senators, Edwin Jacob (Jake) Garn (R) and Orrin G. Hatch (R). Representatives, 3 R.

1984 Presidential Vote

Reagan (R) 469,105 (75%)
Mondale (D) 155,369 (25%)

1980 Presidential Vote

Reagan (R) 439,687 (73%)
Carter (D) 124,266 (21%)
Anderson (I) 30,284 (5%)

GOVERNOR

Gov. Norman H. Bangerter (R)

Elected 1984, term expires Jan. 1989; b. Jan. 4, 1933, Granger; home, West Valley City; Brigham Young U., U. of UT; Mormon; married (Colleen).

Career: Bldg. contractor; UT House of Reps., 1974–84, Speaker, 1980–84.

Office: 210 State Capitol, Salt Lake City 84114, 801-533-5231.

Election Results

1984 gen.	Norman H. Bangerter (R)	351,792	(56%)
	Wayne Owens (D)	275,669	(44%)
1984 prim.	Norman H. Bangerter (R)	94,347	(56%)
	Dan Marriott (R)	72,940	(44%)
1980 gen.	Scott M. Matheson (D)	330,974	(55%)
	Bob Wright (R)	266,578	(44%)

SENATORS

Sen. Edwin Jacob (Jake) Garn (R)

Elected 1974, seat up 1992; b. Oct. 12, 1932, Richfield; home, Park City; U. of UT, B.S. 1955; Mormon; married (Kathleen).

Career: Navy, 1956–60; Insur. exec., 1960–68; Salt Lake City Commissioner, 1968–72; Mayor of Salt Lake City, 1972–74.

Offices: 505 DSOB 20510, 202-224-5444. Also 4225 Fed. Bldg., Salt Lake City 84138, 801-524-5933; 1010 Fed. Bldg., Ogden 84401, 801-625-5676; 88 W. 100 N., Rm. 111, Provo 84601, 801-374-2929; P.O. Box 99, Cedar City 84720, 801-586-8435; and Congressional Office, Energy Bldg., Ste. 1, Moab 84532, 801-259-7188.

Committees: *Appropriations* (5th of 13 R). Subcommittees: Defense; Energy and Water Development; HUD–Independent Agencies (Ranking Member); Interior; Military Construction. *Banking, Housing, and Urban Affairs* (Ranking Member of 9 R). Subcommittees: Housing and Urban Affairs; International Finance and Monetary Policy. *Rules and Administration* (7th of 7 R).

Group Ratings

	ADA	ACLU	COPE	CFA	LCV	ACU	NTU	NSI	COC	CEI
1986	0	7	10	0	0	94	57	100	100	86
1985	0	—	10	7	—	100	65	—	96	—

National Journal Ratings

	1986 LIB — 1986 CONS		1985 LIB — 1985 CONS	
Economic	0% —	84%	27% —	71%
Social	0% —	91%	0% —	83%
Foreign	0% —	86%	0% —	88%

1202   UTAH

Key Votes

1) Ease Gun Cont	FOR	5) Grm-Rdmn Def Red	FOR	9) Rehnquist Nom	—
2) Immig Reform	AGN	6) Contra Aid	FOR	10) Tax Reform	—
3) Lmt Text Imp	FOR	7) SDI Funding	FOR	11) Drug Death Pen	—
4) Aid Tobac Ind	AGN	8) Lmt PAC Contrib	AGN	12) S Africa Sanc	—

Election Results

1986 general	Edwin Jacob (Jake) Garn (R)...........	314,608	(72%)	($752,944)
	Craig S. Oliver (D)...................	115,523	(27%)	($24,508)
1986 primary	Edwin Jacob (Jake) Garn (R) unopposed			
1980 general	Edwin Jacob (Jake) Garn (R)...........	434,675	(74%)	($1,113,061)
	Dan Berman (D).....................	151,454	(26%)	($237,882)

Campaign Contributions and Expenditures

1985–86		Direct Cont. 1985–86		PACS Breakdown 1985–86			
Receipts	$1,025,447	Indiv.	$393,653	Corp.	$384,987	T/M/H	$151,493
Expend.	$752,944	Party	$16,234	Labor	$0	Agr.	$3,012
Unspent	$285,275	PACS	$593,742	Ideo.	$39,166	CWOS	$15,084
		Cand.	$2,498				

Sen. Orrin G. Hatch (R)

Elected 1976, seat up 1988; b. Mar. 22, 1934, Pittsburgh, PA; home, East Midvale; Brigham Young U., B.S. 1959, U. of Pittsburgh, J.D. 1962; Mormon; married (Elaine).

Career: Practicing atty., 1963–76.

Offices: 135 RSOB 20510, 202-224-5251. Also 3438 Fed. Bldg., 125 S. State St., Salt Lake City 84138, 801-524-4380; 109 Fed. Bldg., 88 W. 100 N., Provo 84601, 801-375-7881; 1410 Fed. Bldg., 325 25th St., Ogden 84401, 801-625-5672; and 10 N. Main St., P.O. Box 99, Cedar City 84720, 801-586-8435.

Committees: *Judiciary* (2d of 6 R). Sbcmtees: Antitrust, Monopolies and Business Rights; Constitution; Patents, Copyrights and Trademarks (Ranking Member). *Labor and Human Resources* (Ranking Member of 7 R). Sbcmtees: Children, Family, Drugs and Alcoholism; Education, Arts and Humanities; Employment and Productivity. *Select Cmte. on Intelligence* (3d of 7 R).

Group Ratings

	ADA	ACLU	COPE	CFA	LCV	ACU	NTU	NSI	COC	CEI
1986	5	14	11	0	17	96	52	100	95	82
1985	10	—	10	20	—	91	61	—	86	—

National Journal Ratings

	1986 LIB — 1986 CONS			1985 LIB — 1985 CONS		
Economic	25%	—	86%	24%	—	73%
Social	0%	—	91%	35%	—	62%
Foreign	0%	—	71%	0%	—	88%

Key Votes

1) Ease Gun Cont	FOR	5) Grm-Rdmn Def Red	FOR	9) Rehnquist Nom	FOR
2) Immig Reform	AGN	6) Contra Aid	FOR	10) Tax Reform	AGN
3) Lmt Text Imp	FOR	7) SDI Funding	FOR	11) Drug Death Pen	AGN
4) Aid Tobac Ind	AGN	8) Lmt PAC Contrib	AGN	12) S Africa Sanc	AGN

Election Results

1982 general	Orrin G. Hatch (R).................	309,547	(58%)	($3,838,335)
	Ted Wilson (D).....................	218,895	(41%)	($1,703,170)
1982 primary	Orrin G. Hatch (R) unopposed			
1976 general	Orrin G. Hatch (R).................	290,221	(54%)	($370,517)
	Frank E. Moss (D)	241,948	(45%)	($343,598)

Campaign Contributions and Expenditures

1979-82		Direct Cont. 1979-82		PACS Breakdown			
Receipts	$3,925,739	Indiv.	$2,893,371	Agr	$15,950	Ideo	$67,037
Expend.	$3,838,335	Party	$32,313	Bus	$772,821	Lbr	$2,500
Unspent	$97,122	PACS	$930,420	Hlth	$48,525	Prof	$16,750

FIRST DISTRICT

In the second month of Ulysses S. Grant's first Administration, just four years after a war that left 600,000 Americans dead, a crowd in Promontory Point, Utah, watched several railroad presidents pound a golden spike in the last section of rail connecting the Union Pacific and the Central Pacific, uniting the settled and civilized East with the mostly unsettled and untamed West. Here, beyond sight of the snow-capped mountains the Mormon pioneers crossed to reach Zion, the salt flats stretch endless even today; the rail lines now pass north of here, and Promontory Point lies on uninhabited flat land beside the rising Great Salt Lake. The lake itself kept rising in the middle 1980s, despite state legislation forbidding it to get above a certain level, the local county commissioners called for a day of prayer for drought in May 1986; it rose 11 feet from 1982 to 1986, and if it rises 4 more feet the state will begin pumping water through canals to form a vast new lake in the salt flats to the west.

The 1st Congressional District of Utah on the map is the western half of the state, from Promontory Point down to where the Colorado River flows through Glen Canyon into Arizona in the south; there are national parks (Zion, Bryce Canyon) in the south, mining country in the center, the desert (as it still is at this writing) west of the lake. But 75% of the people of the 1st District live along the Wasatch Front, the thin strip of land between the Wasatch Mountains and the lowlands along the lake. The largest city is Ogden, an old working-class town on the Union Pacific line, the nearest station stop to Promontory Point. North of Ogden the land is agricultural, and the towns north of Ogden—Brigham City and Logan—are mainly farm centers, almost entirely Mormon and heavily conservative. To the south is Davis County, with some high-income spillover from Salt Lake City. Ogden has a Democratic past, but any Democratic votes it casts today (it did give a small margin against Senator Orrin Hatch in 1982) are usually overcome by Davis's Republican majorities. The rest of the voters live in small communities, many almost unanimously Mormon in central and southern Utah.

The congressman from this district is James Hansen, who despite his conservative and Republican record has not held it without challenge. He won the seat in 1980 by beating incumbent Gunn McKay 52%–48%; McKay, after several years heading an LDS mission overseas ran again in 1986 with the same result. McKay argued that he would provide "balance" for Utah and would have clout as he once was a majority member of the Appropriations Committee, where he helped protect Ogden's Hill Air Force Base. But that argument was undercut in the summer when Hansen won a vacant seat on the Armed Services Committee. A former speaker of the Utah House, garrulous and fair-minded, he was respected enough to have been named to Standards of Official Conduct, the House's ethics committee, in his first term; in his second, serving on Interior, he helped pass a compromise Utah Wilderness bill. The interesting question for 1988 is whether he will attract serious competition again or will be reelected routinely as he was in 1982 and 1984.

The People: Pop. 1980: 487,833, up 31.0% 1970–80. Households (1980): 81% family, 51% with

children, 72% married couples; 25.8% housing units rented; median monthly rent: $177; median house value: $58,200. Voting age pop. (1980): 303,406; 3% Spanish origin, 1% Black, 1% Asian origin, 1% American Indian.

1984 Presidential Vote:

Reagan (R) 170,555	(78%)
Mondale (D) 47,364	(22%)

Rep. James V. Hansen (R)

Elected 1980; b. Aug. 14, 1932, Salt Lake City; home, Farmington; U. of UT, B.A. 1960; Mormon; married (Ann).

Career: Navy, Korea; Farmington City Cncl., 1962–72; UT House of Reps., 1972–80, Speaker, 1978–80.

Offices: 1113 LHOB 20515, 202-225-0453. Also 1017 Fed. Bldg., 324 25th St., Ogden 84401, 801-625-5677; and 435 E. Tabernacle, Ste. 105, St. George 84770, 801-628-1071.

Committees: *Armed Services* (16th of 21 R). Subcommittees: Procurement and Military Nuclear Systems; Readiness. *Interior and Insular Affairs* (9th of 15 R). Subcommittees: General Oversight and Investigations; National Parks and Public Lands; Water and Power Resources. *Standards of Official Conduct* (3d of 6 R).

Group Ratings

	ADA	ACLU	COPE	CFA	LCV	ACU	NTU	NSI	COC	CEI
1986	0	10	4	17	16	91	65	100	93	90
1985	5	—	5	17	—	95	70	—	86	—

National Journal Ratings

	1986 LIB — 1986 CONS		1985 LIB — 1985 CONS	
Economic	0% —	94%	16% —	84%
Social	0% —	89%	0% —	76%
Foreign	0% —	86%	0% —	76%

Key Votes

1) Lmt Cln Water Act	FOR	5) Retain Gun Cont	AGN	9) Aid Angola Reb	FOR
2) Rpl Tobac Sub	FOR	6) Contra Aid	FOR	10) Tax Reform	AGN
3) Grm-Rdmn Def Red	FOR	7) Lmt Text Imp	AGN	11) S Africa Sanc	AGN
4) Ban Polygraph	AGN	8) Limit SDI	AGN	12) Immig Reform	—

Election Results

1986 general	James V. Hansen (R)	82,151	(52%)	($419,959)
	Gunn McKay (D)	77,180	(48%)	($244,261)
1986 primary	James V. Hansen (R) unopposed			
1984 general	James V. Hansen (R)	142,952	(71%)	($138,477)
	Milt Abrams (D).	56,619	(28%)	($32,221)

Campaign Contributions and Expenditures

1985-86		Direct Cont. 1985-86		PACS Breakdown 1985-86			
Receipts	$405,790	Indiv.	$165,046	Corp.	$97,965	T/M/H	$73,343
Expend.	$419,959	Party	$11,979	Labor	$0	Agr.	$250
Unspent	$23,561	PACS	$219,381	Ideo.	$44,353	CWOS	$3,470

SECOND DISTRICT

The center of Utah and of the Mormon Church is Temple Square, nestled beneath the towering mountains that flank Salt Lake City. Here you can find the Mormon Tabernacle, home of the famous choir, and the Temple itself, which is entered only by Church members. Two long blocks north is the state Capitol, four blocks south is City Hall, all around are Salt Lake City's impressive array of skyscrapers. Everywhere the snow-capped mountains can be seen towering in the east and the Great Salt Lake to the west shimmering in the waning light of day. Ironically, Salt Lake City is the least Mormon and most cosmopolitan part of Utah: with the state university and businesses bringing in outsiders, some think it now has a gentile (i.e., non-Mormon) majority.

Utah's 2d Congressional District, which includes most of Salt Lake County, has lower percentages of families, children, and married couples per household than the other two Utah districts; there is a tiny slum and a street well enough known for prostitution that when Representative Allan Howe was arrested here in 1976 most people assumed that he was up to no good. The 2d District also includes most of Utah's most affluent people, living in Salt Lake City and suburbs like East Millcreek, Holladay, and Cottonwood, right next to the Wasatch Mountains which rise, right there, to 9,000 feet. It is just an easy drive up or over the mountains, as recruiters for businesses here like to tell prospects, to the ski slopes at Park City and Alta. The district also includes some of the more modest suburbs on the flat land just south of Salt Lake City and east toward the Lake.

Politically the 2d District is as marginal as any, with voters less deeply rooted than in smaller, more heavily Mormon cities; it has had a volatile congressional politics. It has had close races between the parties most years since 1972, when 35-year-old Democrat Wayne Owens attracted attention by walking the district (it went all the way down to the Arizona border then) and upset an incumbent Republican. Owens served on the Judiciary Committee and voted to impeach Richard Nixon in 1974, but he lost the Senate race that year to Jake Garn; Howe held it for the Democrats in 1974 but lost in 1978 to Republican Dan Marriott. Marriott and Owens, returned from an LDS mission to Montreal, were both beaten by Norman Bangerter in the 1984 gubernatorial race, while Republican congressional nominee David Monson, subject of a lawsuit and once a business partner of man accused later of spying for the Soviet Union, nearly lost the House seat to Democratic state Senator Frances Farley.

In 1986 Monson prudently decided to retire from Congress, and Wayne Owens decided to run again in the 2d District. His opponent, Tom Shimizu, is from a family that came here as refugees from the evacuation of Japanese-Americans from the West Coast in World War II. Experienced as a Salt Lake County Comissioner, a supporter of President Reagan, he showed little command of national issues, while Owens was arguing he knew the territory and knew how to raise the awesome sum of $699,000, most of it from PACS. Owens won rather convincingly, 55%–44%. He serves now on the Foreign Affairs and Interior Committees. His voting record is likely to be somewhat less liberal than it was in his first term back in the early 1970s; he is a long way now, and so is Utah, from the days when he served nearly 20 years ago as a top aide to then Senate Democratic Whip Edward Kennedy. There will probably be a serious Republican challenger here in 1988, but Owens has shown strength and will likely be the favorite.

The People: Pop. 1980: 487,475, up 21.3% 1970–80. Households (1980): 72% family, 43% with children, 61% married couples; 35.8% housing units rented; median monthly rent: $200; median house value: $63,100. Voting age pop. (1980): 325,863; 4% Spanish origin, 1% Asian origin, 1% Black, 1% American Indian.

1984 Presidential Vote:

Reagan (R)	144,966	(68%)
Mondale (D)	64,712	(31%)

Rep. Wayne Owens (D)

Elected 1986; b. May 2, 1937, Panquitch; home, Salt Lake City; U. of UT, B.A. 1961, J.D. 1964; Mormon; married (Marlene).

Career: Aide to Sen. Frank Moss, 1965–68; A.A. to Sen. Edward Kennedy, 1971–72; U.S. House of Reps., 1972–74; Pres., Mormon Church Mission, Montreal, Canada, 1975–78; Practicing atty.

Offices: 1728 LHOB 20515, 202-225-3011. Also 125 S. State St., Salt Lake City 84138, 801-524-4394.

Committees: *Foreign Affairs* (26th of 27 D). Subcommittees: Africa; Europe and the Middle East. *Interior and Insular Affairs* (23d of 26 D). Subcommittees: Energy and the Environment; Mining and Natural Resources; Water and Power Resources.

Group Ratings and Key Votes: Newly Elected

Election Results

1986 general	Wayne Owens (R).....................	76,921	(55%)	($704,609)
	Tom Shimizu (D).....................	60,967	(44%)	($373,077)
1986 primary	Wayne Owens (R) unopposed			
1984 general	David S. Monson (R).................	105,540	(49%)	($385,982)
	Frances Farley (D)...................	105,044	(49%)	($349,427)

Campaign Contributions and Expenditures

1985–86		Direct Cont. 1985–86		PACS Breakdown 1985–86			
Receipts	$699,328	Indiv.	$280,929	Corp.	$32,652	T/M/H	$71,246
Expend.	$704,609	Party	$10,999	Labor	$198,792	Agr.	$3,000
Debts	$5,281	PACS	$398,130	Ideo.	$88,693	CWOS	$3,747
		Cand.	$3,000				

THIRD DISTRICT

The heartland of the Mormon Church in America is in a geographically isolated valley between 11,000-foot peaks of the Wasatch Range and the shores of salty Utah Lake. Here is Provo, the home of Brigham Young University, an institution long known for the rigorous and conservative views of its faculty, the old-fashioned moral standards of its students and the thriving skills of its quarterbacks. It is also the home of the Osmond family. Mormonism has always welcomed, and not been hostile to, technological innovation. The Mormon commonwealth, after all, started off with a terrific labor shortage and was willing to use any reasonable means—labor-saving devices, polygamy—to overcome it and prosper. This is an optimistic area, and one with an historical warrant for its optimism: you have only to look at the beautiful but forbidding terrain to understand how much the early Mormon settlers here banked on their own efforts and how much they accomplished.

Utah's 3d Congressional District includes Provo and Utah County and a strip of land about 10 miles wide and less than 40 miles long that runs up along the Jordan River to the modest southwestern suburbs of Salt Lake City. These two urban areas cast nearly two-thirds of the district's votes; the rest are cast in towns scattered amid huge mountains, florid rock formations, and deep canyons from Wyoming down to the Arizona border. Its northernmost point is near Wyoming's Overthrust Belt, site of the greatest American oil and gas strikes of the late 1970s, and it includes the depressed uranium country in the eastern part of the state around Moab. This was the nation's most Republican congressional district in the 1980 presidential election, and was among the leaders in 1984.

The 3d District was created when Utah gained a third seat in the 1980 Census. The congressman here, former Utah House Speaker Howard Nielson, has also been a professor of statistics at Brigham Young. He got a seat on the House Energy and Commerce Committee—a coveted post—and on the Health and the Environment Subcommittee, where he can be expected to resolve conflicts in favor of encouraging economic growth and taking some risks, in situations where the extent of dangers of environmental pollution can't be known for years. In 1985 Nielson took a seat on Government Operations as well, and now serves as ranking Republican on the Housing and Government Activities and Transportation Subcommittee. Nielson is hard-working and has been a force on national legislation. But he also keeps his eye on local matters, seeing if he can't revive the old U.S. Steel Geneva plant in Provo and protecting the Bonneville Unit of the Central Utah water project from cuts by environmentalists.

The decisive contest in this district was the 1982 Republican primary, which Neilson won by a small margin and by virtue of his majority in his home base, Utah County; in the rest of the district he ran even. In the general election he faced an independent running with Democratic endorsement and won 77% of the vote—not far from the standard Republican percentage here. He has been reelected with 75% and 67% of the vote.

The People: Pop. 1980: 485,729, up 70.3% 1970–80. Households (1980): 83% family, 57% with children, 75% married couples; 25.1% housing units rented; median monthly rent: $183; median house value: $58,600. Voting age pop. (1980): 291,663; 3% Spanish origin, 2% American Indian, 1% Asian origin.

1984 Presidential Vote: Reagan (R) 153,584   (77%)
    Mondale (D) 43,293   (22%)

Rep. Howard C. Nielson (R)

Elected 1982; b. Sept. 12, 1924, Richfield; home, Provo; U. of UT, B.S. 1947; U. of OR, M.S. 1949, Stanford U., M.B.A. 1956, Ph.D. 1958; Mormon; married (Julia).

Career: Army, 1943–46; Statistician, 1949–51; Research economist, Stanford Res. Inst., 1951–57; Prof., Brigham Young U., 1957–76, 1978–82, Chmn., Dept. of Statistics, 1960–63; UT House of Reps., 1967–74, Major. Ldr., 1969–70, Spkr., 1973–74.

Offices: 1229 LHOB 20515, 202-225-7751. Also 88 W. 100, N., #105, Provo 84601, 801-377-1776; 92 E. Center St., #1, Moab 84532, 801-259-7188; 2207 Fed. Bldg., 125 S. State, Salt Lake City 84138, 801-524-5301; and 114 Fed. Bldg., 125 E. 100, N., Heber City 84032, 801-654-1144.

Committees: *Energy and Commerce* (13th of 17 R). Subcommittees: Commerce, Consumer Protection and Competitiveness; Telecommunications and Finance. *Government Operations* (6th of 15 R). Subcommittee: Government Activities and Transportation (Ranking Member).

Group Ratings

	ADA	ACLU	COPE	CFA	LCV	ACU	NTU	NSI	COC	CEI
1986	5	15	7	17	16	95	64	100	89	83
1985	5	—	4	17	—	90	69	—	100	—

National Journal Ratings

	1986 LIB — 1986 CONS		1985 LIB — 1985 CONS	
Economic	6%	90%	0%	95%
Social	23%	74%	24%	72%
Foreign	0%	86%	0%	76%

Key Votes

1) Lmt Cln Water Act	FOR	5) Retain Gun Cont	AGN	9) Aid Angola Reb	FOR
2) Rpl Tobac Sub	FOR	6) Contra Aid	FOR	10) Tax Reform	AGN
3) Grm-Rdmn Def Red	FOR	7) Lmt Text Imp	AGN	11) S Africa Sanc	AGN
4) Ban Polygraph	FOR	8) Limit SDI	AGN	12) Immig Reform	FOR

Election Results

1986 general	Howard C. Nielson (R).................	86,599	(67%)	($104,151)
	Dale F. Gardiner (D)...................	42,582	(33%)	($37,279)
1986 primary	Howard C. Nielson (R) unopposed			
1984 general	Howard C. Nielson (R)...............	138,918	(75%)	($177,835)
	Bruce R. Baird (D)...................	46,560	(25%)	

Campaign Contributions and Expenditures

1985-86		Direct Cont. 1985-86		PACS Breakdown 1985-86			
Receipts	$118,151	Indiv.	$21,284	Corp.	$41,600	T/M/H	$42,889
Expend.	$104,659	Party	$3,234	Labor	$0	Agr.	$0
Unspent	$30,659	PACS	$92,614	Ideo.	$5,875	CWOS	$2,250
		Cand.	$1,370				

VERMONT

Clapboard villages and ski condominiums, dairy cows almost as numerous as people and computerized cottages where workers are wired to the whole world: Vermont seems sometimes stuck in the 19th century, sometimes thrust forward into the 21st, seldom tarrying in the 20th. Subtract the automobiles from almost any Vermont landscape, and you're back in the America of 100 years ago: the classic New England town squares are still there; the taciturn Yankee farmers still tap sugar maple trees in early spring; the autumn foliage, perhaps the most magnificent in the world, is seen across landscapes which seem untouched by the technology of the automobile, petrochemical, or silicon revolutions. There are no rows of gas stations on divided highways, franchise restaurants, or shopping malls. Covered bridges seem a more common sight than freeway interchanges.

Vermont has a quaint look to our eyes, as if it were the product of simple, modest rustics. But actually it is solid. The stone office buildings and courthouses, the gold ornament on the Capitol, the solid timbers of big frame houses—these are what remain when the ticky-tack, ramshackle buildings of the 1880s have long since crumbled into dust. Vermont began as an agricultural state, a target of America's northward and eastward migration (as important, for a while, as westward movement), a place where second sons and daughters from small New England farms went starting in the 1790s to scratch out livings from the rocky soil. They did well. As time went on Vermont developed commerce as well as agriculture, it spawned cottage industries—people sewing apparel in their homes, for example, rather than in factories. Vermont accumulated capital, invested it thriftily elsewhere, and used the returns to build the solid buildings that seem the essence of Vermont today.

Vermont also exported people, and aged. Vermont never developed much labor-intensive industry or large factories, and so second sons and daughters left for parts west. The result is that millions of Americans today probably have Vermont blood—far more than the half million who live in the state now, many of whom have no Vermont roots at all. (Two Presidents were born here, but both made their careers elsewhere, Chester Arthur in New York, Calvin Coolidge in Massachusetts.) From 1850 to 1960 Vermont's population hovered between 300,000 and

400,000; only in 1963 were there more people than cows in the state.

Since then Vermont has been changing rapidly. Its economy has been booming, led by the leisure time industries—ski resorts, summer homes—which some see as the harbinger of 21st century growth. IBM, with several big and technologically important installations around Burlington, is now the state's biggest employer. Vermont's tradition of cottage industries continues, with women knitters seeking to overturn union-inspired federal bans on home production. As more Americans get to live where they choose, more choose to live in Vermont. The 1960 population of 390,000 rose to 444,000 by 1970 and 541,000 by 1986.

Demographic change has produced political change. Nineteenth century Vermont was long the most Republican state in the nation; in 1936 Vermont and Maine were the only states to resist Franklin Roosevelt's landslide. Twenty-first century Vermont now has two-party, maybe three-party, politics. Vermont today has one Democratic Senator—the first in its history—and for most of the last generation it has elected Democratic governors. Before 1960 the only areas of Democratic strength were the small Irish and French Canadian communities in Burlington and other towns near the Canadian border; it was almost as if the entire Catholic minority were Democrats and the entire Protestant majority Republicans. Today the old Yankee and Catholic blocs don't always hold together, and the newcomers have increased the environmentalist, generally liberal vote that has helped not only Democrats, but also liberal Republicans and left-wingers like Bernard Sanders, the socialist Mayor of Burlington, who received 14% of the vote for governor in 1986.

Yet there are limits to Vermont's cultural liberalism. In 1986, despite a crackerjack campaign in favor, voters turned down a state Equal Rights Amendment, as voters have in other often culturally liberal states like New York and Iowa. Opponents here as there argued that the amendment's general wording would leave too many important decisions to unpredictable courts. Coincidentally, Vermont got its own court scandal just after the election, when three members of the state Supreme Court were asked to step aside because of alleged unspecified favoritism toward a woman who had been a lay judge in Burlington. Not much of a scandal by Chicago standards; but politics here still has a small town atmosphere.

Vermont has taken precisely the opposite path of its next-door neighbor New Hampshire. In the 1950s they both had low taxes and small government; but New Hampshire has never passed a sales or income tax, while Vermont has raised taxes and spent money on education and environmental protection. Both strategies have been successful, since both states have attracted lots of migrants; increasingly they seem to self-select themselves to fit the state's images and policies and thus reinforce their existing differences. New Hampshire, with most of its population concentrated in the south and a heritage of heavy industry, would seem to have been the likelier candidate for a big-government strategy; but has set itself up as an alternative to nearby Massachusetts. Vermont, on the other hand, has its population scattered all over the state and its largest town up on Lake Champlain nearer Montreal than to any significant U.S. city; it has succeeded in attracting people from farther afield.

Governor. Governor Madeleine Kunin is a symbol of the new Vermont. Born in Switzerland, she grew up in the Berkshires of Massachusetts, moved to Vermont with her husband, and as she raised her four children was a teacher and journalist and got elected to the legislature in 1972. She thus came into government when concern for the environment was sweeping all before it in Vermont politics. In 1978 she was elected lieutenant governor, in 1982 she ran against popular businessman-Governor Richard Snelling and lost. But not badly (55%–44%) and when Snelling retired in 1984 she ran and won. Neither of her victories has been overwhelming. She won 50%–48% in 1984 and 47%–38% in 1986; technically, she was selected by the legislature, which chooses when neither candidate has 50%. But the legislature is controlled by the Democrats and neither Sanders nor Republican Peter Smith was for overturning the obvious verdict of the voters.

Kunin is a liberal Democrat strongly supportive of the environment who argues that the state government can't afford more taxes or great increases in services. Her chief program in 1987

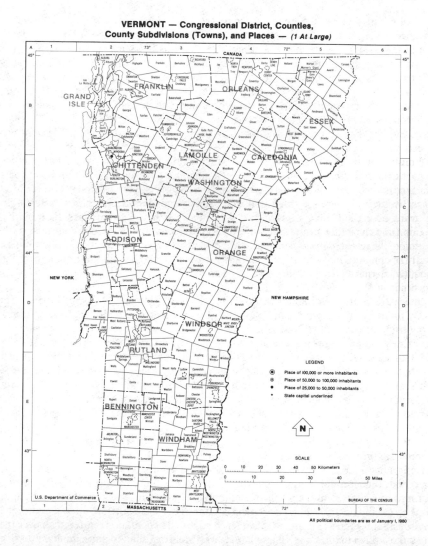

VERMONT — Congressional District, Counties, County Subdivisions (Towns), and Places — *(1 At Large)*

was to equalize education spending across the state by redistributing local property tax revenues from cities and towns with large great lists (the great list is the property tax roll) to those with little money; critics charge this amounts to a statewide property tax. Vermont is one of the last three states to elect its governor every two years; in 1988 Kunin must decide whether to run for a third term or to seek the Senate seat that everyone expects Robert Stafford will vacate.

Senators. Vermont's most durable and successful politician is Robert Stafford, who has held statewide office since 1954. He was elected governor in 1958 and to Congress in 1960; he was appointed Senator when the incumbent died in 1971. Stafford is a taciturn Yankee, neither aggressive nor overbearing; he does not look like a natural politician. Yet he has had his political and policy achievements. On policy, he spent the first six Reagan years as chairman of the Environment and Public Works Committee, where he foiled attempts to relax the Clean Air Act, pushed for a tough acid rain bill (Vermont feels its lakes and snows are polluted by the industrial Great Lakes' coal smoke), and championed a very expansive version of the Superfund. Stafford also proved a roadblock, as a member of the Labor and Human Resources Committee, to many of the changes in labor and welfare laws conservative Republicans wanted.

On other issues, Stafford is not always so liberal; and overall his record and temperament seem well suited to Vermont. But he has not won reelection by overwhelming margins. He beat Governor Thomas Salmon 50%–45% in 1976; in 1982 he won just 46% against two conservative opponents in the Republican primary, and beat a relatively little known Democrat by only 51%–48%. In April 1987 Stafford made it official and announced his retirement after a long and honorable career. Representative James Jeffords had already announced he'd run for the seat if Stafford retired; Snelling took himself out of the race the same week; Kunin said she'd decide by summer. But Jeffords's huge reelection margins and wide popularity made him the immediate favorite for the seat.

Vermont's junior Senator, and the only Democratic Senator in its history, Patrick Leahy, is now a power in Washington. After two sometimes tumultuous years as vice-chairman of the Intelligence Committee, he became chairman of the Agriculture Committee in 1987. He contrasts with the previous chairman, Jesse Helms, not just in positions on issues, but in energy: Helms watched tobacco issues closely, but wasn't well prepared on others and had to be propped up by Bob Dole on occasion; Leahy is more dutiful and hard-working. He comes to the chair in a crisis period, when everyone agrees that farm programs need to cost less and do more; he feels also that the committee can do more to revive rural America. That idea makes sense certainly in Vermont, where agriculture is actually a small segment of the economy, but which sees itself as, and to a substantial extent really is, rural. And Leahy does have his parochial interests too. Vermont is part of the gigantic New York milkshed, and Leahy has spent years carefully tending the dairy programs which are important to so many of his constituents.

Leahy has a record on other issues that is generally liberal, but one which he is also able to claim plausibly is parsimonious. His dovishness is not out of line with state sentiments nor is his liberal stand on most cultural issues; his pro-choice stance on abortion has not hurt him in a state where Democrats' historic base was almost entirely Catholic, perhaps because he is an Irish and Italian Catholic himself. But he has the kind of quiet, thoughtful temperament, combined with a certain zest for life and puckish sense of humor, that seems to be part of the Yankee heritage in Vermont.

Leahy first won the seat in 1974, when that quintessential Vermont Yankee George Aiken retired after 34 years in the Senate. Leahy had made a name for himself as a Burlington area prosecutor who tried all cases personally and attacked the big oil companies during the gasoline price crisis of 1974. Elected by a narrow margin in 1974, he won again by a narrow margin in 1980 in a year when most other vulnerable Democrats lost; Leahy's long-nurtured reputation for thrift got him through a rough year. In 1986 he faced his strongest opponent, former Governor Richard Snelling, a businessman who had been one of the nation's leading authorities on federalism and a thoughtful but sometimes angry critic of the Reagan Administration. But Snelling made all the wrong moves. He seemed reluctant to run, then let himself be manuevered into the race in a way that made him look like the Administration's champion. He launched a harsh negative campaign against the popular Leahy, which allowed Leahy to point out it was orchestrated by the people who had put together Jesse Helms's campaign. He pointed out that he would be chairman of Agriculture if the Democrats took control. In a race which voters began with positive feelings about both candidates, a consensus developed quickly for Leahy, and he won by a 63%–35% margin, carrying every county and all but 10 of Vermont's towns. Does a Democrat have a safe Senate seat in historically Republican Vermont? Looks like it.

Representative. Vermont's congressman-at-large is James Jeffords, a Republican with one of the most liberal records in his party. Even in 1981, when Republicans were voting lockstep for the Reagan economic policies, Jeffords was voting against the Reagan tax plan; by 1982 he was a pretty vocal critic of Reagan budget cuts. The surprise is when he supports an Administration or conservative position, which he does more often on economic than on cultural or foreign issues. First elected in 1974, he is one of the more senior Republicans in the House. He was elbowed aside from the ranking position on the Agriculture Committee in 1982 by Illinois's Edward

Madigan, but he has the ranking position on Education and Labor. His leverage in a closely divided House is potentially great, and he can work with chairman Augustus Hawkins on jobs programs. But his influence with the large majority of House Republicans is very limited indeed, and it is not especially great with Democrats who have gotten used to trying to win majorities with their own votes.

Jeffords long ago announced that he'd run for the Senate if Robert Stafford retired; when Stafford announced in April 1987 that he'd do so, Jeffords was as good as in the race. He will probably have conservative primary opposition, perhaps from one of the conservatives (Stewart Ledbetter, John McClaughry) who have run for the Senate before. But Vermont is one of the few states where the body of registered Republicans covers a broad cross-section of the electorate and where Republican local officials have worked to spend more money on education and to regulate development to protect the environment. So Jeffords's views may not be out of line with those of Republican primary voters and the modesty and austerity of his own lifestyle is very much in tune with Vermont mores. There may be a serious Democratic candidate, especially if Governor Madeleine Kunin runs, but in Vermont the partisan advantage usually goes to the Republicans. So going into 1988 Jeffords has as good a chance of winning a Senate seat as any member of the House.

Presidential politics. James A. Farley had a good laugh on Vermont in 1936 when he updated an adage to say "As goes Maine, so goes Vermont." Vermont still has gone Democratic for President only once, in 1964, but it is now near the median rather than at the heavily Republican end of the spectrum. On cultural issues, there is some resistance to Republicans who take conservative stands: Ronald Reagan won this state in 1980, but with only 44% of the vote; in only six states was his percentage lower. This was also John Anderson's best state (15%), and he did well in the Republican presidential primary, too (29%). In 1984, Reagan carried Vermont by almost precisely his national percentages.

Vermont's presidential primary is early in the season, and the state has tried (but, at this writing, not yet succeeded) to get it scheduled for the same day as New Hampshire's. This is a smaller state and scarcely more typical of the rest of the country than New Hampshire—not to mention any other states which might compete with it for attention.

The People: Est. Pop. 1986: 541,000; Pop. 1980: 511,456, up 3.6% 1980–86 and 15.0% 1970–80; 0.22% of U.S. total, 49th largest. 15% with 1–3 yrs. col., 20% with 4+ yrs. col.; 12.1% below poverty level. Single ancestry: 15% English, 11% French, 5% Irish, 2% German, Italian; 1% Scottish, Polish. Households (1980): 72% family, 40% with children, 61% married couples; 31.3% housing units rented; median monthly rent: $176; median house value: $42,300. Voting age pop. (1980): 366,138; 1% Spanish origin. Registered voters (1986): 327,778; no party registration.

1986 Share of Federal Tax Burden: $1,363,000,000; 0.18% of U.S. total, 51st largest.

1986 Share of Federal Expenditures

	Total		Non-Defense		Defense	
Total Expend	$1,435m	(0.17%)	$1,247m	(0.21%)	$188m	(0.08%)
St/Lcl Grants	334m	(0.30%)	332m	(0.30%)	2m	(1.80%)
Salary/Wages	155m	(0.13%)	121m	(0.21%)	34m	(0.05%)
Pymts to Indiv	754m	(0.21%)	726m	(0.21%)	28m	(0.16%)
Procurement	151m	(0.07%)	28m	(0.05%)	124m	(0.08%)
Research/Other	41m	(0.15%)	41m	(0.15%)	0m	(0%)

Political Lineup: Governor, Madeleine M. Kunin (D); Lt. Gov., Howard Dean (D); Secy. of State, James H. Douglas (R); Atty. Gen., Jeffrey L. Amestoy (R); Treasurer, Emory A. Hebard (R); Auditor, Alexander V. Acebo (R). State Senate, 30 (19 D and 11 R); State House of Representatives, 150 (76 R and 74 D). Senators, Robert T. Stafford (R) and Patrick J. Leahy (D). Representatives, 1 R at large.

1984 Presidential Vote

Reagan (R) 135,865 (58%)
Mondale (D) 95,730 (41%)

1980 Presidential Vote

Reagan (R) 94,628 (44%)
Carter (D) 81,952 (38%)
Anderson (I) 31,761 (15%)

1984 Democratic Presidential Primary

Hart 51,873 (70%)
Mondale 14,834 (20%)
Jackson 5,761 (8%)
Others 1,591 (2%)

1984 Republican Presidential Primary

Reagan 33,218 (99%)
Others 425 (1%)

GOVERNOR

Gov. Madeleine M. Kunin (D)

Elected 1984, term expires Jan. 1989; b. Sept. 28, 1933, Zurich, Switzerland; home, Burlington; U. of MA, B.A. 1956, Columbia U., M.S. 1957, U. of VT, M.A. 1967; Jewish; married (Arthur).

Career: Journalist, college instructor; VT House of Reps., 1973–78; Lt. Gov. of VT, 1979–82; Radio interviewer and talk show host, WJOY, Burlington, 1982–83.

Office: 109 State St., 5th floor, Montpelier 05602, 802-828-3333.

Election Results

1986 gen.	Madeleine M. Kunin (D)	92,379	(47%)
	Peter Smith (R)	75,162	(38%)
	Bernard Sanders (I)	28,430	(14%)
1986 prim.	Madeleine M. Kunin (D) unopposed		
1984 gen.	Madeleine M. Kunin (D)	116,938	(50%)
	John J. Easton (R)	113,264	(48%)

SENATORS

Sen. Robert T. Stafford (R)

Appointed Sept. 15, 1971, elected Jan. 7, 1972, seat up 1988; b. Aug. 8, 1913, Rutland; home, Rutland; Middlebury Col., B.S. 1935, U. of MI, Boston U., LL.B. 1938; Congregational; married (Helen).

Career: Rutland City Prosecuting Atty., 1938–42; Navy, WWII and Korea; Rutland Cnty. States Atty., 1947–51; Dpty. Atty. Gen. of VT, 1953–55; Atty. Gen. of VT, 1955–57; Lt. Gov. of VT, 1957–59; Gov. of VT, 1959–61; U.S. House of Reps., 1961–71.

Offices: 133 HSOB 20510, 202-224-5141. Also 1 Main St., Champlain Mill, #45, Winooski 05404, 802-951-6707; and 27 S. Main St., Rutland 05701, 802-775-5446.

Committees: *Environment and Public Works* (Ranking Member of 7 R). Subcommittees: Environmental Protection: Water Resources, Transportation and Infrastructure. *Labor and Human Resources* (2d of 7 R). Subcommittees: Education, Arts, and Humanities (Ranking Member); Handicapped; Labor. *Veterans' Affairs* (4th of 5 R).

Group Ratings

	ADA	ACLU	COPE	CFA	LCV	ACU	NTU	NSI	COC	CEI
1986	60	76	57	53	100	43	58	50	25	54
1985	45	—	58	53	—	25	49	—	59	—

National Journal Ratings

	1986 LIB — 1986 CONS		1985 LIB — 1985 CONS	
Economic	52%	— 47%	40%	— 59%
Social	48%	— 50%	64%	— 32%
Foreign	53%	— 45%	65%	— 34%

Key Votes

1) Ease Gun Cont	FOR	5) Grm-Rdmn Def Red	AGN	9) Rehnquist Nom	FOR
2) Immig Reform	FOR	6) Contra Aid	AGN	10) Tax Reform	FOR
3) Lmt Text Imp	AGN	7) SDI Funding	AGN	11) Drug Death Pen	—
4) Aid Tobac Ind	AGN	8) Lmt PAC Contrib	FOR	12) S Africa Sanc	FOR

Election Results

1982 general	Robert T. Stafford (R)	83,259	(51%)	($407,340)
	James A. Guest (D)	78,447	(48%)	($282,600)
1982 primary	Robert T. Stafford (R)	26,323	(46%)	
	Stewart M. Ledbetter (R).	19,743	(35%)	
	John McClaughry (R).	10,692	(19%)	
1976 general	Robert T. Stafford (R)	94,481	(50%)	($157,927)
	Thomas P. Salmon (D)	85,682	(45%)	($169,296)

Campaign Contributions and Expenditures

1977-82		Direct Cont. 1977-82		PACS Breakdown			
Receipts	$401,685	Indiv.	$97,512	Corp.	$18,500	T/M/H	$31,199
Expend.	$407,340	Party	$15,811	Labor	$136,320	Agr.	$58,300
Unspent	$3,887	PACS	$295,532	Ideo.	$22,000	CWOS	$7,300

Sen. Patrick J. Leahy (D)

Elected 1974, seat up 1992; b. Mar. 31, 1940, Montpelier; home, Burlington; St. Michael's Col., B.A. 1961, Georgetown U., J.D. 1964; Roman Catholic; married (Marcelle).

Career: Practicing atty., 1964–74; Chittenden Cnty. States Atty., 1966–74.

Offices: 433 RSOB 20510, 202-224-4242. Also 135 Church St., Burlington 05401, 802-863-2525; and Fed. Bldg., Box 933, Montpelier 05602, 802-229-0569.

Committees: *Agriculture, Nutrition, and Forestry* (Chairman of 10 D). *Appropriations* (9th of 16 D). Subcommittees: Defense; Foreign Operations; HUD–Independent Agencies; Interior and Related Agencies. *Judiciary* (6th of 8 D). Subcommittees: Patents, Copyrights, and Trademarks; Technology and the Law (Chairman).

Group Ratings

	ADA	ACLU	COPE	CFA	LCV	ACU	NTU	NSI	COC	CEI
1986	85	85	83	80	100	9	45	0	29	26
1985	70	—	83	87	—	13	31	—	41	—

National Journal Ratings

	1986 LIB — 1986 CONS		1985 LIB — 1985 CONS	
Economic	82% —	16%	74% —	24%
Social	86% —	11%	79% —	20%
Foreign	75% —	0%	88% —	0%

Key Votes

1) Ease Gun Cont	FOR	5) Grm-Rdmn Def Red	FOR	9) Rehnquist Nom	AGN
2) Immig Reform	FOR	6) Contra Aid	AGN	10) Tax Reform	FOR
3) Lmt Text Imp	FOR	7) SDI Funding	AGN	11) Drug Death Pen	AGN
4) Aid Tobac Ind	AGN	8) Lmt PAC Contrib	FOR	12) S Africa Sanc	FOR

Election Results

1986 general	Patrick J. Leahy (D).................	124,123	(63%)	($1,705,099)
	Richard Snelling (R)..................	67,798	(35%)	
1986 primary	Patrick J. Leahy (D) unopposed			
1980 general	Patrick J. Leahy (D).................	104,176	(50%)	($434,644)
	Stewart M. Ledbetter (R).............	101,421	(49%)	($532,904)

Campaign Contributions and Expenditures

1985-86		Direct Cont. 1985-86		PACS Breakdown 1985-86			
Receipts	$1,919,740	Indiv.	$1,024,990	Corp.	$154,225	T/M/H	$210,340
Expend.	$1,705,099	Party	$17,137	Labor	$233,307	Agr.	$29,650
Unspent	$327,768	PACS	$833,356	Ideo.	$193,159	CWOS	$12,675

REPRESENTATIVE

Rep. James M. Jeffords (R)

Elected 1974; b. May 11, 1934, Rutland; home, Rutland; Yale U., B.S.I.A. 1956, Harvard U., LL.B. 1962; Congregationalist; married (Elizabeth).

Career: Navy, 1956–59; Practicing atty.; VT Senate, 1967–68; Atty. Gen. of VT, 1969–73.

Offices: 2431 RHOB 20515, 202-225-4115. Also P.O. Box 676, Montpelier 05602, 802-223-5273; Champlain Mill, 1 Main St., Winooski 05404, 802-951-6732; and P.O. Box 397, 121 West St., Rutland 05701, 802-773-3875.

Committees: *Agriculture* (2d of 17 R). Subcommittees: Conservation, Credit, and Rural Development; Livestock, Dairy, and Poultry (Ranking Member). *Education and Labor* (Ranking Member of 13 R). *Select Committee on Aging* (6th of 26 R). Subcommittee: Retirement Income and Employment.

Group Ratings

	ADA	ACLU	COPE	CFA	LCV	ACU	NTU	NSI	COC	CEI
1986	60	68	48	42	82	14	38	0	56	38
1985	55	—	46	58	—	16	46	—	59	—

National Journal Ratings

	1986 LIB — 1986 CONS		1985 LIB — 1985 CONS	
Economic	42% —	58%	48% —	50%
Social	69% —	28%	72% —	28%
Foreign	75% —	20%	84% —	16%

Key Votes

1) Ease Gun Cont	FOR	5) Grm-Rdmn Def Red	FOR	9) Rehnquist Nom	AGN
2) Immig Reform	AGN	6) Contra Aid	AGN	10) Tax Reform	FOR
3) Lmt Text Imp	FOR	7) SDI Funding	FOR	11) Drug Death Pen	FOR
4) Aid Tobac Ind	FOR	8) Lmt PAC Contrib	FOR	12) S Africa Sanc	FOR

Election Results

1986 general	James M. Jeffords (R)	168,403	(89%)	($86,917)
	Three others	20,320	(11%)	($22,178)
1986 primary	James M. Jeffords (R) unopposed			
1984 general	James M. Jeffords (R)	148,025	(65%)	($53,826)
	Anthony Pollina (D)	60,360	(27%)	($22,178)

Campaign Contributions and Expenditures

1985-86		Direct Cont. 1985-86		PACS Breakdown 1985-86			
Receipts	$178,053	Indiv.	$25,606	Corp.	$19,600	T/M/H	$52,850
Expend.	$86,917	Party	$2,836	Labor	$11,750	Agr.	$31,550
Unspent	$212,676	PACS	$122,300	Ideo.	$3,550	CWOS	$3,000

VIRGINIA

Two hundred years after George Washington presided over the Constitutional Convention, 200 years after the essentials of the soft-spoken and bookish James Madison's plan for a federal government were transformed into a working Constitution that is the longest-lasting governing charter in the world, governing the greatest power on earth; 200 years after these Virginians led the nation, Virginia is once again one of the nation's leaders, in economic growth, in public policy, and perhaps even in political leaders. It has been a long stretch in between. Virginia in 1787 was chronolgically the oldest, geographically the largest, economically probably the richest, and demographically the most populous of the 13 states: if Madison and his pro-Constitution allies had not withstood the frenzied opposition of antifederalist Patrick Henry and prevailed at the state's ratifying convention, it is not clear that the Union could have stayed together.

Yet when the fourth of the presidents of the "House of Virginia," James Monroe, retired in 1825, Virginia's preeminence was already challenged. Its size was dwarfed by the lands being settled across the Appalachians. In population it was surpassed first by Pennsylvania, then New York. The soil was worn out by intensive cultivation of tobacco, and, after the Nat Turner rebellion was suppressed in 1831 and the legislature after long debate rejected proposals for the emancipation of slaves, Virginia east of the Blue Ridge became a vast breeding grounds for slaves. The dazzling brilliance of the generation of Revolutionary leaders gave way to the eccentricity of John Randolph of Roanoke and the unbridled selfishness and general mediocrity of the generation that followed. Virginia had only two more great heroes, Robert E. Lee and Stonewall Jackson, who reluctantly and brilliantly fought for his state rather than his country.

For more than a century after the Civil War, Virginia's public life was scarred by its defeat in war. Virginia lost tens of thousands of young men, its fields and farms were burnt-out battlegrounds, its ablest men were killed or barred from governing. It lost most of its western counties—the coal country, which grew rapidly in the late 19th and early 20th centuries, to the Republican-created state of West Virginia. Industrialization came here and there to Virginia: railroads were built across the state, to ship cotton up from the South and coal to the seaports; textile mills were built in Southside towns and tobacco factories in Richmond; the giant

Newport News Shipbuilding & Dry Dock Company was built by railroad magnate Collis Huntington. But most of the state remained agricultural, sunk in a low-wage economy, ruled by a small class of bankers and lawyers and landholders who worshipped their Revolutionary past and were filled with bitterness over the failure of their Lost Cause. They were pessimists, looking not for economic growth but for stability, bent on maintaining Virginia's segregation and content with its second-class economy, determined to see that the poor masses did not use government to pillage the rich as Yankee troops once had. Organized county courthouse by county courthouse, this class was known as the Byrd machine, led for 40 years, from his election as governor in 1925 to his resignation as Senator in 1965, by Harry F. Byrd, Sr.

Nationally, they lost political battles more often than Lee lost military battles, and less gallantly. But they succeeded in keeping most vestiges of the welfare state and racial equality outside Virginia, even to the point of closing public schools in the late 1950s rather than obey federal court integration orders. But this Massive Resistance collapsed in the late 1950s, Governor Mills Godwin—a Byrd loyalist—accepted integration and upgraded state government in the late 1960s, and, most important, demographic change changed the Old Dominion. As the 20th century advanced, it was the peripheral parts of the state that grew: the coal-mining counties of the far southwest, the Tidewater area around the Navy bases in Norfolk and the shipbuilding yards in Newport News, and the government employee-filled suburbs across the Potomac from Washington, D.C. Courthouse politicians here could no longer carry the vote for the Byrd machine by the middle 1960s: Harry Byrd, Jr., appointed to his father's Senate seat, was nearly beaten in the 1966 Senate primary, and A. Willis Robertson, 20-year veteran of the Senate—and father of televangelist and 1988 presidential hopeful Pat Robertson—was beaten in his primary. Linwood Holton, a Republican and a believer in integration, was elected in 1969. But over the next decade, most of the victories were won by conservatives, some of them Byrd stalwarts turned Republican (like Mills Godwin, returned to the governorship in 1973), some the sons of former insurgent Republicans (like John Dalton, elected governor in 1977) or Republicans with no deep local roots (like John Warner, elected Senator in 1978). The conservatives, using the busing issue or right-to-work or race or whatever came to hand, simply outmaneuvered the liberals; Harry Byrd, Jr., for example, avoided perilous primaries by running as an Independent in 1970 and 1976.

Then suddenly in the early 1980s things began going the other way. The Democrats, shut out in all Virginia presidential elections but one since Byrd, Sr.'s "golden silence" in 1952, won the governorship in 1981 after a 16-year drought, and proceeded to not only to hold onto it four years later but to elect a black lieutenant governor and a woman attorney general. These Democrats had strong black support, they carried the Washington suburbs and the Tidewater and the far western mountains; more important, they carried or ran even in the Richmond area and the rural counties that are geographically and historically the heart of the state. The Democrats won because they no longer represented an attempt to impose a labor-liberal agenda on an unwilling Virginia, but because they argued that they could use government effectively to improve education, build Virginia's economy, and build roads and improve transportation in boom and coal bust areas alike. The catalyst in this change was Governor Charles Robb, elected rather narrowly in 1981, but so popular in 1985 that he would have won near-unanimously if Virginia allowed consecutive terms and he had run. He has impeccable military and Democratic credentials: he is the Marine who married Lynda Bird Johnson and then served in combat in Vietnam. Serious, quiet, he has a demeanor that tradition-minded Virginians trust, even when he promoted blacks and women to leadership positions and spent more money on education. After leaving office Robb became a national figure as head of the Democratic Leadership Council, was ballyhooed as a presidential candidate for 1988, and is widely regarded as a likely winner should he decide to run for the Senate in 1988. He declined to run for President, but is surely on many candidates' short lists of vice presidential nominees.

Governor. The current governor of Virginia, Gerald Baliles, is a Democrat who benefited from Robb's strengths, but has considerable strengths of his own. On the surface he looks grey, quiet,

VIRGINIA — Congressional Districts, Counties, Independent Cities, and Other Selected Places — *(10 Districts)*

Congressional districts established June 12, 1981; all other boundaries are as of January 1, 1980.

even bookish (he is one of the more voracious readers in American politics today), but he has also proved to be a politician who gets what he wants. In 1981 that was the office of attorney general, for which he won upset victories at the Democratic convention and in the general election; in 1985 it was the governorship. There he outmanuevered Lieutenant Governor Richard Davis for convention delegates, by combining support from rural areas (he is from a rural county in the shadow of the Blue Ridge) with votes in northern Virginia (where his pro-choice position on abortion was critical). In the general election, he outcampaigned an attractive Republican, Wyatt Durrette. In office he was almost completely successful with the legislature. He pushed through a transportation program, sorely needed in Virginia's explosively growing suburban areas, including a gas tax and bonds for highway construction—unheard of in the Virginia of Harry Byrd's "pay as you go" tradition. He beefed up Virginia's already impressive system of higher education and promoted international trade. In early 1987 he was calling for changes in the state tax system to adjust to federal tax reform.

Controversy swirled more often around Lieutenant Governor L. Douglas Wilder, who exchanged some abrasive letters with Robb, and Attorney General Mary Sue Terry, who responded slowly with interpretations of the state's conflict-of-interest law. Wilder seems to resent the idea that he won because of Robb's popularity, and understandably; for Wilder himself personally campaigned in dozens of once segregationist rural counties, shaking hands and winning support, and the credit for his victory—the first election of a black lieutenant governor in the South—belongs to him and the voters. Speculation in Richmond pits Wilder and

Terry as candidates for governor in 1989, and both are not far from the evidently popular issue positions of Robb and Baliles; a fight would not necessarily cost the loser his or her current job, since the nominations are made by convention. Other interested Democrats include Representative Norman Sisisky and Delegate Richard Bagley. On the Republican side, two of those who failed to get the 1985 nomination might try again in 1989, though both have weaknesses. Representative Stanford Parris is not well known outside the Washington suburbs, is not universally liked there, and is not known as a hard worker. J. Marshall Coleman, who lost to Robb in 1981, is so distrusted by older party leaders that two-term Governor Mills Godwin personally lobbied the convention to keep him from getting the lieutenant governor nomination in 1985—and came up with a weak candidate who lost to Wilder. This could be a wide-open race.

Senators. Virginia is represented in the Senate by two Republicans with solid conservative records, but with political backgrounds that the late Senator Byrd would have considered odd indeed. Senator John Warner has been fortunate in his marriages: his first wife was a Mellon, one of the world's richest families; his second wife, Elizabeth Taylor, was an effective campaigner for him in 1978. Warner did not actually win the Senate nomination at the Republican convention that year—a gigantic affair, with some 9,000 delegates, probably the largest political convention in American history. But he campaigned hard enough to come in second; and when Richard Obenshain, the nominee and longtime Republican state chairman, was killed in a plane crash, there was no way his supporters could keep from substituting Warner, who had been working hard raising money for the man who beat him. Warner won a hairsbreadth victory in the general election over Democrat Andrew Miller, without convincing Washington observers that he was anything more than a dilettante.

Warner has been something more than that. He served as Secretary of the Navy in the Ford Administration, and is the ranking Republican on the Armed Services Committee now. That is still a position of importance, and he may still end up chairman; the Republicans can still win back the Senate. On the committee Warner has plugged away, working hard to master the issues. He is, as almost every member of Congress from Virginia must be, a Navy man; Virginia's Tidewater region is the East Coast headquarters of the Navy. Warner also serves on the Environment and Public Works Committee, where he supports deregulation of energy prices.

Warner's secret in politics and the Senate has been hard work; Elizabeth Taylor reportedly complained before their divorce that he spent too much time on dull things. Not an original man, he is prone to the most egregious clichés, but he is loyal, and he causes little trouble for his colleagues or his constituents. In effect he won reelection in 1984 without a contest. His sole Democratic opponent, former Delegate Edythe Harrison, was denigrated by state Democratic leaders just as she was announcing her candidacy against a man they shrank from challenging. Harrison is intelligent and her views not much farther out of line with the voters than are those of some Democratic officeholders; nonetheless she was labeled as a nuisance candidate, raised little money, and failed even to carry her home city of Norfolk. Warner has kept working since, often with Governor Gerald Baliles, despite their different party labels; Baliles went out of his way to give Warner credit for successfully pushing through the project to deepen the Hampton Roads port.

Virginia's junior Senator, Paul Trible, is in many ways the unlikeliest of Virginia politicians. He grew up in an affluent suburb of Scranton, Pennsylvania, and after law school worked as an assistant federal prosecutor in the Virginia suburbs of Washington. But his family does have roots there, he attended college and law school in the state, and after his Washington area experience he moved to his family's ancestral home area in the Northern Neck of Virginia—the part of the state northeast of Richmond, and laced with broad estuaries off Chesapeake Bay—to become local prosecutor. From there his upward progress was more rapid than he could have expected. The local congressman retired, unexpectedly, in 1976; Trible ran as a Republican for the seat, and drew an overconfident Democratic opponent; in his first term in the House he was able to make a big issue of Carter Administration plans to renovate the *Saratoga* in Philadelphia, to pay off a political debt, rather than in Newport News, the population center of the district. He went around the state for a year before 1982, anticipating that Senator Byrd might retire; Byrd, against most of his friends' expectations and even after publicly reconsidering at their behest, decided to quit.

Trible then benefited from the Democrats' problems. Chuck Robb had been governor less than a year, and his attempt to choose Tidewater consevrative Owen Pickett, now a congressman, so incensed Douglas Wilder, now lieutenant governor, that Wilder threatened to run as an independent. The upshot was that the Democrats picked Dick Davis, then lieutenant governor, to run, though he had made it plain he wanted to be governor rather than Senator. In many ways he seemed an ideal candidate: a successful mortgage banker and mayor of Portsmouth, with a fine head of white hair, his experience in community affairs was as deep and his Virginia accent as thick as Trible's were shallow and flat. But Trible started earlier and competed more vigorously; Davis challenged his attendance record, but one thing Trible is not is lazy. The low point came when Trible, who never served in the military, ran an ad showing himself in a uniform about to get into a plane.

Senator Trible's greatest national visibility came when Bob Dole named him to the select committee investigating the Iran-contra scandal in late 1986. Until that time he has been scrambling on local issues—protecting the textile industry, Roanoke River flood control, transfer control of Dulles and National Airports to a local authority. He has done his work on national issues as well, compiling a solid if not unvariedly conservative record and serving on important though recently not much publicized committees like Foreign Relations and Commerce. Trible is not naturally popular with reporters: he is prone to speak in platitudes, he holds his cards very close to his chest, he is obviously ambitious, and his conservatism reflects the long-dominant views of the majority in a state which liberals have long loved to hate. But there is nothing in Trible's conservatism of the bitterness and bigotry that suffused so many Byrd machine stalwarts; he worked hard and successfully to win black voters' support in his old House district, and he supported the Martin Luther King birthday holiday. He has conducted dozens of town meetings around the state and kept visible.

Going into 1988, Trible seems to be a clear favorite if not quite a shoo-in for reelection—unless Charles Robb runs. Speculation in early 1987 was that Robb and Baliles would support Ron Dozoretz, a Norfolk psychiatrist who founded a chain of Tidewater psychiatric centers and is vice-chairman of the state Democratic Party; he was raised in New York, but is as deeply rooted in Virginia as Trible was when he first ran. Another possibility is 9th District Representative Frederick Boucher, who has been peppering Trible with criticism and who from his seat on the Energy and Commerce can get a good start on fundraising. But neither would start in a commanding position; Robb would. He is given credit, rightly or wrongly, for much of Virginia's dynamic growth and the confidence and pride that has accompanied it. He begins with overwhelming popularity and a pro-military background which goes together with his willingness to use government on domestic problems aggressively but gingerly. Trible will work hard to hold his seat. But Robb would be the toughest opponent he has ever faced.

Presidential politics. Virginia, prompted for years by Harry Byrd's "golden silences," has voted Republican in every presidential election since except 1964, when it went for Lyndon Johnson (who courted Byrd shamelessly). In 1976 and 1980 it was the most Republican southern state except Oklahoma; in 1984, although four southern states—Florida, Oklahoma, South Carolina and Texas—gave a higher percentage of their vote to Ronald Reagan, Virginia was still overwhelmingly Republican. Its biggest urban areas, which once seemed headed toward the national Democratic party, no longer are: the northern Virginia suburbs of Washington seem increasingly caught up in a free enterprise boom, the Tidewater area is pro-military, and the Richmond area is dominated by conservative suburbanites. Virginia's parties select their national convention delegates through caucus systems. They are to the right of both parties' spectrums.

Congressional districting. One measure of the success of Democrats in Virginia's Chuck Robb era is their progress in House races. In 1980 Virginia elected nine Republican congressmen and only one Democrat, a strong conservative; this was the most conservative delegation in the nation. But Democrats beat two incumbents in 1982 and won two more seats when Republican incumbents retired in the offyears—one in 1982, one in 1986—when Democrats ran better than in presidential years; so now the delegation is 5 to 5.

The People: Est. Pop. 1986: 5,787,000; Pop. 1980: 5,346,818, up 8.2% 1980–86 and 14.9% 1970–80; 2.40% of U.S. total, 13th largest. 15% with 1–3 yrs. col., 19% with 4+ yrs. col.; 11.8% below poverty level. Single ancestry: 15% English, 5% German, 4% Irish, 1% Italian, French, Scottish, Polish. Households (1980): 75% family, 42% with children, 62% married couples; 34.4% housing units rented; median monthly rent: $207; median house value: $48,100. Voting age pop. (1980): 3,872,484; 17% Black, 1% Spanish origin, 1% Asian origin. Registered voters (1986): 2,612,060; no party registration.

1986 Share of Federal Tax Burden: $18,368,000,000; 2.44% of U.S. total, 11th largest.

1986 Share of Federal Expenditures

	Total		Non-Defense		Defense	
Total Expend	$28,039m	(3.38%)	$14,459m	(2.41%)	$13,580m	(5.91%)
St/Lcl Grants	1,995m	(1.77%)	1,990m	(1.77%)	4m	(3.60%)
Salary/Wages	8,705m	(7.22%)	1,785m	(3.04%)	6,920m	(11.18%)
Pymts to Indiv	9,371m	(2.57%)	8,117m	(2.34%)	1,254m	(7.06%)
Procurement	7,260m	(3.53%)	1,858m	(3.34%)	5,403m	(3.60%)
Research/Other	709m	(2.66%)	709m	(2.66%)	0m	(0%)

Political Lineup: Governor, Gerald L. (Jerry) Baliles (D); Lt. Gov., L. Douglas Wilder (D); Atty. Gen., Mary Sue Terry (D). State Senate, 40 (31 D and 9 R); State House of Delegates, 100 (65 D, 33 R, and 2 I). Senators, John W. Warner (R) and Paul S. Trible, Jr. (R). Representatives, 10 (5 R and 5 D).

1984 Presidential Vote

Reagan (R) 1,337,078 (62%)
Mondale (D) 796,250 (37%)

1980 Presidential Vote

Reagan (R) 989,609 (53%)
Carter (D) 752,174 (40%)
Anderson (I) 95,418 (5%)

GOVERNOR

Gov. Gerald L. (Jerry) Baliles (D)

Elected 1985, term expires Jan. 1990; b. July 8, 1940, Patrick Cnty.; home, Richmond; Wesleyan U., B.S. 1963; U. of VA, J.D. 1967; Episcopalian; married (Jeannie).

Career: Asst. Atty Gen., Dpty. Atty. Gen., VA, 1967–75; VA House of Delegates, 1976–82; VA Atty. Gen., 1982–86.

Office: State Capitol, Richmond 23219, 804-786-2211.

Election Results

1985 gen.	Gerald L. (Jerry) Baliles (D) . . .	741,438	(55%)
	Wyatt B. Durette, Jr. (R)	601,652	(44%)
1981 prim.	Gerald L. (Jerry) Baliles (D) nominated by convention		
1981 gen.	Charles S. Robb (D)	760,357	(54%)
	J. Marshall Coleman (R)	659,398	(46%)

SENATORS

Sen. John W. Warner (R)

Elected 1978, seat up 1990; b. Feb. 18, 1927, Washington, DC; home, Middleburg; Wash. & Lee U., B.S., 1949, U. of VA, LL.B. 1953; Episcopalian; divorced.

Career: Navy, WWII, USMC, Korea; Law Clerk to U.S. Crt. of Appeals Chf. Judge E. Barrett Prettyman, 1953–54; Practicing atty., 1954–56, 1960–69; Asst. U.S. Atty., 1956–60; Under Secy. of the U.S. Navy, 1969–72, Secy., 1972–74; Dir., Amer. Rev. Bicentennial Comm., 1974–76.

Offices: 421 RSOB 20510, 202-224-2023. Also 1100 E. Main St., Richmond 23219, 804-771-2579; 805 Fed. Bldg., 200 Granby Mall, Norfolk 23570, 804-441-3079; and 235 Fed. Bldg., 180 E. Main St., Abingdon 24210, 703-628-8158.

Committees: *Armed Services* (Ranking Member of 9 R). *Environment and Public Works* (6th of 7 R). Subcommittees: Nuclear Regulation; Superfund and Environmental Oversight (Ranking Member); Water Resources, Transportation and Infrastructure. *Rules and Administration* (5th of 7 R). *Select Committee on Intelligence* (7th of 7 R).

Group Ratings

	ADA	ACLU	COPE	CFA	LCV	ACU	NTU	NSI	COC	CEI
1986	5	21	13	27	35	73	45	100	79	66
1985	5	—	14	13	—	74	58	—	79	—

National Journal Ratings

	1986 LIB — 1986 CONS		1985 LIB — 1985 CONS	
Economic	0%	— 84%	18%	— 79%
Social	40%	— 59%	45%	— 52%
Foreign	18%	— 77%	12%	— 80%

Key Votes

1) Ease Gun Cont	FOR	5) Grm-Rdmn Def Red	FOR	9) Rehnquist Nom	FOR
2) Immig Reform	FOR	6) Contra Aid	FOR	10) Tax Reform	AGN
3) Lmt Text Imp	FOR	7) SDI Funding	FOR	11) Drug Death Pen	AGN
4) Aid Tobac Ind	FOR	8) Lmt PAC Contrib	FOR	12) S Africa Sanc	FOR

Election Results

1984 general	John W. Warner (R)	1,406,194	(70%)	($2,974,498)
	Edythe C. Harrison (D)	601,142	(30%)	($492,201)
1984 primary	John W. Warner (R) nominated by convention			
1978 general	John W. Warner (R)	613,232	(50%)	($2,897,237)
	Andrew P. Miller (D)	608,511	(50%)	($832,773)

Campaign Contributions and Expenditures

1979-84		Direct Cont. 1979-84				PACS Breakdown		
Receipts	$3,108,607	Indiv.	$1,974,658	Corp.	$537,679	T/M/H	$214,025
Expend.	$2,974,498	Party	$21,422	Labor	$35,348	Agr.	$8,600
Unspent	$44,416	PACS	$883,952	Ideo.	$78,116	CWOS	$2,250
		Cand.	$14,000				

Sen. Paul S. Trible, Jr. (R)

Elected 1982, seat up 1988; b. Dec. 29, 1946, Baltimore, MD; home, Kilmarnock; Hampden-Sydney Col., B.A. 1968, Wash. & Lee U., J.D. 1971; Episcopalian; married (Rosemary).

Career: Law Clerk to U.S. Dist. Judge Albert Bryan, Jr., 1971–72; Asst. U.S. Atty. for East. Dist. of VA, 1972–74; Essex Cnty. Commonwealth's Atty., 1974–76; U.S. House of Reps., 1976–82.

Offices: 517 HSOB 20510, 202-224-4024. Also 113-115 S. 3rd St., Ste. 1-B, Richmond 23219, 804-771-2221; P.O. Box 869, Roanoke 24005, 703-982-4676; Tower Box 59, 2101 Executive Dr., Hampton 23666, 804-838-3309; and 104 S. Union St., Rm. 514, Danville 24541, 804-792-5444.

Committees: *Commerce, Science, and Transportation* (7th of 9 R). Subcommittees: Foreign Commerce and Tourism (Ranking Member); Merchant Marine; Science, Technology and Space. *Foreign Relations* (7th of 9 R). Subcommittees: European Affairs; Western Hemisphere and Peace Corps Affairs. *Governmental Affairs* (6th of 6 R). Subcommittees: Federal Services, Post Office and Civil Service; Investigations.

Group Ratings

	ADA	ACLU	COPE	CFA	LCV	ACU	NTU	NSI	COC	CEI
1986	5	0	11	40	48	78	56	100	79	69
1985	0	—	13	13	—	78	58	—	90	—

National Journal Ratings

	1986 LIB — 1986 CONS		1985 LIB — 1985 CONS	
Economic	25%	— 71%	18%	— 79%
Social	27%	— 70%	17%	— 76%
Foreign	35%	— 62%	12%	— 80%

Key Votes

1) Ease Gun Cont	FOR	5) Grm-Rdmn Def Red	FOR	9) Rehnquist Nom	FOR
2) Immig Reform	FOR	6) Contra Aid	FOR	10) Tax Reform	FOR
3) Lmt Text Imp	FOR	7) SDI Funding	FOR	11) Drug Death Pen	AGN
4) Aid Tobac Ind	FOR	8) Lmt PAC Contrib	FOR	12) S Africa Sanc	FOR

Election Results

1982 general	Paul S. Trible, Jr. (R)................	724,571	(51%)	($2,170,961)
	Richard J. Davis (D).................	690,839	(49%)	($1,192,203)
1982 primary	Paul S. Trible, Jr. (R) nominated by convention			
1976 general	Harry F. Byrd, Jr. (I)	890,778	(57%)	($802,928)
	Elmo R. (Bud) Zumwalt (D)	596,009	(38%)	($443,107)
	Martin H. Perper (I).................	70,559	(5%)	

Campaign Contributions and Expenditures

	1982	Direct Cont. 1982		PACS Breakdown			
Receipts	$2,228,848	Indiv.	$1,414,441	Agr	$14,200	Ideo	$71,225
Expend.	$2,170,961	Party	$33,788	Bus	$523,990	Lbr	$13,714
Unspent	$57,891	PACS	$652,551	Hlth	$20,900	Prof	$10,650
		Cand.	$75,000				

FIRST DISTRICT

The first permanent British settlements in what now is the United States came in Tidewater Virginia, where the waters of the inland sea that is the Chesapeake Bay and the wide estuaries that feed into it provided easy sailing and good anchorages for the tiny wooden vessels that had made it across the Atlantic. There they established a civilization whose elegance is recalled in the craftsmanship of restored Williamsburg and whose coarseness and brutality is brought to life by any narrative of the story of Jamestown or the other beleaguered settlements. Tidewater Virginia brought slavery to America and tobacco to the world, and slave-raised tobacco was the center of its economy in the colonial era and in the years afterward, when its most talented sons left its depleted soil for better opportunities elsewhere.

Now the economy of Tidewater Virginia is based, and the tone of its life is set, by the American military. Hampton Roads, the water that separates Norfolk and Portsmouth from the cities of Hampton and Newport News at the tip of the Peninsula, has the largest concentration of naval bases in the world and one of the world's large ship-manufacturing facilities, the Newport News Shipbuilding and Dry Dock Company. Over the flat neighborhoods that line the baysides you can see the huge ships looming bigger than life; from a distance their turrets and superstructures bristle with armored might. In the years since World War II a giant metropolitan area of more than one million people has grown around the nuclei of military bases and small southern cities and towns, large enough to dominate three Congressional Districts.

One of these is Virginia's 1st Congressional District, which includes Newport News, Hampton, and their Peninsula suburbs, plus Williamsburg and Jamestown, and then goes farther north on both sides of Chesapeake Bay. On the east it includes the southern tip of the Delmarva Peninsula, site of the annual roundup of wild Chincoteague ponies; on the west are the rural Northern Neck counties where George Washington and Robert E. Lee were born, and which in recent years have shown significant population and economic growth for the first time in decades. There is a large black population in all parts of this district, 31% overall; there were big plantations here before the Civil War, and many blacks moved into the industrial Tidewater to find good jobs. Today there is significant integration: the influence of slavery and segregation being overcome by life in the military, the most integrated part of American society.

Historically and in many state elections, this has been a Democratic district; in congressional elections it has been Republican since 1976. The current congressman, Herbert Bateman, won the seat in 1982 when Paul Trible, after six vote-winning years, went on to the Senate. Yet Bateman's career goes farther back than Trible's: he was an old Byrd Democrat who represented Newport News in the Virginia Senate for 15 years and switched parties in 1976. Not especially aggressive, he was outmaneuvered by Trible for the congressional nomination in 1976 and failed to get the Republican lieutenant governor nomination in 1981. But Bateman had the nomination locked up in 1982 and won fairly easily after his first Democratic opponent, Williamsburg legislator George Grayson, withdrew from the race in June. The Democrats replaced him with another young William and Mary professor, John McGlennon, but Bateman won 54%–44%.

Bateman's lack of aggressiveness has showed up since. It took him a term before he got a seat on the Armed Services Committee—a virtual must for representing this area. He also has a seat on Merchant Marine, and has spent time on legislation helping U.S. flag ships. He is a detail man, working hard on measures that will not move the nation very far, but which make a difference to the people and programs affected. He had serious opposition in 1986 from Newport News state Senator Robert Scott, whose record included support of enterprise zones and programs to reduce infant mortality and stressed his strong support of defense spending. Scott won 45% in the Peninsula and held Bateman to 56% overall—not a stunning margin for an incumbent. Scott, incidentally, is black, though elected from a city that is 70% white, and he competed on essentially even terms with Bateman—which tells you how far Tidewater Virginia has come from segregation to military-style integration.

The People: Pop. 1980: 535,092, up 11.3% 1970–80. Households (1980): 76% family, 43% with children, 62% married couples; 33.8% housing units rented; median monthly rent: $180; median house value: $41,600. Voting age pop. (1980): 384,328; 29% Black, 1% Spanish origin, 1% Asian origin.

| 1984 Presidential Vote: | Reagan (R) .... 132,393 | (62%) |
| | Mondale (D) .... 79,051 | (37%) |

Rep. Herbert H. Bateman (R)

Elected 1982; b. Aug. 7, 1928, Elizabeth City, NC; home, Newport News; Col. of William and Mary, B.A. 1949, Georgetown U. Sch. of Law, LL.B. 1956; Presbyterian; married (Laura).

Career: Teacher, Hampton Sch., 1949–51; USAF, 1951–53; Law Clerk to Judge W. Bastian, 1956–57; Practicing atty., 1957–82; VA Senate, 1968–82.

Offices: 1527 LHOB 20515, 202-225-4261. Also 739 Thimble Shoals Blvd., Newport News 23606, 804-873-1132; P.O. Box 1183, Tappahannock 22560, 804-443-4740; and P.O. Box 447, Accomac, 23301, 804-787-7836.

Committees: *Armed Services* (12th of 21 R). Subcommittees: Military Personnel and Compensation (Ranking Member); Seapower and Strategic and Critical Materials. *Merchant Marine and Fisheries* (7th of 17 R). Subcommittees: Fisheries and Wildlife Conservation and the Environment; Merchant Marine; Oceanography.

Group Ratings

	ADA	ACLU	COPE	CFA	LCV	ACU	NTU	NSI	COC	CEI
1986	0	10	5	8	10	68	43	100	78	51
1985	10	—	4	8	—	71	40	—	77	—

National Journal Ratings

	1986 LIB — 1986 CONS		1985 LIB — 1985 CONS	
Economic	16% —	82%	20% —	79%
Social	11% —	85%	30% —	69%
Foreign	23% —	76%	0% —	76%

Key Votes

1) Lmt Cln Water Act	AGN	5) Retain Gun Cont	FOR	9) Aid Angola Reb	FOR
2) Rpl Tobac Sub	AGN	6) Contra Aid	FOR	10) Tax Reform	AGN
3) Grm-Rdmn Def Red	FOR	7) Lmt Text Imp	AGN	11) S Africa Sanc	FOR
4) Ban Polygraph	AGN	8) Limit SDI	AGN	12) Immig Reform	AGN

Election Results

1986 general	Herbert H. Bateman (R) 80,713	(56%)	($602,251)
	Robert C. Scott (D) 63,365	(44%)	($348,485)
1986 primary	Herbert H. Bateman (R) nominated by convention		
1984 general	Herbert H. Bateman (R) 118,085	(59%)	($488,831)
	John J. McGlennon (D) 79,577	(40%)	($265,863)

Campaign Contributions and Expenditures

1985-86		Direct Cont. 1985-86		PACS Breakdown 1985-86			
Receipts	$621,599	Indiv.	$337,857	Corp.	$91,500	T/M/H	$80,004
Expend.	$602,251	Party	$21,695	Labor	$17,626	Agr.	$2,250
Unspent	$31,129	PACS	$224,250	Ideo.	$32,620	CWOS	$250
		Cand.	$18,215				

SECOND DISTRICT

In the quiet days before World War II, Norfolk was a small port city, with 144,000 people and perhaps another 100,000 nearby, a regional industrial center in an economically underdeveloped state, home of several Navy bases but in no way a nationally important or visible city. Today it is the center of the port area with the largest naval installations in the world and the center of a metropolitan area, on both sides of Hampton Roads, with well over one million people. Norfolk and the surrounding cities combine America's antique past with what looks to be its future. The tobacco coast of Chesapeake Bay had its initial growth in the 17th and 18th centuries, and there are here and there in Hampton Roads buildings left from it (as well as restored Williamsburg, a half hour away); the port here languished behind national growth rates in the 19th and much of the 20th centuries; now it has burgeoned with growth that anticipates the 21st. The low-lying land near the wide inlets off the bay has been built up with subdivisions, many pleasantly shaded by fast-growing pines. Near freeway interchanges have sprouted not only shopping centers but such major institution as Pat Robertson's Christian Broadcasting Network and CBN University, housed in gleaming new Georgian buildings larger than any Georgian building ever was.

To the Hampton Roads area the military buildup and economic growth of the last 45 years have brought a population drawn from a wider cross-section of the nation than has traditionally been found in the South. Most people are from some part of the South, but there is no heavy accent here: the brothy Tidewater accent is heard more often farther up the rivers, toward Richmond. Much of Norfolk has the look and feel of a working class town, with shipyard workers, many blacks (35% of the total), and with middle-class neighborhoods out toward the entrance to the bay. East of Norfolk is Virginia Beach, most of it a swamp 40 years ago, with a beachfront honkytonk; now most of the backlands are in pleasant subdivisions, with a large share of the Hampton Roads area's affluent residents, and is only 10% black. Politically, Norfolk is and always has been Democratic; Virginia Beach, the home base of longtime Byrd machine leader Sydney Kellam, has been increasingly Republican.

Norfolk and Virginia Beach together make up Virginia's 2d Congressional District. Once it was solidly Democratic; it even went for Hubert Humphrey in 1968. But the growth of Virginia Beach means that it outvotes Norfolk (with 38% more votes in 1986). Ironically, House elections have gone just the other way. In 1968 the district was captured by Republican William Whitehurst, a thoughtful college professor who served on the Armed Services Committee and was reelected without difficulty until he retired in 1986. That year the district was captured by Democrat Owen Pickett, who may turn out to have a similar House career: he already has the seat on Armed Services.

Pickett had to fight to win the district. Both parties' candidates had represented Virginia Beach in the legislature since 1971. The difference was that Pickett in the House of Delegates was one of those quiet hard workers who get things done, while Republican Joe Canada in the Senate was more of a grandstander—one of the originals of the blow-dried, empty-headed candidate. He was beaten by Charles Robb for lieutenant governor in 1977 and was known for wobbling on the Equal Rights Amendment; in 1986 he was plagued by his close relationship with the head of a bankrupt second mortgage company and his partnership with a Richmond stockbroker sentenced to 25 years in jail for embezzlement and business fraud. Pickett had his own political problems. He is proud to have been a protégé of Kellam, and when he was headed for the U.S. Senate nomination in 1982 he was forced to bow out when Douglas Wilder, now lieutenant governor, said he'd run against him as an independent. Pickett withdrew from the race, tended to his work in Richmond (funding remedial education, divvying up aid to the cities), and by 1986 had solid support from blacks, notably Rev. L. E. Willis, who delivered Norfolk's votes to Jesse Jackson in the 1984 presidential race. Both men raised plenty of money; Pickett lost Virginia Beach 49%–41%, but carried Norfolk 60%–32% for a decisive win. With his political instincts, his Virginia Beach base, and his seat on Armed Services, he seems likely to hold this district.

The People: Pop. 1980: 529,178, up 10.2% 1970–80. Households (1980): 74% family, 44% with children, 58% married couples; 46.1% housing units rented; median monthly rent: $202; median house value: $50,000. Voting age pop. (1980): 383,036; 21% Black, 2% Asian origin, 2% Spanish origin.

1984 Presidential Vote:

Reagan (R)	108,931	(63%)
Mondale (D)	63,616	(37%)

Rep. Owen B. Pickett (D)

Elected 1986; b. Aug. 31, 1930, Richmond; home, Virginia Beach; VA Polytechnic Inst. and State U., B.S. 1952, U. of Richmond, LL.B. 1955; Baptist; married (Sybil).

Career: Practicing atty; VA House of Delegates, 1972–86.

Offices: 1429 LHOB 20515, 202-225-4215. Also Fed. Bldg., Rm. 815, Norfolk 23510, 804-624-9124; and 2710 Virginia Blvd., Virginia Beach 23452, 804-486-3710.

Committees: *Armed Services* (31st of 31 D). Subcommittees: Military Personnel and Compensation; Research and Development; Seapower and Strategic and Critical Materials. *Merchant Marine and Fisheries* (23d of 25 D). Subcommittees: Coast Guard and Navigation; Merchant Marine; Panama Canal and Outer Continental Shelf.

Group Ratings and Key Votes: Newly Elected

Election Results

1986 general	Owen B. Pickett (D)	54,491	(49%)	($607,558)
	A.J. (Joe) Canada, Jr. (R)	46,137	(42%)	($639,598)
	Stephen P. Shao (I)	9,492	(9%)	
1986 primary	G. William Whitehurst (R) nominated by convention			
1984 general	G. William Whitehurst (R)	136,632	(100%)	($67,433)

Campaign Contributions and Expenditures

1985-86		Direct Cont. 1985-86		PACS Breakdown 1985-86			
Receipts	$612,684	Indiv.	$430,235	Corp.	$19,950	T/M/H	$37,650
Expend.	$607,558	Party	$5,098	Labor	$91,250	Agr.	$0
Unspent	$5,125	PACS	$176,529	Ideo.	$25,579	CWOS	$2,100

THIRD DISTRICT

The center of Virginia indisputably remains Richmond. Its metropolitan area is eclipsed in size by the Washington suburbs and by the Tidewater area around Norfolk, but it is still the capital of Virginia nad the home base of most of its major institutions. For years its vested interests—the Virginia Electric and Power Company, the big banks on Main Street and the big law firms like the one that produced Supreme Court Justice Lewis Powell, the Philip Morris tobacco company, and the Richmond newspapers—operating from the capital of the Confederacy kept Virginia very much on the straight and narrow. But Richmond has changed from what it was even a decade ago. Richmond's critics have had the satisfaction of seeing segregation ended and repudiated and the reforms of Democratic Governors Charles Robb and Gerald Baliles endorsed by the voters. Richmond's establishmentarians have had the satisfaction of seeing their state's economy boom and of not seeing it become unionized as the critics wanted.

In the days of Harry Byrd, Sr., Richmond's white majority were conservative Democrats, and its blacks often voted for the more tolerant Republicans. Nowadays the black majority within the city of Richmond is heavily Democratic, but the city is outvoted by the suburbs, which are among the nation's most heavily conservative and Republican. Virginia's 3d Congressional District includes all of Richmond and Henrico County and most of Chesterfield County, which is to say almost all of what has been regarded as the Richmond metropolitan area; although people have been moving farther out to what once were rural counties, and the House district lines may follow them at least a bit in 1990.

The 3d District's congressman, Thomas Bliley, has a similar political history. He was a nominal Democrat as mayor of Richmond between 1970 and 1977; when he ran for Congress in 1980 he became a Republican, got the party's nomination without a primary, and easily won the general election. He has been reelected without difficulty every two years. Bliley is something of a work horse of a legislator, and a thoughtful one. He is a member of the Energy and Commerce Committee, one of the House's most sought-after assignments; on the Health Subcommittee he is predictably a supporter of the tobacco industry and has opposed restrictions on cigarette advertising. He has put forward Congress's leading proposal to ban dial-a-porn phone calls and to require devices that permit parents to limit access to pornographic cable TV channels. He is co-chairman of the Congressional Adoption Caucus, and one of those conservatives who seems genuinely concerned about those in need; as an opponent of abortion, he also favors infant health care and nutrition programs. And he keeps up with local Richmond issues, sponsoring legislation to permit the rehabilitation of the city's Tobacco Row warehouses on East Main Street—a $100 million operation. In the old days Richmond's conservatives seemed inert in government; Bliley, while conservative, seems an activist. He is reelected without difficulty, although he took the trouble of raising and spending about $800,000 in 1986.

The People: Pop. 1980: 533,668, up 12.0% 1970–80. Households (1980): 71% family, 38% with children, 55% married couples; 39.5% housing units rented; median monthly rent: $203; median house value: $47,000. Voting age pop. (1980): 394,810; 26% Black, 1% Spanish origin, 1% Asian origin.

1984 Presidential Vote:

Reagan (R)	155,612	(65%)
Mondale (D)	83,310	(35%)

Rep. Thomas J. Bliley, Jr. (R)

Elected 1980; b. Jan. 28, 1932, Chesterfield Cnty.; home, Richmond; Georgetown U., B.A. 1952; Roman Catholic; married (Mary Virginia).

Career: Navy, 1952–55; Owner, funeral home, 1955–80; Richmond City Cncl., 1968, Vice Mayor, 1968–70, Mayor, 1970–77.

Offices: 213 CHOB 20515, 202-225-2815. Also 4914 Fitzhugh Ave., Ste. 101, Richmond 23230, 804-771-2809.

Committees: *District of Columbia* (3d of 4 R). Subcommittees: Fiscal Affairs and Health; Judiciary and Education (Ranking Member). *Energy and Commerce* (10th of 17 R). Subcommittees: Health and the Environment; Oversight and Investigations; Telecommunications and Finance. *Select Committee on Children, Youth, and Families* (2d of 12 R). Task Forces: Crisis Intervention; Prevention Strategics (Ranking Member).

Group Ratings

	ADA	ACLU	COPE	CFA	LCV	ACU	NTU	NSI	COC	CEI
1986	5	5	11	25	11	73	52	100	88	56
1985	5	—	11	17	—	81	50	—	82	—

National Journal Ratings

	1986 LIB — 1986 CONS		1985 LIB — 1985 CONS	
Economic	15% —	84%	16% —	81%
Social	0% —	89%	0% —	76%
Foreign	27% —	70%	24% —	66%

Key Votes

1) Lmt Cln Water Act	FOR	5) Retain Gun Cont	AGN	9) Aid Angola Reb	FOR
2) Rpl Tobac Sub	AGN	6) Contra Aid	FOR	10) Tax Reform	FOR
3) Grm-Rdmn Def Red	FOR	7) Lmt Text Imp	FOR	11) S Africa Sanc	FOR
4) Ban Polygraph	AGN	8) Limit SDI	AGN	12) Immig Reform	AGN

Election Results

1986 general	Thomas J. Bliley, Jr. (R)...............	74,525	(67%)	($816,159)
	Kenneth E. Powell (D).................	32,961	(30%)	($214,498)
	J. Stephen Hodges (I)..................	3,675	(3%)	($13,545)
1986 primary	Thomas J. Bliley, Jr. (R) unopposed			
1984 general	Thomas J. Bliley, Jr. (R)...............	169,987	(86%)	($243,056)
	Roger L. Coffey (I)...................	28,556	(14%)	

Campaign Contributions and Expenditures

1985–86		Direct Cont. 1985–86		PACS Breakdown 1985–86			
Receipts	$779,700	Indiv.	$465,818	Corp.	$149,334	T/M/H	$120,425
Expend.	$816,159	Party	$15,857	Labor	$4,500	Agr.	$750
Unspent	$8,007	PACS	$296,181	Ideo.	$15,672	CWOS	$5,450

FOURTH DISTRICT

From the Tidewater cities on Hampton Roads to rural counties up above the fall line—a distance it took the first English settlers the better part of a century to explore, clear, and cultivate—stretches the 4th Congressional District of Virginia. This was the scene of some of America's first settlements and of its first revolution, Bacon's Rebellion in 1676; it was the scene also of bitter fighting in the Civil War, as Union troops invested the battlements of the small industrial city of Petersburg, 25 miles south of Richmond. In between are the Tidewater and Petersburg are the flat lands of Southside Virginia fanning south from the James River— tobacco lands when the English first settled them; today they produce Virginia's peanut crop and its Smithfield hams. Today's 4th District has more than half its population in Portsmouth, a Navy port and industrial town with a charming old town section, and the newly developing suburbs of Chesapeake and Suffolk; one-third of the rest is concentrated around Petersburg; the remainder are in rural counties, into a few of which Richmond suburbanites are moving.

More than 300 years ago, planters were bringing in African slaves to work these fields. Today the population of the 4th District is 40% black—the highest percentage of any district in Virginia. Portsmouth has a large and well-established black community, and so does Petersburg; so do many of the tobacco and peanut counties. Politics here for years was run by big landowners, small town bankers, and the like. These people saw themselves as having paternal responsibilities to the community—to help people who are in trouble and, more important to many in Virginia, to keep the community from changing. More recently there has been a kind of plebiscitary democracy which here, in the most Democratic congressional district in Virginia, tends to favor the Democrats.

At least it does when they are as shrewd and politically competent as Representative Norman Sisisky. A Pepsi-Cola distributor from Petersburg, as well as a state legislator with a majority black district, he had the money to finance a big campaign plus a base with black voters to prevent the kind of Independent black candidacies which had sunk some Democratic candidates in the past. All that enabled him in 1982 to beat a landowner-type Republican who had held on for 10 years mostly with pluralities. Since then Sisisky has not had Republican opposition, and doesn't seem likely to given the record he has made in office and the resources he has shown he can bring to a campaign.

In the House, Sisisky began by getting himself assigned to the Armed Services Committee, which is of obvious importance in this base-laden district. He has been critical of the military for spending too much and has asked pointed questions about why the different services pay different amounts for the same items. He has come forward with procurement reforms; but he is also a strong challenger of the Navy's "homeporting" plan which would take some installations from Hampton Roads and scatter them to other ports. Overall, his record is rather conservative on defense and foreign issues, more liberal on cultural and economic issues—a good fit for the 4th District. He is said to be interested in running for governor in 1989, and could make the race without giving up his House seat. But several other strong politicians may also be interested, and it's not clear whether he'll run.

The People: Pop. 1980: 535,703, up 7.1% 1970–80. Households (1980): 79% family, 45% with children, 62% married couples; 32.7% housing units rented; median monthly rent: $145; median house value: $38,900. Voting age pop. (1980): 377,071; 37% Black, 1% Spanish origin, 1% Asian origin.

1984 Presidential Vote:

Reagan (R)	117,579	(56%)
Mondale (D)	91,107	(43%)

Rep. Norman Sisisky (D)

Elected 1982; b. June 9, 1927, Baltimore, MD; home, Petersburg; VA Commonwealth U., B.S. 1949; Jewish; married (Rhoda).

Career: Navy, 1945–46; Pres., Petersburg Pepsi-Cola Bottling Co.; VA House of Delegates, 1974–82.

Offices: 426 CHOB 20515, 202-225-6365. Also Emporia Exec. Ctr., 425-H S. Main St., Emporia 23847, 804-634-5575; VA First Savings and Loan Bldg., Franklin and Adams St., Rm. 607, Petersburg 23803, 804-732-2544; and 801 Water St., Portsmouth 23704, 804-393-2068.

Committees: *Armed Services* (20th of 31 D). Subcommittees: Investigations; Procurement and Military Nuclear Systems; Seapower and Strategic and Critical Materials. *Small Business* (13th of 27 D). Subcommittees: Exports, Tourism and Special Problems; SBA and the General Economy. *Select Committee on Aging* (29th of 39 D). Subcommittee: Health and Long-Term Care.

Group Ratings

	ADA	ACLU	COPE	CFA	LCV	ACU	NTU	NSI	COC	CEI
1986	45	55	61	58	37	48	22	80	36	23
1985	40	—	62	55	—	38	29	—	30	—

National Journal Ratings

	1986 LIB — 1986 CONS	1985 LIB — 1985 CONS
Economic	58% — 41%	53% — 46%
Social	51% — 48%	63% — 33%
Foreign	37% — 62%	42% — 56%

Key Votes

1) Lmt Cln Water Act	AGN	5) Retain Gun Cont	AGN	9) Aid Angola Reb	AGN
2) Rpl Tobac Sub	AGN	6) Contra Aid	FOR	10) Tax Reform	AGN
3) Grm-Rdmn Def Red	FOR	7) Lmt Text Imp	FOR	11) S Africa Sanc	FOR
4) Ban Polygraph	AGN	8) Limit SDI	AGN	12) Immig Reform	FOR

Election Results

1986 general	Norman Sisisky (D)	64,699	(100%)	($53,807)
1986 primary	Norman Sisisky (D) nominated by convention			
1984 general	Norman Sisisky (D)	120,093	(100%)	($105,304)

Campaign Contributions and Expenditures

1985-86		Direct Cont. 1985-86		PACS Breakdown 1985-86			
Receipts	$164,585	Indiv.	$53,063	Corp.	$36,544	T/M/H	$21,750
Expend.	$53,807	PACS	$88,427	Labor	$24,600	Agr.	$1,750
Unspent	$224,269			Ideo.	$3,783	CWOS	$0

FIFTH DISTRICT

Southside Virginia is a geographic name which is also shorthand for a state of mind. In Virginia politics, Southside was always the heartland of segregation, the place where the Byrd machine shut down the public schools, in Prince Edward County in 1957, rather than obey a federal court desegregation order. The 5th Congressional District of Virginia includes most of the Southside region, from Richmond south to the dividing line Colonel William Byrd surveyed in 1728 and from the Tidewater west to the Blue Ridge. Its eastern counties, those nearest Richmond, are flat and humid; they were the frontier in the late colonial period and were plantation country by

1800. Currently about 40% of their residents are black. As you go west into the Piedmont, slowly the land gets hillier. Here you find the textile and furniture manufacturing centers of Danville and Martinsville. Farther west, getting nearer the mountains, you find more livestock and less tobacco, more whites with mountain accents and fewer blacks; the black percentage is about 10%. Altogether the 5th District is 25% black—significantly less than the 40% in the 4th District just to the east.

For years politics here was racially polarized. Before the Voting Rights Act of 1965, it was a stronghold of Byrd Democrats, and its public life was firmly in the hands of big landholders, local bankers, and courthouse lawyers, almost all of whom remembered the Civil War and were dedicated to retaining racial segregation. Since getting the vote, blacks have been solidly Democratic—often the only national Democrats in Southside. But since the election in 1981 of Governor Charles Robb, Southside has become Democratic again in state politics. Robb not only courted old-time Byrd Democrats, like Speaker A. L. Philpott from Henry County, but adopted policies that appealed to rural voters; it didn't hurt in these parts that his successor, Gerald Baliles, comes from Patrick County at the foot of the Blue Ridge.

None of these changes has registered in congressional elections, because the 5th District has been represented since 1968 by Dan Daniel, the last surviving Byrd Democrat in Congress. On most issues Daniel is among the most conservative of House Democrats. He ranks sixth in seniority on the Armed Services Committee, where he generally supports a strong defense and large increases in defense spending; he seems to be temperamentally disposed to accept the recommendations of Defense Department officials and to take for granted their good faith when they assure members of Congress that weapons systems work properly and cost no more money than forecast. He is chairman of the Readiness Subcommittee, where he works to see that military equipment and facilities are properly maintained—a priority that often gets lost in budgeting for new weapons. On the Intelligence Committee, he is the committee Democrat, perhaps the committee member, most inclined to accept the testimony of Administration officials.

Before his election Daniel was an executive at Danville's Dan River Mills, and in 1986 the House ethics committee determined that he violated House rules by accepting free rides on planes belonging to Beech Aircraft, but concluded that he did not intend to violate any law or rule; Daniel apologized, amended his reports, and reimbursed Beech. Daniel seems insulated from present-day politics. His only real contest in the 5th District came in his first election in 1968, when George Wallace was carrying the district, and he had to beat both a Republican and an Independent. Since that time, he has either won easily or been unopposed. Past 70, he gives no sign of retiring.

The People: Pop. 1980: 531,308, up 13.7% 1970–80. Households (1980): 80% family, 43% with children, 67% married couples; 24.0% housing units rented; median monthly rent: $109; median house value: $32,600. Voting age pop. (1980): 382,312; 22% Black, 1% Spanish origin.

1984 Presidential Vote: Reagan (R) 131,912   (65%)
                              Mondale (D) 67,480   (33%)

Rep. W. C. (Dan) Daniel (D)

Elected 1968; b. May 12, 1914, Chatham; home, Danville; Baptist; married (Ruby).

Career: Navy, WWII; Asst. to Bd. Chmn. and other positions, Dan River Mills, Inc., 1939–68; VA House of Delegates, 1959–68.

Offices: 2308 RHOB 20515, 202-225-4711. Also 301 P.O. Bldg., Danville 24541, 804-792-1280; and Abbitt Fed. Bldg., 103 S. Main St., Farmville 23901, 804-392-8331.

Committees: *Armed Services* (6th of 31 D). Subcommittee: Readiness (Chairman). *Permanent Select Committee on Intelligence* (5th of 11 D). Subcommittee: Program and Budget Authorization.

Group Ratings

	ADA	ACLU	COPE	CFA	LCV	ACU	NTU	NSI	COC	CEI
1986	5	7	12	42	38	86	47	100	88	48
1985	10	—	47	25	—	67	45	—	67	—

National Journal Ratings

	1986 LIB — 1986 CONS		1985 LIB — 1985 CONS	
Economic	23% —	76%	40% —	60%
Social	17% —	83%	0% —	76%
Foreign	16% —	79%	0% —	76%

Key Votes

1) Lmt Cln Water Act	AGN	5) Retain Gun Cont	AGN	9) Aid Angola Reb	FOR
2) Rpl Tobac Sub	AGN	6) Contra Aid	FOR	10) Tax Reform	AGN
3) Grm-Rdmn Def Red	FOR	7) Lmt Text Imp	FOR	11) S Africa Sanc	AGN
4) Ban Polygraph	AGN	8) Limit SDI	AGN	12) Immig Reform	AGN

Election Results

1986 general	W. C. (Dan) Daniel (D) 73,085	(82%)	($130,231)
	J. F. (Frank) Cole (I)................... 16,551	(18%)	
1986 primary	W. C. (Dan) Daniel (D) nominated by convention		
1984 general	W. C. (Dan) Daniel (D) 117,738	(100%)	($68,011)

Campaign Contributions and Expenditures

1985-86		Direct Cont. 1985-86		PACS Breakdown 1985-86			
Receipts	$173,552	Indiv.	$43,580	Corp.	$69,725	T/M/H	$22,790
Expend.	$130,231	PACS	$97,015	Labor	$500	Agr.	$1,750
Unspent	$146,097	Cand.	$7,883	Ideo.	$2,250	CWOS	$0

SIXTH DISTRICT

Virginia east of the Blue Ridge was settled by Englishmen coming up the rivers from the Chesapeake, bringing their slaves with them. West of the Blue Ridge the settlers came down the Valley of Virginia on the great Wagon Road from Pennsylvania, and they included not only Englishmen but Highland and Lowland Scots, German Protestants and Mennonites and Moravians, with nary a slave. In the years before the Revolution, while Jefferson was still designing Monticello east of the Blue Ridge, this heterogeneous lot were streaming down the Wagon Road. East of the Blue Ridge lands were planted in tobacco, which required lots of labor and exhausted the soil. West, they were planted in wheat and corn and hay, crops an individual farmer and his family could handle. To the casual traveler today, there is little difference between these two Virginias. Yet their histories in the 1770s were startlingly different—in ways still reflected in politics as we prepare to enter the 1990s.

Thus some of the Valley counties were pro-Union during the Civil War, and in the election returns of the 1980s you can trace the route of the old Wagon Road in the Republican majorities that are cast, even in elections the Democrats win, in the upper part of the Valley around Winchester, down through Harrisonburg and Staunton, and then going over the Blue Ridge in Roanoke down to the still Republican-voting cities of Winston-Salem and Charlotte, North Carolina. For much of the 20th century, Valley Republicanism was an insurgent faith, a credo hospitable to economic assistance to the little guy, and Valley Republicans ran brave campaigns against Harry Byrd's Democrats from time to time; some of them became federal judges during Republican administrations. For 30 years beginning in 1952, the 6th Congressional District, which has included within different boundaries most of the Valley counties, was represented by Republicans.

Now that district, which extends from Roanoke north to Harrisonburg and west to the West Virginia border, and which includes one county and most of the city of Lynchburg east of the Blue Ridge, is represented by a Democrat. He is James Olin, a retired vice president of General Electric, elected in 1982. In that year Olin was a kind of insurgent: Republicans had held the seat for 30 years and the Virginia governorship for 12 of the preceding 13. The Republicans, like southern Democrats of old, were divided; the Democrats united around Olin. He is particularly strong in the Roanoke area; he has lost or carried only barely the upper Valley around Harrisonburg, where the Byrd family still owns the local newspaper.

Olin began his congressional career after a full career of achievement in business, and without the skittishness of some younger members who quiver in fear of their constituents. Olin seems to vote his conscience, which turns out to be pretty liberal on non-economic issues, and does just fine politically. His committees—Agriculture, Small Business—sound like a good match of district concerns. In fact Agriculture has been a panel of great importance, especially in 1985 when the farm bill was rewritten, while Small Business is legislatively almost totally unimportant, bloated in size by politicians who seek a credential useful for reelection but supervising only the most minor (and, if the Reagan Administration had had its way, nonexistent) of federal programs. Olin has been strengthened politically by his vigorous action in speeding flood relief funds to small businesses after the disastrous Roanoke flood of 1985; he initiated also a disaster relief program for southeastern farmers hurt by the 1986 drought. Opposition and age just seem to make him stronger: he was reelected with 69% of the vote in 1986.

The People: Pop. 1980: 538,360, up 8.6% 1970–80. Households (1980): 75% family, 39% with children, 62% married couples; 30.5% housing units rented; median monthly rent: $153; median house value: $38,600. Voting age pop. (1980): 401,356; 10% Black, 1% Spanish origin.

1984 Presidential Vote: Reagan (R) 134,466   (66%)
Mondale (D) 68,311   (33%)

Rep. James R. (Jim) Olin (D)

Elected 1982; b. Feb. 28, 1920, Chicago, IL; home, Roanoke; Deep Springs Col., CA, Cornell U., B.E.E. 1943; Unitarian; married (Phyllis).

Career: U.S. Army Signal Corps., WWII; Plant manager, Vice Pres. and Gen. Mgr., Industrial Electronics Div., General Electric, 1946–82.

Offices: 1207 LHOB 20515, 202-225-5431. Also 406 First St., Rm. 706, Roanoke 24011, 703-982-4672; 925 Main St., 3d Floor, Lynchburg 24504, 804-845-6546; 13 W. Beverly St., 2d Floor, Staunton 24401, 703-885-8178; and Sovran Bank Bldg., Rm. 415, Harrisonburg 22801, 703-433-9433.

Committees: *Agriculture* (18th of 26 D). Subcommittees: Domestic Marketing, Consumer Relations, and Nutrition; Forests, Family Farms, and Energy; Livestock, Dairy, and Poultry. *Small Business* (16th of 27 D). Subcommittees: Regulation and Business Opportunities: SBA and the General Economy.

Group Ratings

	ADA	ACLU	COPE	CFA	LCV	ACU	NTU	NSI	COC	CEI
1986	55	63	52	67	58	14	43	10	56	43
1985	50	—	50	33	—	38	52	—	67	—

National Journal Ratings

	1986 LIB — 1986 CONS		1985 LIB — 1985 CONS	
Economic	42%	57%	43%	57%
Social	63%	37%	57%	42%
Foreign	67%	30%	64%	33%

Key Votes

1) Lmt Cln Water Act	FOR	5) Retain Gun Cont	AGN
2) Rpl Tobac Sub	AGN	6) Contra Aid	AGN
3) Grm-Rdmn Def Red	FOR	7) Lmt Text Imp	FOR
4) Ban Polygraph	FOR	8) Limit SDI	FOR

9) Aid Angola Reb	AGN
10) Tax Reform	AGN
11) S Africa Sanc	FOR
12) Immig Reform	AGN

Election Results

1986 general	James R. (Jim) Olin (D)	88,230	(70%)	($356,857)
	Flo Neher Traywick (R)	38,051	(30%)	($199,880)
1986 primary	James R. (Jim) Olin (D) nominated by convention			
1984 general	James R. (Jim) Olin (D)	105,207	(54%)	($452,636)
	Ray L. Garland (R)	91,344	(46%)	($264,666)

Campaign Contributions and Expenditures

1985-86		Direct Cont. 1985-86		PACS Breakdown 1985-86			
Receipts	$363,604	Indiv.	$196,550	Corp.	$22,607	T/M/H	$54,600
Expend.	$356,857	Party	$3,000	Labor	$54,675	Agr.	$4,200
Unspent	$12,206	PACS	$150,328	Ideo.	$13,196	CWOS	$1,050
		Cand.	$3,000				

SEVENTH DISTRICT

Even as the Constitution was being hammered out in Philadelphia, the rolling green Piedmont of northern Virginia and the fertile mountain-bound lands of the Shenendoah Valley were buzzing with new settlers. From the Piedmont they were coming up the rivers that flow into the Chesapeake, into the Valley from the great Wagon Road south from Pennsylvania, moving onto lands which had been speculated in by George Washington and his peers. But soon the surge of movement propelled new settlers farther west, beyond the Appalachians, and northern Virginia became well-settled, quiet agricultural country—except for the four years of the Civil War, when it was some of the most heavily contested land on the continent.

Now life in the countryside of northern Virginia has changed once again, as metropolitan Washington has moved beyond its old boundaries. Subdivisions are growing up on old fields, and the horse farms of the Piedmont, long the first or second home of some of the richest people in America, have begun to attract a growing population of commuters and weekend residents. What looked like marginal farmlands to the settlers of the early 19th century now looks like something close to heaven for city-dwellers: rolling green hills, with views of the Blue Ridge and other mountains; antique houses and tiny crossroads communities. The region's major towns—Winchester in the valley, Charlottesville and Fredericksburg in the Piedmont, none with a population as large as 40,000—still retain an old-fashioned air at least in the narrow streets of their downtowns, although a McDonald's culture has developed on the bypass roads of their outskirts.

This is the land of the 7th Congressional District of Virginia, which stretches from the outermost Washington suburbs through much of northern Virginia, including Winchester at the northern end of the Shenendoah Valley and Charlottesville, home of the University of Virginia. It was the home of three Presidents (Jefferson, Madison, and Monroe) and, more recently, the home turf of Virginia's Byrd dynasty. In congressional and national elections, the 7th District has switched steadily from Byrd Democrats to conservative Republicans—a switch made easier because often they are the same person.

A case in point is the current 7th District congressman, who sports one of those uneuphonious names that the men who run things in small Virginia towns seem to get saddled with, D. French Slaughter, Jr. He was first elected after a lifetime in and out of politics. He spent 20 years in the state legislature, and there sponsored bills creating Virginia's community college system; he also promoted Virginia's "massive resistance" to integration, in which the state ordered local school systems to close down rather than obey federal court desegregation orders. Asked to comment on that in the 1984 campaign, he allowed that the time had passed for such measures but that he had no regrets of having supported them back then.

Slaughter won the seat in that campaign by a 56%–40% vote. He serves on the Science, Space and Technology Committee, but he seems to have spent much of his legislative energy on another project, a proposal for health care savings accounts—IRAs for health care, in effect, into which people could put tax-free money which they could use later for health care. Slaughter sees this as an alternative to more government involvement, but finds himself opposed by the Reagan Administration's catastrophic health care proposal. He was reelected without opposition in 1986.

The People: Pop. 1980: 535,147, up 31.1% 1970–80. Households (1980): 77% family, 43% with children, 65% married couples; 30.4% housing units rented; median monthly rent: $190; median house value: $48,700. Voting age pop. (1980): 383,878; 11% Black, 1% Spanish origin.

1984 Presidential Vote:
Reagan (R) 142,598	(68%)
Mondale (D) 64,593	(31%)

Rep. D. French Slaughter, Jr. (R)

Elected 1984; b. May 20, 1925, Culpeper; home, Culpeper; VA Military Inst., 1942–43, U. of VA, B.A. 1949, LL.B. 1953; Episcopalian; widowed.

Career: Army, WWII; Practicing atty.; VA House of Del., 1958–78.

Offices: 319 CHOB 20515, 202-225-6561. Also P.O. Box 136, Charlottesville 22902, 804-295-2106; P.O. Box 1075, Culpeper 22701, 703-825-3495; P.O. Box 336, Fredericksburg 22401, 703-373-0536; and P.O. Box 714, Winchester 22601, 703-667-0990.

Committees: *Judiciary* (13th of 14 R). Subcommittees: Courts, Civil Liberties and the Administration of Justice; Immigration, Refugees and International Law. *Science, Space and Technology* (13th of 18 R). Subcommittees: Science Research and Technology; Space Science and Applications. *Small Business* (7th of 17 R). Subcommittees: Antitrust, Impact of Deregulation and Privatization; Exports, Tourism and Special Problems.

Group Ratings

	ADA	ACLU	COPE	CFA	LCV	ACU	NTU	NSI	COC	CEI
1986	0	5	16	25	10	91	58	100	94	63
1985	0	—	12	25	—	86	50	—	95	—

National Journal Ratings

	1986 LIB — 1986 CONS		1985 LIB — 1985 CONS	
Economic	21%	— 77%	12%	— 85%
Social	18%	— 78%	0%	— 76%
Foreign	0%	— 86%	0%	— 76%

Key Votes

1) Lmt Cln Water Act	FOR	5) Retain Gun Cont	FOR	9) Aid Angola Reb	FOR
2) Rpl Tobac Sub	AGN	6) Contra Aid	FOR	10) Tax Reform	FOR
3) Grm-Rdmn Def Red	FOR	7) Lmt Text Imp	FOR	11) S Africa Sanc	AGN
4) Ban Polygraph	AGN	8) Limit SDI	AGN	12) Immig Reform	AGN

Election Results

1986 general	D. French Slaughter, Jr. (R).............	58,927	(98%)	($212,026)
1986 primary	D. French Slaughter, Jr. (R) unopposed			
1984 general	D. French Slaughter, Jr. (R)............	109,110	(56%)	($519,020)
	Lewis M. Costello (D).................	77,624	(40%)	($304,850)

Campaign Contributions and Expenditures

1985-86		Direct Cont. 1985-86		PACS Breakdown 1985-86			
Receipts	$252,801	Indiv.	$149,604	Corp.	$39,140	T/M/H	$34,878
Expend.	$212,026	Party	$6,210	Labor	$7,000	Agr.	$1,000
Unspent	$47,844	PACS	$88,597	Ideo.	$6,813	CWOS	$0
		Cand.	$8,597				

EIGHTH DISTRICT

Two hundred years ago, when George Washington trod the brick sidewalks of Alexandria, Virginia, on his way to market or court or church, this was the largest city in this part of Virginia, dwarfing Georgetown, Maryland, just up the Potomac River; what is now Capitol Hill and downtown Washington were just hills above the river's mud flats. As Washington grew, northern

Virginia just across the river seemed left behind; the District of Columbia retroceded its land south of the Potomac—what is now Alexandria and Arlington—to Virginia in 1846 because it was obvious that the federal government would never need it. It was 97 years before the first federal building was built on the Virginia side, the Pentagon; Franklin Roosevelt wondered out loud what they would do with all that space after the war. When the Pentagon was built, Alexandria and all of the rural countryside of northern Virginia were represented in Congress by Judge Howard W. Smith, a Byrd Democrat, who saw his mission as the maintenance of the standards of Washington, Jefferson, and Robert E. Lee. For him that meant racial segregation, minimal federal government, and control of local affairs by responsible and successful men like himself; as chairman of the House Rules Committee, often controlling the flow of legislation onto the floor, he was able to apply his principles—even after John F. Kennedy and Sam Rayburn packed Rules with a couple of extra Democrats in 1961.

Yet even as Judge Smith kept his law offices in Old Town Alexandria, northern Virginia was changing around him. New subdivision-dwellers, with white-collar jobs and lots of children, wanted schools with good academic programs—not the segregated eighth-grade schoolhouses Judge Smith's friends were willing to finance. They wanted freeways built and traffic lights installed, planning instituted to put limits on sprawl, parks and playgrounds and recreation facilities set aside. Smith's district was moved farther out into the countryside (although even there he was beaten in the 1966 primary), two-party politics came to the suburbs, and local governments got to work.

Today the northern Virginia suburbs of Washington have two congressional districts. The 8th, which is technically the descendant of the district Smith represented for 36 years, begins in Alexandria, and includes not only Old Town but the city's large black population and the two-thirds of its households who live in apartments: this is now a national Democratic city. Beyond Alexandria, in Fairfax County, are the suburbs of Springfield, Annandale, and Mount Vernon, affluent places, with large colonial or, occasionally, contemporary houses built for large families, and with newer townhouse clusters spotting the rolling landscape; voters here are wary both of new developments and of higher taxes, and they have the cautious and sometimes reactionary impulses you find in parents of teenage children. South of Fairfax is Prince William County, where zoning restrictions are less stringent and incomes tend to be lower; and the 8th dips farther south into once rural Stafford County. Growth has slowed in this part of the Washington metro area since the 1960s and 1970s, but continues in its farther reaches at a slower pace. Its affluence is powered by the federal government, whose paychecks have more than doubled since 1960; in the 8th District about 30% of all wage earners take home each payday the familiar green government check.

The congressman from the 8th District is Stanford Parris, a Republican who has proved one of the more resilient if not one of the more accomplished politicians in northern Virginia. He won the district in 1972 when William Scott (once named the dumbest man in Congress) was elected Senator; lost it to Democrat Herb Harris in 1974; came back and beat Harris in 1980; and has held on since. Parris's stock in trade has been to suggest that he shares all the lowest prejudices some suburban residents may harbor, particularly against their black neighbors in the District of Columbia. He is forever inveighing, on the District of Columbia Committee and off, against the District's sieve-like operation of Lorton Prison, in southern Fairfax County, or denouncing the dumping of D.C.'s sludge into the Potomac. What Parris has not done is to follow up his denunciations, or his professions of affection for government workers, with much work. Much of the job of a congressman from the D.C. suburbs comes down to handling constituent complaints and serving the parochial interests of government employees and local communities. Most of the current congressmen, of both parties, work hard at these chores. Parris, however, is known generally as one who dogs it.

Parris has excelled at raising money from Fairfax County developers, not only for House races, but for his unsuccessful race for governor in 1985; he may try to get the Republican convention to nominate him in 1989. After the several close and bitter Parris–Harris races,

Parris won with 56% in 1984 and a record 61% in 1986, when his Democratic opponent was James Boren, a humorous lampooner of bureaucrats. It's still possible he could have a more serious challenger in some future election.

The People: Pop. 1980: 534,366, up 25.6% 1970–80. Households (1980): 73% family, 45% with children, 63% married couples; 36.8% housing units rented; median monthly rent: $312; median house value: $86,000. Voting age pop. (1980): 376,074; 10% Black, 3% Spanish origin, 3% Asian origin.

1984 Presidential Vote: Reagan (R) 141,992   (61%)
Mondale (D) 89,349   (38%)

Rep. Stanford E. Parris (R)

Elected 1980; b. Sept. 9, 1929, Champaign, IL; home, Fairfax Cnty.; U. of IL, B.S. 1950, Geo. Wash. U., J.D. 1958; Episcopalian; married (Marlie).

Career: Air Force, Korea; Commercial pilot; Practicing atty.; Fairfax Cnty. Bd. of Sprvsrs., 1964–67; VA House of Delegates, 1969–72; U.S. House of Reps., 1972–74; Secy., Commonwealth of VA, 1978; Dir., VA Fed. Liaison Ofc., 1978–80.

Offices: 1526 LHOB 20515, 202-225-4376. Also 6901 Old Keene Mill Rd., Ste. 101, Springfield 22150, 703-644-0004; and 14546 Jefferson Davis Hwy., Woodbridge 22191, 703-494-8199.

Committees: *Banking, Finance and Urban Affairs* (5th of 20 R). Subcommittees: Financial Institutions Supervision, Regulation and Insurance; General Oversight and Investigations (Ranking Member); International Finance, Trade, and Monetary Policy. *District of Columbia* (2d of 4 R). Subcommittees: Fiscal Affairs and Health (Ranking Member); Government Operations and Metropolitan Affairs. *Select Committee on Narcotics Abuse and Control* (5th of 10 R).

Group Ratings

	ADA	ACLU	COPE	CFA	LCV	ACU	NTU	NSI	COC	CEI
1986	5	0	25	0	16	83	40	100	71	52
1985	15	—	25	33	—	67	41	—	76	—

National Journal Ratings

	1986 LIB — 1986 CONS		1985 LIB — 1985 CONS	
Economic	29%	— 70%	31%	— 67%
Social	15%	— 84%	0%	— 76%
Foreign	0%	— 86%	0%	— 76%

Key Votes

1) Lmt Cln Water Act	FOR	5) Retain Gun Cont	FOR	9) Aid Angola Reb	FOR
2) Rpl Tobac Sub	AGN	6) Contra Aid	FOR	10) Tax Reform	AGN
3) Grm-Rdmn Def Red	AGN	7) Lmt Text Imp	FOR	11) S Africa Sanc	AGN
4) Ban Polygraph	AGN	8) Limit SDI	AGN	12) Immig Reform	AGN

Election Results

1986 general	Stanford E. Parris (R).	72,670	(61%)	($428,788)
	James H. Boren (D)	44,965	(38%)	($73,981)
1986 primary	Stanford E. Parris (R) nominated by convention			
1984 general	Stanford E. Parris (R).	125,015	(56%)	($863,490)
	Richard L. Saslaw (D)	97,250	(43%)	($292,040)

Campaign Contributions and Expenditures

1985-86		Direct Cont. 1985-86		PACS Breakdown 1985-86			
Receipts	$628,266	Indiv.	$294,273	Corp.	$64,812	T/M/H	$92,764
Expend.	$428,788	Party	$22,334	Labor	$12,000	Agr.	$0
Unspent	$215,092	PACS	$182,499	Ideo.	$11,320	CWOS	$1,603
		Cand.	$119,684				

NINTH DISTRICT

The southwestern corner of Virginia, first settled by farmers in the revolutionary period, streaming down the valleys between the Appalachians on the road to Kentucky, has been a region apart from Virginia since that time. In topography, in settlement, in its economy which still depends much on its coal mines, it has more in common with West Virginia and eastern Kentucky and Tennessee than it does with the great mass of Virginia east of the Blue Ridge. These counties came close to splitting off from Virginia and joining West Virginia during the Civil War; some Virginia counties here spread farther west than any in West Virginia. Mountainous southwestern Virginia has its own cultural traditions: the federal government here can still mean the hated revenuers, and the local music is what you hear from bluegrass banjo pickers and the participants at the Galax Old Time Fiddlers' Convention. Split between secessionists and unionists as the whole mountain region was, southwest Virginia has had a vigorous two-party politics most of the years since the Civil War; and both of the parties have resembled more closely their national counterparts than they have in the rest of Virginia during most of that period.

The 9th Congressional District of Virginia covers all of southwest Virginia west of Roanoke. Over the years it became known as the Fighting Ninth, because of its a taste for raucous, noisy politics: it favored the loud conservatism of William Lloyd Scott in 1972 and the yahooing populism of Henry Howell in 1973; it has elected congressmen loud in their devotion to party and patriotism. It has also changed partisan hands four times in 30 years—in 1952 and 1954, in 1966, and again in 1982—and each time William Wampler, "the bald eagle of the Cumberlands," played a role. As a young Republican Wampler captured the district in 1952 and lost it two years later; he returned to win it again in 1966, and held it until he lost it to Democrat Rick Boucher in 1982. Economic conditions played a major role in the last result: the coal counties on the Kentucky border had high unemployment, and they were just about the only part of the district Boucher carried. He did well enough everywhere else, however, to win a narrow victory.

Boucher, like other Fighting Ninth Democrats, has a record on issues basically in line with national Democratic positions. He is, however, not likely to get way out of line with his district; he is as quick to oppose gun control as he is to champion the interests of coal. In the House he has seats on the Energy and Commerce, Science, Space and Technology, and Judiciary Committees—a full load. He has done useful work on issues ranging from vocational education to criminal statutes. Much of his effort in 1986 and 1987 was aimed at rewriting a criminal statute whose overbroad definition of "racketeering" has caused it to be used by almost any aggrieved party to a business transaction. He is an adept legislator, able to come up with sensible compromises; though he looks young, he was first elected to the Virginia Senate in 1975, and in 1988 he will be in his 13th year as a legislator.

Boucher won one tough race to capture the district and won another tough one, in 1984 against Republican Jeff Stafford, to hold it. By 1986 he was in a strong enough position to be reelected in this highly partisan territory without a Republican opponent. Issues could turn against him, but he seems to have made this a safe district. He has other ambitions, however. He has made it plain he is thinking about running against Senator Paul Trible in 1988, and his work on the racketeering statute has brought him closer to business interests while his record generally continues to endear him to most Democrats. He has made it clear he will defer to former Governor Charles Robb if he decides to run for the Trible seat; it is not so clear whether, as some Democrats would like, he would defer to another potential candidate, Tidewater psychiatrist Ron Dozoretz. If he does decide to run for the Senate, the 9th District will be very much up for grabs.

The People: Pop. 1980: 538,871, up 19.2% 1970–80. Households (1980): 79% family, 44% with children, 68% married couples; 24.9% housing units rented; median monthly rent: $137; median house value: $32,700. Voting age pop. (1980): 388,333; 2% Black, 1% Spanish origin.

1984 Presidential Vote:

Reagan (R)	....	117,088	(58%)
Mondale (D)	....	82,522	(41%)

Rep. Rick Boucher (D)

Elected 1982; b. Aug. 1, 1946, Abingdon; home, Abingdon; Roanoke Col., B.A. 1968, U. of VA, J.D. 1971; United Methodist; single.

Career: Practicing atty., 1971–82; VA Senate, 1975–1982.

Offices: 428 CHOB 20515, 202-225-3861. Also 180 E. Main St., Abingdon 24210, 703-628-1145; 321 Shawnee Ave. E., Big Stone Gap 24319, 703-523-5450; and 112 N. Washington Ave., Pulaski 24301, 703-980-4310.

Committees: *Energy and Commerce* (23d of 25 D). Subcommittee: Oversight and Investigations; Telecommunications and Finance; Transportation, Tourism and Hazardous Materials. *Judiciary* (18th of 21 D). Subcommittees: Courts, Civil Liberties and the Administration of Justice; Criminal Justice. *Science, Space and Technology* (15th of 27 D). Subcommittees: Energy Research and Development. *Select Committee on Aging* (26th of 39 D). Subcommittees: Housing and Consumer Interests; Retirement Income and Employment.

Group Ratings

	ADA	ACLU	COPE	CFA	LCV	ACU	NTU	NSI	COC	CEI
1986	70	87	75	58	60	6	25	10	20	25
1985	60	—	72	67	—	19	34	—	48	—

National Journal Ratings

	1986 LIB — 1986 CONS		1985 LIB — 1985 CONS	
Economic	60% —	40%	59% —	39%
Social	74% —	26%	72% —	27%
Foreign	75% —	20%	68% —	31%

Key Votes

1) Lmt Cln Water Act	AGN	5) Retain Gun Cont	AGN	9) Aid Angola Reb	AGN
2) Rpl Tobac Sub	AGN	6) Contra Aid	AGN	10) Tax Reform	AGN
3) Grm-Rdmn Def Red	FOR	7) Lmt Text Imp	FOR	11) S Africa Sanc	FOR
4) Ban Polygraph	FOR	8) Limit SDI	FOR	12) Immig Reform	FOR

Election Results

1986 general	Rick Boucher (D)	59,864	(100%)	($262,606)
1986 primary	Rick Boucher (D) nominated by convention			
1984 general	Frederick C. (Rick) Boucher (D)	102,446	(52%)	($480,338)
	C. Jefferson Stafford (R)...............	94,510	(48%)	($396,436)

Campaign Contributions and Expenditures

1985-86		Direct Cont. 1985-86		PACS Breakdown 1985-86			
Receipts	$348,320	Indiv.	$152,269	Corp.	$58,855	T/M/H	$66,712
Expend.	$262,606	PACS	$214,037	Labor	$58,525	Agr.	$4,800
Unspent	$119,898			Ideo.	$18,945	CWOS	$6,200

TENTH DISTRICT

For 40 years, suburban Washingtonians have been moving outward from Arlington, the portion of Virginia which was originally part of the District of Columbia but which was ceded back to Virginia in 1846 on the grounds that the capital would never need it, toward the Blue Ridge, creating different kinds of new suburban communities and transforming old ones. Arlington, for example, in the years after World War II filled up with suburbanites, young marrieds with large families, whites fleeing the increasingly black District of Columbia; with rising government salaries and local economic growth, they began to live in affluence that many had never anticipated. Now their children have grown, and most people in Arlington are renters in apartments; it has also a substantial Vietnamese community living in what used to be a decaying white neighborhood. When Arlington was growing, Fairfax County, just beyond its borders, was almost entirely rural. Today it has developed the biggest office building concentration in Virginia, Tysons Corner, plus several smaller city-type nodes; its residential areas, amid hills and runs (the Virginia word for small rivers), are among the most spacious and affluent in the Washington area; the only problem is, the streets are so clogged with traffic and it takes so long to clear the complexly-lighted intersections that no one can get anywhere. Beyond Fairfax, in the flat lands of Loudoun County before you get to the rolling hills around Leesburg and the Blue Ridge, are more modest, crowded subdivisions, filled with young families and tradition-minded churches.

All this land—Arlington, the northern and western half of Fairfax, the tiny cities of Fairfax and Falls Church, and Loudoun, make up Virginia's 10th Congressional District. Its politics have varied with its growth. In the 1950s and 1960s its upwardly mobile families, fearful of Washington's blacks, voted for Republican Joel Broyhill. In 1974, he was beaten by Arlington liberal Democrat Joseph Fisher. In 1980, Fisher lost to Republican Frank Wolf, who has held onto the seat convincingly ever since.

Wolf's politics give some insight into the district's. He is a serious man whose personal attitudes are those of a churchgoing family man; he has a conservative record on national issues generally; but he reserves his greatest fervor for local matters. Once upon a time, the problems of federal employees meant everything here; now the growth of Tysons Corner and other centers has been fueled mostly by private firms (many of them government contractors, however), and Wolf felt free in 1985 to switch off Post Office and Civil Service onto Appropriations. He has worked to fund Washington's Metro subway lines, which now go far out into Virginia, and to build more highways; he has worked to get the federal government to unload National and Dulles Airports to a local authority (which, he and area residents hope, will crack down on noise). Earnest and the opposite of flashy, he listens respectfully to constituents, and has done well at election times. His most impressive victory came in 1986, over John Milliken, a talented Democrat who has headed the Arlington County Board and the Metro Board. Milliken raised lots of money and, interestingly, attacked Wolf for not supporting gun control. He carried Arlington, but only narrowly. Wolf, who raised even more money, ran well there and in the older communities and won 2 to 1 margins in fast-growing, but tradition-minded western Fairfax and Loudoun, for a 60% victory. With hard work, Wolf seems to have converted what has been a marginal district for most of the last 30 years into a safe seat.

The People: Pop. 1980: 535,125, up 15.1% 1970–80. Households (1980): 66% family, 35% with children, 55% married couples; 44.6% housing units rented; median monthly rent: $317; median house

value: $92,900. Voting age pop. (1980): 401,286; 6% Black, 4% Spanish origin, 4% Asian origin.

1984 Presidential Vote: Reagan (R) 154,507   (59%)
Mondale (D) 106,911   (41%)

Rep. Frank R. Wolf (R)

Elected 1980; b. Jan. 30, 1939, Philadelphia, PA; home, Vienna; PA St. U., B.A. 1961; Georgetown U., J.D. 1965; Presbyterian; married (Carolyn).

Career: Army (Reserves), 1962–67; Legis. Asst. to U.S. Rep. Edward Biester, 1968–71; Asst. to Secy. of Interior Rogers Morton, 1971–74; Dpty. Asst. Secy., U.S. Dept. of Interior, 1974–75; practicing atty., 1975–80.

Offices: 130 CHOB 20515, 202-225-5136. Also 1651 Old Meadow Rd., Ste. 115, McLean 22102, 703-734-1500; and 19 E. Market St., Rm. 4B, Leesburg 22075, 703-777-4422.

Committees: *Appropriations* (18th of 22 R). Subcommittees: Transportation; Treasury–Postal Service–General Government. *Select Committee on Children, Youth, and Families* (3d of 12 R). Task Force: Economic Security (Ranking Member).

Group Ratings

	ADA	ACLU	COPE	CFA	LCV	ACU	NTU	NSI	COC	CEI
1986	0	0	16	17	26	86	41	100	20	58
1985	15	—	15	58	—	71	41	—	73	—

National Journal Ratings

	1986 LIB — 1986 CONS			1985 LIB — 1985 CONS		
Economic	31%	—	67%	36%	—	63%
Social	23%	—	74%	24%	—	72%
Foreign	16%	—	79%	0%	—	76%

Key Votes

1) Lmt Cln Water Act	FOR	5) Retain Gun Cont	FOR	9) Aid Angola Reb	FOR
2) Rpl Tobac Sub	AGN	6) Contra Aid	FOR	10) Tax Reform	AGN
3) Grm-Rdmn Def Red	AGN	7) Lmt Text Imp	AGN	11) S Africa Sanc	FOR
4) Ban Polygraph	AGN	8) Limit SDI	AGN	12) Immig Reform	FOR

Election Results

1986 general	Frank R. Wolf (R)	95,724	(60%)	($1,124,866)
	John G. Milliken (D)	63,292	(40%)	($748,918)
1986 primary	Frank R. Wolf (R) nominated by convention			
1984 general	Frank R. Wolf (R)	158,528	(63%)	($624,731)
	John P. Flannery II (D)...............	95,074	(37%)	($425,601)

Campaign Contributions and Expenditures

1985-86		Direct Cont. 1985-86		PACS Breakdown 1985-86			
Receipts	$1,097,358	Indiv.	$731,623	Corp.	$161,368	T/M/H	$109,711
Expend.	$1,124,866	Party	$20,276	Labor	$7,500	Agr.	$250
Unspent	$12,309	PACS	$317,503	Ideo.	$32,724	CWOS	$5,950
		Cand.	$19,375				

WASHINGTON

In 1890, along the flat margin below the hills and next to the waters of Elliott Bay, the first Northern Pacific locomotive steamed into Seattle. Thus was established what was and is the continental United States's closest approach to the Pacific Rim. Seattle is not actually on the Pacific, and would be too rainy and storm-tossed if it were; it sits on one of the inner channels of Puget Sound, the waterways that twist and wind as sinuously as the passage of the inner ear from the open ocean into havens between the mountains sheltered from most (though assuredly not all) of the Pacific's winds and rains. Seattle's victory over Tacoma and Everett in becoming the Pacific Northwest's first railhead assured it primacy, but Seattle itself was anything but prim in its early years. It was a lusty town full of lumbermen and it became a metropolis of miners and prospectors and get-rich-quick operators. Not everyone got rich, of course, and it was in these years that Yesler Way, a street heading down one of Seattle's steep hills to the harborfront area now known as Pioneer Square, became known as Skid Row.

In that booming, young, lusty Seattle there developed a turbulent politics. This was the major center of the Industrial Workers of the World (the IWW or Wobblies) in the years before World War I; Seattle's business and civic leaders decided to exterminate the movement and in brutal fashion did so. Adding to the distinctiveness of the area were its large numbers of Scandinavian immigrants. They rode the Northern Pacific or the Great Northern west from Minneapolis after the long trip from Bergen or Goteberg. The Scandinavians brought with them attitudes favorable to cooperative enterprises (Washington has more businesses owned by workers than any other part of the country). They had no reluctance to encourage public power growth, and Washington, blessed with the hydroelectric resources of the Columbia, became the leader in public power in the United States in the 1930s. Also, despite the experience of the IWW, Washington proved hospitable to the trade union movement from the 1930s on. As early as 1936 its AFL and CIO unions formed a united lobby and struggled mightily over whether to purge Communists from their ranks. Ever since, even in the anti-union 1980s, it has had one of the largest percentages of workers in unions of any state—nearly half its work force in 1970, just before the Boeing payroll was cut from 101,000 to 38,000 when the Senate killed the supersonic transport, more than one-third as late as 1980.

Washington, like the United States generally, is less blue-collar and unionized in the late 1980s than in the early 1970s; but the Pacific Northwest of which Seattle is indubitably the center remains distinctive, as it has been since the 1890s, as the closest major American city to the Orient, middle America's outpost on the Pacific Rim. You can see clearly why on a relief and population map. On both sides of the Pacific, vast numbers of people are squeezed into small margins of level land between the steeply rising volcanic mountains and the sea, or tucked into valleys that are contained sometimes within the eye's sight, or sometimes extend beyond the horizon far up between crevasses of mountains. These islands of settlement are surrounded by vast oceanic wildernesses: desert and mountains, open sea and Arctic vastness—and in another sense by the wildernesses of the totalitarian autarkies of China, Vietnam, and the Soviet Union. Yet the peoples packed into these populated pockets of the Pacific Rim have over the past two or three decades produced more economic growth than anywhere else in the world. This is so even though you are talking about widely diverse, sometimes hostile, ethnic groups: the Japanese and Koreans, the Chinese of Taiwan, Hong Kong, and Singapore. Malays and Fillipinos, and Washington's ethnic mix of Scandinavians and yankees and new migrants attracted by the picturesque hills and outdoorsy atmosphere of Seattle and the communities along island-strewn, ferry-crossed Puget Sound. The valleys in between are dense with factories, warehouses, railroad yards, port facilities: this is one of the great grain- and lumber-shipping ports. Like most of the

WASHINGTON — Congressional Districts, Counties, and Selected Places — (8 Districts)

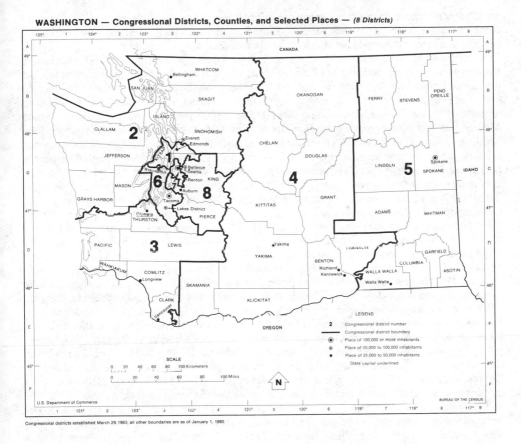

Congressional districts established March 29, 1983; all other boundaries are as of January 1, 1980.

Pacific Rim, and unlike most of the rest of the United States, Washington has a vested interest in free trade.

Yet the economy is vulnerable to slumps in a few industries. One is lumber. When high interest rates discourage homebuilding and construction, or a strong dollar gives Canadian lumber an edge in East Asian markets, Washington's unemployment shoots up. It can spike even higher when Boeing, often America's biggest exporter, has a lull between successful airliners; this happened most spectacularly in the early 1970s and again in the early 1980s. Also, Washington was hurt in the early 1980s by sudden increases in the price of electric power, which for 50 years had been the cheapest in the country. The default of the Washington Public Power Supply System (WPPSS, pronounced whoops), burdened by unwise commitments for huge nuclear plants, was just part of the reason for increased power costs; the major problem is that Washington long ago exhausted its cheap hydroelectric capacity, and all new power costs more. But Washington may be on the way to overcoming these problems. Cheap power doesn't seem any longer the key to attracting industry; Washington's position on the Pacific Rim, its lifestyle, its high competence and high tech type businesses will likely turn out to be more critical in the 1990s. At one time, a state full of apple farmers, fishermen, and dock hands needed to compensate for high freight costs. Now Washington is full of high-skilled people used to a high standard of living and productive enough to sustain it.

Governor. Washington's current governor, Booth Gardner, is the first to establish command over state government since Daniel Evans retired in 1976. Gardner is a Democrat, an heir to a big lumber fortune, former county executive in Tacoma. He stresses the need for Washington to compete economically with other portions of the Pacific Rim and in 1987 proposed extending the sales tax to services to pay for an educational excellence program, and maybe for state health care coverage as well. He has also pushed for workfare-type welfare reforms. Gardner is handicapped, however, because Washington is one of the few states without an income tax; his top tax aide would like to enact one, but that's unlikely: Washington is as averse to the income tax as next-door Oregon is to the sales tax. Gardner won the office in 1984 by beating both parties' 1980 candidates, dispatching liberal Jim McDermott in the primary (in which McDermott had beaten pro-nuclear incumbent Dixy Lee Ray in 1980) and incumbent John Spellman in the general. For 1988 he starts with more strength than either Ray or Spellman, but is likely to have at least some competition. Incidentally, Lieutenant Governor John Cherberg, a former coach, has held his office continuously since 1956 without ever running for governor.

Senators. For many years Washington had two of the nation's most senior and powerful Senators. Warren Magnuson chaired the Commerce Committee, Henry Jackson the Interior Committee; but these two canny politicians got their power from more than chairmanships. They knew their issues, and they knew how to get things done—and everyone knew it. They were also—and this is unusual for Senators of the same party—amiable colleagues in the Congress for 43 years. Magnuson was first elected to the House in 1936 and the Senate in 1944; Jackson was first elected to the House in 1940 and the Senate in 1952.

Today Washington has two of the less senior and, though able, less powerful members of the Senate. Magnuson was defeated in 1980 by Republican Slade Gorton; Jackson died suddenly in 1983, and Governor John Spellman appointed former Governor Daniel Evans to replace him. Gorton and Evans were longtime political allies, Republicans with moderate reputations who are fairly conservative on economic (and union) issues and more liberal on cultural and foreign policy; in many ways they seem perfectly suited to Washington; but both have had close political calls since. Evans was the winner of a special election in November 1983 over liberal Seattle Representative Mike Lowry, by a less-than-expected 55%-49%. Then in 1986 Gorton was upset by former Democratic Representative and Transportation Secretary Brock Adams.

This was one of the most exciting and fiercest battles of 1986, and the outcome was determined by what seems to be peripheral issues. Adams based his campaign primarily on his opposition to a nuclear waste dump near the Hanford Works on the Columbia River. In May 1986 the Hanford site was named as one of three finalists by the Department of Energy; in 1982 Gorton vocally supported nuclear dumping legislation that made this possible. But after Adams ran an ad showing a whistling locomotive coming through with nuclear waste, Gorton claimed first that he had stopped the plan and, after that ad was attacked, that he had stopped it for a year. He wasn't helped, however, when President Reagan came into Washington late in the campaign and refused to rule out the Hanford site. Gorton carried easily the Hanford area, which glories in its nuclear installations; but the issue cost him badly in ecology-conscious metropolitan Seattle. Gorton's other big problem was his switch to vote to confirm Indiana Judge Daniel Manion, in return for the Administration approving an appointment of his, ironically of a liberal Democrat, to a judgeship in Washington. Other Senators might have overcome these handicaps. But Gorton had made a name for himself as a cerebral, brainy, and principled Senator, not given to political manuever, a major force on the Budget Committee, the chief sponsor of the revised Maritime Act. The nuclear waste and Manion issues fatally undermined his strengths.

Brock Adams has by now had a long career in government. He was elected to the House in 1964, put together the Conrail bill, was the first chairman of the House Budget Committee. In 1977 he became Jimmy Carter's Secretary of Transportation, a booster of mass transit and who had doubts about airline and truck deregulation. He was one of the casualties of Carter's Camp David domestic summit in 1979, but resigned before Carter had a chance to fire him. On issues he is likely to be one of the more liberal Democratic Senators. He did not get a seat on Budget, but is on the Commerce, Labor and Foreign Relations Committees.

Dan Evans was in his seventh year of serving as president of Evergreen College in Olympia, after his retirement after a dozen years as governor, when Scoop Jackson's unexpected death suddenly got him back into politics. He beat conservative TV editorialist Lloyd Cooney solidly in the primary; Representative Mike Lowry, a rumpled and rough-hewn politico, was hardly a match in the general for the smooth, pleasant Evans. Evans as a Senator has disappointed many of his backers who thought he would generally oppose Reagan Administration policies; most often he has supported them. Evans has, however, reassured environmentalists and some of the Administration's foreign policy opponents: he landed in the Senate in time to secure passage of the Washington wilderness bill and voted against the Adminsitration's request for aid to the contras. He now serves on two committees of importance to his state: Energy and Natural Resources (Jackson's old panel) and Foreign Relations; he is naturally anxious to promote Washington's interest in Pacific Rim trade.

Evans worked hard for Gorton in 1986, to the point of even changing his vote on the Manion nomination to accommodate his colleague; but it wasn't enough. For 1988 Evans must be wondering whether he too will not get serious competition or perhaps be blindsided by some special issue. Several congressmen—Al Swift, Don Bonker, Norman Dicks—are all looking at this race, and this is one state where the national Republican ticket is not likely to be much of a help. Pleasant and well-intentioned, a proven executive, Evans still does not seem as intent on staying in the Senate as Gorton was; perhaps that will be an advantage. In any case this could be a seriously contested seat.

Presidential politics. The first decades of in-migration after World War II made burly, blue-collar Washington more respectable and more Republican. The next couple of decades disproportionately brought those children of affluence who seek to preserve the natural environment, oppose nuclear power, and want a conciliatory foreign policy. So Washington has moved mildly to the left, movement accentuated by the uncertainties of its economy: together with Oregon and coastal northern California, it has become a kind of New England on the Pacific Rim. Washington cast an above average vote (43%) for Walter Mondale in 1984, even though it has only a handful of black voters. Cultural attitudes have in large part replaced economic status as the main force behind voting behavior. Seattle, once a Democratic stronghold, has grown more white-collar and more prosperous, and it shifts back and forth between the two parties more than it used to.

In a competitive national election, Washington's 10 electoral votes and Oregon's 7 can probably be counted in the Democratic column. This may not be a harbinger of the national result: in the last three close presidential elections, Washington has voted for the loser each time. But of the Democratic trend here there can be little doubt: in 1984 Washington came close to trending toward Walter Mondale, in that same incumbent-prone year it ousted its Republican governor for Democrat Booth Gardner, and in 1986 it ousted Republican Senator Slade Gorton for Democrat Brock Adams. Each race had its own special dynamic, but taken together the results point in one direction.

Congressional districting. Washington gained one House seat in the 1980 Census, and went through a good deal of hassle drawing new district lines. Republicans controlled the legislature and the governorship, but when the legislature passed a partisan plan devised by the conservative Rose Institute, Governor Spellman vetoed it. It would have jeopardized the seats of several Democrats and one Republican congressman, and it was passed just after the delegation, led by Democrat Norman Dicks, had turned the House around and gotten it to approve Export-Import Bank loans for foreign purchases of American airplanes—the key method of financing which accounted for many of Boeing's sales. Practical men of business in the state let the governor know that they were more interested in keeping a savvy delegation that could do that sort of thing in a Democratic House than they were in getting one or two more Republican congressmen out of 435. The plan the legislature did pass ended up giving the Republicans the new seat, which made demographic sense. It was changed slightly for 1984 to meet the objections of a federal judge.

The People: Est. Pop. 1986: 4,463,000; Pop. 1980: 4,132,156, up 8.0% 1980–86 and 21.1% 1970–80; 1.85% of U.S. total, 20th largest (tied with Maryland). 20% with 1–3 yrs. col., 19% with 4+ yrs. col.; 9.8% below poverty level. Single ancestry: 9% English, 8% German, 3% Irish, Norwegian, 2% Swedish, 1% French, Italian, Dutch, Scottish, Polish. Households (1980): 70% family, 38% with children, 59% married couples; 34.4% housing units rented; median monthly rent: $220; median house value: $60,700. Voting age pop. (1980): 2,992,796; 2% Asian origin, 2% Black, 2% Spanish origin, 1% American Indian. Registered voters (1986): 2,230,465; no party registration.

1986 Share of Federal Tax Burden: $14,028,900,000; 1.86% of U.S. total, 18th largest.

1986 Share of Federal Expenditures

	Total		Non-Defense		Defense	
Total Expend	$16,874m	(2.03%)	$11,868m	(1.98%)	$5,006m	(2.18%)
St/Lcl Grants	1,905m	(1.69%)	1,905m	(1.69%)	0m	(0%)
Salary/Wages	2,948m	(2.44%)	1,085m	(1.85%)	1,863m	(3.01%)
Pymts to Indiv	6,736m	(1.85%)	6,118m	(1.76%)	618m	(3.48%)
Procurement	4,761m	(2.31%)	2,237m	(4.02%)	2,524m	(1.68%)
Research/Other	524m	(1.96%)	523m	(1.96%)	0m	(1.21%)

Political Lineup: Governor, William Booth Gardner (D); Lt. Gov., John A. Cherberg (D); Secy. of State, Ralph Munro (R); Atty. Gen., Kenneth (Ken) Eikenberry (R); Treasurer, Robert S. O'Brien (D); Auditor, Robert V. Graham (D). State Senate, 49 (27 D and 22 R); State House of Representatives, 98 (53 D and 45 R). Senators, Daniel Evans (R) and Brock Adams (D). Representatives, 8 (5 D and 3 R).

1984 Presidential Vote

Reagan (R) 1,051,670 (56%)
Mondale (D) 807,352 (43%)

1980 Presidential Vote

Reagan (R) 865,244 (50%)
Carter (D) 650,193 (37%)
Anderson (I) 185,073 (11%)

GOVERNOR

Gov. Booth Gardner (D)

Elected 1984, term expires Jan. 1989; b. Aug. 21, 1936, Tacoma; home, Tacoma; U. of WA, B.A. 1958, Harvard U., M.B.A. 1963; Protestant; married (Jean).

Career: Admin., U. of Puget Sound, 1967–72; WA Senate, 1970–73; Pres., bldg. supply firm, 1972–80; Pierce Cnty. Exec., 1981–84.

Office: Office of the Governor, Olympia 98504, 206-753-6780.

Election Results

1984 gen.	William Booth Gardner (D). . . .	1,006,993	(53%)
	John D. Spellman (R)	881,994	(47%)
1984 prim.	William Booth Gardner (D). . . .	421,087	(64%)
	Jim McDermott (D).	209,435	(32%)
1980 gen.	John D. Spellman (R)	981,083	(57%)
	Jim McDermott (D).	749,813	(43%)

SENATORS

Sen. Daniel J. Evans (R)

Appointed Sept. 12, 1983, elected Nov. 8, 1983, seat up 1988; b. Oct. 16, 1925, Seattle; home, Seattle; U. of CA, U. of WA, B.S. 1948, M.S. 1949; Congregational; married (Nancy).

Career: Engineer, 1954–65; WA House of Reps., 1956–65; Gov. of WA, 1965-77; Pres., Evergreen St. Col., 1977–83.

Offices: 702 HSOB 20510, 202-224-3441. Also 3206 Fed. Bldg., 915 2d Ave., Seattle 98174, 206-442-0350; and 576 U.S. Cthse., W. 920 Riverside, Spokane 99201; 509-456-2507.

Committees: *Energy and Natural Resources* (9th of 9 R). Subcommittees: Energy, Regulation, and Conservation; Energy Research and Development; Water and Power (Ranking Member). *Foreign Relations* (8th of 9 R). Subcommittees: East Asian and Pacific Affairs; International Economic Policy, Trade, Oceans and Environment (Ranking Member); Western Hemisphere and Peace Corps Affairs. *Select Committee on Indian Affairs* (Ranking Member of 3 R).

Group Ratings

	ADA	ACLU	COPE	CFA	LCV	ACU	NTU	NSI	COC	CEI
1986	35	50	21	42	67	23	55	70	67	67
1985	25	—	18	50	—	57	61	—	79	—

National Journal Ratings

	1986 LIB — 1986 CONS	1985 LIB — 1985 CONS
Economic	31% — 68%	30% — 69%
Social	52% — 47%	56% — 38%
Foreign	46% — 53%	45% — 52%

Key Votes

1) Ease Gun Cont	FOR	5) Grm-Rdmn Def Red	FOR	9) Rehnquist Nom	FOR
2) Immig Reform	FOR	6) Contra Aid	AGN	10) Tax Reform	FOR
3) Lmt Text Imp	AGN	7) SDI Funding	AGN	11) Drug Death Pen	FOR
4) Aid Tobac Ind	FOR	8) Lmt PAC Contrib	AGN	12) S Africa Sanc	FOR

Election Results

1983 special	Daniel J. Evans (R)	672,326	(55%)	($1,792,038)
	Michael E. (Mike) Lowry (D)	540,981	(45%)	($1,007,973)
1983 primary	Daniel J. Evans (R)	250,046	(64%)	
	Lloyd E. Cooney (R)	133,799	(34%)	
1982 general	Henry M. (Scoop) Jackson (D)	870,307	(69%)	($1,379,110)
	Doug Jewett (R)	306,522	(24%)	($241,695)

Campaign Contributions and Expenditures

1983-84		Direct Cont. 1983-84		PACS Breakdown 1983-84			
Receipts	$1,931,539	Indiv.	$1,298,595	Corp.	$279,292	T/M/H	$119,450
Expend.	$1,792,038	Party	$23,497	Labor	$13,500	Labor	$3,250
Unspent	$139,400	PACS	$490,837	Ideo.	$75,500	CWOS	$650

Sen. Brock Adams (D)

Elected 1980, seat up 1986; b. Jan. 13, 1927, Atlanta, GA; home, Seattle; U. of WA, B.A. 1949, Harvard U., LL.B. 1952; Episcopalian; married (Elizabeth).

Career: U.S. Atty. Gen., Western WA, 1961–64; U.S. House of Reps., 1964–77; U.S. Secy. of Transportation, 1977–79.

Offices: 513 HSOB 20510, 202-224-2621. Also 2988 Jackson Fed. Bldg., 915 2d Ave., Seattle 98174, 206-442-5545; and 770 U.S. Crthse., W. 920 Riverside Ave., Spokane 99201, 509-456-6816.

Committees: *Commerce, Science and Transportation* (11th of 11 D). Subcommittees: Merchant Marine; Science, Technology and Space; Surface Transportation. *Foreign Relations* (9th of 11 D). Subcommittees: International Economic Policy, Trade, Oceans and Environment; Terrorism, Narcotics and International Communications. *Labor and Human Resources* (8th of 9 D). Subcommittees: Children, Family, Drugs and Alcoholism; Employment and Productivity; Handicapped. *Rules and Administration* (9th of 9 D).

Group Ratings and Key Votes: Newly Elected
Election Results

1986 general	Brock Adams (D)	677,471	(51%)	($1,912,307)
	Slade Gorton (R)	650,937	(49%)	($3,290,072)
1986 primary	Brock Adams (D)	287,258	(92%)	
	Five others (D)	26,027	(8%)	
1980 general	Slade Gorton (R)	936,317	(54%)	($896,532)
	Warren G. Magnuson (D)	792,052	(46%)	($1,614,999)

Campaign Contributions and Expenditures

1985-86		Direct Cont. 1985-86		PACS Breakdown 1985-86			
Receipts	$1,973,142	Indiv.	$1,183,317	Corp.	$107,215	T/M/H	$110,325
Expend.	$1,912,307	Party	$96,569	Labor	$315,150	Agr.	$5,000
Unspent	$86,797	PACS	$718,771	Ideo.	$171,131	CWOS	$9,950

FIRST DISTRICT

If you were sailing up Puget Sound just north of Seattle 40 years ago, much of the shore would have looked undeveloped: stands of Douglas firs and pines on the hills overlooking the water. Since that time, the shoreline and the area inland for perhaps 20 miles has pretty well filled up with subdivisions and people. White-collar families who used to live in small houses in cramped neighborhoods in Seattle have seen their incomes rise and have moved out to more spacious quarters or to a bluff with a view of the Sound or of Lake Washington. Inland you can find subdivisions amid the Washington state vineyards and wineries. As Washington's port cities of Seattle and Everett and Tacoma grew up from their original sites along the docks and the lumber mills, they spread out between and along the hills and ridges that look down on Puget Sound.

The 1st Congressional District of Washington includes most of this territory between Seattle and the much smaller port of Everett. It hugs both sides of Puget Sound and Lake Washington, taking in Bainbridge Island (where you can commute by ferry to downtown Seattle each day and then return to your flannel shirts and L.L. Bean shoes) and part of Kitsap County west of Puget Sound and the comfortable towns of Kirkland and Bothell east of Lake Washington. Although it contains quite a few of Seattle's comfortable neighborhoods and some rural countrysides, it is essentially the northern Seattle suburban district. Its boundaries of this district are rather tortuous, designed to take in most of the Republican precincts in this part of Washington and to exclude most of the Democratic territory. Yet it is only tenuously Republican; its leanings on cultural issues, the environment, and foreign policy leave it pretty close to even in statewide races and leave it vulnerable to Democrats in the House contest.

This was demonstrated conclusively in 1986. Representative John Miller, a Republican first elected in 1984, should by any standard measure have been a shoo-in for reelection. He had won a six-candidate Republican primary in 1984 with 30% of the vote; he got 56% in the general election; he was well known from six years on the Seattle council in the 1970s. In the House he made a liberal record on the environment and was very market-oriented on economics—which suits the district pretty well. Nonetheless, Miller was nearly beaten in 1986. His Democratic opponent, Reese Lindquist, former president of the state teachers' union, attacked him non-stop for his support of aid to the Nicaraguan contras; he added charges that Miller was remote from the district. The foreign policy issue obviously cut deep, and Miller has the problem of any Pacific Northwest representative, that he does most of his work 2,500 miles away from where his constituents live.

This was not expected to be one of 1986's close races, but it was: Miller won 51%–49%. Probably the close result will spur him to keep himself more visible to the voters, and it may make him cautious about supporting contra aid and other controversial Administration foreign policies. In 1987 Miller switched from Government Operations to Foreign Affairs, thus putting himself more on the spot on foreign issues. The close race may also stimulate another serious challenge from Lindquist or one of the other liberal Democrats who are numerous in the area.

The People: Pop. 1980: 516,378, up 20.5% 1970–80. Households: 73% family, 38% with children, 63% married couples; 27.2% housing units rented; median monthly rent: $287; median house value: $74,900. Voting age pop. (1980): 378,407; 3% Asian origin, 1% Spanish origin, 1% Black, 1% American Indian.

1984 Presidential Vote: Reagan (R) 151,870   (57%)
Mondale (D) 112,927   (42%)

Rep. John R. Miller (R)

Elected 1984; b. May 23, 1938, New York City, NY; home, Seattle; Bucknell U., B.A. 1959, Yale U., J.D., M.A. 1964; Jewish; married (June).

Career: Asst. Atty. Gen. of WA, 1965–68; Practicing atty., 1968–72, 1981–84; Seattle City Council, 1972–80; Radio and TV Commentator, KIRO-TV, and KIRO and KSEA Radio, 1981–84.

Offices: 1723 LHOB 20515, 202-225-6311. Also 2888 Fed. Bldg., 915 2d Ave., Seattle 98174, 206-442-4220.

Committees: *Foreign Affairs* (16th of 18 R). Subcommittees: International Economic Policy and Trade; Human Rights and International Organizations. *Merchant Marine and Fisheries* (9th of 17 R). Subcommittees: Fisheries and Wildlife Conservation and the Environment; Merchant Marine.

Group Ratings

	ADA	ACLU	COPE	CFA	LCV	ACU	NTU	NSI	COC	CEI
1986	40	40	29	50	77	55	59	70	67	70
1985	25	—	24	50	—	67	67	—	86	—

National Journal Ratings

	1986 LIB — 1986 CONS			1985 LIB — 1985 CONS		
Economic	6%	—	90%	12%	—	85%
Social	64%	—	34%	59%	—	40%
Foreign	40%	—	59%	46%	—	52%

Key Votes

1) Lmt Cln Water Act	FOR	5) Retain Gun Cont	FOR	9) Aid Angola Reb	FOR
2) Rpl Tobac Sub	FOR	6) Contra Aid	FOR	10) Tax Reform	FOR
3) Grm-Rdmn Def Red	FOR	7) Lmt Text Imp	AGN	11) S Africa Sanc	FOR
4) Ban Polygraph	FOR	8) Limit SDI	AGN	12) Immig Reform	FOR

Election Results

1986 general	John R. Miller (R)	97,969	(51%)	($592,313)
	Reese Lindquist (D)	92,697	(49%)	($397,226)
1986 primary	John R. Miller (R)	44,694	(100%)	
1984 general	John R. Miller (R)	147,926	(56%)	($378,223)
	Brock Evans (D)	115,001	(44%)	($342,678)

Campaign Contributions and Expenditures

1985-86		Direct Cont. 1985-86		PACS Breakdown 1985-86			
Receipts	$594,170	Indiv.	$318,009	Corp.	$58,370	T/M/H	$46,111
Expend.	$592,313	Party	$4,935	Labor	$19,650	Agr.	$1,200
Unspent	$2,800	PACS	$152,734	Ideo.	$26,303	CWOS	$1,100
		Cand.	$100,460				

SECOND DISTRICT

At the far northwest corner of the 48 continental states is the rainiest part of the United States (a small patch of Hawaii excepted). The cold waters of the Pacific evaporate, condense, and then mist or rain down on the hills and mountains that jut up from the ocean or the sides of Puget Sound. The mountains here are always green, the trees that line the inlets towering, the evenness of the climate makes the way of life here steadier and less subject to violent surprise than it can be on the tornado-swept plains of Kansas or the hurricane coasts of Florida.

This land is more thickly populated than you might expect. Most of the people in the 2d Congressional District of Washington, which covers the Olympic Peninsula and both sides of Puget Sound, live in a narrow strip of land just east of the Sound, in or near Bellingham, in Everett with its paper mills and giant Boeing plant, and in the agricultural Skagit Valley. Another 10% here live on the islands in Puget Sound and the Strait of Juan de Fuca, and 34% live along the coast of the Olympic Peninsula and down the Pacific to the lumber mill and fishing town of Hoquiam. This land has attracted some counterculture veterans and young people looking for a more natural, less metropolitan life; there is little hint here of the sophistication of downtown Seattle. This is blue-collar country, where men go out to work at 6 a.m. in air cold enough to see your breath year round, and where there remains a certain surly independence and suspicion of authority. Convicted spy Robert Boyce spent several months here in Port Angeles after escaping from jail and, although some people suspected he was a fugitive, no one turned him in.

The political tradition in most of the lumbering and fishing areas here is Democratic; in the agricultural areas it is sometimes more Republican. For most of the last 50 years the 2d has elected Democratic congressmen. The current incumbent is among the ablest of the bunch— which is saying something, since one was Henry Jackson. Representative Al Swift, the only Washington member on the Energy and Commerce Committee, has become one of the busiest and most knowledgeable of House members, a workhorse with considerable accomplishments.

In the early 1980s, when the Washington Public Power Supply System (WPPSS) was going bankrupt, Swift had to frame the Northwest Power Act, a task which took constant negotiations with regional interests and politicians, and was fraught with political peril: the Northwest was losing its historically low power rates, and many young voters here hate and fear nuclear power. On the Telecommunications Subcommittee, Swift worked on broadcasting deregulation, and he attacked the television network news divisions for projecting the results of presidential elections when the polls were still open on the West Coast. Some congressmen were happy just to bash the networks; Swift—a former newscaster himself—came up with a uniform national poll closing law and got it passed by the House in 1986.

Energy and Commerce's work never ends: Swift got drawn into the Superfund extension fight, with some success. He is ready also to handle local issues, helping clean up a paint dump near Paine Field, urging retaliation against unfair trade practices to help the Northwest's shake and shingle industry, helping Everett become one of the Navy's new home ports and making sure its environment isn't hurt. But Swift's most important contribution in the 100th Congress could be on campaign finance. After the 1984 election, he became chairman of the new House Administration Subcommittee on Elections, which in addition to election day matters has jurisdiction over campaign finance reform measures. Swift has been favorable toward public financing of congressional elections and toward changing the rules on PACs, but he is also a practical politician who is not interested in reporting out a measure that can't pass on the floor. His reputation for hard work and thorough knowledge of the details may help him build trust for any measure he backs.

Swift won the seat narrowly in 1978 after Democrat Lloyd Meeds, whom Swift worked for in between stints on Bellingham TV, retired after being attacked for not being tough enough on Indian fishing rights. Swift has since been reelected easily and seems to be widely popular. In early 1987 he was considering a 1988 Senate race, whether or not, he said, incumbent Daniel Evans runs again. There's every reason to believe that this aggressive, accomplished, and thoughtful legislator would be a strong candidate. Possible successors in the House include Brian Corcoran, the former Jackson aide who lost the 1978 primary to Swift and is now a Snohomish County Councilman, and several state legislators.

The People: Pop. 1980: 516,568, up 33.3% 1970–80. Households (1980): 72% family, 37% with children, 62% married couples; 30.7% housing units rented; median monthly rent: $211; median house value: $58,700. Voting age pop. (1980): 373,304; 2% American Indian, 1% Spanish origin, 1% Asian origin.

1984 Presidential Vote: Reagan (R) 134,985   (55%)
Mondale (D) 107,697   (44%)

Rep. Al Swift (D)

Elected 1978; b. Sept. 12, 1935, Tacoma; home, Bellingham; Whitman Col., 1953–55, Central WA U., B.A. 1957; Unitarian; married (Paula).

Career: Broadcaster and Dir. of Pub. Affairs, KVOS-TV, Bellingham, 1957–62, 1969–77; A. A. to U.S. Rep. Lloyd Meeds, 1965–69, and 1977.

Offices: 1502 LHOB 20515, 202-225-2605. Also Fed. Bldg., Rm. 201, 3002 Colby, Everett 98201, 206-252-3188; and Fed. Bldg., Rm. 308, 104 W. Magnolia, Bellingham 98225, 206-733-4500.

Committees: *Energy and Commerce* (9th of 25 D). Subcommittees: Energy and Power; Telecommunications and Finance. *House Administration* (6th of 12 D). Subcommittees: Accounts; Elections (Chairman).

Group Ratings

	ADA	ACLU	COPE	CFA	LCV	ACU	NTU	NSI	COC	CEI
1986	90	90	82	92	58	9	23	0	18	21
1985	75	—	83	67	—	14	31	—	27	—

National Journal Ratings

	1986 LIB — 1986 CONS	1985 LIB — 1985 CONS
Economic	74% — 23%	85% — 11%
Social	86% — 11%	73% — 23%
Foreign	80% — 0%	75% — 21%

Key Votes

1) Lmt Cln Water Act	AGN	5) Retain Gun Cont	AGN	9) Aid Angola Reb	AGN
2) Rpl Tobac Sub	AGN	6) Contra Aid	AGN	10) Tax Reform	AGN
3) Grm-Rdmn Def Red	FOR	7) Lmt Text Imp	AGN	11) S Africa Sanc	FOR
4) Ban Polygraph	FOR	8) Limit SDI	FOR	12) Immig Reform	FOR

Election Results

1986 general	Al Swift (D)	124,840	(72%)	($239,341)
	Thomas S. Talman (R)	48,077	(28%)	($5,926)
1986 primary	Al Swift (D)	562,131	(100%)	
1984 general	Al Swift (D)	142,065	(59%)	($303,882)
	Jim Klauder (R)	93,472	(39%)	($302,458)

Campaign Contributions and Expenditures

1985-86		Direct Cont. 1985-86		PACS Breakdown 1985-86			
Receipts	$264,928	Indiv.	$88,691	Corp.	$71,450	T/M/H	$47,321
Expend.	$239,341	PACS	$168,246	Labor	$39,825	Agr.	$3,525
Unspent	$56,527			Ideo.	$5,275	CWOS	$850

THIRD DISTRICT

Between the Pacific Ocean and the row of volcanoes, active and inactive, from Mount Rainier to Mount St. Helens to Oregon's Mount Hood, is one of America's most productive lumber areas. The moist air and almost constant rains that are blown in from the Pacific keep the trees on the coast growing rapidly; in the valleys just past the Coast Range there is still plenty of precipitation and fast-growing forests. Then come the high mountains, their snow-capped peaks looking majestically down on the plains—when there aren't clouds in the way. These Cascades are a genuine divide, wrenching almost all the precipitation out of the air, so that the climate eastward for a thousand miles is arid.

The land between the ocean and the Cascades, from the state capital of Olympia on an inlet of Puget Sound south to Vancouver, just across the Columbia River from Portland, Oregon, forms the 3d Congressional District of Washington. Lumber is the biggest industry here, and there are always ferocious demands to stop the export of unfinished timber to East Asia; fishing is also important, and responsible for much export; the port of Portland is America's biggest unloader of Japanese cars. In all, this is one of the United States's biggest exporting congressional districts and perhaps the one most oriented to free trade. But its politics has little of the theoretical about it. The political atmosphere here has not changed much since the turn of the century, when the lumberjacks first attacked the firs, and sawmill towns sprang up along rivers and in bays off Puget Sound and the ocean; there is still a rough-hewn populism, reminiscent of the days when the Industrial Workers of the World were trying to organize the lumber camps. Most voters here are Democrats, and if they are interested in trade issues it is for practical reasons, and their views are typically pugnacious.

Representative Don Bonker is one of those Democrats who first won his seat in 1974, but he is atypical of that year's Watergate class in a number of ways. First is that he won a district long represented by a Democrat; he has no Republican constituency to appeal to. Another is that local issues have always been important for him: he won in 1974 in large part because of his stand against log exports. Third, he is deeply religious, a fundamentalist Christian whose beliefs have led him to oppose what he considers overly aggressive foreign policies and to favor a more generous government at home. As chairman of the Foreign Affairs Subcommittee on Human Rights in the late 1970s and early 1980s, he was ready to criticize even allies for their internal policies, and harshly attacked the Reagan Administration on occasion. More recently he has been emphasizing trade. In 1983 he switched to chair the International Economic Policy and Trade Subcommittee, and in 1985 he was named chairman of the Democratic Caucus Task Force on International Trade. In that capacity he came forward with the Democrats' 1986 trade bill, which included retaliation against countries that restricted American exports. It was attacked in many quarters as protectionist, but Bonker insisted that he was genuinely interested in stimulating international trade, and pointed to other provisions which tended to promote exports by relaxing controls on exports the Pentagon has regarded as strategic, strengthen U.S. export trading companies, and beefing up government export promotion. But he insisted that we may have to get tough if free trade is to prevail. Certainly his district has an economic interest in exports, but it is an interest that is wary of restrictions imposed by East Asian countries and eager to respond aggressively to them.

Bonker has won reelection in this Democratic seat by large margins; his toughest challenge came in the recession year of 1982, and he won 60%–37%. For 1988, he is giving some thought to the Senate race, although he seems unlikely to run if Republican Senator Daniel Evans runs for reelection. If he does run, possible candidates for the 3d District seat include House Speaker Joe King, a Democrat, and the Republican who ran the strong race in 1982, J. T. Quigg.

The People: Pop. 1980: 516,473, up 35.4% 1970–80. Households (1980): 73% family, 41% with children, 63% married couples; 32.1% housing units rented; median monthly rent: $202; median house value: $54,500. Voting age pop. (1980): 360,673; 1% Spanish origin, 1% Asian origin, 1% American Indian, 1% Black.

1984 Presidential Vote: Reagan (R) 117,626   (53%)
Mondale (D) 99,899   (45%)

Rep. Donald L. (Don) Bonker (D)

Elected 1974; b. Mar. 7, 1937, Denver, CO; home, Vancouver; Clark Col., A.A. 1962, Lewis & Clark Col., B.A. 1964, American U., 1964–66; Presbyterian; married (Carolyn).

Career: Coast Guard, 1955–59; Legis. Asst. to U.S. Sen. Maurine B. Neuberger, 1964–66; Clark Cnty. Auditor, 1966–74.

Offices: 434 CHOB 20515, 202-225-3536. Also 207 Fed. Bldg., Olympia 98501, 206-753-9528; and 700 E. Evergreen Blvd., Vancouver 98661, 206-696-7942.

Committees: *Foreign Affairs* (5th of 27 D). Subcommittees: International Economic Policy and Trade (Chairman); Western Hemisphere Affairs. *Merchant Marine and Fisheries* (6th of 25 D). Subcommittees: Fisheries and Wildlife Conservation and the Environment; Merchant Marine. *Select Committee on Aging* (4th of 39 D). Subcommittee: Housing and Consumer Interests (Chairman).

Group Ratings

	ADA	ACLU	COPE	CFA	LCV	ACU	NTU	NSI	COC	CEI
1986	70	89	82	83	71	11	31	0	40	23
1985	85	—	82	83	—	14	35	—	20	—

National Journal Ratings

	1986 LIB — 1986 CONS			1985 LIB — 1985 CONS		
Economic	65%	—	35%	72%	—	27%
Social	85%	—	14%	59%	—	40%
Foreign	63%	—	37%	85%	—	15%

Key Votes

1) Lmt Cln Water Act	AGN	5) Retain Gun Cont	FOR	9) Aid Angola Reb	—
2) Rpl Tobac Sub	FOR	6) Contra Aid	AGN	10) Tax Reform	AGN
3) Grm-Rdmn Def Red	AGN	7) Lmt Text Imp	AGN	11) S Africa Sanc	—
4) Ban Polygraph	FOR	8) Limit SDI	FOR	12) Immig Reform	FOR

Election Results

1986 general	Donald L. (Don) Bonker (D)	114,775	(74%)	($195,212)
	Joe Illing (R).	41,275	(26%)	
1986 primary	Donald L. (Don) Bonker (D)	60,270	(100%)	
1984 general	Donald L. (Don) Bonker (D)	150,432	(71%)	($136,540)
	Herb Elder (R)	61,219	(29%)	($1,713)

Campaign Contributions and Expenditures

1985-86		Direct Cont. 1985-86		PACS Breakdown 1985-86			
Receipts	$186,926	Indiv.	$62,384	Corp.	$52,650	T/M/H	$16,100
Expend.	$195,212	Party	$5,610	Labor	$32,650	Agr.	$1,700
Unspent	$56,752	PACS	$1,715	Ideo.	$14,650	CWOS	$275

FOURTH DISTRICT

Through the arid plateau of Washington, east of the towering Cascades, the Columbia River etches its way. Its waters have rushed downhill from the rugged Canadian Rockies, and they will rush once again through the narrow Columbia Gorge between the Cascades, but in eastern Washington the flow is slower, interrupted and disciplined by dams like the giant Grand Coulee, replenished by tributaries like the Yakima and the Snake, diverted into irrigation channels to make possible a thriving agriculture in an otherwise parched land. Most of the course of the Columbia in eastern Washington falls within the bounds of the state's 4th Congressional District. Much of this is empty land. The majority of the population is in the agricultural valley around Yakima, which is one of America's biggest fruit-producing regions, and, just where the Yakima empties into the Columbia, around the Tri-Cities of Richland, Pasco, and Kennewick. This is the site of one of the major nuclear power areas in the United States; the Hanford Works here house government nuclear projects, and the local economy depends almost entirely on the nuclear industry. For three decades this has been one of the parts of America most enthusiastic about nuclear power and resentful of criticisms of it.

The 4th District has been one of the great beneficiaries of government programs: without Grand Coulee, the Hanford Works, water and agricultural subsidies and aid, it would be unrecognizable. Yet its attitude toward the federal government is more often resentment than gratitude. It grouses as electric power becomes more expensive, partly because the Washington state public power system bungled a huge nuclear plant construction program, partly just because the Columbia's hydroelectric capacity is used up; but the blame goes to the feds. It is angry when farm prices go down or production is low. It is upset at the prospect of reducing the flow of migrant fruitpickers. It is angry when the federal government wants to cut back on nuclear power. And it has even gotten mad—or at least more people here than you would have thought have gotten mad—when the federal government put Hanford on its list of three possible nuclear waste disposal sites in 1983.

The job of articulating these angers and assuaging them belongs to the 4th District's congressman, Sid Morrison. He is a Republican first elected in 1980, but he is not either a free market ideologue or a New Right cultural conservative. He is a fruitgrower and veteran of the Washington legislature who was the co-sponsor with Leon Panetta of California of the amendment to the immigration reform bill allowing growers of perishable products to import foreign laborers—a provision benefitting only a few districts which nonetheless, thanks to skillful politicking, mustered a majority on the floor of the House. Morrison has also been a solid supporter of the nuclear industry and has welcomed most expansions of the Hanford Works because of the jobs they bring to the Tri-Cities. But in 1985 and 1986 he was vociferously opposing the nuclear waste dump proposal proposal and insisting that it made much more sense to put the stuff in Nevada's Yucca Mountains, and he succeeded in 1986 in getting funds cut off for study of the Hanford site. He was also co-sponsoring with Al Swift a bill that would make the federal government fully liable for damages from nuclear waste—a different approach from that used for nuclear plants, whose liability has been limited by federal statute. Morrison is not a dazzlingly articulate legislator, but he has been effective in advancing the interests of his district on the issues it cares about the most. Since he beat Democratic incumbent Mike McCormack in 1980, he has been reelected by wide margins in a district which is, in many elections, the most Republican in the state.

The People: Pop. 1980: 516,426, up 26.5% 1970–80. Households (1980): 74% family, 41% with children, 64% married couples; 33.0% housing units rented; median monthly rent: $186; median house value: $48,100. Voting age pop. (1980): 359,287; 7% Spanish origin, 2% American Indian, 1% Black, 1% Asian origin.

1984 Presidential Vote:

Reagan (R)	134,406	(63%)
Mondale (D)	74,346	(35%)

Rep. Sid Morrison (R)

Elected 1980; b. May 13, 1933, Yakima; home, Zillah; WA St. U., B.S. 1954; United Methodist; married (Marcella).

Career: Army, 1954–56; Orchardist, Morrison Fruit Co., Inc., 1954–81; WA House of Reps., 1966–74; WA Senate, 1974–80.

Offices: 1434 LHOB 20515, 202-225-5816. Also 212 E. E St., Yakima 98901, 509-575-5891; 3311 W. Clearwater, Ste. 105, Kennewick 99336, 509-376-9702; and Morris Bldg., 23 S. Wenatchee Ave., Ste. 210, Wenatchee 98801, 509-662-4294.

Committees: *Agriculture* (9th of 17 R). Subcommittees: Conservation, Credit, and Rural Development; Department Operations, Research, and Foreign Agriculture; Forests, Family Farms, and Energy (Ranking Member). *Science, Space and Technology* (8th of 18 R). Subcommittees: Energy Research and Development (Ranking Member); Science Research and Technology. *Select Committee on Hunger* (3d of 10 R). Task Forces: Domestic Task Force; International Task Force.

Group Ratings

	ADA	ACLU	COPE	CFA	LCV	ACU	NTU	NSI	COC	CEI
1986	25	40	24	25	32	73	31	90	67	54
1985	25	—	22	33	—	71	45	—	82	—

National Journal Ratings

	1986 LIB — 1986 CONS		1985 LIB — 1985 CONS	
Economic	36% —	63%	36% —	63%
Social	39% —	59%	63% —	33%
Foreign	30% —	69%	42% —	56%

Key Votes

1) Lmt Cln Water Act	FOR	5) Retain Gun Cont	AGN	9) Aid Angola Reb	FOR
2) Rpl Tobac Sub	FOR	6) Contra Aid	FOR	10) Tax Reform	FOR
3) Grm-Rdmn Def Red	FOR	7) Lmt Text Imp	AGN	11) S Africa Sanc	FOR
4) Ban Polygraph	AGN	8) Limit SDI	AGN	12) Immig Reform	FOR

Election Results

1986 general	Sid Morrison (R).....................	107,593	(72%)	($105,513)
	Robert Goedecke (D)..................	41,709	(28%)	($5,142)
1986 primary	Sid Morrison (R).....................	57,419	(100%)	
1984 general	Sid Morrison (R).....................	150,322	(76%)	($92,954)
	Mark Epperson (D)...................	47,158	(24%)	

Campaign Contributions and Expenditures

1985-86		Direct Cont. 1985-86		PACS Breakdown 1985-86			
Receipts	$179,274	Indiv.	$90,639	Corp.	$27,975	T/M/H	$28,050
Expend.	$105,513	Party	$3,100	Labor	$1,500	Agr.	$4,300
Unspent	$148,864	PACS	$69,081	Ideo.	$6,000	CWOS	$1,256

FIFTH DISTRICT

The 5th Congressional District of Washington is the easternmost part of the state. Centered on Spokane, Washington's second largest city, this has been called the Inland Empire. Here the Columbia, Spokane, and Snake Rivers wind through and beneath vast plateaus, bringing vast amounts of water from the American and Canadian Rockies to this land of low rainfall. Irrigation systems divert great quantities of the water that lead to the production of some bountiful crop fields, but areas like the Palouse in the southeast corner of the state are so fertile (the topsoil is said to be 200 feet deep) that huge harvests issue just from the rainfall. These rivers are not hospitable streams; they are fast flowing, and in some places lie in great clefts, far below the rest of the landscape. Getting the water out to where it would be useful was a major task—achieved in large part by New Deal projects like the Grand Coulee Dam.

Yet eastern Washington is not particularly enamored of the federal government. This has been very much Reagan country in the last two presidential elections, and would have been before that as well. He carried not only isolated agricultural counties, but also Spokane County, which contains 66% of the district's population, and the county which contains Pullman and Washington State University. Historically and today, voting habits here are in between those of the urbanized Puget Sound area and those in neighboring Rocky Mountain states—which makes some sense, since this part of Washington is physically and economically much more a part of the intermountain basin than of the Pacific coast.

If this district is Republican in most elections, it has nonetheless elected a Democratic congressman, and one of the most important ones, for 20 years. He is Thomas Foley, first elected as a young lawyer in 1964; now he is the House Majority Leader—the number two man in the Democratic leadership—with an excellent chance of being Speaker some day. His path upward has taken an unusual course, running not quite according to the form that was traditional in the days of Sam Rayburn and John McCormack, and not quite according to the folkways that had developed in the House by 1980. He is the product of both seniority and insurgency, of patronage from old leaders and support from younger members of the Democratic Caucus. Thus he was chosen chairman of the Democratic Study Group just after the 1972 election, and just before the Democrats' Watergate surge, when the DSG was an insurgent group dominated by Phillip Burton. Yet by then the DSG was supplanting the leadership under Speaker Carl Albert in important ways, setting the legislative agenda, taking positions on issues, making head counts and whip calls. In the House elected in 1974, controlled by Watergate Democrats, Foley was a natural leader.

So much so that he did not seek leadership positions, but had them thrust upon him. He was voted in, over incumbent Bob Poage, as chairman of the House Agriculture Committee. This was a startling reversal of fortune, since four years before, in 1970, he ranked only eighth in seniority on the committee; but in 1972 three senior Democrats retired and two more were defeated; another was beaten in his 1974 primary; and Poage, though an expert on agricultural legislation, was such a bleak reactionary on every other issue that the post-1974 Democratic Caucus was unwilling to back him, even though Foley himself supported him.

Foley's next elevation came after an election in 1980 which was as disastrous for the Democrats as 1974 was propitious. The House Majority Whip, John Brademas, had lost his seat in Indiana, and Foley, by this time long an ally of the leadership, was chosen for the post by Speaker O'Neill and Majority Leader Jim Wright. Oddly, the post was still appointive (the Democratic Caucus has since decided to make it elective for Foley's would-be successors), and so Foley was climbing up the leadership ladder in the same way O'Neill and others had before him. It is not necessarily a position he would have won had it been elective; Foley might not have pushed himself forward, and he would not necessarily have been the first choice of many factions. But he would have been a strong affirmative choice of almost all.

The last time the Democrats chose a Majority Leader, in 1976, there was a bitter fight. In 1986 Foley won the position unopposed. His fairmindedness and almost judicial temperament leave some of the more partisan Democrats frustrated sometimes, but his unwillingness to take positions unless he can justify both policy and procedure and his ability to see the other side of issues even as he argues his own make him uniquely respected on both sides of the aisle. Calmly, carefully, lucidly, he can explain the most complicated parliamentary tangle clearly enough for any member to understand and fairly enough to permit anyone to rely on it in making up his own mind. Presumably he would like to be Speaker someday. Jim Wright, who sometimes seems insecure, seems certain that he can trust Foley, while those below Foley on the ladder seem to have no thoughts of elbowing their way past him.

Foley appears now to be one of those national leaders of the Democratic party with no problems in his own, not always Democratic, constituency. That was not always so. Thrust suddenly into national prominence in the middle 1970s, he was hard pressed in 1976, 1978, and 1980; it's a tough transition from being the pleasant congressman who sends out all the literature and is identified with only the popular side of issues to the national leader of his party who is saddled with all its locally unpopular stands, and Foley, like others (notably Morris Udall, John Brademas, Jim Corman, Al Ullman), had trouble making the transition. But he seems to have done so. In the 5th District he has raised his percentage from 52% in 1980, to 64% in 1982, 70% in 1984, and 75% in 1986. Evidently he has persuaded eastern Washington voters that they're fortunate to have a congressman as nationally prominent and competent as Foley has proven himself to be.

The People: Pop. 1980: 516,719, up 18.2% 1970–80. Households (1980): 70% family, 37% with children, 59% married couples; 33.4% housing units rented; median monthly rent: $181; median house value: $46,200. Voting age pop. (1980): 373,789; 2% Spanish origin, 1% American Indian, 1% Asian origin, 1% Black.

1984 Presidential Vote:

Reagan (R)	134,923	(60%)
Mondale (D)	86,838	(39%)

Rep. Thomas S. Foley (D)

Elected 1964; b. Mar. 6, 1929, Spokane; home, Spokane; U. of WA, B.A. 1951, LL.B. 1957; Roman Catholic; married (Heather).

Career: Practicing atty., 1957; Spokane Cnty. Dpty. Prosecuting Atty., 1958–60; Instructor, Gonzaga U. Sch. of Law, 1958–60; Asst. Atty. Gen. of WA, 1960–61; Asst. Chf. Clerk and Spec. Counsel, U.S. Sen. Cmtee. on Interior and Insular Affairs, 1961–63.

Offices: 1201 LHOB 20515, 202-225-2006. Also 574 U.S. Crthse., Spokane 99201, 509-456-4680; 12929 E. Sprague, Spokane 99216, 509-926-4434; and 28 W. Main, Walla Walla 99362, 509-522-6370.

Committees: *Majority Leader. Budget* (2d of 21 D).

Group Ratings

	ADA	ACLU	COPE	CFA	LCV	ACU	NTU	NSI	COC	CEI
1986	75	85	80	92	58	14	24	0	33	22
1985	75	—	79	50	—	10	29	—	27	—

National Journal Ratings

	1986 LIB — 1986 CONS			1985 LIB — 1985 CONS		
Economic	69%	—	30%	85%	—	11%
Social	74%	—	23%	69%	—	28%
Foreign	64%	—	34%	64%	—	33%

Key Votes

1) Lmt Cln Water Act	AGN	5) Retain Gun Cont	AGN	9) Aid Angola Reb	AGN
2) Rpl Tobac Sub	AGN	6) Contra Aid	AGN	10) Tax Reform	FOR
3) Grm-Rdmn Def Red	FOR	7) Lmt Text Imp	—	11) S Africa Sanc	FOR
4) Ban Polygraph	FOR	8) Limit SDI	FOR	12) Immig Reform	FOR

Election Results

1986 general	Thomas S. Foley (D)	121,732	(75%)	($481,477)
	Floyd Wakefield (R)	41,179	(25%)	($56,502)
1986 primary	Thomas S. Foley (D)	62,365	(100%)	
1984 general	Thomas S. Foley (D)	154,988	(70%)	($378,158)
	Jack Hebner (R)	67,438	(30%)	($49,819)

Campaign Contributions and Expenditures

1985-86		Direct Cont. 1985-86		PACS Breakdown 1985-86			
Receipts	$599,651	Indiv.	$107,049	Corp.	$182,305	T/M/H	$126,182
Expend.	$481,477	Party	$4,312	Labor	$72,207	Agr.	$14,500
Unspent	$272,193	PACS	$433,261	Ideo.	$20,750	CWOS	$17,317
		Cand.	$60,000				

SIXTH DISTRICT

Looking down from snow-clad Mount Rainier to the cool blue waters of Puget Sound, the city that you would see first is not Seattle, far to the north, but Tacoma. This is the second largest city on Puget Sound, which has always been overshadowed by Seattle. In 1900, just before the state's most explosive decade of growth, Tacoma was still a credible rival—it had 37,000 people to Seattle's 80,000. But in the years that followed, Seattle's growth continued, while Tacoma got itself embroiled in an unsuccessful attempt to rewrite history and change the name of Mount Rainier to Mount Tacoma. Seattle was diversifying, adding white-collar employment to its basic industries of shipping, fishing, lumber, and railroading. Tacoma remained primarily a lumber town, the original base of the giant Weyerhaeuser firm, but with only about one-fourth the population of its larger neighbor. In the middle 1980s, it was losing a meatpacking plant, a shipbuilding firm, a paper mill, and hoping to shift toward white-collar and service employment. With its location, and with the mountain looming over it, it has the potential to do so.

Tacoma is the heart of Washington's 6th Congressional District, which includes the city and virtually all of its suburbs. The 6th also crosses the Puget Sound Narrows (where the Tacoma Straits Bridge collapsed in 1940 and the new bridge, the 5th longest suspension bridge in the world, was opened in 1950) to include most of Kitsap County and its major city, Bremerton, which lies across the Sound from Seattle. Kitsap is bristling with several Navy installations and, the home port of several nuclear submarines, it is one of the major military bases on the West Coast. The 6th is Democratic in most elections. There are white-collar neighborhoods in high lands overlooking the waters, but most of the Tacoma and Bremerton area is blue-collar territory, quite liberal on economic issues, but somewhat more conservative than Seattle on cultural issues, and decidedly hawkish on military issues. In some elections this is the most Democratic congressional district in Washington, though it did go solidly for Ronald Reagan in 1980 and 1984.

The congressman from the 6th is Democrat Norman Dicks. He is a product of the staff of Senator Warren Magnuson, which may have been one of the most competent staffs ever seen on Capitol Hill. He returned back home to Kitsap County to run for Congress in 1976, when the 6th District incumbent finally got the judgeship he had been hankering after for 12 years. Dicks was elected easily that year and reelected easily three times; only in 1980 was the election close, when he was held to 54% of the vote.

In the House Dicks has shown the aggressiveness and political shrewdness that were the hallmarks of the Magnuson staff in its golden days. He won a seat on the Appropriations Committee and is on both the Defense and Military Construction Subcommittees— vital posts for Kitsap County where most workers depend on Pentagon payrolls. He is third in line on Defense, behind Chairman Bill Chappell and Pennsylvania's John Murtha. He took the lead on restoring Export-Import Bank loan authority—Boeing is America's biggest exporter and biggest user of the loans—when the Reagan Administration wanted to cut it, and led a campaign that switched 80 House votes overnight. With Les Aspin and Albert Gore, Jr., he was one of the key House members that lined up support for the MX missile in return for arms control commitments from the Reagan Administration, and felt vindicated when the United States got to the bargaining table. But he also pressed the Administration in 1986 by sponsoring an amendment requiring compliance with the unratified SALT II treaty—a measure that was put aside before the Reykjavik summit when Reagan complained it tied his hands. He is unblushing about getting defense spending for Washington, whether it's getting the military to use Boeing 747s rather than Lockheed C-5s for transport, or getting Boeing's E-6A used for submarine communications, keeping the Tacoma and Bremerton shipbuilding docks busy, or getting the Navy home port for Everett.

Dicks has been mentioned as a candidate for the Senate, but declined to run in 1983 and 1986. It is possible he will decide to run for Senator Daniel Evans's seat in 1988, although he would probably have competition from House colleagues for the Democratic nomination—Al Swift, Don Bonker, and Mike Lowry are thinking of running—and has a particularly crucial position in the House which he would have to give up. If Dicks does run, possible candidates for his House seat include former Tacoma Councilman Tim Strege, Puyallup legislator Dan Grimm and Republican Tacoma Mayor Doug Sutherland.

The People: Pop. 1980: 516,561, up 13.9% 1970–80. Households (1980): 71% family, 39% with children, 59% married couples; 38.9% housing units rented; median monthly rent: $208; median house

value: $53,900. Voting age pop. (1980): 374,063; 6% Black, 3% Asian origin, 2% Spanish origin, 1% American Indian.

1984 Presidential Vote:

Reagan (R) 116,652	(57%)
Mondale (D) 85,889	(42%)

Rep. Norman D. Dicks (D)

Elected 1976; b. Dec. 16, 1940, Bremerton; home, Bremerton; U. of WA, B.A. 1963, J.D. 1968; Lutheran; married (Suzanne).

Career: Ofc. of U.S. Sen. Warren G. Magnuson, Legis. Asst., 1968–73, A. A., 1973–76.

Offices: 2429 RHOB 20515, 202-225-5916. Also One Pacific Bldg., Ste. 201, Tacoma 98402, 206-593-6536; and Great Northwest Bldg., Ste. 307, Bremerton 98310, 206-479-4011.

Committees: *Appropriations* (17th of 35 D). Subcommittees: Defense; Interior; Military Construction.

Group Ratings

	ADA	ACLU	COPE	CFA	LCV	ACU	NTU	NSI	COC	CEI
1986	70	78	83	92	58	23	22	20	28	22
1985	70	—	84	67	—	24	26	—	38	—

National Journal Ratings

	1986 LIB — 1986 CONS		1985 LIB — 1985 CONS	
Economic	77% —	22%	71% —	28%
Social	74% —	23%	73% —	27%
Foreign	60% —	39%	58% —	40%

Key Votes

1) Lmt Cln Water Act	AGN	5) Retain Gun Cont	FOR	9) Aid Angola Reb	AGN
2) Rpl Tobac Sub	AGN	6) Contra Aid	AGN	10) Tax Reform	FOR
3) Grm-Rdmn Def Red	AGN	7) Lmt Text Imp	AGN	11) S Africa Sanc	FOR
4) Ban Polygraph	FOR	8) Limit SDI	FOR	12) Immig Reform	FOR

Election Results

1986 general	Norman D. Dicks (D) 90,063	(71%)	($229,634)
	Ken Braaten (R) 36,140	(29%)	($57,166)
1986 primary	Norman D. Dicks (D) 40,803	(100%)	
1984 general	Norman D. Dicks (D) 124,367	(66%)	($160,903)
	Mike Lonergan (R) 60,721	(32%)	($11,670)

Campaign Contributions and Expenditures

1985-86		Direct Cont. 1985-86		PACS Breakdown 1985-86			
Receipts	$301,848	Indiv.	$95,789	Corp.	$80,675	T/M/H	$30,225
Expend.	$229,634	Party	$20	Labor	$57,500	Agr.	$1,250
Unspent	$198,732	PACS	$179,625	Ideo.	$9,375	CWOS	$600
		Cand.	$641				

SEVENTH DISTRICT

There are scarcely any American cities—maybe there are none—more attractive than Seattle. It rises on steep hills, almost as precipitous as San Francisco's, from crescent-shaped Elliott Bay, an inlet on Puget Sound; and behind the city you can see on a clear day, from almost anywhere, the nimbus of Mount Rainier. Right on the waterfront, below the gleaming high-rises, is the Pike Place market, where you can get fresh salmon and Dungenesse crab; nearby is Pioneer Square, where stores and warehouses from the turn of the century have been restored and renovated. Seattle's upper class, like San Francisco's, continues to be anchored downtown and has kept residential quarters not too far away; but people here are less obsessed with their aristocracy, and many may not realize it exists at all. Seattle's working class has maintained many comfortable neighborhoods of frame houses on steep hillsides. The old ethnic groups are not very distinctive to the untrained eye, because so many people are of Scandinavian ancestry; but Seattle is now getting a significant, although not huge, influx of newcomers of Asian and Mexican background.

Like every city, Seattle is divided into neighborhoods. Its topography—with lots of hills, bays, and lakes—prevents it from having the huge miles-long expanses of homogeneous neighborhoods you find in such cities as Detroit or Houston; there is plenty of variety in almost every mile of Seattle. Generally blue-collar workers live on the south side of the city and in valleys, or midway between Puget Sound and Lake Washington; the factories, warehouses, and railroad yards are concentrated in a flat plain near Puget Sound and south of downtown. The big Boeing factories are located in the plain farther south, and younger blue-collar workers have followed them into the suburban areas directly south of the city: Burien, Tukwila, Kent, and Renton, which lies at the southern end of Lake Washington. More affluent, white-collar workers, and better-educated people tend to live on hills and near the water, and are more likely to be found on the north than the south side.

The 7th Congressional District of Washington includes most of the city of Seattle and many of its suburbs directly to the south. Its boundaries were drawn artfully, however, to corral most of its Democratic voters into this district, to keep them out of the Republican 1st and 8th Districts. So the 7th District doesn't include the north Seattle shores of Puget Sound or Lake Washington, nor the high-income suburb of Mercer Island; it does include the city's small black community (the only significant concentration of blacks in the state) and some of its recent communities of Asian immigrants. Overall, this is a solidly Democratic district and has been the most Democratic district in the state in most elections in the 1980s.

Representative Mike Lowry, one of the House's unblushingly liberal Democrats, won this seat in 1978 by beating a conservative Republican who had won a special election to succeed Brock Adams when he became Secretary of Transportation. Lowry's background is in local and state government; he seems to be not so much an intellectual as he is a doer. His voting record is among the most liberal in the House. Rumpled and rough-hewn, decidedly unelegenic, Lowry decided to make a run for the Senate seat vacated by the sudden death of Scoop Jackson in 1983; and he made a better run of it than almost anyone expected. He beat the popular mayor of Seattle, Charles Royer, in the Democratic primary (and beat him more than 2 to 1 in King County, Royer's backyard and his). Against the suave, much better-known, more moderate Daniel Evans, Lowry won 45% in the November 1983 general election.

Lowry returned, chastened a bit but definitely unbowed, to the House, where his influence has been limited. He is one Democrat who would like to see his party court more confrontations with the Reagan Administration; he would eschew compromise and take some defeats in order to make a record in favor of clear-cut alternatives and then go to the voters with it. It may be a good strategy, but it is not one which appealed in the middle 1980s to most of his fellow Democrats. Lowry is the third-ranking Democrat now on the House Budget Committee, behind chairman William Gray and Majority Leader Thomas Foley, but he has not had much success in making the committee more confrontational or liberal. But he is popular with fellow members even though he does things like buck his fellow Washington members by opposing home port status for Everett. In 1987 he became chairman of the Democratic Study Group, an organization that is less noticed these days mainly because it is so successful. Lowry has been mentioned as a possible candidate against Evans in 1988; given his temperament and his reasonably good showing against Evans last time, and the likelihood he can establish a strong liberal fundraising base, he just may run. Possible successors might include state Senator Jim McDermott, a psychiatrist who lost races for governor in 1980 and 1984, state legislators George Fleming and Jesse Winberry, and County Councilman Ron Sims.

The People: Pop. 1980: 516,531, dn. 5.9% 1970–80. Households (1980): 53% family, 24% with children, 41% married couples; 50.0% housing units rented; median monthly rent: $232; median house value: $62,800. Voting age pop. (1980): 414,472; 8% Black, 7% Asian origin, 2% Spanish origin, 1% American Indian.

1984 Presidential Vote:

Mondale (D) 146,221	(58%)
Reagan (R) 104,330	(41%)

Rep. Michael E. (Mike) Lowry (D)

Elected 1978; b. Mar. 8, 1939, St. John; home, Renton; WA St. U., B.A. 1962; Baptist; married (Mary).

Career: Chf. Fiscal Analyst and Staff Dir., WA Sen. Ways and Means Cmtee., 1969–73; Govt. Affairs Dir., Puget Sound Group Health Coop., 1974–75; King Cnty. Cncl., 1975–78, Chmn., 1977.

Offices: 2454 RHOB 20515, 202-225-3106. Also 318 1st Ave., S., #300, Seattle 98104, 206-442-7170.

Committees: *Budget* (3d of 21 D). Task Forces: Economic Policy (Chairman); Human Resources. *Merchant Marine and Fisheries* (8th of 25 D). Subcommittees: Fisheries and Wildlife Conservation and the Environment; Oceanography (Chairman); Oversight and Investigations; Panama Canal and Outer Continental Shelf.

Group Ratings

	ADA	ACLU	COPE	CFA	LCV	ACU	NTU	NSI	COC	CEI
1986	95	100	81	92	93	5	36	0	7	22
1985	100	—	82	83	—	10	36	—	27	—

National Journal Ratings

	1986 LIB — 1986 CONS		1985 LIB — 1985 CONS	
Economic	54%	— 46%	81%	— 17%
Social	89%	— 0%	85%	— 0%
Foreign	80%	— 0%	92%	— 0%

Key Votes

1) Lmt Cln Water Act	AGN	5) Retain Gun Cont	FOR	9) Aid Angola Reb	AGN
2) Rpl Tobac Sub	AGN	6) Contra Aid	AGN	10) Tax Reform	AGN
3) Grm-Rdmn Def Red	AGN	7) Lmt Text Imp	AGN	11) S Africa Sanc	FOR
4) Ban Polygraph	FOR	8) Limit SDI	FOR	12) Immig Reform	FOR

Election Results

1986 general	Michael E. (Mike) Lowry (D)	124,317	(73%)	($170,979)
	Don MacDonald (R)	46,831	(27%)	($66,103)
1986 primary	Michael E. (Mike) Lowry (D)	57,612	(95%)	
	Demilt Morse (D)	3,345	(5%)	($9,671)
1984 general	Michael E. (Mike) Lowry (D)	174,560	(70%)	($106,498)
	Bob Dorse (R)	71,576	(29%)	($9,671)

Campaign Contributions and Expenditures

1985-86		Direct Cont. 1985-86		PACS Breakdown 1985-86			
Receipts	$200,232	Indiv.	$83,086	Corp.	$17,775	T/M/H	$18,125
Expend.	$170,979	Party	$80	Labor	$41,550	Agr.	$250
Unspent	$53,376	PACS	$90,450	Ideo.	$11,225	CWOS	$1,525
		Cand.	$520				

EIGHTH DISTRICT

In the four decades since World War II, Seattle has spilled out across the hills to the north and south, through the valleys lined with railroads and Boeing facilities, over Puget Sound and across the pontoon bridge over Lake Washington. What was rural territory when the troop ships steamed into Puget Sound after the war is now well-settled suburbia. The 8th Congressional District of Washington, newly created after the 1980 Census, collects together some of this suburban territory. It includes essentially two geographically separate suburban sections of Seattle. One, which accounts for more than half the district's population, consists of the suburbs on the ridges and valleys that run up and down the land just east of Puget Sound, south of Seattle from Tacoma. The latter part includes hilly suburbs starting with Burien and Normandy Park in the north, near Seatac Airport, down to the city limits of Tacoma. This is pleasant middle-income territory, on the average. Politically, Republican and Democratic suburbs seem to alternate, leaving a pretty even balance overall.

Connecting the two parts of the district, almost as a land bridge, is the industrial suburb of Auburn. Running north and east from there, up to and along the east side of Lake Washington, is the second part of the district, with about one-third of its population. The other 10% live in mostly agricultural country, which rises up to Mount Rainier National Park. The largest city here is Bellevue, a high-income suburb; the most prominent suburb is Mercer Island, where contemporary homes are set among the woods on hills overlooking Lake Washington which is connected to Seattle by a once-famous pontoon bridge across the lake. This part of the district is heavily Republican. People here are solidly conservative on economic issues; on cultural matters, particularly environmental issues, they may be more liberal.

The current congressman from this district is Rod Chandler, a former television anchorman and state legislator. He ran in 1982 as a self-described centrist Republican in a multi-candidate primary, and was fortunate enough to have the conservative vote split between two significant opponents; he had little trouble in the general election. In the House, Chandler has proved to be rather conservative on economics and rather liberal on cultural issues; in the climate of the early 1980s, when cultural conservatives really thought they could wipe out abortions, they saw Republicans like Chandler as the enemy. They were angry as well when he voted against aid to the Nicaraguan contras and the MX missile. But as the 1980s have gone on, the conservatives have grown more comfortable with Chandler and he with them. The cultural issues became less important to them; they were settled, one way or the other. Chandler turned out to support the Reagan Administration more often than anticipated, even to the point of switching on contra aid and working out a position he and other moderate Republicans could support.

After the 1986 election, Chandler pulled off a great coup, in the Republican Committee on Committees, when he won a seat on the Ways and Means Committee. He had help from 92

Group moderates, but also from some conservatives; he argued that western Republicans were underrepresented on major committees, and he benefited from a small state alliance on the committee. It helped also that on economic issues he's not so different from the conservatives. Chandler's success in getting on Ways and Means and his reelection by wide margins suggest he has a long House career ahead of him.

The People: Pop. 1980: 516,500, up 40.5% 1970–80. Households (1980): 77% family, 45% with children, 67% married couples; 26.5% housing units rented; median monthly rent: $288; median house value: $75,900. Voting age pop. (1980): 358,801; 2% Asian origin, 1% Spanish origin, 1% Black, 1% American Indian.

1984 Presidential Vote:	Reagan (R)	156,878	(62%)
	Mondale (D)	93,535	(37%)

Rep. Rodney Chandler (R)

Elected 1982; b. July 13, 1942, La Grande, OR; home, Bellevue; OR St. U., B.S. 1968; Presbyterian; married (Joyce).

Career: Correspondent and Anchorman, KOMO-TV, 1968–73; Asst. Vice Pres. for Mktg., WA Mutual Savings Bank, 1973–77; WA House of Reps., 1975–82; Partner, pub. rel. firm, 1977–83.

Offices: 223 CHOB 20515, 202-225-7761. Also 3350 161st Ave. S.E., Bellevue 98008, 206-442-0116; and 1025 S. 320th, Federal Way 98003, 206-593-6371.

Committees: *Ways and Means* (13th of 13 R). Subcommittees: Health; Public Assistance.

Group Ratings

	ADA	ACLU	COPE	CFA	LCV	ACU	NTU	NSI	COC	CEI
1986	20	40	18	17	47	71	51	67	71	66
1985	15	—	17	33	—	67	53	—	95	—

National Journal Ratings

	1986 LIB — 1986 CONS		1985 LIB — 1985 CONS	
Economic	23% —	77%	20% —	79%
Social	44% —	54%	60% —	38%
Foreign	36% —	63%	45% —	55%

Key Votes

1) Lmt Cln Water Act	FOR	5) Retain Gun Cont	AGN	9) Aid Angola Reb	FOR
2) Rpl Tobac Sub	FOR	6) Contra Aid	FOR	10) Tax Reform	AGN
3) Grm-Rdmn Def Red	FOR	7) Lmt Text Imp	AGN	11) S Africa Sanc	FOR
4) Ban Polygraph	AGN	8) Limit SDI	FOR	12) Immig Reform	FOR

Election Results

1986 general	Rodney Chandler (R)	107,824	(65%)	($210,373)
	David Giles (D)	57,545	(35%)	($109,411)
1986 primary	Rodney Chandler (R)	36,654	(100%)	
1984 general	Rodney Chandler (R)	146,891	(62%)	($355,682)
	Bob Lamson (D)	88,379	(38%)	($338,480)

Campaign Contributions and Expenditures

1985-86		Direct Cont. 1985-86		PACS Breakdown 1985-86			
Receipts	$259,317	Indiv.	$125,122	Corp.	$48,795	T/M/H	$56,041
Expend.	$210,373	Party	$2,578	Labor	$4,000	Agr.	$250
Unspent	$73,256	PACS	$118,186	Ideo.	$4,950	CWOS	$4,150
		Cand.	$500				

WEST VIRGINIA

It was the frontier when the Constitution was written 200 years ago, a formidable barrier of range after range of rugged mountains that kept the largest colony and state, Virginia, from expanding straight westward. The empty expanse north and west of the Ohio River was set apart as the Northwest Territory in 1787, the new lands across the mountains split off to become the state of Kentucky in 1792, but the 55 counties that are now West Virginia remained part of Virginia until the Civil War. Even then these counties were distinctive. There were few slaves in the hills, and in the early 1830s legislators from the mountain counties and Jeffersonian aristocrats almost succeeded in abolishing slavery in Virginia as it had been abolished in states to the north. From that time on, the historic heart of Virginia east of the Blue Ridge went one way and the mountain counties the other; one aligned with the South and one the North. When war came they split. The mountain counties opposed secession and continued to send congressmen to Washington. In 1863, after a dispute over the name (the new state was nearly called Kanawha), West Virginia was admitted to the Union. West Virginia emerged from the war a Republican state, and in most of its counties the Civil War heritage may still be seen in today's election results. Democrats, since the coal fields were organized in the 1930s, have become the majority party here. But both parties have large and solid bases; only one politician in the state's history, Robert Byrd, has carried every county in a general election.

West Virginia's history since has been nearly as turbulent. In the late 19th and early 20th centuries West Virginia was far more dynamic than its parent, a part—thanks to its huge coal deposits—of the burgeoning industrial economy while old Virginia was a rural backwater. In recent decades their positions have sometimes seemed precisely reversed. West Virginia's economy depends on coal and the related industries of steel and petrochemicals—industries which over the long run of the past four decades have not grown as fast as the whole economy and which often in the short run have contracted painfully. West Virginia, so mountainous that it's hard to find a level acre anywhere, is at the geographical periphery of the coal-steels-chemicals economy, and while it retains the affections of natives who call it home after lifetimes in Detroit or Akron it has failed to generate enough jobs to employ its sons and daughters.

The old West Virginia is in any case a past no one would want to go back to. The working conditions in the mines were never very good and were sometimes deadly. Lovers of country music know something of life in the coal company towns and the credit practices of company stores, where workers and their families had to buy everything. Immigrant communities in the big cities of the time had some geographical proximity and exposure to other kinds of American life. The coal mining communities of West Virginia, often literally up a creek or a hollow, were connected to the rest of the world only by a rail line that carried coal cars only. Conditions were bad enough that a union movement developed, and during the 1930s John L. Lewis's United Mine Workers organized most of West Virginia's mines—so successfully that for years since West Virginia has been the most heavily unionized state in the nation. But railroads were switching from coal to diesel fuel and houses from coal heating to cheap oil or natural gas, In 1950 Lewis agreed with the companies to allow mechanization of the industry in return for much higher wages and fringe benefits—the opposite of the strategy of the steel and auto unions in the early 1980s, when they tried to maintain high wages and big payrolls, and failed at both. But West Virginia has had trouble replacing lost coal jobs with anything else. In 1950 the state's population was more than 2 million; by 1970, after thousands had left to look for work elsewhere, it was down to 1.7 million. With higher energy prices, the coal industry revived in the 1970s, and West Virginia's population rose above 1.9 million in 1980. But by the middle 1980s, after energy prices collapsed, it was declining again, at the fastest rate in the nation. Coal mines, which in 1950 employed 22% of West Virginia's work force, employed 6% in 1985. For at least two generations has had an aging population, wary of the future and bitter about the past.

In the process old West Virginia institutions and customs have been dying out. The big coal companies have been replaced in importance by small operators; the United Mine Workers, rent by violent faction in the 1970s, represents far fewer workers far less aggressively; the old Democratic machine politicians that produced most of the state's leaders since the days of Franklin D. Roosevelt have not elected a governor in more than 20 years. Men it did not control—Republican Arch Moore, Democrat Jay Rockefeller—have been elected to the governorship now for terms totalling 20 years, and insurgents won a variety of other elections. Neither West Virginia's unions nor its political parties have, over the years, had inspiring leadership; while faraway liberals like to imagine that leaders springing from poor people will represent poor people's interests altruistically, all too often they are interested in representing their own interests first. So the weakness of these institutions has probably elevated the quality of West Virginia's public life.

Will West Virginia in the late 1980s rebound as it has before? The number of jobs started growing again in 1986, the economy seemed a bit more diversified, energy prices started edging up: all good signs. But West Virginia remains vulnerable: its high-sulfur, remote coal can be hurt by acid rain legislation or by a coal slurry pipeline or by another sustained period of low energy prices. West Virginians have a strong attachment to their unique state, where the accent sounds northern and the early-in-the-century factories and houses look northern, where the landscape is rural and the economy industrial. But they are not always able to make their livings there.

Governor. Arch Moore, the man who preceded Jay Rockefeller as governor, has now succeeded him; the two men, who are not at all friendly, have held the governor's office for two decades now. Once upon a time the Republican party used to produce dozens of savvy, instinctive politicians, men who came from (or at least were intimately familiar with) humble backgrounds and understood the way things worked. They could find their way to the pool hall in any small town and knew instinctively when the shifts were about to break. They could jolly up the bankers and businessmen and then go into the next hotel room and make a deal with the sleaziest ward politicians around. Now Arch Moore is one of the last such Republicans in the whole country.

Like most instinctive politicians, Moore is an optimist. He has been winning public office in West Virginia most of his adult life, usually against the odds: beating a Democratic congressman in 1956, winning the governorship in 1968, 1972, and 1984. He has come back from scandal (he was indicted in 1975, but acquitted) and defeat (he lost to Senator Jennings Randolph in 1978 and to Jay Rockefeller, whom he beat in 1972, in 1980). Halfway into his third term, he was claiming credit for $1 billion worth of new jobs and for cuts in taxes, and was calling for more emphasis on higher education, where West Virginia has trailed most southern states.

Senators. Robert Byrd, West Virginia's senior Senator, is the first man in American history to hold the job of Senate Majority Leader, lose it, and then gain it back again. That fact tells us something about his determination, the combination of hard work and ambition which have propelled this coal miner's son to the top ranks of the American Congress. If you go back to the beginning of his career, his rise seems most improbable. He was a meatcutter in a coal town, a former welder in wartime shipyards, when he won his seat in the state House of Delegates in 1946; he campaigned in every hollow in the county, playing his fiddle and even going to the length of joining the Ku Klux Klan (which he quickly quit and has ever since regretted joining)

WEST VIRGINIA — Congressional Districts, Counties, and Selected Places — *(4 Districts)*

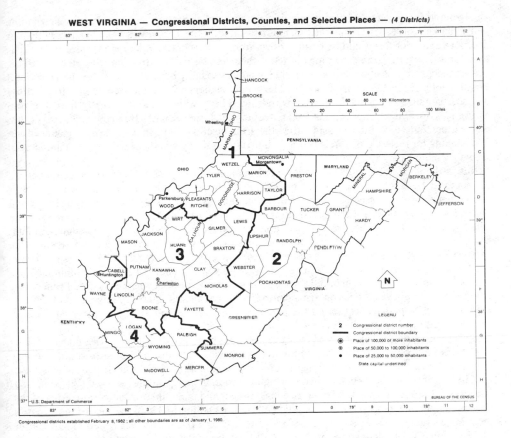

Congressional districts established February 8, 1982 ; all other boundaries are as of January 1, 1980.

to win votes. He worked hard in the legislature, and won a House seat when the incumbent retired in 1952; he made such a name for himself that by 1958, when he was 40, he was elected to the Senate even though the United Mine Workers had been against him and the coal companies were never for him.

The secrets behind his success are hard work and mastery of detail. He cultivated constituents in West Virginia assiduously, keeping card files with thousands of names and telephone numbers and calls constituents every night, to ask their opinions on issues and to find out what is happening back home. He cultivated Senators just as assiduously, and when Edward Kennedy was neglecting his duties as majority whip in 1969 and 1970, after Chappaquiddick, Byrd quietly lined up support and, with Richard Russell's deathbed proxy, won the job himself in 1971. By 1976, when Majority Leader Mike Mansfield was retiring, Byrd was the natural choice for majority leader; Hubert Humphrey ran a quixotic campaign against him, but Byrd had the votes. He was never too busy to attend to the petty details that can make the lives of Senators easier: keeping them informed of the pace of floor debate and the scheduling of upcoming votes, helping them to get amendments before the Senate, arranging pairs, and even getting taxis. This is not mindless work: it means understanding the political situations of each Senator, their strengths and weaknesses, and it means mastering the details of substantive legislation and parliamentary procedure.

By the middle 1980s, however, after the Democrats were in the minority, Byrd was the subject of grumbling and open rebellion. He was too much the technician, it was said; he did not project an attractive image on television; he did not lead the party on issues. He was being criticized for being the kind of leader Democratic Senators wanted in the 1970s, when they expected policy decisions and priorities would be handed down from a Democratic White House and when each Senator was eager to grab credit for himself rather than his party. After the 1984 election, Byrd was challenged by Lawton Chiles of Florida, who was soundly beaten. Before the 1986 election, Bennett Johnston of Louisiana announced he would challenge Byrd; but well before the election his nose-counting persuaded him to withdraw. There were rumors that Byrd had given assurances to Daniel Inouye, his appointee to head the Senate Iran-contra investigating committee, that he would step aside after the 1988 election; Byrd in early 1987 announced he was running for reelection in West Virginia but refused to say whether he'd run for Democratic leader again.

But in the meantime, it is plain that he is responding to the demands of his constituency of Democratic Senators as he has responded to the responsibilities placed on him by every constituency he has served. The detail man has taken the lead on policy, insisting that then Democrats will pursue trade legislation, and with Finance Chairman Lloyd Bentsen shaping what that legislation will be; presenting detailed proposals for arms control agreements; pushing hard for campaign finance reform. None of these is a risk-free position, and all require the mastery of detail he showed, for example, in unravelling the Watergate scandal: it was Byrd who got L. Patrick Gray to admit that John Dean "probably lied" about the affair, an admission that sparked Dean's determination to tell the truth. It remains to be seen whether Senate Democrats, who have been all over the lot on arms control and Reaganomics and tax reform and Gramm-Rudman, can be gotten together on the tough issues Byrd is emphasizing. But it is not wise to underestimate Robert Byrd.

Byrd's voting record has changed over the years; his popularity with West Virginia voters has not. In his early years in the Senate dominated by Lyndon Johnson and Richard Russell, he was almost a Dixiecrat, opposing civil rights laws and conducting vitriolic investigations of D.C. welfare cheaters. He concentrated on bringing government spending to West Virginia, and succeeded. Later, as an elected leader serving younger and more liberal Democratic Senates, he has voted more in line with his Democratic colleagues, and by the 1980s had one of the Senate's most liberal records, especially on economic issues. Byrd's popularity was tested in 1982, after NCPAC ran TV ads against him and Republican Representative Cleveland Benedict spent $1 million on a harshly negative campaign. Byrd raised and spent plenty himself, but more important carried every 54 of 55 counties and 68% of the vote. Four times now Byrd has been reelected with a higher percentage of the vote than any other West Virginia Senate candidate has won even once. 1988 seems likely to be a fifth.

The junior colleague of this coal miner's son is the scion of the richest family in the United States, John D. Rockefeller IV. The fourth in the direct line of eldest sons from the original John D. Rockefeller, Jay Rockefeller was an expert in Asian affairs when he moved to West Virginia in 1964 to work in an antipoverty program. He decided to stay and to enter politics but—unlike his uncles, the governors of New York and Arkansas, as a Democrat rather than as a Republican. He was elected to the legislature in 1966 and to statewide office in 1968. Moore beat him in 1972, when the state was prosperous and his roadbuilding program was humming; Rockefeller became president of West Virginia Wesleyan College for a few years. Rockefeller was elected governor easily in 1976, calling for economic development and—inevitably in this mountainous state—better roads; he promoted coal and removed the sales tax on food. In 1980 he faced Moore again, ran on his record and spent $9 million, and won. His second term was more difficult, as the state's economy shuddered into recession and West Virginia had the nation's highest unemployment rate.

In 1984, barred from a third consecutive term, he ran for the Senate seat Jennings Randolph was vacating. The state's ailing economy made him vulnerable to Republican John Raese, who was originally spurred into the race by what he said was government harassment of his small business and who thought he could match Rockefeller's campaign spending. He couldn't:

Rockefeller spent $12 million, and won a close race while Walter Mondale was losing the state. Rockefeller was snickered at in some quarters for spending hundreds of thousands on Pittsburgh and Washington media to reach a few counties in West Virginia's panhandles. But that may have made the difference. In most counties in the state Rockefeller ran between 1% and 7% ahead of Mondale's 45% showing—not enough on balance to win. But in the northern panhandle and in the eastern counties between Maryland and Virginia, in the Pittsburgh and Washington media markets, he ran (with one exception) between 12% and 18% ahead of Mondale—votes vital to his 52%–48% victory over Raese.

Rockefeller has been mentioned as a possible presidential candidate almost from the time he ran for the House of Delegates in Kanawha County. But he is just on his way to becoming an influential Senator. Wisely, he was quiet his first two years, working on local issues and taking on housekeeping chores. After the 1986 election he got a seat on the Finance Committee, which will help him make his mark on trade laws; with his experience in Japan, he is less interested in barring foreign imports and more interested in spurring American exports than most politicians from the coal-and-steel region. He has been careful not to thrust himself forward as a presidential candidate and seems, as he passes age 50, to be settling in for what could be a long and productive career in the Senate.

Presidential politics. For 50 years West Virginia's partisan preferences were the legacy of two searing decades, the 1860s and 1930s; the question now is whether those preferences still prevail. Although West Virginia stayed with the Union, parts of the state were more sympathetic to it than others, and there are Republican strongholds today—sparsely populated counties in the mountains, cities and towns along the Ohio River—dating from that period. There are also rural Democratic counties as well, like the one around Harpers Ferry, where John Brown was convicted and hanged for storming the arsenal and trying to incite a local slave rebellion. The 1930s saw the coal-mining counties not only unionized, but made heavily Democratic, to the point that the coal counties south of Charleston are one of the most Democratic parts of the nation. But Charleston and Kanawha County, a heavily industrialized area and the most populous part of the state, still go Republican as often as they do Democratic—the Civil War legacy lives on.

On balance, that leaves West Virginia as one of the most Democratic of states. In 1980 it was Jimmy Carter's best state after Georgia, and it was solidly Democratic in the close elections of 1948, 1960, 1968, and 1976. But in the election of 1984, after four years of exceedingly high unemployment figures during a Republican administration, West Virginia went for Ronald Reagan. Have a critical number of West Virginia voters have given up—maybe temporarily, maybe permanently—on the Democrats as the party of prosperity and full employment?

West Virginia's presidential primary was important here only once, in 1960, when John Kennedy seized on it as an opportunity to prove he could beat Hubert Humphrey in a virtually all-Protestant state, spending money freely and in ways that would not be legal today. Otherwise, West Virginia sees little presidential campaigning.

Congressional districting. West Virginia's House delegation is made up of four young Democrats, three of them first elected in 1982, two of them the sons of congressmen, one the son of a successful broadcasting entrepreneur, one the son of a successful lawyer. All four seem to have safe seats.

The People: Est. Pop. 1986: 1,919,000; Pop. 1980: 1,949,644, down 1.6% 1980–86 and up 11.8% 1970–80; 0.80% of U.S. total, 34th largest. 10% with 1–3 yrs. col., 10% with 4+ yrs. col.; 15% below poverty level. Single ancestry: 20% English, 7% German, 5% Irish, 2% Italian, 1% Dutch, Polish, French. Households (1980): 77% family, 42% with children, 65% married couples; 26.4% housing units rented; median monthly rent: $137; median house value: $38,500. Voting age pop. (1980): 1,390,008; 3% Black, 1% Spanish origin. Registered voters (1986): 946,039; 632,087 D (67%); 293,659 R (31%); 20,293 unaffiliated and minor parties (2%).

1986 Share of Federal Tax Burden $4,087,600,000; 0.63% of U.S. total, 34th largest.

1986 Share of Federal Expenditures

	Total		Non-Defense		Defense	
Total Expend	$5,409m	(0.65%)	$5,146m	(0.86%)	$264m	(0.11%)
St/Lcl Grants	1,063m	(0.94%)	1,063m	(0.95%)	1m	(0.90%)
Salary/Wages	486m	(0.40%)	403m	(0.69%)	83m	(0.13%)
Pymnts to Indiv	3,461m	(0.95%)	3,384m	(0.98)	77m	(0.43%)
Procurement	321m	(0.16%)	218m	(0.39%)	103m	(0.07%)
Research/Other	78m	(0.29%)	2m	(4.56%)		

Political Lineup: Governor, Arch A. Moore, Jr. (D); Secy. of State, Ken Hechler (D); Atty. Gen., Charlie Brown (D); Treasurer, A. James Manchin (D); Auditor, Glen B. Gainer (D). State Senate, 34 (27 D and 7 R); State House of Delegates, 100 (78 D and 22 R). Senators, Robert C. Byrd (D) and John D. (Jay) Rockefeller, IV (D). Representatives, 4 D.

1984 Presidential Vote

Reagan (R)	405,483	(55%)
Mondale (D)	328,125	(45%)

1980 Presidential Vote

Carter (D)	367,462	(50%)
Reagan (R)	334,206	(45%)
Anderson (I)	31,691	(4%)

1984 Democratic Presidential Primary

Mondale	198,776	(54%)
Hart	137,866	(37%)
Jackson	24,697	(7%)
Two others	7,906	(2%)

1984 Republican Presidential Primary

Reagan	125,790	(92%)
Stassen	11,206	(8%)

GOVERNOR

Gov. Arch A. Moore, Jr. (R)

Elected 1984, term expires Jan. 1989; b. Apr. 16, 1923, Moundsville; home, Glen Dale; Lafayette Col., WV U., B.A. 1948, LL.B. 1951; United Methodist; married (Shelley).

Career: Practicing atty.; WV House of Delegates, 1953–55; U.S. House of Reps., 1957–69; Gov. of WV, 1969–77.

Office: State Capitol, Charleston 25305, 304-340-1600.

Election Results

1984 gen.	Arch A. Moore, Jr. (R)	394,937	(53%)
	Clyde See (D)	346,565	(47%)
1984 prim.	Arch A. Moore, Jr. (R)	135,877	(100%)
1980 gen.	John D. Rockefeller IV (D)	401,863	(54%)
	Arch A. Moore, Jr. (R)	337,240	(45%)

SENATORS

Sen. Robert C. Byrd (D)

Elected 1958, seat up 1988; b. Nov. 20, 1917, North Wilkesboro, NC; home, Sophia; American U., J.D. 1963; Baptist; married (Erma).

Career: WV House of Reps., 1946–50; WV Senate, 1950–52; U.S. House of Reps., 1953–58; U.S. Sen. Major. Whip, 1971–76, Major. Ldr. 1978–80.

Offices: 311 HSOB 20510, 202-224-3954. Also Fed. Bldg., 500 Quarrier St., Rm. 1006, Charleston 25305, 304-342-5855.

Committees: *Majority Leader. Appropriations* (2d of 16 D). Subcommittees: Defense; Energy and Water Development; Interior (Chairman); Labor, Health and Human Services, Education; Transportation. *Judiciary* (3d of 8 D). *Rules and Administration* (3d of 9 D).

Group Ratings

	ADA	ACLU	COPE	CFA	LCV	ACU	NTU	NSI	COC	CEI
1986	75	57	72	93	50	35	32	70	16	17
1985	65	—	71	80	—	43	20	—	21	—

National Journal Ratings

	1986 LIB — 1986 CONS	1985 LIB — 1985 CONS
Economic	94% — 0%	86% — 11%
Social	79% — 16%	74% — 22%
Foreign	60% — 38%	43% — 56%

Key Votes

1) Ease Gun Cont	FOR	5) Grm-Rdmn Def Red	AGN	9) Rehnquist Nom	AGN
2) Immig Reform	FOR	6) Contra Aid	AGN	10) Tax Reform	FOR
3) Lmt Text Imp	FOR	7) SDI Funding	FOR	11) Drug Death Pen	AGN
4) Aid Tobac Ind	FOR	8) Lmt PAC Contrib	FOR	12) S Africa Sanc	FOR

Election Results

1982 general	Robert C. Byrd (D)	387,170	(69%)	($1,792,573)
	Cleveland K. (Cleve) Benedict (R)	173,910	(31%)	($1,098,218)
1982 primary	Robert C. Byrd (D)	210,523	(100%)	
1976 general	Robert C. Byrd (D)	338,444	(100%)	

Campaign Contributions and Expenditures

1979-82		Direct Cont. 1981-82		PACS Breakdown			
Receipts	$1,869,580	Indiv.	$980,858	Agr	$33,000	Ideo	$102,000
Expend.	$1,792,573	Party	$17,500	Bus	$277,875	Lbr	$260,200
Unspent	$225,313	PACS	$707,641	Hlth	$10,250	Prof	$18,100

Sen. John D. (Jay) **Rockefeller IV (D)**

Elected 1984, seat up 1990; b. June 18, 1937, New York, NY; home, Charleston; Harvard U., A.B. 1961, International Christian U., 1957–60; Presbyterian; married (Sharon).

Career: Natl. Advisory Cncl. of Peace Corps, 1961; Asst. to Peace Corps Dir. Sargent Shriver, 1962–63; VISTA worker, 1964–66; WV House of Delegates, 1966–68; WV Secy. of State, 1968–72; Pres., WV Wesleyan Col., 1973–75; Gov. of WV, 1977–84.

Offices: 241 DSOB 20510, 202-224-6472. Also L and S Bldg., Ste. 200, 812 Quarrier St., Charleston 25301, 304-347-5372; 115 S. Kanawha St., Ste. 1, Beckley 25801, 304-253-9704; and 200 Adams St., Ste. A, Fairmont 26554, 304-367-0122.

Committees: *Commerce, Science, and Transportation* (7th of 11 D). Subcommittees: Foreign Commerce and Tourism (Chairman); Science, Technology, and Space; Surface Transportation. *Finance* (10th of 11 D). Subcommittees: Health; International Debt; International Trade. *Veterans' Affairs* (5th of 6 D).

Group Ratings

	ADA	ACLU	COPE	CFA	LCV	ACU	NTU	NSI	COC	CEI
1986	75	75	92	87	50	13	40	25	32	20
1985	60	—	90	87	—	14	24	—	36	—

National Journal Ratings

	1986 LIB — 1986 CONS	1985 LIB — 1985 CONS
Economic	93% — 6%	81% — 17%
Social	79% — 16%	72% — 27%
Foreign	64% — 33%	72% — 27%

Key Votes

1) Ease Gun Cont	FOR	5) Grm-Rdmn Def Red	FOR	9) Rehnquist Nom	AGN
2) Immig Reform	FOR	6) Contra Aid	AGN	10) Tax Reform	FOR
3) Lmt Text Imp	FOR	7) SDI Funding	AGN	11) Drug Death Pen	AGN
4) Aid Tobac Ind	FOR	8) Lmt PAC Contrib	FOR	12) S Africa Sanc	FOR

Election Results

1984 general	John D. (Jay) Rockefeller IV (D)	374,233	(52%)	($12,055,043)
	John R. Raese (R)	344,680	(48%)	($1,147,123)
1984 primary	John D. (Jay) Rockefeller IV (D)	240,559	(66%)	
	Lacy Wright (D)	51,591	(14%)	
	Ken Auvil (D)	41,408	(11%)	
	Homer L. Harris (D)	29,138	(8%)	
1978 general	Jennings Randolph (D)	249,034	(50%)	($684,605)
	Arch A. Moore, Jr. (R)	244,317	(50%)	($458,823)

Campaign Contributions and Expenditures

1983-84		Direct Cont. 1983-84		PACS Breakdown 1983-84			
Receipts	$12,091,551	Indiv.	$1,271,400	Corp.	$128,050	T/M/H	$90,850
Expend.	$12,055,043	Party	$17,500	Labor	$223,111	Agr.	$8,000
Debts	$10,241,457	PACS	$541,875	Ideo.	$74,895	CWOS	$6,200
		Cand.	$10,250,000				

FIRST DISTRICT

In the heart of America's steel country is West Virginia's northern panhandle, sticking up between western Pennsylvania and the Ohio River: a geographic anomaly created by boundary-drawers who never ventured west of the Appalachians. Geographically, the panhandle is probably the least isolated part of West Virginia. It is part of the Pittsburgh media market, and the terrain is comparatively gentle; it is on main line railroads and interstate highways. Along the Ohio River here are giant blast furnaces in Wheeling and Weirton, many of which are cold, but not all: the workers at the Weirton works took a pay cut in return for a share of the company, and Weirton is now one of the nation's largest worker-owned firms. With the Pittsburgh area, the panhandle is one of the leading glassmaking areas of the country as well. In the early 1970s people here worried about pollution; the air by some measures was the dirtiest in the country. In the early 1980s they worried about the economy, and what they were going to do for a living; the factories were quiet, and it began to appear to people that the props under their communities and their personal lives had been kicked out.

The panhandle forms about one-third of West Virginia's 1st Congressional District. Another third is in the industrialized Monongahela valley, directly south of Pittsburgh, around Clarksburg and Fairmont. This also is coal, steel, and glassmaking country. Finally, about one-third live in the more rural and less industrial hills along the Ohio River, or in the city of Parkersburg. The Panhandle and the Monongahela valley are ordinarily Democratic, though vestiges of Civil War Republicanism remain; the area along the Ohio tends to be Republican.

The incumbent congressman here, Alan Mollohan, is one of two sons of congressmen who won seats themselves in 1982. His father, Robert Mollohan, was elected in 1952 and 1954, defeated by Arch Moore in 1956, then won the seat again when Moore was elected governor in 1968, and kept it until his retirement at age 73 in 1982. He was an old-time Democrat with a liberal record on economic issues and a record as a supporter of military spending increases on the House Armed Services Committee. Alan Mollohan did not win the seat automatically. His main problem was that from 1973 to 1982 he was a Washington, D.C., lawyer, working for, among others, Consolidation Coal. He returned to Fairmont and established a base in the Monongahela valley, but his connection with the district was little closer than that of a British M.P. to a seat his party had assigned him to.

The son of a rough-hewn old politico, Alan Mollohan doesn't look like a successful politician from West Virginia; he looks like a mild-mannered junior associate in a law firm who is reasonably good technically but doesn't bring in much business. Yet he has won two races against serious Republican opponents. In 1982 he beat a former Republican state chairman who had some support from the United Mine Workers; in 1984 he beat a former legislator and decorated Vietnam war veteran, running as he had two years before ahead of his party ticket. Apparently the Republicans were impressed. He had no Republican opponent at all in 1986.

Mollohan is naturally a champion of the steel, coal, and glass industries, and of employee ownership as well. In his third term he got a seat on the Appropriations Committee, where he can work for the U.S. 22 bypass in Weirton, Ohio River projects, and an improved black lung program. He opposes acid rain legislation and favors restrictive trade laws.

The People: Pop. 1980: 488,568, up 6.1% 1970–80. Households (1980): 76% family, 40% with children, 65% married couples; 26.3% housing units rented; median monthly rent: $137; median house value: $38,200. Voting age pop. (1980): 353,283; 2% Black, 1% Spanish origin.

1984 Presidential Vote:

Reagan (R)	111,290	(57%)
Mondale (D)	84,836	(43%)

Rep. Alan B. Mollohan (D)

Elected 1982; b. May 14, 1943, Fairmont; home, Fairmont; Col. of William and Mary, A.B. 1966, WV U., Col. of Law, J.D. 1970; Baptist; married (Barbara).

Career: Practicing atty., 1970–82.

Offices: 516 CHOB 20515, 202-225-4172. Also 603 Deveny Bldg., Fairmont 26554, 304-363-3356; 1117 Fed. Bldg., Parkersburg 26101, 304-428-0493; 316 Fed. Bldg., Wheeling 26003, 304-232-5390; and 209 P.O. Bldg., Clarksburg 26301, 304-623-4422.

Committees: *Appropriations* (35th of 35 D). Subcommitees: Commerce, Justice, State and Judiciary; HUD-Independent Agencies. *Standards of Official Conduct* (4th of 6 D).

Group Ratings

	ADA	ACLU	COPE	CFA	LCV	ACU	NTU	NSI	COC	CEI
1986	50	40	90	50	32	35	15	50	24	11
1985	55	—	87	50	—	38	20	—	23	—

National Journal Ratings

	1986 LIB — 1986 CONS		1985 LIB — 1985 CONS	
Economic	72%	— 27%	81%	— 17%
Social	52%	— 46%	36%	— 60%
Foreign	46%	— 53%	42%	— 56%

Key Votes

1) Lmt Cln Water Act	AGN	5) Retain Gun Cont	AGN	9) Aid Angola Reb	FOR
2) Rpl Tobac Sub	AGN	6) Contra Aid	AGN	10) Tax Reform	FOR
3) Grm-Rdmn Def Red	AGN	7) Lmt Text Imp	FOR	11) S Africa Sanc	FOR
4) Ban Polygraph	FOR	8) Limit SDI	FOR	12) Immig Reform	FOR

Election Results

1986 general	Alan B. Mollohan (D).................	90,715	(100%)	($216,378)
1986 primary	Alan B. Mollohan (D).................	53,018	(100%)	
1984 general	Alan B. Mollohan (D).................	104,639	(54%)	($362,369)
	Jim Altmeyer (R)	87,622	(46%)	($514,096)

Campaign Contributions and Expenditures

1985-86		Direct Cont. 1985-86		PACS Breakdown 1985-86			
Receipts	$243,825	Indiv.	$65,331	Corp.	$34,400	T/M/H	$28,433
Expend.	$216,378	Party	$705	Labor	$50,350	Agr.	$4,500
Debts	$30,284	PACS	$131,105	Ideo.	$13,422	CWOS	$0
		Cand.	$40,000				

SECOND DISTRICT

Eastern West Virginia has some of the loveliest scenery in the United States: gentle hills and rugged mountains, stands of green trees and vistas that stretch to far horizons—"almost heaven," in the words of the song. Yet in most counties you will find, amid scenery primeval and rural, sudden evidence of industrialization: a pulp mill or charcoal factory in a clearing scraped out of the forest; a small factory town, built close to a river in a cleft bordered with hills, its houses built in the same 1910s style as in the factory towns of Pittsburgh; the entrance to an underground coal mine or the exposed brown earth of a strip mine scar. One of America's earliest industrial sites is here, in Harper's Ferry, where the government had one of its arsenals which before the Civil War produced most of America's weapons; this concentration of guns was the reason John Brown chose this as the place for what he hoped would be the center of a slave rebellion, and it was for military reasons that West Virginia's boundaries were extended so far eastward. But this is not the only part of eastern West Virginia that is remote from the state's major population centers. Practically all of it is, because of the continuous chains of mountains and the steep valleys which sometimes, as in 1985, are swept by raging floodwaters.

The 2d Congressional District of West Virginia includes most of the mountainous and sparsely populated eastern part of the state. The district extends from Harpers Ferry south and west to Fayette County, near the state capital of Charleston, and not all that far from the Kentucky line. In the northwestern part of the district, not far from Pittsburgh, is the 2d's largest city, Morgantown, with a population of just 27,000—part of the industrial Monongahela valley and home of West Virginia University. Politically, the 2d Congressional District is a patchwork quilt of partisan preferences. Coal counties have generally been Democratic since the 1930s; counties with relatively few miners trace their partisan ancestry back to the Civil War. The balance generally favors the Democrats, but not overwhelmingly; in many elections, this is the least Democratic of West Virginia's four districts.

The current congressman, Harley Staggers, Jr., is the son of the man who represented this district from 1948 to 1980, and who for more than a decade chaired what now is the House Energy and Commerce Committee. The succession was not automatic, however. When Staggers, Sr., retired in 1980, his son lost the Democratic primary to state Senator Pat Hamilton, who in turn lost the general election to Republican Cleveland Benedict. Benedict, a Procter & Gamble heir, could afford to spend liberally on his races, and he might have held onto the district; but he ran for the Senate, and was devastatingly defeated by Senator Robert Byrd. In the meantime, Harley Staggers, Jr., sought and won a state Senate seat, and when it came time to file for the 2d District in 1982, he had no competition for the Democratic nomination.

That turned out to be tantamount to victory. The Republicans again had a rich self-financing candidate, but he was unable to carry a single one of the district's 20 counties. Benedict himself came back and tried to win the House seat again in 1984. But the response to his negative campaign against Robert Byrd has been a personal repudiation of such proportions that he failed dismally in his comeback bid. Even though Ronald Reagan was carrying the district handily, and losing only 2 of its 20 counties, Benedict won only 44% of the vote and carried only five counties himself.

Staggers has not gotten on his father's old committee, which has become the most sought after committee assignment in the House; he serves on Agriculture and Judiciary which, contrary perhaps to appearances, have no great district significance. He is a pleasant man, who keeps in close touch with his constituency, and seems earnest and determined to do what he thinks is right. Those qualities seem to sell: after two tough races, he was reelected by an impressive margin in 1986, far exceeding usual Democratic percentages in some very partisan hill counties.

The People: Pop. 1980: 487,438, up 20.5% 1970–80. Households (1980): 76% family, 41% with children, 64% married couples; 25.8% housing units rented; median monthly rent: $134; median house value: $36,600. Voting age pop. (1980): 350,168; 3% Black, 1% Spanish origin.

1984 Presidential Vote:

Reagan (R)	107,719	(58%)
Mondale (D)	77,702	(42%)

Rep. Harley O. Staggers, Jr. (D)

Elected 1982; b. Feb. 22, 1951, Washington, DC; home, Keyser; Harvard U., B.A. 1974, WV U., J.D. 1977; Roman Catholic; single.

Career: WV Asst. Atty. Gen., 1977–79; WV Senate, 1980–82.

Offices: 1504 LHOB 20515, 202-225-4331. Also P.O. Box 1096, Keyser 26726, 304-788-6311; P.O. Box 1255, Morgantown 26507, 304-291-6001; 101 N. Court St., Lewisburg 24901, 304-645-3188; and 235 S. Queen St., Martinsburg 25401, 304-267-2144.

Committees: *Agriculture* (15th of 26 D). Subcommittees: Department Operations, Research, and Foreign Agriculture; Domestic Marketing, Consumer Relations, and Nutrition. *Judiciary* (19th of 21 D). Subcommittees: Crime; Monopolies and Commercial Law. *Veterans' Affairs* (9th of 21 D). Subcommittee: Hospitals and Health Care.

Group Ratings

	ADA	ACLU	COPE	CFA	LCV	ACU	NTU	NSI	COC	CEI
1986	80	65	90	92	61	5	28	20	28	14
1985	70	—	87	58	—	19	32	—	38	—

National Journal Ratings

	1986 LIB — 1986 CONS	1985 LIB — 1985 CONS
Economic	84% — 13%	74% — 25%
Social	64% — 34%	54% — 45%
Foreign	64% — 34%	64% — 33%

Key Votes

1) Lmt Cln Water Act	FOR	5) Retain Gun Cont	AGN	9) Aid Angola Reb	AGN
2) Rpl Tobac Sub	AGN	6) Contra Aid	AGN	10) Tax Reform	FOR
3) Grm-Rdmn Def Red	FOR	7) Lmt Text Imp	FOR	11) S Africa Sanc	FOR
4) Ban Polygraph	FOR	8) Limit SDI	FOR	12) Immig Reform	AGN

Election Results

1986 general	Harley O. Staggers, Jr. (D)	76,355	(69%)	($136,766)
	Michele Golden (R)	33,554	(31%)	($67,232)
1986 general	Harley O. Staggers, Jr. (D)	50,533	(86%)	
	D. P. Given (D)	5,513	(10%)	
	Charles Wood (D)	2,473	(4%)	
1984 general	Harley O. Staggers, Jr. (D)	100,345	(56%)	($297,916)
	Cleve Benedict (R)	78,936	(44%)	($322,511)

Campaign Contributions and Expenditures

	1985-86		Direct Cont. 1985-86		PACS Breakdown 1985-86		
Receipts	$158,284	Indiv.	$22,017	Corp.	$14,500	T/M/H	$35,920
Expend.	$136,766	Party	$2,550	Labor	$70,750	Agr.	$1,250
Unspent	$25,537	PACS	$132,279	Ideo.	$8,859	CWOS	$1,000

THIRD DISTRICT

The metropolis of West Virginia is Charleston, an industrial city hemmed in by mountains on the banks of the Kanawha River (pronounced kanAW locally) which might be overlooked in a larger state. But in West Virginia it is central. Along the Kanawha rises West Virginia's Capitol, one of the largest and most beautiful in the country; this is the center of West Virginia's state government and with its two partisan newspapers, the Democratic *Gazette* and the Republican *Daily Mail*, Charleston is the center of West Virginia politics as well. It is also the center of an important part of the economy. In the hills above Charleston are many of West Virginia's coal mines; below, on the banks of the Kanawha in the industrial suburbs, are the large chemical plants that convert coal tar and other feedstocks into products Americans use every day. These plants have been some of America's major polluters of air and water, and Charleston has had some of the nation's nastiest air. Charleston is also West Virginia's white-collar and professional center, with a few downtown skyscrapers and some pleasant affluent residential districts. But the overall atmosphere here is more raw than polished, more tradition-minded than culturally advanced.

Charleston, interestingly, is more Republican than West Virginia as a whole, and far more Republican than the surrounding coal counties. The concentration of management personnel is one reason; another is the permanence of Civil War loyalties; a third may be support from fundamentalists like those who kicked up one of the nation's first fusses over textbook censorship in the 1970s. Charleston and surrounding Kanawha County make up almost half of West Virginia's 3d Congressional District. To the south and west are mining counties, heavily Democratic; to the north and east, toward the Ohio River, are quieter rural counties, with few mine shafts in their hollows, where Civil War loyalties are still very much alive, and which often vote Republican.

The congressman from the 3d District is Bob Wise, a Democratic whose background is a bit unusual for a West Virginia politician—or would have seemed so a generation ago. He is from an affluent Charleston family, went to elite schools, then returned to town to start a law practice geared to low- and middle-income clients; he led a movement to force coal companies to pay higher taxes; in a state where politicians got ahead by relying on ancestral loyalties and smoothing relations with big economic institutions, he has made his way by emphasizing issues on which he opposes the big interests. Wise won the seat after veteran Representative John Slack died and two successors fumbled the chance to hold it. The first was a Democrat who was attacked for hiring an attractive aide for personal reasons and whose wife, it was revealed, wrote a memo insisting that he hire only homely women: he won a 1979 special election but lost in 1980. The second was a Republican who got his start in the textbook controversy and liked to say that he and President Reagan were called by God to help lead the country; he was overconfident and lost in 1982 and then became a Washington lobbyist for the U.S. Chamber of Commerce. Wise was shrewd and popular enough to beat the House of Delegates Majority Leader and a former Kanawha County sheriff in the 1982 primary and then to beat the incumbent soundly in November. He has been reelected easily, seems to have a safe seat, and has been mentioned as a possible candidate for governor in 1988.

In the House Wise has been something of an insurgent, taking to the floor in 1983 to oppose a dam favored by the rest of the West Virginia delegation and stopping it. But he also unblushingly uses his seat on the Public Works Committee to push the Gallipolis and Winfield River navigation projects for coal shipping. He has been a visible participant in efforts by a Government Operations subcommittee (Environment, Energy and Natural Resources) to highlight and correct lax enforcement of reclamation laws by the Office of Surface Mining. He has declined to accept congressional salary increases and uses the money for $1,000-a-year scholarships at 3d District colleges. His voting record is among the more liberal in the House, particularly on economics, but he is no effete easterner: he is a strong West Virginia booster, urging students to make their careers in their native state, and is becoming Congress's most visible promoter of clog dancing.

The People: Pop. 1980: 486,112, up 10.0% 1970–80. Households (1980): 78% family, 42% with children, 67% married couples; 26.8% housing units rented; median monthly rent: $150; median house value: $43,500. Voting age pop. (1980): 347,147; 3% Black, 1% Spanish origin.

1984 Presidential Vote: Reagan (R) 107,004   (56%)
                                Mondale (D) 84,559   (44%)

Rep. Robert E. (Bob) Wise, Jr. (D)

Elected 1982; b. Jan. 6, 1948, Washington, DC; home, Clendenin; Duke U., B.A. 1970, Tulane U. Sch. of Law, J.D. 1975; Episcopalian; married (Sandy).

Career: Practicing atty., 1975–80; Dir., WV for Fair and Equitable Assessment of Taxes, Inc., 1977–80; WV Senate, 1980–82.

Offices: 1421 LHOB 20515, 202-225-2711. Also 107 Pennsylvania Ave., Charleston 25302, 304-347-7170.

Committees: *Education and Labor* (15th of 21 D). Subcommittees: Elementary, Secondary and Vocational Education; Labor Standards. *Government Operations* (12th of 24 D). Subcommittees: Government Activities and Transportation; Legislation and National Security. *Public Works and Transportation* (19th of 32 D). Subcommittees: Surface Transportation; Water Resources. *Select Committee on Aging* (30th of 39 D). Subcommittee: Retirement Income and Employment.

Group Ratings

	ADA	ACLU	COPE	CFA	LCV	ACU	NTU	NSI	COC	CEI
1986	75	70	88	83	60	5	23	0	22	14
1985	70	—	87	58	—	10	32	—	32	—

National Journal Ratings

	1986 LIB — 1986 CONS		1985 LIB — 1985 CONS	
Economic	84%	— 13%	75%	— 22%
Social	74%	— 23%	62%	— 37%
Foreign	75%	— 20%	64%	— 33%

Key Votes

1) Lmt Cln Water Act	AGN	5) Retain Gun Cont	AGN	9) Aid Angola Reb	AGN
2) Rpl Tobac Sub	AGN	6) Contra Aid	AGN	10) Tax Reform	FOR
3) Grm-Rdmn Def Red	FOR	7) Lmt Text Imp	FOR	11) S Africa Sanc	FOR
4) Ban Polygraph	FOR	8) Limit SDI	FOR	12) Immig Reform	FOR

Election Results

1986 general	Robert E. (Bob) Wise, Jr. (D)............	73,669	(65%)	($138,732)
	Tim Sharp (R)	39,820	(35%)	($20,411)
1986 primary	Robert E. (Bob) Wise, Jr. (D)............	52,225	(100%)	
1984 general	Robert E. (Bob) Wise, Jr. (D)...........	125,306	(68%)	($176,627)
	Margaret Peggy Miller (R)..............	59,128	(32%)	($46,941)

Campaign Contributions and Expenditures

1985-86		Direct Cont. 1985-86		PACS Breakdown 1985-86			
Receipts	$147,260	Indiv.	$48,305	Corp.	$21,700	T/M/H	$21,241
Expend.	$138,732	Party	$191	Labor	$47,500	Agr.	$0
Unspent	$41,381	PACS	$96,941	Ideo.	$6,500	CWOS	$0

FOURTH DISTRICT

The heart of America's coal industry is in the mountains of southern West Virginia. Early in this century, this was one of America's boom areas. Into rural farmland and hollows inhabited by the same families since they first came into the mountains a century or so before, came coal company lawyers with minerals rights' leases to sign, coal company engineers to design and sink the mineshafts, and men from other mountain counties and fresh from boats coming from Europe as well to work the mines. Company houses were built; company stores stocked with goods as the company determined; company paymasters kept close tabs on the finances of every employee. Men with the wit and nerve and imagination to do so got rich, and the workers mostly did better than they would have where they came from. But in the process the landscape was spoiled by abandoned mineshafts and piles of tailings, and lives were snuffed out in America's deadliest industry by unpredicted cave-ins or simple carelessness.

Most of the coal counties of southern West Virginia are collected in the state's 4th Congressional District, which also includes the city of Huntington on the Ohio River, set up nearly 100 years ago by railroad magnate Collis P. Huntington. Over the years the eight counties of the 4th District have produced more bituminous coal than any other single congressional district in the United States. But employment in the coal mines has declined drastically in the four decades since World War II, because of labor-saving equipment and because of the United Mine Workers agreement negotiated by John L. Lewis in 1950; and the counties of the 4th District have never entirely replaced the jobs lost in the mines. The population figures tell the story: the counties in today's 4th District had 579,000 people in 1950 and 437,000 in 1970. In the 1970s the economy in this area rebounded somewhat, as coal prices rose and mining—especially strip mining—increased, and by 1980 the population was up to 487,000. But even then the number of coal-mining jobs was still far from its old peak, and in the lengthy recession of the early 1980s was devastating here, and the population fell again.

The politics of this sometimes poverty-stricken area has little of the altruism that some liberal reformers expected when they called in the 1960s for the maximum feasible participation of the poor. In places like southern West Virginia, there are few ways for a bright young man to make money except by owning a coal mine or winning public or union office. Public office is often more lucrative than published salaries suggest; corruption has been common here, and there are still counties where one is supposed to be able to buy votes. Poor people see politics less as a way of helping poor people generally—who can abolish poverty in West Virginia?—than as a way of advancing themselves personally. In the struggle to get ahead, the ordinary politician here has little concern for matters like unsafe mine conditions, black lung disease, or air and water pollution.

The current congressman, Nick Joe Rahall II, did not use politics as a way up from poverty: he is part of a family that owns radio and television stations in such widely dispersed locales as Beckley, West Virginia, and St. Petersburg, Florida, and he has been able and willing to spend his own money in campaigns. This helped him win, at age 27, the decisive 1976 Democratic primary, when incumbent Ken Hechler, a crusader against Tony Boyle's UMW leadership, was running for governor; the 1976 general election, when Hechler came back and ran as an independent; and the 1978 primary, when Hechler tried again to regain the seat. Since then Rahall has won with ease: in 1984 he got 67% of the vote.

In the House Rahall is a member of the Interior and Public Works Committees. You could not find coalier assignments. After the 1984 election, the House leadership placed jurisdiction over mining interests in a new Interior subcommittee (leaving forest management and the Bonneville Power Administration with Jim Weaver of Oregon), and gave Rahall the chairmanship. He works hard for coal's interests, against legislation that would restrict use of eastern coal or encourage use of its competition (oil, natural gas, western coal), against high railroad rates. He urged setting up a Federal Coal Export Commission, and he resisted Administration efforts to increase the coal excise tax that replenishes the Black Lung Trust Fund. He is solidly liberal on economic and foreign issues; on cultural matters, and particularly on environmental issues, his record is mixed. Of Arab descent, he is interested in Middle East issues and critical of Israel. With the three other West Virginia seats held by freshmen, he became in 1982 the dean of the state's House delegation. He has a safe seat and will likely remain in the House for years.

The People: Pop. 1980: 487,526, up 11.4% 1970–80. Households (1980): 79% family, 45% with children, 66% married couples; 26.8% housing units rented; median monthly rent: $135; median house value: $36,000. Voting age pop. (1980): 339,410; 6% Black, 1% Spanish origin.

1984 Presidential Vote:

Mondale (D)	81,060	(50%)
Reagan (R)	79,470	(49%)

Rep. Nick Joe Rahall, II (D)

Elected 1976; b. May 20, 1949, Beckley; home, Beckley; Duke U., A.B. 1971, Geo. Wash. U.; Presbyterian; divorced.

Career: Aide to Sen. Robert C. Byrd, 1972–75; Pres., Mountaineer Tour and Travel Agency, 1974; Pres., WV Broadcasting Corp.

Offices: 343 CHOB 20515, 202-225-3452. Also 110½ Main St., Beckley 25801, 304-252-5000, 304-252-6507; 815 5th Ave., Huntington 25701, 304-522-6425, 304-529-1716; 1005 Fed. Bldg., Bluefield 24701, 304-325-6222; and R.K. Bldg., Logan 25601, 304-752-4934.

Committees: *Interior and Insular Affairs* (6th of 26 D). Subcommittees: Energy and the Environment; Mining and Natural Resources (Chairman); National Parks and Public Lands. *Public Works and Transportation* (7th of 32 D). Subcommittees: Economic Development; Surface Transportation.

Group Ratings

	ADA	ACLU	COPE	CFA	LCV	ACU	NTU	NSI	COC	CEI
1986	90	65	86	83	58	9	24	0	17	8
1985	80	—	85	67	—	5	26	—	18	—

National Journal Ratings

	1986 LIB — 1986 CONS		1985 LIB — 1985 CONS	
Economic	87% —	0%	81% —	17%
Social	69% —	28%	60% —	38%
Foreign	80% —	0%	68% —	31%

Key Votes

1) Lmt Cln Water Act	AGN	5) Retain Gun Cont	AGN	9) Aid Angola Reb	AGN
2) Rpl Tobac Sub	AGN	6) Contra Aid	AGN	10) Tax Reform	FOR
3) Grm-Rdmn Def Red	AGN	7) Lmt Text Imp	FOR	11) S Africa Sanc	FOR
4) Ban Polygraph	FOR	8) Limit SDI	FOR	12) Immig Reform	FOR

Election Results

1986 general	Nick Joe Rahall, II (D)	58,217	(71%)	($68,970)
	Martin Miller, Sr. (R)	23,490	(29%)	
1986 primary	Nick Joe Rahall, II (D)	56,603	(100%)	
1984 general	Nick Joe Rahall, II (D)	98,919	(67%)	($115,277)
	Jess T. Shumate (R)	49,474	(33%)	

Campaign Contributions and Expenditures

1985-86		Direct Cont. 1985-86		PACS Breakdown 1985-86			
Receipts	$212,148	Indiv.	$77,651	Corp.	$36,775	T/M/H	$31,254
Expend.	$68,970	Party	$705	Labor	$47,375	Agr.	$3,500
Unspent	$214,118	PACS	$124,904	Ideo.	$5,000	CWOS	$1,000

WISCONSIN

North of Chicago, west of the Great Lakes, Wisconsin is the first state of the Northwest—the vast stretch of the United States all the way to the Pacific that was more often settled by immigrants from Germany and Scandinavia than by descendants of the New England Yankees and Middle Atlantic settlers who populated the states just to the south. This Germanic origin gives a particular cast to cultural life in Wisconsin and has shaped its politics. The German language is seldom heard any more, the once plainly German beer brands now seem quintessentially American, and not many close ties exist with the old country after two world wars. Yet the tradition that has its origins in Wisconsin's German heritage is a lively one still, and the heritage itself is not totally forgotten: in 1980, 51% of Wisconsin residents volunteered to the Census Bureau that they are of German descent.

To understand that tradition, you need to go back nearly a century, and remember that Germans were the most numerous immigrants of the 19th century, more numerous even than the Irish, and that until the 1880s they were the most distinctive. They often kept their old language, maintained their separate religion, kept old customs from country weddings to drinking beer (a source of friction in temperance-minded America); they established, on the vast empty prairies or in crowded neighborhoods of growing cities, German communities. Politically they were never an entirely monolithic group; their origins were too diverse, and they were spread too widely across the nation. But where they were concentrated, you can see the growth of a distinctive politics, basically American but with echoes of the ideas and movements also seen in German-speaking countries in Europe.

Nowhere was the politics of German-Americans more apparent than in Wisconsin. This is one of the states that gave birth to the Republican party in 1854, and German-Americans, then arriving in vast numbers, heavily preferred its free soil politics to the doughface stands of the Democrats. The German-Americans abhorred slavery; they welcomed the free lands the Republicans were advocating in the Homestead Act, the free educations they were promising by setting up land grant colleges, the transportation routes they were building by subsidizing railroad builders.

At the turn of the century, Wisconsin gave birth to Robert LaFollette's Progressive movement. Elected governor in 1900, LaFollette, previously a conventional Republican politician, completely revamped the state government before going to the Senate in 1906. At a time when Germany was Europe's leader in graduate education and the application of science to government, LaFollette brought in professors from the University of Wisconsin, across town in Madison, to develop the state's workmen's compensation system and income tax. The Progressive movement favored the rational use of government to improve the lot of the ordinary citizen—an idea borrowed, perhaps, from German liberals and adopted by the New Dealers a generation later. LaFollette himself became a national figure, and tried to run for President in 1912 as a Progressive, but was shoved aside by Theodore Roosevelt; in 1924 he finally did run for President as a Progressive and won 18% of the nation's votes. It was the best third-party showing of the last 60 years; he was strongest in the northern tier from Wisconsin to Washington, along the West Coast, and in some hitherto Republican factory towns like Cleveland.

La Follette served in the Senate nearly 20 years as an insurgent reformer, and his sons maintained the traditions of Wisconsin's progressivism. Robert LaFollette, Jr., served in the Senate from 1925 to 1947, and Philip LaFollette was governor of Wisconsin from 1935 to 1939. During the 1930s the LaFollettes ran on the Progressive Party line in Wisconsin and dreamed of forming a national third party. But their foreign policy was not what Americans now think of as progressive at all. The elder Robert LaFollette was a vitriolic opponent of World War I, and voted against both the declaration of war against Germany and the Versailles Treaty; his sons were isolationists in the years before World War II. Once again, their stand was popular with German-Americans, who dreaded a conflict with a country which (in 1917 in most cases, in 1940 far fewer) they regarded sympathetically and as a beacon of enlightened government policy. The Wilson Administration's anti-German campaign in fact destroyed most outward signs of Germano-America in Wisconsin and elsewhere: the teaching of the German language was forbidden widely, half the German language newspapers were shut down and three-quarters of their circulation vanished, people with German names were encouraged to change them and other German words were abolished (sauerkraut became liberty cabbage), and reminders of German culture became something to hide, not something to be proud of.

Inevitably there was a backlash, even after isolationism was politically discredited after Pearl Harbor. One sign was that Senator LaFollette, busy with congressional reorganization in Washington, was upset in the Republican primary in 1946 by one Joseph McCarthy. As Samuel Lubell demonstrated, McCarthy's charges that Communists were influencing American foreign policy fed on the inarticulate convictions of many that we should have been fighting Russia as much as Germany in World War II. After 1945 Wisconsin became for a time a pretty reliable conservative Republican state. Richard Nixon carried it three times; it elected mostly Republicans in the 1940s and 1950s and quite a few in the 1960s and 1970s.

For the last 20 years, Wisconsin has been politically countercyclical, moving in a direction opposite from the rest of the nation. With a Republican heritage, it became one of the most Democratic states as the nation moved mostly Republican. It moved toward, not away from, George McGovern in 1972, and it provided 11 crucial electoral votes for Jimmy Carter in 1976 and came close to supporting him in 1980 as well; it gave 45% of its votes for Walter Mondale in 1984, making it the eighth most Democratic state that year. It has become one of the most dovish states, as if a large number of Wisconsin voters were hit by the same impulse that has led so many voters in West Germany, suddenly in the early 1980s, to start fearing the presence of nuclear weapons and favoring unilateral disarmament. Then, in 1986, when the nation generally appeared to be moving out of the era of Ronald Reagan, Wisconsin seemed to be moving right. It ousted Tony Earl, one of the most liberal governors in America, despite his competence and in a year when most incumbent governors did very well; it was one of the few states to reelect a Reagan landslide Senator, Bob Kasten, who remained strongly identified with Reagan policies, and who also ran under the cloud of a drunken driving conviction when voters generally have strongly approved of cracking down on the offense. It ousted longtime Attorney General Bronson LaFollette.

Environmental issues, which used to work for the Democrats, were overshadowed by concerns that Wisconsin's high taxes were stifling economic growth. The openness to forms of cultural liberation so apparent here in the past seemed replaced by concern about the consequences: Wisconsin passed a trailblazing law making parents, not the state, responsible for supporting the illegitimate children of unmarried teenagers. Yet it's not clear that Wisconsin has moved heavily to the right. The Democrats beefed up their margins in the legislature, and Earl's loss was attributed by some to his inability to get his message out and his reliance on an overly tight-knit staff. If Wisconsin seems unlikely to extend the LaFollette version of the welfare state any further just now, it's not clear that it wants to do away with large parts of it either.

Governor. Wisconsin's Governor, Tommy Thompson, has spent most of his life commuting from the small town of Elroy 80 miles south to Madison, first as a student at the University of Wisconsin, then after his election just after finishing law school to the legislature. There he was

WISCONSIN — Congressional Districts, Counties, and Selected Places — *(9 Districts)*

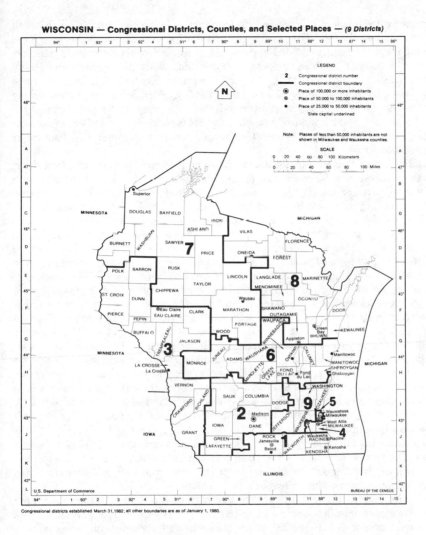

Congressional districts established March 31,1982; all other boundaries are as of January 1, 1980.

part of the minority for nearly 20 years, the minority leader for most of the 1980s, known as "Doctor No." In the 1986 campaign he called for cutting taxes and cutting welfare; Earl was for continued high spending and argued that the state's economy had grown in his term. Earl was also hurt by his support of homosexual rights and a new prison in Milwaukee, by his opposition to the 21-year drinking age, and by his off-the-cuff remark that he'd rather strike than take the 15% pay cut offered to Oscar Mayer workers. Once in office, Thompson turned out to compromise more with the Democratic legislature than expected, backing a small tax rise and insisting on no major cuts in welfare spending, building the prison near Racine rather than up north and accepting a mandatory seat belt law. In the manner of many governors, he began boosting the state constantly, praising its environment and work ethic, and he pointed out sensibly enough that his responsibilities as governor were different from those of a minority party leader in the legislature.

Senators. Wisconsin's senior member of Congress is William Proxmire; indeed, he is now one of the senior members of the Senate. This is not a result many of his colleagues of 20 years ago would have greeted with equanimity; Proxmire was seen then as an uncooperative maverick with a penchant for lost causes. In the 1970s, history started moving his way, and he became more effective, leading the movement that killed government assistance for the supersonic transport in 1970—beating the Nixon Administration and Washington's Warren Magnuson and Henry Jackson in the process. He continued to take on defense contractors with flair and with some success, and to attack domestic spending as well. His monthly "golden fleece" award for wasting federal money has become a Washington tradition. All this gave Proxmire a reputation in some quarters as a liberal; actually, he is more of a pinchpenny. He is consistently rated one of the best Senators by the National Taxpayers Union, which simply notes whether members vote for or against every spending issue.

On non-spending issues Proxmire is not necessarily liberal either. On cultural issues, he is often conservative—a bit of a bluenose. On foreign policy issues, he lines up usually with liberals, but in large part because he opposes spending by the Pentagon and disdains defense contractors. In his committee areas, Proxmire has not been a force for increased spending on housing, and initially was a skeptic rather than a supporter of federal loan guarantees to New York City and the Chrysler Corporation. On Appropriations he is less effective in shaping an overall budget than he might be, because he concentrates on opposing just about every spending item, regardless of importance. (The major exception, naturally, is on dairy price supports: Proxmire is solidly for them.) And this is the major criticism that can be made of his career: that he is a nitpicker, not a man who can move government in a major way in the direction he wants.

Proxmire's greatest success as a legislator came when the public wanted to cut defense spending, didn't care much about increasing or decreasing domestic spending, and was skeptical of foreign involvements—when he was in tune with the times. The 1980s have been more difficult for him: an era of expansive defense spending and of glitter in the society pages. This runs very much against the Proxmire grain. He prizes discipline and hard work above all else: for years he has run the four miles from his home to the Capitol every morning, and he stands rather than sits at a desk. He holds the all-time record for consecutive roll calls answered. He is in superb health and looks years younger than his age. He has an utter disdain for the camaraderie that most politicians enjoy, and is ready to irk the most powerful colleague over the slightest principle; he makes himself exceedingly unpopular by fighting against salary increases (he is independently wealthy himself) and by opposing the gymnasium proposed for the Hart Senate Office Building. The Democrats' loss of the Senate cost him his committee chairmanships, but he had no ties to the newly-dominant Republicans; with the Democrats back in, he is a chairman again but not one influential with his colleagues.

In 1987 Proxmire entered his seventh year as chairman of the Banking Committee. Dire predictions were made when he first became chairman in 1975; few came true. Skeptical of the New York City and Chrysler bailouts, he helped impose such tough conditions on them that they succeeded, and he was at least as constructive on technical (but terribly momentous) banking questions as his successor, Jake Garn, who never got any major banking legislation through. He passed a deregulation bill in 1980, but his lodestar is not market economics, but protecting the little guy, and especially the small town banker; he wants to keep the big banks and Sears from competing with the locals. He is, as you might expect, a stern opponent of greenmail and, more surprisingly, skeptical of hostile takeovers, taking the side of established managements rather than those who can convince investors they'll maximize profits. He brings to issues the perspective of a Waterloo, Wisconsin, businessman, which he once was, not the view of a rich kid from the North Shore suburbs of Chicago and a Harvard Business School graduate, which he also was. He is next in line to chair the Senate Appropriations Committee after John Stennis; here he would probably still pinch pennies, though his lack of give-and-take with his colleagues combined with his advocacy of some Wisconsin projects would limit his leverage. But Robert Byrd, if he gives up the majority leadership, could invoke seniority and take the chair from Proxmire, and there are rumors he might do so in 1989.

At home Proxmire remains one of the most popular and invincible Senators. With his incredible energy, he has continued to work the state hard; the saying is that you can't get into a Green Bay Packers' football game without shaking Proxmire's hand. His reputation as a budget-cutter is helpful in the frugal Upper Midwest and his skepticism about defense budgets has not hurt in a state that has virtually no defense industry or military bases. The numbers suggest, however, that Proxmire's appeal is fading a little: in 1982, at age 67, he was reelected with 64% of the vote—an outstanding percentage but below the 71% and 72% he received in the two preceding elections. That's still an excellent performance, and just about everyone in Wisconsin assumes that Proxmire will win another six-year term in 1988.

Wisconsin's junior Senator, Bob Kasten, has won some upset victories—and taken some lumps. He is a conservative Republican who made his way upward in what was then a liberal Democratic state, winning a House seat in 1974 and 1976, losing the gubernatorial primary in 1978, upsetting Senator Gaylord Nelson in 1980. In the early 1980s he found himself sitting on the Budget and Appropriations Committees, making after his brief apprenticeship in government, key macroeconomic decisions in the richest nation in the world. Now he is back in the minority again. But he has translated his devotion to free-market principles and opposition to what he considers government overregulation and overtaxation into action. He supported the Reagan tax and budget cuts. He was the leading opponent of withholding from savings and brokerage accounts and, though he lost to Bob Dole on the issue in the 1982 tax bill, he worked closely with the banking lobby which generated a massive flood of outraged mail which persuaded an almost unanimous Congress to backtrack in 1983. He was the co-sponsor in 1984 and 1985 of Kemp-Kasten, the Republican alternative to the Bradley-Gephardt tax reform plan, that played a role in producing the historic tax reform of 1986. He was one of those writing the platform at the 1984 Republican National Convention. He introduced the leading measure to federalize liability suits, so as to reduce awards to plaintiffs and, presumably, insurance costs.

Over some time now Kasten has shown solid political skills, including the ability to stick to his guns under heavy pressure. He has made sure to have a positive environmental record and to work to help local governments (unlike the aloof Proxmire). He chaired the Appropriations subcommittee handling foreign aid, supporting aid to Israel and Egypt and Administration policy in Central America. But Kasten also has his foibles. In his first term he got involved in a civil suit involving partnerships he had with a bankrupt real estate speculator who went to jail; in 1985 he was arrested for drunk driving. He lost badly to Al Simpson when he tried to be elected Republican Whip. In 1980 he won in Wisconsin partly because Nelson did not campaign hard; in 1986 he was the winner of one of the year's least edifying brawls. For that much blame must go to Democrat Ed Garvey, the onetime attorney for the National Football League players who got them involved in a long and not very successful strike: Garvey attacked Kasten for being remote from the public and for "drinking on the job" and hired a detective who posed as a reporter to snoop into Kasten's financial affairs; Kasten ran ads opposing those tactics and attacking Garvey's stewardship of the football players' funds. The result was a narrow but decisive Kasten victory; Kasten lost Madison, Kenosha, Milwaukee County (but carried the whole Milwaukee metropolitan area), and a few scattered counties, and won everywhere else.

Presidential politics. Wisconsin was once one of the most influential states in presidential contests. Its presidential primary knocked Wendell Willkie out of the race in 1944 and helped John Kennedy establish his lead over Hubert Humphrey in 1960; Eugene McCarthy was all set to win heavily here in 1968 when Lyndon Johnson withdrew on the Sunday night before the election. The last time Wisconsin was at all important was in 1976 when Morris Udall was barely edged out by Jimmy Carter, but it was overshadowed even then by the New York primary the same day. Now there are so many other primaries before Wisconsin's April contest that it seems unlikely to have much effect. The Democrats have given Wisconsin a special exemption from their rule requiring party registration; the open primary was one of Bob LaFollette's reforms, still cherished in Wisconsin. But they didn't allow it in 1984, which enabled Gary Hart to win the primary but Walter Mondale to win, in party conventions, most of the delegates.

Wisconsin has had a robust Democratic vote in the last four elections, though robust enough to carry the state's 11 electoral votes only once. But if the trend in the 1986 results carries over to national politics, Wisconsin won't be a shoo-in even for a strong Democrat in 1988.

Congressional districting. Wisconsin's congressional district lines were drawn according to a bipartisan plan agreed to by Democrat David Obey and Republican James Sensenbrenner. Interestingly, Obey and Sensenbrenner, at different times, have helped their colleagues and given the hard tasks to themselves: Obey put himself in the same district with a 30-year Republican veteran in 1972, and Sensenbrenner added the Democratic city of Sheboygan to his district in 1982. Both survived handily.

The People: Est. Pop. 1986: 4,785,000; Pop. 1980: 4,705,767, up 1.7% 1980–86 and 6.5% 1970–80; 1.99% of U.S. total, 17th largest. 15% with 1–3 yrs. col., 15% with 4+ yrs. col.; 8.7% below poverty level. Single ancestry: 24% German, 4% Polish, 3% English, Norwegian, 2% Irish, 1% Italian, Swedish, Dutch, French. Households (1980): 73% family, 40% with children, 63% married couples; 31.8% housing units rented; median monthly rent: $186; median house value: $48,600. Voting age pop. (1980): 3,347,947; 3% Black, 1% Spanish origin, 1% American Indian. No state voter registration in Wisconsin.

1986 Share of Federal Tax Burden: $13,918,000,000; 1.85% of U.S. total, 19th largest.

1986 Share of Federal Expenditures

	Total		Non-Defense		Defense	
Total Expend	$12,186m	(1.47%)	$10,855m	(1.81%)	$1,331m	(0.58%)
St/Lcl Grants	2,310m	(2.05%)	2,307m	(2.05%)	3m	(2.70%)
Salary/Wages	941m	(0.78%)	699m	(1.19%)	242m	(0.39%)
Pmnts to Indiv	6,729m	(1.85%)	6,620m	(1.91%)	109m	(.61%)
Procurement	1,604m	(0.78%)	629m	(1.13%)	975m	(0.65%)
Research/Other	602m	(2.26%)	601m	(2.26%)	2m	(4.56%)

Political Lineup: Governor, Tommy G. Thompson (R); Lt. Gov., Scott McCallum (R); Secy. of State, Douglas La Follette (D); Atty. Gen., Donald Hanaway (R); Treasurer, Charles P. Smith (D). State Senate, 33 (20 D and 13 R). State House of Representatives, 99 (54 D and 45 R). Senators, William Proxmire (D) and Robert W. Kasten, Jr. (R). Representatives, 9 (5 D and 4 R).

1984 Presidential Vote

Reagan (R)	1,198,584	(54%)
Mondale (D)	995,740	(45%)

1980 Presidential Vote

Reagan (R)	1,088,845	(48%)
Carter (D)	981,584	(43%)
Anderson (I)	160,657	(7%)

1984 Democratic Presidential Primary

Hart	282,435	(44%)
Mondale	261,374	(41%)
Jackson	62,524	(10%)
Others	29,435	(5%)

1984 Republican Presidential Primary

Reagan	280,608	(95%)
Others	14,205	(5%)

GOVERNOR

Gov. Tommy G. Thompson (R)

Elected 1986, term expires Jan. 1991; b. Nov. 19, 1941, Elroy; home, Elroy; U. of WI, B.A. 1963, J.D. 1966; Roman Catholic; married (Sue Anne).

Career: Practicing Atty; WI Assembly, 1966–86, Asst. Min. Ldr., 1973–81, Flr. Ldr., 1981–86.

Office: State Capitol, 115 E. State Capitol, Madison 53702, 608-266-1212.

Election Results

1986 gen.	Tommy G. Thompson (R)	805,090	(53%)
	Anthony S. Earl (D)	705,578	(46%)
1986 prim.	Tommy G. Thompson (R)	156,875	(52%)
	Jonathan B. Barry (R)	67,114	(22%)
	George Watts (R)	58,424	(19%)
	Albert Wiley (R)	15,233	(5%)
1982 gen.	Anthony S. Earl (D)	896,812	(57%)
	Terry J. Kohler (R)	662,838	(42%)

SENATORS

Sen. William Proxmire (D)

Elected Aug. 1957, seat up 1988; b. Nov. 11, 1915, Lake Forest, IL; home, Madison; Yale U., B.A. 1938, Harvard U., M.B.A. 1940, M.P.A. 1948; United Church of Christ; married (Ellen).

Career: WI Assembly, 1951–53; Dem. Nominee for Gov. of WI, 1952, 1954, 1956; Pres., Artcraft Press, 1953–57.

Offices: 530 DSOB, 202-224-5653. Also Fed. Bldg., 517 E. Wisconsin Ave., Milwaukee 53202, 414-272-0388; and James Wilson Pl., 131 W. Wilson, Ste. 103, Madison 53703, 608-264-5472.

Committees: *Appropriations* (3d of 16 D). Subcommittees: Defense; HUD–Independent Agencies (Chairman); Labor, Health and Human Services, Education; Military Construction; Treasury, Postal Service, and General Government. *Banking, Housing, and Urban Affairs* (Chairman of 11 D). Subcommittees: International Finance and Monetary Policy; Securities. *Joint Economic Committee* (2d of 6 D Sen.). Subcommittees: Fiscal and Monetary Policy; International Economic Policy; National Security Economics (Chairman).

Group Ratings

	ADA	ACLU	COPE	CFA	LCV	ACU	NTU	NSI	COC	CEI
1986	60	64	66	80	100	26	83	10	37	56
1985	60	—	66	67	—	26	77	—	48	—

National Journal Ratings

	1986 LIB — 1986 CONS			1985 LIB — 1985 CONS	
Economic	47%	—	48%	46%	— 52%
Social	58%	—	40%	50%	— 46%
Foreign	75%	—	0%	88%	— 0%

Key Votes

1) Ease Gun Cont	FOR	5) Grm-Rdmn Def Red	FOR	9) Rehnquist Nom	FOR
2) Immig Reform	FOR	6) Contra Aid	AGN	10) Tax Reform	FOR
3) Lmt Text Imp	FOR	7) SDI Funding	AGN	11) Drug Death Pen	FOR
4) Aid Tobac Ind	AGN	8) Lmt PAC Contrib	FOR	12) S Africa Sanc	FOR

Election Results

1982 general	William Proxmire (D)................	983,311	(64%)	
	Scott McCallum (R)................	527,355	(34%)	($119,924)
1982 primary	William Proxmire (D)................	467,214	(86%)	
	Marcel Dandeneau (D)................	75,258	(14%)	
1976 general	William Proxmire (D)...............	1,396,970	(72%)	($697)
	Stanley York (R)....................	521,902	(27%)	($62,210)

Campaign Contributions and Expenditures

Received no campaign contributions and had no expenditures.

Sen. Robert W. Kasten, Jr. (R)

Elected 1980, seat up 1986; b. June 19, 1942, Milwaukee; home, Milwaukee; U. of AZ, B.A. 1964, Columbia U., M.B.A. 1966; Episcopalian; married (Eva).

Career: Air Force, 1967; Businessman; WI Senate, 1972–74; U.S. House of Reps., 1974–78.

Offices: 110 HSOB 20510, 202-224-5323. Also 517 E. Wisconsin Ave., Milwaukee 53202, 414-291-4160; 25 W. Main St., Ste. 775, Madison 53703, 608-264-5366; and Fed. Bldg., Rm. 107, Wausau 54401, 715-842-3307.

Committees: *Appropriations* (7th of 13 R). Subcommittees: Agriculture and Related Agencies; Commerce, Justice, State and Judiciary; Defense; Foreign Operations (Ranking Member); Transportation. *Budget* (7th of 11 R). *Commerce, Science, and Transportation* (6th of 9 R). Subcommittees: Aviation; Consumer; Surface Transportation (Ranking Member). *Small Business* (5th of 9 R). Subcommittee: Government Contracting and Paperwork Reduction (Ranking Member); Rural Economy and Family Farming.

Group Ratings

	ADA	ACLU	COPE	CFA	LCV	ACU	NTU	NSI	COC	CEI
1986	15	7	21	47	67	83	44	100	74	56
1985	10	—	20	40	—	74	47	—	72	—

National Journal Ratings

	1986 LIB — 1986 CONS		1985 LIB — 1985 CONS	
Economic	36% —	60%	41% —	56%
Social	27% —	70%	17% —	76%
Foreign	35% —	62%	31% —	66%

Key Votes

1) Ease Gun Cont	FOR	5) Grm-Rdmn Def Red	FOR	9) Rehnquist Nom	FOR
2) Immig Reform	FOR	6) Contra Aid	FOR	10) Tax Reform	AGN
3) Lmt Text Imp	FOR	7) SDI Funding	FOR	11) Drug Death Pen	—
4) Aid Tobac Ind	AGN	8) Lmt PAC Contrib	FOR	12) S Africa Sanc	FOR

Election Results

1986 general	Robert W. Kasten, Jr. (R)	1,754,537	(51%)	($3,433,870)
	Edward Garvey (D)	1,702,963	(47%)	($1,702,963)
1986 primary	Robert W. Kasten, Jr. (R)	1,248,333	(100%)	
1980 general	Robert W. Kasten, Jr. (R)	1,106,311	(50%)	($686,758)
	Gaylord A. Nelson (D)	1,065,487	(48%)	($897,774)

Campaign Contributions and Expenditures

1985-86		Direct Cont. 1985-86		PACS Breakdown 1985-86			
Receipts	$3,196,099	Indiv.	$1,855,680	Corp.	$555,436	T/M/H	$265,070
Expend.	$3,433,870	Party	$16,958	Labor	$7,000	Agr.	$11,300
Unspent	$125,579	PACS	$1,092,897	Ideo.	$245,479	CWOS	$8,612
		Cand.	$42,420				

FIRST DISTRICT

The southern tier of Wisconsin, just beyond Chicagoland, is the part of Wisconsin least distinctive and most like the rest of the United States. It is a mixture of diverse communities. Kenosha, long the home of American Motors's major assembly plant, has become desperate about its future as first workers refused wage cuts and then the company seemed poised to close the plant altogether. Racine, a slightly bigger industrial town just to the north, rests easier; its big employer is Johnson Wax, a family-owned company that is paternalistic and secure. From these lakefront industrial towns, the 1st District heads straight west, through the affluent resort area around Lake Geneva, over miles of rolling dairy farms, past the smaller factory towns of Janesville and Beloit, and west into more sparsely populated dairy country. Here and there you—in Kenosha or Lake Geneva—you can still find vestiges of the old political struggles between management and labor. But overall this is a marginal district, malleable in its enthusiasms, unmoored to either party: it went for Republican Governor Tommy Thompson in 1986 just as it did for his Democratic predecessor Tony Earl in 1982.

This is the district that elects Les Aspin, chairman of the House Armed Services Committee, one of the most powerful but also one of the most embattled members of the House. Aspin, first elected in 1970, was one of the first of the young generation of anti-Vietnam war Democrats elected to the House, and one of the first to rise to a position of power, when he upset aging Chairman Mel Price in the Democratic Caucus after the 1984 election. But he nearly became one of the first of his generation to fall from such a high position, when in early January 1987 the Caucus voted 130–124 against reconfirming him as chairman. Only when the Caucus voted again three weeks later did he win his chairmanship back, 133–116—on terms that have required from him some changes in operating style and on specific issues. Even so, Aspin remains powerful. On military issues he is pretty close to the fulcrum point in the House, and the positions he takes and the priorities he sets on many, if not most, issues can be decisive.

Aspin's difficulties with the Caucus stem partly from his background. He is much younger than members whose initiation into public events came in World War II, but considerably older and more experienced at a higher level than most of those who came to age in Vietnam. He finished college and studied at Oxford long before the days of student protest. He worked on Senator Proxmire's staff while Eisenhower was still President and for Council of Economic Advisers Chairman Walter Heller in the Kennedy years. When he served in the Vietnam era Army, it was as a high-level staffer for Robert McNamara in the Pentagon, and he was detailed in 1968 to go back home to Wisconsin to manage Lyndon Johnson's hopeless primary campaign against Eugene McCarthy in 1968. While so many other of today's Democratic congressmen were college or high school students demonstrating against the war and worrying whether they would be drafted, Aspin was already part of the power elite, a well-connected young leader confident of his knowledge and connections and his skill at getting things done. From these experiences Aspin brings an intellectual curiosity that sometimes verges on playfulness, an Oxford common room debater's habit of understanding and being able to take any side of an argument, a knowledge of the size and heft of the military establishment and an appreciation that most of it is going to keep on operating as it has been whatever Congress does.

Like so many Democratic policymakers then, Aspin had already turned against the Vietnam war when Johnson pulled out of the race two days before the Wisconsin primary. He returned to Wisconsin, moved to Racine which was represented by an obviously vulnerable Republican congressman, and without difficulty campaigned as an opponent of the war and an advocate of stronger policies against unemployment which was high then; he was sharp enough politically to beat a LaFollette in the primary and to win 61% against an incumbent in the general. In the House of the early 1970s Aspin was clearly an outsider, and even more so on the Armed Services Committee he joined then. Aspin specialized in legislating by press release, attacking high Pentagon spending and wasteful projects and getting plenty of ink in the process.

By the late 1970s this gadfly posture was obsolete, and Aspin was setting forth his own military strategy. He operated from an odd political position: he was far more critical of the military than almost all his fellow members of Armed Services, but far less adolescently negative about his country than many of his Democratic colleagues. By 1983, well before anyone thought he would become chairman any time soon, Aspin was the *de facto* leader of the House on military issues, supporting the nuclear freeze resolution and leading the debate when others stumbled, then becoming a leading supporter of the Scowcroft Commission recommendations for the MX missile. Both times Aspin took a pivotal role, even though he acknowledged intellectual weaknesses in both positions, and even though he had almost completely different sets of allies on each. These performances made him a natural choice for the chair, even though he was only 7th in seniority, in 1984. House Democrats understand that they are represented on national TV by their leading chairmen and may be held responsible by their constituents for how well the chairmen do. Not all of them trusted Aspin, but most figured he would make a better appearance than Price, who was clearly beyond his best years, and they preferred him by a 124–103 vote over the emotional Charles Bennett, even though Bennett led the opposition to the MX.

The standard explanation for Aspin's problems as chairman is that many liberals were angry when he, against what they considered his commitments, supported the MX missile, and that the last blow was his unexpected and unannounced support of aid for the Nicaraguan contras; Armed Services conservatives and elders who never warmed to him joined in, all around the candidacy of Marvin Leath, a Boll Weevil who had done yeoman work helping to craft a budget resolution all Democrats could accept. All correct, as far as it goes. But the liberals' expectations that Aspin would oppose the MX went against his previous prominent position on the weapon, and aid to the contras is not even an issue on Armed Services. Aspin was obviously having trouble straddling the divide between a hawkish committee and a dovish caucus. The trouble was exacerbated by differences in temperament. Aspin's liberal critics oppose the MX and contra aid with an almost religious intensity; when they talk about defense issues they preach rather than argue. To them Aspin seems an agnostic, altogether too fascinated with intricate arguments and lacking in the moral fervor they insist on. Some of the liberals may have mistaken Aspin's silence for their own fervent opposition. He was rescued in January when Don Edwards and Matthew McHugh pointed out how conservative Leath's record was, and after Aspin himself showed contrition. "There are a lot of things I need to do differently with people," he said. "It has to do with the way I deal with my colleagues on a one-to-one basis. I need to be more open, more up front."

What kind of chairman will Aspin be now? Presumably a more open one, and more responsive to Caucus opinion: he voted against contra aid in 1987. But there is still a big gulf between committee and caucus, and there is still a temperamental difference between Aspin and the liberal Democrats who thought he should be their natural ally and resent it when he isn't. Like rebellious teenagers who take for granted the roof over their head, many of Aspin's critics take American security for granted and treat the Pentagon as a major threat to peace; Aspin takes the more adult view, well supported by 20th century history, that the forces of good have no guarantee of surviving, and that sometimes aggressive decisions and serious risks must be taken to maintain peace and freedom. Aspin may well be able to find common ground with most Democrats on weapons systems for the next few years. But he may have a harder time papering over this basic difference in attitude.

Aspin's performance as chairman may not have impressed all his colleagues; it did impress his constituents. His performance at the polls sagged in the late 1970s and was no higher than 56% in 1984. But in 1986 he won 74% of the vote, the best showing of his career. There was once talk that he would run for the Senate, but that seems unlikely so long as he remains Armed Services chairman.

The People: Pop. 1980: 522,838, up 5.1% 1970–80. Households (1980): 75% family, 43% with children, 64% married couples; 30.2% housing units rented; median monthly rent: $188; median house value: $47,900. Voting age pop. (1980): 366,924; 3% Black, 2% Spanish origin.

1984 Presidential Vote:

Reagan (R) 143,113	(55%)
Mondale (D) 114,913	(45%)

Rep. Les Aspin (D)

Elected 1970; b. July 21, 1938, Milwaukee; home, East Troy; Yale U., B.A. 1960, Oxford U., M.A. 1962, M.I.T., Ph.D. 1965; Episcopalian; divorced.

Career: Staff Asst. to U.S. Sen. William Proxmire, 1960; Staff Asst. to Walter Heller, Pres. Cncl. of Econ. Advisers, 1963; Army, 1966–68; Asst. Prof. of Econ., Marquette U., 1969–70.

Offices: 2336 RHOB 20515, 202-225-3031. Also 210 Dodge St., Janesville 53545, 608-752-9074; and 1661 Douglas Ave., Racine 53404, 414-632-4446.

Committees: *Armed Services* (Chairman of 31 D). Subcommittee: Research and Development.

Group Ratings

	ADA	ACLU	COPE	CFA	LCV	ACU	NTU	NSI	COC	CEI
1986	50	77	84	75	69	24	28	60	42	17
1985	65	—	84	75	—	19	22	—	10	—

National Journal Ratings

	1986 LIB — 1986 CONS		1985 LIB — 1985 CONS	
Economic	55% —	44%	89% —	0%
Social	83% —	17%	68% —	31%
Foreign	53% —	46%	56% —	43%

Key Votes

1) Lmt Cln Water Act	AGN	5) Retain Gun Cont	FOR	9) Aid Angola Reb	AGN
2) Rpl Tobac Sub	AGN	6) Contra Aid	AGN	10) Tax Reform	FOR
3) Grm-Rdmn Def Red	AGN	7) Lmt Text Imp	FOR	11) S Africa Sanc	FOR
4) Ban Polygraph	—	8) Limit SDI	FOR	12) Immig Reform	FOR

Election Results

1986 general	Les Aspin (D)	106,288	(74%)	($497,588)
	Iris Peterson (R)	34,495	(24%)	($9,635)
1986 primary	Les Aspin (D)	23,852	(100%)	
1984 general	Les Aspin (D)	127,184	(56%)	($357,813)
	Peter N. Jansson (R)	99,080	(44%)	($368,454)

Campaign Contributions and Expenditures

1985-86		Direct Cont. 1985-86		PACS Breakdown 1985-86			
Receipts	$503,453	Indiv.	$271,292	Corp.	$99,832	T/M/H	$43,071
Expend.	$497,588	Party	$178	Labor	$48,945	Agr.	$3,000
Unspent	$80,127	PACS	$212,948	Ideo.	$17,000	CWOS	$1,100

SECOND DISTRICT

One of the centers of American liberalism, the heart of the progressive tradition in American politics and in American history-writing, is the small midwestern city of Madison, Wisconsin. On the pinched neck of land between two lakes, Madison is home of Wisconsin's state government and of one of the University of Wisconsin, one of the nation's major universities, which was a factor in Wisconsin politics long before the 18-year-old vote of the early 1970s. Its role goes back to 1900, when Madison native Robert LaFollette was elected governor. Once in office, he called on professors from the university to set up the Wisconsin Tax Commission and to draft a workmen's compensation law—both firsts in the nation. Wisconsin's progressive movement, including the *Progressive* magazine, which is published in Madison, has always relied heavily on the university community. The *Madison Capital-Times* continues to be one of the nation's most explicitly liberal newspapers, though it has a Republican rival.

LaFollette was originally a Republican, and he and his sons ran sometimes as Progressives. Their descendants, familial and ideological, have all been Democrats since the early 1950s. Madison produced the state's most successful Democrats, William Proxmire and Gaylord Nelson and Patrick Lucey, who ended his electoral career as John Anderson's running mate in the 1980 presidential election. In the early 1970s, the student vote made Madison and Dane County an especially liberal constituency, but their long tradition has always been progressive and in 1986, when most of Wisconsin was trending Republican, Dane County stood out as the state's leading Democratic bastion.

Madison is the center of Wisconsin's 2d Congressional District; Madison and surrounding Dane County cast two-thirds of the district's votes. The rest are in several rural dairy counties which are all more Republican and conservative; but they've never been enough to outvote Madison. The congressman from the 2d since 1958 has been Robert Kastenmeier, and for most of that time he has been one of the most liberal members of the House.

But not one of the most voluble or flamboyant; quite the contrary. Temperamentally, Kastenmeier is deliberate, quiet, careful, almost plodding. Legislatively, he has specialized in the arcane issue of copyright law, which like so many things is more important than it sounds: just a few words or even a comma in a statute can make millions of dollars of difference for moviemakers or novelists, composers or computer program writers. Kastenmeier carefully and meticulously superintended a major revision of the copyright law in the late 1970s; since then he has worked at accommodating the law to the videotape cassette recorder and the home computer.

Kastenmeier's one moment in the national spotlight came in the 1974 hearings on the impeachment of Richard Nixon. Kastenmeier, as fourth-ranking Democrat, was considered the most senior member absolutely sure to vote for impeachment. He made an important contribution to the proceedings by insisting that each article of impeachment be voted on separately, after evidence pertaining to it was discussed. Some of the Republicans and conservative Democrats favoring impeachment wanted to wait and hold all the roll calls at the end, as if somehow people wouldn't notice then. But Kastenmeier's role ensured an orderly procedure and kept the evidence and the voting closely tied together in people's minds.

Kastenmeier is just the third-ranking Democrat on Judiciary today: Harold Donohue retired in 1974, but Peter Rodino and Jack Brooks remain active. Kastenmeier shoulders the responsibility the position confers. In 1983 and 1984 he helped solve the problem caused by the elevation of bankruptcy referees to the status of federal judges. In 1986 he framed the impeachment resolution against Harry Claiborne, the imprisoned federal judge who refused to resign; Claiborne was impeached by the House and convicted by the Senate. Also in 1986 he got Congress to extend wiretap protections to cellular phone and electronic mail communications.

Kastenmeier's long tenure suggests that he has a safe district. Actually, his percentages in the 2d are sometimes small, well below 60% in 1980 and 1986. The district is very polarized between liberal Dane County and the Republican rural counties. But the balance has always been in Kastenmeier's favor: he may lose the rural counties, but he carries Dane County by a bigger margin. Democrats in their losing races for governor and Senator carried the 2d in 1986; Walter Mondale carried the 2d in 1984 and George McGovern did in 1972. So it seems likely that Kastenmeier will be able to continue his workmanlike and constructive career in the House.

The People: Pop. 1980: 523,011, up 9.8% 1970–80. Households (1980): 68% family, 37% with children, 59% married couples; 37.4% housing units rented; median monthly rent: $211; median house value: $53,900. Voting age pop. (1980): 383,086; 1% Black, 1% Asian origin, 1% Spanish origin.

1984 Presidential Vote:

Mondale (D)	128,947	(51%)
Reagan (R)	124,588	(49%)

Rep. Robert W. Kastenmeier (D)

Elected 1958; b. Jan. 24, 1924, Beaver Dam; home, Sun Prairie; U. of WI, LL.B. 1952; No religious affiliation; married (Dorothy).

Career: Practicing atty., 1952–58.

Offices: 2328 RHOB 20515, 202-225-2906. Also 119 Martin Luther King Blvd., Ste. 505, Madison 53703, 608-264-5206.

Committees: *Judiciary* (3d of 21 D). Subcommittees: Civil and Constitutional Rights; Courts, Civil Liberties, and the Administration of Justice (Chairman). *Permanent Select Committee on Intelligence* (4th of 11 D). Subcommittees: Legislation; Program and Budget Authorization.

Group Ratings

	ADA	ACLU	COPE	CFA	LCV	ACU	NTU	NSI	COC	CEI
1986	100	95	89	92	100	0	31	0	17	21
1985	100	—	90	75	—	5	39	—	24	—

National Journal Ratings

	1986 LIB — 1986 CONS			1985 LIB — 1985 CONS		
Economic	74%	—	23%	79%	—	19%
Social	86%	—	11%	85%	—	0%
Foreign	80%	—	0%	92%	—	0%

Key Votes

1) Lmt Cln Water Act	AGN	5) Retain Gun Cont	FOR	9) Aid Angola Reb	AGN
2) Rpl Tobac Sub	AGN	6) Contra Aid	AGN	10) Tax Reform	FOR
3) Grm-Rdmn Def Red	AGN	7) Lmt Text Imp	FOR	11) S Africa Sanc	FOR
4) Ban Polygraph	FOR	8) Limit SDI	FOR	12) Immig Reform	FOR

Election Results

1986 general	Robert W. Kastenmeier (D)	106,919	(56%)	($385,947)
	Ann Haney (R)	85,156	(44%)	($271,077)
1986 primary	Robert W. Kastenmeier (D)	26,237	(100%)	
1984 general	Robert W. Kastenmeier (D)	159,987	(64%)	($207,882)
	Albert Lee Wiley, Jr. (R)	91,345	(36%)	($96,156)

Campaign Contributions and Expenditures

1985-86		Direct Cont. 1985-86		PACS Breakdown 1985-86			
Receipts	$348,293	Indiv.	$233,958	Corp.	$10,700	T/M/H	$20,042
Expend.	$385,947	Party	$4,613	Labor	$50,523	Agr.	$11,500
Unspent	$32,234	PACS	$111,493	Ideo.	$17,128	CWOS	$1,600

THIRD DISTRICT

The rolling land of western Wisconsin, the knobby hills just east of the Mississippi River, is some of the most placid landscape you can imagine: plenty of green grass and quiet dairy cows. This is the premier dairying region in America, a place where the minerals in the soil produce such good milk and the short length of the growing season precludes other crops, that dairying—producing milk and butter and especially cheese from dairy cows—is the highest and best economic use of this land. It is hard to think of an industry as benign. Dairy products are healthful, they are carefully regulated to guard against spoilage; they are necessities for most babies and growing children. Its waste products are nontoxic and biodegradable; its business is conducted in pleasant surroundings, away from crowded cities; it does not withdraw land from other productive activities. Who can complain?

The taxpayers and the dairy farmers, and not necessarily in that order. For the dairy industry in America is in terrible trouble. First because there's less demand for milk: there are fewer children in this country today than in the 1950s; more adults worry about cholesterol; and it is likely that a lower proportion of Americans are descended from the northern European stock that carries the genes for the enzymes needed for adults to digest milk. Secondly, affluence has reduced the demand for powdered milk and other dairy solids, which used to be one of the country's major products of the dairy industry. The final problem is that the industry has become too productive. It takes fewer cows, which thanks to selective breeding can produce torrents of milk, and fewer farmers to create the same amount of total output as dairy farms did in the 1950s. In these circumstances, dairy farmers have done what any group of American entrepreneurs would do: they have come to the government for aid. Dairy farmers and processors have long been organized in cooperatives, and these co-ops became brilliant lobbyists and campaign contributors by the 1970s; they worked Democrats and Republicans alike to increase dairy subsidies and price supports. As a result, by the early 1980s the government had mountains of cheese and powdered milk it literally could not give away.

The politics of dairy subsidies is nowhere of greater concern than in the 3d Congressional District of Wisconsin, which hugs the eastern bank of the Mississippi River from the Illinois border to the outskirts of Minneapolis–St. Paul. This is probably the nation's number-one dairy district. This is a place north of the main paths of westward migration, and of intensive cultivation; it was settled largely by German and Scandinavian immigrants, and, because the growing season was short and the soil stony with debris left behind by receding glaciers, it was given over mostly to dairy farming. In partisan terms, the district is rather evenly divided: the more German counties in the south tend to be Republican, the more Scandinavian counties north of LaCrosse tend to be Democratic. But the biggest issue here since the dairy industry became dependent on federal help is dairy policy, and it is not one which splits local Democrats and Republicans on party lines.

This is illustrated by the career of Representative Steven Gunderson, a Republican first elected in 1980 at age 29. Gunderson upset Democratic incumbent Al Baldus, who had become chairman of the subcommittee handling the dairy program, and he ran as a supporter of the Reagan economic programs. Gunderson backed Reagan's budget and tax cut measures in 1981, but he also distanced himself very quickly from Administration proposals to cut dairy price supports. And he was able to get himself a place on the Agriculture Committee and on the Livestock, Dairy and Poultry Subcommittee, a body stocked with dairy program lovers. When he went into the Oval Office after voting against the Reagan tax bill in December 1985, he started talking dairy cows and got the President's assurance that he would sign the farm bill before the congressman agreed to support the tax bill.

Gunderson is patently ambitious, a hardworking campaigner who beat a tough incumbent one year and fended off another serious Democrat in the Democratic year of 1982. He ran ahead of Ronald Reagan in 1980 and won despite Reagan's attempts to dismantle the dairy programs in 1982. He probably has statewide ambitions—he said he ran for the House in 1980 because he was too young to serve in the Senate—but he has not pursued them yet. Gunderson won with 68% in 1984, when Ronald Reagan was winning a rather narrow margin over Minnesota neighbor (and longtime dairy program booster) Walter Mondale; he won with 64% in 1986. These performances indicate that Gunderson has mastered the dairy politics of the 3d; the only question is whether he will seek statewide office in some future election.

The People: Pop. 1980: 522,909, up 13.4% 1970–80. Households (1980): 73% family, 40% with children, 64% married couples; 27.3% housing units rented; median monthly rent: $162; median house value: $41,700. Voting age pop. (1980): 374,265.

1984 Presidential Vote:

Reagan (R)	135,466	(55%)
Mondale (D)	108,959	(45%)

Rep. Steve Gunderson (R)

Elected 1980; b. May 10, 1951, Eau Claire; home, Osseo; U. of WI, B.A. 1973, Brown Sch. of Broadcasting, 1974; Lutheran; single.

Career: WI Assembly, 1974–79.

Offices: 227 CHOB 20515, 202-225-5506. Also 438 N. Water St., Black River Falls 54615, 715-284-7431.

Committees: *Agriculture* (10th of 17 R). Subcommittees: Conservation, Credit, and Rural Development; Department Operations, Research, and Foreign Agriculture; Livestock, Dairy, and Poultry. *Education and Labor* (6th of 13 R). Subcommittees: Employment Opportunities (Ranking Member); Postsecondary Education.

Group Ratings

	ADA	ACLU	COPE	CFA	LCV	ACU	NTU	NSI	COC	CEI
1986	40	20	26	33	37	45	50	70	75	48
1985	35	—	20	33	—	43	57	—	72	—

National Journal Ratings

	1986 LIB — 1986 CONS	1985 LIB — 1985 CONS
Economic	35% — 65%	37% — 62%
Social	31% — 67%	24% — 72%
Foreign	46% — 53%	48% — 51%

Key Votes

1) Lmt Cln Water Act	FOR	5) Retain Gun Cont	AGN	9) Aid Angola Reb	FOR
2) Rpl Tobac Sub	AGN	6) Contra Aid	FOR	10) Tax Reform	FOR
3) Grm-Rdmn Def Red	FOR	7) Lmt Text Imp	FOR	11) S Africa Sanc	FOR
4) Ban Polygraph	AGN	8) Limit SDI	FOR	12) Immig Reform	FOR

Election Results

1986 general	Steve Gunderson (R)	104,393	(64%)	($311,707)
	Leland E. Mulder (D)	58,445	(36%)	($62,459)
1986 primary	Steve Gunderson (R)	30,456	(100%)	
1984 general	Steve Gunderson (R)	160,437	(68%)	($242,907)
	Charles F. Dahl (D)	74,253	(32%)	($99,344)

Campaign Contributions and Expenditures

1985-86		Direct Cont. 1985-86		PACS Breakdown 1985-86			
Receipts	$291,040	Indiv.	$136,234	Corp.	$33,747	T/M/H	$64,075
Expend.	$311,707	Party	$9,637	Labor	$200	Agr.	$6,150
Unspent	$6,176	PACS	$121,172	Ideo.	$16,200	CWOS	$800
		Cand.	$10,000				

FOURTH DISTRICT

Criss-crossed by railroads, bounded by the factory zone around the Menomonee River that goes through the center of town and the harbor facing Lake Michigan to the east, the south side of Milwaukee has always been the city's blue-collar side, full of neighborhoods with sturdy houses that have withstood 60 northern winters and streets lined with bars emblazoned with beer signs. Here you can find Milwaukee's prototypical Polish neighborhoods, but they are not the whole south side: more people here claim German ancestry than Polish, and for decades younger families have spread out from the old neighborhoods into the suburbs of Milwaukee County and Waukesha County to the west. The 4th Congressional District of Wisconsin, which has been the south side district since 1892, has also spread out, matching the geographic spread and socioeconomic rise of the children of the south side, to the point that 60% of the people here live outside Milwaukee now. This was long the only securely Democratic part of Wisconsin, and has retained its Democratic preference, though its margins for Democratic presidential candidates lately have been slim.

The congressman from the 4th District is a product of the south side, Gerald Kleczka. He seems to be one of those House members to whom politics comes naturally. He was elected to the Wisconsin Assembly in 1968, at age 24, was elected to the state Senate in 1974, and was co-chairman of the Joint Committee on Finance from 1979 to 1984. When Clement Zablocki, an old-style big city Democrat who served for 35 years and chaired the Foreign Affairs Committee, died suddenly in 1983, Kleczka was an obvious candidate to succeed him. He had serious competition from Clerk of Court Gary Barczak, a former Zablocki aide running as a conservative, from suburban state Senator Lynn Adelman who had run strong races against Bob Kasten in the 1974 general and Zablocki in the 1982 primary; and from Michael McCann, Milwaukee County District Attorney since 1968. Kleczka won the primary with 31% of the vote and has won easily ever since.

So far Kleczka has not been as important a legislator in Washington as he was in Madison. His committee assignments are not generally considered desirable, and he failed to get on the powerful Energy and Commerce Committee in 1987. He does appear, however, to have the luxury of time and the prospect of a long House career.

The People: Pop. 1980: 522,880, dn. 1.0% 1970–80. Households (1980): 73% family, 38% with children, 61% married couples; 38.5% housing units rented; median monthly rent: $210; median house value: $59,900. Voting age pop. (1980): 381,822; 3% Spanish origin.

1984 Presidential Vote:

Mondale (D) 118,528	(52%)
Reagan (R) 109,792	(48%)

Rep. Gerald D. Kleczka (D)

Elected 1984; b. Nov. 26, 1943, Milwaukee; home, Milwaukee; U. of WI; Roman Catholic; married (Bonnie).

Career: Accountant; WI Assembly, 1968–72; WI Senate, 1974–84, Asst. Major. Ldr., 1977–82.

Offices: 226 CHOB 20515, 202-225-4572. Also 5032 W. Forest Home Ave., Milwaukee 53219, 414-291-1140; and 817 Clinton St., Waukesha 53186, 414-549-6360.

Committees: *Banking, Finance and Urban Affairs* (21st of 31 D). Subcommittees: Financial Institutions Supervision, Regulation and Insurance; Housing and Community Development; International Finance, Trade, and Monetary Policy. *Government Operations* (18th of 24 D). Subcommittees: Government Activities and Transportation; Legislation and National Security.

Group Ratings

	ADA	ACLU	COPE	CFA	LCV	ACU	NTU	NSI	COC	CEI
1986	75	88	79	75	68	9	32	10	25	22
1985	75	—	76	83	—	—	14	—	23	—

National Journal Ratings

	1986 LIB — 1986 CONS		1985 LIB — 1985 CONS	
Economic	73% —	26%	67% —	32%
Social	74% —	23%	53% —	46%
Foreign	67% —	30%	80% —	17%

Key Votes

1) Lmt Cln Water Act	AGN	5) Retain Gun Cont	FOR	9) Aid Angola Reb	AGN
2) Rpl Tobac Sub	AGN	6) Contra Aid	AGN	10) Tax Reform	FOR
3) Grm-Rdmn Def Red	FOR	7) Lmt Text Imp	AGN	11) S Africa Sanc	FOR
4) Ban Polygraph	FOR	8) Limit SDI	FOR	12) Immig Reform	AGN

Election Results

1986 general	Gerald D. Kleczka (D) 120,354	(100%)	($93,749)
1986 primary	Gerald D. Kleczka (D) 31,051	(100%)	
1984 general	Gerald D. Kleczka (D) 158,722	(67%)	($394,697)
	Robert V. Nolan (R) 78,056	(33%)	($137,544)

Campaign Contributions and Expenditures

1985-86		Direct Cont. 1985-86		PACS Breakdown 1985-86			
Receipts	$162,267	Indiv.	$47,903	Corp.	$20,510	T/M/H	$33,500
Expend.	$93,749	Party	$362	Labor	$33,450	Agr.	$2,500
Unspent	$111,635	PACS	$102,160	Ideo.	$10,250	CWOS	$1,950

FIFTH DISTRICT

Today the German heritage in not often outwardly visible: you see it in the names of beers and in signs over stores; you can enjoy it in the remaining German restaurants; there is a hint of it in the solidity of the buildings and the order of its streets. But in its time the north side of Milwaukee, above the Menomonee River, was the German-American capital of the United States. German was spoken on the streets and read in newspapers, German beer was brewed in dozens of breweries big and small, German cultural traditions breathed in churches and union halls and parlors. The 5th Congressional District of Wisconsin is made up of the northern side of the city of Milwaukee and Milwaukee County. For most Americans in the late 20th century, mention of German traditions summons up memories of Hitler and junker generals; but there were other German traditions which thrived in Milwaukee and Wisconsin. Germans in the late 19th century pioneered university education, scientific disciplines, technologically advanced industries like chemicals and electric engineering; they also pioneered in social insurance and income taxation, the growth of a humane and vigorous welfare state.

These traditions helped to inspire the Wisconsin progressivism of Robert LaFollette; but they reached their most notable form in Milwaukee's Socialist tradition. Milwaukee elected Socialist mayors for more than 30 years, and they ran businesslike, honest city administrations. To the House the north side 5th District elected Victor Berger in 1910 and in every election from 1918 to 1926. Berger was denied his seat in after the 1918 and 1920 elections because of his opposition to World War I; in 1919 he was sentenced to 20 years in prison for writing antiwar articles. Berger, like the LaFollettes and many German-origin Wisconsin voters, did not want the United States to intervene on the side of Britain and France against Germany, and oppoisition to wars with Germany was a major feature of Wisconsin politics—the root of its isolationism—from 1916 until at least 1946. Feeling in the 5th District was strong enough that Berger was reelected to Congress while his case was on appeal and after he had been denied his seat.

Today some of the north side neighborhoods are black; 28% of 5th District residents were black in 1980, and they made up 81% of Wisconsin's black population. But most of the 5th District, which includes the pleasant, 1950s-ish subdivisions in the far northwest part of Milwaukee, the suburb of Wauwatosa, and a couple of affluent suburbs near the lake shore, are white and middle class. From the city's Socialist and the state's Progressive traditions it has drawn its current Democratic preference.

The 5th District's congressman, Jim Moody, does not have roots in old German Milwaukee. He came to the city as a professor in 1973, was elected to the legislature in 1976, and when Representative Henry Reuss, chairman of the Banking and Joint Economic Committees, retired after 28 years of service in 1982, Moody was one of 11 candidates who ran in the Democratic primary. A loner in Madison, without much support from local politicos, he campaigned hard door to door and, among the six candidates who finished close together, ran ahead with 19% of the vote.

An economics Ph.D., Moody has a liberal record on most issues, but is a little more conservative on economics issues; a man who has had to study microeconomics is probably more respectful of markets than lawyers or lifelong politicians. He has not played backscratching politics: he opposes many of the farm programs which help hold the Democratic party together; on the Public Works Committee he favored cost-sharing on water projects and got beaten 48–2 when he tried to cut out $1.2 in pork barrel highway projects; for Interior he shepherded an Idaho wilderness bill. He is an outspoken opponent of the MX missile system and aid to the contras and co-founded, with Republican John Porter, a congressional caucus on population and development (a former Peace Corps official, he believes that the U.S. should be involved in international family planning). Yet he lobbied the Steering and Policy Committee successfully and won 27 of 30 votes for a seat on Ways and Means in 1987. Will that success mean that Moody puts aside his hopes for a Senate seat and accept what seems to be a good lifetime job?

Maybe, but there is just enough resemblance to William Proxmire—the pinchpenny attitude, the unwillingness to accommodate colleagues—that suggests he might still go for the Senate, and win.

The People: Pop. 1980: 522,854, dn. 10.0% 1970–80. Households (1980): 64% family, 34% with children, 46% married couples; 52.1% housing units rented; median monthly rent: $190; median house value: $50,700. Voting age pop. (1980): 381,248; 22% Black, 2% Spanish origin, 1% Asian origin.

1984 Presidential Vote:

Mondale (D)	146,370	(60%)
Reagan (R)	95,590	(40%)

Rep. Jim Moody (D)

Elected 1982; b. Sept. 2, 1935, Richlands, VA; home, Milwaukee; Haverford Col., B.A. 1957, JFK Sch. of Govt., Harvard U., M.P.A. 1967, U. of CA at Berkeley, Ph.D. 1973; Protestant; single.

Career: Field Rep., CARE, Yugoslavia, 1958–59, Iran, 1960; Country Dir., Peace Corps, Pakistan, 1961; Economist, U.S. Dept. of Transportation, 1967, 1969; Prof., U. of WI, Milwaukee, 1973–82; WI Assembly, 1977–78; WI Senate, 1979–82.

Offices: 1721 LHOB 20515, 202-225-3571. Also 135 W. Wells St., Ste. 618, Milwaukee 53202, 414-291-1331.

Committees: *Ways and Means* (23d of 23 D). Subcommittees: Health; Social Security.

Group Ratings

	ADA	ACLU	COPE	CFA	LCV	ACU	NTU	NSI	COC	CEI
1986	90	94	90	75	80	5	33	0	18	26
1985	80	—	91	92	—	0	39	—	18	—

National Journal Ratings

	1986 LIB — 1986 CONS			1985 LIB — 1985 CONS		
Economic	52%	—	47%	75%	—	22%
Social	89%	—	0%	85%	—	0%
Foreign	80%	—	0%	85%	—	8%

Key Votes

1) Lmt Cln Water Act	AGN	5) Retain Gun Cont	FOR	9) Aid Angola Reb	AGN
2) Rpl Tobac Sub	FOR	6) Contra Aid	AGN	10) Tax Reform	FOR
3) Grm-Rdmn Def Red	AGN	7) Lmt Text Imp	FOR	11) S Africa Sanc	FOR
4) Ban Polygraph	FOR	8) Limit SDI	FOR	12) Immig Reform	FOR

Election Results

1986 general	Jim Moody (D)	109,506	(99%)	($302,442)
1986 primary	Jim Moody (D)	29,703	(100%)	
1984 general	Jim Moody (D)	175,243	(98%)	($141,077)
	William C. Breihan (SWP)	3,364	(2%)	

Campaign Contributions and Expenditures

1985-86		Direct Cont. 1985-86		PACS Breakdown 1985-86			
Receipts	$279,075	Indiv.	$92,952	Corp.	$39,600	T/M/H	$44,151
Expend.	$302,442	Party	$1,688	Labor	$74,387	Agr.	$4,950
Unspent	$4,551	PACS	$175,568	Ideo.	$10,480	CWOS	$2,000

SIXTH DISTRICT

"We went in to the little meeting Whigs, Free Soilers, and Democrats," wrote Alvan Bovay to the *New York Tribune's* Horace Greeley, "We came out Republicans, and we were the first Republicans in the Union." The little meeting took place in a small white schoolhouse in Ripon, Wisconsin, in March 1854, and it is still celebrated by many as the birthplace of the Republican party—though not in Jackson, Michigan, which claims the party was born there. No matter how valid Ripon's claim, the fact is that the party was born—it fielded candidates in the fall elections and nominated its first presidential ticket in 1856—and it has thrived ever since in the countryside around Ripon and places like it all around the United States.

Of course the countryside has changed. Self-sufficient family farms have been replaced by commercial (and heavily subsidized) dairy farms. Crossroads towns have become small factory or paper mill cities, like Manitowoc on Lake Michigan and Oshkosh on Lake Winnebago, recruiting their work force from far afield. The original Protestant settlers have been followed by German and Irish Catholics in large numbers, and others besides. But over the years the Republican party has adapted to the times—less readily in the 1930s than before or since—and the people here have kept voting Republican. The 6th Congressional District of Wisconsin, which cuts a swath across the state from Manitowoc through Oshkosh and Ripon west almost to the Mississippi River is now, as it has been mostly since March 1854, a solidly Republican constituency.

Thomas Petri, the 6th District congressman, first won the seat in an April 1979 special election to replace William Steiger, a talented legislator with the reputation as a Republican liberal whose chief monuments were the all-volunteer army and the 1978 Steiger amendment cutting capital gains tax rates. Petri serves on the Education and Labor and Public Works Committees, which have not always been popular bodies during his tenure; but he is not a backslapping kind of politician. He specializes in thoughtful original proposals which cut across the usual ideological and party lines. In his first term he got passed a law forgiving student loans to those who sign up for military service. He worked on the missing children center and the Job Training Partnership Act. He pushed through a cost-sharing provision requiring local governments to pay part of the cost of federal water projects. He wants to stop the extra AFDC payments that go to under-18 mothers who leave home. He wants to abolish tobacco subsidies. He is solidly conservative on cultural issues, more liberal on foreign policy—points of view in line with the Wisconsin electorate. In 1987 the Republican leadership gave him a seat on the ethics committee—a place most members shun.

Petri won the 1979 special only narrowly, but he has been reelected by wide margins since 1980 and seems solidly entrenched in this very Republican district.

The People: Pop. 1980: 522,477, up 7.5% 1970–80. Households (1980): 75% family, 40% with children, 67% married couples; 25.1% housing units rented; median monthly rent: $158; median house value: $41,100. Voting age pop. (1980): 370,486; 1% Spanish origin.

1984 Presidential Vote:

Reagan (R)	146,218	(62%)
Mondale (D)	88,041	(38%)

Rep. Thomas E. Petri (R)

Elected Apr. 3, 1979; b. May 28, 1940, Marinette; home, Fond du Lac; Harvard U., A.B. 1962, J.D. 1965; Lutheran; married (Anne).

Career: Law Clerk to Federal Judge James Doyle, 1965; Peace Corps, 1966–67; White House Aide, 1969; WI Senate, 1973–79; Practicing atty., 1970–79.

Offices: 2443 RHOB 20515, 202-225-2476. Also Box 1816, Fond du Lac 54935, 414-922-1180.

Committees: *Education and Labor* (4th of 13 R). Subcommittees: Elementary, Secondary and Vocational Education; Labor–Management Relations; Labor Standards (Ranking Member). *Public Works and Transportation* (9th of 20 R). Subcommittees: Aviation; Surface Transportation; Water Resources. *Standards of Official Conduct* (5th of 6 R).

Group Ratings

	ADA	ACLU	COPE	CFA	LCV	ACU	NTU	NSI	COC	CEI
1986	5	5	25	42	74	73	70	90	94	76
1985	30	—	28	75	—	62	65	—	59	—

National Journal Ratings

	1986 LIB — 1986 CONS		1985 LIB — 1985 CONS	
Economic	13%	85%	38%	61%
Social	0%	89%	36%	60%
Foreign	43%	56%	40%	60%

Key Votes

1) Lmt Cln Water Act	AGN	5) Retain Gun Cont	AGN	9) Aid Angola Reb	FOR
2) Rpl Tobac Sub	FOR	6) Contra Aid	FOR	10) Tax Reform	FOR
3) Grm-Rdmn Def Red	FOR	7) Lmt Text Imp	AGN	11) S Africa Sanc	FOR
4) Ban Polygraph	AGN	8) Limit SDI	FOR	12) Immig Reform	AGN

Election Results

1986 general	Thomas E. Petri (R)	124,328	(97%)	($106,394)
	John Richard Daggett (I)	4,268	(3%)	
1986 primary	Thomas E. Petri (R)	43,513	(100%)	
1984 general	Thomas E. Petri (R)	170,271	(76%)	($137,321)
	David L. Iaquinta (D)	54,266	(24%)	($11,920)

Campaign Contributions and Expenditures

1985-86		Direct Cont. 1985-86		PACS Breakdown 1985-86			
Receipts	$204,737	Indiv.	$85,407	Corp.	$34,655	T/M/H	$38,450
Expend.	$106,394	Party	$2,720	Labor	$4,700	Agr.	$11,500
Unspent	$217,162	PACS	$94,275	Ideo.	$3,550	CWOS	$1,420
		Cand.	$1,485				

SEVENTH DISTRICT

The northern reaches of Wisconsin are the northernmost thickly settled land in the United States east of the Mississippi. What brought people up so far was not farmland—there are no acres of industrial-sized wheat farms as in the Red River Valley of Minnesota and North Dakota—as trees. This was one of America's largest virgin timberlands, and the towns on the rivers are dotted with paper mills still. Then there was iron, in the far north near Lake Superior, that brought people to the port of Superior, Wisconsin, right next to Duluth, Minnesota, and to smaller towns on the chilly lake. And finally, there are dairy cows: properly cared for, they can thrive in these northern uplands, and it was natural for the sons of Wisconsin dairymen, many of them immigrants from Germany or Norway, to move their dairy herds farther north. On this base, small cities grew up, and even some big enterprises. The town of Wausau, for example, is the home of the Wausau insurance company, while the entrepreneur who designed the Cray supercomputers has chosen to live and work in Chippewa Falls. Unusual ethnic groups came here, like the Finns of Superior and the Poles of Stevens Point.

All these places are in Wisconsin's 7th Congressional District, which stretches from a point near Green Bay in the southeast up to Superior in the northwest. The politics of northern Wisconsin and the 7th District has always had a rough-hewn quality about it, a certain populist flavor; although this is an ancestrally Republican area, it is also part of the state that always favored the progressivism of the LaFollettes. Superior and Stevens Point are heavily Democratic, while much of the country in between leans Republican.

The congressman from the 7th District is David Obey, one of the most accomplished and effective of his generation of legislators in the House. He is one of those natural politicians who won a seat in the legislature the year he finished graduate school, in 1962 at age 24. He was elected to the House in something of an upset in a 1969 special election, in the seat vacated by Defense Secretary Melvin Laird. By 1972, when he was placed in the same district as a 30-year incumbent Republican with a liberal record, he won with 63% of the vote. Obey is reelected every two years by wide margins, and seems to be widely popular in this district.

Not all of Obey's work has made him popular in the House. He has a prickly personality and a vigorous temper and does not suffer those he considers fools or knaves gladly. Some of the causes he champions are almost guaranteed to be unpopular. In 1977 and 1978 he chaired a special committee on ethics and came up with a new code that was backed by reformers and passed by the House, requiring detailed disclosure of personal finances and limiting outside income to a percentage of the congressional salary. This hit luxury-loving and tuition-paying members where it hurt, and miffed a lot of his colleagues; but he got it through. Starting in 1979 he was the chief sponsor of bills to change the campaign finance laws to limit PAC contributions, and he actually got a bill through the House in the Carter years, only to see it killed in the Senate. For most of the 1980s members have been more interested in collecting PAC funds than in restricting them, but Obey persisted, and in 1987 was on Al Swift's task force looking at the issue once again.

Obey has also been a leader in promoting traditional Democratic economic policies in years when they have been under fierce and often effective attack. In 1979 he was elected head of the liberal Democratic Study Group, just as the tax revolt was beginning and the demand for new domestic spending programs disappearing. After the 1980 elections, he came within one vote of becoming Budget Committee chairman; he finally tied James Jones of Oklahoma twice and finally lost to him on the third ballot by a 121–116 margin. Jones tried to concoct budget resolutions that could pass the House with virtually unanimous Democratic support, a course his successor William Gray has followed. Obey's course, suggested by the budget proposal he presented in 1982, would have been to advance a Democratic plan that contrasted sharply with the Republicans' proposal, to risk losing in the House but having a platform to take before the voters.

In 1985, after Gillis Long died on inauguration day, Obey succeeded to the chair of the Joint Economic Committee. As chairmen of various stripes have done, he used it as a platform for disseminating his views on how the economy is working. Two of the studies he commissioned were cited and used again and again by Democratic leaders: one depicted the decline in family (as opposed to per capita) income since the early 1970s and the other describing what it called a "bicoastal economy," in which the East and West Coasts of America have grown smartly in the 1980s while the vast heartland in between has lagged behind or seen its economy contract. House Speaker Jim Wright has cited the family income study frequently and its finding that young people need a larger percentage of their income to buy a typical new house than they did

20 years ago; Democratic Campaign Chairman Tony Coelho actively publicized the coastal-heartland thesis, at least in heartland races. Some of Obey's studies have been attacked sharply by conservative economists, and one—a study purporting to show an increased concentration of wealth—was withdrawn by the Committee. Another argued that the economy is creating too many low-wage and not enough middle-income jobs, but this was criticized for using as end points two years which present a picture different from those of any other two endpoint years. The Obey JEC did not settle the raging argument over whether the economy of the Reagan years was producing enough growth evenly across the economic strata and geographic regions of the country; but it was a vigorous participant in the debate. What remains to be seen in the late 1980s and 1990s is whether the voters will demand a policy turnaround once again, one which would make the tax structure more progressive and government transfer and aid programs more generous.

Obey's major committee assignment is on the Appropriations Committee, where he is the sixth ranking Democrat, at least 18 years younger than any more senior member; he has every chance to be chairman some day, and for a long time. Since the 1984 election he has chaired the Foreign Operations Subcommittee, a body whose work is often frustrating. It handles the foreign aid bill, which is unpopular with most voters and which channels vast sums to Israel and Egypt. Obey has supported Administration requests for aid to these two countries, and for Pakistan as well (because of its position next to Afghanistan); but he has cut Administration requests for aid to other countries, on the grounds that the Administration's budgets don't provide enough revenue to support it. In addition, the foreign aid appropriation is always in danger of being larded up with mischievous or tricky amendments on everything from human rights to abortions and arms sales. That has put Obey and sometimes the ranking minority member, Jack Kemp, in the midst of some nasty fights, often but not always on opposite sides.

Republicans have sometimes talked of opposing Obey, but have not given him a really hard time in the 7th District since 1972. His 1986 opponent was Kevin Hermening, who as a Marine guard, was one of the hostages at the Tehran embassy; his mother appeared often on TV demanding that President Carter make every possible concession to get him out. A parent's anguish is easy to understand, but it's harder to see why conservatives (or anyone else) should support a candidate whose fame rests on the proposition that a President should concede major American interests in order to protect from any harm a young man who volunteered to serve in a branch of the military that, far from guaranteeing recruits' safety, emphasizes that they will be on the front lines when danger arises. In any case Obey won easily. Some have argued that after almost a decade in which he has been on the defensive fighting for many of the causes he has been on the defensive, he may have grown tired, but the opposite seems to be the case. As he finishes his third decade as a legislator, this busy and angry warrior seems to sense that events are going more his way and that the chances for success on some of the issues he has been working on for years have never been greater.

The People: Pop. 1980: 522,623, up 11.9% 1970–80. Households (1980): 75% family, 41% with children, 66% married couples; 24.0% housing units rented; median monthly rent: $158; median house value: $38,100. Voting age pop. (1980): 366,683; 1% American Indian.

1984 Presidential Vote:	Reagan (R)	126,988	(53%)
	Mondale (D)	114,633	(47%)

Rep. David R. Obey (D)

Elected Apr. 1, 1969; b. Oct. 3, 1938, Okmulgee, OK; home, Wausau; U. of WI, M.A. 1960; Roman Catholic; married (Joan).

Career: Real estate broker; WI Assembly, 1963–69.

Offices: 2217 RHOB 20515, 202-225-3365. Also Fed. Bldg., 317 First St., Wausau 54401, 715-842-5606.

Committees: *Appropriations* (6th of 35 D). Subcommittees: Foreign Operations (Chairman); Labor–Health and Human Services–Education; Legislative. *Joint Economic Committee.* Task Forces: Economic Growth, Trade and Taxes; Economic Resources and Competitiveness (Chairman); National Security Economics.

Group Ratings

	ADA	ACLU	COPE	CFA	LCV	ACU	NTU	NSI	COC	CEI
1986	85	94	86	100	84	10	31	0	12	18
1985	90	—	86	83	—	5	37	—	18	—

National Journal Ratings

	1986 LIB — 1986 CONS	1985 LIB — 1985 CONS
Economic	87% — 0%	81% — 17%
Social	85% — 14%	85% — 0%
Foreign	80% — 0%	92% — 0%

Key Votes

1) Lmt Cln Water Act	AGN	5) Retain Gun Cont	AGN	9) Aid Angola Reb	AGN
2) Rpl Tobac Sub	AGN	6) Contra Aid	AGN	10) Tax Reform	FOR
3) Grm-Rdmn Def Red	AGN	7) Lmt Text Imp	FOR	11) S Africa Sanc	FOR
4) Ban Polygraph	FOR	8) Limit SDI	FOR	12) Immig Reform	FOR

Election Results

1986 general	David R. Obey (D)	106,700	(62%)	($462,535)
	Kevin J. Hermening (R)	63,408	(37%)	($124,210)
1986 primary	David R. Obey (D)	36,682	(100%)	
1984 general	David R. Obey (D)	146,131	(61%)	($202,371)
	Mark G. Michaelsen (R)	92,507	(39%)	($44,273)

Campaign Contributions and Expenditures

1985-86		Direct Cont. 1985-86		PACS Breakdown 1985-86			
Receipts	$473,017	Indiv.	$185,281	Corp.	$24,390	T/M/H	$49,350
Expend.	$462,535	PACS	$254,360	Labor	$123,125	Agr.	$13,950
Unspent	$102,022			Ideo.	$41,495	CWOS	$2,050

EIGHTH DISTRICT

In 1673 the French explorer and priest Father Marquette sailed from the open waters of Lake Michigan into what is now Green Bay, Wisconsin. He hoped he had come upon the Northwest Passage through to the Pacific; actually, what he found was the Fox River, which leads to Lake Winnebago and, after a not-too-difficult portage, the Wisconsin River that flows into the Mississippi. Green Bay and the Fox River Valley remained mostly wilderness and Indian country for more than 150 years. But since they have been settled the Fox River Valley and

Green Bay have been, as surely Father Marquette would like, one of the most heavily Catholic parts of the United States. Economically Green Bay and the towns clustered around Appleton live off the paper mills and high-skill manufacturing; psychically, they live for the triumphs, present and past, of the Green Bay Packers, America's only municipally owned National Football League franchise.

Green Bay and the Fox River Valley make up most of the 8th Congressional District of Wisconsin. It includes also several north woods and dairy counties inland, plus the Door County peninsula that juts out into Lake Michigan and is a favorite summer vacation spot for Chicago and Milwaukee families. Politically, this has always been malleable country. Democrats, especially those with Catholic credentials, can win here: John Kennedy carried the Fox River Valley in the primary and general election in 1960, and the most recent Democratic congressman was Robert Cornell, a priest elected in 1974 and 1976. But the 8th District can go almost ferociously Republican: Appleton was the home of Senator Joseph McCarthy, who did so much to tar the good names of politics, Congress, conservatism, and the Republican party in the early 1950s.

The congressman from the 8th District is Toby Roth, a Republican whose first victory in 1978 was one of the less well-known harbingers of the conservative tide that swept the country in 1980. Roth has played a major role on one important piece of legislation; as ranking Republican on the Subcommittee on International Economic Policy and Trade, he helped frame export control legislation, and he has been the leading congressional advocate for the Pentagon position that severe restrictions are needed on the export of strategic products to the Soviet Union and Eastern Europe. He was successful in frustrating efforts to soften the law. Otherwise, he has worked to earn a reputation as an authority on international trade and a supporter of free trade, stressing Wisconsin's export products. Roth supports conservative and Administration positions on most issues but, in line with Wisconsin's longstanding skepticism about foreign military involvement, he criticized the stationing of U.S. troops in Lebanon in 1983 and the bombing of Libya in 1986. On the Banking Committee, which he joined in 1985, he favors deregulation in several respects of banks and other financial institutions and has opposed and criticized chairman Fernand St Germain's positions. Roth can be a tough partisan; he took on Democrats Michael Barnes and Edward Kennedy and got the House to agree to invite sailors on a Chilean ship to visit the Statue of Liberty for the 1986 Fourth of July celebration; let them see how democracy works, he said.

Roth is a member of Newt Gingrich's Conservative Opportunity Society, but is more conciliatory than many of his allies. He prided himself on waging a positive campaign in 1986, scripting his own positive TV spot, while Wisconsin's Senate candidates Bob Kasten and Ed Garvey were hurling charges at each other. Roth's closest call since his first election was in 1982, when former League of Women Voters president Ruth Clusen held him to 57% of the vote: he won 67% in 1986 and seems to have a safe seat.

The People: Pop. 1980: 523,225, up 12.3% 1970–80. Households (1980): 76% family, 42% with children, 67% married couples; 25.0% housing units rented; median monthly rent: $169; median house value: $43,800. Voting age pop. (1980): 362,554; 2% American Indian.

1984 Presidential Vote:	Reagan (R)	154,397	(63%)
	Mondale (D)	88,909	(37%)

Rep. Toby Roth (R)

Elected 1978; b. Oct. 10, 1938, Strasburg, ND; home, Appleton; Marquette U., B.A. 1961; Roman Catholic; married (Barbara).

Career: Realtor; WI House of Reps., 1973–79.

Offices: 2352 RHOB 20515, 202-225-5665. Also 333 Main St., Ste. 505, Green Bay 54301, 414-433-3931; and 126 N. Oneida St., Appleton 54911, 414-739-4167.

Committees: *Banking, Finance and Urban Affairs* (14th of 20 R). Subcommittees: Economic Stabilization; Financial Institutions Supervision, Regulation and Insurance; Housing and Community Development. *Foreign Affairs* (5th of 18 R). Subcommittees: Asian and Pacific Affairs; International Economic Policy and Trade (Ranking Member).

Group Ratings

	ADA	ACLU	COPE	CFA	LCV	ACU	NTU	NSI	COC	CEI
1986	0	0	14	17	42	82	57	90	81	63
1985	10	—	15	25	—	80	65	—	95	—

National Journal Ratings

	1986 LIB — 1986 CONS		1985 LIB — 1985 CONS	
Economic	16%	— 82%	15%	— 84%
Social	15%	— 84%	0%	— 76%
Foreign	27%	— 70%	24%	— 66%

Key Votes

1) Lmt Cln Water Act	FOR	5) Retain Gun Cont	AGN	9) Aid Angola Reb	FOR
2) Rpl Tobac Sub	AGN	6) Contra Aid	FOR	10) Tax Reform	FOR
3) Grm-Rdmn Def Red	FOR	7) Lmt Text Imp	AGN	11) S Africa Sanc	AGN
4) Ban Polygraph	AGN	8) Limit SDI	AGN	12) Immig Reform	FOR

Election Results

1986 general	Toby Roth (R)	118,162	(67%)	($284,287)
	Paul Willems (D)	57,265	(33%)	($84,037)
1986 primary	Toby Roth (R)	31,014	(100%)	
1984 general	Toby Roth (R)	161,005	(68%)	($220,251)
	Paul Willems (D)	73,090	(31%)	($48,007)

Campaign Contributions and Expenditures

1985-86		Direct Cont. 1985-86		PACS Breakdown 1985-86			
Receipts	$297,407	Indiv.	$131,600	Corp.	$60,272	T/M/H	$56,410
Expend.	$284,287	Party	$6,176	Labor	$1,500	Agr.	$14,750
Unspent	$91,347	PACS	$143,562	Ideo.	$8,478	CWOS	$2,152

NINTH DISTRICT

Out into land once dotted only with dairy cows, past small tiny towns and small cities with long-established high-skill factories, have moved over the past four decades several hundred thousand Milwaukeeans. The standard explanations for suburbanization—white flight, escape from apartments—don't apply much here: there never have been all that many blacks in Milwaukee and there has always been space around its single-family homes. The better explanation is that suburbanization is just the latest form of urbanization, that in a growing city young families will tend to move to the newest subdivisions, where most of the housing available at any one time is, and which tend to be built to their specifications. Moving out in disproportionate numbers will be the affluent. But the subdivisions and garden apartments of Mequon and Brookfield, of Germantown and Menomonee Falls and Pewaukee and Oconomowoc, are by no means entirely filled with the top stratum of society.

They are filled disproportionately, however, with Republicans, as any glance at the election results from the 9th Congressional District of Wisconsin will show. The 9th District is a kind of ring around Milwaukee, including most of its suburbs on the north, northwest, and west sides, and proceeding out past the latest developments a county or two further into small town and dairying country, and including factory towns like West Bend and Sheboygan. About two-thirds of the population is technically within the Milwaukee metropolitan area; but its actual boundary is hazy, and probably a larger percentage than one-third of the residents of this district think of themselves as residents of rural and small-town Wisconsin. This is Wisconsin's most Republican congressional district, the descendant of a seat first created in 1964.

The current congressman, James Sensenbrenner, has been one of the more aggressive Republicans in the House. He started off spending much time on the floor objecting to Democratic moves and measures for his party; he has worked hard on the Judiciary Committee, usually though not always objecting to the Democrats' and the civil rights lobby's versions. He is now the ranking minority member of the Judiciary subcommittee on Civil and Constitutional Rights. This is a hair-shirt assignment for a man of his beliefs; committee chairman Don Edwards holds a solid majority and is not going to let measures he opposes out of the committee if he can help it. Sensenbrenner is by no means always effective, and sometimes he has been in the embarrassing position of seeing his support be the kiss of death for the cause in which he believes. But he perseveres in taking on causes to which he feels committed—like opposing the Legal Services program—regardless of their unpopularity and persists in considering issues on the merits to the point of sometimes joining with his usual adversaries against his usual allies. Most of his dissents from conservatism have been on foreign policy; he has some of the dovishness characteristic of Wisconsin, and made a stir when he opposed the MX missile.

Sensenbrenner was first elected in 1978, when Robert Kasten left the seat to run for governor (he lost that race but was elected Senator in 1980). Sensenbrenner's only tough race was the 1978 primary, in which he barely beat moderate Susan Engeleiter; since then he has won easily, with 78% in 1986.

The People: Pop. 1980: 522,950, up 14.8% 1970–80. Households (1980): 81% family, 46% with children, 73% married couples; 23.2% housing units rented; median monthly rent: $206; median house value: $66,900. Voting age pop. (1980): 360,879; 1% Spanish origin.

1984 Presidential Vote:
Reagan (R)	162,433	(65%)
Mondale (D)	86,439	(35%)

Rep. F. James Sensenbrenner, Jr. (R)

Elected 1978; b. June 14, 1943, Chicago, IL; home, Menomonee Falls; Stanford U., A.B. 1965, U. of WI, J.D. 1968; Episcopalian; married (Cheryl).

Career: Practicing atty.; Staff of U.S. Rep. Arthur Younger, 1965; WI Assembly, 1969–75; WI Senate, 1975–78.

Offices: 2444 RHOB 20515, 202-225-5101. Also 120 Bishops Way, Brookfield 53005, 414-784-1111.

Committees: *Judiciary* (5th of 14 R). Subcommittees: Civil and Constitutional Rights (Ranking Member); Monopolies and Commercial Law. *Science, Space and Technology* (3d of 18 R). Subcommittees: Aviation; International Scientific Cooperation (Ranking Member); Investigations and Oversight. *Select Committee on Narcotics Abuse and Control* (9th of 10 R).

Group Ratings

	ADA	ACLU	COPE	CFA	LCV	ACU	NTU	NSI	COC	CEI
1986	0	20	10	8	48	77	78	80	89	75
1985	20	—	10	50	64	71	80	—	86	—

National Journal Ratings

	1986 LIB — 1986 CONS		1985 LIB — 1985 CONS	
Economic	6%	— 90%	0%	— 95%
Social	0%	— 89%	24%	— 72%
Foreign	34%	— 64%	42%	— 56%

Key Votes

1) Lmt Cln Water Act	FOR	5) Retain Gun Cont	AGN	9) Aid Angola Reb	FOR
2) Rpl Tobac Sub	FOR	6) Contra Aid	FOR	10) Tax Reform	AGN
3) Grm-Rdmn Def Red	FOR	7) Lmt Text Imp	AGN	11) S Africa Sanc	FOR
4) Ban Polygraph	AGN	8) Limit SDI	AGN	12) Immig Reform	AGN

Election Results

1986 general	F. James Sensenbrenner, Jr. (R)	138,766	(78%)	($178,698)
	Thomas G. Popp (D)...................	38,636	(22%)	($10,753)
1986 primary	F. James Sensenbrenner, Jr. (R)	37,099	(100%)	
1984 general	F. James Sensenbrenner, Jr. (R)	180,247	(73%)	($185,011)
	John H. Krause (D)	64,157	(26%)	($26,958)

Campaign Contributions and Expenditures

1985-86		Direct Cont. 1985-86		PACS Breakdown 1985-86			
Receipts	$175,697	Indiv.	$93,096	Corp.	$20,700	T/M/H	$30,300
Expend.	$178,698	Party	$2,522	Labor	$0	Agr.	$7,750
Unspent	$123,693	PACS	$62,750	Ideo.	$3,000	CWOS	$1,000

WYOMING

"Wyoming seems to be the doing of a mad architect—" writes Gretel Ehrlich, who moved here from California, "tumbled and twisted, ribboned with faded, deathbed colors, thrust up and pulled down as if the place had been startled out of a deep sleep and thrown into a pure light." Wyoming is vast, but most of it is not picturesque; it "has a 'lean-to' look. Instead of big, roomy barns and Victorian houses, there are dugouts, low sheds, log cabins, sheep camps, and fence lines that look like driftwood blown haphazardly into place. People here still feel pride because they live in such a harsh place, part of the glamorous cowboy past, and they are determined not to be the victims of a mining-dominated future." But the future of Wyoming is not about to be determined by the mining boom of 1973–83, for it has gone, as booms so often do, quite spectacularly bust. The trailers and tailings left behind seem to be making no greater imprint than the relics of earlier booms: in this improbable place, buildings are only small specks on the landscape, small towns and tiny settlements are just quick blips on the highway. Wyoming was one of leading energy states in the boom years sparked by high oil prices. But it remained then, and still is, the closest state we have to the Old West.

For civilization sits very lightly on this geographical wilderness. Ironically, it is only high technology that makes that civilization possible. After the passing of the open range, the Old West of cattle ranches was made possible only by the barbed wire that could fence in roaming herds of beef and the steam locomotives that could carry them to market back east. This 19th century high tech was brought to Wyoming by some large capitalist operators, like the onetime Texas cowhands and second sons of English landed gentry who started the first big operations and consolidated their power in the Johnson County land war of 1890. The boom of the 1970s and early 1980s, spurred by oil prices, brought the big operators in again: Amoco and other big oil companies planted drilling rigs in the Overthrust belt near Evanston, coal companies mined surface coal up north, and independent oilmen drilled wells all over the state.

The boom also brought in others, increasing Wyoming's population more in the 12 years after 1970 than in the 50 years before (it's declined since 1982). Many workers who flocked here live in grimy trailers, linked precariously to civilization's utilities and unprotected against the winds and snows that come out of the enormous sky. Wyoming simply does not have the infrastructure to protect itself against the pollution that even a small influx of people brings. There is another kind of pollution as well: the mining-camp atmosphere that developed around suddenly sprung-up camps near drilling rigs or mines. Wyoming is one of the few states that has always had more men than women—a sure sign that it never got far from a frontier atmosphere (and also the reason it was the first part of the United States, back in 1869, to give women the vote). In the 1970s around towns like Rock Springs there grew a subculture of prostitution, gambling, and violent crime, which would have been familiar to anyone acquainted with the history of Virginia City, Nevada, or Deadwood, South Dakota.

But there is a settled part of Wyoming as well, in the medium-sized towns that are regarded as the state's largest cities, and dotted across the state are economically hard-pressed livestock (sheep are more important and doing better than beef cattle) ranches and sugar beet farms. This is a small state, one community really, where people remember who played what position, when, for what high school football team; where people regard the hugely successful Wyoming basketball Cowboys, adopted out-of-staters all, as the home town team; and where, because all locals know who your father's cousins are, you mostly live pretty straight. Meanwhile, in partisan politics there has always been an economic and regional split in Wyoming. The big economic interests—cattle ranchers, organized in the Wyoming Stock Growers' Association, and the Union Pacific Railroad—always favored the Republicans, as do the diminishing band of

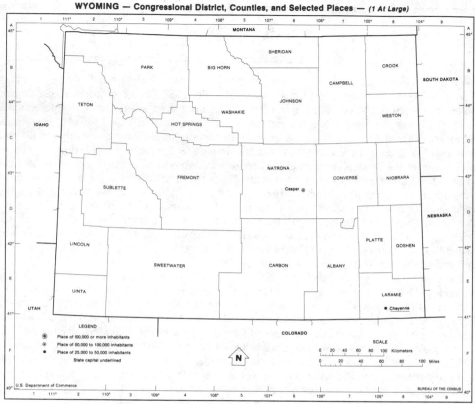

WYOMING — Congressional District, Counties, and Selected Places — *(1 At Large)*

wildcatters, independent producers, and oil company geologists, who want their industry liberated from government controls (except those which prop up prices); the ranching folks north and the oil people around Casper tend to vote Republican. The mainstay for the Democrats, on the other hand, were the Union Pacific railroad workers, who built the first transcontinental line across southern Wyoming in the 1860s and have maintained it ever since; that southern tier of counties, from Cheyenne through Laramie to Evanston, tends to vote Democratic. Historically, the Republicans have been more numerous, though the state was closely contested from the New Deal days through the 1960s.

In the 1980s this has been a very Republican state, regardless of local economic problems, except in governor's races, where it hasn't voted Republican since 1970. But personal campaigning plays the major role in Wyoming politics. Even today there are no cities with as many as 50,000 people here, and Wyoming voters expect to talk with—not just shake hands with, but actually exchange views with—their governor, Senators, and congressman every few years. There is a general agreement that Wyoming needs to build a more diverse economy, and that government should play some role in that. But state government is small and its powers limited; while the federal government, distant, domineering, insensitive to the feel of daily life here, is mistrusted. Wyomingites, with their high tech sophistication in their vast, empty lands, will have to rely mostly on themselves for a solution, as usual.

Senators. Wyoming's congressional delegation does not have great seniority, but man for man it is one of the most talented delegations any state can boast. Its senior member is Malcolm

Wallop, first elected in 1976 and reelected in 1982. On issues Wallop is inclined to go with the Republican right on most but not all matters; temperamentally, he is inclined to go along with the Republican leadership. He is a believer in the free market as an allocator of resources, and he opposes what he sees as intrusive federal regulations. He does, however, take pains to say that he is an environmentalist, or at least one who takes into account environmental considerations when setting public policy.

Wallop's committee assignments are very closely related to matters of great importance to Wyoming. He is a member of the Finance Committee, where he wants to end the windfall profits tax, now a dead letter because oil prices here dropped, but which would return if they go up. He is a member of the Energy and Natural Resources Committee and ranking Republican on the Subcommittee on Public Lands and Reserved Water. Before 1982, he chaired the Senate's Ethics Committee, an assignment which made him the leading advocate of the expulsion of convicted Abscam defendant Harrison Williams; that post was one he happily relinquished. He was disappointed after the 1984 elections when he lost the chairmanship of the National Republican Senatorial Committee to John Heinz of Pennsylvania, who had done so well in 1980 when the Republicans gained the Senate but less well in 1986 when they lost it. Would Wallop have made a difference? A happier time came in October 1984, when Wallop was host to Queen Elizabeth II at his ranch near Sheridan. This was not a state visit, but a private vacation to see horses; Wallop, who for political purposes always styles himself, accurately, as a rancher, is also the brother of Lady Jean Porchester, wife of Lord Henry Porchester, the Queen's racing manager.

Wallop has become a major force on defense and foreign policy. Now an influential proponent of early deployment, he was one of the first backers in the late 1970s of the Strategic Defense Initiative now championed by Ronald Reagan. He is also a vehement supporter of aid to the contras in Nicaragua. He is caustic in debate on such issues and dismissive of the views of opponents; he resembles nothing so much as those English conservatives who take a broad world view of policy, with a long historical perspective. Accordingly, he is convinced that an active, assertive, even aggressive policy against Communism is necessary to preserve the good values of western civilization: he feels he has a mission.

Wallop is perhaps less firmly established than Wyoming's other two members of Congress— but is nonetheless in a position of strength as his second term ends. In 1976 he surprised and upset 18-year Democratic Senator Gale McGee in 1976, featuring an ad showing a cowboy riding a horse out on the range with a portable potty to meet OSHA regulations; he met and quelled a spirited challenge from Democrat Rodger McDaniel in 1982. McDaniel, despite disadvantages—he was 34, managed Edward Kennedy's Wyoming campaign in 1980, favored a lot of national policies that most people in Wyoming oppose, and had far less money to spend than Wallop—held Wallop to 57% of the vote, well below the Reagan level, and kept the Senator from carrying the Union Pacific counties. By all measures, Wallop probably has a safe seat. But it is not expensive to compete in a small state like Wyoming, and personal campaigning can go far; so the Democrats might be looking here for an upset.

Wyoming's junior Senator is Alan Simpson, first elected in 1978, and now the Republican Whip—the second-ranking position in the party's leadership—in the Senate. Moreover, he had the job sewed up in 1984 after just one term in the Senate, in which he took on one of Washington's stickiest issues—and also took on a few Republican Senators. One of Simpson's assets is his sense of humor. This 6'7" giant—taller than Jay Rockefeller or Bill Bradley—has brilliant timing, droll delivery, and a repertoire of jokes that include some that will not find their way into a family almanac. But he is not just a joketeller; he is one of the better extemporaneous speakers in the Senate, one of its sharper debaters, and one of the more aggressive advocates of his positions. Get in his way, and see how funny he is.

He has also received respect for taking on some tough fights. One is immigration reform. This issue fell to him through his committee assignment, and he was not much interested in it. But he studied hard, mastered the facts, made up his mind on what he thought should be done, and tried to get as much of that as he could into legislation that could pass the Senate. Simpson immigration bills passed the Senate in three successive Congresses and, almost miraculously, a bill passed the House and cleared the conference committee in the last moments of the 99th Congress in October 1986. It contains employer sanctions on those who hire illegal immigrants; it provides amnesty for immigrants who arrived here illegally up through the early 1980s; it provides for beefed up border patrolling and has provisions to prevent discrimination against those who may lawfully be employed. The first statistics suggest that illegal border crossings are way down in 1987. But this is not just a measure to keep people out. It is also a measure to see that they get lawfully in, so they can become legitimate contributing members of American society. The quotas allowed in are actually rather high, not all that much lower than the wildly varying and always unreliable estimates of recent immigration. The point is that we ought to regularize immigration and make legitimate those who come here, and not allow the creation of a two-tiered America, one affluent, English-speaking, and legitimate, the other poor, often incompetent in English, and without legitimate status.

That is not the only touchy area Simpson has handled. He chaired the Subcommittee on Nuclear Regulation, a sensitive assignment; Simpson is a cautious but convinced advocate of nuclear power. He was chairman as well of the full Veterans' Affairs Committee, and there was a voice of caution against what he considers jumping to conclusions on issues like Agent Orange; he had to balance the emotional appeal of the case some veterans were making with the fact that no careful scientific study has shown any significant injury yet to have been caused by exposure to the chemical. Simpson has also taken up acid rain legislation, which if enacted would lead many more utilities to burn more low-sulfur Wyoming coal.

His approach on these, and on most issues, is that of an old-fashioned Republican conservative, skeptical of the ability of government to achieve a solution, cautious about spending public money, respectful of local authorities. But he seems decidedly out of sympathy with much of the cultural conservatism of the New Right. In 1982 he leveled a famous outburst at Jesse Helms, who was busy delaying the Senate and contriving roll calls that would embarrass colleagues in the direct mailings his Congressional Club would send out; their differences are rooted in temperament, and in the role they seek to play. Helms is instinctively a complainer, a lamenter that the world is going to the devil; Simpson is a doer, a man who has a definite role to play in this world and tries to get things done. Helms sees himself as part of a hopelessly beleaguered minority; Simpson, in Washington and in Wyoming, considers himself part of a secure majority and also part of the natural aristocracy that Thomas Jefferson saw would develop if meritocratic principles were given a decent chance.

Simpson is, in fact, a member of one of Wyoming's leading political families. His grandfather, a gritty 19th century oldtimer, was one of the state's most influential Democrats. His father, Milward Simpson, served as Republican governor and Senator; always a conservative, he lost one governor's race in Al Simpson's view because of his opposition to capital punishment. The son jumped from the state House of Representatives to the U.S. Senate in 1978 with wonderfully little competition when Senator Clifford Hansen retired. Simpson was reelected with 78% of the vote in 1984, running ran well ahead of President Reagan in this Reagan Republican state. In 1987, the home folks loved Simpson's "stick it in your gazoo" remark to the White House press corps.

Congressman-at-large. Wyoming's one and only congressman is Richard Cheney, who brings to the office an unusual credential and may carry out of it another: he was White House chief of staff under President Ford and he has as good a chance as any Republican of being Speaker of the House some day. In other words, he is used to and attracted to wielding power. Yet at the moment he operates as one of the leaders of the embattled Republican minority in the House.

Of course the White House that Donald Rumsfeld brought Cheney into in 1974, when Cheney was in his early 30s, was beleaguered, too; and the President ended up doing much better than anybody expected come election time. But Ford lost, though narrowly, and Cheney in the ordinary course of things could have been expected to live a comfortable life in

Washington, earning a good living as a lobbyist. Instead he went home to Wyoming and ran for the House of Representatives in 1978. His race was not easy: he had a serious Republican opponent and suffered a mild heart attack during the campaign. Nevertheless he won convincingly.

It looked as if Cheney were moving from a position near the center of power to one very far out on the periphery, as a junior member of the minority party in a House which in general seemed rather disorganized. But it has worked out somewhat differently. In 1981 and for much of 1982, the Republican leadership in effect controlled the House with a solid working majority. Cheney, elected after one term as chairman of the House Republican Policy Committee, was the fourth-ranking member of that leadership. Despite his background in the Ford White House, Cheney was a solid supporter of the Reagan economic program. He believed—which experience in the White House fortified—that government had gotten too large, and was growing larger absent strong countervailing forces; he shared also the President's feeling that American defenses were too weak and the nation's resolve too dubious.

In the second Reagan term, Cheney continued to win support both from traditional Republicans and from the younger aggressive conservatives. He was one of the Republicans who insisted in 1985 and 1986 on not accepting half-a-loaf Democratic compromises on aid to the Nicaraguan contras; he championed the risky course of insisting on an up-or-down vote, which the Republicans initially lost but finally won in 1986, though the victory was jeopardized after the election by the Iran-contra scandal. On tax reform as well he was one of the Republicans who delighted in nearly derailing Dan Rostenkowski's bill in December 1985, both because it cut the tax breaks for business that traditional Republicans have always backed and because it didn't cut personal tax cut rates enough to suit some younger conservatives. On that move as well Cheney was ultimately unsuccessful; the White House twisted arms, and the bill got through. But the Republicans showed they had to be courted, which probably meant that they got more of what they wanted in the final measure. On both issues Cheney showed the aggressiveness that is a hallmark of his leadership style. He is also an authentic scholar; he has finished all the requirements for a Ph.D. but his thesis, and he and his wife Lynne, who has finished her doctorate and is now head of the National Endowment for the Humanities, are co-authors of *Kings of the Hill,* a shrewd and original study of House speakers. But he is less prone to contemplate than to fight.

Cheney also has a sense of judgment tested under fire. Republican leader Robert Michel had no hesitation making Cheney, who has been on the Intelligence Committee, the party's ranking House member on the committee investigating the Iran-contra scandal, and he has cooperated there with Chairman Lee Hamilton. He has the respect of the national press, which sees most House Republicans as crazies but respects Cheney because of his White House experience and obvious competence. His prospects for advancing in the leadership are excellent. He is a generation younger than Michel; Whip Trent Lott may very well run for John Stennis's seat in the Senate in 1988; Jack Kemp has resigned as Conference Chairman because he is running for President. So Cheney has a good chance to become Republican Leader, and the Republicans, if they are treated better in redistricting and with the eventual attrition of the Democrats' large Watergate class, could conceivably end up with a majority in the House. Cheney could be the first Republican speaker since Joseph Martin lost the office in the election of 1954, when Cheney was 13 years old.

Reelected by very large margins, Cheney serves on the Interior Committee and its Water and Power Resources Subcommittee. He tends to Wyoming problems—Indian water claims on the Big Horn River, a wilderness area in the state, grazing fees on federal lands, and a state-federal tax dispute over mineral royalties. Washington observers presume that he must be hungering to run for the Senate, but why should he? Already a very important member of the House, he is clearly a major national politician. Anyway, there aren't likely to be openings in Wyoming Senate seats any time soon.

Governor. Wyoming is one of those Rocky Mountain states which votes Republican for

President and elects nothing, it seems, but Democratic governors. Ed Herschler, a Democrat first elected after the Republicans had a divisive primary in 1974, was an opponent of the coal slurry pipeline (Wyoming feared it would pump away too much of its scarce water) and raised the state's severance tax on minerals by 5%. In 1986 he retired, and most observers expected Pete Simpson, the Senator's brother and winner of a divisive Republican primary that featured charges of dynasty, to win. But Pete was less adept on the stump than Al, and Democrat Mike Sullivan won instead. Once in office, Sullivan, who appears able and certainly has a sunny disposition, called for more economic diversification. This will be tough for a state so isolated and cut off from major markets.

Presidential politics. Wyoming is one state where, in the 1970s, deregulation of oil and natural gas was a policy with genuine popular support. People here felt that federal price controls were hobbling their efforts to find new energy sources, just as they complained that federal regulations, backed by environmentalists living in Portland or San Francisco, prevented them from poisoning the coyotes that were clearly killing their sheep. It became then and remains now one of the most Republican states in the nation in presidential elections. Its national convention delegations are small and have not been seriously contested.

The People: Est. Pop. 1986: 507,000; Pop. 1980: 469,557, up 8.0% 1980–86 and 41.3% 1970–80; 0.21% of U.S. total, 51st largest. 20% with 1–3 yrs. col., 17% with 4+ yrs. col.; 7.9% below poverty level. Single ancestry: 13% German, 11% English, 5% Irish, 2% Swedish, 1% Norwegian, French, Scottish, Italian, Dutch, Polish. Households (1980): 73% family, 43% with children, 65% married couples; 30.8% housing units rented; median monthly rent: $220; median house value: $60,400. Voting age pop. (1980): 324,004; 4% Spanish origin, 1% American Indian, 1% Black. Registered voters (1986): 235,292; 77,136 D (33%), 135,497 R (57%), 22,659 unaffiliated and minor parties (10%).

1986 Share of Federal Tax Burden: $1,625,000,000; 0.22% of U.S. total, 50th largest.

1986 Share of Federal Expenditures

	Total		Non-Defense		Defense	
Total Expend	$1,472m	(0.20%)	$1,270m	(0.25%)	$201m	(0.10%)
St/Lcl Grants	556m	(0.57%)	555m	(0.57%)	1m	(2.08%)
Salary/Wages	240m	(0.22%)	145m	(0.28%)	95m	(0.17%)
Ind Payments	500m	(0.15%)	469m	(0.15%)	31m	(0.19%)
Procurement	139m	(0.08%)	65m	(0.17%)	74m	(0.05%)
Loan/Insurance	371m	(0.26%)	371m	(0.26%)		

Political Lineup: Governor, Mike Sullivan (D); Secy. of State, Kathy Karpan (D); Treasurer, Stan Smith (R); Auditor, Jack Sidi (R). State Senate, 30 (19 R and 11 D), State House of Representatives, 64 (44 R and 20 D). Senators, Malcolm Wallop (R) and Alan K. Simpson (R). Representatives, 1 R at large.

1984 Presidential Vote

Reagan (R) 133,241 (71%)
Mondale (D) 53,370 (28%)

1980 Presidential Vote

Reagan (R) 110,700 (63%)
Carter (D) 49,427 (28%)
Anderson (I) 12,072   (7%)

GOVERNOR

Gov. Michael (Mike) J. Sullivan (D)

Elected 1986, term expires Jan. 1991; b. Sept. 22, 1939, Omaha, NE; home, Casper; U. of WY, B.S., 1961, J.D., 1964; Roman Catholic; married (Jane).

Career: Practicing atty, 1964–86.

Office: State Capitol Bldg., Cheyenne 82002, 307-777-7434.

Election Results

1986 gen.	Michael J. Sullivan (D)	88,879	(54%)
	Pete Simpson (R)	75,841	(46%)
1986 prim.	Michael J. Sullivan (D)	29,266	(71%)
	Pat McGuire (D)	5,406	(13%)
	Keith Brian (D)	4,039	(10%)
	Al Hamburg (D)	2,554	(6%)
1982 gen.	Ed Herschler (D)	106,424	(63%)
	Warren A. Morton (R)	62,119	(37%)

SENATORS

Sen. Malcolm Wallop (R)

Elected 1976, seat up 1988; b. Feb. 27, 1933, New York, NY; home, Big Horn; Yale U., B.A. 1954; Episcopalian; married (French).

Career: Rancher; Army, 1955–57; WY House of Reps., 1969–72; WY Senate, 1973–76.

Offices: 206 RSOB 20510, 202-224-6441. Also 2201 Fed. Bldg., Casper 82601, 307-261-5098; 2009 Fed. Ctr., Cheyenne 82001, 307-634-0626; P.O. Box 1014, Lander 82520, 307-332-2293; 2515 Foothill Blvd., Rock Springs 82901, 307-382-5127; and 40 S. Main, Sheridan 82801, 307-672-6456.

Committees: *Energy and Natural Resources* (5th of 9 R). Subcommittees: Mineral Resources Development and Production; Public Lands, National Parks and Forests (Ranking Member); Water and Power. *Finance* (7th of 9 R). Subcommittees: Energy and Agricultural Taxation (Ranking Member); International Trade; Taxation and Debt Management. *Small Business* (7th of 9 R). Subcommittees: Competition and Antitrust Enforcement (Ranking Member); Export and Expansion.

Group Ratings

	ADA	ACLU	COPE	CFA	LCV	ACU	NTU	NSI	COC	CEI
1986	0	0	8	0	8	100	61	100	95	88
1985	0	—	9	0	—	95	71	—	97	—

National Journal Ratings

	1986 LIB — 1986 CONS		1985 LIB — 1985 CONS	
Economic	0% —	84%	0% —	86%
Social	11% —	87%	0% —	83%
Foreign	0% —	86%	0% —	88%

Key Votes

1) Ease Gun Cont	FOR	5) Grm-Rdmn Def Red	FOR	9) Rehnquist Nom	FOR
2) Immig Reform	FOR	6) Contra Aid	FOR	10) Tax Reform	AGN
3) Lmt Text Imp	AGN	7) SDI Funding	FOR	11) Drug Death Pen	—
4) Aid Tobac Ind	FOR	8) Lmt PAC Contrib	AGN	12) S Africa Sanc	AGN

Election Results

1982 general	Malcolm Wallop (R).................	94,690	(57%)	($1,139,082)
	Rodger McDaniel (D)................	72,453	(43%)	($389,511)
1982 primary	Malcolm Wallop (R) unopposed..........	46,834		
1976 general	Malcolm Wallop (R).................	84,810	(55%)	($301,595)
	Gale McGee (D).....................	70,558	(45%)	($181,028)

Campaign Contributions and Expenditures

1979-82		Direct Cont. 1979-82		PACS Breakdown			
Receipts	$1,151,531	Indiv.	$592,636	Corp.	$14,600	T/M/H	$31,700
Expend.	$1,139,082	Party	$29,125	Labor	$379,044	Agr.	$2,500
Unspent	$19,080	PACS	$472,290	Ideo.	$16,750	CWOS	$15,000
		Cand.	$7,000				

Sen. Alan K. Simpson (R)

Elected 1978, seat up 1990; b. Sept. 2, 1931, Denver, CO; home, Cody; U. of WY, B.S. 1954, J.D. 1958; Episcopalian; married (Ann).

Career: Practicing atty., 1959–78; WY Asst. Atty. Gen., 1959; Cody City Atty., 1959–69; WY House of Reps., 1964–77, Major. Floor Ldr. 1975–76, Speaker Pro-Tem, 1977.

Offices: 261 DSOB 20510, 202-224-3424. Also P.O. Box 430, Cody 82414, 307-527-7121; Fed. Ctr., Ste. 3201, Casper 82601, 307-261-5172; Fed. Ctr., Ste. 2007, Cheyenne 82001, 307-772-2477; 2201 S. Douglas Hwy., P.O. Box 3155, Gillette 82716, 307-682-7091; P.O. Box 335, 209 Grand Ave., Laramie 82070, 307-745-5303; and 2632 Foothills Blvd., Ste. 104, Rock Springs 82901, 307-382-5097.

Committees: *Minority Whip. Environment and Public Works* (3d of 7 R). Subcommittees: Environmental Protection; Hazardous Wastes and Toxic Substances; Nuclear Regulation (Ranking Member). *Judiciary* (3d of 6 R). Subcommittees: Immigration and Refugee Affairs (Ranking Member); Patents, Copyrights and Trademarks. *Veterans' Affairs* (2d of 5 R). *Select Committee on Aging* (2d of 9 R).

Group Ratings

	ADA	ACLU	COPE	CFA	LCV	ACU	NTU	NSI	COC	CEI
1986	10	28	6	7	25	86	49	100	76	73
1985	10	—	6	13	—	78	63	—	90	—

National Journal Ratings

	1986 LIB — 1986 CONS			1985 LIB — 1985 CONS		
Economic	0%	—	84%	0%	—	86%
Social	34%	—	65%	45%	—	52%
Foreign	30%	—	65%	12%	—	80%

Key Votes

1) Ease Gun Cont	FOR	5) Grm-Rdmn Def Red	FOR	9) Rehnquist Nom	FOR
2) Immig Reform	FOR	6) Contra Aid	FOR	10) Tax Reform	AGN
3) Lmt Text Imp	AGN	7) SDI Funding	FOR	11) Drug Death Pen	AGN
4) Aid Tobac Ind	FOR	8) Lmt PAC Contrib	FOR	12) S Africa Sanc	AGN

Election Results

1984 general	Alan K. Simpson (R)	146,373	(78%)	($862,039)
	Victor A. Ryan (D)....................	40,525	(22%)	
1984 primary	Alan K. Simpson (R)	66,178	(88%)	
	Stephen C. Tarver (R)	9,137	(12%)	
1978 general	Alan K. Simpson (R)	82,908	(62%)	($439,805)
	Raymond B. Whitaker (D)	50,456	(38%)	($142,749)

Campaign Contributions and Expenditures

1979-84		Direct Cont. 1979-84		PACS Breakdown 1979-84			
Receipts	$1,071,830	Indiv.	$494,646	Corp.	$269,014	T/M/H	$151,575
Expend.	$862,039	Party	$15,470	Labor	$5,500	Agr.	$2,800
Unspent	$205,615	PACS	$491,437	Ideo.	$44,047	CWOS	$6,500

REPRESENTATIVE

Rep. Richard Bruce (Dick) Cheney (R)

Elected 1978; b. Jan. 30, 1941, Lincoln, NE; home, Casper; U. of WY, B.A. 1965, M.A. 1966, U. of WI, 1968; United Methodist; married (Lynne).

Career: Spec. Asst. to the Dir. of OEO, 1969–70; White House Staff Asst., 1971; Asst. Dir., Cost of Living Cncl., 1971–73; Vice Pres., Bradley, Woods & Co, 1973–74; Deputy Asst. to Pres. Gerald Ford, 1974–75; White House Chief of Staff, 1975–76.

Offices: 104 CHOB, 202-225-2311. Also Fed. Bldg., Rm. 4003, Casper 82601, 307-261-5413; Fed. Bldg., Rm. 2015, Cheyenne 82001, 307-772-2451; and P.O. Box 1357, Green River 82935, 307-875-6969.

Committees: *Interior and Insular Affairs* (5th of 15 R). Subcommittees: National Parks and Public Lands; Water and Power Resources. *Permanent Select Committee on Intelligence* (2d of 6 R). Subcommittee: Program and Budget Authorization (Ranking Member).

Group Ratings

	ADA	ACLU	COPE	CFA	LCV	ACU	NTU	NSI	COC	CEI
1986	0	10	5	8	16	100	64	100	100	84
1985	0	—	5	25	—	100	68	—	95	—

National Journal Ratings

	1986 LIB — 1986 CONS			1985 LIB — 1985 CONS		
Economic	0%	—	94%	5%	—	92%
Social	17%	—	82%	0%	—	76%
Foreign	0%	—	86%	0%	—	76%

Key Votes

1) Lmt Cln Water Act	FOR	5) Retain Gun Cont	AGN	9) Aid Angola Reb	FOR
2) Rpl Tobac Sub	FOR	6) Contra Aid	FOR	10) Tax Reform	AGN
3) Grm-Rdmn Def Red	FOR	7) Lmt Text Imp	AGN	11) S Africa Sanc	AGN
4) Ban Polygraph	AGN	8) Lmt SDI	AGN	12) Immig Reform	FOR

Election Results

1986 general	Richard Bruce (Dick) Cheney (R)	111,007	(69%)	($161,591)
	Rick Gilmore (D)	48,780	(31%)	
1986 primary	Richard Bruce (Dick) Cheney (R)	75,229	(87%)	
	Bob Morris (R)	11,709	(13%)	
1984 general	Richard Bruce (Dick) Cheney (R)	138,234	(74%)	($223,818)
	Hugh B. McFadden, Jr. (D)	45,857	(24%)	($7,549)

Campaign Contributions and Expenditures

1985-86		Direct Cont. 1985-86		PACS Breakdown 1985-86			
Receipts	$249,552	Indiv.	$69,589	Corp.	$92,100	T/M/H	$57,450
Expend.	$161,591	Party	$2,137	Labor	$500	Agr.	$1,050
Unspent	$99,239	PACS	$164,468	Ideo.	$10,800	CWOS	$2,568

PUERTO RICO, VIRGIN ISLANDS, GUAM, AMERICAN SAMOA

Four American insular territories are represented in Congress by elected delegates who—like the District of Columbia representative—have floor privileges and votes on committees but may not vote on the floor. They are Puerto Rico, the Virgin Islands, Guam, and American Samoa, and they are a diverse lot.

Puerto Rico. The largest by far is Puerto Rico, a Caribbean island with more than three million people. (It has about the same population as Connecticut, South Carolina, or Oklahoma.) Puerto Rico was one of Spain's last colonial possessions; the United States gained it in the Spanish-American War of 1898. Until the 1940s it was desperately poor: heavily populated, devoted almost entirely to sugar cultivation. Then in the 1940s, 1950s, and early 1960s Puerto Rico was transformed by Governor Luis Muñoz Marin and his Popular Democratic Party. Muñoz initiated Operation Bootstrap, to lure businesses to Puerto Rico with promises of low-wage labor and government assistance; Puerto Rico is within the United States for trade purposes but is not subject to federal income taxes. Muñoz also developed the Commonwealth form of government (in Spanish, Estado Libre Asociado, free associated state). Under Commonwealth, Puerto Rico is part of the United States for purposes of international trade, foreign policy, and war, but has its own separate laws, taxes, and representative government. Puerto Rico has also developed its own political parties: Muñoz's Popular Democrats; the New Progressives, who favor statehood; and two Independence parties. Muñoz could have been reelected governor for life, but retired in 1964. His death in 1980 was an occasion for an islandwide outpouring of emotion.

The central question in Puerto Rican politics has always been status. Some mainlanders suppose that Puerto Ricans yearn for independence, but in fact in the two referenda on status over the years, independence has been the choice of fewer than 10% of the voters. (Nor is there any large number of independence-minded abstentions. Voter turnout is much higher in the poorest parts of Puerto Rico than on the richest neighborhoods on the mainland.) The argument is between Commonwealth and statehood. In crafting Commonwealth, Muñoz artfully preserved a way for Puerto Rico to retain its Hispanic culture and the advantages of its association with the United States (essentially the same as that enjoyed—or endured—by the District of Columbia). But in the 1970s, when Puerto Rico's economy was hurt badly by the oil crises, and basically stopped growing, people began grumbling about ELA. Puerto Rico has a politics of enthusiasm, in which voters recognize few ambiguities—their own party is right on every issue, the opposition is made up of scoundrels—and Commonwealth—a compromise between two less ambiguous forms of status—started to rankle. Many younger and better educated Puerto Ricans, particularly residents of the growing San Juan metropolitan area, were proud of their American citizenship and wanted their island to become the 51st state. In the 1976 election Carlos Romero Barcelo, of the New Progressive party, upset the Popular Democrats' Rafael Hernandez Colón; although Romero downplayed the status issue, he was clearly trying to move Puerto Ricans toward it. He abandoned the New Progressives' usual association with the Mainland Republicans and backed Jimmy Carter for President (Colón was for Scoop Jackson in 1976 and Ted Kennedy in 1980) and sought a referendum.

He was foiled, however, by the unravelling of a scandal in which police undercover agents shot two terrorists on a hill called Cerro Maravilla in 1978; Romero backed the police in their claim of self-defense, but evidence began accumulating against them. Romero nearly lost to Hernandez in 1980 and his party lost control of the legislature, and in 1984, after 10 policemen were convicted of perjury, Hernandez returned to La Fortaleza, the 16th century governor's mansion. His party ended up winning almost every major office, including the Commonwealth's non-voting delegate position in the House of Representatives. Their victory was, among other things, evidence that a high regard for civil liberties has become deeply rooted in Puerto Rico; few voters shared the terrorists' goals or doubted that their means were wrong, but many were prepared to vote against the authorities who wrongly killed them.

The Popular Democratic party's political problem has been how to adjust ELA to increase Puerto Ricans' enthusiasm for it, how to build Puerto Rican pride without jeopardizing the island's allegiance to the United States. Something more is needed than the cynical (though quite correct) argument that Puerto Ricans do better economically, and did so even in the 1970s and early 1980s, under Commonwealth than they would either as a state or as an independent nation. One reason is the manufacturing jobs brought here by Section 936 of the U.S. commonwealth act, exempting certain manufacturing facilities from U.S. tax but permitting their products entry into U.S. markets. Another reason is Puerto Rico's safety net: for some time more than half its residents have received food stamps, and changes proposed by the Reagan Administration, which have marginal impact on the mainland, can be revolutionary in Puerto Rico. As Hernandez took office both seemed endangered: the safety net seemed to be sapping Puerto Ricans' initiative, while the Administration Treasury II tax bill proposed getting rid of Section 936.

Hernandez responded brilliantly. He tied Section 936 to the Reagan Administration's flagging Caribbean Basin Initiative—which on its own at first seemed to threaten Puerto Rico with more competition—by proposing to use funds that U.S. banks are required by 936 to hold in Puerto Rico to finance "twin plants," with the more complex work done in Puerto Rico and simpler assembly work in Caribbean basin countries. While the tax bill was pending Hernandez got the first agreement with Grenada; Dominica, whose Prime Minister Eugenia Charles had called for the U.S. to intervene in Grenada, added its support. In the past Hernandez was identified with policies of the left, and he once went to the United Nations to testify before the anti-colonialism hearings that Fidel Castro uses to try to embarrass the United States (even though more Puerto Ricans want to be part of the U.S. than Cubans want Communism in Cuba). But in 1987 Hernandez skillfully lobbied both the Democrats on the House Ways and Means Committee and Republicans in the Administration, the Heritage Foundation, and points right. He had concocted a policy that appealed to both sides, and which strengthened Puerto Ricans' allegiance to the United States and to Commonwealth even while it strengthened their own pride as Puerto Ricans—for it emphasized the fact that they are the most economically sophisticated people in the Caribbean, the natural economic leaders of part of the hemisphere.

Working with Hernandez in this project was Puerto Rico's congressional delegate (his official title is resident commissioner), Jaime B. Fuster. Voting in Puerto Rico usually runs along party lines, and when Hernandez won the governorship 48%–45%, Fuster, was elected by a 49%–46% margin. In his early 40s, he has already had a distinguished career as a lawyer and educator, and is part of that class of Puerto Rican leaders familiar with politics and government both on the mainland and in Puerto Rico. He sits in Congress as a Democrat, and has a seat on the Interior and Insular Affairs, as representatives of the territories typically do; it handles most Puerto Rican matters. He also sits on the Foreign Affairs Committee.

Virgin Islands. The United States' other insular area in the Caribbean is the Virgin Islands, a very different sort of place. It is much smaller than Puerto Rico, with a population under 100,000. Puerto Rico is multiracial and not self-conscious about it; most of the Virgin Islanders are black, and there is a pretty clear divide between the races, much resented by the blacks. Puerto Rico has attracted all kinds of light industry; the Virgin Islands has lived off tourism and refineries, industries that have produced higher income levels for its few citizens but have not provided the basis for a mature economy. For years the governor of the Virgin Islands was appointed by the President; more recently contests have had some nasty racial overtones. The delegate from the Virgin Islands is Ron de Lugo, who votes with the Democrats. In 1980, he defeated Melvin Evans, who voted with the Republicans; in 1984 he won by better than 2 to 1. De Lugo is the senior member now from the territories. He serves on the Interior and Insular Affairs Committee, Post Office and Civil Service, and Public Works and Transportation.

Guam. It takes some 19 hours to fly from Washington, D.C., to Guam, the place where, as every viewer of political conventions knows, America's day begins. Guam lies just west of the International Date Line, and it is indeed the early hours of Tuesday there when the rest of us are just trying to get through Monday afternoon. Guam is geographically in the center of the Marianas, but judicially it is separate; Guam is an integral part of the United States, while the Marianas and the islands around them were for years United Nations territories administered by the United States. With a population just over 100,000, Guam is a more advanced society than the Marianas, but economically it is not yet self-supporting. More than two-thirds of the workers are employed by the Guamanian or federal government (there are big defense bases here). The people are of mixed ethnic stock (Spanish and Pacific Islander), their religion is almost always Catholic, and they speak English, Spanish, and a local language called Chamorro.

Guam has a vibrant two-party politics, in which of course personal ties play an important part. One of the more controversial figures is Ricardo Bordallo, a Democrat elected governor in 1974, defeated in 1978, elected again in 1982, indicted just before the election in 1986, beaten for another term, and convicted in February 1987 of bribery and extortion. The new governor is Republican Joseph Ada. Guam is also represented in the U.S. House by a Republican, former Marine Corps General Ben Blaz. In 1984 he upset veteran Democrat Antonio Borja Won Pat by 354 votes; Won Pat died in the spring of 1987. Blaz has a seat on the Armed Services Committee. He seems to have blended in well in the Republican Conference: he was named chairman of the small group of Republican freshmen. Like all the other insular members, he has a seat on the Interior Committee.

American Samoa. In the 1980s, for the first time, American Samoa had representation in Congress. This Southern Pacific Island, unlike Guam, has been little influenced by western settlers; it is almost as Polynesian as it was when the United States took possession in 1900. The delegate is Fofo I.F. Sunia, who served eight years in the American Samoa legislature and for ten years in public office before that. A Democrat, he was reelected in 1986 by 55%-45% margin over Republican Soli Aumoelogo Salanoa. He serves on the Interior and Public Works Committees. As might be expected, he concentrates on legislation affecting American Samoa. He has sponsored bills to get U.S. citizenship for aliens with one American parent and to integrate the American Samoan court system into the federal judiciary; he claims credit for getting Congress to allow fish products to be transported duty-free in the Pacific territories and to allow American Samoans to serve in the (much subsidized) U.S. Merchant Marine.

PUERTO RICO
Gov. Rafael Hernandez Colon (D)

Rep. Jaime B. Fuster (D)

VIRGIN ISLANDS
Rep. Ron de Lugo (D)

GUAM
Rep. Ben Blaz (R)

AMERICAN SAMOA
Rep. Fofo I.F. Sunia (D)

SENATE COMMITTEES

STANDING COMMITTEES

AGRICULTURE, NUTRITION AND FORESTRY

328A RSOB
202-224-2035

Majority (10 D): Leahy (VT), Chmn.; Melcher (MT), Pryor (AR), Boren (OK), Heflin (AL), Harkin (IA), Conrad (ND), Fowler (GA), Daschle (SD), Breaux (LA).
Minority (9 R): Lugar (IN), Dole (KS), Helms (NC), Cochran (MS), Boschwitz (MN), McConnell (KY), Bond (MO), Wilson (CA), Karnes (NE).

SUBCOMMITTEES

AGRICULTURAL CREDIT
Majority (4 D): Boren, Chmn.; Harkin, Daschle, Breaux.
Minority (4 R): Boschwitz, Cochran, McConnell, Karnes.

AGRICULTURAL PRODUCTION AND STABILIZATION OF PRICES
Majority (7 D): Conrad, Heflin, Boren, Fowler, Pryor, Daschle, one vacancy.
Minority (6 R): Helms, Dole, Cochran, McConnell, Bond, Wilson.

AGRICULTURAL RESEARCH, CONSERVATION, FORESTRY AND GENERAL LEGISLATION
Majority (3 D): Melcher, Chmn.; Heflin, Fowler.
Minority (3 R): Bond, Wilson, Karnes.

DOMESTIC AND FOREIGN MARKETING AND PRODUCT PROMOTION
Majority (6 D): Pryor, Chmn., Daschle, Melcher, Conrad, Harkin, Breaux.
Minority (6 R): Cochran, Helms, Bond, Wilson, Boschwitz, Karnes.

NUTRITION AND INVESTIGATIONS
Majority (5 D): Harkin, Chmn.; Melcher, Pryor, Conrad, Breaux.
Minority (3 R): Dole, Boschwitz, Helms.

RURAL DEVELOPMENT AND RURAL ELECTRIFICATION
Majority (2 D): Heflin, Chmn.; Fowler.
Minority (1 R): McConnell.

APPROPRIATIONS

118 DSOB, 202-224-3471

Majority (16 D): Stennis (MS), Chmn.; Byrd (WV), Proxmire (WI), Inouye (HI), Hollings (SC), Chiles (FL), Johnston (LA), Burdick (ND), Leahy (VT), Sasser (TN), DeConcini (AZ), Bumpers (AR), Lautenberg (NJ), Harkin (IA), Mikulski (MD), Reid (NV).
Minority (13 R): Hatfield (OR), Stevens (AK), Weicker (CT), McClure (ID), Garn (UT), Cochran (MS), Kasten (WI), D'Amato (NY), Rudman (NH), Specter (PA), Domenici (NM). Grassley (IA), Nickles (OK).

SUBCOMMITTEES

AGRICULTURE, RURAL DEVELOPMENT AND RELATED AGENCIES
Majority (6 D): Burdick, Chmn.; Stennis, Chiles, Sasser, Bumpers, Harkin.
Minority (5 R): Cochran, McClure, Kasten, Specter, Grassley.

COMMERCE, JUSTICE, AND STATE, THE JUDICIARY AND RELATED AGENCIES
Majority (6 D): Hollings, Chmn.; Inouye, Bumpers, Chiles, Lautenberg, Sasser.
Minority (5 R): Rudman, Stevens, Weicker, Hatfield, Kasten.

DEFENSE
Majority (10 D): Stennis, Chmn., Proxmire, Inouye, Hollings, Chiles, Johnston, Byrd, Leahy, Sasser, DeConcini.
Minority (8 R): Stevens, Weicker, Garn, McClure, Kasten, D'Amato, Rudman, Cochran.

DISTRICT OF COLUMBIA
Majority (3 D): Harkin, Chmn.; Lautenberg, Reid.
Minority (2 R): Nickles, Grassley.

ENERGY AND WATER DEVELOPMENT
Majority (7 D): Johnston, Chmn.; Stennis, Byrd, Hollings, Burdick, Sasser, DeConcini.
Minority (6 R): Hatfield, McClure, Garn, Cochran, Domenici, Specter.

FOREIGN OPERATIONS
Majority (7 D): Inouye, Chmn.; Johnston, Leahy, DeConcini, Lautenberg, Harkin, Mikulski.
Minority (6 R): Kasten, Hatfield, D'Amato, Rudman, Specter, Nickles.

HUD–INDEPENDENT AGENCIES
Majority (6 D): Proxmire, Chmn.; Stennis, Leahy, Johnston, Lautenberg, Mikulski.
Minority (5 R): Garn, D'Amato, Domenici, Grassley, Nickles.

INTERIOR AND RELATED AGENCIES
Majority (8 D): Byrd, Chmn.; Johnston, Leahy, DeConcini, Burdick, Bumpers, Hollings, Reid.
Minority (7 R): McClure, Stevens, Garn, Cochran, Rudman, Weicker, Nickles.

LABOR, HEALTH AND HUMAN SERVICES, EDUCATION AND RELATED AGENCIES
Majority (8 D): Chiles, Chmn.; Byrd, Proxmire, Hollings, Burdick, Inouye, Harkin, Bumpers.
Minority (7 R): Weicker, Hatfield, Stevens, Rudman, Specter, McClure, Domenici.

LEGISLATIVE BRANCH
Majority (3 D): Bumpers, Chmn.; Mikulski, Reid.
Minority (2 R): Grassley, Hatfield.

MILITARY CONSTRUCTION
Majority (4 D): Sasser, Chmn.; Inouye, Proxmire, Reid.
Minority (3 R): Specter, Garn, Stevens.

TRANSPORTATION AND RELATED AGENCIES
Majority (5 D): Lautenberg, Chmn.; Stennis, Byrd, Chiles, Harkin.
Minority (4 R): D'Amato, Cochran, Kasten, Weicker.

TREASURY, POSTAL SERVICE AND GENERAL GOVERNMENT
Majority (3 D): DeConcini, Chmn.; Proxmire, Mikulski.
Minority (2 R): Domenici, D'Amato.

ARMED SERVICES   222 RSOB, 202-224-3871

Majority (11 D): Nunn (GA), Chmn.; Stennis (MS), Exon (NE), Levin (MI), Kennedy (MA),
Bingaman (NM), Dixon (IL), Glenn (OH), Gore (TN), Wirth (CO), Shelby (AL).
Minority (9 R): Warner (VA), Thurmond (SC), Humphrey (NH), Cohen (ME), Quayle (IN),
Wilson (CA), Gramm (TX), Symms (ID), McCain (AZ).

SUBCOMMITTEES

CONVENTIONAL FORCES AND ALLIANCE DEFENSE

Majority (6 D): Levin, Chmn.; Dixon, Glenn, Gore, Wirth, Shelby.
Minority (5 R): Quayle, Thurmond, Cohen, Wilson, Gramm.

DEFENSE INDUSTRY AND TECHNOLOGY

Majority (4 D): Bingaman, Chmn.; Gore, Dixon, Wirth.
Minority (3 R): Gramm, Quayle, Symms.

MANPOWER AND PERSONNEL

Majority (4 D): Glenn, Chmn.; Exon, Kennedy, Shelby.
Minority (3 R): Wilson, Symms, McCain.

PROJECTION FORCES AND REGIONAL DEFENSE

Majority (5 D): Kennedy, Chmn.; Stennis, Exon, Gore, Shelby.
Minority (4 R): Cohen, Humphrey, Symms, McCain.

READINESS, SUSTAINABILITY AND SUPPORT

Majority (5 D): Dixon, Chmn.; Stennis, Levin, Bingaman, Wirth.
Minority (4 R): Humphrey, Thurmond, Gramm, McCain.

STRATEGIC AND THEATER NUCLEAR FORCES

Majority (6 D): Exon, Chmn.; Stennis, Levin, Kennedy, Bingaman, Glenn.
Minority (5 R): Thurmond, Humphrey, Cohen, Quayle, Wilson.

BANKING, HOUSING AND URBAN AFFAIRS   534 DSOB, 202-224-7391

Majority (11 D): Proxmire (WI), Chmn.; Cranston (CA), Riegle (MI), Sarbanes (MD), Dodd
(CT), Dixon (IL), Sasser (TN), Sanford (NC), Shelby (AL), Graham (FL), Wirth (CO).
Minority (9 R): Garn (UT), Heinz (PA), Armstrong (CO), D'Amato (NY), Hecht (NV),
Gramm (TX), Bond (MO), Chafee (RI), Karnes (NE).

SUBCOMMITTEES

CONSUMER AFFAIRS

Majority (4 D): Dodd, Chmn.; Graham, Wirth, Proxmire.
Minority (3 R): Gramm, Chafee, Karnes.

HOUSING AND URBAN AFFAIRS

Majority (6 D): Cranston, Chmn.; Riegle, Sarbanes, Dodd, Dixon, Sasser.
Minority (5 R): D'Amato, Garn, Hecht, Heinz, Chafee.

INTERNATIONAL FINANCE AND MONETARY POLICY

Majority (6 D): Sarbanes, Chmn.; Proxmire, Dixon, Sanford, Graham, Shelby.
Minority (5 R): Heinz, Garn, Armstrong, Gramm, Bond.

SECURITIES

Majority (6 D): Riegle, Chmn.; Cranston, Sasser, Sanford, Shelby, Wirth.
Minority (5 R): Armstrong, Bond, D'Amato, Hecht, Karnes.

BUDGET   621 DSOB, 202-224-0642

Majority (13 D): Chiles (FL), Chmn.; Hollings (SC), Johnston (LA), Sasser (TN), Riegle (MI), Exon (NE), Lautenberg (NJ), Simon (IL), Sanford (NC), Wirth (CO), Fowler (GA), Conrad (ND), Dodd (CT).
Minority (11 R): Domenici (NM), Armstrong (CO), Kassebaum (KS), Boschwitz (MN), Symms (ID), Grassley (IA), Kasten (WI), Quayle (IN), Danforth (MO), Nickles (OK), Rudman (NH).

NO SUBCOMMITTEES

COMMERCE, SCIENCE AND TRANSPORTATION   508 DSOB
                                              202-224-5115

Majority (11 D): Hollings (SC), Chmn.; Inouye (HI), Ford (KY), Riegle (MI), Exon (NE), Gore (TN), Rockefeller (WV), Bentsen (TX), Kerry (MA), Breaux (LA), Adams (WA).
Minority (9 R): Danforth (MO), Packwood (OR), Kassebaum (KS), Pressler (SD), Stevens (AK), Kasten (WI), Trible (VA), Wilson (CA), McCain (AZ).

SUBCOMMITTEES

AVIATION

Majority (5 D): Ford, Chmn.; Exon, Inouye, Kerry, Breaux.
Minority (4 R): Kassebaum, Stevens, Kasten, McCain.

COMMUNICATIONS

Majority (6 D): Inouye, Chmn.; Hollings, Ford, Gore, Exon, Kerry.
Minority (5 R): Packwood, Pressler, Stevens, Wilson, McCain.

CONSUMER

Majority (3 D): Gore, Chmn.; Ford, Breaux.
Minority (2 R): McCain, Kasten.

FOREIGN COMMERCE AND TOURISM

Majority (4 D): Rockefeller, Chmn.; Hollings, Riegle, Bentsen.
Minority (3 R): Trible, Packwood, Wilson.

MERCHANT MARINE

Majority (4 D): Breaux, Chmn.; Inouye, Bentsen, Adams.
Minority (2 R): Stevens, Trible.

NATIONAL OCEAN POLICY STUDY

Majority (8 D): Hollings, Chmn.; Kerry, Inouye, Ford, Gore, Bentsen, Breaux, Adams.
Minority (7 R): Danforth, Stevens, Packwood, Kasten, Trible, Wilson, Pressler.

SCIENCE, TECHNOLOGY AND SPACE

Majority (6 D): Riegle, Chmn.; Gore, Rockefeller, Bentsen, Kerry, Adams.
Minority (4 R): Pressler, Kassebaum, Trible, Wilson.

SURFACE TRANSPORTATION

Majority (5 D): Exon, Chmn.; Riegle, Rockefeller, Hollings, Adams.
Minority (4 R): Kasten, Packwood, Pressler, Kassebaum.

ENERGY AND NATURAL RESOURCES   364 DSOB, 202-224-4971

Majority (10 D): Johnston (LA), Chmn.; Bumpers (AR), Ford (KY), Metzenbaum (OH), Melcher (MT), Bradley (NJ), Bingaman (NM), Wirth (CO), Fowler (GA), Conrad (ND).
Minority (9 R): McClure (ID), Hatfield (OR), Weicker (CT), Domenici (NM), Wallop (WY), Murkowski (AK), Nickles (OK), Hecht (NV), Evans (WA).

SUBCOMMITTEES

ENERGY, REGULATION AND CONSERVATION

Majority (4 D): Metzenbaum, Chmn.; Bradley, Bingaman, Fowler.
Minority (3 R): Nickles, Weicker, Evans.

ENERGY RESEARCH AND DEVELOPMENT

Majority (5 D): Ford, Chmn.; Fowler, Bumpers, Metzenbaum, Melcher.
Minority (4 R): Domenici, Evans, Weicker, Hecht.

MINERAL RESOURCES DEVELOPMENT AND PRODUCTION

Majority (5 D): Melcher, Chmn.; Wirth, Ford, Bingaman, Conrad.
Minority (4 R): Hecht, Nickles, Wallop, Murkowski.

PUBLIC LANDS, NATIONAL PARKS AND FORESTS

Majority (7 D): Bumpers, Chmn.; Bingaman, Melcher, Bradley, Wirth, Fowler, Conrad.
Minority (6 R): Wallop, Weicker, Hatfield, Domenici, Murkowski, Hecht.

WATER AND POWER

Majority (6 D): Bradley, Chmn.; Conrad, Bumpers, Ford, Metzenbaum, Wirth.
Minority (5 R): Evans, Hatfield, Murkowski, Wallop, Nickles.

ENVIRONMENT AND PUBLIC WORKS   458 DSOB, 202-224-6176

Majority (9 D): Burdick (ND), Chmn.; Moynihan (NY), Mitchell (ME), Baucus (MT), Lautenberg (NJ), Breaux (LA), Mikulski (MD), Reid (NV), Graham (FL).
Minority (7 R): Stafford (VT), Chafee (RI), Simpson (WY), Symms (ID), Durenberger (MN), Warner (VA), Pressler (SD).

SUBCOMMITTEES

ENVIRONMENTAL PROTECTION

Majority (6 D): Mitchell, Chmn.; Moynihan, Baucus, Lautenberg, Breaux, Graham.
Minority (5 R): Chafee, Stafford, Simpson, Durenberger, Pressler.

HAZARDOUS WASTES AND TOXIC SUBSTANCES

Majority (5 D): Baucus, Chmn.; Lautenberg, Mikulski, Reid, Graham.
Minority (4 R): Durenberger, Chafee, Simpson, Symms.

NUCLEAR REGULATION

Majority (4 D): Breaux, Chmn.; Moynihan, Mitchell, Reid.
Minority (3 R): Simpson, Symms, Warner.

SUPERFUND AND ENVIRONMENTAL OVERSIGHT

Majority (3 D): Lautenberg, Chmn.; Baucus, Mikulski.
Minority (2 R): Warner, Pressler.

WATER RESOURCES, TRANSPORTATION AND INFRASTRUCTURE

Majority (7 D): Moynihan, Chmn.; Burdick, Mitchell, Breaux, Mikulski, Reid, Graham.
Minority (6 R): Symms, Stafford, Chafee, Durenberger, Warner, Pressler.

FINANCE
205 DSOB, 202-224-4515

Majority (11 D): Bentsen (TX), Chmn.; Matsunaga (HI), Moynihan (NY), Baucus (MT), Boren (OK), Bradley (NJ), Mitchell (ME), Pryor (AR), Riegle (MI), Rockefeller (WV), Daschle (SD).

Minority (9 R): Packwood (OR), Dole (KS), Roth (DE), Danforth (MO), Chafee (RI), Heinz (PA), Wallop (WY), Durenberger (MN), Armstrong (CO).

SUBCOMMITTEES

ENERGY AND AGRICULTURAL TAXATION

Majority (3 D): Boren, Chmn.; Matsunaga, Daschle.
Minority (2 R): Wallop, Armstrong.

HEALTH

Majority (7 D): Mitchell, Chmn.; Bentsen, Baucus, Bradley, Pryor, Riegle, Rockefeller.
Minority (5 R): Durenberger, Packwood, Dole, Chafee, Heinz.

INTERNATIONAL DEBT

Majority (3 D): Bradley, Chmn.; Riegle, Rockefeller.
Minority (3 R): Roth, Dole, Danforth.

INTERNATIONAL TRADE

Majority (10 D): Matsunaga, Chmn.; Bentsen, Moynihan, Baucus, Boren, Bradley, Mitchell, Riegle, Rockefeller, Daschle.
Minority (8 R): Danforth, Packwood, Roth, Chafee, Heinz, Wallop, Armstrong, Durenberger.

PRIVATE RETIREMENT PLANS AND OVERSIGHT
OF THE INTERNAL REVENUE SERVICE

Majority (2 D): Pryor, Chmn.; Bentsen.
Minority (1 R): Heinz.

SOCIAL SECURITY AND FAMILY POLICY

Majority (4 D): Moynihan, Chmn.; Boren, Mitchell, Daschle.
Minority (3 R): Dole, Durenberger, Armstrong.

TAXATION AND DEBT MANAGEMENT

Majority (4 D): Baucus, Chmn.; Matsunaga, Moynihan, Pryor.
Minority (4 R): Chafee, Roth, Danforth, Wallop.

FOREIGN RELATIONS
423 DSOB, 202-224-4651

Majority (11 D): Pell (RI), Chmn.; Biden (DE), Sarbanes (MD), Cranston (CA), Dodd (CT), Kerry (MA), Simon (IL), Sanford (NC), Adams (WA), Moynihan (NY), one vacancy.

Minority (9 R): Helms (NC), Lugar (IN), Kassebaum (KS), Boschwitz (MN), Pressler (SD), Murkowski (AK), Trible (VA), Evans (WA), McConnell (KY).

SUBCOMMITTEES

AFRICAN AFFAIRS

Majority (3 D): Simon, Chmn.; Sanford, Moynihan.
Minority (2 R): Kassebaum, Helms.

EAST ASIAN AND PACIFIC AFFAIRS

Majority (5 D): Cranston, Chmn.; Dodd, Kerry, Adams, one vacancy.
Minority (4 R): Murkowski, Evans, Lugar, McConnell.

EUROPEAN AFFAIRS

Majority (4 D): Biden, Chmn.; Sarbanes, Simon, one vacancy.
Minority (3 R): Pressler, Trible, Boschwitz.

INTERNATIONAL ECONOMIC POLICY, TRADE, OCEANS AND ENVIRONMENT

Majority (4 D): Kerry, Chmn.; Sarbanes, Dodd, Adams.
Minority (3 R): Evans, Murkowski, Lugar.

NEAR EASTERN AND SOUTH ASIAN AFFAIRS

Majority (4 D): Sarbanes, Chmn.; Cranston, Sanford, Moynihan.
Minority (3 R): Boschwitz, McConnell, Pressler.

TERRORISM, NARCOTICS AND INTERNATIONAL COMMUNICATIONS

Majority (2 D): Adams, Moynihan.
Minority (2 R): McConnell, Murkowski.

WESTERN HEMISPHERE AND PEACE CORPS AFFAIRS

Majority (5 D): Dodd, Chmn.; Cranston, Kerry, Sanford, Pell.
Minority (4 R): Lugar, Kassebaum, Trible, Evans.

GOVERNMENTAL AFFAIRS   340 DSOB, 202-224-4751

Majority (8 D): Glenn (OH), Chmn.; Chiles (FL), Nunn (GA), Levin (MI), Sasser (TN), Pryor (AK), Mitchell (ME), Bingaman (NM).
Minority (6 R): Roth (DE), Stevens (AK), Cohen (ME), Rudman (NH), Heinz (PA), Trible (VA).

SUBCOMMITTEES

FEDERAL SERVICES, POST OFFICE AND CIVIL SERVICE

Majority (3 D): Pryor, Chmn.; Sasser, Bingaman.
Minority (2 R): Stevens, Trible.

FEDERAL SPENDING, BUDGET AND ACCOUNTING

Majority (4 D): Chiles, Chmn.; Nunn, Levin, Bingaman.
Minority (3 R): Rudman, Stevens, Heinz.

GOVERNMENTAL EFFICIENCY, FEDERALISM AND THE DISTRICT OF COLUMBIA

Majority (3 D): Sasser, Chmn.; Levin, Mitchell.
Minority (2 R): Heinz, Cohen.

OVERSIGHT OF GOVERNMENT MANAGEMENT

Majority (5 D): Levin, Chmn.; Chiles, Pryor, Bingaman, Mitchell.
Minority (4 R): Cohen, Rudman, Heinz, Stevens.

PERMANENT SUBCOMMITTEE ON INVESTIGATIONS

Majority (7 D): Nunn, Chmn.; Glenn, Chiles, Levin, Sasser, Pryor, Mitchell.
Minority (5 R): Roth, Stevens, Cohen, Rudman, Trible.

JUDICIARY   244 DSOB, 202-224-5225

Majority (8 D): Biden (DE), Chmn.; Kennedy (MA), Byrd (WV), Metzenbaum (OH), DeConcini (AZ), Leahy (VT), Heflin (AL), Simon (IL).

Minority (6 R): Thurmond (SC), Hatch (UT), Simpson (WY), Grassley (IA), Specter (PA), Humphrey (NH).

SUBCOMMITTEES

ANTITRUST, MONOPOLIES AND BUSINESS RIGHTS

Majority (5 D): Metzenbaum, Chmn.; DeConcini, Heflin, Simon, Kennedy.
Minority (4 R): Thurmond, Specter, Humphrey, Hatch.

CONSTITUTION

Majority (4 D): Simon, Chmn.; Metzenbaum, DeConcini, Kennedy.
Minority (2 R): Specter, Hatch.

COURTS AND ADMINISTRATIVE PRACTICE

Majority (3 D): Heflin, Chmn.; Metzenbaum, DeConcini.
Minority (2 R): Grassley, Thurmond.

IMMIGRATION AND REFUGEE AFFAIRS

Majority (2 D): Kennedy, Chmn.; Simon.
Minority (1 R): Simpson.

PATENTS, COPYRIGHTS AND TRADEMARKS

Majority (4 D): DeConcini, Chmn.; Kennedy, Leahy, Heflin.
Minority (3 R): Hatch, Simpson, Grassley.

TECHNOLOGY AND THE LAW

Majority (2 D): Leahy, Chmn.; DeConcini.
Minority (1 R): Humphrey.

LABOR AND HUMAN RESOURCES   428 DSOB, 202-244-5375

Majority (9 D): Kennedy (MA), Chmn.; Pell (RI), Metzenbaum (OH), Matsunaga (HI), Dodd (CT), Simon (IL), Harkin (IA), Adams (WA), Mikulski (MD).
Minority (7 R): Hatch (UT), Stafford (VT), Quayle (IN), Thurmond (SC), Weicker (CT), Cochran (MS), Humphrey (NH).

SUBCOMMITTEES

AGING

Majority (4 D): Matsunaga, Chmn.; Pell, Metzenbaum, Dodd.
Minority (3 R): Cochran, Thurmond, Weicker.

CHILDREN, FAMILY, DRUGS AND ALCOHOLISM

Majority (4 D): Dodd, Chmn.; Pell, Harkin, Adams.
Minority (3 R): Thurmond, Cochran, Hatch.

EDUCATION, ARTS AND HUMANITIES

Majority (6 D): Pell, Chmn.; Metzenbaum, Matsunaga, Dodd, Simon, Mikulski.
Minority (5 R): Stafford, Hatch, Quayle, Thurmond, Weicker.

EMPLOYMENT AND PRODUCTIVITY

Majority (4 D): Simon, Chmn.; Harkin, Adams, Mikulski.
Minority (3 R): Humphrey, Hatch, Quayle.

HANDICAPPED

Majority (4 D): Harkin, Chmn.; Metzenbaum, Simon, Adams.
Minority (3 R): Weicker, Stafford, Cochran.

LABOR

Majority (4 D): Metzenbaum, Chmn.; Matsunaga, Harkin, Mikulski.
Minority (3 R): Quayle, Humphrey, Stafford.

RULES AND ADMINISTRATION   305 RSOB, 202-224-6352

Majority (9 D): Ford (KY), Chmn.; Pell (RI), Byrd (WV), Inouye (HI), DeConcini (AZ), Gore (TN), Moynihan (NY), Dodd (CT), Adams (WA).
Minority (7 R): Stevens (AK), Hatfield (OR), McClure (ID), Helms (NC), Warner (VA), Dole (KS), Garn (UT).

NO SUBCOMMITTEES

SMALL BUSINESS   428A RSOB, 202-224-5175

Majority (10 D): Bumpers (AR), Chmn.; Nunn (GA), Sasser (TN), Baucus (MT), Levin (MI), Dixon (IL), Boren (OK), Harkin (IA), Kerry (MA), Mikulski (MD).
Minority (9 R): Weicker (CT), Boschwitz (MN), Rudman (NH), D'Amato (NY), Kasten (WI), Pressler (SD), Wallop (WY), Bond (MO), Karnes (NE).

SUBCOMMITTEES

COMPETITION AND ANTITRUST ENFORCEMENT

Majority (2 D): Harkin, Chmn.; Bumpers.
Minority (1 R): Wallop.

EXPORT EXPANSION

Majority (4 D): Sasser, Chmn.; Bumpers, Nunn, Harkin.
Minority (3 R): Boschwitz, D'Amato, Wallop.

GOVERNMENT CONTRACTING AND PAPERWORK REDUCTION

Majority (3 D): Dixon, Chmn.; Sasser, Mikulski.
Minority (2 R): Kasten, Rudman.

INNOVATION, TECHNOLOGY AND PRODUCTIVITY

Majority (4 D): Levin, Chmn.; Baucus, Boren, Kerry.
Minority (4 R): Rudman, Weicker, Bond, Karnes.

RURAL ECONOMY AND FAMILY FARMING

Majority (5 D): Baucus, Chmn.; Nunn, Levin, Dixon, Boren.
Minority (4 R): D'Amato, Boschwitz, Kasten, Pressler.

URBAN AND MINORITY-OWNED BUSINESS DEVELOPMENT

Majority (2 D): Kerry, Chmn.; Mikulski.
Minority (1 R): Bond.

VETERANS' AFFAIRS   414 RSOB, 202-224-9126

Majority (6 D): Cranston (CA), Chmn.; Matsunaga (HI), DeConcini (AZ), Mitchell (ME), Rockefeller (WV), Graham (FL).
Minority (5 R): Murkowski (AK), Simpson (WY), Thurmond (SC), Stafford (VT), Specter (PA).

NO SUBCOMMITTEES

SELECT COMMITTEES

SELECT COMMITTEE ON ETHICS   220 HSOB, 202-224-2981

Majority (3 D): Heflin (AL), Chmn.; Pryor (AR), Sanford (NC).
Minority (3 R): Rudman (NH), Vice Chmn.; Helms (NC), Kassebaum (KS).

NO SUBCOMMITTEES

SELECT COMMITTEE ON INDIAN AFFAIRS   838 HSOB, 202-224-2251

Majority (5 D): Inouye (HI), Chmn.; Melcher (MT), DeConcini (AZ), Burdick (ND),
Daschle (SD).
Minority (3 R): Evans (WA), Vice Chmn.; Murkowski (AK), McCain (AZ).

NO SUBCOMMITTEES

SELECT COMMITTEE ON INTELLIGENCE   211 HSOB, 202-224-1700

Majority (8 D): Boren (OK), Chmn.; Bentsen (TX), Nunn (GA), Hollings (SC), Boren (OK),
Bradley (NJ), DeConcini (AZ), Cranston (CA), Metzenbaum (OH).
Minority (7 R): Cohen (ME), Vice Chmn.; Roth (DE), Hatch (UT), Murkowski (AK), Specter
(PA), Hecht (NV), Warner (VA).

NO SUBCOMMITTEES

SELECT COMMITTEE ON SECRET
MILITARY ASSISTANCE TO IRAN
AND THE NICARAGUAN OPPOSITION   901 HSOB, 202-224-9960

Majority (6 D): Inouye (HI), Chmn.; Mitchell (ME), Nunn (GA), Sarbanes (MD), Heflin (AL),
Boren (OK).
Minority (5 R): Rudman (NH), Vice Chmn.; McClure (ID), Hatch (UT), Cohen (ME),
Trible (VA).

NO SUBCOMMITTEES

SPECIAL COMMITTEE

SPECIAL COMMITTEE ON AGING   G41 DSOB, 202-224-5364

Majority (10 D): Melcher (MT), Chmn.; Glenn (OH), Chiles (FL), Pryor (AR), Bradley (NJ),
Burdick (ND), Johnston (LA), Breaux (LA), Shelby (AL), Reid (NV).
Minority (9 R): Heinz (PA), Cohen (ME), Pressler (SD), Grassley (IA), Wilson (CA), Domenici
(NM), Chafee (RI), Durenberger (MN), Simpson (WY).

NO SUBCOMMITTEES

JOINT COMMITTEES OF THE CONGRESS

JOINT ECONOMIC COMMITTEE   G01 DSOB, 202-224-5171

Senate (10): Sarbanes (MD), Chmn.; Proxmire (WI), Bentsen (TX), Kennedy (MA), Melcher (MT), Bingaman (NM), Roth (DE), Symms (ID), D'Amato (NY), Wilson (CA).
House (10): Hamilton (IN), Vice Chmn.; Hawkins (CA), Obey (WI), Scheuer (NY), Stark (CA), Solarz (NY), Wylie (OH), Snowe (ME), Fish (NY), McMillan (NC).

SUBCOMMITTEES

ECONOMIC GOALS AND INTERGOVERNMENTAL POLICY
Senate (4): Melcher, Bentsen, Roth, Wilson.
House (3): Hamilton, Chmn.; Hawkins, Snowe.

ECONOMIC GROWTH, TRADE AND TAXES
Senate (4): Bentsen, Chmn.; Melcher, D'Amato, Roth.
House (4): Hamilton, Obey, Stark, Fish.

ECONOMIC RESOURCES AND COMPETITIVENESS
Senate (3): Melcher, Bingaman, Symms.
House (4): Obey, Chmn.; Scheuer, Wylie, McMillan.

EDUCATION AND HEALTH
Senate (4): Bingaman, Bentsen, Wilson, D'Amato.
House (4): Scheuer, Chmn.; Hawkins, Stark, Snowe.

FISCAL AND MONETARY POLICY
Senate (3): Kennedy, Chmn.; Proxmire, Symms.
House (4): Stark, Solarz, Wylie, McMillan.

INTERNATIONAL ECONOMIC POLICY
Senate (4): Sarbanes, Chmn.; Proxmire, Kennedy, Roth.
House (4): Hamilton, Solarz, Snowe, Wylie.

INVESTMENT, JOBS AND PRICES
Senate (4): Kennedy, Sarbanes, D'Amato, Symms.
House (3): Hawkins, Chmn.; Solarz, Fish.

NATIONAL SECURITY ECONOMICS
Senate (4): Proxmire, Chmn.; Bingaman, Sarbanes, Wilson.
House (4): Obey, Scheuer, McMillan, Fish.

JOINT COMMITTEE ON THE LIBRARY   305 RSOB, 202-224-6352

Senate (5): Pell (RI), Chmn.; DeConcini (AZ), Moynihan (NY), Hatfield (OR), Stevens (AK).
House (5): Annunzio (IL), Vice Chmn.; Oakar (OH), Jones (TN), Gingrich (GA), Roberts (KS).

NO SUBCOMMITTEES

JOINT COMMITTEE ON PRINTING   818 HSOB, 202-224-5241

House (5): Annunzio (IL), Chmn.; Gaydos (PA), Panetta (CA), Badham (CA), Roberts (KS).
Senate (5): Ford (MD), Vice Chmn.; DeConcini (AZ), Gore (TN), Stevens (AK),
  Hatfield (OR).

NO SUBCOMMITTEES

JOINT COMMITTEE ON TAXATION   1015 LHOB, 202-225-3621

House (5): Rostenkowski (IL), Chmn.; Gibbons (FL), Pickle (TX), Duncan (TN), Archer (TX).
Senate (5): Bentsen (TX), Vice Chmn.; Matsunaga (HI), Moynihan (NY), Packwood (OR),
  Dole (KS).

NO SUBCOMMITTEES

HOUSE COMMITTEES

STANDING COMMITTEES

AGRICULTURE
1301 LHOB, 202-225-2171

Majority (26 D): de la Garza (TX), Chmn.; Jones (NC), Jones (TN), Brown (CA), Rose (NC), English (OK), Panetta (CA), Huckaby (LA), Glickman (KS), Coelho (CA), Stenholm (TX), Volkmer (MO), Hatcher (GA), Tallon (SC), Staggers (WV), Evans (IL), Thomas (GA), Olin (VA), Penny (MN), Stallings (ID), Nagle (IA), Jontz (IN), Johnson (SD), Harris (AL), Campbell (CO), Espy (MS).

Minority (17 R): Madigan (IL), Jeffords (VT), Coleman (MO), Marlenee (MT), Hopkins (KY), Stangeland (MN), Roberts (KS), Emerson (MO), Morrison (WA), Gunderson (WI), Lewis (FL), Smith (OR), Combest (TX), Schuette (MI), Grandy (IA), Herger (CA), Holloway (LA).

SUBCOMMITTEES

CONSERVATION, CREDIT AND RURAL DEVELOPMENT

Majority (9 D): Jones (TN), Chmn.; Tallon, Evans, Thomas, Stallings, English, Penny, Nagle, Jontz.

Minority (6 R): Coleman, Jeffords, Morrison, Gunderson, Combest, Grandy.

COTTON, RICE AND SUGAR

Majority (9 D): Huckaby, Chmn.; Espy, Jones (TN), Stallings, Harris, Coehlo, Stenholm, Tallon, English.

Minority (6 R): Stangeland, Emerson, Lewis, Combest, Herger, Holloway.

DEPARTMENT OPERATIONS, RESEARCH AND FOREIGN AGRICULTURE

Majority (8 D): Brown, Chmn.; Panetta, Glickman, Stenholm, Hatcher, Staggers, Espy, Rose.

Minority (5 R): Roberts, Coleman, Morrison, Gunderson, Grandy.

DOMESTIC MARKETING, CONSUMER RELATIONS AND NUTRITION

Majority (6 D): Panetta, Chmn.; Staggers, Huckaby, Glickman, Olin, Espy.

Minority (4 R): Emerson, Coleman, Schuette, Herger.

FORESTS, FAMILY FARMS AND ENERGY

Majority (9 D): Volkmer, Chmn.; Olin, Campbell, Panetta, Hatcher, Stallings, Johnson, Harris, Jontz.

Minority (6 R): Morrison, Marlenee, Smith, Schuette, Herger, Holloway.

LIVESTOCK, DAIRY AND POULTRY

Majority (10 D): Stenholm, Chmn.; Olin, Harris, Campbell, Rose, Coehlo, Volkmer, Johnson, Jones (TN), Nagle.

Minority (6 R): Jeffords, Hopkins, Stangeland, Gunderson, Lewis, Smith.

TOBACCO AND PEANUTS

Majority (7 D): Rose, Chmn.; Jones (NC), Hatcher, Tallon, Thomas, English, Stenholm.

Minority (4 R): Hopkins, Roberts, Combest, Holloway.

WHEAT, SOYBEANS AND FEED GRAINS

Majority (11 D): Glickman, Chmn.; Johnson, English, Huckaby, Evans, Penny, Nagle, Jontz, Volkmer, Espy, Jones (NC).
Minority (7 R): Marlenee, Stangeland, Roberts, Emerson, Smith (OR), Schuette, Grandy.

APPROPRIATIONS   H 218 Capitol, 202-225-2771

Majority (35 D): Whitten (MS), Chmn.; Boland (MA), Natcher (KY), Smith (IA), Yates (IL), Obey (WI), Roybal (CA), Stokes (OH), Bevill (AL), Chappell (FL), Alexander (AR), Murtha (PA), Traxler (MI), Early (MA), Wilson (TX), Boggs (LA), Dicks (WA), McHugh (NY), Lehman (FL), Sabo (MN), Dixon (CA), Fazio (CA), Hefner (NC), AuCoin (OR), Akaka (HI), Watkins (OK), Gray (PA), Dwyer (NJ), Boner (TN), Hoyer (MD), Carr (MI), Mrazek (NY), Durbin (IL), Coleman (TX), Mollohan (WV).
Minority (22 R): Conte (MA), McDade (PA), Myers (IN), Miller (OH), Coughlin (PA), Young (FL), Kemp (NY), Regula (OH), Smith (NE), Pursell (MI), Edwards (OK), Livingston (LA), Green (NY), Lewis (CA), Porter (IL), Rogers (KY), Skeen (NM), Wolf (VA), Lowery (CA), Weber (MN), DeLay (TX), Kolbe (AZ).

SUBCOMMITTEES

COMMERCE, JUSTICE, STATE AND JUDICIARY
Majority (6 D): Smith (IA), Chmn.; Alexander, Early, Dwyer, Carr, Mollohan.
Minority (3 R): Rogers, Regula, Kolbe.

DEFENSE
Majority (7 D): Chappel, Chmn.; Murtha, Dicks, Wilson, Hefner, AuCoin, Sabo.
Minority (4 R): Dade, Young, Miller, Livingston.

DISTRICT OF COLUMBIA
Majority (6 D): Dixon, Chmn.; Natcher, Stokes, Sabo, AuCoin, Hoyer.
Minority (3 R): Coughlin, Green, Regula.

ENERGY AND WATER DEVELOPMENT
Majority (6 D): Bevill, Chmn.; Boggs, Chappell, Fazio, Watkins, Boner.
Minority (3 R): Myers, Smith (NE), Pursell.

FOREIGN OPERATIONS
Majority (8 D): Obey, Chmn.; Yates, McHugh, Lehman, Wilson, Dixon, Gray, Mrazek.
Minority (4 R): Edwards, Kemp, Lewis, Porter.

HUD—INDEPENDENT AGENCIES
Majority (6 D): Boland, Chmn.; Traxler, Stokes, Boggs, Boner, Mollohan.
Minority (3 R): Green, Coughlin, Lewis.

INTERIOR
Majority (6 D): Yates, Chmn.; Murtha, Dicks, Boland, AuCoin, Bevill.
Minority (3 R): Regula, McDade, Loeffler.

LABOR—HEALTH AND HUMAN SERVICES—EDUCATION
Majority (8 D): Natcher, Chmn.; Smith (IA), Obey, Roybal, Stokes, Early, Dwyer, Hoyer.
Minority (5 R): Conte, Pursell, Porter, Young, Weber.

LEGISLATIVE

Majority (6 D): Fazio, Chmn.; Obey, Alexander, Murtha, Traxler, Boggs.
Minority (4 R): Lewis, Conte, Myers, Porter.

MILITARY CONSTRUCTION

Majority (8 D): Hefner, Chmn.; Alexander, Coleman, Bevill, Early, Wilson, Dicks, Fazio.
Minority (4 R): Lowery, Edwards, Kolbe, DeLay.

RURAL DEVELOPMENT, AGRICULTURE AND RELATED AGENCIES

Majority (8 D): Whitten, Chmn.; Traxler, McHugh, Natcher, Akaka, Watkins, Durbin, Smith (IA).
Minority (4 R): Smith (NE), Myers, Skeen, Weber.

TRANSPORTATION

Majority (6 D): Lehman, Chmn.; Gray, Carr, Durbin, Mrazek, Sabo.
Minority (4 R): Coughlin, Conte, Wolf, DeLay.

TREASURY—POSTAL SERVICE—GENERAL GOVERNMENT

Majority (6 D): Roybal, Chmn.; Akaka, Hoyer, Coleman, Boland, Yates.
Minority (3 R): Skeen, Lowery, Wolf.

ARMED SERVICES   2120 RHOB, 202-225-4151

Majority (31 D): Aspin (WI), Chmn.; Price (IL), Bennett (FL), Stratton (NY), Nichols (AL), Daniel (VA), Montgomery (MS), Dellums (CA), Schroeder (CO), Byron (MD), Mavroules (MA), Hutto (FL), Skelton (MO), Leath (TX), McCurdy (OK), Foglietta (PA), Dyson (MD), Hertel (MI), Lloyd (TN), Sisisky (VA), Ray (GA), Spratt (SC), McCloskey (IN), Ortiz (TX), Darden (GA), Robinson (AR), Bustamante (TX), Boxer (CA), Hochbrueckner (NY), Brennan (ME), Pickett (VA).
Minority (21 R): Dickinson (AL), Spence (SC), Badham (CA), Stump (AZ), Courter (NJ), Hopkins (KY), Davis (MI), Hunter (CA), Martin (NY), Kasich (OH), Martin (IL), Bateman (VA), Sweeney (TX), Blaz (GU), Ireland (FL), Hansen (UT), Rowland (CN), Weldon (PA), Kyl (AZ), Ravenel (SC), Davis (IL).

SUBCOMMITTEES

INVESTIGATIONS

Majority (10 D): Nichols, Chmn.; Mavroules, Sisisky, Spratt, McCloskey, Ortiz, Boxer, Stratton, Dellums, Byron.
Minority (6 R): Hopkins, Stump, Kasich, Kyl, Sweeney, Ireland.

MILITARY INSTALLATIONS AND FACILITIES

Majority (10 D): Dellums, Chmn.; Montgomery, Hutto, Skelton, Leath, McCurdy, Foglietta, Hertel, Ortiz, Robinson.
Minority (7 R): Martin (NY), Dickinson, Martin (IL), Blaz, Spence, Ravenel, Weldon.

MILITARY PERSONNEL AND COMPENSATION

Majority (9 D): Byron, Chmn.; Montgomery, Schroeder, Skelton, Dyson, Ray, Bustamante, Pickett, Nichols.
Minority (5 R): Bateman, Kyl, Ravenel, Davis (IL), Weldon.

PROCUREMENT AND MILITARY NUCLEAR SYSTEMS

Majority (11 D): Stratton, Chmn.; Mavroules, Skelton, Leath, Dyson, Lloyd, Ray, Spratt, Bustamante, Bennett.

Minority (8 R): Badham, Courter, Davis (MI), Hopkins, Blaz, Ireland, Hansen, Rowland.

READINESS

Majority (8 D): Daniel, Chmn.; Hutto, Leath, Ray, Darden, Robinson, Hochbrueckner, Nichols.
Minority (5 R): Kasich, Martin (NY), Davis (IL), Hansen, Rowland.

RESEARCH AND DEVELOPMENT

Majority (11 D): Price, Chmn.; Aspin, Schroeder, McCurdy, Hertel, McCloskey, Darden, Boxer, Hochbreuckner, Brennan, Pickett.
Minority (7 R): Dickinson, Courter, Davis (MI), Stump, Hunter, Martin (IL), Sweeney.

SEAPOWER AND STRATEGIC AND CRITICAL MATERIALS

Majority (9 D): Bennett, Chmn.; Hutto, Foglietta, Dyson, Sisisky, Ortiz, Hochbrueckner, Brennan, Pickett.
Minority (5 R): Spence, Hunter, Bateman, Badham, Weldon.

BANKING, FINANCE AND URBAN AFFAIRS   2129 RHOB, 202-225-4247

Majority (30 D): St Germain (RI), Chmn.; Gonzalez (TX), Annunzio (IL), Fauntroy (DC), Neal (NC), Hubbard (KY), LaFalce (NY), Oakar (OH), Vento (MN), Barnard (GA), Garcia (NY), Schumer (NY), Frank (MA), Roemer (LA), Lehman (CA), Morrison (CT), Kaptur (OH), Erdreich (AL), Carper (DE), Torres (CA), Kleczka (WI), Nelson (FL), Kanjorski (PA), Manton (NY), Patterson (SC), McMillen (MD), Kennedy (MA), Flake (NY), Mfume (MD), Price (NC), Pelosi (CA).
Minority (20 R): Wylie (OH), Leach (IA), Shumway (CA), Parris (VA), McCollum (FL), Wortley (NY), Roukema (NJ), Bereuter (NE), Dreier (CA), Hiler (IN), Ridge (PA), Bartlett (TX), Roth (WI), McCandless (CA), McMillan (NC), Saxton (NJ), Swindall (GA), Saiki (HI), Bunning (KY), one vacancy.

SUBCOMMITTEES

CONSUMER AFFAIRS AND COINAGE

Majority (5 D): Annunzio, Chmn.; St Germain, Gonzalez, two vacancies.
Minority (3 R): Hiler, Wylie, Ridge.

DOMESTIC MONETARY POLICY

Majority (4 D): Neal, Chmn.; Barnard, Hubbard, Frank.
Minority (3 R): McCollum, Leach, Saxton.

ECONOMIC STABILIZATION

Majority (14 D): Oakar, Chmn.; LaFalce, Vento, Kaptur, Kanjorski, Barnard, Garcia, Patterson, McMillen, Flake, Mfume, Price, two vacancies.
Minority (9 R): Shumway, Wortley, McCandless, McMillan, Roth, Saxton, Saiki, Swindall, one vacancy.

FINANCIAL INSTITUTIONS SUPERVISION, REGULATION AND INSURANCE

Majority (26 D): St Germain, Chmn.; Annunzio, Hubbard, Barnard, LaFalce, Oakar, Vento, Schumer, Frank, Lehman, Roemer, Kaptur, Nelson, Kanjorski, Manton, Gonzalez, Neal, Morrison, Erdreich, Carper, Torres, Kleczka, Patterson, McMillen, Price, Kennedy.
Minority (17 R): Wylie, Leach, Shumway, McCollum, Wortley, Dreier, Parris, Roukema, Bereuter, Bartlett, Roth, Hiler, Ridge, McCandless, McMillan, Saxton, one vacancy.

GENERAL OVERSIGHT AND INVESTIGATIONS

Majority (10 D): Hubbard, Chmn.; Gonzalez, Barnard, Kanjorski, Roemer, Erdreich, Patterson, Flake, two vacancies.
Minority (6 R): Parris, Dreier, Bartlett, McCandless, McMillan, Bunning.

HOUSING AND COMMUNITY DEVELOPMENT

Majority (23 D): Gonzalez, Chmn.; St Germain, Fauntroy, Oakar, Vento, Garcia, Schumer, Frank, Lehman, Morrison, Kaptur, Erdreich, Carper, Torres, Roemer, Kleczka, Kanjorski, Manton, Neal, Hubbard, Kennedy, Flake, Mfume.
Minority (15 R): Roukema, Wylie, Wortley, McCollum, Bereuter, Dreier, Hiler, Ridge, Bartlett, Roth, Saxton, Swindall, Saiki, Bunning, one vacancy.

INTERNATIONAL DEVELOPMENT INSTITUTIONS AND FINANCE

Majority (9 D): Fauntroy, Chmn.; LaFalce, Torres, Morrison, Schumer, Kennedy, Mfume, two vacancies.
Minority (6 R): Bereuter, Roukema, McCandless, Saiki, Swindall, Bunning.

INTERNATIONAL FINANCE, TRADE AND MONETARY POLICY

Majority (11 D): Garcia, Chmn.; Neal, LaFalce, Fauntroy, Kleczka, Manton, Roemer, Lehman, Carper, two vacancies.
Minority (7 R): Leach, Shumway, Parris, McMillan, Bunning, Swindall, Saiki.

BUDGET   214 House Annex 1, 202-226-7200

Majority (21 D): Gray (PA), Chmn.; Foley (WA), Lowry (WA), Derrick (SC), Miller (CA), Williams (MT), Wolpe (MI), Frost (TX), Fazio (CA), Russo (IL), Jenkins (GA), Leath (TX), Schumer (NY), Boxer (CA), MacKay (FL), Slattery (KS), Atkins (MA), Oberstar (MN), Guarini (NJ), Durbin (IL), Espy (MS).
Minority (14 R): Latta (OH), Gradison (OH), Mark (FL), Goodling (PA), Smith (OR), Boulter (TX), Edwards (OK), Thomas (CA), Rogers (KY), Sundquist (TN), Johnson (CT), Armey (TX), Buechner (MO), Houghton (NY).

TASK FORCES

BUDGET PROCESS

Majority (7 D): Derrick, Chmn.; Miller, Frost, Fazio, MacKay, Atkins, Oberstar.
Minority (8 R): Gradison, Smith, Boulter, Edwards, Thomas, Rogerts, Sundquist, Armey.

COMMUNITY AND NATURAL RESOURCES

Majority (9 D): Wolpe, Chmn.; Williams, Fazio, Jenkins, Slattery, Atkins, Oberstar, Durbin, Espy.
Minority (2 R): Edwards, Armey.

DEFENSE AND INTERNATIONAL AFFAIRS

Majority (12 D): Fazio, Chmn; Miller, Wolpe, Frost, Russo, Leath, Boxer, MacKay, Slattery, Atkins, Oberstar, Guarini.
Minority (7 R): Mack, Smith, Boulter, Edwards, Rogerts, Sundquist, Buechner.

ECONOMIC AND TRADE POLICY

Majority (9 D): Lowry, Chmn.; Derrick, Williams, Russo, Schumer, MacKay, Slattery, Guarini, Espy.
Minority (10 R): Boulter, Gradison, Edwards, Thomas, Rogers, Sundquist, Johnson, Armey, Buechner, Houghton.

HEALTH
Majority (3 D): Frost, Chmn.; Schumer, MacKay.
Minority (4 R): Johnson, Gradison, Fiedler, Mack, Goodling.

HUMAN RESOURCES
Majority (4 D): Williams, Chmn.; Lowry, Durbin, Espy.
Minority (2 R): Goodling, Johnson.

INCOME SECURITY
Majority (4 D): Russo, Chmn.; Miller, Fazio, Boxer.
Minority (5 R): Mack, Gradison, Goodling, Thomas, Houghton.

STATE AND LOCAL GOVERNMENT
Majority (4 D): Miller, Chmn.; Jenkins, Schumer, Boxer.
Minority (1 R): Smith (OR).

DISTRICT OF COLUMBIA   1310 LHOB, 202-225-4457

Majority (8 D): Dellums (CA) Chmn.; Fauntroy (DC), Mazzoli (KY), Stark (CA), Gray (PA), Dymally (CA), Wheat (MO), one vacancy.
Minority (4 R): Parris (VA), Bliley (VA), Combest (TX), Martin (IL).

SUBCOMMITTEES

FISCAL AFFAIRS AND HEALTH
Majority (5 D): Fauntroy, Chmn.; Dellums, Stark, Gray, one vacancy.
Minority (3 R): Bliley, Parris, Combest.

GOVERNMENT OPERATIONS AND METROPOLITAN AFFAIRS
Majority (5 D): Wheat, Chmn.; Gray, Stark, Fauntroy, one vacancy.
Minority (3 R): Combest, Parris, Martin.

JUDICIARY AND EDUCATION
Majority (5 D): Dymally, Chmn.; Mazzoli, Wheat, two vacancies.
Minority (3 R): Martin, Bliley, Parris.

EDUCATION AND LABOR   2181 RHOB, 202-225-4527

Majority (21 D): Hawkins (CA), Chmn.; Ford (MI), Gaydos (PA), Clay (MO), Biaggi (NY), Murphy (PA), Kildee (MI), Williams (MT), Martinez (CA), Owens (NY) Hayes (IL), Perkins (KY), Sawyer (OH), Solarz (NY), Wise (WV), Penny (MN), Richardson (NM), Robinson (AR), Visclosky (IN), Atkins (MA), Jontz (IN).
Minority (13 R): Jeffords (VT), Goodling (PA), Coleman (MO), Petri (WI), Roukema (NJ), Gunderson (WI), Bartlett (TX), Tauke (IA), Armey (TX), Fawell (IL), Henry (MI), Grandy (IA), Ballenger (NC).

SUBCOMMITTEES

ELEMENTARY, SECONDARY AND VOCATIONAL EDUCATION
Majority (15 D): Hawkins, Chmn.; Ford, Kildee, Williams, Martinez, Perkins, Biaggi, Hayes, Sawyer, Solarz, Wise, Richardson, Robinson, Visclosky, Atkins.
Minority (8 R): Goodling, Bartlett, Fawell, Henry, Grandy, Gunderson, Petri, Roukema.

EMPLOYMENT OPPORTUNITIES

Majority (6 D): Martinez, Chmn.; Williams, Hayes, Owens, Atkins, Jontz.
Minority (3 R): Gunderson, Henry, Grandy.

HEALTH AND SAFETY

Majority (4 D): Gaydos, Chmn.; Murphy, Ford, Clay.
Minority (2 R): Henry, Ballenger.

HUMAN RESOURCES

Majority (5 D): Kildee, Chmn.; Sawyer, Biaggi, Solarz, Visclosky.
Minority (3 R): Tauke, Coleman, Grandy.

LABOR–MANAGEMENT RELATIONS

Majority (9 D): Clay, Chmn.; Ford, Kildee, Biaggi, Hayes, Owens, Sawyer, Murphy, Jontz.
Minority (5 R): Roukema, Armey, Fawell, Ballenger, Petri.

LABOR STANDARDS

Majority (5 D): Murphy, Chmn.; Williams, Penny, Wise, Robinson.
Minority (2 R): Petri, Bartlett.

POSTSECONDARY EDUCATION

Majority (9 D): Williams, Chmn.; Ford, Owens, Hayes, Perkins, Gaydos, Martinez, Robinson, Atkins.
Minority (5 R): Coleman, Goodling, Roukema, Tauke, Armey.

SELECT EDUCATION

Majority (3 D): Owens, Chmn.; Williams, Biaggi.
Minority (1 R): Bartlett.

ENERGY AND COMMERCE   2125 RHOB, 202-225-2927

Majority (25 D): Dingell (MI), Chmn.; Scheuer (NY), Waxman (CA), Sharp (IN), Florio (NJ), Markey (MA), Luken (OH), Walgren (PA), Swift (WA), Leland (TX), Collins (IL), Synar (OK), Tauzin (LA), Wyden (OR), Hall, R. (TX), Eckart (OH), Dowdy (MS), Richardson (NM), Slattery (KS), Sikorski (MN), Bryant (TX), Bates (CA), Boucher (VA), Cooper (TN), Bruce (IL).
Minority (17 R): Lent (NY), Madigan (IL), Moorhead (CA), Rinaldo (NJ), Dannemeyer (CA), Whittaker (KS), Tauke (IA), Ritter (PA), Coats (IN), Bliley (VA), Fields (TX), Oxley (OH), Nielson (UT), Bilirakis (FL), Schaefer (CO), Barton (TX), Callahan (AL).

SUBCOMMITTEES

COMMERCE, CONSUMER PROTECTION AND COMPETITIVENESS

Majority (8 D): Florio, Chmn.; Scheuer, Bates, Waxman, Sharp, Collins, Eckart, Richardson.
Minority (5 R): Dannemeyer, Rinaldo, Ritter, Nielson, Barton.

ENERGY AND POWER

Majority (13 D): Sharp, Chmn.; Walgren, Swift, Synar, Tauzin, Richardson, Bryant, Bruce, Markey, Leland, Wyden, Hall, Dowdy.
Minority (8 R): Moorhead, Dannemeyer, Fields, Oxley, Bilirakis, Schaefer, Barton, Callahan.

HEALTH AND THE ENVIRONMENT

Majority (11 D): Waxman, Chmn.; Scheuer, Walgren, Wyden, Sikorski, Bates, Bruce, Leland, Collins, Hall, Dowdy.

Minority (7 R): Madigan, Dannemeyer, Whittaker, Tauke, Coats, Bliley, Fields.

OVERSIGHT AND INVESTIGATIONS

Majority (9 D): Dingell, Chmn.; Wyden, Eckart, Slattery, Sikorski, Boucher, Cooper, Luken, Walgren.

Minority (6 R): Lent, Coats, Bliley, Oxley, Bilirakis, Schaefer.

TELECOMMUNICATIONS AND FINANCE

Majority (14 D): Markey, Chmn.; Swift, Leland, Collins, Synar, Tauzin, Dowdy, Slattery, Bryant, Hall, Eckart, Richardson, Boucher, Cooper.

Minority (9 R): Rinaldo, Moorhead, Tauke, Ritter, Coats, Bliley, Fields, Oxley, Nielson.

TRANSPORTATION, TOURISM AND HAZARDOUS MATERIALS

Majority (8 D): Luken, Chmn.; Florio, Tauzin, Slattery, Sikorski, Bryant, Bates, Boucher.

Minority (5 R): Whittaker, Tauke, Bilirakis, Schaefer, Callahan.

FOREIGN AFFAIRS   2170 RHOB, 202-225-5021

Majority (27 D): Fascell (FL), Chmn.; Hamilton (IN), Yatron (PA), Solarz (NY), Bonker (WA), Studds (MA), Mica (FL), Wolpe (MI), Crockett (MI), Gejdenson (CT), Dymally (CA), Lantos (CA), Kostmayer (PA), Torricelli (NJ), Smith (FL), Berman (CA), Levine (CA), Feighan (OH), Weiss (NY), Ackerman (NY), Udall (AZ), Atkins (MA), Clarke (NC), Fuster (PR), Bilbray (NV), Owens (UT), Sunia (Am. Samoa).

Minority (18 R): Broomfield (MI), Gilman (NY), Lagomarsino (CA), Leach (IA), Roth (WI), Snowe (ME), Hyde (IL), Solomon (NY), Bereuter (NE), Dornan (CA), Smith (NJ), Mack (FL), DeWine (OH), Burton (IN), Meyers (KS), Miller (WA), Lukens (OH), Blaz (Guam).

SUBCOMMITTEES

AFRICA

Majority (6 D): Wolpe, Chmn.; Crockett, Clarke, Bilbray, Sunia, Owens.

Minority (4 R): Burton, Lukens, Blaz, Dornan.

ARMS CONTROL, INTERNATIONAL SECURITY AND SCIENCE

Majority (8 D): Fascell, Chmn.; Berman, Udall, Clarke, Hamilton, Studds, Lantos, Weiss.

Minority (5 R): Broomfield, Leach, Snowe, Hyde, Burton.

ASIAN AND PACIFIC AFFAIRS

Majority (6 D): Solarz, Chmn.; Dymally, Atkins, Sunia, Torricelli, Ackerman.

Minority (4 R): Leach, Blaz, Lagomarsino, Roth.

EUROPE AND THE MIDDLE EAST

Majority (8 D): Hamilton, Chmn.; Lantos, Torricelli, Smith, Levine, Feighan, Ackerman, Owens.

Minority (5 R): Gilman, Meyers, Lukens, Bereuter, Smith.

HUMAN RIGHTS AND INTERNATIONAL ORGANIZATIONS

Majority (6 D): Yatron, Chmn.; Fuster, Lantos, Feighan, Weiss, Ackerman.

Minority (4 R): Solomon, Smith, Meyers, Miller.

INTERNATIONAL ECONOMIC POLICY AND TRADE

Majority (8 D): Bonker, Chmn.; Bilbray, Mica, Wolpe, Gejdenson, Berman, Levine, Feighan.
Minority (5 R): Roth, Bereuter, Miller, Solomon, Dornan.

INTERNATIONAL OPERATIONS

Majority (6 D): Mica, Chmn.; Yatron, Dymally, Kostmayer, Smith, Atkins.
Minority (4 R): Snowe, Gilman, Mack, DeWine.

WESTERN HEMISPHERE AFFAIRS

Majority (8 D): Crockett, Chmn.; Studds, Gejdenson, Kostmayer, Weiss, Fuster, Solarz, Bonker.
Minority (5 R): Lagomarsino, Hyde, Dornan, Mack, DeWine.

GOVERNMENT OPERATIONS   2157 RHOB, 202-225-5051

Majority (24 D): Brooks (TX), Chmn.; Conyers (MI), Collins (IL), English (OK), Waxman (CA), Weiss (NY), Synar (OK), Neal (NC), Barnard (GA), Frank (MA), Lantos (CA), Wise (WV), Owens (NY), Towns (NY), Spratt (SC), Kolter (PA), Erdreich (AL), Kleczka (WI), Bustamante (TX), Matrinez (CA), Sawyer (OH), Slaughter (NY), Grant (FL), Pelosi (CA).
Minority (15 R): Horton (NY), Walker (PA), Clinger (PA), McCandless (CA), Craig (ID), Nielson (UT), DioGuardi (NY), Lightfoot (IA), Boutler (TX), Lukens (OH), Houghton (NY), Hastert (IL), Kyl (AZ), Konnyu (CA), Inhofe (OK).

SUBCOMMITTEES

COMMERCE, CONSUMER AND MONETARY AFFAIRS

Majority (6 D): Barnard, Chmn.; Spratt, Kolter, Erdreich, Bustamante, Martinez.
Minority (4 R): Craig, Konnyu, Inhofe, Houghton.

EMPLOYMENT AND HOUSING

Majority (4 D): Lantos, Chmn.; Slaughter, Grant, Weiss.
Minority (3 R): DioGuardi, Kyl, Konntyu.

ENVIRONMENT, ENERGY AND NATURAL RESOURCES

Majority (6 D): Synar, Chmn.; Towns, Bustamante, Waxman, Martinez, one vacancy.
Minority (3 R): Clinger, Kyl, Boulter.

GOVERNMENT ACTIVITIES AND TRANSPORTATION

Majority (6 D): Collins, Chwn.; Owens, Wise, Kolter, Kleczka, Sawyer.
Minority (3 R): Nielson, Hastert, Lukens.

GOVERNMENT INFORMATION, JUSTICE AND AGRICULTURE

Majority (6 D): English, Chmn.; Slaughter, Grant, Towns, Spratt, one vacancy.
Minority (3 R): McCandless, Houghton, Hastert.

HUMAN RESOURCES AND INTERGOVERNMENTAL RELATIONS

Majority (5 D): Weiss, Chmn.; Sawyer, Conyers, Waxman, Frank.
Minority (3 R): Lightfoot, Konnyu, Inhofe.

LEGISLATION AND NATIONAL SECURITY

Majority (7 D): Brooks, Chmn.; Conyers, Neal, Frank, Wise, Erdreich, Kleczka.
Minority (4 R): Horton, Walker, Boulter, Lukens.

HOUSE ADMINISTRATION

H 326 Capitol, 202-225-2061

Majority (12 D): Annunzio (IL), Chmn.; Gaydos (PA), Jones (TN), Rose (NC), Panetta (CA), Swift (WA), Oakar (OH), Coelho (CA), Bates (CA), Clay (MO), Gejdenson (CT), one vacancy.
Minority (7 R): Frenzel (MN), Dickinson (AL), Badham (CA), Gingrich (GA), Thomas (CA), Vucanovich (NV), Roberts (KS).

SUBCOMMITTEES

ACCOUNTS
Majority (7 D): Gaydos, Chmn.; Swift, Oakar, Coelho, Clay, Gejdenson, Annunzio.
Minority (4 R): Badham, Thomas, Roberts, Vucanovich.

ELECTIONS
Majority (7 D): Swift, Chmn.; Rose, Panetta, Clay, Bates, Coehlo, Annunzio.
Minority (4 R): Thomas, Vucanovich, Roberts, Frenzel.

OFFICE SYSTEMS
Majority (3 D): Rose, Chmn.; Gejdenson, Bates.
Minority (2 R): Thomas, Dickinson.

LIBRARIES AND MEMORIALS
Majority (3 D): Oakar, Chmn.; Swift, Clay.
Minority (2 R): Gingrich, Frenzel.

PERSONNEL AND POLICE
Majority (3 D): Panetta, Chmn.; Jones, Gaydos.
Minority (2 R): Roberts, Dickinson.

PROCUREMENT AND PRINTING
Majority (3 D): Jones, Chmn.; Gaydos, Bates.
Minority (2 R): Gingrich, Badham.

INTERIOR AND INSULAR AFFAIRS

1324 LHOB, 202-225-2761

Majority (26 D): Udall (AZ), Chmn.; Miller (CA), Sharp (IN), Markey (MA), Murphy (PA), Rahall (WV), Vento (MN), Huckaby (LA), Kildee (MI), Coelho (CA), Byron (MD), de Lugo (VI), Gejdenson (CT), Kostmayer (PA), Lehman (CA), Richardson (NM), Sunia (AS), Darden (GA), Visclosky (IN), Fuster (PR), Levine (CA), Clarke (NC), Owens (UT), Lewis (GA), Campbell (CO), DeFazio (OR).
Minority (15 R): Young (AK), Lujan (NM), Lagomarsino (CA), Marlenee (MT), Cheney (WY), Pashayan (CA), Craig (ID), Smith (OR), Hansen (UT), Emerson (MO), Vucanovich (NV), Blaz (Guam), Rhodes (AZ), Gallegly (CA), Baker (LA).

SUBCOMMITTEES

ENERGY AND THE ENVIRONMENT
Majority (13 D): Udall, Chmn.; Miller, Sharp, Markey, Murphy, Rahall, Huckaby, Gejdenson, Darden, Fuster, Levine, Clarke, Owens.
Minority (9 R): Lujan, Young, Pashayan, Craig, Vucanovich, Blaz, Rhodes, Baker.

GENERAL OVERSIGHT AND INVESTIGATIONS
Majority (3 D): Gejdenson, Chmn.; Miller, DeFazio.
Minority (2 R): Smith, Hansen.

INSULAR AND INTERNATIONAL AFFAIRS
Majority (8 D): de Lugo, Chmn.; Udall, Vento, Sunia, Darden, Fuster, Clarke, Lewis.
Minority (4 R): Lagomarsino, Blaz, Gallegly, Baker.

MINING AND NATURAL RESOURCES
Majority (7 D): Rahall, Chmn.; Udall, Miller, Murphy, Kostmayer, Owens, Campbell.
Minority (4 R): Craig, Marlenee, Emerson, Vucanovich.

NATIONAL PARKS AND PUBLIC LANDS
Majority (20 D): Vento, Chmn.; Markey, Rahall, Huckaby, Kildee, Coehlo, Byron, deLugo, Kostmayer, Lehman, Richardson, Sunia, Darden, Visclosky, Fuster, Levine, Clarke, Lewis, DeFazio.
Minority (12 R): Marlenee, Lagomarsino, Cheney, Pashayan, Craig, Hansen, Emerson, Vucanovitch, Blaz, Rhodes, Gallegly.

WATER AND POWER RESOURCES
Majority (14 D): Miller, Chmn.; Udall, Sharp, Markey, Kildee, Lehman, Richardson, Levine, Owens, Campbell, DeFazio.
Minority (9 R): Pashayan, Young, Lujan, Cheney, Craig, Smith, Rhodes, Gallegly, Baker.

JUDICIARY   2137 RHOB, 202-225-3951

Majority (21 D): Rodino (NJ), Chmn.; Brooks (TX), Kastenmeier (WI), Edwards (CA), Conyers (MI), Mazzoli (KY), Hughes (NJ), Synar (OK), Schroeder (CO), Glickman (KS), Frank (MA), Crockett (MI), Schumer (NY), Morrison (CT), Feighan (OH), Smith (FL), Berman (CA), Boucher (VA), Staggers (WV), Bryant (TX), Cardin (MD).
Minority (14 R): Fish (NY), Moorhead (CA), Hyde (IL), Lungren (CA), Sensenbrenner (WI), McCollum (FL), Shaw (FL), Gekas (PA), DeWine (OH), Dannemeyer (CA), Swindall (GA), Coble (NC), Slaughter (VA), Smith (TX).

SUBCOMMITTEES

ADMINISTRATIVE LAW AND GOVERNMENTAL RELATIONS
Majority (6 D): Frank, Chmn.; Brooks, Glickman, Morrison, Berman, Cardin.
Minority (4 R): Shaw, Swindall, Coble, Smith.

CIVIL AND CONSTITUTIONAL RIGHTS
Majority (5 D): Edwards, Chmn.; Kastenmeier, Conyers, Schroeder, Schumer.
Minority (3 R): Sensenbrenner, DeWine, Dannemeyer.

COURTS, CIVIL LIBERTIES AND THE ADMINISTRATION OF JUSTICE
Majority (9 D): Kastenmeier, Chmn.; Synar, Schroeder, Crockett, Morrison, Berman, Boucher, Bryant, Cardin.
Minority (6 R): Moorhead, Hyde, Lundgren, DeWine, Coble, Slaughter.

CRIME
Majority (6 D): Hughes, Chmn.; Mazzoli, Crockett, Feighan, Smith, Staggers.
Minority (4 R): McCollum, Smith, Shaw, Gekas.

CRIMINAL JUSTICE

Majority (5 D): Conyers, Chmn.; Edwards, Synar, Boucher, Bryant.
Minority (3 R): Gekas, Fish, Swindall.

IMMIGRATION, REFUGEES AND INTERNATIONAL LAW

Majority (6 D): Mazzoli, Chmn.; Frank, Schumer, Morrison, Berman, Bryant.
Minority (4 R): Shaw, Swindall, Coble, Smith.

MONOPOLIES AND COMMERCIAL LAW

Majority (9 D): Rodino, Chmn.; Brooks, Edwards, Mazzoli, Hughes, Glickman, Feighan, Smith, Staggers.
Minority (6 R): Fish, Dannemeyer, Moorhead, Hyde, Lungren, Sensenbrenner.

MERCHANT MARINE AND FISHERIES   1334 LHOB, 202-225-4047

Majority (25 D): Jones (NC), Chmn.; Biaggi (NY), Anderson (CA), Studds (MA), Hubbard (KY), Bonker (WA), Hughes (NJ), Lowry (WA), Hutto (FL), Tauzin (LA), Foglietta (PA), Hertel (MI), Dyson (MD), Lipinski (IL), Borski (PA), Carper (DE), Bosco (CA), Tallon (SC), Thomas (GA), Ortiz (TX), Bennett (FL), Manton (NY), Pickett (VA), Brennan (ME), Hochbrueckner (NY).
Minority (17 R): Davis (MI), Young (AK), Lent (NY), Shumway (CA), Fields (TX), Schneider (RI), Bateman (VA), Saxton (NJ), Miller (WA), Bentley (MD), Coble (NC), Sweeney (TX), DioGuardi (NY), Weldon (PA), Saiki (HI), Herger (CA), Bunning (KY).

SUBCOMMITTEES

COAST GUARD AND NAVIGATION

Majority (12 D): Hutto, Chmn.; Hughes, Studds, Lipinski, Carper, Thomas, Pickett, Brennan, Hockbruechner, Hertel, Bennett, Lowry.
Minority (9 R): Davis, Young, Bateman, Coble, Sweeney, DioGuardi, Weldon, Saiki, Bunning.

FISHERIES AND WILDLIFE CONSERVATION AND THE ENVIRONMENT

Majority (14 D): Studds, Chmn.; Bonker, Dyson, Carper, Bosco, Thomas, Ortiz, Manton, Anderson, Hughes, Lowry, Hutto, Tauzin, Hertel.
Minority (11 R): Young, Schneider, Bateman, Saxton, Miller, Sweeney, DioGuardi, Weldon, Saiki, Herger, Bunning.

MERCHANT MARINE

Majority (15 D): Anderson, Biaggi, Foglietta, Hertel, Lipinski, Borski, Tallon, Bennett, Pickett, Brennan, Hochbruckner, Bonker, Dyson, Thomas.
Minority (10 R): Lent, Young, Shumway, Fields, Bateman, Saxton, Miller, Bentley, Coble, Sweeney.

OCEANOGRAPHY

Majority (7 D): Lowry, Chmn.; Foglietta, Borski, Tallon, Studds, Hughes, Bonker.
Minority (6 R): Shumway, Schneider, Saxton, DioGuardi, Saiki, Herger.

OVERSIGHT AND INVESTIGATIONS

Majority (2 D): Jones, Chmn., Lowry.
Minority (2 R): Schneider, Bentley.

PANAMA CANAL AND OUTER CONTINENTAL SHELF

Majority (7 D): Tauzin, Chmn.; Ortiz, Manton, Lowry, Foglietta, Bosco, Brennan.
Minority (6 R): Fields, Shumway, Bentley, Coble, Weldon, Herger.

POST OFFICE AND CIVIL SERVICE   309 CHOB, 202-225-4054

Majority (14 D): Ford (MI), Chmn.; Clay (MO), Schroeder (CO), Solarz (NY), Garcia (NY), Leland (TX), Yatron (PA), Oakar (OH), Sikorski (MN), McCloskey (IN), Ackerman (NY), Dymally (CA), Udall (AZ), de Lugo (VI).
Minority (8 R): Taylor (MO), Gilman (NY), Pashayan (CA), Horton (NY), Myers (IN), Young (AK), Burton (IN), Morella (MD).

SUBCOMMITTEES

CENSUS AND POPULATION
Majority (3 D): Dymally, Chmn.; Garcia, Sikorski.
Minority (2 R): Morella, Burton.

CIVIL SERVICE
Majority (3 D): Schroeder, Chmn.; Solarz, Dymally.
Minority (2 R): Pashayan, Horton.

COMPENSATION AND EMPLOYEE BENEFITS
Majority (3 D): Ackerman, Chmn.; Oakar, Leland.
Minority (2 R): Myers, Morella.

HUMAN RESOURCES
Majority (3 D): Sikorski, Chmn.; Yatron, McCloskey.
Minority (2 R): Burton, Gilman.

INVESTIGATIONS
Majority (3 D): Ford, Chmn.; Yatron, Udall.
Minority (2 R): Taylor, Gilman.

POSTAL OPERATIONS AND SERVICES
Majority (4 D): Leland, Chmn.; Clay, Garcia, de Lugo.
Minority (3 R): Horton, Pashayan, Young.

POSTAL PERSONNEL AND MODERNIZATION
Majority (3 D): McCloskey, Chmn.; Dymally, Ackerman.
Minority (2 R): Young, Myers.

PUBLIC WORKS AND TRANSPORTATION   2165 RHOB, 202-225-4472

Majority (32 D): Howard (NJ), Chmn.; Anderson (CA), Roe (NJ), Mineta (CA), Oberstar (MN), Nowak (NY), Rahall (WV), Applegate (OH), de Lugo (VI), Savage (IL), Sunia (AS), Bosco (CA), Borski (PA), Kolter (PA), Valentine (NC), Towns (NY), Lipinski (IL), Rowland (GA), Wise (WV), Gray (IL), Visclosky (IN), Traficant (OH), Chapman (TX), Lancaster (NC), Slaughter (NY), Lewis (GA), DeFazio (OR), Cardin (MD), Grant (FL), Skaggs (CO), Hayes (LA), Perkins (KY).
Minority (20 R): Hammerschmidt (AR), Shuster (PA), Stangeland (MN), Gingrich (GA), Clinger (PA), Molinari (NY), Shaw (FL), McEwen (OH), Petri (WI), Sundquist (TN), Johnson (CT), Packard (CA), Boehlert (NY), Gallo (NJ), Bentley (MD), Lightfoot (IA), Hastert (IL), Inhofe (OK), Ballenger (NC), Upton (MI).

SUBCOMMITTEES

AVIATION

Majority (17 D): Mineta, Chmn.; de Lugo, Valentine, Visclosky, Chapman, DeFazio, Skaggs, Anderson, Savage, Sunia, Kolter, Towns, Lipinski, Rowland, Cardin, Bosco, Perkins.
Minority (10 R): Gingrich, Shuster, Stangeland, Petri, Sundquist, Packard, Boehlert, Lightfoot, Inhofe, Ballenger.

ECONOMIC DEVELOPMENT

Majority (11 D): Savage, Chmn.; Lewis, Oberstar, Rahall, Applegate, Gray, Hayes, Towns, Lipinski, Traficant, one vacancy.
Minority (7 R): Shaw, Clinger, McEwen, Johnson, Boehlert, Bentley, Ballenger.

INVESTIGATIONS AND OVERSIGHT

Majority (11 D): Oberstar, Chmn.; Roe, Mineta, Nowak, Borski, Kolter, Rowland, Gray, Lancaster, Slaughter, Towns.
Minority (7 R): Clinger, Shuster, Gingrich, Molinari, McEwen, Johnson, Bentley.

PUBLIC BUILDINGS AND GROUNDS

Majority (8 D): Sunia, Chmn.; Lancaster, Lewis, Cardin, Grant, Skaggs, two vacancies.
Minority (4 R): Molinari, Stangeland, Sundquist, Gallo.

SURFACE TRANSPORTATION

Majority (19 D): Anderson, Chmn.; Rahall, Applegate, Bosko, Borski, Kolter, Towns, Lipinski, Rowland, Wise, Gray, Traficant, Lancaster, Slaughter, Grant, Roe, Mineta, Nowak, de Lugo.
Minority (12 R): Shuster, Gingrich, Clinger, Shaw, McEwen, Petri, Packard, Boehlert, Gallo, Lightfoot, Hastert, Upton.

WATER RESOURCES

Majority (21 D): Nowak, Chmn.; Roe, Cardin, Hayes, de Lugo, Borski, Valentine, Wise, Visclosky, Traficant, Chapman, Slaughter, Lewis, DeFazio, Grant, Skaggs, Anderson, Oberstar, Applegate, Bosco, Savage.
Minority (13 R): Stangeland, Molinari, Shaw, Petri, Sundquist, Johnson, Packard, Gallo, Bentley, Lightfoot, Hastert, Inhofe, Upton.

RULES   H 312 Capitol, 202-225-9486

Majority (9 D): Pepper (FL), Chmn.; Moakley (MA), Derrick (SC), Beilenson (CA), Frost (TX), Bonior (MI), Hall (OH), Wheat (MO), Gordon (TN).
Minority (4 R): Quillen (TN), Latta (OH), Lott (MS), Taylor (MO).

SUBCOMMITTEES

THE LEGISLATIVE PROCESS

Majority (5 D): Derrick, Chmn.; Frost, Wheat, Gordon, Pepper.
Minority (2 R): Lott, Taylor.

RULES OF THE HOUSE

Majority (5 D): Moakley, Chmn.; Beilenson, Bonior, Hall, Pepper.
Minority (2 R): Taylor, Lott.

SCIENCE, SPACE AND TECHNOLOGY   2321 RHOB, 202-225-6371

Majority (27 D): Roe (NJ), Chmn.; Brown (CA), Scheuer (NY), Lloyd (TN), Walgren (PA), Glickman (KS), Volkmer (MO), Nelson (FL), , Hall (TX), McCurdy (OK), Mineta (CA), MacKay (FL), Valentine (NC), Torricelli (NJ), Boucher (VA), Bruce (IL), Stallings (ID), Traficant (OH), Chapman (TX), Hamilton (IN), Nowak (NY), Perkins (KY), McMillen (MD), Price (NC), Nagle (IA), Hayes (LA) Skaggs (CO).
Minority (18 R): Lujan (NM), Walker (PA), Sensenbrenner (WI), Schneider (RI), Boehlert (NY), Lewis (FL), Ritter (PA), Morrison (WA), Packard (CA), Smith (NH), Henry (MI), Fawell (IL), Slaughter (VA), Smith (TX), Konnyu (CA), Buechner (MO), Hefley (CO), Morella (MD).

SUBCOMMITTEES

ENERGY RESEARCH AND DEVELOPMENT

Majority (8 D): Lloyd, Chmn.; Boucher, Bruce, Stallings, Walgren, Valentine, Traficant, Chapman.
Minority (5 R): Morrison, Fawell, Smith (TX), Konnyu, Hefley.

INVESTIGATIONS AND OVERSIGHT

Majority (6 D): Roe, Chmn.; Volkmer, Price, Brown, Traficant, one vacancy.
Minority (4 R): Ritter, Sensenbrenner, Packard, Konnyu.

INTERNATIONAL SCIENTIFIC COOPERATION

Majority (6 D): Hall, Chmn.; Lloyd, MacKay, Torricelli, Stallings, Scheuer.
Minority (4 R): Sensenbrenner, Boehlert, Packard, Fawell.

NATURAL RESOURCES, AGRICULTURE RESEARCH AND ENVIRONMENT

Majority (6 D): Scheuer, Chmn.; Valentine, McCurdy, Nowak, McMillen, Brown.
Minority (4 R): Schneider, Smith (NH), Henry, Hefley.

SCIENCE, RESEARCH AND TECHNOLOGY

Majority (14 D): Walgren, Chmn.; MacKay, Hamilton, Nowak, Price, Brown, Mineta, Bruce, Perkins, Nagle, Hayes, Valentine, Chapman, Skaggs.
Minority (9 R): Boehlert, Henry, Schneider, Ritter, Morrison, Slaughter, Smith (TX), Buechner, Morella.

SPACE SCIENCE AND APPLICATIONS

Majority (15 D): Nelson, Chmn.; Brown, Volkmer, Mineta, Torricelli, Traficant, Chapman, Perkins, McMillen, Nagle, Hayes, Scheuer, Hall, MacKay, Skaggs.
Minority (9 R): Walker, Packard, Smith, Slaughter, Konnyu, Buechner, Hefley, Morella, Lewis.

TRANSPORTATION, AVIATION AND MATERIALS

Majority (5 D): McCurdey, Chmn.; Glickman, Nelson, McMillen, Hayes.
Minority (3 R): Lewis, Walker, Sensenbrenner.

SMALL BUSINESS   2361 RHOB, 202-225-5821

Majority (27 D): LaFalce (NY), Smith (IA), Gonzalez (TX), Luken (OH), Skelton (MO), Mazzoli (KY), Mavroules (MA), Hatcher (GA), Wyden (OR), Eckart (OH), Savage (IL), Roemer (LA), Sisisky (VA), Torres (CA), Cooper (TN), Olin (VA), Ray (GA), Hayes (IL), Conyers (MI), Bilbray (NV), Mfume (MD), Flake (NY), Lancaster (NC), Campbell (CO), DeFazio (OR), Price (NC), Martinez (CA).

Minority (17 R): McDade (PA), Conte (MA), Broomfield (MI), Ireland (FL), Hiler (IN), Dreier (CA), Slaughter (VA), Meyers (KS), Gallo (NJ), McMillan (NC), Combest (TX), Baker (LA), Rhodes (AZ), Hefley (CO), Upton (MI), Gallegly (CA), one vacancy.

SUBCOMMITTEES

ANTITRUST, IMPACT OF DEREGULATION AND PRIVATIZATION
Majority (5 D): Eckart, Chmn.; Gonzalez, Luken, Price, Martinez.
Minority (3 R): Hiler, Slaughter, Rhodes.

ENERGY AND AGRICULTURE
Majority (5 D): Hatcher, Chmn.; Ray, Martinez, Bilbray, one vacancy.
Minority (3 R): Dreier, Combest, Gallegly.

EXPORTS, TOURISM AND SPECIAL PROBLEMS
Majority (6 D): Skelton, Chmn.; Bilbray, Lancaster, Campbell, Sisisky, Mfume.
Minority (4 R): Ireland, Slaughter, Gallo, Upton.

PROCUREMENT, INNOVATION AND MINORITY ENTERPRISE DEVELOPMENT
Majority (9 D): Mavroules, Chmn.; Hayes, Conyers, Mfume, Flake, Eckart, Savage, Torres, Lancaster.
Minority (6 R): Conte, Rhodes, Gallo, Upton, Gallegly, one vacancy.

REGULATION AND BUSINESS OPPORTUNITIES
Majority (9 D): Wyden, Chmn.; DeFazio, Price, Luken, Mazzoli, Cooper, Olin, Flake, one vacancy.
Minority (6 R): Broomfield, Meyers, McMillan, Combest, Baker, one vacancy.

SBA AND THE GENERAL ECONOMY
Majority (9 D): LaFalce, Chmn.; Smith, Mazzoli, Savage, Roemer, Sisisky, Torres, Cooper, Olin.
Minority (6 R): McDade, Meyers, McMillan, Baker, Hefley, one vacancy.

STANDARDS OF OFFICIAL CONDUCT   House Terrace 2, Capitol Bldg.
202-225-7103

Majority (6 D): Dixon (CA), Chmn.; Fazio (CA), Dwyer (NJ), Mollohan (WV), Gaydos (PA), Atkins (MA)
Minority (6 R): Spence (SC), Myers (IN), Hansen (UT), Pashayan (CA), Petri (WI), Craig (ID).

NO SUBCOMMITTEES

VETERANS' AFFAIRS   335 CHOB, 202-225-3527

Majority (21 D): Montgomery (MS), Chmn.; Edwards (CA), Applegate (OH), Mica (FL), Dowdy (MS), Evans (IL), Kaptur (OH), Penny (MN), Staggers (WV), Rowland (GA), Bryant (TX), Florio (NJ), Gray (IL), Kanjorski (PA), Robinson (AR), Stenholm (TX), Harris (AL), Kennedy (MA), Patterson (SC), Johnson (SD), Jontz (IN).
Minority (13 R): Solomon (NY), Hammerschmidt (AR), Wylie (OH), Stump (AZ), McEwen (OH), Smith (NJ), Burton (IN), Bilirakis (FL), Ridge (PA), Rowland (CT), Dornan (CA), Smith (NH), Davis (IL).

SUBCOMMITTEES

COMPENSATION, PENSION AND INSURANCE

Majority (5 D): Applegate, Chmn.; Penny, Johnson, Mica, Evans.
Minority (4 R): McEwen, Wylie, Bilirakis, Smith (NH).

EDUCATION, TRAINING AND EMPLOYMENT

Majority (6 D): Dowdy, Chmn.; Patterson, Jontz, Evans, Kaptur, Kennedy.
Minority (4 R): Smith (NJ), Wylie, Ridge, Dornan.

HOSPITALS AND HEALTH CARE

Majority (13 D): Montgomery, Chmn.; Mica, Penny, Staggers, Rowland, Bryant, Florio, Gray, Kanjorski, Robinson, Stenholm, Harris, Kennedy.
Minority (7 R): Hammerschmidt, Stump, McEwen, Smith (NJ), Bilirakis, Ridge, Rowland.

HOUSING AND MEMORIAL AFFAIRS

Majority (5 D): Kaptur, Chmn.; Rowland, Harris, Patterson, Florio.
Minority (4 R): Burton, Rowland, Smith (NH), Davis.

OVERSIGHT AND INVESTIGATIONS

Majority (7 D): Evans, Chmn.; Edwards, Johnson, Applegate, Mica, Dowdy, Florio.
Minority (4 R): Stump, Burton, Dornan, Davis.

WAYS AND MEANS   1102 LHOB, 202-225-3625

Majority (23 D): Rostenkowski (IL), Chmn.; Gibbons (FL), Pickle (TX), Rangel (NY), Stark (CA), Jacobs (IN), Ford (TN), Jenkins (GA), Gephardt (MO), Downey (NY), Guarini (NY), Russo (IL), Pease (OH), Matsui (CA), Anthony (AR), Flippo (AL), Dorgan (ND), Kennelly (CT), Donnelly (MA), Coyne (PA), Andrews (TX), Levin (MI), Moody (WI).
Minority (13 R): Duncan (TN), Archer (TX), Vander Jagt (MI), Crane (IL), Frenzel (MN), Schulze (PA), Gradison (OH), Thomas (CA), McGrath (NY), Daub (NE), Gregg (NH), Brown (CO), Chandler (WA).

SUBCOMMITTEES

HEALTH

Majority (7 D): Stark, Chmn.; Donnelly, Coyne, Pickle, Anthony, Levin, Moody.
Minority (4 R): Gradison, Daub, Gregg, Chandler.

OVERSIGHT

Majority (7 D): Pickle, Chmn.; Anthony, Flippo, Dorgan, Ford, Rangel, Jacobs.
Minority (4 R): Schulze, Frenzel, Thomas, McGrath.

PUBLIC ASSISTANCE AND UNEMPLOYMENT COMPENSATION

Majority (7 D): Ford, Chmn.; Downey, Pease, Matsui, Kennelly, Donnelly, Andrews.
Minority (4 R): Brown, Frenzel, Gradison, Chandler.

SELECT REVENUE MEASURES

Majority (7 D): Rangel, Chmn.; Flippo, Dorgan, Kennelly, Andrews, Stark, Coyne.
Minority (4 R): Vander Jagt, McGrath, Gregg, Brown.

SOCIAL SECURITY

Majority (5 D): Jacobs, Chmn.; Gephardt, Gibbons, Levin, Moody.
Minority (3 R): Archer, Crane, Daub.

TRADE

Majority (9 D): Gibbons, Chmn.; Rostenkowski, Jenkins, Downey, Pease, Russo, Gephardt, Guarini, Matsui.

Minority (5 R): Crane, Archer, Vander Jagt, Frenzel, Schulze.

SELECT COMMITTEES

SELECT COMMITTEE ON AGING   712 House Annex 1, 202-226-3375

Majority (39 D): Roybal (CA), Chmn.; Pepper (FL), Biaggi (NY), Bonker (WA), Downey (NY), Florio (NJ), Ford (TN), Hughes (NJ), Lloyd (TN), Oakar (OH), Luken (OH), Byron (MD), Mica (FL), Waxman (CA), Synar (OK), Derrick (SC), Vento (MN), Frank (MA), Lantos (CA), Wyden (OR), Crockett (MI), Boner (TN), Skelton (MO), Hertel (MI), Borski (PA), Boucher (VA), Erdreich (AL), MacKay (FL), Sisisky (VA), Wise (WV), Richardson (NM), Volkmer (MO), Gordon (TN), Manton (NY), Robinson (AR), Stallings (ID), Clarke (NC), Kennedy (MA), Slaughter (NY).

Minority (26 R): Rinaldo (NJ), Hammerschmidt (AR), Regula (OH), Shumway (CA), Snowe (ME), Jeffords (VT), Tauke (IA), Wortley (NY), Courter (NJ), Schneider (RI), Ridge (PA), Smith (NJ), Boehlert (NY), Saxton (NJ), Bentley (MD), Lightfoot (IA), Fawell (IL), Meyers (KS), Blaz (GU), Swindall (GA), Henry (MI), Schuette (MI), Spence (SC), Clinger (PA), Morella (MD), Saiki (HI).

SUBCOMMITTEES

HEALTH AND LONG-TERM CARE

Majority (18 D): Pepper, Chmn.; Florio, Ford, Oakar, Luken, Mica, Waxman, Synar, Derrick, Vento, Frank, Wyden, Skelton, Hertel, Borski, Erdreich, MacKay, Sisisky.

Minority (13 R): Regula, Rinaldo, Wortley, Courter, Schneider, Ridge, Smith, Boehlert, Saxton, Bentley, Lightfoot, Meyers, Blaz.

HOUSING AND CONSUMER INTERESTS

Majority (9 D): Bonker, Chmn.; Lloyd, Byron, Lantos, Boner, Boucher, Richardson, Volkmer, Gordon.

Minority (7 R): Hammerschmidt, Wortley, Ridge, Boehlert, Schuette, Clinger, Saiki.

HUMAN SERVICES

Majority (10 D): Downey, Biaggi, Florio, Hughes, Lantos, Richardson, Robinson, Clarke, Kennedy, Slaughter.

Minority (8 R): Snowe, Shumway, Meyers, Blaz, Spence, Clinger, Morella, Saiki.

RETIREMENT INCOME AND EMPLOYMENT

Majority (11 D): Roybal, Chmn.; Downey, Lloyd, Oakar, Synar, Crockett, Boucher, Wise, Volkmer, Manton, Stallings.

Minority (8 R): Tauke, Shumway, Jeffords, Fawell, Swindall, Henry, Schuette, Spence.

TASK FORCES

RURAL ELDERLY

Majority (10 D): Synar, Chmn.; Derrick, Wyden, Skelton, Boucher, MacKay, Wise, Richardson, Volkmer, Clarke.

Minority (8 R): Lightfoot, Shumway, Snowe, Jeffords, Tauke, Schuette, Spence, Clinger.

SOCIAL SECURITY AND WOMEN
Majority (9 D): Oakar, Chmn.; Biaggi, Ford, Lloyd, Frank, Boner, Manton, Robinson, Slaughter.
Minority (5 R): Schneider, Snowe, Saxton, Bentley, Saiki.

SELECT COMMITTEE ON CHILDREN, YOUTH AND FAMILIES

385 House Annex 2
202-226-7660

Majority (18 D): Miller (CA), Chmn; Lehman (FL), Schroeder (CO), Boggs (LA), McHugh (NY), Weiss (NY), Anthony (AR), Boxer (CA), Levin (MI), Morrison (CT), Rowland (GA), Sikorski (MN), Wheat (MO), Martinez (CA), Evans (IL), Durbin (IL), Sawyer (OH), Skaggs (CO).
Minority (12 R): Coats (IN), Bliley (VA), Wolf (VA), Johnson (CT), Vucanovich (NV), Kemp (NY), Wortley (NY), Packard (CA), Boulter (TX), Hastert (IL), Holloway (LA), Grandy (IA).

TASK FORCES

CRISIS INTERVENTION
Majority (7 D): Boggs, Chmn.; Anthony, Levin, Sikorski, Weiss, Rowland, Wheat.
Minority (4 R): Johnson, Vucanovich, Grandy, Bliley.

ECONOMIC SECURITY
Majority (7 D): Schroeder, Chmn.; Morrison, Wheat, Martinez, Evans, Sawyer, McHugh.
Minority (4 R): Wolf, Kemp, Boulter, Hastert.

PREVENTION STRATEGIES
Majority (7 D): Lehman, Chmn.; McHugh, Weiss, Boxer, Rowland, Durbin, Skaggs.
Minority (4 R): Bliley, Wortley, Packard, Holloway.

SELECT COMMITTEE ON HUNGER   507 House Annex 2, 202-226-5470

Majority (16 D): Leland (TX), Chmn.; Hall (OH), Traxler (MI), Panetta (CA), Fazio (CA), Gejdenson (CT), Kostmayer (PA), Dorgan (ND), Carr (MI), Penny (MN), Ackerman (NY), Espy (MS), Flake (NY), Bilbray (NV), Mfume (MD), Patterson (SC).
Minority (10 R): Roukema (NJ), Emerson (MO), Morrison (WA), Gilman (NY), Smith (OR), Bereuter (NE), Upton (MI), three vacancies.

TASK FORCES

DOMESTIC TASK FORCE
Majority (8 D): Panetta, Chmn.; Traxler, Ackerman, Espy, Flake, Bilbray, Mfume, Patterson.
Minority (3 R): Emerson, Morrison, Upton.

INTERNATIONAL TASK FORCE
Majority (7 D): Hall, Chmn.; Fazio, Gejdenson, Kostmayer, Dorgan, Carr, Penny.
Minority (4 R): Morrison, Gilman, Smith, Bereuter.

PERMANENT SELECT COMMITTEE ON INTELLIGENCE

H 405 Capitol
202-225-4121

Majority (11 D): Stokes (IN), Chmn.; McCurdy (OK), Beilenson (CA), Kastenmeier (WI), Daniel (VA), Roe (NJ), Brown (CA), McHugh (NY), Dwyer (NJ), Wilson (TX), Kennelly (CT).
Minority (6 R): Hyde (IL), Cheney (WY), Livingston (LA), McEwen (OH), Lungren (CA), Schuster (PA).

SUBCOMMITTEES

LEGISLATION
Majority (6 D): McHugh, Chmn.; Stokes, Kastenmeier, Dwyer, Wilson, Kennelly.
Minority (3 R): Livingston, Schuster, Lungren.

OVERSIGHT AND EVALUATION
Majority (6 D): Beilenson, Chmn.; Dwyer, Wilson, Kennelly, McCurdy, Brown.
Minority (3 R): McEwen, Schuster, Hyde.

PROGRAM AND BUDGET AUTHORIZATION
Majority (6 D): Stokes, Chmn.; McCurdy, Kastenmeier, Daniel, Roe, Brown.
Minority (3 R): Cheney, Hyde, Lungren.

SELECT COMMITTEE ON NARCOTICS ABUSE AND CONTROL

234 House Annex 2
202-226-3040

Majority (15 D): Rangel (NY), Chmn.; Rodino (NJ), Stark (CA), Scheuer (NY), Collins (IL), Akaka (HI), Guarini (NJ), Fascell (FL), Fauntroy (DC), Hughes (NJ), Levine (CA), Ortiz (TX), Smith (FL), Towns (NY), Traficant (OH).
Minority (10 R): Gilman (NY), Coughlin (PA), Shaw (FL), Oxley (OH), Parris (VA), Hunter (CA), DioGuardi (NY), Sensenbrenner (WI), Dornan (CA), one vacancy.

NO SUBCOMMITTEES

SELECT COMMITTEE TO INVESTIGATE COVERT ARMS TRANSACTIONS WITH IRAN

H 419 Capitol
202-225-7902

Majority (9 D): Hamilton (IN), Chmn.; Fascell (FL), Foley (WA), Rodino (NJ), Brooks (TX), Stokes (OH), Aspin (WI), Boland (MA), Jenkins (GA).
Minority (6 R): Cheney (WY), Broomfield (MI), Hyde (IL), Courter (NJ), McCollum (FL), Dewine (OH).

NO SUBCOMMITTEES

DEMOGRAPHICS

Population. All population figures are from the Bureau of the Census, U.S. Department of Commerce, Washington, D.C. 20233, 301-763-4040. The 1980 Census figures regarding population, education, poverty, ancestry, households and voting age can be found in the following publications: Congressional Districts of the 98th Congress, Congressional Districts of the 99th Congress (redistricted states: CA, HI, LA, ME, MS, MT, NJ, NY, TX, and WA), Congressional Districts of the 100th Congress (redistricted state: OH) and Provisional Estimates of Social, Economic and Housing Characteristics. Final figures for the 1970 and 1980 Census counts are as of April 1. The 1986 population figures are provisional estimates as of July 1, 1986.

Voting Age Population. This figure indicates all persons at least 18 years of age who are eligible to vote, including the Armed Forces, aliens and institutional members.

Chart I shows the total U.S. population and total U.S. voting population for 1986 (provisional estimate), 1980 and 1970.

Chart I

Total U.S. Population		Total U.S. Voting Age Population	
July 1, 1986	241,596,000 (est.)	April 1, 1986	178,325,000 (est.)
April 1, 1980	226,545,805	April 1, 1980	163,997,000
April 1, 1970	203,302,031	April 1, 1970	135,290,000

Chart II indicates the range of highest and lowest state population changes in percentage growth and absolute figures for 1970-80. This District of Columbia is included as a state in all of the following charts.

Chart II

1970–80 Population Change
(National Avg.: 11.4%)

State	Highest		State	Lowest	
Nevada	63.8%	(311,755)	District of Columbia	-15.6%	(-118,355)
Arizona	53.1	(942,816)	New York	-3.7	(-683,319)
Florida	43.5	(2,954,906)	Rhode Island	-0.3	(-2,569)
Wyoming	41.3	(137,141)			
Utah	37.9	(401,764)			

Chart III illustrates the highest net in-migration and out-migration for the years 1980-86.

Chart III

1980-86 Population Change: Five Highest and Lowest States
(National Average 6.4%)

State	Highest		State	Lowest	
Alaska	32.8%	132,000	Iowa	-2.2%	(63,000)
Arizona	22.1	601,000	District of Columbia	-1.9	(12,000)
Nevada	20.3	2,456,000	West Virginia	-1.6	(31,000)
Florida	19.8	1,928,000	Michigan	-1.3	(117,000)
Texas	17.3	2,456,000	Ohio	-0.4	(45,000)

Chart IV shows the ten highest and lowest populated states.

Chart IV

1986 U.S. Population: Ten Highest and Lowest States

State	Highest	State	Lowest
California	26,365,000	Wyoming	509,000
New York	17,783,000	Alaska	521,000
Texas	16,370,000	Vermont	535,000
Pennsylvania	11,853,000	Delaware	622,000
Illinois	11,535,000	District of Columbia	626,000
Florida	11,366,000	North Dakota	685,000
Ohio	10,744,000	South Dakota	708,000
Michigan	9,088,000	Montana	826,000
New Jersey	7,562,000	Nevada	936,000
North Carolina	6,255,000	Rhode Island	968,000

Chart V illustrates states with the highest and lowest percentages of citizens completing four or more years of higher education.

Chart V

Persons Living Below Poverty Level (1979)
(National Avg.: 12.4%)

State	Highest	State	Lowest
Mississippi	23.9%	Wyoming	7.9%
Arkansas	19.0	Connecticut	8.0
Alabama	18.9	New Hampshire	8.5
District of Columbia	18.6	Wisconsin	8.7
Louisiana	18.6	Nevada	8.7
Kentucky	17.6	Minnesota	9.5
New Mexico	17.6	New Jersey	9.5

Chart VI lists the states with the highest and lowest average percentages of family households.

Chart VI

1980 Family Households
(National Avg.: 73%)

State	Highest	State	Lowest
Kentucky, South Carolina, Utah	78%	District of Columbia	53%
		Nevada	68
Alabama, Arkansas, Hawaii, North Carolina, Tennessee, West Virginia	77	California	69
		Colorado, New York, Oregon, Washington	70

Chart VII illustrates the states with the highest and lowest average percentages of households with children.

Chart VII

1980 Households with Children
(National Avg.: 40%)

State	Highest	State	Lowest
Utah	50%	District of Columbia	29%
Alaska	49	Florida	33
South Carolina	46	Nevada, Massachusetts	36
Hawaii, Louisiana,	45	California, New York,	37
New Mexico		Oregon	

Chart VIII illustrates the states with the highest and lowest percentages of married-couple households.

Chart VIII

Married-Couple Households
(National Avg.: 60%)

State	Highest	State	Lowest
Utah	69%	District of Columbia	30%
Idaho	67	New York	54
Arkansas, Kentucky, North	65	California	55
Dakota, West Virginia,		Nevada	56
Wyoming		Massachusetts	57

Ethnic Breakdown. The ethnic breakdown illustrates the potential ethnic vote as compared with the overall population. The concept of race as defined by the Census Bureau reflects self-identification and not clear-cut biological or scientific definitions.

Chart IX lists states with Black voting age populations well above the national average of 10.9%. The Black ethnic classification refers to those persons who indicated their race as Black or Negro on the Census questionnaire and includes entries such as Jamaican, Black Puerto Rican, West Indian, Haitian or Nigerian. The percentage of total Black population also includes children under 18 years of age.

Chart IX

1980 Black Population: Total State and Voting Age Population

State	% of voting age pop.	% of total state pop.	State	% of voting age pop.	% of total state pop.
District of Columbia	66%	70.3%	Tennessee	14%	15.8%
Mississippi	31	35.2	Delaware	14	16.1
South Carolina	27	30.4	Arkansas	14	16.3
Louisiana	27	29.4	Illinois	13	14.7
Georgia	24	26.8	New York	12	13.7
Alabama	23	25.6	Michigan	12	12.9
Maryland	21	22.7	Florida	11	13.8
North Carolina	20	22.4	Texas	11	12.0
Virginia	17	18.9			

Chart X illustrates the voting age and the total state population figures for the ten states with the highest Spanish concentration. The Spanish classification refers to those people who indicated Mexican, Puerto Rican and Cuban, as well as those persons from Spain or any Spanish speaking country.

Chart X

1980 Spanish Origin: Total State and Voting Age Population

State	% of voting age pop.	% of total state pop.
New Mexico	33%	36.6%
Texas	18	21.0
California	16	19.2
Arizona	13	16.2
Colorado	10	11.8
Florida	9	8.8
New York	8	9.5
Hawaii	6	6.7
Nevada	6	6.7
New Jersey	6	7.4

Share of Federal Tax Burden. The federal tax burden indicates federal-fund taxes (individual, corporate, alcohol, tobacco, etc.) and trust fund taxes rather than the Treasury Department tax collection data.

Chart XI shows the overall national averages for total tax and per capita burden. The total federal tax burden for 1986 is $752 billion.

Chart XI

Total and Per Capita Federal Tax Burdens

	Total Burden (in millions)		Per Capita Burden	
1987	$822,386	1987	$3,395
1986	752,178	1986	3,133
1985	709,400	1985	2,982
1984	645,043	1984	2,738
1983	580,619	1983	2,490

Chart XII shows the states with the highest and lowest tax burden. Predictably, states with higher populations pay more.

Chart XII

1986 Total Federal Tax Burden
(in billions)

Highest		Lowest	
California	$91.4	Vermont	$1.4
New York	62.9	Wyoming	1.6
Texas	53.6	South Dakota	1.7
Illinois	40.7	North Dakota	2.0
Pennsylvania	36.3	Delaware	2.1
Florida	35.3	Montana	2.2
Ohio	33.5	Idaho	2.3
New Jersey	31.6	Alaska	2.5
Michigan	27.7	District of Columbia	2.7
Massachusetts	21.7	Maine	2.9

Chart XIII shows the states with the highest and lowest per capita federal tax burden. The higher the average income, the higher the per capita federal tax burden.

Chart XIII
1986 Per Capita Federal Tax Burden

Highest		Lowest	
Alaska	$4,907	Mississippi	$1,978
District of Columbia	4,582	Idaho	2,162
Connecticut	4,478	Utah	2,193
New Jersey	4,203	Arizona	2,230
Massachusetts	3,761	West Virginia	2,236
Maryland	3,667	South Carolina	2,317
New York	3,635	Alabama	2,344
Illinois	3,541	Kentucky	2,347
California	3,485	Maine	2,471
Delaware	3,416	New Mexico	2,477

Federal Expenditures by State. For the fiscal year 1986, the Census Bureau compiled statistics on federal expenditures amounting to $830 billion. Not included in this figure is interest on the federal debts, international payments and foreign aid, and expenditures for selected federal agencies (i.e., CIA and National Security Agency). Federal Expenditures by State for fiscal year 1986 (March 1987) by the Department of Commerce contain an in-depth discussion of the categories composing the total federal expenditure. The raw numbers are in millions of dollars. The percentages indicate per capita spending. Defense and All Other Agencies numbers have been rounded and may not equal the total.

Defense numbers reflect amounts earmarked for the Department of Defense only. All other programs, including Veterans Administration benefits, are included in the category All Other Agencies.

Chart XIV shows the highest and lowest federal expenditures for defense by state.

Chart XIV
Federal Expenditures for Defense

	Highest			Lowest	
State	$ (in millions)	% distribution	State	$ (in millions)	% distribution
California	$40,304	17.5%	Vermont	$188	.1%
Texas	16,904	7.4	Wyoming	236	.1
Virginia	13,580	5.9	Montana	238	.1
New York	11,279	4.9	West Virginia	264	.1
Florida	10,366	4.5	Idaho	306	.1

Chart XV shows the highest and lowest federal expenditures for all other agencies by state.

Chart XV

Federal Expenditures for All Other Agencies

State	Highest $ (in millions)	% distribution	State	Lowest $ (in millions)	% distribution
California	$60,556	10.1%	Vermont	$1,247	.2%
New York	48,169	8.0	Wyoming	1,286	.2
Pennsylvania	30.941	5.2	Delaware	1,358	.3
Texas	30,438	7.4	Alaska	1,532	.3
Florida	29,171	4.9	New Hamp.	2,028	.4

Chart XVI shows the highest and lowest per capita federal expenditures for defense by state.

Chart XVI

Per Capita Federal Expenditures for Defense
(U.S. median: $939.11)

State (Highest)	$ per capita	State (Lowest)	$ per capita
District of Columbia	$2,766.41	West Virgina	$137.34
Virginia	2,346.69	Oregon	255.43
Hawaii	2,340.58	Iowa	263.27
Alaska	2,222.94	Wisconsin	278.16
Connecticut	1,879.93	Montana	290.50

Chart XVII shows the highest and lowest per capita federal expenditures for all other agencies by state.

Chart XVII

Per Capita Federal Expenditures for All Other Agencies
(U.S. median: $2,452.83)

State (Highest)	$ per capita	State (Lowest)	$ per capita
District of Columbia	$20,294.88	Texas	1,824.62
New Mexico	3,848.52	North Carolina	1,881.23
North Dakota	3,389.72	New Hampshire	1,975.16
Maryland	3,269.60	Georgia	1,977.06
Montana	3,153.89	Hawaii	2,031.69

CAMPAIGN FINANCE

All data is derived from candidate and party reports as well as other official studies available from the Federal Election Commission located at 999 E Street, N.W., Washington, D.C. 20463, 202-376-4140 (toll free 800-424-9530). For a more detailed explanation of campaign finance, refer to the Guide to Usage.

Chart XVIII shows contributions from Political Action Committees (PACs), total receipts, total expenditures and cash-on-hand (unspent) for all 1985-86 congressional candidates.

Chart XVIII
1985-86 Total Senate Financial Activity: Winners/Losers

	No. of Cand.	Total PAC Contrib.	Total Receipts	Total Expenditures	Latest Cash-on-Hand
Senate	**262**	**$44,999,304**	**$214,021,333**	**$211,082,021**	**$10,793,012**
Democrats	**127**	20,001,296	91,775,796	88,884,265	4,247,943
Incumbents	9	7,277,444	26,290,465	24,414,413	3,120,474
Challengers	75	7,944,268	40,419,960	39,779,421	714,744
Open Seats	43	4,779,584	25,965,371	24,690,431	412,725
Republicans	**92**	24,997,049	122,194,367	122,148,362	6,542,075
Incumbents	18	16,346,957	64,012,012	64,781,363	5,726,223
Challengers	46	2,177,580	26,516,261	26,204,188	341,142
Open Seats	28	6,472,512	31,666,094	31,162,811	474,710
Others	**43**	959	51,170	49,394	2,994

1985-86 Total House Financial Activity: Winners/Losers

	No. of Cand.	Total PAC Contrib.	Total Receipts	Total Expenditures	Latest Cash-on-Hand
House	**1,606**	**$87,178,961**	**$257,427,627**	**$238,967,156**	**$49,447,419**
Democrats	**841**	54,631,391	139,500,941	128,378,639	29,029,929
Incumbents	235	40,962,642	83,732,001	73,380,722	28,077,115
Challengers	430	6,652,409	25,533,843	25,308,685	358,670
Open Seats	176	7,016,340	30,235,097	29,689,232	594,144
Republicans	**596**	32,542,920	117,635,274	110,312,250	20,410,443
Incumbents	161	24,864,949	65,901,124	59,054,984	19,704,941
Challengers	319	2,434,449	23,608,139	23,441,825	346,314
Open Seats	116	5,234,522	28,126,011	27,815,441	359,188
Others	**169**	4,650	291,412	276,267	7,047
Total Senate/House	**1,868**	**$132,178,265**	**$471,448,960**	**$450,049,177**	**$60,240,431**

Chart XIX shows the total financial activity for Senate and House winners since 1975.

Chart XIX

1985-86 Senate/House Winners: Financial Activity
(in millions)

Senate	1985-86	1983-84	1981-82	1979-80	1977-78	1975-76
Receipts	$106.8	$100.9	$ 70.1	$41.7	$43.0	$21.0
Expenditures	104.0	97.5	68.2	40.0	42.3	20.1
PAC Contributions	28.2	20.0	15.6	10.2	6.0	3.1
House						
Receipts	$173.3	$144.8	$123.1	$86.0	$60.0	$42.5
Expenditures	155.4	127.4	114.7	78.0	55.6	38.0
PAC Contributions	72.7	59.5	42.7	27.0	17.0	10.9

Chart XX shows the top ten Senate members and the top twenty House members elected in 1986 in terms of total receipts and total expenditures during the 1985-86 election cycle.

Chart XX

1986 Senate Winners: Top Ten Raisers

1.	Alfonse D'Amato (R-NY)	$11,333,629
2.	Alan Cranston (D-CA)	10,851,596
3.	Bob Packwood (D-OR)	6,725,027
4.	Bob Graham (D-FL)	6,215,911
5.	Kit Bond (R-MO)	5,464,030
6.	Arlen Specter (R-PA)	5,450,763
7.	Terry Sanford (D-NC)	4,181,701
8.	Timothy Wirth (D-CO)	3,819,308
9.	Thomas Daschle (D-SD)	3,515,482
10.	Steve Symms (R-ID)	3,387,726

1986 Senate Winners: Top Ten Spenders

1.	Alfonse D'Amato (R-NY)	$12,914,822
2.	Alan Cranston (D-CA)	11,037,707
3.	Bob Packwood (D-OR)	6,523,492
4.	Bob Graham (D-FL)	6,173,663
5.	Arlen Specter (R-PA)	5,993,230
6.	Kit Bond (R-MO)	5,359,046
7.	Timothy Wirth (D-CO)	4,397,780
8.	Terry Sanford (D-NC)	4,168,509
9.	Thomas Daschle (D-SD)	3,485,870
10.	Bob Kasten (R-WS)	3,433,870

1986 House Winners: Top Twenty Raisers

1.	Jack Kemp (R-NY)	$2,530,981
2.	Joseph P. Kennedy II (D-MA)	1,822,025
3.	Claude Pepper (D-FL)	1,448,167
4.	Ronald Dellums (D-CA)	1,370,820
5.	Joseph DioGuardi (R-NY)	1,280,057
6.	Jim Wright (D-TX)	1,237,895
7.	Bob Dornan (R-CA)	1,190,237
8.	J.J. Pickle (D-TX)	1,151,264
9.	Frank Wolf (R-VA)	1,097,358
10.	Helen Bentley (R-MD)	1,076,329
11.	Lamar Smith (R-TX)	1,066,535
12.	Joe Barton (R-TX)	1,024,246
13.	Jon Kyl (R-AZ)	1,019,967
14.	John Bryant (D-TX)	1,016,970
15.	Sam Gejdenson (D-CT)	975,785
16.	Ernest Konnyu (R-CA)	960,536
17.	Les AuCoin (D-OR)	958,023
18.	Vin Weber (R-MN)	942,499
19.	Sam Gibbons (D-FL)	903,485
20.	Mac Sweeney (R-TX)	901,176

1986 House Winners: Top Twenty Spenders

1.	Jack Kemp (R-NY)	$2,613,605
2.	Joseph P. Kennedy II (D-MA)	1,800,781
3.	Claude Pepper (D-FL)	1,395,549
4.	J. J. Pickle (D-TX)	1,369,912
5.	Joseph DioGuardi (R-NY)	1,264,167
6.	Ron Dellums (D-CA)	1,223,490
7.	Bob Dornan (R-CA)	1,174,637
8.	Frank Wolf (R-VA)	1,124,866
9.	Jim Wright (D-TX)	1,098,252
10.	Helen Bentley (R-MD)	1,070,161
11.	Lamar Smith (R-TX)	1,062,154
12.	Joe Barton (R-TX)	1,034,515
13.	Jon Kyl (R-AZ)	1,010,914
14.	John Bryant (D-TX)	994,285
15.	Sam Gejdenson (D-CT)	987,167
16.	Ernest Konnyu (R-CA)	950,447
17.	Les AuCoin (D-OR)	946,767
18.	Vin Weber (R-MN)	909,607
19.	Bill Boner (D-TN)	909,521
20.	Bill Schuette (R-MI)	897,820

Chart XXI shows the top ten Senate members and the top twenty House members elected in 1986 in terms of the highest cash-on-hand (unspent) during the 1985-86 election cycle.

Chart XXI

1986 Senate Winners:
Top Ten Cash on-Hand

1.	Bob Dole (R-KN)	$2,166,732
2.	John Glenn (R-OH)	818,910
3.	Bob Packwood (R-NH)	692,290
4.	Daniel Inouye (D-HI)	598,388
5.	Charles Grassley (R-IA)	486,432
6.	Alfonse D'Amato (R-NY)	456,293
7.	Alan Dixon (D-IL)	408,427
8.	Dan Quayle (R-IN)	385,126
9.	Don Nickles (R-OK)	375,674
10.	Wendell Ford (D-KY)	360,775

1986 House Winners:
Top Twenty Cash-on-Hand

1.	Dave Dreier (R-CA)	$949,829
2.	Stephen Solarz (D-NY)	812,706
3.	Ronnie Flippo (R-AL)	603,947
4.	Dan Rostenkowski (D-IL)	596,703
5.	Larry Hopkins (R-KY)	547,846
6.	Bill Archer (R-TX)	540,472
7.	John Duncan (R-TN)	512,878
8.	Matthew Rinaldo (R-NJ)	508,842
9.	Charles Schumer (D-NY)	503,941
10.	Carlos Moorhead (R-CA)	460,138
11.	Trent Lott (R-MS)	441,592
12.	Steve Bartlett (R-TX)	438,405
13.	Tom Bevill (D-AL)	437,485
14.	William S. Broomfield (R-MI)	430,594
15.	Doug Barnard (D-GA)	427,257
16.	Dante Fascell (D-FL)	426,393
17.	Billy Tauzin (D-LA)	421,002
18.	Ed Jenkins (D-GA)	416,351
19.	Gene Taylor (R-MO)	411,650
20.	Bob Livingston (D-LA)	403,766

Chart XXII shows the Democratic and Republican Party financial activity for the 1985-86 election cycle.

Chart XXII

1985–86 Party Financial Activity: Democratic/Republican

Democratic	Net Receipts	Net Expenditures	C.O.H. (12-31-86)	Debt Owed By	Contrib. To Cand.	Coordinated Expenditures
DNC Services	$17,235,406	$17,372,276	$155,671	$2,140,743	$ 20,500	$ 343,348
Senatorial	13,397,809	13,533,142	78,911	1,146,003	497,628	6,081,372
Congressional	12,322,969	12,562,666	58,852	865,911	616,086	1,551,926
Assn. of State Dem. Chair.	7,618,834	7,801,818	583,863	0	1,000	0
State and Local	11,178,862	11,451,469	554,101	509,912	498,637	928,250
Totals	**$61,753,000**	**$62,721,371**	**$1,431,398**	**$4,662,569**	**$1,633,851**	**$8,904,896**

Republican	Net Receipts	Net Expenditures	C.O.H. (12-31-86)	Debt Owed By	Contrib. To Cand.	Coordinated Expenditures
RNC	$83,780,156	$84,206,031	$1,240,845	$ 0	$ 350,910	$ 2,100
Senatorial	86,130,776	85,507,590	185,337	5,416,431	675,858	9,960,138
Congressional	39,796,974	41,280,736	275,612	3,098,488	1,699,864	4,101,651
Other Natl. Repub.	86,813	89,202	92	9,855	0	0
State and Local	42,638,196	43,082,442	1,465,813	1,854,837	751,972	280,271
Totals	**$252,432,915**	**$254,166,001**	**$3,167,699**	**$10,379,311**	**$3,478,604**	**$14,344,160**
Grand Total	**$314,186,795**	**$316,887,372**	**$4,599,097**	**$15,042,180**	**$5,112,455**	**$23,249,056**

Chart XXIII shows the total PAC financial activity for the 1985-86 election cycle. For a more detailed explanation of PAC groups, refer to the Guide to Usage.

Chart XXIII
1985–86 PAC Financial Activity

	Total Receipts	Total Expenditures	C.O.H. (12-31-86)	Debts Owed	Contrib. to Candidates
Corporation	$ 82,400,730	$ 79,639,100	$20,302,886	$ 263,243	$ 49,381,959
Labor	66,389,170	58,264,821	19,835,600	122,135	31,004,373
Ideological	115,640,140	115,602,433	10,436,699	8,904,593	19,389,797
Trade/Member-ship/Health	76,071,468	73,533,973	13,682,602	591,187	34,417,897
Agricultural	4,924,010	4,757,081	1,799,678	111,937	2,678,784
Corporation w/out stock	7,492,069	6,500,220	2,294,028	161,016	2,591,892
Total	**$352,917,587**	**$338,297,628**	**$68,351,493**	**$10,154,111**	**$139,465,702**

Chart XXIV shows the PAC contributions in terms of percentages of total receipts since 1979.

Chart XXIV
PAC Contributions as a % to Total Receipts
(in millions)

	1985–86		1983–84		1981–82		1979–80	
	Totals	%	Totals	%	Totals	%	Totals	%
Senate	45.0	21%	29.7	17%	22.5	16%	17.3	17%
House	87.2	34%	75.7	34%	61.1	29%	37.9	26%
Total	**$132.2**	**28%**	**$105.3**	**26%**	**$83.6**	**24%**	**$55.2**	**22%**

Chart XXV shows the top ten Senate members and the top twenty House members elected in 1986 in terms of total PAC receipts during the 1985-86 election cycle.

Chart XXV

1986 Senate Winners:
Top Ten PAC Receipts

1.	Alan Cranston (D-CA)	$1,373,466
2.	Steve Symms (D-ID)	1,371,618
3.	Kit Bond (R-MO)	1,334,222
4.	Arlen Specter (R-PA)	1,313,401
5.	Thomas Daschle (D-SD)	1,205,400
6.	Robert Kasten (R-WI)	1,092,897
7.	Robert Dole (R-KS)	1,036,433
8.	Bob Packwood (R-OR)	963,759
9.	Charles Grassley (R-IA)	959,431
10.	Alan Dixon (D-IL)	958,697

1986 House Winners:
Top Twenty PAC Receipts

1.	Jim Wright (D-TX)	$667,620
2.	Sam Gibbons (D-FL)	571,019
3.	William Gray (R-PA)	457,131
4.	Robert Michel (R-IL)	463,111
5.	Richard Gephardt (D-MO)	455,073
6.	Bob Carr (D-MI)	444,603
7.	Thomas Foley (D-WA)	433,261
8.	Les AuCoin (D-OR)	436,028
9.	Paul Kanjorski (D-PA)	415,829
10.	J. J. Pickle (D-TX)	404,198
11.	John Duncan (R-TN)	405,551
12.	Wayne Owens (D-UT)	398,130
13.	John Dingell (D-MI)	371,815
14.	John Bryant (D-TX)	371,347
15.	Helen Bentley (R-MD)	361,282
16.	James Quillen (R-TN)	359,050
17.	Fortney Stark (D-CA)	354,096
18.	Lane Evans (D-IL)	353,944
19.	Tony Coelho (D-CA)	353,645
20.	Doug Walgren (D-IL)	349,312

Charts XVI-XXXI show the top five raisers and contributors to candidates, broken down into the six categories defined as PACs by the FEC. For a more detailed explanation of these categories, refer to the Guide to Usage.

Chart XXVI

1985-86 Corporate PAC's: Top Five Raisers and Contributors

Raisers

1.	American Telephone and Telegraph Co. Inc PAC (AT&T PAC)	$1,820,939
2.	Philip Morris Political Action Committee (PHIL-PAC)	668,453
3.	AMOCO PAC	647,594
4.	Bear, Stearns and Co. Political Campaign Committee	612,899
5.	United Parcel Service PAC (UPSPAC)	567,328

Contributors

1.	American Telephone and Telegraph Co. Inc PAC (AT&T PAC)	$799,760
2.	Philip Morris Political Action Committee (PHIL-PAC)	559,505
3.	United Parcel Service PAC (UPSPAC)	480,524
4.	Tenneco Employees God Government Fund	447,250
5.	Lockheed Employees PAC	430,858

Chart XXVII

1985-86 Labor PAC's: Top Five Raisers and Contributors

Raisers

1. Democratic Republican Independent Voter Education
    Committee (D.R.I.V.E.) (Teamsters) $4,389,458
2. National Education Association PAC (NEA)   3,196,697
3. UAW-V-CAP (United Auto Workers)   3,054,003
4. Committee on Letter Carriers Political Education   2,070,897
5. Machinists Non-Partisan Political League   2,053,075

Contributors

1. National Education Association PAC (NEA) $2,055,133
2. UAW-V-CAP (United Auto Workers)   1,621,055
3. Committee on Letter Carriers Political Education   1,490,875
4. Democratic Republican Independent Voter Education
    Committee (D.R.I.V.E.) Teamsters   1,457,196
5. Machinists Non-Partisan Political League   1,364,550

Chart XXVIII

1985-86 Ideological PAC's: Top Five Raisers and Contributors

Raisers

1. National Congressional Club $15,364,881
2. Fund for America's Future   9,373,056
3. National Conservative Political Action Committee (NCPAC)   9,319,550
4. National Committee to Preserve Social Security PAC   6,201,412
5. Campaign America   3,347,312

Contributors

1. Auto Dealers for Free Trade PAC $1,016,699
2. National PAC   912,000
3. Fund for America's Future, INC.   809,917
4. National Committee to Preserve Social Security PAC   736,135
5. National Right to Life PAC   695,795

Chart XXIX

1985-86 Trade/Membership/Health PAC's: Top Five Raisers and Contributors

Raisers

1. Realtors Political Action Committee $5,680,419
2. American Medical Association PAC (AMPAC)   4,961,408
3. National Rifle Assn. Political Victory Fund   4,692,544
4. League of Conservative Voters   3,776,005
5. Association of Trial Lawyers PAC (ATLA)   2,970,762

Contributors

1. Realtors Political Action Committee $2,738,338
2. American Medical Association PAC (AMPAC)   2,107,492
3. National Association of Retired Federal Employees PAC (NARFE-PAC) 1,491,895
4. Build PAC of the National Association of Home Builders   1,424,240
5. Association of Trial Lawyers PAC (ATLA)   1,404,000

Chart XXX

1985–86 Agricultural PACs: Top Five Raisers and Spenders

Raisers

1. Committee for Thorough Agricultural Political Education of Associated Milk Producers	$1,569,968
2. Mid-America Dairymen Inc. Agricultural and Dairy Educational PAC	762,459
3. Dairymen Inc. Special Political Agricultural Community Education (DI-PAC)	679,706
4. Conservation Voters Lobby	303,104
5. American Crystal Sugar	248,228

Spenders

1. Committee for Thorough Agricultural Political Education of Associated Milk Producers	$887,200
2. Mid-America Dairymen Inc., Agricultural and Dairy Educational PAC	467,000
3. Dairymen Inc. Special Political Agricultural Community Education (DI-PAC)	231,688
4. American Crystal Sugar	203,112
5. Land O'Lakes Inc. PAC	88,350

Chart XXXI

1985–86 Corporations Without Stock: Top Five Raisers and Contributors

Raisers

1. Council for National Defense Inc.	$1,233,644
2. Commodity Futures Political Fund of the Chicago Mercantile Exchange	1,114,434
3. Aircraft Owners and Pilots Association PAC	942,049
4. American Academy of Ophthalmology Inc. Political Committee (OPHTHPAC)	330,322
5. Handgun Control Inc. PAC (HCI PAC)	299,038

Contributors

1. Commodity Futures Political Fund of the Chicago Mercantile Exchange	$323,950
2. Aircraft Owners and Pilots Association PAC	236,630
3. American Academy of Ophthalmology Inc. Political Committee (OPHTHPAC)	216,150
4. Council for National Defense Inc.	145,528
5. Massachusetts Mutual Life Insurance Co. PAC	130,875

METROPOLITAN MAPS

The maps on the following pages illustrate congressional districts in the metropolitan areas of (in order) San Francisco and Los Angeles, California; Miami, Florida; Chicago, Illinois; Detroit, Michigan; and New York, New York.

CALIFORNIA — Congressional Districts, Counties, and Selected Places

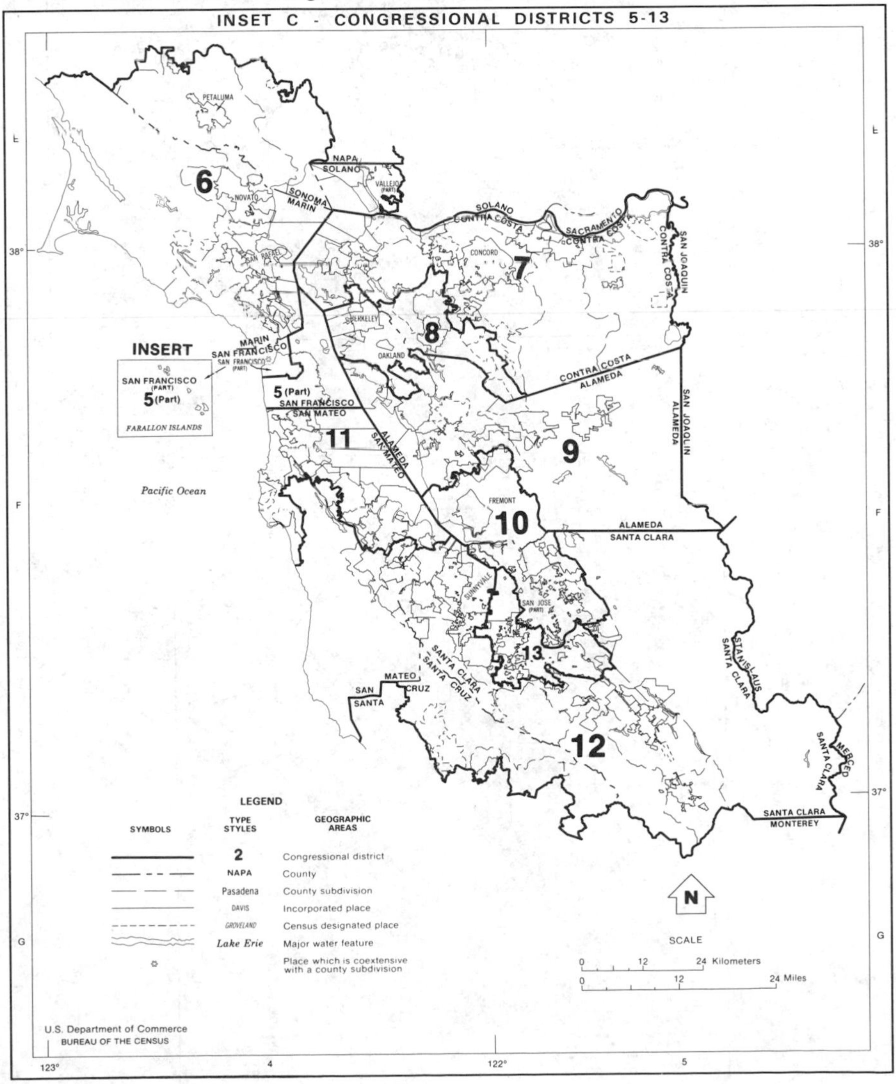

INSET C - CONGRESSIONAL DISTRICTS 5-13

INSERT

SAN FRANCISCO (PART)
5 (Part)

FARALLON ISLANDS

Pacific Ocean

LEGEND

SYMBOLS	TYPE STYLES	GEOGRAPHIC AREAS
	2	Congressional district
	NAPA	County
	Pasadena	County subdivision
	DAVIS	Incorporated place
	GROVELAND	Census designated place
	Lake Erie	Major water feature
○		Place which is coextensive with a county subdivision

U.S. Department of Commerce
BUREAU OF THE CENSUS

N

SCALE

0   12   24 Kilometers
0   12   24 Miles

CALIFORNIA — Congressional Districts, Counties, and Selected Places

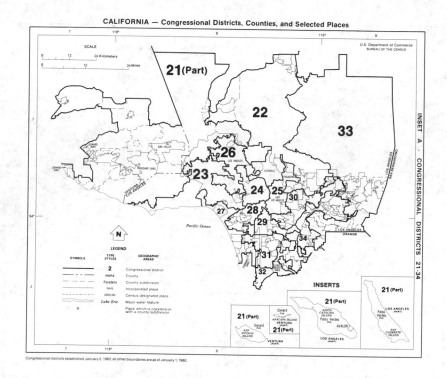

Congressional districts established January 2, 1983; all other boundaries are as of January 1, 1980.

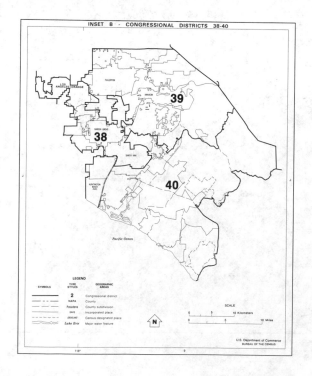

FLORIDA — Congressional Districts, Counties, and Selected Places

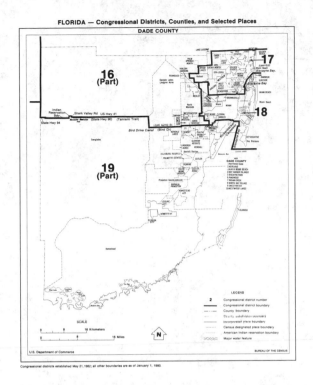

ILLINOIS — Congressional Districts, Counties, and Selected Places

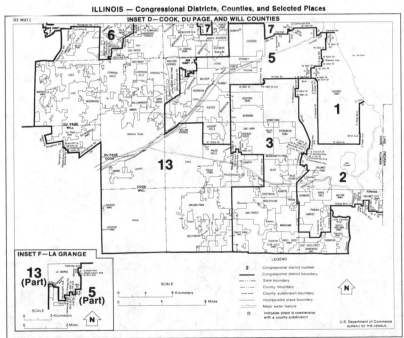

MICHIGAN — Congressional Districts, Counties, and Selected Places

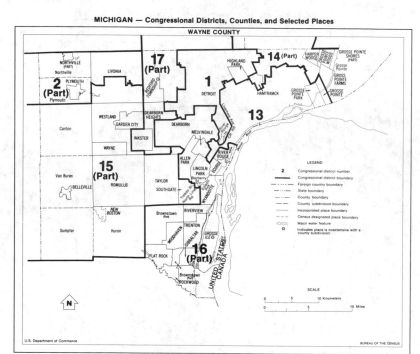

Congressional districts established May 24, 1982; all other boundaries are as of January 1, 1980.

NEW YORK — Congressional Districts, Counties, County Subdivisions, and Places

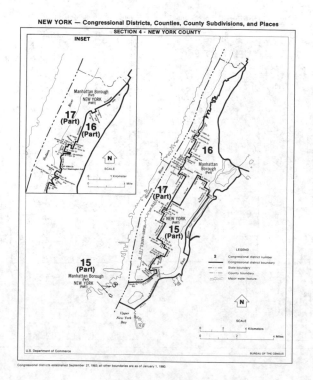

Congressional districts established September 27, 1983; all other boundaries are as of January 1, 1980.

NEW YORK — Congressional Districts, Counties, County Subdivisions, and Places

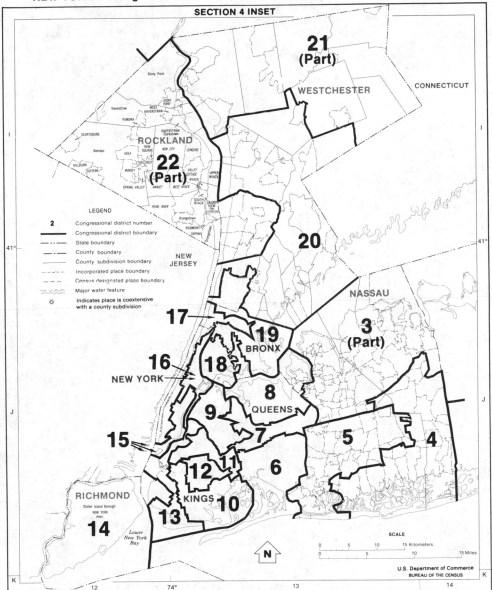

SECTION 4 INSET

21 (Part)

WESTCHESTER

CONNECTICUT

Stony Point

STONY POINT

Haverstraw
WEST
HAVERSTRAW

POMONA

GLOATSOURG

HAVERSTRAW
Clarkstown

ROCKLAND

NEW CITY

CONGERS

RAMAPO

VIOLA

NEW
SQUARE

22
(Part)

HILLBURN

SUFFERN

WILTCREST

MONSEY

VALLEY
COTTAGE
NYACK

UPPER
NYACK

SPRING VALLEY

NANUET

WEST NYACK

PEARL RIVER

SOUTH
NYACK

GRAND
VIEW
HUDSON

Orangetown

LEGEND

2 Congressional district number
    Congressional district boundary
    State boundary
    County boundary
    County subdivision boundary
    Incorporated place boundary
    Census designated place boundary
    Major water feature
    Indicates place is coextensive
    with a county subdivision

PIERMONT

TAPPAN

NEW
JERSEY

41°

20

NASSAU

17

19
BRONX

3
(Part)

16

18

NEW YORK

8
QUEENS

9

41°

J

5

4

7

15

6

12

11

RICHMOND

Staten Island Borough
NEW YORK
(PART)

14

13

10

KINGS

Lower
New York
Bay

N

SCALE

0   5   10   15 Kilometers
0   5   10   15 Miles

U.S. Department of Commerce
BUREAU OF THE CENSUS

12   74°   13   14

K

Congressional districts established September 27, 1983; all other boundaries are as of January 1, 1980.

NEW YORK — Congressional Districts, Counties, County Subdivisions, and Places
SECTION 4 - QUEENS COUNTY

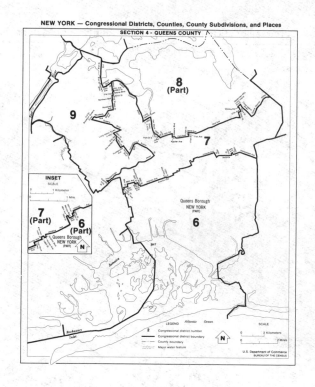

NEW YORK — Congressional Districts, Counties, County Subdivisions, and Places
SECTION 4 - KINGS COUNTY

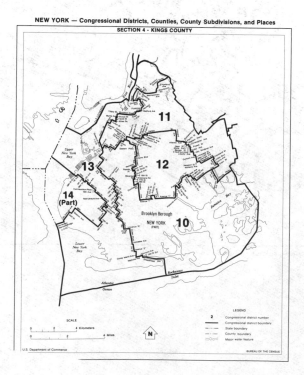

INDEX

The names of Governors, Senators and Representatives appear in boldface type. The number of the page that includes their corresponding biographical, voting and campaign finance information also appears in bold.

THE AUTHORS

MICHAEL BARONE is a senior writer on the editorial staff of *The Washington Post*. He was senior vice president of Peter D. Hart Research Associates Inc., a public opinion research firm. He is a graduate of Harvard College and Yale Law School and is a native of the Detroit area. He lives in Washington, D.C. with his daughter Sarah.

GRANT UJIFUSA, a Japanese-American, is a native of Worland, Wyoming, and a graduate of Harvard College. A senior editor at the Free Press Division of Macmillan, he lives in New York City with his wife Amy and their two sons Steven and Andrew.

THE PUBLISHER

❝The nation's most respected nonpartisan source of information about how Washington's policymaking machinery really works.❞

That's how *Newsweek* described *National Journal*. For 18 years, *National Journal* has reached subscribers with an award-winning weekly magazine noted for its dedication to "facts only" reporting. *National Journal* speaks to people who make it their business to know what's going on in the world's largest business—the United States Government.

Only *National Journal* is exclusively devoted to the coverage and analysis of what the government is doing today, what it's going to do tomorrow, and how its actions affect every facet of our lives.

This 1988 edition of *The Almanac of American Politics* marks the third volume to be published by *National Journal*.

1730 M Street N.W., Washington, D.C. 20036   Telephone (202) 857-1400